THE ENVIRONMENTAL RESOURCE HANDBOOK

2017/18

NINTH EDITION

THE ENVIRONMENTAL RESOURCE HANDBOOK

A Universal Reference Book

GREY HOUSE PUBLISHING

PUBLISHER: Leslie Mackenzie
EDITORIAL DIRECTOR: Laura Mars
STATISTICS EDITOR: David Garoogian

PRODUCTION MANAGER & COMPOSITION: Kristen Hayes
MARKETING DIRECTOR: Jessica Moody

A Sedgwick Press Book
Grey House Publishing, Inc.
4919 Route 22
Amenia, NY 12501
518.789.8700
FAX 845.373.6390
www.greyhouse.com
e-mail: books@greyhouse.com

First edition published 2001
Ninth edition published 2017

Printed in Canada

The environmental resource handbook. – 9th Ed. (2017/18)

Spine title: ERH

1. Environmental protection – United States – Directories. 2. Environmental agencies – United States –Directories. 3. Conservation of natural resources – Societies, etc. – Directories. 4. Nature conservation –Societies, etc. – Directories. 5. Environmental protection – United States – Bibliography. 6. Conservation of natural resources – Bibliography. 7. Nature conservation – Bibliography. I. Grey House Publishing, Inc.

II. Title: ERH.GE20.E5861 363'7 – dc21

RC108 .C645 616' .0025'73 96-640803

ISBN: 978-1-68217-552-1

Table of Contents

Introduction

This ninth edition of *The Environmental Resource Handbook* offers immediate access to a unique combination of more than 6,300 resources and 350 statistical and ranking charts, tables and maps, all revised with the most current information available.

Hailed as a "must-have resource" for environmentalists, educators, researchers and students of environmental studies, this new edition is comprehensive and thoughtfully arranged for easy and efficient use. Our research efforts include Internet, and email campaigns. We've added more than 200 listings and updated thousands, with current email addresses, and key contacts – providing multiple ways to reach exactly who you need.

Section One: Resources

Includes 15 major chapters from **Associations** to **Green Product Catalogs,** and 68 subchapters that further organize the wealth of information in this directory by specific environmental issues from **Air & Climate** to **Water Resources**.

1. Associations & Organizations disseminate information, host seminars, provide educational literature and promote studies. These listings are defined by both national categories and state listings.

2. Awards & Honors list organizations that recognize education and business professionals for excellence in environmental sciences.

3. Conferences & Trade Shows include large conventions, as well as small, specialized conferences. The listings in this section include who, what, when, where and why.

4. Consultants offer information on environmental consulting services – ncluding hazardous material screening, construction requirements, and habitat conservation.

5. Environmental Health addresses health issues caused by the environment. These listings are divided into two sections of Associations – both general and those that focus on environmental issues affecting **Pediatric Health** – plus a third section on pediatric health publications.

6. Environmental Law offers resources that offer legal solutions and advocacy that are needed when environmental issues turn into legal ones.

7. Financial Resources include grants, foundations and scholarships that offer financing for educational programs, research and environmental clean-up programs.

8. Government Agencies & Programs list Federal and State agencies. This section ends with a separate by-state list of National Forests, Parks, and Refuges.

9. Publications include books and periodicals that focus on the environment as a business, course of study, subject of activism, and scientific research. In addition to individual publications, this section includes **Environmental Library Collections** and **Publishers**.

10. Research Centers helps those looking to research environmental issues. The centers listed here are divided into two categories – those that operate within universities, and those that are run by commercial corporations.

11. Educational Programs are divided into two sections – public and private educational institutions, and workshops and camps. These listings offer environmental educational experiences in a wide variety of specific topics for beginning students, professionals new to the work force, and seasoned environmentalists.

12. Industry Web Sites, Online Databases and **Videos** offer ways to connect electronically to environmental resources.

13. Green Product Catalogs lists the best companies for environmentally friendly products for home, office and everything in between, from tree-free paper to cruelty-free aromatherapy products.

Section Two: Statistics & Rankings

Hundreds of tables and charts in this section comprise dozens of main topics from **Agriculture** to **UV Index,** plus valuable **Green Metro Area Rankings.** This section includes the most current data available, as well as a variety of maps, graphs, and pie charts to make the information as accessible as possible.

> *"...Some charts document consumption and production back to the 1940s and will prove valuable to researchers seeking to identify broader trends."*
>
> ***Library Journal***

You will find a great number of state statistics and rankings, making it easy to compile environmental snapshots by state, as well as to compare individual states, counties, and regions of the country. This section is designed to show which communities are taking an active role in protecting our environment and preserving our natural resources. This section helps complete the picture for those doing research, conducting business, or providing education and consulting services. Specific material is listed in the Table of Contents.

Section Three: Appendices

- **Abbreviations & Acronyms**, provided by the Environmental Protection Agency, contains listings that identify and define the political and educational language of the industry.
- **Glossary of Terms**, also from the EPA, defines thousands of commonly used environmental terms in non-technical language.

Section Four: Indexes

- **Entry**: Lists all entries alphabetically, identified by record number.
- **Geographic**: Lists entries alphabetically by state.
- **Subject**: Facilitates search of resources and statistics by environmental categories.

In addition to this print directory, *The Environmental Resource Handbook* is available for subscription on G.O.L.D, Grey House OnLine Databases. This gives you immediate access to the most valuable US environmental contacts, plus offers easy-to-use keyword searches, organization type and subject searches, hotlinks to web sites and emails, and so much more. Call 800-562-2139 for a free trial of the new G.O.L.D OnLine Database, or visit http://gold.greyhouse.com for more information.

User Guide

Descriptive listings in *The Environmental Resource Handbook (ERH)* are organized into 15 chapters and 68 subchapters. You will find the following types of listings throughout the book:

- Associations & Organizations
- Conferences & Trade Shows
- Print & Electronic Media
- Foundations
- Government Agencies
- Research Centers
- Educational Programs
- Catalogs

Below is a sample listing illustrating the kind of information that is or might be included in an Association entry. Each numbered item of information is described in the paragraphs on the following page.

12345 **Water Environment Association of South Central US**
1762 South Major Drive
Suite 200
New Orleans, LA 98087

800-000-0000
058-884-0709
058-884-0568

info@wenvi.com
www.wenvi.com

Barbara Pierce, Executive Director
Diane Watkins, Marketing Director
Robert Goldfarb, Administrative Assistant
Ann Klein, Wastewater Consultant

The mission of the Association is to develop and disseminate information concerning waste quality management and the nature, collection, treatment, and disposal of wastewater. The Association publishes information, including a monthly magazine, manages a web site, and offers workshops and consultation on health and legal issues. A variety of educational programs are offered throughout the year on the history, ecology and culture of local rivers and streams, both on site, and in community schools.

Founded 1964

18 pages

Monthly

User Key

Record Number: Entries are listed alphabetically within each category and numbered, sequentially. Entry numbers, rather than page number, are used in the indexes to refer to listings.

Title: Formal name of company or association. Where association names are completely capitalized, the listing will appear at the beginning of the alphabetized section.

Address: Location or permanent address of the association.

Toll-Free Number: This is listed when provided by the association.

Phone Number: The listed phone number is usually for the main office of the association, but may also be for the sales, marketing, or public relations office as provided.

Fax Number: This is listed when provided by the association.

E-Mail: This is listed when provided, and is generally the main office e-mail.

Web Site: This is listed when provided.

Key Personnel: Names and titles of department heads of the association.

Association Description: This paragraph contains a brief description of the association and their services.

Year Founded: The year in which the association was established or founded. If there has been a name change, the founding date is usually for the earliest name under which it was known.

Number of Pages: Number of pages if the listing is a publication.

Frequency: How often it is published if it is a publication.

Annual Energy Outlook 2017

with projections to 2050

#AEO2017

January 5, 2017
www.eia.gov/aeo

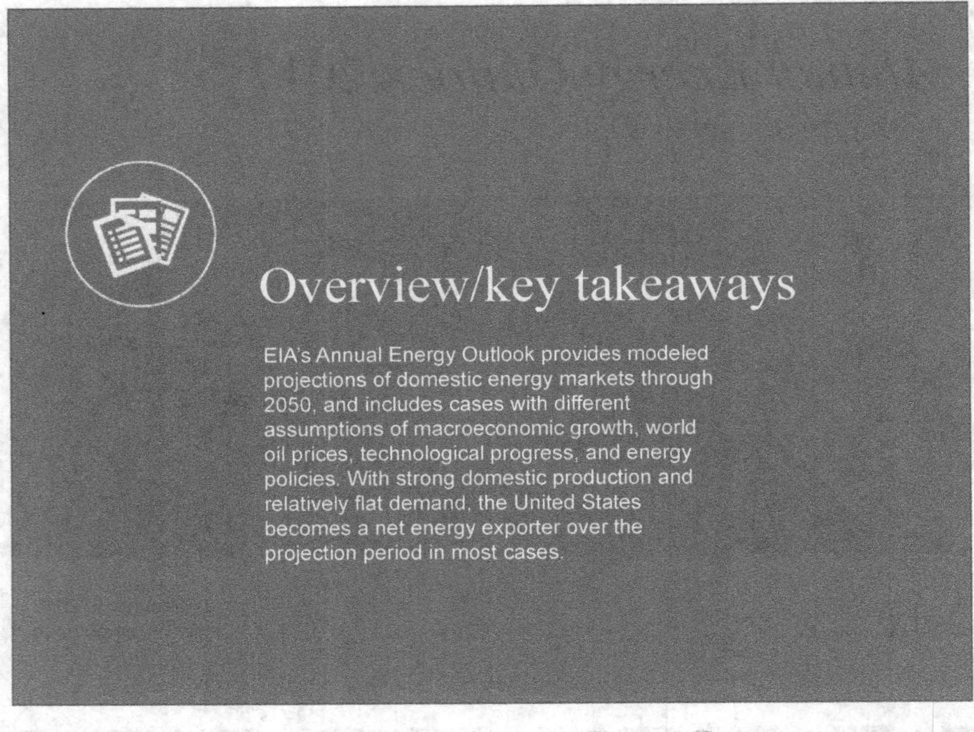

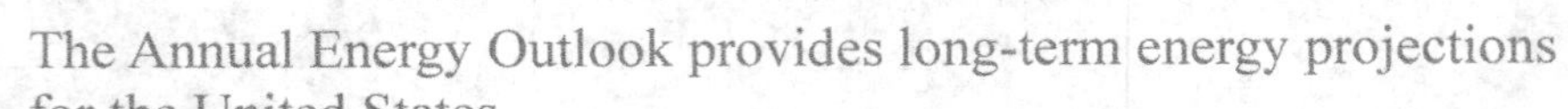

The Annual Energy Outlook provides long-term energy projections for the United States

- Projections in the *Annual Energy Outlook 2017* (AEO2017) are not predictions of what will happen, but rather modeled projections of what may happen given certain assumptions and methodologies.

- The AEO is developed using the National Energy Modeling System (NEMS), an integrated model that aims to capture various interactions of economic changes and energy supply, demand, and prices.

- Energy market projections are subject to much uncertainty, as many of the events that shape energy markets and future developments in technologies, demographics, and resources cannot be foreseen with certainty.

- More information about the assumptions used in developing these projections is available shortly after the release of each AEO.

- The AEO is published pursuant to the Department of Energy Organization Act of 1977, which requires the U.S. Energy Information Administration (EIA) Administrator to prepare annual reports on trends and projections for energy use and supply.

What is the Reference case?

- The Reference case projection assumes trend improvement in known technologies, along with a view of economic and demographic trends reflecting the current central views of leading economic forecasters and demographers.

- It generally assumes that current laws and regulations affecting the energy sector, including sunset dates for laws that have them, are unchanged throughout the projection period.

- The potential impacts of proposed legislation, regulations, or standards are not reflected in the Reference case.

- EIA addresses the uncertainty inherent in energy projections by developing side cases with different assumptions of macroeconomic growth, world oil prices, technological progress, and energy policies.

- Projections in the AEO should be interpreted with a clear understanding of the assumptions that inform them and the limitations inherent in any modeling effort.

U.S. Energy Information Administration #AEO2017 | www.eia.gov/aeo 5

What are the side cases?

- Oil prices are driven by global market balances that are mainly influenced by factors external to the NEMS model. In the High Oil Price case, the price of Brent crude in 2016 dollars reaches $226 per barrel (b) by 2040, compared to $109/b in the Reference case and $43/b in the Low Oil Price case.

- In the High Oil and Gas Resource and Technology case, lower costs and higher resource availability than in the Reference case allow for higher production at lower prices. In the Low Oil and Gas Resource and Technology case, more pessimistic assumptions about resources and costs are applied.

- The effects of economic assumptions on energy consumption are addressed in the High and Low Economic Growth cases, which assume compound annual growth rates for U.S. gross domestic product of 2.6% and 1.6%, respectively, from 2016–40, compared with 2.2% annual growth in the Reference case.

- A case assuming that the Clean Power Plan (CPP) is not implemented can be compared with the Reference case to show how the absence of that policy could affect energy markets and emissions.

U.S. Energy Information Administration #AEO2017 | www.eia.gov/aeo 6

Energy consumption varies minimally across all AEO cases—

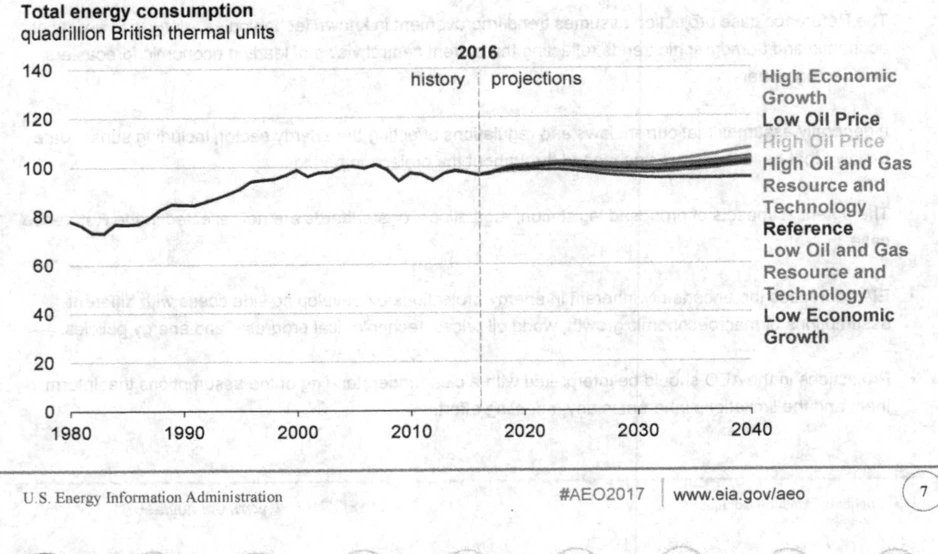

—bounded by the High and Low Economic Growth cases

- In the Reference case, total energy consumption increases by 5% between 2016 and 2040.
- Because a significant portion of energy consumption is related to economic activity, energy consumption is projected to increase by approximately 11% in the High Economic Growth case and to remain nearly flat in the Low Economic Growth case.
- Although the Oil and Gas Resource and Technology cases affect the production of energy, the impact on domestic energy consumption is less significant.
- In all AEO cases, the electric power sector remains the largest consumer of primary energy.
- Projections of total energy consumption (and supply) are sensitive to the conversions used to represent the primary energy content of noncombustible energy resources. AEO2017 uses fossil-equivalence to represent the energy content of renewable fuels.

Domestic energy consumption remains relatively flat in the Reference case—

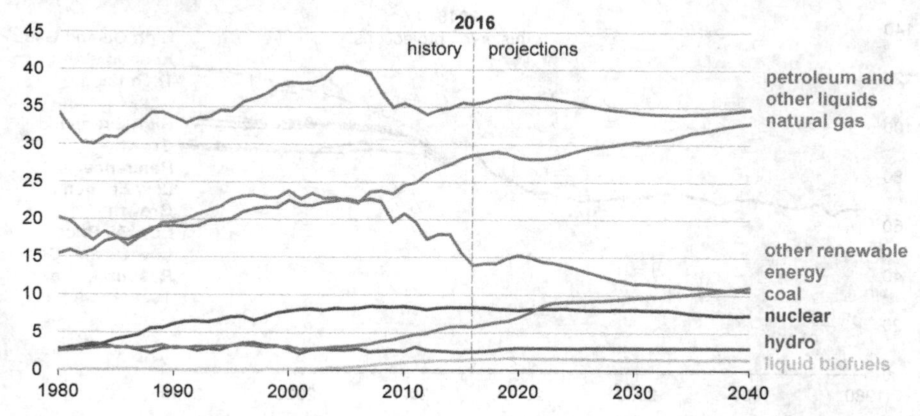

—but the fuel mix changes significantly

- Overall U.S. energy consumption remains relatively flat in the Reference case, rising 5% from the 2016 level by 2040 and somewhat close to its previous peak. Varying assumptions about economic growth rates or energy prices considered in the AEO2017 side cases affect projected consumption.
- Natural gas use increases more than other fuel sources in terms of quantity of energy consumed, led by demand from the industrial and electric power sectors.
- Petroleum consumption remains relatively flat as increases in energy efficiency offset growth in the transportation and industrial activity measures.
- Coal consumption decreases as coal loses market share to natural gas and renewable generation in the electric power sector.
- On a percentage basis, renewable energy grows the fastest because capital costs fall with increased penetration and because current state and federal policies encourage its use.
- Liquid biofuels growth is constrained by relatively flat transportation energy use and blending limitations.

Energy production ranges from nearly flat in the Low Oil and Gas Resource and Technology case—

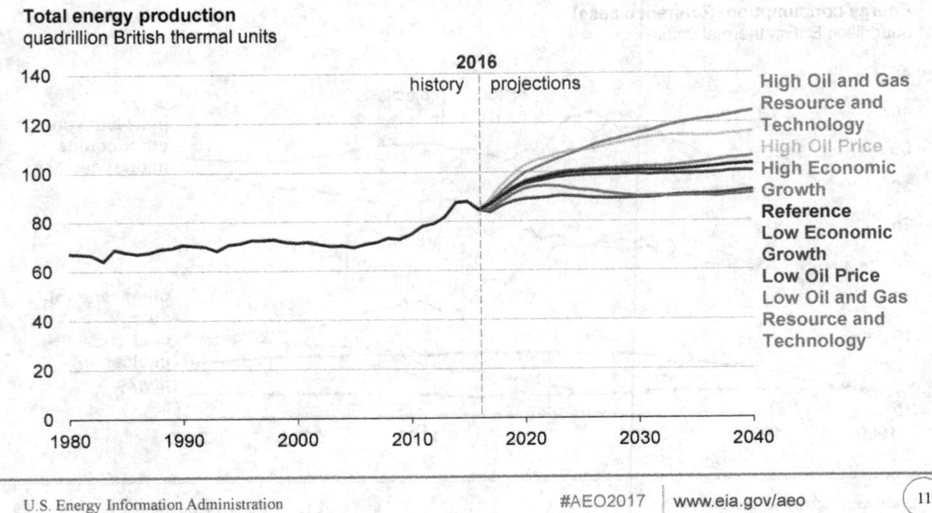

—to continued growth in the High Resource and Technology case

- Unlike energy consumption, which varies less across AEO2017 cases, projections of energy production vary widely.
- Total energy production increases by more than 20% from 2016 through 2040 in the Reference case, led by increases in renewables, natural gas, and crude oil production.
- Production growth is dependent on technology, resources, and market conditions.
- The High Oil and Gas Resource and Technology case assumes higher estimates of unproved Alaska resources; offshore Lower 48 resources; and onshore Lower 48 tight oil, tight gas, and shale gas resources than in the Reference case. This case also assumes lower costs of producing these resources. The Low Oil and Gas Resource and Technology case assumes the opposite.
- The High Oil Price case illustrates the impact of higher world demand for petroleum products, lower Organization of the Petroleum Exporting Countries (OPEC) upstream investment, and higher non-OPEC exploration and development costs. The Low Oil Price case assumes the opposite.

U.S. energy production continues to increase in the Reference case—

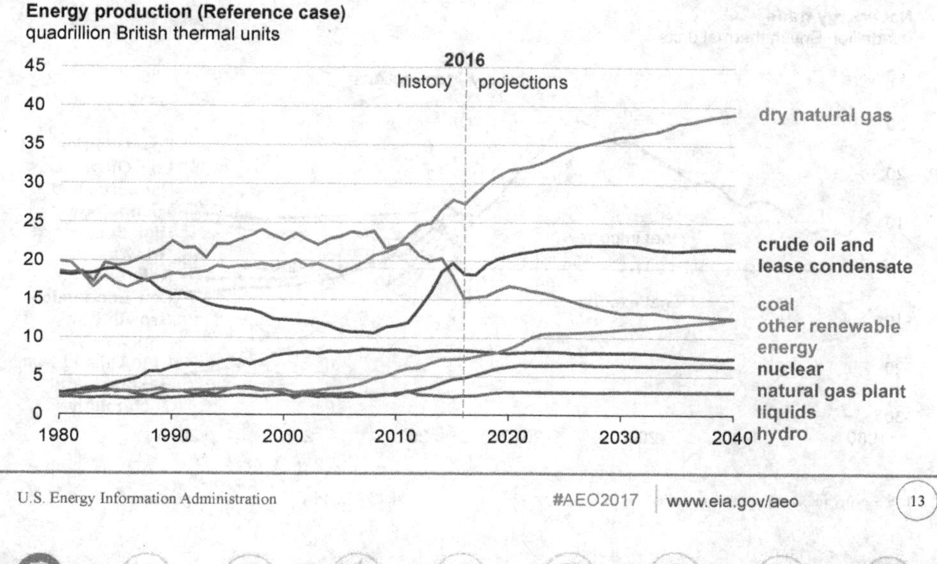

—led by growth in natural gas and renewables

- Natural gas production accounts for nearly 40% of U.S. energy production by 2040 in the Reference case. Varying assumptions about resources, technology, and prices in alternative cases significantly affect the projection for U.S. production.
- Crude oil production in the Reference case increases from current levels, then levels off around 2025 as tight oil development moves into less productive areas. Like natural gas, projected crude oil production varies considerably with assumptions about resources and technology.
- Coal production trends in the Reference case reflect the domestic regulatory environment, including the implementation of the Clean Power Plan, and export market constraints.
- Nonhydroelectric renewable energy production grows, reflecting cost reductions and existing policies at the federal and state level that promote the use of wind and solar energy.
- Nuclear generation declines modestly over 2017–40 in the Reference case as new builds already being developed and plant uprates nearly offset retirements. The decline in nuclear generation accelerates beyond 2040 as a significant share of existing plants is assumed to be retired at age 60.

The United States becomes a net energy exporter in most cases—

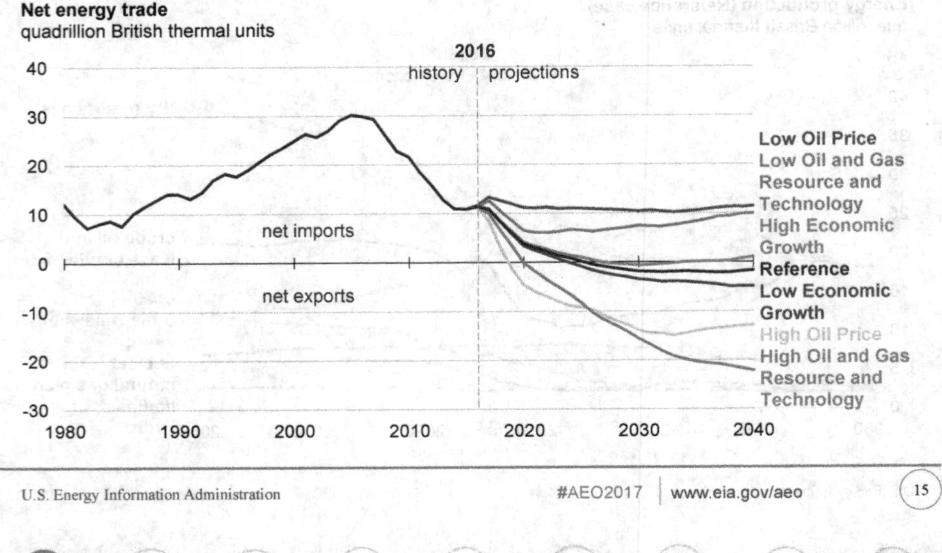

—and under high resource and technology assumptions, net exports are significantly higher than in the Reference case

- The United States is projected to become a net energy exporter by 2026 in the Reference case projections, but the transition occurs earlier in three of the AEO2017 side cases.
- Net exports are highest in the High Oil and Gas Resource and Technology case as favorable geology and technological developments combine to produce oil and natural gas at lower prices.
- The High Oil Price case includes favorable economic conditions for producers, but consumption is lower in response to higher prices. Without substantial improvements in technology and more favorable resource availability, U.S. energy production declines in the 2030s.
- In the Low Oil Price and Low Oil and Gas Resource and Technology cases, the United States remains a net importer over the analysis period.
- In the Low Oil and Gas Resource and Technology case, the conditions are unfavorable for U.S. crude oil production at levels that support exports.
- In the Low Oil Price case, prices are too low to provide a strong incentive for high U.S. production.

The United States becomes a net energy exporter in the Reference case—

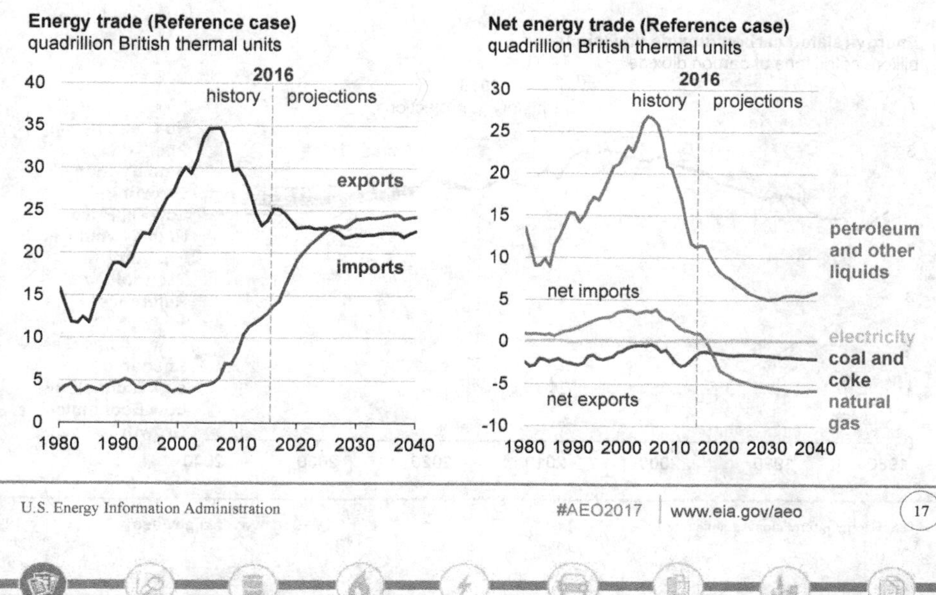

—as natural gas exports increase and net petroleum imports decrease

- The United States has been a net energy importer since 1953, but declining energy imports and growing energy exports make the United States a net energy exporter by 2026 in the Reference case projection.
- Crude oil and petroleum products dominate U.S. energy trade. The United States is both an importer and exporter of petroleum liquids, importing mostly crude oil and exporting mostly petroleum products such as gasoline and diesel throughout the Reference case projection.
- Natural gas trade, which has historically been mostly shipments by pipeline from Canada and to Mexico, is projected to be increasingly dominated by liquefied natural gas exports to more distant destinations.
- The United States continues to be a net exporter of coal (including coal coke), but its exports growth is not expected to increase significantly because of competition from other global suppliers closer to major markets.

Energy-related carbon dioxide emissions decline in most AEO cases—

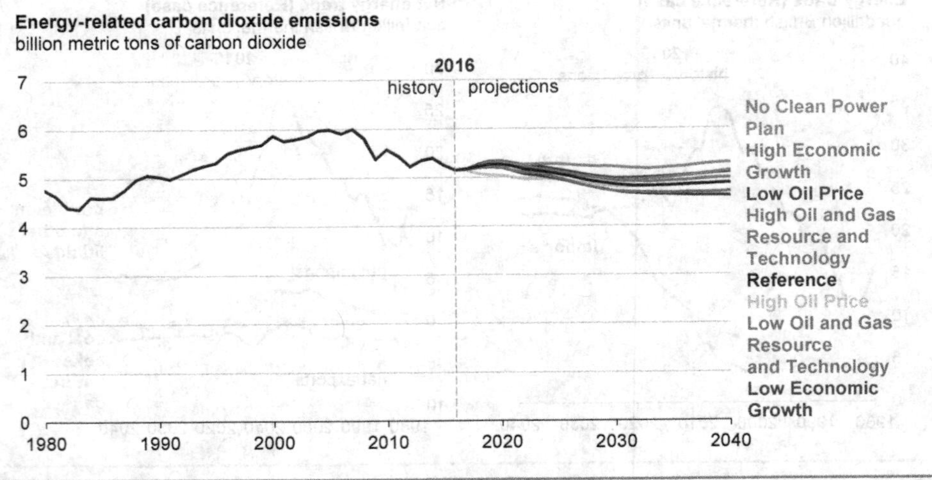

—with the highest emissions projected in the No Clean Power Plan case

- The electric power sector accounted for about 40% of the U.S. total energy-related carbon dioxide (CO2) emissions in 2011, with a declining share in recent years.
- The Clean Power Plan (CPP), which is currently stayed pending judicial review, requires states to develop plans to reduce CO2 emissions from existing generating units that use fossil fuels.
- Combined with lower natural gas prices and the extension of renewable tax credits, the CPP accelerates a shift toward less carbon-intensive electricity generation.
- The Reference case includes the CPP and assumes that states select the mass-based limits on CO2 emissions. An alternative case in AEO2017 assumes that the CPP is not implemented.
- AEO2016 included extensive analysis of the CPP and presented several side cases that examined various compliance options available to states.

Reference case energy-related carbon dioxide emissions fall—

U.S. energy-related carbon dioxide emissions (Reference case)

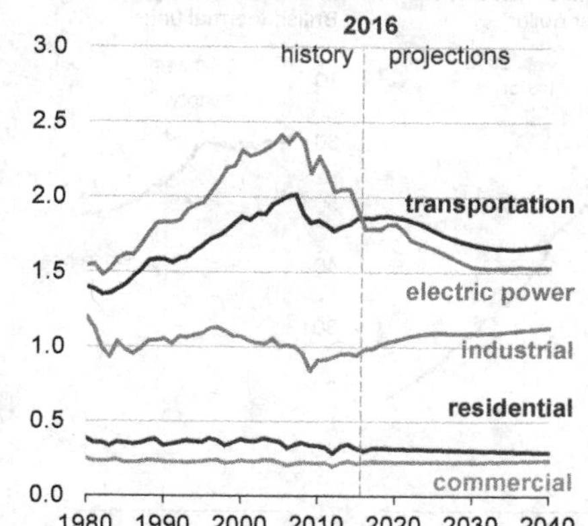

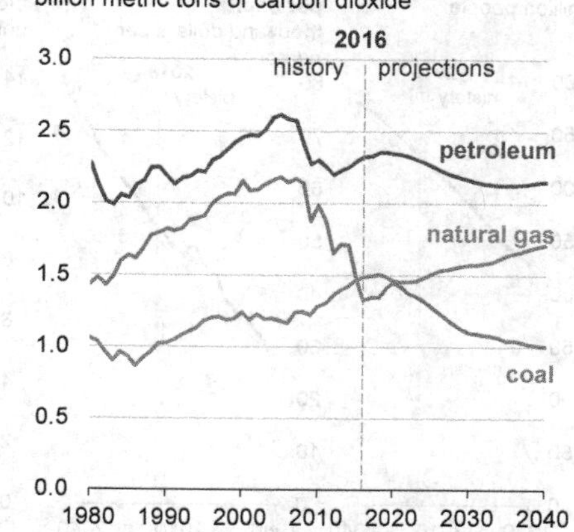

—but at a slower rate than in the recent past

- From 2005 to 2016, energy-related carbon dioxide (CO2) emissions fell at an average annual rate of 1.4%. From 2016 to 2040, energy-related CO2 emissions fall 0.2% annually in the Reference case.
- In the industrial sector, growth in domestic industries, such as bulk chemicals, leads to higher energy consumption and emissions.
- In the electric power sector, coal-fired plants are replaced primarily with new natural gas, solar, and wind capacity, which reduces electricity-related CO2 emissions.
- Direct emissions in the residential and commercial building sectors are largely from space heating, water heating, and cooking equipment. The CO2 emissions associated with the use of electricity in these sectors exceed the direct emissions from these sectors.
- Energy-related CO2 emissions from the transportation sector surpassed those from the electric power sector in 2016. Transportation CO2 emissions remain relatively flat after 2030 as consumption and the carbon intensity of transportation fuels stay relatively constant.

Although population and economic output per capita are assumed to continue rising—

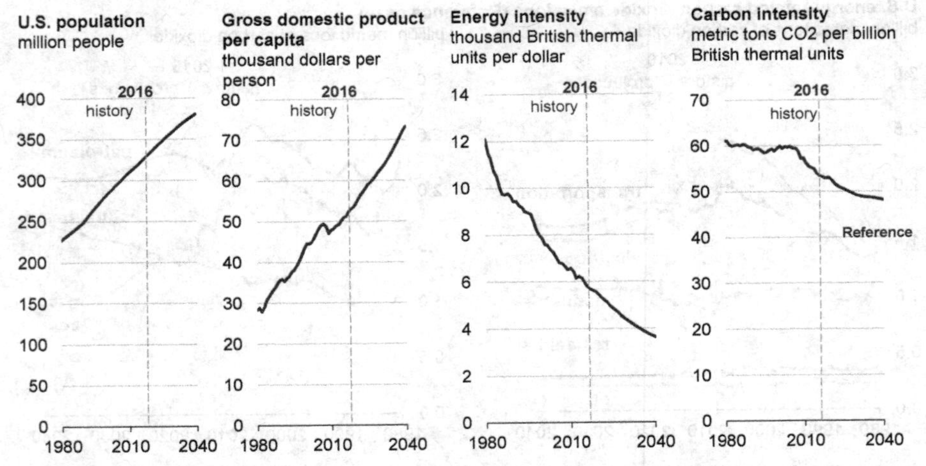

—energy intensity and carbon intensity are projected to continue falling in the Reference case

- In the United States, the amount of energy used per unit of economic growth (energy intensity) has declined steadily for many years, while the amount of CO2 emissions associated with energy consumption (carbon intensity) has generally declined since 2008.
- These trends are projected to continue as energy efficiency, fuel economy improvements, and structural changes in the economy all lower energy intensity.
- Carbon intensity declines largely as a result of changes in the U.S. energy mix that reduce the consumption of carbon-intensive fuels and increase the use of low- or no-carbon fuels.
- By 2040, energy intensity and carbon intensity are 37% and 10% lower than their respective 2016 values in the Reference case, which assumes only the laws and regulations currently in place.

Different macroeconomic assumptions address the energy implications of the uncertainty—

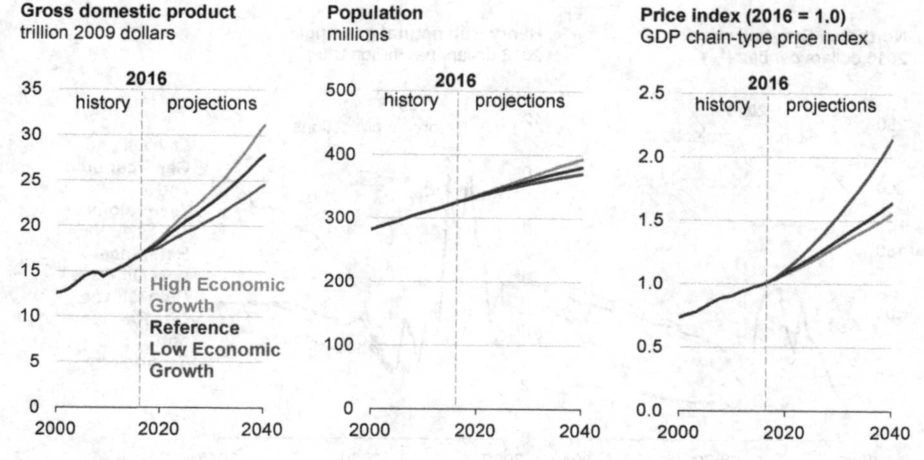

—surrounding future economic trends

- The Reference, High Economic Growth, and Low Economic Growth cases illustrate three possible paths for U.S. economic growth. The High Economic Growth case assumes higher annual growth and lower annual inflation rates (2.6% and 1.9%, respectively) than in the Reference case (2.2% and 2.1%, respectively), while the Low Economic Growth case assumes lower growth and higher inflation rates (1.6% and 3.2%, respectively).
- In general, higher economic growth (as measured by gross domestic product) leads to greater investment, increased consumption of goods and services, more trade, and greater energy consumption.
- Differences among the cases reflect different expectations for growth in population, labor force, capital stock, and productivity. These changes affect growth rates in household formation, industrial activity, and amounts of travel, as well as investment decisions for energy production.
- All three cases assume smooth economic growth and do not anticipate business cycles or large economic shocks.

Reference case oil prices rise from current levels while natural gas prices remain relatively low—

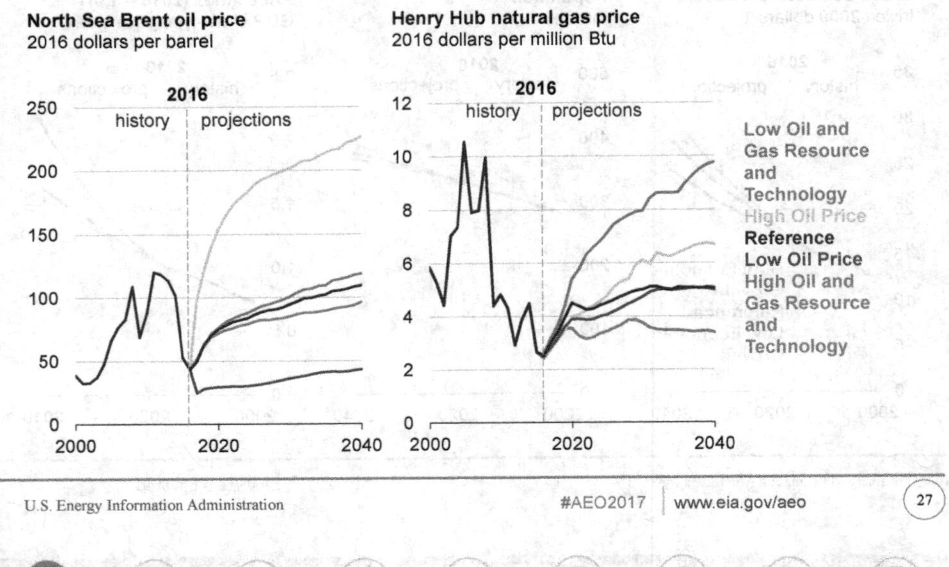

—price paths in the side cases are very different from those in the Reference case

- In real terms, crude oil prices in 2016 (based on the global benchmark North Sea Brent) were at their lowest levels since 2004, and natural gas prices (based on the domestic benchmark Henry Hub) were the lowest since prior to 1990. Both prices are projected to increase over the projection period.
- Crude oil prices in the Reference case are projected to rise at a faster rate in the near term than in the long term. However, price paths vary significantly across the AEO2017 side cases that differ in assumptions about U.S. resources and technology and global market conditions.
- Natural gas prices in the Reference case also rise and then remain relatively flat at about $5 per million British thermal units (MMBtu) over 2030–40, then rise again over the following decade (not shown on the graph). Projected U.S. natural gas prices are highly sensitive to assumptions about domestic resource and technology explored in the side cases.

United States crude oil and natural gas production depends on oil prices—

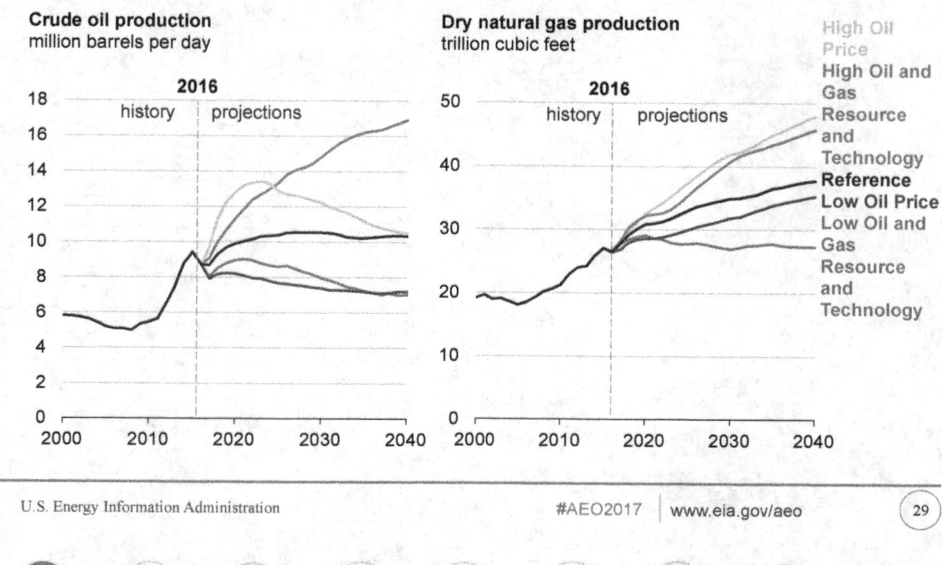

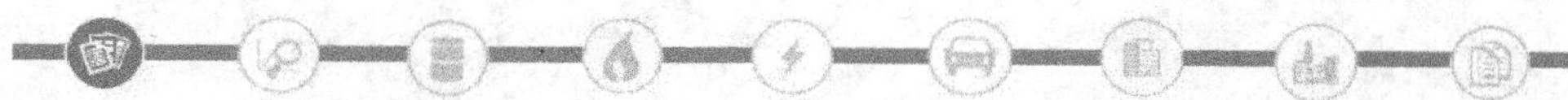

—as well as resource availability and technological improvements

- Projections of tight oil and shale gas production are uncertain because large portions of the known formations have relatively little or no production history, and extraction technologies and practices continue to evolve rapidly. Continued high rates of drilling technology improvement could increase well productivity and reduce drilling, completion, and production costs.
- In the High Oil and Gas Resource and Technology case, both crude oil and natural gas production continue to grow.
- Crude oil prices affect natural gas production primarily through changes in global natural gas consumption/exports, as well as increases in natural gas production from oil formations (associated gas).
- In the High Oil Price case, the difference between the crude oil and natural gas prices creates more incentive to consume natural gas in energy-intensive industries and for transportation, and to export it overseas as liquefied natural gas, all of which drive U.S. production upward. Without the more favorable resources and technological developments found in the High Oil and Gas Resource and Technology case, U.S. crude oil production begins to decline in the High Oil Price case, and by 2040, production is nearly the same as in the Reference case.

"Annual Energy Outlook 2017," U.S. Energy Information Administration. To read the full report please see: https://www.eia.gov/outlooks/aeo.

CLIMATE CHANGE

INDICATORS

IN THE UNITED STATES 2016

EPA United States Environmental Protection Agency

FOURTH EDITION

Introduction

The Earth's climate is changing. Temperatures are rising, snow and rainfall patterns are shifting, and more extreme climate events—like heavy rainstorms and record-high temperatures—are already taking place. Scientists are highly confident that many of these observed changes can be linked to the levels of carbon dioxide and other greenhouse gases in our atmosphere, which have increased because of human activities.

HOW IS THE CLIMATE CHANGING?

Since the Industrial Revolution began in the 1700s, people have added a significant amount of greenhouse gases into the atmosphere, largely by burning fossil fuels to generate electricity, heat and cool buildings, and power vehicles—as well as by clearing forests. The major greenhouse gases that people have added to the atmosphere are carbon dioxide, methane, nitrous oxide, and fluorinated gases. When these gases are emitted into the atmosphere, many remain there for long time periods, ranging from a decade to thousands of years. Past emissions affect our atmosphere in the present day; current and future emissions will continue to increase the levels of these gases in our atmosphere for the foreseeable future.

"Greenhouse gases" got their name because they trap heat (energy) like a greenhouse in the lower part of the atmosphere (see "The Greenhouse Effect" below). As more of these gases are added to the atmosphere, more heat is trapped. This extra heat leads to higher air temperatures near the Earth's surface, alters weather patterns, and raises the temperature of the oceans.

These observed changes affect people and the environment in important ways. For example, sea levels are rising, glaciers are melting, and plant and animal life cycles are changing. These types of changes can bring about fundamental disruptions in ecosystems, affecting plant and animal populations, communities, and biodiversity. Such changes can also affect people's health and quality of life, including where people can live, what kinds of crops are most viable, what kinds of businesses can thrive in certain areas, and the condition of buildings and infrastructure. Some of these changes may be beneficial to certain people and places, as indicators like **Length of Growing Season** point out. Over time, though, many more of these changes will have negative consequences for people and society.[1]

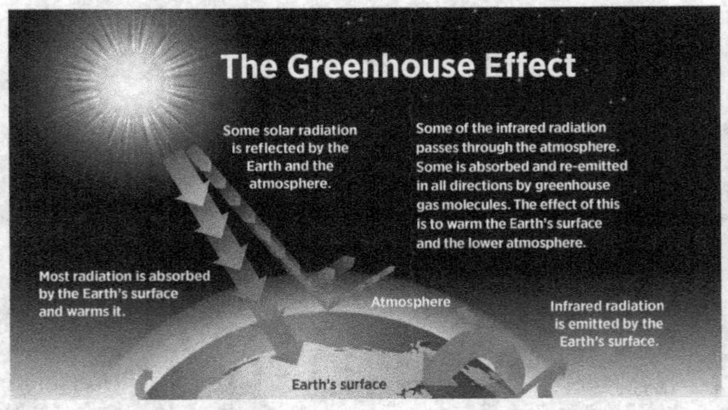
The Greenhouse Effect
Some solar radiation is reflected by the Earth and the atmosphere.
Some of the infrared radiation passes through the atmosphere. Some is absorbed and re-emitted in all directions by greenhouse gas molecules. The effect of this is to warm the Earth's surface and the lower atmosphere.
Most radiation is absorbed by the Earth's surface and warms it.
Atmosphere
Infrared radiation is emitted by the Earth's surface.
Earth's surface

What Is Climate Change?

Climate change refers to any substantial change in measures of climate (such as temperature or precipitation) lasting for an extended period (decades or longer). Natural factors have caused the climate to change during previous periods of the Earth's history, but human activities are the primary cause of the changes that are being observed now.

Global warming is a term often used interchangeably with the term "climate change," but they are not entirely the same thing. Global warming refers to an average increase in the temperature of the atmosphere near the Earth's surface. Global warming is just one aspect of global climate change, though a very important one.

Why Use Indicators?

One important way to track and communicate the causes and effects of climate change is through the use of indicators. An indicator represents the state or trend of certain environmental or societal conditions over a given area and a specified period of time. For example, long-term measurements of temperature in the United States and globally are used as an indicator to track and better understand the effects of changes in the Earth's climate.

How Do the Indicators Relate to Climate Change?

All of the indicators in this report relate to either the causes or effects of climate change. Some indicators show trends that can be more directly linked to human-induced climate change than others. Collectively, the trends depicted in these indicators provide important evidence of "what climate change looks like."

Understanding Greenhouse Gases

MAJOR GREENHOUSE GASES ASSOCIATED WITH HUMAN ACTIVITIES

The major greenhouse gases emitted into the atmosphere are carbon dioxide, methane, nitrous oxide, and fluorinated gases (see the table below). Some of these gases are produced almost entirely by human activities; others come from a combination of natural sources and human activities.

Many of the major greenhouse gases can remain in the atmosphere for tens to thousands of years after being released. They become globally mixed in the lower part of the atmosphere, called the troposphere (the first several miles above the Earth's surface), reflecting the combined contributions of emissions sources worldwide from the past and present. Due to this global mixing, the impact of emissions of these gases does not depend on where in the world they are emitted. Also, concentrations of these gases are similar regardless of where they are measured, as long as the measurement is far from any large sources or sinks of that gas.

Some other substances have much shorter atmospheric lifetimes (i.e., less than a year) but are still relevant to climate change. Important short-lived substances that affect the climate include water vapor, ozone in the troposphere, pollutants that lead to ozone formation, and aerosols (atmospheric particles) such as black carbon and sulfates. Water vapor, tropospheric ozone, and black carbon contribute to warming, while other aerosols produce a cooling effect. Because these substances are short-lived, their climate impact can be influenced by the location of their emissions, with concentrations varying greatly from place to place.

Gases and Substances Included in This Report

This report focuses on most of the major, well-mixed greenhouse gases that contribute to the vast majority of warming of the climate. It also includes certain substances with shorter atmospheric lifetimes (i.e., less than a year) that are relevant to climate change. In addition to several long-lived greenhouse gases, the online version of the **Atmospheric Concentrations of Greenhouse Gases** indicator tracks concentrations of ozone in the layers of the Earth's atmosphere, while Figure 2 of the **Climate Forcing** indicator on EPA's website shows the influence of a variety of short-lived substances.

Several factors determine how strongly a particular greenhouse gas affects the Earth's climate. One factor is the length of time that the gas remains in the atmosphere. A second factor is each gas's unique ability to absorb energy. By considering both of these factors, scientists calculate a gas's global warming potential, which measures how much a given amount of the greenhouse gas is estimated to contribute to global warming over a specific period of time (for example, 100 years) after being emitted. For purposes of comparison, global warming potential values are calculated in relation to carbon dioxide, which is assigned a global warming potential equal to 1. The table below describes sources, lifetimes, and global warming potentials for several important long-lived greenhouse gases.

Major Long-Lived Greenhouse Gases and Their Characteristics

Greenhouse gas	How it's produced	Average lifetime in the atmosphere	100-year global warming potential
Carbon dioxide	Emitted primarily through the burning of fossil fuels (oil, natural gas, and coal), solid waste, and trees and wood products. Changes in land use also play a role. Deforestation and soil degradation add carbon dioxide to the atmosphere, while forest regrowth takes it out of the atmosphere.	see below*	1
Methane	Emitted during the production and transport of oil and natural gas as well as coal. Methane emissions also result from livestock and agricultural practices and from the anaerobic decay of organic waste in municipal solid waste landfills.	12.4 years	28–36
Nitrous oxide	Emitted during agricultural and industrial activities, as well as during combustion of fossil fuels and solid waste.	121 years	265–298
Fluorinated gases	A group of gases that contain fluorine, including hydrofluorocarbons, perfluorocarbons, and sulfur hexafluoride, among other chemicals. These gases are emitted from a variety of industrial processes and commercial and household uses and do not occur naturally. Sometimes used as substitutes for ozone-depleting substances such as chlorofluorocarbons (CFCs).	A few weeks to thousands of years	Varies (the highest is sulfur hexafluoride at 23,500)

This table shows 100-year global warming potentials, which describe the effects that occur over a period of 100 years after a particular mass of a gas is emitted. Global warming potentials and lifetimes come from the Intergovernmental Panel on Climate Change's Fifth Assessment Report.[1]

* *Carbon dioxide's lifetime cannot be represented with a single value because the gas is not destroyed over time, but instead moves among different parts of the ocean–atmosphere–land system. Some of the excess carbon dioxide is absorbed quickly (for example, by the ocean surface), but some will remain in the atmosphere for thousands of years, due in part to the very slow process by which carbon is transferred to ocean sediments.*

Summary of Key Points

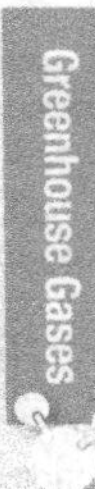

U.S. Greenhouse Gas Emissions. In the United States, greenhouse gas emissions caused by human activities increased by 7 percent from 1990 to 2014. Since 2005, however, total U.S. greenhouse gas emissions have decreased by 7 percent. Electricity generation is the largest source of greenhouse gas emissions in the United States, followed by transportation.

Global Greenhouse Gas Emissions. Worldwide, net emissions of greenhouse gases from human activities increased by 35 percent from 1990 to 2010. Emissions of carbon dioxide, which account for about three-fourths of total emissions, increased by 42 percent over this period.

Atmospheric Concentrations of Greenhouse Gases. Concentrations of carbon dioxide and other greenhouse gases in the atmosphere have increased since the beginning of the industrial era. Almost all of this increase is attributable to human activities.[1] Historical measurements show that the current global atmospheric concentrations of carbon dioxide are unprecedented compared with the past 800,000 years, even after accounting for natural fluctuations.

Climate Forcing. Climate forcing refers to a change in the Earth's energy balance, leading to either a warming or cooling effect over time. An increase in the atmospheric concentrations of greenhouse gases produces a positive climate forcing, or warming effect. From 1990 to 2015, the total warming effect from greenhouse gases added by humans to the Earth's atmosphere increased by 37 percent. The warming effect associated with carbon dioxide alone increased by 30 percent.

Weather & Climate

U.S. and Global Temperature. Average temperatures have risen across the contiguous 48 states since 1901. Average global temperatures show a similar trend, and all of the top 10 warmest years on record worldwide have occurred since 1998. Within the United States, temperatures in parts of the North, the West, and Alaska have increased the most.

High and Low Temperatures. Nationwide, unusually hot summer days (highs) have become more common over the last few decades. Unusually hot summer nights (lows) have become more common at an even faster rate. This trend indicates less "cooling off" at night. Although the United States has experienced many winters with unusually low temperatures, unusually cold winter temperatures have become less common—particularly very cold nights (lows).

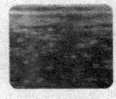

U.S. and Global Precipitation. Total annual precipitation has increased over land areas in the United States and worldwide. Since 1901, precipitation has increased at an average rate of 0.08 inches per decade over land areas worldwide. However, shifting weather patterns have caused certain areas, such as the Southwest, to experience less precipitation than usual.

Heavy Precipitation. In recent years, a higher percentage of precipitation in the United States has come in the form of intense single-day events. The prevalence of extreme single-day precipitation events remained fairly steady between 1910 and the 1980s but has risen substantially since then. Nationwide, nine of the top 10 years for extreme one-day precipitation events have occurred since 1990.

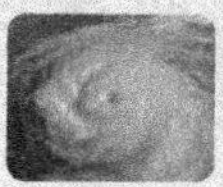

Tropical Cyclone Activity. Tropical storm activity in the Atlantic Ocean, the Caribbean, and the Gulf of Mexico has increased during the past 20 years. Storm intensity is closely related to variations in sea surface temperature in the tropical Atlantic. However, changes in observation methods over time make it difficult to know for sure whether a longer-term increase in storm activity has occurred.

River Flooding. Increases and decreases in the frequency and magnitude of river flood events vary by region. Floods have generally become larger across parts of the Northeast and Midwest and smaller in the West, southern Appalachia, and northern Michigan. Large floods have become more frequent across the Northeast, Pacific Northwest, and parts of the northern Great Plains, and less frequent in the Southwest and the Rockies.

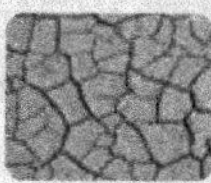

Drought. Over the period from 2000 through 2015, roughly 20 to 70 percent of the U.S. land area experienced conditions that were at least abnormally dry at any given time. However, this index has not been in use for long enough to compare with historical drought patterns.

A Closer Look: Temperature and Drought in the Southwest. The southwestern United States is particularly sensitive to changes in temperature and thus vulnerable to drought, as even a small decrease in water availability in this already arid region can stress natural systems and further threaten water supplies.

Oceans

Ocean Heat. Three independent analyses show that the amount of heat stored in the ocean has increased substantially since the 1950s. Ocean heat content not only determines sea surface temperature, but also affects sea level and currents.

Sea Surface Temperature. Ocean surface temperatures increased around the world during the 20th century. Even with some year-to-year variation, the overall increase is clear, and sea surface temperatures have been consistently higher during the past three decades than at any other time since reliable observations began in the late 1800s.

Sea Level. When averaged over all of the world's oceans, sea level has risen at a rate of roughly six-tenths of an inch per decade since 1880. The rate of increase has accelerated in recent years to more than an inch per decade. Changes in sea level relative to the land vary by region. Along the U.S. coastline, sea level has risen the most along the Mid-Atlantic coast and parts of the Gulf coast, where some stations registered increases of more than 8 inches between 1960 and 2015. Sea level has decreased relative to the land in parts of Alaska and the Pacific Northwest.

A Closer Look: Land Loss Along the Atlantic Coast. As sea level rises, dry land and wetlands can turn into open water. Along many parts of the Atlantic coast, this problem is made worse by low elevations and land that is already sinking. Between 1996 and 2011, the coastline from Florida to New York lost more land than it gained.

Coastal Flooding. Flooding is becoming more frequent along the U.S. coastline as sea level rises. Nearly every site measured has experienced an increase in coastal flooding since the 1950s. The rate is accelerating in many locations along the East and Gulf coasts. The Mid-Atlantic region suffers the highest number of coastal flood days and has also experienced the largest increases in flooding.

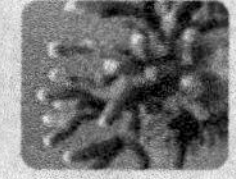

Ocean Acidity. The ocean has become more acidic over the past few decades because of increased levels of atmospheric carbon dioxide, which dissolves in the water. Higher acidity affects the balance of minerals in the water, which can make it more difficult for certain marine animals to build their protective skeletons or shells.

Snow & Ice

Arctic Sea Ice. Part of the Arctic Ocean is covered by ice year-round. The area covered by ice is typically smallest in September, after the summer melting season. The annual minimum extent of Arctic sea ice has decreased over time, and in September 2012 it was the smallest ever recorded. The length of the melt season for Arctic ice has grown, and the ice has also become thinner, which makes it more vulnerable to further melting.

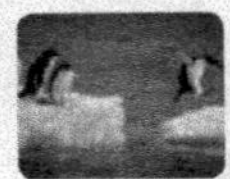

Antarctic Sea Ice. Antarctic sea ice extent in September and February has increased somewhat over time. The September maximum extent reached the highest level on record in 2014—about 7 percent larger than the 1981–2010 average. Slight increases in Antárctic sea ice are outweighed by the loss of sea ice in the Arctic during the same time period, however.

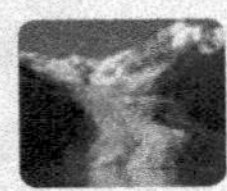

Glaciers. Glaciers in the United States and around the world have generally shrunk since the 1960s, and the rate at which glaciers are melting has accelerated over the last decade. The loss of ice from glaciers has contributed to the observed rise in sea level.

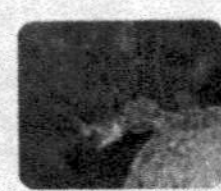

Lake Ice. Lakes in the northern United States are thawing earlier in spring compared with the early 1900s. All 14 lakes studied were found to be thawing earlier in the year, with thaw dates shifting earlier by up to 24 days over the past 110 years.

Community Connection: Ice Breakup in Two Alaskan Rivers. Regions in the far north are warming more quickly than other parts of the world. Two long-running contests on the Tanana and Yukon rivers in Alaska—where people guess the date when the river ice will break up in the spring—provide a century's worth of evidence revealing that the ice on these rivers is generally breaking up earlier in the spring than it once did.

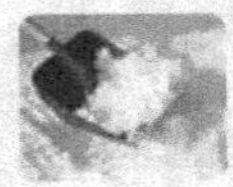

Snowfall. Total snowfall—the amount of snow that falls in a particular location—has decreased in most parts of the country since widespread records began in 1930. One reason for this decline is that nearly 80 percent of the locations studied have seen more winter precipitation fall in the form of rain instead of snow.

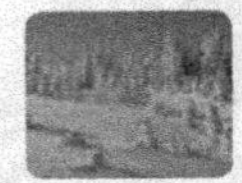

Snow Cover. Snow cover refers to the area of land that is covered by snow at any given time. Between 1972 and 2015, the average portion of North America covered by snow decreased at a rate of about 3,300 square miles per year, based on weekly measurements taken throughout the year. There has been much year-to-year variability, however. The length of time when snow covers the ground has become shorter by nearly two weeks since 1972, on average.

Snowpack. The depth of snow on the ground (snowpack) in early spring decreased at more than 90 percent of measurement sites in the western United States between 1955 and 2016. Across all sites, snowpack depth declined by an average of 23 percent during this time period.

Health & Society

Heat-Related Deaths. Since 1979, more than 9,000 Americans were reported to have died as a direct result of heat-related illnesses such as heat stroke. The annual death rate is higher when accounting for deaths in which heat was reported as a contributing factor, including the interaction of heat and cardiovascular disease. People aged 65+ are a particular concern: a growing demographic group that is several times more likely to die from heat-related cardiovascular disease than the general population. Considerable year-to-year variability and certain limitations of the underlying data for this indicator make it difficult to determine whether the United States has experienced long-term trends in the number of deaths classified as "heat-related."

Heat-Related Illnesses. From 2001 to 2010, a total of about 28,000 heat-related hospitalizations were recorded across 20 states. Annual heat-related hospitalization rates ranged from fewer than one case per 100,000 people in some states to nearly four cases per 100,000 in others. People aged 65+ accounted for more heat-related hospitalizations than any other age group from 2001 to 2010, and males were hospitalized for heat-related illnesses more than twice as often as females.

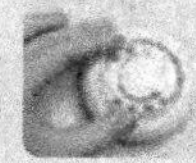

Heating and Cooling Degree Days. Heating and cooling degree days measure the difference between outdoor temperatures and the temperatures that people find comfortable indoors. As the U.S. climate has warmed in recent years, heating degree days have decreased and cooling degree days have increased overall, suggesting that Americans need to use less energy for heating and more energy for air conditioning.

Lyme Disease. Lyme disease is a bacterial illness spread by ticks that bite humans. Tick habitat and populations are influenced by many factors, including climate. Nationwide, the rate of reported cases of Lyme disease has approximately doubled since 1991. The number and distribution of reported cases of Lyme disease have increased in the Northeast and upper Midwest over time, driven by multiple factors.

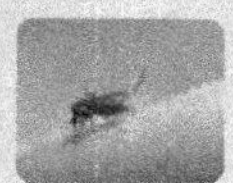

West Nile Virus. West Nile virus is spread by mosquitoes, whose habitat and populations are influenced by temperature and water availability. The incidence of West Nile virus neuroinvasive disease in the United States has varied widely from year to year and among geographic regions since tracking began in 2002. Variation in disease incidence is affected by climate and many other factors, and no obvious long-term trend can be detected yet through this limited data set.

Length of Growing Season. The length of the growing season for crops has increased in almost every state. States in the Southwest (e.g., Arizona and California) have seen the most dramatic increase. In contrast, the growing season has actually become shorter in a few southeastern states. The observed changes reflect earlier spring warming as well as later arrival of fall frosts.

Ragweed Pollen Season. Warmer temperatures and later fall frosts allow ragweed plants to produce pollen later into the year, potentially prolonging the allergy season for millions of people. The length of ragweed pollen season has increased at 10 out of 11 locations studied in the central United States and Canada since 1995. The change becomes more pronounced from south to north.

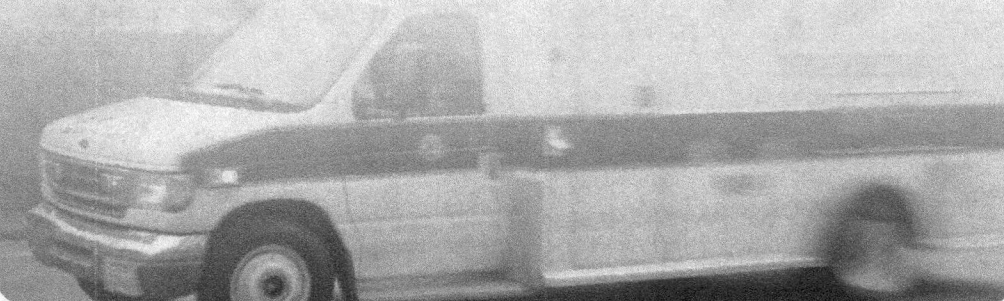

Ecosystems

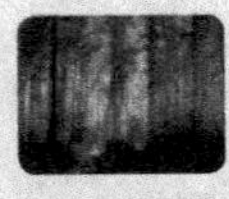

Wildfires. Of the 10 years with the largest acreage burned since 1983, nine have occurred since 2000. Fires burn more land in the western United States than in the East.

Streamflow. Changes in temperature, precipitation, snowpack, and glaciers can affect the rate of streamflow and the timing of peak flow. Over the last 75 years, minimum, maximum, and average flows have changed in many parts of the country—some higher, some lower. Most of the rivers and streams measured show peak winter-spring runoff happening at least five days earlier than it did in the mid-20th century.

Stream Temperature. Stream temperatures have risen throughout the Chesapeake Bay region—the area of focus for this indicator. From 1960 through 2014, water temperature increased at 79 percent of the stream sites measured in the region. Temperature has risen by an average of 1.2°F across all sites and 2.2°F at the sites where trends were statistically significant.

Tribal Connection: Water Temperature in the Snake River. Between 1960 and 2015, water temperatures increased by 1.4°F in the Snake River at a site in eastern Washington. Several species of salmon use the Snake River to migrate and spawn, and these salmon play an important role in the diet, culture, religion, and economy of the region's Native Americans.

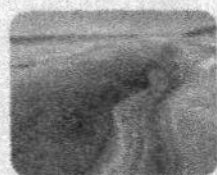

Great Lakes Water Levels. Water levels in most of the Great Lakes appear to have declined in the last few decades. However, the most recent levels are all within the range of historical variation. Water levels in lakes are influenced by water temperature, which affects evaporation rates and ice formation.

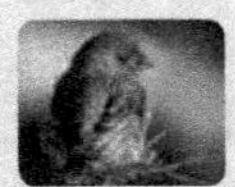

Bird Wintering Ranges. Some birds shift their range or alter their migration habits to adapt to changes in temperature or other environmental conditions. Long-term studies have found that bird species in North America have shifted their wintering grounds northward by an average of more than 40 miles since 1966, with several species shifting by hundreds of miles.

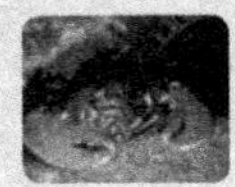

Marine Species Distribution. The average center of biomass for 105 marine fish and invertebrate species along U.S. coasts shifted northward by about 10 miles between 1982 and 2015. These species also moved an average of 20 feet deeper. Shifts have occurred among several economically important fish and shellfish species. For example, American lobster, black sea bass, and red hake in the Northeast have moved northward by an average of 119 miles.

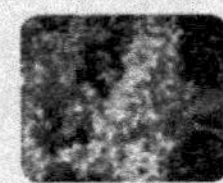

Leaf and Bloom Dates. Leaf growth and flower blooms are examples of natural events whose timing can be influenced by climate change. Observations of lilacs and honeysuckles in the contiguous 48 states suggest that first leaf dates and bloom dates show a great deal of year-to-year variability.

Community Connection: Cherry Blossom Bloom Dates in Washington, D.C. Peak bloom dates of the iconic cherry trees in Washington, D.C., recorded since the 1920s, indicate that cherry trees are blooming slightly earlier than in the past. Bloom dates are key to planning the Cherry Blossom Festival, one of the region's most popular spring attractions.

11

"Climate Change Indicators in the United States 2016," United States Environmental Protection Agency. To read the full report please see: https://www.epa.gov/climate-indicators/downloads-indicators-report.

Associations & Organizations

National: Air & Climate

1 **Air & Waste Management Association**
One Gateway Center, 3rd Floor
420 Fort Duquesne Blvd
Pittsburgh, PA 15222
412-904-6018
info@awma.org
www.awma.org
Professional development organization for environmental professionals.
Founded: 1907
Stephanie Glyptis, Executive Director

2 **American Clean Skies Foundation**
1875 Connecticut Ave NW
Suite 705
Washington, DC 20009
202-682-6294
Fax: 202-682-3050
www.cleanskies.org
Independent non-profit works for cleaner energy in the transportation and electric power sectors.
Founded: 2007
Gregory C. Staple, CEO

3 **American Meteorological Society**
45 Beacon St
Boston, MA 02108-3693
617-227-2425
Fax: 617-742-8718
amsinfo@ametsoc.org
www.ametsoc.org
Professional organization disseminates information about the atmospheric, oceanic and hydrologic sciences.
Founded: 1919 14,000 members
Roger Wakimoto, President-Elect

4 **Center for Clean Air Policy**
750 First St NE
Suite 1025
Washington, DC 20002
202-408-9260
Fax: 202-408-8896
ccap.org
Climate and air quality think tank.
Founded: 1985
Bill Tyndall, CEO
Leila Yim Surratt, COO

5 **Citizens' Climate Lobby**
1330 Orange Ave
Suite 309
Coronado, CA 92118
619-437-7142
citizensclimatelobby.org
Citizens' Climate Lobby is a non-profit, non-partisan, grassroots advocacy organization focused on national policies to address climate change.
Founded: 2007
Ross Astoria, Chairman
George Hetzel, Secretary & Treasurer

6 **Clean Air Council**
135 S 19th Street
Suite 300
Philadelphia, PA 19103
215-567-4004
Fax: 215-567-5791
cleanair.org
Protecting everyone's right to breathe clean air.
Founded: 1967
Joseph Minott, Executive Director

7 **Climate Institute**
1400 16th St NW
Suite 430
Washington, DC 20036
202-552-0163
info@climate.org
climate.org
The Climate Institue seeks to implement innovative and practical solutions to climate change by supporting and collaborating with private, nonprofit and government organizations.
Founded: 1986
John Topping, President
Nasir Khattak, Chief Operating Officer

8 **Conservation International**
2011 Crystal Dr
Suite 500
Arlington, VA 22202
703-341-2400
800-429-5660
www.conservation.org
CI promotes sustainable development and the conservation of earth's ecosystems as keys to solving climate change.
Peter Seligmann, Chair & CEO
Jennifer Morris, COO

9 **Environment America**
294 Washington Street
Suite 500
Boston, MA 02108
617-747-4449
environmentamerica.org
A nonprofit organization dedicated to educating the public on environmental issues through research reports, news conferences, interviews with reporters, op-ed pieces, letters to the editor and more; and to promote sensible solutions.
Margie Alt, Executive Director
Douglas Phelps, President

10 **Institute for Global Environmental Strategies**
3033 Wilson Blvd
Suite 700
Arlington, VA 22201
703-312-0823
Fax: 703-312-8657
info@strategies.org
www.strategies.org
Earth and space science educator.
Nancy Colleton, President

11 **Institute of Clean Air Companies (ICAC)**
3033 Wilson Boulevard
Suite 700
Arlington, VA 22201
571-858-3707
Fax: 703-243-8696
icacinfo@icac.com
www.icac.com
Organization of manufacturers of air pollution monitoring and control systems.
Founded: 1960
Michael Corvese, President
Stan Mack, Vice-President

12 **International Center for Arid and Semiarid Land Studies**
Texas Tech University
International Affairs
601 Indiana Ave
Lubbock, TX 79409-5004
806-742-3667
Fax: 806-742-1286
oia.reception@ttu.edu
www.ttu.edu/departments/icasals.php
Interdisciplinary study of arid and semiarid environments from international perspective.
Founded: 1966

13 **International Research Institute for Climate and Society**
61 Route 9W
Monell Building
Palisades, NY 10964-1000
845-680-4468
info@iri.columbia.edu
iri.columbia.edu
Conducts research to improve understanding of past, present and future climate.
Lisa Goddard, Director
Haresh Bhojwani, Deputy Director

14 **National Association of Clean Air Agencies**
444 N Capitol St NW 202-624-7864
Suite 307 Fax: 202-624-7863
Washington, DC 20001 4cleanair@4cleanair.org
www.4cleanair.org

National, non-partisan, non-profit association of air pollution control agencies.
S. William Becker, Executive Director
Nancy Kruger, Deputy Director

National: Business & Education

15 **ASTM International**
100 Barr Harbor Dr 610-832-9500
PO Box C700 Fax: 610-832-9555
West Conshohocken, PA 19428-2959 www.astm.org
One of the world's largest, and earliest, international standards developing organizations.
Founded: 1898 30K members
Katharine E. Morgan, President

16 **American Association of Zoo Keepers**
8476 E Speedway Blvd 520-298-9688
Suite 204 www.aazk.org
Tucson, AZ 85710-1728
Membership association for animal care professionals, fostering professional development and advancing animal care, animal welfare and conservation.

17 **American Chemical Society**
1155 16th St NW 614-447-3776
Washington, DC 20036 800-333-9511
service@acs.org
www.acs.org

Organization works for the advancement of chemists and the broader chemistry enterprise.
Thomas M. Connelly Jr., Executive Director & CEO

18 **American Chemistry Council**
700 Second St NE 202-249-7000
Washington, DC 20002 Fax: 202-249-6100
www.americanchemistry.com

Industry organization working to enable a more sustainable future.
Founded: 1872
Calvin M. Dooley, President & CEO

19 **American Federation of Teachers**
555 New Jersey Ave NW 202-879-4400
Washington, DC 20001 Fax: 202-879-4597
www.aft.org

Founded to represent the economic, social and professional interests of classroom teachers.
Founded: 1916 1.6 million members
Randi Weingarten, President
Lorretta Johnson, Secretary-Treasurer

20 **American Forest & Paper Association**
1101 K Street NW 202-463-2700
Suite 700 800-878-8878
Washington, DC 20005 info@afandpa.org
www.afandpa.org

The national trade association of the forest, paper, and wood products industry and advances public policies that promote a strong and sustainable US forest products industry in the global marketplace.
Founded: 1993
Donna Harman, President & CEO
Samuel Kerns, VP, Administration & CFO

21 **American National Standards Institute**
1899 L Street NW 202-293-8020
11th Floor Fax: 202-293-9287
Washington, DC 20036 info@ansi.org
www.ansi.org

The Institute's mission is to enhance both the global competitivness of US business and the US quality of life by promoting and facilitating voluntary consensus standards and conformity assessment systems, and safeguarding theirintegrity.
Founded: 1918 3.5 million members
Joe Bhatia, President & CEO

22 **American Public Works Association**
1200 Main St 816-472-6100
Suite 1400 800-848-2792
Kansas City, MO 64105-2100 Fax: 816-472-1610
www.apwa.net

An international educational and professional association of public agencies, private sector companies, and individuals dedicated to providing high quality public works goods and services.
Founded: 1937
Scott Grayson, Executive Director

23 **Association for Educational Communications and Technology**
320 W 8th Street 812-335-7675
Suite 101 877-677-2328
Bloomington, IN 47404-3745 aect@aect.org
aect.site-ym.com

Professional association of educators seeking to improve instruction through technology.
Dr. Phillip Harris, Executive Director

24 **Association of American Geographers**
1710 16th Street NW 202-234-1450
Washington, DC 20009-3198 Fax: 202-234-2744
gaia@aag.org
www.aag.org

Nonprofit, educational society advancing the theory, methods and practice of geography.
Founded: 1904
Douglas Richardson, Executive Director

25 **Association of Environmental and Resource Economists (AERE)**
1616 P Street NW 202-328-5125
Suite 600 Fax: 202-939-3460
Washington, DC 20036 voigt@rff.org
www.aere.org

Offers a way to exhange ideas, stimulate research, and promote graduate training in resource and environmental economics. Members come from academic institutions, the public sector, and private industry.
Founded: 1979 Over 1000 members
Dr. Laura O. Taylor, President
Dr. Andrew Plantinga, Vice President

26 **Association of State Wetland Managers (ASWM)**
32 Tandberg Trail 207-892-3399
Suite 2A Fax: 207-894-7992
Windham, ME 04062 jeanne.christie@aswm.org
www.aswm.org

Nonprofit organization dedicated to the protection and restoration of the nation's wetlands. ASWM's goal is to help public and private wetland decision-makers utilize the best possible scientific information and techniques in wetlanddelineation, assessment, mapping, planning, regulation, acquisition, restoration and other management.
Founded: 1983
Jeanne Christie, Executive Director
Jon Kusler, Associate Director

27 **Association of Zoos and Aquariums (AZA)**
8403 Colesville Road
Suite 710
Silver Spring, MD 20910-3314
301-562-0777
Fax: 301-562-0888
membership@aza.org
www.aza.org

Nonprofit organization dedicated to the advancement of accredited zoos and aquariums in the areas of animal care, wildlife conservation, education and science.
Founded: 1924
Dan Ashe, President/CEO
Kris Vehrs, J.D., Executive Director

28 **Bank Information Center**
1023 15th Street NW
10th floor
Washington, DC 20005
202-737-7752
Fax: 202-737-1155
www.bankinformationcenter.org

The Bank Information Center partners with civil society to help countries influence the World Bank and other international financial institutions to promote social and economic justice and ecological sustainability.
David Hunter, Chairman
Amy Shannon, Vice-chair

29 **Biotechnology Industry Organization (BIO)**
1201 Maryland Avenue NW
Suite 900
Washington, DC 20024
202-962-9200
Fax: 202-488-6301
info@bio.org
www.bio.org

The mission of BIO is to be the champion of biotechnology and the advocate for its member organizations-both large and small.
Founded: 1993
James C Greenwood, President/CEO
Gary Andres, EVP, Public Affairs

30 **Bureau of Land Management (BLM)**
Environmental Education Program
1849 C Street NW
Rm. 5665
Washington, DC 20240
202-208-3801
Fax: 202-208-5242
director@blm.gov
www.blm.gov

Provides public education about public lands resources and management issues. Identifies educational needs and resource gaps and collaborates with partner groups, volunteers, schools, and other agencies. This group also makes productsand programs available to BLM field offices, communities and schools.
Michael D. Nedd, Director
John Ruhs, Deputy Director, Operations

31 **Business for Social Responsibility (BSR)**
5 Union Square W
6th Floor
New York, NY 10003
212-370-7707
Fax: 646-758-8150
connect@bsr.org
www.bsr.org

Works with its global network of more than 250 member companies to develop sustainable business strategies and solutions through consulting, research and cross-sector collaboration.
Founded: 1992
Aron Cramer, President/CEO
Laura Gitman, Sr. Vice-President

32 **CERES (Coalition for Environmentally Responsible Economies)**
99 Chauncy Street
6th Floor
Boston, MA 02111
617-247-0700
info@ceres.org
www.ceres.org

A national network of investors, environmental organizations and other public interest groups working with companies and investors to address sustainability challenges such as global climate change.
Founded: 1989
Anne Stausboll, Chair

33 **CO2 Science**
PO Box 25697
Tempe, AZ 85285-5697
480-966-3719
center@co2science.org
www.co2science.org

Reviews articles, books and other educational materials, attempting to separate reality from rhetoric in the debate that surrounding the subject of carbon dioxide and global change. The Center maintains on-line intructions on how toconduct CO2 enrichment and depletion experiments in its Global Change Laboratory.
Craig D. Idso, Chairman/Founder
Sherwood D. Idso, President

34 **Center for Environmental Philosophy**
University of North Texas
1704 W Mulberry
Suite 370
Denton, TX 76201
940-565-2727
Fax: 940-565-4439
cep@unt.edu.
www.cep.unt.edu

Conducts environmental research and offers environmental education as is relates to decisions made when dealing with environmental issues.
Eugene C. Hargrove, President
J. Baird Callicott, Vice-President

35 **Center for Policy Alternatives**
1875 Connecticut Avenue NW
Suite 710
Washington, DC 20009
202-387-6030
Fax: 202-387-8529
info@cfpa.org
www.stateaction.org

The nation's leading nonpartisan progressive public policy and leadership development center serving state legislators, state policy organizations, and state grassroots leaders. CPA is a 501 (c)(3) nonprofit corporation with thesethree unique programs: Leadership Development; Policy Tools; and Network Building.
Founded: 1976
Nan Grogan-Orrock, Co-Chair
Tim McFeeley, Executive Director

36 **Chelonian Research Institute**
402 South Central Avenue
Oviedo, FL 32765
407-365-6347
Fax: 407-977-5142
chelonianri@gmail.com
chelonianri.org

Dedicated to the study and conservation of turtles and tortoises worldwide. One of the world's leading institutions on the research and conversation of turtles. The 10-acre campus includes offices, a library and a museum to be enjoyedby reseachers, students and dignitaries, as well as the public.
Founded: 1997
Dr. Peter C.H. Pritchard, Founder
Rob Truland, Chairman

37 **Chemical Producers and Distributors Association**
1730 Rhode Island Ave NW
Suite 812
Washington, DC 20036
202-386-7407
Fax: 202-386-7409
www.claraweb.us

The preeminent US based trade association representing the interests of generic pesticide registrants, with a membership that includes manufacturers, formulators, and distributors of pesticide products. Membership also includesmanufacturers and suppliers of inert ingredients used to enhance the delivery and efficacy of pesticide products.
Dr Susan Ferenc, President
Diane Schute, Communications/Programs Dir

38 **Chlorine Institute**
1300 Wilson Boulevard
Suite 525
Arlington, VA 22209
703-894-4140
Fax: 703-894-4130
info@cl2.com
www.chlorineinstitute.org

Exists to support the chlor-alkali industry and serve the public by fostering continuous improvements to safety and the protection of human health and the environment connected with the produc-

tion, distribution and use of chlorine,sodium and potassium hydroxides, and sodium hypochlorite; and the distribution and use of hydrogen chloride.
Founded: 1924 220 Members
Frank Reiner, President
Robyn Kinsley, VP, Transportation

39 **Consumer Specialty Products Association (CSPA)**
1667 K Street NW 202-872-8110
Suite 300 Fax: 202-223-2636
Washington, DC 20006 info@cspa.org
www.cspa.org
To foster high standards for the industry; concern for the health, safety and environmental impacts of its products; address legislative and regulatory challenges at the federal, state and local level; meet the needs of industry fortechnical and legal guidance; provide a forum to share ideas for scientific and marketing excellence.
Founded: 1914
Stephen J. Caldeira, President/CEO
Rick Peluso, Sr. VP/CFO

40 **Corps Network**
1275 K Street NW 202-737-6272
Suite 1050 Fax: 202-737-6277
Washington, DC 20005 msprenkel@corpsnetwork.org
www.nascc.org
A proud advocate and representative of the nation's Service and Conservation Corps. The number one goal is to sustain and grow the Corps movement. The Corps Network's member Service and Conservation Corps operate in 42 state and theDistrict of Columbia. Over 26,000 Corps members, ages 16-25, contribute and generate more than 16 million hours of service annually.
Founded: 1985
Joel D. Holdrop, Chairman
Mickey Fearn, Vice Chairman

41 **Council of State Governments (CSG)**
1776 Avenue of the States 859-244-8000
Lexington, KY 40511 Fax: 859-244-8001
www.csg.org
A region-based forum that fosters the exchange of insights and ideas to help state officials shape public policy. CSG serves the executive, judicial and legislative branches of state government through leadership education, researchand information services.
Founded: 1933
David Akins, Executive Director/CEO
Gov. Kate Brown, President

42 **Earth First!**
PO Box 964 561-320-3840
Lake Worth, FL 33460 collective@earthfirstjournal.org
earthfirstjournal.org
Earth First! was first created in response to a compromising and increasingly corporate environmental community. Earth First! publish Earth First! Journal. Earth First! Journal highlights radical environmental movements and causes. Earth First! pride themselves on being a grassroots organization fighting to save lives and the evironment.
Founded: 1979

43 **EarthShare**
7735 Old Georgetown Road 240-333-0300
Suite 900 800-875-3863
Bethesda, MD 20814 Fax: 240-333-0301
info@earthshare.org
www.earthshare.org
Mission is to engage individuals and organization in creating a healthy and sustainable environment.
Founded: 1988
Meri-Margaret Deoudes, President/CEO
Mary MacDonald, Sr. VP

44 **Ecological Society of America**
1990 M Street NW 202-833-8773
Suite 700 Fax: 202-833-8775
Washington, DC 20036 esahq@esa.org
www.esa.org
To promote ecological science by improving communication among ecologists; raise the public's level of awareness of the importance of ecological science; increase the resources available for the conduct of ecological science.
Founded: 1915
David Lodge, President
Rich Pouyat, President-Elect

45 **Environmental Council of the States**
50 F Street NW 202-266-4920
Suite 350 Fax: 202-266-4937
Washington, DC 20001 ecos@ecos.org
www.ecos.org
National non profit and non partisan association of state and territorial environmental agency leaders. Its purpose is to improve the capability of state environmental agencies and their leaders to proteect and improve humanhealth andthe environment of the United States of America.
Founded: 1993
Alexandra Dapolito Dunn, Executive Director/GC
Carolyn Hanson, Deputy Director

46 **Environmental Industry Associations**
4301 Connecticut Avenue NW 202-244-4700
Suite 300 800-424-2869
Washington, DC 20008 Fax: 202-966-4824
info@wasterecycling.org
wasterecycling.org
The Environmental Industry Associations (EIA) is the parent organization for the National Solid Waste Management Association and the Waste Equipment Technology Association. Through these two associations, EIA represents companies andindividuals who manage solid and medical wastes; manufacture and distribute waste equipment; and to provide environmental managment, consulting and pollution-prevention-related services.
Sharon H. Kneiss, President and CEO
Sheila R. Alkire, Director, Education

47 **Environmental Media Association (EMA)**
8909 W Olympic Boulevard 323-556-2790
Suite 200 Fax: 877-849-4891
Beverly Hills, CA 90211 ema@ema-online.org
www.green4ema.org
Dedicated to the broadcast of balanced news about the environment. Through celebrity role modeling, campaign work, year-round programs and annual events EMA looks to promote environmental progress and innovation.
Founded: 1989
Debbie Levin, President
Asher Levin, Executive Director

48 **Executive Office of Energy and Environmental Affairs**
Environmental Education
100 Cambidge Street 617-626-1000
Suite 900 Fax: 617-626-1181
Boston, MA 02114 env.internet@state.ma.us
www.mass.gov/eea
A resource for environmental literacy, whose goal is to reconnect people to the natural world, and to inspire a sense of public responsibility.
Kate McKeever, General Counsel
Peter Lorenz, Director of Communications

49 **Federal Wildlife Officer's Association**
1501 India Street 949-355-6449
Suite 103-93 sobesurf@gmail.com
San Diego, CA 92102 www.fwoa.net

Dedicated to the protection of wildlife, the enforcement of federal wildlife law, the fostering of cooperation and communication among federal wildlife officers, and the perpetuation, enhancement and defense of the wildlife enforcementprofession.
$40/Year
Dave Hubbard, President
Roger Turnell, Jr., Secretary

50 Federation of Environmental Technologists (FET)
W175 N11081 Stonewood Drive 262-437-1700
Suite 203 Fax: 262-437-1702
Germantown, WI 53022 info@fetinc.org
www.fetinc.org
A nonprofit organization formed to assist industry in interpretation of and compliance with environmental regulations. FET is dedicated to educate its members and other environmental professionals on regulatory compliance andtechnological developments in a cost-effective manner through training, professional development and networking.
Founded: 1982 600-700 Members
Jeffrey Nettesheim, Board Chair/Director
Cheryl Moran, President/Director

51 Florida Center for Environmental Studies
3200 College Avenue 954-236-1104
Building DW, Rm. 311 cpolsky@fau.edu
Davie, FL 33458 www.ces.fau.edu
Represents the ten state universities and the major private universities in regard to environmental studies and research.
Founded: 1995
Dr. Colin Polsky, Director
Dr. John D. Baldwin, Associate Director

52 Forestry Conservation Communications Association (FCAA)
424 E. Middle Street 717-398-0815
Rear Unit 844-458-0298
Gettysburg, PA 17325 Fax: 717-778-4237
lloyd.mitchell@fcca-usa.org
www.fcca-usa.org
The FCCA is a national organization. Its main function is to assist federal, state and local governments in public safety two-way radio operations by locating suitable frequencies within specified operating areas, recommending theirassignment to the FCC for licensing, and protecting them once licensed.
Lloyd M. Mitchell, President
Roy Mott, Vice-President

53 Get America Working!
1700 N Moore Street
Arlington, VA 22209 info@getamericaworking.org
A nonprofit national organization whose mission is to create 70 million jobs through structural changes in the US economy.

54 Global Environmental Management Initiative (GEMI)
1156 15th Street NW 202-296-7449
Suite 800 info@gemi.org
Washington, DC 20005 www.gemi.org
Business helping business improve EHS performance, shareholder value and corporate citizenship.
Founded: 1990
Bill Gill, Chairman
Dan Daggett, Vice-Chairman

55 Green America
1612 K Street NW
Suite 600 800-584-7336
Washington, DC 20006 Fax: 202-331-8166
info@greenamerica.org
www.greenamerica.org
Formerly known as Co-op America, whose mission is to harness economic power-the strength of consumers, investors, businesses, and the marketplace-to create a socially just and environmentally sustainable society.
Founded: 1982
Alisa Gravitz, President/CEO
Davina Ewtaroo, Executive Assistant

56 Green Seal
1001 Connecticut Avenue NW 202-872-6400
Suite 827 Fax: 202-872-4324
Washington, DC 20036-5525 greenseal@greenseal.org
www.greenseal.org
An independent nonprofit organization dedicated to safeguearding the environment and transforming the marketplace by promoting the manufacture, purchase, and use of environmentally responsible products and services.
Founded: 1989
Joanne Fox-Przeworski, Ph.D., Chairman
Paul Bateman, Treasurer

57 Greenpeace USA
702 H Street NW 202-462-1177
Suite 300 800-722-6995
Washington, DC 20001 Fax: 202-462-4507
info@wdc.greenpeace.org
www.greenpeace.org
Greenpeace is the leading independent campaigning organization that uses non-violent direct action and creative communication to expose global environmental problems and to promote solutions that are essential to a green and peacefulfuture.
Founded: 1971
Annie Leonard, Executive Director
Nathan Santry, Actions Director

58 H. John Heinz III Center for Science, Economics and the Environment
900 17th Street NW 202-737-6307
Suite 700 Fax: 202-737-6410
Washington, DC 20006 info@heinzctr.org
www.heinzctr.org
The Center is a nonpartisan, nonprofit institute dedicated to improving the scientific and economic foundation for environmental policy through nmultisectoral collaboration. The Heinz Center fosters collaboration among industry,environmental organizations, academia, and all levels of government in each of its program areas.
Founded: 1995
Conn Nugent, President
Matthew Grason, Fundraising Coordinator

59 Halogenated Solvents Industry Alliance, Inc. (HSIA)
3033 Wilson Boulevard 703-875-0683
Suite 700 info@hsia.org
Arlington, VA 22201 www.hsia.org
The mission is to represent the users and producers of chlorinated solvents - trichloroethylene, perchloroethylene and methylene chloride. To promote the continued safe use of these products and the use of sound science in assessingtheir potential health effects.
Founded: 1980
Faye Graul, Executive Director

60 Honor the Earth
607 Main Avenue 218-375-3200
PO Box 63 info@honorearth.org
Callaway, MN 56521 www.honorearth.org
Honor the Earth is a Native-led organization, addressing the two primary needs of the Native environmental movement: the need to break the geographic and political isolation of Native commu-

nities and the need to increase financialresources for organizing and change.
Founded: 1993
Winona LaDuke, Founder
Amy Ray, Founder

61 **Institute for Earth Education**
Cedar Cove 304-832-6404
Greenville, WV 24945 Fax: 304-832-6077
info@ieetree.org
www.eartheducation.org
The Institute for Earth Education is the world's alternative agency-and industry-sponsored supplemental environmental education. IEE develops and disseminates instructional programs aimed at helping people live more lightly,harmoniously, and joyously with the natural world.
Founded: 1974

62 **Institute of Clean Air Companies (ICAC)**
3033 Wilson Boulevard 571-858-3707
Suite 700 Fax: 703-243-8696
Arlington, VA 22201 icacinfo@icac.com
www.icac.com
Organization of manufacturers of aor pollution monitoring and control systems.
Founded: 1960
Michael Corvese, President
Stan Mack, Vice-President

63 **Institute of Environmental Sciences and Technology (IEST)**
1827 Walden Office Square 847-981-0100
Suite 100 Fax: 847-981-4130
Schaumburg, IL 60173 information@iest.org
www.iest.org
An international professional society that serves the environmental sciences in the areas of contamination control in electronics manufacturing and pharmaceutical processes, design, test and evaluation of commercial and militaryequipment and product reliability issues.
Ahmad Soueid, President
Gordon Ely, President-elect

64 **Institute of Hazardous Materials Management (IHMM)**
11900 Parklawn Drive 301-984-8969
Suite 450 Fax: 301-984-1516
Rockville, MD 20852-2624 info@ihmm.org
www.ihmm.org
A nonprofit organization that protects the environment and the public's health and safety through the administration of credentials recognizing professionals who have demonstrated a high level of knowledge, expertise, and excellence inthe management of hazardous materials.
Founded: 1984
Allison A. King, Chairman
Glenn Fellman, Executive Director

65 **International Center for the Solution of Environmental Problems (ICSEP)**
5120 Woodway Drive 713-527-8711
Suite 8009 Fax: 713-961-5157
Houston, TX 77056-5157 icsep@airmail.net
To anticipate and detect environmental problems and either solve the problems or design and demonstrate their solutions using scientific methods in concert with nature. To provide environmental information.
Founded: 1975
Joseph L. Goldman, Ph.D., CCM, Technical Director

66 **Interstate Mining Compact Commission (IMCC)**
445A Carlisle Drive 703-709-8654
Herndon, VA 20170 Fax: 703-709-8655
bbotsis@imcc.isa.us
www.imcc.isa.us
A multi-state governmental organization that represents the natural resource interests of its members. They work closely with several Federal agencies such as Office of Surface Mining Reclamation and Enforcement, US EPA and US Bureauof Land Management.
Founded: 1970
Gregory E. Conrad, Executive Director
Beth A. Botsis, Deputy Executive Director

67 **Jane Goodall Institute**
1595 Spring Hill Road 703-682-9220
Suite 550 Fax: 703-682-9312
Vienna, VA 22182 www.janegoodall.org
A tax-exempt, nonprofit corporation, founded to concentrate on research, education and conservation of wildlife, pursuant to the life work of Jane Goodall.
Jane Goodall, Ph.D., DBE, Founder
Carlos Drews, Ph.D., Executive Director

68 **Land Improvement Contractors of America**
3080 Ogden Avenue 630-548-1984
Suite 300 Fax: 630-548-9189
Lisle, IL 60532 nlica@aol.com
www.licanational.com
Organization composed primarily of small contractors whose activities related to the conservation, use and improvement of land and water resources ranging from grading, excavating, paving, landscaping, wetland development, drainage,and site preparation. Strives to improve the climate within which members conduct their businesses by working for better legislation and regulations.
Founded: 1951
David Rule, Chairman
Brad McArdle, President

69 **National Association for Environmental Management (NAEM)**
1612 K Street NW 202-986-6616
Suite 1002 800-391-6236
Washington, DC 20006 Fax: 202-530-4408
programs@naem.org
www.naem.org
Provides peer-to-peer networking for EHS managers; develop EHS professionals as leaders; advance the integration of EHS into business as a value driver; and promote the growth and implementation of EHS management systems worldwide; so,as to offer tangible benefits to the regulated entity and other stakeholders.
Founded: 1990
Carol Singer Neuvelt, Executive Director
Virginia Hoekenga, Deputy Director

70 **National Association of Biology Teachers (NABT)**
PO Box 3363 703-264-9696
Warrenton, VA 20188 888-501-6228
Fax: 703-435-4390
office@nabt.org
www.nabt.org
Includes more than 9,000 educators who share experience and expertise with colleagues from around the globe; keep up with trends and developments; and grow professionally. The NABT empowers educators to provide the best biology andlife science education for all students.
Susan Finazzo, Ph.D., President
Elizabeth Cowles, Ph.D., President-elect

71 **National Association of Environmental Professionals (NAEP)**
PO Box 460 856-283-7816
Collingswood, NJ 08108 Fax: 856-210-1619
naep@bowermanagementservices.com
www.naep.org

NAEP is a multidisciplinary association dedicated to the advancement of environmental professionals in the US and abroad, and a forum for state-of-the-art information on environmental planning, research and management. A network ofprofessional contacts and a resource for structured career development, this organization is a strong proponent of ethics and the highest standards of practice in the environmental professions.
Marie Campbell, President
Betty Dehoney, CEP, PMP, ENV SP, Vice-President

72 **National Conference of State Legislatures (NCSL)**
7700 East First Place 303-364-7700
Denver, CO 80230 800-659-2656
Fax: 303-364-7800
ncslnet-admin@ncsl.org
www.ncsl.org

The National Conference of State Legislatures serves the legislators and staffs of the nation's 50 states and its commonwealths and territories. NCSL is a bipartisan organization with three objectives: to improve the quality andeffectiveness of state legislatures; to foster interstate communications and cooperation; and to ensure states a strong cohesive voice in the federal system.
Founded: 1975
Sen. Curt Bramble, President
Jean Cantrell, Vice-President

73 **National Council for Science and the Environment**
1101 17th Street NW 202-530-5810
Suite 250 www.ncseglobal.org
Washington, DC 20036

National nonprofit organization working to improve the scientific basis for making decisions on environmental issues. The Council promotes a new crosscutting approach to environmental science that integrates interdisciplinary research,scientific assessment, environmental education and communication of science-based information to decision makers and the public.
James Buizer, Ph.D., Chairman
Michelle Wyman, Executive Director

74 **National Energy Foundation**
4516 South 700 East 801-327-9500
Suite 100 800-616-8326
Salt Lake City, UT 84107 Fax: 801-908-5400
nefl.org

A nonprofit educational organization dedicated to the development, dissemination and implementation of supplemental educational materials and programs primarily related to the environment, conservation, science, energy, water andnatural resources.
Founded: 1976
Elissa Richards, President/CEO
Anne Lowe, Vice-President, Operations

75 **National Environmental Education Foundation (NEEF)**
4301 Connecticut Avenue NW 202-833-2933
Suite 160 Fax: 202-261-6464
Washington, DC 20008-2326 www.neefusa.org

Provides objective environmental information and education to help Americans live better. Environmental education programs include those tailored to the adult public, for health professionals, and in the schools.
Carlos Alcazar, Chairman
Diane W. Wood, President

76 **National Environmental Trust**
Washington, DC 20004 202-552-2000
Fax: 202-552-2299
info@pewtrusts.org

Informs citizens about environmental problems and how they affect human health and quality of life. The Trust uses public education campaigns and modern communication techniques to localize the impacts of national problems.
Founded: 1994
Rebecca W. Rimel, President
Rebecca A. Cornejo, Senior Officer

77 **National FFA Organization**
6060 FFA Drive 317-802-6060
PO Box 68960 888-332-2668
Indianapolis, IN 46268-0960 Fax: 800-366-6556
orders@ffa.org
www.ffa.org

The organization (formerly Future Farmers of America) is dedicated to making a positive difference in the lives of young people by developing their potential for premier leadership, personal growth and career success throughagricultural education.
Founded: 1928
Mark Poeschl, CEO
Joshua Bledsoe, COO

78 **National Geographic Society**
1145 17th Street NW 202-862-8638
Washington, DC 20036 800-373-1717
Fax: 202-429-5709
givinginfo@ngs.org
www.nationalgeographic.com

Its mission, in a nutshell, is to inspire people to care about the planet. Programs support scientific fieldwork and expeditions; encourage geography education for students; and promote natural and cultural conservation.
Founded: 1888
John Fahey, Chairman/CEO
Terrence B. Adamson, Executive VP

79 **National Governors Association (NGA)**
444 North Capitol Street 202-624-5300
Suite 267 Fax: 202-624-5313
Washington, DC 20001-1512 webmaster@nga.org
www.nga.org

The Association works closely with the administration and Congress on state and federal policy issues, serves as a vehicle for sharing knowledge of innovative programs among states, and provides technical assistance and consultantservices to governors on a wide range of management and policy issues. Part of the organization is the Center for Best Practices which undertakes demonstration projects and provides anticipatory research on important policy issues.
Founded: 1908
Scott Pattison, Executive Director/CEO
Stan Czerwinski, COO

80 **National Institute for Global Environmental Change**
University of California, Davis
2850 Spafford Street 530-757-3350
Suite A Fax: 530-756-6499
Davis, CA 95618 nigec@ucdavis.edu

Sponsored by the Office of Science at the US Department of Energy, the institute is operated by the University of California under a cooperative agreement. Its overall mission is to assist the nation in its response to human-inducedclimate and environmental change.
Dr Lawrence B Coleman, Interim National Director
Thanos Toulopoulos, Program & Info Systems

81 National Network of Forest Practitioners (NNFP)
8 North Court Street 740-593-8733
Suite 411 colin@nnfp.org
Athens, OH 45701 www.nnfp.org
Promotes the mutual well-being of workers, rural communities and forests by supporting individuals and groups that build sustainable relationships between forests and people.
Colin Donohue, Executive Director
Chris Demel, Financial Manager

82 National Parent Teachers Association
1250 N. Pitt Street 703-518-1200
Alexandria, VA 22314 800-307-4782
Fax: 703-836-0942
info@pta.org
www.pta.org
Part of the mission of the National PTA is to support and speak on behalf of children and youth in the school, in the community and before governmental bodies and other organizations. School Construction and Environmental Health is oneof the program focuses where the National PTA aims to ensure that facilities are free from health and environmental hazards.
Laura Bay, President
Jim Accomando, President-elect

83 National Religious Partnership for the Environment
110 Maryland Avenue, NE 212-532-7436
Suite 203 Fax: 413-253-1414
Washington, DC 20002 nrpe@nrpe.org
www.nrpe.org
The mission of the National Religious Partnership for the Environment is to permanently integrate issues of environmental sustainability and justice across all aspects of organized religious life.
Rabbi Steve Gutow, Chairman
Dr. Jonathan Reyes, Vice Chairman

84 National Waste & Recycling Association
Environmental Industry Associations
1550 Crystal Drive 202-244-4700
Suite 804 800-424-2869
Arlington, VA 22202 Fax: 202-966-4824
info@wasterecycling.org
wasterecycling.org
The trade association that represents the private scetor companies in North America that provide solid, hazardous and medical waste collection, recycling and disposal services, and companies that provide professionals and consultingservices to the waste services industry.
Founded: 1962
Bret Biggers, Director
Anne Germain, Director

85 Nature's Classroom
19 Harrington Road 508-248-2741
Charlton, MA 01507 800-433-8375
Fax: 508-248-2745
info@naturesclassroom.org
www.naturesclassroom.org
Nature's Classroom is a residential environmental education program, at fifteen wonderful sites in New York and New England. They give students, and teachers, the chance to experience education from another perspective, outside thewalls of the classroom. After spending time in Nature's Classroom, living and learning together, students develop a sense of community, a confidence in themselves and an appreciation for others that carries over to the school community.
Dr. John Santos, Director

86 Netcentric Campaigns
1875 Connecticut Avenue NW 202-570-4325
10th Floor info@greenmediatoolshed.org
Washington, DC 20009 www.netcentriccampaigns.org
Netcentric Campaigns transforms advocacy for foundations and nonprofits by building networks of people to move change forward.
Founded: 2000
Marty Kearns, Founder/President
Dawn Arteaga, Vice-President

87 Noise Free America
P.O. Box 2754
Chapel Hill, NC 27515 877-664-7366
noisefree@hotmail.com
www.noisefree.org
A national nonprofit organization aimed at reducing noise pollution in the community. Their main focus is on noises from boom cars, leaf blowers, motorcycles and car alarms.
Founded: 2001

88 North American Association for Environmental Education (NAAEE)
2000 P Street NW 202-419-0412
Suite 540 Fax: 202-419-0415
Washington, DC 20036 jbraus@naaee.org
www.naaee.org
A professional association that promotes excellence in environmental education and serves environmental educators for the purpose of achieving environmental literacy to allow present and future generations to benefit from a safe andhealthy environment.
Founded: 1971
Jose Marcos-Iga, President
Judy Braus, Executive Director

89 Orion Society
187 Main Street 413-528-4422
Great Barrington, MA 01230 888-909-6568
orionmag@pcspublink.com
orionmagazine.org
A nonprofit organization supported by donations from individuals, families and foundations, and corporate and government grants. Mission is to inform, inspire, and engage individuals and grassroots organizations in becoming asignificant cultural force for healing nature and community.
Founded: 1982
Christopher Nye, Chair
H.Emerson Blake, Executive Director

90 Public Citizen
1600 20th Street NW 202-588-1000
Washington, DC 20009 member@citizen.org
www.citizen.org
A consumer advocacy organization founded to represent consumer interests in Congress, the executive branch, and the courts.
Founded: 1971
Robert Weissman, President
Margrete Strand Rangnes, Executive Vice-President

91 Public Employees for Environmental Responsibility (PEER)
962 Wayne Avenue 202-265-7337
Suite 610 Fax: 202-265-4192
Silver Spring, MD 20910 info@peer.org
www.peer.org
A national nonprofit alliance of local, state and federal scientists, law enfornement officers, land managers and other professionals dedicated to upholding environmental laws and values.
Frank Buono, Chairman
Jeff Ruch, Executive Director

92 Renew America
1200 18th Street NW 202-721-1545
Suite 1100 Fax: 202-467-5780
Washington, DC 20036

Renew America is a nonprofit organization founded in 1989. They coordinate a network of community and environment groups, businesses, government leaders and civic activists to exchange ideas and expertise for improving the enviroment.By finding and promoting programs that work, Renew America helps inspire communities and businesses to meet today's environmental challenges.
Founded: 1989
Kenneth Brown, Executive Director
L Hunter Lovins, President

93 **Renewable Fuels Association**
425 3rd Street SW 202-289-3835
Suite 1150 Fax: 202-289-7519
Washington, DC 20024 info@ethanolrfa.org
www.ethanolrfa.org
The national trade association for the US ethanol industry, promotes policies, regulations and research and development initiative that will lead to the increased production and use of fuel ethanol.
Founded: 1981
Bob Dinneen, President/CEO
Geoff Cooper, Executive VP

94 **Roger Tory Peterson Institute of Natural History**
311 Curtis Street 716-665-2473
Jamestown, NY 14701 800-758-6841
Fax: 716-665-3794
pbeeson@rtpi.org
rtpi.org
Nature education organization that works on the national level, with an audience of primarily adults who are interested in gaining skills for educating young people about the natural world. RTPI also houses the life's work of RogerTory Peterson.
Founded: 1984
Twan Leenders, President
Linda Pierce, Director, Development

95 **Silicones Environmental, Health and Safety Center**
American Chemistry Council (ACC)
700 2nd Street NE 703-788-6535
Washington, DC 20002 Fax: 202-249-6100
sehsc@americanchemistry.com
sehsc.americanchemistry.com
An organization of North America silicone chemical producers and importers. It promotes the safe use of silicones through product stewardship and environmental, health and safety research. It focuses on coordinating research andsubmitting it for peer review through independent advisory boards and publication of peer-reviewed literature.
Karluss Thomas, Executive Director

96 **Smithsonian Institution**
Smithsonian Information
SI building, Room 153, MRC 010 202-633-1000
PO Box 37012 866-868-7774
Washington, DC 20013-7012 info@si.edu
www.si.edu
Independent trust instrumental of the United States holding more than 140 million artifacts and specimens in its trust for the public interest and knowledge. Also a center for research dedicated to public education, national service,and scholarship in the arts, sciences, and history.
Founded: 1846
Dr. David J. Skorton, Secretary
Cathy Helm, Inspector General

97 **Society of American Foresters**
10100 Laureate Way 301-897-8720
Bethesda, MD 20814-2198 866-897-8720
Fax: 301-897-3690
membership@safnet.org
www.eforester.org
To advance the science, education, technology, and practice of forestry; to enhance the competency of its members; to establish professional excellence; and to use the knowledge, skills, and conservation ethic of the profession toensure the continued health and use of forest ecosystems present and future of availability of forest resources to benefit society.
Founded: 1900
Frederick W. Cubbage, CF, President
David S. Lewis, Vice President

98 **Society of Chemical Manufacturers and Affiliates (SOCMA)**
1400 Crystal Drive 571-348-5100
Suite 630 Fax: 571-348-5138
Arlington, VA 22202 eo@socma.com
www.socma.com
The leading international trade association serving the small and mid-sized batch chemical manufacturers. Advocates flexible policies grounded in sound science and works to ensure that Congress and the regulatory agencies do not adopta one-size fits-all approach to the industry.
Founded: 1921
Jennifer L. Abril, President/CEO

99 **Student Pugwash USA**
1015 18th Street NW 202-429-8900
Suite 704 800-969-2784
Washington, DC 20036 Fax: 202-429-8905
spusa@spusa.org
www.spusa.org
Promotes social responsibility in science and technology. Prepare science, technology and policy students to make social responsibility a guiding focus of their academic and professional endeavors.
Sharlissa Moore, President
Kyle Gracey, Vice-President

100 **U.S. Global Change Research Program**
1800 G St NW 202-223-6262
Suite 9100 Fax: 202-223-3065
Washington, DC 20006 www.globalchange.gov
The U.S. Global Change Research Program (USGCRP) was established by Presidential Initiative to "assist the Nation and the world to understand, assess, predict, and respond to human-induced and natural processes of global change."
Founded: 1989
Dr. Ann Bartuska, Chair
Dr. Michael Kuperberg, Executive Director

101 **United Nations Environment Programme New York Office**
2 UN Plaza, Room DC2-803 212-963-8210
323 E. 44th Street Fax: 212-963-7341
New York, NY 10017 unepnyo@un.org
www.unep.org/newyork
Provides leadership and to encourage partnership in caring for the environment by inspiring, informing, and enabling nations and peoples to improve their quality of life without compromising that of future generations.
Founded: 1972
Elliot C. Harris, Director

102 **Welder Wildlife Foundation**
10429 Welder Wildlife 361-364-2643
PO Box 1400 Fax: 361-364-2650
Sinton, TX 78387 welderwildlife.org
A private non profit organization that has gained international recognition through its research program. The mission of the Foundation is to conduct research and education in the fields of

wildlife management and conservation andother closely related fields.
Founded: 1954
Dr. Terry Blankenship, Director
Dr. Selma Glasscock, Assistant Director

National: Design & Architecture

103 **ABS Group**
American Bureau of Shipping
16855 Northchase Drive
Houston, TX 77060
281-673-2800
Fax: 281-877-5946
info@abs-group.com
www.abs-group.com
A subsidiary of American Bureau of Shipping offering risk management, safety, quality and environmental consulting and certification services to a wide range of industries and companies throughout the world.
Founded: 1990
Todd Grove, President/CEO
Thomas Adams, Vice-President

104 **American Society of Landscape Architects**
636 Eye Street NW
Washington, DC 20001-3736
202-898-2444
888-999-2752
Fax: 202-898-1185
info@asla.org
www.asla.org
To lead, to educate and to participate in the careful stewardship, wise planning and artful design of cultural and natural environments.
Founded: 1899
Vaughn B. Rinner, FASLA, President
George A. Miller, FASLA, President-Elect

105 **Environmental Action Foundation Associated General Contractors of America**
2300 Wilson Boulevard
Suite 300
Arlington, VA 22201
703-548-3118
800-242-1767
Fax: 703-548-3119
info@agc.org
www.agc.org
The mission is to demonstrate the construction industry's commitment to improving the environment and quality of life through: improving environmental education, supporting sensible application of environmental laws, promotingenvironmental awareness campaigns and assisting in environmental litigation.
Founded: 1999
Art Daniel, President
Eddie Stewart, Senior Vice-President

106 **Environmental Design Research Association (EDRA)**
1000 Westgate Drive
Suite 252
St. Paul, MN 55114
651-379-7306
Fax: 651-290-2266
headquarters@edra.org
www.edra.org
Advances and disseminates behavior and design research toward improving understanding of the relationships between people and their environments.
Founded: 1968
Lynne Manzo, Chair
Jeremy Wells, Chair-Elect

107 **Green Building Initiative**
7805 SW 40th Avenue
Suite 80010
Portland, OR 97219
503-274-0448
info@thegbi.org
thegbi.org
The Green Building Initiative (GBI) is a nonprofit organization dedicated to accelerating the adoption of building practices that result in energy-efficient, healthier and environmentally sustainable buildings.
Founded: 2004
Vicki Worden, Executive Director
Richard Mitchell, Chairman

108 **Land Improvement Contractors of America**
3080 Ogden Avenue
Suite 300
Lisle, IL 60563
630-548-1984
Fax: 630-548-9189
nlica@aol.com
www.licanational.com
Organization composed primarily of small contractors whose activities related to the conservation, use and improvement of land and water resources ranging from grading, excavating, paving, landscaping, wetland development, drainage,and site preparation. Strives to improve the climate within which members conduct their businesses by working for better legislation and regulations.
Founded: 1951
David Rule, Chairman
Brad McArdle, President

109 **Rocky Mountain Institute**
22830 Two Rivers Road
Basalt, CO 81621
970-927-3851
Fax: 970-927-3420
www.rmi.org
An independent, entrepreneurial, nonprofit think and do tank. Envisage a world thriving, verdant, and secure, for all.
Edward D. White, Chair
Jules Kortenhorst, CEO

110 **U.S. Green Building Council (USGBC)**
2101 L Street NW
Suite 500
Washington, DC 20037
202-742-3792
800-795-1747
education@usgbc.org
usgbc.org
USGBC is a nonprofit organization that promotes sustainability in buildings design, construction, and operation. They work in collaboration with industry experts, market research publications and LEED professional credentials.
Founded: 1993
Warren Weisberg, President
Olusola Dosunmu, Project Manager

National: Disaster Preparedness & Response

111 **Cultural Survival**
2067 Massachusetts Avenue
Cambridge, MA 02140
617-441-5400
Fax: 617-441-5417
culturalsurvival@cs.org
www.culturalsurvival.org
Provides a worldwide connection for a better global environment through effective letter-writing campaigns. Empowers people of all ages, cultures, and nationalities to protect the environment by creating partnerships for effectivecitizen action.
Sarah Fuller, President
Duana Champagne, Vice-President

112 **DRI International**
119 West 23rd Street
Suite 704
New York, NY 10011
866-542-3744
drii.org
DRI International is the non-profit that helps organizations prepare for and recover from disasters. DRI also serves continuity professionals through conferencing, outreach, and volunteerism.
Founded: 1988
Chloe Demrovsky, President
Traci O'Neal, Sr Director of Operations

113 **International Association of Emergency Managers**
201 Park Washington Court 703-538-1795
Falls Church, VA 22046-4527 Fax: 703-241-5603
info@iaem.com
iaem.com
The International Association of Emergency Managers (IAEM) is a nonprofit educational organization dedicated to Emergency Management and representing those professionals whose goals are saving lives and protecting property and theenvironment during emergencies and disasters.
Elizabeth B. Armstrong, Chief Executive Officer
Clay D. Tyeryar, Deputy Executive Director

114 **International Association of Wildland Fire**
1418 Washburn Street 406-531-8264
Missoula, MT 59801 888-440-4293
execdir@iawfonline.org
www.iawfonline.org
A professional association representing members of the global wildland fire community. It facilitates communication and provides leadership for the wildland fire community.
Tom Zimmerman, President
Alen Slijepcevic, Vice-President

115 **National Association of Flood and Stormwater Management Agencies (NAFSMA)**
PO Box 56764 202-289-8625
Washington, DC 20040 Fax: 202-530-3389
info@nafsma.org
www.nafsma.org
NAFSMA is an organization of public agencies whose function is the protection of lives, property and economic activity from the adverse impacts of storm and flood waters. The mission of the association is to advocate public policy,encourage technologies and conduct education programs which facilitate and enhance the achievement of the public service functions of its members.
Founded: 1978
Steve Fitzgerald, President
Janet Bly, Vice-President

116 **National Council on Radiation Protection and Measurements**
7910 Woodmont Avenue 301-657-2652
Suite 400 Fax: 301-907-8768
Bethesda, MD 20814-3095 ncrp@ncrponline.org
ncrponline.org
The National Council on Radiation Protection and Measurements (NCRP) seeks to formulate and widely disseminate information, guidance and recommendations on radiation protection and measurements which represent the consensus of leadingscientific thinking.
Founded: 1964
John D. Boice, Jr., President
Kathyrn D. Held, Executive Director

117 **National Fire Protection Association (NFPA)**
1 Batterymarch Park 617-770-3000
Quincy, MA 02169-7471 800-344-3555
Fax: 800-593-6372
www.nfpa.org
Reduces the worldwide burden of fire and other hazards on the quality of life by providing and advocating consensus codes and standards, research, training and education.
Founded: 1896 81,000 members
Randolph W. Tucker, Chair
Jim Pauley, President

118 **Natural Hazards Center**
University of Colorado Boulder
1440 15th Street 303-492-6818
Boulder, CO 80302-0483 Fax: 303-492-2151
hazctr@colorado.edu
hazards.colorado.edu
Advances and communicates knowledge on hazards mitigation and disaster preparedness, response, and recovery. Using an all-hazards and interdisciplinary framework, the Center fosters information sharing and integration of activitiesamong researchers, practitioners, and policy makers from around the world; supports and conducts research; and provides educational opportunities for the next generation of hazards scholars and professionals.
Founded: 1976
Lori Peek, Director
Liesel Ritchie, Associate Director

119 **Office of Response and Restoration-NOAA**
National Oceanic and Atmospheric Administration
1305 East-West Highway 240-533-0391
Silver Spring, MD 20910 orr.webmaster@noaa.gov
response.restoration.noaa.gov
Protects coastal and marine resources, mitigates threats, reduces harm, restores ecological function and provides comprehensive solutions to environmental hazards caused by oil, chemicals and marine debris.
Amy V. Uhrin, Chief Scientist
Kristin Rusello, Foreign Affairs Specialist

120 **Safety Equipment Institute (SEI)**
1307 Dolley Madison Boulevard 703-442-5732
Suite 3A Fax: 703-442-5756
McLean, VA 22101 Info@SEInet.org
www.seinet.org
A private, nonprofit organization established to administer the first non-governmental, third-party certification program to test and certify a broad range of safety equipment products.
Founded: 1981
James W. Platner, Chairman
Patricia A. Gleason, President

National: Energy & Transportation

121 **Advanced Energy**
909 Capability Drive 919-857-9000
Suite 2100 advancedenergy.org
Raleigh, NC 27606
Advanced Energy is a nonprofit energy consulting firm. They work with electric utilities, government and a wide variety of public and private organizations in the residential, commercial and industrial, solar, motors and drives andelectric vehicle markets. They provide energy efficient services through research, testing, training, consulting and program design.
Founded: 1980
Robert Koger, President/Executive Director
Brian Coble, Vice-President

122 **Alliance to Save Energy**
1850 M St NW 202-857-0666
Suite 610 Fax: 202-331-9588
Washington, DC 20036 www.ase.org
This organization is a non-profit collective of business, government, environmental and consumer leaders with the mission of promoting energy efficiency worldwide to achieve a healthier economy, environment and greater energy security.
Founded: 1977
Kateri Callahan, President
Daniel Bresette, VP, Policy & Research

123 **Alternative Energy Resources Organization**
302 N Last Chance Gulch 406-443-7272
Suite 309 Fax: 406-442-9120
Helena, MT 59601 aero@aeromt.org
aeromt.org
A nonprofit organization dedicated to promoting sustainable living in Montana by nuturing individuals and communities through

programs that support sustainable agriculture, renewable energy and access to healthy food.
Founded: 1974
Jenn Battles, Executive Director
Corrie Williamson, Outreach Director

124 American Coal Ash Association
15200 East Girard Avenue
Suite 3050
Aurora, CO 80014
720-870-7897
Fax: 720-870-7889
info@acaa-usa.org
www.acaa-usa.org

ACAA's mission is to advance the management and use of coal combustion products in ways that are environmentally responsible, technically sound, commercially competitive and more supportive of a sustainable global community.
Thomas Adams, Executive Director
Alyssa Barto, Member Liaison

125 American Council for an Energy-Efficient Economy
529 14th Street NW
Suite 600
Washington, DC 20045-1000
202-507-4000
Fax: 202-429-2248
industry@aceee.org
aceee.org

A nonprofit organization dedicated to advancing energy efficiency by promoting policies, programs, technologies and sustainable living. ACEEE employs a number of strategies to accomplish this goal, such as conducting technical andpolicy assessments, advising governments, publishing books, holding conferences, generating research reports and more.
Founded: 1980
Carl Blumstein, Chairman
Penni McLean-Conner, President

126 American Gas Association
400 North Capitol Street NW
Suite 450
Washington, DC 20001
202-824-7000
Fax: 202-824-7115
tburleson@aga.org
www.aga.org

The Association represents over 200 local energy companies responsible for delivering natural gas throughout the United States.
Founded: 1918
Pierce Norton, Chairman
Dave McCurdy, President & CEO

127 American Petroleum Institute
1220 L Street NW
Washington, DC 20005-4070
202-682-8000
www.api.org

API is the major national trade association representing all aspects of America's oil and natural gas industry. With over 625 corporate members (including producers, refiners, pipeline operators, and service companies) the associationoffers a broad range of programs including advocacy, research and statistics, certification, operating standards and education.
Founded: 1911
Jack Gerard, President & CEO
Kyle Isakower, Vice President

128 American Public Power Association
2451 Crystal Drive
Suite 1000
Arlington, VA 22202-4804
202-467-2900
Fax: 202-467-2910
mrufe@appanet.org
www.publicpower.org

The American Public Power Association (APPA) provides the nation with more than 2,000 community-owned electric utilities serving over 48 million Americans. It is a non-profit organization. APPA aims to advance the public policyinterests of its members and consumers through services that create reliable, affordable electricity while keeping environmental health in mind.
Founded: 1940
Andrew Boatright, Chair
Walter Haase, Chairman Elect

129 American Solar Energy Society
2525 Arapahoe Ave
Suite E4-253
Boulder, CO 80302
303-443-3130
Fax: 303-443-3212
info@ases.org
www.ases.org

The American Solar Energy Society (ASES) is a national organizationdedicated to advancing the use of solar energy for the benefit of US citizens a nd the global environment. The organization promotes this goal by offering education,events and resources to communities.
Founded: 1954
Elaine Hebert, Chair
Lucas Dixon, Vice Chair

130 Association of Energy Engineers
3168 Mercer University Drive
Atlanta, GA 30341
770-447-5083
Fax: 770-446-3969
info@aeecenter.org
www.aeecenter.org

The Association of Energy Engineers is a nonprofit professional society that promotes the scientific and educational interests of those in the energy industry. The association offers conferences, journals, books and certificationprograms in support of sustainable development.
Founded: 1977
Albert Thumann, Executive Director
Ruth Whitlock, Executive Administrator

131 Association of Energy Engineers (AEE)
3168 Mercer University Drive
Atlanta, GA 30341
770-447-5083
Fax: 770-446-3969
whit@aeecenter.org
www.aeecenter.org

A nonprofit professional society that promotes the scientific and educational interests of those engaged in the energy industry and fosters action for sustainable development.
Ruth Whitlock, Executive Administrator
Albert Thumann, Executive Director

132 Clean Fuels Development Coalition
4641 Montgomery Avenue
Suite 350
Bethesda, MD 20814
301-718-0077
Fax: 301-718-0606
CFDCInc@aol.com
www.cleanfuelsdc.org

The Clean Fuels Development Coalition is an organization that aims to support the production and use of fuels helping to reduce air pollution and oil imports.
Douglas Durante, Executive Director

133 Compressed Gas Association
14501 George Carter Way
Suite 103
Chantilly, VA 20151
703-788-2700
Fax: 703-961-1831
cga@cganet.com
www.cganet.com

The mission of the CGA is to promote the safe manufacture, transportation, storage, transfilling, and disposal of industrial and medical gases and their containers. Strategies employed by the CGA include developing standards andpractices, working with other organizations, providing safety training and more.
Founded: 1913
Jerrold Sameth, Technical Manager
Laura Brumsey, Director of Operations

134 Consumer Energy Council of America
2737 Devonshire Place NW
Suite 102
Washington, DC 20008
info@cecarf.org
www.cecarf.org

The CECA is an organization in the US focusing on supporting clean, affordable energy services for consumers.
Founded: 1973
Rich Aiken, President
Ellen Berman, CEO

135 Institute for Energy and Environmental Research (IEER)
6935 Laurel Ave.
Suite 201
Takoma Park, MD 20912
301-270-5500
Fax: 301-270-3029
info@ieer.org
www.ieer.org

IEER's aim is to provide scientific information about environmental issues in an easy to understand format for use by activists, policy-makers, journalists and the public. The educational material covers emissions-free energy systems,energy equity, energy democracy, nuclear weapons security and more.
Founded: 1987
Arjun Makhijani, President
Sadaf Rassoul Cameron, Vice President

136 International Association for Energy Economics
28790 Chagrin Boulevard
Suite 350
Cleveland, OH 44122
216-464-5365
iaee@iaee.org
www.iaee.org

A non-profit, professoinal organization that provides an interdisciplinary forum for the exchage of ideas, experiences and issues among professionals interested in the field of energy economics.
Founded: 1977
Ricardo Raineri, President
David H. Knapp, President Elect

137 Interstate Oil and Gas Compact Commission
900 NE 23rd Street
PO Box 53127
Oklahoma City, OK 73152
405-525-8380
Fax: 405-525-3592
communications@iogcc.ok.gov
www.iogcc.state.ok.us

A multi-state government agency that maximizes oil and natural gas resources in order to protect the nation's health, safety and environment.
Founded: 1935
Asa Hutchinson, Chairman
Mike Smith, Executive Director

138 Midwest Energy Efficiency Alliance
20 N Wacker Drive
Suite 1301
Chicago, IL 60606
312-587-8390
sparadis@mwalliance.org
mwalliance.org

The Midwest Energy Efficiency Alliance (MEEA) is a collaborative network advancing energy efficiency in the Midwest for sustainable economic development and environmental stewardship.
Stacey Paradis, Executive Director
William Angelos, Deputy Director

139 NW Energy Coalition
811 1st Avenue
Suite 305
Seattle, WA 98104
206-621-0094
Fax: 206-621-0097
nwec@nwenergy.org
www.nwenergy.org

The Coalition promotes renewable energy development, energy conservation, consumer protection, low-income energy assistance, and fish and wildlife restoration.
Founded: 1981
Ben Otto, Chair
Nancy Hirsh, Executive Director

140 National Energy Foundation
4516 South 700 East
Suite 100
Salt Lake City, UT 84107
801-908-5400
800-616-8326
Fax: 801-908-5400
info@nefl.org
nefl.org

A nonprofit educational organization dedicated to the development and implementation of educational opportunities and programs related to the environment, conservation, science, energy, water, and natural resources.
Founded: 1976
Elissa Richards, President

141 Northwest Energy Efficiency Alliance (NEEA)
421 SW 6th Avenue
Suite 600
Portland, OR 97204
503-688-5400
800-411-0834
Fax: 503-688-5447
www.neea.org

A non-profit organization working to maximize energy efficiency in the Pacific Northwest through the acceleration and adoption of energy-efficient products, services and practices.
John Francisco, Chair
Cory Scott, Vice Chair

142 Northwest Power and Conservation Council
851 SW 6th Avenue
Suite 1100
Portland, OR 97204
503-222-5161
800-452-5161
Fax: 503-820-2370
info@nwcouncil.org
www.nwcouncil.org

Develops and maintains a regional power plan and a fish and wildlife program to balance the Northwest's environment and energy needs.
Henry Lorenzen, Chair
Bill Booth, Vice Chair

143 Renewable Fuels Association
425 Third Street, SW
Suite 1150
Washington, DC 20024
202-289-3835
Fax: 202-289-7519
info@ethanolrfa.org
www.ethanolrfa.org

The national trade association for the US ethanol industry. Promotes policies, regulations, research and development initiatives that will lead to the increased production and use of fuel ethanol.
Founded: 1981
Mick Henderson, Chairman
Neil Koehler, Vice Chairman

144 Rocky Mountain Institute
1820 Folsom St
Boulder, CO 80302
303-567-8541
Fax: 970-927-3420
www.rmi.org

Aims to create a prosperous, low-carbon future through the efficient and restorative use of resources with help from business, government, and nonprofit partners.
Founded: 1982
Jules Kortenhorst, CEO
Edward D. White, Chair

145 Western Electricity Coordinating Council
431 Charmany Drive
Madison, WI 53719
800-969-9322
Fax: 608-249-0339
weccinfo@weccusa.org
weccusa.org

WECC is a nonprofit organization dedicated to the development of energy efficiency and renewable energy programs. They partner with local and state governments, regulatory agencies, and other organizations to provide cost-efficientsolutions that help both consumers and businesses conserve energy.
Founded: 1980
Peter Kilde, Chair
David Donovan, Chair

National: Environmental Engineering

146 American Academy of Environmental Engineers & Scientists
147 Old Solomons Island Road
Suite 303
Annapolis, MD 21401
410-266-3311
Fax: 410-266-7653
www.aaees.org

Dedicated to excellence in the practice of environmental engineering and science by providing professional opportunities for students and protecting the environment and public health.
Founded: 1955
Burk Kalweit, Executive Director
Robert C. Williams, President

147 American Institute of Chemical Engineers
120 Wall Street 203-702-7660
FL 23 800-242-4363
New York, NY 10005-4020 Fax: 203-775-5177
www.aiche.org

The world's leading organization for chemical engineering professionals. Provides resources, leadership and career development opportunities for members.
Founded: 1908 50,000 Members
T. Bond Calloway, President
Chritine Seymour, President Elect

148 American Institute of Chemists
315 Chestnut Street 215-873-8224
Philadelphia, PA 19106-2702 Fax: 215-629-5224
info@theaic.org
www.theaic.org

To advance the chemical sciences by establishing high professional standards of practice and to emphasize the professional, ethical, economic, and social status of its members for the benefit of society as a whole.
Founded: 1923
Dr. David M. Manuta, President
Dr. Jerry Jasinski, Chairman

149 American Society for Engineering Education
1818 N Street NW 202-331-3500
Suite 600 Fax: 202-265-8504
Washington, DC 20036-2479 board@asee.org
asee.org

The American Society for Engineering Education is a nonprofit organization of individuals and institutions committed to furthering education in engineering and engineering technology.
Founded: 1893
Louis A. Martin-Vega, President
Bevlee Watford, President-Elect

150 American Society of Agricultural and Biological Engineers
2950 Niles Road 269-429-0300
St Joseph, MI 49085 800-371-2723
Fax: 269-429-3852
hq@asabe.org
www.asabe.org

An educational and scientific organization dedicated to the advancement of agricultural, food, and biological systems.
Founded: 1907 9,000 Members
Maynard Herron, President
Darrin J. Drollinger, Executive Director

151 American Society of Civil Engineers
1801 Alexander Bell Drive 703-295-6000
Reston, VA 20191 703-295-6300
800-548-2723
Fax: 703-295-6333
customercare@asce.org
www.asce.org

Represents members of the civil engineering profession worldwide, and aims to protect and restore the natural environment.
Founded: 1852 150,000 Members
Norma Jean Mattei, President
Kristina L. Swallow, President Elect

152 American Society of Safety Engineers
520 N. Northwest Hwy 847-699-2929
Park Ridge, IL 60068 Fax: 847-768-3434
customerservice@asse.org
www.asse.org

The oldest and largest professional safety organization whose members are dedicated to creating safer work environments and protecting people, property, and the environment.
Founded: 1911 36,000 Members
James D. Smith, CSP, President
Rixio E. Medina, CSP, President Elect

153 American Society of Sanitary Engineering
18927 Hickory Creek Drive 708-995-3019
Suite 220 Fax: 708-479-6139
Mokena, IL 60448 info@asse-plumbing.org
www.asse-plumbing.org

A nonprofit organization that is comprised of individuals and sustaining members who represent all disciplines of the Plumbing Industry.
Founded: 1906
Dana Colombo, President
Tom Palkon, Executive Director

154 Association for Environmental Health and Sciences
150 Fearing Street 413-549-5170
Amherst, MA 01002 Fax: 413-549-0579
paul@aehs.com
www.aehsfoundation.org

The AEHS was created to facilitate communication among professionals concerned with soil protection and water assessment.
Founded: 2009
Paul Kostecki, Executive Director
Ed Calabrese, Editor in Chief

155 Association of Energy Engineers
3168 Mercer University Drive 770-447-5083
Atlanta, GA 30341 Fax: 770-446-3969
info@aeecenter.org
www.aeecenter.org

The Association of Energy Engineers is a nonprofit professional society that promotes the scientific and educational interests of those in the energy industry. The association offers conferences, journals, books and certificationprograms in support of sustainable development.
Founded: 1977 17,500 Members
Ruth Whitlock, Executive Administrator
Albert Thumann, Executive Director

156 Association of Environmental Engineering and Science Professors
AEESP Business Office 202-640-6591
1211 Connecticut Ave NW, Suite 650 Fax: 217-355-9232
Washington, DC 20036 joanne@aeesp.org
www.aeesp.org

The association is made up of professors who provide education in the sciences and technologies of environmental protection.
Founded: 1963
Gregory W. Characklis, President
Peter J. Vikesland, President Elect

157 Association of Ground Water Scientists and Engineers
601 Dempsey Road 614-898-7791
Westerville, OH 43081 800-551-7379
Fax: 614-898-7786
ngwa@ngwa.org
www.ngwa.org

A not-for-profit society and trade association for the global groundwater industry, working to advance groundwater knowledge.
Founded: 1948
Todd Hunter, President
David Henrich, President Elect

158 **Environmental and Engineering Geophysical Society**
1720 South Bellaire Street 303-531-7517
Suite 110 Fax: 303-820-3844
Denver, CO 80222-4303 staff@eegs.org
www.eegs.org
An applied scientific organization that promotes the science of geophysics as it is applied to environmental and engineering problems.
Founded: 1992 650 Members
Laura Sherrod, President
Rick A. Hoover, President Elect

159 **Institute for Alternative Futures**
100 North Pitt Street 703-684-5880
Suite 235 Fax: 703-684-0640
Alexandria, VA 22314 futurist@altfutures.com
www.altfutures.com
A nonprofit research and educational organization that specializes in aiding individuals to choose and create their preferred futures.
Founded: 1977
Jonathan Peck, President
Clement Bezold, Chairman

160 **Institute of Noise Control Engineering**
11130 Sunrise Valley Drive 703-234-4124
Suite 350 Fax: 703-435-4390
Reston, VA 20191 ibo@inceusa.org
www.inceusa.org
A non-profit professional organization that promotes noise control solutions to environmental, product, machinery, industrial and other noise problems.
Rick Kolano, President
Steve E. Marshall, President Elect

161 **Inter-American Association of Sanitary and Environmental Engineering**
USAIDIS 703-247-8730
PO Box 7737 Fax: 703-243-9004
McLean, VA 22106 turnerje@cdm.com
www.aidisnet.org/html/eng/index_eng.html
To further the goals of AIDIS Interamericana through programs and services that promote sound environmental practices, policies, management, and education to improve the quality of life throughout the Americas.
Dr. Pilar Tello Espinoza, President
Jacqueline Rose, Senior Vice President

162 **National Registry of Environmental Professionals (NREP)**
PO Box 2099 847-724-6631
Glenview, IL 60025-6099 Fax: 847-724-4223
customerservice@nrep.org
www.nrep.org
The NREP are dedicated to enhancing the recognition of those who possess the education and experience as qualified environmental and safety professionals.
Founded: 1987 15,000 Members
Scott Spear, Chairperson
Richard Young, Executive Director

163 **NatureServe**
4600 N. Fairfax Dr. 703-908-1800
7th Floor Fax: 703-229-1670
Arlington, VA 22203 info@natureserve.org
www.natureserve.org
Provides the scientific basis for conservation action. Collects and manages local information on plants, animals and ecosystems and develops related information products, data management tools and conservation services.
Gregory A. Miller, President & CEO
Nicole Firlotte, Chair

National: Environmental Health

164 **Bonneville Environmental Foundation**
240 SW 1st Avenue 503-248-1905
Portland, OR 97204 866-233-8247
Fax: 503-248-1908
info@b-e-f.org
www.b-e-f.org
Strives to protect the globe against climate change and the degradation of world freshwater resources through products, programs, and custom solutions for businesses.
Founded: 1998
Angus Duncan, Founder & President
Todd Reeve, CEO

165 **Greenguard Environmental Institute**
2211 Newmarket Parkway 770-984-9903
Suite 110 888-485-4733
Marietta, GA 30067 Fax: 770-980-0072
environment@ul.com
www.greenguard.org
The Greenguard Environmental Institute aims to protect human health by creating interior products that will improve air quality and reduce exposure to chemicals and other pollutants.
Founded: 2001
Henning Bloech, Executive Director
Dr. Marilyn Black, Founder

166 **Group Against Smog & Pollution**
1133 South Braddock Avenue 412-924-0604
Suite 1A info@gasp-pgh.org
Edgewood, PA 15218 gasp-pgh.org
The Group Against Smog and Pollution is a nonprofit organization dedicated to the improvement of air quality through public meetings, engagement with the press, educational events, permit reviews, and other means.
Founded: 1969
Rachel Fillipini, Executive Director
Suzanne Seppi, Project Manager

167 **Inform, Inc.**
PO Box 320403
Brooklyn, NY 11232 ramsey@informinc.org
www.informinc.org
A non-profit environmental organization that uses media and published reports to educate the public about the environmental effects of consumer products.
Founded: 1973
Virginia Ramsey, Executive Producer
Joanna Underwood, Founder

168 **Soil Health Institute**
2803 Slater Road 919-230-0303
Suite 115 soilhealthinstitute.org
Morrisville, NC 27560

The Soil Health Institue is an independent, nonprofit organization focused on fundamental and applied research and ensuring its adoption.
William Buckner, CEO
Constance Cullman, President

National: Gaming & Hunting

169 Action Volunteers for Animals (AVA)
P.O. Box 18233
RPO Steeple Hill
Pickering, ON L1V-0B8
416-439-8770
www.actionvolunteersforanimals.com
A volunteer-run animal rescue dedicated to helping stray and feral animals.
Founded: 1972

170 American Bass Association
402 N Prospect Ave
Redondo Beach, CA 90277
310-376-1026
Fax: 310-376-5072
feedback@americanbass.com
www.americanbass.co/index.php
American Bass develops programs that will protect and improve the environment and natural resources while providing high value to sponsors and advertisers through quality run events and promotions. They are also involved in stockingbass in public lakes, planting trees, protection of natural spawning and juvenile fish.
Founded: 1983
David Plotnik, President & Founder

171 American Birding Association
93 Clinton Street
Suite ABA; P.O. Box 744
Delaware City, DE 19706
302-838-3660
800-850-2473
Fax: 302-838-3651
info@aba.org
www.aba.org
The Association represents the interests of birdwatchers and helps birders increase their knowledge and skills of birding. ABA also contributes to bird conservation and promotes field-birding skills through meetings, workshops,equipment, and guided involvement in birding, promoting national and international birders networks and publications.
Founded: 1969
Jeffrey A. Gordon, President/CEO
Bill Stewart, Director

172 American Eagle Foundation
PO Box 333
Pigeon Forge, TN 37868
865-429-0157
800-232-4537
Fax: 865-429-4743
eaglemail@eagles.org
www.eagles.org
Not-for-profit organization of concerned citizens and professionals who develop and conduct bald eagle and environmental recovery programs in the United States and assist private, state and federal projects that do the same.
Founded: 1985
Al Louis Cecere, Founder/President
Laura Sterbens, Director, Operations

173 American Fisheries Society
425 Barlow Place
Suite 110
Bethesda, MD 20814-2144
301-897-8616
Fax: 301-897-8096
main@fisheries.org
www.fisheries.org
The American Fisheries Society (AFS) is the oldest and largest organization devoted to fisheries. AFS promotes the research and management of fisheries resources, is dedicated to the advancement of fisheries sciences and professionals,and the sustainability of aquatic ecosystems.
Founded: 1870 8,000 Members
Douglas Austen, Executive Director
Daniel Cassidy, Deputy Executive Director

174 American Humane Association
1400 16th Street NW
Suite 360
Washington, DC 20036
303-792-9900
800-227-4645
Fax: 303-792-5333
info@americanhumane.org
www.americanhumane.org
The American Humane Association is committed to preventing cruelty,abuse, neglect and exploitation of children and animals and to assure that their interests and well-being are fully, effectively, and humanely guaranteed by an awareand caring society.
Founded: 1877
Robin R. Ganzert, President/CEO
Audrey Lang, Senior VP & COO

175 American Livestock Breeds Conservancy
33 Hillsboro St
PO Box 477
Pittsboro, NC 27312
919-542-5704
Fax: 919-545-0022
info@livestockconservancy.org
www.albc-usa.org
Protects the genetic diversity of livestock and poultry species through the conservation of endangered breeds.
Founded: 1977
John Metzer, Chairman
Allison Martin, Director

176 American Medical Fly Fishing Association
PO Box 768
Lock Haven, PA 17745
570-769-7375
www.amffa.org
The Association began with the idea of combining professional medical interests with the interest of fly fishing to promote conservation of the natural resources as pertains to the sport and support the causes and efforts orientedtowards these intersts.
Founded: 1969
Veryl F. Frye MD, Secretary/Treasurer

177 American Pheasant and Waterfowl Society
6220 Bullbeggar Road
Withams, VA 23488
757-824-5828
www.apwsbirds.com
To promote the rights and interest of the members to keep and rear upland aquatic and ornamental birds while collecting pertinent and scientific data and information relating to these rights.
Founded: 1936 $25/Year
Jim Bleurer, President
Don Steurer, Vice President

178 American Society of Ichthyologists and Herpetologists
PO Box 1897
Lawrence, KA 66044-8897
785-843-1235
800-627-0326
Fax: 785-843-1274
asih@allenpress.com
www.asih.org
ASIH is dedicated to the scientific study of fishes, amphibians and reptiles. Its mission is to increase knowledge about these organisms through publications, conferences, and symposia, and to encourage young scientists who will makefuture advances in these fields.
Founded: 1913
Carole Baldwin, President
Brian Crother, President Elect

179 American Society of Mammalogists
PO Box 7060
Lawrence, KS 66044
785-550-6904
800-627-0629
Fax: 785-843-1274
cclassi@mammalsociety.org
www.mammalsociety.org

Established for the purpose of promoting interest in the conservation, education and resource management of mammals.
Founded: 1919 4,500 Members
Robert S. Sikes, President
Felisa A. Smith, Vice President

180 Animal Welfare Institute
900 Pennsylvania Ave SE
Washington, DC 20003
202-337-2332
Fax: 202-446-2131
awi@awionline.org
www.awionline.org
AWI works to alleviate the suffering inflicted on animals by humans including factory farming, experimentation, commercial whaling, as well as the impact on endangered species and their habitat.
Founded: 1951
Cathy Liss, President
Cynthia Wilson, Chair & Vice President

181 Birds of Prey Foundation
2290 South 104th Street
Broomfield, CO 80020
303-460-0674
raptor@birds-of-prey.org
www.birds-of-prey.org
Fosters compassion and seeks protecton for injured and orphaned raptors such as eagles, hawks, falcons and owls, and improves the quality of care through education, observation, and invention.
Founded: 1981
Sigrid Ueblacker, Founder

182 Born Free USA
P.O. Box 32160
Washington, DC 20007
202-450-3168
800-348-7387
Fax: 202-450-3581
info@bornfreeusa.org
www.bornfreeusa.org
A national animal advocacy nonprofit organization established to advocate for the protection of animals from cruelty and exploitation. Its primary campaign areas include: farmed animals, companion animals, compassionate consumerism, wildlife protection, and animals used in entertainment.
Founded: 1968
Sean Cassidy, Chairman
Errol Antzis, Treasurer

183 Cetacean Society International
65 Redding Road-0953
Georgetown, CT 06829-0953
203-770-8615
Fax: 860-561-0187
Info@csiwhalesalive.org
www.csiwhalesalive.org
All volunteer, nonprofit conservation, educational and research organization to benefit whales, dolphins, porpoises and the marine environment. Promotes education and conservation programs, including whale and dolphin watching, andnoninvasive, benign research.
Founded: 1974
David Kaplan, President
Cynde McInnis, Vice-President

184 EcoHealth Alliance
460 West 34th Street
17th Floor
New York, NY 10001-2320
212-380-4460
Fax: 212-380-4465
homeoffice@ecohealthalliance.org
www.ecohealthalliance.org
Works in the United States and worldwide to save threatened species from extinction, safeguard human health from the emergence of diesease, and promote conservation by protecting ecosystems.
Founded: 1971
Ellen Shedlarz, Chairman
Peter Daszak, President

185 Federal Wildlife Officers Association
1501 India St
#103-93
San Diego, CA 92102
949-355-6449
sobesurf@gmail.com
www.fwoa.org
An organization dedicated to the protection of wildlife, the enforcement of federal wildlife law, the fostering of cooperation and communication among federal wildlife officers, and the perpetuation, enhancement and defense of thewildlife enforcement profession.
Dave Hubbard, President
Roger Turnell, Secretary

186 Friends of the Australian Koala Foundation
112 East 17th Street
Suite #1W
New York, NY 10003
212-967-8200
Fax: 212-967-7292
akf@savethekoala.com
www.savethekoala.com
The AFK is a non profit organization dedicated to the conservation, management, research, and community education of koalas and their habitat.
Founded: 1986
Deborah Tabart, CEO, Chairman
Lorraine O'Keefe, Director

187 Friends of the Earth
1100 15th Street NW
11th Floor
Washington, DC 20005
202-783-7400
877-843-8687
Fax: 202-783-0444
foe@foe.org
www.foe.org
National nonprofit advocacy organization dedicated to protecting the planet from environmental degradation; preserving biological, cultural and ethnic diversity, and empowering citizens to have an influential voice in decisionsaffecting the quality of their environment and their lives.
Founded: 1969
Erich Pica, President
Michelle Chan, Vice-President, Programs

188 Fund for Animals
200 West 57th Street
New York, NY 10019
212-246-2096
866-482-3708
Fax: 212-246-2633
info@fundforanimals.org
www.fundforanimals.org
The Fund for Animals was founded by author/humanitarian Cleveland Amory and in 2005 merged with The Humane Society of the United States. It is dedicated to protecting animals and providing veterinary and rehabilitative needs.
Founded: 1967
Marian G. Probst, Chair
Holly Hazard, President

189 Game Conservancy USA
49 Locust Ave
Suite 104
New Canaan, CT 06840
203-966-4187
Fax: 203-661-7997
info@gcusa.org
www.gcusa.org
Seeks to increase support for reserach of the conservation of game and wildlife habitats in the US and UK through an expanding membership base.
Bruce D. Sargent, President
Robert Hatch, Director

190 Hawk Migration Association of North America
P.O. Box 721
Plymouth, NH 03264
info@hmana.org
www.hmana.org
To conserve raptor populations through the scientific study, enjoyment and appreciation of raptor migration.
Founded: 1974
Carolyn Hoffman, Chair
Laurie Goodrich, Vice Chair

191 HawkWatch International
2240 South 900 East
Salt Lake City, UT 84106
801-484-6808
800-726-4295
Fax: 801-484-6810
hwi@hawkwatch.org
hawkwatch.org

HawkWatch International is a non-profit organization that works to protect raptors and their environment through scientific research and public education.
Founded: 1986
Paul Parker, Executive Director
Joseph Dane, Marketing Director

192 Humane Society of the United States
1255 23rd Street, NW
Suite 450
Washington, DC 20037
202-452-1100
866-720-2676
Fax: 202-778-6132
corprelations@hsus.org
www.humanesociety.org

HSUS is the nation's largest animal-protection organization. It is dedicated to promoting the humane treatment of animals, to foster respect, understanding, and compassion for all creatures.
Founded: 1954
Wayne Pacelle, President/CEO
Michael Markarian, Chief Operating Officer

193 International Association for Bear Research and Management
1300 College Road
Fairbanks, AK 99071
907-459-7238
Fax: 907-451-9723
www.bearbiology.com

A volunteer organization open to professional biologists, wildlife managers and others dedicated to the conservation of all species of bears. Supports the scientific management of bears through research and distribution of information.
Founded: 1968
Andreas Zedrosser, President
Marty Obbard, Vice President

194 International Society for Endangered Cats
3070 Riverside Drive
Suite 160
Columbus, OH 43221
614-487-8760
Fax: 614-487-8769
education@isec.org
www.isec.org

A not-for-profit organization dedicated to the conservation of wild cats throughout the world. The society's goals are to raise public understanding and knowledge of wild cats and support and facilitate research on ecology, captivebreeding and reintroduction of cats to their native habitats.
Founded: 1988
Bill Simpson, President
Patricia Currie, Executive Director

195 International Wild Waterfowl Association
500 Sylvian Heights Park Way
P.O Box 11
Scotland Neck, NC 27874
252-826-3186
Fax: 425-397-8136
info@shwpark.com
www.wildwaterfowl.org

IWWA is committed to protecting and enhancing wild waterfowl habitats. Supports the captive breeding and restoration of endangered species, and the establishment and maintenance of genetically diverse and disease-free captivepopulations of endangered waterfowl.
Founded: 1958
Arnold Schouten, President
Edward Asper, 1st Vice President

196 International Wildlife Coalition
Whale Adoption Program
70 East Falmouth Highway
PO Box 388
East Falmouth, MA 02536
508-548-8328
Fax: 508-548-8542
iwchq@iwc.org

Aims to prevent cruelty, killing and destruction of wildlife and their habitat.
Founded: 1984
Daniel J Morast, President

197 International Wildlife Conservation Society
PO Box 34
Pacific Palisades, CA 90272
310-476-9305
Fax: 212-220-7114
peterb@internationalwildlife.org
www.internationalwildlife.org

The Society has created a Wildlife Reserve that provides habitat to a variety of mammals, birds, fish and reptiles. The Society continues to increase the awareness of wildlife conservation, preservation and research.
Founded: 1968
Peter Byrne, Founder

198 International Wolf Center
1396 Highway 169
Ely, MN 55731
218-365-4695
Fax: 763-560-7368
officmgr@wolf.org
www.wolf.org

The International Wolf Center advances the survival of the wolf populations by teaching the public about wolves and their relationship to wildlands and humans for the benefit of their future.
Founded: 1985
Nancy Jo Tubbs, Chair
L. David Mech, Vice Chair

199 Last Chance Forever
PO Box 460993
San Antonio, TX 78246-0993
210-499-4080
Fax: 210-499-4305
info@lastchanceforever.org
www.lastchanceforever.org

Dedicated to the rehabilitation of sick, injured and orphaned birds of prey, scientific investigation, and educating the public.
Founded: 1978
John A Karger, Executive Director, Founder
Melissa Hill, President

200 Muskies
P.O Box 1509
Waukesha, WI 53187-1509
701-239-9540
888-710-8286
info@muskiesinc.org
www.muskiesinc.org

Supports growth and interest in the sport of muskie fishing. Works to protect existing fisheries, to develop new fisheries, and to support conservation practices and research.
Founded: 1966
Greg Wells, President

201 NOAA Fisheries
1315 East-West Highway
Silver Spring, MD 20910
301-713-2322
Fax: 301-713-0376
jim.lecky@noaa.gov
www.nmfs.noaa.gov

Provides conservation for protected resources, productive and sustainable fisheries and healthy ecosystems for the nation's marine resources and their habitats.
Founded: 1871
Jim Lecky, Director
Melanie King, Foreign Affairs Specialist

202 National Bison Association
8690 Wolff Ct. #200
Westminster, CO 80031
303-292-2833
Fax: 303-845-9081
info@bisoncentral.com
www.bisoncentral.com

A nonprofit association which promotes the preservation, production and marketing of bison. NBA activities and services serve to better inform and educate the general public about bison and to create and sustainable future for theindustry.
Founded: 1995
Roy Liedtke, President
Dick Gehring, Vice President

203 **National Endangered Species Act Reform Coalition**
1050 Thomas Jefferson Street NW 202-333-7481
6th Floor Fax: 202-338-2416
Washington, DC 20007 nesarc@vnf.com
www.nesarc.org
Dedicated to promoting effective legislative and administrative improvements to the ESA that protect fish, wildlife and plant populations as well as responsible land, water and resource management.
Jordan A. Smith, Executive Director
Joseph B. Nelson, Lead Counsel

204 **National Hunters Association**
PO Box 820 919-365-7157
Knightdale, NC 27545 Fax: 919-366-2142
admin@nationalhunters.com
www.nationalhunters.com
Dedicated to preserving the rights of hunters, promoting hunter safety among youth and all hunters by demanding game controls and hunting laws, maintaining the rights to use and own firearms, protecting the environment and maintaininghealthy habitats.
Debbie Smith, President
Faye Smith, Secretary/Treasurer

205 **National Rifle Association of America**
11250 Waples Mill Road 703-267-1000
Fairfax, VA 22030 800-672-3888
Fax: 703-267-3909
www.nra.org
Gun rights organization that serves to protect the Second Amendment rights of Americans as well as offer firearm educational programs.
Founded: 1871
Pete Brownell, Preident
Wayne LaPierre, Executive Vice President

206 **National Shooting Sports Foundation**
11 Mile Hill Road 203-426-1320
Newtown, CT 06470-2359 Fax: 203-426-1087
portal@nssf.org
www.nssf.org
Leading trade association of the firearms and recreational shooting sports industry. The NSSF manages a variety of programs designed to promote a better understanding of and a more active participaqtion in the shooting sports.
Founded: 1961
Stephen L Sanetti, President & CEO
Hugh C. Wiley, COO

207 **National Trappers Association**
2815 Washington Avenue 812-277-9670
Bedford, IN 47421 866-680-8727
Fax: 812-277-9672
ntaheadquarters@nationaltrappers.com
www.nationaltrappers.com
To promote conservation, legislation and administrative procedures; to save and faithfully defend from waste the natural resources of the United States; to promote environmental education programs; and to promote a continued annual furharvest using the best tools.
Founded: 1959
Chris McAllister, President
John Daniel, Vice President

208 **National Walking Horse Association**
P.O Box 7111 859-252-6942
4059 Iron Works Pkwy #4 Fax: 859-252-0640
Jacksonville, NC 28540 office@nwha.com
www.nwha.com
An alliance of people committed to preserving and fostering the natural abilities and welfare of the Walking Horse while improving the lives of horses and people by encouraging responsibility and sportsmanship.
Amy Spinelli, President
Kimberly O'Connor, CEO

209 **National Wildlife Federation**
11100 Wildlife Center Drive 202-797-6800
Reston, VA 20190 800-822-9919
Fax: 202-797-6646
friends@nwf.org
www.nwf.org
The National Wildlife Federation is the largest member-supported conservation group, uniting individuals, organizations, businesses and government to protect wildlife, wild places and the environment.
Founded: 1936
Kathy Hadley, Chair
Collin O'Mara, President/CEO

210 **National Wildlife Federation: Office of Federal and International Affairs**
1400 16th Street NW 202-797-6800
Washington, DC 20036 Fax: 202-797-6646
A field office of the NWF staffed by people experienced on policy issues, grassroots outreach, law, government affairs, and media. The Office educates, mobilizes and advocates to preserve and strengthen protection for wildlife and wildplaces.

211 **Native American Fish and Wildlife Society**
From The Eagle's Nest
1055 7th Ave Ste 91 303-466-1725
Longmont, CO 80501 866-890-7258
Fax: 303-466-5414
Fax: 866-889-4956
klynch@nafws.org
www.nafws.org
A Native American non-profit organization assisting with the conservation, protection, and enhancement of fish and wildlife resources through conferences, training, summer youth programs and information dissemination.
Founded: 1983
Donald F. Matt, Executive Director
Ronald D. Rodgers, Deputy Director

212 **North American Bear Center**
1926 Highway 169 218-365-7879
PO Box 161 877-365-7879
Ely, MN 55731 www.bear.org/website
To advance the long-term survival of bears by replacing misconceptions with scientific facts about their role in ecosystems and their relations with humans.
Lynn Rogers, Chair
Joe Edlund, Vice Chair

213 **North American Native Fishes Association**
info@nanfa.org
www.nanfa.org
NANFA is dedicated to the enjoyment, study and conservation of the continent's native fishes. Strives to disseminate knowledge about fishes and their habitats and to promote the conservation and the restoration of natural habitats.
Fritz Rohde, President
Brian Zimmerman, Vice President

214 Organization of Wildlife Planners
517-284-6199
wildlifeplanners@gmail.com
www.wildlifeplanners.org
A professional organization concerned with the management and future of government agencies that manage fish and wildlife populations and habitat. The purpose of OWP is to improve the management of fish and wildlife agencies.
Founded: 1978
Ann LeClaire-Mitchell, President
Bill Romberg, Treasurer

215 PAWS Wildlife Rehabilitation Center & Hospital
15305 44th Avenue West 425-787-2500
PO Box 1037 Fax: 425-742-5711
Lynnwood, WA 98087 kparker@paws.org
www.paws.org/wildlife
Rehabilitating injured and orphaned wildlife, provides shelter and adoption for animals. PAWS educates people to recognize the intrinsic value of animals and make choices that demonstrate compassion and respect.
Founded: 1967
Leslie Chandler, President
Damian King, Vice President

216 Pacific Whale Foundation
300 Maalaea Road 808-249-8811
612 Front St, Lahaina, HI 800-942-5311
Wailuku, HI 96793 Fax: 808-243-9021
info@pacificwhale.org
www.pacificwhale.org
Mission is to promote appreciation, understanding and protection of whales, dolphins, coral reefs, and our planet's oceans by educating the public from a scientific perspective about the marine environment.
Founded: 1980
Paul Forestell, PhD, Chairperson
Mark Orams, Director

217 People for the Ethical Treatment of Animals
501 Front Street 757-622-7382
Norfolk, VA 23510 Fax: 757-622-0457
info@peta.org
www.peta.org
PETA is the largest animal rights organization in the world. Dedicated to establishing and protecting the rights of all animals. Operates under the principal that animals are not ours to eat, wear, experiment on, or use forentertainment.
Founded: 1980
Ingrid Newkirk, President
Tracy Reiman, Executive Vice President

218 Pheasants Forever
1783 Buerkle Circle 651-773-2000
St. Paul, MN 55110 877-773-2070
Fax: 651-773-5500
contact@pheasantsforever.org
www.pheasantsforever.org
A non profit organization dedicated to the protection and enhancement of pheasant and other wildlife populations in North America. This mission is carried out through habitat improvement, land management, public awareness, andeducation.
Founded: 1983 149,000 Members
Tim Kessler, Chairman
Shefali Mehta, Vice Chairman

219 Pope and Young Club
273 Mill Creek Road NW 507-867-4144
PO Box 548 www.pope-young.org
Chatfield, MN 55923
One of North America's leading bowhunting and conservation organizations. The Club advocates and encourages responsible bowhunting by promoting quality, fair chase hunting, and sound conservation practices.
Founded: 1961
Donald Ace Morgan, President

220 Purple Martin Conservation Association
301 Peinsula Drive 814-833-7656
Suite 6 Fax: 814-833-2451
Erie, PA 16505 generalinfo@purplemartin.org
www.purplemartin.org
The only organization devoted exclusively to the scientific study of purple martins, their biology, and habitat requirements.
Founded: 1987
James R. Hill, Founder
Ellen Brockwell, Executive Director

221 Safari Club International
4800 West Gates Pass Road 520-620-1220
Tucson, AZ 85745-9490 888-486-8724
Fax: 520-622-1205
www.safariclub.org/
A leader in wildlife conservation, hunter education, and protecting the freedom to hunt.
Warren A. Sackman, President
Craig L. Kauffman, Vice President

222 Scientists Center for Animal Welfare
2660 NE Highway 20 301-345-3500
Suite 610-115 Fax: 541-383-4655
Bend, OR 97701 INFO@SCAW.COM
www.scaw.com
A nonprofit educational association of individuals whose mission is to promote humane care, use, and management of animals involved in research, testing or education in laboratory, agricultural, wildlife or other settings.
Founded: 1978
Randall J. Nelson, President
Paul G. Braunschweiger, Vice President

223 Sea Shepherd Conservation Society
PO Box 8626 212-220-2302
Alexandria, VA 22306 Fax: 818-279-0707
www.seashepherd.org
This organization is committed to mammal protection and conservation with an immediate goal of shutting down illegal whaling and sealing operations, poaching, shark finning, unlawful habitat destruction, and violations of establishedlaws in the world's oceans.
Founded: 1977
Paul Watson, President, Founder
Pritam Singh, Vice President

224 Society of Tympanuchus Cupido Pinnatus
PO Box 320487 414-559-4278
Franklin, WI 53132 www.prairiegrouse.org/stcp
The oldest organization dedicated to conserving and restoring native prairie grouse populations in North America.
Founded: 1961
Peter D. Ziegler, President
Greg Septon, Executive Director

225 Sportsmans Network
111 S Main Street 859-824-6526
PO Box 257 800-680-8058
Dry Ridge, KY 41035 Fax: 606-824-0556
To raise awareness of animal wildlife conservation issues through various forms of public media and to address the subject in all appropriate ways including hunting, fishing, trapping, and related activities.
William Krebs, Treasurer

226 **Trout Unlimited**
1777 N. Kent Street
Suite 100
Arlington, VA 22209-2404
703-522-0200
800-834-2419
Fax: 703-284-9400
trout@tu.org
www.tu.org

This organization seeks to conserve, protect and restore North America's trout and salmon fisheries and their watersheds.
Founded: 1959
Jim Asselstine, Chairman
Nancy Mackinnon, Secretary

227 **Trumpeter Swan Society**
12615 Rockford Road
Plymouth, MN 55441-1248
763-441-1994
Fax: 763-557-4943
ttss@trumpeterswansociety.org
www.trumpeterswansociety.org

Private, nonprofit organization dedicated to assuring the vitality and welfare of wild Trumpeter Swan populations, and to restoring the species to as much of its former range as possible.
Founded: 1968
Carey Smith, President
Dave Hoffman, Vice President

228 **Turtle Island Restoration Network**
9255 Sir Francis Drake Blvd
P.O Box 370
Olema, CA 94938
415-663-8590
Fax: 415-663-9534
info@seaturtles.org
www.seaturtles.org

Fights to protect endangered sea turtle populations in ways that meet the ecological needs of the sea turtles and the oceans and inland watersheds that sustain them.
Founded: 1989
Donna Howe, Board Chair
Todd Steiner, Executive Director

229 **US Sportsmen's Alliance**
801 Kingsmill Parkway
Columbus, OH 43229
614-888-4868
Fax: 614-888-0326
info@sportsmensalliance.org
www.sportsmensalliance.org

The US Sportsmen's Alliance is a national non-profit association that protects hunting, fishing and trapping and scientific wildlife management programs.
Founded: 1978
Evan Heusinkveld, President/CEO
Gordon Pry, Chief Financial Officer

230 **Waterfowl USA**
P.O Box 500
Oak Forest, IL 60452
803-637-5767
Fax: 803-637-6983
nwfusa@yahoo.com
www.waterfowlusa.org

National non profit, conservation organization dedicated to using funds for local and state waterfowl projects.
Founded: 1983
Mark Judge, President
Tabatha Cloutier, Executive Director

231 **Whitetails Unlimited**
2100 Michigan Street
PO Box 720
Sturgeon Bay, WI 54235
920-743-6777
800-274-5471
Fax: 920-743-4658
www.whitetailsunlimited.com

A national conservation organization that dedicates their resources to the betterment of the white-tail deer and its environment.
Founded: 1982
Jeffrey Schinkten, President
Peter J. Gerl, Executive Director

232 **Wild Sheep Foundation**
720 Allen Avenue
412 Pronghorn Trail, Bozeman, MT
Cody, WY 82414-3402
307-527-6261
Fax: 307-527-7117
info@wildsheepfoundation.org
www.wildsheepfoundation.org

The Foundation's mission is to promote and enhance populations of indigenous wild sheep in North America, and to fund programs for the professional management of these populations.
Founded: 1977
Brett Jefferson, Chairman
Jim Wilson, Vice Chairman

233 **Wilderness Society**
1615 M Street NW
Washington, DC 20036
202-833-2300
800-843-9453
action@tws.org
www.wilderness.org

Conservation organization working to protect the nation's shared wildlands and to inspire Americans to care for the wilderness.
Founded: 1935
Jamie Williams, President
Melyssa Watson, Vice President

234 **Xerces Society for Invertebrate Conservation**
628 NE Broadway
Suite 200
Portland, OR 97232
503-232-6639
855-232-6639
Fax: 503-233-6794
info@xerces.org
www.xerces.org

An international non profit organization dedicated to protecting biological diversity through inverterate conservation. Core programs focus on endangered species, protecting pollinators and watershed health.
Founded: 1971
David F. Johnson, President
Robert M. Pyle, Founder

National: Habitat Preservation & Land Use

235 **Agricultural Resources Center**
CB #3456 Manning Hill
Chapel Hill, NC 27599-3456
919-833-5333
877-667-7729
info@PESTed.org

With the belief that everybody deserves the right to clean air and water, the Agricultural Resources Center works in partnership with communities, supplying them with the knowledge and resources required to prevent or cleanup pollutionat the local level.
Paul Jones, Director
Cristobal Palmer, Technical Director

236 **Aldo Leopold Foundation**
E13701 Levee Road
PO Box 77
Baraboo, WI 53913-0077
608-355-0279
Fax: 608-356-7309
mail@aldoleopold.org
www.aldoleopold.org

The Aldo Leopold Foundation is a 501 (c)3 nonprofit organization that works to promote the philosophy of Aldo Leopold and the land ethic he so eloquently defined in his writing. The foundation actively integrates programs on landstewardship, environmental education and scientific research to promote care of natural resources and have an ethical relationship between people and land.
Founded: 1982
Levrett Nelson, Chair
Buddy Huffaker, President

237 **America the Beautiful Fund**
725 15th Street NW 202-638-1649
Suite 605 Fax: 202-638-2175
Washington, DC 20005
America the Beautiful Fund encourages volunteer citizen efforts to protect the natural and historic beauty of America. Programs include Operation Green Plant:Free Seeds! which provides free seeds and bulbs for environmental educationand preservation, community gardens and hunger relief.
Founded: 1965
Nanine Bilski, President/CEO
Kay Lautman, VP

238 **American Cave Conservation Association**
119 E Main Street 270-786-1466
PO Box 409 Fax: 270-786-1467
Horse Cave, KY 42749 hiddenrivercave@gmail.com
hiddenrivercave.com
A national nonprofit association dedicated to the protection of caves, karstlands and groundwater. The ACCA operates the American Cave Museum and Karst Center, an educational center that includes the American Cave Museum and HiddenRiver Cave.
Founded: 1978
David G Foster, Executive Director
Peggy A Nims, Community Outreach

239 **American Geological Institute**
4220 King Street 703-379-2480
Alexandria, VA 22302-1502 Fax: 703-379-7563
agi@americangeosciences.org
www.americangeosciences.org
Comprised of more than 50 scientific and professional associations that represent more than 120,000 geologists, geophysicists, and other earth scientists. Provides information services to geoscientists, serves as a voice of sharedinterests in the profession, plays a major role in strengthening geoscience education, and strives to increase public awareness of the vital role the geosciences play in society's use of resources and interaction with the environment.
Founded: 1948
Allyson K. Anderson Book, Executive Director

240 **American Institute of Fishery Research Biologists**
1315 East West Highway
Silver Spring, MD 20910 www.aifrb.org
A professional organization that pusrues the conservation and proper utlization of fishery resources. In dedication to the cause AIFRB develops and promotes advancements in the theory, practice and application of fishery biology andrelated sceinces.
Tom Keegan, President
Steve Cadrin, Past President

241 **American Littoral Society**
18 Hartshorne Drive 732-291-0055
Suite 1 Fax: 732-291-3551
Highlands, NJ 07732 www.littoralsociety.org
The American Littoral Society is an environmental organization concerned about issues that affect the littoral zone: that area on the beach between low and high tide. The American Littoral Society is a national, nonprofit,public-interest organization comprised of over 6,000 professional and amateur naturalists.
Tim Dillingham, Executive Director
Stevie Thorsen, Education Director

242 **American Public Gardens Association**
351 Longwood Road 610-708-3010
Kennett Square, PA 19348 Fax: 610-444-3594
info@publicgardens.org
publicgardens.org
Formerly the American Association of Botanical Gardens and Arboreta. APGA is committed to increasing the knowledge of public garden professionals through information sharing, professional development, education, research and plantconservation.
Founded: 1940
William M. LeFerve, President
Casey Sclar, Ph.D., Executive Director

243 **American Shore and Beach Preservation Association (ASBPA)**
5460 Beaujolais Lane 239-489-2616
Fort Myers, FL 33919 Fax: 239-362-9771
derek.brockbank@asbpa.org
asbpa.org
Dedicated to preserving, protecting and enhancing the beaches, shores and other coastal resources of America, recognizing their important quality-of-life assets.
Founded: 1926
Anthony P. Pratt, President
Derek Brockbank, Executive Director

244 **Animal Welfare Institute - Save The Whales**
900 Pennsylvania Avenue SE 202-337-2332
Washington, DC 20003 Fax: 202-446-2131
awionline.org
Save the Whales' purpose is to educate children and adults about marine mammals, their environment and their preservation. Founded in 1977, Save the Whale is a 801(c)(3) Educational Nonprofit Corporation.
Founded: 1951
Cathy Liss, President
Cynthia Wilson, Chair & Vice President

245 **Antarctica Project**
1320 19th Street, NW 202-234-2480
5th Floor Fax: 202-387-4823
Washington, DC 20036 secretariat@asoc.org
www.asoc.org
The only conservation organization in the world that works exclusively for Antarctica. Leads domestic and international campaigns to protect Antarctica's pristine wilderness and environment, as the international secretariat for theAntarctic and Southern Ocean Coalition (ASOC). ASOC is a global coalition with 214 member organizations working in 44 countries on six continents.
Mark Bauman, Chair
Scott Hajost, Vice Chair

246 **Association for Conservation Information**
1000 Assembly Street 843-762-5032
PO Box 167 Fax: 843-734-3951
Columbia, SC 29202 www.aci-net.org
ACI, the Association for Conservation Information, is a nonprofit association of information and education professionals representing state, federal and Canadian agencies and private conservation organizations.
Kim Nix, President
Jenifer Wisniewski, Vice-President

247 **Association for Environmental Health and Sciences**
150 Fearing Street 413-549-5170
Amherst, MA 01002 Fax: 413-549-0579
info@aehs.com
www.aehsfoundation.org
The AEHS was created to facilitate communication and foster cooperation among professionals concerned with the challenge of soil protection and cleanup. Members represent the many disciplines involved in making decisions and solvingproblems affecting soils. AEHS recognizes that widely acceptable solutions to the problem can be found only through the integration of scientific and technological discovery, social and political judgement and hands on practice.
Founded: 1989
Paul Kostecki, Ph.D., Executive Director
Brenna Lockwood, Managing Director

248 **Association for Natural Resources Enforcement Training**
Missouri Department of Conservation 573-751-4115
Box 180
Jefferson City, MO 65102
Dave Windsor, Vice-President

249 **Association of Consulting Foresters of America, Inc**
312 Montgomery Street 703-548-0990
Suite 208 membership@acf-foresters.org
Alexandria, VA 22314 www.acf-foresters.org
To protect the public welfare and property in the practice of forestry. To raise the professional standards and work of ACF Consultants and all other consulting foresters. To develop and expand the services of ACF Consultants.
Edward G. Tugwell, President
Michael R. Wetzel, President-Elect

250 **Association of Field Ornithologists**
University of Maine at Machias
116 O'Brien Avenue
Machias, ME 04654 afonet.org
Society of professional and amateur ornithologists dedicated to the scientific study and dissemination of information about birds in their natural habitats. Especially active in bird-banding and development of field techniques.Encourages participation of amateurs in research, and emphasizes conservation biology of birds.
Founded: 1922
Charles Duncan, President

251 **Association of Great Lakes Outdoor Writers**
PO Box 548
Knox, IN 46534 877-472-4569
aglowinfo.org
Dedicated to communicating the outdoor experience in word and image. AGLOW provide grants, scholarships and awards to writers and students who promote the outdoors in their own work.
Brandon Butler, President
Dan Stefanich, Vice-President

252 **Association of State Wetland Managers (ASWM)**
32 Tandberg Trail 207-892-3399
Suite 2A Fax: 207-894-7992
Windham, ME 04062 jeanne.christie@aswm.org
www.aswm.org
Nonprofit organization dedicated to the protection and restoration of the nation's wetlands. ASWM's goal is to help public and private wetland decision-makers utilize the best possible scientific information and techniques in wetlanddelineation, assessment, mapping, planning, regulation, acquisition, restoration and other management.
Founded: 1983
Jeanne Christie, Executive Director
Jon Kusler, Associate Director

253 **Bat Conservation International**
PO Box 162603 512-327-9721
Austin, TX 78716 800-538-2287
batinfo@batcon.org
www.batcon.org
Dedicated to preserving and restoring bat populations and habitats around the world. Uses a non-confrontational approach to educate the public about the ecological and economic value of bats, advance scientific knowledge about bats andthe ecosystems that rely on them and preserve critical bat habitats through win-win solutions that benefit both humans and bats.
Founded: 1982 $30/Yr
Cullen Geiselman, Chair
Steven P. Quarles, Vice Chair

254 **Big Thicket Association**
700 North Street 409-790-5399
Suite 79 director@bigthicket.org
Beaumont, TX 77701 www.bigthicket.org
Formed to save remnants of the once extensive historic Big Thicket forests with its remarkable diversity. A 501(c)3 organization, the Big Thicket Association established the Big Thicket National Preserve, a preserve that is nowdesignated as one of America's Ten Most Endangered National Parks.
Founded: 1964
Kathy Smartt, President
Bruce Walker, Executive Director

255 **Birds of Prey Foundation**
2290 South 104th Street 303-460-0674
Broomfield, CO 80020 raptor@birds-of-prey.org
www.birds-of-prey.org
The foundation seeks protection for raptors in the wild through education, invention and intervention; treats injured and orphaned wildlife; and works continuously to improve the quality of care and housing of captive raptorseverywhere.
Founded: 1984
Heidi Bucknam, Executive Director

256 **Blue Frontier**
P.O. Box 19367 202-387-8030
Washington, DC 20036 Fax: 202-234-5176
bluefront.org
The Blue Frontier is a nonprofit organization working towards preserving oceans and marine wildlife by providing resources to other organizations and communities.
Founded: 2003
Isis Schwartz, President
Scott Fielder, Treasurer

257 **BlueVoice.org**
10 Sunnfish Drive
St. Augustine, FL 32080 contact@bluevoice.org
bluevoice.org
BlueVoice.org is an ocean conservation organization seeking to protect dolphins, save the whales, and other marine mammals and to raise popular awareness about toxic chemicals in the oceans.
Founded: 2000
Hardy Jones, Executive Director

258 **Boone and Crockett Club**
250 Station Drive 406-542-1888
Missoula, MT 59801 888-840-4868
Fax: 406-542-0784
bcclub@boone-crockett.org
www.boone-crockett.org
Organization founded by Theodore Roosevelt with the vision of establishing a coalition of dedicated conservationists and sportsmen to provide leadership in the issues affecting hunting, wildlife and wildlife habitat.
Founded: 1887
B.B. Hollingsworth, Jr., President
James F. Arnold, Exec. VP, Conservation

259 **Brotherhood of the Jungle Cock**
1877 Trudeau Drive
Forest Hill, MD 21050 bosleywright@hotmail.com
bojcmd.wordpress.com
A member based organization focused on upholding the traditions of angling and fishing in Maryland's Hunting Creek. Campfire, an annual event, takes place to pass on to the youth of today the knowledge, skills and love for angling andthe outdoors. The parent chapter is located in Maryland with new chapters located in Michigan, New York, Ohio, Pennsylvania and Virginia.
Founded: 1938 $25/Year
James Mackley, President
Steve Lewis, Vice-President

260 **Campfire Conservation Fund Inc.**
230 Campfire Road 914-769-5508
Chappaqua, NY 10514-2419 Fax: 914-923-0977
The fund is a wildlife and habitat conservation organization that has been around for over 100 years.
Gordon Whiting, President

261 **Canyonlands Field Institute**
1320 South Highway 191 435-259-7750
PO Box 68 800-860-5262
Moab, UT 84532 Fax: 435-259-2335
info@cfimoab.org
cfimoab.org
To increase understanding of, connection to and care for the Colorado Plateau, expand perception of and appreciation for the beauty and integrity of the natural world, improve the quality of field oriented, experiential teaching andlearning for students and adults and to encourage individuals to be involved in the care of their own home places.
Founded: 1984
Sue Bellagamba, Chair
Karla VanderZanden, Executive Director

262 **Carrying Capacity Network**
1629 K Street NW 202-296-4548
Suite 300 info@carryingcapacity.org
Washington, DC 20006 carryingcapacity.org
An information exchange network. Interests include resource conservation, population stabilization and environmental protection.

263 **Center for Clean Air Policy**
750 First Street NE 202-408-9260
Suite 1025 Fax: 202-408-8896
Washington, DC 20002 communications@ccap.org
ccap.org
A leader in climate and air quality policy, it advances cost-effective and pragmatic policies. International and domestic programs focus on these four major areas: GHG Emission and Mitigation Economics; Emerging Technologies andTechnology Investment; Transportation and Land Use; and Adaptation.
Founded: 1985
Jim Maddy, Chair
Bill Tyndall, CEO

264 **Center for Humans and Nature**
20 N. Wacker Drive 312-629-5060
Suite 2807 Fax: 312-629-5061
Chicago, IL 60606 www.humansandnature.org
Works to explore and promote human responsibilities in relation to nature.
Founded: 2003
Gerald Adelmann, Chair

265 **Center for Plant Conservation**
15600 San Pasqual Valley Road 760-796-5686
Escondido, CA 92027-7000 info@saveplants.org
www.saveplants.org
The CPC is a consortium of 28 American botanical gardens and arboreta whose mission is to conserve and restore the rare native plants of the US To meet this end, they are involved in plant conservation, research and education. Thissite includes information about the National Collection of Endangered Plants, which is maintained by the group.
Dr. Peter Raven, Chair
John R. Clark, Ph.D., President/CEO

266 **Center for Wildlife Information**
PO Box 8289 406-239-2315
Missoula, MT 59807 bearinfo@cfwi.org
www.centerforwildlifeinformation.org
A resource that provides information on ways to interact and enjoy wildlife safely and responsibly. The objective is to reduce conflcits between humans and wildlife, in particular with bears, alligators and cougars.
Chuck Bartlebaugh, Contact

267 **Center for the Study of Tropical Birds**
218 Conway 210-214-9292
San Antonio, TX 78209 Fax: 210-828-9732
admin@cstbinc.org
www.cstbinc.org
Devoted to the conservation of neotropical birdlife through collaborative programs of research and education.
Jack Eitniear, President/Chairman
Thomas Rueckle, Treasurer

268 **Clean Sites**
228 S Washington Street 703-519-2135
Alexandria, VA 22314 Fax: 703-548-8733
www.cleansites.com
Clean Sites applies sound project management principles, real-world experience, and cost control measures to find creative solutions to environmental remediation and land reuse problems.

269 **Conservation International**
2011 Crystal Drive 703-341-2400
Suite 500 800-429-5660
Arlington, VA 22202 Fax: 202-887-5188
community@conservation.org
www.conservation.org
Their mission is to conserve the Earth's living natural heritage, our global biodiversity, and to demonstrate that human societies are able to live harmoniously with nature.
Peter Seligmann, Chairman/CEO
Jennifer Morris, President

270 **Conservation Management Institute**
Virginia Tech
1900 Kraft Drive 540-231-7348
Suite 250 Fax: 540-231-8825
Blacksburg, VA 24061 cmiinfo@vt.edu
www.cmi.vt.edu
To better address multi-disciplinary research questions that affect conservation management effectiveness in Virginia, North America and the world. Faculty from research institutions work collaboratively on projects ranging fromendangered species propagation to natural resource-based satellite imagery interpretation.
Founded: 2000
Scott D. Klofper, Executive Director

271 **Conservation Treaty Support Fund**
3705 Cardiff Road 301-654-3150
Chevy Chase, MD 20815 800-654-3150
Fax: 301-652-6390
CTSF's mission is to support the major inter-governmental treaties which conserve wild natural resources and habitat for their own sake and the benefit of people. These include the Endangered Species Convention and the InternationalWetlands Convention. CTSF raises support for treaty projects from individuals, corporations, foundations and government agencies. It also develops educational and informational materials including videos and the CITES Endangered Species Book.
Founded: 1986
George A. Furness,Jr., President

272 **Counterpart International**
2345 Crystal Drive 571-447-5700
Suite 301 Fax: 703-412-5035
Arlington, VA 22202 communications@counterpart.org
www.counterpart.org

Promotes socioeconomics, health care, biodiversity, and natural resource management in over 60 countries.
Raul Herrera, Chair
Joan Parker, President/CEO

273 **Defenders of Wildlife**
1130 17th Street NW 202-682-9400
Washington, DC 20036 800-385-9712
Fax: 202-682-1331
memberservices@defenders.org
www.defenders.org
Dedicated to the protection of all native wild animals and plants in their natural communities. Focus is placed on the accelerating rate of extinction of species and the associated loss of biological diversity, and habitat alterationand destruction.
Judith Posnikoff, Ph.D., Chair
Jamie Rappaport Clark, President/CEO

274 **Delta Wildlife**
433 Stoneville Road 662-686-3370
PO Box 276 Fax: 662-686-3382
Stoneville, MS 38776 trey@deltawildlife.org
deltawildlife.org
Recognizing the need for an agressive, but reasonable effort to develop wildlife, in 1990, one-hundred agri-business leaders, representing every country in Mississippi Delta, had the vision and dedication to form Delta Wildlife so theyand others could do more for conservation.
Randy Sewall, Chair
Paul D. Dees, President

275 **Department of Fisheries, Wildlife and Conservation Biology**
University of Minnesota
2003 Upper Buford Circle 612-624-3600
135 Skok Hall Fax: 612-301-1852
St. Paul, MN 55108 myfwcb@unm.edu
fwcb.cfans.umn.edu
Fosters a high quality natural environment by contributing to the management, protection, and sustainable use of fisheries and wildlife resources through teaching, research and outreach.
Founded: 1972

276 **Desert Fishes Council**
PO Box 337 520-221-0354
Bishop, CA 93515 phildesfish@verizon.net
www.desertfishes.org
The mission of the Desert Fishes Council is to preserve the biological integrity of desert aquatic ecosystems and their associated life forms, to hold symposia to report related research and management endeavors, and to effect rapiddissemination of information concerning activities of the Council and its members.
Founded: 1965
Michael Bogan, President
Phil Pister, Executive Secretary

277 **Desert Protective Council**
PO Box 3635 619-228-6316
San Diego, CA 92163-1635 indy@dpcinc.org
www.dpcinc.org
To safeguard for wise and reverent use by this and succeeding generations those desert areas of unique scenic, scientific, historical, spiritual or recreational value and to educate children and adults to a better understanding of thedeserts.
Founded: 1954
Janet Anderson, President
Larry Klaasen, Treasurer

278 **Desert Tortoise Council**
4654 East Avenue S
Suite 257B mojotort@yahoo.com
Palmdale, CA 93552 www.deserttortoise.org
The Council is a private, nonprofit organization made up of hundreds of professionals, and lay-persons from all walks of life, from across the United States, and several continents.These people come together from a shared fascinationwith wild desert tortoises and environments they depend upon.
Founded: 1976
Bruce Palmer, Chair
Michael Tuma, Chair-Elect

279 **Dragonfly Society of the Americas**
University Of Alabama Museums
335 Mary Harmon Bryant
PO Box 870340 jabbott1@ua.edu
Tuscaloosa, AL 35487 www.dragonflysocietyamericas.org
The Dragonfly Society of the Americas was organized in 1988. It is a nonprofit society whose purpose is to encourage scientific research, habitat preservation and aesthetic enjoyment of Odonata (dragon flies.)
Founded: 1988 $15/Year
R. DuBois, President
B. Pfeiffer, President-Elect

280 **Ducks Unlimited**
One Waterfowl Way 901-758-3825
Memphis, TN 38120 800-453-8257
Fax: 847-438-9236
www.ducks.org
The mission is to fulfill the annual life cycle needs of North American waterfowl by protecting, enhancing, restoring and managing important wetlands and associated uplands.
Rogers Hoyt, Jr., President
Dale Hall, CEO

281 **Eagle Nature Foundation Ltd.**
300 East Hickory Street 815-594-2306
Apple River, IL 61001 Fax: 815-594-2305
eaglenature.tni@juno.com
eaglenature.com
A nonprofit organization dedicated to the preservation of the bald eagle, America's national symbol, and other endangered species from extinction and to increase public awareness of unique endangered plants and animals. They monitorbald eagle and other endangered species populations, strive to preserve habitiat essential to their survival, and develops materials for schools to inform students about the needs of the bald eagle.
Founded: 1995
Terrence N Ingram, Founder/President
Eugene Small, Vice-President

282 **Earth Ecology Foundation**
4175 S. Decatur 702-778-9930
Las Vegas, NV 89103 erikwunstell@aol.com
www.westvegas.com/earth_ecology_foundation.html
Exploring natural and human environments by imagining futuristic ecological technolgies, and encouraging discoveries in theoretical physics and applies sciences.
Erik Wunstell, Director

283 **Earth Island Institute**
2150 Allston Way 510-859-9100
Suite 460 Fax: 510-859-9091
Berkeley, CA 94704-1375 www.earthisland.org
A nonprofit, public interest, membership organization that supports people who are creating solutions to protect the shared planet.
Founded: 1982
Josh Floum, President
Kenneth Brower, Vice-President

284 Earthworks
1612 K Street NW
Suite 904
Washington, DC 20006
202-887-1872
Fax: 202-887-1875
info@earthworksaction.org
www.earthworksaction.org

Mining causes serious environmental problems for local communities across the United States and throughout the world. From the perpetual water pollution caused by mine drainage to cyanide spills and heavy metals contamination; from thedesecration of sacred sites to the creation of toxic waste, rock mining creates devastating environmental consequences. EARTHWORKS carries out research and publishes comprehensive reports on the environmental impacts of mining.
Bill McNeill, D.D.D., Chair
Jennifer Krill, Executive Director

285 Endangered Species Coalition
PO Box 65195
Washington, DC 20035
240-353-2765
www.stopextinction.org
The Coalition is one of the most unique organizations in the United States. An organization of ogranizations that supports endangered species issues for over 430 environmental, religious, scientific, humane, and business groups aroundthe country. The vast majority of its member groups are small, local grassroots organizations, who struggle to protect species and habitats in their region.
Jon Ellenbogen, Chair
Brock Evans, President

286 Endangered Wolf Center
PO Box 760
Eureka, MO 63025
636-938-5900
info@endangeredwolfcenter.org
www.endangeredwolfcenter.org

A private nonprofit conservation organization dedicated to the preservation of the wolf and other endangered canids through education, research and captive breeding.
Founded: 1971
Jermiah Dellas, Chair
Ginny Busch, Executive Director

287 Ford Foundation
1440 Broadway
New York, NY 10017
212-573-5000
Fax: 212-351-3677
www.fordfoundation.org
Concerned with natural resource preservation. Provides funding for environmental projects throughout the world.
Kofi Appenteng, Chair
Darren Walker, President

288 Forest Guild
2019 Galisteo Street
Suite N7
Santa Fe, NM 87505
505-983-8992
Fax: 505-986-0798
info@forestguild.org
www.forestguild.org
The Forest Trust merged with Forest Stewards Guild to form Forest Guild. The practice of conservation forestry and the promotion of stewardship are central to the guild's mission.
Founded: 1984
Rick Morrill, Chair
Eric Holst, Vice Chair

289 Forest History Society
701 William Vickers Avenue
Durham, NC 27701-3162
919-682-9319
Fax: 919-682-2349
stevena@duke.edu
www.foresthistory.org

A nonprofit educational institution that links the past to the future by identifying, collecting, preserving, interpreting and disseminating information on the history of people, forests and their related resources.
Founded: 1946
Chris Zinkhan, Chair
Steven Anderson, President

290 Friends of Acadia
43 Cottage Street
PO Box 45
Bar Harbor, ME 04609
207-288-3340
800-625-0321
Fax: 207-288-8938
info@friendsofacadia.org
www.friendsofacadia.org
The mission of Friends of Acadia is to preserve and protect the outstanding natural beauty, ecological vitality and cultural distinctiveness of Acadia National Park and the surrounding communities. Their methods are: raises and donatesprivate funds to park and communities; advocates before legislatures and agencies; counters threats to park; and represents users in betterment of its operations.
Founded: 1986
Edward L. Samek, Chair
John Fassak, Vice Chair

291 Friends of the Sea Otter
PO Box 223260
Carmel, CA 93922
831-915-3275
info@seaotters.org
www.seaotters.org
Friends of the Sea Otter is a nonprofit organization founded in 1968 dedicated to the protection of a threatened species, the Southern Sea Otter, as well as Sea Otters throughout their north pacific range, and all sea otter habitat.
Jennifer Covert, Chair
Michael DeLapa, Interim Executive Director

292 Garden Club of America
14 East 60th Street
3rd Floor
New York, NY 10022
212-753-8287
Fax: 212-753-0134
gca@gcamerica.org
www.gcamerica.org

To stimulate the knowledge and love of gardening, to share the advantages of association by means of educational meetings, conferences, correspondence and publications, and to restore, improve, and protect the quality of theenvironment through educational programs and action in the fields of conservation and civic improvement.
Frederik Hansen, President

293 George Wright Society
PO Box 65
Hancock, MI 49930
906-487-9722
Fax: 906-487-9405
info@georgewright.org
www.georgewrightsociety.org
Concerned with the preservation of natural and cultural parks in the United States.
Nathalie Gagnon, President
Jennifer Palmer, Executive Director

294 Global Coral Reef Alliance
37 Pleasant Street
Cambridge, MA 02139
617-864-4226
goreau@bestweb.net
www.globalcoral.org

A nonprofit organization for the protection and sustainable management of coral reef.
Founded: 1990
Dr. Thomas J Goreau, President

295 Gopher Tortoise Council
303 Main Street
Suite 241
Safety Harbor, FL 34695
850-921-1030
www.gophertortoisecouncil.org
Formed by a group of biologists and others concerned about the range-wide decline of the gopher tortoise.
Founded: 1978
Will Dillman, Co-Chair
Dick Franz, Co-Chair

296 **Grand Canyon Trust**
2601 N. Fort Valley Road
Flagstaff, AZ 86001
928-774-7488
888-428-5550
Fax: 928-774-7570
info@grandcanyontrust.org
www.grandcanyontrust.org

The mission of The Grand Canyon Trust is to protect and restore the canyon country of the Colorado Plateau. The vision for this unique region 100 years from now is of a landscape still characterized by vast open spaces, dominated bywildness and healthy and restored natural ecosystems.

Founded: 1985
Steve Martin, Chair
Jim Enote, Vice-Chair

297 **Grassland Heritage Foundation**
PO Box 394
Shawnee Mission, KS 66201
785-748-0955
grasslandheritage@gmail.com
www.grasslandheritage.org

Grassland Heritage Foundation is a nonprofit membership organization to prairie preservation and education.

Founded: 1976
Andrea Repinsky, President
Megan Withiam, Vice-President

298 **Great Bear Foundation**
802 E. Front Street
PO Box 9383
Missoula, MT 59807-9383
406-829-9378
gbf@greatbear.org
www.greatbear.org

The Foundation was established to promote conservation of wild bears and their natural habitat worldwide.

Dr. Frank Tyro, President
Shannon Donahue, Executive Director

299 **HawkWatch International**
2240 South 900 East
Salt Lake City, UT 84106
801-484-6808
800-726-4295
Fax: 801-484-6810
hwi@hawkwatch.org
hawkwatch.org

HawkWatch International is a nonprofit organization that works to protect raptors and their environment through scientific research and public education.

Founded: 1986
Natalie Kaddas, Chair
Paul Parker, Executive Director

300 **Holy Land Conservation Fund**
805 Third Avenue
New York, NY 10022
Founded: 1972

301 **Humane Society of the United States**
1255 23rd Street NW
Washington, DC 20037
202-452-1100
866-720-2676
donorcare@humanesociety.org
www.humanesociety.org

HSUS is the nation's largest animal-protection organization with more than 5 million constituents. The HSUS was founded in 1954 to promote the humane treatment of animals, to foster respect, understanding, and compassion for allcreatures. Today their message of care and protection embraces not only the animal kingdom but also the Earth and its environment.

Founded: 1954
Wayne Pacelle, President/CEO
Michael Markarian, COO

302 **Hummingbird Society**
6560 State Route 179
Suite 124
Sedona, AZ 86351
928-284-2251
800-529-3699
Fax: 928-284-2251
info@hummingbirdsociety.org
www.hummingbirdsociety.org

Nonprofit corporation organized for the purpose of encouraging international understanding and conservation of hummingbirds by publishing and disseminating information, promoting and supporting scientific study and protecting habitat.

Founded: 1996
Cletus Toschlog, President
Dr. Robert L. Gell, Vice-President

303 **Inland Bird Banding Association**
1409 Childs Road East
Bellevue, NE 68005
419-447-0005
www.ibbainfo.org

Inland Bird Banding Association was organized in 1922, and now supports the largest membership of any bird banding association in America. Inland Bird Banding Association is an organization for all individuals interested in the seriousstudy of birds, their life-history, ecology, and conservation.

Founded: 1922
Vernon Kleen, President
Linda Tossing, 1st Vice-President

304 **Institute for Conservation Leadership**
6930 Carroll Avenue
Suite 1050
Takoma Park, MD 20912
301-270-2900
Fax: 301-270-0610
info@icl.org
www.icl.org

The mission of this Institute is to train and empower volunteer leaders and to build volunteer institutions that protect and conserve the Earth's environment. They lend a helping hand to dedicated partners in pursuit of a better worldfor everyone.

Mauricio Vel squez, Chair
Diane Russell, President

305 **International Association for Bear Research and Management**
1300 College Road
Fairbanks, AK 99071
907-459-7238
www.bearbiology.com

A volunteer organization open to professional biologists, wildlife managers and others dedicated to the conservation of all species of bears. Supports the scientific management of bears through research and distribution of information.

Founded: 1968
Andreas Zedrosser, President
Marty Obbard, Vice-President

306 **International Bird Rescue**
PO Box 2171
Long Beach, CA 90801
707-207-0380
Fax: 707-207-0395
gifts@bird-rescue.org
www.bird-rescue.org

Dedicated to mitigating the human impact on aquatic birds and other wildlife worldwide. The Rescue provides emergency response and planning, wildlife rehabilitation, research and education.

Founded: 1971
Ron Morris, Chair
J.D. Bergeron, Executive Director

307 **International Crane Foundation**
E11376 Shady Lane Road
PO Box 447
Baraboo, WI 53913
608-356-9462
info@savingcranes.org
www.savingcranes.org

Works worldwide to conserve cranes and the wetland and grasslands communities on which they depend. Dedicated to providing

experience, knowledge, and inspiration to involve people in resolving threats to these ecosystems.
Founded: 1973
Richard Beilfuss, President/CEO
James Brumm, Chair

308 International Erosion Control Association

3401 Quebec Street
Suite 3500
Denver, CO 80207
303-640-7554
800-455-4322
Fax: 866-308-3087
ecinfo@ieca.org
www.ieca.org

An organization dedicated to minimizing accelerated soil erosion. IECA offers an annual conference, chapter events, training courses as well as a variety of topic specific publications and a quarterly news letter.
Founded: 1972
Thomas W. Schneider, CPESC, President
Sharan Wilson, Executive Director

309 International Fund for Animal Welfare

290 Summer Street
Yarmouth, MA 02675
508-744-2000
800-932-4329
Fax: 508-744-2009
info@ifaw.org
www.ifaw.org

The International Fund for Animal Welfare (IFAW) aims to improve the welfare of wild and domestic animals throughout the world by reducing commercial exploitation of animals in distress, primarily by motivating the public to preventcruelty to animals and promoting animal welfare and conservation policies that advance the well-being of both animals and people.
Kathleen Savesky Buckley, Chair
Azzedine Downes, President/CEO

310 International Osprey Foundation

PO Box 250
Sanibel, FL 33957
tiof@ospreys.com
www.ospreys.com

Nonprofit corporation dedicated to the continuing recovery and preservation of the osprey, others in the raptor family, wildlife and the environment as a whole. Conducts monitoring activities and accumulates data specific to thebreeding activities of the osprey population. Publishes newsletter, issues grants for researchers whose studies involve environmental concerns. Directs and participates in all areas of wildlife and habitat maintenance and restoration.
Jim Griffith, President
Anne Mitchell, Vice-President

311 International SeaKeepers Society

255 Aragon Avenue
Third Floor
Coral Gables, FL 33134
305-448-7089
800-435-7352
crrobinson@seakeepers.org
seakeepers.org

The International SeaKeepers Society promotes oceanographic research, conservation, and education through direct involvement with the yachting community. SeaKeepers enables the yachting community to take full advantage of their uniquepotential to advance marine sciences and to raise awareness about global ocean issues.
Richard Snow, President/CEO
Carolyn Ruth Robinson, Operations & Administration

312 International Society for the Protection of Mustangs and Burros

PO Box 55
Lantry, SD 57636-0055
605-430-2088
ispmb@lakotanetwork.com
www.ispmb.org

Dedicated to preserving wild horses/burros and their habitats. They also run a rescue program and purchase slaughter bound wild horses and burros, placing them in permanent loving homes, or transporting entire herds of horses.
Karen Sussman, Director

313 International Society of Limnology Theoretical and Applied

5020 Swepsonville-Saxapahaw Road
Granham, NC 27253
www.limnology.org

To further the study and understanding of all aspects of limnology. Promotes and communicates new and emerging knowledge among limnologists to advance the understanding of inland aquatic ecosystems and their management.
Founded: 1922
Prof. Dr. Yves Prairie, President
Prof. Dr. David Livingstone, Vice-President

314 International Union for Conservation of Nature and Natural Resources

1630 Connecticut Avenue NW
3rd Floor, Suite 300
Washington, DC 20009
202-387-4826
+41-22-9990000
Fax: 202-387-4823
Fax: +41-22-9990002
deborah.good@iucn.org
www.iucn.org

Founded: 1948
Inger Andersen, Director General
Frank Hawkins, Director, Washington DC

315 International Wildlife Rehabilitation Council

PO Box 3197
Eugene, OR 97403
866-871-1869
Fax: 408-876-6153
office@theiwrc.org
theiwrc.org

A nonprofit organization that works to enhance the integrity of native wildlife systems and conserve biological diversity worldwide, through rehabilitation of wildlife, support of rehabilitators, public education and advocacy.
Founded: 1972
Susan Wylie, President
Adam Grogan, Vice President

316 Island Conservation

2100 Delaware Avenue
Suite 1
Santa Cruz, CA 95060
831-359-4787
info@islandconservation.org
www.islandconservation.org

Island Conservation look to maintain wildlife by removing invasive species from islands. Islands across the world are where biodiversity and species exstinction is the greatest.
Founded: 1994
Angus Parker, Chair
Mike Sweeney, Vice Chair

317 Izaak Walton League of America

707 Conservation Lane
Gaithersburg, MD 20878
301-548-0150
800-453-5463
Fax: 301-548-0146
info@iwla.org
www.iwla.org

The mission is to conserve, maintain, protect and restore the soil, forest water and other natural resources of the United States and other lands; to promote means and opportunities for the education of the public with respect to suchresources and their enjoyment and wholesome utilization.
Founded: 1922
Jeff Deschamps, President
Scott Kovarovics, Executive Director

318 Life of the Land

76 N. King Street
Suite 203
Honolulu, HI 96817
808-533-3454
Fax: 808-533-0993
www.lifeofthelandhawaii.org

Hawaii's own environmental and community action group protecting fragile natural and cultural resources through research, education, advocacy and litigation.
Founded: 1970
Kapua Sproat, President
Henry Curtis, Executive Director

319 Lighthawk
PO Box 2710
Telluride, CO 81435
970-797-9355
terriwatson@lighthawk.org
www.lighthawk.org
Nonprofit organization addressing critical environmental issues by providing an aerial perspective on areas of concern in the US, Canada and Central America. Using small aircrafts, they fly partner organizations, elected officials,industry and media representatives, activists, and indigenous groups over protected and threatened regions.
Founded: 1979
Terri Watson, CEO
Emilie Ryan, CFO

320 Marin Conservation League
175 N. Redwood Drive
Suite 135
San Rafael, CA 94903
415-485-6257
Fax: 415-485-6259
mcl@conservationleague.org
www.conservationleague.org
The Marin Conservation League is an a nonprofit organization founded in 1934 to preserve, protect and enhance the natural assets of Marin County for all people. MCL is Marin's oldest, locally based environmental organization,championing a sound balance between the needs of Marin's citizens and its beautiful and fragile environment.
Founded: 1934
Kate Powers, President
Linda Novy, 1st Vice-President

321 Marine Conservation Alliance
PO Box 1030
Poulsbo, WA 98370
360-626-1140
Fax: 206-260-3639
marineconservationalliance.org
MCA seeks to provide proactive management of ecosystems and fisheries to ensure sustainable seafood providers.
Lori Swanson, Executive Director
Anne Vanderhoeven, President

322 Marine Conservation Institute
4010 Stone Way N
Suite 210
Seattle, WA 98103-8099
206-686-1455
Fax: 206-686-1460
info@marine-conservation.org
marine-conservation.org
The Marine Conservation Institute is an nonprofit organization dedicated to ensuring permanent protection for the ocean's survival. The Institute works with scientists, politicians, government officials and other organizations toidentify key threats to areas in marine ecosystems and build workable solutions.
Founded: 1996
Lance Morgan, President
David Johns, Chair

323 Mountain Institute
3000 Connecticut Avenue NW
Suite 101
Washington, DC 20008
202-234-4050
Fax: 202-234-4054
summit@mountain.org
www.mountain.org
The Mountain Institute's objectives are to conserve high priority mountain eco-systems; increase environmentally and culturally sustainable livelihoods for mountain communities; and promote support for mountain cultures and issuesthrough advocacy, education and outreach.
Founded: 1972
Andrew Taber, Executive Director
Jennifer Drenning, Director of Development

324 Mountain Lion Foundation
PO Box 1896
Sacramento, CA 95812
916-442-2666
800-319-7621
Fax: 916-442-2871
info@mountainlion.org
www.mountainlion.org
A national nonprofit conservation and education organization dedicated to protecting the mountain lion, its habitat and the wildlife that shares that habitat.
Founded: 1986
Toby Cooper, Chair
Elizabeth Sullivan, Vice Chair

325 Mustangs Of America Foundation
1895 Crockett Lane
Gardnerville, NV 89410
775-790-0207
kjleach2004@yahoo.com
www.mustangsofamericafoundation.org
MAF is dedicated to promoting mustang and burro adoption, training, facilitating public education, rescue and prevention of cruelty to animals. MAF is committed to working with the Bureau of Land Management, Department of Agricultureand other nonprofit organizations to increase the number of successful adoptions by providing information and education to the public about adoption, rescue and training programs.
Kathy Leach, President
Lynda Sanford, Director/Secretary

326 National Association of Conservation Districts
509 Capitol Court NE
Washington, DC 20002-4937
202-547-6223
Fax: 202-547-6450
info@nacdnet.org
www.nacdnet.org
A non-governmental, nonprofit organization representing 3000 local soil and water conservation districts as well as the 17,000 that serve on their governing boards. Among its goals are: provide useful information to the districts andtheir state associations; represent them as a national unified voice; analyze programs and policy issues that have an impact on local districts; and offer needed and cost-effective services.
Founded: 1946
Brent Van Dyke, President
Jeremy Peters, CEO

327 National Audubon Society
225 Varick Street
7th Floor
New York, NY 10014
212-979-3000
844-428-3826
Fax: 212-979-3188
audubon@emailcustomerservice.com
www.audubon.org
The National Audubon Society is one of the oldest, largest, and most powerful nature appreciation and conservation organizations in the country. NAS works on a broad range of concerns related to the protection of the world'secosystems; preserving wetlands, population planning, eliminating acid rain and reducing air pollution, promoting environmental justice, and protecting water quality.
Founded: 1905
David Yarnold, President/CEO
John Beavers, Vice President

328 National Audubon Society: Project Puffin
311 Main Street
Rockland, ME 04841
207-596-5566
877-478-3346
puffin@audubon.org
projectpuffin.audubon.org
Established to learn how to restore puffins to historic nesting islands in the Gulf of Maine. Although puffins are abundant in Newfoundland, Iceland and Britain, they are rare in Maine. Project Puffin has a year round staff of sixwhich increases to include more than 50 biologists and researchers during the seabird breeding season in spring and summer.
Founded: 1973
Stephen W. Kress, Director
Rosalie Borzik, Associate Director

329 National Fish and Wildlife Foundation

1133 15th Street, NW
Suite 1000
Washington, DC 20005
202-857-0166
Fax: 202-857-0162
info@nfwf.org
www.nfwf.org

The National Fish and Wildlife Foundation is a nonprofit organization dedicated to the conservation of fish, wildlife, and plants and the habitats on which they depend. Among its goals are species habitat protection, environmentaleducation, public policy development, natural resource management, habitat and ecosystem rehabilitation and restoration, and leadership training for conservation professionals.

Founded: 1984
John V. Faraci, Jr., Chair
Jeff Trandahl, CEO/Executive Director

330 National Forest Foundation

Fort Missoula Road
Building 27, Suite 3
Missoula, MT 59804
406-542-2805
Fax: 406-542-2810
www.nationalforests.org

The official nonprofit partner of the USDA Forest Service. To accept and administer private contributions, undertaking activities that further the purposes for which the National Forest System was established and conductingeducational, technical, and other activities that support the multiple use, research, and forestry programs administered by the Forest Service.

Craig R. Barrett, Chair
Mary Mitsos, President

331 National Garden Clubs

4401 Magnolia Avenue
St. Louis, MO 63110
314-776-7574
800-550-6007
Fax: 314-776-5108
headquarters@gardenclub.org
www.gardenclub.org

National Garden Clubs is a nonprofit educational organization with its headquarters in St. Louis, Missouri, US. It is composed of 50 State Garden Clubs and the National Capital Area, 8,858 member garden clubs and 235,316 members. Inaddition, NGC proudly recognizes 200 Internationl Affiliates from Canada to Mexico and South America.

Founded: 1891
Nancy L. Hargroves, President
Gay Austin, First Vice-President

332 National Grange

1616 H Street NW
Washington, DC 20006
202-628-3507
888-447-2643
Fax: 202-347-1091
info@nationalgrange.org
www.nationalgrange.org

The Grange is a family based community organization with a special interest in agriculture and rural America, as well as in legislative efforts regarding these issues.

Founded: 1867
Betsy Huber, President
Stephanie Tiller, Director, Operations

333 National Military Fish and Wildlife Association (NMFWA)

12428 Pinecrest Lane
Newburg, MD 20664
540-663-4186
Fax: 540-663-4016
nicole.olmsted@fe.navy.mil
www.nmfwa.net

NMFWA recognizes the critical need for enhanced awareness of natural resource conservation requirements to provide for both long term sustainability of resource diversity and the successful accomplishment of the military trainingmission on public lands. Members include biologists, botanists, ecologists, range conservationists, foresters, cultural resource managers and law enforcement agents.

Elizabeth Neipert, President
Eric Britzke, Vice-President

334 National Park Foundation

1110 Vermont Avenue, NW
Suite 200
Washington, DC 20005
202-796-2500
888-467-2757
Fax: 202-796-2509
ask-npf@nationalparks.org
www.nationalparks.org

Mission is to strengthen the connection between the American people and their National Parks by raising private funds, making strategic grants, creating innovative parnerships and increasing public awareness.

Al Baldwin, Chair
Will S. Shafroth, President/CEO

335 National Park Trust (NPT)

401 E. Jefferson Street
Suite 207
Rockville, MD 20850
301-279-7275
866-281-5971
Fax: 301-279-7211
npt@parktrust.org
www.parktrust.org

Dedicated to preserving parks today and creating stewards for tomorrow, because NPT believes everyone deserves a American Park Experience. Building awareness and appreciation for American national parks and other public lands andwaters.

Founded: 1983
Grace Lee, Executive Director
Maryann Kearns, Director, Development

336 National Parks Conservation Association

777 6th Street NW
Suite 700
Washington, DC 20001-3723
202-223-6722
800-628-7275
Fax: 202-454-3333
npca@npca.org
www.npca.org

The National Parks Conservation Association is the voice of the American people fighting to safeguard the scenic beauty, wildlife, and historical and cultural treasures of their American homeland.

Founded: 1919
W. Clark Bunting, President/CEO
Theresa Pierno, COO

337 National Recreation and Park Association

Parks and Recreation Magazine
22377 Belmont Ridge Road
Ashburn, VA 20148-4501
703-858-0784
800-626-6772
Fax: 703-858-0794
customerservice@nrpa.org
www.nrpa.org

The NRPA is a national nonprofit organization devoted to advancing park, recreation and conservation efforts that enhance the quality of life for all Americans. The Association works to extend social, health, cultural and economicbenefits of parks and recreation through its network of 23,000 recreation and park professionals and civic leaders. NRPA encourages recreation initiatives for youth in high-risk environments.

Founded: 1965
Stephen Eckelberry, Chair
Barbara Tulipane, President/CEO

338 National Speleological Society

6001 Pulaski Pike
Huntsville, AL 35810-1122
256-852-1300
Fax: 256-851-9241
nss@caves.org
caves.org

Founded for the purpose of advancing the study, conservation, exploration, and knowledge of caves. More than 12,000 members in 200 grottos conduct regular meetings to bring cavers

trogether within their general area to coordinateactivities which may include mapping, cleaning and investigating sensitive caves.
Geary Schindel, President
Curt Harler, Executive VP

339 National Trust for Historic Preservation
2600 Virginia Avenue NW 202-588-6000
Suite 1100 800-944-6847
Washington, DC 20037 Fax: 202-588-6038
info@savingplaces.org
savingplaces.org
Provides leadership, education, resources and advocacy to save America's diverse historic places and revitalize its communities.
Founded: 1949
Stephanie Meeks, President/CEO
David J. Brown, Chief Preservation Officer

340 National Wildflower Research Center
4801 La Crosse Avenue 512-232-0100
Austin, TX 78739 877-945-3357
Fax: 512-232-0156
www.wildflower.org
Combines native plants with local culture, reflecting the specifics and peculiarities of Central Texas Hill Country ecosystems. Walking through the center, you'll find native plants in gardens and natural areas, an unparalledrainwater collection and storage system, recycled building materials, American folk art, environmentally conscious construction and engaging educational faciltities—all designed to learn to live more gently on the land.
Founded: 1897
Patrick Newman, Executive Director

341 National Wildlife Federation
11100 Wildlife Center Drive
Reston, VA 20190 800-822-9919
www.nwf.org
Gives voice to the wildlife conservation values that are part of the country's heritage.
Founded: 1936
Kathy Hadley, Chair
Collin O'Mara, President/CEO

342 National Wildlife Refuge Association
1001 Connecticut Avevenue NW 202-417-3803
Suite 905 nwra@refugeassociation.org
Washington, DC 20036 refugeassociation.org
The National Wildlife Refuge Association is the only conservation organization solely dedicated to protecting and enhancing the National Wildlife Refuge System, the world's largest network of lands and waters set aside for wildlifeconservation.
Founded: 1975
Rebecca Rubin, Chair
Geoffrey Haskett, President

343 National Wildlife Rehabilitators Association
2625 Clearwater Road 320-230-9920
Saint Cloud, MN 56301 Fax: 320-230-3077
nwra@nwrawildlife.org
www.nwrawildlife.org
The National Wildlife Rehabilitators Association is a nonprofit international membership organization committed to promoting and improving the integrity and professionalism of wildlife rehabilitation and contributing to thepreservation of natural ecosystems.
Founded: 1982
Richard Grant, President
Jennifer Convey, Vice-President

344 National Woodland Owners Association
374 Maple Avenue East 703-255-2700
Suite 310 Fax: 703-281-9200
Vienna, VA 22180 info@woodlandowners.org
www.nwoa.net
NWOA is independent of the forest products industry and forestry agencies. They work with all organizations to promote non-industrial forestry and the best interests of woodland owners.
Founded: 1983
Dick Couter, Chairman
Keith A. Argow, President

345 Natural Areas Association
PO Box 594 724-995-8466
Ligonier, PA 15658 info@naturalareas.org
naturalareas.org
To advance the preservation of natural diversity. To inform, unite and support persons engaged in identifying, protecting, managing, and studying natural areas and biological diversity across landscapes and ecosystems.
Founded: 1980
Lisa Smith, Executive Director
Joe Walko, Operations Manager

346 Natural Resources Defense Council
40 West 20th Street 212-727-2700
11th Floor Fax: 212-727-1773
New York, NY 10011 nrdcinfo@nrdc.org
www.nrdc.org
The NRDC focuses on issues impacting climate change, ocean pollution, water management and treatment, clean energy, and the conservation of wildlife.
Founded: 1990
Rhea . Suh, President
Mitchell Bernard, Chief Counsel

347 Neighborhood Parks Council
1663 Mission Street 415-621-3260
Suite 320 Fax: 415-703-0889
San Francisco, CA 94103 feedback@sfparksalliance.org
www.sfparksalliance.org
Neighborhood Parks Council (NPC) advocates for a superior, equitable and sustainable park and recreation system. NPC provides leadership and support to park users through community-driven stewardship, education, planning and research.
Founded: 1996
Drew Becher, CEO

348 Nicodemus Wilderness Project
PO Box 40712
Albuquerque, NM 87196-0712 mail@wildernessproject.org
www.wildernessproject.org
The Nicodemus Wilderness Project was founded because of the need for environmental restoration, stewardship, and projection of neglected public lands.
Robert K. Dudley, President/Executive Director
Yih Ming Hsu, VP, Program Manager

349 North American Bluebird Society (NABS)
PO Box 7844 330-359-5511
Bloomington, IN 47407 Fax: 330-359-5455
info@nabluebirdsociety.org
www.nabluebirdsociety.org
Nonprofit conservation, education and research organization, promotes the recovery of the bluebirds and other native cavity-nesting bird species. NABS supports conservation through such continent wide programs as the TranscontinentalBluebird Trail and the NABS Nestbox Approval Process. NABS also produces award-winning educational materials.
Founded: 1977
Bernie Daniel, President
Phil Berry, First VP

350 North American Crane Working Group
E-11376 Shady Lane Road
Baraboo, WI 53913-0447
www.nacwg.org
NACWG is an organization of professional biologists, aviculturists, land managers and other interested individuals dedicated to the conservation of cranes and their habitats in North America. They sponsor a North American CraneWorkshop every 3-4 years, promulgates technical information including a published Proceedings of a North American Workshop and a semi-annual newsletter, address conservation issues affecting cranes and their habitat, promote appropriate research oncrane conservation.
Richard Urbanek, President

351 North American Falconers Association
7828 Hood Street
Fort Worth, TX 76135
www.n-a-f-a.com
Provides communication among and disseminates relevant information to interested members; scientific study of raptorial species, their care, welfare and training; promotes conservation of the birds of prey and an appreciation of theirvalue in nature and in wildlife conservation programs; urges recognition of falconry as a legal field sport; and establishs traditions which will aid, perpetuate and further the welfare of falconry and raptors it employs.
Founded: 1961
Scott McNeff, President
Sheldon Nicolle, Vice-President

352 North American Wildlife Park Foundation Wolf Park
4004 East 800 North
Battle Ground, IN 47920
765-567-2265
Fax: 765-567-4299
admin@wolfpark.org
wolfpark.org
Wolf Park is a 501(c)(3) not-for-profit organization. Their mission is to improve public understanding of wolves and the value they provide to the environment.
Founded: 1972
Dana Drenzek, Manager
Pat Goodmann, Senior

353 Ocean Alliance
32 Horton Street
Gloucester, MA 01930
978-281-2814
whale.org
Ocean Alliance is a nonprofit organization dedicated to increasing public awareness of the importance of whale and ocean health through research and public education.
Founded: 1971
Roger Payne, President
Iain Kerr, Chief Executive Officer

354 Oceanic Preservation Society
336 Bon Air Center
Suite 384
Greenbrae, CA 94904
info@opsociety.org
opsociety.org
The Oceanic Preservation Society is dedicated to the conservation of marine ecosystems and promote advocacy through the use of film, photography, social media, and collaboration.
Louie Psihoyos, Founder/CEO
Samara Stein, Ceif Operating Officer

355 Open Space Institute
1350 Broadway
Suite 201
New York, NY 10018
212-290-8200
Fax: 212-244-3441
webmaster@osiny.org
www.openspaceinstitute.org
Protects land for public benefit and supports the efforts of citizen activists working to improve environmental regulations in their communities.
Christopher J. Elliman, President/CEO
Robert K. Anderberg, Sr. VP/General Counsel

356 Openlands Project
25 East Washington Street
Suite 1650
Chicago, IL 60602
312-863-6250
Fax: 312-863-6251
info@openlands.org
openlands.org
Openlands Project is an independent, nonprofit organization dedicated to preserving and enhancing public open space in northeastern Illinois. Openlands bridges political boundaries and build consensus on open space goals and regionalgrowth strategies.
Founded: 1963
Carrie C. McNally, Chair
Gerald W. Adelmann, President/CEO

357 Organization for Bat Conservation
75 West Huron Street
Pontiac, MI 48342
248-294-7370
800-276-7074
Fax: 248-294-7373
info@batconservation.org
batconservation.org
A nonprofit organization with the mission to preserve bats and their habitats through education, collaboration and research. The organization also works with local health departments and government agencies to aid in public healthissues associated with bats.
Founded: 1997
Danielle Todd, President
Rob Mies, Executive Director

358 Ozark Society
PO Box 2914
Little Rock, AR 72203
479-466-3077
bobcross610@gmail.com
www.ozarksociety.net
The Ozark Society has remained a strong regional organization because is has not allowed itself to be diverted from its principal purpose: the preservation of wild and scenic rivers, wilderness and unique natural areas. Its primaryfocus is the Ozark-Ouachita region and its associated bottom land habitat.
Founded: 1962
David Peterson, President
Lucas Parsch, Vice-President

359 Pacific Marine Mammal Center
20612 Laguna Canyon Road
Laguna Beach, CA 92651
949-494-3050
info@pacificmmc.org
www.pacificmmc.org
Formerly Friends of the Sea Lion Marine Mammal Center, Pacific Marine Mammal Center is a nonprofit organization staffed by dedicated volunteers and funded by donations. Its mission is to rescue, medically treat and rehabilitate sealsand sea lions that are stranded along Orange County, California beaches due to injury and illness; release healthly animals back to their natural habitat; and increase public awareness of the marine environment through education and research.
Keith Matassa, Executive Director

360 Panthera
8 West 40th Street
18th Floor
New York, NY 10018
646-786-0400
info@panthera.org
panthera.org
Panthera is an international nonprofit organization devoted to the conservation of the world's 40 wild cat species and their ecosystems.
Founded: 2006
Thomas S. Kaplan, Founder/Chairman
Alan Rabinowitz, Chief Executive Officer

361 Partners in Parks
PO 362
Tustin, CA 92781
714-393-8506
www.partnersinparks.org

Organize and direct volunteers for work in city parks and trails. Outdoor work can be as simple as litter pick-up to trail cleaning and tree planting.
Founded: 1988

362 Peregrine Fund
5668 West Flying Hawk Lane
Boise, ID 83709
208-362-3716
Fax: 208-362-2376
tpf@peregrinefund.org
www.peregrinefund.org

The Peregrine Fund was founded to restore the Peregrine Falcon, which was removed from the U.S. Endangered Species List in 1999. That success has encouraged the organization to expand its focus and apply its experience andunderstanding to raptor conservation efforts on behalf of 87 species in 61 countries worldwide, including the California Condor and Aplomado Falcon in the United States. The organization is non-political, solution-oriented, and hands-on.
Founded: 1970
Richard Watson, President/CEO
Tom Cade, Founding Chairman

363 Point Blue
3820 Cypress Drive
Suite 11
Petaluma, CA 94954
707-781-2555
Fax: 707-765-1685
jholton@pointblue.org
pointblue.org

Point Blue's mission is to conserve birds, other wildlife and ecosystems through science, partnerships, and outreach.
Founded: 1965
Jeffrey Holton, Facilities Manager
Ellie M. Cohen, President/CEO

364 Prairie Grouse Technical Council
North American Grouse Partnership
39177 Flamingo Street NW
Stranchfield, MN 58050

The Prairie Grouse Technical Council is an organization of people who appreciate and enjoy grouses and their habitats. The group meets in odd numbered years.
Greg Hoch, Treasurer

365 Project AWARE
301541 Tomas
Suite 200
Rancho Santa Margarita, CA 92688
949-858-7657
projectaware.org

Project AWARE is a nonprofit organization dedicated to engaging divers and activists around the world in marine conservation with a focus on sharks and marine debris.
Founded: 1992
Tiffany Leite, Director
Ania Duziak, Associate Director

366 Public Lands Alliance
2401 Blueridge Ave
Suite 303
Silver Spring, MD 20902
301-946-9475
Fax: 301-946-9478
publiclandsalliance.org

Formely known as Association of Partners for Public Lands (APPL), Public Lands Alliance work to create understanding and appreciation for America's public lands by partnering with nonprofit organizations.
Founded: 1977
David Poteet, President
Christine Muldoon, Vice-President

367 Public Lands Foundation
PO Box 7226
Arlington, VA 22207-0916
703-935-0916
866-985-9636
Fax: 888-204-9814
info@publicland.org
publicland.org

The Public Lands Foundation (PLF) is a national non-profit membership organization that advocates and works for the retention of America's National System of Public Lands (NSPL) in public hands, professionally and sustainably managedby the Bureau of Land Management (BLM) for responsible use and enjoyment by everyone.
Founded: 1987
Jesse Juen, President
Don Simpson, Vice-President

368 Quail Forever
1783 Buerkle Circle
St. Paul, MN 31701
651-209-4981
866-457-8245
contact@quailforever.org
www.quailforever.org

Quail Forever is a division of Pheasant Forever. Quail Forever is a grassroots, volunteer, membership-based organization that sets out to preserve and replenish quail habitats and quail populations acros North America.
Howard K. Vincent, President/CEO
Bob St. Pierre, Vice-President, Marketing

369 Rainforest Alliance
233 Broadway
28th Floor
New York, NY 10279
212-677-1900
Fax: 212-677-2187
info@ra.org
www.rainforest-alliance.org

Dedicated to tropical forest conservation for the benefit of the global community. Rainforest Alliance works with farmers, foresters and tourism entrepreneurs. Through education and training they believe they can show people how tominimize environmental impact, while earning a stable income.
Founded: 1987
Daniel R. Katz, Chairman
Roger Deromedi, Vice Chair

370 Raptor Education Foundation (REF)
PO Box 200400
Denver, CO 80220
303-680-8500
Fax: 720-685-9988
raptor2@usaref.org
www.usaref.org

Raptors refer to birds with hoooked beakes; eagles, hawks, falcons and owls are all raptors. REF provides environmental literacy to schools, corporations, conventions and gatherings of all sizes. They use live, non-releasable raptorsin their seminars and programs to better demonstrate environmental concepts.
Founded: 1980
Peter Reshetniak, Chairman
Ann Price, Secretary

371 Rare
1310 North Courthouse Road
Suite 110
Arlington, VA 22201
703-522-5070
Fax: 703-522-5027
info@rare.org
www.rare.org

Rare is an organization that focuses on the things that are working in environmental conservation. Rare's methodology revolves around locally-led solutions, bright spots, and repeat them in communities around the globe.
Founded: 1973
Brett Jenks, President/CEO
Taufiq Alimi, Vice-President

372 Ruffed Grouse Society
451 McCormick Road
Coraopolis, PA 15108
412-262-4044
888-564-6747
Fax: 412-262-9207
rgs@ruffedgrousesociety.org
www.ruffedgrousesociety.org

The Ruffed Grouse Society's role in conservation of wildlife habitat is to enhance the environment for the Ruffed Grouse, Ameri-

can Woodcock, and other forest wildlife that require or utilize thick, young forests.
Founded: 1961
Terry Wilson, Chair
John Eichinger, President/CEO

373 **Save the Dunes Council**
444 Barker Road 219-879-3564
Michigan City, IN 46360 Fax: 219-872-4875
office@savedunes.org
savedunes.org

The Save the Dunes Council of northwest Indiana was founded in 1952, one of the oldest grassroots conservation organizations in the country. Its objectives are to maintain and restore the integrity and quality of the naturalenvironment of the Indiana Dunes region. The hard work of their members led to the establishment of the Indiana Dunes National Lakeshore in 1966; the group continues to work on a wide variety of issues concerning the Dunes and the environmentalquality of the area.
Founded: 1952
Tom Conway, President
Natalie Johnson, Executive Director

374 **Save the Manatee Club**
500 N. Maitland Avenue 407-539-0990
Maitland, FL 32751 800-432-5646
Fax: 407-539-0871
membership@savethemanatee.org
www.savethemanatee.org

Save the Manatee Club is a nonprofit organization, established in 1981 by US Senator Bob Graham and singer/songwriter Jimmy Buffett so the general public could participate in conservation efforts to save endangered manatees fromextinction. The purpose of SMC is to promote public awareness and education; fund manatee research, rescue, and rehabilitation efforts; lobby for the protection of manatees and their habitat, and take appropriate legal action.
Founded: 1981
Jimmy Buffett, Co-Chair
Helen Digges Spivey, Co-Chair

375 **Scenic America**
1307 New Hampshire Avenue NW 202-463-1294
Washington, DC 20036 Fax: 202-463-1299
max.ashburn@scenic.org
www.scenic.org

A national nonprofit organization dedicated solely to protecting natural beauty and distinctive community character. They provide technnical assistance across the nation and through their state affiliates on scenic byways, billboardand sign control, context sensitive highway design, wireless telecommunications tower location, transportation enhancements, and other scenic conservation. Scenic's number one goal is to build a citizen movement for scenic conservation througheducation.
Ronald Lee Fleming, Chair
Mark Falzone, President

376 **Sea Turtle Conservancy**
4424 NW 13th Street 352-373-6441
Suite B-11 Fax: 352-375-2449
Gainesville, FL 32609 stc@conserveturtles.org
www.conserveturtles.org

Strives to ensure the survival of sea turtles within the Wider Caribbean basin abd Atlantic through research, education, training, advocacy and protection of habitats. CCC was the first marine turtle conservation organization in theworld, and has more than 40 years of experience in national and international sea turtle conservation, research and educational endeavors.
Founded: 1959
Landon T. Clay, Chairman
Laura Forte, President

377 **Seacology**
1623 Solano Avenue 510-559-3505
Berkeley, CA 94707 Fax: 510-559-3506
islands@seacology.org
seacology.org

Seacology is a nonprofit organization whose mission is to work with islanders around the world to protect threatened ecosystems and help their local communities.
Founded: 1990
Michael Burbank, President
Paul Alan Cox, Chair

378 **Secore International**
4673 Northwest Parkway
Hilliard, OH 43026 info@secore.org
secore.org

Secore International is a nonprofit organization dedicated to the protection and restorarion of coral reefs.
Dirk Petersen, Founder/Executive Director
Kathy Shank, Administrative Manager

379 **Sierra Club**
2101 Webster Street 415-977-5500
Suite 1300 Fax: 510-208-3140
Oakland, CA 94612 information@sierraclub.org
www.sierraclub.org

To advance the preservation and protection of the natural environment by empowering the citizenry with charitable resources to further the cause of environmental protection.
Founded: 1892
Loren Blackford, President
Susana Reyes, Vice-President

380 **Smithsonian Institution**
Smithsonian Information
SI Building, Room 153, MRC 010 202-633-1000
PO Box 37012 866-868-7774
Washington, DC 20013-7012 info@si.edu
www.si.edu

Independent trust instrumental of the United States holding more than 140 million artifacts and specimens in its trust for the public interest and knowledge. Also a center for research dedicated to the public education, nationalservice, and scholarship in the arts, sciences, and history.
Dr. David J. Skorton, Secretary
Cathy Helm, Inspector General

381 **Snow Leopard Trust**
4649 Sunnyside Avenue North 206-632-2421
Suite 325 Fax: 206-632-3967
Seattle, WA 98103 info@snowleopard.org
www.snowleopard.org

The trust is dedicated to the conservation of the endangered Snow Leopard and its mountain ecosystem. Since its founding by Helen Freeman, ISLT has worked on more than 100 projects with local people throughout Central Asia. Focus is onsmall, creative and sustainable programs to make conservation happen now and in the future. Has hosted snow leopard symposia and developed the Snow Leopard Information Management System. This allows for range-wide comparison and sharing ofinformation.
Founded: 1981
Rhetick Sengupta, President
Gayle Podrabsky, Vice-President

382 **Society for Conservation Biology**
1133 15th Street, NW 202-384-4133
Suite 300 Fax: 855-523-6070
Washington, DC 20005 info@conbio.org
conbio.org

The Society for Conservation Biology (SCB) is an international professional organization dedicated to promoting the scientific study of the phenomena that affect the maintenance, loss, and restoration of biological diversity. TheSociety's membership com-

prises a wide range of people interested in the conservation and study of biological diversity: resource managers, educators, government and private conservation workers, and students make up the more than 5,000 membersworld-wide.
Founded: 1985
Debborah Luke, Executive Director
Mike Mascia, President

383 **Society for Marine Mammalogy**
4006 Castilleja Place
Anacortes, WA 98221
admin@marinemammalscience.org
www.marinemammalscience.org
To evaluate and promote the educational, scientific and managerial advancement of marine mammal science. Gather and disseminate to members of the Society, the public and private institutions, scientific, technical and managementinformation through publications and meetings. Provide scientific information, as required, on matters related to the conservation and management of marine mammal resources.
Founded: 1981
Jay Barlow, President
Ann Pabst, President-Elect

384 **Sonoran Institute**
100 N. Stone Avenue
Suite 400
Tucson, AZ 85701
520-290-0828
Fax: 520-290-0969
tbullington@sonoraninstitute.org
www.sonoraninstitute.org
Nonprofit organization that works collaboratively with local people and interests to conserve and restore important natural landscapes in western North America, engaging partners such as landowners, public land managers, local leaders,commuunity residents and nongovernmental organizations. Community Stewardship is an innovative approach to conservation.
Founded: 1990
Chris Perez, Chair
Stephanie Sklar, CEO

385 **Tall Timbers Research Station**
13093 Henry Beadel Drive
Tallahassee, FL 32312
850-893-4153
Fax: 850-668-7781
talltimbers.org
Dedicated to protecting wildlands and preserving natural habitats. Promotes public education on the importance of natural disturbances to the environment and the subsequent need for wildlife and land management. Conducts fire ecologyresearch and other biological research programs through the Tall Timbers Research Station. Operates museum.
Founded: 1958
Tom L. Rankin, Chair
William E. Palmer, President/CEO

386 **Territorial Seed Company**
PO Box 158
Cottage Grove, OR 97424
541-942-9547
800-626-0866
Fax: 888-657-3131
info@territorialseed.com
www.territorialseed.com
Focuses on the genetic diversity of rare and endangered food crops. Offers varieties grown using only certified organic or biodynamic farming methods.
Founded: 1975
Tom Johns, Owner
Julie Johns, Owner

387 **Theodore Roosevelt Conservation Partnership**
529 14th Street NW
Suite 500
Washington, DC 20045
202-639-8727
Fax: 202-639-8728
info@trcp.org
www.trcp.org
Mission to preserve America's quality places to hunt and fish. TRCP supports federal policy and funding solutions by uniting its partners and making the voices of American sportsmen and women heard.
Founded: 1991
F. Weldon Baird, Chair
Whit Fosburgh, President/CEO

388 **Tread Lightly!**
500 N. Marketplace Drive
Suite 240
Centerville, UT 84014
801-627-0077
800-966-9900
treadlightly@treadlightly.org
www.treadlightly.org
National nonprofit organization dedicated to proactively protecting recreation access and opportunities through education and stewardship.
Founded: 1985
Kevin Lund, Chair
Casey Snider, COO

389 **TreePeople**
12601 Mulholland Drive
Beverly Hills, CA 90210
818-753-4600
Fax: 818-753-4635
info@treepeople.org
www.treepeople.org
To inspire the people of Los Angeles to take personal responsibility for their environment, training and supporting them as they plant and care for trees and improve the neighborhoods in which they live, work and play. Througheducation, planting projects, policy development and research, the organization is helping lead the promotion of integrated urban watershed management.
Founded: 1973
Andy Lipkis, President/Founder
Cindy Monta□ez, CEO

390 **Trees for Life**
3006 W. St Louis
Wichita, KS 67203
316-945-6929
Fax: 316-945-0909
info@treesforlife.org
www.treesforlife.org
Empowers people by demonstrating that in helping each other, they can unleash extraordinary power that impacts lives. By planting fruit trees in developing countries, Trees for Life protect the environment and provide a low-cost,self-renewing source of food for a large number of people. Activities include three elements: education, health and environment.
Founded: 1984
Balbir S. Mathur, Chair/Founder
Simmi Dalla, President

391 **Trust for Public Land**
101 Montgomery Street
Suite 900
San Francisco, CA 94104
415-495-4014
800-714-5263
info@tpl.org
www.tpl.org
A national nonprofit land conservation organization working to protect land for human enjoyment and well-being. Initiatives include: Parks for People; Working Lands; Natural Lands; Heritage Lands; and Land & Water.
Founded: 1972
Adrian Benepe, Sr. VP/Director
Raymond Christman, Sr. VP/Director

392 **Turtle Island Restoration Network**
9255 Sir Francis Drake Blvd
Olema, CA 94950
415-663-8590
800-859-7283
Fax: 415-663-9534
info@seaturtles.org
seaturtles.org
Turtle Island is a nonprofit organization and leading advocate for oceans' health and marine wildlife, including sea turtles, whale sharks and coho salmon.
Founded: 1987
Todd Steiner, Executive Director
Donna Howe, Board Chair

393 UNEP:United Nations Environment Programme/ Regional Office for North America
900 17th Street, NW 202-974-1300
Suite 506 unep.rona@unep.org
Washington, DC 20006 www.unep.org
Its mission is to provide leadership and encourage partnership in caring for the environment by inspiring, informing, and enabling nations and peoples to improve their quality of life.
Achim Steiner, Executive Director

394 Unexpected Wildlife Refuge: New Beaver Defende rs
PO Box 765 856-697-3541
Newfield, NJ 08344-0765 Fax: 856-697-5081
info@unexpectedwildliferefuge.org
www.unexpectedwildliferefuge.org
Providing sanctuary for animals and plants indigenous to New Jersey Pinelands.
Nedim C. Buyukmihci, VP, Interim Director
Helga Tacreiter, President

395 Waitt Institute
P.O. Box 1948 858-551-4437
La Jolla, CA 92038-1948 waittinstitute.org
The Waitt Institute endeavors to ensure ecologically, economically, and culturally sustainable use of ocean resources. The Institute partners with governments committed to developing and implementing comprehensive, science-based,community-driven solutions for sustainable ocean management. They aim to benefit coastal communities while restoring fish populations and habitats.
Ted Waitt, Founder/Chairman
Dave Russell, Vice-Chairman

396 Way of Nature Spiritual Fellowship
PO Box 268 520-730-8271
Crestone, CO 81131 info.wayofnature@gmail.com
www.sacredpassage.com
Way of Nature is now a global fellowship of people of all ages and nationalities. Founded by John P. Milton, Milton has guided thousands of people into the wilderness, sharing with them different ways to connect with nature on a deepand spiritual level.
John P. Milton, President

397 Western Hemisphere Shorebird Reserve Network (WHSRN)
125 Manomet Point Road 508-224-6521
PO Box 1770 Fax: 508-224-9220
Manomet, MA 02345 whsrn@manomet.org
www.whsrn.org
WHSRN is a voluntary, community-based coalition of over 185 organizations across the US and other countries in the Western Hemisphere that have joined together to protect, restore and manage critical wetland habitats for migratorybirds.
John Cecil, Chair
Dr. Rob P. Clay, Director

398 Western Society of Naturalists
PO Box 247
Bodega Bay, CA 94923 secretariat@wsn-online.org
www.wsn-online.org
A scientific society with a strong focus on ecology, evolution, natural history and marine biology. Its memebers are predominantly from the west coast. The society organizes one or two meetings each year for its members.
Founded: 1916
Jenn Caselle, President
Ginny Eskert, President-Elect

399 Whooping Crane Conservation Association
2950 7th Avenue
Port Albert, BC V9Y-2J4 whoopingcrane.com
The mission is to advance conservation, protection and propagation of the whooping crane population, to prevent its extinction, to establish and maintain a captive management program for the perpetuation of the species. They collectand disseminate knowledge of this species; and advocate and encourage public appreciation and understanding of the whooping crane's educational, scientific and economic values.
Walt Sturgeon, President
Dr. James Lewis, Treasurer

400 Wild Oceans
P.O. Box 258 703-777-0037
Waterford, VA 20197 wildoceans.org
Wild Oceans (formerly the National Coalition for Marine Conservation or NCMC) is a nonprofit organization dedicated to the protection of fish by bringing conservation-minded fishermen and pro-fishing environmentalists together topromote a broad, ecosystems approach to fisheries management.
Founded: 1973
Tim Choate, Chairman
Rick Weber, Vice-Chairman

401 Wilderness Society
1615 M Street, NW 202-833-2300
Washington, DC 20036 800-843-9453
action@tws.org
wilderness.org
Protects the wilderness and inspires Americans to care for the wild places. Devoted to protecting the nation's well-known icons and hidden gems, because the wilderness provides clean air and water; abundant wildlife; havens forrecreation, solitude and sources of renewable energy; and vital natural resources.
Founded: 1935
David Churchill, Chair
Jamie Williams, President

402 Wilderness Watch
PO Box 9175 406-542-2048
Missoula, MT 59807 wild@wildernesswatch.org
wildernesswatch.org
Leading the nation as an organization whose sole focus in the preservation and proper stewardship of lands and rivers included in the National Wilderness Preservation System (NWPS). Established out of the concern that already existingWilderness and rivers are largely ignored.
Founded: 1989
Louise Lasley, President
Howie Wolke, VP

403 Wildlife Action
405 N. Main Street 843-464-8473
PO Box 866 800-753-2264
Mullins, SC 29574 Fax: 843-464-8859
wlaceo@bellsouth.net
www.wildlifeaction.com
Raises public awareness about wildlife habitat, security, protection and management; protects the rivers and wetlands from unnecessary destruction and development and works to reduce poaching, trespassing and other illegal outdooractivities.
Founded: 1977
Rivers Anderson, National President
Gil Wiggins, National VP

404 Wildlife Conservation Society (WCS)
2300 Southern Boulevard 718-220-5100
Bronx, NY 10460 Fax: 718-220-2685
www.wcs.org
WCS is at work in 53 nations across Africa, Latin America and North America, protecting wild landscapes that are home to a variety of species from butterflies to tigers. They uniquely combine

the resources of wildlife parks in New Yorkwith field projects around the globe to inspire care for nature, provide leadership in environmental eduation, and help sustain our planet's biological diversity.
Founded: 1895
Cristi n Samper, President/CEO
Robert G. Menzi, Executive VP/COO

405 Wildlife Disease Association
PO Box 7065 785-865-9403
Lawrence, KS 66044-7065 800-627-0326
Fax: 785-843-6153
wda@allenpress.com
www.wildlifedisease.org
Their mission is to acquire, disseminate and apply knowledge of the health and diseases of wild animals in relation to their biology, conservation and interactions with human and domestic animals.
Founded: 1952
Marcela Uhart, President
Debra Miller, Vice-President

406 Wildlife Forever
2700 Freeway Boulevard 763-253-0222
Suite 1000 www.wildlifeforever.org
Brooklyn Center, MN 55430-1779
Wildlife Forever conserves America's wildlife heritage through preservation of habitat, conservation education and management of fish and wildlife.
Founded: 1987
Douglas H. Grann, President/CEO

407 Wildlife Habitat Council
8737 Colesville Road 301-588-8994
Suite 800 whc@wildlifehc.org
Silver Spring, MD 20910 www.wildlifehc.org
The Wildlife Habitat Council is a nonprofit groups of corporations, conservations, and individuals dedicated to protecting and enhensing wildlife habitat.
Founded: 1998
Margaret O'Gorman, President
Josiane Bonneau, Sr. Director

408 Wildlife Management Institute (WMI)
1440 Upper Bermudian Road 717-677-4480
Gardners, PA 17324 info@wildlifemgt.org
wildlifemanagement.institute
WMI is a private, nonprofit, scientific and educational organization. It is committed to the conservation, enhancement and professional management of North America's wildlife and other natural resources.
Founded: 1911
Douglas Painter, Chairman
Stephen A. Williams, President

409 Wildlife Society
425 Barlow Place 301-897-9770
Suite 200 tws@wildlife.org
Bethesda, MD 20814 wildlife.org
A nonprofit scientific and educational organization that serves professionals such as government agencies, academia, industry, and non-government organizations in all areas related to the conservation of wildlife and natural resourcesmanagement.
Founded: 1937
Bruce C. Thompson, President
Darren A. Miller, Vice-President

410 Wilson Ornithological Society
1109 Geddes Avenue 734-764-0457
Ann Arbor, MI 48109-1079 www.wilsonsociety.org
World-wide organization of approximately 2,500 people who share a curiosity about birds.
Founded: 1888
Dr. Mark Deutschlander, President
Dr. Jameson Chace, 1st Vice-President

411 Wolf Education and Research Center
PO Box 12604
Portland, OR 97212 888-422-1110
info@wolfcenter.org
www.wolfcenter.org
Dedicated to providing public education concerning the gray wolf and its habitat in the Northern Rocky Mountains. Provides the public with the rare opportunity to observe and learn about wolves in their natural habitat.
Chris Anderson, President
Jeremy Heft, Director

412 Wolf Haven International
3111 Offut Lake Road SE 360-264-4695
Tenino, WA 98589 800-448-9653
Fax: 360-264-4639
info@wolfhaven.org
wolfhaven.org
Wolf Haven International's mission is: conserve and protect wolves and their habitat. They are nationally and internationally certified sanctuary for captive-born and displaced wolves. Wolf Haven offers a variety of educationalprograms in English and Spanish about wolves and the value of all wildlife. Guided 50-minute sanctuary visits offer guests an opportunity to learn more about wolves and their role in the wild.
Founded: 1982
Diane Gallegos, Executive Director
Patt Poinsett, Director of Development

413 World Bird Sanctuary
125 Bald Eagle Ridge Road 636-225-4390
Valley Park, MO 63088 Fax: 636-861-3240
info@worldbirdsanctuary.org
www.worldbirdsanctuary.org
The World Bird Sanctuary's mission is to preserve the earth's biological diversity and to secure the future of threatened bird species in their natural environment. They work to fulfill that mission through education, propagation,field studies and rehabilitation.
John Kemper, President
Bill Berthold, Vice-President

414 World Forestry Center (WFC)
4033 SW Canyon Road 503-228-1367
Portland, OR 97221 Fax: 503-228-4608
www.worldforestry.org
They educate and inform people about the world's forests and trees and their importance to all life, in order to promote a balanced and sustainable future. The WFC also operates a museum in Portland, OR, with local, national, andinternational programs and three demonstration forests.
Founded: 1964
Sara Wu, Interim Executive Director
Darlene Boles, CPA, Financial Director

415 World Wildlife Fund
1250 24th Street NW 202-293-4800
PO Box 97180 800-225-5993
Washington, DC 20037 Fax: 202-293-9211
membership@wwfus.org
www.worldwildlife.org
Dedicated to protecting endangered species and their habitats through field work, advocacy, policy engagement, pioneering work and education. The largest multinational conservation organization in the world. WWF works in 100 countriesand is sup-

ported by 1.2 million members in the US and almost 5 million members globally.
Founded: 1960
Carter Roberts, President/CEO
Marcia Marsh, COO

National: Recycling & Pollution Prevention

416 **Acoustical Society of America**
1305 Walt Whitman Road 516-576-2360
Suite 300 Fax: 631-923-2875
Melville, NY 11747-4300 asa@acousticalsociety.org
acousticalsociety.org

For years the society has been involved in studies of noise as far as measurements, effects, and ways of reducing noise to improve the human environment.
Founded: 1929
Michael R. Stinson, President
Ronald A. Roy, Vice-President

417 **Air and Waste Management Association**
420 Fort Duquesne Boulevard 412-232-3444
One Gateway Center, 3rd Floor 800-270-3444
Pittsburgh, PA 15222-1435 Fax: 412-232-3450
info@awma.org
www.awma.org

The Air and Waste Management Association (A&WMA) is a nonprofit, nonpartisan professional organization that provides information, networking opportunities, public educational and professional development to more than 9,000environmental professionals in 65 countries.
Founded: 1907
Scott A. Freeburn, P.E., President
Chris Nelson, President-Elect

418 **Association of Battery Recyclers (ABR)**
PO Box 667
Troy, AL 36081 www.associationofbatteryrecyclers.com

To keep members abreast of environmental, health, and safety requirements that affect the industry. The association meets two times a year and membership consists of recyclers of lead-acid batteries and their components, manufacturersand environmental consulting services.
Founded: 1984

419 **Association of State and Territorial Solid Waste Management Officials**
1101 17th Street NW 202-640-1060
Suite 707 Fax: 202-331-3254
Washington, DC 20036 daniar@astswmo.org
www.astswmo.org

To enhance and promote effective state and territorial waste management programs, and affect national waste management policies.
Founded: 1974
Mark de Bie, President
Ken Kloo, Vice-President

420 **College & University Recycling Coalition**
admin@curc3r.org
curc3r.org

The College & University Recycling Coalition is a nonprofit organization dedicated to helping higher education institutions facilitate the exchange of technical knowledge and best practices on recycling and waste reduction programs.CURC represents a community of over 900 recycling and sustainability professionals in higher education led by a Board of Directors made up of recycling, zero waste and sustainability managers in North America.
Larry Cook, Chair
Kris Jolley, Vice-Chair

421 **Container Recycling Institute**
4361 Keystone Avenue 310-559-7451
Culver City, CA 90232 info@container-recycling.org
www.container-recycling.org

A nonprofit organization that studies and promotes policies and programs that increase recovery and recycling of beverage containers, and shift the social and environmental costs associated with manufacturing, recycling and disposal ofcontainer and packaging waste from government and taxpayers to producers and consumers.
Founded: 1991
Susan V. Collins, President

422 **Environmental Industry Associations**
4301 Connecticut Avenue NW 202-244-4700
Suite 300 800-424-2869
Washington, DC 20008 Fax: 202-966-4818
www.envasns.org

The Environmental Industry Associations (EIA) is the parent organization for the National Solid Waste Management Association and the Waste Equipment Technology Association. It supports these through research and administrative, legal,federal affairs and public relations resources.
Bruce Parker, President

423 **Environmental Technology Council**
Environmental Technology Council
1112 16th Street NW 202-783-0870
Suite 420 Fax: 202-737-2038
Washington, DC 20036 mail@etc.org
www.etc.org

The Environmental Technology Council (ETC) is a trade association of commercial environmental firms the recycle, treat and dispose of industrial and hazardous wastes; and firms involved in cleanup of contaminated sites.
Founded: 1982
David R Case, Executive Director
Scott Slesunger, VP Goverment Affairs

424 **Get Oil Out**
914 Anacapa Street 805-965-1519
Santa Barbara, CA 93102 www.getoilout.org

A Santa Barbara public group dedicated to the protection of the Santa Barbara Channel and coastline from the environmental, economic and esthetic impact of oil development. The organization was formed in response to a 1969 accidentthat blackened the beaches, poisoned the ocean's water and killed many creatures that depend on clean water for survival.
John Abraham Powell, President

425 **Global Links**
700 Trumbull Drive 412-361-3424
Pittsburgh, PA 15205 Fax: 412-875-6150
globallinks.org

Global Links is a medical relief and development organization dedicated to supporting health improvement initiatives in resource-poor communities and promoting environmental stewardship in the US healthcare system. The organization iscommited to environmental and sustainable practices and ensures recycling and reuse of medical surplus and deliver them to resource-poor communities.
Founded: 1989
Jeffrey Ford, Chair
Charles Vargo, Vice-Chair

426 **GrassRoots Recycling Network**
672 Robinson Road 707-321-7883
Sebastopol, CA 95472 www.grrn.org
A national network of waste reduction activists and recycling professionals. The voice calling for Zero Waste in the United States by promoting the message that individuals must go beyond recycling and go upstream to the headwaters ofthe waste stream which is the industrial designer's desk.
Rick Anthony, Board President
Portia Sinnott, Program Director

427 **Institute of Clean Air Companies (ICAC)**
3033 Wilson Boulevard 571-858-3707
Suite 700 Fax: 703-243-8696
Arlington, VA 22201 icacinfo@icac.com
www.icac.com
Organization of manufacturers of air pollution monitoring and control systems.
Founded: 1960
Michael Corvese, President
Stan Mack, Vice-President

428 **Institute of Scrap Recycling Industries**
1250 H Street 202-662-8500
Suite 400 Fax: 202-624-9256
Washington, DC 20005 isri@isri.org
www.isri.org
Its membership is made up of manufacturers and processors, brokers and industrial consumers of scrap commodities, including ferrous and nonferrous metals, paper, electronics, rubber, plastics, glass and textiles. ISRI's associatemembers include equipment and service providers to the scrap recycling industry.
Mark Lewon, Chair
Robin K. Wiener, President

429 **Kids Against Pollution**
8096 Boonville Road 315-942-4492
Boonville, NY 13309 contact@kids-against-pollution.org
www.kids-against-pollution.org
Nonprofit organization of active youth dedicated to solving and preventing pollution problems through educational projects and events in order to protect children's health and the planet.
Founded: 1987

430 **Manufacturers of Emission Controls Association (MECA)**
2200 Wilson Boulevard 202-296-4797
Suite 310 Fax: 202-331-1388
Arlington, VA 22201 asantos@meca.org
www.meca.org
Offers current and relevant technical information on emission control technology thereby facilitating strong state, federal and local air quality programs that promote public health, environmental quality and industrial progress.
Founded: 1976
Bruce I. Bertelsen, Executive Director

431 **Municipal Waste Management Association**
1620 I Street NW 202-293-7330
Washington, DC 20006 info@usmayors.org
www.usmayors.org/uscm/mwma
MWMA promotes operational efficiencies, facilitates information, fosters innovation and promotes legislation advocacy around Superfund, brownfields redevlopment, clean air and water and waste energy regulations.
Founded: 1982
Keith S. Hackett, President
Harry J. Hayes, 1st Vice-President

432 **NORA An Association of Responsible Recyclers**
7250 Heritage Village Plaza 703-753-4277
Suite 201 Fax: 703-753-2445
Gainesville, VA 20155 sparker@noranews.org
www.noranews.org
A trade association that represents almost 200 leading companies in the liquid recycling industry. It defends and promotes the liquid recycling industry and business.
Bill Hinton, President
Chris Bergstrom, EVP

433 **National Association for PET Container Resources**
7310 Turfway Road 859-372-6635
Suite 550 n4mayshun@napcor.com
Florence, KY 41042 www.napcor.com
A trade association formed in 1987, that helps communities establish recycling programs and conducts promotional and educational activities to promote PET plastic container recycling. The members of NAPCOR are manufacturers ofpolyester resins and bottles.
Founded: 1987
Rick Moore, Executive Director
Kate Eagles, Project Director

434 **National Association of Chemical Recyclers**
1900 Main Street NW 202-296-1725
Suite 750 Fax: 202-296-2530
Washington, DC 20036
The National Association of Chemical Recyclers is comprised of companies that recycle solvents and other chemicals for reuse by industry. Its members include both large conglomerates and smaller companies. The association's responsiblerecycling program ensures that all recyclers adhere to the same standards and regulations members in the assocation pledge to meet the ten principles of responsible recycling.
Brenda Pulley, Executive Director
Christopher Goebel, Director

435 **National Association of Clean Air Agencies**
444 North Capitol Street NW 202-624-7864
Suite 307 Fax: 202-624-7863
Washington, DC 20001 4cleanair@4cleanair.org
www.4cleanair.org
State and local air pollution control officials formed NACAA (formerly STAPPA/ALAPCO) to improve their effectiveness as managers of air quality programs. It encourages the exchange of information among officials, enhances communicationand cooperation among federal, state and local regulatory agencies, and promotes good management of air resources.
Dave Klemp, Co-President
Craig Kenworthy, Co-President

436 **National Center for Electronics Recycling**
161 Studio Lane 304-699-1008
Vienna, WV 26105 jlinnell@electronicsrecycling.org
electronicsrecycling.org
The National Center for Electronics Recycling (NCER) is a nonprofit organization dedicated to the development and enhancement of a national infrastructure for the recycling of used electronics in the U.S. through the coordination ofinitiatives, participation in pilot projects to advance and encourage electronics recycling, and the development of programs that reduce the burden of government through private management of electronics recycling systems.
Founded: 2005
Jason Linnell, Executive Director
Heather Smith, Senior Manager

437 **National Council for Air and Stream Improvements (NCASI)**
1513 Walnut Street 919-941-6400
Suite 200 administrator@ncasi.org
Cary, NC 27511 www.ncasi.org

The Council is a technical organization devoted to finding solutions to environmental protection problems in the manufacture of pulp, paper, and wood products in industrial forestry. It now has about 75 member companies.
Founded: 1943

438 National Recycling Coalition, Inc. (NRC)
727 East Washington Street 202-618-2107
Syracuse, NY 13210 nrcrecycles.org
Nonprofit advocacy group with members from all aspects of the waste reduction, reuse and recycling industries. It is dedicated to the advancement and improvement of recycling, waste prevention, composting and reuse.
Founded: 1978
David Freeman, Chair
Bob Gedert, President

439 Noise Pollution Clearinghouse
PO Box 1137
Montpelier, VT 05601-1137 888-200-8332
npc@nonoise.org
www.nonoise.org
A national nonprofit organization with extensive online noise related resources. Creates more civil cities and more natural rural and wilderness areas by reducing noise pollution at the source.

440 Public Citizen
1600 20th Street NW 202-588-1000
Washington, DC 20009 member@citizen.org
www.citizen.org
A consumer advocacy organization founded to represent consumer interests in Congress, the executive branch, and the courts.
Founded: 1971
Robert Weissman, President
Margrete Strand Rangnes, Executive Vice-President

441 Secondary Materials and Recycled Textiles Association (SMART)
3465 Box Hill Corp. Center Drive 443-640-1050
Suite H Fax: 443-640-1086
Abingdon, MD 21009 amrtinfo@kingmgmt.org
www.smartasn.org
SMART has represented the interests of companies dealing with pre-consumer and post-consumer recyclable textile materials. This material includes fibers, remnants, recycled clothing and shoes, and other related materials. SMART membersalso manufacture and distribute industrial and commercial wipers.
Founded: 1932
Eric Stubin, President
David Bloovman, Vice-President

442 Solid Waste Association of North America
1100 Wayne Avenue
Suite 650 800-467-9262
Silver Spring, MD 20910 Fax: 301-589-7068
info@swana.org
swana.org
Professional organization for the advancement of responsible solid waste management.
Founded: 1965
David Biderman, Executive Director/EO

443 Southeast Recycling Development Council
638 Spartanburg Hwy
Suite 70-152 will.sagar@serdc.org
Hendersonville, NC 28792 serdc.org
The Southeast Recycling Development Council is an\ nonprofit dedicated to unite industry, government, and non-government organizations to promote sustainable recycling in the Southeast.
Will Sagar, Executive Director
Nicole Smith, Chairman

444 Steel Recycling Institute
680 Andersen Drive 412-922-2772
Pittsburgh, PA 15220 800-937-1226
Fax: 412-922-3213
jimw@recycle-steel.org
www.recycle-steel.org
The Steel Recycling Institute, a unit of the American Iron and Steel Institute, is an industry association that promotes and sustains the recycling of all steel products. The SRI educates the solid waste industry, government, bussinesand ultimately the consumer about the benefit of steel's infinite recycling cycle.
Founded: 1988
Bill Heenan, President
Gregory L Crawford, VP Operations

National: Sustainable Development

445 Alliance for Sustainability
2801 21st Avenue S 612-250-0389
Suite 100 Fax: 612-379-9004
Minneapolis, MN 55407 sean@afors.org
www.afors.org
The Mission of the Alliance is to bring about personal, organizational and planetary sustainability through support of projects that are ecologically sound, economically viable, socially just and humane.
Founded: 1983
Collie Graddick, Chair
Terry Gips, President

446 American Forest Foundation
2000 M Street, NW 202-765-3660
Suite 550 Fax: 202-827-7924
Washington, DC 20036 info@forestfoundation.org
www.forestfoundation.org
A nonprofit 501 (C)(3) conservation and education organization that strives to ensure the sustainability of America's family forests for present and future generations. The vision is to create a future where North American forests aresustained by the public which understands and values the social, economic, and environmental benefits they provide to the communities, the nation, and the world.
Founded: 1982
Daniel P. Beard, Chair
Tom Martin, President

447 American Forests
1220 L Street NW 202-737-1944
Suite 750 Fax: 202-737-2457
Washington, DC 20005 info@americanforests.org
www.americanforests.org
Works to protect, restore and enhance the natural capital of trees and forests. Healthy forest filter water, remove air pollution, catch carbon, and provide homes for wildlife.
Founded: 1875
Scott Steen, President/CEO
Jad Daley, VP, Conservative Programs

448 American Planning Association
205 N. Michigan Avenue 312-431-9100
Suite 1200 Fax: 312-786-6700
Chicago, IL 60601 www.planning.org
The American Planning Association is a nonprofit public interest and research organization representing 30,000 practicing officials, and citizens involved with urban and rural planning issues. Sixty-five percent of APA's members areemployed by state and local government agencies. These members are involved, on a day-to-day basis, in formulating planning policies and preparing land use regulations.
James Drinan, CEO
Ann Simms, COO/CFO

449 American Society of Agronomy (ASA)
5585 Guilford Road
Madison, WI 53711-5801
608-273-8080
membership@agronomy.org
www.agronomy.org
ASA is dedicated to development of agricultural interests in harmony with environmental and human values. The society supports scientific, educational and professional activities that enhance communication and technology transfer amongagronomists and those in related disciplines on topics of local, regional, national and international significance.
Jessica Davis, President
Steven Evett, President-Elect

450 Ancient Forest International (AFI)
PO Box 1850
Redway, CA 95560
707-923-4475
Fax: 707-923-4475
www.asis.com/users/afi/about_afi
Ancient Forest International has been instrumental in the protection of primary forests around the world. With the help of its international ancient forest network, AFI develops opportunities for wildlands philanthropists andcommunities to work together to acquire and protect strategic and invaluable forestlands.
Founded: 1989

451 Association of Fish and Wildlife Agencies (AFWA)
1100 First Street, NE
Suite 825
Washington, DC 20002
202-838-3474
Fax: 202-350-9869
info@fishwildlife.org
www.fishwildlife.org
Representing North America's fish and wildlife agencies, they advance science-based management with the goal to conserve fish and wildlife and the habitats they depend on. The Association represents its state agency members on CapitolHill and before the Administration creating a clear and collective voice.
Founded: 1902
Nick Wiley, President
Ron Regan, Executive Director

452 Audubon Florida
4500 Biscayne Boulevard
Suite 350
Miami, FL 33137
305-371-6399
flconservation@audubon.org
fl.audubon.org
Audobon Florida is one of the many branches of the Audobon Society. Audubon Florida unites sanctuary management, ecosystem science and environmental education programs to lead the state as a voice for conservation.
Founded: 1886
Eric Draper, Executive Director

453 CONCERN
PO Box 5892
Washington, DC 20016
202-328-8160
Fax: 202-387-3378
concern@sustainable.org
www.sustainable.org
CONCERN is a national nonprofit environmental education organization with a focus on sustainable communities. CONCERN disseminates examples of successful initiatives, offers numerous resources and guidelines for action, serves as aclearinghouse for information and collaborates with others to carry out its programs. Through its Sustainable Communities Network CONCERN seeks to increase public understanding of and participation in initatives that are environmentally and sociallysound.
Founded: 1970
Susan Boyd, Director

454 Center for Ecoliteracy
2150 Allston Way
Suite 270
Berkeley, CA 94704-1377
510-845-4595
info@ecoliteracy.org
www.ecoliteracy.org
The Center for Ecoliteracy is dedicated to fostering a profound understanding of the natural world, grounded in direct experience that leads to sustainable patterns of living.
Wendy Williams, Chair
Zenobia Barlow, Executive Director

455 Conservation Fund
1655 N. Fort Myer Drive
Suite 1300
Arlington, VA 22209-3199
703-525-6300
Fax: 703-525-4610
webmaster@conservationfund.org
www.conservationfund.org
Forges partnerships to protect America's legacy of land and water resources. Through land acquisition, community initiatives and leadership training, the Fund and its partners demonstrate sustainable conservation solutions emphasizingthe integration of economic and environmental goals.
Founded: 1985
R. Michael Leonard, Chair
Lawrence A. Selzer, President/CEO

456 CropLife America (CLA)
1156 15th Street NW
Washington, DC 20005
202-296-1585
Fax: 202-463-0474
info@croplifeamerica.org
www.croplifeamerica.org
CLA promotes the environmentally sound use of crop protection products for the economical production of safe, high-quality food, fiber and renewable fuel.
Founded: 1933
Jay Vroom, President/CEO
Dr. Janet Collins, Executive VP

457 Earth Island Institute
2150 Allston Way
Suite 460
Berkeley, CA 94704-1375
510-859-9100
Fax: 510-859-9091
www.earthisland.org
A nonprofit, public interest, membership organization that supports people who are creating solutions to protect the shared planet.
Founded: 1982
Josh Floum, President
Kenneth Brower, Vice-President

458 Environmental Policy Center Global Cities Project
2962 Fillmore Street
San Francisco, CA 94123
415-775-0791
Fax: 415-775-4159
epc@globalcities.org
www.globalcities.org
Provides assistance and information on sustainable development and environmental conservation to communities within North America.

459 Environmental and Energy Study Institute (EESI)
1112 16th Street NW
Suite 300
Washington, DC 20036-4819
202-628-1400
Fax: 202-204-5244
info@eesi.org
www.eesi.org
They are a nonprofit organization dedicated to promoting environmentally sustainable societies. EESI believes meeting this goal requires transitions to social and economic patterns that sustain people, the environment and the naturalresources upon which present and future generations depend.
Founded: 1984
Jared Blum, Chair
Carol Werner, Executive Director

460 Forest History Society
701 William Vickers Avenue
Durham, NC 27701-3162
919-682-9319
Fax: 919-682-2349
stevena@duke.edu
www.foresthistory.org

A nonprofit educational institution that links the past to the future by identifying, collecting, preserving, interpreting and disseminating information on the history of people, forests and their related resources.
Founded: 1946
Chris Zinkham, Chair
Steven Anderson, President

461 Friends of the Earth
1100 15th Street NW 202-783-7400
11th Floor 877-843-8687
Washington, DC 20005 Fax: 202-783-0444
foe@foe.org
www.foe.org
National nonprofit advocacy organization dedicated to protecting the planet from environmental degradation; preserving biological, cultural and ethnic diversity, and empowering citizens to have an influential voice in decisionsaffecting the quality of their environment and their lives.
Founded: 1969
Erich Pica, President
Michelle Chan, Vice-President, Programs

462 Institute for Agriculture and Trade Policy (IATP)
2105 First Avenue South 612-870-0453
Minneapolis, MN 55404 Fax: 612-870-4846
www.iatp.org
IATP works locally and globally at the intersection of policy and practice to ensure fair and sustainable food, farm and trade systems.
Founded: 1980
Harriet Barlow, Chair

463 Institute for Sustainable Communities
535 Stone Cutters Way 802-229-2900
Montpelier, VT 05602 www.iscvt.org
Promotes sustainable environmental practices in the US and around the world. It leads transformative communtiy-driven projects for environmental problem solving and other challenges.
Founded: 1991
Richard D. Paisner, Chair
George Hamilton, Presdient

464 International Society of Arboriculture (ISA)
2101 West Park Court 217-355-9411
PO Box 3129 888-472-8733
Champaign, IL 61826-3129 Fax: 217-355-9516
isa@isa-arbor.com
www.isa-arbor.com
Through research, technology, and education ISA is able to promote the professional practice of arboriculture and foster a greater public awareness of the benefits of trees.
Founded: 1924
Michelle Mitchell, President
Paul Ries, President-Elect

465 Interstate Mining Compact Commission (IMCC)
445A Carlisle Drive 703-709-8654
Herndon, VA 20170 Fax: 703-709-8655
bbotsis@imcc.isa.us
www.imcc.isa.us
A multi-state governmental organization that represents the natural resource interests of its members. They work closely with several Federal agencies such as Office of Surface Mining Reclamation and Enforcement, US EPA and US Bureauof Land Management.
Founded: 1970
Gregory E. Conrad, Executive Director
Beth A. Botsis, Deputy Executive Director

466 Kids for Saving Earth Worldwide
37955 Bridge Road 763-559-1234
North Branch, MN 55056 Fax: 651-674-5005
kse@kidsforsavingearth.org
www.kidsforsavingearth.org/
A nonprofit organization inspired by Clinton Hill, who died at the young age of eleven. The organization dreams of a healthy planet and provides "Education into Action" curriculum to thousands of teachers, parents and kids to helpinspire envirnmnetal awareness.
Tessa Hill, President

467 Land Institute
2440 E Water Well Road 785-823-5376
Salina, KS 67401 Fax: 785-823-8728
info@landinstitute.org
landinstitute.org
A non profit organization working to develop science-based alternatives to current destructive agricultural practices. In particular, they are focused on advancing perennial grain crops and polyculture farming solutions, instead ofheavy chemical application and petroleum consumption.
Founded: 1976
Petes Ferrell, Chair
Fred Iutzi, President

468 Land Trust Alliance
1250 H Street NW 202-638-4725
Suite 600 Fax: 202-638-4730
Washington, DC 20055 info@lta.org
www.landtrustalliance.org
The Land Trust Alliance is a national conservation organization that works to influence the conservation movement, by promoting voluntary land conservation across the country and providing resources, leadership and training to thenation's 1,200+ nonprofit, grassroots land trusts, helping them to protect important open spaces.
Founded: 1982
Andrew Bowman, President
Wendy Jackson, Executive VP

469 Manomet
125 Manomet Point Road 508-224-6521
PO Box 1770 Fax: 508-224-9220
Plymouth, MA 02345 info@manomet.org
www.manomet.org
Manomet aims to conserve natural resources for the benefit of wildlife and human populations. Through research and collaboration, Manomet builds science-based, cooperative solutions to environmental problems.
Founded: 1970
Dean H. Steeger, Chair
John Hagan, President

470 Manufacturers of Emission Controls Association (MECA)
2200 Wilson Boulevard 202-296-4797
Suite 310 Fax: 202-331-1388
Arlington, VA 22201 asantos@meca.org
www.meca.org
Offers current and relevant technical information on emission control technology thereby facilitating strong state, federal and local air quality programs in promoting public health, environmental quality and industrial progress.
Founded: 1976
Bruce I. Bertelsen, Executive Director

471 Mountain Research and Development (MRD)
810 East 10th Street
Lawrence, KS 66044 mrd-journal@peertrack.net
www.mrd-journal.org
MRD is devoted to preserving mountains and their surrounding lowlands where communities are often marginalized. Through

peer-reviewed, interdisciplinary, disciplinary and transdisciplinary research MRD are strengthening networks withinthe mountain community. Their content is all available through open access.
Thomas Breu, Editor-in-chief
David Molden, Editor-in-chief

472 **National Association of State Departments of Agriculture (NASDA)**
4350 North Fairfax Drive 202-296-9680
Suite 910 Fax: 703-880-0509
Arlington, VA nasda@nasda.org
www.nasda.org
NASDA is a ten member Board of Directors whose objectives include growing and enhancing agricultural practices and procedures by forging partnerships and creating consensuses to achieve sound policy outcomes.
Founded: 1916
Michael Strain, President
Steven Reviczky, Vice-President

473 **National Association of State Land Reclamationists (NASLR)**
186 Enterprise Drive 814-342-8116
Phlipsburg, PA 16866 jmeitrott@pa.gov
naslr.org
With its beginnings in Illinois, NASLR holds anuual conferences across America. NASLR sponsors awards and programs in the pursuit to support the reclamation lands and waters across America.
Founded: 1972
Janet Yates l, President
Ed Coleman, Vice-President

474 **National Environmental Development Association**
1440 New York Avenue NW 202-638-1230
Suite 300 Fax: 202-639-8685
Washington, DC 20005
Companies and others concerned with balancing environmental and economic interests to obtain both a clean environment and a strong economy.
Andrew McElwaine, Director

475 **National FFA Organization**
6060 FFA Drive 317-802-6060
PO Box 68960 888-332-2668
Indianapolis, IN 46268-0960 Fax: 800-366-6556
www.ffa.org
The organization (formerly Future Farmers of America) is dedicated to making a positive difference in the lives of young people by developing their potential for premier leadership, personal growth and career success throughagricultural education.
Founded: 1928
Dr. Steve A. Brown, Chair
Mark Poeschl, CEO

476 **National Forestry Association**
374 Maple Avenue East 703-255-2700
Suite 310 800-476-8733
Vienna, VA 22180 Fax: 703-281-9200
www.nationalforestry.net
Nation's largest referral program to link up private forest owners with professional foresters. To be supplemented with a new innovative Forest Practices Certification program for landowners. Landowners who complete the review processand follow designated practices will be certified by the National Forestry Association.
Founded: 1981
Keith A. Argow, President/CEO
Dale Zoug, Treasurer

477 **National Gardening Association**
237 Commerce Street 802-863-5251
Suite 101 Fax: 802-864-6889
Williston, VT 05945 www.garden.org
The mission of the National Gardening Association is to sustain and renew the fundamental links between people, plants and the earth. NGA achieves its mission through youth and community gardening programs, industry research, freegardening information and memberships.
Founded: 1973
Bruce Lisman, Chair
Jennifer Tedeschi, Executive Director

478 **National Mining Association**
101 Constitution Avenue NW 202-463-2600
Suite 500 East Fax: 202-463-2666
Washington, DC 20001 nma.org
The mission of the National Mining Association is to create and maintain a broad base of political support in Congress, the Administration and the media for the mining industry of the US. In doing so, a secondary goal is to help thenation and the world realize the full promise and potential of the natural resources derived from America's mining industry.
Founded: 1917
Kevin Crutchfield, Chair
Hal Quinn, President/CEO

479 **Native Forest Council (NFC)**
PO Box 2190 541-688-2600
Eugene, OR 97402 Fax: 541-461-2156
info@forestcouncil.org
forestcouncil.org
The Native Forest Council (NFC) aims to provide visionary leadership and to ensure the integrity of public land ecosystems without compromising people or forests.
Founded: 1987
Timothy Hermach, President/Founder
Ed Dorsch, Vice President

480 **Native Seeds/SEARCH**
3061 N. Campbell Avenue 520-622-5561
Tucson, AZ 85719 Fax: 520-622-0829
info@nativeseeds.org
www.nativeseeds.org
Promote the use of ancient crops and their wild relatives by gathering, safeguarding, and distributing their seeds, while sharing benefits with tradtional communities. Work to preserve knowledge about their uses. Through research,training, and community education, works to protect biodiversity and to celebrate cultural diversity.
Founded: 1983
Janos Wilder, Chair
Joy Hought, Executive Director

481 **Natural Land Institute**
320 South 3rd Street 815-964-6666
Rockford, IL 61104 Fax: 815-964-6661
info@naturalland.org
www.naturalland.org
From Illinois, functioning as a nonprofit organization dedicated to preserving land and natural diversity for future generations, and helping residents of northern Illinois conserve the land they cherish.
Founded: 1958
Kerry Leigh, Executive Director
Jill Kennay, Assistant Director

482 **Natural Resources Council of America**
11100 Wiodlise Centre Drive 703-438-6000
Reston, VA 20190 Fax: 703-438-3570
www.naturalresourcescouncil.org
The Council dedicated to strengthing the conservation movement as a whole. For more than 50 years the Council has been the

Crossroads of Conservation, keeping conservationists connected, informed and prepared to face the challenges ofthe future. The Council provides their membership- more than 85 conservation groups and nearly 100 individual supporters- with unique networking opportunities, valuable leadership training and cost-saving services.
Founded: 1946
Andrea Yank, Executive Director
Carlton Gleed, Program Coordinator

483 Negative Population Growth
2861 Duke Street 703-370-9510
Suite 36 Fax: 703-370-9514
Alexandria, VA 22314 npg@npg.org
www.npg.org
Leader in the movement for a sound population policy and advocates a smaller and truly sustainable population through voluntary incentives for smaller families and reduced immigration levels.
Founded: 1972
Donald Mann, President
Craig Lewis, Executive Vice President

484 New England Coalition for Sustainable Population
PO Box 1163 603-283-6686
Montpelier, VT 05601 plumb.george@gmail.com
Provides progressive leadership and programs to educate the public about population stabilization and its beneficial relationship to environmental conservation, human rights and sustainable economic development.
George Plumb, Co-Chair
Linn Duvall Harwell, Co-Chair

485 Old-Growth Forest Network
PO Box 21 410-251-1800
Easton, MD 21601 joan@oldgrowthforest.net
oldgrowthforest.net
Old-Growth Forest Network is a nonprofit organization dedicated to the preservation and sustainable management of forests.
Founded: 2007
Joan Maloof, Executive Director
Susan Barnett, Administrative Assistant

486 PCI Media Impact
777 United Nations Plaza 212-687-3366
5th Floor Fax: 212-661-4188
New York, NY 10017 info@mediaimpact.org
mediaimpact.org
PCI's mission is to work creatively with the media and other organizations to motivate individuals and communities to make choices that influence population trends encouraging sustainable development and environmental protection.
Founded: 1985
Sean Southey, CEO
David J. Andrews, Director, Development

487 Pacific Institute for Studies in Development, Environment and Security
654 13th Street 510-251-1600
Preservation Park Fax: 510-251-2203
Oakland, CA 94612 info@pacinst.org
pacinst.org
Nonprofit policy research group, bringing knowledge to power on issues of environmental, economical development, and international peace and security.
Founded: 1987
Olivier J. Marie, Chair
Jason Morrison, President

488 Panos Institute
1322 18th Street,NW 202-429-0730
Suite 26 Fax: 202-223-7947
Washington, DC 20036 www.panosinst.org
Founded in 1986, the Panos Institute is an international, nonprofit, nongovernmental organization with offices in Budapest, London, Paris, and Washington DC, working to raise public understanding of sustainable development issues.
Founded: 1986
Melanie Oliviero, Executive Director

489 Pinchot Institute for Conservation
1400 16th Street NW 202-797-6580
Suite 350 www.pinchot.org
Washington, DC 20036
Strives to advance conservation and sustainable natural resource management by developing innovative, practical, and broadly-supported solutions to conservation challenges and opportunities. This is accomplished through nonpartisanresearch, education and technical assistance.
Founded: 1963
William C. Price, President
Jennifer Yeager, CFO

490 Population Connection
2120 L Street NW 202-332-2200
Suite 500 800-767-1956
Washington, DC 20037 Fax: 202-332-2302
info@populationconnection.org
www.populationconnection.org
A national nonprofit organization working to slow population growth and achieve a sustainable balance between the Earth's people and its resources. They seek to protect the environment and ensure a high quality of life for present andfuture generations.
Founded: 1965
Estelle Raboni, Chair
John Seager, President/CEO

491 Population Crisis Committee
1120 19th Street NW 202-659-1833
Washington, DC 20036 Fax: 202-293-1795
J Joseph Speidel, President

492 Population Institute
107 2nd Street NE 202-544-3300
Washington, DC 20002 888-787-0038
Fax: 202-544-0068
info@populationinstitute.org
www.populationinstitute.org
The Population Institute is the World's largest independent nonprofit, educational organization dedicated exclusively to achieving a more equitable balance between the worlds population, environment, and resources. Established in 1969,the Institute, with members in 172 countries, is headquartered on Capitol Hill in Washington DC. The Institute uses a variety of resources and programs to bring its concerns about the consequences of rapid poulation growth to the forefront of thenational agenda.
Founded: 1969
Robert Walker, President
William Ryerson, Chairman, CEO

493 Population Reference Bureau
1875 Connecticut Avenue NW 202-483-1100
Suite 520 800-877-9881
Washington, DC 20009-5728 Fax: 202-328-3937
popref@prb.org
www.prb.org
PRB informs policymakers, educators, the media, and concerned citizens working in the public interest around the world through a broad range of activities, including publications, information

services, seminars and workshops, andtechnical support. They work with both public-sector and private-sector partners.
Founded: 1929
Jeffrey Jordan, President/CEO
James Scott, CFO/COO

494 **Population Resource Center**
15 Roszel Road
Princeton, NJ 08540
609-452-2822
Fax: 609-452-0010
www.prcdc.org
The mission of the Population Resource Center is to promote the use of accurate population data and sound, objective analysis of these data in the making of public policy.
Founded: 1985
Jane S De Lung, President
Linda Rosen, Director of Policy Analysis

495 **Population: Environment Balance**
1629 K Street NW
Suite 300
Washington, DC 20006
202-955-5700
800-866-8269
Fax: 202-955-6161
info@balance.org
www.balance.org
Population Environment Balance is a national, nonprofit membership organization dedicated to maintaing the quality of the United States population stabilization.
Founded: 1973
Aaron Beckwith, Vice President

496 **Population: Environmental Council**
1629 K Street NW
Suite 300
Washington, DC 20006
202-955-5700
Fax: 202-955-6161
info@balance.org
www.balance.org
Population-Environment Balance is dedicated to public education regarding the adverse effects of population growth on the environment. Founded in 1973, Population-Environment Balance has 8,800 members. It advocates measures that wouldencourage population stabilization.
Founded: 1973
Aaron Beckwith, Vice President

497 **Quebec-Labrador Foundation (QFL)**
QLF-Atlantic Center for the Environment
4 South Main Street
Suite 4
Ipswich, MA 01938
978-356-0038
Fax: 978-268-5310
qlf@qlf.org
www.qlf.org
A not-for-profit corporation in the United States and a registered Charity in Canada. QLF exissts to support the rural communities and environment of eastern Canada and New England and to create models for stewardship of naturalresources and cultural heritage that can be applied worldwide.
Founded: 1961
Elizabeth Alling, President/CEO
Brett Mitchell, Sr. Vice-President

498 **Rainforest Relief**
PO Box 8451
Jersey City, NJ 07308
917-543-4064
info@rainforestrelief.org
www.rainforestrelief.org
Rainforest Relief works to end the loss of the world's tropical and temperate rainforests by reducing the demand for materials for which rainforests are destroyed. These include rainforest woods such as mohogany, lauan and cedar,agricultural products such as bananas, chocolate, coffee and cut flowers, and mining products such as petroleum, gold, aluminum and copper. Rainforest relief works through research, education and non-violent direct action campaigns.
Founded: 1989

499 **Rural Advancement Foundation International USA (RAFI USA)**
PO Box 640
274 Pittsboro Elementary School Road
Pittsboro, NC 27312
919-542-1396
Fax: 919-542-0069
rafiusa.org
RAFI USA is a nonprofit organization promoting community, equity and sustainability for family farmers and rural communities. Our headquarters serves as a model for green building. In addition to daylighting, solar and energyconservation features, the building showcases the use of salvaged materials from the deconstruction of an 1830s farmhouse.
Founded: 1990
Alex Hitt, Board President
Scott Marlow, Executive Director

500 **Save America's Forests**
4 Library Court SE
Washington, DC 20003
202-544-9219
Fax: 202-544-7462
webmaster@saveamericasforests.org
www.saveamericasforests.org
A nationwide campaign to end clearcutting and protect and restore America's wild and natural forests. A coalition of groups through America working together to protect local forests, national forests and forests throughout the world.
Founded: 1994
Carl Ross, Executive Director

501 **Society for Ecological Restoration (SER)**
1133 15th Street NW
Suite 300
Washington, DC 20005
202-299-9518
info@ser.org
www.ser.org
SER is dedicated to reversing the damage done to aquatic, marine and terrestrial environments and restoring the earth for the benefit of humans and nature. Restoration embraces the interrelationships between nature and culture byengaging all sectors of society and enabling full and effective participation.
Founded: 1987
Al Unwin, Chair
Bethanie Walder, Executive Director

502 **Society of American Foresters**
10100 Laureate Way
Bethesda, MD 20814-2198
301-897-8720
866-897-8720
Fax: 301-897-3690
membership@safnet.org
www.eforester.org
To advance the science, education, technology, and practice of forestry; to enhance the competency of its members; to establish professional excellence; and to use the knowledge, skills, and conservation ethic of the profession toensure the continued health and use of forest ecosystems present and future of availability of forest resources to benefit society.
Founded: 1900
Frederick W. Cubbage, CF, President
David S. Lewis, Vice President

503 **Society of Chemical Manufacturers and Affiliates (SOCMA)**
1400 Crystal Drive
Suite 630
Arlington, VA 22202
571-348-5100
Fax: 571-348-5138
co@socma.com
www.socma.com
The leading international trade association serving the small and mid-sized batch chemical manufacturers. Advocates flexible policies grounded in sound science and works to ensure that Congress and the regulatory agencies do not adopta one-size fits-all approach to the industry.
Founded: 1921
Jennifer L. Abril, President/CEO

504 **Soil Science Society Of America**
5585 Guilford Road 608-273-8080
Madison, WI 53711-5801 Fax: 608-273-2021
membership@soils.org
soils.org
The Soil Science Society of America (SSSA) is a progressive international scientific society that fosters the transfer of knowledge and practices to sustain global soils. The Society provides information about soils in relation to cropproduction, environmental quality, ecosystem sustainability, bioremediation, waste management, recycling, and wise land use.
Founded: 1936
Andrew N. Sharpley, President
Richard P. Dick, President-Elect

505 **Southface Energy Institute**
241 Pine Street NE 404-872-3549
Atlanta, GA 30308 Fax: 404-872-5009
info@southface.org
www.southface.org
An environmental nonprofit working to promote sustainable homes, workplaces and communities through education, research, advocacy and technical assistance.
Founded: 1978
Barry R. Goldman, Chair
Andrea Pinabell, President

506 **Sustainable Forestry Initiative**
2121 K Street, NW 202-596-3450
Suite 750 Fax: 202-596-3451
Washington, DC 20037 info@sfiprogram.org
sfiprogram.org
SFI is an independent, nonprofit organization dedicated to sustainable forest management across the United States and Canada.
Kathy Abusow, President/CEO
Nadine Block, Chief of Operations

507 **World Environment Center**
734 15th Street NW 202-312-1370
Suite 720 Fax: 202-637-2411
Washington, DC 20005 info@wec.org
www.wec.org
The World Environment Center is an independent, global non-profit, non-advocacy organization that advances sustainable development worldwide through the business practices of member companies and in partnership with governments,multi-lateral organizations, private sector organizations, universities and other stakeholders.
Founded: 1974
Francisco Su rez Hern ndez, Chair
Dr. Terry F. Yosie, President/CEO

508 **Worldwatch Institute**
1400 16th Street NW 202-745-8092
Suite 430 Fax: 202-478-2534
Washington, DC 20036 worldwatch@worldwatch.org
www.worldwatch.org
The Worldwatch Institute is an independent, nonprofit environmental research organization in Washington DC. Its mission is to foster a sustainable society in which human needs are met in ways that do not threaten the health of thenatural environment or future generations. To this end, this Institute conducts interdisciplinary research on emerging global issues, the results of which are published and disseminated to decision-makers and the media.
Founded: 1974
Ed Groark, Acting Interim President
Barbara Fallin, Director, Finance

National: Travel & Tourism

509 **American Hiking Society (AHS)**
8605 Second Avenue 301-565-6704
Silver Spring, MD 20910 800-972-8608
Fax: 301-565-6704
info@americanhiking.org
americanhiking.org
AHS is a recreation based conservation organization working to cultivate a nation of hikers dedicated to establishing, protecting, and maintaning foot trails in America. The more than 10,000 individual members and hiking club memberscontribute to this national effort.
Founded: 1976
Jack Hess, Chair
Kathryn Van Waes o, Executive Director

510 **American Recreation Coalition (ARC)**
1200 G Street NW 202-682-9530
Suite 650 Fax: 202-682-9529
Washington, DC 20005-3832 bnasta@funoutdoors.com
www.funoutdoors.com
Washington based nonprofit that partners public and private organizations to enhance and protect outdoor recreational opportunities and resources. ARC also monitors legislative and regulatory proposals that influence recreation.
Founded: 1979
Derrick Crandall, President
Ben Nasta, Director, Communications

511 **American Whitewater**
PO Box 1540 828-586-1930
Cullowhee, NC 28723 866-262-8429
Fax: 828-586-2840
info@americanwhitewater.org
www.americanwhitewater.org
Restores rivers adversely affected by hydropower dams, eliminates water degradation, improves public land management and protects public access to rivers for responsible recreational use.
Founded: 1954
Courtney Wilton, President
Christopher Hest, Vice-President

512 **Association of Outdoor Recreation and Education**
1100 North Main Street 810-299-2782
Suite 101 Fax: 810-299-3436
Ann Arbor, MI 48104 nationaloffice@aore.org
aore.org
The Association of Outdoor Recreation and Education (AORE) is a nonprofit organization serving the needs of recreation and education professionals.AORE promotes ecologically sound stewardship of the natural environment and serves as acollective voice for its members regarding topics of regional and national concern.
Jeannette Stawski, Executive Director
Lance Haynie, President

513 **Association of Zoos and Aquariums**
8403 Colesville Road 301-562-0777
Suite 710 Fax: 301-562-0888
Silver Spring, MD 20910-3314 membership@aza.org
www.aza.org
Nonprofit organization dedicated to the advancement of accredited zoos and aquariums in the areas of animal care, wildlife conservation, education and science.
Founded: 1924
Dan Ashe, President/CEO
Kris Vehrs, J.D., Executive Director

514 **Federation of Western Outdoor Clubs (FWOC)**
1864 SE Anspach Street 503-653-1394
Oak Grove, OR 97267 sylviamilne@msn.com
www.federationofwesternoutdoorclubs.org

The Federation is composed of organizations that engage in hiking, camping, birding and other similar activities that rely on an outdoor environment where natural conditions predominate. Organizations in the West that have suchprograms, and that have an active interest in protecting the natural environment are invited to affiliate.
Founded: 1932
George Milne, President
Jan Walker, Vice-President

515 **Green Hotels Association**
1611 Mossy Stone Drive 713-789-8889
Houston, TX 77242-0212 Fax: 713-789-9786
green@greenhotels.com
www.greenhotels.com

Bringing together hotels that are interested in environmental issues by informing its members of the latest green and environmentally friendly procedurs and products that help hotels save money and time, and preserve the environment.
Founded: 1993
Patricia Griffin, President/Founder

516 **Lighthawk**
PO Box 2710 970-797-9355
Telluride, CO 81435 terriwatson@lighthawk.org
www.lighthawk.org

Nonprofit organization addressing critical environmental issues by providing an aerial perspective on areas of concern in the US, Canada and Central America. Using small aircrafts, they fly partner organizations, elected officials,industry and media representatives, activists, and indigenous groups over protected and threatened regions.
Founded: 1979
Terri Watson, CEO
Emilie Ryan, CFO

517 **National Association of State Outdoor Recreation Liaison Officers (NASORLO)**
University of Missouri
105 H, ABNR Building 573-353-2702
Columbia, MO 65211 Fax: 573-882-9526
nasorlo@gmail.com
www.nasorlo.org

An association representing the states and territories as a liason to the National Park Service. Their primary objective is to promote and advocate for the State Assistance program of the Land and Water Conservation Fund.
Lauren Imgrund, President
Doug Eiken, Executive Director

518 **National Council of State Tourism Directors (NCSTD)**
U.S. Travel Association
1100 New York Avenue NW 202-408-2147
Suite 450
Washington, DC 20005

NCSTD represents all U.S. states, territories and districts providing a voice on critical public policy, offering learning opportunities to furhter the professionalism and effectiveness of state tourism offices, facilitating internaland external communication and supporting domestic and international marketing efforts.
Jim Hagen, Chair
Duane Parrish, Vice Chair

519 **North Country Trail Association**
229 East Main Street 616-897-5987
Lowell, MI 49331 866-445-3628
Fax: 616-897-6605
hq@northcountrytrail.org
northcountrytrail.org

The North Country Trail Association (NCTA) unites individuals, affiliated trail groups, local chapters, corporate sponsors and others linked in support of building and maintaining the North Country National Scenic Trail, and tellingits story.
Ruth Dorrough, President
Jaron Nyhof, First Vice-President

520 **Outdoor Industry Association**
4909 Pearl East Circle 303-443-353
Suite 300 Fax: 303-444-3284
Boulder, CO 80301 info@outdoorindustry.org
outdoorindustry.org

The Outdoor Industry Association is a membership-driven trade organization for the outdoor recreation industry.
Amy Roberts, Executive Director
Travis Campbell, President

521 **Pacific Crest Trail Association**
1331 Garden Highway 916-285-1846
Sacramento, CA 95833 Fax: 916-285-1865
info@pcta.org
pcta.org

PCTA is a nonprofit organization singularly focused on preserving , protecting, and promoting the Pacific Crest Trail.
Liz Bergeron, Executive Director
John E. Crawford, Board Chair

522 **Rails-to-Trails Conservancy**
2121 Ward Court NW 202-331-9696
5th Floor 866-202-9788
Washington, DC 20037 Fax: 202-223-9257
www.railstotrails.org

A nonprofit organization working with communities to preserve unused rail corridors by transforming them into trails, enhancing the health of American's environment, economy, neighborhoods and people.
Founded: 1986
Keith Laughlin, President
Cindy Dickerson, COO

523 **Safari Club International (SCI)**
4800 West Gates Pass Road 520-620-1220
Tucson, AZ 85745-9490 888-486-8724
Fax: 520-622-1205
www.safariclub.org

A leader in wildlife conservation, hunter education, and protecting the freedom to hunt.

524 **Society of Health and Physical Educators (SHAPE)**
1900 Association Drive 703-476-3400
Reston, VA 20191-1598 800-213-7193
Fax: 703-476-9527
www.shapeamerica.org

SHAPE America serves recreation professionals, practitioners, educators and students by encouraging and facilitating healthy living through physical activity.
Founded: 2005
Fran Cleland, President
Judy LoBianco, President-Elect

525 **Society of Outdoor Recreation Professionals (SORP)**
PO Box 221 814-927-8212
Marienville, PA 16239 Fax: 814-927-6659
brenda@recpro.org
www.recpro.org

Dedicated to serving the outdoor recreation profession. Acts as the nation's leading association of outdoor recreation and related professionals who strive to protect natural and cultural resources. SORP uses research, planning,management and policy develop-

ment to meets its mission to serve outdoor recreatio professionals.
Founded: 1983
Rachel Franchina, President
Maren Murphy, VP of Operation

526 Wilderness Education Association (WEA)
PO Box 601 740-607-9759
Dresden, OH 43821 nationaloffice@weainfo.org
www.weainfo.org
WEA provides professional instruction, leadership training and wilderness travel. Promoting safe, ethical and professional wilderness leaders.
Founded: 1977
Kelli McMahan, President
Francois Guilleux, President-Elect

National: Water Resources

527 Adopt-A-Stream Foundation (AASF)
Northwest Stream Center 425-316-8592
600 - 128th Street SE Fax: 425-338-1423
Everett, WA 98208 aasf@streamkeeper.org
www.streamkeeper.org
The mission of the AASF is to teach people how to become stewards of their watershed. That mission is carried out by conducting classes, producing environmental education materials, and providing local communitites stram and wetlandrestoration technical assistance.
Founded: 1985
Daryl Williams, President
Tom Murdoch, Executive Directors

528 Alliance for Water Efficiency
33 N. LaSalle Street 733-360-5100
Suite 2275 866-730-A4WE
Chicago, IL 60602 Fax: 773-345-3636
allianceforwaterefficiency.org
The Alliance for Water Efficiency is a nonprofit organization dedicated to the efficient and sustainable use of water. It provides information and assistance on water conservation efforts.
Pete DeMarco, Chair
Kirk Stinchcombe, Vice-Chair

529 American Canal Society
117 Main Street 610-691-0956
Freemansburg, PA 18017 dgbarber@cs.com
www.americancanals.org
Dedicated to Historic Canal Research, Preservation, Restoration, and Parks. Promotes the wise use of America's many historic canal resources through research, preservation, restoriation, recreation, and parks. Acts as a nationalclearing house of canal information and co-operates with local, state, and international canal societies, groups, and individuals to identify historic canal resources, to publicize canal history, activities, and problems, and to take action onthreatened canals and sites
Founded: 1972
David G. Barber, President

530 American Ground Water Trust
50 Pleasant Street 603-228-5444
Concord, NH 03301 agwt.org
A not-for-profit education organization. Promotes opportunity, cooperation and action among individuals, groups and organizations in order to educate the public, and further its mission: to protect ground water, promote publicawareness of the environment and economic importance of groundwater and provide accurate information to assist public participation in water resources decisions and management.
Founded: 1986
David Kill, Chair
Andrew Stone, Executive Director

531 American Rivers
1101 14th Street NW 202-347-7550
Suite 1400 877-347-7550
Washington, DC 20005 feedback@americanrivers.org
www.americanrivers.org
The only national organization that is dedicated to protecting and restoring rivers nationwide. Founded over 30 years ago it now has over 65,000 members and supports nationwide and two regional and six field offices.
Founded: 1973
William Robert Irwin, President

532 American Shore and Beach Preservation Association (ASBPA)
5460 Beaujolais Lane 239-489-2616
Fort Myers, FL 33919 Fax: 239-362-9771
derek.brockbank@asbpa.org
asbpa.org
Dedicated to preserving, protecting and enhancing the beaches, shores and other coastal resources of America, recognizing their important quality-of-life assets.
Founded: 1926
Anthony P. Pratt, President
Derek Brockbank, Executive Director

533 American Sportfishing Association (ASA)
1001 North Fairfax Street 703-519-9691
Suite 501 Fax: 703-519-1872
Alexandria, VA 22314 asacomm@asafishing.org
asafishing.org
A sportsfishing industry trade association that consider tackle manufacturers' business interests. ASA's members include sportfishing and boating manufacturers and the people who use their products.
Founded: 1933
Mike Nussman, President/CEO
Diane Carpenter, VP, Operations/CFO

534 American Water Resources Association (AWRA)
PO Box 1626 540-687-8390
Middleburg, VA 20118 Fax: 540-687-8395
info@awra.org
www.awra.org
AWRA advances water resources research, planning, development, management and education. AWRA takes a balanced, professional approach to solving water resources challenges by establishing discourse between physical, biological, andsocial scientists, engineers, and other persons concerned with water resources.
Founded: 1964
Kenneth D. Reid, President
Michael J. Kowalski, Director of Operations

535 American Water Works Association (AWWA)
6666 W. Quincy Avenue 303-794-7711
Denver, CO 80235 800-926-7337
Fax: 303-347-0804
service@awwa.org
www.awwa.org
The AWWA is an international, nonprofit, scientific and educational society motivated to providing water solutions that assure the effective management of water. The Association is the largest organization of water supply professionalsin the world with its

membership accounting for 3,900 utilities that supplies roughly 80 percent of the nation's drinking water.
Founded: 1881
David B. LaFrance, CEO
Paula I. Macllwaine, Deputy CEO

536 **Association of Metropolitan Water Agencies (AMWA)**
1620 I Street NW 202-331-2820
Suite 500 Fax: 202-785-1845
Washington, DC 20006 info@amwa.net
www.amwa.net
An organization of the largest publicly owned drinking water systems in the nation. AMWA is focused on putting forth policy to aid its members who supply drinking water to the population.
Founded: 1981
Scott Potter, President
Diane VanDe Hei, CEO

537 **Association of State Floodplain Managers (ASFM)**
575 D'Onofrio Drive 608-828-3000
Suite 200 Fax: 608-828-6319
Madison, WI 53719 asfpm@floods.org
www.floods.org
The Association is an organization of professionals involved in floodplain management, flood hazard mitigation, the National Flood Insurance Program, and flood preparedness, warning and recovery.
Founded: 1977
Ceil Strauss, Chair
Maria Cox Lamm, Vice Chair

538 **Association of State Wetland Managers (ASWM)**
32 Tandberg Trail 207-892-3399
Suite 2A Fax: 207-894-7992
Windham, ME 04062 jeanne.christie@aswm.org
www.aswm.org
Nonprofit organization dedicated to the protection and restoration of the nation's wetlands. ASWM's goal is to help public and private wetland decision-makers utilize the best possible scientific information and techniques in wetlanddelineation, assessment, mapping, planning, regulation, acquisition, restoration and other management.
Founded: 1983
Jeanne Christie, Executive Director
Jon Kusler, Associate Director

539 **CEDAM International**
2 Fox Road 914-271-5365
Croton-on-Hudson, NY 10520 susansammon@gmail.com
cedarinternational.com
Conservation, Education, Diving, Awareness and Marine research International is a nonprofit organization dedicated to the understanding, protection and preservation of the world's marine resources.They continue to offer the LloydBridges Scholarship which allows teachers and educators to have a chance to participate in a REEF field survey.
Founded: 1967
Susan Sammon, Director

540 **Center for Coastal Studies**
5 Holway Avenue 508-487-3623
Provincetown, MA 02657 800-900-3622
ccs@coastalstudies.org
coastalstudies.org
Private nonprofit organization for research, conservation and education in the coastal and marine environments.
Founded: 1976
Bill Bonn, Chair
Richard Delaney, President/CEO

541 **Center for Marine Conservation (CMC)**
2029 K Street, NW 202-429-5609
Washington, DC 20006 800-519-1541
Fax: 202-872-0619
info@oceanconservancy.org
www.cmc-ocean.org
The mission of the CMC is to protect ocean ecosystems and conserve the global abundance and diversity of marine wildlife. Through sciencebased advocacy, research and public education, CMC informs, inspires and empowers people to speakand act for the oceans.
Roger Rufe Jr, President
Thomas J Tepper, Senior VP Operations

542 **Center for Watershed Protection**
3290 North Ridge Road 410-461-8323
Suite 290 Fax: 410-461-8324
Ellicott City, MD 21043 center@cwp.org
www.cwp.org
The center is a nonprofit 501(c)3 organization dedicated to finding new ways to protect and restore the nation's streams, lakes, rivers and estuaries. The center publishes numerous technical publications on all aspects of watershedprotection, including stormwater management, watershed planning and better site design. Publications are available online.
Founded: 1992
Carlton G. Epps, Sr., President
Hye Yeong Kwon, Executive Director

543 **Clean Water Action**
1444 I Street NW 202-895-0420
Suite 400 Fax: 202-895-0438
Washington, DC 20005 www.cleanwateraction.org
National citizens' organization working for clean, safe and affordable water, prevention of health-threatening pollution, creation of environmentally-safe jobs and businesses, and empowerment of people to make democracy work.Organizes strong grassroots groups, coalitions and campaigns to protect the environment, health, economic well-being and community quality of life.
Founded: 1972
Robert Wendelgass, President/CEO

544 **Clean Water Fund**
1444 I Street 202-895-0420
Suite 400 Fax: 202-895-0438
Washington, DC 20005 www.cleanwaterfund.org
Brings diverse communities together to work for changes that improve our lives, promoting sensible solutions for people and the environment.
Founded: 1972
Robert Wendelgass, President/CEO

545 **Clean Water Network**
1200 New York Avenue NW 202-298-2421
Suite 400 Fax: 202-289-1060
Washington, DC 20005 info@cwn.org
www.cleanwaternetwork.org
A nonprofit network of over 1,000 organizations that deal with clean water issues covered by the Clean Water Act. Our member organizations consist of a variety of organizations representing environmentalists, family farmers, recreationanglers, commercial fishermen, surfers, boaters, faith communities, labor unions and civic associations. We publish a monthly newsletter and various reports.
Natalie Roy, Executive Director

546 **Coastal Conservation Association**
6919 Portwest 713-626-4234
Suite 100 800-201-3474
Houston, TX 77024 Fax: 713-626-5852
ccantl@joincca.org
www.joincca.org

A national nonprofit organization of 17 coastal state chapters dedicated to the conservation and preservation of marine resources.
Founded: 1977
Patrick D. Murray, President
Robert G. Hayes, Vice-President

547 **Coastal Society**
PO Box 3590 757-565-0999
Williamsburg, VA 23187-3590 Fax: 757-565-0922
coastalsoc@aol.com
www.thecoastalsociety.org

Organization of private sector, academic, government professionals and students dedicated to actively addressing emerging coastal issues by fostering dialogue, forging partnerships and promoting communication and education.
Founded: 1975
Lewis Lawrence, President
Megan D. Bailiff, President-Elect

548 **Cook Inletkeeper**
3734 Ben Walters Lane 907-235-4068
Homer, AK 99603 888-694-6538
Fax: 907-235-4069
inletkeeper.org

Dedicated to protecting the vast Cook Inlet watershed and the life it sustains; it is a community-based nonprofit organization that combines education, advocacy and science to reach this goal.
Founded: 1995
Bob Shavelson, Executive Director
Sue Mauger, Science Director

549 **Coral Reef Alliance**
1330 Broadway 510-370-0500
Suite 1602 info@coral.org
Oakland, CA 94612 coral.org
Unites and empowers communities to save coral reefs. Provides tools, education and inspiration to residents of coral reef destinations to support local projects that benefit both reefs and people.
Founded: 1994
Dr. Michael Webster, Executive Director
Dr. Madhavi Colton, Program Director

550 **Earth Island Institute**
2150 Allston Way 510-859-9100
Suite 460 Fax: 510-859-9091
Berkeley, CA 94704-1375 www.earthisland.org
A nonprofit, public interest, membership organization that supports people who are creating solutions to protect our shared planet.
Founded: 1982
Josh Floum, President
Kenneth Brower, Vice-President

551 **Ecological Society of America (ESA)**
1990 M Street NW 202-833-8773
Suite 700 Fax: 202-833-8775
Washington, DC 20036 esahq@esa.org
www.esa.org
To promote ecological science by improving communication among ecologists; raise the public's level of awareness of the importance of ecological science; increase the resources available for the conduct of ecological science; andensure the appropriate use of ecological science in environmental decision making by enhancing communication between the ecological community and policy-makers.
Founded: 1915
David Lodge, President
Rich Pouyat, President-Elect

552 **Freshwater Society**
2424 Territorial Road 651-313-5800
Suite B Fax: 651-666-2569
St. Paul, MN 55114 freshwater@freshwater.org
freshwater.org

Founded by the late Dick Gray, the late Hib Hill and Dr. Richard Caldecott, the Freshwater Society sets out to promote the conservation, protection and restoration of all freshwaterresources across the United States.
Founded: 1968
Rick Bateson, Chair
Steve Woods, Executive Directors

553 **Gaia Institute**
440 City Island Avenue 718-885-1906
Bronx, NY 10464 Fax: 718-885-0882
thegaiainstitute.org

Named after the Gaia hypothesis, the Gaia Institute believes the planet's well-being is connected to the activities of organisms. The Gaia Institute partners with eager and bright people who are creating new solutions in greentechnology.
Founded: 1972
Paul Mankiewicz, Executive Director

554 **Global Water Policy Project (GWPP)**
107 Larkspur Drive
Amherst, MA 01002 info@globalwaterpolicy.org
www.globalwaterpolicy.org

Global Water Policy Projects aims to promote the preservation and sustainable use of Earth's fresh water through research, writing, outreach, and public speaking.
Founded: 1994
Sandra Postel, Founder/Director

555 **Groundwater Foundation**
3201 Pioneers Boulevard 402-434-2740
Suite 105 800-858-4844
Lincoln, NE 68502 Fax: 402-434-2742
info@groundwater.org
www.groundwater.org
The Groundwater Foundation is a nonprofit organization that is dedicated to informing the public about one of our greatest hidden resources, groundwater. Since 1985, our programs and publications present the benefits everyone receivesfrom groundwater and the risks that threaten groundwater quality. We make learning about groundwater fun and understandable for kids and adults alike.
Founded: 1985
Andy Belenger, President
Jane Grffin, Vice-President

556 **International Association for Environmental Hydrology (IAEH)**
2607 Hopeton Drive 201-984-7583
San Antonio, TX 78230 Fax: 703-564-8581
hydroweb@gmail.com
www.hydroweb.com

IAEH tries to share its knowledge and expertise in hydrology and to provide a source of inexpensive tools and resources for hydrologists all over the world.

557 **International Desalination Association (IDA)**
94 Central Street, Suite 200 978-887-0410
PO Box 387 Fax: 978-887-0411
Topsfield, MA 01983 info@idadesal.org
idadesal.org

IDA is committed to the development and promotion of the appropriate use of desalination and desalination technology worldwide. We endeavor to carry out these goals by encouraging

research and development, exchanging, promotingcommunication and disseminating information.
Founded: 1972
Dr. Emilio Gabbrielli, President
Shannon McCarthy, 1st Vice-President

558 International Rivers
2054 University Avenue 510-848-1155
Suite 300 Fax: 510-848-1008
Berkeley, CA 94704-2644 contact@internationalrivers.org
www.internationalrivers.org
International Rivers works with an international network of dam-affected people, grassroots organizations, environmentalists, human rights advocates and others who are committed to stopping destructive river projects and promotingbetter options.
Founded: 1985
Scott Spann, Chair
Kate Horner, Executive Director

559 Interstate Council on Water Policy (ICWP)
505 North Ivy Street 573-303-6644
Arlington, VA 22220-1707 www.icwp.org
The ICWP is the national organization of state and regional water resource management agencies. It provides a means to exchange information, ideas, and experience and to work with Federal agencies which share water managementresponsibilities. In particular, ICWP focuses on water quality and water quantity issues, and on the dynamic interface state and Federal roles.
Founded: 1959
Dru Buntin, Chair
Ryan Mueller, Executive Director

560 Marine Technology Society
1100 H Street NW 202-717-8705
Suite LL 100 Fax: 202-347-4302
Washington, DC 20005 membership@mtsociety.org
www.mtsociety.org
Addresses coastal zone management, marine mineral and energy resources, marine environmental protection, and ocean engineering issues.
Founded: 1963
Kevin Traver, Executive Director

561 National Association of Clean Water Agencies (NACWA)
1816 Jefferson Place NW 202-833-2672
Washington, DC 20036 Fax: 888-267-9505
info@nacwa.org
www.nacwa.org
The NACWA is a recognized leader in environmental policy and a technical resource on water quality and ecosystem protection issues. It represents the interests of the country's wastewater treatment agencies and true environmentalpractioners.
Raymond J. Marshall, President
Adam Krantz, CEO

562 National Association of Flood and Stormwater Management Agencies (NAFSMA)
PO Box 56764 202-289-8625
Washington, DC 20040 Fax: 202-530-3389
info@nafsma.org
www.nafsma.org
NAFSMA is an organization of public agencies whose function is the protection of lives, property and economic activity from the adverse impacts of storm and flood waters. The mission of the association is to advocate public policy,encourage technologies and conduct education programs which facilitate and enhance the achievement of the public service functions of its members.
Founded: 1978
Steve Fitzgerald, President
Janet Bly, Vice-President

563 National Boating Federation
PO Box 4111
Annapolis, MD 21403-4111 Fax: 866-239-2070
info@n-b-f.org
www.n-b-f.org
Nonprofit, volunteer organization that represents over 2 million of America's boaters. It is an alliance of yacht and boating clubs, recreational boating organizations and includes associate and individual members.
Founded: 1966
Keith Christopher, President
Ed Payne, Vice-President

564 National Council for Air and Stream Improvements (NCASI)
1513 Walnut Street 919-941-6400
Suite 200 administrator@ncasi.org
Cary, NC 27511 www.ncasi.org
The Council is a technical organization devoted to finding solutions to environmental protection problems in the manufacture of pulp, paper, and wood products in industrial forestry. It now has about 75 member companies.
Founded: 1943

565 National Ground Water Association (NGWA)
601 Dempsey Road 614-898-7791
Westerville, OH 43081 800-551-7379
Fax: 614-898-7786
ngwa@ngwa.org
www.ngwa.org
The National Ground Water Association (NGWA) works to provide and protect the world's ground water resources; enhance the skills and credibility of all ground water professionals; develop and exchange industry knowledge and promote theground water industry and understanding of ground water resources.
Founded: 1948
Todd Hunter, President
David Henrich, President-Elect

566 National Institutes for Water Resources
niwr@mail.wvu.edu
niwr.info
The National Institutes for Water Resources is a network of Research Institutes in every state. They conduct basic and applied research to solve water problems unique to their area. The programmatic responsibilities stipulated by theWater resources Research Act provide a unified focus for the federal and non-federal components of the Institute Program.
Founded: 1970
Dr. John Tracy, Secretary-Treasurer

567 National Water Center
Eureka Springs, AR 479-244-0985
lwater@nationalwatercenter.org
www.nationalwatercenter.org
Strives to look at water with the broadest ideas of ecological balance and harmony. Support appropriate technology, bioregionalism, composting toilets, dowsing, ecology, flow forms, stream monitoring, vibrational water, watershedplanning.

568 National Water Resources Association (NWRA)
4 E Street Southeast 202-698-0693
Washington, DC 20003 nwra@nwra.org
www.nwra.org
The NWRA consists of individuals and groups, such as irrigation districts, canal companies and conservancy districts, municipalities and the public in general, who are interested in water resource development projects. It now hasabout 5,000 members.
Founded: 1932
Ron Thompson, President
Ian Lyle, Vice-President

569 National Watershed Coalition
PO Box 566 405-627-0670
Pawnee, OK 74058 nwchdqtrs@sbcglobal.net
A nonprofit Coalition made up of national, regional, state, and local organizations, associations, and individuals, that advocate dealing with natural resource problems and issues using watersheds as the planning and implementationunit.
Founded: 1989

570 National Waterways Conference
1100 North Glebe Road 703-224-8007
Suite 1010 Fax: 866-371-1390
Arlington, VA 22201 info@waterways.org
www.waterways.org
Coalition of trade and regional associations that have an interest in national waterways policy issues.
Founded: 1960
Amy W. Larson, President
Carole Wright, Dir., Internal Operations

571 North American Lake Management Society (NAMLS)
PO Box 5443 608-233-2836
Madison, WI 53705-0443 info@nalms.org
www.nalms.org
NAMLS's focus is on lake management for a wide variety of uses, but they are also involved with other issues on a watershed level: land, streams, wet lands, and estuaries. The society forges partnerships among citizens, scientists andprofessionals to foster the management and protection of lakes and reservoirs.
Founded: 1980
Frank Wilhelm, President
Frank Browne, President-Elect

572 Ocean Champions
202 San Jose Avenue 831-462-2539
Capitola, CA 95010 Fax: 831-462-2542
info@oceanchampions.org
www.oceanchampions.org
Environmental organization connected to a political action committee focused solely on oceans and ocean wildlife. Ocean Champions works to build a broad, bipartisan base of supporters to create a strong group of people who willchampion policy that supports ocean conservation.
Founded: 2003
Michael Sutton, Chair
David Wilmot, Ph.D., President/Co-Founder

573 Ocean Conservancy
1300 19th Street NW 202-429-5609
8th Floor 800-519-1541
Washington, DC 20036 membership@oceanconservancy.org
oceanconservancy.org
By working with millions of volunteers of all ages, from all around the world, Ocean Conservancy is able to organize International Coastal Cleanup.
Founded: 1972
Andreas Merkl, President
Janis Searles Jones, CEO

574 Ocean Foundation
1320 19th Street NW 202-887-8996
Washington, DC 20036 info@oceanfdn.org
www.oceanfdn.org
The Ocean Foundation sets out to aid in every way possible the preservation and strengthening of ocean environmnets around the world. Workig with donors to get resources out to marine conservation intiatives is one of the many ways TheOcean Foundation works to preserve the oceans.
Mark J. Spalding, Chair/President
Karen Muir, Vice-President

575 Oceana USA
1350 Connecticut Avenue NW 202-833-3900
5th Floor 877-762-3262
Washington, DC 20036 Fax: 202-833-2070
info@oceana.org
usa.oceana.org
Established by a group of leading foundations with the mission to achieve measurable change by conducting specific, science-based campaigns with fixed deadlines and articulated goals. Oceana is an international, nonprofit organizationwith chapters all over the world.
Founded: 2001
Simon Sidamon-Eristoff, Chair
Keith Addis, President

576 Oceanic Society
PO Box 844 415-256-9604
Ross, CA 94957 800-326-7491
www.oceanic-society.org
Founded for the protection of the marine environment, environmental education and conservation-based field research.
Founded: 1969
Zachary Rabinor, Chair
Roderic Mast, President/CEO

577 River Network
PO Box 21387 303-736-2724
Boulder, CO 80308 info@rivernetwork.org
www.rivernetwork.org
River Network is a national nonprofit organization for citizen groups working for river and watershed protection. Thier mission is to help people understand, protect and restore rivers and their watersheds. They provide conservationpartners with with information training, consultation, grants, referrals to other service organizations and networking opportunities.
Founded: 1988
Lynn Boaddus, Chair
Nicole Silk, President

578 Safina Center
80 North Country Road 631-675-1984
Setauket, NY 11733 admin@safinacenter.org
safinacenter.org
Formerly Blue Ocean Institute, the Safiina Center, named after its founder is inspired to do great work in the sciences by fostering relationships with science communicators and bringing forward discussion about the planet's ecologicalconcerns.
Founded: 2003
B. Eric Graham, Chair
Dr. Carl Safina, Founder/President

579 Scientific Committee on Oceanic Research (SCOR)
University of Delaware
Newark, DE 19716
secretariat@scor-int.org
www.scor-int.org
SCOR is an international nonprofit organization whose purpose is to encourage international cooperation in ocean research.
Founded: 1957
Edward R. Urban Jr., Executive Director

580 Seacoast Anti-Pollution League (SAPL)
PO Box 1136 603-431-5089
Portsmouth, NH 03802 sapl.info@comcast.net
saplnh.org
A nonprofit environmental group that monitor threats to public health and safety, wildlife, and ecosystems in the community.
Founded: 1969
Doug Bogen, Executive Director

581 Society for Freshwater Science (SFS)
Stroud Water Reserach Center

970 Spencer Road 610-268-2153
Avondale, PA 19311 webeditor@freshwater-science.org
www.freshwater-science.org

Previously North American Benthological Society, SFS specializes in stream insect ecology along with other scientific endeavors including; environmental impact assessments; taxonomy of microbes, algae, invertebrates and fish; carbonand nutrient dynamics; watershed dynamics; hydrology and geomorphology; conservation and restoration.
Founded: 1953

582 **Soil and Water Conservation Society**
945 SW Ankeny Road 515-289-2331
Ankeny, IA 50023-9723 800-THE-SOIL
Fax: 515-289-1227
swcs@swcs.org
www.swcs.org

Their mission is to foster the science and art of natural resource conservation. Their work targets the conservation of soil, water, and related natural resources.
Founded: 1943
Clare Lindahl, CEO
Rex Martin, President

583 **Steamboaters**
PO Box 41266 541-688-4980
Eugene, OR 97404 Fax: 541-607-3763
steamboaters@hotmail.com
www.steamboaters.org

Nonprofit organization dedicated to work to restore the North Umpqua river system's wild fish stocks, particularly steelhead, to a sustainable level that is consistent with optimum natural population levels. Protect, preserve andrestore fish habitat, including adequate and consistent flows of high quality water in the North Umpqua and its tributaries.
Founded: 1975
Tim Goforth, President
Jeff Dose, Vice-President

584 **Surfrider Foundation**
942 Calle Negocio 949-492-8170
Suite 350 Fax: 949-492-8142
San Clemente, CA 92673 info@surfrider.org
www.surfrider.org

A nonprofit organization that works to protect the world's oceans, waves and beaches. The organization largely focuses on issues such as; water quality, beach access, beach and surf spot preservation and sustaining marine and coastalecosystems.
Founded: 1984
Dr. Chad Nelsen, CEO
Michelle Kremer, COO

585 **Water Environment Federation (WEF)**
601 Wythe Street 703-684-2400
Alexandria, VA 22314-1304 800-666-0206
www.wef.org

A nonprofit technical and educational organization with members from varied disciplines who work toward the WEF vision of preservation and enhancement of the global water environment.
Founded: 1928
Rick Warner, P.E., President
Jenny Hartfelder, P.E., PMP, President-Elect

586 **Water Quality Association (WQA)**
4151 Naperville Road 630-505-0160
Lisle, IL 60532-3696 Fax: 630-505-9637
info@mail.wqa.org
www.wqa.org

Nonprofit international trade association representing the water treatment industry. Members include manufacturers, suppliers, dealers and distributors of water quality improvement products and services.
Founded: 1974
Pauli Undesser, Executive Director
Scott Parker, Associate Exective Director

587 **Water Resources Congress**
2300 Claredon Boulevard 703-525-4881
Suite 404 Fax: 703-527-1693
Arlington, VA 22201
Kathleen A Phelps, Executive Director

588 **Watershed Management Group**
1137 N Dodge Blvd 520-396-3266
Tuscon, AZ 85716 Fax: 520-300-6700
watershedmg.org

Watershed Management Group (WMG) is a nonprofit organization that develops community-based solutions to ensure the long-term prosperity of people and health of the environment.
Founded: 2002
Bill Wilkening, President
Jennifer Mills, Treasurer

589 **Western Hemisphere Shorebird Reserve Network (WHSRN)**
125 Manomet Point Road 508-224-6521
PO Box 1770 Fax: 508-224-9220
Manomet, MA 02345 whsrn@manomet.org
www.whsrn.org

WHSRN is a voluntary, community-based coalition of over 185 organizations across the US and other countries in the Western Hemisphere that have joined together to protect, restore and manage critical wetland habitats for migratorybirds.
John Cecil, Chair
Dr. Rob P. Clay, Director

590 **Wild Oceans**
PO Box 258 703-777-0037
Waterford, VA 20197 wildoceans.org
Previously National Coalition for Marine Conservation, Wild Oceans is dedicated exclusively to conserving ocean fish, preventing overfishing, reducing bycatch and protecting marine habitat.
Founded: 1973
Tim Choate, Chair
Ken Hinman, President

591 **Wildlands Conservancy**
3701 Orchid Place 610-965-4397
Emmaus, PA 18049 info@wildlandspa.org
www.wildlandspa.org
Wildlands Conservancy is a nonprofit organization dedicated to preserving precious lands, restoring rivers, maintaing healthy waterways, teaching the community about nature and caring for orphaned or injured wildlife.
Founded: 1973
Lona Farr, Chair
Christopher M. Kocher, President

592 **World Aquaculture Society (WAS)**
143 JM Parker Coliseum 225-578-3137
Baton Rouge, LA 70803 Fax: 225-578-3493
carolm@was.org
www.was.org

The World Aquaculture Society is an international nonprofit society, whose commitment to excellence in science, technology, education and information exchange, contribute to progressive and sustainable development of aquaculturethroughout the world.
Founded: 1970
Dr. William Daniels, President
Dr. Maria Celia Portella, President-Elect

Alabama

593 **Alabama Association of Soil & Water Conservation Committee**
100 North Union Street 334-242-2620
PO Box 304800 Fax: 334-242-0551
Montgomery, AL 36104 debra.brooks@swcc.alabama.gov
www.alconservationdistricts.gov
The committee is committed to conserving Alabama's natural resources to promote healthy soil, fishable and drinkable water, sustainable forests, and clean air for prosperous farming industries and quality of life for Alabama citizens.
Founded: 1937
William E. Puckett, PhD, Executive Director
Charles A. Holmes, Chairman

594 **Alabama Environmental Council**
4330 1st St Avenue S 205-252-7581
Birmingham, AL 35222 info@aeconline.org
www.aeconline.org
The AEC gives voice to those interested in protecting the rights to have a clean and safe environment. Their efforts are focused towards sustainable living through reducing the impacts of global warming, educating through environmentalliteracy and recycling.
Founded: 1967
Julie Danley, President
Laney DeJonge, Vice President

595 **Alabama National Safety Council: Birmingham**
2125 Data Office Drive 205-328-7233
Suite 102 800-457-7233
Birmingham, AL 35244 Fax: 205-328-1467
info@nsc.org
www.nsc.org/Pages/Alabama.aspx
The National Safety Council eliminates preventable deaths at work, in homes, communities and on the road through leadership, research, education and advocacy. Provides training, conferences, workshops, consultations newletters, updatesand safety support materials.
Founded: 1913
Donny Ward, Executive Director
Janet Froetscher, President, CEO

596 **Alabama Solar Association**
PO Box 143 256-650-5120
Huntsville, AL 35804-143 Fax: 256-650-5119
isimon1027@aol.com
al-solar.wixsite.com/a-s-a
A non-profit organization advocating and promoting green, renewable and solar energy conservation.
Doug Elgin, President
Al Orilion, Founder

597 **Alabama Waterfowl Association**
1346 Country Road #11 205-259-2509
Scottsboro, AL 35768
www.sites.google.com/site/alabamawaterfowlassociation
Dedicated to increasing waterfowl populations, natural wetland and upland waterways. AWA networks with other state waterfowl associations in the North American Waterfowl Federation for wetlands conservation.
Founded: 1989
Jerry Davis, CEO
Gary Benefield, Executive Director

598 **Alabama Wildlife Federation**
3050 Lanark Rd 334-285-4550
Millbrook, AL 36054 800-822-9453
Fax: 334-285-4959
awf@alabamawildlife.org
www.alabamawildlife.org
Mission is to promote the conservation of Alabama's wildlife and natural resources, as a basis for the social and economic prosperity, through responsible use and stewardship of wildlife, forests, fish, soils, water and air.
Founded: 1935
Angus R. Cooper, President
Ed Leigh McMillan, Vice President

599 **American Lung Association of Alabama**
1678 Montgomery Highway 205-603-1540
Suite 104-355 alaal@LungSE.org
Birmingham, AL 35216 www.lung.org
The American Lung Association of Alabama works to prevent lung disease and promote lung health; offering a wide variety of lung health services to the people of Alabama.
Martha C. Bogdan, Executive VP, Southeast
Willie L. Bythwood, Jr, CFO

600 **American Society of Landscape Architects: Alabama Chapter**
202-898-2444
888-999-2752
Fax: 202-898-1185
info@asla.org
www.alabamaasla.com
The professional association representing landscape architects who lead, educate and participate in the careful stewardship, planning, and artful design of cultural and natural environments.
Lois S. Mash, President
Jane Reed Ross, President-Elect

601 **BASS Anglers Sportsman Society**
3500 Blue Lake Drive 334-272-9530
Suite 330 877-227-7872
Birmingham, AL 35243 Fax: 334-270-7148
bassmaster@emailcustomerservice.com
www.bassmaster.com
B.A.S.S. is dedicated to enhancing the sport of bass fishing by advocating for access, conservation and youth fishing.
Founded: 1967
Gary Jones, Federation Director

602 **National Safety Council: Tennessee Valley Office**
2042 Beltline Road SW 256-308-1133
Building A, Suite 110 Fax: 256-308-1161
Decatur, AL 35601 alabama@nsc.org
Conducts safety, health and environmental efforts at the community level in order to eliminate preventable deaths at work, in homes, communities and on the road.
Donny Ward, Executive Director

603 **Sierra Club: Alabama Chapter**
4075 Lawson Gap Rd 256-572-0400
Boaz, AL 35956-6507 jonathonmeeks@gmail.com
www.sierraclub.org/alabama
The Alabama Chapter of the Sierra Club fights for clean water, educates the public and creates political action to protect Alabama's wilderness to make Alabama a cleaner and safer place.
Founded: 1908 3,000 Members
Loren Blackford, President
Susana Reyes, Vice President

Alaska

604 **Alaska Conservation Alliance**
810 N St #203 907-258-6171
P.O Box 100660 Fax: 907-258-6177
Anchorage, AK 99501-3271 info@akvoice.org
nwtoxiccommunities.org
Statewide non-profit organization whose primary mission is to protect Alaska's natural environment through voter education, engagement and advocacy.
Founded: 1997
Kate Troll, Principal Officer

605 **Alaska Natural Resource & Outdoor Education**
200 W. 34th Street 907-292-1772
Suite 1007 Fax: 907-207-1795
Anchorage, AK 99503 anroeak@gmail.com
www.anroe.net
Mission is to promote and implement excellence in natural resource, outdoor, and environmental education for Alaskans.
Founded: 1986
Marilyn Sigman, President
Elizabeth Trowbridge, Treasurer

606 **Alaska Wildlife Alliance**
PO Box 202022 907-277-0897
Anchorage, AK 99520 Fax: 907-277-7423
info@akwildlife.org
www.akwildlife.org
Advocates for scientifically managed and healthy ecosystems to protect wildlife for present and future generations.
Founded: 1978
Ed Schmitt, President
Richard Hoskins, Vice President

607 **American Lung Association of Alaska**
500 W Intl Airport Rd A 907-664-6400
Anchorage, AK 99518 Fax: 907-565-5587
marge.stoneking@lung.org
www.aklung.org
Promoting lung health awareness amd preventing lung diseases in Alaska.
Founded: 1934
Kathryn A. Forbes, CPA, Chair
John F. Emanuel, JD, Vice Chair

608 **American Lung Association of Alaska: Fairbanks**
529 6th Avenue 907-891-7451
Suite 203 maegan.weltzin@lung.org
Fairbanks, AK 99701 www.aklung.org

609 **American Lung Association of Alaska: Wasilla**
1075 S Check Street 907-891-7445
Suite 205 ashley.peltier@lung.org
Wasilla, AK 99654 www.aklung.org

610 **American Society of Landscape Architects: Alaska Chapter**
800 F St 907-343-8368
PO Box 196650 888-999-2752
Anchorage, AK 99519 Fax: 907-343-8088
aslaak.web@gmail.com
www.akasla.org
Supports the knowledge and practice of landscape architecture as a means to protect and enhance the natural and built environments of Alaska.
Founded: 1978
Ed Leonetti, President
Eliza Cink, Vice President, Interior

611 **Audubon Alaska**
Nation Audubon Society
431 West 7th Ave 907-276-7034
Suite 101 Fax: 907-276-5069
Anchorage, AK 99501 audubonalaska@audubon.org
ak.audubon.org
Working to conserve Alaska's natural ecosystems, birds, wildlife, and their habitats by using science to identify conservation priorities and support conservation actions and policies.
Founded: 1977
David Yarnold, President/CEO
Milo Burcham, Chair

612 **Bureau of Land Management**
222 West 7th Ave #13 907-271-5960
Anchorage, AK 99513 Fax: 907-271-3684
AK_AKSO_Public_Room@blm.gov
www.blm.gov/alaska
The Bureau of Land Management in Alaska focuses on land transfer, energy development, Trans-Alaska pipeline system and fire management.
Mark Spencer, District Manager
Bonnie Million, Field Manager

613 **National Wildlife Federation Alaska Regional Center**
750 W. 2nd Avenue 206-285-8707
Anchorage, AK 99501 800-937-2026
Fax: 206-285-8698
www.nwf.org/pacific-region/alaska.aspx
Focuses on global warming, renewable energy, wildlife, sustainable tourism and youth education.
Founded: 1988
Beth Pratt, Director
Jennifer Murck, Manager

614 **Northern Alaska Environmental Center**
830 College Road 907-452-5021
Fairbanks, AK 99701-1535 Fax: 907-452-3100
info@northern.org
www.northern.org
Promotes conservation of the environment in Interior and Arctic Alaska through advocacy, education, and sustainable resource stewardship.
Founded: 1971
Elisabeth Dabney, Executive Director
Frank Williams, President

615 **Sierra Club Alaska Chapter**
750 W 2nd Ave 907-258-6807
Suite 100 Fax: 907-258-6807
Anchorage, AK 99501 dan.ritzman@sierraclub.org
www.sierraclub.org/alaska
The Alaska Chapter of the Sierra Club works to protect the Last Frontier from the damage of logging and drilling. It strives for renewable energy, sustainable use of resources, preservation of wild places, and the smart growth of urbanareas.
Founded: 1892
Dan Ritzman, Program Director
Yasuhiro Ozuru, Chair

616 **Trustees for Alaska**
1026 W 4th Avenue 907-276-4244
Suite 201 Fax: 907-276-7110
Anchorage, AK 99501 ecolaw@trustees.org
www.trustees.org
A public interest law firm that provides legal counsel to sustain and protect Alaska's natural environment.
Founded: 1974
Michelle Meyer, Chair
Chase Hensel, Vice Chair

617 Wildlife Society: Alaska Chapter
1271 Lowbush Lane 907-456-8682
Fairbanks, AK 99709 Fax: 907-257-2774
twsalaska@gmail.com
www.wildlife.org/alaska
A nonprofit organization of professional wildlife biologists dedicated to excellence in conserving wildlife and their habitats and wildlife sterwardship through science and education.
Founded: 1971
Scott Brainerd, President
Nate Svoboda, President-Elect

Arizona

618 American Lung Association of Arizona
102 West McDowell Rd 602-258-7505
2819 East Boradway Blvd 800-586-4872
Phoenix, AZ 85003 Fax: 877-276-2108
AZInfo@Lungs.org
www.lung.org
The mission of the American Lung Association is to prevent lung disease and promote lung health.
Founded: 1912
Lynn Rosenbach, Chair, CEO
Susan Cordier, COO

619 American Lung Association of Arizona: Tucson
2819 East Broadway Bouelvard 520-323-1812
Tucson, AZ 85716 AZInfo@Lungs.org
www.lung.org/about-us/local-associations/arizona.html

620 Arizona ASLA: American Society of Landscape Architects
PO Box 28393 602-258-8668
Tempe, AZ 85285 Fax: 602-273-6814
www.azasla.org
The Arizona state affiliate of the American Society of Landscape Architects are dedicated to educate and participate in the planning and design of cultural and natural environments.
Rick Campbell, President
Laura Paty, President Elect

621 Arizona Automotive Recyclers Association
1030 E. Baseline Rd. 480-609-3999
#105-1025 admin@aara.com
Tempe, AZ 85283 www.aara.com
A group of automotive recyclers that are committed to serving Arizona with quality recycled auto parts, to help customers, communities and the environment.
Founded: 1910
Mike Pierson Jr, President
Leroy Liebermann, Secretary/Treasurer

622 Arizona BASS Chapter Federation
P.O Box 11448 480-304-1033
Chandler, AZ 85248 Fax: 480-773-7019
info@azbassfederation.com
www.azbassfederation.com
Bass fishing tournament organization, facilitators of recruiting youth fishers and help conserve natural habitats.
Founded: 1972
Gregory Krueger, President
Steven Boyce, Vice President

623 Arizona Chapter, National Safety Council
1606 West Indian School Road 602-264-2394
Phoenix, AZ 85015-5232 Fax: 602-277-5485
main@acnsc.org
www.acnsc.org
To protect life and promote health through accident and injury prevention at home, work, school and on the road.
Founded: 1949
John Keeler, President
Margaret Cather, Executive Director

624 Arizona Recycling Coalition
24 West Camelback Road 408-254-1922
Suite A-492 info@arizonarecyclingcoalition.org
Phoenix, AZ 85013 arizonarecyclingcoalition.org
The Arizona Recycling Coalition (AzRC) is a membership-based, non-profit organization dedicated to promoting waste reuse, reduction and recycling throughout Arizona and our southwestern region.
Alana Levine, Chairperson
Terry Gellenbeck, Vice-Chair

625 Arizona Solar Energy Industries Association
Solar Energy Industries Association
2122 W. Lone Cactus Dr 602-559-4769
Suite 2 info@ariseia.org
Phoenix, AZ 85027 www.ariseia.org
A non-profit trade organization that aims to deploy solar energy technologies in an ethical manner.
Founded: 1997
Tom Harris, President
Court Rich, Vice President

626 Arizona Water Well Association
950 E. Baseline Rd. 480-609-3999
#104-1025 Fax: 480-609-3939
Tempe, AZ 85283 admin@azwwa.org
www.azwwa.org
Promotes protection and wise development of underground water resources.
Founded: 1957
Nate Little, President
David Williams, President Elect

627 Arizona-Sonora Desert Museum
2021 N Kinney Road 520-883-2702
Tucson, AZ 85743 Fax: 520-883-2500
info@desertmuseum.org
www.desertmuseum.org
Museum, zoo, botanical garden, art gellery and aquarium. Also helps to conserve the Sonoran Desert.
Founded: 1952
Craig Ivanyi, Executive Director
Holly Swangstu, Art Institute Director

628 Center for Biological Diversity
PO Box 710 520-623-5252
Tucson, AZ 85702-0710 866-357-3349
Fax: 520-623-9797
center@biologicaldiversity.org
www.biologicaldiversity.org
Works through science, law and creative media to secure a future for all species on the brink of extinction.
Marcey Olajos, Chair
Kieran Suckling, Exe. Dir., Co-Founder

629 Sierra Club: Arizona Chapter
514 W. Roosevelt St 602-253-8633
Phoenix, AZ 85003 grand.canyon.chapter@sierraclub.org
www.sierraclub.org/arizona
The Grand Canyon Chapter utilizes conservation, political and legislative activism, administrative work and outings to protect the state and its natural resources.
Founded: 1965
Jim Vaaler, Chair
Sandy Bahr, Outreach Director

Arkansas

630 **American Society of Landscape Architects: Arkansas Chapter**
P.O. Box 3343 202-898-2444
Fayetteville, AR 72702 800-999-2752
Fax: 202-898-1185
www.arasla.org
Promotes the profession of landscappe architecture and advances the practive through advocacy, education, communication and fellowship.
Founded: 1899
Allison Thurmond Quinlan, President
Alan Ostner, Treasurer

631 **Arkansas Association of Conservation Districts**
101 East Capitol 501-682-2915
Suite 350 Fax: 501-682-3991
Little Rock, AR 72201 rockyharrell@sbcglobal.net
www.aracd.org
The Arkansas Association of Conservation Districts assists the conservation districts of Arkansas in their efforts to serve the soil and water conservation needs of the people of Arkansas.
Founded: 1937
Debbie Moreland, Program Administrator
Martha Manley, President

632 **Arkansas Environmental Federation**
415 N. McKinley St 501-374-0263
Suite 835 Fax: 501-374-8752
Little Rock, AR 72205 cmiller@environmentark.org
www.environmentark.org
The AEF is a non-profit education association that provides training for environmental professionals and advocates with a focus on practical laws and regulations based on science, a teamwork approach to compliance, waste minimizationand pollution prevention.
Founded: 1967
Tom Fox, President
Kelley Crouch, President-Elect

633 **Arkansas Respiratory Health Association**
211 Natural Resources Drive 501-224-5864
Little Rock, AR 72205 800-880-5864
Fax: 501-224-5645
lcollers@lungark.org
www.arkresp.org
Mission of the Arkansas Respiratory Health Association is to prevent lung disease and promote lung health through education, advocacy and research.

634 **Sierra Club: Arkansas Chapter**
1308 West 2nd St 501-301-8280
Little Rock, AR 72201 glen.hooks@sierraclub.org
www.sierraclub.org/arkansas
To practice and promote responsible use of the earth's ecosystems and resources; educate the public to protect and restore the quality of the natural environment. The Arkansas Chapter focuses on protecting the wilderness of Arkansasand clean energy and water.
Founded: 1982
Loren Blackford, President
Susana Reyes, Vice President

California

635 **American Lung Association of California**
American Lung Association
333 Hegenberger Rd 510-638-5864
Suite 450 Fax: 510-638-8984
Oakland, CA 94621 cainfo@lung.org
www.lung.org/about-us/local-associations/california.html
Focuses on lung cancer, air quality, lung diesease, the elimination of tobacco and related diseases and fundraising.
Founded: 1904
Stephen R. O'Kane, Secretary, Treasurer
Cheryl A. Calhoun, Managing Director

636 **American Lung Association of California: Bakersfield**
2025 Westwind Drive 661-847-4700
Suite C maria.jaime@lung.org
Bakersfield, CA 93301
www.lung.org/about-us/local-associations/california.html

637 **American Lung Association of California: Chico**
25 Jan Court 530-345-5864
Chico, CA 95928 shelly.brantley@lung.org
www.lung.org/about-us/local-associations/california.html

638 **American Lung Association of California: Fresno**
1680 W Shaw Avenue 559-772-3307
Fresno, CA 93711 justina.felix@lung.org
www.lung.org/about-us/local-associations/california.html

639 **American Lung Association of California: Los Angeles**
3325 Wilshire Boulevard 213-384-5864
Suite 900 ana.martinez@lung.org
Los Angeles, CA 90010
www.lung.org/about-us/local-associations/california.html

640 **American Lung Association of California: Orange County**
513 E 1st Street 714-835-5864
Suite B ana.martinez@lung.org
Tustin, CA 92780
www.lung.org/about-us/local-associations/california.html

641 **American Lung Association of California: Sacramento**
1531 I St 916-554-5864
Sacramento, CA 95814 cainfo@lung.org
www.lung.org/about-us/local-associations/california.html

642 **American Lung Association of California: San Berardino**
441 Mac Kay Drive 909-884-5864
San Bernardino, CA 92408 clarissa.mprales@lung.org
www.lung.org/about-us/local-associations/california.html

643 **American Lung Association of California: San Diego**
2020 Camino Del Rio N 619-297-3901
Suite 200 ellen.sherwood@lung.org
San Diego, CA 92108
www.lung.org/about-us/local-associations/california.html

644 **American Rivers: California Region: Fairfax**
2150 Allston Way 510-809-8010
Suite 320 outreach@americanrivers.org
Berkeley, CA 94704 www.americanrivers.org

American Rivers is the only national organization standing up for healthy rivers so communities can thrive.
Founded: 1973
Bob Irvin, President
Chris Williams, Senior V.P, Conservation

645 American Rivers: California Region: Nevada City
120 Union St 530-478-0206
Nevada City, CA 95959 Fax: 530-478-5849
outreach@americanrivers.org
www.americanrivers.org
The conservation organization stands up for healthy rivers so communities can thrive. American Rivers protects and restores America's rivers for the benefit of people, wildlife and nature.
Founded: 1973 65,000 Members
Bob Irvin, President
Chris Williams, Senior V.P, Conservation

646 American Society of Landscape Architects: Northern California Chapter
3130 Balfour Road 415-974-5490
Suite D #275 Fax: 415-543-2112
Brentwood, CA 94513 www.asla-ncc.org
To advance the profession of Landscape Architecture for the public's appreciation and awareness.
Founded: 1899
Elizabeth Boults, President
Carolyne Orazi, President-Elect

647 American Society of Landscape Architects: San Diego Chapter
1050 Rosecrans St 619-283-8818
Suite B Fax: 619-222-8154
San Diego, CA 92106 aslasd@sbcglobal.net
www.asla-sandiego.org
To lead, educate and participate in the careful stewardship, planning and artful design of cultural and natural environments.
Nate Magnusson, President
Michael D. Brennan, President Elect

648 American Society of Landscape Architects: Sierra Chapter
1400 S St 916-447-7400
Suite 100 Fax: 916-447-8270
Sacramento, CA 95811 webmaster@asla-sierra.org
www.asla-sierra.org
Strives for the advancement of knowledge, education and skill in the art and science of landscape architecture.
Jessica McWilliams, President
Andrew Wickham, President-Elect

649 American Society of Landscape Architects: Southern California Chapter
360 E. First St 714-838-3615
Suite 371 877-378-6726
Tustin, CA 92780 Fax: 714-730-6296
vphillipy@socal-asla.org
www.socal-asla.org
Promotes landscape architecture through knowledge, ecducation, communication, advocacy and skill.
Duane Border, President
Pamela Brief, President Elect

650 Asian Pacific Environmental Network
426 17th St 510-834-8920
Suite 500 Fax: 510-834-8926
Oakland, CA 94612 info@apen4ej.org
www.apen4ej.org
The Asian Pacific Environmental Network (APEN) empowers low-income Asian Pacific Islander (API) communities to take action on environmental and social justice issues. APEN builds organizations in dis-empowered API communities todevelop lasting capacity and to achieve solutions to problems affecting people's lives.
Founded: 1991
Nayantara Mehta, Board Chair
Joanne Kim, Board Vice Chair

651 Bio Integral Resource Center
PO Box 7414 510-524-2567
Berkeley, CA 94707 Fax: 510-524-1758
birc@igc.org
www.birc.org
The goal of the Bio Integral Resources Center is to reduce pesticide use by educating the public about effective, less toxic alternatives for pest problems.
Founded: 1979
Dr. William Quarles, Executive Director

652 Breathe California Golden Gate Public Health Partnership
1 Sutter St 650-994-5868
Suite 225 Fax: 415-445-3000
San Francisco, CA 94014 info@ggbreathe.org
www.ggbreathe.org
Breathe California fights lung disease, advocates for clean air and advances public health through grassroots education, advocacy and services.
Founded: 1908
Tanya Stevenson, President/CEO
Elias Trevino, Vice President, Operations

653 Breathe California Of Los Angeles County
5858 Wilshire Blvd 323-935-8050
Suite 300 Fax: 323-935-1873
Los Angeles, CA 90036 info@breathela.org
www.breathela.org
Dedicated to providing communities in Los Angeles County with the resources needed to promote clean air initiatives through its continued commitment to research, education and advocacy.
Founded: 1903
Steven L. Bryson, Esq., Chair
Fernando Del Rio, Chair Elect

654 Breathe California of the Bay Area: Alameda, Santa Clara And San Benito Counties
1469 Park Ave 408-998-5865
San Jose, CA 95126 Fax: 408-998-0578
info@lungsrus.org
www.lungsrus.org
Fights lung disease and works with communities to promote lung health.
Founded: 1904
Scott McLarty, Chair
Abhay Tewari, Founder, CEO

655 California Academy of Sciences Library
55 Music Concourse Drive 415-379-8000
Golden Gate Park Fax: 415-321-8633
San Francisco, CA 94118 info@calacademy.org
www.calacademy.org
The California Academy of Sciences is dedicated to exploring, explaining, and sustaining life on Earth. Includes an aquarium, natural history museum, planetarium and rainforest.
Founded: 1853
Jonathan Foley, PhD, Executive Director
Mike McGee, Chief Financial Officer

656 California Air Resources Board
State of California

1001 I St
PO Box 2815
Sacramento, CA 95814
916-322-2990
800-242-4450
Fax: 916-445-5025
helpline@arb.ca.gov
www.arb.ca.gov

The California ARB is the state agency charged with coordinating efforts to attain and maintain ambient air quality standards, conduct research into the causes and solutions to air pollution and its health impacts. Their mission is topromote and protect public health, welfare and ecological resources.

Founded: 1967
Mary D. Nichols, Chairman
Sandra Berg, Vice Chair

657 **California Association of Environmental Health**
3700 Chaney Court
Carmichael, CA 95608
530-676-0715
Fax: 530-676-0515
justin@ccdeh.com
www.ccdeh.com

Environmental Health Departments provide the delivery of Local Environmental Health Programs.

Justin Malan, Executive Director
Sheryl Baldwin, CCDEH Manager

658 **California Association of Resource Conservation Districts**
801 K St, MS 14-15
Sacramento, CA 95814
916-457-7904
Fax: 916-457-7934
info@carcd.org
www.carcd.org

CARCD is a voluntary association whose primary purpose is to enhance the effectiveness of local Resource Conservation Districts (RCDs) so as to implement strong and locally-led conservation efforts of natural resources and agriculturein California.

Karen Buhr, Executive Director
Paul Williams, President

659 **California BASS Federation**
13350 Racquet Court
Poway, CA 92064
858-748-9459
californiabassorg@gmail.com
www.californiabass.org

Dedicated to promoting bass fishing through youth, conservation, public awareness, and local support. Regional tournaments are held throughout California.

Founded: 1969
Scott Sweet, President
Larry Wilson, VP

660 **California Birth Defects Monitoring Program**
1615 Capitol Ave
Sacramento, CA 95814
916-558-1784
Fax: 916-650-0305
mchinet@cdph.ca.gov
www.cdph.ca.gov/Programs/CFH/DGDS/Pages/cbdmp/about.aspx

The California Birth Defects Monitoring Program is a public health program devoted to finding the causes of birth defects in order to prevent them.

Founded: 1982
Karen L. Smith, Director
Kate Clayton, Health Promotion, Chief

661 **California Certified Organic Farmers**
2155 Delaware Avenue
Suite 150
Santa Cruz, CA 95060
831-423-2263
Fax: 831-423-4528
ccof@ccof.org
www.ccof.org

Promotes and supports organic food and agriculture through an organic certification program, trade support, producer and consumer education, and political advocacy.

Founded: 1973
Phil LaRocca, Chair
Malcolm Ricci, Vice Chair

662 **California Council for Environmental and Economic Balance**
101 Mission St
Suite 1440
San Francisco, CA 94105
415-512-7890
Fax: 415-512-7897
cceeb@cceeb.org
www.cceeb.org

A coalition of California business, labor and public leaders that strive to make environmental and economic balance a reality.

Founded: 1976
Walter McGuire, Chairman
Jerry Secundy, President/CEO

663 **California Renewable Fuels Council**
1516 Ninth St
MS-29
Sacramento, CA 95814-5512
916-654-4287
844-421-6229
renewable@energy.ca.gov
www.energy.ca.gov/renewables

As part of the California Energy Commission, the California Renewable Fuels Council is committed to reducing energy costs and the environmental impacts of energy use.

Founded: 2002
Robert B. Weisenmiller, Chair
Kourtney Vaccaro, Chief Counsel

664 **California Resource Recovery Association**
915 L Street
Suite C-216
Sacramento, CA 95814
916-441-2772
ccra.com

The California Resource Recovery Association (CRRA) is California's statewide recycling association dedicated to achieving environmental sustainability in and beyond California through Zero Waste strategies including productstewardship, waste prevention, reuse, recycling and composting.

Founded: 1974
Jenna Abbott, Executive Director
Rob Hilton, Conference Program Chair

665 **California Solar Energy Industries Association**
1107 9th St
Suite 820
Sacramento, CA 95814
916-228-4567
Fax: 707-374-4767
info@calseia.org
www.calseia.org

Promotes the expanding use of solar technologies in California and the growth of the solar industry.

Founded: 1977
Ed Murray, President
Jeanine Cotter, Vice President

666 **California State University East Bay**
California State University
California State University
25800 Carlos Bee Blvd
Hayward, CA 94542
510-885-3000
Fax: 510-885-4747
www.csueastbay.edu

The University's mission is to provide an academically rich, multicultural learning experience that prepares its students to realize their goals, pursue meaningful lifework, and to be socially responsible contributors to theircommunities.

Leroy M. Morishita, President
Bill Johnson, Vice President

667 **California Trappers Association (CTA)**
907 Holmes Flat Road
Redcrest, CA 95525
707-772-4259
chris.adamski@fwmedia.com
www.californiatrappers.com

CTA's primary concern is California's fur bearing mammals and small predatory mammals.

Founded: 1863
John Clark, President
James C Schmerker Jr, Vice President

668 California Waterfowl Association
1346 Blue Oaks Blvd
Roseville, CA 95678
916-648-1406
Fax: 916-648-1665
www.calwaterfowl.org

A statewide nonprofit organization whose principal objectives are the preservation, protection, and enhancement of California's waterfowl resources, wetlands, and associated hunting heritage.
Founded: 1945
John Carlson Jr., President
Rob Plath, Chair

669 California Wildlife Foundation
428 13th St
Suite 10A
Oakland, CA 94612
510-763-0211
Fax: 510-268-9948
info@californiawildlifefoundation.org
www.californiawildlifefoundation.org

Committed to protecting the state's wildlife species by acquiring, restoring, and managing sufficient habitat to sustain healthy populations over time.
Founded: 1990
Ellen Maldonado, Secretary
James Lightbody, Treasurer

670 Californians for Population Stabilization (CAPS)
P.O Box 90409
Santa Barbara, CA 93101
805-564-6626
Fax: 805-564-6636
info@capsweb.org
www.capsweb.org

A nonprofit, public interest organization that works to protect California's environment and quality of life by stabilizing the population.
Founded: 1986
Ben Zuckerman, President
Judith F. Smith, Vice President

671 Central California Safety Council
6004 N. El Dorado St
Stockton, CA 95207-4349
209-472-7233
www.californiasafety.org

To promote health and safety at home, in travel and in the workplace. Provides community health and safety programs, information and educational materials on health and safety-related topics and products.
Founded: 1934
Lynndee Riley, Secretary

672 Colorado River Board of California
770 Fairmont Ave
Suite 100
Glendale, CA 91203-1068
818-500-1625
Fax: 818-543-4685
crb@crb.ca.gov
www.crb.ca.gov

Established to protect California's rights and interests in the resources provided by the Colorado River and to represent California in discussions and negotiations regarding the Colorado River and its management.
Founded: 1937
Christopher Harris, Executive Director

673 Communities for a Better Environment
6325 Pacific Blvd Suite 300
120 Broadway Suite 2
Huntington Park, CA 90255
323-826-9771
Fax: 323-588-7079
cbeca@mail.com
www.cbecal.org

Nonprofit statewide, urban environmental health and justice organization that works with urban communities and grassroots organizations to prevent air and water pollution, eliminate toxic hazards and improve public health using sciencebased research, legal tactics and strategies.
Founded: 1978
Suma Peesapati, President
Adrian Martinez, Vice President

674 Concerned Citizens of South Central Los Angeles
4707 South Central Avenue
PO Box 11337
Los Angeles, CA 90011
323-846-2500
Fax: 323-846-2508
info@ccscla.org
www.ccscla.org

The mission of the Concerned Citizens of South Central Los Angeles is to fight for social, economic and environmental justice and to encourage resident participation in the process.
Founded: 1985
Robin Cannon, President
Noreen McClendon, Executive Director & VP

675 Desert Tortoise Preserve Committee
Tortoise T-R-A-C-K-S
4067 Mission Inn Ave
Riverside, CA 92501
951-683-3872
Fax: 951-683-6949
dtpc@pacbell.net
www.tortoise-tracks.org

A non-profit organization formed to promote the welfare of the desert tortoise in its native wild state.
Founded: 1974
Ron Berger, President
Robert Wood, Vice President

676 Earth Island Institute
2150 Allston Way
Suite 460
Berkeley, CA 94704-1375
510-859-9100
Fax: 510-859-9091
johnknox@earthisland.org
www.earthisland.org

A non-profit, public interest organization that supports people who create solutions to protect our planet.
Founded: 1982
Josh Floum, President
Kenneth Brower, Vice President

677 Environmental Defense Center
906 Garden St
Santa Barbara, CA 93101
805-963-1622
Fax: 805-962-3152
EDC@EnvironmentalDefenseCenter.org
www.environmentaldefensecenter.org

The Environmental Defense Center is a nonprofit, public interest organization that provides legal, educational and advocacy support to advance the environmental quality of California's south central coast.
Founded: 1977
Judy Pirkowitsch, President
Dave Davis, Vice President

678 Environmental Health Coalition
2727 Hoover Ave
Suite 202
National City, CA 91950
619-474-0220
Fax: 619-474-1210
ehc@environmentalhealth.org
www.environmentalhealth.org

Uses social change strategies to achieve environmental and social justice. Organizes and advocates to protect public health and the environment threatened by toxic pollution.
Founded: 1980
Margaret Godshalk, President
Enrique Medina, Vice President

679 Environmental Health Network
PO Box 1155
Larkspur, CA 94977-1155
415-541-5075
fdadockets@oc.fda.gov
www.ehnca.org

Nonprofit, volunteer organization, whose main goal is to promote public awareness of environmental sensitivities and causative factors. EHN's focus is on issues of access and developments relating to the health and welfare of theenvironmentally sensitive.
Connie Barker, Board President
Cyndi Norwitz, Board Vice President

680 Environmental Protection Information Center
145 G Street
Suite A
Arcata, CA 95521
707-822-7711
Fax: 707-822-7712
epic@wildcalifornia.org
wildcalifornia.org

The Environmental Protection Information Center (EPIC) advocates for science-based protection and restoration of Northwest California's forests, using an integrated, science-based approach, combining public education, citizen advocacy,and strategic litigation.
Founded: 1977
Shawnee Alexandri, President
Robert Shearer, Vice President

681 Friends of the River
1418 20th St
Suite 100
Sacramento, CA 95811
916-442-3155
888-464-2477
Fax: 916-442-3396
info@friendsoftheriver.org
www.friendsoftheriver.org

Friends of the River is dedicated to preserving and restoring California's rivers, streams and watersheds as well as advocating for sustainable water management.
Founded: 1973
Eric Wesselman, Executive Director
John Yost, Treasurer

682 Heal the Bay
1444 9th St
Santa Monica, CA 90401
310-451-1500
Fax: 310-496-1902
www.healthebay.com

A nonprofit organization dedicated to protecting Santa Monica Bay and all Southern California coastal waters and watersheds.
Founded: 1985
Shelley Luce, President, CEO
Sarah Abramson Sikich, Vice President

683 Hopland Research and Extension Center
4070 University Road
Hopland, CA 95449
707-744-1424
Fax: 707-744-1040
karodrigues@ucanr.edu
hrec.ucanr.edu

The Hopland Research and Extension Center (HREC) is a multi-disciplinary research and education facility for agriculture and natural resources in the North Coast region run by the University of California.
Founded: 1951
Kimberly A. Rodriques, Director

684 Institute of International Education
Institute of International Education
530 Bush St
Suite 1000
San Francisco, CA 94108
415-362-6520
Fax: 415-392-4667
iiesf@iie.org
www.iie.org

An independent non-profit organization that works to advance international education and access to education worldwide.
Founded: 1919
Allen E. Goodman, President, CEO
Mary Karam McKey, Director

685 League to Save Lake Tahoe
2608 Lake Tahoe Blvd
South Lake Tahoe, CA 96150
530-541-5388
Fax: 530-541-5454
info@keeptahoeblue.org
www.keeptahoeblue.org

Focused on the preservation and restoration of the Tahoe Basin's waters, forests, wildlife and landscape for present and future generations.
Founded: 1957
Ash Daggs, President
David Brandenburger, Vice President

686 Marine Mammal Center
2000 Bunker Rd
Fort Cronkite
Sausalito, CA 94965-2619
415-289-7325
Fax: 415-289-7333
info@tmmc.org
www.marinemammalcenter.org

Veterinary research hospital and educational center dedicated to the rescue and rehabilitation of ill and injured marine mammals.
Founded: 1975
Dr. Jeffrey R. Boehm, Executive Director
Marci Davis, CFO

687 Mendocino County Resource Conservation District
410 Jones Street
Suite C-3
Ukiah, CA 95482
707-462-3664
mcrcd.org

The Mendocino County Resource Conservation District is a non-profit organization that helps communities voluntarily conserve, protect, and restore wild and working landscapes in Mendocino County. They provide technical assistance,education and outreach programs, monitoring and assessment services, and funding opportunities to help land managers improve the long-term stewardship of the county's natural resource base.
Dave Koball, Chair
Craig Blencowe, Vice Chair

688 Mendocino Land Trust
P.O. Box 1094
330 N. Franklin Street, Suite 7
Fort Bragg, CA 95437
707-962-0470
admin@mendocinolandtrust.org
mendocinolandtrust.org

The mission of the Mendocino Land Trust is to conserve important natural resources of Mendocino County including working farmlands and forests, wildlife habitat, open space, scenic vistas, watersheds, and to facilitate public access.
Founded: 1976
Terry Gross, President
Richard Strom, Vice President

689 Mendocino Wildlife Association
45090 Little Lake Street
Mendocino, CA 95460
707-357-5693
707-984-6363
info@mendowildass.org
mendowildlife.com

Mendocino Wildlife Association (MWA) is a non-profit organization dicated to public education about wildlife, using non-lethal wildlife management practices, and wildlife rescue and rehabilitation.
Traci Pellar, Administrator

690 National Institute for Global Environmental Change: Western Regional Center
University of Califonia-Davis
1 Shields Avenue
Davis, CA 95616
530-752-1011
Fax: 530-752-7302
www.ucdavis.edu

This overview provides insight into the major environmental programs and permitting requirements governing industrial processes and activities.
Founded: 1990
Dr. Susan Ustin, Director

691 NorCal Solar/Northern California Solar Energy Society
PO Box 3008
Berkeley, CA 94703
510-592-7136
info@norcalsolar.org
www.norcalsolar.org

A non-profit educational organization whose mission is to accelerate the use of solar energy technology through the exchange of information.
Founded: 1974
Eric Larson, President

692 Northcoast Environmental Center
415 I St
Arcata, CA 95521
707-822-6918
Fax: 707-822-6980
nec@yournec.org
www.yournec.org

A nonprofit educational organization devoted to conserving and protecting the terrestrial, aquatic and marine ecosystems of Northern California. Their goal is to promote the importance of the relations between people and the biosphere.
Founded: 1971
Larry Glass, President
Dan Sealy, Vice-President

693 Outdoor Programs
University of California San Francisco
Milberry Union 125 West
500 Parnassus Ave
San Francisco, CA 94143-0234
415-476-1115
Fax: 415-502-5887
outdoors@cls.ucsf.edu
campuslifeservices.ucsf.edu/fitnessrecreation

Paddling, hiking, climbing, aquatics, personal training, and pilates available for students, families in the UCSF community and the public.
Founded: 1970
Kirk McLaughlin, Outdoor Programs Manager
Colleen Massey, Mission Bay Prog. Supervisor

694 Pesticide Action Network North America
161 Telegraph Ave
Suite 1200
Oakland, CA 94612
510-788-9020
panna@panna.org
www.panna.org

Pesticide Action Network North America advocates the adoption of ecologically sound practices in place of hazardous pesticide use in order to create a thriving food system.
Founded: 1984
Denise O'Brien, President
Virginia Nesmith, Vice President

695 Pesticide Education Center
PO Box 225279
San Francisco, CA 94122-5279
415-391-8511
Fax: 415-391-9159
pec@igc.org
old.cehn.org/pesticide_education_center

To educate the public about the health effects of exposure to pesticides in the home, community and at work.
Founded: 1988
Marion Moses, President

696 Rainforest Action Network
425 Bush St
Suite 300
San Francisco, CA 94108
415-398-4404
Fax: 415-398-2732
ran@ran.org
www.ran.org

Rainforest Action Network works to protect the Earth's rainforest and support the rights of their inhabitants through education, grassroots organizing and non-violent direct action.
Founded: 1985
Anna Hawken, Chair
James D. Gollin, President

697 Redwood Empire Solar Living Association
c/o Solar Living Institute
P.O Box 836
Hopland, CA 95449
707-472-2450
Fax: 707-472-2498
sli@solarliving.org
www.solarliving.org

The Solar Living Institute promotes sustainable living through environmental education. Offers professional solar training and a wide array of sustainability courses.
Founded: 1998
John Schaeffer, President
Karen Kallen, Executive Director

698 San Diego Renewable Energy Society (SDRES)
PO Box 927203
San Diego, CA 92192
info@sdres.org
sdres.org

Dedicated to increasing the use of renewable and sustainable energy technologies in San Diego County.
Jamaal Knight, Chairman
Jake Lincoln, Treasurer

699 Save San Francisco Bay Association
1330 Broadway
Suite 1800
Oakland, CA 94612-2519
510-463-6850
Fax: 510-463-6851
info@saveSFbay.org
www.savesfbay.org

Save the Bay works to protect and restore the San Francisco Bay from pollution, fill, shoreline destruction and fresh water diversion.
Founded: 1961
David Lewis, Executive Director
Samuel N. Luoma, Chair

700 Scenic California
CA
510-883-0390
Fax: 510-883-0391
www.scenic.org

Nonprofit organization dedicated to protecting natural beauty and distinctive community character through scenic conservation.
Mark Falzone, President
Ronald L. Fleming, Chair

701 Sierra Club: Angeles Chapter
3250 Wilshire Blvd
Suite 660
Los Angeles, CA 90010-1904
213-387-4287
Fax: 213-387-5383
info@angeles.sierraclub.org
www.angeles.sierraclub.org

To advance the preservation and protection of the natural environment by empowering the citizenry with charitable resources to further the cause of environmental protection.
Founded: 1920
Loren Blackford, President
Susana Reyes, Vice President

702 Sierra Club: Kern Kaweah Chapter
PO Box 3357
Bakersfield, CA 93385-3357
661-496-6585
harold.wood@sierraclub.org
www.kernkaweah.sierraclub.org

To advance the preservation and protection of the natural environment by empowering democratically-based grassroots organizations, with charitable resources to further the cause of environmental protection.
Founded: 1952
Loren Blackford, President
Susana Reyes, Vice President

703 Sierra Club: Loma Prieta Chapter
3921 East Bayshore Rd
Suite 204
Palo Alto, CA 94303
650-390-8411
Fax: 650-390-8497
loma.prieta.chapter@sierraclub.org
www.lomaprieta.sierraclub.org

To advance the preservation and protection of the natural environment by empowering the citizenry with charitable resources to further the cause of environmental protection.
Founded: 1933
James Eggers, Chapter Director
Barbara Kelsey, Chapter Coordinator

704 Sierra Club: Los Padres Chapter
PO Box 31241
Santa Barbara, CA 93130-1241
805-965-9719
davidgold4@aol.com
www.lospadres.sierraclub.org

To advance the preservation and protection of the natural environment by empowering the citizenry with charitable resources to further the cause of environmental protection.
Loren Blackford, President
Susana Reyes, Vice President

705 **Sierra Club: Mother Lode Chapter**
909 12th St
Suite 202
Sacramento, CA 95814
916-557-1100
Fax: 916-557-9669
info@mlc.sierraclub.org
www.sierraclub.org/mother-lode
Focused on tackling issues regarding fracking, the management of wolf populations, protecting old growth forests, forest clearcutting, climate change, and water management.
Dyane Osorio, Chapter Director
Andy Sawyer, Chair

706 **Sierra Club: Redwood Chapter**
55A Ridgeway Ave
PO Box 466
Santa Rosa, CA 95402
707-544-7651
Fax: 707-544-9861
www.redwood.sierraclub.org
The Redwood Chapter contends with climate change, works for sustainable communities, and defends land, water and wildlife while creating opportunities for the exploration and enjoyment.
Victoria Brandon, Chair
Ed Robey, Vice Chair

707 **Sierra Club: San Diego Chapter**
8304 Clairemont Mesa Blvd
Suite 101
San Diego, CA 92111
858-569-6005
Fax: 619-299-1742
san-diego.chapter@sierraclub.org
www.sandiego.sierraclub.org
To advance the preservation and protection of the natural environment by empowering the citizenry with charitable resources to further the cause of environmental protection.
11,000 Members
Loren Blackford, President
Susana Reyes, Vice President

708 **Sierra Club: San Francisco Bay Chapter**
2530 San Pablo Ave
Suite I
Berkeley, CA 94702-2000
510-848-0800
Fax: 510-345-2518
info@sfbaysc.org
www.sanfranciscobay.sierraclub.org
To advance the preservation and protection of the natural environment by empowering the citizenry with charitable resources to further the cause of environmental protection.
Founded: 1924
Igor Tregub, Chair
Jennifer Ong, Vice Chair

709 **Sierra Club: San Gorgonio Chapter**
P.O Box 5452
Riverside, CA 92517
951-684-6203
Fax: 951-684-6172
ruizmaryann@gmail.com
www.sangorgonio.sierraclub.org
Advocates for the San Bernardino Mountains and forests, energy conservation, habitat and land use preservation and the congestion of urban cities and inland valleys.
Mary Ann Ruiz, Chair
Kim Floyd, Conservation Chair

710 **Sierra Club: Tehipite Chapter**
PO Box 5396
Fresno, CA 93755-5396
559-229-4031
robertsturner52@gmail.com
www.tehipite.sierraclub.org
To advance the preservation and protection of the natural environment by empowering the citizenry with charitable resources to further the cause of environmental protection.
Bruce Gray, Chapter Chair
Trudy Tucker, Vice Chair

711 **Sierra Club: Ventana Chapter**
PO Box 5667
Carmel, CA 93921
831-624-8032
Fax: 831-624-3371
chapter@ventana.sierraclub.org
www.ventana.sierraclub.org
Committed to protecting 127 miles of coastline, hundreds of thousands of acres of wild lands and dwindling water supplies.
Joel Weinstein, Chair
Scott Waltz, Vice Chair

712 **Society for the Conservation of Bighorn Sheep**
PO Box 94182
Pasadena, CA 91109
310-339-4677
sheepsociety.com
Strives for the full restoration of the California Desert Bighorn to its habitat and the establishment of self-sustaining populations.
Founded: 1964
Steve Marschke, President
Bob Burke, 1st Vice President

713 **Southern California Chapter: American Solar Energy Society**
P.O Box 2532
Seal Beach, CA 90740
714-794-7795
info@ocrenewables.org
www.ocrenewables.org
The official local chapter of the American Solar Energy Society (ASES). Provides the SoCal community a local resource to learn about solar energy, energy efficiency and sustainability.
Adam Plesniak, Managing Director
Mike Kilroy, Associate Director

714 **Southwestern Herpetologists Society**
PO Box 7469
Van Nuys, CA 91409
818-503-2052
peggywu@ca.rr.com
www.swhs.org
Promotes the conservation of repitiles and amphibians while educating the public about the role of reptiles and amphibians in the natural world.
Founded: 1954
Wes Pollock, President
Grayson Kent, Vice President

715 **The Nature Conservancy: California**
201 Mission St 4th Fl
San Francisco, CA 94105-1832
415-777-0487
Fax: 415-777-0244
nature.org/california
Protects California's important lands and waters with a focus on freshwater, climate change, renewable energy, oceans and migratory birds.
Mark R. Tercek, President/CEO
Thomas J. Tierney, Chairman

716 **Urban Habitat Program**
Presido Station
2000 Franklin St
Oakland, CA 94612
510-839-9510
Fax: 510-788-5406
info@urbanhabitat.org
www.urbanhabitat.org
Dedicated to building a multicultural majority that provides urban environmental leadership in order to create socially just, ecologically sustainable communities in the Bay Area.
Founded: 1989
Joe Brooks, Board Chair
Tamar Dorfman, Board Treasurer

717 **Western Occupational and Environmental Medical Association**
575 Market St
Suite 2125
San Francisco, CA 94105
415-764-4918
Fax: 415-764-4915
woema@woema.org
www.woema.org

To represent and be a resource to members in the profession and practice of occupational and environmental medicine and to enhance their efforts to promote and improve health in the workplace.
Founded: 1941
Scott C. Levy, Chairman
Robert C. Blink, President

718 Yellowstone Grizzly Foundation
2515 Wilshire Blvd — 307-734-8643
5006 Coolidge Ave, Culver City — www.grizzlypeople.com
Santa Monica, CA 90403
A non-profit organization dedicated to the conservation of the threatened grizzly bear and their wilderness habitat in the greater Yellowstone Ecosystem.
Louisa Willcox, President
Timothy Treadwell, Founder

Colorado

719 American Lung Association of Colorado
5600 Greenwood Plaza Boulevard — 303-388-4327
Suite 100 — COInfo@lungs.org
Greenwood Village, CO 80111-2116
www.lung.org/about-us/local-associations/colorado.html
Works to prevent lung disease and to promote lung health by fighting for cleaner air.
Founded: 1904
Cheryl A. Calhoun, Managing Director
Linn P. Bilingsley, Vice President

720 American Society of Landscape Architects: Colorado Chapter
PO Box 200822 — 303-748-0321
Denver, CO 80220 — Fax: 303-220-5833
info@aslacolorado.org
www.aslacolorado.org
Serves as the state professional society representing landscape architects in Colorado and Wyoming. Promotes the landscape architecture profession and advances the practice through advocacy, education, communication and networking.
Founded: 1973
Brian Nicholson, President
Craig Stoffel, President-Elect

721 Aspen Global Change Institute
104 Midland Ave — 970-925-7376
Suite 205 — Fax: 970-925-7097
Basalt, CO 81621 — agcimail@agci.org
www.agci.org
A Colorado nonprofit dedicated to furthering the understanding of Earth systems and global environmental change through interdisciplinary science meetings, publications and educational programs.
Dr. Marty Hoffert, Chairman
Ken Caldeira, Vice President

722 Association of Midwest Fish and Game Law Enforcement Officers
Division of Wildlife
6060 Broadway — 303-291-7223
Denver, CO 80216 — secretary@midwestgamewarden.org
www.midwestgamewarden.org
Lead group among wildlife enforcement organizations in the development and maintenance of training for field officers that protects the resource and benefit citizens.
Founded: 1944
Bob Thompson, Executive Secretary
Bill Hale, Audit Committee

723 B.A.S.S Nation: Colorado Chapter
4485 Enchanted Circle North — 719-597-2304
Colorado Springs, CO 80917 — info@coloradobassnation.com
www.coloradobassnation.com
Stimulates public awareness of bass fishing as a major sport and to offer the Colorado Department of Wildlife and other organizations moral and political support and encouragement.
Audrey McKenney, President
Jack Chaney, Vice President

724 Colorado Association of Conservation Districts
P.O. Box 1175 — 719-686-0020
Lamar, CO 81052 — executivedirector4cacd@gmail.com
www.coloradoacd.org
Colorado's 76 conservation districts ensure the health, safety and general welfare of the citizens through the conservation of natural resources and a responsible conservation ethic.
Don McBee, President
Anthony Lobato, Vice President

725 Colorado Forestry Association
P.O Box 270132 — 970-531-9421
Ft. Collins, CO 80527 — walt.bigkid@gmail.com
www.coloradoforestry.org
Strives for the renewal of forests through conservation, management, forestry legislation, public education and the creation of forest reserves.
Founded: 1884
Walt Plese, President
Ed Olmstead, Treasurer

726 Colorado Renewable Energy Society
430 Myrtle St — 303-806-5317
Fort Collins, CO 80521 — info@cres-energy.org
www.cres-energy.org
Nonprofit membership organization that works for the advancement of cost-effective energy efficient and renewable energy technologies for economic development.
Founded: 1996
Alex Blackmer, Board President
Janna West-Heiss, Vice President

727 Colorado Safety Association
1114 West 7th Ave — 303-373-1937
Suite 150 — 800-727-0519
Denver, CO 80204 — Fax: 303-373-1955
melodye@coloradosafety.org
www.coloradosafety.org
Not-for-profit educational organization specializing in occupational safety and health issues.
Founded: 1968
Liz Couture, Executive Director
Chris Baker, Program Director

728 Colorado Solar Energy Industries Association
1536 Wynkoop St — 303-333-7342
Suite 104 — Fax: 303-604-6988
Denver, CO 80202 — info@coseia.org
www.coseia.org
Promote the use of solar energy technologies to improve the environment and create a sustainable future.
Founded: 1989
Taylor Henderson, President
Todd Stewart, Vice President

729 Colorado Trappers Association
PO Box 397 — 970-268-5554
Empire, CO 80438 — Dan@coloradoridacritter.com
www.coloradotrapper.com

An organization dedicated to promoting wildlife education and management, and upholding the ideals of their unique trapping heritage.
Founded: 1975
Dan Gates, President, Director
Joe Herrman, Vice President

730 Colorado Water Congress
1580 Logan St — 303-837-0812
Suite 700 — Fax: 303-526-3864
Denver, CO 80203 — info@cowatercongress.org
www.cowatercongress.org
Protects and conserves Colorado's water resources by means of advocacy and education.
Founded: 1958
Sam Susuras, President
Erin Wilson, Vice President

731 Colorado Wildlife Federation
1410 Grant St — 303-987-0400
Suite C-313 — Fax: 303-987-0200
Denver, CO 80203 — cwfed@coloradowildlife.org
www.coloradowildlife.org
Promotes the conservation, management and sustainable use of Colorado's wildlife and wildlife habitats through education and advocacy.
Founded: 1953
Suzanne O'Neill, Executive Director
Kent Ingram, Chair

732 Keystone Center and Keystone Science School
Keystone Center & Science School
1053 Soda Ridge Rd — 970-468-2098
Keystone, CO 80435 — Fax: 970-262-0152
salexander@keystone.org
www.keystonescienceschool.org
Strives to develop creative problem-solving processes and to provide qualified science education through hands-on inquiry of the natural world for youth and adults.
Founded: 1975
Ellen Reid, Executive Director
Douglas D. Sims, Chairman

733 National Wildlife Federation: Rocky Mountain Regional Center
303 E 17th Ave — 303-786-8001
Suite 15 — 800-822-9919
Denver, CO 80203 — Fax: 303-786-8911
www.nwf.org/Rocky-Mountain-Region.aspx
Protects and restores wildlife habitat on tribal lands, conserves iconic Western species, fights climate change and water issues and inspire new generations.
Meaghan Olwell, Operations Manager
Brian Kurzel, Regional Executive Director

734 Sierra Club: Rocky Mountain Chapter
1536 Wynkoop Street — 303-861-8819
Suite 312 — Fax: 303-449-6520
Denver, CO 80202 — rocky.mountain.chapter@sierraclub.org
www.sierraclub.org/colorado
Works directly on activism and advocacy with a grassroots, citizen-based leadership to protect Colorado and engages with the public through a leadership outings program.
Jim Alexee, Chapter Director
Bryce Carter, Conservation Program Manager

735 The Nature Conservancy: Colorado Field Office
2424 Spruce St — 303-444-2950
Boulder, CO 80302 — Fax: 303-444-2986
colorado@tnc.org
www.nature.org/colorado
The mission of the Nature Conservancy is to preserve plants, animals and natural communities that represent the diversity of life on Earth.
Founded: 1965
Mark R. Tercek, President/CEO
Thomas J. Tierney, Chairman

Connecticut

736 American Association in Support of Ecological Initiatives
45 Wyllys Avenue — 860-685-2000
Middletown, CT 06459 — Fax: 860-347-8459
admission@wesleyan.edu
www.wesleyan.edu
AASEI is a US 501 nonprofit organization which supports international environmental initiatives in Russian Nature Reserves. In cooperation with Russia and foreign scientists, students, and universities, AASEI organizes scientificresearch projects, academic internships, work camps, environmental exchanges, and eco-tourism. Our aim is to provide practical support to Russian Reserves, expand opportunities for international scientific research, and promote internationalunderstanding.
Founded: 1994
Michael S. Roth, President
Brendan Sweeney, President

737 American Lung Association of Connecticut
45 Ash Street — 860-289-5401
East Hartford, CT 06108-3272 — 800-586-4872
Fax: 860-289-5405
info@lungne.org
www.lung.org/about-us/local-associations/connecticut.html
The American Lung Association of Connecticut offers a wide variety of lung health services to the people of Connecticut.
Founded: 1904
Kim Lacina, National VP, Marketing
Harold P. Wimmer, President, CEO

738 American Society of Landscape Architects: Connecticut Chapter
370 James Street — 203-966-7071
4th Floor — 800-878-1474
New Haven, CT 06513 — Fax: 203-972-0770
executivedirector@ctasla.org
www.ctasla.org
As a chapter of the American Society of Landscape Architects (ASLA), it aims to lead, educate and participate in the careful stewardship, wise planning, and artful design of cultural and natural environments.
275 Members
Debra De Vries-Dalton, President
Jeffrey H. Mills, Executive Director

739 Connecticut Audubon Society
314 Unquowa Road — 203-259-0416
Fairfield, CT 06824 — Fax: 203-254-7673
fairfield@ctaudubon.org
www.ctaudubon.org
A statewide, nonprofit, membership organization dedicated to conserving the Connecticut environment through science-based education and adocacy focused on the state's bird populations and habitats. Each year, through school programs,teacher training workshops, youth activities, adult and family trips, community events and legislative initiatives, the Society reaches more than 200,000 people.
Founded: 1898
Nelson North, Executive Director
Tom Andersen, Director, Communications

740 **Connecticut Botanical Society**
PO Box 9004 860-246-2077
New Haven, CT 06532-0004 yyih@wesleyan.edu
www.ct-botanical-society.org
A group of amateur and professional botanists who share an interest in the plants and habitats of Connecticut and the surrounding region. The goals are to increase knowledge of the state's flora, to accumulate a permanent botanicalrecord, and to promote conservation and public awareness of the state's rich natural heritage.
Founded: 1903 $15/Year
David Yih, President

741 **Connecticut Forest & Park Association**
16 Meriden Road 860-346-2372
Rockfall, CT 06481-2372 Fax: 860-347-7463
info@ctwoodlands.org
www.ctwoodlands.org
The Connecticut Forest & Park Association (CFPA) is a nonprofit organization dedicated to connecting people to the land in order to protect forests, parks, walking trails, and open spaces in Connecticut.
Founded: 1895
Eric Lukingbeal, President
Starr Sayres, Vice President

742 **Connecticut Fund for the Environment & Save the Sound**
900 Chapel Street 203-787-0646
Upper Mezzanine Fax: 203-787-0246
New Haven, CT 06510 protect@cfenv.org
www.ctenvironment.org
A nonprofit legal champion for the environment and water of the regiom. The CFE merged with Save the Sound and utilizes law, science and education to better air and water quality, control toxic contamination, minimize the adverseimpacts of highways and traffic congestion, protect public water supplies, and preserve the open space and wetlands so crucial to both the state's citizens and its wildlife.
Founded: 1978
Donald S. Strait, President
Curt Johnson, Executive Director

743 **Friends of Animals**
777 Post Road 203-656-1522
Suite 205 800-321-7387
Darien, CT 06820 Fax: 203-656-0267
info@friendsofanimals.org
www.friendsofanimals.org
A non-profit, international animal advocacy organization that works to cultivate a respectful view of non-human animals, free-living and domestic.
Founded: 1957
Priscilla Feral, President
Donna Berlanda, VP, Administration

744 **Sierra Club: Connecticut Chapter**
2074 Park Street 860-236-4405
Suite 308 connecticut.chapter@sierraclub.org
Hartford, CT 06106 www.sierraclub.org/connecticut
To advance the preservation and protection of the natural environment by empowering the citizenry with charitable resources to further the cause of environmental protection.
Martha Klein, Chair & Communications Chair
John D. Calandrelli, Chapter Coordinator

745 **The Berkshire-Litchfield Environmental Council**
PO Box 668, The Roraback Building 860-824-7247
115 Main Street wml61@comcast.net
North Canaan, CT 06018 www.berklitchfieldenviro.org
The Berkshire-Litchfield Environmental Council (BLEC) is a group of citizens acting together as an advocate for the natural environment, to promote an understanding of both the environmental and economic needs, and of the preservationand conservation issues, within the bioregion.
Founded: 1970
Ellery Sinclair, Executive Secretary
B.Blake Levitt, Communications Director

District of Columbia

746 **Alliance to Save Energy**
1850 M Street NW 202-857-0666
Suite 610 Fax: 202-331-9588
Washington, DC 20036 www.ase.org
This organization is a non-profit collective of business, government, environmental and consumer leaders with the mission of promoting energy efficiency worldwide to achieve a healthier economy, environment and greater energy security.
Founded: 1977
Ben Evans, VP, Government Affairs
Kateri Callahan, President

747 **American Lung Association Of the District of Columbia**
1331 Pennsylvania Avenue NW 202-747-5541
Suite 1425 lhale@lunginfo.org
Washington, DC 20004 www.lung.org/about-us/local-associations/washington.html
The American Lung Association of the District of Columbia works to prevent lung disease and promote lung health. Offering a wide variety of lung health services to the people of the District of Columbia.

748 **American Rivers**
1101 14th Street NW 202-347-7550
Suite 1400 www.americanrivers.org
Washington, DC 20005
American Rivers protects wild rivers, restores damaged rivers, and conserves clean water for people and nature.
200,000 Members
William Robert Irvin, President & CEO
Bruce Leathwood, Senior Director, Membership

749 **American Society of Landscape Architects: Potomac Chapter**
Washington, DC 202-827-7380
info@potomacasla.org
www.potomacasla.org
As a chapter of the American Society of Landscape Architects (ASLA), it aims to lead, educate and participate in the careful stewardship, wise planning, and artful design of cultural and natural environments. The Potomac Chapter of theALSA represents nearly 400 landscape architects and affiliates in the Greater Washington DC metro area.
Stephen K. Cook, President

750 **Association of Occupational and Environmental Clinics**
1010 Vermont Avenue NW 202-347-4976
#513 888-347-2632
Washington, DC 20005 Fax: 202-347-4950
aoec@aoec.org
www.aoec.org
The Association of Occupational and Environmental Clinics (AOEC), is a non-profit organization of over 60 clinics and 250 individuals, committed to improving the practice of occupational and environmental health through informationsharing and collaborative research.
Founded: 1987 $500/Year
Katherine Kirkland, Executive Director
Ingrid Denis, Program Coordinator

751 **Casey Trees**
3030 12th Street NE 202-833-4010
Washington, DC 20017 Fax: 202-833-4092
friends@caseytrees.org
caseytrees.org
A nonprofit, working to restore, enhance and protect the tree canopy of Washington D.C. Working with public and private affiliates, Casey Trees plants, maintains, monitors and advocates for the trees of Washington D.C.
Founded: 2002
Mark Buscaino, Executive Director
Omolara Fatiregun, COO

752 **Environmental Working Group**
1436 U Street NW 202-667-6982
Suite 100 www.ewg.org
Washington, DC 20009
The Environmental Working Group is a leading content provider for public interest groups and concerned citizens who are campaigning to protect the environment.
Founded: 1993
Ken Cook, President
Monica Amarelo, Director, Communications

753 **Institute of Scrap Recycling Industries**
1250 H Street 202-662-8500
Suite 400 Fax: 202-624-9256
Washington, DC 20005 isri@isri.org
www.isri.org
Its membership is made up of manufacturers and processors, brokers and industrial consumers of scrap commodities, including ferrous and nonferrous metals, paper, electronics, rubber, plastics, glass and textiles. ISRI's associatemembers include equipment and service providers to the scrap recycling industry.
Founded: 1987
Robin K. Wiener, President
Margie Erinle, CFO

754 **National Parks Conservation Association**
777 6th Street NW
Suite 700 800-628-7275
Washington, DC 20001-3723 npca@npca.org
www.npca.org
The National Parks Conservation Assocaition (NPCA) works to protect and enhance America's National Parks. The NPCA is an independent, nonpartisan organization with members from all across the United States.
Founded: 1919 1 Million Members
Theresa Pierno, President & CEO
Robin Martin Mckenna, Executive VP

755 **Resources for the Future**
1616 P Street NW 202-328-5000
Suite 600 Fax: 202-939-3460
Washington, DC 20036 info@rff.org
www.rff.org
Resource for the Future (RFF) is a nonprofit and nonpartisan organization that conducts independent research and analysis, rooted primarily in economics, to help leaders make decisions and policies regarding natural resources and theenvironment.
Founded: 1952
Richard G. Newell, President & CEO
Peter Nelson, Director, Communications

756 **Sierra Club: DC Chapter**
50 F Street NW 202-675-2391
Washington, DC 20001 washingtondc.chapter@sierraclub.org
dc.sierraclub.org
The more than 3,600 members of the DC Chapter are actively involved in local conservation and political efforts in conjunction with the national Sierra Club mission.
Rebekah Whilden, Chapter Organizer
Mark Rodeffer, Chair

757 **The Climate Reality Project**
750 9th Street NW
Suite 520 www.climaterealityproject.org
Washington, DC 20001
The Climate Reality Project, is a nonprofit organization dedicated to the education and advocacy of climate change. Formerly known as the Alliance for Climate Protection, The Climate Reality Project is working to cause a global shiftaway from fossil fuels towards renewable resources
Founded: 2011
Ken Berlin, President & CEO
Stacie Paxton Cobos, Senior VP, Communications

Delaware

758 **American Lung Association of Delaware**
630 Churchmans Road 302-737-6414
Suite 202 www.lung.org/about-us/local-associations/delaware.html
Newark, DE 19702
The American Lung Association of Delaware works to prevent lung disease and promote lung health. Offering a wide variety of lung health services to the people of Delaware.
Deborah Brown, Executive VP, Mid-Atlantic

759 **American Lung Association of Delaware: Dover**
422 S Governor's Avenue 302-737-6414
Dover, DE 19904 www.lung.org/about-us/local-associations/delaware.html

760 **Atlantic Flyaway Council**
Division of Fish and Wildlife
89 Kings Highway 302-739-5295
Dover, DE 19901 Fax: 302-739-6157
www.flyways.us/flyways/atlantic
Committed to the preservation and advancement of waterfowl.
Founded: 1948
William C Wagner II, Chairman

761 **B.A.S.S Nation: Delaware Chapter**
DE 302-698-9257
800-463-6062
Fax: 720-302-1230
delawarebass1@verizon.net
www.delawarebassnation.com
The Delaware Chapter of BASS Nation works to stimulate public awareness of bass fishing as a major sport and encourages sportsmanship, courtesy and boating safety at all levels. The Chapter promotes the full adherence to allconservation codes, adequate water quality standards and legal enforcement of existing regulatory standards.
Founded: 1975
Ron Horton, President
Shawn Taylor, Vice President

762 **Delaware Greenways**
1910 Rockland Road 302-655-7275
Wilmington, DE 19803 info@delawaregreenways.org
www.delawaregreenways.org
Delaware Greenways promotes, protects and advocates for the development of outdoor trails, byways and natural open spaces.
Founded: 1989
Mary Roth, Executive Director
Leslie Hubbard, Marketing & Communication

763 **Delaware Nature Society**
Delaware Nature Society
PO Box 700 302-239-2334
Hockessin, DE 19707 dnsinfo@delawarenaturesociety.org
www.delawarenaturesociety.org

Delaware Nature Society (DNS) works to improve the environment through conservation, advocacy and education. DNS manages over 2,000 acres of land, including four nature preserves, and operates three educational nature centers, it isthe state affiliate of the National Wildlife Federation.
Founded: 1964
Brian Winslow, Executive Director
Ginger North, Director, Conservation

764 National Association of Conservation Districts:Delaware
NACD Headquarters
509 Capitol Court NE 202-547-6223
Washington, DC 20002-4937 Fax: 202-547-6450
www.nacdnet.org/state/delaware
The National Association of Conservation Districts (NACD) is the nonprofit organization that represents America's 3,000 conservation districts. Conservation districts are local units of government established under state law to carryout natural resource management programs and protection of land and water resources at the local level.
Robert Emerson, State Association President

765 Sierra Club: Delaware Chapter
100 West 10th Street 302-468-4550
Suite 106 delaware.chapter@sierraclub.org
Wilmington, DE 19801 delaware.sierraclub.org
The Delaware Chapter of the Sierra Club works to protect the Delaware River, Delaware's wetlands including critical habitat areas and the coastal zone.
Jamie Watts, Membership Committee Chair
Dee Durham, Vice Chair

Florida

766 American Fisheries Society: Agriculture Economics Section
University of California
PO Box 240 352-392-4991
Gainsville, FL 32611 Fax: 352-392-3646
adams@fred.ifas.ufl.edu
Committed to the preservation and advancement of Florida's natural resources.
Charles Adams, President

767 American Lung Association of Florida
6852 Belfort Oaks Place 904-743-2933
Jacksonville, FL 32216 alaf@lungse.org
www.lung.org/about-us/local-associations/florida.html
The American Lung Association of Florida works to prevent lung disease and promote lung health. Offering a wide variety of lung health services to the people of Florida.
Martha C. Bogdan, Executive VP, Southeast

768 American Lung Association of Florida: Fort Lauderdale
2020 South Andrews Avenue 954-524-4657
Fort Lauderdale, FL 33316-3430 alafsouth@lungse.org
www.lung.org/about-us/local-associations/florida.html
Martha C. Bogdan, Executive VP, Southeast

769 American Lung Association of Florida: Fort Meyers
PO Box 07142 239-908-2680
Fort Meyers, FL 33919 alafgcfm@lungse.org
www.lung.org/about-us/local-associations/florida.html
Martha C. Bogdan, Executive VP, Southeast

770 American Lung Association of Florida: Orlando
851 Outer Road 407-425-5864
Orlando, FL 32814-6652 central@lungse.org
www.lung.org/about-us/local-associations/florida.html
Martha C. Bogdan, Executive VP, Southeast

771 American Lung Association of Florida: Palm Beach & Treasure Coast
2701 North Australian Avenue 561-659-7644
Suite 100 alafse@lungse.org
West Palm Beach, FL 33407-4526
www.lung.org/about-us/local-associations/florida.html
Martha C. Bogdan, Executive VP, Southeast

772 American Lung Association of Florida: Tampa
100 South Ashley Drive 813-712-2307
Suite 275 alafgc@lungse.org
Tampa, FL 33602-6652
www.lung.org/about-us/local-associations/florida.html
Martha C. Bogdan, Executive VP, Southeast

773 American Society of Landscape Architects: Florida Chapter
1390 Timberlane Road 850-222-6000
Tallahassee, FL 32312 www.flasla.org
The Florida Chapter of the American Society of Landscape Architects(FLASLA), is a nonprofit association representing the landscape architecture profession throughout the state of Florida.
Founded: 1959
Deena Bell Llewellyn, President

774 Association of Battery Recyclers
PO Box 290286 813-626-6151
Tampa, FL 33687 Fax: 813-622-8388
info@associationofbatteryrecyclers.com
www.americasbatteryrecyclers.com
To keep members abreast of environmental, health, and safety requirements that affect our industry.
Founded: 1984
Earl Cornette, President
Joyce Morales Caramella, Secretary

775 Audubon of Florida
Travenier Science Center
4500 Biscayne Blvd 305-371-6399
Suite 205 Fax: 305-371-6398
Miami, FL 33137 wmones@audubon.org
fl.audubon.org
The science center is the research arm of the Everglades Campaign. The mission of Audubon of Florida is to ensure the restoration and conservation of the Greater Everglades Ecosystem in order to achieve an ecologically and economicallysustainable South Florida. Our Everglades Conservation office has a five-part program including science, education, advocacy, outreach and grassroots action.
Founded: 1938
Eric Draper, Executive Director
Victoria Johnston, Donor Relations Manager

776 Citizens for Scenic Florida
4401 Emerson Street 904-396-0037
Suite 10 Fax: 904-744-2940
Jacksonville, FL 32207 www.scenicflorida.org
Citizens for Scenic Florida is a nonprofit corporation that enhances, protects and preserves the visual environment of Florida as mandated by the Scenic Beauty clause of the Florida Constitution.
Bill Jonson, President
Trudy Barker, Vice Chairman & Executive VP

777 Fish & Wildlife Foundation of Florida
2574 Seagate Drive

Suite 100
Tallahassee, FL 32301
850-922-1066
800-988-4889
info@wildlifeflorida.org
www.fishwildlifeflorida.org

Working closely with Florida Fish and Wildlife Conservation Commission, the Fish & Wildlife Foundation of Florida is a non-profit organization that is dedicated to providing assistance, funding and promotional support for the habitatsand resources of Florida's fish and wildlife.
Founded: 1994
Andy Walker, President & CEO
Will Bradford, CFO

778 Florida Defenders of the Environment
309 State Road 26
Melrose, FL 32666
352-475-1119
floridadefenders@gmail.com
www.fladefenders.org

The Florida Defenders of the Environment work to protect fresh-water resources, conserve public lands and provide environmental education.
Founded: 1969
Jim Gross, Executive Director
Tracy Marinello, Executive Assistant

779 Florida Environmental Health Association
P.O. Box 350356
Jacksonville, FL 32235
407-790-0347
Contact_Us@feha.org
www.feha.org

The Florida Environmental Health Association, Inc (FEHA) is a nonprofit group of over 500 professionals that promotes and protects the health of Florida's resident and visitors. The FEHA is an affiliate of the National EnvironmentalHealth Association, Inc.
Founded: 1967
Trisha Dall, Director
Michael Crea, President

780 Florida Forestry Association
402 East Jefferson Street
Tallahassee, FL 32301
850-222-5646
Fax: 850-222-6179
info@forestfla.org
www.floridaforest.org

A statewide membership organization, the Florida Forestry Association advocates and promotes the responsible and sustainable use of Florida's forest resources.
Founded: 1923
Alan Shelby, Executive VP
Debbie Bryant, Director, Member Services

781 Florida Keys Wild Bird Rehabilitation Center
Mission Wild Bird
92080 Overseas Highway
Tavernier, FL 33070
305-852-4486
Fax: 305-852-3186
info@keepthemflying.org
www.keepthemflying.org

The Florida Keys Wild Bird Center is a nonprofit conservation organization dedicated to the rescue, rehabilitation, and release of native and migratory wild birds that have been harmed or displaced. The Florida Keys Wild Bird Centerprovides or locates a humane shelter for birds that cannot be released and educates the public on the importance of coexistence with all wild bird species.
Founded: 1988
Kayla Gainer, Wildlife Rehab Manager

782 Florida Oceanographic Society
890 NE Ocean Boulevard
Stuart, FL 34996
772-225-0505
mperry@floridaocean.org
floridaocean.org

Florida Oceanographic Society is a non-profit organization with a mission to inspire environmental stewardship of Florida's coastal ecosystems through education, research and advocacy.
Founded: 1964
Mark D. Perry, Executive Director
Allen Herskowitz, Chairman

783 Florida Ornithological Society
www.fosbirds.org

The Florida Ornithological Society (FOS) promotes field ornithology and facilitates contact between ameteur and professional ornithologists.
Founded: 1972
Adam Kent, President
Emilynne Angell, Vice President

784 Florida Public Interest Research Group
3110 1st Avenue North
Suite 2K
St. Petersburg, FL 33713
727-431-9686
800-838-6554
info@floridapirg.org
www.floridapirg.org

Statewide, nonprofit, public interest advocacy organization that focuses primarily on environmental and consumer protection.
Steve Blackledge, Director, Pubic Health
Ed Mierzwinski, Consumer Program Director

785 Florida Renewable Energy Association
PO Box 560272
Orlando, FL 32856-272
407-710-8705
freainformation@gmail.com
www.cleanenergyflorida.org

The Florida Renewable Energy Association (FREA), is a non-profit organization that promotes the development of clean renewable energy in Florida through public education, political advocacy, and individual networking opportunities. FREAis the Florida Chapter of the American Solar Energy Society (ASES).
Founded: 2006 $30/Year
Bill Young, President
Mehdi Zeyghami, Vice President

786 Florida Solar Energy Industries Association
2555 Porter Lake Drive
Suite 106
Sarasota, FL 34240
407-339-2010
800-426-5899
Fax: 941-366-7433
wendy@FlaSEIA.org
www.flaseia.org

The Florida Solar Energy Industries Association (FlaSEIA) is a nonprofit professional association of companies, dedicated to protecting and promoting the interests of Florida's solar energy industry.
Founded: 1977
Wendy Parker Barsell, Executive Director
Michelle D'Aiuto, Membership Coordinator

787 Florida Trail Association
5415 SW 13th Street
Gainesville, FL 32608
352-378-8823
fta@floridatrail.org
www.floridatrail.org

The Florida Trail Association (FTA) develops, maintains, protects and promotes a network of hiking trails across the state. With 18 statewide chapters, the FTA provides environmental education and opportunities for the public toparticipate in outdoor recreation.
Founded: 1964
Janet Akerson, Administrative Director
Alex Stigliano, Trail Program Director

788 International Association for Hydrogen Energy
5794 SW 40 Street
303
Miami, FL 33155
info@iahe.org
www.iahe.org

The International Association for Hydrogen Energy promotes the use of hydrogen energy as the global clean energy source. The Association works to achieve this goal by exchanging hydrogen energy information through publications andinternational workshops.
Founded: 1974
T. Nejat Veziroglu, President
John W. Sheffield, Executive Vice President

789 **International Game Fish Association**
300 Gulf Stream Way 954-927-2628
Dania Beach, FL 33004 Fax: 954-924-4299
hq@igfa.org
www.igfa.org
The International Game Fish Association is a nonprofit organization committed to the conservation of game fish and the promotion of responsible, ethical angling practices through science, education, rulemaking and record keeping.
Founded: 1939
Rob Kramer, President
Michael J. Myatt, COO

790 **Keep Florida Beautiful**
3324 Charleston Road
Tallahassee, FL 32309 keepflbeautiful@gmail.com
www.keepfloridabeautiful.org
Keep Florida Beautiful (KFB) is Florida's largest volunteer-based community action and education organization. With more than 40 county and city affiliates, KFB is working to educate people about recycling and litter reduction. KFB isthe state affiliate of Keep America Beautiful (KAB).
Kim Brunson, Chair
Mary Jean Yon, Executive Director

791 **National Wildlife Federation: Everglades Project**
PO Box 1583 239-643-4111
Merrifield, VA 22116-1583 800-822-9919
Fax: 239-643-5130
adamsk@nwf.org
www.nwf.org
To advocate and support restoration of the greater Everglades ecosystem and protection of the western Everglades through planning, education and management activities. To re-create a more natural hydrologic flow through the greaterEverglades that ensures the long-term viability of native habitats, threatened and endangered species and associated wildlife.
Founded: 1934
Kathy Hadley, Chair
Collin O'Mara, President

792 **Reef Relief**
631 Greene Street 305-294-3100
Key West, FL 33040 Fax: 305-293-9515
reefrelief@gmail.com
www.reefrelief.org
Reef relief is a nonprofit membership organization, dedicated to protecting, preserving and improving Florida's coral reef. Through education, advocacy and eco-tourism, the organization works to increase awareness about coral reefecosystems.
Founded: 1987
Bob Cardenas, President & CEO
Tricia Coyne, Vice President

793 **Sanibel-Captiva Conservation Foundation**
3333 Sanibel-Captiva Road 239-472-2329
Sanibel, FL 33957 sccf@sccf.org
www.sccf.org
The Sanibel - Captiva Conservation Foundation (SCCF) is committed to the conservation of coastal habitats and aquatic resources on Sanibel and Captiva and it surrounding watershed. The SCCF is known as a land trust and is the largestprivate landowner on Sanibel Island managing over 1,200 acres of land on Sanibel with another 600 acres on Captiva Island.
Founded: 1967
Erick Lindblad, Executive Director
Karen Nelson, Communications Coordinator

794 **Seaside Seabird Sanctuary**
18328 Gulf Boulevard 727-391-6211
Indian Shores, FL 33785 800-406-3400
Fax: 727-399-2923
seabird@seabirdsanctuary.com
www.seabirdsanctuary.com
The sanctuary is the largest wild bird hospital in the United States dedicated to the rescue, repair, rehabilitation and hopeful release of sick and injured native birds. Over 600 birds permanently reside at our beachfront sanctuary.We are open free of charge to the public 365 days a year. Tours and educational programs are available.
Founded: 1971
Brian Max Tharp, Business Manager
Eddie Gayton, Operations Manager

795 **Sierra Club: Florida Chapter**
1990 Central Avenue 727-824-8813
St. Petersburg, FL 33712 frank.jackalone@sierraclub.org
florida.sierraclub.org
Comprising of 16 Club Groups across the state, the Florida Chapter of the Sierra Club promotes and practices the responsible use of Florida's ecosystems and natural resources.
35,200 Members
Mark Walters, Chair
Kristine Cunningham, Vice Chair

796 **Society of Environmental Toxicology and Chemistry**
SETAC North America
229 South Baylen Street 850-469-1500
2nd Floor Fax: 888-296-4136
Pensacola, FL 32502 setac@setac.org
www.setac.org
The Society of Environmental Toxicology and Chemistry (SETAC), is a global nonprofit professional society, that promotes the development of principles and practices designed to protect, enhance and manage a sustainable environment.SETAC provides a forum for scientists, managers and other professionals to exchange information and ideas, for the development and application of multidisciplinary scientific principles in order to manage and conserve natural resources.
Founded: 1979 6,000 Members
Greg E. Schiefer, Executive Director

797 **South Florida Chapter, National Safety Council**
4171 West Hillsborro Boulevard 954-422-5757
Suite 5 800-392-5101
Coconut Creek, FL 33073 Fax: 954-418-9290
Not-for-profit, non-governmental, public service organization dedicated to the safety and health of the Broward, Dade, Palm Beach and surrounding communities.
Michael Walters, VP Operations

798 **Tallahassee Museum of History and Natural Science**
3945 Museum Drive 850-575-8684
Tallahassee, FL 32310 Fax: 850-574-8243
www.tallahasseemuseum.org
The Tallahassee Museum, is a 52-acre nonprofit outdoor museum. Combining a natural habitat zoo of indigenous wildlife, collection of historical building and artifacts and an environmental science center, the museum is dedicated topromoting the knowledge and understanding of the Big Bend's cultural history and natural environment.
Founded: 1957
Russell S. Daws, President/CEO
Rebekka K. Wade, Director, Finance

Georgia

799 **Agency for Toxic Substances and Disease Registry**
ATSDR Division of Community Health Investigations
4770 Buford Highway NE 770-488-0706
Atlanta, GA 30341-3717 800-232-4636
Fax: 770-488-1544
www.atsdr.cdc.gov
As an agency of the US Department of Health and Human Services, the Agency for Toxic Substances and Disease Registry (ATSDR) aims to prevent exposure, adverse human health effects and diminished quality of life associated with exposureto hazardous substances from waste sites, unplanned releases and other sources of pollution present in the environment.
Founded: 1987
Ileana Arias, Director
Socorro Zandueta, Administratuve Support

800 **American Academy of Sanitarians**
GA 678-518-4028
gnoonan@charter.net
www.sanitarians.org
The American Academy of Sanitarians (AAS) is dedicated to improving the environmental health status of individuals through the certification process of environmental health professionals. The AAS works to elevate the standards, improvethe practice of and promote ethical conduct among sanitarians in all fields of environmental health. Certification is open to any persons who have attained high professional stature through leadership and accomplishment in the field of environmentalhealth.
Founded: 1966
Gary P. Noonan, Executive Secretary-Teasurer

801 **American Lung Association of Georgia**
2452 Spring Road SE 770-434-5864
Smyrna, GA 30080 alaga@lungse.org
www.lung.org/about-us/local-associations/georgia.html
The American Lung Association of Georgia works to prevent lung disease and promote lung health. Offering a wide variety of lung health services to the people of Georgia.
Martha C. Bogdan, Executive VP, Southest

802 **American Society of Landscape Architects: Georgia Chapter**
PO Box 18622 202-898-2444
Atlanta, GA 31126 www.gaasla.org
The Georgia Chapter of the American Society of Landscape Architects (ASLA) represents over 450 landscape architects and affiliates across the state, who are dedicated to the promotion of the landscape profession through advocacy,education and communication.
450 Members
Ben Kent, Section Chair
Matt Cherry, President

803 **Center for a Sustainable Coast**
221 Mallery Street 912-506-5088
Suite B Fax: 912-638-3615
St. Simons Island, GA 31522 susdev@gate.net
www.sustainablecoast.org
A nonprofit member organization that works to improve, protect, conserve and promote the responsible use of Georgia's coastal resources.
Founded: 1997
Steve Willis, President
David Kyler, Executive Director

804 **Centers for Disease Control and Prevention**
1600 Clifton Road
Atlanta, GA 30329-4027 800-232-4636
www.cdc.gov
To promote health and quality of life by preventing and controlling disease, injury and disability. The CDC seeks to accomplish its mission by working with partners throughout the nation and world to monitor health; detect andinvestigate health problems; conduct research to enhance prevention; develop and advocate sound public health policies; implement prevention strategies; promote healthy behaviors; foster safe and healthful environments and provide leadership andtraining.
Founded: 1946
Brenda Fitzgerald, Director
Sherri A. Berger, COO

805 **Chattahoochee Riverkeeper**
3 Puritan Mill 404-352-9828
916 Joseph E. Lowery Boulevard NW Fax: 404-352-8676
Atlanta, GA 30318 www.chattahoochee.org
An nonprofit environmental advocacy organization dedicated to the protection preservation and restoration of the Chattahoochee River, its lakes and tributaries. The Chattahoochee Riverkeeper (CRK) is part of the internationalWaterkeeper Alliance.
Founded: 1994 7,200 Members
Juliet Cohen, Executive Director
Chris Manganiello, Water Policy Director

806 **Coastal Conservation Association of Georgia**
Coastal Conservation Association
2807-A Roger Lacey Avenue 912-660-8440
Savannah, GA 31404 www.ccaga.org
A state affiliate of the Coastal Conservation Association (CCA), the Georgia Chapter is a nonprofit association dedicated to promoting the preservation, conservation, restoration and protection of the marine fisheries and habitats ofthe Georgia coast both onshore and offshore, for the benefit and responsible utilization by the general public.
Founded: 1986
Tom Rood, State Chairman
Ron Winders, Secretary

807 **Coosa River Basin Initiative**
408 Broad Street 706-232-2724
Rome, GA 30161 Fax: 706-235-9066
jcook@coosa.org
www.coosa.org
Cossa River Basin Initiative (CRBI) also known as the Upper Cossa Riverkeeper, is a nonprofit grassroots organization working to inform and empower citizens to become involved in creating a clean, healthy and economically viable CoosaRiver Basin. The CRBI is also a member of the International Waterkeeper Alliance, which works to enforce the Clean Water Act, the Georgia Water Coalition and Alabama Rivers Alliance.
Founded: 1992 3,000 Members
Joe Cook, Communication Coordinator
Jesse Demonbruen-Chapman, Executive Director

808 **Council of State and Territorial Epidemiologists (CSTE)**
CSTE National Office
2872 Woodcock Boulevard 770-458-3811
Suite 250 Fax: 770-458-8516
Atlanta, GA 30341 fellowship@cste.org
www.cste.org
The Council of State and Territorial Epidemiologists (CSTE) is an organization of epidemiologists working to advance public health policy, epidemiologic capacity and the establishment of more effective relationships among state andother health agencies. The CTSE provides education, information, and developmental support of practicing epidemiologists. It also provides technical advice and assistance to partner and federal public health organizations.
Founded: 1992
Jeff Engel, Executive Director
Shundra Clinton, Member Services Coordinator

809 EarthShare of Georgia
100 Peachtree Street NW — 404-873-3173
Suite 1960 — Fax: 404-873-3135
Atlanta, GA 30303 — info@earthsharega.org
www.earthsharega.org

EarthShare of Georgia works to protect, conserve and enhance, air, land and water quality by connecting people to trusted nonprofit organizations dedicated to creating a healthy and sustainable environment.
Founded: 1992
Madeline L. Reamy, Executive Director
Linette Singleton, Operations Manager

810 Environment Georgia
108 E. Ponce De Leon Avenue — 404-370-1764
Suite 210 — 800-401-6511
Decatur, GA 30030 — www.environmentgeorgia.org

Environment Georgia is a citizen advocacy group of Environment America. Through research and education, Environment Georgia is dedicated to conserving the air, water and land of Georgia.
Jennette Gayer, Director

811 Forest Landowners Association
3300 Highlands Parkway — 404-325-2954
Suite 200 — 800-325-2954
Smyrna, GA 30082 — Fax: 404-325-2955
info@forestlandowners.com
www.forestlandowners.com

The Forest Landowners Association (FLA) advocates and promotes the rights of all private landowners. The FLA provides its members with education, information and national grassroots advocacy enabling them to maintain their forestlands.
Founded: 1941
Scott Rowland, President
Scott P. Jones, CEO

812 Georgia Association of Conservation District
PO Box 1134 — 706-542-3065
Ringgold, GA 30736 — info@gacd.us
www.gacd.us

Representing 40 Soil and Water Conservation Districts in Georgia, the Georgia Association of Conservation Districts (GACD) is a nonprofit organization dedicated to advocating for the conservation of Georgia's natural resources. Throughleadership and a unified strategic direction GACD works to conserve, support partner agencies, sustain Georgia's land and educate the public across the state.
Woody Snell, President
Marty McLendon, Vice-President

813 Georgia Association of Water Professionals
1655 Enterprise Way — 770-618-8690
Marietta, GA 30067 — Fax: 770-618-8695
www.gawp.org

Georgia Association of Water Professionals (GAWP) is a nonprofit organization focused on providing education and training opportunities for people working in the water and wastewater industr.
Pam Burnett, Executive Director
Susana Lanier, Member Services

814 Georgia Conservancy
230 Peachtree Street NW — 404-876-2900
Suite 1250 — Fax: 404-872-9229
Atlanta, GA 30303 — mail@gaconservancy.org
www.georgiaconservancy.org

The Georgia Conservancy is a statewide member organization committed to the conservation of Georgia's natural resources.
Founded: 1967
Robert Ramsay, President
Monica Thornton, Vice President

815 Georgia Environmental Health Association
397 Eastman Highway — 706-595-5478
Hawkinsville, GA 31036 — www.geha-online.org

A non-profit, professional organization, dedicated to promoting, supporting, training, and registering individuals working in environmental health fields throughout government, academia, industry and business.
$25/Year
Jessica Baldour, Secretary
Angie Corder, President

816 Georgia Solar Energy Association
1199 Euclid Ave — 404-522-4775
Atlanta, GA 30307 — admin@gasolar.org
www.gasolar.org

The Georgia Solar Energy Association (GA Solar), is a nonprofit organization comprised of solar energy experts working to support the development of the solar industry in Georgia through advocacy, education and outreach.
Founded: 2002
Don Moreland, Chair
Norene Quinn, Executive Director

817 Georgia Trappers Association
9969 GA Highway 102 W
Mitchell, GA 30820 — info@gatrappersassoc.com
www.gatrappersassoc.com

The Georgia Trappers Association (GTA) promotes the education and growth of hunting,fishing and trapping while maintaining the highest standards of sportsmanship. The GTA encourages public conservation, protection, restoration andmanagement of the environment.
$25/Year
Dan Eaton, President
Brian Igou, Executive Director

818 Georgia Wildlife Federation
11600 Hazelbrand Road — 770-787-7887
Covington, GA 30014 — Fax: 770-787-9229
info@gwf.org
www.gwf.org

As Georgia's oldest and largest member supported conservation organization, Georgia Wildlife Federation (GWF), is working to encourage the protection, restoration and rehabilitation of Georgia's water, wildlife, forests and fields.
Founded: 1936
Mike Worley, President & CEO
DeAnna Harris, Conservation & Outreach Mngr

819 Human Ecology Action League (HEAL)
PO Box 509
Stockbridge, GA 30281 — HEALNatnl@aol.com
www.healnatl.org

The Human Ecology Action League Inc (HEAL) is a nonprofit organization committed to serving those whose health has been adversely affected by environment exposures; to provide information to those who are concerned about the healtheffects of chemicals; and to alert the general public about the potential dangers of chemicals
Founded: 1977

820 Mountain Conservation Trust of Georgia
104 North Main Street — 706-253-4077
Suite B3 — conserve@mctga.org
Jasper, GA 30143 — www.mctga.org

The Mountain Conservation Trust of Georgia (MCT) is an accredited land trust focused on the permanent conversation of the natural resources and scenic beauty of the North Georgia foothills and mountains.
Founded: 1991
George Kimberly, Executive Director
Jessica Pfiel, Office Manager

821 National Wildlife Federation: Southeast Regional Center
730 Peachtree Street NE 404-876-8733
Suite 1000 queenc@nwf.org
Atlanta, GA 30308 www.nwf.org
The Southeast Regional Center of the National Wildlife Federation, covers 7 states, Puerto Rico and the U.S. Virgin Islands. The center is dedicated to restoring and rehabilitating Longleaf pine forest and the Gulf of Mexico.
Carly Queen, Campus Field Coordinator

822 Sierra Club: Georgia Chapter
743 E College Avenue 404-607-1262
Suite B georgia.chapter@sierraclub.org
Decatur, GA 30030 georgia.sierraclub.org
The Georgia Chapter of the Sierra Club, is a grassroots environmental organization in the state dedicated to forest protection, transportation and clean energy.
45,000 Members
Ted Terry, Chapter Director
Jessica Morehead, Chapter Coordinator

823 The Nature Conservancy: Georgia Chapter
100 Peachtree NW 404-873-6946
Suite 2250 Fax: 404-873-6984
Atlanta, GA 30303 comment@tnc.org
www.nature.org
The Georgia Chapter of The Nature Conservancy, works to protect Georgia's woods, water and coast. It manages 15 nature preserves and more than 338,000 acres of land and water.
Founded: 1951
Mark R. Tercek, President/CEO
Thomas J. Tierney, Chairman

824 Trees Atlanta
225 Chester Avenue SE 404-522-4097
Atlanta, GA 30316 www.treesatlanta.org
Trees Atlanta is a nationally recognized nonprofit citizens' group committed to protecting and improving Atlanta's urban forest through planting trees, conservation and education.
Founded: 1985
Connie Veates, Co-Executive Director & COO
Greg Levine, Co-Executive Director & CPO

Hawaii

825 American Lung Association Of Hawaii
810 Richards Street 808-537-5966
Suite 750 bev.stewart@lung.org
Honolulu, HI 96813 www.ala-hawaii.org
The American Lung Association of Hawaii works to prevent lung disease and promote lung health. Offering a wide variety of lung health services to the people of Hawaii.
Allison Hickey, Exec. VP, Mountain Pacific
Tony Peterson, CFO

826 American Society of Landscape Architects: Hawaii Chapter
1253 South Beretania Street #3006
Honululu, HI 96814 www.hawaiiasla.org
The Hawaii Chapter of the American Society of Landscape Architects, is a nonprofit association representing the landscape architecture profession throughout the state of Hawaii.
Grace Zheng, President
Rachel Katzman, Secretary

827 Earth Trust
Windward Environmental Center
1118 Manuawili Road 415-662-3264
Kailua, HI 96734 Fax: 206-202-3893
info@earthtrust.us
www.earthtrust.org
Earth Trust is a nonprofit organization focused on solving global environmental issues through advocacy and innovative strategy.
Founded: 1976
Don White, President

828 Greenpeace Foundation
Windward Environmental Center
1118 Manawili Road 415-689-9931
Kailua, HI 96734 Fax: 206-202-3893
email@gpfdn.com
www.greenpeacefoundation.org
Greenpeace Foundation is a nonprofit organization committed to the advocacy of species conservation and biodiversity; with a focus is on the marine ecosystem and how human interaction changes it. The Foundation is dedicated to solvingand preventing environmental crises.
Founded: 1976

829 Hawaii Association of Conservation Districts
Po Box 1411 808-214-5388
Wailuku, HI 96793 hacdhawaii@gmail.com
www.nacdnet.org/hawaii
The state chapter of the National Association of Conservation Districts, the Hawaii Association of Conservation Districts (HCAD), works to conserve the Soil and Water Conservation Districts of Hawaii.
Founded: 1954
Michelle Watkins, State Executive Director
Brenda lokepa-Moses, State President

830 Hawaii Nature Center
875 Iao Valley Road 808-244-6500
Wailuku, HI 96793 hncinfo@hawaiinaturecenter.org
www.hawaiinaturecenter.org
The Hawaii Nature Center is a private nonprofit organization specializing in environmental education field program for children, adults and families. Its mission is to foster awareness appreciation and understanding of Hawaii andencourage wise stewardship of the Islands. The Nature Center provides full day field trips for more than 15,000 students on two islands each year and features an interactive nature museum at its field site on Maui.
Founded: 1981
Dee Dee Letts, President
Jeeyun Lee, Executive Director

831 Sierra Club: Hawaii Chapter
1164 Bishop Street 808-538-6616
Suite 1512 hawaii.chapter@sierraclub.org
Honolulu, HI 96813 www.hi.sierraclub.org
The Hawaii Chapter of the Sierra Club is one of the oldest grassroots environmental organization in the islands. It is made up of a four regional groups, that work toward water security, energy independence, food security, a zero wastefuture and the defense of special places.
Founded: 1968 16,000 Members
Marti Townsend, Director
Kirsten Fujitani, Communications Coordinator

832 The Nature Conservancy: Hawaii Chapter
923 Nuuanu Avenue 808-537-4508
Honolulu, HI 96817 hawaii@tnc.org
www.nature.org
The Hawaii Chapter of the Nature Conservancy, is a nonprofit organization focused on climate change, coral reefs, forests and invasive species. With over 200,000 acres of natural land and 10 conservancy preserves, the Hawaii Chapterworks to protect the threatened species that are native to the state of Hawaii.
Grady Timmons, Directo, Communications
Evelyn Wight, Senior Communications Mngr

Idaho

833 American Lung Association of Idaho
1412 W Idaho Street 208-345-5864
Suite 100 liz.hall@lung.org
Boise, ID 83702
http://www.lung.org/about-us/local-associations/idaho.html
The American Lung Association of Idahon works to prevent lung disease and promote lung health. Offering a wide variety of lung health services to the people of Idaho.
Allison Hickey, Exec. VP, Mountain Pacific
Tony Peterson, CFO

834 American Society of Landscape Architects: Idaho/Montana Chapter
PO Box 8224 208-321-2389
Boise, ID 83707 Fax: 208-321-4819
tottens@amsidaho.com
www.idmtasla.org
As a chapter of the American Society of Landscape Architects(ASLA), it aims to lead, educate and participate in the careful stewardship, wise planning, and artful design of cultural and natural environments.
Jay Gibbons, President
Jennie Meinershagen, VP of Montana

835 Idaho Association of Soil Conservation Districts
55 SW 5th Avnue 208-895-8928
Suite 100 Fax: 208-888-4586
Meridian, ID 83642 benjamin@amgidaho.com
www.iascd.org
Provides action at the local level for promoting wise and beneficial conservation of natural resources with emphasis on soil and water.
Founded: 1944
Kit Tillotson, President
Benjamin Kelly, Executive Director

836 Idaho Conservation League
710 North 6th Street 208-345-6933
Boise, ID 83702 Fax: 208-344-0344
icl@wildidaho.org
www.idahoconservation.org
The Idaho Conservation League (ICL) works to preserve Idaho's clean water, wilderness and quality of life through citizen action, public education, and professional advocacy.
Founded: 1973
Rick Johnson, Executive Director
Justin Hayes, Program Director

837 Northwest Management, Inc.
233 E. Palouse River Drive 208-883-4488
PO Box 9748 nwmanage@nmi2.com
Moscow, ID 83843 www.consulting-foresters.com
Northwest Management Inc. is a leader in forest and environmental management, with expertise in forestry, wildfire, water resources, hazard management and planning.
Founded: 1983
Vincent Corrao, President & CEO
Brock Purvis, Forest Inventory Manager

838 Sierra Club: Idaho Chapter
503 W Franklin Street 208-384-1023
Boise, ID 83702 zack.waterman@sierraclub.org
idaho.sierraclub.org
The Idaho Chapter of the Sierra Club works to secure the permanent protection of wildlands and endangered species in Idaho and advocates for the use of clean energy sources.
Zack Waterman, Chapter Director
Casey Mattoon, Conservation Coordinator

Illinois

839 Alliance for the Great Lakes
150 N Michigan Avenue 312-939-0838
Suite 700 alliance@greatlakes.org
Chicago, IL 60601 www.greatlakes.org
Dedicated to the preservation and restoration of the Great Lakes. The Alliance for the Great Lakes, formerly known as the Lake Michigan Federation, uses advocacy, volunteering, education and research to ensure the health and safety ofthe Great Lakes.
Founded: 1970
Joel Brammeier, President & CEO
Stephanie Smith, VP, Operations

840 American College of Occupational and Environmental Medicine
25 Northwest Point Boulevard 847-818-1800
Suite 700 Fax: 847-818-9266
Elk Grove Village, IL 60007-1030 www.acoem.org
Made up of over 4,500 physicians and other healthcare professionals in industry, government, academia, private practice and military. The American College of Occupational Environmental Medicine (ACOEM) promotes the health of workersthrough preventive medicine, clinical care, research and education.
Founded: 1916
Charles M. Yarborough, President
William G. Buchta, President Elect

841 American Fisheries Society: North Central Division: Illinois Chapter
IL
JT-Lamer@wiu.edu
www.illinoisamericanfisheriessociety.weebly.com
The Illinois Chapter of the American Fisheries Society, is part of the American Fisheries Society (AFS) North Central Division. Working to further to the goals of the AFS through research, education, and professional development, thechapter is committed to the conservation, development, and wise use of fishery resources, and the global protection and sustainability of aquatic ecosystems.
Jim Lamer, President
Phil Willink, Secretary

842 American Lung Association of Illinois
55 W Wacker
Suite 800 312-781-1100
Chicago, IL 60601 info@lungil.org
www.lung.org/about-us/local-associations/illinois.html
The American Lung Association of Illinois works to prevent lung disease and promote lung health. Through education, advocacy, support and campaigns, such as Smokefree Illinois; the Association offers a wide variety of lung healthservices to the people Illinois.
Kristen Young, Executive Director, Chicago
Lewis Bartfield, Executive VP, Upper Midwest

843 American Lung Association of Illinois: Springfield
3000 Kelly Lane 217-787-5864
Springfield, IL 62711 info@lungil.org
www.lung.org/about-us/local-associations/illinois.html
Lewis Bartfield, Executive VP, Upper Midwest

844 **American Society of Landscape Architects: Illinois Chapter**
PO Box 4566 630-833-4516
Oak Brook, IL 60522-4566 info@il-asla.org
www.il-asla.org
The Illinois Chapter of the American Society of Landscape Architects, is a nonprofit association representing the landscape architecture profession throughout the state of Illinois.
Susan Ragaishis, Executive Director
John Pizzo, President

845 **Association of Illinois Soil and Water Conservation Districts**
4285 North Walnut Street 217-744-3414
Springfield, IL 62707 Fax: 217-744-3420
www.aiswcd.org
The Association of Illinois Soil and Water Conservation Districts (AISWCD) is a grassroots organization committed to reprsenting and empowering the 97 soil and water conservation districts of Illinois.
Founded: 1948
Kelly Thompson, Executive Director
Steve Stierwalt, President

846 **Chicago Chapter: National Safety Council**
1121 Spring Lake Drive 630-285-1121
Suite 100 800-621-7615
Itasca, IL 60143-3201 Fax: 630-285-1434
customerservice@nsc.org
www.chicago.nsc.org
The National Safety Council saves lives by preventing injuries and deaths at work, in homes and communities, and on the roads through leadership, research, education and advocacy.
Jeffrey J. Woodbury, NSC Board Chairman
Deborah Hersman, President & CEO

847 **Chicago Zoological Society**
Brookfield Zoo 708-688-8000
3300 Golf Road bzadmin@brookfieldzoo.org
Brookfield, IL 60513 www.czs.org/Chicago-Zoological-Society
The Chicago Zoological Society is a nonprofit operating out of Brookfield Zoo. The society is committed to inspiring conservation leadership by connecting people with wildlife and nature.
Founded: 1934
Stuart D. Strahl, President & CEO
Richar G. Gamble, COO

848 **Eagle Nature Foundation,Ltd.**
300 East Hickory Street 815-594-2306
Apple River, IL 61001 Fax: 815-594-2305
eaglenature.tni@juno.com
www.eaglenature.com
An international, nonprofit organization dedicated to the development and implementation of habitat preservations strategies for endangered species. The Eagle Nature Foundation (ENF) utilizes nature education and awareness programs tofund research and advocate for the bald eagle and other endangered species.
Founded: 1995
Terrence N. Ingram, Chief Executive Officer
Eugene Small, Vice President

849 **Environmental Education Association of Illinois**
Enivronmental Education Association of Illinois
Anita Purves Nature Center
1505 N. Broadway EEAssociation.Illinois@gmail.com
Urbana, IL 61801 www.eeai.net
The Environment Education Association of Illinois (EEAI), is nonprofit association focused on the advancement of environmental education throughout the state. The EEAI is the Illinois affiliate of the North American Association forEnvironmental Education (NAAEE).
Jennifer Tariq, President
Kirsten Hope Walker, Treasurer

850 **Great Lakes Sport Fishing Council**
PO Box 297 630-941-1351
Elmhurst, IL 60126 www.great-lakes.org
The Great Lakes Sport Fishing council is a nonprofit confederation of organizations and individuals representing the Great Lakes region. Dedicated to the advocacy of the present and future state of sport fishing, the council promotes,protects and conserves the regions aquatic resources.
Founded: 1971 325,000 Members
Dan Thomas, President
Robert Mitchell, Vice President

851 **Illinois Association of Environmental Professionals**
9575 West Higgins Road
Suite 600 info@iaepnetwork.org
Rosemont, IL 60018 www.iaepnetwork.org
A nonprofit organization focused on enhnacing environmental awareness and quality for the businesses, communities and citizens of Illinois.
Founded: 1975
Caroline Levenda, President
Larry Falbe, VP

852 **Illinois Audubon Society**
IL 217-544-2473
www.illinoisaudubon.org
The Illinois Audubon Society (IAS), is a member organization with 16 chapters throughout the state. The IAS is dedicated to the preservation of Illinois wildlife and the habitats which support them.
Founded: 1897 $25/Year
Jim Herkert, Executive Director
Jodie Owen, Accounts Manager

853 **Illinois Environmental Council**
230 Broadway 217-544-5954
Suite 150 Fax: 217-544-5958
Springfield, IL 62701 iec@ilenviro.org
www.ilenviro.org
Known as the IEC, the Illinois Environmental Council is made up of the Illinois Environmental Council Education Fund and the Illinois Environmental Council. The Education Fund provides education, outreach and a forum forenvironmentalists and the Council serves as the voice for the environmental community of Illinois. The IEC represents 60 environmental and community organizations and close to 300 individuals from across the state.
Founded: 1975
Jennifer Walling, Executive Director
Matt Steffen, Director, Communications

854 **Illinois Prairie Path**
P.O. Box 1086 630-752-0120
Wheaton, IL 60187 info@ipp.org
www.ipp.org
The Illinois Prairie Path (IPP), is a nonprofit corporation working to preserve, enhance and advocate for the Illinois Prairie Path. The path was the first successful U.S. "rails-to-trails" path, in which the abandoned route ofChicago's Aurora and Elgin Electric rail line was converted to a public path, starting the "rails-to-trails" movement of the 1960's. The IPP is for non-motorized public use.
Founded: 1963

855 **Illinois Recycling Association**
PO Box 6957 708-358-0050
Villa Park, IL 60181 info@illinoisrecycles.org
www.illinoisrecycles.org

A collective voice for waste management in the state of Illinois, the Illinois Recycling Association (IRA) is a nonprofit organization consisting of municipal, county, and state recycling coordinators. The IRA is dedicated to theadvocacy of the responsible use of resources through the promotion of waste reduction, re-use and recycling.
Founded: 1980 100 Members
Kris Kaar, President

856 **Illinois Solar Energy Association**
C/O Shamrock Electirc
1281 E Brummel Avenue 312-376-8245
Elk Grove Village, IL 60007 Fax: 630-420-1517
contactisea@illinoissolar.org
www.illinoissolar.org

The Illinois Solar Energy Association (ISEA) is a nonprofit organization using education and advocacy to promote the widespread use of solar and other renewable energy sources.
Founded: 1975
Nicola Brown, Program Development
Lesley McCain, Executive Director

857 **Iowa-Illinois Safety Council**
1501 42nd Street 515-276-4724
Suite 100 800-568-2495
West Des Moines, IA 50266 Fax: 515-276-8038
iiscadmin@iisc.org
www.iisc.org

The Iowa-Illinois Safety Council (IISC) is a nonprofit resource organization that helps business and industry with safety, health and environmental programs. As of 1980, the IISC is a chapter of the National Safety Council.
Founded: 1953 1,000 Members
Adam Lathrop, Executive Director
Dawn Gunderson, Director, Communications

858 **Midwest Pesticide Action Center**
35 E Upper Wacker Drive 773-878-7378
Suite 1200 general@pesticideaction.org
Chicago, IL 60601 www.midwestpesticideaction.org
Working at the local, state and regional level, the Midwest Pesticide Action Center, uses advocacy, education, and outreach to reduce the health risks and environmental impact of pesticides and promote safer alternatives.
Founded: 1994
Ruth Kerzee, Executive Director
Ryan Anderson, Program Manager

859 **Prairie Rivers Network**
1902 Fox Drive 217-344-2371
Suite G Fax: 217-344-2381
Champaign, IL 61820 info@prairierivers.org
www.prairierivers.org

Working at a local, state and federal level, Prairie Rivers Networks champions the protection, conservation and restoration of rivers and lakes; promoting healthy waterways and safe drinking water for people, fish and wildlife.
Founded: 1967
Jon McNussen, President
Carol Hays, Executive Director

860 **Respiratory Health Association**
1440 W Washington Boulevard 312-243-2000
Chicago, IL 60607 888-880-5864
Fax: 312-243-3954
info@lungchicago.org
www.lungchicago.org

The Respiratory Health Association (RHA) works to prevent lung disease, promote clean air and help people live better. Through education, research and policy change, the RHA is a public health leader in metropolitan Chicago with afocus on asthma, COPD, lung cancer, tobacco control and air quality.
Founded: 1906
Beth Ritter Ruback, Director, Communications
Joel Africk, President & CEO

861 **Sierra Club: Illinois Chapter**
70 E Lake Street 312-251-1680
Suite 1500 Fax: 312-251-1780
Chicago, IL 60601 firstname.lastname@sierraclub.org
illinois.sierraclub.org

With 14 local groups, the Illinois Chapter of the Sierra Club encompasses the entire state of Illinois plus a small part of Iowa. In conjunction with the National Sierra Club's mission, the Illinois Chapter protects and promotes cleanenergy, air and water.
Founded: 1959
Jack Darin, Chapter Director
Kady McFadden, Deputy Director

862 **The Nature Conservancy: Illinois Chapter**
8 S Michigan Avenue 312-580-2100
Suite 900 Fax: 312-346-5606
Chicago, IL 60603 illinois@tnc.org
www.nature.org

The Illinois Chapter of The Nature Conservancy is dedicated to protecting the land and water of Illinois. With over 100 sites across the state, the Illinois Chapter is working to preserve the diverse habitats of the prairies, savannas,forests, wetlands and rivers found in Illinois.
Michelle Carr, State Director
Georgie Geraghty, Chief of Staff

Indiana

863 **Acres Land Trust**
1802 Chapman Road 260-637-2273
PO Box 665 Fax: 260-637-2273
Huntertown, IN 46748 acres@acreslandtrust.org
www.acreslandtrust.org

Acres Land Trust is the largest and oldest local land trust, covering 32 counties across northeast Indiana and Michigan. Dedicated to the protecting, promotion, and education of local land. Acres Land Trust acquires, owns, manages andprotects the working land, forests, wetlands, native grasslands, unique geological formations and habitats of the rare, threatened and endangered species of Indiana.
Founded: 1960
Steven Hammer, President
Jason Kissel, Executive Director

864 **American Fisheries Society: North Central Division: Indiana Chapter**
IN
bmiller2@dnr.in.gov
www.indianaafs.org

The Indiana Chapter of the American Fisheries Society (IAFS), is part of the American Fisheries Society (AFS) North Central Division. Working to further to the goals of the AFS through research, education, and professional development,the chapter is committed to the conservation, development, and wise use of fishery resources in Indiana.
Ben Miller, President
Briana Ciara, Secretary & Treasurer

865 **American Lung Association of Indiana**
115 West Washington Street 317-819-1181
Suite 1180 South info@lungin.org
Indianapolis, IN 46204
http://www.lung.org/about-us/local-associations/indiana.html

The American Lung Association of Indiana works to prevent lung disease and promote lung health. Through education, advo-

cacy,and campaigns, such as the Indiana Tuberculosis Education program; the Association offers a wide variety oflung health services to the people Illinois.
Tanya Husain, Executive Director, Indiana
Lewis Bartfield, Executive VP, Upper Midwest

866 American Society of Landscape Architects: Indiana Chapter
PO Box 441195
Indianapolis, IN 46244-1195
office@inasla.org
www.inasla.org
As a chapter of the American Society of Landscape Architects (ASLA), it aims to lead, educate and participate in the careful stewardship, wise planning, and artful design of cultural and natural environments.
Founded: 1972 200 Members
April Westcott, President
Jon Ruble, VP

867 Conservation Technology Information Center
3495 Kent Avenue
Suite L100
West Lafayette, IN 47906
765-494-9555
Fax: 765-463-4106
ctic@ctic.org
www.ctic.purdue.edu
Conservation Technology Information Center (CTIC) is dedicated the promotion and provision of information on technologies and sustainable agricultural systems that conserve and enhance soil, water, air and wildlife resources.
Chad Watts, Executive Director
Tammy Taylor, Director, Operations

868 Dj Case & Associates
317 E Jefferson Boulevard
Mishawaka, IN 46545
574-258-0100
info@djcase.com
www.djcase.com
Specializing in conservation and natural resources communication, DJ Case & Associates is made up of social scientists, biologists, strategic communication planners, storytellers, video producers and web application developers.Working with state, federal and private natural resource agencies, DJ Case & Associates are dedicated to implementing positive, measurable and effective communication using conservation engagement and digital tools.
Founded: 1986
Dave Case, President
Phil Seng, Vice President

869 Indiana Audubon Society
3499 S Bird Sanctuary Road
Connersville, IN 47331
765-827-5109
president@indianaaudubon.org
indianaaudubon.org
The Indiana Audubon Society (IAS) is dedicated to stimulating interest in and promoting the protection of resident and migrant bird species and their habitats, both in Indiana and other regions. The organization also strives to supporteducational efforts to assist future generations in continuing this tradition.
Founded: 1898
Brad Bumgardner, Executive Director
Jeff Canada, Board President

870 Indiana State Trappers Association
ISTA C/O Ms. Georgia Gifford Treasurer
921 S Locke Street
Kokomo, IN 46901
765-438-3630
www.indianatrappers.org
The Indiana State Trappers Association (ISTA) is a public charity working to conserve Indiana's fur resources, preserve the rights, history and heritage of trappers, educate those interested in trapping and increasing public awarenessof trapping issues and benefits.
Fred Philips, President
Tom Setser, VP

871 Indiana Water Environment Association
8909 Purdue Road
Suite 130
Indianapolis, IN 46268
317-686-2664
Fax: 317-686-2672
kylee@indianawea.org
www.indianawea.org
The Indiana Water Environment Association is dedicated to perserving and protecting Indiana's waterways through the education of it members and the general public. The Indiana Water Environment Association is an affiliate of the WaterEnvironment Federation (WEF).
$35/Year
Kylee Dycus, Association Coordinator
Julia Whitson, Executive Director

872 Indiana Woodland Steward
IN
steward1@inwoodlands.org
www.inwoodlands.org
The Indiana Woodland Steward is made up of 11 member organizations with the purpose of promoting the wise use of Indiana's forest resources.
Dan Shaver, President
Lynn Andrews, Treasurer

873 Sierra Club: Indiana Chapter
1100 W 42nd Street
Suite 140
Indianapolis, IN 46208
317-822-3750
sierra@netdirect.net
www.hoosier.sierraclub.org
To advance the preservation and protection of the natural environment by empowering the citizenry with charitable resources to further the cause of environmental protection.
Founded: 1975 8,000 Members
Loren Blackford, President
Susana Reyes, Vice President

874 The Wildlife Society: Indiana Chapter
IN
www.intws.org
The Indiana Chapter of the the Wildlife Society is dedicated to enhancing the ability of wildlife professionals, conserve diversity, sustained productivity and ensuring the responsible use of wildlife resources.
Founded: 1968 $12 for Membership

Iowa

875 American Fisheries Society: North Central Division: Iowa Chapter
IA
jonathan.meerbeek@dnr.iowa.gov
www.iowa.fisheries.org
The Iowa Chapter of the American Fisheries Society, is part of the American Fisheries Society (AFS) North Central Division. Working to further to the goals of the AFS through research, education, and professional development; the IowaChapter is a scientific and professional society focused on the encouragement of exchanging information by members working in, living in or have an interest in the state of Iowa.
Founded: 1969
Jonathan Meerbeek, President
Ryan Hupfeld, Secretary & Treasurer

876 American Lung Association of Iowa
2530 73rd Street
Des Moines, IA 50322
515-309-9507
info@lungia.org
www.lung.org/about-us/local-associations/iowa.html
The American Lung Association of the Iowa works to prevent lung disease and promote lung health. Offering a wide variety of lung health services to the people of Iowa.
Micki Sandquist, Executive Director, Iowa
Lewis Bartfield, Executive VP, Upper Midwest

877 **American Society of Landscape Architects: Iowa Chapter**
200 W. 2nd Avenue
Indianola, IA 50125
515-442-2451
Fax: 866-442-6751
ia-asla@assocserv.com
www.iaasla.org
The chapter organizes educational and social activities for its more than 155 members.
Founded: 1899
Laura Peters, President
Jim Harbaugh, President Elect

878 **Asla Iowa Chapter**
200 W. 2nd Avenue
Indianola, IA 50125
515-442-2451
Fax: 866-442-6751
ia-asla@assocserv.com
www.iaasla.org
The chapter organizes educational and social activities for its more than 155 members.
Laura Peters, President
Jim Harbaugh, President Elect

879 **B.A.S.S Nation: Iowa Chapter**
IA
319-393-1481
bobgarman@aol.com
www.iabass.com
The Iowa Chapter of BASS Nation is dedicated to the promotion of the sport of bass fishing, fishing tournaments and conservation initiatives to preserve the states natural resources.
Bob Garman, President
Harry Heines, Vice President

880 **Indian Creek Nature Center**
6665 Otis Road SE
Cedar Rapids, IA 52403
319-362-0664
Fax: 319-362-2876
naturecenter@indiancreeknaturecenter.org
www.indiancreeknaturecenter.org
A private nonprofit organization open to the public. The Nature Center provides about 300 acres of natural land and provides an array of educational programs.
Founded: 1973
John Myers, Executive Director
Dana Wood, Office Manager

881 **Iowa Academy of Science**
Iowa Academy of Science
BRC 50
University of Northern Iowa
Cedar Falls, IA 50614-0508
319-273-2581
Fax: 319-273-2807
iascience@uni.edu
www.scienceiniowa.org
Iowa Academy of Science is a professional scientific organization.
Founded: 1875
Craig Johnson, Executive Director
Cory Davis, Office Manager

882 **Iowa Association of Soil and Water Conservation District Commissioners**
945 SW Ankeny Road
Suite A
Ankeny, IA 50023
515-289-8300
clare.lindahl@cdiowa.org
www.cdiowa.org
Bernie Bolton, Secretary

883 **Iowa Native Plant Society**
Iowa State University
Botany Department, 341A Bessey Hall
Iowa State University
Ames, IA 50011
515-294-9499
Fax: 515-294-1337
pubmaster@iastate.edu
www.public.iastate.edu
An organization of amateur and professional botanists and native plant enthusiasts who are interested in the scientific, educational and cultural aspects, as well as the preservation and conservation of the native plants of Iowa. TheSociety was organized in 1995 to create a forum where plant enthusiasts, gardners and professional botanists could exchange ideas and coordinate activities such as field trips, work shops, and restoration of natural areas.
Larissa Mottl, President
Connie Mutel, Vice President

884 **Iowa Prairie Network**
IA
www.iowaprairienetwork.org
The Iowa Prairie Network is a grass-roots, volunteer, non-profit, organization that is dedicated to the preservation of Iowa's prairie heritage.
Mark Wilson, President
Jon Judson, Vice President

885 **Iowa Renewable Fuels Association**
5505 NW 88th Street
100
Johnston, IA 50131-2948
515-252-6249
Fax: 515-225-0781
info@IowaRFA.org
www.iowarfa.org
Brings together ethanol and biodiesel producers to promote the development and growth of the state's renewable fuels industry through education and infrastructure development.
Brian Cahill, President
Monte Shaw, Executive Director

886 **Iowa Trappers Association**
Gene Purdy
122 2nd Street
Fontanelle, IA 50846
641-682-3937
Fax: 641-682-9092
hightoweria@aol.com
www.iowatrappers.com
Craig Sweet, President
Randy Mitchell, Vice President

887 **Iowa Wildlife Rehabilitators Association**
328 Main Street
Suite 208
Ames, IA 50010
515-233-1379
www.iowawildlifecenter.org
Terry VanDeWalle, President
Marlene Ehresman, Executive Director

888 **Iowa-Illinois Safety Council**
1501 42nd Street
Suite 100
West Des Moines, IA 50266
515-276-4724
800-568-2495
Fax: 515-276-8038
iiscadmin@iisc.org
www.iisc.org
The Iowa-Illinois Safety Council (IISC) is a nonprofit resource organization that helps business and industry with safety, health and environmental programs. As of 1980, the IISC is a chapter of the National Safety Council.
1,000 Members
Adam Lanthrop, Executive Director
Dawn Gunderson, Director, Communications

889 **Macbride Raptor Project**
309 S. Madison Street
Iowa City, IA 52242
319-335-9293
Fax: 319-398-4493
rec-services@uiowa.edu
www.macbrideraptorproject.org
A nonprofit organization jointly sponsored by the University of Iowa and Kirkwood Community College. The project has two main facilities, the educational display facility and rehabilitation flight cage at the Macbride NatureRecreational Area and the medical clinic on the Kirkwood Campus.
Founded: 1985
Jodeane Cancilla, Project Coordinator
Brian Baxter, Senior Associate Director

890 Practical Farmers of Iowa
600 Fifth Street
Suite 100
Ames, IA 50010
515-232-5661
Fax: 515-232-5649
info@practicalfarmers.org
www.practicalfarmers.org
Teresa Opheim, Executive Director
Erica Andorf, Office Manager

891 Sierra Club: Iowa Chapter
3839 Merle Hay Road
Suite 280
Des Moines, IA 50310
515-277-8868
iowa.chapter@sierraclub.org
iowa.sierraclub.org
To advance the preservation and protection of the natural environment by empowering the citizenry with charitable resources to further the cause of environmental protection.
Founded: 1972
Loren Blackford, President
Susana Reyes, Vice President

892 Soil and Water Conservation Society
945 SW Ankeny Road
Ankeny, IA 50023-9723
515-289-2331
800-THE-SOIL
Fax: 515-289-1227
swcs@swcs.org
www.swcs.org
Their mission is to foster the science and art of natural resource conservation. Their work targets the conservation of soil, water, and related natural resources.
Founded: 1943
Clare Lindahl, CEO
Rex Martin, President

893 State of Iowa Woodlands Associations
204 Park Rd
Iowa City, IA 52246
515-233-1161
Fax: 515-233-1131
Al Wagner, President
Chuck Semler, VP

894 The Nature Conservancy: Iowa Chapter
505 5th Ave
Suite 930
Des Moines, IA 50309
515-244-5044
800-628-6860
Fax: 515-244-8890
iowa@tnc.org
nature.org
To preserve the plants, animals and natural communities that represent the diversity of life on Earth by protecting the lands and waters they need to survive.
Founded: 1951
Jan Glendening, State Director

Kansas

895 American Fisheries Society: North Central Division: Kansas Chapter
KS
josh.jagels@ksoutdoors.com
www.ksfisheries.org
The Kansas Chapter of the American Fisheries Society, is part of the American Fisheries Society (AFS) North Central Division. Working to further to the goals of the AFS through research, education, and professional development, thechapter is committed to the conservation, development, and wise use of fishery resources, and protection and sustainability of aquatic ecosystems.
Founded: 1975 $10/Year
Josh Jagels, President
Eric Johnson, Secretary

896 American Lung Association of Kansas
8400 W 110th Street
Suite 130
Overland Park, KS 66210
913-353-9165
kansas@lung.org
http://www.lung.org/about-us/local-associations/kansas.html
The American Lung Association of Kansas works to prevent lung disease and promote lung health through direct assistance, education programs, advocacy and research.
Linda Crider, Executive Director, Kansas
Lewis Bartfield, Executive VP, Upper Midwest

897 Arkansas River Compact Administration
KS
www.co-ks-arkansasrivercompactadmin.org
The Arkansas River Compact Administration (ARCA), is a committee that settles disputes over the Arkansas River between Arkansas and Colorado.
James Rizzuto, Chairman
Randy Hayzlett, Vice-Chairman

898 Audubon of Kansas
210 Southwind Place
Manhattan, KS 66503
785-537-4385
Fax: 785-537-4395
aok@audubonofkansas.org
www.audubonofkansas.org
The Audubon of Kansas, Inc (AOK) is a nonprofit grassroots statewide organization. The AOK is dedicated to promoting the appreciation and stewardship of the ecosystems of Kansas, with a focus on birds, wildlife, prairies and otherhabitats.
Founded: 1999
Ron Klataske, Executive Director
Monica Goss, Director, Development

899 B.A.S.S Nation: Kansas Chapter
KS
joelbassman87@yahoo.com
www.ksbassnation.com
Kansas BASS Nation works to stimulate public awareness of bass fishing as a major sport and encourages sportsmanship, courtesy and boating safety at all levels. Kansas BASS Nation promotes the full adherence to all conservation codes,adequate water quality standards and legal enforcement of existing regulatory standards.
Evan Hartnett, Director
Joel Porter, President

900 Heartland Renewable Energy Society
9844 Georgia Avenue
Kansas City, KS 66109
913-299-4474
info@heartlandrenewable.org
www.heartlandrenewable.org
As a chapter of the American Solar Energy Society, the Heartland Renewable Energy Society (HRES) is a volunteer based organization working to support and further develop the use of renewable energy and energy efficient techniques inbusiness. HRES promotes businesses using renewable energy and educates the public about clean, safe and renewable energy.
Founded: 2000
Craig Wolfe, President
Shauna Zahner, Secretary

901 Kansas Academy of Science
KS
785-231-1010
sam.leung@washburn.edu
www.kansasacademyscience.org
The Kansas Academy of Science (KAS) is dedicated to encouraging science and science education in the State of Kansas. KAS is a member of the National Association of Academies of Science and is affiliated with the American Associationfor the Advancement of Science and the US National Academy of Science.
Founded: 1868
David McKenzie, President
Sam Leung, Secretary

902 Kansas Association for Conservation and Environmental Education
2610 Claflin Road 785-532-1902
Manhattan, KS 66502-2743 Fax: 785-532-3305
info@kacee.org
www.kacee.org
The Kansas Assocaition for Conservation and Environmental Education (KACEE) is a statewide nonprofit dedicated to promoting quality sound, non-brased environmental education in Kansas through professional development and technical assistance.
Melissa Arthur, Director, Operations
Laura Downey, Executive Director

903 Kansas Native Plant Society
Kansas Native Plant Society
R.L McGregor Herbarium 785-864-3453
2045 Constant Avenue email@ksnps.org
Lawrence, KS 66047-3729 www.kansasnativeplantsociety.org
Formerly known as the Kansas Wildflower Society, the Kansas Native Plant Society (KNPS) is a nonprofit organization working to encourage awareness and appreciation of the states native plants, their habitats and landscapes througheducation, stewardship and scientific knowledge.
Founded: 1978
Dwight Platt, President
Cynthia Ford, Secretary

904 Kansas Natural Resources Council
PO Box 2635 785-840-8104
Topeka, KS 66601 lerick@ksu.edu
www.knrc.weebly.com
A nonprofit, member organization the Kansas Natural Resource Council (KNRC) is dedicated to educating Kansans about the natural resources of the state and advocating for the wise use and conservation of these natural resources. KNRCprotects the quality of the water and air of Kansas.
Founded: 1981
Larry Erickson, President
Sharon Ashworth, Program Manager

905 Kansas Rural Center
4021 SW 10th Street
#337 866-579-5469
Topeka, KS 66604 info@kansasruralcenter.org
www.kansasruralcenter.org
Kansas Rural Center Inc. (KRC), is a nonprofit organization committed to promoting the long-term health of the land and the people of Kansas through community based research, education and advocacy. By working directly with Kansasfarmers, communities and leaders, KRC seeks to advance a sustainable farm and food system that is ecologically sound, economically viable and socially just in the state.
Founded: 1979
Mary Fund, Executive Director
Natalie Fullerton, Project Director

906 Kansas Wildscape Foundation
2500 W 6th 785-843-9453
Suite G 866-655-4377
Lawrence, KS 66049 Fax: 785-843-6379
charlieblack@sunflower.com
www.kansaswildscape.org
The Kansas Wildscape Foundation is a private, nonprofit organization working to conserve the land and wild species of the state. Wildscape promotes outdoor recreation and public land use, through projects such as the Kansas WetlandsEducational Center, the Cabins Project and the Milford Wetlands Restoration.
Founded: 1991
Charlie Black, Executive Director
Debbie Brandt, Director, Member Services

907 Safety and Health Council of Western Missouri& Kansas
5829 Troost Avenue 816-842-5223
Kansas City, MO 64110 Fax: 816-842-6226
shc@safetycouncilmoks.com
www.safetycouncilmoks.com
A private nonprofit community service organization dedicated to preventing unintentional injuries where ever they occur through education and outreach
Julian H. Harvey, President
H.L. Goodwin, Secretary & Treasurer

908 Sierra Club: Kansas Chapter
9844 Georgia Avenue 913-707-3296
Kansas City, KS 66109 info@kansas.sierraclub.org
kansas.sierraclub.org
To advance the preservation and protection of the natural environment by empowering the citizenry with charitable resources to further the cause of environmental protection.
Loren Blackford, President
Susana Reyes, Vice President

909 The Wildlife Society: Kansas Chapter
Kansas State University
205 Ackert 758-532-0978
Manhattan, KS 66506 justin.hamilton@ksoutdoors.com
www.wildlife.org/kansas-chapter
The Kansas Chapter of The Wildlife Society provides an avenue for professionals in wildlife management and natural resource fields a way to connect and work with their peers, in order to further advance professional natural resourcemanagment.
$10/Year
Justin Hamilton, President
Kent Fricke, Secretary & Treasurer

Kentucky

910 American Lung Association of Kentucky
4100 Churchman Avenue 502-363-2652
Louisville, KY 40215 barry.gottschalk@lung.org
www.lung.org/about-us/local-associations/kentucky.html
The American Lung Association of Kentucky works to prevent lung disease and promote lung health through direct assistance, education programs, advocacy and research.
Patricia J. Volz, VP, Communication
Barry Gottschalk, Executive VP, Midland States

911 American Society of Landscape Architects: Kentucky Chapter
KY
www.kyasla.com
The Kentucky Chapter seeks to represent and further the aims and policies of the American Society of Landscape Architects as they fall within the domain of the Chapter.
John Swontosky, Trustee
Josh DeSpain, President

912 Friends of Land Between The Lakes
345 Maintenance Road
Murray, KY 42211 800-455-5897
information@friendsoflbl.org
www.friendsoflbl.org
Friends of Land Between The Lakes is a private nonprofit organization that provides educational programs at the Woodlands Nature Station, Golden Pond Planetarium and Observatory, and The Homeplace 1850's Working Farm. Friends of LandBetween The Lakes is a partner of the Forest Service at the Land Between the Lakes National Recreation Area.
John Rufli, Executive Director
Jim Taylor, Director, Operations

913 **Kentucky Association for Environmental Education**
PO Box 1208
Frankfort, KY 40602
programs@kaee.org
www.kaee.org
The first affiliate of the North American Association for Environment Education, the Kentucky Association for Environment Education (KAEE) is nonprofit, professional membership organization and of the country's oldest association. KAEEis dedicated to the promotion of excellence in environmental education through the support and networking the the states environmental educators.
Ashley Hoffman, Executive Director
Brittany Wray, Operations Coordinator

914 **Kentucky Audubon Council**
KY
president@kentuckyaudubon.org
www.kentuckyauduboncouncil.org
The Kentucky Audubon Council is an organization acting as the facilitator for the Audubon chapters in the state, including: the Central Kentucky, Daviess County, Frankfort, Jackson Purchase, Little River and Louisville Audubon Society.The council is comprised of a member from each chapter and is actively working to conserve and restore natural ecosystems with a focus on birds, other wildlife and their habitats.
Angela Myers, President
Robin Antenucci, VP

915 **Kentucky Audubon Council: Central Kentucky Audubon Society**
KY
859-299-9421
president@centralkentuckyaudubon.org
www.centralkentuckyaudubon.org
The Central Kentucky Audubon Society serves 10 central Kentucky counties and promotes conservation education and awareness.
Founded: 1968 $20/Year
Tony Brusate, President
David Lang, VP

916 **Kentucky Audubon Council: Daviess County Audubon Society**
Owensboro, KY 42303
270-926-2202
dcas@daviessaudubon.net
www.daviessaudubon.net
The Daviess County Audubon Society works to support the mission of the National Audubon Society and is involved in commuity outreach and education.
David Stratton, President
Mike Henshaw, Director, Program

917 **Kentucky Audubon Council: Frankfort Audubon Society**
844-428-3826
FrankfortAudubonChapter@gmail.com
www.sites.google.com/site/frankfortaudubon/
The Frankfort Audubon Society works to connect people with nature through education and wildlife conservation.
Robin Antenucci, President
Don Stosberg, Treasurer

918 **Kentucky Audubon Council: Jackson Purchase Audubon Society**
Office or Chapter J59
Paducah, KY 42001
www.audubon.org/location/jackson-purchase-audubon-society

919 **Kentucky Audubon Council: Little River Audubon Society**
Office or Chapter J61
PO Box 352
Hopkinsville, KY 42240
www.audubon.org/location/little-river-audubon-society

920 **Kentucky Audubon Council: Louisville Audubon Society**
PO Box 22162
Louisville, KY 40222
louisvilleaudubon@gmail.com
www.louisvilleaudubon.org
Kathy Dennis, President
Charon Morales, VP

921 **Kentucky Department of Fish & Wildlife Resources**
1 Sportsman's Lane
Frankfort, KY 40601
800-858-1549
info.center@ky.gov
fw.ky.gov
The Kentucky Department of Fish & Wildlife Resources is dedicated to the conservation and enhancement of fish and wildlife resources. The Department provides education and opportunities for hunting, fishing, trapping, boating and otherwildlife related activities.
Dr. Johathan W. Gassett, Commissioner

922 **Kentucky Resources Council**
PO Box 1070
Frankfort, KY 40602
502-875-2428
Fax: 502-875-2845
FitzKRC@aol.com
www.kyrc.org
The Kentucky Resource Council (KRC) is a nonprofit member organization committed to protecting the states natural resources and promoting healthy communities by providing legal and technical guidance to individuals, communities andorganizations.
Founded: 1982
Tom Fitzserald, Director

923 **Scenic Kentucky**
PO Box 23317
Louisville, KY 40223-0317
502-574-3768
Fax: 502-489-5278
info@scenickentucky.org
www.scenickentucky.org
Scenic Kentucky is the state affiliate of Scenic America dedicated to protecting, preserving and enhancing the scenic character of the state. Working at the local, state and federal level, Scenic Kentucky uses advocacy to protect thescenic heritage of the Commonwealth of Kentucky.
Paul Bergmann, Executive Director
Marlene Grissom, President

924 **Sierra Club: Kentucky Chapter**
PO Box 1368
Lexington, KY 40588-1368
859-444-4338
alicehowell@insightbb.com
kentucky.sierraclub.org
To advance the preservation and protection of the natural environment by empowering the citizenry with charitable resources to further the cause of environmental protection.
Founded: 1968
Loren Blackford, President
Susana Reyes, Vice President

925 **The Nature Conservancy: Kentucky Chapter**
114 Woodland Ave
Lexington, KY 40502
859-259-9655
Fax: 859-259-9678
kentucky@tnc.org
www.nature.org

In conjunction with the mission of the Nature Conservancy, the Kentucky Chapter protects 50,000 acres of private and public land across the state, including 18 miles of public use nature trail.
David Phemister, State Director
Lisa Morris, Office Manager

Louisiana

926 American Lung Association of Louisiana
2325 Severn Avenue 504-828-5864
Suite 8 alala@lungse.org
Metairie, LA 70001-6918
http://www.lung.org/about-us/local-associations/louisiana.html
The American Lung Association of Louisiana works to prevent lung disease and promote lung health through direct assistance, education programs, advocacy and research.
Martha C. Bogdan, Executive VP, Southeast
Willie L. Bythwood, Jr, CFO

927 American Society of Landscape Architects: Louisiana Chapter
541 South Eugene Street
Baton Rouge, LA 70806 www.lcasla.org
As the Louisiana Chapter of the American Society of Landscape Architects (LCASLA), it aims to lead, educate and participate in the careful stewardship, wise planning, and artful design of cultural and natural environments. The LCASLArepresents landscape architects from across the state and provides its members with networking, social and volunteer opportunities.
150 Members
Shannon Blakeman, Trustee
Michael Petty, Secretary

928 B.A.S.S Nation: Louisiana Chapter
603 Terri Drive 985-785-9069
Luling, LA 70070 kevgobear@cox.net
www.louisianabass.com
The Louisiana Chapter of BASS Nation is dedicated to the promotion of the sport of bass fishing, fishing tournaments and conservation initiatives to preserve the states natural resources.
Kevin Gaubert, President
Tracy Noble, VP

929 Calcasieu Parish Animal Control & Protection Department
5500-A Swift Plant Road 337-721-3730
Lake Charles, LA 70615 Fax: 337-721-4188
cpas@cppj.net
www.cppj.net/services/animal-services-and-adoption
The Calcasieu Parish Animal Control & Protection Department provides education and intervention surrounding public and animal safety. The Department is dedicated to preventing animal abuse and neglect.
Nathan Areno, Director
Jerry Roy, Operations Supervisor

930 LACD: Louisiana Association of Conservation Districts
825 Kaliste Saloom Road 337-262-5777
Brandywine III, Suite 220 Fax: 337-262-5486
Lafayette, LA 70508 www.laconservationdistricts.org
The Louisiana Association of Conservation Districts(LACD) is charged with the conservation and regulation of the states oil, gas, and lignite resources.

931 LACD: Monroe
24 Accent Drive 318-362-3111
Suite 104 Fax: 318-362-5227
Monroe, LA 71202 www.laconservationdistricts.org

932 LACD: Shreveport
1525 Fairfield Avenue 318-676-7585
Suite 668 Fax: 318-676-7486
Shreveport, LA 71101-4327 www.laconservationdistricts.org

933 Louisiana Wildlife Federation
337 S Acadian Thruway 225-344-6707
Baton Rouge, LA 70806 Fax: 225-344-6707
lwf@lawildlifefed.org
www.lawildlifefed.org
The Louisiana Wildlife Federation (LWF) is a statewide, nonprofit conservation education and advocacy organization dedicated to the restoration, preservation, and development of birds, fish, game, forestry, wild flowers and wildliferesources of the state.
Founded: 1940
Rebecca Triche, Executive Director
Stacy Ortego, Outreach Coordinator

934 National Safety Council: ArkLaTex Chapter
8101 Kingston Road 318-687-7550
Suite 107 800-595-7550
Shreveport, LA 71108 Fax: 318-687-7298
info@nscaltchapter.org
www.nscaltchapter.org
The National Safety Council: ArkLaTex Chapter is a nonprofit corporation that advocates and offers compliance training on safety, health, and environmental issues, with a heavy emphasis on industrial requirements, occupationaltraining, First Aid/CPR, OSHA and supervisor development. The ArkLaTex Chapter is the regional chapter of the National Safety Council.
Larry Holbert, President & CEO
Dana Gunn, Director, Operations

935 Sierra Club: Delta Chapter of Louisiana
PO Box 52503 337-298-8380
Lafayette, LA 70505 hrmartin2sc@gmail.com
www.sierraclub.org/louisiana
The Delta Chapter is comprised of 5 regional groups working to conserve Louisiana's environment through lobbying efforts, education campaigns and the protection of the Atchafalaya Basin.
3,000 Members
Martin Haywood, Chair
Diana Morgan, Vice Chair

936 Sierra Club: New Orleans/Gulf of Mexico Regional Office
716 Adams Street 504-861-4834
New Orleans, LA 70118 Fax: 504-861-4441
daryl.malek-wiley@sierraclub.org
www.sierraclub.org/louisiana
Daryl Malek-Wiley, Regional Representative
Grace Morris, Conservation Organizer

937 The Nature Conservancy: Louisiana Chapter
PO Box 4125 225-338-1040
Baton Rouge, LA 70821 lafo@tnc.org
www.nature.org
The Louisiana Chapter of the Nature Conservancy works to conserve the natural resources of the state with multiple locations and the management of 5 nature preserves.

938 The Nature Conservancy: Louisiana Chapter: Cypress Island
PO Box 317 337-342-2475
Breaux Bridge, LA 70517 www.nature.org

939 The Nature Conservancy: Louisiana Chapter: Grande Isle
PO Box 675 985-787-3599
Grand Isle, LA 70358 www.nature.org

940 **The Nature Conservancy: Louisiana Chapter: New Orleans**
320 Hammond Highway
Suite 404
Metairie, LA 70005
504-831-9689
www.nature.org

941 **The Nature Conservancy: Louisiana Chapter: Northeast Louisiana**
4276 Front Street
Winnsboro, LA 71295
318-412-0472
www.nature.org

942 **The Nature Conservancy: Louisiana Chapter: Southwest Louisiana**
12 Williamsburg Street
Lake Charles, LA 70605
337-480-9393
www.nature.org

943 **The Nature Conservancy: Louisiana Chapter:Northshore Field Office**
PO Box 1657
Abita Springs, LA 70420
985-809-1414
www.nature.org

944 **The Nature Conservancy:Louisiana Chapter:Northwest Louisiana**
PO Box 72299
Bossier City, LA 71125
318-560-5725
www.nature.org

945 **The Wildlife Society: Louisiana Chapter**
LA 70808
www.wildlife.org/tag/louisiana

The LouisianaCchapter of the the Wildlife Society,is a nonprofit scientific and educational organization that serves professionals such as government agencies, academia, industry and non-government organizations in all areas related tothe conservation of wildlife and natural resources management.

946 **Tulane Environment Law Clinic**
6329 Freret Street
New Orleans, LA 70118
504-865-5789
Fax: 504-862-8721
www.tulane.edu/~telc/

Part of Tulane University's Law School, the Tulane Environmental Law Clinic was founded in order to offer students real world experience in representing clients in order to resolve disputes under state and federal environmental laws.The Clinic is Louisiana's premier public interest environmental legal services organization, providing free legal representation and community outreach to community organizations, lower-income individuals and local governments.
Founded: 1989
Lisa Lavie Jordan, Director
Corinne Van Dalen, Clinic Instructor

Maine

947 **American Lung Association of Maine**
122 State Street
Augusta, ME 04330
207-622-6394
info@lungne.org
www.lung.org/about-us/local-associations/maine.html

The American Lung Association of Maine works to prevent lung disease and promote lung health through direct assistance, education programs, advocacy and research.
Jeff Seyler, Executive VP, Northeast
Adam Shuster, CFO

948 **Atlantic Salmon Federation**
PO Box 807
Calais, ME 04619-0807
506-529-4581
506-529-1033
800-565-5666
Fax: 506-529-1070
Fax: 506-529-4438
savesalmon@asf.ca
www.asf.ca

The Atlantic Salmon Federation is an international nonprofit organization that promotes the conservation and wise management of wild Atlantic salmon and their habitat.
Bill Taylor, President & CEO
Robert Otto, COO

949 **Maine Association of Conservation Commissions**
665 Western Avenue
Manchester, ME 04351
207-623-1217
fws319@aol.com
www.meaccme.org

The Maine Association of Conservation Commissions is committed to connecting the communities of Maine to the natural resources of the state, including its water, woods and wildlife.
Founded: 1973
Robert C Cummings, Executive Director
Marcel Polak, Cons. Resource Advisor

950 **Maine Association of Conservation Districts**
Portland, ME
207-878-0857
tomgordon@avportland.com
www.maineconservationdistricts.com

Reprsenting Maine's 16 Soil & Water Conservation distircts. The Maine Association of Conservation Districts, works to strengthn the states ability to conserve natural resources.
Founded: 1949
Andy Reed, President
Steve Follette, Vice President

951 **Maine Audubon**
20 Gilsland Farm Road
Falmouth, ME 04105
207-781-2330
Fax: 207-781-0974
info@maineaudubon.org
maineaudubon.org

Maine Audubon works to conserve Maine's wildlife and wildlife habitat by engaging people of all ages in education, conservation and action.
Founded: 1843
Andrew Beahm, Executive Director
Eric Topper, Director of Education

952 **Maine Coast Heritage Trust**
1 Bowdoin Mill Island
Suite 201
Topsham, ME 04086
207-729-7366
Fax: 207-729-6863
info@mcht.org
www.mcht.org

Maine Coast Heritage Trust (MCHT) is a statewide nonprofit organization working to conserve and promote the natural places of Maine. Through land trusts, communities,and partnerships MCHT protects over 146,000 acres of land and morethan 322 costal islands
Founded: 1970
Tim Glidden, President
Richard Knox, Director, Communications

953 **Maine Coast Heritage Trust: Aldermere Farm**
70 Russel Avenue
Rockport, ME 04856
207-236-2739
Fax: 207-230-2582
info@mcht.org
www.mcht.org

Tim Glidden, President
Richard Knox, Director, Communications

954 Maine Coast Heritage Trust: Downeast Field Office
13A Willow Street
East Machias, ME 04630
207-259-5040
info@mcht.org
www.mcht.org

Tim Glidden, President
Richard Knox, Director, Communications

955 Maine Coast Heritage Trust: Mount Desert Island
PO Box 669
Mount Desert, ME 04660
201-244-5100
Fax: 207-244-5200
info@mcht.org
www.mcht.org

Tim Glidden, President
Richard Knox, Director, Communications

956 Maine Woodland Owners
153 Hospital Street
PO Box 836
Augusta, ME 04332-0836
207-626-0005
877-467-9626
info@mainewoodlandowners.org
www.swoam.org

Formerly known as the Small Woodland Owners Association of Maine, the Woodland Owners of Maine, is a nonprofit organization working to promote the stewardship of Maine's woodland resources and provide information for better forestmanagement. Maine Woodland Owners is a statewide organization with 10 regional chapters.
Founded: 1975
Thomas C. Doak, Executive Director
Bill S. Williams, Deputy Executive Director

957 Sierra Club: Maine Chapter
44 Oak Street
Suite 301
Portland, ME 04101-3936
207-761-5616
Fax: 207-773-6690
maine.chapter@sierraclub.org
maine.sierraclub.org

To advance the preservation and protection of the natural environment by empowering the citizenry with charitable resources to further the cause of environmental protection.
Loren Blackford, President
Susana Reyes, Vice President

Massachusetts

958 Alternatives for Community & Environment
2201 Washington Street
Suite 302
Roxbury, MA 02119
617-442-3343
Fax: 617-442-2425
info@ace-ej.org
www.ace-ej.org

The Alternatives for Community & Environment organization works to support and build the communities of color and lower income communities in New England by pursuing systematic change in order to eliminate environmental racism,classism and achieve environmental justice.
Founded: 1994
Sue Heilman, Interim Executive Director
Lee Matsueda, Political Director

959 American Lung Association of Massachusetts
14 Beacon Street
Suite 717
Boston, MA 02108
781-890-4262
info@lungne.org
www.lung.org/about-us/local-associations/massachusetts.html

The American Lung Association of Massachusetts works to prevent lung disease and promote lung health; offering a wide variety of lung health services to the people of Massachusetts.
Jeff Seyler, Executive VP, Northeast
Adam Shuster, CFO

960 American Lung Association of Massachusetts: Framingham
1661 Worcester Road
Suite 301
Framingham, MA 01701
781-890-4262
info@lungne.org
http://www.lung.org/about-us/local-associations/massachusetts.html
Jeff Seyler, Executive VP, Northeast
Adam Shuster, CFO

961 American Lung Association of Massachusetts: Springfield
393 Maple Street
Springfield, MA 01105
413-737-3506
info@lungne.org
www.lung.org/about-us/local-associations/massachusetts.html
Jeff Seyler, Executive VP, Northeast
Adam Shuster, CFO

962 Association for Environmental Health and Sciences Foundation
150 Fearing Street
Amherst, MA 01002
413-549-5170
Fax: 413-549-0579
anina@aehsfoundation.org
www.aehsfoundation.org

The Association for Environment Health and Sciences Foundation, Inc. is a nonprofit, member supported, professional organization working to facilitate the communication and cooperation among environmental professionals. The Foundationworks to help the international community adopt and maintain environmentally sound and sustainable practices.
Founded: 1990 600 Members
Paul Kostecki, Ph.D, Executive Director
Brenna Lockwood, Managing Director

963 Boston Society of Landscape Architects
PO Box 262047
Boston, MA 02196
chapteroffice@bslanow.org
www.bslaweb.org

The Boston Society of Landscape Architects (BSLA) is the state affiliate of the American Society of Landscape Architects, it is the oldest and largest chapter of the ASLA. The BSLA is focused on supporting the success of its membersand their supporters through member benefits, career and skill development and scholarship programs.
Founded: 1913
Chris Moyles, President
Jeanne Lukenda, Trustee

964 Earthwatch Institute
114 Western Avenue
Boston, MA 02134
978-461-0081
800-776-0188
Fax: 978-461-2332
info@earthwatch.org
earthwatch.org

Earthwatch Institute is an international environmental conservation organization, dedicated to scientific field research and education in the promotion and creation of a sustainable environment. Working with the general public,scientists, communities, educators, students and other organizations, Earthwatch has over 50 scientific research expeditions in over 40 countries focused on ocean health, climate change, habitat and ecosystems, and cultural heritage.
Founded: 1971
Kristen Kusek, COO, Comm.& Development
Scott Kania, CEO, United States

965 Environmental League of Massachusetts
14 Beacon Street
Suite 714
Boston, MA 02108
617-742-2553
Fax: 617-742-9656
info@environmentalleague.org
www.environmentalleague.org

The Environmental League of Massachusetts (ELM) is a nonprofit educational and advocacy organization. ELM focuses its

resources on the state level and works to combat climate change and protect the land, water and public health ofMassachusetts.
Founded: 1898
Elizabeth Turnbull, President
Nancy Goodman, VP, Policy

966 **Mass Audubon**
208 South Great Road 781-259-9500
Lincoln, MA 01773 mass_audubon@massaudubon.org
www.massaudubon.org
Mass Audubon is the largest nonprofit nature conservation in Massachusetts, it works to protect nature for the people and wildlife of the state. Through education and advocacy, the Mass Audubon is protecting over 37,000 acres of land,including the habitats of over 150 endangered and threatened native species.
Founded: 1896 125,000 Members
Gary Clayton, President
Bancroft Poor, VP, Operations

967 **Massachusetts Association of Conservation Commissions**
10 Juniper Road 617-489-3930
Belmont, MA 02478 staff@maccweb.org
www.maccweb.org
The Massachusetts Association of Conservation Commissions (MACC) is a statewide, nonprofit organization dedicated to the protection of Massachusetts natural resources by supporting Conservation Commissions. Through education andadvocacy, MACC provides training and assistance for more than 2,000 conservation commissioners protecting wetlands, open space and biological diversity across the state.
Founded: 1961
Eugene B. Benson, Executive Director
Michele Girard, Associate Director

968 **Massachusetts Association of Conservation Districts**
319 Littleton Road 978-692-9395
Suite 205 Fax: 978-392-1305
Westford, MA 01886 jobbagymacd@gmail.com
www.massacd.wordpress.com
The Massachusetts Association of Conservation Districts (MACD) represents the 14 conservation districts of the state. MACD works to protect wildlife, restore habitats, conserve soil and improve the water quality of Massachusetts.
Jane Obbagy, Executive Director
Joseph Smith, President

969 **Massachusetts Environmental Education Society**
c/O Environmental Business Council
375 Harvard Street
Suite 2 info@massmees.org
Brookline, MA 02446 www.massmees.org
The Massachusetts Environmental Education Society (MEES) is committed to the promotion, preservation, and improvement of environmental education in the state and region. MEES provides tools to environmental educators, including accessto online resources, professional development through an annual conference and social media connection.
Founded: 1977
Ann Gisinger, President
Erin Kelly, Treasurer

970 **Massachusetts Forest Alliance**
249 Lakeside Avenue 617-455-9918
Marlborough, MA 01752-4503 nletoile@massforestalliance.org
www.massforestalliance.net
The Massachusetts Forest Alliance (FLA) represents and advocates for citizens and businesses who support a strong, sustainable forest economy. Working on a local, regional and state level the FLA promotes the understanding of forestmanagement, provides educational opportunities for landowners, foresters, timber harvesters and public officials and ensures a sensible legal and regulatory environment.
Founded: 2012
Nathan L'Etoile, Executive Director
Gregory Cox, Program Director

971 **Massachusetts Public Interest Research Group**
294 Washington St 617-292-4800
Suite 500 800-838-6554
Boston, MA 02108 www.masspirg.org
Massachusetts Public Interest Research Group (MASSPIRG) is a statewide, nonprofit, public interest advocacy organization; that focuses primarily on environmental, health, safety, financial and consumer protection.
Founded: 1972
Janet Domenitz, Executive Director
Deirdre Cummings, Legislative Director

972 **Massachusetts Trappers Association**
c/o Marie Barras
PO Box 476
Leominster www.masstrappers.com
, MA 01453
The Massachusetts Trappers Association works to perserve, promote and educate on the tradition of fur harvesting.

973 **Massachusetts Water Pollution Control Association**
PO Box 60 774-276-9722
Rochdale, MA 01542 Fax: 774-670-9956
mwpca2011@yahoo.com
www.mwpca.org
The Massachusetts Water Pollution Control Association (MWPCA) is a nonprofit organization that provides education, training, and promotes the exchange of information among operators and water quality professionals.
Founded: 1965
Lynn Foisy, Executive Director
Tom Azevedo, Program Coordinator

974 **Mount Grace Land Conservation Trust**
1461 Old Keene Road 978-248-2043
Athol, MA 01331 Fax: 978-248-2053
landtrust@mountgrace.org
www.mountgrace.org
The Mount Grace Land Trust is a regional land trust serving 23 towns in Worcester and Franklin counties. The Trust protects natural, agricultural, and scenic areas through the promotion and encouragement of stewardship.
Founded: 1986 1,200 Members
Leigh Youngblood, Executive Director
David Graham Wolf, Deputy Director

975 **New England Water Environment Association**
10 Tower Office Park 781-939-0908
Suite 601 Fax: 781-939-0907
Woburn, MA 01801-2155 mail@newea.org
www.newea.org
A not-for-profit organization whose objective is the advancement of fundamental knowledge and technology of design, construction, operation and management of waste treatment works and other water pollution contral activities anddedication to the preservation of water quality and water resources.
Founded: 1929
Mary Barry, Executive Director
Janice Moran, Program Coordinator

976 **Northeast Sustainable Energy Association**
50 Miles Street 413-774-6051
Greenfield, MA 01301 Fax: 413-774-6053
nesea@nesea.org
www.nesea.org

The Northeast Sustainable Energy Association (NESA) is the region's leading membership organization promoting the use of sustainable energy in the built environment.
Founded: 1974
Jennifer Marrapese, Executive Director
Miriam Aylward, Director,Program Development

977 **Save the Harbor/Save the Bay**
Boston Fish Pier
212 Northern Avenue 617-451-2860
Suite 304 West Fax: 617-451-0496
Boston, MA 02210 info@savetheharbor.org
www.savetheharbor.org
Save the Harbor/Save the Bay is nonprofit public interest organization using education and advocacy to restore and protect the Boston Harbor, Massachusetts Bay and the marine environment.
Founded: 1986
Joseph P. Newman, Chairman
Mark Chrisos, Vice Chair

978 **Sierra Club: Massachusetts Chapter**
10 Milk Street 617-423-5775
Suite 417 Fax: 617-423-5858
Boston, MA 02108-4600 office@sierraclubmass.org
www.sierraclubmass.org
To advance the preservation and protection of the natural environment by empowering the citizenry with charitable resources to further the cause of environmental protection.
Cathy Ann Buckley, Chair
Elisa Campbell, Vice Chair

979 **Walden Woods Project**
The Thoreau Institute at Walden Woods
44 Baker Farm Road 781-259-4700
Lincoln, MA 01773-3004 Fax: 781-259-4710
wwproject@walden.org
www.walden.org
The Walden Woods Project is a nonprofit organization committed to preserving the land, literature, and legacy of Henry David Thoreau through conservation, education, research and advocacy.
Founded: 1990
Matthew Burne, Conservation Director
Samantha Corron, Social Media Coordinator

Maryland

980 **Alliance for the Chesapeake Bay**
501 Sixth Street 443-949-0575
Annapolis, MD 21403 Fax: 443-949-0673
contact@allianceforthebay.org
www.allianceforthebay.org
The Alliance for the Chesapeake Bay leads and supports local collaborative action in order to restore and protect Chesapeake Bay and its surrounding watershed. The Alliance has programs in all 6 Chesapeake Bay watershed states and theDistrict of Columbia, that work to restore, conserve, and clean up local rivers and streams.
Founded: 1971
Al Todd, Executive Director
Lou Etgen, Deputy & State Director

981 **American Fisheries Society**
425 Barlow Place 301-897-8616
Suite 110 Fax: 301-897-8096
Bethesda, MD 20814-2144 main@fisheries.org
www.fisheries.org
The American Fisheries Society (AFS) is an international organization working to strengthen the fisheries profession, advance fisheries science and conserve fisheries resources. The AFS encourages the education and professionaldevelopment of fisheries professionals and its members come from diverse backgrounds including fisheries managers, biologists, professors, ecologists, aquaculturists, economists, engineers, geneticists, and social scientists.
Founded: 1870 8,000 Members
Douglas Austen, Executive Director
Daniel Cassidy, Deputy Executive Director

982 **American Lung Association of Maryland**
211 East Lombard Street #260 804-302-5740
Baltimore, MD 21202 lungmd@lunginfo.org
www.lung.org/about-us/local-associations/maryland.html
The American Lung Association of Maryland works to prevent lung disease and promote lung health through direct assistance, education programs, advocacy and research.
Deborah Brown, Executive VP, Mid-Atlantic
Joy Meyer, VP, Community Impact

983 **American Society of Landscape Architects: Maryland Chapter**
Baltimore, MD
www.marylandasla.org
The Maryland Chapter of the American Society of Landscape Architects (MDASLA), is a nonprofit association representing the landscape architecture profession throughout the state of Maryland.
Founded: 1972 370 Members
Larissa Torres, President
Jennifer Kirschnick, Exectuive Director

984 **Audubon Naturalist Society**
Woodend Sanctuary
8940 Jones Mill Road 301-652-9188
Chevy Chase, MD 20815 www.anshome.org
Through education, advocacy and outdoor experiences, the Audubon Naturalist Society (ANS) works to inspire the community of the greater Washington, DC region to appreciate, understand and protect the natural environment.
Founded: 1897
Lisa Alexander, Executive Director
Jacky Wershbale, Director, Development

985 **B.A.S.S Nation: Maryland Chapter**
MD 410-426-2343
teamroger@aol.com
www.mdbass.com
Dedicated to the promotion of the sport of bass fishing. The Maryland BASS nation is comprised of 50 bass fishing clubs organized into four separate regions.
Roger Trageser, President
Denis Schanberger, Secrtary

986 **Center for Chesapeake Communities**
192 Duke Of Gloucester Street 410-267-8595
Annapolis, MD 21401 Fax: 410-267-8597
www.chesapeakecommunities.org
Technical assistance on environmental, land use, energy and water quality issues for local government in Chesapeake Bay Watershed.
Gary Allen, Executive Director

987 **Chesapeake Bay Environmental Center**
600 Discovery Lane 410-827-6694
PO Box 519 jwink@bayrestoration.org
Grasonville, MD 21638 www.bayrestoration.org
The Chesapeake Bay Environmental Center (CBEC) is a nonprofit membership organization dedicated to the promotion of stewardship and sustainability through environmental education and habitat restoration. The CBEC is an environmentcenter located on a 510 acre wildlife habitat surrounded by the Chesa-

peake Bay, where research, education, and restoration of the Bay occurs.
Founded: 1979
Judy Wink, Executive Director
Vicki Paulas, Assistant Director

988 **Chesapeake Bay Foundation**
Philip Merrill Environmental Center
6 Herndon Avenue 410-268-8816
Annapolis, MD 21403 888-728-3229
Fax: 410-268-6687
chesapeake@cbf.org
www.cbf.org
Through education, advocacy and litigation, the Chesapeake Bay Foundation (CBF) is the largest nonprofit, independent conservation organization, dedicated solely to the protection and restoration of Chesapeake Bay and its watersheds.
Founded: 1967
Alison Prost, Executive Director, Maryland
Tom Zopler, Assitant Director, Media

989 **Chesapeake Wildlife Heritage**
CWH and Western Maryland Division
c/o Ned Gerber 410-822-5100
PO Box 1745 Fax: 410-822-4016
Easton, MD 21601 info@cheswildlife.org
www.cheswildlife.org
Dedicated to creating, restoring and protecting wildlife habitat and establishing a more sustainable agriculture through direct action, education and research in partnership with private landowners.
Founded: 1980
John E. (Ned) Gerber, Director
Ralph V. Partlow III, President & Treasurer

990 **Eastern Shore Land Conservancy**
114 S Washington Street 410-690-4603
Suite 101 info@eslc.org
Easton, MD 21601 www.eslc.org
Eastern Shore Land Conservancy (ESLC) is a private, nonprofit organization committed to preserving and sustaining the communities of Eastern Shore, their lands and water. Through the promotion of sound land use, planning and ESLC LandProtection Program, the ESLC has protected nearly 60,000 acres of the regions natural habitats and farmland.
Founded: 1990
Robert Etgen, Executive Director
Laura Sanford, Director of Advancement

991 **Institute of Hazardous Materials Management**
11900 Parklawn Drive 301-984-8969
Suite 450 Fax: 301-984-1516
Rockville, MD 20852-2624 info@ihmm.org
www.ihmm.org
The Institute of Hazardous Materials Management (IHMM), is a nonprofit organization committed to protecting the environment and the public's health, safety and security through the recognition and administration of credentials forprofessionals who have demonstrated excellence in the management of hazardous materials.
Founded: 1984
Glenn Fellman, Executive Director
M. Patricia Buley, Director, Certification

992 **Izaak Walton League of America**
707 Conservation Lane 301-548-0150
Gaithersburg, MD 20878 info@iwla.org
www.iwla.org
The Izaak Walton League of America, is one of the oldest and most respected conservation organizations in the United States. With local chapters across the US, the League works to conserve, restore, and promote the sustainable use ofnatural resources.
Founded: 1922 43,000 Members
Scott Kovarovics, Executive Director
Dawn Merritt, Director, Communications

993 **Maryland Association of Soil Conservation Districts**
209 Jarman Branch Drive 443-262-8491
Centreville, MD 21617 Fax: 410-956-0161
lindsay.mdag@gmail.com
www.mascd.net
The Maryland Association of Soil Conservation Districts (MASCD) is a nonprofit organization representing the 24 soil and water conservation districts of the state. The MASCD provides a forum for training, policy-making and the exchangeof information while promoting the practical and effective use of soil and water.
Founded: 1956
Danielle Bauer, Program Assitant
Lindsay Thompson, Executive Director

994 **Maryland Native Plant Society**
PO Box 4877
Silver Spring, MD 20914 info@mdflora.org
www.mdflora.org
Through education, research, advocacyand service activities the Maryland Native Plant Society, promotes awareness, appreciation, and conservation of the states native plants and their habitats.
Founded: 1992
Kristen Johnson, President
Karyn Molines, VP

995 **Maryland Recyclers Network**
c/o Mariner Management 443-741-8740
PO Box 1046 Fax: 301-238-4579
Laurel, MD 20725 info@marylandrecyclingnetwork.org
www.marylandrecyclingnetwork.org
The Maryland Recycling Network (MRN) serves as an educational resource providing information regarding the 3 "R's" to professionals in the recycling industry and the publi;, through a combonation of programs, advocacy activities andtechnical assitance the MRN promotes the sustainable reduction, reuse and recycling in Maryland.
Peter Houstle, Executive Director
Brian Ryerson, President

996 **Multiple Chemical Sensitivity Referral and Resources**
MD 410-889-6666
adonnay@mcsrr.org
www.mcsrr.org
A non-profit organization engaged in professional outreach, patient support and public advocacy devoted to the diagnosis, treatment, accommodation and prevention of Multiple Chemical Sensitivity disorders.
Albert Donnay MHS, Co-Founder/Exe. Director

997 **Rachel Carson Council**
8600 Irvington Avenue 301-214-2400
Bethesda, MD 20817 office@rachelcarsoncouncil.org
rachelcarsoncouncil.org
An association seeking to inform and advise the public about the effects of pesticides that threaten the health, welfare, and survival of living organisms and biological systems. Special attention is given to the areas of globalclimate change, renewable energy, toxic chemicals and sustainable food.
Founded: 1965
Roger Christie, Chairman
Robert K. Musil, Ph.D., President & CEO

998 Sierra Club: Maryland Chapter
7338 Baltimore Avenue 301-277-7111
#102 Fax: 301-277-6699
College Park, MD 20740 josh.tulkin@sierraclub.org
maryland.sierraclub.org
To advance the preservation and protection of the natural environment by empowering the citizenry with charitable resources to further the cause of environmental protection.
Founded: 1865
Baird Straughan, Chair
Josh Tulkin, State Director

999 The Nature Conservancy: Maryland/DC Chapter
425 Barlow Plae 301-897-8570
Suite 100 800-628-6860
Bethesda, MD 20814 Fax: 301-897-0858
www.nature.org/maryland
The Maryland/DC Chapter of The Nature Conservancy uses advocacy and on the ground conservation work to protect the region's natural resources. Primarily focused on clean water and climate resilience, the Maryland/DC Chapter manages75,000 acres of private and public lands, including 13 nature preserves.
Mark Bryer, Acting Executive Director
Severn Smith, Director, Comm. & Marketing

1000 The Wildlife Society: Maryland - Delaware Chapter
MD 20814 301-897-9770
Fax: 301-530-2471
mddechapter@gmail.com
www.mddechapter.wixsite.com/mdde
The Maryland-Delaware Chapter is a local membership organization of The Wildlife Society, the Chapter is dedicated to the promotion and development of sound stewardship of wildlife resources and the surrounding environment.
Founded: 1977 80 Members
Jennifer Murrow, President
Trevor Michaels, Vice President

1001 White Lung Association
MD
info@whitelung.org
www.whitelung.org
A nonprofit organization dedicated to the education of the public to the hazards of asbestos exposure. Has developed programs of public education and consults with victims of asbestos exposure, school boards, building owners,government agencies and others interested in identifying asbestos hazards and developing control programs.

Michigan

1002 American Fisheries Society: North Central Division: Michigan Chapter
MI
keiperw@michigan.gov
www.michigan.fisheries.org
The Michigan Chapter of the American Fisheries Society, is part of the American Fisheries Society (AFS) North Central Division, it is a professional organization comprised of around 400 members from different fishery backgrounds.Working to further to the goals of the AFS through research, education, and professional development, the Chapter's primary focus is to provide a forum for the discussion of fishery issues and raise awareness regarding aquatic resources in Michigan.
Founded: 1973 $10/ Year
Justin Chiotti, President
William Keiper, Secretary & Treasurer

1003 American Lung Association of Michigan
1475 E 12 Mile Road 248-784-2000
Madison Heights, MI 48071 midland@lung.org
www.lung.org/about-us/local-associations/michigan.html
The American Lung Association of Michigan works to prevent lung disease and promote lung health through direct assistance, education programs, advocacy and research.
Patricia J. Volz, VP, Communication
Barry Gottschalk, Executive VP, Midland States

1004 American Lung Association of Michigan: Flint
PO Box 966
Grand Blanc, MI 48480 800-586-4872
www.lung.org/about-us/local-associations/michigan.html
Barry Gottschalk, Executive VP, Midlant States
Patricia J. Volz, VP, Communication

1005 American Society of Landscape Architects: Michigan Chapter
1000 W St Joseph Highway 517-485-4116
Suite 200 Fax: 517-485-9408
Lansing, MI 48915 manager@michiganasla.org
www.michiganasla.org
The Michigan Chapter of the American Society of Landscape Architects (MiASLA), is a nonprofit association representing the landscape architecture profession throughout the state of Michigan. Through advocacy, education, communicationand fellowship, the MiASLA promotes and advances the profession of landscape architecture.
330 Members
Ben Baker, President
Dana Hernalsteen, VP, Membership

1006 B.A.S.S Nation: Michigan Chapter
MI 248-909-5750
webtech@michiganbass.net
www.michiganbassnation.com
Dedicated to the promotion of the sport of bass fishing.The Michigan BASS Nation is focused on building youth programs, fishing tournaments and conservation initiatives to preserve the states natural resources.
Founded: 1973 600 Members
Paul Rambo, President
Jason Hurst, Director, Membership

1007 Ecology Center
339 E Liberty Street 734-663-2400
Suite 300 info@ecocenter.org
Ann Arbor, MI 48104 www.ecocenter.org
Through education, the Ecology Center educates consumers, advocates for clean energy and provides services in the promotion of an environment, food and products that are safe and healthy.
Founded: 1970
Katy Adams, Education Director
Mike Garfield, Director

1008 Great Lakes Commission
Eisenhower Corporate Park
2805 S Industrial Highway 734-971-9135
Suite 100 Fax: 734-971-9150
Ann Arbor, MI 48104-6791 www.glc.org
A binational public agency dedicated to the use, management and protection of the water, land and other natural resources of the Great Lakes-St Lawrence system.
Founded: 1955
Jon W. Allan, Chair
John Linc Stine, Vice Chair

1009 Great Lakes Renewable Energy Association
MI 313-655-7945
info@glrea.org
www.glrea.org

The Great Lakes Renewable Energy Association (GLREA), is a nonprofit member association that represents individuals, organizations, and businesses that support the use and expansion of clean and renewable energy, such as wind and solarin Michigan. GLREA uses education, training and advocacy to promote the increased use of renewable energy.
Founded: 1991
Dave Konkle, President
Sarah Mulkoff, VP

1010 Michigan Association of Conservation Districts
3001 Coolidge Road
Suite 250
East Lansing, MI 48823
517-324-5274
Fax: 517-324-4435
lori.phalen@macd.org
www.macd.org
A nonprofit, non-governmental organization the Michigan Association of Conservation Districts (MACD) represents and provides services to Michigan's 78 Conservation Districts. Working at a state level with legislators, agencies andspecial interest groups, MACD advocates for the management and conservation of the states natural resources.
Lori Phalen, Executive Director
Angela Sandusky, Coordinator

1011 Michigan Forest Association
15851 S US 27
Suite 16
Lansing, MI 48906-1987
517-816-7879
info@michiganforests.org
www.michiganforests.org
The Michigan Forest Association (MFA) is a nonprofit organization that represents and educates Michigan forest owners and citizens about forest management and sustainability.
Founded: 1972
Debra Huff, Executive Director
Lisa Parker, Associate Director

1012 Michigan United Conservation Clubs
2101 Wood Street
Lansing, MI 48912
517-371-1041
muccpolicy@mucc.org
www.mucc.org
The largest statewide conservation organization in the United States, Michigan United Conservation Clubs, is a nonprofit working to conserve Michigan's natural resources and outdoor heritage. Through its membership of over 40,000hunters, anglers, conservationists and 200 local clubs, Michigan United Conservation Clubs uses advocacy, education and on the ground work to conserve, protect, and enhance Michigan's natural resources.
Founded: 1937
Ron Burris, President
Dan Eichinger, Executive Director

1013 Midwest Association of Fish & Wildlife Agencies
PO Box 30028
Lansing, MI 48909
517-284-6367
www.mafwa.org
The Midwest Association of Fish & Wildlife Agencies (MAFWA) is an organization made up of 13 state and 3 Midwest fish and wildlife agencies. MAFWA works to provide a forum for the exchange of information and ideas and initiate actionto protect and conserve fish and wildlife resources of the Midwest.
Founded: 1934
Jim Douglas, President
Terry Steinwand, First VP

1014 National Wildlife Federation: Great Lakes Regional Center
213 W Liberty
Suite 200
Ann Arbor, MI 48104
734-769-3351
greatlakes@nwf.org
www.nwf.org/greatlakes
The Great Lakes Regional Center of the National Wildlife Federation works to protect and restore the Great Lakes for the people and wildlife dependant upon them.
Founded: 1982
Anna Brunner, Communications Coordinator
Mike Shriberg, Regional Executive Director

1015 Scenic Michigan
445 E Mitchell Street
Petoskey, MI 49770
231-347-4929
Fax: 231-347-1185
info@scenicmichigan.org
www.scenicmichigan.org
The state affiliate of Scenic America, Scenic Michigan works to preserve and enhance the aesthetic amenities of the state. Primarily a grassroots organization, Scenic Michigan uses education, legislature and lobbying to improvecommunity appeareance.
Founded: 1996
Abby Dart, Executive Director
Jim Lagowski, President

1016 Sierra Club: Michigan Chapter
109 E Grand River Avenue
Lansing, MI 48906-4348
517-484-2372
Contact.Us@michigan.sierraclub.org
www.michigan.sierraclub.org
With 10 regional volunteer groups and conservation committees, the Michigan Chapter of the Sierra Club is dedicated to the promotion of better environmental stewardship in the state. The Michigan Chapter is focused on the longevity ofnatural resources and works to preserve and enhance the quality of water and air in Michigan communities and promotes the use of renewable energy sources.
Founded: 1967 150,000 Members
Cecilla J. Garcia, Administrative Assitant
Gail Philbin, State Director

1017 The Nature Conservancy: Michigan Chapter
101 East Grand River Avenue
Lansing, MI 48906
517-316-0300
Fax: 517-316-9886
michigan@tnc.org
www.nature.org/michigan
The Michigan Chapter of the Nature Conservancy is dedicated to protecting the land and water, including the Great Lakes, of the state. Through the development of broad and innovative strategies that can be applied to large naturalenvironment systems, the Michigan Chapter has been able to put these strategies into effect throughout the 20 nature preserves the chapter manages.
Founded: 1952
Danielle Basgall, Conservation Coordinator
Sharon Mascola, Office Manager

1018 The Wildlife Society: Michigan Chapter
MI
www.michigantws.wixsite.com/mitws
The state chapter of The Wildlife Society, it works to promote the sound stewardship of Michigan's wildlife and environmental resources and increase the appreciation of wildlife.
Founded: 1982
Lori Sargent, Secretary & Treasurer
Sonja Christensen, President

1019 Wildflower Association of Michigan
Lansing, MI
www.wildflowersmich.org
The Wildflower Association of Michigan (WAM) is a nonprofit, membership based organization that encourages the preservation and restoration of Michigan's native plants through advocacy and the education of Michigan's citizens.
Founded: 1986
Chad Hughson, President
Trish Hacker-Hennig, 1st Vice President

Minnesota

1020 American Fisheries Society: North Central Division: Minnesota Chapter
MN
pgafs2012@gmail.com
www.mnafs.org
The Minnesota Chapter of the American Fisheries Society (MNAFS), is part of the American Fisheries Society (AFS) North Central Division. Working to further to the goals of the AFS through research, education, and professionaldevelopment, the chapter is committed to the conservation, development, and wise use of fishery resources, and protection and sustainability of aquatic ecosystems.
Founded: 1967 $10/ Year
Paul Glander, President
Calub Shavlik, Secretary & Treasurer

1021 American Lung Association in Minnesota
490 Concordia Avenue 651-227-8014
Saint Paul, MN 55103 info@lungmn.org
www.lung.org/about-us/local-associations/minnesota.html
The American Lung Association of Minnesota works to prevent lung disease and promote lung health. Through education, advocacy,and campaigns, such as Teens Against Tobacco Use (TATU); the Association offers a wide variety of lung healthservices to the people Minnesota.
Lewis Bartfield, Executive VP, Upper Midwest
Greg Voss, Executive Dir. Minnesota

1022 American Lung Association of Minnesota: Duluth
424 W Superior Street 218-726-4721
Suite 202 info@lungmn.org
Duluth, MN 55802 www.lung.org/about-us/local-associations/minnesota.html
Lewis Bartfield, Executive VP, Upper Midwest
Greg Voss, Executive Dir. Minnesota

1023 American Society of Landscape Architects: Minnesota Chapter
International Market Square
275 Market Street 612-339-0797
Suite 54 Fax: 612-338-7981
Minneapolis, MN 55405-1627 info@asla-mn.org
www.asla-mn.org
The Minnesota Chapter of the American Society of Landscape Architects (ASLA-MN) represents over 300 landscape architects and affiliates across the state, who are dedicated to the promotion of the landscape profession through advocacy,education and communication.
David Motzenbecker, President
Nicole Peterson, Director, Communications

1024 B.A.S.S Nation: Minnesota Chapter
MN 55349 218-390-9973
dpirila@mnbfn.org
www.mnbfn.org
Minnesota BASS Nation works to stimulate public awareness of bass fishing as a major sport and encourages sportsmanship, courtesy and boating safety at all levels. Minnesota BASS Nation promotes the full adherence to all conservationcodes, adequate water quality standards and legal enforcement of existing regulatory standards.
Peter Perovich, President
Mark Gomez, VP

1025 Institute for Agriculture and Trade Policy
2105 1st Avenue South 612-870-0453
Minneapolis, MN 55404 Fax: 612-870-4846
iatp@iatp.org
www.iatp.org
Promotes resilient family farms, rural communitites and ecosystems around the world through research and education, science and technology, and advocacy.
Founded: 1987
Juliette Majot, Executive Director
Josh Wise, Director, Development

1026 Minnesota Association of Soil and Water Conservation Districts
Soil and Water Conservation Districts
255 Kellogg Boulevard East 651-690-9028
Suite 101 Fax: 651-690-9065
St. Paul, MN 55101 www.maswcd.org
The Minnesota Association of Soil and Water Conservation Districts (MASWCD) is a nonprofit organization representing Minnesota soil and water conservation districts. MASWCD is committed to maintaining a positive, results-oriented relationship with rulemaking agencies,partners and legislators; expanding education opportunities for the districts so they may carry out effective conservation programs.
Founded: 1952
LeAnn Buck, Executive Director
Sheila Vanney, Assitant Director

1027 Minnesota Conservation Federation
542 Snelling Avenue 651-690-3077
#104 info@mncf.org
Saint Paul, MN 55116 www.mncf.org
The Minnesota Conservation Federation (MCF) is an organization of dedicated hunters, anglers and other environmentally conscious individuals, working to educate and promote the enjoyment of, and ethical use of Minnesota's naturalresources. The MCF is an affiliate of the National Wildlife Federation.
Joe Hoffmann, President
Gary Botzek, Executive Director

1028 Minnesota Ground Water Association
4779 126th Street N
White Bear Lake, MN 55110 office@mgwa.org
www.mgwa.org
The Minnesota Ground Water Association (MGWA) is a non-profit, volunteer organization dedicated to the promotion and encouragement of scientific and public policy regarding ground water. MGWA provides a forum for ground waterprofessionals and educates the public about ground water.
Founded: 1982
Ellen Considine, President
Andrew Retzler, Secretary

1029 Minnesota Renewable Energy Society
2928 5th Avenue South 612-308-4757
Minneapolis, MN 55408 info@mnRenewables.org
www.mnrenewables.org
A nonprofit, member-run organization the Minnesota Renewable Energy Society (MRES) promotes, advocates and encourages the use of renewable energy in Minnesota.
Founded: 1978
Kitty (Kitrina) Stratton, Director
Mark Weber, Director

1030 Parks and Trails Council of Minnesota
275 E 4th Street 651-726-2457
Suite 250 800-944-0707
St. Paul, MN 55101-1626 Fax: 651-726-2458
info@parksandtrails.org
www.parksandtrails.org
Parks and Trails Council of Minnesota seeks to aquire, protect andsustain long-term statewide land.
Founded: 1954
Julie Gugin, President
Bob Biersheid, Vice President

1031 Raptor Center
University Of Minnesota
College of Veterinary Medicine 612-624-4745
1920 Fitch Avenue Fax: 612-624-8740
St.Paul, MN 55108 raptor@umn.edu
www.raptor.cvm.umn.edu

Specializes in the medical care, rehabilitation, and conservation of eagles, hawks, owls and falcons. In addition to treating approximately 800 birds a year, the internationally known program reaches more than 240,000 people each yearthrough public education programs and events, provides training in avian medicine and surgery for veterinarians from around the world, and identifies emerging issues related to raptor health and populations.
Founded: 1974
Dr Julia Ponder, Executive Director
Lori Arent, Clinic Manager

1032 Sierra Club: North Star Chapter
2327 East Franklin Avenue 612-659-9124
Suite 1 Fax: 612-659-9129
Minneapolis, MN 55406-1024 north.star.chapter@sierraclub.org
www.sierraclub.org/minnesota

In conjunction with the national mission of the Sierra Club, the North Star Chapter is the leading volunteer organizations working to protect and preserve Minnesota's environment.
Margaret Levin, State Director
Alexis Boxer, Associate Organizing Rep.

1033 The Nature Conservancy: Minnesota Chapter
1101 West River Parkway 612-331-0750
Suite 200 Fax: 612-331-0770
Minneapolis, MN 55415-1291 minnesota@tnc.org
www.nature.org/minnesota

The Minnesota Chapter of The Nature Conservancy uses science to implement effective environmental strategies in order to protect and conserve the over 50 nature preserves in the state.
Founded: 1958
Wendy Bennet, Chair
Jack Dempsey, Vice Chair

1034 The Nature Conservancy: Minnesota Chapter: Central Minnesota
7163 Bear Road 218-575-3032
Cushing, MN 56443-1291 Fax: 218-212-1320
minnesota@tnc.org
www.nature.org/minnesota

Wendy Bennet, Chair
Jack Dempsey, Vice Chair

1035 The Nature Conservancy: Minnesota Chapter: Mississippi River
PO Box 422 612-867-3140
Brainerd, MN 56401-1291 minnesota@tnc.org
www.nature.org/minnesota

Wendy Bennet, Chair
Jack Dempsey, Vice Chair

1036 The Nature Conservancy: Minnesota Chapter: Northeast Minnesota
394 Lake Avenue S 218-727-6119
Suite 308 Fax: 218-727-0882
Duluth, MN 55802-1291 minnesota@tnc.org
www.nature.org/minnesota

Wendy Bennet, Chair
Jack Dempsey, Vice Chair

1037 The Nature Conservancy: Minnesota Chapter: Tallgrass Aspen Parkland
202 N Main Street 218-436-3455
PO Box 139 Fax: 218-436-3454
Karlstad, MN 56732 minnesota@tnc.org
www.nature.org/minnesota

Wendy Bennet, Chair
Jack Dempsey, Vice Chair

1038 The Nature Conservancy: Minnesota Chapter:Northern Tallgrass Prairie Ecoregion
15337 28th Avenue S 218-498-2679
Glyndon, MN 56547-9561 Fax: 218-498-2325
minnesota@tnc.org
www.nature.org/minnesota

Wendy Bennet, Chair
Jack Dempsey, Vice Chair

Mississippi

1039 American Lung Association of Mississippi
438 Kathrine Drive 601-206-5810
Suite C alams@lungse.org
Flowood, MS 39232
www.lung.org/about-us/local-associations/mississippi.html
The American Lung Association of Mississippi works to prevent lung disease and promote lung health through direct assistance, education programs, advocacy and research.
Martha C. Bogdan, Executive VP, Southeast
Willie L. Bythwood, Jr, CFO

1040 American Lung Association of Mississippi: Bay St. Louis
7060 Stennis Airport Road 228-282-2622
Kiln, MS 39556 alams@lungse.org
www.lung.org/about-us/local-associations/mississippi.html
Martha C. Bogdan, Executive VP, Southeast
Willie L. Bythwood, Jr, CFO

1041 American Lung Association of Mississippi: Biloxi
1141 Bayview Avenue 228-282-2622
Biloxi, MS 39530 alams@lungse.org
www.lung.org/about-us/local-associations/mississippi.html
Martha C. Bogdan, Executive VP, Southeast
Willie L. Bythwood, Jr, CFO

1042 American Lung Association of Mississippi: Pascagoula
4502 Lt. Eugene J Manure Drive 678-478-0314
Pascagoula, MS 39581 alams@lungse.org
www.lung.org/about-us/local-associations/mississippi.html
Martha C. Bogdan, Executive VP, Southeast
Willie L. Bythwood, Jr, CFO

1043 American Society of Landscape Architects: Mississippi Chapter
MS
ahoops601@gmail.com
www.msasla.wordpress.com

The Mississippi Chapter of the American Society of Landscape Architects, is a nonprofit association representing the landscape architecture profession throughout the state of Mississippi.
Jim Jackson, President
Alan Hoops, Advocacy Chair

1044 Mississippi Flyway
MI
www.mississippi.flyways.us

The Mississippi Flyway Council works to coordinate the management of migratory game birds and their resources to ensure longevity. The Council is composed of representatives from Alabama, Arkansas, Indiana, Illinois, Iowa, Kentucky, Louisiana, Michigan, Minnesota, Mississippi, Missouri, Ohio, Tennessee, and Wisconsin, and the Canadian provinces of Saskatchewan, Manitoba and Ontario.
Founded: 1952
Ed Penny, Mississippi Representative

1045 **Mississippi Wildlife Federation**
517 Cobblestone Court 601-605-1790
Suite 2 Fax: 601-605-1794
Madison, MS 39110-7570 www.mswildlife.org
The Mississippi Wildlife Federation works to advance the protection of wildlife in Mississippi, the conservation of natural resources and the environmental quality of hunting, fishing and outdoor recreation.
Founded: 1946
Brad Young, Executive Director
Melanie Starnes, Office Manager

1046 **Sierra Club: Mississippi Chapter**
921 North Congress Street 601-624-3503
Jackson, MS 39202 louie.miller@sierraclub.org
mississippi.sierraclub.org
The Mississippi Chapter of the Sierra Club is comprised of three regional groups. The Chapter works in coordination with the mission of the National Sierra Club to protect and conserve the natural resources of Mississippi.
Louie Miller, State Director

1047 **The Crosby Arboretum**
P.O. Box 1639 601-799-2311
Picayune, MS 39466 Fax: 601-799-2372
drackett@ext.msstate.edu
www.crosbyarboretum.msstate.edu
Owned by Mississippi State University and operated the MSU Extension Service, The Crosby Arboretum is dedicated to education the public about the environment they live in. The Arboretum preserves, protects and displays plants native tothe Pearl River Drainage Basin ecosystem of Mississippi and Louisiana, providing research opportunities and offering cultural, scientific and recreational programs.
Founded: 1986
Patricia Drackett, Director
Kimberly Johnson, Customer Service

Missouri

1048 **American Fisheries Society: North Central Division: Missouri Chapter**
MO
gregndonna8286@gmail.com
www.moafs.org
The Missouri Chapter of the American Fisheries Society (MOAFS), is part of the AFS' North Central Division. MOAFS works to further to the goals of the AFS and is committed to the conservation, development, and wise use of fisheryresources and the distribution and exchange of information pertaining to aquatic sciences.
Greg Pitchford, President
Alex Prentice, Treasurer

1049 **American Lung Association of Missouri**
7745 Carondelet Avenue 314-645-5505
Suite 305 missouri@lung.org
Clayton, MO 63105-3196
http://www.lung.org/about-us/local-associations/missouri.html
The American Lung Association of Missouri works to prevent lung disease and promote lung health through direct assistance, education programs, advocacy and research.
Angela Wiseman, Executive Director, Missouri
Lewis Bartfield, Executive VP, Upper Midwest

1050 **American Society of Landscape Architects: Prairie Gateway Chapter**
Center for Architecture & Design:c/O PGASLA
1801 McGee Street 816-421-1054
Suite 100 president@pgasla.org
Kansas City, MO 64108 www.pgasla.org
The Prairie Gateway Chapter of The American Society of Landscape Architects (PGASLA) represents those in the landscape architecture profession throughout Kansas and Western Missouri. The PGASLA is dedicated to the promotion of thelandscape architecture profession through advocacy, education and communication with its members working to enhance natural and built environments.
Christopher Cline, President
Chad Weinand, VP, Communications

1051 **American Society of Landscape Architects: St. Louis Chapter**
St. Louis, MO 63105 314-206-4313
exdir@stlouisasla.org
www.stlouisasla.org
The St. Louis Chapter of the American Society of Landscape Architects represents the eastern half of Missouri. Through advocacy, education and communication the chapter is dedicated to the promotion of the landscape architectureprofession in the St. Louis region.
Cory Murner, President
Chris Sanders, VP, Membership

1052 **Audubon Society of Missouri**
2101 W Broadway
PO Box 122 webmaster@mobirds.org
Columbia, MO 65203-1261 www.mobirds.org
The Audubon Society of Missouri is dedicated to the preservation and protection of birds and other wildlife; to education and appreciation of the natural world; and to effective wildlife and habitat conservation practices.
Founded: 1990
Mark Haas, President
Bill Eddelman, VP

1053 **Missouri Forest Products Association**
505 East State Street 573-634-3252
Jefferson City, MO 65101 laura@moforest.org
www.moforest.org
The Missouri Forest Products Association (MFA) serves and promotes the forest products industry in the state, advocating for the sustainable management of Missouri's forests. The MFA represents the primary and secondary wood industry,suppliers and service industries, loggers, and landowners.
Founded: 1970 300 Members
Brian Brookshire, Executive Director
Laura Brookshire, Communications Manager

1054 **Missouri Prairie Foundation**
PO Box 200
Columbia, MO 65205 888-843-6739
info@moprairie.com
www.moprairie.org
A nonprofit organization dedicated to the permanent protection of prairie habitat. The Missouri Prairie Foundation works with public and private partners to protect and restore prairie and native grassland communities through landacquisition, management, education and research.
Founded: 1966
Carol Davit, Executive Director
Dorris Sherrick, President

1055 **Missouri Public Interest Research Group**
10 S Euclid Ave 314-454-1713
Suite H info@mopirg.org
Saint Louis, MO 63108 www.mopirg.org
The Missouri Public Interest Research Group (MoPIRG) is a statewide, nonprofit, public interest advocacy organization that uses investigative research, media exposes, grassroots organization and litigation to inform, represent andeducate the public. MoPIRG focuses primarily on environmental, health, safety, financial and consumer protection.
Founded: 1972
Kathryn Lee, Digital Campaigner
Ed Mierzwinski, Consumer Program Director

1056 **Missouri Stream Team**
2901 W Truman Boluevard
Jefferson City, MO 65109 800-781-1989
streamteam@mdc.mo.gov
www.mostreamteam.org
Part of the Missouri Department of Conservation, the Missouri Stream Team endeavours to conserve the 110,000 miles of Missouri's streams through education, stewardship and advocacy. By partnering with citizens, the Stream Team is ableto execute campaigns and on the ground action work to protect Missouri's streams and watersheds.
Founded: 1989
Chris Riggert, Stream Team, Coordinator
Sherry Fischer, Streams & Watershed Chief

1057 **Scenic Missouri**
607 Dougherty Terrace Drive
Ballwin, MO 63021 info@scenicmo.org
scenicmo.org
Scenic Missouri is a statewide, nonprofit dedicated to protecting, preserving and enhancing the scenic character of the state. Scenic Missouri provides education and technical services to communities throughout the state to assist inaesthetic issues.
John Hock, President
Karl Kruse, Director, Emeritus

1058 **Sierra Club: Missouri Chapter**
2818 Sutton Boulevard 314-644-1011
St. Louis, MO 63143 800-628-5333
missouri.chapter@sierraclub.org
missouri.sierraclub.org
To advance the preservation and protection of the natural environment by empowering the citizenry with charitable resources to further the cause of environmental protection.
Jim Turner, Chair
Carolyn Amparan, Vice Chair

1059 **Society for Environmental Geochemistry and Health**
MO 573-341-4831
Fax: 303-556-4822
seghwebmaster@gmail.com
www.segh.net
The Society for Environmental Geochemistry and Health (SEGH) provides a forum for scientists from various disciplines, to work together in order to understand the interaction between the geochemical environment and the health ofplants, animals, and humans.
Founded: 1971
Chaosheng Zhang, President
Anthea Brown, Treasurer

Montana

1060 **American Lung Association of Montana**
936 S 2nd Street West 406-214-5700
Missoula, MT 59801 ronni.flannery@lung.org
www.lung.org/about-us/local-associations/montana.html
The American Lung Association of Montana works to prevent lung disease and promote lung health through direct assistance, education programs, advocacy and research.
Allison Hickey, Exec. VP, Mountain Pacific
Tony Peterson, CFO

1061 **Chemical Injury Information Network**
PO Box 301 406-547-2255
White Sulphur Springs, MT 59645 Fax: 406-547-2455
chemicalinjury@ciin.org
www.ciin.org
A nonprofit support and advocacy organization, the Chemical Injury Information Network (CIIN) deals with Multiple Chemical Sensitivities (MCS). CIIN is run by the chemically injured for the benefit of the chemically injured andprimarily focuses on education, research and support of the chemically injured.
Founded: 1990

1062 **Craighead Institute**
201 S Wallace Avenue 405-585-8705
Suite B2D info@craigheadresearch.org
Bozeman, MT 59715 craigheadresearch.org
The Craighead Institute, formerly Craighead Environmental Research Institute, is an applied science and research organization dedicated to the designing and managing research projects to help conserve the Northern Rockies.
Founded: 1964
Frank Lance Craighead, PhD, Executive Director
Brent Brock, Research Associate

1063 **Foundation for Research on Economics & the Environment (FREE)**
PO Box 555 406-585-1776
Gallatin Gateway, MT 59730 www.free-eco.org
FREE mission is to advance conservation and environmental values consistent with individuals freedom and responsibility. The Foundation's intellectual entrepreneurs develop environmental policies featuring private property rights,market incentives, and voluntary organizations. FREE achieves its mission by working with leaders in universities, businesses, environmental groups, government, the media, and think tanks.
John A. Baden, Chairman
John A. Von Kannon, VP

1064 **Greater Yellowstone Coalition**
215 South Wallace Avenue 406-586-1593
Bozeman, MT 59715 800-775-1834
Fax: 406-556-2839
gyc@greateryellowstone.org
www.greateryellowstone.org
The Greater Yellowstone Coalition works to permanently protect the 4.5 million acres in the Greater Yellowstone Ecosystem. With offices in Montana, Wyoming and Idaho, the Greater Yellowstone Coalition engages in local, regional andnational efforts to protect the land, water, and wildlife found within the Greater Yellowstone Ecosystem.
Founded: 1983
Caroline Byrd, Executive Director
Scott Christensen, Director, Conservation

1065 **Montana Association of Conservation Districts**
1101 11th Avenue 406-443-5711
Helena, MT 59601 Fax: 406-443-0174
mail@macdnet.org
www.macdnet.org

The Montana Association of Conservation Districts represents the 58 conservation districts of the state. The Association works to protect the natural resources of the state, conserve soil and improve the water quality of Montana. TheMontana Association of Conservation Districts works with the National Association of Conservation Districts to advocate legislature on a federal and congressional level.
Founded: 1942
Elena Evansm, Executive Director
Jeff Tiberi, Director, Policy

1066 Montana Audubon
PO Box 595 406-443-3949
Helena, MT 59624 Fax: 406-443-7144
mtaudubon@mtaudubon.org
www.mtaudubon.org
The Montana Audubon is nonprofit organization, with 9 chapters throughout the state. Through public policy and education program the Montana Audubon is dedicated to the appreciation, knowledge, and conservation of Montana's nativebirds and wildlife.
Founded: 1976
Norane Freistadt, Interim Director
Janet Johnston, Office Manager

1067 Montana Environmental Information Center
107 W Lawrence St #N-6 406-443-2520
Helena, MT 59601 Fax: 406-443-2507
meic@meic.org
www.meic.org
The Montana Environmental Information Center (MEIC) is a nonprofit, environmental advocacy organization dedicated to protectionn and restoration of Montana's natural environment. MEIC works to monitor and contribute to theenvironmental decisions and activities of the government on a state, local and federal level, educate individuals and assist individuals and other nonprofit organizations in the conservation of Montana's natural environment.
5,000 Members
Jim Jensen, Executive Director
Sara Marino, Director, Development

1068 Montana Land Reliance
324 Fuller Avenue 406-443-7027
PO Box 355 Fax: 406-443-7061
Helena, MT 59624-0355 info@mtlandreliance.org
www.mtlandreliance.org
Working with private landowners, the Montana Land Reliance (MLR) is dedicated to the permanent protection of Montana's agricultural lands, fish, wildlife and open space. The MLR has conserved over 958, 000 acres of land in over 820voluntary easement agreements across the state.
Founded: 1978
Rock Ringling, Managing Director
Lois Delger-DeMars, Managing Director

1069 Montana Wildlife Federation
PO Box 1175 406-458-0227
Helena, MT 59601 800-517-7256
Fax: 406-458-0373
mwf@mtwf.org
www.montanawildlife.com
The Montana Wildlife Federation (MWF), is the oldest and largest conservation organization in the state. Comprised of state and national members, including 15 local affiliate clubs, the MWF is committed to the conservation of Montana'swild rivers, natural lands, fish, wildlife and public access outdoor recreation land.
Founded: 1936
Dave Chadwick, Executive Director
Nick Gevock, Director, Conservation

1070 Rocky Mountain Elk Foundation
5705 Grant Creek 406-523-4500
PO Box 8249 800-225-5355
Missoula, MT 59808 www.rmef.org
Committed to conserving, restoring and enhancing natural habitats; promoting the sound management of wild, free-ranging elk, which may be hunted or otherwise enjoyed; fostering cooperation among federal, state, tribal and privateorganizations and individuals in wildlife management and habitat conservation; and educating members and the public about habitat conservation, the value of hunting, hunting ethics and wildlife management.
Founded: 1984
M David Allen, President & CEO
Rod Triepke, COO

1071 Sierra Club: Montana Chapter
PO Box 7201 406-549-1142
Missoula, MT 59807 sierraclubmt@gmail.com
montana.sierraclub.org
The Montana Chapter of the Sierra Club is made up of 4 local groups in Missoula, Bozeman, Helena and Billings. The Chapter works in conjunction with the Sierra Club's national efforts and is committed to addressing the environmentalissues of the state.
Jonathan Matthews, Chair
David Merrill, Senior Organizing

1072 The Wildlife Society: Montana Chapter
MT
mttws.secretary@gmail.com
www.wildlife.org/montana-chapter
The Montana Chapter of The Wildlife Society works to serve and represent wildlife life professionals in all areas of wildlife conservation and management in the state of Montana.
Founded: 1962
Kelvin Johnson, President
Dan Bachen, Secretary

Nebraska

1073 American Fisheries Society: North Central Division: Nebraska Chapter
NE
mike.archer@Nebraska.gov
www.nebraskaafs.org
The Nebraska Chapter of the American Fisheries Society, is part of the American Fisheries Society (AFS) North Central Division, it is a professional organization with its members coming from diverse fishery backgrounds. Working tofurther to the goals of the AFS through research, education, and professional development, the chapter is committed to the conservation, development, and wise use of fishery resources, and protection and sustainability of aquatic ecosystems.
Founded: 1970 $10/ Year
Mike Archerr, President
Dave Adams, Secretary & Treasurer

1074 American Lung Association of Nebraska
8990 West Dodge 402-502-4950
Suite 226 info@lungnb.org
Omaha, NE 68114 www.lung.org/about-us/local-associations/nebraska.html
The American Lung Association of Nebraska works to prevent lung disease and promote lung health through direct assistance, education programs, advocacy and research.
Julia McCarville, Executive Director, Nebraska
Lewis Bartfield, Executive VP, Upper Midwest

1075 American Society of Landscape Architects: Great Plains Chapter
NE
Regan.Pence@LRA-INC.com
www.gpcasla.org

Representing Nebraska, North Dakota and South Dakota, the Great Plains Chapter of the American Landscape Society works to expand the profession of landscape architecture in these states. The Chapter advocates and provides professionaleducational and developmental programs for its members
Regan Pence, President
Chad Kucker, Secretary & Treasurer

1076 B.A.S.S Nation: Nebraska Chapter
NE 402-563-2297
jlcitta@nppd.com
www.nebraskabass.com
Dedicated to the promotion of the sport of bass fishing. The Nebraska Chapter of BASS Nation also known as Nebraska BASS federation, is focused on building youth programs, fishing tournaments and conservation initiatives to preservethe states natural resources.
Joe Citta Jr., President
Dave Knuth, Vice President

1077 Nebraska Association of Resource Districts
601 S 12th Street 402-471-7670
Suite 201 Fax: 402-471-7677
Lincoln, NE 68508 nard@nrdnet.org
www.nrdnet.org
The Nebraska Association of Resources Districts (NARD) is the trade association representing Nebraska's 23 Natural Resource Districts. NARD works to assist in the coordination of Nebraska's Natural Resource Districts, in order toprovide a collective voice for state and federal policies and to further enhance conservation and improvement efforts in the state.
Dean E. Edson, Executive Director
Jeanne Dryburgh, Office Manager

1078 Nebraska Wildlife Federation
PO Box 81437 402-477-1008
Lincoln, NE 68501 Info@NebraskaWildlife.org
www.nebraskawildlife.org
A statewide, nonprofit membership organization dedicated wildlife and wild places through environmental education, fish and wild life conservation, and public policy. The Nebraska Wildlife Federation is the state affiliate of TheNational Wildlife Federation.
J.J. Johnson, President
Duane Hovorka, Executive Director

1079 Sierra Club: Nebraska Chapter
PO Box 4664
Omaha, NE 68104-664 www.sierraclub.org/nebraska
The Nebraska Chapter of the Sierra Club is made up of the MoValley Group and Bluestem Group and is working in the state to fulfill the goals of the National Sierra Club.
3,000 Members
Candy Bless, Chapter Chair
David Corbin, Chapter Vice Chair

1080 The Nature Conservancy: Nebraska Chapter
1007 Leavenworth Street 402-342-0282
Omaha, NE 68102 Fax: 402-342-0474
nebraska@tnc.org
www.nature.org/nebraska
The Nebraska Chapter of The Nature Conservancy works to to preserve the plants, animals and natural communities of Nebraska by protecting the lands and waters needed to sustain these ecosystems.
Founded: 1915
Mace Hack, State Director
Katie Torpy Carroll, Operations Coordinator

1081 The Nature Conservancy: Nebraska Chapter: Derr House
13650 South Platte River Drive 308-583-2294
Wind River, NE 68883 Fax: 308-583-0102
nebraska@tnc.org
www.nature.org/nebraska
Nelson Winkle, Prserve Management Assistant
Mace Hack, State Director

1082 The Nature Conservancy: Nebraska Chapter: Eastern Nebraska Project Office
1228 L Street 402-694-4191
PO Box 438 Fax: 402-694-4191
Aurora, NE 68818 nebraska@tnc.org
www.nature.org/nebraska
Chris Helzer, Director, Science
Mardell Jasnowski, Operations Assistant

1083 The Nature Conservancy: Nebraska Chapter: Niobrara Valley Preserve
42269 Morel Road 402-722-4440
Johnstown, NE 69214 Fax: 402-722-4203
nebraska@tnc.org
www.nature.org/nebraska
Rich Walters, Jr., Director, Stewardship
Mace Hack, State Director

1084 The Nature Conservancy: Nebraska Chapter: Platte River Project Office
112 W 8th Street 308-784-5336
PO Box 144 Fax: 308-784-5326
Cozad, NE 69130 nebraska@tnc.org
www.nature.org/nebraska
Jacob Fritton, Irrigation Coordinator
Mace Hack, State Director

1085 The Wildlife Society: Nebraska Chapter
NE
matt.steffle@nebraska.gov
www.wildlife.org/nebraska
The Nebraska Chapter of the Wildlife Society (NE-TWS) is a professional organzation of biologists, educators, and administrators working in the field of wildlife management. NE-TWS is dedicated to the promotion of sound stewardship ofwildlife resource and habitats in Nebraska.
Founded: 1966
Matt Steffl, President
Melvin Nenneman, Secretary

Nevada

1086 American Lung Association of Nevada
3552 West Cheyenne Avenue 702-431-6333
Suite 130 nvinfo@lungs.org
Las Vegas, NV 89032-8920 www.lung.org/about-us/local-associations/nevada.html
The American Lung Association of Nevada works to prevent lung disease and promote lung health. Through direct assistance, advocacy and education programs, such as Addressing COPD in Nevada; the Association offers a wide variety of lunghealth services to the people Nevada.
Bill Pfeifer, Executive VP, Southwest
Kristina Crawford, Executive Director

1087 American Society of Landscape Architects: Nevada Chapter
PO Box 97986
Las Vegas, NV 89193 info@nvasla.com
www.nvasla.com

The Nevada Chapter of the American Society of Landscape Architects (NVASLA) is dedicated to the continuous education of its members and the public in the service of promoting sound stewardship of the environment.
Laura Miller, President
Nicole Hoffmann, Association Assitant

1088 Nevada Wildlife Federation
PO Box 71238
Reno, NV 89570
775-677-0927
Fax: 775-885-0405
nvwf@nvwf.org
www.nvwf.org

The Nevada Wildlife Federation (NvWF) is an all volunteer organization dedicated to sustaining Nevada's natural resources for the states wildlife. The NvWF is an affiliate of the National Wildlife Federation.
Robert Gaudet, President
Tammi Gaudet, Treasurer

1089 Sierra Club: Toiyabe Chapter
PO Box 8096
Reno, NV 89507
toiyabe.chapter@gmx.com
nevada.sierraclub.org

The Toiyabe Chapter of the Sierra Club is the largest grassroots conservation organization of the region. Made of the 4 local groups, the Great Basin Group, Range of Light Group, Southern Nevada Group and the Tahoe Area Group, theChapter is primarily focused on the conservation of water, public lands, and wilderness, the promotion of renewable energy and environmental legislation in Nevada.
David Von Seggern, Chapter Chair
David Gibson, Chapter Vice Chair

1090 Solar NV
817 S Main St
Las Vegas, NV 89101
Fax: 702-507-0093
contact@solarnv.org
www.solarnv.org

Solar NV is a nonprofit, volunteer organization dedicated to the promotion, education and use of solar and renewable energy in Nevada. Solar NV is the Southern Nevada chapter of the American Solar Energy Society.
Founded: 2004 $24/Year

1091 Sunrise Sustainable Resources Group
PO Box 19074
Reno, NV 89511
775-348-7192
president@sunrisenevada.org
www.sunrisenevada.org

Empowers Nevadans to use resources responsibly through education, advocacy and community.
Founded: 1996
KC Mares, President
Roger Jacobson, VP

1092 Tahoe Regional Planning Agency
128 Market Street
PO Box 5310
Stateline, NV 89449
775-588-4547
Fax: 775-588-4527
trpa@trpa.org
www.trpa.org

Tahoe Regional Planning Agency (TRPA) was the first bi-state environmental planning agency in the United States. Leading through cooperative efforts TRPA is dedicated to the preservation, restoration and the enhancement of the uniquenatural and human environments in the Lake Tahoe Region.
Joanne Marchetta, Executive Director
John Hester, COO

New Hampshire

1093 American Lung Association of New Hampshire
Cove Workspace
36 Maplewood Avenue
Portsmouth, NH 03801
603-369-3977
info@lungne.org
www.lung.org/about-us/local-associations/new-hampshire.html

The American Lung Association of New Hampshire works to prevent lung disease and promote lung health; offering a wide variety of lung health services to the people of New Hampshire.
Jeff Seyler, Executive VP, Northeast
Adam Shuster, CFO

1094 B.A.S.S Nation: New Hampshire Chapter
235 Ridgeview Road
Weare, NH 03281
603-529-2642
www.nhbassfednation.com

Dedicated to the promotion of the sport of bass fishing.The New Hampshire Chapter of BASS Nation is focused on building youth programs, fishing tournaments and conservation initiatives to preserve the states natural resources.
John Foster, President
Brian Emerson, Secretary & Webmaster

1095 Breathe New Hampshire
145 Hollis Street
Unit C
Manchester, NH 03101
603-669-2411
800-835-8647
Fax: 603-645-6220
info@breathenh.org
www.breathenh.org

A nonprofit organization, Breather New Hampshire, is dedicated to the elimination of lung disease and the improvement in the quality of life for those living with lung disease in the state. Through educational programs, advocacy, andresearch, Breathe New Hampshire is focused on the issues related to lung health, including tobacco use, COPD, asthma, air quality and lung cancer.
Founded: 1916
Daniel Fortin, President/CEO
Allyssa Thompson, Director, Programs

1096 New Hampshire Association of Conservation Commissions
54 Portsmouth Street
Concord, NH 03301
603-224-7867
Fax: 603-228-0423
info@nhacc.org
www.nhacc.org

The New Hampshire Association of Conservation Commissions is a private, nonprofit association of 216 Conservation Commissions. Its purpose is to foster conservation and appropriate use of New Hampshire's natural resources by providingassistance to conservation commissions, facilitating communication and cooperation among commissions, and helping to create a climate in which commissions can be successful.
Founded: 1970
Rep. Michele Peckham, President
Barbara Richter, Executive Director

1097 New Hampshire Association of Conservation Districts
PO Box 2311
Concord, NH 03302-2311
603-796-2615
Fax: 603-796-2600
nhenvirothon@gmail.com
www.nhacd.net

The New Hampshire Association of Conservation Districts (NHACD) works collaboratively with county districts, federal, state and local nonprofit agencies to conserve, protect and promote the responsible use of New Hampshire's naturalresources. The NHACD, provides statewide coordination and representation for the Conservation Districts of New Hampshire.
Founded: 1946
Sue Kessler, NH Envirothon Coordinator
Lisa M. Morin, Soil Judging Coordinator

1098 New Hampshire Audubon
84 Silk Farm Road
Concord, NH 03301
603-224-9909
Fax: 603-226-0902
nha@nhaudubon.org
www.nhaudubon.org

A statewide, nonprofit membership organization dedicated to the conservation of wildlife and habitat throughout the New Hampshire. The New Hampshire Audubon (NHA) offers environmental education, convservation, land protection andenviornmental policy programs. The NHA is independent of the National Audubon Society.

Founded: 1914
Doug Bechtel, President
Shelby Bernier, Director, Education

1099 New Hampshire Lakes Association
14 Horseshoe Pond Lane
Concord, NH 03301
603-226-0299
Fax: 603-224-9442
info@nhlakes.org
www.nhlakes.org

The New Hampshire Lake Association (NH LAKES) is a member supported, nonprofit organization dedicated to the protection of the states 1,000 lakes.

Founded: 1992
Tom O'Brien, President
Erin Grichen, Membership Coordinator

1100 New Hampshire Wildlife Federation
54 Portsmouth Street
Concord, NH 03301
603-224-5953
ed@nhwf.org
www.nhwf.org

Through education, legislation, conservation, community organizations and affiliates, the New Hampshire Wildlife Federation promotes and protects hunting, fishing, trapping and the conservation and access to fish and wildlife habitats.The New Hampshire Wildlife Federation is an affiliate of the National Wildlife Federation.

Founded: 1933
James Morse, President
Ron Sowa, Executive Director

1101 Northeast Resource Recovery Association
2101 Dover Road
Epsom, NH 03234
603-736-4401
800-223-0150
Fax: 603-736-4402
info@nrra.net
www.nrra.net

The Northeast Resource Recovery Association is a pro-active nonprofit working with its membership to make their recycling programs strong, efficient, and financially successful by providing cooperative marketing, cooperativepurchasing, education and networking opportunities; developing innovative recycling programs; creating sustainable alternatives to reduce the volume and toxicity of the waste, and educating and informing local officials about recycling and solidwaste issues.

Founded: 1981
Duncan P. Watson, President
John Hurd, Vice President

1102 The Nature Conservancy: New Hampshire Chapter
22 Bridge Street
4th Floor
Concord, NH 03301
603-224-5853
Fax: 603-228-2459
kelly.buchanan@tnc.org
www.nature.org/newhampshire

The New Hampshire Chapter of The Nature Conservancy, works to protect New Hampshire's lands and natural resources. Through science based projects and conservation efforts, the chapter protects 280,000 acres of the states naturalresources.

Founded: 1961
Mark Zankel, State Director
Kelly Buchanan, Operations Assistant

1103 The Nature Conservancy:New Hampshire Chapter:Great Bay Office
112 Bay Road
Newmarket, NH 03857
603-659-2678
Fax: 603-659-2729
kelly.buchanan@tnc.org
www.nature.org/newhampshire

Mark Zankel, State Director
Kelly Buchanan, Operations Assistant

1104 The Nature Conservancy:New Hampshire Chapter:Northern New Hampshire Office
24 Reporter Court, 2nd Floor
PO Box 310
North Conway, NH 03860
603-356-8833
Fax: 603-356-2434
kelly.buchanan@tnc.org
www.nature.org/newhampshire

Mark Zankel, State Director
Kelly Buchanan, Operations Assistant

New Jersey

1105 American Bass Association of Eastern Pennsylvania & New Jersey
NJ
abapanj@gmail.com
www.bestbassteams.com

The American Bass Association of PA & NJ is dedicated to the promotion of bass fishing as a major sport, to conserve the future of fishing through the protection and enhancement of fishery resources and to introduce fishing to Americanyouth.

Founded: 1974
Fred Eurick, President
Mark Dilatush, VP

1106 American Lung Association of New Jersey
PO Box 10188,37214
Newark, NJ 07101
908-685-8040
Klsky@lunginfo.org
www.lung.org/about-us/local-associations/new-jersey.html

The American Lung Association of New Jersey works to prevent lung disease and promote lung health; offering a wide variety of lung health services to the people of New Jersey.

Deborah Brown, Executive VP, Mid-Atlantic
Joy Meyer, VP, Community Impact

1107 American Society of Landscape Architects: New Jersey Chapter
414 River View Plaza
Trenton, NJ 08611-3420
609-393-7500
Fax: 609-393-9891
info@njasla.org
www.njasla.org

As the New Jersey Chapter of the American Society of Landscape Architects (NJASLA), it aims to lead, educate and participate in the careful stewardship, wise planning, and artful design of cultural and natural environments. The NJASLArepresents landscape architects from across the state and provides its members with networking, social and volunteer opportunities.

Founded: 1901
John M. Thomas, President

1108 Association of New Jersey Environmental Commissions
Morris County Cultural Center
300 Mendham Road
PO Box 157
Mendham, NJ 07945
973-539-7547
Fax: 973-539-7713
info@anjec.org
www.anjec.org

The Association of New Jersey Environmental Commissions (ANJEC) promotes the responsible and sustainable use of New

Jersey's natural resources and the protection of the states environmental health. ANJEC is a statewide, nonprofitorganization.
Jennifer M. Coffey, Executive Director
Elizabeth Ritter, Deputy Director

1109 B.A.S.S Nation: New Jersey Chapter
NJ
201-584-9387
rjrjob@verizon.net
www.njbassnation.org
The New Jersey BASS Nation is the state affiliate of BASS Nation, the New Jersey chapter works to provide an association between anglers for the advancement and promotion of sport bass fishing.
Founded: 1917
Randy Baran, President
Billy Tyger, Vice President

1110 Clean Ocean Action
18 Hartshorne Dr
Suite 2
Highlands, NJ 07732
732-872-0111
Fax: 732-872-8041
info@cleanoceanaction.org
www.cleanoceanaction.org
COA staff research pollution in the New York Bight then organize campaigns to clean up and protect the waters of the New York and New Jersey coasts.
Founded: 1984
Cindy Zipf, Executive Director

1111 Environmental and Occupational Health Science Institute
Rutgers University
170 Frelinghuysen Road
Piscataway, NJ 08854
848-445-0200
Fax: 732-445-0131
info@eohsi.rutgers.edu
eohsi.rutgers.edu
Sponsors research, education and service programs in a setting that fosters interaction among experts in environmental health, toxicology, occupational health, exposure assessment, public policy and health education. The Institute alsoserves as an unbiased source of expertise about environmental problems for communities, employers and government in all areas of occupational and environmental health, toxicology and risk assessment.
Kenneth Reuhl, Interim Director
Howard Kipen, Associate Director

1112 New Jersey Environmental Lobby
204 W State Street
Trenton, NJ 08608
njel@earthlink.net
The New Jersey Environmental Lobby (NJEL) is a nonpartisan, independent organization committed to lobbying on behalf of the environment. Primarily focused on environmental efforts in New Jersey, such as the expansion of mass transitand legislature for the control of single use plastic bags, the NJEL collaborates with other organizations to advocate and educate for the conservation of New Jersey's environment.
Founded: 1969
Anne O. Poole, President
Noemi de la Puente, Executive Director

1113 New Jersey Public Interest Research Group
104 Bayard St.
6th Floor
New Brunswick, NJ 08901
609-394-8155
info@njpirg.org
www.njpirg.org
The New Jersey Public Interest Research Group (NJPIRG) is a statewide, nonprofit, public interest advocacy organization that uses investigative research, media exposes, grassroots organization and litigation to inform, represent andeducate the public. NJPIRG focuses primarily on environmental, health, safety, financial and consumer protection.
Dan Xie, Organizing Director
Ed Mierzeinkski, Consumer Program Director

1114 New York/New Jersey Trail Conference
600 Ramapo Valley Road
Mahwah, NJ 07430-1199
201-512-9348
office@nynjtc.org
www.nynjtc.org
A federation of 104 hiking clubs and environmental organizations and 10,000 individuals dedicated to building and maintaining marked hiking trails and protecting related open spaces in the bi-state region.
Edward Goodell, Executive Director
Joshua Howard, Deputy Executive Director

1115 Passaic River Coalition
330 Speedwell Avenue
Morristown, NJ 07960
973-532-9830
Fax: 973-889-9172
www.passaicriver.org
A nonprofit organization, the Passaic River Coalition (PRC) is dedicated to the preservation and protection of the Passaic River and its watersheds. The PRC focuses on improvements in land-water resource management and public healthissues by advising citizens, environmental organizations, governments and businesses.
Founded: 1969
Laurie Howard, Chair
Russell Furnari, Treasurer

1116 Sierra Club: New Jersey Chapter
145 West Hanover Street
Trenton, NJ 08618
609-656-7612
Fax: 609-656-7618
jeff.tittel@SierraClub.org
newjersey.sierraclub.org
The New Jersey Chapter of the Sierra Club is comprised of 12 regional groups. The Chapter works in coordination with the mission of the National Sierra Club to protect and conserve the natural resources of New Jersey.
20,000 Members
Jeff Tittel, Senior Chapter Director
Toni Granato, Program Assistant

New Mexico

1117 American Lung Association of New Mexico
5911 Jefferson Stree NE
Albuquerque, NM 87109
800-586-4872
NMInfo@lungs.org
www.lung.org/about-us/local-associations/new-mexico.html
The American Lung Association of New Mexico works to prevent lung disease and promote lung health; offering a wide variety of lung health services to the people of New Mexico.
Terry Huertaz, Executive Director
Kathy Moseley, Program Manager

1118 American Society of Landscape Architects: New Mexico
NM
jlent@asla.org
www.nmasla.org
The New Mexico Chapter of the American Society of Landscape Architects (NMASLA), is a nonprofit association representing the landscape architecture profession throughout the state of New Mexico.
Julia Lent, Director, Chapter Services
Justin Weathermon, President

1119 Holistic Management International
5941 Jefferson Street NE
Suite B
Albuquerque, NM 87109
505-842-5252
Fax: 505-843-7900
hmi@holisticmanagement.org
www.holisticmanagement.org
Holistic Management International (HMI) helps communities to grow through the education of family farmers and ranchers. HMI focuses on regenerative agriculture to help enhance the effi-

ciency, natural health, productivity andprofitability of farm land and to help protect and improve local wildlife habitats.
Founded: 1984
Kelly Sidoryk, Board Chair
Ben Bartlett, Director

1120 New Mexico Association of Conservation Districts
163 Trail Canyon Road 505-981-2400
Carlsbad, NM 88220 Fax: 505-981-2400
conserve@hughes.net
www.nmacd.org
The New Mexico Association of Conservation Districts (NMACD), is a private nonprofit organization working with New Mexico Legislature, Congressional Delegations, and related governmental agencies to provide statewide coordination andrepresentation for the 48 Soil and Water Conservation Districts of New Mexico.
Founded: 1946
Debbie Hughes, Executive Director
Mary Lou Ballard, Executive Assistant

1121 New Mexico Rural Water Association
8336 Washington Place NE 505-884-1031
Albuquerque, NM 87113 800-819-9893
Fax: 505-884-1032
info@nmrwa.org
www.nmrwa.org
A state affiliate of the National Rural Water Association, the New Mexico Rural Water Association (NMRWA) is a nonprofit organization committed to ensuring communities have safe drinking water and wastewater services . NMRWA offerson-site technical assistance and specialized training.
Bill Conner, Executive Director
Jose E. Terrones, President

1122 New Mexico Solar Energy Association
PO Box 3434 505-246-0400
Albuquerque, NM 87190 info@NMSolar.org
www.nmsolar.org
New Mexico Solar Energy Association (NMSEA) is a nonprofit, educational organization. Made of up 7 regional chapters, the NMSEA promotes the use of clean and renewable energy and sustainability in New Mexico.
Founded: 1972
Jim DesJardins, Chapter Leader

1123 New Mexico Solar Energy Association: Alamgordo Chapter
Alamgordo, NM
ronnoffley@gmail.com
www.nmsolar.org/alamagordo/
Ron Offley, Chapter Leader

1124 New Mexico Solar Energy Association: Las Vegas Chapter
Las Vegas, NM
lgoding@hughes.net
www.nmsolar.org/las-vegas-chapter/
Also known as Sustainable Las Vegas
Lloyd Goding, Chapter Leader
Cheryl Zebrowski, Chapter Secretary

1125 New Mexico Solar Energy Association: Los Alamos Chapter
Los Alamos, NM
ekarenp@gmail.com
www.nmsolar.org/los-alamos-chapter/
Also known as the Los Alamos Sustainable Energy Network.
Karen Paramanandam, Chapter President

1126 New Mexico Solar Energy Association: Santa Fe Chapter
Santa Fe, NM
cjpavel@me.com
www.nmsolar.org/santa-fe-chapter
Claudia Pavel, Chapter Contact

1127 New Mexico Solar Energy Association: Silver City Chapter
Silver City, NM
laimansmith@gmail.com
www.nmsolar.org/silver-city-chapter
Lydia Aiman-Smith, Chapter Co-President
Mike Sauber, Chapter Co-President

1128 New Mexico Solar Energy Association: Taps Chapter
Taos, NM 575-758-5338
greenbuilderstaos@gmail.com
www.nmsolar.org/taos-chapter
Scott Evans, Chapter President

1129 Sierra Club: Rio Grande Chapter
142 Truman NE 505-243-7767
Albuquerque, NM 87108 Fax: 505-243-7771
daniel.lorimier@sierraclub.org
nmsierraclub.org
To advance the preservation and protection of the natural environment by empowering the citizenry with charitable resources to further the cause of environmental protection.
Founded: 1892
John Buchser, Chair
Norma McCallan, Vice Chair

1130 The Nature Conservancy: New Mexico Chapter
212 E Marcy Street 505-988-3867
Santa Fe, NM 87501 Fax: 505-988-4095
nm@tnc.org
www.nature.org
The New Mexico Chapter of The Nature Conservancy, works to protect New Mexico's land, water and wildlife. The New Mexico Chapter protects more than 1.4 million acres of land, including 6 nature preserves.
Founded: 1951
Priscilla Ornelas, Director, Operations
Terry Sullivan, State Director

1131 The Wildlife Society: New Mexico Chapter
NM
twsnewmexico@gmail.com
www.wildlife.org/nm-chapter/
The New Chapter of The Wildlife Society works to serve and represent wildlife life professionals in all areas of wildlife conservation and management in the state of New Mexico.
$8/Year
Scott Carleton, Chapter President
Dan Collins, Treasurer

New York

1132 Adirondack Council
103 Hand Avenue, Suite 3 518-873-2240
PO Box D-2 info@adirondackcouncil.org
Elizabethtown, NY 12932 www.adirondackcouncil.org
Through cooperative collaboration, the Adirondacks Council uses science, the law and knowledge of political decision making

in order to educate and motivate the public to protect the Adirondack Park.
Founded: 1975
William C. Janeway, Executive Director
Diane W. Fish, Deputy Director

1133 Adirondack Council: Albany Office
342 Hamilton Street 518-432-1770
First Floor info@adirondackcouncil.org
Albany, NY 12210 www.adirondackcouncil.org
William C. Janeway, Executive Director
Diane W. Fish, Deputy Director

1134 Adirondack Mountain Club
814 Goggins Road 518-668-4447
Lake George, NY 12845-1738 800-395-8080
Fax: 518-668-3746
info@adk.org
www.adk.org
The Adirondack Mountain Club (ADK) is composed of 27 regional chapters spanning through the state, dedicated to the protection and responsible recreational use of the New York State's wildlands and water.
Founded: 1922 30,000 Members
Neil Woodworth, Executive Director
Wes Lampman, COO

1135 American Council on Science and Health
110 East 42nd Steet 212-362-7044
Suite 1300 acsh@acsh.org
New York, NY 10017-5882 www.acsh.org
A consumer education organization based in New York City that promotes scientifically balanced evaluations of food, chemicals and the environment, and their relationship to human health.
Founded: 1978
Hank Campbell, President
Erik Lief, Director, Communications

1136 American Lung Association of New York
21 West 38th Street 212-889-3370
3rd Floor info@lungne.org
New York, NY 10018 www.lung.org/about-us/local-associations/new-york.html
The American Lung Association of New York works to prevent lung disease and promote lung health through direct assistance, education programs, advocacy and research.
Jeff Seyler, Executive VP, Northeast
Adam Shuster, CFO

1137 American Lung Association of New York: Albany
418 Broadway 518-465-2013
1st Floor info@lungne.org
Albany, NY 12207 www.lung.org/about-us/local-associations/new-york.html
Jeff Seyler, Executive VP, Northeast
Adam Shuster, CFO

1138 American Lung Association of New York: Hauppauge
700 Veterans Memorial Highway 631-265-3848
Hauppauge info@lungne.org
Albany, NY 11788 www.lung.org/about-us/local-associations/new-york.html
Jeff Seyler, Executive VP, Northeast
Adam Shuster, CFO

1139 American Lung Association of New York: Rochester
1595 Elmwood Avenue 585-442-4260
Rochester, NY 14620 info@lungne.org
www.lung.org/about-us/local-associations/new-york.html
Jeff Seyler, Executive VP, Northeast
Adam Shuster, CFO

1140 American Lung Association of New York: White Plains
237 Mamaroneck Avenue 585-442-4260
Suite 205 info@lungne.org
White Plains, NY 10605 www.lung.org/about-us/local-associations/new-york.html
Jeff Seyler, Executive VP, Northeast
Adam Shuster, CFO

1141 American Society of Landscape Architects: New York Upstate Chapter
The Rivers Organization 585-586-6906
P.O. Box 227 asla@riversorg.com
East Rochester, NY 14445 www.nyuasla.org
The New York Upstate Chapter of the American Society of Landscape Architects is a nonprofit association representing the landscape architecture profession throughout Upstate New York. The Chapter is dedicated to the promotion of thelandscape architecture profession through advocacy, education and communication.
Founded: 1954 16,000
Nick Schwartz, President
Rick Rivers, Chapter Executive Director

1142 American Society of Landscape Architects: New York Chapter
205 East 42nd Street 212-269-2984
14th Floor director@aslany.org
New York, NY 10017 www.nyasla.org
The New York Chapter of the American Society of Landscape Architects (ASLA-NY) is a nonprofit association representing the landscape architecture profession throughout 5 New York City boroughs, Nassau and Suffolk counties on LongIsland, and Westchester, Putnam, Dutchess, Orange, and Rockland counties. The Chapter is dedicated to the promotion of the landscape architecture profession through advocacy, education and communication.
Founded: 1914 500 Members
Jennifer Nitzky, President
Kathy Shea, Executive Director

1143 Catskill Forest Association
43469 State Highway 28 845-586-3054
PO Box 336 Fax: 845-586-4071
Arkville, NY 12406 cfa@catskill.net
www.catskillforest.org

Catskill Forest Association, Inc. is dedicated to protecting the health and environmental well being of the forests and the forests ecosystem, through knowledge promotion, understanding forest ecology, promotion of long-term forestmanagement and education of the public in a six-country region in Central New York State.
Founded: 1982
Ryan Trapani, Director, Forest Operations
Kathy Fox, Office Administrator

1144 Clean Ocean Action
18 Hartshorne Dr 732-872-0111
Suite 2 Fax: 732-872-8041
Highlands, NJ 07732 info@cleanoceanaction.org
www.cleanoceanaction.org
COA staff research pollution in the New York Bight then organize campaigns to clean up and protect the waters of the New York and New Jersey coasts.
Founded: 1984
Cindy Zipf, Executive Director

1145 Cornell Lab of Ornithology
159 Sapsucker Woods Road 607-254-2437
Ithaca, NY 14850 800-843-2473
www.birds.cornell.edu
The Cornell Lab of Ornithology is a nonprofit environmental organization concerned with the study, appreciation and conserva-

tion of birds. Using scientific knowledge and technological innovation, the Cornell Lab has become a worldleader in advancing the understanding of nature and engaging people of all ages in learning about birds and protecting the planet. The Cornell Lab is a unit of Cornell University.
Founded: 1915
John Fitzpatrick, Executive Director
Ron Rohrbaugh, Assitant Director

1146 Great Camp Sagamore
Sagamore Road 315-354-5311
PO Box 40 info@greatcampsagamore.org
Raquette Lake, NY 13436 www.greatcampsagamore.org
A nonprofit corporation dedicated to the stewardship of Great Camp Sagamore, and its use for educational and interpretive purposes.
Founded: 1973
Garet D. Livermore, Executive Director
Frances Parent, Associate Director

1147 Hudsonia Limited
30 Campus Road 845-758-7053
PO Box 5000 Fax: 845-758-7033
Annandale, NY 12504 www.hudsonia.org
Hudsonia Ltd., is a nonprofit, non advocacy, public interest organization. Hudsonia is committed to research, education, and technical assistance in the environmental sciences; helping people and professionals makes the most informeddecision regarding the environment and natural resources based on the available data
Founded: 1981
Erik Kiviat PhD, Executive Director
Robert E. Schmidt PhD, Associate Director

1148 In Our Backyards
540 President Street 917-464-4515
1st Floor hello@ioby.org
Brooklyn, NY 11215 www.ioby.org
Strives to deepen civic engagement in cities by connecting individuals directly to community-led, crowdfunded projects in their neighborhoods.
Founded: 2008
Erin Barnes, Co-Founder & Exec. Director
Brandon Whitney, Co-Founder & COO

1149 New York Association of Conservation Districts
415 W Morris Street
Bath, NY 14810 blanche_13335@yahoo.com
www.nyacd.org
The New York Association of Conservation Districts (NYACD) provides statewide coordination and representation for the Soil and Water Conservation Districts of New York. The NYACD provides a platform for relationships, networking,advocacy, training, and education and promotes the wise use of soil, water and natural resources throughout the state.
Founded: 1958
Dan Farrand, President
Blanche Hurlbutt, Executive Director

1150 New York Forest Owners Association
PO Box 541
Lima, NY 14485 800-836-3566
info@nyfoa.org
www.nyfoa.org
The New York Forest Owners Association (NYFOA) is a nonprofit organization comprised of 10 regional chapters working to promote sustainable forestry and improved stewardship of privately owned woodlands across the state.
Charles Stackhouse, President
Liana Gooding, Office Administrator

1151 New York Healthy Schools Network
NY 518-462-0632
info@healthyschools.org
www.healthyschools.org
Healthy Schools Network is a nonprofit, responsible for the start of the national healthy school environments movement. The Healthy Schools Network supports collaborative research, policy development, and systemic reform for thepromotion of a healthier school environment for children.
Founded: 1995
Chip Halverson, President
Linda Mendonca, VP

1152 New York State Department of Environmental Conservation
625 Broadway
Albany, NY 12233-1 contact@dec.ny.gov
www.dec.ny.gov
The New York State Department of Environmental Conservation (DEC) protects, improves and conserves the state's land, water, air, fish, wildlife and other resources to enhance the health, safety and welfare of the people and theiroverall economic and social well-being.
Founded: 1970
Kenneth Lynch, Exec. Deputy Commissione
Basil Seggos, Commissioner

1153 New York State Ornithological Association
NYSOA, Inc.
PO Box 296
Somers, NY 10589 president1@nybirds.org
www.nybirds.org
Formerly the Federation of New York State Birds, the New York State Ornithological Association (NYSOA) is dedicated to the documentation and protection of New York State's birds and their habitats and to the promotion of interest inand appreciation of birds.
Joan Collins, President
Andy Mason, Treasurer

1154 New York Turtle and Tortoise Society
1214 W Boston Post Road
PO Box 267 www.nytts.org
Mamaroneck, NY 10543
A nonprofit organization dedication to the conservation, preservation of habitat, and the promotion of proper husbandry and captive propagation of turtles and tortoises.
Founded: 1970

1155 New York Water Environment Association
525 Plum Street 315-422-7811
Suite 102 877-556-9932
Syracuse, NY 13204 Fax: 315-422-3851
pcr@nywea.org
www.nywea.org
The New York Water Environment Association is a nonprofit educational association dedicated to the development and dissemination of information concerning water quality management and the nature, collection, treatment, and disposal ofwastewater.
Founded: 1929 2,500 Members
Paul McGarvey, President
Geoffrey Baldwin, President Elect

1156 Parks and Trails New York
29 Elk Street 518-434-1583
Albany, NY 12207 Fax: 518-427-0067
ptny@ptny.org
www.ptny.org
The only organization working statewide to protect New York's parks and help communities create new parks. A non-profit organization whose mission is to expand, protect and promote a net-

work of parks, trails, and open spaces throughoutour state for use and enjoyment by all.
Founded: 1985
A. Joseph Scott, Chairman
Richard H. Remmer, Vice Chairman

1157 **Riverkeeper**
20 Secor Road
Ossining, NY 10562
800-217-4837
info@riverkeeper.org
www.riverkeeper.org

Riverkeeper works to protect the environmental, recreational, and commercial integrity of the Hudson River and its tributaries. Riverkeeper is a global leader in water keeper programs and is New York's clean water advocate.
Founded: 1966
Deborah Brown, Chief of Staff
Paul Gallay, President

1158 **Scenic Hudson**
1 Civic Center Plaza
Suite 200
Poughkeepsie, NY 12601
845-473-4440
Fax: 845-473-2648
info@scenichudson.org
www.scenichudson.org

Scenic Hudson works to protect and restore the Hudson River. Through land preservation, citizen-based advocacy, and the creation of parks; Scenic Hudson is the largest environmental organization focused on the Hudson River Valley,preserving 40,000 acres and creating or enhancing 65 parks in the region.
Founded: 1963
Steve Rosenberg, Senior VP
Ned Sullivan, President

1159 **Selikoff Clinical Center for Occupational & Environmental Medicine**
Mount Sinai School of Medicine
Department of Community Medicine
1 Gustave Levy Place, Box 1043
New York, NY 10029-6574
212-241-6500
Fax: 212-241-6696
www.mssm.edu/cpm

Internationally respected diagnostic referral center and an important interface between the research programs of the Division of Environmental Health Science and populations exposed to environmental hazards.

1160 **Sierra Club: Atlantic Chapter**
744 Broadway
Albany, NY 12207
518-426-9144
atlantic.chapter@sierraclub.org
www.atlantic2.sierraclub.org

The Atlantic Chapter applies the principles of the national Sierra Club to the environmental issues facing New York State.
Rogers Downs, Director, Conservation
Caitlin Ferrante, Chapter Coordinator

1161 **Sierra Club: New York City Chapter**
NY
info@nyc.sierraclub.org
www.nyc.sierraclub.org

The New York City Chapter applies the principles of the national Sierra Club to the environmental issues facing New York City.
Founded: 1892
Allison Tupper, Chair
Bonnie Lane Webber, Vice Chair

1162 **The Nature Conservancy: New York Chapter**
195 New Karner Road
Suite 200
Albany, NY 12205
518-690-7850
Fax: 518-869-2332
natureny@tnc.org
www.nature.org/newyork

In conjunction with the mission of the The Nature Conservancy, which started in New York, the New York Chapter protects more than 815,000 acres of land across the state. This chapter was the first state chapter to establish acomprehensive program for fresh water, oceans and cities.
Founded: 1955 90,000 Members

1163 **The Nature Conservancy: New York Chapter: Long Island The Center for Conservation**
142 Route 114
PO Box 5125
East Hampton, NY 11937
631-329-7689
Fax: 631-329-0215
natureny@tnc.org
www.nature.org/newyork

1164 **The Nature Conservancy: New York Chapter: Adirondacks**
Adirondack Land Trust
PO Box 65
Keene Valley, NY 12943
518-576-2082
adirondacks@tnc.org
www.nature.org/newyork

Tim Barnett, VP, Special Programs
Dirk Bryan, Director, Conservation

1165 **The Nature Conservancy: New York Chapter: Central & Western New York**
274 N Goodman Street
Suite B261
Rochester, NY 14607
585-546-8030
Fax: 585-546-7825
natureny@tnc.org
www.nature.org/newyork

Jim Howe, Executive Director
Darran Crabtree, Director, Conservation

1166 **The Nature Conservancy: New York Chapter: Long Island Uplands Farm Sanctuary**
250 Lawrence Hill Road
Cold Spring Harbor, NY 11724
631-367-3225
Fax: 631-367-4715
natureny@tnc.org
www.nature.org/newyork

1167 **The Nature Conservancy: New York Chapter: New York City**
322 8th Avenue
16th Floor
New York, NY 10001
212-997-1880
Fax: 212-997-8451
natureny@tnc.org
www.nature.org/newyork

1168 **Tug Hill Tomorrow Land Trust**
1 Thompson Park
PO Box 6063
Watertown, NY 13601
315-779-8240
thtomorr@northnet.org
www.tughilltomorrowlandtrust.org

A regional, private, nonprofit organization, Tug Hill Tomorrow Land Trust works to protect the 2,100 square mile region. Tug Hill Tomorrow Land Trust uses publications, education, and community programs to increase the awareness,appreciation, and conservation of the Tug Hill region land.
Founded: 1991
Linda Garrett, Executive Director
Lianna Lee, Manager, Communications

1169 **Waterkeeper Alliance**
180 Maiden Lane
Suite 603
New York, NY 10038
212-747-0622
info@waterkeeper.org
www.waterkeeper.org

The Waterkeeper Alliance provides global coordination and networking for local waterkeeper organizations and affiliates. A nonprofit organization, the Waterkeeper Alliance works to conserve, protect, and promote water quality fordrinkable, fishable, and swimmable water.
Marc Yaggi, Executive Director
Mary Beth Postman, Deputy Director

1170 **West Harlem Environmental Action**
1854 Amsterdam Avenue 212-961-1000
2nd Floor Fax: 212-961-1015
New York, NY 10031 info@weact.org
www.weact.org

A nonprofit, community-based, environmental organization dedicated to building community power to help end environmental racism and improve environmental health, protection and policy in communities of color and low incomeneighborhoods.
Peggy M Shepard, Executive Director
Cecill D. Corbin-Mark, Deputy Director

North Carolina

1171 **American Lung Association of North Carolina**
514 Daniels Street 919-792-1641
Suite 109 alanc-r@lungse.org
Raleigh, NC 27605 www.lungnc.org
The American Lung Association of North Carolina works to prevent lung disease and promote lung health through direct assistance, education programs, advocacy and research.
Martha C. Bogdan, Executive VP, South East
Willie L. Bythwood, Jr, CFO

1172 **American Lung Association of North Carolina: Charlotte**
401 Hawthrone Lane 980-237-6611
Suite 110 #298 alanc@lungse.org
Charlotte, NC 28204 www.lungnc.org
Martha C. Bogdan, Executive VP, South East
Willie L. Bythwood, Jr, CFO

1173 **American Society of Landscape Architects: North Carolina Chapter**
c/o Blue Star Services
5201 Albemarle Drive 919-215-3117
Oriental, NC 28571 manager@ncasla.org
www.ncasla.org
The North Carolina Chapter of the American Society of Landscape Architects (NCASLA) is a nonprofit association representing the landscape architecture profession throughout North Carolina. The Chapter is dedicated to the promotion ofthe landscape architecture profession through advocacy, education and communication.
Founded: 1899
Debora Steenson, Chapter Co-Manager
George Steenson, Chapter Co-Manager

1174 **Carolina Bird Club**
1809 Lakepark Drive 910-791-9034
Raleigh, NC 27612 Fax: 910-791-7228
hq@carolinabirdclub.org
www.carolinabirdclub.org
A nonprofit education and scientific association, open to anyone interested in the study and conservation of wildlife, particularly birds. Through its website, publications, meetings, workshops, trips, and partnerships, the CarolinaBird Club supports the birding community in the Carolinas.
Founded: 1937
Christine Stoughton-Root, President
Paul Dayer, Treasurer

1175 **Environmental Educators of North Carolina**
PO Box 4904 919-250-1050
Chapel Hill, NC 27515-4904 Fax: 919-250-1058
communicationseenc@gmail.com
www.eenc.org
A nonprofit organization, dedicated to promoting excellence, professional development, and to facilitate networking opportunities, in order to foster greater environmental education among the community and environmental educators.
Founded: 1987
Jonathan Marchal, President
Chris Goforth, Communications Chair

1176 **Forest History Society**
701 Williams Vickers Avenue 919-682-9319
Durham, NC 27701-3162 www.foresthistory.org
The Forest History is a nonprofit educational institution that links the past to the future by indentifying, collecting, preserving, interpreting, and disseminating information on the history of people, forests, and their relatedresources, contributing to the informed decision making concering natural resources.
Founded: 1946
Steven Anderson, President & CEO
Andrea H. Anderson, Administrative Assistant

1177 **NC Sustainable Energy Association**
4800 Six Forks Road 919-832-7601
Suite 300 info@energync.org
Raleigh, NC 27609 www.energync.org
Composed of individuals, businesses, government, and nonprofits, the NC Sustainable Energy Association (NCSEA) is a nonprofit membership organization working to change policy and market development to create clean energy jobs, economicopportunities, and affordable energy in North Carolina.
Founded: 1978
Ivan Urlaub, Executive Director
Ward Lenz, Director, Development

1178 **North Carolina Association of Soil & Water Conservation Districts**
PO Box 27943 919-715-6104
Raleigh, NC 27611 ncaswcd@gmail.com
www.ncaswcd.org
An independent nonpartisan conservation organization created to represent the interests of 96 local soil and water conservation districts and the 492 district supervisors who direct their local district's conservation programs.
Founded: 1944
Chris Hogan, President
Dietrich Kilpatrick, First Vice President

1179 **North Carolina Coastal Federation**
3609 N.C. 24 Ocean 252-393-8185
Newport, NC 28570 Fax: 252-393-7508
nccf@nccoast.org
www.nccoast.org
Working with citizens to safeguard the state's coastal rivers, creeks, sounds and beaches. The state's only nonprofit organization focused exclusivley on protecting and restoring the coast of Nort Carolina through education, advocacy,and habitat preservation and restoration.
Founded: 1982
Todd Miller, Executive Director
Lauren Kolodij, Deputy Director

1180 **North Carolina Coastal Federation: Northeast Office**
637 Harbor Road 252-473-1607
PO Box 276 Fax: 252-473-2402
Wanchese, NC 27981 nccf@nccoast.org
www.nccoast.org

Founded: 1982
Todd Miller, Executive Director
Lauren Kolodij, Deputy Director

1181 **North Carolina Coastal Federation: Southeast Office**
Wrightsville Beach Historic Square

309 W Salisbury Street 910-509-2838
Wrightsville Beach, NC 28480 Fax: 910-509-2840
nccf@nccoast.org
www.nccoast.org

Founded: 1982
Todd Miller, Executive Director
Lauren Kolodij, Deputy Director

1182 North Carolina Museum of Natural Sciences
11 W Jones Street 919-707-9800
Raleigh, NC 27601 www.naturalsciences.org
The North Museum of Natural Sciences, is a free admission museum working to highlight the interdependent relationship between the natural environment and humanity.
Founded: 1985
Angela Baker-James, Executive Director
Emlyn Koster, Director

1183 North Carolina Native Plant Society
PO Box 10815
Greensboro, NC 27404 jean@ncwildflower.org
www.ncwildflower.org
A nonprofit organization dedicated to the promotion, enjoyment and conservation of North Carolina's native plants and their habitats through education, protection, and propagation.
Founded: 1951
Jean Woods, President
John Clarke, VP

1184 Sierra Club: North Carolina Chapter
19 W. Hargett Street 919-833-8467
Suite 210 info@sierraclub-nc.org
Raleigh, NC 27601 www.sierraclub.org/north-carolina
The North Carolina Chapter of the Sierra Club, is composed of 12 local groups that work to advocate across the state in order to protect the land and environment of North Carolina.
Founded: 1970 70,000 Members
Molly Diggins, State Director
Margaret Lillard, Communications Coordinator

1185 Southeastern Association of Fish and Wildlife Agencies
27 Sylwood Place 601-668-6916
Jackson, MS 39209 crayhopkins@bellsouth.net
www.seafwa.org
The Southeastern Association of Fish and Wildlife Agencies (SEAFWA) is an organization whose members are the state agencies with primary responsibility for management and protection of the fish and wildlife resources in 15 states.
Curtis R. Hopkins, Executive Secretary
Alvin Taylor, President

1186 The Wildlife Society: North Carolina Chapter
NC
admin@nctws.org
www.nctws.org/wordpress
The North Carolina Chapter of The Wildlife Society works to serve and represent wildlife life professionals in all areas of wildlife conservation and management in the state of North Carolina.
Founded: 1983
Colleen Olfenbuttel, President
Brandon Sherrill, Treasurer

North Dakota

1187 American Fisheries Society: North Central Division: Dakota Chapter
ND
Steven.Chipps@sdstate.edu
www.dakota.fisheries.org
The Dakota Chapter of the American Fisheries Society, is part of the American Fisheries Society (AFS) North Central Division. The Dakota Chapter works to further to the goals of the AFS and is committed to the conservation,development, and wise use of fishery resources, the chapter provides several annual awards to fishery professionals, conservation groups, and students.
Steve Chipps, President
Michael Johnson, Secretary & Treasurer

1188 American Lung Association in North Dakota
212 North 2nd Street 701-223-5613
Bismarck, ND 58501 info@lungnd.org
www.lung.org/about-us/local-associations/north-dakota.html
The American Lung Association of North Dakota works to prevent lung disease and promote lung health through direct assistance, education programs, advocacy and research.
Penny Fena, Chief Mission Officer
Lewis Bartfield, Executive VP,Upper Midwest

1189 American Society of Landscape Architects: Great Plains Chapter
NE
Regan.Pence@LRA-INC.com
www.gpcasla.org
Representing North Dakota, South Dakota, and Nebraska the Great Plains Chapter of the American Landscape Society works to expand the profession of landscape architecture in these states. The Chapter advocates and provides professionaleducational and developmental programs for its members
Regan Pence, President
Chad Kucker, Secretary & Treasurer

1190 International Association for Impact Assessment
1330 23rd Street South 701-297-7908
Suite C Fax: 701-297-7917
Fargo, ND 58103-3705 info@iaia.org
www.iaia.org
The International Association for Impact Assessment (IAIA) is an interdisciplinary society dedicated to developing international capacity to anticipate, plan and manage the consequences of development. IAIA seeks to ensure thatpolitical, environmental, social and technological dimensions of decisions are understood by those making them.
Founded: 1980
Jill Baker, Executive Director
Kayla Deitch, Administrative Assistant

1191 North Dakota Association of Soil Conservation Districts
3310 University Drive 701-223-8518
Bismarck, ND 58504 kathy@lincolnoakes.com
ndascd.org
The North Dakota Association of Soil Conservation Districts (NDASD) works to promote the widespread application of sound and practical soil and water conservation practices in the state.
Richard Knopp, President
Kathy Hendrickson, Association Secretary

Ohio

1192 American Fisheries Society: North Central Division: Ohio Chapter
OH
kristin.arend@dnr.state.oh.us
www.ohio.fisheries.org
The Ohio Chapter of the American Fisheries Society (OCAFS), is part of the American Fisheries Society (AFS) North Central Division. Working to further to the goals of the AFS through research, education, and professional development,the chapter is committed to the conservation, development, and wise use of fishery resources, and the protection and sustainability of aquatic ecosystems.
Founded: 1970 $10/ Year
Kristi Arend, President
Jo Ann Banda, Secretary & Treasurer

1193 American Lung Association of Ohio
4050 Executive Park Drive 513-985-3990
402 midland@lung.org
Cincinatti, OH 45241 www.lung.org/about-us/local-associations/ohio.html
The American Lung Association of Ohio works to prevent lung disease and promote lung health through direct assistance, advocacy and education programs. Due to the unique partnership between the American Lung Association of Ohio andpublic television stations in Daytona and Cincinnati, the ALA of Ohio established the project CAARE for care providers, dedicated to managing childhood asthma in daycare centers.
Barry Gottschalk, Executive VP, Midland States
Patricia J. Volz, VP, Communication

1194 American Lung Association of Ohio: Columbus
5900 Wilcox Place 614-279-1700
Dublin, OH 43016 midland@lung.org
www.lung.org/about-us/local-associations/ohio.html
Barry Gottschalk, Executive VP, Midland States
Patricia J. Volz, VP, Communication

1195 American Lung Association of Ohio: Independence
6100 Rockside Wood 216-524-5864
Suite 260 midland@lung.org
Independence, OH 44131 www.lung.org/about-us/local-associations/ohio.html
Founded: 1901
Barry Gottschalk, Executive VP, Midland States
Patricia J. Volz, VP, Communication

1196 American Lung Association of Ohio: Sandusky
PO Box 415 419-663-5864
Sandusky, OH 44871 pat.volz@lung.org
www.lung.org/about-us/local-associations/ohio.html
Barry Gottschalk, Executive VP, Midland states
Patricia J. Volz, VP, Communication

1197 American Society of Landscape Architects: Ohio Chapter
PO Box 776
Worthington, OH 43085 info@ohioasla.org
www.ohioasla.org
The Ohio Chapter of the American Society of Landscape Architects is a nonprofit association representing the landscape architecture profession throughout the state. The Chapter is dedicated to the promotion of the landscapearchitecture profession through advocacy, education and communication.
Ashley Solether, President
Eugenia M. Martin, Chapter Trustee

1198 B.A.S.S Nation: Ohio Chapter
OH
www.ohiobassnation.com
The Ohio Chapter of BASS Nation is dedicated to the promotion of the sport of bass fishing, fishing tournaments and conservation initiatives to preserve the states natural resources.
Al Evans, President
Danny Ryan, VP

1199 Cincinnati Nature Center
4949 Tealtown Road 513-831-1711
Milford, OH 45150 cnc@cincynature.org
www.cincynature.org
To inspire passion for nature and promote environmentally responsible choices through experience and education. The Cincinnati Nature Center is 1,600 acres of forests, fields, streams and ponds.
Founded: 1965
Paul F. Haffner, Chair
Michael R. Mauch, Vice Chair

1200 Green Energy Ohio
7870 Olentangy River Road 614-985-6131
Suite 304 Fax: 614-888-9716
Columbus, OH 43235 geo@greenenergyohio.org
www.greenenergyohio.org
Green Energy Ohio is a statewide nonprofit that promotes the use of renewable energy and policies.
Barry Adler, Operations Coordinator
Jane Harf, Executive Director

1201 Holden Arboretum
9500 Sperry Road 440-946-4400
Kirtland, OH 44094 editor@holdenarb.org
www.holdenarb.org
The Holden Arboretum is a living museum that covers over 3,600 acres. The Arboretum promotes the importance of a trees and woodlands and connecting with nature, allowing the public to walk through themed gardens, hiking trails, picnicareas, and receive guided tours.
Founded: 1931
Paul Abbey, Interim President & CEO
Patricia Roberts, VP, Operations

1202 League of Ohio Sportsmen
642 West Broad Street 614-224-8970
Columbus, OH 43215 Fax: 614-224-8971
president@leagueofohiosportsmen.org
www.leagueofohiosportsmen.org
Dedicated to supporting conservation, restoration, and education that promotes the wise use and enjoyment of our natural resources including wildlife management.
Founded: 1908
Larry Mitchell Sr, President
John Hobbs, Vice President

1203 Ohio Energy Project
200 E. Wilson Bridge Road 614-785-1717
Suite 320 Fax: 614-785-1731
Worthington, OH 43085 dyerkes@ohioenergy.org
www.ohioenergy.org
An nonproft organization, created by teachers for teachers that provides energy and energy efficiency education using current complete and unbiased information, as well as hands-on, engaging and innovative techniques.
Debby Yerkes, Executive Director
Sue Tenney, Education Coordinator

1204 Ohio Environmental Council
Chesapeake Warehouse
1145 Chesapeake Avenue 614-487-7506
Suite I Fax: 614-487-7510
Columbus, OH 43212 OEC@theOEC.org
www.theoec.org

Through legislative initiatives, legal action, science , and statewide partnerships the Ohio Environmental Council is dedicated to advocating for healthier air, land, and water in Ohio.
Jodi Segal, COO
Heather Taylor-Miles, Executive Director

1205 Ohio Federation of Soil and Water Conservation Districts
8995 E Main Street 614-784-1900
Reynoldsburg, OH 43068 www.ofswcd.org
Working to provide leadership and support to the board supervisors, soil and water conservation districts, and their partners through grassroots programs that promote natural resource stewardship.
Founded: 1943
Harold Neuenschwander, President
Bob Short, First VP

1206 Ohio Parks and Recreation Association
1069-A West Main Street 614-895-2222
Westerville, OH 43081 800-238-1108
Fax: 614-895-3050
opra@opraonline.org
www.opraonline.org
A nonprofit, public interest organization representing over 1,700 professionals and citizen board members involved in providing leisure facilities and opportunities to all Ohioans as well as the tourists who visit the state each year.Dedicated to the promotion of parks and recreation services for all Ohioans and the sound stewardship of Ohio's natural resources.
Founded: 1934
Woody Woodward, Executive Director
Mindy McInturf, Business Manager

1207 Sierra Club: Ohio Chapter
Columbus, OH
www.sierraclub.org/ohio
To advance the preservation and protection of the natural environment by empowering the citizenry with charitable resources to further the cause of environmental protection.
Guy Marentette, Chapter Chair
Jen Miller, Chapter Director

1208 The Native Plant Society of Northeastern Ohio
OH
www.nativeplantsocietyneo.org
As the Northeastern Chapter of The Ohio Native Plant Society, the chapter works to promote the conservation of Ohio's native plants and native plant communities through habitat protection.
Kathy Hanratty, President
Judy Barnhart, VP

1209 The Nature Conservancy: Ohio Chapter
6375 Riverside Drive 614-717-2770
Suite 100 877-862-6446
Dublin, OH 43017 ohio@tnc.org
www.nature.org/ohio
The Ohio Chapter of The Nature Conservancy is dedicated to protecting Ohio's streams, wetlands and forests. With more than 15 nature preserves and over 60,000 acres of natural land protected, The Nature Conservancy of Ohio works toconserve the natural resources across the state of Ohio.
Founded: 1958
Josh Knights, Executive Director
Julia Gehring, Conservation Coordinator

1210 The Nature Conservancy: Ohio Chapter: Coastal Programs Office
2900 Columbus Avenue 419-627-7564
Sadusky, OH 44870 877-862-6446
ohio@tnc.org
www.nature.org/ohio

1211 The Nature Conservancy: Ohio Chapter: Edge of Appalachia Preserve - Eulett Center
4274 Waggoner Riffle Road 937-544-2188
West Union, OH 45693 877-862-6446
ohio@tnc.org
www.nature.org/ohio

1212 The Nature Conservancy: Ohio Chapter: Grand Rivers Conservation Campus
3973 Callender Road 440-563-3081
Rock Creek, OH 44084 877-862-6446
ohio@tnc.org
www.nature.org/ohio

1213 The Nature Conservancy: Ohio Chapter: Northeast Ohio Coastal Project
416 West Prospect Street 847-641-1129
Painesville, OH 44077 877-862-6446
ohio@tnc.org
www.nature.org/ohio

1214 The Nature Conservancy: Ohio Chapter: Oak Openings Region
10420 Old State Line Road 419-867-1521
Swanton, OH 43558 877-862-6446
ohio@tnc.org
www.nature.org/ohio

1215 The Nature Conservancy: Ohio Chapter: Western Lake Erie Basin Agriculture Project Office
210 Clinton Street 614-570-0034
Defiance, OH 43512 877-862-6446
ohio@tnc.org
www.nature.org/ohio

1216 The Wildlife Society: Ohio Chapter
OH
www.wildlife.org/ohio
The Ohio Chapter of The Wildlife Society works to serve and represent wildlife life professionals in all areas of wildlife conservation and management in the state of Ohio.
Geoff Westerfield, President
Gabe Karns, Secretary

Oklahoma

1217 American Fisheries Society: Fisheries Management Section
OK
www.fms.fisheries.org
A section of the American Fisheries Society, Fisheries Management is composed of people dedicated to developing, applying, and evaluating effective fishery management concepts or techniques. The section sponsors workshops andsymposiums in promotion of the exchange of information among fishery professionals, students, and individuals or groups interested in fish.

1218 American Lung Association of Oklahoma
730 Wilshire Boulevard 405-748-4674
Suite 105 www.lung.org/about-us/local-associations/oklahoma.html
Oklahoma City, OK 73116
The American Lung Association of Oklahoma works to prevent lung disease and promote lung health through direct assistance, education programs, advocacy and research.
Terri Bailey, Executive Director
Cassidy Fallik, Program Coordinator

1219 **B.A.S.S Nation: Oklahoma Chapter**
OK
580-761-8094
limit5mike@yahoo.com
www.okbassnation.com
The Oklahoma Chapter of BASS Nation works to stimulate public awareness of bass fishing as a major sport and encourages sportsmanship, courtesy and boating safety at all levels. The Chapter promotes the full adherence to allconservation codes, adequate water quality standards and legal enforcement of existing regulatory standards.
Founded: 1972
Mike Myers, President
Chuck Boso, Secretary

1220 **Oklahoma Association of Conservation Districts**
PO Box 2775
Oklahoma City, OK 73101-2775
info@okconservation.org
www.okconservation.org
Working to provide leadership, resources, and partnership opportunities for the 88 conservation districts and those who manage the land to enhance the natural resources of Oklahoma.
Founded: 1950
Jimmy Emmons, President
Sarah Blaney, Director

1221 **Oklahoma Ornithological Society**
OK
www.okbirds.org
The Oklahoma Ornithological Society (OOS) is an independent, nonprofit educational organization, dedicated to the observation, study, and conservation of birds in Oklahoma.
Founded: 1951
Jimmy Woodard, President
Doug Wood, Secretary

1222 **Sierra Club: Oklahoma Chapter**
Oklahoma City, OK
johnson.bridgwater@sierraclub.org
www.oklahoma.sierraclub.org
Composed of local groups from across the state, the Oklahoma Chapter of the Sierra Club organizes outdoor activities, social events, conservation activities, and education outreach efforts in support of the national Sierra Club'smission.
Founded: 1972 3,000 Members
Johnson Bridgwater, Chapter Director
Michael Belifuss, Chapter Chair

1223 **The Nature Conservancy: Oklahoma Chapter**
10425 South 82nd East Avenue
918-585-1117
Suite 104
Fax: 888-267-5904
Tulsa, OK 74133
www.nature.org/oklahoma
In conjunction with the mission of the The Nature Conservancy, the Oklahoma Chapter conserves nearly 100,00 acres land and unique biodiversity across the state.
Mike Fuhr, State Director
Ashley Dubriwny, Director, Operations

1224 **The Nature Conservancy: Oklahoma Chapter: Oklahoma City**
408 NW 7th Street
405-858-8557
Oklahoma City, OK 73102
Fax: 888-267-5904
www.nature.org/oklahoma
Katie Hawk, Director, Communications
Melissa Nagel Shackford, Director, Land Protection

Oregon

1225 **American Lung Association of Oregon**
16037 SW Upper Boones Ferry Road
503-924-4094
Suite 165
InfoMTP@lung.org
Tigard, OR 97224
www.lung.org/about-us/local-associations/oregon.html
The American Lung Association of Oregon works to prevent lung disease and promote lung health through direct assistance, education programs, advocacy and research.
Allison Hickey, Exec. VP, Mountain Pacific
Tony Peterson, CFO

1226 **American Rivers: Pacific Northwest Region: Portland**
317 SW Alder Street
503-827-8648
Suite 900
www.americanrivers.org/region/pacific
Portland, OR 97204
The Pacific Northwest Region of American Rivers works according to the mission of American Rivers, and promotes and applies innovative water and river management.
Founded: 1992

1227 **American Society of Landscape Architects: Oregon Chapter**
147 SE 102nd Avenue
503-227-6156
Portland, OR 97216
Fax: 503-253-9172
info@aslaoregon.org
www.aslaoregon.org
The Oregon Chapter of the American Society of Landscape Architects, is a nonprofit association representing the landscape architecture profession throughout the state of Oregon.
Andreas Stavropoulos, President
Jamie Hendrickson, VP Chapter Services

1228 **Columbia Basin Fish and Wildlife Authority**
851 SW Sixth Avenue, Suite 260
503-229-0191
Pacific Centre
Fax: 503-229-0443
Portland, OR 97204
www.cbfish.org
A non-profit corporation to provide an opportunity for the Agencies and Tribes of the Pacific Northwest to become directly involved in the fiscal, administrative and managerial aspects of jointly funded activities.
Founded: 1993
Jann Eckman, President
Dave Statler, Vice President

1229 **Ecotrust**
Jean Vollum Natural Capital Center
721 NW 9th Avenue
503-227-6225
Portland, OR 97209
contact@ecotrust.org
www.ecotrust.org
Working to inspire innovative thinking that creates economic opportunity, social equity and environmental well-being.
Founded: 1991
Jeremy Barnicle, Executive Director
Laura Ford, Director, Communications

1230 **Northwest Center for Alternatives to Pesticides**
Eugene Headquarters
211 W 5th Avenue
541-344-5044
PO Box 1393
info@pesticide.org
Eugene, OR 97440
www.pesticide.org
Protects the health of people and the environment by advancing alternatives to pesticides.
Founded: 1977
Kim Leval, Executive Director
Edward Winter, COFO

1231 Northwest Power and Conservation Council
851 SW Sixth Avenue 503-222-5161
Suite 1020 800-452-5161
Portland, OR 97204-1347 Fax: 503-820-2370
info@nwcouncil.org
www.nwcouncil.org
The council develops and maintains a regional power plan and a fish and wildlife program to balance the Northwest's environment and energy needs.
Bill Bradbury, Council Chair

1232 Oregon Refuse and Recycling Association
727 Center Street NE, Suite 350 503-588-1837
PO Box 2186 800-527-7624
Salem, OR 97308 Fax: 503-399-7784
orrainfo@orra.net
www.orra.net
A 200 member voluntary association of solid waste management companies and businesses which specialize in offering equipment and services important to the industry. ORRA provides legislative advocacy, education, group insurance,meeting facilities and advice on regulatory matters to its memebers.
Founded: 1965
Kristan Mitchell, Executive Director
Kimera Coady, Executive Assistant

1233 Oregon State Public Interest Research Group
1536 SE 11th Avenue 503-231-4181
Suite A info@ospirg.org
Portland, OR 97214 www.ospirg.org
OSPIRG's mission is to deliver persistent, result-oriented public interest activism that protects consumers, encourages a fair, sustainable economy, and fosters responsive democratic government.
Founded: 1983
Dave Rosenfeld, Executive Director
Jesse Ellis O'Brien, Health Care Advocate

1234 Oregon Trout
65 SW Yamhill Street 503-222-9091
Suite 200 Fax: 503-222-9187
Portland, OR 97204 info@thefreshwatertrust.org
www.ortrout.org
A statewide non-profit organization headquartered in Portland, Oregon with satellite offices in Bandon, Bend, Corvallis and Medford. Oregon Trout works to restore freshwater health through innovation and education.
Founded: 1983
Joe S. Whitworth, President
Alan Horton, Managing Director

1235 Oregon Water Resources Congress
437 Union Street NE 503-363-0121
Salem, OR 97301 Fax: 503-371-4926
owrc_info@yahoo.com
www.owrc.org
To promote the protection and use of water rights and the wise stewarship of water resources.
Founded: 1912
April Snell, Executive Director
Ken Crick, Office Manager

1236 Oregon Wild
5825 N. Greeley Ave. 503-283-6343
Portland, OR 97217 Fax: 503-283-0756
info@oregonwild.org
www.oregonwild.org
Formerly Oregon Natural Resources Council, Oregon Wild works to protect and restore Oregon's wildlands, wildlife and waters as an enduring leagacy for all Oregonians.
Founded: 1974
Daniel Robertson, President
Brett Sommermeyer, VP

1237 Pacific Rivers Council
PO Box 10798 541-345-0119
Eugene, OR 97440 Fax: 541-345-0710
info@pacrivers.org
www.pacrivers.org
One of the most influential river conservation organizations in the United States. The mission is to protect and restore rivers, their watersheds, and native aquatic species.
Founded: 1987
Holly Spencer, Acting Executive Director

1238 Rising Tide North America
268 Bush St
Box # 3717 networking@risingtidenorthamerica.org
San Francisco, CA 94101 www.risingtidenorthamerica.org
An international, all-volunteer, grassroots network of groups and individuals who organize locally, promote community-based solutions to the climate crisis and take direct action to confront the root causes of climate change.

1239 Sierra Club-Oregon Chapter
1821 SE Ankeny St 503-238-0442
Portland, OR 97214-1521 Fax: 503-238-6281
oregon.chapter@sierraclub.org
oregon.sierraclub.org
To advance the preservation and protection of the natural environment by empowering the citizenry with charitable resources to further the cause of environmental protection.
Amanda Caffall, Chair
Mary Fifield, Vice Chair

1240 Solar Oregon
1231 NW Hoyt St. 503-231-5662
Suite 402 info@SolarOregon.org
Portland, OR 97209 solaroregon.org
A non-profit membership organization providing public education and community outreach to encourage Oregonians to choose solar energy
Alan Scott, President
Lisa Logie, Executive Director

1241 University of Oregon Environmental Studies Program
5223 University of Oregon 541-346-5257
Eugene, OR 97403-5223 Fax: 541-346-5954
ecopeers@uoregon.edu
envs.uoregon.edu
Environmental Studies crosses the boundaries of traditional disciplines, challenging faculty and students to look at the relationship between humans and their environment from a new perspective. They are dedicated to gaining greaterunderstanding of the natural world from an ecological perspective; devising policy and behavior that address contemporary environmental problems; and promoting a rethinking of basic cultural premises, ways of structuring knowledge and the rootmetaphors of society.
Founded: 1983
Richard York, Program Director
Monica Guy, Office Manager

1242 Wildlife Society
PO Box 2378 541-937-2131
Corvallis, OR 97339 Fax: 541-937-3401
To promote wise conservation and management of wildlife resources in Oregon by serving and representing wildlife professionals.
Mark Penninger, President

Pennsylvania

1243 **Air and Waste Management Association**
One Gateway Center, 3rd Floor 412-232-3444
420 Fort Duquesne Boulevard 800-270-3444
Pittsburgh, PA 15222-1435 Fax: 412-232-3450
info@awma.org
www.awma.org

The Air and Waste Management Association (A&WMA) is a nonprofit, nonpartisan professional organization that provides information, networking opportfessional development, networking opportunities, public education, and outreach unities,public educational and professional development to more than 9,000 envies global environmental responsibility and increases the effectiveness of organironmental professionals in 65 countries.
Founded: 1907
Scott A. Freeburn, President
Chris Nelson, President Elect

1244 **Alliance for the Chesapeake Bay**
3310 Market Street 717-737-8622
Suite A Fax: 717-737-8650
Camp Hill, PA 17011 contact@allianceforthebay.org
www.allianceforthebay.org
Founded: 1971
David Bancroft, President

1245 **American Bass Association of Eastern Pennsylvania & New Jersey**
NJ
abapanj@gmail.com
www.bestbassteams.com

The American Bass Association of PA & NJ is dedicated to the promotion of bass fishing as a major sport, to conserve the future of fishing through the protection and enhancement of fishery resources and to introduce fishing to Americanyouth.
Founded: 1974
Fred Eurick, President
Mark Dilatush, VP

1246 **American Lung Association of Pennsylvania**
3001 Old Gettysburg Road 717-541-5864
Camp Hill, PA 17011 ckillinger@lunginfo.org
www.lung.org/about-us/local-associations/pennsylvania.html

The American Lung Association of Pennsylvania works to prevent lung disease and promote lung health through direct assistance, education programs, advocacy and research.
Deborah Brown, Excutive VP, Mid-Atlantic
Joy Meyer, VP, Community Impact

1247 **American Lung Association of Pennsylvania: Allentown**
2200 W Hamilton Street 610-253-5060
Suite 318 kwerkheiser@lunginfo.org
Allentown, PA 18104 www.lung.org/about-us/local-associations/pennsylvania.html
Deborah Brown, Excutive VP, Mid-Atlantic
Joy Meyer, VP, Community Impact

1248 **American Lung Association of Pennsylvania: Pittsburgh**
810 River Avenue 412-321-4029
Suite 140 pschnarrs@lunginfo.org
Pittsburgh, PA 15212 www.lung.org/about-us/local-associations/pennsylvania.html
Deborah Brown, Excutive VP, Mid-Atlantic
Joy Meyer, VP, Community Impact

1249 **American Lung Association of Pennsylvania: Plymouth Meeting & Scranton**
527 Plymouth Road 610-941-9595
Suite 415 jkeith@lunginfo.org
Plymouth Meeting, PA 19462 www.lung.org/about-us/local-associations/pennsylvania.html
Deborah Brown, Excutive VP, Mid-Atlantic
Joy Meyer, VP, Community Impact

1250 **American Rivers: Mid-Atlantic Region**
1 Danker Avenue 518-482-2631
Albany, NY 12206 Fax: 518-482-2632
www.americanrivers.org
Stephanie Lindloff, Director

1251 **American Society of Landscape Architects: Pennsylvania/Delaware Chapter**
908 North Second Street 717-441-6041
Harrisburg, PA 19102 www.padeasla.org
Founded: 1899
Adam Supplee, President
John D Wanner, Executive Director

1252 **Appalachian States Low-Level Radioactive Waste Commission**
Rachel Carson State Office Building 410-537-3345
400 Market Street, 13th Floor Fax: 410-537-4133
Harrisburg, PA 17101 kmcginty@state.pa.us
www.dep.state.pa.us

The commission was ratified by Maryland, Delaware, Pennsylvania and West Virginia to assure intertstate cooperation for the proper packaging and transportation of low-level radioactive waste. Pennsylvania is the host state and handlesthe administrative duties of the commission at this time.
Founded: 1986
Kathleen A McGinty, Chair/Executive Director
Richard R Janati, Administrator

1253 **Audubon Society of Western Pennsylvania at the Beechwood Farms Nature Reserve**
614 Dorseyville Road 412-963-6100
Pittsburgh, PA 15238 Fax: 412-963-6761
aswp@aswp.org
www.aswp.org/

To inspire and educate the people of southwesterm Pennsylvania to be respectful and responsible stewards of the natural world.
Founded: 1916
Sally Tarhi, President
Jim Bonner, Executive Director

1254 **B.A.S.S Nation: Pennsylvania Chapter**
PA
president@pabassnation.com
www.pabassnation.com

The Pennsylvania Chapter of BASS Nation is dedicated to the promotion of the sport of bass fishing, fishing tournaments and conservation initiatives to preserve the states natural resources.
Josh Giran, President
Derek Severns, VP

1255 **Brandywine Conservancy**
PO Box 141 610-388-2700
Chadds Ford, PA 19317 Fax: 610-388-1197
emc@brandywine.org
www.brandywineconservancy.org

The Conservancy is a nonprofit land and water conservation organization protecting natural resources in southeastern PA and northern DE. It provides conservation services to landowners, farmers and municipalities through acomprehensive approach to cutting-edge environmental planning and management. Through conservation easements, historic preservation, and water protec-

tion efforts, the Conservancy has been instrumental in permanently protecting more than 43,000 acresof land.
Founded: 1967
Joel E. Necowitz, Director of Finance
Andrew Stewart, Director of Marketing

1256 **Global Education Motivators**
9601 Germantown Avenue 215-248-1150
Philadelphia, PA 19118 877-451-7925
Fax: 215-248-7056
gem@chc.edu
A non-profit organization to help schools meet the complex challenges of living in a global society.
Founded: 1981
Wayne Jacoby, President
Sabrina Cusimano, Director of Programs

1257 **Hawk Mountain Sanctuary Association**
1700 Hawk Mountain Road 610-756-6961
Kempton, PA 19529 Fax: 601-756-4468
www.hawkmountain.org
To conserve birds of prey worldwide by providing leadership in raptor conservation science and education, and by maintaining Hawk Mountain Sanctuary as a model observation, research and education facility.
Wendy Mclean, Chairman
Frederick Beste, III, Vice Chairman

1258 **Nature Conservancy: Pennsylvania Chapter**
Nature Conservancy
2101 North Front Street 717-232-6001
Building # 1 Suite 200 866-298-1267
Harrisburg, PA 17110 Fax: 717-232-6061
pa_chapter@tnc.org
nature.org/wherewework/northamerica/states/pennsylvania
To preserve the plants, animals and natural communities that represent the diversity of life on Earth by protecting the lands and waters they need to survive.
Founded: 1951
Bill Kunze, State Director
Nels Johnson, Deputy State Director

1259 **Penn State Institutes of Energy and the Environment**
100 Land and Water Research Buildin 814-863-0291
University Park, PA 16802 Fax: 814-865-3378
www.environment.psu.edu
The mission is to expand Penn State's capacity to pursue the newest frontiers in energy and environmental research by encouraging cooperation across disciplines and the participation of local, state, federal and internationalstakeholders.
Tom Richard, Director
Jenni Evans, Acting Director

1260 **Pennsylvania Association of Accredited Environmental Laboratories**
316 Roosevelt Street 570-888-4768
Sayre, PA 18840 Fax: 570-882-8538
judygraves@paael.org
www.paael.org
A non-profit association of PA DEP accredited laboratories and related industry representatives which takes a leadership role in promoting the advancement of environmental laboratories by: providing educational opportunities,professional development, and a forum for information exchange; providing an arena for memebers to effectively interact with state and national regulatory agencies; and encouraging ethical conduct of environmental laboratories.
Founded: 1987
Twila Dixon, President
Judy Graves, Executive Director

1261 **Pennsylvania Association of Conservation Districts**
25 North Front Street 717-238-7223
Harrisburg, PA 17101 Fax: 717-238-7201
pacd@pacd.org
www.pacd.org
A nonprofit organization that supports, enhances and promotes Pennsylvania's Conservation Districts and their programs. PACd provides districts with education and information to help them in their work in land and water conservation.
Founded: 1950
Robert Maiden, Executive Director

1262 **Pennsylvania Environmental Council**
3915-917 Union Deposit Road 717-230-8044
Harrisburg, PA 17109 Fax: 717-230-8045
bhill@pecpa.org
www.pecpa.org
Protects and restores the natural and built environments through innovation, collaboration, education and advocacy.
Carol F. McCabe, Chair
Jolene Chinchilli, Vice Chair

1263 **Pennsylvania Forestry Association**
116 Pine Street 717-766-5371
5th Floor 800-835-8065
Harrisburg, PA 17101 thePFA@paforestry.org
pfa.cas.psu.edu
A broad-based citizens organization, provides leadership in sound forest management advice and education and promotes wise stewardship to private land owners, resulting in benefits for the resident of the Commonwealth.
Founded: 1886
Robert W. Piper, Jr., President
Gene F. Odato, Vice President

1264 **Pennsylvania Resources Council**
3606 Providence Road 610-353-1555
Newtown Square, PA 19073 Fax: 610-353-6257
infoeast@prc.org
www.prc.org
To promote conservation of our natural resources and protection of scenic beauty through public education and outreach in a collaborative effort with government agencies, business, charitable foundations and other nonprofitorganizations.
Founded: 1939
Tomlinson Fort, President
Robert Jondreau, Executive Director

1265 **Pocono Environmental Education Center**
538 Emery Road 570-828-2319
Dingsman Ferry, PA 18328-9614 Fax: 570-828-9695
peec@peec.org
www.peec.org
PEEC enhances environmental awareness, knowledge, and appreciation through hands-on experience in a natural outdoor classroom. Located in the Delaware Water Gap Nat'l Rec Area, PEEC is open year-round and welcomes school groupsfamilies, retreats, and volunteers.
Founded: 1972
Ed Winters, Development Director
Jeff Rosalsky, Executive Director

1266 **Rodale Institute**
611 Siegfriedale Road 610-683-1400
Kutztown, PA 19530-9320 Fax: 610-683-8548
info@rodaleinst.org
www.rodaleinstitute.org
Works with people worldwide to achieve a regenerative food system thaty renews environmental and human health working with the philosophy that healthy soil = healthy food = healthy people.
Mark Smallwood, Executive Director
Dr. Kristine Nichols, Chief Scientist

1267 **Sierra Club: Pennsylvania Chapter**
PO Box 606 717-232-0101
Harrisburg, PA 17108 Fax: 717-238-6330
pennsylvania.chapter@sierraclub.org
pennsylvania.sierraclub.org

Includes 10 local Sierra Club groups. Emphasis is on state environmental policy advocacy, outings, education and local environmental protection efforts.

Joanne Kilgour, Esq. , Director
Deb Nardone, Director

1268 **Western Pennsylvania Conservancy**
800 Waterfront Drive 412-288-2777
Pittsburgh, PA 15222 866-564-6972
Fax: 412-231-1414
info@paconserve.org
www.paconserve.org

Protects, conserves and restores land and water for the diversity of the region's plants, animals and their ecosystems. Through science-based strategies, collaboration, leadership and recognition of the relationship between humankindand nature, WPC achieves tangible conservation outcomes for present and future generations.

Susan Fitzsimmons, Chairman
Stephen G Robinson, Vice Chairman

Rhode Island

1269 **American Lung Association of Rhode Island**
260 West Exchange Street 401-421-6487
Suite 102 B info@lungne.org
Providence, RI 02903
www.lung.org/about-us/local-associations/rhode-island.html

The American Lung Association of Rhode Island works to prevent lung disease and promote lung health through direct assistance, education programs, advocacy and research.

Jeff Seyler, Executive VP, Northeast
Adam Shuster, CFO

1270 **American Society of Landscape Architects: Rhode Island Chapter**
www.riasla.org

The purpose shall be the advancement of knowledge, education, and skill in the art and science of landscape architecture as an instrument of service in the public welfare.

Jennifer Judge, President
Kurt Van Dexter, President-Elect

1271 **Audubon Society of Rhode Island**
12 Sanderson Road 401-949-5454
Smithfield, RI 02917 Fax: 401-949-5788
audubon@asri.org
www.asri.org

An independent, nonprofit, state organization dedicated to the conservation of wildlife habitat, the education of young and old about natural ecosystems and the need to preserve them, and advocacy in order to promote continued effortsat preserving our natural heritage.

Founded: 1897
Cynthia J. Warren, Esq., President
Deborah Linnell , VP

1272 **Nature Conservancy: Rhode Island Chapter**
159 Waterman Street 401-331-7110
Providence, RI 02906 Fax: 401-273-4902
ri@tnc.org
www.nature.org

An international nonprofit organization dedicated to preserving the plants, animals and natural communities that represent the diversity of life on Earth by protecting the lands and waters they need to survive.

John Cook, Regional Managing Director

1273 **Sierra Club: Rhode Island Chapter**
42 Rice Street 401-521-4734
Providence, RI 02907 chair@risierraclub.org
rhodeisland.sierraclub.org

To advance the preservation and protection of the natural environment by empowering the citizenry with charitable resources to further the cause of environmental protection.

2500 Members
Dana Goodman, Chair
Peter Galvin, Treasurer

South Carolina

1274 **American Lung Association of South Carolina**
44-A Markfield Drive 843-556-8451
Charleston, SC 29407 Fax: 843-766-3294
costal@lungse.org
www.lung.org/about-us/local-associations/south-carolina.html

The American Lung Association of South Carolina works to prevent lung disease and promote lung health through direct assistance, education programs, advocacy and research.

Martha C. Bogdan, Executive VP, Southeast
Willie L. Bythwood, Jr, CFO

1275 **American Lung Association of South Carolina: Upstate**
2030 North Church Place 864-764-1777
Spartanburg, SC 29303 upstate@lungse.org
www.lung.org

Martha C. Bogdan, Executive VP, Southeast
Willie L. Bythwood, Jr, CFO

1276 **American Rivers: Southeast Region**
215 Pickens Street 803-771-7114
Columbia, SC 29205 Fax: 803-771-7580
www.americanrivers.org

Jeremy Diner, Clean Water Supply Associate
Ben Emanuel, Associate Dir, Water Supply

1277 **American Society of Landscape Architects: South Carolina Chapter**
7 Lafayette Place 843-681-6618
Hilton Head Island, SC 29926 Fax: 843-681-7086
www.scasla.org

Jesse McClung, President
Jamie Hairfield, President Elect

1278 **B.A.S.S Nation: South Carolina Chapter**
SC
www.scbassfed.org

The South Carolina Chapter of BASS Nation is dedicated to the promotion of the sport of bass fishing, fishing tournaments and conservation initiatives to preserve the states natural resources

Randy Mosley, President
Chris Jones, VP

1279 **Carolina Recycling Association**
PO Box 1296 877-972-0007
Greenville, SC 29602 Fax: 919-545-9060
staff@cra-recycle.org
www.cra-recycle.org

Conserves resources by advancing waste reducation and recycling throughout the Carolinas
Founded: 1989
Amanda Kain, Board President
Harris Deloach III, Board VP

1280 Friends of the Reedy River
PO Box 9351 864-255-8946
Greensville, SC 29604 www.friendsofthereedyriver.org
The Reedy River is an economic and social resource for the community that impacts our quality of life. Maintaining and protecting its health, above and below the surface, is pivotal in maintaining the natural, social and economicalhealth of the Upstate of South Carolina.
Nikki Grumbine, President
Bob Lloyd, Vice President

1281 Nature Conservancy: South Carolina Chapter
2231 Devine Street, Suite 100 803-254-9049
P.O. Box 5475 Fax: 803-252-7134
Columbia, SC 29205 southcarolina@tnc.org
www.nature.org
To preserve the plants, animals and natural communities that represent the diversity of life on Earth by protecting the lands and waters they need to survive.
Mark Robertson, Executive Director
Serena Hunter, Director of Operations

1282 Sierra Club: South Carolina Chapter
1314 Lincoln Street 803-256-8487
Suite 211 Fax: 803-256-8448
Columbia, SC 29202 southcarolina.sierraclub.org
To advance the preservation and protection of the natural environment by empowering the citizenry with charitable resources to further the cause of environmental protection.
Kurt Henning, Chapter Coordinator

1283 South Atlantic Fishery Management Council
1314 Lincoln Street, Suite 211 803-256-8487
P O Box 2388 866-SAF-C 10
Columbia, SC 29201 Fax: 843-769-4520
safmc@safmc.net
www.safmc.net
Responsible for the conservation and management of fish stocks within the federal 200-mile limit of the Atlantic off the coasts of North Carolina, South Carolina, Georgia and east Florida to Key West.
Robert Mahood, Executive Director
Gregg Waugh, Deputy Executive Director

1284 South Carolina Native Plant Society
PO Box 1324
Greenville, SC 29602 jeffbeacham@gmail.com
www.scnps.org
A non-profit ogranization committed to the preservation and protection of native plant communities in South Carolina.
Jeff Beacham, President
Thomas Angell, Vice-President

1285 South Carolina Solar Council
PO Box 402 803-691-4576
Columbia, SC 29201 scsolarcouncil@gmail.com
www.scsolarcouncil.org

Todd Delello, Chairman
Ron Sebeczek, Treasurer

1286 Southern Appalachian Botanical Society: Gastanea
Newberry College
2100 College Street 803-321-5257
Newberry, SC 29108 Fax: 803-321-5636
charles.horn@newberry.edu
www.sabs.us
This is a professional organization for those interested in botanical research, especially in the areas of ecology, floristics and systematics. To this end, they publish a journal, CASTANEA, and a newsletter, CHINQUAPIN.
Founded: 1936
Charles Horn, President
Kunsiri Grubbs, Treasurer

South Dakota

1287 American Fisheries Society: North Central Division: Dakota Chapter
SD
Steven.Chipps@sdstate.edu
www.dakota.fisheries.org
The Dakota Chapter of the American Fisheries Society, is part of the American Fisheries Society (AFS) North Central Division. The Dakota Chapter works to further to the goals of the AFS and is committed to the conservation,development, and wise use of fishery resources, the chapter provides several annual awards to fishery professionals, conservation groups, and students.
Steve Chipps, President
Michael Johnson, Secretary & Treasurer

1288 American Lung Association of South Dakota
490 Concordia Avenue 651-227-8014
St. Paul, MN 55103 info@lungsd.org
www.lung.org/about-us/local-associations/south-dakota.html
The American Lung Association of South Dakota works to prevent lung disease and promote lung health through direct assistance, education programs, advocacy and research.
Lewis Bartfield, Executive VP, Upper Midwest
Penny Fena, Chief Mission Officer

1289 American Society of Landscape Architects: Great Plains Chapter
NE
Regan.Pence@LRA-INC.com
www.gpcasla.org
Representing South Dakota, North Dakota, and Nebraska the Great Plains Chapter of the American Landscape Society works to expand the profession of landscape architecture in these states. The Chapter advocates and provides professionaleducational and developmental programs for its members
Regan Pence, President
Chad Kucker, Secretary & Treasurer

1290 Great Plains Native Plant Society
PO Box 461 605-745-3397
Hot Springs, SD 57747 Fax: 605-745-3397
info@gpnps.org
www.gpnps.org
Mission is to engage in scientific research regarding plants of the Great Plains of North America; to disseminate this knowledge through the creation of one or more educational botanic gardens of plants of the Great Plains, featuringbut not limited to Barr's discoveries; and to engage in any educational activities which may further public familiarity with plants of the Great Plains, their uses and enjoyment.
Founded: 1984

1291 Sierra Club: South Dakota Chapter
PO Box 1624 605-348-1345
Rapid City, SD 57709 Fax: 605-348-1344
southdakota.sierraclub.org

To advance the preservation and protection of the natural environment by empowering the citizenry with charitable resources to further the cause of environmental protection.
Dana Loseke, Chair
Michelle Loseke, Secretary

1292 South Dakota Association of Conservation Districts
116 N Euclid Avenue 605-895-4099
Pierre, SD 57501 800-729-4099
www.sdconservation.org
Mission is to lead, represent and assist South Dakota's conservation districts in promoting a healthy environment. Specific areas of concern include wind and water erosion, water quality and quantity including preservation of theMissouri main stem dams, air quality, forestry, rangeland, wildlife and recreation.
Founded: 1942
Angela Ehlers, Executive Director
Karl Jensen, President

1293 South Dakota Ornithologists Union
Sioux Falls, SD 57105
www.sdou.org
To encourage the study of birds in South Dakota and to promote the study of orinthology by more closely uniting the students of this branch of natural science.
Founded: 1949
Kent C. Jensen, President
Scott Stolz, Vice President

1294 South Dakota Wildlife Federation
PO Box 7075 605-224-7524
Pierre, SD 57501 Fax: 605-224-7524
sdwf@mncomm.com
www.sdwf.org
Represents the interests of all South Dakotans in wildelife, outdoor recreation, natural resources, and a quality environment.
Founded: 1945
Rich Widman, President
Mark Widman, 1st Vice-President

1295 Wildlife Society
Box 218 605-854-9105
DeSmet, SD 57231 paul.coughlin@state.sd.us
A nonprofit scientific and educational organization that serves professionals such as government agencies, academia, industry, and non-government organizations in all areas related to the conservation of wildlife and natural resourcesmanagement.
Founded: 1937
Will Morlock, South Dakota State President

Tennessee

1296 American Lung Association of Tennessee
1466 Riverside Drive 423-629-1098
Suite D Gail.Bost@lung.org
Chattanooga, TN 37406 www.lung.org/about-us/local-associations/tennessee.html
The American Lung Association of Tennessee is dedicated to preventing lung disease and promoting lung health through direct assistance, education programs, advocacy and research.
Barry Gottschalk, Executive VP, Midland States
Patricia J. Volz, VP, Communication

1297 American Lung Association of Tennessee: Nashville
One Vantage Way 615-329-1151
Suite C 120 Gail.Bost@lung.org
Nashville, TN 37228 www.lung.org/about-us/local-associations/tennessee.html
Barry Gottschalk, Executive VP, Midland States
Patricia J Vloz, VP, Communication

1298 American Society of Landscape Architects: Tennessee Chapter
hollie@tnasla.org
www.tnasla.org
Allen Jonest, President
Alisha Eley, President-Elect

1299 Environmental Toxicology Laboratory
PO Box 2008 865-574-9387
Oak Ridge, TN 37831 www.ornl.gov/content/environmental-toxicology-laboratory
Oak Ridge National Laboratory's Environmental Toxicology Laboratory provides toxicity testing for the DOE, DoD and other Federal agencies.
Mark Greeley Jr., Contact

1300 Kids for a Clean Environment
PO Box 158254 615-331-7381
Nashville, TN 37215 Fax: 615-333-9879
kidsface@mindspring.com
www.kidsface.org
Established to help children who wanted to learn more about the world in which they live, provide a way for children to be involved in the protection of nature and connect children with other children who share their concerns aboutglobal environmental issues.
Founded: 1989
Melissa Poe, Founder

1301 Nature Conservancy: Tennessee Chapter
2021 21st Avenue South 615-383-9909
Suite C-400 800-628-6860
Nashville, TN 37212 Fax: 615-383-9717
tennessee@tnc.org
www.nature.org
To preserve the plants, animals and natural communities that represent the diversity of life on Earth by protecting the lands and waters they need to survive.
Founded: 1951
Gina Hancock, State Director
Paul Kingsbury, Communications Manager

1302 Scenic Tennessee
45 Burris Court 615-758-8647
Mount Juliet, TN 37122 margedavis@comcast.net
The only organization in the state devoted exclusively to issues of scenic beauty.
Marge Davis Ph D, President
Jay Nevans, Vice President

1303 Sierra Club: Tennessee Chapter
3712 Ringgold Road 615-837-3773
#156 tennessee.sierraclub.org
Chattanooga, TN 37412-1638
To advance the preservation and protection of the natural environment by empowering the citizenry with charitable resources to further the cause of environmental protection.
Keven Routon, Chair
Angela Garrone, Vice Chair

1304 Tennessee Association of Conservation Districts
PO Box 107 731-764-2909
Hickory Valley, TN 38042 Fax: 731-658-6726
tnacd.org
Founded: 1982
Ray Weaver, President
John Leeman, Vice President

1305 **Tennessee Citizens for Wilderness Planning**
130 Tabor Road
Oak Ridge, TN 37830
865-481-0286
groton87@comcast.net
www.tcwp.org

Dedicated to achieving and perpetuating protection of natural lands and waters by means of public ownership, legislation, or cooperation of the private sector.
Founded: 1966
Jimmy Groton, President
Sandra Goss, Executive Director

1306 **Tennessee Environmental Council**
One Vantage Way
Suite E-250
Nashville, TN 37228
615-248-6500
Fax: 615-248-6500
tec@tectn.org
www.tectn.org

The mission of the Tennessee Environmental Council is to educate and advocate for the conservation and improvement of Tennessee's environment, communities, and public health.
Founded: 1970
Pat Van Ryckeghem, Chairman
Mary Mastin, Board Secretary

1307 **Tennessee Woodland Owners Association**
PO Box 1400
Crossville, TN 38557
615-484-5535
Fax: 915-484-1924
reharrison@multipro.com

Robert Harrison, Secretary/Treasurer

1308 **Wildlife Society**
554 University Street
PO Box 40747
Martin, TN 38238
731-881-7000
mdodson@fs.fed.us
www.utm.edu/TN-TWS

A nonprofit scientific and educational organization that serves professionals such as government agencies, academia, industry, and non-government organizations in all areas related to the conservation of wildlife and natural resourcesmanagement.
Founded: 1968 $10/Year
Ed Warr, President
Tim White, President-Elect

Texas

1309 **American Environmental Health Foundation**
8345 Walnut Hill Lane
Suite 225
Dallas, TX 75231
214-361-9515
800-428-2343
Fax: 214-361-2534
aehf@aehf.com
www.aehf.com

The Environmental Health Foundation's mission is two-fold: to fund scientific and/or medical research into the causes of environmentally linked disease; and to educate the public about environmentally linked illness and how to preventexposure through lifestyle changes.
Founded: 1975
William Rea, Founder
David Hicks, Director

1310 **American Lung Association of Texas**
1349 Empire Central Drive
Suite 280
Dallas, TX 75247
214-631-5864
TXInfo@lungs.org
www.lung.org/about-us/local-associations/texas.html

The American Lung Association of Texas is dedicated to preventing lung disease and promoting lung health through direct assistance, education programs, advocacy and research.
Holly Torres, Executive Director
Kellye Stephens, Program Coordinator

1311 **American Lung Association of Texas: Houston**
2030 North Loop West
Suite 250
Houston, TX 77018
713-476-9882
TXInfo@lungs.org
www.lung.org/about-us/local-associations/texas.html
Katie Jones, Executive Director
Dr. Rubina Abrol, MD, Program Manager

1312 **American Lung Association of Texas: San Antonio & Austin**
8207 Callaghan Road
Suite 140
San Antonio, TX 78230
210-308-8978
TXInfo@lungs.org
www.lung.org/about-us/local-associations/texas.html
Bill Pfeifer, Executive VP, Southwest
Robbie Moore, Office Assistant

1313 **American Society of Landscape Architects: Texas Chapter**
P O Box 170125
Austin, TX 78725
512-627-4570
Fax: 512-249-9885
jennifer@texasasla.org
www.texasasla.org

Tim Bargainer, President
Jennifer Fontana,CAE, Executive Director

1314 **Association of Texas Soil and Water Conservation Districts**
4311 South 31st Street
Suite 125
Temple, TX 76502
254-773-2250
800-792-3485
Fax: 254-773-3311
bwhite@tsswcb.state.tx.us
www.tsswcb.state.tx.us/swcds/atswcd

The nonprofit organization attempts to make owners and operators of agricultural land aware of the need to conserve and protect the soil and water resources in Texas. It promotes SWCDs (soil and water conservation districts) througheducational, scientific, charitable, and religious activities.
Scott Buckles, President

1315 **Big Bend Natural History Association**
PO Box 196
Big Bend National Park, TX 79834
432-477-2236
Fax: 432-477-2234
info@bigbendbookstore.org
www.bigbendbookstore.org

The association's goal is to educate the public and increase their appreciation of the Big Bend Area. It conducts seminars, publishes and supplies books, maps and other materials.
Founded: 1956
Mike Boren, Executive Director

1316 **Center for Environmental Philosophy**
University of North Texas
1155 Union Circle # 310980
Denton, TX 76203
940-565-2727
Fax: 940-565-4439
www.cep.unt.edu

Publishes the journal Environmental Ethics, maintains a reprint book series in environmental philosophy, promotes education in the field of environmental philosophy, sponsors conference, workshops.
Founded: 1979
Eugene C Hargrove, President
Alexandria K. Poole, Associate Director

1317 **National Wildlife Federation Gulf States Natural Resource Center**
44 East Avenue
Suite 200
Austin, TX 78701
512-610-7761
Fax: 512-476-9810
dayanandap@nwf.org
www.nwf.org

The focus of the four state region (TX, LA, OK, MO) is to restore clean rivers and estuaries, conserve wetlands and natural river

systems, protect wildlife populations, promote sustainable land and water use, and educate the public onthese issues.
Praween Dayananda, Campus Field Coordinator
Lacey McCormick, Communications Manager

1318 Nature Conservancy: Texas

www.tnc.org/texas/

The Nature Conservancy of Texas conserves habitat for native wildlife, using science based research and a cooperative approach to protect the animals and plants that represent Texas' precious natural heritage.

1319 North Plains Groundwater Conservation District
603 E 1st Street
PO Box 795
Dumas, TX 79029
806-935-6401
Fax: 806-935-6633
www.npwd.org
Founded: 1949
Steven Walthour, General Manager
Casey Tice, Compliance Coordinator

1320 Scenic Texas
3015 Richmond Ave
Suite 220
Houston, TX 77098
713-629-0481
Fax: 713-629-0485
scenic@scenictexas.org
www.scenictexas.org

Scenic Texas is a nonprofit organization dedicated to the preservation and enhancement of the tstate's visual environemnt. It seeks and supports public policies which promote scenic conservation and beautification and limits harmfulactions to the visual environment.
Founded: 1967
Don Glendenning, President
Margaret Lloyd, Vice President

1321 Sierra Club: Lone Star Chapter
PO Box 1931
Austin, TX 78767-1931
512-477-1729
Fax: 512-477-8526
lonestar.chapter@sierraclub.org
texas.sierraclub.org

The Lone Star Chapter consists of over 25,000 members and serves as the grassroots communications center. The chapter also represents memebers as they fight at the state level to protect and conserve Texas' diverse natural heritage.
Founded: 1965
Reggie James, Director
Cyrus Reed, Conservation Director

1322 Texas Conservation Alliance
PO Box 822554
Dallas, TX 75382-2554
512-327-4119
TCA@TCAtexas.org
tconr.org

Formerly the Texas Committee on Natural Resources. A statewide conservation organization protecting native wildlife habitat and urging the wise and efficient use of natural resources.
Founded: 1970
Mack Turner, Chairman
Richard LeTourneau, Vice Chair

1323 Texas Environmental Health Association
PO Box 889
Wolfforth, TX 79382
806-855-4277
Fax: 806-855-4277
www.myteha.org

A professional nonprofit educational organization that was originally founded as the Texas Association of Sanitarians and then merged with the National Environmental Health Association and changed its name in 1971. TEHA provides aprofessional organization for Sanitarians and Environmental Health Professionals, designed to serve as the focal point for their education and professional status.
Founded: 1956
J. Victor Baldovinos, President
Russell O'Brien, President Elect

1324 Texas Solar Energy Society
PO Box 1447
Austin, TX 78767
512-326-3391
800-465-5049
Fax: 512-444-0333
info@txses.org
www.txses.org

Their mission is to increase the awareness of the potential of solar and other renewable energy applications and promote the wise use of these sustainable and non-polluting resources.
Lucy Stolzenburg, Executive Director
Scot Arey, Chairman

1325 Texas State Soil and Water Conservation Board (TSSWCB)
4311 South 31st Street
Suite 125
Temple, TX 76502
254-773-2250
800-792-3485
Fax: 254-773-3311
www.tsswcb.state.tx.us

The state agency that administers Texas' soil and water conservation laws and coordinates conservation and nonpoint source pollution abatement programs through the State. The Board is composed of 7 members, 2 Governor appointed and 5landowners, from across Texas, and is the lead state agency for planning, management, and abatement of agricultural and silvicultural (forestry) nonpoint source pollution, and administers the Texas Brush Control Program. There are regional officesthroughout Texas.
Founded: 1939
Marty H. Graham, Chairman
Scott Buckles, Vice Chairman

1326 Texas Water Conservation Association
3755 S. Capital of Texas Highway
Suite 105
Austin, TX 78704
512-472-7216
Fax: 512-472-0537
admin@twca.org
www.twca.org

The Texas Water Conservation Association consists of water professionals and organizations in the state of Texas who represent river authorities, municipalities, navigation and flood control districts, drainage and irrigationdistricts, utility districts, municipalities, groundwater conservation districts, all kinds of water users, and general/environmental water interests.
Founded: 1944
Michael J. Baldovinos, President
Hope Wells, President-Elect

Utah

1327 American Fisheries Society: Water Quality Section
324 25th Street
Ogden, UT 84401
801-625-5358
Fax: 801-625-5756
glampman@fs.fed.us

Section objectives are to: maintain an association of persons involved in the protection of watersheds, water quality, and aquatic habitat, and the abatement of water pollution and aquatic habitat and water deterioration.
Gina Lampman, President

1328 American Lung Association Of Utah
3920 South 1100 East
Suite 240
Salt Lake City, UT 84124
801-484-4456
UTInfo@Lungs.org
www.lung.org/about-us/local-associations/utah.html

The American Lung Association of Utah is committed to preventing lung disease and promoting lung health, through education, research, and advocacy.
Founded: 1904
Bill Pfeifer, Executive VP, Southwest
Kelly Smith, Senior VP,Programs

1329 American Society of Landscape Architects: Utah Chapter
636 Eye Street NW
Washington, DC 20001
202-898-2444
888-999-2752
Fax: 202-898-1185
info@asla.org
host.asla.org/chapters/utahasla

1330 Grand Canyon Trust: Utah Office
390 Castle Creek Lane
Moab, UT 84532
435-259-5284
info@grandcanyontrust.org
www.grandcanyontrust.org
A regional, non-profit conservation organization that advocates for collaborative, common sense solutions to the significant problems affecting the natural resources of the greater Grand Canyon region of northern Arizona, as well asthe forests and red rock country of central and southern Utah.
Bill Hedden, Executive Director
Ethan Aumack, Conservation Director

1331 Jack H Berryman Institute
Utah State University
5230 Old Main Hill NR 206
Logan, UT 84322-5271
435-797-2436
Fax: 435-797-1871
www.berrymaninstitute.org
The Berryman Institute is a national organization based in the Department of Wildland Resources at Utah State University and the Department of Wildlife & Fisheries at Mississippi State University. The Berryman Institute is dedicatedto improving human-wildlife relationships and resolving human-wildlife conflicts through teaching, research, and extension.
Dr. Terry A. Messmer, Director
Dr. Mike Conover, Editor in Chief

1332 Nature Conservancy: Utah Chapter
559 E South Temple
Salt Lake City, UT 84102
801-531-0999
Fax: 801-531-1003
utah@tnc.org
www.tnc.org/utah
To preserve the plants, animals and natural communities that represent the diversity of life on Earth by protecting the lands and waters they need to survive.
Founded: 1951
Dave Livermore, State Director
Ian Mathias, Marketing Manager

1333 Sierra Club: Utah Chapter
423 W 800 S STE A103
Salt Lake City, UT 84101-4803
801-467-9294
utah.chapter@sierraclub.org
utah.sierraclub.org
To advance the preservation and protection of the natural environment by empowering the citizenry with charitable resources to further the cause of environmental protection.
Founded: 1892
Marion Klaus, Chair
Leslie Hugo, Secretary

1334 Southern Utah Wilderness Alliance
425 East 100 South
Salt Lake City, UT 84111
801-486-3161
info@suwa.org
www.suwa.org
The mission is the preservation of the outstanding wilderness at the heartof the Colorado Plateau, and the mangement of these lands in their natural state for the benefit of all Americans.
Founded: 1983
Darrell Knuffke, Chair
Richard Ingebretsen, Vice-Chair & Secretary

1335 Utah Association of Conservation Districts
PO Box 4117
Logan, UT 84323
435-881-7688
www.uacd.org
A nonprofit corporation representing Utah's 38 soil conservation districts. Provides technicians and planners to design conservation projects for private landowners, staff to coordinate watershed and conservation district projects andconservation education outreach.
Bob Barry, President
Allen Henrie, Vice President

1336 Utah Association of Soil Conservation Districts
40 West Cache Valley Blvd.
Building 8C
Logan, UT 84341
435-753-6029
Fax: 435-753-4037
www.uacd.org
William Rigby, Executive Board Member

1337 Utah Division of Wildlife Resources
1594 West North Temple
Suite 2110 Box 146301
Salt Lake City, UT 84114-6301
801-538-4700
Fax: 801-538-4745
dwrcomment@utah.gov
wildlife.utah.gov
Serve people of Utah as trustee and guardian of the state's wildlife.

1338 Utah Solar Energy Association
7414 S State
PO Box 25263
SLC, UT 84125
801-566-5620
Fax: 801-566-0708
info@UTSOLAR.org
utsolar.org
Organized to promote the usage of renewable energy, with a focus on solar energy, through education, public outreach, participation in policy development and other activities to accomplish the goals of the organization.

Vermont

1339 American Lung Association of Vermont
372 Hurricane Lane
Suite 101
Williston, VT 05495
802-876-6500
info@lungne.org
www.lung.org/about-us/local-associations/vermont.html
The American Lung Association of Vermont is dedicated to preventing lung disease and promoting lung health through direct assistance, education programs, advocacy and research.
Jeff Seyler, Executive VP, Northeast
Adam Shuster, CFO

1340 American Society of Landscape Architects: Vermont Chapter
PO Box 1844
Chester
Burlington, VT 05401
info@vtasla.org
www.vtasla.org
The chapter holds monthly meetings to encourage dialogue among practioners and members, collaborate with those in related fields, and embrace professional guidelines.
Scott Wunderle, President
Hannah Loope, President Elect

1341 Bluebirds Across Vermont Project
The Birdhouse Network

255 Sherman Hollow Road
Green Mountain Abdubon Society
Huntington, VT 05462
802-434-3068
Fax: 802-434-4686
bluebirdhousing@ellijay.com
www.cornell.edu

Elizabeth Garrett, President

1342 Conservation and Research Foundation
PO Box 909
Shelburne, VT 05482
913-268-0076
Fax: 913-268-0076
www.conservationresearch.wordpress.com
Founded: 1953
Mary Wetzel, President
Myron Sopher, Treasurer

1343 National Wildlife Federation Northeastern Natural Resource Center
149 State Street
Suite 1
Montpelier, VT 05602
802-229-0650
800-822-9919
Fax: 802-229-4532
www.nwf.org
The Northeastern Field Office works with state-based affiliates and like-minded organizations to protect valuable woods, water and wildlife resources across New England through education, advocacy and research.
Curtis Fisher, Regional Executive Director
Catherine Bowes, Senior Manager

1344 Noise Pollution Clearinghouse
PO Box 1137
Montpelier, VT 05601
888-200-8332
www.nonoise.org
A national non-profit organization with extensive online noise related resources. The mission of the Clearinghouse is to create more civil cities and more natural rural and wilderness areas by reducing noise pollutions at the source.

1345 Northeast Recycling Council
139 Main Street
Suite 401
Brattleboro, VT 05301
802-254-3636
info@nerc.org
www.nerc.org
NERC's mission is to To advance an environmentally sustainable economy by promoting source and toxicity reduction, recycling, and the purchasing of environmentally preferable products and services.
Robert Isner, President
Kaley Laleker, Vice President

1346 Sierra Club: Vermont Chapter
4 Saint Paul St.
Montpelier, VT 05602
802-229-6399
sierraclub.vt@gmail.com
vermont.sierraclub.org
To advance the preservation and protection of the natural environment by empowering the citizenry with charitable resources to further the cause of environmental protection.
Mark Nelson , Chair
David Ellenbogen, Vice-Chair

1347 Vermont Association of Conservation Districts
PO Box 566
Waitsfield, VT 05673-2057
802-496-5162
Fax: 802-329-2057
jill.arace@vacd.org
www.vacd.org
A non-profit organization of Vermont's 14 Conservation Districts whose mission is to help the Districts carry out natural resource oriented programs at the local level.
Jonathan Chamberlin, President
D. Jill Arace, Executive Director

1348 Vermont Haulers and Recyclers Association
PO Box 976
Williston, VT 05495
802-864-3615
Fax: 802-660-8553

1349 Vermont Land Trust
8 Bailey Avenue
Montpelier, VT 05602
802-223-5234
800-639-1709
Fax: 802-223-4223
info@vlt.org
www.vlt.org
One of the most effective land trusts in the country. Its primary focus is on permanently conserving productive, recreational, and scenic lands vital to Vermont's and rural economy and environment.
Founded: 1977
Gil Livingston, President
Rick Provost, Director of Finance

1350 Vermont Public Interest Research Group
141 Main Street
Suite 6
Montpelier, VT 05602
802-223-5221
Fax: 802-223-6855
vpirg@vpirg.org
www.vpirg.org
The largest nonprofit consumer and environmental advocacy organization in the state, with approximately 20,000 members and supporters. VPIRG's mission is to promote and protect the health of Vermont's people, environment andlocally-based economy by informing and mobilizing citizens statewide.
Founded: 1972
Paul Burns, Executive Director
Colleen Thomas, Associate Director

1351 Vermont State-Wide Environmental Education Programs
P.O. Box 412
Lincoln, MA 00177
802-985-8686
info@neeea.org
vermontsweep.org

Heather Durkel, Co-Chair
Jenna Guarino, Co-Chair

Virginia

1352 American Bird Conservancy
4249 Loudoun Ave
PO Box 249
The Plains, VA 20198-2237
540-253-5780
888-247-3624
Fax: 540-253-5782
www.abcbirds.org
A not-for-profit organization whose mission is to conserve native birds and their habitats throughout the Americas.
George H Fenwick, President
Warren F Cooke, Chairman

1353 American Dream
PO Box 797
Suite 101
Charlottesville, VA 22902
301-891-3683
newdream@newdream.org
www.newdream.org
New Dream empowers individuals, communities, and organizations to transform their consumption habits to improve the well-being of people and the planet.
Founded: 1997
Guinevere Higgins, Strategic Partnerships
Casey Williams, Operations & Outreach

1354 American Lung Association of Virginia
9702 Gayton Road,#110
Richmond, VA 23238
804-302-5740
kkoon@lunginfo.org
www.lung.org/about-us/local-associations/virginia.html
The American Lung Association of Virginia is dedicated to preventing lung disease and promoting lung health through direct assistance, education programs, advocacy and research.
Deborah Brown, Executive Director
Joy Meyer, VP, Community Impact

1355 American Society of Landscape Architects: Virginia Chapter
2415-B Westwood Avenue 804-523-2901
Richmond, VA 23230 Fax: 804-288-3551
mary.kidd@vaasla.org
www.vaasla.org

Founded: 1899
Barry Frankenfield, President
Jimmy Shepherd, President-Elect

1356 Arlington Outdoor Education Association
Phoebe Hall Knipling Outdoor Laboratory
PO Box 5646 703-228-7650
Arlington, VA 22205 Fax: 540-349-3336
arlingtonoutdoorlab@gmail.com
www.outdoorlab.org
Founded to own and operate the Phoebe Hall Knipling Outdoor Laboratory. Its primary purpose is to provide a facility and support a school program designed to give urban school children who live in Arlington, Virginia, an opportunity tolearn science, outdoor skills, arts and humanities in a natural setting.
Founded: 1967
Mike Nardolilli, President
Bob Schrider, Vice President

1357 Ashoka
1700 N Moore Street 703-527-8300
Suite 2000, 20th Floor Fax: 703-527-8383
Arlington, VA 22209 info@ashoka.org
www.ashoka.org
Strives to shape a global, entrepreneurial, competitive citizen sector: one that allows social entrepreneurs to thrive and enables the world's citizens to think and act as changemakers.
Bill Drayton, CEO/Chair
Diana Wells, President

1358 Association for Facilities Engineering
12801 Worldgate Drive 571-203-7171
Suite 500 Fax: 571-766-2142
Herndon, VA 20170 info@AFE.org
www.afe.org
The premier organization for facility engineers and maintenance personnel. Unites a large community of likeminded professionals for networking opportunities, knowledge-sharing, and support, as well as offers members a world variety ofeducational opportunities, training, and certification for career advancement.
Dennis M. Hydrick, President & Chairman
Wayne P. Saya, Sr., CPE, Executive Director

1359 Audubon Society of Northern Virginia
11100 Wildlife Center Drive 703-438-6008
Suite 100 info@audubonva.org
Reston, VA 20190 www.audubonva.org
To conserve and restore natural ecosystems. ASNV carries out conservation, education and advocacy programs throughout the region from Alexandria to Manassas in Fairfax, Prince William, Loudoun and Arlington counties, and beyond.
Founded: 1980
Terrence Liercke, President
Bill Brown, Treasurer

1360 Center for Health, Environment and Justice
PO Box 6806 703-237-2249
Falls Chruch, VA 22040-6806 chej@chej.org
www.chej.org
Works to build healthy communities, with social justice, economic well-being, and democratic governance. Through training, coalition-building and one-on-one technical and organizing assistance, the Center works to level the playingfield so that people can have a say in the environmental policies and decisions that affect their health and well-being.
Founded: 1981
Louis Marie Gibbs, Executive Director
Sharon Franklin, Finance/Administration Direc

1361 Chesapeake Bay Foundation
Capitol Place
1108 E Main Street 804-780-1392
Suite 1600 Fax: 804-648-4011
Richmond, VA 23219 chesapeake@cbf.org
www.cbf.org

Founded: 1964
William C. Baker, President
Fay R. Nance, Chief Financial Officer

1362 Citizens Clearinghouse for Hazardous Waste
PO Box 6806 703-237-2249
Falls Church, VA 22040-6806 chej@chej.org
www.chej.org
Nonprofit organization serves citizens' groups, individuals and small municipalities working to solve hazardous and solid waste problems. Supplies information needed to understand, prevent, reduce or eliminate exposure to toxicchemicals through customized assistance, both in-house and on referral, a research library and service, publications and newsletters.
Founded: 1981
Louis Marie Gibbs, Executive Director
Sharon Franklin, Finance/Admin Director

1363 Mid Atlantic Solar Energy Society
Attn: John R. Essig, Chair
PO Box 3333 301-880-7045
Fairfax, VA 22038 866-477-5369
john.essig@mases.org
www.mases.org
Formerly known as the Potomac Region Solar Energy Association, the Mid Atlantic Solar Energy Society (MASES) is a nonprofit organization working to further the development of, use of, and support solar energy. MASES is the regionalchapter of the American Solar Energy Society and serves Maryland, Washington DC and Virginia.
John Essig, Chair

1364 Nature Conservancy
4245 North Fairfax Drive 703-841-5300
Suite 100 800-628-6860
Arlington, VA 22203-1606 mlipford@tnc.org
www.nature.org
To preserve the plants, animals and natural communities that represent the diversity of life on Earth by protecting the lands and waters they need to survive.
Michael L Lipford, Executive Director

1365 Potomac Appalachian Trail Club
118 Park Street SE 703-242-0315
Vienna, VA 22180-4609 Fax: 703-242-0968
info@patc.net
www.patc.net
A volunteer-based organization, founded by the men and women who planned and built the Appalachian Trail. The Club now manages over 1000 miles of hiking trails in the Mid-Atlantic region, along with cabins, shelters, and hundreds of acres of conserved land.
Founded: 1927
Brewster Thhackeray, Staff Director
Heidi Forrest, Management Coordinator

1366 Scenic Virginia
4 East Main Street
Suite 2A
Richmond, VA 23219
804-643-8439
Fax: 804-643-8438
email@scenicvirginia.org
scenicvirginia.org

The sole statewide organization in the Commonwealth dedicated to the preservation, protection and enhancement of Virginia's scenic beauty and community character. Promotes and sponsors programs that enhance landscapes, promote tourismand economic development, encourage natural beauty in the environment, preserve historical and cultural resources, and improve community appearance.

Founded: 1998
Cecelia S Howell, Chair
Barry W Starke, President

1367 Sierra Club: Virginia Chapter
422 East Franklin Street
Suite 302
Richmond, VA 23219
804-225-9113
Fax: 804-225-9114
glen.besa@sierraclub.org
virginia.sierraclub.org

To advance the preservation and protection of the natural environment by empowering the citizenry with charitable resources to further the cause of environmental protection.

Glen Besa, Director
Eileen Levandoski, Assistant Director

1368 Spill Control Association of America
103 Oronoco Street
Suite 200
Alexandria, VA 22314
571-451-0433
info@scaa-spill.org
www.scaa-spill.org

Organized to actively promote the interests of all groups within the spill response community. The organization represents spill response contractors, manufacturers, distributors, consultants, instructors, government & traininginstitutions and corporation working in the industry.

Founded: 1973
Rick Lewis, President
Devon Grennan, Vice President

1369 Student Conservation Association
4245 North Fairfax Drive
Suite 825
Arlington, VA 22203
703-524-2441
Fax: 603-543-1828
dcinfo@thesca.org
www.thesca.org

To build the next generation of conservation leaders and inspire lifelong stewardship of our environment and communities by engaging young people in hands-on service to the land.

Founded: 1957
Martha H Talbot, Co-Founder
Elizabeth Titus Putnam, Founding President

1370 Teratology Society
1821 Michael Faraday Drive
Suite 300
Reston, VA 20190
703-438-3104
Fax: 703-438-3113
tshq@teratology.org
teratology.org/

A multidisciplinary scientific society founded in 1960, the members of which study the causes and biological processes leading to abnormal development and birth defects at the fundamental and clinical level, and appropriate measuresfor prevention.

1371 Trout Unlimited
1777 N. Kent Street
Suite 100
Arlington, VA 22209
703-522-0200
800-834-2419
Fax: 703-284-9400
trout@tu.org
www.tu.org

This organization seeks to conserve, protect and restore North America's trout and salmon fisheries and their watersheds.

Founded: 1959
Jim Asselstine, Chairman
Nancy Mackinnon, Secretary

1372 Virginia Association of Soil and Water Conservation Districts
7308 Hanover Green Drive
Suite 100
Mechanicsville, VA 23111
804-559-0324
Fax: 804-559-0325
info@vaswcd.org
www.vaswcd.org

The Virginia Association of Soil and Water Conservation Districts (VASWCD) is a private nonprofit association of 47 soil and water conservation districts in Virginia. It is a voluntary, nongovernmental association of Virginia'sdistricts that provides and promotes leadership in the conservation of natural resources through stewardship and education programs.

Founded: 1930
Steven Meeks, President
Kendall Elaine Tyree, Executive Director

1373 Virginia Conservation Network
409 East Main Street
Suite 104
Richmond, VA 23219
804-644-0283
Fax: 804-644-0286
vcn@vcna.org
www.vcnva.org

Devoted to advancing a common, environmentally sound vision for Virginia. The network's membership is comprised of more than 115 member organizations committed to protecting Virginia's natural resources.

Founded: 1990
Jacob Powell, Executive Director
Kelley Galownia, Communications Manager

1374 Virginia Forestry Association
3808 Augusta Avenue
Richmond, VA 23230
804-278-8733
Fax: 804-278-8774
vfa@vaforestry.org
www.vaforestry.org

VFA promotes stewardship and wise use of the Commonwealth's forestresources for the economic and environmental benefits of all Virginians. Membership consists of forest landowners, forest product businesses, forestry professionals, anda variety of individuals and groups who are concerned about the future and well-being of Virginia's forest resources.

Founded: 1943
John Carroll, President
Brad Fuller, Vice President

1375 Virginia Native Plant Society
400 Blandy Farm Lane
Unit 2
Boyce, VA 22620
540-837-1600
Fax: 540-837-1523
vnpsofa@shentel.net
www.vnps.org

A statewide organization with approximately 2000 members supported primarily by dues and contributions. The Society's programs emphasize public education, protection of endangered species, habitat preservation, and encouragement ofappropriate landscape use of natice plants.

Founded: 1982
Sally Anderson, President

1376 Virginia Waste Industries Association
508 Somerset Avenue
Richmond, VA 23226
757-686-5960
Fax: 757-686-0010
www.vwia.com

To promote the management of waste in a manner that is environmentally responsible, efficient, profitable, and ethical while benefiting the public and protecting the employees.

Mike Dobson, Manager

1377 **Water Environment Federation**
601 Wythe Street
Alexandria, VA 22314-1994
703-684-2400
800-666-0206
Fax: 703-684-2492
inquiry@wef.org
www.wef.org

A not-for-profit technical and educational organization with 32,000 individual members and 80 affiliated Member Associations representing and additional 50,000 water quality professionals throughout the world. WEF and its memberassociations proudly work to achieve our mission of preserving and enhancing the global water environment.
Founded: 1928
Rick Warner, President

Washington

1378 **American Lung Association of Washington**
5601 6th Avenue
Suite 460
Seattle, WA 98108
206-441-5100
InfoMTP@Lung.org
www.lung.org/about-us/local-associations/washington.html

The American Lung Association of Washington works to prevent lung disease and promote lung health; offering a wide variety of lung health services to the people of Washington.
Allison Hickey, Exec. VP, Mountain Pacific
Tony Peterson, CFO

1379 **American Rivers: Pacific Northwest**
P.O. Box 1234
Bellingham, WA 98227
206-213-0330
877-347-7550
www.americanrivers.org

American Rivers protects and promotes rivers across the United States through national advocacy, innovative solutions and networking with strategic partners. The Pacific Northwest chapter focuses on the conservation of the coastalrivers of Washington and Oregon.
Founded: 1992
Wendy McDermott, Associate Director

1380 **American Society of Landscape Architects: Washington Chapter**
2150 N. 107th St.
Suite 205
Seattle, WA 98133-9009
206-443-9484
Fax: 206-367-8777
office@wasla.org
www.wasla.org

Mission is to lead, to educate and to participate in the careful stewardship, wise planning and artful design of our cultural and natural environments.
Founded: 1973
Laura Thompson, President
Dean W. Koonts, Treasurer

1381 **Conservation Northwest**
1208 Bay Street
Suite 201
Bellingham, WA 98225-4301
360-671-9950
www.conservationnw.org

A nonprofit organization protecting old-growth forests and other wildlands, connecting a larger landscape and vital natural habitats and restoring native wildlife.
Founded: 1988
Bill Donnelly, President
Lisa McShane, Vice President

1382 **Environmental Education Association of Washington**
Environmental Education Association of Washington
210 South Hudson Street
Seattle, WA 98134
info@e3washington.org
www.e3washington.org

Dedicated to increasing the awareness of and support for environmental education in the state of Washington.
Founded: 1991
Ron Harris-White, President
Gillia Bakie, Foundation Manager

1383 **Friends of Discovery Park**
PO Box 99662
Seattle, WA 98139
friendsdiscoverypark@gmail.com
www.seattlediscoverypark.org

An all-volunteer group formed to defend the integrity of Discovery Park and to create and protect there an open space of quiet and tranquility, a sanctuary where the words of man are minimized.
Founded: 1970
Gary Gaffner, President
David Sinclair, Secretary/Treasurer

1384 **Friends of the San Juans**
PO Box 1344
Friday Harbor, WA 98250
360-378-2319
friends@sanjuans.org
www.sanjuans.org

Mission is to protect and preserve the San Juan Islands and Salish Sea for people and for nature.
Founded: 1979
San Olson, President
Stephanie Buffum, Executive Director

1385 **Great Peninsula Conservancy**
423 Pacific Ave
Suite 401
Bremerton, WA 98337
360-373-3500
info@greatpeninsula.org
www.greatpeninsula.org

The Great Peninsula Conservancy is a private nonprofit land trust dedicated to protecting the rural landscapes, natural habitat and open spaces of the Great Peninsula region.
Founded: 2000
Sandr S Bortner, Executive Director
Kate Kuhlman, Operations Director

1386 **International Bicycle Fund**
4887 Columbia Drive South
Seattle, WA 98108-1919
206-767-0848
ibike@ibike.org
www.ibike.org

A non-governmental, nonprofit, advocacy organization, promoting sustainable transport and international understanding. Major areas of activity are non-motorized urban planning, economic development, bike safety education, responsibletravel and bicycle tourism, and cross-cultural, educational programs.
Founded: 1983
David Mozer, President
John Dowlin, Executive Director

1387 **Issaquah Alps Trails Club**
PO Box 351
Issaquah, WA 98027
844-392-4282
contact@issaquahalps.org
www.issaquahalps.org

Mission is to act as custodian of the trails and the lush, open tree-covered mountaintops known as the Issaquah Alps. Offers free guided hikes and a voice for protection of our open spaces, trails, and quality of life.
Founded: 1979
Kirt Lenard, President
David Kappler, Vice President

1388 **Mountaineers Conservation Division**
The Mountaineers
7700 Sand Point Way NW
Seattle, WA 98115
206-521-6000
800-573-8484
Fax: 206-523-6763
info@mountaineers.org
www.mountaineers.org

Mission is to be the premier outdoor recreation club, dedicated to the responsible employment and protection of natural areas.
Founded: 1906
Geoff Lawrence, President
Lorna Corrigan, Vice President

1389 Nature Conservancy: Washington Chapter
74 Wall Street
Seattle, WA 98121
206-343-4345
800-964-0636
Fax: 206-343-5608
washington@tnc.org
www.washingtonnature.org
The Nature Conservancy in Washington is dedicated to sustaining and enhancing a healthy relationship between people and nature.
Founded: 1951
Mike Stevens, Director
Melissa Garvey, Deputy Director

1390 North Cascades Conservation Council
PO Box 95980
Seattle, WA 98145-2980
ncccinfo@northcascades.org
www.northcascades.org/wordpress
The North Cascades Conservation Council (NCCC) keeps government officials, environmental organizations and the general public informed about issues affecting the Greater North Cascade Ecosystem. Action is pursued through legislative,legal and public participation channels to protect the lands, waters, plants and wildlife.
Founded: 1957
Tom Hammond, President
Tom Brucker, Treasurer

1391 Olympic Park Associates
P.O. Box 27560
Seattle, WA 98165-2560
olympicparkassociates.org
An organization working to preseve Olympic Park's wilderness, beauty and spelndor.
Founded: 1948
Donna Osseward, President
John Bridge, Secretary

1392 Olympic Region Clean Air Agency
2940 Limited Lane
Olympia, WA 98502
360-539-7610
800-422-5623
Fax: 360-491-6308
info@orcaa.org
www.orcaa.org
A local government agency charged with regulatory and enforcement authority for air quality issues. It is one of the seven such regional air pollution control agencies in Washington State. The agency also administers laws andregulations regarding such programs as solid fuel burning devices, asbestos abatement, and open burning. ORCAA's jurisdiction: Clallam, Grays Harbor, Jefferson, Mason, Pacific and Thurston Counties.
Founded: 1968
Jim Cooper, Chairman
Cynthia Pratt, Vice Chair

1393 People for Puget Sound
1402 3rd Avenue
Suite 1400
Seattle, WA 98101
206-631-2600
info@wecprotects.org
www.pugetsound.org
People for Puget Sound is a regional citizen's organization founded to educate and involve people in protecting and restoring the land and waters of Puget Sound. People for Puget Sound's programs are based on partnership andcollaborations, scientific credibility, creative use of communications and technology, and a hands-on-style. The organization publishes a quarterly newsletter, and many scientific publications.
Founded: 1991
Joan Crooks, CEO
Rein Attemann, Advocacy Manager

1394 Sea Shepherd: Seattle Chapter
Seattle, WA
seattle@seashepherd.org
www.seashepherd.org
An international non-profit, marine wildlife conservation organization whose mission is to end the destruction of habitat and slaughter of wildlife in the world's oceans in order to conserve and protect ecosystems and species. TheSeattle Chapter focuses on Orcas, Salmon, whales, seals, birds and other marine life and ocean habitats of the Puget Sound and Salish Sea.
Founded: 1977
Paul Watson, President
Peter Rysman, Secretary / Treasurer

1395 Sierra Club: Cascade Chapter
180 Nickerson Street
Suite 202
Seattle, WA 98109
206-378-0114
Fax: 206-378-0034
cascade.chapter@sierraclub.org
cascade.sierraclub.org
To advance the preservation and protection of the natural environment by empowering the citizenry with charitable resources to further the cause of environmental protection.
Margie V Cleve, Chairman
Ken Gersten, Vice Chairman

1396 Solar Washington
PO Box 3832
Seattle, WA 98124
206-618-3620
www.solarwashington.org
A private not-for-profit 501(c)3 association of solar energy equipment manufacturers, system integrators, distributors, dealers, designers, consultants, students, and interested people
David Nicol, President
Robert Ransom, Vice President

1397 Student Conservation Association Northwest
1265 S Main Street
Suite 210
Seattle, WA 98144
412-325-1851
Fax: 206-324-4998
webmaster@thesca.org
www.thesca.org/
SCA is a national organization with regional offices in Seattle, Oakland, Pittsburg, Washington DC and headquartered in Charlestown NH. Our mission is to build the next generation of conservation leaders and inspire lifelongstewardship of our environment and communities by engaging young people in hands-on service to the land. We offer a wide range of internships and crew based programs for ages 16 years and up.
Founded: 1957
Dale M Penny, President/CEO
Jay A Satz, Vice President

1398 Washington Association of Conservation Districts
185 Beebe Road
Goldendale, WA 98620
509-773-5065
Fax: 509-773-5600
wacd@ncia.com
www.wacd.org
A non-profit organization representing Washington's 48 Conservation Districts, whos mission is to advance the purposes of Conservation Districts and their constituents by providing leadership, information, and representation.
Alan Stromberger, President
Mark Craven, Vice President

1399 Washington Environmental Council
1402 Third Avenue
Suite 1400
Seattle, WA 98101
206-631-2600
800-561-8294
Fax: 206-622-8113
wec@wecprotects.org
www.wecprotects.org
Protects what Washingtonians care about- our land and water, fish, and wildlife, and our special way of life. We engage the pub-

lic and decision makers to improve and enforce protections for the health and well-being of our communities.
Founded: 1967
Jay Manning, President

1400 Washington Public Interest Research Group
1402 Third Avenue 206-568-2854
Suite 715 800-213-7383
Seattle, WA 98101 Fax: 206-568-2858
www.washpirg.org
When consumers are cheated or the voices of ordinary citizens are drowned out by special interest lobbyists, WashPIRG speaks up and takes action.
Steve Blackledge, Regional Director

1401 Washington Recreation and Park Association
2150 N 107th St 360-459-9396
#205 888-459-0009
Seattle, WA 98133 Fax: 206-367-8777
www.wrpatoday.org
A not-for-profit professional and public interest organization which is dedicated to enhancing and promoting parks, recreation and arts pursuits in Washington State.
Brad Case, President
Cheryl Fraser, President Elect

1402 Washington Refuse and Recycling Association
4160 6th Avenue SE 360-943-8859
Suite 205 866-788-9772
Lacey, WA 98503 Fax: 360-357-6958
office@wrra.org
www.wrra.org
Represents Washington's diverse and multifaceted solid waste handling industry, providing its members with general legal support, educational seminars, workshops, and representation before regulatory agencies and the Legislature.
Jay Alexander, President
Mark Wash, Vice-President

1403 Washington Toxics Coalition
4649 Sunnyside Avenue N 206-632-1545
Suite 540 800-844-7233
Seattle, WA 98103 Fax: 206-632-8661
webmaster@watoxics.org
www.watoxics.org
Washington Toxics Coalition protects public health and the environment by eliminating toxic pollution. WTC promotes alternatives, advocates policies, empowers communities, and educates people to create a healthy environment.
Founded: 1981
Jesseca Brand, President
Laurie Valeriano, Executive Director

1404 Washington Wilderness Coalition
305 North 206-633-1992
83rd Street 800-627-0062
Seattle, WA 98103 Fax: 206-633-1996
info@wawild.org
www.wawild.org
Mission is to preserve and restore wild areas of Washington State throuh citizen empowerment, support for grassroots community groups and advocacy and public education.
Founded: 1979
Roger Mellem, President
Doug North, Vice President

1405 Washington Wildlife Federation
PO Box 1656 206-769-5627
Bellevue, WA 98009 www.washingtonwildlife.org
To preserve, enhance, and perpetuate Washington's fish, wildlife and habitat through education and conservation programs.
Ronni McGlenn, President

West Virginia

1406 American Lung Association of West Virginia
2102 Kanawha Boulevard E 304-342-6600
Charleston, WV 253[illegible] www.lung.org/about-us/local-associations/west-virginia.html
The American Lung Association of West Virginia works to prevent lung disease and promote lung health; offering a wide variety of lung health services to the people of West Virginia.
Deborah Brown, Executive VP, Mid-Atlantic
Joy Meyer, VP, Community Impact

1407 Sierra Club: West Virginia Chapter
PO Box 4142
Morgantown, WV 26504-4142 melwaggy@gmail.com
westvirginia.sierraclub.org
To advance the preservation and protection of the natural environment by empowering the citizenry with charitable resources to further the cause of environmental protection.
Jim Kotcon, Chair
Mel Waggy, Secretary

1408 West Virginia Department of Health and Human Resources
West Virginia Department of Health and Human Reso
One Davis Square 304-558-0684
Suite 100 East Fax: 304-558-1130
Charleston, WV 25301 DHHRSecretary@wv.gov
www.dhhr.wv.gov
This organization provides life-saving services to West Virginia residents, and has a specific focus on protecting children in West Virginia.
Bill J. Crouch, Cabinet Secretary
Cynthia Dellinger, Assistant General Counsel

1409 West Virginia Forestry Association
1776 Parkersburg Road 304-372-1955
PO Box 718 Fax: 304-372-1957
Ripley, WV 25271 wvfa@wvfa.org
www.wvfa.org
The West Virginia Forestry Association is a non-profit organization funded by its membership. Our members include individuals and businesses involved in forest management, timber production and wood product manufacturing. Our membersare concerned with protecting the environment, as well as enhancing the future of West Virginia's forests through multiple-use management.
Mark Haddix, President
Dane Moore, First Vice President

1410 West Virginia Highlands Conservancy
P.O. Box 306
Charleston, WV 25321 info@wvhighlands.org
www.wvhighlands.org
One of the state's oldest environmental activist organizations. A coalition of recreational users of the West Virginia Highlands working together to address the host of environmental threats to the state.
Founded: 1967
Cynthia Ellis, President
Larry Thomas, Senior Vice President

1411 West Virginia Woodland Owners Association
374 Maple Avenue East 703-255-2700
Suite 310 Fax: 703-281-9200
Vienna, VA 22180 woodlandowners.org

A nonprofit membership organization started and continues to be operated exclusively by independent West Virginia woodland owners.
Keith Argow, President
Dick Courter, Chairman

Wisconsin

1412 **American Fisheries Society: North Central Division: Wisconsin Chapter**
WI
Secretary-treasurer@wi-afs.org
www.wi-afs.org
The Wisconsin Chapter of the American Fisheries Society , is part of the American Fisheries Society (AFS) North Central Division. Working to further to the goals of the AFS through research, education, and professional development, thechapter is committed to the conservation, development, and wise use of fishery resources, and the protection and sustainability of aquatic ecosystems.
Founded: 1969 $10/ Year
Derek Ogle, President
Ted Treska, Secretary & Treasurer

1413 **American Lung Association of Wisconsin**
13100 W Lisbon Road
262-703-4200
Suite 700
info@lungwi.org
Brookfield, WI 53005
www.lung.org/about-us/local-associations/wisconsin.html
The American Lung Association of Wisconsin works to prevent lung disease and promote lung health; offering a wide variety of lung health services to the people of Wisconsin.
Linda Witucki, Executive Directo, Wisconsin
Lewis Bartfield, Executive VP, Upper Midwest

1414 **American Society of Landscape Architects: Wisconsin Chapter**
11801 W. Silver Spring Drive
414-930-1797
Suite 200
president@wiasla.com
Milwaukee, WI 53225
www.wiasla.com
The Wisconsin state chapter supports professional development, visibility and network working opportunities in the field of landscape architecture.
Cody Axness, President
Jonathan Bronk, President-Elect

1415 **Botanical Club of Wisconsin**
Wisconsin Academy of Science, Arts, & Letters
8166 Highway 57
Baileys Harbor, WI 54202
botanicalclubofwisconsin@gmail.com
sites.google.com/site/botanicalclubofwisconsin
The Botanical Club serves the interests of amateurs and professionals working towards a common goal of learning more about the state's diverse vegitation.
Chris Tyrrell, Treasurer

1416 **Central Wisconsin Environmental Station (CWES)**
10186 County Road MM
715-346-2937
Amherst Junction, WI 54407
Fax: 715-346-2493
tquinn@uwsp.edu
www.uwsp.edu/cnr/cwes/
Mission is to foster the appreciation, understanding, skill development, and motivation needed to help build a sustainable balance between the environment, economy, and community.
Founded: 1975
Tom Quinn, Director
Sheri Trzebiatowski, Office Manager

1417 **Midwest Renewable Energy Association**
7558 Deer Road
715-592-6595
Custer, WI 54423
info@midwestrenew.org
www.midwestrenew.org
A non profit organization promoting renewable energy, energy efficiency, and sustainable living through education and demonstration. There are over 3200 active international members representing 39 states and 3 foreign countries.
Founded: 1990
Nick Hylla, Executive Director
Amiee Wetmore, Operations Director

1418 **River Alliance of Wisconsin**
147 S. Butler Street
608-257-2424
Suite 2
info@wisconsinrivers.org
Madison, WI 53703
www.wisconsinrivers.org
Mission is to advocate for the protection, enhancement and restoration of Wisconsin's rivers and watersheds.
Tamara Dean, Chair
Ronald G. Anderson, Vice Chair

1419 **Sierra Club: John Muir Chapter**
754 Williamson Street
608-256-0565
Madison, WI 53703
john.muir.chapter@sierraclub.org
wisconsin.sierraclub.org
To advance the preservation and protection of the natural environment by empowering the citizenry with charitable resources to further the cause of environmental protection.
Bill Davis, Director
Elizabeth Ward, Coordinator

1420 **Sixteenth Street Community Health Center**
1032 South Cesar E Chavez Drive
414-672-1353
Milwaukee, WI 53204
www.sschc.org
The mission of the Sixteenth Street Community Health Center is to improve the health and well-being of Milwaukee's Near South Side residents by providing quality, family-based health care, health education and social services, freefrom linguistic, cultural and economic barriers.
Founded: 1969
Liz Claudio, VP of Operations
Julie B. Schuller, President/CEO

1421 **Trees for Tomorrow Natural Resources Educational Center**
519 Sheridan Street
715-479-6456
PO Box 609
Fax: 715-479-2318
Eagle River, WI 54521
learning@treesfortomorrow.com
www.treesfortomorrow.com
Accredited natural resource specialty school. Hosts workshops for middle/high school students during the school year. Workshops emphasize conservation, proper land management and environmental basics.
Founded: 1944
Kelley Knoerr, President
Bill O'Brion, Vice President

1422 **Upper Mississippi River Conservation Committee**
9053 Route 148
608-783-8432
Marion, IL 62959
neal_jackson@fws.gov
www.umrcc.org
An organization of natural resource managers from IL, IA, MN, MO, and WI, created to promote a continuing cooperation between conservation agencies on the Upper Mississippi River. This is accomplished through workshops, publicationsand annual meetings.
Founded: 1943
Neal Jackson, UMRCC Coordinator
Janet Sternburg, Chairperson

1423 Wildlife Society
425 Barlow Place 301-897-9770
Suite 200 tws@wildlife.org
Bethesda, MD 20814 www.wildlife.org/Wisconsin/home
A nonprofit scientific and educational organization that serves professionals such as government agencies, academia, industry, and non-government organizations in all areas related to the conservation of wildlife and natural resourcesmanagement.
Bruce C. Thompson, President
Darren A. Millier, Vice President

1424 Wisconsin Association for Environmental Education
P.P. Box 418 715-570-2587
Stevens Point, WI 54481 admin@waee.org
www.waee.org
A non-profit organization that sponsors conferences, workshops, and gatherings to promote professional growth and networking opportunities in environmental studies.
Founded: 1975
Lynn Karbowski, Administor

1425 Wisconsin Association of Lakes
147 S. Butler Street 608-661-4313
Madison, WI 53703 info@wisconsinlakes.org
www.wisconsinlakes.org
The Wisconsin Association of Lakes is the only statewide non-profit organization working exclusively to protect and enhance the quality of Wisconsin's 15,000 lakes.
Mary Knipper, President
Derek Kavanaugh, Vice President

1426 Wisconsin Land and Water Conservation Association
131 W. Wilson Street 608-441-2677
Suite 601 Fax: 608-441-2676
Madison, WI 53703 info@wisconsinlandwater.org
wisconsinlandwater.org
To assist county Land Conservation Committees and Departments with the protection, enhancement and sustainable use of Wisconsin's natural resources and to represent them through education and governmental interaction.
Jim VandenBrook, Executive Director
Kirsten Moore, Office Manager

1427 Wisconsin Society for Ornithology
654 W Hillcrest Road 414-416-3272
Apt 202 treasurer@wsobirds.org
Saukville, WI 53080 www.wsobirds.org
Emphasizes all of the many aspects of birding and to support the research and habitat protection necessary to preserve Wisconsin's birdlife.
Founded: 1939
Michael John Jaeger, President
Andy Cassini, Vice President

1428 Wisconsin Wildlife Federation
213 North Main Street 608-635-0600
P.O. Box 460 800-897-4161
Poynette, WI 53955 office@wiwf.org
www.wiwf.org
The mission of the Wisconsin Wildlife Federation is to conserve Wisconsin's wildlife, natural resources and outdoor sporting heritage through conservation education and advocating for strong conservation policies on state and nationallevels.
Bill Tollard, President
Gary Dieckd, First Vice President

1429 Wisconsin Woodland Owners Association
PO Box 285 715-346-4798
Stevens Point, WI 54481 wwoa@uwsp.edu
www.wisconsinwoodlands.org
The Wisconsin Woodland Owners Association is a nonprofit educational organization seeking to advance the interests of woodland owners and the cause of forestry; develop public appreciation for the value of Wisconsin's woodlands andtheir importance in the economy and overall welfare of the state; foster and encourage wise use and management of Wisconsin's woodlands for timber production, wildlife habitat and recreation; and to educate those interested in managing the woodlands.
Founded: 1979
Steven Ring, President
David Congos, Vice President

Wyoming

1430 American Lung Association of Wyoming
c/o American Lung Association
822 John Street 206-441-5100
Seattle, WA 98109 InfoMTP@Lung.org
www.lung.org/about-us/local-associations/wyoming.html
The American Lung Association of the Wyoming works to prevent lung disease and promote lung health; offering a wide variety of lung health services to the people of Wyoming.
Allison Hickey, Exec. VP, Mountain Pacific
Tony Peterson, CFO

1431 Jackson Hole Conservation Alliance
685 S. Cache Street 307-733-9417
PO Box 2728 info@jhalliance.org
Jackson, WY 83001 www.jhalliance.org
An organization dedicated to responsible land stewardship in Jackson Hole, Wyoming to ensure that human activities are in harmony with the area's irreplaceable wildlife, scenery and other natural resources.
Founded: 1979
Carter Cox, Development Director
Dawn Webster, Operations Manager

1432 Nature Conservancy: Wyoming Chapter
Nature Conservancy
258 Main Street 307-335-2120
Suite 200 Fax: 307-332-2974
Lander, WY 82520 pplatt@tnc.org
www.nature.org
The leading conservation organization working around the world to protect ecologically important lands and waters for nature and people.
Founded: 1950
Milward Simpson, State Director
Arlen Lancaster, Conservation Director

1433 Powder River Basin Resource Council
934 North Main Sreet 307-672-5809
Sheridan, WY 82801 Fax: 307-672-5800
info@powderriverbasin.org
www.powderriverbasin.org
Committed to the preservation and enrichment of Wyoming's agricultural heritage and rural lifestyle; the conservation of Wyoming's land, mineral, water and clean air resources, consistent with responsible use of those resources tosustain the vitality of present and future generations; the education and empowerment of Wyoming's citizens to raise a coherent voice in decisions. They are the only group in Wyoming that addresses both agricultural and conservation issues.
Bob LeResche, Chairman
Joyce Evans, Vice Chairman

1434 Sierra Club: Wyoming Chapter
PO Box 1736 307-742-0056
Laramie, WY 82501 Fax: 307-460-8046
connie.wilbert@sierraclub.org
www.wyoming.sierraclub.org

To advance the preservation and protection of the natural environment by empowering the citizenry with charitable resources to further the cause of environmental protection.
Founded: 1984
Connie Wilbert, Chapter Director
Lloyd Dorsey, Conservation Director

1435 Western Association of Fish and Wildlife Agencies
522 Notre Dame Court 307-631-4536
Cheyenne, WY 82009 Fax: 307-638-1470
larry.kruckenberg@wyo.gov
www.wafwa.org

The Western Association of Fish and Wildlife Agencies represents 23states and Canadian provinces and supports resource management to conserve wildlife.
Curt Melcher, President
Keith Sexton, 1st Vice President

1436 Wyoming Association of Conservation Districts
517 E 19th Street 307-632-5716
Cheyenne, WY 82001 Fax: 307-638-4099
bobbie.frank@conservewy.com
www.conservewy.com

Mission is to provide leadership for the conservation of Wyoming's soil and water resources; promote the controll of soil erosion; promote and protects the quality of Wyomings's waters; reduce siltation of stream channels andreservoirs; promote wise use of Wyoming's water and other natural resources; preserve and enhance wildlife habitat; protect the tax base and promote the health, safety and general welfare of the citzens of the state through a responsible conservationethic.
Founded: 1945
Bobbie Frank, Executive Director
Shaun Sims, President

1437 Wyoming Native Plant Society
P.O. Box 2449
Laramie, WY 82073 wynps@wynps.org
www.wynps.org

Goals are to encourage the appreciation and conservation of the native flora and plant communities of Wyoming through education, research, and communication.
Founded: 1981
Charmaine Delmatier, President
Katy Duffy, Vice President

1438 Wyoming Wildlife Federation
PO Box 1312 307-335-8633
Lander, WY 82520 800-786-5434
Fax: 307-335-8690
info@wyomingwildlife.org
www.wyomingwildlife.org

The Wyoming Wildlife Federation is Wyomings oldest and largest conservation group advocating sportsmen and sportswomen. The Federation's mission is to work for hunters, anglers and other wildlife enthusiasts to protect and enhancehabitat; propetuate quality hunting and fishing; protect citizens rights to use public lands and waters; and promote ethical hunting and fishing.
Founded: 1937
Dwayne Meadows, Executive Director
Joy Bannon, Field Director

Awards & Honors

Environmental

1439 Adirondack Council Conservationist of the Year
103 Hand Avenue 518-873-2240
P.O. Box D-2, Suite 3 877-873-2240
Elizabethtown, NY 12932 Fax: 518-873-6675
info@adirondackcouncil.org
www.adirondackcouncil.org

This is awarded to the individual or organization who has provided the greatest contribution towards protecting the health of Adirondack Park. The award is presented each year at the Council's Forever Wild Day, and winners receive aspecailly commissioned, museum-quality, hand-carved common loon in recognition of their achievements.
Ann E. Carmel, Chair
Kevin Arquit, Vice-Chair

1440 Aerospace Medical Association
Aerospace Medicine and Human Performance
320 S Henry Street 703-739-2240
Alexandria, VA 22314-3579 Fax: 703-739-9652
rrayman@asma.org
www.asma.org

AsMA is dedicated to uniting the world's professionals in aviation, space and environmental medicine; advancing the frontiers of aerospace medicineand ensuring the highest level of safety, health and performance of those involved inaerospace. AsMA offers a number of awards outstanding contributors to fields such as aerospace physiology, spatial disorientation, and longstanding education and development of Aerospace Medicine.
Jeffrey Sventek, Executive Director
Fredrick Bonato, Editor-in-Chief

1441 Air Force Association
1501 Lee Highway 703-247-5800
Arlington, VA 22209-1198 800-727-3337
Fax: 703-247-5853
membership@afa.org
www.afa.org

The Air Force Association's mission is to advocate aerospace power and a strong national defense; to support the United States Air Force and Air Force Family; and to promote aerospace education to the American people. The associationhonors the outstanding achievments and contributions of men and women to the United States Air Force. They present over two dozen awards each year.
Kathy Hartness, Industry Relations

1442 Air and Waste Management Association
1 Gateway Center, 3rd Floor 412-232-3444
420 Fort Duquesne Blvd 800-270-3444
Pittsburgh, PA 15222 Fax: 412-232-3450
info@awma.org
www.awma.org

The Air and Waste Management Association is a nonprofit, nonpartisan professional organization that provides training, information and networking opportunites to thousands of environmental professionals in 65 countries. The associationhonors achivements made in leadership and contributions to environmental causes such as air pollution, waste management and further continuing the eduction on air and waste management.
Scott Freeburn, President
Chris Nelson, President Elect

1443 American Association of Engineering Societies
1801 Alexander Bell Dr 202-296-2237
Reston, VA 20191 Fax: 202-296-1151
info@aaes.org
www.aaes.org

Multidisciplinary organization dedicated to advancing the knowledge, understanding and practice of engineering in the public interest. Its members represent the mainstream of US engineering-affecting over 1,000,000 engineers inindustry, government and education. Through its councils, commissions, committees and task forces, the AAES addresses questions relating to the engineering profession. AAES offer their members awards in celebration of their accomplishments inengineering and leadership.
Melissa Prelewicz, Ass. Executive Director

1444 American Chemical Society
American Chemical Society
1155 16th Street NW 614-447-3776
Washington, DC 20036 800-227-5558
webmaster@acs.org
www.chemistry.org

The American Chemical Society is a self-governed individual membership organization that consists of more than 158,000 members in the field of chemistry. The organizations provides a broad range of opportunities for peer intereactionand career development, regardless of professional or scientific interests. They also offer grants and scholarships and awards to honor achivements made in field.
Allison A. Campbell, President
Peter K. Dorhout, President-Elect

1445 American Conference of Governmental Industrial Hygienists
1330 Kemper Meadow Dr 513-742-2020
Cincinnati, OH 45240 Fax: 513-742-3355
mail@acgih.org
www.acgih.org

ACGIH is a member-based organization and community of professionals that advances worker health and safety through education and the development and dissemination of scientific and technical knowledge. The organization honors itsmembers with six awards each year for exceptional leadership and dedication.
Sheryl A. Milz, Chair
Alan Rossner, Treasurer

1446 American Forest and Paper Association
1101 K Street NW 202-463-2700
Suite 700 800-878-8878
Washington, DC 20005 info@afandpa.org
afandpa.org

The American Forest and Paper Association (AF&PA) is the national trade association of the forest, pulp, and paperboard wood products industry. The association represents member companies engaged in growing, harvesting and processingwood and wood fibers, manufacturing paper products from both virgin and recycled fiber, and producing engineered and traditional wood products. They offer the Sustainability Award to a group of exceptional individuals for their work in the field.
Linda Massman, Chairman
John Rooney, First Vice Chairman

1447 American Institute of Chemical Engineers
120 Wall Street 212-591-8100
FL 23 800-242-4363
New York, NY 10005-4020 Fax: 203-775-5177
www.aiche.org

A professional association of more than 50,000 members that provides leadership in advancing the chemical engineering profession. Fosters and disseminates chemical engineering knowledge, supports the professional and personal growth ofits members, and applies the expertise of its members to address societal needs through the world. It offers over 60 awards including certificates, medals, scholarships, and more.
T. Bond Calloway, President
Christine Seymour, President-Elect

1448 American Institute of Mining, Metallurgical and Petroleum Engineers
12999 East Adam Aircraft Circle 303-325-5185
Englewood, CO 80112 Fax: 888-702-0049
aime@aimehq.org
www.aimehq.org
Organized and operated exclusively to advance, record and disseminate significant knowledge of engineering and the arts and sciences involved in the production and use of minerals, metals, energy sources and materials. AIME funds 25awards, including medals and scholarships, every year to honor those who have contributed exceptional work to the AIME disciplines.
L. Michele Lawrie-Munro, Executive Director

1449 American Nuclear Society
555 North Kensington Ave 708-352-6611
La Grange Park, IL 60526 800-323-3044
Fax: 708-352-0499
nucleus@ans.org
www.ans.org
The American Nuclear Society is a not-for-profit, international, scientific and educational organization. It was established by a group of individuals who recognized the need to unify the professional activities within the diversefields of nuclear science and technology.
Robert N. Coward, President
Robert C. Fine, Executive Director

1450 American Society of Civil Engineers
1801 Alexander Bell Dr
Reston, VA 20191 703-295-6300
800-548-2723
Fax: 703-295-6222
www.asce.org
The American Society of Civil Engineers represents more than 137,500 members of the civil engineering profession worldwide, and is America's oldest national engineering society. The organization funds over a hundred awards tocommemorate the achievements and contribution of its members in the field.
Norma Jean Mattei, President
Kristina L. Swallow, President-Elect

1451 American Society of Heating, Refrigerating and Air-Conditioning (ASHRAE)
1791 Tullie Circle NE 404-636-8400
Atlanta, GA 30329 800-527-4723
Fax: 404-321-5478
ashrae@ashrae.org
www.ashrae.org
ASHRAE is an international organization of some 50,000 persons. ASHRAE fulfills its mission of advancing heating, ventilation, air conditioning and refrigeration to serve humanity and promote a sustainable world through reserach,standards writing, publishing and continuing education. The organization offers a number of awards and certificates in recognition of the dedication demonstrated by its members.
Jeff Littleton, Executive Vice President

1452 American Sportfishing Association
1001 North Fairfax St 703-519-9691
Suite 501 Fax: 703-519-1872
Alexandria, VA 22314 info@asafishing.org
www.asafishing.org
The sportfishing industry's trade association, committed to looking out for the interests of the entire sportfishing community. Provides a unified voice, speaking out on behalf of the industry, state and federal natural resourceagencies, conservation organizations, advocacy groups and outdoor journalists. The association gives out 26 awards at their annuel exhibit for innovation and entrepreneurship within the industry.
Mike Nussman, President/CEO
Scott Gudes, VP

1453 American Water Resources Association
4 West Federal St 540-687-8390
PO Box 1626 Fax: 540-687-8395
Middleburg, VA 20118 terry@awra.org
www.awra.org
A nonprofit professional association dedicated to the advancement of men and women in water resources management, research, and education. AWRA's membership is multidisciplinary. It employs water resources experts including engineers,educators, foresters, biologists, ecologists, geographers, managers, regulators, hydrologists and attorneys. AWRA funds ten awards to acknowledge excellence and contributions within the water management field.
Rafael Frias III, President
Brenda Bateman, President-Elect

1454 Association for Conservation Information
1000 Assembly St 843-762-5032
PO Box 167 Fax: 843-734-3951
Columbia, SC 29202 www.aci-net.org
ACI is a nonprofit association of information and education professionals representing state, federal and Canadian agencies and private conservation organizations. Provides natural resource, environmental, wildlife and otherinformation and education to the public through a variety of means, many of which are continental in scope. Each year, the association honors a group of indivudals who demonstrate excellence and innitiative in support of conservation work.
Kim Nix, President
Jenifer Wisniewski, VP

1455 Association of Conservation Engineers
PO Box 180
Jefferson City, MO 65109 conversationengineers@gmail.com
www.conservationengineers.org
Association of conservation engineers and technicians who are working to conserve and improve the nation's natural heritage. It employs experts in the conservation of fish, wildlife, natural resource protection, parks, forests, andrecreation fields.
Holly Bentze, President
Natalie Little, President-Elect

1456 Association of Consulting Foresters of America
312 Montgomery St 703-548-0990
Suite 208 Fax: 703-548-6395
Alexandria, VA 22314 director@acf-foresters.org
www.acf-foresters.org
ACF protects the public welfare and property in the practice of forestry, raises the professional standards, and works with consulting foresters.
Edward G. Tugwell, President
Michael R. Wetzel, President Elect

1457 Audubon Naturalist Society of Central Atlantic
8940 Jones Mill Rd 301-652-9188
Chevy Chase, MD 20815 Fax: 301-951-7179
contact@audubonnaturalist.com
www.audubonnaturalist.com
The Audubon Naturalist Society is an independent environmental education and conservation organization with over 10,000 members in the Washington DC area. The society offers a wide variety of natural history classes and campaigns forthe protection and renewal of the Mid-Atlantic regions natural resources. ANS grants the Paul Bartsch Award for distinguished contributions to natural history.
Leslie Catherwood, President
Paul D'Andrea, Vice President

1458 Audubon Society of New Hampshire
84 Silk Farm Rd 603-224-9909
Concord, NH 03301 Fax: 603-226-0902
asnh@nhaudubon.org
www.nhaudubon.org

The Audubon Society of New Hampshire, a nonprofit statewide membership organization, is dedicated to the conservation of wildlife and habitat throughout the state. Independent of the National Audubon Society, ASNH offers programs inwildlife conservation, land protection, environmental policy and environmental education.
Douglas A. Bechtel, President
Helen Dalbeck, Executive Director

1459 Audubon of Florida: Center for Birds of Prey

1101 Audubon Way 407-644-0190
Maitland, FL 32751 Fax: 407-644-8940
fl.audubon.org/chapters-centers/audubon-center-birds-prey

Audubon of Florida aims to conserve and restore natural ecosystems, focusing on birds and other wildlife for the benefit of humanity and the earth's biological diversity. The Center for Birds of Prey is dedicated to promoting astewardship ethic towards Florida's birds of prey and their habitats through medical rehabilitation, interactive education and practical research.
Katie Warner, Program Manager

1460 Botanical Society of America

PO Box 299 314-577-9566
St. Louis, MO 63166-0299 Fax: 314-577-9515
bsa-manager@botany.org
www.botany.org

This organization promotes botany, the field of basic science dealing with the study and inquiry into the form, function, reproduction, evolution, and the use of plants and their interactions within the biosphere. The society offers anumber of awards to scientists and students in both research and active field work, as well as grants and buseries.
Loren Rieseberg, President

1461 Chicago Community Trust

225 North Michigan Ave 312-616-8000
Suite 2200 Fax: 312-616-7955
Chicago, IL 60601 info@cct.org
www.cct.org

The Chicago Community Trust is a foundation that assists nonprofit organizations through the development of grants and other resources.
Terry Mazany, President/CEO
Michelle Hunter, Director of Strategy

1462 Connecticut River Watershed Council

15 Bank Row 413-772-2020
Greenfield, MA 00130 Fax: 413-772-2090
afisk@ctriver.org
www.ctriver.org

The Connecticut River Watershed Council (CRWC) is the only broad-based citizen advocate for the environmental well-being of the entire Connecticut River. Their mission is to promote improvement of water quality and the restoration,conservation, wise development and use of the natural resources of the Connecticut River watershed.
Andrew Fisk, Executive Director
Colleen Bent, Development Director

1463 Department of the Interior

1849 C Street NW 202-208-3100
Washington, DC 20240 feedback@ios.doi.gov
www.doi.gov

The Department of the Interior protects and manages the Nation's natural resources and cultural heritage; provides scientific and other information about those resources; and honors its trust responsibilities or special commitments toAmerican Indians, Alaska Natives, and affiliated island communities.
Ryan Zinke, Secretary

1464 Ecological Society of America

1990 M Street NW 202-833-8773
Suite 700 Fax: 202-833-8775
Washington, DC 20036 esahq@esa.org
www.esa.org

To promote ecological science by improving communication among ecologists; raise the public's level of awareness of the importance of ecological science; increase the resources available for the conduct of ecological science.
David Lodge, President
Rich Pouyat, President-Elect

1465 Federal Aviation Administration

Office of Public Affairs
800 Independence Avenue SW 202-267-3883
Washington, DC 20591 Fax: 202-267-5047
www.faa.gov

The major roles of the Federal Aviation Administration (a part of the Department of Transportation) include regulation, development, and research in the areas of civil aviation, civil aeronautics, and U.S. commercial spacetransportation. The FAA funds awards for airport safety, aerospace medicine, and more.
Michael Huerta, Administrator
Dan Elwell, Deputy Administrator

1466 Fly Fishers International

5237 U.S. Highway 89 South 406-222-9369
Suite 11 Fax: 406-222-5823
Livingston, MT 59047 ceo@flyfishersinternational.org
www.flyfishersinternational.org

Fly Fishers International seeks to cultivate and advance the art science and sport of flyfishing; to promote conservation of recreational resources; to facilitate and improve the knowledge of fly fishing; and to elevate the standard ofintegrity, honor and courtesy of anglers. Each year, awards are given to various individuals and groups who exemplify the mission and values of the IFFF.
Len Zickler, President/CEO
Rhonda Sellers, Operations Manager

1467 Frank A Chambers Award

Air and Waste Management Association
One Gateway Center, 3rd Floor 412-232-3444
420 Fort Duquesne Blvd 800-270-3444
Pittsburgh, PA 15222 Fax: 412-232-3450
www.awma.org

This award is for outstanding achievement in the science and art of air pollution control. It requires accomplishment of a technical nature on the part of the recipient which is considered to be a major contribution to the science andart of air pollution control.
Dallas Baker, President
Brad Waldron, President Elect

1468 German Marshall Fund of the United States

1744 R Street NW 202-683-2650
Washington, DC 20009 Fax: 202-265-1662
info@gmfus.org
www.gmfus.org

This organization seeks to stimulate the exchange of ideas and promote cooperation between the United States and Europe in the spirit of the postwar Marshall Plan. They recognizes excellence in leadership and innovation through theirawards, grants, and fellowship program.
Craig Kennedy, President

1469 Golden Gate Audubon Society

2530 San Pablo Avenue 510-843-2222
Suite G Fax: 510-843-5351
Berkeley, CA 94702 ggas@goldengateaudubon.org
goldengateaudubon.org

A conservation and education organization that seek to protect birds and wildlife and their natural habitat in San Francisco and East Bay.
Cindy Margulis, Executive Director
Hana DeBare, Communications Director

1470 Goldman Environmental Foundation
160 Pacific Avenue 415-249-5800
Suite 200 Fax: 415-772-9137
San Francisco, CA 94111 info@goldmanprize.org
www.goldmanprize.org
Goldman Environmental Prizes are awarded for sustained and important efforts to preserve the natural environment, including, but not limited to: protecting endangered ecosystems and species, combatting destructive development projects,promoting sustainability, influencing environmental policies and striving for environmental justice.
John D. Goldman, President
Susan R. Gelman, Vice President

1471 Great Lakes Commission
2805 S Industrial Highway 734-971-9135
Suite 100 Fax: 734-971-9150
Ann Arbor, MI 48104-6791 eschmidt@glc.org
www.glc.org
Binational agency that promotes the orderly, integrated and comprehensive development, use and conservation of the water and related natural resources of the Great Lakes basin and St Lawrence River. The Great Lakes Commission offersthe Sea Grant Fellowship which is a year-long position focusing on environmental quality and sustainable economic development in the Great Lakes region.
Jon W. Allan, Chair
John Linc Stine, Vice Chair

1472 Green Watch
Capital Research Center
1513 16th Street NW 202-483-6900
Washington, DC 20036 Fax: 202-483-6990
contact@capitalresearch.org
www.capitalresearch.org/gw
Green Watch is an online database and information clearinghouse providing factual information on over 500 nonprofit environmental groups. This free service identifies the location, leadership and membership of each profiled group.Green Watch also produces timely news reports and analyses of the environmental movement.
Terrence Scanlon, Chairman

1473 Honorary Membership
Air and Waste Management
1 Gateway Center, 3rd Floor 412-232-3444
420 Fort Duquesne Blvd 800-270-3444
Pittsburgh, PA 15222 Fax: 412-232-3450
info@awma.org
www.awma.org
This honorary membership may be conferred upon persons who have attained eminence in some field related to Air and Waste management and have rendered valuable service to the Association of Air and Waste Management.
Scott A. Freeburn, President
Chris Nelson, President Elect

1474 Institute of Environmental Sciences and Technology
1827 Walden Office Square 847-981-0100
Suite 100 Fax: 847-981-4130
Schaumburg, IL 60173 iest@iest.org
www.iest.org
An international professional society that serves the environmental sciences in the areas of contamination control in electronic manufacturing and pharmaceutical processes, design, test and evaluation of commercial and militaryequipment and product reliability issues. IEST recognizes outstanding achievements in technological advances, contamination control, and leadership through their awards program. They also offer scholarships and fellows.
Ahmad Soueid, President
Gordon Ely, President-elect

1475 International Desalination Association
PO Box 387 978-887-0410
94 Central Street, Suite 200 Fax: 978-887-0411
Topsfield, MA 01983 info@idadesal.org
www.idadesal.org
IDA is committed to the development and promotion of the appropriate use of desalination and desalination technology worldwide. The association encourages research and development, promotes communication and disseminates information.
Dr. Emilio Gabbrielli, President
Shannon McCarthy, First Vice President

1476 International Wildlife Film Festival: Media Center
718 S Higgins Avenue 406-728-9380
Missoula, MT 59801 Fax: 406-728-2881
iwff@wildlifefilms.org
www.wildlifefilms.org
An organization showcasing the world's best wildlife films and television programs, providing educational resources and event seminars, workshops, field classes, film tours and many hands-on activities that emphasize the mostup-to-date, factual and ethical scienced based information. Their goal is to promote awareness, knowledge and understanding of wildlife, habitat, people and nature through the medium of film, television and media.
Mike Steinberg, Executive Director

1477 Irrigation Association
8280 Willow Oaks Corporate Drive 703-536-7080
Suite 400 Fax: 703-536-7019
Fairfax, VA 22031 webmaster@irrigation.org
www.irrigation.org
This associate seeks to improve the products and practices used to manage water resources and to help shape the worldwide business environment of the irrigation industry. Each year the Irrigation Association recognizes individuals andorganizations that have made significant contributions to the irrigation industry with the presentation of six awards.
Gregory R. Hunter, President
Warren S. Gorowitz, Vice President

1478 John Burroughs Association
15 West 77th Street 212-769-5169
New York, NY 10024 lbreslof@amnh.org
research.amnh.org/burroughs
Each year a medal is awarded to the author of a distinguished book of natural history, a list of exceptional national history books for young readers is selected, and an outstanding nature essay is identified.
Jeff Walker, President
Dave Liddell, First Vice President

1479 Keep America Beautiful
1010 Washington Boulevard 203-659-3000
Stamford, CT 00690 Fax: 203-659-3001
info@kab.org
www.kab.org
Nonprofit organization whose network of local, statewide and international affiliate progams educates individuals about litter prevention and ways to reduce, reuse, recycle and properly manage wase materials. KAB recognizesachievements made by individuals, communities, and corperations in the field of environmental sustainability, innovation, litter prevention and more.
Carey Hamilton, Executive Director
Beth Buehler, Chief Operating Officer

1480 Keep North Carolina Beautiful
1663 Edgewood Drive 843-427-4969
Little River, NC 29566 nckab@carolina.rr.com
keepncbeautiful.org

Keep North Carolina Beautiful is a nonprofit public education organization dedicated to enhancing the natural beauty of North Carolina communities, improving waste handling practices and empowering individuals to take greaterresponsibility for improving community environments.
Brenda Ewadinger, Executive Director

1481 Lawrence K Cecil Award
American Institute of Chemical Engineers
120 Wall Street
FL 23 212-591-8100
New York, NY 10005-4020 800-242-4363
Fax: 203-775-5177
awards@aiche.org
www.aiche.org

Recognizes an individual's outstanding chemical engineering contribution and achievement in the preservation or improvement of the environment.
T. Bond Calloway, President
Christine Seymour, President-Elect

1482 Lyman A Ripperton Award
Air and Waste Management Association
One Gateway Center, 3rd Floor 412-232-3444
420 Fort Duquesne Boulevard Fax: 412-232-3450
Pittsburgh, PA 15222 info@awma.org
www.awma.org

Awarded for distinguished achievement as an educator in some field of air pollution control. Awarded to an individual, who by precept and example, has inspired students to achieve excellence in all their professional and socialendeavors.
Scott A. Freeburn, President
Chris Nelson, President Elect

1483 NSF International
789 N Disboro Road 734-769-8010
PO Box 130140 Fax: 734-769-0109
Ann Arbor, MI 48105 info@nsf.org
www.nsf.org

NSF International, The Public Health and Safety Company, is an independent, not-for-profit organization providing a wide range of services around the world. NSF is committed to public health, safety and protection of the enviroment.NSF recognizes outstanding professionals in the fields of environmental health and food safety with two annual awards, including the Food Safety Leadership award and the Walter F. Snyder award which celebrates achievement in attaining environmentalquality.
Kevan P. Lawlor, President/CEO
Jesse Ahrendt, Executive Director

1484 National Association of Conservation Districts
509 Capitol Court, NE 202-547-6223
Washington, DC 20002-4937 Fax: 202-547-6450
beth-mason@nacdnet.org
www.nacdnet.org

The association's annual Awards Program recognizes individuals and organizations for outstanding work and leadership in soil and water conservation. Awards include: NACD Friend of Conservation; Distinguished Service; President's;Excellence in Communications; District Excellence; and Collaborative Conservation.
Jeremy Peters, CEO
Rich Duesterhaus, Director of Projects

1485 National Audubon Society
National Audubon Society
225 Varick Street 212-979-3196
7th Floor Fax: 212-979-3188
New York, NY 10014 audubon@emailcustomerservice.com
www.audubon.org

The mission of the National Audubon Society is to conserve and restore natural ecosystems, focusing on birds and other wildlife for the benefit of humanity and the earth's biological diversity. Awards include: the Callison Award, theRachel Carson Award, and the Audubon Photography Awards.
David Yarnold, President and CEO
John Beavers, Vice President

1486 National Bison Association
The National Bison Association
8690 Wolff Ct 303-292-2833
Suite 200 Fax: 303-845-9081
Westminster, CO 80031 info@bisoncentral.com
www.bisoncentral.com

A nonprofit association which promotes the preservation, production and marketing of bison. NBA activities and services serve to better inform andeducate the general public about bison and to create and sustainable future fortheindustry. The association offers scholarships for university students persuing bison related studies.
Roy Liedtke, President
Dick Gehring, Vice President

1487 National Environmental, Safety And Health Training Association
584 Main Street 207-771-9020
South Portland, MN 04106 neshta@neshta.org
neshta.org

The National Environmental Training Assoication, is a nonprofit international organization of enviromental, health and safety, and other technical training professionals.
Myrtle I. Turner-Harris, Executive Director
Jeffery K. Dennis, President

1488 National Ocean Industries Association
National Ocean Industries Association
1120 G Street NW 202-347-6900
Suite 900 Fax: 202-347-8650
Washington, DC 20005 jwilliams@noia.org
www.noia.org

The National Ocean Industries Assoication represents all facets of the domestic offshore and related industries. More than 300 member companies are dedicated to the development of offshore oil and natural gas. Annual awards include theCulture of Safety Award and the Safety Practice Award.
Cindy Taylor, Chairman
Kevin Mcevoy, Vice Chairman

1489 National Press Club
National Press Club
529 14th Street NW 202-662-7500
13th Floor info@press.org
Washington, DC 20045 www.press.org
Professional organization of reporters, writers and newspeople employed by newspapers, wire services, magazines, radio and television stations, and other forms of news media. They publish a weekly newsletter. Awards include: ConsumerJournalism Award; Washington Regional Reporting Award; Arthur Rowse Award for Press Criticism; Edwin M. Hood Award for Diplomatic Correspondence; Newsletter Journalism Award; Joan M. Friedenberg Online Journalism Award; and eight more.
Jeffrey Ballou, President

1490 National Recreation and Park Association
National Recreation And Park Association
22377 Belmont Ridge Road 703-858-0784
Ashburn, VA 20148-4501 800-626-6772
Fax: 703-858-0794
info@nrpa.org
www.nrpa.org

The mission of the National Recreation and Park Association is to a advance parks, recreation and environmental conservation efforts that enhance the quality of life for all people. The associa-

tion recognizes individual achievementswithin the field through scholarships and fellows, and awards including the Gold Medal Award for Excellence in Park and Recreation Management, the NRPA National Award, and induction into the NRPA Robert C. Crawford Hall of Fame.
Barbara Tulipane, President/CEO
Stephen Eckelberry, Chair

1491 National Recycling Coalition
National Recycling Coalition
1220 L St NW — 202-618-2107
Suite 100-155 — Fax: 202-789-1431
Washington, DC 20005 — info@nrc-recycle.org
www.nrc-recycle.org
NRC is a not-for-profit organization dedicated to the advancement and improvement of recycling, source reduction, composting, and reuse by providing technical information, education, training, outreach, and advocacy services to itsmembers in order to conserve resources and benefits the environment. Awards include: NRCs's Lifetime Achievement Award; Bill Heenan Emerging Leader Award; Outstanding Recycling Organization; Outstanding Community or Government Program ; and threemore.
Bob Gedert, President
Marjie Griek, Vice President

1492 National Water Resources Association (NWRA)
4 E Street Southeast — 202-698-0693
Washington, DC 20003 — Fax: 202-698-0694
nwra@nwra.org
www.nwra.org
The NWRA consists of individuals and groups, such as irrigation districts, canal companies and conservancy districts, municipalities and the public in general, who are interested in water resource development projects. The NWRA offersseven awards for achievements within the field, including Distinguished Service Award, the Water Buffalo Award, the Lifetime Achievement Award, the President's Award, the John M. Sayre Award, Water Statesman Award, and the John F. Sullivan/G. ThomasChoules Award.
Ron Thompson, President
Ian Lyle, Vice-President

1493 National Wild Turkey Federation
770 Augusta Road — 803-637-3106
PO Box 530 — 800-843-6983
Edgefield, SC 29824-530 — Fax: 803-637-0034
nwtf@nwtf.net
www.nwtf.org/
The NWTF, an international nonprofit conservation and education organization dedicated to conserving wild turkeys and preserving hunting traditions. The NWTF funs over 30 different awards including invidual achievements in preservingheritage, communication, law enforecement, forest services, volunteering, wildlife preservation, education, and sportmenship.
Becky Humphries, CEO
Vern Ross, Chairman

1494 National Wildlife Federation
11100 Wildlife Center Drive
Reston, VA 20190 — 800-822-9919
www.nwf.org
The National Wildlife Federation represents the power and commitment of over five million members and supporters joined by affiliated wildlife organizations throughout the states and territories. The NWF honors three individuals everyyear at their annual luncheon through the Jay N. "Ding" Darling Conservation Award, Conservationist of the Year, and the National Conservation Achievement Award.
Collin O'Mara, President/CEO
Kathy Hadley, Chair

1495 Natural Resources Defense Council
40 West 20th Street — 212-727-2700
11th Floor — Fax: 212-727-1773
New York, NY 10011 — nrdcinfo@nrdc.org
www.nrdc.org
The NRDC focuses on issues impacting climate change, ocean pollution, water management and treatment, clean energy, and the conservation of wildlife. The NRDC funds the the Growing Green Awards to celebrate America's most influentialleaders in sustainable food market.
Rhea Suh, President
Mitchell Bernard, Chief Counsel

1496 Nature Conservancy
4245 N Fairfax Drive — 703-841-5300
Suite 100 — 800-628-6860
Arlington, VA 22203-1606 — www.nature.org
The Nature Conservancy is an international, nonprofit organization dedicated to preserving plant life. animals and natural communities by protecting the lands and waters they need to survive. Awards funded by this organization includeConservation Leadership, Volunteer Excellence, and Special Recognition.
Mark R. Tercek, President/CEO
Thomas J. Tierney, Chairman

1497 New England Wildflower Society
180 Hemenway Road — 508-877-7630
Framingham, MA 01701-2699 — 508-877-3658
Fax: 508-877-3658
information@newenglandwild.org
www.newenglandwild.org
New England Wild Flower Society is a recognized leader in native plant conservation. Its purpose is to promote the conservation of temperate North American plants through key programs-conservation and research, education, horticultureand habitat preservation. They publish two magazines annually. The society offers three awards: the Founder's Medal, the Regional Impact Award, and the Service to the Society Award.
Debbi Edelstein, Executive Director
Alan Smith, Chair, Board of Trustees

1498 New York Botanical Garden
2900 Southern Boulevard — 718-817-8700
Bronx, NY 10458-5126 — Fax: 718-562-8474
www.nybg.org
The Garden is one of the world's largest collection of plants, an educational center for gardening and horticulture, and an international center for plant research. The NYBG honors persons whose committment to botanical research isinfluencial with the Gold Medal.
Maureen Chilton, Chairman
Gregory Long, President

1499 North American Association for Environmental Education
2000 P Street NW — 202-419-0412
Suite 540 — Fax: 937-335-5623
Washington, DC 20036 — judybraus@naaee.org
www.naaee.org
The North American Association for Environmental Education is a network of professionals, students and volunteers working in the field of environmental education. NAAEE takes a cooperative, nonconfrontational, scientifically-basedapproach to promoting education about environmental issues. Awards funded by the NAAEE include: Walter E. Jeske Award, Rosa Parks and Grace Lee Boggs Outstanding Service, K-12 Educator of the Year, Outstanding Affiliate Organization; and more.
Jose Marcos-Iga, President
Judy Braus, Executive Director

1500 Outdoor Writers Association of America
615 Oak Street
Suite 201
Missoula, MT 59801
406-728-7434
800-692-2477
Fax: 406-728-7445
krhoades@owaa.org
www.owaa.org

The mission of the Outdoor Writers Association of America is to improve the professional skills of its members, encourage public enjoyment and conservation of natural resources, and be mentors for the next generation of professionaloutdoor communicators. It funds a number of scholarships and fellows; and honors its memebers' achievements with five awards, which include: the Excellence in Craft Award, the Outstanding Board Member award, the Ham Brown Award, and Jackie PfeifferMemorial Award.
Brett Prettyman, President
Phil Bloom, First Vice President

1501 Sea Grant Association
University Of Maine
PO Box 1950
Ocean Springs, ME 03956-1950
608-262-0905
jphurley@wisc.edu
www.sga.seagrant.org

SGA is a non-profit organization dedicated to furthering the Sea Grant program concept. SGA provides the mechanism for academic institutions to coordinate their activities, set program priorities at both the regional and nationallevel, and to be a unified voice for the institutions on issues of importance to the oceans and coasts. The association funds six awards, including: the Distinguished Service Award, the President's Award, and the Sea Grant Association Award.
James Hurley, President
Fredrika Moser, President-Elect

1502 Sierra Club
2101 Webster Street
Suite 1300
Oakland, CA 94612
415-977-5500
Fax: 510-208-3140
information@sierraclub.org
www.sierraclub.org

To advance the preservation and protection of the natural environment by empowering the citizenry with charitable resources to further the cause of environmental protection. The Sierra Club honors its volunteers and staff membersthrough its awards program. Awards include: the John Muir award, the Distinguished Achievement Award, the Special Service Award, the One-Club Award, The Roy Family Award for Environmental Partnership, and many more.
Loren Blackford, President
Susana Reyes, Vice President

1503 Society of American Foresters
10100 Laureate Way
Bethesda, MD 20814-2198
301-897-8720
866-897-8720
Fax: 301-897-3690
membership@safnet.org
www.eforester.org

To advance the science, education, technology, and practice of forestry; to enhance the competency of its members; to establish professional excellence; and to use the knowledge, skills, and conservation ethic of the profession toensure the continued health and use of forest ecosystems present and future of availability of forest resources to benefit society. Awards are offered for communication, journalism, forest science, technoly, leadership, and outstanding achievments inforestry.
Frederick W. Cubbage, CF, President
David S. Lewis, Vice President

1504 Society of American Travel Writers
7044 South 13th Street
Oak Creek, WI 53154
414-908-4949
Fax: 414-768-8001
satw@satw.org
www.satw.org

SATW is a professional association whose purpose is to promote responsible journalism, provide professional support and development for its members and encourage the conservation and preservation of travel resources worldwide. Awardsoffered by SATW include: the Lowell Thomas Award, the Marco Polo Status, the Phoenix Award, the Muster Photo Competition; as well as writing and photography awards.
Catharine Hamm, President
Barbara Ramsay, President-Elect

1505 Society of Petroleum Engineers
222 Palisades Creek Drive
PO Box 833836
Richardson, TX 75080
972-952-9393
Fax: 972-952-9435
spedal@spe.org
www.spe.org

This organization represents and serves managers, engineers, scientists and other professionals worldwide in the oil and gas industry. The SPE celebrates its members with over 30 awards, including: Anthony F. Lucas Technical LeadershipGold Medal, Drilling Engineering Award, Production and Operations Award, Distinguished Lifetime Achievement Award, Young Member Outstanding Service Award, Health, Safety, Security, Environment, and Social Responsibility Award, and many more.
Janeen Judah, President
Roland Moreau, VP, Finance

1506 Soil and Water Conservation Society
945 Sw Ankeny Road
Ankeny, IA 50023-9723
515-289-2331
800-THE-SOIL
Fax: 515-289-1227
swcs@swcs.org
www.swcs.org

Foster the science and the art of soil, water and related natural resource management to achieve sustainability. To promote and practice an ethic recognizing the interdependence of the people in the environment. Awards include afellowship, the Outstanding Service Award, the Commendation Award, the Conservation Research Award, the Hugh Hammond Bennett Award, the Harold-Kay Scholl Excellence in Conservation Award, and the Merit and Honor awards.
Clare Lindahl, CEO
Rex Martin, President

1507 Solar Energy Industries Association
600 14th Street NW
Suite 400
Washington, DC 20005
202-682-0556
Fax: 202-628-7779
info@seia.org
www.seia.org/

SEIA seeks to expand the use of solar technologies in the global marketplace. National members combined with chapter members in 22 states exceed 500 compines providing solar thermal and solar electric products and services. It honorsachievments in the field of solar energy with their annual Solar Champion Awards.
Abigail Ross Hopper, President
Tom Starrs, Chair

1508 The Wildlife Society Awards
5410 Grosvenor Lane
Suite 200
Bethesda, MD 20814-2144
301-897-9770
Fax: 301-530-2471
wildlife.org/engage/awards

TWS Awards Program honors individuals and groups who have made notable contributions to wildlife conservation. With more than a dozen awards in all, visit thieir website for full details and nomination information. Some included areAldo Leopold Memorial Award, Chapter of the Year Award, Distinguished Service Award, Caesar Kleberg Award For Excellence in Applied Wildlife Research, Donald H. Rusch Memorial Game Bird Research Scholarship, Wildlife Publication Awards, and more.
Bruce C. Thompson, President
Darren A. Miller, Vice President

1509 Trout Unlimited
1777 N. Kent Street
Suite 100
Arlington, VA 22209
703-522-0200
800-834-2419
Fax: 703-284-9400
trout@tu.org
www.tu.org

This organization seeks to conserve, protect and restore North America's trout and salmon fisheries and their watersheds. Trout Unlimited offer five awards including: State Council Award for Excellence, Gold and Silver Trout ChapterAwards, Mortensen Award for Outstanding Volunteer Leadership, Trout Conservation Award: Professional, Partner Organization/Business, Communications, and Distinguished Service Award: Conservation, Leadership, Communications, Youth Education, andVeteran's Services.

Jim Asselstine, Chairman
Nancy Mackinnon, Secretary

1510 US Army Corps of Engineers
441 G Street NW
Washington, DC 20314-1000
202-761-0011
webmaster@usace.army.mil
www.usace.army.mil/

The US Army Corps of Engineers provides quality, responsive engineering services to the nation including: planning, desiging, building and operating water resources and other civila works projects. The organization honors its membersin over 40 catagories including: Civilian of the Year, Enginner of the Year, Leadership in Contracting, project management, research, excellence in safety, Architect of the Year, Green Innovation, sustainability, human resources, enviornmentalengineering, and more.

Todd T. Semonite, Commander/Chief Engineers
Richard L. Stevens, Major General

1511 US Department of Energy
1000 Independence Avenue SW
Washington, DC 20585
202-586-5000
800-dia-ldoe
Fax: 202-586-4403
www.energy.gov

The Department of Energy's mission is to advance the national, economic and energy security of the US; to promote scientific and technological innovation; and to ensure the environmental cleanup of the national nuclear weapons complex.The department honors students across the country who demonstrate commitment and excellence.

Dr. Ernest Moniz, Secretary of Energy
Dr. Elizabeth Sherwood-Randall, Deputy Secretary of Energy

1512 US Environmental Protection Agency
Ariel Rios Building
1200 Pennsylvania Ave Nw
Washington, DC 20460
800-438-2474
www.epa.gov

The mission of the EPA is to protect human health and the environment. Awards include: Organizational Leadership Award, Excellence in Greenhouse Gas Management, and Innovative Partnership Certificate.

Scott Pruitt, Administrator
Mike Flynn, Deputy Administrator

1513 Underwater Society of America
PO Box 628
Daly City, CA 94017
650-583-8492
Fax: 408-294-3496
www.underwater-society.org/

This organization focuses on diving, marine ecology, safety, legislation, and marine conservation. Awards include: the NOGI, The Regional Divers of the Year Award, and the Women Divers Hall of Fame.

Carol Rose, President

1514 Washington Journalism Center
P.O. Box 15603
Washington, DC 20003-603
202-296-8455
Fax: 808-588-365
terrymichael@wcpj.org
www.wcpj.org

National Award for Environmental Reporting recognizes excellence in journalism and promoting awareness to environmental issues.

Joe Foote, President

1515 Water Environment Federation
601 Wythe Street
Alexandria, VA 22314
800-666-0206
Fax: 703-684-2400
inquiry@wef.org
www.wef.org

The Water Environment Federation (WEF) is a not-for-profit technical and educational organization with members from varied disciplines who work toward the preservation and enhancement of the global water environment. The Awards Programprovides an opportunity to recognize individuals and organizations that have made outstanding contributions to the water environment profession. Catergories include: graduate studies scholarships, environmental engineering, excellence in safety andoperations.

Jenny Hartfelder, President-Elect
Rick Warner, President

1516 Whooping Crane Conservation Association
715 Earl Drive
Lawrenceburg, TN 38464
337-234-6339
www.whoopingcrane.com

To advance conservation, protection and propagation of the Whooping Crane population, to prevent its extinction, to establish and maintain a captive management program for the perpetuation of the species. The Whooping CraneConservation Award is for lifetime achievement through exceptional dedication and significant contributions to the conservation and/or collective knowledge of the whooping crane.

Walt Strugeon, President

1517 Wilderness Society
1615 M Street NW
Washington, DC 20036
202-833-2300
800-THE-WILD
member@tws.org
www.wilderness.org

The Wilderness Society seeks to achieve clean air and water; and preserve forestry and ecosystems. Ansel Adams Conservation Award is presented to a current or former federal official who has shown exceptional commitment to the cause ofconservation and the fostering of an American land ethic. The The Robert Marshall Award is The Wilderness Society's highest award presented to a private citizen who has never held federal office but has devoted long-term service to and has had anotable influence.

Jamie Williams, President
Thomas Tepper, Vice President

1518 Willowbrook Wildlife Haven Preservation
National Wildlife Rehabilitation Association
2625 Clearwater Road
Suite 110
St. Cloud, MN 56301
320-230-9920
Fax: 320-230-3077

The National Wildlife Rehabilitators Association is a nonprofit international membership organization committed to promoting and improving the integrity and professionalism of wildlife rehabilitation and contributing to thepreservation of natural ecosystems.

Elaine M. Thrune, President
Richard Grant, President Elect

1519 World Environment Center
734 15th Street NW 202-312-1370
Suite 720 Fax: 202-637-2411
Washington, DC 20005 info@wec.org
www.wec.org

The World Environment Center is an independent, global non-profit, non-advocacy organization that advances sustainable development worldwide through the business practices of member companies and in partnership with governments,multi-lateral organizations, private sector organizations, universities and other stakeholders. The Gold Medal Award is presented annually to a global company that has demonstrated a unique example of sustainability in business practice.

Francisco Su rez Hern ndez, Chair
Dr. Terry F. Yosie, President/CEO

1520 World Wildlife Fund
1250 24th Street NW 202-293-4800
PO Box 97180 800-225-5993
Washington, DC 20037 Fax: 202-293-9211
membership@wwfus.org
www.worldwildlife.org

Dedicated to protecting endangered species and their habitats through field work, advocacy, policy engagement, pioneering work and education. The largest multinational conservation organization in the world. Awards funded by theorganization include: The Duke of Edinburgh Conservation, the International President's Award, WWF Award for Conservation Merit, the Gift to the Earth award, Leaders for a Living Planet, and External Recognition of WWF.

Carter Roberts, President/CEO
Marcia Marsh, COO

Conferences & Trade Shows

Environmental

1521 Air and Waste Management Association Annual Conference and Exhibition
1 Gateway Center, 3rd Floor 412-232-3444
420 Fort Duquesne Boulevard 800-270-3444
Pittsburgh, PA 15222 Fax: 412-232-3450
info@awma.org
www.awma.org

Environmental professionals from all sectors of the economy including colleges, universities, natural resource manufacturing and process industries, consultants, local state, provincial, regional and federal governments, construction,utilities industries gather to work together to improve community health and protect the environment.
Scott Freeburn, President
Chris Nelson, President Elect

1522 American Academy of Environmental Medicine Conference
6505 E. Central Avenue 316-684-5500
Suite 296 Fax: 888-411-1206
Wichita, KS 67206 defox@aaemonline.org
www.aaemonline.org

Aims to support physicians and other professionals in serving the public through education about the interaction between humans and their environment, and to promote optimal health through prevention and safe, effective treatment ofthe causes, not the illness.
35+ booths with 200 attendees and 35+ exhibits
Gregg Govett, M.D., President
Derek Lang, D.O., President Elect

1523 American Board of Industrial Hygiene Professional Conference
American Board of Industrial Hygiene
6005 West St Joseph 517-321-2638
Suite 300 Fax: 517-321-4624
Lansing, MI 48917 abih@abih.org
www.abih.org

Industrial hygiene certification organization. Certified industrial hygienist is offered based on education, experience and examination.
Robert DeHart II, Director
Cynthia Hanko, Director

1524 American Conference of Governmental Industrial Hygienists
1330 Kemper Meadow Drive 513-742-2020
Cincinnati, OH 45240 Fax: 513-742-3355
mail@acgih.org
www.acgih.org

ACGIH is a charitable scientific organization that aims to advance occupational and environmental health through education and the development and dissemination of scientific and technical knowledge.
3,000 Members
90 booths
Sheryl A. Milz, Chair
Alan Rossner, Treasurer

1525 American Industrial Hygiene Association Conference and Exposition
3141 Fairview Park Drive 703-849-8888
Suite 777 Fax: 703-207-3561
Falls Church, VA 22042 infonet@aiha.org
www.aiha.org

AIHA promotes, protects and enhances industrial hygienists and other occupational health, safety and environmental professionals in their efforts to improve the health and well-being of workers, the community and the environment.
Deborah Imel Nelson, President
Cynthia A. Ostrowski, President-elect

1526 American Solar Energy Society Conference
American Solar Energy Society
2525 Arapahoe Ave 303-443-3130
Ste E4-253 info@ases.org
Boulder, CO 80302 www.ases.org
The American Solar Energy Society (ASES) is natioal nonprofit organization dedicated to advancing the use of solar energy for the benefit of uS citizens and the global environment. The organization promotes this goal by offeringeducation, events and resources to communities.
Elaine Hebert, Chair
Lucas Dixon, Vice-Chair

1527 American Water Resources Association Conference
4 West Federal Street 540-687-8390
PO Box 1626 Fax: 540-687-8395
Middleburg, VA 20118 terry@awra.org
www.awra.org

The American Water Resources Association is a nonprofit professional association dedicated to the advancement of men and women in water resources management, research and education.
Rafael Frias III, President
Brenda Bateman, President Elect

1528 Arkansas Association of Conservation Districts Annual Conference
101 East Capitol 501-682-2915
Suite 350 Fax: 501-682-3991
Little Rock, AR 72201 debbiepinreal@aol.com
www.aracd.org

Affiliated with the National Association of Conservation Districts.The AACD is dedicated to educating the public about conservation work.

November
Martha Manley, President
William Bailey, First Vice President

1529 Atlantic States Marine Fisheries Commission Annual Meeting
150 N Highland Street 703-842-0740
Suite 200 A-N Fax: 703-842-0741
Arlington, VA 22201 info@asmfc.org
www.asmfc.org

The Atlantic States Marine Fisheries Commission serves as a deliberative body, coordinating the conservation and management of the states shared near shore fishery resources-marine, shell, and anadromous-for sustainable use.
Robert E. Beal, Executive Director
Tina L. Berger, Director of Communications

1530 Children's Environmental Health: Research, Practice, Prevention and Policy
110 Maryland Avenue NE 202-543-4033
Suite 404 Fax: 202-543-8797
Washington, DC 20002 cehn@cehn.org
www.cehn.org

Children's Environmental Health Network is a national nonprofit organization focused on environmental health. The work of the work focuses on promoting pediatric research, prevention and practice. The organization hosts a AnniversaryGala every year to raise awareness for the cause.
Nsedu Obot Witherspoon, Executive Director
Kristie Trousdale, Program Manager

1531 Civilian Conservation Corps Legacy
P.O. Box 341 540-984-8735
Edinburg, VA 22824 ccc@ccclegacy.org
www.ccclegacy.org

Provides educational programs to perserve the heritage of the California Conservation Corp alumni and their conservation efforts.

10 booths
Jean Martin, President

1532 Coastal Society Conference
PO Box 3590 757-565-0999
Williamsburg, VA 23187-3590 Fax: 757-565-0922
coastalsoc@aol.com
www.thecoastalsociety.org

The Coastal Society is an organization of private sector, academic, and government professionals and students dedicated to actively addressing emerging coastal issues by fostering dialogue, forging partnerships, and promotingcommunication and education.
Lewis Lawrence, President
Megan D. Bailiff, President-Elect

1533 Colorado Water Congress Annual Meeting
1580 Logan Street 303-837-0812
Suite 700 Fax: 303-526-3864
Denver, CO 80203 cwc@cowatercongress.org
www.cowatercongress.org

Protects and conserves Colorado's water resources by means of advocacy and education.

January
350 attendees and 9 exhibits
Sam Susuras, President
Erin Wilson, Vice President

1534 Connecticut Forest & Park Association Annual Meeting
16 Meriden Road 860-346-TREE
Rockfall, CT 06481-2372 info@ctwoodlands.org
www.ctwoodlands.org

The Connecticut Forest & Park Association (CFPA) is a nonprofit organization dedicated to connecting people to the land in order to protect forests, parks, walking trails, and open spaces in Connecticut.

Spring
Eric Lukingbeal, President
Starr Sayres, Vice President

1535 Environmental Technology Expo
Association of Energy Engineers
3168 Mercer University Drive 770-447-5083
Atlanta, GA 30341 Fax: 770-446-3969
whit@aeecenter.org
www.aeecenter.org

AEE is a source of information in the field of energy efficiency, utility deregulation, facility management, plant engineering, and environmental compliance. Outreach programs include technical seminars, conferences, books, joblistings and certification programs.
Ruth Whitlock, Executive Administrator
Albert Thumann, Executive Director

1536 Federation of Environmental Technologists
W175 N11081 Stonewood Dr 262-437-1700
Ste 203 Fax: 262-437-1702
Germantown, WI 53022 info@fetinc.org
www.fetinc.org

A nonprofit organization dedicated to educate its members and other environmental professionals on regulatory compliance and technological developments in a cost-effective manner through training, professional development andnetworking. FET accomplishes this through seminars, conferences, workshops, publications and other activities that address new and evolving regulations and policies in a non-advocacy format.

March
200 attendees and 70 exhibits
Jeffrey Nettesheim, Chair
Cheryl Moran, President/Director

1537 Forestry Conservation Communications Association Annual Meeting
Fcca
424 E. Middle Street 717-398-0815
Rear Unit 844-458-0298
Gettysburg, PA 17325 Fax: 717-778-4237
nfc@fcca-usa.org
www.fcca-usa.org

The FCCA is a national organization. Its main function is to assist federal, state and local governments in public safety two-way radio operations by locating suitable frequencies within specified operating areas, recommending theirassignment to the FCC for licensing, and protecting them once licensed.
Ralph Haller, Executive Director
Lloyd M. Mitchell, President

1538 GlobalCon
Association of Energy Engineers
3168 Mercer University Drive 770-447-5083
Atlanta, GA 30340 Fax: 770-446-3969
info@aeecenter.org
www.globalconevent.com

Presented by the Association of Energy Engineers (AEE) the conference is designed to provide hands-on, up-to-the-minute information to improve energy management programs, and get up to speed on the current generation of innovativetechnologies.
Craig White, President
Albert Thumann, Executive Director

1539 Greenprints: Sustainable Communities by Design
Southface Energy Institute
241 Pine Street Northeast 404-872-3549
Atlanta, GA 30308 Fax: 404-872-5009
info@southface.org
www.southface.org

Southface promotes sustainable homes, workplaces and communities through education, research, advocacy and technical assistance. Greenprints is a conference and trade show produced by the Southface Energy Institute.

March
100 booths with 1200 attendees
Linda Bolan, Vice President
Barry R. Goldman, Chair

1540 HydroVision International
Pennwell Publications
501 S College Street 918-831-9160
Charlotte, SC 28202 888-299-8016
registration@pennwell.com
www.hydroevent.com

Hydrovision Int'l provides a week of informative hydropower focused meetings including perspectives on the role of hydropower and issues affecting hydro resources. It will also help participants develop a vision to meet challenges andensure the future sustainability of hydro.
Andrea Harner, Conference Manager
Elizabeth Ingram, Conference Committee Chair

1541 Institute of Environmental Sciences and Technology
Institute of Environmental Sciences & Technology

1827 Walden Office Square
Suite 100
Schaumburg, IL 60173
847-981-0100
Fax: 847-981-4130
information@iest.org
www.iest.org

An international professional society that serves the environmental sciences in the areas of contamination control in electronics manufacturing and pharmaceutical processes, design, test and evaluation of commercial and militaryequipment and product reliability issues.

April
50 booths with 500 attendees
Ahmad Soueid, President
Gordon Ely, President-elect

1542 Institute of Scrap Recycling Industries Convention

1250 H Street
Suite 400
Washington, DC 20005
202-662-8500
Fax: 202-624-9256
robinwiener@isri.org
www.isri.org

Its membership is made up of manufacturers and processors, brokers and industrial consumers of scrap commodities, including ferrous and nonferrous metals, paper, electronics, rubber, plastics, glass and textiles. ISRI's associatemembers include equipment and service providers to the scrap recycling industry.

Robin Wiener, President
Mark Lewon, Chair

1543 International Association for Energy Economics Conference

International Association for Energy Economics
28790 Chagrin Boulevard
Suite 350
Cleveland, OH 44122
216-464-5365
iaee@iaee.org
www.iaee.org

The IAEE is a nonprofit professional organization that provides a forum for the exchange of ideas and experiences among energy professionals. The conference attracts delegates governmental, corporate and academic energydecision-makers.

Ricardo Raineri, President
David H. Knapp, President-Elect

1544 International Conference on Solid Waste

Widener University, Civil Engineering
One University Place
Chester, PA 19013-5792
610-499-4042
Fax: 610-499-4461
solid.waste@widener.edu
solid-waste.org

An annual conference on solid waste technology and management. Over 150 speakers from 40 countries present their work.

March
Ronald L Mersky, Chair

1545 Maryland Recyclers Coalition Annual Conference

Maryland Recyclers Coalition
PO Box 1640
Columbia, MD 21044
443-741-8740
Fax: 301-238-4579
www.marylandrecyclingnetwork.org

MRC's mission is to promote sustainable reduction, reuse and recycling of materials otherwise destined for disposal and promote and increase buying products made with recycled material content. Maryland recycling and solid wastemanagement professionals gather each year to discuss topics such as changing waste management and recycling models, policy & regulation, commodities markets, new technologies & more.

June
Kemrey Kidd, President
Peter Houstle, Executive Director

1546 Massachusetts Association of Conservation Commissions Conference

10 Juniper Road
Belmont, MA 02478
617-489-3930
Fax: 617-489-3935
staff@maccweb.org
www.maccweb.org

MACC hosts an Annual Environmental Conference, the largest in New England, with over 40 workshops and nearly 50 exhibitors.

March
1100 attendees and 50 exhibits
Jennifer Carlino, Board President
Michael Howard, First Vice President

1547 Massachusetts Water Pollution Control Association Annual Conference

P.O. Box 60
Rochdale, MA 01542
774-276-9722
Fax: 774-670-9956
mwpca2011@yahoo.com
www.mwpca.org

The Massachusetts Water Pollution Control Association (MWPCA) is a non profit organization that provides education, training, and promote the exchange of information among operators and water quality professionals.

September
Bob Greene, President
Eric Smith, President-Elect

1548 Michigan Association of Conservation Districts Annual Meeting

3001 Coolidge Road
Suite 250
East Lansing, MI 48823
517-324-5274
Fax: 517-324-4435
macd@macd.org
www.macd.org

The Michigan Association of Conservation Districts is a non-governmental, non-profit organization, established to represent and provide services to Michigan's 76 Conservation Districts. The Association represents its members at thestate level by working with legislators, cooperating agencies, and special interest groups whose programs affect the care and management of Michigan's natural resources, especially on private lands.

November
Art Pelon, President
Lori Phalen, Executive Director

1549 Michigan Forest Association Annual Meeting

6120 South Clinton Trail
Eaton Rapids, MI 48827
517-663-3423
www.michiganforests.com

The Association seeks to promote good management on all forest land, to educate its members about good forest practices and stewardship of the land, and to inform the general public about forestry issues and the benefits of good forestmanagement.

Summer
William Botti, Executive Director

1550 Minnesota Association of Soil and Water Conservation Districts Annual Meeting

255 Kellogg Boulevard East
Ste 101
St. Paul, MN 55101
651-690-9028
Fax: 651-690-9065
www.maswcd.org

MASWCD is a nonprofit organization which exists to provide leadership and a common voice for Minnesota's soil and water conservation districts and to maintain a positive, results-oriented relationship with rule making agencies,partners and legislators; expanding education opportunities for the districts so they may carry out effective conservation programs.

December
Kurt Beckstorm, President
Roland Celevland, Vice President

1551 Montana Association of Conservation Districts Annual Meeting
1101 11th Avenue 406-443-5711
Helena, MT 59601 Fax: 406-443-0174
mail@macdnet.org
www.macdnet.org
The Montana Association of Conservation Districts provides assistance to the state's 58 conservation districts by helping local people match their needs with technical and financial resources.

November
Jeff Wivholm, President
Mark Suta, Vice President

1552 Montana Water Environment Association Annual Meeting
601 Wythe Street 800-666-0206
Alexandria, VA 22314 Fax: 703-684-2400
wef.org
A division of the Water Environment Federation, the Montana Water Environment Association (MWEA) is a non-profit organization dedicated to the preservation and enhancement of Montana's water environment. The Association is committed toadvancing science and education, disseminating technical information, increasing public understanding and promoting sound public policy in the water quality and water resources field.

Spring
Starr Sullivan, President
Herb Bartle, Vice-President

1553 NEHA Annual Educational Conference and Exhibition
National Environmental Health Association
720 South Colorado Boulevard 303-756-9090
Suite 1000 N 866-956-2258
Denver, CO 80246 Fax: 303-691-9490
staff@neha.org
www.neha.org
The NEHA AEC and Exhibition is a six-day educational event consisting of nine different environmental health and protection conferences and a two-day exhibition. It is the only conference that emcompasses all areas of environmentalhealth and protection, including, but not limited to: food protection, onsite wastewater, chemical and bioterrorism preparedness, indoor air quality, hazardous waste, and drinking water.

Late June-Early July
900 booths with 1300 attendees
Adam London, President
Vince Radke, President-Elect

1554 NESEA BuildingEnergy Conference
50 Miles Street 413-774-6051
Greenfield, MA 01301 Fax: 413-774-6053
nesea@nesea.org
www.nesea.org
This conference is the oldest and largest regional building energy and renewable energy conference and trade show for practitioners in the Northeast.

March
4000 attendees and 150 exhibits
Martine Dion, Vice-Chair
Paul Eldrenkamp, Treasurer

1555 National Association of Environmental Professionals
40747 Baranda Court 760-636-0065
Palm Desert, CA 92260 Fax: 760-674-2479
lbynder@naep.org
www.naep.org
NAEP is a multidisciplinary association dedicated to the advancement of environmental professionals in the US and abroad, and a forum for information on environmental planning, research and management; a network of professionalcontacts and a resource for structured career development.
Marie Campbell, President
Betty Dehoney, Vice President

1556 National Conference of Local Environmental Health Administrators
University of Washington
1010 South Third Street 509-382-2181
Dayton, WA 99328 Fax: 360-382-2942
david_riggs@co.columbia.wa.us
depts.washington.edu/clehaweb
The NCLEHA's purpose is to provide a forum for local administrators to share common concerns and solutions to mutual problems, and to provide a professional organization for environmental health administrators, focused on the issuesand problems of local environmental health programs.
Dave Riggs, Chair

1557 National Environmental Balancing Bureau Meeting
National Environmental Balancing Bureau
8575 Grovemont Circle 301-977-3698
Gaithersburg, MD 20877 877-800-5147
Fax: 301-977-9589
tiffany@nebb.org
www.nebb.org
The NEBB is a nonprofit organization founded by contractors in the heating, ventilating and air conditioning (HVAC) industry. NEBB exists to help architects, engineers, building owners and contractors produce great buildings with HVACsystems that perform in ways they have visualized and designed.
Jim Kelleher, President
Donald E. Hill, President Elect

1558 National Environmental, Safety and Health Training Association
584 Main Street 207-771-9020
South Portland, MN 04106-1147 neshta@neshta.org
neshta.org
NESHTA is a non-profit international society for environmental, safety, health and other technical training and adult education professionals. NESHTA promotes trainer competency through training and education standards, voluntarycertification, and peer networking. They partner with the National Partnership for Environmental Technology Education to host education and training conferences.
Myrtle I. Turner-Harris, President
Jeffery K. Dennis, Vice President

1559 National Recycling Congress Show
1220 L St NW 202-618-2107
Suite 100 Fax: 202-789-1431
Washington, DC 20005 www.nrc-recycle.org
The National Recycling Coalition, Inc. provides technical education, disseminates public information on selected recycling issues, shapes public and private policy on recycling and operates programs that encourage recycling markets andeconomic development.
Bob Gebert, President
Marjie Griek, Vice President

1560 National Solar Energy Conference
2525 Arapahoe Ave 303-443-3130
Ste E4-253 Fax: 303-442-3212
Boulder, CO 80302 info@ases.org
www.ases.org
The American Solar Energy Society (ASES) presents the Conference along with Green Energy Ohio. The event combines a premiere technical conference, plenary and forum sessions, a Renewable Energy Products and Services exhibit, work-

shops,tours and special events of interest to professionals and consumers.

October
750 attendees and 75-100 exhibits
Elaine Hebert, Chair
Paulette Middleton, Chair

1561 National Water Resources Association Annual Conference
4 E Street Southeast 202-698-0693
Suite 4 Fax: 202-698-0694
Washington, DC 20003 nwra@nwra.org
www.nwra.org
The NWRA consists of individuals and groups, such as irrigation districts, canal companies and conservancy districts, municipalities and the publicin general, who are interested in water resource development projects. It now has about5,000 members.
Ron Thompson, President
Ian Lyle, Vice-President

1562 Natural Resources Districts Annual Conference
Nebraska Association of Resources Districts
601 South 12th Street 402-471-7670
Suite 201 Fax: 402-471-7677
Lincoln, NE 68508 nard@nrdnet.org
www.nrdnet.org
The Nebraska Association of Resources Districts (NARD) is the trade association for Nebraska's 23 Natural Resources Districts. Its mission is to coordinated effort to accomplish collectively what may not be accomplished individually toconserve, sustain, and improve our natural resources and environment.

September
Jim Bendfeldt, President
Larry Reynolds, Vice President

1563 New England Water Environment Association Annual Meeting
NEWEA
10 Tower Office Park 781-939-0908
Suite 601 Fax: 781-939-0907
Woburn, MA 00180-2155 mail@newea.org
www.newea.org
We are a regional member association of the Water Environmental Federation. We provide technical and education for the waste water industry.

150+ booths with 1500 attendees
Mary Barry, Executive Director
Janice Moran, Program Coordinator

1564 New Hampshire Association of Conservation Commissions Annual Meeting
54 Portsmouth Street 603-224-7867
Concord, NH 03301 info@nhacc.org
www.nhacc.org
The New Hampshire Association of Conservation Commissions is a private, non-profit association of municipal conservation commissions. Its purpose is to foster conservation and appropriate use of New Hampshire's natural resources byproviding assistance to conservation commissions, facilitating communication and cooperation among commissions, and helping to create a climate in which commissions can be successful.

November
Rep. Michele Peckham, President
Bruce Allen, Vice President

1565 New Jersey Society for Environmental Economic Development Annual Conference
222 West State Street 609-695-3481
Trenton, NJ 08608 Fax: 609-695-0151
www.njslom.org
Servicing the local municiple government and providing resources to improve the quality of living for its citizens.

November
16,000 attendees and 700+ exhibits
Albert B. Kelly, President
James Cassella, 1st Vice President

1566 New Jersey Water Environment Association Conference
Fair Lawn, NJ
john.corkery@pumpingservices.com
www.njwea.org
The New Jersey Water Environment Association is a nonprofit educational organization dedicated to preserving and enhancing the water environment.
Francis Bonaccorso, President
John Corkery, Secretary

1567 New Mexico Association of Soil and Water Conservation Annual Conference
New Mexico Association Of Conservation Districts
163 Trail Canyon Road 575-981-2400
Carlsbad, NM 88220 conserve@hughes.net
www.nmacd.org
The mission of NMACD is to facilitate conservation of the natural resources in New Mexico by providing opportunities and quality support to local conservation districts through representation and leadership.

Fall
Jim Berlier, President
John Arrington, Vice President

1568 New York Water Environment Association Semi-Annual Conferences
Nywea
525 Plum Street 315-422-7811
Suite 102 877-556-9932
Syracuse, NY 13204 Fax: 315-422-3851
pcr@nywea.org
www.nywea.org
The New York Water Environment Association is a nonprofit educational association dedicated to the development and dissemination of information concerning water quality management and the nature, collection, treatment, and disposal ofwastewater.
2,500 Members
Winter and Summer
Paul McGarvey, President
Geoffrey Baldwin, President Elect

1569 North American Lake Management Society International Symposium
PO Box 5443 608-233-2836
Madison, WI 53705-0443 Fax: 608-233-3186
www.nalms.org
NAMLS's focus is on lake management for a wide variety of uses, but they are also involved with other issues on a watershed level: land, streams, wet lands, and estuaries. The society forges partnerships among citizens, scientists andprofessionals to foster the management and protection of lakes and reservoirs.

October and November
100 booths with 850 attendees and 50 exhibits
Frank Wilhelm, President
Frank Browne, President-Elect

1570 North Carolina Association of Soil and Water Conservation Districts Annual Conference
Po Box 27943 919-715-6104
Raleigh, NC 27611 ncaswcd@gmail.com
www.ncaswcd.org
The association is an indepented, nonpartisan conservation organization presenting the interests of the 96 local soil and water conservation districts and the 492 district supervisors who direct their local district's conservationprograms.

January
Chris Hogan, President
Dietrich Kilpatrick, First Vice-President

1571 North Dakota Association of Soil Conservation Districts Annual Conference
Lincoln Oaks Nursurey
3310 University Drive 701-223-8575
Bismarck, ND 58504 Fax: 701-223-1291
bismarcknursery@lincolnoakes.com
www.lincolnoakes.com

The purpose of the North Dakota Association of Soil Conservation Districts is to further the widespread application of sound and practical soil and water conservation practices in North Dakota.

November
Bill Elhard, Nursery Manager
Shirley Christenson, Nursery Tech

1572 Northeast Recycling Council Conference
139 Main Street 802-254-3636
Suite 401 info@nerc.org
Brattleboro, VT 05301 www.nerc.org
NERC's mission is to To advance an environmentally sustainable economy by promoting source and toxicity reduction, recycling, and the purchasing of environmentally preferable products and services.

March and November
Robert Isner, President
Kaley Laleker, Vice President

1573 Northeast Resource Recovery Association Annual Conference
2101 Dover Road 603-736-4401
Epsom, NH 03234 800-223-0150
Fax: 603-736-4402
info@nrra.net
www.nrra.net
The Northeast Resource Recovery Association is a pro-active nonprofit working with its membership to make their recycling programs strong, efficient, and financially successful by providing cooperative marketing, cooperativepurchasing, education and networking opportunities; developing innovative recycling programs; creating sustainable alternatives to reduce the volume and toxicity of the waste, and educating and informing local officials about recycling and solidwaste issues.

June
Duncan P. Watson, President
John Hurd, Vice President

1574 Pacific Fishery Management Council Conferences
7700 Northeast Ambassador Place 503-820-2280
Suite 101 866-806-7204
Portland, OR 97220 Fax: 503-820-2299
pfmc.comments@noaa.gov
www.pcouncil.org
The Pacific Council has developed fishery management plans for salmon, groundfish and coastal species in the US Exclusive Economic Zone off the coast of Washington, Oregon and California.

5x year
Chuck Tracy, Executive Director
Mike Burner, Deputy Director

1575 Parks and Trails Council of Minnesota Annual Meeting
275 E 4th Street 651-726-2457
Suite 250 800-944-0707
St. Paul, MN 55101-1626 Fax: 651-726-2458
info@parksandtrails.org
www.parksandtrails.org
Parks and Trails Council of Minnesota seeks to aquire, protect and sustain long-term statewide land.

March
Julie Gugin, President
Bob Biersheid, Vice President

1576 Plant and Facilities Expo
Association of Energy Engineers
3168 Mercer University Drive 770-447-5083
Suite 420 Fax: 770-446-3969
Atlanta, GA 30341 info@aeecenter.org
www.aeecenter.org
The Association of Energy Engineers is a nonprofit professional society that promotes the scientific and educational interests of those in the energy industry. The association offers conferences, journals, books and certificationprograms in support of sustainable development.
Ruth Whitlock, Exe. Administrator
Albert Thumann, Exe. Director

1577 Renewable Energy Roundup & Green Living Fair
PO Box 1447 512-345-5446
Austin, TX 78767-1447 800-465-5049
info@txses.org
www.txses.org
Organized by the Texas Solar Energy Society and Texas Renewable Energy Industries Association featuring solutions to global warming such as rainwater harvesting, green and sustainable building, alternative transporation, and energyconservation.

September
Lucy Stolzenburg, Executive Director
Russel Smith, Event Coordinator

1578 Solar Cookers International World Conference
2400 22nd Street 916-455-4499
Suite 210 info@solarcookers.org
Sacramento, CA 95818 www.solarcookers.org
Solar Cookers International's mission is to spread solar thermal cooking technology to benefit people and environments.
James G. Moose, President
Monica Woods, Vice President

1579 South Dakota Association of Conservation Districts Conference
116 N Euclid Avenue 605-895-4099
Pierre, SD 57501 800-729-4099
www.sdconservation.org
Mission is to lead, represent and assist South Dakota's conservation districts in promoting a healthy environment. Specific areas of concern include wind and water erosion, water quality and quantity including preservation of theMissouri main stem dams, air quality, forestry, rangeland, wildlife and recreation.

September
Angela Ehlers, Executive Director
Karl Jensen, President

1580 South Dakota Environmental Health Association Annual Conference
State Department of Health
PO Box 2275A
Pierre, SD 57007
605-773-3361
800-738-2301
office@sdpublichealth.org
sdpublichealth.org
The South Dakota Public Health Association is the only trade association in South Dakota for public health professionals, whose mission is to promote and protect the health of individuals, families and the communities.

April
Kimberly Wilson-Sweebe, President
Wyatt Pickner, Vice President

1581 Southeastern Association of Fish and Wildlife Agencies Annual Meeting
27 Sylwood Place
Jackson, MS 39209
601-668-6916
crayhopkins@bellsouth.net
www.seafwa.org
The SEAFWA conducts an annual conference each fall to provide a forum for presentation of information and exchange of ideas regarding the management and protection of fish and wildlife resources throughout the nation with emphasis onthe southeast.

October/November
Curtis R Hopkins, Executive Secretary
Alvin Taylor, President

1582 Take it Back
Raymond Communications
P.O. Box 4311
Silver Spring, MD 20914-4311
301-879-0628
circulation@raymond.com
www.raymond.com
Raymond Communications provides news and insight on environmental legislative and regulatory developments from around the world. Their Take It Back conferences focus on recycling and waste management programs.

250 attendees
Bruce Popka, President

1583 Texas Environmental Health Association Annual Education Conference
PO Box 889
Wolfforth, TX 79382
806-855-4277
Fax: 806-855-4277
www.myteha.org
TEHA provides a professional organization for Sanitarians and Environmental Health Professionals, designed to serve as the focal point for their education and professional status. They host educational meetings each year for membersand their guests and to promote the exchange of ideas and update techniques in the profession.

March
J. Victor Baldovinos, President
Russell O'Brien, President Elect

1584 Texas Water Conservation Association Annual Conference
3755 S. Capital of Texas Highway
Suite 105
Austin, TX 78704
512-472-7216
Fax: 512-472-0537
admin@twca.org
www.twca.org
The Texas Water Conservation Association consists of water professionals and organizations in the state of Texas who represent river authorities, municipalities, navigation and flood control districts, drainage and irrigationdistricts, utility districts, municipalities, groundwater conservation districts, all kinds of water users, and general/environmental water interests.

March
Michael J. Booth, President
Hope Wells, President-Elect

1585 Utah Association of Conservation Districts Annual Conference
PO Box 4117
Logan, UT 84323
435-881-7688
uacd.org
The Utah Association of Conservation Districts is a nonprofit corporation representing Utah's 38 soil conservation districts. By working with landowners, organizations and government, the conservation districts work through voluntary,incentive-based programs to protect soil, water quality and other natural resources.

November
Bob Barry, President
Allen Henrie, Vice President

1586 Virginia Association of Soil and Water Conservation Districts Annual Conference
7308 Hanover Green Drive
Suite 100
Mechanicsville, VA 23111
804-559-0324
Fax: 804-559-0325
info@vaswcd.org
www.vaswcd.org
The Virginia Association of Soil and Water Conservation Districts (VASWCD) is a private nonprofit association of 47 soil and water conservation districts in Virginia. It is a voluntary, nongovernmental association of Virginia'sdistricts that provides and promotes leadership in the conservation of natural resources through stewardship and education programs.

December
Steven Meeks, President
Kendall Elaine Tyree, Executive Director

1587 Virginia Forestry Association Annual Conference
3308 Augusta Avenue
Richmond, VA 23230
804-278-8733
Fax: 804-278-8774
www.vaforestry.org
VFA promotes stewardship and wise use of the Commonwealth's forest resources for the economic and environmental benefits of all Virginians. Membership consists of forest landowners, forest product businesses, forestry professionals,and a variety of individuals and groups who are concerned about the future and well-being of Virginia's forest resources.

Late Spring
John Hancock, President
Carl Garrison, Vice President

1588 WEFTEC Show
Water Environment Federation
601 Wythe Street
Alexandria, VA 22314
800-666-0206
Fax: 703-684-2400
inquiry@wef.org
www.wef.org
North America's largest annual water quality conference and exposition. The WEFTEC covers a wide spectrum of critical water quality issues.

Fall
16,000 attendees and 800+ exhibits
Rick Warner, President
Jenny Harfelder, President-Elect

1589 Waste Expo
Waste360

Las Vegas Convention Center 312-840-8408
3150 Paradise Road wasteexpo.com
Las Vegas, NV
This conference focuses on education and training on recycling programs and waste management, including topics such as bioplastics, composting, equipment leasing and financing, fire safety, food waste reduction, operating landfills,Zero Waste strategies and practices, and more.

April
Mark Hickey, Market Leader
Catherine E. Campfield, Show Coordinator

1590 West Virginia Forestry Association
1776 Parkersburg Road 304-372-1955
PO Box 718 Fax: 304-372-1957
Ripley, WV 25271 wvfa@wvfa.org
www.wvfa.org

The West Virginia Forestry Association is a non-profit organization funded by its membership. Our members include individuals and businesses involved in forest management, timber production and wood product manufacturing. Our membersare concerned with protecting the environment, as well as enhancing the future of West Virginia's forests through multiple-use management.

Summer
Mark Haddix, President
Dane Moore, First Vice President

1591 Western Association of Fish and Wildlife Agencies Annual Meeting
522 Notre Dame Court 307-631-4536
Cheyenne, WY 82009 Fax: 307-638-1470
larry.kruckenberg@wyo.gov
www.wafwa.org

The Western Association of Fish and Wildlife Agencies represents 23 states and Canadian provinces and supports resource management to conserve wildlife.

July
Curt Melcher, President
Keith Sexton, 1st VP

1592 Western Forestry and Conservation Association Conference
4033 SW Canyon Road 503-226-4562
Portland, OR 97221 Fax: 503-226-2515
richard@westernforestry.org
westernforestry.org

Offers continuing education workshops and seminars for professional foresters throughout the west.

January/February
Richard Zabel, Executive Director

1593 Western Society of Naturalists Annual Meeting
San Diego State University Department Of Biology
P.O. Box 247
Bodega Bay, CA 94923 secretariat@wsn-online.org
www.wsn-online.org
Members include researchers, educators, academics and others with an interest in the area's biology, particularly its marine life.
Jenn Caselle, President
Brian Gaylord, Secretary

1594 Wildlife Habitat Council Annual Symposium
Wildlife Habitat Council
8737 Colesville Road 301-588-8994
Suite 800 whc@wildlifehc.org
Silver Spring, MD 20910 www.wildlifehc.org

The Wildlife Habitat Council is a nonprofit, group of corporations, conservation organizations, and individuals dedicated to restoring and enhancing wildlife habitat.
Margaret O'Gorman, President
Michael Shaw, Coordinator

1595 Wildlife Society Annual Conference
Wildlife Society
425 Barlow Place 301-897-9770
Suite 200 tws@wildlife.org
Bethesda, MD 20814 www.wildlife.org
Annual conference of wildlife professionals, organized by the Wildlife Society.

September
50 booths with 1400 attendees
Ed Thompson, Executive Director/CEO
Bruce C. Thompson, President

1596 Wisconsin Association for Environmental Education Annual Conference
2100 Main Street 715-346-0123
University of Wisconsin webmaster@uwsp.edu
Stevens Point, WI 54481-3897 www.uwsp.edu
WAEE is a statewide non-profit organization promoting responsible environmental action through education in the classroom and in the community. Each year WAEE hosts an Annual Conference where environmental educators from across thestate gather to learn from one another, meet others in the field.

Fall
Rebecca Franzen, Instructor

1597 Wisconsin Land and Water Conservation Association Annual Conference
131 W. Wilson St. 608-441-2677
Suite 601 Fax: 608-441-2676
Madison, WI 53703 info@wisconsinlandwater.org
wisconsinlandwater.org
To assist county Land Conservation Committees and Departments with the protection, enhancement and sustainable use of Wisconsin's natural resources and to represent them through education and governmental interaction.

December
Ken Dolata, Executive Director

1598 Wisconsin Woodland Owners Association Annual Conference
PO Box 285 715-346-4798
Stevens Point, WI 54481 wwoa@uwsp.edu
www.wisconsinwoodlands.org
The Wisconsin Woodland Owners Association is a nonprofit educational organization seeking to advance the interests of woodland owners and the cause of forestry; develop public appreciation for the value of Wisconsin's woodlands andtheir importance in the economy and overall welfare of the state; foster and encourage wise use and management of Wisconsin's woodlands for timber production, wildlife habitat and recreation; and to educate those interested in managing the woodlands.

October
Steven Ring, President
David Congos, Vice President

1599 World Energy Engineering Congress
Association of Energy Engineers
3168 Mercer University Drive 770-447-5083
Suite 420 Fax: 770-446-3969
Atlanta, GA 30341 info@aeecenter.org
www.aeecenter.org

The Association of Energy Engineers is a nonprofit professional society that promotes the scientific and educational interests of

those in the energy industry. The association offers conferences, journals, books and certificationprograms in support of sustainable development.

September
Albert Thumman, Executive Director
Ruth Whitlock, Executive Administrator

Consultants

Environmental

1600 AAA Lead Consultants and Inspections
1307 West 6th Street
Suite 134
Corona, CA 92882
951-582-9071
Fax: 951-582-9073
aaalead@sbcglobal.net
aaalead.com

This organization offers quality consulting, inspections, monitoring and project design for lead based paint.
Michael Cohn, Owner

1601 AB2MT Consultants
9400 South Dadeland Boulevard
Suite 370
Miami, FL 33156
305-670-1011
Fax: 305-670-1016

AB2MT offers environmental and engineering consulting, in areas such as hazardous waste and water testing.

1602 ABCO Construction Services
6901 South Yosemite Street
Suite 205
Centennial, CO 80112
303-220-8220
Fax: 303-796-0810
info@abco-corp.com
www.abco-corp.com

Provides a full spectrum of engineering and environmental services pertaining to both new construction and existing buildings. Services include Property Condition Assessment Reports, Phase I Environmental Assessments, Quality ControlReports and other technical support services relating to buildings and building systems.
Joe Johnson, President

1603 ABS Consulting
16855 Northchase Drive
Houston, TX 77060
281-673-2800
Fax: 281-877-5946
info@abs-group.com
www.abs-group.com

ABS Consulting provides risk management consultation services for the Oil, Gas and Chemical, Power, Marine, Offshore and Government sectors. Services offered include technical inspection, risk compliance analysis, asset performance,management system certification and more.
Tony Nassif, President
David Walker, Chief Operating Officer

1604 ACC Environmental Consultants
7977 Capwell Drive
Suite 100
Oakland, CA 94621
510-638-8400
800-525-8838
Fax: 510-638-8404
general@accenv.com
www.accenv.com

This organization is an employee-owned environmental and energy consulting firm, assisting companies and public agencies throughout California to identify and manage environmental hazards and comply with environmental policies. ACCoffers a number of services: asbestos consulting, site assessments for real estate businesses, environmental management software and more.
Jim Wilson, President & CEO
Heather Sobky, Chief Operating Officer

1605 ACRT Environmental Specialists
1333 Home Avenue
Akron, OH 44310
330-945-7500
800-622-2562
Fax: 330-945-7200
support@acrtinc.com
www.acrtinc.com

ACRT is an international consulting service and training organization providing research and educational services relating to urban forestry, arboricultural, and horticultural fields. One of main services offered is the utilityvegetation management (UVM) program.
Michael B. Weidner, President & CEO
Todd Jones, Chief Operations Officer

1606 ACV Enviro
928 East Hazelwood Avenue
Rahway, NJ 07065
732-815-0220
800-876-9699
Fax: 732-815-9892
marketing@acvenviro.com
www.acvenviro.com

Provider of industrial and environmental waste management services: cleaning and maintenance, tank and oil processing, waste disposal, transportation and more.
Jeffrey Keenan, Executive Chairman
Dan Coon, Chief Financial Officer

1607 ADS LLC
340 The Bridge Street
Suite 204
Huntsville, AL 35806
256-430-3366
800-633-7246
Fax: 256-430-6633
adssales@idexcorp.com
www.adsenv.com

ADS LLC develops and provides technology-based hardware and software products and services for the water, wastewater, gas, and hydroelectric industries through three divisions: ADS environmental services, hydra-stop and accusonictechnologies. ADS pioneered the industry's first flow monitoring hardware and software products over 32 years ago.
Hal Kimbrough, General Manager

1608 AECOS
45-939 Kamehameha Highway
Suite 104
Kaneohe, HI 96744
808-234-7770
Fax: 808-234-7775
aecos@aecos.com
www.aecos.com

Environmental consulting firm providing the services of scientists and facilities in the environmental sciences to clients throughout the Pacific area. AECOS specializes in aquatic (both fresh water and marine) biology and waterquality, with expertise in analytical chemistry, oceanography, water pollution, and marine and fresh water ecology.
Eric B. Guinther, President
Susan Burr, Environmental Scientist

1609 AKT Peerless Environmental Services
6600 Peachtree Dunwoody Road
Bldg 400 #108
Atlanta, GA 30328
404-256-1779
800-985-7633
info@aktpeerless.com
www.aktpeerless.com

Provides environmental services to facilitate real estate transfer, development, and redevelopment. Services include phase I ESA, subsurface investigation, remediation, Brownfield's redevelopment and Brownfield's financial incentives.
Tony R. Anthony, Principal
Robert W. Lambdin, Senior VP, Operations

1610 ALS Environmental
10450 Stancliff Road
Suite 210
Houston, TX 77099
360-577-7222
800-695-7222
Fax: 360-636-1068
www.caslab.com

Areas of expertise and services include environmental testing of air, water, soil, hazardous waste, sediments and tissues; process and quality control testing; analytical method development; sampling and mobile laboratory services; andconsulting and data management services.
Raj Naran, CEO & Managing Director
Lan Le, Technical Director

1611 AM Kinney
150 E 4th Street 513-421-2265
Cincinnati, OH 45202 800-265-3682
Fax: 513-281-1123
nielseng@amkinney.com
www.amkinney.com

Provides creative and cost effective solutions in the planning, design and delivery of clients' projects. Areas covered include mechanical, electrical, structural, civil, industrial and chemical engineering, architectural design andconstruction management.
A.M. Kinney, Chairman & Owner
George L. Nielsen, Senior Architect

1612 ANA-Lab Corporation
2600 Dudley Road 903-984-0551
P.O. Box 9000 Fax: 903-984-5914
Kilgore, TX 75663
corp@ana-lab.com
www.ana-lab.com

ANA-Lab is an environmental testing laboratory providing analytical testing of wastewater, groundwater, and solid waste. Areas tested cover heavy metals, priority pollutants, herbicides, pesticides, and PCBs.
Scott Moss, Vice President, Operations
Bill Peery, Executive Vice President

1613 APEC-AM Environmental Consultants
2525 NW Expressway 405-840-9327
Suite 301d Fax: 405-840-9328
Oklahoma City, OK 73112

APEC is a petroleum and environmental consulting firm providing oil and gas exploration services.
Saleem Nizami, Founder

1614 ARCADIS
630 Plaza Drive 720-344-3500
Suite 200 866-287-7373
Highlands Ranch, CO 80129 Fax: 720-344-3535
AUSInternet@arcadis.com
www.arcadis.com

A leading global, knowledge-driven service provider for the fields of infrastructure, environment and buildings. ARCADIS offers feasibility studies, design, engineering, project management, implementation and facility managementservices, as well as legal and financial support.
Joachim Ebert, CEO
Gary Coates, Chief Operating Officer

1615 ATS-Chester Engineers
1555 Coraopolis Heights Road 412-809-6600
Moon Township, PA 15108 Fax: 412-809-6611
www.chesterengineers.com

Provides services in waste water treatment and air pollution control.
Robert Agbede, President & CEO

1616 Aarcher
2635 Riva Road 410-897-9100
Suite 100 Fax: 410-897-9104
Annapolis, MD 21401 cschwartz@aarcherinc.com
www.aarcherinc.com

Aarcher provides environmental management, assessment and planning services nationwide. Services provided include environmental compliance audits, NEPA analysis and documentation, resource management planning, site assessment, plansand permits and environmental liability assessment.
Craig J Schwartz, President

1617 Abacus Environment
3440 Fordham Road 214-363-0099
Dallas, TX 75216 Fax: 214-363-3919
www.abacusae.com

Full service environmental and occupational safety and health consulting firm. Services include project management, indoor air quality and industrial hygiene, asbestos and lead project management, expert witness testimony and allaspects of workplace safety.
Donald Weekes, President

1618 Abonmarche Environmental
95 West Main Street 269-927-2295
Benton Harbor, MI 49022 Fax: 269-927-4639
aci@abonmarche.com
www.abonmarche.com

Full-service architectural, engineering, land surveying and planning firm.
Christopher Cook, President & CEO
John Linn, Chairman

1619 AccuTech Environmental Services
43 West Front Street 732-739-6444
Suite D 800-644-ISRA
Keyport, NJ 07735 Fax: 732-739-0451

Manages environmental sampling and cleanup programs in compliance with New Jersey's Environmental Cleanup Responsibility Act.
James Bartley, Owner

1620 Acheron Engineering Services
147 Main Street 207-368-5700
Newport, ME 04953 Fax: 207-368-5120
WBall@AcheronEngineering.com
www.acheronengineering.com

Provides solutions to uncommon engineering, environmental and geologic issues. Some services offered include water supply engineering, contingency plans, design, site planning, endangered species searches, licensing and permits, labtesting and more.
William B Ball, President
Kirk Ball, Project Engineer

1621 Activated Carbon Services
409 Meade Drive 724-457-6576
Coraopolis, PA 15108 800-367-2587
Fax: 724-457-1214
Henry@pacslabs.com
pacslabs.com

Provides short courses in spectrocopy, chomatography, quality, safety, environment and management. Also provided are professional manuals, software products, laboratory testing and consulting services.
Henry G Nowicki PhD/MBA, President
Barbara Sherman MS/MBA, Manager of Operations

1622 Acumen Industrial Hygiene
1032 Irving Street 415-242-6060
Suite 922 Fax: 415-242-6006
San Francisco, CA 94122 info@acumen-ih.com
www.acumen-ih.com

Offers hygiene consultation for industrial fields. Services include air and noise monitoring programs, injury and illness prevention programs, building inspections, hazardous materials investigation, employee safety training and more.
Paul Spillane, Owner

1623 Advanced Chemistry Labs
3039 Amwiler Road 770-409-1444
Suite 100 Fax: 770-409-1844
Atlanta, GA 30360 acl@acl-labs.net
www.advancedchemistrylabs.com

Environmental testing laboratory specializing in the analysis of trace level organic and inorganic contaminants in water, wastewater, soil, sediment, sludge, oil, waste and air.
John Andros, Owner

1624 **Advanced Resources International**
4501 Fairfax Drive 703-528-8420
Suite 910 Fax: 703-528-0439
Arlington, VA 22203 ari-info@adv-res.com
www.adv-res.com

Consulting, research and development firm providing services in the areas of unconventional gas, oil recovery and carbon capture.
Vello A Kuuskraa, President
Jonathan R. Kelafant, Senior Vice President

1625 **Advanced Waste Management Systems**
6430 Hixson Pike 423-843-2206
PO Box 100 Fax: 423-843-2310
Hixson, TN 37343 info@awm.net
www.awm.net

Provides a wide range of environmental and engineering services to domestic and international clients such as governments, corporations, and private citizens. Some of these services include GHG verification, industrial wastemanagement, project management and auditing.
Richard A. Ellis, PhD, Chairman
Jim Mullican, PE, President

1626 **Aerosol Monitoring and Analysis**
1331 Ashton Road 410-684-3327
Hanover, MD 21076 Fax: 410-684-3384
www.amatraining.com

Aerosol Monitoring & Analysis provides industrial hygiene, environmental and health & safety services to government agencies, institutions, building owners, property managers, architects and engineers.
Todd M. Woerner, President
Joseph A. Coco, Senior Vice President

1627 **Aguirre Roden**
10670 N Central Expwy 972-788-1508
6th Floor Fax: 972-788-1583
Dallas, TX 75231 www.aguirreroden.com
Aguirre Roden is an environmental engineering firm offering services such as architectural planning and design, plumbing, construction and program management.
Gary Roden, President
Pedro Aguirre, CEO

1628 **Air Consulting, Environmental, & Safety**
9597 Jones Rd. 713-253-0901
Suite 132 info@aces-llc.com
Houston, TX 77065 aces-llc.com
Provider of air pollution testing services, as well as solutions for waste management and water quality issues.
Bob Shary, President
Pat Patrick, Vice President

1629 **Air Sciences**
150 Capital Drive 303-988-2960
Suite 320 Fax: 303-988-2968
Golden, CO 80401 air@airsci.com
airsci.com

Air Sciences specializes in air pollution consulting services. Some of its work has included mineral extraction and refining, natural gas processing, chemical manufacturing, pesticide formulation, environmental compliance, firemissions modeling and more.
Kevin Lewis, President
Mark Schaaf, Vice President

1630 **Aires Consulting Group**
1550 Hubbard Avenue 630-879-3006
Batavia, IL 60510 800-247-3799
Fax: 630-879-3014
info@airesconsulting.com
www.airesconsulting.com

Offers services in occupational hygiene, environmental engineering and building sciences.
Rich Rapacki, Business Development
Kevin Bannon, Marketing Director

1631 **Airtek Environmental Corporation**
39-37, 29th Street 718-937-3720
New York City, NY 11101 Fax: 718-937-3721
www.airtekenv.com
Firm offering consulting services to the real estate community in New York, specializing in the areas of laws and liability. Services include mold and bacteria testing, air quality testing, lead paint management, industrial hygiene,biosafety, industry training and more.
Saad Zouak, President

1632 **Alan Plummer Associates**
1320 South University Drive 817-806-1700
Suite 300 Fax: 817-870-2536
Fort Worth, TX 76107 aplummer@apaienv.com
www.apaienv.com

Organization offering civil and environmental engineering consulting.
Alan Tucker, President & CEO
James Naylor, Senior Project Manager

1633 **All 4 Inc**
2393 Kimberton Road 610-933-5246
PO Box 299 Fax: 610-933-5127
Kimberton, PA 19442 jegan@all4inc.com
www.all4inc.com

An environmental consulting company specializing in air quality services, primarily assisting clients with complex air permitting, modeling, continuous monitoring, and regulation compliance.
John Egan, Principal Consultant
Dan Holland, Senior Consultant

1634 **AllWest Environmental**
2141 Mission Street 415-391-2510
Suite 100 Fax: 714-541-5303
San Francisco, CA 94110 info@allwest1.com
www.allwest1.com
Business-oriented consulting firm specializing in Environmental and Engineering sectors, offering expertise to the real estate industry. AllWest assists clients in understanding and managing potential environmental and buildingliabilites, and in advocating their interests through the discovery and mitigation process.
Marc Cunningham, President
Kevin Reeve, Business Development

1635 **Allee, King, Rosen and Fleming**
440 Park Avenue South 212-696-0670
7th Floor 800-899-2573
New York, NY 10016 Fax: 212-779-9721
nycinfo@akrf.com
www.akrf.com

Offers services in the areas of environmental regulations, engineering, planning, air quality, cultural resources, environmental impact assessment, natural resources, permits, compliance, site assessment and more.
Debra Allee, Founder
Edward Applebome, Senior Vice President

1636 **Allied Engineers**
2303 Camino Ramon 925-867-4646
Suite 290 Fax: 925-867-4474
San Ramon, CA 94583 info@alliedengineersinc.com
www.alliedengineersinc.com

Provides consulting services in wastewater and industrial waste, including emissions testing.
Robert Dawyot, President
Vlasta Cejna, Vice President

1637 Alpha-Omega Environmental Services
933 Northwest 31 Avenue 954-969-5906
Pompano Beach, FL 33069 866-969-6653
Fax: 954-969-5232
dave@aomegagroup.com
www.aomegagroup.com
Organization offering services for water damage mitigation, mold remediation, smoke and odor removal, hoarding and other emergency needs.

1638 Alternative Resources
1732 Main Street 978-371-2054
Concord, MA 01742 Fax: 978-371-7269
info@alt-res.com
alt-res.com
Alternative Resources is an independent consulting firm providing management, engineering, environmental, economic and financial solutions in the fields of water and wastewater treatment, solid waste management and renewable energygeneration.
James Osborn, President
Susan Higgins, Director

1639 Ambient Engineering
P.O. Box 670 978-798-0999
Hingham, MA 02043 888-262-6232
Fax: 978-369-8380
info@ambient-engineering.com
ambient-engineering.com
An environmental engineering and consulting firm providing site civil engineering, hazardous waste cleanup, regulatory compliance, site assessments, hydrological assessments and more.
Thomas J. Stevenson, PhD, President & CEO
David Bramley, Lead Engineer

1640 American Archaeology Group LLC
PO Box 534 512-556-4100
Lampasas, TX 76550 Fax: 512-556-3373
Archaeological consulting firm offering archaeological investigations, historical research, and archival research during construction projects.
Michael Bradle, President

1641 American Engineering Testing
550 Cleveland Avenue North 651-659-9001
St. Paul, MN 55114 800-972-6364
Fax: 651-659-1379
rkaiser@amengtest.com
www.amengtest.com
Provides engineering, testing and laboratory services for environmental, geotechnical and construction purposes.
Robert Kaiser, VP, Environmental Division
Gail Cederberg, VP, Environmental Services

1642 Andco Environmental Processes
415 Commerce Drive 716-691-2100
Amherst, NY 14228 Fax: 716-691-2880
andco@localnet.com
Manufacturers of waste disposal treatment systems.
William Waytena, Chairman

1643 Andersen 2000

1644 Anderson Consulting Group
PO Box 407 610-918-7461
Downingtown, PA 19335 Fax: 610-918-9469
Anderson Consulting Group helps companies and public agencies to manage project development risk and reduce construction costs, while offering environmental and geotechnical services as well as engineering solutions tailored to theirneeds.

1645 Apollo Energy Systems
4100 North Powerline Road 954-969-7755
Building D3 Fax: 954-969-7788
Pompano Beach, FL 33073 electricauto@electricauto.com
www.electricauto.com
Developer of environmentally friendly batteries, fuel cells and systems.
Robert Aronsson, Chairman
Raymond Douglas, CEO

1646 Applied Ecological Services
17921 Smith Road 608-897-8641
Brodhead, WI 53520 Fax: 608-897-8486
info@appliedeco.com
www.appliedeco.com
AES is an ecological consulting, contracting and restoration firm providing services to foundations, government units, corporations and commercial and residential developers nationwide. Consultations are provided in the areas ofwetlands, natural resources, endangered species, site design, watershed planning and more.
Steven Apfelbaum, Founder & Chairman
Steven Dischler, President & CEO

1647 Applied Geoscience and Engineering
150-C Love Road 610-777-5027
Reading, PA 19607 Fax: 610-777-4276
lmullis@appliedgeoscience.com
www.appliedgeoscience.com
Specializes in the areas of geotechnical engineering, soils laboratory testing, and environmental services for civil engineers.
M. Ayub Iqbal, Ph.D, P.E., President
Drew M. Kurtz, P.E., Senior Geotechnical Engineer

1648 Applied Marine Ecology
1359 South West 22nd 305-757-0018
Terrace 1
Miami, FL 33145
Marine ecology research and environmental conservation firm.
Anitra Thorhaug, President

1649 Applied Science Associates
55 Village Square Drive 401-789-6224
South Kingstown, RI 02879 Fax: 401-789-1932
asacontact@asascience.com
asascience.com
A global science and technology solutions company. Through consulting, environmental modeling, and application development, ASA serves a diverse range of clients in government, industry, and academia. Some of their areas of expertiseinclude oil and gas, impact assessments, ocean observing, coastal resilence, software development and more.
Paul Hall, Senior Project Manager
Kelly Knee, Environmental Engineer

1650 Aqua Sierra
9094 US Highway 285 303-697-5486
Morrison, CO 80465-8950 800-524-3474
Fax: 303-697-5069
info@aqua-sierra.com
www.aqua-sierra.com
Aqua Sierra offers consulting services for managing aquatic resources by combining a broad base of experience in all aspects of fisheries, aquatic ecology, and water quality management. Some of their services include water qualitytesting, aquatic treatment, lake and stream design, biofouling control, aquaculture and more.
Bill Logan, President
Kendra Holmes, VP, Operations

1651 Aqua Survey
469 Point Breeze Road
Flemington, NJ 08822
908-788-8700
Fax: 908-788-9165
mail@aquasurvey.com
www.aquasurvey.com

Aqua Survey is a full service ecotoxicology company providing laboratory testing, field sampling and consulting services in the areas of sediment vibracoring, water quality, benthic grab sampling and taxonomy, toxicity identification,geophysical and hydrographic surveys, sediment toxicology and more.
Ken Hayes, President
Jon Doi, Executive Vice President

1652 Aqualogic
30 Devine Street
North Haven, CT 06473
203-248-8959
800-989-8959
Fax: 203-288-4308
waterservices@aqualogic.com
www.aqualogic.com

Provider of equipment for wastewater treatment. Some of their products include carbon and particle filters, water filters, acid recovery systems and more.
Nick Papa, General Manager
Richard Heller, Sales Engineer

1653 Arctech
14100 Park Meadow Drive
Chantilly, VA 20151
703-222-0280
Fax: 703-222-0299
info@arctech.com
www.arctech.com

Arctech provides cost-effective solutions and products for the energy, environmental and agriculture markets. These products help to create economical clean energy, clean water and environments, safer foods, effective waste managementprocesses and the reduction of greenhouse gas emissions.
Daman Walia, President & CEO

1654 Ardea Consulting
10 1st Street
Woodland, CA 95695
530-669-1645
birdtox1@ardeacon.com
www.ardeacon.com

Ardea Consulting provides avian and wildlife toxicology and ecological risk assessments guidance to engineering and environmental firms, government agencies, businesses and non-governmental organizations.
Joseph P Sullivan, PhD, Sr. Consultant

1655 Arro Consulting
108 West Airport Road
Lititz, PA 17543
717-569-7021
Fax: 717-560-0577
info@thearrogroup.com
www.thearrogroup.com

Offers services in the areas of waste water management, planning, geosciences, environmental site assessments and more.
G. Matthew Brown, P.E., President & CEO
Susan L. Long, EVP & CFO

1656 Arro Laboratory
425 Caton Farm Road
Crest Hill, IL 60431
815-727-5436
Fax: 815-740-3234
info@arrolab.com
www.arrolab.com

Provides environmental and chemical testing services for wastewater, drinking water and biosolids.
Joan Serdar, Laboratory Director

1657 Artemel International
218 North Lee Street
Suite 316
Alexandria, VA 22314
703-683-3838
Fax: 703-836-1370
aiusa@artemel.com
www.artemel.com

Artemel International offers planning, project development and financing services for the environment sector as well as other sectors.
Engin Artemel, President

1658 Athena Environmental Sciences
1450 South Rolling Road
Baltimore, MD 21227
410-455-6319
888-892-8408
Fax: 410-455-1155
athenaes@athenaenvironmental.com
www.athenaes.com

Designs and develops biotechnology products that represent environmentally responsible and economically sound solutions to environmental problems. Products include the company's own Spill Pill (TM) - a proprietary cleaning agent forpetroleum contamination on concrete and other building surfaces - and Bilge Tech Inc.'s Bilge Pill (TM), a cleaning agent for removing oil and dirt buildup in boat bilges.
Sheldon Broedel, PhD, CEO

1659 Atlantic Testing Laboratories
6431 US Highway 11
Canton, NY 13617
315-386-4578
Fax: 315-386-1012
info@atlantictesting.com
www.atlantictesting.com

ATL is a full-service engineering support firm offering environmental services, subsurface investigations, geoprobe services, water-based investigations, geotechnical engineering, construction materials testing and engineering, specialinspections, nondestructive testing and surveying.
Marijean B. Remington, CHMM, CEO
James J. Kuhn, PE, President

1660 Atlas Environmental Engineering
3185 Airway Avenue
Suite D-1
Costa Mesa, CA 92626
714-890-7129
Fax: 714-890-7149
karl@aeei.com
www.aeei.com

Atlas Environmental Engineering provides cost effective site assessments, investigations, risk-based corrective actions, groundwater monitoring, soil remediation and more.
Karl Kerner, Senior Engineer
Jasmine Senn, Technical Support

1661 Ayres Associates
3433 Oakwood Hills Parkway
Eau Claire, WI 54701-7698
715-834-3161
800-666-3103
Fax: 715-831-7500
ayrescontact@ayresassociates.com
www.ayresassociates.com

Ayres Associates is an architectural/engineering consulting firm providing services in aerial mapping, architecture, land surveying, structural design, water resources, levee and river engineering, environmental science, siteinspections and more.
Thomas Pulse, PE, President
Richard Schoenthaler, Chief Financial Officer

1662 BCI Engineers and Scientists
2000 East Edgewood Drive
Suite 215
Lakeland, FL 33803
863-667-2345
Fax: 863-667-2662
ctownsend@bcieng.com
www.amecfw.com

BCI provides solutions to complex engineering and environmental challenges through services in consultancy, engineering, project management, operations and construction, specialised power equipment, oil and gas processing and more.
John Connolly, Chairman
Jonathan Lewis, CEO

1663 BHE Environmental
11733 Chesterdale Road 513-326-1500
Cincinnati, OH 45246 Fax: 513-326-1550
BHE's mission is to provide a full range of environmental consulting and remediation services in the areas of environmental engineering, sciences, and management.

1664 BJAAM Environmental
472 Elm Ridge Avenue 330-854-5300
PO Box 523 800-666-5331
Canal Fulton, OH 44614 Fax: 330-854-5340
info@bjaam.com
bjaam.com
Provides environmental consulting and contracting services, as well as industrial wastewater pre-treatment systems.
Brett Urian, President
Jason Grecco, Executive Director

1665 BRC Acoustics & Audiovisual Design
1932 First Avenue 206-270-8910
Suite 620 800-843-4524
Seattle, WA 98101 Fax: 206-270-8690
brc@brcacoustics.com
www.brcacoustics.com
A Seattle-based acoustical and technology consulting firm serving public and private clients throughout the United States. Services include architectural and mechanical acoustics, vibration measurement and analysis, and noise contourmapping for environmental noise control projects.
Daniel C Bruck, Ph.D, President
Roger Andrews, General Manager

1666 Bac-Ground
3216 Georgetown 713-664-8452
Houston, TX 77005 Fax: 713-664-2629
ebaca@bac-ground.com
www.bac-ground.com
Independent consultation service for groundwater pollution concerns. Bac-Ground offers water, soil, and waste material sampling, surface and borehole geophysical surveys, and aquifer tests.
Ernesto Baca

1667 Badger Laboratories and Engineering Company
501 West Bell Street 920-729-1100
Neenah, WI 54956-4868 800-776-7196
Fax: 920-729-4945
information@badgerlabs.com
www.badgerlabs.com
Badger Laboratories and Engineering provides customers with analytical, engineering and technical services focusing on the environmental field. The labs specialize in the testing and sampling of drinking water, groundwater, wastewater,solids and hazardous waste.
Richard Larson, President
Jeff Wagner, Lab Manager

1668 Barco Enterprises
11200 Pulaski Highway 410-335-0660
PO Box 0074 800-832-7538
White Marsh, MD 21162 Fax: 410-335-0790
www.barcoenterprises.com
Offers cleaning and restoration services. Some services include asbestos and lead paint abatement, dry ice blasting, air conveyance system cleaning, mold remediation; fire, smoke & water damage restoration; infrared inspections,hazardous materials disposal and more.
Bart Harrison, President
John King, VP, Operations

1669 Barer Engineering
199 Main Street 518-236-7070
Suite 600 800-878-2806
Burlington, VT 05401-8339 Fax: 518-236-5796
info@barer.com
www.barer.com
Produces machine tools and fabricating equipments that assist in air pollution control.

1670 Baron Consulting Company
181 Research Drive 203-874-5678
Suite 1 Fax: 203-874-7863
Milford, CT 06460 analyze@baronconsulting.com
www.baronconsulting.com
Chemical, environmental and biological consulting firm offering testing for products and materials. Some services include checking air quality for metals, solvents, and toxins. Types of materials tested include parmaceuticals, medicaldevices, cosmetic products and fragrances, plastic and polymers, speciality chemicals, rubber products and more.
Harry Agahigian, Technical Director

1671 Barr Engineering Company
4300 Market Pointe Drive 952-832-2600
Suite 200 800-632-2277
Minneapolis, MN 55435 Fax: 734-922-4401
askbarr@barr.com
www.barr.com
Barr provides engineering, environmental, and information technology services to clients across the nation and around the world. Services include engineering support, natural resources management, site assessment, groundwater modeling,water quality control and more.
Steve Kapeller, Sr Environmental Engineer
David Hibbs, Senior Civil Engineer

1672 Batta Environmental Associates
6 Garfield Way 302-737-3376
Newark, DE 19713-5817 800-543-4807
Fax: 302-737-5764
bcbatta@battaenv.com
www.battaenv.com
BATTA provides in-house expertise in the scientific disciplines of geology, hydrogeology, civil and environmental engineering, chemistry, toxicology, health and safety, project design and construction management. BATTA also offers labtesting for toxins and water filtration equipment.
Naresh C Batta, President
Neeraj K Batta, Vice President

1673 Baxter and Woodman
8678 Ridgefield Road 815-459-1260
Crystal Lake, IL 60012 Fax: 815-455-0450
info@baxterwoodman.com
www.baxterwoodman.com
Provides Municipal waste, water, transportation, control systems, and mapping services. Attention is given to the planning, design and construction of public infrastructure.
Derek Wold, Vice President
Louis Haussmann, Chief Operating Officer

1674 Baystate Environmental Consultants
296 North Main Street 413-525-3822
East Longmeadow, MA 01028 Fax: 413-525-8348
BEC offers a wide range of civil engineering, water resources and environmental expertise. The consultants specialize in lake and pond restoration services, environmental assessment under MEPA/NEPA and wetland science.
Tom Jenkins, Senior Engineer

1675 **Beals and Thomas**
144 Turnpike Road 508-366-0560
Southborough, MA 01772 Fax: 508-366-4391
info@btiweb.com
www.bealsandthomas.com
Beals and Thomas is a multidisciplinary consulting firm providing services to support the development and conservation of land and water resources throughout New England and the northeastern United States. Services include constructionplanning, waste management, water quality sampling, the issuing of permits, sustainable design and more.
George G. Preble, PE, President
Richard P. Kosian, PE, Executive Vice President

1676 **Bear West Company**
8 East Broadway 801-364-0525
Suite 300 Fax: 801-364-0676
Salt Lake City, UT 84111 logansimpson.com
Consultants providing expertise in environmental planning and permitting services.

1677 **Becher-Hoppe Associates**
330 North Fourth Street 715-845-8000
Wausau, WI 54403-5417 Fax: 715-845-8008
www.becherhoppe.com
Becher-Hoppe Associates is a consulting firm of engineers, architects, scientists, real estate specialists and surveyors. Services offered include airport, highway, municipal and facilities maintainance; solid waste and wastewatermanagement; agriculture management; and environmental projects.
Randy W. Van Natta, PE, President
Bonnie L. Stange, CPA, Corporate Controller

1678 **Benchmark Environmental Consultants**
6333 E. Mockingbird Lane 214-363-5996
Suite 147-913 Fax: 214-363-5994
Dallas, TX 75214 info@benchmarkenviro.com
www.benchmarkenviro.com
An environmental consulting firm offering site assessments, subsurface and geotechnical investigations, environmental permitting and compliance, archaeological surveys, spill prevention and control, endangered species & wildlifehabitat assessment and more.
Kelly Walker, President
Dustin Cox, Operations Manager

1679 **Bendix Environmental Research**
1950 Addison Street
Suite 202 home.earthlink.net/~bendix/
Berkeley, CA 94704
Specializes in toxicology, hazardous materials management, and preparation of environmental documents dealing with hazardous materials. Bendix provides expert witness services and litigation research and support for toxic tort cases,such as workplace and environmental exposures to harmful chemicals.
Selina Bendix, Ph.D, President
Gilbert G. Bendix, Vice President

1680 **Beta & Associates**
30 Macintosh Boulevard 416-736-1886
Unit 11 Fax: 919-545-0481
Concord, ON L4K-4P1 info@betaandassociates.ca
betaandassociates.ca
A professional organization which provides complete problem analysis, skilled engineers and design services for construction projects.

1681 **Better Management Corporation of Ohio**
4321 State 330-921-4301
Route 7 877-293-4300
New Waterford, OH 44445 Fax: 330-482-9242
www.bmcbulk.com
Provides bulk transportation and disposal of solid waste to the oil, gas, steel and waste management industries.
Craig Stacy, President & CEO
Paul Wilson, Vice President

1682 **Bhate Environmental Associates**
1608 13th Avenue South 205-918-4000
Suite 300 800-806-4001
Birmingham, AL 35205 Fax: 205-918-4050
www.bhate.com
The association provides support in the areas of environmental compliance, investigations, remedial action, restoration, energy conservation, information technology, industrial hygiene, hazardous substance exposure and more.
Sam Bhate, President
Kimberly Nemmers, Program Manager

1683 **Bioengineering Group**
1555 Coraopolis Heights Rd. 412-809-6600
Moon Township, PA 15108 Fax: 978-740-0097
mail@bioengineering.com
www.chesterengineers.com
Provides a full range of consulting services in the field of bioengineering for erosion control, water quality, habitat restoration and stormwater management.

1684 **Biological Monitoring**
1800 Kraft Drive 540-953-2821
Suite 101 877-953-2821
Blacksburg, VA 24060 Fax: 540-951-1481
bmi@biomon.com
www.biomon.com
Offers consulting on issues related to water quality and toxicology.
David Gruber, President

1685 **Biospec Products**
PO Box 788 918-336-3363
Bartlesville, OK 74005 800-617-3363
Fax: 918-336-6060
info@biospec.com
biospec.com
Producers of laboratory scientific equipment. Products include homogenizers & cell disrupters, pulverizers, tissue dispersers, bio mixers, beads, vials, tissue grinders and more.
Tim Hopkins, President

1686 **Bison Engineering**
1400 11th Avenue 406-442-5768
Helena, MT 59601 800-571-7346
Fax: 406-449-6653
hrobbins@bison-eng.com
www.bison-eng.com
Bison Engineering is an environmental consulting firm with extensive experience in air quality permitting, air emissions testing and ambient air monitoring.
Jeffrey T. Chaffee, PE, President
Harold W. Robbins, Executive Manager

1687 **Black and Veatch**
11401 Lamar Avenue 913-458-2000
Overland Park, KS 66211 Fax: 913-458-2934
info@bv.com
www.bv.com
Consultants specializing in energy resources, water quality controland communication techology.
Steven L. Edwards, Chairman & CEO
Karen L. Daniel, Executive Director & CFO

1688 Block Environmental Services
2451 Estand Way
Pleasant Hill, CA 94523
925-682-7200
800-682-7255
Fax: 925-686-0399
dblock@blockenviron.com
www.blockenviron.com

An environmental consulting firm specializing in risk assessment and toxicology, hazardous waste compliance, and indoor air quality.
David Block, President
Ron Block, Chief Financial Officer

1689 Bollyky Associates
31 Strawberry Hill Avenue
Stamford, CT 06902
203-967-4223
Fax: 203-967-4845
ljbbai@bai-ozone.com
www.bai-ozone.com

Engineering firm specializing in Ozone technology, water and wastewater treatment and treatability studies.
L Joseph Bollyky, President

1690 Braun Intertec Corporation
11001 Hampshire Avenue South
Minneapolis, MN 55438
952-995-2000
800-279-6100
Fax: 952-995-2020
info@braunintertec.com
braunintertec.com

An engineering firm providing consulting, management and testing services to clients in the commercial, industrial and residential real estate, institutional, retail, financial and government markets. Some services includeenvironmental and geothermal consulting, geospacial operations, construction materials testing, structures evaluation and more.
Jon Carlson, CEO
Robert Janssen, President

1691 Breedlove, Dennis and Associates
330 West Canton Avenue
Winter Park, FL 32789
407-677-1882
Fax: 407-657-7008
bda-inc.com

Offers environmental and natural resources consulting. Services include environmental impact assessments, aquatic resources analyses, endangered species mitigation, natural resource and wildlife management, wetland delineation, waterresources planning, landscape planning, analytical software, litigation support and more.
Michael W Dennis, Ph.D, President
Jeffrey W Pardue, Vice President

1692 Brinkerhoff Environmental Services
1805 Atlantic Avenue
Manasquan, NJ 08736
732-223-2225
800-246-7358
Fax: 732-223-3666
info@brinkenv.com
brinkenv.com

Offers consulting services dealing with groundwater remediation, environmental site assessments, hazardous materials, permitting, indoor air quality, underground storage tank management, preservation of open space, field oversight andsensitive area mapping.
Laura Brinkerhoff, President & CEO
John Checchio, VP, Technical Services

1693 Brown, Vence and Associates
115 Sansome Street
Suite 800
San Francisco, CA 94104
415-434-0900
Fax: 415-956-6220
bvamail@brownvence.com
www.brownvence.com

Waste and energy management consulting firm.

1694 Buck, Seifert and Jost
65 Oak Street
Suite 201
Norwood, NJ 07648-0415
201-767-3111
877-867-1071
Fax: 201-767-3178
bsjinc@bsjinc.com
www.bsjinc.com

Consultancy for the water and wastewater industries. Services include water supply treatment, industrial waste management, site development, permits, environmental planning and design and more.
Ronald von Autenried, PE, President
Guido von Autenried, PE, Director & Chief Engineer

1695 Bureau Veritas
100 Northpointe Parkway
Buffalo, NY 14228
716-505-3300
Fax: 716-505-3301
www.bureauveritas.com

Specializes in the testing, inspection and certification of workplace safety. Some of the industries served include marine, mining, oil and gas, transport and infrastructures, agriculture and food.
Didier Michaud-Daniel, Chief Executive Officer
Nicolas Tissot, Finance

1696 Burk-Kleinpeter
4176 Canal Street
New Orleans, LA 70119
504-486-5901
Fax: 504-488-1714
mjackson@bkiusa.com
www.bkiusa.com

A full service consulting firm providing services such as transportation systems, flood protection, wastewater management, electrical systems, environmental compliance consulting and more.
George C. Kleinpeter, Jr., President & CEO
J. W. Bill Giardina, Jr., Principal

1697 Burns and McDonnell
9400 Ward Parkway
Kansas City, MO 64114
816-333-9400
Fax: 816-333-3690
busdev@burnsmcd.com
www.burnsmcd.com

A multidisciplinary engineering, architectural, construction and environmental service firm. Services are offered in the areas of aviation, construction, environmental engineering, oil and gas, power, water, industrial management andtransportation.
Melissa Lavin-Hickey, Director of Marketing

1698 C&H Environmental Technical Services
P.O. Box 334
Pittsfield, MA 01202
413-464-4815
Fax: 413-499-4510
www.chenvironmental.com

Environmental consulting firm providing services in demolition projects, excavation, asbestos abatement, industrial hygiene, waste management and construction for water facilities.
John Crow, President

1699 CA Rich
17 Dupont Street
Plainview, NY 11803
516-576-8844
Fax: 516-576-0093
info@carichinc.com
carichinc.com

An independently owned, private consulting firm providing hydrogeologic and environmental engineering services. CA Rich also assists in the conception, development, design, implementation, documentation and defense of site evaluationsand remedial action.
Charles A Rich, Founder & President
Richard J Izzo, Vice President

1700 CBA Environmental Services
57 Park Lane
Hegins, PA 17938
570-682-8742
Fax: 570-682-8915
info@cbaenvironmental.com
www.cbaenvironmental.com
Provides environmental solutions from general plant maintenance and cleaning to large-scale soil remediation projects. Services also include groundwater treatment, storage tank management and training.
Bruce L Bruso, Principal

1701 CBI
2103 Research Forest Drive
The Woodlands, TX 77380
832-513-1000
Fax: 832-513-1005
www.cbi.com
Provides consultations in technology and infrastructure for the energy industry.
Patrick K. Mullen, President & CEO
Michael S. Taff, VP, Chief Financial Officer

1702 CDS Laboratories
75 Suttle Street
PO Box 2605
Durango, CO 81302
303-247-4220
800-553-6266
Fax: 303-247-4227
Specializes in analytical analysis and testing, consulting, QA, environmental and dyes.

1703 CEDA
567 W. Lake Street
Suite 1200
Chicago, IL 60661
312-782-2332
800-571-2332
webmaster@cedaorg.net
www.cedaorg.net
Provides solutions to clients' energy needs.
Ronald Bean, Chairman
Martha Martinez, Vice Chairman

1704 CIH Environmental Solutions
425 SW 17 Avenue
Miami, FL 33135
610-372-6692
888-860-0101
Fax: 610-372-0862
info@cihenvironmental.com
www.cihenvironmental.com
Provides services in indoor air quality, industrial hygiene and mold/bacterial contaminations.
Armando Chamorro, President

1705 CIH Services
7148 Creekside Lane
Indianapolis, IN 46250
317-797-7768
Fax: 317-913-1895
cihservices@juno.com
www.cih-services.com
Offers services in indoor air quality and industrial hygiene.
John Beltz, Sr. Industrial Hygienist

1706 CII Engineered Systems
6767 Forrest Hill Avenue
Suite 100
Richmond, VA 23225
804-320-1405
800-768-2545
Fax: 804-320-9625
cii.richmond@ciiservice.com
www.ciiservice.com
Provides services in energy management.
Dorothy Thacker, Chairman
Robert Ranson, President

1707 CK Environmental
1020 Turnpike Street
Suite 8
Canton, MA 02021
781-828-5200
888-253-0303
Fax: 781-828-5380
www.ckenvironmental.com
Purveyor of air quality testing in compliance with environmental policies.
Michael F. Kelley, QSTI, President & Cofounder
Stephen J. Phillips, QSTI, Sr. Project Manager

1708 CRB Geological and Environmental Services
8744 SW 133rd Street
Miami, FL 33176
305-447-9777
Fax: 305-567-2853
info@crbgeo.com
www.crbgeo.com
Environmental consulting firm offering site assessments, treatment of waste water, air quality assessments, asbestos abatement, mold testing and environmental permits.
Fred Baddour, Owner
Victor Rossinsky, Vice President

1709 CTI and Associates
28001 Cabot Drive
Suite 250
Novi, MI 48377
248-486-5100
800-284-8632
Fax: 248-486-5050
info@cticompanies.com
www.cticompanies.com
Environmental engineering firm offering services in site remediation, environmental compliance, industrial hygiene, waste management, renewable energy, geotechnical engineering and more.
Morgan Subbarayan, Owner & President
Christopher Winkeljohn, Senior Vice President

1710 CZR Incorporated
825 S US Highway 1
Suite 110
Jupiter, FL 33477
561-747-7455
Fax: 561-747-7576
czrinc@czr-inc.com
www.czr-inc.com
Environmental impact studies, wetlands delineation, threatened species surveys, environmental resource permitting.
Susan Hudgens-Moore, President
Thomas F. Fucigna, Jr., Sr. Environmental Scientist

1711 Cabe Associates
5400 Limestone Road
Wilmington, DE 19808
302-239-6634
877-732-9633
Fax: 302-239-8485
cabe.com
Environmental consulting for pollution control, environmental copliance, regulatory permitting, sustainable site design, lab testing, geotechnical solutions and more.
Lee J. Beetschen, Principal

1712 California Environmental Protection Agency
1001 I Street
P.O. Box 2815
Sacramento, CA 95812
916-323-2514
cepacomm@calepa.ca.gov
calepa.ca.gov
Specializes in consulting for industrial safety and hygiene, air quality monitoring and pesticide regulation.
Matthew Rodriquez, Secretary
Gordon Burns, Undersecretary

1713 California Geo-Systems
1545 Victory Boulevard
2nd Floor
Glendale, CA 91201
818-500-9533
Fax: 818-500-0134
geosys@pacbell.net
www.geosys1.com
Offers Geotechnical environmental services such as site assessments, groundwater monitoring, engineering investigations, soil sampling and more.
Vince Carnegie, Chief Geologist
Rachel Fischer, Senior Geologist

1714 Cambridge Environmental
75 State Street 617-452-6180
Suite 701 info@cambridgeenvironmental.com
Boston, MA 02109 www.cambridgeenvironmental.com
Consulting and research firm that assesses and works to minimize risks to health and the environment. Some services offered include interpretation of scientific studies and policies, data analysis, regulatory compliance, permitting andsafety checks.
Laura Green, Ph.D., President
Stephen G. Zemba, Ph.D., Senior Engineer

1715 Camiros Limited
411 South Wells Street 312-922-9211
Suite 400 Fax: 312-922-9689
Chicago, IL 60607 info@camiros.com
www.camiros.com
Camiros offers services in planning, zoning, urban design, economic development, and landscape architecture. The firm has drafted land use plans and zoning ordinances that pay careful attention to environmental issues.
Bill James, AICP, Principal
Arista Strungys, AICP, Principal

1716 Camo Pollution Control
1610 State Route 376 845-463-7310
Wappingers Falls, NY 12590
Producer of water purification and sewage treatment systems.
George P. Cacchio, President

1717 Canin Associates
500 Delaney Avenue 407-422-4040
Suite 404 Fax: 407-425-7427
Orlando, FL 32801 www.canin.com
Provides environmental services: urban planning, landscape architecture and building design.
Brian Canin, President
Myrna Canin, Vice President

1718 CannonDesign
2170 Whitehaven Road 716-773-6800
Grand Island, NY 14072 www.cannondesign.com
Provides informational services for sustainable development, promoting environmentally friendly engineering. Topics covered include renewable energy, clean water and more.
Bradley A. Lukanic, AIA, CEO
David M. Carlino, Finance

1719 Cape Environmental Management
500 Pinnacle Court 877-422-7350
Suite 100 800-488-4372
Norcross, GA 30071 Fax: 770-908-7219
pferroni@cape-inc.com
www.cape-inc.com
Consulting firm offering construction, environmental remediation and industrial services.
Fernando Rios, CEO
Luis Terry, Project Manager

1720 Capital Environmental Enterprises
3440 South Post Road 317-240-8085
Indianapolis, IN 46239 888-376-4315
Fax: 317-241-4180
info@capitalenvironmentalenterprises.com
www.capitalenvironmentalenterprises.com
Environmental consulting professionals with a focus on asbestos, underground storage tank installation, and material testing.
Davies Batterton, President

1721 Cardinal Environmental
3303 Paine Avenue 920-459-2500
Sheboygan, WI 53081 800-413-7225
Fax: 920-459-2503
redbird@cardinalenvironmental.com
www.cardinalenvironmental.com
Environmental testing laboratory and consulting firm offering services in air permitting, asbestos inspections, health and safety training programs, industrial hygiene, wastewater sampling and more.
Scott A Hanson, President
Jennifer Beimel, Vice President

1722 Cardno ATC
10004 Park Meadows Drive 720-257-5800
Suite 300 Fax: 720-257-5801
Lone Tree, Denver, CO 80124 www.cardno.com
Environmental consulting firm offering services in environmental design, planning, software, construction management, material testing and more.
Michael Alscher, Chairman
Neville Buch, CEO

1723 Carpenter Environmental Associates
610 County Route 1 845-781-4844
Unit 2F Fax: 845-782-5591
Pine Island, NY 10969 mail@cea-enviro.com
www.ceaenviro.com
Provides environmental engineering and assessment services, including wastewater and storm water management, wetlands and ecological investigations, site assessments, environmental compliance and contingency planning, permittingservices, and litigation support.
Kim Bell Hosea, President
Ralph E Huddleston, Jr., Sr Environmental Scientist

1724 Carr Research Laboratory
17 Waban Street 781-235-3132
Wellesley, MA 02482
Environmental consulting research laboratory providing wetlands delineation, wildlife habitat evaluation, groundwater impact study, soil testing, water quality monitoring and more.
Jerome Carr, Ph.D, President

1725 Catlin Engineers and Scientists
220 Old Dairy Road 910-452-5861
Wilmington, NC 28405 Fax: 910-452-7563
info@catlinusa.com
www.catlinusa.com
Specializes in providing quality services in the fields of environmental, civil, and geotechnical engineering. Services include soil and ground water remediation, wastewater treatment system design, public infrastructure,environmentally secure landfills, and clean water supplies.
Richard Catlin, President

1726 Central States Environmental Services
2206 Horns Mill Road, SE 740-681-9902
Lancaster, OH 43130 800-837-8064
Fax: 740-681-1389
www.bbuenvironmental.com
Environmental clean-up contractor offering transportation services for hazardous and non-hazardous liquid and solid waste.
Steve Schmelzer, President

1727 Challenge Environmental Systems
2270 Worth Lane 479-927-1008
Suite D Fax: 479-927-1000
Springdale, AR 72764 kent@challenge-sys.com
challenge-sys.com

Challenge Environmental Systems manufactures environmental equipment (Respirometers) for testing wastewater, and other material testing equipment.
Mark Kuss, President

1728 Chapman Engineering
P.O. Box 1305
Boerne, TX 78006
800-375-7747
830-816-3311
Fax: 830-816-1753
info@chapmanengr.com
www.chapman.engineering

Offers environmental engineering services: pipeline corrosion assessment, environmental compliance, spill prevention and control, water pollution control and more.
Cal Chapman, P.E., President
Mikes Ames, Vice President

1729 Chelsea Group
733 Bishop Street
Suite 181
Honolulu, HI 96813
800-626-6722
Fax: 808-356-0992
info@chelsea-grp.com
chelsea-grp.com

Specializes in consulting for the enhancement of building infrastructure, considering areas such as air quality, property condition, energy planning and more.
George Benda, Chairman & CEO
Dave Munn, PE, Senior Engineering Advisor

1730 Chemical Data Management Systems
6516 Trinity Court
Suite 201
Dublin, CA 94568
925-551-7300
800-735-1761
Fax: 925-829-3886
info@cdms.com
www.cdms.com

Provides a full range of hazardous material and OSHA regulatory compliance services, including implementing compliance programs, submitting necessary reports to all regulatory agencies, employee training, noise monitoring, spillprevention and more.
Michele McSweeney, CEO & Owner
Raschelle Mullette, Business Manager

1731 Chicago Chem Consultants Corporation
14 North Peoria Street
Suite 2C
Chicago, IL 60607-2609
312-226-2436
Fax: 312-226-8886
info@chichem.com
www.chichem.com

Provides a range of risk protective environmental and engineering services: energy management, chemical process design, forensics, equipment evaluation and more.
Jeffrey P. Perl, Ph.D, President
Stanley Yoslov, Senior Associate

1732 Cigna Loss Control Services
900 Cottage Grove Road
Bloomfield, CT 06002
800-997-1654
www.cigna.com

Provides services in the field of industrial hygiene and corporate responsibility.
David Cordani, President & CEO
Lisa Bacus, Executive Vice President

1733 Clean Air Engineering
500 West Wood Street
Palatine, IL 60067
800-553-5511
800-627-0033
Fax: 847-991-3300
info@cleanair.com
www.cleanair.com

Environmental consulting for air quality management. Clean Air Engineering also offers permitting services, process engineering, equipment rental and manufacture, measurement and analytical services.
Allen Kephart, President & CEO
Anthony Milianti, Project Engineer

1734 Clean Environments
2800 NE Loop 410
Suite 105
San Antonio, TX 78218
210-349-7242
800-299-7242
Fax: 210-349-1132
sales@cleanenvironments.com
www.cleanenvironments.com

Environmental consulting firm offering mold and asbesto control services.
John Lavoie, President
Ray Keeble, Senior Project Manager

1735 Clean World Engineering
1737 S Naperville Road
Suite 200
Wheaton, IL 60189
630-260-0200
800-761-9603
Fax: 630-260-0797

An environmental engineering firm specializing in developing practical solutions in compliance with environmental regulations. Services include asbestos and lead inspections, indoor air quality testing, site assessments, industrialhygiene, waste management and more.
Rita Kapur, President

1736 Cohen Group
3 Waters Park Drive
Suite 226
San Mateo, CA 94403-1169
650-349-9737
Fax: 650-349-3378
admin@thecohengroup.com
www.thecohengroup.com

Provides a complete range of environmental health and safety services to businesses and governments, covering indoor air quality, asbestos, respiratory protection, and industrial hygiene safety.
Joel M. Cohen, President
Timothy Bormann, Vice President

1737 Cohrssen Environmental
2970 Pine Street
San Francisco, CA 94115
415-775-1105

Offers industrial hygiene services.
Barbara Cohrssen, President

1738 Community Conservation
120 Sunset Ridge Avenue
Suite 114
Gays Mills, WI 54631
608-735-4717
Fax: 512-519-8494
cc@communityconservation.org
www.communityconservation.org

Works together with local rural people to aid in the protection of their wildlife and forests. Projects undertaken have mainly been in India, Belize and Wisconsin with an emphasis on primates and other species. The organization offersservices such as project management, land use assessment, zoning plans, resource monitoring, publicity and more.
Keefe Keeley, President
Terry Beck, Ph.D, Vice President

1739 Compass Environmental
1751 McCollum Parkway, NW
Kennesaw, GA 30064
770-499-7127
Fax: 770-423-7402
staff@compassenv.com
www.compassenv.com

Offers services in asbestos control, indoor air quality investigations, industrial hygiene surveys and audits, and guidance in environmental regulatory compliance.
Eva M Ewing, CIH, Senior Industrial Hygienist
William M Ewing, CIH, Technical Director

1740 **Comprehensive Environmental**
225 Cedar Hill Street 508-281-5160
Marlborough, MA 01752 800-725-2550
Fax: 508-281-5136
hr@ceiengineers.com
ceiengineers.com
Provides water, wastewater and hazardous waste services: flood and drainage management, stormwater engineering, testing of water quality in lakes and rivers, environmental compliance and more.
Eileen Pannetier, President & CEO

1741 **Conservtech Group**
5875 Rickenbacker Road 323-867-9044
Commerce, CA 90040 Fax: 323-867-9045
bob@conservtechgroup.com
www.conservtechgroup.com
Offers solutions for environmental challenges through pollution control systems, site assessment, waste management services, civil engineering planning and design, air quality analysis and more.
Robert MacDonald, President
Bruce Charest, Sr. Environmental Engineer

1742 **Consultox**
PO Box 1239 207-563-2300
Damariscotta, ME 04543 800-566-2301
Fax: 207-563-8990
www.consultox.com
Consultation services offered by an expert toxicologist in the areas of industry placement and implementation, product safety, trade association representation, drug and cosmetic registration, litigation support, occupational safetyassessment and more.
Richard A Parent, Ph.D, President
Michael J Siener, BS, Information Systems Manager

1743 **Continental Shelf Associates**
8502 SW Kansas Avenue 772-219-3000
Stuart, FL 34997 csa@conshelf.com
www.conshelf.com
Environmental consulting firm specializing in marine sciences and offering related services such as environmental impact analysis, researching energy resources, infrastructure programs, permitting, marine surveys, marine operations andmore.
Kevin Peterson, President & CEO
Dan White, Chief Technology Officer

1744 **Converse Consultants**
717 South Myrtle Avenue 626-930-1200
Monrovia, CA 91016 Fax: 626-930-1212
converse@converseconsultants.com
www.converseconsultants.com
Environmental consulting and engineering firm offering services in geotechnical engineering, materials testing, water resource management, workplace safety, site assessments, hazardous materials management, laboratory testing servicesand more.
Hashmi S Quazi, Ph.D., Chairman
Ruben L Romero, MBA, Chief Financial Officer

1745 **Cook, Flatt and Strobel Engineers**
2930 SW Woodside Drive 785-272-4706
Topeka, KS 66614 Fax: 785-272-4736
www.cfse.com
Consulting services for transportation, wastewater management, geotechnical engineering, solid waste disposal, site development, landscape architecture, land planning, construction inspection and administration and more.
Kenneth Blair, PE, Chairman
Robert Chambers, PE, President

1746 **Cornerstone Environmental, Health and Safety**
880 Lennox Court 317-733-2637
Zionsville, IN 46077 800-285-2568
Fax: 317-733-2481
info@corner-enviro.com
www.corner-enviro.com
Provides environmental and safety compliance services such as chemical management, site assessment, software, employee safety training and more.
Mark Miller, President
Kevin Mallin, Senior Project Manager

1747 **Corporate Environmental Advisors**
127 Hartwell Street 508-835-8822
Suite 2 800-358-7960
West Boylston, MA 01583 Fax: 508-835-8812
cea-inc.com
Environmental consulting firm specializing in environmental compliance and engineering, health and safety training, hazardous building material assessments and more.
Joseph S Campisi, President

1748 **Cultural Resource Consultants, International Archaeology & Ecology**
PO Box 315 979-530-0331
Chappell Hill, TX 77426 www.culturalresource.com
Provides services for environmentally sensitive projects: archaeology investigations, permitting, computer graphics and mapping, mineral exploration and development, ground penetrating radar, land reclamation, environmental design, andmore.
John Griggs, Ph.D., Sr. Principal Investigator
Robert B d'Aigle, MA, Sr. Principal Investigator

1749 **Custom Environmental Services**
233 Forest Drive 805-968-2112
Santa Barbara, CA 93117 Fax: 805-968-2137
contact@custom-env.com
www.custom-env.com
Environmental compliance consulting firm providing services that help individuals and companies comply with environmental laws, including the Clean Air Act, Clean Water Act, and Medical Waste Management Act.
Rosalie Skefich, Founder & President

1750 **D'Appolonia**
701 Rodi Road 412-856-9440
2nd Floor Fax: 412-856-9535
Pittsburgh, PA 15235 info@dappolonia.com
www.dappolonia.com
Provides engineering, scientific and construction management services for projects involving large civil works and special earth/structure interaction issues. Some of the areas covered include power generation, mining, dams andwaterways, geophysics, forensic studies and more.
Robert Shusko, President
Aaron Antell, Principal Engineer

1751 **DPRA**
10215 Technology Drive 785-539-3565
Suite 201 865-218-4824
Knoxville, TN 37932-4304 Fax: 785-539-5353
info@dpra.com
www.dpra.com
Offers environmental consulting services with a focus on compliance, sustainable practices, records management and more.
Denis O'Keefe, CEO
Mary J Carter, Executive Vice President

1752 Datanet Engineering
11416 Reisterstown Road
Owings Mills, MD 21117
410-654-1800
Fax: 410-654-3711
info@datanetengineering.com
www.datanetengineering.com

Provides services for the fuel systems industry: corrosion engineering, cathodic protection, construction and training, system installations and more.
Andrew Cignatta, President
John V Cignatta, Ph.D, PE, VP, Principal Engineer

1753 DeVany Industrial Consultants
14507 NW 19th Avenue
Vancouver, WA 98685
360-546-0999
Fax: 360-546-0777
mdevany@earthlink.net

Provides a full custom range of safety and industrial hygiene services.
Mary DeVany, President

1754 Detail Associates: Environmental Engineering Consulting
300 Grand Avenue
Englewood, NJ 07631
201-569-6708
Fax: 201-569-4378
stephenj@daienviro.com
www.daienviro.com

Offers consulting services in asbestos assessment, project management, lead surveys, air quality testing, environmental audits, environmental design and more.
Steve Jaraczewski, Principal

1755 Dunn Development Corporation
316 Douglass Street
2nd Floor
Brooklyn, NY 11217
718-388-9407
Fax: 718-388-0638
info@dunndev.com
www.dunndev.com

Development consulting firm for affordable housing building projects. Dunn Development incorporates sustainable design and green building into their projects. Areas covered include property acquisition, building design, assetmanagement, construction supervision and more.
Martin Dunn, President
Stephen Viafore, Finance Director

1756 Durand & Anastas Environmental Strategies
250 Northern Avenue
Suite 400
Boston, MA 02210
617-860-2556
info@durandanastas.com
www.durandanastas.com

Provides consulting services in environmental impact assessments, regulatory compliance, public outreach and media strategies. The agency specializes in issues affecting inland resources, the coastal zone, and offshore waters.
Bob Durand, President
Chuck Anastas, Managing Partner

1757 ESS Group
100 Fifth Avenue
5th Floor
Waltham, MA 02451
781-419-7696
Fax: 781-622-2612
info@essgroup.com
www.essgroup.com

ESS is a multi-disciplinary environmental consulting and engineering firm offering services in the areas of energy generation and transmission, coastal engineering and marine sciences, water resources, natural resources, environmentalcompliance and more.
Charles Natale, President & CEO
Deirdra Taylor, VP, Chief Operating Officer

1758 ETS Environmental Services
1401 Municipal Road NW
Roanoke, VA 24012-1309
540-265-0004
Fax: 540-265-0131
jmck@etsi-inc.com
www.etsi-inc.com

ETS is a full-service fabric filter baghouse consulting and training firm specializing in air emissions control, testing, training, testimony and troubleshooting services.
John McKenna, Ph.D, Principal
Terry Williamson, VP, Laboratory Operations

1759 Earth Science Associates
4300 Long Beach Blvd
Suite 310
Long Beach, CA 90807
562-428-3181
Fax: 562-428-3186
contactESA@earthsci.com
www.earthsci.com

Consulting company serving the oil and gas industry. ESA specializes in resource assessment, economic evaluation, risk studies and the development of custom geographic information systems.
John D Grace, President

1760 EcoLogic Systems
7977 Capwell Drive
Suite 150
Oakland, CA 94621
510-635-7400
800-223-0609
Fax: 510-635-7402
sales@ecologicsystems.com
www.ecologicsystems.com

Developer of software for hazardous material management and environmental health and safety compliance. Some of their programs include Asbestos Inventory and Document Management, Indoor Air Quality and Analytical Data Management,Employee Health and Safety Records Management, Equipment Maintenance Management and more.
Jim Wilson, President & CEO

1761 Ecology and Environment
368 Pleasant View Drive
Lancaster, NY 14086
716-684-8060
Fax: 716-684-0844
info@ene.com
www.ene.com

Ecology and Environment is an environmental science and engineering company providing environmental consulting services and litigation support. Areas covered include engineering, restoration, water treatment, regulatory compliance,permitting, environmental impact assessments, air and noise studies, field studies and more.
Mye John, Chief Financial Officer
Cheryl Karpowicz, Sr VP, Development

1762 Elinor Schwartz
318 South Abingdon Street
Arlington, VA 22204
703-920-5389
Fax: 703-920-5402
es@elinorschwartz.com

Offering representation services for state agencies and providing research on natural resources, energy and environmental issues.
Elinor Schwartz, Washington Representative

1763 EnSafe
5724 Summer Trees Drive
Memphis, TN 38134
901-372-7962
800-588-7962
Fax: 901-372-2454
www.ensafe.com

Provides consulting services such as the implementation of occupational health and safety programs, worker's compensation programs, and environmental management systems meant to decrease accident frequency and accident costs.
Phillip G Coop, Chairman
Don Bradford, President & CEO

1764 EnviroTest Laboratories
315 Fullerton Avenue
Newburgh, NY 12550
845-562-0890
Fax: 845-562-0841
customerservice@envirotestlaboratories.com
www.envirotestlaboratories.com

Laboratory testing for soil and water.
Renee Cusack, Laboratory Director
Samuel Cohen, General Manager

1765 Environmental Compliance Consultants
1500 North Post Road 907-644-0428
Anchorage, AK 99501 888-644-0428
Fax: 907-677-9328
www.eccalaska.com
Environmental consultants offering services in waste management, UST/AST services, regulatory compliance, emergency response, natural resource management, site restoration, risk assessment and more.
Mark Goodwin, President

1766 Environmental HELP
PO Box 222320 661-260-2260
Santa Clarita, CA 91322-2320 800-750-0622
Fax: 661-253-3555
bj@environmentalhelp.net
www.environmentalhelp.net
Offers consultation services for environmental health and safety compliance. Areas of expertise include environmental assessments and audits, granting permits, waste water management and more.
BJ Atkins, President

1767 Environmental Resource Associates
16341 Table Mountain Parkway 303-431-8454
Golden, CO 80403 800-372-0122
Fax: 303-421-0159
info@eraqc.com
www.eraqc.com
Provides products and consultation services for laboratories in the areas of water pollution, chemistry, microbiology, soil testing and more.
Chris Ackerman, Life Science Sales

1768 Environmental Resources Management
3352 128th Avenue 616-399-3500
Holland, MI 49424 Fax: 616-399-3777
www.erm.com
Provides consulting services such as sustainability planning, health and safety, risk assessment, data management, asset management and environmental compliance.
Robin Bidwell, Executive Chair

1769 Environmental Risk Management
3702 S. Expressway 281 956-383-6569
PO Box 3213 Fax: 956-383-6568
Edinburg, TX 78542 scott@enrisk.com
www.enrisk.com
Provides experienced environmental consulting to South Texas. Services include Phase I, II and III environmental site assessments, leaking petroleum storage tank assessments and project management, underground fuel system assessmentsand remedial services for environmental projects.
Mark Barron, President
Scott Boyd, Vice President

1770 Environmental Science Associates
550 Kearney Street 415-896-5900
Suite 800 Fax: 415-896-0332
San Francisco, CA 94108 www.esassoc.com
Environmental Science Associates is a consulting firm committed to helping clients meet the challenges of environmental projects, planning, assessment and regulatory compliance.
Leslie Moulton, President & CEO
Albert Cuisinot, Chief Financial Officer

1771 Environmental Strategy Consultants
1528 Walnut Street 215-731-4200
Suite 500 Fax: 215-731-4207
Philadelphia, PA 19102 info@envirostrat.com
www.envirostrat.com
Environmental consulting, management, and engineering firm specializing in identifying potential or actual environmental liabilities and preventing or remediating them. Some services include emergency planning, wastewater management,compliance assessment, health and safety training and more.
Lorna M Velardi, President
Elaine Feldman, PE, Senior Consultant

1772 Enviroplan Consulting
155 Route 46 West 973-575-2555
Suite 109 Fax: 973-575-6617
Wayne, NJ 07470 contact@enviroplan.com
www.enviroplan.com
Meteorological and air pollution consulting company specializing in three areas: air pollution consulting including greenhouse gas emmissions, inventory development and mitigation, meteorological monitoring programs and wind resourceanalyses.
Howard Ellis, Ph.D, President
Allen Dittenhoefer, Ph.D, Sr Vice President

1773 Epcon Industrial Systems
17777 I-45 South 936-273-3300
P.O. Box 7060 800-447-7872
Conroe, TX 77385 Fax: 936-273-4600
epcon@epconlp.com
www.epconlp.com
Provides a broad line of technology advanced, yet user friendly air pollution control products, finishing systems and heat processing equipment.
Aziz Jamaluddin, President & CEO
Tasha Jamaluddin, Managing Director

1774 GBMC & Associates
219 Brown Lane 501-847-7077
Suite 215 Fax: 501-847-7943
Bryant, AK 72022 vblubaugh@gbmcassoc.com
GBMC & Associates is a consulting firm providing strategic environmental services to industrial clients in the form of air permitting support, water quality and toxicity studies, storm water management, environmental programdevelopment and reporting.
Chuck Campbell, PE, Principal & Sr. Engineer
Jonathan Brown, Project Manager

1775 GEO/Plan Associates
30 Mann Street 781-740-1340
Hingham, MA 02043 Fax: 617-740-1340
Consultation company offering geology petroleum expert witness service.
Michu Tcheng, Managing Partner

1776 GHD USA
1240 North Mountain Road 717-541-0622
Harrisburg, PA 17112 Fax: 717-541-8004
news@ghd.com
www.ghd.com
Offers engineering, architecture, environmental and construction services such as agricultural impact assessments, air quality monitoring, construction engineering, waste management and more.
Rob Knott, Chairman
Ashley Wright, CEO

1777 **Gabbard Environmental Services**
7611 Hope Farm Road 260-493-2982
Fort Wayne, IN 46815-654 Fax: 260-493-4043
wdgabbard@aol.com
www.gabbardenvironmentalservices.com
Consulting services for environmental affairs such as permitting, compliance, hazardous material transportation, inspections and audits, employee safety training, indoor air quality checks and written programs.
William D Gabbard, President

1778 **Galson Corporation**
6601 Kirkville Road 315-432-0506
East Syracuse, NY 13057 888-432-5227
Fax: 315-437-0509
www.galsonlabs.com
Offerings consulting services in industrial hygiene analysis with the aim of preventing hazardous exposures in the workplace. Methods utilized include air quality analysis and air quality monitoring.
Joe Unangst, VP, Industrial Hygiene
Kevin Kuppel, Finance Director

1779 **Geo-Marine Technology**
101 South California Street 406-721-1599
Suite B Fax: 406-926-1379
Missoula, MT 59801 services@geomarinetech.com
www.geomarinetech.com
Provides geological, geophysical and hydrographic survey consultancy services to offshore oil and gas industries, offshore survey industries, and governments.
John Rietman, President & Founder
Beau Pallister, Vice President

1780 **Gradient Corporation**
20 University Road 617-395-5000
Cambridge, MA 02138 Fax: 617-395-5001
info@gradientcorp.com
gradientcorp.com
A consulting firm offering services in toxicology, epidemiology, contaminants, industrial hygiene, geographic information systems, environmental sciences and forensic chemistry.
Teresa S Bowers, Ph.D, Principal
Barbara D Beck, Ph.D, Principal

1781 **Greeley-Polhemus Group**
1310 Birmingham Road 610-793-9440
West Chester, PA 19382
Specializes in providing consulting services to the United States Army Corps of Engineers and to other Corps Districts. Services are provided in the aras of project planning, economics, finance, institutional strategy development, andenvironmental studies related to flood control, land use, recreation, water supply, and navigation.
Maureen Polhemus, President & Owner

1782 **Ground/Water Treatment and Technology**
627 Mt. Hope Road 973-983-0901
Wharton, NJ 07885 800-770-0901
Fax: 973-983-0903
sales@gwttllc.com
www.gwttllc.com
Develops advanced technologies for environmental restoration of contaminated sites. The organization offers bioremedial technology for rapid cleanup of soil and groundwater.
Robert Kunzel, President & CEO
Matthew Phillips, Vice President, Sales

1783 **HDR**
8404 Indian Hills Drive 402-399-1000
Omaha, NE 68114-4098 800-366-4411
Fax: 402-548-5015
www.hdrinc.com
Environmental engineering and consulting firm offering services such as site design, asset management, commissioning plans, funding, environmental remediation, impact analysis, compliance, natural resources management, permitting andmore.
George A Little, PE, Chairman & CEO

1784 **HYGIENETICS Environmental Services**
432 Columbia Street 617-621-0363
Suite 16A Fax: 617-621-1609
Cambridge, MA 02141
Hygienetics provides comprehensive analysis, design, and program management services to a diverse group of private sector customers. Primary areas of expertise include environmental site assessments, remedial and compliance services,industrial hygiene and asbestos/lead management.
Greg Youngblood, VP, National Sales

1785 **Harold I Zeliger PhD**
25 River Place Drive 207-747-4040
Suite 25-14 hiz@zeliger.com
South Portand, ME 04106 www.zeliger.com
Consultant offering expertise in occupational and environmental exposure to toxic and flammable chemicals, hazard communication, chemical formulating and processing and forensic investigations.
Harold I Zeliger, Ph.D, Principal

1786 **Hart Crowser**
3131 Elliott Avenue 206-324-9530
Suite 600 Fax: 206-328-5581
Seattle, WA 98121 www.hartcrowser.com
Hart Crowser provides a full range of services from initial site studies through regulatory permitting design and construction. Areas covered include environmental site cleanup, biological surveys, regulatory compliance, naturalresources, geotechnical, environmental engineering and oil and gas.
David Winter, President & CEO

1787 **Hasbrouck Geophysics**
12 Woodside Drive 928-778-6320
Prescott, AZ 86305 Fax: 928-778-6320
jim@hasgeo.com
www.hasgeo.com
Offers consulting in the areas of groundwater, engineering, environment and mining. Services offered include geophysical consulting, field supervision, data processing; surface, airborne, and borehole geophysical methods; radiometricsand more.
Jim Hasbrouck, Principal

1788 **HazMat Environmental Group**
60 Commerce Drive 716-827-7200
Buffalo, NY 14218-1040 Fax: 716-827-7217
jwhite@hazmatinc.com
www.hazmatinc.com
Offers transportation services for hazardous materials and hazardous waste.
John Stewart, President
Eric Hoxsie, Chief Financial Officer

1789 **Heritage Environmental Services**
7901 West Morris Street 317-243-0811
Indianapolis, IN 46231 877-436-8778
Fax: 317-486-5085
webmaster@heritage-enviro.com
www.heritage-enviro.com
Provides environmental services such as emergency response, data management, industrial cleaning, site remediation, regula-

tory compliance training, hazardous waste management, waste disposal and more.
Ken Price, Chairman & CEO
Angie Martin, Vice President

1790 Hermann and Associates
4603 North Galena Road 309-687-5566
Peoria Heights, IL 61616 Fax: 309-687-0571
info@hermannassoc.com
www.hermannassoc.com
Consulting firm offering services in transportation and municipal engineering. Services include traffic studies, drainage studies and design, asbestos inspection and air quality sampling, roadway reconstruction and more.
Alicia Hermann, PE, Principal & Project Manager
Jeff Hermann, PE, Senior Project Engineer

1791 Huff and Huff
915 Harger Road 630-684-9100
Suite 330 Fax: 630-684-9120
Oak Brook, IL 60523-1486 info@huffnhuff.com
www.huffnhuff.com
Consulting firm providing environmental, civil, and biological engineering services in the areas of natural resource assessments, wetlands, remediation, wastewater, stream surveys, site assessments, air quality, underground storagetanks, hazardous waste management and more.
Linda Huff, PE, Senior Vice President
James Huff, PE, Senior Vice President

1792 Hydrogeologic
11107 Sunset Hills Road 703-478-5186
Suite 400 Fax: 703-471-4180
Reston, VA 20190 www.hgl.com
Offers environmental consulting for environmental, infrastructure and natural resource challenges. Services offered include remediation, Military Munitions response, mining reclamation, water resource management and more.
Peter S Huyakorn, President
Linda Soller, Director, Human Resources

1793 Integrated Chemistries
PO Box 10558 651-426-3224
White Bear Lake, MN 55110 Fax: 651-426-3114
info@integratedchemistries.com
integratedchemistries.com
Develops cleaning and extraction systems for the decontamination of buildings. The equipment targets hazardous and non-hazardous waste.
Jim Nash, President

1794 Integrated Environmental Management
118 North Peters Road 865-588-9180
Suite 178 nsd@plexsci.com
Knoxville, TN 37923 www.iem-inc.com
Provides strategic consulting and services in the areas of radiation, radioactivity and the environment.
Ronald Duff, Vice President

1795 International Certification Accreditation Board
6263 North McCormick Road 847-724-6631
Suite 318 www.icab-usa.org
Chicago, IL 60659
Accreditation organization providing credentialing programs to environmental, safety, medical, pharaceutical, information technology, educational, industrial and training organizations.
Adrian Estes, Ph.D, Health & Safety

1796 International Cotton Advisory Committee
1629 K Street North West 202-463-6660
Suite 702 Fax: 202-463-6950
Washington, DC 20006 secretariat@icac.org
www.icac.org
An organization with the mission of encouraging a healthy cotton economy by providing information about world cotton production, consumption, trade and stocks.
Rebecca Pandolph, Statistician

1797 Interpoll Laboratories
4500 Ball Road NE 763-786-6020
Circle Pines, MN 55014 Fax: 763-786-7854
interpoll@interpoll-labs.com
www.interpoll-labs.com
Environmental laboratory offering analyses of air, soil, water, fuel, hazardous and nonhazardous wastes and pharmaceuticals.
Dan Despen, President
Gregg Holman, VP & Laboratory Manager

1798 JJ Keller and Associates
3003 Breezewood Lane 877-564-2333
P.O. Box 368 Fax: 800-727-7516
Neenah, WI 54957 sales@jjkeller.com
www.jjkeller.com
Offers services in regulatory compliance, best practices and training for environmental, safety, and transportation issues.
Robert L. Keller, Chairman
James J. Keller, Vice Chairman & Treasurer

1799 James M Anderson and Associates
104 Oak Street 912-764-2002
PO Box 894 800-829-4250
Statesboro, GA 30459 Fax: 912-489-6635
mattanderson@frontier.com
www.georgiacarolinasurveyors.com
Land surveying company offering services such as construction planning, GPS surveying, mapping, wetland surveys, 3D machine control and more.
James Anderson, Principle & Owner

1800 James W Sewall Company
136 Center Street 207-827-4456
PO Box 433 800-648-4202
Old Town, ME 04468-0433 Fax: 207-827-3641
scott.graham@sewall.com
www.sewall.com
Sewall provides services in forestry appraisal and inventory, aerial imagery, GIS consulting and engineering, natural resources mapping and more.
David Edson, LPF, President & CEO
Scott Graham, PE, Vice President

1801 John Zink Hamworthy Combustion
11920 East Apache 918-234-1800
Tulsa, OK 74116 800-421-9242
Fax: 918-234-2700
info@johnzink.com
www.johnzink.com
Offers technologically advanced equipment and systems for the clean and efficient combustion of fossil fuels, chemical processing, automobile manufacturing, food processing, waste management and more. Some equipments include process,boiler and duct burners; flare systems; thermal oxidation; vapor control technolgy and more.
Scott Fox, Vice President
Jason Cardoza, VP, Operations

1802 Kimre Clean Air Technology
744 South West 1st Street
Homestead, FL 33030
305-233-4249
Fax: 305-233-8687
sales@kimre.com
www.kimre.com

Produces technology for cleaning air through pollution control features. Products include mist eliminators, scrubbers, liquid coalescers, drift eliminators and aerosol separation systems.
Mary R Keenan, President
George C Pedersen, CEO

1803 LA Weaver Company
308 East Jones Street
Raleigh, NC 27601-1028
919-832-6242
aweaver1@bellsouth.net

Occupational and environmental safety consulting services.
Al Weaver, President

1804 LSI Industries
10000 Alliance Road
Cincinnati, OH 45242
513-793-3200
Fax: 513-984-1335
lsi.solutions@lsi-industries.com
www.lsi-industries.com

Produces LED technology for energy-efficient lighting, as well as custom graphic products. Some of their products include printed graphics, illuminated menu boards and decorations, structural graphics, LED products, digital signagesystems and more.
Bob Ready, Chairman & CEO
Scott Ready, President

1805 Landau Associates
130 2nd Avenue South
Edmonds, WA 98020
425-778-0907
Fax: 425-778-6409
information@landauinc.com
www.landauinc.com

Provides environmental engineering and geotechnical consulting services such as site assessments, hazardous materials assessment, water quality analysis, habitat restoration, geologic hazards assessment, permitting, air qualityanalyses and more.
Jay Bower, PE, President & CEO
Brian Butler, Principal Geologist

1806 Les A Cartier and Associates
PO Box 338
Laconia, NH 03247
603-366-7356
Fax: 603-483-8986

Offers environmental consulting for regulatory compliance, permitting, hazardous materials education and training, and site assessments.
Diane Cartier, Principal

1807 Louis Berger Group
412 Mount Kemble Avenue
PO Box 1946
Morristown, NJ 07962-1946
973-407-1000
Fax: 973-267-6468
communication@louisberger.com
www.louisberger.com

Offers professional services in environmental engineering and infrastructure development. Services include program management, planning, environmental sciences, cultural resources, information services, economics, policy and managementanalysis, and construction management.
Ernest A Portfors, Ph.D, Chairman
Jim Stamatis, PE, CEO

1808 Louis DeFilippi
208 Edgewood Lane
Palatine, IL 60067
847-925-8524
louisdef@expertbiochemist.com
www.expertbiochemist.com

Independent consulting firm offering consulting services in biochemistry, biocatalysis, bioprocessing, and biotransformations. Services cover the topics of regulatory compliance and hazardous waste treatment.
Louis DeFilippi, Ph.D, President

1809 Marc Boogay Consulting Engineer
1584 Whispering Palm Drive
Oceanside, CA 92056
760-407-4000
Fax: 760-407-4004
claudia@boogay.com
www.boogay.com

Consulting firm offering services such as investigations, sampling surveys, remediation designs, abatement monitoring, risk assessment and expert witness testimony.
Marc Boogay, PE, Principal
Claudia Padilla, Engineering Technician

1810 McVehil-Monnett Associates
9250 East Costilla Avenue
Suite 630
Greenwood Village, CO 80112
303-790-1332
Fax: 303-790-7820
gmcvehil@mcvehil-monnett.com
www.mmaaqs.com

Consulting firm providing services in air quality monitoring, permitting, litigation support, environmental management systems, compliance and more. Industries served include the mining, oil and gas, electricity and manufacturingindustries.
Bill Monnett, President
George McVehil, Principal

1811 Meteorological Evaluation Services Company
165 Broadway
Amityville, NY 11701
631-691-3395
Fax: 631-691-3550
www.mesamity.com

Consultants in Applied Meteorology, Air Quality and the Environment.

1812 Miceli Kulik Williams and Associates
39 Park Avenue
Rutherford, NJ 00707
201-933-7809
Fax: 201-933-8702
info@mkwla.com
www.mkwla.com

Offers complete services covering the various aspects of landscape architecture, site planning, and urban design. Present scope of work includes neighborhood rehabilitation, housing and community development, park, recreational andopen space planning, landscape architecture, impact assessment, educational, municipal, commercial and industrial commissions. Project involvement extends throughout the Eastern States.

1813 Michael Baker Corporation
Airside Business Park
100 Airside Drive
Moon Township, PA 15108
412-269-6300
800-553-1153
CorpCom@mbakercorp.com
www.mbakercorp.com

Michael Baker Corporation provides engineering and operations and maintenance services for its clients' most complex challenges worldwide. The firm's primary practice areas are aviation, environmental, facilities, geospatialinformation technologies, linear utilities, transportation, water/wastewater, and oil & gas. With approximately 4,500 employees in over 400 offices across the U.S. and internationally, Baker is focused on providing services that span the completelife cycle of infrastucture.
David Higie, VP Corporate Communications

1814 Michael Brandman Associates
250 Commerce
Suite 250
Irvine, CA 92602
714-508-4100
888-826-5814
Fax: 714-508-4110
www.brandman.com

Michael Brandman Associates is a comprehensive environmental planning services firm specializing in environmental documentation, planning, and natural resources management.
Michele Carchman, Vice President
Robert Francisco, President

1815 Micro-Bac
3200 North Interstate Highway 35 512-310-9000
Round Rock, TX 78681-2410 877-559-1800
Fax: 512-310-8800
mail@micro-bac.com
www.micro-bac.com
Delvelops and manufactures biological products for remediation of contaminated substances; reduction of waste and odor in food processing, agriculture, and sewage; and control of paraffin in oil production.

1816 Midstream Farm
20004 Sterling Creek Lane 804-749-8720
Rockville, VA 23146 804-317-0777
usaclem@erols.com
www.usaclem.com
Clement Mesavage Jr, Proprietor

1817 Mostardi Platt Environmental
888 Industrial Drive 630-993-2100
Elmhurst, IL 60126-1121 Fax: 630-993-9017
www.mostardiplattenv.com
Mostardi Platt Environmental-your full service environmental management partner. Offers innovative solutions and strategies to assist our clients comply with environmental, health and safety regulations and develop environmentalprograms that save long-term costs. We understand our clients need the best possible compliance options. We evaluate a wide variety of technical and economic concerns and work with our clients to establish the best path towards compliance.
Joseph J Macak III, President
Robert A Gere, Engineering Consultant

1818 NTH Consultants
41780 6 Mile Rd. 248-553-6300
Northville, MI 48168 800-736-6842
Fax: 248-324-5179
paspalding@nthconsultants.com
www.nthconsultants.com
NTH Consultants has provided consulting engineering services to clients throughout the United States since 1968. Headquartered in Farmington Hills, MI, NTH has maintained an office in downtown Detroit since 1980, a regional,full-service office in Exton, PA and offices in Lansing and Grand Rapids, MI since 1992.
Keith M. Swaffar, Chairman
Kevin B. Hoppe, President and CEO

1819 National Environment Management Group
PO Box 5131 708-771-7350
River Forest, IL 60305 Fax: 312-733-2478
www.nema.go.ke
Environmental consulting.
Maluki Mwendwa, Chairman
Geoffrey Wahungu, Director General

1820 National Environmental
1019 W Manchester Boulevard 310-645-4516
Suite 102 800-870-1719
Inglewood, CA 90301 Fax: 310-645-0148
www.neeri.res.in
Training school. Training in use of lead, asbestos and hzardous materials.
James McFarland, President
David P Fuller, VP

1821 National Institute for Urban Wildlife
10921 Trotting Ridge Way 301-596-3311
Columbia, MD 21044 urbanwildlifegroup.org
Promotes the preservation of wildlife in urban settings, providing support to individuals and organizations invloved in maintaining a place for wildlife in expanding American cities and suburbs. The Institute conducts researchexploring the relationship between humans and wildlife in these habitats, publicizes urban wildlife management methods, and raises public awareness of the value of wildlife in city settings. The Institute also provides consulting services.
Nils Peterson, President Elect
Liza Watson Lehrer, Secretary/Treasurer

1822 National Sanitation Foundation
789 North Dixboro Road 734-769-8010
PO Box 130140 800-NSF-MARK
Ann Arbor, MI 48105 Fax: 734-769-0109
info@nsf.org
www.nsf.org
NSF International, The Public Health and Safety Company, is an independent, not for profit organization providing a wide range of services around the world. For more than 55 years, NSF has been committes to public health, safety andprotection of the environment.
Lori Bestervelt, Sr. Vice President
Kevan P. Lawlor, President/CEO

1823 National Society of Environmental Consultants
303 West Cypress Street 856-283-7816
PO Box 460 800-486-3676
Collingswood, NJ 00810 Fax: 856-210-1619
NAEP@bowermanagementservices.com
www.naep.org
The mission is to encourage an awareness of environmental risk and the regulations regarding their impact on real property value, to advocate reponsible use and development of real estate resources in harmony with the environment, toelevate the competency of the membership through information and education and to promote the development of ethics and standards of professional practice for the speciality of environmental consultants
Brock Hoeqh, President
David Dickson, Vice President

1824 Natural Resources Consulting Engineers
131 Lincoln Avenue 970-224-1851
Suite 300 Fax: 970-224-1885
Fort Collins, CO 80524 office@nrce.com
www.nrce.com
Water supply investigations. Native American water rights expert witness testimony.

1825 Navigant
150 North Riverside Plaza 312-583-5700
Suite 2100 Fax: 312-583-5701
Chicago, IL 60606 www.navigant.com/energy
Consulting firm offering services to the energy industry such as planning, data analysis, operations and asset management and more.
Julie M. Howard, Chairman & CEO
Lucinda Baier, Exe. VP & CFO

1826 Network Environmental Systems
1141 Sibley Street
Folsom, CA 95630 800-637-2384
Fax: 916-353-2375
office@nesglobal.net
www.nesglobal.net
Network Environmental Systems was incorporated in 1988 to privide high quality professional industrial hygiene and environmental management services through customer service excellence.
Jerry Bucklin, President/CEO
Donald Rothenbaum, Senior Vice President

1827 Ninyo and Moore
5710 Ruffin Road 858-576-1000
San Diego, CA 92123 Fax: 858-576-9600
nminquiries@ninyoandmoore.com
www.ninyoandmoore.com

As a leading geotechnical and environmental scieces engineering and consulting firm, Ninyo & Moore provides specialized services to clients in both public and private sectors.
Avram Ninyo, Principal Engineer

1828 Nordlund and Associates
813 East Ludington Avenue 231-843-3485
Ludington, MI 49431 Fax: 231-843-7676
Nordlund@T-one.net
www.nordlundandassociates.com

Water systems, wastewater treatment, sanitary landfills and hydrogeological studies.
Holly A. Mulherin, P.E., President
James T. Nordlund, Jr., P.E., Vice President

1829 Noresco United Technologies
1 Research Drive 508-614-1000
Suite 400C Fax: 508-836-9988
Westborough, MA 01581 info@archenergy.com
www.noresco.com

Provides energy efficiency and sustainable design consulting services for building owners, architects and engineers. Services offered include energy auditing, commissioning and retro-commissioning, energy & daylighting analysis, LEED©certification consulting and sustainability planning.
Neil Petchers, President & CEO
David G Mannherz, Chief Financial Officer

1830 Normandeau Associates
25 Nashua Road 603-472-5191
Bedford, NH 03110-5500 Fax: 603-472-7052
marketing@normandeau.com
www.normandeau.com

Normandeau Associates is an employee owned natural resources management consulting and testing services firm that provides: permit assistance, water quality studies, aquatic and terrestrial ecology, environmental impact assessments,property transfer site assessments, wetlands services, contamination studies and biological laboratory services.
Pamela Hall, President
Peter Kinner, Senior VP

1831 Norton Associates
136 Estelle Drive 508-528-3357
Naples, FL 34112 774-244-1248
Fax: 508-758-4759
norton@designofmachinery.com
www.designofmachinery.com

Professor Norton and his associates have been providing engineering consulting services since 1970. Areas of expertise include: cam design and analysis, linkage design and analysis, street analysis, vibrations in machinery, dynamicsignal analysis, machinery monitoring, and machine dynamic analysis. We also can provide short courses and seminars on site in cam design, dynamic signal analysis and machinery vibrations.
Robert L Norton, President

1832 NuChemCo
5765-F Burke Centre Parkway 703-548-3200
#149 800-682-4362
Burke, VA 22015 Fax: 703-978-0642
info@nuchemco.com
www.nuchemco.com

Neil B Jurinski
Joseph B Jurinski

1833 OCCU-TECH
4151 N. Mulberry Drive 816-231-5580
Suite 275 800-950-1953
Kansas City, MO 64116 Fax: 816-231-5641
service@occutec.com
www.occutec.com

OCCU-TECH is a leading safety, health and environmental services company. From OSHA to EPA issues, safety assessments to program development, asbestos inspections to environmental management, our expertise has been relied on for over16 years.

1834 Oak Creek
60 Oak Creek 207-929-0856
Buxton, ME 00409-6616 Fax: 207-929-6374
jssmith@oak-creek.net
James S Smith Jr, PhD, President/Toxicologist
Brad House, Senior Scientist

1835 OccuSafe
14144 Regency Place 214-662-6005
Dallas, TX 75254 occusafe@occusafeinc.com
occusafeinc.com

OCUSAFE is an industrial hygiene consulting firm specializing in the evaluation of employee exposures to chemicals and noise, and indoor air quality.
Gary Ticker, President

1836 Occupational Health and Safety Management
117 La Farge 303-665-8528
Louisville, CO 80027 Fax: 303-673-0785
Industrial hygiene/safety consulting.
Mary Ann Heaney

1837 Occupational Safety and Health Consultants
12000 6th Street East 727-345-1552
Saint Petersburg, FL 33706 Fax: 727-363-8151
webmaster@oshc.com
www.oshc.com

Air pollution control/industrial hygiene.

1838 Occupational and Environmental Health Consultiing Services
6877 Bonillo Dr 630-325-2083
Las Vegas, NV 89103 Fax: 630-325-2098
bobb@safety-epa.com
www.safety-epa.com

A full service regulatory, safety, industrial hygiene, and environmental engineering consulting firm. Specialize in assisting all sizes of companies and corporations. Clients include very small businesses up to Fortune 100corporations.
Bob Brandys PhD,MPH,PE,CIH, President

1839 Ocean City Research
1055 W. Smith Road 330-723-5082
Medina, OH 44256 Fax: 330-722-7654
www.corrpro.com

Ocean City Research Corporation, incorporated in 1963, is a wholly owned subsidiary of Corrpro Companies, Collectively, the Corrpro affiliated companies represent the largest, independent consulting corrosion engineering organizationin the world.
J Peter Ault, PE

1840 Omega Waste Management
957 Colusa Street 530-824-1890
PO Box 495 www.omegawaste.com
Corning, CA 96021

A consulting firm, whose unique and innovative approach to waste removal and recycling has made it one of the largest volume purchasers of waste services in the nation.
Robert O'Connor, President
Karen O'Connor, Chief Financial Officer

1841 **Owen Engineering and Management Consultants**
5353 West Dartmouth Avenue 530-677-5286
Suite 402 Fax: 303-969-9394
Denver, CO 80227
Water/Wastewater design systems.
Webster J Owen, President

1842 **PACE Analytical Services**
1800 Elm Street SE 612-607-6400
Minneapolis, MN 55414 Fax: 612-607-6444
info@pacelabs.com
www.pacelabs.com
Provider of air, water, soil and environmental testing services.
Michael R. Prasch, EVP/CFO
Jack Dullaghan, SVP/COO

1843 **PAR Environmental**
1906 21st Street 916-739-8356
Sacramento, CA 95811 Fax: 916-739-0626
mlmaniery@aol.com
www.paraenvironmental.com
PAR Environmantal Services mission is to provide technical reports on time, within budget, and with meticulous attention to detail.
Mary L Maniery, CEO

1844 **PBR HAWAII**
1001 Bishop Street, ASB Tower 808-521-5631
Suite 650 Fax: 808-523-1402
Honolulu, HI 96813-3484 sysadmin@pbrhawaii.com
www.pbrhawaii.com
Consulting services in environmental studies, permitting land planning, lanscape architecture and graphic design.
Thomas S Witten, ASLA, Chairman
Frank Brandt, FASLA, Chairman Emeritus

1845 **PBS Environmental Building Consultants**
4412 SW Corbett Ave 503-248-1939
Portland, OR 97239 888-371-7891
Fax: 866-727-0140
www.pbsenv.com
PBS specializes in program development, identification, assessment, testing and corrective action consultation in the areas of: Environmental Engineering, Geotechnical Engineering, Hazardous Materials Management, Industrial HygieneServices, Natural Resources Studies, Training and Laboratory.
Guy Neal, President
Ron Petti, Principal/CEO

1846 **PEER Consultants**
888 17th Street N. W. 202-478-2060
Suite 850 Fax: 202-478-2050
Washington, DC 20006 peercpc@peercpc.com
www.peercpc.com
For nearly a quarter of a century, PEER Consultants has provided civil, sanitary, and environmental engineering consulting services for public and private sector clients nationwide.
Lilia Abron, President
C. Davis Venn, Vice President/Chief Enginee

1847 **PELA GeoEnvironmental**
PO Box 2310 205-752-5543
Tuscaloosa, AL 35403 Fax: 205-752-4043
info@pela.com
www.pela.com
For over three decades, PELA's integration of qualified personnel, up-to-date technology, and sound management has established PELA as an international leader in the environmental consulting field. PELA's expertise in hydrogeology,geotechnical analysis, design and construction management, remediation, computer graphics and models, and permitting can get your project on two feet quicker than you might think.
James Jim La Moreaux, Chairman Of Board
James M Lee, President

1848 **Pacific Soils Engineering**
13331 Garden Grove Blvd 714-703-1347
Suite N Fax: 714-220-9589
Garden Grove, CA 92843 info@pacificsoils.com
pacificsoils.com
Services include: Geotechnical Services, Laboratory Testing, Field Observation and Testing, Consultation and Review of Geotechnical Reports.
Daniel Martinez, President

1849 **Parish and Weiner Inc**
297 Knollwood Road 914-997-7200
Suite 315 Fax: 914-997-7201
White Plains, NY 10607 www.parishweiner.com
Consulting firm which prepares environmental impact studies, traffic studies, zoning and site plan studies for private developers, non-profit organizations, governmental entities. Also provide expert consultation to lawyers forlitigation and hearings.
Nat Parish, President

1850 **Pavia-Byrne Engineering Corporation**
7443 Obyx St. 504-288-8406
New Orleans, LA 70184 Fax: 504-283-4090
Provides services for environmental control and water treatment including definition, process development, and start up services.
Edgar H Pavia, President

1851 **Perry-Carrington Engineering Corporation**
214 West Second Street 715-384-2133
Suite 201 Fax: 715-384-9797
Marshfield, WI 54449 2perryear@temet.com
www.msa-ps.com
Water pollution control systems.
Gill Hnatz, President

1852 **Petra Environmental**
10550 North 6th Avenue 715-536-7870
Merrill, WI 54452 800-458-3772
Fax: 715-536-7890
info@petraenvironmental.net
www.petraenvironmental.net
PETRA Environmental Consultants, is an environmental engineering firm specializing in environmental compliance, hydrogeological investigations, and environmental assessments.
David Treis, Vice President/ General Mana
Mark Glendenning, CEO

1853 **Phase One**
23282 Mill Creek Drive 714-669-8055
Suite 160 800-524-8877
Laguna Hills, CA 92653 Fax: 714-669-8025
info@phasei.com
www.phasei.com
A focused environmental consulting practice that specializes in real property assessments for any type of property transfer, leasing development, special uses, and/or financing purposes. Founded in response to the business community'sneed for affordable, standardized and consistently high quality assessment reports that provide recommendations for sound real estate decisions.
Eric D Kieselbach, President/CEO

1854 **Planning Resources**
402 W Liberty Drive 630-668-3788
Wheaton, IL 60187 Fax: 630-668-4125
webmaster@planres.com
www.planres.com

Land use and environmental planning.
Keven Graham, COO/ Director

1855 **Post, Buckley, Schuh and Jernigan**
2001 Northwest 107th Avenue 305-592-7275
Miami, FL 33172 Fax: 305-599-3809
PBS&J was founded in 1960 by four respected engineers who joined forces to help develop Florida's first planned community. Their tenacity in meeting production schedules, commitment to client service, and ability to provide innovativesolutions to difficult challenges quickly earned our firm a reputation for excellence and laid the foundation for future grouth.
Todd J Kenner, President

1856 **Presnell Associates**
1046 East Chestnut Street 502-719-7900
Louisville, KY 40204 800-928-2222
www.qk4.com
The professional practice of Prenell encompasses a variety of services directly related to preserving the environment, including potable water system planning and design, municipal and industrial wastewater treatment, solid wastemanagement, landfill siting, asbestos management, contamination screening assessments, indoos air quality, and lead paint abatement.
David Smith, President/CEO

1857 **Priester and Associates**
1345 Garner Lane 803-798-4377
Suite 105 877-798-4377
Columbia, SC 29210 Fax: 803-798-4378
Provides personalized environmental services ranging from short-term consulting to extensive remediation and management activities.
LE Priester, President

1858 **Process Applications**
2627 Redwing Road 215-493-9361
Suite 340 Fax: 970-223-5786
Fort Collins, CO 80526 info@palpaperchem.com
www.palpaperchem.com
Produces specialty performance chemicals for Paper Industry machines, for high quality performance with lower energy consumption.
Bob Hegg, President

1859 **Professional Analytical and Consulting Services (PACS)**
409 Meade Drive 724-457-6576
Coraopolis, PA 15108 800-367-2587
Fax: 724-457-1214
web@pacslabs.com
www.pacslabs.com
Training courses and conferences. Provides short courses in spectrocopy, chomatography, quality, safety, environmental, and management. Provides professional manuals and software products. Provides laboratory testing and consultingservices. Company also goes by the following names: Activated Carbon Services, PACS Testing and Consulting, PACS Courses and Conferences. PACS provides: Testing, Training, R & D Conferences, and software for activated carbon users.
Henry G Nowicki PhD/MBA, President
Barbara Sherman, Manager of Operations

1860 **Psomas and Associates**
1500 Lowa Avenue 951-787-8421
Suite 210 info@psomas.com
Riverside, CA 92507 www.psomas.com
Psomas is a leading consulting engineering firm offering services in land development, water and natural resources, transportaion, public works, survey and information systems to public and private sector clients.
Ryan McLean, CEO/President
Loren Sokolow, CFO

1861 **QORE**
4201 Pleasant Hill Road Northwest 770-232-0235
Suite A 877-767-3462
Duluth, GA 30096 Fax: 770-232-0238
www.qore.net
Consultants in property science, in fields of geology, geotechnical and environmental engineering.
Richard D Heckel, PE, President
Ed Heustess, Chief Financial Officer

1862 **RDG Geoscience and Engineering**
10360 Sapp Brothers Drive 402-894-2678
Omaha, NE 68138 888-260-0893
Fax: 402-894-9043
www.rdgge.com
Is an earth science and engineering consulting firm that has completed over 1200 projects throughout the mid-west and mountain west of US.
Jon Gross, President
Robert Kalinski, Vice President

1863 **RGA Environmental**
1466 66th Street 510-547-7771
Emeryville, CA 94608 800-776-5696
Fax: 510-547-1983
rga@rgaenv.com
www.rgaenv.com
Founded in 1985, RGA Environmental is a specialty consultant in the environmental sciences. Our mission is to provide high-quality environmental engineering, health & safety consulting services to meet the special needs of our clients.
Steven C Rosas, COO, Director of Business

1864 **RMT**
1212 Deming Way 608-831-4444
Suite 200 800-283-3443
Madison, WI 53717 Fax: 608-831-3334
info@rmtinc.com
www.rmtinc.com
Serves industrial compaines throughout the world who value environmental and engineering solutions that improve productivity and profitability. RMT's diversified staff of over 550 engineers, scientists and technicians takesresponsibility for managing environmental issues so clients can concentrate on their core business.
Paul M. Daily, CEO
John Kennedy, President

1865 **RMT Inc.**
1212 Deming Way 608-831-4444
Suite 200 800-283-3443
Madison, WI 53717 Fax: 608-831-3334
info@rmtinc.com
www.rmtinc.com
RMT delivers environmental engineering health and safety and construction solutions that help industrial companies solve complex problems while improving their bottom line.
Paul M. Daily, CEO
John Kennedy, President

1866 **Ramboll ENVIRON**
4350 North Fairfax Drive 703-516-2300
Suite 300 Fax: 703-516-2345
Arlington, VA 22203 www.ramboll.com

Health and environmental sciences consultants providing services in air quality management, site solutions, urban planning, energy, environmental compliance, water treatment and more.
Mark J Nielsen, Principal
Jose Fernandez, VP, Market Director

1867 Raterman Group
9000 Crow Canyon Road 866-545-0111
Suite 364 Fax: 925-555-1233
Danville, CA 94506 susan@ratermangroup.com
www.ratermangroup.com

Industrial hygiene and environmental assessments.
Susan M Raterman, President

1868 Reclamation Services Unlimited
701 Temple Street 270-754-3976
Central City, KY 42330 Fax: 270-754-4374
scardwel@muhlon.com
www.total-testing.com

Environmental consulting services.
Sue Poole Cardwell, President

1869 Redniss and Mead
22 1st Street 203-327-0500
Stamford, CT 00690-5101 800-404-2060
Fax: 203-357-1118
a.mead@rednissmead.com
www.rednissmead.com

Redniss & Mead, Inc. provides land surveying, civil engineering and land planning services.
Aubrey E Mead, Jr., PE, VP
Raymond L Redniss, PLS, Senior Vice President

1870 Refuse Management Systems
99 Tulip Avenue 516-354-1212
#303 800-346-5926
Floral Park, NY 11001 Fax: 516-354-2434
Environmental consultants.
Harvey Podolsky, President

1871 Regional Services Corporation
3200 Sycamore Court 403-794-4000
P.O. Box 638 Fax: 403-794-4051
Brooks, AB T1R 1 info@nrsc.ca
www.nrsc.ca

Solid waste disposal.
Mark Richards, President

1872 Regulatory Management
6190 Lehman Drive 719-531-6883
Suite 106 Fax: 719-599-4410
Colorado Springs, CO 80918 maxlab@usa.net
Environmental consulting group.
James T Egan, President

1873 Remtech Engineers
200 Cobb Parkway North 770-427-7766
Suite 208 800-377-3648
Marietta, GA 30062 Fax: 314-678-6610
webmaster@remtech-eng.com
www.remtech-eng.com

Provices services in spill response, environmental remediation, hazardous waste management, industrial cleaning, environmental engineering and disaster response.
Mark D Ryckman, PE, Founder & CEO
Larry K Seabolt, Vice President

1874 Resource Applications
9291 Old Keene Mill Road 703-644-0401
Burke, VA 22015 Fax: 703-644-0404

Hazardous waste management, pollution prevention/site remediation.
Damons G Barber, President & CEO

1875 Resource Concepts
340 North Minnesota Street 775-883-1600
Carson City, NV 89703 Fax: 775-883-1656
john@rci-nv.com
www.rci-nv.com

RCI has years of experience and demonstrated accomplisjment working with environmentally sensitive projects. Combining technical abilities and excellent working relationships with regulatory agencies results in highly effective projectplanning and permitting services.
Bruce R Scott, Principal
John McLain, Principal

1876 Resource Decisions
934 Diamond Street 415-282-5330
San Francisco, CA 94114 mfeldman@resourcedecisions.net
www.resourcedecisions.net

Assisting clients to evaluate trade-offs which foster the wise allocation of resources is primary mission of Resource Decisions. To accomplish this mission we apply a wide range of economic and decision-making tools.
Marvin Feldman, PhD, Principal

1877 Resource Management
625 Chapin Road 803-345-0200
Chapin, SC 29036 Fax: 803-345-6520
resourc9@winusa.com

Hazardous waste management.
Don Dicus, President

1878 Resource Technology Corporation (RTC)
248 East Calder Way 307-742-5452
Suite 305 877-489-0199
State College, PA 16801 Fax: 814-237-1769
rtc@sial.com
www.resourcetec.com

They offer Laboratory Proficiency Testing for drinking water, waste water and USEPA RCCRA Program. Certified analytical standards and Certified Reference Materials.
Jeffrey R. Kern, Senior Appraiser

1879 Respec Engineering
3824 Jet Drive 605-394-6400
Rapid City, SD 57703-4757 877-737-7321
www.respec.com

Since our founding in 1969, RESPEC has remained committed to its original purpose of providing clients with high-quality technical and advisory services.

1880 Reston Consulting Group (RCG)
462 Herndon Parkway 703-834-1155
Suite 203 Fax: 703-834-3086
Herndon, VA 20170 info@rcg.com
www.rcg.com

Rosemarie Franz, Director

1881 Rich Tech
2600 S Rainbow Blvd 815-229-1122
Suite 103 Fax: 815-229-1525
Las Vegas, NE 89146 sales@richtechsystem.com
www.richtechsystem.com

Water pollution control.
Gail Rivitts, President
Rich Rivitts, Vice President

1882 **Rizzo Associates**
16 Serra Street
Corte Madera, CA 94925
415-290-1670
Fax: 866-220-6889
www.rizzoassociates.com
A leading engineering, transportation, and environmental engineering firm. We work with you throughout the development process to reslove the challenges that arise in planning, permitting, design, and construction phases of complexprojects.
James Rizzo, Founder

1883 **Robert B Balter Company**
18 Music Fair Road
Owings Mills, MD 21117
410-363-1555
Fax: 410-363-8073
mknowles@balterco.com
www.balterco.com
Environmental consultation.
Michael F. Knowles, Marketing Director

1884 **Rockwood Environmental Services Corporation**
50 Kearney Road
Needham, MA 00249-2508
781-449-8740
Fax: 781-449-8741
bwhite@rockwood-enviro.com
www.rockwood-enviro.com
Rockwood specializes in solving the problems of hazardous waste management and disposal for New England generators. By shipping wastes directly to ultimate disposal sites on a regular basis, Rockwood reduces current disposal costs andreduces long-term liability exposure.
William A White III, President

1885 **Rodriguez, Villacorta and Weiss**
8765 Springs Cypress
Suite L#177
Spring, TX 77379
281-379-4005
mbrooks@rvw.net
rvw.net/
Our mission is to provide cost-effective and thorough work product for claims services and loss control. Maximum integration of all in-house and affiliated expertise will guarantee prompt service, nurturing strong client relationshipsbased on dependability, trust and competence.
Richard Rodriguez, Principal Associate

1886 **Roux Associates**
209 Shafter Street
Islandia, NY 11749
631-232-2600
800-322-Roux
Fax: 631-232-9898
sales@rouxinc.com
www.rouxinc.com
Environmental Consulting and Management.
Steve Sadiker, Vice President
Doug Swanson, CEO/President

1887 **SCS Engineers**
3900 Kilroy Airport Way
Suite 100
Long Beach, CA 90806-6816
562-426-9544
800-767-4727
Fax: 562-427-0805
service@scsengineers.com
www.scsengineers.com
Delivers economically and environmentally sound solutions for solid waste management and site remediation projects throughout the world. Services provided include engineering, construction, and contract operations services to privateand public sector clients through a network of more than 70 offices and 800 professional staff working in the US and abroad.
Jim Walsh, President & CEO
Mike McLaughlin, Sr VP, Environmental Service

1888 **SGS Accutest Laboratories**
201 Route 17 North
Rutherford, NJ 07070
201-508-3000
Fax: 732-329-3499
infonj@accutest.com
www.accutest.com
Testing laboratory delivering legally defensible data and providing a full range of environmental analytical services to industrial, engineering/consulting and government clients throughout the United States. Testing includes analysisof water, soil, air, waste characterization, energetics and explosives.
Charles Tate, Director of Finance
Charles Hartke, Quality Assurance Director

1889 **SLC Consultants/Constructors**
295 Mill Street
Lockport, NY 14094
716-433-0776
800-932-0157
Fax: 716-433-0802

1890 **SLR Environmental Consultants**
597-599 Industrial Drive
Suite 211
Carmel, IN 46032
317-876-3940
americaswebenquiry@slrconsulting.com
slrconsulting.com/na/
Environmental consulting firm offering solutions for issues relating to oil and gas, environmental engineering, mining, infrastructure and energy.
Graham Love, Non-Executive Chairman
Neil Penhall, CEO

1891 **Safe at Work**
2123 University Park Drive
Suite 130
Okemos, MI 48864
517-349-8066
Fax: 517-349-7870
support@safe-at-work.com
www.safe-at-work.com
Provides noise control, sound exposure, and hearing loss prevention services and software.

1892 **Safina**
953 N Plum Grove Road
Suite A-1
Schaumburg, IL 60173
847-605-8319
Fax: 847-956-8619
safinacenter.org
Environmental due diligence.
Sanjiv Pillai, General Manager

1893 **Schneider Instrument Company**
8115 Camargo Road
74226 Nordheim
Cincinnati, OH 45243
513-561-6803
Fax: 513-527-4375
schneidxcompany@aol.com
www.as-schneider.com
G L Schneider, Vice President

1894 **Schoell and Madson**
12800 Whitewater Drive
Suite 300
Minnetonka, MN 55343
763-476-6010
Fax: 763-476-8532
sambatek@sambatek.com
www.sambatek.com
We are dedicated to creatively serving our clients by meeting or exceeding their needs in a responsive and cost-effective manner while providing an interesting and rewarding experience for our employees.

1895 **SciComm**
7735 Old Georgetown Road
12th Floor
Bethesda, MD 20814
301-652-1900
www.scicomm.com
A professional services firm specializing in communications, engineering, environmental, and information management services. Organized to carry out the interest, expertise, and vision of co-founder Laura Chen and Dan Lewis.
Laura Chen, President

1896 **SevernTrent Laboratories**
4101 Shuffel Drive NW
North Canton, OH 44720
866-785-5227
webmaster@testamericainc.com
www.stl-inc.com

The two compaines merged as Wadsworth/Alert Laboratories in early 1980's and the core business focused on environmental testing, with a specialization in on-site and emergency response projects. Mobile Labs were placed as far north asMichigan, and south to Florida, east to New York, and west to Missouri.
James Hyman, CEO

1897 Shaw Environmental
2103 Research Forest Drive 832-513-1000
The Woodland, TX 77380 general@shawgrp.com
Hazardous waste remediation.
Ron Prann, Division Manager

1898 Shell Engineering and Associates
2403 West Ash Street 573-445-0106
Columbia, MO 65203 Fax: 573-445-0137
info@shellengr.com
www.shellengr.com
Shell Engineering provides services firm specializing in communications, engineering, environmental monitoring and engineering. Shell Engineering has completed hundreds of projects since 1975 throughout the United States, Canada.Centeral America, South America, Asia and Africa.
Harvey D Shell, CEO/Chairman
Charles A Shell, President

1899 Sierra Geological and Environmental Consultants
91 South Main Street 800-769-7437
PO Box 136 Fax: 616-678-5149
Kent City, MI 49330 info@sierraconsultants.net
www.sierraconsultants.net
A full service environmental consulting firm providing assassment, investigation, and cleanup services throughout Michigan and the Great Lakes States.

1900 Slakey and Associates
375 Village Square 925-254-4164
PO Box 944 Fax: 925-254-0679
Orinda, CA 94563
Consulting, civil, mechanical, environmental engineers with 40 years experience in indoor air quality, air pollution control. Design of systems and equipment for collection abatement of fugitive and source missions of dusts, odor andfumes. Industrial clients only.
Philip Slakey, President

1901 Slosky & Company
999 18th Street 303-825-1911
Suite 2400 S Fax: 303-892-3882
Denver, CO 80202-2499 Lslosky@slosky.com
www.slosky.com
Full service environmental consulting firm.
Leonard Slosky, President

1902 Snyder Research Company
330Twin Dolphin Drive 408-414-5950
Suite # 101 Fax: 408-275-6219
Redwood City, CA 94065 info@sdforum.org
www.sdforum.org

1903 Staunton-Chow Engineers
5 Pen Plaza 212-683-8865
23rd Floor Fax: 212-695-6307
New York, NY 10001 www.stauntonchow.com
Known widely as a small premiere multidisciplined engineering/architectural consulting firm providing professional services for new construction, repair, alterations, and maintenance for nearly 50 years.
Kin Chow, President

1904 Strata Environmental Services
110 Perimeter Park 517-676-6900
Suite E Fax: 517-676-8834
Knoxville, TN 37922 strata@acd.net
www.strataenv.com
Founded to provide consulting services in geosciences, engineering, air quality, water quality, regulatory compliance, and environmental due diligence.
Charles W. Ferst, CEO

1905 TECHRAD Environmental Services
8440 East Washington Street 405-528-7016
#207 800-375-7016
Chagrin Falls, OH 44023 Fax: 405-528-3346
www.testingpartners.com
Analytical laboratory, environmental site assessments, underground storage tank management and remediation, industrial hygiene, stormwater and hazardous waste management, asbestos consulting and analysis and regulatory compliance.
Edward M Wall, President/CEO

1906 THP
100 E Eightth Street 533-241-3222
Ste 300 Fax: 513-241-2981
Cincinnati, OH 45202-2129 www.thpltd.com
Engineering traffic and engineering planning consulting firm.
E James Miller, President

1907 Technos
10430 Northwest 31st Terrace 305-718-9594
Miami, FL 33172 Fax: 305-718-9621
info@technos-inc.com
A geologic and geophysical consulting firm specializing in subsurface site characterization for geotechnical, environmental, and groundwater projects.
Lynn Yuhr, President
Ron Kaufmann, VP

1908 Terracon Consultants, Inc.
611 Lunken Park Drive 513-321-5816
Cincinnati, OH 45226 Fax: 513-321-0294
cincinnati@hcnutting.com
www.hcnutting.com
Materials tesing company, geotechnical and environmental engineering firm.
Jack Scott, President

1909 Terranext
1660 South Albion 303-399-6145
Suite 900 Fax: 303-399-6146
Denver, CO 80222 kmartin@terranext.net
www.terranext.net
Provides environmental consulting and engineering services. Focus areas include environmental remediation, science and consulting, environmental engineering, energy reduction and more.
Kim Martin, CPA, President & CEO
Christopher Kinn, P.G., Senior Geophysicist

1910 Terryn Barill
301 N Harrison
Suite 484 800-718-6690
Princeton, NJ 00854 Fax: 609-243-8703
terryn1@mail.com
Audits/assessments, training, implementation and facilitation.

1911 Tetra Tech
3475 East Foothill Boulevard 802-658-3890
Pasadena, CA 91107 Fax: 802-658-4247
ard@ardinc.com
www.tetratech.com

Provides consulting and engineering services with a focus on environment. Some of its services include assessment, data analytics, resource management, energy and developments, lab services, geotechnical engineering, constructionmanagement, water management, government consulting and more.
Dan L. Batrack, President & CEO
Steven M. Burdick, Chief Financial Officer

1912 Theil Consulting
1136 South Fort Thomas Avenue 859-781-2651
Fort Thomas, KY 41075 Fax: 859-781-2356
Experts in industrial process exhausts—especially submicron particles created by heat or other high energy in a process.
Greg Theil, Technical Director
Larry Olson, Sales Manager

1913 Titan Corp. Ship and Aviation Engineering Group
11955 Freedom Drive 703-434-4000
Reston, VA 20190 Fax: 703-434-5075
www.titan.com
TITAN provides a wide range of engineering and environmental services. Experience includes ISO 14001 and ISO 9000 series and its implementation, pollution prevention planning, hazardous materials/waste management, database management.
Gene W Ray, Chairman of the Board
Lawrence J Delaney, VP of Operations

1914 Tradet Laboratories
8 Industrial Park Drive 304-233-9060
Wheeling, WV 26003 Fax: 304-233-9063
info@tra-det.com
www.tra-det.com
Coal, analytical and environmental services.
G William Kald, President

1915 Transviron
1624 York Road 410-321-6961
Lutherville, MD 21093 Fax: 410-494-9321
transviron.com

1916 Trinity Consultants
12770 Merit Drive 972-661-8100
Suite 900 800-229-6655
Dallas, TX 75251 Fax: 972-385-9203
information@trinityconsultants.com
www.trinityconsultants.com
An environmental consulting company that assists industrial facilities with issues related to regulatory compliance and environmental management. Founded in 1974, this nationwide firm has particular expertise in air quality issues.Trinity also sells environmental software and professional education. T3, a Trinity Consultants Company, provides EH&S management information systems (EMIS) implementation and integration services.
Jay Hofmann, President/CEO
Dave Larsen, CFO

1917 Troppe Environmental Consulting
24 N. High Street 330-375-1900
Akron, OH 44308 Fax: 330-375-1904
Provides level I and level II assessments, water and oil testing, and amtm standards.
Fred Troppe, President

1918 Versar
6850 Versar Center 703-750-3000
Springfield, VA 22151 800-283-7727
Fax: 703-642-6807
info@versar.com
www.versar.com
Versar is a public-held, international professional services firm that applies technology, science, and management skills to enhance its customers' performance.
Anthony L Otten, CEO

1919 Water and Air Research
6821 SW Archer Road 352-372-1500
Gainesville, FL 32608 800-242-4927
Fax: 352-378-1500
www.waterandair.com
Mission is to be an international environmental consulting firm that achieves extraordinary results by partnering with clients that to make informed and responsible decisions regarding the environment.
William C Zegel, President
William Kinser, Director/Manager

1920 Waypoint Analytical
2790 Whitten Road 901-213-2400
Memphis, TN 38133 800-264-4522
Fax: 901-213-2440
supporttn@waypointanalytical.com
www.waypointanalytical.com
Agricultural laboratory group specializing in soil tests.
Michael Sterling, Chief Financial Officer

1921 Weavertown Group Optimal Technologies
2 Dorrington Road 724-746-4850
Carnegie, PA 15106 800-746-4850
Fax: 724-746-9024
www.weavertown.com
We are an environmental engineering and consulting firm.
Dawn Fuchs, President

1922 Wenck Associates
1800 Pioneer Creek Center 763-479-4200
PO Box 249 800-472-2232
Maple Plain, MN 55359 Fax: 763-479-4242
wenckmp@wenck.com
www.wenck.com
Our mission is to provide our customers strategic advice and technical excellence.

1923 Weston Solutions, Inc
1400 Weston Way 610-701-3000
Box 2653 800-7WE-STON
West Chester, PA 19380-903 Fax: 610-701-3186
contactweston@westonsolutions.com
www.westonsolutions.com
Weston is a leading infrastructure redevelopment services firm delivering integrated environmental engineering solutions to industry and government worldwide. With an emphasis on creating lasting economic value for its clients, thecompany provides services in site remediation, redevelopment, infrastructure operations and knowledge management.
George Mackenzie, Chairman
William L. Robertson, CEO/President

1924 Wilcox Environmental Engineering
1552 Main Street 317-472-0999
Suite 100 Fax: 317-472-0993
Speedway, IN 46224 info@wilcoxenv.com
www.wilcoxenv.com
Provides a full range of environmental services in the areas of engineering, geology, chemistry, environmental science, air analysis, industrial compliance and hygiene, and health and safety. Services include site investigation andcorrective action, solid and hazardous waste management and more.
Steve Wilcox, President
Jim Nance, VP, Industrial Services

1925 **Zapata Engineering, Blackhawk Division**
6302 Fairview Road 704-358-8240
Suite 600 888-529-7243
Charlotte, NC 28210 Fax: 704-358-8342
zapata@zapatainc.com
www.zapatainc.com
High quality geophysical contracting and consulting services over the full spectrum of geophysical technologies, and to apply the geophysical technologies to several cross-cutting areas of engineering and exploration.
Manuel L. Zapata, P.E., President

Environmental Health

Associations

1926 ALS Environmental
10450 Stancliff Road
Suite 210
Houston, TX 77099
360-577-7222
800-695-7222
Fax: 360-636-1068
www.caslab.com

Areas of expertise and services include environmental testing of air, water, soil, hazardous waste, sediments and tissues; process and quality control testing; analytical method development; sampling and mobile laboratory services; andconsulting and data management services.
Raj Naran, CEO & Managing Director
Lan Le, Technical Director

1927 Acadia Environmental Society
626 Old Students' Union Building
Wolfville, NS B4P-2R6
902-585-2149
Fax: 902-542-3901
aes@acadiau.ca

Provides resources on environmental issues. The Society's goal is to encourage and help the Acadia community to adopt and maintain environmentally sound and sustainable practices.
Hillary Barter, Coordinator

1928 Acid Rain Foundation
11 Bay St
Suite 1B
Easton, MD 21601
919-828-9443
Fax: 919-515-3593
www.chesbay.org
James E. Price, President

1929 Action on Smoking and Health
701 4th St. NW
Washington, DC 20001
202-659-4310
Fax: 202-289-7166
info@ash.org
ash.org

Organized to use the power of the law to protect the rights of nonsmokers. Emphasis is placed on legal efforts to protect nonsmokers and to get courts to support the rights of nonsmokers. Also conducts educational and awarenesscampaigns regarding the problem of smoking and the rights of nonsmokers.
Laurent Huber, Executive Director
Chris Bostic, Deputy Director

1930 Advanced Foods & Materials Network
8911 Jubilee Rd E
Suite 310
Summerland, BC V0H-1Z5
519-822-6253
Fax: 519-824-8453
info@afmcanada.ca

Canada's front line of research and development in the area of advanced foods and bio-materials, including new, low-cost antibiotics, improved frozen food quality, and fast healing wound dressings.
Dr. Larry Milligan, Chairman
Rickey Yada, Scientific Director

1931 Agency for Toxic Substances and Disease Registry
4770 Buford Highway NE
Atlanta, GA 30341
800-232-4636
Fax: 888-232-6348
www.atsdr.cdc.gov

The mission of the agency is to prevent exposure and adverse human health effects and diminished quality of life associated with exposure to hazardous substances from waste sites, unplanned releases, and other sources of pollutionpresent in the enviroment. ATSDR is an operating division of the US Department of Health and Human Services. It divids its activities between those related to a particular site and those related to a specific hazardous substance.
Julie L. Gerberding, MD, MPH, Administrator
Howard Frumkin, MD, DrPH, Director

1932 Air and Waste Management Association
1 Gateway Center, 3rd Floor
420 Fort Duquesne
Pittsburgh, PA 15222
412-232-3444
800-270-3444
Fax: 412-232-3450
info@awma.org
www.awma.org

The Air & Waste Management Association (A&WMA) is a nonprofit, nonpartisan professional organization that provides training, information, and networking opportunities to thousands of environmental professionals in 65 countries.
Scott A. Freeburn, President
Chris Nelson, President Elect

1933 Alliance for Acid Rain Control and Energy Policy
444 N Capitol Street
Suite 602
Washington, DC 20001
202-624-5475
Fax: 202-508-3829

1934 Alternatives for Community and Environment
2201 Washington Street
Suite 302
Roxbury, MA 00211
617-442-3343
Fax: 617-442-2425
info@ace-ej.org
www.ace-ej.org

ACE is a community-based, nonprofit, environmental justice, law and education center. ACE works in partnership with community groups from low income communities and communities of color to help them address their environmental andenvironmental heath issues by providing free legal, educational and organizing services.
Kalila Barnett, Executive Director
Eugene B Benson, Program Director

1935 American Academy of Environmental Medicine
6505 E. Central Avenue
Suite 296
Wichita, KS 67206
316-684-5500
Fax: 888-411-1206
defox@aaemonline.org
www.aaemonline.org

The Academy focuses on the study of interactions between human individuals and their environment, and the environmental impact on human health. The Academy is comprised primarily of medical professionals who sponsor publications,seminars and courses. A newsletter and journal are among the organization's publications.
Gregg Govett, President
De Rodgers Fox, Executive Director

1936 American Association for the Support of Ecological Initiatives
150 Coleman Road
Middletown, CT 00645
860-346-2967
Fax: 860-347-8459
Wwasch@wesleyan.edu
www.wesleyan.edu

AASEI is a US 501 nonprofit organization which suports international environmental initiatives in Russian Nature Reserves. In cooperation sith Russia and foreign scientists, students, and universities, AASEI organizes scientificresearch projects, academic internships, work camps, environmental exchanges, and eco-tourism. Our aim is to provide practical support to Russina Reserves, expand opportunities for international scientific research, and promote internationalunderstanding.
Brendan Sweeney, President/Founder
Stephanie Hitztaler, Executive Director

1937 American Association of Poison Control Centers
515 King Street
Suite 510
Alexandria, VA 22314
703-894-1858
800-222-1222
Fax: 703-683-2812
info@aapcc.org
www.aapcc.org

A non-profit national organization that represents the poison control centers of the United States and the interests of poison prevention and treatment of poisoning.
Debbie Carr, M Ed., Executive Director

1938 American Board of Environmental Medicine
65 Wehrle Drive 716-833-2213
Buffalo, NY 14225 Fax: 716-833-2244
www.americanboardofenvironmentalmedicine.org
To establish and maintain the educational and testing criteria for board certification to ensure optimal standard and quality of the environmental physician.
Dr. Phil Ranhein, President

1939 American Board of Industrial Hygiene
6005 W St Joseph Highway 517-321-2638
Suite 300 Fax: 517-321-4624
Lansing, MI 48917 abih@abih.org
www.abih.org
Premier organization for certifying professionals in the practice of industrial hygiene. Responsible for ensuring high-quality certification application and examination processes, certifcation maintenance and ethics governance andenforcement.
Robert DeHart II, Director
Cynthia Hanko, Director

1940 American Cancer Society
PO Box 22718 800-227-2345
Oklahoma, OK 73123-1718 www.cancer.org
The American Cancer Society is the nationwide, community-based, voluntary health organization dedicated to eliminating cancer as a major health problem by preventing cancer, saving lives, and diminishing suffering from cancer throughresearch, education, advocacy and service.
John R Seffrin PhD, CEO

1941 American College of Occupational and Environmental Medicine
25 NW Point Blvd 847-818-1800
Suite 700 Fax: 847-818-9266
Elk Grove Village, IL 60007-1030 mdreger@acoem.org
www.acoem.org
Made up of physicians in industry, government, academia, private practice and the military, who promote the health of workers through preventive medicine, clinical care, research and education.
Marl A. Roberts, President
James A. Tacci, President-Elect

1942 American Conference of Governmental Industrial Hygienists
1330 Kemper Meadow Drive 513-742-2020
Cincinnati, OH 45240 Fax: 513-742-3355
mail@acgih.org
www.acgih.org
ACGIH is a member-based organization and community of professionals that advances worker health and saftey through education and the development and dissemination of scientific and technical knowledge.
90 pages Magazine
Sheryl A. Milz, Chair
Alan Rossner, Treasurer

1943 American Council on Science and Health
1995 Broadway 212-362-7044
Suite 202 866-905-2694
New York, NY 10023-5882 Fax: 212-362-4919
acsh@acsh.org
www.acsh.org
A consumer education consortium concerned with issues related to food, nutrition, chemicals, pharmaceuticals, lifestyle, the environment and health.
Elizabeth M Whelan, President
Gilbert Ross MD, Medical/Executive Director

1944 American Indian Environmental Office
1200 Pennsylvania Avenue NW 202-564-0303
Washington, DC 20460 Fax: 202-564-0298
www.epa.gov/indian
Coordinates the US environmental Protection Agency-wide effort to strengthen public health and environmental protection in Indian Country, with a special emphasis on building Tribal capacity to administer their own environmentalprograms.
Felicia Wright, Acting Director

1945 American Industrial Hygiene Association
3141 Fairview Park Drive 703-849-8888
Suite 777 Fax: 703-207-3561
Falls Church, VA 22042 infonet@aiha.org
www.aiha.org
To promote the highest quality of occupational and environmental health and safety within the workplace and the community through advocacy and the provision of services and tools to enhance the professional practice of our members.
Deborah Imel Nelson, President
Cynthia A. Ostrowski, President-Elect

1946 American Institute of Biological Sciences
1800 Alexander Bell Drive 703-674-2500
Suite 400 Fax: 703-674-2509
Reston, VA 20191 www.aibs.org
AIBS facilities communication and interactions among biologists, biological societies, and biological disciplines in order to serve and advance the interests of organismal and integrative biology in the broader scientific community andother components of society on issues related to research, education, and public policy.
Joseph Travis, President
Karen Schmaling, Vice President

1947 American Lung Association
55 W. Wacker Drive 212-315-8700
Suite 1150 Fax: 202-452-1805
Chicago, IL 60601 www.lungusa.org
The American Lung Association has been fighting lung disease in all its forms with emphasis on environmental health, asthma, and tobacco control. The work continues as they strive to make breathing easier for everyone througheducation, community service, advocacy and research programs.
Kathryn A. Forbes, Chair
John F. Emanuel, Vice Chair

1948 American Medical Association
330 N. Wabash Ave. 312-464-5000
Chicago, IL 60611-5885 800-621-8335
Fax: 312-464-4184
www.ama-assn.org
Mission: To promote the art and science of medicine and the betterment of public health.
Jmaes L. Madara, CEO/Executive Vice President

1949 American Public Health Association
800 I Street NW 202-777-2742
Washington, DC 20001 Fax: 202-777-2534
comments@apha.org
www.apha.org
Aims to protect all Americans and their communities from preventable, serious health threats and strives to assure community-based health promotion and disease prevention activities

and preventive health services are universallyaccessible in the United States.
Georges C Benjamin, Executive Director
Kemi Oluwafemi, Finance & System Controller

1950 American Society for Microbiology
1752 N Street NW 202-737-3600
Washington, DC 20036-2904 Fax: 202-942-9333
service@asmusa.org
www.asm.org
A scientific society of individuals interested inthe microbiological sciences. The mission is to advance microbiological sciences through the pursuit of scientific knowledge and dissemination of the results of fundamental and appliedresearch.
43,000 Members
Lynn Enquist, President
Joseph M. Campos, Secretary

1951 American Society of Safety Engineers
520 N. Northwest Hwy 847-699-2929
Park Ridge, IL 60068 Fax: 847-768-3434
customerservice@asse.org
www.asse.org
ASSE is a global association providing professional development and representation for those engaged in the practice of safety, health and environmental issues. Provides services to the private and public sectors to protect people,property and the environment.
James R. Thornton, Chairman
David L. Heidorn, Manager of Gov't Affairs

1952 Appalachian States Low-Level Radioactive Waste Commission
Pennsylvania DEP/BRP 717-783-2300
400 Market Street, 13th Floor kmcginty@state.pa.us
Harrisburg, PA 17101 www.dep.state.pa.us
The commission was ratified by Maryland, Delaware, Pennsylvania and West Virginia to assure intertstate cooperation for the proper packaging and transportation of low-level radioactive waste. Pennsylvania is the host state and handlesthe administrative duties of the commission at this time.
Darrin Bodner, Executive Deputy Secretary
Chris Abruzzo, Acting Secretary

1953 Asbestos Information Association of North America
PO Box 2227 703-560-2980
Arlington, VA 22202 Fax: 703-560-2981
aiabjpigg@aol.com
The Asbestos Information Association/North America was founded in 1970 to represent the interest of the asbestos industry and to collect and disseminate information about asbestos and asbestos products, with emphasis on safety, health,and environmental issues. The Association appears before Federal regulatory bodies and works with Government agencies to develop and implement standards for worker protection.
Bob Pigg, President

1954 Asian Pacific Environmental Network
426 17th Street 510-834-8920
Suite 500 Fax: 510-834-8926
Oakland, CA 94612 info@apen4ej.org
www.apen4ej.org
The Asian Pacific Environmental Network (APEN) empowers low-income Asian Pacific Islander (API) communities to take action on environmental and social justice issues. APEN builds organizations in dis-empowered API communities todevelop lasting capacity of the community to achieve solutions to problems affecting people's lives.
Roger Kim, Executive Director
Rachel Shigekane, Board Secretary

1955 Association for Environmental Health and Sciences
150 Fearing Street 413-549-5170
Amherst, MA 00100 Fax: 413-549-0579
www.aehs.com
The Association for Environmental Health and Sciences (AEHS) was created to facilitate communication and foster cooperation among professionals concerned with the challenge of soil protection and cleanup.
Paul Kostecki, Executive Director
Marc A Nascarella, Managing Ed/Conference Coor

1956 Association of American Pesticide Control Officials
PO Box 466 302-422-8152
Milford, DE 19963 Fax: 302-422-2435
www.aapco.org
Organization formed to provide a rational forum and representation for state pesticide control officials in the development, implementation, and communication of parties and programs related to the sale, transport, application anddisposal of pesticide.
Jeff Comstock, President
Tim Drake, President-Elect

1957 Association of Battery Recyclers
PO Box 290286 813-626-6151
Tampa, FL 33687 Fax: 813-622-8388
info@batteryrecyclers.com
www.batteryrecyclers.com
The Association of Battery Recyclers is a non-profit trade association. ABR strives to keep its members abreast on environmental and health matters and also provides a means for communication with government officials on issuesaffecting the lead recycling industry.
Joyce Morales, Contact

1958 Association of Occupational and Environmental Clinics
1010 Vermont Ave. NW 202-347-4976
#513 888-347-2632
Washington, DC 20005 Fax: 202-347-4950
aoec@aoec.org
www.aoec.org
The Association of Occupational and Environmental Clinics (AOEC), is a non-profit organization of over 60 clinics and 250 individuals, committed to improving the practice of occupational and environmental health through informationsharing and collaborative research.
$500/Year
Ingrid Denis, Program Coordinator
Katherine H Kirkland, Executive Director

1959 Association of State and Territorial Health Officials
2231 Crystal Drive 202-371-9090
Suite 450 Fax: 571-527-3189
Arlington, VA 22202 pjarris@astho.org
www.astho.org
Dedicated to formulating and influencing sound public health policy, and to assuring excellence in state-based public health practice.
Jewel Mullen, President
Edward Ehlinger, President-Elect

1960 Asthma and Allergy Foundation of America
8201 Corporate Drive 202-466-7643
Suite 1000 800-727-8462
Landover, MD 20785 Fax: 202-466-8940
info@aafa.org
www.aafa.org
AAFA provides practical information, community based services and support through a national network of chapters and support groups. AAFA develops health education, organizes state and na-

tional advocacy efforts and funds research tofind better treatments and cures.
William Mclin, M. Ed., President
Jacqui Vok, Programs & Services Director

1961 Beyond Pesticides
701 E Street SE 202-543-5450
Suite 200 Fax: 202-543-4791
Washington, DC 20003 info@beyondpesticides.org
www.beyondpesticides.org
Beyond Pesticides works with allies in protecting public health and the environment to lead the transition to a world free of toxic pesticides.
Routt Reigart, M.D., President
Lani Malmberg, Vice-President

1962 Bio Integral Resource Center
PO Box 7414 510-524-2567
Berkeley, CA 94707 Fax: 510-524-1758
birc@igc.org
www.birc.org
The goal of the Bio Integral Resources Center is to reduce pesticide use by educating the public about effective, less toxic alternatives for pest problems.
Dr. William Quarles, Executive Director

1963 Bison World
National Bison Association
8690 Wolff Ct 303-292-2833
Suite 200 Fax: 303-845-9081
Westminster, CO 80031 info@bisoncentral.com
www.bisoncentral.com
An organization of bison producers dedicated to awareness of the healthy properties of bison meat and bison production.
Dave Carter, Executive Director

1964 BlueGreen Alliance
1300 Godward Street NE 612-466-4479
Suite 2625 info@bluegreenalliance.org
Minneapolis, MN 55413 bluegreenalliance.org
The BlueGreen Alliance unites America's largest labor unions and its most influential environmental organizations to solve today's environmental challenges in ways that create and maintain quality jobs and build a stronger, fairereconomy.
Kim Glas, Executive Director
Eric Steen, Director of Communications

1965 Center for Health, Environment and Justice Library
150 S Washington Street, Ste 300 703-237-2249
PO Box 6806 Fax: 703-237-8389
Falls Church, VA 22040-6806 chej@chej.org
www.chej.org
The Center for Health, Environment and Justice works to build healthy communities, with social justice, economic well-being, and democratic governance. We believe this can happen when individuals from communities have the power to playan integral role in promoting human health and environmental integrity. Our role is to provide the tools to build strong, healthy communities where people can live, work, learn, play and pray.
Lois Marie Gibbs, Executive Director
Sharon Franklin, Finance/Admin Director

1966 Center for Science in the Public Interest
1220 L St. N. W. 202-332-9110
Suite 300 Fax: 202-265-4954
Washington, DC 20005 cspi@cspinet.org
www.cspinet.org
Mission: To provide useful, objective information to the public and policymakers and to conduct research on food, alcohol, health, the environment, and other issues related to science and technology; to represent the citizen'sinterests before regulatory, judicial and legislative bodies on food, alcohol, health, the environment, and other issues; and to ensure that science and technology are used for the public good and to encourage scientists to engage in public-interestactivities.
Michael F. Jacobson, Executive Director
Don Allen, Director of Finance

1967 Center for the Evaluation of Risks to Human Reproduction
110 Maryland Avenue NE 202-543-4033
Suite 402 Fax: 202-543-8797
Washington, DC 20002 cehn@cehn.org
The Center's mission includes the following: to provide timely and unbiased, scientifically sound assessments of reproductive health hazards associated with human exposure to naturally occurring and man-made chemicals; to make theseassessments readily available to the public, to state and federal agencies and to the scientific community; and to build an electronic resource for providing, or directing one to, information of public interest concerning human reproductive health.
Dr. Michael D Shelby

1968 Centers for Disease Control & Prevention
National Center for Environmental Health
1600 Clifton Road 800-232-4636
Atlanta, GA 30329-4027 Fax: 800-232-6348
www.cdc.gov/nceh
To provide national leadership, through science and service, to promote health and quality of life by preventing and controlling disease and death resulting from interactions between people and their environment.
Robin Ikeda, Director
Donna Knutson, Deputy Director

1969 Chemical Injury Information Network
PO Box 301 406-547-2255
White Sulphur Springs, MT 59645 Fax: 406-547-2455
chemicalinjury@ciin.org
www.ciin.org
Nonprofit tax-exempt support and advocacy organization run by the chemically injured for the benefit of the chemically injured. CIIN serves an international membership, and focuses primarily on eductaion, credible multiple sensitivityresearch and the empowerment of the chemically injured.
Cinthia Wilson, Executive Director
Al Gore, Vice President

1970 Chlorine Institute
1300 Wilson Boulevard 703-894-4140
Suite 525 Fax: 703-894-4130
Arlington, VA 22209 www.chlorineinstitute.org
Exists to support the chlor-alkali industry and serve the public by fostering continuous improvements to safety and the protection of human health and the environment connected with the production, distribution and use of chlorine,sodium and potassium hydroxides, and sodium hypochlorite; and the distribution and use of hydrogen chloride.
Robyn Kinsley, Director
Anna Belousovitch, Project Coordinator

1971 Commonweal
PO Box 316 415-868-0970
Bolinas, CA 94924 Fax: 415-868-2230
commonweal@commonweal.org
www.commonweal.org
A health and environment research institute that conducts programs that contribute to human and ecosystem health. The Commonweal Health and Environment Program focuses on environmental contaminants.
Michael Lerner, President
Waz Thomas, General Manager

1972 **Communities for a Better Environment**
1904 Franklin Street 510-302-0430
Suite 600 Fax: 510-302-0437
Oakland, CA 94612 cbeca@mail.com
www.cbecal.org
Mission: To achieve environmental health and justice by building grassroots power in and with communities of color and working-class communities.
Bill Gallegos, Executive Director
Rev. Daniel Buford, Board Vice President

1973 **Community-Based Hazard Management Program**
George Perkins Marsh Institute
Clark University 508-793-7711
950 Main Street otaylor@clarku.edu
Worcester, MA 00161 www.clarku.edu
The Community-Based Hazardous Management Program (formerly the Childhood Cancer Research Institute) is engaged in capacity building in communities affected by nuclear weapons production and testing and also specializes in radiationhealth risk assessment and management.
Davis Baird, Vice President

1974 **Cork Forest Conservation Alliance**
565 Oxford Street 503-931-9690
Salem, OR 97302 info@corkforest.org
corkforest.org
The Cork Forest Conservation Alliance campaigns globally for the protection and preservation of the Mediterranean cork forests, its inhabitants and biodiversity, through education, direct action, and partnerships with communities,businesses and governments.
Patrick Spencer, Executive Director

1975 **Corporate Accountability International**
10 Milk Street 617-695-2525
Suite 610 800-688-8797
Boston, MA 00210 Fax: 617-695-2626
info@stopcorporateabuse.org
www.stopcorporateabuse.org
For more than 30 years, Corporate Accountability International has successfully challenged corporations like GE, NestlS, and Philip Morris to halt abusive practices that threaten public health, the environment and our democracy. Todayour campaigns challenge the dangerous practices of some of the world's most powerful industries.
Kelle Louaillier, Executive Director
Nick Guroff, Communications Director

1976 **Council of State and Territorial Epidemiologists (CSTE)**
2872 Woodcock Boulevard 770-458-3811
Suite 250 Fax: 770-458-8516
Atlanta, GA 30341 www.cste.org
CSTE promotes the effective use of epidemiologic data to guide public health practice and improve health. CSTE accomplishes this by supporting the use of effective public health surveillance and good epidemiologic practice throughtraining, capacity development, and peer consultation, developing standards for practice, and advocating for resources and scientifically based policy.
Joseph McLaughlin, President
Alfred DeMaria, Vice President

1977 **Dangerous Goods Advisory Council**
7501 Greenway Center Drive 202-289-4550
Suite 760 Fax: 202-289-4074
Greenbelt, MD 20770 info@dgac.org
www.hmac.org
DGAC, also known as the Hazardous Materials Advisory Council, promotes improvement in the safe transportation of hazardous materials/dangerous goods globally by: providing education, assistance, and information to the private andpublic sectors; through our unique status with regulatory bodies; and the adversity and technical strengths of our membership.
Vaughn Arthur, President
Barbara Lantry-Miller, Chairman

1978 **EPA Environmental Protection Agency**
1200 Pennsylvania Avenue, NW 202-564-4700
Washington, DC 20460 www.epa.gov
An agency supporting research, monitoring, and regulation activities that ensure environmental regulations are followed. The agency also offers education to the public on environmental topics such as chemicals and toxins, wastemanagement, environmental science and more.
Scott Pruitt, EPA Administrator
Mike Flynn, Deputy Administrator

1979 **Earth Regeneration Society**
1442A Walnut Street 510-527-9716
57 www.newenergymovement.org
Berkeley, CA 94709
The Earth Regeneration Society does research and education on climate change, ozone, and pollution, and calls for full employment and full social support based on surival programs and national and international networking.
Alden Bryant, President

1980 **EarthSave International**
20555 Devonshire St. 415-234-0829
Suite 105 Fax: 818-337-1957
Chatsworth, CA 91311 info@earthsave.org
www.earthsave.org
Educates people on the powerful effects that our food choices have on the environment, our health, and all life on Earth, and supports people in moving toward a plant-based diet. Founded by John Robbins, author of Diet for a NewAmerica.
Patricia Carney, Executive Director

1981 **Environmental Defense Fund**
1875 Connecticut Avenue 212-505-2100
Suite 600 Fax: 212-505-2375
Washington, DC 20009 members@edf.org
www.edf.org
Dedicated to protecting the environmental rights of all people, including future generations. Among these rights are clean air, clean water, healthy, nourishing food and a flourishing ecosystem. Advocates solutions based on science,even when it leads in unfamiliar directions. Works to create solutions that win lasting political, economic and social support because they are bipartisan, efficient and fair.
Fred Krupp, President
Liza Henshaw, Chief Operating Officer

1982 **Environmental Hazards Management Institute**
10 New Market Road 603-868-1496
Durham, NH 03821 800-558-3464
Fax: 603-868-1547
info@ehmi.org
www.ehmi.org
An independent, nonprofit organization dedicated to understanding enhancement and preservation of our environment. A catalyst for informed environmental decision making by gathering, refining, and disseminating objective information toall stakeholders with emphasis on the role played by individuals and communities of individuals.
Alan John Borner, Chief Executive Officer

1983 **Environmental Health Coalition**
2727 Hoover Avenue 619-474-0220
Suite 202 Fax: 619-474-1210
National City, CA 91950 ehc@environmentalhealth.org
www.environmentalhealth.org

One of the oldest and most effective grassroots organizations in the US, using social change strategies to achive environmental and social justice. We believe that justice is accomplished by empowered communities acting together tomake social change. We organize and advocate to protect public health and the environment threatened by toxic pollution. EHC supports broad efforts that create a just society which foster a healthy and sustainable quality of life.
Margaret Godshalk, President
Enrique Medina, Vice President

1984 **Environmental Health Education Center**
655 West Lombard Street 410-706-1849
Room 665 Fax: 410-706-0295
Baltimore, MD 21201
Mission: Supporting nursing professionals seeking accurate, timely and credible scientific information on environmental health and nursing. The ultimate goal is to prevent environmental disease by increasing the numbers of nursingprofessionals who can recognize environmental etiologies and risk factors of disease, promote health through risk reduction and control strategies and empower individuals, families and communities through partnering, advocacy and education.
Nsedu Obot Witherspoon, MPH, Executive Director
Kristie Trousdale, MPH, Program Associate

1985 **Environmental Health Network**
PO Box 1155 415-541-5075
Larkspur, CA 94977-1155 www.ehnca.org
Nonprofit, volunteer organization, whose main goal is to promote public awareness of evironmental sensitivities and causative factors. EHN's focus is on issues of access and developments relating to the health and welfare of theenvironmentally sensitive.
Janet Harmon, Manager

1986 **Environmental Health Strategy Center**
565 Congress St. 207-699-5795
Suite 204 Fax: 207-699-5790
Portland, ME 00410 info@preventharm.org
www.preventharm.org
The Environmental Health Strategy Center works to protect human health by reducing exposure to toxic chemicals, expanding the use of safer alternatives, and building partnerships that focus on the environment as a public healthpriority.
Michael Belliveau, Executive Director
Jenny Rottman, Managing Director

1987 **Environmental Information Association**
6935 Wisconsin Avenue 301-961-4999
Suite 306 888-343-4342
Chevy Chase, MD 20815 Fax: 301-961-3094
info@eia-usa.org
www.eia-usa.org
A nonprofit organization dedicated to providing environmental information to individuals, members, and industry. They specialize in the dissemination of information about the abatement of asbestos and lead based paint, and about safetyand health issues, analytical issues and environmental site assessments.
Kevin Cannan, President
Steve Fulford, Vice President

1988 **Environmental Integrity Project**
1000 Vermont Avenue NW 202-296-8800
Suite 1100 Fax: 202-296-8822
Washington, DC 20005 info@environmentalintegrity.org
environmentalintegrity.org
The Environmental Integrity Project is a nonpartisan, nonprofit watchdog organization that advocates for effective enforcement of environmental laws comprised of former EPA enforcement attorneys, public interest lawyers, analysts,investigators, and community organizers.
John Dawes, President
Wesley P. Warren, Treasurer

1989 **Environmental Justice Resource Center**
223 James P. Brawley Drive SW 404-880-6911
Atlanta, GA 30314 Fax: 404-880-6909
ejrc@cau.edu
Since 1994, a research, policy and information clearinghouse on issues related to environmental justice, race and the environment, civil rights, facility siting, land use planning, brownfields, transportation equity, suburban sprawland Smart Growth. The overall goal of the center is to assist, support, train and educate people of color, students, professionals and grassroots community leaders with the goal of facilitating their inclusion into the mainstream of environmentaldecision-making.
Robert D Bullard PhD, Director

1990 **Environmental Mutagenesis and Genomics Society**
12627 San Jose Blvd 904-289-3410
Suite 202 bobbk@emgs-us.org
Jacksonville, FL 32223 www.emgs-us.org
The Environmental Mutagenesis and Genomics Society's mission is to foster scientific research and education on the causes and mechanistic bases of DNA damage and repair, mutagenesis, heritable effects, epigenetic alterations in genomefunction, and their relevance to disease; to promote the application and communication of this knowledge to genetic toxicology testing, risk assessment, and regulatory policy-making to protect human health and the environment.
Bob Bevans-Kerr, Executive Director
Thomas E. Wilson, President

1991 **Environmental Resource Center**
471 Washington Ave. N 208-726-4333
PO Box 819 Fax: 208-726-1531
Ketchum, ID 83340 molly@ercsv.org
www.ercsv.org
An oraganization offering environmental education for the community.
Kingsley Murphy, Chair
Michael Schlatter, Treasurer

1992 **Environmental Resource Management (ERM)**
2211 Rimland Drive 360-647-3900
Suite 210 Fax: 360-312-4183
Washington, BE 98226 www.erm.com
ERM works around the world with the private sector assessing how their business is likely to be impacted by environmental and social issues, new regulations, consumer concerns and supply chain issues and help companies developappropriate policies and management systems to manage these business risks.
John Alexander, Chief Executive
David Mcarthur, CEO

1993 **Environmental Safety**
1700 North Moore Street 703-527-8300
Suite 2000 (20th Floor) Fax: 703-527-8383
Arlington, VA 22209 info@ashoka.org
www.ashoka.org
Ashoka's mission is to shape a citizen sector that is entrepreneurial, productive and globally integrated, and to develop the profession of social entrepreneurship around the world. Ashoka identifies and invests in leading socialentrepreneurs-extraordinary individuals and unprecedented ideas for change in their communities-supporting the individual, idea and institution through all phases of their career. Once elected to Ashoka, Fellows benefit from being part of the globalfellowship for life.
Dr. Iman Bibars, Regional Director
Romanus Berg, CIO

1994 **Environmental Technology Council**
1112 16th Street NW 202-783-0870
Suite 420 Fax: 202-737-2038
Washington, DC 20036 www.etc.org

The Environmental Technology Council (ETC) is a trade association of commercial firms that recycle, treat and dispose of industrial and hazardous wastes; and firms involved in cleanup of contaminated sites.
David R Case, Executive Director
Scott Slesunger, VP Goverment Affairs

1995 **Environmental Working Group**
1436 U Street Northwest 202-667-6982
Suite 100 Fax: 202-232-2592
Washington, DC 20009 www.ewg.org
Mission: To use the power of public information to protect public health and the environment
Ken Cook, President
Heather White, Executive Director

1996 **Environmental and Occupational Health Science Institute**
Rutgers University
170 Frelinghuysen Road 848-445-0200
Piscataway, NJ 00885 Fax: 732-445-0131
www.eohsi.rutgers.edu
Environmental and Occupational Health Sciences Institute sponsors research, education and service programs in a setting that fosters interaction among experts in environmental health, toxicology, occupational health, exposureassessment, public policy and health education. The Institute also serves as an unbiased source of expertise about environmental problems for communities, employers and government in all areas of occupational and environmental health, toxicology andrisk assessment.
Howard Kipen, M.D, MPH, Associate Director
Kenneth Reuhl PhD, Interim Director

1997 **Food Safety and Inspection Service**
Food Safety Education Office
1400 Independence Avenue SW 202-720-7025
Washington, DC 20250-3700 Fax: 202-205-0158
fsis.webmaster@usda.gov
www.fsis.usda.gov
The Food Safety and Inspection Services (FSIS) is the public health agency in the U.S. Department of Agriculture responsible for ensuring that the nation's commercial supply of meat, poultry, and egg products is safe, wholesome, andcorrectly labeled and packaged.
Alfred V. Almanza, Deputy Under Secretary
Carmen Rottenberg, Deputy Administrator

1998 **Food and Drug Administration**
US Department of Health and Human Services
10903 New Hampshire Avenue
Silver Spring, MD 20993 888-463-6332
www.fda.gov
The FDA is responsible for protecting the public health by assuring the safety, efficacy, and security of human and veterinary drugs, biological products, medical devices, our nation's food supply, cosmetics, and products that emitradiation.
Scott Gottlieb, Commissioner
Anna Abram, Deputy Commissioner

1999 **Friends of the River**
1418 20th Street 916-442-3155
Suite 100 888-464-2477
Sacramento, CA 95811 Fax: 916-442-3396
info@friendsoftheriver.org
www.friendsoftheriver.org
Friends of the River educates, organizes, and advocates to protect and restore California rivers, streams, and watersheds.
Corley Phillips, Chair
John Yost, Treasurer

2000 **Halogenated Solvents Industry Alliance, Inc. (HSIA)**
3033 Wilson Boulevard 703-875-0683
Suite 700 info@hsia.org
Arlington, VA 22201 www.hsia.org
The mission is to represent the users and producers of chlorinated solvents - trichloroethylene, perchloroethylene and methylene chloride. To promote the continued safe use of these products and the use of sound science in assessingtheir potential health effects.
Faye Graul, Executive Director

2001 **Holistic Management International**
5941 Jefferson St. NE 505-842-5252
Suite B Fax: 505-843-7900
Albuquerque, NM 87109 hmi@holisticmanagement.org
www.holisticmanagement.org
Enhance the efficiency, natural health, productivity and profitability of their land; increase natural annual profits; provide a framework for family, owners, managers, foreman, communal agriculturalists and other ranch/farmstakeholders to work together toward a common future; and enable development agencies working with marginalized farmers or pastoral people to break the cycle of food and water insecurity.
Peter Holter, CEO
Tracy Favre, Sr Director Contract Sales

2002 **Human Ecology Action League (HEAL)**
PO Box 509 770-389-4519
Stockbridge, GA 30281 Fax: 770-389-4520
HEALNatnl@aol.com
www.healnatl.org
The Human Ecology Action League Inc (HEAL) is a nonprofit organization founded in 1977 to serve those whose health has been adversely affected by environment exposures; to provide information to those who are concerned about the healtheffects of chemicals; and to alert the general public about the potential dangers of chemicals. Referrals to local HEAL chapters and other support groups are available from the League.
John Heal, Contact

2003 **INFORM**
PO Box 320403 212-361-2400
Brooklyn, NY 11232 Fax: 212-361-2412
ramsey@informinc.org
www.informinc.org
Dedicated to educating the public about the effects of human activity on the environment and public health. The goal is to empower citizens, businesses and government to adopt practices and policies that will sustain our planet forfuture generations.
Virginia Ramsey, President
Marina Belesis Casoria, Chair

2004 **Institute for Agriculture and Trade Policy**
2105 First Avenue South 612-870-0453
Minneapolis, MN 55404 Fax: 612-870-4846
www.iatp.org
The mission of the Institute for Agriculture and Trade Policy is to foster socially, economically and environmentally sustainable rural communities and regions.
Harriet Barlow, Board Chair
Becky Glass, Board Secretary-Treasurer

2005 **Institute of Hazardous Materials Management**
11900 Parklawn Drive 301-984-8969
Suite 450 Fax: 301-984-1516
Rockville, MD 20852-2624 ihmminfo@ihmm.org
www.ihmm.org
Mission is to provide recognition for professionals engaged in the managment and engineering control of hazardous materials who have attained the required level of education, experience and competence; foster continued professionaldevelopment of Certified Hazardous Materials Managers (CHMM).
John H Frick, PhD, CHMM, Executive Director
Betty Fishman, Assistant Executive Director

2006 MCS Referral and Resources
618 Wyndhurst Avenue #2 410-889-6666
Baltimore, MD 21210 Fax: 410-889-4944
adonnay@mcsrr.org
www.mcsrr.org
The mission of MCS Refferal and Resources is to further the diagnosis, treatment, accomodation and prevention of multiple chemical sensitivity (MCS) disorders.
Dr. Anne McCampbell

2007 Midwest Center for Environmental Science and Public Policy
One East Hazelwood Drive
Champaign, IL 61820 800-407-0261
glrppr@istc.illinois.edu
www.glrppr.org
A professional organization dedicated to promoting information exchange and networking to P2 professionals in the Great Lakes regions of the United States and Canada
Bob Iverson, Contact

2008 Midwest Pesticide Action Center
35 E Upper Wacker Drive 773-878-7378
Suite 1200 general@pesticideaction.org
Chicago, IL 60601 www.midwestpesticideaction.org
Working at the local, state and regional level, the Midwest Pesticide Action Center, uses advocacy, education, and outreach to reduce the health risks and environmental impact of pesticides and promote safer alternatives.
Ruth Kerzee, Executive Director
Ryan Anderson, Program Manager

2009 Mount Sinai School of Medicine: Division of Environmental Health Science
Department of Community and Preventive Medicine
1 Gustave Levy Place 212-241-6500
Box 1057 Fax: 212-241-6696
New York, NY 10029-6574 www.mssm.edu/cpm
The Division's ultimate goal is the protection of the public's health by understanding, elucidating and preventing diseases that arise from environmental exposures.
Philip J Landrigan M.D., Chair

2010 National Alliance for Hispanic Health
1501 16th Street NW 202-387-5000
Washington, DC 20036 Fax: 202-797-4353
www.hispanichealth.org
The mission of the National Alliance for Hispanic Health is to improve the health and well-being of Hispanics. Issues covered include the full range of health and human services issues, including environmental health.
Jane L. Delgado, President and CEO
Adolph P. Falcon, Senior Vice President

2011 National Association of City and County Health Officials
1100 17th Street NW 202-783-5550
Seventh Floor Fax: 202-783-1583
Washington, DC 20036 info@naccho.org
www.naccho.org
The National Assoication of County and City Health Officials is a nonprofit, membership organization serving all 3,000 local health departments nationwide. NACCHO is dedicated to improving the health of people and communities byassuring an effective local public health system. As the Voice of local public health officials at the national level, NACCHO is able to promote the local perspective on national health programs and policies.
Georgia Heise, President

2012 National Association of Noise Control Officials
53 Cubberly Road 609-586-2684
West Windsor, NJ 00855-3400 Fax: 609-799-2616
www.arcat.com
The association consists of employees of the federal and state governments, consultants, scientists, and students concerned with acoustical control in the environment. It now has about 70 members.
Edward J DiPolzere, Executive Director

2013 National Association of Physicians for the Environment
6410 Rockledge Drive 307-571-9790
Suite 412 Fax: 301-530-8910
Bethesda, MD 20817
The National Association of Physicians for the Environment works to involve physicians and other health care professionals, particularly through their geographic and medical specialty organizations, to deal with the impact ofpollutants on organs and systems of the human body.
Betty Farley, Executive Assistant

2014 National Cancer Institute
National Institutes of Health
BG 9609 MSC 9760 301-496-6641
9609 Medical Centre Drive 800-422-6237
Bethesda, MD 20892-9760 Fax: 301-496-0846
ncipressofficers@mail.nih.gov
www.cancer.gov
Leads the Nation's fight against cancer by supporting and conducting ground-breaking research in cancer biology, causation, prevention, detection, treatment and survivorship.
John E Niederhuber, Director
Joseph V. Simone, MD, Chairman

2015 National Capital Poison Center
3201 New Mexico Avenue NW 202-362-3867
Suite 310 800-222-1222
Washington, DC 20016 Fax: 202-362-8377
pc@poison.org
www.poison.org
This mission of the Poison Center is to prevent poisonings, save lives, and limit injury from poisoning. In addition, the Center decreases health care costs of poisoning cases. The Center provides 24-hour telephone guidance, teachingmaterials, and professional education.

2016 National Center for Disease Control and Prevention
1600 Clifton Road 404-639-3311
Atlanta, GA 30333-4027 800-232-4636
www.cdc.gov
Mission: To promote health and quality of life by preventing and controlling disease, injury, and disability.
Lynn Austin, Chief of Staff

2017 National Center for Environmental Health Strategies
1100 Rural Avenue 856-429-5358
Voorhees, NJ 00804 Fax: 856-816-8820
marylamielle@ncehs.org
www.ncehs.org/
Fosters the development of creative solutions to environmental health problems with a focus on indoor air quality, chemical sensitivites and environmental disabilities.
Mary Lamielle, Executive Director

2018 National Center for Healthy Housing
10320 Little Patuxent Parkway 410-992-0712
Suite 500 877-312-3046
Columbia, MD 21044 Fax: 443-539-4150
www.centerforhealthyhousing.org
Formerly known as the National Center for Lead-Safe Housing, it deveops and promotes practical methods to protect children fron

environmental health hazards in homes while preserving affordable housing.
Rebecca L Morley, Executive Director
Jonathan W Wilson, Deputy Director

2019 National Conference of Local Environmental Health Administrators
University of Washington
Department of Environmental Health 509-382-2181
1010 South Third Street Fax: 360-382-2942
Dayton, WA 99328 ctreser@u.washington.edu
depts.washington.edu/clehaweb
The NCLEHA's purpose is to provide a forum for local administrators to share common concerns and solutions to mutual problems, and to provide a professional organization for environmental health administrators, focused on the issuesand problems of local environmental health programs.
David Riggs, Chair
Charles D Treser, Treasurer

2020 National Conference of State Legislatures
7700 E First Place 303-364-7700
Denver, CO 80230 Fax: 303-364-7800
www.ncsl.org
The National Conference of State Legislatures serves the legislators and staffs of the nation's 50 states and its commonwealths and territories. NCSL is a bipartisan organization with three objectives: to improve the quality andeffectiveness of state legislatures; to foster interstate communications and cooperation; and to ensure states a strong cohesive voice in the federal system.
Debbie Smith, President
Mike Gronstal, Vice President

2021 National Education Association Health Information Network
1201 16th Street NW 202-822-7570
Suite 216 800-718-8387
Washington, DC 20036-3290 Fax: 202-822-7775
info@neahin.org
The National Education Association Health Information Network believes that sound public education must begin with school employees and students who are healthy and free of preventable diseases and supported with information, materialsand training opportunities that reaffirm these values.
Jim Bender, Executive Director
Annelise Cohon, Program Coordinator

2022 National Environmental Coalition of Native Americans
PO Box 988 918-342-3041
Claremore, OK 74018 noteno_84@hotmail.com
necona.indigenousnative.org
Nonprofit organization formed to educate Indians and Non-Indians about the health dangers of radioactivity and the transport of nuclear waste on America's rails and roads. Networks with environmentalists to develop grassrootscounter-movement to the efforts of the nuclear industry and develop Tribal nuclear free zones across the nation.
Grace Thorpe, President

2023 National Environmental Health Association (NEHA)
720 S Colorado Boulevard 303-756-9090
Suite 1000-N 866-956-2258
Denver, CO 80246 Fax: 303-691-9490
staff@NEHA.org
www.neha.org

NEHA is the only national association that represents all of environmental health and protection from terrorism and all-hazards preparedness, to food safety and protection and on site wastewater systems. Over 4500 members and theprofession are served by the association through its Journal of Environmental Health, Annual Education Conference and Exhibition credentialing programs, research and development activities and other services.
Bob Custard, President
David E. Riggs, President-Elect

2024 National Environmental Health Science and Protection Accreditation Council
PO Box 66057 206-522-5272
Suite 394 Fax: 206-985-9805
Burien, WA 98166 ehacinfo@aehap.org
www.ehacoffice.org
The National Environmental Health Science and Protection Accreditation Council promotes a high quality education for persons studying environmental health science and protection; promotes commonality in coverage of basic concepts ofenvironmental health science and protection education; and promotes undergraduate curricula of a quality and content compatible with admission prerequisites of graduate programs in environmental health science and protection.
Yalonda Sinde, Executive Director

2025 National Environmental Trust
1200 18th Street NW 202-887-8800
5th Floor Fax: 202-887-8877
Washington, DC 20036 cdelany@net.org
Manages comprehensive media and public policy campaigns around national environmental issues.
Kymberly Escobar, Director

2026 National Institute for Global Environmental Change
University of California, Davis
2850 Spafford Street 530-757-3350
Suite A Fax: 530-756-6499
Davis, CA 95618 www.ucdavis.edu
Mission: To assist the nation in its response to human-induced climate and environmental change.
Lawrence B Coleman, Interim National Director

2027 National Institute of Environmental Health Sciences
111 T.W. Alexander Drive 919-541-3345
Durham, NC 27709 Fax: 301-480-2978
webcenter@niehs.nih.gov
www.niehs.nih.gov
The mission of the National Institute of Environmental Health Sciences is to reduce the burden of environmentally associated diseases and dysfunctions.
Linda S. Birnbaum, Ph.D, Director
Richard Woychik, Deputy Director

2028 National Oceanic & Atmospheric Administration
1401 Constitution Avenue NW
Room 5128 webmaster@noaa.gov
Washington, DC 20230 www.noaa.gov
The Administration's mission is to explore, map, and chart the global ocean and its living resources and to manage, use, and conserve those resources; to describe, monitor, and predict conditions in the atmosphere, ocean, sun,and spaceenvironment; to issue warnings against impending destructive natural events; to assess the consequences of inadvertent environmental modification over several scales of time, and to manage and disseminate long-term environmental information.
Benjamin Friedman, Under Secretary

2029 National Pesticide Information Center Oregon State University
310 Weniger Hall
Corvallis, OR 97331 800-858-7378
Fax: 541-737-0761
npic.orst.edu
Provides objective, science-based information about a wide variety of pesticide-related topics, including: pesticide product information, information on the recognition and management of

pesticide poisonings, toxicology andenvironmental chemistry. Highly trained specialists can also provide referrals for the following: investigation of pesticide incidents, emergency treatment information, safety information, health and environmental effects, and clean-up and disposalprocedures.
Jeff Jenkins, Director
Amy Hallman, Project Coordinator

2030 National Religious Partnership for the Environment
49 South Pleasant Street 413-253-1515
Suite 301 Fax: 413-253-1414
Amherst, MA 00100 www.nrpe.org
The mission of the National Religious Partnership for the Environment is to permanently integrate issues of environmental sustainability and justice across all aspects of organized religious life.
Cassandra Carmichael, Executive Director

2031 National Safety Council
Environmental Health Center
1121 Spring Lake Dr. 202-293-2270
Suite 1210 800-621-7615
Itasca, IL 60143-3201 Fax: 630-285-1434
info@nsc.org
www.nsc.org
The Mission of the Environmental Health Center is to foster improved public understanding of significant health risk and challenges facing modern society. This goal reinforces the National Safety Council's commitment to increased andmore effective citizen involvement in safety, health and environmental decision-making.
Jeffrey Shavelson, Policy Analyst

2032 Natural Resources Defense Council
40 West 20th Street 212-727-2700
New York, NY 10011 Fax: 212-727-1773
nrdcinfo@nrdc.org
www.nrdc.org
The NRDC focuses on issues impacting climate change, ocean pollution, water management and treatment, clean energy, and the conservation of wildlife.
Rhea Suh, President
Mitchell Bernard, Chief Counsel

2033 Navy & Marine Corps Public Health Center
620 John Paul Jones Circle 757-953-0700
Suite 1100 NMCPHC-PAO@med.navy.mil
Portsmouth, VA 23708-2103 www.med.navy.mil/sites/nmcphc/Pages/Home.aspx
The Navy and Marine Corps Center for Public Health Services provides leadership and expertise to ensure mission readiness through disease prevention and health promotion in support of the National Military Strategy.
Todd L. Wagner, Commanding Officer
Robert Hawkins, Executive Officer

2034 Navy and Marine Corps Public Health Center
620 John Paul Jones Circle 757-953-0700
Suite 1100 ask-nmcphc@med.navy.mil
Portsmouth, VA 23708
The Navy and Marine Corps center for public health services that provides leadership and expertise to ensure mission readiness through disease prevention and health promotion in support of the National Military Strategy.
CAPT Bruce A Cohen MC USN, Commanding Officer
CAPT Mike Henderson MSC USN, Executive Officer

2035 Noise Pollution Clearinghouse
PO Box 1137
Montpelier, VT 05601-1137 888-200-8332
webmaster@nonoise.org
www.nonoise.org
The Noise Pollution Clearinghouse is a nonprofit organization with extensive online noise related resources. The mission is to create more civil cities and more natural rural and wilderness areas by reducing noise pollution and itssources.

2036 North American Association for Environmental Education
2000 P Street NW 202-419-0412
Suite 540 Fax: 202-419-0415
Washington, DC 20036 judybraus@naaee.org
www.naaee.org
A professional association that promotes excellence in environmental education and serves environmental educators for the purpose of achieving environmental literacy to allow present and future generations to benefit from a safe andhealthy environment.
Jose Marcos-Iga, President
Judy Braus, Executive Director

2037 Northwest Coalition for Alternatives to Pesticides
PO Box 1393 541-344-5044
Eugene, OR 97440 Fax: 541-344-6923
info@pesticide.org
www.pesticide.org
The Northwest Coalition for Alternatives to Pesticides protects the health of people and the environment by advancing alternatives to pesticides.
Tony Brand, President
Kim Leval, Executive Director

2038 Novozymes North America Inc
77 Perry Chapel Church Road 919-494-3000
Franklinton, NC 27525 Fax: 919-494-3450
enzymesna@novozymes.com
www.novozymes.com/en
Novozymes is the biotech bases world leader in enzymes and microorganisms. Using nature's own technologies, they continuously expand the frontiers of biological solutions to improve industrial performance everywhere.
Henrik Gurtler, CEO

2039 Occupational Safety and Health Administration: US Department of Labor
Office of Administrative Services
200 Constitution Avenue NW
Room N-310 800-321-6742
Washington, DC 20210 www.osha.gov
Mission: To assure the safety and health of America's workers by setting and enforcing standards; providing training, outreach, and education; establishing partnerships; and encouraging continual improvement in workplace safety andhealth.
Loren Sweatt, Deputy Assistant Secretary
Thomas Galassi, Deputy Assistant Secretary

2040 Pesticide Action Network North America
1611 Telegraph Avenue 510-788-9020
Suite 1200 www.panna.org
Oakland, CA 94612
Pesticide Action Network North American advocates the adoption of ecologically sound practices in place of hazardous pestices in place of pesticide use. PANNA works with more than 100 affiliated oragnizations in Canada, Mexico and US,as well as with Pesticide Action Network partners around the world to demand that development agencies and governments redirect support from pesticides to safe alternatives.
Susan Baker, President
Mary Brune, Vice President

2041 Physicians for Social Responsibility
1111 14th St., NW
Suite 700
Washington, DC 20005
202-667-4260
Fax: 202-667-4201
psrnatl@psr.org
www.psr.org

A non-profit advocacy organization that is the medical and public health voice for policies to prevent nuclear war and proliferation and to slow, stop and reverse global warming and toxic degradation of the environment.
Catherine Thomasson MD, Executive Director
Martin Fleck, Program Director

2042 Plastic Pollution Coalition
2150 Allston Way
Suite 460
Berkeley, CA 94704
323-936-3010
dianna@plasticpollutioncoalition.org
plasticpollutioncoalition.org

The Plastic Pollution Coalition is a nonprofit association dedicated to finding a sustainable solution for plastic pollution through strategic planing and global communication.
Dianna Cohen, Chief Executive Officer
Jane Patton, Managing Director

2043 Public Citizen
1600 20th Street NW
Washington, DC 20009
202-588-1000
member@citizen.org
www.citizen.org

A consumer advocacy organization founded to represent consumer interests in Congress, the executive branch and the courts.
Robert Weissman, President
Margrete Strand Rangnes, Executive Vice-President

2044 Rachel Carson Center for Natural Resources
Churchill High School
1850 Bailey Hill Road
Eugene, OR 97405
541-687-3421
haberman@4j.lane.edu
schools.4j.lane.edu/carson/

Offers an alternative to the traditional high school curriculum, providing students with experience, knowledge, and skills that relate to the natural environment.
Helen Haberman, Environmental Instructor
Tim Whitley, Director

2045 Rachel Carson Council
8600 Irvington Avenue
Bethesda, MD 20817
301-214-2400
office@rachelcarsoncouncil.org
rachelcarsoncouncil.org

Independent nonprofit scientific organization dedicated to protecting the environment against toxic and chemical threats, particularly those of pesticides.
Roger Christie, Chairman
Robert K. Musil, Ph.D., President & CEO

2046 Rene Dubos Center
The Rene Dubos Center
279 Bronxville Road
Bronxville, NY 10708
914-337-1636
Fax: 914-771-5206
www.dubos.org

The Rene Dubos Center for Human Environments is a non-profit education and research organization focused on the social and humanistic aspects of environmental problems.
Ruth A Eblen, President

2047 Rodale Institute
611 Siegfriedale Road
Kutztown, PA 19530-9320
610-683-1400
Fax: 610-683-8548
info@rodaleinst.org
www.rodaleinstitute.org

The Institute offers creative opportunities and solutions that contribute to regenerating environmental and human health worldwide. Their mission statement is clear: The Rodale Institute works worldwide to achieve a regenerative foodsystem that improves environmental and human health.
Anthony Rodale, Chairman
Paul A. McGinley, Co-chairman

2048 Second Nature Inc.
Consortium for Environmental Education in Medicine
18 Tremont Street
Suite 930
Boston, MA 00210
617-722-0036
Fax: 320-451-1612
info@secondnature.org
www.secondnature.org

Dedicated to advancing our quality of life by demostrating the close links between human health and the environment. The center's goal is to make the relationship of environment to human health an integral part of medical education.
Richard J Cook, Chair
James L Buizer, Vice Chair

2049 Silicones Environmental, Health and Safety Council of North America
700 2nd Street NE
Washington, DC 20002
202-249-7000
Fax: 202-249-6100
sehsc@americanchemistry.com
sehsc.americanchemistry.com

An organization of North America silicone chemical producers and importers. It promotes the safe use of silicones through product stewardship and environmental, health and safety research. It focuses on coordinating research andsubmitting it for peer review through independent advisory boards and publication of peer-reviewed literature.
Calvin M Dooley, President & CEO
Karluss Thomas, Executive Director

2050 Society of Chemical Manufacturers and Affiliates (SOCMA)
1400 Crystal Drive
Suite 630
Arlington, VA 22202
571-348-5100
Fax: 571-348-5138
co@socma.com
www.socma.com

The leading international trade association serving the small and mid-sized batch chemical manufacturers. Advocates flexible policies grounded in sound science and works to ensure that Congress and the regulatory agencies do not adopta one-size fits-all approach to the industry.
Jennifer L. Abril, President/CEO

2051 Society of Environmental Toxicology and Chemistry
SETAC N America Office
229 South Baylen Street
2nd Floor
Pensacola, FL 32502
850-469-1500
Fax: 850-469-4136
setac@setac.org
www.setac.org

Mission: To support the development of principles and practices for protection, enhancement and management of sustainable environmental quality and ecosystem integrity.
Greg Schiefer, Executive Director
Jason Anderson, IT Manager

2052 Teratology Society
1821 Michael Faraday Drive
Suite 300
Reston, VA 20190
703-438-3104
Fax: 703-483-3113
tshq@teratology.org
www.teratology.org

A multidisciplinary scientific society founded in 1960, the members of which study the causes and biological processes leading to abnormal development and birth defects at the fundamental and clinical level, and appropriate measuresfor prevention.
Tacey E.K. White, President
Sonja A. Rasmussen, Vice President

2053 The Natural Step
251 Bank Street
Suite 526
Ottawa, ON K2P-1X3
613-748-3001
Fax: 613-748-1649
info@naturalstep.ca
naturalstep.ca

The Natural Step is a Canadian nonprofit organization dedicated to science-based sustainable development, working internationally with other organizations, researchers, and local communities.
Tim Broadhead, Director
Karen Clarke-Whistler, Vice-Chair

2054 US Consumer Product Safety Commission
4330 East West Highway 800-638-2772
Bethesda, MD 20814 Fax: 301-504-0124
info@cpsc.gov
www.cpsc.gov
The U.S. Consumer Product Safety Commission (CPSC) is an independent federal regulatory agency that aims to protect the public against unreasonable risks of injuries and deaths associated with consumer products.
Ann Marie Buerkle, Acting Chairman

2055 US Nuclear Regulatory Commission
U.S Nuclear Regulatory Commission 301-415-7000
Washington, DC 20555-0001 800-368-5642
oca_web@nrc.gov
www.nrc.gov
The Nuclear Regulatory Commission focuses on reactor safety oversight and liscense renewal of existing plants, materials safety oversight and liscencing, as well as high and low-level waste management.
Kristine L. Svinicki, Chairman
Jeff Baran, Commissioner

2056 US Public Interest Research Group
218 D Street SE 202-546-9707
1st Floor Fax: 202-546-2461
Washington, DC 20003 www.pirg.org
Mission: To deliver persistent, result-oriented public interest activism that protects our environment, encourages a fair, sustainable economy, and fosters responsive, democratic government.
Douglas H Phelps, President
Andre Delattre, Executive Director

2057 US-Mexico Border Health Association
211 N. Florence 915-532-1006
Suite101 866-785-9867
El Paso, TX 79901 Fax: 915-833-7840
bhc@borderhealth.org
www.borderhealth.org
Promotes public and individual health along the United States-Mexico border through reciprocal technical cooperation.
Rebeca Ramos, Interim Executive Director

2058 Water Environment Federation
601 Wythe Street 703-684-2400
Alexandria, VA 22314-1994 800-666-0206
Fax: 703-684-2492
inquiry@wef.org
www.wef.org
Nonprofit international membership organization that develops and disseminates technical information on the nature, collection, treatment and disposal of domestic and industrial wastewater.
Rick Warner, President
Jenny Hartfelder, President-Elect

2059 Western Forest Genetics Association
1731 Research Park 530-759-1742
Davis, CA 95618 fsl.orst.edu/wfga
The Western Forest Genetics Association (WFGA) comprises professionals, researchers, and students involved in forest genetics issues in the western US and Canada.
Jessia W. Wright, Vice President
Andrew D. Bower, Treasurer

2060 Western Occupational and Environmental Medical Association
575 Market Street 415-764-4918
Suite 2125 Fax: 415-764-4915
San Francisco, CA 94105 woema@woema.org
www.woema.org
The mission is to represent and be a resource to members in the profession and practice of occupational and environmental medicine and to enhance their efforts to promote and improve health in the workplace and the community.
Ellyn G. McIntosh, Chairman
Peter J. Vasquez, President

2061 White Lung Association
PO Box 1483 410-243-5864
Baltimore, MD 21203 Fax: 410-243-5234
www.whitelung.org
National nonprofit organization dedicated to the education of the public to the hazards of asbestos exposure. Has developed programs of public education and consults with victims of asbestos exposure, school boards, building owners,government agencies and others interested in identifying asbestos hazards and developing control programs.
James Fite, Executive Director

Pediatric Health: Associations

2062 Academic Pediatric Association
6728 Old McLean Village Drive 703-556-9222
McLean, VA 22101 Fax: 703-556-8729
info@academicpeds.org
www.academicpeds.org
The mission of the APA is to foster the health and well-being of children and their families by: promoting health services, education and research in general pediatrics; affecting public and governmental policies regarding issues vitalto child health and to education and research in general pediatrics; and supporting the professional growth and development of faculty in general pediatrics.
David Keller, MD, President
Connie Mackay, Executive Director

2063 Allergy and Asthma Network: Mothers of Asthmatics
8229 Boone Boulevard
Suite 260 800-878-4403
Vienna, VA 22182 Fax: 703-288-5271
www.allergyasthmanetwork.org
Our mission is to eliminate suffering and death due to asthma and allergies through education, advocacy, community outreach and research.
Nancy Sander, President
Mary McGowan, Executive Director

2064 American Academy of Pediatrics: Committee on Environment Health
141 NW Point Boulevard 847-434-4000
Elk Grove Villiage, IL 60007-1098 800-433-9016
Fax: 847-434-8000
www.aap.org
The AAP is commited to the attainment of optimal physical, mental and social health for all infants, children, and young adults. This mission will be accomplished by engaging in the following activities: professional education,advocacy for children and youth, advocacy for pediatricians, public education, membership service and research.
Sandra Hassink, President
Benard P. Dreyer, President Elect

2065 American Federation of Teachers
555 New Jersey Avenue NW 202-879-4400
Washington, DC 20001 Fax: 202-879-4597
www.aft.org
The American Federation of Teachers is a union that represents K-12 teachers and other school employees, health care professionals and public employees. The union considers itself an advocacy organization for children and the public.
Randi Weingarten, President
Mary Cathryn Ricker, Executive Vice President

2066 Association of Maternal and Child Health Program
2030 M Street 202-775-0436
Suite 350 Fax: 202-775-0061
Washington, DC 20036 www.amchp.org
AMCHP accomplishes its mission through the active participation of its members and vital partnerships with government agencies, families and advocates, health care purchasers and providers, academic and research professionals, andothers at the national, state and local levels.
Millie Jones, President
Lori Tremmel Freeman, Chief Executive Officer

2067 Childhood Lead Poisoning Prevention Program
Ohio Department of Health
246 N High Street 614-728-9454
Columbus, OH 43215 Fax: 614-728-6793
BCFHS@odh.ohio.gov
The mission of Ohio's Childhood Lead Poisoning Prevention Program is to eliminate childhood lead poisoning through screening, environmental inspection, abatement, education and case management.
Alvin D Jackson, Director

2068 Children's Defense Fund
25 E Street NW
Washington, DC 20001 800-233-1200
cdfinfo@childrensdefense.org
www.childrensdefense.org
Mission: To ensure every child a healthy start, a head start, a fair start, a safe start, and a moral start in life and successful passage to adulthood with the help of caring families and communities.
Marian Wright Edelman, President
Melanie Hartzog, Executive Director

2069 Children's Environmental Health Network
110 Maryland Avenue NE 202-543-4033
Suite 404 Fax: 202-543-8797
Washington, DC 20002 cehn@cehn.org
www.cehn.org/
Mission is to promote a healthy environment and to protect the fetus and child from environmental hazards. Three areas of concentration for the Network are education, research and policy. Network's goals are: to promote the developmentof sound public health and child-focused national policy; to stimulate prevention-oriented research; to educate health professionals, policymakers and community members in preventive strategies; and to elevate public awareness of environmentalhazards to children.
James R. Roberts, M.D., M.P.H, Chair
Dick J Batchelor, Vice Chair

2070 Children's Hopsital at Montefiore
111 E 210th Street 718-920-5016
Bronx, NY 10467 Fax: 718-920-4377
www.montefiore.org
The Montefiore Lead Poisoning Prevention Program addresses all aspects of childhood lead poisoning from diagnosis and treatment to education and research. Their mission is to treat lead-poisoned children and their families and toeducate families at risk, other medical providers and local, state and national legislators and policy makers.
Steven M Safyer, President & CEO
Philip O Ozuah, Chief Operating Officer

2071 Coalition for Clean Air
800 Wilshire Blvd. 213-223-6860
Suite 1010 Fax: 213-223-6862
Los Angelos, CA 90017 NICHOLAS@CCAIR.ORG
www.coalitionforcleanair.org
The Coalition for Clean Air is committed to restoring clean, healthy air to all of California and strengthening the environmental movement by promoting broad-based community involvement, advocating responsible public policy andproviding technical expertise.
Erik Neandross, Board Chair
Joseph K Lyou, Ph.D, President & CEO

2072 Genesis Fund/National Birth Defects Center: Pregnancy Environmental Hotline
1347 Main Street 781-890-4282
Second Floor 800-322-5014
Waltham, MA 00245 Fax: 781-487-2361
www.thegenesisfund.org
General information service that provides information regarding exposure to environmental factors during pregnancy and the effects on the developing fetus.
Matthew Hoffman, Chairman
Erica D Agostino, Executive Director

2073 Healthy Child Healthy World
8383 Wilshire Blvd 424-343-0020
Suite 800 Fax: 310-820-2070
Beverly Hills, CA 90211 info@healthychild.org
www.healthychild.org
Healthy Child Healthy World is dedicated to protecting the health and well being of children from harmful environmental exposures. We educate parents, support protective policies, and engage communities to make responsible decisions,simple everyday choices, and well-informed lifestyle improvements to create healthy environments where children and families can flourish.
Megan Boyle, Editorial Director
Kelly Herman, Program Director

2074 Healthy Mothers, Healthy Babies
4401 Ford Avenue 703-838-7552
Suite 300 Fax: 703-664-0485
Alexandria, VA 22302 info@hmhb.org
www.hmhb.org
Healthy Mothers, Healthy Babies is a coalition of national, state and local providers, advocates and administrators concerned about health of pregnant women, infants and families. The coalition serves as a forum for informationexchange and as a catalyst to encourage collaborative partnerships amoung its members and colleagues.
Janice Frey-Angel, CEO
Jennifer Sharp, Authorized Executive

2075 Healthy Schools Network
773 Madison Avenue 518-462-0632
Albany, NY 12208 202-543-7555
Fax: 518-462-0433
www.healthyschools.org
HSN is a nationally recognized state-based advocate for the protection of children's environmental health in schools. Engages in research, education, outreach, technical assistance and coalition building to create schols that areenvironmentally responsible to children, and to their communities. Publishes a quarterly newsletter and maintains an Information Clearinghouse and Referral Service.
Chip Halverson, President
Laura Anderko, Vice President

2076 **Institute of Medicine: Board on Children, Youth and Families**
500 Fifth Street, NW 202-334-2000
Washington, DC 20001 Fax: 202-334-3829
bocyf@nas.edu
The Board on Children, Youth and Families addresses a variety of policy-relevant issues related to the health and development, of children, youth and families. It does so by convening experts to weigh in on matters from the perspectiveof the behavioral, social, and health sciences. The Board operates under the National Research Council and the Institute of Medicine of the National Academies.
Kimber Bogard, Director
Morgan Ford, Senior Program Officer

2077 **Kids for Saving Earth Worldwide**
37955 Bridge Road 763-559-1234
North Branch, MN 55056 Fax: 651-674-5005
kse@kidsforsavingearth.org
www.kidsforsavingearth.org/
To help protect the Earth through kids and adults. To educate and inspire them to participate in Earth-saving actions.
Tessa Hill, President and Director

2078 **Kids for a Clean Environment**
PO Box 158254 615-331-7381
Nashville, TN 37215 Fax: 615-333-9879
kidsface@mindspring.com
www.kidsface.org
Mission: To provide information on environmental issues to children, to encourage and facilitate youth's involvement with effective environmental action and to recognize those efforts which result in the improvement of nature.
Melissa Poe, Founder

2079 **March of Dimes Birth Defects Foundation**
1275 Mamaroneck Avenue 914-997-4488
White Plains, NY 10605 www.marchofdimes.org
The mission of the March of Dimes Birth Defects Foundation is to improve the health of babies by preventing birth defects and reducing infant mortality. The March of Dimes carries out the mission through research, community service,education and advocacy.
Ann Umemoto, Associate Director

2080 **National Institute of Child Health and Human Development**
31 Center Drive 800-370-2943
Building 31, Room 2A32 Fax: 866-760-5947
Bethesda, MD 20892-2425 NICHDInformationresourcecenter@mail.nih.gov
www.nichd.nih.gov
National Institute of Child Health and Human Development conducts and supports basic, translational, and clinical research in the biomedical, behavioral, and social sciences related to child and maternal health, in medicalrehabilitation, and in the reproductive sciences.
Diana Bianchi, Director
John N. Kennedy, President

2081 **National Parent Teachers Association**
1250 N. Pitt Street 703-518-1200
Alexandria, VA 22314 800-307-4782
Fax: 703-836-0942
info@pta.org
www.pta.org
The mission of the National PTA is to support and speak on behalf of children and youth in the school, in the community and before governmental bodies and other organizations; to assist parents in developing the skills they need toraise and protect their children and to encourage parent and public involvement in the public schools.
Laura Bay, President
Jim Accomando, President Elect

2082 **Office of Children's Health Protection**
US Environmental Protection Agency
Ariel Rios Building 202-564-2188
1200 Pennsylvania Avenue NW Fax: 202-564-2733
Washington, DC 20460 www.epa.gov
The mission of the Office of Children's Health Protection is to make the protection of children's health a fundamental goal of public health and environmental protection in the United States.
Dr. Ruth A. Etzel, M.D., Ph.D, Director

2083 **Oklahoma Childhood Lead Poisioning Prevention Program**
Oklahoma Department of Health
1000 Northeast 10th Street 405-271-5600
Room 711 800-522-0203
Oklahoma, OK 73117-1299 Fax: 405-271-4971
oklppp@health.ok.gov
lpp.health.ok.gov
Mission: To reduce blood lead levels to below a level of concern in all Oklahomans.

Pediatric Health: Publications

2084 **Child Health and the Environment**
Oxford University Press
198 Madison Avenue 212-726-6000
New York, NY 10016 800-445-9714
Fax: 919-677-1303
custserv.us@oup.com
global.oup.com
A publication on environmental threats to child health. The first three chapters provide overviews of key children's environmental health issues as well as the role of environmental epidemiology and risk assessment in child healthprotection. Later chapters address the health affects of metal, PCBs, dioxins, pesticides, hormonally active agents, radiation, indoor and outdoor air pollution, and water contaminants.
416 pages
ISBN: 0-195135-59-8
Donald T Wigle, Author

2085 **Children's Defense Fund**
25 E Street NW 202-628-8787
Washington, DC 20001 800-233-1200
cdfinfo@childrensdefense.org
www.childrensdefense.org
Mission: To ensure every child a healthy start, a head start, a fair start, a safe start, and a moral start in life and successful passage to adulthood with the help of caring families and communities.
Marian Wright Edelman, President
Lori Wood, Vice President for Field

2086 **Handbook of Pediatric Environmental Health**
American Academy of Pediatrics
141 NW Point Boulevard 847-434-4000
Elk Grove Village, IL 60007-1098 800-433-9016
Fax: 847-434-8000
www.aap.org
The AAP is committed to the attainment of optimal physical, mental and social health for all infants, children, and young adults. This mission will be accomplished by engaging in the following activities: professional education,advocacy for children

and youth, advocacy for pediatricians, public education, membership service and research.
723 pages
ISBN: 1-581100-29-9
Sandra Hassink, President
Benard P. Dreyer, President Elect

2087 Handle with Care: Children and Environmental Carcinogens
Natural Resources Defense Council
40 West 20th Street 212-727-2700
New York, NY 10011 Fax: 212-727-1773
nrdcinfo@nrdc.org
www.nrdc.org
Mission: To safeguard the Earth: its people, its plants and animals, and the natural systems on which all life depends.
50 pages
Daniel R. Tishman, Chairman
Patricia Bauman, Vice Chairman

2088 Kids Count Data Book: State Profiles of Child Well-Being
701 St. Paul Street 410-547-6600
Baltimore, MD 21202 Fax: 410-547-6624
webmail@aecf.org
www.aecf.org/work/kids-count
Kids Count is national and state-by-state effort to provide makers and citizens with benchmarks of child well-being. It includes variables such as percentage of low birth-weight babies, child death rates, percentage of childern inpoverty, and percentage of childern without health insurance.
Patrick McCarthy, President & CEO
Ryan Chao, Vice President

2089 Pesticides and the Immune System: Public Health Risks
10 G Street NE 202-729-7600
Suite 800 Fax: 202-729-7686
Washington, DC 20002 lzelin@wri.org
www.wri.org
Brings together for the frist time an extensive body of experimental and epidemiological research from around the world documenting the the effects of widely used pesticides on the immune system and the attendent health risks. In sodoing, it documents that pesticide-related health risks are much more serious than genrally known, especially in developing countries where exposure is widespread and infectious diseases take a heavy toll.
100 pages
ISBN: 1-569730-87-3
Andrew Steer, President & CEO
Manish Bapna, EVP/Managing Director

2090 Resource Guide on Children's Environmental Health
600 Grant Street 303-861-5165
Suite 800 Fax: 303-861-5315
Denver, CO 80203 info@cchn.org
www.cchn.org
The Children's Environmental Health Network has developed the Resource Guide on Childern's Environmental Health to assist community leaders, policy makers, health and environmental specialists, members of the advocacy community andmedia, and the general public in identifying and accessing key resources in childern's environmental health.
Annette Kowal, CEO
Polly Anderson, Chief Operating Officer

Environmental Law

Associations

2091 Atlantic States Legal Foundation
658 West Onondaga Street
Syracuse, NY 13204
315-475-1170
Fax: 315-475-6719
atlantic.states@aslf.org
www.aslf.org

Atlantic States Legal Foundation was established in 1982 to provide legal, technical, and organizational assistance on environment issues to citizen organizations (NGOs), individuals, local governments, and others.
Robin Chanay, Chair
Martha Loew, Vice Chair

2092 Business & Legals Reports
100 Winners Circle
Suite 300
Brentwood, TN 37027
860-510-0100
800-727-5257
Fax: 860-510-7220
service@blr.com
www.blr.com

Provides essential tools for safety and environmental compliance and training needs.
Guy Crossley, Chief Operating Officer
Dan Oswald, Chief Executive Officer

2093 Center for Community Action and Environmental Justice
PO Box 33124
Riverside, CA 92519
951-360-8451
Fax: 951-360-5950
Jean.k@ccaej.org
www.ccaej.org

The Center for Community Action and Environmental Justice serves as a resource center for community groups working on environmental justice issues.
Maggie Hawkins, President
Gwen D'Arcangelis, President-Elect

2094 Center for Health, Environment and Justice Library
105 Rowell Court
1st Floor
Falls Church, VA 22046-6806
703-237-2249
Fax: 703-237-8389
chej@chej.org
www.chej.org

The Center for Health, Environment and Justice works to build healthy communities, with social justice, economic well-being, and democratic governance. We believe this can happen when individuals from communities have the power to playan integral role in promoting human health and environmental integrity. Our role is to provide the tools to build strong, healthy communities where people can live, work, learn, play and pray.
Lois Marie Gibbs, Executive Director
Holly Gibson, Corporate Secretary

2095 Center for International Environmental Law
1350 Connecticut Avenue NW
Suite 1100
Washington, DC 20036
202-785-8700
Fax: 202-785-8701
info@ciel.org
www.ciel.org

The Center for International Environmental Law (CIEL) is a nonprofit organization working to use international law and institutions to protect the environment, promote human health, and ensure a just and sustainable society. We providea wide range of services including legal counsel, policy research, analysis, advocacy, education, training, and capacity building.
Carroll Muffett, President & CEO
Cameron Aishton, Administrator

2096 Center for Investigative Reporting
2927 Newbury Street
Suite A
Berkeley, CA 94703
510-809-3160
Fax: 510-849-1813
center@cironline.org
www.muckraker.org

The only independent, nonprofit organization in the country dedicated to investigative reporting in the public interest on a broad range of issues.
Tom Goldstein, President
Christa Scharfenberg, Acting Executive Director

2097 Communities for a Better Environment
1904 Franklin Street
Suite 600
Oakland, CA 94612
510-302-0430
Fax: 510-302-0437
cbeca@mail.com
www.cbecal.org

Mission: To achieve environmental health and justice by building grassroots power in and with communities of color and working-class communities.
Suma Peesapati, Board President
Adrian Martinez, Board Vice President

2098 Community Environmental Council
26 West Anapamu Street
2nd Floor
Santa Barbara, CA 93101
805-963-0583
Fax: 805-962-9080
cecadmin@cecmail.org
www.cecsb.org

The Community Environmental Council is a nonprofit environmental organization headquartered in Santa Barbara, California. Our community involvement includes managing two recycling centers, a household hazardous waste facility, anurban farm, and three community gardens as well as the environmental education program Art From Scrap. In addition CEC provides research, technical assistance and education on local and statewide land use planning, and solid waste and integrated pestmanagement.
Dave Davis, President & CEO
Laura Burton Capps, Vice President

2099 Community Rights Counsel
1301 Connecticut Avenue NW
Suite 502
Washington, DC 20036
202-296-6889
Fax: 202-296-6895
crc@communityrights.org
www.communityrights.org

A nonprofit public interest law firm that was formed in 1997 to assist communities in protecting their health and welfare by regulating permissible land uses, and that provides strategic assistance to state and local governmentattorneys in defending land use laws.
Douglas T Kendall, Founder/Executive Director
Timothy J Dowling, Chief Counsel

2100 Conservation Law Foundation
62 Summer Street
Boston, MA 00211
617-350-0990
Fax: 617-350-4030
www.clf.org

A nonprofit, member-supported organization that works to solve the environmental problems that threaten the people, natural resources and communities of New England. CLF's advocates use law, economics and science to design andimplement strategies that conserve natural resources, protect public health and promote vital communities in our region.
Peter Shelley, Interim President
Priscilla Brooks, Vice President

2101 Earthjustice
50 California Street
Suite 500
San Francisco, CA 94111
415-217-2000
800-584-6460
Fax: 415-217-2040
info@earthjustice.org
www.earthjustice.org

Nonprofit public interest law firm dedicated to protecting the magnificent places, natural resources, and wildlife of this earth and to defending the right of all people to a healthy environment.

It enforces and strengthensenvironmental laws on behalf of hundreds of organizations and communities.
Trip Van Noppen, President
Minna Jung, Vice President

2102 Environmental Defense Fund
257 Park Avenue South 212-505-2100
17th Floor 800-684-3322
New York, NY 10010 Fax: 212-505-2375
members@edf.org
www.edf.org

Dedicated to protecting the environmental rights of all people, including future generations. Among these rights are clean air, clean water, healthy, nourishing food and a flourishing ecosystem. Advocates solutions based on science,even when it leads in unfamiliar directions. Works to create solutions that win lasting political, economic and social support because they are bipartisan, efficient and fair
Fred Krupp, President
David Yarnold, Executive Director

2103 Environmental Law Alliance Worldwide
1877 Garden Avenue 541-687-8454
Eugene, OR 97403 Fax: 541-687-0535
elawus@elaw.org
www.elaw.org

E-LAW advocates serve low income communities around the world, helping citizens strengthen and enforce laws to protect communities from toxic pollution and environmental degradation.
Bern Johnson, Executive Director
Lori Maddox, Associate Director

2104 Environmental Law Institute
1730 M Street, NW 202-939-3800
Suite 700 Fax: 202-939-3868
Washington, DC 20036 law@eli.org
www.eli.org

Community Education and Training Program provides citizens and grassroots groups with information on environmental law and policy that can help them participate effectively in the decisions that impact public health and the environmentin their communities. Program's activities have included training courses on right-to-know laws and a series of workshops in demystifying the law, which focus on using the tools of public participation to address issues ranging from hazardous wasteto land use.
Scott Schang, President
Scott Fulton, President Elect

2105 Environmental Law and Policy Center
35 East Wacker Drive 312-673-6500
Suite 1600 ELPCinfo@ELPC.org
Chicago, IL 60601 elpc.org
Organization responsible for developing advocacy campaigns to protect environmental quality and ensure the availability of clean air, transportation, energy and water.
Daniel Levin, Chairman
Howard A Learner, President

2106 Environmental Law and Policy Center of the Midwest
35 E Wacker Drive 312-673-6500
Suite 1600 Fax: 312-795-3730
Chicago, IL 60601 www.elpc.org
Howard A. Learner, President/Executive Director
Kevin Brubaker, Deputy Director

2107 Environmental Support Center
PO Box 1816 202-331-9700
Alexandria, VA 22313 Fax: 202-331-8592
envirosupport@hotmail.com
www.envsc.org/

The mission of the Environmental Support Center is to promote the quality of the natural environment, human health, and community sustainability by increasing the organizational effectiveness of local, state, and regional organizationsworking on environmental issues and for environmental justice. To be eligible for assistance, your organization must be a local, state or regional nonprofit organization with a portion of its resources devoted to environmental issues.
Judy Hatcher, Interim Co-Director
Yudi Kidokoro, Chair

2108 Federation of Environmental Technologists
W 175 N 11081 Stonewood Dr 262-437-1700
Suite 203 Fax: 262-437-1702
Germantown, WI 53022 info@fetinc.org
www.fetinc.org

A nonprofit organization formed to assist industry in interpretation of and compliance with environmental regulations. FET is dedicated to educate its members and other environmental professionals on regulatory compliance andtechnological developments in a cost-effective manner through training, professional development and networking.
Jeffrey Nettesheim, Chair
Cheryl Moran, President/Director

2109 Getches-Wilkinson Center for Natural Resources, Energy, and The Environment
University of Colorado
2450 Kittredge Loop Road 303-492-8047
Boulder, CO 80309 Fax: 303-492-1297
gwc@colorado.edu
www.colorado.edu

To promote sustainability in the rapidly changing American West by informing and influencing natural resources policies, and decisions.
Alice Madden, Executive Director
Shaun LaBarre, Program Manager

2110 Greenpeace
702 H Street NW 202-884-7615
Suite 300 800-722-6995
Washington, DC 20001 info@WDC.greenpeace.org
www.Greenpeaceusa.org

Greenpeace is an independent campaigning organization which uses non-violent creative confrontation to expose global environmental problems, and to force solutions that are essential to a green and peaceful future.
Phil Radford, Executive Director
David Barre, Communication Director

2111 Harvard Environmental Law Society
Harvard Law School
1585 Massachusetts Avenue 617-495-3125
Cambridge, MA 00213 els@mail.law.harvard.edu
www.law.harvard.edu/students/orgs/els

The Harvard Environmental Law Society was founded by three Harvard Law students who perceived a pressing need for the Law School, and the law in general, to respond more effectively to the nation's environmental problems. To this end,they created an organization that was committed to preparing students to creatively and intelligently use the law in the service of the environment.
Alice Cherry, Co-President
Kelsey Skaggs, Co-President

2112 Humane Society Legislative Fund
2100 L Street NW 202-676-2314
Suite 310 866-720-2676
Washington, DC 20037 humanesociety@hslf.org
www.hslf.org

Humane Society Legislative Fund (HSLF) is a social welfare organization. HSLF works to pass animal protection laws at the

state and federal level, to educate the public about animal protection issues, and to support humane candidatesfor office.
Michael Markarian, President
Wayne Pacelle, Executive Vice President

2113 International Land Conservation Network
617-661-3016
landconservationnetwork.org
The International Land Conservation Network connects organizations around the world that focus on the conservation, management, and development of land and water resources. They provide research, training, information regardingfinance, law, organization, stewardship and regional capacity building.
Laura Johnson, Director
Jivan Sobrinho-Wheeler, Project Coordinator

2114 LandWatch Monterey County
PO Box 1876 831-759-2824
Salinas, CA 93902-1876 Fax: 831-759-2825
landwatch@mclw.org
www.landwatch.org
LandWatch is a nonprofit membership organization, founded in 1997. LandWatch works to promote and inspire sound land use legislation at the city, country, and regional lands, through grassroots community action.
Chris Fitz, President
Amy White, Executive Director

2115 League of Conservation Voters
1920 L Street NW 202-785-8683
Suite 800 Fax: 202-835-0491
Washington, DC 20036 seth_stein@lcv.org
www.lcv.org
Works to create a Congress more responsive to your environmental concerns. As the nonpartisan political voice for over nine million members of environmental and conservation groups, LCV is the only national environmental organizationdedicated full-time to educating citizens about the environmental voting records of Members of Congress.
Carol Browner, Chair
Gene Karpinski, President

2116 League of Women Voters of the United States
1730 M Street NW 202-429-1965
Suite 1000 Fax: 202-429-0854
Washington, DC 20036-4508 lwv@lwv.org
www.lwv.org
The League of Women Voters, a nonpartisan political organization, encourages the informed and active participation of citizens in government, works to increase understanding of major public policy issues and influences public policythrough education and advocacy.
Elisabeth MacNamara, President
Toni Larson, Vice President

2117 Legacy International
1020 Legacy Drive 540-297-5982
Bedford, VA 24523 Fax: 540-297-1860
mail@legacyintl.org
www.legacyintl.org
Creates environments where people can address personal, community, and global needs while developing skills and effective responses to change.Whether working with youths, corporate leaders, educational professionals, entrepreneurs, orindividuals on opposing sides of a conflict, our goal is the same. Programs provide experiences, skills, and strategies that enable people to build better lives for themselves and others around them.
J E Rash, President
Shanti Thompson, VP/Director of Training

2118 National Association of Conservation Districts League City Office
509 Capitol Ct NE 202-547-6223
Washington, DC 20002 Fax: 202-547-6450
www.nacdnet.org
To serve conservation districts by providing national leadership and a unified voice for natural resource conservation.
David Guenther, President
Jeremy Peters, Chief Executive Officer

2119 Natural Resources Defense Council
40 West 20th Street 212-727-2700
New York, NY 10011 Fax: 212-727-1773
nrdcinfo@nrdc.org
www.nrdc.org
The NRDC focuses on issues impacting climate change, ocean pollution, water management and treatment, clean energy, and the conservation of wildlife.
Rhea Suh, President
Mitchell Bernard, Chief Counsel

2120 New Mexico Environmental Law Center
1405 Luisa Street 505-989-9022
Suite 5 Fax: 505-989-3769
Santa Fe, NM 87505 nmelc@nmelc.org
www.nmenvirolaw.org
The New Mexico Environmental Law Center works to protect New Mexico's communities and their environments through public education, legislative initiatives, administrative negotiations and litigation.
Douglas Meiklejohn, Executive Director
Shelbie Knox, Development Officer

2121 Southern Environmental Law Center
201 W Main Street 434-977-4090
Suite 14 Fax: 434-977-1483
Charlottesville, VA 22902 selcva@selcva.org
www.southernenvironment.org
Dedicated to protecting the natural resources of Alabama, Georgia, North Carolina, South Carolina, Tennessee and Virginia. Works with more than 100 partner groups to safeguard southern forests, wetlands, coastal resources, rivers, airand water quality, wildlife habitat and rural landscapes through policy reform, public education, and direct legal action.
Dennis M. Crumpler, President
Rick Middleton, Executive Director

2122 Stanford Environmental Law Society
559 Nathan Abbott Way 650-723-4421
Stanford, CA 94305-8610 elj.stanford.edu/
Provides students with a unique set of opportunities to tap into structured programs or to create and pursue their own projects. Both organizations complement the Stanford Environmental and Natural Reources Law and Policy Program.
Zachary Fabish, Co-President
Craig Segall, Co-President

2123 Student Environmental Action Coalition
PO Box 31909 215-222-4711
Philadelphia, PA 19104 webteam@seac.org
Student and youth run national network of progressive organizations and individuals whose aim is to uproot environmental injustices through action and education. Works to create progressive social change on both the local and globallevels.
Matt Reitmann, Working Comte Coordinator

2124 US Public Interest Research Group
294 Washington St 617-747-4370
Suite 500 Fax: 202-546-2461
Boston, MA 00210 webmaster@pirg.org
www.uspirg.org

Mission: To deliver persistent, result-oriented public interest activism that protects our environment, encourages a fair, sustainable economy, and fosters responsive, democratic government.
Douglas H Phelps, President
Andre Delattre, Executive Director

2125 Western Environmental Law Center
1216 Lincoln Street
Eugene, OR 97401
541-485-2471
Fax: 541-485-2457
info@westernlaw.org
www.westernlaw.org

The Western Environmental Law Center is a non-profit public interest law firm that works to protect and restore western wildlands and advocates for healthy environments on behalf of communities throughout the West.
Lori Maddox, President
Karin P. Sheldon, Vice President

Publications

2126 A Guide to Environmental Law in Washington DC
Environmental Law Institute
1730 M Street, NW
Suite 700
Washington, DC 20036
202-939-3800
Fax: 202-939-3868
law@eli.org
www.eli.org
Community Education and Training Program provides citizens and grassroots groups with information on environmental law and policy that can help them participate effectively in the decisions that impact public health and the environmentin their communities. Program's activities have included training courses on right-to-know laws and a series of workshops in demystifying the law, which focus on using the tools of public participation to address issues ranging from hazardous wasteto land use.
Scott Schang, President
Scott Fulton, President Elect

2127 Buying Green: Federal Purchasing Practices and the Environment
Government Printing Office
732 North Capitol Street NW
Washington, DC 20401-0001
202-512-1800
866-512-1800
Fax: 202-512-2104
ContactCenter@gpo.gov
www.gpo.gov

Jim Breadley, Deputy Director
Andrew M. Sherman, Cheif of Staff

2128 Clean Water Act Twenty Years Later
Island Press
2000 M Street NW
Suite 650
Washington, DC 20036
202-232-7933
Fax: 202-234-1328
info@islandpress.org
www.islandpress.org

333 pages
ISBN: 1-559632-65-8
Richard W Alder; Jessica C Landman; Diane Cameron, Author
Charles C. Savitt, President
David Miller, SVP/Editor

2129 Comparative Environmental Law and Regulation
Oceana Publications, Inc
198 Madison Avenue
New York, NY 10016
800-334-4249
Fax: 212-726-6476
oxfordonline@oup.com
www.oceanalaw.com
Key environmental laws, regulations and implementation systems and agencies of 37 countries from around the world.
2 vol pages Semi-Annual
ISBN: 0-379012-51-0
Nicholas A Robinson, Editor

2130 Environmental Defense Fund
257 Park Avenue South
17th Floor
New York, NY 10010
212-505-2100
800-684-3322
Fax: 212-505-2375
members@edf.org
www.edf.org
Dedicated to protecting the environmental rights of all people, including future generations. Among these rights are clean air, clean water, healthy nourishing food and a flourishing ecosystem. Advocates solutions based on science,even when it leads in unfamiliar directions. Works to create solutions that win lasting political, economic and social support because they are bipartisan, efficient and fair.
Fred Krupp, President
David Yarnold, Executive Director

2131 Environmental Defense Newsletter
257 Park Avenue South
17th Floor
New York, NY 10010
212-505-2100
800-684-3322
Fax: 212-505-2375
members@edf.org
www.edf.org

Dedicated to protecting the environmental rights of all people, including future generations. Among these rights are clean air, clean water, healthy, nourishing food and a flourishing ecosystem. The solutions we advocate will be basedon science, even when it leads in unfamiliar directions. We will work to create solutions that win lasting political, economic and social support because they are bipartisan, efficient and fair.
Fred Krupp, President
David Yarnold, Executive Director

2132 Environmental Law and Compliance Methods
Oceana Publications, Inc
198 Madison Avenue
New York, NY 10016
800-334-4249
Fax: 212-726-6476
www.oceanalaw.com

Presents practical information tailored to professionals responsible for day-to-day compliance with the environmental laws of the US.
678 pages One Time
ISBN: 0-379214-26-1
Edward E Shea, Author

2133 Environmental Politics and Policy
Congressional Quarterly Press
1255 22nd Street NW
Suite 400
Washington, DC 20037
202-729-1800
366 pages
ISBN: 1-568028-78-4
Walker A Rosenbaum, Author

2134 Environmental Regulatory Glossary
Government Institutes
4 Research Place
Suite 200
Rockville, MD 20850
301-921-2300
Fax: 301-921-0373
623 pages
Thomas F P Sullivan, Author

2135 How Wet is a Wetland?: The Impacts of the Proposed Revisions to the Federal Wetlands Manual
Environmental Defense Fund
257 Park Avenue South
17th Floor
New York, NY 10010
212-505-2100
Fax: 212-505-2375
members@edf.org
www.edf.org
To prevent environmentally induced harm to human populations.
Fred Krupp, President
David Yarnold, Executive Director

2136 Insider's Guide to Environmental Negotiation
Lewis Publishers
PO Box 72264
Albany, GA 31708
229-432-1781
tlewis@lewispub.com
www.lewispub.com
242 pages
ISBN: 0-873715-09-8
Dale M Gorczynski, Author

2137 International Environmental Policy: From the Twentieth to the Twenty-First Century
Duke University Press
905 W Main Street, Ste 18-B
Durham, NC 27701
919-688-5134
888-651-0122
Fax: 919-688-2615
www.dukepress.com
496 pages
Ken Wissoker, Editor in Chief
Courtney Berger, Assistant Editor

2138 Making Development Sustainable: Redefining Institutions, Policy, and Economics
Island Press
2000 M Street NW
Suite 650
Washington, DC 20036
202-232-7933
Fax: 202-234-1328
info@islandpress.org
www.islandpress.org
362 pages
ISBN: 1-559632-13-5
Johan Holmberg, Author
Charles C. Savitt, President
David Miller, SVP/Editor

2139 Managing Planet Earth: Perspectives on Population, Ecology and the Law
Greenwood Publishing Group
130 Cremona Drive
Santa Barbara, CA 93117
805-968-1911
800-368-6868
Fax: 866-270-3856
CustomerService@abc-clio.com
www.abc-clio.com
184 pages
ISBN: 0-897892-16-X
Miguel A Santos, Author
Vince Burns, Vice President

2140 Natural Resources Policy and Law: Trends and Directions
Island Press; Natural Resources Law Center
2000 M Street NW
Suite 650
Washington, DC 20036
202-232-7933
Fax: 202-234-1328
info@islandpress.org
www.islandpress.org
255 pages
ISBN: 1-559632-46-1
Lawrence J MacDonnell; Sarah F Bates, Author
Charles C. Savitt, President
David Miller, SVP/Editor

2141 New Mexico Environmental Law Center: Green Fire Report
1405 Luisa Street
Suite 5
Santa Fe, NM 87505
505-989-9022
Fax: 505-989-3769
nmelc@nmelc.org
www.nmenvirolaw.org
A publication from the organization dedicated to protecting New Mexico's natural environment and communities from pollution and degradation. Over 80 percent of our clients are indigenous Native American or Hispanic and low income.Cases often include mining issues, growth impacts, water protection, air pollution, public lands protection or indigenous land claims. The organization is supported by grants from foundations, contributions from individuals and fees.
12 pages Quarterly
Douglas Meiklejohn, Executive Director
Shelbie Knox, Development Officer

2142 Oversight of Implementation of the Clean Air Act Amendments of 1990
Government Printing Office
1616 P Street NW
Washington, DC 20036
202-328-5000
Fax: 202-939-3460
contactcenter@gpo.gov
www.rff.org
ISBN: 0-160388-26-0
Dana Yanocha, Development Officer
Adrienne Young, Managing Editor

2143 People for the Ethical Treatment of Animals
501 Front Street
Norfolk, VA 23510
757-622-7382
Fax: 757-622-0457
info@peta.org
www.peta.org
People for the Ethical Treatment of Animals, with more than seven hundred members, is the largest animal rights organization in the world. Founded in 1980, PETA is dedicated to establishing and protecting the rights of all animals.PETA operates under the simple principle that animals are not ours to eat, wear, experiment on, or use for entertainment.
Kathy Guillermo, Senior Vice President, Labor
Tracy Reiman, Executive Vice President

2144 Renewable Resource Policy: The Legal-Institutional Foundation
Island Press
2000 M Street NW
Suite 650
Washington, DC 20036
202-232-7933
Fax: 202-234-1328
info@islandpress.org
www.islandpress.org
572 pages
ISBN: 1-559632-25-9
Charles C. Savitt, President
David Miller, SVP/Editor

2145 Saving All the Parts: Reconciling Economics and the Endangered Species Act
Island Press
2000 M Street NW
Suite 650
Washington, DC 20036
202-232-7933
Fax: 202-234-1328
info@islandpress.org
www.islandpress.org
280 pages
ISBN: 1-559632-02-X
Rocky Barker, Author
Charles C. Savitt, President
David Miller, SVP/Editor

2146 Searching Out the Headwaters: Change and Rediscovery in Western Policy
Island Press

2000 M Street NW
Suite 650
Washington, DC 20036
202-232-7933
Fax: 202-234-1328
info@islandpress.org
www.islandpress.org

253 pages
ISBN: 1-559632-17-8
Sarah F Bates, et al, Author
Charles C. Savitt, President
David Miller, SVP/Editor

2147 Setting National Priorities: Policy for the Nineties

Brookings Institution
1775 Massachusetts Ave., NW
Washington, DC 20036
202-797-6000
800-275-1447
Fax: 202-797-6004
www.brookings.edu

Strobe Talbott, President
Martin S Indyk, Executive Vice President

2148 Trade and the Environment: Law, Economics and Policy

Island Press
2000 M Street NW
Suite 650
Washington, DC 20036
202-232-7933
Fax: 202-234-1328
info@islandpress.org
www.islandpress.org

333 pages
ISBN: 1-559632-67-4
Charles C. Savitt, President
David Miller, SVP/Editor

2149 Understanding Environmental Administration and Law

Island Press
2000 M Street NW
Suite 650
Washington, DC 20036
202-232-7933
Fax: 202-234-1328
info@islandpress.org
www.islandpress.org

239 pages
ISBN: 1-559634-74-X
Susan J Buck, Author
Charles C. Savitt, President
David Miller, SVP/Editor

Financial Resources

Foundations & Charities

2150 AMETEK Foundation
1100 Cassatt Road 610-647-2121
PO Box 1764 800-473-1286
Berwyn, PA 19312 Fax: 215-323-9337
webmaster@ametek.com
www.ametek.com
AMETEK is a global manufacturer of electronic insturments and electric motors. The AMETEK Foundation provides funding for community programs such as science education for children. The products made by this company supportenvironmental sustainability, the production of renewable fuels and solar energy.
Frank S. Hermance, Chairman
David A. Zapico, CEO

2151 ARCO Foundation
515 South Flower Street 213-486-3342
Los Angeles, CA 90071 www.southlandarchitecture.com
The foundation awards education grants both on the national and regional level. Education programs that are national in scope are funded through the headquarters located in Los Angeles. Regional grants are made to nonprofitorganizations in states where ARCO has facilities and personnel.
Russell Sakaguchi, Program Officer

2152 Abelard Foundation
2530 San Pable Avenue 510-644-1904
Suite B
Berkeley, CA 94702
A family foundation with a 40 year history of progressive funding. The foundation is committed to supporting grassroots social change organizations which engage in community organizing.
Leah Brumer, Executive Director

2153 Acid Rain Foundation
1410 Varsity Drive 919-828-9443
Raleigh, NC 27606 Fax: 919-515-3593
Designed to significantly reduce emissions responsible for acid deposition.
Dr. Harriet S Stubbs, Executive Director

2154 African Wildlife Foundation
1400 Sixteenth Street, NW 202-939-3333
Suite 120 888-494-5354
Washington, DC 20036 Fax: 202-939-3332
africanwildlife@awf.org
www.awf.org
The African Wildlife Foundation, together with the people of Africa, work to ensure the wildlife and wild lands of Africa will endure forever. The AFW is the leading international conservation organization focused soley on Africa. Webelieve that protecting Africa's wildlife and wild landscapes is the key to the future prosperity of Africa and its people.
Jef Dupain, Director
Fiesta Warinwa, Program Director

2155 Amax Foundation
200 Park Avenue 212-856-4250
New York, NY 10166
Sonja Michaud, President

2156 American Association of Petroleum Geologists Foundation
1444 S. Boulder 918-584-2555
Tulsa, OK 74119 800-364-2274
Fax: 918-560-2665
info@aapg.org
www.aapg.org
News for explorationists of oil, gas and minerals as well as for geologists with environmental and water well concerns.
John R Hogg, President
Paul W Britt, President Elect

2157 American Electric Power
1 Riverside Plaza 614-716-1000
Columbus, OH 43215-2372 corpcomm@aep.com
www.aep.com
One of the largest electric utilities in the United States, delivering electricity to more then 5 million customers in 11 states. AEP ranks among the nations largest generators of electricity, owning more then 38,000 megawatts ofgenerating capacity in the US.
Nicholas K. Akins, President & CEO
Robert P. Powers, Executive Vice President

2158 American Rivers
1101 14th Street NW 202-347-7550
Suite 1400 877-347-7550
Washington, DC 20005 Fax: 202-347-9240
outreach@americanrivers.org
www.americanrivers.org
Support and donations for the protection and restoration of America's rivers for the benefit of people, fish and wildlife.
William Robert (Bob) Irvin, President
Sandra Adams, Senior VP Advertising

2159 Amoco Foundation
501 Westlake Park Boulevard 312-856-6306
Houston, TX 77079 bpconsum@bp.com
www.bp.com
The BP Amoco awards grants for education, primarily in the field of science and engineering, as well as community organizations in BP Amoco communities.
Dr. Brian Gilvary, CFO
Bernard Looney, COO Production

2160 Andrew W. Mellon Foundation
140 East 62nd Street 212-838-8400
New York, NY 10065 Fax: 212-888-4172
inquiries@mellon.org
www.mellon.org
The foundation concentrates most of its grantmaking in a few areas. Institutions and programs receiving support are often leaders in fields of Foundation activity, but they may also be promising newcomers, or in a position todemonstrate new ways of overcoming obstacles to achieve program goals.
Earl Lewis, President
Mariët Westermann, Vice President

2161 Asthma and Allergy Foundation of America
8201 Corporate Drive 202-466-7643
Suite 1000 800-727-8462
Landover, MD 20785 Fax: 202-466-8940
info@aafa.org
www.aafa.org
Dedicated to improving the quality of life for people with asthma and allergies through education, advocacy and research.
Heidi Bayer, Chair
James Flood, Chair, Finance & Treasurer

2162 Atherton Family Foundation
827 Fort Street Mall
Honolulu, HI 96813
808-566-5524
888-731-3863
Fax: 808-521-6286
foundations@hcf-hawaii.org
www.athertonfamilyfoundation.org

The Atherton Family Foundation is now one of the largest endowed grantmaking private resource in the State of Hawaii, devoted exclusively to the support of charutabe activities. It perpetuates the philanthropic commitment expressedduring the lifetime of Juliette M. Atherton and Frank C. Atherton, and of the family who have followed them.

Judith M. Dawson, President
Frank C. Atherton, Vice President & Treasurer

2163 Audubon Naturalist Society of the Central Atlantic States
8940 Jones Mill Road
Chevy Chase, MD 20815
301-652-9188
Fax: 301-951-7179
contact@audubonnaturalist.org
www.audubonnaturalist.org

The Audubon Naturalist Society is an independent environmental education and conservation organization with over 10,000 members in the Washington DC area. The society offers a wide variety of natural history classes and campaigns forprotection and renewal of the Mid-Atlantic regions natural resources.

Lee Babcock, President
Leslie Catherwood, Vice President

2164 BP America
501 Westlake Park Boulevard
Houston, TX 77079
281-366-2000
bpconsum@bp.com
www.bp.com

The purpose is to provide products that satisfy human needs, fuel progress and economic growth and to maintain and invest in a sustainable environment.

Dr. Brian Gilvary, CFO
Bernard Looney, COO Production

2165 Baltimore Gas & Electric Foundation
PO Box 1475
Baltimore, MD 21203
410-265-4100
800-685-0123
Fax: 410-234-7123
corporate.communications@bge.com
www.bge.com

The mission is to safely, economically, reliably, and profitably deliver gas and electricity to our customers. The vision is to be a recognized leader in energy delivery by enhancing our customer's quality of life, our shareholdersvalue, and our team's well being.

Stephen J Woerner PE, President & COO
Calvin G Butler, Chief Executive Officer

2166 Bauman Foundation
2040 S Street, NW
Washington, DC 20009
202-328-2040
Fax: 202-328-2003
www.baumanfoundation.org

The Bauman Foundation was funded by the estate of Lionel R. Bauman, a New York City lawyer and businessman. He was a partner in the real estate development firm of Eugene M. Grant & Co. The foundation is managed by Lionel's daughter.Patricia Bauman.

Patricia Bauman, President
John Landrum Bryant, Vice President & Treasurer

2167 Bay and Paul Foundations, The
17 West 94th Street
1st Floor
New York, NY 10025
212-663-1115
Fax: 212-932-0316
info@bayandpaul.org
www.bayandpaulfoundations.org

The Bay and Paul Foundations Inc. was formed in January 2005 by the merger of 2 foundations. The Bay Foundation and the Josephine Bay Paul and C. Michael Paul Foundation.

David Bury, Chairman
Fred Bay, President & CEO

2168 Blandin Foundation
100 North Pokegama Avenue
Grand Rapids, MI 55744
218-326-0523
877-882-2257
Fax: 218-327-1949
www.blandinfoundation.org

Blandin Foundation is focused on the economic viability of rural Minnesota communities, as part of our mission to help strengthen rural Minnesota and the Grand Rapids area, our home.

Annette Kathy, President
Wade Fauth, Vice President

2169 Boise Cascade Corporation
1111 West Jefferson Street
Suite 300
Boise, ID 83728-5389
208-384-6161
Fax: 208-384-7189
bcweb@bc.com
www.bc.com

As we focus on delivering the best return for our investors, we can be trusted to do what we say and take responsibility for our actions, which we base on values and principles.

Duane McDougall, Chairman
Thomas Carlile, CEO

2170 Cape Branch Foundation
5 Independence Way
Princeton, NJ 00854
609-987-0300
Fax: 609-452-1024

A private foundation which provides grant support for higher education, museums, and land conservation in the New Jersey area. There are no grants to individuals.

Dorothy Frank, Partner

2171 Cargill Foundation
PO Box 9300
Minneapolis, MN 55440-9300
952-742-2546
800-227-4455
Fax: 952-742-7224
www.cargill.com

Cargill is an international provider of food, agricultural and risk management products and services. With 158,000 employees in 66 countries, the company is committed to using its knoweldge and experience to collaborate with customersto help them succeed.

Gregory R. Page, Chairman & CEO
David W MacLennan, President, COO & CFO

2172 Caribbean Conservation Corporation
4424 NW 13th Street
Suite B-11
Gainesville, FL 32609
352-373-6441
800-678-7853
Fax: 352-375-2449
stc@conserveturtles.org
www.conserveturtles.org

Caribbean Conservation Corporation is a nonprofit membership organization based in Gainesville. CCC was the first marine turtle conservation organization in the world, and has more than 40 years of experience in national andinternational sea turtle conservation, research and educational endeavors.

Landon T. Clay, Chairman
Laura Forte, President

2173 Carolyn Foundation
1917 Logan Avenue South
Minneapolis, MN 55403
612-596-3266
612-596-3279
Fax: 612-979-2670
berdahl@carolynfoundation.org
www.carolynfoundation.org

The Carolyn Foundation is a small general foundation. Please check out our website www.carolynfoundation.org for the most

up-to-date information regarding funding priorities, guidelines and application process.
Becky Erdahl, Executive Director
Caroline Partoll, Administrator

2174 Caterpillar Foundation
501 Southwest Jefferson Avenue 309-675-1000
Peoria, IL 61630 888-614-4328
www.caterpillar.com
Provides funding and support from a corporate perspective. Formed in 1952, the Foundation has distributed almost $200 million to support education, health and human services, and civic, cultural, and environmental causes.
Doug Oberhalman, Chairman & CEO
Edward J Scott, Treasurer

2175 Charles Engelhard Foundation
645 5th Avenue 212-935-2430
7th Floor
New York, NY 10022
Provides funding to a wide range of causes including education, medical research, cultural institutions, and wildlife conservation.
Elaine Catterall, Secretary

2176 Chesapeake Bay Foundation
6 Herndon Avenue 410-268-8816
Annapolis, MD 21403 Fax: 410-268-6687
chesapeake@cbf.org
www.cbf.org
The only independent organization dedicated soley to restoring and protecting the Chesapeake Bay and its tributary rivers.
William C Baker, President
Katharene Snavely, Vice President, Development

2177 Chevron Corporation
6001 Bollinger Canyon Road 925-842-1000
San Ramon, CA 94583 chevweb@chevron.com
www.chevron.com
As a global enterprise that is highly competitive across all energy sectors, Chevron brings together a wealth of talent, shared values and a strong commitment to developing vital energy resources worldwide.
John S Watson, Chairman
Alexander B Cummings, Executive Vice President

2178 Clean Water Action
1444 Eye Street NW 202-895-0420
Suite 400 Fax: 202-895-0438
Washington, DC 20005 cwa@cleanwater.org
www.cleanwateraction.org
Clean Water Action is a national organization of diverse people and groups working together for clean water, protecting health, creating jobs and making democracy work.
David Tykulsker, Chair
Robert Wendelgass, President

2179 Collins Foundation
1618 SW 1st Avenue 503-227-7171
Suite 505 Fax: 503-295-3794
Portland, OR 97201 information@collinsfoundation.org
www.collinsfoundation.org
An independent private foundation, exists to improve, enrich and give greater expression to the religious, educational, cultural, and scientific endeavors in the state of Oregon and to assist in improving the quality of life in thestate.
Truman W. Collins Jr., President
Cynthia G Adams, Executive Vice President

2180 Compton Foundation
101 Montgomery Street 415-391-9001
Suite 850 Fax: 415-391-9005
San Francisco, CA 94104 info@comptonfoundation.org
www.comptonfoundation.org
Seeks to foster human and ecological security by addressing contemporary threats to these inalienable rights. We support responsible stewardship that respects the rights of future generations to a balanced and healthy ecology, bothpersonal and global, allowing for the full richness of human experience.
Rebecca DiDomenico, President
Rebecca DiDomenico, Vice President

2181 Conservation International
2011 Crystal Drive 703-341-2400
Suite 500 800-429-5660
Arlington, VA 22202 Fax: 202-887-5188
community@conservation.org
www.conservation.org
Our mission is to conserve the Earth's living natural heritage, our global biodiversity, and to demonstrate that human societies are able to live harmoniously with nature.
Peter A Seligmann, Chairman of the Board

2182 Conservation Treaty Support Fund
3705 Cardiff Road 301-654-3150
Chevy Chase, MD 20815 800-654-3150
Fax: 301-652-6390
CTSF's mission is to support the major inter-governmental treaties which conserve wild natural resrouces and habitat for their own sake and the benefit of the people. These includ the Endangered Species Convention and the InternationalWetlands Convention. CTSF raises support for treaty projects from indivudals, corporations, foundations and government agencies. It also develops educational and informational materials including videos and the CITES Endangered Species Book.
1986 pages
George A Furness Jr, President

2183 Conservation and Research Foundation
PO Box 909 913-268-0076
Shelburne, VT 05482 Fax: 913-268-0076
conservationresearch.wordpress.com
Dr Mary Wetzel, President
Philip M Lintilhac, Secretary

2184 Cooper Industries Foundation
1000 Eaton Boulevard 713-209-8400
Cleveland, OH 44122 Fax: 713-209-8982
www.cooperindustries.com
Cooper was primarily a one-market company, manufactguring power and compression equipment for the transmission of natural gas. Eventually broadening its product lines to include petroleum and industrial equipment, electrical powerequipment, automotive products tools and hardware.
Alexander M Cutler, Chairman & CEO
Kenneth F Davis, President, Vehicle Group

2185 Cricket Foundation
Exchange Place 617-570-1130
Suite 2200 Fax: 617-523-1231
Boston, MA 00210
Dedicated to improving the quality of life
George W Butterworth III, Counsel

2186 Curtis and Edith Munson Foundation
1320 19th Street 202-887-8992
Suite 500 Fax: 202-887-8987
Washington, DC 20036 info@munsonfdn.org
www.munsonfdn.org
Over the past 15 years, we have emphasized partnerships, collaborations, and seed funding for new projects and organizations

within the framework of our programs as defined by our guidelines.
C Wolcott Henry III, President
Angel Braestrup, Executive Director

2187 Deer Creek Foundation
20701 N. MacArthur Blvd 314-241-3228
Edmond, OK 73012 dcsfoundation.org
Projects should focus on the preservation and advancement of majority rule in our society, including the protection of basic rights
Rich DiAngelo, President
Gerald Elrod, Vice President

2188 Defenders of Wildlife
1130 17th Street NW 202-682-9400
Washington, DC 20036 800-385-9712
Fax: 202-682-1331
defenders@mail.defenders.org
www.defenders.org
Dedicated to the protection of all native wild animals and plants in their natural communities. Focus is placed on what scientists consider two of the most serious environmental threats to the planet: the accelerating rate ofextinction of species and the associated loss of biological diversity, and habitat alteration and destruction. Long known for leadership on endangered species issues.
Jamie Rappaport Clark, President & CEO

2189 Dunspaugh-Dalton Foundation
1501 Venera Avenue 305-668-4192
Suite 312 Fax: 305-668-4247
Coral Gables, FL 33146 ddf@dunspaughdalton.org
www.dunspaughdalton.com
Supports educational, social, medical and cultural institutions in Florida, California and North Carolina.
Sarah Lane Bonner, President
Aexina H Lane, Vice President

2190 Earth Society Foundation
238 E 58th Street 212-832-3659
Suite 2400 Fax: 212-826-6213
New York, NY 10022 earthsociety1@hotmail.com
earthsocietyfoundation.org
Started the original Earth Day, which is devoted to peace, justice and the care of earth. It invites everyone to think and act as trustees of earth.
Thomas C Dowd, President
Helen Garland, Chairperson

2191 EarthShare
7735 Old Georgetown Road 240-333-0300
Suite 900 800-875-3863
Bethesda, MD 20814 Fax: 240-333-0301
info@earthshare.org
www.earthshare.org
A nationwide network of America's leading non-profit environmental and conservation organizations, works to promote environmental education and charitable giving through workplace giving campaigns.
Marci Reed, Executive Director
Don Kandel, CFO

2192 Echoing Green
462 Seventh Avenue 212-689-1165
Thirteenth Floor Fax: 212-689-9010
New York, NY 10001 info@echoinggreen.org
www.echoinggreen.org
Echoing Green is a global science venture fund that provides seed funding and support to visionary leaders with bold new ideas for social change.
David C Hodgson, Chairman
Maya Ajmera, Co-Chairman

2193 Edward John Noble Foundation
Po Box 954 203-438-5690
Ridgefield, CT 00687
EJ Noble Smith, Executive Director

2194 Energy Foundation
301 Battery Street 415-561-6700
5th Floor Fax: 415-561-6709
San Francisco, CA 94111 energyfund@ef.org
www.ef.org
The Energy Foundation is a partnership of major donors interested in solving the world's energy problems by promoting energy efficiency and renewable energy.
Eric Heitz, CEO & Co-Founder
Mark Burget, VP, Regional Director

2195 Environmental Law Institute
1730 M Street, NW 202-939-3800
Suite 700 Fax: 202-939-3868
Washington, DC 20036 law@eli.org
www.eli.org
Provides information services, advice, publications, training courses, seminars, research programs and policy recommendations to engage and empower environmental leaders the world over.
Scott Schang, President
Scott Fulton, President Elect

2196 Exxon Education Foundation
225 E John W Carpenter Freeway 972-444-1000
Room 1429 www.exxon.com
Irving, TX 75062
It is ExxonMobil's longstanding belief that education is the key to progress, development and economic growth, and we are committed to being a responsible partner in the communities where we operate.
Leonard Fleischer, Mgr. Corporate Contributions

2197 First Hawaiian Foundation
999 S Bishop Street 808-525-7000
29th Floor www.fhb.com
Honolulu, HI 96813
First Hawaiian Foundation is the charitable arm of First Hawaiian Bank. The foundation funds educational opportunities, access to health care, services for children and youth, human service needs, and the many ways that the arts enrichour lives.
Herbert E Wolff, Secretary

2198 First Interstate Bank of Nevada Foundation
PO Box 11007 775-784-3844
Reno, NV 89520 www.firstinterstatebank.com
Kevin Day, President

2199 FishAmerica Foundation
1001 North Fairfax St. 703-519-9691
Suite 501 Fax: 703-519-1872
Alexandria, VA 22314 fafgrants@asafishing.org
www.fishamerica.org
Unites the sportfishing industry with conservation groups, government natural resource agencies, corporations, and charitable foundations to invest in fish and habitat conservation and research across the country.
Jeff Marble, Chairman
Patrick Egan, Grants Manager

2200 FishAmerica Foundation.
Grant Guidelines
1001 North Fairfax St. 703-519-9691
Suite 501 Fax: 703-519-1872
Alexandria, VA 22314 fafgrants@asafishing.org
www.fishamerica.org

The FishAmerica Foundation provides funding for local, hands-on projects to enhance fish populations, restore fisheries habitat, improve water quality, and advancing fisheries research in North America; thereby increasing theopportunity for sportfishing success.
Jeff Marble, Chairman
Patrick Egan, Grants Manager

2201 Friends of the Earth Foundation
1100 15th Street NW 202-783-7400
11th Floor 877-843-8687
Washington, DC 20005 Fax: 202-783-0444
foe@foe.org
www.foe.org

National nonprofit advocacy organization dedicated to protecting the planet from environmental degradation; preserving biological, cultural and ethnic diversity, and empowering citizens to have an influential voice in decisionsaffecting the quality of their environment and their lives.
Erich Pica, President
Michelle Chan, Vice-President, Programs

2202 Frost Foundation
511 Armijo 505-986-0208
Suite A info@frostfound.org
Santa Fe, NM 87501 www.frostfound.org
Created to be operated exclusively for educational, charitable and religious purposes. The foundation possesses all powers, rights, privileges, capacities and immunities which non profit corporations are authorized to possess.
Mary Amelia Whited-Howell, President
Philip B. Howell, Executive Vice President

2203 Fund for Animals
200 West 57th Street 212-246-2096
New York, NY 10019 866-482-3708
Fax: 212-246-2633
info@fundforanimals.org
www.fundforanimals.org/about/

The Fund for Animals was founded in 1967 by author/humanitarian Cleveland Amory to speak for those who can't. In 2005, The Fund for Animals merged with The Humane Society of the United States, to avoid duplication of program andincrease strength and coordination in the areas of legislation, litigation, humane education and disaster relief.
Marian G Probst, Chair
Michael Markarian, President

2204 Fund for Preservation of Wildlife and Natural Areas
Boston Safe Deposit and Trust Company
1 Boston Place 617-722-7340
Boston, MA 00210 Fax: 617-722-7129
Accounting services for mutual fund companies.
Sylvia Salas, Director

2205 George B Storer Foundation
220 South King Street 307-733-0800
Jackson, WY 83001 info@storerfoundation.org
storerfoundation.org

Provides support for higher education and social services, especially for the blind, youth organizations, conservation, hospitals, and cultural programs.
Peter Storer, Chairman
Elizabeth Storer, President & CEO

2206 Georgia Pacific Foundation
133 Peachtree Street NE 404-652-4000
Atlanta, GA 30303 www.gp.com
Invests in educational efforts that empower youth, and provide workers with job readiness training. We also invest in scholarships and technical programs that give workers the skills necessary for today's workplace.
Curley M Dossman, President
Michael E. Adams, SVP, Sourcing

2207 Geraldine R. Dodge Foundation
14 Maple Avenue 973-540-8442
Suite 400 Fax: 973-540-1211
Morristown, NJ 00796 info@grdodge.org
www.grdodge.org

The mission of the Geraldine R. Dodge Foundation is to support and encourage those educational, cultural, social and environmental values that contribute to making our society more humaine and our world more liveable.
Chris Daggett, President & CEO
Cynthia Evans, Chief Financial Officer

2208 Greensward Foundation
Po Box 610 Lenox Hill Station 917-655-9491
New York, NY 10021 help@echonyc.com
www.echonyc.com

The Greensward Foundation, through its local branches, celebrates and suppports our communities's public parks. We are nonprofit. We receive no public funding, subsisting entirely on private grants and member contributions.
Robert M Makla, Director

2209 HKH Foundation
275 Madison Avenue 212-682-7522
33rd Floor
New York, NY 10016
Gives a major portion of its funding to the Adirondack Historical Association. Additional funding is distributed to the disarmament and prevention of war, civil liberties and human rights, and environmental protection.
Harriet Barlow, Adv.

2210 Helen Clay Frick Foundation
7227 Reynolds Street 412-371-0600
PO Box 86190
Pittsburgh, PA 15208
Devoted to the interpretation of the life and times of Henry Clay Frick.
DeCoursey E McIntosh, Executive Director

2211 Henry L and Consuelo S Wenger Foundation
100 Renaissance Center 313-567-1212
Detroit, MI 48226
Shelly Raines, Principal Manager

2212 Hoffman-La Roche Foundation
340 Kingsland Street 973-235-5000
Nutley, NJ 00711
Hoffman-La Roche is the US prescription drug unit of the Roche Group, one of the world's leading research-oriented health care groups with core businesses in pharmaceuticals and diagnostics.
Dr Christoph Franz, Chairman
Dr Severin Schwan, CEO

2213 INFORM
PO Box 320403 212-361-2400
Brooklyn, NY 11232 Fax: 212-361-2412
www.informinc.org
INFORM is an independent research organization that examines the effects of business practices on the environment and on human health. Our goal is to identify ways of doing business that en-

sure environmentally sustainable economicgrowth. Our reports are used by government, industry, and environmental leaders around the world.
Verginia Ramsey, President
Jon Parks, Co Chair

2214 International Primate Protection League
PO Box 776 843-871-2280
Summerville, SC 29484 Fax: 843-871-7988
info@ippl.org
www.ippl.org/gibbon
An organization that works worldwide for the conservation and protection of apes and monkeys.
Dr Shirley McGreal, Executive Director
Barbara Allison, Office Manager

2215 International Wildlife Coalition
634 N Falmouth Highway 508-457-1898
Box 388 Fax: 508-457-1898
North Falmouth, MA 00255 www.iwc.org
A federally recognized, non-profit tax-exempt charitable organization. The Coalition is dedicated to public education, research, resuce, rehabilitation, litigation, legislation and international treaty negotiations concerning globalwildlife and natural habitat protection issues.
Daniel J Morast, President

2216 International Wildlife Conservation Society
Grants Management Association
2300 Southern Boulevard 718-220-5100
Bronx, NY 10460 membership@wcs.org
www.wcs.org
Saves wildlife and wetlands. We do so through careful science, international conservation, education, and the management of the world's largest system of urban wildlife parks, led by the flagship Bronx Zoo.
Ward W Woods, Chair of the Board
Christian Samper, President & CEO

2217 Jessie Smith Noyes Foundation
122 East 42nd St. 212-684-6577
Suite 2501 Fax: 212-689-6549
New York, NY 10168 noyes@noyes.org
www.noyes.org
Promotes a sustainable and just social and natural system by supporting grassroots organizations and movements committed to this goal.
Victor DeLuca, President
Margaret Segall, Director of Administration

2218 John D and Catherine T MacArthur Foundation
140 S Dearborn Street 312-920-6285
Suite 1100 Fax: 312-920-6258
Chicago, IL 60603-5285 4answers@macfound.org
www.macfound.org
A private independent grantmaking institution dedicated to helping groups and individuals foster lasting improvement in the human condition.
Robert L Galluci, President

2219 Jules and Doris Stein Foundation
PO Box 30 323-276-2101
Beverly Hills, CA 90213
Founded the Jules Stein Eyes Institute at UCLA in the 1960's. Founded as a multidisciplinary center for vision science.
Linda L Valliant, Secretary

2220 Kangaroo Protection Foundation
1900 L Street NW 202-452-1100
Suite 526
Washington, DC 20036
Marian Newman, Program Director

2221 Keep America Beautiful
1010 Washington Boulevard 203-659-3000
Stamford, CT 00690 Fax: 203-659-3001
info@kab.org
www.kab.org
Nonprofit organization whose network of local, statewide and international affiliate programs educates individuals about litter prevention and ways to reduce, reuse, recycle and properly manage waste materials. Through partnershipsand strategic alliances with citizens, businesses and government, Keep America Beautiful's programs motivate millions of volunteers annually to clean up, beautify and improve their neighborhoods, thereby creating healthier and safer communityenvironments.
Carey Hamilton, Executive Director
Beth Buehler, Chief Operating Officer

2222 Kraft General Foods Foundation
Kraft Court 877-535-5666
Unit 2W 800-543-5335
Glenview, IL 60025 www.kraftfoods.com
Based on the values of innovation, quality, safety, respect, integrtity and openness. These values are what we stand for, the standard of conduct we hold ourselves to and our commitment to the people who work with us, invest in us andpurchase our products.
Pamela Hollie, Dir. Corporate Contributions

2223 Kroger Company Foundation
1014 Vine Street 513-762-4443
PO Box 1199 866-221-4141
Cincinnati, OH 45202-1100 www.kroger.com
Spans many states with store formats that include grocery and multi-department store, convenience stores and mall jewelry stores. We operate under nearly 2 dozen banners, all of which share the same belief in building strong local tiesand brand loyalty with our customers.
Paul Bernish, VP/Secretary

2224 Liz Claiborne Foundation
1441 Broadway Avenue
New York, NY 10018
Established to serve as the Company's center for charitable activiteis. Works to meet the needs of the communities where the major facilities of Liz Claiborne, Inc. are located. Projects focus primarily on helping disadvantaged womengain their self-sufficiency through job training and microenterprise development. The Foundation also provides ongoing support to many artistic and cultural institutions which enhance the livability of our communities.
Paul R Charron, Chairman of the Board/CEO
Angela J Ahrendts, Executive Vice President

2225 Liz Claiborne and Art Ortenberg Foundation
650 5th Avenue 212-333-2536
15th Floor Fax: 212-956-3531
New York, NY 10019 www.lcaof.org
The Foundation has 2 primary program interests: mitigation of conflict between the land and resources needs of local communities and conservation of biological diversity in rural landscapes outside of parks and reserves; implementationof relevant, field based scientific, technical and practical training programs for local people. The Foundation typically funds modest, carefully designed field activities-primarily in developing countries and the Northern Rockies.
James Murtaugh, Director
Jim Murtaugh, Program Director

2226 Louis and Anne Abrons Foundation
437 Madison Avenue 212-756-3376
New York, NY 10017 fdo.foundationcenter.org
Richard Abrons, President and Director

2227 Louisiana Land and Exploration Company
PO Box 60350 504-566-6500
New Orleans, LA 70160
One of the largest independent oil and gas exploration compaines in the United States. It operates a crude oil refinery and conducts exploration and production operations in the United States and selected foreign countries.
Karen A Overson, Contributions Coordinator

2228 MNC Financial Foundation
10 Light Street 301-244-5000
PO Box 987-MS251001
Baltimore, MD 21203
Geeorge BP Ward Jr, Secretary/Treasurer
Alfred Lerner, Chairman

2229 Mark and Catherine Winkler Foundation
4900 Seminary Road 703-998-0400
Alexandria, VA 22311 Fax: 703-578-7899
Lynne Ball, Executive Director

2230 Mars Foundation
2156 Vail Avenue 515-480-6610
Williams, IA 50271 wcande@wcande.com
www.multiple-sclerosis-mf.org
The mission of the MARS foundation is to be committed to finding a cure for multiple sclerosis by funding medical research.
Roger G Best, Secretary

2231 Marshall and Ilsley Foundation
770 North Water Street 414-765-7835
Milwaukee, WI 53201
Provides comprehensive financial products and services and unparalleled customer service to personal, business, corporate and institutional customers nationwide.
Diana L Sebion, Secretary

2232 Mary Reynolds Babcock Foundation
2920 Reynolda Village 336-748-9222
Winston-Salem, NC 27106 Fax: 336-777-0095
www.mrbf.org
Our mission is to help people and places to move out of poverty and achieve greater social and economic justice.
Justin Maxson, Executive Director
Jennifer Barksdale, Finance Officer

2233 Max McGraw Wildlife Foundation
PO Box 9 847-741-8000
Dundee, IL 60118 Fax: 847-741-8157
www.mcgrawwildlife.org
The foundation's mission: education, research, and land management. Currently, the Foundation is invovled in over 15 research and land management projects through the Chicago region, including participation in the Chicago Wildernessinitiative. Situated on 1,225 acres, the Foundation property is managed by professional land management staff.
Stanley W Koenig, Executive Director
John Thompson, Director Research

2234 Max and Victoria Dreyfus Foundation
2233 Wisconsin Avenue NW 202-337-3300
Suite 414 Fax: 202-337-3302
Washington, DC 20007 info@mvdreyfusfoundation.org
www.mvdreyfusfoundation.org
A leading figure in the music publishing business, the Foundation's grantmaking supports organizations in the arts, education, health care, hospitals, social services, civic affairs, and religion.
Lucy Gioia, Administrative Assistant

2235 May Stores Foundation
611 Olive Street 314-342-6300
St. Louis, MO 63101 Fax: 314-342-4461
www.lordandtaylor.com
James Abrams, VP Corporate Communications

2236 McIntosh Foundation
15840 Meadows Wood Drive 202-720-7871
Wellington, FL 33414 Fax: 202-234-0745
mcf@aol.com
www.activistfacts.com
The McIntosh foundation began in 1949 who founded the Great Atlantic & Pacific Tea Company...later renamed A&P
Michael A McIntosh, President
Hunter H. McIntosh, Director

2237 Nathan Cummings Foundation
475 Tenth Avenue 212-787-7300
14th Floor Fax: 212-787-7377
New York, NY 10018 contact@nathancummings.org
www.nathancummings.org
The Nathan Cummings Foundation is rooted in the Jewish tradition and committed to democratic values and social justice, including fairness, diversity, and community. They seek to build a socially and economically just society thatvalues nature and protects the ecological balance for future generations; promotes humane health care; and fosters arts and cultures that enriches communities.
Adam N. Cummings, Chair
Roberta Friedm Cummings, Vice Chair

2238 National Arbor Day Foundation
100 Arbor Avenue 402-474-5655
Nebraska City, NE 68410 888-448-7337
Fax: 402-474-0820
info@arborday.org
www.arborday.org
A nonprofit educational, environmental organization that helps people plant and care for trees. We are committed to tree-planting and environmental stewardsip. Newsletter free with $10.00 annual membership.
8 pages Bi-Monthly
John Rosenow, President
Gary Brienzo, Info. Coordinator

2239 National Audubon Society
225 Varick Street 212-979-3000
New York, NY 10014 800-274-4201
Fax: 212-979-3188
jbianchi@audubon.org
www.audubon.org
The mission of the National Audubon Society is to conserve and restore natural ecosystems, focusing on birds and other wildlife for the benefit of humanity and the earth's biological diversity. Founded in 1905, the National AudubonSociety is named for John James Audubon, famed orinthologist, exployer, and wildlife artist.
David Yarnold, President
Susan Lunden, Chief Operating Officer

2240 National Fish and Wildlife Foundation
1133 Fifteenth St. 202-857-0166
Suite 1100 Fax: 202-857-0162
Washington, DC 20005 www.nfwf.org

Sustains, restores and enhances the Nation's fish, wildlife, plants, and habitats.
John V. Faraci, Chairman
Patsy Ishiyama, Vice Chairman

2241 National Forest Foundation
Bldg 27, Ste 3 406-542-2805
Fort Missoula Rd Fax: 406-542-2810
Missoula, MT 59804 bpossiel@nationalforests.org
www.nationalforests.org
The official nonprofit partner of the USDA Forest Service. To accept and administer private contributions, undertaking activities that further the purposes for which the National Forest System was established and conductingeducational, technical, and other activities that support the multiple use, research, and forestry programs administered by the Forest Service.
Craig R. Barrett, Chair
John Hendricks, Vice Chair

2242 National Geographic Society Education Foundation
1145 17th Street NW 202-857-7310
Washington, DC 20036 Fax: 202-429-5701
foundation@ngs.org
The mission is to motivate and enable each new generation to become geographically literate.
John M. Fahey, Jr.,, Chairman
Patrick F. Noonan, Vice Chairman

2243 National Parks Conservation Association
777 6th Street 202-223-6722
Suite 700 800-628-7275
Washington, DC 20001-3723 Fax: 202-454-3333
npca@npca.org
www.npca.org
Mission is to protect and enhance America's National Parks for present and future generations.
Thomas F. Secunda, Chairman
W Clark Bunting, President & CEO

2244 National Wildlife Federation
11100 Wildlife Center Drive 202-797-6800
Reston, VA 20190 800-822-9919
Fax: 202-797-6646
www.nwf.org
The National Wildlife Federation is the largest member-supported conservation group, uniting individuals, organizations, businesses and government to protect wildlife, wild places and the environment.
Kathy Hadley, Chair
Collin O'Mara, President and CEO

2245 Nature Conservancy
4245 North Fairfax Drive 703-841-5300
Suite 100 800-628-6860
Arlington, VA 22203-1606 Fax: 703-841-1283
member@tnc.org
www.nature.org
The mission is to preserve plants, animals and natural communities that represent the diversity of life on Earth by protecting the lands and waters they need to survive.
John C Sawhill, President

2246 New England Biolabs Foundation
240 Country Road 978-998-7990
Ipswich, MA 00193 Fax: 978-356-3250
info@nebf.org
www.nebf.org
NEBF funds grass roots organizations in developing countries that focus on environmental issues and education.
Jessica Brown, Executive Director
David Comb, Trustees

2247 New York Times Company Foundation
620 Eighth Avenue 212-556-1982
New York, NY 10018 Fax: 212-556-3690
danielle.rhoades-ha@nytimes.com
www.nytco.com
This foundation provides funds to organizations that are involved in journalism, education, culture or environmentalism.
Danielle Rhoades Ha, Vice President
Eileen M. Murphy, SVP, Communications

2248 New-Land Foundation
1114 Avenue of the Americans 212-479-6086
46th Floor Fax: 212-841-6275
New York, NY 10036 www.rlch.org
Seeks to foster positive change throughout the global community through its grant making.
Robert Wolf, President

2249 Norcross Wildlife Foundation
Caller Box 611 212-362-4831
New York, NY 10024 Fax: 212-812-4783
www.norcrosswildlife.org
A place of refuge where all wildlife is encouraged not just to survive but also to proliferate naturally, and where certain species, now threatned with extinction, may again attain more normal distribution and benefit the public bytheir survival.
Angel Braestrup, Chair
Jennifer Grossman, Vice Chair

2250 Northwest Area Foundation
60 Plato Boulevard E 651-224-9635
Suite 400 Fax: 651-225-3881
St. Paul, MN 55107 info@nwaf.org
www.nwaf.org
Committed to helping communities reduce poverty for the long term.
Kevin Walker, President/CEO
Millie Acamovic, Vice President

2251 Oliver S and Jennie R Donaldson Charitable Trust
US Trust Company of New York
114 W 47th Street 212-852-3683
New York, NY 10036 Fax: 212-852-3377
Philantropic organization working to promote social change that contributes to a more just, sustainable and peaceful world.
Anne L Smith-Ganey, Secretary

2252 Overbrook Foundation
60 East 42nd Street 212-603-9996
Suite 565 Fax: 212-661-8664
New York, NY 10165 www.overbrook.org
The Overbrook Foundation strives to improve the lives of people by supporting projects that protect human and civil rights, advance the self-sufficiencey and well being of individuals and their communities, and conserve the naturalenvironment.
Aaron Labaree, Chair
Carolyn J. Cole, Vice Chair

2253 Pacific Whale Foundation
101 N Kihei Road 808-879-8811
Suite 25 800-942-5311
Kihei, HI 96753 Fax: 808-879-2615
www.pacificwhale.org
Mission is to promote appreciation, understanding and protection of whales, dolphins, coral reefs and our plantet's oceans. We accomplish this by educating the public from a scientific perspective about the marine environment. Wesupport and conduct responsible marine research and address marine conservation issues in Hawaii and the Pacific. Through educational ecotours, we

model and promote sound ecotourism practices and responsible wildlife watching.
Paul Forestell, Co-Chairperson
Mark Orams, Co-Chairperson

2254 Patrick and Anna Cudahy Fund
70 E. Lake St., 312-422-1442
Suite 1120 Fax: 312-641-5736
Chicago, IL 60601 laurenkrieg@cudahyfund.org
cudahyfund.org
Types of support: general/operating support; continuing support; annual campaigns; building/renovation; equipment; program development; seed money; technical assistance; matching funds.
Lauren Krieg, Executive Director

2255 Pew Charitable Trusts
2005 Market Street Suite 1800 215-575-9050
Suite 2800 Fax: 215-575-4939
Philadelphia, PA 19103-7077 info@pewtrusts.org
www.pewtrusts.org
Driven by the power of knowledge to solve today's most challenging problems. Pew applies a rigorous, analytical approach to improve public policy, inform the public and stimulate civic life.
Rebecca W. Rimel, President/CEO
Melissa Skolfield, Senior Vice President

2256 Providence Journal Charitable Foundation
75 Fountain Street 401-277-7000
Providence, RI 02902 help@providencejournal.com
www.providencejournal.com
Focuses on offering local and regional news, information, advertising and interactive opportunities for our audience.
Phil Kukielski, Managing Editor
John Kostrzewa, Business Editor

2257 RARE Center for Tropical Bird Conservation
1529 Walnut Street 215-568-0420
Philadelphia, PA 19102
Works globally to equip people in the world's most threatened natural areas with the tools and motivation they need to care for their natural resources.
John Guarnaccia, Executive Director

2258 Rainforest Action Network
425 Bush Street 415-398-4404
Suite 300 Fax: 415-398-2732
San Francisco, CA 94108 answers@ran.org
www.ran.org
Rainforest Action Network works to protect the Earth's rainforests and support the rights of their inhabitants through education, grassroots organizing and non-violent direct action.
André Carothers, Board Chair
James D. Gollin, President

2259 Rainforest Alliance
233 Broadway 212-677-1900
28th Floor 888-693-2784
New York, NY 10279 Fax: 212-677-2187
info@ra.org
www.rainforest-alliance.org
Works to conserve biodiversity and ensure sustainable livelihoods by transforming land-use practices, business practices and consumer behavior.
Daniel R Katz, Chairman
Roger Deromedi, Vice Chairman

2260 Raytheon Company
870 Winter Street 781-552-3000
Waltham, MA 00245 www.raytheon.com
Raytheon is a technology leader specializing in defense, homeland security, and other government markets throughout the world.
Thomas A Kennedy, Chairman/CEO
John D Harris, Vice President

2261 Richard Lounsberry Foundation
601 Thirteenth Street 202-872-8080
Suite 1030N Fax: 202-872-9292
Washington, DC 20005 foundation@rlounsbery.org
www.rlounsbery.org
Aims to enhance national strengths in science and technology through support programs in the areas of science and technology components of key US policy issues, elementary and secondary science and math education, historical studiesand contemporary assessments of key trends in the physical and biomedical sciences and start up assistance for establishing the infrastructure of research projects.
William Happer, Chairman
Jesse H Ausubel, Vice Chairman

2262 Rockefeller Brothers Foundation
475 Riverside Drive 212-812-4200
Suite 900 Fax: 212-812-4299
New York, NY 10115 communications@rbf.org
www.rbf.org
A philantropic organization working to promote social change that contributes to a more just, sustainable and peaceful world. The Fund's programs are intended to develop leaders, strenghten institutions, engage citizens, buildcommunity, and foster partnerships that include government, business, and civil society.
Stephen Heintz, President
Judy Clark, Executive Director

2263 Rockefeller Family Fund
475 Riverside Drive 212-812-4252
Suite 900 Fax: 212-812-4299
New York, NY 10115 www.rffund.org
For thirty years, the Rockefeller Family Fund has worked at the cutting edge of advocacy in such areas as environmental protection, advancing the economic rights of women, and holding public and private institutions accountable fortheir actions.
David Kaiser, President
Wendy Gordon, Vice President

2264 Safari Club International Foundation
4800 West Gates Pass Road 520-620-1220
Tucson, AZ 85745-9450 800-377-5399
Fax: 520-622-1205
www.scifirstforhunters.org
Safari Club Internation Foundation is a charitable organization that funds and manages worldwide programs dedicated to wildlife conservation, outdoor education and humanitarian services.
Larry B Higgins, President
Paul D Babaz, Vice President

2265 Samuel Roberts Noble Foundation
2510 Sam Noble Parkway 508-223-5810
Ardmore, OK 73401 Fax: 508-224-6217
www.noble.org
One of the largest international offshore drilling contractors in the world.
Bill Buckner, President & CEO
Billy Cook, Senior Vice President

2266 Save the Redwoods League
111 Sutter Street 415-362-2352
11th Floor 888-836-0005
San Francisco, CA 94104 Fax: 415-362-7017
info@savetheredwoods.org
www.savetheredwoods.org

Guided by their science-based master plan to save redwoods throughout their natural ranges, the Leagues purchases priority pieces of land and donates or sells the property to government agencies for protection as parks and reserves.The league funds restoration, supports research to expand knowledge of redwood forest dynamics, and educates the public about redwoods and their ecosystems, in order to reconnect people with the peace and beauty of these wonders of the natural world.
James Larson, President
Melinda Thomas, Vice President

2267 Scherman Foundation

16 E 52nd Street
Suite #601
New York, NY 10022
212-832-3086
Fax: 212-838-0154
mpratt@scherman.org
www.scherman.org

The giving program of the Foundation emphasizes long-term general support, reflecting the director's commitment to sustained support for current grantees, and the belief that strong non-profit leaders who are closest to the issues canbest decide on the most effective use of grant funds.
Karen R. Sollins, Chair
Mr Mike Pratt, President

2268 Sequoia Foundation

1250 Pacific Avenue
Suite 870
Tacoma, WA 98402
253-627-1634
Fax: 253-627-6249
grants@grantmakerconsultants.com
www.sequoiafound.org

A private non-profit organization dedicated to the identification and reduction of environmental threats to public health. We seek to support the efforts of local, state, national-and international-public health agencies in promotingand implimenting effective public health policy. This mission is achieved through research collaborations with local, state, federal, and international agencies, community-based organizations, and hospitals and universities.
John S. Petterson Ph.D., Executive Director
Pam Petree, Contracts Manager

2269 Sierra Club Foundation

85 Second Street
Suite 750
San Francisco, CA 94105
415-995-1780
Fax: 415-995-1791
foundation@sierraclub.org
www.sierraclubfoundation.org

To advance the preservation and protection of the natural environment by empowering the citizenry with charitable resources to further the cause of environmental protection.
Steven Berkenfeld, Chair
Allison Chin, Vice Chair

2270 Social Justice Fund NW

1904 Third Avenue
Suite 806
Seattle, WA 98101
206-624-4081
Fax: 206-382-2640
info@socialjusticefund.org
www.socialjusticefund.org

Progressive foundation dedicated to creating a more just society. Funds grass-roots community-based organizations in Idoho, Montana, Wyoming, Washington, and Oregon.
Jessan Hutchison-Quillian, Chair
Abel Valladares, Vice Chair

2271 Switzer Foundation New Hampshire Charitable Foundation

Po Box 293
Belfast, ME 00491
207-338-5654
800-464-6641
Fax: 603-225-1700
info@switzernetwork.org
www.switzernetwork.org

Identifies and nurtures environmental leaders who have the ability and determination to make a significant impact, and supports initiatives that will have direct and measurable results to improve environmental quality.
Judith Burrows, Director Student Aid
Joe Aldy, Assistant professor

2272 Texaco Foundation

2000 Westchester Avenue
White Plains, NY 10650
914-701-0320
www.texaco.com

The foundation focuses on early childhood education in math and science through its Early Notes (music) program and its Touch Science program, which supports scientific discovery through hands-on learning.
Maria Mike-Mayer, Secretary

2273 Threshold Foundation

Po Box 29903
San Francisco, CA 94129-0903
415-561-6400
Fax: 415-561-6401
threshold@tides.org
www.thresholdfoundation.org

A progressive foundation and a community of individuals united through wealth, mobilizing money, people and power to create a more just, joyful and sustainable world.
Terrence Meck, President
Reid Williams, Treasurer

2274 Times Mirror Foundation

202 W First Street
Los Angeles, CA 90012
213-237-3945
Fax: 213-237-2116
www.timesmirrorfoundation.org

The Times Mirror Foundation, an affiliate of Tribune Company, is dedicated to supporting nonprofit organizations that measurably improve the quality of life in communities we serve. The Foundation focuses its support on programs thatimprove the quality of journalism, education and literacy, strengthen the fabric of the community, and enhance cultural appreciation and understanding.
Cassandra Malry, Treasurer

2275 Tinker Foundation Inc

55 E 59th Street
New York, NY 10022
212-421-6858
Fax: 212-223-3326
tinker@tinker.org
www.tinker.org

Endeavors to promote better understanding among the peoples of the US, Latin America, and Iberia. In the environmental policy program area, grants are awarded to to 501(c)(3) or equivalent organizations for projects addressingresource-based economic activities and for improving the formulation of effective environmental governance.
Renate Rennie, Chairman/President
Alan Stoga, Secretary

2276 Town Creek Foundation

121 N West Street
Easton, MD 21601
410-763-8171
Fax: 410-763-8172
info@towncreekfdn.org
www.towncreekfdn.org

A private philanthropic foundation dedicated to a sustainable environment
Stuart Clarke, Executive Director
Jennifer Stanley, President

2277 TreePeople

12601 Mulholland Drive
Beverly Hills, CA 90210
818-753-4600
Fax: 818-753-4635
info@treepeople.org
www.treepeople.org

A nonprofit organization that has been serving the Los Angeles area for over three decades. Simply put, our work is about helping nature heal our cities.
Andy Lipkis, Founder and President
Caryn Bosson, Interim Executive Director

2278 Trout Unlimited
1300 North 17th Street
Suite 100
Arlington, VA 22209
703-522-0200
800-834-2419
Fax: 703-284-9400
trout@tu.org
www.tu.org
This organization seeks to conserve, protect and restore North America's trout and salmon fisheries and their watersheds.
Jim Asselstine, Chairman
Nancy Mackinnon, Secretary

2279 True North Foundation
508 Westwood Drive
Fort Collins, CO 80524
970-223-5285
Fax: 970-495-0892
Committed to preventing damage to the natural systems, water, air, and land on which all life depends.
Kerry K Anderson, President

2280 Turner Foundation
133 Luckie Street NW
2nd Floor
Atlanta, GA 30303
404-681-9900
Fax: 404-681-0172
www.turnerfoundation.org
This Foundation is committed to preventing damage to the natural systems, water, air and land, on which all life depends.
Ted Turner, Chairman
Laura Turner Seydel, Director

2281 US-Japan Foundation
145 East 32nd Street
New York, NY 10016
212-481-8753
Fax: 212-481-8762
info@us-jf.org
www.us-jf.org
Committed to promoting stronger ties between Americans and Japanese by supporting projects that foster mutual knowledge and education, deepen understanding, create effective channels of communication, and address common concerns in anincreasingly interdependent world.
James W. Lintott, Chairman
Dr. George R. Packard, President

2282 USF and G Foundation
100 Light Street
Baltimore, MD 21202
410-685-3047

2283 Union of Concerned Scientists
2 Brattle Square
Cambridge, MA 00213-3780
617-547-5552
Fax: 617-864-9405
ucs@ucsusa.org
www.ucsusa.org
The Union of Scientists is the leading science-based nonprofit organization working for a healthy environment and a safer world. Since 1969. we've used rigorous scientific analysis, innovative policy development, and tenacious citizenadvocacy to advance practical solutions for the environment.
James J. McCarthy, Chair
Peter A. Bradford, Vice Chair

2284 Unitarian Universalist Veatch Program at Shelter Rock
48 Shelter Rock Road
Manhasset, NY 11030
516-627-6560
Fax: 516-627-6596
uucsr@uucsr.org
www.uucsr.org
Supports Unitarian Universalist organizations that foster the growth and development of the denomination and that increase the involvement of Unitarian Universalists in social action and non-denominational organizations whose goalsreflect UU principles.
Ned Wight, Executive Director

2285 Victoria Foundation
31 Mulberry Street
5th Floor
Newark, NJ 00710
973-792-9200
Fax: 973-792-1300
info@victoriafoundation.org
www.victoriafoundation.org
A private grantmaking institution. Since the early 1960's the Foundation's trustees have targeted giving to programs that impact the cycle of poverty in Newark, New Jersey.
Frank Alvarez, President
Margaret H. Parker, Vice President

2286 Vidda Foundation
250 West 57th Street
Suite 1928
New York, NY 10107
212-696-4052
Fax: 212-889-7791
www.vidda.org
The Vidda Foundation is a private non-operating foundation interested in supporting programs that will have lasting impact in the areas of conservation, education, healthcare, human services, and the arts.
Gerald E Rupp, Chairman
John A. Downey, MD

2287 Virginia Environmental Endowment
Three James Center
1051 East Cary Street
PO Box 790
Richmond, VA 23218-790
804-644-5000
info@vee.org
www.vee.org
Mission is to improve the quality of the environment by using its capital to encourage all sectors to work together to prevent pollution, conserve natural resources, and promote environmental literacy.
Gerald P McCarthy, Executive Director

2288 W Alton Jones Foundation
232 East High Street
Charlottesville, VA 22902
804-295-2134
Fax: 804-295-1648
Helps to fund hundreds of environmental groups.
Dr. JP Meyers, Director

2289 Wallace Genetic Foundation
4910 Massachusetts Avenue NW
Suite 221
Washington, DC 20016
202-966-2932
Fax: 202-966-3370
wgfdn@aol.com
www.wallacegenetic.org
Committed to funding a variety of interests including agricultural research, preservation of farmland, ecology, conservation and sustainable development.
John D Murray, President
David W Douglas, Vice President, Treasurer

2290 Weeden Foundation
P.O. Box 606
Bedford Hills, NY 10507-0606
914-864-1375
Fax: 914-864-1377
info@weedenfoundation.org
www.weedenfoundation.org
A foundation dedicated to the protection of biodiversity through the financial support of conservation-centered organizations.
Norman Weeden, Ph.D., President
Don A. Weeden, Executive Director

2291 Wilderness Society
1615 M Street NW
Washington, DC 20036
202-833-2300
800-843-9453
action@tws.org
www.wilderness.org
Deliver to future generations an unspoiled legacy of wild places, with all the precious values they hold: Biological diversity; clean air and water; towering forests, rushing rivers, and sage-sweet, silent deserts.
Jamie Williams, President
Thomas Tepper, Vice President

2292 Wildlife Preservation Trust International
3400 West Girard Avenue 215-222-3636
Philadelphia, PA 19104 Fax: 215-222-2191
www.wildlifeconservationtrust.org
Empowers local conservation scientists worldwide to protect nature and safeguard ecosystem and human health.
Dr. Mary Pearl

2293 William Bingham Foundation
1111 Superior Avenue 216-363-6482
Suite 700 info@wbinghamfoundation.org
Cleveland, OH 44114 www.foundationcenter.org
Supports organizations in in education, science, health and human servces and the arts.
Kari Blakley, Grants Manager
Daniel L Horn, Secretary

2294 William H Donner Foundation
520 White Plains Road 914-524-0404
Suite 500 Fax: 914-524-0407
Tarrytown, NY 10591 donner.org
When we build let us...build forever. Let it not be for present delight nor for present alone. Let it be such work as our descendants will thank us for.
Timothy E Donner, President
Cristina Winsor, Vice President

2295 William Penn Foundation
Two Logan Square 11th Floor 215-988-1830
100 North 18th Street Fax: 215-988-1823
Philadelphia, PA 19103-2757 grants@williampennfoundation.org
www.williampennfoundation.org
To improve the quality of life in the greater Philadelphia region through efforts that foster rich cultural expression, strenghten children's futures, and deepen connections to nature and community. In partnerships with others, we workto advance a vital, just and caring community.
Janet Haas, Chair
Leonard C. Haas, Vice Chair

2296 William and Flora Hewlett Foundation
2121 Sand Hill Road 650-234-4500
Menlo Park, CA 94025 Fax: 650-234-4501
www.hewlett.org
The Foundation concentrates its resources on activities in education, environment, global development, performing arts and population. In addition, the Foundation has programs that make grants to advance the field of philanthropy, andto support disadvantaged communities in the San Francisco Bay Area.
Stephen C Neal, Chairman
Larry D Kramer, President

2297 Winston Foundation for World Peace
2040 S Street, NW 202-483-4215
Washington, DC 20009 Fax: 202-483-4219
winstonfoun@igc.apc.org
John H. Adams, Director

2298 Wisconsin Energy Corporation Foundation
231 W. Michigan St. 414-221-2345
Milwaukee, WI 53203 Fax: 414-221-2554
www.wecenergygroup.com
Wisconsin Energy's principal business is providng electric and natural gas service to customers across Wisconsin and the Upper Peninsula of Michigan.
David L Hughes, Assistant Treasurer
Gale E Klappa, Chairman, President & CEO

2299 World Parks Endowment
1616 Place Street NW 202-939-3808
Suite 200 Fax: 202-939-3868
Washington, DC 20036 info@worldlandtrust.org
www.worldlandtrust.org
The World Parks Endowment provides the opportunity to buy rainforest land and establish new protected areas that conserve rainforests and other sites of high biodiversity value. Our projects target lands that conserve rare orendangered species, and are low price, so the minimum amount of the funds protect high priority areas.
John A Burton, Chief Executive Officer
Roger Wilson, Senior Conservationist

2300 World Research Foundation
P.O. Box 20828 928-284-3300
Sedona, AZ 86341 Fax: 928-284-3530
info@wrf.org
www.wrf.org
The purpose of the foundation is to locate, gather, codify, evaluate, classify and disseminate information dealing with health and the environment. All countries are contacted to collect the best information in an unbiased, neutral andindependent manner.
LaVerne Boeckmann, Vice President/Founder

2301 World Resources Institute
10 G Street, NE 202-729-7600
Suite 800 Fax: 202-729-7686
Washington, DC 20002 www.wri.org
An independent nonprofit organization with a staff of more than 100 scientists, economists, policy experts, business analysts, statistic analysists, mapmakers and communicators working to protect the Earth and improve people's lives.Our four goals are: protect the Earth's living systems, increase access to information, create sustainable enterprise and opportunity and reverse global warming.
James A Harmon, Chairman
Harriet C Babbitt, Vice Chairman

2302 World Society for the Protection of Animals
450 Seventh Avenue 646-783-2200
31st Floor 800-883-9772
New York, NY 10123 Fax: 212-564-4250
wspa@wspausa.org
www.wspa-usa.org
The world's largest alliance of animal welfare organization whose vision is a world where animal welfare matters and animal cruelty ends. We strive to bring about change from grassroots to government levels to benefit animals. WSPAsupports and develops high-profile campaigns, scientifically-backed projects and innovative education initiatives. Its work is recognized by the United Nations and Council of Europe.
Annie Lieberman, USA Executive Director
John Bowen, President

2303 World Wildlife Fund
1250 24th Street NW 202-293-4800
PO Box 97180 800-225-5993
Washington, DC 20037 Fax: 202-293-9211
membership@wwfus.org
www.worldwildlife.org
Dedicated to protecting endangered species and their habitats through field work, advocacy, policy engagement, pioneering work and education. The largest multinational conservation organization in the world. WWF worls in 100 countriesand is supported by 1.2 million members in the US and almost 5 million members globally.
Carter Roberts, President/CEO
Marcia Marsh, COO

2304 **Xerces Society**
628 NE Broadway
Suite 200
Portland, OR 97232
503-232-6639
855-232-6639
Fax: 503-233-6794
info@xerces.org
www.xerces.org
Works with farmers, land managers, golf course staff, public agencies, and gardners to promote the conservation and recovery of native pollinator insects and their habitat.
David Frazee Johnson, President
Logan Lauvray, Vice President

Scholarships

2305 **AGI Minority Geoscience Scholarship**
American Geological Institute
4220 King Street
Alexandria, VA 22302-1502
703-379-2480
800-336-4764
Fax: 703-379-7563
pleahy@agiweb.org
www.americangeosciences.org
Provides information services, serves as a voice of shared interests in our profession, plays a major role in strengthening geoscience education, and strives to increase public understanding of the vital role in geosciences play insociety's use of resources and interaction with the environment.
Patrick Leahy, Executive Director
Edward C. Robeck, Education, Outreach Director

2306 **Abundant Life Seed Foundation**
930 Lawrence Street
PO Box 772
Port Townsend, WA 98368
425-385-5660
Fax: 360-385-7455
www.abundantlifeseed.org
A nonprofit organization dedicated to the preservation of rare, heirloom and native seeds. ALSF grows and distributes open-pollinated seeds and offers them for sale in an annual catalog. Seeds are also sent to people in need throughthe World Seed Fund. ALSF teaches seed saving through workshops, appreticeships and school programs.
Matthew Dillon, Executive Director
Elsa Golts, Board President

2307 **Alexander Hollaender Distinguished Postdoctoral Fellowships**
PO Box 117
Oak Ridge, TN 37831-117
865-576-3146
Fax: 865-241-2923
www.orau.gov/orise/contacts.htm
Prepares and distributes program literature to universities and laboratories across the country, accepts application, convenes a panel to make award recommendation, and issues stipend checks.
Andy Page, Director
Dan Standley, Director

2308 **American Association for the Advancement of Science**
1200 New York Avenue NW
Washington, DC 20005
202-326-6400
Fax: 202-289-4950
www.aaas.org
An international non-profit organization dedicated to advancing science around the world by serving as an educator, leader, spokesperson and professional association.
Gerald Fink, Chair
Geraldine Richmond, President

2309 **American Geophysical Union Member Programs Division**
2000 Florida Avenue NW
Washington, DC 20009
202-462-6900
800-966-2481
Fax: 202-328-0566
service@agu.org
membership.agu.org
Organized to represent the US in the International Research Council's International Union Of Geodesy and Geophysics and to serve as the National Research Council Committee on Geophysics.
Eric A Davidson, Chair
Robin Elizabeth Bell, Vice Chair

2310 **American Indian Science and Engineering Society**
PO Box 9828
Albuquerque, NM 87119-9828
505-765-1052
Fax: 505-765-5608
info@aises.org
www.aises.org
The mission is to increase substantially the representation of American Indian and Alaskan Natives in engineering, science and other related technology disciplines.
Sarah Echohawk, CEO
Shirley LaCourse, Business Development Officer

2311 **American Museum of Natural History**
Central Park West at 79th Street
New York, NY 10024-5192
212-769-5100
Fax: 212-769-5427
www.amnh.org
Mission is to discover, interpret, and disseminate-through scientific research and education, knowledge about human cultures, the natural world, and the universe.
Lewis W Bernard, Chairman
Ellen V Futter, President

2312 **American Nuclear Society**
555 North Kensington Ave
La Grange Park, IL 60526
708-352-6611
800-323-3044
Fax: 708-352-0499
www.ans.org
Not-for-profit, international, scientific and educational organization. Established by a group of individuals who recognized the need to unify the professional activities within the diverse fields of nuclear science and technology.
Robert N. Coward, President
Robert C. Fine, Executive Director

2313 **American Society of Naturalists**
Queens College - CUNY
Department of Biology
Flushing, NY 11367
718-997-3426
asn@press.uchicago.edu
www.amnat.org
Purpose is to advance and to diffuse knowledge of organic evolution and other broad biological principals so as to enhance the conceptual unification of the biological sciences.
Ellen Ketterson, President

2314 **American Sport Fishing Association**
1001 North Fairfax St.
Suite 501
Alexandria, VA 22314
703-519-9691
Fax: 703-519-1872
info@asafishing.org
www.asafishing.org
Unites more then 650 members of the sportfishing and boating industries with state fish and wildlife agencies, federal land and water management agencies, conservation organizations, angler advocacy groups and outdoor journalists. Wesafeguard and promote the enduring social, economic and conservation values of sportfishing.
Mike Nussman, President And CEO
Glenn Hudges, Vice President

2315 **Apple Computer Earth Grants: Community Affairs Department**
1 Infinite Loop
Cupertino, CA 95014
408-996-1010
800-692-7753
www.apple.com
Beverly Long, Program Manager

2316 Beldon Fund
99 Madison Avenue
8th Floor
New York, NY 10016
212-616-5600
800-591-9595
Fax: 212-616-5656
beldoninfo@yahoo.com
www.beldon.org

Mission is by supporting effective, nonprofit, advocacy organizations, the Beldon Fund seeks to build a national consensus to achieve and sustain a healthy planet.
John Hunting, Chair
Lael Stegall, Vice Chair

2317 Beldon II Fund: Old Kent Bank and Trust Company
99 Madison Avenue
8th Floor
New York, NY 10016
212-616-5600
800-591-9595
Fax: 212-616-5656
beldoninfo@yahoo.com
www.beldon.org

John R Hunting, Chair
Lael Stegall, Vice Chair

2318 Charles A. and Anne Morrow Lindbergh Foundation
PO Box 861
Berkeley Springs, WV 25411
763-576-1596
Fax: 763-576-1664
info@thelindberghfoundation.org
www.lindberghfoundation.org

Each year, the Charles A. and Anne Morrow Lindbergh Foundation provides grants to men and women whose individual initiative and work in a wide spectrum of disciplines furthers the Lindbergh's vision of a balance between the advance oftechnology and the perservation of the natural/human environment.
John Peterson, Chairman
Gregg E Maryniak, Vice Chairman

2319 Cousteau Society
4 East 27th Street
New York, NY 10001
212-532-2588
800-441-4395
Fax: 757-722-8185
communication@cousteau.org
www.cousteau.org

Mission is to educate people to understand, to love and to protect the water systems of the planet, marine and fresh water, for the wellbeing of future generations.
Francine Cousteau, President

2320 DRB Communications
1234 Summer Street
Stamford, CT 00690
800-323-1550
Fax: 203-324-7175

Robyn DeWolf

2321 Delmar Publishers Scholarship
National FAA Foundation
6060 FFA Drive
PO Box 68960
Indianapolis, IN 46268
317-802-6060
Fax: 317-802-6061
Carrie Powers, Contact

2322 Du Pont de Nemours and Company
1007 Market Street
Room 8065
Wilmington, DE 19898
302-774-2036
800-441-7515
info@dupont.com
www.dupont.com

Creating sustainable solutions essential to a better, safer, healthier, life for people everywhere.
Peter C Morrow, Mgr. Corporate Contributions

2323 Earth Island Institute-Brower Youth Awards
2150 Allston Way
Suite 460
Berkeley, CA 94704-1375
510-859-9100
Fax: 510-859-9091
bya@earthisland.org
www.earthisland.org

Incubates and supports over 30 projects working on environmental issues worldwide. Publishes quarterly Earth Island Journal. Project support programs help aspiring and veteran activists alike put ideas into action. Youth programincreases the visibility, effectiveness and influence of youth leadership in the environmental movement, inspiring other young people to work for the Earth.
Michael Mitrani, President
Martha Davis, Vice President

2324 Environmental Defense Fund
1875 Connecticut Ave
Suite 600
New York, NY 20009
212-505-2100
800-684-3322
Fax: 212-505-2375
members@edf.org
www.edf.org

Dedicated to protecting the environmental rights of all people, including future generations. Among these rights are clean air, clean water, healthy, nourishing food and a flourishing ecosystem. Advocates solutions based on science,even when it leads in unfamiliar directions. Works to create solutions that win lasting political, economic and social support because they are bipartisan, efficient and fair.
Fred Krupp, President
Liza Henshaw, Chief Operating Officer

2325 Environmental Grantmakers Association
475 Riverside Drive
Suite 960
New York, NY 10115
212-812-4310
Fax: 212-812-4311
ega.org

Mission is to help member organizations become more effective environmental grantmakers through information sharing, collaboration and networking.
Scott Cullen, Chair
Paul Beaudet, Vice Chair

2326 Environmental Protection Agency: Grants Administration Division
Grants Operation Branch
401 M Street SW
Washington, DC 20460
202-260-5260

Programs include air and water pollution controll, toxic substances, pesticides, and drinking water regulation, wetlands protection, hazardous waste management, hazardous waste site cleanup and some regulation of radioactive materials.

2327 Environmental and Engineering Fellowship
American Association for the Advancement
1333 H Street NW
Washington, DC 20005
202-326-6600
Fax: 202-289-4950

Aimed at postdoctoral to midcareer professionals from any discipline of science, engineering or any relevant interdisciplinary fields.

2328 Financial Support for Graduate Work
Women's Seamen's Friend Society of Connecticut
300 Boston Post Road
West Haven, CT 00651
800-342-5864
skaplan@newhaven.edu
www.newhaven.edu/academics/10844/

Restricted to Connecticut residents who are students at state maritime schools, or Connecticut residents majoring in Marine Sciences at any college or university or residents of any state majoring in Marine Sciences at a Connecticutcollege or university.
Steven H. Kaplan, President

2329 Ford Motor Company Fund
320 East 212-573-5000
43rd Street Fax: 212-351-3677
New York, NY 10017
Ford Motor Company Fund is a not-for-profit corporation organized in 1949. Made possible by Ford Motor Company profits, Ford Motor Company Fund supports initiatives and institutions that enhance and improve opportunities for those wholive in the communities where Ford Motor Company operates.
Kofi Appenteng, Chair
Darren Walker, President

2330 Forest History Society
701 William Vickers Avenue 919-682-9319
Durham, NC 27701-3162 Fax: 919-682-2349
coakes@duke.edu
www.foresthistory.org
The Forest History Society is a non-profit educational institution that links the past to the future by identifying, collecting, preserving, interpreting, and disseminating information on the history of people, forests, and theirrelated resources.
Hayes Brown, Chairman
Kent Gilges, Co-vice chairman

2331 Garden Club of America
14 East 60th Street 212-753-8287
3rd Floor Fax: 212-753-0134
New York, NY 10022 gca@gcamerica.org
www.gcamerica.org
Purpose is to stimulate the knowledge and love of gardening, to share the advantages of association by means of educational meetings, conferences, correspondence and publications, and to restore, improve, and protect the quality of theenvironment through educational programs and action in the fields of conservation and civic improvement.
Katherine Astor, Honorary Member
Anne Butler, Receptionist

2332 Georgia M. Hellberg Memorial Scholarships
National Future Federation of America
6060 FFA Drive 317-802-6060
PO Box 68960 888-332-2668
Indianapolis, IN 46268-0960 Fax: 317-802-6061
webmaster@ffa.org
www.ffa.org
Steve A. Brown, Advisor
Sherene R. Donaldson, Executive Secretary

2333 German Marshall Fund of the United States
1744 R Street NW 202-683-2650
Washington, DC 20009 Fax: 202-265-1662
info@gmfus.org
www.gmfus.org
A nonpartisan American public policy and grantmaking institution dedicated to promoting greater cooperation and understanding between the United States and Europe.
Craig Kennedy, President

2334 Great Lakes Protection Fund
1560 Sherman Avenue 847-425-8150
Suite 880 Fax: 847-424-9832
Evanston, IL 60201 info@glpf.org
www.glpf.org
A private non profit organization formed by the Govenors of the Great Lakes States. It is a permanent environmental endowdment that supports collaborative actions to improve the health of the Great Lakes ecosystem.
Russell Van Herik, Executive Director
J. David Rankin, Program Director

2335 Hawk Mountain Sanctuary Association
1700 Hawk Mountain Road 610-756-6961
Kempton, PA 19529 Fax: 610-756-4468
info@hawkmountain.org
www.hawkmountain.org/contact/contact-us~form.aspx
Mission is to conserve birds of prey worldwide by providing leadership in raptor conservation science and education, and my maintaining Hawk Mountain Sanctuary as a model observation, research and education facility.
Wendy Mclean, Chairman
Peter Bennett, Vice Chairman

2336 Hazardous Waste Reduction Loan Program
California Department of Commerce
1001 I Street 916-341-6181
PO Box 4025 www.calrecycle.ca.gov
Sacramento, CA 95812
Loans assist small business to redude waste generation or to reduce the hazardous properties of waste generated. Proceeds can only be used to finance hazardous waste equipment acquistion, installation and processes.
Scott Smithline, Director
Ken DaRosa, Chief Deputy Director

2337 Heller Charitable and Educational Fund
244 California Street 415-434-3160
San Francisco, CA 94111 Fax: 415-434-3807
Mission is to protect and improve the quality of life through support of programs in the environment, human health, education, and the arts.
Ruth B Heller, Correspondence Secretary

2338 JM Kaplan Fund
120 East 23rd Street 212-767-0630
5th Floor Fax: 212-767-0639
New York, NY 10010 info@jmkfund.org
www.jmkfund.org
Support for the arts, the environment, human rights, and a robust civil society. New interests emerged in programs to support New York City neighborhoods parks and libraries as well as historic preservation and municipal design work inLower Manhattan.
Peter Davidson, Chairman
Joan K. Davidson, President

2339 Jessie Ball duPont Religious, Charitable and Educational Fund
40 East Adams Street 904-353-0890
Suite 300 800-252-3452
Jacksonville, FL 32202-3302 Fax: 904-353-3870
contactus@dupontfund.org
www.dupontfund.org
A private grantmaking foundation limited in its giving to approximately 330 eligible organizations to which Mrs. duPont personnally contributed to in a five year period 1960-1964. The duPont fund accomplishes its mission by workingcreatively with these organizations and their partners.
Sherry Magill, PhD, President
Mark D. Constantine, Senior Vice President

2340 Johnson's Wax Fund
1525 Howe Street 800-494-4855
Racine, WI 53403 www.scjohnson.com
Through the SC Johnson Fund, in the US, we donate, on average, 5% pre-tax profits every year to increase local and global well-being. Our contributions are targeted to advancing the three legs of sustainability: economic vitality,social progress, and a healthy environmnet.

2341 Joint Oceanographic Institutions
1201 New York Avenue NW

Suite 400
Washington, DC 20005
202-232-3900
Fax: 202-265-4409
info@joiscience.org
oceanleadership.org

A consortium of 20 premier oceanographic research institutions that serves the US scientific community through management of large scale, global research programs in the fields of marine geology and geophysics and oceanography.
Steven Bohlen, President
Amy Castner, Executive Program Associate

2342 LSB Leakey Foundation
1003B O'Reilly Avenue
San Francisco, CA 94129
415-561-4646
Fax: 415-561-4647
info@leakeyfoundation.org
www.leakeyfoundation.org/

The mission of the Leakey Foundation is to increase scientific knowledge and public understanding of human origins and evolution.
Dr. Francis Brown, Co-Chairman
Dr. Richard G. Klein, Co-Chairman

2343 MJ Murdock Charitable Trust
703 Broadway
Suite 710
Vancouver, WA 98660
360-694-8415
Fax: 360-649-1819
www.murdock-trust.org

The mission is to enrich the quality of life in the Pacific Northwest by providing grants organizations that seek to strenghten the region's educational and cultural base in creative and sustainable ways.
Steve Moore, Executive Director

2344 Mary Flagler Cary Charitable Trust
122 East 42nd Street
Room 3505
New York, NY 10168
212-953-7700
Fax: 212-953-7720
www.carytrust.org/

The Trust was established as a testamentary, charitable trust by the will of the late Mary Flagler Cary. The trustees have worked to use the assets of the Trust to carry forward Mrs. Cary's interests, and to elaborate on them in lightof new circumstances and needs. A major part of the Trust's assets continue to be devoted to special commitments relating to the origins of the Trust, especially the Institute of Ecosystem Studies at the Mary Flagler Cary Arboretum in Millbrook, NewYork.

2345 Maryland Sea Grant
University of Maryland
4321 Hardwick Road
Suite 300
College Park, MD 20740
301-405-7500
Fax: 301-314-5780
moser@mdsg.umd.edu
www.mdsg.umd.edu

Supports innovative marine research and education, with a special focus on the Chesapeake Bay.
Dr Fredrika Moser, Director

2346 National Academy of Sciences
500 Fifth Street, NW
Washington, DC 20001
202-334-2000
Fax: 202-334-2158
www.nasonline.org

The National Academy of Sciences (NAS) is an honorific society of distinguished scholars engaged in scientific and engineering research, dedicated to the furtherance of science and technology and to their use for the general welfare.
Ralph J. Cicerone, President
Diane Griffin, Vice President

2347 National Center for Atmospheric Research
PO Box 3000
Boulder, CO 80307-3000
303-497-1601
Fax: 303-497-1314
ncar.ucar.edu

NCAR provides the university research and teaching community with tools such as aircraft and radar to observe the atmosphere and with the technology and assistance to interpret and use these observations, including supercomputeraccess, computer models, and user support.
Michael Thompson, Interim President
Jim Hurrell, Director

2348 National Environmental Health Association NEHA/AAS Scholarships
720 S Colorado Boulevard
Suite 1000-N
Denver, CO 80246-1926
303-756-9090
866-956-2258
Fax: 303-691-9490
staff@neha.org
www.neha.org

Mission is to advance the environmental health and protection professional for the purpose of providing a healthful environment for all.
Elizabeth Landeen, Assistant Manager

2349 Needmor Fund
42 South Saint Clair Street
Toledo, OH 43604-8736
419-255-5560
Fax: 419-255-5561
www.needmorfund.org/

Mission is to work with others to bring about social justice. The Needmor Fund supposrt people who work together to change the social, economic or politcal conditions which bar their access to participation in a democratic society.
Abby Staranahan, Chair
Ken Rolling, Vice Chair

2350 Nixon Griffis Fund for Zoological Research: New York Zoological Society
Bronx Zoo
185th Street & Southern Boulevard
Bronx, NY 10460
212-220-5152
Fax: 212-220-7114

Supports research in zoology, conservation, and marine science. Grants lilmited to $3,000. Grants made four times a year. Applications reviewed by selected US zoo personnel.
John Behler, Contact

2351 North American Loon Fund Grants
PO Box 329
Holderness, NH 03245
603-528-4711
800-462-5666

The North American Loon Fund's mission is to promote the preservation of loons and their lake habitats through research, public education, and the involvement of people who share their lakes with loons.
Linda O'Bara, Director

2352 Oak Ridge Institute Science & Engineering Education Division
MC100-44
PO Box 117
Oak Ridge, TN 37831-0117
865-576-3146
Fax: 865-241-2923
communications@orau.org
www.orau.org

Strive to advance scientific research and education by creating mutually beneficial collaborative partnerships involving academe, government, and industry.
Andy Page, President & CEO
Eric Abelquist, Executive Vice President

2353 Resources for the Future
1616 P Street NW
Suite 600
Washington, DC 20036
202-328-5000
Fax: 202-939-3460
info@rff.org
www.rff.org

Resource for the Future (RFF) is a nonprofit and nonpartisan organization that conducts independent research and analysis, rooted primarily in economics, to help leaders make decisions and policies regarding natural resources and theenvironment.
Richard G. Newell, President & CEO

2354 The Center for Environmental Biotechnology at the University of Tennessee at Knoxville
1416 Circle Drive, 676 Dabney Hall 865-974-8080
Knoxville, TN 37996 Fax: 865-974-8086
cebweb@utk.edu
www.ceb.utk.edu

One of the nations oldest and largest university-based multidisciplinary research units devoted to environmental analysis. The CEB is a leader in the development of whole cell bioluminescent bioreporters for the detection of organicand inorganic pollutants including environmental endocrine disruptors and toxicants.
Gary S Sayler, Professor & Director
Lee Barham, Research Assistant

2355 University of Colorado: Boulder
Campus Box 216 303-492-1143
Boulder, CO 80309 Fax: 303-492-1149
www.colorado.edu

Recognized as one of the outstanding public universities in the United States. The Boulder campus has 5 colleges and 4 schools, offering 3,400 courses in about 150 areas of study.
Dr. Robert Sievers, Director

2356 WERC Undergraduate Fellowships
New Mexico State University 575-646-2038
Box 30001, MSC WERC 800-523-5996
Las Cruces, NM 88003 Fax: 505-646-4149
iee@nmsu.edu
www.ieenmsu.com/werc-2

WERC a consortium for environmental education and technology development. The consortium's mission is to develop the human resources and technologies needed to address environmental issues.
Abbas Ghassemi, Director
Barbara Valdez, Program Coordinator

2357 Water Environment Federation
601 Wythe Street 703-684-2492
Alexandria, VA 22314-1994 800-666-0206
inquiry@wef.org
www.wef.org

The Water Environment Federation (WEF) is a not-for-profit technical and educational organization with members from varied disciplines who work toward the preservation and enhancement of the global water environment.
Rick Warner, President
Jenny Hartfelder, President Elect

2358 Weston Institute
1400 Weston Way 610-701-3000
Po Box 2653 800-7WE-STON
West Chester, PA 19380 Fax: 610-701-3186
contactweston@westonsolutions.com
www.westonsolutions.com

A leading environmental and redevelopment firm focused on restoring efficiency to your essential resources: air, land, water, people, and facilities. We can help you develop solutions that maximize resource value and turn environmentalresponsibility into economic growth.
William L. Roberston, President/CEO

2359 Wildlife Conservation Society
2300 Southern Blvd 718-220-5100
Bronx, NY 10460 Fax: 718-365-3694
www.wcs.org

The Wildlife Conservation Society saves wildlife and wild lands. We do so through careful science, internation conservation, education, and the management of the world's largest system of urban wildlife parks, led by the flagship BronxZoo. Together, these activities change individual attitudes toward nature and help people imagine wildlife and humans living in sustainable interaction on both a local and a global scale.
Ward W Woods, Chair
Antonia M. Grumbach, Vice Chair

2360 Women's Seamen's Friend Society of Connecticut
P.O. Box 83100 203-777-2165
New Haven, CT 07868-3100 Fax: 203-777-5774
C. Marshall Davidson, Executive Director

2361 Yale Institute for Biospheric Studies (YIBS)
21 Sachem Street 203-432-9856
Rooms 132 and 136 Fax: 203-432-9927
New Haven, CT 00651 roserita.riccitelli@yale.edu
www.yale.edu/yibs

The Yale Institute for Biospheric Studies (YIBS) serves as a principal focus for Yale University's research and training efforts in the environmental sciences, and is committed to the teaching of environmental studies to futuregenerations. It provides physical and intellectual centers for research and education that address fundamental questions that will inform the ability to generate solutions to the biosphere's most critical environmental solutions.
Rose Rita Riccitelli, Assistant Director
Oswald Schmitz, Director

Government Agencies & Programs

Federal

2362 **Acid Rain Program (ARP)**
Clean Air Markets Division
1200 Pennsylvania Avenue NW 202-343-9429
Mail Code 6204M www.epa.gov/airmarkets/acid-rain-program
Washington, DC 20460

The Acid Rain Program is a part of the Clean Air Markets Division of the EPA and works toward emissions reductions of sulfur dioxide and nitrogen oxides, precursors of acid rain, from the power sector.
Reid Harvey, Director, Clean Air Markets

2363 **Advisory Committee on Reactor Safeguards**
US Nuclear Regulatory Commission
Washington, DC 20555-0001 301-415-7000
800-368-5642
Fax: 301-415-5575
www.nrc.gov

This committee's primary purposes are to review and report on safety studies and license applications; to advise the Commission on the hazards of proposed and existing production and utilization facilities; to initiate reviews ofnuclear facility safety; and to provide advice in the areas of health physics and radiation protection.
Dennis Bley, Chairman
Michael L. Corradini, Vice Chairman

2364 **Advisory Council on Historic Preservation**
401 F Street NW 202-517-0200
Suite 308 Fax: 202-517-6381
Washington, DC 20001-2637 achp@achp.gov
www.achp.gov

Mission: To promote the preservation, enhancement, and productive use of the nation's historic resources, and advise the President and Congress on national historic preservation policy.
John M. Fowler, Executive Director
Valerie Hauser, Director

2365 **Agency for Toxic Substances and Disease Registry**
Centers for Disease Control and Prevention
4770 Buford Highway NE
Atlanta, GA 30341 800-232-4636
ATSDRIC@cdc.gov
www.atsdr.cdc.gov

This agency provides leadership and direction to programs and activities designed to protect both the public and workers from exposure or adverse health effects of hazardous substances in storage sites or released in fires, explosions,or transportation accidents. The agency also collects, maintains, analyzes and disseminates information relating to serious diseases, mortality and human exposure to toxic or hazardous substances.
Robin Ikeda, Director
Donna Knutson, Deputy Director

2366 **American Farmland Trust**
1150 Connecticut Ave NW 202-331-7300
Suite 600 800-431-1499
Washington, DC 20036 Fax: 202-659-8339
info@farmland.org
www.farmland.org

American Farmland Trust aims to stop the loss of productive farmland, and to promote sound farming practices that lead to a healthy environment and keeps farmers on the land.
John Piotti, President
Jimmy Daukas, VP/Operations

2367 **American Indian Environmental Office**
1200 Pennsylvania Avenue NW 202-564-0303
Washington, DC 20460 Fax: 202-564-0298
tribal.portal@epa.gov
www.epa.gov/indian/

Coordinates the US Environmental Protection Agency-wide effort to strengthen public health and environmental protection in Indian Country, with a special emphasis on building Tribal capacity to administer their own environmentalprograms.
Felicia Wright, Acting Director

2368 **American Membrane Technology Association**
2409 SE Dixie Highway 772-463-0820
Stuart, FL 34996 Fax: 772-463-0860
custsrv@amtaorg.com
www.amtaorg.com/

AMTA's mission is to advocate for and advance the understanding and application of membrane technology to create safe, affordable and reliable water supplies, and to treat municipal, industrial, agricultural and waste waters forbeneficial use.
Brent Alspach, Presiednt

2369 **Animal and Plant Health Inspection Service Protection Quarantine**
1400 Independence Avenue SW 202-720-5601
Whitten Building, Room 302-E Fax: 202-690-0472
Washington, DC 20250 aelder@aphis.usda.gov
www.aphis.usda.gov

Mission: To protect the health and value of American agriculture and natural resources by promoting U.S. agricultural health, regulating genetically engineered organisms, administering the Animal Welfare Act and carrying out wildlifedamage management activities.
Michael C. Gregoire, Associate Administrator
Kevin Shea, Administrator

2370 **Antarctica Project and Southern Ocean Coalition**
1320 19th Street, NW, 202-234-2480
5th Floor Fax: 202-387-4823
Washington, DC 20036 secretariat@asoc.org
www.asoc.org

Concerned with educating the public about environmental problems in the arctic regions. Conducts research pertaining to Antarctica.
Claire Christian, Interim Executive Director

2371 **Aquatic Nuisance Species Task Force**
5275 Leesburg Pike 703-358-2466
Falls Church, VA 22041 Fax: 703-358-2487
david_hoskins@fws.gov
www.anstaskforce.gov/taskforce.php

An intergovernmental organization dedicated to preventing and controlling aquatic nuisance species. The task force consists of 10 federal agency reps and 12 ex-officio members
David Hoskins, Co-Chairman
Jennifer Lukens, Co-Chairman

2372 **Argonne National Laboratory**
9700 S Cass Avenue 630-252-2000
Argonne, IL 60439 webmaster@anl.gov
www.anl.gov/

One of the US Department of Energy's largest research centers that develops and researches solutions in areas such as sustainable energy, environmental health, and national safety.
Matthew Tirrell, Deputy Director
Paul Kearns, Interim Director

2373 **Army Corps of Engineers**
441 G Street NW 202-761-0011
Washington, DC 20314-1000 hq-publicaffairs@usace.army.mil
www.usace.army.mil

The Army Corps of Engineers manages and executes civil works programs, including research and development, planning, design, construction, operation and maintenance, and real estate activities related to rivers, harbors and waterways;administers laws for protection and preservation of navigable waters and related resources such as wetlands, and assists in recovery from natural disasters.
Todd T. Semonite, Commander/Chief Engineers
Richard L. Stevens, Major General

2374 Aspen Institute
One Dupont Circle, NW 202-736-5800
Suite 700 Fax: 202-467-0790
Washington, DC 21658 www.aspeninstitute.org
An education and policy studies organization that seeks to foster intellectual inquiry, create diverse leadership, and provides a nonpartisan forum for solutions on vital public policy issues in a number of areas, including engergy andthe environment.
Walter Isaacson, President/CEO
Elliot Gerson, Executive Vice President

2375 Atlantic States Marine Fisheries Commission
1050 North Highland Street 703-842-0740
Suite 200A-N Fax: 703-842-0741
Arlington, VA 22201 tberger@asmfc.org
www.asmfc.org
The Atlantic States Marine Fisheries Commission serves as a deliberative body, coordinating the conservation and management of the states shared near shore fishery resources-marine, shell, and anadromous-for sustainable use.
Robert E. Beal, Executive Director
Tina L. Berger, Director of Communications

2376 Bureau of Economic Analysis
4600 Silver Hill Road 301-278-9004
Washington, DC 20230 Fax: 301-763-4149
CustomerService@bea.gov
www.bea.gov
The mission of The Bureau of Economic Analysis (BEA) is to promote a better understanding of the US economy by providing timely, relevant, objective, and accurate economic accounts data through research, analysis, estimationmethodologies, and dissemtination of statistics to both the public and business professionals.
Brian C Moyer, Director
Sarahelen Thompson, Deputy Director

2377 Bureau of Land Management, Land & Renewable Resources
1849 C Street NW 202-208-3801
Room 5665 Fax: 202-208-5242
Washington, DC 20240 director@blm.gov
www.blm.gov
The mission of the Bureau of Land Management is to sustain the health, diversity, and productivity of the public lands for the use and enjoyment of present and future generations. Offers environmental education, news about theactivities of the Bureau, events, and regulations.
Michael D. Nedd, Director
John Ruhs, Deputy Director

2378 Bureau of Land Management: Division of Fish and Wildlife Conservation
1849 C Street NW 202-208-3801
Room 5665 Fax: 202-208-5242
Washington, DC 20240 www.blm.gov/programs/fish-and-wildlife
This division of the Bureau of Land Management aims to promote the restoration, enhancement, and protection of fish, wildlife, and invertebrate species and their habitats. More than 3,000 species of wildlife live on BLM-managed lands.
Michael D. Nedd, Acting Director
John Ruhs, Acting Deputy Director

2379 Bureau of Land Management: Soil, Air, and Water Program
Bureau of Land Management
1849 C Street NW 202-208-3801
Room 5665 Fax: 202-208-5242
Washington, DC 20240 director@blm.gov
www.blm.gov
Integrates soil, water, and air information with other disciples to support the BLM's multiple use and sustained yield mission.
Michael D. Nedd, Director
John Ruhs, Deputy Director

2380 Bureau of Land Management: Threatened and Endangered Species Program
1849 C Street NW 202-208-3801
Room 5665 Fax: 202-208-5242
Washington, DC 20240 www.blm.gov/programs/fish-and-wildlife
The Threatened and Endangered Species Program works to manage lands that provide a habitat for threatened and endangered species, helps to recover listed animal and plant species to remove them from the List of Threatened andEndangered Species, and collaborates with other federal agencies such as the U.S. Fish and Wildlife Service.
Michael D. Nedd, Acting Director
John Ruhs, Acting Deputy Director

2381 Bureau of Land Management: Wildlife Program
1849 C Street NW 202-208-3801
Room 5665 Fax: 202-208-5242
Washington, DC 20240 www.blm.gov/programs/fish-and-wildlife/wildlife
The BLM's Wildlife program helps support habitat maintenance and restoration to ensure the self-sustaining, abundant and diverse populations of wildlife on public lands.
Michael D. Nedd, Acting Director
John Ruhs, Acting Deputy Director

2382 Bureau of Oceans International Environmental & Scientific Affairs
US Department of State
2201 C Street NW 202-347-6950
Washington, DC 20520 www.state.gov/e/oes/
OES coordinates US international oceans, environmental and health policy, integrating US domestic concerns with geopolitical concerns. OES promotes the full range of US interests in the oceans to advance national security, facilitatecommerce, manage fish resources, foster scientific understanding and protect the marine environment through bilateral, regional and multilateral fora.
Rex W. Tillerson, Secretary of State
Judth G. Garber, Acting Assisstant Secretary

2383 Center for Environmental Finance: Environmental Finance Center Network (EFC)
Environmental Protection Agency
1200 Pennsylvania Ave (2710A) 202-564-4700
Washington, DC 20460 Fax: 202-564-1714
ocfoinfo@epa.gov
www.epa.gov/waterfinancecenter
Part of the EPA's EFP, the EFC is a network of 8 university-based programs in ten EPA regions that delivers techincal assistance and solutions to help manage costs of environmental financing.
Mike Flynn, Chief of Staff

2384 Centers for Disease Control and Prevention
National Center for Environmental Health
1600 Clifton Road
Atlanta, GA 30329-4027 800-232-4636
www.cdc.gov/nceh
To provide national leadership, through science and service, to promote health and quality of life by preventing and controlling

disease and death resulting from interactions between people and their environment.
Robin Ikeda, Director
Donna Knutson, Deputy Director

2385 Chemical, Bioengineering, Environmental & Transport Systems
National Science Foundation
4201 Wilson Boulevard 703-292-8320
Arlington, VA 22230 800-877-8339
www.nsf.gov/dir/index.jsp?org=ENG
CBET supports research and education in the rapidly evolving fields of bioengineering and environmental engineering and in areas that involve the transformation and/or transport of matter and energy by chemical, thermal, or mechanicalmeans.
Dr. JoAnne S. Lighty, Division Director
France A. Cordova, Director, NSF

2386 Chesapeake Bay Critical Areas Commission
1804 West Street 410-260-3460
Suite 100 Fax: 410-974-5338
Annapolis, MD 21401 dnr.maryland.gov/criticalarea/Pages/default.aspx
Develops criteria used by local jurisdictions to develop individual Critical Area programs and amend local comprehensive plans, zoning ordinances and subdivision regulations. Programs are designed to address the unique characteristicsand needs of each county and municipality and together they represent a comprehensive land use strategy for preserving and protecting Maryland's most important natural resource, the Chesapeake Bay.
Kate Charbonneau, Executive Director
Charles Deegan, Chairman

2387 Chief of Engineers Environmental Advisory Board
441 G Street NW 202-761-7690
Washington, DC 20314-1000 Fax: 202-761-1683
hq-publicaffairs@usace.army.mil
www.usace.army.mil
Serves the Armed Forces and the Nation by providing vital engineering services and capabilities, as a public service, across the full spectrum of operations; from peace to war; in support of national interests.
5 to 10 members
Once or twice a year
Todd T. Semonite, Commander/Chief of Engineers
Richard L. Stevens, Major General

2388 Children's Health Protection Advisory Committee (CHPAC)
Office of Children's Health Protection
1200 Pennsylvanie Avenue NW 202-564-2188
Mail Code 1107-T Fax: 202-564-2733
Washington, DC 20460 www.epa.gov/children
Advises, consults with and makes recommendations to EPA on issues associated with the development of regulations to address prevention of adverse health effects to children. The Committee also carries out related functions such ascollecting information and data to inform Agency decisions and serves to improve the breadth and depth of analyses related to the rules.

2 or 3 times a year
Martha Berger, Designated Federal Officer
Barbara Morrissey, Committee Chair

2389 Civil Division: Consumer Protection Branch
950 Pennsylvania Avenue NW 202-307-0066
Washington, DC 20530-0001 Civil.Feedback@usdoj.gov
www.justice.gov/civil
The Civil Division's Office of Consumer Litigation is responsible for criminal and civil litigation and related matters arising under a variety of federal statutes administered by its client agencies that protect public health andsafety.
Chad A. Readler, Acting Attorney General

2390 Clean Air Scientific Advisory Committee
US Environmental Protection Agency
1200 Pennsylvania Avenue NW 202-564-4700
Washington, DC 20460 www.epa.gov
The Clean Air Scientific Advisory Committee (CASAC) has a statutorily mandated responsibility to review and offer scientific advice on the air quality criteria and regulatory documents which form the basis for the National Ambient AirQuality Standards (NAAQS), which are currently lead, particulate matter (PM), ozone and other photochemical oxidants (O3), carbon monoxide (CO), nitrogen oxides (NOx) and sulfur oxides (SOx).
Ana V. Diez Roux, Chair

2391 Clean Air Status and Trends Network (CASTNET)
Clean Air Markets Division
1200 Pennsylvania Avenue NW 202-343-9429
Mail Code 6204M www.epa.gov/castnet
Washington, DC 20460
Esablished under the 1991 Clean Air Act Amendments, CASTNET is a national network that asseses trends in pollutant concentrations, atmospheric depositions, and ecological effect of changes in pollutant emissions.
Reid Harvey, Director

2392 Coast Guard
245 Muray Lane SW 202-372-4630
Washington, DC 20528-0075 www.uscg.mil
Its core roles are to protect the public, the environment, and US ecomonic and security interests in any maritime region in which those interests may be at risk, including international waters and America's coasts, ports, and inlandwaterways.
Admiral Paul Zukunft, Commandant
Admiral Charles Michel, Vice Commandant

2393 Coastal States Organization
444 N Capitol Street NW 202-508-3860
Suite 638 Fax: 202-508-3843
Washington, DC 20001 cso@coastalstates.org
www.coastalstates.org
Mission: To support the shared vision of the coastal states, commonwealths and territories for the protection, conservation, responsible use and sustainable economic development of the nation's coastal and ocean resources.
Mary Munson, Executive Director
Bradley Watson, Deputy Director

2394 Committee on Agriculture, Nutrition, and Forestry
328A Russell Senate Office Building 202-224-2035
Washington, DC 20510 Fax: 202-228-2125
agriculture.senate.gov
The Committee aims to help establish, guide, and examine agricultural policies both in America and abroad. The Committee deals with trade, research, food stafety, nutrition, conservation, and commodity price and income supports.
Debbie Stabenow, Ranking Member
Pat Roberts, Chairman

2395 Committee on Commerce
Committee on Energy and Commerce
2125 Rayburn House Office Building 202-225-2927
Washington, DC 20515 Fax: 202-225-1919
commerce@mail.house.gov
www.house.gov/commerce
The oldest standing legislative committee in the U.S. House of Representatives, the Committee on Engery and Commerce is responsible for things such as environmental quality, energy policy, and food and drug safety. The Committee onEnergy on Commerce also oversees the Departments of Engery, the Environmental Protection Agency, and others.
Greg Walden, Chairman
Joe Barton, Vice Chair

2396 Committee on Commerce, Science, and Transportation
512 Dirksen Senate Office Building 202-224-0411
Washington, DC 20510 www.commerce.senate.gov
The Committee on Commerce, Science, and Transportation studies and reviews all matters relating to science and technology, oceans policy, transportation, communications, and comsumer affairs. It is comprised of 6 subcommittees thatoversee any issues under their jurisdiction.
26 members
John Thune, Chairman
Bill Nelson, Ranking Member

2397 Committee on Energy and Natural Resources
304 Dirksen Senate Building 202-224-4971
Washington, DC 20510 Fax: 202-224-6163
energy.senate.gov
The Committee on Energy and Natural Resources considers, reports, and oversees legislation in areas such as energy resources, including regulation and conservation; nuclear energy; Indian affairs; territories and insular possessions;water resources; surface mining, Federal coal, oil, gas, and other mineral leasing.
Lisa Murkowski, Chairman
Maria Cantwell, Ranking Member

2398 Committee on Environment and Public Works Republicans
410 Dirksen Senate Office Bldg 202-224-6176
Washington, DC 20510-6175 epw.senate.gov
John Barrasso, Chair

2399 Committee on Government Reform and Oversight
2157 Rayburn House Office Building 202-225-5074
Washington, DC 20515 Fax: 202-225-3974
oversight.house.gov
The Committee acts as the voice of hard working taxpayers, by ensuring the efficieny, effectivness, and accountability of the federal government.
Trey Gowdy, Chairman
Elijah Cummings, Ranking Member

2400 Committee on Natural Resources
US House of Representatives
1324 Longworth House Office Bldg. 202-225-2761
Washington, DC 20515 Fax: 202-225-5929
naturalresources.house.gov
Composed of 26 Republicans and 18 Democrats, the Committee on Natural Resources considers legislation regarding energy production, mineral lands and mining, fisheries and wildlife, public lands, oceans, Native Americans, irrigation andreclamation. The Committee is divided into 5 subcommittes on Energy and Natural Resources; Federal Lands; Water, Power and Oceans; Oversight and Investiagtions; and Indian, Insular and Alaska Native Affairs
44 members
Rob Bishop, Chair

2401 Committee on Science and Technology
2321 Rayburn House Office Building 202-225-6371
Washington, DC 20515 Fax: 202-226-0113
science.house.gov
The Committee on Science and Technology deals with all research, development, demonstrations, and projects relating to environmental research, marine research, astronautical research and development, exploration of outer space, civilaviation research and development, and more.
Lamar Smith, Chair

2402 Committee on Small Business and Entrepreneurship: US Senate
428A Russell Senate Office Building 202-224-5175
Washington, DC 20515 Fax: 202-224-5619
sbc.senate.gov
Founded in 1981 and composed of 10 Republican and 9 Democrat members, the Committee on Small Business Entrepreneurship refers to all proposed legisaltion, messages, petitions, memorials, and other matters relating to the Small BusinessAdministration (SBA). They also investigate all problems of small business enterprises.
19 members
James Risch, Chair
Jeanne Shaheen, Ranking Member

2403 Committee on Small Business: House of Representatives
Small Business Committee
2361 Rayburn House Office Bldg. 202-225-5821
Washington, DC 20515 Fax: 202-226-5276
smbiz@mail.house.gov
smallbusiness.house.gov
The Small Business Committee protects and assists small business in matters of financial aid, regulatory flexibility, and paperwork reduction.Additionally, they have legisaltive authority over the Small Business Administration (SBA).
Steve Chabot, Chair
Nydia Velazquez, Ranking Member

2404 Committee on Transportation and Infrastructure
2251 Rayburn House Office Building 202-225-9446
Washington, DC 20515 Fax: 202-225-6782
Transport@mail.house.gov
transportation.house.gov
The Committee on Transportation has jurisdiction over all modes of transportation, including aviation, maritime and waterborne transportation; federal agencies, including the Department of Transportation, the U.S. Coast Guard, and theEnvironmental Protection Agency. They also deal with clean water and waste water management, flood damage reduction, and hazardous materials transportation.
Bill Shuster, Chair
Peter A. DeFazio, Ranking Member

2405 Cooperative Forestry Research Advisory Council
US Forest Service
1400 Independence Avenue SW
Washington, DC 20250-0003 800-832-1355
www.fs.fed.us/research/about
The Forestry Research Advisory Council (FRAC) provides advice to the Secretary of Agricultre on the McIntire-Stennis Act of 1962, and deals with regional and national forestry research planning and coordination within Federal and Stateagencies, forestry schools, forest industries, and non-governmental organizations.
20 members
Anually
Shibu Jose, Chair
Nicole D. Cavender, Chair-Elect

2406 Council for the Conservation of Migratory Birds
US Fish & Wildlife Service
1849 C Street NW 202-208-1050
Room 3331 800-344-9453
Washington, DC 20240-0001 Fax: 202-482-3716
www.fws.gov/
The Council was created by the Secretary of the Interior to oversee the implementation of an Executive order that deals with the responsibilities of Federal Agencies to protect migratory birds.
Jim Kurthway, Deputy Director
Greg Sheehan, Acting Director

2407 Council on Environmental Quality
730 Jackson Place, Northwest
Washington, DC 20503
202-395-5750
Fax: 202-456-6546
www.whitehouse.gov/CEQ/

The Council on Environmental Quality coordinates federal environmental efforts and works closely with agencies and other White House offices in the development of environmental policies and initiatives.

2408 Dangerous Goods Advisory Council
7501 Greenway Center Drive
Suite 760
Greenbelt, MD 20770
202-289-4550
Fax: 202-289-4074
info@dgac.org
www.dgac.org

DGAC, also known as the Hazardous Materials Advidosry Council, is an international, nonprofit, educational organization that promotes safety in the transportation of hazardous materials and dangerous goods, including hazardoussubstances and hazardous wastes.

Barbara Lantry-Miller, Chairman
Todd Strobel, Vice Chairman

2409 Department of Agriculture
USDA Forest Service
1400 Independence Avenue SW
Washington, DC 20250-1111
800-832-1355
www.fs.fed.us

The mission of the Department of Agriculture's Forest Service is to promote sustainable forest management and biodiversity concervation, and to help sustain the health and diversity of the nation's forests and grasslands.

Thomas L. Tidwell, Chief
Dan Jiron, Associate Chief

2410 Department of Agriculture: Research Department, Forest Environment Research
1400 Independence Avenue SW
Washington, DC 20250-0003
800-832-1355
www.fs.fed.us/research

The Research Department of the USDA works to improve the health of the nation's forests and grasslands, and to research and promote the sustainbale management of the nation's forests and rangelands.

Thomas L. Tidwell, Chief
Dan Jiron, Associate Chief

2411 Department of Agriculture: Agricultural Research Service (ARS)
Jamie L. Whitten Building
1400 Independence Avenue SW
Room 302A
Washington, DC 20250
202-720-3656
Fax: 202-720-5427
www.ars.usda.gov/

ARS is a scientific research agency that is part of the USDA. They conduct research to develop and transfer solutions to agricultural problems of high national priority.

Chavonda Jacobs-Young, Administrator
Steven M. Kappes, Associate Administrator

2412 Department of Agriculture: Forest Inventory and Analysis Program
USDA Forest Service
1400 Independence Avenue SW
Washington, DC 20250-1111
703-605-4177
800-832-1355
greams@fs.fed.us
www.fs.fed.us/research

The Forest Inventory and Analysis Program (FIA) provides census information on the nation's forest. They report on things such as status and trends in forest area and location; the species, size, and health of trees; total tree growth,mortality, and removals; and in forest land ownership.

Greg Reams, National Program Manager
Brad Smith, Associate Program Manager

2413 Department of Agriculture: Forest Service Public Affairs
1400 Independence Avenue SW
Washington, DC 20250-1111
202-205-1296
800-832-1355
webmaster@fs.fed.us
www.fs.fed.us

Thomas L. Tidwell, Chief
Dan Jiron, Associate Chief

2414 Department of Agriculture: Natural Resources State and Private Forestry Division
US Forest Service State and Private Forestry
1400 Independence Avenue SW
Washington, DC 20250-0003
202-205-1657
800-832-1355
www.fs.fed.us/spf

Links forestry and conservation with people from the inner city to the rural countryside. Connects people to resources and provides technical and financial assitance to landowners and resource managers in order to help sustain thenation's forests.

Vicki Christiansen, Deputy Chief
Jane Darnell, Associate Deputy Chief

2415 Department of Agriculture: Research Department Fire Sciences Program
Boise Aquatic Sciences Lab
322 East Front Street
Suit 401
Boise, ID 83702
208-373-4340
Fax: 208-373-4391
www.fs.fed.us/recreation

This project conducts research on the reestablishment of native vegetation after wildfires.

Thomas L. Tidwell, Chief
Dan Jiron, Associate Chief

2416 Department of Agriculture: Water, Air, and Soil Research
US Forest Service Research & Development
1400 Independence Avenue SW
Washington, DC 20250-0003
202-205-1657
800-832-1355
www.fs.fed.us/research/water-air-soil

This research builds on 100 years of research to better understand various interactions of weather patterns, changing land uses, and pollution levels on the nation's forests and their water, air, and soil resources.

Thomas L. Tidwell, Chief
Dan Jiron, Associate Chief

2417 Department of Commerce: National Oceanic & Atmospheric Administration
1401 Constitution Avenue NW
Room 5128
Washington, DC 20230
www.noaa.gov

The mission of the NOAA is to understand changes in climate, weather, oceans and coasts; to share that knowledge and information with the public; and to foster the conservation and management of coastal and marine ecosystems.

Benjamin Friedman, Under Secretary of Commerce
Dr. Stephen Volz, Assistant Secretary

2418 Department of Commerce: National Marine Fisheries Service
1315 East West Highway
Silver Spring, MD 20910
301-713-2379
Fax: 301-713-2385
www.nmfs.noaa.gov

Mission: Stewardship of living marine resources through science-based conservation and management and the promotion of healthy ecosystems.

Chris Oliver, Assistant Administrator

2419 Department of Commerce: National Ocean Service
Office of Ocean Resources Conservation/Assessment

1305 East-West Highway 301-713-3066
Silver Spring, MD 20910 Fax: 301-713-4389
nos.info@noaa.gov
www.oceanservice.noaa.gov
The National Ocean Service works to observe, understand, and manage our nation's coastal and marine resources.
Russell Callender, Assistant Administrator

2420 Department of Energy: Office of Electricity Delivery and Energy Reliability
U.S. Department of Energy
1000 Independence Avenue SW 202-586-1411
Washington, DC 20585 Fax: 202-586-1472
OEwebmaster@hq.doe.gov
energy.gov/
The Office of Electricity Delivery and Energy Reliability works to ensure that the Nation's energy is secure and reliable, as well as developing new technologies that improve existing systems that bring electricity into homes andbusinesses. The office also assists with grid restoration when major energy disruptions occur.
Patricia A. Hoffman, Deputy Assistant Secretary
Terri T. Lee, Chief Operating Officer

2421 Department of Energy: Office of Fossil Energy
U.S. Department of Energy
1000 Independence Avenue SW 202-586-6660
Forrestal Building energy.gov/fe/office-fossil-energy
Washington, DC 20585
This office is responsible for the research, development, and demonstration efforts on advanced carbon capture and storage technologies. They aim to ennsure that the nation can continue to rely on traditional resources for clean andaffordable energy while enhancing environmental protection.
Douglas Hollett, Deputy Assisstant Secretary

2422 Department of Energy: Office of NEPA Policy and Compliance
1000 Independence Avenue SW 202-586-4600
EH-42 800-472-2756
Washington, DC 20585 Fax: 202-586-7031
AskNEPA@hq.doe.gov
energy.gov/nepa/office-nepa-policy-and-compliance
This office serves as the contact point for NEPA matters for the US Department of Energy, and ensures that any proposed actions comply with NEPA requirements.
Brian Costner, Director

2423 Department of Energy: Office of Nuclear Energy
U.S. Department of Energy 202-586-2240
1000 Independence Avenue SW energy.gov/ne/office-nuclear-energy
Washington, DC 20585
The Office of Nuclear Energy's (NE) primary mission is to advance nuclear power as a resource capable of making major contributions in meeting the Nation's energy supply, environmental, and energy security needs.
Edward McGinnis, Acting Assistant Secretary
Raymond Furstenau, Acting Principal Deputy

2424 Department of Energy: Transportation and Alternative Fuels
Office of Energy Efficiency and Renewable Energy
1000 Independence Avenue SW 202-586-8302
EE-1 Fax: 202-586-9811
Washington, DC 20585 energy.gov/eere/transportation
Researches how to make transportation cleaner and more efficient through green technology and alternative fuelss.
Daniel Simmons, Assistant Secretary

2425 Department of Justice: Environment and Natural Resources Division
US Department of Justice
950 Pennsylvania Avenue NW 202-514-2701
Washington, DC 20530-0001 webcontentmgr.enrd@usdoj.gov
www.justice.gov/enrd
The ENRD is responsible for prosecuting violations of civil and criminal pollution control laws, defending environmental challenges to government programs, and representing the US in the stewardship of the nation's natural resourcesand public lands.
Jeffrey H. Wood, Acting Attorney General

2426 Department of State: Bureau of Economic and Business
2201 C Street NW Room 3529 202-647-4000
Washington, DC 20520 Fax: 202-647-8758
www.state.gov/e/eb/
The Bureau of Economic and Business Affairs works to create jobs for Americans at home while increasing economic opportunities overseas, such as opening new export opportunities for farmers and ranchers.
Patricia M. Haslach, Assistant Secretary

2427 Department of State: Office of Conservation and Water
US Department of State
2201 C Street NW 202-347-6950
Washington, DC 20520 www.state.gov/e/oes/ecw/index.htm
Coordinates and leads the formulation of policies on conserving and sustainably managing ecologically and economically important ecosystems.
Judith G. Garber, Acting Assistant Secretary

2428 Department of State: Office of Global Change
Office of Global Change 202-347-6950
OES/EGC, US Department State ClimateComms@State.gov
Washington, DC 20520 www.state.gov/e/oes/climate/
Leads the US in a variety of international panels and forums, coordinates bilateral and regional partnerships on climate change, and US forign assistance on clean energy, adaptation, and sustainable landscapes.
Judith G. Garber, Acting Assistant Secretary

2429 Department of State: Office of Marine Conservation
US Department of State
Office of Marine Conservation 202-347-6950
2201 C Street NW, Room 5806 www.state.gov/e/oes/ocns/fish/index.htm
Washington, DC 20520
The Office of Marine Conservation is responsible for US policy on the conservation and management of living marine resources.
Judith G. Garber, Acting Assistant Secretary

2430 Department of Transportation: Office of Marine Safety, Security & Environmental
Maritime Administration
1200 New Jersey Avenue, SE 202-366-4000
Washington, DC 20590 webmaster.marad@dot.gov
www.marad.dot.gov/environment_safety_landing_page/environmen
Ensures a safe, secure, efficient and environmentally sustainable maritime transportation system.
John P. Quinn, Associate Administrator

2431 Department of Transportation: Office of Pipeline Safety
1200 New Jersey Avenue SE 202-366-4433
East Building 2nd Floor Fax: 202-366-3666
Washington, DC 20590 phmsa.administrator@dot.gov
www.phmsa.dot.gov/pipeline
Mission: To protect people and the environment from the risks of hazardous materials transportation by establishing national poli-

cies, enforcing standards, educating the public, and conducting research.
Vasiliki Tsaganos, Chief Counsel
Howard McMillan, Deputy Administrator

2432 Department of the Interior
1849 C Street NW 202-208-3100
Washington, DC 20240 feedback@ios.doi.gov
www.doi.gov
The Department of the Interior protects and manages the Nation's natural resources and cultural heritage; provides scientific and other information about those resources; and honors its trust responsibilities or special commitments toAmerican Indians, Alaska Natives, and affiliated island communities.
Ryan Zinke, Secretary

2433 Department of the Interior: National Parks Service
1849 C Street NW 202-208-6843
Washington, DC 20240 www.nps.gov
The National Park Service preserves unimpaired the natural and cultural resources and values of the national park system for the enjoyment, education, and inspiration of this and future generations. The Park Service cooperates withpartners to extend the benefits of natural and cultural resource conservation and outdoor recreation throughout this country and the world.
Michael T. Reynolds, Director
Lena McDowell, Deputy Director

2434 Department of the Interior: Bureau of Land Management
1849 C Street Northwest 202-208-3801
Room 5665 Fax: 202-208-5242
Washington, DC 20240 director@blm.gov
www.blm.gov
To sustain the health, diversity, and productivity of America's public lands for the use and enjoyment of present and future generations.
John Ruhs, Acting Deputy Director
Michael D. Nedd, Acting Director

2435 Department of the Interior: Division of Parks and Wildlife
Office of the Solicitor
1849 C Street NW 202-208-4344
Washington, DC 20240 www.doi.gov/solicitor/headquarters
To provide legal counsel on matters such as the administration of programs and activities of the National Park Service, the Fish and Wildlife Service, and the biological research functions of the Geological Survey.
Ryan Zinke, Secretary, DOI

2436 Department of the Interior: Office of the Solicitor
1849 C Street Northwest 202-208-4423
Washington, DC 20240 www.doi.gov/solicitor
To provide legal counsel and representation to the Secretary, the Assistant Secretaries, and the Bureau Directors.
Ryan Zinke, Sectretary, DOI

2437 Department of the Interior: Office of the Secretary
1849 C Street NW 202-208-3100
Interior Building, Room 6156 feedback@ios.doi.gov
Washington, DC 20240 www.doi.gov
The Secretary of the Interior is responsible for leading an agency of over 70,000 empolyees. The department oversees the responsible development of conventional and renewable energy supplies on public lands and waters and upholds trustresponsibilities to the 567 federally recognized American Indian Tribes and Alaska Natives.
Ryan Zinke, Secretary of the Interior

2438 Department of the Interior: U.S. Fish & Wildlife Service
1849 C Street NW 202-208-4717
Room 3331 800-344-9453
Washington, DC 20240-0001 Fax: 202-208-6965
www.fws.gov
Mission: Working with others, to conserve, protect and enhance fish, wildlife, and plants and their habitats for the continuing benefit of the American people.
Greg Sheehan, Acting Director
Jim Kurth, Deputy Director

2439 Department of the Interior: Water and Science, Water Resources Division
US Geological Survey
12201 Sunrise Valley Drive 703-648-4557
Reston, VA 20192 usgsnews@usgs.gov
water.usgs.gov/about_WRD.html
Provides reliable, impartial, timely information to understand the water resources of the United States.
Donald Cline, Associate Director
William Guertal, Deputy Associate Director

2440 Department of the Interior: Water and Science Bureau of Reclamation
1849 C Street NW 202-513-0501
Washington, DC 20240-0001 Fax: 202-513-0309
www.usbr.gov
To manage, develop, and protect water and related resources in an environmentally and economically sound manner in the interest of the American public.
Alan Mikkelsen, Commissioner
James Hess, Chief of Staff

2441 Department of the Interior: Wild Horses and Burros
Bureau of Land Management
1849 C Steet NW 775-861-6614
Room 5665 866-468-7826
Washington, DC 20240 wildhorse@blm.gov
www.blm.gov
The BLM protects, manages, and controls wild horses and burros under the authority of the Wild Free-Roaming Horses and Burros Act of 1971 to ensure that healthy herds thrive on healthy rangelands.
Brian Lombard, BLM Public Affairs
Jason Lutterman, Public Affairs

2442 Dept. of Agriculture: National Forest Watershed and Hydrology
USDA Forest Service
1400 Independence Avenue SW 202-205-8333
Washington, DC 20250-1111 800-832-1355
webmaster@fs.fed.us
www.fs.fed.us
The Watershed Team leads programs dealing with watershed restoration, surface water, and groundwater to conserve and protect the soil, water and aquatic resources of national forests and grasslands.
Thomas L. Tidwell, Chief
Kate P. Walker, Assistant Director

2443 EPA: Office of Land and Emergency Management
1200 Pennsylvania Ave NW 202-566-0200
Washington, DC 20460 www.epa.gov
Develops guidelines for land disposal of hazardous waste, provides assistance in the establishment of safe waste management practices, supports the redevelopment of contaminated sites, and respondes to abandoned and active hazardouswaste sites.
Brad Breen, Assistant Administrator

2444 EPA:Science Advidsory Committee on Chemicals
Environmental Protection Agency
1200 Pennsylvania Ave. NW 202-260-5495
Washington, DC 20460-0001
Established in 2016, the SACC provides scientific advice to the EPA on risk assessments, methodologies, and pollution prevention for chemicals regulated by the Toxic Substances Control Act (TSCA).
18 members
Dr. Kenneth Portier, Chair

2445 Economic Research Service
United States Department of Agriculture
1400 Independance Avenue SW 202-694-5139
Mail Stop 1800 www.ers.usda.gov
Washington, DC 20250-0002
The USDA's Economic Research Service anticipates trends and emerging issues in agriculture, food, and the environment, and conducts objective economic reasearch to inform the public.
Mary Bohman, Administrator
Greg Pompelli, Associate Administrator

2446 Environment and Natural Resources: Environmental Crimes Section
Department of Justice
950 Pennsylvania Avenue NW 202-514-2701
Washington, DC 20530-0001 webcontentmgr.enrd@usdoj.gov
www.justice.gov/enrd
To bring criminal cases against individuals and organizations that break the laws that protect our nation's ecological and wildlife resources
Deborah L. Harris, Chief

2447 Environmental Change and Security Program: Woodrow Wilson International Center for Scholars
1300 Pennsylvania Avenue NW 202-691-4000
Washington, DC 20004-3027 www.wilsoncenter.org/ecsp
The ECSP provides specialists and interested individuals with a road-map to the myriad conceptions, activities and policy initiatives related to environment, population and security. The project pursues three basic activities:gathering information on related international academic and policy initiatives; organizing meetings of experts and public seminars; and publishing the ECSP Report, The China Environment Series and related papers.ECSP explores a wide range ofenvironment related issues.
Thomas R. Nides, Chairman

2448 Environmental Financial Advisory Board (EFAB)
US EPA, Office of Wastewater Management
1200 Pennsylvania Avenue NW 202-564-1151
Washington, DC 20460 www.epa.gov/waterfinancecenter/efab
The EFAB provides advice to the Environmental Protection Agency's Administrator and program offices around the financial aspects of environmental protection. They are a federally chartered advisory committee operating under the FederalAdvisory Committee Act.
Aurel M. Arndt, General Manager, CEO
James McGoff, Director

2449 Environmental Health Sciences Review Committee
National Institute of Envronmental Health Services
111 T.W. Alexander Drive 919-541-3345
Durham, NC 27709 Fax: 301-480-2978
www.niehs.nih.gov/index.cfm
SRB is responsible for the initial scientific and technical merit review of grant applications and contract proposals submitted to the NIH
21 members
Thomas J. Montine, Chair
Linda K. Bass, Scientific Review Officer

2450 Environmental Management
US Department of Energy 202-586-7709
1000 Independence Ave SW EM.WebContentManager@em.doe.gov
Washington, DC 20585 www.em.doe.gov
The Office of Environmental Management deals with the safe cleanup of decades worth of nuclear weapons development and nuclear energy research.
James M. Owendoff, Assistant Secretary
Stacy Charboneau, Associate Principal Deputy

2451 Environmental Management Advisory Board
Office of Environmental Management
1000 Independence Avenue SW 202-586-7709
Washington, DC 20585 EM.WebContentManager@em.doe.gov
energy.gov
The mission of the Environmental Management Advisory Board is to provide advice, information and recommendations to the Assistant Secretary for Environmental Management regarding environmental restoration and waste management issues.
David W. Swindle Jr., Chair
Paul M. Dabbar, Board Member

2452 Environmental Protection Agency
1200 Pennsylvania Avenue NW 202-564-4700
Washington, DC 20460 www.epa.gov
EPA's mission is to protect human health and to safeguard the natural environment- air, water and land- upon which life depends. Since 1970, EPA has been working for a cleaner, healthier environment for the American people.
Scott Pruitt, Administrator
Mike Flynn, Deputy Administrator

2453 Environmental Protection Agency Climate Change Division
Office of Atmospheric Programs (OAP)
Ariel Rios Building 202-349-9140
1200 Pennsylvania Avenue www.epa.gov
Washington, DC 20460
EPA's Climate Change Division works to assess and address global climate change and the associated risks to human health and the environment.
Scott Pruitt, Administrator
Mike Flynn, Deputy Administrator

2454 Environmental Protection Agency Ground Water and Drinking Water
Ariel Rios Building 202-564-3750
1200 Pennsylvania Avenue grevatt.peter@epa.gov
Washington, DC 20460 www.epa.gov/ground-water-and-drinking-water
Mission: To protect public health by ensuring safe drinking water and protecting ground water.
Peter C. Grevatt, Director
Jennifer McLain, Deputy Director

2455 Environmental Protection Agency Resource Conservation and Recovery Act
Ariel Rios Building 202-564-4700
1200 Pennsylvania Avenue www.epa.gov/rcra
Washington, DC 20460
RCRA is a public law that gives EPA the authority to control hazardous waste from the cradle-to-grave. This includes the generation, transportation, treatment, storage, and disposal of hazardous waste.
Scott Pruitt, Administrator
Mike Flynn, Deputy Administrator

2456 Environmental Protection Agency: Indoor Air Division
Office of Radiation and Indoor Air

Ariel Rios Building 202-343-9370
1200 Pennsylvania Avenue NW indoorair@epa.gov
Washington, DC 20460 www.epa.gov
Mission: To protect the public and the environment from the risks of radiation and indoor air pollution.
David Rowson, Director

2457 Environmental Protection Agency: Office of Pollution Prevention & Toxics
Pollution Prevention Division
1200 Pennsylvania Avenue NW 202-564-3810
Mail Code 7401-M oppt.homepage@epa.gov
Washington, DC 20460 www.epa.gov/oppt
To manage programs under the Toxic Substances Control Act
Jeffrey Morris, Director
Barbara Cunningham, Deputy Director

2458 Environmental Protection Agency: Water
Environmental Protection Agency
Ariel Rios Building 202-564-5700
1200 Pennsylvania Avenue NW
Washington, DC 20460
The Office of Water is responsible for implementing the Clean Water Act and Safe Drinking Water Act. They also help to restore and maintain the health of oceans, watersheds, and aquatic ecosystems.
Michael H. Shapiro, Assistant Administrator
Dennis Lee Forsgren Jr., Deputy Asst Administrator

2459 Farm, Ranch, and Rural Communities Committee (FRRCC)
Federal Advisory Committee Management Division
1200 Pennsylvania Avenue NW 202-564-2294
Mail Code 1601M www.epa.gov/faca/frrcc
Washington, DC 20460
Provides advice and recommendations to the Administrator on environmental issues and programs that impact, or are of concern to, farms, ranches, and rural communities

Twice a year
David Petty, Deputy Chair
Steven Balling, Chair

2460 Federal Aviation Administration
800 Independence Avenue, SW
Washington, DC 20591 866-835-5322
www.faa.gov
The major roles of the Federal Aviation Administration (a part of the Department of Transportation) include regulation, development, and research in the areas of civil aviation, civil aeronautics, and U.S. commercial spacetransportation. The FAA funds awards for airport safety, aerospace medicine, and more.
Michael P. Huerta, Administrator
Dan Elwell, Deputy Administrator

2461 Federal Energy Regulatory Commission
888 1st Street NE 202-502-6088
Washington, DC 20426 866-208-3372
customer@ferc.gov
www.ferc.gov
FERC is an independent commission within which has retained many of the functions of the Federal Power Commission, such as setting rates and charges for the transporation and scale of natural gas and for the transmission and sale ofelectricity and the licensing of hydroelectric power projects. In addition, the commission establishes rates or charges for the transportation of oil by pipeline, as well as the valuation of such pipelines.
Cheryl A. LaFleur, Chairman

2462 Federal Highway Administration
1200 New Jersey Avenue SE 202-366-4000
Washington, DC 20590 web.master@fhwa.dot.gov
www.fhwa.dot.gov
Mission: Enhancing mobility through innovation, leadership, and public service.
Walter C. Waidelich Jr., Deputy Administrator
Gloria M. Shepherd, Executive Director

2463 Federal Insecticide, Fungicide, and Rodenticide Act Scientific Advisory Panel
Office of Science Coordination and Policy
1200 Pennsylvanie Avenue NW 202-564-0103
Mail Stop 7201M knott.steven@epa.gov
Washington, DC 20460-0001 www.epa.gov/sap
Provides independent scientific advice on pesticides and pesticide-related issues and analyzes the impacts of EPA's pesticide-related regulatory actions.
Steven Knott, Designated Federal Officer
James McManaman, Chair

2464 Federal Railroad Administration
1200 New Jersey Avenue, SE 202-493-6000
Washington, DC 20590 webmaster@fra.dot.gov
www.fra.dot.gov
Created by the Department of Transportation Act in 1966, the FRA ensures the safe and efficient movement of people and goods in the present and future.
Patrick T. Warren, Executive Director
Heath Hall, Acting Administrator

2465 Federal Transit Administration
US Department of Transportation
1200 New Jersey Avenue SE 202-366-4043
4th & 5th Floor, East Building 866-377-8642
Washington, DC 20590 www.fta.dot.gov
Provides financial and technical assitance to local public transit systems, and oversees safety measures.
Matthew Welbes, Executive Director
Dana Nifosi, Acting Chief Counsel

2466 Food Safety and Inspection Service
1400 Independence Ave SW 202-720-7025
Washington, DC 20250-3700 Fax: 202-205-0158
fsis.webmaster@usda.gov
www.fsis.usda.gov
The Food Safety and Inspection Service (FSIS) is the public health agency in the U.S. Department of Agriculture responsible for ensuring that the nation's commercial supply of meat, poultry, and egg products is safe, wholesome, andcorrectly labeled and packaged.
Carmen Rottenberg, Deputy Administrator
Alfred V Almanza, Deputy Under Secretary

2467 Food and Drug Administration
US Department of Health and Human Services
10903 New Hampshire Avenue
Silver Spring, MD 20993-0002 888-463-6332
www.fda.gov
Mission: Responsible for protecting the public health by assuring the safety, efficacy, and security of human and veterinary drugs, biological products, medical devices, our nation's food supply, cosmetics, and products that emitradiation. The FDA is also responsible for advancing the public health by helping to speed innovations that make medicines and foods more effective, safer, and more affordable.
Scott Gottlieb, Commissioner
Anna Abram, Deputy Commissioner

2468 Forest Health Protection
Forest Service-USDA

1400 Independance Avenue SW 705-605-5344
Stop Code 1110 www.fs.fed.us/foresthealth/
Washington, DC 20250-1110
Forest Health Protection protects and improves the health of America's rural, wildland, and urban forests by providing technical assistance on forest health-related matters.
Rick Cooksey, Acting Director

2469 General Services Administration
1800 F Street, NW
Washington, DC 20405 844-472-4111
fbo.support@gsa.gov
www.gsa.gov
The GSA's mission is to provide the best value in real estate, acqusition, and technology services to the government and the American people.
Timothy O. Horne, Administrator
Anothony Costa, Deputy Administrator

2470 Global Learning and Observations to Benefit the Environment
3300 Mitchell Lane 303-497-2620
Boulder, CO 80301 800-858-9947
help@globe.gov
www.globe.gov
Mission: To promote the teaching and learning of science, enhance environmental literacy and stewardship, and promote scientific discovery.
Dr. Tony Murphy, Director
Hanne Mauriello, Senior Advisor

2471 Good Neighbor Environmental Board (GNEB)
1200 Pennsylvania Avenue NW 202-564-2130
Mail Code 1601-M Fax: 202-564-8129
Washington, DC 20460 joyce.mark@epa.gov
www.epa.gov/faca/gneb
GNEB is an independent federal advisory committee that reports to and advises the President and Congress about environmental and infrastructure isses and needs within the US states contiguous to Mexico in order to improve the qualityof life of persons residing along the US border.
Mark Joyce, Designated Federal Officer

2472 Greenhouse Gas Reporting Program (GHGRP)
EPA: Climate Change Division
1200 Pennsylvania Avenue NW 202-343-9876
Washington, DC 20460 www.epa.gov/ghgreporting
This program, a part of the Climate Change Division of the EPA, requires reporting of greenhouse gas data from large greenhouse gas emission sources, fuel and industrial gas suppliers, and CO2 injection sites. The data gathered canthen be used by businesses, states, cities, and communities to take a number of actions including tracking greenhouse gas emissions, minimized wasted energy, and identify opportunities to cut pollution.
Paul Gunning, Director, Climate Change

2473 House Committee on Agriculture
1301 Longworth House Office Bldg 202-225-2171
Washington, DC 20515 Fax: 202-225-4464
www.agriculture.house.gov
The House Committee on Agriculture presently deals with issues such as farm economy, agricultural conservation, food transparency, agricultural innorvation, and more.
K. Michael Conaway, Chairman
Collin C. Peterson, Ranking Member

2474 House Committee on Foreign Affairs
2170 Rayburn House Office Building 202-225-5021
Washington, DC 20515 Fax: 202-225-5394
www.foreignaffairs.house.gov
The Committee is charged with overseeing US foreign policy programs and agencies. They manage legislation regarding foreign policy, State Department management, foreign assistance, trade promotion, export controls, foreign arms sales,student exchanges, international broadcasting and many other issues.
Ed Royce, Chairman
Eliot Engel, Ranking Member

2475 Installation Management Command
Army Public Affairs Office
1500 Army Prentagon 703-220-9044
Room 1E475 Fax: 703-697-2159
Washington, DC 20310-1500 help@us.army.mil
www.army.mil
This office integrates and delivers base support to enable readiness for a globally responsive Army.
Kenneth R. Dahl, Commanding General

2476 Inter-American Foundation
1331 Pennsylvania Ave. NW, 202-360-4530
Suite 1200 inquiries@iaf.gov
Washington, DC 20004 www.iaf.gov
The Inter-American Foundation (IAF) is an independent foreign assistance agency of the United States government, working to promote equitable, responsive, and participatory self-help development in Latin America and the Caribbean.
Paloma Adams-Allen, President, CEO
Eddy Arriola, Chairman

2477 International Joint Commission
1717 H Street, NW 202-736-9000
Suite 801 Fax: 202-632-2006
Washington, DC 20006 commission@washington.ijc.org
www.ijc.org
Mission: Prevents and resolves disputes between the United States and Canada, and pursues the common good of both countries as an independent and objective advisor to the two governments.
Lana Pollack, Chair
Rich Moy, Commissioner

2478 Land and Minerals Office of Surface Mining Reclamation & Enforcement
Department of the Interior
1951 Constitution Avenue NW 202-208-2565
Washington, DC 20240 osm-getinfo@osmre.gov
www.osmre.gov
Their mission is to carry out the requirments of the Surface Mining Control and Reclamation Act in cooperation with States and Tribes. Their primary objectives are to ensure that coal mines are operated in a manner that protectscitizens and the environment during mining and assures that the land is restored to beneficial use following mining, and to mitigate the effects of past mining by aggressively pursuing reclamation of abandoned coal mines.

Glenda Owens, Acting Director

2479 Local Government Advisory Committee (LGAC)
Environmental Protection Agency
1200 Pennsylvania Avenue NW 202-564-5200
Washington, DC 20460 scales.wuanisha@epa.gov
www.epa.gov/ocir
Composed mainly of elected and appointed local officials, several state representatives, and environmental interest groups, this committee advises, consults with, and makes recommendations to EPA on matters related to theimplementation of federal environmental requirements by local governments.
Bob Dixson, Chair
Jill Duson, Vice Chair

2480 Manpower, Reserve Affairs, Installations and Environment
Environment, Safety and Occupational Health

1665 Air Force Pentagon 703-697-3039
Washington, DC 20330 www.af.mil
This office provides guidance, direction, and oversight for the department on all matters pertaining to the environment, safety, and occupational health.
Gabe Camarillo, Assistant Secretary

2481 Marine Mammal Commission
4340 East West Highway 301-504-0087
Suite 700 Fax: 301-504-0099
Bethesda, MD 20814 mmc@mmc.gov
www.mmc.gov
Developing, reviewing and making recommendations on domestic and international actions and policies with respect to marine mammal protection, conservation and with carrying out a research program. Primary objective is to ensure thatfederal programs are being administered in ways that maintain the health and stability of marine ecosystems and do not disadvantage marine mammal populations or species.
Daryl J. Boness, Chairman
Michael F. Tillman, Commissioner

2482 Marine Minerals Program
1849 C Street NW 202-208-6474
Washington, DC 20240 MarineMinerals@boem.gov
www.boem.gov/Marine-Minerals-Program/
The MMP works with communities to address erosion along the Nation's coastal beaches, dunes, barrier islands, and wetlands.
Dr. Walter Cruickshank, Director

2483 Marine Protected Areas Federal Advisory Committee
1305 East West Highway 301-713-7265
Silver Spring, MD 20910-3281 Fax: 301-713-3110
Lauren.Wenzel@noaa.gov
marineprotectedareas.noaa.gov/fac/
The Marine Protected Areas (MPA) Federal Advisory Committee advises NOAA and the Department of the Interior on ways to strengthen the nation's system of MPAs.
John Anderson, Committee Member
Lauren Wenzel, Designated Federal Officer

2484 Maritime Administration
Maritime Administration (MARAD)
1200 New Jersey Avenue, SE 202-366-4000
Washington, DC 20590 www.marad.dot.gov
The Maritime Administration is an agency within the Department of Transportation that promotes the use of waterborne transportation and maintains the health of the merchant marine. The administation works in a number of areas,including environment, national security, safety, port operation, and more.
Joel Szabat, Executive Director
Rand Pixa, Chief Counsel

2485 Migratory Bird Conservation Commission
5275 Leesburg Pike 703-358-1716
MS: 3N053 realty@fws.gov
Falls Church, VA 22041-3803 www.fws.gov/refuges/realty/mbcc.html
The Migratory Bird Conservation Commission (MBCC) is responsible for considering and approving for acquistion areas of migratory bird habitat (other than waterfowl production areas) that have been submitted by regional offices andrecommended by the Secretary. The MBCC is composed of representatives from the Legislative and Executive Branches of government, fixes the price at which such areas may be purchased or rented, and meets three times a year.
Thad Cochran, Member
A. Eric Alvarez, Secretary

2486 Mine Safety and Health Administration
201 12th Street South 202-693-9400
Suit 401 AskMSHA@dol.gov
Arlington, VA 22202-5450 www.msha.gov
The mission of the Mine Safety and Health Administration is to administer the provisions of the Federal Mine Safety and Health Act of 1977 and to enforce compliance with mandatory safety and health standards as means to eliminate fatalaccidents; to reduce the frequency and severity of nonfatal accidents; to minimize health hazards; and to promote improved safety and health conditions in the Nation's mines. MSHA carries out the mandates of the Mine Act at all mining and mineralprocessing areas.
Patricia W. Silvey, Deputy Assistant Secretary

2487 NOAA Office of National Marine Sanctuaries
1305 East-West Highway 301-713-3125
11th Floor Fax: 301-713-0404
Silver Spring, MD 20910 sanctuaries@noaa.gov
sanctuaries.noaa.gov
Mission: To serve as the trustee for the nation's system of marine protected areas; to conserve, protect and enhance the biodiversity, ecological integrity and cultural legacy of America's ocean and Great Lakes waters.
Dr. Stephen Volz, Assistant Secretary
Benjamin Friedman, Under Secretary Of Commerce

2488 NTSB Office of Railroad, Pipeline and Hazardous Materials Investigations
National Transportation Safety Board
490 L'Enfant Plaza East, SW 202-314-6000
Washington, DC 20594 www.ntsb.gov/Pages/default.aspx
Made up of four divisions, this office investigates accidents involving railroads, pipelines, and the transportation of hazardous materials and informs the NTSB of their findings so that the NTSB can make safety recommendations tofederal and state regulatory industries, and a variety of other organizations and individuals.
Robert Hall, Director
Sandy Rowlett, Deputy Director

2489 National Aeronautics and Space Administration
NASA
300 E. Street SW 202-358-0001
Suite 5R30 Fax: 202-358-4338
Washington, DC 20546 public-inquiries@hq.nasa.gov
www.nasa.gov
NASA conducts scientifc research and innovations on topics such as aeronautics, human exploration, science, and space discovery.
Robert M. Lightfoot Jr., Administrator
Lesa Roe, Deputy Administrator

2490 National Association of State Foresters
444 N Capitol Street NW 202-624-5415
Suit 540 Fax: 202-624-5407
Washington, DC 20001 www.stateforesters.org/
The National Association of State Foresters provides management assistance and protection services for more than two thirds of America's forests.
Tom Boggus, Chair
Bill O'Neill, President

2491 National Atmospheric Deposition Program (NADP)
Illinois State Water Survey
2204 Griffith Drive 217-333-7871
Champaign, IL 61820-7495 nadp.sws.uiuc.edu/
This program involves the cooperation of federal, state, tribal and local governmental agencies, educational institutions, private companies, and non-governmental agencies to measure atmospheric deposition and study its effects on theenvironment.
David Gay, Program Coordinator

2492 National Cancer Institute: Cancer Epidemiology and Genetics Division
9609 Medical Center Drive 240-276-7150
MSC 9776 800-422-6237
Bethesda, MD 20892 www.dceg.cancer.gov/about
The National Cancer Institute expands existing scientific knowledge on cancer cause and prevention as well as on the diagnosis, treatment, and rehabilitation of cancer patients. This division conducts research on cancer epdiemiologyand genetics.
Stephen J. Chanock, Director
Montserrat Garcia-Closes, Deptuy Director

2493 National Center for Health Statistics
National Center for Health Statistics
3311 Toledo Road
Hyattsville, MD 20782-2064 800-232-4636
www.cdc.gov/nchs/
The mission of the National Center for Health Statistics (NCHS) is to provide statistical information that will guide actions and policies to improve the health of the American people. As the Nation's principal health statisticsagency, NCHS leads the way with accurate, relevant, and timely data.
Charles Rothwell, Director
Jennifer H. Madans, Associate Director, Science

2494 National Centers for Environmental Education
SSMC3, 4th Floor 828-271-4800
1315 East West Highway Fax: 828-271-4876
Silver Spring, MD 20910-3282 ncei.info@noaa.gov
www.ncei.noaa.gov/
Provides access to one of the most signifact archives of oceanic, atmospheric, and geophysical data, and also provides products and services to businesses, the government, and the general public.
Benjamin Friedman, Under Secretary of Commerce
Dr. Stephen Volz, Assistant Secretary, NOAA

2495 National Council on Radiation Protection and Measurements
7910 Woodmont Avenue 301-657-2652
Suite 400 800-229-2652
Bethesda, MD 20814-3095 Fax: 301-907-8768
ncrp@ncrponline.org
www.ncrponline.org
The National Council on Radiation Protection and Measurements (NCRP) seeks to formulate and widely disseminate information, guidance and recommendations on radiation protection and measurements which represent the consensus of leadingscientific thinking.
John D. Boice, President
Jerrold T. Bushberg, Senior Vice President

2496 National Drinking Water Advisory Council
EPA Office of Ground and Drinking Water
1200 Pennsylvania Avenue NW 202-564-3750
Mail Code 4601M www.epa.gov/ndwac
Washington, DC 20460
This council was established under the Safe Drinking Water Act of 1974 and provides EPA with advice and recommendations related to the national drinking water program.

Carrie M. Lewis, Chairperson Superintendant

2497 National Environmental Education Advisory Council
Office of Environmental Education
1200 Pennsylvania Avenue NW 202-564-2642
Mail Code 1704-A education@epa.gov
Washington, DC 20460 www.epa.gov/enviroed/FTFmemws.html
Comprised of representatives from organizations other than the federal goverment, NEEAC provides the EPA with advice on environmental education and an understanding of the needs of schools, universities, state departments, andeducational organizations.
Javier Araujo, Designated Federal Officer

2498 National Environmental Justice Advisory Council
1200 Pennsylvania Avenue NW 202-564-2515
Mail Code 2201A 800-962-6215
Washington, DC 20460 Fax: 202-501-0740
environmental-justice@epa.gov
www.epa.gov/environmentaljustice
A federal advisory committee established by charter to provide independent advice, consultation and recommendations to the Administrator of the US Environmental Protection Agency on matters related to environmental justice.
Richard Moore, Chair
Jill Witkowski Heaps, Vice Chair

2499 National Environmental Satellite Data & Information Service
National Oceanic and Atmospheric Administration
1335 East-West Highway 301-713-3578
SSMC1, 8th Floor Fax: 301-713-1249
Silver Spring, MD 20910 John.Leslie@noaa.gov
www.nesdis.noaa.gov
The National Environmental Satellite, Data and Information Service operates a national environmental satellite system. It acquires, stores and disseminates worldwide environmental data through its data centers.
Stephen Volz, Assistant Administrator
Mark S. Paese, Deputy Assistant Admin.

2500 National Health Information Center (NHIC)
US Department of Health and Human Services
1101 Wootton Parkway 301-565-4167
Suit LL100 Fax: 240-453-8281
Rockville, MD 20852 www.health.gov/nhic
A health information referral line. NHIC links consumers and health professionals who have health questions and organizations best able to provide reliable health information. Maintains an online directory of more than than 1600 healthorganizations that can provide provide information. The database is accessible to the public through the healthfinder web site.
Don Wright, Deputy Assistant Secretary

2501 National Institute for Occupational Safety and Health
395 E Street SW, Suite 9200 202-245-0625
Patriots Plaza Building 800-232-4636
Washington, DC 20201 Fax: 513-533-8347
www.cdc.gov/niosh
Ensures that safe and healthy working conditions for all working people are met, develops occupational safety and health standards, and conducts research to reduce worker illness and injury.
Frank Hearl, Chief of Staff
John Howard, Director

2502 National Institute of Environmental Health Sciences
111 T.W. Alexander Drive 919-541-3345
Durham, NC 27709 Fax: 301-480-2978
webcenter@niehs.nih.gov
www.niehs.nih.gov
NIEHS' mission is to discover how the environment affects people in order to promote healthier lives, and to provide global leadership for research that improves public health.
Linda S. Birnbaum, Director
Richard Woychik, Deputy Director

2503 National Institutes of Health
9000 Rockville Pike 301-496-4000
Bethesda, MD 20892 NIHinfo@od.nih.gov
www.nih.gov
The National Institutes of Health conducts, supports and promotes biomedical research to improve the health of the American

people by increasing the understanding of processes underlying human health, disability and disease. Theinstitutes advance knowledge concerning the health effects of interactions between humans and the environment.
Francis S. Collins, Director
James M. Anderson, Deputy Director

2504 National Lead Information Center
422 South Clifton Avenue
Rochester, NY 14620
800-424-5323
Fax: 585-232-3111
leadinfo@epa.gov
www.epa.gov/lead/pubs/nlic.htm
Provides the general public and professionals with information about lead hazards and their prevention.
Scott Pruit, Administrator, EPA
Mike Flynn, Deputy Administrator, EPA

2505 National Marine Fisheries Service
National Oceanic & Atmospheric Administration
1315 East West Highway
Silver Spring, MD 20910
www.nmfs.noaa.gov
NMFS conducts an integrated program of management, research and services for the protection and rational use of living marine resources. It also is responsible for the protection of marine mammals.
Chris Oliver, Assistant Administrator
Brian Pawlak, Deputy Assistant Admin.

2506 National Oceanic & Atmospheric Administration
1401 Constitution Avenue, NW
Room 5128
webmaster@noaa.gov
Washington, DC 20230
www.noaa.gov/
The Administration's mission is to explore, map, and chart the global ocean and its living resources and to manage, use, and conserve those resources; to describe, monitor, and predict conditions in the atmosphere, ocean, sun, andspace environment; to issue warnings against impending destructive natural events; to assess the consequences of inadvertent environmental modification over several scales of time, and to manage and disseminate long-term environmental information.

Benjamin Friedman, Under Secretary

2507 National Organic Standards Board Agricultural Marketing Service
USDA/AMS
1400 Independence Avenue SW
202-720-8998
Washington, DC 20250 AMSAdministratorOffice@ams.usda.gov
www.ams.usda.gov/nop
The AMS creates national and international marketing opportunities for US producers of food, and provides the agricultural industry with services that ensure the quality and abundance of wholesome food for consumers.
Bruce Summers, Administrator
Erin Morris, Associate Administrator

2508 National Park Service: Fish, Wildlife and Parks
National Park Service
1849 C Street NW
202-208-6843
Washington, DC 20240
nps_director@nps.gov
www.nps.gov
The National Park Service preserves unimpaired the natural and cultural resources and values of the national park system for the enjoyment, education, and inspiration of this and future generations. The Park Service cooperates withpartners to extend the benefits of natural and cultural resource conservation and outdoor recreation throughout this country and the world.
Michael T. Reynolds, Acting Director
Lena McDowell, Deputy Director

2509 National Petroleum Council
1625 K Street NW
202-393-6100
Suite 600
Fax: 202-331-8539
Washington, DC 20006
info@npc.org
www.npc.org
The purpose of the NPC is solely to represent the views of the oil and natural gas industries in advising, informing, and making recommendations to the Secretary of Energy with respect to any matter relating to oil and natural gas, orto the oil and gas industries submitted to it or approved by the Secretary. The NPC does not concern itself with trade practices, nor does it engage in any of the usual trade association activities.

Twice a year
Gregory L. Armstrong, Acting Chair
Marshall W. Nichols, Executive Director

2510 National Science Foundation
4201 Wilson Boulevard
703-292-5111
Arlington, VA 22230
800-877-8339
info@nsf.gov
www.nsf.gov
It is the National Science Foundation's mission to promote the progress of science; to advance the national health, prosperity, and welfare; and to secure the national defense.
Joan Ferrini-Mundy, Chief Operating Officer
France A. Cordova, Director

2511 National Science Foundation Office of Polar Programs
4201 Wilson Boulevard
703-292-8030
Room 755 S
Fax: 703-292-9081
Arlington, VA 22230
info@nsf.gov
www.nsf.gov/div/index.jsp?div=OPP
OPP promotes creative and innovative scientific research, engineering, and education in and about the polar regions, catalyzing fundamental discovery and understanding of polar systems and their global interactions to inform the nationand advance the welfare of all people, and shares in the vision and goals expressed in NSF's strategic plan.
Pawnee C. Maiden, Administrative Officer
Kelly K. Falkner, Office Director

2512 National Science and Technology Council (NSTC)
Office of Science and Technology Policy
1650 Pennsylvania Avenue
202-456-4444
Washington, DC 20504
www.whitehouse.gov/ostp/nstc
Established by Executive Order in 1993, this Cabinet-level Council aims to establish clear national goals for Federal science and technology investments, and to coordinates policies across the many entities that make up the Federalresearch and development enterprise.
Donald J. Trump, Chair, President of the US

2513 National Urban and Community Forestry Advisory Council
USDA Forest Service
1400 Independence Avenue SW
Washington, DC 20250-1111
800-832-1355
nucfac@fs.fed.us
www.fs.fed.us/managing-land/urban-forests/ucf
This council is a Congressionally designated advisory council to the Secretary of Agriculture on urban forestry and related issues. They were created by the 1990 Farm Bill to bring together various voices concerned about the presentand future health of America's urban forests.
Lance Davisson, Chair

2514 Natural Resources Conservation Service
1400 Independence Ave., SW
202-720-7246
Room 5105-A
Fax: 202-720-7690
Washington, DC 20250
www.nrcs.usda.gov

Provides leadership in a partnership effort to help people conserve, maintain and improve America's natural resources and environment. NRCS is the technical delivery arm of USDA and provides conservation information, incentive programsand technical assistance at the state and county levels.
Leslie Deavers, Chief of Staff
Kaveh Sadeghzadeh, Director, Public Affairs

2515 Naval Sea Systems Command
1333 Isaac Hull Avenue SE 202-781-0000
Washington Navy Yard, DC 20376 800-356-8464
Fax: 202-781-4495
NSSC_Public_Affairs@navy.mil
www.navsea.navy.mil
The Naval Sea Systems Command provides material support to the Navy and Marine Corps, and for mobilization purposes to the Department of Defense and Department of Transportation, for ships, submarines, and other sea platforms,shipboard combat systems and components, other surface and undersea warfare and weapons systems, and ordinance expendables not specifically assigned to other system commands.
Thomas Moore, Commander
Jim Smerchansky, Executive Director

2516 Navy and Marine Corps Public Health Center
620 John Paul Jones Circle 757-953-0700
Suite 1100 NMCPHC-PAO@med.navy.mil
Portsmouth, VA 23708-2103 www.med.navy.mil/sites/nmcphc/Pages/Home.aspx
The Navy and Marine Corps Center for Public Health Services provides leadership and expertise to ensure mission readiness through disease prevention and health promotion in support of the National Military Strategy.
Todd L. Wagner, Commanding Officer
Robert Hawkins, Executive Officer

2517 New Forests Project
1001 North Carolina Avenue SE 202-285-4328
Washington, DC 20003 info-newforests@theintlcenter.org
www.newforestsproject.org/
The New Forest Project strives to protect, conserve and enhance the health of the Earth's ecosystems along with the people depending on them, by supporting integrated grassroots efforts in agroforestry, reforestation, protection ofwatersheds, water and sanitation and renewable energy initiatives.
Viginia B. Foote, President
Catalina Serna-Valencia, Chief Executive Officer

2518 Nuclear Materials, Safety, Safeguards & Operations
U.S. Nuclear Regulatory Commission 301-415-7000
Washington, DC 20555-0001 800-368-5642
www.nrc.gov
The Office of Nuclear Materials Safety and Safeguards at the NRC has the responsibility for NRC's principal rulemaking and guidance development, licensing, inspection, event response and regulatory activities for material licensedunder the Atomic Energy Act of 1954, as amended, to ensure safety and quality associated with the possession, processing, and handling of nuclear material.
Marc Dapas, Director
Scott Moore, Deputy Director

2519 Occupational Safety and Health Administration: US Department of Labor
Office of Administrative Services
200 Constitution Avenue NW
Room N3626 800-321-6742
Washington, DC 20210 www.osha.gov
OSHA's mission is to send every worker home whole and healthy every day by enforcing healthful working conditions, enforcing standards, and providing training, education, and outreach.
Loren Sweatt, Deputy Assistant Secretary
Thomas Galassi, Deputy Assistant Secretary

2520 Oceanic and Atmospheric Research Office
National Oceanic and Atmospheric Administration
1315 East West Highway 301-713-2458
Silver Spring, MD 20910 www.oar.noaa.gov
The Office of Oceanic and Atmospheric Research is where much of the work is done that results in better weather forecasts, longer warning lead times for natural disasters, new products from the sea, and greater understanding of ourclimate, atmosphere, and oceans.
Craig McLean, Assistant Administrator
Ko Barrett, Deputy Asst Administrator

2521 Office Of Air Quality Planning and Standards
Environmental Protection Agency
1200 Pennsylvania Avenue, NW 919-541-5616
Washington, DC 20460 www.epa.gov/aboutepa/about-office-air-and-radiation-oar
The Ofice of Air Quality Planning and Standards (OAQPS) mission is to improve and preserve air quality in the US.
Steve Page, Director
Bill Harnett, Associate Director

2522 Office Of Air and Radiation (OAR)
Environmental Protection Agency
1200 Pennsylvania Avenue NW 202-564-4700
Washington, DC 20460 866-411-4372
Fax: 202-501-0826
www.epa.gov/environmental-topics/air-topics
The Office of Air and Radiation (OAR) develops national programs, policies, and regulations for controlling air pollution and radiation exposure.
Scott Pruitt, Administrator
Mike Flynn, Acting Deputy Administrator

2523 Office of Chemical Safety and Pollution Prevention
U.S. Environmental Protection Agency
1200 Pennsylvania Avenue NW 202-564-2901
Mail Code 7101M www.epa.gov/environmental-topics/chemicals-and-toxics-topics
Washington, DC 20460
The Office of Chemical Safety and Pollution aims to protect Americans, their families, and the environment from risks related to pesticides and toxic chemicals.
Wendy Cleland-Hamnett, Assistant Administrator
Nancy B. Beck, Assistant Administrator

2524 Office of Civil Enforcement: Water Enforcement Division
Environmental Protection Agency
US Env. Protect. Agency, Water Enf. 202-564-4001
1200 Pennsylvania Avenue www.epa.gov
Washington, DC 20460
Enforces ther equirements under the Clean Water Act and the Safe Drinking Water Act.
Mark Pollins, Director, Water Enforcement
Susan Shinkman, Director, Civil Enforcement

2525 Office of Research & Engineering
National Transportation Safety Board
490 L'Enfant Plaza East SW 202-314-6000
Washington, DC 20594 www.ntsb.gov
This office provides support to accident investigations and conducts safety studies for all modes of transportation. There are four divisions that make up this office: the Safety Research Division, the Vehicle Performance Division, theVehicle Recorder Division, and the Materials Laboratory Division.
Barbara Czech, Deputy Director
Jim Ritter, Director

2526 Office of Surface Mining, Reclamation and Enforcement
1951 Constitution Avenue NW 202-208-2565
Washington, DC 20240 osm-getinfo@osmre.gov
www.osmre.gov

The Office of Surface Mining is responsible for protecting society and the environment from negative effects of surface coal mining, and ensuring that the land is restored after mining is finished. OSMRE also is responsible forreclaiming and restoring lands and water damaged by mining operations before 1977.
Glenda Owens, Director

2527 Office of the Chief Economist
12th & Jefferson Drive SW 202-720-5447
Room 112, Whitten Building scarter@oce.usda.gov
Washington, DC 20250 www.usda.gov/oce
The Office of the Chief Economist advises the Secretary on the economic implications of policies and programs affecting the US food and fiber systems and rural areas. The Chief Economist coordinates, reviews, and approves theDepartment's commodity and farm sector forecast.
Warren Preston, Deputy Chief Economist
Robert Johansson, Chief Economist

2528 Office of the General Counsel
1401 Constitution Avenue NW 202-482-4772
Washington, DC 20230 Fax: 202-482-0042
GeneralCounsel@doc.gov
ogc.commerce.gov/
The Office of the General Counsel provides legal services for all programs, operations and activities of the department.
Michelle O. McClelland, Deputy General Counsel
Katherine Keller, Deputy General Counsel

2529 Office of the Secretary of Energy
1000 Independence Avenue SW 202-586-5000
Washington, DC 20585 Fax: 202-586-4403
The.Secretary@hq.doe.gov
www.doe.gov
The Secretary of Energy provides the framework for a comprehensive and balanced national energy plan through the coordination and administration of the energy functions of the federal government. The Secretary is also responsible formainting the a safe and secure nuclear deterrent, carrying out envirnmental cleanup from the Cold War nuclear mission, and managing 17 National Laboratories.
Rick Perry, Secretary

2530 Office of the Secretary of Health and Human Services
200 Independence Avenue SW 202-690-7000
Hubert H Humphery Building 877-696-6775
Washington, DC 20201 www.hhs.gov
The Secretary of Health and Human Services advises the President on health, welfare, and income security plans, policies, and programs of the federal government.
Thomas E. Price, Secretary
John A. Bardis, Assistant Secretary

2531 Office of the Solicitor
1849 C Street NW 202-208-4423
Washington, DC 20240 feedback@ios.doi.gov
www.doi.gov/solicitor
Mission: To provide legal counsel and representation to the Secretary, the Assistant Secretaries, and the Bureau Directors.

2532 Office of the US Trade Representative
600 17th Street NW 202-395-6850
Washington, DC 20508 Fax: 202-395-4656
correspondence@ustr.eop.gov
www.ustr.gov
This division of the Office of the US Trade Representative is responsible for the direction of all trade negotiations and the formulation of trade policy for the United States as related to the environment and natural resources.
Jamieson L. Greer, Chief of Staff
Robert E. Lighthizer, US Trade Representative

2533 Peace Corps
Paul D. Coverdell Peace Corps
1111 20th Street NW
Washington, DC 20526 855-855-1961
www.peacecorps.gov
The goal of the Peace Corps is to help people of interested countries in meeting their need for trained men and women, to promote a better understanding of Americans on the part of people served and to help promote a betterunderstanding of other peoples on the part of Americans.
Kathy Stroker, Acting Deputy Director
Sheila Crowley, Acting Director

2534 Pesticide Program Dialogue Committee (PPDC)
EPA: Office of Pesticide Programs
1200 Pennsylvania Avenue NW 312-353-6344
Mail Code: 7506C www.epa.gov/environmental-topics/chemicals-and-toxics-topics
Washington, DC 20460
This committee provides feedback to the EPA on various pesticide regulatory, policy, and program implementation issues.

Twice per year
Jack E. Housenger, Chair
Dea Zimmerman, Designated Federal Officer

2535 Regional Haze Program
US EPA
109 TW Alexander Drive 919-541-5616
Research Triangle Park, NC 27709 www.epa.gov/visibility
This program enforces the Regional Haze Rule, which calls for state and federal agencies to work to improve visibility in 156 national parks and wilderness areas by developing and implementing air quality protection plans that helpreduce the lack of visibility caused by pollution.
Steve Page, Director
Bill Harnett, Associate Director

2536 Research, Education and Economics
U.S. Department of Agriculture
1400 Independence Avenue SW 202-720-2791
Washington, DC 20250 www.ree.usda.gov
Mission: Federal leadership responsibility for the discovery of knowledge spanning the biological, physical, and social sciences, and involving agricultural research, economic analysis, statistics, outreach, and higher education.
Ann Bartuska, Acting Under Secretary
Michele Esch, Acting Chief of Staff

2537 Research, Education, and Economics National Agricultural Statistics Service
1400 Independence Avenue SW
Washington, DC 20250 800-727-9540
nass@nass.usda.gov
www.nass.usda.gov
Mission: Provides timely, accurate, and useful statistics in service to US agriculture.
Hubert Hamer, Administrator
Renee Picanso, Assoiciate Administrator

2538 Risk Assessment and Cost Benefit Analysis Office
Office of the Chief Economist
1400 Independance Avenue SW 202-720-8022
Room 4032, South Building scarter@oce.usda.gov
Washington, DC 20250-3811 www.usda.gov/oce/risk_assessment
ORACBA's primary role is to ensure that major regulations proposed by USDA are based on sound scientific and economic analysis.
Linda Abbott, Director
Mark R. Powell, Risk Scientist

2539 Rural Utilities Service
USDA Rural Development
1400 Independence Avenue SW 202-720-9540
Room 5135 www.usda.gov/rus
Washington, DC 20250-1510
RUS administers programs that provide infrastructure to rural communities, including water and waste treatment and electric power.
Christopher A. McLean, Acting Administrator
Catherine Early, Executive Assistant

2540 Safe Ocean Network
US Department of State
2201 C Street NW 202-347-6950
Washington, DC 20520 www.state.gov/e/oes/ocns/fish/safeoceannetwork/index.htm
The Safe Ocearn Network is focused on building a global community and increasing collaboration between countries and organizations to combat illegal fishing.
Rex W. Tillerson, Secretary of State
Judith G. Garber, Assistant Secretary, OES

2541 Saint Lawrence Seaway Development Corporation
US Department of Transportation
1200 New Jersey Avenue SE 202-366-0091
Suite W32-300 800-785-2779
Washington, DC 20590 Fax: 202-366-7147
slsdc@dot.gov
www.seaway.dot.gov
Saint Lawrence Seaway Development Corporation operates and maintains the Great Lakes/St. Lawrence System, which encompasses the St. Lawrence River and the five Great lakes.
Wayne A. Williams, Chief of Staff
Craig H. Middlebrook, Deputy Administrator

2542 Science Advisory Board Environmental Protection Agency
Environmental Protection Agency
1200 Pennsylvania Avenue NW 202-564-2221
Washington, DC 20460-4164 Fax: 202-564-2098
sab@epa.gov
www.epa.gov/sab
The SAB was established by Congress to provide independent scientific and engineering advice to the EPA Administrator on the technical basis for EPA regulations. SAB reviews and gives advice on scientific issues and EPA programs, aswell as performs special assignments as requested by Agency officials.
Peter S. Thorne, Chair

2543 Science and Technology Policy Office
Eisenhower Executive Office Bldg 202-456-4444
1650 Pennsylvania Avenue www.whitehouse.gov/administration/eop/ostp
Washington, DC 20504
The Science and Technology Policy Office serves as a source of scientific, engineering, and technological analysis and judgement for the President with respect to major policies, plans, and programs of the federal government. Incarrying out this mission, the office advises the President of scientific and technological considerations involved in areas of national concern, including the economy, national security, health, foreign relations, and the environment.

2544 Senate Committee on Appropriations
The Capitol 202-224-7257
Room S-28 www.appropriations.senate.gov
Washington, DC 20510
The largest committee in the U.S. Senate, The Senate Committee on Appropriations writes the legislation that allocates federal funds to numerous goverment agencies, departments, and organizations. Twelve subcomittees are tasked withcreating legislation to allocate funds to government agencies within their juristictions, hearing testsiomies from goverment officials, and drafting spending plans for the fiscal year.
30 members
Thad Cochran, Chair
Patrick Leahy, Vice Chairman

2545 Senate Committee on Foreign Relations
423 Dirksen Senate Office Building 202-224-4651
Washington, DC 20510-6225 Fax: 202-224-3612
Web_Inquiry@foreign.senate.gov
www.foreign.senate.gov
Established as one of the original ten standing committees, the TheSenate Foreign Relations Committee develops and influences US foreign policy, debates and reports treaties and legislation, holds jurisdiction over all diplomaticnominations, and assists in the negotiation of treaties.
Bob Corker, Chairman
Ben Cardin, Ranking Member

2546 Smithsonian Tropical Research Institute
Smithsonian Institution Research Department
1100 Jefferson Drive 202-633-4014
Suite 3123 Fax: 202-786-2557
Washington, DC 20013-7012 www.stri.org
The STRI is a bureau of the Smithsonian Insititution based outside the US in Panama, and is dedicated to understanding biological diversity.
Matthew C. Larsen, Director
William Wcislo, Deputy Director

2547 Technology Administration: National Institute of Standards & Technology
Technology Policy Office
100 Bureau Drive 301-975-2758
Gaithersburg, MD 20899-1070 inquiries@nist.gov
www.nist.gov
The National Institute of Standards and Technology assists industries in the development of technology needed to improve product quality, modernize manufacturing processes, ensure product reliability, and facilitate rapidcommercialization of products based on new scientific discoveries. NIST's primary mission is to promote US economic growth by working with industries to develop and apply technology, measurements, and standards.
Kent Rochford, Director
James Olthoff, Associate Director

2548 US Agency for International Development Information Center
Office of Inspector General
1300 Pennsylvania Avenue NW 202-712-1150
Washington, DC 20523 Fax: 202-216-3047
www.usaid.gov
Aids in the development of urban environmental programs, works toward ending extreme poverty, and promotes the development of democratic societies.
Wade Warren, Administrator
William R. Steiger, Chief Of Staff

2549 US Consumer Product Safety Commission
4330 East West Highway 301-504-7923
Bethesda, MD 20814 800-638-2772
Fax: 301-504-0124
info@cpsc.gov
www.cpsc.gov
The U.S. Consumer Product Safety Commission (CPSC) is an independent federal regulatory agency that aims to protect the public against unreasonable risks of injuries and deaths associated with consumer products.
Ann Marie Buerkle, Chairman

2550 US Customs & Border Protection
1300 Pennsylvania Avenue NW 202-325-8000
Washington, DC 20229 877-227-5511
www.cbp.gov
Mission: Safeguard the American homeland at and beyond our borders, while enhancing the Nation's global economic competitiveness by enable legitimate trade and travel.
Ronald D. Vitello, Acting Deputy Commissioner
Kevin K. McAleenan, Acting Commissioner

2551 US Department of Agriculture
1400 Independence Avenue SW 202-720-2791
Washington, DC 20250 www.usda.gov
USDA Mission: Enhance the quality of life for the American people by supporting production of agriculture: ensuring a safe, affordable, nutritious, and accessible food supply; caring for agricultural, forest, and range lands;supporting sound development of rural communities; providing economic opportunities for farm and rural residents; expanding global markets for agricultural and forest products and services; and working to reduce hunger in America and throughout theworld.
Sonny Perdue, Secretary

2552 US Department of Education
400 Maryland Avenue SW
Washington, DC 20202 800-872-5327
answers.ed.gov
www.ed.gov
Mission: To strengthen the Federal commitment to assuring access to equal educational opportunity for every individual; improve the coordination of Federal education programs; improve the management of Federal education activities; andincrease the accountability of Federal education programs to the President, the Congress, and the public
Betsy DeVos, Secretary

2553 US Department of Housing and Urban Development
451 7th Street SW 202-708-1112
Washington, DC 20410 portal.hud.gov/hudportal/HUD
HUD's mission is to create strong, sustainable, inclusive communities and quality affordable homes for all, and is working towards strengthening the housing market to bolster the economy and protect consumers.
Ben Carson, Secretary
Janet Golrick, Deputy Secretary

2554 US Department of Housing and Urban Development Office of Lead Hazard Control & Healthy Homes
Office of Lead Hazard Control
451 7th Street SW 202-708-1112
Washington, DC 20410 portal.hud.gov/hudportal/HUD
The office provides funds to state and local governments to develop cost-effective ways to reduce lead-based hazards, enforces lead-based paint regulations, provides public outreach, and conducts studies to aid children and familiesfrom health/safety hazards in the home.
Jon Gant, Director
Michelle Miller, Deputy Director

2555 US Department of Labor
200 Constitution Avenue NW 202-693-6000
Washington, DC 20210 866-487-2365
webmaster@dol.gov
www.dol.gov/
To foster, promote, and develop the welfare of the wage earners, job seekers, and retirees of the United States; improve working conditions; advance opportunities for profitable employment; and assure work-related benefits and rights.
Wayne Palmer, Chief of Staff
R. Alexander Acosta, Secretary of Labor

2556 US Department of Treasury
1500 Pennsylvania Avenue NW 202-622-2000
Washington, DC 20220 Fax: 202-622-6415
www.treasury.gov
Maintain a strong economy and create economic and job opportunities by promoting the conditions that enable economic growth and stability at home and abroad, strengthen national security by combating threats and protecting theintegrity of the financial system, and manage the U.S. Government's finances and resources effectively
Stephen Terner Mnuchin, Secretary

2557 US Department of the Army: Office of Public Affairs
Army Public Affairs Office
1500 Army Pentagon 703-220-9044
Room 1E475 Fax: 703-697-2159
Washington, DC 20310-1500 help@us.army.mil
www.army.mil
Mission: Public Affairs fulfills the Army's obligation to keep the American people and the Army informed, and helps to establish the conditions that lead to confidence in America's Army and its readiness to conduct operations inpeacetime, conflict and war.
Michael P. Brady, Principal Deputy Chief
Omar J. Jones IV, Chief of Public Affairs

2558 US Environmental Protection Agency Office of Children's Health Protection
Office of Children's Health Protection
1200 Pennsylvania Avenue NW 202-564-2188
Mail Code 1107T Fax: 202-564-2733
Washington, DC 20460 www.epa.gov/children
The mission of this office is to make the protection of children's environmental health a fundamental goal of public health and environmental protection in the US.
Dr. Ruth A. Etzel, M.D., Ph.D, Director

2559 US Environmental Protection Agency: Clean Air Markets Division
1200 Pennsylvania Avenue NW 202-343-9429
Mail Code 6204M www.epa.gov/airmarkets
Washington, DC 20460
Through regulatory programs, The Clean Air Market's division regulates air pollution from power plants that contribute to environmental problems such as acid rain, ozone and particle pollution.
Reid Harvery, Director

2560 US Environmental Protection Agency: Office of Environmental Justice
1200 Pennsylvania Avenue NW 202-564-2515
Mail Code: 2201A 800-962-6215
Washington, DC 20460-1 environmental-justice@epa.gov
www.epa.gov
Serves as a focal point for ensuring that indigenous and low income communities receive protection under environmental laws, and works to protect the health of the environment in communities burdened by pollution.
Matthew Tejada, Director
Sheila Lewis, Deputy Director

2561 US Forest Service
U.S. Dept. of Agriculture
1400 Independence Avenue SW 202-205-8333
Washington, DC 20250-1111 800-832-1355
webmaster@fs.fed.us
www.fs.fed.us.
Manages 140 National Forests and 20 Grasslands. Provides assistance to private forest operators, and helps to sustain the health, diversity, and productivity of the nation's forests and grasslands for present and future generations.
Thomas L. Tidwell, Chief
Dan Jiron, Associate Chief

2562 US Forest Service: Forest Legacy Program
US Forest Service
1400 Independence Avenue SW
Washington, DC 20250-1111 800-832-1355
www.fs.fed.us/spf/coop/programs/loa/flp.shtml

The Forest Legacy Program is a federal program that supports state efforts to protect environmentally sensitive forest lands by encouraging the protection of privately owned forest lands, supporting property aquisition, and helpingstates carry out conservation plans.

Dan Jiron, Associate Chief
Thomas L. Tidwell, Chief

2563 US Geological Survey: Wetlands and Aquatic Research Center
700 Cajundome Boulevard 337-266-8500
Lafayette, LA 70506-3152 Fax: 337-266-8513
nwrcinfo@usgs.gov
www.nwrc.usgs.gov

The research center's mission is to develop and disseminate scientific information needed for understanding the ecology and values of the nation's wetlands and other aquatic and coastal ecosystems, and to manage and restore wetland,coastal, and aquatic habitats and associated plant and animal communtities.

Thomas Doyle, Deputy Director
Kenneth Rice, Center Director

2564 US Nuclear Regulatory Commission
U.S Nuclear Regulatory Commission 301-415-7000
Washington, DC 20555-0001 800-368-5642
oca_web@nrc.gov
www.nrc.gov

The Nuclear Regulatory Commission focuses on reactor safety oversight and liscense renewal of existing plants, materials safety oversight and liscencing, as well as high and low-level waste management.

Jeff Baran, Commissioner
Kristine L. Svinicki, Chairman

2565 Urban and Community Forestry Program
USDA Forest Service
1400 Intependence Avenue SW
Washington, DC 20250-1111 800-832-1355
www.fs.fed.us/managing-land/urban-forests/ucf

The Urban and Community Forestry Program (UCF) is a cooperative program that focuses on the stewardship of urban natural resources by providing technical, financial, research and educational services to local government, nonprofitorganizations, community groups, educational institutions, and tribal governments.

Jim Hubbard, Deputy Chief
Jan Davis, Assisstant Director

Alabama

2566 Agriculture and Industries Department
Pesticide Laboratory
1445 Federal Drive 334-240-7171
Montgomery, AL 36107 800-642-7761
www.agi.stste.al.us/

Mission: To provide timely, fair and expert regulatory control over product, business entities, movement, and application of goods and services for which applicable state and federal law exists and strive to protect and provide serviceto Alabama consumers.

John McMillan, Commissioner
Brett Hall, Deputy Commissioner

2567 Alabama Cooperative Extension System
224 Duncan Hall Annex 334-844-5270
Auburn University, AL 36849 Fax: 334-844-5276
webmaster@aces.edu
www.aces.edu

Operates as the primary outreach organization for the land-grant function of Alabama A&M University and Auburn University. Identifies statewide educational needs, audiences, and optimal educational programs that are delivered through anetwork of public and private partners supported by county, state, and federal governments.

Paul Waddy, Extension Coordinator

2568 Alabama Department of Environmental Management
1400 Coliseum Boulevard 334-271-7700
PO Box 301463 Fax: 334-271-7950
Montgomery, AL 36110-2400 webmaster@adem.state.al.us
www.adem.state.al.us

Alabama Department of Environmental Management is the state agency responsible for the adoption and fair enforcement of rules and regulations set to protect and improve the quality of Alabama's environment and the health of all itscitizens. Monitor environmental conditions in Alabama and recommend changes in state law or revise regulations as needed to respond appropriately to changing environmental conditions.

Lance LeFleur, Director
Marilyn G. Elliott, Deputy Director

2569 Alabama Forestry Commission
513 Madison Avenue 334-240-9300
Montgomery, AL 36104 Fax: 334-240-9390
www.forestry.state.al.us

Mission: To serve Alabama by protecting and sustaining our forest resources using professionally applied stewardship principles and education. We will ensure Alabama's forests contribute to abundant timber and wildlife, clean air andwater, and a healthy economy.

Tommy Thompson, Chair
Jerry Dwyer, Vice Chairman

2570 Conservation and Natural Resources Department
64 North Union Street 334-242-3486
Suite 468 Fax: 334-242-0999
Montgomery, AL 36130 www.outdooralabama.com

N.Gunter Guy Jr., Commissioner
Curtis Jones, Deputy Commissioner

2571 EPA: National Air and Radiation Environmental Laboratory
540 S Morris Avenue 334-270-3400
Montgomery, AL 36115-2600 Fax: 334-270-3454
petko.charles@epa.gov
www.epa.gov/narel/

The National Air and Radiation Environmental Laboratory is a comprehensive environmental laboratory, and provides services to a wide range of clients, including other EPA offices, Federal agencies, and, in somes cases, the privatesector. The mission is the commitment to developing and applying the most advanced methods for measuring environmental radioactivity and evaluating its risk to the public.

Gina McCarthy, Administrator
Tom Reynolds, Office of Public Affairs

2572 Geological Survey of Alabama, Agency of the State of Alabama
University of Alabama
420 Hackberry Lane 205-349-2852
P.O. Box 869999 Fax: 205-349-2861
Tuscaloosa, AL 35486-6999 info@gsa.state.al.us
www.gsa.state.al.us

To survey and investigate the mineral, energy, water, and biological resources of the state, to maintain adequate geological, topographic, hydrologic, and biologic databases, and to prepare maps

and reports on the state's naturalresources to encourage the safe and prudent development of Alabama's natural resources while providing for the safety, health and well-being of all Americans.
Dr. Berry H. Tew Jr., State Geologist
Dr. Patrick O'Neil, Deputy Director

Alaska

2573 Alaska Cooperative Fish and Wildlife Research Unit
University of Alaska
209 Irving 1 907-474-7661
PO Box 757020 Fax: 907-474-7872
Fairbanks, AK 99775-7020 uaf-iab-akcfwru@alaska.edu
www.akcfwru.uaf.edu
The Alaska Unit is a part of a nationwide program created to foster college-level research and graduate student training in support of science-based management of fish and wildlife, and their habitats. The Unit exists by cooperativeagreement between the AK Department of Fish and Game, University of Alaska Fairbanks, US Geological Survey, Wildlife Management Institute, and US Fish and Wildlife Service. The Unit is staffed by 5 USGS scientists, who are also research faculty.
Kathleen Pearse, Administrative Assistant

2574 Alaska Department of Fish and Game
PO Box 115526 907-465-4100
1255 W. 8th Street www.adfg.alaska.gov
Juneau, AK 99811-5526
Aims to manage, protect, maintain and improve the fish, game and aquatic plant resources of Alaska. The primary goals are to ensure that Alaska's renwable fish and wildlife resources and their habitats are conserved and managed on thesustained yield prinicpal, and the use of development of these resources are in the best interest of the economy and well-being of the people of the state.
Cora Campbell, Commissioner
Sunny Haight, Director

2575 Alaska Department of Public Safety
5700 E Tudor Road 907-269-5511
Anchorage, AK 99507 www.dps.state.ak.us
Provides functions relative to the protection of life, property and wildlife resources.
Joseph A. Masters, Commissioner
Terry Vrabec, Deputy Commissioner

2576 Alaska Division of Forestry: Central Office
550 W 7th Avenue 907-269-8400
Suite 1260 Fax: 907-269-8901
Anchorage, AK 99501-3557 forestry.alaska.gov
Mission: To develop, conserve, and enhance Alaska's forests to provide a sustainable supply of forest resources for Alaskans.
Chris Maisch, State Forester/Director
Dean Brown, Deputy State Forester

2577 Alaska Division of Forestry: Coastal Region Office
2417 Tongass Ave 907-225-3070
Suite 213 Fax: 907-247-3070
Ketchikan, AK 99901 forestry.alaska.gov
Mission: To develop, conserve, and enhance Alaska's forests to provide a sustainable supply of forest resources for Alaskans.
Chris Maisch, State Forester/Director
Mike Curran, Regional Forester

2578 Alaska Division of Forestry: Delta Area Office
Mi. 267.5 Richardson Highway 907-895-4225
PO Box 1149 Fax: 907-895-2125
Delta Junction, AK 99737 forestry.alaska.gov
Mission: To develop, conserve, and enhance Alaska's forests to provide a sustainable supply of forest resources for Alaskans.
Chris Maisch, State Forester/Director
Dean Brown, Deputy State Forester

2579 Alaska Division of Forestry: Fairbanks Area Office
3700 Airport Way 907-451-2600
Fairbanks, AK 99709-4699 Fax: 907-458-6895
forestry.alaska.gov
Mission: To develop, conserve, and enhance Alaska's forests to provide a sustainable supply of forest resources for Alaskans.
Chris Maisch, State Forester/Director
Paul Maki, Acting Area Forester

2580 Alaska Division of Forestry: Kenai/Kodiak Area Office
42499 Sterling Highway 907-260-4200
Mi. 92.5 Sterling Hwy. Fax: 907-260-4205
Soldotna, AK 99669 forestry.alaska.gov
Mission: To develop, conserve, and enhance Alaska's forests to provide a sustainable supply of forest resources for Alaskans.
Chris Maisch, State Forester/Director
Hans Rinke, Area Forester

2581 Alaska Division of Forestry: Mat-Su/Southwest Area Office
101 Airport Road 907-761-6300
Palmer, AK 99645 Fax: 907-761-6319
forestry.alaska.gov
Mission: To develop, conserve, and enhance Alaska's forests to provide a sustainable supply of forest resources for Alaskans.
Chris Maisch, State Forester/Director
Rick Jandreau, Area Forester

2582 Alaska Division of Forestry: Northern Region Office
3700 Airport Way 907-451-2670
Fairbanks, AK 99709-4699 Fax: 907-451-2690
forestry.alaska.gov
Mission: To develop, conserve, and enhance Alaska's forests to provide a sustainable supply of forest resources for Alaskans.
Chris Maisch, State Forester/Director
Tim Dabney, Regional Forester

2583 Alaska Division of Forestry: State Forester's Office
550 W 7th Avenue 907-451-8463
Suite 1450 Fax: 907-451-8931
Anchorage, AK 99501-3566 forestry.alaska.gov
Mission: To develop, conserve, and enhance Alaska's forests to provide a sustainable supply of forest resources for Alaskans.
Chris Maisch, State Forester/Director
Dean Brown, Deputy State Forester

2584 Alaska Division of Forestry: Tok Area Office
Mile 123 Glenn Highway 907-883-1400
PO Box 10 Fax: 907-883-5135
Tok, AK 99780 forestry.alaska.gov
Mission: To develop, conserve, and enhance Alaska's forests to provide a sustainable supply of forest resources for Alaskans.
Chris Maisch, State Forester/Director
Jeff Hermanns, Area Forester

2585 Alaska Division of Forestry: Valdez/Copper River Area Office
Mile 110 Richardson Highway 907-822-5534
Box 185 Fax: 907-822-8600
Glennallen, AK 99588 forestry.alaska.gov
Mission: To develop, conserve, and enhance Alaska's forests to provide a sustainable supply of forest resources for Alaskans.
Chris Maisch, State Forester/Director
Gary Mullen, Area Forester

2586 Alaska Health Project
3601 C Street
Suite 902
Anchorage, AK 99503-5923
907-276-2864
Fax: 907-279-3089
AhelpRequest@Alaska.gov
www.ahelp.org

Provides information to professionals and the general public about occupational safety and health, hazardous materials management and waste reduction at work and in the community

Carl Hild, Executive Director
Valerie Davidson, Commissioner

2587 Alaska Oil and Gas Conservation Commission
333 W 7th Avenue
Suite 100
Anchorage, AK 99501
907-279-1433
Fax: 907-276-7542
aogcc.customer.svc@alaska.gov
www.doa.alaska.gov/ogc/

Protecting the oil and gas of Alaska.

Dan Seamount, Commissioner
John Norman, Commissioner

2588 Alaska Resource Advisory Council
Bureau of Land Management
222 W 7th Avenue
Suite 13
Anchorage, AK 99513
907-271-5555
Fax: 907-271-3684
www.blm.gov

A statewide resource advisory council that advises BLM on land management issues for 80 million acres of federal public lands in Alaska. Membership is comprised of representatives from industry, conservation, recreation, Alaska Nativeorganizations, an elected offical, and the public at large. The council meets three times a year.

Thomas P Lonnie, BLM/AK State Director
Sharon Wilson, Alaska RAC Coordinator

2589 Anchorage Office: Alaska Department of Environmental Conservation
555 Cordova Street
Anchorage, AK 99501-2617
907-269-7553
Fax: 907-269-7649
Jennifer.Roberts@alaska.gov
www.dec.state.ak.us

The people and industries that operate in our state have both the corporate conscience and the technical ability to work with us on constuctive solutions to basic environmental management and public health issues. We anticipate,collaborate, negotiate, educate and communicate to address the most important environmental and public health risks to Alaska and Alaskans. Investigation, legislation, regulation and litigation are available tools, but not the first tools of choice.

Larry Hartig, Commissioner

2590 Cooperative Extension Service: University of Alaska Fairbanks
308 Tanana Loop
Room 101
Fairbanks, AK 99775-6180
907-474-5211
Fax: 907-474-2631
snre-web@alaska.edu
www.uaf.edu/coop-ext

Mission: To interpret and extend relevant research-based knowledge in an understandable and usable form; and to encourage the application of this knowledge to solve the problems and meet the challenges that face the people of Alaska;and, to bring the concerns of the community back to the university.

Pete Pinney, Interim Director

2591 Fairbanks Office: Alaska Department of Environmental Conservation
610 University Avenue
Fairbanks, AK 99709-3643
907-451-2125
Fax: 907-451-2362
tom.deruyter@alaska.gov
www.dec.state.ak.us

Nancy Sonafrank, Program Manager

2592 Juneau Office: Alaska Department of Environmental Conservation
410 Willoughby Avenue
Suite 303
Juneau, AK 99811-1800
907-465-5066
Fax: 907-465-5070
www.dec.state.ak.us

Larry Hartig, Commissioner

2593 Kenai Office: Alaska Department of Environmental Conservation
43335 Kalifornsky Beach Road
Suite 11, Red Diamond Center
Soldotna, AK 99669-9792
907-262-5210
Fax: 907-262-2294
www.dec.state.ak.us

Kristin Ryan, Director

2594 Kodiak Office: Alaska Department of Environmental Conservation
PO Box 515
Kodiak, AK 99615-515
907-486-3350
Fax: 907-486-5032
www.dec.state.ak.us

Kristin Ryan, Director

2595 Natural Resources Department Public Affairs Information Office
550 West 7th Avenue
Suite 1260
Anchorage, AK 99501-3557
907-269-8400
Fax: 907-269-8901
www.dnr.alaska.gov

Kathy Johnson, Manager

2596 Palmer Office: Alaska Department of Environmental Conservation
500 S Alaska Street
Suite A
Palmer, AK 99645
907-747-3236
www.dec.state.ak.us

2597 Sitka Office: Alaska Department of Environmental Conservation
901 Halibut Point Road
Suite 3
Sitka, AK 99835-7106
907-747-8614
Fax: 907-747-7419
www.dec.state.ak.us

Kristin Ryan, Director

2598 Subsistance Resource Commission Cape Krusenstern National Monument
National Park Service
PO Box 1029
Kotzebue, AK 99752
907-442-3890
Fax: 907-442-8316
www.nps.gov/cakr

Frank Hays, Superintendent

2599 Subsistence Resource Gates of the Artic National Park
National Park Service
National Park Service-Fairbanks HQ
4175 Geist Road
Fairbanks, AK 99709
907-457-5752
Fax: 907-455-0601
www.nps.gov/gaar

Susan Holly, Administrative Assistant

2600 United States Department of the Army: US Army Corps of Engineers
441 G Street NW
Washington, DC 20314-1000
202-761-0011
www.usace.army.mil

Design and constructs military projects for the Army, Air Force, civil works and water resources development projects for coastal communities. Conducts military Real Estate transactions, is responsible for Emergency Operationsinvolving national emergency and natural disaster, and regulates development in

navigable waters, and placement of fill material in waters and wetlands.
Thomas P. Bostick, Commanding General
Richard L. Stevens, Deputy Commanding General

Arizona

2601 Arizona Department of Agriculture: Animal Services Division
1688 West Adams Street 602-542-4373
Phoenix, AZ 85007 www.azda.gov/ASD/asd.htm
Mission: Protect consumers from contagious and infectious disease in livestock, poultry, commercially raised fish, meat, milk, and eggs; enforce laws concerning the movement, sale, importation, transport, slaughter, and theft oflivestock.
Donald Butler, Director

2602 Arizona Department of Environmental Quality
1110 West Washington Street 602-771-2300
Phoenix, AZ 85007 800-234-5677
www.azdeq.gov/
The Arizona Department of Environmental Quality was established in 1987 to preserve, protect and enhance the environmental and public health through the maintenance of air, land and water resources. The department oversees compliancewith state and federal environmental regulations and works with industry and local governments.
Henry R. Darwin, Director
Misael Cabrera, Deputy Director

2603 Arizona Game & Fish Department
5000 W. Carefree Highway 602-942-3000
Phoenix, AZ 85086-5000 azgfdportal.az.gov
Aims to conserve, enhance and restore Arizona's diverse wildlife resources and habitats through aggressive protection and management programs, and to provide wildlife resources and safe watercraft and off-highway vehicle recreation forthe enjoyment, appreciation, and use by present and future generations.
Larry D. Voyles, Director
Ty Gray, Deputy Director

2604 Arizona Game & Fish Department: Region I
2878 East White Mountain Blvd 928-367-4281
Pinetop, AZ 85935 azgfdportal.az.gov
Aims to conserve, enhance and restore Arizona's diverse wildlife resources and habitats through aggressive protection and management programs, and to provide wildlife resources and safe watercraft and off-highway vehicle recreation forthe enjoyment, appreciation, and use by present and future generations.
Larry D. Voyles, Director
Ty Gray, Deputy Director

2605 Arizona Game & Fish Department: Region II
3500 South Lake Mary Road 928-774-5045
Flagstaff, AZ 86005 azgfdportal.az.gov
Aims to conserve, enhance and restore Arizona's diverse wildlife resources and habitats through aggressive protection and management programs, and to provide wildlife resources and safe watercraft and off-highway vehicle recreation forthe enjoyment, appreciation, and use by present and future generations.
Larry D. Voyles, Director
Ty Gray, Deputy Director

2606 Arizona Game & Fish Department: Region III
5325 North Stockton Hill Road 928-692-7700
Kingman, AZ 86409 azgfdportal.az.gov
Aims to conserve, enhance and restore Arizona's diverse wildlife resources and habitats through aggressive protection and management programs, and to provide wildlife resources and safe watercraft and off-highway vehicle recreation forthe enjoyment, appreciation, and use by present and future generations.
Larry D. Voyles, Director
Ty Gray, Deputy Director

2607 Arizona Game & Fish Department: Region IV
9140 East 28th Street 928-342-0091
Yuma, AZ 85365 azgfdportal.az.gov
Aims to conserve, enhance and restore Arizona's diverse wildlife resources and habitats through aggressive protection and management programs, and to provide wildlife resources and safe watercraft and off-highway vehicle recreation forthe enjoyment, appreciation, and use by present and future generations.
Larry D. Voyles, Director
Ty Gray, Deputy Director

2608 Arizona Game & Fish Department: Region V
555 North Greasewood Road 520-628-5376
Tucson, AZ 85745 azgfdportal.az.gov
Aims to conserve, enhance and restore Arizona's diverse wildlife resources and habitats through aggressive protection and management programs, and to provide wildlife resources and safe watercraft and off-highway vehicle recreation forthe enjoyment, appreciation, and use by present and future generations.
Larry D. Voyles, Director
Ty Gray, Deputy Director

2609 Arizona Game & Fish Department: Region VI
7200 East University 480-981-9400
Mesa, AZ 85207
Aims to conserve, enhance and restore Arizona's diverse wildlife resources and habitats through aggressive protection and management programs, and to provide wildlife resources and safe watercraft and off-highway vehicle recreation forthe enjoyment, appreciation, and use by present and future generations.
Larry D. Voyles, Director
Ty Gray, Deputy Director

2610 Arizona Geological Survey
416 W Congress Street 520-770-3500
Suite 100 Fax: 520-770-3505
Tucson, AZ 85701-1381 web@azgs.az.gov
www.azgs.state.az.us
The Arizona Geological Survey aims to inform and advise the public about the geologic character of Arizona in order to foster understanding and prudent development of the State's land, water, mineral and energy resources.
M Lee Allison, Director
Cindy Castro, Fiscal Services Specialist

2611 Arizona State Parks
1300 West Washington 602-542-4174
Phoenix, AZ 85007 800-285-3703
Fax: 602-542-4188
azstateparks.com
Walter D. Armer Jr., Chair
Bryan Martyn, Executive Director

2612 Arizona Strip District-US Department of Interior Bureau of Land Management
345 E Riverside Drive 435-688-3200
St George, UT 84790-6714 Fax: 435-688-3528
www.blm.gov
Manages nearly 2 million acres in northwestern Arizona, including the Vermilion Cliffs National Monument.
Timothy J. Burke, District Manager
Lorraine Christian, Acting Field Manager

2613 Environmental and Analytical Chemistry Laboratory
Arizona Department of Health 602-542-1025
150 North 18th Avenue Fax: 602-542-0883
Phoenix, AZ 85007 piowebmaster@azdhs.gov
www.azdhs.gov

State public health laboratory both in chemistry and microbiology. Supports investigations into environmental contamination by analyzing water, soil, air, hazardous materials, food and miscellaneous items for the presence of hazardousand toxic chemicals. Microbiology tests for pathogens and/or indicator organisms.
Will Humble, Director

2614 Gila Box Riparian National Conservation Area BLM Safford District Office
711 14th Avenue 928-348-4400
Safford, AZ 85546 Fax: 928-348-4450
www.az.blm.gov

There are more than 14 million acres of public lands in Arizona that people have put in our trust. It's an awesome responsiblity, and one that we take very seriously. We don't try to do it alone. Every day, we work with people to helpmake sure we are doing what is right for Arizona's envrionment, wildlife, culture, and history... for the people who rely upon the land to earn a living or to manufacture the things which make our lives a little easier...and most importantly, forArizona's future.
Tim Shannon, District Manager
Scott Cooke, Field Manager

2615 Phoenix District Advisory Council: BLM
21605 North 7th Avenue 623-580-5500
Phoenix, AZ 85027-2929 Fax: 623-580-5580
www.az.blm.gov

Manages public lands and resources in central Arizona, and supports related statewide initiatives and functions to sustain their health, diversity and productivity while providing for customer service and meeting public demandresulting from the expanding Phoenix metropolitan area and growth of adjoining communities.
Mary D'Aversa, District Manager
Rem Hawes, Field Manager

Arkansas

2616 Arkansas Department of Parks and Tourism
One Capitol Mall 501-682-7777
Little Rock, AR 72201 www.arkansas.com

To provide optimum quality state park recreation facilities conveniently located and in sufficient quantity to meet the needs of all state citizens and visitors
Richard W. Davis, Executive Director

2617 Arkansas Fish and Game Commission
2 Natural Resources Drive 501-223-6300
Little Rock, AR 72205 800-364-4263
askAGFC@agfc.state.ar.us
www.agfc.com

The Arkansas Game and Fish Commission plays an important role in keeping The Natural State true to its name.
Ronald Pierce, Commissioner
Ty Patterson, Commissioner

2618 Arkansas Natural Heritage Commission
323 Center Street 501-324-9619
St. 1500 Fax: 501-324-9618
Little Rock, AR 72201 www.arkansasheritage.com/

The Arkansas Natural Heritage Commission (ANHC) is responsible for maintaining the most up-to-date and comprehensive source of information concerning the rare plant and animal species, and high-quality natural communities of Arkansas.
Mark Karnes, Chairman
Robert Bevis, Vice Chairman

2619 Arkansas State Plant Board
1 Natural Resources Drive 501-225-1598
Little Rock, AR 72205 Fax: 501-219-1697
info@aspb.ar.gov
www.plantboard.org

Mission: To protect and serve the citizens of Arkansas and the agricultural and business communities by providing information and unbiased enforcement of laws and regulations thus ensuring quality products and services.
Darryl Little, Director

2620 Department of Environmental Quality
5301 Northshore Drive 501-682-0744
North Little Rock, AR 72118-5317 888-233-0326
www.adeq.state.ar.us

Mission: To protect, enhance and restore the natural environment for the well-being of Arkansas.
Teresa Marks, Director

California

2621 American Cetacean Society
PO Box 1391 310-548-6279
San Pedro, CA 90733-1391 Fax: 310-548-6950
acsoffice@acsonline.org
www.acsonline.org

A non profit organization that is the oldest whale conservation group in the world. Founded to protect whales, dolphins, porpoises, and their habitats through public education, research grants, and conservation actions.
Diane Glim, President
Barbara Bennett, Secretary

2622 California Department of Education Office of Environmental Education
1430 North Street 916-319-0800
Suite 5602 www.cde.ca.gov
Sacramento, CA 95814

Mission: Guiding principles, goals, and objectives of the California Department of Education.
Tom Torlakson, Superintendent
Richard Zeiger, Chief Deputy Superintendent

2623 California Department of Fish and Game
1416 9th Street 916-445-0411
12th Floor Webmaster@wildlife.ca.gov
Sacramento, CA 95814 www.wildlife.ca.gov

Manages California's diverse fish, wildlife, and plant resources, and the habitats upon which they depend, for their ecological values and for their use and enjoyment by the public.
Charlton H. Bonham, Director
Thomas Gibson, General Counsel

2624 California Department of Water Resources
1416-9th Street 916-653-5791
Room 1104-1 Fax: 916-653-3310
Sacramento, CA 95814 www.dwr.water.ca.gov

Mission: To manage the water resources of California in cooperation with other agencies, to benefit the State's people, and to protect, restore, and enhance the natural and human environments.
Mark W. Cowin, Director
Laura King Moon, Deputy Director

2625 California Desert District Advisory Council Bureau of Land Management
California State Office

2800 Cottage Way
Suite W-1623
Sacramento, CA 9582-1886
916-78 -400
Fax: 916-978-4416
www.ca.blm.gov
Mission: To protect the natural, historic, recreation and economic riches, and scenic beauty of the California Desert.

2626 California Environmental Protection Agency
1001 I Street
P.O. Box 2815
Sacramento, CA 95812-2815
916-323-2514
cepacomm@calepa.ca.gov
calepa.ca.gov
Agency with a focus on restoring, protecting and enhancing the environment through air quality control and pollution control.
Matthew Rodriquez, Secretary
Gordon Burns, Undersecretary

2627 California Pollution Control Financing Authority
915 Capitol Mall, Room 457
Sacramento, CA 95814
916-654-5610
Fax: 916-657-4821
cpcfa@treasurer.ca.gov
www.treasurer.ca.gov/cpcfa
Bill Lockyer, Chairman
Renee Webster-Hawkins, Executive Director

2628 Department of Agriculture: Forest Service, Pacific Southwest Region
1323 Club Drive
Vallejo, CA 94592-1110
707-562-8737
Fax: 707-562-9130
www.fs.fed.us/r5
Randy Moore, Regional Forester
Barnie Gyant, Deputy Regional Forester

2629 Energy Commission
1516 9th Street
MS-29
Sacramento, CA 95814-5512
916-654-4287
www.energy.ca.gov
Promoting Efficiency and Conservation, Supporting Cutting-Edge Research, and Developing Our Renewable Energy Resources
Robert B. Weisenmiller, Ph.D., Chair
Karen Douglas, Commissioner

2630 Environmental Protection Agency Region IX
75 Hawthorne Street
San Francisco, CA 94105
415-947-8000
866-EPA-WEST
www.epa.gov/region09/
Region 9 covers Arizona, California, Hawaii, Nevada, the Pacific Islands subject to US law, and approximately 140 Tribal Nations. We work together with state, local, and tribal governments in the region to carry out the nationsenvironmental laws.
Wayne Nastri, Regional Administrator

2631 Environmental Protection Office: Hazard Identification
Environmental Health Hazard Assessment Office
1001 Street
Sacramento, CA 95814
916-445-6900
Fax: 916-323-8803
P65Public.comments@oehha.ca.gov
www.oehha.ca.gov/prop65/hazard_ident/092812HID.html
The mission of the Office of Environmental Health Hazard Assessment (OEHHA) is to protect and enhance public health and the environment by objective scientific evaluation of risks posed by hazardous substances.
Sam Delson, Deputy Director
Laura August, Staff

2632 Environmental Protection Office: Toxic Substance Control Department
1001 I Street
PO Box 806
Sacramento, CA 95814-2828
916-323-9723
800-728-6942
Fax: 916-323-3215
webcoord@dtsc.ca.gov
www.dtsc.ca.gov
The Department's mission is to restore, protect and enhance the environment, to ensure public health, environmental quality and economic vitality by regulating hazardous waste, conducting and overseeing cleanups, and developing andpromoting pollution prevention.
Barbara A. Lee, Director
Miriam B. Ingenito, Chief Deputy Director

2633 Golden Gate National Recreation Area
Fort Mason
Building 201
San Francisco, CA 94123-22
415-561-4700
www.nps.gov/goga
The Golden Gate National Recreation Area (GGNRA) is the largest urban national park in the world. The total park area is 74,000 acres of land and water. Approximately 28 miles of coastline line within its boundaries. It is nearly twoand one-half times the size of San Francisco.
Frank Dean, General Superintendent
Aaron Roth, Deputy Superintendent

2634 Inter-American Tropical Tuna Commission
8601 La Jolla Shores Drive
La Jolla, CA 92037-1508
858-546-7100
Fax: 858-546-7133
webmaster@iattc.org
www.iattc.org/homeeng.htm
The IATTC, established by international convention in 1950, is responsible for the conservation and management of fisheries for tunas and other species taken by tuna-fishing vessels in the eastern Pacific Ocean. The IATTC also hassignificant responsibilities for the implementation of the International Dolphin Conservation Program (IDCP), and provides the Secretariat for that program.
Guillermo Compean, Director
Richard B. Deriso, Chief Scientist

2635 InterEnvironment Institute
PO Box 99
Claremont, CA 91711
909-621-9018
Mail@InterEnvironment.org
www.interenvironment.org
A forum for policy dialogue and research on California and international environmental issues.
Thaddeus C Trzyna, President
Michael Paparian, Secretary-Treasurer

2636 Klamath Fishery Management Council US Fish & Wildlife Service
1829 South Oregon Street
Yreka, CA 96097
530-842-5763
Fax: 530-842-4517
yreka@fws.gov
www.fws.gov/yreka/kfmc.htm
To manage harvests and ensure continued viable populations of anadromous fish in the Klamath Basin
Phil Detrich, Supervisor

2637 Native American Heritage Commission
1550 Harbor Blvd
Suite 100
Sacramento, CA 95691
916-373-3710
Fax: 916-373-5471
nahc@pacbell.net
www.nahc.ca.gov
The mission of the Native American Heritage Comm. is to provide protection to Native American burials from vandalism and inadvertent destruction, provide a procedure for the notification of most likely descendents regarding thediscovery of Native American human remains and associated grave goods, bring legal action to prevent severe and irreparable damage to sacred shrines,

ceremonial sites, sanctified cemeteries and place of worship on pub. property, and maintain aninventory of sacred places.
Cynthia Gomez, Executive Secretary
James Ramos, Chair

2638 Pesticide Regulation, Environmental Monitoring and Pesticide Management
1001 I Street 916-445-4300
PO Box 4015 Fax: 916-324-1452
Sacramento, CA 95812-4015 cdprweb@cdpr.ca.gov
www.cdpr.ca.gov
Mission: Protect human health and the environment by regulating pesticide sales and use, and by fostering reduced-risk pest management.
Rudy Artau, Branch Chief
Charles Andrews, Associate Director

2639 Resources Agency: California Coastal Commission
45 Fremont Street 415-904-5250
Suite 2000 Fax: 415-904-5400
San Francisco, CA 94105 www.coastal.ca.gov
Mission: To protect, conserve, restore, and enhance environmental and human-based resources of the California coast and ocean for environmentally sustainable and prudent use by current and future generations.
Mary K. Shallenberger, Chair
Steve Kinsey, Vice Chairman

2640 Resources Agency: California Conservation Corps
1719 24th Street 916-341-3100
Sacramento, CA 95816 800-952-5627
Fax: 916-323-8922
www.ccc.ca.gov
Engages young men and women in meaningful work, public service educational activities that assist them in becoming more responsible citizens, while protecting and enhancing California's environment, human resources and communities.
David Muraki, Director
Jeffrey Schwarzchild, Chief Counsel

2641 Resources Agency: State Coastal Conservancy
1330 Broadway 510-286-1015
13th Floor Fax: 510-286-0470
Oakland, CA 94612-2530 dwayman@scc.ca.gov
www.scc.ca.gov
The Coastal Conservancy acts with others to preserve, protect and restore the resources of the California Coast.
Quarterly Magazine
Samuel Schuchat, Executive Officer
Mary Small, Deputy Executive Officer

2642 Southwestern Low-Level Radioactive Waste Commission
1731 Howe Ave #611 916-448-2390
Sacramento, CA 95825 Fax: 916-720-0144
kathydavis@swllrwcc.org
www.swllrwcc.org
The Southwestern Low-Level Radioactive Waste Commission is the governing body for the Southwestern Low-Level Radioactive Waste Disposal Compact, consisting of Arizona, California, North Dakota, and South Dakota. Created by public law100-712 in 1988, its key duties include controlling the importation and exportation of low-level waste into and out of the region. The Commission has no authority over disposal facility siting, but can make recommendations and comments to ensure safedisposal.
Kathy A David, Executive Director

2643 United States Department of Agriculture Research Education and Economics
800 Buchanan Street 510-559-6060
Albany, CA 94710 Fax: 510-559-5779
www.ree.usda.gov
Mission: Dedicated to the creation of a safe, sustainable, competitive US food and fiber system and strong, healthy communities, families, and youth through integrated research, analysis and education.
John King, Director
Cathie Woteki, Undersecretary

Colorado

2644 Bureau of Land Management
Department of the Interior
2850 Youngfield Street 303-239-3600
Lakewood, CO 80215-7093 Fax: 303-239-3933
www.blm.gov
Manages 8.3 million acres of public lands in Colorado. These lands are managed for a multitude of uses including, but not limited to, recreation, mining, wildlife habitat and grazing. Along with these 8.3 million acres, BLM oversees27.3 million subsurface acres for mineral development.
Ruth Welch, State Director
Greg Shoop, Associate State Director

2645 Bureau of Land Management: Little Snake Field Office
Little Snake Field Office 970-826-5000
455 Emerson Street Fax: 970-526-5002
Craig, CO 81625 swiser@blm.gov
www.blm.gov
Encompasses 4.2 million acres of federal, state and private lands in Moffat, Routt, and Rio Blanco counties.
Wendy Reynolds, Field Manager

2646 Canon City District Advisory Council
Royal Gorge Field Office 719-269-8500
3028 East Main Street Fax: 719-269-8599
Canon City, CO 81212 www.co.blm.gov/ccdo/canon.htm
This office administers over 680,000 surface acres of public land along the Front Range and 6.8 million sub-surface acres

2647 Cheyenne Mountain Zoological Park
4250 Cheyenne Mountain Zoo Road 719-633-9925
Colorado Springs, CO 80906 Fax: 719-633-2254
info@cmzoo.org
www.cmzoo.org
Mission: To foster an appreciation and respect for all living things. Actifely provide survival assistance for species in peril. Provide a high quality recreational experience. Be source of pride and economic strength.
Erica Meyer, PR Manager

2648 Colorado Department of Agriculture
305 Interlocken Parkway 303-239-4100
Suite 4000 Fax: 303-239-4125
Broomfield, CO 80021 vital.records@state.co.us
www.colorado.gov/ag
Mission: To strengthen and advance Colorado's agriculture industry; ensure a safe, high quality, and sustainable food supply; and protect consumers, the environment, and natural resources.
John R Stulp, Commisioner
Dr. Larry Wolk, Executive Director

2649 Colorado Department of Natural Resources
1313 Sherman Street 303-866-3311
Room 718 800-536-5308
Denver, CO 80203 Fax: 303-866-2115
dnr.edoassist@state.co.us
cdnr.us
Mike King, Executive Director
Bob Randall, Deputy Director

2650 Colorado Department of Natural Resources: Division of Water Resources
1313 Sherman Street 303-866-3581
Room 818 Fax: 303-866-3589
Denver, CO 80203 firstname.lastname@state.co.us
www.water.state.co.us

The Colorado Division of Water Resources is an agency of the State of Colorado, Department of Natural Resources, operating under the direction of specific state stautes, court decrees, and interstate compacts. The DWR is empowered toadminister all surface and ground water rights throughout the state and ensure that the doctrine of prior appopiation is enforced.
Dick Wolfe, State Engineer
Scott Cuthbertson, Assistant State Engineer

2651 Colorado Department of Public Health Environment Consumer Protection Division
4300 Cherry Creek Drive South 303-692-3620
Denver, CO 80246 Fax: 303-753-6809
www.cdphe.state.co.us/cp

The Consumer Protection Division assumes the responsiblity for protecting Colorado residents and visitors by prevention of a wide array of health hazards.

2652 Colorado Department of Public Health and Environment
4300 Cherry Creek Drive South 303-692-2000
Denver, CO 80246 800-886-7689
cdphe.information@state.co.us
www.cdphe.state.co.us

Mission: Committed to protecting and preserving the health and environment of the people of Colorado.
Dr. Larry Wolk, Executive Director/CMO
Karin McGowan, Deputy Executive Director

2653 Colorado River Basin Salinity Control Program
US Bureau of Land Reclamation
125 S State Street 801-524-3753
Room 7311 Fax: 801-524-3847
Salt Lake City, UT 84138-1147 kjacobson@usbr.gov
www.usbr.gov

The Colorado River and its tributaries provide municipal and industrial water to about 27 million people and irrigation to nearly four million acres of land in the US. The river also serves about 2.3 million people and 500,000 acres inMexico. The threat of salinity is a major concern in both the US and Mexico. Salinity affects agricultural, municipal and industrial water users. We work to control the salinity of the Colorado river and thereby to protect the land and people.
Kib Jacobson, Program Manager
Brad Parry, Program Coordinator

2654 Colorado State Forest Service
Colorado State University
5060 Campus Delivery 970-491-8660
Fort Collins, CO 80523-5060 Fax: 970-491-8645
CSFS_FortCollins@mail.colostate.edu
www.csfs.colostate.edu

Mission: To provide for the stewardship of forest resources and to reduce related risks to life, property and the environment for the benefit of present and future generations.
Boyd Lebeda, District Forester

2655 Environmental Protection Agency Region VIII (CO, MT, ND, SD, UT, WY)
1595 Wynkoop Street 303-312-6312
Denver, CO 80202-1129 800-227-8917
www.epa.gov/region8/

To restore and protect the ecological integrity of the mountains, plains and deserts and to protect the health of their inhabitants.
Shaun McGrath, Regional Administrator

2656 Governors Office of Energy, Management and Conservation: Colorado
1580 Logan Street 303-866-2100
Suite 100 800-632-6662
Denver, CO 80203 Fax: 303-866-2930
geo@state.co.us
www.colorado.gov/pacific/energyoffice

Supports cost-effective programs, grants and partnerships that benefit Colorado's economic and natural environment.
Jeff Ackermann, Director
Nancey Steinheimer, Assistant to the Director

2657 Minerals Management Service/Minerals Revenue Management
PO Box 25165 303-231-3162
Denver, CO 80225

Mission: To manage the ocean energy and mineral resources on the Outer Continental Shelf and Federal and Indian mineral revenues to enhance public and trust benefits, promote responsible use, and realize fair value.
Randall B Luthi, Director

2658 Natural Resources Department: Air Quality Division
Department of the Interior
PO Box 25287 303-969-2070
Denver, CO 80225-287 Fax: 303-969-2822
christine_shaver@nps.gov
www.nature.nps.gov/air/who/npsStaff.cfm

To protect air quality and resources affected by air pollution under the NPS Organic Act and the Clean Air Act
Carol McCoy, Division Chief
Chris Havermann, Office Manager

2659 Natural Resources Department: Oil & Gas Conservation Commission
1120 Lincoln Street Suite 801 303-894-2100
Denver, CO 80203 Fax: 303-894-2109
dnr_dnr.ogcc@state.co.us

To foster the responsible development of Colorado's oil and gas natural resources
M. Lepore, Director
J. Missey, Executive Assistant

2660 Natural Resources Department: Wildlife Division
6060 Broadway 303-291-7227
Denver, CO 80216 www.wildlife.state.co.us

Manages the state's 960 wildlife species. Regulates hunting and fishing activities by issuing licenses and enforcing regulations. Conducts research to improve wildlife management activities, provides technical assistance to private andother land owners concerning wildlife and habitat management and develops programs to protect and recover threatened and endangered species.
Mark B Konishi, Acting Director

2661 Office of Surface Mining Reclamation & Enforcement
1999 Broadway 303-293-5000
Suite 3320 Fax: 303-844-1546
Denver, CO 80202-3050 osm-wrWeb@osmre.gov
www.wrcc.osmre.gov/

Al Klein, Regional Director
Jeffrey Fleischman, Field Manager

2662 Rocky Mountain Low-Level Radioactive Waste Board
1313 Sherman Street 303-825-1912
6th Floor Fax: 303-892-3882
Denver, CO 80203-1264 sreynolds@rmllwb.us
www.cpw.state.co.us

Gary Baughman, Director
Leonard C. Slosky, Executive Director

2663 United States Forest Service: United States Department of Agriculture
740 Simms Street 202-205-8333
Golden, CO 80401 800-832-1355
www.fs.fed.us/r2
Mary Wagner, Associate Chief
Thomas L. Tidwell, Chief

Connecticut

2664 Connecticut Department of Agriculture
165 Capitol Avenue 860-713-2500
Hartford, CT 00610 Fax: 860-713-2514
www.ct.gov/doag/site/default.asp
Steven K Reviczky, Commissioner

2665 Connecticut Department of Environmental Protection
Department of Environmental Protection
79 Elm Street 860-424-3000
Hartford, CT 00610 dep.webmaster@po.state.ct.us
www.ct.gov/deep/site/default.asp
Mission: To conserve, improve and protect the natural resources and environment of the State of Connecticut in such a manner as to encourage the social and economic development of Connecticut while preserving the natural environmentand the life forms it supports in a delicate, interrelated and complex balance, to the end that the state may fulfill its responsibility as trustee of the environment for present and future generations.
Daniel C. Esty, Commissioner

2666 Connecticut Department of Public Health
410 Capitol Avenue 860-509-8000
PO Box 340308 www.ct.gov/dph/site/default.asp
Hartford, CT 00613
Has long recognized the adverse public health impact of environmental sources of lead in many of Connecticut's childern. Established dedicated staff to evaluate these environmental sources and began funding local programs in the1970's. The Childhood Lead Posioning Prevention Program has continued to be active in addressing this issue by implementing additional state and community programs, especially in towns that have been identified as high risk.
Jewell Mullen, Commissioner
Norma Gyle, Deputy Commissioner

District of Columbia

2667 District of Columbia State Extension Services
4200 Connecticut Avenue 202-274-5000
Building 352, Suite 322 Fax: 202-274-7130
Washington, DC 20008 alumni@udc.edu
www.udc.edu

Delaware

2668 Delaware Association of Conservation Districts
PO Box 242 302-739-9921
Dover, DE 19903-242 Fax: 302-739-6724
Martha.Pileggi@state.de.us
www.nacdnet.org
Coordinates the three state conservation districts.
Wendy Baker, President
Robert Emerson, Vice President

2669 Delaware Cooperative Extension
University of Delaware
531 South College Avenue 302-831-2504
113 Townsend Hall Fax: 302-831-6758
Newark, DE 19716-2103 mrodgers@udel.edu
www.extension.udel.edu
Contact person Janice A Seitz's title is Associate Dean for Extension and Outreach Director of Extension College of Agriculture and Natural Resources.
Michelle Rogers, Director
Alice Moore, Administrative Assistant

2670 Delaware Department of Agriculture
2320 S DuPont Highway 302-698-4500
Dover, DE 19901 800-282-8685
www.dda.delaware.gov
As part of the state government, the department's mission is to sustain and promote the viability of food, fiber and agricultural industries in Delaware through quality services that protect and enhance the environment, health andwelfare of the general public.
Ed Kee, Secretary
E. Austin Short, Deputy Secretary

2671 Delaware Department of Natural Resources and Environmental Control
DNREC
89 Kings Highway 302-739-9400
Dover, DE 19901 Fax: 302-739-3106
dnrec.alpha.delaware.gov
Protects and manages the state's vital natural resources, protects public health and safety, provides quality outdoor recreation, and serves and educates the citizens of the First State about the wise use, conservation and enhancementof Delaware's environment.
Collin O'Mara, Secretary

2672 Delaware Sea Grant Program
University of Delaware 302-831-8083
222 South Chapel Street www.deseagrant.org/
Newark, DE 19716-3530
Using Technology, Innovation, and Cooperation to Tackle Coastal Challenges
Nancy Targett, Director
Jennifer Adkins, Executive Director

2673 Department of the Interior: U.S. Fish & Wildlife Service - Delaware Bay Estate Project
Delaware Bay Estuary Project
2610 Whitehall Neck Road 302-653-9152
Smyrna, DE 19977-2910 Fax: 302-653-9421
R5ES_DPEP@fws.gov
www.fws.gov/delawarebay/
Delaware Bay Estate Project is a field office of the US Fish & Wildlife service's coastal program.
Gregory Breese, Project Leader
Richard McCorkle, Biologist

2674 Mid-Atlantic Fishery Management Council
800 North State Street 302-674-2331
Suite 201 Fax: 302-674-5399
Dover, DE 19901 contact@mafmc.org
www.mafmc.org
The Mid-Atlantic Fishery Management Council is responsible for management of fisheries in federal waters which occur predominantly off the mid-Atlantic coast.
Richard B. Robins, Chairman
Lee Anderson, Vice Chairman

Florida

2675 Department of Commerce National Oceanic & Atlantic Oceanographic & Meteorological Laboratory
4301 Rickenbacker Causeway 305-361-4420
Miami, FL 33149 Fax: 305-361-4449
www.aoml.noaa.gov

Robert M Atlas, Director
Dr. Molly Baringer, Deputy Director

2676 Fish & Wildlife Conservation Commission
620 South Meridian Street 850-488-4676
Tallahassee, FL 32399 www.myfwc.com/
Mission: Managing fish and wildlife resources for their long-term well-being and the benefit of the people.
Rodney Barreto, Chair

2677 Florida Department of Agriculture & Consumer Service
The Capitol, Pl 10 850-488-3022
400 South Monroe Street Fax: 850-488-7585
Tallahassee, FL 32399-800 www.freshfromflorida.com
Mission: To safeguard the public and support Florida's agriculture economy by: ensuring the safety and wholesomeness of food and other consumer products through inspection and testing programs; protecting consumers from unfair anddeceptive business practices and providing consumer information; assisting Florida's farmers and agriculture industries with the production and promotion of agriculture products; and conserving and protecting the state's agriculture and naturalresources.
Adam H. Putnam, Commissioner

2678 Florida Department of Environmental Protection
3900 Commonwealth Boulevard 850-245-2118
M.S. 49 Fax: 850-245-2128
Tallahassee, FL 32399-3000 www.dep.state.fl.us
Mission: To promote the efficient and effective operation of the Agency consistent with its Administratice and statutory responsibilities.
Rick Scott, Governor
Herschel Vinyard, Jr., Secretary

2679 Florida State Department of Health
2585 Merchants Row Blvd 850-245-4444
Tallahassee, FL 32399 www.doh.state.fl.us
Mission: To promote and protect the health and safety of all people in Florida through the delivery of quality public health services and the promotion of health care standards.
J. Martin Stubblefield, Deputy Secretary
Kim Barnhill, Chief of Staff

2680 Gulf of Mexico Fishery Management Council
2203 North Lois Avenue 813-348-1630
Suite 1100 888-833-1844
Tampa, FL 33607 Fax: 813-348-1711
gulfcouncil@gulfcouncil.org
www.gulfcouncil.org
The Gulf of Mexico Fishery management Council is one of eight regional Fishery Management Councils which were established by the Fishery conservation and Management Act in 1976 (now called the Magnuson-Stevens Fishery Conservation andMagnuson Act). The Council prepares fishery plans which are designed to manage fishery resources from where state waters end to the 200 mile limit of the Gulf of mexico.
Wayne E Swingle, Executive Director
Rick Leard, Deputy Executive Director

2681 Lee County Parks & Recreation
3410 Palm Beach Boulevard 239-533-7275
Fort Myers, FL 33916 Fax: 239-485-2300
LeeParks@leegov.com
www.leeparks.org/
Our mission is to provide safe, clean and functional Parks & Recreation facilities; to provide programs and services that add to the quality of life for all Lee County residents and visitors; to enhance tourism through special eventsand attractions. We are committed to fulfilling this mission through visionary leadership, individual dedication and the trustworthy use of available resources.
Dana Kasler, Director
Dana Kasler, Deputy Director

2682 Natural Resources Department: Recreation & Parks Division
3900 Commonwealth Boulevard 850-245-2157
Tallahassee, FL 32399 www.dep.state.fl.us/parks
Mission: To provide resource-based recreation while preserving, interpreting and restoring natural and cultural resources. Our goal is to help create a sense of place by showing park visitors the best of Florida's diverse natural andcultural heritage sites.
Donald V. Forgione, Director

2683 Southwest Florida Water Management District
2379 Broad Street 352-796-7211
Brookville, FL 34604-6899 800-423-1476
Fax: 352-754-6885
info@watermatters.org
www.swfwmd.state.fl.us
Manages the water and water-related resources within its boundaries. Maintains balance between the water needs of current and future users while protecting and maintaining the natural systems that provide the District with its existingand future water supply. The Conservation Projects Section, in the Resource Conservation and Development Department, is reponsible for managing water conservation, reclaimed water and other alternative source projects, and estimating future waterdemands.
Michael A. Babb, Chairman
Randall S. Maggard, Vice Chairman

Georgia

2684 Board of Scientific Counselors: Agency for Toxic Substance and Disease Registry
4770 Buford Hwy NE 800-232-4636
Atlanta, GA 30341 800-232-4636
Fax: 404-562-1790
www.atsdr.cdc.gov
Serves the public by using the best science, taking responsive public health actions, and providing trusted health information to prevent harmful exposures and diseases related to toxic substances
Robin Ikeda, Director
Thomas Sinks, Deputy Director

2685 Georgia Department of Agriculture
19 Martin Luther King Jr Drive SW 404-656-3600
Atlanta, GA 30334 800-282-5852
www.agr.georgia.gov
Mission: To provide excellence in services and regulatory functions, to protect and promote agriculture and consumer interests, and to ensure an abundance of safe food and fiber for Georgia, America and the world by usingstate-of-the-art technology and a professional workforce.
Gary W. Black, Commissioner
James Sutton, Chief Administration Officer

2686 Georgia Department of Education
205 Jesse Hill Jr. Drive SE 404-656-2800
Atlanta, GA 30334 Fax: 404-651-8737
askdoe@gadoe.org
www.gadoe.org
To function as a service oriented and policy driven agency that meets the needs of local school systems as they go about the business of preparing all students for college or a career in a safe and drug free environment where we ensurethat no chils is left behind.
Joel Thorton, Chief of Staff
Mike Buck, Chief Academic Officer

2687 Georgia Department of Natural Resources: Historic Preservation Division
2610 GA Hwy 155, SW 404-656-2840
Stockbridge, GA 30281 Fax: 770-389-7844
www.georgiashpo.org
To promote the preservation and use of historic places for a better Georgia.
Ray Luce, Director

2688 Georgia Department of Natural Resources: Pollution Prevention Assistance Division
2 Martin Luther King Jr. Drive 404-651-5120
SE Suite 1252 800-685-2443
Atlantic, GA 30334 Fax: 404-651-5130
www.gadnr.org/
Lauren Travis, Program Manager
David Gipson, Assistant Director

2689 Georgia Sea Grant College Program
University of Georgia
220 Marine Science Building 706-542-6009
Athens, GA 30602 Fax: 706-542-3652
www.georgiaseagrant.uga.edu
Goal is to better understand the complex interactions between the physical, chemical, biological and geological processes that are manifested in the area where land and sea come together, and to make that knowledge available and usefulto Georgia's citizens. Sea Grant strives to deepen our understanding of coastal and estuarine ecology, the critical role of fresh water interaction and to expand our knowledge of action beyond the marshes and estuaries and into the life of the riversand streams.
Charles Hopkinson, Director
David Bryant, Assistant Director

2690 National Center for Environmental Health
1600 Clifton Road
Atlanta, GA 30329-4027 800-232-4636
Fax: 770-488-7042
www.cdc.gov/nceh
Mission: Plans, directs, and coordinates a national program to maintain and improve the health of the American people by promoting a healthy environment and by preventing premature death and avoidable illness and disability caused bynon-infectious, non-occupational and related factors.
Robin Ikeda, Director

2691 Natural Resource Department
2 Martin Luther King Jr Drive SE 404-656-3500
Suite 1252 East Tower www.state.ga.us/dnr/
Atlanta, GA 30334
The mission of the Department of Natural Resources is to sustain, enhance, protect and conserve Georgia's natural, historic and cultural resources for present and future generations, while recognizing the importance of promoting thedevelopment of commerce and industry that utilize sound environmental practices.
Noel Holcomb, Commissioner

2692 Natural Resources Department: Air Protection
4244 International Parkway 404-363-7000
Suite 120 Fax: 404-363-7100
Atlanta, GA 30354 james.capp@dnr.state.ga.us
www.georgiaair.org
The Air Protection Branch helps provide Georgia's citizens with clean air and works closely with other branches of Georgia's Environmental Protection Division to assure compliance with environmental laws so that, in addition to clearair, we have clean water, healthy lives and productive land.
James A Capp, Branch Chief

2693 Natural Resources Department: Coastal Resources Division
1 Conservation Way 912-264-7218
Brunswick, GA 31520 Fax: 912-262-3143
www.coastalgadnr.org
Spud Woodward, Director
Brad Jane, Ecological Services Chief

2694 Natural Resources Department: Environmental Protection Division
2 Martin Luther King Jr Drive 404-657-5947
Suite 1152 East Tower 888-373-5947
Atlanta, GA 30334 askepd@gaepd.org
www.gaepd.org
Provides Georgia's citizens with clean air, clean water, healthy lives and productive land by assuring compliance with environmental laws and by assisting others to do their part for a better environment.
Judson H. Turner, Director

2695 United States Department of the Army US Army Corps of Engineers
US Army Engineer Distric 912-652-5279
100 W Oglethorpe Ave cesas-cco@usace.army.mil
Savannah, GA 31401 www.sas.usace.army.mil
Mission: To provide quality, responsive engineering services to the nation including: planning, designing, building and operating water resources and other civil works projects; designing and managing the construction of militaryfacilities for the Army and Air Force; and providing design and construction management support for other defense and federal agencies.
Jeffrey M. Hall, District Commander
Ronald L Johnson, Deputy Commander

2696 Wassaw National Wildlife Refuge
1000 Business Center Drive 912-832-4608
Suite 10 savannahcoastal@fws.gov
Savannah, GA 31405 www.fws.gov/wassaw
The most primitive of Georgia's barrier islands, the 10,053 acre refuge, includes beaches with rolling dunes, live oak and slash pine woodlands, and vast salt marshes. The island supports rookeries for egrets and herons, and a varietyof leading birds are abundant in the summer months. Wassaw also provides prime nesting habitat for the loggerhead seaturtles. Refuge visitors may enjoy recreational activities such as birdwatching, beachocombing, hiking, and general nature studies.
Jane Griess, Project Leader
Kimberley Hayes, Refuge Manager

Hawaii

2697 Agriculture Department
1428 South King Street 808-973-9560
Honolulu, HI 96814 www.agricoop.nic.in/
Sandra Lee Kunimoto, Chair

2698 College of Tropical Agriculture and Human Resources
University of Hawaii
3050 Maile Way — 808-956-8131
Gilmore 202 — Fax: 808-956-9105
Honolulu, HI 96822 — gallom@ctahr.hawaii.edu
www.ctahr.hawaii.edu/site/

Mission: Committed to the preparation of students and all citizens of Hawaii for life in the global community through research and educational programs supporting tropical agriculture systems that foster viable communities, adiversified economy, and a healthy environment.
Maria Gallo, Dean/Director
Wimmie Wong Lui, Assistant

2699 Department of Land and Natural Resources Division of Water Resource Management
1151 Punchbowl Street — 808-587-0214
Room 227 — Fax: 808-587-0219
Honolulu, HI 96813 — dlnr.cwrm@hawaii.gov
www.dlnr.hawaii.gov

W. Roy Hardy, P.E., Deputy Director
William J. Aila, Chair

2700 Environmental Center
University of Hawaii
2500 Dole Street — 808-956-7361
Krauss Annex 19 — Fax: 808-956-3980
Honolulu, HI 96822 — envctr@hawaii.edu
www.hawaii.edu/envctr

The Center's three areas of focus are education, research and service. The education function of the Center includes the administration of the Environmental Studies Major Equivalent and Certificate program. It fulfills its researchfunction by identifying and addressing environmentally related research needs, particularly those pertinent to Hawaii. The service function primarily involves the coordination and transfer of technical information from the University community togovernment agencies.
Charlotte Kato, Secretary

2701 Hawaii Department of Agriculture
1428 South King Street — 808-973-9560
Honolulu, HI 96814 — www.hawaii.gov/hdoa
Contains devisions such as: Administrative; Animal Industry; Marketing; Measurement Standards; and Plant Industry. Carries out programs to conserve, develop and utilize the agricultural resources of the state. Enforces laws, andformulates and enforces rules and regulation to further control the management of these resources.
Sandra Lee Kunimoto, Chairperson

2702 Hawaii Institute of Marine Biology University of Hawaii
PO Box 1346 — 808-236-7401
Kane'ohe, HI 96744 — Fax: 808-236-7443
www.hawaii.edu/HIMB
Jo-Ann C Leong, Director

2703 Health Department: Environmental Quality Control
235 S Beretania Street — 808-586-4185
Room 702 — Fax: 808-586-4186
Honolulu, HI 96813 — oeqc@doh.hawaii.gov
health.hawaii.gov
The office is tasked to implement Chapter 343, Hawaii Revised Statues and Title 11, Chapter 200. This is a systematic process to ensure consideration is given to the environmental consequences of actions proposed within our state. Thereview process offers many opportunities to prevent environmental degradation and protect human communities through decreased citizen involvement and informed decision making.
Virgina Pressler, M.D., Director

2704 State of Hawaii: Department of Land and Natural Resources
Kalanimoku Building — 808-587-0400
1151 Punchbowl Street — Fax: 808-587-0390
Honolulu, HI 96813 — dlnr@hawaii.gov
www.hawaii.gov/dlnr
State agency.
Suzanne D. Case, Chairperson
Kekoa Kaluhiwa, First Deputy

2705 Water Resources Research Center University of Hawaii
2540 Dole Street — 808-956-7847
Holmes Hall 283 — Fax: 808-956-5044
Honolulu, HI 96822 — wrrc@hawaii.edu
www.wrrc.hawaii.edu
The Water Resources Research Center was organized under the federal Water Resources Research Act of 1964. The Center is supported by university funds, external grants, contracts and a small annual federal grant. WRRC faculty coverthe areas of engineering, hydrology, microbiology, ecology, economics and zoology. Cooperating faculty come from numerous other disciplines. WRRC is open to consideration of any question related to water supply or water quality.
James Moncur, Director

Idaho

2706 Department of the Interior: Bureau of Land Management - Idaho
1387 South Vinnell Way — 208-373-4000
Boise, ID 83709 — blm_id_stateoffice@blm.gov
www.blm.gov/idaho
The BLM manages a variety of resources in Idaho with an emphasis on recreation, grazing and fire management on nearly 12 million acres of public lands (nearly 1/4 of the state's total land area).

2707 Idaho Association of Soil Conservation Districts
55 SW 5th Ave — 208-895-8928
Suite 100 — Fax: 208-376-6858
Meridian, ID 83642 — kent.foster@agri.idaho.gov
www.iascd.org
Provides action at the local level for promoting wise and beneficial conservation of natural resources with emphasis on soil and water.
Kit Tillotson, President
Billie J. Brown, Vice President

2708 Idaho Cooperative Extension
875 Perimeter Drive — 208-885-5883
MS 2338 — Fax: 208-885-6654
Moscow, ID 83844-2338 — extension@uidaho.edu
www.uidaho.edu/extension/
Barbara Petty, Interim Director

2709 Idaho Department of Environmental Quality: Pocatello Regional Office
444 Hospital Way #300 — 208-236-6160
Pocatello, ID 83201 — 888-655-6160
Fax: 208-236-6168
www.state.id.us
Mission: To protect human health and preserve the quality of Idaho's air, land, and water for use and enjoyment today and in the future.
Toni Hardesty, Director

2710 Idaho Department of Environmental Quality: State Office
1410 North Hilton 208-373-0502
Boise, ID 83706 Fax: 208-373-0417
john.tippets@deq.idaho.gov
www.deq.idaho.gov
Mission: To protect human health and preserve the quality of Idaho's air, land, and water for use and enjoyment today and in the future.
John Tippets, Director
Jess Byrne, Deputy Director

2711 Idaho Department of Environmental Quality: Idaho Falls Regional Office
900 N Skyline 208-528-2650
Suite B 800-232-4635
Idaho Falls, ID 83402 Fax: 208-528-2695
www.state.id.us
Mission: To protect human health and preserve the quality of Idaho's air, land, and water for use and enjoyment today and in the future.
Toni Hardesty, Director

2712 Idaho Department of Fish & Game: Clearwater Region
3316 16th Street 208-799-5010
Lewiston, ID 83501 Fax: 208-799-5012
Mission: All wildlife, including all wild animals, wild birds, and fish, within the state of Idaho, is hereby declared to be the property of the state of Idaho.
Virgil Moore, Director
Sharon Kiefer, Deputy Director

2713 Idaho Department of Fish & Game: Headquarters
600 S Walnut Street 208-334-3700
PO Box 25 Fax: 208-334-2114
Boise, ID 83707 www.fishandgame.idaho.gov
Mission: All wildlife, including all wild animals, wild birds, and fish, within the state of Idaho, is hereby declared to be the property of the state of Idaho.
Virgil Moore, Director
Sharon Kiefer, Deputy Director

2714 Idaho Department of Fish & Game: Magic Valley Region
324 South 417 East 208-324-4359
Suite 1 Fax: 208-324-1160
Jerome, ID 83338 www.fishandgame.idaho.gov
Mission: All wildlife including all wild animals, wild birds, and fish, within the state of Idaho, is hereby declared to be the property of the state of Idaho.
Virgil Moore, Director
Sharon Kiefer, Deputy Director

2715 Idaho Department of Fish & Game: McCall
555 Deinhard Lane 208-634-8137
McCall, ID 83638 Fax: 208-634-4320
www.fishandgame.idaho.gov
Mission: All wildlife, including all wild animals, wild birds, and fish, within the state of Idaho, is hereby declared to be the property of the state of Idaho.
Virgil Moore, Director
Sharon Kiefer, Deputy Director

2716 Idaho Department of Fish & Game: Panhandle Region
2885 West Kathleen Avenue 208-769-1414
Coeur d'Alene, ID 83815 Fax: 208-769-1418
www.fishandgame.idaho.gov
Mission: All wildlife, including all wild animals, wild birds, and fish, within the state of Idaho, is hereby declared to be the property of the state of Idaho.
Virgil Moore, Director
Sharon Kiefer, Deputy Director

2717 Idaho Department of Fish & Game: Salmon Region
99 Highway 93 N 208-756-2271
PO Box 1336 Fax: 208-756-6274
Salmon, ID 83467 www.fishandgame.idaho.gov
Mission: All wildlife, including all wild animals, wild birds, and fish, within the state of Idaho, is hereby declared to be the property of the state of Idaho.
Virgil Moore, Director
Sharon Kiefer, Deputy Director

2718 Idaho Department of Fish & Game: Southeast Region
1345 Barton Road 208-232-4703
Pocatello, ID 83204 Fax: 208-233-6430
www.fishandgame.idaho.gov
Mission: All wildlife, including all wild animals, wild birds, and fish, within the state of Idaho, is hereby declared to be the property of the state of Idaho.
Virgil Moore, Director
Sharon Kiefer, Deputy Director

2719 Idaho Department of Fish & Game: Southwest Region
3101 S Powerline Road 208-465-8465
Nampa, ID 83686 Fax: 208-465-8467
www.fishandgame.idaho.gov
Mission: All wildlife, including all wild animals, wild birds, and fish, within the state of Idaho, is hereby declared to be the property of the state of Idaho.
Virgil Moore, Director
Sharon Kiefer, Deputy Director

2720 Idaho Department of Fish & Game: Upper Snake Region
4279 Commerce Circle 208-525-7290
Idaho Falls, ID 83401 Fax: 208-523-7604
www.fishandgame.idaho.gov
Mission: All wildlife, including all wild animals, wild birds, and fish, within the state of Idaho, is hereby decalred to be the property of the state of Idaho.
Virgil Moore, Director
Sharon Kiefer, Deputy Director

2721 Idaho Department of Lands
300 N 6th Street, Suite 103 208-334-0200
Po Box 83720 Fax: 208-334-3698
Boise, ID 83720-0050 public_records_request@idl.idaho.gov
www.idl.idaho.gov
Mission: To manage endowment trust lands to maximize long-term financial returns to the benficiary institutions and provide protection to Idaho's natural resources.
Tom Schultz, Director
Kathy Opp, Deputy Director

2722 Idaho Department of State Parks and Recreation
PO Box 83720 208-334-4199
Boise, ID 83720 Fax: 208-334-5232
Manages 27 state parks. We also run the registration program for snowmobiles, boats and off-highway vehicles. Money from registrations and other sources goes to develop and maintain trails, facilities and programs statewide for thepeople who use those vehicles.
Robert L Meinen, Director

2723 **Idaho Department of Water Resources**
322 E Front Street 208-287-4800
Boise, ID 83720-98 Fax: 208-287-6700
IDWRInfo@idwr.idaho.gov
www.idwr.idaho.gov/about/
Working for a controlled development and wise management of Idaho's resources. Documents and reports on topics of public interest such as drought, salmon, wilderness and the Snake River Basin.
Roger Chase, Chairman
Jeffrey Raybould, Vice Chair

2724 **Idaho Geological Survey**
University of Idaho
Morrill Hall 208-885-7991
3rd Floor Fax: 208-885-5826
Moscow, ID 83844-3014 igs@uidaho.edu
www.idahogeology.org
Roy M Breckenridge, Director
Kurt L Othberg, Director

2725 **Idaho State Department of Agriculture**
2270 Old Penitentiary Road 208-332-8500
Boise, ID 83712 Fax: 208-334-2170
info@agri.idaho.gov
www.agri.idaho.gov
Celia R Gould, Director
Brian Oakey, Deputy Director

2726 **Lands Department: Soil Conservation Commission**
Po Box 790 208-332-8650
Boise, ID 83701
Responsibilities of the Commission are: organize Districts and provide assistance, coordination, information and training to Disrict supervisors; ensure that Districts function legally and properly as local subdivisions of stategovernment; administer general funds appropriated by the Idaho Legislature to Districts so they can install resource conservation practices and provide technical assistance personnel to Districts administering water quality projects and conductingsoil surveys.
Jerry Nicolescu, Administrator

Illinois

2727 **Construction Engineering Research Laboratory**
US Army Engineer Research and Development Center
PO Box 9005 217-352-6511
Champaign, IL 61826 800-USA-CERL
www.erdc.usace.army.mil/Locations/CERL
CERL conducts research to support sustainable military installations. Research is directed toward increasing the Army's ability to more efficiently construct, operate and maintain its installations and ensure environmental quality andsafety at a reduced life-cycle cost. Excellent facilities support the Army's training, readiness, mobilization and sustainability missions.
Ilker Adiguzel, Director

2728 **Department of Natural Resources: Division of Education**
Illinois Department of Natural Resources
One Natural Resources Way 217-524-4126
Springfield, IL 62702-1271 Fax: 217-782-9552
valerie.keener@illinois.gov
www.dnr.illinois.gov
Responsible for the development and dissemination of educational programs and materials and for training in their use. The website provides contests for students, loan materials, education materials, and grant information, in additionto graduate program information, podcasts and workshops. Overall, an excellent resource for education professionals, parents, and students.
Valerie Keener, Administrator

2729 **Environmental Protection Agency Bureau of Water**
Water Bureau
4500 South Sixth Street Road 312-814-8199
Springfield, IL 62706 www.epa.state.il.us/water
Mission: To ensure that Illinois' rivers, streams and lakes will support all uses for which they are designated including protection of aquatic life, recreation and drinking water supplies; ensure that every illinois Public Watersystem will provide water that is consistently safe to drink; and protect Illinois' groundwater resource for designated drinking water and other beneficial uses.
Lisa Bonnett, Director
Elmo Dowd, Associate Director

2730 **Environmental Protection Agency: Region 5**
77 West Jackson Boulevard 312-353-2000
Chicago, IL 60604-3590 800-621-8431
www.epa.gov/region5
Susan Hedman, Region Administrator

2731 **Illinois Conservation Foundation**
One Natural Resources Way 217-785-2003
Springfield, IL 62702 Fax: 217-785-8405
www.ilcf.org
Established by law, the ILCF is a volunteer group with a 13-member Board, chaired by the Director of the IL Dept of Natural Resources. The role of the ILCF and its partners is to preserve and enhance our precious natural resources bysupporting and fostering ecological, educational, and recreational programs for the benefit of all citizens of Illinois and for future generations.
Wayne Rosenthal, Chairman
Barbara Ducey, Secretary

2732 **Illinois Department of Agriculture Bureau of Land and Water Resources**
PO Box 19281 217-782-2172
Springfield, IL 62794-9281 Fax: 217-785-4505
www.agr.state.il.us
Charles A Hartke, Director

2733 **Illinois Department of Transportation**
2300 S Dirksen Parkway 217-782-7820
Springfield, IL 62764-1 www.idot.illinois.gov
Provides cost-effective, safe and efficient transportation for the people who live, work, visit and do business in Illinois, and ensures that the system supports the state's economic growth.
Ann L Schneider, Director
Vincent E Rangel, Deputy Director

2734 **Illinois Nature Preserves Commission**
One Natural Resources Way 217-785-8686
Springfield, IL 62702 Fax: 217-785-2438
kelly.neal@illinois.gov
www.dnr.illinois.gov
Assists private and public landowners in protecting high quality natral areas and habitats of endangered and threatened species through voluntary dedication or registration of such lands into the Illinois Nature Preserves Systems. TheCommission also provides leadership in the areas of stewardship, management and protection.
Donald R. Dann, Chair
Kelly L. Neal, Stewardship Project Manager

2735 **United States Department of the Army US Army Corps of Engineers**
US Army Engineer District

Clock Tower Building
PO Box 2004
Rock Island, IL 61204
309-794-5729
Fax: 309-794-5793
www.usace.army.mil
Thomas Bostick, Commanding General
Todd T. Semonite, Deputy Commanding General

Indiana

2736 Indiana Department of Natural Resources
402 West Washington Street
Indianapolis, IN 46204
317-232-4020
Fax: 317-232-8036
www.ai.org/dnr
Protects, enhances, preserves, and wisely uses natural, cultural, and recreational resources for the benefit of Indiana's citizens through professional leadership, management and education.
Robert E Carter, Director
Todd Tande, Deputy Director

2737 Indiana State Department of Agriculture, Soil Conservation
One North Capitol Avenue
Suite 600
Indianapolis, IN 46204
317-232-8770
Fax: 317-232-1362
www.in.gov/isda
Mission: To facilitate the protection and enhancement of Indiana's land and water.
Ted McKinney, Director
Melissa Rekeweg, Deputy Director

2738 Indiana State Department of Health
2 N Meridan Street
Indianapolis, IN 46204
317-233-1325
www.in.gov/isdh/
Mission: To support Indiana's economic prosperity and quality of life by promoting, protecting and providing for the health of Hoosiers in their communities.
Judith A Monroe, State Health Commissioner
Mary L Hill, Deputy State Health Commiss.

2739 Natural Resources Department: Fish & Wildlife
402 West Washington Street RMW273
Indianapolis, IN 46204
317-232-4080
Fax: 317-232-8150
dfw@dnr.in.gov
www.in.gov/dnr/fishwild
Mission: To professionally manage Indiana's fish and wildlife for present and future generations, balancing ecological, recreational, and economic benefits.

Iowa

2740 Iowa Association of County Conservation Boards
405 SW 3rd Street
Suite 1
Ankeny, IA 50023
515-963-9582
Fax: 515-963-9582
iaccb@ecity.net
www.ecity.net/iaccb
IACCB is a nonprofit organization assisting member county conservation boards in areas of board member education, public relations and legislation. The association's main purposes are to promote the objectives and supplement theactivities of conservation boards, exchange information, assist boards and members in program development and provide a unified voice in the legislature. IACCB is governed by a nine-member board elected by member counties.

2741 Iowa Department of Agriculture, and Land Stewardship Division of Soil Conservation
502 E 9th
Wallace State Office Building
Des Moines, IA 50319
515-281-5321
Fax: 515-281-6170
www.iowaagriculture.gov/
The Division of Soil Conservation is responsible for state leadership in the protection and management of soil, water and mineral resources, assisting soil and water conservation districts and private landowners to meet theiragricultural and environmental protection needs.
Chuck Gipp, Director
Karen Fynaardt, Administrative Assistant

2742 Iowa Department of Natural Resources Administrative Services Division
502 E 9th Street
Wallace Office Building
Des Moines, IA 50319-34
515-281-5918
Fax: 515-281-8895
www.iowadnr.com
Aims to manage, protect, conserve and develop Iowa's natural resources in cooperation with other public and private organizations and individuals, so that the quality of life for Iowans is significantly enhanced by the use, enjoymentand understanding of those resources.

2743 Iowa State Extension Services
2150 Beardshear Hall
Ames, IA 55011-2031
515-294-6192
Fax: 515-294-4715
jlpease@iastate.edu
www.extension.iastate.edu/
Dr James L Pease, Specialist

2744 Natural Resource Department
502 E 9th Street
Des Moines, IA 50319-34
515-281-5385
Fax: 515-281-8895
www.iowadnr.com
Mission: To conserve and enhance our natural resources in cooperation with individuals and organizations to improve the quality of life for Iowans and ensure a legacy for future generations.
Richard Leopold, Director
Liz Christiansen, Deputy Director

Kansas

2745 Emporia Research and Survey Office Kansas Department of Wildlife & Parks
1830 Merchant
512 SE 25th Ave
1830 Merchant
Emporia, KS 67124-1525
620-672-5911
www.ksoutdoors.com
Randy Doll, Commissioner
Robert J. Wilson, Commissioner

2746 Environmental Protection Agency: Region 7, Air & Toxics Division
11201 Renner Blvd.
Lenexa, KS 66219
913-551-7003
Fax: 913-551-7066
www.epa.gov/region7/
Responsible for management of programs for air, hazardous waste, toxic substances, radiation and pollution prevention in Iowa, Kansa, Missouri and Nebraska as required by the following legistlation: The Clean Air Act, The ResourceConservation and Recovery Act, the Toxic Substances Control Act and the Emergency planning and Community Right-to Know Act.
Patrick Bustos, Director
Hattie Thomas, Deputy Director

2747 Health & Environment Department: Air & Radiation
1000 SW Jackson
Suite 310
Topeka, KS 66612
785-296-1593
Fax: 785-296-8464
jmitchell@kdheks.gov
www.kdheks.gov/bar
Mission: To protect the public from the harmful effects of radiation and air pollution and conserve the natural resources of the

state by preventing damage to the environment from releases of radioactive materials or air contaminants.
Rick Bruneti, Director

2748 Health & Environment Department: Environment Division
1000 SW Jackson Street 785-296-1535
Suite 400 Fax: 785-296-8464
Topeka, KS 66612-1367 jmitchell@kdheks.gov
www.kdheks.gov/environment
The mission of the Division of Environment is the protection of the public health and environment. The division conducts regulatory programs involving public water supplies, industrial discharges, wastewater treatment systems, solidswaste landfills, hazardous waste, air emissions, radioactive materials, asbestos removal, refined petroleum storage tanks and other sources which impact the environment.
John Michtell, Director
Sam Brownback, Secretary

2749 Health & Environment Department: Waste Management
1000 SW Jackson 785-296-1600
Suite 320 Fax: 785-296-8909
Topeka, KS 66612-1366 www.kdheks.gov/waste
Regulates landfills, HHW, Hazardous Waste Permitting, Solid Waste Permitting, Public Outreach, Illegal Dumps.
John Michtell, Director
Sam Brownback, Secretary

2750 Kansas Cooperative Fish & Wildlife Research Unit
Kansas State University
205 Leasure Hall 785-532-6070
Manhattan, KS 66506 Fax: 785-532-7159
kscfwru@ksu.edu
www.k-state.edu/kscfwru
Unit Research contributes to understanding ecological systems within the Great Plains. Unit staff, collaborators, and graduate students conduct research with both natural and altered systems, particularly those impacted by agriculture.Unit projects investigate ways to maintain a rich diversity of endemic wild animals and habitats while meeting the needs of people. The Unit focuses on projects that involve graduate students, and the research needs of cooperators are given priority.
David Haukos, Leader
Jack Cully Jr, Assistant Leader

2751 Kansas Corporation Commission Conservation Division
266 N. Main St. 316-337-6200
Ste 220 Fax: 316-337-6211
Wichita, KS 67202-1513 www.kcc.state.ks.us
State of Kansas oilfield regulatory agency. The KCC is responsible for the preservation of Kansas' hydro and carbo resources, protection of corrullative right and the prevention and remediation of oil field pollution.
Shari Feist, Chair
Jay Scott Emler, Commissioner

2752 Kansas Department of Health & Environment
1000 SW Jackson Street 785-296-1500
Topeka, KS 66612 Fax: 785-368-6368
info@kdhe.state.ks.us
www.kdheks.gov
An organization dedicated to optimizing the promotion and protection of the health of Kansas through efficient and effective public health programs and services and through preservation, protection and remediation of natural resourcesof the environment.
Susan Brownback, Secretary
Aaron Dunkel, Deputy Secretary

2753 Kansas Department of Wildlife & Parks Region 2
300 SW Wanamaker Road 785-273-6740
Topeka, KS 66606 Fax: 785-273-6757
www.ksoutdoors.com/
Manages and promotes the wildlife and natural resources of Kansas. Administered by a secetary of Wildlife and Parks and is advised by a seven-member Wildlife and Parks Commission.
Randy Doll, Commissioner
Robert J. Wilson, Commissioner

2754 Kansas Department of Wildlife & Parks Region 3
1001 McArtor Drive 620-227-8609
Dodge City, KS 67801-6024 Fax: 620-227-8600
www.ksoutdoors.com/
Randy Doll, Commissioner
Robert J. Wilson, Commissioner

2755 Kansas Department of Wildlife & Parks Region 4
6232 E 29th Street N 316-683-8069
Wichita, KS 67220 www.ksoutdoors.com/
Randy Doll, Commissioner
Robert J. Wilson, Commissioner

2756 Kansas Department of Wildlife & Parks Region 5
1500 W 7th Street 620-431-0380
Po Box 777 Fax: 620-431-0381
Chanute, KS 66720-777 www.ksoutdoors.com/
This region is made up of 18 counties in the southeastern corner of the state. This area is dominated by the Osage Questas physiographic region, which is characterized by rolling grasslands, limestone bluffs, and heavily timberedbottomlands.
Randy Doll, Commissioner
Robert J. Wilson, Commissioner

2757 Kansas Department of Wildlife and Parks
512 SE 25th Avenue 620-672-5911
Topeka, KS 66612-1327 Fax: 620-672-2972
www.ksoutdoors.com
Randy Doll, Commissioner
Robert J. Wilson, Commissioner

2758 Kansas Geological Survey
University of Kansas
1930 Constant Avenue 785-864-3965
Lawrence, KS 66047-3724 Fax: 785-864-5317
webadmin@kgs.ku.edu
www.kgs.ku.edu
Conducts geological studies and research and collects, correlates, preserves and disseminates information leading to a better understanding of the geology of Kansas, with special emphasis on nautral resources of economic value, waterquality and quantity and geologic hazards. This information is published in books and maps both technical and educational and also provides computer programs and data bases derived from geologic investigations.
Rex C. Buchanan, Director & State Geologist

2759 Kansas Health & Environmental Laboratories
6810 SE Dwight Street 785-296-0801
Building 740 Fax: 785-296-1641
Topeka, KS 66620-1401 www.kdhe.state.ks.us/labs
Provides timely and accurate analytical information for public health benefit in Kansas and assures the quality of statewide laboratory sevices though certification and improvement programs.
Leo Hanning, Interim Director
N. Myron Gunsalus, Jr., Director

2760 Kansas Water Office
901 S Kansas Avenue 785-296-3185
Topeka, KS 66612 888-526-9283
Fax: 785-296-0878
kwo-info@kwo.ks.gov
www.kwo.org

Works to achieve proactive solutions for resource issues of the state and to ensure good quality water to meet the needs of the people and the environment of Kansas. Evaluates and develops public policies, coordinating the waterresource operations of agencies at all levels of government.

Tracy Streeter, Director
Earl Lewis, Assistant Director

2761 Pratt Operations Office Kansas Department of Wildlife & Parks
512 SE 25th Avenue 620-672-5911
Pratt, KS 67124 www.ksoutdoors.com
Randy Doll, Commissioner
Robert J. Wilson, Commissioner

Kentucky

2762 Attorney General's Office Civil and Environmental Law Division
700 Capitol Avenue 502-696-5300
Capitol Building, Suite 118 ag.ky.gov/civil/uninsured.htm
Frankfort, KY 40601
Jack Conway, Attorney General
Margaret Everson, Asst Deputy Attorney General

2763 Department for Energy Development & Independence
500 Mero Street 502-564-7192
12th Floor Capital Plaza Tower Fax: 502-564-7484
Frankfort, KY 40601 amanda.cook@ky.gov
www.energy.ky.gov

Provides leadership to maximize the benefits of energy effeciency and alternate energy through awareness, technology development, energy preparedness and new partnerships and resources.

Greg Guess, Director
John Davies, Deputy Commissioner

2764 Department for Environmental Protection
300 Fair Oaks Lane 502-564-0323
Frankfort, KY 40601 Fax: 502-564-4245
envhelp@ky.gov
www.dep.ky.gov

Mission: To protect and enhance Kentucky's environment. This mission is important because it has a direct impact on Kentucky's public health, our citizens' safety and the quality of Kentucky's valuable natural resources-ourenvironment.

Robert W Logan, Commisioner

2765 Division of Mine Reclamation and Enforcement
Two Hudson Hollow Road 502-564-2340
Frankfort, KY 40601 Fax: 502-564-5848
j.hamon@ky.gov
www.dmre.ky.gov

The Division of Mine Reclamation and Enforcement is responsible for inspecting all surface and underground coal mining permits in the state to assure compliance with the 1977 Federal Surface Mining Control Act. The DMRE is alsoresponsible for regulating and enforcing the surface mining reclamation laws for non-coal mining sites in the state, including limestone, sand, gravel, clay, shale and the surface effects of dredging river sand and gravel.

2766 Economic Development Cabinet: Community Development Department Brokerage Division
Old Capitol Annex 502-564-7140
300 West Broadway 800-626-2930
Frankfort, KY 40601 Fax: 502-564-3256
econdev@ky.gov
www.thinkkentucky.com

Responsible for encouraging job creation and retention, and new investment in the state

Larry Hayes, Secretary
Hollie Spade, Chief of Staff

2767 Environmental Protection Department: Waste Management Division
200 Fair Oaks Lane 502-564-6716
4th Floor Fax: 502-564-4049
Frankfort, KY 40601 waste@ky.gov
www.waste.ky.gov

Mission: To protect human health and the environment by minimizing adverse impacts on all citizens of the commonwealth through the development and implementation of fair, equitable and effective waste management programs.

Anthony Hatton, Director
Jon Maybriar, Assistant Director

2768 Environmental Protection Department: Water Division
200 Fair Oaks Lane 502-564-6716
4th Floor Fax: 502-564-4049
Frankfort, KY 40601 water@ky.gov
www.water.ky.gov

To manage, protect and enhance the quality of the Commonwealth's water resources for present and future generations through voluntary, regulatory and educational programs

Anthony Hatton, Director
Jon Maybriar, Assistant Director

2769 Fish and Wildlife Resources Department: Fisheries Division
1 Sportsman's Lane 502-564-3596
1 Sportsman's Lane 800-858-1549
Frankfort, KY 40601 Fax: 502-564-6501
info.center@ky.gov
www.fw.ky.gov

Mission: To conserve and enhance fish and wildlife resources and provide opportunity for hunting, fishing, trapping, boating and other wildlife related activities.

John Gassett, Commissioner
Benjy T Kinman, Fisheries Director

2770 Kentucky Department for Public Health
275 E Main Street 502-564-5497
Franfort, KY 40621 800-372-2973
Fax: 502-564-9523
www.chfs.ky.gov/dph

Stephanie Mayfield Gibson, Commissioner

2771 Kentucky Environmental and Public Protection Cabinet
500 Metro Street 502-564-3350
Capital Plaza Tower, 5th Floor Fax: 502-564-3354
Frankfort, KY 40601

Provides a safe, clean environment in the Commonwealth, while working with business and industry to help ensure adequate jobs and a strong economy.

Teresa J Hill, Secretary

2772 Kentucky State Cooperative Extension Services
University of Kentucky

S-107 Agricultural Science Bldg N 859-257-4302
Lexington, KY 40546-91 Fax: 859-257-3501
jimmy.henning@uky.edu
www.ca.uky.edu/ces

Jimmy Henning, Director
Gary Palmer, Assistant Director

2773 Kentucky State Nature Preserves Commission
801 Schenkel Lane 502-573-2886
Frankfort, KY 40601 Fax: 502-573-2355
naturepreserves@ky.gov
www.naturepreserves.ky.gov

Aims to protect Kentucky's natural heritage by identifying, acquiring and managing natural areas that represent the best known occurrences of rare native species and natural communities and working together to protect biologicaldiversity.
Don Dott, Director

2774 Natural Resources Department: Conservation Division
#2 Hudson Hollow 502-564-2320
Frankfort, KY 40601 Fax: 502-564-6079
www.conservation.ky.gov

Assists Kentucky's local conservation districts in the development and implementation of sound soil and water conservation programs to manage, enhance, and promote the wise use of the Commonwealth's natural resources.
Stephen A Coleman, Director

2775 Natural Resources Department: Division of Forestry
500 Mero Street 502-564-2674
Capital Plaza Tower Fax: 502-564-6553
Frankfort, KY 40601 www.eqc.ky.gov
Steve Coleman, Chairman
Amrita Gadson, Executive Director

2776 Natural Resources and Environment Protection Cabinet: Environmental Quality Commission
500 Mero Street 502-564-2674
Capital Plaza Tower eqc@ky.gov
Frankfort, KY 40601 www.eqc.ky.gov

To serve as an advisory board to the governor and other state officials on environmental matters
Steve Coleman, Chairman
Steve Coleman, Vice Chairman

2777 Tourism Cabinet: Parks Department
Capital Plaza Tower 22nd floor 502-564-4930
500 Metro Street 800-225-8747
Frankfort, KY 40601 www.kentuckytourism.com/stateparks
Mike Mangeot, Commissioner
Hank Phillips, Deputy Commissioner

Louisiana

2778 Agriculture & Forestry: Soil & Water Conservation
Louisiana Department of Agriculture and Forestry
5825 Florida Blvd 866-927-2476
Baton Rouge, LA 70821-3554 Fax: 225-922-2577
www.ldaf.state.la.us

To sustain and conserve water quality and soil stability on croplands, woodlands, grasslands, wetlands and waterways of Louisiana
Mike Strain, Commissioner
Brad Spicer, Assistant Commissioner

2779 Culture, Recreation and Tourism
PO Box 94361 225-342-8115
Baton Rouge, LA 70802 Fax: 225-342-3207
ltgov@crt.la.gov
www.crt.state.la.us

Desireé W. Honoré, Undersecretary
Shirley S Johnson, Executive Assistant

2780 Department of Natural Resources: Office of Mineral Resources
617 North Third Street 225-342-4615
PO Box 2827 Fax: 225-342-4527
Baton Rouge, LA 70821-2827 www.dnr.louisiana.gov/MIN/

Provides staff support to the State Mineral Board in granting and administering leases on state-owned lands and waterbottoms for the production and development of minerals, primarily oil and gas, for the purpose of optimizing revenueto the state from the royalties, bonuses and rentals generated therefrom.
Stacey Talley, Deputy Assistant Secretary

2781 Louisana Department of Natural Resources
PO Box 94396 225-342-4500
Baton Rouge, LA 70804-9396 Fax: 225-342-5861
www.dnr.louisiana.gov/

To preserve and enhance the nonrenewable natural resources of the state, consisting of land, water, oil, gas, and other minerals, through conservation, regulation, management and development to ensure that the state of Louisianarealizes appropriate economic benefit from its asset base
Stephen Chustz, Secretary
Lori LeBlanc, Deputy Secretary

2782 Louisiana Cooperative Extension Services
101 J. Norman Efferson Hall 225-578-4161
110 LSU Union Square Fax: 225-578-4225
Baton Rouge, LA 70803-106 www.lsuagcenter.com/

To provide the people of Louisiana with research-based educational information that will improve their lives and economic well-being
Bill Richardson, Chancellor

2783 Louisiana Department of Natural Resources Office of Coastal Restoration and Management
617 North Third Street 225-342-7591
Baton Rouge, LA 70821 800-267-4019
Fax: 225-342-9439
www.dnr.louisiana.gov/

Develops, implements and monitors costal vegetated wetland restoration, creation and conservation measures. Preforms engineering, planning and monitoring functions essential to successful development and implementation of wetlandconservation and restoration plans and projects as directed by the Costal Wetlands Conservation and Restoration Plan.
Keith Lowell, Acting Assistant Secretary

2784 Natural Resources: Conservation Office
617 N 3rd Street 225-342-5540
PO Box 94275 Fax: 225-342-3705
Baton Rouge, LA 70802 www.dnr.louisiana.gov

Regulatory oil and gas agency, State of Louisiana.
James H Welsh, Commissioner of Conservation
Gary P Ross, Asst. Commissioner, Conserva

2785 Natural Resources: Injection & Mining Division
PO Box 94275 225-342-5515
Baton Rouge, LA 70804 Fax: 225-342-3094
Injection-Mining@la.gov
www.dnr.louisiana.gov

Has the responsibility for implementation of major environmental programs statutorily charged to the Office of Conservation. Administers a regulatory and permit program to protect underground sources of drinking water fromendangerment; is respon-

sible for regulating exploration, development and surface mining operations for coal and lignite; and protection of state and private lands.
Joseph S Ball Jr, Director
Laurence Bland, Assistant Director

Maine

2786 Maine Cooperative Fish & Wildlife Research Unit
University of Maine
USGS Biological ResourcesDiscipline 207-581-2862
5755 Nutting Hall Fax: 207-581-2858
Orono, ME 00446 www.wle.umaine.edu
Mission: To facilitate and strengthen professional education and training of fisheries and wildlife scientists; carry out research programs of aquatic, mammalian, and avian organisms and their habitats; and disseminate research resultsthrough the appropriate media, especially peer-review scientific articles.
Dr Cyndy Loftin, Leader

2787 Maine Department Of Inland Fisheries & Wildlife
284 State Street 207-287-8000
41 State House Station Fax: 207-287-6395
Augusta, ME 00433-0041 www.maine.gov/ifw
The Department of Inland Fisheries & Wildlife was established to ensure that all species of wildlife and aquatic resources in the State of Maine are maintained and perpetuated for their intrinsic and ecological values, for theireconomic contribution, and for their recreational, scientific and educational use by the people of the State. The Department is also responsible for the establishment and enforcement of rules and regulations.
Chandler E. Woodcock, Commissioner
Andrea Erskine, Deputy Commissioner

2788 Maine Department of Environmental Protection: Augusta
17 State House Station 207-287-7688
28 Tyson Drive 800-452-1942
Augusta, ME 00433-17 Fax: 207-287-7826
www.maine.gov/dep
Responsible for environmental protection and regulation in the state of Maine. Engages in a wide range of activities, makes reccomendations to the Legistlature regarding measures to minimize and eliminate environmental pollution,grants licenses, initiates enforcement actions, and provides information and technical assistance.
Robert A. Foley, Chair
Alvin K. Ahlers, Director

2789 Maine Department of Conservation
22 State House Station 207-287-3200
Augusta, ME 00433 Fax: 207-287-2400
DACF@Maine.gov
www.maine.gov/doc
To oversee the management, development and protection of some of Maine's most special places: 17 million acres of forest land, 10.4 million acres of unorganized territory, 48 parks and historic sites and more than 590,000 acres ofpublic-reserved and non-reserved land
Walter E. Whitcomb, Commissioner

2790 Maine Department of Conservation: Ashland Regional Office
45 Radar Road 207-435-7963
Ashland, ME 00473 Fax: 207-435-7184
DACF@Maine.gov
www.maine.gov/doc
To oversee the management, development and protection of some of Maine's most special places: 17 million acres of forest land, 10.4 million acres of unorganized territory, 48 parks and historic sites and more than 590,000 acres ofpublic-reserved and non-reserved land
Don Cote, Compliance Investigator
Billie J. MacLean, Regional Representative

2791 Maine Department of Conservation: Bangor Regional Office
106 Hogan Road 207-941-4014
BMHI Complex Fax: 207-941-4222
Bangor, ME 00440 DACF@Maine.gov
www.maine.gov/doc
To oversee the management, development and protection of some of Maine's most special places: 17 million acres of forest land, 10.4 million acres of unorganized territory, 48 parks and historic sites and more than 590,000 acres ofpublic-reserved and non-reserved land

2792 Maine Department of Conservation: Bolton Hill Regional Office
22 State House Station 207-624-3700
Augusta, ME 00433-22 Fax: 207-287-8534
DACF@Maine.gov
www.maine.gov/doc
To oversee the management, development and protection of some of Maine's most special places: 17 million acres of forest land, 10.4 million acres of unorganized territory, 48 parks and historic sites and more than 590,000 acres ofpublic-reserved and non-reserved land
Walter E. Whitcomb, Commissioner

2793 Maine Department of Conservation: Bureau of Parks & Lands
22 State House Station 207-287-3821
2nd & 1st Floors Fax: 207-287-3823
Augusta, ME 00433-22 DACF@Maine.gov
www.maine.gov/doc
To oversee the management, development and protection of some of Maine's most special places: 17 million acres of forest land, 10.4 million acres of unorganized territory, 48 parks and historic sites and more than 590,000 acres ofpublic-reserved and non-reserved land
Walter E. Whitcomb, Commissioner

2794 Maine Department of Conservation: Entomology Laboratory
22 State House Station 207-287-2431
Augusta, ME 00433-22 Fax: 207-287-2432
DACF@Maine.gov
www.maine.gov/doc
To oversee the management, development and protection of some of Maine's most special places: 17 million acres of forest land, 10.4 million acres of unorganized territory, 48 parks and historic sites and more than 590,000 acres ofpublic-reserved and non-reserved land
Walter E. Whitcomb, Commissioner

2795 Maine Department of Conservation: Farmington Regional Office
129 Main Street 207-778-8231
PO Box 327 Fax: 207-778-5932
Farmington, ME 00493 DACF@Maine.gov
www.maine.gov/doc
To oversee the management, development and protection of some of Maine's most special places: 17 million acres of forest land, 10.4 million acres of unorganized territory, 48 parks and historic sites and more than 590,000 acres ofpublic-reserved and non-reserved land

2796 Maine Department of Conservation: Greenville Regional Office
43 Lakeview Street 207-695-2466
PO Box 1107 Fax: 207-695-2380
Greenville, ME 00444-1107 DACF@Maine.gov
www.maine.gov/doc

To oversee the management, development and protection of some of Maine's most special places: 17 million acres of forest land, 10.4 million acres of unorganized territory, 48 parks and historic sites and more than 590,000 acres ofpublic-reserved and non-reserved land
Keith Smith, Regional Representative

2797 Maine Department of Conservation: Hallowell Regional Office
Winthrop Street 207-624-6080
Stevens Complex Fax: 207-287-5081
Hallowell, ME 00433 DACF@Maine.gov
www.maine.gov/doc

To oversee the management, development and protection of some of Maine's most special places: 17 million acres of forest land, 10.4 million acres of unorganized territory, 48 parks and historic sites and more than 590,000 acres ofpublic-reserved and non-reserved land

2798 Maine Department of Conservation: Jonesboro Regional Office
Route 1A 207-434-2627
PO Box 130 Fax: 207-434-2624
Jonesboro, ME 00464 DACF@Maine.gov
www.maine.gov/doc

To oversee the management, development and protection of some of Maine's most special places: 17 million acres of forest land, 10.4 million acres of unorganized territory, 48 parks and historic sites and more than 590,000 acres ofpublic-reserved and non-reserved land

2799 Maine Department of Conservation: Land Use Regulation Commission
22 State House Station 207-287-2631
4th Floor Fax: 207-287-7439
Augusta, ME 00433-22 DACF@Maine.gov
www.maine.gov/doc

The Maine Land Use Regulation Commission meets monthly in various locations throughout the state to discuss jurisdiction-related issues and to act upon pending cases.
Walter E. Whitcomb, Commissioner

2800 Maine Department of Conservation: Millinocket Regional Office
191 Main Street 207-746-2244
East Millinocket, ME 00443 Fax: 207-746-2243
DACF@Maine.gov
www.maine.gov/doc

To oversee the management, development and protection of some of Maine's most special places: 17 million acres of forest land, 10.4 million acres of unorganized territory, 48 parks and historic sites and more than 590,000 acres ofpublic-reserved and non-reserved land
Marc Russell, Regional Representative

2801 Maine Department of Conservation: Old Town Regional Office
87 Airport Road 207-827-1800
PO Box 415 Fax: 207-827-6295
Old Town, ME 00446 DACF@Maine.gov
www.maine.gov/doc

To oversee the management, development and protection of some of Maine's most special places: 17 million acres of forest land, 10.4 million acres of unorganized territory, 48 parks and historic sites and more than 590,000 acres ofpublic-reserved and non-reserved land

2802 Maine Department of Conservation: Rangeley Regional Office
133 Fyfe Road 207-670-7493
PO Box 307 Fax: 207-864-5252
West Farmington, ME 00499 DACF@Maine.gov
www.maine.gov/doc

To oversee the management, development and protection of some of Maine's most special places: 17 million acres of forest land, 10.4 million acres of unorganized territory, 48 parks and historic sites and more than 590,000 acres ofpublic-reserved and non-reserved land
Sara Brusila, Regional Representative

2803 Maine Department of Environmental Protection: Presque Isle
744 Main Street 207-764-2105
Skyway Park 888-769-1053
Presque Isle, ME 00476 Fax: 207-764-2035
DACF@Maine.gov
www.maine.gov/doc

2804 Maine Department of Environmental Protection: Portland
17 State House Station 207-287-7688
28 Tyson Drive 888-769-1036
Augusta, ME 00433-17 Fax: 207-287-7826
www.maine.gov/dep

Robert A. Foley, Chair
Alvin K. Ahlers, Director

2805 Maine Natural Areas Program
22 State House Station 207-287-3200
Augusta, ME 00433-93 Fax: 207-287-2400
dacf@maine.gov
www.maine.gov/dacf

Mission: To ensure the maintenance of Maine's natural heritage for the benefit of present and future generations. MNAP facilitates informed decision-making in development planning, conservation, and natural resources management. TheProgram's success relies upon using consistent and objective methods to collect, organize, and interpret information.
Molly Docherty, Director

2806 Maine Sea Grant College Program
University of Maine
5784 York Complex 207-581-1435
The University of Maine Fax: 207-581-1426
Orono, ME 00446-5784 umseagrant@maine.edu
www.seagrant.umaine.edu

Paul Anderson, Director
Beth Bisson, Assistant Director

2807 Northeastern Forest Fire Protection Compact
P.O. Box 6192 207-968-3782
21 Parmenter Terrace Fax: 207-968-3782
China Village, ME 00492 info@nffpc.org
www.nffpc.org

The mandate of the Northeastern Forest Fire Protection Commission is to provide the means for its member states and provinces to cope with fires that might be beyond the capabilities of a singler member through infromation, technologyand resources sharing activities.
Tom Parent, Executive Director

2808 University of Maine Cooperative Extension Forestry & Wildlife Office
5741 Libby Hall 207-581-3188
Room 105 Fax: 207-581-3466
Orono, ME 00446-5741 extension@maine.edu
www.extension.umaine.edu/

Catherine Elliott, Wildlife Specialist
Les Hyde, Extension Educator

Massachusetts

2809 Connecticut River Salmon Association
16 Forest Road 860-519-7451
West Hartford, CT 06119 info@ctriversalmon.org
www.ctriversalmon.org

To support the effort to restore Atlantic salmon in the Connecticut River basin.
Tom Chrosniak, President
Richard Bell, Vice President

2810 Department of Agricultural Resources
251 Causeway Street 617-626-1700
Suite 500 Fax: 617-626-1850
Boston, MA 00211 dwebber@state.ma.us
www.mass.gov/eea/agencies/agr/

The Bureau of Animal Health focuses its efforts on ensuring the health and safety of the Commonwealth's domestic animals. Through diligent inspection, examination, licensing, quarantine, and enforcement of laws, regulations and ordersand the provision of technical assistance the Bureau promotes the welfare of companion and food-producing animals in Massachusetts.
John Lebeaux, Commissioner

2811 Department of Environmental Protection
100 Cambridge Street 617-626-1000
Suite 900 Fax: 617-626-4900
Boston, MA 00211 env.internet@state.ma.us
www.mass.gov/eea

The Department of Environmental Protection is the state agency responsible for ensuring clean air and water, the safe management of toxics and hazards, the recycling of solid and hazardous wastes, the timely cleanup of hazardous wastesites and spills, and the preservation of wetlands and coastal resources.
Arleen O'Donnell, Acting Commissioner

2812 Department of Fish & Game
251 Causeway Street 617-626-1500
Suite 400 Fax: 617-626-1505
Boston, MA 00211 www.wildlife.ca.gov/

The Department of Fish & Game works to preserve the state's natural resources and people's right to conservation of those resources, as protected by Article 97 of the Massachusetts Constitution. To carry out this mission, theDepartment exercises responsibility over the Commonwealth's marine and freshwater fisheries, wildlife species, plants, and natural communities, as well as the habitats that support them.
Mary B Griffin, Commissioner

2813 EPA: Region 1, Air Management Division
5 Post Office Square 888-372-7341
Suite 100 888-372-7341
Boston, MA 00201-3912 Fax: 617-918-1112
www.epa.gov/region1

The mission of the US Environmental Protection Agency is to protect human health and to safeguard the natural environment- air, water and land- upon which life depends.
H. Curtis Spalding, Region Administrator

2814 Environmental Affairs Bureau of Markets
251 Causeway Street 617-626-1750
Suite 500 Fax: 617-626-1850
Boston, MA 00211 www.massdfa.org/agricult.html

2815 Environmental Affairs: Hazardous Waste Facilities Site Safety Council
100 Cambridge Street 617-727-6629
Boston, MA 00220
www.environment.gov.za/branches/chemiclas_wastemanagement

2816 Environmental Protection Agency Region 1 (CT, ME, MA, NH, RI, VT)
5 Post Office Square 888-372-7341
Suite 100 888-372-7341
Boston, MA 00201-3912 Fax: 617-918-1112
www.epa.gov/region1

The mission of the US Environmental Protection Agency is to protect human health and to safeguard the natural environment- air, water and land- upon which life depends.
H. Curtis Spalding, Region Administrator

2817 Executive Office of Energy & Environmental Affairs
Executive Office of Environmental Affairs
100 Cambridge Street 617-626-1000
Suite 900 Fax: 617-626-4900
Boston, MA 00211 env.internet@state.ma.us
www.mass.gov/envir/eoea.htm

Richard K. Sullivan, Secretary
Kathleen Baskin, Director of Water Policy

2818 Massachusetts Highway Department
10 Park Plaza 857-368-4636
Suite 4160 877-623-6846
Boston, MA 00211 Fax: 857-368-0601
www.massdot.state.ma.us/highway/Main.aspx

To deliver excellent customer service to people who travel in the Commonwealth, and provide our nation's safest and most reliable transportation system in a way that strengthens our economy and quality of life
Luisa Paiewonsky, Commissioner
Charlie Baker, Governor

2819 New England Interstate Water Pollution Control Commission
650 Suffolk Street 978-323-7929
Suite 410 Fax: 978-323-7919
Lowell, MA 00185 mail@neiwpcc.org
www.neiwpcc.org

The New England Interstate Water Pollution Control Commission, a nonprofit interstate agency established by an Act of Congress, serves and assist its members states individually and collectively by providing coordination, publiceducation, training and leadership in the management and protection of water quality in the New England Region and New York.
Peter LaFlamme, Chair
Yvonne Bolton, Vice Chairman

2820 United States Department of the Army US Army Corps of Engineers
696 Virginia Road 978-318-8220
Concord, MA 00174 Fax: 978-318-8821
www.usace.army.mil

Thomas Bostick, Commanding General
Todd T. Semonite, Deputy Commanding General

2821 Waquoit Bay National Estuarine Research Reserve
131 Waquoit Highway 508-457-0495
PO Box 3092 Fax: 617-727-5537
Waquoit, MA 00253 www.waquoitbayreserve.org

In 1979, The Commonwealth of Massachusetts designated Waquoit Bay as an Area of Critical Environment Concern (ACEC) in recognition of its significant natural resources. The designation provides a state-wide umbrella of protection andoversight under the exisiting regulations of different state agencies which include higher standards of protection for ACEC's. The Waquoit Bay ACEC includes parts of the Bay proper. Although the ACEC covers 2522 acres, including Washburn Island andSouth Cape Beach.
Alison Leschen, Reserve Manager
Sheri Proft, Fiscal Administrator

Maryland

2822 Chesapeake Bay Executive Council
410 Severn Avenue 410-267-5700
Suite 112 800-908-7229
Annapolis, MD 21403 Fax: 410-267-5777
www.chesapeakebay.net
The Chesapeake Bay Executive Council establishes the policy direction for the restoration and protection of the Chesapeake Bay and its living resources. A series of Directives, Agreements, and Amendments signed by the ExecutiveCouncil set goals and guide policy for the Bay restoration. The Council meets annually.
Nicholas DiPasquale, Chairman
Greg Barranco, Coordinator

2823 Interstate Commission on the Potomac River Basin
30 West Gude Drive 301-984-1908
Suite 450 Fax: 301-984-5841
Rockville, MD 20850 info@icprb.org
www.potomacriver.org
The Interstate Commission on the Potomac River Basin is an interstate compact agency established to help protect the Potomac River and its 14,670-square-mile watershed. Its mission is to enhance, protect, and conserve the water andassociated land resources of the Potomac River and its tributaries through regional and interstate cooperation.
Carlton Haywood, Executive Director
Bo Park, Administrative Officer

2824 Maryland Department of Agriculture
50 Harry S Truman Parkway 410-841-5700
Annapolis, MD 21401 800-492-5590
Fax: 410-841-5914
www.mda.state.md.us
Established on the basis of agriculture's growing importance and impact to the economy of the state. Many activities are regulatory in nature, others are assigned to a category of public service and some are educational or promotionalin scope. All are intended to provide the maximum protection possible for the consumer as well as promote the economic well-being of farmers, food and fiber processors and businesses engage in agricultural related operations.
Earl F Hance, Secretary

2825 Maryland Department of Agriculture: State Soil Conservation Committee
50 Harry S Truman Parkway 410-841-5863
Annapolis, MD 21401 Fax: 410-841-5736
www.mda.state.md.us
Bill Giese, Chair
Charles Rice, Vice Chairman

2826 Maryland Department of Health and Mental Hygiene
201 W Preston Street 410-767-6500
Baltimore, MD 21201 877-463-3464
Fax: 410-767-6489
dhmh.healthmd@maryland.gov
www.dhmh.maryland.gov
The Maryland Department of Health and Mental Hygiene's mission is to protect and promote health and prevent disease and injury. This is accomplished through the provision of population-based health services and core public health;assessment, assurance and policy development.
Joshua M. Sharfstein, Secretary

2827 Maryland Department of the Environment: Water Management Field Office
160 South Water Street 301-689-5756
Frostburg, MD 21532 Fax: 301-689-6544
mdecambr@intercom.net
www.mde.state.md.us
To restore and maintain the quality of the State's ground and surface waters, protect wetland habitats throughout the State, and manage the utilization of Maryland's mineral resources.
Scott Boylan, Program Chief
Tamara Davis, Manager

2828 Maryland Department of the Environment/Water Management: Nontidal Wetlands & Waterways
201 Baptist Street 410-713-3680
Suite 15 Fax: 410-713-3681
Salisbury, MD 21801 www.mde.state.md.us
Jay Bozman, Manager

2829 Maryland Department of the Environment: Air & Radiation Management Field Office
201 Baptist Street 410-713-3680
Suite 15 Fax: 410-713-3681
Salisbury, MD 21801 awilliams@mde.state.md.us
www.mde.state.md.us
Jay Bozman, Manager

2830 Maryland Department of the Environment: Air and Radiation Management Main Field Office
160 South Water Street 301-689-5756
Frostburg, MD 21532 Fax: 301-689-6544
www.mde.state.md.us
Tamara Davis, Manager

2831 Maryland Department of the Environment: Field Operations Office
416 Chinquapin Round Road 443-482-2700
Annapolis, MD 21401 www.mde.state.md.us
John Steinfort, Manager

2832 Maryland Department of the Environment: Main Office
1800 Washington Blvd 410-537-3000
Baltimore, MD 21230 800-633-6101
www.mde.state.md.us
To protect and restore the quality of Maryland's air, land, and water resources, while fostering economic development, healthy and safe communities, and quality environmental education for the benefit of the environment, public health,and future generations.
Robert Summers, Secretary
David Costello, Deputy Secretary

2833 Maryland National Capital Park & Planning Commission
6611 Kenilworth Avenue 301-454-1740
Riverdale, MD 20737 Fax: 301-454-1750
mcp-infocounter@mncppc-mc.org
www.mncppc.org
Is a bi-county agency empowered by the State of Maryland to acquire, develop, maintain and administer a regional system of parks withing Montgomery and Prince George's Counties, and to

prepare and administer a general plan for thephysical development of the two counties.
Patricia Barney, Executive Director
Joseph Zimmerman, Secretary-Treasurer's Office

2834 NOAA Chesapeake Bay Office
410 Severn Avenue 410-267-5660
Suite 207-A Fax: 410-267-5666
Annapolis, MD 21403 www.chesapeakebay.noaa.gov
NOAA Chesapeake Bay Office works to help protect and restore the Chesapeake Bay through programs in fisheries management, habitat restoration, coastal observations, and education.
Sean Corson, Acting Director

Michigan

2835 Great Lakes Environmental Research Laboratory
4840 S. State Rd 734-741-2235
Ann Arbor, MI 48108-9719 Fax: 734-741-2055
www.glerl.noaa.gov
Conducts integrated, interdisciplinary environmental research in support of resource management and environmental services in coastal and estuarine waters with a special emphasis on the Great Lakes. Laboratory performs field,analytical, and laboratory investigations to improve understanding and prediction of coastal and estuarine processes and the interdependencies with the atmosphere and sediments.
Marie C. Colton, Director
John Bratton, Deputy Director

2836 Great Lakes Fishery Commission
2100 Commonwealth Boulevard 734-662-3209
Suite 100 Fax: 734-741-2010
Ann Arbor, MI 48105 info@glfc.org
www.glfc.org
The Great Lakes Fishery Commision was established by the Convention on Great Lakes Fisheries between Canada and the US in 1955. It has two major responsibilities: to develop coordinated programs of research on the Great Lakes and, onthe basis of the findings, to recommend measures which will permit the maximum sustained productivity in stocks of fish of common concern; and to formulate and implement a program to eradicate or minimize sea lampry populations in the Great Lakes.
Michael Hansen, Chairman
David Ullrich, Commissioner

2837 Michigan Department of Community Health
Capitol View Building 517-335-9030
201 Townsend Street 800-649-3777
Lansing, MI 48913 Fax: 517-335-8509
www.michigan.gov/mdch
A state agency which continually and diligently endeavors to prevent disease, prolong life and promote the public health.
James K. Haveman, Director
Angela Awrey, Deputy Director/ COO

2838 Michigan Department of Environmental Quality
525 W Allegan Street, 6th Floor 517-373-7917
PO Box 30473 800-662-9278
Lansing, MI 48909-7973 www.michigan.gov/deq
Promotes wise management of Michigan's air, land, and water resources to support a sustainable environment, healthy communities, and vibrant economy
Dan Wyant, Director
Jim Kasprzak, State Bureau Administrator

2839 Michigan Department of Natural Resources
PO Box 30028 517-241-7427
Lansing, MI 48909 Fax: 517-241-7428
www.michigan.gov/dnr
Committed to the conservation, protection, management, use and enjoyment of the state's natural and cultural resources for current and future generations
Keith Creagh, Director
Dennis Knapp, Chief of Staff

2840 Michigan State University Extension
Agriculture Hall 517-355-2308
Room 108 Fax: 517-355-6473
East Lansing, MI 48824 www.msue.msu.edu/msue/
Michigan State University Extension helps people improve their lives through an educational process that applies knowledge to critical issues, needs and opportunities.
Thomas G Coon, Director
Stephen B. Lovejoy, Associate Director

2841 Natural Resources: Wildlife Division
PO Box 30444 517-373-1263
Lansing, MI 48909-7944 Fax: 517-373-1547
www.michigan.gov/dnr
Committed to the conservation, protection, management, use and enjoyment of the state's natural and cultural resources for current and future generations
Keith Creagh, Director
Terry Minzey, Regional Supervisor

Minnesota

2842 Minnesota Board of Water & Soil Resources
520 Lafayette Road North 651-296-3767
St Paul, MN 55155 Fax: 651-297-5615
www.bwsr.state.mn.us
The Minnesota Board of Water and Soil Resources assists local governments to manage and conserve their irreplaceable water and soil resources.
Brian Napstad, Chairman of the Board
Tom Loveall, Co-Commissioner

2843 Minnesota Department of Agriculture
625 Robert Street North 651-201-6000
St Paul, MN 55155-2538 800-967-2474
Fax: 651-297-5522
www.mda.state.mn.us
The MDA's mission is to work toward a diverse ag industry that is profitable as well as environmentally sound; to protect the public health safety regarding food and ag products; and to ensure orderly commerce in agricultural and foodproducts. We have two major branches of the department to accomplish this mission: regulatory divisions and non-regulatory divisions.
Dave Frederickson, Commissioner
Jim Boerboom, Deputy Commissioner

2844 Minnesota Department of Natural Resources
500 Lafayette Road 651-296-6157
Box 21 888-646-6367
St. Paul, MN 55155-4040 Fax: 651-297-4946
www.dnr.state.mn.us
The DNR vision hinges on the concept of sustainability. To DNR, sustainability means protecting and restoring the natural environment while enhancing economic opportunity and community well-being. DNR endorsed ecosystem-basedmanagement as its method to achieve sustainability goals. Sustainability addresses three related elements: the environment, the economy and the community. The goal is to maintain all three elements in a healthy state indefinitely.
Tom Landwehr, Commissioner
Bob Meier, Policy/Government Relations

2845 Minnesota Environmental Quality Board
520 Lafayette Road North 651-757-2014
St Paul, MN 55155 Fax: 651-296-6334
www.eqb.state.mn.us
The mission of the Environmental Quality Board is to lead Minnesota environmental policy by responding to key issues, providing appropriate review and coordination, serving as a public forum and developing long-range strategies toenhance Minnesota's environmental quality. The Environmental Quality Board consists of 10 state agency commissioners or directors and five citizen members. It was established by the Minnesota Legislature in 1973.
Dave Frederickson, Chair
Brian Napstad, Vice Chair

2846 Minnesota Pollution Control Agency
520 Lafayette Road North 651-296-6300
St. Paul, MN 55155-4194 800-657-3864
Fax: 651-296-7923
www.pca.state.mn.us
Established in 1967 to protect Minnesota's environment through monitoring environmental quality and enforcing environmental regulations.
John Linc Stine, Commissioner
Michelle Beeman, Deputy Commissioner

2847 Minnesota Pollution Control Agency: Duluth
525 S Lake Avenue 218-723-4660
Suite 400 800-657-3864
Duluth, MN 55802 Fax: 218-723-4727
www.pca.state.mn.us
MPCA staff at Duluth and the other six agency offices: identify environmental problems through testing, monitoring, inspections and research; develop environmental priorities; set standards and propose rules to protect people and theenvironment; develop permits; provide technical assistance; respond to emergencies and encourage pollution prevention and sustainability.
Suzanne Hanson, Manager

2848 Minnesota Sea Grant College Program
University of Minnesota
144 Chester Park 218-726-8106
31 W College Street Fax: 218-726-6556
Duluth, MN 55812 seagr@d.umn.edu
www.seagrant.umn.edu
Minnesota Sea Grant is dedicated to providing the tools and technology for responsible management and policy decisions to maintain and enhance Lake Superior and Minnesota's inland aquatic economies and resources. We involveuniversities, federal and state agencies, the public and industry in a partnership to understand the complex nature of the multidisciplinary problems facing us, and then help in the development of the infrastructure necessary for innovativesolutions.
Jeffrey Gunderson, Acting Director
Judy Zomerfelt, Executive Secretary

2849 United States Department of the Army US Army Corps of Engineers
190 5th Street East 651-290-5200
Suite 401 Fax: 651-290-5752
St. Paul, MN 55101-1638 www.usace.army.mil
Deliver vital public and military engineering services; partnering in peace and war to strengthen our Nation's security, energize the economy and reduce risks from disasters
Thomas P. Bostick, Commanding General
Todd T. Semonite, Deputy Commanding General

Mississippi

2850 Gulf Coast Research Laboratory
703 E Beach Drive 228-872-4200
Ocean Springs, MS 39564 Fax: 228-872-4204
www.usm.edu/gcrl
Operates centers of excellence and national research and development programs in fisheries, geospatial technologies, marine aquaculture, environmental assessment and marine toxicology
Eric N. Powell, Director
Dr Jeffrey M Lotz, Chair

2851 Mississippi Alabama Sea Grant Consortium
703 East Beach Drive 228-818-8836
Ocean Springs, MS 39564 Fax: 228-818-8841
swanndl@auburn.edu
www.masgc.org
A federal state partnership that is dedicated to activities that foster the conservation and sustainable development of coastal and marine resources in Mississippi and Alabama.
Dr La Don Swann, Director
Stephen Sempier, Deputy Director

2852 Mississippi Department Agriculture & Commerce
121 North Jefferson Street 601-359-1100
Jackson, MS 39201 Fax: 601-354-6290
WebMaster@mdac.ms.gov
www.mdac.state.ms.us/Index.asp
The mission of the Mississippi Department of Agriculture and Commerce is to regulate and promote agricultural-related businesses within the state and to promote Mississippi's products throughout both the state and the rest of the worldfor the benefit of all Mississippi citizens.
Cindy Hyde-Smith, Commissioner

2853 Mississippi Department of Environmental Quality
PO Box 2261 601-961-5171
Jackson, MS 39225 888-786-0661
charles-chisolm@deq.state.ms.us
www.deq.state.ms.us
Mission: To safeguard the health, safety, and welfare of present and future generations of Mississippians by conserving and improving our environment and fostering wise economic growth through focused research and responsibleregulation.
Trudy D Fisher, Executive Director
Martha Dairymple, Chairman

2854 Mississippi Department of Wildlife, Fisheries and Parks
1505 Eastover Drive 601-432-2400
Jackson, MS 39211 www.mdwfp.com
It is the mission of the Mississippi Department of Wildlife, Fisheries and Parks to conserve and enhance Mississippi's natural resources, to provide continuing outdoor recreational opportunities, to maintain the ecological integrityand aesthetic quality of the resources and to ensure socioeconomic and educational opportunities for present and future generations.
Jerry Munro, Chairman
Sam Polles, Executive Director

2855 Mississippi Forestry Commission
660 North Street 601-359-1386
Suite 300 Fax: 601-359-1349
Jackson, MS 39202 www.mfc.ms.gov
Mission: To provide active leadership in forest protection, forest management, forest inventory and effective forest information distribution, necessary for Mississippi's sustainable forset-based economy.
Floyd Hobbs, Chairman
Joseph E. Pettigrew, Vice Chair

2856 **Mississippi State Department of Health Bureau of Child/Adolescent Health**
570 East Woodrow Wilson Drive 601-576-7464
Post Office Box 1700 866-453-4948
Jackson, MS 39216 www.msdh.state.ms.us
The Mississippi Department of Health's mission is to promote and protect the health of the citizens of Missippi. Geographic focus: Missippi other organizational activies, not directed specifically toward children; advocacy, directservice delivery, education, organizing, regulation, social services
Sam Valentine, Director

2857 **United States Department of the Army US Army Corps of Engineers**
4155 Clay Street 601-631-5972
Vicksburg, MS 39180 www.usace.army.mil
Deliver vital public and military engineering services; partnering in peace and war to strengthen our Nation's security, energize the economy and reduce risks from disasters
Thomas P. Bostick, Commanding General
Todd T. Semonite, Deputy Commanding General

Missouri

2858 **Missouri Conservation Department**
3500 East Gans Road 573-815-7901
Columbia, MO 65201 Fax: 573-815-7902
mdc.mo.gov

2859 **Missouri Department of Natural Resources**
PO Box 176 573-751-3443
Jefferson City, MO 65102 800-361-4827
Fax: 573-751-7627
contact@dnr.mo.gov
www.dnr.mo.gov
The Department of Natural Resources preserves, protects and enhances Missouri's natural, cultural and energy resources and works to inspire their enjoyment and responsible use for present and future generations. Our staff work toensure that our state enjoys clean air to breathe, clean water for drinking and recreation and land that sustains a diversity of life.
Sara Parker Pauley, Director

2860 **Natural Resources Department: Air Pollution Control**
PO Box 176 573-751-4817
Jefferson City, MO 65102 800-334-6946
Fax: 573-751-8656
cleanair@dnr.mo.gov
www.dnr.mo.gov
Mission: To maintain the purity of Missouri's air to protect the health, general welfare and property of the people.
Jack Baker, Chairman
Gary Pendergrass, Vice Chair

2861 **Natural Resources Department: Energy Center**
PO Box 176 573-751-3443
Jefferson City, MO 65102 800-361-4827
Fax: 573-751-6860
energy@dnr.mo.gov
www.dnr.mo.gov
A nonregulatory state agency that works to protect the environment and stimulate the economy through energy efficiency and renewable energy resources and technologies.

2862 **Natural Resources Department: Environmental Improvement and Energy Resources Authority**
PO Box 744 573-751-4919
Jefferson City, MO 65102 Fax: 573-635-3486
eiera@dnr.mo.gov
www.dnr.mo.gov
A quasi-governmental agency that serves as the financing arm for the Missouri Department of Natural Resources.
Deron Cherry, Director
Andy Dalton, Director

2863 **United States Department of the Army US Army Corps of Engineers**
US Army Engineer District
601 E 12th Street 816-389-3486
Room 736 www.usace.army.mil
Kansas City, MO 64106
Deliver vital public and military engineering services; partnering in peace and war to strengthen our Nation's security, energize the economy and reduce risks from disasters
Thomas P. Bostick, Commanding General
Todd T. Semonite, Deputy Commanding General

Montana

2864 **Butte District Advisory Council**
106 N Parkmont 406-533-7600
Butte, MT 59702 Fax: 406-533-7660
mt_butte_fo@blm.gov
www.mt.blm.gov/bdo/
Jamie Conell, State Director
Theresa Hanley, Deputy State Director

2865 **Crown of the Continent Research Learning Center - Glacier National Park**
PO Box 128 406-888-7863
West Glacier, MT 59936 Fax: 406-888-7903
tara_carolin@nps.gov
www.nps.gov/rlc/crown/index.htm
Designed to increase the effectiveness and communication of research and science results in national parks through facilitating the use of parks for scientific inquiry, supporting science-informed decision making, communicating therelevance of and providing access to knowledge gained through scientific research, and promoting science literacy and resource stewardship
Tara Carolin, Director
Melissa Sladek, Science Comm Specialist

2866 **Environmental Quality Council**
State Capitol, Room 171 406-444-3742
PO Box 201704 Fax: 406-444-3971
Helena, MT 59620-1704 teverts@mt.gov
www.leg.mt.gov/lepo.asp
The EQC is a state legislative committee create by the 1971 Montana Environmental Policy Act. As outlined in MEPA, the EQC'S purpose is to encourage conditions under which people can coexist with nature in productive harmony. TheCouncil fulfills this purpose by assisting the Legislature in the development of natural resource and environmental policy, by conducting studies on related issues and by serving in an advisory capacity to the state's natural resource programs.
Jim Keane, Chairman
Duane Ankney

2867 **Lewiston District Advisory Council Bureau of Land Management**
920 Northeast Main Street 406-538-1900
PO Box 1160 Fax: 406-538-1904
Lewistown, MT 59457 www.blm.gov
Manages approximately 750,300 surface acres of public land scattered across eight counties in central Montana

2868 **Montana Department of Agriculture**
302 North Roberts 406-444-3144
Helena, MT 59620-0201 Fax: 406-444-5409
www.agr.mt.gov

Mission: To protect producers and consumers and to enhance and develop agriculture and allied industries.
Ron de Yong, Acting Director

2869 Montana Natural Heritage Program
1515 East 6th Avenue 406-444-5354
Helena, MT 59620-1800 Fax: 406-444-0266
mtnhp@mt.gov
www.mtnhp.org
The Montana Natural Heritage Program is the state's source for information on the status and distribution of our native animals and plants, emphasizing species of concern and high quality habitats such as wetlands.
Allan Cox, Lead Program Manager
Darlene Patzer, Finance/Grants Administrator

2870 Natural Resources & Conservation Department
1625 11th Avenue 406-444-2074
Helena, MT 59601 Fax: 406-444-2684
www.dnrc.mt.gov
To help ensure that Montana's land and water resources provide benefits for present and future generations
John Tubbs, Director

Nebraska

2871 Central Interstate Low-Level Radioactive Waste Commission
PO Box 4770 402-476-8247
Lincoln, NE 68504-770 Fax: 402-476-8205
rita@cillrwcc.org
www.cillrwcc.org
Rita Houskie, Administrator

2872 Department of Agriculture: Natural Resources Conservation Service
National Soil Survey Center
100 Centennial Mall N Room 152 402-437-5499
Lincoln, NE 68508-3866 Fax: 402-437-5336
www.soils.usda.gov
Developing and maintaining soil survey data and information systems; assistance in planning regional work planning conferences; liaison to NCSS Regional Agriculture Experiment Station Soil Survey Committees; and technical coordinationat the national level
Jonathan W. Hempel, Director
Linda M. Bouc, Administrative Assistant

2873 Department of Natural Resources
301 Centennial Mall S 402-471-2341
PO Box 94676 Fax: 402-471-6876
Lincoln, NE 68509-4947 www.dnr.ne.gov
State Natural Resources Agency
Ann Saloman Bleed, Director
Brian P Dunnigan, Deputy Director

2874 Nebraska Department of Agriculture
301 Centennial Mall S 402-471-2341
PO Box 94947 800-831-0550
Lincoln, NE 68509-4947 Fax: 402-471-6876
agr.webmaster@nebraska.gov
www.nda.nebraska.gov
The Nebraska Department of Agriculture is a regulatory state agency.
Greg Ibach, Director
Mat Habrock, Assistant Director

2875 Nebraska Department of Environmental Quality
1200 N Street Suite 400 402-471-2186
PO Box 98922 Fax: 402-471-2909
Lincoln, NE 68509 www.deq.state.ne.us
Mission: To protect the quality of Nebraska's environment-our air, land, and water resources. Enforce regulations and provide assistance.

2876 Nebraska Ethanol Board
301 Centennial Mall S 402-471-2941
PO Box 94922 Fax: 402-471-2470
Lincoln, NE 68509 www.ne-ethanol.org
The Nebraska Ethanol Board assists ethanol producers with programs and strategies for marketing ethanol and related co-products. The Board supports organizations and policies that advocate the increased use of ethanol fuels, andadministers public information, education and ethanol research projects. The Board also assists companies and organizations in the development of ethanol production facilities in Nebraska.
Paul Kenney, Chair
Mike Thede, Vice Chair

2877 Nebraska Game & Parks Commission: Fisheries Division
2200 N 33rd Street 402-471-0641
PO Box 30370 Fax: 402-471-4992
Lincoln, NE 68503 Donna.Waller@nebraska.gov
www.outdoornebraska.ne.gov
Mission: Stewardship of the state's fish, wildlife, park, and outdoor recreation resources in the best long-term interests of the people and those resources
James Douglas, Director
Tim McCoy, Deputy Director

2878 Nebraska Games & Parks Commission
2200 North 33rd Street 402-471-0641
Lincoln, NE 68503 www.outdoornebraska.ne.gov
Mission: Stewardship of the state's fish, wildlife, park, and outdoor recreation resources in the best long-term interests of the people and those resources
James Douglas, Director
Tim McCoy, Deputy Director

2879 Nebraska Games & Parks: Wildlife Division
2200 N 33rd Street 402-471-0641
PO Box 30370 Fax: 402-471-4992
Lincoln, NE 68503 jim.douglas@nebraska.gov
www.outdoornebraska.gov
Mission: Stewardship of the state's fish, wildlife, park, and outdoor recreation resources in the best long-term interests of the people and those resources
James Douglas, Director
Tim McCoy, Deputy Director

2880 United States Department of the Army US Army Corps of Engineers
US Army Engineer District
215 N 17th Street 402-995-2417
Omaha, NE 68102-4978 Fax: 402-221-4626
www.usace.army.mil
Deliver vital public and military engineering services; partnering in peace and war to strengthen our Nation's security, energize the economy and reduce risks from disasters
Thomas P. Bostick, Commanding General
Todd T. Semonite, Deputy Commanding General

Nevada

2881 Bureau of Land Management
Department of the Interior

702 N. Industrial Way 775-289-1800
HC 33 Box 33500 Fax: 775-289-1910
Ely, NV 89301 eyfoweb@blm.gov
www.blm.gov

2882 Bureau of Reclamation - Great Plains Region
Great Plains Regional Office
PO Box 36900 406-247-7610
Billings, MT 59101 www.usbr.gov/gp/
One of five Bureau Reclamation Regions dedicated to the management and protection of water and related resources.
Michael Ryan, Regional Director

2883 Bureau of Reclamation - Lower Colorado Region
Lower Colorado Regional Office
PO Box 61470 702-293-8000
Boulder City, NV 89006 Fax: 702-293-8333
www.usbr.gov/lc/
One of five Bureau Reclamation Regions dedicated to the management and protection of water and related resources.
Terry Fulp, Regional Director

2884 Bureau of Reclamation - Mid-Pacific Region
Mid-Pacific Regional Office
Federal Office Building 916-978-5001
2800 Cottage Way Fax: 916-978-5005
Sacramento, CA 95825-1898 www.usbr.gov/mp/
One of five Bureau Reclamation Regions dedicated to the management and protection of water and related resources.
David Murillo, Regional Director

2885 Bureau of Reclamation - Pacific Northwest Region
Pacific Northwest Regional Office
1150 North Curtis Rd
Suite 100 www.usbr.gov/pn/
Boise, ID 83706-1234
One of five Bureau Reclamation Regions dedicated to the management and protection of water and related resources.
Lorri Gray, Regional Director

2886 Bureau of Reclamation - Upper Colorado
Upper Colorado Regional Office
125 South State St
Room 8100 ucpao@usbr.gov
Salt Lake City, UT 84138-1147 www.usbr.gov/uc/
One of five Bureau Reclamation Regions dedicated to the management and protection of water and related resources.
Brent Rhees, Regional Director

2887 Carson City Field Office Advisory Council
Bureau of Land Management
5665 Morgan Mill Road 775-885-6000
Carson City, NV 89701 Fax: 775-885-6147
ccfoweb@blm.gov
www.blm.gov
A Federal Land Management Agency.

2888 Conservation and Natural Resources Department
Wildlife Division, Conservation Education
901 South Stewart Street 775-684-2700
Suite1003 Fax: 775-684-2715
Carson City, NV 89701 www.dcnr.nv.gov
The Department of Conservation and Natural Resources (DCNR) is responsible for the establishment and administration of goals, objectives and priorities for the preservation of the State's natural resources.
Leo Drozdoff, Director
Kay Scherer, Deputy Director

2889 Conservation and Natural Resources: Water Resources Division
901 South Stewart Street 775-684-2800
Suite 2002 Fax: 775-684-2811
Carson City, NV 89701 hricci@wr.state.nv.us
www.water.nv.gov
To conserve, protect, manage and enhance the State's water resources for Nevada's citizens through the appropriation and reallocation of the public waters
Jason King, State Engineer
Tracy Taylor, Deputy

2890 Las Vegas Bureau of Land Management
4701 N Torrey Pines Drive 702-515-5000
Las Vegas, NV 89130 www.nv.blm.gov
The Bureau of Land Management's mission is to help sustain the health, diversity and productivity of public lands so they can be used and enjoyed by both present and future generations.

2891 Nevada Bureau of Mines & Geology
University of Nevada
Mail Stop 178 775-784-6691
Reno, NV 89557 Fax: 775-784-1709
nbmg@unr.edu
www.nbmg.unr.edu
Research and public service unit of the University of Nevada and is the state geological survey
James E. Faulds, Director/State Geologist

2892 Nevada Department of Wildlife
1100 Valley Road 775-688-1500
Reno, NV 89512 Fax: 775-688-1207
ndowinfo@ndow.org
www.ndow.org
Responsible for the restoration and management of fish and wildlife resources, and the promotion of boating safety on Nevada's waters
Tony Wasley, Director
Rich Haskins, Deputy Director

2893 Nevada Natural Heritage Program
901 South Stewart Street 775-684-2900
Suite 5002 Fax: 775-684-2909
Carson City, NV 89701 www.heritage.nv.gov
The mission is to develop and maintain a cost-effective central information source and inventory of locations, biology, and status of all threatened, endangered, rare and at-risk plants and animals in Nevada.
Jennifer Newmark, Administrator
Jessica Sanders, Office Manager

2894 Tahoe Regional Planning Agency (TRPA) Advisory Planning Commission
PO Box 5310 775-588-4547
Stateline, NV 89449 Fax: 775-588-4527
trpa@trpa.org
www.trpa.org
The TRPA leads the cooperative effort to preserve, restore and enhance the natural and human environment of the Lake Tahoe Region. The Code of Ordinances regulates, among other things, land use, density, rate of growth, land coverage,excavation and scenic impacts. These regulations are designed to bring the region into compliance with the threshold standards established for water quality, air quality, soil conservation, wildlife habitat, vegetation, noise, recreation and scenicresources.
Joanne Marchetta, Executive Director
Marja Ambler, Management Assistant

New Hampshire

2895 New Hampshire Department of Environmental Services
29 Hazen Drive 603-271-3503
PO Box 95 Fax: 603-271-2867
Concord, NH 03302-0095 www.des.nh.us
The New Hampshire Department of Environmental Services aims to protect, maintain and enhance environmental quality and public health in New Hampshire.
Tom Burack, Commissioner
Vicki V. Quiram, Assistant Commissioner

2896 New Hampshire Fish and Game Department
11 Hazen Drive 603-271-3421
Concord, NH 03301 Fax: 603-271-1438
info@wildlife.nh.gov
www.wildnh.com
As the guardian of the states fish, wildlife and marine resources, the department works with the public to: conserve, manage and protect these resources and their habitats; inform and advise the public about these resources; providethe public with opportunities to use and appreciate these resources.
Gelnn Normandeau, Executive Director
Tanya L Haskell, Administrative Assistant

2897 New Hampshire State Conservation Committee
PO Box 3907 603-271-1092
Concord, NH 03302 www.nh.gov/scc
Coordinates the work of the ten county conservation districts in the state of New Hampshire.
Jim Raynes, Chairman

2898 Resources & Development Council: State Planning
Department of Resources & Economic Development
172 Pembroke Road 603-271-2411
P.O. Box 1856 Fax: 603-271-2629
Concord, NH 03302-1856 www.dred.state.nh.us
Promoting the principles of smart growth at the state, regional, and local levels through the municipal and regional planning assistance program
Victoria Cimino, Director
Michele Zydel, Administrative Secretary

2899 University of New Hampshire Cooperative Extension
Taylor Hall 603-862-1520
59 College Road Fax: 603-862-1585
Durham, NH 03824 ce.webinfo@unh.edu
www.extension.unh.edu
The University of New Hampshire Cooperative Extension provides New Hampshire citizens with research-based education and information, enhancing their ability to make informed decisions that strengthen youth, families and communities,sustain natural resources, and improve the economy.
John Pike, Dean/Director
Lisa Townson, Assistant Director

New Jersey

2900 New Jersey Department of Agriculture
PO Box 330 609-292-3976
Trenton, NJ 00862 Fax: 609-292-3978
The New Jersey Department of Agriculture is an agency which oversees programs that serve virutally all New Jersey citizens. A major priority of the NJDA is to promote, protect and serve the Garden State's diverse agriculture andagribusiness industries.
Douglas H. Fisher, Secretary

2901 New Jersey Department of Environmental Protection
401 E State Street 609-777-3373
7th Floor, E Wing 866-337-5669
Trenton, NJ 00862 Fax: 609-292-7695
www.nj.gov/dep/
A state department dedicated to protecting New Jersey's air, land, water and natural resources.
Bob Martin, Commissioner
Irene Kropp, Deputy Commissioner

2902 New Jersey Department of Environmental Protection: Site Remediation Program
401 E State Street 609-292-1250
PO Box 420 Fax: 609-777-1914
Trenton, NJ 00862-0420 www.state.nj.us/dep/srp
Kenneth Kloo, Director
David Sweeney, Assistant Commissioner

2903 New Jersey Division of Fish & Wildlife
501 E State Street, 3rd Fl 609-292-2965
PO Box 420 Fax: 609-292-8207
Trenton, NJ 00862-0420 www.njfishandwildlife.com
Our mission is to protect and manage the state's fish and wildlife to maximize their long-term biological, recreation and economic values for all New Jerseyans.
David Chanda, Director
Larry Herrighty, Assistant Director of Operat

2904 New Jersey Geological Survey
PO Box 420 609-292-1185
Mail Code:29-01 Fax: 609-633-1004
Trenton, NJ 00862-0420 njgsweb@dep.state.nj.us
www.njgeology.org
State agency that maps, interprets and provides geoscience information to the public on geology and ground water resources.
Karl Muessig, State Geologist

2905 New Jersey Pinelands Commission
PO Box 7 609-894-7300
15 Springfield Road Fax: 609-894-7330
New Lisbon, NJ 00806 info@njpines.state.nj.us
www.state.nj.us/pinelands/
Mission: To preserve, protect, and enhance the natural and cultural resourcse of the Pinelands National Reserve, and to encourage compatible economic and other human activities consistent with that purpose.
Mark S. Lohbauer, Chairman
Nancy Wittenberg, Executive Director

New Mexico

2906 Albuquerque Bureau of Land Management
435 Montano Road NE 505-761-8700
Albuquerque, NM 87107-4935 Fax: 505-761-8911
www.nm.blm.gov
Ed Singleton, District Manager
Ernest J Chavez, Assistant District Manager

2907 Attorney General
Environmental Enforcement
PO Drawer 1508 505-827-6000
Santa Fe, NM 87504-1508 Fax: 505-827-5826
Gary King, Attorney General

2908 **Department of the Interior: U.S. Fish & Wildlife Service - New Mexico**
500 Gold Avenue SW 505-248-6911
P.O. Box 1306 RDTuggle@fws.gov
Albuquerque, NM 87102-1306 www.fws.gov/southwest/
Aim to protect endangered and threatened species, migratory birds, freshwater fish and wildlife habitats in New Mexico; work with many other private and public partners to preserve and protect living resources of the New Mexicoecosystems.
Benjamin Tuggle, Director

2909 **Energy, Minerals & Natural Resources: Energy Conservation & Management Division**
1220 South Street 505-476-3310
Francis Drive www.emnrd.state.nm.us/ecmd/
Santa Fe, NM 87505
Encourages efficient energy use in New Mexico by offerin programs and information for state agencies, companies and induviduals.
Louise N. Martinez, Director

2910 **Energy, Minerals and Natural Resources Department**
1220 S St. Francis Drive 505-476-3200
Santa Fe, NM 87505 Fax: 505-476-3220
www.emnrd.state.nm.us
Mission is to provide leadership in the protection, conservation, management and responsible use of New Mexico's natural resources.
David Martin, Cabinet Secretary
Brett F. Woods, Deputy Cabinet Secretary

2911 **New Mexico Bureau of Geology & Mineral Resources**
801 Leroy Place 505-835-5420
Socorro, NM 87801-4796 Fax: 505-835-6333
scholle1@nmt.edu
www.geoinfo.nmt.edu
A service and research division of the New Mexico Institute of Mining and Technology. Acts as the geological survey of New Mexico.
Paul Bauer, Principal Geologist, Assoc.
Bruce Allen, Sr. Field Geologist

2912 **New Mexico Cooperative Fish & Wildlife Research Unit**
New Mexico University MSC 4901 505-646-6053
PO Box 30003 Fax: 505-646-1281
Las Cruces, NM 88003 www.coopunits.org/New_Mexico/
The New Mexico Research Unit conducts, research on problems of mutual concern to cooperators; graduate academic training; technical assistance in fish and wildlife management; and conservation education through publications, lectures,and demonstrations.
Colleen Caldwell, Leader
Louis Bender, Assisstant Unit Leader

2913 **New Mexico Department of Game & Fish**
1 Wildlife Way 505-476-8000
Santa Fe, NM 87507 888-248-6866
ispa@state.nm.us
www.wildlife.state.nm.us
To conserve, regulate, propagate and protect the wildlife and fish within the state of New Mexico using a flexible management system that ensures sustainable use for public food supply, recreation and safety; and to provide foroff-highway motor vehicle recreation that recognizes cultural, historic, and resource values while ensuring public safety
Jim Lane, Director
Alexa Sandoval, Chief

2914 **New Mexico Environment Department**
1190 St. Francis Drive 505-827-2855
Suite N4050 800-219-6157
Santa Fe, NM 87505 www.nmenv.state.nm.us
The New Mexico Environment Department's mission is to provide the highest quality of life throughout the state by promoting a safe, clean, and productive environment.
Ryan Flynn, Cabinet Secretary
Butch Tongate, Deputy Secretary

2915 **New Mexico Soil & Water Conservation Commission**
163 Trail Canyon Road 505-646-2642
Carlsbad, NM 88242 Fax: 505-646-1540
acoleman@nmda.nmsu.edu
www.nmacd.org/state-agencies
Serves as the state entity providing guidance and policy direction to the local soil and water conservation districts.
Jim Berlier, President
John Arrington, Vice President

2916 **Roswell District Advisory Council: Bureau of Land Management**
2909 W 2nd Street 505-627-0272
Roswell, NM 88201-2019 Fax: 505-627-0276
www.nm.blm.gov/rfo/index.htm
Larry Ashley, Engine Module Leader

New York

2917 **Adirondack Park Agency**
1133 NYS Route 86 518-891-4050
PO Box 99 Fax: 518-891-3938
Ray Brook, NY 12977 www.apa.state.ny.us
Mission: To protect the public and private resources of the Park through the exercise of the powers and duties provided by law.
Leilani Ulrich, Chair
Richard Booth, Commissioner

2918 **Department of Environmental Conservation**
625 Broadway 518-402-8545
Albany, NY 12233-0001 800-847-7332
Fax: 518-402-8541
dpaeweb@gw.dec.state.ny.us
www.dec.ny.gov
Mission: To conserve, improve, and protect New York State's natural resources and environment, and control water, land and air pollution, in order to enhance the health, safety and welfare of the people of the state and their overalleconomic and social well being.
Joe Martens, Commissioner
Marc Gerstman, Executive Dep Commissioner

2919 **Department of Environmental Conservation: Division of Air Resources**
625 Broadway 518-402-8452
Albany, NY 12233-0001 DARWeb@gw.dec.state.ny.us
www.dec.ny.gov/about/644.html
Maintains and improves New York State air quality through research, permitting and enforcement.
Jared Snyder, Assistant Commissioner

2920 **Department of Environmental Conservation: Division of Mineral Resources**
625 Broadway 518-402-8076
3rd Floor Fax: 518-402-8060
Albany, NY 12233-0001 dmninfo@gw.dec.state.ny.us
www.dec.ny.gov/about/636.html
The Division of Mineral Resources is responsible for ensuring the environmentally sound, economic development of New

York's non-renewable energy and mineral resources for the benefit of current and future generations. To carry out thismission, we regulate the extraction of oil and gas, and require the reclamation of land after mining.
Bradley J. Field, Director
Kathleen F. Sanford, Assistant Director

2921 New York Cooperative Fish & Wildlife Research Unit
Cornell University, Fernow Hall 607-255-2839
Natural Resources Department Fax: 607-255-1895
Ithaca, NY 14853-3001 dnrcru-mailbox@cornell.edu
www.coopunits.org/New_York/index.html
Pays particular attention to the resource problems and issues of the Northeastern States with New York as its focal point
William Fisher, Unit Leader
Mitchell Eaton, Assistant Leader

2922 New York Department of Health
Corning Tower 518-402-7500
Empire State Plaza Fax: 518-402-7509
Albany, NY 12237 www.health.state.ny.us
Working together and committed to excellence, we protect and promote the health of New Yorkers through prevention, science and the assurance of quality health care delivery.
Nirav R. Shah, Commissioner

2923 New York State Office of Parks, Recreation and Historic Preservation
Empire State Plaza 518-474-0456
Agency Building 1 www.nysparks.com
Albany, NY 12238
The agency operates 168 parks offering a wide variety of recreational, cultural and education activities, and 35 state historic sites; sponsors boating and snowmobiling, nature study and outreach programs; manages grant programs forboating and snowmobiling enforcement and aid to zoos, botanical gardens, aquariums; and administers funds for federal historical preservation and parks programs, the Environmental Protection Fund and the 1996 Clean Water/Clean Air Bond act.
Rose Harvey, Commissioner

2924 New York State Soil and Water Conservation Committee
10B Airline Drive 518-457-3738
Albany, NY 12235 Fax: 518-457-3412
www.nys-soilandwater.org
The New York State Soil and Water Conservation Committee is composed of voting and advisory members who represent a wide range of agricultural, environmental and other interests. The Committee operates through a network of partnershipsbetween state, federal and local agencies, as well as citizen interests and the private sector. The mission of the Committee is to develop and oversee and agriculatural nonpoint source water quality program for New York State.
Michael Latham, Director
Brian Steinmuller, Assistant Director

2925 Tug Hill Tomorrow Land Trust
PO Box 6063 315-779-8240
Watertown, NY 13601 Fax: 315-782-6192
thtomorr@northnet.org
www.tughilltomorrowlandtrust.org
A regional, private, nonprofit founded by a group of Tug Hill residents to serve the region of 2,100 square miles serving portions of Jefferson, Lewis, Oneida & Oswego Counties. The mission is two-fold: increase awareness andappreciation of the Tug Hill Rgion through education; and to help retain the forest, farm, recreation, and wild land of the region through voluntary, private land protection efforts.
Bob Quinn, Chairman
George Bibbins, Vice Chair

2926 United States Department of the Army US Army Corps of Engineers
1776 Niagara Street
Buffalo, NY 14207-3199 800-833-6390
www.lrb.usace.army.mil
Delivers world class engineering solutions to the Great Lakes Region, the Army, and the Nation in order to ensure national security, environmental sustainability, water resource management, and emergency assistance during peace and war
LTC Karl D. Jansen, Commander and District Engin
MAJ Michael A. Busby, Deputy Commander

North Carolina

2927 Carolina Tiger Rescue
1940 Hanks Chapel Road 919-542-4684
Pittsboro, NC 27312 Fax: 919-542-4454
info@carolinatigerrescue.org
carolinatigerrescue.org
Is a wildlife sanctuary, offering unique opportunities to learn about these animals and their critical importance to our quality of life on Earth.
Pam Fulk, Executive Director
Amanda Byrne, IT Administrator

2928 Department of Agriculture & Consumer Services
2 West Edenton Street 919-707-3000
Raleigh, NC 27601 www.ncagr.com
Mission: To improve the state of agriculture in North Carolina by providing services to farmers and agribusinesses, and to serve the citizens of North Carolina by providing services and enforcing laws to protect consumers.
Steve Troxler, Commissioner

2929 North Carolina Board of Science and Technology
301 North Wilmington Street 919-715-0303
1326 Mail Service Center Fax: 919-733-8356
Raleigh, NC 27699-1326 tguffey@nccommerce.com
www.nccommerce.com
Encourages, promotes, and supports scientific, engineering, and industrial research applications in North Carolina.
John Hardin, Executive Director
Trudy Guffey, Executive Assistant

2930 North Carolina Department of Environment and Natural Resources
1601 Mail Service Center 919-733-4984
Raleigh, NC 27699-1601 877-623-6748
Fax: 919-715-3060
www.ncdenr.gov/web/guest
John E. Skvarla, III, Secretary
Lacy Presnell, General Counsel

2931 United States Department of the Army US Army Corps of Engineers
69 Darlington Avenue 910-251-4626
PO Box 1890 910-251-4185
Wilmington, NC 28403 www.saw.usace.army.mil
Provides quality planning, design, construction, and operations products and services to meet the needs of civilian and military customers.
Colonel Kevin Landers, Commander
Major R.J. Hughes, Deputy Commander

North Dakota

2932 Dakotas Resource Advisory Council: Department of the Interior
Bureau of Land Management
99 23rd Avenue West 701-227-7700
Suite A Fax: 701-227-7701
Dickinson, ND 58601 www.blm.gov
The Dakotas Council currently has 15 members. It is structured to provide a balance of membership by area of expertise, training, and experience. It consists of five individuals in each of three categories.

2933 ND Game and Fish Department
100 N Bismarck Expressway 701-328-6300
Bismarck, ND 58501-5095 Fax: 701-328-6352
ndgf@nd.gov
www.gf.nd.gov
To protect, conserve and enhance fish and wildlife populations and their habitats for sustained public consumptive and nonconsumptive use.
Terry Steinwand, Director
Scott Peterson, Deputy Director

2934 North Dakota Forest Service
307 First Street E 701-228-5422
Bottineau, ND 58318-1100 Fax: 701-228-5448
forest@nd.gov
www.nd.gov
The ND Forest Service administers forestry programs statewide. The agency operates a nursery at Towner specializing in the production of conifer tree stock. The nursery is the sole supplier of evergreen seedlings in North Dakota.Technial assistance relating to the management of private forest lands, state forest lands, urban and community forests, tree planting and wildland fire protection is provided by the agency. The ND Forest Service also owns and manages app. 13,278acres of state lands.
Larry Kotchman, State Forester
Kathy Wyman, Administrative Assistant

2935 North Dakota Parks and Recreation Department
1600 E Century Ave. 701-328-5357
Suite 3 Fax: 701-328-5363
Bismarck, ND 58503
The state government agency charged with managing North Dakota's state parks and recreation areas; the state's nature preserves and natural area programs; motorized and non-motorized trail programs; recreational grants and state-widerecreation planning; and state scenic byways program.
Douglass A Prchal, Director
Dorothy Streyle, Coordinator

Ohio

2936 Division of Environmental Services
Ohio EPA
8955 East Main Street 614-644-4247
Reynoldsburg, OH 43068 Fax: 614-644-4272
web.requests@epa.ohio.gov
www.epa.state.oh.us/des
The Division of Environmental Services provides biological and chemical data and technical assistance to other divisions within Ohio EPA, state and local agencies, and private entities in order to help monitor and protect human healthand the environment to ensure a high quality of life in Ohio.
Steve Roberts, Quality Assurance Supervisor
Jennifer Kraft, Chief

2937 Environmental Protection Agency: Ohio Division of Surface Water
50 West Town Street
Suite 700 800-282-9378
Columbus, OH 43215 Fax: 614-644-2745
www.epa.state.oh.us/dsw
To protect, enhance and restore all waters of the state for the health, safety and welfare of present and future generations. We accomplish this mission by monitoring the aquatic environment, permitting, enforcing environmental laws,using and refining scientifically sound methods and regulations, planning, coordinating, educating, providing technical assistance and encouraging pollution prevention practices.
George Elmaraghy, Division Chief
Brian Hall, Assistant Chief

2938 Lead Poisoning Prevention Program
Ohio Department of Health
246 N High Street 614-466-5332
Columbus, OH 43215 877-532-3723
Fax: 614-728-6793
lead@odh.ohio.gov
The Lead Poisoning Prevention Program ensures the public receives safe and proper lead abatement, detection, and analytical services by requiring those services be conducted according to federal and state regulations, and by trainedand licensed personnel.
Chris Alexander, Program Supervisor
Pam Blais, Environmental Supervisor

2939 Ohio Department of Natural Resources Division of Geological Survey
2045 Morse Rd 614-265-6576
Bldg C Fax: 614-447-1918
Columbus, OH 43229-6693 geo.survey@dnr.state.oh.us
www.ohiodnr.com
Provides geologic information and services for responsible management of Ohio's natural resources. Geologic maps, reports and data files developed by the division can be used by individuals, educators, industry, business andgovernment.
Thomas J. Serenko, Division Chief
Mike P. Angle, Assistant Chief

2940 Ohio Environmental Protection Agency
50 West Town Street
Suite 700 800-282-9378
Columbus, OH 43215 Fax: 614-644-2329
www.epa.state.oh.us
Mission: To protect the environment and public health by ensuring compliance with environmental laws and demonstrating leadership in environmental stewardship.
Scott J. Nally, Director
Laura Factor, Assistant Director

2941 Ohio River Valley Water Sanitation Commission
5735 Kellogg Avenue 513-231-7719
Cincinnati, OH 45230 Fax: 513-231-7761
info@orsanco.org
www.orsanco.org
ORSANCO operates programs to improve water quality in the Ohio River and its tributaries, including: setting waste water discharge standards; performing biological assessment; monitoring for the chemical and physical properties of thewaterways; and conducting special surveys and studies. Also coordinates emergency response activities for spills or accidental discharges to the river and promotes public participating programs.
Kenneth Komoroski, Chairman
Toby Frevert, Vice-Chairman

2942 Ohio Water Development Authority
480 South High Street 614-466-5822
Columbus, OH 43215 Fax: 614-644-9964
www.owda.org

Provides financial assistance for environmental infrastructure from the sale of municipal revenue bonds through loans to local governments in Ohio and issuing Industrial Revenue Bonds for qualified projects. The vision of OWDA is tocontinue to provide assistance for environmental infrastructure by being responsive to the needs of local government agencies, enhancing the provision of financial and technical assistance and developing new financial assistance products for theprivate sector.
James P. Joyce, Chairman
Steve Grossman, Executive Director

Oklahoma

2943 Oklahoma Department of Environmental Quality
707 N Robinson 405-702-0100
PO Box 1677 800-869-1400
Oklahoma City, OK 73101-1677 Fax: 405-702-1001
www.deq.state.ok.us
Administers environmental laws considering both the economy of today and the environment of tomorrow.

2944 Oklahoma Department of Health
1000 Northeast 10th Street 405-271-5600
Oklahoma, OK 73117 800-522-0203
Fax: 405-271-6199
AskVR@health.ok.gov
www.ok.gov/triton
The Oklahoma State Department of Health is to protect and promote the health of citizens of Oklahoma and to prevent disease and injury, and to assure the conditions by which our citizens can be healthy.
Terry L. Cline, Commissioner

2945 Salt Plains National Wildlife Refuge
71189 Harper Road 580-626-4794
Jet, OK 73749 Fax: 580-626-4793
fw2_rw_saltplains@fws.gov
www.fws.gov/refuge/Salt_Plains
Provide quality habitat for migratory waterfowl
Debbie Pike, Park Ranger

2946 Water Quality Division
5225 N Shurtel 405-702-8100
Oklahoma City, OK 73118 800-869-1400
Fax: 405-810-1046
www.deq.state.ok.us/WQDNew
Larry Edmison, Director

Oregon

2947 Burns District: Bureau of Land Management
Department of the Interior
28910 Highway 20 West 541-573-4400
Hines, OR 97738 BLM_OR_BU_Mail@blm.gov
www.blm.gov
Dana Shuford, Manager
Melissa Towers, Administrative Officer

2948 Department of Transportation
355 Capitol St. NE
Salem, OR 97301-3871 888-275-6368
Fax: 503-986-3432
www.oregon.gov/odot
Mission: To provide a safe, efficient transportation system that supports economic opportunity and livable communities for Oregonians.
Pat Egan, Chairman
David Lohman, Commissioner

2949 Eugene District: Bureau of Land Management
Department of the Interior
3106 Pierce Parkway 541-683-6600
Suite E 888-442-3061
Springfield, OR 97477 Fax: 541-683-6981
OR_Eugene_Mail@blm.gov
www.blm.gov
The Eugene District manages several ecosystems ranging from coastal inlands to dense Douglas-fir, hemlock, and cedar forests. The wide variation in the lands managed by the District offers the perfect compromise between the urban parksin the cities and the high elevation recreation opportunities in the adjacent Willamette, Siuslaw and Umpqua National Forest.
Ginnie Grilley, Manager

2950 Klamath River Compact Commission
280 Main Street 541-882-4436
Klamath Falls, OR 97601-6331
Created by the Klamath River Compact in 1957, KRCC is a three member commission whose purpose, with respect to the water of the Klamath River Basin, is to faciliate and promote the orderly, integrated, and comprehensive developement,use, conservation and control of water for development of lands by irrigation, protection of fish and wildlife, domestic and industrial use, hydropower, navigation, and flood protection.

2951 Lakeview District: Bureau of Land Management
Department of the Interior
1301 South G Street 541-947-2177
Lakeview, OR 97630 Fax: 541-947-6399
BLM_OR_LV_Mailbox@blm.gov
www.blm.gov

2952 Medford District: Bureau of Land Management
3040 Biddle Road 541-618-2200
Medford, OR 97504 BLM_OR_MD_Mail@blm.gov
www.blm.gov
The Bureau of Land Management's Medford District oversees approximately 862,000 acres of scattered public lands between the Cascade and Siskiyou mountain ranges and from the Oregon/California border to Canyon Creek and southern DouglasCounty. This large land base is divided into four Resource Areas: Ashland, Butte Falls, Grants Pass and Glendale.

2953 Oregon Department of Environmental Quality
811 SW Sixth Avenue 503-229-5696
Portland, OR 97204-1390 800-452-4011
Fax: 503-229-6124
deq.info@deq.state.or.us
www.oregon.gov/deq
Mission: To be a leader in restoring, maintaining and enhancing the quality of Oregon's air, land and water.
Dick Pederson, Director
Joni Hammond, Deputy Director

2954 Oregon Department of Fish and Wildlife
4034 Fairview Industrial Drive SE 503-947-6000
Salem, OR 97303 800-720-6339
odfw.info@state.or.us
www.dfw.state.or.us
Commissioners formulate general state programs and policies concerning management and conservation of fish wildlife resources and establishes seasons, methods and bag limits for recreational and commercial take.
Roy Elicker, Director
David Lane, Deputy Administrator-Informa

2955 Oregon Department of Forestry
2600 State Street 503-945-7200
Salem, OR 97310 800-437-4490
Fax: 503-945-7212
www.oregon.gov/odf
Mission: To serve the people of Oregon by protecting, managing, and promoting stewardship of Oregon's forests to enhance environmental, economic, and community sustainability.
Doug Decker, State Forester
Paul Bell, Deputy State Forester

2956 Oregon Department of Land Conservation and Development
635 Capitol Street NE 503-373-0050
Suite 150 Fax: 503-378-5518
Salem, OR 97301-2540 www.oregon.gov/LCD
Mission: Support all of our partners in creating and implementing comprehensive plans that reflect and balance the statewide planning goals, the vision of citizens, and the interests of local, state, federal and tribal governments.
Jim Rue, Director
Caroline Maclaren, Deputy Director

2957 Oregon Water Resource Department
725 Summer Street Northeast 503-986-0900
Suite A Fax: 503-986-0904
Salem, OR 97301 webmaster@wrd.state.or.us
www.oregon.gov/owrd
Mission: To serve the public by practicing and promoting responsible water management through two key goals: to directly address Oregon's water supply needs; and to restore and protect streamflows and watersheds in order to ensure thelong-term sustainability of Oregon's ecosystems, economy, and quality of life.
Tom Byler, Director
Brenda Bateman, Public Information Officer

2958 Prineville District: Bureau of Land Management
Department of the Interior
3050 NE Third Street 541-416-6700
Prineville, OR 97754 Fax: 541-416-6798
BLM_OR_PR_Mail@blm.gov
www.blm.gov
Debbie Henderson-Norton, Manager
Steve Robertson, Associate Manager

2959 Roseburg District: Bureau of Land Management
Department of the Interior
777 NW Garden Valley Boulevard 541-440-4930
Roseburg, OR 97471 Fax: 541-440-4948
BLM_OR_RB_Mail@blm.gov
www.blm.gov
Public lands of the Roseburg District, located in southwestern Oregon, contain some of the most productive forests in the world. An important mainstay of the local economy, which acquires timber from both private and federal lands inthe region. The district is criss-crossed with streams and rivers that support sport fishing. With Interstate 5 running through the middle of the district, and east-west state highways connecting Crater Lake to the Pacfic coast, the district drawsmany tourists.

2960 Salem District: Bureau of Land Management
Department of the Interior
1717 Fabry Road Southeast 503-375-5646
Salem, OR 97306 Fax: 503-375-5622
BLM_OR_SA_Mail@blm.gov
www.blm.gov
BLM Mission: to sustain the health, diversity and productivity of the public lands for the use and enjoyment of present and future generations. Salem District manages 400,000 acres scattered across 13 counties. Seventy three percent ofOregon's population live within the boundries of this district. Their major focus is an ecosystem management approach involving many different disciplines. Salem employs 200 full-time employees working in forestry, land surveying, wildlife biology,hydrology, etc.
Aaron Horton, Manager
Don Hollenkamp, Associate Manager

2961 United States Department of the Army: US Army Corps of Engineers
US Army Engineer Division
PO Box 2946 503-808-5150
Portland, OR 97208 www.army.mil/

2962 Vale District: Bureau of Land Management
Department of the Interior
100 Oregon Street 541-473-3144
Vale, OR 97918 Fax: 541-473-6213
BLM_OR_VL_Mail@blm.gov
www.blm.gov
The Vale District of the Bureau of Land Management manages 4.9 million acres of public land in eastern Oregon. The mission of the BLM is to sustain the health, diversity, and productivity of the public lands for the use and enjoymentof present and future generations.
Dave Henderson, Manager
Larry Frazier, Associate Manager

Pennsylvania

2963 Allegheny National Forest
US Forest Service
4 Farm Colony Road 814-723-5150
Warren, PA 16365 Fax: 814-726-1465
r9_allegheny_nf@fs.fed.us
www.fs.fed.us/r9/allegheny
An organization dedicated to providing advice for development of the corridor management plan for the northern section of the Allegheny River that has been designated as a National Wild and Scenic River.
Erin Connelly, Forest Supervisor

2964 Childhood Lead Poisoning Prevention Program
Pennsylvania Department of Health
PO Box 90 717-783-8451
Harrisburg, PA 17108 Fax: 717-772-0323
www.cehn.org
The mission of the Pennsylvania Department of Health, Childhood Lead Poisoning Prevention Program is to make the citizens of the Commonwealth aware of the dangers of lead poisoning and to reduce the number of children who becomelead-poisoned.

2965 Citizens Advisory Council
Pennsylvania Department Environmental Protection
13th Floor, RCSOB 717-787-4527
PO Box 8459 Fax: 717-787-2878
Harrisburg, PA 17105-8549 mahughes@pa.gov
Advises the Department of Environmental Protection, the Governor and the General Assembly on environmental issues and the work of the Department.
Susan Wilson, Executive Director
Joyce Hatala, Chair

2966 Environmental Protection Agency: Region III
1650 Arch Street 215-814-5000
Philadelphia, PA 19103-2029 800-438-2474
www.epa.gov/region03
Region III is responsible for federal environmental programs in Delaware, Maryland, Pennsylvania, Virginia, West Virginia and District of Columbia. Programs include air and water pollution control; toxic substances, pesticides, anddrinking water regulation; wetlands protection; hazardous waste management, hazard-

ous waste dump site cleanup; and some aspects of radioactive materials regulation.
Shawn M. Garvin, Administrator

2967 Lacawac Sanctuary Foundation
94 Sanctuary Road 570-689-9494
Lake Ariel, PA 18436 Fax: 570-689-2017
info@lacawac.org
www.lacawac.org
A nature preserve and historic site in northeastern PA's Pocono Mountains. The main function is the protection of its natural areas and historic buildings, including the pristine glacial Lake Lacawac. Research space is available forvisiting researchers, and participants in the Pocono Comparative Lakes Program.
Craig Lukatch, President/Executive Director
Lesley Knoll, Director of Research & Edu

2968 Pennsylvania Department of Conservation and Natural Resources
Rachel Carson State Office Building 717-787-2869
400 Market Street, PO Box 8767 Fax: 717-772-9106
Harrisburg, PA 17105-8767 ra-askdcnr@state.pa.us
www.dcnr.state.pa.us
Mission: To maintain, improve and preserve state parks; to manage state forest lands to assure their long-term health, sustainability and economic use; to provide information on Pennsylvania's ecological and geological resources; andto administer grant and technical assistance programs that will benefit rivers conservation, trails and greenways, local recreation, regional heritage conservation and environmental education programs across Pennsylvania.
Ellen Ferretti, Secretary
Jennifer Stepulitis, Executive Secretary

2969 Pennsylvania Fish & Boat Commission: Northeast Region
5566 Main Road 570-477-5717
Sweet Valley, PA 18656 Fax: 570-477-3221
ra-needureach@pa.gov
www.fishandboat.com
Mission: To protect, conserve, and enhance the Commonwealth's aquatic resources and provide fishing and boating opportunities.
Steven M. Ketterer, President
G. Warren Elliott, Vice-President

2970 Pennsylvania Forest Stewardship Program
PO Box 8552 717-787-2106
Harrisburg, PA 17105 www.enr.gov.nt.ca/
Forest stewardship is a US Forest Service program with the goal of helping private landowners manage their lands for various objectives. Landowners participating in the Forest Stewardship Program work with a private forestry consultantto depelop a customized plan for their land and objetives. Studies show that landowners that work with professionals and follow their customized plan are more likely to engage in practices that sustain forest values.

2971 Pennsylvania Game Commission
2001 Elmerton Avenue 717-787-4250
Harrisburg, PA 17110-9797 Fax: 717-772-0542
www.pgc.state.pa.us
The Pennsylvania Game Commission has the specific responsibility of acting as steward of the Commonwealth's wild birds and wild animals for the benefit of present and future generations. In carrying out this state constitutionalmandate, the Pennsylvania Game Commission will: Protect, conserve and manage the diversity of wildlife and their habitats; Provide wildlife related education, services, and recreational opportunities for both consumptive and non-consumptive uses ofwildlife.
Thomas Boop, President
Roxane Palone, Vice President

2972 Susquehanna River Basin Commission
4423 North Front Street 717-238-0423
Harrisburg, PA 17110 Fax: 717-238-2436
srbc@srbc.net
www.srbc.net
The responsibility of SRBC is to enhance public welfare through comprehensive planning, water supply allocation & management of the water resources of the Susquehanna River Basin. The SRBC works to reduce damages caused by floods;provide for the reasonable & sustained development & use of surface & ground water for municipal, agricultural, recreational, commercial & industrial purposes; protect & restore fisheries, wetlands & aquatic habitat; protect water quality & instreamuses.
Paul O Swartz, Executive Director
Thomas W. Beauduy, Deputy Executive Director

2973 United States Department of the Army US Army Corps of Engineers
US Army Engineer District
1000 Liberty Avenue 412-395-7500
Pittsburgh, PA 15222-4186 Fax: 412-644-2811
www.usace.army.mil
Michael P Crall, District Engineer
Peter A Steinig, Deputy District Engineer

Rhode Island

2974 Division of Parks and Recreation
2321 Hartford Avenue 401-222-2632
Johnston, RI 02919 Fax: 401-934-6010
www.riparks.com
The objective of the Division of Parks & Recreation is to provide all Rhode Island Residents and Visitors the opportunity to enjoy a diverse mix of well-maintained, scenic, safe, accessible areas and facilities within our park systemand to offer a variety of outdoor recreational opportunities and programming which may benefit and enhance our Quality of Life.

2975 Environmental Management: Division of Fish and Wildlife
82 Smith Street 401-222-2357
Room 217 Fax: 401-222-1356
Providence, RI 02903-1120 www.sos.ri.gov
Agency manages the fish and wildlife resources of the State of Rhode Island inluding marine fisheries. The division has 60 employees and is located in 4 stations statwide.
Michael Lapisky, Chief

2976 Rhode Island Department of Environmental Management
235 Promenade Street 401-222-6800
Providence, RI 02908 www.dem.ri.gov
We are committed to preserving the quality of Rhode Island's environment, maintaining and safety of its residents and protecting the natural systems upon which life depends. Together with many partners, we offer assistance toindividuals, business and municipalities, conduct research, find solutions, and enforce laws created to protect the environment.
W Michael Sullivan, Director

2977 Rhode Island Department of Evironmental Management: Forest Environment
1037 Hartford Pike 401-647-4389
North Scituate, RI 02857 Fax: 401-647-3590
www.dem.ri.gov
Coordinates a statewide forest fire protection plan, provides forest fire protection on state lands, assists rural volunteer fire departments, and develops forest and wildlife management plans for private landowners who choose tomanage their property in ways that will protect these resources on their land. The program

promotes public understanding of environmental conservation, enforces Department rules and regulations on DEM lands.
Catherine Sparks, Chief

2978 Rhode Island Water Resources Board
1 Capitol Hill 401-574-8400
3rd Floor Fax: 401-574-8401
Providence, RI 02908 www.wrb.state.ri.us
An executive agency of state government charged with managingther proper development, utilization and conservation of water resources. The primary responsibility is to ensure that sufficient water supply is available for present andfuture generations, apportioning available water to all areas of the state.
Daniel W Varin, Chairman
Juan Mariscal, General Manager

South Carolina

2979 Blackbeard Island National Wildlife Refuge
694 Beech Hill Lane 843-784-2468
Hardeeville, SC 29927 Fax: 843-784-2465
savannahcoastal@fws.gov
www.fws.gov/blackbeardisland
This Georgia barrier island's 5,618 acres includes maritime forest, saltmarsh, freshwater marsh, and beach habitat, 3,000 of which has been set aside as National wilderness of variety of recreational activities are availableyear-round, including wildlife observation, birdwatching, hiking and beachcombing.
Jane Griess, Project Leader
Kimberley Hayes, Refuge Manager

2980 Department of Interior: U.S. Fish & Wildlife Service - South Carolina
Clemson University
261 Lehotsky Hall 864-656-2432
Clemson, SC 29634 Fax: 864-656-1350
southeast@fws.gov
www.fws.gov/southeast
Cindy Dohner, Regional Director

2981 Department of Parks, Recreation and Tourism
1205 Pendleton Street 803-734-1700
Edgar A Brown Building 866-224-9339
Columbia, SC 29201 www.scprt.com
Mission: To learn more about our purpose, mission, and vision.
Pam Benjamin, Director of Human Resources

2982 Office of Environmental Laboratory Certification
PO Box 72 803-896-0970
State Park, SC 29147 Fax: 803-896-0850
We offer certification to any environmental laboratory wishing to analyze samples for South Carolina's Department of Health and Environmental Control [DHEC]. This scope of certification covers the Safe Drinking Water Act (SDWA), theClean Water Act (NPDES), and solid & hazardous wastes including RCRA and CERCLA requirements (SW846 methodologies).

2983 South Atlantic Fishery Management Council
4055 Faber Place Drive 843-571-4366
Suite 201 Fax: 843-769-4520
North Charleston, SC 29405 safmc@safmc.net
www.safmc.net
The South Atlantic Fishery Management Council is headquartered in Charleston, SC, and is responsible for the conservation and management of fish stocks within the 200-mile limit of the Atlantic off the coasts of North Carolina, SouthCarolina, Georgia, and east florida to Key West.
David M. Cupka, Chairman
Ben C. Hartig, Vice Chairman

2984 South Carolina Department of Health and Environmental Control
2600 Bull Street 803-898-3432
Columbia, SC 29201
Mission: We promote and protect the health of the public and the environment.

2985 South Carolina Department of Natural Resources
1000 Assembly Street 803-734-4007
Rembert C Dennis Building Fax: 803-734-4300
Columbia, SC 29201 webmaster@dnr.sc.gov
www.dnr.state.sc.us
Mission: To serve as the principal advocate for and steward of South Carolina's natural resources.
Glenn McFadden, Chairman
Cary L. Chastain, Vice Chairman

2986 South Carolina Forestry Commission
5500 Broad River Road 803-896-8800
Columbia, SC 29212 Fax: 803-798-8097
www.trees.sc.gov
The mission of the Forestry Commission is to protect, promote, enhance and nurture the forest lands of South Carolina in a manner consistent with achieving the greatest good for its citizens. Responsibilities extend to all forestlands, both rural and urban, and to all associated forest values and amenities including, but not limited to: timber, wildlife, water quality, air quality, soil protection, recreation and aesthetics.
Henry E Kodama, State Forester
Tom Patton, Deputy State Forester

2987 United States Department of the Army US Army Corps of Engineers
69A Hagood Avenue 843-329-8000
Charleston, SC 29403 Fax: 843-329-2332
CESAC-PAO@usace.army.mil
www.sac.usace.army.mil
The Charleston District (USACE), South Atlantic Division serves the citizens of South Carolina, the Region, and the Nation by providing quality water resources, value engineering/value management, environmental, and international andinteragency projects and services.
Lt. Col. Edward Chamberlayne, Commander
Maj. John O'Brien, Deputy Commander

South Dakota

2988 Attorney General's Office
1302 East Highway 14 605-773-3215
Suite 1 Fax: 605-773-4106
Pierre, SD 57501-8501 atghelp@state.sd.us
www.atg.sd.gov
The Natural Resources Division of the South Dakota Attorney General's Office provides specialized legal counsel to state agencies in environmental, agricultural, financial, Indian law and natural resource matters. It focuses on (1)state boards and agencies which issue environmental, water, and agricultural permits and the lease of state mineral lands; (2) environmental litigation before boards and agencies and in the courts; and (3) jurisdictional disputes.
Marty J. Jackley, Attorney General

2989 Department of Environment & Natural Resources
523 E Capitol Avenue 605-773-3151
Pierre, SD 57501 Fax: 605-773-6035
denrinternet@state.sd.us
www.extension.psu.edu/natural-resources
Our mission is to provide environmental and natural resources assessment, financial assistance, and regulation in a customer service manner that protects the public health, conserves natural

resources, preserves the environment andpromotes economic development.
Steven M. Pirner, Secretary of the Department

2990 Department of Wildlife and Fisheries Sciences
South Dakota State University
Box 2140b
Brookings, SD 57007
605-688-6121
Fax: 605-688-4515
terri.symens@sdstate.edu
www.sdstate.edu/nrm/

David Willis, Department Head
Nels Troelstrup, Assistant Department Head

2991 South Dakota Department of Game, Fish & Parks
523 E Capitol Avenue
Pierre, SD 57501
605-773-3485
Fax: 605-773-5842
wildinfo@state.sd.us
www.gfp.sd.gov

The purpose of the Department of Game, Fish and Parks is to perpetuate, conserve, manage, protect and enhance South Dakota's wildlife resources, parks and outdoor recreational opportunities for the use, benefit and enjoyment of thepeople of this state and its visitors, and to give the highest priority to the welfare of this states's wildlife and parks, and their environment, in planning and decisions.
Susie Knippling, Chairwoman
John Cooper, Vice Chair

2992 South Dakota Department of Health
600 E Capitol Avenue
Pierre, SD 57501-2536
605-773-3361
800-738-2301
Fax: 605-773-5683
DOH.info@state.sd.us
www.doh.sd.gov/

Mission: To prevent disease and promote health, ensure access to needed, high-quality health care, and to efficiently manage public health resources.
Kim Malsam Rysdon, Secretary
Joan Adam, Division Director, Administr

2993 South Dakota State Extension Services
South Dakota State University
Box 2207D
Brookings, SD 57007
605-688-4792
Fax: 605-688-6733
www.sdstate.edu/sdsuextension/index.cfm

Extension serves the people of South Dakota by helping them apply unbiased, scientific knowledge to improve their lives. Extension also offers educational information, programs, and services in response to local issues and needs.
Barry Dunn, Extension Director
Karla Trautman, Associate Director

Tennessee

2994 Obed Wild & Scenic River
PO Box 429
Wartburg, TN 37887
423-346-6294
Fax: 423-346-3362
rebecca_schapansky@nps.gov
www.nps.gov/obed/

Approximately 45 miles of wild and scenic river are comprised of the Obed River, Clear Creek, Daddy's Creek and Emory River. These water courses have cut rugged gorges leaving exciting whitewater gorges with bluffs as high as 500 feetabove the water.
Niki Stephanie Nicholas, Superintendent
Barbara Olmstead, Administrative Officer

2995 Tennessee Department of Agriculture
Ellington Agricultural Center
Melrose Station, PO Box 40627
Nashville, TN 37204
615-837-5103
Fax: 615-837-5333
TN.Agriculture@TN.gov
www.tennessee.gov/agriculture

Mission: To serve the citizens of Tennessee by promoting wise uses of our agriculture and forest resources, developing economic opportunities, and ensuring safe and dependable food and fiber.
Julius Johnson, Commissioner
Jai Templeton, Deputy Commissioner

2996 Tennessee Department of Environment and Conservation
401 Church Street
L&C Annex, 1st Floor
Nashville, TN 37243
615-532-0109
888-891-8332
ask.TDEC@tn.gov
www.state.tn.us/environment

Safeguarding the health and safety of Tennessee citizens from environmental hazards
Robert J. Martineau, Jr., Commissioner
Shari Meghreblian, Deputy Commissioner

2997 Tennessee Valley Authority
400 W Summit Hill Drive
Knoxville, TN 37902-1499
865-632-2101
tvainfo@tva.com
www.tva.gov

TVA generates prosperity in the Tennessee Valley by promoting economic development, supplying low-cost, reliable power and supporting a thriving river system.
Bill Johnson, President/CEO
Janet Hernin, Executive Vice President

2998 United States Army Engineer District: Memphis
167 N Main Street
Memphis, TN 38103
901-544-4109
800-317-4156
MemphisPAO@usace.army.mil
www.mvm.usace.army.mil

Provides flood control, navigation, environmental stewardship, emergency operations, and other authorized civil works to benefit the region and the Nation.
Col. Vernie L. Reichling, Jr., Commander
Lt. Col. Thomas Patton, Deputy Commander

2999 University of Tennessee Extension
2621 Morgan Circle
121 Morgan Hall
Knoxville, TN 37996
865-974-7114
Fax: 865-974-1068
tlcross@utk.edu

Statewide educational organization that brings research-based information about agriculture, family and consumer sciences, and resource development to the people of Tennessee where they live and work.
Tim L. Cross, Dean
Shirley W. Hastings, Deputy Dean

3000 Wildlife Resources Agency
440 Hogan Rd
Nashville, TN 37220
615-781-6500
Fax: 615-741-4606
Ask.TWRA@tn.gov
www.state.tn.us/twra

The Tennessee Wildlife Resources Agency develops, manages and maintains sound programs of hunting, fishing, trapping, boating, and other wildlife related outdoor recreational activities.
Ed Carter, Executive Director

3001 Wildlife Resources Agency: Fisheries Management Division
440 Hogan Rd 615-781-6500
PO Box 40747 Fax: 615-781-6667
Nashville, TN 37220 Ask.TWRA@tn.gov
www.state.tn.us/twra
Ed Carter, Executive Director

Texas

3002 Attorney General of Texas Natural Resources Division (NRD)
300 W 15th Street 512-463-2100
PO Box 12548 Fax: 512-475-2994
Austin, TX 78711-2548 www.texasattorneygeneral.gov
The NRD represents the enviromental and energy agencies of the State of Texas in court. NRD's primary activity is the prosecution of lawsuits, referred by state agencies, that involve violations of the state's enviromental and naturalresources protection laws. NRD also defends permits issued by agencies uder those laws and defends challenges to the statues and regulations themselves.NRD also has primary enforcement responsibility for protecting the public's access to Texasbeaches.
Greg Abbott, Attorney General

3003 Bureau of Economic Geology
University of Texas at Austin
10100 Burnet Rd., Bldg 130 512-471-1534
Box X 888-839-4365
Austin, TX 78713-8924 Fax: 512-471-0140
begmail@beg.utexas.edu
www.beg.utexas.edu
The Bureau provides wide-ranging advisory, technical, informational, and research-based services to industries, nonprofit organizations, and Federal, State, and local agencies.
Scott W Tinker, Director
Jay Kipper, Associate Director

3004 Chihuahuan Desert Research Institute
43869 Hwy 118 432-364-2499
PO Box 905 Fax: 432-364-2686
Fort Davis, TX 79734 www.cdri.org
Conducts research on the Chihuahuan Desert.
Rick Herman, Executive Director Interim
Rusty Brockman, Vice chair

3005 Environmental Protection Agency: Region VI
1445 Ross Avenue 214-665-2760
Suite 1200 800-887-6063
Dallas, TX 75202 www.epa.gov/region06
Region 6 encompasses the ecologically, demographically and economically diverse of states of Arkansas, Louisiana, New Mexico, Oklahoma and Texas. The regional vision is to meet the environmental needs of a changing world.
Ron Curry, Regional Administrator
Larry Starfield, Deputy Administrator

3006 Guadalupe: Blanco River Authority
933 E Court Street 830-379-5822
Seguin, TX 78155 Fax: 830-379-9718
comments@gbra.org
www.gbra.org
Aims to conserve and protect the water resources of the Guadalupe River basin and make them available for beneficial use. Services include water and wastewater treatment, water quality testing, the management of water rights anddelivery of stored water, the production of electricity from seven hydroelectric plants and engineering design support.
Thomas Mathews, Chair
James Murphy, Executive Manager

3007 Parks & Wildlife: Public Lands Division
4200 Smith School Road 512-389-4800
Austin, TX 78744 800-792-1112
Fax: 512-389-4960
www.tpwd.state.tx.us
In 1963 the Parks Board merged with the game and Fish Commission to form the Texas Parks and Wildlife Department. The merger created the Parks Division, currently the Public Lands Division. In 1967 park acquisition and developmentincreased with the passage of a $75 million parks bond authorization and the dedication of a portion of the state's cigarette tax to the development of state and local parks.
Carter Smith, Executive Director
Joe Carter, Internal Affairs

3008 Parks & Wildlife: Resource Protection Division
4200 Smith School Road 512-389-4864
Austin, TX 78744 www.tpwd.state.tx.us
The Resource Protection Division protects Tezas fich, wildlife, plant and mineral resources from degradation or depletion. The division investigates any environmental contamination that may cause loss of fish or wildlife. It providesinformation and recommendations to other government agencies and participates in administrative and judicial proceedings concerning pollution incidents, development, development projects and other actions that may affect fish and wildlife.
Carter Smith, Executive Director
Joe Carter, Internal Affairs

3009 Pecos River Commission
PO Box 969 432-729-3225
Marfa, TX 79843 Fax: 432-729-3224
tatecattle@sbcglobal.net
www.tceq.state.tx.us
The Pecos River Compact Commission administers the Pecos River Compact to ensure that Texas receives its equitable share of quality water from the Pecos River and its tributaries as appointed by the Compact. The Compact includes thestates of New Mexico and Texas.
Frederic Tate, Commissioner

3010 Rio Grande Compact Commission
P.O. Box 13087 915-834-7075
Ste. 560 Fax: 915-834-7080
Austin, TX 79843-3087 www.tceq.state.tx.us
The Rio Grande Compact Commission administers the Rio Grande Compact to ensure that Texas receives its equitable share of quality water from the Rio Grande and its tributaries as appointed by the Compact. The Compact includes thestates of Colorado, New Mexico, and Texas.
Patrick R Gordon, Commisioner

3011 Sabine River Compact Commission
P.O. Box 13087 409-988-9428
Austin, TX 79843-3087 gary.gagnon@att.net
The Sabine River Compact Commission administers the Sabine River Compact to ensure that Texas receives its equitable share of quality water from the Sabine River and its tributaries as apportioned by the Compact. The Compact includesthe states of Texas and Louisiana.
Gary E Gagnon, Commissioner
Jerry F. Gipson, Commissioner

3012 Texas Animal Health Commission
2105 Kramer Lane 512-719-0700
Austin, TX 78758 800-550-8242
Fax: 512-719-0719
www.tahc.state.tx.us
TAHC works to keep pests from reoccurring as major livestock health hazards. Ultimately, the TAHC mission and role is the assurance of marketability and mobility of Texas livestock. TAHC works to sustain and continue to make a vitalcontribution to a

wholesome and abundant supply of meat, eggs, and dairy products at affordable costs.
Dee Ellis, Executive Director
Gene Snelson, General Counsel

3013 Texas Cooperative Extension
Jack K Williams Administration Bldg 979-845-7800
Room 112, 7101 TAMU Fax: 979-845-9542
College Station, TX 77843
Edward G Smith, Director

3014 Texas Department of Agriculture
PO Box 12847 512-463-7476
Austin, TX 78711-2847 800-835-5832
Fax: 888-223-8861
Customer.Relations@TexasAgriculture.gov
www.texasagriculture.gov
TDA's mission is to partner with all Texans to make Texas the nation's leader in agriculture, fortify our economy, empower rural communities, promote healthy lifestyles, and cultivate winning strategies for rural, suburban and urbanTexas through exceptional service and the common threads of agriculture in our daily lives
Sid Miller, Commissioner
Jason Fearneyhough, Deputy Commissioner

3015 Texas Department of Health
1100 W 49th Street 512-776-7111
Austin, TX 78756-3199 888-963-7111
Fax: 512-458-7686
customer.service@dshs.state.tx.us
www.dshs.state.tx.us
The Texas Department of Health is the state government agency charged with protecting and promoting the health of the public.
David L. Lakey, Commissioner
Kirk Cole, Associate Commissioner

3016 Texas Forest Service
301 Tarrow 979-458-6606
Suite 364 Fax: 979-458-6610
College Station, TX 77840 texasforestservice.tamu.edu
The mission is to provide statewide leadership and professional assistance to assure the states's forest, tree and related natural resources are wisely used, nurtured, protected and perpetuated for the benefit of all Texans.
Thomas G. Boggus, Director

3017 Texas Natural Resource Conservation Commission
12100 Park 35 Circle 512-239-1000
Austin, TX 78753 Fax: 512-239-4430
www.tceq.state.tx.us/
The Texas Natural Resource Conservation Commission strives to keep our state's human and natural resources consistent with sustainable economic development. Our goal is clean air, clean water and the safe management of waste.

3018 Texas Parks & Wildlife Department
4200 Smith School Road 512-389-4800
Austin, TX 78744 800-792-1112
Fax: 512-389-4814
webcomments@tpwd.state.tx.us
www.tpwd.state.tx.us
Mission: To manage and conserve the natural and cultural resources of Texas and to provide hunting, fishing and outdoor recreation opportunities for the use and enjoyment of present and future generations.
Carter Smith, Executive Director
Joe Carter, Internal Affairs

3019 Texas State Soil and Water Conservation Board (TSSWCB)
4311 South 31st Street 254-773-2250
Suite 125 800-792-3485
Temple, TX 76502 Fax: 254-773-3311
www.tpwd.state.tx.us
The state agency that administers Texas' soil and water conservation laws and coordinates conservation and nonpoint source pollution abatement programs through the State. The Board is composed of 7 members, 2 Governor appointed and 5landowners, from across Texas, and is the lead state agency for planning, management, and abatement of agricultural and silvicultural (forestry) nonpoint source pollution, and administers the Texas Brush Control Program. There are regional officesthroughout Texas.
Marty H. Graham, Chairman
Scott Buckles, Vice-Chairman

3020 United States Department of the Army: US Army Corps of Engineers
819 Taylor Street 817-886-1306
Fort Worth, TX 76102-0300 www.usace.army.mil
Thomas Bostick, Commander
Richard Stevens, Deputy Chief Of Engineers

Utah

3021 Cedar City District: Bureau of Land Management
Department of the Interior
176 East D.L. Sargent Drive 435-865-3000
Cedar City, UT 84721 Fax: 435-865-3053
utccmail@blm.gov
www.blm.gov
Responsible for administering about 2.1 million acres of public lands located in Iron and Beaver counties in southwestern Utah
Todd S Christiansen, Field Manager

3022 Colorado River Basin Salinity Control Advisory Council: Upper Colorado Region
US Bureau of Reclamation
125 S State Street 801-524-3774
Room 6107 Fax: 801-524-3856
Salt Lake City, UT 84138 www.usbr.gov/uc
Rick Gold, Director

3023 Moab District: Bureau of Land Management
Department of the Interior
82 East Dogwood 435-259-2100
Moab, UT 84532 Fax: 435-259-2106
www.blm.gov
The BLM is committed to providing the highest possible level of access to its facilities, programs, services, and activities on the public lands for persons with disabilities
Maggie Wyatt, Manager

3024 Richfield Field Office: Bureau of Land Management
Department of the Interior
150 E 900 N 435-896-1500
Richfield, UT 84701 Fax: 435-896-1550
utrfmail@blm.gov
www.blm.gov
Cornell Christensen, Manager

3025 Salt Lake District: Bureau of Land Management
Department of the Interior
2370 S. Decker Lake Blvd 801-977-4300
West Valley City, UT 84119 www.blm.gov
The BLM administers public lands within a framework of numerous laws. The most comprehensive of these is the Federal Land

Policy and Management Act of 1976. All Bureau policies, procedures and management actions must be consistent withFLPMA and the other laws that govern use of the public lands. It is their mission to sustain the health, diversity and productivity of the public lands for the use and enjoyment of present and future generations.
Glenn Carpenter, Manager

3026 Upper Colorado River Commission
355 S 400 E Street 801-531-1150
Salt Lake City, UT 84111-2969 Fax: 801-531-9750
dostler@ucrcommission.com
www.usbr.gov/uc/rm/amp/amwg/amwgbioALT_ostler.html
The Upper Colorado River Commission is an interstate compact administration agency created by the Upper Colorado River Basin Compact of 1948. Since its inception, the Commission (made up of Commissioners appointed by the Governor ofeach Upper Division State and one appointed by the President of the United States) has actively participated in the development, utilization and conservation of the water resources of the Colorado River Basin.
Don Ostler, Executive Director

3027 Utah Department of Agriculture and Food
350 N Redwood Road 801-538-7100
PO Box 146500 Fax: 801-538-7126
Salt Lake City, UT 84114-6500 agriculture@utah.gov
www.ag.utah.gov
The Utah Department of Agriculture and Food is one of the state's oldest agencies, overseeing dozens of legislatively mandated programs that promote the healthy growth of Utah agriculture, the conservation of natural resources and theprotection of food supply.
LuAnn Adams, Commissioner
Scott Ericson, Deputy Commissioner

3028 Utah Geological Survey
1594 W North Temple, Suite 3110 801-537-3300
PO Box 146100 Fax: 801-537-3400
Salt Lake City, UT 84114-6100 www.geology.utah.gov
The Utah Geological Survey is an applied scientific agency that creates, interprets and provides information about Utah's geologic environment, resources and hazards to promote safe, beneficial and wise use of land.
Bill Loughlin, Chair
Mark D. Bunnell, Co-Chair

3029 Utah Natural Resources: Water Resources Section
1594 W North Temple, Room 310 801-538-7230
Salt Lake City, UT 84116 Fax: 801-538-7229
www.water.utah.gov
Mission: Plan, conserve, develop and protect Utah's water resources.
N.Gawain Snow, Chairman
Jim Lemmon, Vice Chairman

3030 Utah Natural Resources: Wildlife Resource Division
1594 W N Temple, Suite 2110 801-538-4700
Salt Lake City, UT 84116 Fax: 801-538-4745
www.wildlife.utah.gov
Mission: To serve the people of Utah as trustee and guardian of the state's wildlife and to ensure its future and values through management, protection, conservation and education.
Greg Sheehan, Director
Mike P. Fowlks, Deputy Director

3031 Utah State Department of Natural Resources: Division of Forestry, Fire, & State Lands
1594 W North Temple, Suite 3520 801-538-5555
PO Box 145703 Fax: 801-533-4111
Salt Lake City, UT 84114-5703 www.ffsl.utah.gov
The Division of Forestry, Fire & State Lands manages, sustains and strengthens Utah's forests, rangelands, sovereign lands and watersheds for its citizens and visitors
Dick Buehler, State Forester/Director
Brian Cottam, Deputy Director

3032 Vernal District: Bureau of Land Management
Department of the Interior
170 South 500 East 435-781-4423
Vernal, UT 84078 Fax: 435-781-4410
BLM_UT_Vernal_Comments@blm.gov
Bill Stringer, Manager

Vermont

3033 Department of Forests, Parks, and Recreation
1 National Life Drive 802-241-3670
Davis 2 Fax: 802-244-1481
Montpelier, VT 05620-3801 www.fpr.vermont.gov
Mission: To practice and encourage high quality stewardship of Vermont's environment by: monitoring and maintaining the health, integrity and diversity of important species, natural communities, and ecological processes; managingforests for sustainable use; providing and promoting opportunities for compatible outdoor recreation; and furnishing related information, education, and service.
Michael C. Snyder, Commissioner
Tracy Zeno, Executive Assistant

3034 Vermont Agency of Agriculture, Food and Markets
116 State Street 802-828-2430
Montpelier, VT 05620-2901 www.vermontagriculture.com
To facilitate, support and encourage the growth and viability of agriculture while protecting the working landscape, human health, animal health, plant health, consumers and the environment
Chuck Ross, Secretary
Jolinda LaClair, Deputy Secretary

3035 Vermont Agency of Natural Resources
1 National Life Drive, Davis 2 802-828-1294
Montpelier, VT 05620-3901 Fax: 802-244-1102
www.anr.state.vt.us
To draw from and build upon Vermonters' shared ethic of responsibility for our natural environment, an ethic that encompasses a sense of place, community and quality of life, and understanding that we are an integral part of theenvironment and that we must all be responsible stewards for this and future generations
Deb Markowitz, Secretary

3036 Vermont Department of Health
108 Cherry Street 802-863-7200
PO Box 70 800-464-4343
Burlington, VT 05402 Fax: 802-865-7754
www.healthvermont.gov
The Vermont Department of Health, the state's public health agency, works to protect and improve the health of our population through core public health functions. Core public health functions are those activities that lay thegroundwork for healthy communities.
Harry Chen MD, Commissioner

Virginia

3037 Commerce and Trade: Mines, Minerals and Energy Department
Depart. Mines, Minerals & Energy 804-692-3200
9th St Office Bldg, 202 North 9th Street Fax: 804-692-3200
Richmond, VA 23219 www.mme.state.va.us/
Mission: To enhance the development and conservation of energy and mineral resources in a safe and environmentally sound manner in order to support a more productive economy in Virginia.
George P. Willis, Director

3038 Conservation & Development of Public Beaches Board
Virginia Department of Conservation & Recreation
600 E. Main St., 24th Floor 804-786-2064
Richmond, VA 23219 pco@dcr.virginia.gov
Helps localities maintain and improve public beaches to enhance recreation for Virginia's citizens and visitors
Mark E. Smith, Chair
W. Bruce Wingo, Vice-Chairman

3039 Department of Conservation & Recreation: Division of Dam Safety
600 E. Main St., 24th Floor 804-786-6124
Richmond, VA 23219 Fax: 804-786-0536
pco@dcr.virginia.gov
www.dcr.virginia.gov
The program's purpose is to provide for safe design, construction, operation and maintenance of dams to protect public safety.
Mark E. Smith, Chair
W. Bruce Wingo, Vice-Chairman

3040 Division of Mineral Resources
Washington Building , 8th Floor 804-692-3200
1100 Bank Street Fax: 804-692-3237
Richmond, VA 23219 www.dmme.virginia.gov
Mission: To enhance the development and conservation of energy and mineral resources in a safe and environmentally sound manner to support a more productive economy in Virginia. DMR generates, collects, complies, and evaluates geologicdata, creates and publishes geologic maps and report, works cooperatively with other state and federal agencies, and is the primary source of information on geology, minerla and energy resources, and geologic hazards for both the mineral and energyindustries.
Ed Erb, Director

3041 Division of State Parks
Virginia Department of Conservation & Recreation
600 E. Main St., 24th Floor 804-786-6124
Richmond, VA 23219 800-933-7275
Fax: 804-786-9294
pco@dcr.virginia.gov
www.dcr.virginia.gov

3042 Secretary of Commerce and Trade
1111 East Broad Street 804-786-7831
PO Box 1475 Fax: 804-371-0250
Richmond, VA 23218 mdd@mme.state.va.us
www.commerce.virginia.gov
The secretayr of Commerce and Trade oversees the economic, community, and workforce development of the Commonwealth. Each of the 13 Commerce and Trade agencies actively contributes to the Commonwealth's economic strength and highquality of life.
Maurice A. Jones, Sec of Commerce & Trade
Carry Roth, Deputy Secretary

3043 US Geological Survey
12201 Sunrise Valley Drive 703-648-4000
Reston, VA 20192 va.water.usgs.gov
Mission: The Unites States Geological Survey serves the Nation by providing reliable scientific information to describe and understand the Earth; minimize loss of life and property from natural disasters; manage water, biological,energy, and mineral resources; and enhance and protect our quality of life.
Mark D Myers, Director
Bob Doyle, Deputy Director

3044 Virginia Cooperative Fish & Wildlife Research Unit
Virginia Polytechnic Institute & State Unversity
106 Cheatham Hall 540-231-4934
Blacksburg, VA 24061 www.coopunits.org
A field station of the US Geological Survey, dedicated to research and management of fish and wildlife resources in Virginia and surrounding states. Expertise includes freshwater fish and mollusks and large game mammals. The unitincludes 3 research scientists.
Ken Williams, Chief
Jim Fleming, Supervisor

3045 Virginia Department of Environmental Quality
629 E Main Street 804-698-4000
PO Box 1105 800-592-5482
Richmond, VA 23218 Fax: 804-698-4500
vanaturally@deq.virginia.gov
www.deq.virginia.gov
Virginia's regulatory state agency for air, water waste management and coastal resources. The department is also the coordinating clearinghouse for environmental education and information; and maintains the state's gateway.
David K Paylor, Director
James Golden, Deputy Director

3046 Virginia Department of Game & Inland Fisheries: Wildlife Division
P.O. Box 90778 804-367-1000
Henrico, VA 23228-778 Fax: 804-367-9147
dgifweb@dgif.virginia.gov
www.dgif.virginia.gov
Bob Duncan, Executive Director
Angele Goff, Executive Assistant

3047 Virginia Department of Game & Inland Fisheries Fisheries Division
P.O. Box 90778 804-367-1000
Henrico, VA 23228-778 Fax: 804-367-9147
dgifweb@dgif.virginia.gov
www.dgif.virginia.gov
Bob Duncan, Executive Director
Angele Goff, Executive Assistant

3048 Virginia Department of Game and Inland Fisheries
P.O. Box 90778 804-367-1000
Henrico, VA 23228-778 Fax: 804-364-9147
dgifweb@dgif.virginia.gov
www.dgif.virginia.gov
To manage Virginia's wildlife and inland fish to maintain optimum population of all species to serve the needs of the commonwealth; to provide opportunity for all to enjoy wildlife, inland fish, boating and related outdoor recreation;to promote safety for persons and property in connection with boating, hunting and fishing.
Bob Duncan, Executive Director
Angele Goff, Executive Assistant

3049 Virginia Department of Health Commissioners Office
2001 Maywill Street 804-786-3561
Richmond, VA 23230 Fax: 804-786-4616
www.vdh.state.va.us
Cynthia C. Romero, Commissioner

3050 Virginia Department of Mines, Minerals & Energy: Division of Mined Land Reclamation
3405 Mountain Empire Road 276-523-8100
Big Stone Gap, VA 24219 Fax: 276-523-8148
www.dmme.virginia.gov
Responsible for ensuring the reclamation of land affected by surface and underground coal mining activity
Randy Casey, Director

3051 Virginia Department of Mines, Minerals and Energy: Division of Mineral Resources
900 Natural Resources Drive 434-951-6310
Ste. 400 Fax: 434-951-6325
Charlottesville, VA 22903 www.dmme.virginia.gov
Mission: To enhance the development and conservation of energy and mineral resources in a safe and environementally sound manner to support a more productive economy in Virginia.

3052 Virginia Museum of Natural History
21 Starling Avenue 276-634-4141
Martinsville, VA 24112 Fax: 276-634-4199
information@vmnh.virginia.gov
www.vmnh.net
We are a state museum of natural history with research scientists in marine biology, vertebrate and invertebrate paleontology, archaeology, earth sciences, entomology, and mammalogy. Creates education programs, exhibits, and fieldtrips focused on natural history and environmental issues. Its publishing division specializes in works by natural scientists and environmental educators in the US and abroad. Writing, editorial, and design services available for books, reports, textbooks, etc..
Joe Keiper, Executive Director
Gloria Niblett, Director of Administration

3053 Virginia Sea Grant Program
1208 Greate Road 804-684-7530
PO Box 1346 rickards@virginia.edu
Gloucester Point, VA 23062 www.virginia.edu
Virginia Sea Grant facilitates research, educational, and outreach activities promoting sustainable management of marine resources.
William DuPaul, Interim Director
Cynthia L Suchman, Assistant Director

Washington

3054 Department of Commerce: Pacific Marine Environmental Laboratory
7600 Sand Point Way NE 206-526-6239
Seattle, WA 98115 Fax: 206-526-6815
pmel.info@noaa.gov
www.pmel.noaa.gov
PMEL carries out interdisciplinary scientific investigations in oceanography and atmospheric science.
Christopher Sabine, Director
Dan Simon, Associate Director

3055 Department of Fish and Wildlife
1111 Washington Street SE 360-902-2200
Olympia, WA 98501 Fax: 360-902-2947
www.wdfw.wa.gov
To preserve, protect and perpetuate fish, wildlife and ecosystems while providing sustainable fish and wildlife recreational and commercial opportunities
Jim Unsworth, Director

3056 Environmental Protection Agency: Region 10 Environmental Services
1200 6th Avenue 206-553-1200
Seattle, WA 98101 800-424-4372
Fax: 206-553-1809
epa-seattle@epa.gov
www.epa.gov/r10earth
Dennis Mclerran, Regional Administrator

3057 Julia Butler Hansen Refuge for the Columbian White-Tailed Deer
46 Steamboat Slough Rd 360-795-3915
Cathlamet, WA 98612-566 Fax: 360-795-0803
willapa@fws.gov
www.fws.gov/refuge/julia_butler_hansen/
Offers critical habitat for the endangered Columbian white-tailed deer. The refuge also provides a wintering area for tundra swans, Canada geese, mallards, American wigeon and pintails. Deer and elk are easily observed and photographedfrom the country road that circles the mainland portion of the refuge. Evenings and mornings are the best time to spot animals. Open year-round. No fees charged.

3058 Washington Cooperative Fish & Wildlife Research Unit
University of Washington
Box 355020 206-543-6475
Seattle, WA 98195 washcoop@u.washington.edu
www.coopunits.org
Chris Grue, Unit Leader
David Beauchamp, Assistant Unit Leader

3059 Washington Department of Ecology
300 Desmond Drive 360-407-6000
Lacey, WA 98503 Fax: 360-407-6989
www.ecy.wa.gov
The mission is to protect, preserve and enhance Washington's environment and to promote the wise management of our air, land and water.
Maia D. Bellon, Director

3060 Washington Department of Fish & Wildlife: Fish and Wildlife Commission
600 Capitol Way N 360-902-2267
Olympia, WA 98501-1091 Fax: 360-902-2448
commission@dfw.wa.gov
www.wdfw.wa.gov/commission
The Fish and Wildlife Commission's primary role is to establish policy and direction for fish and wildlife species and their habitats in Washington and to monitor the Department's implementation of the goals, policies and objectivesestablished by the Commission. The Commission also classifies wildlife and establishes the basic rules and regulations governing the time, place, manner, and methods used to harvest or enjoy fish and wildlife.
Miranda Wecker, Chair
Bradley Smith, Vice Chair

3061 Washington Department of Fish & Wildlife: Habitat Program
600 Capitol Way N 360-902-2534
Olympia, WA 98501 Fax: 360-902-2946
habitatprogram@dfw.wa.gov
www.wdfw.wa.gov
Includes Maps and Digital Info Requests.
Phil Anderson, Director

3062 Washington Department of Natural Resources: Southeast Region
713 Bowers Road
Ellensburg, WA 98926-9301
509-925-8510
Fax: 509-925-8522
southeast.region@dnr.wa.gov
www.dnr.wa.gov

In partnership with citizens and governments, the Washington State DNR provides innovative leadership and expertise to ensure environmental protection, public safety, perpetual funding for schools and communities, and a rich quality oflife
Peter Goldmark, Commissioner

3063 Washington Dept. of Natural Resources: Northwest Division
919 North Township Street
Sedro Woolley, WA 98284-9384
360-856-3500
Fax: 360-856-2150
northwest.region@dnr.wa.gov
www.dnr.wa.gov

In partnership with citizens and governments, the Washington State DNR provides innovative leadership and expertise to ensure environmental protection, public safety, perpetual funding for schools and communities, and a rich quality oflife
Peter Goldmark, Commissioner

3064 Washington Dept. of Natural Resources: South Puget Sound Region
950 Farman Avenue North
Enumclaw, WA 98022-9282
360-825-1631
Fax: 360-825-1672
southpuget.region@dnr.wa.gov
www.dnr.wa.gov

In partnership with citizens and governments, the Washington State DNR provides innovative leadership and expertise to ensure environmental protection, public safety, perpetual funding for schools and communities, and a rich quality oflife
Peter Goldmark, Commissioner

3065 Washington Sea Grant Program
University of Washington
3716 Brooklyn Avenue NE
Seattle, WA 98105-6716
206-543-6600
Fax: 206-685-0380
seagrant@uw.edu
www.wsg.washington.edu/

Mission: Washington Sea Grant serves communities, industries and the people of Washington state, the Pacific Northwest and the nation through research, education and outreach by: identifying and addressing important marine issues;providing better tools for management of the marine environment and use of its resources; and initiating and supporting strategic partnerships within the marine community.
Penelope D Dalton, Director
Raechel Waters, Associate Director

3066 Washington State Parks & Recreation Commission: Eastern Region
7150 Cleanwater Drive SW
PO Box 42650
Olympia, WA 98504
360-902-8844
infocent@parks.wa.gov
www.parks.wa.gov

The Washington State Parks and Recreation Commission aquires, operates, enhances and protects a diverse system of recreational, cultural, historical, and natural sites. The Commission fosters outdoor recreation and education statewideto provide enjoyment and enrichment for all and a valued legacy to future generations.
Rex Derr, Director
Judy Johnson, Deputy Director

West Virginia

3067 Capitol Conservation District
418 Goff Mountain Road
Suite 102
Cross Lanes, WV 25313
304-759-0736
Fax: 304-776-5326
ccd@wvca.us
www.wvca.us

Walt Helmick, Commissioner
Daniel J. Robinson, Commissioner

3068 Gauley River National Recreation Area Advisory National Park Service
PO Box 246
Glen Jean, WV 25846
304-465-0508
Fax: 304-465-0591
katy_miller@nps.gov
www.nps.gov

Located in the southern West Virginia, New River Gorge National River was established in 1978 to conserve and protect 53 miles of the New River as a free-flowing waterway. This unit of the National Park System encompasses over 70,000acres of land along the New River between the towns of Hinton and Fayetteville. New River Gorge National River and Bluestone National Scenic River are both managed by our same office in Glen Jean, WV.
Lorrie Sprague, Public Information Officer

3069 West Virginia Cooperative Fish & Wildlife Research Unit USGS
322 Percival Hall West Virginia Un
PO Box 6125
Morgantown, WV 26506-6125
304-293-3794
Fax: 304-293-4826
wvcoop@wvu.edu
www.coopunits.org

Patricia Mazik, Unit Leader Fisheries
Petra Wood, Assistant Leader Wildlife

3070 West Virginia Department of Environmental Protection
WV Dpt of Environmental Protection
601 57th Street South East
Charleston, WV 25304
304-926-0440
Fax: 304-926-0446
dhhrsecretary@wv.gov
www.wvdep.org

Promotes compliance with environmental policies in the areas of hazardous waste management, air quality, water pollution, underground storage tanks, dam safety, land reclamation and more.
Randy Huffman, Cabinet Secretary
Bill Crouch, Cabinet Secretary

3071 West Virginia Division of Natural Resources
324 4th Avenue
South Charleston, WV 25303
304-558-2754
Fax: 304-558-2768
www.wvdnr.gov

Frank Jezioro, Director
Harry F Price, Executive Secretary

3072 West Virginia Geological & Economic Survey
1 Mont Chateau Road
Morgantown, WV 26508-8079
304-594-2331
Fax: 304-594-2575
www.wvgs.wvnet.edu

Michael Hohn, Director/State Geologist
Earl Ray Tomblin, Governor

Wisconsin

3073 Great Lakes Indian Fish and Wildlife Commission
72682 Maple Street
PO Box 9
Odanah, WI 54861
715-682-6619
Fax: 715-682-9294
www.glifwc.org

Mission: To help ensure significant, off-reservation harvests while protecting the resources for generations to come.
James Zorn, Executive Administrator
Gerald DePerry, Deputy Administrator

3074 Natural Resources Department
101 S. Webster Street 888-936-7463
PO Box 7921 Fax: 608-261-4380
Madison, WI 53707-7921 www.dnr.wi.gov
Mission: To protect and enhance our natural resources; to provide a healthy, sustainable environment; to ensure the right of all people; to work with people; and to consider the future and generations to follow.
P Scott Hassett, Secretary

3075 Wisconsin Cooperative Fishery Research Unit
University of Wisconsin
College of Natural Resources 715-346-2178
Stevens Point, WI 54481 Fax: 715-346-3624
coopfish@uwsp.edu

3076 Wisconsin Department of Agriculture Trade & Cosumer Protection: Land & Water Resources Bureau
2811 Agriculture Drive 608-224-5012
PO Box 8911 Fax: 608-224-4615
Madison, WI 53708-8911 www.datcp.state.wi.us
Ben Brancel, Secretary

3077 Wisconsin Geological & Natural History Survey
University of Wisconsin Extension
3817 Mineral Point Road 608-262-1705
Madison, WI 53705 Fax: 608-262-8086
www.wisconsingeologicalsurvey.org
Mission: The survey conducts earth-science surveys, field studies, and research. We provide objective scientific information about the geology, mineral resources, water resources, soil, and biology of Wisconsin. We collect, interpret,disseminate, and archive natural resource information. We communicate the results of our activities through publications, technical talks, and responses to inquiries from the public.
William G. Batten, State Geologist & Director

3078 Wisconsin State Extension Services Community Natural Resources & Economic Development
University of Wisconsin Extension
432 N Lake Street 608-263-2781
Madison, WI 53706 Fax: 606-262-9166
www.uwex.edu/ces/
Rick Klemme, Dean

Wyoming

3079 Casper District: Bureau of Land Management
Department of the Interior
2987 Prospector Drive 307-261-7600
Casper, WY 82604 Fax: 307-261-7587
casper_wymail@blm.gov
www.blm.gov

3080 Environmental Quality Department
122 W 25th Street 307-777-7937
Herschler Building Fax: 307-777-7682
Cheyenne, WY 82002 keith.guille@wyo.gov
www.michigan.gov/deq
DEQ contributes to Wyoming's quality of life through a combination of monitoring, permitting, inspection, enforcement and restoration/remediation activities which protect, conserve and enhance the environment while supportingresponsible stewarship of our state's resources.
Todd Parfitt, Director

3081 Rock Springs Field Office: Bureau of Land Management
Department of the Interior
280 Highway 191 N 307-352-0256
Rock Springs, WY 82901 Fax: 307-352-0329
www.blm.gov
BLM's Rock Springs Field Office is a federal agency in the USA that manages over 3.6 million acres of public land surface and 3.5 million acres of public sub-surface minerals in the southwestern part of the great State of Wyoming. Forthese public lands, BLM administers a variety of programs including mineral exploration and development, wildlife habitat, outdoor recreation, wild horses, lifestock grazing and historic trails.

3082 Wyoming Cooperative Fish and Wildlife Research Unit
University of Wyoming
1000 East University Avenue 307-766-5415
Dept. 3166 Fax: 307-766-5400
Laramie, WY 82071 www.wyocoopunit.org/index.php/test/
Unit conducts fish and wildlife research for the state of Wyoming conservation, fish department and federal agencies.
Matthew K. Kauffman, Leader

3083 Wyoming State Board Of Land Commissioners
Herschler Building 3W 307-777-7331
122 West 25th Street Fax: 307-777-2980
Cheyenne, WY 82002 slfmail@wyo.gov
lands.wyo.gov
Manages all land sales, acquisitions and exchanges, agricultural and commercial leasing, recreations, natural resources and minerals management in the state of Wyoming.
Jason Crowder, Assistant Director
Benjamin Bump, Assistant Director

3084 Wyoming State Forestry Division
5500 Bishop Blvd 307-777-7586
Cheyenne, WY 82002-0060 Fax: 307-777-5986
slf-forestry@wyo.gov
www.wsfd.wyo.gov/
The Forestry Division's general reposnsibility and objectives are to promote and assist the multiple use management and protection of Wyoming's 270,000 acres of state and 1.9 million acres of private forest lands; to provide forestryassistance and information to landowners, industry, communities and public agencies; and to help provide rural, range, and forest land fire protection, equipment and training.
Bill Crasper, State Forester
Dan Perko, Deputy State Forester

3085 Wyoming State Geological Survey
PO Box 1347 307-766-2286
Laramie, WY 82073 Fax: 307-766-2605
wsgs-info@uwyo.edu
www.wsgs.uwyo.edu
The Wyoming State Geological Survey's mission is to promote the beneficial and environmentally sound use of Wyoming's vast geologic, mineral, and energy resources while helping to protect the public from geologic hazards.
Thomas Drean, Director
Kathy Olson, Administrative Officer

Alabama: US Forests, Parks, Refuges

3086 Bon Secour National Wildlife Refuge
12295 State Highway 180 — 251-540-7720
Gulf Shores, AL 36542 — Fax: 251-540-7301
bonsecour@fws.gov
www.fws.gov/refuge/Bon_Secour
Gulf Shores offer nature enthusiasts much to explore. The Bon Secour NWR, which lies just 6 miles west of Gulf Shores, caters equally to the angler, the hiker and the birder. The refuge encourages guests to enjoy a leisurely hikethrough the grounds or a fishing excursion on the 40-acre fresh water Gator Lake. Pack a picnic lunch and your binoculars, park your blanket on one of the many secluded beaches and savor the scenery. Call 1-866-SEA TURTLE to report sea turtleactivity.

3087 Choctaw National Wildlife Refuge
PO Box 150 — 251-843-5238
Gilbertown, AL 36908 — Fax: 251-843-2568
choctaw@fws.gov
www.fws.gov/choctaw
The objectives of the Refuge are: to manage habitat for wintering waterfowl, maintain habitat and provide protection for threatened and endangered species, manage wood duck nest boxes and brood rearing habitat, maintain wildlifediversity, manage forest to be productive bottomland hardwoods, and to provide wildlife dependent recreation.
Robert Dailey, Manager

3088 Little River Canyon National Preserve
4322 Little River Trail NE — 256-845-9605
Suite 100 — Fax: 256-997-9129
Fort Payne, AL 35967 — sandra_arther@nps.gov
www.nps.gov
Little River flows for most of its length atop Lookout Mountain in northeast Alabama. The river and canyon systems are Appalachian Plateau landscapes, made up of forested uplands, waterfalls, canyon rims and bluffs, stream riffles andpools, boulders and sandstone cliffs. Natural resources and cultural heritage come together to tell the story of the preserve, a special place in the Southern Appalachians.
Steve Black, Superintendent
Cheri Killam-Bomhard, Facility Manager

3089 Wheeler National Wildlife Refuge Complex
2700 Refuge Headquarters Road — 256-353-7243
Decatur, AL 35603 — Fax: 256-340-9728
wheeler@fws.gov
www.fws.gov/wheeler/
The 35,000 acre wildlife refuge was established in 1938 The refuge is located between Decatur and Huntsville in the Tennessee River Valley of northern Alabama.
Dwight Cooley, Project Leader

3090 William B Bankhead National Forest
Bankhead Ranger District — 205-489-5111
1070 Hwy 33 — Fax: 205-489-3427
Double Springs, AL 35553
www.forestcamping.com/dow/southern/bankinfo.htm
The William B Bankhead national Forest covers 180,000 acres in Franklin, Winston and Lawrence counties. Within the forest are the 26,000 acre Sipsey Wilkderness and the Sipsey Wild and Scenic River, offering 61.4 miles of seasonalcanoeing.

Alaska: US Forests, Parks, Refuges

3091 Alagnak Wild River Katmai National Park
1000 Silver Street, Bldg. 603 — 907-246-3305
PO Box 245 — Fax: 907-246-2116
King Salmon, AK 99613 — www.nps.gov/alag
The Alagnak river offers 69 miles of outstanding white-water floating. The river is also noted for abundant wildlife and sport fishing for five species of salmon.

3092 Alaska Maritime National Wildlife Refuge
95 Sterling Highway — 907-235-6546
Suite 1 — Fax: 907-235-7783
Homer, AK 99603 — alaskamaritime@fws.gov
www.fws.gov/refuge/alaska_maritime
To administer a national network of lands and waters for the conservation management and where appropiate, restoration of the fish, wildlife, and plant resources and their habitats within the US for the benefit of present and futuregeneration of Americans.
Steve Delehanty, Refuge Manager

3093 Alaska Peninsula National Wildlife Refuge
P.O. Box 298 — 907-246-3339
King Salmon, AK 99613 — Fax: 907-246-6696
becharof@fws.gov
www.fws.gov/refuges/profiles

3094 Becharof National Wildlife Refuge
PO Box 277 — 907-246-3339
4 Bear Road — Fax: 907-246-6696
King Salmon, AK 99613 — becharof@fws.gov
becharof.fws.gov
Daryle Lons, Manager

3095 Chugach National Forest
161 East 1st Avenue — 907-743-9500
Door 8 — Fax: 907-743-9476
Anchorage, AK 99501 — www.fs.fed.us/r10/chugach

3096 Denali National Park and Preserve
PO Box 9 — 907-683-2294
Denali Park, AK 99755-0009 — Fax: 907-683-9612
denali_info@nps.gov
www.nps.gov/dena

3097 Innoko National Wildlife Refuge
101 Front Street — 907-656-1231
P.O. Box 287 — 800-656-1231
Galena, AK 99741-287 — Fax: 907-656-1708
innoko@fws.gov
www.fws.gov/refuge/innoko
The Innoko National Wildlife Refuge was established December 2, 1980, with the passage of the Alaska National Interest Lands Conservation Act. This 3.85 million acre refuge supports a large nesting waterfowl population, and is wellpopulated with moose, bear, and other animals, as well as a variety of game birds and neotropical bird species and is a relatively flat plain covering much of the drainage area of the Innoko and Iditarod rivers. The vegetation of the reguse is atransition zone.
Kenton Moos, Manager
Bob Rebarchik, Deputy Refuge Manager

3098 Izembek National Wildlife Refuge
Box 127 — 907-532-2445
MS 515 — 877-837-6332
Cold Bay, AK 99571-127 — Fax: 907-532-2549
izembek@fws.gov
www.fws.gov/refuge/izembek/
Established to conserve fish, wildlife and habitats in their natural diversity including, waterfowl, shorebirds, other migratory birds, brown bears and salmon; to fulfill treaty obligations; to provide the opportunity for continuedsubsistence uses by local residents consistent with the purposes previously mentioned; and to ensure necessary water quality and quantity.
Nancy Hoffman, Wildlife Refuge Manager

3099 Kanuti National Wildlife Refuge
101 12th Avenue
MS 555 Room 262
Fairbanks, AK 99701
907-456-0329
877-220-1853
Fax: 907-456-0506
kanuti_refuge@fws.gov
www.fws.gov/refuge/kanuti/

Mike Spindler, Manager

3100 Katmai National Park and Preserve
PO Box 7
King Salmon, AK 99613
907-246-3305
Fax: 907-246-2116
www.nps.gov/katm

3101 Kenai Fjords National Park
PO Box 1727
Seward, AK 99664
907-422-0500
Fax: 907-422-0571
www.nps.gov/kefj

This park encompasses over 600,000 acres of wild coastal Alaska. The Harding Icefield dominates most of the park. This 300-square mile bowl of ice spills out into numerous glaciers at its edges. Tidewater glaciers and the amazingmarine wildlife of the park can be viewed from boat or air. Humpback whales, orca, many species of sea birds, Steller sea lions and other marine wildlife come here because of the rich variety of foods. Sea birds and sea lions also raise their youngon the rocky sites.

3102 Kenai National Wildlife Refuge
PO Box 2139
Soldotna, AK 99669-2139
907-262-7021
Fax: 907-487-2144
kenai@fws.gov
www.fws.gov/refuge/Kenai

3103 Kobuk Valley National Park
PO Box 1029
Kotzebue, AK 99752
907-442-3890
Fax: 907-442-8316
NWAK_superintendant@nps.gov
www.nps.gov/kova

Mission: Cooperative stewardship for the conservation and understanding of natural and cultural resources in Northwest Alaska.

3104 Kodiak National Wildlife Refuge
1390 Buskin River Road
MS 559
Kodiak, AK 99615
907-487-2600
888-408-3514
Fax: 907-487-2144
kodiak@fws.gov
www.fws.gov/refuge/kodiak/

Kodiak National Wildlife Refuge was established to conserve Kodiak brown bears, salmon, sea otters, sea lions, other marine mammals, and migratory birds; to fulfill treaty obligations; to provide for continued subsistence uses; and toensure necessary water quanlity and quantity.
Gary Wheeler, Manager
Jason Osles, Park Ranger

3105 Koyukuk and Nowitna National Wildlife Refuge
101 Front Street
PO Box 287
Galena, AK 99741-0287
907-656-1231
800-656-1231
Fax: 907-656-1708
r7kynwr@fws.gov
www.fws.gov/refuges/profiles/

Approximately 200 miles west of Fairbanks, the refuge lies within a solar basin encircled by rolling hills capped by alpine tundra. The Nowitna River, a nationally designated Wild River, bisects the refuge and forms a broad meanderingfloodplain. The river passes through a scenic 15 mile canyon with peaks up to 2,100 feet.
Kenton Moos, Manager

3106 Lake Clark National Park and Preserve
2181 Kachemak Dr.
Suite 236
Homer, AK 99603
907- 23- 790
Fax: 907-644-3810
www.nps.gov/lacl

Lake Clark National Park and Preserve was created to protect scenic beauty, populations of fish and wildlife, watersheds essential for red salmon, and the traditional lifestyle of local residents.
Dick Proenneke, Wilderness Steward

3107 Selawik National Wildlife Refuge
160 2nd Avenue
PO Box 270
Kotzebue, AK 99752
907-442-3799
800-492-8848
Fax: 907-442-3124
selawik@fws.gov
www.fws.gov/refuge/Selawik/contact.html

Selawik National Wildlife Refuge was established to conserve the Western Arctic caribou herd, waterfowl, shorebirds, other migratory birds, salmon, and sheefish; to fulfill treaty obligations; to provide for continued subsistence uses;and to ensure necessary water quality and quantity.
LeeAnne Ayres, Manager
Tina Moran, Deputy Refuge Manager

3108 Tetlin National Wildlife Refuge
PO Box 779
Tok, AK 99780
907-883-5312
Fax: 907-883-5747
tetlin@fws.gov
www.fws.gov/refuge/tetlin/

Shawn Bayless, Refuge Manager
Jerry Hill, Deputy Refuge Manager

3109 Togiak National Wildlife Refuge
PO Box 270
MS 569
Dillingham, AK 99576
907-842-1063
800-817-2538
Fax: 907-842-5402
togiak@fws.gov
www.fws.gov/refuge/togiak/

Established to conserve fish and wildlife populations and habitats in their natural diversity including salmon, marine birds, mammals, migrating birds and large mammals, to fulfill international treaty obligations; to provide forcontinued subsistence uses; and to ensure necessary water quality and quantity.
Paul Liedberg, Manager

3110 Tongass National Forest: Chatham Area
204 Siginaka Way
Sitka, AK 99835-7316
907-747-6671
Fax: 907-747-4331
www.fs.fed.us/r10/tongass

The Tongass National Forest is a forest of islands and trees and rain. It also abounds in animals and birds and fish, with unsurpassed scenery. It's a place where eagles are commonplace, most every road is a deer crossing, and bearsuse the trails too. The spirituality and scenery demands respect.
Fred Salinas, Forest Supervisor

3111 Tongass National Forest: Ketchikan Area
Federal Building
648 Mission Street
Ketchikan, AK 99901-6591
907-225-3101
Fax: 907-228-6215
www.fs.fed.us/r10/tongass

The Tongass National Forest is a forest of islands and trees and rain. It also abounds in animals and birds and fish, with unsurpassed scenery. It's a place where eagles are commonplace, most every road is a deer crossing, and bearsuse the trails too. The Tongass is a wild place, where the natural world is a strong presence that nurtures spirituality and materially demands respect.

3112 Tongass National Forest: Stikine Area
123 Scow Bay Loop Road
PO Box 309
Petersburg, AK 99833-0309
907-772-3841
Fax: 907-772-5895
www.fs.fed.us/r10/tongass

The Tongass National Forest is a forest of islands and trees and rain. It also abounds in animals and birds and fish, with unsurpassed scenery. It's a place where eagles are commonplace, most every road is a deer crossing, and bearsuse the trails too. The Tongass is a wild place, where the natural world is a strong presence that nurtures spirituality and materially demands respect.

3113 Yukon Delta National Wildlife Refuge
807 Chief Eddie Hoffman Road 907-543-3151
PO Box 346 MS 535 Fax: 907-543-4413
Bethel, AK 99559 yukondelta@fws.gov
www.fws.gov/refuge/yukon_delta

Yukon Delta National Wildlife Refuge was established to conserce shorebirds, seabirds, whistling swans, emperor, white-fronted and Canada geese, black brant and other migratory birds, salmon, muskox, and marine mammals; to fulfilltreaty obligations; to provide for continued subsistence uses; and to ensure necessary water quality and quantity.
Michael Rearden, Manager

3114 Yukon Flats National Wildlife Refuge
101 12th Avenue 907-456-0440
Room 264 MS 575 800-531-0676
Fairbanks, AK 99701 Fax: 907-456-0447
yukonflats@fws.gov
www.fws.gov/refuge/yukon_flats/

Located about 100 air miles north of Fairbanks, encompassing about 12 million acres along the Yukon River. In the spring, millions of migrating birds converge on the refuge. With its 40,000 lakes and other wetlands, it has one of thehighest waterfowl nesting densities in North America for ducks, geese, sandhill cranes, loons, grebes and songbirds. Each year, the Yukon Flats is a major contributor to the migrations that occur along the North American flyways.
Robert Jess, Refuge Manager
Wennona Brown, Deputy Refuge Manager

3115 Yukon-Charley Rivers National Preserve
PO Box 167 907-547-2233
Eagle, AK 99738 Fax: 907-547-2247
www.nps.gov/yuch

Arizona: US Forests, Parks, Refuges

3116 Apache-Sitgreaves National Forest
PO Box 640 928-333-4301
Springerville, AZ 85938 Fax: 928-333-5966
www.fs.fed.us/r3/asnf

Taking care of the land while making the forest resources available to all shareholders. Resources include: high quality water, wilderness, and outdoor recreation; quality habitat for many plants and animals; wood for paper, homes, andhundreds of other uses; forage for wildlife and livestock; a source of minerals.
Chris Knopp, Forests Supervisor
Pam Baltimore, Public Affairs Officer

3117 Bill Williams River National Wildlife Refuge
60911 Highway 95 928-667-4144
Parker, AZ 85344 Fax: 928-667-3402
dick_gilbert@fws.gov
www.billwilliamsriver.org

Bill Williams River National Wildlife Refuge is located along the Bill Williams River in La Paz and Mojave Counties, Arizona, with the river as the dividing line between the two counties. The refuge was established in 1941 as part ofHavasu NWR as mitigation for the Boulder and Parker Dam projects. In 1993, the two refuges were seperated and the Bill W Unit became the Bill Williams River NWR.
Larry Voyles, Member
Dave Weedman, Member

3118 Buenos Aires National Wildlife Refuge
PO Box 109 520-823-4251
Sasabe, AZ 85633 Fax: 520-823-4247
Daniel_Peterson@fws.gov
www.fws.gov/refuge/Buenos_Aires

3119 Cabeza Prieta National Wildlife Refuge
1611 N 2nd Avenue 520-387-6483
Ajo, AZ 85321 Fax: 520-387-5359
cabezaprieta@fws.gov
Roger Di Rosa, Manager

3120 Chiricahua National Monument
12856 East Rhyolite Creek Road 520-824-3560
Wilcox, AZ 85643 Fax: 520-824-3421
www.nps.gov/chir

The monument is mecca for hikers and birders. At the intersection of the Chiricahuan and Sonoran deserts, and the southern Rocky Mountains and northern Sierra Madre in Mexico, Chiricahua plants and animals represents one of the premierareas for biological diversity in the northern hemisphere.

3121 Coconino National Forest
1824 South Thompson Street 928-527-3600
Flagstaff, AZ 86001 Fax: 928-527-3620
www.fs.fed.us/r3/coconino/

The Coconino National Forest is one of the most diverse National Forests in the country with landscapes ranging from the famous Red Rocks of Sedona to Ponderosa Pine Forests, to alpine tundra

3122 Coronado National Forest
300 W Congress Street 520-388-8300
Tucson, AZ 85701 www.fs.fed.us/r3/coronado

The Coronado National Forest covers 1,780,000 acres of southeastern Arizona and southwestern New Mexico. Elevations range from 3,000 feet to 10,720 feet in 12 widely scattered mountain ranges or sky islands that rise dramatically fromthe desert floor, supporting plant communities as biologically diverse as those encountered on a trip from Mexico to Canada. The views are spectacular from these mountains, and visitors may experience all four seasons during a single day's journey.
Jim Upchurch, Forest Supervisor

3123 Glen Canyon National Recreation Area
Glen Canyon NRA 928-608-6200
PO Box 1507 Fax: 928-608-6259
Page, AZ 86040 GLCA_CHVC@nps.gov
www.nps.gov/glca

Glen Canyon National Recreation Area offers unparalleled opportunities for water-based & backcountry recreation. The recreation area stretches for hundreds of miles from Lees Ferry in Arizona to the Orange Cliffs of southern Utah,encompassing scenic vistas, geologic wonders, and a panorama of human history. Additionally, the controversy surrounding the construction of Glen Cayon Dam and the creation of Lake Powell contributed to the birth of modern day environmental movement.

3124 Grand Canyon National Park
PO Box 129 928-638-7888
Grand Canyon, AZ 86023 Fax: 928-638-7797
www.nps.gov/grca

3125 Imperial National Wildlife Refuge
PO Box 72217 928-783-3371
Yuma, AZ 85365 Fax: 928-783-0652
FW2_RW_Imperial@fws.gov

Imperial National Wildlife Refuge protects wildlife habitat along 30 miles of the lower Colorado River in Arizona and California, including the last unchannelized section before the river enters Mexico.
Elaine Johnson, Manager

3126 Kaibab National Forest
800 South Sixth Street
Williams, AZ 86046
928-635-8200
Fax: 928-635-8208
www.fs.fed.us/r3/kai/

3127 Kofa National Wildlife Refuge
9300 East 28th Street
Yuma, AZ 85365
928-783-7861
Fax: 928-783-8611
www.fws.gov/refuge/Kofa

Refuge dedicated to protecting the desert bighorn sheep and other native wildlife of Arizona.
Lydia Morton, Volunteer Coordinator

3128 Organ Pipe Cactus National Monument
10 Organ Pipe Drive
Ajo, AZ 85321
520-387-6849
orpi_information@nps.gov
www.nps.gov/orpi

Organ Pipe Cactus National Monument celebrates the life and landscape of the Sonoran Desert. Here, in this desert wilderness of plants and animals and dramatic mountains and plains scenery, you can drive a lonely road, hike abackcountry trail, camp beneath a clear desert sky, or just soak in the warmth and beauty of Southwest.

3129 Petrified Forest National Park
1 Park Road
PO Box 2217
Petrified Forest, AZ 86028
928-524-6228
Fax: 928-524-3567
PEFO_superintendant@nps.gov
www.nps.gov/pefo

Petrified Forest is a surprising land of scenic wonders and fascinating science. The park is located in northeast Arizona and features one of the world's largest and most colorful concentrations of petrified wood. Also included in thepark's 93,533 acres are the multihued badlands of the Chinle Formation known as the Painted Desert, historic structures, archeological sites and displays of 225 millio-year-old fossils.

3130 Prescott National Forest
344 S Cortez Street
Prescott, AZ 86303
928-443-8000
www.fs.fed.us/r3/prescott

This involves taking care of the land while making the forest resources available to all shareholders. Resources include high quality water, wilderness and outdoor recreation; quality habitat for many plants and animals; wood forpaper, homes and hundreds of other uses; forage for wildlife and livestock; and minerals.

3131 Saguaro National Park
3693 S Old Spanish Trail
Tuscon, AZ 85730-5601
520-733-5153
Fax: 520-733-5183
www.nps.gov/sagu

This unique desert is home to the most recognizable cactus in the world, the majestic saguaro. Visitors of all ages are fascinated and enchanted by these desert gaints, especially their many interesting and complex interrelationshipswith other desert life. With the average life span of 150 years, a mature saguaro may grow to the height of 50 feet and weigh over 10 tons.

3132 San Bernardino/Leslie Canyon National Refuge
PO Box 3509
Douglas, AZ 85607
520-364-2104
Fax: 520-364-2130
Bill Radke, Manager

3133 Sunset Crater Volcano National Monument
6400 N. Hwy 89
Flagstaff, AZ 86004
928-526-0502
Fax: 928-714-0565
www.nps.gov/sucr

Welcome to the Flagstaff Area National Monuments! There is something for everyone: prehistoic cliff dwellings at Walnut Canyon, the mountain scenery and geology of Sunset Crater Volcano, and the painted desert landscape and masonrypueblos of Wupatki National Monument. Here at Sunset Crater Volcano, amid lava and cinders, one can imagine a landscape still hot to the touch. Imagine the thoughts of the prehistoric people who lived here when the eruption occured.

3134 Tonto National Forest
2324 East McDowell Road
Phoenix, AZ 85006
602-225-5200
Fax: 602-225-5295
www.fs.fed.us/r3/tonto

The Tonto National Forest occupies about 2.8 million acres which generally lie northeast of Phoenix, Ariz., to the Mogollon Rim and east to the San Carlos and Fort Apache Indain Reservations. The west side approximately interstate 17which stretches north of Phoenix to Flagstaff. The lower elevations are of the Sonoran Desert type while the northern portion of the Forest is generally Pinon, Juniper, and Ponderosa Pine types.

3135 Walnut Canyon National Monument
6400 N. Hwy 89
Flagstaff, AZ 86004
928-526-1157
Fax: 928-526-4259
www.nps.gov/waca

Hike down into Walnut Canyon and walk in the footsteps of people who lived here over 900 years ago. Built under limestone overhangs, these dwellings were occupied from about 1100 to 1250. Look down into the canyon and imagine the creekrunning through. Visualize a woman hiking up from the bottom with a pot of water on her back. Imagine the men on the rim farming corn or hunting deer. Think of a cold winter night with your family huddled around the fire.

3136 Wupatki National Monument
25137 N Wupatki Loop
Flagstaff, AZ 86004
928-679-2365
Fax: 928-679-2349
www.nps.gov

Wupatki, comprised of big skies, open grassland, and desert scrub, with Painted Desert to the east and San Francisco Peaks to the west. A visit to this beautiful landscape will remind you what life was like in this region 900 yearsago.
Chuck Sypher, District Ranger

Arkansas: US Forests, Parks, Refuges

3137 Bald Knob National Wildlife Refuge
1439 Coal Chute Road
Bald Knob, AR 72010
501-724-2458
Fax: 501-724-2460
paul_provence@fws.gov
www.fws.gov/baldknob

The refuge facts established in 1993 has 14,800 acres and the location is in White County, Ar approximately two miles south of Bald Knob, AR on Coal Chute Road. It provides habitat for migratory waterfowl and other birds. And also forendangered species recreational and environmental education opportunities.
Bald Knob, Refuge Manager

3138 Buffalo National River
402 N Walnut
Suite 136
Harrison, AR 72601
870-365-2700
Fax: 870-365-2701
buff_information@nps.gov
www.nps.gov/buff

One of the few remaining unpolluted, free-flowing rivers in the lower 48 states offering both swift-running and placid stretches. The river encompasses 135 miles of the 150 mile long river. It begins as a trickle in the BostonMountains 15 miles above the park boundary. Following what is likely an ancient riverbed, the Buffalo cuts its way through massive limestone bluffs traveling eastward throug the Ozarks and into the Whtie River.

3139 Felsenthal National Wildlife Refuge
5531 Highway 82 West
Crossett, AR 71635
870-364-3167
Fax: 870-364-3757
felsenthal@fws.gov
www.fws.gov/refuge/felsenthal

65,000 acre national wildlife refuge with abuntant water resources - 15,000 acres, and vast bottomland hardwood forest that rises to the pine uplands.
Bernard J Petersen, Project Leader

3140 Greers Ferry National Fish Hatchery
349 Hatchery Road 501-362-3615
Heber Springs, AR 72543 Fax: 501-362-4007
greersferry@fws.gov
www.fws.gov/greersferry
Through self-guided tours at the hatchery, visitors can observe techniques of trout production, view information exhibits in the aquarium, and see trout in the outdoor raceways. Adjacent to the hatchery, visitors can camp at JFK Parkand trout fish the Little Red River. Nearby, the US Army Corps of Engineers has a visitor center, two mini-hiking trails and an overlook of Greers Ferry Dam. Greers Ferry Lake on the other side of the dam offers camping, swimming, fishing and otherwater sports.
Sherri Shoults, Hatchery Manager
Eric Thompson, Assistant Hatchery Manager

3141 Holla Bend National Wildlife Refuge
10448 Holla Bend Road 479-229-4300
Dardanelle, AR 72834 Fax: 479-229-4302
hollabend@fws.gov
www.fws.gov/refuge/holla_bend
Part of a system of over 475 national wildlife refuges located across the country. Administered by US Fish and Wildlife Service, this system of refuges, the finest in the world, protects important habitat needed to provide a home for awide variety of wildlife. These refuges also provide the public with valuable opportunities to see and learn about wildlife and to enjoy outdoor activities such as hunting and fishing. Holla Bend's main purpose is to provide a winter home for ducksand geese.
Durwin Carter, Manager

3142 Hot Springs National Park
101 Reserve Street 501-620-6715
Hot Springs, AR 71901 Fax: 501-624-3458
HOSP_Interpretation@nps.gov
www.nps.gov/hosp
The park protects eight historic bathhouses with the former luxurious Fordyce Bathhouse housing the park visitor center. The entire Bathhouse Row area is national Historic Landmark District that contains the grandest collection ofbathhouses of its kind in North America. By protecting the 47 hot springs and their watershed, the National Park Service continues to provide visitors with historic leisure activities such as hiking, picnicking and scenic drives.
Josie Fernandez, Superintendent
Mardi Arce, Deputy Superintendent

3143 Ouachita National Forest
100 Reserve Street 501-321-5202
PO Box 1270 Fax: 501-321-5305
Hot Springs, AR 71902 www.fs.usda.gov/ouachita/
Mission: To sustain the ecological health and productivity of lands and waters entrusted to our care and provide for human uses compatible with that goal. We understand that our greatest asset is the land, our greatest strength is ourworkforce, and our greatest challenge is achieving public understanding, trust, and confidence in all that we do.

3144 Overflow National Wildlife Refuge
3858 Highway 8 East 870-473-2869
Parkdale, AR 71661 Fax: 870-473-5191
www.fws.gov
Refuge objectives are to: provide a diversity of habitat types for migratory waterfowl and other birds; provide habitat and protection for the delisted bald eagle; provide opportunities for environmental and ecological research;provide a variety of recreational opportunities consistent with primary wildlife objectives; and expand the public's understanding of and appreciation for the environment with special emphasis on natural resources.
Lake Lewis, Manager

3145 Ozark-St. Francis National Forest
605 W Main Street 479-964-7200
Russleville, AR 72801 www.fs.usda.gov/osfnf
The Ozark-St. Francis National Forests are really two separate Forests with many differences. They are distinct in their own topographical, geological, biological, cultural and social differences, yet each makes up a part of theoverall National Forest system.
Judi Henry, Forest Supervisor

3146 Pond Creek National Wildlife Refuge
1958 Central Road 870-289-2126
Lockesburg, AR 71846 Fax: 870-289-2127
www.fws.gov
Pond Creek National Wildlife Refuge plans to: protect the area's wetland and bottomland hardwood hbitat for natural diversity of wildlife; provide habitat for neo-tropical migratory birds; provide wintering habitat for migratorywaterfowl; provide breeding and nesting habitat for wood ducks; and to provide opportunities for compatible public outdoor recreation.
Paul Gideon, Manager

3147 Wapanocca National Wildlife Refuge
178 Hammond Avenue Highway 42 East 870-343-2595
PO Box 279 Fax: 870-343-2416
Turrell, AR 72384 jared_nance@fws.gov
www.fws.gov/wapanocca/
The 5,484 acre refuge is an important stopover for waterfowl traveling the Mississippi Flyway and for songbirds as they migrate to and from Central and South America. The refuge is open to limited small and big game hunting. Auto tourroutes offers excellent wildlife observation, photography and hiking opportunities. An observation platform is located on the east side of the 600 acre Wapanocca Lake.
Jared Nance, Refuge Manager

3148 White River National Wildlife Refuge
57 South CC Camp Road 870-282-8200
PO Box 205 Fax: 870-282-8234
St Charles, AR 72140 whiteriver@fws.gov
www.fws.gov/whiteriver
Refuge objectives are to provide: optimum habitat for migratory birds; habitat and protection for endangered species: a natural diversity of wildlife common to the White River bottoms; opportunities and facilities for wildlife orientedrecreation and environmental education; cooperation with other water and land managing agencies and private interests to foster proper management of the White River Basin's resources; and preservation of appropriate wooded areas in their naturalcondition.
Keith Weaver, Project Leader

California: US Forests, Parks, Refuges

3149 Angeles National Forest
701 North Santa Anita Avenue 626-574-1613
Arcadia, CA 91006 Fax: 626-574-5207
www.fs.usda.gov/angeles/
The Angeles National Forest covers 650,000 acres and is the backyard playground to the huge metropolitan area of Los Angeles. The Los Angeles National Forest manages the watersheds eithin its boundaries to provide valuable water tosouthern California and to protect surrounding communities from catastrophics floods.
Tom Contreras, Forest Supervisor

3150 Bear Valley National Wildlife Refuge
4009 Hill Rd 916-667-2231
Tulelake, CA 96134 Fax: 916-667-3299
ron_cole@fws.gov
www.fws.gov
Refuge was established to protect a major winter night roost site for bald egales. The acquisition program was completed in 1991. Klamath Basin hosts the largest wintering popluation of blad eagles in the contiguous United States, withnumbers some years approaching 1,000. Refuge serves as one of serveral eagle roots in the Basin. It consists of large stands of old-growth tinmber, which protects the birds at night from the harsh winter weather.
Ron Cole, Refuge Manager

3151 Bitter Creek National Wildlife Refuge
Hopper Mountain NWR 805-644-5185
Po Box 5839 Fax: 805-644-1732
Ventura, CA 93005 www.fws.gov/hoppermountain/BitterCreekNWR
The primary wildlife traditional feeding and roosting habitat for the California condor. Also provides habitat for the San Joaquin kit fox, golden eagle, Southern bald eagle and American peregrine falcon. 14,000 contiguous acres,mostly annual grasslands with some juniper and scrub oak with grass understory. Public use is severely limited because of the sensitive situation of the California condor. The refuge can be viewed from the Cerro Noroeste Road.
Dan Tappe, Refuge Manager

3152 Blue Ridge National Wildlife Refuge
Kern NWR 805-644-5185
PO Box 5839 Dan_Tappe@fws.gov
Ventura, CA 93005 www.fws.gov/refuge/blue_ridge/
Primary wildlife area is a traditional summer roosting site for the endangered Califorina condor. The habitat includes 897 acres of rugged mountains, rock outcroppings, chaparral and coniferous trees. The refuge is closed to publicaccess due to the sensitivity of California condors and its isolation and difficulty in access.
Dan Tappe, Refuge Manager

3153 Castle Rock National Wildlife Refuge
Humboldt Bay NWR 707-733-5406
PO Box 576 Fax: 707-733-1946
Loleta, CA 95551 www.fws.gov/refuge/castle_rock/
The Refuge is a 14-acre offshore rock with steep cliffs and sparse vegetation. It was established in 1981 to protect an important migration staging area of the threatened Aleutian Canada goose. Over 21,000 of these roost on the island,which contains the second largest seabird breeding colony in California. Haul-out for a variety of marine mammals, including California sea lion, Stellar sea lion and northern elephant seal. Not open to the public, but wildlife can be observed fromshore.

3154 Channel Islands National Park
1901 Spinnaker Drive 805-658-5730
Ventura, CA 93001 Fax: 805-658-5799
chis_interpretation@nps.gov
www.nps.gov
Encompasses five of the eight California Channel Islands and their ocean environment, preserving and protecting a wealth of natural and cultural resources. Marine life ranges from microscopic plankton to the blue whale, the largestanimal to live on Earth. Archeological and cultural resources span a period of more than 10,000 years of human habitation.

3155 Clear Lake National NWR Wildlife Refuge

3155 Clear Lake National Wildlife Refuge
Klamath Basin NWR Complex 916-667-2231
Route 1 Box 74 Fax: 916-667-3299
Tulelake, CA 96134 klamathbasinrefuges.fws.gov
Clear Lake National Wildlife Refuge plans to: maintain habitat for endangered, threatened and sensitive species; provide and enhance habitat for fall and spring migrant waterfowl; protect native habitats and wildlife representativeofthe natural biological diversity of the Klamath Basin; integrate the maintenance of productive wetland habitats and sustainable agriculture; and to provide high quality wildlife-dependent visitor services.

3156 Cleveland National Forest
10845 Rancho Bernardo Road 858-673-6180
Suite 200 Fax: 858-673-6192
San Diego, CA 92127 www.fs.usda.gov/cleveland/

3157 Coachella Valley National Wildlife Refuge
906 W Siclair Road 760-348-5278
PO Box 120 Fax: 760-348-7245
Calipatria, CA 92233 christian_schoneman@fws.gov
www.fws.gov
Contains 13,000 acres consisting of palm oasis woodlands, perennial desert pools and blow-sand habitat. This habitat is critical for the Coachella Valley fringe-toed lizard (Uma inornata) and flat-tailed horned lizard. These threatenedspecies are restricted to the refuge dune system and a few other small areas. Also has the state's second largest grove of native fan palms and the Coachella milk-vetch, a species of special concern.
Christian Schoneman, Project Leader

3158 Death Valley National Park
PO Box 579 760-786-3200
Death Valley, CA 92328 Fax: 760-786-3246
deva_superintendant@nps.gov
www.nps.gov/deva/index.htm
Death Valley National Park has more than 3.3 million acres of spectacular desert scenery, interesting and rare desert wildlife, complex geology, undisturbed wilderness and sites of historical and cultural interest. The National ParkService is dedicated to the protection and preservation of this park's unique resources for everyone to enjoy now and for future generations.

3159 Delevan National Wildlife Refuge
Sacramento NWR Complex 530-934-2801
752 County Road 99W Fax: 530-934-7814
Willows, CA 95988 www.fws.gov/sacramentovalleyrefuges
Delevan NWR is part of the Sacramento NWR Complex and is located in the Sacramento Valley of north-central California. The refuge consists of nearly 5,800 acres comprised of seasonal marsh, permanent ponds, watergrass and uplands inColusa County.

3160 Devil's Postpile National Monument
PO Box 3999 760-934-2289
Mammoth Lakes, CA 93546 Fax: 760-934-4780
www.nps.gov/depo
The geologic formation that is the Postpile is the world's finest example of unusual columnar basalt. Its columns of lava, with their four to seven sides, display of honeycomb pattern of order and harmony. Another jewel in the Monumentis the San Joaquin River.

3161 Eldorado National Forest
100 Forni Road 530-622-5061
Placeville, CA 95667 Fax: 530-621-5297
www.fs.usda.gov/eldorado/
Situated near the California gold discovery site on the American River at Coloma, this forest still boast numerous gold-bearing rivers and streams.Fishing opportunities are abundant. Only 34 miles of waterways are stocked, theremainder contain resident trout. Winter sports are cross country ski, sonowmobile and snowshoe. Backcountry exploration takes place year round in the Desolation and Mokelumme wildernesses.
Kathy Hardy, Forest Supervisor

3162 Ellicott Slough National Wildlife Refuge
San Andreas Rd 510-792-0222
Watsonville, CA 94560 sfbaynwrc@fws.gov
www.fws.gov

3163 Havasu National Wildlife Refuge
317 Mesquite Ave 760-326-3853
Needles, CA 92363 Fax: 760-326-5745
linda_l_miller@fws.gov
www.fws.gov/southwest/refuges/arizona/havasu
Benjamin Tuggle, Regional Director

3164 Hopper Mountain National Wildlife Refuge
2493 Portola Rd. 805-644-5185
Suite A Fax: 805-644-1732
Ventura, CA 9300 hoppermountain@fws.gov
www.fws.gov/refuge/hopper_mountain
The area is a traditional feeding site for the endangered California condor. Condors use the area frequently from October through May. A variety of other birds occur during migration and year round. The habitat includes 2,471 acres ofgrassland, chaparral and coastal sage scrub. There is a small, 350 acre area of intact California black walnut groves, some of the last remaining in southern California.
Dan Tappe, Refuge Manager

3165 Inyo National Forest
317 Mesquite Avenue 760-326-3853
Suite 200 Fax: 760-326-5745
Needles, CA 9236 www.fws.gov
The Inyo National Forest is a unique and special area of public land located along the aestern edge of California and Sierra Nevada. Extending 165 miles along the California/Nevada border between Los Angeles and Reno, the Inyo Nationalforest includes 1.9 million acres of pristine lakes, fragile meadows, winding streams, rugged Sierra Nevada peaks, and arid Great Baisn Mountains. Elevations range frome 4,000 to 14,495 feet, providing diverse habitats that support vegetationpatterns ranging.

3166 Joshua Tree National Park
74485 National Park Drive 760-367-5500
Twentynine Palms, CA 92277-3597 Fax: 760-367-6392
JOTR_info@nps.gov
www.nps.gov/jotr
Joshua Tree National Park's 794,000 acres span the transition between the Mojave and Colorado deserts of Southern California. Proclaimed a National Monument in 1936 and a Biosphere Reserve in 1984, Joshua Tree was designated a NationalPark In 1994. The area possesses a rich human history and a pristine natural environment.

3167 Kern National Wildlife Refuge
PO Box 670 661-725-2767
Delano, CA 93216-0670 Fax: 661-725-6041
www.natureali.org/KNWR.htm
David Hardt, Manager

3168 Kings Canyon National Park
Sequoia & Kings Canyon National Park
47050 Generals Highway 559-565-3341
Three Rivers, CA 93271-9700 Fax: 559-565-3730
www.nps.gov/seki
Kings Canyon National Park, located in California's Sierra Nevada Mountains, is a park most famous for its pristine stands of Giant Sequoia trees. Visitors explore Grant Grove along a network of easy trails. For the more adventurous,longer trails including those in the remote Kings Canyon Backcountry provide a greater challenge.

3169 Klamath Basin National Wildlife Refuges
Tulelake, CA 96134 530-667-2231
Fax: 530-667-8337
r8kbwebmaster@fws.gov
www.fws.gov/klamathbasinrefuges/
The Klamath Basin National Wildlife Refuges Complex consists of six refuges in Northern California and Southern Oregon. The refuges support the largest concentration of migratory water fowl on the west coast and the largest winteringnumbers of bald eagles in the lower 48 states.
Ron Cole, Refuge Manager
Greg Austin, Assistant Refuge Manager

3170 Klamath National Forest
1711 South Main Street 530-842-6131
Yreka, CA 96097-9549 www.fs.usda.gov/klamath/
The Klamath National Forest covers an area of 1,700,000 acres located in Siskiyou County, Northern California and Jackson County, Oregon. The forest comprises some five wilderness areas, Marble Mountain, Russian Wilderness Area,Trinity Alps, Red Buttes Wilderness Area and Siskiyou Wilderness Area.
Peg Boland, Forest Supervisor
Patricia A Grantham, Deputy Forest Supervisor

3171 Lake Tahoe Basin Management Unit
35 College Drive 530-543-2600
S Lake Tahoe, CA 96150 Fax: 530-573-2693
www.fs.usda.gov/ltbmu/
Majestic sceenery and diverse recreation oppotunities draw millions of visitors to the Lake Tahoe Basin annually. Changing colors throughout the year afford a brilliant backdrop to the many available activities in all seasons. TheBasin is home to a rich diversity of plants and animals that can be viewed during walks at interpertive sites and on many forest trails.

3172 Lassen National Forest
2550 Riverside Drive 530-257-2151
Susanville, CA 96130 www.fs.usda.gov/lassen/
Lassen National Forest lies at the heart of a fascinating part of California, a crossroads of people and nature. This is where the Sierra Nevada, the Cascades, the Modoc Plateau and the Great Basin meet. Within Lassen National Forest,you can explore a lava tube or the land of Ishi, the last survivor of the Yahi Tana Native American tribe: watch prong-horn antelope glide across sage flats; drive four-wheel trails into granite country appointed with sapphire lakes or discoverwildflowers on foot.

3173 Lava Beds National Monument
1 Indian Well Headquarters 530-667-8113
Tulelake, CA 96134 Fax: 530-667-2737
LABE_SUperintendent@nps.gov
www.nps.gov/labe
Volcanic eruptions on the Medicine Lake shield volcano have created an incredibly rugged landscape punctuated by cinder cones, lava flows, spatter cones, lava tube caves and pit craters. During the Modoc War of 1872-1873, the ModocIndains used these tortuous lava flows to their advantage. Under the leadership of Captain Jack, the Modocs took refuge in Captain Jack's Stronghold, a natural lava fortress.

3174 Los Padres National Forest
6755 Hollister Avenue 805-968-6640
Suite 150 www.fs.usda.gov/lpnf/
Goleta, CA 93117
Los Padres National Forest encompasses nearly 2 million acres of the central coastal mountains of California.
Ken Heffner, Forest Supervisor
Ann Garland, Deputy Forest Supervisor

3175 Lower Klamath National Wildlife Refuge
4009 Hill Rd 530-667-2231
Box 74 r8kbwebmaster@fws.gov
Tulelake, CA 96134 www.fws.gov/refuge/lower_klamath
The objectives of the refuge are to: maintain habitat for endangered, threatened and sensitive species; provide and enhance habitat for fall and spring migrant waterfowl; protect native habitats and wildlife representative of thenatural biological diversity of the Klamath Basin; integrate the maintenance of productive wetland habitats and sustainable agriculture; provide high quality wildlife-dependent visitor services.

3176 Mendocino National Forest
825 North Humboldt Avenue 530-934-3316
Willows, CA 95988 mailroom_r5_mendocino@fs.fed.us
www.fs.usda.gov/mendocino/
The Mendocino national Forest was set aside by President Roosevelt in 1907. It was frist named the Stony Creek Reserve and then the Stony Creek National Forest. It was later named the California National Forest and in 1932 became theMendocino National Forest. The MNF straddles the eastern spur of the Coastal Mountain Range in northernwestern Califonia, just a three hour drive north of San Francisco and Sacramento.
Tom Contreras, Forest Supervisor

3177 Modoc National Forest
225 West 8th Street 530-233-5811
Alturas, CA 96101 Fax: 530-233-8709
www.fs.usda.gov/modoc/
A land of contrasts and unspoiled vaction-hideaway settings. Nestled in the extreme northeastern corner of California, The Modoc National Forest is 140 miles east of Redding on Highway 299, and 169 miles north of Reno, Nevada, viahighway 395. The Modoc National Forest features several mountain areas. The Warner Mountains, on its east, are the western edge of Great Basin Province, the Medicine Lake Highlands, to northwest, are a couthern spur of the Cascade Range.
Stanley G Sylva, Forest Supervisor

3178 Modoc National Wildlife Refuge
PO Box 1610 530-233-3572
Alturas, CA 96101-1610 Fax: 530-233-4143
modoc@fws.gov
www.fws.gov/refuge/modoc/
A 7,000+ acre refuge established to manage and protect migratory waterfowl.
Steve Clay, Refuge Manager
Sean Cross, Assistant Refuge Manager

3179 Pinnacles National Monument
5000 Highway 146 831-389-4485
Paicines, CA 95043 Fax: 831-389-4489
www.nps.gov/pinn
Rising out of the chaparral-covered Gabilan Mountains, east of central California's Salinas Valley, are the spectacular remains of an ancient volcano. Massive monoliths, spires, sheer-walled canyons and talus passages define millionsof years of erosion, faulting and tectonic plate movement is reowned for the beauty and variety of its spring wildflowers. Hiking, rock climbing, picnicing and sildlife observation can be enjoyed throughout the year.

3180 Pixley National Wildlife Refuge
Kern NWR 661-725-2767
Po Box 670 www.fws.gov
Delano, CA 93216
Pixley national Wildlife Refuge provides for the endangered San Joaquin kit fox, Tipton kangaroo rat, and blunt-nosed leopard lizard.

3181 Plumas National Forest
159 Lawrence Street 530-283-2050
Quincy, CA 95971-6025 Fax: 530-283-7746
www.fs.usda.gov/plumas/
The Plumas National Forest has fresh conifer forests, rugged cayons, crystal clear lakes, grassy meadows, trout filled streams and brilliant star-filled skies. Located where the Sierra Nevada and Cascade Mountain ranges meet, thisforest has more than 100 lakes, 1,000 miles of rivers and streams, and over a million acres of National Forest.
Alice Carlton, Forest Supervisor

3182 Redwood National Park
1111 2nd Street 707-465-7335
Crescent City, CA 95531 Fax: 707-464-1812
www.nps.gov/redw
The world's tallest living trees can found along the northern California coast. Of the coast redwood forests still around today, almost one half of them can be found within the projected boundaries of Redwood National and State Parks.In 1994, the National Park Service and the California State Parks joined forces to manage four parks: Redwood National, Jebediah Smith, Del Norte Coast, and Prairie Creek Redwoods State Parks collectively known as Redwood National and State Parks.

3183 Sacramento National Wildlife Refuge Complex
752 County Road 99 West 530-934-2801
Willows, CA 95988 Fax: 530-934-7814
sacramentovalleyrefuges@fws.gov
www.fws.gov
The Complex consists of five national wildlife refuges and three wildlife management areas that comprise over 35,000 acres of wetlands and uplands in the Sacramento Valley of California. In addition there are over 30,000 acres ofconservation easements in the Complex. The refuges and easements serve as resting and feeding areas for nearly half the migratory birds on the Pacific Flyway.

3184 Salinas River National Wildlife Refuge
PO Box 524 510-792-0222
Newark, CA 94560 www.fws.gov
367 acres of diverse habitats including ocean, beach, dunes, grassland, river, lagoon, and salt marsh.

3185 San Bernardino National Forest
602 South Tippecanoe Avenue 909-382-2600
San Bernardino, CA 92408 www.fs.usda.gov/sbnf/
In the San Bernardino Mountains, the forest service has developed an extensive network of campgrounds and dozens of picnic areas for families and groups who want to enjoy a day in the mountains. The forest offers camping, picnicking,fishing, boating, swimming, hiking, horseback riding and more. During the winter, visitors come to the forest to cross-contry and down ski, snowboard and snowmobile.
Jeanne Wade Evans, Forest Supervisor
Max Copenhagen, Deputy Forest Supervisor

3186 San Francisco Bay National Wildlife Refuge Complex
1 Marshlands Rd 510-792-0222
Fremont, CA 94555 sfbaynwrc@fws.gov
www.fws.gov/sfbayrefuges
The San Francisco Bay National Refuge Complex is a collection of seven National Wildlife Refuges administered by the US Fish and Wildlife Service-Antioch Dunes National Wildlife Refuge, Don Edwards San Francisco Bay National Wildliferefuge, Ellicott Slough National Wildlife Refuge, Farallon National Wildlife Refuge, Marin Islands National Wildlife Refuge, Salinas River National Wildlife Refuge, and San Pablo National Wildlife Refuge.

3187 San Luis National Wildlife Refuge
7376 S. Wolfsen Road 209-826-3508
PO Box 2176 Fax: 209-826-1445
Los Banos, CA 93635
Mission: Working with others, to conserve, protect and enhance fish, wildlife, and plants and their habitats for the continuing benefit of the American people.

3188 San Pablo Bay National Wildlife Refuge
7715 Lakeville Highway 707-769-4200
Petaluma, CA 94954 www.pickleweed.org
San Pablo Bay National Wildlife Refuge protects and preserves habitat critical to the survival of the endangered California clapper rail and salt marsh harvest mouse. The Refuge and surrounding San Pablo Bay area also provide winteringhabitat for millions

of shorebirds and thousands of waterfowl, including the largest wintering population of canvasbacks on the west coast.
Francesca Demgen, President
Debra Green, Vice President

3189 Santa Monica Mountains National Recreation
401 West Hillcrest Drive 805-370-2301
Thousand Oaks, CA 91360 Fax: 805-370-2351
www.nps.gov/samo
Santa Monica Mountains rise above Los Angeles, widen to meet the curve of Santa Monica Bay and reach their highest peaks facing the ocean, forming a beautiful and multi-faceted landscape. Santa Monica Mountains National Recreation Areais a cooperative effort that joins federal, state and local park agencies with private preserves and landowners to protect the natural and cultural resources of this transverse mountain range and seashore.

3190 Sequoia National Forest
1839 South Newcomb Street 559-784-1500
Porterville, CA 93257 Fax: 559-781-4744
www.fs.usda.gov/sequoia/
The Sequoia National Forest is at the southern tip of the Sierra Nevada range. Its highest point is 12,432 foot Florence Peak in the Golden Trout Wilderness. The forest has five wildernesses, a scenic byway and four wild and scenicrivers. About 10,000 cows graze on the forest land. Camping, water sports, hiking, downhill and cross-country skiing and horseback riding are amoung the forest's many recreational activities.

3191 Shasta-Trinity National Forest
3644 Avtech Parkway 530-226-2500
Redding, CA 96002 Fax: 530-226-2470
www.fs.usda.gov/stnf/
J Sharon Heywood, Forest Supervisor

3192 Sierra National Forest
1600 Tollhouse Road 559-297-0706
Clovis, CA 93611 dkohut@fs.fed.us
www.fs.usda.gov/sierra/
Edward C Cole, Forest Supervisor

3193 Six Rivers National Forest
1330 Bayshore Way 707-442-1721
Eureka, CA 95501 Fax: 707-442-9242
www.fs.usda.gov/srnf/
Six Rivers National Forest lies east of Redwood State and National Parks in northwestern California, and stretches southward from the Oregon border for about 140 miles.
Tyrone Kelley, Forest Supervisor
Will Metz, Deputy Forest Supervisor

3194 Sonny Bono Salton Sea National Wildlife Refuge Complex
906 W Sinclair Road 760-348-5278
Calipatria, CA 92233 saltonsea.fws.gov
The Refuge is composed of two disjunctive units, separated by 18 miles of private lands. Each unit contains managed wetland habitat, agricultural fields, and tree rows. The courses of the New and Alamo rivers run through the Refuge,providing freshwater inflow to the Salton Sea.

3195 Stanislaus National Forest
19777 Greenley Road 209-532-3671
Sonora, CA 95370 Fax: 209-533-1890
www.fs.usda.gov/stanislaus/
The Stanislaus National Forest, created on February 22, 1897, is among the oldest of the National Forests. It is named for the Stanislaus River whose headwaters rise within Forest boundaries. The Spanish explorer Gabriel Moraga namedthe river Our Lady of Guadalupe during an 1806 expedition. Later, the river was renamed in honor of Estanislao, an Indian leader.

3196 Sutter National Wildlife Refuge
Sacramento NWR Complex 530-934-2801
752 County Road 99W Fax: 530-934-7814
Willows, CA 95988 www.fws.gov

3197 Tahoe National Forest
631 Coyote Street 530-265-4531
Nevada City, CA 95959 www.fs.usda.gov/tahoe/
The Tahoe National Forest straddles the crest of the Sierra Nevada mountains in northern California, and encompasses a vast territory, from the golden foothills on the western slope to the high peaks of the Sierra crest.

3198 Tijuana Slough National Wildlife Refuge
Tijuana River NERR 619-575-2704
301 Caspian Way Fax: 619-575-6913
Imperial Beach, CA 91932 www.fws.gov
Established in 1980 to conserve and protect endangered and threatened fish, wildlife and plant species. Conservation of the light-footed clapper rail was the primary impetus for the creation of the refuge. The refuge is part of alarger unit called the Tijuana River National Estuarine Research Reserve, which is administered by the National Oceanographic and Atmospheric Administration.

3199 Tule Lake National Wildlife Refuge
4009 Hill Road 530-667-2231
Tulelake, CA 96134 Fax: 530-667-3299
The objectives of Tule Lake are to: maintain habitat for endangered, threatened and sensitive species; provide and enhance habitat for fall and spring migrant waterfowl; protect native habitats and wildlife representative of thenatural biological diversity of the Klamath Basin; integrate the maintenance of productive wetland habitats and sustainable agriculture; and ensure that the refuge agricultural practices confirm to the principles of integrated pest management.

3200 Yosemite National Park
PO Box 577 209-372-0200
Yosemite National Park, CA 95389 www.nps.gov
Yosemite National Park embraces a spectacular tract of mountain-and-valley scenery in the Sierra Nevada, which was set aside as a national park in 1890. The park harbors a grand collection of waterfalls, meadows, and forests thatinclude groves of giant sequoias, the world's largest living things. Highlights of the park include Yosemite Valley, and its high cliffs and waterfalls;Wawona's history center and historic hotel; the Mariposa Grove, which contains hundreds of ancientgiant sequoias.

Colorado: US Forests, Parks, Refuges

3201 Alamosa/Monte Vista/ Baca National Wildlife Refuge Complex
9383 El Rancho Lane 719-589-4021
Alamosa, CO 81101 Fax: 719-587-0595
alamosa@fws.gov
www.fws.gov/refuge/alamosa
The Valley extends over 100 miles from north to south and 50 miles from east to west, with dwarfing mountains in three directions. The surrounding mountains feed the arid valley with precious surface water, as well as replenish anexpansive underground reservoir. This liquid wealth has made two National Wildlife Refuges possible in the San Luis Valley: Alamosa and Monte Vista.

3202 Arapaho National Wildlife Refuge
953 JC Rd 32 970-723-8202
Walden, CO 80480 Fax: 970-723-8528
arapaho@fws.gov
www.fws.gov/refuge/Arapaho
Arapaho National Wildlife Refuge supports diverse wildlife habitats including sagebrush grassland uplands, grassland meadows, willow riparian areas, wetlands and mixed conifer and aspen woodland. This refuge is one in a system of over500 National Wildlife Refuges, a network of lands set aside and managed specifically for wildlife. It is administered by the US Fish and Wildlife Service.

3203 Browns Park National Wildlife Refuge
1318 Highway 318 970-365-3613
Maybell, CO 81640 Fax: 970-365-3614
brownspark@fws.gov
www.fws.gov/refuge/browns_park
The primary purpose of Browns Park Refuge is to provide high quality nesting and migration habitat for the Great Basin Canada Goose, ducks and other migratory birds. Before Flaming Gorge Dam was constructed in 1962, the Green Riverflooded annually, creating excellent waterfowl nesting, feeding and resting marshes in the backwater sloughs and old stream meanders. The dam stopped the flooding, eliminating much of this waterfowl habitat.

3204 Colorado National Monument
1750 Rim Rock Drive 970-858-3617
Fruita, CO 81521 Fax: 970-858-0372
COLM_Info@nps.gov
www.nps.gov/colm
Colorado National Monument consists of geological features including: towering red sandstone monoliths, deep sheer-walled canyons and a variety of wildlife.

3205 Curecanti National Recreation Area
102 Elk Creek 970-641-2337
Gunnison, CO 81230 Fax: 970-641-3127
CURE_Vis_Mail@nps.gov
www.nps.gov/cure
Three reservoirs, named for corresponding dams on the Gunnison River, form the heart of Curecanti National Recreation Area; Blue Mesa Reservoir, Morrow Point Reservoir and the Crystal Reservoir.

3206 Dinosaur National Monument
4545 East Highway 40 970-374-3000
PO Box 128 Fax: 970-374-3003
Dinosaur, CO 81610 www.nps.gov/dino
Dinosaur Monument protects a large deposit of fossil dinosaur bones that lived millons of years ago.

3207 Florissant Fossil Beds National Monument
PO Box 185 719-748-3253
Florissant, CO 80816 Fax: 719-748-3164
FLFO_Information@nps.gov
www.nps.gov/flfo
Huge petrified redwoods and incredibly detailed fossils of ancient insects and plants reveal a very different Colorado of long ago. A lake formed in the valley and the fine-grained sediments at its bottom became the final resting-placefor thousands of insects and plants. These sediments compacted into layers of shale and preserved the delicated details of these organisms as fossils.

3208 Great Sand Dunes National Park & Preserve
11999 Highway 150 719-378-6399
Mosca, CO 81146 Fax: 719-378-6310
www.nps.gov/grsa
These dunes are the tallest in North America, rising 750 feet from the valley floor. The dunes are home to some unique and spectacular species of flora and fauna. Besides a large variety of birds, there are quite a few species ofmammals that visit or reside within the dunes. Few reptiles are found here due to the high altitude.

3209 Rio Grande National Forest
1803 W US Highway 160 719-852-5941
Monte Vista, CO 81144 www.fs.usda.gov/riogrande
The Rio Grande National Forest is 1.86 million acres located in southwestern Colorado and remains one of the true undiscovered jewels of Colorado. The Continental Divide runs for 236 miles along most of the western border of theForest. The Forest present myraid ecosystems; from 7600-ft alpine desert to over 14,300-ft in the majestic Sangre de Cristo Wilderness on the eastern side.

3210 Rocky Mountain National Park
1000 Highway 36 970-586-1206
Estes Park, CO 80517 Fax: 970-586-1256
ROMO_informatin@nps.gov
www.nps.gov/romo

3211 San Juan National Forest
15 Burnett Court 970-247-4874
Durango, CO 81301 Fax: 970-385-1243
www.fs.usda.gov/sanjuan
San Jaun National Forest, a region of forested mountains, 14,000-foot peaks, scenic roads, geological wonders, hisoric and prehistoric communities, and a narrow-gauge railroad.
Mark Stiles, Forest Supervisor
Howard Sargent, Deputy Forest Supervisor

3212 White River National Forest
900 Grand Avenue 970-945-2521
PO Box 948 Fax: 970-945-3266
Glenwood Springs, CO 81602 www.fs.usda.gov/wps
The two and one quarter million acre White River National Forest is located in the heart of the Colorado Rocky Mountains, approximately two to four hours west of Denver on Interstate 70. The scenic beauty of the area, along with ampledeveloped and undeveloped recreation opportunities on the forest, accounts for the fact the White River consistently ranks as one of the top five Forests nationwide for total recreation use.

Connecticut: US Forests, Parks, Refuges

3213 Stewart B McKinney National Wildlife Refuge
733 Old Clinton Road 860-399-2513
Westbrook, CT 00649 Fax: 860-399-2515
fw5rw_sbmnwr@fws.gov
www.fws.gov/refuge/stewart_b_mckinney

Delaware: US Forests, Parks, Refuges

3214 Bombay Hook National Wildlife Refuge
2591 Whitehall Neck Road 302-653-6872
Smyrna, DE 19977 fw5rw_bhnwr@fws.gov
www.fws.gov/refuge/bombay_hook/
Stretching about eight miles along Delaware Bay and covering nearly 16,000 acres, Bombay Hook NWR was established as a refuge for migratory waterfowl. Today, the Refuge provides habitat for a diversity of wildlife. The refuge offersauto tours, walking trails, observation towers, and interpretive displays for the visiting public.

3215 Prime Hook National Wildlife Refuge
11978 Turkle Pond Road 302-684-8419
Milton, DE 19968 Fax: 302-684-8504
FW5RW_PHNWR@fws.gov
primehook.fws.gov

The Prime Hook National Wlidlife Refuge spans about 10,000 acres along the western Delaware Bay. The marshes of the refuge are ideal habitat for thousands of migrating ducks, geese, and shorebirds. The refuge is also home to woodlandand grassland birds, reptiles, amphibians, and mammals, including the endangered Delmarva Peninsula Fox Squirrel. Avid photographers can enjoy the beauty of wildlife from a photography blind and wheel-chair accessible observation platform.

District of Columbia: US Forests, Parks, Refuges

3216 **Battleground National Cemetery**
6625 Georgia Avenue, NW 202-426-6924
Washington, DC 20240 Fax: 202-426-1845
www.nps.gov
Battleground National Cemetery, located at 6625 Georgia Avenue NW, was established shortly after the Battle of Fort Stevens in the summer of 1864. The battle, which lasted two days (July 11-12, 1864) marked the defeat of General JubalA Early's Confederate campaign to launch an offensive action against the poorly defended Nation's Capital. Near the entrance are monuments commemorating those units which fought at Fort Stevens.

Florida: US Forests, Parks, Refuges

3217 **Arthur R Marshall Loxahatchee National Wildlife Refuge**
10216 Lee Road 561-734-8303
Boynton Beach, FL 33437 Fax: 561-369-7190
www.fws.gov/refuge/arm_loxahatchee
Welcome to the Arthur R. Marshall Loxahatchee National Wildlife Refuge, the last northernmost portion of the unique Everglades. With over 221 square miles of Everglades habitat, A.R.M. Loxahatchee National Wildlife Refuge is home tothe American alligator and the endangered Everglades snail kite. In any given year, as many as 257 species of birds may use the refuge's diverse wetland habitats.

3218 **Big Cypress National Preserve**
33100 Tamiami Trail East 239-695-1201
Ochopee, FL 34141 Fax: 239-695-3901
bob_degross@nps.gov
www.nps.gov/bicy
The 729,000 acre Big Cypress National Preserve was set aside to ensure the preservation, conservation, and protection of the natural scenic, floral and faunal, and recreational values of the Big Cypress Watershed. The importance ofthis watershed to the Everglades National Park was a major consideration for its establishment. The name Big Cypress refers to the large size of this area. Vast expanses of cypress strands span this unique landscape.

3219 **Biscayne National Park**
9700 SW 328 Street 305-230-7275
Homestead, FL 33033 Fax: 305-230-1190
BISC_Information@nps.gov
www.nps.gov/bisc
Turquoise waters, emerald islands and fish-bejeweled reefs make Biscayne National Park a paradise for wildlife-watching, snorkeling, diving, boating, fishing and other activities. Within the park boundaries are the longest stretch ofmangrove forest left on Florida's east coast, the clear shallow waters of Biscayne Bay, over 40 of the northernmost Florida Keys, and a spectacular living coral reef. Superimposed on all of this natural beauty is 10,000 years of human history.

3220 **Canaveral National Seashore**
212 South Washington Avenue 321-267-1110
Titusville, FL 32796 Fax: 321-264-2906
cana_resource_management@nps.gov
www.nbbd.com/godo/cns/
Canaveral National Seashore is a step into the past, protection for the present and a doorway into the future. The 100 Native American Archeological sites that are within our boundaries are evidence of past generations of people thatlived here. Canaveral National Seashore covers 57,000 acres and is the longest stretch (24 miles) of undeveloped beach on Florida's east coast. Fourteen endangered species make their home within Canaveral's boundaries.
Carol Clark, Superintendent

3221 **Chassahowitzka National Wildlife Refuge Complex**
1502 SE Kings Bay Drive 352-563-2088
Crystal River, FL 34429 Fax: 352-795-7961
chassahowitzka@fws.gov
chassahowitzka.fws.gov
A complex of 5 National Wildlife Refuges on the Gulf Coast of Florida including Crystal River NWR. Established in 1983 for the protection of the endangered West Indian manatee. Office hours are from 7:30 AM to 4:00 PM Monday thruFriday. The office is also open Saturdays and Sundays during the winter months (November 15 - March 31) please call the office at 352-563-2088 for more information.
James Kraus, Manager

3222 **Dry Torgus National Park & Everglades National Park**
P.O. Box 6208 305-242-7700
Key West, FL 33041 Fax: 305-242-7711
drto_information@nps.gov
www.nps.gov/drto
Recognized for its near-pristine natural resources including sea grass beds, fisheries, and sea turtle and nesting habit. The area also lays claim to a rich cultural heritage with a diverse array of themes. Fort Jefferson, on GardenKey, is the park's central cultural feature and one of the largest 19th century American masonry coastal forts.
Dan Kimball, Superintendent
Keith Whisenant, Deputy Superintendent

3223 **Egmont Key National Wildlife Refuge**
1502 SE Kings Bay Drive 352-563-2088
Crystal River, FL 34429 Fax: 352-795-7961
CrystalRiver@fws.gov
www.fws.gov/refuge/Egmont_Key
This barrier island refuge is approximately 350 acres and was established to provide nesting, feeding and resting habitat for brown pelicans and other migratory birds. The combined resources of the US Fish and Wildlife Service andFlorida Park Service provide protection for Egmont Key and its wildlife, as well as an enjoyable experience for the visitor.
James Kraus, Manager

3224 **Everglades National Park**
40001 State Road 9336 305-242-7700
Homestead, FL 33034-6733 Fax: 305-242-7711
EVER_Information@nps.gov
www.nps.gov/ever
The largest subtropical wilderness in the United States, boasts rare and endangered species. It has been designated a World Heritage Site, international Biosphere Reserve, and Wetland of International Importance, significant to allpeople of the world.
Dan Kimball, Superintendent
Keith Whisenant, Deputy Superintendent

3225 Florida Panther National Wildlife Refuge
12085 SR 29 South 239-657-8001
Suite 300 Fax: 239-657-8002
Immokalee, FL 34142 floridapanther@fws.gov
www.fws.gov/floridapanther
Mission: To conserve and manage lands and waters in concert with other agency efforts within the Big Cypress Watershed, primarily for the Florida Panther, other endangered and threatened species, natural diversity, and culturalresources for the benefit of the American people.
Layne Hamilton, Manager

3226 Hobe Sound National Wildlife Refuge and Nature Center
13640 U.S. Highway 1 772-546-6141
PO Box 645 Fax: 772-545-7572
Hobe Sound, FL 33475-645 hobesound@fws.gov
www.fws.gov/refuge/hobe_sound
Refuge objectives are to: maintain and restore diverse habitats designed to achieve refuge purposes and wildlife population objectives; maintain viable diverse populations of native flora and fauna consistent with sound biologicalprinciples; manage natural and cultural resources through land protection and partnership; and develop and implement wildlife dependent recreation and environmental education that leads to enjoyable recreation experiences and a greater understandingof resources.
Margo Stahl, Refuge Manager
Debbie Fritz-Quincy, Nature Center Director

3227 JN Darling National Wildlife Refuge
1 Wildlife Drive 239-472-1100
Sanibel, FL 33957 Fax: 239-472-4061
dingdarling@fws.gov
www.fws.gov/dingdarling
The refuge on Sanibel Island is a subtropical barrier island in the Gulf of Mexico hemmed by mangrove trees, shallow bays and white sandy beaches. The 6,300-acre refuge is connected to the mainland by a three-mile causeway. Named in1967 for Jay Norwood (Ding) Darling, an editorial cartoonist, pioneer conservationist and originator of the federal Duck Stamp Program. Darling, who was the first director of what is now the US Fish and Wildlife Service, wintered on neighboringCaptiva Island.
Paul Leader, Project Ledaer
Joyce Palmer, Deputy Refuge Mnanager

3228 Lake Woodruff National Wildlife Refuge
2045 Mud Lake Road 904-985-4673
DeLeon Springs, FL 32130 Fax: 904-985-0926
lakewoodruff@fws.gov
www.fws.gov/lakewoodruff
Encompasses two large lakes offering sights of diverse habitats and a variety of wildlife. Fishing and boating are the primary recreational activities.
Harold Morrow, Project Leader

3229 National Key Deer Refuge
28950 Watson Blvd. 305-872-2239
Big Pine Key Plaza Fax: 305-872-2154
Big Pine Key, FL 33043 keydeer@fws.gov
www.fws.gov/refuge/National_Key_Deer_Refuge
Refuge objectives are: to protect and preserve Key deer and other wildlife resources in the Florida Keys; to conserve endangered and threatened fish, wildlife and plants; to provide habitat and protection for migratory birds; and toprovide opportunities for environmental education and public viewing of refuge wildlife and habitats.
Anne Morkill, Manager

3230 Pelican Island National Wildlife Refuge
1339 20th Street 772-562-3909
Vero Beach, FL 32960 Fax: 772-299-3101
pelicanisland@fws.gov
www.fws.gov/pelicanisland
Charlie Pelizza, Refuge Manager
Nick Wirwa, Refuge Manager

3231 St. Marks National Wildlife Refuge
1255 Lighthouse Road 850-925-6121
St Marks, FL 32355 saintmarks@fws.gov
www.fws.gov/saintmarks
Saint Marks National Wildlife Refuge is in Wakulla, Jefferson and Taylor counties along the Gulf coast of north Florida. The refuge is approximately 25 miles south of Tallahassee. The refuge encompasses 65,000 acres of divided tidalflats; and freshwater impoundments harbor a large variety of wildlife, including 434 verebrate species, excluding fish. Over quarter million vistors enjoy a variety of outdoor recreation opportunities annually.

3232 St. Vincent National Wildlife Refuge
3100 County Road 30A 850-653-8808
Port St. Joe, FL 32456 Fax: 850-653-9893
saintvincent@fws.gov
www.fws.gov/saintvincent
The historic St Vincent National Wildlife Refuge is a large barrier island, four miles wide and nine miles long. It was inhabited as early as 240A.D. and is known to have been visited by Franciscan friars in the early 1600s. Over itshistory, private landowners developed the island into a preserve housing Asian and African wildlife and an assortment in between. The US Fish and Wildlife Service purchased the island in 1968 bringing an end to the exotic jungle.
Monica Harris, Manager

3233 Timucuan Ecological & Historic Preserve
12713 Fort Caroline Road 904-221-5568
Jacksonville, FL 32225 Fax: 904-221-5248
www.nps.gov/timu
The 46,000 acre Timucan Ecological and Historic Preserve was established to protect one of the last unspoiled coastal wetlands on the Atlantic Coast and to preserve historic and prehistoric sites within the area. The estuarineecosystem includes aslt marsh, coastal dunes, hardwood hammock, as well as salt, fresh, and brackish waters, all rich in native vegetation and animal life.
Barbara Goodman, Superintendent

Georgia: US Forests, Parks, Refuges

3234 Chattahoochee-Oconee National Forest
1755 Cleveland Highway 770-297-3000
Gainesville, GA 30501 Fax: 770-297-3011
www.fs.usda.gov/main/conf/
Together, these forest offer more than ten wilderness areas, six beaches, and thousands of acres of lakes and stream. The forest is real draw for history buffs, who can get absorbed in tracing events such as the Trail of Tears and manya Civil War battle.

3235 Cumberland Island National Seashore
101 Wheeler Street 912-882-4336
P.O. Box 1203 Fax: 912-882-2651
Saint Marys, GA 31558 www.nps.gov/cuis
Cumberland Island is 17.5 miles long and totals 36,415 acres of which 16,850 are marsh, mud flats, and todal crreks. Well know for its sea turtles, abundant shore bierds, dune fields, maritime forest, salt marshes, and historicstructures.

3236 Okefenokee National Wildlife Refuge
2700 Suwannee Canal Road 912-496-7836
Folkston, GA 31537 okefenokee@fws.gov
www.fws.gov/okefenokee
Okefenokee NWR was established in 1937 to preserve the 438,000 acre Okefenokee Swamp. Presently the refuge encompasses approximately 406,000 acres of which 353,000 are designated as Wilderness. Habitats include open wet prairies,cypress forests, scrub-shrub, oak hammocks and longleaf pine forests. The prosperity and survival of the swamp, and the species dependent on it, is directly tied to maintaining the integrity of complex ecological processes, including hydrology andfire.
Michael Lusk, Refuge Manager

3237 Piedmont National Wildlife Refuge
718 Juliette Road 478-986-5441
Hillsboro, GA 31038 Fax: 478-986-9646
piedmont@fws.gov
www.fws.gov/piedmont
35,000 acre national wildlife refuge with hiking trails, gravel roads throughout, wildlife drive, hunting and fishing opportunties, bird watching.

3238 Pinckney Island National Wild Refuge
Savannah Coastal Refuges
694 Beech Hill Lane 843-784-2468
Suite 10 Fax: 912-652-4385
Hardeeville, SC 29927 savannahcoastal@fws.gov
www.fws.gov/refuge/pinckney_island
A group of islands and small hammocks, the 4,053-acre refuge includes a variety of land types: saltmarsh, forestland, brushland, fallow fields and freshwater ponds. Pinckney, the largest of the refuge islands, is 3.8 miles long and1.75 miles across at its greatest width. Boaters who navigate the refuge's estuarine waters may view shore and wading birds, including the endangered wood stork, that feeds on mudflats, oysterbeds and shores.

3239 Savannah National Wildlife Refuge
694 Beech Hill Lane 843-784-2468
Suite 10 Fax: 912-652-4385
Hardeeville, SC 29927 savannacoastal@fws.gov
www.fws.gov/refuge/pinckney_island
Refuge objectives are to provide: a refuge and feeding ground for native birds and wild animals; habitat and protection for threatened and endangered plants and animals; habitat and sanctuary for migratory birds consistent with theobjectives of the Atlantic Flyway; habitats for other species of indigenous wildlife and fishery resources; management of furbearers, deer and other upland animals; and opportunities for environmental education, interpretation and recreation for thevisiting public.

Hawaii: US Forests, Parks, Refuges

3240 Haleakala National Park
PO Box 369 808-572-4400
Makawao, HI 96768 www.nps.gov/hale
The Park preserves the outstanding volcanic landscape of the upper slopes of Haleakala on the island of Maui and protects the unique and fragile ecosystems of Kipahulu Valley, the scenic pools along Oheo gulch, and many rare andendangered species. Haleakala National Park was designated an International Biosphere Reserve.

3241 Hawaii Volcanoes National Park
1 Crater Rim Drive 808-985-6000
PO Box 52 Fax: 808-985-6004
Hawaii National Park, HI 96718-52 www.nps.gov/havo
Established in 1916, this 333,000 acre National Park encompasses coastal lava plains, rain forests and deserts. It preserves and protects active volcanoes, rare and endangered plants and animals, and Hawaiian archeological sites.

3242 Huleia National Wildlife Refuge: Kauai
PO Box 1128 808-828-1413
Kilauea Fax: 808-828-6634
Kauai, HI 96754 jennifer_waipa@fws.gov
www.fws.gov/refuge/huleia/
Located on the southeast side of Kauai, lies adjacent to the famous Menehune Fish Pond, a registered National Historic Landmark. The Huleia Refuge is approximately 241 acres of wetlands which provides habitat for five endangeredHawaiian waterbirds.
Shannon Smith, Refuge Manager
Mike Mitchell, Deputy Refuge Manager

3243 James Campbell National Wildlife Refuge
Oahu Refuge Complex 808-637-6330
66-590 Kam Highway, Rm 2C Fax: 808-637-3578
Haleiwa, HI 96712 sylvia_pelissa@fws.gov
James Campbell NWR lies at the northernmost tip of Oahu near the community of Kahuku and serves as a strategic landfall for native and migratory birds coming from as far away as Alaska, Siberia, and Asia. The specific purpose of theRefuge is to provide habitat for Hawaii's four endemic, endangered waterbirds and other native wildlife, as well as migratory waterfowl and shorebirds. A total of 102 bird species have been documented on the Refuge since its creation.
Sylvia R Pelizza, Manager

3244 Kauai National Wildlife Refuge Complex
PO Box 1128 808-828-1413
Kilauea, HI 96754 Fax: 808-828-1414
Kauai is also known as the Garden Isle for its lush vegetation and spectacular waterfalls. It is the oldest of the Hawaiian islands chain and is approximately 553 square miles in size. The Kauai National Wildlife Refuge Complexconsists of Kilauea Point, Hanalei, and Huleia National Wildlife Refuges.

3245 Kealia Pond National Wildlife Refuge
300 Ala Moana Boulevard 808-792-9400
Room 3-122, Box 50088 Fax: 808-792-9580
Honolulu, HI 96850 www.fws.gov/pacificislands
Glynnis Nakai, Manager

3246 Kilauea Point National Wildlife Refuge
PO Box 1128 808-828-1413
Kilauea, HI 96754 Fax: 808-828-1414
This National Wildlife Refuge provides nesting habitat for seabirds; notably red-footed boobies, Laysan albatross and wedge-tailed shearwaters. The Refuge is also home to the historic Kilauea Point Lighthouse and native marine coastalplant communities. In winter, the 180 foot high precipice provides an ideal site for viewing humpback whales in offshore waters.
Mike Hawkes, Refuge Manager

3247 Oahu National Wildlife Refuge Complex
66-590 Kamehameha Highway 808-637-6330
Room 2C Fax: 808-637-3578
Haleiwa, HI 96712 www.fws.gov/pacificislands
Sylvia Pelizza, Manager

3248 Pearl Harbor National Wildlife Refuge
66-590 Kamehameha Highway 808-637-6330
Room 2C Fax: 808-637-3578
Haleiwa, HI 96712 www.fws.gov/pacificislands
Sylvia Pelizza, Manager

Idaho: US Forests, Parks, Refuges

3249 Bear Lake National Wildlife Refuge
322 North 4th St. 208-847-1757
Montpelier, ID 83254-1019 Fax: 208-847-1319
annette_deknijf@fws.gov
www.fws.gov/refuge/bear_lake/
18,000 acres of marsh and uplands north of Bear Lake proper. Approx 7 miles south of Montpelier. White-faced ibis, Franklin's gulls, sandhill cranes, lots of ducks, Canada geese, Trumpeter swans.
Annette deKniff, Refuge Manager

3250 Boise National Forest
1249 S Vinnell Way 208-373-4100
Boise, ID 83709 r4_boise_info@fs.fed.us
www.fs.usda.gov/boise
The predominantly Ponderosa pine and Douglas fir ecosystem provides homes for fish and wildlife; fiber for wood and paper products; forage for cows and sheep; precious metals for industrial and personal use; and an unlimited menu ofyear round opportunities. The Boise National Forest also contains a number of unique sites, including the Experimental Forest, the Lucky Peak Nursery and Bogus Basin Ski Area.

3251 Camas National Wildlife Refuge Southeast Idaho Refuge Complex
2150 E 2350 N 208-662-5423
Hamer, ID 83425 www.fws.gov/pacific/refuges
Cama NWR is 36 miles north of Idaho Falls in southeast Idaho, in the Cama Creek floodplain. Elevation is 4,800 feet. About half of its acreage consists of lakes, ponds and marshlands; the remainder is grass sagebrush uplands, meadowsand farm fields. Camas Creek flows for 8 miles through the length of the refuge and is the source of water for many of the lakes and ponds. Tall cottonwood trees along the creek attract a wide variety of songbirds.

3252 Caribou-Targhee National Forest
1405 Hollipark Drive 208-524-7500
Idaho Falls, ID 83401 jjbennett@fs.fed.us
www.fs.usda.gov/ctnf
The Caribou National Forest was created to help preserve wilderness land in an area marked by mining activity and westward migration. The forest now covers more than 1 million acres in southeast Idaho, with small portions in Utah andWyoming. Several north-south mountain ranges of the Overthrust Belt dominate the landscape. Caribou National Park offers a wide variety of outdoor activities, including camping, hiking, fishing, climbing, skiing and horseback riding.
Larry Timchak, Supervisor
Lynn Ballard, Public Affairs

3253 Clearwater National Forest
903 3rd Street 208-935-2513
Kamiah, ID 83536 Fax: 208-476-8329
www.fs.usda.gov/nezperceclearwater/
The Clearwater National Forest covers 1.8 million acres from the jagged peaks of the Bitterroot Mountains in the east to the river canyons and rolling hills of the Palouse Prairie in the west. The North Fork of the Clearwater & theLochsa rivers provide miles of tumbling white water interspersed with quiet pools for migratory and resident fish. The mountains provide habitat for elk, moose, whitetail & mule deer, gray wolf, cougar, mountain goats, and many smaller mammals.
Tom Reilly, Forest Supervisor
Kimberly Nelson, Public Affairs

3254 Craters of the Moon National Monument & Preserve
PO Box 29 208-527-3257
Arco, ID 83213 Fax: 208-527-3073
www.nps.gov/crmo
A sea of lava flows with scattered islands of cinder cones and sagebrush characterizes this wierd and scenic landscape known as Craters of the Moon. Craters of the Moon National Monument and Preserve contains three young lava fieldscovering almost half a million acres. These remarkably well preserved volcanic features resulted from geologic events that appear to have happened yesterday and will likely continue tomorrow.

3255 Deer Flat National Wildlife Refuge
13751 Upper Embankment Road 208-467-9278
Nampa, ID 83686 Fax: 208-467-1019
deerflat@fws.gov
www.fws.gov/refuge/deer_flat/
One of the nation's oldest refuges. It includes the Lake Lowell sector and the Snake River Islands sector. The refuge provides a mix of wildlife habitats, including open waters, wetland edges around the lake, sagebrush uplands,grasslands and riparian forests. More than 250 birds and 30 mammals have been seen on the refuge, providing excellent wildlife observation and photography opportunities.

3256 Grays Lake National Wildlife Refuge
74 Grays Lake Road 208-574-2755
Wayan, ID 83285 www.fws.gov/pacific/refuges
Twenty-seven miles north of Soda Springs in southeast Idaho, the refuge lies in a high mountain valley at 6,400 feet. Grays Lake is actually a large, shallow marsh with dense vegetation and little open water. Most of the marshvegetation is bulrush and cattail. Adjacent lands are primarily wet meadows and grasslands.

3257 Idaho Panhandle National Forest
3815 Schreiber Way 208-765-7223
Coeur d'Alene, ID 83815 Fax: 208-765-7307
www.fs.usda.gov/ipnf/

3258 Kootenai National Wildlife Refuge
287 Westside Rd 208-267-3888
Bonners Ferry, ID 83805 Fax: 208-267-5570
fw1KootenaiNWR@fws.gov
www.fws.gov/refuge/kootenai
The 2,774 acre refuge is located in the northern panhandle of Idaho, and serves as a resting and feeding area for migratory birds.

3259 Minidoka National Wildlife Refuge
961 E Minidoka Dam 208-436-3589
Rupert, ID 83350 www.fws.gov/pacific/refuges
Lying 12 miles northeast of Rupert in the Snake River Valley in south-central Idaho, the refuge extends upstream about 25 miles from the Minidoka Dam along both shores of the Snake River and includes all of Lake Walcott. Over half therefuge is open water, with some small marsh area.

3260 Nez Perce National Forest
1005 Highway 13 208-983-1950
Grangeville, ID 83530 Fax: 208-983-4099
www.fs.fed.us/r1/nezperce
The Forest is best known for its wild character. Nearly half of the Forest is designated wilderness. It also sports two rivers popular with thrill-seeking floaters-the Selway and the Salmon.
Jane Cottrell, Forest Supervisor

3261 Payette National Forest
500 N Mission St Building 2 208-634-0700
McCall, ID 83638 webmaster@fs.fed.us
www.fs.usda.gov/payette/
Payette National Forest spans over 2.3 million acres of some of west-central Idaho's most beautiful and diverse country. In one day you can travel from hot desert grasslands through cool conifer forests to snow-capped peaks. Thespecacular land is bordered by two of the deepest canyons in North America— the Salmon River Canyon On the north and Hells Canyon of the Sake River on

the west. To the east lies 2.4 million-acre the largest Congressionally designated wilderness inthe lower 48 states.
Suzanne Rainville, Forest Supervisor

3262 Sawtooth National Forest
2647 Kimberly Road E 208-737-3200
Twin Falls, ID 83301-7976 Fax: 208-737-3236
www.fs.usda.gov/sawtooth/
The Sawtooth National Forest encompasses 2.1 million acres of some of the nation's most magnificent country. Managed and protected by the US Department of Agriculture's Forest Service, the Sawtooth National Forest is working, producingforest that has been providing goods and services to the American people since its establishment in 1905.
Jane Kollmeyer, Forest Supervisor

3263 Southeast Idaho National Wildlife Refuge Complex
4425 Burley Drive 208-237-6615
Suite A
Chubbuck, ID 83202

Illinois: US Forests, Parks, Refuges

3264 Mark Twain National Wildlife Refuge Complex
1704 N 24th Street 217-224-8580
Quincy, IL 62301 Dick_Steinbach@fws.gov
www.fws.gov/Midwest/planning/marktwain
Administrative office over five refuges; Port Louisa NWR, Great River NWR, Clarence Common NWR, Two Rivers NWR, and Middle Mississippi River NWR.
Richard Steinbach, Manager

3265 Shawnee National Forest
50 Highway 145 South 618-253-7114
Harrisburg, IL 62946 800-699-6637
Fax: 618-253-1060
www.fs.usda.gov/shawnee/
The Shawnee National Forest lies in the rough, unglaciated areas known as the Illinois Ozark and Shawnee Hills. The geology is spectacular and divergent, with numerous stone bluffs and overlooks transcending to lowland areas.
Rebecca Banker, Public Affairs

3266 Upper Mississippi River National Wildlife & Fish Refuge: Savanna District
Riverview Road 815-273-2732
Thomson, IL 61285 Fax: 815-273-2960
uppermississippiriver@fws.gov
www.fws.gov/refuge/upper_mississippi_river
The Upper Mississippi River National Wildlife and Fish Refuge covers nearly 240,000 acres and extends along 281 miles of the Mississippi River. This Refuge is home to a diverse collection of wildlife, including bald eagles, great blueherons, sandhill cranes and spectacular concentrations of waterfowl. Local residents and visitors enjoy a wide array of opportunties throughout the year such as fishing, hunting, wildlife observation, photography, interpretation and environmentaleducation.
Sabrina Chandler, Refuge Manager
Timothy Yager, Assistant Refuge Manager

Indiana: US Forests, Parks, Refuges

3267 Indiana Dunes National Lakeshore
1100 N Mineral Springs Road 219-926-7561
Porter, IN 46304 Fax: 219-395-1767
www.nps.gov/indu
Indiana Dunes National Lakeshore, authorized by Congress in 1996, is located approximately 50 miles southeast of Chicago, Illinois in the counties of Lake, Porter and LaPorte in Northwest Indiana. The national lakeshore runs for nearly25 miles along southern Lake Michigan, bordered by Michigan City, Indiana on the east and Gary on the west. The park contains approximately 15,000 acres, 2,182 of which are located in Indiana Dunes State Park managed by the Indiana Department ofNatural Resources.

Iowa: US Forests, Parks, Refuges

3268 DeSoto National Wildlife Refuge
1434 316th Lane 712-388-4800
Missouri Valley, IA 51555 Fax: 712-388-4808
DeSoto@fws.gov
www.fws.gov/refuge/desoto
DeSoto Refuge is located along the Missouri River, 25 miles north of Omaha, NE. Popular activities include fishing, picnicking, mushroom-picking, hiking, boating, and wildlife observation. Peak viewing of 500,000 waterfowl inmid-November. The DeSoto Visitor Center houses over 200,000 artifacts from the 1860's steamboat Bertrand.
Larry Klimek, Refuge Manager
Mindy Sheets, Assistant Refuge Manager

3269 McGregor District Upper: Mississippi River National Wildlife & Fish Refuge
PO Box 460 563-873-3423
McGregor, IA 52157 Fax: 563-873-3803
uppermississippiriver@fws.gov
www.fws.gov/midwest/uppermississippiriver
Sabrina Chandler, Refuge Manager
Timothy Yager, Assistant Refuge Manager

Kansas: US Forests, Parks, Refuges

3270 Kirwin National Wildlife Refuge
702 East Xavier Road 785-543-6673
Kirwin, KS 67644 kirwin@fws.gov
www.fws.gov/refuge/kirwin
Brad Krohn, Refuge Manager
Melisa Johnson, Budget Technician

Kentucky: US Forests, Parks, Refuges

3271 Daniel Boone National Forest
1700 Bypass Road 859-745-3100
Winchester, KY 40391 Fax: 859-744-1568
www.fs.usda.gov/dbnf/
The mission is to achive quality land management under the sustainable multiple-use management concept to meer the diverse need of people.

3272 Mammoth Cave National Park
1 Mammoth Cave Parkway 270-758-2180
PO Box 7 MACA_Park_information@nps.gov
Mammoth Cave, KY 42259 www.nps.gov/maca
Established to preserve the cave system, including Mammoth Cave, the scenic river valleys of the Green and Nolin Rivers, and a section of the hilly country of south central Kentucky. This is the longest recorded cave system in theworld with more than 360 miles explored and mapped. Established July 1, 1941. Designated a World Heritage Site October 27, 1981. Designated a Biosphere Reserve in 1990.
Patrick Reed, Superintendent
Bruce Powell, Deputy Superintendent

Louisiana: US Forests, Parks, Refuges

3273 Atchafalaya National Wildlife Refuge
PO Box 127 318-566-2251
Krotz Springs, LA 70750 www.fws.gov/atchafalaya
The State of Louisiana's Sherburne Wildlife Management Area is located in the upper third of the Atchafalaya River Basin between Interstate Highway 10 and US Highway 190. It covers approximately 11,780 acres and was established in 1983by the Louisiana Department of Wildlife and Fisheries. The area supervisor's headquaters is located east of Krotz Springs, Louisiana, on LA 975 approximately three miles south of US Highway 190.

3274 Cameron Prairie National Wildlife Refuge
3599 Bayou Black Drive 985-853-1078
Houma, LA 70630 Fax: 985-853-1079
southeastlouisianarefuges@fws.gov
The refuge contains 9,621 acres of fresh marsh, coastal prairie and old rice fields. East Cove Unit of the refuge contains 14,927 acres of brackish and salt marsh. Seasonal visitors include the Peregrine falcon, alligators, whitetailed deer, wading and shorebirds, ducks and geese and various migratory birds.
Glen Harris, Manager

3275 Catahoula National Wildlife Refuge
P.O. Box 120 318-992-5261
Rhinehart, LA 71363-201 Fax: 318-992-6023
catahoula@fws.gov
catahoula.fws.gov
The objectives of the refuge are: to provide wintering habitat for migratory waterfowl consistent with Mississippi Flyway objectives; to provide habitat and protection for endangered species; preserve bottomland hardwoods and providehabitat necessary for wildlife diversity; provide opportunities for environmental education, interpretation and wildlife oriented recreation.
Greg Harper, Manager

3276 D'Arbonne National Wildlife Refuge
11372 Highway 143 318-726-4400
Farmerville, LA 71363 Fax: 318-726-4667
northlarefuges@fws.gov
www.fws.gov/darbonne
The Refuge provides habitat for a diversity of migratory birds and resident wildlife species, provides habitat and protection for endangered species such as the bald eagle, wood stork and red-cockaded woodpecker and providesopportunities for wildlife-oriented recreation, environmental education and interpretation.
Kelby Ouchley, Manager

3277 Kisatchie National Forest
2500 Shreveport Highway 318-473-7160
Pineville, LA 71360-2009 www.fs.usda.gov/kisatchie
The Kisatchie National Forest has a lot to offer vistors, such as 355 miles of trails for hiking, camping, mountain biking, horseback riding, ORV riding. Other recreational opportunites include four lakes, an 8700 acre Wilderness anddozens of caming sites. The forest also provides opportunities to hunt and fish.

3278 Lacassine National Wildlife Refuge
209 Nature Road 337-774-5923
Lake Arthur, LA 70549 Fax: 337-774-9913
lacassine@fws.gov
www.fws.gov/swlarefugecomplex/lacassine
The nearly 35,000 acre refuge is mostly freshwater marsh habitat. It preserves one of the major wintering grounds for waterfowl in the US. Wintering populations of ducks and geese at Lacassine are among the largest in the NationalWildlife Refuge System. Portions of the refuge are open year-round from one hour before sunrise until one hour after sunset. Please consult refuge brochures or contact the refuge office for more details. A vicinity map and refuge map are available.
Larry Narcisse, Manager

3279 Sabine National Wildlife Refuge
3000 Holly Beach Highway 337-762-3816
Hackberry, LA 70645 Fax: 337-762-3780
sabine@fws.gov
www.fws.gov/sabine/
The objectives of the refuge is to provide habitat for migratory waterfowl and other birds, to preserve and enhance coastal marshes for fish and wildlife, and to provide outdoor recreation and environmental education for the public.
Don Voros, Project Manager
Terence Delaine, Refuge Manager

Maine: US Forests, Parks, Refuges

3280 Acadia National Park
20 McFarland Hill Drive 207-288-8800
PO Box 177 Fax: 208-288-8813
Bar Harbor, ME 00460-177 Acadia_Information@nps.gov
www.nps.gov/acad/faqs.htm
The purpose of the commission is to consult with the Secretary of the Interior, or his designee, on matters relating to the management and development of the park, including but not liited to the acquisition of lands and interests inlands and termination of rights of use and occupancy.

3281 Sunkhaze Meadows National Wildlife Refuge
PO Box 453 207-827-6138
Old Town, ME 00446 Fax: 207-827-6099
FriendsofSunkhazeNWR@gmail.com
www.sunkhaze.org
Sunkhaze Meadows NWR was established to protect a large peat bog and its associated wildlife. There are three divisions of the refuge, totalling 11,772 acres. The areas are open to wildlife-dependent recreation.

Maryland: US Forests, Parks, Refuges

3282 Antietam National Battlefield
PO Box 158 301-432-5124
Sharpsburg, MD 21782 Fax: 301-432-4590
www.nps.gov/anti

3283 Assateague Island National Seashore
7206 National Seashore Lane 410-641-1441
Berlin, MD 21811 Fax: 410-641-1099
www.nps.gov
Natural resource management and environmental education related to coastal resources in general and Assateague Island in particular.
Trish Kicklighter, Superintendent

3284 Patuxent Research Refuge
230 Bald Eagle Drive 301-497-5770
Laurel, MD 20724 Fax: 301-497-5515
Jennifer_Hill@fws.gov
www.fws.gov/refuge/Patuxent
One of over 500 refuges in the National Wildlife Refuge System, a network of lands and waters specifically for the protection of wildlife and wildlife habitat.
Brad Knudsen, Project Leader/Manager

Massachusetts: US Forests, Parks, Refuges

3285 **Boston National Historical Park**
Charleston Navy Yard 617-242-5642
Boston, MA 02212 Fax: 617-242-6006
www.nps.gov/bost
Boston National Historical Park tells the story of the events that led to the American Revolution and the Navy that kept the nation strong.

3286 **Cape Cod National Seashore**
99 Marconi Station Site Road 508-349-3785
Wellfleet, MA 00266 Fax: 508-349-9052
CACO_Superintendent@nps.gov
www.nps.gov
Cape Cod National Seashore comprises 43,604 acres of shoreline and upland landscape features, including a forty-mile long stretch of pristine sandy beach, dozens of clear, deep, freshwater kettle ponds, and upland scenes that depictevidence of how people have used the land. A variety of historic structures are within the boundary of the Seashore, including lighthouses, a lifesaving station, and numerous Cape Cod style houses.

3287 **Great Meadows National Wildlife Refuge**
73 Weir Hill Road 978-443-4661
Sudbury, MA 00177 Fax: 978-443-2898
fw5rw_emnwr@fws.gov
www.fws.gov/refuge/great_meadows
The Sudbury office serves as the headquarters for the eight refuge Eastern Massachusetts National Wildlife Refuge Complex. Public use opportunities are available at a number of the complex's refuges.
Libby Herland, Complex Manager

3288 **Silvio O Conte National Fish & Wildlife Refuge**
2 Avenue A 413-863-3676
Turners Falls, MA 00137 Fax: 802-962-5006
www.fws.gov/refuge/Silvio_O_Conte
The Connecticut River Watershed, 7.2 million acres in four states, is larger and more heavily populated than areas usually considered when creating a refuge. The refuge's purposes are also much broader than usual. The new scientificand social challenge of protecting natural diversity cannot be met by land acquistion alone. The refuge's primary action is to involve people of the watershed, especially landowners and land managers, in environmental education programs andcooperative management.

Michigan: US Forests, Parks, Refuges

3289 **Hiawatha National Forest**
2727 North Lincoln Road 906-786-4062
Escanaba, MI 49829 Fax: 906-789-3311
www.fs.fed.us/r9/forests/hiawatha
Located in the central and easter Upper Peninsula of Michigan, the firest affords visitors access to white sand, scenic beaches and relatively undeveloped shorelines along three of Americas's Inland Seas, Lake Superior, Michigan andHuron.

3290 **Huron-Manistee National Forest**
1755 S Mitchell Street 231-775-2421
Cadillac, MI 49601 800-821-6263
Fax: 231-775-5551
www.fs.usda.gov/hmnf/
The Huron-Manistee National Forest comprise almost a million acres of public lands extending across the northern lower peninsula of Michigan. The Huron-Manistee national Forest provide recreation opportunities for visitors, habitat forfish and wildlife, and resources for local industry.

3291 **Ottawa National Forest**
E6248 US Highway 2 906-932-1330
Ironwood, MI 49938 Fax: 906-932-0122
www.fs.usda.gov/ottawa/
The almost one million acres of the Ottawa National Forest are located in the western Upper Peninsula of Michigan. It extends from the south shore of Lake Superior down to Wisconsin and the Nicolet National Forest. The area is rich inwildlife viewing opportunities; topography in the northern portion is the most dramatic with breathtaking views of rolling hills dotted with lakes, rivers and spectacular waterfalls.

3292 **Pictured Rocks National Lakeshore**
N8391 Sand Point Road 906-387-2607
PO Box 40 Fax: 906-387-4025
Munising, MI 49862 www.nps.gov
Multicolored sandstone cliffs, beaches, and dunes, waterfalls, inland lakes, wildlife and the forest of Lake Superior shoreline beckon visitors to explore this 73,000+ acre park. Attractions include a lighthouse and former Coast Guardlife-saving stations along with old farmsteads and orchards. The park is a four season recreational destination where hiking, camping, hunting, nature study, and winter activities abound.

3293 **Seney National Wildlife Refuge**
1674 Refuge Entrance Road 906-586-9851
Seney, MI 49883 Fax: 906-586-3800
seney@fws.gov
www.fws.gov/refuge/seney
Seney National Wildlife Refuge was established as a refuge and breeding ground for migratory birds and other wildlife. Today, Seney supports a variety of wildlife, including protected and reintroduced species. Bald eagles, commonloons, and trumpeter swans are regularly seen during the summer months, especially June and July, when they are raising their young.
Sara Siekierski, Refuge Manager
Greg McClellan, Assistant Refuge manager

3294 **Shiawassee National Wildlife Refuge**
6975 Mower Road 989-777-5930
Saginaw, MI 48601 Fax: 989-777-9200
shiawassee@fws.gov
www.fws.gov/refuge/Shiawassee
The refuge is comprised of over 9400 acres of wetlands, uplands, and bottomland hardwood forests. Four rivers flow through. Over 12 miles of hiking trails, bank fishing sites, and two photography blinds are available. Environmentaleducation progrms are offered at Green Point Environmental Learning Center in Saginaw.
Steve Kahl, Manager
Ed DeVries, Assistant Manager

3295 **Sleeping Bear Dunes National Lakeshore**
9922 Front Street 231-326-5134
Empire, MI 49630 Fax: 231-326-5382
www.nps.gov/slbe
Sleeping Bear Dunes National Lakeshore encompasses a 60 km stretch of Lake Michigan's eastern coastline, as well as North and South Manitou Islands. The park was established primarily for its outstanding natural features, includingforests, beaches, dune formations and ancient glacial phenomena. The Lakeshore also contains many cultural features including an 1871 lighthouse, three former Life-Saving Service (Coast Guard) Stations and an extensive rural historic farm district.

Minnesota: US Forests, Parks, Refuges

3296 **Agassiz National Wildlife Refuge**
22996 290th Street Northeast 218-449-4115
Middle River, MN 56737-9653 Fax: 218-449-3241
agassiz@fws.gov
www.fws.gov/refuge/agassiz

The National Refuge provides resting, nesting and feeding habitat for waterfowl and other migratory birds. Agassiz NWR is designated a Globally Important Bird Area by the American Bird Conservancy. It protects endangered and threatenedspecies. It also provides for biodiversity, public opportunities for outdoor recreation and environmental education.
Margaret Anderson, Manager

3297 Big Stone National Wildlife Refuge
44843 County Road 19 320-273-2191
Odessa, MN 56276 Fax: 320-273-2231
BigStone@fws.gov
www.fws.gov/refuge/big_stone
Fig Stone NWR is one of more than 545 National Wildlife Refuges administered as part of the National Wildlife Refuge System by the US Fish and Wildlife Service. The Refuge now overlays 11,585.8 acres of the Minnesota River Valley inwestern Minnesota. A unique visual and geological feature of the Refuge is the red, lichen covered granite outcrops for which the Refuge was named. The Refuge offers an auto tour route, nature trails, wildlife observation, hunting and fishingopportunities.
Alice Hanley, Manager

3298 Chippewa National Forest
200 Ash Avenue Northwest 218-335-8600
Cass Lake, MN 56633 www.fs.fed.us/r9/chippewa/
The Chippewa was the first National Forest established east of the Mississippi. The Forest boundary encompasses 1.6 millon, of which over 666,618 acres are managed by the USDA Forest Service. Aspen, birch, pines, balsam fir and maplesblanket the uplands. Water is abundant, with over 1300 lakes, 923 miles of rivers and streams, and 400,000 acres of wetlands.
Robert M Harper, Forest Supervisor

3299 Crane Meadows National Wildlife Refuge
19502 Iris Road 320-632-1575
Little Falls, MN 56345 Fax: 320-632-5471
cranemeadows@fws.gov
www.fws.gov/refuge/crane_meadows
Crane Meadows National Wildlife Refuge was established in 1992 to preserve a large, natural wetland complex. The refuge is located in central Minnesota and serves as an important stop for many species of migrating birds.

3300 Detroit Lakes Wetland Management District
26624 N Tower Road 218-847-4431
Detroit Lakes, MN 56501 Fax: 218-847-4156
DetroitLakes@fws.gov
www.fws.gov/Midwest.detroitlakes/
The district covers approximately 6000 square miles. From east to west, these are: the Red River Valley floodplain, the glacial moraine/prairie pothole region, and the hardwood/coniferous forest. Land acquisition and managementefforts are focused in the prairie pothole region of the WMD, with a goal of providing habitat for nesting waterfowl.
Scott Kahan, Manager

3301 Mille Lacs National Wildlife Refuge
36289 State Highway 65 218-768-2402
McGregor, MN 55760 Fax: 218-768-3040
ricelake@fws.gov
www.fws.gov/refuge/mille_lacs
Comprised of two small islands in Mille Lacs Lake in central Minnesota. The islands are boulder and gravel outcrops for colonial nesting birds including common terns and ring-billed gulls.
Walt Ford, Manager

3302 Minnesota Valley National Wildlife Refuge
3815 American Blvd East 612-854-5900
Bloomington, MN 55425 Fax: 612-725-3279
minnesotavalley@fws.gov
www.fws.gov/refuge/minnesota_valley
Mission: To restore and manage the ecological communities of the Lower Minnesota River Valley and its watershed while providing environmental education and wildlife dependent recreation.
Thomas Larson, Manager

3303 Rice Lake National Wildlife Refuge
36289 State Highway 65 218-768-2402
McGregor, MN 55760 Fax: 218-768-3040
ricelakes@fws.gov
www.fws.gov/refuge/rice_lake
Walt Ford, Manager

3304 Rydell National Wildlife Refuge
17788 349th Street Southeast 218-687-2229
Erskine, MN 56535 Fax: 218-687-2225
dave_bennett@fws.gov
Dave Bennett, Manager

3305 Sherburne National Wildlife Refuge
17076 293rd Avenue 763-389-3323
Zimmerman, MN 55398 Fax: 763-389-3493
sherburne@fws.gov
Mission: To represent a diverse biological community characteristic of the transition zone between tallgrass prairie and forest.

3306 Superior National Forest
8901 Grand Avenue Place 218-626-4300
Duluth, MN 55808 Fax: 218-626-4398
www.fs.usda.gov/superior/
Located in northeastern tip of Minnesota, the Superior National Forest stretches 150 miles along the US-Canadian border, encompassing 3.85 million acres. This hilly deep pine forest is home to moose, wolves, black bears, loons andmigratory birds. More than 2,250 miles of stream flow within the forest, including the renowned Boundary Waters Canoe Area, where you can canoe, portage and camp in the spirit of the French Canadian voyagers of 200 years ago.
Jim Sanders, Forest Supervisor

3307 Tamarac National Wildlife Refuge
35704 County Highway 26 218-847-2641
Rochert, MN 56578 Fax: 218-847-9141
tamarac@fws.gov
www.fws.gov/refuge/tamarac
Established in 1938, Tamarac Refuge is dedicated to providing a breeding ground and sanctuary for migratory birds and other wildlife. Situated at a unique transitional zone where hardwood forest, boreal forest and tallgrass prairiemeets. Tamarac provides boundless opportunities for visitors to observe wildlife in their natural surroundings. Spring and fall migrations of songbirds and waterfowl can be spectacular. Their visitor center offers interpretive displays and programs.

3308 Voyageurs National Park
360 Highway 11 East 218-283-6600
International Falls, MN 56649 Fax: 218-285-7407
www.nps.gov/voya
The park lies in the southern part of the Canadian Shield, representing some of the oldest exposed rock formations in the world. This bedrock has been shaped and carved by at least four periods of glaciation. The topography of the parkis rugged and varied; rolling hills are interspersed between bogs, beaver ponds, swamps, islands, small lakes and four large lakes.

3309 Winona District National Wildlife Refuge Upper Mississippi River National Wildlife and Fish
51 E 4th Street 507-452-4232
Winona, MN 55987 Fax: 507-452-0851
uppermississippiriver@fws.gov
www.fws.gov/refuge/upper_mississippi_river

Refuge objectives are to: protect and preserve one of America's premier fish and wildlife areas; provide habitat for migratory birds, fish, plants and resident wildlife; protect and enhance habitat for endangered species; provideinterpretation, environmental education and wildlife-oriented recreational public use opportunities; and conserve a diversity of plant life.
Sabira Chandler, Refugee Manager
Timothy Yager, Asst. Refuge Manager

Mississippi: US Forests, Parks, Refuges

3310 Bienville National Forest
200 S. Lamar St. 601-965-1600
Suite 500-N www.fs.usda.gov/mississippi/
Jackson, MS 39201
The forest offers camping, picnicking, swimming, hiking, fishing and historic sites. Bienville boasts the largest known cluster of old growth pine forest in Mississippi in the 180-acre Bienville Pines Scenic Area. Here visitors canwander among towering loblolly and shortleaf pines, many more than two centuries old. The 23-mile Shockaloe Horse Trail, a national recreation trail, starts near the town of Forest.

3311 Mississippi Sandhill Crane National Wildlife Refuge
7200 Crane Lane 228-497-6322
Gautier, MS 39553 Fax: 228-497-5407
mississippisandhillcrane@fws.gov
www.fws.gov/refuge/mississippi_sandhill_crane
Located in southeast Mississippi in Jackson County, the refuge was established to protect the endangered Mississippi Sandhill Cranes and the wet pine savanna habitat they prefer. The refuge features exhibits, informational videos, anda walking trail where you can view carnivorous plants.
Jereme Phillips, Complex Manager
Danny Moss, Refuge Manager

3312 Noxubee National Wildlife Refuge
13723 Bluff Lake Road 662-323-5548
Brooksville, MS 39739 Fax: 662-323-6390
noxubee@fws.gov
Established in 1940 to protect and enhance habitat for the conservation of migratory birds, endangered species and other wildlife. The recreational and educational opportunities provided on the refuge help the public experience natureand learn how sound management ensures that future generations continue to enjoy fish and wildlife and their habitats.

3313 Panther Swamp National Wildlife Refuge
12595 Mississippi Highway 149 662-836-3004
Yazoo City, MS 39194 Fax: 662-836-3009
yazoo@fws.gov
www.fws.gov/refuge/panther_swamp
Refuge objectives are: to provide resting, nesting and feeding habitat for waterfowl and other migratory birds; to provide habitat for resident wildlife; to protect endangered and threatened species; and to provide public useopportunities for outdoor recreation and environmental education.
Bo Sloan, Refuge Manager

Missouri: US Forests, Parks, Refuges

3314 Mark Twain National Forest
401 Fairgrounds Road 573-364-4621
Rollo, MO 65401 Fax: 573-364-6844
www.fs.fed.us/r9/forests/marktwain
The Mark Twain National forest is located in southern and central Missouri, and extends from the St Francois Mountains in the southeast to glades in the southwest, from the southwest, from the prairie lands the Missouri River to thenation's most ancient mountains in the south.

3315 Mingo National Wildlife Refuge
24279 State Highway 51 573-222-3589
Puxico, MO 63960 Fax: 573-222-6343
mingo@fws.gov
www.fws.gov/refuge/mingo
Established as a resting and wintering area for migratory waterfowl and other birds. The 21,592-acre Refuge contains approximately 15,000 acres of bottomland hardwood forest, 3,500 acres of marsh and water, 506 acres of cropland, 704acres of seasonally flooded impoundments, and 474 acres of grassy openings.

3316 Ozark National Scenic Riverways
404 Watercress Drive 573-323-4236
PO Box 490 Fax: 573-323-4140
Van Buren, MO 63965 ozar_superintendent@nps.gov
www.nps.gov/ozar
Missouri's largest National Park and America's first to preserve a free flowing river in its wild state. Covers some 80,000 acres along 134 miles of the Current and Jacks Fork Rivers. Staff provide elementary level environmentaleducation programs on natural history, with an emphasis on karst and water issues. Publishes More Than Skin Deep, a Teacher's Guide to Caves and Groundwater, a curriculum guide suitable for grades K-12.

3317 Swan Lake National Wildlife Refuge
16194 Swan Lake Avenue 660-856-3323
Sumner, MO 64681 Fax: 660-856-3687
john_benson@fws.gov
www.fws.gov/refuge/swan_lake
Steve Whitson, Project Director

Montana: US Forests, Parks, Refuges

3318 Beaverhead-Deerlodge National Forest
200 East Broadway 406-329-3511
P.O. Box 7669 Fax: 406-329-3347
Missoula, MT 59807-7669 www.fs.usda.gov/r1
Bruce Ramsey, Forest Supervisor
Thomas D Osen, District Ranger

3319 Benton Lake National Wildlife Refuge
922 Bootlegger Trail 406-727-7400
Great Falls, MT 59404 Fax: 406-727-7432
bentonlake@fws.gov
www.fws.gov/refuge/benton_lake
Kathleen Burchett, Project Leader
Robert F Johnson Jr, Deputy Manager

3320 Bighorn Canyon National Recreation Area
5 Avenue B 406-666-2412
PO Box 7458 Fax: 406-666-2415
Fort Smith, MT 59035-7458 www.nps.gov/bica
This dam, named after the famous Crow chairman Robert Yellowtail, harnessed the waters of the Bighorn River and turned this variable stream into a magnificent lake. The Afterbay Lake below the Yellowtail Dam is a good spot for troutfishing and wildlife viewing for ducks, geese and other animals. The Bighorn River below the Afterbay Dam is a world class trout fishing area. Bighorn Canyon National Recreation Area boasts breath-takign scenery, countless varieties of wildlife.

3321 Bitterroot National Forest
1801 N First Street 406-363-7100
Hamilton, MT 59840 Fax: 406-363-7106
rl_bitterroot_comments@fs.fed.us
www.fs.fed.us
The 1.6 million acre Bitterroot National Forest, in west central Montana and east central Idaho, is part of the Norther Rocky Mountains. National Forest land begins above the foothills of the

Bitterroot River Valley in two mountainranges—the Bitterroot Mountains on the west and the Sapphire Mountains on the east side of the valley.

3322 **Bowdoin National Wildlife Refuge: Refuge Manager**
194 Bowdoin Auto Tour Road 406-654-2863
Malta, MT 59538 Fax: 406-654-2866
bowdoin@fws.gov
www.fws.gov/refuge/bowdoin
Bowdoin National Wildlife Refuge was established in 1936 as a migratory bird refuge. It is located in the short and mixed greens prairie region of North-central Montana and encompasses 15,551 acres.

3323 **Custer National Forest**
1310 Main Street 406-657-6200
Billings, MT 59105 Fax: 406-657-6222
www.fs.fed.us/r1/custer/
The Custer national Forest is made up of 1.2 million acres of high alpine mountain country, and small pockets of timbered buttes and grasslands scattered across two states, Montana and South Dakota.
Mary C Erickson, Acting Forest Supervisor
Chris C Worth, Deputy Forest Supervisor

3324 **Flathead National Forest**
650 Wolfpack Way 406-758-5208
Kalispell, MT 59901 Fax: 406-758-5379
www.fs.usda.gov/flathead/
The 2.3 million-acre Flathead national Forest is bordered by Canada to the north, Glacier National Park to the north and east and Clark National Forest to the east, the Lolo national Forest to the south, and the Kootenai NationalForest to the west.

3325 **Gallatin National Forest**
10 East Babcock Ave. 406-587-6701
PO Box 130 Fax: 406-587-6758
Bozeman, MT 59771 www.fs.usda.gov/main/custergallatin

3326 **Helena National Forest**
2880 Skyway Drive 406-449-5201
Helena, MT 59602 Fax: 406-449-5436
www.fs.usda.gov/helena/
The Helena National Forest offers close to one million acres of diverse landscapes and wildland opportunities. Located in west central Montana, the Helena National Forest boasts some of the most vivid glimpses into the past of thishistorically rich area.

3327 **Kootenai National Forest**
31374 Highway 2 West 406-293-6211
Libby, MT 59923-3022 Fax: 406-283-7709
www.fs.usda.gov/kootenai/
The Kootenai National Forest, conataining 2.2 million acres, is located in the extreme northwest corner of Montana, Bordered on the north by Canada and on the west by Idaho. Of the total acres, 50,384 are in the state of Idaho. Accessinto the forest is available from US highways 2 and 93, and Montana State Highways 37, 56, 200, and 508.
Paul Bradford, Forest Supervisor

3328 **Lee Metcalf National Wildlife Refuge**
4567 Wildfowl Lane 406-777-5552
Stevensville, MT 59870 Fax: 406-777-2489
lee_metcalf@fws.gov
www.fws.gov/refuge/lee_metcalf/
Mission is to manage habitat for a diversity of wildlife species with emphasis on migratory birds and endangered and threatened species.
Tom Reed, Manager
Kim Pennington, Admin. Asst.

3329 **Lewis & Clark National Forest**
1101 15th Street N 406-791-7700
Great Falls, MT 59401 www.fs.usda.gov/lcnf
The 1.8 million acres of the Lewis and clark National Forest are scatteered into seven separate mountain ranges. The Forest is situated i west central Montana. The boundaries spread eastward from the rugged, mountainous ContinentalDivide onto the plains. When looking at a map, the National Forest System lands appear as islands of forest within oceans of prairie. Because of its wide-ranging land pattern, the forest is separated into two divisions: the Rocky Mountain and theJefferson.

3330 **Lolo National Forest**
24 Fort Missoula Road 406-329-3750
Missoula, MT 59804 www.fs.usda.gov/lolo/
Of the 15 National Forests in the Northern Region of the USDA Forest Service, the Lolo National Forest is estimated to be the third largest. It is located in western Montana. Several major tributaries to the Clark Fork River of theColumbia River Basin flow through the Forest. Its 2.1 million acres of diverse and spectacular mountainous country extend into seven counties.
Debbie Austin, Forest Supervisor
Paul Matter, District Ranger

3331 **Medicine Lake National Wildlife Refuge Complex**
223 North Shore Road 406-789-2305
Medicine Lake, MT 59247 Fax: 406-789-2350
medicinelake@fws.gov
www.fws.gov/refuge/medicine_lake
Medicine Lake National Wildlife Refuge is located on the heavily glaciated rolling plains of northeaster Montana, between Missouri River and the Canadian Border.

3332 **National Bison Range**
58355 Bisons Range Road 406-644-2211
Moiese, MT 59824 Fax: 406-644-2211
bisonrange@fws.gov
www.fws.gov/refuge/national_bison_range
The National Bison Range provides conservation of habitat for the American bison, as well as wildlife viewing for the public.
Jeff King, Project Leader
Bob Rebarchik, Deputy Project leader

3333 **Red Rocks Lakes National Wildlife Refuge**
27650B South Valley Road 406-276-3536
Lima, MT 59739 Fax: 406-276-3538
redrocks@fws.gov
www.fws.gov/refuge/red_rock_lakes
Primarily a high elevation mountain wetland-riparian area. Red Rock Creek flows through the upper end of the Centennial Valley, within which the Refuge lies, creating the impressive Upper Red Rock Lake, River Marsh and Lower Red RockLake marshlands. The rugged Centennial Mountains border the Refuge on the south, catching the snows of winter that replenish the Refuge's lakes and marshes.

Nebraska: US Forests, Parks, Refuges

3334 **Crescent Lake National Wildlife Refuge**
10630 Road 181 308-762-4893
Ellsworth, NE 69340 Fax: 308-762-7606
crescentlake@fws.gov
www.fws.gov/refuge/crescent_lake
Located in the panhandle of Western Nebraska, Crescent Lake consists of 45,818 acres of rolling sandhills interspersed with numberous shallow wetlands and lakes. Plant and animal species call Crescent Lake home, while visitors canparticipate in a variety of public use activities.

3335 **Fort Niobrara National Wildlife Refuge**
Fort Niobrara/Valentine NWR Complex

39983 Refuge Road 402-376-3789
Nebraska, NE 69201 Fax: 402-376-3217
fortniobrara@fws.gov
www.fws.gov/refuge/fort_niobrara
National Wildlife Refuge Complex includes Fort Niobrara NWR, Valentine NWR and Seier NWR. Complex lands include riverine, riparian, marshland, hand prairie, and sandhills prairie habitats.
Steven A Hicks, Project Leader

3336 Nebraska & Samuel R McKelvie National Forest
125 N Main Street 308-432-0300
Chadron, NE 69337 nnf_info@fs.fed.us
www.fs.usda.gov/nebraska
There is an unusual combination of the native ponderosa pine forest of the Nebraska and Samuel R. McKelvie National Forests and mixed grass prairies on the Buffalo Gap, Fort Pierre, and Oglala National Grasslands
Jane Darnell, Supervisor
Stephen Lenzo, Deputy Supervisor

Nevada: US Forests, Parks, Refuges

3337 Ash Meadows National Wildlife Refuge
610 Springs Meadows Road 775-372-5435
Amargosa Valley, NV 89020 Fax: 775-372-5436
Daniel_Balduini@fws.gov
www.fws.gov/refuge/ash_meadows/
Refuge staff are responsible for managing the 22,117 acre refuge, most of which is spring-fed wetland and alkaline desert upland The refuge area habitat for at least 24 plants and animals found nowhere else in the world. Four fishesand one plant are currently listed as endangered. Species found on the refuge include numerous endemic species, the greatest concentration in the US and the second greatest in all of North America.
Sharon McKelvey, Manager

3338 Desert National Wildlife Refuge Complex
16001 Corn Creek Road 702-879-6110
Las Vegas, NV 89124 www.fws.gov/refuge/desert
Established in 1936 for perpetuating the desert bighorn sheep. Two threatened, and twenty-nine species of concern can be found at the refuge. Wildlife observation is one of the most popular refuge activities. Big game hunting is verylimited, but also very popular. Bird watching is another popular activity. A growing program provides additional opportunities and students are able to earn college credits through an internship at the refuge.

3339 Great Basin National Park
100 Great Basin National Park 775-234-7331
Baker, NV 89311 Fax: 775-234-7269
www.nps.gov/grba
Great Basin National Park includes streams, lakes, alpine plants, abundant wildlife, a variety of forest types including groves of ancient bristlecone pines, and numerous limestone caverns, including beatiful Lehman Caves.

3340 Humboldt-Toiyabe National Forest
100 Midas Canyon Road 775-964-2671
P.O. Box 130 Fax: 775-964-1451
Austin, NV 89310 www.fs.usda.gov/htnf/
The Humboldt-Toiyabe National Forest encompasses all of Nevada and the far Eastern edge of California. The Humboldt-Toiyabe is the largest forest in the lower 48 states.
Bill Dunkelberger, Forest Supervisor
Jack Isaacs, Deputy Forest Supervisor

3341 Lake Mead National Recreation Area (NRA)
601 Nevada Way 702-293-8990
Boulder City, NV 89005 Fax: 702-293-8936
LAME_Interpretation@nps.gov
www.nps.gov/lame
Lake Mead NRA, which includes Lake Mohave, offers a wealth of things to do and places to go year-round. Its huge lakes cater to boaters, swimmers, sunbathers and fishermen while its desert rewards hikers, wildlife photographers androadside sightseers. Three of America's four desert ecosystems: the Mojave, the Great Basin and the Sonoran Desert meet in here. As a result, this seemingly barren area contains a surprising variety of plants animals, some of which may be foundnowhere else.

3342 Moapa Valley National Wildlife Refuge
4701 N Torrey Pines Drive 702-515-5450
Las Vegas, NV 89130 Fax: 702-515-5460
To secure habitat for the endangered Moapa dace, a small fish commonly found throughout the headwaters of the Muddy River system
Amy Lavoie, Refuge Manager

3343 Pahranagat National Wildlife Refuge
PO Box 510 775-725-3417
Alamo, NV 89001 Fax: 775-725-3389
amy_lavoie@fws.gov
www.fws.gov/refuge/Pahranagat/
Refuge staff are responsible for managing the 5,380 acre refuge, a mixture of desert, open water, native grass meadows, cropland and marsh. The refuge provides habitat for migratory birds of the Pacific Flyway and several speciesabound at this desert oasis. Wildlife observation is one of the most popular refuge activities. Waterfowl and small game hunting are also very popular, as is bird watching. A growing program provides additional opportunities, including internshipsfor college students.
Rob Vinson, Refuge Manager
Annji Greenwood, Deputy Refuge Manager

3344 Stillwater National Wildlife Refuge Complex
1020 New River Parkway 775-423-5128
Suite 305 Fax: 775-423-0416
Fallon, NV 89406 stillwater@fws.gov
The Stillwater NWRC includes three National Wildlife Refuges: Anaho Island, Fallon, and Stillwater NWRs. They work to conserve American white pelican nesting colonies, as well as double crested cormorant, great blue heron, and gullnesting olonies. The Fallon NWR conserves large expanses of playa and native shrub/scrub high desert habitat within the Carson Sink of the Great Basin. Stillwater NWR conserves and manages a network of wetlands at the terminal end of the CarsonRiver.

New Hampshire: US Forests, Parks, Refuges

3345 Lake Umbagog National Wildlife Refuge
PO Box 240 603-482-3415
2756 Dam Road Fax: 603-482-3308
Errol, NH 03579 lakeumbagog@fws.gov
www.fws.gov/northeast/lakeumbagog/
Northern Forest refuge of New Hampshire and Maine provides long-term conservation of important wetland/upland habitats for wildlife, migratory birds and protected species.

3346 White Mountain National Forest
200 East Broadway 414-297-3600
P.O. Box 7669 Fax: 603-528-8783
Missoula, MT 59807-7669 www.fs.usda.gov/r9
The White Mountain National Forest is located in northern New Hampshire and southwestern Maine, and lies within Carroll,

Coos, and Grafton Counties in New Hampshire, and Oxford County in Maine.
Tom Wagner, Forest Supervisor

New Jersey: US Forests, Parks, Refuges

3347 Cape May National Wildlife Refuge
24 Kimbles Beach Road 609-463-0994
Cape May Courthouse, NJ 00821 Fax: 609-463-1667
capemay@fws.gov
www.fws.gov/refuge/cape_may

3348 Great Swamp National Wildlife Refuge
241 Pleasant Plains Road 973-425-1222
Basking Ridge, NJ 00792 Fax: 973-425-7309
greatswamp@fws.gov
www.fws.gov/refuge/great_swamp
Swamp woodland, hardwood ridges, cattail marsh and grassland are typical of this approximately 7,800 acre refuge. The Swamp contains many large old oak and beach trees, stands of mountain laurel, mosses, ferns and species of many otherplants of both Northern and Southern botanical zones.
William Koch, Refuge Manager
Steve Henry, Deputy Refuge Manager

New Mexico: US Forests, Parks, Refuges

3349 Bitter Lake National Wildlife Refuge
4200 East Pine Lodge Road 505-622-6755
Roswell, NM 88201 Fax: 505-623-9039
steve_alvarez@fws.gov
www.fws.gov/refuge/bitter_lake/
Native grasses, sand dunes, brushy bottomlands, seven lakes and a red-rimmed plateau make up Bitter Lake National Wildlife Refuge, winter home for thousands of migratory birds. The Lakes on the refuge were formed within the ancientriver beds of the Pecos River. These lakes store about 1,000 acres of water at their highest levels, while nearby marshland, mudflats and the Pecos Rriver provide an additional 24,500 acres of habitat.
Floyd Truetken, Refuge Manager

3350 Bosque del Apache National Wildlife Refuge
1001 Highway 1 505-835-1828
P.O. Box 280 Fax: 505-835-0314
San Antonio, NM 87832 fw2_rw_bosque_del_apache@fws.gov
www.fws.gov/southwest/refuges/newmex/bosque/
Bosque del Apache NWR is located in south-central New Mexico, along the Rio Grande in the northern reach of the Chihuahuan Desert. Habitats include cottonwood forests, seasonally managed wetlands, farm fields, saltgrass meadows, anddesert uplands. The refuge features large concentrations of sandhill cranes, light geese, and migrating waterfowl in fall and winter, shorebirds and songbirds travel through in spring and fall, and hummingbirds are abundant in summer.

3351 Capulin Volcano National Monument National Park Service
46 Volcano Rd. 505-278-2201
PO Box 40 Fax: 505-278-2211
Capulin, NM 88414 www.nps.gov/cavo
Capulin Volcano is long extinct, and today the forested slopes provide habitat for mule deer, wild turkey, black bear and other wildlife. Abundant displays of wildflowers bloom on the mountain each summer. A two mile paved roadspiraling to the volcano rim makes Capulin Volcano one of the most accessible volcanos in the world. Trails leading around the rim allow exploration of this classic cinder cone.
, Superintendent, Park Ranger

3352 Carlsbad Caverns National Park
3225 National Parks Highway 505-785-2232
Carlsbad, NM 88220 Fax: 505-785-2133
cave_park_information@nps.gov
www.nps.gov/cave
Established to preserve Carlsbad Cavern and numerous other caves within a Permian-age fossil reef, the park contains over 100 known caves, including Lechuguilla Cave-the nation's deepest limestone cave and third longest. CarlsbadCavern, with one of the world's largest underground chambers and countless formations, is highly accessible, with a variety of tours offered year-round.
John Benjamin, Superintendent
Chuck Barat, Deputy Superintendent

3353 Carson National Park
208 Cruz Alta Road 505-758-6200
Taos, NM 87571 Fax: 505-758-6213
mailroom_r3_carson@fs.fed.us
www.fs.usda.gov/carson
Some of the finest mountain scenery in the southwest is found in the 1.5 million acres covered by the Carson National Forest. Elevations rise from 6,000 feet to 13,161 feet. The scenic Sangre de Cristo Mountains include Wheeler Peak,the highest peak in New Mexico.

3354 Cibola National Forest
2113 Osuna Road Northeast Suite A 505-346-3900
Albuquerque, NM 87113 Fax: 505-346-3901
www.fs.fed.us/r3/cibola
Cibola, pronounced See'-bo-lah, is thought to be the original Zuni Indian name for their group of pueblos or tribal lands. Later, the Spanish interpreted the word to mean, buffalo. Valued for its recreation opportunities, naturalbeauty, timber, watersheds, water, forage, and wilderness resources, the forest is managed to give the American people the greatest benefits that can be produced on a permanent basis.
Elaine Kohrman, Forest Supervisor
Ruth Sutton, Public Affairs

3355 El Malpais National Monument
1900 E Santa Fe Avenue 505-876-2783
201 E Roosevelt Fax: 505-285-5661
Grants, NM 87020 Leslie_DeLong@nps.gov
www.nps.gov/elma/
This monument preserves 114,277 acres of which 109,260 acres are federal and 5,017 acres are private. Volcanic features such as lava flows, cinder cones, pressure ridges and complex lava tube systems dominate the landscape. Sandstonebluffs and mesas border the eastern side, providing to vast wilderness.
Douglas E Eury

3356 Las Vegas National Wildlife Refuge
Route 1 Box 399 505-425-3581
Las Vegas, NM 87701 Fax: 505-454-8510
www.fws.gov/refuge/Las_Vegas
8,672 acres consisting of native grassland, cropland, marshes, ponds, forested canyons, and streams.
Joe B Rodriguez, Manager

3357 Lincoln National Forest
3463 Las Palomas Rd. 575-434-7200
Alamogordo, NM 88310 Fax: 575-434-7218
www.fs.fed.us/r3/lincoln/
The Lincoln consists of three ranger districts: Sacramento, Smokey Bear and Guadalupe
Travis Moseley, Forest Supervisor
Karla Eldridge, Administrative Officer

3358 **Maxwell National Wildlife Refuge**
168 Lake 13 Road 575-375-2331
PO Box 276 Fax: 575-375-2331
Maxwell, NM 87728 fw2_rw_maxwell@fws.gov
www.fws.gov/refuge/maxwell/
At an altitude of 6,050 feet, the refuge is made up of more than 3,000 acres of gently rolling prairie, playa lakes and farmland for waterfowl. Rangeland and reclaimed farmland on the refuge are made up of a variety of grassesincluding blue grama, galleta, sand dropseed, threeawn and buffalo grass, as well as fourwing saltbush and cactus. Several lakes provide approximately 700 acres of roosting and feeding habitat for waterfowl. Supports waterfowl nesting and is alsobeneficial to shore birds.
Leann Wilkins, Refuge Manager

3359 **San Andres National Wildlife Refuge**
5686 Santa Gertrudis Dr. 505-382-5047
Las Cruces, NM 88012 Fax: 505-382-5454
lorie_hardin@fws.gov
www.fws.gov/southwest/refuges/newmex/sanandres/index.html
Refuge not open to the public due to its location within the boundaries of U.S. Department of Army, White Sands Missile Range. Primary emphasis has been focused on restoring a remnant population of desert bighorn sheet (OvisCanadensis Mexicana)
Kevin Cobble, Refuge Manager

3360 **Sevilleta National Wildlife Refuge**
PO Box 1248 505-864-4021
Socorro, NM 87801 Fax: 505-864-7761
Jeannine_Kimble@fws.gov
www.fws.gov/refuge/sevilleta/
Home to over 1200 species of plants, 89 species of mammals, 225 species of birds and 15 species of amphibians. More commonly seen species include mule deer, coyotes, pronghorns, red-tailed hawks, northern harriers, western diamondbackrattlesnakes, roadrunners, sandhill cranes and many different types of waterfowl and migrating shorebirds. Bobcats, elk, bighorn sheep and an occasional mountain lion also roam the hillsides.
Kathy Granillo, Manager
Renee Robichaud, Deputy Refuge Manager

3361 **White Sands National Monument**
PO Box 1086 505-479-6124
Holloman Air Force Base, NM 88330 Fax: 505-479-4333
whsa_interpretation@nps.gov
www.nps.gov/whsa/
White Sands National Mounment preserves a major portion of this gypsum dune field, along with the plants and animals that have successfully adapted to this constantly changing environment.
Dennis L Ditmanson

New York: US Forests, Parks, Refuges

3362 **Fire Island National Seashore**
120 Laurel Street 631-687-4750
Patchogue, NY 11772-3596 Fax: 631-289-4898
fiis_interpretation@nps.gov
www.nps.gov/fiis/
There are 32 miles of sandy beaches and saltwater marshes, a sunken forest of 300 year old holly trees, hiking trails, a wilderness area and many other sites on the Fire Island National Seashore.
Michael T Reynolds, Superintendent
K Christopher Soller, Superintendent

3363 **Gateway National Recreation Area**
210 New York Avenue 718-354-4606
Staten Island, NY 10305 Fax: 718-354-4764
carole_silano@nps.gov
www.nps.gov/gate/
Gateway NRA is a 26,000 acre recreation area located in the heart of the New York metropolitan area. The park extends through three New York City boroughs and into northern New Jersey. Parks sites offer a variety of recreationopportunities, along with a chance to explore many significant cultural resources.
Kevin Buckley, Supt

3364 **Iroquois National Wildlife Refuge**
1101 Casey Road 585-948-5445
Basom, NY 14013 Fax: 585-948-9538
iroquois@fws.gov
www.fws.gov/refuge/iroquois/
Iroquois National Wildlife Refuge lies within the rural township of Alabama, New York, midway between Buffalo and Rochester. Part of what the locals call the Alabama Swamps, its 10,818 acres of freshwater marshes, and hardwood swampsbounded by woods, forest, pastures and wet meadows, serve the habitat needs of many animals as a major stopover for migrating birds and as a year-round residence.
Robert Lamayr, Refuge Manager

3365 **Montezuma National Wildlife Refuge**
3395 Routes 5 & 20 East 315-568-5987
Seneca Falls, NY 13148 Fax: 315-568-8835
andrea_vanbeusichem@fws.gov
www.fws.gov/r5mnwr
Montezuma is the premiere refuge in New York State. View bald eagles year-round. Spring and fall bring tens of thousands of migrating ducks and geese. View Shaebirds in early spring and late summer. May and June are great for warblerwatching. Volunteer opportunities available Spring- Fall.
Tom Jasikoff, Manager
Andrea VanBeusichem, Visitor Services Manager

3366 **Seatuck National Wildlife Refuge: Long Island National Wildlife Refuge Complex**
340 Smith Road 631-286-0485
Shirley, NY 11967 Fax: 516-581-2003
R5RW_STKNWR@fws.gov
www.fws.gov/refuge/Seatuck
Located along the southern shore of Long Island, the Refuge consists of half salt marsh and half freshwater wetlands, ponds and sparsely wooded areas. It is part of the larger Great South Bay, which is a significant coastal habitat formigrating birds. Limited recreation includes viewing wildlife and bird watching.
Charles Stenvall, Manager

3367 **Target Rock National Wildlife Refuge Long Island National Wildlife Refuge Complex**
340 Smith Road 631-286-0485
Shirley, NY 11967 Fax: 516-286-4003
www.fws.gov/refuge/target_rock
The refuge was established in 1967. It consists of mixed upland forest, a half mile of rocky beach, a brackish and several vernal ponds. The offshore, beach and pond habitats provide foraging areas for piping plover, winteringwaterfowl and fish species.

North Carolina: US Forests, Parks, Refuges

3368 **Alligator River National Wildlife Refuge**
PO Box 1969 252-473-1131
Manteo, NC 27954 Fax: 252-473-1668
alligatorriver@fws.gov
www.fws.gov/alligatorriver
Provide habitat and protection for endangered species such as red wolves, red-cockaded woodpeckers, and American alligators
Mike Bryant, Refuge Manager
Scott Lanier, Deputy Refuge Manager

3369 Cape Hatteras National Seashore
1401 National Park Drive 252-473-2111
Manteo, NC 27954 Fax: 252-473-2595
CAHA_Information@nps.gov
www.nps.gov/caha/
A thin broken strand of islands curves out into the Atlantic Ocean and then back again in a sheltering embrace of North Carolina's mainland coast and its offshore sounds. These are the Outer Banks of North Carolina. Today their longstretches of beach, sand dunes, marshes and woodlands are set aside as Cape Hatteras National Seashore.
Lawrence A Belli, Superintendent

3370 Cape Lookout National Seashore
131 Charles Street 252-728-2250
Harkers Island, NC 28531 Fax: 252-728-2160
CALO_information@nps.gov
www.nps.gov/calo
The seashore is a 56 mile long section of the Outer Banks of North Carolina running from Ocracoke Inlet on the northeast to Beafort Inlet on the southeast. The four undeveloped barrier island, make up the seashore- North Core Banks,South Core Banks, Middle Core Banks and Shackleford Banks- may seem barren and isolated but they offer many natural and historical features that can make a visit very rewarding.
Robert A Vogel, Superintendent
Donna O Tiptor, Administrative Officer

3371 Cedar Island National Wildlife Refuge
85 Mattamuskeet Road 252-926-4021
Swan Quarter, NC 27885 Fax: 252-926-1743
mattamuskeet@fws.gov
www.fws.gov/refuge/cedar_island
Provide habitat and protection for endangered species such as American alligators and brown pelicans
Peter Campbell, Refuge Manager
Jerry Fringeli, Deputy Refuge Manager

3372 Currituck National Wildlife Refuge
316 Marsh Causeway 919-429-3100
PO Box 39 Fax: 919-429-3185
Knotts Island, NC 27950-0039 mackayisland@fws.gov
www.fws.gov/refuge/currituck/
The purpose of the Refuge is to preserve and protect a portion of the Outer Banks habitat for wintering waterfowl, endangered species, other migratory birds, and native wildlife

3373 Mattamuskeet National Wildlife Refuge
85 Mattamuskeet Road 919-926-4021
Box N-2 mattamuskeet@fws.gov
Swan Quarter, NC 27885 www.fws.gov/refuges
Located in eastern North Carolina in Hyde County, the Mattamuskeet Refuge consists of more than 50,000 acres of water, marsh, timber and crop lands. The refuge's most significant feature is lake Mattamuskeet, the largest natural lakein North Carolina. The lake is 18 miles long and five to 6 miles wide, encompassing approximately 40,000 acres, but averages 2 feet in depth.
Don Temple, Manager

3374 Nantahala National Forest
160-A Zillicoa Street 828-257-4200
Asheville, NC 28801 Fax: 828-257-4263
www.fs.usda.gov/recarea/nfsnc
The National Forests of North Carolina include four national forests covering 1.2 million acres from the mountains to the sea. The Nantahala is located in the Appalachians of southwest North Carolina. The Nantahala is the largest ofthe four forests, totaling 528,541 acres. The Nantahala sits adjacent to Great Smokey Mountains National Park.

3375 Pea Island River National Wildlife Refuge
PO Box 1969 252-473-1131
Manteo, NC 27954 Fax: 252-473-1668
alligatorriver@fws.gov
www.fws.gov/peaisland
Provide nesting, resting, and wintering habitat for migratory birds, including the greater snow geese and other migratory waterfowl, shorebirds, wading birds, raptors, and neotropical migrants
Mike Bryant, Refuge Manager
Scott Lanier, Deputy Refuge Manager

3376 Pee Dee National Wildlife Refuge
5770 U.S. Hwy. 52 North 704-694-4424
Wadesboro, NC 28170 Fax: 704-694-6570
fw4_rw_pee_dee@fws.gov
www.fws.gov/peedee/
Refuge objectives are to: provide habitat for migratory waterfowl and song birds; to provide habitat and protection for an endangered species, the red-cockaded woodpecker; to provide recreation, environmental education andinterpretation for the public; to engage in dynamic partnering.
J.D Bricken, Refuge Manager
Greg Walmsley, Assistant Refuge Manager

3377 Pocosin Lakes National Wildlife Refuge
205 South Ludington Dr 252-796-3004
PO Box 329 Fax: 252-796-3010
Columbia, NC 27925 pocosinlakes@fws.gov
www.fws.gov/pocosinlakes/
The 112,000 acre refuge was established to protect and ehnhance a unique habitat called a pocosin and contains a variety of wildlife including endangered species such as the red wolf, bald eagle, peregrine falcon and red-cockadedwoodpecker as well as natural vegetation and scenic areas.
Howard Philips, Refuge Manager
David Kitts, Deputy Manager

3378 Roanoke River National Wildlife Refuge
114 W Water Street 252-794-3808
PO Box 430 Fax: 252-794-3780
Windsor, NC 27983 roanokeriver@fws.gov
www.fws.gov/roanokeriver/
Refuge objectives are: to provide habitat for migratory waterfowl, neo-tropical migrants and other birds; to provide migrating, spawning and nursery habitat for anadromous fish; (i.e. blueback herring, alewife, hickory shad and stripedbass); to enhance and protect forested wetlands consisting of bottomland hardwoods and swamps; to protect and manage for endangered and threatened wildlife; and to provide recreation and environmental education for the public
Matt Connolly, Refuge Manager
Jean Richer, Biologist

3379 Swanquarter National Wildlife Refuge
85 Mattamuskeet Road 252-926-4021
Swan Quarter, NC 27885 Fax: 252-926-1743
mattamuskeet@fws.gov
www.fws.gov/swanquarter/
Provide habitat for endangered species such as bald eagles, peregrine falcons, and American alligators.
Peter Campbell, Refuge Manager
Jerry Fringeli, Deputy Refuge Manager

North Dakota: US Forests, Parks, Refuges

3380 Crosby Wetland Management District
10100 Hwy 42 NW 701-965-6488
Crosby, ND 58730 crosbywetlands@fws.gov
Previously a part of the Des Lacs NWR Complex, the Crosby WMD includes of 17,000 acres of Waterfowl Production Areas

(WPAs), numerous grassland and wetland easment contracts, and the 3,219 acre Lake Zahl NWR.
Tim K Kessler, WMD Manager

3381 Des Lacs National Wildlife Refuge
42000 520th Street NW 701-385-4046
Kenmare, ND 58746 Fax: 701-385-3214
deslacs@fws.gov
www.fws.gov/refuge/des_lacs/
Previously a part of the old Des Lacs NWR complex, the Des Lacs NWR is a smaller parcel that is home to wildlife and water fowl. The Lakes no longer encompass the the wetlands that are part of Crosby Wetlands district.

3382 Devils Lake Wetland Management District
221 2nd Street NW 701-662-8611
Suite #2 Fax: 701-662-8612
Devils Lake, ND 58301 devilslake@fws.gov
www.fws.gov/refuge/devils_lake_wmd/
Located in the heart of the Prairie Pothole Region of the US. The northeastern North Dakota counties of Towner, Cavalier, Pembina, Benson, Ramsey, Walsh, Nelson and Grand Forks are included in the District. Managed by the US Fish andWildlife Service, the district provides wetland areas needed by waterfowl in the spring and summer for nesting and feeding. Hundreds of thousands of waterfowl also use these wetlands in the spring and fall for feeding and resting during longmigratory flights.
Roger Hollevoet, Project Leader
Jim Alfonso, Deputy Project leader

3383 Lake Ilo National Wildlife Refuge
489 102 Avenue SW 701-548-8110
Dunn Center, ND 58626 Fax: 701-548-8108
lakeilo@fws.gov
www.fws.gov/lakeilo
Located near the center of Dunn County in west central North Dakota, the refuge habitat is made up of native prairie, planted grasslands and wetlands. The uplands are characterized by gently sloping hills and terraces with creeks andan occasional slough. The average rainfall of 16.8 inches supports a prairie environment with a climate of hot dry summers, occasional thunderstorms and cold winters.
Kory Richardson, Refuge Manager

3384 Long Lake National Wildlife Refuge
12000 353rd Street 56 701-387-4397
Moffit, ND 58560 Fax: 701-387-4767
longlake@fws.gov
www.fws.gov/refuge/long_lake/
The Refuge is about 18 miles long and contains 22,300 acres. The Refuge attracts a diversity and abundance of animals and waterfowl, both resident and migratory. Over 200 species of birds use the Refuge for breeding, rearing theiryoung and as a migratory stop. Long Lake Refuge is open for birdwatching, fishing, photography, boating, hiking and regulated hunting.

3385 Lostwood National Wildlife Refuge
8315 Highway 8 701-848-2722
Kenmare, ND 58746-9046 Fax: 701-848-2702
Lostwood@fws.gov
www.fws.gov/refuge/lostwood/
Lies in the highly productive pothole region that produces more ducks than any other region in the lower 48 states. The refuge is a land of rolling hills mantled in short-grass and mixed with grass prairie interspersed with numerouswetlands. Established to preserve a unique wildlife habitat, Lostwood is an important link in our nation's system of more than 410 wildlife refuges.

3386 Theodore Roosevelt National Park
315 Second Avenue 701-623-4466
PO Box 7 Fax: 701-623-4840
Medora, ND 58645-0007 susan_recce@nps.gov
www.nps.gov/thro/
Here in the North Dakota badlands, where many of his personal concerns first gave rise to his later environmental efforts, Roosevelt is remembered with a national park that bears his name and honors the memory of this greatconservationist. Theodore Roosevelt NAtional Park is colorful North Dakota badlands and is home to a variety of plants and animals, including bison, prairie dogs, and elk.

Ohio: US Forests, Parks, Refuges

3387 Cuyahoga Valley National Park
15610 Vaughn Road 216-524-1497
Brecksville, OH 44141 800-445-9667
Fax: 440-546-5989
cuva_canal_visitor_center@nps.gov
www.nps.gov/cuva
Cuyahoga Valley National Park protects 33,000 acres along the Cuyahoga River between Cleveland and Akron, Ohio. Managed by the National Park Service, CVNP combines cultural, historical, recreational and natural activities in onesetting. Visitors can hike, bike, birdwatch, golf, fish, ski, ride Cuyahoga Valley Scenic Railroad, explore the history of the Ohio and Erie Canal on a 20 mile section of the Towpath Trail, and attend national park ranger-guided programs, concerts,art exhibits and more.
Mary Pat Doorley, Media contact

3388 Ottawa National Wildlife Refuge
14000 W State Route 2 419-898-0014
Oak Harbor, OH 43449 Fax: 419-898-7895
ottawa@fws.gov
www.fws.gov/refuge/ottawa
Refuge objectives are: to restore optimum acreage to a natural floodplain condition; to improve and restore wetland habitat, to improve fishery and wildlife resources, to provide for biodiversity; and to provide public opportunitiesfor outdoor recreation and environmental education.
Dan Frisk, Refuge Manager

Oklahoma: US Forests, Parks, Refuges

3389 Deep Fork National Wildlife Refuge
21844 S. 250 Road 918-652-0456
PO Box 816 Fax: 918-652-3427
Okmulgee, OK 74447 lori_jones@fws.gov
Protecting important wetlands along the Deep Fork River, Deep Fork National Wildlife Refuge in eastern Oklahoma is a newcomer to the National Wildlife Refuge System. Established in 1993, the 9,000 acre refuge is subject to flooding atleast once a year. This flooding results in excellent conditions for waterfowl, including mallard, blue-winged teal, shoveler, pintail and wood ducks.
Darrin B Unruh, Manager

3390 Little River National Wildlife Refuge
PO Box 340 405-584-6211
Broken Bow, OK 74728 Fax: 405-584-2034
www.fws.gov/refuge/little_river/
13,000 acres of bottomland hardwoods within the floodplain of Little River.
Berlin A Heck, Manager

3391 Oklahoma Bat Caves National Wildlife Refuge
16602 CR 465 918-773-5251
Colcord, OK 74338 Fax: 918-773-5252
shea_hammond@fws.gov
www.fws.gov/refuge/ozark_plateau/

The endangered status of wildlife species and the delicate (and hazardous) nature of the habitat precludes any recreational use. Approved studies can be done under proper supervision.
Shea Hammond, Deputy Refuge Manager

3392 Optima National Wildlife Refuge
20834 east 940 Road 580-664-2205
Butler, OK 73625-5001 Fax: 580-664-2206
washita@fws.gov
www.fws.gov/refuge/optima
Located in the middle of the Oklahoma panhandle, the 4,333-acre refuge is made up of grasslands and wooded bottomland on the Coldwater Creek arm of the Army Corps of Engineers Optima Reservoir Project.
Daniel Moss, Refuge Manager

3393 Sequoyah National Wildlife Refuge
107993 S. 4520 Rd 918-773-5251
Vian, OK 74962-9304 Fax: 918-773-5598
www.fws.gov/refuge/Sequoyah
Sequoyah National Wildlife Refuge is home to wildlife as unique as the bald eagle and as elusive as the bobcat
Jeff Haas, Refuge Manager
Scott Gilje, Assistant Refuge Manager

3394 US Fish & Wildlife Service Tishomingo National Wildlife Refuge
12000 S Refuge Road 580-371-2402
Tishomingo, OK 73460 Fax: 580-371-9312
fw2_rw_tishomingo@fws.gov
www.fws.gov/refuge/tishomingo
The 16,464-acre Refuge lies at the upper Washita arm of Lake Texoma and is administered for the benefit of migratory waterfowl in the Central Flyway. It offers a variety of aquatic habitats for wildlife. The murky water of theCumberland Pool provides abundant nutrients for innumerable microscopic plants and animals. Seasonally flooded flats and willow shallows lying at the Pool's edge also provide excellent wildlife habitat.
Kris Patton, Refuge Manager

3395 Washita National Wildlife Refuge
20834 E 0940 Road 405-664-2205
Butler, OK 73625-5001 Fax: 580-664-2206
washita@fws.gov
www.fws.gov/refuge/washita/
Provides habitat for migrating/wintering waterfowl. Endangered species managed include the bald eagle, whooping crane, and interior least tern.
Jon M Brock, Manager

Oregon: US Forests, Parks, Refuges

3396 Ankeny National Wildlife Refuge
2301 Wintel Road 503-327-2444
2301 Wintel Road Fax: 541-757-4450
Jefferson, OR 97352-9758 willamettevalley@fws.gov
www.fws.gov/refuges
Refuge's primary management goal is to provide vital wintering habitat for dusky Canada geese. The refuge includes flat to gently rolling land near the confluence of the Willamette and Sanitiam rivers. The refuge's fertile farmedfields, hedgerows, forests, and wetlands provide a variety of wildlife habitats. the refuge is open to limited opportunites for wildlife-oriented education and recreation. Ducks, geese, and swans are commonly seen in refuge fields and ponds throughthe fall and winter.

3397 Bandon Marsh National Wildlife Refuge
83673 North Bank Lane 541-347-1470
2127 SE Marine Science Drive Fax: 541-347-9376
Bandon, OR 97411 oregoncoast@fws.gov
www.fws.gov/refuge/bandon_marsh/

3398 Baskett Slough National Wildlife Refuge
Western Oregon NWR Complex 503-757-7236
26208 Finley Refuge Road www.fws.gov/refuge/baskett_slough/
Corvallis, OR 97333
Includes 2,492 acres typical of Willamette Valley's irrigated hillsides, oak-covered knolls and grass fields. Wetlands include Morgan Lake and Baskett Slough. The refuge's objective is the protection and management of winteringhabitat for dusky Canada geese. Several species of waterfowl, herons, hawks, quail , shorebirds, mourning doves, woodpeckers and a variety of songbirds frequent the area, as well as mammals, amphibians and reptiles. Recreation includes observation,study and photography.
Richard Guadagno, Manager

3399 Cape Meares National Wildlife Refuge
2127 SE Marine Science Drive 541-867-4550
26208 Finley Refuge Road oregoncoast@fws.gov
Newport, OR 97365 www.fws.gov/refuge/cape_meares/

3400 Cold Springs National Wildlife Refuge
PO Box 239 541-992-3232
Umatilla, OR 97882 gary_hagedorn@fws.gov
www.gorp.com
Cold Springs NWR lies in sharp contrast with the arid desert surroundings of northeastern Oregon. The refuge, a tree-lined reservoir, lies 7 miles east of the agricultural community of Hermiston. The variety of refuge habitats attractsan abundance of wildlife. Cold Springs supports peak populations of over 45,000 winter waterfowl comprised mainly of mallards and Canada geese.

3401 Columbia River Gorge National Scenic Area
902 Wasco Avenue 541-386-2333
Waucoma Center, Suite 200 www.fs.fed.us/r6/columbia/
Hood River, OR 97031
The Columbia River Gorge is a espaectacular river canyon cutting the only sea-level route through the Cascade Mountain Range. It's 80 miles long and to 4,00 feet deep with the north canyon walls in Washington State and the south canyonwalls in Oregon State.

3402 Crater Lake National Park
Highway 62 541-594-3000
PO Box 7 Fax: 541-594-3010
Crater Lake, OR 97604 www.nps.gov
During the summer, visitors may navigate the Rim Drive around the lake, enjoy boat tours, stay in the historic Crater Lake Lodge Camp or hike some of the park's various trails. The winter brings some of the heaviest snowfall in thecountry, averaging 533 inches per year. Although park facilities mostly close for the snow season, visitors may view the lake during fair weather, enjoy cross-country skiing, and participate in weekend snowshoe hikes.
Dave Morris, Supt

3403 Deschutes National Forest
63095 Deschutes Market Road 541-383-5300
Bend, OR 97701 Fax: 541-383-5531
www.fs.usda.gov/main/deschutes
Scenic backdrop of volcanic attraction, evergreen forest, mountain lakes, caves, desert areas and alpine meadows.

3404 Fremont Winema National Forest
1301 South G Street 541-947-2151
Lakeview, OR 97630 Fax: 541-947-6399
www.fs.usda.gov/fremont-winema

Located in Oregon's Outback, the forest provides the self reliant recreationist the opportunity to discover nature in a rustic environment.

3405 Malheur National Forest
431 Patterson Bridge Road 541-575-1731
PO Box 909 jtrosclair02@fs.fed.us
John Day, OR 97845 www.fs.usda.gov/malheur/
The 1,460,000 acre Malheur National Forest is located in the blue Mountains of Eastern Oregon. The diverse and beautiful scenery of the forest includes high desert grasslands, sage and juniper, pine, fir and other tree species, and thehidden gem of alpine lakes and meadows. Elevations vary from about 4000feet (1200 meters) to the 9038 foot (2754 meters) top Strawberry Mountain. The Strawberry Mountain range extends east to west through the center of the forest.
Bonnie J Wood, Forest Supervisor

3406 Malheur National Wildlife Refuge
36391 Sodhouse Lane 541-493-2612
Princeton, OR 97721 Fax: 541-493-2405
tim_bodeen@fws.gov
www.fws.gov/refuge/malheur
Tim Bodeen, Manager

3407 McKay Creek National Wildlife Refuge
Umatilla NWR Complex 503-922-3232
PO Box 239
Umatilla, OR 97882

3408 Mount Hood National Forest
16400 Champion Way 503-668-1700
Sandy, OR 97055 Fax: 503-668-1641
www.fs.usda.gov/mthood/
Located 20 miles east of the city of Portland and the northern Willamette River valley, Mt Hood National Forest extends south from the strikingly beautiful Columbia River Gorge across more than sixty miles of forested mountains, lakesand streams to OlAllie Scienic Area, a high lake basin under the slopes of Mt Jefferson. Our many visitors enjoy fishing, caming, boating and hiking in the summer, hunting in the fall, skiing and other snow sports in the winter.

3409 National Park Service: John Day Fossil Beds National Monument
32651 Highway 19 541-987-2333
Kimberly, OR 97845-9701 Fax: 541-987-2336
joda_interpretation@nps.gov
www.nps.gov/joda
Within the heavily eroded volcanic deposits of the scenic John Day Fossil Basin is a great diversity of well-preserved plant and animal fossils. This remarkably complete record spans more than 40 of the 65 million years of the CenozoicEra (the Age of Mammals). The monument was established in 1975.
John Fiedor, Chief Visitor Services

3410 Ochoco National Forest
1220 SW 3rd Ave 503-808-2468
Portland, OR 97204 Fax: 541-416-6695
www.fs.fed.us/r6/centraloregon
With a total of almost 1,500 square miles, the Ochoco National Forest is endowed with vast natural resources, scenic grandeur and tremendous recreation opportunities. People are drawn to the Ochoco for its majestic ponderosa pinestands, picturesque rimrock vantage points, deep canyons, unique geologic formations, abundant wildlife and plentiful sunshine.

3411 Oregon Caves National Monument
19000 Caves Highway 541-592-2100
Cave Junction, OR 97523 Fax: 541-592-3981
www.nps.gov/orca
Oregan Caves National Monument is small in size, 480 acres, but rich in diversity. Above ground, the monument encompasses a remnant old-growth coniferous forest. It harbors a fantastic array of plants, and a Douglas-fir tree with thewildest known girth in Oregon. Three hiking trails access this forest. Below ground is an active marble cave created by natural forces over hundreds of thousands of years in one of the world's most diverse geologic realms.
Vicki Snitzler, Superintendent

3412 Oregon Coastal Refuges
2127 SE OSU Drive 541-867-4550
Newport, OR 97365 Fax: 541-867-4551
oregoncoast@fws.gov
575 acres of rocks and islands located offshore along the length of the Oregon coast. Most of the refuge is included in the Oregon Islands Wilderness.
Nancy Morrissey, Manager

3413 Oregon Islands National Wildlife Refuge
c/o Oregon Coast NWR Complex 541-867-4550
2127 SE Marine Science Drive Fax: 541-867-4551
Newport, OR 97365 oregoncoast@fws.gov
www.fws.gov/refuge/oregon_islands/
575 acres of rocks and islands located offshore along the length of the Oregon coast. Most of the refuge is included in the Oregon Islands Wilderness.

3414 Rogue River National Forest
3040 Biddle Road 541-858-2200
Medford, OR 97504 Fax: 541-858-2220
www.fs.fed.us/r6/rogue
Rob MacWhorter, Forest Supervisor
Tracy Tophooven, Deputy Forest Supervisor

3415 Sheldon National Wildlife Refuge
US Fish and Wildlife Service- Pacific Region
20995 Rabbit Hill Road 503-947-3315
PO Box 111 Fax: 503-947-4414
Lakeview, OR 97630 Sheldon-Hart@fws.gov
www.fws.gov/sheldonhartmtn/sheldon/
Provide habitat for pronghorn antelope, the primary species, and populations of native secondary species (e.g., mule deer, sage-grouse, and song birds) in such numbers as may be necessary to maintain a balanced wildlife population
Brian Day, Manager
John Kasbohm, Project Leader

3416 Siskiyou National Forest
3040 Biddle Road
Medford, OR 9750 866-296-3823
Fax: 541-471-6514
www.fs.usda.gov/rogue-siskiyou/
The Siskiyou National Forest embodies the most complex soils, geology, landscape, and plant communities in the Pacific Northwest. World-class rivers, biological diversity, fisheries, and complex watersheds rank the Siskiyou high in theNation as an outstanding resource.
Roy Bergstrom, District Ranger

3417 Siuslaw National Forest
3200 SW Jefferson Way 541-750-7000
Corvallis, OR 97331 Fax: 541-750-7234
www.fs.usda.gov/siuslaw
The Siuslaw National Forest encompasses one of the most productive and diverse landscapes in the world from fertile soils, which support tall stands of Douglas fir, western hemlock and Sitka spruce forests laced with miles of riversand streams, to miles of open sand dunes. These rich settings from habitats for a broad array of plants and animals and provide endless opportunities for learning.
Jerry Ingersoll, Forest Supervisor

3418 Three Arch Rocks National Wildlife Refuge
Western Oregon NWR Complex 541-867-4550
2127 SE Marine Science Drive oregoncoast@fws.gov
Newport, OR 97365 www.fws.gov/refuge/three_arch_rocks/
Large numbers of nesting common murres, tufted puffins, and Brandt's and pelagic cormorants use the area. Northern and California seal lions and harbor seals.

3419 Umatilla National Forest
72510 Coyote Road 541-278-3716
Pendleton, OR 97801 www.fs.usda.gov/umatilla
The Umatilla National Forest, located in the Blue Mountains of southeast Wasington and northeast Oregon, covers 1.4 million acres of diverse landscapes and plant communities. The forest has some mountainous terrain, but most of theforest consists of v-shaped valleys separated by narrow ridges or plateaus.
Kevin Martin, Forest Supervisor

3420 Umpqua National Forest
2900 NW Stewart Parkway 541-957-3200
PO Box 1008 Fax: 541-957-3495
Roseburg, OR 97471 jcaplan@fs.fed.us
www.fs.usda.gov/umpqua/
The Umpqua National Forest covers nearly one million acres and is located in the western slopes of the Cascades in Southwest Oregon. The forest encommpasses a diverse area of rugged peaks, high rolling meadows, sparkling rivers andlakes and deep canyons producing a wealth of water resources, timber, forage, minerals, wildlife and outdoor recreation opportunities.
Kelly Miller, Information Assistant

3421 Wallowa-Whitman National Forest
1500 Dewey Avenue 541-523-6391
PO Bos 907 Fax: 541-523-1315
Baker, OR 97814 www.fs.usda.gov/wallowa-whitman/
The Wallowa-Whitman National Forest contains 2.3 million acres ranging in elevation from 875 feet in Hells Canyon, to 9845 feet in the Eagle Cap Wilderness. Our varied forests are managed as sustainable ecosystems providing cleanwater, wildlife habitat and valuable forest products. For things to do and places to be, the Wallowa-Whitman is the setting for a variety of year-round recreation. You are welcome at the Wallowa-Whitman National Forest.

3422 William L Finley National Wildlife Refuge
26208 Finley Refuge Road 503-757-7236
Corvallis, OR 97333 www.fws.gov/refuge/william_l_finley/
Primary objective for the refuge is the protection and management of wintering habitat for dusky Canada geese. In addition to geese, other migratory and resident animals use refuge lands

3423 Winema National Forest
1301 South G Street 541-947-2151
Lakeview, OR 97630 Fax: 541-883-6709
www.fs.usda.gov/fremont-winema
The 1.1 million acre Winema National Forest lies on the eastern slopes of the Cascade Mountain Range in South Central Oregon, an area noted for its year-round sunshine. The Forest borders Crater Lake National Park near the crest of theCascades and stretches eastward into the Klamath River Basin. Near the floor of the Basin the Forest gives way to vast marshes and meadows assoicated with Upper Klamath Lake and the Williamson River.

Pennsylvania: US Forests, Parks, Refuges

3424 Allegheny National Forest
4 Farm Colony Road 814-723-5150
Warren, PA 16365-6100 Fax: 814-726-1465
r9_allegheny_nf@fs.fed.us
www.fs.usda.gov/allegheny/
An organization dedicated to providing advice for development of the corridor management plan for the northern section of the Allegheny River that has been designated as a National Wild and Scenic River.
Erin Connelly, Forest Supervisor

3425 Delaware National Scenic River: Delaware Water Gap National Recreation Area
Delaware Water Gap National Recreation Area
HQ River Road - Route 209 570-588-2435
Bushkill, PA 18324 Fax: 570-588-2780
www.nationalparksgallery.com/

3426 Erie National Wildlife Refuge
11296 Wood Duck Lane 814-789-3585
Guys Mills, PA 16327 Fax: 814-789-2909
erie@fws.gov
www.fws.gov/refuge/erie/
A haven for migratory birds consisting of two divisions: the Sugar Lake Division and the Seneca Division. Refuge management objectives include: providing waterfowl and other migratory birds with nesting, feeding, brooding, and restinghabitat; providing habitat to support a diversity of other wildlife species; and enhancing opportunities for wildlife-oriented public recreation and environmental education.
Patty Nagel, Deputy Refuge Manager

3427 Gettysburg National Military Park
1195 Baltimore Pike, Suite 100 717-334-1124
Gettysburg, PA 17325-2804 Fax: 717-334-1891
gett_superintendant@nps.gov
www.nps.gov/gett/index.htm
A unit of the national park service preserving 6000 acres of Gettysburg battlefield, and the Soldiers' National Cemetery, site of Lincoln's Gettysburg Address.

3428 John Heinz National Wildlife Refuge at Tinicum
8601 Lindbergh Boulevard 215-365-3118
Philadelphia, PA 19153 Fax: 215-365-2846
JohnHeinzNWR@fws.gov
www.fws.gov/refuge/John_Heinz
The John Heinz National Wildlife Refuge at Tinicum is administered by the Department of Interior's U.S. Fish and Wildlife Service and is located in Philadelphia and Delaware Counties, Pennsylvania. The refuge protects the last 200acres of freshwater tidal marsh in Pennsylvania. The refuge has become a resting and feeding area for more than 20 species of birds, 80 of which nest here. Fox, deer, muskrat, turtles, fish, frogs and a wide variety of wildflowers and plants callthe refuge home.

3429 Upper Delaware Scenic & Recreational River
274 River Road 570-729-7134
Beach Lake, PA 18405 Fax: 570-729-8565
www.nps.gov/upde
As a part of the National Wild and Scenic Rivers System, upper Delaware Scenic and Recreational River stretches 73.4 miles (118.3 km) along the New York/Pennsylvania border. The longest free flowing river in the Northeast, it includesriffles and Class I and II rapids between placid pools eddies. Public fishing and boating accesses are provided, although most land along the river is privately owned. Wintering bald eagles are among the wildlife that may be seen here.
Dave Forney, Superintendent
Michael Reubet, Chief Resource Management

Rhode Island: US Forests, Parks, Refuges

3430 Rhode Island National Wildlife Refuge Complex
3769 D Old Post Road 401-364-0170
PO Box 307 Fax: 401-364-0170
Charlestown, RI 02813 fw5rw_rinwr@fws.gov
www.fws.gov/northeast/ri.htm
Charles Vandemoer, Complex Refuge Manager
Gary M Andres, Deputy Refuge Manager

South Carolina: US Forests, Parks, Refuges

3431 Ace Basin National Wildlife Refuge
PO Box 848 843-889-3084
Hollywood, SC 29449 Fax: 843-889-3282
www.fws.gov/acebasin/
The Ace Basin National Wildlife Refuge was established in 1990 to assist in preserving the nationally significant wildlife and related habitats within the 350,000-acre Ashepoo, Combahee and South Edisto (ACE) rivers basin. The wetlandshabitat of the area has been preserved during the last several centuries through careful management by private landowners. An antebellum mansion that survived the Civil War now serves in part as office space for the refuge.
Jane Griess, Refuge Manager

3432 Cape Romain National Wildlife Refuge
5801 Highway 17 North 843-928-3264
Awendaw, SC 29429 Fax: 843-928-3803
caperomain@fws.gov
www.fws.gov/refuge/cape_romain
Refuge objectives are to: provide habitat for waterfowl, shorebirds, wading birds and resident species; provide habitat and management of endangered and threatened species; provide protection of Class I Wilderness Area; and provideenvironmental education and recreation for the public.
Sarah Dawsey, Refuge Manager
Raye Nilius, Project Leader

3433 Carolina Sandhills National Wildlife Refuge
23734 U.S. Highway 1 803-335-8350
McBee, SC 29101 Fax: 803-335-8406
carolinasandhills@fws.gov
www.fws.gov/refuge/Carolina_Sandhills/
Richard P Ingram, Manager

3434 Francis Marion-Sumter National Forest
4931 Broad River Road 803-561-4000
Columbia, SC 29212 Fax: 803-561-4004
www.fs.usda.gov/scnfs
Headquaters in the capital city of Columbia, both forests are managed for many uses; including timber and wood production, watershed protection and improvement, habitat for wildlife and fish species, wilderness area management,minerals leasing and outdoor recreation.
Paul Bradley, Forest Supervisor

3435 Santee National Wildlife Refuge
2125 Fort Watson Road 803-478-2217
Summerton, SC 29148 Fax: 803-478-2314
santee@fws.gov
www.fws.gov/santee
Wildlife viewing opportunities available at the refuge on hiking, biking, canoeing/kayaking, and driving trails. A refuge visitor center is open Tuesday thru Saturday from 8-4. Located off of I-95 at exit 102 in Summerton, SC, SanteeNational Wildlife offers something for everybody.
Marc Epstein, Refuge Manager
Christopher Spivey, Refuge Officer

South Dakota: US Forests, Parks, Refuges

3436 Badlands National Park
25216 Ben Reifel Road 605-433-5361
PO Box 6 Fax: 605-433-5404
Interior, SD 57750 www.nps.gov/badl/
Consists of acres of sharply eroded buttes, pinnacles and spires blended with the largest protected mixed grass prarie in the US. The Badlands Wilderness Area covers 64,000 acres and is the site of the reintroduction of theblack-footed ferret, the most endangered land mammal in North America. The Stronghold Unit is co-managed with the Oglala Sioux Tribe and includes site of 1890s Glost Dances. Over 11,000 years of human history pale to the ages old paleontologicalresources.
William R Supernaugh, Superintendent

3437 Black Hills National Forest
1019 N. 5th Street 605-673-9200
Custer, SD 57730 Fax: 605-673-9350
r2_blackhills_webinfo@fs.fed.us
www.fs.usda.gov/blackhills
Eleven reservoirs, 30 campgrounds, 2 scenic byways, 1300 miles of streams, 13,000 acres of wilderness, 353 miles of trails, and much more. The forest is managed for multiple use so don't be surprised to see mining, logging, cattlegrazing, and summer homes on your travel.

3438 Huron Wetland Management District
20721 392nd Ave 605-352-5894
Hwy 14 Fax: 605-352-6709
Wolsey, SD 57384 huronwetlands@fws.gov
www.fws.gov/refuge/huron_wmd
The public lands of the HWMD, called Waterfowl Production Areas, are part of the National Wildlife Refuge System. The refuges and WPAs are vitally important to wildlife and people. They provide food, water, cover and space for hundredsof species of birds, mammals, reptiles, amphibians, fish and plants. Managed to benefit endangered species, migratory birds and other wildlife and provide places to learn about and enjoy wildlife. HWMD's mission is to preserve wetlands and managehabitat.
harris Hoisted, Project Leader

3439 Jewel Cave National Monument
11149 U.S. Highway 16 605-673-8300
Building B12 Fax: 605-673-8301
Custer, SD 57730 www.nps.gov/jeca/
With more than 125 miles sureyed, jewel cave is recognized as the third longest cave in the world. Airflow within its passages indicates a vast area yet to be explored. Cave tours provide opportunities for viewing this pristine cavesystem and its wide varitey of speleothems including stalactites, stalagmites, draperies, frostwork, flowstone, boxwork and hydromagnesite balloons. The cave is an important hibernaculum for several species of bats.
Kate Cannon, Superintendent

3440 Sand Lake National Wildlife Refuge
39650 Sand Lake Drive 605-885-6320
Columbia, SD 57433 Fax: 605-885-6333
sandlake@fws.gov
www.fws.gov/sandlake/
Sand Lake Refuge is haven for wildlife and those who enjoy it. Home to more than 266 species of birds, 40 mammal species and a variety of fish, reptiles and amphibians, this 22,000 acre refuge is a mosaic of wildlife and the wildplaces they need. Sand Lake is also a very popular recreation spot. Wildlife observation, fishing, hunting, photography, interpretation and environmental education are all popular activities at the refuge.

3441 Wind Cave National Park
26611 US Highway 385 605-745-4600
Hot Springs, SD 57747-6027 Fax: 605-745-4207
www.nps.gov/wica

One of the world's longest and most complex caves lies beneath the 28,295 acres of rolling, mixed grass prairie ecosystems of Wind Cave National Park. The park is home to a large variety of prairie wildlife such as bison, pronghornantelope and prairie dogs. The cave is famous for the rare cave formation called boxwork.
Vidal Davila, Park Superintendent

Tennessee: US Forests, Parks, Refuges

3442 Big South Fork National River Recreation Area
4564 Leatherwood Road 423-569-9778
Onieda, TN 37841 Fax: 423-569-5505
www.nps.gov/biso/

The free-flowing Big South Fork of the Cumberland River and its tributaries pass through 90 miles of scenic gorges and valleys containing a wide range of natural and historic features. The area offers a broad range of recreationalopportunities including camping, whitewater rafting, kayaking, canoeing, hiking, horseback riding, mountain biking, hunting and fishing, The US Army Corps of Engineers, with its experience in managing river basins, was charged with land acquisition,planning and deve
William K Dickinson, Superintendent

3443 Cherokee National Forest
2800 N Ocoee Street NW 423-476-9700
Po Box 2010 Fax: 423-476-9721
Cleveland, TN 37312-5374 www.fs.usda.gov/cherokee

The Cherokee is steeped in colorful history and rich in the grandeur of the Appalachian Mountains. The forest is separated into two sections by Great Smoky Mountains Park and shares other boundaries with national forest in Georgia,North Carolina and Virginia.
Tom Speaks, Forest Supervisor

3444 Chickasaw National Wildlife Refuge
1505 Sand Bluff Road 731-635-7621
Ripley, TN 38063 Fax: 731-635-0178
www.fws.gov/refuge/chickasaw

Established to provide essentail habitat for migratory birds in the Lower Mississippi Valley. The refuge supports a variety of wildlife. Visitors can see large numbers of migratory wasterfowl in the winter. Neotropical migratory birdsand shorebirds are a common site yearround. The refuge is open to hunting and fishing-special regulations apply. Please contact the refuge manager for current regulations.
Bryan Woodward, Refuge Manager
Randy Cook, Refuge Complex Manager

3445 Cross Creeks National Wildlife Refuge
643 Wildlife Road 931-232-7477
Dover, TN 37058 Fax: 931-232-5958
crosscreeks@fws.gov
www.fws.gov/refuge/Cross_Creeks

Its primary purpose is to provide feeding and resting habitat for migratory birds with an emphasis placed on providing habitat for wintering waterfowl.
Vicki C Grafe, Manager

3446 Great Smokey Mountains National Park
107 Park Headquarters Road 865-436-1200
Gatlinburg, TN 37738 Fax: 865-436-1220
grsm_smokies_information@nps.gov
www.nps.gov/grsm

The national park, in the state of North Carolina is world renowned for the diversity of its plant and animal resources, the beauty of its ancient mountains, the quality of its remnants of Southern Appalachian mountain culture, and thedepth and integrity of the wilderness sanctuary within its boundaries, it is one the largest protected areas in the east.
Randall R Pope, Supt

3447 Hatchie National Wildlife Refuge
6772 Highway 76 South 731-772-0501
Stanton, TN 38069-8322 Fax: 731-772-7839
hatchie@fws.gov
www.fws.gov/refuge/hatchie

The dominant habitat type is 9,400 acres of seasonally flooded bottomland hardwoods. Other habitats include 400 acres of upland forest; 534 acres of open water, including 9 oxbow lakes; and 1,100 acres of agricultural areas managed ascropland, moist soil and old field habitats.
James B. Roberts, Manager

3448 Lower Hatchie National Wildlife Refuge
1505 Sand Bluff Road 901-635-7621
Ripley, TN 38063 Fax: 901-635-7621
r4rw_tn.rlf@fws.gov
www.fws.gov/refuge/Lower_Hatchie

The Refuge's primary purposes are to be a sanctuary for migratory birds and to preserve a representative portion of the fast vanishing bottomland hardwood forests as habitat for wintering waterfowl and other migratory birds.

3449 Reelfoot National Wildlife Refuge
4343 Highway 157 731-538-2481
Union City, TN 38261 Fax: 901-538-9760
r4rw_tn.rlf@fws.gov
www.fws.gov/refuge/reelfoot/

Reelfoot Lake is approximately 13,000 acres and provides numerous recreational opportunities including sport fishing and hunting.
Randy Cook, Manager

3450 Tennessee National Wildlife Refuge
1371 Wildlife Drive 901-642-2091
Springville, TN 38256 Fax: 901-644-3351
www.fws.gov/refuge/tennessee/

The refuge provides habitat for more than 226 species of birds, 47 species of mammals, 90 species of reptiles and amphibians and 109 species of fish.
John Taylor, Manager

Texas: US Forests, Parks, Refuges

3451 Alibates Flint Quarries National Monument: Lake Meredith National Recreation Area
PO Box 1460 806-857-3151
Fritch, TX 79036 Fax: 806-857-2319
www.nps.gov/alfl

ALIBATES: The only national monument in Texas. Preserves over 700 archeological sites. The monument can only be viewed by ranger-led guided tours. LAKE MEREDITH: A 45,000 acre recreation area that includes a 10,000 acre reservoirwhere visitors can enjoy water and land recreational activities such as hunting, fishing, boating, horseback riding, off-road vehicles, jetskies and the like.
Karren Brown, Supt

3452 Amistad National Recreation Area
4121 Veterans Blvd. 830-775-7491
Del Rio, TX 78840-9350 Fax: 830-778-9248
interpretation@nps.gov
www.nps.gov/amis

Situated on the United States-Mexico border, is know primarily for excellent year round, water-based recreation including: fishing , boating, swimming, suba diving. Also provides opportuni-

ties for picnicking, camping and hinting. Thereservoir, at the confluence of the Rio Grande, Devils and Pecos rivers, was created by Amistad Dam in 1969, This area is reach in technology and rock art, and contains a wide variety of plant and animal life.
Alan W. Cox, Supt

3453 Angelina National Forest
111 Walnut Ridge Road 936-897-1068
Zavalla, TX 75904 Fax: 936-639-8588
mailroom_r8_texas@fs.fed.us
www.fs.usda.gov/texas
The Angelina National Forest is located in the heart of Texas. The reservoir, a 114,500 acre lake on the Angelina River is noted for its fishing, boating and water skiing.

3454 Big Bend National Park
PO Box 129 915-477-2251
Big Bend National Park, TX 79834 Fax: 915-477-1175
www.nps.gov/bibe/
The Big Bend National Park is situated on the boundary with Mexico along the Rio Grande. It is a place where countries and cultures meet, also a place that merges natural environments, from desert to mountains. It's a place where southmeets north and east meets west, creating a great diversity of plants and animals. The park covers over 801,000 acres of west Texas in the place where the Rio Grande makes a sharp turn - the Big Bend.
Robert Arnberger, Supt

3455 Big Thicket National Preserve
6044 FM 420 409-951-6800
Kountze, TX 77625 Fax: 409-951-6714
BITH_Administration@nps.gov
www.nps.gov/bith
The Preserve consists of nine land units and six water corridors encompassing more than 97,000 acres. Big Thicket was the first Preserve in the National Park System and protects and area of rich biological diversity. A convergence ofecosystems occured here during the last Ice Age. It brought together, in one geographical location, the eastern hardwood forests, the Gulf coastal plains and the midwest praries.
Ronald Switzer, Supt

3456 Grulla National Wildlife Refuge
1531 County Road 1248 806-946-3341
P.O. Box 549 Fax: 806-946-3317
Muleshoe, TX 79347 jude_smith@fws.gov
www.fws.gov/southwest/refuges/newmex/grulla/index.html
Located in Roosevelt County, New Mexico, near the small town of Arch, approximately 25 miles northwest of Muleshoe National Wildlife Refuge. Grulla NWR, which is managed by the staff at Muleshoe NWR, has 3,236 acres, more than 2,000 ofwhich make up the saline lake bed of Salt Lake. The rest of the refuge is grassland. When the lake holds sufficient water, Grulla NWR is a wintering area for lesser sandhill cranes. Ring-necked pheasant, scaled quail and lesser prairie chickens maybe seen.
Jude Smith, Refuge Manager

3457 Guadalupe Mountains National Park
400 Pine Canyon Drive 915-828-3251
Salt Flat, TX 79847-9400 Fax: 915-828-3269
GUMO_Superintendent@nps.gov
www.nps.gov/gumo
This mountain mass contains portions of the world's most extensive and significant Permian limestone fossil reef, earth fault peaks, unusual flora and fauna. Guadalupe Peak, highest point in Texas at 8,749 feet.
John Lujan, Superintendent
Fred Armstrong, Chief of Resource Management

3458 Hagerman National Wildlife Refuge
6465 Refuge Road 903-786-2826
Sherman, TX 75092 Fax: 903-786-3327
gayle_ellis@fws.gov
www.fws.gov/refuge/hagerman/
Hagerman NWR lies on the Big Mineral Arm of Lake Texoma, on the Red River between Oklahoma and Texas. Established in 1946, the refuge includes 3,000 acres of marsh and water and 8,000 acres of upland and farmland. During fall, winterand spring, the marshes and waters are in constant use by migrating and wintering waterfowl.
Kathy Whaley, Manager

3459 Padre Island National Seashore
PO Box 181300 361-949-8068
Corpus Christi, TX 78480-1300 Fax: 361-949-8023
www.nps.gov/pais
Encompassing 130,434 acres, the longest remaining undeveloped stretch of barrier island in the world, and offers a wide variety of flora and fauna as well as recreation.

3460 Santa Ana National Wildlife Refuge
3325 Green Jay 956-784-7500
Box 202A Fax: 956-787-8338
Alamo, TX 78516 christine_donald@fws.gov
www.fws.gov/refuge/santa_ana/
The 2,088 acre refuge along the banks of the lower Rio Grande was established in 1943 for the protection of migratory birds. Considered the jewel of the refuge system, this essential island of thorn forest habitat is host or home tonearly 400 different types of birds and a myriad of other species, including the indigo snake, malachite butterfly and the endangered ocelot. Provides habitat for thousands of migrating birds and about one half of all butterfly species found in NorthAmerica.
Jeff Howland, Refuge Manager

Utah: US Forests, Parks, Refuges

3461 Arches National Park
PO Box 907 435-719-2299
Moab, UT 84532-0907 Fax: 435-719-2300
archinfo@nps.gov
www.nps.gov/arch/
Arches National Park preserves over two thousand natural sandstone arches and a variety of other unique geological resources. The extraordinary features of the park are highlighted by a striking environment of contrasting colors,landforms and textures. Administered by Canyonlands National Park
Laura Jess, Supt

3462 Ashley National Forest
355 North Vernal Avenue 435-789-1181
Vernal, UT 84078 Fax: 435-781-5295
www.fs.usda.gov/ashley
Remarkable features include Kings Peak (highest peak in Utah), Flaming Gorge National Recreation Area, Flaming Gorge-Uintas National Scenic Byway, The Green River Corridor
Rowdy Muir, District Ranger

3463 Bear River Migratory Bird Refuge
58 S 435-723-5887
Brigham City, UT 84302 Fax: 435-723-8873
bearriver@fws.gov
www.fws.gov/refuge/bear_river_migratory_bird_refuge/
To date, close to 1 million cubic yards of earth has been moved to restore and enhance the refuge. Forty-seven primary water control structures have been restored along with over forty-seven miles of dikes. Through volunteer efforts,debris has been removed from the old headquaters site and a new pavilion,

restroom, demonstration pond, and kiosk have been built on the site. The 12-mile auto tour route has been reopened to the public.
Alan K Trout, Manager

3464 Bryce Canyon National Park
PO Box 640201 435-834-5322
Bryce Canyon, UT 84764-0201 Fax: 435-834-4102
www.nps.gov/brca
Consists of 37,277 acres of scenic colorful rock formations and desert wonderland. Bryce Canyon National Park is named for one of a series of horseshoe-shaped amphitheaters carved from the eastern edge of the Paunsaugunt Plateau insouthern Utah. Erosion has shaped colorful Claron limestones, sandstones and mudstones into thousands of spires, fins, pinnacles and mazes. Collectively called hoodoos, these unique formations are whimsically arranged and tinted with colors toonumerous to name.
Craig C Axtell

3465 Canyonlands National Park
2282 S West Resource Boulevard 435-719-2313
Moab, UT 84532 Fax: 435-719-2300
canyinfo@nps.gov
www.nps.gov/cany/index.htm
Canyonlands National Park preserves a stunning landscape of sedimentary sandstones eroded into countless canyons, mesas and buttes by the Colorado River and its tributaries. Largely undeveloped, the park is a popular backcountrydestination and scientific research site.

3466 Capitol Reef National Park
HC 70 Box 15 435-425-3791
Torrey, UT 84775-9602 Fax: 435-425-3026
care_administration@nps.gov
www.ehow.com/fashion
The Waterpocket Fold, a 100 mile long wrinkle in the earth's know as a monoclide, extends from nearby Thousand Lakes Mountain to the Colorado River. Capitol Reef National Park was established to protect this grand and colorful geologicfeature, as well as the unique historical and cultural history found in the area.
Albert J Hendricks, Supt

3467 Cedar Breaks National Monument
2390 W Highway 56 435-586-9451
Suite 11 Fax: 435-586-3813
Cedar City, UT 84720 www.nps.gov/cebr/
Millons of years of sedimentation, uplift and erosion continue to create a deep canyon of rock walls, fins, spires and columms, that spans some three miles, and over 2,000 feet deep. The rim of the canyon is over 10,000 feet above sealevel, and is forested with islands of Englemann spruce, subalpine fir and aspen: separated by broad meadows of brillant summertime wild flowers.
Denny Davies, Supt
Ateve Robinson, Chief Ranger

3468 Dixie National Forest
1789 N Wedgewood Ln 435-865-3700
Cedar City, UT 84721 Fax: 435-865-3791
www.fs.usda.gov/dixie
The Dixie is located adjacent to three National Parks, Bryce Canyon, Zion and Capitol Reef.The red sandstone formations of Red Canyon rival those of Bryce Canyon National park. From the top of Powell Point, it is possible to see farinto three different states. Boulder Mountain and the many different lakes provide opportunities for hiking, fishing and viewing outstanding scenery.
Mary Wagner, Forest Supervisor

3469 Fish Springs National Wildlife Refuge
PO Box 568 435-693-3122
Dugway, UT 84022 Fax: 435-693-9933
fishsprings@fws.gov
www.fws.gov/refuge/fish_springs
Located at the southern end of the Great Salt Lake Desert in western Utah, Fish Springs National Wildlife Refuge encompasses 17,992 acres between two small mountain ranges. Five major springs and several lesser springs and seeps flowfrom a faultline at the base of the eastern front of the Fish Springs Mountain Range, These warm, saline springs provide virtually all of the water for the Refuge's 10,000-acre marsh system.
Jerry Bana, Manager

3470 Fishlake National Forest
115 E 900 N 435-896-9233
Richfield, UT 84701 Fax: 435-896-9347
www.fs.usda.gov/fishlake
The Fishlake National Forest in central Utah features majestic stands of aspen encircling open mountain meadows that are lush with a diverse community of forbs and grasses. The mountains of the Fishlake are a source of water for manyof the neighboring communities and agricultural valleys in the region. Hunting, fishing and OHV use are among the most popular forms of recreation enjoyed by forest visitors.
Allen Rowley, Forest Supervisor

3471 Natural Bridges National Monument
HC 60 435-692-1234
Box 1 Fax: 435-692-1111
Lake Powell, UT 84533 nabrinfo@nps.gov
www.nps.gov/nabr
Natural Bridges protects some of the finest examples of ancient stone architecture in the southwest. The monument is located in the southeast Utah on a pinyon-juniper covered mesa bisected by deep canyons of Permian age Ceder MesaSandstone. Where meandering streams cut through the cayon walls, three natural bridges formed: Kachina, Owachomo and Sipapu.
Coralee S Hays, Superintendent

3472 Ouray National Wildlife Refuge
HC 69 Box 232 435-545-2522
Randlett, UT 84063 Fax: 435-545-2369
Ouray@fws.gov
www.fws.gov/refuge/ouray/
This organization is dedicated to the conservation of wildlife and endangered species. They provide and maintain safe habitats for these animals.
Dan Schaad, Refuge Manager
Sonja Jahrsdoerfer, Project Leader

3473 Timpanogos Cave National Monument
Rural Route 3 Box 200 801-756-5239
American Fork, UT 84003 Fax: 801-756-5661
www.nps.gov/tica
Timpanogos Cave Natioanl Monument sits high in the Wasatch Mountains. The cave system consists of three spectacularly decorated caverns. Each cavern has unique colors and formations. Helicitites and anthodites are just a few of themany dazzling formations to be found in the many chambers. As visitors climb to the cavern entrance, on a hike gaining over 1,000 feet in elevation, they are offered incredible views of American Fork Canyon.
Dennis Davis, Superintendent

3474 Uinta National Forest
857 West South Jordan 801-342-5100
South Jordan, UT 84095 Fax: 801-342-5144
uwc-info@fs.fed.us
www.fs.usda.gov/uwcnf
The Uinta National Forest ranges from high western desert at Vernon to lofty mountain peaks such as Mount Nebo (elevation 11,877 feet, the highest peak in the Wasatch Range) and Mount Timpanogos (elevation 11,750 feet). The forestcontains three wilderness areas: the Lone Peak, the Mount Timpanogos and the Mount Nebo Wildernesses. The Forest surrounds the Timpanogos Cave National Mounment.
Peter Karp, Forest Supervisor

3475 Wasatch-Cache National Forest
857 West South Jordan 801-466-6411
South Jordan, UT 84095 Fax: 801-524-3172
uwc-info@fs.fed.us
www.fs.usda.gov/uwcnf
Wasatch-Cache National Forest lands are located in three major areas: the northern and western slopes of the Uinta Mountains. The Wasatch Front from Lone Peak north to the Idaho border including the Wasatch, Monte cristo, and BearRiver Ranges. The Stansbury Range, in the Great Basin.
Tom Tidwell, Forest Supervisor

3476 Zion National Park
Star Route 9 435-772-3256
Springdale, UT 84767-1099 Fax: 435-772-3426
zion_park_information@nps.gov
www.nps.gov/zion
Protected within Zion National Park's 229 square miles (593.1 km) is a spectacular cliff-and-cayon landscape and wilderness full of the unexpected including the world's largest arch -Kolob Arch- with a span that measures 310 feet(94.5m). Wildlife such as mule deer, golden eagles, and mountain lions also inhabit the park. Mukuntuweap National Monument proclaimed July 31, 1909; incorporated in Zion National Monument March 18, 1918; established as national park Nov. 19, 1919.
Ron Terry, Public Information Officer

Vermont: US Forests, Parks, Refuges

3477 Green Mountains & Finger Lakes National Forest
231 North Main Street 802-747-6700
Rutland, VT 05701 Fax: 802-747-6766
www.fs.usda.gov/greenmountain

3478 Missisquoi National Wildlife Refuge
29 Tabor Road 802-868-4781
Swanton, VT 05488 Fax: 802-868-2379
missisquoi@fws.gov
www.fws.gov/refuge/missisquoi
The 6,592-acre refuge includes most of the Missisquoi River delta where it flows into Missisquoi Bay. The refuge consists of quiet waters and wetlands which attract large flocks of migratory birds.
Mark Sweeny, Manager

Virginia: US Forests, Parks, Refuges

3479 George Washington National Forest
5162 Valleypointe Parkway
PO Box 233 888-265-0019
Roanoke, VA 24019 Fax: 540-265-5145
www.fs.usda.gov/gwj
Outstanding hiking trails, campsites, fishing and canoeing are the hallmarks of George Washington Forest in Virginia and West Virginia, part of the George Washington and Jefferson National Forest.

3480 Jefferson National Forest
5162 Valleypointe Parkway
Roanoke, VA 24019 888-265-0019
www.fs.usda.gov/gwj
The Jefferson National Forest is prize Appalachia country: tumbling waterfalls, rare wildflowers, vividly colored hills and Virginia's highest peak. Jefferson National Forest spreads 690,000 acres of hardwood and conifer forest acrosswest-central Virginia, West Virgina and Kentucky, including the ridge province of the Blue Ridge mountains.

3481 Mason Neck National Wildlife Refuge
12638 Darby Brooke Ct. 703-490-4979
Woodbridge, VA 22192 potomacriverrefuges@fws.gov
www.fws.gov/refuge/mason_neck/
The refuge, the Mason Neck State Park, the Northern Virginia Park Authority, the Gunston Hall Plantation and the Virginia Department of Game and Inland Fisheries are cooperating in the management of their combined 5,000+ acres on theMason Neck peninsula. This cooperation provides a wide variety of recreational activities while protecting natural resources. The primary objective of the refuge is to protect essential nesting, feeding and roosting habitat for bald eagles.
J Frederick Milton, Manager

3482 Shenandoah National Park
3655 US Highway 211 East 540-999-3500
Luray, VA 22835 Fax: 540-999-3601
www.nps.gov/shen/index.htm
Shenandoah National park lies astride a beautiful section of the blue rige mountains, which from the eastern rampart of the Appalachian Mountains between Pennsylvania and Georgia. The Shenandoah River flows through the valley to thewest, with Massanutten Mountain, 40 miles long, standing between the river's north and south forks. The rolling Piedmont country lies to the east of the park. Skyline Drive, a 105- mile road that winds along the crest of the mountainsthrough thelength of the park.
William Wade, Supt

Washington: US Forests, Parks, Refuges

3483 Colville National Forest
255 W. 11th Avenue Kettle Falls 509-684-7000
Coleville, WA 99114 Fax: 509-684-7280
www.fs.usda.gov/colville
The Colville National Forest encompasses over one million acres in northeastern Washington. The Sherman Pass National Scenic Byway leads through a portion of the Forest, with camping, fishing, hiking, picnicking, mountain biking,cross-country skiing, sonowmobiling and other recreational activities. 49 Degrees North, a full service ski resort, is located east of Chewelah, about one hour north of Spokane. The Salmo-Prist Wilderness Area sits in the northeast corner of theforest.

3484 Conboy Lake National Wildlife Refuge
PO Box 5 509-546-8300
Glenwood, WA 98619 Fax: 509-364-3667
mcriver@fws.gov
www.fws.gov/refuge/conboy_lake/
Located in the northwest corner of Klickitat County, Washington, the refuge was established primarily for waterfowl. The broad range of habitat diversity provides for a broad diversity of resident wildlife species.
Harold E Cole, Manager

3485 Gifford Pinchot National Forest
10600 N.E. 51st Circle 360-891-5000
Vancouver, WA 98682 Fax: 360-891-5045
www.fs.usda.gov/giffordpinchot/
The Gifford Pinchot National Forst is one of the oldest National Forests in the United States. Include as part of The Mount Rainier Forest Reserve in 1897, this area was set aside as the columbia National Forest in 1908, and renamedthe Gifford Pinchot National Forest in 1949. The Forest, located in southwest Washington State, now contains 1,312,000 acres and includes the 110,000- acre Mount St. Helens National Volcanic Mounument established by congress in 1982.

3486 Lewis & Clark National Wildlife Refuge
46 Steamboat Slough Rd 360-795-3915
PO Box 566 willapa@fws.gov
Cathlamet, WA 98612 www.fws.gov/refuges/profiles/

3487 McNary National Wildlife Refuge
64 Maple Road 509-546-8300
PO Box 544 Fax: 509-546-8303
Burbank, WA 99323 mcriver@fws.gov
www.fws.gov/mcnary/
A resting and feeding area for up to 100,000 migrating waterfowl. It includes 3,629 acres of water and marsh, croplands, grasslands, trees and shrubs.
Robyn Thorson, Regional Manager
Richard Hannon, Deputy Regional Manager

3488 Mount Baker-Snoqualmie National Forests
2930 Wetmore Avenue 425-783-6000
Suite 3A 800-627-0062
Everett, WA 98201 www.fs.usda.gov/mbs
An urban forest, extending over 140 miles along the western slopes of the Cascade Mountains from the Canadian border to Mount Rainier National Park.
Jennifer Eberlien, Forest Supervisor

3489 Mount Rainier National Park
55210 238th Avenue East 253-569-2211
Ashford, WA 98304 Fax: 360-569-2170
MORAInfo@nps.gov
www.nps.gov/mora/
Established in 1899. 235,625 acres (97% is designated Wilderness). Includes mount Rainier (14,410'), an active volcano encased in over 35 square miles of snow and ice. The park contains outstanding examples of old growth forests andsubalpine meadows. Designated a National Historic landmark District in 1997 as a showcase for the NPS Rustic style architecture of the 1920s and 1930s.
William Briggle, Supt

3490 North Cascades National Park Service Complex
810 State Route 20 360-854-7200
Sedro-Woolley, WA 98284 Fax: 360-856-1934
NOCA_Interpretation@nps.gov
www.nps.gov/noca

3491 Okanogan National Forest
1240 S 2nd Avenue 509-826-3275
PO Box 950 Fax: 509-826-3789
Okanogan, WA 98840 www.fs.usda.gov/okawen/
There is a variety of country from craggy peaks to rolling meadows, to rich old growth forest and classic groves of ponderosa pine. We're called the Sunny Okanogan and for good reason: summers here are hot and dry, and our winters arefamous for brilliant clear skies and plenty of snow.

3492 Okanogan and Wenatchee National Forests Headquarters
215 Melody Lane 509-664-9200
Wenatchee, WA 98801 Fax: 509-664-9280
www.fs.usda.gov/okawen
The 2.2 million acre Wenatchee National Forest extends about 135 miles along the east side of the crest of the Cascade Mountains in Washington State. This National Forest is most noted for its wide range of recreation opportunities.There truly is something for everyone who likes to have fun in the outdoors.
Rebecca Heath, Forest Supervisor

3493 Olympic National Forest
1835 Black Lake Boulevard SW 360-956-2402
Olympia, WA 98512 www.fs.fed.us/r6/olympic
The National Forests are part of America's great outdoors and are public lands. They are managed for the multiple uses of recreation, wildlife, timber, gazing, mining, oil and gas, watershed and wilderness. The Olympic National Forestis over 632,000 acres in size and is divided into two Ranger Districts: Hood Canal and Pacific.

3494 Olympic National Park
600 East Park Avenue 360-565-3000
Port Angeles, WA 98362 Fax: 360-565-3015
www.nps.gov/olym
Often referred to as three parks in one, Olympic National Park encompasses three distinctly different ecosystems-rugged glacier capped mountains, over 73 miles of wild Pacific coast and magnificent mountains are still largely pristinein character and are Olympic's gift to you.
Karen Gustin, Superintendent

3495 Ross Lake National Recreation Area North Cascades National Park
810 State Route 20 360-854-7200
Sedro Woolley, WA 98284 Fax: 360-856-1934
www.nps.gov/rola
The most accessible part of the North Cascades National Park Service Complex. Is also the corridor for scenic Washington State Route 20, the North Cascades Highway, and includes three reserviors.

3496 Toppenish National Wildlife Refuge
State Route 97 509-546-8300
Toppenish, WA 98948 800-344-9453
mcriver@fws.gov
www.fws.gov/refuge/toppenish/
An important migration and wintering area for waterfowl in the Yakima Valley of eastern Washington. Wetland impoundments along Toppenish Creek provide natural foods for wintering mallards and other ducks. Ducks and other water birdsbreed in the wetland impoundments during the summer. Native shrub-steppe communities and riparian areas along Toppenish and Snake creeks provide habitat for many other species of birds. The refuge has active hunting and wildlife-viewing programs.
George J Fenn, Manager

3497 Umatilla National Wildlife Refuge
Mid-Columbian River Refuges
64 Maple Street 509-546-8300
Burbank, WA 99323 Fax: 509-546-8303
mcriver@fws.gov
www.fws.gov/mcriver/
The refuge is a varied mix of open water, sloughs, shallow marsh, seasonal wetlands, cropland, islands, and shrub-steppe upland habitats
Morris C LeFever, Manager

3498 Willapa National Wildlife Refuge
3888 State Route 101 206-484-3482
Ilwaco, WA 98624 willapa@fws.gov
www.fws.gov/willapa/
Located on Willapa Bay in Pacific County, the southernmost coastal county in Washington. The upland forest varies in successional stages from recently logged areas to a unique remnant of virgin, coastal cedar-hemlock forest home todeer, bear, elk, grouse, beaver and numerous songbirds and small mammals.
James A Hidy, Manager

West Virginia: US Forests, Parks, Refuges

3499 Monongahela National Forest
200 Sycamore Street 304-636-1800
Elkins, WV 26241 Fax: 304-636-1875
www.fs.usda.gov/mnf
The Monongahela National Forest was established following passage of the 1911 Weeks Act. This act authorized the purchase of land for long-term watershed protection and natural resource

management following massive cutting of theEastern forests in the late 1800's and at the turn of the century.

3500 Ohio River Islands National Wildlife Refuge
3982 Waverly Road 304-375-2923
Williamstown, WV 26187 Fax: 304-422-0754
OhioRiverIslands@fws.gov
www.fws.gov/refuge/ohio_river_islands/
The refuge extends 362 river miles from Shippingport, Pennsylvania to Manchester, Ohio along one of the nation's busiest waterways. The Ohio River Islands and their back channels have long been recognized for high quality fish andwildlife, recreation, scientific and natural heritage values.
Michael Schramm, Visitor Services Manager

Wisconsin: US Forests, Parks, Refuges

3501 Apostle Islands National Lakeshore
415 Washington Street 715-779-3397
Route 1, Box 4 Fax: 715-779-3049
Bayfield, WI 54814 APIS_Webmaster@nps.gov
www.nps.gov/apis/index.htm
The national lakeshore includes 21 islands and 12 miles of mainland Lake Superior shoreline, featuring pristine stretches of sand beach, spectacular sea caves, remnant old growth forests, resident bald eagles and black bears and thelargest collection of lighthouses anywhere in the National Park System.
Robert J Krumenaker, Superintendant

3502 Chequamegon National Forest
1170 4th Avenue S 715-762-2461
Park Falls, WI 54552 Fax: 715-762-5179
www.fs.usda.gov/cnnf
Shaped principally by glacial action some 10,000 years ago, the forest offers a variety of hiking, ATV, and cross-country ski trails at different levels of difficulty. These campgrounds are located on either a lake or a river and offerfishing and boating.

3503 Ice Age National Scientific Reserve
PO Box 7921 608-266-2183
Madison, WI 53707 Fax: 608-267-7474
info@iceagetrail.org
www.wildernet.com
This first national scientific reserve contains nationally significant features of continental glaciation. State parks in the area are open to the public.
Tom Gilbert, Supt

3504 Nicolet National Forest
500 Hanson Lake Road 715-362-1300
Rhinelander, WI 54501 Fax: 715-362-1359
www.fs.usda.gov/cnnf
Located in Wisconsin's Northwoods where towering pine and hardwood forests are interspersed with hundreds of crystal clear lakes and streams, the Nicolet offers you many opportunities to enjoy the outdoors. Within a day's drive of theChicago, Milwaukee, St. Paul and Minneapolis metropolitan areas, the forest is a place where urban dwellers can truly get away from it all in the scenic beauty of the northwoods.

3505 St Croix National Scenic Riverway
401 N Hamilton Street 715-483-3284
St Croix Falls, WI 54024 Fax: 715-483-3288
www.nps.gov/sacn/index.htm
The St. Croix National Scenic Riverway is home to the endangered Higgins Eye and Winged Mapleleaf mussels, bald eagles, gray wolves, and the prehistoric paddlefish. The 252 miles of Riverway provide numerous recreational opportunitiesfor boaters, canoeists, kayakers and others.
Tom Bradley, Superintendent
Ron Erickson, Education Team Manager

Wyoming: US Forests, Parks, Refuges

3506 Bighorn National Forest
2013 Eastside 2nd Street 307-674-2600
Sheridan, WY 82801 Fax: 307-674-2668
www.fs.usda.gov/bighorn
The forest has 32 campgrounds, 14 picnic areas, 2 visitor centers, 2 ski areas, 7 lodges, 2 recreation lakes, 3 scenic byways and over 1500 miles of trails. The Bighorn National Forest is 80 miles long and 30 miles wide. The mostcommon tree is the lodgepole pine. The Bighorn River, flowing along the west side of the forest was first named by American Indians due to the great herds of bighorn sheep at its mouth.
Bill Bass, Forest Supervisor

3507 Bridger-Teton National Forest
340 N Cache-Forest Service Bldg 307-739-5500
PO Box 1888 Fax: 307-739-5010
Jackson, WY 83001 r4_b-t_info@fs.fed.us
www.fs.fed.us/btnf/
With it's 3.4 million acres, it is the second largest National Forest outside Alaska. Included are more than 1.2 million acres of wilderness in the Bridger, Gros Ventre, and Teton Wildernesses. The Bridger-Teton is a land of variedrecreational opportunities, beautiful vistas, and abundant wildlife. Its crystal blue skies are puctuated by awesome mountain ranges which include the Gros Ventre, Teton, Salt River, Wind River, and Wyoming Mountain Ranges.
Jacque Buchanan, Forest Supervisor
Pamela Bode, Resources Staff Officer

3508 Devils Tower National Monument
PO Box 10 307-467-5283
Devils Tower, WY 82714-0010 Fax: 307-467-5350
deto_interpretation@nps.gov
www.nps.gov
This unit of the National Park Service protects the nearly vertical monolith known as Devil's Tower. The rolling hills of this 1347 acre park are covered with pine forests, deciduous woodlands, and prairie grasslands. Known byseveral northern plains tribes as Bear Lodge, it is sacred to many American Indians. Devil's Tower was proclaimed in September, 1906 as the nation's first national monument by President Theodore Roosevelt.
Dorothy FireCloud, Superintendent

3509 Fossil Butte National Monument
PO Box 592 307-877-4455
Kemmerer, WY 83101 Fax: 307-877-4457
FOBU_Superintendent@nps.gov
www.nps.gov/fobu
Located in southwest Wyoming, Fossil Butte National Monument represents one of the richest fossil localities in the world. Fifty million-year-old fish, insects, birds, reptiles, and plants are nearly perfectly preserved in limestone.
David E McGinnis, Superintendent
Marcia Fagnant, Park Ranger

3510 Grand Teton National Park
PO Box 170 307-739-3300
Moose, WY 83012-0170 GRTE_info@nps.gov
www.nps.gov/grte
Grand Teton National Park seeks to protect the mountains and wildlife habitats in National Park Wyoming.

3511 Medicine Bow National Forest
2468 Jackson Street 307-745-2300
Laramie, WY 82070 Fax: 307-745-2398
www.fs.usda.gov/mbr

The Medicine Bow National Forest dates back to May 22, 1902, with the establishment of the Medicine Bow Forest Reserve by President Theodore Roosevelt. In 1929, the former Hayden National Forest along the Continental Divide wasformerly a War Department target and maneuver reservation under joint administration by the Forest Service and the War Department. In 1959, the area formerly used by the military was added to the Medicine Bow National Forest.

3512 **National Elk Refuge**
PO Box 510 307-733-9212
Jackson, WY 83001 Fax: 307-733-9729
nationalelkrefuge@fws.gov
www.fws.gov/refuge/national_elk_refuge
More than 7,500 elk make the winter range of National Elk Refuge their home from October until May. Adjacent to the north side of Jackson, Wyoming, the 25,000-acre refuge includes nearly 1600 acres of open water and marsh lands, 47different mammals and nearly 175 species of birds.
Mike Hedrick, Manager

3513 **Seedskadee National Wildlife Refuge**
37 miles north on Hwy 372 307-875-2187
PO Box 700 Fax: 307-875-4425
Green River, WY 82935 Seedskadee@fws.gov
www.fws.gov/refuge/seedskadee/
Fishery resource is managed cooperatively with the state G&F and includes a special regulations area to promote catch and release fishing for trophy trout (brown, Snake River cutthroat and rainbow trout). Refuge lands are rich inhistorical and cultural resources as the area was utilized by nomadic Indian tribes, fur trappers, early pioneers and travelers heading for the better life of California and Oregon. Many of the old campsites, river crossings and early structuresstill exist.

3514 **Shoshone National Forest**
808 Meadow Lane 307-527-6241
Cody, WY 82414 Fax: 307-578-1212
www.fs.usda.gov/shoshone
The Shoshone consists of 2.4 million acres of varied terrain ranging from sagebrush flats to rugged mountain peaks and includes portions of the Absaroka, Wind River, and Beartooth Mountain Ranges. Elevations on the Shoshone range from4,600 feet at the mouth of the spectacular Clarks Fork Canyon to 13,804 feet on ganneett Peak, Wyoming's highest point. Geologists delightedly call the Shoshone's varied topography an open book.
Joe Alexander, Forest Supervisor

3515 **Yellowstone National Park**
PO Box 168 307-344-7381
Yellowstone National Park, WY 82190-0168 Fax: 307-344-2014
yell_visitor_services@nps.gov
www.nps.gov
Established on March 1, 1872, Yellowstone National Park is the first and oldest national park in the world. Preserved within Yellowstone are Old Faithful Geyser and some 10,000 hot springs and geysers, the majority of the plant'stotal. These geothermal wonders are evidence of one of the world's largest active volcanoes; its last eruption created a crater or caldera that spans almost half of the park.
Suzanne Lewis, Superintendent

Publications

Directories & Handbooks: Air & Climate

3516 **Acid Rain**
Watts, Franklin
1201 Constitution Avenue 202-343-9790
Washington, DC 20004 800-621-1115
Fax: 203-797-3657
www.epa.gov/acidrain
Lists over 4,000 citations, with abstracts, to the worldwide literature on the sources of acid rain and its effects on the environment.

3517 **Weather America**
Grey House Publishing
4919 Route 22 518-789-8700
P.O. Box 56 800-562-2139
Amenia, NY 12501-56 Fax: 518-789-0556
books@greyhouse.com
www.greyhouse.com
Provides extensive climatological data for over 4,000 national and cooperative weather stations throughout the US. Includes a new major storms section and a nationwide ranking section that provides rankings for maximum and minimumtemperatures, precipitation, snowfall, fog, humidity and wind speed. Each of 50 state sections contains a city index for locating the nearest weather station to the city/county being researched and a narrative description of the state's climaticconditions.
Publication Date: 2010 2,013 pages
ISBN: 1-891482-29-7
Leslie Mackenzie, Publisher
David Garoogian, Editor

Directories & Handbooks: Business

3518 **American Caves**
American Caves Conservation Association
119 E Main Street 270-786-1466
PO Box 409 Fax: 270-786-1467
Horse Cave, KY 42749 acca@cavern.org
www.hiddenrivercave.com
A bi-annual membership publication. Published by the American Caves Conservation Association and available by subscription to nonmembers.
David Foster, Executive Director/Author
Debra Heavers, Editor

3519 **Associations Canada**
Grey House Publishing Canada
555 Richmond Street West 416-644-6479
2nd Floor 866-433-4739
Toronto, Ontario M5V 3B1 Fax: 416-644-1904
info@greyhouse.ca
www.greyhouse.ca
Annual directory of Canadian associations and environmental groups including industry, commerical and professional organizations.
Publication Date: 2011 1200 pages
Bryon Moore, General Manager

3520 **Business and the Environment: A Resource Guide**
Island Press
2000 M Street NW 202-232-7933
Suite 650 800-828-1302
Washington, DC 20036 Fax: 202-234-1328
info@islandpress.org
www.islandpress.org
Includes more than 1,000 references to material from scholarly journals, government agencies, case clearing-houses, research organizations, trade magazines and the popular press. It was the most current (1992) listing of research onself-monitoring and compliance programs and environmental performance strategies for corporate competitiveness.
Publication Date: 1992 382 pages
ISBN: 1-559631-59-7
Katie Dolan, Chair
Pamela Murphy, Vice Chair

3521 **California Certified Organic Farmers: Membership Directory**
2155 Delaware Ave. 831-423-2263
Suite 150 Fax: 831-423-4528
Santa Cruz, CA 95060 ccof@ccof.org
www.ccof.org
Annual
Phil LaRocca, Chair
Malcolm Ricci, Vice Chair

3522 **Directory of Environmental Information Sources**
Government Institutes
4 Research Place 301-907-1000
Suite 200A Fax: 301-921-2362
Rockville, MD 20850
Over 1,400 federal and state government agencies, professional and scientific organizations and trade associations are profiled.
322 pages

3523 **Directory of New York City Environmental Organizations**
Council on the Environment of New York City
100 Gold Street 212-788-7900
Room 3035 Fax: 212-788-7913
New York, NY 10038 conyc@cenyc.org
www.cenyc.org
Promotes environmental awareness and solutions to environmental problems.
Marcel Van Ooyen, Executive Director
Julie A. Walsh, Assistant Director

3524 **Directory of Professional Services**
Professional Services Institute
7918 Jones Branch Drive 703-556-7172
Suite 300 800-424-2869
McLean, VA 22102 Fax: 703-506-3266
www.resolve.org/resources
RESOLVE is dedicated to improving the lives of women and men living with the disease of infertility

3525 **Directory of Socially Responsible Investments**
Funding Exchange
4200 Connecticut Ave. NW 202-274-5000
Suite 500 Fax: 212-982-9272
Washington, DC 20008 alumni@udc.edu
www.udc.edu
Network of 15 community foundations around the country with a national office in New York City. Staff at the national office are responsible for three main program areas: grantmaking, donor programs and member fund services.

3526 **EPA Information Resources Directory**
National Technical Information Service
5301 Shawnee Road 703-605-6000
Alexandria, VA 2231 800-533-6847
helpdesk@ntis.gov
www.ntis.gov
Supports the nation's economic growth and job creation by providing access to information that stimulates innovation and discovery. NTIS accomplishes this mission through two major programs: information collection and dissemination tothe public and production and other services to federal agencies.

3527 EnviroSafety Directory
IEI Publishing Division
1635 W Alabama St 713-529-1616
Houston, TX 77006 800-654-1480
Fax: 281-529-0936
www.oilonline.com
Approximately 6,000 environmental services, state agencies and EPA/Superfund sites within the EPA regions 4, 6 and 9.
Kelli Lauletta, Editor
Janis Johnson, Managing Editor

3528 Environment: Books by Small Presses of the General Society of Mechanics & Tradesmen
Small Press Center
P.O. Box 422460 212-764-7021
Palm Coast, FL 32142 Fax: 212-840-2046
smallpress@aol.com
www.pw.org/small_presses
Publication Date: 1992 250 pages
ISBN: 0-962276-93-6
Paula Matta, Author
Elliot Figman, Executive Director
Melissa Ford Gradel, Managing Director

3529 Environmental Address Book: The Environment's Greatest Champions and Worst Offenders
Perigee Books
200 Madison Avenue 212-951-8400
New York, NY 10016 www.penguin.com

3530 Fibre Market News: Paper Recycling Markets Directory
Recycling Media Group GIE Publishers
4012 Bridge Avenue 216-961-4130
Cleveland, OH 44113 800-456-0707
Fax: 216-961-0364
A list of over 2,000 dealers, brokers, packers and graders of paper stock in the US and Canada.
Dan Sandoval, Internet/Senior Editor
Jim Keefe, Group Publisher

3531 Greenpeace Guide to Anti-Environmental Organizations
Odonian Press
PO Box 776 510-486-0313
Berkeley, CA 94701 800-326-0959
Fax: 415-512-8699
Corporations, foundations and public relations firms determined to be anti-environmental despite their attempts to project the green image.
Publication Date: 1993 112 pages
ISBN: 1-878825-05-3
Carl Deal, Author

3532 Guide to Curriculum Planning in Environmental Education
125 S Webster Street 608-266-2188
PO Box 7841 800-441-4563
Madison, WI 53707-7841 Fax: 608-267-9110
sandi.mcnamer@dpi.state.wi.us
www.pubsales.dpi.wi.gov
Provides a direction in planning a comprehensive environmental education program based on perceptual awareness knowledge, environmental ethics, citizen action skills and citizen action experience.
Publication Date: 1994 167 pages Book
Sandi McNamer, Publications Director

3533 Handbook on Air Filtration
IEST
2340 S. Arlington Heights Road 847-981-0100
Suite 620 Fax: 847-981-4130
Arlington Heights, IL 60005-4501 www.iest.org
Covers a broad range of applications for users who require removal of airborn particulate contamination for maximum air cleanliness.
ISBN: 1-877862-60-6
Shawn Windley, President
Wei Sun, President Elect

3534 Harbinger File
Harbinger Communications, Inc
5 N Union Street 847-622-0905
Elgin, IL 60123 800-320-7206
Fax: 847-622-0830
www.harbingeronline.com

3535 National Environmental Data Referral Service
US National Environmental Data Referral Service
1825 Connecticut Avenue NW 202-606-4089
Washington, DC 20235
More than 22,200 data resources that have available data on climatology and meteorology, ecology and pollution, geography, geophysics and geology, hydrology and limnology, oceanography and transmissions from remote sensing satellites.

3536 National Environmental Organizations
US Environmental Directories
1201 New York Avenue
PO Box 65156
St Paul, MN 20005

3537 New Jersey Environmental Directory
Youth Environmental Society
PO Box 441 609-655-8030
Cranbury, NJ 00851 www.nj.gov/dep
Environmental education and leadership programs for high school students in New Jersey.

3538 Opportunities in Environmental Careers
VGM Career Books
601 N. Mechanic Street 847-679-5500
Suite 306 800-323-4900
Franklin, VA 23851 Fax: 847-679-2494
www.environmentalcareer.com/
Odom Fanning, Author

3539 Research Services Directory
Grey House Publishing
4919 Route 22 518-789-8700
Amenia, NY 12501 800-562-2139
Fax: 518-789-0556
books@greyhouse.com
www.greyhouse.com
Provides access to well over 8,000 corporate and independent commercial research firms and laboratories offering contract services for hands-on, basic or applied research in environmental and other areas. Provides the company's nameand addresses, as well as a company description and research and technical fields served.
Publication Date: 2003 1,200 pages
ISBN: 1-891482-30-0
Leslie Mackenzie, Publisher
Richard Gottlieb, Editor

3540 State Environmental Agencies on the Internet
Government Institutes
16855 Northchase Drive 281-877-5800
Suite 200A Fax: 301-921-2362
Houston , TX 77060 www.govinst.com

Provides a concise profile of each state agency's requirements and resources-including hard-to-find online laws, rules, and regulations-in one quick-reference guide.

3541 Water Environment & Technology Buyer's Guide and Yearbook
Water Environment Federation
601 Wythe Street
Alexandria, VA 22314 800-666-0206
Fax: 703-684-2492
inquiry@wef.org
www.wef.org

Founded in 1928, the Water Environment Federation (WEF) is a not for profit technical and educational organization with members from varied disciplines who work toward the WEF vision of preservation and enhancement of the global waterenvironment. The WEF network includes water quality professionals from 76 Member Associations in 30 countries.
Ed Mc Comick, President
Paul Bowen, President-Elect

3542 World Directory of Environmental Organizations Online
California Institute of Public Affairs
PO Box 189040 916-442-2472
Sacramento, CA 95818 www.interenvironment.org
A guide to governmental and nongovernmental organizations and programs concerned with protecting the earth's resources. It also covers national and international organizations throughout the world. Only available online.

Directories & Handbooks: Design & Architecture

3543 Directory of International Periodicals and Newsletters on Built Environments
Van Nostrand Reinhold

More than 1,400 international periodicals and newsletters that cover architectural design and the building industry and the aspects of the environment that deal with the industry are covered.
Publication Date: 1992 175 pages
ISBN: 0-442230-03-6
Frances C Gretes, Author

Directories & Handbooks: Disaster Peparedness & Response

3544 Association of State Floodplain Managers
Association of State Floodplain Managers
575 D'Onofrio Drive 608-828-3000
Suite 200 Fax: 608-828-6319
Madison, WI 53719 asfpm@floods.org
www.floods.org
A complete name/address/phone listing for all key floodplain managers in the nation, comprehensive summary of ASFPM's activities of past year and planned future directions, key federal agency programs, much more. Free to currentmembers.
Ceil Strauss, Chair
Marica CoxLamm, Vice Chair

3545 EI Environmental Services Directory Online
Environmental Information Limited
8525 Arjons Drive 858-695-0050
Suite H Fax: 952-831-6550
San Diego, CA 92126 ei@enviro-information.com
www.envirobiz.com

The most comprehensive, largest directory of environmental services in the United States. Coverage includes asbestos & lead abatement, consulting, laboratories, transportation, industrial cleaning, municipal solid waste facilities,hazardous waste facilities, indsutrial waste facilities, well drilling, soil boring, drum reconditioning, spill response, and remediation services.
Cary Perket

3546 Floodplain Management: State & Local Programs
Association of State Floodplain Managers
575 D'Onofrio Drive 608-828-3000
Suite 200 Fax: 608-828-6319
Madison, WI 53719 asfpm@floods.org
www.floods.org

The most comprehensive source assembled to date, this report summarizes and analyzes various state and local programs and activities.
Publication Date: 2005
Ceil Strauss, Chair
Marica CoxLamm, Vice Chair

3547 Hazardous Materials Regulations Guide
JJ Keller
3003 West Breezewood Lane 920-722-2848
PO Box 368 877-564-2333
Neenah, WI 54957 Fax: 800-727-7516
sales@jjkeller.com
www.jjkeller.com

A complete reference guide of hazardous materials regulations.
May/Novemeber
ISBN: 0-934674-94-9
Tom Ziebell, Editor

3548 Institute of Chemical Waste Management Directory of Hazardous Waste Treatment
National Solid Wastes Management Assn.
4301 Connecticut Ave. 202-244-4700
Suite 1000 800-424-2869
Washington, DC 20008 Fax: 202-966-4824
www.nswma.org

3549 Pesticide Directory: A Guide to Producers and Products, Regulators, and Researchers
Thomson Publications
Box 9335 559-266-2964
Fresno, CA 93791 Fax: 559-266-0189
www.agbook.com
This directory is for the person who needs to know anything about the US pesticide industry. It includes basic manufacturers and formulators along with their products, key personnel, managers, district/regional offices and otherpertinent information. Other sections include Universities, State Extension Centers, USDA, EPA, National Organizations, US Forest Service, Poison Control Centers and much more.
Publication Date: 1987 153 pages Biannual
ISBN: 0-913702-45-5
WT Thomson, Author
Susan Heflin, President/Owner

3550 SEEK
520 Lafayette Rd N. 651-757-2700
St. Paul, MN 55155 800-657-3864
Minnesotas's interactive directory of environmetal education resources.

3551 The Homeland Security Directory
Grey House Publishing
4919 Route 22 518-789-8700
Amenia, NY 12510 800-562-2139
Fax: 518-789-0556
books@greyhouse.com
www.greyhouse.com

A comprehensive, annual resource for national, state and local officials responsible for homeland security along with manufacturers of homeland security products and services.
Publication Date: 2011 900 pages
Leslie Mackenzie, Publisher
Jessica Moody, Marketing Director

3552 **Tracking Toxic Wastes in CA: A Guide to Federal and State Government Information Sources**
INFORM
120 Wall Street — 212-361-2400
14th Floor — Fax: 212-361-2412
New York, NY 10005 — www.dtsc.ca.gov/HazardousWaste/

Directories & Handbooks: Energy & Transportation

3553 **Alternative Energy Network Online**
Environmental Information Networks
119 South Fairfax Street — 703-683-0774
Alexandria, VA 22314 — Fax: 703-683-3893
Reports on news of all energy sources designed as alternatives to conventional fossil fuels, including wind, solar and alcohol fuels.

3554 **Current Alternative Energy Research and Development in Illinois**
Department of Energy & Natural Resources
325 W Adams — 217-785-2800
Room 300 — 800-252-8955
Springfield, IL 62704 — Fax: 217-785-2618

3555 **Department of Energy Annual Procurement and Financial Assistance Report**
US Department of Energy
Mail Stop 142
Washington, DC 20585 — 800-342-5303
Fax: 202-586-4403
Offers a list of universities, research centers and laboratories that represent the Department of Energy.

3556 **Directory of Solar-Terrestrial Physics Monitoring Stations**
Air Force Geophysics Laboratory
Department of Defense — 781-377-3977
Hanscom Air Force Base, MA 00173 — Fax: 781-377-4498

3557 **Energy Science and Technology**
US Department of Energy
1 Science Gov Way — 865-576-1188
Oak Ridge, TN 37831 — Fax: 865-576-2865
ISTIWebmaster@osti.gov
www.osti.gov
To collect, preserve, disseminate, and leverage the scientific and technical information (STI) resources of the Department of Energy to provide access to national and global STI for use by DOE, the scientific research community,academia, US industry, and the public to expand the knowledge base of science and technology.

3558 **Energy Statistics Spreadsheets**
Institute of Gas Technology
3424 S State St — 312-842-4100
Chicago, IL 60616 — Fax: 773-567-5209
The coverage of this database encompasses worldwide energy industry statistics, including production, consumption, reserves, imports and prices.

3559 **Interstate Oil Compact Commission and State Oil and Gas Agencies Directory**
Interstate Oil & Gas Compact Commission
2101 N. Lincoln Blvd. — 405-521-2302
Oklahoma City, OK 73105 — 800-822-4015
Fax: 405-521-3099
iogcc@iogcc.state.ok.us
www.iogcc.oklaosf.state.ok.us
A directory of members and in the back is a list of state oil and gas agencies

3560 **Women's Council on Energy and the Environment Membership Directory**
816 Connecticut Ave NW — 202-997-4512
Suite 200 — Fax: 202-478-2098
Washington, DC 20006 — info@wcee.org
www.wcee.org
Offers valuable information on over 800 members representing consulting firms, private industry and the environmental community.
Publication Date: 1980
Robin Cantor, President
Mary Brosnan-Sell, Vice President

Directories & Handbooks: Environmental Engineering

3561 **Association of Conservation Engineers: Membership Directory**
Engineering Section Alabama Dept. of Conservation
573-522-2323
Fax: 573-522-2324
www.conservationengineers.org/

3562 **Energy Engineering: Directory of Software for Energy Managers and Engineers**
Fairmont Press
700 Indian Trail — 770-925-9388
Liburn, GA 30047 — Fax: 770-381-9865
linda@fairmontpress.com
www.fairmontpress.com
Directory of services and supplies to the industry.
Publication Date: 1904 80 pages Bimonthly
ISSN: 0199-8895
Wayne C Turner, Author
Wayne C Turner, Editor

3563 **NEPA Lessons Learned**
Office of NEPA Policy & Compliance
1000 Independence Avenue SW — 202-586-4600
EH-42 — 800-472-2756
Washington, DC 20585 — Fax: 202-586-7031
denise.freeman@eh.doe.gov
www.eh.doe.gov/nepa
Publication Date: 1994 Quarterly
Carol M Borgstrom, Director

3564 **Pollution Abstracts**
Cambridge Scientific Abstracts
7200 Wisconsin Avenue — 301-961-6700
Suite 601 — 800-843-7751
Bethesda, MD 20814 — Fax: 301-961-6720
sales@csa.com
www.csa.com
This database provides fast access to the environmental information necessary to resolve day to day problems, ensure ongoing compliance, and handle emergency situations more effectively.
James P McGinty, President
Ted Caris, Publisher

Directories & Handbooks: Environmental Health

3565 American Academy of Environmental Medicine
American Academy of Environmental Medicine
6505 E. Central Avenue
Suite 296
Wichita, KS 67206
316-684-5500
Fax: 888-411-1206
defox@aaemonline.org
www.aaemonline.org

To support physicians and other professionals in their work through education about the interaction between humans and their environment. The academy also promotes optimal health through preventative treatments for illnesses induced byenvironmental and chemical pollutants.
Publication Date: 1965
Gregg Govett, President
De Rodgers Fox, Executive Director

3566 Canadian Environmental Resource Guide
Grey House Publishing Canada
555 Richmond Street West
5th Floor
Toronto, ON M5V-3B1
416-644-6479
866-433-4739
Fax: 416-644-1904
info@greyhouse.ca
www.greyhouse.ca

Canada's only national listing of environmental products & services companies, as well as major environmental corporations, law firms with environmental specialties, and municipal government information. Online access is alsoavailable, with additional resources such as federal and provincial governments, associations, and special libraries.
900 pages Annual
Bryon Moore, General Manager

3567 Directory of NEHA Credentialed Professionals
720 S Colorado Boulevard
Suite 1000-N
Denver, CO 80246
303-756-9090
Fax: 303-691-9490
staff@neha.org
www.neha.org

This is a directory of all NEHA credentialed professionals. It is available to NEHA credentialed professionals only.
Catalog 569

3568 Ecosystem Change and Public Health: A Global Perspective
Johns Hopkins University Press
2715 N Charles Street
Baltimore, MD 21218
410-516-6900
800-537-5487
Fax: 410-516-6968
www.press.jhu.edu/books

The strength of the John Hopkins University Press' publications in medicine is in part a reflection of the university and medical institution's excellence and long term tradition of exceptional research and clinical care. Joan Aron'sEcosystem Change and Public Health is the first textbook devoted to this emerging field. The book covers such topics as global climate change, stratospheric ozone depletion, water resources management, ecology and infectious disease. Paperback
Publication Date: 2001 526 pages
ISBN: 0-801865-82-4
Joan Aron, Author
Joan Aron, Editor
Jonathan Pratz, Editor

3569 Environmental Encyclopedia
Thomson Gale
27500 Drake Road
Farmington Hills, MI 48331
248-699-4253
877-363-4253
Fax: 800-414-5043
www.cengage.com

Consisting of nearly 1,300 signed articles and term definitions. The encyclopedia provides in-depth, worldwide coverage of environmental issues. Each article written in a nontechnical style and provides current status, analysis andsuggests solutions whenever possible.
Publication Date: 2002 2000 pages
ISBN: 0-787654-86-8
Virginia Regish, Contact

3570 Environmental Guidebook: A Selective Guide to Environmental Organizations and Related Entities
Environmental Frontlines
PO Box 43
Menlo Park, CA 94026
650-323-8452
info@envirofront.org
www.envirofront.org

Designed to serve as an essential reference book profiling nearly 500 national organizations and other entities actively engaged in environmental issues in the US and beyond.
312 pages
ISBN: 0-972068-50-3
Jeff Staudinger, Author

3571 Environmental Key Contacts and Information Sources
Government Institutes
16855 Northchase Drive
Suite 200A
Houston, TX 77060
281-877-5800
Fax: 301-921-2362
www.govinst.com

An updated and revised compilation of Government Institutes' two previous directories, this reference contains more than 400 pages of contact information for more than 2,700 federal, state, and local environmental agencies andorganizations. This directory also includes contacts for information concerning environmental protection, hazardous waste materials, clean water and air, environmental assessment and management, pesticides, pollution control, recycling, naturalresources and conservation.
Publication Date: 1998 424 pages
ISBN: 0-865876-39-8
Charlene Ikonomou and Diane Pacchione, Author

3572 Pesticide Directory: A Guide to Producers and Products, Regulators, and Researchers
Thomson Publications
Box 9335
Fresno, CA 93791
559-266-2964
Fax: 559-266-0189
www.agbook.com

This directory is for the person who needs to know anything about the US pesticide industry. It includes basic manufacturers and formulators along with their products, key personnel, managers, district/regional offices and otherpertinent information. Other sections include Universities, State Extension Centers, USDA, EPA, National Organizations, US Forest Service, Poison Control Centers and much more.
Publication Date: 1987 153 pages Biannual
ISBN: 0-913702-45-5
WT Thomson, Author
Susan Heflin, President/Owner

Directories & Handbooks: Habitat Preservation & Land Use

3573 Alliance for Wildlife Rehabilitation and Education Wildlife Care Directory
1441 Broadway
5th Floor
New York, NY 10018
646-569-5860
info@wildlifealliance.org
www.wildlifealliance.org/

3574 Biodiversity Action Network
1630 Connecticut Avenue
3rd Floor
Washington, DC 20009
202-547-8902
Fax: 202-265-0222

An information exchange network launched by the Center for International Environmental Law.

3575 Conservation Directory 2004: The Guide to Worldwide Environmental Organizations

National Wildlife Federation
PO Box 1583
Merrifield, VA 22116-1583 800-822-9919
www.nwf.org/conservationDirectory/

Your guide to thousands of environmental non-profit, education, commercial, and government groups operating across the planet.
Robin Assa, Sales Assistant

3576 County Conservation Board Outdoor Adventure Guide

Iowa Association of County Conservation Boards
405 SW 3rd Street 515-963-9582
Suite 1 Fax: 515-963-9582
Ankeny, IA 50021 www.dickinsoncountyconservationboard.com/

Includes a map of each county with the area to be shaded in or a pinpoint of the location, and has information on cabin rentals, camping, shelters, playgrounds, swimming, fishing, boating, boat rental, sports and fields, hunting,nature centers, praires, historic sites, wildlife exhibits and more.
184 pages
Don Brazelton, Contact

3577 DOCKET

US Environmental Protection Agency
US EPA Region 3 215-814-2993
1650 Arch Street (3PM52) Fax: 215-814-5102
Philadelphia, PA 19103 teller.lawrence@epa.gov
www.epa.gov

This database offers the complete text of summaries of all justice cases filed by the US Department of Justice on behalf of the US Environmental Protection Agency.
Gina McCarthy, Administrator
Stan Meiburg, Deputy Administrator

3578 Directory of Resource Recovery Projects and Services

Institute of Resource Recovery
1730 Rhode Island Avenue NW 202-659-4613
Suite 1000 Fax: 202-775-5917
Washington, DC 20036

3579 Ecology Abstracts

Cambridge Scientific Abstracts
7200 Wisconsin Avenue 301-961-6700
Suite 601 800-843-7751
Bethesda, MD 20814 Fax: 301-961-6720
sales@csa.com
www.csa.com

This large database updated continuously, offers over 150,000 citations, with abstracts, to the worldwide literature available on ecology and the environment.
James P McGinty, President
Theodore Caris, Publisher

3580 Environmental Bibliography

International Academy at Santa Barbara
5385 Hollister Avenue 805-683-8889
#210 Fax: 805-965-6071
Santa Barbara, CA 93111 info@iasb.org
www.ifrs.org

Over 615,000 citations are offered in this database, aimed at scientific, technical and popular periodical literature dealing with the environment.

ISSN: 1053-1440

3581 Environmental Concerns: Directory of the Environmental Industry in Colorado

Business Research Division-Univ. of Colorado
995 Regent Drive 303-492-8397
419 UCB Fax: 303-492-3620
Boulder, CO 80309-0419 leeds.colorado.edu/brd

Approximately 1,300 private businesses, government organizations and corporations in Colorado that contribute to environmental protection and rehabilitation.

ISBN: 1-883226-02-3
Gin Hayden, Editor
Sean Shepherd, Editor

3582 Environmental Guide to the Internet

Government Institutes
16855 Northchase Drive 281-877-5800
Suite 200A Fax: 301-921-2362
Houston , TX 77060 www.govinst.com

Provides information for the best sites in the internet dealing with the preservation and protection of the environment, ecology, and conservation and offers over 320 new listings and addresses. Writin for environmental consultants,industry professionals, researchers, lawyers, educators, and students, contains the top 1,200 environmental internet resources, including, newletters and journals, and world wide web sites
Publication Date: 1997 384 pages
ISBN: 0-865875-78-2
Carol Briggs-Erickson and Toni Murphy, Author

3583 Environmental Guidebook: A Selective Guide to Environmental Organizations and Related Entities

Environmental Frontlines
PO Box 43 650-323-8452
Menlo Park, CA 94026 info@envirofront.org
www.envirofront.org

Designed to serve as an essential reference book profiling nearly 500 national organizations and other entities actively engaged in environmental issues in the US and beyond.
312 pages
ISBN: 0-972068-50-3
Jeff Staudinger, Author

3584 Helping Out in the Outdoors: A Directory of Volunteer Opportunities on Public Lands

American Hiking Society
1424 Fenwick Lane 301-565-6704
Silver Spring, MD 20910 Fax: 301-565-6714
info@americanhiking.org
www.americanhiking.org

Mary Margaret Sloan, President

3585 Hospitality Directory

Human Ecology Action League (HEAL)
PO Box 29629 404-248-1898
Atlanta, GA 30359 Fax: 404-248-0162
HEALNatnl@aol.com
www.lifestream.aol.com

Nonprofit organization founded in 1977 to serve those whose health has been adversely affected by environment exposures; to provide information to those who are concerned about the health effects of chemicals; and to alert the generalpublic about the potential dangers of chemicals.
Katherine P Collier, Contact

3586 Human Ecology Action League Directory

Human Ecology Action League
PO Box 29629 404-248-1898
Atlanta, GA 30359 Fax: 404-248-0162
HEALNatnl@aol.com

The Human Ecology Action League Inc (HEAL) is a nonprofit organization founded in 1977 to serve those whose health has been affected by environmental exposures; to provide information to those who are concerned about the health effectsof chemicals; and to alert the general public about the potential dangers of chemicals. Referrals to local HEAL chapters and other support groups are available from the League.
Katherine P Collier, Contact

3587 Hummingbird Connection
6560 Highway 179
6560 State Route 179 928-284-2251
Suite 124 800-529-3699
Sedona, AZ 86351 info@hummingbird.org
www.hummingbirdsociety.org

Published by the Hummingbird Society.
Publication Date: 1992 16 pages Quarterly
ISSN: 1097-3427
H Ross Hawkins, Author/Editor

3588 International Society of Tropical Foresters: Membership Directory
5400 Grosvenor Lane 301-897-8720
Bethesda, MD 20814 Fax: 301-897-3690
www.istf-bethesda.org/

The International Society of Tropical Foresters, Inc. (ISTF) is a nonprofit organization committed to the protection, wise management and rational use of the world's tropical forests. Established in 1950, ISTF was reactivated in 1979.It has about 1500 members in more than 100 countries. Financial support comes from membership dues, donations and grants. ISTF sponsors meetings, promotes chapters in other countries, maintains a web site and has chapters at universities.
Warren T Doolittle, President

3589 Journal of Wildlife Rehabilitation
International Wildlife Rehabilitation Council
PO Box 8187 408-271-2685
San Jose, CA 95155 Fax: 408-271-9285
office@iwrc-online.org
www.theiwrc.org

A peer reviewed scientific journal that has served as a primary reference for wildlife rehabilitators and others involved in the care and conservation of wildlife. Features articles, columns and reviews, with topics ranging from allaspects of wildlife care to administration, fundraising, education programs, case studies, environmental issues, legalities, ethics and more. And is also a benefit of membership to IWRC.
Publication Date: 1978 40 pages Quarterly
Susan Wylie, President
Adam Grogan, Vice President

3590 LEXIS Environmental Law Library
Lexis Nexis Group
PO Box 933 937-865-6800
Dayton, OH 45401 800-227-9597
Fax: 937-865-6909
www.lexis-nexis.com

This database contains decisions related to environmental law from the Supreme Court and other legislative bodies.

3591 Learning About Our Place
311 Curtis Street 716-665-2473
Jamestown, NY 14701 800-758-6841
Fax: 716-665-3794
mail@rtpi.org
www.rtpi.org

47 lesson plans that connect learning to nature and the outdoors
15-30 pages Quarterly
Jim Berry, President

3592 Managed Area Basic Record
The Nature Conservancy
4245 N. Fairfax Drive 703-841-5300
Suite 100 Fax: 804-979-0370
Arlington, VA 22203-1606 cmullen@tnc.org
www.nature.org

3593 Minienvironments
IEST
2340 South Arlington Heights Road 847-981-0100
Suite 620 Fax: 847-981-4130
Arlington Heights, IL 60005-4510 iest@iest.org
www.iest.org

The purpose of this document is to provide a framework for describing minienvironments for microelectronics and similar applications.
Publication Date: 2002 28 pages
ISBN: 1-877862-83-5
Shawn Windley, President
Wei Sun, President Elect

3594 Morrison Environmental Directory
PO Box 2312 316-262-0100
Wichita, KS 67201

ISSN: 1060-488

3595 National Directory of Conservation Land Trusts
Land Trust Alliance
1660 L St. NW 202-638-4725
Suite 1100 Fax: 202-638-4730
Washington, DC 20036 info@lta.org
www.landtrustalliance.org

More than 1,200 nonprofit land conservation organizations at the local and regional levels are profiled.
210 pages
Lise Aangeenbrug, Executive Director
Maria Elena Campisteguy, Executive Vice President

3596 New York State Department of Environmental Conservation Personnel Directory: Internet Only
NYS Department of Environmental Conservation
625 Broadway 518-402-8013
Albany, NY 12233 Fax: 518-402-9036
dinnelson@gw.dec.state.ny.us
www.dec.ny.gov

Internet only, this directory includes DEC's executive management and division directors. Executive managers are appointed by the Governor to carry out the policies of the state. Division directors have direct management responsibilityfor the department's programs.
Mary A Kadlecek, Chief Internet Publications

3597 Nonprofit Sample and Core Repositories Open to the Public in the United States
Branch of Sedimentary Processes
MS 939 Federal Center 303-236-5760
Denver, CO 80225 Fax: 303-236-0459
Walter E Dean, Contact

3598 Range and Land Management Handbook
Wyoming Association of Conservation Districts
517 E 19th Street 307-632-5716
Cheyenne, WY 82001 Fax: 307-638-4099
www.conservewy.com

This publication is intended for people from all walks of life who want to gain an appreciation of rangelands. This publication is also an introduction to the various fields of range management.
Annual

3599 Takings Litigation Handbook: Defending Takings Challenges to Land Use Regulations
American Legal Publishing Corporation
One West Fourth Street
Ste. 300 800-445-5588
Cincinnati, OH 45202 Fax: 513-763-3562
customerservice@amlegal.com
www.amlegal.com
No government attorney, land use planner or other local official can effectively protect their community from harmful land use without a working knowledge of takings law. Developers and other landowners increasingly are attempting touse takings litigation, or the mere threat of takings litigation, to convince government agencies to relax or abandon vital protections for our neighborhoods and natural environment.
Publication Date: 2000 404 pages
Kendall, Dowling and Schwartz, Author
Douglas Kendall, Executive Director

3600 Trout Unlimited Chapter and Council Handbook
Trout Unlimited
1777 N. Kent Street
Suite 100 800-834-2419
Arlington, VA 22209 Fax: 703-284-9400
trout@tu.org
www.tu.org
This organization seeks to conserve, protect and restore North America's trout and salmon fisheries and their watersheds.
Jim Asselstine, Chairman
Nancy Mackinnon, Secretary

3601 Turtle Help Network
New York Turtle and Tortoise Society
PO Box 878 212-459-4803
Orange, NJ 00705 www.turtle.net/

3602 Wilson Journal of Ornithology
OSNA
5400 Bosque Blvd 254-399-9636
Suite 680 business@osnabirds.org
Waco, TX 76710 www.wilsonsociety.org/
Scholarly journal consisting of articles on bird studies, orinthological news, reviews of new bird books and related subjects.
Quarterly
Dr Doris J Watt, President
John A Smallwood, Secretary

3603 Wisconsin Department of Public Instruction
125 S Webster Street
PO Box 7841 800-441-4563
Madison, WI 53707-7841 Fax: 608-267-9110
sandi.mcnamer@dpi.state.wi.us
www.pubsales.dpi.wi.gov
State education department publisher of K-12 curriculum planning guides in 25 subject areas including environmental education and science.
Sandi McNamer, Publications Director

Directories & Handbooks: Recycling & Pollution Prevention

3604 A Glossary of Terms and Definitions Relating to Contamination Control
IEST
2340 South Arlington Heights Road 847-981-0100
Suite 620 Fax: 847-981-4130
Arlington Heights, IL 60005-4510 information@iest.org
www.iest.org
A publication from the Institute of Environmental Science and Technology.
Publication Date: 1995 32 pages
ISBN: 1-877862-28-2
Shawn Windley, President
Wei Sun, President Elect

3605 American Recycling Market Directory: Reference Manual
Recycling Data Management Corp.
PO Box 577 315-471-0707
Ogdensburg, NY 13669 800-267-0707
Fax: 613-471-3258
Comprehensive directory/reference manual to materials recycling markets. Helps individuals locate buyers and sellers of recyclable materials on a regional basis throughout North America. Contains 20,000 cross-referenced company andagency listings. Sections include: scrap metals, waste paper, paper mills, auto dismantlers, demolition, glass, oil, rubber and textiles recyclers, recycling centers, MRF's composting, equipment and consulting services, industry references UBC specsand more.

3606 Analysis of the Stockholm Convention on Persistent Organic Pollutants
Oceana Publications, Inc
198 Madison Ave
New York, NY 10016 800-334-4249
Fax: 212-726-6476
oxfordonline@oup.com
www.oceanalaw.com
This book analyzes the Stockholm Convention on Persistent Organic Pollutants. Prepared under the auspices of the UN Environment Programme Chemical Division.
Publication Date: 2003 200 pages One Time
ISBN: 0-379215-06-3
Mario Antonio Olsen, Author

3607 Criteria Pollutant Point Source Directory
North American Water Office
3394 Lake Elmo Ave 651-770-3861
Lake Elmo, MN 55042 Fax: 651-770-3976
gwillc@mtn.org
www.nawo.org

3608 Directory of Municipal Solid Waste Management Facilities
The Institute of Solid Waste Disposal
1730 Rhode Island Avenue NW 202-659-4613
Suite 1000 Fax: 202-296-7915
Washington, DC 20036

3609 EI Environmental Services Directory
Environmental Information Networks
8525 Arjons Drive 858-695-0050
Suite H Fax: 952-831-6550
San Diego, CA 92126 www.envirobiz.com
Waste-handling facilities, transportation and spill response firms, laboratories and the broad scope of environmental services. Online versions are also available.

ISSN: 1053-475N
Cary Perket

3610 Environmental Encyclopedia
Thomson Gale
27500 Drake Road 248-699-4253
Farmington Hills, MI 48331 800-877-4253
Fax: 800-414-5043
www.galegroup.com
Consisting of nearly 1,300 signed articles and definitions. The encyclopedia provides in depth, worldwide coverage of environ-

mental issues. Each article written in a non technical style and provides current status, analysis andsuggests solutions whenever possible.
Publication Date: 2002 2000 pages
ISBN: 0-787654-86-8
Virginia Regish, Contact

3611 Environmental Guide to the Internet
Government Institutes
16855 Northchase Drive 281-877-5800
Suite 200A Fax: 301-921-2362
Houston , TX 77060 www.govinst.com
Provides information for the best sites on the internet dealing with the preservation and protection of the environment, ecology, and conservation and offers over 320 new listings and addresses. Writin for environmental consultants,industry professionals, researchers, lawyers, educators, and students, contains the top 1,200 environmental internet resources, including, newletters and journals, and world wide web sites
Publication Date: 1997 384 pages
ISBN: 0-865875-78-2
Carol Briggs-Erickson and Toni Murphy, Author

3612 Environmental Guidebook: A Selective Guide to Environmental Organizations and Related Entities
Environmental Frontlines
PO Box 43 650-323-8452
Menlo Park, CA 94026 www.envirofront.org
Designed to serve as an essential reference book profiling nearly 500 national organizations and other entities actively engaged in environmental issues in the US and beyond.
312 pages
ISBN: 0-972068-50-3
Jeff Staudinger, Author

3613 Fibre Market News: Paper Recycling Markets Directory
Recycling Media Group GIE Publishers
4012 Bridge Avenue 216-961-4130
Cleveland, OH 44113 800-456-0707
Fax: 216-961-0364
A list of over 2,000 dealers, brokers, packers and graders of paper stock in the US and Canada.
Dan Sandoval, Editor

3614 Hazardous Materials Regulations Guide
JJ Keller
3003 West Breezewood Lane
PO Box 368 877-564-2333
Neenah, WI 54957 Fax: 800-727-7516
sales@jjkeller.com
www.jjkeller.com
A complete reference guide of hazardous materials regulations.
May/November
ISBN: 0-934674-94-9
Tom Ziebell, Editor

3615 How-To: 1,400 Best Books on Doing Almost Everything
R.R. Bowker Company
630 Central Ave. 908-286-1090
New Providence, NJ 00797 888-269-5372
www.bowker.com

3616 Institute of Chemical Waste Management Directory of Hazardous Waste Treatment and Disposal
National Solid Wastes Management Assn.
4301 Connecticut Avenue NW 202-244-4700
Suite 300 Fax: 202-966-4824
Washington, DC 20008 www.nswma.org

3617 International Handbook of Pollution Control
Greenwood Publishing Group
P.O. Box 1911 203-226-3571
Santa Barbara, CA 93116-1911 webmaster@greenwood.com
www.abc-clio.com
Publication Date: 1989 482 pages
ISBN: 0-313240-17-5
Edward J Kormondy, Author

3618 List of Water Pollution Control Administrators
Assn. of State and Interstate Water Pollution Con.
1221 Connecticut Ave. NW 202-898-0905
2nd Floor Fax: 202-898-0929
Washington, DC 20036 admin1@asiwpca.org
www.asiwpca.org

Roberta Savage, Executive Director
Linda Eichmiller, Deputy Director

3619 Nebraska Recycling Resource Directory
Nebraska Dept of Environmental Quality
1200 N Street Suite 400 402-471-2186
PO Box 98922 877-253-2603
Lincoln, NE 68509 Fax: 402-471-2909
www.deq.state.ne.us

Publication Date: 1986 139 pages Bi-Annually
Steve Danahy, Unit Supervisor

3620 Pesticide Directory: A Guide to Producers and Products, Regulators, and Researchers
Thomson Publications
Box 9335 559-266-2964
Fresno, CA 93791 Fax: 559-266-0189
This directory is for the person who needs to know anything about the US pesticide industry. It includes basic manufacturers and formulators along with their products, key personnel, managers, district/regional offices and otherpertinent information. Other sections include Universities, State Extension Centers, USDA, EPA, National Organizations, US Forest Service, Poison Control Centers and much more.
Publication Date: 1987 153 pages Biannual
ISBN: 0-913702-45-5
WT Thomson, Author
Susan Heflin, President/Owner

3621 Pollution Abstracts
Cambridge Scientific Abstracts
7200 Wisconsin Avenue 301-961-6700
Suite 601 800-843-7751
Bethesda, MD 20814 Fax: 301-961-6720
www.csa.com
This database provides fast access to the environmental information necessary to resolve day to day problems, ensure ongoing compliance, and handle emergency situations more effectively.
James P McGinty, President
Ted Caris, Publisher

3622 Product Cleanliness Levels and Contamination Control Program
IEST
2340 South Arlington Heights Road 847-981-0100
Suite 620 Fax: 847-981-4130
Arlington Heights, IL 60005-4510 information@iest.org
www.iest.org

Intended to provide a basis for specifying product cleanliness levels and contamination control program requirments with emphasis on contaminants that affect product performance.
Publication Date: 2002 20 pages
ISBN: 1-877862-82-7
Shawn Windley, President
Wei Sun, President Elect

3623 Recycling Related Newsletters, Publications And Periodicals
Continnuus
PO Box 416 303-575-5676
Denver, CO 80201 Fax: 970-292-2136

3624 Recycling Today: Recycling Products & Services Buyers Guide
Recycling Today GIE Publishers
5811 Canal Road 216-961-4130
#201 800-456-0707
Valley View, OH 44125 Fax: 216-961-0364
jkeefe@gie.net
www.recyclingtoday.com
Directory of services and supplies to the industry.
Dan Sandoval, Internet/Senior Editor
James Keefe, Group Publisher

3625 Scholastic Environmental Atlas of the United States
Scholastic
4333 Brooklyn Avenue NE 206-543-4050
Seattle, NY 98195-9570 Fax: 206-543-3932
hfscustserv@press.jhu.edu
www.washington.edu/uwpress/

3626 Tracking Toxic Wastes in CA: A Guide to Federal and State Government Information Sources
INFORM
P.O. Box 320403 212-361-2400
Floor 19 Fax: 212-361-2412
Brooklyn, NY 11232 www.informinc.org

3627 Waste Age: Resource Recovery Acitivities Update Issue
National Solid Wastes Management Assn.
1730 Rhode Island Avenue NW 202-659-4613
Suite 1000
Washington, DC 20036

3628 Waste Age: Waste Industry Buyer Guide
National Solid Wastes Management
1730 Rhode Island Avenue NW 202-659-4613
Suite 1000 800-424-2869
Washington, DC 20036 Fax: 202-659-0925

3629 Wastes to Resources: Appropriate Technologies for Sewage Treatment and Conversion
National Center for Appropriate Techology
3040 Continental Drive 406-494-4572
Butte, MT 59701 800-275-6228
Fax: 406-494-2905
4info@ncat.org
www.ncat.org

Kathy Hadley, Executive Director

Directories & Handbooks: Sustainable Development

3630 Solar Energy Resource Guide/SERG
NorCal Solar
PO Box 3008 530-852-0354
Berkeley, CA 94703 info@norcalsolar.org
www.norcalsolar.org
Articles and resources on solar electric, solar thermal, financial analysis, etc. Also a guidebook for education on the workings and intstallation of solar technology.
96 pages
Claudia Wentworth, President
Liz Merry, Program Manager

Directories & Handbooks: Travel & Tourism

3631 Access America: An Atlas and Guide to the National Parks for Visitors with Disabilities
Northern Cartographic
4050 Williston Road 802-860-2886
South Burlington, VT 05403 Fax: 802-865-4912
info@ncarto.com

Publication Date: 1988
ISBN: 0-944187-00-5

3632 Audubon Society Field Guide to the Natural Places of the Northeast
National Audubon Society
700 Broadway 212-979-3000
New York, NY 10003 Fax: 212-979-3188
www.audubon.org

3633 Complete Guide to America's National Parks: The Official Visitor's Guide
National Park Foundation
11 Dupont Circle NW 202-238-4200
Suite 600 800-285-2448
Washington, DC 20036 Fax: 202-234-3103
ask-npf@nationalparks.org

3634 Field Guide to American Windmills
University of Oklahoma Press
2800 Venture Drive 405-325-2000
Norman, OK 73069 800-627-7377
Fax: 405-364-5798
This guide to America's windmills is both a complete general history of turbine wheel mills and an identification guide to the 112 most common models, which still dot landscapes today.
Publication Date: 1985 528 pages
T Lindsay Baker, Author

3635 Guide to the National Wildlife Refuges
Macmillan Publishing Company
National Wildlife Guide 212-832-2101
590 Madison Avenue
New York, NY 10022
More than 500 National Wildlife Refuges and satellite refuges are listed.
684 pages

3636 National Parks Visitor Facilities and Services
Conference of National Park Concessioners
PO Box 29041 480-967-6006
Phoenix, AZ 85038 www.nps.gov

Within the parks, private businesses provide accommodations and services for visitors under concession contracts.
Rex G Maughan, Chairman

3637 National Parks: National Park Campgrounds Issue
National Parks Conservation Association
777 6th Street, NW
Suite 700 800-628-7275
Washington, DC 20001-3723 Fax: 202-659-0650
npca@npca.org
www.npca.org

To safeguard the scenic beauty, wildlife, and historical and cultural treasures of the largest and most diverse park system in the world.
W.Clark Buntimg, President
Theresa Pierno, Chief Operating Officer

3638 National Wildlife Refuges: A Visitor's Guide
Fish and Wildlife Services, Interior Department
1849 C Street NW 703-358-2043
Washington, DC 20242 webteam@ios.doi.gov
www.fws.gov

Contains a map showing national wildlife refuges that provide recrational and educational opportunities. Provides tips for visiting national wildlife refuges. Also list refuges in all 50 States, Puerto Rico and the Virgin Islans, withthe best wildlife viewing season and the features of each refuge.

ISBN: 0-160617-00-6

3639 Nature Center Directory
Wisconsin Association for Environmental Education
2100 Main Street Stevens Point 715-346-0123
University of Wisconsin-Stevens Point Fax: 715-346-3835
Stevens Point, WI 54481-3897 webmaster@uwsp.edu
Annual

3640 Rails-to-Trails Magazine
2121 Ward Court, NW 202-331-9696
5th Floor Fax: 202-223-9257
Washington, DC 20037 www.railstotrails.org/magazine

Official magazine of the Rails-to-Trails Conservancy (RTC). The RTC is a national nonprofit organization dedicated to creating a nationwide network of trails from former rail lines and connecting corridors. It does not own or manageany rail trails.
Quarterly
Keith Laughlin, President
Elizabeth Thorstensen, VP Trail Development

3641 Recreation Sites in Southwestern National Forests
USDA Forest Service
Public Affairs Office 505-842-3292
333 Broadway Blvd SE Fax: 505-842-3106
Albuquerque, NM 87102 www.fs.usda.gov/r3

Listings for all recreation sites for Arizona and New Mexico.
72 pages
Corbin Newman, Regional Forester

3642 Sierra Club Guide to the Natural Areas of California
Sierra Club
85 2nd Street 415-977-5500
2nd Floor Fax: 415-977-5799
San Francisco, CA 94105 information@sierraclub.org
www.sierraclub.org

Revised and updated, this comprehensive guide makes more than 200 wilderness areas in California, including many lesser known natural areas, accessible to the outdoor enthusiast.
Publication Date: 1997 352 pages
ISBN: 0-871568-50-0
John Perry and Jane Greverus Perry, Author
Loren Blackford, President
Susana Reyes, Vice President

3643 Thermal Springs of Wyoming
Wyoming State Geological Survey
PO Box 1347 307-766-2286
Laramie, WY 82073 Fax: 307-766-2605
wsgs-info@uwyo.edu
www.wsgs.uwyo.edu

Ronald C Surdam, Agency Director
Richard W Jones, Editor

3644 Traveler's Guide to the Smoky Mountains Region
Harvard Common Press
535 Albany Street 617-423-5803
Boston, MA 00211 Fax: 619-695-9794
info@harvardcommonpress.com
www.harvardcommonpress.com

Features museums, events of the South Appalachians of Tennessee, North Carolilna, Virginia and Georgia
Publication Date: 1985 288 pages
ISBN: 0-916782-64-6
Valerie Cimino, Executive Editor
Christine Alaimo, Associate Publisher

3645 Wild Places & Open Spaces Map
Division of Fish and Wildlife
PO Box 420 609-292-2965
Trenton, NJ 00862 Fax: 609-292-8207
www.njfishandwildlife.com

Designed similar to a road map, offers the outdoors person a welath of information on locating and exploring New Jersey's open spaces in compact and easy to read format. Showcasing a full color map of New Jersey, with more than 700,000acres of public open space.
David Chanda, Director
Larry Herrighty, Assis Dir of Operations

Directories & Handbooks: Water Resources

3646 Citizen's Directory for Water Quality Abuses
Izaak Walton League of America
707 Conservation Lane 301-548-0150
Gaithersburg, MD 20878 800-453-5463
Fax: 301-548-0146
info@iwla.org
www.iwla.org

It is working to advance conservation, engage people in outdoor recreation, and safeguard natural resources for the future in communities across the country
Shawn Gallagher, President
Jeff Deschamps, Vice President

3647 Coordination Directory of State and Federal Agency Water Resources Officials: Missouri Basin
Department of Water Resources
5231 South 19th Street 402-328-4100
Lincoln, NE 68512 ne.water.usgs.gov

It operates the most extensive satellite network of stream-gaging stations in the state, many of which form the backbone of flood-warning systems.

3648 How Wet is a Wetland?: The Impacts of the Proposed Revisions to the Federal Wetlands Manual
Environmental Defense Fund
257 Park Avenue South 212-505-2100
New York, NY 10010 800-684-3322
Fax: 212-505-0892
media@environmentaldefense.org
www.edf.org

The mission is to preserve the natural systems on which all life depends.
Publication Date: 1992
Carl Ferenbach, Chair
Shelby W. Bonnie, Vice Chair

3649 **Hydro Review: Industry Source Book Issue**
HCI Publications
410 Archibald Street 847-763-9540
Kansas City, MO 64111 Fax: 816-931-2015
hr@halldata.com
www.hydroworld.com
List of over 800 manufacturers and suppliers of products and services to the hydroelectric industry in the US and Canada.
January
David Appleyard, Editor-In-Chief
Elizabeth Ingram, Managing Editor

3650 **List of Water Pollution Control Administrators**
Assn. of State and Interstate Water Pollution Con.
1221 Connecticut Ave. NW 202-898-0905
2nd Floor Fax: 202-898-0929
Washington, DC 20036
Roberta Savage, Executive Director
Linda Eichmiller, Deputy Director

3651 **Water Environment & Technology Buyer's Guide and Yearbook**
Water Environment Federation
601 Wythe Street 703-684-2400
Alexandria, VA 22314 800-666-0206
Fax: 703-684-2492
inquiry@wef.org
www.wef.org
Founded in 1928, the Water Environment Foundation (WEF) is a not for profit technical and educational organization with members from varied disiplines who work toward the WEF vision of preservation and enhancement of the globalwaterenvironment. The WEF network includes water quality professionals from 76 Member Associations in 30 countries.
Eileen O'Neill, Executive Director
Ed McCormick, President

Periodicals: Air & Climate

3652 **Air/Water Pollution Report**
Business Publishers
2222 Sedwick Drive 301-589-5103
Durham, NC 27713 800-223-8720
Fax: 800-508-2592
custserv@bpines.com
www.bpinews.com
Regulatory activities and governmental legislation and litigation are covered in this pulication.
Publication Date: 1963 Monthly
Leonard Eiserer, Publisher

3653 **Bulletin of the American Meteorological Society**
45 Beacon Street 617-227-2425
Boston, MA 00210 Fax: 617-742-8718
amsinfo@ametsoc.org
www.ametsoc.org
The American Meteorological Society promotes the development and dissemination of information and education on the atmospheric and related oceanic and hydrologic sciences and the advancement of their professional applications.
Publication Date: 1919 Monthly
Alexander E. MacDonald, President
Frederick H. Carr, President-Elect

3654 **Climate Institute: Climate Alert**
Coping with Climate Change
1400 16th St., NW 202-552-0163
Suite 430 Fax: 202-547-0111
Washington, DC 20036 info@climate.org
www.climate.org
The Climate Institute works to protect the balance between climate and life on earth by facilitating dialogue among scientists, policy makers, business executives and citizens. In all its efforts, the institute strives to be a sourceof objective, reliable information.
Publication Date: 1988 8-12 pages Quarterly
ISSN: 1071-3271
John Topping, President/CEO
Nasir Khattak, Chief Operating Officer

3655 **EarthShare of Georgia Newsletter**
100 Peachtree Street NW 404-873-3173
Suite 1960 Fax: 404-873-3135
Atlanta, GA 30303 info@earthsharega.org
www.earthsharega.org
Nonprofit federation of local, national and global environmental groups addressing the critical environmental issues. ESGA raises funds for these groups through workplace giving campaigns, special events and individual contributions.
Publication Date: 1992 Bi-Monthly
Madeline Reamy, Executive Director
Trecinia Wiggins, Development Coordinator

3656 **Environmental Policy Alert**
Inside Washington Publishers
1919 South Eads Street 703-416-8500
Suite 201 800-424-9068
Arlington, VA 22202 Fax: 703-416-8543
iwp@iwpnews.com
www.iwpnews.com
Addresses the legislative news and provides reports on the federal environmental policy process.
Publication Date: 1980
Paul Finger, Publisher

3657 **Journal of the Air Pollution Control Association**
Air Pollution Control Association
420 Fort Duquesne 412-232-3444
Boulevard #3 www.awma.org
Pittsburgh, PA 15222
A comprehensive journal offering information to the environment and conservation industry.
Dallas Baker, President
Brad Waldron, President Elect

3658 **Journal of the Air and Waste Management Association**
Air and Waste Management Association
420 Fort Duquesne Blvd. 412-232-3444
Pittsburgh, PA 15222 800-270-3444
Fax: 412-232-3450
info@awma.org
www.awma.org
Published for the working environmental professional and carries peer-reviewed technical papers on a variety of topics form control technology to science.
Publication Date: 1951 Monthly
Scott A. Freeburn, President
Chris Nelson, President Elect

3659 Population Reference Bureau: Household Transportation Use and Urban Pollution
1875 Connecticut Avenue NW 202-483-1100
Suite 520 800-877-9881
Washington, DC 20009 Fax: 202-328-3937
popref@prb.org
www.prb.org

Publication Date: 1929
Jeffrey Jordan, President and CEO
James Scott, CFO, COO

3660 Population Reference Bureau: Population & Environment Dynamics
1875 Connecticut Avenue NW 202-483-1100
Suite 520 800-877-9881
Washington, DC 20009 Fax: 202-328-3937
popref@prb.org
www.prb.org

PRB publishes the quarterly Population Bulletin, the annual World Population Data Sheet, and PRB Reports on America, as well as specialized publications covering population and public policy issues in the U.S. and abroad, particularlyin developing countries.
Publication Date: 1929
Jeffrey Jordan, President and CEO
James Scott, CFO, COO

3661 Population Reference Bureau: Water
1875 Connecticut Avenue NW 202-483-1100
Suite 520 800-877-9887
Washington, DC 20009 Fax: 202-328-3937
popref@prb.org
www.prb.org

Publication Date: 1929
Jeffrey Jordan, President and CEO
James Scott, CFO, COO

3662 Trinity Consultants Air Issues Review
12770 Merit Drive 972-661-8100
Suite 900 800-229-6655
Dallas, TX 75251 Fax: 972-385-9203
information@trinityconsultants.com
www.trinityconsultants.com

An environmental consulting company that assists industrial facilities with issues related to regulatory compliance and environmental management. Founded in 1974, this nationwide firm has particular expertise in air quality issues.Trinity also sells environmental software and professional education. T3, a Trinity Consultants Company, provides EH&S management information systems (EMIS) implementation and integration services.
Publication Date: 1990 8 pages Quarterly
John Hofmann, President and CEO
Dave Larsen, Chief Financial Officer

3663 Weather & Climate Report
Nautilus Press
1054 National Press Building 202-347-6643
Washington, DC 20045
Reports on federal actions which impact weather, climate research and global changes in climate.
Monthly
ISSN: 0730-8256
John R Botzum, Editor

3664 World Resource Review
SUPCON International
PO Box 50303 630-910-1551
Palo Alto, CA 94303 Fax: 630-910-1561
syshen@megsinet.net
www.globalwarming.net

For business and government readers, provides expert worldwide reviews of global warming and extreme events in relation to the management of natural, mineral and material resources. Subjects include global warming impacts onagriculture, energy, and infrastructure, monitoring of changes in resources using remote sensing, actions of national and international bodies, global carbon budget, greenhouse budget and more.
Publication Date: 1990 Quarterly
ISSN: 1042-8011
Dr. Sinya Shen, Production Manager

3665 World Watch
Worldwatch Institute
1400 16th Street NW 202-745-8092
Suite 430 Fax: 202-478-2534
Washington, DC 20036 worldwatch@worldwatch.org
www.worldwatch.org

Magazine on global environmental issues.
Publication Date: 1975 40 pages
ISSN: 0896-0615
Ed Ayres, Author
Ed Groark, Chair/Acting Interim Pres
Robert Charles Friese, Vice Chair

Periodicals: Business

3666 AFE Journal
8200 Greensboro Drive 571-395-8777
Suite 400 Fax: 571-766-2142
McLean, VA 22102 info@afe.org
www.afe.org

AFE Journal is a bimonthly publication from the Association for Facilities Engineering.
48 pages Bimonthly
ISSN: 1088-5900
Gabriella Jacobs, Author
Dennis M. Hydrick, President & Chairman
Wayne P. Saya, Executive Director

3667 ALBC News
American Livestock Breeds Conservancy
PO Box 477 919-542-5704
Pittsboro, NC 27312 Fax: 919-545-0022
www.livestockconservancy.org

ALBC News is a bi-monthly newsletter published by the American Livestock Breeds Conservancy.
Publication Date: 1987 20 pages Bi-Monthly
ISSN: 1064-1599
Cindy Rubel, Author
Cindy Rubel, Editor

3668 Abstracts of Presentations
Wildlife Society
5410 Grosvenor Lane 301-897-9770
Suite 200 Fax: 301-530-2471
Bethesda, MD 20814 tws@wildlife.org
www.wildlife.org

A yearly publication of the Wildlife Society.
Publication Date: 1994 300 pages Yearly
Rick Baydack, President
Bruce Thompson, Vice President

3669 Advisor
Great Lakes Commission
Eisenhower Corporate Park 734-665-9135
2805 South Industrial Hwy, Suite 100 Fax: 734-971-9150
Ann Arbor, MI 48104 www.glc.org
Covers economic and environmental issues of the Great Lakes region with a special focus on activities of the Great Lakes Commission.
Publication Date: 1955 12 pages Bi-Monthly
Kelvin Burch, Chairman
Tim A. Eder, Executive Director

3670 Agribusiness Fieldman
Western Agricultural Publishing Company
4969 E Clinton Way 559-252-7000
Suite 104 Fax: 559-252-7387
Fresno, CA 93727
Aimed at keeping the professional agriculture consultant posted on changes in the agricultural-chemical industry. Provides news about pests and control measures for all segments of the agricultural-chemical industry.
Paul Baltimore, Publisher
Margi Katz, Editor

3671 American Environmental Laboratory
International Scientific Communications
PO Box 870 203-926-9300
Shelton, CT 00648 Fax: 203-926-9310
www.iscpubs.com
Laboratory activities, new equipment, and analysis and collection of samples are the main topics.
Bi-Monthly
Brian Howard, Publisher/Editor-in-Chief

3672 Annual Newsletter and Report
The Peregrine Fund
5668 W Flying Hawk Lane 208-362-3716
Boise, ID 83709 Fax: 208-362-2376
tpf@peregrinefund.org
www.peregrinefund.org
Yearly publication from The Peregrine Fund. Free with $25 membership fee.
Publication Date: 1970 Yearly
William Burnham, Author
Carl A. Navarre, Chairman
J. Peter Jenny, President

3673 Bison World
National Bison Association
8690 Wolff Ct. 303-292-2833
Suite 200 Fax: 303-845-9081
Westminster, CO 80031 info@bisoncentral.com
www.bisoncentral.com
Published by the NBA, an organization of bison producers dedicated to awareness of the healthy properties of bison meat and bison production.
Publication Date: 1975 100 pages Quarterly
Dave Carter, Executive Director
Jim Matheson, Assistant Director

3674 Business and the Environment
Cutter Information Corporation
37 Broadway 781-648-8700
Suite 1 800-888-8939
Arlington, MA 00247 Fax: 781-648-8707
service@cutter.com
www.cutter.com
Environmental investment trends, deals and market developments.
Karen Fine Coburn, President & CEO
Paul Bergeron, CFO & COO

3675 CAC Annual Reports
Citizens Advisory Council
13th Floor, RCSOB 717-787-4527
PO Box 8459 Fax: 717-787-2878
Harrisburg, PA 17105 mioff.stephanie@state.pa.us
www.cacdep.state.pa.us
Publisher by the Citizens Advisory Council.
Publication Date: 1977 20-40 pages Annual
Susan Wilson, Executive Director
Stephanie Mioff, Administrative Assistant

3676 Chemosphere
Pergamon Press
660 White Plains Road 914-524-9200
Tarrytown, NY 10591 Fax: 914-592-3625
Related to environmental affairs. Accepts advertising.
100 pages
T Stephen, Editor
Rosemarie Fazzolari, Advertising

3677 Connecticut Sea Grant
1080 Shennecossett Road 860-405-9128
Groton, CT 00634 Fax: 860-405-9109
peg.vanpatten@uconn.edu
www.seagrant.uconn.edu
Based at the University of Connecticut, CT Sea Grant is part of the National Sea Grant network, whose mission is the conservation and wise use of coastal and marine resources through research, education and outreach.
Jeffrey Seeman, Chair
Bonnie Burr, Advisory Board

3678 Earth First! Journal
PO Box 964 561-320-3840
Lake Worth, FL 33460 Fax: 413-254-0057
collective@earthfirstjournal.org
www.earthfirstjournal.org/
Earth First! Journal was founded in 1979 in response to a lethargic, compromising and increasingly corporate environmental community. Earth First! takes a decidedly different tack toward environmental issues. We believe in using allthe tools in the toolbox, ranging from grassroots organizing and involvement in the legal process to civil disobedience and monkeywrenching.
Publication Date: 1979 64 pages Bimonthly
ISSN: 1055-8411

3679 Earth Island Journal
Earth Island Institute
2150 Allston Way 510-859-9100
Suite 460 Fax: 510-859-9091
Berkeley, CA 94704-1375 editor@earthisland.org
www.earthisland.org
Publication from the Earth Island Institute - cutting-edge news, analysis and commentary on vital international environmental news.
Publication Date: 1987 64 pages Quarterly
ISSN: 1041-0406
Michael Mitrani, President
Martha Davis, Vice President

3680 Economic Opportunity Report
Business Publishers
2222 Sedwick Drive 301-589-5103
Durham, NC 27713 800-223-8720
Fax: 800-508-2592
www.bpinews.com
Regulatory activities and governmental legislation and litigation are covered in this pulication.
Publication Date: 1963
Leonard Eiserer, Publisher
Beth Early, Operations Director

3681 Environmental Business Journal
ZweigWhite
4452 Park Blvd. 508-651-1559
Suite 306 800-466-6275
San Diego, CA 92116 Fax: 800-842-1560
info@zweigwhite.com
EBJ is the leading business newsletter for the environmental industry, providing competive strategies, new business opportuni-

ties, and up-to-date market trends and data. Now published by ZweigWhite, the EBJ comes out every month.
Publication Date: 1988 16+ pages Monthly
Grant Ferrier, President and CEO
George Stubbs, Senior Editor

3682 Environmental Compliance Update
High Tech Publishing Company
PO Box 1275 413-534-4500
Amherst, MA 00100
Identifies and analyzes the issues and business and economic impact of environmental compliance laws and regulations. Monitors the relevant changes due to legislation, court decisions, private rulings and technology.
Lori Reilly, Editor

3683 Environmental News
CA Business Publications
PO Box 3359 817-924-5301
Fort Worth, TX 76113 Fax: 817-922-8893
txenv@aol.com
Follows the progress of public environmental stock companies, provides updates on environmental contract opportunities, news of international environmental opportunities, and profiles innovative new companies.
Carolyn Ashford, Publisher/Editor

3684 Environmental Packaging
Thompson Publishing Group
P.O. Box 41868 202-872-4000
Austin, TX 78704 800-677-3789
Fax: 800-999-5661
www.thompson.com
A newletter aimed at the environmental regulatory specialist, product development managers, purchasing managers, legal counsel and package designers covering state-by-state regulations and the FCA guidelines and enforcement.
Publication Date: 1972
Daphne Musselwhite, Publisher

3685 Florida Forests Magazine
Florida Forestry Association
PO Box 1696 850-222-5646
Tallahassee, FL 32302 Fax: 850-222-6179
info@forestfla.org
www.floridaforest.org
A publication of the Florida Forestry Association.
Publication Date: 1997 26-32 pages Quarterly
J Doran, Executive VP

3686 George Miksch Sutton Avian Research Center Sutton Newsletter
PO Box 2007 918-336-7778
Bartlesville, OK 74005 Fax: 918-336-7783
info@suttoncenter.org
www.suttoncenter.org
Newsletter published by George Miksch Sutton Avian Research Center.
Publication Date: 1990 8-10 pages Semiannual
Steve Sherrod, Director of Conservation
Lena C. Larsson, Assistant Director

3687 Green Business Letter
Tilden Press
6 Hillwood Place 202-332-1700
Oakland, CA 94610 Fax: 202-332-3028
www.greenbiz.com
Hands-on journal for environmentally conscious companies, covering management strategies, facilities management, personnel policies and procurement with environmental consciousness. Emphasis on products, resources and how-toinformation.
8 pages
ISSN: 1056-490X
Joel Makower, Chairman & Executive Editor
Heather Clancy, Senior Writer

3688 In Business: The Magazine for Sustainable Enterprises and Communities
JG Press, Inc
419 State Avenue 610-967-4135
Emmaus, PA 18049 advert@jgpress.com
www.biocycle.net
It is the go-to magazine and website on composting, organics recycling, anaerobic digestion and renewable energy.
Jerome Goldstein, Editor

3689 International Environment Reporter
Bureau of National Affairs
1231 25th Street NW 202-452-4200
Washington, DC 20037 800-372-1033
Fax: 202-822-8092
www.bna.com
A four-binder information and reference service covering international environmental law and developing policy in the major industrial nations.
William A Beltz, Publisher

3690 International Environmental Systems Update
BSI Management Systems
12110 Sunset Hills Road 703-437-9000
Suite 200 800-862-4977
Reston, VA 20190 Fax: 703-435-7979
Provides accurate, up-to-date and useful information for environmental professionals around the globe. Monthly publication brings current environmental events into the limelight, dissecting complex issues, helping hundreds oforganizations improve their environmental and business preformance.
Publication Date: 1994 24 pages Monthly
ISSN: 1079-0837
Marcus Darby, Publisher

3691 McCoy's RCRA Unraveled
McCoy & Associates
12596 West Bayaud Avenue 303-526-2674
Suite 210 Fax: 303-526-5471
Lakewood, CO 80228 info@mccoyseminars.com
www.mccoyseminars.com
This book addresses the most troublesome areas in 40 CFR Parts 261 and 262 of the federal regulations. Our engineers have researched every scrap of guidance EPA has ever issued on these troublesome topics, studied the Federal Registerpreamble language, and talked to thousands of people who attented our RCRA seminars and shared their real-world experiences. It includes a keyword index with more than 1,300 entries, 200 probing examples from EPA's own guidance documents and ahelpful acronym list.
Publication Date: 2005 828 pages Yearly
Paul Gallagher, President
Nancy Pribble, Marketing Manager

3692 NFPA Journal
One Batterymarch Park 617-770-3000
Quincy, MA 00216 Fax: 617-770-0700
www.nfpa.org
A bi-monthly journal published by the National Fire Protection Association.
Bi-Monthly
Jim Pauley, President
Melinda Collins, Executive Administrator

3693 **NSS News**
National Speleological Society
6001 Pulaski Pike
Huntsville, AL 35810
256-852-1300
Fax: 256-851-9241
nss@caves.org
www.caves.org

Published by the National Speleological Society.
Publication Date: 1942 Monthly
ISSN: 0027-7010
Dave Bunnell, Editor
Wm Shrewsbury, President

3694 **Newsleaf**
4949 Tealtown Road
Milford, OH 45150
513-831-1711
Fax: 513-831-8052
cnc@cincynature.org
www.cincynature.org

Newsleaf is a quarterly publication for Cincinatti Nature Center members. This publication provides informative articles that teach readers about native flora and fauna.
Publication Date: 1965 20-24 pages Quarterly
Bill Hopple, Executive Director
Amy Johnson, Executive Assistant

3695 **Proceedings of the Desert Fishes Council**
Desert Fishes Council
PO Box 337
Bishop, CA 93515
760-872-8751
www.desertfishes.org
Yearly publication from Desert Fishes Council.
Publication Date: 1969 Yearly
ISSN: 1068-0381
E P Pister, Executive Secretary
Kathryn Boyer, President

3696 **Proceedings of the Southeastern Association of Fish and Wildlife Agencies**
27 Sylwood Place
Jackson, MS 39209
601-668-6916
Fax: 850-893-6204
crayhopkins@bellsouth.net
www.seafwa.org
Proceedings of the SEAFWA - an annual publication.
Publication Date: 1947 4-900 pages Yearly
Curtis R Hopkins, Executive Secretary

3697 **Pumper**
COLE Publishing
1720 Maple Lake Dam Road
PO Box 220
Three Lakes, WI 54562
715-546-3346
800-257-7222
Fax: 715-546-3786
info@pumper.com
www.pumper.com

Emphasis on companies, individuals and industry events while focusing on customer service, environmental issues and employment trends.
Publication Date: 1947
Ken Lowther, Editor

3698 **Regulatory Update**
Arkansas Environmental Federation
1400 W Markham Street
Suite 302
Little Rock, AR 72201
501-374-0263
Fax: 501-374-8752
cmiller@environmentark.org
www.environmentark.org

The AEF focuses on practical, common-sense laws and regulations based on sound science; a teamwork approach to compliance; waste minimization and pollution prevention. The AEF enables information to be exchanged on a daily basisbetween its members, government regulators, and policy makers.
Publication Date: 1967 Semi-Annual
Charles Miller, Executive Director
Marge Brookins, Office Manager

3699 **Risk Policy Report**
Inside Washington Publishers
1225 South Clark Street
Suite 1400
Arlington, VA 22202
703-416-8500
800-424-9068
iwp@iwpnews.com
www.iwnews.com

Contains analysis, great perspectives, industry news, policymaking profiles and a calendar of events.
Monthly
David P Clarke, Publisher/Editor

3700 **Semillero**
731 8th Street SE
Washington, DC 20003
202-547-3800
Fax: 202-546-4784
etoledo@newforestsproject.com
www.newforestsproject.com

Our electronic publication has more than 2500 subscribers in the US and Latin America. It provides useful information and references to specifice resources regarding agro-forestry, rural development and grant information.
Publication Date: 1982
Erick Toledo and Catalina Serna, Author
Erick Toledo, Director

Periodicals: Design & Architecture

3701 **LICA News**
Land Improvement Contractors of America
3080 Ogden Avenue
Suite 300
Lisle, IL 60532
630-548-1984
Fax: 630-548-9189
nlica@aol.com
www.licanational.com

Official publication of Land Improvement Contractors of America.
Bob Clark, Chairman
Steve Anderson, President

3702 **MSW Management**
Forester Communications
PO Box 3100
Santa Barbara, CA 93130
805-682-1300
Fax: 805-682-0200
www.mswmanagement.com

Provides general news on facility construction, financing, new equipment and revenue issues.
Publication Date: 1991 7 Times Yearly
Daniel Waldman, Publisher

Periodicals: Disaster Preparedness & Response

3703 **Hazard Technology**
EIS International
555 Herndon Parkway
Herndon, VA 20170
703-478-9808
Fax: 703-787-6720

Application of technology to the field of emergency and environmental management to save lives and protect property.
James W Morentz PhD, Publisher
Leslie Atkin, Managing Editor

3704 **Hazardous Materials Newsletter**
Hazardous Materials Publishing
243 West Main Street
Kutztown, PA 19530
610-683-6721
Fax: 610-683-3171
lfricker@hazmat-tsp.com
www.hazmatpublishing.com

Focuses on response to and control of hazardous materials emergencies. Particularly appropriate tools, equipment, materials, methods, procedures, strategies and lessons learned. Addresses

leak, fore and spill control for incidentcommanders and experienced responders, including incident clauses, prevention and remedial actions; decisionmaking; scene management; control and containment; response teams; and product identification and hazards.
12 pages

3705 Natural Hazards Observer
Natural Hazards Center
University of Colorado 303-492-6818
482 UCB Fax: 303-492-2151
Boulder, CO 80309 hazctr@colorado.edu
www.colorado.edu/hazards

A periodical of the Natural Hazards Center that covers current disaster issues; new international, national, and local disaster management, mitigation, and education programs; hazards research; political and policy developments; newinformation sources and Web sites; upcoming conference; and recent publications
Bi Monthly
Liesel Ritchie, Associate Director
Kathleen Tierney, Director

Periodicals: Energy & Transportation

3706 AERO SunTimes
Alternative Energy Resources Organization
432 N Last Chance Gulch 406-443-7272
Helena, MT 59601 Fax: 406-442-9120
aero@aeromt.org

The SunTimes is the newsletter for AERO. The organization is a statewide grassroots group whose members work together to strengthen communities through promoting sustainable agriculture, local food production and citizen-based SmartGrowth community planning.
Publication Date: 1978 4-24 pages Quarterly
ISSN: 1046-0993
Kiki Hubbard, Editor
Jean Duncan, Editor

3707 Butane-Propane News
Butane-Propane News, Inc
PO Box 660698 626-357-2168
Arcadia, CA 91066 800-214-4386
Fax: 626-303-2854
arey@bpnews.com
www.bpnews.com

Offers information to professionals that are involved in the distribution, production, shipping and sales of butane and propane in the US and internationally. $32 for US one year subscription; $60 for international one yearsubscription.
Publication Date: 1939 48-96 pages Monthly
ISSN: 0007-7259
Natalie Peal, Publisher
John Needham, Editor

3708 Cars of Tomorrow
Northeast Sustainable Energy Association
50 Miles Street 413-774-6051
Greenfield, MA 00130 Fax: 413-774-6053
nesea@nesea.org
www.nesea.org

Offers a look at the energy options of vehicles of the future.
Curriculum
Jennifer Marrapese, Executive Director
Gina Sieber, Business Manager

3709 E&P Environment
Pasha Publications
1600 Wilson Boulevard 703-528-1244
Suite 600 800-424-2908
Arlington, VA 22209 Fax: 703-528-1253

Reports on environmental regulations, advances in technology and litigation aimed specifically at the exploration and production segments of the oil and gas industry.
Harry Baisden, Group Publisher
Michael Hopps, Editor

3710 Energy Engineering
Association of Energy Engineers
3168 Mercer University Drive 770-447-5083
Atlanta, GA 30341 Fax: 770-446-3969
webmaster@aeecenter.org
www.aeecenter.org

Engineering solutions to cost efficiency problems and mechanical contractors who design, specify, install, maintain, and purchase non-residential heating, ventilating, air conditioning and refrigeration equipment and components.
Jennifer Vendola, Controller
Ruth Whitlock, Executive Administrator

3711 Energy Journal
International Association for Energy Economics
28790 Chagrin Boulevard 216-464-5365
Suite 350 Fax: 216-464-2737
Cleveland, OH 44122 iaee@iaee.org
www.iaee.org

Promotes the advancement and dissemination of new knowledge on energy matters and related topics. Topics include: transportation, electricity markets, environmental issues, natural gas topics, and carbon emissions reduction.
Publication Date: 1980 200 pages Quarterly
David L Williams, Executive Director
Peter R. Hartley, President

3712 Getting Around Clean & Green
Northeast Sustainable Energy Association
50 Miles Street 413-774-6051
Greenfield, MA 00130 Fax: 413-774-6053
nesea@nesea.org
www.nesea.org

This interdisciplinary science/social studies curriculum allows students to explore the transportation and environmental issues in their own lives. Activities cover: transportation systems, health impacts, environmental andtransportation histories, carpooling, and mass transit.
90 pages Curriculum
Jennifer Marrapese, Executive Director
Gina Sieber, Business Manager

3713 Getting Around Without Gasoline
Northeast Sustainable Energy Association
50 Miles Street 413-774-6051
Greenfield, MA 00130 Fax: 413-774-6053
nesea@nesea.org
www.nesea.org

An interdisciplinary unit that explores the feasibility of getting around without using gasoline. Students can conduct various activities to compare powering vehicles with gasoline versus electricity.
60 pages S & H Only
Jennifer Marrapese, Executive Director
Gina Sieber, Business Manager

3714 Heliographs
Illinois Solar Energy Association
1281 E. Brummel Ave 630-260-0424
Elk Grove Village, IL 60007 contactisea@illinoissolar.org
www.illinoissolar.org

It is a non-profit organization that promotes the widespread application of solar and other forms of renewable energy through our mission of education and advocacy
Publication Date: 1975 12 pages Quarterly
Lesley McCain, Executive Director
Shannon Fulton, President

3715 **IAEE Membership Directory**
International Association for Energy Economics
28790 Chagrin Boulevard 216-464-5365
Suite 350 Fax: 216-464-2737
Cleveland, OH 44122 iaee@iaee.org
www.iaee.org
One of the three periodicals put out by the International Association for Energy Economics (IAEE). It lists members contact information and affiliation and general association information. Also available online.
Annual
David L Williams, Executive Director
Peter R. Hartley, President

3716 **IAEE Newsletter**
International Association for Energy Economics
28790 Chagrin Boulevard 216-464-5365
Suite 350 Fax: 216-464-2737
Cleveland, OH 44122 iaee@iaee.org
www.iaee.org
Association information including: upcoming events, conferences, special reports, affiliate activities, and chapter news.
Quarterly
David L Williams, Executive Director
Peter R. Hartley, President

3717 **International Journal of Hydrogen Energy**
5794 SW 40 Street 305-284-4666
#303 Fax: 305-284-4792
Miami, FL 33155 info@iahe.org
www.iahe.org
A monthly publication serving to inform scientists and the public of advances made in hydrogen energy research and development.
Publication Date: 1976 120 pages Monthly
ISSN: 0360-3199
T Nejat Veziroglu, Author
T Neja Veziroglu, President
Matthew M. Mench, Executive Vice President

3718 **Midwest Renewable Energy Association Newsletter**
7558 Deer Road 715-592-6595
Custer, WI 54423 Fax: 715-592-6596
info@the-mrea.org
www.midwestrenew.org
ReNews includes articles on energy issues, book reviews, case studies, and other general information about renewable energy.
Quarterly
Nick Hylla, Executive Director
Kaitlyn Kohl, Administrative Assistant

3719 **Northeast Sun**
Northeast Sustainable Energy Association
50 Miles Street 413-774-6051
Greenfield, MA 00130 Fax: 413-774-6053
nesea@nesea.org
www.nesea.org
Promotes responsible use of energy for a stronger economy and cleaner environment. Northeast Sun is a bi-annual Spring and Fall publication that includes articles by leading authorities on sustainable energy practices, energyefficiency and renewable energy, and each Fall issue includes the Sustainable Green Pages Directory of engery professionals in the Northeast. Subscription is free with membership.
Bi-Annual
Jennifer Marrapese, Executive Director
Gina Sieber, Business Manager

3720 **Nuclear Waste News**
Business Publishers
2222 Sedwick Drive 301-589-5103
Durham, NC 27713 800-223-8720
Fax: 800-508-2592
custserv@bpinews.com
www.bpinews.com
Worldwide coverage of the nuclear waste management industry, including waste generation, radiological environmental remediation, packaging, transport, processing and disposal.
Weekly
Leonard A Eiserer, Publisher
Beth Early, Associate Publisher

3721 **Radwaste Magazine**
American Nuclear Society
555 North Kensington Avenue 708-352-6611
LaGrange Park, IL 60526 800-323-3044
Fax: 708-352-0499
TMarc@ans.org
www.ans.org
Addresses issues in all fields of radioactive waste management, removal, handling, disposal, treatment, cleanup and environmental restoration.
6x per Year
Robert C. Fine, Executive Director
Patricia Schroeder, Manager

3722 **ReNews**
Midwest Renewable Energy Association
PO Box 249 715-592-6595
Amherst, WI 54406 Fax: 715-592-6596
www.midwestrenew.org
ReNews is a quarterly newsletter that includes articles on energy issues, book reviews, case studies, and other general information about renewable energy.
Quarterly
Nick Hylla, Executive Director
Kaitlyn Kohl, Administrative Assistant

3723 **Solar Energy**
Elsevier Science
360 Park Avenue South 212-989-5800
11th Floor Fax: 212-633-3990
New York, NY 10010 usinfo-f@elsevier.com
www.elsevier.com
It is a world-leading provider of information solutions that enhance the performance of science, health, and technology professionals, empowering them to make better decisions, deliver better care, and sometimes make groundbreakingdiscoveries that advance the boundaries of knowledge and human progress.
Ron Mobed, Chief Executive Officer
Stuart Whayman, Chief Financial Officer

3724 **Solar Energy Report**
1107 9th St. 949-837-7430
Suite 820 Fax: 949-709-8043
Sacramento, CA 95814 www.calseia.org
It advances the common interests of the California solar industry, helping make California's solar market the most robust in the United States
Bi-Monthly
Aaron Thurlow, Secretary
Cecilia Aguillon, Vice President

3725 **Solar Reflector**
Texas Solar Energy Society
PO Box 1447 512-326-3391
Austin, TX 78767 800-465-5049
Fax: 512-444-0333
info@txses.org
www.txses.org

A Texas Solar Energy Society publication. Promotes the wise use of sustainable and non-polluting resources.
Quarterly
Lucy Stolzenburg, Executive Director
Scot Arey, Chairman

3726 Solar Today
American Solar Energy Society
2525 Arapahoe Ave 303-443-3130
Ste E4-253 Fax: 303-443-3212
Boulder, CO 80302 info@ases.org
www.ases.org
Provides information and case histories and reviews of a variety of renewable energy technologies, including solar, wind, biomass and geothermal.
Carly Rixham, Executive Director
Brooke Simmons, Managing Editor

3727 Sustainable Green Pages Directory
Northeast Sustainable Energy Association
50 Miles Street 413-774-6051
Greenfield, MA 00130 Fax: 413-774-6053
nesea@nesea.org
www.nesea.org
The SPG Directory lists over 30 categories of sustainable energy professionals working throughout the Northeast, including architects, engineers, builders, energy auditors, consultants and renewable energy installers and manufacturers.It is the largest directory of its kind and the only one that targets the Northeastern USA. Published in the Northeast Sun magazine and onlines.
September Annual
Jennifer Marrapese, Executive Director
Gina Sieber, Business Manager

Periodicals: Environmental Engineering

3728 Air and Waste Management Association's Magazine for Environmental Managers
Air and Waste Management Association
One Gateway Center 412-232-3444
420 Fort Duquesne Blvd., 3rd Floor 800-270-3444
Pittsburgh, PA 15222 Fax: 412-232-3450
info@awma.org
www.awma.org
A magazine that contains sections of Washington and Canadian reports, a calendar of events, government affairs, news focus, campus research, business briefs, district control news, porfessional development programs, professionalservices and other issues facing the environmental professionals.
Scott A. Freeburn, President
Chris Nelson, President-Elect

3729 Asbestos & Lead Abatement Report
Business Publishers
2222 Sedwick Drive 301-589-5103
Durham, NC 27713 800-223-8720
Fax: 800-508-2592
custserv@bpinews.com
www.bpinews.com
Tracks the major legal, legislative, regulatory, business and technological developments in the asbestos and lead abatement industries.
Weekly
Leonard A Eiserer, Publisher
Beth Early, Associate Publisher

3730 Defense Cleanup
Business Publishers
2222 Sedwick Drive 301-589-5103
Durham, NC 27713 800-223-8720
Fax: 800-508-2592
custserv@bpinews.com
www.bpinews.com
Covers the latest news and analysis of defense cleanup activity. Including base remediation and closure, contract awards and site cleanups.
Weekly
Leonard A Eiserer, Publisher
Beth Early, Associate Publisher

3731 EI Digest
Environmental Information
8525 Arjons Drive 858-695-0050
Suite H Fax: 952-831-6550
San Diego, CA 92126 www.envirobiz.com
Contains market studies of commercial hazardous waste management companies with in-depth analysis of trends in policy, regulations, technology and business.
Publication Date: 1983
ISSN: 1042-251X
Cary Perket, Editor

3732 Environment
Helen Dwight Reid Educational Foundation
325 Chestnut Street 215-625-8900
Suite 800 800-354-1420
Philadelphia, PA 19106 customer.service@taylorandfrancis.com
www.heldref.org
Provides environment professionals and concerned citizens with authoritative yet accessible articles that provide critical analysis of environmental science and policy issues, book recommendations, commentaries, news briefs and reviewson environmental websites and major governmental and institutional reports.
Publication Date: 1958 48 pages Monthly
ISSN: 0013-9157
Douglas Kirkpatrick, Executive Director
Barbara T Richman, Managing Editor

3733 Environment 21
Florida Environments Publishing
4010 Newberry Road 352-373-1401
#F Fax: 352-373-1405
Gainesville, FL 32607
Regulations, wildlife, hazard waste/materials, ground/surface/drinking water and other issues concerning Florida's environment are emphasized in this publication for the environmental management team.
Dave Newport, Publisher

3734 Environmental Engineer Magazine
American Academy of Environmental Engineers
130 Holiday Court 410-266-3311
Suite 100 Fax: 410-266-7653
Annapolis, MD 21401 www.aaee.net
Official magazine of the American Academy of Environmental Engineers. It addresses issues and practice with: updates on legal developments affecting environmental engineering, documentation of the profession's heritage, articles onenvironmental policy, and profiles of leading environmental engineers.
Quarterly
Lawrence C Pencak, Executive Director
Yolanda Y Moulden, Production Manager

3735 **Environmental Engineering Science**
Mary Ann Liebert
140 Huguenot Street 914-740-2100
3rd Floor 800-MLI-EBER
New Rochelle, NY 10801 Fax: 914-740-2101
info@liebertpub.com
www.liebertpub.com

The focus is on pollution control of the suface, ground, and drinking water, and highlight research news and product developments that aid in the fight against pollution.
Bi-Monthly
ISSN: 1092-8758
Mary Ann Liebert, Publisher
Dumpnico Grosso PhD, Editor-in-Chief

3736 **Environmental Manager**
Air and Waste Management Association
420 Fort Duquesne Blvd 412-232-3444
3rd Floor 800-270-3444
Pittsburgh, PA 15222 Fax: 412-232-3450
info@awma.org
www.awma.org

Features timely articles on business, regulatory, and technical issues of interest to the environmental industry.
Dallas Baker, President
Nancy Meilahn Fowler, Treasurer

3737 **Environmental and Energy Study Institute**
1112 16th Street, NW 202-628-1400
Suite 300 Fax: 202-204-5244
Washington, DC 20036 eesi@eesi.org
www.eesi.org

A nonprofit organization dedicated to promoting environmentally sustainable societies. EESI believes meeting this goal requires transitions to social and economic patterns that sustain people, the environment and the natural resourcesupon which present and future generations depend. EESI produces credible, timely information and innovative public policy initiatives that lead to these transitions. These products take the form of publications, briefings, work shops and taskforces.
Publication Date: 1984
Jared Blum, Chair
Shelley Fidler, Secretary/Treasurer

3738 **Federation of Environmental Technologists**
W175 N11081 Stonewood Dr 262-437-1700
Ste 203 Fax: 262-437-1702
Germantown, WI 53022 info@fetinc.org
www.fetinc.org

A nonprofit organization formed to assist industry in interpretation of and compliance with environmental regulations. FET is dedicated to educate its members and other environmental professionals on regulatory compliance andtechnological developments in a cost-effective manner through training, professional development and networking.
Publication Date: 1982 Monthly
Jeffrey Nettesheim, Chair/Director
Renee Bashel, President/Director

3739 **Food Protection Trends**
International Association for Food Protection
6200 Aurora Avenue 515-276-3344
Suite 200W 800-369-6337
Des Moines, IA 50322 Fax: 515-276-8655
info@foodprotection.org
www.foodprotection.org

Published as the general membership publication by the International Association for Food Protection, each issue contains refereed articles on applied research, applications of current technology and general interest subjects for foodsafety professionals. Regular features include industry and association news, an industry related product section and a calendar of meetings, seminars and workshops.Updates of government regulations and sanitary design is also featured. All membersreceive FPT.
Publication Date: 1981 80+ pages Monthly
ISSN: 1043-3546
David W Tharp, Executive Director
Lisa K Hovey, Assistant Director

3740 **Hazardous Materials Intelligence Report**
World Information Systems
129 Mount Auburn 617-491-5100
Cambridge, MA 00223 Fax: 617-492-3312
Provides news analysis on environmental business, hazardous materials, waste management, pollution prevention and control. Covers regulations, legislation and court decisions, new technology, contract opportunities and awards andconference notices.
Richard S Golob, Publisher
Roger B Wilson Jr, Editor

3741 **Hazmat Transport News**
Business Publishers
2222 Sedwick Drive 301-589-5103
Durham, NC 27713 800-223-8720
Fax: 800-508-2592
custserv@bpinews.com
www.bpinews.com

Reports on the regulatory, enforcement, legislative and litigation developments affecting hazardous materials transportation.
Monthly
Leonard A Eiserer, Publisher
Beth Early, Associate Publisher

3742 **Integrated Waste Management**
McGraw Hill
1221 Ave. of the Americas 212-904-2000
New YorK, NY 10020 www.mhfi.com
Articles geared toward integration of solid waste management.
8 pages
Deirdre Borrego, VP and General Manager
Tina Morris, Operations Director

3743 **International Journal of Phytoremediation**
Taylor & Francis Inc
150 Fearing Street 413-549-5170
Amherst, MA 00100 Fax: 413-549-0579
www.aehs.com

An official journal of the Association for Environmental Health and Sciences (AEHS). Dedicated to current laboratory and field research on how to use plant systems to remediate contaminated environments.
6 Issues Yr
ISSN: 1522-6514
Jason White, Managing Editor

3744 **Iowa Academy of Science Journal**
Iowa Academy of Science
UNI - 175 Baker Hall 319-273-2021
2607 Campus Street Fax: 319-273-2807
Cedar Falls, IA 50614-0508 iascience@uni.edu
www.scienceiniowa.org

A non-profit organization whose mission is to further scientific research, science education, public understanding of science and to recognize excellence in these endeavors.
Quarterly

Craig Johnson, Executive Director

3745 **Journal of Environmental Engineering**
American Society of Civil Engineers
1801 Alexander Bell Drive 703-295-6300
Reston, VA 20191 Fax: 703-295-6211
onlinejls@asce.org

The journal of Environmental Engineering presents a collection of broad interdisciplinary information on the practice and status of research in environmental engineering science, systems engineering, and sanitation.
Publication Date: 1875
Raymond A Ferrara, Editor
Melissa Junior, Director, Journals

3746 Journal of Environmental Quality
American Society of Agronomy
5585 Guilford Road 608-273-8080
Madison, WI 53711 Fax: 608-273-2021
membership@agronomy.org
www.agronomy.org

Written for university, government and industry scientists interested in the impacts of environmental perturbations on the biological and physical sciences. Domestic member price: $50 (Int'l $103); Domestic non-member price: $650(Int'l $703).
Bi-Monthly
Wes Meixelsperger, Chief Financial Officer
Susan Ernst, Managing Editor

3747 Journal of Environmental and Engineering Geophysics: JEEG
1720 South Bellaire Street 303-531-7517
Suite 110 Fax: 303-820-3844
Denver, CO 80222 staff@eegs.org
www.eegs.org

A peer reviewed journal of the EEGS made available to members and a variety of libraries.
Publication Date: 1992 Quarterly
ISSN: 1083-1363
Kathie Barstnar, Executive Director
Janet Simms, Editor

3748 Journal of IEST
Institute of Environmental Sciences & Technology
2340 S. Arlington Heights Rd 847-981-0100
Suite 100 Fax: 847-981-4130
Arlingotn Heights, IL 60005 www.iest.org
An annual journal published by the Institute of Environmental Sciences & Technology.
Publication Date: 1957 185 pages Annual
ISSN: 1098-4321
Shawn Windley, President
Wei Sun, President-elect

3749 Kennedy-Jenks Consultants: Alert Newsletter
303 Second Street 415-243-2150
Suite 300 S Fax: 415-896-0999
San Francisco, CA 94107 www.kennedyjenks.com
Environmental engineering consulting company.
Publication Date: 1990 6 pages 3 times/year
Gary Carlton, Chair
Keith London, President and CEO

3750 Kennedy-Jenks Consultants: Spotlights
303 Second Street 415-243-2150
Suite 300 S Fax: 415-896-0999
San Francisco, CA 94107 www.kennedyjenks.com
Environmental engineering consulting company.
Publication Date: 1981 12 pages 3 times/year
Gary Carlton, Chair
Keith London, President and CEO

3751 Lead Detection & Abatement Contractor
IAQ Publications
7920 Norfolk Avenue 301-913-0115
Suite 900 Fax: 301-913-0119
Bethesda, MD 20814 iaqpubs@aol.com
www.iaqpubs.com

Feature articles include new on legislation, operational and safety issues that affect the removal of lead and lead by-products from paint, water, soil, and air.
Susan Valenti, Editor

3752 Leading Edge
Society of Exploration Geophysicists
8801 South Yale Avenue 918-497-5500
Tulsa, OK 74137 Fax: 918-497-5557
jlawnick@seg.org
www.seg.org

Addresses a broad spectrum of topics related to applied geophysics. Material immediately accessible to a broad audience.
Publication Date: 1930 116 pages
ISSN: 1070-485X
Dean Clark, Editor
Linda Holeman, Associate Editor

3753 McCoy's CAA Unraveled
McCoy & Associates
12596 W Bayaud AvenueRoad 303-526-2674
Suite 210 Fax: 303-526-5471
Lakewood, CO 80228 info@mccoyseminars.com
www.mccoyseminars.com

It is an environmental engineering firm founded in 1982 by Drew McCoy. Our mission is to provide our customers current, accurate environmental compliance information in plain English
414 pages

3754 McCoy's RCRA Reference
McCoy & Associates
12596 W Bayaud AvenueRoad 303-526-2674
Suite 210 Fax: 303-526-5471
Lakewood, CO 80228 info@mccoyseminars.com
www.mccoyseminars.com
It is an environmental engineering firm founded in 1982 by Drew McCoy. Our mission is to provide our customers current, accurate environmental compliance information in plain English
1190 pages

3755 Medical Waste News
Business Publishers
2222 Sedwick Drive 301-589-5103
Durham, NC 27713 800-223-8720
Fax: 800-508-2592
custserv@bpinews.com
www.bpinews.com
Reports on the rapidly evolving legislative and regulatory actions in medical waste management. Includes coverage of incineration, laboratory wastes, infection control, liability and legal issues and waste transport.
Publication Date: 1963
Leonard A Eiserer, Publisher
Beth Early, Operations Director

3756 New York State Conservationist
NYS Department of Environmental Conservation
625 Broadway 518-402-8047
2nd Floor 800-678-6399
Albany, NY 12233 Fax: 518-402-9036
dinnelson@gw.dec.state.ny.us
www.dec.ny.gov
An informative and entertaining full-color bi-monthly magazine featuring New York State's natural resources and peoples' enjoyment of those resources.
Bi-Monthly
ISSN: 0010-650X
David Nelson, Editor

3757 Noise Control Engineering Journal
Institute of Noise Control Engineering

12100 Sunset Hills Rd., 703-234-4073
Suite 130 Fax: 703-435-4390
Reston, VA 20190 ibo@inceusa.org
www.inceusa.org

The technical publication of the Institute of Noise Control Engineering. It contains technical articles on all aspects of noise control engineering.
Bi-Monthly
ISSN: 0736-2501
Joseph M Cuschieri, Executive Director
Courtney Burroughs, Editor in Chief

3758 Noise Regulation Report
Business Publishers
2222 Sedwick Drive 301-589-5103
Durham, NC 27713 800-223-8720
Fax: 800-508-2592
custserv@bpinews.com
www.bpinews.com

Exclusive coverage of airport, highway, occupational and open space noise, noise control and mitigation issues.
Publication Date: 1963
Leonard A Eiserer, Publisher
Beth Early, Operations Director

3759 Plumbing Standards
American Society of Sanitary Engineering
18927 Hickory Creek Drive 708-995-3019
Suite 220 Fax: 708-479-6139
Mokena, IL 60448 info@asse-plumbing.org
www.asse-plumbing.org

Disseminates industry-wide technical information on standards, updates, water, wastewater, plumbing design, and other topics related to the water industry.
Douglas A. Marian, President
Dana Colombo, Vice President

3760 Pollution Engineering
Cahners Business Information
2000 Clearwater Drive 630-320-7000
Oak Brook, IL 60523 Fax: 630-288-8282
www.pollutionengineering.com

Serves the field of pollution control in manufacturing industries, utilities, consulting engineers and constructors. Also serves government agencies including administration of federal, state and local environmental programs.

ISSN: 0032-3640
Barbara Olsen, Publisher
Roy Bigham, Managing Editor

3761 RMT Newsletter
744 Heartland Trail 608-831-4444
PO Box 8923 800-283-3443
Madison, WI 53717 Fax: 608-831-3334
info@rmtinc.com
www.rmtinc.com

Global engineering and management consulting firm that develops environmental solutions for industry. With a 600 person staff and 20 offices throughout the US and Europe helping clients sustain the environment while meeting theirbusiness objectives. Engineers, scientists and construction managers can take a project from conception through successful completion. Expertise includes air, water and waste permitting, remediation, hazardous/solid waste management, air pollutioncontrol and more.
8 pages Quarterly
Jodi Burmester, Marketing Communications

3762 SPAC Newsletter
Soil and Plant Analysis Council
347 North Shores Circle 970-686-5702
Windsor, CO 80550 Fax: 402-476-0302

Quarterly newsletter.
Quarterly
Rao Mylavarapu, President
Robert Miller, Secretary/Treasurer

3763 Sludge
Business Publishers
2222 Sedwick Drive 301-589-5103
Durham, NC 27713 800-223-8720
Fax: 800-508-2592
custserv@bpinews.com
www.bpinews.com

Premier insider guide to the biosolids industry. Follows developments in and management of beneficial use and wastewater residuals, with practical information about industrial sludge, incineration, special wastes, permits andlandfills.
BiWeekly
Leonard A Eiserer, Publisher
Beth Early, Operations Director

3764 Soil & Sediment Contamination:An International Journal
Taylor & Francis Inc
150 Fearing Street 413-549-5170
Amherst, MA 00100 Fax: 413-549-0579
www.aehs.com

An official journal of the Association for Environmental Health and Sciences (AEHS). An internationally peer-reviewed publication that focuses on sediment and soil contamination.
Bi Monthly
ISSN: 1532-0383
James Dragun, Editor-in-Chief
Paul Kostecki, Managing Editor

3765 Solid Waste Report
Business Publishers
2222 Sedwick Drive 301-589-5103
Durham, NC 27713 800-223-8720
Fax: 800-508-2592
custserv@bpinews.com
www.bpinews.com

Comprehensive news and analysis of legislation, regulation and litigation in solid waste management. Regularly features federal rules, congressional actions, state updates and business trends.
Weekly
Leonard A Eiserer, Publisher
Beth Early, Associate Publisher

3766 Waste News
Crain Communications
1725 Merriman Road 330-836-9180
#300 Fax: 330-836-1692
Akron, OH 44313

Editorial content focuses on waste management and recycling issues, primarily how businesses deal with the waste they generate. Covers waste management service providers, legistlative and regulatory environmental issues, emergingtechnologies, municipal recycling and waste issues, commodity market price, mergers, aquisitions and expansions.
Publication Date: 1995 Bi-Weekly
ISSN: 1091-699
Allan Gerlat, Editor
Brennan Lafferty, Managing Editor

3767 Widener University: International Conference on Solid Waste Proceedings
One University Place 610-499-4042
Chester, PA 19013 Fax: 610-499-4461
solid.waste@widener.edu
solid-waste.org

Publication of the annual conference on solid waste technology and management. Over 100 speakers from 35 countries present their work. Proceedings available.
Publication Date: 1983 Quarterly
ISSN: 1088-1697
James T. Harris III, Ed, President
Stephen C. Wilhite, Dphil, Provost of Academic Affairs

Periodicals: Environmental Health

3768 American College of Toxicology
1821 Michael Faraday Drive 703-547-0875
Suite 300 Fax: 703-438-3113
Reston, VA 20190 acthq@actox.org
www.actox.org

The American College of Toxicology is a 501-0-3 nonprofit organization. It is not a degree-granting organization. The American College of Toxicology is dedicated to providing an interactive forum for the advancement and exchange oftoxicologic information between industry, goverment, and academia. There is an annual meeting in November each year. The ACT publiches a journal, International Journal of Toxicology on a bi-monthly basis.

ISSN: 1091-5818
Mary Ellen Cosenza, President
Hanan Ghantous, President Elect

3769 American Journal of Public Health
American Public Health Association
800 I Street NW 202-777-2742
Washington, DC 20001 888-320-2742
Fax: 202-777-2533
ellen.meyer@apha.org
www.apha.org

Peer-reviewed journal of the American Public Health Association (APHA) for public health workers and academics. Its emphasis is on research and practioners experiences.
12 Issues/Yr
Georges C. Benjamin, MD, Executive Director
James Carbo, Executive Office

3770 Applied and Environmental Microbiology
American Society for Microbiology
1752 N Street NW 202-737-3600
Washington, DC 20036 Fax: 202-942-9333
service@asmusa.org
www.asm.org

Contains current significant research in industrial microbiology, microbial ecology, biotechnology, public health microbiology and food microbiology.
Lynn Enquist, President
Joseph M. Campos, Secretary

3771 Asbestos & Lead Abatement Report
Business Publishers
2222 Sedwick Drive 301-589-5103
Durham, NC 27713 800-223-8720
Fax: 800-508-2592
custserv@bpinews.com
www.bpinews.com

Contains articles on regulation compliance, environmental trends and business opportunities.
Leonard A Eiserer, Publisher

3772 Aviation, Space and Environmental Medicine
Aerospace Medical Association
320 S Henry Street 703-739-2240
Alexandria, VA 22314 Fax: 703-739-9652
pday@asma.org
www.asma.org

Provides contact with physicians, life scientists, bioengineers, and medical specialists working in both basic medical research and in its clinical applications.
Publication Date: 1929 962 pages Monthly
ISSN: 0095-6562
Sarah A Nunneley MD, Author
Kris Belland, President
David Gradwell, President Elect

3773 Bio Integral Resource Center: Common Sense Pest Control
PO Box 7414 510-524-2567
Berkeley, CA 94707 Fax: 510-524-1758
birc@igc.org
www.birc.org

Features least toxic solutions to pest problems of the home and garden. Those who are chemically sensitive and looking for alternatives may find what they need in the Quarterly.
Publication Date: 1984 24 pages Quarterly
ISSN: 8756-7881
Dr. William Quarles, Executive Director

3774 Bio Integral Resource Center: IPM Practitioner
PO Box 7414 510-524-2567
Berkeley, CA 94707 Fax: 510-524-1758
birc@igc.org
www.birc.org

Focuses on management alternatives for pests such as insects, mites, ticks, vertebrates, weeds and plant pathogens.
Publication Date: 1979 24 pages 10 Times a Year
ISSN: 0738-969x
Dr. William Quarles, Executive Director

3775 Center for Statistical Ecology & Environmental Statistics: Environmental & Ecological Statistics
Kluwer Academic Publishers
Pennsylvania State University 814-865-9442
421 Thomas Building, Dept of Statistics Fax: 814-865-1278
University Park, PA 16802 gpp@stat.psu.edu
sites.stat.psu.edu/~gpp

The Center is the first of its kind in the world and enjoys national and international reputation. They have an ongoing program of research that integrates statistics, ecology and the environment. The emphasis is on the environment andcollaborative research, training and exposition on improving the quantification and communication of man's impact on the environment. Major interest also lies in statistical investigations of the impact of the environment on man. Contact them forfull listings.
Publication Date: 1984 110 pages Quarterly
ISSN: 1352-8505
Ganapati P Patil, Editor-in-Chief

3776 EH&S Software News Online
Donley Technology
220 Garfield Avenue 804-224-9427
PO Box 152 Fax: 804-224-7958
Colonial Beach, VA 22443 donleytech@donleytech.com
www.donleytech.com

Reports on news and upgraded software products, database, and on-line systems from commercial developers and government resources.
Quarterly
John Donley, Editor
Elizabeth Donley, Managing Editor/Publisher

3777 Enterprise Software: Essential EH&S
Essential Technologies
1401 Rockville Pike 301-284-3000
#500 Fax: 301-284-3001
Rockville, MD 20852 www.essential-technologies.com

Integrated solutions for emissions management, hazard communication, compliance management, occupational health and safety and contingency management.
James Morentz, Publisher

3778 **Environmental Connections**
Connecticut College
270 Mohegan Avenue 860-439-5417
Box 5293 Fax: 860-439-2418
New London, CT 00632 ccbes@conncoll.edu
Publication Date: 1998 10 pages 2 times per year
Robert Askins, Director
Diane Whitelaw, Assistant Director

3779 **Environmental Dimensions**
Trine Publishers
C/O Blogar & Partners 919-653-2581
14600 Weston Parkway, Suite 300 866-541-3841
Cary, NC 27513 Fax: 919-678-8696
ehponline@niehs.nih.gov
ehp.niehs.nih.gov
Provides the environmental professionals with news and information on current environmental health issues, solution, and hazards, as well as examining governmental policies, legal news and Canada's environmental preformance.
22 times per year
Shaun R. Halloran, Operations Manager
Rita B. Hanson, Managing Editor

3780 **Environmental Health Letter**
Business Publishers
2222 Sedwick Drive 301-589-5103
Durham, NC 27713 800-223-8720
Fax: 800-508-2592
custserv@bpinews.com
www.bpinews.com
Comprehensive coverage of the latest policies and ground-breaking research that explores the potential links between environmental factors and human health.
8 pages
Leonard A Eiserer, Publisher
Beth Early, Operations Director

3781 **Environmental Health perspectives**
National Inst. of Environmental Health Sciences
C/O Blogar & Partners 919-653-2581
14600 Weston Parkway, Suite 300 866-541-3841
Cary, NC 27513 Fax: 919-678-8696
ehponline@niehs.nih.gov
ehp.niehs.nih.gov
Annual subscription.
224 pages Monthly
Shaun R. Halloran, Operations Manager
Rita B. Hanson, Managing Editor

3782 **Florida Journal of Environmental Health**
Florida Environmental Health Association
P.O. Box 350356 904-384-0838
Jacksonville, FL 32235 Contact_Us@feha.org
www.feha.org
Promotes public health by means of advanced environmental control.
Quarterly
ISSN: 0897-1823
Trisha Dall, President
Garry Schneider, President Elect

3783 **Healthy Schools Network Newsletter**
773 Madison Avenue 518-462-0632
Albany, NY 12208 Fax: 518-462-0433
info@healthyschools.org
www.healthyschools.org
HSN is a nationally recognized state-based advocate for the protection of children's environmental health in schools. Engages in research, education, outreach, technical assistance and coalition building to create schols that areenvironmentally responsible to children, and to their communities. Publishes a quarterly newsletter and maintains an Information Clearinghouse and Referral Service.
Quarterly
Claire L Barnett, Executive Director

3784 **Human Ecology Action League Magazine**
2250 N Druid Hills Road NE 404-248-1898
Atlanta, GA 30329 Fax: 404-248-0162
HEALNatnl@aol.com
lifestream.aol.com
The Human Ecology Action League Inc (HEAL) is a nonprofit organization founded in 1977 to serve those whose health has been adversely affected by environment exposures; to provide information to those who are concerned about the healtheffects of chemicals; and to alert the general public about the potential dangers of chemicals. Referrals to local HEAL chapters and other support groups are available from the League.
Publication Date: 1977 35 pages Quarterly
ISSN: 8755-7878
Diane Thomas, Editor

3785 **Indoor Environment Review**
IAQ Publications
7920 Norfolk Avenue 301-913-0115
Suite 900 Fax: 301-913-0119
Bethesda, MD 20814
New technology, research and legislation concerning all indoor air and water quality issues.
Robert Morrow, Editor

3786 **Industrial Health and Hazards Update**
InfoTeam
PO Box 15640 954-473-9560
Plantation, FL 33318 Fax: 954-473-0544
infoteamma@aol.com
Covers occupational safety, health hazards, and disease; mitigation and control of hazardous situations; waste recycling and treatment.
20 pages
Dr. David Allen, Associate Editor

3787 **Journal of Environmental Health**
National Environmental Health Association
720 S Colorado Boulevard 303-756-9090
Suite 1000-N 866-956-2258
Denver, CO 80246 Fax: 303-691-9490
staff@neha.org
www.neha.org
A practical journal containing information on a variety of environmental health issues.
Publication Date: 1937 70-76 pages 10 Times a Year
ISSN: 0022-0892
Dr. David Dyjack, Executive Director
Rance Baker, Program Administrator

3788 **Journal of Medical Entomology**
Journal of Entomology
3 Park Place 301-731-4535
Ste 307 Fax: 301-731-4538
Annapolis, MD 21401 esa@entsoc.org
www.entsoc.org
Contributions report on all phases of medical entomology and medical acarology, including the systematics and biology of insects, acarines, and other arthropods of public health and veterinary significance.
David Gammel, Executive Director
Neil Willoughby, Director of Finance

3789 Journal of Pesticide Reform
PO Box 1393 541-344-5044
Eugene, OR 97440 Fax: 541-344-6923
info@pesticide.org
www.pesticide.org

Pesticide factsheets, alternatives factsheets for common pest problems, and helpful information on how to take action for change are featured in this journal. Each issue also includes updates on NCAP's work, news on pesticide issues,and reviews of books and videos.

Publication Date: 1984 24 pages Quarterly
Jeremy Olsen, Assistant Director
Kim Leval, Executive Director

3790 Nation's Health, The
American Public Health Association
800 I Street NW 202-777-2742
Washington, DC 20001 888-320-2742
Fax: 202-777-2533
www.apha.org

Monthly newspaper of the American Public Health Association (APHA). It focuses on the latest public health news that public health professionals need to know such as food safety, racial and ethnic disparities, patients' rights,environmental issues, and health screening.

10 Issues/Yr
Georges C. Benjamin, MD, Executive Director
James Carbo, Executive Office

3791 National Institute of Environmental Health Sciences Journal
111 T.W. Alexander Drive 919-496-2433
Research Triangle Park, NC 27709 Fax: 919-496-8276
www.niehs.nih.gov

The National Institute of Environmental Health Sciences is the principal federal agency for basic biomedical research on the health effects of environmental agents. It is the headquarters for the National Toxicology Program whichcoordinates toxicology studies within the Department of Health and Human Services.

Publication Date: 1972 150 pages Monthly
ISSN: 0091-6765
Kenneth Olden PhD, Director

3792 Natural Resources Council of America: Environmental Resource Handbook
Universal Reference Publications
1616 P Street 202-232-6631
NW Suite 340 Fax: 240-465-0467
Washington, DC 20036 www.NaturalResourcesCouncil.org

Environmental Resource Handbook updates.

4 pages
Laura Seal, Membership Coordinator

3793 Natural Resources Council of America: Conservation Voice
1616 P Street 202-232-6631
NW Suite 340 Fax: 240-465-0467
Washington, DC 20036 www.naturalresourcescouncil.org

Charts the news, events, and personnel that shape the face of the conservation movement and includes the quarterly supplemental publication NEPA news.

Publication Date: 1958 6-8 pages Bi-Monthly
Andrea Yank, Executive Director

3794 Natural Resources Council of America: NEPA News
1616 P Street 202-232-6631
NW Suite 340 Fax: 240-465-0467
Washington, DC 20036

Publication Date: 1994 8 pages Quarterly
Andrea Yank, Executive Director

Periodicals: Gaming & Hunting

3795 American Bass Association Newsletter
402 N Prospect Avenue 310-376-1026
Redondo Beach, CA 90277 Fax: 310-376-5072
www.americanbass.com

Publication Date: 1989 24 pages Quarterly
Jason Sutherland, Director
Larry Mantle, Director

3796 IPPL News
PO Box 776 843-871-2280
Summerville, SC 29484 Fax: 843-871-7988
info@ippl.org
www.ippl.org/gibbon

Educates readers in more than 50 countries about action that can be taken to protect primates.

Publication Date: 1974 32 pages 3 Times a Year
ISSN: 1040-3027
Dr Shirley McGreal, Chairperson
Barbara Allison, Office Manager

3797 International Game Fish Association Newsletter
300 Gulf Stream Way 954-927-2628
Dania Beach, FL 33004 Fax: 954-924-4299
hq@igfa.org
www.igfa.org

Founded as record-keeper and to maintain fishing rules. Today, emphasis is on conservation and education. Newsletters published are World Record Game Fish, annually and The International Angler, bi-monthly.

Bi-Monhtly
Rob Kramer, President
Michael J. Myatt, Chief Operating Officer

3798 JAKES Magazine
770 Augusta Road 803-637-3106
PO Box 530 800-THE-NWTF
Edgefield, SC 29824 Fax: 803-637-0034
nwtf@nwtf.net
www.nwtf.org

JAKES (Juniors Acquiring Knowledge, Ethics and Sportsmanship) is a magazine which provides fun and educational articles focusing on young hunters, outdoor activities, the environment and other items of interest to readers 17 years oldand younger. Free with membership.

Quarterly
Vern Ross, President
Marvin Hartley, Vice President

3799 Mid-Atlantic Fishery Management Council Newsletter
800 North State Street 302-674-2331
Suite 201 877-446-2362
Dover, DE 19901 Fax: 302-674-5399
contact@mafmc.org
www.mafmc.org

It is responsible for the conservation and management of fishery resources within the federal 200-mile limit of the Atlantic off the coasts of New York, New Jersey, Pennsylvania, Delaware, Maryland, Virginia and North Carolina.

Publication Date: 1998 8 pages Quarterly
Christopher M. Moore, Executive Director
Rich Seagraves, Senior Scientist

3800 Turkey Call
770 Augusta Road 803-637-3106
PO Box 530 800-THE-NWTF
Edgefield, SC 29824 Fax: 803-637-0034
nwtf@nwtf.net
www.nwtf.org

A magazine for turkey hunting enthusiasts, provides articles to help you improve your hunting skills and learn how to enhance your land for wildlife. Free with membership.
Bi-Monthly
Vern Ross, President
Marvin Hartley, Vice President

3801 Wheelin' Sportsmen
770 Augusta Road 803-637-3106
PO Box 530 800-THE-NWTF
Edgefield, SC 29824 Fax: 803-637-0034
nwtf@nwtf.net
www.nwtf.org
Magazine for all disabled people and their able-bodied partners who are interested in the outdoors, especially recreational shooting, hunting and fishing. Free with membership.
Quarterly
Vern Ross, President
Marvin Hartley, Vice President

3802 Women in the Outdoors
770 Augusta Road 803-637-3106
PO Box 530 800-THE-NWTF
Edgefield, SC 29824 Fax: 803-637-0034
www.nwtf.org
Magazine that delivers features on a variety of outdoor topics of interest to the novice and experienced outdoorswoman. Free with membership.
Quarterly
Vern Ross, President
Marvin Hartley, Vice President

Periodicals: Habitat Preservation & Land Use

3803 ANJEC Report
Association/New Jersey Environmental Commissions
PO Box 157 973-539-7547
Mendham, NJ 00794 Fax: 973-539-7713
info@anjec.org
www.anjec.org
Nonprofit organization promoting public interest in natural resorce protection and supporting municipal environmental commissions throughout New Jersey.
Publication Date: 1970 32 pages Quarterly
Jennifer M. Coffey, Executive Director
Kerry Miller, Assistant Director

3804 Afield
4705 University Drive 919-403-8558
Suite 290 Fax: 919-403-0379
Durham, NC 27707 northcarolina@tnc.org
www.nature.org/northcarolina
Published by The Nature Conservancy, saving the last great places of North Carolina.
Quarterly Newsletter
Craig O. McCaw, Chairman
James E. Rogers, Vice Chair

3805 Aldo Leopold Foundation: The Leopold Outdoor
E13701 Levee Road 608-355-0279
Baraboo, WI 53913 Fax: 608-356-7309
mail@aldoleopold.org
www.aldoleopold.org
A nonprofit organization founded in 1982, works to promote the philosophy of Aldo Leopold and the land ethic he so eloquently defined in his writing. The foundation actively integrates programs on land stewardship, environmentaleducation and scientific research to promote care of natural resources and have an ethical relationship between people and land.
Publication Date: 1999 8 pages Quarterly
Steve Swenson, Ecologist
Buddy Huffaker, Executive Director

3806 American Association for Advancement of Science: Animal Keeper's Forum
1200 New York Avenue Northwest 202-326-6400
Washington, DC 20005 Fax: 202-289-4985
webster@aaas.org
www.aaas.org
The American Association for the Advancement of Science is the world's largest general science and publisher of the peer-reviewed journal. With more than 138,000 members and 275, AAAS serves as an authoritative source for informationon the latest developments in science and bridges gaps among scientists, policy- makers and the public to advance science and science education.
Publication Date: 1947 54 pages Monthly
ISSN: 0164-9531
Gerald Fink, Chair
Geraldine Richmond, President

3807 American Birding Association: Birding
P.O. Box 744 302-838-3660
Delaware City, DE 19706 800-850-2473
Fax: 302-838-3651
info@aba.org
www.aba.org
The American Birding Association represents the interests of birdwatchers in various arenas, and helps birders increase their knowledge, skills, and enjoyment of birding. ABA also contributes to bird conservation by linking the skillsof its members to on-the-ground projects. ABA promotes field-birding skills through meetings, workshops, equipment, and guided involvement in birding, promoting national and international birders networks and publications.
Publication Date: 1972 8 pages Bi Monthly
Jeffrey A. Gordon, President
Lisa Slocum, Accountant

3808 American Birding Association: Winging It
P.O. Box 744 302-838-3651
Delaware City, DE 19706 800-850-2473
Fax: 302-838-3651
info@aba.org
www.aba.org
The American Birding Association represents the interests of birdwatchers in various arenas, and helps birders increase their knowledge, skills, and enjoyment of birding. ABA also contributes to bird conservation by linking the skillsof its members to on-the-ground projects. ABA promotes field-birding skills through meetings, workshops, equipment, and guided involvement in birding, promoting national and international birders networks and publications.
Publication Date: 1989 24 pages Bi Monthly
Jeffrey A. Gordon, President
Lisa Slocum, Accountant

3809 American Entomologist
Journal of Entomology
3 Park Place 301-731-4535
Ste 307 Fax: 301-731-4538
Annapolis, MD 21401 esa@entsoc.org
www.entsoc.org
American Entomologist is a quarterly, general interest entomology magazine written for both scientists and nonscientists. It publishes colorful, illustrated feature articles, peer-reviewed

scientific reports, provocative and humorouscolumns, letters, book reviews, and obituaries.
Publication Date: 1955 64 pages Quarterly
ISSN: 1046-2821
David Gammel, Executive Director
Neil Willoughby, Director of Finance

3810 American Forests Magazine
1220 L Street NW 202-737-1944
Suite 750 800-368-5748
Washington, DC 20005 Fax: 202-955-4588
info@amfor.org
www.americanforests.org
Published by American Forests, the oldest national citizens conservation organization in the US.
Quarterly
Ann Nichols, Chair
Bruce Lisman, Vice Chair

3811 Annals of the Entomological Society of America
Journal of Entomology
3 Park Place
Ste 307 Fax: 301-731-4538
Annapolis, MD 21401 esa@entsoc.org
www.entsoc.org
Contributions report on the basic aspects of the biology of anthropods and are divided into categories by subject matter; systematics; ecology and population biology; arthropods in relation to plant disease; conservation biology andbiodiversity; physiology, biochemistry, and toxicology; morphology, history, and fine sructure; genetics and behavior.
Bi-Monthly
David Gammel, Executive Director
Neil Willoughby, Director of Finance

3812 Annual Review of Entomology
Annual Reviews
3 Park Place
Ste 307 Fax: 301-731-4538
Annapolis, MD 21401 esa@entsoc.org
www.entsoc.org
This is published in Januray and made available through ESA on a regular subscription basis. The series occupies a special place within the field of entomology. Authoritative critical reviews by eminent scientists provide a valuableresource for students, teachers, and researchers: specialists and nonspecialists.
Yearly
David Gammel, Executive Director
Neil Willoughby, Director of Finance

3813 Appalachian Mountain Club
Appalachian Mountain Club Books
5 Joy Street 617-523-0636
Boston, MA 00210 800-262-4455
Fax: 617-523-0722
information@outdoors.org
www.outdoors.org
The AMC, founded in 1876, promotes the protection, enjoyment, and wise use of the mountains, rivers and trails of the Northeast. We encourage people to enjoy and protect the natural world because we believe that successful conservationdepends on this experience. The AMC publishes an award-winning magazine and more than 60 guide books to the Northeast.
Wayne Thornbrough, Chair
Rol Fessenden, Vice Chair

3814 Arthropod Management Tests
Journal of Entomology
3 Park Place
Ste 307 Fax: 301-731-4538
Annapolis, MD 21401 esa@entsoc.org
www.entsoc.org
This is published in late spring. The purpose is to promote timely dissemination of information on preliminary and routine screening tests on management of arthropods, both beneficial and harmful. Pest management methods tested andreported may include the use of chemical pesticides as well as other materials or agents, such as insect growth regulators, pheromones, natural enemies for biological control, or pest-resistant plants/animals. Reports are based on tests conducted byreseachers.
Yearly
David Gammel, Executive Director
Neil Willoughby, Director of Finance

3815 Biodiversity Institute Newsletter
University of Kansas
Dyche Hall 785-864-4540
Lawrence, KS 66045 Fax: 785-864-5335
A comprehensive research, graduate education and public service institution dedicated to biodiversity science and collections. Collections of more than 7 million plant and animal specimens, with particular strengths in neotropicalamphibians, great plains, flora, bees and antarctic plant fossils.
Publication Date: 1978 6 pages Quarterly
Dr Leonard Krishtalka, Director

3816 Blowhole
3625 Brigantine Boulevard 609-266-0538
PO Box 773 Fax: 609-266-6300
Brigantine, NJ 00820 mmsc@verizon.net
mmsc.org
A quarterly newsletter published by the Marine Mammal Stranding Center.
Publication Date: 1978 8 pages Quarterly
Robert C Schoelkopf, President
Kenneth Schaffer, Chairman

3817 Carolina Bird Club
1809 Lakepark Drive 910-791-5726
Raleigh, NC 27612 Fax: 910-791-7228
hq@carolinabirdclub.org
www.carolinabirdclub.org
A nonprofit educational and scientific association, open to anyone interested in the study and conservation of wildlife, particularly birds. Meets each winter, spring and fall. Meeting sites are selected to give participants anopportunity to see many different kinds of birds. Guided field trips, informative programs and business sessions are combined for an exciting weekend of meeting with people who share an enthusiasm and concern for birds.
Publication Date: 1937 Quarterly
ISSN: 0009-1987
Irvin Pitts, President
Don Seriff, Editor

3818 Coalition for Education in the Outdoors
P.O. Box 2000 607-753-2011
Cortland, NY 13045 Fax: 607-753-5982
www.outdooredcoalition.org
A network of organizations, business, institutions, centers, agencies, and associations linked and communicating in support of the broad purpose of education in, for, and about the outdoors. Takes a board view of outdoor education andseeks not to duplicate or compete with the work of organizations, but to provide services not easily performed by other groups.
Publication Date: 1987 48-52 pages Bi-Annual
ISSN: 1065-5204
Erik J. Bitterbaum, President
Peter Perkins, VP Institutional Advancement

3819 College of Tropical Agriculture and Human Resources: Impact Report
University of Hawaii

3050 Maile Way
Gilmore 119
Honolulu, HI 96822
808-956-7056
Fax: 808-956-5966
ocs@ctahr.hawaii.edu
www.ctahr.hawaii.edu

The vision of the college is to be the premier resource for tropical agricultural systems and resource management in the Asia-Pacific region. Its mission outlines a commitment to the preparation of students and all citizens of Hawaiifor life in a global community through research and education programs supporting tropical agricultural systems that foster viable communities, a diversified economy and a healthy environment.

Annual
Maria Gallo, Dean/Director
Wimmie Wong Lui, Assistant to the Dean

3820 Connecticut Woodlands
Middlefield
16 Meriden Road
Rockfall, CT 00648
860-346-2372
Fax: 860-347-7463
info@ctwoodlands.org
www.ctwoodlands.org

Quarterly publication of the Connecticut Forest and Park Association, an organization for forest and wildlife conservation. Develops outdoor recreation and natural resources. Provides forest management, construction of hiking trailsand consultation in the areas of forestry and environment.

Quarterly
Lori Paradis Brant, Education Director
Teresa Peters, Office Manager

3821 Conservancy of Southwest Florida
Eye On The Issues
1495 Smith Preserve Way
Naples, FL 34102
232-262-0304
Fax: 232-262-0672
info@conservancy.org
www.conservancy.org

It aims to protect the quality of life in the region

8 pages Quarterly
Rob Moher, President/CEO
Lynn Slabaugh, Board Chair

3822 Conservation & Natural Resources: Water Resources Division, Nevada Wildlife Almanac
901 S. Stewart Street
Suite 2002
Carson City, NV 89701
775-681-2800
Fax: 775-684-2811
ndwr.state.nv.us

The mission is to conserve, protect, manage and enhance the State's water resources for Nevada's citizens through the appropriation and reallocation of the public waters.

Publication Date: 1996 12 pages Twice/year
Hugh Ricci, State Engineer

3823 Conservation Commission News
New Hampshire Association of Conservation Comm.
54 Portsmouth Street
Concord, NH 03301
603-224-7867
info@nhacc.org
www.nhacc.org

Encourage conservation and appropriate use of New Hampshire's natural resources by providing assistance to New Hampshire's municipal conservation commissions and by facilitating communication among commissions and between commissionsand other public and private agencies involved in conservation.

8 pages
G. Wesley Robertson, President
Tom Duston, Secretary

3824 Conservation Communique
Wyoming Association of Conservation Districts
517 East 19th Street
Cheyenne, WY 82001
307-632-5716
Fax: 307-638-4099
www.conservewy.com

It provides leadership for the conservation of Wyoming's soil and water resources, promotes the control of soil erosion, promotes and protects the quality of Wyoming's waters, reduce siltation of stream channels and reservoirs, promotewise use of Wyoming's water, and all other natural resources, preserve and enhance wildlife habitat, protect the tax base and promote the health, safety and general welfare of the citizens of this state through a responsible conservation ethic.

Quarterly
Kelly Brown, Program Specialist
Bobbie Frank, Executive Director

3825 Conservation Conversation
Montana Association of Conservation Districts
3001 Coolidge Road
Suite 250
East Lansing, MI 48823-6362
517-324-5274
Fax: 517-324-4435
macd@macd.org
www.macd.org

It is Working to strengthen Michigan's Conservation Districts through leadership, information and representation at the state level.

Quarterly
Lori Phalen, Executive Director
Waynette Ginter, Bookkeeper

3826 Conservation Leader
Utah Association of Conservation Districts
1860 North 100 East
Logan, UT 84341
435-753-6029
Fax: 435-755-2117

Quarterly

3827 Conservation Notes: New England Wildflower Society
180 Hemenway Road
Framingham, MA 00170
508-877-7630
508-877-6553
Fax: 508-877-3658
information@newenglandwild.org
www.newenglandwild.org

The mission is to conserve and promote the region's native plants to ensure healthy, biologically diverse landscapes.

36 pages Yearly
Debbi Edelstein, Executive Director
Deirdre C. Menoyo, Chair, Board of Trustees

3828 Conservation Partner
Arkansas Association of Conservation Districts
101 E Capitol
Suite 350
Little Rock, AR 72201
501-682-2915
Fax: 501-682-3991
www.aracd.org

The purpose and mission is to assist the conservation districts of the state of Arkansas in their efforts to serve the soil and water conservation needs of the people of Arkansas.

Quarterly
Debbie Moreland, Program Administrator
Rocky Harrell, President

3829 Conservation Visions
Nebraska Association of Resources Districts
601 S 12th Street
Suite 201
Lincoln, NE 68508
402-471-7670
Fax: 402-471-7677
nard@nrdnet.org
www.nrdnet.org

The mission is to assist NRDs in a coordinated effort to accomplish collectively what may not be accomplished individually to conserve, sustain, and improve our natural resources and environment.

Bi-Monthly
Terry Martin, President
Jim Bendfeldt, Vice President

3830 Conservogram
Soil and Water Conservation Society

945 Southwest Ankeny Road 515-289-2331
Ankeny, IA 50023 Fax: 515-289-1227
pubs@swcs.org
www.swcs.org

Published for the professionals in the natural resource fields, and contains highlights on the news and ideas in the preservation of natural resources.
Monthly
Mark Berkland, President
Cheryl Simmons, Vice President

3831 Consultant
Assoc of Consutling Foresters of America, Inc
312 Montgomery Street 703-548-0990
Suite 208 888-540-8733
Alexandria, VA 22314 Fax: 703-548-6395
director@acf-foresters.org
www.acf-foresters.org

Publication from Association of Consulting Foresters of America, Inc.
Publication Date: 1948
Lynn C Wilson, Executive Director
Clifford J. Barnhart, President

3832 Cornell Lab of Ornithology: Birdscope
Birdscope
159 Sapsucker Woods Road 607-254-2451
Ithaca, NY 14850 Fax: 607-254-2415
cornellbirds@cornell.edu
www.birds.cornell.edu

It is a world leader in the study, appreciation, and conservation of birds.
Quarterly,Newsletter
Alex Chang, Communications Director
Gustave Axelson, Editorial Director

3833 Cornell Lab of Ornithology: Living Bird
Birdscope
159 Sapsucker Woods Road 607-254-2475
Ithaca, NY 14850 Fax: 607-254-2415
cornellbirds@cornell.edu
www.birds.cornell.edu

It is a world leader in the study, appreciation, and conservation of birds.
Quarterly, Magazine
Alex Chang, Communications Director
Gustave Axelson, Editorial Director

3834 Department of Natural Resources
301 Centennial Mall South 402-471-2363
PO Box 94676 Fax: 402-471-2900
Lincoln, NE 68509
Quarterly
Roger K Patterson, Director

3835 District Connection Newsletter
North Carolina Assoc. of Soil/Water Cons. Dist.
1614 Mail Service Center 919-733-2302
Raleigh, NC 27699 Fax: 919-715-3559
Monthly
David Williams, Acting Director

3836 E Magazine
Doug Moss
28 Knight St 203-854-5559
Norwalk, CT 00685 Fax: 203-866-0602
www.emagazine.com

A comprehensive magazine dealing with environmental issues and national conservation concerns.
Publication Date: 1990 64 pages Bimonthly
Doug Moss, Publisher/Executive Director
Roddy Scheer, Executive Director/Editor

3837 ESA Newsletter
Journal of Entomology
3 Park Place
Ste 307 301-731-4538
Annapolis, MD 21401 esa@entsoc.org
www.entsoc.org
Monthly
David Gammel, Executive Director
Neil Willoughby, Director of Finance

3838 Eagle Nature Foundation Ltd: Bald Eagle News
Bald Eagle News
300 E Hickory 815-594-2306
Apple River, IL 61001 Fax: 815-594-2305
eaglenature.tni@juno.com
eaglenature.com

A quarterly publication from the Eagle Nature Foundation.
Publication Date: 1992 20 pages Quarterly
Terrence N Ingram, Executive Director
Angelina Rodriguez, Secretary

3839 Earth Steward
Michigan Association of Conservation Districts
3001 Coolidge Road 517-324-5274
Suite 250 Fax: 517-324-4435
East Lansing, MI 48823-6362 macd@macd.org
www.macd.org

Quarterly membership newsletter
Quarterly
Waynette Ginter, Bookkeeper
Lori Phalen, Executive Director

3840 Ecosphere
Forum International
91 Gregory Lane 925-997-1864
Suite 21 800-252-4475
Pleasant Hill, CA 94523 Fax: 925-946-1500
fti@foruminternational.com
www.foruminternational.com

Accepts advertising. The first ever environmental/ecological magazine. It is dedicated to the interrelations of man in nature and a balanced approach of its biological, economic, socio-political and spiritual components. Since 1965.
Publication Date: 1965 16-48 pages Bi Monthly
Dr. Nicolas Hetzer, Production Manager
J McCormack, Circulation Director

3841 Elm Leaves
Elm Research Institute
11 Kit Street 603-358-6198
Keene, NH 03431 800-367-3567
Fax: 603-358-6305
libertyelm@webryders.com

A semi annual publication published by the Elm Research Institute. Free with membership.
Publication Date: 1967 4-9 pages Semi-Annually
John Hansel, Editor/Executive Director
Yvonne Spalthoff, Assistant Director

3842 Environmental Concern: The Wonders of Wetlands, an Educators Guide
POW-The Planning of Wetlands
201 Boundary Lane 410-745-9620
PO Box P Fax: 410-745-3517
St Michaels, MD 21663 order@wetland.org
www.wetland.org

Since its founding in 1972, EC has been specializing in consulting, planning design, education services, construction services and research related to all aspects of wetlands. As wetlands and contiguous upland forests and meadows areinteracting ecosystems EC specializes in consulting, planning, design, and project

supervision services for such upland ecosystem constructions and restorations for the purpose of wetland buffers, reforestation, wildlife habitat and critical areas ofpreservation.
Publication Date: 1995 Quarterly
ISSN: 1095-2063
Suzanne Pittengar Slear, President
Chuck Barbour, Nursery Manager

3843 **Environmental Entomology**
Journal of Entomology
3 Park Place
Ste 307
Annapolis, MD 21401
301-731-4535
Fax: 301-731-4538
esa@entsoc.org
www.entsoc.org
Contributions report on the interaction of insects with biological, chemical, and physiological and chemical ecology (abiotic effects, pheromonea, effects of miscellaneous pollutants), community/ecosystem ecology (trophic-levelsstudies, associations), population ecology (mating, reproduction, movement, behavior, parasitism, predation, microbial ecology, insect-plant relations), pest management and sampling (integrated pest management, sampling, distribution), and biologicalcontrol.
Bi-Monthly
David Gammel, Executive Director
Neil Willoughby, Director of Finance

3844 **Everglades Reporter**
Friends of the Everglades
11767 South Dixie Highway
#232
South Miami, FL 33156
305-669-0858
Fax: 305-669-0858
www.everglades.org
Protecting the Everglades. A bi-annual publication from Friends of the Everglades.
Publication Date: 1971 8 pages Quarterly
Alan Farago, President
Connie Washburn, Vice-President

3845 **Fisheries**
American Fisheries Society
5410 Grosvenor Lane
Bethesda, MD 20814
301-897-8616
Fax: 307-897-8096
main@fisheries.org
www.fisheries.org
Peer-reviewed articles that address contemporary issues and problems, techniques, philosophies and other areas of interest to the general fisheries profession. Monthly features include letters, meeting notices, book listings andreviews, environmental essays and organization profiles.
Donna L. Parrish, President
Ronald J. Essig, President-Elect

3846 **Fisheries Focus: Atlantic**
Atlantic States Marine Fisheries Commission
1050 N. Highland Street
Suite 200
Arlington, VA 22201
703-842-0740
Fax: 703-842-0741
info@asmfc.org
www.asmfc.org

12 pages Monthly
Robert E. Beal, Executive Director
Tina L Berger, Director of Communications

3847 **Forest History Society**
701 William Vickers Avenue
Durham, NC 27701
919-682-9319
Fax: 919-682-2349
coakes@duke.edu
www.foresthistory.org
The Forest History Society is a non-profit educational institution that links the past to the future by identifying, collecting, preserving, interpreting, and disseminating information on the history of people, forests, and theirrelated resources.
Publication Date: 1946
Jason Howard, Librarian
Steven Anderson, President

3848 **Forest Voice**
Native Forest Council
PO Box 2190
Eugene, OR 97402
541-688-2600
Fax: 541-461-2156
info@forestcouncil.org
www.forestcouncil.org
Quarterly publication from Native Forest Council.
Publication Date: 1989 16 pages Quarterly
ISSN: 1069-2002
Timothy Hermach, President
Bill Barton, Board Member

3849 **Forestry Source**
Society of American Foresters
5400 Grosvernor Lane
Bethesada, MD 20814
301-897-8720
866-897-8720
Fax: 301-897-3690
www.safnet.org
Tabloid newsletter covering important information regarding critical issues in forestry research and technology, legislative updates and news about SAF programs and activities on a national and local level.
20 pages Monthly
Matt Walls, Editor

3850 **Game & Fish Commission Wildlife Management Division Newsletter**
2 Natural Resources Drive
Little Rock, AR 72205
501-223-6300
800-364-4263
Fax: 501-223-6452
askAGFC@agfc.state.ar.us
www.agfc.com
Dedicated to managing wildlife in the state of Arkansas.
Publication Date: 1920 33-35 pages 5x year
Mike Knoedl, Director
Andrew Bass, Assistant Deputy Director

3851 **Golden Gate Audubon Society**
2530 San Pablo Avenue
Suite G
Berkeley, CA 94702
510-843-2222
Fax: 510-843-5351
ggas@goldengateaudubon.org
www.goldengateaudubon.org
Monthly publication from Golden Gate Audubon Society. Published 10 times yearly.
Publication Date: 1917 12 pages Monthly
ISSN: 0164-971x
Cindy Margulis, Executive Director
Ilana DeBare, Communications Director

3852 **Great Plains Native Plant Society Newsletter**
P.O. Box 461
Hot Springs, SD 57747
605-745-3397
Fax: 605-745-3397
info@gpnps.org
www.gpnps.org
The Society's mission is to engage in scientific research regarding plants of the Great Plains of North America; to disseminate this knowledge through the creation of one or more educational botanical garders of such flora, featuringbut not limited to Barr's discoveries; and to engage any educational activities which may further public familiarity with the plants of the Great Plains, their uses and enjoyment.
Publication Date: 1984 4-8 pages Intermittant
Cynthia Reed, President

3853 **Green Space**
New York Parks and Conservation Association

29 Elk Street
Albany, NY 12207
518-434-1583
Fax: 518-427-0067
ptny@ptny.org
www.nypca.org

Semi-Annual
Robin Dropkin, Executive Director

3854 Habitat Hotline
Atlantic States Marine Fisheries Commission
1050 N. Highland Street
Suite 200
Arlington, VA 22201
703-842-0740
Fax: 703-842-0741
info@asmfc.org
www.asmfc.org

6 pages Quarterly
Robert E. Beal, Executive Director
Tina L Berger, Director of Communications

3855 Illinois Audubon Society
PO Box 2547
Springfield, IL 62708
217-544-BIRD
Fax: 217-544-7433
ias@illinoisaudubon.org
www.illinoisaudubon.org

A membership organization dedicated to the preservation of Illinois Wildlife and the habitats which support them. Has sanctuaries, conservation education and land acquisition programs and publishes quarterly magazines and newsletters.
Publication Date: 1916 28 pages Quarterly
ISSN: 1061-9801
Tom Clay, Executive Director
Jodie Owen, Accounts Manager

3856 Illinois Environmental Council: IEC Bulletin
230 Broadway
Suite 150
Springfield, IL 62701
217-544-5954
Fax: 217-544-5958
iec@ilenviro.org
www.ilenviro.org

The IEC is a coalition of over 70 environmental, conservation and health groups.
Bi-Monthly
Jonathan Goldman, Executive Director
Jennifer Sublett, Outreach Coordinator

3857 In Brief
50 California Street
Suite 500
San Francisco, CA 94111
800-584-6460
Fax: 415-217-2040
headquarters@earthjustice.org
www.earthjustice.org

Newsletter of Earthjustice, a nonprofit public interest law firm dedicated to protecting the magnificent places, natural resources and wildlife of this earth and to defending the right of all people to a healthy environment. We bringabout far-reaching change by enforcing and strengthening environmental laws on behalf of hundreds of organizations and communities.
Quarterly
Trip Van Noppen, President
DARRELL BYERS, Vice President, Development

3858 Iowa Cooperative Fish & Wildlife Research Unit: Annual Report
Iowa State University
Science Hall II
Ames, IA 50011
515-294-3056
Fax: 515-294-5468
Publication Date: 1932 50 pages Annual

3859 Iowa Native Plant Society Newsletter
Iowa State University
Botany Department
Ames, IA 50011
515-294-9499
Fax: 515-294-1337
dlewis@iastate.edu

An organization of amateur and professional botanists and native plant enthusiasts who are interested in the scientific, educational and cultural aspects, as well as the preservation and conservation of the native plants of Iowa. TheSociety was organized in 1995 to create a forum where plant enthusiasts, gardners and professional botanists could exchange ideas and coordinate activities such as field trips, work shops, and restoration of natural areas.
Publication Date: 1995 12 pages 3/4 times X year
Tom Rosburg, President
Deb Lewis, Contact Person

3860 Journal of Caves & Karst Studies
National Speleological Society
6001 Pulaski Pike
Huntsville, AL 35810
256-852-1300
Fax: 256-851-9241
nss@caves.org
www.caves.org

A quarterly journal published by the National Speleological Society.
Quarterly
ISSN: 1090-6924
Stephanie Searles, Operations Manager
Dave Bunnell, Editor

3861 Journal of Economic Entomology
Journal of Entomology
3 Park Place
Ste 307
Annapolis, MD 21401
301-731-4535
Fax: 301-731-4538
esa@entsoc.org
www.entsoc.org

Contributions report on the economic significance of insects and are divided into categories by subject matter: apiculture and social insects; arthropods in relation to plant disease; biological and microbial disease; ecology andbehavior; ecotoxicology; extension; field and forage crops; forest entomology; horticultural entomology; household and structural insects; insecticide resistance and resistance management; medical entomology; plant resistance; sampling andbiostatistics.
Bi-Monthly
David Gammel, Executive Director
Neil Willoughby, Director of Finance

3862 Land Use Law Report
Business Publishers
2222 Sedwick Drive
Durham, NC 27713
301-587-6300
800-223-8720
Fax: 800-508-2592
custserv@bpinews.com
www.bpinews.com

Provides timely news on court decisions, legislation and regulations that impact today's most pressing land-use policy planning and legal issues.
Biweekly
James D Lawlor, Author
Adam Goldstein, Publisher
James D Lawlor, Editor

3863 Land and Water Magazine
Land and Water
320 A Street
Fort Dodge, IA 50501
515-576-3191
Fax: 515-576-2606
landandwater@frontiernet.net
www.landandwater.com

Edited for contractors, engineers, architects, government officials and those working in the field of natural resource management and restoration from idea stage through project completion and maintenance.
Publication Date: 1974 72 pages Bimonthly
ISSN: 0192-9453
Amy Dencklau, Publisher/Editor

3864 Leaves Newsletter
Michigan Forest Association

6120 S. Clinton Trail 517-663-3423
Eaton Rapids, MI 48827 mfa@i-star.com
www.michiganforests.com

A monthly publication from the Michigan Forest Association.
Monthly
McClain B Smith Jr, Executive Director

3865 MACC Newsletter

Alba Press
10 Juniper Road 617-489-3930
Belmont, MA 00247 Fax: 617-489-3935
staff@maccweb.org
www.maccweb.org

Published six times a year, each issue features carefully chosen technical and interpreative articles, updates on government actions and policies, notices of workshops and meetings, publications, listings and a professional directory.
16 pages Bi-Monthly
Lindsay Martucci, Editor
Eugene Benson, Executive Director

3866 Michigan Forests Magazine

Michigan Forest Association
6120 S. Clinton Trail 734-665-8279
Eaton Rapids, MI 48827 Fax: 734-913-9167
www.michiganforests.com

A quarterly magazine published by the Michigan Forest Association.
Quarterly
McClain B Smith Jr, Executive Director

3867 Minnesota Plant Press

Minnesota Native Plant Society
P.O. Box 20401
Bloomington, MN 55420 president@mnnps.org
www.mnnps.org

A nonprofit organization dedicated to the conservation of the native plants of Minnesota through public education and advocacy. Offered are monthly meetings, field trips, symposia and a regular newsletter.
4 per year
Mike Lynch, President
Shirley Mah Kooyman, Vice President

3868 Monitor

Florida Defenders of the Environment
PO Box 357086 352-475-1119
Gainesville, FL 32635 Fax: 352-377-0869
floridadefenders@gmail.com
www.fladefenders.org

Newsletter of Florida Defenders of the Environment, one of the oldest and most accomplished conservation organizations in Florida with a network of scientists, economists and other professionals dedicated to preserving and protectingthe state's natural resources. FDE's top priority is currently the restoration of a 16-mile stretch of the Ocklawaha River and its 9,000-acre floodplain forest by removal of Rodman Dam- the last vestige of the Cross-Florida Barge Canal.
Publication Date: 1982 6-8 pages Bi-Annually
Thomas Hawkins, Executive Director
Tracy Marinello, Office Manager

3869 Montana Land Reliance Newsletter

324 Fuller Avenue 406-443-7027
PO Box 355 Fax: 406-443-7061
Helena, MT 59624 info@mtlandreliance.org
www.mtlandreliance.org

Montana's only private, statewide land trust, an apolitical, nonprofit corporation. Our mission is to provide permanent protection for private lands that are ecologically significant for agricultural production, fish and wildlifehabitat and scenic open space. We publish a newsletter twice per year.
8 pages Spring/Fall
George Olsen, President
Carol Bibler, Vice President

3870 NACD News & Views

National Association of Conservation Districts
509 Capitol Court, NE 202-547-6223
Washington, DC 20002 Fax: 202-547-6450
www.nacdnet.org

Newsletter of the nonprofit organization that represents the nation's 3,000 conservation districts and 17,000 men and women who serve on their governing boards. Conservation districts, local units of government established under statelaw to carry out natural resource management programs at the local level, work with more than 2.5 million cooperating landowners and operators to help them amange and protect land and water resources on nearly 98% of the private lands in the UnitedStates.
Publication Date: 1952 8 pages Bi-Monthly
Jeremy Peters, CEO
Rich Duesterhaus, Director of Projects

3871 National Gardener Magazine

National Garden Clubs, Inc
4401 Magnolia Avenue 314-776-7574
St Louis, MO 63110 800-550-6007
Fax: 314-776-5108
headquarters@gardenclub.org
www.gardenclub.org

National Garden Clubs, Inc publishes The National Gardener Magazinequarterly.
Publication Date: 1970 48 pages Quarterly
ISSN: 0027-9331
Susan Davidson, Author
Sandra H. Robinson, President
Shirley Tetreault, Secretary

3872 National Grange Newsletter

1616 H Street Northwest 202-628-3507
Washington, DC 20006 888-447-2643
Fax: 202-347-1091
rweiss@nationalgrange.org
www.nationalgrange.org

The Grange is a family based community organization with a special interest in agriculture and rural america as well as in legislative efforts regarding these issues.
6 pages Bi-Monthly
Ed Luttrell, President
Duane Scott, Secretary

3873 National Recreation and Park Association, (NRPA): Parks & Recreation Magazine

Parks and Recreation Magazine
22377 Belmont Ridge Road 703-858-0784
Ashburn, VA 20148 Fax: 703-858-0794
info@nrpa.org
www.nrpa.org

The NRPA, headquartered in Ashburn Virginia, is a national nonprofit organization devoted to advancing park, recreation and conservation efforts that enhance the quality of life for all Americans. The Association works to extendsocial, health, cultural and economic benefits of parks and recreation, through its network of 23,000 recreation and park professionals and civic leaders. NRPA encourages recreation initiatives for youth in high-risk environments.
100 pages Monthly
ISSN: 0031-2215
Mike Abbat,, Director
Sonia Myrick, Managing Editor

3874 National Wildlife Magazine

National Wildlife Federation

PO Box 1583
Merrifield, VA 22116 800-822-9919
www.nwf.org

The official member magazine of the National Wildlife Federation.

6 Issues/Yr
Collin O'Mara, President/CEO
Bruce Wallace, Chair

3875 National Woodlands Magazine
National Woodland Owners Association
374 Maple Avenue E 703-255-2700
Suite 310 800-476-8733
Vienna, VA 22180 Fax: 703-281-9200
argow@nwoa.net
www.nationalwoodlands.org

Provides timely information about forestry and forest practices with news from Washington, DC and state capitals. Written for non-industrial, private woodland owners. Includes state landowner association news.

28 pages Quarterly
Keith A Argow, President
Eric Johnson, Editor

3876 Natural Resources Department: Fish & Wildlife Newsletter
402 West Washington Street RMW273 317-232-4080
Indianapolis, IN 46204 Fax: 317-232-8150
www.state.in.us/dnr/fishwild/index.htm

Publication Date: 1985 12 pages Quarterly

3877 Nature Conservancy: Nebraska Chapter Newsletter
4245 North Fairfax Drive 703-841-5300
Suite 100 Fax: 402-342-0474
Arlington, VA 22203-1606 member@tnc.org
nature.org

The mission of the Nature Conservancy is to preserve the plants, animals and natural communities that represent the diversity of life on Earth by protecting the lands and waters they need to survive.

Publication Date: 1987 12 pages Quarterly
Thomas J. Tierney, Chairman
Mark R. Tercek, President and CEO

3878 Nature's Voice, The DNS Online Newsletter
Delaware Nature Society
PO Box 700 302-239-2334
Hockessin, DE 19707 Fax: 302-239-2473
dnsinfo@delawarenaturesociety.org
www.delawarenaturesociety.org

Now only available online, the newsletter offers trail information, nature center updates and programs, volunteer opportunities and more about what's happening in the outdoors of Delaware.

Brian Winslow, Executive Director
Christine Carlisle Odom, President

3879 New England WildFlower: New England Wildflower Society
180 Hemenway Road 508-877-7630
Framingham, MA 00170 Fax: 508-877-3658
information@newenglandwild.org
www.newenglandwild.org

36 pages Twice a Year
Debbi Edelstein, Executive Director
Christine Bennett, Office Manager

3880 New Jersey Environmental Lobby News
204 W State Street 609-396-3774
Trenton, NJ 00860 Fax: 609-396-4521
njel@earthlink.net
www.njenvironment.org

Quarterly publication from New Jersey Environmental Lobby.

Publication Date: 1971 8 pages Quarterly
ISSN: 1535-2021
Anne Poole, President
Noemi de la Puente, Executive Director

3881 North Dakota Association of Soil Conservation Districts Newsletter
3310 University Drive 701-223-8518
Bismarck, ND 58504 Fax: 701-223-1291
kathy@lincolnoakes.com
www.ndascd.org

Quarterly
Roger Christenson, President
Brian Johnston, CEO

3882 Outdoors Unlimited
615 Oak St. 406-728-7434
Ste. 201 Fax: 406-728-7445
Missoula, MT 59801 owaa@montana.com
www.owaa.org

Magazine of the Outdoor Writers Association of America. Membership fees are $175.00 (individual), $325.00 (supporting), $40.00 (student)

Publication Date: 1962 35 pages Monthly
Tom Sadler, Executive Director
Lisa Ballard, President/Board Chair:

3883 Pacific Fishery Management Council Newsletter
7700 NE Ambassador Place 503-820-2280
Suite 101 866-806-7204
Portland, OR 97220 Fax: 503-820-2299
pfmc.comments@noaa.gov
www.pcouncil.org

The Pacific Council has developed fishery management plans for salmon, groundfish and coastal species in the US Exclusive Economic Zone off the coast of Washington, Oregon and California.

24 pages 5x Year
Chuck Tracy, Executive Director
Mike Burner, Deputy Director

3884 Parks and Trails Council of Minnesota: Newsletter
275 E 4th Street 651-726-2457
Suite 250 800-944-0707
Saint Paul, MN 55101 Fax: 651-726-2458
info@parksandtrails.org
www.parksandtrails.org

Parks and Trails Council of Minnesota seeks to aquire, protect and sustain long-term statewide land.

Quarterly
Julie Gugin, President
Bob Biersheid, Vice President

3885 Powder River Basin Resource Council: Powder River Breaks Newsletter
934 North Main 307-672-5809
Sheridan, WY 82801 Fax: 307-672-5800
info@powderriverbasin.org
www.powderriverbasin.org

Committed to the preservation and enrichment of Wyoming's agricultural heritage and rural lifestyle; the conservation of Wyomings unique land, mineral, water and clean air resources, consistent with responsible use of those resourcesto sustain the vitality of present and future generations; the education and empowerment of Wyoming's citizens to raise a coherent voice in decisions. They are the only group in Wyoming that addresses both agricultural and conservation issues.

Publication Date: 1973 8-12 pages 6x year
Stephanie Avey, Office Administrator
Kevin Lind, Director

3886 Prairie Naturalist Magazine
600 Park Street 785-628-4214
Department of Biological Sciences Fax: 316-341-5607
Hays, KS 67601 efinck@fhsu.edu
www.fhsu.edu
Published by the North Dakota Natural Science Society, a regional organization with interests in the natural history of grasslands and the Great Plains.
Publication Date: 1968 260 pages Quarterly
ISSN: 0091-0376
Elmer J Finck, Editor

3887 Reef Line
Reef Relief Environmental Center
PO Box 430 305-294-3100
Key West, FL 33041 Fax: 305-293-9515
info@reefrelief.org
www.reefrelief.org
Reef Line is a quarterly publication from Reef Relief.
Publication Date: 1986 16 pages Quarterly
Bob Cardenas, President
Dave Kirwan, Vice President

3888 SWOAM News
Small Woodland Owners Association of Maine
153 Hospital Street 207-626-0005
PO Box 836 877-467-9626
Augusta, ME 00433 Fax: 207-626-7992
info@swoam.com
www.swoam.com
Monthly
Tom Doak, Executive Director
Bill S. Williams, Deputy Executive Director

3889 Save San Francisco Bay Association: Watershed Newsletter
1330 Broadway 510-463-6850
Suite 1800 Fax: 510-463-6851
Oakland, CA 94612 info@savesfbay.org
www.savesfbay.org
Save the Bay has worked for over 40 years to protect the San Francisco Bay-Delta from pollution, fill, shoreline destruction and fresh water diversion. We have launched a century of renewal to restore bay fish and wildlife, reclaimtidal wetlands and make the bay safe and accessible to all.
8-10 pages 3-4 times/year
David Lewis, Executive Director
Jackie Richardson, Development Coordinator

3890 Scenic America Newsletter
Scenic America
1307 New Hampshire Ave NW 202-463-1294
Washington, DC 20005 Fax: 202-463-1297
tracy@scenic.org
www.scenic.org
12 pages 3 Times Per Year
Mary Tracy, President
Mark McCrummen, Accountant

3891 Shore and Beach
5460 Beaujolais Lane 239-489-2616
Fort Myers, FL 33919 Fax: 239-489-9917
ExDir@asbpa.org
www.asbpa.org
A quarterly publication from the American Shore and Beach Preservation Association.
24 pages Quarterly
ISSN: 0037-4237
Ken Gooderham, Managing Directors
Derek Brockbank, Executive Director

3892 Sierra Club, NJ Chapter: The Jersey Sierran
85 Second Street 415-977-5500
2nd Floor Fax: 415-977-5797
San Francisco, CA 94105
The Sierra Club is our country's oldest and most effective grassroots environmental organization. Hikes and outings are scheduled throughout the year. We are dedicated to fighting sprawl and over-development.
Publication Date: 1992 14 pages Quarterly
Jeff Tittle, Director
Dennis Schvejda, Conservation Coordinator

3893 Sierra Club: Pennsylvania Chapter Newsletter
600 North 2nd Street 717-232-0101
Suite 300A Fax: 717-238-6330
Harrisburg, PA 17101 www.sierraclub.org
The Pennsylvania chapter includes 11 local Sierra Club groups. Emphasis is on state environmental policy advocacy, outings, education and local environmental protection efforts.
18 pages Quarterly
Jeff Schmidt, Sr. Chapter Director

3894 Southern Appalachian Botanical Society: Gastanea
Newberry College
2100 College Street 803-321-5257
Newberry, SC 29108 Fax: 803-321-5636
charles.horn@newberry.edu
www.sabs.us
This is a professional organization for those interested in botanical research, especially in the areas of ecology, floristics and systematics. To this end, they publish a journal, CASTANEA, and a newsletter, CHINQUAPIN.
Publication Date: 1936 350 pages Quarterly
ISSN: 0008-7475
Charles Horn, President
Kunsiri Grubbs, Treasurer

3895 Tidbits Newsletter
Minnesota Association/Soil and Water Cons. Dist.
255 Kellogg Boulevard East 651-690-9028
Ste 101 Fax: 651-690-9065
St. Paul, MN 55101 leann.buck@maswcd.org
www.maswcd.org
Quarterly
Le Ann Buck, Executive Director
Ian Cunningham, President

3896 Tide
Coastal Conservation Association
4801 Woodway Drive 713-626-4234
Houston, TX 77056 800-201-FISH
ccantl@joincca.org
TIDE is the official bimonthly magazine of the Coastal Conservation Association. It has received local, state and national acclaim for writing, photography and layout and currently boasts a circulation of more than 70,000. TIDE isavailable only to members of the Coastal Conservation Association.

3897 Upper Mississippi River Conservation Committee Newsletter
4469 48th Avenue Court 309-793-5800
Rock Island, IL 61201 Fax: 309-793-5804
mississippi-river.com/umrcc
A bimonthly newsletter published by the Upper Mississippi River Conservation Committee.
10 pages Bi monthly
Mike McGhee, Chairman

3898 Urban Land Magazine
Urban Land Institute

1025 Thomas Jefferson Street NW 202-624-7000
Suite 500 W 800-321-5011
Washington, DC 20007 Fax: 202-624-7140
www.uli.org

Nonprofit research and education organization dedicated to improving land use policy and development practice. Publishes a monthly magazine, several quarterly publications and books. Topics relate to real estate development includinggovernment sensitive development, smart growth, sustainable development and city parks.

Monthly
Randall Rowe, Chairman
Patrick L. Phillips, Global CEO

3899 Utah Geological Survey: Survey Notes
1594 W N Temple Suite 3110 801-537-3300
PO Box 146100 Fax: 801-537-3400
Salt Lake City, UT 84114

The Utah Geological Survey is an applied scientific agency that creates, interprets and provides information about Utah's geologic environment, resources and hazards to promote safe, beneficial and wise use of land. This is theirpublication, which is issued three times yearly.

Publication Date: 1964 3 Times Yearly
ISSN: 1061-7930
Richard Allis, Director

3900 Virginia Forests Magazine
Virginia Forestry Association
3808 Augusta Avenue 804-278-8733
Richmond, VA 23255 Fax: 804-320-1447
www.vaforestry.org

Quarterly magazine published by the Virginia Forestry Association.

Quarterly
Paul Howe, VFA Executive Vice President

3901 WAEE Bulletin
Wisconsin Association for Environmental Education
8 Nelson Hall 715-346-2796
University of Wisconsin waee@uwsp.edu
Stevens Point, WI 54481

Quarterly
Carol Weston, Administrative Assistant

3902 Western Pennsylvania Conservancy Newsletter
800 Waterfront Drive 412-288-2777
Pittsburgh, PA 15222 866-JOI-NWPC
Fax: 412-231-1414
info@paconserve.org
waterlandlife.org

WPC, working together to save the places we care about, protects natural lands, promotes healthy and attractive communities, and preserves Fallingwater, Frank Lloyd Wright's masterwork in Mill Run, which was entrusted to theConservancy in 1963. Since its inception in 1932, the Conservancy has protected more than 280,000 acres of natural lands in Pennnsylvania. We continue to work to secure lands of ecological significance that frequently offer recreational and scenicvalues.

16 pages Quarterly
Susan Fitzsimmons, Chair
Stephen G. Robinson, Vice Chair

3903 Western Proceedings Newsletter
Western Association of Fish and Wildlife Agencies
5400 Bishop Boulevard 307-777-4580
Cheyenne, WY 82006 Fax: 307-777-4650
bob.lanka@wyo.gov
wildlife.org

Annual

3904 Western Society of Naturalists: Newsletter
San Diego State University Biology Department
P.O. Box 247 818-677-3256
Bodega Bay, CA 94923 Fax: 818-677-2034
secretariat@wsn-online.org
www.westsocnat.com

A scientific society with a strong focus on ecology, evolution, natural history and marine biology. Its memebers are predominantly from the west coast. The society organizes one or two meetings each year for its members.

Jenn Caselle, President
Brian Gaylord, Secretary

3905 Wetlands in the United States
American Ground Water Trust
50 Pleasant Street Ste 2 603-228-5444
Concord, NH 03301 Fax: 603-228-6557
trustinfo@agwt.org
www.agwt.org

15 pages Quarterly
Andrew Stone, Director

3906 Whalewatcher
PO Box 1391 310-548-6279
San Pedro, CA 90733 Fax: 310-548-6950
info@acsonline.org
www.acsonline.org

A bi-annual publication from the American Cetacean Society. Cost included with membership fees.

Publication Date: 1967 30 pages Bi-Annual
Diane Alps, President
Kaye Reznick, Editorial Consultant

3907 Wilderness Education Association
2150 N 107th St 206-209-5275
Ste 205 Fax: 206-367-8777
Seattle, WA 98133 nationaloffice@weainfo.org
www.weainfo.org

Publication Date: 1976 4-6 pages 3 Times Per Year
Ricky Haro, President
Kelli McMahan, President-elect

3908 Wildfowl Trust of North America: Newsletter
Wildfowl Trust of North America
600 Discovery Lane 410-827-6694
PO Box 519 Fax: 410-827-6713
Grasonville, MD 21638 jwink@bayrestoration.org
www.bayrestoration.org

Published by the Wildfowl Trust of North America.

Publication Date: 1995 8 pages Qaurterly
Judy Wink, Executive Director
Katey Nelson, Education Manager

3909 Wildlife Law News Quarterly and Weekly Alerts
University of New Mexico School of Law
MSC 11 6060rd NE 505-277-5006
One University of New Mexico Fax: 505-277-7064
Albuquerque, NM 87131 musgrave@unm.edu

A quarterly publication from the New Mexico Center for Wildlife Law.

Publication Date: 1993 16 pages Quarterly
ISSN: 1085-7338
R Musgrave, Editor
D Macke, Editor

3910 Wildlife Society Bulletin
Wildlife Society
5410 Grosvenor Lane 301-897-9770
Suite 200 Fax: 301-530-2471
Bethesda, MD 20814 tws@wildlife.org
www.wildlife.org

A quarterly publication from the Wildlife Society.
Publication Date: 1973 Quarterly
ISSN: 0091-7648
Rick Baydack, President
Bruce Thompson, Vice President

3911 Woodland Management Newsletter
Wisconsin Woodland Owners Association
PO Box 285 715-346-4798
Stevens Point, WI 54481 Fax: 715-346-4821
wwoa@uwsp.edu
www.wisconsinwoodlands.org
Quarterly
Paul Kienitz, President
Marilyn Steele, VICE PRESIDENT

3912 Woodland Report
National Woodland Owners Association
374 Maple Avenue E 703-255-2700
Suite 310 800-476-8733
Vienna, VA 22180 Fax: 703-281-9200
argow@nwoa.net
www.nationalwoodlands.org
Provides timely information about forestry and forest practices with news from Washington, DC and state capitals. Written for non-industrial, private woodland owners. Includes state landowner association news.
2 pages
Keith A Argow, President
Eric Johnson, Editor

3913 World Wildlife Fund: US Focus
1250 24th Street NW 202-293-4800
Suite 500 www.worldwildlife.org
Washington, DC 20037
WWF projects.
8 pages
Carter Roberts, President & CEO
Marcia Marsh, Chief Operating Officer

Periodicals: Recycling & Pollution Prevention

3914 AARA Newsletter
Arizona Automotive Recyclers Association
950 E. Baseline Rd. 480-609-3999
#104-1025 admin@aara.com
Tempe, AZ 85283 www.aara.com
Quarterly newsletter of the AARA, a select group of recyclers providing quality recycled parts for the benefit of our customers, communities and environment. There are 90 member companies. AARA is affiliated with the AutomotiveDismantlers and Recyclers Association.
Quarterly
Mike Pierson Jr, President
Leroy Liebermann, Secretary/Treasurer

3915 Air/Water Pollution Report
Business Publishers
2222 Sedwick Drive 301-589-5103
Durham, NC 27713 800-223-8720
Fax: 800-508-2592
custserv@bpinews.com
www.bpinews.com
Provides comprehensive coverage of economic, political, legislative, regulatory and domestic and international implications of air and water pollution.
Weekly
Leonard A Eiserer, Publisher
Beth Early, Associate Publisher

3916 American Waste Digest
Carasue Moody
226 King Street 610-326-9480
Pottstown, PA 19464 800-442-4215
Fax: 610-326-9752
awd@americanwastedigest.com
www.americanwastedigest.com
Provides reviews on new products, profiles on sucessful waste removal businesses, and provides discussion on legislation on municipal regulations on recycling.
100 pages Monthly
Carasue Moody, Publisher/Editor
Marlene Lowder, Sales Administrator

3917 BNA's Environmental Compliance Bulletin
Bureau of National Affairs
3 Bethesda Metro Center 202-452-4200
Suite 250 800-372-1033
Bethesda, MD 20814-5377 Fax: 800-253-0332
www.bna.com
Cover the water and air pollution, waste management and regulatory updates, as well as a summary of selected regulatory actions and a list of key environmental compliance dates.
Gregory C. McCaffery, President & CEO
Sue Martin, COO

3918 Bio-Integral Resource Center: IPM Practitioner
PO Box 7414 510-524-2567
Berkeley, CA 94707 Fax: 510-524-1758
birc@igc.org
www.birc.org
The goal of the Bio Integral Resources Center is to reduce pesticide use by educating the public about effective, least-toxic alternatives for pest problems.
Publication Date: 1979 6-12 pages
ISSN: 0738-968x
Dr. William Quarles, Executive Director

3919 C&D Recycler
Gie Publishing
5811 Canal Road 216-961-4130
Valley View, OH 44125 800-456-0707
Fax: 216-525-0515
btaylor@gie.net
www.cdrecycler.com
Brian Taylor, Editor

3920 Common Sense Pest Control Quarterly
PO Box 7414 510-524-2567
Berkeley, CA 94707 Fax: 510-524-1758
birc@igc.org
www.birc.org
A quarterly publication published by the Bio Integral Resource Center
Publication Date: 1984 24 pages Quarterly
ISSN: 8756-7881
Dr. William Quarles, Executive Director

3921 Composting News
McEntee Media Corporation
9815 Hazelwood Avenue 440-238-6603
Cleveland, OH 44149 Fax: 440-238-6712
ken@recycle.cc
www.recycle.cc
New composting projects, research, regulations and legislation, as well as the latest news in the composting industry.
Publication Date: 1992 Monthly
Ken McEntee, Publisher

3922 Daily Environment Report
Bureau of National Affairs
3 Bethesda Metro Center 202-452-4200
Suite 250 800-372-1033
Bethesda, MD 20814-5377 Fax: 800-253-0332
www.bna.com

A 40-page daily report providing comprehensive, in-depth coverage of national and international environmental news. Each issue contains summaries of the top news stories, articles, and in-brief items, and a journal of meetings, agencyactivities, hearings and legal proceedings. Coverage includes air and water pollution, hazardous substances, and hazardous waste, solid waste, oil spills, gas drilling, pollution prevention, impact statements and budget matters.

40 pages
ISSN: 1060-2976
Gregory C. McCaffery, President & CEO
Sue Martin, COO

3923 E-Scrap News
Resource Recycling
PO Box 42270 503-233-1305
Portland, OR 97242 Fax: 503-233-1356
info@resource-recycling.com
www.resource-recycling.com

64 pages
ISSN: 0744-4710
Jerry Powell, Executive Editor
Dylan de Thomas, Editorial Director

3924 Earth Preservers
PO Box 6 908-654-9293
Westfield, NJ 00709

Award winning monthly environmental newspaper for school children aged 7 to 15.

4 pages
Bill Paul, Publisher

3925 Environment Reporter
Bureau of National Affairs
3 Bethesda Metro Center 202-452-4200
Suite 250 800-372-1033
Bethesda, MD 20814-5377 Fax: 800-253-0332
www.bna.com

A weekly notification and reference service covering the full-spectrum of legislative, administrative, judicial, industrial and technological developments affecting pollution control and environmental protection.

ISSN: 0013-9211
Gregory C. McCaffery, President & CEO
Sue Martin, COO

3926 Environmental Engineering Science
Mary Ann Liebert
140 Huguenot Street 914-740-2100
3rd Floor 800-MLI-EBER
New Rochelle, NY 10801 Fax: 914-740-2101
info@liebertpub.com
www.liebertpub.com

The focus is on pollution control of the suface, ground, and drinking water, and highlight research news and product developments that aid in the fight against pollution.

Bi-Monthly
ISSN: 1092-8758
Mary Ann Liebert, Publisher
Dumpnico Grosso PhD, Editor-in-Chief

3927 Environmental Notice
75 Aupuni Street 808-974-6006
#201 Fax: 808-974-6000
Hilo, HI 96720 oeqc@doh.hawaii.gov
health.hawaii.gov

A bi-monthly publication from the Health Department Environmental Quality Control division.

Publication Date: 1978 24 pages Bi monthly
Keith Y. Yamamoto, Deputy Director
Virginia Pressler, Director of Health

3928 Environmental Regulation
State Capitals Newsletters
PO Box 7376 703-768-9600
Alexandria, VA 22307 Fax: 703-768-9690
newsletters@statecapitals.com
www.statecapitals.com

Weekly news from the state capitals keeps you informed on state programs, recycling, wetlands, ground water protection, beach renourishment, land management, greenspace laws, brownfields, livestock regulation, wilderness preservation,urban sprawl and solid waste.

Publication Date: 1946 4-10 pages Newsletter 48x/Yr
ISSN: 1061-9682
Ellen Klein, Editor

3929 Environmental Regulatory Advisor
JJ Keller
3003 W Breezewood Lane
PO Box 368 877-564-2333
Neenah, WI 54957 Fax: 800-727-7516
sales@jjkeller.com
www.jjkeller.com

Covers developments at the EPA.

12 pages
ISSN: 1056-3164
Robert L. Keller, Chair
James J. Keller, Vice Chairman & Treasurer

3930 Environmental Science and Technology
American Chemical Society
1155 16th Street NW 800-221-5558
Washington, DC 20036 Fax: 202-872-4615
help@acs.org
www.acs.org

Articles on pollution control, waste treatment, climate changes and various other environmental interests.

110 pages Semi-Monthly
Diane Grob Schmidt, President
Pat N. Confalone, Chair

3931 Environmental Systems Corporation Newsletter
10801 N Mopac Bldg 1-200 865-688-7900
Austin, TX 78759 Fax: 512-258-5836
escsales@envirosys.com
www.envirosys.com

Data acquisition and reporting systems for electric power producers and industrial sources, ESC is the leading supplier of CEM and ambient data systems in the US Newsletter is free.

Publication Date: 1994 4 pages Quarterly
Jeff Rabensteine, President
Mmark Shell, Chief Engineer

3932 Environmental Times
Environmental Assessment Association
1224 N Nokomis NE 320-763-4320
Alexandria, MN 56308 Fax: 320-763-9290
eaa@iami.org
www.iami.org/eaa.cfm

This publication contains environmental conferences and expos, industry trends, federal regulations related to the environment and industry assessments.

Robert Johnson, Publisher/Editor

3933 From the Ground Up
Ecology Center

117 Division Street 734-761-3186
Ann Arbor, MI 48104 Fax: 734-663-2414
Progressive environmental news from southeast Michigan.
32 pages
Michael Garfield, Editor

3934 Full Circle
Northeast Resource Recovery Association
PO Box 721 603-798-5777
Concord, NH 03302 Fax: 603-798-5744
www.recyclewithus.org

Bi-Monthly
Elizabeth Bedard, Executive Director

3935 Hauler
Hauler Magazine
166 South Main Street 215-997-3622
PO Box 508 800-220-6029
New Hope, PA 18938 Fax: 215-862-3455
mag@thehauler.com
www.thehauler.com
This magazine serves as an advertising guide to new products in the waste management, recycling, and environmental industries.
Publication Date: 1978 Monthly
Thomas N Smith, CEO
Leslie T. Smith, Publisher

3936 HazMat Management
Business Information Group
80 Valleybrook Drive 416-442-2223
Toronto, ON M3B2S 888-702-1111
Fax: 416-510-5133
amadden@bizinfogroup.ca

Solutions for the environment.
Publication Date: 1989 Bi-Annual
ISSN: 0843-9303
Brad O'Brien, Publisher
David Nesseth, Editor

3937 Hazardous Waste News
Business Publishers
2222 Sedwick Drive 301-589-5103
Durham, NC 27713 800-223-8720
Fax: 800-508-2592
custserv@bpinews.com
www.bpinews.com
Comprehensive federal, state and local coverage of legislation and regulation affecting all aspects of the hazardous waste industry including Superfund, Resource Conservation and Recovery Act, US EPA, incineration, land disposal andmore.
8 pages
Leonard A Eiserer, Publisher
Beth Early, Operations Director

3938 Hazardous Waste/Superfund Week
Business Publishers
2222 Sedwick Drive 301-589-5103
Durham, NC 27713 800-223-8720
Fax: 800-508-2592
custserv@bpinews.com
www.bpinews.com
Provides comprehensive coverage on hazardous waste disposal and cleanup, behind-the-scenes coverage of congressional action, EPA initiatives, Superfund sites, regulatory changes, court cases, enforcement news, contract opportunities,new technologies, research findings and business developments.
Weekly
Leonard A Eiserer, Publisher
Beth Early, Associate Publisher

3939 Hazmat Transportation News
Bureau of National Affairs
3 Bethesda Metro Center
Suite 250 800-372-1033
Bethesda, MD 20814-5377 Fax: 800-253-0332
www.bna.com
A two-binder service containing the full-text of rules and regulations governing shipment of hazardous material by rail, air, ship, highway and pipeline, including DOT's Hazardous Materials Tables and EPA's rules for its hazardouswaste tracking system.
Gregory C. McCaffery, President & CEO
Sue Martin, COO

3940 Inside EPA
Inside Washington Publishers
1919 South Eads Street 703-416-8500
Suite 201 800-424-9068
Arlington, VA 22202 Fax: 703-415-8543
custsvc@iwpnews.com
www.iwpnews.com
Gives timely information on all facets of waste, water, air, and other environmental regulatory programs.
Publication Date: 1980 Weekly
Al Sosenko, Publisher

3941 Institute of Scrap Recycling Industries
1615 L Street NW 202-662-8500
Suite 600 Fax: 202-626-0900
Washington, DC 20036 kentkiser@scrap.org
www.isri.org
Its membership is made up of manufacturers and processors, brokersand industrial consumers of scrap commodities, including ferrous and nonferrous metals, paper, electronics, rubber, plastics, glass and textiles. ISRI's associatemembers include equipment and service providers to the scrap recycling industry.
Publication Date: 1988 148 pages Bi monthly
ISSN: 0036-9527
Robin K. Wiener, President
Mark Lewon, Chair

3942 Journal of Environmental Education
Heldref Publications
325 Chestnut Street 215-625-8900
Suite 800 Fax: 202-296-5149
Philadelphia, PA 19106 customer.service@taylorandfrancis.com
www.heldref.org
The issues featured are case studies, environmental philosophy and policy discussions, new research evaluations and information on environmental education.
Douglas Kirkpatrick, Publisher/Executive Director

3943 KIND News
National Assn for Humane & Environmental Education
2100 L St., NW 202-452-1100
Washington, DC 20037 Fax: 860-434-6282
www.humanesociety.org
Classroom newspaper for kids in grades K-6. It features articles, puzzles and celebrity interviews that teach children the value of showing kindness and respect to animals, the environment, and one another.
Publication Date: 1985 4 pages 9 per year
William Pacelle, President and CEO
Betsy Liley, Chief Development Officer

3944 Legislative Bulletin
Arkansas Environmental Federation
1400 W Markham Street 501-374-0263
Suite 302 Fax: 501-374-8752
Little Rock, AR 72201 cmiller@environmentark.org
www.environmentark.org

Publication Date: 1967
Charles Miller, Executive Director
Rebecca Neely, Communications Director

3945 Minnesota Pollution Control Agency Minnesota Environment Magazine
520 Lafayette Road North 651-296-6300
St. Paul, MN 55155 800-657-3864
Fax: 651-296-7923
vicki.schindeldecker@pca.state.mn.us
www.pca.state.mn.us
Established in 1967 to protect Minnesota's environment through monitoring environmental quality and enforcing environmental regulations.
Publication Date: 2000 16-20 pages Quarterly
Paul Eger, Comm./Chair Citizens' Board

3946 Northeast Recycling Council Bulletin
139 Main Street 802-254-3636
Suite 401 info@nerc.org
Brattleboro, VT 05301 www.nerc.org
NERC's mission is to To advance an environmentally sustainable economy by promoting source and toxicity reduction, recycling, and the purchasing ofenvironmentally preferable products and services.
Monthly
Robert Isner, President
Lynn Rubinstein, Executive Director

3947 Northeast Recycling Council News
139 Main Street 802-254-3636
Suite 401 Fax: 802-254-5870
Brattleboro, VT 05301 info@nerc.org
www.nerc.org
NERC's mission is to To advance an environmentally sustainable economy by promoting source and toxicity reduction, recycling, and the purchasing ofenvironmentally preferable products and services.
3x Year
Lynn Rubenstein, Executive Director
Mary Ann Remolador, Assistant Director

3948 Oregon Refuse and Recycling Association Newsletter
PO Box 2186 503-588-1837
Salem, OR 97308 800-527-7624
Fax: 503-399-7784
orrainfo@orra.net
www.orra.net
Monthly
Kristan Mitchell, Executive Director
Kimera Coady, Executive Assistant

3949 Plastics Recycling Update
Resource Recycling
PO Box 42270 503-233-1305
Portland, OR 97242 Fax: 503-233-1356
subscriptions@resource-recycling.com
www.resource-recycling.com
Monthly
Jerry Powell, Executive Editor
Dylan de Thomas, Editorial Director

3950 Pollution Equipment News
Rimbach Publishing
8650 Babcock Boulevard 412-364-5366
Pittsburgh, PA 15237 800-245-3182
Fax: 412-369-9720
info@rimbach.com
www.rimbach.com
Provides information to those responsible for selecting products and services for air, water, wastewater and hazardous waste pollution control.
Publication Date: 1967 64 pages Bi-Monthly
ISSN: 0032-3659
Raquel Rimbach, Owner

3951 Pollution Prevention News
US EPA
1200 Pennsylvania Avenue, NW 202-272-0167
Washington, DC 20460 Fax: 202-260-2219
www.epa.gov
Articles include recent information on source reduction and sustainable technologies in industry, transportation, consumer, agriculture, energy, and the international sector.
Gina McCarthy, Administrator
Stan Meiburg, Acting Deputy Administrator

3952 Recharger Magazine
Recharger Magazine
15335 Don Julian Road 626-961-2688
Hacienda Heights, CA 91745 Fax: 626-961-2788
info@rechargermag.com
greenprojectinc.com
Information including articles that cover business and marketing, technical updates, association and industry news, and company profiles. On the remanufactured imaging supplies industry, related features focus on the importance ofrecycling, government legislation, and product comparisons. Annual trade event in Las Vegas.
Publication Date: 1989 300+ pages Monthly
ISSN: 1053-7503
Julie Kerrane, Author
Phyllis Gurgevich, Publisher
Amy Turner, Managing Editor

3953 Recycled News
Maryland Recyclers Coalition
PO Box 1046
Laurel, MD 20725 888-496-3196
Fax: 301-238-4579
info@marylandrecyclers.org
www.marylandrecyclers.org
2 pages Bi-Monthly
Jackie King, Executive Director

3954 Recycling Laws International
Raymond Communications
P.O. Box 4311 301-879-0628
Silver Spring, MD 20914-4311 Fax: 301-345-4768
circulation@raymond.com
www.raymond.com
Covers recycling, takeback and green labeling policy for business in 38 countries. Available online.
Publication Date: 1995 Bi-Monthly
Bruce Popka, Vice President

3955 Recycling Markets
NV Business Publishers Corporation
43 Main Street 732-502-0500
Avon by the Sea, NJ 00771 Fax: 732-502-9606
lprazych@nvpublications.com
www.nvpublications.com
Contains profiles on recycling mills, as well as large users and generators of recycled materials for the broker, dealers and processors of paper stock, scrap metal, plastics and glass.
Jim Curley, Editor
Anna Dutko Rowley, Managing Editor

3956 Recycling Product News
Baum Publications
124-2323 Boundary Rd 604-291-9900
Vancouver, Can, BC V5M Fax: 604-291-1906
webadmin@baumpub.com
www.baumpub.com
Published for the recycling center operators and other waste mangers, articles discuss technology and new products.
Engelbert J Baum, President
Keith Barker, Editor

3957 Recycling Today
GIE Media
5811 Canal Road
Valley View, OH 44125
800-456-0707
Fax: 216-525-0515
dtoto@gie.net
www.recyclingtoday.com

Published for the secondary commodity processing/recycling market.
James R Keefe, Group Publisher
Brian Taylor, Editor

3958 Resource Recovery Report
5313 38th Street NW
PO Box 3356
Warrenton, VA 20188
540-347-4500
800-627-8913
Fax: 540-348-4540
rwill@coordgrp.com

Covers all alternatives to landfills, i.e., recycling, energy recovery, composting in North America, Government, industry, associations, universities, etc. are included.
12 pages
Richard Will, Production Manager

3959 Resource Recycling Magazine
Resource Recycling
PO Box 42270
Portland, OR 97242
503-233-1305
Fax: 503-233-1356
info@resource-recycling.com
www.resource-recycling.com

Monthly
Jerry Powell, Executive Editor
Dylan de Thomas, Editorial Director

3960 Reuse/Recycle Newsletter
Technomic Publishing Company
PO Box 3535
Lancaster, PA 17601
717-291-5609
800-233-9936
Fax: 717-295-4538

Provides news and information on important developments in both industrial and municipal recycling, and focuses on large-scale post-consumer, post-commercial, and post-industrial waste recycling.
8 pages
ISSN: 0048-7457
Susan E Selke, Author
Amy Flannery, Marketing

3961 Scrap
Institute of Scrap Recycling Industries
1615 L Street NW
Suite 600
Washington, DC 20036
202-662-8500
Fax: 202-626-0900
ellenross@scrap.org
www.isri.org

Serves the scrap processing and recycling industry. Subscription: $32.95 (US), $38.95 (Canada/Mexico) & $104.95 (all other international)
Bi-Monthly
Kent Kiser, Publisher/Editor-in-Chief
Marian Weiss, Production Manager

3962 Solid Waste & Recycling
Southam Environment Group
80 Valleybrook Drive
Toronto M3B2S
416-442-5600
800-268-7742
Fax: 416-510-5130
amadden@bizinfogroup.ca
www.solidwastemag.com

Published to emphasize on municipal and commercial aspects of collection, handling, transportation, hauling, disposal and treatment of solid waste , including incineration, recycling and landfill technology.
Brad O'Brien, Publisher
David Nesseth, Editor

3963 Solid Waste Report
Business Publishers
2222 Sedwick Drive
Durham, NC 27713
301-589-5103
800-223-8720
Fax: 800-508-2592
custserv@bpinews.com
www.bpinews.com

Comprehensive news and analysis of legislation, regulation and litigation in solid waste management including resource recovery, recycling, collection and disposal. Regularly features international news, state updates and businesstrends.
Bi-Weekly
Leonard A Eiserer, Publisher
Beth Early, Operations Director

3964 State Recycling Laws Update
Raymond Communications
P.O. Box 4311
Silver Spring, MD 20914-4311
301-879-0628
Fax: 301-345-4768
circulation@raymond.com
www.raymond.com

Provides coverage of recycling legislation affecting business, as well as the outlook on future legislation across the US and Canada.
Bruce Popka, Vice President

3965 Waste Age
Environmental Industry Associations
4301 Connecticut Avenue NW
#300
Washington, DC 20008
202-244-4700
800-424-2869
Fax: 202-966-4868
ptom@primediabusiness.com
www.wasteage.com

Contents focus on new system technologies, recycling, resource recovery and sanitary landfills with regular features on updates in the status of government regulations, new products, guides, company profiles, exclusive surveyinformation, legislative implications and news.
Warren Bimblick, Group President
David Bodamer, Executive Director

3966 Waste Age's Recycling Times
Environmental Industry Associations
4301 Connecticut Avenue NW
#300
Washington, DC 20008
202-244-4700
800-424-2869
Fax: 202-966-4868
www.wasteage.com

Features municipalities, recycling goals and rates, program innovations, waste habits, and new materials being recycled.
Warren Bimblick, Group President
David Bodamer, Executive Director

3967 Waste Handling Equipment News
Lee Publications
6113 State Highway 5
PO Box 121
Palatine Bridge, NY 13428
518-673-3237
800-218-5586
Fax: 518-673-2381
mstanley@leepub.com
www.leepub.com

Dicusses the latest developments in woodwaste, C&D, scrapmetal, concrete, asphalt, recycling and composting with the emphasis on equipment.
Publication Date: 1993 50 pages Monthly
Coyle Rockwell, Author
Colleen Suo, Editor
Matt Stanley, Editor

3968 Waste Recovery Report
Icon/Information Concepts
211 S 45th Street
Philadelphia, PA 19104
215-349-6500
Fax: 215-349-6502
wasterec@aol.com
www.icodat.com

Contains information on waste-to-energy, recycling, composting and other technologies.
Publication Date: 1975 6 pages Monthly
ISSN: 0889-0072
Alan Krigman, Publisher/Editor

Periodicals: Sustainable Development

3969 AERO SunTimes
Alternative Energy Resources Organization
432 N Last Chance Gulch 406-443-7272
Helena, MT 59601 Fax: 406-442-9120
aero@aeromt.org
www.aeromt.org

The SunTimes is the newsletter for AERO. The organization is a statewide grassroots group whose members work together to strengthen communities through promoting sustainable agriculture, local food production and citizen-based SmartGrowth community planning.
Publication Date: 1978 4-24 pages Quarterly
ISSN: 1046-0993
Jennifer Hill-Hart, Executive Director
Corrie Williamson, Communications

3970 California Association of Resource Conservation Districts- CCP News
801 K Street 916-457-7094
Suite 1415 Fax: 916-457-7934
Sacramento, CA 93101 www.carcd.org
Quarterly
Karen Buhr, Executive Director
Emily Sutherland, Office Manager

3971 Californians for Population Stabilization: CAPS News
1129 State Street 805-564-6626
Suite 3-D Fax: 805-564-6636
Santa Barbara, CA 93101 info@capsweb.org
www.capsweb.org

A nonprofit, public interest organization that works to protect California's environment and quality of life by turning the tide of population growth.
Publication Date: 1986 8 pages 3x year
Dick Schneider, Chairman
Ben Zuckerman PhD, Vice President

3972 Cultivar
Center for Agoecology
1156 High Street 831-459-2506
Santa Cruz, CA 95064 Fax: 831-459-2867
www.agroecology.org

Publication Date: 1985 9-12 pages Bi-Yearly
Steven Gliessman, Professor Agroecology
Martha Brown, Editor

3973 Ecosphere
Forum International
91 Gregory Lane
Suite 21 800-252-4475
Pleasant Hill, CA 94523 Fax: 925-946-1500
www.foruminternational.com

Accepts advertising. The first ever environmental/ecological magazine. It is dedicated to the interrelations of man in nature and a balanced approach of its biological, economic, socio-political and spiritual components. Since 1965.
Publication Date: 1965 16-48 pages Bi-monthly
Dr. Nicolas Hetzer, Production Manager
J McCormack, Circulation Director

3974 EnviroNews
600 Forbes Avenue 412-396-6000
331 Fisher Hall 800-456-0590
Pittsburgh, PA 15282 Fax: 412-396-4092
bembic@duq.edu
www.science.duq.edu

Educating environmental professionals for the twenty-first century is the focus of the Duquesne University Environmental Science and Management (ESM) Masters Degree Program. The program grew out of the perceived need to combine depthof knowledge in environmental science with a comprehensive understanding of the business, legal and policy implications surrounding environmental issues.
4 pages Semester Newsletter
Charles Dougherty, President
Linda Drago, J.D., University Secretary

3975 Environmental News
Arkansas Environmental Federation
1400 W Markham Street 501-374-0263
Suite 302 Fax: 501-374-8752
Little Rock, AR 72201 cmiller@environmentark.org
www.environmentark.org

Charles Miller, Executive Director
Marge Brookins, Office Manager

3976 Forest Magazine
Forest Service Employees for Environmental Ethics
PO Box 11615 541-484-2692
Eugene, OR 97440 Fax: 541-484-3004
fseee@fseee.org
www.fseee.org

FSEEE is the largest forest watchdog organization in the nation. Since 1989, FSEEE has defended the rights and responsibilities of brave scientists and resource professionals working to assure the long-term health and vitality of ournational forests. FSEEE publishes Forest Magazine quarterly to educate the public on forest issues.
Publication Date: 1989 50 pages Bi-Monthly
ISSN: 1534-9284
Andy Stahl, Executive Director
Matt Rasmussen, Editor

3977 Forest Service Employees for Environmental Ethics
PO Box 11615 541-484-2692
Eugene, OR 97440 Fax: 541-484-3004
fseee@fseee.org
www.fseee.org

FSEEE is the largest forest watchdog organization in the nation. Since 1989, FSEEE has defended the rights and responsibilities of brave scientists and resource professionals working to assure the long-term health and vitality of ournational forests. FSEEE publishes Forest Magazine quarterly to educate the public on forest issues.
Andy Stahl, Executive Director
Matt Rasmussen, Editor

3978 Greens/Green Party USA Green Politics Green Politics
PO Box 408316 978-682-4353
Chicago, IL 60640 866-GRE-ENS2
Fax: 978-682-4318
info@greenparty.org
www.greenparty.org

Is a national non-profit membership organization dedicated to advancing the Green Ten Key Values as a guiding force in American society and politics.
12 pages Quarterly
Don Fitz, Editor

3979 International Boreal Forest Newsletter
Institute for World Resource Research

PO Box 50303 630-910-1551
Palo Alto, CA 94303 Fax: 630-910-1561
www.globalwarming.net

Covers all phases of developments in forestry and reforestation of northern nations including the US, Canada, Russia, Sweden, Finland, Norway, China, Japan and others. Its goal is to increase the worldwide understanding of theecological and economic roles of the northern forest regions of the world.

Dr. Yuan Lee, Editor-in-Chief
BJ Jefferson, Advertising/Sales

3980 International Society of Tropical Foresters: ISTF Notices

5400 Grosvenor Lane 301-897-8720
Bethesda, MD 20814 Fax: 301-897-3690
istfi@igc.apc.org
www.istf-bethesda.org

The International Society of Tropical Foresters, Inc. (ISTF) is a nonprofit organization committed to the protection, wise management and rational use of the world's tropical forests. Established in 1950, ISTF was reactivated in 1979.It has about 1500 members in more than 100 countries. Financial support comes from membership dues, donations and grants. ISTF sponsors meetings, promotes chapters in other countries, maintains a web site and has chapters at universities.

Gary S. Harshorn, President
Roger R. B. Leakey, Vice President

3981 Jackson Hole Conservation Alliance: Alliance News

685 S. Cache St 307-733-9417
PO Box 2728 Fax: 307-733-9008
Jackson, WY 83001 info@jhalliance.org
www.jhalliance.org

An organization dedicated to responsible land stewardship in Jackson Hole, Wyoming to ensure that human activities are in harmony with the area's irreplaceable wildlife, scenery and other natural resources.

20 pages Quarterly
Craig M. Benjamin, Executive Director
David Hardie, Co-Chair

3982 Leopold Letter

Iowa State University
209 Curtiss Hall 515-294-3711
513 Farm House Lane Fax: 515-294-9696
Ames, IA 50011-1054 leocenter@iastate.edu
www.leopold.iastate.edu

A newsletter informing diverse audiences about Leopold Center programs and activities, with the purpose of encouraging interest in and use of sustainable farming practices as well as stimulating public discussion on sustainableagriculture in Iowa.

Publication Date: 1987 12 pages Quarterly
ISSN: 1065-2116
Doug Gronau, Chair
Mark Rasmussen, Director

3983 Minnesota Department of Agriculture: MDA Quarterly

625 Robert St. N. 651-201-6000
St Paul, MN 55155 800-967-2474
Fax: 651-297-5522
webinfo@mda.state.mn.us
www.mda.state.mn.us

The MDA's mission is to work toward a diverse ag industry that is profitable as well as environmentally sound; to protect the public health safety regarding food and ag products; and to ensure orderly commerce in agricultural and foodproducts. We have two major branches of the department to accomplish this mission: regulatory divisions and non-regulatory divisions.

Publication Date: 2000
Dave Frederickson, Commissioner
Jim Boerboom, Deputy Commissioner

3984 Mountain Research and Development

PO Box 1978 530-752-8330
Davis, CA 95617 www.mrd-journal.org

The leading journal specifically devoted to the world's mountains. It has been published since 1981 and has established itself as a renowned international publication containing well-researched, peer-reviewed scientific articles byauthors from around the world.

Professor Hans Hurni, Editor-in-Chief

3985 Northeast Sun

Northeast Sustainable Energy Association
50 Miles Street 413-774-6051
Greenfield, MA 00130 Fax: 413-774-6053
nesea@nesea.org
www.nesea.org

Promotes responsible use of energy for a stronger economy and cleaner environment. Northeast Sun is a bi-annual Spring and Fall publication that includes articles by leading authorities on sustainable energy practices, energyefficiency and renewable energy, and each Fall issue includes the Sustainable Green Pages Directory of engery professionals in the Northeast. Subscription is free with membership.

Bi-Annual
Jennifer Marrapese, Executive Director
Gina Sieber, Business Manager

3986 Pinchot Letter

1616 P Street NW 202-797-6580
Suite 100 Fax: 202-797-6583
Washington, DC 20036 pinchot@pinchot.org
www.pinchot.org

A tri-annual newsletter published by the Pinchot Institute for Conservation, an independent nonprofit organization that works collaboratively with all Americans-from federal and state policymakers to citizens in rural communities-tostrengthen forest conservation by advancing sustainable forest management, developing conservation leaders and providing science-based solutions to natural resource issues.

Publication Date: 1995 20 pages Tri-Annual
Dr V Alaric Sample, President
Jennifer Yeager, Chief Financial Officer

3987 Population Institute Newsletter

107 2nd Street NE 202-544-3300
Suite 207 188-787-0038
Washington, DC 20002 Fax: 202-544-0068
info@populationinstitute.org
www.populationinstitute.org

The Population Institute is the World's largest independent nonprofit, educational organization dedicated exclusively to achieving a more equitable balance between the worlds population, environment, and resources. Established in 1969,the Institute, with members in 172 countries, is headquartered on Capitol Hill in Washington DC. The Institute uses a variety of resources and programs to bring its concerns about the consequences of rapid poulation growth to the forefront of thenational agenda.

Publication Date: 1988 8 pages Bi-Monthly
Werner Ryerson, Chair/CEO
Robert Walker, President

3988 Population Reference Bureau: World Population Data Sheet

1875 Connecticut Avenue NW 202-483-1100
Suite 520 800-877-9881
Washington, DC 20009 Fax: 202-328-3937
popref@prb.org
www.prb.org

Up-to-date demographic data and estimates for all the countries and major regions of the world.

Jeffrey Jordan, President/CEO
Linda A. Jacobsen, VP, U.S. Programs

3989 Reporter
Population Connection
2120 L Street NW 202-332-2200
Suite 500 Fax: 202-332-2302
Washington, DC 20037 info@populationconnection.org
www.populationconnection.org
Looks at the connections between overpopulation and the environment around the world and features reports from our activists on Capitol Hill Days 2005. This publication is included in your $25.00 memberhsip fee.
Publication Date: 1972 24 pages Quarterly
ISSN: 0199-0071
John Seager, President/CEO
Jessica Duarte, Membership Manager

3990 Resource Development Newsletter
University of Tennessee
PO Box 1071 865-974-7448
Knoxville, TN 37901 Fax: 423-974-7448
Community development information.
4 pages
Dr Alan Barefield, Publisher

3991 Restoration Ecology Magazine
Blackwell Science
350 Main Street 781-388-8200
Commerce Place Fax: 781-388-8210
Malden, MA 00214 info@wiley.com
as.wiley.com
Provides the most recent developments in the ecological and biological restoration field for both the fundamental and practical implications of restorations.
Mark Mark Allin, President/CEO
Peter Booth Wiley, Chair

3992 Society of American Foresters Information Center Newsletter
5400 Grosvenor Lane 301-897-8720
Bethesda, MD 20814 866-897-8720
Fax: 301-897-3690
membership@safnet.org
www.eforester.org
An organization that represents the forestry profession in the United States. Its mission is to advance the science, education, technology and practice of forestry.
Publication Date: 1996 24 pages Monthly
Michael T Goergen, Jr, EVP/CEO

3993 Solar Energy Magazine
Elsevier Science
360 Park Avenue S 212-989-5800
11th Floor Fax: 212-633-3680
New York, NY 10010
Devoted exclusively to the science and technology of solar energy applications.
Publication Date: 1957
ISSN: 0380-92X
D Yogi Goswami, Editor-in-Chief

3994 Solar Energy Report
California Solar Energy Industries Association
1107 9th St. 916-747-6987
Ste 820 Fax: 707-374-4767
Sacramento, CA 95814 info@calseia.org
www.calseia.org
Bi-Monthly
Rick Reed, President
Cecilia Aguillon, Vice President

3995 Southface Journal of Sustainable Building
Southface Energy Institute
241 Pine Street NE 404-872-3549
Atlanta, GA 30308 Fax: 404-872-5009
info@southface.org
www.southface.org
Contains articles on numerous sustainable building topics. Free to members and available online.
Publication Date: 1978 24 pages Quarterly
Linda Bolan, Chair
Barry R. Goldman, Vice Chair

3996 Sustainable Green Pages Directory
Northeast Sustainable Energy Association
50 Miles Street 413-774-6051
Greenfield, MA 00130 Fax: 413-774-6053
nesea@nesea.org
www.nesea.org
The SPG Directory lists over 30 categories of sustainable energy professionals working throughout the Northeast, including architects, engineers, builders, energy auditors, consultants and renewable energy installers and manufacturers.It is the largest directory of its kind and the only one that targets the Northeastern USA. Published in the Northeast Sun magazine and online.
September Annual
Jennifer Marrapese, Executive Director
Gina Sieber, Business Manager

3997 Tall Timbers Research Station: Bulletin Series
13093 Henry Beadel Drive 850-893-4153
Tallahassee, FL 32312 Fax: 850-668-7781
rose@ttrs.org
www.talltimbers.org
Dedicated to protecting wildlands and preserving natural habitats. Promotes public education on the importance of natural disturbances to the environment and the subsequent need for wildlife and land management. Conducts fire ecologyresearch and other biological research programs through the Tall Timbers Research Station. Operates museum.
Publication Date: 1962
ISSN: 0496-7631
William E. Palmer, Ph.D., President/CEO
Jennifer Roberts, Administrative Assistant

3998 Tall Timbers Research Station: Fire Ecology Conference Proceedings
13093 Henry Beadel Drive 850-893-4153
Tallahassee, FL 32312 Fax: 850-668-7781
rose@ttrs.org
www.talltimbers.org
Dedicated to protecting wildlands and preserving natural habitats. Promotes public education on the importance of natural disturbances to the environment and the subsequent need for wildlife and land management. Conducts fire ecologyresearch and other biological research programs through the Tall Timbers Research Station. Operates museum.
Publication Date: 1962
ISSN: 0082-1527
William E. Palmer, Ph.D., President/CEO
Jennifer Roberts, Administrative Assistant

3999 Tall Timbers Research Station: Game Bird Seminar Proceedings
13093 Henry Beadel Drive 850-893-4153
Tallahassee, FL 32312 Fax: 850-668-7781
rose@ttrs.org
www.talltimbers.org
Dedicated to protecting wildlands and preserving natural habitats. Promotes public education on the importance of natural disturbances to the environment and the subsequent need for wildlife and land management. Conducts fire ecologyresearch

and other biological research programs through the Tall Timbers Research Station. Operates museum.
Publication Date: 1980
ISSN: 1087-4372
William E. Palmer, Ph.D., President/CEO
Jennifer Roberts, Administrative Assistant

4000 Tall Timbers Research Station: Miscellaneous Series
13093 Henry Beadel Drive 850-893-4153
Tallahassee, FL 32312 Fax: 850-668-7781
rose@ttrs.org
www.talltimbers.org
Dedicated to protecting wildlands and preserving natural habitats. Promotes public education on the importance of natural disturbances to the environment and the subsequent need for wildlife and land management. Conducts fire ecologyresearch and other biological research programs through the Tall Timbers Research Station. Operates museum.
Publication Date: 1961
ISSN: 0494-764x
William E. Palmer, Ph.D., President/CEO
Jennifer Roberts, Administrative Assistant

4001 Totally Tree-Mendous Activities
Northeast Sustainable Energy Association
50 Miles Street 413-774-6051
Greenfield, MA 00130 Fax: 413-774-6053
nesea@nesea.org
www.nesea.org
Resource for teachers and parents that offers creative and fun tree-based projects for students.
40 pages
Jennifer Marrapese, Executive Director
Gina Sieber, Business Manager

4002 Woodland Steward
Massachusetts Forestry Association
270 Jackson Street 413-323-7326
Belchertown, MA 00100 Fax: 413-323-9594
This publication is full of information about Massachusett's forest and ways that landowners can manage their woodlands to achieve their goals in an environmentally sustainable manner. Free with membership.
Bi-Monthly
Gregory Cox, Executive Director

4003 Worldwatch Institute: State of the World
1400 16th Street NW 202-745-8092
Suite 430 Fax: 202-478-2534
Washington, DC 20036 worldwatch@worldwatch.org
www.worldwatch.org
The most authorative go-to resource for those who understand the importance of nuturing a safe, sane and healthy global environment through both policy and action.
Annual
ISBN: 0-393326-66-7
Ed Groark, Chair/Acting Interim Pres
John Robbins, Treasurer

4004 Worldwatch Institute: Vital Signs
1400 16th Street NW 202-745-8092
Suite 430 Fax: 202-478-2534
Washington, DC 20036 worldwatch@worldwatch.org
www.worldwatch.org
Provides comprehensive, user-friendly information on key trends and includes tables and graphs that help readers access the developments that are changing their lives for better or for worse.
Annual
ISBN: 0-393326-89-6
Ed Groark, Chair/Acting Interim Pres
John Robbins, Treasurer

4005 Worldwatch Institute: World Watch
1400 16th Street NW 202-745-8092
Suite 430 Fax: 202-478-2534
Washington, DC 20036 worldwatch@worldwatch.org
www.worldwatch.org
The Worldwatch Institute is an independent, nonprofit environmental research organization in Washington DC. Its mission is to foster a sustainable society in which human needs are met in ways that do not threaten the health of thenatural environment or future generations. To this end, this Institute conducts interdisciplinary research on emerging global issues, the results of which are published and disseminated to decision-makers and the media.
Bi-Monthly
Ed Groark, Chair/Acting Interim Pres
John Robbins, Treasurer

4006 Worldwatch Institute: Worldwatch Papers
1400 16th Street NW 202-745-8092
Suite 430 Fax: 202-478-2534
Washington, DC 20036 worldwatch@worldwatch.org
www.worldwatch.org
Provides cutting-edge analysis on an environmental topic that is making - or is about to make - headlines worldwide.
50-70 pages 5x times year
Ed Groark, Chair/Acting Interim Pres
John Robbins, Treasurer

Periodicals: Travel & Tourism

4007 New York State Parks, Recreation and Historic Preservation
Empire State Plaza 518-474-0456
Agency Building 1 Fax: 518-486-2924
Albany, NY 12238 www.nysparks.com
Publishes New York State Boat Launching Guide, Camping/Cabin Reservation Info, Snowmobiling Guide and Preservation Magazine.
Bernadette Castro, Commissioner

4008 Parks and Recreation Magazine
National Recreation and Park Association
22377 Belmont Ridge Road 703-858-0784
Ashburn, VA 20148 Fax: 703-858-0794
info@nrpa.org
www.npca.org/articles/magazine
Informs, motivates and inspires professionals, civic leaders and citizens to elevate the value of parks and recreation as a public service.
Monthly
John Thorner, Exectutive Director
Rachel Roberts, Editor

4009 Potomac Appalachian
118 Park Street SE 703-242-0315
Vienna, VA 22180 Fax: 703-242-0968
info@patc.net
www.patc.net
Published by the Potomac Appalachian Trail Club, which through volunteer efforts, education and advocacy, acquires, maintains and protects the trail and lands of the Appalachian Trail, other trails and related facilities in theMid-Atlantic Region for the enjoyment of present and future hikers. PATC publishes hiking guides, maps and history books of the Appalachian Trail and other trails in our area of responsibility. The monthly newsletter is sent to members and uponrequest. Free to members.
16-20 pages Monthly
ISSN: 098 -8154
Richard Hostelley, President
Rachel Levin, Editor

4010 Sam D. Hamilton Noxubee National Wildlife Refuge
13723 Bluff Lake Road 662-323-5548
Brooksville, MS 39739 Fax: 662-323-6390
noxubee@fws.gov
www.fws.gov/refuge/noxubee
Noxubee National Wildlife Refuge was established to protect and enhance habitat for the conservation of migratory birds, endangered species and other wildlife. The recreational and educational opportunities provided on the refuge helpthe public experience nature and learn how sound management ensures that future generations continue to enjoy fish and wildlife and their habitats.
Publication Date: 1940 2 pages Bi-Annual

Periodicals: Water Resources

4011 Air Water Pollution Report's Environment Week
Business Publishers
2222 Sedwick Drive 301-589-5103
Durham, NC 27713 800-223-8720
Fax: 800-508-2592
custserv@bpinews.com
www.bpinews.com
Provides a balanced, insightful update on the week's most important environmental news from Washington, DC.
Leonard A Eiserer, Publisher
David Goeller, Editor

4012 Air/Water Pollution Report
Business Publishers
2222 Sedwick Drive 301-589-5103
Durham, NC 27713 800-223-8720
Fax: 800-508-2592
custserv@bpinews.com
www.bpinews.com
Regulatory activities and governmental legislation, in addition to litigation are covered in this pulication.
Leonard A Eiserer, Publisher
David Goeller, Editor

4013 America's Priceless Groundwater
American Ground Water Trust
50 Pleasant Street Ste 2 603-228-5444
Concord, NH 03301 Fax: 603-228-6557
trustinfo@agwt.org
www.agwt.org
15 pages Quarterly
Kevin McGinnis, Chairman
Andrew Stone, Executive Director

4014 American Fisheries Society: Water Quality Matters
324 25th Street 801-625-5358
Ogden, UT 84401 Fax: 801-625-5756
glampman@fs.fed.us
8 pages 1-2 per year
Georgina Lampman, President
Gregg Lomincky, Editor

4015 American Water Resources Association: Journal of the American Water Resources Association
4 West Federal Street 540-687-8390
PO Box 1626 Fax: 540-687-8395
Middleburg, VA 20118 terry@awra.org
www.awra.org
AWRA is a nonprofit, scientific educational association for individuals and organizations involved in all aspects of water resources. Its goal is to advance multidisciplinary water resources management and research through itsconferences, publications, technical commettees, state sections and student chapters.
Publication Date: 1964 Bi-Monthly
ISSN: 1093-474X
Rafael Frias III, President
Brenda Bateman, President-Elect

4016 American Water Resources Association: Water Resources IMPACT
4 West Federal Street 540-687-8390
PO Box 1626 Fax: 540-687-8395
Middleburg, VA 20118 terry@awra.org
www.awra.org
AWRA is a nonprofit, scientific educational association for individuals and organizations involved in all aspects of water resources. Its goal is to advance multidisciplinary water resources management and research through itsconferences, publications, technical commettees, state sections and student chapters.
Bi-Monthly
ISSN: 1093-474X
Rafael Frias III, President
Brenda Bateman, President-Elect

4017 Arsenic and Groud Water Home
American Ground Water Trust
50 Pleasant Street Ste 2 603-228-5444
Concord, NH 03301 Fax: 603-228-6557
trustinfo@agwt.org
www.agwt.org
15 pages Quarterly
Kevin McGinnis, Chairman
Andrew Stone, Executive Director

4018 Bacteria and Water Wells
American Ground Water Trust
50 Pleasant Street Ste2 603-228-5444
Concord, NH 00330 Fax: 603-228-6557
trustinfo@agwt.org
www.agwt.org
15 pages Quarterly
Kevin McGinnis, Chairman
Andrew Stone, Executive Director

4019 Blue Planet Magazine
The Ocean Conservancy
1300 19th Street, NW 202-429-5609
8th Floor 800-519-1541
Washington, DC 20036 Fax: 202-429-0056
www.oceanconservancy.org
To educate peoeple about ocean issues; inspire readers with the beauty and wonder of oceans; encourage dedication to appreciating and protecting marine resources; and enlist new volunteers in the ocean community. Free with membershipfee of $25.00
46 pages Quarterly
Andreas Merkl, CEO
Janis Searles Jones, President

4020 Clean Water Network: CWN Status Water Report
Spills and Kills
1200 New York Avenue, NW 202-289-2421
Suite 400 Fax: 202-289-1060
Washington, DC 20005
A nonprofit network of over 1,000 organizations that deal with clean water issues covered by the Clean Water Act. Our member organizations consist of a variety of organizations representing environmentalists, family farmers, recreationanglers, commercial fishermen, surfers, boaters, faith communities, labor unions and civic associates. We publish a monthly newsletter and various reports.
8-12 pages Monthly
Katherine Smitherman, Executive Director

4021 Clean Water Report Newsletter
Business Publishers
2222 Sedwick Drive 301-589-5103
Durham, NC 27713 800-223-8720
Fax: 800-508-2592
custserv@bpinews.com
www.bpinews.com

Follows the latest news from the EPA, Congress, the states, the courts, and private industry. A key information source for environmental professionals, covering the important issues of ground and drinking water, wastewater treatment,wetlands, drought, coastal protection, non-point source pollution, agrichemical contamination and more.

8 pages Bi-Weekly
ISSN: 0009-8620
Leonard A Eiserer, Publisher
Louise Harris, Editor

4022 Clearwaters Magazine
New York Water Environment Association
525 Plum Street 315-422-7811
Suite 102 877-556-9932
Syracuse, NY 13204 Fax: 315-422-3851
pcr@nywea.org
www.nywea.org

Published by The New York Water Environment Association, a nonprofit educational association dedicated to the development and dissemination of information concerning water quality management and the nature, collection, treatment, anddisposal of wastewater. Founded in 1929, the Association has over 2,500 members. The NYWEA is a member association of the Water Environment Federation.

Quarterly
Patricia Cerro-Reehil, Executive Director
Maggie Hoose, Administrative Manager

4023 Colorado Department of Natural Resources: Division of Water Resources: StreamLines
1313 Sherman Street 303-866-3581
Room 818 Fax: 303-866-3589
Denver, CO 80203 www.water.state.co.us

The Colorado Division of Water Resources is an agency of the State of Colorado, Department of Natural Resources, operating under the direction of specific state stautes, court decrees, and interstate compacts. The DWR is empowered toadminister all surface and ground water rights throughout the state and ensure that the doctrine of prior appropiation is enforced.

Publication Date: 1988 4-8 pages Quearterly
Hal D Simpson, Director Water Resources
Russell George, Executive Director

4024 Colorado Water Rights
1580 Logan Street 303-837-0812
#700 Fax: 303-526-3864
Denver, CO 80203 cwc@cowatercongress.org
www.cowatercongress.org

This newsletter helps the Colorado Water Congress protect and conserve Colorado's water resouces by educating its readers.

Publication Date: 1982 4-16 pages Quarterly
Meg Meyer, Associate Director
Doug Kemper, Executive Director

4025 Confluence
Texas Water Conservation Association
221 E 9th Street 512-472-7216
Suite 206 Fax: 512-472-0537
Austin, TX 78701 drobbins@twca.org

The official newsletter of the Texas Water Conservation Association. For those interested in water issues from river authorities to industrial concerns.

Quarterly
Robert J. Brandes, President
John W. Grant, President-Elect

4026 Domestic Water Treatment for Homeowners
American Ground Water Trust
50 Pleasant Street Ste 2 603-228-5444
Concord, NH 00330 Fax: 603-228-6557
trustinfo@agwt.org
www.agwt.org

15 pages Quarterly
Kevin McGinnis, Chairman
Andrew Stone, Executive Director

4027 Environmental Policy Alert
Inside Washington Publishers
1919 South Eads Street 703-416-8500
Suite 201 800-424-9068
Arlington, VA 22202 Fax: 703-416-8543
custsvc@iwpnews.com
www.iwpnews.com

Is a reliable resource for all regulatory, congressional and litigation developments in air quality, waste cleanup, clean water and other environmental quality issues. Also provides a special focus on efforts to reinvent environmentalpolicies.

Publication Date: 1984 Bi-Weekly
Jeremy Bernstein, Editor

4028 Georgia Water and Pollution Control Association: Operator
2121 New Market Parkway 770-618-8690
Suite 144 Fax: 770-618-8695
Marietta, GA 30067 info@gwpca.org
www.gawponline.org

The GW+PCA is dedicated to education, dissemination of technical and scientific information, increased public understanding and promotion of sound public laws and programs in the water resources and related environmental fields.Founded in 1932.

Publication Date: 1970 56-68 pages Quarterly
Jack C Dozier, PE, Executive Director

4029 Georgia Water and Pollution Control Association: News & Notes
2121 New Market Parkway 770-618-8690
Suite 144 Fax: 770-618-8695
Marietta, GA 30067 info@gwpca.org

The GW+PCA is dedicated to education, dissemination of technical and scientific information, increased public understanding and promotion of sound public laws and programs in the water resources and related environmental fields.Founded in 1932.

Publication Date: 1970 20-28 pages Monthly
Jack C Dozier, PE, Executive Director

4030 Groundwater: A Course of Wonder
American Ground Water Trust
50 Pleasant Street Ste 2 603-228-5444
Concord, NH 00330 Fax: 603-228-6557
trustinfo@agwt.org
www.agwt.org

15 pages Quarterly
Kevin McGinnis, Chairman
Andrew Stone, Executive Director

4031 Gulf of Mexico Science
Dauphin Island Sea Lab
101 Bienville Boulevard 251-861-2141
Dauphin Island, AL 36528 Fax: 251-861-4646
www.disl.org

Journal devoted to disemminating knowledge of the Gulf of Mexico and adjacent areas. Appropriate topics of consideration for publication include all areas of marine science.

2x Year
ISSN: 1087-688X
Lisa Young, Public Relations Consultant
Katy Blankenhorn, Scheduling Coordinator

4032 **International Desalination and Water Reuse Quarterly**
Lineal Publishing Company
306 Eagle Dr 561-451-9429
Jupiter, FL 33477 Fax: 561-451-9435
www.desalination.biz
Disseminates technical information, reviews and analyzes regional developments in the field, as well as new products and processes. The publication provides, on a continuing basis, a major vehicle in which to promote desalination andwater reuse technologies, equipment, and design to potential users.
Trevor Loveday, Editor
John Gould, Publisher

4033 **Journal of Soil and Water Conservation**
Soil & Water Conservation Society
945 SW Ankeny Road 515-289-2331
Ankeny, IA 50023 800-THE-SOIL
Fax: 515-289-1227
swcs@swcs.org
www.swcs.org
Publication includes a variety of conservation subjects, as well as international conservation issues.
Clare Lindahl, CEO
Jody Thompson, Editorial Assistant

4034 **Journal of the American Shore and Beach Preservation Association**
American Shore & Beach Preservation Association
5460 Beaujolais Lane 239-489-2616
Fort Myers, FL 33919 Fax: 239-489-9917
exdir@asbpa.org
www.asbpa.org
Peer-reviewed journal of the ASBPA. It provides sound, interesting technical information concerning shores and beaches of the nation and worldwide.
24 pages Quarterly
ISSN: 0037-4237
Kate & Ken Gooderham, Managing Directors
Derek Brockbank, Executive Director

4035 **Journal of the New England Water Environment**
New England Water Environment Association
10 Tower Office Park 781-939-0908
Suite 601 Fax: 781-939-0907
Woburn, MA 01801 mail@newea.org
www.newea.org
Quarterly publication from New England Water Environment Association.
Publication Date: 1929 150 pages Bi-Annual
ISSN: 1077-3002
Mary Barry, Executive Director
Janice Moran, Program Coordinator

4036 **Journal of the North American Benthological Society**
North American Benthological Society
PO Box 7065
Lawrence, KS 66044 www.benthos.org
The society is an international scientific organization that promotes better understanding of biotic communities of lake and stream bottoms and their role in aquatic ecosystems. The journal includes articles that promote the furtherunderstanding of benthic communities and helps members to keep current on interests.
Quarterly
ISSN: 0887-3593
N LeRoy Poff, President

4037 **Mass Waters**
Massachusetts Water Pollution Control Association
P.O. Box 60 774-276-9722
Rochdale, MA 00154 Fax: 774-670-9956
mwpca2011@yahoo.com
www.mwpca.org
Quarterly
Mike Foisy, President
Lynn Foisy, Executive Director

4038 **Mono Lake Committee Newsletter**
Corner of Hwy 395 & 3rd Street 760-647-6595
PO Box 29 Fax: 760-647-6377
Lee Vining, CA 93541 info@monolake.org
www.monolake.org
Nonprofit citizen's group dedicated to: protecting and restoring the Mono Basin ecosystem; educating the public about Mono Lake and the impacts on the environment of excessive water use; promoting cooperative solutions that protectMono Lake and meet real water needs without transferring environmental problems to other areas.
Publication Date: 1978 28 pages Quarterly
Geoffrey McQuilkin, Executive Director
Arya Degenhardt, Communications Director

4039 **Montana Environmental Training Center Newsletter**
Hagener Science Center
8336 Washington Place NE 505-884-1031
Albuquerque, NM 87113 Fax: 505-884-1032
boylej@msun.edu
www.nmrwa.org
METC is a cooperative effort between Montana State University-Northern and the Montana Department of Environmental Quality. Basic, advance training, and continuing education in the areas of water and wastewater operation, maintenance,safety, process control, cross connection and backflow prevention along with courses in basic water science and watershed awareness define the training activities of METC. A newsletter and Training Announcement are published quarterly.
Quarterly
David Kenneke, President
Jose E. Terrones, Vice-President

4040 **Montana Environmental Training Center Training Announcement**
Hagener Science Center
8336 Washington Place NE 505-884-1031
Albuquerque, NM 87113 Fax: 505-884-1032
www.nmrwa.org
METC is a cooperative effort between Montana State University-Northern and the Montana Department of Environmental Quality. Basic, advance training, and continuing education in the areas of water and wastewater operation, maintenance,safety, process control, cross connection and backflow prevention along with courses in basic water science and watershed awareness define the training activities of METC. A newsletter and Training Announcement are published quarterly.
Quarterly
David Kenneke, President
Jose E. Terrones, Vice-President

4041 **New Mexico Rural Water Association Newsletter**
8336 Washington Place NE 505-884-1031
Albuquerque, NM 87113 800-819-9893
Fax: 505-884-1032
www.nmrwa.org
To provide top quality, responsive technical assistance and training for rural water and wastewater systems in New Mexico.
Quarterly
David Kenneke, President
Jose E. Terrones, Vice-President

4042 New York Water Environment Association Clearwaters
525 Plum Street
Suite 102
Syracuse, NY 13204
315-422-7811
877-556-9932
Fax: 315-422-3851
pcr@nywea.org
www.nywea.org

Contains articles on environmental issues, regulatory changes, technological advances as well as, updates on members and activities.
50 pages Quarterly
Paul McGarvey, President
Geoffrey Baldwin, President Elect

4043 Oregon Water Resources Congress Newsletter
437 Union St. NE
Salem, OR 97301
503-363-0121
Fax: 503-371-4926
www.owrc.org

Is to promote the protection and use of water rights and the wise stewardship of water resources.
Quarterly
April Snell, Executive Director
Ken Crick, Office Manager

4044 Ozark National Scenic Riverways
Ozark National Scenic Riverways
PO Box 490
Van Buren, MO 63965
573-323-4236
Fax: 573-323-4140
ozar_superintendent@nps.gov
www.nps.gov/ozar

Missouri's largest National Park and America's first to preserve a free flowing river in its wild state. Covers some 80,000 acres along 134 miles of the Current and Jacks Fork Rivers. Staff provide elementary level environmentaleducation programs on natural history, with an emphasis on karst and water issues. Publishes More Than Skin Deep, a Teacher's Guide to Caves and Groundwater, a curriculum guide suitable for grades K-12.
Publication Date: 1964 Annual
Noel Poe, Superintendent

4045 Pacific Rivers Council: Freeflow
PO Box 10798
Eugene, OR 97440
541-345-0119
Fax: 541-345-0710
www.pacrivers.org

Promoting the protection and restoration of rivers, their watersheds, and native aquatic species.
Quarterly
David Bayles, Executive Director
Holly Spencer, Editor

4046 Puerto Rico Water Resources and Environmental Research Institute Newsletter
University of Puerto Rico
College of Engineering
PO Box 9000
Mayaguez, PR 00681
787-833-0300
Fax: 787-833-3985
PRWRERI@uprm.edu
www.ece.uprm.edu/rumhp/prwrri

Its objectives are to: conduct research aimed at resolving local and national water resources problems; train scientists and engineers through hands-on participation in research; and to facilitate the incorporation of research resultsin the knowledge base of water resources professionals.
Publication Date: 1990 4 pages Quarterly/thru Email
Walter Silva Araya, Associate Director
Jesenia Carrero, Administrative Assistant

4047 Runoff Rundown
Center for Watershed Protection
3290 North Ridge Road
Suite 290
Ellicott City, MD 21043
410-461-8323
Fax: 410-461-8324
center@cwp.org
www.cwp.org

Electronic newsletter published by the Center for Watershed Protection, a nonprofit 501(c)3 organization dedicated to finding new ways to protect and restore our nation's streams, lakes, rivers and estuaries. The center publishesnumerous technical publications on all aspects of watershed protection, including stormwater management, watershed planning and better site design.
Publication Date: 2000 Quarterly
Hye Yeong Kwon, Executive Director
Bill Stack, Deputy Director of Programs

4048 Save San Francisco Bay Association: Watershed Newsletter
1330 Broadway
Suite 1800
Oakland, CA 94612
510-463-6850
Fax: 510-463-6851
info@saveSFbay.org
www.savesfbay.org

Save the Bay has worked for over 40 years to protect the San Francisco Bay-Delta from pollution, fill, shoreline destruction and fresh water diversion. We have launched a century of renewal to restore bay fish and wildlife, reclaimtidal wetlands and make the bay safe and accessible to all.
8-10 pages 3-4 times/year
David Lewis, Executive Director
Jackie Richardson, Development Coordinator

4049 South Carolina Sea Grant Consortium
287 Meeting Street
Charleston, SC 29401
843-727-2078
Fax: 843-727-2080
www.scseagrant.org

A state agency that supports coastal and marine research, education, outreach, and one technical assistance program that fosters sustainable economic development and resource conservation. The consortium represents eight university andstate research organizations and induces a number of information products on coastal and marine resource topics.
Publication Date: 1982 16 pages
M Richard DeVoe, Executive Director

4050 TCS Bulletin
P. O. Box 3590
Williamsburg, VA 23187
757-565-0999
Fax: 757-565-0922
coastalsoc@aol.com
www.thecoastalsociety.org

Organization of private sector, academic, government professionals and students dedicated to actively addressing emerging coastal issues by fostering dialogue, forging partnerships and promoting communication and education. Thispublication covers issues of aquaculture-related law and coastal management research.
Publication Date: 1975 24 pages Yearly
Thomas Bigford, President
Susannah Sheldon, Secretary

4051 Tide
Coastal Conservation Association
6919 Portwest
Suite 100
Houston, TX 77024
713-626-4234
800-201-FISH
Fax: 713-626-5852
ccantl@joincca.org
www.joincca.org

TIDE is the official bimonthly magazine of the Coastal Conservation Association. It has received local, state and national acclaim for writing, photography and layout and currently boasts a circulation of more than 70,000. TIDE isavailable only to members of the Coastal Conservation Association.
Bi-Monthly
Degraaf Adams, Board Member
Bruce Arendale, Board Member

4052 Utah Watershed Review
Utah Association of Conservation Districts

40 West Cache Valley Blvd 435-374-4444
Building 8C Fax: 435-755-2117
Logan, UT 84341 www.uacd.org
Provides information about what's new in Utah and watershed volunteer work and management.
Bi-Monthly
Gordon Younker, EVP
Jack Wilbur, Editor

4053 Water & Wastes Digest
Scranton Gillette Communications
3030 W. Salt Creek Lane 847-391-1000
Suite 201 Fax: 847-390-0408
Arlington Heights, IL 60005 webmaster@sgcmail.com
www.scrantongillette.com
This serves readers in the water and/or wastewater industries. These people work for municipalities, in industry, or as engineers. They design, specify, buy, operate and maintain equipment, chemicals, software and wastewater treatmentservices.
128 pages
ISSN: 0043-1181
Dennis Martyka, Publisher
Tim Gregorski, Editorial Director

4054 Water Conservation in Your Home
American Ground Water Trust
50 Pleasant Street Ste 2 603-228-5444
Concord, NH 00330 Fax: 603-228-6557
trustinfo@agwt.org
www.agwt.org
15 pages Quarterly
Kevin McGinnis, Chairman
Andrew Stone, Executive Director

4055 Water Quality Products
Scranton Gillette Communications
3030 W. Salt Creek Lane 847-391-1000
Suite 201 Fax: 847-390-0408
Arlington Heights, IL 60005 webmaster@sgcmail.com
www.scrantongillette.com
Provides balanced editorial content including developments in water conditioning, filtration and disinfection for residential, commercial and industrial systems.
68 pages
ISSN: 1092-0978
Dennis Martyka, Publisher
Tracy Fabre, Editor

4056 Water Resource Center: Minnegram
University of Minnesota
173 McNeal 1985 Buford Avenue 612-624-9282
St Paul, MN 55108 Fax: 612-625-1263
Fax: '
ander045@umn.edu
Four University water programs, Extension Water Quality Program, Center for Hydrocultural Impacts on Water Quality, Water Resources Research Center and Water Resources Science Graduate Program make up the Water Resources Center. Thecenter sponsors and coordinates programs in research, graduate education, outreach and service to address water resource management issues.
Publication Date: 1986 Quarterly
Jim Anderson, Co-Director
Debra Swackhamer, Co-Director

4057 WaterMatters
Southwest Florida Water Management District
2379 Broad Street 352-796-7211
Brookville, FL 34604 Fax: 352-754-6885
www.swfwmd.state.fl.us
Newletter of the Southwest Florida Water Management District, which manages the water and water-related resources within its boundaries. Maintains balance between the water needs of current and future users while protecting andmaintaining the natural systems that provide the District with its existing and future water supply. The Conservation Projects Section, is reponsible for managing water conservation, reclaimed water, other alternative source projects, and estimatingfuture water demands.
2 pages Monthly
Michael A. Babb, Chair
Randall S. Maggard, Vice Chair

Books: Air & Climate

4058 Air Pollution Control and the German Experience: Lessons for the United States
Center for Clean Air Policy
750 1st Street NE 202-408-9260
Suite 940 Fax: 202-408-8896
Washington, DC 20002 communications@ccap.org
www.ccap.org
Ned Helme, President
Stacey Davis, Senior Program Manager

4059 Caring for Our Air
Enslow Publishers, Inc
101 West 23rd Street 908-771-9400
Suite #240 800-398-2504
New York, NY 10011 Fax: 877-980-4454
customerservice@enslow.com
www.enslow.com
Publication Date: 1976

4060 Center for Resource Economics
2000 M Street NW 202-232-7933
Suite 650 Fax: 202-234-1328
Wasington, DC 20036 info@islandpress.org
www.islandpress.org
Works to educate the public about global environmental issues. Methods include publishing literature on environmental concerns.
Charles C. Savitt, President
Shaina Lange, Executive Assistant

4061 Confronting Climate Change: Strategies for Energy Research and Development
National Academy Press
500 5th Street NW 202-334-3313
Lockbox 285 888-624-8373
Washington, DC 20055 Fax: 202-334-2451
www.nap.edu
Publication Date: 1990 144 pages
ISBN: 0-309043-47-6

4062 Fight Global Warming: 29 Things You Can Do
Environmental Defense Fund
257 Park Avenue South 212-505-2100
17th Floor 800-684-3322
New York, NY 10010 Fax: 212-505-2375
members@edf.org
www.edf.org
Fred Krupp, President
David Yarnold, Executive Director

4063 Fundamentals of Stack Gas Dispersion
Milton R. Beychok Consulting
1126 Colony Plaza 949-718-1360
Newport Beach, CA 92660 Fax: 949-718-1360
mbeychok@air-dispersion.com
The most comprehensive single-source reference book on dispertion modeling of continuous buoyant pollution plumes.
Milton R Beychok, Principal

4064 Healing the Planet: Strategies for Resolving the Environmental Crisis
Addison-Wesley Publishing Company
75 Arlington Street
Suite 300
Boston, MA 00211
617-848-7500
www.aw.com

4065 Indoor Air Quality: Design Guide Book
Fairmont Press
700 Indian Trail
Liburn, GA 30047
770-925-9388
Fax: 770-381-9865
linda@fairmountpress.com
www.fairmontpress.com

4066 Ozone Depletion and Climate Change: Constructing a Global Response
SUNY Press
22 Corporate Woods Boulevard
3rd Floor
Albany, NY 12211
518-472-5000
866-430-7869
Fax: 518-472-5038
info@sunypress.edu
www.sunypress.edu

Available in both soft and hardcover, this book offers solutions that address climate change from a global viewpoint.
Publication Date: 2005 276 pages
Matthew J Hoffman, Author
Tom Baker, Editorial Board
Sue Books, Editorial Board

4067 Politics of Air Pollution: Urban Growth, Ecological Modernization, and Symbolic Inclusion
SUNY Press
22 Corporate Woods Boulevard
3rd Floor
Albany, NY 12211
518-472-5000
866-430-7869
Fax: 518-472-5038
info@sunypress.edu
www.sunypress.edu

Available in both soft and hardcover, this title addresses the relationship between urban growth and pollution.
Publication Date: 2005 152 pages
George A Gonzalez, Author
Tom Baker, Editorial Board
Sue Books, Editorial Board

4068 To Breath Free: Eastern Europe's Environmental Crisis
John Hopkins University Press
3400 N Charles Street
Baltimore, MD 21218
410-516-6900
800-537-5487
Adam Glazer, Promotions Manager

Books: Business

4069 Environmental Career Guide: Job Opportunities with the Earth in Mind
J Wiley & Sons
111 River Street
Hoboken, NJ 00703-5774
212-850-6000
Fax: 212-850-6088
info@wiley.com
as.wiley.com

Publication Date: 1991 208 pages
ISBN: 0-471534-13-7
Nicholas Basta, Author
Mark Mark Allin, President/CEO
Peter Booth Wiley, Chair

4070 Environmental Disputes: Community Involvement in Conflict Resolution
Island Press
PO Box 7
Covelo, CA 95428
707-983-6432
800-828-1302
Fax: 707-983-6414

A book published by Island Press which helps citizen groups, business and government understand how Envionmental Dispute Settlement-a set of procedures for settling disputes over environmental policies without litigation-can work forthem.
Publication Date: 1990 295 pages
ISBN: 0-933280-74-2
James E Crowfoot, Julia Wondolleck, Author

4071 Globalization and the Environment: Greening Global Political Economy
SUNY Press
22 Corporate Woods Boulevard
3rd Floor
Albany, NY 12211
518-472-5000
866-430-7869
Fax: 518-472-5038
info@sunypress.edu
www.sunypress.edu

Also in hardcover, 40.00.
Publication Date: 2004 175 pages
Gabriela Kutting, Author
Tom Baker, Editorial Board
Sue Books, Editorial Board

4072 Shopping for a Better Environment: Brand Name Guide to Environmentally Responsible Shopping
Meadowbrook Press
6110 Blue Circle Drive
Suite 237
Minnetonka, MN 55343
800-338-2232
Fax: 952-930-1940
info@meadowbrookpress.com
www.meadowbrookpress.com

Books: Design & Architecture

4073 Designing Healthy Cities
Krieger Publishing Co.
1725 Krieger Drive
Malabar, FL 32950
321-724-9542
800-724-0025
Fax: 321-951-3671
info@krieger-publishing.com
www.krieger-publishing.com

Krieger Publishing Company produces quality books in various fields of interest. We have an extensive Natural Science listing.
Publication Date: 1998 158 pages
ISBN: 0-894649-27-2
Cheryl Stanton, Advertising

4074 Indoor Air Quality: Design Guide Book
Fairmont Press
700 Indian Trail
Liburn, GA 30047
770-925-9388
Fax: 770-381-9865
www.fairmontpress.com

Books: Disaster Preparedness & Response

4075 Acceptable Risk?: Making Decisions in a Toxic Environment
University of California Press
210 American Drive
Jackson, TN 38301
510-642-4247
800-343-4499
Fax: 800-351-5073
Orderentry@perseusbooks.com
www.ucpress.edu

Alison Mudditt, Director

4076 Borrowed Earth, Borrowed Time: Healing America's Chemical Wounds
Plenum Publishers
233 Spring Street 212-460-1500
New York, NY 10013 Fax: 212-460-1575
support@apress.com
www.plenum.com

Publication Date: 1991
Derk Haank, CEO
Martin Mos, COO

Books: Energy & Transportation

4077 Coming Clean: Breaking America's Addiction to Oil And Coal
Sierra Club Books
85 Second Street 415-977-5500
2nd Floor Fax: 415-977-5797
San Francisco, CA 94105 information@sierraclub.org
www.sierraclub.org

As Americans awaken to their addiction to oil and coal, we want to take action towards a cleaner path. This title provides the road map, showing how we can promote real solutions, and collectively pressure government and corporationsto change their energy priorities.
256 pages
Michael Brune, Author

4078 Confronting Climate Change: Strategies for Energy Research and Development
National Academy Press
500 5th Street NW 202-334-3313
Washington, DC 20055 888-624-8373
Fax: 202-334-2451
www.nap.edu

Publication Date: 1990 144 pages
ISBN: 0-309043-47-6

4079 Energy & Environmental Strategies for the 1990's
Fairmont Press
700 Indian Tr. 770-925-9388
Lilburn, GA 30047 Fax: 770-381-9865
linda@fairmontpress.com
www.fairmontpress.com

4080 Energy Management and Conservation
National Conference of State Legislatures
7700 E First Place 303-364-7700
Denver, CO 80230 Fax: 303-364-7800
www.ncsl.org

Senator Pamela Althoff, President
Jean Cantrell, Vice President

4081 Getting Around Clean & Green
Northeast Sustainable Energy Association
50 Miles Street 413-774-6051
Greenfield, MA 00130 Fax: 413-774-6053
nesea@nesea.org
www.nesea.org

This interdisciplinary science/social studies curriculum allows students to explore the transportation and environmental issues in their own lives. Activities cover: transportation systems, health impacts, environmental andtransportation histories, carpooling, and mass transit.
90 pages Curriculum
Jennifer Marrapese, Executive Director
Gina Sieber, Business Manager

4082 Getting Around Without Gasoline
Northeast Sustainable Energy Association
50 Miles Street 413-774-6051
Greenfield, MA 00130 Fax: 413-774-6053
nesea@nesea.org
www.nesea.org

An interdisciplinary unit that explores the feasibility of getting around without using gasoline. Students can conduct various activities to compare powering vehicles with gasoline versus electricity.
60 pages S & H Only
Jennifer Marrapese, Executive Director
Gina Sieber, Business Manager

4083 Global Science: Energy, Resources, Environment
Kendall-Hunt Publishing Company
4050 Westmark Drive 563-589-1000
PO Box 1840 800-772-9165
Dubuque, IA 52004 Fax: 563-589-1046
orders@kendallhunt.com
www.kendallhunt.com

4084 Oil, Globalization, and the War for the Arctic Refuge
SUNY Press
22 Corporate Woods Boulevard 518-472-5000
3rd Floor 866-430-7869
Albany, NY 12211 Fax: 518-472-5038
info@sunypress.edu
www.sunypress.edu

Also in hardcover, 71.50.
Publication Date: 2006 227 pages
David M Stanlea, Author
Tom Baker, Editorial Board
Sue Books, Editorial Board

4085 Transporting Atlanta: The Mode of Mobility Under Construction
SUNY Press
22 Corporate Woods Boulevard 518-472-5000
3rd Floor 866-430-7869
Albany, NY 12211 Fax: 518-472-5038
info@sunypress.edu
www.sunypress.edu

Publication Date: 2009 220 pages
Miriam Konrad, Author
Tom Baker, Editorial Board
Sue Books, Editorial Board

Books: Environmental Engineering

4086 Principles of Environmental Science and Technology
Elsevier Science Publishers
360 Park Avenue South 212-989-5800
New York, NY 10010 Fax: 212-633-3990
www.elsevier.com

Ron Mobed, Chief Executive Officer
Youngsuk Chi, Chairman

Books: Environmental Health

4087 Ecologue: The Environmental Catalogue and Consumer's Guide for a Safe Earth
Prentice Hall Press (Simon & Schuster Division)
1 Gulf & Western Plaza 212-373-8500
New York, NY 10023 800-223-1360
www.pearsonhighered.com

4088 **Wetlands: Development, Progress, and Environmental Protection Under The Changing Law**
American Law Institute
4025 Chestnut St 215-243-1600
Philadelphia, PA 19104 Fax: 215-243-1636
ali@ali.org
www.ali.org

A book about environmental law.
Stephanie Middleton, Deputy Director

Books: Gaming & Hunting

4089 **Better Trout Habitat: A Guide to Stream Restoration**
Island Press
2000 M Street NW 202-232-7933
Suite 650 Fax: 202-234-1328
Wasington, DC 20036 info@islandpress.org
www.islandpress.org

Charles C. Savitt, President
Shaina Lange, Executive Assistant

Books: Habitat Preservation & Land Use

4090 **50 Simple Things Kids Can Do to Save the Earth**
Andrews and McMeel
4520 Main Street 816-932-6700
Suite 700 Fax: 816-932-6706
Kansas City, MO 64111

4091 **Access EPA: Clearinghouses and Hotlines**
National Technical Information Service
5301 Shawnee Road 703-605-6000
Alexandria, VA 22312 800-553-6847
info@ntis.gov
www.ntis.gov

Publication Date: 1991 57 pages
John J. Regazzi, Board Member
Judith C. Russell, Board Member

4092 **Access EPA: Library and Information Services**
National Technical Information Service
5301 Shawnee Road 703-605-6000
Alexandria, VA 22312 800-553-6847
info@ntis.gov
www.ntis.gov

Publication Date: 1990 110 pages
John J. Regazzi, Board Member
Judith C. Russell, Board Member

4093 **After Earth Day: Continuing the Conservation Effort**
University of North Texas Press
1155 Union Circle 940-565-2142
#311336 800-826-8911
Denton, TX 76203 Fax: 940-565-4590
rchrisman@unt.edu
www.unt.edu/untpress

Publication Date: 1992 241 pages
ISBN: 1-574414-44-0
Karen DeVinney, Managing Editor
Ronald Chrisman, Director

4094 **Agatha's Feather Bed: Not Just Another Wild Goose Story**
Peachtree Publishers
1700 Chattahoochee Avenue 404-876-8761
Atlanta, GA 30318 Fax: 404-875-2578
hello@peachtree-online.com
www.peachtree-online.com

32 pages
ISBN: 1-561450-08-1

4095 **America in the 21st Century: Environmental Concerns**
Population Reference Bureau
1875 Connecticut Avenue, NW 202-530-5810
Suite 520 800-877-9881
Washington, DC 20009 Fax: 202-328-3937
popref@prb.org
www.prb.org

Jeffrey Jordan, President and CEO
Linda A. Jacobsen, VP U.S. Programs

4096 **Ancient Ones: The World of the Old-Growth Douglas Fir**
Sierra Club Books
85 2nd Street 415-977-5500
2nd Floor Fax: 415-977-5797
San Francisco, CA 94105 information@sierraclub.org
www.sierraclub.org

A children's book that offers insight on one of the oldest species of trees.
32 pages
ISBN: 0-871566-82-6
Barbara Bash, Author
Suzanne Head, Editor
Robert Heinzman, Editor

4097 **Association of State Wetland Managers Symposium**
Association of State Wetland Managers
32 Tandberg Trail 207-892-3399
Suite 2A Fax: 207-892-3089
Windham, ME 00406 aswm@aswm.org
www.aswm.org

Jeanne Christie, Executive Director
Jon Kusler, Associate Director

4098 **At Odds with Progress: Americans and Conservation**
University of Arizona Press
1510 E. University Blvd. 520-621-1441
P.O. Box 210055 800-621-2736
Tucson, AZ 85721 Fax: 520-621-1441
www.uapress.arizona.edu

Publication Date: 1991 255 pages
ISBN: 0-816509-17-4
Bret Wallach, Author
Kathryn Conrad, Director
Allyson Carter, Editor in Chief

4099 **Balancing on the Brink of Extinction**
Island Press
2000 M Street NW 202-232-7933
Suite 650 Fax: 202-232-1328
Wasington, DC 20036 info@islandpress.org
www.islandpress.org

Publication Date: 1991 329 pages
Kathryn A Kohm, Author
Charles C. Savitt, President
Shaina Lange, Executive Assistant

4100 **Beyond the Beauty Strip: Saving What's Left of Our Forests**
Tilbury House Publishers

12 Starr Street
Thomaston, ME 00486
207-582-1899
800-582-1899
Fax: 202-582-8227
tilbury@tilburyhouse.com
www.tilburyhouse.com

Joanne Parkin, Office Manager
Tristram Coburn, Co-Publisher

4101 Biodiversity and Ecosystem Function
Springer-Verlag
233 Spring Street
New York, NY 10013
212-460-1500
800-777-4643
Fax: 212-460-1575
service-ny@springer-sbm.com
www.springer.com

Publication Date: 1994 528 pages
Derk Haank, CEO
Martin Mos, COO

4102 Bioemediation
McGraw-Hill
1221 Avenue of the Americas
New York, NY 10020
212-512-2000
800-722-4726
www.magraw-hill.com

4103 Bluebird Bibliography
North American Bluebird Society
PO Box 7844
Bloomington, IN 47407
812-988-1876
Fax: 330-359-5455
info@nabluebirdsociety.org
www.nabluebirdsociety.org

Bernie Daniel, President
Kathy Kremnitzer, Secretary

4104 Butterflies of Delmarva
Delware Nature Society and Tidewater Publishers
PO Box 700
Hockessin, DE 19707
301-239-2334
Fax: 302-239-2473
www.delawarenaturesociety.org

The result of the author's lifelong interest in the 61 adult butterfly species that naturally occur on the Delmarva Peninsula, this field guide clearly identifies the adult, larva and pulpa stages, discusses the differences in colorand wing patterns between sexes, as well as the habitat, range, and food sources of each species. 132 full-color photographs illustrate the text. Includes general butterfly information, and how to attrract them to your garden. Paperback
Publication Date: 1998 138 pages 2nd Edition
ISBN: 0-870334-53-0
Brian Winslow, Executive Director
Christine Carlisle Odom, President

4105 Clean Sites Annual Report
Clean Sites
46161 West Lake Drive
Suite 230-B
Potomac Falls, VA 20165
703-519-2140
Fax: 703-519-2141
cses@cleansites.com
www.cleansites.com

We apply sound project management principles, real-world experience, and cost control measures to find creative solutions to environmental remediation and land reuse problems.
Douglas Ammon, Contact

4106 Connections: Linking Population and the Environment Teaching Kit
Population Reference Bureau
1875 Connecticut Avenue NW
Suite 520
Washington, DC 20009
202-483-1100
800-877-9881
Fax: 202-328-3937
popref@prb.org
www.prb.org

Jeffrey Jordan, President and CEO
Linda A. Jacobsen, VP U.S. Programs

4107 Conservation and Research Foundation Five Year Report
Conservation and Research Foundation
PO Box 909
Shelburne, VT 00548
913-268-0076
Fax: 913-268-0076

Publication from Conservation and Research Foundation which is published every five years and distributed to contributors. This publication is also available upon request.
Publication Date: 1998 43 pages
Dr Mary Wetzel, President

4108 Decade of Destruction: The Crusade to Save the Amazon Rain Forest
Henry Holt and Company
175 Fifth Avenue
New York, NY 10010
646-307-5095
Fax: 212-633-0748
publicity@hholt.com
www.henryholt.com

215 pages
Adrian Cowell, Author

4109 Discordant Harmonies: A New Ecology for the Twenty-first Century
Oxford University Press
198 Madison Avenue
New York, NY 10016
212-679-7300
Fax: 212-725-2972
global.oup.com

Publication Date: 1992 254 pages
ISBN: 0-195074-69-6
Daniel B Botkin, Author

4110 Earth Keeping
Zondervan Publishing House
5300 Patterson Avenue SE
Grand Rapids, MI 49530
616-698-6900
Fax: 616-698-3439
www.zondervan.com

4111 Earthright
Prima Publishing & Communications
PO Box 1260BK
Rocklin, CA 95677
916-786-0426
800-632-8676
Fax: 916-632-4405
www.primagames.com

4112 Ecology of Greenways: Design and Function of Linear Conservation
University of Minnesota Press
111 Third Avenue South
Suite 290
Minneapolis, MN 55401
612-627-1970
800-388-3863
Fax: 612-627-1980
www.upress.umn.edu

Publication Date: 1994 238 pages
ISBN: 0-816621-57-8
Daniel S Smith, Paul Cawood Hellmund, Author

4113 Eli's Songs
MacMillan Publishing Company
866 3rd Avenue
New York, NY 10022
212-702-2000
800-257-5755
www.macmillian.com

4114 Endangered Kingdom: The Struggle to Save America's Wildlife
John Wiley & Sons
605 3rd Avenue 212-850-6890
New York, NY 10158 800-825-7550
Fax: 212-850-8800
info@wiley.com
as.wiley.com

Publication Date: 1991 241 pages
ISBN: 0-471528-22-6
Roger L DiSilvestro, Author
Mark Mark Allin, President/CEO
Peter Booth Wiley, Chair

4115 Environment in Peril
Smithsonian Institution Press
SI Building, Room 153, MRC 010 202-633-1000
PO Box 37012 800-782-4612
Washington, DC 20013 Fax: 202-633-5285
info@si.edu
www.si.edu

Deron Burba, Chief Information Officer
Chandra P. Heilman, Ombudsman

4116 Environmental Concern in Florida and the Nation
University of Florida Press
15 NW 15th Street 352-392-1351
Gainesville, FL 32611 800-226-3822
Fax: 352-392-0590
press@upf.com
www.upf.com

Publication Date: 1997 144 pages
ISBN: 0-813010-56-X
Lance Dehaven-Smith, Author
Marthe Walters, Assistant Managing Editor
Judith Knight, Editor at Large

4117 Environmental Concern: A Comprehensive Review of Wetlands Assessment Producers
POW-The Planning of Wetlands
201 Boundary Lane 410-745-9620
PO Box P Fax: 410-745-3517
St Michaels, MD 21663 order@wetland.org
www.wetland.org

Since its founding in 1972, EC has been specializing in consulting, planning design, education services, construction services and research related to all aspects of wetlands. As wetlands and contiguous upland forests and meadows areinteracting ecosystems EC specializes in consulting, planning, design, and project supervision services for such upland ecosystem constructions and restorations for the purpose of wetland buffers, reforestation, wildlife habitat and critical areas ofpreservation.
Publication Date: 1999 Quarterly
ISBN: 1-883226-04-x
Suzanne Pitenger Slear, President
Katelin Frase, Education Director

4118 Environmental Concern: Evaluation for Planned Wetlands
POW-The Planning of Wetlands
201 Boundary Lane 410-745-9620
PO Box P Fax: 410-745-3517
St Michaels, MD 21663 order@wetland.org
www.wetland.org

Since its founding in 1972, EC has been specializing in consulting, planning design, education services, construction services and research related to all aspects of wetlands. As wetlands and contiguous upland forests and meadows areinteracting ecosystems EC specializes in consulting, planning, design, and project supervision services for such upland ecosystem constructions and restorations for the purpose of wetland buffers, reforestation, wildlife habitat and critical areas ofpreservation.
Publication Date: 1994 Quarterly
ISBN: 1-883226-03-1
Suzanne Pittenger Slear, President
Katelin Frase, Education Director

4119 Environmental Concern: The Wonders of Wetlands
POW-The Planning of Wetlands
201 Boundary Lane 410-745-9620
PO Box P Fax: 410-745-3517
St Michaels, MD 21663 order@wetland.org
www.wetland.org

Since its founding in 1972, EC has been specializing in consulting, planning design, education services, construction services and research related to all aspects of wetlands. As wetlands and contiguous upland forests and meadows areinteracting ecosystems EC specializes in consulting, planning, design, and project supervision services for such upland ecosystem constructions and restorations for the purpose of wetland buffers, reforestation, wildlife habitat and critical areas ofpreservation.
Publication Date: 1995
ISBN: 1-888631-00-7
Suzanne Pittenger Slear, President
Katelin Frase, Education Director

4120 Environmental Crisis: Opposing Viewpoints
Greenhaven Press
10650 Toebben Drive 858-485-9549
Independence, KY 41051 800-354-9706
Fax: 800-487-8488
solutions.cengage.com/greenhaven

4121 Environmental Profiles: A Global Guide to Projects and People
Garland Publishing
717 5th Avenue 212-751-7447
25th Floor Fax: 212-308-9399
New York, NY 10022 www.garlandpub.com
Publication Date: 1993 1112 pages
ISBN: 0-815300-63-8

4122 Friends of the Earth Foundation Annual Report
Friends of the Earth Found.
30 Sir Francis Drake Blvd 415-256-9604
P.O. Box 437 800-326-7491
Ross, CA 94957 Fax: 202-543-4710
www.oceanic-society.org

Roderic Mast, President and CEO
Brian Hutchinson, Director of Outreach

4123 Future Primitive
University of North Texas Press
1155 Union Circle 940-565-2142
#311336 800-826-8911
Denton, TX 76203 Fax: 940-565-4590
rchrisman@unt.edu
www.unt.edu/untpress
Publication Date: 1996 223 pages
ISBN: 1-574410-07-5
Ronald Chrisman, Director
Karen DeVinney, Managing Editor

4124 Going Green: A Kid's Handbook to Saving the Planet
Puffin Books
375 Hudson Street 212-366-2403
New York, NY 10014 www.puffin.co.uk
Out of print—limited availability.
Publication Date: 1990
ISBN: 0-140345-97-3

4125 Guide to Spring Wildflower Areas
Minnesota Native Plant Society
1520 St. Olaf Avenue 507-786-2222
Northfield, MN 55057 www.stolaf.edu
Updated its guide to over 40 wildflower sites in the Twin Cities area. The guide contains a description and location for each.
4 per year

4126 Guide to Urban Wildlife Management
National Institute for Urban Wildlife
10921 Trotting Ridge Way 301-596-3311
Columbia, MD 21044

4127 Information Please Environmental Almanac
Houghton Mifflin Company
222 Berkeley Street 617-725-5000
30th Floor www.hmco.com
Boston, MA 00211
Publication Date: 1992 704 pages
ISBN: 0-395637-67-8

4128 International Protection of the Environment
Oceana Publications, Inc
198 Madison Avenue
New York, NY 10016 800-334-4249
Fax: 212-726-6476
global.oup.com/uk/goto/oceana
This set provides the documents which form the framework of softlaw administrative instruments for the implementation of international environment treaties under Agenda 21.
Publication Date: 1995 7 vol pages Bi-Monthly
ISBN: 0-379102-95-1
Nicholas A Robinson & Wolfgang Burhenne, Author

4129 International Society for Endangered Cats
3070 Riverside Drive Suite 160 614-487-8760
Columbus, OH 43221 Fax: 614-487-8769
Publication Date: 1990 237 pages
ISBN: 0-816019-44-4
Bill Simpson, President
Patricia Currie, Executive Director

4130 Just A Dream
Houghton Mifflin Company
Beacon Street 617-725-5000
30th Floor
Boston, MA 00210

4131 Krieger Publishing Company: Wildlife Habitat Management of Wetlands
Krieger Publishing Co.
1725 Krieger Drive 321-724-9542
Malabar, FL 32950 800-724-0025
Fax: 321-951-3671
info@krieger-publishing.com
www.krieger-publishing.com
Krieger Publishing Company produces quality books in various fields of interest. We have an extensive Natural Science listing.
Publication Date: 1992 572 pages
ISBN: 1-575240-89-0
Cheryl Stanton, Advertising

4132 Krieger Publishing Company: Wildlife Habitat Management of Forestlands/Rangelands/Farmlands
Krieger Publishing Co.
1725 Krieger Drive 321-724-9542
Malabar, FL 32950 800-724-0025
Fax: 321-951-3671
info@krieger-publishing.com
www.krieger-publishing.com
Krieger Publishing Company produces quality books in various fields of interest. We have an extensive Natural Science listing.
Publication Date: 1994 868 pages
ISBN: 1-575240-93-9
Cheryl Stanton, Advertising

4133 Last Extinction
MIT Press
5 Cambridge Center 617-253-5646
Cambridge, MA 00214 Fax: 617-258-6779
Today there is a new and more widespread awareness of what some consider to be the great tragedy of our time - organisms which took many thousands or even millions of years to evolve are being snuffed out permanently owing to humanactivity.
Publication Date: 1993
Les Kaufman, Kenneth Mallory, Author

4134 National Wildlife Rehabilitators Association Annual Report
National Wildlife Rehabilitators Association
2625 Clearwater Rd 320-230-9920
Suite 110 Fax: 320-230-3077
St Cloud, MN 56301 nwra@nwrawildlife.org
www.nwrawildlife.org
Elaine M. Thrune, President
Richard Grant, President Elect

4135 Nature and the American: Three Centuries of Changing Attitudes
Unviersity of Nebraska Press
1111 Lincoln Mall 402-472-3581
Lincoln, NE 68588 Fax: 402-472-6214
pressmail@unl.edu
www.nebraskapress.unl.edu
Kristen Elias Rowley, Editor
Donna Shear, Director

4136 Ordinance Information Packet
Scenic America
1307 New Hampshire Ave NW 202-463-1294
Washington, DC 20036 Fax: 202-463-1297
www.scenic.org
Mary Tracy, President
Max Ashburn, Communications Director

4137 Ozone Diplomacy: New Directions in Safeguarding the Planet
Harvard University Press
79 Garden Street 617-495-2600
Cambridge, MA 00213 Fax: 617-495-5898
botref@oeb.harvard.edu
www.hup.harvard.edu
Offers an insider's view of the politics, economics, science and diplomacy involved in creating the precedent-setting treaty to protect the Earth: the 1987 Montreal Protocol on Substances That Deplete the Ozone Layer.
Richard Elliot Benedick, Author

4138 Practical Guide to Environmental Management
1616 P Street NW 202-939-3800
Suite 200 Fax: 202-939-3868
Washington, DC 20036

4139 Preserving the World Ecology
H W Wilson Company
950 University Avenue 718-588-8400
Bronx, NY 10452 Fax: 718-588-6365
www.hwwilson.com

4140 **Protecting Our Environment: Lessons from the European Union**
SUNY Press
22 Corporate Woods Boulevard 518-472-5000
3rd Floor 866-430-7869
Albany, NY 12211 Fax: 518-472-5038
info@sunypress.edu
www.sunypress.edu
Available in both hard and soft cover, this title deals with the environment as a global issue.
Publication Date: 2005 204 pages
Janet R Hunter, Zachary A Smith, Author
Tom Baker, Editorial Board
Sue Books, Editorial Board

4141 **Quill's Adventures in Grozzieland**
John Muir Publications
PO Box 613 505-982-4078
Santa Fe, NM 87504 800-888-7504
Fax: 505-988-1680

4142 **RARE Center for Tropical Conservation Annual Report**
Rare Center for Tropical Conservation
1616 Walnut Street 215-735-3510
Suite 911 Fax: 215-735-3615
Philadelphia, PA 19103 www.rarecenter.org

4143 **Resource Conservation and Management**
Wadsworth Publishing Company
10 Davis Drive 415-595-2350
Belmont, CA 94002 Fax: 415-637-7544
www.wadsworth.com

4144 **Revolution for Nature: From the Environment to the Connatural World**
University of North Texas Press
1155 Union Circle 940-565-2142
#311336 800-826-8911
Denton, TX 76203 Fax: 940-565-4590
rchrisman@unt.edu
www.unt.edu/untpress

145 pages
ISBN: 1-574417-0X-
Ronald Chrisman, Director
Karen DeVinney, Managing Editor

4145 **Saving Sterling Forest: The Epic Struggle to Preserve New York's Highlands**
SUNY Press
22 Corporate Woods Boulevard 518-472-5000
3rd Floor 866-430-7869
Albany, NY 12211 Fax: 518-472-5038
info@sunypress.edu
www.sunypress.edu

Also in hardcover, 59.50.
Publication Date: 2007 216 pages
Ann Botshon, Author
Tom Baker, Editorial Board
Sue Books, Editorial Board

4146 **Seed Listing**
Native Seeds/SEARCH
3061 N. Campbell Ave. 520-622-5561
Tucson, AZ 85719 Fax: 520-622-5591
info@nativeseeds.org
www.nativeseeds.org

Cynthia Anson, Chair
Carolyn Niethammer, Vice-Chair

4147 **Statement of Policy and Practices for Protection of Wetlands**
National Wildlife Fed. Corporate Conservation Coun
1400 16th Street NW 202-797-6870
Washington, DC 20036 Fax: 202-797-6871

4148 **Student Conservation Association Northwest: Lightly on the Land**
1265 S Main Street 206-324-4649
Suite 210 Fax: 206-324-4998
Seattle, WA 98144 www.thesca.org
SCA is a national organization with regional offices in Seattle, Oakland, Pittsburg, Washington DC and headquartered in Charlestown NH. Our mission is to build the next generation of conservation leaders and inspire lifelongstewardship of the environment by engaging young people in hands-on environmental service. We offer a wide range of internships and crew based programs for ages 16 years and up.
Publication Date: 1996 267 pages
ISBN: 0-898869-91-7
Jaime Berman Matyas, President/CEO
Laura Herrin, SVP Programs

4149 **Transactions of Annual North American Wildlife and Natural Resources Conference**
Wildlife Management
1101 14th Street NW 202-371-1808
Suite 801 Fax: 202-408-5059
Washington, DC 20005

4150 **Urban Wildlife Manager's Notebook**
National Institute for Urban Wildlife
10921 Trotting Ridge Way 301-596-3311
Columbia, MD 21044

4151 **Wetlands Protection: The Role of Economics**
Environmental Law Institute
1616 P Street NW 202-939-3800
Suite 200 Fax: 202-939-3868
Washington, DC 20036

4152 **Whales**
Simon & Schuster Children's Publishing
1230 6th Ave
New York, NY 10020 866-506-1949
www.simonandschuster.com
A book studying the characteristics, behavior, and migration habits of the humpback whale.
Publication Date: 1993 24 pages
Cousteau Society, Author

4153 **Wilderness Society Annual Report**
1615 M Street NW 202-833-2300
Washington, DC 20036 800-THE-WILD
action@tws.org
www.wilderness.org
Deliver to future generations an unspoiled legacy of wild places, with all the precious values they hold: Biological diversity; clean air and water; towering forests, rushing rivers, and sage-sweet, silent deserts.
Jamie Williams, President
Thomas Tepper, VP Finance/Administration

4154 **Wildlife Conservation in Metropolitan Environments**
National Institute for Urban Wildlife
10921 Trotting Ridge Way 301-596-3311
Columbia, MD 21044

4155 Wildlife Habitat Relationships in Forested Ecosystems
Timber Press
133 SW 2nd Avenue
Suite 450
Portland, OR 97204
503-227-2878
800-327-5680
Fax: 503-227-3070
www.timber-press.com

Available by special order.
Publication Date: 1997
David R Patton, Author

4156 Wildlife Research and Management in the National Parks
University of Illinois Press
1325 S Oak Street
Champaign, IL 61820
217-333-0950
Fax: 217-244-8082
uipress@uillinois.edu
www.press.uillinois.edu

Publication Date: 1992 240 pages
ISBN: 0-252018-24-9
Gerald R Wright, Author
Willis G. Regier, Director
Laurie Matheson, Editor-in-Chief

4157 Wildlife-Habitat Relationships: Concepts and Applications
University of Wisconsin Press
114 N Murray Street
Madison, WI 53715
608-262-8782

Anyone working with wildlife must be concerned with its habitat identification, measurement and analysis. Wildlife-Habitat Relationships goes beyond introductory wildlife biology texts and specialized studies of single species toprovide a broad but advanced understanding of habitat relationships applicable to all terrestrial species.
Publication Date: 1998 416 pages
ISBN: 0-299156-40-0
Michael L Morrison, Bruce G Marcot, Author

Books: Recycling & Pollution Prevention

4158 An Ontology of Trash: The Disposable and Its Problematic Nature
SUNY Press
22 Corporate Woods Boulevard
3rd Floor
Albany, NY 12211
518-472-5000
866-430-7869
Fax: 518-472-5038
info@sunypress.edu
www.sunypress.edu

Also in hardcover, 65.00.
Publication Date: 2008 238 pages
Greg Kennedy, Author
Tom Baker, Editorial Board
Sue Books, Editorial Board

4159 Aunt Ipp's Museum of Junk
HarperCollins
195 Broadway
New York, NY 10007
212-207-7000
800-424-6234
Fax: 212-207-7433
orders@harpercollins.com
www.harpercollins.com

Brian Murray, President and CEO
Larry Nevins, EVP, Operations

4160 Beyond 40 Percent: Record-Setting Recycling and Composting Programs
Island Press
2000 M Street NW
Suite 650
Wasington, DC 20036
202-232-7933
Fax: 202-234-1328
info@islandpress.org
www.islandpress.org

Publication Date: 1991 280 pages
ISBN: 1-559630-73-6
Charles C. Savitt, President
Shaina Lange, Executive Assistant

4161 Borrowed Earth, Borrowed Time: Healing America's Chemical Wounds
Plenum Publishers
233 Spring Street
New York, NY 10013
212-460-1500
Fax: 212-460-1575
www.springer.com

Publication Date: 1991
Derk Haank, CEO
Martin Mos, COO

4162 Caring for Our Air
Enslow Publishers
101 West 23rd Street
Suite #240
New York, NY 10011
908-771-9400
800-398-2504
Fax: 877-980-4454
customerservice@enslow.com
www.enslow.com

4163 Community Recycling: System Design to Management
Prentice Hall
101 West 23rd Street
Suite #240
New York, NY 10011
908-771-9400
800-398-2504
Fax: 877-980-4454
customerservice@enslow.com
www.enslow.com

A guide for getting into the growing business of community recycling, for those with little or no previous experience with the technical details of recycling. Discusses marketing, management, equipment, profit comparisons of variousprocessing methods and legal considerations.
Publication Date: 1992 240 pages
ISBN: 0-131557-89-0
Nyles V Reinfeld, Carl M Layman, Author

4164 Garbage and Recycling
Kingfisher Publications
1 Gulf & Western Plaza
New York, NY 10023
212-373-8500
800-223-1360
home.pearsonhighered.com

Publication Date: 1995 32 pages
ISBN: 1-856976-15-7
Rosie Harlow, Sally Morgan, Author

4165 Hey Mr. Green: Sierra Magazine's Answer Guy Tackles Your Toughest Green Living Questions
Sierra Club Books
85 Second Street
2nd Floor
San Francisco, CA 94105
415-977-5500
Fax: 415-977-5797
information@sierraclub.org
www.sierraclub.org

When is the right time to replace an old refridgerator? Is it more environmentally correct to buy your beer in bottles or cans? And is it okay to knit a sweater with acrylic (pertoleum-based) yarn? Bob Schildgen has been Mr. Green inSierra Magazine for several years now, providing fact-backed replies to reader's questions. Well organized, funny, and supremely useful, this title offers green-living tips for everyday.
Publication Date: 2009 224 pages
ISBN: 1-578051-43-4
Bob Schildgen, Author

4166 How On Earth Do We Recycle Glass?
Millbrook Press
2 Old New Milford Road 203-740-2220
PO Box 335 800-462-4703
Brookfield, CT 00680 Fax: 203-740-2526
www.millbrookpress.com

4167 Let's Talk Trash: The Kids' Book About Recycling
Waterfront Books
85 Crescent Road 802-658-7477
Burlington, VT 00540

4168 Plastic: America's Packaging Dilemma
Island Press
2000 M Street NW 202-232-7933
Suite 650 Fax: 202-234-1328
Wasington, DC 20036 info@islandpress.org
www.islandpress.org

Charles C. Savitt, President
Shaina Lange, Executive Assistant

4169 Pollution Knows No Frontiers
Paragon House of Publishers
3600 Labore Road 651-644-3087
Suite 1 Fax: 651-644-0997
St. Paul, MN 55110 info@paragonhouse.com
www.paragonhouse.com

4170 Recycle!: A Handbook for Kids
Little, Brown & Company
1271 Avenue of the Americas
New York, NY 10020 800-759-0190
Fax: 212-522-0885
Publication Date: 1996 32 pages
Gail Gibbons, Editor

4171 Recycling Paper: From Fiber to Finished Product
TAPPI Press
15 Technology Parkway South 770-446-1400
Norcross, GA 30092 Fax: 770-446-6947
memberconnection@tappi.org
www.tappi.org

4172 Reducing Toxics
Island Press
2000 M Street NW 202-232-7933
Suite 650 Fax: 202-234-1328
Wasington, DC 20036 info@islandpress.org
www.islandpress.org

Publication Date: 1995 460 pages
Charles C. Savitt, President
Shaina Lange, Executive Assistant

Books: Sustainable Development

4173 Biodiversity Prospecting: Using Genetic Resources for Sustainable Development
World Resources Insitute
10 G Street NE 202-729-7600
Suite 800 Fax: 202-729-7610
Washington, DC 20002 www.wri.org
Andrew Steer, President/CEO
Lawrence MacDonald, VP, Communications

4174 Building Sustainable Communities: An Environmental Guide for Local Government
Global Cities Project
One Rockefeller Plaza 212-618-6345
Suite 1134 info@globalcities.org
New York, NY 10020 www.globalcities.org
Frances Arricale, Board Member
Carol Bellamy, Board Member

4175 Center for Ecoliteracy
2150 Allston Way 510-845-4595
Suite 270 Fax: 510-845-1439
Berkeley, CA 94704 info@ecoliteracy.org
www.ecoliteracy.org
The Center for Ecoliteracy is dedicated to fostering a profound understanding of the natural world, grounded in direct experience that leads to sustainable patterns of living.
Publication Date: 2000 90 pages Paperback
ISBN: 0-967565-23-5
Zenobia Barlow, Executive Director
Nate Evans, Finance Manager

4176 Constructing Sustainable Development
SUNY Press
194 Washington Avenue 518-472-5000
Suite 305 800-666-2211
Albany, NY 12210 Fax: 518-472-5038
Publication Date: 2000 188 pages
Neil E Harrison, Author

4177 Ecological Literacy: Educating Our Children for a Sustainable World
Sierra Club Books
85 Second Street 415-977-5500
2nd Floor Fax: 415-977-5797
San Francisco, CA 94105 information@sierraclub.org
www.sierraclub.org
256 pages
ISBN: 1-578051-53-3
Michael K Stone and Zenobia Barlow, Author

4178 Environmental Defense Annual Report
Environmental Defense
257 Park Avenue South 212-505-2100
17th Floor 800-684-3322
New York, NY 10010 Fax: 212-505-2375
members@edf.org
www.edf.org
Environmental Defense believes that a sustainable environment will require economic and social systems that are equitable and just.
Fred Krupp, President
David Yarnold, Executive Director

4179 Environmental Integration: Our Common Challenge
SUNY Press
22 Corporate Woods Boulevard 518-472-5000
3rd Floor 866-430-7869
Albany, NY 12211 Fax: 518-472-5038
info@sunypress.edu
www.sunypress.edu

Also in hardcover, 85.00.
Publication Date: 2009 290 pages
Ton Buhrs, Author
Tom Baker, Editorial Board
Sue Books, Editorial Board

4180 Environmental Policy Making: Assessing the Use of Alternative Policy Instruments
SUNY Press
22 Corporate Woods Boulevard 518-472-5000
3rd Floor 866-430-7869
Albany, NY 12211 Fax: 518-472-5038
info@sunypress.edu
www.sunypress.edu

Also in hardcover, 85.00.
Publication Date: 2005 276 pages
Michael T Hatch, Author
Tom Baker, Editorial Board
Sue Books, Editorial Board

4181 Environmental Profiles: A Global Guide to Projects and People
Garland Publishing
717 5th Avenue 212-751-7447
25th Floor Fax: 212-308-9399
New York, NY 10022 www.garlandpub.com
Publication Date: 1993 1112 pages
ISBN: 0-815300-63-8

4182 Global Environment
Jones and Bartlett Publishers
5 Wall Street
Burlington, MA 00180 800-832-0034
Fax: 978-443-8000
info@jblearning.com
www.jblearning.com

4183 Gnat is Older than Man: Global Environment and Human Agenda
Princeton University Press
41 William Street 609-258-4900
Princeton, NJ 00854 800-777-4726
Fax: 609-258-6305
press.princeton.edu

Peter Dougherty, Director
Patrick Carroll, Associate Director

4184 Implementation of Environmental Policies in Developing Countries
SUNY Press
22 Corporate Woods Boulevard 518-472-5000
3rd Floor 866-430-7869
Albany, NY 12211 Fax: 518-472-5038
info@sunypress.edu
www.sunypress.edu
A Case of Protected Areas and Tourism in Brazil. Also in hardcover, 50.00.
Publication Date: 2008 150 pages
Jose Antonio Puppim de Oliveira, Author
Tom Baker, Editorial Board
Sue Books, Editorial Board

4185 Managing Sustainable Development
Earthscan Publications
8-12 Camden High Street 207-387-8558
London Fax: 207-387-8998
Publication Date: 2001 304 pages
Michael Carley, Editor

4186 Practice of Sustainable Development
Urban Land Institute
1025 Thomas Jefferson Street NW 202-624-7000
Suite 500 W Fax: 202-624-7140
Washington, DC 20007 customerservice@uli.org
www.uli.org

Publication Date: 2000 160 pages
ISBN: 0-874208-31-9
Douglas R Porter, Author
Randall Rowe, Global Chair
Patrick L. Phillips, Global CEO

4187 Sustainable Planning and Development
WIT Press
25 Bridge Street, 978-667-5841
Billerica, MA 01821 Fax: 978-667-7582
salesUSA@witpress.com
www.witpress.com

Publication Date: 2003 1048 pages
ISBN: 1-853129-85-2
Simon Ibbotson, Marketing Co-ordinator
Dee Halzack, Marketing Manager

4188 The Incompleat Eco-Philosopher:Essay from the Edges of Environmental Ethics
SUNY Press
22 Corporate Woods Boulevard 518-472-5000
3rd Floor 866-430-7869
Albany, NY 12211 Fax: 518-472-5038
info@sunypress.edu
www.sunypress.edu

Also in hardcover for 65.50
Publication Date: 2009 210 pages
Anthony Weston, Author
Tom Baker, Editorial Board
Sue Books, Editorial Board

4189 Urban Sprawl, Global Warming, and the Empire of Capital
SUNY Press
22 Corporate Woods Boulevard 518-472-5000
3rd Floor 866-430-7869
Albany, NY 12211 Fax: 518-472-5038
info@sunypress.edu
www.sunypress.edu

Also in hardcover, 60.00.
Publication Date: 2009 170 pages
George A Gonzalez, Author
Tom Baker, Editorial Board
Sue Books, Editorial Board

4190 Who Gets What? Domestic Influences on International Negotiations Allocating Shared Resources
SUNY Press
22 Corporate Woods Boulevard 518-472-5000
3rd Floor 866-430-7869
Albany, NY 12211 Fax: 518-472-5038
info@sunypress.edu
www.sunypress.edu

Also in hardcover, 60.00.
Publication Date: 2008 192 pages
Aslaug Asgeirsdottir, Author
Tom Baker, Editorial Board
Sue Books, Editorial Board

4191 Worldwatch Paper 101: Discarding the Throwaway Society
Worldwatch Intitutes

1400 16th Street NW
Suite 430
Washington, DC 20036
202-745-8092
Fax: 202-478-2534
worldwatch@worldwatch.org
www.worldwatch.org

Ed Groark, Chair/Acting Interim Pres
John Robbins, Treasurer

Books: Travel & Tourism

4192 Appalachian Mountain Club
Appalachian Mountain Club Books
5 Joy Street
Boston, MA 00210
617-523-0636
800-262-4455
Fax: 617-523-0722
information@outdoors.org
www.outdoors.org

The AMC, founded in 1876, promotes the protection, enjoyment, and wise use of the mountains, rivers and trails of the Northeast. We encourage people to enjoy and protect the natural world because we believe that successful conservationdepends on this experience. The AMC publishes an award-winning magazine and more than 60 guide books to the Northeast.
Wayne Thornbrough, Chair
Rol Fessenden, Vice Chair

4193 Prospect Park Handbook
Greensward Found
Lenox Hill Station
PO Box 610
New York, NY 10021
212-473-6283
www.greenswardparks.org

Books: Water Resources

4194 And Two if By Sea: Fighting the Attack on America's Coasts
Coast Alliance
202-546-9609

This book is the benchmark in the effort to save the coasts.
Publication Date: 1986

4195 Comparative Health Effects Assessment of Drinking Water Treatment Technologies
Government Institutes Division
16855 Northchase Drive
Houston, TX 77060
281-673-2800

The report evaluates the public health impact of the most widespread drinking water treatment technologies, with particular emphasis on disinfection.
Publication Date: 1988 20 pages

4196 Dying Oceans
Gareth Stevens, Inc
111 East 14th Street
Suite #349
New York, NY 10003
414-332-3520
800-542-2595
Fax: 877-542-2596
www.garethstevens.com

Publication Date: 1991
ISBN: 0-836804-76-7

4197 Freshwater Resources and Interstate Cooperation: Strategies to Mitigate an Environmental Risk
SUNY Press
22 Corporate Woods Boulevard
3rd Floor
Albany, NY 12211
518-472-5000
866-430-7869
Fax: 518-472-5038
info@sunypress.edu
www.sunypress.edu

Also in hardcover, 60.00.
Publication Date: 2008 184 pages
Frederick D Gordon, Author

4198 Living Waters: Reading the Rivers of the Lower Great Lakes
SUNY Press
22 Corporate Woods Boulevard
3rd Floor
Albany, NY 12211
518-472-5000
866-430-7869
Fax: 518-472-5038
info@sunypress.edu
www.sunypress.edu

Also in hardcover for 45.00
Publication Date: 2009 213 pages
Margaret Wooster, Author

4199 Managing Troubled Water: The Role of Marine Environmental Monitoring
Duke University Press
905 W Main Street
Suite 18B
Durham, NC 27701
919-687-3600
Fax: 919-688-4574
Publication Date: 1990

4200 Turning the Tide: Saving the Chesapeake Bay
Island Press
2000 M Street NW
Suite 650
Wasington, DC 20036
707-983-6432
800-828-1302
info@islandpress.org
www.islandpress.org

The Chesapeake Bay is one of the most productive and important ecosystems on earth, and as such is a model for other estuaries facing the demands of commerce, tourism, transportation, recreation and other uses. Turning the Tidepresents a comprehensive look at two decades of efforts to save the bay, outlining which methods have worked and which have not.
Publication Date: 2003 352 pages
ISBN: 1-559635-48-7
Tom Horton, Author
Katie Dolan, Chair
Pamela Murphy, Vice Chair

4201 Using Common Sense to Protect the Coasts: The Need to Expand Coastal Barrier Resources
Coast Alliance
PO Box 505
Sandy Hook, NJ 00773
732-872-0111
coast@coastalliance.org
www.coastalliance.org

This report gives a common sense approach to protecting coastal areas from unwise development that would benefit American taxpayers.
Publication Date: 1990

Library Collections

4202 3M: 201 Technical Library
3M Center
St. Paul, MN 55133
651-575-1300
Fax: 651-736-3940
www.3M.com

High-tech library that manages its collection with 3M digital identification.

4203 Acres International Library
100 Sylvan Parkway
Amherst, NY 14228
716-689-3737
Fax: 716-689-3749

Serves clients in the hydroelectric power, highways and bridges, mining, heavy industrial, civil/geotechnical and environmental and hazardous waste sectors.
Marion D'Amboise, Librarian

4204 Alaska Department of Fish and Game Habitat Library
333 Raspberry Road 907-267-2189
Anchorage, AK 99518 Fax: 907-349-1723
dfg.dwc.mcneil-info@alaska.gov
www.adfg.alaska.gov
Celia Rozen, Contact

4205 Alaska Resources Library and Information Services
ARLIS Suite 111 Library Building 907-272-7547
3211 Providence Drive Fax: 907-786-7652
Anchorage, AK 99508 reference@arlis.org
www.arlis.org
ARLIS is the mother lode of Alaska resources information. ARLIS has served as the central library for rresource information supporting management of 235 million acres of federal and 100 million acres of state and water resourcesthroughout Alaska.
Publication Date: 1997
Carrie Holba, Reference Services Coord

4206 American Academy of Pediatrics
141 NW Point Boulevard 847-434-4000
PO Box 747 800-433-9016
Elk Grove Village, IL 60007 Fax: 847-434-8000
www.aap.org
Dedicated to the health of all children.

4207 American Water Works Association
6666 W Quincy Avenue 303-794-7711
Denver, CO 80235 Fax: 303-347-0804
www.awwa.org
Dedicated to the promotion of public health and welfare in the provision of drinking water of unquestionable quality and sufficient quantity. AWWA must be proactive and effective in advancing the technology, science, management andgovernment policies relative to the stewardship of water.
Jack W Hoffbuhr, Executive Director

4208 Aquatic Research Institute: Aquatic Sciences and Technology Archive
2242 Davis Court 510-782-4058
Hayward, CA 94545 Fax: 510-784-0945
Library and data base in aquatic sciences and technologies also research faculty in aquatic sciences.
V Parker, Archv

4209 Arizona State Energy Office Information Center
3800 N Central 602-280-1402
Suite 1200 Fax: 602-280-1445
Phoenix, AZ 85012
Maxine Robertson, Assistant Director

4210 Arizona State University Architecture and Environmental Design Library
College of Architecture and Environmental Design
4300 480-965-6400
Tempe, AZ 85287 Fax: 480-727-6965
deborah.koshinsky@asu.edu
www.asu.edu
Deborah H Koshinsky, Director

4211 Arkansas Energy Office Library
1 State Capitol Mall 501-682-1370
Little Rock, AR 72201 Fax: 501-682-2703
cbenson@1800arkansas.com

4212 Atmospheric Sciences Model Division Library
US Environmental Protection Agency
1200 Pennsylvania Avenue N.W. 202-272-0167
Washington, DC 20004 www.epa.gov
Serves the NOAA Division assigned to support the EPA National Exposure Laboratory and Office of Air Quality Planning and Standards. The major field of interest is the meteorological aspects of air pollution, including numerical andphysical model development and application.
Evelyn M Poole-Kober, Tech. Pubns.

4213 Belle W Baruch Institute for Marine Biology and Coastal Research Library
607 EWS Building 803-777-5288
Columbia, SC 29208 Fax: 803-777-3935

4214 Bickelhaupt Arboretum Education Center
340 S 14th Street 319-242-4771
Clinton, IA 52742

4215 Brown University Center for Environmental Studies Library
85 Waterman Street 401-863-3449
Box 1951 Fax: 401-863-3839
Providence, RI 00291 envstudies@brown.edu
www.brown.edu
The Center for Environmental Studies at Brown University was established with the primary aim of educating individuals to solve challenging environmental problems both at the local and global levels. It also works directly to improvehuman well-being and environmental quality through community, city, and state partnerships in service and research.
J Timmons Roberts, Program Director

4216 Burroughs Audubon Center and Library
Burroughs Audubon Society
21905 SW Woods Chapel Road 816-795-8177
Independence, MO 64050

4217 CH2M Hill
Corvallis Regional Office Library
9191 South Jamaica Street 720-286-2000
Englewood, CO 80112 www.ch2m.com
The firm's solutions keep sustainability always in mind, along with government regulations, environmental concerns, maintenance requirements, and public perceptions. A team of experts brings the knowledge gained from a wide range ofprojects around the world, rigourous attention to detail, and a capability to create innovative solutions that are also models for the industry.
Shirley Fisher, COO

4218 California Energy Commission Library
1516 9th Street 916-654-4292
MS 10 Fax: 916-654-4046
Sacramento, CA 95814 library@energy.state.ca.us
www.energy.ca.gov
The state's central repository for information on all forms of energy. The collection consists of more than 22,000 titles on energy policy, energy conservation, energy consumption, electric utilities, environmental issues, petroleum,natural gas, solar, wind, biomass, nuclear power and related subjects. The Library serves Energy Commission staff, California state government agencies, the Legislature and its staff, and members of the public.
Robert Weisenmiller, Ph.D., Chair
Karen Douglas, J.D., Commissioner

4219 California State Resources Agency Library
1416 9th Street 916-653-2225
Room 117 Fax: 916-653-1856
Sacramento, CA 95814 www.water.ca.gov/about/contacts.cfm
Contains books, documents and subscriptions on topics including: flood control; natural resources (in California); endangered species (in California); soil conservation; water; water pollution; water quality; water resources;conservation and water supply.
Mark W. Cowin, Director
Laura King Moon, Chief Deputy Director

4220 Center for Coastal Fisheries and Habitat Research: Rice Library
101 Pivers Island Road 252-728-8713
Beaufort, NC 28516 Fax: 252-838-0809
patti.marraro@noaa.gov
Ensures the delivery of scientific, technical, and legistlative information to library users including NOAA staff, general public, academia, industry, and governmental agencies. Houses comprehensive coverage of marine fisheries,fisheries statistics, habitat restoration, mapping and remote sensing, marine chemistry, pollution and toxicology, living marine resources, protected species, and oceanography.
Patti M Marraro, Technical Info Specialist

4221 Center for Health, Environment and Justice Library
150 S Washington Street, Ste 300 703-237-2249
PO Box 6806 Fax: 703-237-8389
Falls Church, VA 22040-6806 chej@chej.org
www.chej.org
Works to build healthy communities, with social justice, economic well-being, and democratic governance. We believe this can happen when individuals from communities have the power to play an integral role in promoting human health andenvironmental integrity. Our role is to provide the tools to build strong, healthy communities where people can live, work, learn, play and pray.
Lois Marie Gibbs, Executive Director

4222 Clinton River Watershed Council Library
1115 W. Avon Road 248-601-0606
Rochester, MI 48309 Fax: 248-601-1280
contact@crwc.org
www.crwc.org
Susan Kelsey, President
Jeff Bednar, 1st Vice President

4223 Colorado River Board of California
770 Fairmont Avenue 818-500-1625
Suite 100 Fax: 818-543-4685
Glendale, CA 91203 crb@crb.ca.gov
www.crb.ca.gov
Tanya M. Trujillo, Executive Director

4224 Columbia River Inter-Tribal Fish Commission
StreamNet Library
700 NE Multnomah 503-238-0667
Ste 1200 Fax: 503-235-4228
Portland, OR 97232 oftl@critfc.org
www.streamnetlibrary.org
Serving the scientific and environmental community of the Pacific Northwest, The StreamNet Library works in cooperation with the region's fish and wildlife recovery efforts. The library provides access to technical information on theColumbia Basin fisheries, ecosystem and other relevant subjects for states in the Pacfic Northwest. The library collections emphasize less commonly available grey literature, such as consultant's reports, state documents and nonprofit organizations'reports.
Lenora Oftedahl, Librarian
Todd Hannon, Assistant Librarian

4225 DER Research Library
Pennsylvania Department of Environmental Resources
Box 8458 717-787-9647
Harrisburg, PA 17105 Fax: 717-772-0288

4226 Dawes Arboretum Library
7770 Jacksontown Road SE 740-323-2355
Newark, OH 43056 800-44D-AWES
Fax: 740-323-4058
www.dawesarb.org
Luke Messinger, Executive Director
Laura Appleman, PR/Marketing Director

4227 Delaware River Basin Commission Library
25 State Police Drive 609-883-9500
Box 7360 Fax: 609-883-9522
West Trenton, NJ 00862 www.nj.gov/drbc
The Commission is a federal/interstate agency responsible for managing the water resources at the Delaware River Basin.
Steve Tambini, Executive Director
Paula Schmitt, Secretary

4228 Division of Water Resources Library
Kansas Department of Agriculture
109 SW 9th Street 785-296-3717
2nd Floor Fax: 785-296-1176
Topeka, KS 66612

4229 Duke University Biology: Forestry Library
Duke University
411 Chapel Drive 919-660-5880
Box 90193 Fax: 919-660-5923
Durham, NC 27708 asklib@duke.edu
www.lib.duke.edu
Shawn Miller, Director

4230 Earthworm Recycling Information Center
35 Medford Street 617-628-1844
Somerville, MA 00214 Fax: 617-628-2773
info@earthwormrecycling.org
www.earthwormrecycling.org
Jeff Coyne, Executive Director

4231 Eastern States Office Library
US Bureau of Land Management
7450 Boston Boulevard 703-440-1561
Springfield, VA 22153 Fax: 703-440-1599
Terry Lewis, Contact

4232 Eastern Technical Associates Library
PO Box 1009 919-878-3188
Garner, NC 27529 Fax: 919-872-5199
tomrose@eta-is-opacity.com
www.eta-is-opacity.com
Environmental consulting firm. Research results published in government reports.
Publication Date: 1979
Thomas H Rose, President

4233 Ecology Center Library
2530 San Pablo Avenue 510-548-2220
Berkeley, CA 94702 Fax: 510-548-2240
info@ecologycenter.org
www.ecologycenter.org
Provides educational materials with special focus on the environmental concerns of the California Bay Area. Some topics covered include renewable energy, permaculture, gardening, recycling,

environmental education, sustainabledevelopment, climate action, and environmental justice.
Raquel Pinderhughes, President
Becca Prager, Secretary

4234 Environment and Natural Resources Branch Library
US Department of Justice
One Congress Street 617-918-1807
Suite 1100 Fax: 617-918-1810
Boston, MA 00211 friedman.fred@epa.gov
Research library for Solid Wasteto conduct research and answer questions in the subject fields of nonhazarodus solid waste and recycling.
Leola Decker, Librarian

4235 Environmental Action Coalition Library: Resource Center
625 Broadway 212-677-1601
2nd Floor Fax: 212-505-8613
New York, NY 10012 www.enviro-action.org
Paul Berizzi, Executive Director

4236 Environmental Coalition on Nuclear Power Library
433 Orlando Avenue 814-237-3900
State College, PA 16803 Fax: 814-237-3900
Dr Judith Johnsrud, Executive Officer

4237 Environmental Contracting Center Library
ENSR Consulting and Engineering
Box 2105 970-493-8878
Fort Collins, CO 80522 800-722-2440
www.aecom.com
Michael Bruke, Chairman
Carla Christofferson, Executive Vice President

4238 Environmental Research Associates Library
PO Box 219 610-449-7400
Villanova, PA 19085 Fax: 610-449-7404
Research and consulting ecologists and testing firm. Research results published in professional journals. Research results for private clients.
Publication Date: 1970
M H Levin PhD, Director

4239 Federated Conservationists of Westchester County (FCWC) Office Resource Library
78 N Broadway 914-422-4053
White Plains, NY 10603 Fax: 914-289-0539
info@fcwc.org
www.fcwc.org
Jason Klien, Co-President
Sara Goddard, Vice President

4240 Fish and Wildlife Reference Service
5430 Grosvenor Lane 301-492-6403
Suite 110 800-582-3421
Bethesda, MD 20814 Fax: 301-564-4059
To provide policy guidance regarding the operation and use of the Fish and Wildlife Reference Service.
Paul E Wilson, Project Manager

4241 Florida Conservation Foundation
1191 Orange Avenue 407-644-5377
Winter Park, FL 32789

4242 Forest History Society Library and Archives
701 William Vickers Avenue 919-682-9319
Durham, NC 27701 Fax: 919-682-2349
coakes@duke.edu
www.foresthistory.org
The Forest History Society is a non-profit educational institution that links the past to the future by identifying, collecting, preserving, interpreting, and disseminating information on the history of people, forests, and theirrelated resources.
Publication Date: 1946
Cheryl Oakes, Librarian
Steven Anderson, President

4243 Galveston District Library
US Army Corps of Engineers
Box 1229 409-766-3196
Galveston, TX 77553 Fax: 409-766-3905
clark.bartee@usace.army.mil
www.swg.usace.army.mil
Clark Bartee

4244 Georgia State Forestry Commission Library
PO Box 819 912-751-3480
Macon, GA 31202 Fax: 912-751-3465
Fred Allen, Director

4245 Glen Helen Association Library
405 Corry Street 937-767-7375
Yellow Springs, OH 45387 www.glenhelen.org

4246 Great Lakes Environmental Research Laboratory
2205 Commonwealth Boulevard 734-741-2235
Ann Arbor, MI 48105 Fax: 734-741-2055
www.glerl.com
Conducts integrated interdiciplinary environmental research in support of resource management and environmental services in costal and esturine water with special emphasis on the Great Lakes.

4247 Huxley College of Environmental Studies
516 High Street 360-650-3000
Bellingham, WA 98225 huxley.wwu.edu
One of the oldest environmental studies colleges in the nation. Innovative and indisciplinary academic programs reflect a broad view of the physical, biological, social and cultural world.
Hailey Outzs, Coordinater

4248 Illinois State Water Survey Library
208 Water Survey Research Center 217-244-5459
2204 Griffith Drive Fax: 217-333-6540
Champaign, IL 61820 info@isws.illinois.edu
www.sws.uiuc.edu/chief
The Illinois State Water Survey, a division of the office of Scientific Research and Analysis of the Illinois Department of Natural Resources and affiliated with the University of Illinois, is the primary agency in Illinois concernedwith water and atmosheric resources.
Patricia G Morse, Librarian
Dr. Misganaw Demissie, Director

4249 Institute of Ecosystem Studies
2801 Sharon Turnpike 845-677-5343
Millbrook, NY 12545 Fax: 845-677-5976
www.caryinstitute.org
Ecology research and education institution; independent; international.
Jill Cadwallader, Public Information Officer

4250 International Academy at Santa Barbara Library
800 Garden Street 805-965-5010
Suite D Fax: 805-965-6071
Santa Barbara, CA 93101
Susan J Shaffer, Office Manager

4251 International Game Fish Association
300 Gulf Stream Way 954-927-2628
Dania Beach, FL 33004 Fax: 954-924-4299
hq@igfa.org
www.igfa.org
The International Game Fish Association is a nonprofit organization committed to the conservation of game fish and the promotion of responsible, ethical angling practices through science, education, rulemaking and record keeping.
Publication Date: 1939
Rob Kramer, President

4252 Interstate Oil and Gas Compact Commission Library
900 NE 23rd Street 405-525-3556
Box 53127 Fax: 405-525-3592
Oklahoma City, OK 73152 iogcc@iogcc.state.ok.us
W Timothy Dowd, Executive Director

4253 Lake Michigan Federation
150 N. Michigan Ave. 312-939-0838
Suite 700 Fax: 312-939-2708
Chicago, IL 60601 alliance@greatlakes.org
www.greatlakes.org
Works to restore fish and wildlife habitat, conserve land and water, and eliminate pollution in the watershed of America's largest lake. We achieve these through education, research, law, science, economics and strategic partnerships.
Lori Colman, Chair
Sanjiv Sinha , Ph.D., Vice Chairman

4254 Lionael A Walford Library
74 Magruder Road 732-872-3035
Highlands, NJ 00773 Fax: 732-872-3088
Claire L Steimle, Librarian

4255 Los Angeles County Sanitation District Technical Library
PO Box 4998 562-699-7411
Whittier, CA 90607 Fax: 562-699-5422
info@lacsd.org
www.lacsd.org

4256 Louisiana Department of Environmental Quality Information Resource Center
7290 Bluebonnet Boulevard 225-765-0169
2nd Floor Fax: 225-765-0222
Baton Rouge, LA 70810
To promote a healthy environment by providing a specialized environmental library to meet the informational and educational needs of the DEQ employees and the citizens of Louisiana.
Patty Birkett, Tech. Librarian

4257 Marine Environmental Sciences Consortium
Dauphin Island Sea Lab
101 Bienville Boulevard 251-861-2141
Dauphin Island, AL 36528 Fax: 251-861-4646
lpritchett@disl.org
www.disl.org
Carolyn Wood, Assistant Editor
Dr. Just Cebrian, Senior Marine Scientist III

4258 Massachusetts Audubon Society's Berkshire Wildelife Sanctuaries
Pleasant Valley Wildlife Sanctuary
472 W Mountain Road 413-637-0320
Lenox, MA 00124 Fax: 413-637-0499
berkshires@massaudubon.org
The Massachusetts Audubon Society is an environmental organization with emphases in conservation, advocacy and education. The advocacy effort is statewide and features a legislative team in Boston.
Publication Date: 1896
Rene Laubach, Sanctuary Director

4259 Minneapolis Public Library and Information Center
Technology and Science Department
300 Nicolet Mall 612-372-6570
Minneapolis, MN 55401 Fax: 312-372-6546
www.hclib.org/about/locations/minneapolis-central
The varied collection in the Technology/Science/Government Documents department runs from agriculture to zoology, computers to cooking, engineering to handicrafts, medicine to motorcycle repair to military science. Special resourcesinclude a complete US Patent and Trademark collection and the CASSIS Patent Trademark Databases, a collection of US industrial standards, including publications from ANSI (American National Standards Institutes).

4260 Minnesota Department of Natural Resources DNR Library
500 Lafayette Road 651-259-5506
Box 21 Fax: 651-297-4946
St. Paul, MN 55155 www.dnr.state.mn.us/library/index.html
15,000 titles on natural resource subjects available on interlibrary loan.
Jo Ann Musumeci, Librarian
Denise Legato, Administrator

4261 Minnesota Department of Trade and Economic Development Library
500 Metro Square 651-296-8902
121 7th Place E Fax: 651-296-1290
St. Paul, MN 55101
Pat Fenton, Sr. Librarian

4262 Minot State University Bottineau Library
105 Simrall Boulevard 701-228-5454
Bottineau, ND 58318 Fax: 701-228-5468
Jan Wysocki, Library Director

4263 Mississippi Department of Environmental Quality Library
P. O. Box 2261 601-961-5024
Jackson, MS 39225 Fax: 601-354-6965
ronnie_sanders@deq.state.ms.us
www.deq.state.ms.us
Geology and environmental reference library. Holdings in geosciences, hydrology, pollution control, paleontology, petroleum geology, land and water resources. Special collections; Topographic maps, United States, State andInternational Geoloical survey publications.
Ronnie Sanders, Librarian
Gray Rikard, Executive Director

4264 Missouri Department of Natural Resources Geological Survey & Resource Assessment Division
Box 250 573-368-2101
Rolla, MO 65401 Fax: 573-368-2111
Mimi Garstang, Director/State Geologist

4265 **National Audubon Society: Aullwood Audubon Center and Farm Library**
1000 Aullwood Road 937-890-7360
Dayton, OH 45414 Fax: 937-890-2382
aullwood@gemair.com
web4.audubon.org/local/sanctuary/aullwood
Known as the Miami Valley's first educational farm, here visitors will discover a variety of native grasses and flowers, 300 year old oak trees and threatened bird species.

4266 **National Institute for Urban Wildlife Library**
10921 Trotting Ridge Way 301-596-3311
Columbia, MD 21004 www.webdirectory.com/wildlife/
Louise E Dove, Wildlife Biology

4267 **Native Americans for a Clean Environment Resource Office**
Box 1671 918-458-4322
Tahlequah, OK 74465 Fax: 918-458-0322
NACE is to raise the consciousness of Indian people and the general public about environment hazards, with an emphasis on the nuclear industry.
Lance Hughes, Executive Director

4268 **Nature Conservancy Long Island Chapter**
Uplands Farm Environmental Center
250 Lawrence Hill Road 516-367-3225
Cold Spring Harbor, NY 11724 Fax: 516-367-4715
To preserve the plants, animals and natural communities that represent the diversity of life on Earth by protecting the lands and waters they need to survive.
Mark R. Tercek, President/CEO
Thomas J. Tierney, Chairman

4269 **Nebraska Natural Resources Commission Planning Library**
301 Centennial Mall S 402-471-2081
Box 94876 Fax: 402-471-3132
Lincoln, NE 68509 www.nrc.state.ne.us/

4270 **New England Coalition on Nuclear Pollution Library**
PO Box 545 802-257-0336
Brattleboro, VT 00530 energy@necnp.org
www.necnp.org

4271 **New England Governors' Conference Reference Library**
76 Summer Street 617-423-6900
Boston, MA 00211 Fax: 617-423-7327
www.negc.org

4272 **Occupational Safety and Health Library**
1111 3rd Avenue 206-553-5930
Suite 715 Fax: 206-553-6499
Seattle, WA 98101

4273 **Ohio Environmental Protection Agency Library**
1200 Pennsylvania Avenue N.W. 202-272-0167
Washington, DC 20004 www.epa.state.oh.us
Ruth Ann Evans, Librarian

4274 **Peninsula Conservation Foundation Library of the Environment**
3921 E Bayshore Road 650-962-9876
Palo Alto, CA 94303 Fax: 650-962-8234

4275 **People, Food and Land Foundation Library**
PO Box 314 559-855-3710
Prather, CA 93651 mail@sunmt.org
www.sunmt.org

4276 **Rainforest Action Network Library**
221 Pine Street 415-398-4404
Suite 500 Fax: 415-398-2732
San Francisco, CA 94104
Rainforest Action Network works to protect the Earth's rainforests and support the rights of their inhabitants through education, grassroots organizing and non-violent direct action.
Michael Brune, Executive Director
Mrtha DiSario, Director

4277 **Region 2 Library**
US Environmental Protection Agency
1200 Pennsylvania Avenue N.W. 202-272-0167
Washington, DC 20004 www.epa.gov
Is a research and reference library for use by EPA staff, EPA contractors, other government agencies, and the public. The library contains or has access to scientific and technical materials in paper and electronic media related to awide variety of environmental issues, with and emphasis on EPA's Region 2.
Eveline M Goodman, Head Librarian

4278 **Region 9 Library**
US Environmental Protection Agency
1200 Pennsylvania Avenue N.W. 202-272-0167
Washington, DC 20004 www.epa.gov/region9/library
Deborra Samuels, Head Librarian & Coordinator

4279 **Rob and Bessie Welder Wildlife Foundation Library**
Walker Wildlife Foundation 361-364-2643
PO Box 1400 Fax: 361-364-2650
Sinton, TX 78387 www.members.aol.com/welderwf/welderhome
Private, nonprofit operation foundation which conducts research and education in wildlife management and related fields. Funds graduate fellowships and conducts its reserach and education program on its 7,800 acre wildlife refuge inthe surrounding South Texas region and throughout the United States.
Dr. D Lynn Drawe, Director
Vandra Davis, Librarian

4280 **Schuylkill Center for Environmental Education**
8480 Hagy's Mill Road 215-482-7300
Philadelphia, PA 19128 Fax: 215-482-8158
scee@schuylkillcenter.org
www.schuylkillcenter.org

Karin James, Resource Librarian
Barbara Baumgartner, Environmental Educator

4281 **Society of American Foresters Information Center**
5400 Grosvenor Lane 301-897-8720
Bethesda, MD 20814 866-897-8720
Fax: 301-897-3690
membership@safnet.org
www.eforester.org

An organization that represents the forestry profession in the United States. Its mission is to advance the science, education, technology and practice of forestry.
Jeff Ghannam, Director Media Relations

4282 **Solartherm Library**
1315 Apple Avenue 301-587-8686
Silver Spring, MD 20910 Fax: 301-587-8688
www.solartherm.com

4283 Solid Waste Association of North America
1100 Wayne Avenue
Suite 700 800-467-9262
Silver Spring, MD 20910 Fax: 301-589-7068
info@swana.org
www.swana.org

Nonprofit trade association designed to serve the municipal solid waste industry in cutting-edge informational and technilogical practices.
Dr John Skinner, Executive Director
Michelle P. Leonard, Vice President

4284 Southeast Fisheries Laboratory Library
75 Virginia Beach Drive 305-361-4229
Miami, FL 33149 Fax: 305-361-4499
www.sefsc.noaa.gov/library

4285 Southwest Research and Information Center
105 Stanford SE 505-262-1862
PO Box 4524 Fax: 505-262-1864
Albuquerque, NM 87106 Info@sric.org
www.sric.org

SRIC exists to provide timely, accurate information to the public on matters that affect the environment, human health, and communities in order to protect natural resources, promote citizen participation, and ensure environmental andsocial justice now and for future generations.
Dan Hancock, Administrator
Annette Aguayo, Information Specialist

4286 St Paul Plant Pathology Library
395 Borlaug Hall 612-625-9777
St Paul Campus
St Paul, MN 55108

Subject oriented library, specializing in plant diseases, plant virology, mycology, mycotoxicology and the effects of air pollution on vegetation. The collection contains approximately 8000 volumes of books, periodicals and PlantPathology theses. Over 50 current periodicals are recieved.

4287 St. Paul Forestry Library
University of Minnesota
499 Wilson Library 612-624-3321
309 19th Avenue South Fax: 612-624-3733
Minneapolis, MN 55455 heroL228@umn.edu
www.lib.umn.edu/naturalresources

Houses a general collection of books, journals, government documents, maps, and pamphlets relating to the subjects of forestry, forest products, outdoor recreation, range management, and remote sensing. There is also a small generalrefernce section. Also compiles and maintains four databases focused on aspects of forestry: Social Sciences in Forestry, Urban Forestry, Tropical Conservation and Development, Trails Planning Construction and Maintenance Planning.
Philip Herold, Librarian

4288 State University of New York
College of Environmental Science and Forestry
Environamental Science and Forestry 315-470-6715
Syracuse, NY 13210 Fax: 315-470-6512
www.esf.edu/moonlib

Moon Library supports the SUNY College of Environmental Science and Forestry where students major in Engineering, Chemistry, Biology, Landscape Architecture, Forest Resources Management and Environmental Studies.
Stephen Weiter, Director/College Libraries

4289 Staten Island Institute of Arts and Sciences
William T Davis Education Center
75 Stuyvesant Place 718-987-6233
State Island, NY 10301 Fax: 718-273-5683
www.statenislandmuseum.org

Ralph Branca, Chairperson
Doloerss Morris, Vice Chairperson

4290 Texas Water Commission Library
PO Box 13087 512-463-7834
Austin, TX 78711

4291 Turner, Collie and Braden Library
Box 130089 713-267-2826
Houston, TX 77219 Fax: 713-780-0838
rushbrookd@tcbhou.com

David Rushbrook, Librarian
Renee Miller, Library Assistant

4292 US Bureau of Land Management
California State Office
2135 Butano Drive 916-978-4400
Sacramento, CA 95825 Fax: 916-978-4305

It is the mission of the Bureau of Land management to sustain the health, diversity and productivity of the public lands for the use an employment of present and future generations.

4293 US Bureau of Land Management Library
Denver Federal Center Building 50 303-236-6650
Box 25047 Fax: 303-236-4810
Denver, CO 80225 blm_library@blm.gov
www.blm.gov

The BLM Library serves the information and research needs of BLM personnel. The library also serves as the point of contract for bureau publications and information with other federal agencies and the public. The collection covers allaspects of land management and natural resources.
Barbara Campbell, Director

4294 US Department of Agriculture: National Agricultural Library, Water Quality Info Center
10301 Baltimore Boulevard 301-504-6077
Beltsville, MD 20705 Fax: 301-504-6409
wqic.nal.usda.gov

Collects, organizes and communicates the scientific findings, educational methologies and public policy issues related to water and agriculture.
Joseph R Makuch, Coord. WQIC

4295 US Geological Survey: Great Lakes Science Center
1451 Green Road 734-994-3331
Ann Arbor, MI 48105 Fax: 734-994-8780
GS-B-GLSC-Webmaster@usgs.gov
www.glsc.usgs.gov

The USGS Great Lakes Science Center exists to meet the Nation's need for scientific information for restoring, enhancing, managing, and protecting living resources and their habitats in the Great Lakes. The center is headquartered inAnn Arbor, Michigan, and has biological research stations and vessels located throughout the Great Lakes basin.
Russell Strach, Center Director
Jacqueline F Savino, Deputy Center Director

4296 US Geological Survey: Upper Midwest Environmental Sciences Center Library
2630 Fanta Reed Road 608-783-6451
La Crosse, WI 54603 Fax: 608-783-6066
www.umesc.usgs.gov

A federal library with technical holdings mainly in aquatic sciences, bird and amphibean materials.
Kathy Mannstedt, Librarian

4297 US Geological Survey: Water Resources Division Library
375 S Euclid Avenue 520-670-6201
Tucson, AZ 85719

4298 US Geological Survey: Wetland and Aquatic Research Center
700 Cajundome Boulevard 337-266-8500
Lafayette, LA 70506-3152 Fax: 337-266-8513
nwrcinfo@usgs.gov
www.nwrc.usgs.gov

The Wetland and Aquatic Reseach Center, created in 2015 from the merger of two US science biology centers, develops and disseminates scientific information needed for understanding the ecology and values of the nation's wetlands andother aquatic and coastal ecosystems, and manages and restores wetland, coastal, and aquatic habitats and associated plant and animal communities.
Publication Date: 2015
Thomas Doyle, Deputy Director
Kenneth Rice, Cetner Director

4299 Unexpected Wildlife Refuge Library
17314 McCourtney Ave 530-477-1757
Grass Valley, CA 95949 info@animalplace.org
www.animalplace.org

Kim Sturla, Executive Director
Marji Beach, Education Director

4300 University of California
1 Shields Avenue 530-752-1011
Davis, CA 95616 ucdavis.edu

4301 University of Florida Coastal Engineering Archives
209 Yon Hall 352-392-2710
Gainesville, FL 32611 Fax: 352-392-2710
Twedell@coastal.ufl.edu

Helen Twedell, Archivist
Kimberly Hunt, Sr. Library Technical Asst

4302 University of Hawaii at Manoa Water Resources Center
2540 Dole Street 808-956-7847
Homes Hall 283 Fax: 808-956-5044
Honolulu, HI 96822 morav@hawaii.edu
www.wrrc.hawaii.edu

Coordinates and conducts research to identify, characterize and quantify water/environmental related problems in the state of Hawaii. Based on the research WRRC makes recommendations to all agencies and organizations withresponsibilities to manage the water/ environmental resources in Hawaii.
Phillip Morakik, Technology Transfer Spec
James Moncur, Director

4303 University of Illinois at Chicago
Energy Resource Center
851 S Morgan Street 312-996-4490
12th Floor Fax: 312-996-5420
Chicago, IL 60607 uic.edu

The Energy Resources center is an interdiciplinary public service, research, and special projects organization dedicated to improving energy efficiency and the environment. Conducts studies in the fields of energy and environment andprovides industry, utilities, government agencies and the public with assistance, information, and advice on new technologies, public policy, and professional development training.
James Hartnett, Director

4304 University of Maryland: Center for Environmental Science Chesapeake Biological Lab
P.O. BOX 775 410-228-9250
Cambridge, MD 21613 Fax: 410-326-7302
boesch@umces.edu
www.umces.edu/cbl

Kathleen A Heil, Librarian
Thomas Miller, Director

4305 University of Montana Wilderness Institute Library
32 Campus Drive 406-243-5361
Missoula, MT 59812 Fax: 406-243-4845
wi@cfc.umt.edu
www.cfc.umt.edu/wi

Natalie Dawson, Director
Rachel James, Assistant Director

4306 Vermont Institute of Natural Sciences Library
27023 Church Hill Road 802-457-2779
Woodstock, VT 00509 Fax: 802-457-2779

4307 Voices from the Earth
105 Stanford SE 505-262-1862
PO Box 4524 Fax: 505-262-1864
Albuquerque, NM 87196 Info@sric.org
www.sric.org

SRIC exists to provide timely, accurate information to the public on matters that affect the environment, human health, and communities in order to protect natural resources, promote citizen participation, and ensure environmental andsocial justice now and for future generations.
Dan Hancock, Administrator
Annette Aguayo, Information Specialist

4308 Wasserman Public Affairs Library
University of Texas at Austin
General Libraries 512-495-4400
Sid Richardson Hall 3243 Fax: 512-495-4347
Austin, TX 78712 pal@lib.utexas.edu
www.lib.utexas.edu/pal

Stephen Littrell, Head Librarian
Ester Bolmey, Library Technical Assistant

4309 Western Ecology Division Library
US Environmental Protection Agency
1200 Pennsylvania Avenue N.W. 202-272-0167
Washington, DC 20004 www.epa.gov
Publication Date: 1966
Kathy Martin, Program Analyst
Mary O'Brien, Librarian

4310 Wildlife Management Institute Library
1440 Upper Bermudian Road 717-677-4480
Gardners, PA 17324 Fax: 202-408-5059
www.wildlifemanagementinstitute.org

Richard E McCabe, Sec./Dir., Pubns.

4311 Wisconsin Department of Natural Resources Library
Box 7921 608-266-8933
Madison, WI 53707 Fax: 608-266-5226
dnr.wi.gov

Contains books, journals, and EPA reports on air pollution, geology, hazardous waste, natural resources management, recycling, soil pollution, solid waste, toxic substances, waste minimization, wastewater, water pollution, andwetlands.
Erin Matiszik, Librarian

4312 Wisconsin's Water Library at UW Madison
University of Wisconsin

1975 Willow Drive, Floor 2 608-262-3069
Madison, WI 53706 Fax: 608-262-0591
AskWater@aqua.wisc.edu
www.aqua.wisc.edu/waterlibrary

Wisconsin's Water Library is a collection of materials that cover all major topics in water resources, but is particularly strong in Wisconsin and Great Lakes water issues, groundwater protection, wetlands issues, and the impacts ofagricultural chemicals. The collection consists of over 31,000 hard copy and microfiche documents, over 35 journals and 130 newsletters.
Anne K Moser, Special Librarian

4313 Yale University School of Forestry and Environmental Studies Library
205 Prospect Street 203-432-5132
New Haven, CT 00651 Fax: 203-432-5942
www.library.yale.edu/scilib/forestl.html

A part of the Yale University Library System, the library serves the resource needs of the graduate students and faculty of Yale's 100 year old school of Forestry and Environmental Studies.
Carla Heister, Librarian

Publishers

4314 Academic Press: New York
Academic Press
15 E 26th Street 212-592-1000
15th Floor
New York, NY 10010

4315 Adison Wesley Longman
Pearson
330 Hudson St 212-641-2400
New York, NY 10013 800-563-9196
Fax: 800-263-7733
pearson.com

One integrated and diverse company offering learning resources on an extraordinary level. Pearson has an estblished reputation for producing market-leading educational products and services as well as a comprehensive range ofbest-selling consumer, environmental technical and professional titles.
Glen Moreno, Chairman
John Fallon, Chief Executive

4316 Blackwell Publishers
Blackwell Publishers
350 Main Street 781-388-8200
Malden, MA 00214 Fax: 781-388-8210
as.wiley.com/WileyCDA/Section/id-301698.html

Blackwell Publishers are dedicated to serving the global academic community. We recognize that publishing is about making connections. Knowledge is not constrained by national or liguistic boundries. Many academics are engaged in bothteaching and research. Our readers are often our authors as well. We develop books for students which take account of the latest research and we aim to make the journals we publish as acessible as possible.

4317 Boxwood Press
183 Ocean View Boulevard 408-375-9110
Pacific Grove, CA 93950 Fax: 408-375-0430
boxwood@boxwoodpress.com

Publishes significant titles in the areas of Natural History, Area Studies, General Sciences and Local and Special Interest. Founded in 1952, it first published lab manuals, then expanded to include a variety of mainly biologicaltitles.

4318 CABI Publishing
CAB International 617-395-4056
875 Massachusetts Ave, 7th Floor 800-552-3083
Cambridge, MA 00213 Fax: 617-354-6875
cabi-nao@cabi.org
www.cabi.org

CABI publishing is a leading international, nonprofit publisher in applied life sciences, including animal science, nutrition, integrated crop management and forestry. Our products have a global reputation for quality, relevance andauthority, and are used in over 100 countries. Our long-established print publishing activities include a substantial book and reference work list, and an expanding primary and review journal program.

4319 CRC Press
CRC Press
2000 NW Corporate Boulevard 561-994-0555
Boca Raton, FL 33431 800-272-7737
Fax: 800-374-3401
www.crcpress.com

CRC Press LLC is recognized as a leader in scientific, medical, environmental science, engineering, business, technical, mathamatical, and statistics publishing. CRC Press LLC publishes books, journals, newsletters and databases.Customers have access to publications through individual purchases, bookstores, libraries and on-line acess at www.crcpress.com

4320 Chelsea Green Publishing Company
85 N Main Street 802-295-6300
PO Box 428 800-639-4099
White River Junction, VT 00500 Fax: 802-295-6444
publicity@chelseagreen.com
www.chelseagreen.com

Chelsea Green publishes information that helps us lead pleasurable lives on a planet where human activities are in harmony and balance with nature.Free catolog listing over 250 titles on sustainable living, innovative shelter andorganic gardening.
Alice Blackmer, Publicity Director

4321 DK Publishing
DK Publishing
95 Madison Avenue 212-213-4800
New York, NY 10016 Fax: 212-213-5240

Dorling Kindersley is an international publishing company specialising in the creation of high quality, illustrated information books, interactive software, TV programs and online resources for childern and adults. Founded in London1974, DK now has offices in the UK, USA, Australia, South Africa, India France, Germany and Russia.
Publication Date: 1974

4322 Elsevier Science
Elsevier Sciences
655 Avenue of the Americas 212-633-3730
New York, NY 10010 Fax: 212-633-3680
usinfo-f@elsevier.com

Our focus will be entirely on scientific, technical and medical publishing. Together we can offer customers choice across our portfolio, with outstanding platforms for the delivery of electronic services and a high level of investmentto ensure the development of leading electronic products.

4323 Environmental Working Group
1436 U Street 202-667-6982
Suite 100 www.ewg.org
Washington, DC 20009

The Environmental Working Group is a leading content provider for public interest groups and concerned citizens who are campaigning to protect the environment. Offers reports, articles, technical assistance and the development ofcomputer databases and Internet resources.
Ken Cook, President
Heather White, Executive Director

4324 **Global and Environmental Education Resources**
Global Change Research Information
Suite 250 1717 202-223-6262
Pennsylvania Ave NW Fax: 202-223-3065
Washington, DC 20006 information@gcrio.org
www.gcrio.org/edu.html
Multidisciplinary and international in scope, this collection of resources was selected for its relevance to global change and environmental education. Included is a wide range of resources in a variety of formats for educators andstudents at all levels (K-12 and higher education), librarians, citizens and community groups.

4325 **Grey House Publishing**
4919 Route 22 518-789-8700
P.O. Box 56 800-562-2139
Amenia, NY 12501 Fax: 518-789-0556
books@greyhouse.com
www.greyhouse.com
Directories, handbooks and reference works for public, high school and academic libraries and the business and health communities. Publishes environmental directories for US and Canadian markets.
Leslie Mackenzie, Publisher
Richard Gottlieb, Editor

4326 **Grey House Publishing Canada**
555 Richmond Street West 416-644-6479
2nd Floor 866-433-4739
Toronto, Ontario M5V 3B1 Fax: 416-644-1904
info@greyhouse.ca
www.greyhouse.ca
Canada's largest developer, publisher and distributor of value-added reference information for the academic, library, government and corporate markets. Our mission is to be Canada's one stop shop for information products and services.We license content from media, government and other sources and organize, abstract and compile this content into databases. Through a combination of technology expertise and a full service approach, our solutions provide access to a wide range ofinformation.
Bryon Moore, General Manager

4327 **Institute for Food and Development Policy**
398 60th Street 510-654-4400
Oakland, CA 94618 Fax: 510-654-4551
foodfirst@foodfirst.org
www.foodfirst.org
Publishes books on poverty, agriculture and development, also backgrounders, policy briefs and development reports.
Publication Date: 1975
Eric Holt-GimèNez, Executive Director
Alexandra Toledo, Development Director

4328 **Island Press**
Distribution Center
PO Box 7 707-983-6432
Covelo, CA 95428 800-828-1302
Fax: 707-983-6414
service@islandpress.com
www.islandpress.com
Mission-oriented nonprofit publisher organized in 1984 to help meet the need for accessible, solutions-oriented information through a unique approach that addresses the multidisciplinary nature of environmental problems. Our program isdesigned to translate technical information from a range of disciplines into a book format that is accessible and informative to citizen activists, educators, students and professionals involved in the study or management of environmental problems.
Bernice Hiatt, Customer Service

4329 **It's Academic**
29 West 35th Street 212-216-7800
New York, NY 10001 Fax: 212-564-7854
A tool for teachers who use Routledge books in their classes. To aid in finding the books best suited for your needs, we offer: pages which highlight books designed specifically for your courses, a list of conferences at which wedisplay our books, journal information, a forum for instructors to send us their comments, supplements available on line and a subject search menu.

4330 **Kluwer Academic Publishers**
101 Philip Drive 781-871-6600
Assinippi Park Fax: 781-871-6528
Norwell, MA 00206
A sector of the Wolters Kluwer publishing group. Operates world-wide from offices in Dordrecht, Boston, New York and London. All over the world, scientists and professionals hold our publications in high esteem.

4331 **Krieger Publishing Company**
Krieger Publishing Co.
1725 Krieger Drive 321-724-9542
Malabar, FL 32950 800-724-0025
Fax: 321-951-3671
info@krieger-publishing.com
www.krieger-publishing.com
Krieger Publishing Company produces quality books in various fields of interest. We have an extensive Natural Science listing.
Cheryl Stanton, Advertising

4332 **MIT Press**
One Rogers Street 617-253-5646
Cambridge, MA 00214 Fax: 617-258-6779
mitpress.mit.edu
The only university press in the US whose list is based in science and technology. Our environment list is strong in policy and the social sciences. We are committed to the edges and frontiers of the world - to exploring new fields andnew modes of inquiry. We publish about 200 new books a year and over 40 journals including Global Environmental Politics. We have a long-term commitment to both design excellence and the efficient and creative use of new technologies.
Amy Brand, Director
Bill Trippe, Director of Technology

4333 **McGraw-Hill Education**
The McGraw-Hill Companies
P.O. Box 182605 212-512-2000
Columbus, OH 43218 800-338-3987
Fax: 609-308-4480
customer.service@mheducation.com
www.mheducation.com
A global leader in educational materials and professional information, with offices in more than 30 countries and publications in more than 40 languages, we develop products that influence people's lives from preschool through career.The scope of our operations, the quality of our editorial product and the pace at which we are developing new media to fulfill our customers' information requirements are increasing.
David Levin, President/ CEO
Angelo T. DeGenaro, Chief Information Officer

4334 **National Information Service Corporation**
NISC USA, Wyman Towers 410-243-0797
3100 St. Paul Street Fax: 410-243-0982
Baltimore, MD 21218 www.nisc.com
Publishes information products for access through BiblioLine, our Web search service, or on CD-ROM. Some of our abstract and index services are available in print. NISC's bibliographic and full-text databases cover a wide range oftopics in the natural and social sciences, arts and humanities. Some titles provide comprehensive coverage of particular geographic regions, such as Latin America, Africa, South-East Asia or the Arctic and Antarctic.

4335 O'Reilly & Associates
101 Morris Street
Sebastopol, CA 95472
800-998-9938
Fax: 707-829-0104

Premier information source for leading-edge computer technologies. We offer the knowledge of experts through our books, conferences and web sites. Our books, known for their animals on the covers, occupy a treasured place on theshelves of developers building the next generation of software. Conferences and summits bring innovators together to shape the ideas that spark new industries. From the Internet to the web, Linux, Open Source and peer-to-peer networking, we puttechnologies on the map.

4336 Random House
1540 Broadway
New York, NY 10036
212-782-9000
Fax: 212-302-7985

The world's largest English-language general trade book publisher. It is a division of the Bertelsmann Book Group of Bertelsmann AG, one of the foremost media companies in the world.

4337 Simon & Schuster
1230 Avenue of the Americas
New York, NY 10020
212-698-7000
Fax: 212-698-2359
www.simonandschuster.biz

Carolyn Reidy, President
Jon Anderson, Executive Vice President and

4338 Solano Press Books
Solano Press
PO Box 773
Point Arena, CA 95468
800-931-9373
Fax: 707-884-4109
spbooks@solano.com
www.solano.com

Solano Press Books is a California publishing house specializing in land use, planning law, urban affairs, and environmental subjects. Publications also offer readers detailed guidance on policy matters and instructions on implementingand complying with specific programs and procedures.
Publication Date: 1988
Ling-Yen Jones, Publisher

4339 Springer-Verlag New York
175 Fifth Avenue
New York, NY 10010
212-460-1500
Fax: 212-473-6272

Founded in 1964 and maintained its position last year as the Springer Group's largest foreign subsidiary. In 1999, 426 new titles were released. In addition, 50 journals were published, most of them available in electronic form as wellas via the Springer information system LINK. The number of license agreements in the North American market has increased fivefold due to the increasing demand for this leading Online Library.

4340 Virginia Museum of Natural History
1001 Douglas Avenue
Martinsville, VA 24112
540-666-8600
Fax: 540-632-6487
www.vmnh.org

Our publishing division specializes in works by natural scientists and environmental educators in the US and abroad. Writing, editorial, and design services available for books, reports, manuals, text books, presentations, fieldguides.
24 pages Quarterly
ISSN: 1085-5084
Susan Felker, Managing Editor\Outreach

4341 WW Norton & Company
500 5th Avenue
New York, NY 10110
212-354-5500
Fax: 212-869-0856
wwnorton.com

The oldest and largest publishing house owned wholly by its employees, strives to carry out the imperative of its founder to publish books of long-term value in the areas of fiction, nonfiction and poetry. The roots of the company dateback to 1923, when William Warder Norton and his wife, M.D. Herter Norton, began publishing lectures delivered at the People's Institute, the adult education division of New York City's Cooper Union.
Diane Ackerman, Author
Dalton Conley, Author

4342 Wiley North America
605 3rd Avenue
New York, NY 10158
212-850-6000
Fax: 212-850-6088

The company was founded in 1807, during the Jefferson presidency. In the early years, Wiley was best known for the works of Washington Irving, Edgar Allen Poe, Herman Melville and other 19th century American literary giants. By theturn of the century, Wiley was established as a leading publisher of scientific and technical information.

Research Centers

Corporate & Commercial Centers

4343 AAA & Associates
28 West Adams
Suite 1511
Detroit, MI 48226
313-961-4122
Fax: 313-588-6232
Katherine Banicki, President

4344 AB Gurda Company
6061 Whitnall Way
Hales Corners, WI 53130
414-529-3116
Environmental testing and analysis firm.

4345 ABC Research Corporation
3437 SW 24th Avenue
Gainesville, FL 32607
352-372-0436
866-233-5883
Fax: 352-378-6483
info@abcr.com
Research and analysis laboratory. Research results published in scientific journals.
Dr William L Brown, President
Dr Peter Bodnaruck, VP

4346 ACRES Research
6621 W Ridgeway Avenue
Cedar Falls, IA 50613
319-277-6661
Fax: 319-266-7569
www.acresresearch.com
Environmental research and testing.
Bert Schou PhD, President

4347 ACZ Laboratories, Inc
2773 Downhill Drive
Steamboat Springs, CO 80487
970-879-6590
800-334-5493
Fax: 815-301-3857
sales@acz.com
www.acz.com
A full service environmental analytical lab with inorganic, organic and radiochemical capabilities. We perform analysis on a wide variety of matrices including water, wastewater, waste, soil, plant and animal tissue as well as fishtissue.
Sue Webber, Project Manager
Tony Antalek, Project Manager

4348 ADA Technologies
8100 Shaffer Parkway
Suite 130
Littleton, CO 80127-4107
303-792-5615
800-232-0296
Fax: 303-792-5633
ada@adatech.com
www.adatech.com
Product development and testing of environmental technologies.
James P. Budimlya, President & CEO
Russell Farmer, Executive Vice President

4349 AECOM
10 Iverness Center Parkway
Suite 120
Birmingham, AL 35242
205-980-0054
800-722-2440
Fax: 205-980-1509
askenvironment@aecom.com
www.aecom.com
AECOM is a global provider of environmental and energy development services to industry and government. As a full-service environmental firm, AECOM's professionals provide clients with consulting, engineering, remediation, and relatedservices from over 24 countries.
Michael S. Bruke, Chairman & CEO
Carla Christofferson, Executive Vice President

4350 AER
131 Hartwell Avenue
Lexington, MA 00242
781-761-2288
Fax: 781-761-2299
ross@aer.com
www.aer.com
Ron Isaacs, CEO
David B. Hogan, CTO/SVP

4351 AMA Analytical Services
4475 Forbes Boulevard
Lanham, MD 20706
301-459-2640
800-346-0961
Fax: 301-459-2643
info@amalab.com
www.amalab.com
Environmental research. Asbestos, lead and explosives analysis.
David P Hood, CEO

4352 ANA-Lab Corporation
2600 Dudley Road
PO Box 9000
Kilgore, TX 75663
903-984-0551
Fax: 903-984-5914
corp@ana-lab.com
www.ana-lab.com
Environmental laboratory specializing in the testing of wastewater, groundwater, and solid waste for pollutants, herbicides, pesticides, and PCBs.
Scott Moss, Vice President, Operations
Bill Peery, Executive Vice President

4353 APC Lab
13760 Manolia Avenue
Chino, CA 91710
909-590-1828
Fax: 909-590-1498
apcl@apclab.com
Environmental and industrial testing laboratory. Research results published in journals and conference reports.
Irene Huang, Public Relations

4354 APS Technology
7 Laser Lane
Wallingford, CT 00649
860-613-4450
Fax: 203-284-7428
contact@aps-tech.com
www.aps-tech.com
Product development, conceptual design, engineering, prototype manufacture and test analysis.
William E Turner, CEO
Denis Bigin, VP

4355 ARDL
400 Aviation Drive
Mount Vernon, IL 62864
618-244-3235
Fax: 618-244-1149
techserv@ardlinc.com
www.ardlinc.com
Environmental sampling and testing laboratory; Research Development Engineering. Alternate Name: Applied Research and Development Laboratories, Inc.
Larry Gibbons PhD, President
Don Gillespie, Marketing Manager

4356 ASW Environmental Consultants
20 N Plains Industrial Road
PO Box 495
Wallingford, CT 00649
203-265-0509
Fax: 203-265-1476
Jason J Sarojak, PE

4357 ATC Associates
5415 SW Westgate Drive
Suite 100
Portland, OR 97221
503-419-2500
Fax: 503-419-2600
www.cardno.com
Technical engineering research and environmental consulting firm.
John Marlay, Chairman
Richard Wankmuller, CEO & Mnanaging Director

4358 ATC Environmental
720 E Benson Road 605-338-0555
Sioux Falls, SD 57103
Donald Beck

4359 ATL
2921 N. 30th Avenue 602-241-1097
Phoenix, AZ 85017-5402 Fax: 602-277-1306
tatafcr@ATL-quality.com
www.atl-quality.com
Technical engineering evaluation firm. Research results published in test summaries and project reports.
Frank C Rivera, President
David P Hayes, VP

4360 AW Research Laboratories
16326 Airport Road 218-829-7974
Brainerd, MN 56401 Fax: 218-829-1316
awlab@awlab.com
www.awlab.com
A.W. Research Laboratories provides environmental consulting services and water quality analysis, specializing in the use of remote sensing techniques for lake analysis and management.
Sara Ahlers, CEO
Sarah Fogderud, Chief Financial Officer

4361 AZTEC Laboratories
6402 Stadium Drive 816-921-3922
PO Box 7953
Kansas City, MO 64129
Data collection and analysis, systems design and product development firm.

4362 Aaron Environmental
189 Atwater Street 860-276-1201
Plantsville, CT 00647 800-372-2766
Fax: 860-276-1233
info@aaronenvironmental.com
www.aaronenvironmental.com
Joyce Kogut, President
Mike Bolegh, Business Manager

4363 Accurate Engineering Laboratories
4831 S. Whipple Ave. 773-523-3100
Chicago, IL 60632 Fax: 773-384-8681
www.accu-labs.com
Environmental engineering laboratory.
Noel Buczkowski, President

4364 Accutest Laboratories
2235 Route 130 S 732-329-0200
Building B Fax: 732-329-3499
Dayton, NJ 00881 www.accutest.com
Environmental testing firm.
Phillip B. Rooney, Chairman & CEO
Gene Malloy, President & COO

4365 Acts Testing Labs
25 Anderson Rd 716-505-3300
Buffalo, NY 14228 Fax: 716-505-3301
Global consumer products testing organization providing quality assurance testing, inspections and consulting services.
Tom Fatta, Contact

4366 Adelaide Associates
7 Holland Avenue 914-949-3109
White Plains, NY 10603 Fax: 914-949-8103
Environmental health consulting and testing firm. Additional offices: White Plains, NY, Poughkeepsie, NY and Perth Amboy, NJ.
Ron Birlinski, CEO

4367 Adelaide Environmental Health Associates
1511 Route 22 845-278-7710
Suite C24 Fax: 845-278-7750
Brewster, NY 10509 www.adelaidellc.com
Stephanie A. Soter, President
John W. Soter, Vice President

4368 Adirondack Environmental Services
314 N Pearl Street 518-434-4546
Albany, NY 12207 800-848-4983
Fax: 518-434-0891
aes@adirondackenvironmental.com
www.adirondackenvironmental.com
Analytical medical laboratory.

4369 Adirondack Lakes Survey Corporation
Route 86 518-897-1354
PO Box 296 Fax: 518-897-1364
Ray Brook, NY 12977 info@adirondacklakessurvey.org
www.adirondacklakessurvey.org
Determines the extent and magnitude of acidification of lakes and ponds in the Adironack region.

4370 Advance Pump and Filter Company
10 Calef Highway 603-868-3212
Lee, NH 00382 800-863-3212
Fax: 603-868-3230
info@advanceh2o.com
www.advancepumpandfilter.com
Services include water treatment, submersible pumps, jet pumps, water tanks, sewage and sump systems.
Cathleen Pleadwell, Business Manager

4371 Advanced Terra Testing
833 Parfet Street 303-232-8308
Unit A 888-859-8378
Lakewood, CO 80215 Fax: 303-232-1579
info@terratesting.com
www.terratesting.com
Geotechnical and geosynthetic testing firm.
Chris Wienecke, Co-Owner
Duke C. Wilson, Co-Owner

4372 AeroVironment
181 West Huntington Drive 626-357-9983
Suite 202 Fax: 626-359-9628
Monrovia, CA 91016 info@avinc.com
www.avinc.com
Research, service and consulting firm specializing in the environment, alternative energy and aerodynamic design. Research results published in project reports and technical journals.
Tim Conver, CEO
Raymond Cook, CFO

4373 Aerosol Monitoring & Analysis
1331 Ashton Road 410-684-3327
Hanover, MD 21076 Fax: 410-684-3384
www.amatraining.com
Environmental services firm.
Todd M. Woerner, President
Joseph A. Coco, Senior Vice President

4374 Agvise Laboratories
604 Highway 15 West 701-587-6010
PO Box 510 Fax: 701-587-6013
Northwood, ND 58267 www.agvise.com

Applied and product research in environmental applications.
Bob Deutsch, President
Bob Wallace, CEO/CFO

4375 Alan Plummer and Associates
1320 South University Drive 817-806-1700
Suite 300 Fax: 817-870-2536
Fort Worth, TX 76107-5737
Civil and environmental engineering consulting.
Alan H Plummer Jr, President

4376 Alar Engineering Corporation
9651 West 196th Street 708-479-6100
Mokena, IL 60448 Fax: 708-479-9059
www.alarcorp.com
Alex Doncer, President

4377 Alden Research Laboratory
30 Shrewsbury Street 508-829-6000
Holden, MA 00152 Fax: 508-829-5939
info@aldenlab.com
www.aldenlab.com
Hydraulic engineering firm solving air and water flow problems using physical and CFD models and field testing, for areas such as fish passage/protection systems, free surface and closed conduit flow, pump/turbine performance,hydraulic structures, environmental hydraulics, fluid equipment, 3D air flow, and flow meter calibration.
Stuart A. Cain, President
David K. Anderson, Vice President

4378 Allied Laboratories
716 North Iowa 630-279-0390
Villa Park, IL 60181 Fax: 630-279-3114
Irving I Domsky, Director

4379 Alloway Testing
1101 N Cole Street 419-223-1362
Lima, OH 45805 800-436-1243
Fax: 419-227-3792
www.alloway.com
Environmental sampling and analysis laboratory.
John R Hoffman, President
Lana Jackson, Labrotary Manager

4380 Alpha Manufacturing Company
100 Old Barnwell Road 803-739-4500
PO Box 2809 Fax: 803-739-0517
West Columbia, SC 29170 young@alphamfg.com
www.alphamfg.com
Physical testing of environmental testing and repair services, and instrument design.
Patricia O. Young, President & CEO
Dean Young, General Manager

4381 Alton Geoscience
650 Suffolk Street 978-970-5600
Wannalancit Mills Fax: 978-453-1995
Lowell, MA 01854 www.trcsolutions.com
Environmental remediation and consulting firm.
Thomas W. Bennet, Jr., Chief Financial Officer
Larry Farrington, Contact

4382 Amalgamated Technologies
13901 N 73rd Street 480-991-2901
Suite 208
Scottsdale, AZ 85260
Firm providing metals and materials development, processing and testing.
Roy E Beal, President

4383 American Environmental Network
9151 Rumsey Road 410-730-8525
Suite 150 Fax: 410-997-2586
Columbia, MD 21045
Paul Jackson, Marketing Manager

4384 American Testing Laboratory
11 Industrial Road 201-489-8573
Pequannock, NJ 00744 800-488-4951
Fax: 201-489-9365
info@mytestlab.com
www.americantestinglaboratory.com
Multidisciplinary testing laboratory offering a wide range of confidential testing services including environmental simulations (humidity, high/low temperature extremes).
Daniel Narbone, Manager

4385 American Waste Processing
2100 West Madison Street 630-506-9977
Maywood, IL 60153 Fax: 888-607-7441
www.americanrecyclingdisposal.com
Non-hazardous waste management, disposal/transfer, station/recycling, roll off containers.
William Vajdik, President

4386 Analab
One Omega Circle 856-467-4555
Bridgeport, NJ 00801 800-262-5229
Fax: 856-467-1212
info@analab1.com
Compliance lab services for EMC/EMI, safety and ESD.
Jason Smith, Director/Manager

4387 Analyte Laboratories
2121 Cedar Circle Drive 410-747-3844
Catonsville, MD 21228 Fax: 410-747-4007

4388 Analytical Laboratories and Consulting
361 West 5th Avenue
Eugene, OR 97401 541-485-8404
Fax: 541-484-5995
Rory E White, Sr. Analyst

4389 Analytical Process Laboratories
8222 W Calumet Road 414-355-3909
Milwaukee, WI 53223 800-236-3909
Fax: 414-355-3099
www.apl-inc.net
Materials analysis laboratory and environmental engineering.
Jitendra Shah, President
Rakesh Shah, Vice President

4390 Analytical Resources
4611 S 134th Place 206-695-6200
Tukwila, WA 98168-3240 Fax: 206-695-6201
www.arilabs.com
Environmental testing and analysis laboratory.
Mark Weidner, President
Stephanie Lucas, Project Manager

4391 Analytical Services
110 Technology Parkway 770-734-4200
Nocross, GA 30092 800-ASI-7227
Fax: 770-734-4201
www.asi-lab.com
Environmental testing and analysis firm.
G Wyn Jones, President

4392 Anametrix
1961 Concourse Drive 408-432-8192
Suite E Fax: 408-432-8198
San Jose, CA 95131-1708
Doug Robbins, President

4393 AndCare
PO Box 14566 Parkway 919-544-8220
Research Triangle Park, NC 27709 Fax: 919-544-9808
Development and commercialization of low cost, simple to use diagnostic devices and tests for medical, environmental, and laboratory markets.
Dr. Steven Wagner, PhD, President

4394 Anderson Engineering Consultants
10205 W Rockwood Road 501-455-4545
Little Rock, AR 72204 Fax: 501-455-4552
aecigeo@comcast.net
www.aecigeo.com
Firm providing engineering, inspection, and testing services specializing in geotechnology and materials, and environmental sciences. Services include site studies, soil testing, engineering surveys, specification evaluation, andfailure investigation.

4395 Andrea Aromatics
PO Box 3091 609-695-7710
Princeton, NJ 00854 Fax: 609-392-8914
orders@andreaaromatics.com
www.andreaaromatics.com
Natural essential oils, fragrances, deodorants, odor neutralizers.
Michael D'Andrea, VP
Richard D'Andrea, President

4396 Anlab
1910 S Street 916-447-2946
Sacramento, CA 95814

4397 Anteon Corporation
3211 Jermantown Road 703-246-0200
Suite 200 Fax: 703-246-0797
Fairfax, VA 22030-2201
Joseph M. Kampf, CEO

4398 Applied Biomathematics
100 N Country Road 631-751-4350
Setauket, NY 11733 Fax: 631-751-3435
admin@ramas.com
www.ramas.com
Environmental and ecological software development firm.
Lev Ginzburg, President

4399 Applied Coastal Research & Engineering
766 Falmouth Road 508-539-3737
Suite A-1 Fax: 508-539-3739
Mashpee, MA 00264 info@appliedcoastal.com
www.appliedcoastal.com
Environmental analysis.
Mark Bynes PhD, President
John S. Ramsey, Senior Coastal Engineer

4400 Applied Technical Services
1049 Triad Court 770-423-1400
Marietta, GA 30066 888-287-5227
Fax: 770-514-3299
www.atslab.com
Environmental, chemical, and mechanical testing and consulting company.
Jim F Hill, President

4401 Aquatec Chemical International
408 Auburn Avenue 313-334-4747
Pontiac, MI 48342
Douglas Schwartz, President

4402 Ardaman & Associates
8008 S Orange Avenue 407-855-3860
Orlando, FL 32809 800-683-SOIL
Fax: 407-859-8121
mmongeau@ardaman.com
www.ardaman.com
Geotechnical, environmental and materials consultants.
Mark L Mongeau PE, Vice President

4403 Arete Associates
9301 Corbin Avenue 818-885-2201
Northridge, CA 91324 Fax: 818-885-2210
info@arete.com
www.arete.com
Environmental research.
John Mclean, President & CEO
David Kane, Vice President

4404 Aroostook Testing & Consulting Laboratory
160 Airport Drive 207-762-5771
Presque Isle, ME 00476 Fax: 207-764-8123
www.aroostooktesting.com
Toxiological and environmental laboratory.
G Noel Currie III, President

4405 Arro
Caton Farm Road 815-727-5436
PO Box 686 Fax: 815-740-3234
Joliet, IL 60434 info@arrolab.com
www.arrolab.com
Robert J Rolih, President

4406 Artesian Laboratories
630 Churchmans Road 302-266-9121
Newark, DE 19702 Fax: 302-454-8720
Environmental sampling and testing laboratory. Research results published in methods reports to clients.

4407 Association of Ecosystem Research Centers
730 11th Street NW 202-628-1500
Washington, DC 20001 Fax: 202-628-1509
aerc@culter.colorado.edu
www.ecosystemresearch.org
Brings together 39 US research programs in universities and private, state and federal laboratories that conduct research, provide training and analyze policy at the ecosystem level of environmental science and natural resourcesmanagement. Although AERC is an association of professional scientists rather than environmental activists, its goals and interest complement those of conservation organizations.
John A. Arnone III, President
Lucinda Johnson, Secretary

4408 Astro-Chem Services
4102 2nd Avenue W 701-572-7355
PO Box 972 800-568-6614
Williston, ND 58801 Fax: 701-774-3907
info@astrochemlab.com
www.astrochemlab.com
A modern analytical laboratory that specializes in the in the petroleum and agricultural industry
David Zander, President
Bruce Kyllo, Lab Manager

4409 Astro-Pure Water Purifiers
1441 SW 1st Way 954-422-8966
Deerfield Beach, FL 33441 Fax: 954-422-8966
Manufacturers complete line of water treatment equipment, purifiers, De Calcifiers, R.O., V.V., iron filters, chemical feed equipment. Sizes for portable, point of use, central commercial and industrial. Manufacturers and privatelabels counter top units.
RL Stefl, President

4410 Atlantic Testing Laboratories
6431 US Highway 11 315-386-4578
Canton, NY 13617 Fax: 315-386-1012
info@atlantictesting.com
www.atlantictesting.com
Engineering firm offering environmental services: subsurface investigations, geoprobe services, water-based investigations, geotechnical engineering, construction materials testing and engineering, surveying and more.
Marijean B. Remington, CHMM, CEO
James J. Kuhn, PE, President

4411 Atlas Weathering Services Group
45601 N 47th Avenue 623-465-7356
Phoenix, AZ 85087 800-255-3738
Fax: 623-465-9409
atlas.info@ametek.com
atlas-mts.com
Technical research firm specializing in environmental testing. Research results published in reports to clients and in archival journals.
Jack Martin, President

4412 Atmospheric & Environmental Research
131 Hartwell Avenue 781-761-2288
Lexington, MA 00242 Fax: 781-761-2299
aer@aer.com
www.aer.com
Firm providing research, consulting, and assessment on atmospheric chemistry, meteorology, climate, and air quality.
Ron Isaacs, President & CEO
David B. Hogan, Executive Vice President

4413 Axiom Laboratories
24 Tobey Road 860-242-6291
Bloomfield, CT 00600 Fax: 860-286-0634
Environmental and materials analytical testing services.
William AG Macke, President

4414 B&P Laboratories
5635 Delridge Way SW 206-937-3644
Seattle, WA 98106 Fax: 206-937-1348
mail@bplabs.net
www.bplabs.net
Environmental testing and chemical laboratory water analyses (ICP);Mercury analyzer sulfates, fluorides, chlorides (DIONEX); cyandes (CONTES); storm waters; fats, oil & grease (FOG); Karl Fischer corrosion testing; process solutions
Victor Broto, President

4415 BC Analytical
4100 Atlas Court 661-327-4911
Bakersfield, CA 93308 Fax: 661-327-1918
www.bclabs.com
Lab capabilities include diversified sample matrices for drinkg waters, ground water monitoring and waste acceptance. Diversified analytical methods include general chemistry and field services including field analysis, sampling andcourier service.
Carolyn Jackson, President
Richard Eglin, Vice President

4416 BC Laboratories
4100 Atlas Court 661-327-4911
Bakersfield, CA 93308 Fax: 661-327-1918
www.bclabs.com
Chemical analysis and environmental monitoring of hazardous waste. Research results published in project reports.
Carolyn Jackson, President
Richard Eglin, Vice President

4417 BC Research
200 Granville Street 604-224-4331
Suite 1800 Fax: 604-224-0540
Vancouver, BC V6C1S info@bcri.ca
www.bcri.ca
Research results published in scientific journals and trade magazines.
Hassan Hamza, President
Kevin Dodds, CFO

4418 BCI Engineers & Scientists
2000 Edgewood Drive 863-667-2345
Suite 215 877-550-4224
Lakeland, FL 33807 Fax: 863-667-2262
www.bcieng.com
Environmental and civil engineering, geotechnical processes, and chemical research and development firm.
Rick Powers, President/CEO
Wendy Lee, Chief Financial Officer

4419 BCM Engineers
5415 SW Westgate Drive 503-419-2500
Suite 100 Fax: 503-419-2600
Portland, OR 97221 www.cardno.com
Services include environmental, geotechnical and materials, remedial design, industrial hygiene and hazardous management planning.
Richard Wankmuller, CEO & Managing Director
Trevor Johnson, General Manager

4420 Babcock & Wilcox Company
13024 Ballantyne Corporate Place 704-625-4900
Suite 700 Fax: 704-625-4910
Charlotte, NC 22827 www.babcock.com
Deliver innovative technologies and solutions to fulfill the needs of our customers
E.James Ferland, President
Jenny L. Apker, Vice President

4421 Badger Laboratories & Engineering Company
501 West Bell Street 920-729-1100
Neenah, WI 54956 800-776-7196
Fax: 920-729-4945
information@badgerlabs.com
www.badgerlabs.com
Specializes in the testing and sampling of drinking water, groundwater, waste water and hazardous wastes.
Richard Larson, President
Jeff Wagner, Lab Manager

4422 Baird Scientific
532 Oak Street 417-358-5567
Carthage, MO 64836
Gary Baird, President/Owner

4423 Baker Environmental
420 Rouser Road 412-269-6000
Coraopolis, PA 15108 Fax: 412-269-2534
Environmental engineering company.
Andrew P Paja, President

4424 Baker-Shiflett
5701 East Loop 820 South 817-478-8254
Fort Worth, TX 76119 Fax: 817-478-8874
Larry Gardner, Administrative Manager

4425 Barnebey & Sutcliffe Corporation
835 North Cassady Avenue 614-258-9501
PO Box 2526 Fax: 614-258-0222
Columbus, OH 43216 www.bscairfiltration.com
Unparalleled technical assistance in selection of the most cost-effective activated carbon for the application
Amanda L Fisher, Marketing Coordinator

4426 Barton & Loguidice
443 Electronics Parkway 315-457-5200
Liverpool, NY 13088 800-724-1070
Fax: 315-451-0052
info@BartonandLoguidice.com
www.BartonandLoguidice.com
B&L helps communities throughout the Northeast and Mid-Atlantic states meet their engineering, environmental science, planning, and landscape architecture needs. Provides planning, funding procurement, site design, engineering, andconstruction phase services for projects involving facilities, sustainable design, green infrastructure, recreational facilities, renewable energy, site utilities, water and wastewater, solid waste, transportation, community revitalization, andenvironmental issues.
John F. Brusa Jr., President/CEO
John A. Benson, Sr. Vice President

4427 Baxter and Woodman
8678 Ridgefield Road 815-459-1260
Crystal Lake, IL 60012 Fax: 815-455-0450
info@baxterwoodman.com
www.baxterwoodman.com
Environmental engineering firm offering services in waste management, construction, resource management, and infrastructure.
Derek Wold, Vice President
Louis Haussmann, Chief Operating Officer

4428 Bell Evaluation Laboratory
17300 Mercury Drive 281-488-3701
Houston, TX 77058 Fax: 281-488-8543
www.bellabs.com
Coating testing and evaluation firm.
Bob Bell, Contact
Monte Middlebrooks, Contact

4429 Belle W Baruch Institute for Marine Biology and Coastal Research
607 EWS Building 803-777-5288
Columbia, SC 29208 Fax: 803-777-3935
Conducts basic and applied research in marine and coastal environments.
Jim Morris, Director
Margaret Bergin, Business Manager

4430 Beltran Associates
1133 East 35th Street 718-338-3311
Brooklyn, NY 11210 Fax: 718-253-9028
info@beltrantechnologies.com
www.beltrantechnologies.com
A leader in advanced gas cleaning and air pollution control for a broad spectrum of industrial processes and emission requirements. Our reputation is based on 50 years of successful research, development and problem solving leading tomore than 1000 installations worldwide.
Mike Beltran, President
Swapan Mitra, Sales Manager

4431 Benchmark Analytics
4777 Saucon Creek Road 610-974-8100
Center Valley, PA 18034-9004 Fax: 610-974-8104
f.adamsky@benchmarkanalyticslabs.com
Benchmark Analytics is an independent analytical testing laboratory. Benchmark analyzes many types of samples including drinking water, wastewater and soil in addition to testing food, mold, sludge, soot, air samples and industrialproducts.
Fiona Adamsky, General Manager

4432 Bendix Environmental Research
1950 Addison Street
Suite 202 home.earthlink.net/~bendix/
Berkeley, CA 94704
Specializes in toxicology, hazardous materials management, and preparation of environmental documents dealing with hazardous materials.
Selina Bendix, Ph.D, President
Gilbert G. Bendix, Vice President

4433 Bhate Environmental Associates
1608 13th Ave S 205-918-4000
#300 Fax: 615-661-4226
Birmingham, AL 35205 www.bhate.com
Environmental consulting.

4434 Bio-Chem Analysts Inc
4940 North Memorial Pkwy 256-859-2161
PO Box 3270 Fax: 256-859-9222
Huntsville, AL 35810
Environmental testing of water, wastewater, air, soil, and hazardous waste.
Vijay Thakore, President

4435 Bio-Science Research Institute
4813 Cheyenne Way 909-628-3007
Chino, CA 91710 Fax: 909-590-8948
Independent environmental testing laboratory.

4436 Bio/West
1063 West 1400 North 435-752-4202
Logan, UT 84321-2291 Fax: 435-752-0507
www.bio-west.com
Using scientific principles, making sound resource decisions, and providing context-sensitive solutions for more than 35 years
Darren Oslen, President
Ed Oborny, Vice President

4437 Biomarine
16 E Main Street 978-281-0222
PO Box 1153 Fax: 978-283-6296
Gloucester, MA 00193 www.biomarinelab.com
Provides water and seafood analysis and consulting for the public, private companies and government.
Jim Groleau, Laboratory Director
John Marletta, Vice President

4438 Bionetics Corporation Analytical Laboratories
20 Research Drive 757-865-0880
Hampton, VA 23666 Fax: 757-865-8014
Joseph A Stern, President

4439 Bioscience
966 Postal Road 484-245-5232
Suite 200 800-627-3069
Allentown, PA 18109 Fax: 484-245-5236
bioscience@bioscienceinc.com
www.bioscienceinc.com

Specialized microbes for wastewater and hazardous waste, biological treatment. BOD and COD monitoring instruments and test kits for water and wastewater analysis.
Thomas G Zitrides, President
Richard Bleam, Director of Technical Svc.

4440 Biospherics
12051 Indian Creek Court
Beltsville, MD 20705
301-419-3900
Fax: 301-210-4909
Gilbert V Levin, PhD, President

4441 Black Rock Test Lab
5 Eastgate Plaza
Morgantown, WV 26501
304-296-8347

4442 BlazeTech Corporation
29B Montvale Ave
Woburn, MA 00180
781-759-0700
Fax: 781-759-0703
office@blazetech.com
www.blazetech.com
An engineering consulting firm specializing in fire, explosion, environmental safety and homeland defense. They have developed specialized software for the chemical, petroleum, aerospace and power industries: ADORA, BLAZETANK andothers.
Albert Moussa, President

4443 Bollyky Associates
31 Strawberry Hill Avenue
Stamford, CT 06902
203-967-4223
Fax: 203-967-4845
ljbbai@bai-ozone.com
www.bai-ozone.com
Engineering firm specializing in Ozone technology, water and wastewater treatment and treatability studies.
L Joseph Bollyky, President

4444 Braun Intertec Corporation
11001 Hampshire Avenue South
Minneapolis, MN 55438
952-995-2000
800-279-6100
Fax: 952-995-2020
info@braunintertec.com
braunintertec.com
Full-service engineering, environmental and infrastructure consulting and testing organization.
Robert Janssen, President
John Carlson, CEO

4445 Braun Intertec Northwest
11001 Hampshire Avenue S
Minneapolis, MN 55438
952-995-2000
800-279-6100
Fax: 952-995-2020
info@braunintertec.com
www.braunintertec.com
Testing and quality control monitoring laboratory specializing in construction inspections, materials testing, soils engineering and geological services.
Robert J Janssen PE, President
John A. Carlson, CEO

4446 Briggs Associates
2300 Holcomb Bridge Road
Suite 103, #366
Roswell, GA 30076
770-993-4559
Fax: 781-871-7982
briggscentral@briggsassociates.org
www.briggsassociates.org
Environmental engineering and testing facility.
Meet David Kimmel, President/COO
Meet Al Blackwelder, COO

4447 Brighton Analytical
2105 Pless Drive
Brighton, MI 48114
810-229-7575
Fax: 810-229-8650
bai-brighton@sbcglobal.net
www.brightonanalytical.net
Specializes in the area of Environmental Laboratory Testing Services.
J Shawn Letwin, Laboratory Director

4448 Brooks Companies
3900 Essex Ln
Suite 555
Houston, TX 77027
713-337-2222
866-454-1900
Fax: 713-337-2239
www.brookecompanies.com
Margaret Y Brooks PhD, President

4449 Brotcke Engineering Company
750 Merus Court
PO Box 1168
Fenton, MO 63026-2028
636-343-3029
800-969-3029
Fax: 636-343-3773
www.brotcke.com
Professional engineering firm that provides well drilling and pump services.
Paul Brotcke, President

4450 Buchart-Horn
3700 Koppers Street
Suite 540
Baltimore, MD 21227
717-852-1400
800-274-2224
ckinney@bh-ba.com
www.bh-ba.com
This company provides environmental engineering, consulting, civil engineering, facility design and planning as well as laboratory and testing services.
Brian S. Funkhouser, President/CEO
Stephanie A. Schaefer, Regional Manager

4451 Burt Hill Kosar Rittelmann Associates
400 Morgan Center
101 East Diamond Street
Butler, PA 16001
724-285-4761
Fax: 724-285-6815
www.burthill.com
John Brock, Chief Operating Office/Vice
Michael Carter, Principal

4452 Business Health Environmental Lab
33 E 7th Street
300 Doctors Building
Covington, KY 41011
859-431-6224
Fax: 859-431-6228
Dan Moos, President

4453 C L Technology Division of Microbac Lab
101 Bellevue Road
Suite 301
Pittsburgh, PA 15229-2132
412-459-1060
Fax: 866-515-4668
microbac_info@microbac.com
www.microbac.com
Research and development laboratory specializing in analysis and testing. Services include: air quality; environmental testing, consulting and analysis; nutraceutical testing and analysis; consumer products testing; food producttesting; fuel and manufactured products testing.
J Trevor Boyce, Chairman/CEO
James Nokes, President

4454 CDS Laboratories
52 Biomedical Education Building
South Campus
Buffalo, NY 14214
716-829-2797
Fax: 716-829-3979
cdsdept@buffalo.edu
arts-sciences.buffalo.edu/cds/about.html

The department of Communicative Disorders and Sciences offers basic and clinical research from the molecular level to patient oriented diagnostic and rehabilitative research.
Carol M. Altman, Sr. Administrative Assistant
MaryAnn L. Doskocz, Department Administrator

4455 CENSOL
582 Hawthorne 416-219-6950
L9T-4N8 Fax: 905-878-8775
Milton, ON L9T4N contactme@censol.ca
www.laughton.ca
Environmental consulting and testing firm. Research results published in technical association papers.

4456 CET Environmental Services
7032 South Revere Parkway 720-875-9115
Englewood, CO 80112 Fax: 720-875-9114
Provides environmental consulting, engineering, remediation & construction servies. There are three primary segments: Industrial services, environmental remediation & government. programs.
Steven H Davis, President & CEO
Dale W Bleck, CFO

4457 CPAC
2364 Leicester Road 585-382-3223
PO Box 175 800-828-6011
Leicester, NY 14481 Fax: 585-382-3031
cpacinfo@cpac.com
www.cpac.com
CPAC, Inc. manages holdings in two industries: Cleaning and Personal Care and Imaging. The Fuller Brands segment develops, manufactures, and markets over 2799 branded and private lavel products for commercial cleaning, householdcleaning, and personal care. CPAC Imaging manufactures, packages, and distrubtes branded and private label chemicals for photographic, health care, and graphic arts markets as well as associated imaging equipment and silver refining services.
Thomas N Hendrickson, President

4458 Cardno ATC
10004 Park Meadows Drive 720-257-5800
Suite 300 Fax: 720-257-5801
Lone Tree, Denver, CO 80124 www.cardno.com
Environmental consulting firm offering services in environmental design, planning, software, construction management, material testing and more.
Michael Alscher, Chairman
Neville Buch, CEO

4459 Cascadia Research
218 1/2 W 4th Avenue 360-943-7325
Olympia, WA 98501 800-747-7329
calambokidis@cascadiaresearch.org
www.cascadiaresearch.org
Nonprofit tax-exempt scientific and educational organization founded to conduct research needed to manage and protect threatened marine mammals.

4460 Cedar Grove Environmental Laboratories
1401 Gallagherville Road 610-269-6977
Downingtown, PA 19335 Fax: 610-269-6965
www.cgelab.com
Environmental analysis firm serving agriculture and industry.

4461 Ceimic Corporation
10 Dean Knauss Drive 401-782-8900
Narragansett, RI 00288 Fax: 401-782-8905
www.ceimic.com
Environmental testing for water and soil.
Margaret Marple, Marketing
John McGarry, President

4462 Center for Solid & Hazardous Waste Management
1929 Stadium Road Nuclear Science 352-392-6264
Bldg 634, Room No. 528 Fax: 352-846-0183
Gainesville, FL 32611 rogersrd@ufl.edu
www.hinkleycenter.org
The center serves the citizens of Florida by providing leadership in the field of waste management research and by supporting the Florida Department of Environmental Protection in its mission to preserve and protect the state's naturalresources.
Nandra Weeks, Chairman
Sumpter H. Barker, President

4463 Center for Technology, Policy & Industrial Development
77 Massachusetts Avenue 617-324-7103
Building E38-600 Fax: 617-258-7845
Cambridge, MA 00213-4307 ssrcinfo@mit.edu
Environmental research.
Deborah Nightingale, Director
Nicolene Hengen, Assistant Director for Strat

4464 Central Virginia Laboratories and Consultants
3109 Odd Fellows Road 804-847-2852
PO Box 10938 Fax: 804-847-2830
Lynchburg, VA 24506
Adrian K Mood, President

4465 Century West Engineering Corporation
5331 SW Macadam Ave 503-419-2130
Suite 207 Fax: 503-639-2710
Portland, OR 97239 www.centurywest.com
Matt MacRostie, Project Manager
Ron Weigel, Project Manager

4466 Chas. T Main: Environmental Division
Prudential Center 617-262-3200
Boston, MA 00219 Fax: 781-401-2575
Environmental consulting firm specializing in site assessments, surveys, and tests and analysis.

4467 Chemical Resource Processing
2525 Battleground Road 281-930-2525
PO Box 1914 Fax: 281-930-2535
Deer Park, TX 77536
Environmental consulting and chemical processing firm.

4468 Chemical Waste Disposal Corporation
4214 19th Avenue 718-274-3339
Astoria, NY 11105 Fax: 718-726-7917
Environmental waste disposal and consulting company.

4469 Chemir Analytical Services
2672 Metro Boulevard 314-291-6620
Maryland Heights, MO 63043 800-659-7659
Fax: 314-291-6630
info@chemir.com
www.chemir.com
Provides a wide range of chemical analysis and chemical testing services. Experienced at solving difficult problems including product failure analysis, materials identification, plastic testing or reverse engineering. An independenttesting lab with scientists that can provide litigation support such as expert witness testimony in intellectual property or products liability cases.
Dr Shri Thanedar, President

4470 Chesner Engineering
38 West Park Avenue 516-431-4031
Suite 200 Fax: 516-717-2621
Long Beach, NY 11561 cemail@chesnerengineering.com
www.chesnerengineering.com

Civil, environmental, and waste management firm that provides professional services to industry and government. Specializes in the areas of waste and by-product material recycling and stabliization, marine and dredge environmentalmanagement, risk assessment and environmental modeling, environmental database program development, remedial site investigations and cleanup management, and water and wastewater treatment.
Warren Chesner, President

4471 Chihuahuan Desert Research Institute
43869 SH 118 432-364-2499
PO Box 905 Fax: 432-364-2686
Fort Davis, TX 79734 www.cdri.org

Conducts research on the Chihuahuan Desert.
Shirley Powell, President
Rick Herrman, Executive Director

4472 ChromatoChem
2837 Fort Missoula Road 406-728-5897
Missoula, MT 59801 Fax: 406-728-5924

Biotechnology firm. Research results published in proposals to the Environmental Protection Agency.
Bob Perciasepe, Administrator
Arthur A. Elkins, Jr. Inspector General

4473 Chyun Associates
267 Wall Street 609-924-5151
Princeton, NJ 00854

4474 Clark Engineering Corporation
621 Lilac Drive N 763-545-9196
Minneapolis, MN 55422-4609 877-246-9196
Fax: 763-541-0056
info@clark-eng.com
www.clark-eng.com

Offer structural engineering, civil engineering, and land surveying services throughout the world.
Dr. Abi Assadi, PE, President
Doug Fell, PE, Executive VP/CEO

4475 Clark's Industrial Hygiene and Environmental Laboratory
1801 Route 51 S 412-387-1001
Building 9 888-325-8517
Jefferson Hills, PA 15025 Fax: 412-387-1027
info@clarktesting.com
www.clarktesting.com

General industrial hygiene consulting and field services laboratory that provides support to the environmental efforts of industry, both light and heavy, refineries, power industry, aluminum, steel and environmental consulting firms.Maintains AIHA (American Industrial Hygiene Association) accreditation for asbestos (PLM and PCM), metals, organic solvents, diffusive samplers and silica.
Paul Heffernan, CEO
Lee Rogers, Quality Assurance Manager

4476 Clean Air Engineering
500 West Wood Street 800-553-5511
Palatine, IL 60067 800-627-0033
Fax: 847-991-3300
info@cleanair.com
www.cleanair.com

Offers environmental consulting and permitting, process engineering, equipment rental and manufacture, measurement and analytical services.
Allen Kephart, President & CEO
Anthony Milianti, Project Engineer

4477 Clean Harbors
42 Longwater Drive 781-792-5000
PO Box 9149 800-282-7158
Norwell, MA 00206-9149 Fax: 781-282-0058
www.cleanharbors.com

Environmental consulting firm specializing in soil analysis, site assessments, and water sample testing.
Alan S. Mckim, Chairman & CEO
James M. Rutledge, Vice Chairman

4478 Clean Water Systems
2322 Marina Drive 541-882-9993
Klamath Falls, OR 97601-146 Fax: 541-882-9994
sales@cleanwatersysintl.com
www.cleanwatersysintl.com

Environmental research firm. Designs, develops and manufactures ultra-violet electronic water purification units and systems and electronic measuring systems. The Company has developed lines of proprietary electronic monitoring andcontrol systems and electronic ballast.
Charles Romary, President

4479 Coastal Resources
25 Old Solomons Island Road 410-956-9000
Annapolis, MD 24101 Fax: 410-956-0566
coastal@coastal-resources.net
www.coastal-resources.net

Environmental impact assessments and nontidal wetlands identification expert testimony. Also conducts field investigations for a broad range of natural resources including soils, wetlands, streams, water quality, forests, wildlife,habitats and rare, threatened and endangered species.
Betsy M Weinkam, President/Enviro Biologist
Chuck Weinkam, Sr Environmental Scientist

4480 Colorado Analytical
240 S Main Avenue 303-659-2313
PO Box 507 Fax: 303-659-2315
Brighton, CO 80601 info@coloradolab.com
www.coloradolab.com

Agricultural consulting and testing laboratory. Research results published in project reports and test summaries.

4481 Colorado Research Associates
4118 148th Ave NE 425-556-9055
Redmond, WA 98052-5164 Fax: 425-556-9099
info@nwra.com
www.nwra.com

Environmental research.
Debbi Bardsley, Manager Of HR
Marie Barrington, Accounts Receivable

4482 Columbus Instruments International
950 N Hague Avenue 614-276-0861
Columbus, OH 43204 800-669-5011
Fax: 614-276-0529
sales@colinst.com
www.colinst.com

Manufacturer of biomedical and environmental research equipment which includes respirometers and gas analysis monitoring systems.
Jan Czekdjewski, President
Ken Kober, Sales Manager

4483 **Columbus Water and Chemical Testing Laboratory**
4628 Indianola Avenue 614-262-4372
Columbus, OH 43214

4484 **Commonwealth Technology**
1263 E. New Circle Road 859-294-3911
Lexington, KY 40505 800-755-5672
Fax: 859-276-4374
www.commonwealthtechnology.com
Environmental engineering and analysis firm.
Troy W. Turner, President
Patricia Ulrich, Vice President

4485 **CompuChem Environmental Corporation**
501 Madison Avenue 919-379-4100
Cary, NC 27513 800-833-5097
Fax: 919-379-4050
markross@compuchemlabs.com
Environmental testing laboratory.
Kenneth Grzybowski, Vice President
Mark Ross, VP of Sales & Marketing

4486 **Conjun Laboratories**
9283 Highway 15 606-633-8027
Isom, KY 41824

4487 **Conservation Foundation**
1919 M Street NW 202-912-1000
Suite 600 Fax: 202-912-0765
Washington, DC 20036 www.conservation.org
Conducts research and develops knowledge and techniques to improve the quality of the environment.
Peter A. Seligmann, Chairman of the Board
Rob Walton, Chairman of Executive Commit

4488 **Container Testing Laboratory**
P.O. Box 60508 805-683-5825
Santa Barbara, CA 93106 Fax: 805-683-5625
sales@containertechnology.com
www.containertechnology.com
Independent third party testing laboratory.
Anton Cotaj, Laboratory Director/Manager

4489 **Contaminated Site Clean-Up Information**
William Jefferson Clinton Federal B 703-603-8733
1200 Pennsylvania Avenue, N.W 800-527-3272
Washington, DC 20460-2298 Fax: 703-603-9135
www.clu-in.org
CLU-IN, a US Environmental Protection Agency forum, provides information about innovative treatment and site characterization technologies while acting as a forum for all waste remediation stakeholders.
Pamela Barr, Division Director
Jeff Heimerman, Associate Division Director

4490 **Conti Testing Laboratories**
3190 Industrial Blvd 412-833-7766
PO Box 174 Fax: 412-854-0373
Bethel Park, PA 15102 contilab@verizon.net
www.contitesting.com
Analytical commerical laboratory, fuel analysis (coal, coke, alternative fuels), metals, ore barge gauging, customize analysis.
Patricia A Otroba, President
Timothy Otrobe, CEO

4491 **Continental Systems**
7870 Deering Avenue 818-340-3217
Canoga Park, CA 91304 Fax: 818-340-2405
Environmental laboratory specializing in soil and water analysis.
Janis Butler, President

4492 **Controlled Environment Corporation**
Gorham Industrial Park 207-854-9126
29 Sanford Drive 800-569-5444
Gorham, ME 00403 Fax: 207-854-4357
ceec@ceecusa.com
www.ceecusa.com
Firm providing research, design, and development services relating to clean rooms and contamination control.
Matthew F Pec, President

4493 **Controls for Environmental Pollution**
1925 Rosina Street 505-982-9841
Box 5351 800-545-2188
Santa Fe, NM 87502 Fax: 505-982-9289
James J Mueller, President

4494 **Converse Consultants**
622 State Route 10 West 973-428-0934
Whippany, NJ 07981 Fax: 973-428-0713
whippany@converseconsultants.com
www.converseconsultants.com
Applied and product research in environmental studies.
Hashmi S Quazi, Ph.D, Chairman
Ruben L Romero, MBA, Chief Financial Officer

4495 **Copper State Analytical Lab**
1050 Spire Drive Suite I 928-443-5227
Prescott, AZ 86305 Fax: 928-443-5277
info@prescottlab.com
www.prescottlab.com
Hazardous waste characterization, organic and inorganic waste oil characterization, waste water analysis, potable water analysis, microbiology, general waters and soil chemistry.
D.A. Shah, President
Andrew Shah, Lab Manager

4496 **Corning**
1 Riverfront Plaza 607-974-9000
Corning, NY 14831 Inquiries@corning.com
www.corning.com
Corning is one of the world's leading innovators in materials science. For more than 160 years, Corning has applied its unparalleled expertise in speciality glass, ceramics, and optical physics to develop products that have created newindustries and transformed people's lives.
Wendell P. Weeks, Chairman/CEO
James B. Flaws, Vice Chair/CFO

4497 **Corrosion Testing Laboratories**
60 Blue Hen Drive 302-454-8200
Newark, DE 19713 Fax: 302-454-8204
web@corrosionlab.net
www.corrosionlab.com
Corrosion testing laboratory. Research results published in technical journals and conference proceedings.
Randy Nixon, President/Senior Consultant
Bradley D. Krantz, Vice President

4498 **Coshocton Environmental Testing Service**
709 Main Street 740-622-3328
Coshocton, OH 43812 800-870-6570
Fax: 740-622-3368
cets1@hotmail.com
www.cets1.com
Environmental testing service.

4499 Crane Environmental
2650 Eisenhower Avenue
Bldg 100A
Trooper, PA 19403
610-631-7700
800-828-2447
Fax: 610-631-6800
www.craneenv.com

Industrial water treatment equipment.

4500 Crosby & Overton
1610 W 17th Street
Long Beach, CA 90813
562-432-5445
800-827-6729
Fax: 562-436-7540
rangeles@crosbyoverton.com
www.crosbyoverton.com

Fully permitted RCRA Part B TSD facility located in Southern California. The Facility can process both bulk and drummed waste, including lab-packs. Crosby & Overton can process a wide variety of D,F,K,P and U listed RCRA waste.
Bob Ritter, Sales Manager
Raquel Angeles, Customer Service

4501 Curtis & Tompkins
2323 5th Street
Berkeley, CA 94710
510-486-0900
Fax: 510-486-0532
www.curtisandtompkins.com

C Bruce Godfrey, President
Maggie Chan, CFO

4502 Cyberchron Corporation
33 Corporate Park Drive
Suite 'A'
Hopewell Junction, NY 12533
845-765-8120
Fax: 845-765-8119
cybersales@cyberchron.com
www.cyberchron.com

Computer manufacturing firm specializing in the development of computers designed to withstand extreme travel, environmental, and work conditions.
Christopher R. Fadden, Vice President

4503 Cyrus Rice Consulting Group
1200 Fourth Avenue
Coraopolis, PA 15108
412-269-2468
Fax: 412-375-7507
support@cyrusrice.com
www.cyrusrice.com

Al Owens, VP

4504 DE3
2800 Woods Hollow Road
Madison, WI 53711
608-274-4330
800-356-9526
Fax: 608-277-2516
custserv@promega.com

Environmental engineering research and testing firm.
Harold N Danto, President

4505 DLZ
1425 Keystone Avenue
PO Box 22127
Lansing, MI 48911
517-393-6800
800-336-5352
Fax: 517-272-7390
www.dlzcorp.com

Consulting structural engineers.
Vikram (Raj) Rajadhyaksha, P.E., Chairman/CEO
Robert Kirkley, P.E., L.S., President

4506 DLZ Laboratories - Cleveland
614 W Superior Avenue
Suite 1000
Cleveland, OH 44113
216-771-1090
800-336-5352
Fax: 216-771-0334
dlzroundabouts.com
www.dlz.com

DLZ, a minority-owned business enterprise, is a full-service, multidisciplinary professional corporation that provides complete architectural, engineering, and environmental services to both the public and private sectors. Researchstudies are published in professional journals and project reports.
Vikram Rajadhyaksha, Chairman
Ram Rajyadhyaksha, Vice President

4507 DLZ Laboratories - Columbus/Corporate
6121 Huntley Road
Columbus, OH 43229
614-888-0040
800-336-5352
Fax: 614-436-0161
dlzroundabouts.com
www.dlz.com

DLZ, a minority-owned business enterprise, is a full-service, multidisciplinary professional corporation that provides complete architectural, engineering, and environmental services to both the public and private sectors. Researchstudies are published in professional journals and project reports.
Vikram Rajadhyaksha, Chairman
Ram Rajyadhyaksha, Vice President

4508 DLZ Laboratories - Cuyahoga Falls
1 Canal Square Plaza
Suite 1300
Akron, OH 44308
330-923-0401
800-336-5352
Fax: 330-928-1029
dlz.com

DLZ, a minority-owned business enterprise, is a full-service, multidisciplinary professional corporation that provides complete architectural, engineering, and environmental services to both the public and private sectors. Researchstudies are published in professional journals and project reports.
Vikram Rajadhyaksha, P.E., Chairman
Ram Rajadhyaksha, P.E., Vice President

4509 DOWL HKM
4041 B Street
Anchorage, AK 99503
907-562-2000
Fax: 800-865-9847
www.dowl.com

Serves clients' needs in the areas of environmental planning, National Environmental Policy Act (NEPA) documentation, permitting, engineering and public involvement. Environmental studies and analyses include wetland delineation andfunction and values assessment, vegetation mapping, GIS mapping and analysis, environmental site assessment, air and noise impact analysis. Section 106 consultation, hydrology studies, and secondary and cumulative impact analysis.
Dayton H. Alsaker P.E., Wyoming Region Manager
Raymond L. Armstrong P.E., BCEE, Senior Project Manager

4510 DW Ryckman and Associates REACT Environmental Engineers
1120 S 6th Street
St. Louis, MO 63104-3628
314-678-1398
800-325-1398
Fax: 314-678-6610
stewart_ryckman@reactenvironmental.com
www.reactenvironmental.com

D.W. Ryckman & Associates, Inc., d.b.a. REACT Environmental Engineers, was founded in 1975 to provide rapid response and remediation services for environmental and hazardous contamination problems.
SE Ryckman, President

4511 Daily Analytical Laboratories
1621 West Candletree Drive
Peoria, IL 61614
309-692-5252
Fax: 309-692-0488
Kurt Stepping, Chief Chemist

4512 Dan Raviv Associates
57 E Willow Street
Millburn, NJ 00704
973-564-6006
Fax: 973-564-6442
www.danraviv.com

Environmental consulting firm specializing in environmental impact studies, waste management, site assessment and litigation support.
Dan D Raviv PhD, President
John J Trela PhD, Director/Manager

4513 Danaher Corporation
2200 Pennsylvania Avenue NW 202-828-0850
Suite 800 W Fax: 202-828-0860
Washington, DC 20037 www.danaher.com
Development of process and environmental controls, tools and components.
Thomas P. Joyce, President
Daniel L. Comas, Executive VP/CFO

4514 Datachem Laboratories
960 W Levoy Drive 801-266-7700
Salt Lake City, UT 84123 Fax: 801-268-9992
Brent.Stephens@alsglobal.com
www.alsglobal.com
Analytical laboratory provides lab analysis of soil, water, air and asbestos samples.
Greg Kilmister, Managing Director/CEO
Nerolie Withnall, BA, LLB, FAICD, Chairman

4515 Davis Research
23801 Calabasas Rd. 818-591-2408
Suite 1036 Fax: 818-591-2488
Calabasas, CA 91302-1595 info@davisresearch.com
www.davisresearch.com
Agricultural, food and environmental testing and research firm.
Bill Davis, CEO
Bob Davis, Chief Technical Officer

4516 Dellavalle Laboratory
1910 W McKinley Avenue 559-233-6129
Suite 110 800-228-9896
Fresno, CA 93728 Fax: 818-591-2488
www.dellavallelab.com
Agricultural laboatory analyzes plant, soil, manure and water (ag, domestic, wastewater). Certified Professional Soil Scientits/Agronomists/Crop Advisors and others provide consultation on nutrient and fertilizer management, cropfeasibility, regulatory compliance, troubleshooting and related areas.
Hugh A Rathbun, President
Bill Davis, CEO

4517 Douglass Environmental Services
8649 Bash Street 317-595-9108
Indianapolis, IN 46256 Fax: 317-822-8362
Environmental engineering and testing firm.

4518 Duke Solutions
1 Winthrop Square 617-482-8228
Boston, MA 00211 Fax: 617-482-3784

4519 Dynamac Corporation
CSS-Dynamac, 10301 Democracy Lane 703-691-4612
Suite 300 800-888-4612
Fairfax, VA 22030 Fax: 703-691-4615
ibaumel@dynamac.com
www.css-dynamac.com
A scientific research, engineering, and information technology company, conducting state of the art field and laboratory research, and providing scientific and technical support to federal and state environmental programs.
Jolanda Janczewski, Chairman
W. Dennis Lauchner, CEO

4520 E&A Environmental Consultants
11629 Central Street 781-344-6446
Stoughton, MA 00207 Fax: 781-575-8915
members.aol.com/eaenviron/index.html
An environmental consulting firm, E&A provides waste management solutions through the utilization of alternative and innovative management and treatment techniques. E&A has developed expertise in all aspects of composting and organicwaste utilization. Research results are published in presentations, journals, and newsletters.
Eliot Epstein PhD, Ch. Environmental Scientist
Charles M Alix PE, Senior Engineer

4521 E&S Environmental Chemistry
PO Box 609 541-758-5777
Corvallis, OR 97339-609 Fax: 541-758-4413
www.esenvironmental.com
Environmental research.
Tim Sullivan, President
Jayne Charles, Office Manager

4522 EA Engineering, Science, and Technology, Inc., PBC
225 Schilling Circle 410-584-7000
Suite 400 Fax: 410-771-1625
Hunt Valley, MD 21031 info@eaest.com
www.eaest.com
Provides environmental, compliance, natural resources, and infrastructure engineering and management solutions to a wide range of public and private sector clients.
Ian D. MacFarlane, President

4523 EADS Group
1126 8th Avenue 814-944-5035
Altoona, PA 16602 800-626-0904
Fax: 814-944-4862
ibelsel@eadsgroup.com
www.eadsgroup.com
The EADS Group has experienced personnel that provide environmental risk assessments and site investigations, wetlands delineation and mitigation, and all related permitting. The scope of services covers terrestrial and aquaticecology, water resources, threatened and endangered species, vegetation and wetlands, soils and geology, air quality, noise, hazardous waste, socioeconomics and land use. The EADS Group has five offices in Pennsylvania and one in Maryland.
Dennis M Stidinger, President
David M. Yahner, P.E., Office Manager

4524 EAI Corporation
1308 Continental Drive 410-676-1449
Suite J Fax: 410-671-7241
Abingdon, MD 21009 www.eaicorp.com
Environmental engineering and scientific firm. Research results published in private reports to clients.
Charles Speranzella, President
Tom Albro, VP

4525 EMCO Testing & Engineering
PO Box 266 860-886-0697
Taftville, CT 00638 Fax: 860-886-0697
emco@99main.com
Water treatment and environmental research and consulting, including: storm water pollution prevention; well water contamination investigation; property contamination investigation; solar energy application to commercial andresidential buildings.
Dr Ernie Cohen, President/R&D

4526 EMCON Alaska
201 E 56th Avenue 907-562-3452
Suite 300 Fax: 907-563-2814
Anchorage, AK 99518
Environmental engineering firm.

4527 EMMES Corporation
401 North Washington Street
Suite 700
Rockville, MD 20850
301-251-1161
Fax: 301-251-1355
info@emmes.com
www.emmes.com
Firm providing medical data management and statistical support services. Research results published in scientific literature.
Brian Hochheimer, VP and CFO
Anne Laindblad, President

4528 EMS Laboratories, Inc.
117 W Bellevue Drive
Pasadena, CA 91105-2503
626-568-4065
800-675-5777
Fax: 626-796-5282
www.emslabs.com
Environmental testing lab services. Asbestos/Lead/,I.H. testing. Fully accreditted AIHA lab for metal waste characterization.
Bernadine Kolk, President
Anthony Kolk, CEO

4529 EN-CAS Analytical Laboratories
2359 Farrington Point Drive
Winston-Salem, NC 27107
336-785-3252
Fax: 336-785-3262
info@en-cas.com
www.en-cas.com
Chemical and environmental testing and analysis company.
Tim Ballard, President

4530 ENSR-Anchorage
700 G Street
Suite 500
Anchorage, AK 99501-3439
907-562-3366
800-662-7232
Fax: 907-562-1297
AECOMInvestorRelations@aecom.com
www.ensr.aecom.com
ENSR is a global provider of environmental and energy development services to industry and government. As a full-service environmental firm, ENSR's professionals provide clients with consulting, engineering, remediation, and relatedservices from over 15 countries.
Michael S. Burke, Chairman/CEO
Daniel R. Tishman, Director, Vice Chairman

4531 ENSR-Billings
207 North Broadway
Suite 315
Billings, MT 59101
406-652-7481
800-662-7232
Fax: 406-652-7485
AECOMInvestorRelations@aecom.com
www.ensr.aecom.com
ENSR is a global provider of environmental and energy development services to industry and government. As a full-service environmental firm, ENSR's professionals provide clients with consulting, engineering, remediation, and relatedservices from over 15 countries.
Michael S. Burke, Chairman/CEO
Daniel R. Tishman, Director, Vice Chairman

4532 ENSR-Carmel
4030 Vincennes Road
Suite 250
Indianapolis, IN 46268
317-297-6200
800-662-7232
Fax: 317-293-4295
AECOMInvestorRelations@aecom.com
www.ensr.aecom.com
ENSR is a global provider of environmental and energy development services to industry and government. As a full-service environmental firm, ENSR's professionals provide clients with consulting, engineering, remediation, and relatedservices from over 15 countries.
Michael S. Burke, Chairman/CEO
Daniel R. Tishman, Director, Vice Chairman

4533 ENSR-Chicago
303 East Wacker Drive
Suite 1400
Chicago, IL 60601
312-373-7700
800-662-7232
Fax: 312-373-6800
AECOMInvestorRelations@aecom.com
www.ensr.aecom.com
ENSR is a global provider of environmental and energy development services to industry and government. As a full-service environmental firm, ENSR's professionals provide clients with consulting, engineering, remediation, and relatedservices from over 15 countries.
Michael S. Burke, Chairman/CEO
Daniel R. Tishman, Director, Vice Chairman

4534 ENSR-Columbia (MD)
9755 Patuxent Woods Drive
Suite 300
Columbia, MD 21046
410-423-2500
800-662-7232
Fax: 410-423-2570
AECOMInvestorRelations@aecom.com
www.ensr.aecom.com
ENSR is a global provider of environmental and energy development services to industry and government. As a full-service environmental firm, ENSR's professionals provide clients with consulting, engineering, remediation, and relatedservices from over 15 countries.
Michael S. Burke, Chairman/CEO
Daniel R. Tishman, Director, Vice Chairman

4535 ENSR-Fort Collins
1601 Prospect Parkway
Fort Collins, CO 80525-9769
970-493-8878
800-662-7232
Fax: 970-493-0213
AECOMInvestorRelations@aecom.com
www.ensr.aecom.com
ENSR is a global provider of environmental and energy development services to industry and government. As a full-service environmental firm, ENSR's professionals provide clients with consulting, engineering, remediation, and relatedservices from over 15 countries.
Michael S. Burke, Chairman/CEO
Daniel R. Tishman, Director, Vice Chairman

4536 ENSR-Harvard
325 Ayer Road
Harvard, MA 00145
978-772-2345
800-662-7232
Fax: 978-772-4956
AECOMInvestorRelations@aecom.com
www.ensr.aecom.com
ENSR is a global provider of environmental and energy development services to industry and government. As a full-service environmental firm, ENSR's professionals provide clients with consulting, engineering, remediation, and relatedservices from over 15 countries.
Michael S. Burke, Chairman/CEO
Daniel R. Tishman, Director, Vice Chairman

4537 ENSR-Kalamazoo
400 Monroe Street
Suite 270
Detroit, MI 48226-2977
313-961-9797
800-662-7232
Fax: 313-961-3480
AECOMInvestorRelations@aecom.com
www.ensr.aecom.com
ENSR is a global provider of environmental and energy development services to industry and government. As a full-service environmental firm, ENSR's professionals provide clients with consulting, engineering, remediation, and relatedservices from over 15 countries.
Michael S. Burke, Chairman/CEO
Daniel R. Tishman, Director, Vice Chairman

4538 ENSR-Minneapolis
800 LaSalle Avenue 612-376-2000
Suite 500 800-662-7232
Minneapolis, MN 55402 Fax: 612-376-2271
AECOMInvestorRelations@aecom.com
www.ensr.aecom.com

ENSR is a global provider of environmental and energy development services to industry and government. As a full-service environmental firm, ENSR's professionals provide clients with consulting, engineering, remediation, and relatedservices from over 15 countries.
Michael S. Burke, Chairman/CEO
Daniel R. Tishman, Director, Vice Chairman

4539 ENSR-New Orleans
1555 Poydras Street 504-586-8111
Suite 2700 800-662-7232
New Orleans, LA 70112 Fax: 504-582-0554
AECOMInvestorRelations@aecom.com
www.ensr.aecom.com

ENSR is a global provider of environmental and energy development services to industry and government. As a full-service environmental firm, ENSR's professionals provide clients with consulting, engineering, remediation, and relatedservices from over 15 countries.
Michael S. Burke, Chairman/CEO
Daniel R. Tishman, Director, Vice Chairman

4540 ENSR-Norcross
2 Sun Court at Technology Park 770-441-2364
Suite 200 800-662-7232
Norcross, GA 30092 Fax: 678-966-0751
AECOMInvestorRelations@aecom.com
www.ensr.aecom.com

ENSR is a global provider of environmental and energy development services to industry and government. As a full-service environmental firm, ENSR's professionals provide clients with consulting, engineering, remediation, and relatedservices from over 15 countries.
Michael S. Burke, Chairman/CEO
Daniel R. Tishman, Director, Vice Chairman

4541 ENSR-Portland (ME)
500 Southborough Drive 207-775-2800
South Portland, ME 00410-3209 800-662-7232
Fax: 207-775-4820
AECOMInvestorRelations@aecom.com
www.ensr.aecom.com

ENSR is a global provider of environmental and energy development services to industry and government. As a full-service environmental firm, ENSR's professionals provide clients with consulting, engineering, remediation, and relatedservices from over 15 countries.
Michael S. Burke, Chairman/CEO
Daniel R. Tishman, Director, Vice Chairman

4542 ENSR-Sacramento
2870 Gateway Oaks Drive 916-679-2000
Suite 150 800-662-7232
Sacramento, CA 95833-4308 Fax: 916-679-2900
AECOMInvestorRelations@aecom.com
www.ensr.aecom.com

ENSR is a global provider of environmental and energy development services to industry and government. As a full-service environmental firm, ENSR's professionals provide clients with consulting, engineering, remediation, and relatedservices from over 15 countries.
Michael S. Burke, Chairman/CEO
Daniel R. Tishman, Director, Vice Chairman

4543 ENSR-Shawnee Mission
6400 Glenwood Street 913-362-8444
Suite 105 800-662-7232
Shawnee Mission, KS 66202 Fax: 913-362-1044
AECOMInvestorRelations@aecom.com
www.ensr.aecom.com

ENSR is a global provider of environmental and energy development services to industry and government. As a full-service environmental firm, ENSR's professionals provide clients with consulting, engineering, remediation, and relatedservices from over 15 countries.
Michael S. Burke, Chairman/CEO
Daniel R. Tishman, Director, Vice Chairman

4544 ENSR-St Petersburg
10210 Highland Manor Drive 813-630-2500
Suite 350 800-662-7232
Tampa, FL 33610 Fax: 813-621-2300
AECOMInvestorRelations@aecom.com
www.ensr.aecom.com

ENSR is a global provider of environmental and energy development services to industry and government. As a full-service environmental firm, ENSR's professionals provide clients with consulting, engineering, remediation, and relatedservices from over 15 countries.
Michael S. Burke, Chairman/CEO
Daniel R. Tishman, Director, Vice Chairman

4545 ENSR-Stamford
500 Enterprise Drive 860-263-5800
Suite 1A 800-662-7232
Rocky Hill, CT 00606 Fax: 860-263-5777
AECOMInvestorRelations@aecom.com
www.ensr.aecom.com

ENSR is a global provider of environmental and energy development services to industry and government. As a full-service environmental firm, ENSR's professionals provide clients with consulting, engineering, remediation, and relatedservices from over 15 countries.
Michael S. Burke, Chairman/CEO
Daniel R. Tishman, Director, Vice Chairman

4546 ENVIRO Tech Services
910 54th Avenue 970-346-3900
Suite 230 800-369-3878
Greeley, CO 80634 Fax: 785-827-8765
www.envirotechservices.com

Developing superior road and surface solutions to manage all environments; both natural and man-made.
Roger Knoph, President/CEO
Kevin Whyrick, CFO

4547 ESA Laboratories
Laboratories, 22 Alpha Road 978-250-7150
Chelmsford, MA 00182 Fax: 978-250-7171
Environmental and biological testing laboratory.

4548 ESS Group
100 Fifth Avenue 781-419-7696
5th Floor Fax: 781-622-2612
Waltham, MA 02451 info@essgroup.com
www.essgroup.com

The ESS team of scientists, engineers, and regulatory specialists provides a comprehensive range of services related to energy facility development, land and waterfront development, water resource management and ecology, and industrialpermitting and compliance.
Charles Natale, President & CEO
Deirdra Taylor, VP, Chief Operating Officer

4549 ETTI Engineers and Consultants
1000 Rand Road
Unit 210
Wauconda, IL 60084
847-526-1606
Fax: 847-526-7443
solutions@ettinc.com
www.ettinc.com
Engineering research and testing laboratory specializing in construction services and environmental needs. Research results published in project reports and test summaries.
Wes Scott, President

4550 Eaglebrook Environmental Laboratories
1152 Junction Avenue
Schererville, IN 46375
219-322-0450
Fax: 219-322-0440
Environmental testing service.

4551 Earth Dimensions
1091 Jamison Road
Elma, NY 14059
716-655-1717
Fax: 716-655-2915
Geotechnical soil investigations and wetland delineations.
Don Owens, President
Brian Bartron, Geologist/Drilling Manager

4552 Earth Tech
4135 Technology Parkway
PO Box 1067
Sheboygan, WI 53083
920-458-8711
Fax: 920-458-0537
www.aecom.com
Specializes in the planning, design, and construction management and observation of environmental and infrastructure projects including water/wastewater; solid, hazardous and process waste facilities; environmental restoration;transportation; and architecture. The company's staff size, multiple office locations and comprehensive mix of expertise and experience combined iwht an in-depth knowledge of technical and regulatory issues, provide our clients with a valuableresource for solutions.
Diane Creel, President

4553 Earth Technology Corporation
300 Oceangate
Suite 700
Long Beach, CA 90802
562-951-2000
Fax: 562-951-2100
www.earthtech.com/
Alan P. Krusi, President

4554 Earthwatch International
114 Western Ave
Boston, MA 00213
978-461-0081
800-776-0188
Fax: 978-461-2332
info@earthwatch.org
earthwatch.org
Engages people worldwide in scientific research and education to promote the understanding and action necessary for a sustainable environment.
Larry Mason, CEO
Schott Kania, COO

4555 East Texas Testing Laboratory
1717 E Erwin Street
Tyler, TX 75702
903-595-4421
Fax: 903-595-6113
www.ettlinc.com
Engineering research and testing laboratory specializing in construction services and environmental needs. Research results published in project reports and test summaries.
Darrell Flatt, President
Thomas R. McLemore, CFO

4556 Eastern Technical Associates
PO Box 1009
Garner, NC 27529
919-878-3188
Fax: 919-872-5199
tomrose@eta-is-opacity.com
www.eta-is-opacity.com
Environmental consulting firm services of which include visible emissions training & certification. Research results published in government reports.
Jody Monk, General Manager
Sherri Sigworth, Office Manager

4557 Eberline Analytical, Lionville Laboratory
264 Welsh Pool Road
Exton, PA 19341
610-280-3060
800-841-5487
Fax: 610-280-3041
info@eberlineservices.com
www.eberlineservices.com
Analytical, consulting, and field services offer broad capabilities in: radiological characterization and analyses; environmental chemical analyses; hazardous, radioactive, and mixed waste management; and environmental, safety, andhealth management.
Carter Nulton, Laboratory Manager
William F Niemeyer, Business Development Manager

4558 Eberline Services - Albuquerque
10400 Academy NE
Ste 300
Albuquerque, NM 87111
505-262-2694
877-477-8989
Fax: 505-262-2698
info@eberlineservices.com
www.eberlineservices.com
Provides analytical, consulting and field services, offering broad capabilities in radiological characterizaion and analysis; hazaradous, radioactive, and mixed waste management; and environmental, safety, and health management. Inaddition, Eberline Services provides onsite staff and services for site characterization and remediation, decontamination and decommissioning, waste management, and facility operations.
Leva Jensen, Laboratory Manager
William F Niemeyer, Project Manager

4559 Eberline Services - Los Alamos
183 Central Park Square
Los Almos, NM 87544
505-262-2694
877-477-8989
Fax: 505-262-2698
info@eberlineservices.com
www.eberlineservices.com
Provides analytical, consulting and field services, offering broad capabilities in radiological characterizaion and analysis; hazaradous, radioactive, and mixed waste management; and environmental, safety, and health management. Inaddition, Eberline Services provides onsite staff and services for site characterization and remediation, decontamination and decommissioning, waste management, and facility operations.
Leva Jensen, Laboratory Manager
William F Niemeyer, Project Manager

4560 Eberline Services - Oak Ridge
601 Scarboro Road
Oak Ridge, TN 37830-7371
865-481-0683
877-477-8989
Fax: 865-483-4621
info@eberlineservices.com
www.eberlineservices.com
Provides analytical, consulting and field services, offering broad capabilities in radiological characterizaion and analysis; hazaradous, radioactive, and mixed waste management; and environmental, safety, and health management. Inaddition, Eberline Services provides onsite staff and services for site characterization and remediation, decontamination and decommissioning, waste management, and facility operations.
Leva Jensen, Laboratory Manager
William F Niemeyer, Project Manager

4561 Eberline Services - Richland
3200 George Washington Way
Richland, WA 99352
509-420-0841
877-477-8989
Fax: 505-262-2698
info@eberlineservices.com
www.eberlineservices.com

Provides analytical, consulting and field services, offering broad capabilities in radiological characterizaion and analysis; hazaradous, radioactive, and mixed waste management; and environmental, safety, and health management. Inaddition, Eberline Services provides onsite staff and services for site characterization and remediation, decontamination and decommissioning, waste management, and facility operations.
Leva Jensen, Laboratory Manager
William F Niemeyer, Project Manager

4562 Eberline Services - Richmond
2030 Wright Avenue 510-235-2633
Richmond, CA 94804-3849 800-841-5487
Fax: 510-235-0438
info@eberlineservices.com
www.eberlineservices.com

Analytical, consulting, and field services offer broad capabilities in: radiological characterization and analysis; hazardous, radioactive, and mixed waste management; and environmental, safety, and health management.
Leva Jensen, Laboratory Manager
William F Niemeyer, Program Manager

4563 Eco-Analysts
1420 S. Blaine 208-882-2588
Suite 14 Fax: 208-883-4288
Moscow, ID 83843 eco@ecoanalysts.com
www.ecoanalysts.com

Specializes in Aquatic Taxonomy and Bioassessment. An independent environmental consulting firm located in Moscow, Idaho. Experienced in the identification of freshwater organisms; macroinvertebrates, periphyton, plankton, and fish.Offer aquatic bioassessment and biological monitoring services.
Gary Lester, President/CEO
Scott Lindstrom, CFO

4564 EcoTest Laboratories
575 Broadhollow Rd. 631-694-3040
Melville, NY 11747-5076 Fax: 631-422-5770
www.h2mlabs.com

Environmental testing laboratory.
John J. Molloy, President and CEO
Joann M. Slavin, SVP, Laboratory Manager

4565 Ecological Engineering Associates
508 Boston Post Road 978-369-9440
PO Box 415 Fax: 508-748-9740
Weston, MA 00249-0003 info@ecological-engineering.com
www.ecological-engineering.com

Ecological Engineering Group is a unique engineering and design practice combining conventional engineering, innovative ecological design, and permitting know-how.
Bruce Strong, Operations Manager

4566 Ecology and Environment
368 Pleasant View Drive 716-684-8060
Lancaster, NY 14086 Fax: 716-684-0844
info@ene.com
www.ene.com

Ecology and Environment is an environmental science and engineering company providing environmental consulting services and litigation support in the areas of engineering, water treatment, regulatory compliance, permitting,environmental impact assessments, air and noise studies and more.
Mye John, Chief Financial Officer
Cheryl Karpowicz, Sr VP, Development

4567 Economists
2121 K Street, NW 202-223-4700
Suite 1100 Fax: 202-296-7138
Washington, DC 20037 info@ei.com
www.ei.com

Firm providing economic analysis and public policy evaluation, with emphasis on private antitrust litigation, communications regulation, and the Environment.
David Argue, President
Peter Greenhalgh, Director

4568 Ecotope
4056 9th Avenue NE 206-322-3753
Seattle, WA 98105 Fax: 206-325-7270
www.ecotope.com

Energy efficiency research, architecture, and engineering.
David Baylon, President
Jonathan Heller, Principal/Lead Mechanical En

4569 Eder Associates
480 Forest Avenue 516-671-8440
Locust Valley, NY 11560 Fax: 516-671-3349

Environmental engineering and consulting firm.
Leonard J Eden, President

4570 Eichleay Corporation of Illinois
11919 S Avenue O 773-731-7010
Chicago, IL 60617

Environmental consulting firm.

4571 El Dorado Engineering
2964 W 4700 South 801-966-8288
Suite 109 Fax: 801-966-8499
Salt Lake City, UT 84129 rfrandsen@eldoradoengineering.com
www.eldoradoengineering.com

Established in 1981, El Dorado Engineering (EDE) is a small business with the flexibility to meet the clients needs. In addition to the specialty work in Demilitarization, Environmental, Thermal Disposal, of energetics, EDE hasengineering experience that covers a wide variety of applications.
Bob Hayes, President/CEO
Ralph Hayes, Director, BD

4572 Electron Microprobe Laboratory Bilby Research Center
Northern Arizona University 928-523-9565
PO Box 6013 Fax: 928-523-7290
Flagstaff, AZ 86011 james.wittke@nau.edu
www4.nau.edu

The primary goal at the Bilby Research Center is to promote research across the Northern Arizona University campus. Research support services include professional editing; imaging services include illustration, photography, andvideography; and website design.
James H Wittke, Director
Marcelle Coder, Project Director

4573 Element Houston
222 Cavalcade Street 713-692-9151
PO Box 8768 888-786-7555
Houston, TX 77009 Fax: 713-696-6307
info.houston@element.com
www.element.com

Analysis and testing laboratory offering environmental control services including materials testing; nondestructive testing; polymer testing and polymeric materials testing; electrical and thermal testing; failure analysis;construction materials testing and engineering; product evaluation; surface testing, and air emissions.
Peter T Regan, Chairman
Charles Noall, President/CEO

4574 Element Materials Technology
1200 Westinghouse Boulevard 704-588-1131
Suite A 888-786-7555
Charlotte, NC 28273 Fax: 704-588-5412
info.charlotte@element.com
www.element.com

Analysis and testing laboratory offering environmental control services including mechanical, metallurgical, and chemical analysis in addition to materials testing, nondestructive testing, failure analysis and product evaluation.
Peter T Regan, Chairman
Charles Noall, President/CEO

4575 Elm Research Institute
11 Kit Street 603-358-6198
Keene, NH 00343 800-367-3567
Fax: 603-358-6305
libertytreesociety@gmail.com
www.libertytreesociety.org

A nonprofit organization dedicated to the restoration and preservation of the American Elm. Provides disease-resistant American Liberty Elms to municipalities, colleges and volunteer nonprofit groups for public planting. Distributionof Elm Fungicide for treatment of Dutch Elm Disease.
John Hansel, Executive Director
Yvonne Spalthoff, Assistant Director

4576 Emcon Baker-Shiflett
5701 E Loop S 817-478-8254
Fort Worth, TX 76119 Fax: 817-478-8874
Consulting engineers providing research services to the construction industry.
Larry Gardner, Contact

4577 Endyne Labs
160 James Brown Drive 802-879-4333
Williston, VT 00549 Fax: 802-879-7103
info@endynelabs.com
www.endynelabs.com

Endyne Labs is a full-service environmental testing laboratory that specializes in the analysis of organic, inorganic, metals and microbiological contaminants in a variety of matrices including drinking water, wastewater, soil,hazardous waste and air.
Harry B Locker PhD, President

4578 Energetics
7067 Columbia Gateway Drive 410-290-0370
Columbia, MD 21046 Fax: 410-290-0377
webmaster@energetics.com
www.energetics.com

Environmental engineering firm.
Nancy Margolis, President
Christopher Kelley, VP

4579 Energy & Environmental Technology
400 Perimeter Center Terrace NE 770-558-1205
Suite 105 Fax: 770-628-0459
Atlanta, GA 30346 Jaye@EandETech.com
www.eandetech.com

Environmental research.
Jack Locke, President
Russel Jones, VP

4580 Energy Conversion Devices
2956 Waterview Drive 248-293-0440
Rochester Hills, MI 48309 800-528-0617
Fax: 248-844-1214
www.ovonic.com

Maintained a strong core competence in materials research and advanced product development throughout its forty plus year history. The company protects the results of these efforts through an extensive patent collection.
Stanford Ovshinsky, President/CTO
Iris Ovshinsky, Vice President

4581 Energy Laboratories
400 West Boxelder Road 307-686-7175
Gillette, WY 82718 866-686-7175
Fax: 307-682-4625
casper@energylab.com
www.energylab.com

Environmental data collection, testing and analysis firm.
Tracey Archer, Project Manager
Alyson Degnan, Project Manager

4582 Energy and Environmental Analysis
9300 Lee Highway 703-934-3603
Fairfax, VA 22031-1207 800-532-4783
Fax: 703-934-3740
info@icfi.com
www.icfi.com

Consulting firm offering technical, analytical, and managerial services in the energy/environmental field.
Sudhakar Kesavan, Chairman/CEO
John Wasson, President/COO

4583 Engineering & Environmental Management Group
11251 Roger Bacon Drive 703-318-4522
Reston, VA 20910 Fax: 703-318-4729
Environmental applications.

4584 Engineering Analysis
715 Arcadia Circle 256-533-9391
Huntsville, AL 35801 Fax: 256-533-9325
eai@mindspring.com
www.mindspring.com/~eai/

Environmental and safety research and analysis organization. Research results published in client and technical reports and professional journals.
Frank B Tatom, President
Theodore (Ted) Sumrall, Consultant

4585 Entek Environmental & Technical Services
3 Agway Drive 518-269-3170
Rensselaer, NY 12144 800-888-9200
Fax: 518-283-4031
uhlig@entek-env.com
www.entek-env.com/

Environmental consulting and engineering firm.
Patrick J McDonough, Director/Manager

4586 Entropy
PO Box 90067 919-781-3550
Raleigh, NC 27675 800-486-3550
Fax: 919-787-8442
www.entropyinc.com

Provides air emission testing services.
Robert Drew, President

4587 Enviro Dynamics
1340 Old Chain Bridge Road 703-760-0023
Suite 300 Fax: 703-760-9382
Mc Lean, VA 22101
Occupational and environmental health analysis and consulting firm.
William J Keanet, President

4588 Enviro Systems
1 Lafayette Road
PO Box 778
Hampton, NH 00384
603-926-3345
Fax: 603-926-3521
pkarbe@envirosystems.com
www.envirosystems.com
Environmental compliance testing services, specializing in analytical chemistry and environmental toxicity testing with fresh and salt water, soil and sediment.
Petra Karbe, VP Marketing

4589 Enviro-Bio-Tech
4693 19th St. Court East
Bradenton, FL 34203
941-757-2591
800-314-6263
Fax: 941-757-2592
info@environmentalbiotech.com
www.environmentalbiotech.com
Chemical analysis firm.
Harpal Singh, President

4590 Enviro-Lab
45-10 Court Square
Long Island City, NY 11101
718-392-0185
Fax: 718-392-8654
www.envirolab.com
Environmental Toxicology Laboratory (ETL) is a research, development and testing laboratory; concentrating its efforts on new approaches to toxicity testing. The mission of ETL is the further advancement of the Tetramitis Assay aswell as the promotion and commercialization of the test.
Dr. Robert L Jaffe, Ph.D, Director of Lab. Science

4591 Enviro-Sciences
781 Route 15 South
Hopatcong, NJ 00784
973-398-8183
Fax: 973-398-8037
info@enviro-sciences.com
www.enviro-sciences.com
Environmental sciences firm.
Irving D Cohen, CEO
Glenn Lechner, Marketing Manager

4592 EnviroAnalytical
286 Mask Island Drive
Barry's Bay, ON K0J 1
613-756-0101
800-427-8591
Fax: 613-756-0909
www.enviro-analytical.com
Environmental compliance analysis, R&D, personnel training and analytical method development.
Dr S Sethi, Job Director

4593 Enviroclean Technology
1000 N.W. 57th Court
Suite 360
Miami, FL 33126
305-267-6667
Fax: 888-418-3181
www.erm.com
Environmental laboratory service company.
John Alexander, CEO
David McArthur, Director of Acquisitions

4594 Envirodyne Engineers
303 E Wacker Drive
Suite 600
Chicago, IL 60601
312-938-0300
Fax: 312-938-1109
Environmental science research firm.

4595 Environ Laboratories
9725 Girard Avenue S
Minneapolis, MN 55431
952-888-7795
800-826-3710
Fax: 952-888-6345
Laboratory providing environmental and physical testing of products and materials to commercial and military specifications.
Alan G Thompson, President

4596 Environment Associates
9604 Variel Avenue
Chatsworth, CA 91311
818-709-0568
800-354-1522
Fax: 818-709-8914
Andrews@Eatest.com
www.eatest.com
Provides a full spectrum of environmental test services to Aerospace, Military and commercial manufacturers including temperature, humidity, altitude, thermal vacuum, shock, vibration, corrosive atmosphere, a DSCC approved connectortest lab, hydraulic and pneumatic test capabilities, flow testing firewall testing, EMMI/EMC testing and more. Services also include test procedure development formal test reports, certification and test fixture modifications and adaptations.
William Spaulding, President
Andrew Spaulding, Sales

4597 Environment/One Corporation
2773 Balltown Road
Niskayuna, NY 12309-1090
518-346-6161
Fax: 518-346-6188
eone@eone.com
www.eone.com
Environmental analysis and instrumentation firm. Research results published in technical journals.
George A. Vorsheim, Communications Director

4598 Environmental Acoustical Research
PO Box 18888
Boulder, CO 80308
303-447-2619
800-525-2690
Fax: 303-447-2637
info@earinc.com
www.earinc.com
Specialized hearing protection and enhancement systems.
Garry G. Gordon, President/Audiologist
Andrew Gordon, Lab/Marketing Director

4599 Environmental Analysis
3278 N Highway 67
Florissant, MO 63033
314-921-4488
Fax: 314-921-4494
Environmental analytical laboratory.
R M Ferris, President

4600 Environmental Analytical Laboratory
95 Beaver Street
Waltham, MA 00245
781-893-8330
Fax: 781-893-4414
Info@hubtesting.net
www.hubtesting.net
Environmental testing services company specializing in asbestos consulting and analysis, waste water, soils and surveys. Also mold remediation and screening.
Frederick Boyle, President

4601 Environmental Audits
11327 W. Lincoln Ave.
West Allis, WI 53227
414-226-5563
Fax: 414-231-9374
info@environmentalaudits.net
Consulting firm specializing in environmental science.
John R Ruetz, President

4602 Environmental Chemical
1240 Bayshore Highway
Burlingame, CA 94010
650-347-1555
Fax: 650-347-8789
www.ecc.net
Research and testing firm.

4603 Environmental Consultants
391 Newman Avenue
Clarksville, IN 47129
812-282-8481
Fax: 812-282-8554
Environmental consulting firm.
Robert E Fuchs, President

4604 Environmental Consulting Laboratories
1005 Boston Post Road 203-245-0568
Madison, CT 00644 800-246-9624
eclinc@aol.com
Environmental testing and consulting firm.

4605 Environmental Consulting Laboratories, Inc.
1005 Boston Post Road 203-245-0568
Madison, CT 00644 800-246-9624
Fax: 203-318-0830
eclinc@aol.com
Environmental testing and consulting firm. Specializing in Micro Biology and aquatic tixicity.
David Barris, President/Lab Director

4606 Environmental Control
6525 North Mineral Drive 208-772-8200
Coeur d'Alene Fax: 505-232-0942
Idaho, ID 83815-8788 www.environmentcontrol.com
Environmental consulting and analytical laboratory. Research results published in project reports and test summaries.
Reid Warner, Owner
James J Meuller, President

4607 Environmental Control Laboratories
38818 Talyor Industrial Parkway 440-353-3700
North Ridgeville, OH 44039 800-962-0118
Fax: 440-353-3773
E.C. Labs does environmental testing, such as: waste water, soil, asbestos, remediation and constrution projects.
Ron Schiedel, Marketing Manager
Phyllis Conley, Lab Manager

4608 Environmental Data Resources
6 Armstrong Road 203-783-0300
4th Floor 800-352-0050
Shelton, CT 00648 Fax: 800-231-6802
www.edrnet.com
Applied and product research in environmental applications.
Dan Gottlieb, CEO
Tom Flynn, CFO

4609 Environmental Elements Corporation
333 West Camden St. 410-333-1560
Suite 500 877-637-8234
Batlimore, MD 21201 Fax: 410-333-1888
msa@mdstad.com
www.EEC1.com
Environmental Elements Corporation, the leading supplier of air pollution control systems for over 50 years, designs, installs, and maintains electrostatic precipitators, fabric filters, gas, and particulate scrubbing andAmmonia-on-Demand (AOD) Systems. EEC technologies enable customers in a broad range of power and generation, pulp, and paper, waste-to-energy, rock products, metals and petrochemical industries to operate their facilities in compliance withparticulate and gaseous emissions.
Robert L. McKinney, Chairman
Alison L. Asti, Executive Director

4610 Environmental Health Sciences Research Laboratory
127 New Market Street 504-394-2233
PO Box 379 Fax: 504-394-7982
Belle Chasse, LA 70037

4611 Environmental Innovations
9600 West Flag Avenue 414-358-7760
Milwaukee, WI 53225 Fax: 414-358-7770
Environmental engineering and consulting firm.

4612 Environmental Laboratories
1 United Nations Plaza 212-963-6010
Room DC-1-1155 Fax: 917-367-4046
New York, NY 10017 iaeany@un.org
www.iaea.org
Yukiya Amano, Director General
Janice Dunn Lee, Head, Dept of Management

4613 Environmental Management: Guthrie
5200 N.E. Highway 33 405-282-8510
PO Box 700 800-510-8510
Guthrie, OK 73044 Fax: 405-282-8533
www.emiok.com
Full service environmental firm provides emergency response remediation routine waste management for hazardous and non hazardous materials and consulting. The firm owns the transportation and remediation equipment along with providinga full technical staff.
Terry Bobo, President
Keeton Hill, Health and Safety Officer

4614 Environmental Management: Waltham
95 Beaver Street 781-893-8330
Waltham, MA 00245 Fax: 781-893-4414
Info@hubtesting.net
www.hubtesting.net
Environmental testing services, consulting services, environmental abatement services, water quality/chemical testing, asbestos remediation monitoring and inspections, mold testing/mold remediation, industrial hygiene services.
Susan Boyle, Vice President

4615 Environmental Measurements
2660 California Street 415-567-8089
San Francisco, CA 94115 Fax: 415-398-7664
sales@langan.net

4616 Environmental Monitoring Laboratory
59 N Plains Industrial Road 203-284-0555
Suite A Fax: 203-284-2064
Wallingford, CT 00649
Laboratory providing environmental chemistry services including analysis, bioassays, product efficacy and research and development in the areas of water and wastewater, agricultural chemicals, protective coatings, petroleum products,metals and chemicals.
Jan D Dunn PhD, Director/Manager

4617 Environmental Quality Protection Systems Company
5150 Keele Street 601-961-5650
Jackson, MS 39206 Fax: 601-354-6612
Environmental engineering and science firm.

4618 Environmental Research Associates
16341 Table Mountain Parkway 303-421-0122
Golden, CO 80403 800-372-0122
Fax: 303-431-8454
info@eraqc.com
www.eraqc.com
Research and consulting ecologists and testing firm. Research results published in professional journals. Research results for private clients.
M H Levin PhD, Director

4619 Environmental Resource Associates
16341 Table Mountain Parkway 303-431-8454
Golden, CO 80403 800-372-0122
Fax: 303-421-0159
info@eraqc.com
www.eraqc.com

Provides products and consultation services for laboratories specializing in environmental research.
Chris Ackerman, Life Science Sales

4620 Environmental Risk: Clifton Division
1373 Broad Street 973-773-8322
Suite 301 Fax: 973-243-9055
Clifton, NJ 00701
Environmental engineering and consulting services.

4621 Environmental Science & Engineering
1200 E. California Blvd 626-795-6070
MC 131-24 Fax: 626-795-6028
Pasadena, CA 91125 www.ese.caltech.edu
Comprehensive environmental and engineering consulting firm.
Nora Oshima, Grants Manager
Elizabeth Boyd, Academic Assistant

4622 Environmental Services International
6404 Maccorkle Avenue 304-768-2233
Saint Albans, WV 25177 Fax: 304-768-9988
esi@citynet.net
Consulting, engineering, and analytical firm. Research results published in reports to clients.

4623 Environmental Systems Corporation
10801 N Mopac Bldg 1-200 512-250-7900
Austin, TX 78759 Fax: 512-258-5836
support@envirosys.com
www.envirosys.com
Data acquisition and reporting systems for electric power producers and industrial sources, ESC is the leading supplier of CEM and ambient data systems in the US.
Rachael Morgan, VP
Jeff Rabenteine, President

4624 Environmental Technical Services
834 Castle Ridge Road 512-327-6672
Austin, TX 78746 Fax: 512-327-1974
www.wetlands.com/
Firm conducts sewer rehabilitation and tank testing.

4625 Environmental Testing Services
95 Beaver Street 781-893-8330
Waltham, MA 00245 Fax: 781-893-4414
Info@hubtesting.net
www.hubtesting.net
Environmental testing services company specializing in asbestos consulting and analysis, waste water, soils and surveys. Also mold remediation and screening.
Frederick Boyle, President

4626 Environmental Working Group
1436 U St. NW 202-667-6982
Suite 100 Fax: 202-232-2592
Washington, DC 20009 www.ewg.org
Cutting-edge research on health and the environment.
Carol Mcdonnell, Director, Chair
Ami Aronson, Director

4627 Enviropro
9765 Eton Avenue 818-998-7197
Chatsworth, CA 91311 Fax: 818-998-7258
Environmental engineering services. Spcialize in: Site investigation/remediation; Real Estate transfers: Phase I and II assessments; feasibility studies; clean-up of contaminated property, soil and groundwater; Methane gasinvestigations.
Zvia Uziel, President
Dr Michael Uziel, Director/Manager

4628 Enviroscan Inc
1051 Columbia Avenue 717-396-8922
Lancaster, PA 17603 Fax: 717-396-8746
email@enviroscan.com
www.enviroscan.com
Specializes in non-intrusive, non-deestructive land marine and borhole geophysics for engineers, environmental consultants, architects, industry, government and others. Geophysics is the earth science equivalent of medical radiology,and is used to locate subsurface objects such as utilities, underground storage tanks, drums, bedrock depths, sinkholes, contaminant plumes, fractures, graves, downed aircraft(in oceans, lakes) and submerged items.
Felicia Kegel Bechtel, President
Geoffrey T. Stankiewicz, Vice President

4629 Envisage Environmental
PO Box 152 440-526-0990
Richfield, OH 44286 Fax: 440-526-8555
Environmental engineering firm.

4630 Eppley Laboratory
12 Sheffield Avenue 401-847-1020
PO Box 419 Fax: 401-847-1031
Newport, RI 00284 info@eppleylab.com
www.eppleylab.com
Produces radiometer, pyranometers, pyrheliometers and pyrgeometers that measure solar and terrestrial radiation.
George L Kirk, President

4631 Era Laboratories
4730 Oneota Street 218-727-6380
Duluth, MN 55807-2719 800-727-6380
Fax: 218-727-3049
info@eralabs.com
Environmental laboratory serving the agricultural industry through chemical analysis and sampling.
Robert D Manuson, President

4632 Ernaco
3740 Capulet Terr. 301-598-5025
Silver Spring, MD 20906
Firm offers biomedical, health and environmental research services.
Dr Muriel M Lippman, President

4633 Eureka Laboratories
4701 S. Whipple Street 773-847-9672
Chicago, IL 60632 Fax: 773-847-9675
Shao-Pin Yo, Laboratory Director

4634 Eurofins QC
1205 Industrial Highway 215-355-3900
P.O. Box 514 800-289-8378
Southampton, PA 18966-514 Fax: 215-355-7231
www.qclaboratories.com
Environmental testing lab.

4635 Eurofins SFA Laboratories
2345 South 170th Street 262-754-5300
New Berlin, WI 53151 800-300-6700
Fax: 262-754-5310
dkliber@sflabs.com
www.eurofinsus.com
Environmental and materials testing laboratory.
David L Kliber, President/CEO

4636 Eustis Engineering Services, LLC
3011 28th Street
Metairie, LA 70002
504-834-0157
800-966-0157
Fax: 504-834-0354
info@eustiseng.com
www.eustiseng.com

Geotechnical firm performing complete investigations, dynamic pile testing, cone penetrometer testing, CQC and materials testing and environmental services.
William W Gwyn, President
John R Eustis, Executive Vice President

4637 Evans Cooling Systems
1 Mountain Rd
Suffield, CT 00607
860-668-1114
Fax: 860-668-2757
tech@evanscooling.com
www.evanscooling.com

Environmental applications.
J. Thomas Light, President/CEO
Jeff Bye, VP/COO

4638 Everglades Laboratories
1602 Clare Avenue
West Palm Beach, FL 33401
561-833-4200
Fax: 561-833-7280
info@evergladeslabs.com
www.evergladeslabs.com/

EVERGLADES Laboratories, Inc. is a Florida state certified and NELAC accredited independent environmental and analytical testing laboratory.
Dr. Ben Martin, Director

4639 Excel Environmental Resources
111 North Center Drive
New Brunswick, NJ 00890
732-545-9525
800-810-3923
Fax: 732-545-9425
info@excelenv.com
www.excelenv.com

Environmental research.
Laura J. Dodge, President
Ron Harwood, Executive VP

4640 First Coast Environmental Laboratory
8818 Arlington Expressway
Jacksonville, FL 32211
904-725-4847
Fax: 904-725-2215

Analytical laboratory.
Adolph W Wollitz, Director/Manager

4641 Fishbeck, Thompson, Carr & Huber, Inc.
1515 Arboretum Drive, SE
Grand Rapids, MI 49546
616-575-3824
Fax: 616-464-3993
info@ftch.com
www.ftch.com

Environmental consulting and engineering firm.
Ryan Eversole, Sr. Structural Engineer
Julia Smith, Sr. Mechanical Engineer

4642 Flowers Chemical Laboratories
481 Newburyport Avenue
PO Box 150597
Altamonte Springs, FL 32701
407-339-5984
800-669-5227
Fax: 407-260-6110
jeff@flowerslabs.com
www.flowerslabs.com

Analytical consulting firm. Research results published in reports to clients. Displays report in a pdf or html format.
Dr Jefferson Flowers, President

4643 Forensic Engineering
1439 Legion Road
Burlington, ON L7S1T
905-632-3040
800-263-6351
Fax: 905-632-2131
www.forensiceng.ca

Joe M Beard, President

4644 Fredericktowne Labs
3020 Ventrie Court
PO Box 245
Myersville, MD 21778
301-293-3340
800-332-3340
Fax: 301-293-2366
info@Fredericktownelabs.com
www.Fredericktownelabs.com

Environmental testing lab performing analyses on drinking water, waste water and natural waters for microbiological, inorganic, metal and organic contaminants. State certified laboratory. State certified sample collectors.Consulting services.
Mary Miller, PhD, Laboratory Director
Kathy Ryan, Special Projects Coordinator

4645 Free-Col Laboratories: A Division of Modern Industries
613 West 11th ST.
Erie, PA 16501
814-455-8061
Fax: 814-453-4382
johnp@modernind.com
www.modernind.com

Full service environmental laboratory - drinking water, waste water, solid waste, industrial hygiene testing; materials testing & engineering; non-destructive testing; mechanical testing; chemical analysis; failure analysis;consulting.
John Paraska, Director

4646 Froehling & Robertson
3015 Dumbarton Road
Richmond, VA 23228
804-264-2701
Fax: 804-264-1202
www.fandr.com

Environmental and construction materials testing lab.
Daniel K. Shaefer, VP
Scott Sutton, Business Development

4647 Froehling & Robertson, Inc.
3015 Dumbarton Road
Richmond, VA 23228
804-264-2701
Fax: 804-264-1202
jmingus@fandr.com
www.fandr.com

Independent testing laboratory whose mission is to provide excellent client service with its scope of both engineering and chemical services.
Bob Hill, PE, Branch Manager
Scott Sutton, Business Development

4648 FuelCell Energy
3 Great Pasture Road
Danbury, CT 00681
203-825-6000
www.fce.com

Developer and manufacturer of clean and efficient electric power generators. Products are designed for distributed generation users including schools, data centers, hospitals, buildings, waste water treatment plants and othercommercial and industrial applications.
Arthur Chipp Bottone, President/CEO
Michael Bishop, Sr. VP/CFO/Treasurer

4649 Fugro McClelland
6100 Hillcroft
Houston, TX 77081
713-369-5600
Fax: 512-444-3996
www.fugrogeoconsulting.com

Environmental, geotechnical, marine geoscience and environmental engineering firm.
Frank Marshall, President

4650 G&E Engineering
P.O. Box 3592 405-840-0301
Olympic Valley, CA 96146-3592 Fax: 405-840-4307
eidinger@earthlink.net
www.geengineeringsystems.com
Environmental impact assessment firm.
Richard Adams, President
John Eidinger

4651 GE Osmonics: GE Water Technologies
4636 Somerton Road 952-933-2277
Trevose, PA 19053 866-439-2837
Fax: 952-933-0141
www.gewater.com
Water and process technologies from GE Osmonics provide water, wastewater and process systems solutions.
Yuvbir Singh, General Manager
Heiner Markhoff, President/CEO

4652 GEO Plan Associates
30 Mann Street 781-740-1340
Hingham, MA 00204-1316 Fax: 781-740-1340
geoplanassoc@gmail.com
Scientific and technical consulting, environmental planning and analysis firm. Experienced in coastal and shallow marine geology, land-use planning, and transportation.
Peter S Rosen PhD, Partner
Michu Tcheng, Partner

4653 GEO-CENTERS
4805 Westway Park Blvd. 281-443-8150
Houston, TX 77041 Fax: 281-443-8010
mmohr@geocenter.com
Provider of WMD homeland security preparedness services and products with major strengths in chemical and biological research.
Sukhie Hyare, President
John Asma, VP of Marketing

4654 GKY and Associates
4229 Lafayette Ctr Dr 703-870-7000
Suite 1850 Fax: 703-870-7039
Chantilly, VA 21051 sstein@gky.com
www.gky.com
Civil and environmental systems engineering consulting organization. Research results published in project reports, government publications, and professional journals.
Stuart Stein, President
Brett Martin, VP

4655 GL Applied Research
142 Hawley Street 847-223-2220
PO Box 187 Fax: 847-223-2287
Grayslake, IL 60030 glapplied@glappliedresearch.com
www.glappliedresearch.com
Analytical and process control instrumentation development and manufacture; photometric analyzers.
Edgar Watson Jr, President

4656 GSEE
599 Waldron Road 615-793-7547
La Vergne, TN 37086 Fax: 615-793-5070
gsee@gseeinc.com
www.gseeinc.com
GSEE provides environmental engineering and technical services for municipal, industrial and governmental clientele as well as other engineering consultants and manufacturers throughout the United States and abroad. GSEE offersexisting plant evaluations, process engineering, detail engineering, and operations training.
Wendy Ingram, Lab Director

4657 GZA GeoEnvironmental
249 Vanderbilt Avenue 781-278-3700
Norwood, MA 00206 Fax: 781-278-5701
info@gza.com
www.gza.com
Geotechnical and geohydrological testing and analysis firm.
William Hadge, CEO
Joseph P Hehir, CFO

4658 Gabriel Environmental Services
1421 North Elston 773-486-2123
Chicago, IL 60642 Fax: 773-486-0004
gabriel@gabrielenvironmental.com
www.gabrielenvironmental.com
Gabriel Environmental Services is a multi-disciplinary environmental consulting firm headquartered just northwest of downtown Chicago. They have been providing site assessment services, environmental testing and monitoring, andlaboratory analysis to a wide variety of clients since 1973.
William Gray, VP
Steve Sawyer, Evecutive VP

4659 Galson Laboratories
6601 Kirkville Road 315-432-5227
PO Box 369 888-432-5227
East Syracuse, NY 13057 Fax: 315-437-0509
pweaver@galsonlabs.com
www.galsonlabs.com
Environmental industrial hygiene and biological testing service.
Mary Unangst, VP Operations
Joe Unangst, VP

4660 Gas Technology Institute
1700 S Mount Prospect Road 847-768-0500
Des Plaines, IL 60018 Fax: 847-768-0501
info@gastechnology.org
www.gastechnology.org
Energy and environmental research.
David Carroll, President/CEO
Ronald Snedic, VP

4661 Gaynes Labs
9708 Industrial Drive 708-223-6655
Bridgeview, IL 60455 Fax: 708-233-6985
Gayneslabs@aol.com
www.gaynestesting.com
Research laboratories. Research results published in confidential test summaries and project reports. Services include environmental testing, atmospheric simulations, frequency vibration testing, temperature and humidity simulationtesting.
Philip Ross, Material Testing Manager

4662 General Engineering Labs
2040 Savage Road 843-556-8171
PO Box 30712 Fax: 843-766-1178
Charleston, SC 29417 grm@gel.com
www.gel.com
Environmental testing lab.
James M. Stelling, President/CEO
Kathleen S. Stelling, Chairman

4663 General Oil Company/GOC-Waste Compliance Services
35796 Veronica Street 734-266-6500
PO Box 1204 800-323-9905
Livonia, MI 48150 Fax: 734-266-6400
twesterdale@generaloilco.com
Waste Compliance Services (WCS) is an analytical laboratory, serving the industrial community. WCS services a broad client base that includes manufacturing industries, environmental consultants, independent contractors, andindividuals. Services include effluent management programs (permit negotiation and

management, sampling, self monitoring reports and waste treatment assistance) and analytical testing services.
Timothy A Westerdale, President/CEO
Adam Westerdale, VP/Chief Operating Officer

4664 General Sciences Corporation
205 Schoolhouse Rd. 215-723-8588
Souderton, PA 18964 Fax: 215-723-8875
Consulting and research firm specializing in environmental sciences.
Jeffrey Chen, President

4665 General Systems Division
1025 West Nursery Road 410-636-8700
Suite 120 Fax: 410-636-8708
Linthicum Heights, MD 21090 www.nct-active.com
Environmental studies.
Michael Parella, President

4666 Geo Environmental Technologies
103 E. Lemon Ave. 626-305-0400
Suite 212 Fax: 401-751-8613
Monrovia, CA 91016 jcouture@geoenvironment-technologies.com
www.geoenvironment-technologies.com
Environmental testing and consulting company.
Jeff Couture, Contact Person

4667 Geo-Con
1250 Fifth Avenue 724-335-7273
New Kensington, PA 15068 Fax: 412-373-3357
lmartin@geocon.net
www.geocon.net
Environmental services firm provides soil remediation by mixing soil with chemicals designed to eliminate the contaminants.
James Brannigan, VP of Opertaions
Loren Martin, Business Development Manager

4668 GeoPotential
22323 E Wild Fern Lane 503-622-0154
Brightwood, OR 97011 Fax: 503-492-4404
geopotential@aol.com
www.members.aol.com/resiii/geomain.htm
GeoPotential provides subsurface mapping surveys to locate underground objects such as underground storage tanks, utilities, geology, etc. They use geophysical methods consisting of ground penetrating radar, magnetics,electromagnetics and gravity.
Ralph Soule, President

4669 Geological Sciences & Laboratories
3133 N Main Street 606-439-3373
Hazard, KY 41701

4670 Geomatrix
210 East High Street 732-579-8283
Bound Brook, NJ 00880 Fax: 732-579-8305
info@geosoftinc.com
www.geosoftinc.com
Environmental engineering and consulting firm.

4671 Geophex
605 Mercury Street 919-839-8515
Raleigh, NC 27603 Fax: 919-839-8528
info@geophex.com
www.geophex.com
Environmental services firm.
IJ Won, President

4672 George Miksch Sutton Avian Research Center
PO Box 2007 918-336-7778
Bartlesville, OK 74005-2007 Fax: 918-336-7783
gmsarc@aol.com
www.suttoncenter.org
Finding cooperative conservation solutions for birds and the natural world through science and education.
George Kamp, Chairman
Lee Holcombe, President

4673 Geotechnical and Materials Testing
693 Plymouth Ave NE 616-456-5469
Grand Rapids, MI 49505 800-968-8378
Fax: 616-456-5784
www.mtc-test.com
Environmental engineering and consulting firm.
Ahmed N Elrefai, President

4674 Gerhart Laboratories
Route 219 814-634-0820
Garrett, PA 15542
Environmental testing laboratory.
Michael Gerhart, President

4675 Giblin Associates
PO Box 6172 707-528-3078
Santa Rosa, CA 95406 Fax: 707-528-2837
Environmental and geotechnical engineering firm.
Jere A Giblin, President

4676 Global Geochemistry Corporation
Station A 902-453-0061
PO Box 9469 Fax: 902-453-0061
Halifax, NS B3K5S www.global-geoenergy.com
Consulting firm in the fields of geochemistry and environmental sciences. Research results published by the firm's scientists in journals.
Prasanta Mukhopadhyay, President

4677 Globetrotters Engineering Corporation
300 S Wacker Drive 312-922-6400
Suite 400 Fax: 312-922-2953
Chicago, IL 60606 marketing@gec-group.com
www.gec-group.com
Globetrotters helps its clients achieve their goals by understanding their needs and offering high quality, sustainable, and value added professional services that are specifically tailored to each project.
Niranjan S Shah, Chair/CEO/Co-founder
Michael J. McMurray, ESQ., President

4678 GoodKind & O'Dea
31 Saint James Avenue 617-695-3400
Suite 1601 Fax: 617-695-3310
Boston, MA 00211
Architectural and engineering consulting firm.
David K Blake, Contact

4679 Gordon & Associates
1 Gateway Center 617-227-2707
Suite 312 Fax: 617-916-9218
Newton, MA 00245 jsanders@gordonassociates.com
www.gordonassociates.com
Environmental consulting firm specializing in waste residuals.
Howard J. Gordon, President
Robert S. Kamanitz, Sr. VP

4680 Gordon Piatt Energy Group
7811 Baumgart Road 800-848-8197
Evansville, IN 47725 800-848-8197
Fax: 812-867-0760
sales@ciciboilers.com
www.gordonpiattparts.com

Jim Salomon, President

4681 Grand Junction Laboratories
435 North Avenue 970-242-7618
Grand Junction, CO 81501 Fax: 970-243-7235
Brian Bauer, Director

4682 Greeley-Polhemus Group
1310 Birmingham Road 610-793-9440
West Chester, PA 19382
Environmental engineering and economic analysis firm.
Maureen Polhemus, President & Owner

4683 Green Globe Laboratories
1860 Arthur Road 630-231-0680
West Chicago, IL 60185 Fax: 630-957-4394
rajan@therightstuff.com
www.therightstuff.com
Environmental testing and consulting firm.
Robert Fitzsimmons, President

4684 Ground Technology
14227 Fern Drive 281-597-8866
Houston, TX 77079 Fax: 281-597-8308
A multi-disciplinary engineering firm specializing in environmental services, geotechnical engineering, and construction materials and inspection services. GTI is a woman owned business enterprise as well as minority/disadvantagedenterprise certified by TxDOT, METRO, the State of Texas, and City of Houston, HISD, and the Houston Minority Business Council.
Ruma Acharya, President

4685 Groundwater Specialists
3806 Telluride Place 303-494-8122
Boulder, CO 80305 Fax: 303-494-5443
gws@qwest.net
Groundwater exploration; dewatering; waterwell design; mitigation of high groundwater problems.
William H Bellis, Hydrologist

4686 Gruen, Gruen & Associates
1160 Mission Street 415-433-7598
#2204 Fax: 415-989-4224
San Francisco, CA 94103 jlofton@ggassoc.com
www.ggassoc.com
The urban economists, sociologists, market and financial analysts, demographers and statisticians of Gruen Gruen + Associates (GG+A) are dedicated to helping make the best use of land, real property and urban and environmentalresources.
Nina J Gruen, Principle Sociologist
Claude Gruen, Ph.D., Principal Economist

4687 Guanterra Environmental Services
1721 S Grand Avenue 714-258-8610
Santa Ana, CA 92705 Fax: 714-258-0921
Chemical analysis technical and consulting research firm. Research results published in project reports and professional journals.

4688 Guardian Systems
1108 Ashville Road NE 205-699-6647
PO Box 190 866-729-7211
Leeds, AL 35094 Fax: 205-699-3882
awilliams@gsilab.com
www.gsilab.com
Laboratory division provides a full range of analysis for inorganic, organicand physical testing of drinking water, wastewater, groundwater sediments, sludge, waste materials and soils. Industrial Hygiene division provides equipmentand analysis to meet OSHA requirements. Bio-Assay division can accommodate Aquatic Toxicity monitoring requirement.
Linda Miller, President
Gerald Miller, CEO

4689 Gulf Coast Analytical Laboratories
7979 Innovation Park Drive 225-769-4900
Baton Rouge, LA 70820 Fax: 225-767-5717
edg@gcal.com
www.gcal.com
Environmental and industrial testing laboratory.
Randy K. Whittington, CEO
Mark Peterman, IT Director

4690 Gutierrez, Smouse, Wilmut and Associates
11117 Shady Trl 972-620-1255
Dallas, TX 75229 Fax: 972-620-8028
Environmental engineering consulting firm. Research results published in project reports and technical journals.
Charles G Wilmut, President

4691 H John Heinz III Center for Science
900 17th Street NW 202-737-6307
Suite 700 Fax: 202-737-6410
Washington, DC 20006 info@heinzctr.org
www.heinzctr.org
The Center is a nonpartisan, nonprofit institute dedicated to improving the scientific and economic foundation for environmental policy through nmultisectoral collaboration. The Heinz Center fosters collaboration among industry,environmental organizations, academia, and all levels of government in each of its program areas.
Conn Nugent, President
Matthew Grason, Fundraising Coordinator

4692 H2M Group: Holzmacherm McLendon & Murrell
575 Broad Hollow Road 631-694-3040
Melville, NY 11747-5076 Fax: 631-694-4122
www.h2mlabs.com
Engineers, hydrogeologists, geologists and scientists strive to balance society's dynamic industrial and commercial growth with appropriate development and conservation of natural and man-made resources.
John J Molloy, President
Joann M. Slavin, Sr. VP

4693 HDR
8404 Indian Hills Drive 402-399-1000
Omaha, NE 68114-4098 800-366-4411
Fax: 402-548-5015
www.hdrinc.com
Consulting firm offering services in site design, asset management, environmental remediation, impact analysis, compliance, natural resources management, permitting and more.
George A Little, PE, Chairman & CEO

4694 HTS
416 Pickering Street 713-692-8373
Houston, TX 77091
Ron Langston, President

4695 HWS Consulting Group
PO Box 80358 402-479-2200
Lincoln, NE 68501 Fax: 402-479-2276
James Linderholm, President

4696 Hach Company
PO Box 389 970-669-3050
Loveland, CO 80539-389 800-227-4224
Fax: 970-669-2932
techhelp@hach.com
www.hach.com
Offers water quality product for government buyers.
Bruce Hach, President

4697 Haley & Aldrich
70 Blanchard Road 617-886-7400
Suite 204 Fax: 619-285-7169
Burlington, MA 00180 info@haleyaldrich.com
www.haleyaldrich.com
Haley & Aldrich provides leading edge underground engineering and environmental consulting services, nationally and internationally. The staff encompass a wide range of disciplines, offering their clients integrated solutions.Environmental services include corrective action; environmental management, health and safety consulting; and environmental site assessment/due diligence.
Lawrence Smith, President/CEO
Ellie Haddad, Market Segment Leader

4698 Halliburton Company
3000 N. Sam Houston Pkwy E. 281-871-4000
Houston, TX 77032 Fax: 214-978-2611
www.halliburton.com
One of the world's largest providers of products and services to the oil and gas industries.
Milton Carroll, Chairman
David J. Lesar, Chairman of the Board

4699 Hamilton Research, Ltd.
80 Grove Street 914-631-9194
Tarrytown, NY 10591 Fax: 914-631-6134
Hamilton Research is a consulting firm specializing in environmental physiology. Our focus is mainly on exposure of people to pressures less and greater than atmospheric, and involves dealing with different breathing gases, especiallyhigh and low levels of oxygen, and the consequences of changes in pressure, especially decompression. Another important area of interest is hyperbaric oxygen therapy.
R W Hamilton, President

4700 Hampton Roads Testing Laboratories
611 Howmet Drive 757-826-5310
Hampton, VA 23661
Independent third party testing laboratory. Performs sampling and analysis in accordance with the required ASTM or ISO Standards.

4701 Handex Environmental Recovery
500 Campus Drive 732-536-8500
PO Box 451 Fax: 732-536-7751
Morganville, NJ 00775
Environmental management and analysis firm.
CL Smith, CEO

4702 Hart Crowser
1700 Westlake Avenue North 206-328-5581
Suite 200 Fax: 206-324-9530
Seattle, WA 98109-6212 rick.moore@hartcrowser.com
www.hartcrowser.com
Hart Crowser, Inc. provides a full range of services from initial site studies through regulatory permitting, design, and construction. They integrate thses services as required by each project. They know what kind of information isimportant, how to collect it and apply it to the selection of viable solutions, and how actions are perceived by regulatory agencies and the public. Consequently, they design an appraoch that is practical, cost-effective, and client-oriented.
Mike Bailey, CEO
Jeff Barrett, Principal

4703 Hatch Mott MacDonald
833 Rt 9 North 609-465-9377
Cape May, NJ 0 800-832-3272
Fax: 973-376-1072
www.hatchmott.com
Hatch Mott MacDonald is a client-focused consulting firm providing planning, investigation, design and management capabilities in engineering disciplines and environmental sciences. Areas of expertise include industrial wastewater,site utilities engineering, hazardous and solid waste management and environmental site assessments.
Nicholas DeNichilo, President/CEO
Albert Beninato, East Unit MD

4704 Hatcher-Sayre
905 Southlake Boulevard 804-794-0216
Richmond, VA 23236 Fax: 804-379-8934
Environmental consulting and engineering services firm.

4705 Havens & Emerson
700 Bond Court Building 216-621-2407
1300 E 9th Street Fax: 216-621-4972
Cleveland, OH 44114
Environmental engineering firm.
Gary Siegel, President/CEO

4706 Hayden Environmental Group
561 Congress Park Drive 937-438-3010
Dayton, OH 45459 Fax: 937-438-3020
www.heg.com
Testing, sampling, and analysis service.
Patrick Purvermuller, Group CEO
Andrear Palm, CEO Mass Hosting

4707 Hayes, Seay, Mattern & Mattern
PO Box 13446 540-857-3100
Roanoke, VA 24034 Fax: 540-857-3296
Troy S Kincer, PE, Principal Associate
Guy E Slagle, PE, LS, Vice President

4708 HazMat Environmental Group
60 Commerce Drive 716-827-7200
Buffalo, NY 14218-1040 Fax: 716-827-7217
jwhite@hazmatinc.com
www.hazmatinc.com
Offers transportation services for hazardous materials and hazardous waste.
John Stewart, President
Eric Hoxsie, Chief Financial Officer

4709 Henry Souther Laboratories
24 Tobey Road 860-242-6291
Bloomfield, CT 00600 Fax: 860-286-0634
Richard J Lombardi, VP

4710 Heritage Laboratories
560 North Rogers Road 913-764-1045
Olathe, KS 66062 Fax: 913-764-3372
Environmental testing laboratory.

4711 **Heritage Remediation Engineering**
4925 Heller Street 502-473-0638
Louisville, KY 40218 Fax: 502-459-4988
Environemtal management and remediation company.

4712 **Hess Environmental Services**
6057 Executive Centre Drive 901-377-9139
Suite 6 Fax: 901-377-9150
Memphis, TN 38134
Hess Environmental Services, Inc. (HES) is an environmental consulting/engineering firm. Their primary activities are: Indoor air quality (IAQ) (Mold and Bacterial) Investigations; Title V Air and Other Permit Applications; Phase I,II, III Property Assessments; Remedial Investigations, Audits, Enviromental Health and Safety, Storm Water, Wastewater, Air Monitoring, Asbestos Inspection and Sampling.
Connie Hess, President
Gary Siebenschuh, VP

4713 **Hidell-Eyster Technical Services**
PO Box 325 781-749-8040
Accord, MA 00201 Fax: 781-749-2304
Info@hidelleyster.com
www.hidelleyster.com
Environmental and bottled water assessment and consulting company.
Henry R Hidell, Founder/Chairman
Carroll S. Keim, President/CEO

4714 **Hillmann Environmental Company**
1600 Route 22 East 908-377-5644
Suite 107 Fax: 908-686-2636
Union, NJ 00708 www.hillmannconsulting.com
Hillmann Consulting, LLC is a full-service Environmental and Engineering Consulting firm providing an array of customized Remediation Support, Environmental Health and Occupational Safety, Sustainability Consulting, Environmental DueDiligence, Geotechnical, and Laboratory Analysis services.
Christopher Hillmann, Founder
Joseph Hillmann, Executive VP

4715 **Honeywell Technology Center**
3660 Technology Drive 480-353-3020
Minneapolis, MN 55418 877-841-2840
Fax: 612-951-7438
www.honeywell.com
Parent holding company with numerous high-tech units involved in environmental, energy, computer hardware and industrial automation research and development.
David M. Cote, CEO/Chairman
Andreas Kramvis, Vice Chairman

4716 **Hoosier Microbiological Laboratory**
912 West McGalliard 765-288-1124
Muncie, IN 47303 Fax: 765-288-8378
Donald A Hendrickson, Owner

4717 **Horner & Shifrin**
401 S. 18th St. 314-531-4321
Ste. 400 Fax: 314-531-6966
Saint Louis, MO 63103 www.hornershifrin.com
Civil, structural, and environmental engineering firm.
Duane L. Siegfried, President
Gino E.B. Bernardez, VP

4718 **Houston Advanced Research Center**
4800 Research Forest Drive 281-364-6000
The Woodlands, TX 77381 Fax: 281-363-7914
www.harc.edu
Environmental studies
Lina Gonzalez, VP/COO
Jim Lester, President/CEO

4719 **Humphrey Energy Enterprises**
One Beacon Street 617-720-5222
Suite 2320 Fax: 617-720-5507
Boston, MA 00210 info@humphreyenterprises.com
www.humphreyenterprises.com
Humphrey Enterprises, LLC is a private equity investment firm focused on three primary industry sectors: automotive, healthcare, and training and education.
John W. Humphrey, Chairman/Principal
James Humphrey, CEO/Principal

4720 **Huntingdon Engineering & Environmental**
1940 Orange Tree Lane 909-793-2691
Redlands, CA 92374 800-285-1653
Fax: 909-793-1704
www.dell.com/outlet
Offers the following service(s): Environmental remediation, engineering services, environmental consultant, environmental research, petroleum, mining, and chemical engineers and sanitary engineers.
Michael S. Dell, Chairman/CEO
Jeffrey W. Clarke, President/VP Operations

4721 **Hydro Science Laboratories**
320 West Water Street 732-349-9692
Toms River, NJ 00875 800-624-3100
Fax: 732-349-9729
info@HydroscienceInc.com
www.hydroscienceinc.com
Environmental testing and analysis laboratory.
Robert Salt, Director of Business Dvlpmt

4722 **Hydro-logic**
1927 North 1275 Road 785-550-6474
Eudora, KS 66025 Fax: 785-542-3971
info@hydro-logic.com
www.hydro-logic.com
Offers professional environmental services, specializing in hydraulic soil and groundwater sampling. Maintains a multidisiplinary team of geologists, hydrologists, chemists, and regulatory compliance specialists.
Thomas Barr, President

4723 **Hydrocomp**
13 Jenkins Court 603-868-3344
Suite 200 Fax: 603-868-3366
Durham, NH 00382 info@hydrocompinc.com
www.hydrocompinc.com
Responding to the growth in desktop computing during the mid-1980s, HydroComp introduced the first version of the NavCad® software in 1987. NavCad is still HydroComp's flagship product, with users in all corners of the world fromdesign to construction to academia.
Jill Aaron, Managing Director
Donald MacPherson, Technical Director

4724 **Hydrologic Purification Systems**
370 Encinal Street 888-426-5644
Suite 150 888-426-5644
Santa Cruz, CA 95060 Fax: 831-336-9840
marco@hydrologicsystems.com
www.hydrologicsystems.com
Manufactures water purification systems.
Richard Gellert, President
Jenifer Ringel, Accounting Manager

4725 IAS Laboratories Inter Ag Services
2515 E University Drive 602-273-7248
Phoenix, AZ 85034 Fax: 602-275-3836
www.iaslabs.com
IAS is an international agricultural laboratory and research facility serving that provides a variety of environmental services including: soil fertility and water suitability testing; ASTM, AASHTO, ADOT & CDOT testing; quality controltesting for the fertilizer industry; and plant tissue, petiole and soil analysis for agriculture and farmers.
Paul J Eberhardt PhD, President
Sheri K McLane, Laboratory Manager

4726 IC Laboratories
3253 Grapevine St. 951-681-4422
Mira Loma, CA 91752 Fax: 951-681-4404
iclabs@iclabs.net
www.iclabs.net
Firm providing qualitative and quantitative materials analysis through X-ray diffraction. Studies focus on powders, metals, fibers, and clays, including analysis of crystallinity, thin films, environmental dusts, geological materials,and fabrics. Also provides limited research and development and consulting.

4727 ICS Radiation Technologies
8416 Florence Avenue 562-923-1837
Suite 207 Fax: 562-923-3609
Downey, CA 90240
Testing, engineering and consulting firm specializing in radiation effects in semiconductor devices.
Dr Michael K Gauthier, President

4728 IHI Environmental
4685 S. Ash Ave. 480-897-8200
Suite H-4 Fax: 480-897-1133
Temple, AZ 85282
ihi@ihi-env.com
www.ihi-env.com/

William T. Hopkins, Chairman
Donald E. Marano, President

4729 INFORM
P.O. Box 320403 212-361-2400
Brooklyn, NY 11232 Fax: 212-361-2412
inform@informinc.org
www.informinc.org
INFORM is an independent research organization that examines the effects of business practices on the environment and on human health. Our goal is to identify ways of doing business that ensure environmentally sustainable economicgrowth. Our reports are used by government, industry, and environmental leaders around the world.
Virginia Rramsay, Executive Producer
Marina Belesis Casoria, Chairman

4730 Ike Yen Associates
867 Marymount Lane 714-621-2302
Claremont, CA 91711

4731 Image
4525 Kingston Street 303-371-3338
Denver, CO 80239 Fax: 303-371-3299
Biochemistry and environmental research firm. Research results published in professional journals.

4732 ImmuCell Corporation
56 Evergreen Drive 207-878-2770
Portland, ME 00410 800-466-8235
Fax: 207-878-2117
mail@immucell.com
www.immucell.com
Biotechnology testing kits, animal health products and environment water testing.
Michael F Brigham, President

4733 Industrial Laboratories
4046 Youngfield Street 303-287-9691
Wheat Ridge, CO 80033 800-456-5288
Fax: 303-287-0964
kinman@industriallabs.net
www.industriallabs.net
Provides quality laboratory analysis and consultation. ICP Mineral Analysis.
Petra Hartmann, Director
Lisle Goeldner, Controller

4734 Informatics Division of Bio-Rad
2000 Market Street 267-322-6931
Suite 1460 888-524-6723
Philadelphia, PA 19102-1737 Fax: 267-322-6932
informatics.usa@bio-rad.com
www.bio-rad.com

Richard Shaps, Division Manager

4735 Innovative Biotechnologies International
335 Lang Boulevard 716-773-4232
Grand Island, NY 14702 Fax: 716-773-4257
www.ibi.cc
Manufacturing technology of biosensing technology.

4736 Inprimis
500 West Cypress Creek Road 954-556-4020
Suite 1 Fax: 954-556-4031
Fort Lauderdale, FL 33309 info@ener1.com
www.inprimis.com/
Provides hardware and software technology, communications solutions that enbale data transmission, connectivity of devices, and access to applications and information via the Internet, personal computers, and/or server-basedenvironments. Also designs, manufactures, markets, and supports quality, innovative products that have a cost, performance, and time-to-market advantage.
Kevin P. Fitzgerald, Chairman/CEO
Ronald N. Stewart, Executive VP

4737 Institute for Alternative Agriculture
9200 Edmonston Road 301-441-8777
Suite 117 Fax: 301-220-0164
Greenbelt, MD 20770
The Wallace Institute advances this goal by providing the leadership, and policy research and analysis necessary to influence national agriculturalpolicy. It is a contributing member of a growing national alternaative agriculturenetwork, and works directly with government agencies, educational and research institutions, producer groups, farmers, scientists, advocates, and other organizations that provide agricultural research, education, and information services.
Dr. I Garth Youngberg, Executive Director

4738 Institute for Applied Research
103 W. Lockwood 314-968-9625
Suite 200 contact@iarstl.org
St. Louis, MO 63119 www.iarstl.org
The Institute of Applied Research (IAR) is an independent research and consulting organization with offices in St. Louis, Missouri. Founded in 1978, the Institute has specialized in providing research and technical assistance servicesto state governments and agencies and other public service and community organizations.

4739 Institute for Environmental Education
16 Upton Drive 978-658-5272
Wilmington, MA 00188 800-823-6239
Fax: 978-658-5435
sales@ieetrains.com
www.ieetrains.com
IEE is New England's largest environmental training provider with over 57 classes in Asbestos, OSHA, Lead-paint and Environmental Health and Safety.
Martin Wood, President
Roy Teresky, VP Marketing

4740 Integral System
5200 Philadelphia Way 443-539-5330
Suite A Fax: 301-577-1982
Lanham, MD 20706 www.integ.com
Custom computer systems for satellite control; environmental monitoring.
John Byme, Director of Engineering

4741 Inter-Mountain Laboratories
1673 Terra Avenue 307-672-8945
Sheridan, WY 82801 Fax: 307-672-6053
ebrandjord@imlinc.com
www.intermountainlabs.com
Provides high-quality analytical, engineering and field services to industry and governmental agencies.
Kevin Chartier, President
Eric Brandjord, Business Development

4742 International Asbestos Testing Laboratories
9000 Commerce Parkway 856-231-9449
Suite B 877-428-4285
Mount Laurel, NJ 00805 Fax: 856-231-9818
info@iatl.com
www.iatl.com
An environmental laboratory specializing in asbestos, lead and mold analysis. Provides environmental laboratory services to environmental consultants, engineers, building owners and govt. agencies throughout the US, Canada and othercountries. Accredited by numerous agencies including the National Voluntary Laboratory Accreditation Program (NVLAP) and the American Industrial Hygiene Association (AIHA).
Eric M. Snyder, President
Christine Davis, Office Manager

4743 International Maritime, Inc
1250 24th Street N.W. 202-333-8501
Suite 350 Fax: 202-318-8114
Washington, DC 20037 imaassoc@msn.com
www.imastudies.com
International Maritime Associates (IMA) is a firm of business consultants specializing in market analysis and strategic planning for companies in the marine and offshore sectors.
Jim McCaul, Founder

4744 International Science and Technology Institute
1820 North Fort Myer Drive 703-807-2080
Suite 600 Fax: 703-807-1126
Arlington, VA 22209
Provides technical assistance in project design, implementation, and evaluation; database development and maintenance; institutional and human resource development; policy and economic analysis, methodological research and analysis;strategic planning; and workshop and conference design and organization.
BK Wesley Copeland, Vice Chair

4745 International Society of Chemical Ecology
University of California
Department of Entomology 909-787-5821
Riverside, CA 92521 Fax: 909-787-3086
jocelyn.millar@ucr.edu
www.isce.ucr.edu/Society/
ISCE is organized specifically to promote the understanding of interactions between organisms and their environment. Research areas include the chemistry, biochemistry and function of natural products, their importance at all levels ofecological organization, their evolutionary origin and their practical application.
John Hildebrand, President

4746 Interpoll Laboratories
4500 Ball Road NE 763-786-6020
Circle Pines, MN 55014 Fax: 763-786-7854
interpoll@interpoll-labs.com
www.interpoll-labs.com
Environmental laboratory providing clients with a range of environmental testing services including stationary source testing, laboratory analysis, groundwater monitoring, ambient air monitoring and pharmaceutical analysis.
Dan Despen, President
Gregg Holman, VP & Laboratory Manager

4747 Invensys Climate Controls
191 East North Avneue 630-260-3400
Carol Stream, IL 60188 www.invensyscontrols.com
Formely the Robertshaw Controls Company. Founded after a successfully designing and manufacturing a line of top quality smoke alarms for the residential smoke alarm market.
Jean-Pascal Tricoire, Chairman/CEO
Jullo Rodriguez, Executive VP

4748 J Dallon and Associates
16 Fox Hollow Road 201-825-4574
Ramsey, NJ 00744
Research and consulting firm specializing in hortoculture.
Dr Joseph Dallon Jr, President

4749 J Phillip Keathley: Agricultural Services Division
25330 Ruess Avenue 209-599-2800
Ripon, CA 95366
Dr. J Phillip Keathley, President

4750 JABA
2766 North Country Club Road 520-327-7440
Tucson, AZ 85716 Fax: 520-327-7450
Mining exploration and environmental analysis firm.
James A Briscoe, President

4751 JH Kleinfelder & Associates
6700 Koll Center Parkway 925-484-1700
Suite 120 Fax: 925-484-5838
Pleasanton, CA 94566 www.kleinfelder.com
Geotechnical and environmental Engineering firm.
William C. Siegel, President
Michael P. Kesler, COO

4752 JH Stuard Associates
22 Tanglewood Drive 802-878-5171
Woodstock, VT 00509
Environmental Consulting firm.
Joe Shockcor, President

4753 JK Research Associates
86 Gold Hill Road 970-453-1760
Breckenridge, CO 80424

4754 **JL Rogers & Callcott Engineers**
PO Box 5655 864-232-1556
Greenville, SC 29606-5655 866-805-9596
Fax: 864-233-9058
rogers.callcott@rogersandcallcott.com
www.rogersandcallcott.com
Environmental engineering research firm.

4755 **JM Best**
119 S College Street 724-222-2102
Washington, PA 15301
Performs geologic, economic and engineering evaluations for oil and gas well drilling. Also provides completion operations, environmental studies, map preparations and investigative studies.

4756 **JR Henderson Labs**
123 Seaman Avenue 732-341-1211
Beachwood, NJ 00872 Fax: 732-505-1658
www.jrhendersonlabs.com
Environmental laboratory.
Elmer Hemphill, President

4757 **JWS Delavau Company**
10101 Roosevelt Blvd 215-671-1400
Philadelphia, PA 19154-2105 Fax: 215-671-1401
www.delavau.com
International environmental and technical company.
David L Sokol, President

4758 **James R Reed and Associates**
770 Pilot House Drive 757-873-4703
Newport News, VA 23606 800-873-4703
Fax: 757-873-1498
claiborne@jrreed.com
www.jrreed.com
Full service environmental testing facility offering quality analysis and reliable technical services to industry, local and federal government, engineers and private citizens. Areas of expertise include organic and inorganic chemicalanalyses, microbiological testing, and aquatic toxicity monitoring. Certificationto include NELAC Certification for the State of Virginia.
Han Ping Huang, President
Elaine Claiborne, Laboratory Director

4759 **James W Bunger and Associates**
PO Box 520037 801-975-1456
Salt Lake City, UT 84152-0037 Fax: 801-975-1530
jwba@jwba.com
www.jwba.com
Energy research and development firm specializing in environmental and oil remediation.
Christopher P. Russell, Director
Donald E. Cogswell, Process Development

4760 **Jane Goodall Institute for Wildlife Research, Education and Conservation**
1595 Spring Hill Rd 703-682-9220
Suite 550 800-99C-HIMP
Vienna, VA 22182 Fax: 703-682-9312
www.janegoodall.org
A tax-exempt, nonprofit corporation, founded in 1977 focusing on Jane Goodall.
Jane Goodall, Founder
Donald Kendall, Vice-Chair

4761 **John D MacArthur Agro Ecology Research Center**
300 Buck Island Ranch Road 863-699-0242
Lake Placid, FL 33852 Fax: 863-699-2217
info@archbold-station.org
www.maerc.org
The MacArthur Agro Ecology Research Center at Buck Island Ranch is dedicated to a mission of long-term research, education and outreach related to the ecological and social value of subtropical grazing lands. The Center is at a 10,300acre cattle ranch on a long-term lease to Archbold Biological Station from the John D and Catherine T MacArthur Foundation. Provides researchers the opportunity to evaluate the relationship between economic and ecological factors and how these changeover time.
Elizabeth H. Boughton, Program Director
Gene Lollis, Ranch Manager

4762 **Johnson Company**
100 State Street 802-229-4600
Suite 600 Fax: 802-229-5876
Montpelier, VT 00560 info@jcomail.com
www.johnsonco.com
Environmental science and engineering consulting
Guy Wm. Vaillancourt, President
Glen A. Kirkpatrick, VP

4763 **Johnson Controls**
5757 N Green Bay Avenue 414-524-1200
P.O. Box 591 Fax: 414-228-2446
Milwaukee, WI 53201 www.johnsoncontrols.com
Research in environmental controls.
David Abney, CEO
Natalie A. Black, Sr. VP

4764 **Johnson Research Center**
University of Alabama at Huntsville 256-890-6343
Huntsville, AL 35899 Fax: 256-890-6848
Environmental research.
Dr. Michael Eley, CEO

4765 **Jones & Henry Laboratories**
2567 Tracy Road 419-666-0411
Northwood, OH 43619 Fax: 419-666-1657
jhlabs@glasscity.net
www.jhlaboratories.com
Environmental sampling and testing laboratory.
Fred W Doering, President
David Collins, Marketing Manager

4766 **Joyce Engineering, Inc.**
1604 Ownby Lane 804-355-4520
Richmond, VA 23220 Fax: 804-355-4282
info@joyceengineering.com
www.joyceengineering.com
Joyce Engineering, Inc. is a full-service consulting firm. They specialize in providing engineering and environmental solutions for clients throughout the southeastern United States. From siting to post-closure monitoring, managementplanning, construction services, landfill gas services, operator training and operations consulting, or environmental remediation, they provide expertise.
Connie Morrison, VP

4767 **KAI Technologies**
16 Marin Way 603-778-1888
Stratham, NH 00388 Fax: 603-778-0700
info@kaitechnologies.com
www.kaitechnologies.com
Applied and product research in the environment.
Bruce L. Cliff, Director

4768 **KCM**
3475 East Foothill Boulevard 626-470-2439
Pasadena, CA 91107-6024 Fax: 626-351-5291
info@tetratech.com
www.tetratech.com

Applied and product research in the environment.
Dan L. Batrack, Chairman/President/CEO
Steven M. Burdick, Executive VP

4769 KE Sorrells Research Associates
8100 National Drive 501-562-8139
Little Rock, AR 72209 800-331-8139
Fax: 501-562-7025
Analytical chemistry and applied research company providing consulting services in water technology and stream ecology.
KE Sorrells, President
Cecil Sorrells, CEO

4770 KLM Engineering
3394 Lake Elmo Avenue N 651-773-5111
PO Box 897 888-959-5111
Lake Elmo, MN 55042 Fax: 651-773-5222
www.klmengineering.com
Structural engineering and inspection firm specializing in the industry of steel and concrete plate structures.
Jack R Kollmer, President/Principal
Shawn A Mulhern, Vice President-Sales/Mktg.

4771 Kag Laboratories International
2323 Jackson Street 920-426-2222
Oshkosh, WI 54901 800-356-6045
Fax: 920-273-6128
akkhwaja@aol.com
www.kaglab.com/
An independent agricultural testing and consulting laboratory. Professional scientific services for agriculture, soil, feed, plant, water and other fields. Total farm management services including high value crops such as cranberry,stevia, blueberry, ginseng, strawberry, herbs, etc. Consultation and recommendation to increase net yield. Available for contractual applied research for all agribusiness industries in Wisconsin, North America and world-wide.
Dr. Akhtar Khwaja, President
Ruma Roy, Vice President/Chemist

4772 Kansas City Testing Laboratory
1308 Adams Street 913-321-8100
Kansas City, KS 66103 Fax: 913-321-8181
www.kctesting.com
Consulting engineering firm employed in geotechnical, materials, and environmental engineering. Research results published in Project reports.
Elisabeth DeCoursey, President/Co-Owner
Scott Martens, VP/Co-Owner

4773 Kar Laboratories
4425 Manchester Road 269-381-9666
Kalamazoo, MI 49001 Fax: 269-381-9698
info@karlabs.com
www.karlabs.com
Environmental testing laboratory, wastewater, drinking water, hay waste, soil and air.
William Rauch, President
Jayne Rauch, Marketing Manager

4774 Kemper Research Foundation
122 Main Street 513-249-2489
Milford, OH 45150
Richard Kemper, Director

4775 Kemron Environmental Services
2343-A State Route 821 740-373-4308
Marietta, OH 45750 Fax: 740-376-2536
mzumbro@kemron.com
Environmental testing and analysis firm.
Juan J. Gutierrez, President/CEO
John Dwyer, Executive VP

4776 Kennedy-Jenks Consultants
303 Second Street 415-243-2150
Suite 300 Fax: 415-896-0999
San Francisco, CA 94107 info@kennedyjenks.com
www.kennedyjenks.com
Environmental engineering consulting company.
Gary Carlton, Chair
Keith London, President/CEO

4777 Kentucky Resource Laboratory
Highway 421 606-598-2605
Manchester, KY 40962 Fax: 606-598-1544
Environmental testing firm.
Roy Rice, President

4778 Kenvirons
452 Versailles Road 502-695-4357
Frankfort, KY 40601 Fax: 502-695-4363
kenvirons.com/About/tabid/96/Default.aspx
A multi-disciplined environmental and civil engineering firm. Offers engineering services in a range of areas to include water and wastewater related studies and system design, dam design, hydrological studies, environmentalassessments, air and water quality studies, urban and industrial planning, solid waste management, energy-environment interface, computer technology and laboratory services.
Randall Russell, President
Douglas Griffin, Chair

4779 Keystone Labs
600 East 17th Street South 800-858-5227
Suite B 800-858-5227
Newton, IA 50208 Fax: 641-792-7989
www.keystonelabs.com
Keystone Laboroatories, Inc. is a full service environmental laboratory committed to providing the highest quality services at competitive prives.
Jodi King, President
Jerry Dawson, Manager

4780 Kinnetic Laboratories
307 Washington Street 831-457-3950
Santa Cruz, CA 95060 Fax: 831-426-0405
kkronsch@kinneticlabs.com
www.kineticlabs.com
Offers environmental consulting services in the areas of marine science, toxicology, water quality, biological research and more.
Patrick Kinney, President
Mark Savoie, Vice President

4781 Kleinfelder
981 Garcia Avenue 925-427-6477
Suite A Fax: 925-427-6478
Pittsburg, CA 94565 www.kleinfelder.com
Laboratories testing.
William C. Siegel, President
Michael P. Kesler, COO

4782 Konheim & Ketcham
175 Pacific Street 718-330-0550
Brooklyn, NY 11201 Fax: 718-330-0582
csk@konheimketcham.com
www.konheimketcham.com
Environmental and transportation planning.
Carolyn S Konheim, President
Brian T. Ketcham, Executive VP

4783 **Kraim Environmental Engineering Services**
11437 Etiwanda Avenue 818-363-0952
Northridge, CA 91326 Fax: 818-363-0492
luftmench@msn.com

Environmental engineering firm.
Jerry Kraim, President

4784 **Kramer & Associates**
20801 Biscayne Blvd 505-881-0243
Suite #403 800-281-1400
Miami, FL 33180 Fax: 505-881-7738
eservice@kramerandassociates.com
www.kramerandassociates.com

Environmental monitoring firm. Research results published in conference proceedings.
Lyn Kramer, MD/Partner
Gary Kramer, Contact

4785 **Ktech Corporation**
10800 Gibson S E 505-998-5830
Albuquerque, NM 87123 Fax: 505-998-5848
rswanson@ktech.com
www.ktech.com/corporate/history.cfm

Ktech Corporation, an employee-owned company based in Albuquerque, New Mexico, is dedicated to providing outstanding technical support services, sound scientific and engineering work, and proven management expertise to a wide varietyof government and industry clients.
Steven E Downie, President
Robert E Swanson, VP/Chief Operations Officer

4786 **LaBella Associates P.C.**
300 State Street 872-626-6606
Suite 201 Fax: 585-454-3066
Rochester, NY 14614 labweb@labellapc.com
www.labellapc.com

Civil and environmental engineering firm.
Salvatore A. LaBella, Founder
Robert Healy, President

4787 **LaQue Center for Corrosion Technology**
521 Fort Fisher Blvd, North 910-256-2271
Kure Beach, NC 28449 Fax: 910-256-9816
www.laque.com

Corrosion technology firm. Research results published in trade journals and presented at technical association meetings.
W T Raines, President
D G Melton, VP

4788 **Laboratory Corporation of America Holdings**
1904 Alexander Drive 919-572-6900
Research Triangle Park, NC 27709 800-533-0567
www.labcorp.com

Whether the needs are large or small, routine or complex, physicians and patients can depend on them for access to a full range of the highest quality diagnostic testing.
Mark E. Breacher, CMO/SVP/Discipline Director
James K. Fleming, Div. Medical Director

4789 **Laboratory Services Division of Consumers Energy**
135 W Trail Street 517-788-2238
Jackson, MI 49201 Fax: 517-788-1104
naserafin@cmsenergy.com
www.laboratoryservices.com

Laboratory Services is a full-service testing laboratory. Services include: calibration, nondestructive testing, metallurgy, materials testing and chemistry. They are A2LA accredited (ISO/IEC 17025)-request scope-and 10CFR50 AppendixB authorized.
Nick Serafin, Marketing Manager

4790 **Lancaster Laboratories**
2425 New Holland Pike 717-656-2300
Lancaster, PA 17601 Fax: 717-656-2681
pha@lancasterlabs.com
www.lancasterlabs.com

Premier contract testing laboratory serving environmental, pharmaceutical and biophamaceutical clients worldwide. Offers a broad range of high quality analytical services in full compliance with EPA and FDA regulations and clientrequirements.
Gilles Martin, Chairman
Valerie Hanote, Board Member

4791 **Lancy Environmental**
181 Thorn Hill Road 724-772-0044
Warrendale, PA 15086 Fax: 724-772-1360
Gerald Rogers, President

4792 **Land Management Decisions**
3048 Research Drive 814-231-1248
State College, PA 16801 Fax: 814-231-1253
Dr. Dale E Baker, President

4793 **Land Management Group Inc**
3805 Wrightsville Avenue 910-452-0001
Suite 15 886-LMG-1078
Wilmington, NC 28403 Fax: 910-452-0060
rbrant@LMGroup.net
www.lmgroup.net

LMG provides environmental servicesin the following discplines: wetland delineations and permitting; soil mapping and waste water suitability studies; phase I & II environmental site assiessments; EA and EIS land use and ecologicalstudies; wetland mitigations; and coastal management (CAMA) permitting assistance.
Robert L Moul, Founder/President
Craig Turner, VP

4794 **Land Research Management**
1300 N Congress Avenue 561-686-2481
Suite C Fax: 561-684-8709
West Palm Beach, FL 33409 lrmi@bellsouth.net
Land planning and zoning, environmental assessments and market analysis firm. Research results published in reports.
Kevin McGinley, President

4795 **Lark Enterprises**
2665 Ellwood Road 724-658-5676
New Castle, PA 16101 Fax: 508-943-8833
rjlark@aol.com
www.larkenterprises.org

Environmental research.
Justin Bruce, President
Roger Zallon, VP

4796 **Laticrete International**
1 Laticrete Park N 203-393-0010
91 Amity Road Fax: 203-393-1684
Bethany, CT 00652-3423 www.laticrete.com
Firm providing chemical, mechanical, and environmental simulation testing of concrete and aggregrate building materials.
Henry M. Rothberg, Chairman/Founder
David A. Rothberg, Chairman/CEO

4797 **Law & Company of Wilmington**
1711 Castle Street 910-762-7082
Wilmington, NC 28403 Fax: 910-762-8785
Richard W Spivey, President

4798 Lawrence Berkeley Laboratory: Structural Biology Division
1 Cyclotron Road 510-486-4311
Mail Stop 3-0226 Fax: 510-486-6059
Berkeley, CA 94720 www.lbl.gov
Paul Alivisatos, Director
Horst Simon, Deputy Director

4799 Lawrence G Spielvogel
21506 Valley Forge Circle 610-783-6350
King of Prussia, PA 19406 Fax: 610-783-6349
A consulting engineer who specializes in energy management and procurement and problem solving in buildings.
Lawrence G Spielvogel, President

4800 Ledoux and Company
359 Alfred Avenue
Teaneck, NJ 00766-5755 800-758-1201
Fax: 201-837-1235
info@ledoux.com
Ledoux & Company is an independent commercial metallurgical chemical laboratory, which has been family owned and operated since 1880.
A.R. Ledoux, Founder
LA Ledoux, President

4801 Lee Wilson and Associates
105 Cienega Street 505-988-9811
Santa Fe, NM 87501 Fax: 505-986-0092
Environmental consulting firm. Research results published in project reports.
Lee Wilson, President

4802 Leighton & Associates
17781 Cowan Street 949-250-1421
Irvine, CA 92614 Fax: 949-250-1114
www.leightongeo.com
Geotechnical and environmental engineering firm.
F. Beach Leighton, Founder
Bruce Clark, Contact

4803 Life Science Resources
Post Office Box 379 808-553-3211
Hoolehua, HI 96729 800-543-3211
Fax: 808-553-5033
Support@LifescienceResources.com
www.lifescienceresources.com
Biomedical and environmental sciences research firm.

4804 Life Systems
916-C Old Liverpool Road 315-378-4338
Liverpool, NY 13088 Fax: 315-299-5090
info@lifesysteminternational.com
www.lifesysteminternational.com
Environmental engineering research and consulting organization. Research results published In project reports and in technical journals.
R Wynveen, President

4805 Los Alamos Technical Associates
6501 Americas Parkway NE 505-884-3800
Suite 200 800-952-5282
Albuquerque, NM 87110 Fax: 505-880-3560
info@lata.com
www.lata.com
Environmental studies.
Dale Goralczyk, Contracts Manager
Bob Kingsbury, President/COO

4806 Louisville Testing Laboratory
1401 West Chestnut Street 502-584-5914
Louisville, KY 40203 Fax: 502-584-5914
Kenneth Smith Jr, President

4807 Lowry Systems
146 South Street
Blue Hill, ME 00461 800-434-9080
Fax: 207-374-3503
info@lowryh2o.com
www.lowryh2o.com
Environmental research.
Sylvia Lowry, President

4808 Lycott Environmental Inc
600 Charlton Street 508-765-0101
Southbridge, MA 00155 800-462-8211
Fax: 508-765-1352
lycottine@aol.com
www.lycott.com
Environmental science and ecological planning consultant and research firm. Research results published in project reports.
Lee D Lyman, President

4809 Lyle Environmental Management
1507 Chambers Road 614-488-1022
Columbus, OH 43212 Fax: 614-488-1198
Chemical research and consulting service.

4810 Lyle Laboratories
1507 Chambers Road 614-488-1022
Columbus, OH 43212 Fax: 614-867-5265
manager@lylelabs.com
www.lylelabs.com
They offer a wide range of testing and remediation services. They can test for biological contaminants, organic compounds, industrial pollutants, carcinogens, etc., and can do so in residential or commercial settings.
Dr. Thomas Eggers, Director

4811 Lynntech
2501 Earl Rudder Freeway South 979-764-2200
Suite 100 Fax: 979-764-2343
College Station, TX 77845 requests@lynntech.com
www.lynntech.com
Lynntech scientists and engineers develop world-class technology solutions for aerospace, defense and human health.
Oliver J Murphy, President
Jenifer Cross, Life Sciences Unit

4812 MBA Labs
340 South 66th Street 713-928-2701
Houston, TX 77261 800-472-1485
Fax: 281-292-7492
www.mbalabs.com
Independently owned and operated since 1968, mba Labs serves industry, government agencies and private citizens in Houston, the continental US and even across the globe. Conform to standards established by the EPA, the TNRCC and meetthe equivalent of ISO 9000 requirements for laboratories through their accreditation by NELAC.
Herman J Kresse

4813 MBA Polymers
500 West Ohio Avenue 510-231-9031
Richmond, CA 94804 Fax: 510-231-0302
info@mbapolymers.com
www.mbapolymers.com/
Environmental research.
Mike Biddle, Founder/President
Nigel Hunton, CEO

4814 MBC Applied Environmental Sciences
3000 Redhill Avenue 714-850-4830
Costa Mesa, CA 92626 Fax: 714-850-4840
info@mbcnet.net
www.mbcnet.net
Environmenatl consultants since 1969. Specializing in marine biology and ecology, oceanography, EIR, EIS, EA, toxicity testing, technical meetings, expert witnesses. MBE/DBE certified.
Shane Beck, President
Charles T. Mitchell, VP

4815 META Environmental
2200 West 25th Street 785-842-6382
Lawrence, KS 66047 800-444-6382
Fax: 785-842-6993
info@metaworldwide.com
www.metaenvironmental.net
Environmental testing lab offering site assessments.
Thomas Bradford Mayhew, Founder/Chairman
Fernando Ipanaque, CEO/General Manager

4816 MWH Global
380 Interlocken Crescent 303-533-1900
Suite 200 Fax: 303-533-1901
Broomfield, CO 80021 webinfo@mwhglobal.com
www.mwhglobal.com
MWH, globally driving the wet infrastructure sector, is leading the world in results-oriented management services, technical engineering, construction services and solutions to create a better world. The wet infrastructure sectorencompasses a full range of water related projects and programs from water supply, treatment and storage, dams, water management for the natural resources industry and coastal restoration to renewable power and environmental services.
Joseph D. Adams, President
Paul F. Boulos, President

4817 MWH Laboratories
750 Royal Oaks Drive 626-386-1100
Suite 100 800-566-5227
Monrovia, CA 91016 Fax: 626-386-1101
mwhlabs@mwhglobal.com
www.mwhlabs.com
Environmental testing laboratory that provides water and wastewater analyses including: drinking water synthetic organic and volatile organic tests; recycled water tests; organic disinfection byproduct and precursor analyses; inorganicdisinfection byproducts and precursors; inorganic tests including a complete suite of metals to low-reporting levels; microbiological analyses ; and radiochemical analyses.
Andrew Eaton Ph.D, Technical Director
Ed Wilson, Laboratory Director

4818 Mabbett & Associates: Environmental Consultants and Engineers
5 Alfred Circle 888-748-6024
Bedford, MA 00173 800-877-6050
Fax: 781-275-5651
info@mabbett.com
www.mabbett.com
Mabbett & Associates (M&A) provides multi-disciplinary environmental, health and safety services to manufacturing and commercial industry, institutions and public agencies. M&A's services include pollution prevention and wasteminimization, site assessment and remediation, environmental pollution control, environmental management systems and auditing, training and occupational safety and health.
Arthur N Mabbett, Chairman/CEO
Paul D. Stelnberg, President

4819 Mack Laboratories
1163 Nicole Court 909-394-9007
Glendora, CA 91740 Fax: 909-394-9411
info@macklabs.com
www.macklabs.com
Mackenzie Laboratories, Inc. has been manufacturing and supplying American made products of the highest quality since 1954.

4820 Magma-Seal
10116 Aspen Street 512-836-4936
Austin, TX 78758 Fax: 512-836-4936
Develops materials (plastic and rubber) to withstand severe environmental conditions.
Earl Dumitro, President

4821 Malcolm Pirnie
630 Plaza Drive 720-344-3500
Suite 200 800-478-6870
Highlands Ranch, CO 80129 Fax: 720-344-3535
AUSInternet@arcadis-us.com
Provides environmental engineering, science and consulting services to over 3,000 public and private clients.
John Jastrem, CEO
Joachim Ebert, COO

4822 Maryland Spectral Services
1500 Caton Center Drive 410-247-7600
Suite G Fax: 410-247-7602
Baltimore, MD 21227 labman@mdspectral.com
www.mdspectral.com
Maryland Spectral Services, Inc. (MSS) is a privately owned, independent laboratory, which was incorporated in 1988, that provides environmental organic analytical services.
Samuel Hamner, VP

4823 Massachusetts Technological Lab
330 Pleasant Street 617-484-7314
Belmont, MA 00217
Applies research in the following areas: telecommunications and Internet.
Dr Ta-Ming Fang, President

4824 Mateson Chemical Corporation
1025 E Montgomery Avenue 215-423-3200
Philadelphia, PA 19125 Fax: 215-423-1164
www.matesonchemical.com
Environmental, toxic, materials, hazerdous waste research.

4825 McCoy & McCoy Laboratories
825 Industrial Road 270-821-7375
Madisonville, KY 42431 Fax: 270-444-6572
www.mccoylabs.com
Environmental assessment laboratory.
Bonnie Hewlett, Project Manager
Mike Baumgardner, Laboratory Operations

4826 McIlvaine Company
191 Waukegan Road 847-784-0012
Suite 208 Fax: 847-784-0061
Northfield, IL 60093 editor@mcilvainecompany.com
www.mcilvainecompany.com
Environmental research and consulting firm. Research results published in manuals updated by newsletters and abstracts.
Robert W McIlvaine, President
Marilyn McIlvaine, Marketing Manager

4827 McLaren-Hart
3039 Kilgore Road 916-638-3696
Rancho Cordova, CA 95670 Fax: 916-638-6840
Environmental research.

4828 McNamee Advanced Technology
3135 S State Street 734-665-5553
Suite 301 Fax: 734-665-2570
Ann Arbor, MI 48108
Environmental engineering firm, offering environmental consulting and environmental testing services.

4829 McVehil-Monnett Associates
9250 East Costilla Avenue 303-790-1332
Suite 630 Fax: 303-790-7820
Greenwood Village, CO 80112 gmcvehil@mcvehil-monnett.com
www.mmaaqs.com
Consulting firm offering services in air quality monitoring, environmental management systems, litigation support, environmental compliance, permitting and more.
Bill Monnett, President
George McVehil, Principal

4830 McWhorter and Associates
33 Bull Street 912-234-8891
Suite 500 Fax: 912-234-8892
Savannah, GA 31401-9419 info@tankcarrobot.com
www.mcwhorterassoc.com
The company designs, builds, and installs robotic tools that clean residuals and strip linings from the interiors of rail tank cars and tanker trucks.
Thomas McWhorter, President

4831 Mega Engineering
10800 Lockwood Drive 301-681-4778
Silver Spring, MD 20901 Fax: 301-681-5683
Richard E Dame, PE

4832 Membrane Technology & Research Corporate Headquarters
39630 Eureka Drive 650-328-2228
Newark, CA 94560 Fax: 650-328-6580
sales@mtrinc.com
www.mtrinc.com
Supplier of membrane-based hydrocarbon recovery systems natural gas treatment systems and hydrogen recovery systems. Company capabilities include membrane and module manufacturing, process and system design, project engineering andcommissioning services.
Dr. Hans Wijmans, President
Nick Wynn, Commercial Operations

4833 Merck & Company
2000 Galloping Hill Road 908-740-4000
Kenilworth, NJ 00703 Fax: 732-594-3810
www.merck.com
The mission is to discover, develop and provide innovative products and services that save and improve lives around the world.
Kenneth C. Frazier, Chairman/President/CEO
Leslie A. Brun, Chairman/CEO

4834 Merrimack Engineering Services
66 Park Street 978-533-1659
Andover, MA 00181 Fax: 978-475-1448
merreng@aol.com
www.merrimackengineering.com
Research of all forms of environmental studies.
Stephen Stapinski, President

4835 Metro Services Laboratories
6309 Fern Valley Pass 502-964-0865
Louisville, KY 40228 Fax: 502-241-4347
Environmental testing laboratory offering air, water and soil testing services.

4836 Michael Baker Jr: Civil and Water Division
100 Airside Drive 412-269-6300
Moon Township, PA 15108 800-553-1153
Fax: 724-495-4017
hchakrav@mbakercorp.com
www.mbakercorp.com
Michael Baker International is a leading provider of engineering, development, intelligence and technology solutions with global reach and mobility.
Thomas J. Campbell, Chairman
T. Gail Dady, Executive VP

4837 Michael Baker Jr: Environmental Division
101 Airside Drive 720-514-1100
Moon Township, PA 15109 Fax: 720-514-1120
www.mbakercorp.com
Michael Baker International is a leading provider of engineering, development, intelligence and technology solutions with global reach and mobility.
Thomas J. Campbell, Chairman
T. Gail Dady, Executive VP

4838 Mickle, Wagner & Coleman
3434 Country Club Avenue 479-649-8484
PO Box 1507 Fax: 479-649-8486
Fort Smith, AR 72903 info@mwc-engr.com
www.mwc-engr.com/
Provides civil and environmental engineering services, offering clients a broad range of plan designs and development capabilities from water, sewer, and drainage to streets, bridges, and dams, airports, recreational facilities, andresidential subdivisions.
Patrick J Mickle, PE, Chief Engineer

4839 Microseeps, Inc
220 William Pitt Way 412-826-5245
Pittsburgh, PA 15238 800-659-2887
Fax: 412-826-3433
www.microseeps.com
A full service, NELAP certified environmental laboratory which specializes in the evaluation of groundwater geochemistry for use in in-situ remediation processes.
Robert J Pirkle, President
Thomas W Hill, Sr. VP

4840 Microspec Analytical
3352 128th Avenue 616-399-6070
Holland, MI 49424 Fax: 616-399-6185
Environmental research and resting firm. Research results published in journals and client reports.
Tom Beamish, President

4841 Midwest Environmental Assistance Center
6561 N Seeley Avenue 773-973-4850
Chicago, IL 60645 Fax: 773-973-4851
meac2@aol.com
Noise pollution research firm.
Howard R Schechter, President

4842 Midwest Laboratories
13611 B Street 402-334-7770
Omaha, NE 68144 Fax: 402-334-9121
getinfo@midwestlabs.com
www.midwestlabs.com
Midwest Laboratories offers analytical services to agriculture, industry and municipal entities throughout the US and Canada. Using wet chemistry methods, the labs test soil, water, feed, food, plants, fertilizers and residues.
Brent Pohlman, President
Traci Grummert, Marketing Director

4843 Midwest Research Institute
425 Volker Boulevard
Kansas City, MO 64110-2241
816-753-7600
Fax: 816-753-8420
info@mriresearch.org
www.mriresearch.org

Midwest Research Institute is an independent, not-for-profit organization that performs contract research for clients in business, industry and government. MRI conducts programs in the areas of environment, health, engineering,technology development and energy research.

Dr. John Stanley, Business Development
Dr. Dan Kuchynka, Technical Enquires

4844 MikroPul Environmental Systems Division of Beacon Industrial Group
17 Wachung Avenue
Chatham, NJ 00792
704-908-2604
800-892-7278
Fax: 973-635-0678
info@mikropul.com
www.mikropul.com

Established in 1929, MikroPul is a manufacturer of dust control and product recovery products, from small unit collectors to complete engineered systems, for industrial applications worldwide.

Lacy Hayes, President/Beacon Ind Group
Richard Bearse, Chairman/Beacon Ind Group

4845 Miller Engineers
PO Box 422
Manlius, NY 13104
315-682-0028
Fax: 920-458-0369
DougMiller@MillerEngineers.com
www.millerengineers.com

Civil and environmental engineering firm.

Roger G Miller, President

4846 Minnesota Valley Testing Laboratories
1126 N Front Street
New Ulm, MN 56073
507-354-8517
800-782-3557
Fax: 507-359-1231
crc@mvtl.com
www.mvtl.com

Independent bacteriological and chemical analysis firm, with services in environmental, agricultural, and energy fields. Research results published in project reports.

Jerry Balbach, President
Thomas R. Berg, CEO

4847 Mirage Systems
PO Box 820
DeLand, FL 32721
386-740-9222
Fax: 386-740-9444
info@miragesys.com
www.miragesys.com

Environmental research.

Robert S Ziernicki, President

4848 Montgomery Watson Mining Group
380 Interlocken Crescent
Suite 200
Broomfield, CO 80021
303-533-1900
Fax: 303-533-1901
www.mwhglobal.com

Mine engineering and environmental services firm.

Joseph D. Adams, President
Alan J. Krause, CEO

4849 Mycotech
100 Commons Road
Ste 7354
Dripping Springs, TX 78620
406-782-2386
800-272-3716
Fax: 406-782-9912
mbi@mycotechbiological.com
www.mycotechbiological.com

Clifford Bradley, Director R&D

4850 Myra L Frank & Associates
811 W 7th Street
Suite 800
Los Angeles, CA 90017
213-627-5376
Fax: 213-627-6853

Environmental impact analysis firm. Architectural historic surveys.

Florence Williams

4851 Mystic Air Quality Consultants
1204 North Road
Route 117
Groton, CT 00634
860-449-8903
800-247-7746
Fax: 860-449-8860
maqc2@aol.com
www.mysticair.com

Indoor air quality and industrial hygiene services.

Chris Eident, CEO

4852 NET Pacific
3qb ODC International Plaza
219 salcedo St. Legaspi Village
Makati City, PH 01229
632-893-9306
Fax: 632-812-4852
www.netpacific.net

Net Pacific is an award-winning, full-service telecommunications, data communications, and electrical systems provider.

4853 National Institute for Urban Wildlife
10921 Trotting Ridge Way
Columbia, MD 21044
301-596-3311

Promotes the preservation of wildlife in urban settings, providing support to individuals and organizations invloved in maintaining a place for wildlife in expanding American cities and suburbs. The Institute conducts researchexploring the relationship between humans and wildlife in these habitats, publicizes urban wildlife management methods, and raises public awareness of the value of wildlife in city settings. The Institute also provides consulting services.

4854 National Loss Control Service Corporation
1 Kemper Drive
Long Grove, IL 60049
847-320-2488
Fax: 847-320-4331

Environmental science laboratory.

Joan Wronski, Laboratory Manager

4855 National Oceanic & Atmospheric Administration
1401 Constitution Avenue, NW
Room 5128
Washington, DC 20230
webmaster@noaa.gov
www.noaa.gov

Earth system research including climate, weather, and atmospheric chemistry, space weather research and forecasts.

Benjamin Friedman, Under Secretary

4856 National Renewable Energy Laboratory/NREL
15013 Denver West Parkway
Golden, CO 80401
303-275-3000
Fax: 303-275-4053
www.nrel.gov

The National Renewable Energy Laboratory/NREL began operating in 1977 as the Solar Energy Research Institute. It was designated a national laboratory of the U.S. Department of Energy (DOE) in September 1991 and its name changed toNREL. NREL develops renewable energy and energy efficiency technologies and practices, advances related science and engineering, and transfers knowledge and innovations to address the nation's energy and environmental goals.

Dan Arvizu, Director
Dana Christensen, Deputy Lab Director

4857 Neilson Research Corporation
245 South Grape Street
Medford, OR 97501
541-770-5678
800-600-5227
Fax: 541-770-2901
www.nrclabs.com

Provides analytical services to support environmental projects including testing of drinking water, wastewater, ground and surface water, foods soils, sediments, sludges, filters, air, and hazardous waste samples.
John WT Neils, CEO

4858 Neponset Valley Engineering Company
378 Page Street 781-297-7040
Suite 10 Fax: 781-297-7050
Stoughton, MA 00207
Environmental engineering analysis and consulting firm.

4859 New England Testing Laboratory
1254 Douglas Avenue 888-863-8522
North Providence, RI 00290 888-863-8522
Fax: 401-354-8951
rich.warila@newenglandtesting.com
www.newenglandtesting.com
New England Testing Laboratory provides environmental analytical services to the consulting engineering community, municipal utilities, private industry and commercial concerns, as well as state and federal agencies.
Richard Warila, VP
Mark Bishop, VP Operations

4860 New York Testing Laboratories
375 Rabro Drive 631-761-5555
Hauppage, NY 11788 800-281-3329
Fax: 718-657-3902
jhicks@mtllab.com
www.mtllab.net
Consulting on a range of disciplines including environmental.
Charles Realmuto, Director Marketing

4861 Newport Electronics
2229 South Yale Street 714-540-4914
Santa Ana, CA 92704-4401 800-639-7678
Fax: 203-968-7311
info@newportus.com
www.newportus.com
Manufacturer of industrial and environmental instrumentation including signal conditioners, digital panel meters, PID controllers and temperature sensors.
Milton Hollander, President

4862 Nobis Engineering
18 Chenell Drive 603-224-4182
Concord, NH 00330 Fax: 603-224-2507
www.nobisengineering.com
Environmental engineering consulting firm.

4863 Noresco United Technologies
1 Research Drive 508-614-1000
Suite 400C Fax: 508-836-9988
Westborough, MA 01581 www.noresco.com
Provides energy and sustainable design services such as LEED© certification consulting, building commissioning, energy auditing and diagnostic testing, energy analysis software and data acquisition equipment.
Neil Petchers, President & CEO
David G Mannherz, Chief Financial Officer

4864 Normandeau Associates
1019B Cherokee Avenue, Northwest 803-644-6262
Aiken, SC 29801 Fax: 803-644-6965
marketing@normandeau.com
www.normandeau.com
Normandeau Associates, Inc. is one of the nation's largest science-based environmental consulting firms with over 250 employees located in 19 offices in 12 states.
Jean Eidson
Bob Hasevlat

4865 North American Environmental Services
2848 Banwick Road 614-487-1109
Columbus, OH 43232 Fax: 614-291-8682
www.northamericanenviro.com
Environmental science research firm.
D Craig Kissock, President

4866 Northeast Test Consultants
587 Spring Street 207-854-3939
Westbrook, ME 00409-3918 Fax: 207-854-3658
info@netest.com
www.netest.com
Asbestos and lead testing/industrial hygiene.
Stephen Broadhead, Laboratory Manager

4867 Northern Lights Institute
210 N Higgins #326 406-721-7415
PO Box 8084 Fax: 406-721-7415
Missoula, MT 59807
Donald Snow, Program Director

4868 Nuclear Consulting Services
7000 Huntley Road 614-846-5710
Columbus, OH 43229 Fax: 614-431-0858
Joseph C Enneking, VP

4869 O'Brien & Gere Engineers
Box 4873 315-956-6100
Syracuse, NY 13221-4873 Fax: 315-463-7554
www.obg.com
R. Leland Davis, President
Timothy J. Barry, Sr. VP

4870 OA Laboratories and Research, Inc.
4717 North Shadeland Avenue 317-639-2626
Indianapolis, IN 46202-2628 Fax: 317-377-1924
oalabs@dajanigroup.com
OA Laboratories and Research, Inc. serves customers in Indiana and throughout the United States by meeting their Analytical needs.
Usama H. Dajani, President/CEO
Lisa K. Mesalam, Executive Secretary/Office M

4871 Oak Ridge Institute for Science and Education
1299 Bethel Valley Road 865-241-5947
Bldg SC-200 Fax: 865-576-5576
Oak Ridge, TN 37830 communications@orau.org
www.orau.org
As a consortium of major Ph.D.–granting academic institutions, ORAU cultivates collaborative partnerships that enhance the scientific research and education enterprise of our nation.
Andy Page, Director
Eric Abelquist, Executive VP

4872 Occupational Health Conservation
5118 N 56th Street 813-626-8156
Tampa, FL 33610 800-229-8156
Fax: 813-623-6702
Environmental impact assessment firm.
James F Rizk, President

4873 Ogden Environment & Energy Services Company
4455 Brookfield Corporate Drive 703-488-3700
Suite 100 Fax: 703-488-3701
Chantilly, VA 20151
Environmental engineering and consulting company.
J Mark Elliot, President

4874 Ogden Environment & Energy Services Company
5510 Morehouse Drive 858-458-9044
San Diego, CA 92121 Fax: 858-458-0943
Scientific and environmental engineering; analytical chemistry.
Mike Nienberg, Executive VP

4875 Oil-Dri Corporation of America
410 N Michigan Avenue 312-321-1515
Suite 400 800-645-3747
Chicago, IL 60611 Fax: 312-321-1271
info@oildri.com
www.oildri.com
Absorbents for consumers, industrial, agricultural, environmental and fluid purification.
Richard M. Jaffree, Chairman
Daniel S. Jafree, President/CEO

4876 Olver
1116 S Main Street 540-552-5548
Blacksburg, VA 24060 Fax: 540-552-5577
Engineering research and consulting firm specializing in environmental design and analysis. Research results published in project reports.

4877 Omega Thermal Technologies
21 Elbo Lane 610-572-2332
Mount Laurel, NJ 00805 Fax: 610-664-1258
contact@ottusa.com
www.ottusa.com
Technology consultants, designers and constructors offering technical expertise and hardware design for thermal processing and environmental studies.
Kenneth W Hladun, President
Peter V. Hewka, VP

4878 Oneil M Banks
336 S Main Street 410-879-4676
Suite 2D Fax: 410-836-8685
Bel Air, MD 21014
Industrial and environmental hygiene and toxicology consulting company.

4879 Online Environs
201 Broadway 617-577-0202
Suite 7 Fax: 617-577-0772
Cambridge, MA 00213
Telecommunications and Internet research.
Anrew Yu, President

4880 Operational Technology Corporation
4100 NW Loop 410 Street 210-731-0000
Suite 230 800-677-8072
San Antonio, TX 78229-4255 Fax: 210-731-0008
www.otcorp.com
Employment research firm providing information technologies, computer sales and service and environmental services.
John Fernandez, CEO

4881 Orlando Laboratories
820 Humphries Avenue 407-896-6645
Orlando, FL 32814 Fax: 407-898-6588
Independent environmental testing and analysis laboratory.

4882 Ostergaard Acoustical Associates
200 Executive Drive 973-731-7002
Suite 350 Fax: 973-731-6680
West Orange, NJ 00705 info@acousticalconsultant.com
www.acousticalconsultant.com
Environmental, acoustic and noise control testing and analysis firm. Research results published in project reports.
R Kring Herbert, Principal
Edward M. Clark, Principal

4883 Ozark Environmental Laboratories
PO Box 806 573-364-8900
Rolla, MO 65402 Fax: 573-341-2040
Firm providing construction materials testing on soils, aggregates, and asphaltic and portland cement concrete; water and wastewater physical and chemical analysis; and quality control studies encompassing physical measurements andchemical analysis.

4884 P&P Laboratories
2025 Woodlynne Avenue 856-962-6188
Oaklyn, NJ 00810
Environmental testing and chemical toxicology laboratory.

4885 PACE
100 Marshall Drive 724-772-0610
Warrendale, PA 15086 Fax: 724-772-1686
Environmental testing and analysis firm.

4886 PACE Analytical Services
1700 Elm Street 612-607-0151
Suite 200 Fax: 612-607-6444
Minneapolis, MN 55414 nathan.eklund@pacelabs.com
www.pacelabs.com
Provider of air, water, soil and environmental testing services.
Steve A Vanderboom, President/CEO
Michael R. Prasch, VP/CFO

4887 PACE Environmental Products
5240 West Coplay Road 610-262-3818
Whitehall, PA 18052 800-303-4532
Fax: 610-262-4445
www.paceenvironmental.com
Manufacturer and Integrator of continuous emissions monitoring systems (EMS). Regulatory, process, and certification stack testing. In-shop analyzer repair, CEMS field service. Parts, sales, rentals, repairs and service.
Damian Gaiotti, Sales Manager

4888 PACE Resources, Incorporated
40 S Richland Avenue 717-852-1300
York, PA 17404 800-711-8075
Fax: 717-852-1301
pace40@aol.com
This company is the parent of units involved in environmental engineering and consulting, civil engineering, architectural planning, data processing, printing and other services.
Russell E Horn, Jr, President

4889 PARS Environmental
500 Horizon Drive 609-890-7277
Suite 540 800-959-1119
Robbinsville, NJ 00869 Fax: 609-890-9116
info@parsenviro.com
www.parsenviro.com
Environmental consulting company.
HS Gill, President

4890 PCCI
300 North Lee Street
Suite 201
Alexandria, VA 22314
703-684-2060
Fax: 703-684-5343
thudon@pccii.com
www.pccii.com

Provides sensible solutions to difficult engineering and environmental problems in coastal, ocean and inland environments. Specialties include: environmental compliance; all hazards emergency response planning, trainings, drills andexercises; and marine engineering.
Robert Urban, President
Frank Marcinkowski, VP

4891 PDC and AREA Companies
4700 N Sterling Avenue
Peoria, IL 61615
309-688-0760
Fax: 309-692-9689
www.pdcarea.com

Environmental laboratory performs air sample analysis, soil analysis, and potential toxic waste analysis.

4892 PEI Associates
11499 Chester Road
Suite 200
Cincinnati, OH 45246
513-782-4700
Fax: 513-782-4807
Environmental consulting firm. Research results published in government publications.

4893 PELA
PO Box 2310
Tuscaloosa, AL 35403
205-752-5543
Fax: 205-752-4043
info@pela.com
www.pela.com

For over three decades, PELA's integration of qualified personnel, up to date technology, and sound management has established PELA as an international leader in the environmental consulting field. PELA's expertise in hydrology,geotechnical analysis, design and construction management, remediation, computer graphics and models, and permitting can get your project on the two feet quicker than you might think.
James Lee, President/CFO
Dr. Bashir Memon, Executive VP

4894 PELA GeoEnvironmental
PO Box 2310
Tuscaloosa, AL 35403
205-752-5543
Fax: 205-752-4043
www.pela.com
Consulting hydrologists, geologists, engineers, and environmental scientists. Research results published in brochures, pamphlets, news releases, speeches, seminars, studies, and reports.
James Lee, President/CFO
Dr. Bashir Memon, PhD., P.G., Executive VP

4895 PRC Environmental Management
233 N Michigan Avenue
Suite 1621
Chicago, IL 60601
312-938-0300
Fax: 312-931-1109
Robert Banosten, VP

4896 PRD Tech
1776 Mentor Avenue
Suite 400-A
Cincinnati, OH 45212
513-731-1800
Fax: 513-984-5710
prdbiofilter@aol.com
www.prdtechinc.com
Biological and chemical research and commercial technology development firm, serving primarily the baking, brewing, and other food industry segments with their environmental control needs - odor and volatile organic compound (VOC)control applications.
Ramesh Melarkode, President

4897 PSC Environmental Services
2337 N. Penn Road
Hatfield, PA 19440
215-822-2676
800-292-2510
Fax: 215-997-1315
www.pscnow.com

Environmental services
Bruce Roberson, President/CEO
Jeffrey Stocks, Sr. VP/CFO

4898 PSI
1901 South Meyers Road
Suite 400
Oakbrook Terrace, IL 60181
630-691-1587
800-548-7901
Fax: 630-691-1587
info@psiusa.com
www.psiusa.com
Distinguished as a leader in environmental consulting, geotechnical engineering, and construction testing services, PSI is nationally recognized in several disciplines, including: construction services, materials testing, roofconsulting and asbestos management.

4899 Pace
2400 Cumberland Drive
Valparaiso, IN 46383
219-464-2389
Fax: 219-462-2953
Environmental testing laboratory.
Les Arnold, President

4900 Pace Laboratory
9893 Brewers Court
Laurel, MD 20723
301-490-9860
Environmental testing laboratory.
Eric Holinger
Steve Marquez

4901 Pace New Jersey
284 Raritan Center Parkway
Edison, NJ 00883
973-257-9300
Fax: 973-257-0777
Environmental analytical laboratory and data management firm.

4902 Pacific Gamefish Research Foundation
47-381 Kealakehe Parkway
PO Box 4800
Kailua Kona, HI 96740
808-329-6105
Fax: 808-329-1148

4903 Pacific Northwest National Lab
902 Battelle Boulevard
PO Box 999
Richland, WA 99352
509-375-2121
888-375-7665
Fax: 509-375-2491
inquiry@pnl.gov
www.pnl.gov
Contract research and development for the government environmental restoration, energy, national security and health.
Mike Kluse, Lab Director
Steve Ashby, Deputy Director

4904 Pacific Northwest Research Institute
720 Broadway
Seattle, WA 98122
206-726-1200
800-745-1527
Fax: 206-726-1206
info@pndri.org
www.pnri.org
Established as Pacific Northwest Research Foundation in 1956 by Dr. William B Hutchinson, Sr. as the first private nonprofit biomedical and clinical research institute in the Northwest. As founder and first director, Dr. Hutchinson'sprimary objective was to provide a facility for basic and clinical research dedicated to the improvement of patient care. Sponsors basic science efforts in biochemistry, molecular biology and immunology as they pertain to the clinical areas of cancerand diabetes.
Erik Iverson, JD LLM, Chair
John Wecker, PH.D., President/CEO

4905 Pacific Nuclear
2525 West 10th St.
Antioch, CA 94509-9111
925-706-8300
800-706-3395
Fax: 925-706-8396
www.pacificnucleartechnology.com

4906 Package Research Laboratory
21 Pine Street
Suite 105
Rockaway, NJ 00786
973-627-4405
Fax: 973-627-4407
info@package-testing.com
www.package-testing.com

Packaged product testing facility. Research results published in reports, videos and pictures. Custom tests designed. DOT/UN certification on hazardous materials. Extreme environment testing. Pallet load and pallet merchandizingtesting. Design and packaging development, consulting, package analysis, project management, and vendor audits.
David Dixon, VP
Brian Berg, R&D

4907 PamLab
4099 Highway 190 East Service Rd
Covington, LA 70433
985-893-4097
844-639-9725
Fax: 985-893-6195
pamlab@pamlab.com
www.pamlab.com/

Pharmaceutical manufacturer.
Samuel Camp, Chairman
Kenny Ladner, President

4908 Pan Earth Designs
16525 103rd Street SE
Suite A
Yelm, WA 98597
360-458-9173
Fax: 360-458-9123
Environmental research firm.

4909 Par Environmental Services
1906 21st Street
PO Box 160756
Sacramento, CA 95816-756
916-739-8356
Fax: 916-739-0626
mlmaniery@yahoo.com
www.parenvironmental.com

Environmental research firm.
Mary Maniery, President/CEO

4910 Parsons Engineering Science
100 W Walnut Street
Pasadena, CA 91124
626-440-2000
Fax: 626-440-2630
erin.kuhlman@parsons.com
www.parsons.com

Environmental engineering testing and consulting company with expertise in advanced wastewater treatment.
Mark K. Holdsworth, Co-Founder
Kenneth C. Dahlberg, Chairman

4911 Peoria Disposal Company
2231 West Altorfer Drive
Peoria, IL 61615
800-752-6651
Fax: 309-688-0881
www.pdclab.com

Environmental services firm, especially hazardous waste testing.

4912 Pharmaco LSR
Mettlers Road
Box 2360
East Millstone, NJ 00887
732-873-2550
Fax: 732-873-3992
Dr. Geoffrey K Hogan, President

4913 Philip Environmental Services
210 W Sand Bank Road
PO Box 230
Columbia, IL 62236
618-281-7173
Fax: 618-281-5120
www.philipinc.com
Environmental research and analysis firm.
Jenny Penland, President

4914 Physical Sciences
20 New England Business Center
Andover, MA 00181-1077
978-689-0003
Fax: 978-689-3232
contact@psicorp.com
www.psicorp.com

PSI focuses on providing contract research and development services in a variety of technical areas to both government and commercial customers. Our interests range from basic research to technology development, with an emphasis onapplied research.
George.E Caledonia, Chairman
David Green, President/CEO

4915 Pittsburgh Mineral & Environmental Technology
700 5th Avenue
New Brighton, PA 15066-1837
724-843-5000
Fax: 724-843-5353
info@pmet-inc.com
www.pmet-inc.com

A full service company specializing in metals and mineral processing, coal ash utilization, waste stream management, and precision analysis. Also develops technologies dedicated to waste minimibation, treatment, and conversion tosafe,usable, profitable products.
Thomas E Weyand, President
William F Sutton, EVP

4916 Planning Concepts
1920 E. Northland Avenue
Appleton, WI 54911
920-730-3333
800-798-5722
Fax: 920-731-7401
cindy@planningconcepts.net
www.planningconcepts.net
Environmental impact assessment firm.
Richard Gasman, President
Randall Schmitz, VP

4917 Planning Design & Research Engineers
2000 Lindell Avenue
Nashville, TN 37203-5509
615-298-2065
Fax: 615-269-4119
pdre@pdre.net
www.PDRE.net
Environmental engineers, asbestos, lead paint design, testing underground tanks, hazardous waste projects, Phase I and II site assessments.
Teresa Tichenor, Office Manager

4918 Planning Resources
402 W Liberty Drive
Wheaton, IL 60187
630-668-3788
Fax: 630-668-4125
webmaster@planres.com
www.planres.com

Land use and environmental planning.
Darrell E Garrison, CEO
Keven L. Graham, COO/Director

4919 Plant Research Technologies
525 Del Rey Avenue Unit C
PO Box 6008
Sunnyvale, CA 94086
408-245-4423
Fax: 408-245-8043
Contact research organization which provides agricultural and analytical applied services.
Basil Burke PhD, President

4920 Plasma Science & Fusion Center
77 Massachusetts Avenue 617-253-7232
North West 17 Fax: 617-253-0570
Cambridge, MA 02139 psfc-info@mit.edu
www.psfc.mit.edu
Center for plasma science and technology and plasma fusion energy research. The mission of the center is to invent alternative energy resources that are more environmentally friendly.
Dennis G Whyte, Director
Martin Greenwald, Deputy Director

4921 Polaroid Corporation
549 Technology Square 617-577-2000
Cambridge, MA 00213 Fax: 617-577-5618
www.polaroid.com

4922 Polyengineering
1935 Headland Avenue 334-793-4700
PO Box 837 888-793-4700
Dothan, AL 36302 Fax: 334-793-9015
info@polyengineering.com
www.polyengineering.com
Offers a broad range of professional engineering and architectural services as well as financial services and administrative support.
Max A. Mobley, Chairman
Bruce Bradley, P.E., President

4923 Polytechnic
3740 W Morse Avenue 847-677-0450
Lincolnwood, IL 60712 Fax: 847-677-0480

4924 Porter Consultants
4400 Old William Penn Highway 412-380-7500
Suite 200 Fax: 412-380-6899
Monroeville, PA 15146 info@portercs.com
www.porter-consulting.com
Executive recruiting firm specializing in national and international placement of Sales, Marketing, Management, Executive-level, and Technical Support professionals within a wide rang of industries including High Tech, Exhibit.Telecommunications, Medical, and Pharmaceutical.
William Porter, Founder/President
Art Floro, Sr.VP/Executive Recruiter

4925 Powell Labs Limited
1915 Aliceanna Street 410-558-3540
Baltimore, MD 21231
Provides services in the specialty fields of metallurgical investigations, failure analysis, metal overheating and corrosion failures, remaining life assessments of high temperature components, identification of casting andmanufacturing defects, microbiological investigations, alloy identification, cycle water, cooling water, drinking water, high purity water, industrial process water, waste water, water and stream formed deposits, field examinations and training.

4926 Precision Environmental
2945 Townsgate Road 805-500-3713
Suite 200 800-375-7786
Westlake Village, CA 91361 Fax: 805-648-6999
info@precisionenv.com
www.precisionenv.com
Precision Environmental, Inc. was founded at Stanford University with the purpose of providing quality environmental contracting services to clients with asbestos contamination problems. State licensed and registered.

4927 Princeton Energy Resources International
2275 Research Blvd 301-881-0650
Suite200 Fax: 301-230-1232
Rockville, MD 20850 www.perihq.com
Engineering and consulting firm: engineering and environmental technology, environmental management and global climate change issues, economic research, aviation economics, and human factors
Adolfo Menendez, Chairman/CEO
Nicholas P. Cheremisinoff, VP

4928 Priorities Institute
3233 Vallejo Street 303-477-3792
#3B Fax: 303-838-8105
Denver, CO 80211 mail@priorities.org
www.priorities.org
Nonprofit, educational research organization that explores issues of critical importance that are not adequately researched by existing educational, media, research, governmental or other organizations.
Logan Perkins, Director/Founder

4929 Professional Service Industries
1901 S. Meyers Road 913-310-1600
Suite 400 800-548-7901
Oakbrook Terrace, IL 60181 Fax: 913-310-1601
www.psiusa.com
Elizabeth Noakes, Department Manager

4930 Professional Service Industries Laboratory
4106 NW Riverside Drive 816-741-9466
Riverside, MO 64150 Fax: 816-587-2996
Engineering test laboratory.
Stephen Fitzer, President

4931 Professional Service Industries/Jammal & Associates Division
1675 Lee Road 407-645-5560
Winter Park, FL 32789 Fax: 407-645-1320
William N Phillips, Executive VP

4932 Q-Lab
1005 SW 18th Avenue 305-245-5600
PO Box 349490 Fax: 305-245-5656
Homestead, FL 33034-1725 q-lab@q-lab.com
www.q-panel.com
Firm providing environmental simulation testing.
George Grossman, Founder
Doug Grossman, President

4933 Quantum Environmental
167 Little Lake Drive 734-930-2600
Ann Arbor, MI 48104 Fax: 734-930-2798
info@quantumenvironmental.com
www.quantumenvironmental.com
Environmental remediation firm.

4934 RESPEC
3824 Jet Drive 605-394-6400
Rapid City, SD 57703-4757 877-737-7321
Fax: 605-394-6456
www.respec.com
RESPEC is an integrated consulting and services firm with over 210 full-time employees and annual revenue over $30 million. Since our founding in 1969, RESPEC has remained committed to its original purpose of providing clients withhigh-quality technical and advisory services. Because of this commitment, we place particular emphasis on personnel experience and expertise, as well as the reliability and quality of our services.
Tom Zeller, VP Finance
Daniel B. Adams, Sr. Project Manager

4935 RMC Corporation Laboratories
55 Charles St. East 416-633-4123
Suite 101 Fax: 416-633-9503
Toronto, ON 65775 info@reitter.com
www.reitter.com
Environmental waste studies. Research results published in journals.
Bert Reitter, President
Lianne Reitter, Vice Prsident/Director

4936 RMT
1212 Deming Way 608-831-4444
Suite 1200 800-283-3443
Madison, WI 53717 Fax: 608-831-3334
www.rmtinc.com
Global engineering and management consulting firm that develops environmental solutions for industry. With a 600 person staff and 20 offices throughout the US and Europe helping clients sustain the environment while meeting theirbusiness objectives. Engineers, scientists and construction managers take a project from conception through successful completion. Expertise includes air, water and waste permitting, remediation, hazardous/solid waste management, air pollutioncontrol and more.
John Kennedy, President
Katherine Martin, VP

4937 Radian Corporation
1601 Market Street 800-523-1988
Philadelphia, PA 19103 877-723-4261
Fax: 512-388-0966
www.radian.biz
Environmental science and industrial safety research and consulting firm. Research results published in project reports and in professional journals.
Teresa Bryce Bazemore, President
S.A. Ibrahim, CEO

4938 Ralph Stone and Company
10954 Santa Monica Boulevard 310-478-1501
Los Angeles, CA 90025 800-813-9613
Fax: 310-478-7359
rstoneco@aol.com
www.ralphstoneco.com
Environmental - Phase 1&2; Remediation; Geology
Richard Kahle, President
James Rowlands, VP

4939 Ramco
3150 Brunswick Pike 609-620-4800
Suite 130 800-472-6261
Lawrenceville, NJ 00864 Fax: 609-620-4860
www.ramco.com
P R Venketrama Raja, Vice Chairman
Virender Aggarwal, CEO

4940 RapidView
1828 W Olson Road 574-224-5426
Rochester, IN 46975 800-656-4225
Fax: 574-223-7953
info@rapidview.com
www.rapidview.com
Developing and providing unique inspection solutions to the nuclear, petrochemical, industrial and municipal sewer industries.
Rex Robinson, President/CEO
Matt Sutton, VP, Sales & Marketing

4941 Raytheon Company
870 Winter Street 781-522-3000
Waltham, MA 00245 Fax: 781-522-3001
cjkovalsky@raytheon.com
www.raytheon.com
An environmental testing firm, one of Raytheon's unique testing resources is the Andover Environmental Test Laboratory (ETL), a full-service, state-of-the-art facility. ETL specializes in performing static, dynamic (vibration, shock,and acceleration) and climatic test procedures, as well as comprehensive failure analysis studies.
Thomas A. Kennedy, Chairman/CEO
Daniel J. Crowley, Vice President

4942 Recon Environmental Corporation
1927 5th Avenue 619-308-9333
San Diego, CA 92101-2358 Fax: 619-308-9334
www.recon-us.com
Environmental engineering, consulting, and laboratory services. Research results published in project reports and government publications.
Robert MacAller, President
Bobbi Herdes, Private Team Leader

4943 Recon Systems
5815 Willowdale Ave. SE 330-484-8444
Waynesburg, OH 44688 Fax: 330-484-8555
www.reconsystems.com
Dr. Norman J Weinstein, President

4944 Reed and Associates
269 Germantown Bend Cove 847-718-0101
Memphis, TN 38018 Fax: 847-718-0202
www.myreedhome.com
Environmental testing laboratory.

4945 Reid, Quebe, Allison, Wilcox & Associates
4755 Kingsway Drive 317-255-6060
Suite 400 Fax: 317-255-8354
Indianapolis, IN 46205
Architectural and environmental engineering research firm.
J Edward Doyle, President

4946 Reliance Laboratories
2001 Young Court 304-842-5285
Racine, WI 53404 800-634-6155
Fax: 304-842-5351
neil_czarnecki@reliancelaboratories.com
www.reliancelaboratories.com
William F Kirk Jr, President

4947 Remtech
110 12th Street NW 205-682-7900
Suite E 106 Fax: 205-682-7953
Birmingham, AL 35203
Systems design and engineering firm specializing in energy and environmental control applications. Research results published in project reports and are presented in papers at conferences.
Gene Fuller, President

4948 Research Planning
1121 Park Street 803-256-7322
PO Box 328 Fax: 803-254-6445
Columbia, SC 29201 www.researchplanning.com
Scientific consulting firm specializing in the environment and natural resource assessment. Extensive experience in field surveys, EIS, spatial data analysis, and international work in Central America, West Africa and the Middle East.Research results pub-

lished in professional journals, proceedings, and project reports. Woman-owned, small business concern.
Miles O. Hayes, Chairman
Jacqueline Michel, President

4949 Resource Technologies Corporation
248 E Calder Way 877-489-0199
Suite 305 877-489-0199
State College, PA 16801 Fax: 814-237-1769
appraisals@resourcetec.com
www.resourcetec.com

An independent research, development and technical services firm located in central Pennsylvania. Specializes in appraisal and assessment services, information system development, assessment appeals and digitalmapping, web basedapplications, geotechnical services, environmental and ecological analysis and planning and management services.
Jeffrey R Kern, Senior Appraiser
Patrick J. Federinko, Field Development Geologist

4950 Resources for the Future
1616 P Street NW 202-328-5000
Suite 600 Fax: 202-939-3460
Washington, DC 20036 info@rff.org
www.rff.org

RFF is a nonprofit and nonpartisan think tank located in Washington DC that conducts independent research-rooted primarily in economics and other social sciences on environmental and natural resource issues. RFF was founded in 1952.
Richard L. Schmalensee, Chair
Philip R. Sharp, President

4951 Responsive Management
130 Fraklin Street 540-432-1888
Harrisonburg, VA 22801 Fax: 540-432-1892
mark@responsivemanagement.com
www.responsivemanagement.com

Responsive Management is a Virginia-based public opinion polling and survey research firm specializing in fisheries, wildlife, natural resource, outdoor recreation and environmental issues.
Mark Damian Duda, Executive Director
Steven J. Bissell, Qualitative Research Analyst

4952 Revet Environmental and Analytical Lab
181 Cedar Hill Street 508-460-7600
Marlborough, MA 00175 Fax: 508-460-7777
Environmental analysis and consulting laboratory.
V Taylor, President

4953 Ricerca Biosciences LLC
7528 Auburn Road 440-357-3300
Concord, OH 44077 888-742-3722
Fax: 440-354-6276
www.ricerca.com

Ricerca, a premier solution provider, offers expertise in both biology and chemistry to enable life sciences companies to fully leverage integrated, cost-effective, best practices approach to lead optimization and drug development.Services include in-vitro/in-vivo ADME, pharmacology, toxicology, medicinal, process, analytical chemistry, cGMP API scale-up production, regulatory support.
Dorothie L Okleson, Vice President
Clifford W . Croley, CEO

4954 Rich Technology
PO Box 4886 805-523-3415
Glen Allen, VA 23058 Fax: 815-229-1525
www.richtech.com

Environmental engineering research firm.
Robby Demeria, Executive Director
Tracy Dickerson, Financial & Ops Manager

4955 Riviana Foods: RVR Package Testing Center
1702 Taylor Street 713-861-8221
Houston, TX 77007 Fax: 713-861-9939
Lejo C Brana, Director Packaging

4956 Robert Bosch Corporation
32104 State Road 2 574-237-2100
New Carlisle, IN 46552 Fax: 219-654-8755
Controlled-road environmental testing of automotive components for passenger cars, trucks, buses, tractor-trailers and off-road vehicles; certification to federal brake commission and fuel economy requirements.

4957 Robert D Niehaus
140 E Carrillo Street 805-962-0611
Santa Barbara, CA 93101 Fax: 805-962-0097
Daniel@rdniehaus.com
www.rdniehaus.com

Socioeconomic and environmental planning organization. Research results published in reports.
Daniel Brown, Business Development Manager
Jessica Solis, Market Analyst

4958 Rone Engineers
8908 Ambassador Row 214-630-9745
Dallas, TX 75247 Fax: 214-630-9819
www.roneengineers.com

Provider of Geotechnical, Construction Materials Testing and Environmental Consulting services throughout Texas and the Southwest.
Richard Leigh, President
Mark D. Gray, VP

4959 Roux Associates
209 Shafter Street 631-232-2600
Islandia, NY 11749 800-322-ROUX
Fax: 631-232-9898
sales@rouxinc.com
www.rouxinc.com

Environmental Consulting and Management.
Paul Roux, Chairman
Doug Swanson, President/CEO

4960 Rummel, Klepper & Kahl
81 Mosher Street 410-728-2900
Baltimore, MD 21217 800-787-3755
Fax: 410-728-2992
www.rkk.com

Civil, site, transpotation, environmental, structural engineering services.
Ken Goon, AICP, Senior Director, Transportat
Bob Andryszak, PE, Director, Wastewater

4961 SGI International
1200 Prospect Street 858-551-1090
Suite 325 Fax: 858-551-0247
La Jolla, CA 92037
Environmental applications.
Michael L Rose, President

4962 SGS Environmental Services Inc
201 Route 17 North 201-508-3000
Rutherford, NJ 00707 Fax: 201-508-3183
julie.shumway@sgs.com
www.sgsgroup.us.com

Environmental laboratory services.
Olivier Coppey, Executive Vice President
Frankie NG, CEO

4963 SHB AGRA
3232 W Virginia Avenue
Phoenix, AZ 85009
602-995-3916
Fax: 602-995-3921
Geotechnical and environmental research firm.

4964 SP Engineering
45 Congress Street, Building 4
PO Box 848, Shetland Park
Salem, MA 00197
978-745-4569
Fax: 978-745-4881
brucepoolesp@aol.com
www.spengineeringinc.com
SP Engineering specializes in all areas of environmental compliance. Services include testing for chemical or bacterial contamination of well water and assessments for the presence of petroleum products or hazardous waste, in additionto performing environmental audits insuring owners that all the tenants in their industrial complexes are in compliance with government regulations relative to hazardous waste disposal.
Bruce Poole, Executive Director

4965 SPECTROGRAM Corporation
287 Boston Post Road
Madison, CT 00644
203-318-0535
Fax: 203-318-0535
spectrogram@msn.com
www.spectrogram.com
Research, development and manufacturing firm which produces analytical instrumentation and systems in the fields of analytical chemistry (environmental) and elastomeric physical testing (rubber and plastics). Also offers a line ofproducts, each of which is involved in on-line environmental monitoring for the detection of an accidental release of petroleum products (oil spills).
HR Gram, President/CEO

4966 STL Denver
4955 Yarrow Street
Arvada, CO 80002
303-736-0100
800-572-8958
Fax: 303-431-7171
Testing and analysis services.

4967 STS Consultants
750 Corporate Woods Parkway
Vernon Hills, IL 60061
847-279-2500
800-859-7871
Fax: 847-279-2510
stsltd.com
Consulting engineering firm offering an integrated package of services in geotechnical engineering, waste management, environmental management, and construction technology.
Thomas W Wolf, CEO

4968 STS Consultants
111 Pfingsten Road
Northbrook, IL 60062
630-272-6520
Fax: 847-498-2721
Mike Russell, President

4969 Saint Louis Testing Laboratories
2810 Clark Avenue
Saint Louis, MO 63103
314-531-8080
Fax: 314-531-8085
testlab@labinc.com
www.labinc.com/
Research and testing laboratory specializing in chemical, metallurgical, nondestructive and environmental testing and field services. Research results published in project reports.
W Trowbridge, President

4970 Samtest
3730 James Savage Road
Midland, MI 48642
989-496-3610
Fax: 989-496-3190
Geotechnical and environmental services firm.

4971 Sari Sommarstrom
PO Box 219
Etna, CA 96027
530-467-5783
Fax: 530-467-3623
sari@sisqtel.net

4972 Savannah Laboratories
PO Box 13548
Savannah, GA 31416
912-354-7854
Fax: 912-352-0165
Environmental and biological research and testing laboratory with expertise in fish farming technology.

4973 Scitest
1110 E. Collins Blvd.
Suite 130
Richardson, TX 75081
972-479-1300
Fax: 972-479-1301
info@scitest.com
www.scitest.com
Environmental testing and analysis laboratory.
Brandon Bailey, Vice President

4974 Separation Systems Technology
100 Nightingale Ln
Gulf Breeze, FL 32561
850-932-1433
Fax: 850-934-8642
office@separationsystems.com
www.separationsystems.com
Environmental research.
Robert L Riley, President

4975 Shannon & Wilson
400 N 34th Street
PO Box 300303
Seattle, WA 98103
206-632-8020
Fax: 206-695-6777
info-seattle@shanwil.com
www.shannonwilson.com
Environmental research.

4976 Sheladia Associates
15825 Shady Grove Road
Suite 100
Rockville, MD 20850
301-590-3939
Fax: 301-948-7174
www.sheladia.com
Consulting firm specializing in environmental studies. Research results published in research reports for the government.
A Moytayek, President

4977 Shell Engineering and Associates
2403 West Ash
Columbia, MO 65203
573-445-0106
Fax: 573-445-0137
charles@shellengr.com
www.shellengr.com
Harvey D Shell, Founder/Chairman
Charles Shell, President/CEO

4978 Sherry Laboratories
9301 Innovation Drive
Suite 103
Daleville, IN 47334-569
765-378-4101
800-737-2378
Fax: 765-378-4107
Analytical environmental laboratory.
Mel Burnell, President

4979 Shive-Hattery Engineers & Architects
316 2nd Street SE
Suite 500
Cedar Rapids, IA 52406-1803
319-364-0227
800-798-0227
Fax: 319-364-4251
shivecr@shive-hattery.com
www.shive-hattery.com
Jim Lee, President
Mark Anderson, Vice President/Office Direct

4980 Siebe Appliance Controls
2809 Emerywood Parkway
Richmond, VA 23294
804-756-6500
Fax: 804-756-6563

Automatic temperature, environmental, electronic appliance, heating, cooling and gas safety controls and valves; thermostats and oven burners.

4981 Siemens Water Technologies
10 Technology Drive 978-614-7156
Lowell, MA 00185 800-224-9474
Fax: 978-934-9499
Products and services includes: environmental devices and controls; system troubleshooting/diagnostics; system startup; instrumentation calibration and commissioning, and radio topographic path analysis.
Ursula Boehm, VP
Reudiger Knauf, VP

4982 Simpson Electric Company
520 Simpson Ave. 715-588-3311
PO Box 99 Fax: 715-588-3326
Lac Du Flambeau, WI 54538 www.simpsonelectric.com
Analog and digital panel meters, meter relays, controllers, volt-ohm-milliammeters, scopes and industrial and environmental test instruments.

4983 Skinner and Sherman Laboratories
1st Avenue 781-890-7200
Waltham, MA 00245 Fax: 781-890-7003

4984 Smith & Mahoney
540 Broadway 518-463-4107
PO 22047 Fax: 518-463-3823
Albany, NY 12201
Michael W McNarney, President

4985 Soil Engineering Testing/SET
2401 West 66th Street 612-353-5770
Richfield, MN 55423 Fax: 651-760-4312
labinfo@soilengineeringtesting.com
www.soilengineeringtesting.com/
A comprehensive soil mechanics laboratory facility for engineering disciplines, environmental and hydrological applications. Scope of services includes: water content; unit mass; liquid limit; sieve analysis; specific gravity; pH;organic content; unconfined compression; and expansion index.
Slade Olson, President
John Whelan, VP

4986 Solar Testing Laboratories
1125 Valley Belt Road 216-741-7007
Cleveland, OH 44131 Fax: 216-741-7011
www.stlohio.com
Geotechnical, environmental engineering, materials testing, and construction inspection laboratory. Services include environmental site assessments, assisting in the selection and coordination of the work of remediation contractors,asbestos inspection and abatement supervision, micro purgegroundwater sampling, sediment control inspection, landfill closure quality assurance, radiological assessments, U.S.T. closures and RCRA closures and facility investigation.
George J Ata PE, President

4987 Southeastern Engineering & Testing Laboratories
4761 SW 51st Street 954-584-4322
Davie, FL 33314 Fax: 954-584-4338
jack@seetl.com
www.seetl.com
Geotechnical and environmental engineering consulting firm and construction materials engineering laboratory.
Jack Krouskroup, Director

4988 Southern Petroleum Laboratory/SPL
8850 Interchange Drive 713-660-0901
PO Box 20807 877-775-5227
Houston, TX 77054 Fax: 713-660-8975
HRBrown@spl-inc.com
www.spl-inc.com
SPL provides technical and analytical services to the oil and gas industry including environmental and hydrocarbon analytical services as well as field (gas & liquid measurement) services.
Christopher F Brown, President
Steve Grenda, CEO

4989 Southern Research Institute COBRA Training Facility Center for Domestic Preparedness
2000 Ninth Avenue South 205-581-2000
P.O. Box 55305 Fax: 800-967-6774
Birmingham, AL 35255-5305 secrist@southernresearch.org
www.southernresearch.org
Southern Research Institute is an independent research corporation with established capabilities in pharmaceutical discovery and development, engineering, chemical and biological defense, environmental and energy-related sciences.Research is conducted through contracts and grants with government and commerical clients.
Ray L. Watts M.D, Chairman
Arthur J. Tipton, Ph.D., President/CEO

4990 Southern Research Institute Corporate Office: Life Sciences/Environment/Energy
757 Tom Martin Drive 205-581-2000
PO Box 55305 800-967-6774
Birmingham, AL 35211-5305 Fax: 800-967-6774
secrist@southernresearch.org
www.southernresearch.org
Southern Research Institute is an independent research corporation with established capabilities in pharmaceutical discovery and development, engineering, chemical and biological defense, environmental and energy-related sciences.Research is conducted through contracts and grants with government and commerical clients.
Ray L. Watts M.D, Chairman
Arthur J. Tipton, Ph.D., President/CEO

4991 Southern Research Institute: Carbon To Liquids Development Center
31972 Highway 25 North 205-670-5068
Wilsonville, AL 35186 800-967-6774
Fax: 205-670-5843
secrist@southernresearch.org
www.southernresearch.org
Southern Research Institute is an independent research corporation with established capabilities in pharmaceutical discovery and development, engineering, chemical and biological defense, environmental and energy-related sciences.Research is conducted through contracts and grants with government and commerical clients.
Ray L. Watts M.D, Chairman
Arthur J. Tipton, Ph.D., President/CEO

4992 Southern Research Institute: Chemical Defense Training Facility-Missouri
5201 International Drive 919-282-1050
PO Box 55305 800-967-6774
Durham, CA 27712-5305 Fax: 573-596-0722
secrist@southernresearch.org
www.southernresearch.org
Southern Research Institute is an independent research corporation with established capabilities in pharmaceutical discovery and development, engineering, chemical and biological defense, environmental and energy-related sciences.Research is conducted through contracts and grants with government and commerical clients.
Ray L. Watts M.D, Chairman
Arthur J. Tipton, Ph.D., President/CEO

4993 Southern Research Institute: Engineering Research Center
757 Tom Martin Drive 205-581-2000
Birmingham, AL 35211 800-967-6774
Fax: 205-581-2726
secrist@southernresearch.org
www.southernresearch.org

Southern Research Institute is an independent research corporation with established capabilities in pharmaceutical discovery and development, engineering, chemical and biological defense, environmental and energy-related sciences.Research is conducted through contracts and grants with government and commerical clients.
Ray L. Watts M.D, Chairman
Arthur J. Tipton, Ph.D., President/CEO

4994 Southern Research Institute: Environment & Energy Research
994 Ellington Field 256-726-9334
Houston, AL 77034 Fax: 256-726-9340
secrist@southernresearch.org
www.southernresearch.org

Southern Research Institute is an independent research corporation with established capabilities in pharmaceutical discovery and development, engineering, chemical and biological defense, environmental and energy-related sciences.Research is conducted through contracts and grants with government and commerical clients.
Ray L. Watts M.D, Chairman
Arthur J. Tipton, Ph.D., President/CEO

4995 Southern Research Institute: Infectious Disease Research Facility
431 Aviation Way 301-694-3232
Frederick, MD 21701 Fax: 301-694-7223
secrist@southernresearch.org
www.southernresearch.org

Southern Research Institute is an independent research corporation with established capabilities in pharmaceutical discovery and development, engineering, chemical and biological defense, environmental and energy-related sciences.Research is conducted through contracts and grants with government and commerical clients.
Ray L. Watts M.D, Chairman
Arthur J. Tipton, Ph.D., President/CEO

4996 Southern Research Institute: Power Systems Development Facility
31972 Highway 25 North 205-670-5068
Wilsonville, AL 35186 Fax: 205-670-5843
secrist@southernresearch.org
www.southernresearch.org

Southern Research Institute is an independent research corporation with established capabilities in pharmaceutical discovery and development, engineering, chemical and biological defense, environmental and energy-related sciences.Research is conducted through contracts and grants with government and commerical clients.
Ray L. Watts M.D, Chairman
Arthur J. Tipton, Ph.D., President/CEO

4997 Southern Testing & Research Laboratories
317 Covered Bridge Road 252-237-4175
Catersville, GA 30120 Fax: 252-237-9341
www.southerntesting.com

Full-service laboratory with over 75 chemists, microbiologists and support personnel that provides personalized service to clients. Capabilities include pharmaceutical, foods and feeds, environmental, industrial hygiene, agriculturaland microbiological sciences. Laboratory is FDA-inspected GLP/cGMP laboratory utilizing AOAC, USP, EPA, USDA, AACC, AOCS, ISO, client and in-house validated methods.
Robert Dermer, Managing Director
Walter Hogg, Business Development

4998 Spears Professional Environmental & Archeological Research Services
13858 S Highway 170 479-839-3663
West Fork, AR 72774 Fax: 479-839-2575
SPEARSC@aol.com

Archeological research service. The company conducts cultural resources studies including background studies for Environmental Impact Studies, archeological surveys, significance testing, and data recovery/excavation. Large multi-yearprojects have included cultural resources surveys for timber sales and studies for proposed interstates and utilities.
Carol S Spears, President/Owner

4999 Spectrochem Laboratories
545 Commerce Street 201-337-4774
Franklin Lakes, NJ 00741 Fax: 201-337-1255
www.spectrochem.in

Research and development firm specializing in environmental sciences and inorganic chemistry. Research results published in proceedings at technical conferences.
Irene Van Dren, President

5000 Spectrum Sciences & Software
91 Hill Avenue NW 850-796-0909
Fort Walton Beach, FL 32548 Fax: 850-244-9560
www.specsci.com

An environmental research firm, Spectrum provides diversified capabilities of a large business in a number of advanced technologies. Services include all the disciplines and technologies relevant to operations and maintenance; computerand system sciences; manufacturing; comprehensive planning and environmental assessment technology; and system design testing and evaluation.
Jeremy Maines, Information Technology
Dwight Howard, VP Business Development

5001 Spotts, Stevens and McCoy
1047 North Park Road 610-621-2000
PO Box 6307 Fax: 610-621-2001
Reading, PA 19610-307 information@ssmgroup.com
www.ssmgroup.com

An engineering and consulting firm, serving business, industry, and government, SSM provides consulting services in the areas of environmental health and safety, regulatory compliance and training. In addition, SSM provides costeffective, well-engineered solutions to environmental health and safety issues facing facility owners in industry, education, healthcare and local government.
Eileen Kaley, Marketing Director

5002 Standard Testing and Engineering - Corporate
3400 N. Lincoln Boulevard 405-528-0541
Oklahoma City, OK 73105-5106 800-725-0541
Fax: 405-528-0559
bburris@stantest.com
www.stantest.com

Standard Testing and Engineering Company was founded in 1951 as a professional engineering firm specializing in materials testing and engineering for the construction and manufacturing industries. Standard Testing also providesenvironmental services such as groundwater studies. Standard Testing's capabilities include a wide variety of specialties such as environmental engineering, and industrial hygiene.
Thomas J Kelly, President
Richard W Mudd, Vice President

5003 Standard Testing and Engineering - Enid
902 Trails West Loop
Enid, OK 73703-6336
580-725-3130
800-725-3130
Fax: 580-237-3211
bburris@stantest.com
www.stantest.com

Standard Testing and Engineering Company was founded in 1951 as a professional engineering firm specializing in materials testing and engineering for the construction and manufacturing industries. Standard Testing also providesenvironmental services such as groundwater studies. Standard Testing's capabilities include a wide variety of specialties such as environmental engineering, and industrial hygiene.
Thomas J Kelly, President
Richard W Mudd, Vice President

5004 Standard Testing and Engineering - Lawton
202 S.E.
J Ave.
Lawton, OK 73501-2481
580-353-0872
800-725-0872
Fax: 580-353-1263
bburris@stantest.com
www.stantest.com

Standard Testing and Engineering Company was founded in 1951 as a professional engineering firm specializing in materials testing and engineering for the construction and manufacturing industries. Standard Testing also providesenvironmental services such as groundwater studies. Standard Testing's capabilities include a wide variety of specialties such as environmental engineering, and industrial hygiene.
Thomas J Kelly, President
Richard W Mudd, Vice President

5005 Standard Testing and Engineering - Oklahoma City Environmental Services Division
4300 N Lincoln Boulevard
Oklahoma, OK 73105-5106
405-424-8378
800-725-8378
Fax: 405-424-8129
tjkelly@stantest.com
www.stantest.com

Standard Testing and Engineering Company was founded in 1951 as a professional engineering firm specializing in materials testing and engineering for the construction and manufacturing industries. Standard Testing also providesenvironmental services such as groundwater studies. Standard Testing's capabilities include a wide variety of specialties such as environmental engineering, and industrial hygiene.
Thomas J Kelly, President
Richard W Mudd, Vice President

5006 Standard Testing and Engineering - Tulsa
10816 E. Newton St.
Suite 110
Tulsa, OK 74116
918-439-9539
800-725-4592
Fax: 918-437-0853
www.stantest.com

Standard Testing and Engineering Company was founded in 1951 as a professional engineering firm specializing in materials testing and engineering for the construction and manufacturing industries. Standard Testing also providesenvironmental services such as groundwater studies. Standard Testing's capabilities include a wide variety of specialties such as environmental engineering, and industrial hygiene.
Thomas J Kelly, President
Richard W Mudd, Vice President

5007 Stanford Technology Corporation
1010 N. Normandie
Suite 301
Spokane, WA 99201
203-348-4080
866-717-7363
Fax: 203-327-5225
stctestlab@aol.com
www.stanfordtechnology.com

High technology research firm. Research results published in confidential project reports.
Charles C Cullari, President
Gerald T Ciccone, VP

5008 Stantec Consulting Services
4875 Riverside Drive
Macon, GA 31210
780-917-7000
Fax: 478-474-8933
media@stantec.com
www.stantec.com

Stantec, founded in 1954, provides professional design and consulting services in planning, engineering, architecture, surveying, economics, and project management. Stantec supports public and private sector clients in a diverse rangeof markets in the infrastructure and facilities sector at every stage, from initial concept and financial feasibility to project completion and beyond.
Anton Germishuizen, VP/Business Leader
Bill Shelley, VP/Business Leader

5009 Steven Winter Associates - New York NY
307 7th Avenue
Suite 1701
New York, NY 10001
212-564-5800
Fax: 212-741-8673
swa@swinter.com
www.swinter.com

New York client base includes City, State, and Federal agencies, and owners of a wide array of buildings from small residential to well-known sustainable buildings, such as Battery Park City, 4 Times Square, AOL/Time Warner and HearstHeadquarters. SWA is working with many developers, architects, engineers, and building scientists to help deliver higher performance buildings throughout the NYC metropolitan area and in the surrounding region.
Steven Winter, President

5010 Steven Winter Associates - Norwalk CT
61 Washington Street
Norwalk, CT 00685
203-857-0200
Fax: 203-852-0741
swa@swinter.com
www.swinter.com

Founded in 1972, Steven Winter Associates, Inc. (SWA) provides a variety of services including: building system assessment, green materials and product specifications, LEED assessments and certification, green building commissioning,accessibility conformance, energy auditing capabilities, builder/operator training, preparation of green guidelines, HVAC troubleshooting, indooor air quality analysis and testing, solar and PV design engineering.
Steven Winter, President

5011 Steven Winter Associates - Washington DC
1001 G Street NW
Suite 800
Washington, DC 20001
202-628-6100
Fax: 202-393-5043
swadc@swinter.com
www.swinter.com

Located just a few blocks from the White House in the historic downtown section, SWA/DC focuses on technology transfer, buildings-related policy analysis, information dissemination, media outreach & publishing, association management,classroom and web-based training, and buildings research work on behalf of U.S. DOE, HUD, EPA, and the national energy laboratories. SWA/DC also provides logistical support to HUD's Office of Native American Programs (ONAP).
Steven Winter, President

5012 Stone Environmental
535 Stone Cutters Way
Montpelier, VT 00560
802-229-4541
603-273-9250
Fax: 802-229-5417
sei@stone-env.com
www.stone-env.com

Environmental consulting services and technologies that include: environmental planning and documentation; environmental compliance; waste management; environmental spatial analysis; remediation. Scientific disciplines include: civilengineering; environmental engineering and chemistry; for-

est biology; hydrogeology; geology; soil science; and geographic information systems.
Christopher Stone, President
David Healy, Vice President

5013 Suburban Laboratories
1950 S. Batavia Ave Ste 150 708-544-3260
Geneva, IL 60134 800-783-5227
Fax: 708-544-8587
Info@suburbanlabs.com
www.suburbanlabs.com
Environmental laboratory providing chemical, chromatographic, and spectrographic analysis of biological materials, including water and groundwater, soil, and hazardous materials for priority pollutants, metals, and pesticide residues.
Jarrett Thomas, President/CEO
Shane Clarke, Business Development Manager

5014 Sunsearch
PO Box 590 203-453-6591
393A Soundview Road 800-338-0258
Guilford, CT 00643 Fax: 203-458-9011
www.sunsearchinc.com
Designs, installs and services solar energy systems. Additional services includes: feasibility studies; inspections or assessments of existing systems; repair and redesign of existing systems; service agreements and evaluation ofcomplex systems.
Everett M Barber Jr, President

5015 Systech Environmental Corporation
3085 Woodman Drive 937-643-1240
Suite 300 800-888-8011
Dayton, OH 45420 Fax: 937-643-1203
www.go2systech.com
Provider of alternative fuels to cement kilns.
Erica Hawk, Corporate Mktg Specialist

5016 TAKA Asbestos Analytical Services
PO Box 208 631-261-2117
Greenlawn, NY 11740 Fax: 631-261-2120
TAKA provides environmental consultation, testing and analytical services for the assessment and detection of onsite asbestos materials. The president and owner of TAKA, Dr. Thomas A. Kubic, has extensive experience with forensicmicroscopy and advanced techniques in sampling and evaluation of airborne asbestos particles using Polarized Light Microscopy.
Thomas A Kubic PhD/MS/JD/FABC, President/Owner

5017 TRAC Laboratories
16969 North Texas Ave. 281-461-7886
Suite 300 Fax: 940-566-2698
Webster, TX 77598 info@traclabs.com
www.traclabs.com
Provide multi-disciplinary problem-solving approaches to environmental and public health issues.
David Kortenkamp, President/CEO
Bryn Wolfe, Director of Communication

5018 TRC Environmental Corporation-Alexandria
8550 United Plaza Blvd. 225-216-7483
Suite 502 Fax: 225-216-0732
Baton Rouge, LA 70809 cobrien@trcsolutions.com
www.trcsolutions.com
A provider of engineering, financial, risk management and construction services to large industrial and government customers throughout the United States, TRC provides customer focused solutions in three primary markets: environmental,energy and infrastructure. Environmental services include project development, resolving legacy environmental issues, ensuring compliance for continuing operations, and identifing and mitigating future environmental risks.
Christopher P Vincze, Chairman/CEO
John A. Carrig, President/COO

5019 TRC Environmental Corporation-Atlanta
4155 Shackleford Road. 770-270-1192
Norcross, GA 30093 Fax: 770-270-1392
cobrien@trcsolutions.com
www.trcsolutions.com
A provider of engineering, financial, risk management and construction services to large industrial and government customers throughout the United States, TRC provides customer focused solutions in three primary markets: environmental,energy and infrastructure. Environmental services include project development, resolving legacy environmental issues, ensuring compliance for continuing operations, and identifing and mitigating future environmental risks.
Christopher P Vincze, Chairman/CEO
John A. Carrig, President/COO

5020 TRC Environmental Corporation-Augusta
14 Gabriel Drive 207-621-7000
Augusta, ME 00433 Fax: 207-621-7001
cobrien@trcsolutions.com
www.trcsolutions.com
A provider of engineering, financial, risk management and construction services to large industrial and government customers throughout the United States, TRC provides customer focused solutions in three primary markets: environmental,energy and infrastructure. Environmental services include project development, resolving legacy environmental issues, ensuring compliance for continuing operations, and identifing and mitigating future environmental risks.
Christopher P Vincze, Chairman/CEO
John A. Carrig, President/COO

5021 TRC Environmental Corporation-Boston
2 Liberty Square 617-350-3444
6th Floor Fax: 617-350-3443
Boston, MA 00210 cobrien@trcsolutions.com
www.trcsolutions.com
A provider of engineering, financial, risk management and construction services to large industrial and government customers throughout the United States, TRC provides customer focused solutions in three primary markets: environmental,energy and infrastructure. Environmental services include project development, resolving legacy environmental issues, ensuring compliance for continuing operations, and identifing and mitigating future environmental risks.
Christopher P Vincze, Chairman/CEO
John A. Carrig, President/COO

5022 TRC Environmental Corporation-Bridgeport
10 Middle St 203-876-1453
Suite 600 Fax: 203-876-1486
Bridgeport, CT 00660 cobrien@trcsolutions.com
www.trcsolutions.com
A provider of engineering, financial, risk management and construction services to large industrial and government customers throughout the United States, TRC provides customer focused solutions in three primary markets: environmental,energy and infrastructure. Environmental services include project development, resolving legacy environmental issues, ensuring compliance for continuing operations, and identifing and mitigating future environmental risks.
Christopher P Vincze, Chairman/CEO
John A. Carrig, President/COO

5023 TRC Environmental Corporation-Chicago
230 West Monroe Street 312-269-5800
Suite 2370 Fax: 312-578-0877
Chicago, IL 60606 cobrien@trcsolutions.com
www.trcsolutions.com

A provider of engineering, financial, risk management and construction services to large industrial and government customers throughout the United States, TRC provides customer focused solutions in three primary markets: environmental,energy and infrastructure. Environmental services include project development, resolving legacy environmental issues, ensuring compliance for continuing operations, and identifing and mitigating future environmental risks.
Christopher P Vincze, Chairman/CEO
John A. Carrig, President/COO

5024 TRC Environmental Corporation-Ellicott City
4425 Forbes Blvd 301-306-6981
Lanham, MD 20706 Fax: 301-306-6986
cobrien@trcsolutions.com
www.trcsolutions.com

A provider of engineering, financial, risk management and construction services to large industrial and government customers throughout the United States, TRC provides customer focused solutions in three primary markets: environmental,energy and infrastructure. Environmental services include project development, resolving legacy environmental issues, ensuring compliance for continuing operations, and identifing and mitigating future environmental risks.
Christopher P Vincze, Chairman/CEO
John A. Carrig, President/COO

5025 TRC Environmental Corporation-Henderson
1009 Whitney Ranch Drive 702-248-6415
Henderson, NV 89014 Fax: 702-248-0626
cobrien@trcsolutions.com
www.trcsolutions.com

A provider of engineering, financial, risk management and construction services to large industrial and government customers throughout the United States, TRC provides customer focused solutions in three primary markets: environmental,energy and infrastructure. Environmental services include project development, resolving legacy environmental issues, ensuring compliance for continuing operations, and identifing and mitigating future environmental risks.
Christopher P Vincze, Chairman/CEO
John A. Carrig, President/COO

5026 TRC Environmental Corporation-Honolulu
1600 Kapiolani Blvd 808-728-4111
Suite 717 Fax: 808-638-5649
Honolulu Oahu, HI 96814 cobrien@trcsolutions.com
www.trcsolutions.com

A provider of engineering, financial, risk management and construction services to large industrial and government customers throughout the United States, TRC provides customer focused solutions in three primary markets: environmental,energy and infrastructure. Environmental services include project development, resolving legacy environmental issues, ensuring compliance for continuing operations, and identifing and mitigating future environmental risks.
Christopher P Vincze, Chairman/CEO
John A. Carrig, President/COO

5027 TRC Environmental Corporation-Indianapolis
10475 Crosspoint Blvd 317-517-2616
Suite 250 Fax: 651-686-4434
Indianapolis, IN 46256 cobrien@trcsolutions.com
www.trcsolutions.com

A provider of engineering, financial, risk management and construction services to large industrial and government customers throughout the United States, TRC provides customer focused solutions in three primary markets: environmental,energy and infrastructure. Environmental services include project development, resolving legacy environmental issues, ensuring compliance for continuing operations, and identifing and mitigating future environmental risks.
Christopher P Vincze, Chairman/CEO
John A. Carrig, President/COO

5028 TRC Environmental Corporation-Irvine
9685 Research Drive 949-727-9336
Irvine, CA 92618 Fax: 949-727-7311
dzarider@trcsolutions.com
www.trcsolutions.com

A provider of engineering, financial, risk management and construction services to large industrial and government customers throughout the United States, TRC provides customer focused solutions in three primary markets: environmental,energy and infrastructure. Environmental services include project development, resolving legacy environmental issues, ensuring compliance for continuing operations, and identifing and mitigating future environmental risks.
Christopher P Vincze, Chairman/CEO
John A. Carrig, President/COO

5029 TRC Environmental Corporation-Jackson
1540 Eisenhower Place 734-971-7080
Ann Arbor, MI 48108 Fax: 734-971-9022
cobrien@trcsolutions.com
www.trcsolutions.com

A provider of engineering, financial, risk management and construction services to large industrial and government customers throughout the United States, TRC provides customer focused solutions in three primary markets: environmental,energy and infrastructure. Environmental services include project development, resolving legacy environmental issues, ensuring compliance for continuing operations, and identifing and mitigating future environmental risks.
Christopher P Vincze, Chairman/CEO
John A. Carrig, President/COO

5030 TRC Environmental Corporation-Kansas City
Livestock Exchange Building 816-474-1500
1600 Genessee Street, Suite 416 Fax: 816-474-1853
Kansas City, MO 64102-1039 cobrien@trcsolutions.com
www.trcsolutions.com

A provider of engineering, financial, risk management and construction services to large industrial and government customers throughout the United States, TRC provides customer focused solutions in three primary markets: environmental,energy and infrastructure. Environmental services include project development, resolving legacy environmental issues, ensuring compliance for continuing operations, and identifing and mitigating future environmental risks.
Christopher P Vincze, Chairman/CEO
John A. Carrig, President/COO

5031 TRC Environmental Corporation-Lexington
670 Morrison Road 614-655-5360
Suite 220 Fax: 614-866-4359
Guhanna, OH 43230 cobrien@trcsolutions.com
www.trcsolutions.com

A provider of engineering, financial, risk management and construction services to large industrial and government customers throughout the United States, TRC provides customer focused solutions in three primary markets: environmental,energy and infrastructure. Environmental services include project development, resolving legacy environmental issues, ensuring compliance for continuing operations, and identifing and mitigating future environmental risks.
Christopher P Vincze, Chairman/CEO
John A. Carrig, President/COO

5032 TRC Environmental Corporation-Littleton
7761 Shaffer Parkway 970-419-4364
Suite 100 Fax: 303-792-0122
Littleton, CO 80127 cobrien@trcsolutions.com
www.trcsolutions.com

A provider of engineering, financial, risk management and construction services to large industrial and government customers throughout the United States, TRC provides customer focused solutions in three primary markets: environmental,energy and infrastructure. Environmental services include project development, resolving legacy environmental issues, ensuring compliance for continuing operations, and identifing and mitigating future environmental risks.
Christopher P Vincze, Chairman/CEO
John A. Carrig, President/COO

5033 TRC Environmental Corporation-Lowell
650 Suffolk Street 978-970-5600
Lowell, MA 00185 Fax: 978-453-1995
gharkness@trcsolutions.com
www.trcsolutions.com

A provider of engineering, financial, risk management and construction services to large industrial and government customers throughout the United States, TRC provides customer focused solutions in three primary markets: environmental,energy and infrastructure. Environmental services include project development, resolving legacy environmental issues, ensuring compliance for continuing operations, and identifing and mitigating future environmental risks.
Christopher P Vincze, Chairman/CEO
John A. Carrig, President/COO

5034 TRC Environmental Corporation-Phoenix
650 Suffolk Street 978-970-5600
Lowell, MA 00185 Fax: 978-453-1995
gharkness@trcsolutions.com
www.trcsolutions.com

A provider of engineering, financial, risk management and construction services to large industrial and government customers throughout the United States, TRC provides customer focused solutions in three primary markets: environmental,energy and infrastructure. Environmental services include project development, resolving legacy environmental issues, ensuring compliance for continuing operations, and identifing and mitigating future environmental risks.
Christopher P Vincze, Chairman/CEO
John A. Carrig, President/COO

5035 TRC Environmental Corporation-Princeton
Research Park 609-497-1379
322 Wall Street Fax: 609-497-1879
Princeton, NJ 00854 cobrien@trcsolutions.com
www.trcsolutions.com

A provider of engineering, financial, risk management and construction services to large industrial and government customers throughout the United States, TRC provides customer focused solutions in three primary markets: environmental,energy and infrastructure. Environmental services include project development, resolving legacy environmental issues, ensuring compliance for continuing operations, and identifing and mitigating future environmental risks.
Christopher P Vincze, Chairman/CEO
John A. Carrig, President/COO

5036 TRC Environmental Corporation-San Francisco
505 Sansome Street 415-434-2600
Suite 1600 Fax: 415-434-2321
San Francisco, CA 94111 cobrien@trcsolutions.com
www.trcsolutions.com

A provider of engineering, financial, risk management and construction services to large industrial and government customers throughout the United States, TRC provides customer focused solutions in three primary markets: environmental,energy and infrastructure. Environmental services include project development, resolving legacy environmental issues, ensuring compliance for continuing operations, and identifing and mitigating future environmental risks.
Christopher P Vincze, Chairman/CEO
John A. Carrig, President/COO

5037 TRC Environmental Corporation-West Palm Beach
1665 Palm Beach Lakes Boulevard 561-681-3494
Suite 720 Fax: 561-681-3496
West Palm Beach, FL 33401 cobrien@trcsolutions.com
www.trcsolutions.com

A provider of engineering, financial, risk management and construction services to large industrial and government customers throughout the United States, TRC provides customer focused solutions in three primary markets: environmental,energy and infrastructure. Environmental services include project development, resolving legacy environmental issues, ensuring compliance for continuing operations, and identifing and mitigating future environmental risks.
Christopher P Vincze, Chairman/CEO
John A. Carrig, President/COO

5038 TRC Environmental Corporation-Windsor
21 Griffin Road North 860-298-9692
Windsor, CT 00609 Fax: 860-298-6399
czoephel@trcsolutions.com
www.trcsolutions.com

A provider of engineering, financial, risk management and construction services to large industrial and government customers throughout the United States, TRC provides customer focused solutions in three primary markets: environmental,energy and infrastructure. Environmental services include project development, resolving legacy environmental issues, ensuring compliance for continuing operations, and identifing and mitigating future environmental risks.
Christopher P Vincze, Chairman/CEO
John A. Carrig, President/COO

5039 TRC Garrow Associates
3772 Pleasantdale Road 770-270-1192
Suite 200 Fax: 770-270-1392
Atlanta, GA 30340

TRC Garrow Associates provides business consulting services focusing on environmental analysis, planning and development.
Barbara Garrow, President

5040 Talos Technology Consulting
3336 Fern Hollow Place 703-715-3500
Suite 100 Fax: 703-715-0189
Herndon, VA 20171 information@talos.com

An environmental computer company, Talos works with businesses and government organizations to help them capitalize upon emerging technologies and achieve their organizational objectives. Talos professionals perform strategic planning;requirements analysis; design documentation; software trade surveying; system security planning; cost-benefit analysis; and surveys of technology markets.
Scott Little, Strategic Development
Rob Smith

5041 Taylor Engineering
10151 Deerwood Park Blvd. 904-731-7040
Bldg. 300, Suite 300 Fax: 904-731-9847
Jacksonville, FL 32256 www.taylorengineering.com

Services in coastal engineering consulting, dredging and dredged material management, hydrology and hydraulics, environmental services, and construction support services.
Terrence Hall P.E., President

5042 Tellus Institute
11 Arlington Street
Boston, MA 00211-3411
617-266-5400
Fax: 617-266-8303
www.tellus.org

Environmental research and strategic development firm. Services include: analyzing energy systems and environmental impacts; evaluating policies for transition to efficient and renewable energy technology; formulating strategies formitigating and adapting to climate change; evaluating long-term solutions that balance competing freshwater needs for basic services; and developing methods to support comprehensive river basin assessment.

Paul D Raskin PhD, President
David McAnulty, Administrative Director

5043 Terracon Consultants, Inc.
611 Lunken Park Drive
Cincinnati, OH 45226
513-321-5816
800-593-7777
Fax: 513-321-0294
corporate@terracon.com
www.terracon.com

A materials testing company, geotechnical and environmental engineering firm.

Jess Schroeder
George Webb

5044 TestAmerica-Austin
14050 Summit Drive
Suite A100
Austin, TX 78728
866-785-5227
Fax: 512-244-0160
webmaster@testamericainc.com
www.testamericainc.com

Environmental engineering research and consulting firm. Testing capabilities include chemical, physical and biological analyses of a variety of matrices, including aqueous, solid, drinking water, waste, tissue, air and saline/estuarinesamples. Specialty capabilities include air toxics testing, mixed waste testing, tissue preparation and analysis, aquatic toxicology, dioxin/furan testing and microscopy.

Rachel Brydon Jannetta, Chairman/CEO
James Miller, VP National Accounts & Progr

5045 TestAmerica-Buffalo
25 Kraft Ave.
Albany, NY 12205
866-785-5227
Fax: 518-438-8150
webmaster@testamericainc.com
www.testamericainc.com

Environmental engineering research and consulting firm. Testing capabilities include chemical, physical and biological analyses of a variety of matrices, including aqueous, solid, drinking water, waste, tissue, air and saline/estuarinesamples. Specialty capabilities include air toxics testing, mixed waste testing, tissue preparation and analysis, aquatic toxicology, dioxin/furan testing and microscopy.

Rachel Brydon Jannetta, Chairman/CEO
James Miller, VP National Accounts & Progr

5046 TestAmerica-Burlington
30 Community Drive
Suite 11
South Burlington, VT 00540
866-785-5227
Fax: 802-660-1919
webmaster@testamericainc.com
www.testamericainc.com

Environmental engineering research and consulting firm. Testing capabilities include chemical, physical and biological analyses of a variety of matrices, including aqueous, solid, drinking water, waste, tissue, air and saline/estuarinesamples. Specialty capabilities include air toxics testing, mixed waste testing, tissue preparation and analysis, aquatic toxicology, dioxin/furan testing and microscopy.

Rachel Brydon Jannetta, Chairman/CEO
James Miller, VP National Accounts & Progr

5047 TestAmerica-Chicago
2417 Bond Street
University Park, IL 60484
866-785-5227
Fax: 708-534-5211
webmaster@testamericainc.com
www.testamericainc.com

Environmental engineering research and consulting firm. Testing capabilities include chemical, physical and biological analyses of a variety of matrices, including aqueous, solid, drinking water, waste, tissue, air and saline/estuarinesamples. Specialty capabilities include air toxics testing, mixed waste testing, tissue preparation and analysis, aquatic toxicology, dioxin/furan testing and microscopy.

Rachel Brydon Jannetta, Chairman/CEO
James Miller, VP National Accounts & Progr

5048 TestAmerica-Connecticut
19 Old Kings Highway South
Suite 100
Darien, CT 00682
866-785-5227
Fax: 203-929-8142
webmaster@testamericainc.com
www.testamericainc.com

Environmental engineering research and consulting firm. Testing capabilities include chemical, physical and biological analyses of a variety of matrices, including aqueous, solid, drinking water, waste, tissue, air and saline/estuarinesamples. Specialty capabilities include air toxics testing, mixed waste testing, tissue preparation and analysis, aquatic toxicology, dioxin/furan testing and microscopy.

Rachel Brydon Jannetta, Chairman/CEO
James Miller, VP National Accounts & Progr

5049 TestAmerica-Corpus Christi
1733 N Padre Island Drive
Corpus Christi, TX 78408
866-785-5227
Fax: 361-289-2471
webmaster@testamericainc.com
www.testamericainc.com

Environmental engineering research and consulting firm. Testing capabilities include chemical, physical and biological analyses of a variety of matrices, including aqueous, solid, drinking water, waste, tissue, air and saline/estuarinesamples. Specialty capabilities include air toxics testing, mixed waste testing, tissue preparation and analysis, aquatic toxicology, dioxin/furan testing and microscopy.

Rachel Brydon Jannetta, Chairman/CEO
James Miller, VP National Accounts & Progr

5050 TestAmerica-Denver
4955 Yarrow Street
Arvada, CO 80002
866-785-5227
Fax: 303-431-7171
webmaster@testamericainc.com
www.testamericainc.com

Environmental engineering research and consulting firm. Testing capabilities include chemical, physical and biological analyses of a variety of matrices, including aqueous, solid, drinking water, waste, tissue, air and saline/estuarinesamples. Specialty capabilities include air toxics testing, mixed waste testing, tissue preparation and analysis, aquatic toxicology, dioxin/furan testing and microscopy.

Rachel Brydon Jannetta, Chairman/CEO
James Miller, VP National Accounts & Progr

5051 TestAmerica-Edison
3000 Lincoln Drive East
Suite A
Marlton, NJ 00805
866-785-5227
Fax: 732-549-3679
webmaster@testamericainc.com
www.testamericainc.com

Environmental engineering research and consulting firm. Testing capabilities include chemical, physical and biological analyses of a variety of matrices, including aqueous, solid, drinking water, waste, tissue, air and saline/estuarinesamples. Specialty capabil-

ities include air toxics testing, mixed waste testing, tissue preparation and analysis, aquatic toxicology, dioxin/furan testing and microscopy.
Rachel Brydon Jannetta, Chairman/CEO
James Miller, VP National Accounts & Progr

5052 TestAmerica-Houston
6310 Rothway Street
Houston, TX 77040 866-785-5227
Fax: 713-690-5646
webmaster@testamericainc.com
www.testamericainc.com
Environmental engineering research and consulting firm. Testing capabilities include chemical, physical and biological analyses of a variety of matrices, including aqueous, solid, drinking water, waste, tissue, air and saline/estuarinesamples. Specialty capabilities include air toxics testing, mixed waste testing, tissue preparation and analysis, aquatic toxicology, dioxin/furan testing and microscopy.
Rachel Brydon Jannetta, Chairman/CEO
James Miller, VP National Accounts & Progr

5053 TestAmerica-Knoxville
2960 Foster Creighton Drive
Nashville, TN 37204 866-785-5227
Fax: 615-726-3404
webmaster@testamericainc.com
www.testamericainc.com
Environmental engineering research and consulting firm. Testing capabilities include chemical, physical and biological analyses of a variety of matrices, including aqueous, solid, drinking water, waste, tissue, air and saline/estuarinesamples. Specialty capabilities include air toxics testing, mixed waste testing, tissue preparation and analysis, aquatic toxicology, dioxin/furan testing and microscopy.
Rachel Brydon Jannetta, Chairman/CEO
James Miller, VP National Accounts & Progr

5054 TestAmerica-Los Angeles
17461 Derian Ave.
Suite 100 866-785-5227
Irvine, CA 92614-5843 Fax: 949-260-3299
webmaster@testamericainc.com
www.testamericainc.com
Environmental engineering research and consulting firm. Testing capabilities include chemical, physical and biological analyses of a variety of matrices, including aqueous, solid, drinking water, waste, tissue, air and saline/estuarinesamples. Specialty capabilities include air toxics testing, mixed waste testing, tissue preparation and analysis, aquatic toxicology, dioxin/furan testing and microscopy.
Rachel Brydon Jannetta, Chairman/CEO
James Miller, VP National Accounts & Progr

5055 TestAmerica-Mobile
1870 W. Prince Road
Suite 59 866-785-5227
Tucson, AZ 85705 Fax: 251-666-6696
webmaster@testamericainc.com
www.testamericainc.com
Environmental engineering research and consulting firm. Testing capabilities include chemical, physical and biological analyses of a variety of matrices, including aqueous, solid, drinking water, waste, tissue, air and saline/estuarinesamples. Specialty capabilities include air toxics testing, mixed waste testing, tissue preparation and analysis, aquatic toxicology, dioxin/furan testing and microscopy.
Rachel Brydon Jannetta, Chairman/CEO
James Miller, VP National Accounts & Progr

5056 TestAmerica-New Orleans
6113 Benefit Dr
Baton Rouge, LA 70809 866-785-5227
Fax: 225-755-3080
webmaster@testamericainc.com
www.testamericainc.com
Environmental engineering research and consulting firm. Testing capabilities include chemical, physical and biological analyses of a variety of matrices, including aqueous, solid, drinking water, waste, tissue, air and saline/estuarinesamples. Specialty capabilities include air toxics testing, mixed waste testing, tissue preparation and analysis, aquatic toxicology, dioxin/furan testing and microscopy.
Rachel Brydon Jannetta, Chairman/CEO
James Miller, VP National Accounts & Progr

5057 TestAmerica-North Canton
4738 Gateway Circle
Dayton, OH 45440 866-785-5227
Fax: 937-499-1249
webmaster@testamericainc.com
www.testamericainc.com
Environmental engineering research and consulting firm. Testing capabilities include chemical, physical and biological analyses of a variety of matrices, including aqueous, solid, drinking water, waste, tissue, air and saline/estuarinesamples. Specialty capabilities include air toxics testing, mixed waste testing, tissue preparation and analysis, aquatic toxicology, dioxin/furan testing and microscopy.
Rachel Brydon Jannetta, Chairman/CEO
James Miller, VP National Accounts & Progr

5058 TestAmerica-Orlando
8010 Sunport Drive
Suite 116 866-785-5227
Orlando, FL 32809 Fax: 407-856-0886
webmaster@testamericainc.com
www.testamericainc.com
Environmental engineering research and consulting firm. Testing capabilities include chemical, physical and biological analyses of a variety of matrices, including aqueous, solid, drinking water, waste, tissue, air and saline/estuarinesamples. Specialty capabilities include air toxics testing, mixed waste testing, tissue preparation and analysis, aquatic toxicology, dioxin/furan testing and microscopy.
Rachel Brydon Jannetta, Chairman/CEO
James Miller, VP National Accounts & Progr

5059 TestAmerica-Pensacola
6301 NW 5th Way
Suite 2850 866-785-5227
Ft. Lauderdale, FL 33309 Fax: 954-776-8485
webmaster@testamericainc.com
www.testamericainc.com
Environmental engineering research and consulting firm. Testing capabilities include chemical, physical and biological analyses of a variety of matrices, including aqueous, solid, drinking water, waste, tissue, air and saline/estuarinesamples. Specialty capabilities include air toxics testing, mixed waste testing, tissue preparation and analysis, aquatic toxicology, dioxin/furan testing and microscopy.
Rachel Brydon Jannetta, Chairman/CEO
James Miller, VP National Accounts & Progr

5060 TestAmerica-Phoenix / Aerotech Environmental Laboratories
4645 East Cotton Center Blvd
Building 3, Suite 189 866-785-5227
Phoenix, AZ 85040 Fax: 602-454-9303
webmaster@testamericainc.com
www.testamericainc.com
Environmental engineering research and consulting firm. Testing capabilities include chemical, physical and biological analyses of a variety of matrices, including aqueous, solid, drinking water,

waste, tissue, air and saline/estuarinesamples. Specialty capabilities include air toxics testing, mixed waste testing, tissue preparation and analysis, aquatic toxicology, dioxin/furan testing and microscopy.
Rachel Brydon Jannetta, Chairman/CEO
James Miller, VP National Accounts & Progr

5061 TestAmerica-Pittsburgh
301 Alpha Drive
RIDC Park
Pittsburgh, PA 15238
866-785-5227
Fax: 412-963-2468
webmaster@testamericainc.com
www.testamericainc.com
Environmental engineering research and consulting firm. Testing capabilities include chemical, physical and biological analyses of a variety of matrices, including aqueous, solid, drinking water, waste, tissue, air and saline/estuarinesamples. Specialty capabilities include air toxics testing, mixed waste testing, tissue preparation and analysis, aquatic toxicology, dioxin/furan testing and microscopy.
Rachel Brydon Jannetta, Chairman/CEO
James Miller, VP National Accounts & Progr

5062 TestAmerica-Richland
2800 George Washington Way
Richland, WA 99354
866-785-5227
Fax: 509-375-5590
webmaster@testamericainc.com
www.testamericainc.com
Environmental engineering research and consulting firm. Testing capabilities include chemical, physical and biological analyses of a variety of matrices, including aqueous, solid, drinking water, waste, tissue, air and saline/estuarinesamples. Specialty capabilities include air toxics testing, mixed waste testing, tissue preparation and analysis, aquatic toxicology, dioxin/furan testing and microscopy.
Rachel Brydon Jannetta, Chairman/CEO
James Miller, VP National Accounts & Progr

5063 TestAmerica-San Francisco
1220 Quarry Lane
Pleasanton, CA 94566
866-785-5227
Fax: 925-600-3002
webmaster@testamericainc.com
www.testamericainc.com
Environmental engineering research and consulting firm. Testing capabilities include chemical, physical and biological analyses of a variety of matrices, including aqueous, solid, drinking water, waste, tissue, air and saline/estuarinesamples. Specialty capabilities include air toxics testing, mixed waste testing, tissue preparation and analysis, aquatic toxicology, dioxin/furan testing and microscopy.
Rachel Brydon Jannetta, Chairman/CEO
James Miller, VP National Accounts & Progr

5064 TestAmerica-Savannah
5102 LaRoche Avenue
Savannah, GA 31404
866-785-5227
Fax: 912-352-0165
webmaster@testamericainc.com
www.testamericainc.com
Environmental engineering research and consulting firm. Testing capabilities include chemical, physical and biological analyses of a variety of matrices, including aqueous, solid, drinking water, waste, tissue, air and saline/estuarinesamples. Specialty capabilities include air toxics testing, mixed waste testing, tissue preparation and analysis, aquatic toxicology, dioxin/furan testing and microscopy.
Rachel Brydon Jannetta, Chairman/CEO
James Miller, VP National Accounts & Progr

5065 TestAmerica-St Louis
13715 Rider Trail North
Earth City, MO 63045
866-785-5227
Fax: 314-298-8757
webmaster@testamericainc.com
www.testamericainc.com
Environmental engineering research and consulting firm. Testing capabilities include chemical, physical and biological analyses of a variety of matrices, including aqueous, solid, drinking water, waste, tissue, air and saline/estuarinesamples. Specialty capabilities include air toxics testing, mixed waste testing, tissue preparation and analysis, aquatic toxicology, dioxin/furan testing and microscopy.
Rachel Brydon Jannetta, Chairman/CEO
James Miller, VP National Accounts & Progr

5066 TestAmerica-Tacoma
5755 8th Street E
Tacoma, WA 98424
866-785-5227
Fax: 253-922-5047
webmaster@testamericainc.com
www.testamericainc.com
Environmental engineering research and consulting firm. Testing capabilities include chemical, physical and biological analyses of a variety of matrices, including aqueous, solid, drinking water, waste, tissue, air and saline/estuarinesamples. Specialty capabilities include air toxics testing, mixed waste testing, tissue preparation and analysis, aquatic toxicology, dioxin/furan testing and microscopy.
Rachel Brydon Jannetta, Chairman/CEO
James Miller, VP National Accounts & Progr

5067 TestAmerica-Tallahassee
2846 Industrial Plaza Drive
Suite 100
Tallahassee, FL 32301
866-785-5227
Fax: 850-878-9504
webmaster@testamericainc.com
www.testamericainc.com
Environmental engineering research and consulting firm. Testing capabilities include chemical, physical and biological analyses of a variety of matrices, including aqueous, solid, drinking water, waste, tissue, air and saline/estuarinesamples. Specialty capabilities include air toxics testing, mixed waste testing, tissue preparation and analysis, aquatic toxicology, dioxin/furan testing and microscopy.
Rachel Brydon Jannetta, Chairman/CEO
James Miller, VP National Accounts & Progr

5068 TestAmerica-Tampa
6712 Benjamin Road
Suite 100
Tampa, FL 33634
866-785-5227
Fax: 813-885-7049
webmaster@testamericainc.com
www.testamericainc.com
Environmental engineering research and consulting firm. Testing capabilities include chemical, physical and biological analyses of a variety of matrices, including aqueous, solid, drinking water, waste, tissue, air and saline/estuarinesamples. Specialty capabilities include air toxics testing, mixed waste testing, tissue preparation and analysis, aquatic toxicology, dioxin/furan testing and microscopy.
Rachel Brydon Jannetta, Chairman/CEO
James Miller, VP National Accounts & Progr

5069 TestAmerica-Valparaiso
2400 Cumberland Drive
Valparaiso, IN 46383
866-785-5227
Fax: 219-462-2953
webmaster@testamericainc.com
www.testamericainc.com
Environmental engineering research and consulting firm. Testing capabilities include chemical, physical and biological analyses of a variety of matrices, including aqueous, solid, drinking water, waste, tissue, air and saline/estuarinesamples. Specialty capabil-

ities include air toxics testing, mixed waste testing, tissue preparation and analysis, aquatic toxicology, dioxin/furan testing and microscopy.
Rachel Brydon Jannetta, Chairman/CEO
James Miller, VP National Accounts & Progr

5070 TestAmerica-West Sacramento
880 Riverside Parkway
West Sacramento, CA 95605 866-785-5227
Fax: 916-372-1059
webmaster@testamericainc.com
www.testamericainc.com

Environmental engineering research and consulting firm. Testing capabilities include chemical, physical and biological analyses of a variety of matrices, including aqueous, solid, drinking water, waste, tissue, air and saline/estuarinesamples. Specialty capabilities include air toxics testing, mixed waste testing, tissue preparation and analysis, aquatic toxicology, dioxin/furan testing and microscopy.
Rachel Brydon Jannetta, Chairman/CEO
James Miller, VP National Accounts & Progr

5071 TestAmerica-Westfield
53 Southampton Road
Westfield, MA 00108 866-785-5227
Fax: 413-572-3707
webmaster@testamericainc.com
www.testamericainc.com

Environmental engineering research and consulting firm. Testing capabilities include chemical, physical and biological analyses of a variety of matrices, including aqueous, solid, drinking water, waste, tissue, air and saline/estuarinesamples. Specialty capabilities include air toxics testing, mixed waste testing, tissue preparation and analysis, aquatic toxicology, dioxin/furan testing and microscopy.
Rachel Brydon Jannetta, Chairman/CEO
James Miller, VP National Accounts & Progr

5072 Testing Engineers & Consultants (TEC) - Ann Arbor
3985 Varsity Drive 734-971-0030
Ann Arbor, MI 48108 Fax: 734-971-3721
tec@tectest.com
www.tectest.com

TEC specializes in environmental and geotechnical engineering, materials testing, roof systems management, facility asset management, and indoor air quality. Environmental services include: baseline assessments; contaminationassessments; expert testimony; feasibility studies; hazardous materials surveys; and hyrogeological/groundwater investigations.
John Banicki, Founder/Chairman
Katherine Banicki, President

5073 Testing Engineers & Consultants (TEC) - Detroit
601 W Fort Street 313-837-8464
Suite 440 800-835-2654
Detroit, MI 48226 Fax: 313-837-1305
tec@tectest.com
www.tectest.com

TEC specializes in environmental and geotechnical engineering, materials testing, roof systems management, facility asset management, and indoor air quality. Environmental services include: baseline assessments; contaminationassessments; expert testimony; feasibility studies; hazardous materials surveys; and hyrogeological/groundwater investigations.
John Banicki, Founder/Chairman
Katherine Banicki, President

5074 Testing Engineers & Consultants (TEC) - Troy
1343 Rochester Road 248-588-6200
Troy, MI 48083 Fax: 248-588-6232
tec@tectest.com
www.tectest.com

TEC specializes in environmental and geotechnical engineering, materials testing, roof systems management, facility asset management, and indoor air quality. Environmental services include: baseline assessments; contaminationassessments; expert testimony; feasibility studies; hazardous materials surveys; and hyrogeological/groundwater investigations.
John Banicki, Founder/Chairman
Katherine Banicki, President

5075 Testing Laboratories of Canada, Inc.
1840 Argentia Road 905-812-7783
Missssauga, ON L5N1P Fax: 905-812-3271
canada@consumertesting.com
www.consumertesting.com

Research in textiles, safety wear.
Stewart A. Satter, Chief Executive Officer

5076 Tetra Tech
3475 East Foothill Boulevard 802-658-3890
Pasadena, CA 91107 Fax: 802-658-4247
ard@ardinc.com
www.tetratech.com

Provides management consulting and technical services in resource management, infrastructure and communication. Tetra Tech's services include research and development, applied science and technology, engineering design, programmanagement, construction management, and operations and maintenance.
Dan L. Batrack, President & CEO
Steven M. Burdick, Chief Financial Officer

5077 Thermo Fisher Scientific
81 Wyman Street 781-622-1000
Waltham, MA 00245 800-678-5599
Fax: 781-622-1207
www.thermofisher.com

Provides a wide range of products, services and solutions for research, analysis, discovery and diagnostics using advanced technologies ranging from mass spectrometry and elemental analysis to chromatography, molecular spectroscopy,and microanalysis. Additional services includes automated systems and technologies from standalone robots to complete liquid handling systems.
Marc N. Casper, President/CEO
Lori Gorski, Media Relations

5078 ThermoEnergy Corporation
10 New Bond Street 508-854-1628
Worcester, MA 00160 Fax: 508-854-1753
technology@thermoenergy.com
www.thermoenergy.com

ThermoEnergy Corporation is an integrated technologies company seeking to develop and commercialize patented water treatment and clean energy technologies. Products and services solutions include removing nitrogen from wastewaterstreams, converting sewage sludge to a renewable high-energy fuel, and enabling the conversion of coal and other hydrocarbon fuels into energy with zero air emissions.
James F. Wood, Chairman/President/CEO
Gregory M. Landegger, VP/COO/CFO

5079 Thermotron Industries
291 Kollen Park Drive 616-393-4580
Holland, MI 49423 800-409-3449
Fax: 616-392-5643
info@thermotron.com
www.thermotron.com

Manufacturers and suppliers of environmental testing, test system integration, screening, simulation equipment, and vibration equipment for transportation and screening test requirements. Additional services includes integrated testingsolutions with Research & Development and Total Quality Control to help insure product reliability and performance.
Mark Lamers, Technical Manager
Kevin Ewing, Marketing/Sales Manager

5080 Thompson Engineering
2970 Cottage Hill Road 251-666-2443
Suite 190 Fax: 251-666-6422
Mobile, AL 36606 info@thompsonengineering.com
www.thompsonengineering.com
A multi disciplined engineering design, environmental consulting, construction management, construction inspection and materials testing firm. The Environmental Division is comprised of a diverse team of professionals with significantknowledge and experience in environmental compliance and permitting, audits and assessments, engineering design, and monitoring and supervision of remedial activities.
Henry R. Seawell III, Chairman
John H. Baker III, President

5081 Thornton Laboratories Testing and Inspection Services, Inc.
Thornton Laboratories
1145 E Cass Street 813-223-9702
PO Box 2880 Fax: 813-223-9332
Tampa, FL 33602 steve.fickett@thorntonlab.com
www.thorntonlab.com
Environmental & fertilizer sampling and testing laboratory and general analytical testing lab.
Stephen B. Fickett, President
Hugh B. Rodriques, COO/VP lab Operations

5082 Tighe & Bond
4 Barlows Landing Road 508-564-7285
Unit 15 Fax: 413-562-5317
Pocasset, MA 00255 info@tighebond.com
www.tighebond.com
Tighe & Bond provides engineering and consulting services to a wide variety of clients, from some of the largest municipalities in the country to small, privately-held businesses. Areas of expertise includes water supply, wastewatermanagement, buildings, roadways, environmental permitting, remediation, health and safety training.
David E. Pinsky, President
Jeffrey P Bibeau, Environmental Manager

5083 Timber Products Inspection - Conyers
1641 Sigman Road 770-922-8000
Conyers, GA 30012 Fax: 770-922-1290
info@tpinspection.com
www.tpinspection.com
Timber Products Inspection, Inc. (TP) is an independent inspection, testing and consulting company with expertise in all phases of the wood products industry. TP provides quality auditing services in the areas of sawmilling, drying,component fabrication as well as value added processes such as pressure treating and gluing.
Donna Whitaker, Chairman
Bill Howard, Vice-Chairman

5084 Timber Products Inspection - Vancouver
1641 Sigman Road 770-922-8000
Conyers, GA 30012 Fax: 770-922-1290
info@tpinspection.com
www.tpinspection.com
Timber Products Inspection, Inc. (TP) is an independent inspection, testing and consulting company with expertise in all phases of the wood products industry. TP provides quality auditing services in the areas of sawmilling, drying,component fabrication as well as value added processes such as pressure treating and gluing.
Donna Whitaker, Chairman
Bill Howard, Vice-Chairman

5085 Tox Scan
42 Hangar Way 831-724-4522
Watsonville, CA 95076 Fax: 831-761-5449
Environmental bioassay and bioacoumulation testing.
David B. Lewis, Director

5086 Transviron
1624 York Road 410-321-6961
Lutherville, MD 21093 Fax: 410-949-9321
Transviron@comcast.net
www.transviron.com
Civil and environmental engineering firm. Technical consulting services includes: water supply and distribution; storm water management; highways and bridges; hazardous waste management; water and wastewater treatment plant operationsand construction management; wastewater collection and treatment.
Charles S. Bao, President
Michelle Ireland, Marketing Coordinator

5087 Tri-State Laboratories
2870 Salt Springs Road 330-797-8844
Youngstown, OH 44509 800-523-0347
Fax: 330-797-3264
www.tristatelabs.net
Environmental testing laboratory services of which include: asbestos testing; field services; forensic analysis and court testimony; hazardous waste analysis; inorganics/wet chemistry, metals, and organic analysis.
A Bari Lateef PhD, CEO
Wendy Hanna, COO

5088 Turner Laboratories
2445 North Coyote Drive 520-882-5880
Suite 104 Fax: 520-882-9788
Tucson, AZ 85745 sales@turnerlabs.com
www.turnerlabs.com
Turner Laboratories is an advanced, full-service environmental testing laboratory specializing in providing a wide range of analytical services including: inorganic, organic, wet chemistry and microbiological testing on soils/solids,drinking water, wastewater and groundwater.
Nancy D Turner, President
Michael McGovern, Executive VP

5089 URS
600 Montgomery Street 415-774-2700
26th Floor 888-877-7752
San Francisco, CA 94111-2728 Fax: 415-398-1905
media_contact@urs.com
www.urscorp.com
An environmental analysis and comprehensive engineering service firm, URS provides a full range of planning, design, program and construction management services to a wide variety of private and public sector clients. URS hasapproximately 30,000 employees in a network of more than 370 offices and contract-specific job sites in 20 countries.
Martin M Koffel, Chairman/CEO
Thomas W Biship, VP/Strategic Development

5090 US Public Interest Research Group
294 Washington St 617-747-4370
Suite 500 Fax: 617-292-8057
Boston, MA 00210 info@uspirg.org
www.uspirg.org
US PIRG is an advocate for the public interest. We uncover threats to public health and well-being and fight to end them, using the time-tested tools of investigative research, media exposes, grassroots organizing, advocacy andlitigation.
Douglas H Phelps, President/Chairman
Andre Delattre, Executive Director

5091 US Public Interest Research Group - Washington
218 D Street SE — 202-546-9707
1st Floor — Fax: 202-546-2461
Washington, DC 20003 — www.uspirg.org

US PIRG is an advocate for the public interest. We uncover threats to public health and well-being and fight to end them, using the time-tested tools of investigative research, media exposes, grassroots organizing, advocacy andlitigation.

Douglas H Phelps, President/Chairman
Andre Delattre, Executive Director

5092 USDA Forest Service: Pacific Southwest Research Station
800 Buchanan Street — 510-883-8830
West Annex Building — Fax: 510-559-6440
Albany, CA 94710-11 — psw_webmaster@fs.fed.us
www.fs.fed.us/psw/

A Governmental Research Organization specializing in research on forest ecosystems, including fire, watersheds, forest genetics and diversity, wildlife, forest diseases, and urban forestry.

Jim Baldwin, Project Manager
Marilyn Hartley, Communications Director

5093 Umpqua Research Company
125 Volunteer Way — 541-863-7770
PO Box 609 — Fax: 541-863-7775
Myrtle Creek, OR 97457 — info@urcmail.net
www.urc.cc

UMPQUA Research Company (URC), founded in 1973 by David F. Putnam and Gerald V. Colombo, offers technical services in four primary areas: Drinking Water and Environmental Analysis; Air and Water Purification Related EngineeringServices (including NASA Flight Hardware); Research & Development; and Materials Testing. The staff includes chemical, electrical, and mechanical engineers, chemists, physicists, and biological scientists.

William F Michalek PE, President
James R. Akse, VP

5094 United Environmental Services
86 Hillside Drive — 570-788-8180
Drums, PA 18222 — Fax: 856-227-6578
www.unitedenvironmental.com

An environmental testing and analysis firm providing a full range of construction, remedial and maintenance services at landfills, commercial and industrial sites, including Brownfield re-development projects.

Rod Sterner, VP
Walter Meck, CEO

5095 Universal Environmental Technologies
87 Technology Way — 603-883-9312
Nashua, NH 00306 — Fax: 603-883-9314

An environmental research firm, Universal Environmental Technologies specializes in the design, fabrication and installation of integrated groundwater and soil remediation systems that are used on retail petroleum sites, industrialmanufacturing sites, EPA Superfund sites and U.S. military bases.

Sharon McMillin, VP/Remedial Services

5096 Upstate Laboratories
6034 Corporate Drive — 315-437-0255
East Syracuse, NY 13057 — Fax: 315-437-1209
enalyticsupport@enalytic.com
www.enalytic.com

Testing laboratory specializing in environmental and organic/synthetic analysis. Services include certification and air quality (mycology).

Anthony J Scala, President/CEO/Chemist
Corey Niland, Quality Assurance & Control

5097 Vara International: Division of Calgon Corporation
Calgon Carbon Corporation — 412-787-6700
3000 GSK Drive — 800-4CA-BON
Moon Township, PA 15108 — Fax: 412-787-6676
info@calgoncarbon-us.com
www.calgoncarbon.com

An environmental and industrial process research firm, Vara International is a global manufacturer and supplier of granular activated carbon, innovative treatment systems, value added technologies and services for optimizing productionprocesses and safely purifying the environment.

Randall S. Dearth, President/CEO
Robert P. O'Brien, EVP/Chief Operating Officer

5098 Versar
6850 Versar Center — 703-750-3000
PO Box 1549 — 800-283-7727
Springfield, VA 22151 — Fax: 703-642-6825
info@versar.com
www.versar.com

Engineering and environmental research organization. Research results published in project reports, government publications, books, articles, and technical reports.

Jeffrey A. Wagonhurst, President/COO
Cynthia A. Downes, Executive VP/CFO

5099 Vista Leak Detection
755 N Mary Avenue — 408-830-3300
Sunnyvale, CA 94085 — Fax: 408-830-3399
info@VistaLD.com

Vista Research provides leak detection products and services to airport, oil industry and military clients for ensuring the integrity of underground/aboveground pipeline and tank systems.

William W Pickett, VP/Operations
Cody Freeman, Contracts Administrator

5100 Volumetric Techniques, Ltd. / VTEQE
317 Bernice Drive — 631-472-4848
Bayport, NY 11705-1304 — Fax: 631-472-4991
Sandy@vteqeltd.com
vteqeltd.com/137.html

Full service environmental engineering organization, VTEQE specializes in all aspects of the environmental services industry, including assessments (ESA Phase 1,2), site engineering, investigations/reports, remediation/cleanupstrategies, Phase 3, and bottled water facility licensing dealing with contaminated water, groundwater, soil, also engineering design, construction management, and full revitalization management.

Sander Sternig, President/CEO/Chairman
Benito San Pedro, Professional Engineer

5101 WERC: Consortium for Environmental Education & Technology Development
New Mexico State University
PO Box 30001 — 575-646-2038
Las Cruces, NM 88003-8001 — 800-523-5996
Fax: 505-646-5474
iee@nmsu.edu
www.ieenmsu.com

A consortium focusing on environmental education and technology development. The consortium's mission is to develop the human resources and technologies needed to address environmental issues. WERC's program aims to achieveenvironmental excellence through education, public outreach and technology development and deployment.

Abbas Ghassemi PhD, Executive Director
Patricia Pines, Administrative Asst.

5102 Waid & Associates - Austin/Corporate
10800 Pecan Park Blvd — 512-255-9999
Suite 300 — Fax: 512-255-8780
Austin, TX 78750 — information@waid.com
www.waid.com

Waid & Associates is an engineering and environmental services firm that specializes in air quality services, particularly emissions control, permits, and compliance. Additional services include wastewater/waste management andenvironmental information management systems.
Jay R Hoover PE, President/Principal Engineer
Sara A. Hutson, Principal Engineer

5103 Waid & Associates - Houston
2600 South Shore Blvd. 281-333-9990
Suite 300 Fax: 512-255-8780
League City, TX 77573 information@waid.com
www.waid.com
Waid & Associates is an engineering and environmental services firm that specializes in air quality services, particularly emissions control, permits, and compliance. Additional services include wastewater/waste management andenvironmental information management systems.
Jay R Hoover PE, President/Principal Engineer
Sara A. Hutson, Principal Engineer

5104 Waid & Associates - Permian Basin
24 Smith Road 432-682-9999
Suite 304 Fax: 432-682-7774
Midland, TX 79705 information@waid.com
www.waid.com
Waid & Associates is an engineering and environmental services firm that specializes in air quality services, particularly emissions control, permits, and compliance. Additional services include wastewater/waste management andenvironmental information management systems.
Jay R Hoover PE, President/Principal Engineer
Sara A. Hutson, Principal Engineer

5105 Waste Water Engineers
210 Coy Court 248-236-9800
Oxford, MI 48371 Fax: 248-236-9870
www.wastewatereng.com
Environmental science research consultant. Research results published in project reports. Environmental civil engineering consultant.
Thomas H Patton Jr, President

5106 Water and Air Research
6821 SW Archer Road 352-372-1500
Gainesville, FL 32608 800-242-4927
Fax: 352-378-1500
lmosura-bliss@waterandair.com
www.waterandair.com
Environmental research and consulting firm. Research results published in client reports.
William C Zegel, President
Connie Bieber, Director/Manager

5107 Watkins Environmental Sciences
PO Box 6655 315-446-4763
Syracuse, NY 13217 Fax: 315-446-4764
awatkins3@gmail.com
www.watkinsenvironmental.com
Environmental assessments, septic system designs, residential water sampling and testing services, home inspections, radon, foundation designs & inspections.
Andrew A Watkins PE, President

5108 Waypoint Analytical
2790 Whitten Road 901-213-2400
Memphis, TN 38133 800-264-4522
Fax: 901-213-2440
supporttn@waypointanalytical.com
www.waypointanalytical.com
Environmental laboratory service specializing in soil testing.
Michael Sterling, Chief Financial Officer

5109 Weather Services Corporation
131A Great Road 781-275-8860
Bedford, MA 00173 Fax: 781-271-0178
Michael Leavitt, President

5110 West Coast Analytical Service
9240 Santa Fe Springs Road 562-948-2225
Santa Fe Springs, CA 90670 Fax: 562-948-5850
DJ Northington, PhD, President
Eric Lindsay, General Manager

5111 West Michigan Testing
815 E Ludington Avenue 231-843-3353
Ludington, MI 49431 Fax: 231-843-7676
We provide soil borings, geotechnical services, environmental assessments, construction materials testing and asbestos inspection.
James T Nordlund Jr, Vice President

5112 West More Mechanical Testing and Research
221 Westmoreland Drive 724-537-3131
PO Box 388 Fax: 724-537-3151
Youngstown, PA 15696-388 us.sales@wmtr.com
www.wmtr.com
Don Rossi, President
Mike Rossi, Vice President

5113 Western Environmental Services
913 N Foster Road 307-234-5511
Casper, WY 82601 800-545-5711
Fax: 307-234-8324
aroylance@testair.com
www.testair.com
Air emission testing.
James Meador, Founder/Project Manager
Alan Roylance, President

5114 Western Michigan Environmental Services
1007 Lake Drive 616-451-3051
Grand rapids, MI 49505 Fax: 616-451-3054
www.wmeac.org
Christine Helms, President
David Rein, VP

5115 Westinghouse Electric Company
1000 Westinghouse Drive 412-244-2000
Suite 572A 888-943-8442
Cranberry Township, PA 16066 Fax: 412-642-4985
www.westinghousenuclear.com
Danny Roderick, President/Chief Executive Of
Jim Brennan, Sr. VP

5116 Westinghouse Remediation Services
675 Park N Boulevard 404-298-7101
Suite F-100 Fax: 404-296-9752
Clarkston, GA 30021
Environmental remediation firm.

5117 Weston Solutions, Inc
1400 Weston Way 610-701-3000
Box 2653 800-7WE-STON
West Chester, PA 19380 Fax: 610-701-3186
info@westonsolutions.com
www.westonsolutions.com
Weston is a leading infrastructure redevelopment services firm delivering integrated environmental engineering solutions to industry and government worldwide. With an emphasis on creating lasting economic value for its clients, thecompany provides ser-

vices in site remediation, redevelopment, infrastructure operations and knowledge management.
Alan J. Solow, President/Chief Executive Of
Vincent A. Laino, Sr. VP/CFO

5118 Whibco
87 East Commerce Street 856-455-9200
Bridgeton, NJ 00830 Fax: 856-455-9009
www.whibco.com
Andrew R Strelczyk, Director Quality Control

5119 Wik Associates
PO Box 230 302-322-2558
New Castle, DE 19720 Fax: 302-322-8921
Environmental testing and analysis firm.

5120 William T Lorenz & Company
3541 Norwegian Hollow Road 608-935-9285
Dodgeville, WI 53533 Fax: 608-935-2010
Environmental and water resources marketing, consulting, and product research firm.

5121 William W Walker Jr
1127 Lowell Road 978-369-8061
Concord, MA 00174-5522 Fax: 978-369-8061
bill@wwwalker.net
www.wwwalker.net
William W Walker, Jr, Environmental Engineer

5122 Woods End Research Laboratory
290 Belgrade Rd 207-293-2457
PO Box 297 800-451-0337
Mount Vernon, ME 00435 Fax: 207-293-2488
www.woodsend.org
Compost analysis; bioremediation design; solvita test kits for soil and compost. Quality Seal of Approval Program for Compost Products.
William Brinton, President

5123 World Resources Company
1600 Anderson Road 703-734-9800
Suite 200 Fax: 703-790-7245
Mc Lean, VA 22102 www.worldresourcescompany.com
World Resources Company (WRC) is a highly specialized environmental risk management company that designs, implements and manages recycling activities and provides environmental services for non-ferrous metal industries nationally andinternationally. This support includes regulatory, environmental, transportation, production, and all other aspects of business inherent to recycling services.
Peter T Halpin, CEO

5124 Yellowstone Environmental Science
65-1116 Hoku'ula Rd. 808-885-4194
PO Box 2709 Fax: 808-885-4114
Kamuela, HI 96743 yes@yestech.com
www.yestech.com
Mary M Hunter, President
Robert M. Hunter, Director

5125 Yes Technologies
65-1116 Hoku'ula Rd. 808-885-4194
PO Box 2709 Fax: 808-885-4114
Kamuela, HI 96743 yes@yestech.com
www.yestech.com
Environmental and public health research and development. Patent consulting.
Mary M Hunter, President
Robert M. Hunter, Director

5126 Zimpro Environmental
301 West Military Road 715-359-7211
Rothschild, WI 54474 Fax: 715-355-3219
William Copa, VP Technical Services

5127 Zurn Industries
1801 Pittsburgh Avenue 855-663-9876
Erie, PA 16502 800-997-3876
Fax: 919-775-3541
sean.martin@zurn.com
www.zurn.com
Environmental systems including air, land, thermal and water; energy systems including steam and heat; mechanical systems.
Sean Martin, VP Marketing & Sales
Michael Boone, General Manager

University Centers

5128 ASME
University of Florida
Two Park Avenue 973-882-1170
New York, NY 10016-5990 800-843-2763
Fax: 352-392-1071
CustomerCare@asme.org
www.asme.org
Has uniquely influenced the development of solar energy and renewable energy conversion systems all over the world through its research, education and training. Has pioneered research in many areas of solar energy, energy conversionand conservation. The lab has been designated as an ASME National Landmark.
Julio Guerrero, President
Thomas G. Loughlin, Executive Director

5129 Adirondack Ecological Center
SUNY College of Environmental Science & Forestry
1 Forestry Drive 315-470-6500
Syracuse, NY 13210 Fax: 518-582-2181
aechwf@esf.edu
www.esf.edu
Provides the organizational framework for research, instructional, and public service activities thoughout the Adriondack region.
Vita DeMarchi, Chair
Matthew J. Marko, Vice Chair

5130 Agricultural Research and Development Center
University of Nebraska
1071 County Road G 402-624-8000
Ithaca, NE 68033 Fax: 402-624-8010
ardc@unl.edu
ardc.unl.edu
Serves as the primary site for field based reseach with 5,000 acres of row crops and 5,000 domestic farm animals used for teaching and research.
Mark Schroeder, Director
Ruby Urban, Asst. Director

5131 Akron Center for Environmental Studies
University of Akron
215 Crouse Hall 330-972-7111
Akron, OH 44325-4102 Fax: 330-972-7611
ids@uakron.edu
www.uakron.edu
Jonathan T. Pavloff, Chair
Jennifer E. Blickle, Vice Chair

5132 Albrook Hydraulics Laboratory
Washington State University

PO Box 641227 509-335-3564
Pullman, WA 99164 Fax: 509-335-7632
rhh@wsu.edu
www.wsu.edu
Research laboratory capable of performing projects with physically scaled hydraulic models. 15,000 square feet of floor space, discharge capacity up to 70 cubic feet per second, modern instrumentaion and shop facilities.
Elson S. Floyd, President
Daniel Bernardo, Vice President

5133 **Alternative Energy Institute**
Texas A&M University 806-656-2296
WTAMU Box 60248 Fax: 806-656-2733
Canyon, TX 79016 aeimail@wtamu.edu
Byungik Chang, Director
Ken Starcher, Associate Director

5134 **American Petroleum Institute University**
1220 L Street NW 202-682-8000
Washington, DC 20005-4070 Fax: 202-682-8232
training@api.org
www.api-u.org
API, through its university, provides training materials to help those in the oil and natural gas business meet regulatory requirements and industry standards. It works with the National Science Teachers Association and othereducational groups to impart scientific literacy and develop critical thinking skills in the classroom.
Jack N. Gerard, President/CEO
Kyle Isakower, Vice President

5135 **American Society of Primatologists**
University of Washington
PO Box 357330 206-543-0440
Seattle, WA 98195 Fax: 206-685-0305
www.asp.org
Conducts research on primates.
Marilyn A. Norconk, President
Justin McNulty, Executive Secretary

5136 **Applied Energy Research Laboratory**
North Carolina State University 919-515-5236
Raleigh, NC 27695 www.mae.ncsu.edu
Dr. John A Edwards, Director

5137 **Aquatic Research Laboratory**
Lake Superior State University
650 W Easterday Avenue 906-635-1949
Sault Sainte Marie, MI 49783 888-800-LSSU
Fax: 906-635-2266
Administered through the college of Arts and Sciences.
Prof Alex Litvinov, Director

5138 **Architecture Research Laboratory**
University of Arizona
College of Architecture 520-621-6751
Tucson, AZ 85721 Fax: 520-621-8700
www.architectureresearchlab.com
Provides assistance in the areas of education, applied research and public service.
Alexandra Fenton, Co-Founder
Michael S Bergin, Co-Founder

5139 **Biological Reserve**
Denison University 740-587-6261
Granville, OH 43023 stocker@denison.edu
Enhances the education of students in Biology and the Environmental Sciences by providing opportunities for field studies.
Dr. John E Fauth, Contact

5140 **Caesar Kleberg Wildlife Research Institute**
Texas A&M University
700 University Boulevard 361-595-3922
MSC 218 Fax: 361-593-3924
Kingsville, TX 78363 www.ckwri.tamuk.edu
Facilitates complex wildlife-related research studies. Includes modern high-tech facilities, specially designed wildlife pens, and rangeland tracts.
Henry R. Hamman, Chairman
Gus T. Canales, Co-Chairs

5141 **California Sea Grant College Program**
University of California
9500 Gilman Drive 858-534-4440
Deptartment 0232 Fax: 858-534-2231
La Jolla, CA 92093-0232 caseagrant@ucsd.edu
caseagrant.ucsd.edu
Offers products and services related to coastal and marine science, such as fellowship opportunities, grant administration services, library services and networking with Sea Grant experts and partners. The purpose of the programs is topromote conservation of coastal and marine resources.
James E. Eckman, Director
Caitlin Coomber, Marketing Communications

5142 **Cedar Creek Natural History Area**
University of Minnesota
2660 Fawn Lake Drive NE 763-434-5131
Bethel, MN 55005 Fax: 763-434-7361
Twenty-two hundred hectare experimental ecological reserve.

5143 **Center for Applied Energy Research**
University of Kentucky
2540 Research Park Drive 859-257-0200
Lexington, KY 40511-8479 Fax: 859-257-0220
rodney.andrews@uky.edu
www.caer.uky.edu
An applied research and development center with an international reputation, focusing on the optimal use of Kentucky's energy resources for the benefit of its people.
Jim Tracy, Vice President
Rodney Andrews, Director

5144 **Center for Applied Environmental Research**
University of Michigan
130 Mumford Hall 573-882-7458
Columbia, MO 65211 Fax: 573-884-2199
fulcherc@missouri.edu
Chris Barnett, Co-Director
Chris Fulcher, Co-Director

5145 **Center for Aquatic Research and Resource Management**
Florida State University
319 Stadium Drive 850-644-3700
Tallahassee, FL 32306-4295 Fax: 850-645-8447
livingston@bio.fsu.edu
Conducts research designed to answer aquatic resource-management questions posed by government agencies and private concerns. Research is conducted in lakes, rivers, and near-shore coastal systems throughout the southeastern UnitedStates with a multi-disciplinary approach to topics such as light, nutrients, primary productivity, fate and effects of storm water pollutants, sediment-water interactions, community assemblages of fish and invertebrates in various habitats andtrophic dynamics.
Dr. Robert J Livingston, Director

5146 **Center for Cave and Karst Studies**
Western Kentucky University

1906 College Heights Blvd. 270-745-0111
Bowling Green, KY 42101-3576 Fax: 270-745-3961
wku@wku.edu
www.wku.edu

Promotes research on all aspects of cave and karst studies with emphasis upon solving environmental problems associated with karst.
Gary A. Ransdell, President
Dr. Phillip W. Bale, Regent

5147 Center for Crops Utilization Research
Iowa State University of Science & Technology
1041 Food Sciences Building 515-294-0160
Iowa State University Fax: 515-294-6261
Ames, IA 50011 ccur@iastate.edu
www.ccur.iastate.edu

Incorporates various aspects of new product and product research, applications development, and technology transfer. Activities focus on developing technologies for producing food and industrial products from agricultural materials,developing agricultural substitutes for petrochemicals, and exploring and modifying the functional properties of crop-derived materials.
Dr. Lawrence A Johnson, Director
Peggy Best, Admin Specialist

5148 Center for Earth & Environmental Science
SUNY Plattsburgh
723 West Michigan Street 317-274-7154
SL 118 877-554-1041
Indianapolis, IN 46202 Fax: 317-274-7966
cees@iupui.edu
www.cees.iupui.edu

Undergraduate degree programs in environmental science, geology, planning and geography, with special emphasis on watershed science, remote sensing and geographic information systems, and aquatic and terrestrial ecology. The center isone of the oldest and largest environmental programs in the US, with 16 full-time interdisciplinary faculty and diverse field sites.
Dr. Pamela A. Martin, Director
Jessica Davis, Assistant Director

5149 Center for Environmental Communications (CEC)
Rutgers University
31 Pine Street 732-932-1966
New Brunswick, NJ 00890 Fax: 732-932-9544
cec@aesop.rutgers.edu

The CEC, located on the Cook College Campus, brings together university investigators to provide a social science perspective to environmental problem solving. CEC has gained international recognition for responding to environmentalcommunication dilemmas with research, training, and public service. Established in 1986, CEC is now jointly sponsored by the New Jersey Agricultural Experiment Station and the Edward J. Bloustein School of Planning and Public Policy.
Caron Chess, Director

5150 Center for Environmental Health Sciences
Massachusetts Institute of Technology
77 Massachusetts Avenue 617-253-1000
Building 16-743 Fax: 617-258-9344
Cambridge, MA 00213-4307 web.mit.edu
L. Rafael Reif, President
Israel Ruiz, Executive VP

5151 Center for Environmental Medicine Asthma & Lung Biology
University of North Carolina
554 Human Studies Facility 919-962-0126
CB# 7310, 104 Mason Farm Road 866-962-4457
Chapel Hill, NC 27599-7310 Fax: 919-966-9863
slshaw@med.unc.edu
www.med.unc.edu

The CEMALB are a group of investigators with diverse research interests that include cardiopulmonary medicine, immunology, lung physiology, cell biology, cell and molecular immunology, molecular toxicology and epidemiology. We conductresearch studies involving human volunteers that are aimed at understanding the negative health effects of air pollution on the lung and heart.
Philip A Bromberg, MD, Scientific Director
William L. Roper MD, MPH, Dean

5152 Center for Environmental Research Education
SUNY Buffalo
1300 Elmwood Avenue 716-878-4000
Upton Hall, Room 314 Fax: 716-878-6644
Buffalo, NY 14222 zolnowsa@buffalostate.edu
www.buffalostate.edu

Marsha D. Jackson, President
Father Robert J Pecoraro, VP

5153 Center for Environmental Studies
Williams College
Hopkins Hall, 880 Main Street 413-597-3131
Williamstown, MA 00126 Fax: 413-597-3489
www.williams.edu

Provides students with the opportunity to learn how environmental issues are interconnected with many traditional fields of study. Offered as a concentration, the program encourages students to become well grounded in a single field bypersuing a major in a traditional discipline or department, while focusing several of their elective courses on the interdisciplinary study of the environment.
Karen Merrill, Director
Sarah Gardner, Associate Director

5154 Center for Environmental Toxicology and Technology
Colorado State University 970-491-7051
1601 Campus Delivery Fax: 970-491-8304
Fort Collins, CO 80523-1601 dvmadmissions@colostate.edu
Mark Stetter, Dean
Chris Haase, Asst. to Dean

5155 Center for Field Biology
Austin Pay State University
PO Box 4718 931-221-7019
Clarksville, TN 37044 Fax: 931-221-6372
fieldbiology@apsu.edu
www.apsu.edu/field_biology

The Center of Excellence for Field Biology at Austin Peay State University brings together scholars and students from various biological disciplines to conduct research on topics in field biology and ecology, including toxicology,population and community ecology, and the ecology and biology of rare, threatened and endangered species. Major research efforts have focused on the ecology and biology of the flora and fauna of the Land Between the Lakes.
Dr. Steve Hamilton, Director
Michelle Rogers, Project Manager

5156 Center for Global & Regional Environmental Research
University of Iowa
The University of Iowa 319-335-3333
424 IATL Fax: 319-335-3337
Iowa City, IA 52242 www.cgrer.uiowa.edu
Greg Carmichael, Co-Director
Jerry Schnoor, Co-Director

5157 Center for Global Change Science (MIT)
Massachusetts Institute of Technology

77 Massachusetts Avenue 617-253-4902
Room 54-1312 Fax: 617-253-0354
Cambridge, MA 00213-4307 cgcs@mit.edu
cgcs.mit.edu

Addresses long-standing scientific problems whose solution is necessary for accurate prediction of changes in the global environment. The CGCS is interdisciplinary and interdepartmental, and builds on research and educational programsin earth sciences and engineering. The Center is also involved in substantial cooperative efforts focused on climate modeling, and on climate-policy research.

Ronald Prinn, Director
Anne Slinn, Executive Director

5158 Center for Groundwater Research (CGR)

Oregon Health & Science University
20000 NW Walker Road 503-748-1070
Beaverton, OR 97006-8921 Fax: 503-748-1273
cgr.ieh.ohsu.edu

The CGR coordinates a range of projects relating to the transport and fate of contaminants in soils and groundwater. The scope of the Center includes: the development of new sampling and site characterization techniques; thedevelopment of new analytical techniques; and other improved groundwater remediation techniques.

Richard L. Johnson, Director
Dr. James Pankow, Professor

5159 Center for Hazardous Substance Research

Kansas State University 785-532-6519
Ward Hall 104 Fax: 785-532-5985
Manhattan, KS 66506-2502 chsr@k-state.edu
www.engg.ksu.edu/CHSR

Dr. Larry E. Erickson, Director
Blase A. Leven, Associate Director

5160 Center for International Development Research

Duke University
PO Box 8500 613-236-6163
Ottawa, ON K1G3H Fax: 613-238-7230
info@idrc.ca
www.idrc.ca

Denis Desautels, Chairperson
Morton Solberg, Vice President

5161 Center for International Food and Agricultural Policy

University of Minnesota
University of Minnesota 612-625-8713
332 Classroom Office Bldg, 1994 Buford A Fax: 612-625-6245
St. Paul, MN 55108-6040 cifap@umn.edu
www.cifap.umn.edu

With its interdisciplinary approach, CIFAP uses its research and education activities to increase international understanding about food, agriculture, nutrition, natural and human resources, and the environment, and to positivelyaffect the policies of both developed and developing countries.

Terry Roe, Director
Marc Bellemare, Assistant Professor

5162 Center for Lake Superior Ecosystem Research

Michigan Technological University
1400 Townsend Drive 906-487-2769
Houghton, MI 49931 wkerfoot@mtu.edu
www.mtu.edu

An interdisiplinary center with goals to promote and strengthen ecological research and graduate programs at MTU through developing and applying technological advances to ecological problems, to advocate an ecosystem perspective forstudying aquatic and terrestrial portions of the Lake Superior watershed and to become a resource center for basic information on watershed and lake properties.

5163 Center for Marine Biology

University of New Hampshire
85 Adams Point Road 603-862-1234
The University of New Hampshire Fax: 603-862-1101
Durham, NH 00382 ray.grizzle@unh.edu
marine.unh.edu

The Center for Marine Biology (CMB) fosters excellence in marine biological research and education. Its primary goals are to strengthen and focus research and graduate education in modern marine biology and to encourage the developmentof high-quality undergraduate programs in all aspects of marine biology. The center helps faculty members compete for external grant funds and fosters coordination of marine research efforts, both with the life sciences and in other disciplines.

Larry Mayer, Director
Jonathan Pennock, Deputy Director

5164 Center for Population Biology

University of California
One Shields Avenue 530-752-1274
2320 Storer Hall Fax: 530-752-1449
Davis, CA 95616 cpb.ucdavis.edu

Founded in 1989, the Center for Population Biology unites UC Davis' population biologists. The center's membership comprises graduate students enrolled in the http://www-eve.ucdavis.edu/popbio.htm, graduate students interested inpopulation biology who are earning their degrees in graduate programs such as ecology or entomology, postdoctoral researchers, from nine academic departments and sections, 17 of whom have faculty appointments in the division.

John J. Stachowicz, Director
Theresa Garcia, Graduate Group Coordinator

5165 Center for Resource Policy Studies

University of Wisconsin
1450 Linden Drive 608-262-8254
Room 240
Madison, WI 53706

The Center for Resource Policy Studies and Programs uses interdisciplinary research, teaching and extension efforts to analyze resource policies and development programs. This center gives particular emphasis to the social scienceaspects of natural resource policy issues.

5166 Center for Statistical Ecology & Environmental Statistics

Pennsylvania State University
Dept of Statistics 814-865-9442
421 Thomas Building Fax: 814-865-1278
University Park, PA 16802 gpp@stat.psu.edu
www.stat.psu.edu/~gpp/aims_scope.htm

The Center is the first of its kind in the world and enjoys national and international reputation. They have an ongoing program of research that integrates statistics, ecology and the environment. The emphasis is on the environment andcollaborative research, training and exposition on improving the quantification and communication of man's impact on the environment. Major interest also lies in statistical investigations of the impact of the environment on man.

Ganapati P Patil, Director

5167 Center for Streamside Studies

University of Washington
Box 352100 206-543-6920
Seattle, WA 98195 Fax: 206-543-3254
www.washington.edu/cssuw/

The mission of the Center for Streamside Studies is to provide scientific information necessary for the resolution of management issues related to the production and protection of forest, fish, wildlife, and water resources associatedwith the streams and rivers in the Pacific Northwest.

Robert J Naiman, Director

5168 Center for Tropical Agriculture
University of Florida
Km 17, Recta Cali-Palmira 650-833-6625
Apartado Aéreo 6713 Fax: 650-833-6626
Cali, CO AA671 ciat@cgiar.org
www.ciat.cgiar.org
Enhances research and education on tropical agriculture between University of Florida and tropical countries.
Wanda Collins, Board Chair
Geoffrey Hawtin, Vice Chair

5169 Center for Water Resources and Environmental Research (CWRER)
The City College of New York
160 Convent Avenue 212-650-7000
New York, NY 10031 www.ccny.cuny.edu
The Center investigates pollution movement, surface water and groundwater cleanup, wetland preservation, watershed management, hydraulics and hydrology of natural flow systems, ecology preservation and the technical and sociopoliticaloutcomes.
Dr. Lisa Staiano-Coico, President
Dr. Maurizio Trevisan, Provost

5170 Center for the Management, Utilization and Protection of Water Resources
Tennessee Technological University
P.O. Box 5033 931-372-3507
Cookeville, TN 38505 800-255-8881
Fax: 931-372-6346
sdodson@tntech.edu
www.tntech.edu/research/centers/wrc/
The Center for the Management, Utilization and Protection of Water Resources at Tennessee Technological University is dedicated to the vision of enhancing environmental education through research. Using interdisciplinary teams ofresearchers, the Center focuses its work in the core areas of environmental resource management and protection, environmental hazards, and environmental information.
Philip Oldham, President
Sandy Dodson, Academic Support Associate 3

5171 Clean Energy Research Institute
University of Miami
4202 East Fowler Avenue 813-974-7322
Mail Stop ENB118 Fax: 813-974-2050
Tampa, FL 33620 stefanak@eng.usf.edu
Acts as the focal point of energy and environmental related activities in the College of Engineering. Its goals are to conduct research and to generate research proposals to investigate energy and environmental problems; to organizeseminars, workshops and conferences using researchers within and without the University; to assemble, compile, publish and disseminate information on every aspect of energy and environmental problems; and to cooperate with other organs of theUniversity.
Elias (Lee) Stefanakos, Director
Yogi D. Goswami, Director

5172 Cobbs Creek Community Environment Educational Center (CCCEEC)
700 Cobbs Creek Parkway 215-685-1900
63rd & Catharine Streets Fax: 215-764-1586
Philadelphia, PA 19143 cobbscreekinfo@gmail.com
www.cobbscreekcenter.org
CCCEEC is designated to institutionalize the practice of Urban Environmental Education. Their mission is to preserve the quality for residents living in the Cobbs Creek area of Philadelphia through the establishment of a center foreducating and informing people about the issues affecting their environment.
Carole Williams-Green, Founder
Sharon Williams-Losier, President

5173 College of Forest Resources
University of Washington
College of Forest Resources 206-543-2730
PO Box 352100 Fax: 206-685-0790
Seattle, WA 98195-2100 sefsuw@u.washington.edu
www.cfr.washington.edu
The University of Washington College of Forest Resources is dedicated to generating and disseminating knowledge for the stewardship of natural and managed environments and the sustainable use of their products and services throughteaching, research and outreach.
Tom DeLuca, Director
Acker Steven, Associate Professor

5174 Colorado Cooperative Fish & Wildlife Research Unit
Colorado State University
1474 Campus Delivery 970-491-5396
Fort Collins, CO 80523-1474 Fax: 970-491-1413
www.warnercnr.colostate.edu
The Colorado Cooperative Wildlife Research Unit was founded in 1947, and the Colorado Cooperative Fishery Research Unit was established in 1963. The two Units were combined in 1984 into the Colorado Cooperative Fish and WildlifeResearch Unit. This unit is staffed, supported, and coordinated by the Colorado Division of Wildlife, Colorado State University, the United States Geological Survey , and the Wildlife Management Insistute.
David Anderson, Program Director/Chief Scien
Denise Culver, Research Associate

5175 Cooperative Fish & Wildlife Research Unit
University of Missouri
Colorado State University 970-491-5020
1474 Campus Delivery Fax: 970-491-5091
Fort Collins, CO 80523-1474 www.warnercnr.colostate.edu
David Anderson, Program Director
Carroll Bjork, Illustrator I

5176 Cornell Waste Management Institute
Department of Crop and Soil Science 607-255-1187
817 Bradfield Hall Fax: 607-255-8207
Ithaca, NY 14853 cwmi@cornell.edu
cwmi.css.cornell.edu
Conduct applied research and outreach focused on composting and land application of sewage sludges.
Jean Bonhotal, Director
Murray B. McBride, Professor

5177 ERI Earth Research Institute
University of California
6832 Ellison Hall 805-893-4885
University of California Fax: 805-893-2578
Santa Barbara, CA 93106-3060 webmaster@eri.ucsb.edu
www.eri.ucsb.edu
Purpose is to increase our understanding of the geological processes and evolution of the earth's crust and lithosphere, and the impact these processes have on society.
Susannah Porter, Director
David Siegel, Director

5178 Eagle Lake Biological Field Station
California State University
Department of Biology Sciences 530-898-4143
California State University Fax: 530-898-5060
Chico, CA 95929-0040 publicaffairs@csuchico.edu
www.csuchico.edu
The Eagle Lake Biological Field Station, located 26 miles northwest of Susanville in Lassen County, California is a ten building facility on the eastern shore of Eagle Lake. The field station is administered by California StateUniversity, Chico and the CSUC Foundation with support from the University of California Natural Reserve System and UC Davis. The ELBFS is open to any indi-

vidual or group whose purpose is primarily academic and whose activities are consistent withthe isolation.
Raymond J Bogiatto, Director
Jeffrey Bell, Chair, Biology

5179 Earth Science & Observation Center
University of Colorado Boulder
University of Colorado at Boulder 303-492-8773
216 UCB Fax: 303-492-1149
Boulder, CO 80309-216 lornay.hansen@colorado.edu
www.cires.colorado.edu/esoc
We advance scientific and societal understanding of the Earth System based on innovative remote sensing research. Through our research, we provide fundamental insights into how the Earth system functions, how it is changing, and whatthose changes mean for life on earth, for the benefit of human kind.
Dr Waleed Abdalati, Director
Tom Chase, Associate Professor

5180 Ecology Center
2530 San Pablo Avenue 510-548-2220
Suite H Fax: 510-548-2240
Berkeley, CA 94702 info@ecologycenter.org
ecologycenter.org
The Utah State University Ecology Center supports and coordinates ecological research and graduate education in the science of ecology. Also offered by the center are services such as farmers' markets, produce stands, residentialcurbside recycling, classes and workshops, Youth Environmental Academy, help desk and hotline, book & DVD library and more.
Raquel Pinderhughes, President
Becca Prager, Secretary

5181 Energy Resources Center
Univeristy of Illinois at Chicago
The University of Illinois at Chica 312-996-4490
1309 South Halsted Street, 2nd Fl, Suit Fax: 312-996-5620
Chicago, IL 60607 uic.edu
The Center is a University of Illinois at Chicago interdiciplinary research and public service organization. It was established in 1973 by the University's Board of Trustees to conduct studies in the field of energy and to providelocal, state and federal governments and the public with current information on energy technology and policy.
Cliff Haefke, Acting Director
Henry C. Kurth, Associate Director

5182 Energy, Environment & Resource Center
University of Tennesse at Knoxville
University of Tennessee, Knoxville 865-974-8080
676 Dabney Hall Fax: 865-974-8086
Knoxville, TN 37996-1605 cebweb@utk.edu
www.ceb.utk.edu
Gary S Sayler, Founding Director
Sabine Nabenfuehr, Administrative Assistant

5183 Environmental & Water Resources Engineering
Texas A&M University
Civil Engineering Department 512-471-4921
301 E. Dean Keeton St. Stop C1700 Fax: 979-862-1542
Austin, TX 78712 www.ce.utexas.edu/ewre
Jessica Treptow, Graduate Coordinator
Dr. Desmond Lawler, Graduate Advisor

5184 Environmental Center
University of Hawaii
2500 Dole Street 808-956-7361
Krauss Annex 19 Fax: 808-956-3980
Honolulu, HI 96822 www.hawaii.edu/envctr
The Center's three areas of focus are education, research and service. The education function of the Center includes the administration of the Environmental Studies Major Equivalent and Certificate program. It fulfills its researchfunction by identifying and addressing environmentally related research needs, particularly those pertinent to Hawaii. The service function primarily involves the coordination and transfer of technical information from the University community togovernment agencies.
Chittaranjan Ray, Director
John Cusick, Assistant Specialist

5185 Environmental Chemistry and Technology Program
University of Wisconsin at Madison
1415 Engineering Drive 608-263-3264
Room 122 Fax: 608-262-0454
Madison, WI 53706-1481 mcpossin@wisc.edu
www.engr.wisc.edu
Marc A. Anderson, Professor and Chair
Anders W. Andren, Professor Research

5186 Environmental Exposure Laboratory
University of California
1000 Veterans Avenue 310-825-2739
Rehabilitation Center, Room A163
Los Angeles, CA 90024
Dr. Henry Gong Jr, Director

5187 Environmental Human Toxicology
University of Florida
Bldg 471 Mowry Road 352-294-4514
PO Box 110885 Fax: 352-392-4707
Gainesville, FL 32611
The Center serves as an interface between basic research and its applications for evaluation of human health and environmental risk. The research and teaching activities of the Center provide a resource to identify and reduce riskassociated with environmental pollution, food contamination, and workplace hazards. The center provides a forum for the discussion of specific and general problems concerning the potential adverse human health effects associated with chemicalexposure.
Dr. Stephen Roberts, Director
Dr. Steve Roberts, Director

5188 Environmental Institue and Water Resources Research Institute
Auburn University
1090 South Donahue Drive 334-844-4132
Auburn, AL 36849 Fax: 334-844-4462
info@alabamawaterwatch.org
Samuel Fowler, Director
Dr Upton Hatch, Director

5189 Environmental Institute of Houston
University ofg Houston
University of Houston-Clear Lake 281-283-3950
2700 Bay Area Blvd., MC 540, North Offic Fax: 281-283-3953
Houston, TX 77058-1002 eih@uhcl.edu
www.eih.uhcl.edu
The mission of EIH is to help people in the Houston region participate more effectively in environmental improvement. Information and technology will be obtained and disseminated from research supported by EIH in critical areasincluding pollution prevention, natural resource conservation, public policy and societal issues. EIH will seek to expand balanced environmental education based on objective scholarship to empower the community to make sound decisions onenvironmental issues.
Sheila Brown, Board Member
Alecya Gallaway, Board Member

5190 Environmental Remote Sensing Center
University of Wisconsin
1225 W Dayton Street 608-263-3251
Floor 12 Fax: 608-262-5964
Madison, WI 53706 sventura@wisc.edu

A university research center focused on application of remote sensing and attending geospatial technologies in government, business and science. Particular heritage in the application of remote sensing in natural resource managementand environmental monitoring. A NASA-sponsored Affiliated Research Center.
Prof Thomas Lillesand, Director

5191 Environmental Research Institute
University of Idaho
875 Perimeter Drive 208-885-6111
PO Box 444264 888-8UI-DAHO
Moscow, ID 83844-4264 Fax: 208-885-9119
info@uidaho.edu
www.uidaho.edu

The faculty, associated with the institute, perform multidisciplinary research in environmental molecular ecology, restoration of contaminated soils and waters, and microbial genomics related to environmental processes.
Chuck Staben, President
Brenda Helbling, Executive Assistant

5192 Environmental Resource Center
San Jose Southern University
101 Center Pointe Drive 919-469-1585
Cary, NC 27513-5706 800-537-2372
Fax: 919-342-0807
service@ercweb.com
www.ercweb.com

The Environmental Resource Center is a nonprofit information and outreach organization within the Environmental Studes department at San Jose Southern University, serving the San Jose community since 1971.
Annemarie Vallesteros, Executive Director

5193 Environmental Science & Engineering Program
Clarkson University
1200 E California Blvd. MC 131-24 626-395-6070
Pasadena, CA 91125 Fax: 626-795-6028
www.ese.caltech.edu

Elizabeth Boyd, Associate Academic Assistant
Nora Oshima, Grants Manager

5194 Environmental Studies Institute
University of Pennsylvania
The University of Texas at Austin 512-471-5847
2275 Speedway, Mail Code C9000 Fax: 512-232-1913
Austin, TX 78712 banner@jsg.utexas.edu
www.esi.utexas.edu

The Institute for Environmental Studies is dedicated to improving the understanding of key scientific, economic, and political issues that underlie environmental problems and their management. The mission of the Institute is to bringscholars together from across the University in order to promote collaborations in education and research endeavors in the area of environmental issues. These collaborative endeavors span basic and applied sciences, engineering and the social andhuman sciences.
Jay L. Banner, Director
Eric W. James, Program Coordinator

5195 Environmental Systems Application Center
Indiana University
107 S Indiana Avenue 812-855-4848
Bloomington, IN 47405

The goals of the Center are to promote excellence in environmental science research and to foster increased interdisciplinary collaboration among environmental science faculty on the Indiana University-Bloomington campus. The Centerhas no degree programs. The Center can be listed as an affiliation of the associated faculty in publications and in correspondence.

5196 Environmental Systems Engineering Institute
University of Central Florida
University of Central Florida 407-823-2841
4000 Central Florida Boulevard Fax: 407-823-3315
Orlando, FL 32816-2450 www.cece.ucf.edu
Dr. Steven J. Duranceau, Associate Professor & Dir
Maria Pia Real-Robert, Laboratory Manager

5197 Environmental Toxicology Center
University of Wisconsin
1300 University Avenue 608-263-4580
1530 MSC Fax: 608-262-5245
Madison, WI 53706

Environmental Toxicology is the study of the adverse effects on individual life forms and ecosystems of environmental agents (chemical, physcial, biological) whether of natural origin or released through human activity, and origins andcontrol of these harmful agents.
Christopher A. Bradfield, Director
Prof. Colin R Jefcoate, Director

5198 Environmental and Occupational Health Science Institute
Rutgers University
170 Frelinghuysen Road 848-445-0202
PO Box 1179 Fax: 732-445-0131
Piscataway, NJ 00885 info@eohsi.rutgers.edu
www.eohsi.rutgers.edu

The major objectives of the institute are to: improve understanding of the impact of environmental chemicals on human health; to find ways to quantify and prevent exposure to hazardous substances; and develop methods to identify andtreat people adversely affected by environmental agents. Devises approaches for educating the public about the relative risks from chemical exposure. Trains professionals to accomplish these tasks.
Kenneth Reuhl, Ph.D., Interim Director
Howard Kipen, M.D., M.P.H., Assoc Director

5199 Feed and Fertilizer Laboratory
Louisiana State University
Department Agriculture and Forestry 208-332-8500
PO Box 790 Fax: 208-334-2170
Boise, ID 83701-790 info@agri.idaho.gov
www.agri.idaho.gov

Celia R. Gould, Director
Brian J. Oakey, Deputy Director

5200 Field Station & Ecological Reserves
University of Kansas
c/o Kansas Biological Survey 785-864-1500
2101 Constant Ave. Fax: 785-864-5093
Lawrence, KS 66047-3759 biosurvey@ku.edu
biosurvey.ku.edu

The KSR is dedicated to field-based environmental reseach and education. KSR is located within the transition zone (ecotone) between the eastern deciduous forest and tallgrass prairie biomes. The 3,000 acres of diverse native andmanaged habitats, experimental systems, support facilities, and longterm databases are used to undertake an outstanding array of scholarly activities. Environmental stewardship is a stong emphasis as high-quality natural areas are preserved for thefuture.
Ed Martinko, Ph.D., Director
Jerry deNoyelles, Ph.D., Deputy Director

5201 Fitch Natural History Reservation
University of Kansas
Kansas Biological Survey 785-864-1500
2101 Constant Avenue Fax: 785-864-1534
Lawrence, KS 66047 biosurvey@ku.edu
biosurvey.ku.edu

Ed Martinko, Ph.D., Director
Jerry deNoyelles, Ph.D., Deputy Director

5202 Florida Cooperative Fish and Wildlife Research Unit
University of Florida
University of Florida 352-846-0643
110 Newins-Ziegler Hall, PO Box 110430 Fax: 352-846-0841
Gainesville, FL 32611-0430 mghale@ufl.edu
www.wec.ufl.edu
The Cooperative Research Unit has three facets to its mission: education—Cooperative Unit scientists teach university courses at the graduate level, provide academic guidence to graduate students, and serve on academic committees;research—Cooperative Unit scientists conduct research that is designed to meet the information needs expressed by unit cooperators; technical Assistance— unit provides technical assistance and training to State and federal personnel and othernatural resources.
James D Austin, Associate Professor
Benjamin Baiser, Assistant Professor

5203 Florida Museum of Natural History
University of Florida
Dickinson Hall, 1659 Museum Road 352-392-1721
PO Box 117800 Fax: 352-392-8783
Gainesville, FL 32611-7800 gdshaak@flmnh.ufl.edu
www.flmnh.ufl.edu
The Florida Museum of Natural History, on the University of Florida Campus, is one of the leading university natural history museums in the nation. With over 30 million specimens and artifacts in its permanent collections, it is thelargest collection-based museum in the southeastern US. The museum was established by the Legislature in 1917 at the University of Florida where it functions in a dual capacity as the official state museum of Florida and the University Museum.
Dr Douglas S Jones, Director
Dr Beverly Sensbach, Associate Director

5204 Formaldehyde Institute
1330 Connecticut Avenue NW 202-833-2131
Washington, DC 20036 Fax: 202-659-1699
John F Murray, Executive Director

5205 Gannett Energy Laboratory
Florida Institute of Technology
207 Senate Avenue 717-763-7211
Harrisburg, PA 17011-2316 800-233-1055
www.gannettfleming.com
Bill Stout, Chairman/CEO
Bob Scaer, President/COO

5206 Global Change & Environmental Quality Program
University of Colorado
University of Colorado at Boulder 303-492-1411
Campus Box 214 Fax: 303-492-1414
Boulder, CO 80309 bob.sievers@colorado.edu
www.colorado.edu
In addition to addressing CU's overall objectives, the Global Change and Environmental Quality Program is pursuing three main goals; studying environmental issues at the local level, including the cleanup and restoration of toxicsites, such as Rocky Flats, the Rocky Mountain Arsenal, and mine tailing sites; waste treatment and water quality; and land use.
Bob Sievers, Director
Rosella Chavez, Admin Asst.

5207 Graduate Program in Community and Regional Planning
University of Texas
Main Building 512-471-0134
Austin, TX 78701 Fax: 512-471-0716
The CRP provides its graduates with the theoretical foundations, specific skills and practical experience to succeed in professional planning and related policy careers. They strive to create a diverse student body and program and arecommitted to building a professional planning community that rese,bles those where graduates will work. The program has a strong focus on sustainable development processes and practices. Finding paths that balance growth with improved environmentalperformance.
Jane Shaughness, Graduate Admissions Coor.

5208 Great Lakes Coastal Research Laboratory
Purdue University
School of Civil Engineering 765-494-4600
West Lafayette, IN 47907

5209 Great Lakes/Mid-Atlantic Hazardous Substance Research Center
University of Michigan
One Potomac Yard (South Building) 734-763-2274
2777 South Crystal Drive www.epa.gov
Arlington, VA 22202
The mission of the Great Lakes Mid- Atlantic Center for Hazardous Substances Research is to foster and support integrated, intersdisciplinary, and collaborative efforts that advance the science and technology of hazardous substancemanagement to benefit human and environmental health and well-being.
Gina McCarthy, Administrator
Stan Meiburg, Deputy Administrator

5210 Great Plains: Rocky Mountain Hazardous Substance Research Center
Kansas State University
Kansas State University 785-532-6519
104 Ward Hall 800-798-7796
Manhattan, KS 66506-2502 Fax: 785-532-5985
hsrc@ksu.edu
www.engg.ksu.edu/HSRC
Conducts research and transfers technology on hazardous substance management, and remediation of contaminated soil and water.
Dr. Larry Erickson, Center Director
Dr. Richard B. Hayter, Technology Transfer & Traini

5211 Greenley Research Center
University of Missouri
64399 Greenley Place 660-739-4410
Novelty, MO 63460 Fax: 660-739-4500
bradleytl@missouri.edu
greenley.cafnr.org
Located in the claypan soil region of northeast Missouri, this Center evaluates efficient and profitable crop production while emphasizing soil conservation, water quality and energy efficiency.
Jesse Schwanke, Chairman
Harold Beach, Vice-chairman

5212 HT Peters Aquatic Biology Laboratory
Sattgast 230 218-755-2001
1500 Birchmont Drive NE #27 800-475-2001
Bemidji, MN 56601-2699 Fax: 218-755-4107
dcloutman@bemidjistate.edu
www.bemidjistate.edu
Dr. Richard Hansen, President
Bill Maki, VP

5213 Harry Reid Center for Environmental Studies
University of Las Vegas
4505 Maryland Parkway 702-895-3382
Box 454009 Fax: 702-895-3094
Las Vegas, NV 89154-4009
The HRC was started in 1981 under UNLV's Marjorie Barrick Museum of Natural History. HRC currently includes 65 staff members and a 65,000 square foot building with four laboratories.
Dr. Oliver A. Hemmers, Executive Director
Leisa Baldwin-Rodriguez, Finance Director

5214 **Harvard NIEHS Center for Environmental Health**
Harvard University
665 Huntington Avenue 617-432-1271
Boston, MA 00211 ddockery@hsph.harvard.edu
www.hsph.harvard.edu

Serves as the focus for research and training activities in environmental health at the Harvard School of Public Health and elsewhere in the University. The Center was established in 1958 to promote interactions among biologicalscientists, physical scientists and engineers working on environmental problems of human health concern.
Douglas Dockery, Center Director
Julie Goodman, Center Coordinator

5215 **Hawaii Cooperative Fishery Research Unit**
University of Hawaii at Manoa
12201 Sunrise Valley Drive MS303 703-648-4260
Reston, VA 20192-2279 Fax: 703-648-4269
kkhardin@hawaii.edu
www.coopunits.org

John F. Organ, Chief
Suzanne Cartagirone, Admin Ops Assistant

5216 **Hawaii Undersea Research Laboratory**
University of Hawaii at Manoa
1 Sand Island Access Road 808-842-9813
Marine Science Building (MSB) 303 888-800-0460
Honolulu, HI 96819 Fax: 808-842-9833
www.soest.hawaii.edu

One of six research centers funded by NOAA's National Undersea Research Program. HURL operates two 2000-meter Pisces submersibles and a remotely operated vehicle. Research projects include fisheries research, geology and biology of thedeepsea around the Hawaiian Islands.
Diane Apau, Admin Officer
Karynne Chong Morgan, Admin Officer

5217 **Henry S Conrad Environmental Research Area**
1210 Grinnell College 641-269-4000
Grinnell, IA 50112-1690 Fax: 641-269-4984
bakermar@grinnell.edu

Paula V. Smith, Vp Academic Affairs
Retta Kelley, Administrative Asst. II

5218 **Highlands Biological Station**
University of North Carolina
265 N Sixth Street 828-526-2602
PO Box 580 Fax: 828-526-2797
Highlands, NC 28741 hbs@email.wcu.edu
www.highlandsbiological.org

The Highlands Biological Station is an interinstitutional center of the University of North Carolina administered by Western Carolina University. Through support of field biology research, immersive field courses, and an extensiveoutreach program, their mission is to foster understanding and appreciation of the natural heritage of the southern Appalachian region.
James T. Costa, Executive
Sarah W. Workman, Associate Director

5219 **Hudsonia**
30 Campus Rd 845-758-7053
PO Box 5000 Fax: 845-758-7033
Annandale, NY 12504-5000 kiviat@bard.edu
www.hudsonia.org

Since 1981 Hudsonia has conducted environmental research, education, training and technical assistance to protect the Hudson River Valley's natural heritage. Nonpartisan and non-ideological, Hudsonia serves as a neutral voice in thechallenging process of land conservation.
Erik Kiviat PhD, Executive Director
Robert E. Schmidt PhD, Associate Director

5220 **Huntsman Environmental Research Center**
Utah State University 435-797-1000
4105 Old Main Hill Fax: 435-797-1248
Logan, UT 84322-1400 herc@usu.edu
www.herc.usu.edu

The establishement of the Hunts man Environmental Research Center recognized the fundamental interdependence of the health of man and the health of the environment. The HERC's mission is to engage in research in the key areas ofrecycling, degradability, improvement of air and water quality and conservation of trees. The center purpose is to solve environmental problems and to provide realistic and comprehensive research solutions for our environment.
Stan L. Albrecht, President
Raymond T. Coward, Executive VP

5221 **INFORM**
PO Box 320403 212-361-2400
Brooklyn, NY 11232 Fax: 212-361-2412
www.informinc.org

INFORM is an independent research organization that examines the effects of business practices on the environment and on human health. Our goal is to identify ways of doing business that ensure environmentally sustainable economicgrowth. Our reports are used by government, industry, and environmental leaders around the world.
Thomas C.T. Brokaw, Co-Chair
Marina Belesis-Casoria, Co-Chair

5222 **Idaho Cooperative Fish & Wildlife Research Unit**
University of Idaho
875 Perimeter Drive 208-885-6111
PO Box 444264 888-8UI-DAHO
Moscow, ID 83844-4264 Fax: 208-885-9119
info@uidaho.edu
www.uidaho.edu

The faculty, associated with the institute, perform multidisciplinary research in environmental molecular ecology, restoration of contaminated soils and waters, and microbial genomics related to environmental processes.
Chuck Staben, President
John Wiencek, Provost/EVP

5223 **Institute for Biopsychological Studies of Color, Light, Radiation, Health**
San Jose State University
One Washington Square 408-924-1000
Psychology Department Fax: 408-924-1018
San Jose, CA 95192 www.sjsu.edu
Dr Paul Lanning, VP
Dr Reginald Blaylock, VP for Student Affairs

5224 **Institute for Ecological Infrastructure Engineering**
Losuisiana State University
College of Engineering 225-578-1399
102 ELAB Fax: 225-578-8662
Baton Rouge, LA 70803
Institute for Ecological Infrastructure Engineering integrates engineering with science (physical, chemical, life & social) for the co-development of society and nature (ecosystems).
Lily A Rusch, Director

5225 **Institute for Environmental Science**
University of Texas at Dallas
Arlington Place One 847-981-0100
2340 South Arlington Heights Road, Suite Fax: 847-981-4130
Arlington, IL 60005-4510 information@iest.org
www.iest.org

Shawn Windley, President
Kevin Stultz, Fiscal VP

5226 **Institute for Lake Superior Research**
University of Minnesota
University of Wisconsin-Superior 715-394-8101
Belknap & Catlin, PO Box 2000 relations@uwsuper.edu
Superior, WI 54880 www.uwsuper.edu
Janet Hanson, Vice Chancellor
Jeff Kahler, Budget & Policy Analyst

5227 **Institute for Regional and Community Studies**
Western Illinois University 309-298-1566
Tillman Hall 413B
Macomb, IL 61455

5228 **Institute for Urban Ports and Harbors**
School of Marine and Atmospheric Sciences
Stony Brook University 631-632-8700
Endeavor Hall, Room 145 Fax: 631-632-8820
Stony Brook, NY 11794-5000 somas@stonybrook.edu
www.somas.stonybrook.edu
Minghua Zhang, Dean/Director
R. Lawrence Swanson, Associate Dean

5229 **Institute of Analytical and Environmental Chemistry**
University of New Haven
300 Boston Post Road 203-932-7171
West Haven, CT 00651 800-342-5864
www.newhaven.edu
Steven H. Kaplan, President
Lourdes Alvarez, Dean

5230 **Institute of Chemical Toxicology**
Wayne State University
Wayne State University 313-577-2424
42 W. Warren Ave. Fax: 313-577-0082
Detroit, MI 48202 www.wayne.edu
Gary S. Pollard, Chair
M. Roy Wilson, President

5231 **Institute of Ecology**
University of California
Davis 1 Shields Avenue Davis 530-752-1011
Davis, CA 95616 Fax: 530-752-3350
aking@ucdavis.edu
www.ucdavis.edu
Linda P.B. Katehi, Chancellor
Ralph Hexter, Provost/Executive Vice Chanc

5232 **Interdisciplinary Center for Aeronomy & Other Atmospheric Sciences**
University of Florida
317, Bryant Space Science Center 352-392-2001
PO Box 112050 Fax: 352-392-2003
Gainesville, FL 32611-2050 aesgreen@ufl.edu
Prof. Alex ES Green, Director

5233 **Iowa Cooperative Fish & Wildlife Research Unit**
Iowa State University
NREM-ICFWRU 515-294-3056
339 Science II Fax: 515-294-5468
Ames, IA 50011-3221 coppunit@iastate.edu
www.cfwru.iastate.edu
The Iowa landscape and economy are dominated by production agriculture. Game and non-game wildlife species inhabinting the state are influenced by the destruction, degradation and frgamentation of wetland, prairie, and forest habitatscaused by intensified agricultural practices. This Unit is designed to identify, and emaphsize these effects through research and education programs.
Robert W Klaver, Unit Leader
Clay L Pierce, Assistant Unit leader

5234 **Iowa Waste Reduction Center**
University of Northern Iowa
113, BCS Building 319-273-8905
University of Northern Iowa 800-422-3109
Cedar Falls, IA 50614 Fax: 319-273-6582
www.iwrc.org
A service of the University of Northern Iowa, it provides free and confidential environmental regulatory assistance to Iowa small businesses. The IWRC has also developed two products available to the painting and coating industry:LaserPaint and VirtualPaint.
Diane Albertson, IT Specialist
Michael Bolick, Comm/PR Manager

5235 **James H Barrow Field Station**
Hiram College Biological Station 330-527-2141
Garrettsville, OH 44231 Fax: 330-527-3187
The James H Barrow Field Station was established in 1967 to provide Hiram College students the opportunity to supplement classroom activities with hands-on learning experiences. Over the Last 32 years the Station has grown anddeveloped into an active research and educational facility that not only echances the College's science and environmental studies programs, but also provides a means for the general public to increase their understanding and appreciation of Ohio'snatural history.

5236 **John F Kennedy School of Government Environmental and Natural Resources Program**
Harvard University
79 John F Kennedy Street 617-495-1351
Cambridge, MA 00213 Fax: 617-495-1635
enrp@ksg.harvard.edu
Henry Lee, Director

5237 **Juneau Center School of Fisheries & Ocean Sciences**
University of Alaska Fairbanks
17101 Point Lena Loop Rd 907-796-5441
UAF Fisheries Division Fax: 907-796-5447
Juneau, AK 99801-8344 www.sfos.uaf.edu
JCSFOS has the primary responsibility within the University for education, research and public service in support of fisheries related areas of oceanography, marine biology and limnology with emphasis on Alaskan waters and the Arctic.The school's goal is to maintain and develop the broad expertise among its faculty and students needed to contribute to the wise use of Alaska's natural resources.
Joan Braddock, Dean
Adkison Milo, Professor

5238 **Laboratory for Energy and the Environment**
Massachusetts Institute of Technology
Massachusetts Institute of Technolo 617-258-8891
77 Massachusetts Avenue, E19-307 Fax: 617-253-8013
Cambridge, MA 00213-4307 thill@mit.edu
The LFEE at the Massachusetts Institute of Technology brings together collaborating faculty and staff in 13 departments to address the complex interrelationships between energy and the environment, and other global environmentalchallenges.
Prof. Robert C. Armstrong, Director
Prof. Angela M. Belcher, Professor

5239 **Leopold Center for Sustainable Agriculture**
Iowa State University
209 Curtiss Hall 515-294-3711
513 Farm House Lane Fax: 515-294-9696
Ames, IA 50011-1054 leocenter@iastate.edu
www.leopold.iastate.edu
The center was created by the Iowa Groundwater Protection Act with the mission to identify and reduce adverse environmental impacts of farming practices while developing profitable farming systems that conserve natural resources.
Doug Gronau, Chair
Mark Rasmussen, Director

5240 **Living Marine Resources Institute**
Stony Brook University 631-632-6000
Stony Brook, NY 11794 Fax: 631-632-9441
Loreen.Brandes@stonybrook.edu
www.stonybrook.edu
LIMRI is one of several specialized institutes subsumed within the Marine Sciences Research Center of Stony Brook University. LIMRI's program of research includes investigations on marine fisheries, harmful algal blooms, marine law &policy, and aquaculture. The Institute operates the Flax Pond Marine Laboratory, a seaside, seawater-equipped facility for experimental work, located 5 miles north of the main campus on a tidal pond adjacent to Long Island Sound.
Samuel L. Stanley, President
William Arens, Vice Provost

5241 **Long-Term Ecological Research Project**
University of Colorado
1 University of New Mexico 505-277-2649
Albuquerque, NM 87131 Fax: 303-492-0434
tech-support@lternet.edu
www.lternet.edu
Scott Collins, Chair
Bob Waide, Executive Director

5242 **Louisiana Sea Grant College Program**
Louisiana State University
Sea Grant Building 225-578-6564
Baton Rouge, LA 70803 Fax: 225-578-6331
www.laseagrant.org
Works to promote stewardship of the state's coastal resources through a combination of research, education and outreach programs critical to the cultural, economic, and environmental health of Louisiana's coastal zone. Part of theNational Sea Grant Program, it is one of 32 programs located in coastal, Great Lakes, and Puerto Rican coast areas.
Robert R. Twilley, Executive Director
Matthew Bethel Ph.D., Assistant Executive Director

5243 **MIT Sea Grant College Program**
Massachusetts Institute of Technology
77 Massachusetts Ave. 617-253-7131
E 38-300 Fax: 617-258-5730
Cambridge, MA 00213 chrys@mit.edu
Chrys Chryssostomidis, Director
Stefano Brizzolara, Asst Director

5244 **Marine Science Institute**
University of Texas
The University of Texas 361-749-6711
750 Channel View Drive Fax: 361-749-6777
Port Aransas, TX 78373 www.utmsi.utexas.edu
The Marine Institute is an organized research unit of The University of Texas at Austin. Institute scientists are engaged in both multi-investigator, multi-disciplinary studies and individual research projects in the local area andthroughout the world. Many of these projects are combinations of field and laboratory investigations. The Institute receives an operating budget annually that is based on a two-year advanced budget approval by the state legislature.
Perry R. Bass, Chair
Robert W. Dickey Ph.D., Director

5245 **Massachusetts Cooperative Fish & Wildlife Unit**
University of Massachusetts
12201 Sunrise Valley Drive MS303 703-648-4260
PO Box 34220 Fax: 703-648-4269
Reston, VA 20192-4220 sdestef@eco.umass.edu
www.coopunits.org
John F. Organ, Chief
Suzanne Cartagirone, Admin Ops Assistant

5246 **Masschusetts Water Resources Research Center**
University of Massachusetts
Blaisdell House 413-545-5531
113 Grinnell Way Fax: 413-253-1309
Amherst, MA 00100 wrrc@cns.umass.edu
The Center has three objectives: 1) to develop, through research, new technology and more efficient methods for resolving local, state and national water resources problems; 2) to train water scientists and engineers through on-the-jobparticipation in water resources research and outreach; 3) to facilitate water research coordination and the application of research results by means of information dissemination, technology transfer and outreach.
Paula Rees, Director
Marie-Françoise Hatte, Assoc. Director

5247 **Millar Wilson Laboratory for Chemical Research**
Jacksonville University
2800 University Boulevard N 904-744-3950
Jacksonville, FL 32211 Fax: 904-744-0101
Lsonnen@ju.edu

5248 **Mining and Mineral Resources Research Center**
205 Particle Science & Technology 352-846-1194
Gainesville, FL 32611 Fax: 352-846-1196
info@perc.ufl.edu
www.perc.ufl.edu/mrrc
Brij M. Moudgil, Director
B. Koopman, Affiliated Faculty

5249 **Mississippi Cooperative Fish & Wildlife Research Unit**
Mississippi State University
12201 Sunrise Valley Drive MS303 703-648-4260
Reston, VA 20192 Fax: 703-648-4269
www.coopunits.org
John F. Organ, Chief
Suzanne Cartagirone, Admin Ops Assistant

5250 **Mississippi State Chemical Laboratory**
Mississippi State University
262 Lee Boulevard 662-325-3742
PO Box BQ Fax: 662-325-4039
Mississippi State, MS 39762 www.msstate.edu
Mark E. Keenum, President
Jerome A. Gilbert, Provost/Executive Vice Presi

5251 **Montana Cooperative Fishery Research Unit**
Montana St University Dept Ecology 406-994-2672
100 Culbertson Hall, PO Box 172000 Fax: 406-994-7479
Bozeman, MT 59717-2000 www.montana.edu
Dr. Waded Cruzado, President
Wanda DeMay, Manager

5252 **Monterey Bay Watershed Project**
California State University
100 Campus Center 831-582-3689
Watershed Institute Building 42 Fax: 831-582-5114
Seaside, CA 93955-8001 laura_lienk@csumb.edu
www.watershed.csumb.edu
The Watershed Institute is a direct action, community based coalition of researchers, restoration ecologists, educators, students, planners and area volunteers dedicated to restoring the watersheds of the Monterey Bay region throughrestoration, education and research. Their policy is to work with state and federal agencies, private landowers and local planners to gain access to critical lands. Institute staff are involved in local land and water planning.
Laura Lee Lienk, Co-Director
Doug Smith, Co-Director/Professor

5253 **Museum of Zoology**
University of Massachusetts
Zoology Department 413-545-2287
Amherst, MA 00100 web@admin.umass.edu
www.umass.edu

Kumble R. Subbaswamy, Chancellor
James V. Staros, Provost/Vice Chancellor

5254 **National Center for Ground Water Research**
University of Oklahoma
660 Parrington Oval 405-325-0311
Norman, OK 73019 Fax: 405-325-7596
canter@ou.edu

Dr Larry Canter, Director

5255 **National Center for Vehicle Emissions Control & Safety**
Colorado State University
1584 Campus Delivery 970-491-7240
Fort Collins, CO 80523 Fax: 970-491-7801
ncvecs@cahs.colostate.edu
www.colostate.edu

NCVECS is a nationally and internationally recognized university based research and training center devoted to motor vehicle emission issues. NCVECS primarily assists states with research and training related to their local vehicleinspection program. In addition, research is conducted on OBDII systems, alternative fuels and diesel vehicle issues.
Dr Lenora Bohren, Director
Joe Beebe, Automotive Emissions Testing

5256 **National Institute for Global Environmental Change: South Central Regional Center**
Tulane University
605 Lindy Boggs Center 504-865-5250
New Orleans, LA 70118 Fax: 504-865-6745
nigec@tulane.edu

Dr Stathis Michaelides, Director
Valentina M. Tournier, Regional Assistant

5257 **National Mine Land Reclamation Center: Eastern Region**
State University of Pennsylvania
106 Land & Water Resources Building 814-863-0291
University Park, PA 16802 Fax: 814-865-3378
www.wvmdtaskforce.com

Ben Greene, Chairman/President
Buddy Beach, VP

5258 **National Mine Land Reclamation Center: Midwest Region**
Southern Illinois University
1201 W Gregory 618-453-2496
Carbondale, IL 62901 Fax: 217-333-8816
www.wvmdtaskforce.com

Ben Greene, Chairman/President
Buddy Beach, VP

5259 **National Mine Land Reclamation Center: Western Region**
Highway 6 S 701-777-5217
Mandan, ND 58554 jsolc@eerc.und.nodak.edu
www.wvmdtaskforce.com

Ben Greene, Chairman/President
Buddy Beach, VP

5260 **National Park Service Cooperative Unit: Athens**
University of Georgia
Institute of Ecology 706-542-8301
Athens, GA 30602
Dr. Stephen Cover-Shabica, Contact

5261 **National Research Center for Coal and Energy (NRCCE)**
West Virginia University 304-293-4974
PO Box 6064 Fax: 304-293-3749
Morgantown, WV 26506 Paul.Ziemkiewicz@mail.wvu.edu
www.wvwri.org

A research and training center at West Virginia University, advances innovations for energy and the environment by working with research faculty across WVU and with other university, government, and private sector researchersnationwide. The center is organized into a variety of multidisciplinary programs, centers, and institutes focusing on topics such as clean energy production, energy distribution, energy efficiency, alternative fuels, watershed restorationandpreservation.
Paul F. Ziemkiewicz, PhD, Director
Tamara F. Vandivort, Associate Director

5262 **Natural Energy Laboratory of Hawaii Authority**
73-4460 Queen Kaahumanu Hwy. #101 808-327-9585
Kailua Kona, HI 96740-2637 Fax: 808-327-9586
nelha.hawaii.gov

The Natural Energy Laboratory of Hawaii Authority (NELHA) operates facilities at Keahole Point on Hawaii Island that pump ashore cold deep and warm surface seawater for commercial and research tenants from the private and publicsectors. Tenants utilize the seawater and NELHA's high sunlight and consistant temperatures in a wide range of aquaculture and energy projects.
Ron Baird, CEO

5263 **New Hampshire Sea Grant College Program**
University of New Hampshire
The University of New Hampshire 603-862-1234
Main Street 800-735-2964
Durham, NH 00382 Fax: 603-743-3997
www.seagrant.unh.edu

A component of the National Sea Grant College Program, NH Sea Grant works toward the conservation, wise use and development of marine resources in the state and region.
Mark W. Huddleston, President
John Aber, Provost

5264 **New York Cooperative Fish & Wildlife Research Unit**
Cornell University
211 Fernow Hall 607-255-2839
Ithaca, NY 14853-3001 Fax: 607-255-1895
meaton@usgs.gov
www.coopunits.org/New_York

Angela Fuller, Unit Leader
Mitchell Eaton, Asst. Unit Leader

5265 **New York State Water Resources Institute**
Cornell University
204A Rice Hall 607-255-5941
Ithaca, NY 14853 Fax: 607-255-5945
sjr4@cornell.edu

Susan J. Riha, Director
Brian G. Rahm, Post Doctoral Associate

5266 **Northwoods Field Station**
Hiram College
11715 Garfield Road 330-569-3211
Hiram, OH 44234 800-362-5280
www.hiram.edu

Lori E. Varlotta Ph.D, President
Gay Cull Addicott, President

5267 Occupational & Environmental Health Laboratory
University of North Alabama
2206 East Mall 604-822-2772
Vancouver, BC V6T1Z Fax: 604-822-4994
mha.program@ubc.ca
www.spph.ubc.ca

Dr. David Patrick, Director
Cecilia Gruber, Asst. Director

5268 Ocean & Coastal Policy Center
University of California
Woolley-5134 805-893-8393
Santa Barbara, CA 93106 Fax: 805-893-8062
Dr. Michael Vincent, Conratct

5269 Ocean Engineering Center
Massachusetts Institute of Technolo 617-253-9344
77 Massachusetts Avenue, Room 5-228 Fax: 603-862-0241
Cambridge, MA 00213 oe@mit.edu
Geoff Fox, Administrative Assistant II
Mary Mullowney, Administrative Assistant II

5270 Oceanic Institute
Makapuu Point 808-259-3102
41-202 Kalanianaole Highway Fax: 808-259-5971
Waimanalo, HI 96795 oi@oceanicinstitute.org
www.oceanicinstitute.org
Oceanic Institute is a not-for-profit organization dedicated to research, development and transfer of oceanographic, marine Environmental, and aquaculture technologies. Oceanic Institute is a world leader in conducting appliedresearch in aquaculture production and marine resource conservation. Its mission is to develop and transfer environmentally responsible technologies to increase aquatic food production while promoting the sustainable use of ocean resources.
Dr. Geoffrey Bannister, Chairman
James A. Ajello, Board Of Trustees

5271 Oregon Cooperative Fishery Research Unit
Oregon State University
Oregon State University 541-737-1000
104 Nash Hall Fax: 541-737-3590
Corvallis, OR 97330 OSU.Provost@oregonstate.edu
www.oregonstate.edu

Pat Reser, Chair
Darry Callahan, Vice Chair

5272 Oregon Cooperative Park Studies Unit
Oregon State University
3200 Jefferson Way 541-737-2056
Corvallis, OR 97331 www.cof.orst.edu/
Dr Edward E Starkey, Codirector

5273 Oregon Sea Grant College Program
Oregon State University
Oregon State University 541-737-1000
Suite 350 Fax: 541-737-7958
Corvallis, OR 97330 www.seagrant.oregonstate.edu
Pat Reser, Chair
Darry Callahan, Vice Chair

5274 Pennsylvania Cooperative Fish & Wildlife Research Unit
Pennsylvania State University
117 Forest Resources Bldg 814-865-7541
University Park, PA 16802 Fax: 814-865-3725
www.ecosystems.psu.edu

Michael G. Messina Ph.D., Head /Professor
Marc David Abrams Ph.D, Professor

5275 Permaculture Gap Mountain
9 Old County Road 603-532-6877
Jaffrey, NH 00345

5276 Pesticide Research Center
Michigan State University
Michigan State University 517-353-4647
426 Auditorium Rd, Board of Trustees Roo 800-500-1554
East Lansing, MI 48824-1046 Fax: 51- 35- 467
beekman@msu.edu
www.msu.edu

Joel I. Ferguson, Chairperson
Mitch Lyons, Vice Chairperson

5277 Planning Institute
University of Southern California
University of Southern California 213-740-2311
Los Angeles, CA 90089 Fax: 213-740-1801
sppd@usc.edu
www.usc.edu

Wallis Annenberg, Chairman
C.L. Max Nikias, President

5278 Program for International Collaboration in Agroecology
University of California Santa Cruz
MS: PICA 831-459-4051
1156 High Street Fax: 831-459-2867
Santa Cruz, CA 95064 gliess@ucsc.edu
Researches, develops, and advances sustainable food and agricultural systems that are environmentally sound, economically viable, socially responsible, nonexploitive, and that serve as a foundation for future generations. A specialfocus on promoting an international network of training programs in agroecology.
Stephen R. Gliessman, Professor of Agroecology
Vivan Vadakan, PICA Program Manager

5279 Program in Freshwater Biology
University of Mississippi
University of Mississippi 662-915-2787
P.O. Box 1848 Fax: 662-915-5144
University, MS 38677 biology@olemiss.edu
www.olemiss.edu

Dr. James Kushlan, Chairman
Daniel W. Jones, Chancellor

5280 Randolph G Pack Environmental Institute
1 Forestry Drive 315-470-6500
107 Marshall Hall Fax: 315-470-6915
Syracuse, NY 13210 envsty@esf.edu
www.esf.edu
The Institute seeks to advance scholoarly and popular knowledge of key contemporary issues related to environmental policy and regulartion. It focuses on how democratic public decisions affecting the natural environment are made,concentrating on such topics as public participation, environmental equity, and sustainable development.
Vita DeMarchi, Chair
Dr. Quentin Wheeler, President

5281 Rare and/or Endangered Species Research Center
215 Mitchell Street 256-760-4429
Florence, AL 35630

5282 Red Butte Garden and Arboretum
300 Wakara Way 801-585-0556
Salt Lake City, UT 84108 www.redbuttegarden.org
David Gee, Chair
Tom Ramsey, Vice Chair

5283 Remote Sensing/Geographic Information Systems Facility
Geography Building 517-353-7195
673 Auditorium Road Fax: 517-353-1821
East Lansing, MI 48824 boothj@msu.edu
www.rsgis.msu.edu

Dr Susan Berta, Interim Chairperson
Justin Booth, Director

5284 Renew America
1200 18th Street Northwest 202-721-1545
Suite 1100 Fax: 202-467-5780
Washington, DC 20036 www.renewamerica.com
Stephen Stone, President
Matt C. Abbott, Columnist

5285 Research Triangle Institute
3040 Cornwallis Road 919-541-6000
PO Box 12194 Fax: 919-541-7155
Research Triangle Park, NC 27709-2194 listen@rti.org
www.rti.org
Clients around the world rely on RTI to conduct innovative, multidisciplinary research to meet their R and D challenges. RTI's staff of more then 1,850 people represents a diverse set of technical capabilities in health and medicine,environmental protection, technology commercialization, decision support systems and education and training.
William M. Moore, Chair
Richard H. Brodhead, President

5286 Resources for the Future
1616 P Street Northwest 202-328-5000
Suite 600 Fax: 202-939-3460
Washington, DC 20036 info@rff.org
www.rff.org
RFF is a nonprofit and nonpartisan think tank located in Washington DC that conducts independent research-rooted primarily in economics and other social sciences on environmental and natural resource issues. RFF was founded in 1952.
Richard L. Schmalensee, Chair
Philip R. Sharp, President

5287 Resources for the Future: Energy & Natural Resources Division
1616 P Street, Northwest 202-328-5000
Suite 600 Fax: 202-939-3460
Washington, DC 20036 info@rff.org
www.rff.org

Richard L. Schmalensee, Chair
Philip R. Sharp, President

5288 Resources for the Future: Quality of the Environment Division
1616 P Street, Northwest 202-328-5000
Suite 600 Fax: 202-939-3460
Washington, DC 20036 info@rff.org
www.rff.org

Richard L. Schmalensee, Chair
Philip R. Sharp, President

5289 River Studies Center
University of Wisconsin
University of Wisconsin-La Crosse 608-785-8000
1725 State Street Fax: 608-785-6460
La Crosse, WI 54601 www.uwlax.edu
Bob Hetzel, Vice Chancellor
Vickie Baer, University Exec Staff Assis

5290 Robert J Bernard Biological Field Station
1400 N Amherst Avenue 909-398-1751
Claremont, CA 91711 wallace.meyer@pomona.edu
www.bfs.claremont.edu/

Robert J. Bernard, Biological Field Station
Dr. Wallace Meyer III, Director

5291 Rocky Mountain Biological Laboratory
PO Box 519 970-349-7231
Crested Butte, CO 81224 Fax: 970-349-7481
admin@rmbl.org
www.rmbl.org
High-altitude field station whose principal purpose is to provide quality research and teaching facilities for biologists and biology students of all diciplines who can benefit personally and intellectually from studying at thislocation. An important further purpose of the Laboratory is to promote the understanding and protection of the high altitude ecosystems of Colorado and the watershed of the Gunnison River through through the professional activities of its members.
Scott Wissinger, President
Carol M. Johnson, VP

5292 Rocky Mountain Mineral Law Foundation
9191 Sheridan Boulevard #203 303-321-8100
Westminster, CO 80031 Fax: 303-321-7657
info@rmmlf.org
www.rmmlf.org

Phillip R. Clark, President
Jonathan A. Hunter, Vice President

5293 Romberg Tiburon Centers
San Francisco State University
3152 Paradise Drive 415-338-6063
PO Box 855 Fax: 415-435-7120
Tiburon, CA 94920 jviale@sfsu.edu
www.rtc.sfsu.edu

Karina Nielsen, Director
Sheldon Axler, Dean

5294 Roosevelt Wildlife Station
1 Forestry Drive 315-470-6764
405 Illick Hall Fax: 315-470-6934
Syracuse, NY 13210 jpgibbs@syr.edu
www.esf.edu

Dr. James P. Gibbs, Director
Jacqueline L Frair, Associate Director

5295 Salt Institute
700 N. Fairfax St 703-549-4648
Suite 600 Fax: 703-548-2194
Alexandria, VA 22314-2040 info@saltinstitute.org
www.saltinstitute.org
The Salt Institute is an international trade association of salt producers. It has information about the environmental impacts of salt production and use.
Lori Roman, President
Morton Satin, VP

5296 School for Field Studies
100 Cummings Center 978-741-3567
Suite 534-G 800-989-4435
Beverly, MA 00191 Fax: 978-922-3835
sfs@fieldstudies.org
www.fieldstudies.org
Students conduct hands-on, community-focused environmental field work around the world. Addresses critical environmental issues including preserving entire ecosystems or individual species, balancing economic development andconservation, and

finding ways to manage and maintain wildlife, marine and agricultural resources.
James A. Cramer, President
Katlyn Osgood Armstrong, Vice President

5297 School of Marine Affairs (SMA)
University of Washington
University of Washington 206-543-7004
36 Gerberding Hall Fax: 206-543-1417
Seattle, WA 98195-6715 uwsmea@uw.edu
www.depts.washington.edu
SMA is a masters-level, professional school within the University of Washington specializing in the interdisciplinary teaching and research on contemporary coastal and ocean resources, environmental and developmental problems.
Suanty Kaghan, Admin Specialist
Tiffany Dion, Program Advisor

5298 Science and Public Policy
Rockefeller University 212-327-8000
1230 York Avenue, Box 234 Fax: 212-327-7974
New York, NY 10065-6399 www.rockefeller.edu
David Rockefeller, Honorary Chair
Russel L. Carson, Chair

5299 Seatuck Foundation: Seatuck Research Program
Seatuck Environmental Association 631-581-6908
PO Box 31 staff@seatuck.org
Islip, NY 11751 www.seatuck.org
Anthony Graves, President
Lucinda Mullin, Co-VP

5300 Society for Ecological Restoration
1017 O Street NW 202-299-9518
Washington, DC 20001 Fax: 520-622-5491
info@ser.org
www.ser.org
Cara R. Nelson, Chair
Alan Unwin, Vice Chair

5301 Society for the Application of Free Energy
1315 Apple Avenue 301-587-8686
Silver Spring, MD 20910 Fax: 301-587-8688

5302 Soil and Water Research
4115 Gourrier Avenue 225-757-7726
Baton Rouge, LA 70808 Fax: 225-757-7728
mse.ars.usda.gov/la/btn/swr/
Mission is to characterize and quantify the transport and fate of agrochemicals in high water table soils, develop integrated soil, water, and agrochemical management systems that provide profitable yields and improve water table soilsin the humid, warm temperature areas of the US and develop improved soil and water management systems and operational procedures that enhance crop production conditions and increase the efficiency of conducting farming operationsin a timely manner.
Dr. James Fouss, Research Leader

5303 Solar Energy Group
University of Chicago
1835 E 6th Street 480-884-1603
Suite 24 Fax: 480-884-1888
Tempe, AZ 85281 solareg@gmail.com

5304 South Carolina Agromedicine Program
Medical University of South Carolin 843-792-2211
179 Ashley Avenue, Colcock Hall 800-922-5250
Charleston, SC 29425 Fax: 843-792-4702
Simpsowm@musc.edu
www.musc.edu
Information, consultation, referral service for professional and lay persons involved in or in contact with agriculture or agricultural products.
Raymond G. Greenberg, President
Dr. Mark Sothmann, VP for Academic Affairs/Prov

5305 South Carolina Sea Grant Consortium
287 Meeting Street 843-953-2078
Charleston, SC 29401 Fax: 843-953-2080
www.scseagrant.org
A state agency that supports coastal and marine research, education, outreach, one technical assistance program that foster sustainable economic development and resource conservation. The consortium represents eight university andstate research organizations and induces a number of information products on coastal and marine resource topics.
16 pages
Alvin A. Taylor, Board Chair/Director
David A DeCenzo, Ph.D., President

5306 Southern California Pacific Coastal Water Research Project
3535 Harbor Blvd 714-755-3200
Suite 110 Fax: 714-755-3299
Costa Mesa, CA 92626 www.sccwrp.org
SCCWRP is a joint powers agency focusing on marine environmental research. A joint powers agency is one that is formed when several government agencies have a common mission that can be better addressed by pooling resources andknowledge. In our case, the common mission is to gather the necessary scientific information so that our member agencies can effectively and cost-efficiently protect the Southern California marine environment.
Dr. Stephen Weisberg, Executive Director
Ken Schiff, Deputy Director

5307 Southwest Consortium on Plant Genetics & Water Resources
New Mexico State University 575-646-0111
Box 3GL 800-662-6678
Las Cruces, NM 88003 admissions@nmsu.edu
www.nmsu.edu
Dr. John D Kemp, Chairman
Garrey Carruthers, President

5308 Strom Thurmond Institute of Government & Public Affairs, Regional Development Group
Clemson University 864-656-4700
Clemson, SC 29634
Jeffrey S. Allen, Director
Carolyn Benson, Administrative Analyst

5309 Stroud Water Research Center
970 Spencer Road 610-268-2153
Avondale, PA 19311 Fax: 610-268-0490
webmaster@stroudcenter.org
www.stroudcenter.org
The Stroud Water Research Center seeks to understand streams and rivers and to use the knowledge gained from its research to promote environmental stewardship and resolve freshwater challenges throughout the world.
Bernard W. Sweeney, President/Director/Sr. Resea
David B. Arscott, VP

5310 Sustainable Agriculture Research & Education Program
ASI at UC Davis

One Shields Avenue
Davis, CA 95616
530-752-3915
Fax: 530-752-2829
asi@ucdavis.edu
www.sarep.ucdavis.edu

Tom Tomich, Director
Raoul Adamchak, CSA Coordinator

5311 Tennessee Cooperative Fishery Research Unit

Tennessee Technological University
PO Box 5114
Cookeville, TN 38505
931-372-3094
Fax: 931-372-6257
jim_layzer@tntech.edu
www.tntech.edu

Betty Harris, Administrative Associate 3
Kendall Moles, Research Assistant 3

5312 Texas Center for Policy Studies

707 Rio Grande
Suite 200
Austin, TX 78701
512-474-0811
Fax: 512-474-7846
tcps@texascenter.org
www.texascenter.org

David Hall, Chair/Board Member
Cyrus Reed, Treasurer/Board Member

5313 Texas Water Resources Institute

500 Research Parkway A110
2260 TAMU
College Station, TX 77843-2260
979-845-1851
Fax: 979-845-0662
twri@tamu.edu

Roel Lopez, Interim Director
Kevin Wagner, Assoc. Director

5314 The Natural History Museum & Biodiversity Research Center

University of Kansas
Dyche Hall
1345 Jayhawk Boulevard
Lawrence, KS 66045-7593
785-864-4540
Fax: 785-864-5335
naturalhistory@ku.edu

At the UK Natural History Museum & Biodiversity Research Center, they study the life of the planet for the benefit of the earth and its inhabitants. They document the diverse life of the earth, uncover its patters and document theresearch in order to better understand the natural environments, enhance power to predict environmental phenomena, and provide knowledge for natural resource management. Their ability to discover, document and diesseminate their research leads thenation.

Dr. Leanord Krishtalka, Director-Admin
Linda Trueb, Assoc. Director

5315 Throckmorton-Purdue Agricultural Center

615 West State Street
US 231
West Lafayette, IN 47907-2053
765-494-8392
Fax: 765-538-3423
jayyoung@purdue.edu
www.ag.purdue.edu

Jay Akridge, Sample Dean of Agriculture
Marcos . Fernandez, Associate Dean

5316 Toxic Chemicals Laboratory

Cornell University
Cornell University, Tower Road
New York State College of Agriculture
Ithaca, NY 14853
607-255-4538

5317 US Forest Service: Wildlife Habitat & Silviculture Laboratory

USDA Forest Service, Southern Resea
P.O. Box 3516 UAM
Monticello, AR 71656
870-367-3464
Fax: 870-367-1164
www.srs.fs.usda.gov

We assess impacts of forest management practices on wildlife populations and their habitats and provide guide lines to land managers for improving their management to accommodate wildlife.

Cory K. Adams, Wildlife Biologist
Gina Franke, Support Services Specialist

5318 USDA Forest Service: Northern Research Station

11 Campus Blvd.
Suite 200
Newtown Square, PA 19073
610-557-4017
610-557-4132
Fax: 517-355-5121
rhaack@fs.fed.us
www.nrs.fs.fed.us

Michael T Rains, Director
Deb Dietzman, Assistant Director

5319 USDA Forest Service: Rocky Mountain Research Station

240 West Prospect
Fort Collins, CO 80526
970-498-1100
Fax: 970-295-5927
www.fs.fed.us

We seek to be an unbiased source of scientific information; provide tools that consider the multidisciplinary nature of natural resource decisions and recognize that resource managers need scientific information that is integrated anddeveloped for application. Research results are made available through a variety of technical reports, seminars, demonstrations, exhibits and personal consultations. These help resource managers and planners balance economic and environmental demandsworldwide.

Cloetta Schroeder, AD Operations
Angela Baca, Director

5320 UVA Institute for Environmental Negotiation

University of Virginia
The Institute for Environmental Neg
PO Box 400179
Charlottesville, VA 22904-4179
434-924-1970
Fax: 434-924-0231
ed7k@virginia.edu
www.virginia.edu/ien

The Institute for Environmental Negotiation is committed to building a sustainable future for Virginia's communities and beyond by: bringing people together to develop sustainable solutions; providing people with learning opportunitiesto be creative and collaborative leaders; and building understanding of best collaborative practices.

Dr E Franklin Dukes PhD, Director
Tanya Denckla Cobb, Associate Director

5321 University Forest

University of Missouri
2600 Bay Area Boulevard
Houston, TX 77058
281-286-5959
Fax: 281-286-2095
info@universityforestUHCL.com
www.universityforestuhcl.com

Lawrance Samaranayake, Manager
Steven Fance, Maintenance Assistant

5322 VT Forest Resource Center and Arboretum

University of Tennessee
901 S Illinois Avenue
Oak Ridge, TN 37830
865-483-3571
Fax: 865-483-3572
utforest@utk.edu

The UT Forestry Experiment Station mission is to:(1) provide the land and supporting resources necessary for conducting modern and effective forestry, wildlife, and associated social, biological and ecological research programs;(2)demonstrate the application of optimal forest and wildlife management technologies; and (3) assist with transfer of new technology to forest land owners and industries.

Kevin P. Hoyt, Center Director
Lynne Lucas, Administrative Specialist I

5323 Vantuna Research Group

Moore Laboratory of Zoology

Occidental College
1600 Campus Road
Los Angeles, CA 90041
323-259-2500
Fax: 323-259-2958
admission@oxy.edu
www.oxy.edu

John S Stephens, Director

5324 Virginia Center for Coal & Energy Research
Virginia Tech
Mail Code 0411
Blacksburg, VA 24061
540-231-5038
Fax: 540-231-4078
vccer@vt.edu
www.energy.vt.edu

Created by an Act of the VA General Assembly in 1977 as a study, research, information and resource facility for the commonwealth of VA, and is located at VA Tech. The mission involves four primary functions: research in energy andcoal related issues of interest to the Commonweatlth; coordination of coal and energy research at VA Tech; dissemination of coal and energy data to users in the Commonwealth; examination of socio-economic implications and environmental impacts ofcoal and energy.
K. Scott Keim, President
John R. Craynon, Director

5325 Washington Cooperative Fishery Research Unit
University of Washington
Box 355020
Seattle, WA 98195-5020
206-543-6475
www.depts.washington.edu
Dr. Christian Grue, Unit Leader
Dr. Glenn VanBlaricom, Asst. Unit Leader

5326 Waste Management Education & Research Consortium
New Mexico State University
Box 30001, MSC WERC
Las Cruces, NM 88003
505-646-2038
800-523-5996
Fax: 505-646-4149
iee@nmsu.edu
www.ieenmsu.com

A key component of WERC is higher education degree programs. To support this component, WERC administers a Fellowship Program at each academic partner institution. The primary objective for the WERC Fellowship program is to helpstudents develop a program which will lead to environmental related career opportunities upon graduation.
Barbara Valdez, Program Facilitator
Paul K. Anderson, Associate Professor

5327 Waste Management Research & Education Institute
University of Tennessee
The EERC & the University of Tennes
676 Dabney Hall
Knoxville, TN 37996
865-974-1000
Fax: 865-974-8086
ceb@utk.edu
Jack N. Barkenbus, Executive Director
Kim Davis, Asst. Director

5328 Water Quality Laboratory
Western Wyoming Community College
PO Box 428
Rock Springs, WY 82901
307-382-1662
www.wwcc.cc.wy.us/
Craig Thompson, Director

5329 Water Resource Center
University of Minnesota
173 McNeal Hall
1985 Buford Avenue
St Paul, MN 55108
612-624-9282
Fax: 612-625-1263
umwrc@umn.edu
www.wrc.umn.edu

The center coordinatoes research, education and extension programs on water resource issues. Administrative responsibility for Water Resource Sciences Graduate Program. Is the Water Resources Institute for Minnesota.
Faye Sleeper, Co-Director
Deborah L. Swackhamer, Co-Director

5330 Water Resources Institute
University of Wisconsin
1975 Willow Drive
Floor 2
Madison, WI 53706-1103
608-262-0905
Fax: 608-262-0591
hurley@aqua.wisc.edu
www.wri.wisc.edu

The University of Wisconsin Water Resources Institute's primary mission is to plan, develop and coordinate research programs that address present and emerging water-and land-related issues. It has developed a broadly based statewideprogram of basic and applied research that has effectively confronted a spectrum of societal concerns. It is one of 54 institutes or centers located at the Land Grant College in each state.
James Hurley, Director
Terri Liebmann, Assistant Director/Accountin

5331 Water Resources Research Institute at Kent University
Kent State University
800 E. Summit St.
PO Box 5190
Kent, OH 44240
330-672-3000
Fax: 330-672-4834
info@kent.edu
www.kent.edu

The institute fosters a broad-based approach to the evaluation and analysis of environmental problems related to water use. WRRI is a resouce for citizens, governmental agencies and policy makers, providing reliable scientificinformation on which to base decisions related to the wise use and management of water and land management, water policy decisions and environmental conservation.
Beverly Warren, President
Edward G. Mahon, Vice President

5332 Water Resources Research of the University of North Carolina
North Carolina State University
1575 Varsity Drive, Module 7
NCSU Campus Box 7912
Raleigh, NC 27695-7912
919-515-2815
Fax: 919-515-2839
www.ncsu.edu

One of 54 state water institutes authorized to administer and promote federal/state partnerships in research and information transfer on water-related issues. Identifies and supports research needed to help solve water quality andwater resources problems in NC. Publishes peer-reviewed reports on completed research projects. Sponsors educational seminars and conferences and provides public information on water issues through publication of a newsletter.
William R. Woodson, Chancellor
Kevin D. Howell, Assistant to the Chancellor

5333 Water Testing Laboratory
Morehead State University
150 University Blvd.
Morehead, KY 40351
606-783-2961
800-585-6781
Rita Wright, Contact

5334 Weather Analysis Center
University of Michigan
Space Research Building
2455 Hayward Street
Ann Arbor, MI 48109
734-936-0482
Fax: 734-763-0437
dbaker@umich.edu

Atmospheric, planetary and space science engineering.
Dr Dennis Baker, Director

5335 West Virginia Water Research Institute
West Virginia University
Room 202 NRCCE
Box 6064
Morgantown, WV 26506
304-293-4974
Fax: 304-293-7822
pziemkie@wvu.edu
www.wvwri.org

The West Virginia Water Research Institute (WVWRI) has served as a statewide vehicle for performing research related to water issues. WVWRI serves as the coordinating body for the following programs: the National Mine Land ReclamationCenter, Appalachian Clean Streams Initiatve, Acid Drainage Technology Initiative, Northern WV Brownfields Assistant Center, Hydrogeology Research Center, State Water Institutes, and more.
Paul F. Ziemkiewicz, PhD, Director
Tamara F. Vandivort, Assoc. Director

5336 Western Research Farm
36515 Highway 34 E 712-885-2802
Castana, IA 51010 wroush@iastate.edu
Wayne B Roush, Ag Specialist

5337 Wetland Biogeochemistry Institute
University of Florida 352-392-1803
106 Newell Hall, Box 110510 Fax: 225-388-6423
Gainesville, FL 32611
William H Patrick Jr, Director
K. Ramesh Reddy

5338 Wilderness Institute: University of Montana
School of Forestry 406-243-5361
32 Campus Drive 800-462-8636
Missola, MT 59812 Fax: 406-243-4845
wi@cfc.umt.edu
www.cfc.umt.edu

Mission is to further understand wilderness and its stewardship through education, outreach, and scholarship. Activity is guided by the philosophy that wildlands are increasingly significant, ecologically and socially, and educateddialogue about the role of wild places in our nation's future should be promoted. Engaged in undergraduate education, graduate student research, the dissemination of wilderness information and the promotion of scholarship on wilderness issues.
Wayne Freimund, Director
Michael Patterson, Associate Dean

5339 Wilderness Research Center
University of Idaho
College of Natural Resources 208-885-7911
Room 18a Fax: 208-885-6226
Moscow, ID 83844-1139 wrc@uidaho.edu

The mission of the WRC is to study the human dimensions of wilderness ecosystems. The WRC conducts research and teaches courses on the use of wilderness for personal growth, therapy, education, and leadership development.
Steve Hollenhorst, Ph.D, Director
Lilly Steinhorst, Administrative Assistant

5340 Wisconsin Applied Water Pollution Research Consortium: University of Wisconsin-Madison
University of Wisconsin
3232 Engineering Hall 608-263-7773
1415 Engineering Drive Fax: 608-262-5199
Madison, WI 53706-1691 harringt@engr.wisc.edu
www.engr.wisc.edu

This consortium seeks effective and economical solutions to water supply problems and pollution control in Wisconsin. It conducts innovative practical research that cannot be carried out effectively by individual organizations.
Ian M. Robertson, Dean
James P. Blanchard, Executive Associate Dean

5341 Wisconsin Rural Development Center
USDA Rural Development-WI
P.O. Box 66889 715-345-7600
St. Louis, MO 63166 800-414-1226
Fax: 314-457-4431
RD.Webmaster@wi.usda.gov
www.rd.usda.gov/wi

Lisa Mensah, Under Secretary
Edna Primrose, Deputy Administrator

5342 Wisconsin Sea Grant Institute
University of Wisconsin
1975 Williw Drive 608-262-0905
Floor 2 Fax: 608-262-0591
Madison, WI 53706-1103 hurley@aqua.wisc.edu
www.seagrant.wisc.edu

The University of Wisconsin Sea Grant Institute is a statewide program of basic and applied research, education, and technology transfer dedicated to the wise stewardship and sustainable use of Great Lakes and ocean resources. It ispart of a national network of 30 university-based programs.
James Hurley, Director
Terri Liebmann, Assistant Director/Accountin

5343 Yale Institute for Biospheric Studies (YIBS)
21 Sachem Street 203-432-9856
PO Box 208105 Fax: 203-432-9927
New Haven, CT 00652-8105 roserita.riccitelli@yale.edu
www.yale.edu/yibs

Oswald J. Schmitz, Director
Toya Sealy Cotto, Sr. Administrative Assistant

Educational Resources & Programs

Universities

5344 Academy for Educational Development
Center for Environmental Strategies
1825 Connecticut Avenue NW
Washington, DC 20009
202-884-8000
Fax: 202-884-8400
web@aed.org
www.fhi360.org

Develops sustainable solutions to global environmental protection and natural resource management problems through individual and institutional behavior change, education, training and communication strategies. Efforts are driven by astrong commitment to improve or maintain environmental quality as well as the quality of life for diverse communities and groups through the provision of technical assistance, guided practice and capacity building support.
Patrick C. Fine, Chief Executive Officer
Robert S. Murphy, MBA, Chief Financial Officer

5345 Allegheny College
Environmental Science/Studies
520 North Main Street
Meadville, PA 16335
814-332-3100
info@allegheny.edu
www.allegheny.edu

Offers the study of interrelationships between human activities and the environment. Two major programs: 1) Environmental Science. Core courses include biology, chemistry, geology, and mathematics. Upper level courses synthesize,integrate and apply basic sciences toward solving real environmental problems; 2) Environmental Studies. Objective is to study the concept of sustainability in an integrated way.
Barbara D. Riess, Chairperson
Richard J Cook, President

5346 Antioch College
Glen Helen Outoor Education Center
1075 State Route 343
1 Morgan Place
Yellow Springs, OH 45387
937-319-6082
Fax: 937-767-6655
www.antiochcollege.org

Training in residential naturalist instruction for upper elementary aged students. Classes and field experience in outdoor education methods and natural history. Care for hawk or owl in Raptor Center.
Mark Roosevelt, President
Hassan Rahmanian, VP

5347 Antioch University/New England
Environmental Studies
40 Avon Street
Keene, NH 00343-3516
800-553-8920
Fax: 603-357-0718
admissions@antiochne.edu
www.antiochne.edu

For those committed to scholarly excellence and wish to design, implement and evaluate research regarding crucial environmental issues. The PhD program cultivates a dynamic learning community of environmental practioners who addresscomplex regional, national, and global issues responsibly, creatively, and compassionately.
Charlton MacVeagh, Chair
Stephen B. Jones, President

5348 Antioch University/Seattle
Center for Creative Change
2326 Sixth Avenue
Seattle, WA 98121
206-441-5352
www.antiochseattle.edu

Approches environmental concerns by emphasizing social science perspectives and natural science literacy. The program is part of the Center for Creative Change, an integrated professional studies center.
Dan Hocoy, President
Tsegereda Giorgis, Director of Finance

5349 Arkansas Tech University
Wildlife Conservation Program
1605 Coliseum Drive
Suite 141
Russellville, AR 72801
479-968-0389
800-582-6953
sdonnell@atu.edu
www.atu.edu

A two-year preparatory program in Wildlife Conservation with an outlined Wildlife Curriculum was developed at Arkansas Tech University in 1956. Two years later, plans were made to elevate this program to a four-year program. During the1959-1960 academic year, a full slate of courses was developed that provided the foudation for degree that specialized in fisheries and wildlife management.
Shauna Donnell, Vice President
Robin E. Bowen, President

5350 Auburn University
Environmental Institute
1090 South Donahue Drive
Auburn, AL 36849
334-844-4132
Fax: 334-844-4462
kochafr@auburn.edu
www.auburn.edu

Serves faculty, governments, and the general public in a coordinating role to bring together teams to develop acceptable and economically feasible means of enhancing the environmental quality of the state and nation.
Samuel Fowler, Director
M. Kay Stone, Program Administrator

5351 Ball State University
Natural Resources and Environmental Management
2000 West University
Muncie, IN 47306
765-289-1241
800-382-8540
Fax: 765-285-2606
nrem@bsu.edu
www.bsu.edu/nrem

The Natural Resources and Environmental Management Department enhances scientific competence and prepares students for a variety of environmental careers. Programs focus on air, energy, land, parks, recreation, soil, waste management,and water and emergency management.
Rick Hall, Chairperson
Paul W. Ferguson, President

5352 Bard College
Environmental and Urban Studies
PO Box 5000
Annandale-on-Hudson, NY 12504-5000
845-758-6822
admission@bard.edu
www.bard.edu

This program focuses on both the lived and built environments. Its goal is to involve students in empirically-based studies that bridge the divisions between natural and artificial, given and created. This approach is designed to buildon the transformations within a range of social and natual sciences, ranging from systems theory to enviornmental toxicology.
Sanjib Baruah, Director
Felicia Keesing, Professor

5353 Bemidji State University
Center for Environmental, Earth & Space Studies
1500 Birchmont Drive NE
Bemidji, MN 56601-2699
218-755-2001
800-475-2001
Fax: 218-755-4048
fchang@bemidjistate.edu
www.bemidjistate.edu/

The Center for Environmental, Earth and Space Studies (CEESS) offer a unique variety of interdisciplinary degree programs. Degrees in Environmental Studies include both B.S. and M.S., and a

B.S. or B.A. with geology minor is alsoavailable. Students in the CEESS program are concerned with both the technological problems and social apects of enviromental issues.
Dr. Richard Hanson, President
Karen Snorek, VP Finance

5354 Bradley University
Geological Sciences Program
1501 West Bradley Avenue 309-676-1000
Peoria, IL 61625 800-447-6460
www.bradley.edu/admissions
Aims to develop an awareness of the Earth as a dynamic and unified system in time and space. Curriculum is preparatory for careers in geology, engineering geology, geophysics, hydrogeology, oceanography or secondary Earth scienceteaching.
Dr. Stan Liberty, Interim President
Dr. Joan Sattler, Interim Provost

5355 Brooklyn College
Environmental Studies
PO Box 8102 718-951-4159
Pittsburgh, PA 15217 Fax: 718-951-4546
yklein@brooklyn.cuny.edu
www.envirolink.org
Program is aimed at educating students to be fluent in social and physical sciences as related to the environment. In addition, the program draws from other courses in humanities, social sciences, mathematics, and sciences. Thisinterdisciplanary approach is designed to introduce the field of environmental studies and to apply this knowledge to various careers.
Yehuda Klein, Deputy Director

5356 Brown University
Center for Environmental Studies
135 Angel Street 401-863-1000
Box 1943 Fax: 401-863-3503
Providence, RI 00291 janet_blume@brown.edu
www.brown.edu
The Center for Environmental Studies at Brown University was established with the primary aim of educating individuals to solve challenging environmental problems both at the local and global levels. It also works directly to improvehuman well-being and environmental quality through community, city, and state partnerships in service and research.
Crystal Caesar, Financial Coordinator
Mariella DaSilva, Administrative Assistant

5357 California Polytechnic State University
Institute for City & Regional Planning
California Polytechnic State Univer 805-756-1111
San Luis Obispo, CA 93407-283 Fax: 805-756-1340
www.planning.calpoly.edu
Developed to coordinate interdisciplinary projects and research relating to the management of watersheds, urban areas, marine environments and related natural and human resources. The Institute offers specialists in various areas suchas biological science, business administation, city and regional planning, civil and environmental engineering, economics, geology, landscape architecture, natural resources management, political science and soil science.
Hemalata C. Dandekar, Department Head
Kathy Lehmkuhl, Administrative Support Coord

5358 California State University/Fullerton
Environmental Studies
PO Box 34080 714-278-2011
Fullerton, CA 92834-9480 arwebmaster@fullerton.edu
www.fullerton.edu
The Environmental Studies program is an interdisciplinary program that broadens environmental knowledge and awareness. It's designed to prepare students as professionals in the environmental field by providing an opportunity to learnapplicable skills and to develop an appropriate body of knowledge.
Mildred Garcia, President
Danny C. Kim, VP Finance/CFO

5359 California State University/Seaside
Capstone Project Program
100 Campus Center 831-582-3689
Building 42 laura_lienk@csumb.edu
Seaside, CA 93955-8001
Capstone Projects encompass a broad array of student interests, primarily within the programs of Earth Systems Science and Policy. A Capstone Project is similar to a senior thesis project at other universites, and showcases mastery ofESSP skills. They follow a set of outcome based, interdisciplinary criteria used to measure the competence of participants.
Laura Lee Lienk, Co-Director
Doug Smith, Co-Director

5360 California University of Pennsylvania
Biological & Environmental Sciences
250 University Avenue 724-938-4000
California, PA 15419 www.calu.edu
Department includes intensive scientific curricula that prepare students for graduate work in the biological and environmental sciences and career work in related areas.
Guido M. Pichini, Chairman
Geraldine M. Jones, Interim President

5361 Carnegie Mellon University
Civil and Environmental Engineering Program
5000 Forbes Avenue 412-268-2940
119 Porter Hall Fax: 412-268-7813
Pittsburgh, PA 15213 www.ce.cmu.edu
A major function of the Environmental Institute is to enable Carnegie Mellon to play a leadership role in developing educational programs on environmental issues. These include initiatives at both undergraduate and graduate levels.
Irving Oppenheim, Interim Department Head
Deborah Lange, Executive Director

5362 Clark University
Environmental Science & Policy
950 Main Street 508-793-7711
Worcester, MA 00161 idce@clarku.edu
www.clarku.edu/
An interdisciplinary approach that emphasizes policy questions involving the environment and use and misuse of science and technology. Its goal is to enable individuals to deal with technical and environmental issues in social andpolitical areas. Topics addresses deal with urgent and important issues, including assessment and management of environmental risks to humans and ecosystems, capacity for sustainable development in third world countriie, and integrated watershedmanagement.
David P. Angel, President
Davis Baird, Provost/VP for Academic Affa

5363 Clemson University
Environmental Engineering and Earth Sciences
Clemson University 864-656-3311
Clemson, SC 29634 www.clemson.edu
Programs in the environmental field focus on environmental process engineering, hydrogeology, environmental health physics and radiochemistry, environmental chemistry and sustainable systems.
Esin Gulari, Dean

5364 Colby-Sawyer College
Community & Environmental Studies
541 Main Street 603-526-3000
New London, NH 00325 www.colby-sawyer.edu

Bachelor of Science degree in Community and Environmental Studies. A minor in CES is also available.
Thomas C. Csatari, Chair
Thomas C. Galligan, President

5365 College of Natural Resources
Conservation Management Institute
1900 Kraft Drive
Suite 250
Blacksburg, VA 24061
540-231-7348
Fax: 540-231-7019
CMIinfo@vt.edu
www.cmi.vt.edu
Offers multi-disciplinary research that addresses conservation management effectiveness throughout the world. Faculty from far reaching research institutions work collaboratively on projects ranging from endangered species propagationto natural resource-based satellite imagery interpretation.
Scott D Klopfer, Director
Caitlin Carey, Research Fishery? Biologist

5366 College of William and Mary
Center for Conservation Biology
PO Box 1346
1375 Greate Road
Gloucester Point, VA 23062-1346
804-684-7000
Fax: 804-684-7097
wmaster@vims.edu
www.vims.edu/
The Center for Conservation Biology is an organization dedicated to discovering innovative solutions to environmental problems that are both scientifically sound and practical within today's social context. It has been a leader inconservation issues throughout the mid-Atlantic region with a philosophy that uses a general systems approach to locate critical information needs and to plot a deliberate course of action to reach goals.
John T. Wells, Dean And Director
Jennifer Latour, CFO/CAO

5367 Colorado Mountain College
Natural Resource Management Program
802 Grand Avenue
Glenwood Springs, CO 81601
970-945-8691
800-621-8559
Fax: 970-947-8324
servicedesk@coloradomtn.edu
www.coloradomtn.edu
The Natural Resource Management program grew out of the Environmental Technology, which was one of the most well established programs of its kind in the country. It specializes in helping students graduate with entry-level skills in avariety of environmental fields, while combining aquatic and terrestrial resource management. Students are trained in career fields of environmental site assessment, hydrology, soil science, environmental law and others.
Ken Brenner, Treasurer
Glenn Davis, President

5368 Colorado School of Mines
Environmental Engineering & Applied Science
1500 Illinois Street
Golden, CO 80401
303-273-3000
800-446-9488
www.mines.edu
This public research university devoted to engineering and applied science, offers a curriculum and research program that is geared toward responsible stewardship of the earth and its resources. It has broad expertise in resourceexploration, extration, production and utilization. The programs at Mines are central to balancing resource availability with environmental protection.
James Spaanstra, Chairman
Richard Truly, Vice Chairman

5369 Colorado State University
College of Natural Resouses
101 Natural Resources Building
Campus Delivery 1401
Fort Collins, CO 80523-1401
970-491-6675
Fax: 970-491-0279
www.warnercnr.colostate.edu
The College of Natural Resources is one of the most comprehensive environment and natural resources programs in the nation. With four departments and eight undergraduate majors, 9 minors and 13 concentrations, students address the mostcurrent issues in environment and natural resources, including endangered species, water quality, biological diversity, parks forests and wildlife management, recreation and environmental and ecosystem sciences.
Joyce Berry, Dean
Scott Webb, Director of Development

5370 Columbia University
Public Admin in Environmental Science & Policy
116th and Broadway
New York, NY 10027
212-854-1754
www.columbia.edu
The program is designed to train sophisticated public managers and policymakers who apply innovative, system-based thinking to environmental issues. It emphasizes practical skills and is enriched by ecological and plantatary science.
Lee C. Bollinger, President
John H. Coatsworth, Provost

5371 Connecticut College
Goodwin Niering Center for Conservation Biology
270 Mohegan Avenue
Box 5293
New London, CT 06320
860-447-1911
Fax: 860-439-5277
info@conncoll.edu
www.conncoll.edu
A comprehensive, interdisciplinary program aimed at understanding contemporary ecological challenges. Its Certificate Program offers students the opportunity to blend thier interest in the environment with a non-science major and is ofparticular interest to those planning careers in environmental policy, law, economies or education.
Ulysses B. Hammond, VP for Administration
Glenn Dreyer, Executive Director

5372 Conservation Leadership School
117 Forest Resources Building
University Park, PA 16802
814-865-7541
877-778-2937
Fax: 814-865-3725
www.ecosystems.psu.edu
A one-week residential program for high school students to learn about the world around them through exploration and hands-on activities. The classroom includes over 700 acres of forest, fields, wetlands, and streams, and learningabout the environment includes having fun, meeting new friends and learning leadership skills.
Michael G. Messina, Head/Professor
Linda Spangler, Manager

5373 Cornell University
Center for the Environment
Day Hall Lobby
Cornell University
Ithaca, NY 14853
607-254-4636
Fax: 607-254-6225
info@cornell.edu
www.cornell.edu
Offers opportunities for graduate study in the ecology, management, and policy of fishery, forest, wetland, wildlife, and other environmental resources. There also are opportunities to focus on conservation biology, agroforestry,environmetnal change, and conservation and sustainable development.
Elizabeth Garrett, President
Michael I. Kotlikoff, Provost

5374 Dartmouth College
Department of Earth Sciences
Dartmouth College
Hanover, NH 00375
603-646-1110
cantact@dartmouth.edu
www.dartmouth.edu/
Offers opportunities for learning and research in all major disciplines devoted to the study of the earth, including its structure and development, the oceans and atmosphere, weather and climate.

Teaching and research at a moreadvanced level emphasize watershed processes, environmental biogeochemistry, geophysics and mechanics, sedimentology, paleontology, economic geology, end remote sensing of the earth from aircraft and satellites.
Philip J. Hanlon '77, President
Martin N. Wybourne, Interim Provost/Vice Provost

5375 **Delaware Valley College**
Agronomy & Environmental Science
700 East Butler Avenue 215-345-1500
Doylestown, PA 18901 800-233-5825
webmaster@delval.edu
www.delval.edu
The Department of Agronomy and Environmental Science offers courses designed to give a broad, workable background in the plant, soil, turf or environmental sciences. Focusing on the environmental issues facing society today, thesecourses provide the knowledge and training necessary to be successful in the field or to move on to the graduate level.
Dorothy Prisco, Vice President

5376 **Drake University**
Environmental Science & Policy Program
2507 University Avenue 515-271-2011
Olin Hall 800-443-7253
Des Moines, IA 50311-4505 Fax: 515-271-3702
thomas.rosburg@drake.edu
www.drake.edu
Environmental Science and Policy Program is an interdisciplinary program that awards BS and BA degrees in both Environmental Science and Environmental Policy.
Joe Lenz, Interim Provost
Deneese Jones, Immediate Past Provost

5377 **Duke University/Marine Laboratory**
Nicholas School of the Environment
Marine Laboratory 252-504-7502
135 Duke Marine Lab Road Fax: 252-504-7648
Beaufort, NC 28516-9721 WEBMANAGER@NICHOLAS.DUKE.EDU
www.nicholas.duke.edu/marinelab
The Laboratory is a campus of Duke University and a unit within the Nicholas School of the Environment. The mission is education, research, and service to understand marine systems, including the human component, and to developapproaches for marine conservation and restoration.
Belinda Williford, Administrator
Cindy Van Dover, Director

5378 **Duquesne University**
Environmental Science & Management Program
600 Forbes Avenue 412-396-6000
Pittsburgh, PA 15282 www.duq.edu
Educating environmental professionals for the twenty-first century is the focus of this program, which grew out of the need to combine depth of knowledge in environmental science with a comprehensive understanding of the business,legal and policy implications surrounding environmental issues.
Charles J. Dougherty, President
Madelyn A. Reilly, J.D., VP for Legal Affairs & Gener

5379 **Eastern Illinois University**
Aquatic and Fisheries Program
600 Lincoln Avenue 217-581-5000
Charleston, IL 61920 877-581-2348
admissions@eiu.edu
www.eiu.edu
Offers aquatic ecology, fisheries biology, and physiological ecology. Specific areas of concentration include community analysis of stream fishes, life history and demographics of fish, bioenergetics of development and life historyphenomena, and lipid storage and utilization patterns of fish.
William L. Perry, President
Blair M. Lord, Provost

5380 **Eastern Michigan University**
Kresge Environmental Education Center
202 Welch Hall 734-487-1849
Ypsilanti, MI 48197 800-468-6368
Fax: 734-487-6559
tkasper@emich.edu
www.emich.edu
The Kresge Environmental Education Center is located in Mayfield, about six miles north east of the city of Lapeer. The main buildings are located on Fish Lake Road in the middle of the center's 240 acres. These 240 acres sit next to7,000 acres of state land.
Mike Morris, Chair
Mary Treder, Vice Chair

5381 **Eastern Nazarene College**
Eastern Environmental Program
23 East Elm Avenue 617-745-3000
Quincy, MA 00217 800-88E-NC88
Fax: 617-745-3907
jonathan.e.twining@enc.edu
www.enc.edu
Cross-disciplinary program which provides for students strong pereparation in the several scientific disciplines involved in the study of environmental issues. The program is jointly sponsored by the Department of Biology andChemistry in order to provide the appropriate basis in all the sciences for students wishing to pursue environmental careers or graduate school.
Elizabeth Buckley, Chair
Dr. Corlis McGee, President

5382 **Fairleigh Dickinson University**
Environmental Studies/System Science
1000 River Road 973-443-8500
Teaneck, NJ 00766 800-338-8803
Fax: 973-443-8921
www.fdu.edu
This program offers students a wide variety of 18 concentrations, including envionmental chemistry, environmental risk assessment, water treatment, environmental planning, groundwater hydrology, environmental remediation, soil science,land-use planning and air pollution.
Patrick J. Zenner, Chair
Sheldon Drucker, President

5383 **Ferrum College**
Environmental Science
PO Box 1000 540-365-2121
Ferrum, VA 24088 800-868-9797
Fax: 540-365-4203
webmaster@ferrum.edu
www.ferrum.edu
Offers programs in environmental science that includes informationon air pollutant deposition in the Great Lakes and the formulation of membrances for ion-selective electrodes. The program also includes participation in a water qualitymonitoring project on Smith Mountain Lake that uses a geographical information system to model soil loss in its watershed.
Samuel L. Lionberger, Chair
Jennifer L. Braaten, President

5384 **Field Station & Ecological Reserves**
University of Kansas
C/O Kansas Biological Survey 785-864-1500
2101 Constant Avenue Fax: 785-864-1534
Lawrence, KS 66047 biosurvey.ku.edu
The KSR is dedicated to field-based environmental reseach and education. KSR is located within the transition zone (ecotone) between the eastern deciduous forest and tallgrass prairie biomes. The 3,000 acres of diverse native andmanaged habitats, experimental systems, support facilities, and longterm databases are used to undertake an outstanding array of scholarly activities.

Environmental stewardship is a stong emphasis as high-quality natural areas are preserved for thefuture.
LeeAnn Bennett, Senior Research
Kirsten Bosnak, Communications Director

5385 Florida State University
Environmental Studies
600 W. College Avenue 850-644-2525
Tallahassee, FL 32306 Fax: 850-644-9936
admissions@admin.fsu.edu
www.fsu.edu
Offers the study of environmental issues as they relate to geological phenomena, which include volcanic and earthquake hazards, resource and land- use planning, air and water pollution, waste disposal, glaciation and sea-level change,landslides, flooding, shoreline erosion, and global change issues.
Eric J. Barron, President
Dr. Garnett S. Stokes, Provost

5386 George Washington University
International Environmental Policy & Management
2121 1st Street NW 202-994-1000
Washington, DC 20052 www.gwu.edu/
Offers a program on International Environmental Policy and Management and Marketing Management, held in various locations around the world
Steven Knapp, President
Steven R. Lerman, Provost

5387 Georgetown University - Environmental Studies
Environmental Studies
37th O Streets NW 202-687-0100
Washington, DC 20057 webmaster@georgetown.edu
www.georgetown.edu
Environmental Studies is an interdisciplinary program designed to allow an undergraduate of the college majoring in any discipline to learn about environmental issues. Environmental Studies provides a framework for the study offundamental mechanisms of ecosystems and human interaction with the Earth, encompassing the humanities, social sciences and natural sciences as they relate to environmental questions.
John J DeGioia, Ph.D, President
Christopher Augostini, Sr. VP & COO

5388 Hocking College
Environmental Restoration Technology Program
3301 Hocking Parkway 740-753-3591
Nelsonville, OH 45764 877-462-5464
Fax: 740-753-7065
admissions@hocking.edu
www.hocking.edu
Growing concern for the environment has increased the need for technicians qualified in the restoration of environmentally unstable land, water, and air. Hocking College's Environmental Restoration technology prepares students for thatchallenge.
Tammy Andrews

5389 Idaho State University
Geochemistry & Hydrogeology Program
921 South Eighth Avenue 208-282-0211
Pocatello, ID 83209 webmaster@isu.edu
www.isu.edu/
Emphasizes environmental geochemistry and hydrogeology. This specialty is ideal in southern Idaho where problems of nuclear and toxic waste clean-up at the Idaho National Environmental Engineering Laboratory will require study andgenerate research monies for years to come.
Robert A. Wharton, Provost And Vice President

5390 Indiana State University
Department of Ecology & Organismal Biology
200 North Seventh Street 812-237-4000
Terre Haute, IN 47809-1902 800-468-6478
Fax: 812-237-8525
www.indstate.edu/
This department conducts research in the areas of ecology, evolution, and conservation. The M.S. and Ph.D degrees garnered in state-of-the-art laboratories and local field stations enable students to conduct innovative research andplay significant roles as well-trained evnironmentists.
Dr. Daniel J. Bradley, President
David Campbell, Secretary

5391 Iowa State University
Environmental Studies Program
100 Enrollment Services Center 515-294-5836
Ames, IA 50011-2011 800-262-3810
Fax: 515-294-2592
contact@iastate.edu
www.iastate.edu
The Environmental Studies Program deals with the relationship between humans and nature, or between humans and natural systems. The curriculum is designed to give students an understanding of regional and global environmental issuesand an appreciation of different perspectives regarding these issues. Courses are provided for both students pursuing careers related to the environment and those with an interest in environmental issues.

5392 Johns Hopkins University
Department of Geography/Environmental Engineering
Wyman Park Building, 4th Floor 410-516-4050
3400 N Charles Street www.jhu.edu/
Baltimore, MD 21218
Concerned with understanding the nature and dynamics of ecosystems, engineered systems, and societies. Offers a broad range of graduate programs including the natural, social and engineering sciences.
Ronald J. Daniels, President
Jonathan A. Bagger, Interim Provost/Sr. VP for A

5393 Kansas State University
Department of Agricultural Economics
342 Waters Hall 785-532-6011
Manhattan, KS 66506 Fax: 785-532-6897
k-state@k-state.edu
www.k-state.edu
The Department of Agricultural Economics has a rich tradition of services to agriculture and related fields. The department has a history of succes in its land-grant mission, teaching, research, and extension outreach, maintaininglarge and diverse programs in undergraduate and graduate instruction, as well as research and extension outreach.
Kirk H Schulz, President
Dana Hastings, Administrative Assistant

5394 Keene State College
Environmental Studies
229 Main Street
Keene, NH 00343 800-572-1909
agagnon@keene.edu
www.keene.edu
Environmental Studies is an interdisciplinary program comprised of courses in Biology, Chemistry, Economics, Geography, Geology, and Political Science. Two concentration options are Environmental Policy and Enviromental Science, bothof which will prepare students for a wide range of environment-related career opportunities.
Anne E. Huot, President
Barbara A. Hall, Administrative Assistant

5395 Lake Erie College
Environmental Management Program

391 West Washington Street 440-296-1856
Painesville, OH 44077 800-533-4996
Fax: 440-375-7005
webmaster@lec.edu

Interdisciplinary major, grounded in the sciences and liberal arts,designed for those who want to pursue career paths utilizing environmental science in decision making. Courses include environmental management, biology, chemistry,mathamatics and business. Program is designed to help students build a solid knolwledge base in regional and global environmental issues.
Elizabeth Abraham, Owner/CEO
Richard J. Kessler, Treasurer

5396 **Louisiana State University**
Environmental Sciences Program
1271 Energy, Coast and Environment Building 225-578-9421
Fax: 225-578-4286
Baton Rouge, LA 70803 cstrom4@lsu.edu
www.environmental.lsu.edu

Environmental Sciences program is designed to provide a broad-based graduate education to prepare students for careers in industrial, government, and academia. The program builds on a strong undergraduate background in the sciences.
Larry Rouse, Chair/Assoc. Professor
Edward Laws, Interim Chair

5397 **Louisiana Tech University**
Wildlife Conservation Program
305 Wisteria Street 318-257-4287
PO Box 10197 ANSmail@ans.latech.edu
Ruston, LA 71272 www.ans.latech.edu/

The Wildlife Conservation degree program meets the certification requirements of the Wildlife Society, and graduates may apply for certification as an Associate Wildlife Biologist.
Sally Strickland, Administrative Coordinator
Betty T. Jensen, Administrative Assistant

5398 **Miami University**
Institute of Environmental Sciences
501 E. High St. 513-529-2531
Oxford, OH 45056-3434 admission@muohio.edu
miamioh.edu

Offers a masters degree in Environmental Science. This interdisciplinary program stresses problem solving and community service, and provides practical experience in many potential areas of concentration, preparing students for avariety of practical careers in public and private sector jobs.
David C. Hodge, President
Phyllis Callahan, Provost

5399 **Michigan Technological University**
Applied Technology & Environmental Science
1400 Townsend Drive 906-487-1885
Houghton, MI 49931-1295 800-966-3764
Fax: 906-487-2915
forest@mtu.edu
www.mtu.edu

A degree in Applied Ecology and Environmental Sciences prepares students to address complex environmental problems posed by the use of natural resources. Students learn how to protect the integrity of ecosystems and help assure thatnatural resources will be managed wisely for generations of sustainable use.
Glenn Mroz, President
Max Seel, Professor, Physics

5400 **Middlebury College**
Environmental Studies
121a South Main Street 802-443-5000
Middlebury, VT 00575 Fax: 802-443-2060
admissions@middlebury.edu
www.middlebury.edu

Explores the relationship between humans and their environment. Students pursuing the ES major work in a variety of disciplines, including biology, chemistry, economics, geography, geology, literature, the performing arts, philosophy,political science, religion and sociology.
Gregory B. Buckles, Dean of Admissions
Susan Campbell, Provost

5401 **Montana State University**
Montana Environmental Training Center
2100 16th Avenue South 406-265-3730
Great Falls, MT 59405 800-662-6132
webmaster@msun.edu
www.msun.edu/

A cooperative effort between Montana State University/Northern and the Montana Department of Environmental Quality. Offers basic, advance training, and continuing education in the areas of water and wastewater operation, maintenance,safety, process control, cross connection and backflow prevention along with courses in basic water science and watershed awareness. A newsletter and Training Announcement are published quarterly.
Greg Kegel, Chancellor
Marianne Hamilton, Administrative Assistant

5402 **Natural Resources and Environmental Science - Purdue University**
Purdue University, College of Agriculture
Lilly Hall of Life Sciences 765-496-9024
915 West State Street 888-398-4636
West Lafayette, IN 47907-2054 Fax: 765-494-5876
nres@purdue.edu
www.ag.purdue.edu

An interdisciplinary program at the Purdue School of Agriculture designed to prepare students to work with environmental problems which impact our basic natural resources: specifically land, air and water. NRES is a flexible programthat allows students, working closely with an academic advisor, to develop their personal curriculum to meet individual career goals.
Linda Prokopy, Ph.D, Co-Director
Tami J Borror, Academic Advisor

5403 **New Mexico State University**
Department of Geological Sciences
Box 30001 575-646-2708
MSC 3AB Fax: 575-646-1056
Las Cruces, NM 88003 geology@nmsu.edu
www.nmsu.edu

Offers both undergraduate and graduate study leading to advanced degrees in geological science. Advanced training qualifies students for employment in such branches of geological science as mining, petroleum, environmental andengineering geology, government service or for further graduate study. The education experience may include sedimentology, geochemistry, volcanology, stratigraphy, geotectonics and paleontology.
Lee Hubbard, Administrative Department
Dr. Nancy S. McMillan, Department Head

5404 **North Dakota State University**
Department of Biological Sciences
PO Box 6050 701-231-8011
Fargo, ND 58108-6050 Fax: 701-231-7149
www.ndsu.nodak.edu

Department offers undergraduate and graduate degrees in biological disciplines, including environmental and conservation sciences.
Dean Bresciani, President
Barb Pederson, Executive Assistant

5405 **Northeastern Illinois University**
International Center for Tropical Ecology
5500 N St. Louis 773-583-4050
Chicago, IL 60625-4699 Fax: 773-442-4900
admrec@neiu.edu
www.neiu.edu

The International Center for Tropical Ecology provides a focal point for interdisciplinary research and graduate education in all aspects of the conservation of tropical ecosystems. The Center, formed in collaboration with the MissouriBotanical Garden, supports a network in the United States of students, scientists, and conservationists from tropical countries to study issues related to biodiversity conservation.
Sharon Hahs, President
Richard J. helldobler, Provost/VP for Academic Affa

5406 Northern Arizona University
Environmental Sciences
South San Francisco Street 928-523-9011
Flagstaff, AZ 86011 Fax: 928-523-6023
www.nau.edu/
Designed to offer students a technically rigorous foundation and broad exposure to the environmental science. The core courses in environmental sciences are interdisciplinary, and team taught by scientists with different backgroundsand specialties, providing multiple perspectives and rich learning experiences.
John D. Haeger, President
Tom Acker, Professor of Mechanical Engi

5407 Northern Michigan University
Environmental Studies
1401 Presque Isle Avenue 906-227-1000
Marquette, MI 49855-5301 Fax: 906-227-2249
www.nmu.edu
Research focuses on the Upper Peninsula environment, ethnic groups, economy, politics, folklore and literature.
L. Garnet Lewis, Chair
Richard M. Popp, Vice Chair

5408 Northland College
Environmental Studies
1411 Ellis Avenue S 715-682-1699
Ashland, WI 54806 800-753-1840
Fax: 715-682-1308
info@northland.edu
www.northland.edu
Offers a comprehensive range of environmental programs that integrate traditional study with a keen eye toward problem-solving and environmental impact.
Karen Halbersleben, President
Rick Fairbanks, Provost

5409 Ohio State University
School of Environment and Natural Resources
2021 Coffey Road 614-292-2265
210 Kottman Hall Fax: 614-292-7432
Columbus, OH 43210 geise.1@osu.edu
www.senr.osu.edu
Focuses on the science and management of natural resources and the environment. A variety of integrated undergraduate programs of study provide the foundation to a variety of career paths dealing with natural resources and theenvironment. Graduates are employed as environmental and ecosystem scientists; forest, wildlife and fisheries reserchers and biologists; environmental educators, communicators and naturalists; and park, forest, and wildlife managers.
Olivia Ameredes, Fiscal Manager
Laura Hughes, Office Associate

5410 Oregon State University
Environmental Sciences
Corvallis, OR 97331 541-737-1000
Fax: 541-737-3590
OSU.Provost@oregonstate.edu
www.oregonstate.edu
Offers programs that are central to the mission of the university, which includes wise use of natural resources. Recognized as a Land, Sea, and Space Grant institution, OSU has exceptional strength in many of the disciplines that arerequired to provide a high-quality interdisciplinary education for future environmental scientists.
Dr. Edward J. Ray, President
Sabah U. Randhawa, Provost

5411 Pennsylvania State University
Center for Statistical Ecology
323 Thomas Building 814-865-1348
University Park, PA 16802 Fax: 814-863-7114
www.stat.psu.edu
This ground-breaking program enjoys national and international recognition. With an ongoing program of research that integrates statistics, ecology and the environment, the emphasis is on the environment and collaborative research,training and exposition on improving the quantification and communication of human impact on the environment. Studies also include statistical investigations of the impact of the environment on man.
Bonnie Cain, Financial Secretary
Barbara Freed, Administrative Assistant

5412 Portland State University
Environmental Sciences & Resources Program
PO Box 751 503-725-3000
Portland, OR 97207 Fax: 503-725-4882
psuinfo@pdx.edu
www.pdx.edu
Environmental studies are central to the mission of Portland State University, which serves the state's major urban center. The Environmental Sciences and Resources program offers both undergraduate and graduate degrees.
Win Wiewel, President
John Reuter, Program Director

5413 Prescott College
Department of Environmental Studies
220 Grove Avenue
Prescott, AZ 86301 877-350-2100
Fax: 928-776-5242
admissions@prescott.edu
www.prescott.edu/
Prescott College is a private liberal arts collage offering a resident BA and limited residency BA, MA, and PhD. Small groups of students work actively on real-world projects with faculty who are leaders in the field of environmentalstudies. Offers dynamic and active laboratories for students and gives them the opportunity to be on the cutting edge of environmental and sustainabilty research.
Paul Burkhardt, President/Ececutive VP
Frank Cardamone, Provost

5414 Rensselaer Polytechnic Institute
Lally School of Management and Technology
110 8th Street 518-276-2812
Pittsburgh Building www.lallyschool.rpi.edu
Troy, NY 12180
Committed to integrating green business strategy throughout all management curriculum. An MBA with an Environmental Management and Policy Concentration is truly designed as an interdisciplinary degree, enabling graduates to work intraditional business settings with the knowledge and skill to help these businesses realize environmental, health and safety strategy.
Thomas Begley, Dean
Chaina Porter, Administrative Coordinator

5415 Rice University
Urban & Environmental Policy Program
6100 Main 713-348-7423
PO Box 1892 800-527-OWLS
Huston, TX 77251 www.rice.edu

This program is designed to introduce students to how environmental policies are developed and how science and engineering issues are included in effective policy.
David W. Leebron, President
David K. Vassar, Sr. Asst. to the President

5416 Roger Williams University
Center for Environmental Development
One Old Ferry Road
Bristol, RI 00280
401-253-1040
800-458-7144
Fax: 401-254-3310
www.rwu.edu/
Undergraduate program in marine biology combining chemistry, biology, physics, and mathmatics. Designed to keep and develop interest in the sciences by using field research and laboratory experimentation.
Rodney A. Butler, Chairman
Donald J. Farish, President

5417 SUNY/Cortland
Coalition for Education in the Outdoors
Park Center
PO Box 2000
Cortland, NY 13045-900
607-753-4971
Fax: 607-753-5982
outdoored@outdooredcoalition.org
www.outdooredcoalition.org
A nonprofit network of outdoor and environmental education centers, nature centers, conservation and recreation organizations, outdoor education and experimential education associations, public and private schools and fish and wildlifeagencies. All those involved in the coalition share the desire to support and encourage environmental and outdoor education and its goals.
Erik J. Bitterbaum, President
Mark Prus, Provost

5418 SUNY/Fredonia
Environmental Sciences
280 Central Avenue
Fredonia, NY 14063
716-673-3111
800-252-1212
Fax: 716-673-3249
admissions@fredonia.edu
www.fredonia.edu/
Rigorous, interdisciplinary program in environmental science with 68 semester hours of core courses in mathematics, biology, chemistry, environmental sciences, and geosciences. Students are prepared to pursue graduate studies,professional certifications, or employment in the private or public sector.
Ginny Horvath, President
Mrs. Denise Szalkowski, Assistant to the President

5419 SUNY/Plattsburgh
Environmental Science
101 Broad Street
Plattsburgh, NY 12901
518-564-2000
One of the largest and most established environmental science programs in the US, with 20 interdisciplinary faculty and nearly 300 majors among five degree programs. Opportunities for hands-on work and practical experience are providedby close proximity to the Adirondack Mountains State Forest Preserve, Plattsburgh's location on the banks of Lake Champlain, and affiliations with the Miner Agricultural Research Institute and more.
John Ettling, President
Dr. James Liszka, Provost

5420 SUNY/Syracuse
College of Environmental Science & Forestry
One Forestry Drive
106 Bray Hall
Syracuse, NY 13210
315-470-6500
800-777-7373
Fax: 315-470-6933
esfinfo@esf.edu
www.esf.edu
As part of its education mission, SUNY offers an accredited engineering undergraduate program in Forest Engineering and graduate programs at both the masters and doctoral levels. The Faculty also conducts research and public serviceprograms that study how a variety of events affect our environment.
Vita DeMarchi, Chair
Matthew J. Marko, Vice Chair

5421 School for Field Studies
Environmental Field Studies
100 Cummings Center
Suite 534-G
Beverly, MA 00191
978-741-3567
800-989-4418
Fax: 978-922-3835
sfs@fieldstudies.org
www.fieldstudies.org
Teaches students to address critical environmental problems using an interdisciplinary experimental approach to education.
Terry Andreas, Chairman
James A. Cramer, President

5422 Slippery Rock University
Environmental Geosciences
1 Morrow Way
Slippery Rock, PA 16057
724-738-2015
800-929-4778
Fax: 724-738-2913
asktherock@sru.edu
www.sru.edu/
Prepares students for ocupations with industrial laboratories concerned with air, water and soil pollution control, engineering firms that study industrial pollution and prepare environmental impact statements, and state and federalagencies charged with monitoring the environment.
James Hathaway, Chair
Michael May, Director of Admissions

5423 Sonoma State University
Environmental Studies & Planning Program
1801 E Cotati Avenue
Rohnert Park, CA 94928-3609
707-664-2880
Fax: 707-644-4060
cynthia.jowers@sonoma.edu
www.sonoma.edu
Founded as an interdisciplinary program during a period of growing environmental concern. The department has evolved and matured, now stressing the development of a global prespective by synthesizing knowledge from a variety ofscientific and academic disciplines, the acquisition of specific professional skills through a focused course of study, and the application of knowledge and skills through effective strategies for environmental management.
Dr. Ruben Arminana, President
Lauren Furukawa-Schlereth, CFO and Vice President

5424 Southern Connecticut State University
Environmental Education Program
501 Crescent Avenue
Jennings Hall, Room 342
New Haven, CT 00651
203-392-7278
888-500-SCSU
Fax: 203-392-6614
information@southernct.edu
www.southernct.edu
This program focuses on practicality and application of theory bringing about environmental change through educational processes. The objective is to prepare well informed people who are dedicated to improving environmental conditions.
Cheryl J Norton, President
Susan Cusato, Chair Department of Science

5425 Southern Oregon University
Environmental Education Program
1250 Siskiyou Boulevard
Siskiyou Environmental Center
Ashland, OR 97520
541-552-6600
855-470-3377
Fax: 541-552-6614
presidentsoffice@sou.edu
www.sou.edu/
Designed to promote a better understanding of the environment and environmental issues, including an awarenesss and knowledge of biodiversity and ecosystem complexity. Seeks to prepare

students for active roles in education and socialchange related to resolution of environmental problems and conflicts affecting present and future generations.
Mary Cullinan, President
James M. Klein, Provost/VP for Academic Affa

5426 St. Lawrence University
Environmental Studies
23 Romoda Drive 315-229-5011
Canton, NY 13617 800-285-1856
icania@stlawu.edu
www.stlawu.edu
Programs offer ten options for combining environmental studies with traditional disciplines (eg. biology, economics) plus B.A. program in Environmental Studies.
Ms. Jacquelyn M Bouchard, President
Ms. Dayle B. Burgess, Assistant to the President

5427 Stanford University
Center for Environmental Studies
Building - MC 4205 650-736-8688
473 Via Ortega Fax: 650-725-3402
Stanford, CA 94305 environment@stanford.edu
woods.stanford.edu
Focuses on significant environmental problems and draws methods and analyses from multiple diciplines.
Luis Tam, Assosciate Director
Pam Sturner, ExecutiveDirector

5428 Sterling College
Center for Northern Studies
Sterling College Admissions 802-586-7711
PO Box 72 800-648-3591
Craftsbury Common, VT 00582 Fax: 802-586-2596
admissions@sterlingcollege.edu
www.sterlingcollege.edu
Center for Northern Studies is part of a small, undergraduate teaching and research institution located in Wolcott, Vermont. Its program is interdisciplinary in nature, integrating social and natural sciences, humanities and resourceissues in the Circumpolar North.
Matthew Allen Derr, President
Melissa Fisher '00, COO

5429 Tennessee Technological University
Bioenvironmental Sciences
1 William L Jones Dr 931-372-3101
Cookeville, TN 38505 800-255-8881
visit@tntech.edu
www.tntech.edu
Prepares graduates for high-level careers in various areas of biology and bioenvironmentl sciences.
Philip Oldham, President
Mark Stephens, Interim Provost/VP for Acade

5430 Texas A & M University
Center for Natural Resource Information Technology
113 Administration Building 979-845-1060
College Station, TX 77843 Fax: 409-845-6430
admissions@tamu.edu
www.tamu.edu
Serves as a point of contact for external organizations seeking cooperative efforts to assemble and disseminate information, create information technologies, and research critical natural resource concepts. The center strives tofacilitate technology transfer through training of end users and establishing necessary information infrastructures.
Michael K. Young, President
Dr. Karan L. Watson, Provost/Executive VP for Aca

5431 Texas Christian University
Environmental Science Program
PO Box 298830 817-257-7270
Fort Worth, TX 76129 Fax: 817-257-7789
m.slattery@tcu.edu
www.ensc.tcu.edu
A program helping students to understand the connection between science and the earth.
Michael C. Slattery, Director
John Breyer, Director

5432 Treasure Valley Community College
Biology Department
650 College Boulevard 541-881-8822
Ontario, OR 97914 888-987-8822
Fax: 541-881-2721
www.tvcc.cc
Offers several courses for those seeking careers in natural resource management including range management, wildland fire management, and forest management.
Dana M. Young, President
Randy Griffin, VP of Administrative Service

5433 Tulane University
Environmental Health & Sciences
6823 St. Charles Avenue 504-865-5000
New Orleans, LA 70118 800-873-9283
Fax: 504-862-8715
website@tulane.edu
www.tulane.edu
Environmental Health Sciences offers several graduate degree programs, including Public Health and Science. Graduates will be prepared to meet the needs of public health professionals such as environmental health and health officers,as well as undertake responsible positions in government, industrial facilities, research, or edeational institutions.
Scott S. Cowen, President
Yvette M. Jones, Executive VP

5434 UCLA - University of California/Los Angeles
Earth, Planetary, and Space Sciences
595 Charles Young Drive E 310-825-3880
PO Box 951567 Fax: 310-825-2779
Los Angeles, CA 90095 info@epss.ucla.edu
epss.ucla.edu
Offers programs in the study of soil mechanics and foundation engineering in light of geologic conditions, recognition, prediction, control or abatement of subsidence, landslides, earthquakes, and other geologic aspects of urbanplanning.
Vassilis Angelopoulos, Professor
Jonathan Aurnou, Professor

5435 University of Arizona
Soutywest Environmental Health Sciences Center
1501 Campbell Avenue 520-626-4555
PO Box 245018 Fax: 602-827-2074
Tucson, AZ 85721 admissions@arizona.edu
www.arizona.edu
This center serves as a platform to promote the study of health effects of environmental agents. The SWEHSC promotes interdisciplinary research collaborations driven by cutting-edge technologies. Research in the SWEHSC is focused onmechanisms of action of environmetnal agents in living systems.
Ann Weaver Hart, President
Keith A. Joiner, Vice Provost

5436 University of California/Berkeley
Environmental Management Program
1995 University Avenue 510-642-4111
Suite 110 extension-info@berkeley.edu
Berkeley, CA 94704-7000 extension.berkeley.edu/

The Environmental Management Program prepares students to take on significant leadership roles in the environmental community.
Diana Wu, Acting Dean
Scott Shireman, CFO

5437 University of California/Santa Barbara

Bren School of Environmental Studies
Bren Hall 805-893-2968
Room 4312 Fax: 805-893-8686
Santa Barbara, CA 93106-4160 esprogram@es.ucsb.edu
www.es.ucsb.edu

Program provides students with the scholarly background and intellectual skills necessary to understand complex environmental problems and formulate decisions that are environmentally sound. Academic process is interdisciplinary,drawing upon not only environmental science faculty, but also the resources of a variety of related departments and disciplines.
Dr. Carla D'Antonio, Chair
Cheryl Hutton, Financial Manager

5438 University of California/Santa Cruz

Environmental Studies
1156 Hight Street 831-459-2634
Santa Cruz, CA 95064 envs.ucsc.edu

Offers programs that prepare students to make significant contributions in the various fields of environmental study, whether pursing a career with private or non-profit institutions.
George Blumenthal, Chancellor
Alison Galloway, Provost/Executive Vice Chanc

5439 University of Colorado

Environmental Engineering Program
Regent Administrative Center 125 303-492-8908
552 UCB apply@colorado.edu
Boulder, CO 80309 www.colorado.edu

Environmental Engineering Progam in the Department of Civil, Environmental, and Architectural Engineering at the University of Colorado in Boulder welcomes students, alumni, and colleagues in environmental engineering with aninvitation to explore areas of environmental emphasis, B.S., M.S., and Ph.D programs, research, and facilities.
Philip P. DiStefano, Chancellor
Bob Sievers, Director

5440 University of Florida

College of Natural Resources & Environment
103 Black Hall 352-392-9230
PO Box 116455 Fax: 352-392-9748
Gainesville, FL 32611 kbray@ufl.edu
www.snre.ufl.edu

Science based, multidisciplinary and academically rigorous, the College of Natural Resources & Environment has students and a curriculum that includes 200 courses taught in 56 departments of other colleges. The 290 affiliate facultyhave their primary appointments in discipline-centered departments of other colleges.
Jack Payne, Chair
Joseph Glover, Provost/Sr. VP for Academic

5441 University of Florida/Gainesville

School of Forest Resources and Conservation
118 Newins-Ziegler Hall 352-392-3261
PO Box 110410 Fax: 352-392-1707
Gainesville, FL 32611 www.ufl.edu

Offers baccalaureate (BSFRC) and graduate (PhD, MS, MFRC, MFAS, incl. a joint JD with the College of Law and a co-major with Dept of Statistics) degree programs; conducts fundamental and applied research; and provides public servicethrough extension programs. Programs include forestry, geomatics, fisheries, and aquatic sciences, natural resource economics, management, and policy, as well as related programs in natural resource education, ecotourism, and agroforestry.
C. David Brown, II, Chair
Dr. W. Kent Fuchs, President

5442 University of Georgia

Savannah River Ecology Laboratory
P.O. Drawer E 803-725-2472
Aiken, SC 29802 Fax: 803-725-3309
srel.uga.edu

Our goal is to attract collaborating scientists from across the DOE complex and the nation for collaborative work at the interface of fundamental and applied environmental research. We strive to improve the management of contaminatedstites. The staff and facilities of AACES are available to researchers in environmental science and engineering and to practitoneers from industry, government, academia and private foundations.
Olin E. Rhodes, Director
John Seaman, Assistant Director

5443 University of Hawaii/Manoa

Oceanography & Global Environmental Sciences
1000 Pope Road 808-956-9154
MSB 205 Fax: 808-956-9152
Honolulu, HI 96822 ocean@soest.hawaii.edu
www.soest.hawaii.edu

Bachelor of Science degree in Global Environmental Science offered through the Department of Oceanography, University of Hawaii at Manoa.
Brain Taylor, Dean
Chip Fletcher, Associate Dean

5444 University of Idaho

College of Natural Resources
875 Perimeter Drive 208-885-6111
Moscow, ID 83844 Fax: 208-885-5534
info@uidaho.edu
www.uidaho.edu

Consists of 5 departments which together form a comprehensive educational program on the study and management of natural resources. Each department has several degree options to provide students with a flexible curriculum for theirdegree. We educate resource professionals with truly integrated resource management skills using innovative instructional programs. Our education occurs in a residential setting and provides a balance between theoretical and pratical experiences.
Chuck Staben, President
Donald L. Burnett, Interim President

5445 University of Illinois/Springfield

Environmental Studies
One University Plaza 217-206-6600
MS UHB 1080 888-977-4847
Springfield, IL 62703 admissions@uis.edu
www.uis.edu/

Goal of the environmental studies program is to enhance society's ability to create an environmentally acceptable future. Program faculty with diverse backgrounds in social and natural sciences and humanities are committed todeveloping interdisciplinary approaches to environmental problem solving. The primary objective is to educate citizens and professionals who are aware of environmental issues and their origins, causes, effects, and resolutions.
Susan J. Koch, Chancellor
Patricia Sanchez, Executive Assistant

5446 University of Illinois/Urbana

Department of Natural Resources and Environment
1102 South Goodwin Avenue 217-333-2770
W-503 Turner Hall Fax: 217-244-3219
Urbana, IL 61801 nres@illinois.edu
nres.illinois.edu

Establishes and implements research and educational programs that enhance environmental stewardship in the management and use of natural, agricultural, and urban systems in a socially responsible manner.
Bruce Branham, Associate Prof/Interim Head
Jason Emmert, Assistant Dean

5447 **University of Iowa**
MacBride Raptor Project
309 S. Madison Street 319-335-9293
Iowa City, IA 52242 Fax: 319-335-6655
rec-services@uiowa.edu
www.recserv.uiowa.edu
Jointly sponsored by the University of Iowa and Kirkwood Community College, the project has two main facilities. Classes are held at the educational display facility and rehabilitation flight cage at the Macbride Nature RecreationalArea, and at the Raptor Clinic and educational display at KCC. The project is dedicated to the preservation of birds of prey and their habitats through rehabilitation of injured raptors, public education programs and raptor reseach.
Mark J. Braun, Interim VP for strategic Com
David Drake, Sr. Associate

5448 **University of Maine**
Environmental Studies
23 University Street 207-834-7500
Fort Kent, ME 00474 888-879-8635
Fax: 207-834-7466
umfkadm@maine.edu
www.umfk.maine.edu
Offers a broad knowledge of the natural and social sciences, with the ability to focus of an area of personal interest. Students learn to critically identify environmental problems, collect and interpret data, communicate complexenvironmental issues, and explore creative solutions, while working closely with an interdisciplinary group of faculty with expertise in biology, chemistry, forestry, the social sciences and the humanities.
Steven Selva, Professor

5449 **University of Maryland**
Environmental Policy Programs
2101 Van Munching Hall 301-405-1000
College Park, MD 20742 Fax: 301-403-4675
jbanders@umd.edu
www.umd.edu
This part-time degree program is intented for highly ambitious mid-career professionals who are ready to advance within the field, understand the importance and value of a professional degree and able to attend one or two classes perweek for two years. A minimum of 5 years of policy related work experience is required. For-profit, nonprofit and public sector work will be considered. A minimum udergraduate GPA of 3.0 is required.
Wallace D. Loh, President
Mary Ann Rankin, Provost

5450 **University of Maryland/Baltimore**
Environmental Science Studies
1000 Hilltop Circle 410-455-2274
Baltimore, MD 21250 800-UMB-C4US
Fax: 410-455-1094
adnmissions@umbc.edu
www.umbc.edu
The goal of the MEES program is to train students with career interests in environmental science involving terrestrial, freshwater, marine, or estuarine systems. The program is university-wide and interdisciplinary, allowing studentsto use facilities and interact with all faculty in order to plan a program best suited to their particular interests.
Freeman A. Hrabowski, III, President
Philip Rous, Provost & SVP

5451 **University of Maryland/College Park**
Environmental Chemistry
0107 Chemistry Building 301-405-1788
College Park, MD 20742-4454 Fax: 301-314-9121
chem-web@umd.edu
www.chem.umd.edu
The combined Chemistry and Biochemistry Departments offers specialized training at the graduate level in environmental chemistry. In addition to course work in traditional chemistry subjects, students in this specialty take specificenvironmental courses and do research under the guidance of faculty members specializing in this area.
Michael Doyle, Professor & Chair
Herman Ammon, Associate Chair/Professor

5452 **University of Miami**
Rosenstiel School of Marine & Atmospheric Science
4600 Rickenbacker Causeway 305-421-4000
Miami, FL 33149-1098 Fax: 305-421-4711
dean@rsmas.miami.edu
www.rsmas.miami.edu/
Established as the Marine Laboratory of the University of Miami. It has grown from its modest beginnings in a boathouse to one of the nations leading institutions for oceanographic research and education.
Ron Avissar, Dean
Ramon Alfonso, Director

5453 **University of Minnesota/St. Paul**
College of Agriculatural & Environmental Sciences
3 Morrill Hall 612-625-2008
100 Church St. S.E. 800-752-1000
Minneapolis, MN 55455-213 Fax: 612-626-1693
spccc@umn.edu
www1.umn.edu
The programs offered through this college are designed to prepare students for work in a variety of environmental disciplines, specifically those that relate to the agriculture industry
Eric W. Kaler, President
Karen Hanson, Provost/Sr. VP for Academic

5454 **University of Montana**
Environmetal Studies
32 Campus Drive 406-243-0211
Missoula, MT 59812 david.micus@umontana.edu
www.umt.edu
Interdisciplinary graduate and undergraduate program in environmental studies.
Royce C. Engstrom, President
Perry J. Brown, Provost/Sr. VP for Academic

5455 **University of Nebraska**
Environmental Studies Program
1400 R Street 402-472-7211
Lincoln, NE 68588 hperlman1@unl.edu
www.unl.edu
The Environmental Studies Program is designed to serve a variety of students concerned about environmental issues and change. The program provides a thorough, holistic view of the environment and human-environmental interaction and thetechnical skills for active participation in an environmental career.
Harvey Perlman, Chancellor

5456 **University of Nevada/Las Vegas**
Department of Civil & Environmental Engineering
4505 S Maryland Parkway 702-895-3701
Box 454015 Fax: 702-895-3936
Las Vegas, NV 89154-4015 www.unlv.edu
Department of Civil and Environmental Engineering offers programs leading to a Master of Science in Engineering and Doctor of Philosophy, with concentration in six areas: environmental engineering; fluid mechanics and hydraulics;geotechnical engi-

neering; structural engineering; construction engineering; and transportation systems.
Donald Hayes, Chair/Professor
Allen Sampson, Sr Development Tech

5457 University of Nevada/Reno
Civil & Environmental Engineering
1664 N. Virginia Street
Reno, NV 89557-208
775-784-1110
866-2NE-ADA
Fax: 775-784-4466
www.unr.edu

Offers an educational program in environmental engineering. Environmental engineers have taken an increasingly important role in the application on engineering and scientific principles to protect and preserve human health andenvironment. The curriculum is designed with the goal of providing each student with the necessary fundamentals and background in engineering science and design to address many different challenges.
Dr Manos Maragakis, Dean
Dr Indira Chatterjee, Professor/Assoc. Dean

5458 University of New Haven
Environmental Science
300 Boston Post Road
Westhaven, CT 00651
203-932-7319
800-342-5864
adminfo@newhaven.edu
www.newhaven.edu

The bachelor of science program in environmental science is designed to give students a strong foundation in the fudamental sciences, including biology, chemistry, physics, and geology, and how they relate to our environmentalconcerns.
Steven H. Kaplan, President
Lourdes Alvarez, Dean

5459 University of North Carolina/Chapel Hill
Environmental Science & Studies
153A Country Club Road
Jackson Hall
Chapel Hill, NC 27514
919-966-3621
Fax: 919-962-3045
unchelp@admissions.unc.edu
www.admissions.unc.edu

The Environmental Science and Studies program leads to degrees in Environmental Science or Environmental Studies. Students investigate the relationship between the environment and society, focusing on environmental management, law andbusiness. The programs combines traditional classroom teaching with extensive use of interdisciplinary, team-based field projects, internships, study abroad and research.
Holden Thorp, Chancellor
Jim Dean, Provost

5460 University of Oregon
Environmental Studies
5223 University of Oregon
Eugene, OR 97403-5223
541-346-2549
Fax: 541-346-6056
adickman@uoregon.edu

Environmental Studies crosses the boundaries of traditional disciplines, challenging faculty and students to look at the relationship between humans and their environment from a new perspective. They are dedicated to gaining greaterunderstanding of the natural world from an ecological perspective; devising policy and behavior that address contemporary environmental problems; and promoting a rethinking of basic cultural premises, ways of structuring knowledge and the rootmetaphors of society.
Alan Dickman, Program Director
Monica Guy, Office Manager

5461 University of Pennsylvania
Natural Resource Conservation Program
3451 Walnut Street
Philadelphia, PA 19104
215-898-5000
webmaster@upenn.edu
www.upenn.edu

The mission of our department is to bring the time perspective of the Earth scientist/historian to bear on contemporary problems of natural resource conservation and environmental quality.
Dr. Amy Gutmann, President
Vincent Price, Provost

5462 University of Pittsburgh
Department of Geology & Planetary Science
4107 O'Hara Street
200 SRCC Building
Pittsburgh, PA 15260-3332
412-624-8780
Fax: 412-624-3914
mookie@pitt.edu
www.geology.pitt.edu

Equips students with an understanding of earth systems and the impact of humans on the biosphere, atmosphere and hydrosphere. Courses in the natural and social sciences, humanities, and schools of law, business, and public healthprovide a comprehensive, interdisciplinary background in environmental issues and public policy.
Patricia DeMarco, Executive Director
Mark Ambott, Department Chair

5463 University of Redlands
Environmental Studies
1200 E Colton Avenue
PO Box 3080
Redlands, CA 92373
909-793-2121
Fax: 909-793-2029
kerry_robles@redlands.edu
www.redlands.edu

Designed to promote a new way of thinking and acting about our relationship to the world, including graduating students who are environmentally literate, sensitive to competing demands and conflicting values of each issue and finally,and have the creativity, confidence and conviction to begin effecting change.
Dr. Ralph W. Kuncl, President
Bradley N. Adams '93, Managing Director

5464 University of South Carolina
Belle Baruch Institute of Marine Costalsciences
Petigru College
Room 300
Columbia, SC 29208
803-777-7161
Fax: 803-777-4532
artsandsciences.sc.edu

Environmental research and programs are focused on estuarine systems and their associated watersheds. More than 160 investigators representing 30 academic institutes and agencies are affiliated with over 100 projects. The lab providessupport for undergraduate classes, graduate students, and senior scientists. Long-term environmental monitoring, training programs and outreach activities are sponsored by the North-inlet-Winyah Bay National Estuarine research reserve.
Dr. Roger Sawyer, Executive Dean
Dr. Anne Bezuidenhout, Sr. Associate Dean

5465 University of Southern California
Environmental Sciences, Policy/Engineering Program
University Park Campus
Hancock Building, Room 232
Los Angeles, CA 90089
213-740-2311
www.usc.edu

This multidisciplinary doctoral training program is funded by the National Science Foundation, and prepares students to confront, analyze and resolve the challenges posed by problems of urban sustainablilty. Engineering SustainableCities is high on the list of goals of the program, which allows students to transcend disciplines, and conduct policy-relevant research on major environmental problems.
Wallis Annenberg, Chairman
Wanda M. Austin, President & CEO

5466 University of Southern Mississippi
Environmental Science Program
118 College Drive
Building #5018
Hattiesburg, MS 39406-0001
601-266-0001
Fax: 601-266-5797
admissions@usm.edu
www.usm.edu

The Environmental Science concentration focuses on industrial problems related to the working environment, pollution control, and safety. Courses address major industrial issues, including environmental impact statements, industrialhygiene and environmental laws and regulations.
Frank Moore, Chair
Rodney D. Bennett, President

5467 University of Tennessee

Geoscience Program
554 University Street — 731-881-7000
Martin, TN 38238 — 800-829-utm1
Fax: 901-587-7029
admitme@utm.edu
www.utm.edu

This program focuses on the application of geology to the interaction between man and the environment. Topics include geohazards, chemical and nuclear contamination of soils and water, remediation of environmental problems andgovernmental environmental agencies and laws.
Tom Rakes, Chancellor
Nancy Yarbrough, Interim Vice Chancellor

5468 University of Virginia

Department of Environmental Sciences
291 McCormick Road — 434-924-7761
PO Box 400123 — Fax: 434-982-2137
Charlottesville, VA 22904-4123 — ralph@virginia.edu
www.evsc.virginia.edu

Offers instruction and research opportunities in Ecology, Geosciences, Hydrology, and Atmospheric Sciences. The research endeavors of both faculty and graduate students, whether disciplinary or interdisciplinary, deal largely withproblems of fundamental scientific interest and with applied sciences, management or policy making.
Allen Cindy, Asst to Dept/Chair/Clark
Sheila Riddle, Administrative Support Speci

5469 University of Washington

Environmental Science
18115 Campus Way NE — 425-352-5000
Bothell, WA 98011-8246 — Fax: 425-352-5455
info@uwb.edu
www.uwb.edu

Primary goal of this program is to train a new generation of interdisciplinary scientists who are able to work in both the public and private sectors to address some of the pressing environmental issues that face our society.
Bjong Wolf Yeigh, Chancellor
Marilyn Cox, Vice Chancellor

5470 University of West Florida

Environmental Studies
11000 University Parkway — 850-474-2000
Pensacola, FL 32514 — Fax: 850-474-3131
web@uwf.edu
www.uwf.edu

The program in Environmental Studies consists of a multi-disciplinary approach that combines natural science and resource management. Students learn to analyze physical and socioeconomic environments and to reach decisions concerningenvironmental use and protection. It offers a core curriculum that is designed to provide the student with a solid foundation in earth and life sciences, as well as in modern methods and techniques.
Lewis Bear, Chair
Judy A. Bense, President

5471 University of Wisconsin/Green Bay

Environmental Science
2420 Nicolet Drive — 920-465-2000
Green Bay, WI 54311 — uwgb@uwgb.edu
www.uwgb.edu

This program is interdisciplinary, emphasizing an integrated approach to knowledge in the field. Because the study of the environmental science major is grounded in the natural sciences and mathematics, the curriculum includes a socialscience component, enabling students to gain an understanding of environmental economic and policy issues. Field experiences, internships and practicums are emphasized.
Thomas K. Harden, Chancellor
Julia E. Wallace, Provost/Vice Chancellor for

5472 University of Wisconsin/Madison

Environmental Monitoring Program
212 Agricultural Hall — 608-261-1432
1450 Linden Drive — Fax: 608-265-9534
Madison, WI 53706 — waes@cals.wisc.edu
www.cals.wisc.edu

Remote sensing and geographic information systems offer sophisticated and powerful tools for monitoring the environment on large geographic scales over time. Students in the Environmental Monitoring Program learn to employ thesetechnologies in fields of their choice, from forestry to urban planning to environmental engineering.
Kathryn VandenBosch, Dean/Director
Angela Seitler, Assistant Director

5473 University of Wisconsin/Stevens Point

Environmental Task Force Progeam
2100 Main Street — 715-346-0123
Stevens Point, WI 54481-3897 — Fax: 715-346-2561
webmaster@uwsp.edu
www.uwsp.edu/

This program involves two water chemistry labs which tests for organics and inorganics. This is staffed by five full time workers, plus a part time faculty director, and about 40 students are hired and/or trained each year. Samplingis performed with state-of-the-art field sampling and laboratory analytical equipment nutrients, pesticides, polynuclear aromatic hydrocarbons, polychlorinated biphenyls, and volatile organic compounds.
Bernie L. Patterson, Chancellor
Greg Summers, Provost/Vice Chancellor

5474 University of the South

Environmental Studies
735 University Avenue — 931-598-1000
Sewanee, TN 37383 — 800-522-2234
Fax: 931-598-1667
collegeadmission@sewanee.edu
www.sewanee.edu

Brings together students, faculty, and staff from thirteen academic departments to study, discuss, and research environmental issues at local, national, and international scales. The program's goal is to expose students to a variety ofviewpoints concerning environmental issues, and to offer the interdisciplinary tools they need to become environmental problem solvers before they graduate from Sewanee.
John McCardell, Vice Chancellor
John Swallow, Provost

5475 Utah State University

Berryman Institute
Wildland Resources Department — 435-797-0242
5230 Old Main Hill — Fax: 435-797-3796
Logan, UT 84322 — www.berrymaninstitute.org

The Berryman Institute is a functional component of the Department of Wildland Resources and the College of Natural Resources. Its faculty members hold academics appointments in various departments throughout Utah State University andother universities. This multidisciplinary approach is calculated to speed the discovery and development of innovative methods to solve human wildlife conflict.
Dr. Terry A. Messmer, Director
Lana Barr, Assistant to the Director

5476 **Vanderbilt University**
Vanderbilt Center for Environmental Management
2301 Vanderbilt Place 615-322-7311
Nashville, TN 37240 Fax: 615-343-7177
mark.a.cohen@vanderbilt.edu
www.vanderbilt.edu

VCEMS provides guidance and support for the interdisciplinary study of environmental issues. The Center brings faculty and students together from various disciplines for collaborative study and research on topics such as environmentalrisk assessment, management and communication, policy analysis, civil and criminal liability, environmentally conscious manufacturing and technology management, and global environmental studies.
Nicholas S. Zeppos, Chancellor
Dr. Mark Cohen, Co-Director

5477 **Vermont Law School**
Environmental Law Center
164 Chelsea Street 802-831-1000
PO Box 96 800-227-1395
South Royalton, VT 00506 www.vermontlaw.edu

The Environmental Law Center administers three different degrees in Environmental Law, each adaptable to career objectives in both public and private sectors. The school's mission is to educate for stewardship, to teach an awareness ofunderlining environmental issues and values, to provide a solid knowledge of environmental law and to develop skills to administer and improve policies.
J. Scott Cameron, Chair
Margaret Martin Barry, Professor of Law/Associate D

5478 **Virginia Polytechnic Institute**
Environmental Science
965 Prices Fork Road 540-231-6267
Blackburg, VA 24061 Fax: 540-231-3242
vtadmiss@vt.edu
www.vt.edu

This program deals with crop production, soil utilization, and environmental stewardship. Its professionals are concerned with helping to feed the world and protect the environment, and include women and men who work to grow crucialcommodities, improve water quality, develop environmentally acceptable methods for protecting crops from pests, and advise municipalities on use of the land resource.
Timothy D. Sands, President
Mark G. McNamee, Provost

5479 **Virginia Tech**
925 Prices Fork Road 540-231-6267
Blacksburg, VA 24061 Fax: 540-231-3242
admissions@vt.edu
www.vt.edu

Provides a B.S. degree for environmental professionals needed in the private and public sector and by nonprofit organizations. Virginia Tech offers a rigorous interdisciplinary curriculum that stresses the basic sciences, environmentaltechnologies, soils, and analytical skills. Graduates are in high demand in the environmental arena.
Timothy D. Sands, President
M. Dwight Shelton, Chief Financial Officer

5480 **Warren Wilson College**
Natural & Social Sciences
Warren Wilson College 828-298-3325
PO Box 9000 800-934-3536
Asheville, NC 28815-9000 Fax: 828-299-4841
admit@warren-wilson.edu
www.warren-wilson.edu

Combines rigorous courses in the natural and social sciences with abundant natural resources near the classrooom. Courses and work crews give students a balance of theory, first hand knowledge and field experience. Successful programsmost often result when students, with the help of an advisor, begin planning course work and indentifying goals during their first year.
Alice C. Buhl, Chair
Steven L. Solnick, President

5481 **Washington State University**
Environmental Science
PO Box 642812 509-335-3009
Pullman, WA 99164-2812 Fax: 509-335-3700
sees@wsu.edu
cahnrs.wsu.edu/soe/

The students in this diverse program are encouraged to specialize in their specific interest, including agricultural ecology, biological science, environmental education, environmental quality (air and water), natural resourcemanagement, systems, environmental/land use planning or hazardous waste management.
Elson Floyd, President
Stephen Bollens, Director

5482 **West Virginia University**
Environmental Geosciences Program
1168 Agricultural Sciences Building 304-293-2395
PO Box 6108 Fax: 304-293-3740
Morgantown, WV 26506-6108 www.davis.wvu.edu

The Environmental Geosciences program features an interdisciplinary approach to environmental issues. Graduates will be well prepared to face the environmental challenges, whether in government or in the corporate world.
Dan Robison, Dean
Dennis K. Smith, Assoc. Dean

5483 **Western Montana College**
Environmental Sciences Program
710 S Atlantic Street 406-683-7331
Dillon, MT 59725 877-683-7331
Fax: 406-683-7331
admissions@umwestern.edu
www.umwestern.edu

The mission of the environmental sciences programs is to provide students with an in-depth understanding of the natural processes which create and shape our environment. Students will become informed, critical thinkers capable ofscientifically evaluating complex issues involving the environment. Student development will occur through interdisciplinary, field-based research projects that have societal relevance.
Roxanne Engellant, Foundation Director
Kelly Allen, Administrative Assistant

5484 **Williams College**
Center for Environmental Studies
Hopkins Hall 413-597-3131
880 Main Street Fax: 412-597-3489
Williamstown, MA 00126 szepke@williams.edu
www.williams.edu

The Environmental Studies program provides students with tools, ideas, and opportunities to engage constructively with the environmental and social issues brought about by changes in population, economic activity, and values. Theenvironmental studies program is interdisciplinary and broad, including the coditions of inner-city poverty as well as the magnificent scenery of wildlands, encompassing the view of planet earth from near space as well as from culturalanthropologists.
Hank Art, Director

5485 **Yale University**
Office of Public Affairs
265 Church Street 203-432-1345
Suite 901 Fax: 203-432-1323
New Haven, CT 00651 undergraduate.admission@yale.edu
www.yale.edu

Our mission is to provide the leadership and knowledge needed to restore and sustain both the health of the biosphere and the well-being of its people. Believing that human enterprise can and

must be conducted in harmony with theenvironment, we are committed to using natural resources in ways that sustain both resources and ourselves. Solving environmental problems must incorporate human values and motivations and a deep respect for both human and natural communities.
Richard Charles Levin, President

Workshops & Camps

5486 A Closer Look at Plant Life
Educational Images
PO Box 3456 607-732-1090
Westside Station 800-527-4264
Elmira, NY 14905-456 Fax: 607-732-1183
edimages@edimages.com
www.educationalimages.com
Access a wealth of information on every major group of vascular and nonvascular plants. Includes details on plant microanatomy; external and internal structures; life cycles; and processes such as growth transpiration andphotosynthesis.
Charles R Belinky, Ph.D, CEO

5487 A Closer Look at Pondlife - CD-ROM
Educational Images
PO Box 3456 607-732-1090
Westside Station 800-527-4264
Elmira, NY 14905-456 Fax: 607-732-1183
edimages@edimages.com
www.educationalimages.com
Through the wonders of close-up photography, this unique CD-ROM brings students face-to-face with the inner workings of a freshwater pond, the myriad creatures and plants that reside there, and the dynamic interactions that go onbeneath the surface. This disk features a library of reference information, images, illustrations, clip art, video clips and more!
Charles R Belinky, Ph.D, CEO

5488 Abbott's Mill Nature Center
Delaware Nature Society
3511 Barley Mill Road 302-239-2334
PO Box 700 Fax: 302-239-2473
Hockessin, DE 19707 dnsinfo@delawarenaturesociety.org
www.delawarenaturesociety.org
Abbott's Mill Nature Center features education programs for families, school classes and public groups, walking trails through fields, pine woods and streams, and a historic, fully-operating gristmill.
Peter H. Flint, President
Sharon Struthers, VP

5489 Air and Waste Management Association
One Gateway Center 3rd Floor 412-232-3444
420 Fort Duquesne Blvd. Fax: 412-232-3450
Pittsburg, PA 15222 info@awma.org
www.awma.org
The Air and Waste Management Association is a non-profit, nonpartisan professional organization that provides training, information and networking ortunities to 12,000 environmental professionals in 65 countries. TheAssociatiopportunities to thousands of environmental professionals in 65 countries.
Scott A. Freeburn, President
Chris Nelson, President-Elect

5490 American Academy of Clinical Toxicology
6728 Old McLean Village Drive 571-488-6000
McLean, VA 22101 admin@clintox.org
www.clintox.org
Offers programs such as the American Board of Medical Toxicology to provide physicians with certification in the field of clinical toxicology. The mission of the academy is to research and educate people about the prevention andtreatment of diseases caused by chemicals, drugs and toxins.
Robert Palmer, Ph.D, President
Mark Kostic, MD, President-Elect

5491 American Museum of Natural History
Center for Biodiversity and Conservation
Central Park West 212-769-5100
79th Street Fax: 212-769-5427
New York, NY 10024-5192 biodiversity@amnh.org
www.amnh.org
Conducts research and field projects based on information provided by Museum departments.
Lewis W. Bernard, Chairman
Ellen V. Futter, President

5492 Animal Tracks and Signs
Educational Images
PO Box 3456 607-732-1090
Westside Station 800-527-4264
Elmira, NY 14905-456 Fax: 607-732-1183
edimages@edimages.com
www.educationalimages.com
Presents various animal tracks and signs throughout the seasons, and provides useful information about the special characteristics and natural history of the animals that left the signs. Footprints, scratch marks, nesting places,wallows, scats and signs of food gathering are all detailed. Coverage includes deer, fox, porcupine, rabbit, bear, mink, otter, owl, woodpecker, killdeer, wild turkey, sapsucker and grouse.
Charles R Belinky, Ph.D, CEO

5493 Annotated Invertebrate Clipart CD-ROM
Educational Images
PO Box 3456 607-732-1090
Westside Station 800-527-4264
Elmira, NY 14905-456 Fax: 607-732-1183
edimages@edimages.com
www.educationalimages.com
780 colorful graphics of invertebrates from protists through urochordates, supported by extensive written annotations in addition to traditional labels. Includes presentation graphics and page after page of supplemental information onclassification, anatomy, evolution, development, reproduction, etc.
Charles R Belinky, Ph.D, CEO

5494 Annotated Vertebrate Clipart CD-ROM
Educational Images
PO Box 3456 607-732-1090
Westside Station 800-527-4264
Elmira, NY 14905-456 Fax: 607-732-1183
edimages@edimages.com
www.educationalimages.com
792 colorful graphics of vertebrates from urochordates and tunicates through mammals, supported by extensive written annotations in addition to traditional labels. Includes presentation graphics and page after page of supplementalinformation on classification, organ systems, anatomy, evolution, development, reproduction, etc.
Charles R Belinky, Ph.D, CEO

5495 Argonne National Laboratory
9700 S Cass Avenue 630-252-2000
Argonne, IL 60439 webmaster@anl.gov
www.anl.gov/
One of the US Department of Energy's largest research centers that develops and researches solutions in areas such as sustainable energy, environmental health, and national security.
Matthew Tirrell, Deputy Director
Paul Kearns, Interim Director

5496 Ashland Nature Center
Delaware Nature Society
3511 Barley Mill Road 302-239-2334
PO Box 700 Fax: 302-239-2473
Hockessin, DE 19707 dnsinfo@delawarenaturesociety.org
www.delawarenaturesociety.org

Open year round, seven days a week, Ashland is headquarters of the Delaware Nature Society. Ashland Nature Center offers self-guided nature trails traversing 81 acres of rolling terrain, through meadows, woodlands, and marshes.Programs for all ages are offered, including schools and groups.
Peter H. Flint, President
Sharon Struthers, VP

5497 Aspen Global Change Institute
104 Midland Ave 970-925-7376
Suite 205 Fax: 970-925-7097
Basalt, CO 81621 www.agci.org

A Colorado nonprofit dedicated to furthering the understanding of Earth systems through interdisciplinary science meetings, publications, and educational programs about global environmental change.
Dr. Martin Hoffert, Chairman
John Katzenberger, President

5498 Association for Environmental Health and Sciences
150 Fearing Street 413-549-5170
Amherst, MA 00100 Fax: 413-549-0579
www.aehs.com

Created to facilitate communication and foster cooperation among professionals concerned with the challenge of soil protection and cleanup. Experience over the past decades has revealed the need for a consistent and reliable networkfor the exchange of information derived from multiple sources and disciplines among people who, because of different disciplinary affiliations and interests, may not have easy access to significant portions of the information map.
Paul Kostecki, Executive Director

5499 Audubon Expedition Institute
29 Everett Street 617-868-9600
Cambridge, MA 00213 800-999-1959
info@lesley.edu
www.lesley.edu/

Students challenge themselves and their assumptions through experimental learning and direct contact with social, natural, historical and urban environments. Subjects are studied and integrated through real life experiences.
Deborah Schwartz Raizes, Chair
Hans D. Strauch, Vice Chair

5500 Bio-Integral Resource Center
PO Box 7414 510-524-2567
Berkeley, CA 94707 Fax: 510-524-1758
birc@igc.org
www.birc.org

The goal of the Bio Integral Resources Center is to reduce pesticide use by educating the public about effective, least-toxic alternatives for pest problems.
Dr. William Quarles, Executive Director

5501 Biosystems and Agricultural Engineering
Univerity of Kentucky
128 C.E Barnhart Building 859-257-9000
University of Kentucky Fax: 859-257-5671
Lexington, KY 40546-276 gates@bae.uky.edu
www.uky.edu/bae/

Biosystems and Agricultural Engineering provides an essential link between the biological sciences and the engineering profession. The linkage is necessary for the development of food and fiber production and processing systems whichpreserves our natural resources base.
Dr. Sue E. Nokes, Chair
Dr. Czarena Crofcheck, Director of Undergraduate St

5502 Bishop Resource Area
3000 E. Line St. 760-873-4344
Bishop, CA 93514 Fax: 760-873-7830
wmrcinfo@ucla.edu
www.wmrc.edu

The Bishop Resource Area has facilitated aerial photo interpretation and remote sensing programs in local schools through corporate and public partnerships. The program incorporates aerial photo interpretation, its relationship tomapping and land use history.
Antony Orme, Director
Glen MacDonald, Director

5503 Bog Ecology
Educational Images Ltd
306 Academy Pl 607-732-1090
Elmira, NY 14901

A comprehensive program that explores the origin and formation of bogs, common plants and animals, and compares bogs to other types of wetlands. Bog succession is illustrated by use of diagrams and photographs. Includes 74 frames andguide.

5504 Camp Fire USA
1100 Walnut Street 816-285-2010
Suite 1900 800-669-6884
Kansas City, MO 64106-2197 Fax: 816-285-9444
info@campfireusa.org
www.campfireusa.org

Not-for-profit, youth development organization, Camp Fire USA provides fun, coeducational programs for approximately 650,000 youth from birth to age 21. Helps boys and girls learn and play side by side in comfortable, informalsettings.
Ms. Elizabeth Darling, President/CEO
Richard Goldfarb, Sr. VP

5505 Camp Habitat Northern Alaska Environmental Center
830 College Road 907-452-5021
Fairbanks, AK 99701-1535 Fax: 907-452-3100
info@northern.org
www.northern.org

Camp Habitat is a nature education program for young people ages 4-17 sponsored by the Northern Alaska Environmental Center, Friends of Creamer's Field, and Alaska Department of Fish & Game. The mission of Camp Habitat is to provideyoung people with guided explorations of their natural surroundings through interactive, hands-on activities. Skilled instructors and resource specialists lead small groups through new outdoor activities focusing on the habitats of Interior Alaska.
Frank Williams, President
Carol Norton, Treasurer

5506 Center for Geography and Environmental Education
311 Conference Center Building 865-974-1000
University of Tennessee Fax: 865-974-1838
Knoxville, TN 37996 mckeowni@utk.edu
tennessee.edu

A research and outreach center at the University of Tennessee. The CGEE focuses on environmental and geography education contributions to education for sustainable development. CGEE is responsible for the Tennessee Solid WasteEducation Project.
Dr. Rosalyn McKeown-Ice, Director

5507 Center for Mathematical Services
4202 East Fowler Avenue 813-974-2011
Adm 147 Fax: 974-974-2700
Tampa, FL 33620 www.usf.edu

Mission is to help prepare students of all levels to effectively use mathematics as a tool to analyze situations and resolve problems. In the field of mathematical sciences it serves as an interface for the University with thesecondary schools in the area served by the University of South Florida. By means of this interface special programs in the mathematics, science, and engineering are offered at the University of South Florida for secondary students.
Ralph Wilcox, Provost/VP
Dr. Dwayne Smith, Sr. Vice Provost

5508 Cetacean Society International
65 Redding Road 203-770-8615
PO Box 953 Fax: 860-561-0187
Georgetown, CT 00682-953 Info@csiwhalesalive.org
www.csiwhalesalive.org
All volunteer, nonprofit conservation, educational and research organization to benefit whales, dolphins, porpoises and the marine environment. Promotes education and conservation programs, including whale and dolphin watching, andnoninvasive, benign research. Advocates for laws and treaties to prevent commercial whaling, habitat destruction and other harmful or destructive human interactions. CSI's world goal is to minimize cetacean killing and captures and to enhance publicawareness.
A. Daniel Knaub, President
Brent Hall, VP

5509 Chicago Botanic Garden
1000 Lake Cook Road 847-835-5440
Glencoe, IL 60022 www.chicagobotanic.org
The Chicago Horticultural Society has been promoting gardens and gardening since 1890. Generations of Chicagoans have been touched by the Society's flower shows, victory gardens, horticultural lectures and more. The mission encompassesthree important components: collections, programs and research. A living museum, the Chicago Botanic Garden serves both a public and a scientific community.
Robert F. Finke, Chair
John L. Howard, Vice Chair/Secretary

5510 Cleaner and Greener Environment
PO Box 5425 608-280-0255
Madison, WI 53705-425 877-977-9277
Fax: 608-255-7202
info@cleanerandgreener.org
www.cleanerandgreener.org
Cleaner and Greener Environment is a program of Leonardo Academy, a 501 environmental nonprofit organization. Leonardo Academy reports reductions in emissions, and promotes the development of markets for the emission reductions thatresult from energy efficiency, renewable energy, and other emission reduction action.

5511 Climate Change Program
Dade County Dept. of Env. Res. Mgm. 305-372-6825
701 NW 1st Court Fax: 305-372-6954
Miami, FL 33136
Receives monies from sources such as fees from pollution prevention events, grants, allocations, appropriations and workshop fees. These funds are then used in developing, promoting and conducting environmental workshops, expositions,symposia, conferences and other forms of public information for the purpose of educating industry, government and the public about pollution prevention.
Nichole Hefty, Coordinator

5512 Coastal Resources Center
University of Rhode Island
220 South Ferry Road 401-874-6224
Narragansett, RI 00288 Fax: 401-874-6920
info@crc.uri.edu
www.crc.uri.edu
Mobilizes governments, business and communities around the world to work together as stewards of coastal ecosystems. With partners we strive to define and achieve the health, equitable allocation of wealth, and sustainable intensitiesof human activity at the transition between the land and sea.
Brian Crawford, Director
Lesley Squillante, Asst. Director

5513 Columbia Environmental Research Center
1200 Amsterdam Avenue 212-854-8179
New York, NY 10027-5557 Fax: 212-854-8188
eices@columbia.edu
www.cerc.columbia.edu
CERC, a consortium of five education and research institutions, was created in response to critical environmental concerns facing the Earth. Within the next fifty years human influence will affect every place on the planet. That impactwill almost certainly result in species extinctions, ecosystem degradation and a loss of the benefits those species and ecosystems provide to people.
Shahid Naeem, Director
Alexandra Varga, Deputy Director

5514 Comet Halley: Once in a Lifetime!
Educational Images
PO Box 3456 607-732-1090
Westside Station 800-527-4264
Elmira, NY 14905-456 Fax: 607-732-1183
edimages@edimages.com
www.educationalimages.com
Particularly relevant because of the recent appearance of Hale-Bopp, this program presents the reactions to comets in ancient, historic and relatively modern times, press coverage of the 1910 Halley return, superstitions and beliefs,current scientific knowledge and research, and much more.
Charles R Belinky, Ph.D, CEO

5515 Cooch-Dayett Mills
Delaware Nature Society
3511 Barley Mill Road 302-239-2334
PO Box 700 Fax: 302-239-2473
Hockessin, DE 19707 dnsinfo@delawarenaturesociety.org
www.delawarenaturesociety.org
Programming provided by the delaware nature society features environmental education and natural history for families, classes, groups and the public. The historic roller mills, along with natural features of the site, become theclassroom.
Peter H. Flint, President
Sharon Struthers, VP

5516 Cooperative Institute for Research in Environmental Sciences: K-12 and Public Outreach
University of Colorado
449 UCB 303-492-5670
PO Box 700 Fax: 303-492-1149
Boulder, CO 80309-449 info@cires.colorado.edu
www.cires.colorado.edu/education/outreach
We educate people about Earth and environmental science issues that are relevant to our everyday lives, through outreach to the public and to the K-12 education community.
Waleed Abdalati, Director
William M. Lewis, Jr., Assoc. Director

5517 Coverdale Farm
Delaware Nature Society
3511 Barley Mill Road 302-239-2334
PO Box 700 Fax: 302-239-2473
Hockessin, DE 19707 dnsinfo@delawarenaturesociety.org
www.delawarenaturesociety.org
School students and guests of all ages participate in seasonal programs, learning about the farm cycle of life and humans' dependence on soil, water, plants and animals for survival.
Peter H. Flint, President
Sharon Struthers, VP

5518 **Deep Portage Conservation Reserve**
2197 Nature Center Drive NW 218-682-2325
Hackensack, MN 56452 888-280-9908
Fax: 218-682-3121
portage@uslink.net
www.deep-portage.org

Deep Portage serves schools, groups, organizations, research teams, area residents and visitor with resident environmental education programs, weekly classes, interpretive programs, wildflower garden displays, land use demonstrations,summer youth camps and recreation opportunities of birding, hiking, hunting and skiing.

Dale Yerger, Executive Director
Molly Malecek, Assistant Director

5519 **Department of Energy and Geo-Environmental Engineering**
116 Deike Building 814-865-6546
University Park, PA 16802 Fax: 814-863-7708
contact@ems.psu.edu
www.ems.psu.edu

Through education, research and service, EGEE aspires to insure that socisty is provided with an affordable supply of energy and minerals, concomitant with protecting the environment.

William E. Easterling, Dean
John Hellmann, Associate Dean

5520 **DuPont Environmental Education Center**
Delaware Nature Society
3511 Barley Mill Road 302-239-2334
PO Box 700 Fax: 302-239-2473
Hockessin, DE 19707 dnsinfo@delawarenaturesociety.org
www.delawarenaturesociety.org

Programming provided by the delaware nature society features environmental education and natural history for families, classes, groups and the public. The historic roller mills, along with natural features of the site, become theclassroom.

Peter H. Flint, President
Sharon Struthers, VP

5521 **Earth Day Network**
1616 P Street NW 202-518-0044
Suite 340 Fax: 202-518-8794
Washington, DC 20036 buchanan@earthday.org
www.earthday.net

This nonprofit network was created to be a vehicle for increased awareness & responsibility through the promotion of Earth Day. Offers workshops.

Denis Hayes, Board Chair/President/CEO
Gerald Torres, Vice Chair

5522 **Earth Force**
2555 W 34th Avenue 303-433-0016
PO Box 1228 Fax: 888-899-5324
Denver, CO 80211 earthforce@earthforce.org
www.earthforce.org

Earth Force offers educators innovatove programs and resources. The young graduates of these programs create lasting solutions to environmental problems in their communities. Earth Force's goal is to help youth become environmentalproblem solvers.

James Macgregor, Chairman
Chris Chopyak, President

5523 **Ecological & Environmental Learning Services**
46 Back Bone Hill Road 732-577-5599
Clarksburg, NJ 00851 800-206-6672
Fax: 732-577-5598

Ecological & Environmental Learning Services provides K-12 education consulting for teacher professional development, curriculum development and education programs and assemblies. EELS has the expertise and experience to providesolutions for enhancing the academic excellence of students in the following areas: Science (particularly in science research); Ecology; Environmental Science; and Environmental Education.

5524 **Ecology and Environmental Sciences**
5703 Alumni Hall 207-581-1512
Suite 200 877-486-2364
Orono, ME 00446 Fax: 207-581-1517
president@umaine.edu
www.umaine.edu

Faculty from five different academic departments, covering biological, physical and social sciences, work together to offer a broad educational experience for our students. Since these faculty have active research programs, studentsnot only get access to the most up-to-date information, but also get employment opportunities in their fields of study during the academic year and the summer months.

Susan J. Hunter, President

5525 **Economic Development/Marketing California Environmental Business Council**
UC Extention 408-748-2170
3120 De La Cruz Fax: 408-748-2189
Santa Clara, CA 95054 br1027@aol.com

The CEBC is a nonprofit trade and business assoication that promotes and assists California's environmental technology and services industry at the state, national, and international levels. Founded in 1994, the CEBC currently has morethan 100 member compines and other organizations throughout the state that represent all segments of the environmental industry.

5526 **Energy Thinking for Massachusetts**
Northeast Sustainable Energy Association
50 Miles Street 413-774-6051
Greenfield, MA 00130 Fax: 413-774-6053
nesea@nesea.org
www.nesea.org

CD

Jennifer Marrapese, Executive Director
Mary Biddle, Deputy Executive Director

5527 **Energy Thinking for Pennsylvania**
Northeast Sustainable Energy Association
50 Miles Street 413-774-6051
Greenfield, MA 00130 Fax: 413-774-6053
nesea@nesea.org
www.nesea.org

CD

Jennifer Marrapese, Executive Director
Mary Biddle, Deputy Executive Director

5528 **Environmental Data Resources**
6 Armstrong Road 203-783-0300
4th Floor 800-352-0050
Shelton, CT 00648 Fax: 800-231-6802
resinfo@edrnet.com
www.edrnet.com

Applied and product research in environmental applications.

Guy Tassinari, Managing Director
Tom Flynn, Chief Financial Officer

5529 **Environmental Education Council of Ohio**
PO Box 1004 740-653-2649
Lancaster, OH 43130-1004 800-992-6682
Fax: 330-823-8531
director@eeco-online.org
www.eeco.wildapricot.org

EECO believes that: we are all learners interacting with others in lifelong process, education is vital for individuals to reach their full potential as members of our global community, a healthy and sustainable environment isessential to the survival of the planet. It is the mission of EECO to lead in facilitating and promoting en-

vironmental education which nurtures knowledge, attitudes and behaviors that foster global stewardship.
Denise Natoli Brooks, President
Brenda Metcalf, Executive Director

5530 Environmental Education K-12
Archbold Biological Station 863-465-2571
123 Main Dr. Fax: 863-699-1927
Venus, FL 33960 archbold@archbold-station.org
Archbold Biological Station provides environmental education programs to help people af all ages discover and understand the unique and endangered Florida scrib. Several programs for children Grades K-12 are offered each year. Theprogram goals are; promote a sound foundation in ecological principles, nurture a sense of stewardship for Florida scrub habitat, demostrate the value of scientific research, and develop a deeper understanding of the importance of natural habitatsfor investigation.
Dr. Hilary Swain, Executive Director
Frances C. James, Advisor

5531 Environmental Forum of Marin
PO Box 151546 415-484-8336
San Rafael, CA 94915 board@MarinEFM.org
www.marinefm.org
Dedicated to protecting and enhancing the environment by educating its members and the Marin citizenry on environmental issues. In futherance of this goal, the Environmental Forum of Marin conducts annual training programs onenvironmental matters, provides continuing education for its members and public, and supports citizen action to influence environmental decision-making and public policy.
Vicki Rupp, President
Kathryn Olson, Vice President

5532 Environmental Law Institute
1730 M Street, NW 202-939-3800
Suite 700 Fax: 202-939-3868
Washington, DC 20036 law@eli.org
www.eli.org
Jose R Allen, Partner
Paul J Allen, Senior Vice President

5533 Environmental Resources
700 W Virginia Street 414-289-9505
Suite 601 Fax: 414-289-9552
Milwaukee, WI 53204 www.erm.com
Owner and co-founder of Moraine Multimedia, and Environmental Resources developes continuing education programs.
Shawn Doherty, Global Commercial Director
David McArthur, Regional CEO

5534 Environmental Sciences
900 University Ave. 951-827-1012
Riverside, CA 92521 Fax: 951-827-3993
enviro@eas.slu.edu
www.envisci.ucr.edu
Environmental Sciences is concerned with the near-surface realm of Earth and the way humans interact with that environment. Environmental scientist are concerned with water availability and equal, waste disposal, the use of Earth'slimited resources, and natural hazards such as earthquakes, landslides, and floods. Environmental scientists use the principles of geology, physics, chemistry, and biology to understand these phenomena and solve environmental problems.
Janice Border, Finance Officer
RC Sutton, Financial Operations Manager

5535 Exploring Animal Life - CD-ROM
Educational Images
PO Box 3456 607-732-1090
Westside Station 800-527-4264
Elmira, NY 14905-456 Fax: 607-732-1183
edimages@edimages.com
www.educationalimages.com
A curriculum oriented presentation and an instant encyclopedia, filled with superb photographs, informative text, exciting video clips, printable diagrams and illustrations, and lab activities. Provides a fascinating survey of themajor divisions of animal life and their characteristics: sponges, molluscs, insects, arthropods, fish, reptiles, birds and mammals are fully presented in the order in which you teach them.
Charles R Belinky, Ph.D, CEO

5536 Exploring Environmental Science Topics
Educational Images
PO Box 3456 607-732-1090
Westside Station 800-527-4264
Elmira, NY 14905-456 Fax: 607-732-1183
edimages@edimages.com
www.educationalimages.com
Provides a curriculum oriented presentation, an instant encyclopedia, superb photographs, video clips, informative text, printable diagrams & illustrations, & lab activities. This program offers a fascinating survey of environmentaltopics & concerns such as the environmental costs of energy; acid rain; energy flow and the greenhouse effect; oil spills; tundra, chaparral, desert, grassland and forest biomes; the hydrological cycle and water pollution; and the recycling elementsin the biosphere.
CD-Rom
Charles R Belinky, Ph.D, CEO

5537 Exploring Freshwater Communities
Educational Images
PO Box 3456 607-732-1090
Westside Station 800-527-4264
Elmira, NY 14905-456 Fax: 607-732-1183
edimages@edimages.com
www.educationalimages.com
A complete resource for studying freshwater biomes. It provides a fascinating survey of the ecology of swamps, bogs, marshes, wetlands, streams, ponds, lakes and the Everglades. There is even an introduction to fish restoration andwater pollution.
CD-Rom
Charles R Belinky, Ph.D, CEO

5538 Five Winds International
Hauptstraße 111-113 711-341- 170
Echterdingen, ON 70771 Fax: 711-341- 172
www.thinkstep.com
Five Winds helps companies and organizations understand sustainability to improve their performance and succeed in the marketplace.
Christoph Wilfert, CEO
Thomas Dollhoph, CFO

5539 Fossil Rim Wildlife Center
2155 County Road 2008 254-897-2960
PO Box 2189 888-775-6742
Glen Rose, TX 76043 Fax: 254-897-3785
vistor-services@fossilrim.org
www.fossilrim.org
Fossil Rim Wildlife Center is dedicated to conservation of species in peril, scientific research, training of professionals, creative management of natural resources, and impactful public education. Through these activities we providea diversity of compelling learning experiences which invoke positive change in the way people think, feel and act environmentally. Also provides scenic drives and lodgings for visitors, and is open all seasons.
Billie Kinnard, Marketing/PR Director
Lisa Roberts, Membership Director

5540 GLOBE Program
Mailstop T28H
Moffett Field, CA 94035
800-858-9947
Fax: 650-604-1913
help@globe.gov
www.globe.gov

GLOBE is a worldwide hands-on, primary and secondary school based science and education program.

5541 Glacier Institute
137 Main Street
PO Box 1887
Kalispell, MT 59903
406-755-1211
Fax: 406-755-7154
register@glacierinstitute.org
www.glacierinstitute.org

The Glacier Institute serves adults and children as an educational leader in the Crown of the Continent ecosystem with Glacier National Park at its center. Emphasizing field based learning experiences, the Institute provides anobjective and science based understanding of the area's ecology and its interaction with people. Through this non advocacy approach to outdoor education, participants can be better prepared to make informed and constructive decisions which impactthis & other ecosystems.

Joyce H Baltz, Executive Director
Dawn Glynn, Office Administrator

5542 Global Nest
Michigan State University
281 State Route 79
Suite 208
Morganville, NJ 00775
732-333-5848
Fax: 732-333-5946
info@globalnest.com
www.globalnest.com

The Global Nest constitutes an international association of scientists, technologists, engineers and other interested groups involved in all scientific and technological aspects of the environment as well as in application techniquesaiming at the development of sustainable solutions. Its main target is to support and assist the dissemination of information regarding the most contemporary methods for improving quality of life through the development and application oftechnologies.

5543 Gore Range Natural Science School
318 Walking Mountains Lane
PO Box 9469
Avon, CO 81620
970-827-9725
Fax: 970-827-9730
info@walkingmountains.org
www.walkingmountains.org

Offers summer day and overnight programs for students in 3rd grade up. During the academic school year GRNSS provides integrated field science education to local and visiting schools. Its mission is to raise environmental awareness andinspire stewardship of the Eagle River watershed.

Alix Berglund, Director
Hans Berglund, Advisory Director

5544 Groundwater Foundation
The Groundwater Foundation
3201 Pioneers Blvd
Suite 105
Lincoln, NE 68502
402-434-2740
800-858-4844
Fax: 402-434-2742
info@groundwater.org
www.groundwater.org

the groundwater foundation is a non profit organization, that is dedicated to informing the public about one of our greatest hidden resources, groundwater since 1985 our program and publications presents the benefits everyone recievesfrom groundwater,and the risks that threaten groundwater quality. we make learning about ground water fun and understandable for kids and adults alike.

Cathy Lotzer, Chair
Andy Belanger, Vice Chair

5545 Hazardous Chemicals: Handle With Care
Educational Images
PO Box 3456
Westside Station
Elmira, NY 14905-456
607-732-1090
800-527-4264
Fax: 607-732-1183
edimages@edimages.com
www.educationalimages.com

Shows the importance of hazardous chemicals in our daily lives and problems caused by ignorance, mistakes, accidents and occasionally, recklessness in their use. Four case studies show how toxic chemicals were introduced into theenvironment causing serious health and environmental effects. Video, 56 page guide with lesson plans, projects, reproducible handouts.

Charles R Belinky, CEO

5546 Hidden Villa
26870 Moody Road
Los Altos Hills, CA 94022
650-949-8650
Fax: 650-948-4159
info@hiddenvilla.org
www.hiddenvilla.org

Hidden Villa is a nonprofit educational organization that uses its organic farm, wilderness, and community to provide learning opportunities about the environment and social justice.

Chris Overington, Executive Director
Ken Ebbitt, Chair

5547 ISPTR-PARD
72902 Raymond Way
Twentynine Palms, CA 92277
310-303-9050
pard_expeditions@yahoo.com

ISPTR-PARD is a partnership between The International Society for the Preservation of the Tropical Rainforest and Pink Amazon River Dolphin Expedition. The organization is focused on conserving the Peruvian Amazon Rainforest and theAmazon pink river dolphin. Educational resources are also offered on their website for those that want to learn more.

Roxanne Kremer, Executive Director

5548 Ice Age Relicts: Living Glaciers and Signs of Ancient Ice Sheets
Educational Images
PO Box 3456
Westside Station
Elmira, NY 14905-456
607-732-1090
800-527-4264
Fax: 607-732-1183
edimages@edimages.com
www.educationalimages.com

Glaciers, living relicts of the ice age, are still important today. They hold much of the earth's fresh water, sculpted much of North America, and promise an early return to finish their work. Provides a coherent picture of howglaciers work, and what they did. 26 page guide. Video or filmstrips.

Charles R Belinky, Ph.D, CEO

5549 International Center for Earth Concerns
Centennial Valley, MT
805-649-3535
Fax: 805-649-1757
earthconcerns@earthconcerns.org
www.earthconcerns.org

Dedicated to providing for public use, a world class botanic garden, outdoor learning-ecology center and a 50-passenger all-electric floating classroom on Lake Casitas. These facilities are used to promote a better understanding ofman's place in the environment, as well as to help develop a sense of respect, responsibility and compassion for animals and nature.

John Hoyt, Founding President
John Taft, Chairman

5550 Invertebrate Animal Videos
Educational Images
PO Box 3456
Westside Station
Elmira, NY 14905-456
607-732-1090
800-527-4264
Fax: 607-732-1183
edimages@edimages.com
www.educationalimages.com

Four part series. Each a 40-minute multimedia presentation with easy going narration and hundreds of interactive links. Part I:

sponges, anemones, corals and flatworms. Part II: molluscs, segmented worms and minor phyla. Part III:the insects. Part IV: noninsect arthropods and echinoderms.
Charles R Belinky, Ph.D, CEO

5551 Jones & Stokes

11820 Northup Way
Suite E300
Bellevue, WA 98005
425-822-1077
Fax: 425-822-1079

An employee-owned company, Jones & Stokes is the best consulting source for integrated environmental planning and natural resources management services in the western United States.
Grant Bailey

5552 Killer Whales: Lords of the Sea

Educational Images
PO Boc 3456
Westside Station
Elmira, NY 14905-456
607-732-1090
800-527-4264
Fax: 607-732-1183
edimages@edimages.com
www.educationalimages.com

Separates facts from myth about these majestic, maligned and usually misrepresented seagoing mammals: both wild and captive killer whales, their mental and physical powers, their feeding and reproductive behavior, physiology,sociology and echolocation. Information on other cetaceans is presented for comparison and better understanding. Provides scientific information and reports on ongoing research.
Charles R Belinky, Ph.D, CEO

5553 Legacy International

1020 Legacy Drive
Bedford, VA 24523
540-297-5982
Fax: 540-297-1860
mail@legacyintl.org
www.legacyintl.org

Creates environments where people can address personal, community, and global needs while developing skills and effective responses to change.Whether working with youths, corporate leaders, educational professionals, entrepreneurs, orindividuals on opposing sides of a conflict, our goal is the same. Programs provide experiences, skills, and strategies that enable people to build better lives for themselves and others around them.
JE Rash, President/Founder
Shanti Thompson, VP

5554 Lesley/Audubon Environmental Education Programs

Lesley University
29 Everett Street
Cambridge, MA 00213
617-868-9600
info@lesley.edu
www.lesley.edu

In partership with Audubon Expedition Institute in Belfast, Lesley University offers a Bachelor of Science degree in Environmental Studies, a Master of Science degree in Environmental Education and a Master of Science in EcologicalTeaching and Learning. Students travel throughout the US earning academic credit and gaining first-hand experience of environmental issues.
Donald Perrin, Chair

5555 Let's Grow Houseplants

Educational Images
Po Box 3456
Westside Station
Elmira, NY 14905-456
607-732-1090
800-527-4264
Fax: 607-732-1183
edimages@edimages.com
www.educationalimages.com

Details different kinds of plants and their needs, when to water, selection, how to start from seeds and cuttings, how to make inexpensive pots, etc. Perfect to initiate an elementary classroom gardening project. 74 frames and guide.For elementary and preschool.
Charles R Belinky, Ph.D, CEO

5556 Lost Valley Educational Center

81868 Lost Valley Lane
Dexter, OR 97431
541-937-3351
info@lostvalley.org
www.lostvalley.org

Offers a wide variety of programs, including residential interships, educational workshops that emphasize hands on, experiential learning and personal/spiritual growth workshops. The Center also provides a supportive and nourishingplace to hold individuals and organizations who share our vision for an environmentally sound, pollution free world to hold conferences, retreats and workshops.
Dianne Brause, Co-Founder
Justin Michelson, Executive Director

5557 MacKenzie Environmental Education Center

Wisconsin Department of Natural Resources
W7303 County Road CS & Q
Poynette, WI 53955
608-635-8105
Fax: 608-635-2743
info@naturenet.com
www.mackenziecenter.com

Located only 20 miles north of Madison, the MacKenzie Center offers a wide array of outdoor experiences. Five themed nature trails, prairie restorations, picnic area, nature study, three museums and a wildlife exhibit containing liveanimals that are native to Wisconsin, are here to help you gain a better understanding of our natural resources.
Ruth Ann Lee, Director
Derek A. Duane, Maintenance

5558 Marine Biological Laboratory

7 Mbl Street
Woods Hole, MA 00254
508-548-3705
Fax: 508-457-1924
mdonovan@mbl.edu
www.mbl.edu

For more than a century, scientists from around the world have been gathering in Woods Hole. The best students from the best universities, the brightest young faculty, the most succesful scientists working at the pinnacle of theprofession, an unmatched collection of researchers and educators congregates every year in the seaside village whose name has become synonimous with science.
John W. Rowe, Chairman
Huntington F. Willard, Director

5559 Microscopic Pond

Educational Images
PO Box 3456
Westside Station
Elmira, NY 14905-456
607-732-1090
800-527-4264
Fax: 607-732-1183
edimages@edimages.com
www.educationalimages.com

Introduces students to both the micrscopic plant and animal life of a pond. Various groups of algae are discussed and illustrated, including desmids, Pediastrum, Pithophora, Spyrogyra, Volvox, Nostac, calothrix, Bacillariophyseae,Dinophyseae, and amoebas (includeing Amoeba proteus), Arcella, the testaceans, and many others. With only a few exceptions, all of the organisms in this program were photographed live.
Charles R Belinky, Ph.D, CEO

5560 Mote Environmental Services

1600 Ken Thompson Parkway
Sarasota, FL 34236
941-388-4441
800-691-6683
www.mote.org

Mote Environmental Services offers consulting services focused on marine and coastal issues, where our expertise is strongest. We provide superior, results-oriented investigations and management planning service within our areas oftechnical and policy specialty. MESI is a wholly owned subsidiary of Mote Marine Laboratory, an independent, nonprofit research and public education institution dedicated to excellence in marine and environmental sciences.
Eugene Beckstein, Chairman
Dr. Michael P. Crosby, President & CEO

5561 National Environmental Health Association (NEHA)
720 South Colorado Boulevard 303-756-9090
Suite 1000-N 866-956-2258
Denver, CO 80246-1926 Fax: 303-691-9490
staff@neha.org
www.neha.org

NEHA is the only national association that represents all of environmental health and protection from terrorism and all-hazards preparedness, to food safety and protection and onsite wastewater systems. Over 4500 members and theprofession are served by the association through its Journal of Environmental Health, Annual Educational Conference & Exhibition, credentialing programs, research and development activities and other services.
Bob Custard, President
David E. Riggs, President-Elect

5562 National Institute of Environmental Health Sciences
111 TW Alexander Drive 919-541-3345
PO Box 12233 Fax: 919-541-4395
Durham, NC 27709 webcenter@niehs.nih.gov
www.niehs.nih.gov

The National Institute of Environmental Health Sciences is the principal federal agency for basic biomedical research on the health effects of environmental agents. It is the headquarters for the National Toxicology Program whichcoordinates toxicology studies within the Department of Health and Human Services.
Linda S. Birnbaum, Director
Richard Woychik, Deputy Director

5563 National PTA: Environmental Project
1250 N. Pitt Street Alexandria 703-518-1200
Alexandria, VA 22314 800-307-4782
Fax: 703-836-0942
info@pta.org
www.pta.org

The mission of the National PTA is to support and speak on behalf of children and youth in the school, in the community and before governmental bodies and other organizations; to assist parents in developing the skills they need toraise and protect their children and to encourage parent and public involvement in the public schools. Engages in advocacy and education, including workshops and lobbying.
Laura Bay, President
Otha Thornton, President-Elect

5564 Natural Resources Conservation and Management
Lexindton Convention And Visitors Bureau
301 East Vine Street 859-244-7706
Lexington, KY 40507 800-845-3959
lexadmin@visitlex.com

As a trained professional, you will have a variety of challenging employment opportunities in public agencies and industry to contribute to sustained productivity and equality of all of our natural resources. In addition, some studentsfind that the Natural Resource Conservation and Management program satisfies their desire for a career in environmental education or environmental journalism.
David Lord, President

5565 Nielsen Environmental Field School
9600 Achenbach Canyon Road 575-532-5535
Las Cruces, NM 88011 Fax: 575-532-5978
info@envirofieldschool.com
www.envirofieldschool.com

In 1990, the Nielsen Environmental Field School was created in reponse to a demand from the environmental industry for practically oriented, hands-on environmental field training.
David M. Nielsen, Co-Founder
Gillian L. Nielsen, Co-Founder

5566 Northwest Environmental Education Council
Northwest Environmental Education Council
650 S. Orcas Street 206-762-1976
Suite 220 Fax: 206-762-1979
Seattle, WA 98108 www.nweec.org

The Northwest Environmental Education Council increases environmental awareness, appreciation and stewardship by providing environmental education and science training opportunities for youth and adults.
Tasya Gray, President
Lief Horwitz, Vice President

5567 Northwest Interpretive Association
Northwest Interpretive Association
164 South Jackson Street 206-220-4140
Seattle, WA 98104 877-874-6775
www.discovernw.org

Works with public and management agencies to operate educational bookstores. Our mission is to provide visitors with information they need to learn about the nature and natural history of public lands so they can make wise choicesabout the lands use, preservation and protection. We accomplish our mission by selling educational and interpretive materials directly to visitors as well as returning net proceeds to the site where they were guaranteed to help fund other programs.
Lori Brockman, Chair
Jim Caplan, Vice Chair

5568 Office of Energy and Environmental Industries
1401 Constitution Ave, NW 202-482-5225
Washington, DC 20230 800-usa-trad
Fax: 202-482-5665
www.ita.doc.gov

The Office of Energy and Environmental Industries (OEEI) is the principal resource and key contact point within the US Department of Commerce for American environmental technology companies. OEEI's goal is to facilitate and increasecexports of environmental technologuies-goods and services-by providing support and guidance to US exporters.
Adam O'Malley, Office Director
Man Cho, Team Leader, Energy

5569 Perkiomen Watershed Conservancy
1 Skippack Pike 610-287-9383
Schwenksville, PA 19473 Fax: 610-287-9237
pwc@perkiomenwatershed.org
www.perkiomenwatershed.org/

A nonprofit organization founded in 1964 by local citizens that works to protect the watershed of the Perkiomen Creek and its tributaries. This is accomplished through environmental education, conservation programs and watershedstewardship activities.
Michael Stokes, Chairman
Andrew Meadows, Vice Chairman

5570 Primary Ecological Succession
Educational Images
PO Box 3456 607-732-1090
Westside Station 800-527-4264
Elmira, NY 14905-456 Fax: 607-732-1183
edimages@edimages.com
www.educationalimages.com

An illustrated explanation of basic concepts of primary succession: the pioneer community; tolerant vs. intolerant species; stabilization; stratification and the climax community. Concise overview followed by classic, specificexamples of succession - on bare rock, on the sand dunes of Lake Michigan, on the outer banks of North Carolina - all explored in detail. 72 frames and guide.
Charles R Belinky, Ph.D, CEO

5571 Project Oceanology
University Of Connecticut

Avery Point Campus 860-445-9007
1084 Shennecossett Road 800-364-8472
Groton, CT 00634 Fax: 860-449-8008
projecto@oceanology.org
www.oceanology.org

Project Oceanology is owned and operated by Interdistrict Committee for Project Oceanology and association of 25 educational institutions in Massachusetts, Rodhe Island, Connecticut and New York. Members of this associations includepublic school districts, private schools, states university, public and private colleges, a maritime museum and an aquarium. The project is governed by an assembly of delegates representing the member institutions.

Thaxter Tewksbury, Director
Lauren Rader, Chief Instructor

5572 Project WILD

5555 Morningside Drive 713-520-1936
Suite 212 Fax: 713-520-8008
Houston, TX 77005 info@councilforee.org
www.projectwild.org

Project WILD is one of the most widely-used conservation and environmental education programs among educators of students in kindergarten through high school. Project WILD is based on the premise that young people and educators have avital interest in learning about natural world.

Mark LeFebre, Senior Program Manager
Josetta Hawthorne, Executive Director

5573 Resource-Use Education Council

The Virginia Natural Resources Education Guide
PO Box 11104 804-698-4442
Richmond, VA 23230 Fax: 804-698-4522

In the mid 1950s, representatives from Virginia and federal natural resource agencies, along with professors in the colleges of education and resource management, came together as the Virginia Resource Use Education Council. For 35years, the VRUEC sponsored a summer conservation course for teachers at four of Virginia's colleges.

Ann Regn, Chairman

5574 Risk Management Internet Services

Managerial Technologies Corporation
2400 East Main Street 630-221-9116
Suite 103- 319 Fax: 312-602-4935
St Charles, IL 60174 info@rmis.com
rmis.com

Dedicated to bringing risk management related professions together with the consultants, developers and providers who service them.

5575 Ross & Associates Environmental Consulting,Ltd

1218 Third Avenue 206-447-1805
Suite 1207 Fax: 206-447-0956
Seattle, WA 98101

Ross and Associates environmental consulting, is a small group of highly motivated professionals committed to helping environmental and natural resources agencies improve management programs and achieve better environmental results.

Rob Greenwood, Principal
Tim Larson, Principal

5576 SEEK

520 Lafayette Rd. N. 651-757-2700
St. Paul, MN 55155-4194 800-857-3864
seek.pca@state.mn.us
www.seek.state.mn.us

The SEEK directory works as a clearinghouse for all types of environmental education resources, from articles to lesson plans, from performances to displays, and many more. These resources come a variety of organizations throughoutMinnesota, including schools and colleges, government agencies, libraries and businesses.

Lee Ann Landstrom, Chair
Karen Balmer, Board of Teaching

5577 Sacramento River Discovery Center

1000 Sale Lane 530-527-1196
Red Bluff, CA 96080 Fax: 530-527-1312

The mission of the Sacramento River Discovery Center is to educate the public's school programs. Teacher professional development, camping, rafting and tourist events are available.

Lupe Green, Executive Director
Anna Draper, Program Manager

5578 Save the Dolphins Project Earth Island Institute

2150 Allston Way 510-859-9100
Suite 460 Fax: 510-859-9091
Berkeley, CA 94704-1375 johnknox@earthisland.org
www.earthisland.org

Martha Davis, President
Kenneth Brower, VP

5579 Schlitz Audubon Nature Center

1111 E Brown Deer Road 414-352-2880
Milwaukee, WI 53217 Fax: 414-352-6091
smanning@sanc.org
www.schlitzauduboncenter.com

A unique urban area of green just 15 minutes north of downtown Milwaukee, we are located along the shore of Lake Michigan. Escape from the world of concrete to hike seven miles of trails, walk along the beach and feel far away from thecity or view forests and wildlife from the 60-foot observation tower. Remember to bring your binoculars, you never know what you may want to take a closer look at while visiting the Center.

Margarete R. Harvey, President
Stuart D. Findlay, Treasurer

5580 School of Public & Environmental Affairs

Indiana University
1315 East Tenth Street 812-855-4848
Bloomington, IN 47405 800-765-7755
www.spea.indiana.edu

The School of Public Environmental Affairs offer environmental science summer programs to high school students and middle/high school teachers who want answers to environmental questions.

Michael McRobbie, President
Mary Anna Weber, VP

5581 Science House

909 Capability Drive 919-515-6118
Suite 1200 Fax: 919-515-7545
Raleigh, NC 27606 science_house@ncsu.edu
www.thesciencehouse.org

The activities of The Science House is itself a partership of facultu and stuff from science and education departments across the NC State campus, and collaborates with many other k-12 support organization in North Carolina.

5582 Seacamp Association, Inc

Newfound Harbor Marine Institute
1300 Big Pine Avenue 305-872-2331
Big Pine Key, FL 33043 877-SEA-AMP
Fax: 305-872-2555
info@seacamp.org
www.seacamp.org

To create awareness of the complex and fragile marine world and to foster critical thinking and informed decision making about man's use of natural resources. One of the few organizations in

the US providing experiential education inmarine studies to students aged 8 to 21 years.
Irene Hooper, President
Betty Rein, VP

5583 Setting Up a Small Aquarium
Educational Images
PO Box 3456 607-732-1090
Westside Station 800-527-4264
Elmira, NY 14905-456 Fax: 607-732-1183
Details the exact procedure to be followed in setting up either a marine or freshwater aquarium successfully. Methods are scientifically sound, well documented, and up-to-date.
Charles R Belinky, Ph.D, CEO

5584 Sierra Club
85 Second Street 415-977-5500
2nd Floor Fax: 415-977-5797
San Francisco, CA 94105 information@sierraclub.org
www.sierraclub.org
Aims to explore, enjoy, and protect the wild places of the earth, to practice and promote the responsible use of the earth's ecosystems and resources, to educate and enlist humanity to protect and restore the quality of the naturaland human environment, and to use all lawful means to carry out these objectives.
Loren Reyes, Vice President
Loren Blackford, President

5585 Smithsonian Environmental Research Center
Po Box 28 443-482-2200
647 Contees Wharf Road Fax: 443-482-2380
Edgewater, MD 21037-28 hollyj@si.edu
www.serc.si.edu
The Smithsonian Environmental Research Center advances stewardship of the biosphere through interdisciplinary research and educational outreach. SERC's scientists study a variety of interconnected ecosystems at the Center's primaryresearch site here in Maryland, and at affiliated sites around the world.
Suzanne H. Woolsey, Chairperson
V.K. Holtzendorf, VP

5586 Society of Environmental Toxicology and Chemistry
SETAC N America Office
229 South Baylen Street 850-469-1500
2nd Floor Fax: 850-469-9778
Pensacola, FL 32502 setac@setac.org
www.setac.org
The Society of Environmental Toxicology and Chemistry provides a forum for the examination of environmental issues by environmental professionals from industry, academia, government, and public-interest groups.
Patrick D. Guiney, President
Kurt J. Maier, VP

5587 Southwest Environmental Health Sciences: Community Outreach and Education Program
University Of Arizona College Of Pharmacy
Room 244 520-626-5594
Po Box 210207 Fax: 520-626-6944
Tucson, AZ 85721-207
The COEP goals are to review, develop, and disseminate quality environmental health science curricula. Develop and host K-12 teacher training workshops, communicate with the general public about local and common environmental healthscience concerns, share research results from SWEHSC investigators with the COEP target audiences.
Marti Lindsey, Director
Stephanie Nardei, Information Specialist

5588 Spiders in Perspective: Their Webs, Ways and Worth
Educational Images
PO Box 3456 607-732-1090
Elmira, NY 14905 800-527-4264
Fax: 607-732-1183
Comprehensive coverage of the nature of spiders, their diversity of structures, and their remarkable behavior patterns. Presents the unique world of creatures you may have ignored before, but probably never will again. Coverslocomotion, the various perceptual senses, silk production, camouflage and mimicry, webs, hunting, predation by wasps, kleptoparasitism, courtship and reproduction, population densities, impact on humans, etc. 2 parts, 76 & 78 frames. Video, slidesor filmstrip.
Charles R Belinky, Ph.D., CEO

5589 Student Conservation Association
Po Box 550 603-543-1700
689 River Road Fax: 603-543-1828
Charlestown, NH 00360 internships@thesca.org
www.thesca.org
America's largest and oldest provider of conservation service opportunities, outdoor education and career training for youth. SCA is building the next generation of conservation leaders and inspire lifelong stewardship of ourenvironment and communities.
Dale Penny, President/CEO
Valrie Bailey, Executive VP/Chaief of Staff

5590 The Groundwater Foundation
5561 S 48th Street 402-434-2740
Suite 215 800-858-4844
Lincoln, NE 68516 Fax: 402-434-2742
info@groundwater.org
www.groundwater.org
The Groundwater Foundation is a nonprofit organization that is dedicated to informing the public about one of our greatest hidden resources, groundwater. Since 1985, our programs and publications present the benefits everyone receivesfrom groundwater and the risks that threaten groundwater quality. We make learning about groundwater fun and understandable for kids and adults alike.
James Burks, Chair
Jay Beaumont, Vice Chair

5591 The Nelson Institute for Environmental Studies
UW Madison, 550 N Park Street 608-262-7996
70 Science Hall Fax: 608-262-2273
Madison, WI 53706-1491 nelson@mailplus.wisc.edu
www.nelson.wisc.edu
Few institutions can match the University of Wisconsin-Madison's expertise in environmental studies. Literally hundreds of professors teach and conduct research in environmentally related subjects ranging from agriculture to zoology.Their scholarship and achievement are widely recognized. In dozens of academic fields, the university is consistently rated the nation's best and most prolific.
Janet Silbernagel, Program Chairs, Conservation
Jess Gilbert, Program Chairs, Culture, His

5592 Thorne Ecological Institute
1466 N 63rd Street 303-499-3647
PO Box 19107 Fax: 720-565-3873
Boulder, CO 80308 info@thornenature.org
www.thornenature.org
Offers hands-on environmental education for young people along the Front Range of Colorado.
Melissa Amold, Chair
Mike Moelter, Vice Chair

5593 Trees for Tomorrow
519 Sheridan Street 715-479-6456
PO Box 609 800-838-9472
Eagle River, WI 54521 Fax: 715-479-2318
learning@treesfortomorrow.com
www.treesfortomorrow.com

Private, nonprofit natural resource education school that uses a combination of field studies and classroom presentations to teach conservation values, as well as demonstrate the benefits of modern resource management.
Maggie Bishop, Executive Director
Sheri Buller, Assistant Director

5594 Triumvirate Environmental
200 Inner Belt Road
Somerville, MA 00214
800-966-9282
Fax: 617-628-8099
contactus@triumvirate.com
www.triumvirate.com

Triumvirate Environmental is a full-service environmental management firm headquartered in eastern Massachusetts. Serving the environmental and hazardous waste needs of clients throughout the northeast in the areas of biotechnology andpharmaceuticals, education, health care, metal platers and finishers, manufacturing, and utilities, Triumvirate Environmental is the industry leader in personalized service.

5595 Tropical Forest Foundation
2121 Eisenhower Avenue
Suite 200
Alexandria, VA 22314
703-518-8834
Fax: 703-518-8974
www.tropicalforestfoundation.org

A non-profit educational institution dedicated to the conservation of tropical forests through sustainable forestry. Its Board of Directors includes representatives from industry, government, science, academia and conservation.
Shawn Draper, Chairman
Steve Tourek, President

5596 US Environmental Protection Agency: Great Lakes National Program Office
77 West Jackson Boulevard
G-17
Chicago, IL 60604-3511
312-353-2117
800-621-8431
Fax: 312-886-6869
www.epa.gov/greatlakes

The focus for the State of the Lakes Ecosystem Conference (SOLEC) 1996 is the nearshore zone of the Great Lakes. Nearshore ecosystems are complex and dynamic with many measurable parameters. The nearshore area is extremely important tooverall ecosystem function. It is the most productive zone within each of the Great Lakes and is the area most affected by human activity. Nearshore zones include embayments, tributaries and tributary mouths, marshes and other wetlands, and dunes.

5597 Water Resources Management
550 N Park Street
122 Science Hall
Madison, WI 53706-1491
608-265-5296
Fax: 608-262-0014
nelsongrad@mailplus.wisc.edu
www.nelson.wisc.edu

The program addresses the complex, interdisciplinary aspects of managing resources by helping students integrate the biological and phisical sciences with engineering and law and the social sciences. The workshop provides anopportunity for students to work outside of the textbook environment and tackle a rea-world problem.
Eileen Hanneman, Sr. Administrative Program S
Carol Enseki, Department Administrator

5598 Western Forestry and Conservation Association
4033 SW Canyon Road
Portland, OR 97221
503-226-4562
Fax: 503-226-2515
richard@westernforestry.org
westernforestry.org

Offers continuing education workshops and seminars for professional foresters. The association awards medals for distinguished service to forestry at their annual conference.
Richard Zabel, Executive Director

5599 Wilderness Education Association
2150 N 107th Street
Suite 205
Seattle, WA 98133
206-367-8704
800-572-3015
Fax: 206-367-8777
nationaloffice@weainfo.org
www.weainfo.org

Mike McGowan, President
Ricky Haro, VP

5600 Windows on the Wild
World Wildlife Fund
1250 24th Street Northwest
Po Box 97180
Washington, DC 20037
202-293-4800
800-225-5993
Fax: 202-293-9211
www.windowsonthewild.com

Provides educators with interdisciplinary curriculum materials and training programs. By using biodiversity as its organizing theme, WOW provides students with a unique window for exploring a range of topics including science,economics, social studies, language arts, geography and civics.
Jennifer A Zadwick, Program Information Coord.

5601 World Resources Institute
10 G Street, NE
Suite 800
Washington, DC 20002
202-729-7600
Fax: 202-729-7610
www.wri.org

WRI provides information, ideas, and solutions to global environmental problems. Our mission is to move human society to live in ways that protect the environment for current and future generations, with programs that meet globalchallenges by using knowledge to catalyze public and private action. Goals include safeguarding earth's climate from further harm, protecting the ecosystems, and reducing the use of materials and generation of wastes in the production of goods andservices.
James Gustave Speth, Founder/Trustee
James A. Harmon, Chairman

5602 Young Entomologists Society
6907 West Grand River Avenue
Lansing, MI 48906
517-886-0630
Fax: 517-886-0630
www.members.@aol.com/YESbugs/mainmenu.html

To provide young people with a combination of programs, publications, and educational materials that enrich their insect and spider studies through dynamic, innovative, and enjoyable learning experience.
Gary Dunn, Director Of Education

Industry Web Sites

Environmental

5603 ABS Group

www.abs-group.com/Training

ABS Group offers training programs that deliver information on safety, risk and compliance services. Provide advanced engineering support and certify management systems for the marine; offshore oil, gas & chemical; and power sectors.

5604 Academy of Natural Sciences of Drexel University

www.ansp.org

The Academy of Natural Sciences of Drexel University is a natural history museum dedicated to advancing research, education and public engagement in biodiversity and environmental science, while aiming to promote positive human impactsthrough the communication and application of rigorous science.
George Gephart, President & CEO
Robert Peck, Curator of Art & Artifacts

5605 ActiveSet.org

www.activeset.org

ActiveSet.org allows professionals involved in all aspects of environmental air quality testing, monitoring and management to easily research and contact emissions testing firms, services and products either by state, region, or usingthe site's built-in search engine.

5606 Adirondack Council

www.adirondackcouncil.org

The Adirondack Council is a non-profit environmental group working to protect the open space resources of New York's six million acre Adirondack Park and to help sustain the natural and human communities of the region. It monitorsdevelopment on private lands and ensures the mandated constitutional protection of public lands.

5607 Advanced Buildings

www.advancedbuildings.org

A community resource pertaining to green residential and commerical construction information. The organization aims to provide insights on individual green consturction methods that improve energy efficiency, conserve natural resourcesand preserve the environment.

5608 Advanced Recovery, Inc

www.advancedrecovery.com

Advanced Recovery, based in New Jersey, concentrates on the proper disposal and recycling of all scrap, but are particularly interested in the disposal of electronic equipment, such as computer monitors containing lead.

5609 Advanced Technology Environmental Education Center

www.ateec.org

The Advanced Technology Environmental Education Center (ATEEC) aims to advance environmental technology education through curriculum development, professional development and program improvement in the nation's community colleges andhigh schools. ATEEC is funded by the National Science Foundation and is a partnership of the Hazardous Materials Training and Research Institute, the National Partnership for Environmental Technology Education and the University of Northern Iowa.

5610 African Environmental Research and Consulting Group

www.africanenviro.org

The African Environmental Research and Consulting Group (AERCG) is a non-profit organization headquartered in Kansas City with regional offices in Africa. The group, consisting of native African expatriates who are professionals in theenvironmental industry, focuses on improving the quality of life, mitigating environmental hazards and protecting human health in Africa. They are also involved in promoting sustainable development in African communities.

5611 Agency for Toxic Substances and Disease Registry

www.atsdr.cdc.gov

As an agency of the US Department of Health and Human Services, theAgency for Toxic Substances and Disease Registry (ATSDR) aims to prevent exposure and adverse human health effects and diminished quality of life associated withexposure to hazardous substances from waste sites, unplanned releases and other sources of pollution present in the environment.

5612 Agriculture Network Information Collaborative

www.agnic.org

AgNIC is a voluntary alliance of the National Agricultural Library, land-grant universities and other agricultural organizations in cooperation with citizen groups and government agencies. They focus on providing agriculturalinformation in electronic format via the Internet.

5613 Air Force Center for Environmental Excellence

www.usaf.com/orgs/environmental.htm

The Center for Environmental Excellence provides Air Force leaders with the comprehensive expertise they need to protect, preserve, restore, develop and sustain America's environmental and installation resources.

5614 Air and Waste Management Association

www.awma.org

The Air and Waste Management Association is a non-profit, nonpartisan professional organization that provides training, information and networking opportunities to thousands of environmental professionals in 65 countries.

5615 Alabama Department of Environmental Management

www.adem.state.al.us

The Alabama Department of Environmental Management (ADEM) provides environmental stewardship through the implementation of authorized environmental statutes, advocating statutory change as needed.

5616 Alaska Chilkat Bald Eagle Preserve

dnr.alaska.gov/parks/units/eagleprv.htm

The Alaska Chilkat Bald Eagle Preserve was created by the State of Alaska in June 1982 to protect and perpetuate the world's largest concentration of bald eagles and their critical habitat. It also sustains and protects the naturalsalmon runs.

5617 Alfred Wegener Institute for Polar and Marine Research

www.awi.de/en.html

The Alfred Wegener Institute conducts research in the Arctic, the Antarctic and at temperate latitudes. It coordinates Polar research in Germany and provides both the necessary equipment and the essential logistic back up for polarexpeditions.

5618 Alliance for Environmental Technology

www.aet.org

The Alliance for Environmental Technology is an international association of chemical manufacturers dedicated to improving the environmental performance of the pulp and paper industry. AET was established to gather and distributeeducational and technical resources relating to Chlorine Dioxide and its use in papermaking.

5619 American Academy of Environmental Engineers & Scientists

www.aaees.org

The American Academy of Environmental Engineers & Scientists is dedicated to excellence in the practice of environmental engineering to ensure public health, safety and welfare and enable humankind to co-exist in harmony with nature.

5620 American Chemical Society

www.acs.org

The American Chemical Society aims to promote a positive public perception and understanding of chemistry and the chemical sciences through public outreach programs and public awareness campaigns; involve the Society's 163,000+ membersin improving the public's perception of chemistry.

5621 American Conference of Governmental Industrial Hygienists

www.acgih.org

ACGIH is a charitable scientific organization that aims to advance occupational and environmental health through education and the development and dissemination of scientific and technical knowledge.

5622 American Council for an Energy-Efficient Economy

www.aceee.org

The American Council for an Energy-Efficient Economy is a non-profit organization dedicated to advancing energy efficiency as a means of promoting both economic prosperity and environmental protection.

5623 American Farmland Trust

1150 Connecticut Ave NW — 202-331-7300
Suit 600 — 800-431-1499
Washington, DC — Fax: 202-659-8339
info@farmland.org
www.farmland.org

American Farmland Trust is a private non-profit organization that aims to stop the loss of productive farmland and to promote farming practices that lead to a healthy environment.

John Piotti, President
Jimmy Daukas, VP/Operations

5624 American Forests

www.americanforests.org

American Forests aims to inspire and advance the conservation of forests, which they do through protecting and restoring threatened forest ecosystems; promoting and expanding urban forests; and increasing public understanding of theimportance of forests.

5625 American Geophysical Union

sites.agu.org

The American Geophysical Union is dedicated to the furtherance of Earth and space sciences, and to communicating science's ability to benefit humanity. They promote cooperation among scientific organizations involved in geophysics andrelated disciplines, and initiate and participate in geophysical research programs.

5626 American Hydrogen Association

www.clean-air.org

The American Hydrogen Association aims to close the information gap between researchers, industries and the public concerning solar hydrogen technologies that will eliminate economic, environmental and energy hardships caused byburning fossil fuels.

5627 American Rivers

www.americanrivers.org

American Rivers is a national non-profit conservation organization dedicated to protecting and restoring America's rivers and to fostering a river stewardship ethic.

5628 American Solar Energy Society

www.ases.org

The American Solar Energy Society (ASES) is a national organization dedicated to advancing the use of solar energy for the benefit of US citizens and the global environment. ASES promotes the widespread near-term and long-term use ofsolar energy.

5629 Ames Laboratory: Environmental & Protection Sciences Program

www.ameslab.gov/epsci/epsci-home

The Ames Laboratory's Environmental & Protection Sciences Program aims to exploit expertise and developing sciences for the benefit of problems associated with environmental characterization and monitoring.

5630 Antarctic and Southern Ocean Coalition

www.asoc.org

The Antartic and Southern Ocean Coalition is a collaborative effort by conservation organizations from around the world to defend the integrity of Antarctic and Southern Ocean ecosystems from encroaching human activities. Responsiblefor national and international campaigns to protect the biological diversity and pristine wilderness of Antartica, including its oceans and marine life.

5631 Argonne National Laboratory

9700 S Cass Avenue — 630-252-2000
Argonne, IL 60439 — www.anl.gov

Argonne National Laboratory is one of the US Department of Energy's largest research centers and focuses on topics ranging from ways to obtain affordable clean energy to methods of protecting the environment and its inhabitants.

Matthew Tirrell, Deputy Director
Paul Kearns, Interim Director

5632 Arizona Geological Survey

www.azgs.state.az.us

The Arizona Geological Survey aims to inform and advise the public about the geologic character of Arizona in order to foster understanding and prudent development of the State's land, water, mineral and energy resources.

5633 **Arkansas Natural Heritage Commission**

www.naturalheritage.org

The Arkansas Natural Heritage Commission (ANHC) is responsible for maintaining the most up-to-date and comprehensive source of information concerning the rare plant and animal species, and high-quality natural communities of Arkansas.

5634 **Asia Pacific Centre for Environmental Law**

law.nus.edu.sg/apcel

The Asia acific Centre for Environmental Law (APCEL) was established in response to the need for capacity-building in environmental legal education and the need for promotion of awareness in environmental issues. It is currentlyworking closely with the International Union for Conservation of Nature's Commission on Environmental Law.

5635 **Association of Energy Engineers**

www.aeecenter.org

The Association of Energy Engineers is a non-profit professional society that promotes the scientific and educational interests of those engaged in the energy industry, while fostering action for sustainable development.

5636 **Association of State Floodplain Managers**

www.floods.org

The Association of State Floodplain Managers promotes common interest in flood damage abatement, supports environmental protection for floodplain areas, provides education on floodplain management practices and policy and urgesincorporating multi-objective management approaches to solve local flooding problems.

5637 **Associations of University Leaders for a Sustainable Future**

ulsf.org

The mission of the Association of University Leaders for a Sustainable Future is to make sustainability a major focus of teaching, research, operations and outreach at colleges and universities worldwide. ULSF pursues this missionthrough advocacy, education, research, assessment, membership support and international partnerships to advance education for sustainability.

5638 **Atlantic Salmon Federation**

www.asf.ca

The Atlantic Salmon Federation is an international non-profit organization that promotes the conservation and wise management of wild Atlantic salmon and their habitat.

5639 **Audubon Society of Missouri**

mobirds.org

The Audubon Society of Missouri is dedicated to the preservation and protection of birds and other wildlife; to education and appreciation of the natural world; and to effective wildlife and habitat conservation practices.

5640 **Australian Ocean Data Network**

portal.aodn.org.au

The Australian Ocean Data Network provides access to all available Australian marine and climate science data and provides primary access to IMOS data, including access to IMOS metadata.

5641 **Bat Conservation International**

www.batcon.org

Bat Conservation International is dedicated to the preservation and restoration of bat populations and their habitats around the world.

5642 **Battelle Memorial Institute**

www.battelle.org

Battelle Memorial Institute is a multidimensional organization providing research and development across a number of fields. Their Environmental Services division handles air quality & regulatory compliance; analytical chemistry;contaminated sites; ecological sampling & analysis; and sediment assessment & management. Their Environmental & Analytical Services division deals with reducing risk, increasing sustainability and mitigating environmental impacts in sensative anddeepwater environments.

5643 **Bellona Foundation**

www.bellona.org

The Bellona Foundation is an independent non-profit organization that aims to meet and fight climate challenges through identifying and implementing sustainable environmental solutions. Although they are headquarted in Norway, withoffices in Belgium and Russia, they are engaged in a broad spectrum of current national and international environmental questions that have a global impact.

5644 **Bioelectromagnetics Society**

www.bems.org

The Bioeletromagnetics Society is an independent organization of biological and physical scientists, physicians and engineers interested in the interactions of non-ionizing radiation within biological systems.

5645 **Birdingonthe.Net**

www.birdingonthe.net

Birdingonthe.net serves as a resource for birdwatchers who may be interested in joining mailing lists including comprehensive archive indexes of birds and rare bird alerts. Also provides information about birdwatching worldwide.

5646 **Brookhaven National Laboratory**

www.bnl.gov/world

Brookhaven National Laboratory is a multipurpose research institution funded primarily by the US Department of Energy's Office of Science. Brookhaven conducts research in physical, biomedical and environmental sciences, as well as inenergy technologies; it also builds and operates major facilities available to university, industrial and government scientists.

5647 **Brown is Green**

www.brown.edu/initiatives/brown-is-green/

The Brown is Green website (BIG) is the Energy & Environmental Initiatives office's primary communication medium to report progress on Brown University's sustainability programs and related goals. It is not, however,a reliable sourceof information for students, faculty and staff working on campus environmental programs.

5648 **Bureau of International Recycling**

www.bir.org

The Bureau of International Recycling (BIR) is an international trade federation representing the world's recycling industry, specifically focusing on ferrous and non-ferrous metals, paper and textiles. Plastics, rubber, tires andglass are also studied and traded by some BIR members.

5649 Bureau of Transportation Statistics

www.bts.gov

The Bureau of Transportation Statistics focuses on data collection, analysis and reporting and aims to ensure the most cost-effective use of transportation-monitoring resources. They strive to increase public awareness of the nation'stransportation system and its implications.

5650 California Conservation Corps

www.ccc.ca.gov

The California Conservation Corps is a state agency that puts young people and the environment together to help improve California's natural resources; they also assist with emergency responses, including fighting fires, floods,earthquakes and pest infestations.

5651 California Energy Commission

www.energy.ca.gov

The California Energy Commission is the state's primary energy policy and planning agency. It was created by the Legislature in 1974 and located in Sacramento.

5652 California Environmental Protection Agency

calepa.ca.gov

The California Environmental Protection Agency aims to restore, protect and enhance the environment, to ensure public health, environmental quality and economic vitality. The agency offers a number of services including air qualitymonitoring and pesticide control.

5653 California League of Conservation Voters

www.ecovote.org

The California League of Conservation Voters mobilizes California voters to support environmentally responsible candidates and issues and serves as a watchdog to hold elected officials accountable for their environmental votes.

5654 California Resources Agency

resources.ca.gov

The California Resources Agency is responsible for the conservation, enhancement and management of California's natural and cultural resources, including land, water, wildlife, parks, minerals and historic sites. The CaliforniaEnvironmental Resources Evaluation System is an initative within the agency.

5655 California/Nevada Amphibian Populations Task Force

www.canvamphibs.com

The California/Nevada Working Group seeks to understand and reverse amphibian population declines in California and Nevada, and to provide for the continued existance of both declining and non-declining species.

5656 Canadian Chlorine Chemistry Council

www.cfour.org

The Canadian Chlorine Chemistry Council aims to facilitate dialogue and promote coordinated action in Canada among key stakeholders in order to bring about a balanced view of chlorine chemistry to enable society to make informed,science based decisions on issues involving chlorine.

5657 Canadian Council of Ministers of the Environment

www.ccme.ca

The Canadian Coucil of Ministers of the Environment (CCME) works to promote cooperation on and coordination of interjurisdictional issues such as waste management, air pollution and toxic chemicals. CCME members proposenationally-consistent environmental standards and objectives to help achieve a high level of environmental quality across the country.

5658 Canadian Environmental Assessment Agency

www.ceaa.gc.ca

The Canadian Environmenal Assessment Agency provides Canadians with high quality environmental assessments that contribute to informed decision-making in support of sustainable development.

5659 Canadian Institute for Environmental Law and Policy

www.cielap.org

The Canadian Institute for Environmental Law and Policy (CIELAP) provides leadership in the research and development of environmental law and policy that promotes public interest and principles of sustainability.

5660 Carnegie Mellon University: Department of Civil & Environmental Engineering

www.cmu.edu/cee

Carnegie Mellon's Department of Civil and Environmental Engineering is a part of the engineering college, Carnegie Institute of Technology. The department maintains a commitment to excellence and innovation in education and research.

5661 Center for Environmental Biotechnology

www.ceb.utk.edu

The Center for Environmental Biotechnology at the University of Tennessee, Knoxville was established to foster a multidisciplinary approach for training the next generation of environmental scientists and solving environmental problemsthrough biotechnology.

5662 Center for Environmental Design Research

www.cedr.berkeley.edu

The Center for Environmental Design Research is an Organized Research Unit of the University of California at Berkeley. The Center encourages research in environmental planning and design, in order to increase the factual content ofdesign decisions and to promote systematic approaches to design decision making.

5663 Center for Environmental Philosophy

www.cep.unt.edu

The Center for Environmental Philosophy, a non-profit organization affiliated with the University of North Texas, is responsible for the publication of the Environmental Ethics journal, as well as the training and promotion of researchin environmental ethics through workshops and conferences.

5664 Center for Environmental and Regulatory Information Systems

ceris.purdue.edu/ceris

The Center for Environmental and Regulatory Information Systems (CERIS) is a center within the Entomology Department at Purdue University and is home to a collection of databases concerning pesticides, plant export/import requirementsand exotic pest tracking. Some of the databases include the National Pesticide Information Retrieval System (NPIRS), the National Agricultural Pest Information System (NAPIS) and the National Plant Diagnostic Network (NPDN).

5665 Center for Health Effects of Environmental Contamination

www.cheec.uiowa.edu

The University of Iowa's Center for Health Effects of Environmental Contamination supports and conducts research to identify, measure and prevent adverse health outcomes related to exposure to environmental toxins. CHEEC organizes andparticipates in educational and outreach programs; provides environmental health expertise to local, state and federal entities and serves as a resource to Iowans in the field of environmental health.

5666 Center for International Earth Science Information Network

www.ciesin.org

The Center for International Earth Science Informatio nNetwork (CIESIN) works at the intersection of the social, natural and information services, specializing in online data and information management; spatial data integration andtraining and interdisciplinary research related to human interactions in the environment.

5667 Center for International Environmental Law

www.ciel.org

The Center for International Environmental Law is a public interest non-profit environmental law firm founded in 1989 to strengthen international and comparative environmental law and policy around the world. CIEL provides a full rangeof environmental legal services in both international and comparative national law.

5668 Center for Plant Conservation

www.saveplants.org

The Center for Plant Conservation is dedicated solely to preventing the extinction of native US plant species. The CPC is a network of more than 40 leading botanic institutions that are involved in plant conservation, research andeducation.

5669 Center for Renewable Energy and Sustainable Technology

thecrestproject.com

The Center for Renewable Energy and Sustainable Technology (CREST) aims to accelerate the use of renewable energy by providing credible information, insightful analysis and innovative strategies amid changing energy markets andmounting environmental needs. The combined CREST organization boasts a strong platform for research, publication and dissemination of timely information regarding sustainable energy.

5670 Centers for Disease Control and Prevention

1600 Clifton Road
Atlanta, GA

800-232-4636
www.cdc.gov

To promote health and quality of life by preventing and controlling disease, injury and disability. The CDC seeks to accomplish its mission by working with partners throughout the nation and world to monitor health; detect andinvestigate health problems; conduct research to enhance prevention; develop and advocate sound public health policies; implement prevention strategies; promote healthy behaviors; foster safe and healthful environments and provide leadership andtraining.

Brenda Fitzgerald, Director
Anne Schuchat, Deputy Director

5671 Central European Environmental Data Request Facility

www.cedar.at/sitemap.htm

The Cebntral European Environmental Data Request Facility (CEDAR) was created to provide computing and Internetworking facilities to support international data exchange with the Central and Eastern European environmental community.Focusing at first on mainly Central and Eastern European countries, CEDAR's activities expanded quickly to an audience all over the world.

5672 Centre for Environmental Data Analysis

www.ceda.ac.uk

The Centre for Environmental Data Analysis serves the environmental sciences community through four data centres, data anaylsis environments and participation in a host of relevant research projects.

5673 Cetacean Society International

csiwhalesalive.org

The Cetacean Society International is a non-profit conservation, education and research organization based in the USA, with volunteer representatives in 26 countries around the world. Their stance is that it is no longer justifiablefor cetaceans to be captured or maintained in captivity for exhibition, research or educational purposes.

5674 Charles Darwin Foundation

www.darwinfoundation.org/en

The Charles Darwin Foundation conducts scientific research and provides environmental education about conservation and natural resource management in the Galapagos archipelago and its surrounding Marine Reserve.

5675 Chicago Wilderness

www.chicagowilderness.org

Chicago Wilderness is a regional organization that aims to preserve, improve and expand nature and quality of life in parts of Illinois, Indiana, Wisconsin and Michigan. The alliance covers projects that tackle invasive speciesremoval, land regeneration, childhood education and volunteer initiatives.

5676 China Council for International Cooperation on Environment and Development

www.cciced.net/cciceden

The main goals of the China Council for International Cooperation on Environment & Development include exchanging and disseminating international successful experience; studying key environment and development issues of China;providing forward-looking, strategic and early warning policies; facilitating the implementation of sustainable development strategies and the development of a resource-saving and environment-friendly society in China.

5677 Chlorine Chemistry Council

c3.org

The Chlorine Chemistry Council, a business council of the American Chemistry Council, represents the manufacturers and users of chlorine and chlorine-related products. Chlorine is widely used as a disease-fighting disinfection agent,as a basic component in pharmaceuticals and a myriad other products that are essential to modern life.

5678 **City Farmer News**

www.cityfarmer.info
City Farmer News is a non-profit society that promotes urban food production and environmental conservation by teaching people how to grow food in the city, compost their waste and take care of their home landscape in anenvironmentally responsible way.

5679 **Coastal Conservation Association**

www.joincca.org
The Coastal Conservation Association conserves, promotes and enhances the present and future available resources for the benefit of the general public.

5680 **Colorado Department of Natural Resources**

cdnr.us
The Colorado Department of Natural Resources was created to develop, protect and enhance Colorado's natural resources for the use and enjoyment of the state's present and future residents, as well as for visitors to the state.

5681 **Colorado School of Mines**

www.mines.edu
The Colorado School of Mines is a public research university devoted to engineering and applied sciences with a curriculum and research program geared towards responsible stewardship of the earth and its resources.

5682 **Commission for Environmental Cooperation**

www.cec.org
The Commission for Environmental Cooperation (CEC) is an international organization created by Canada, Mexico and the US under the North American Agreement on Environmental Cooperation. The CEC was established to address regionalenvironmental concerns, help prevent potential trade and environmental conflicts and to promote the effective enforcement of environmental law.

5683 **Connecticut Department of Energy and Environmental Protection**

www.ct.gov/deep/site/default.asp
Connecticut's Department of Energy and Environmental Protection aims to conserve, improve and protect the natural resources and environment of the State of Connecticut while preserving the natural environment and the life forms itsupports in a delicate, interrelated and complex balance, to the end that the state may fulfill its responsibility as trustee of the environment for present and future generations.

5684 **Conservation International**

www.conservation.org
Conservation International aims to protect vital natural resources such as food, fresh water, livelihoods and a stable climate.

5685 **Consortium on Green Design and Manufacturing**

cgdm.berkeley.edu
The Consortium on Green Design and Manfacturing is an interdisciplinary research initiative at the University of California, Berkeley. The CGDM is an industry/government/university partnership that develops linkages betweenmanufacturing and design and their environmental effects while integrating engineering information, management practices and government policy-making.

5686 **Consultative Group on International Agricultural Research**

www.cgiar.org
The Consultative Group on International Agricultural Research aims to contribute to food security and poverty eradication in developing countries through research, partnerships, capacity building and policy support. CGIAR promotessustainable agricultural development based on the environmentally sound management of natural resources.

5687 **Contaminated Site Clean-Up Information**

www.clu-in.org
CLU-IN, a US Environmental Protection Agency forum, provides information about innovative treatment and site characterization technologies while acting as a forum for all waste remediation stakeholders.

5688 **Coral Health and Monitoring Program**

www.coral.noaa.gov
The goal of the Coral Health and Monitoring Program is to provide services to help improve and sustain coral reef health throughout the world.

5689 **Coral Reef Alliance**

coral.org
The Coral Reef Alliance is a member supported, non-profit organization dedicated to keeping coral reefs alive around the world. The Alliance works with marine park managers, businesses and communities to help increase their capacity toprotect their local coral reefs.

5690 **Council for Agricultural Science & Technology**

www.cast-science.org
The Council for Agricultural Science & Technology is a non-profit organization composed of scientific societies and many individual, student, company, nonprofit and associate society members. CAST assembles, interprets and communicatesscience based information regionally, nationally and internationally on food, fiber, agricultural, natural resources and related environmental issues to stakeholders.

5691 **Council on Environmental Quality**

730 Jackson Place NW 202-395-5750
Washington, DC 20503 www.whitehouse.gov/CEQ/
The Council on Environmental Quality coordinates federal environmental efforts and works closely with agenices and other White House offices in the development of environmental policies and initiatives.

5692 **Coweeta Long Term Ecological Research**

coweeta.uga.edu
The Coweeta LTER Program was developed to support research of ecological phenomena that occur on time scales of decades or centuries.

5693 **CropLife Canada**

croplife.ca
CropLife Canada aims to support sustainable agriculture in Canada, in cooperation with others, by building trust and appreciation for plant life science technologies.

5694 **David R. Atkinson Center for a Sustainable Future**

www.atkinson.cornell.edu

Cornell University's David R. Atkinson Center for a Sustainable Future is committed to research, teaching and outreach focused on environmental issues, with the goals of enhancing the quality of life, encouraging economic vitality andpromoting the conservation of natural resources for sustainable future.

5695 **Defenders of Wildlife**

www.defenders.org

Defenders of Wildlife is dedicated to the protection of all native wild animals and plants and their natural communities. Their focus is placed on the accelerating rate of extinction of species and the associated loss of biologicaldiversity, and habitat alteration and destruction.

5696 **Delaware Department of Natural Resources and Environmental Control**

dnrec.alpha.delaware.gov

Delaware's Department of Natural Resources and Environmental Control aims to protect and manage the state's vital natural resources, protect public health and safety, provide quality outdoor recreation and to serve and educate thecitizens of the state about the wise use, conservation and enhancement of Delaware's environment.

5697 **Department of the Interior**

1849 C Street NW 202-208-3100
Washington, DC 20240 feedback@ios.doi.gov
www.doi.gov

The Department of the Interior protects and manages the US' natural resources and cultural heritage; provides sceintific and other information about these resources; and honors its trust responsibilities or special commitments toAmerican Indians, Alaska Natives and affiliated island communities.

Ryan Zinke, Secretary

5698 **EARTHWORKS**

www.earthworksaction.org

EARTHWORKS is a non-profit organization dedicated to protecting communities and the environment from the adverse impacts of mineral and energy development while promoting sustainable solutions.

5699 **EAWAG Biocatalysis/Biodegradation Database**

eawag-bbd.ethz.ch

This database contains information on microbial biocatalytic reations and biodegradation pathways for primarily xenobiotic, chemical compounds. The goal of the EAWAG-BBD is to provide information on microbial enzyme catalyzed reactionsthat are important for biotechnology.

5700 **ECOLOGIA**

www.ecologia.org

ECOLOGIA, or ECOlogists Linked for Organizing Grassroots Initiatives and Action, is a private non-profit organization providing information, training and technical support for grassroots environmental groups. ECOLOGIA offers technicaland humanitarian assistance to individuals and organizations working to solve ecological problems at the local, regional, national and global levels.

5701 **Earth Day Network**

www.earthday.org

Earth Day Network is a non-profit coordinating body of worldwide Earth Day activities that aims to promote environmental awareness by providing educational materials and publications and by organizing events, activities and annualcampaigns. The network includes more than 5,000 organizations in 184 countries.

5702 **Earth Resources Laboratory at MIT**

erlweb.mit.edu

MIT's Earth Resources Laboratory, brings together faculty, staff and students dedicated to research in applied geophysics that will further understanding of the Earth, its resources and the environment.

5703 **EarthVote**

www.earthvote.org

EarthVote is the purveyor of the idea of Common Planet, a plan to end global poverty, homelessness, Masters, war & nuclear Weapons.

5704 **EarthWatch Institute**

earthwatch.org

The EarthWatch Institute aims to engage people worldwide in scientific field research and education to promote the understanding and action necesary for a sustainable environment.

5705 **EcoInternet**

ecointernet.org

EcoInternet provides people, families and businesses with tools, services and information pertaining to green living and the environmental sustainability movement.

5706 **Ecology Action Centre**

ecologyaction.ca

The Ecology Action Centre has been working at the local, regional, national and more recently, international level to build a healthier and more sustainable world while working closely with communities, social and natural scientists.

5707 **Edison Electric Institute**

www.eei.org

The Edison Electric Institute is the association that represents all US investor-owned electric companies; providing electricity for over 220 million Americans.

5708 **Edwards Aquifer Research and Data Center**

www.eardc.txstate.edu

The Edwards Aquifer Research and Data Center was established in 1979 by the Southwest Texas State University to provide a public service in the study, understanding and use of the Edwards Aquifer System.

5709 **Electric Power Research Institute**

www.epri.com

The Electric Power Research Institute (EPRI) is a non-profit organization committed to providing science and technology-based energy solutions of indispensable value to global energy customers.

5710 Elsevier

www.elsevier.com

Elsevier provides information and analytics that help institutions and professionals progress science, advance healthcare and improve performance.

5711 Endangered Species Recovery Program

esrp.csustan.edu

California State University, Stanislaus' Endangered Species Recovery Program aims to facilitate endangered species recovery and resolve conservation conflicts through scientifically based recovery planning and implementation.

5712 Energy & Environmental Research Center

www.eerc.und.nodak.edu

The Energy & Environmental Research Center (EERC) is dedicated to moving promising technologies out of the laboratory and into the marketplace to produce energy cleanly and efficiently, minimizing enviromental impacts and conservingprecious natural resources.

5713 Energy Technology Data Exchange

www.etde.org

The Energy Technology Data Exchange (ETDE) was a multilateral energy information exchange initiative under the International Energy Agency from 1987-2014. ETDE's World Erergy Base's content remains freely available online.

5714 EnergyIdeas Clearinghouse

www.energyideas.org/products.aspx

EnergyIdeas Clearinghouse is a database comprised of a series of publications that addressed the energy saving claims of products and technologies of interest to electric utility staff in the Pacific Northwest. Although the WSUExtension Energy Program, from which these publications resulted, became inactive in 2008, the publications are still accesible online.

5715 Enviro-access: GHG Experts

www.enviroaccess.ca

Enviro-access is an investor in the development of environmental technologies by supplying companies in the environemtal sector with the professional services required during the various steps of bringing their products and services tothe marketplace.

5716 Enviro.BLR.com

enviro.blr.com

The environment division of Buisness & Legal Resources aims to provide the public with the most comprehensive state and federal environmental compliance information available.

5717 EnviroCitizen.org

www.envirocitizen.org

EnviroCitizen.org encourages college students to be environmental citizens and is dedicated to educating, training and organizing a diverse national network of young leaders to protect the environment.

5718 EnviroLink

www.envirolink.org

EnviroLink is an online community that is dedicated to providing comprehensive, up-to-date environmental information and news.

5719 EnviroOne

www.enviroone.org

EnviroOne is a non-profit company that promotes sustainable environmental and agricultural activities in the US and around the world.

5720 Environmental Alliance for Senior Involvement

www.easi.org

The Environmental Alliance for Senior Involvement aims to build, promote and utilize the environmental ethic, expertise and commitment of older persons to expand citizen involvement in protecting and caring for the environment forpresent and future generations.

5721 Environmental Assessment Association

www.eaa-assoc.org

The Environmental Assessment Association is an international organization dedicated to providing members with information and education in the environmental industry in respect to environmental inspections and testing.

5722 Environmental Contaminants Encyclopedia

www.nature.nps.gov/hazardssafety/toxic/index.cfm

The Environmental Contaminants Encyclopedia summarizes information about 118 environmental contaminants and serves as a quick reference for determining whether or not concentrations of potential contaminants are above levels that mightaffect living things. Important to note: last update was in 1998.

5723 Environmental Defense Fund

www.edf.org

Environmental Defense Fund is dedicated to protecting the environmental rights of all people, including future generations. Among these rights are clean and water; healthy, nourishing food and flourishing ecosystem.

5724 Environmental News Network

www.enn.com

The Environmental News Network works to inform, educate, enable and create a platform for global environmental action. Aims to be provide a collection of resources, teachers, experts and tools to provide onjective information andknowledge about the increasingly complex field of environmental science.

5725 Environmental Protection

www.eponline.com

Environmental Protection provides online content pertaining to pollution and waste treatment solutions for environmental professionals.

5726 Environmental Resource Center

www.ercweb.com/home

Environmental Resource Center is a full-service environmental consulting firm that has been serving the needs of industry, academia and federal and state government agencies with the goal of helping its clients effectively comply withenvironmental, safety and health regulations.

5727 Environmental Resources Management

www.erm.com

Environmental Resources Management is a global provider of environmental, health, safety, risk and sustainability consulting services that delivers innovative solutions to industrial and non-industrial clients.

5728 Environmental Simulations, Inc.

www.groundwatermodels.com

Environmental Simulations, Inc. (ESI) specializes in software, consulting and training for groundwater modeling.

5729 Environmental Treaties and Resource Indicators

sedac.ciesin.columbia.edu/entri/

Environmental Treaties and Resource Indicators (ENTRI), a database of searchable treaties and resource indicators, is provided by the Center for International Earth Science Information Network of the Earth Institute of ColumbiaUniversity.

5730 Environmental Working Group

www.ewg.org

The Environmental Working Group is a leading content provider for public interest groups and concerned citizens who are campaigning to protect the environment.

5731 European Centre for Nature Conservation

www.ecnc.org

The European Centre for Nature Conservation (ECNC) is an independent European expertise centre for biodiversity and sustainable development that promotes an integrated approach that actively stimulates the internation between science,society and policy.

5732 European Forest Institute

www.efi.int

The European Forest Institute (EFI) aims to promote, conduct and co-operate in research of forests, forestry and forest products at the pan-European level; and to make the results of the research known to all interested parties,notably in the areas of policy formulation and implementation, in order to promote the conservation and sustainable management of forests in Europe.

5733 Everglades Digital Library

everglades.fiu.edu

The Everglades Information Network & Digital Library at Florida International University Libraries is a program of library and information services in support of research, restoration, and resource management of the south Floridaenvironment. The EIN serves researchers, resource managers, educators, students, researchers, decision makers, and concerned citizens both within south Florida and around the world.

5734 Federal Emergency Management Agency

www.fema.gov

The Federal Emergency Management Agency (FEMA) supports citizens and first responders to ensure that the nation works together to build, sustain and improve capabilities to prepare for, protect against, respond to, recover from andmitigate all hazards.

5735 Federal Geographic Data Committee

www.fgdc.gov

The Federal Geographic Data Committee is an interagency committee composed of representatives from the Executive Office of the President, Cabinet-level and independent agencies. The FGDC is developing the National Spatial DataInfrasturcture (NSDI) in cooperation with organizations from state, local and tribal governments, the academic community and the private sector.

5736 Florida Center for Environmental Studies

www.ces.fau.edu

The Florida Center for Environmental Studies at Florida Atlantic University is dedicated to advancing Florida's sustainability by promoting collaborative research, education and community engagaement activities.

5737 Florida Department of Environmental Protection

www.dep.state.fl.us

The Florida Department of Environmental Protection promotes the idea of: More Protection, Less Process, which is accomplishes by providing stewardship of Florida's ecosystems so that the state's unique quality of life may be preservedfor present and future generations.

5738 Florida Wildlife Extension

www.wec.ufl.edu/extension

The Florida Wildlife Extenstion serves, advises and develops educational programs for Florida citizens in conjunction with county extension agents and other state, county and local organizations interested in wildlife issues.

5739 Forest History Society

www.foresthistory.org

The Forest History Society is a non-profit educational institution that links the past to the future by identifying, collecting, preserving, interpreting, and disseminating information on the history of people, forests, and theirrelated resources.

5740 Forest Service Employees for Environmental Ethics

www.fseee.org

Forest Service Employess for Environmental Ethics is a non-profit organization whose goal is to forge a socially responsible value system for the Forest Service based on a land ethic that ensures ecologically and economicallysustainable resource management.

5741 Fresh Energy

fresh-energy.org

Fresh Energy is working to shape and drive realistic, visionary energy policies by promoting energy efficiency and the sound use of renewable energy resources. Through program research, public education and intervention in the decisionmaking process, Fresh Energy seeks to develop and build a consensus for energy vision that will ensure the well being of future generations.

5742 Friends of the Earth International

www.foei.org

Friends of the Earth International is a worldwide federation of national environmental organizations that aims to protect the earth against futher deterioration and repair damage inflicted upon the environment by human activities andnegligence; preserve the earth's ecological, cultural and ethic diversity.

5743 GLOBE Program

www.globe.gov

GLOBE, or Global Learning and Observations to Benefit the Environment, is an international science and education program that provides students and the public with the opportunity to participate in data collection and contributemeaningfully to the understanding of the Earth system and global environment.

5744 **GRID-Arendal**

www.grida.no

GRID-Arendal provides environmental information, communications and capacity buildings services for information management and assessment. Established to strengthen the United Nations through its Environmental Program, its focus is tomake credible, science-based knowledge understandable to the public and to decision makeing personnel for sustainable development.

5745 **GeoHydrodynamics and Environment Research**

modb.oce.ulg.ac.be

GeoHydrodynamics and Environment Research (GHER) is a research group based out of the University of LiŠge (Belgium) devoted to marine and environmental study and modelling in sites such as the North Sea, the Black Sea, the Aral Sea,the South China Sea, the Bering Sea, the PeErsian Gulf and the Mediterranean Sea.

5746 **Georgia Department of Natural Resources**

www.gadnr.org

The Georgia Department of Natural Resources aims to sustain, enhance, protect and conserve Georgia's natural, historic and cultural resources for present and future generations, while recognizing the importance of promoting thedevelopment of commerce and industry that utilize sound environmental practices.

5747 **Geotechnical & Geoenvironmental Software Directory**

www.ggsd.com

The Geotechnical & Geoenvironmental Software Directory (GGSD) catalogues over 1750 programs in the fields of Geotechnical Engineering, Soil Mechanics, Rock Mechanics, Engineering Geology, Foundation Engineering, Hydogeology,Geoenvironmental Engineering, Environmental Engineering, Data Alaysis and Data Visualization.

5748 **Global Change Master Directory**

gcmd.gsfc.nasa.gov

The Global Change Master Directory (GCMD) aims to assist the scientific community in the discovery of and linkage to Earth science data, as well as to provide data holders a means to advertise their data to the Earth Science Community.

5749 **Global Ecovillage Network**

ecovillage.org

The Global Ecovillage Network (GEN) builds bridges between policy-makers, governments, NGOs, academics, entrepreneurs, activists, community networks and ecologically-minded individuals across the globe in order to develop strategiesfor a global transition to sustainable communities and cultures.

5750 **Global Energy and Water Cycle Exchanges**

www.gewex.org

The Global Energy and Water Cycle Exhcnages (GEWEX) Project is dedicated to understanding Earth's water cycle and energy fluxes at the surface and in the atmosphere.

5751 **Global Network on Environmental Science and Technology**

www.gnest.org

The Global Network on Environmental Science and Technology (NEST) constitutes an international association of scientists, technologists, engineers and other interested groups involved in all scientific and technological aspects of theenvironment as well as in application techniques aimed at the development of sustainable solutions.

5752 **Great Lakes Fishery Commission**

www.glfc.org

The Great Lakes Fishery Commission facilitates successful cross-border cooperation that ensures Canada and the United States work together to improve and perpetuate the Greak Lakes fishery.

5753 **Great Lakes Information Network**

www.great-lakes.net

The Great Lakes Information Network (GLIN) is a partnership that provides information relating to the binational Great Lakes-St. Lawrence region of North America. GLIN offers a wealth of data and information about the region'senvironment, economy, tourism, education and more.

5754 **Green Mountain Institute for Environmental Democracy**

www.gmied.org

The Green Mountain Institute for Environmental Democracy (GMI) works to reinvigorate the essential connections among the public, government and information necessary for effective improvements in environmental quality and the long-termvitality of communities and regions.

5755 **Green Seal**

www.greenseal.org

Green Seal is an independent non-profit organization dedicated to protecting the environment by promoting the manufacture and sale of enviromentally responsible consumer products. It sets environmental standards and awards a Green Sealof Approval to products that cause less harm to the environment than other similar products.

5756 **Greenbelt Alliance**

www.greenbelt.org

The Greenbelt Alliance's goal is to make the San Francisco Bay Area a better place to live by protecting the region's greenbelts and improving the livability of its cities and towns. They work in partnership with diverse coalitions onpublic policy development, advocacy and education.

5757 **Groundwater Remediation Technologies Analysis Center**

www.gwrtac.org

The Groundwater Remediation Technologies Analysis Center (GWRTAC) compiles, analyzes and disseminates information on innovative groundwater remediation technologies. GWRTAC prepares reports by technical teams selectively chosen fromConcurrent Technologies Corporation, the University of Pittsburgh and other supporting institutions, while also maintaining an active outreach program.

5758 **Harbor Branch Oceanographic Institute**

The Harbor Branch Oceanographic Institute of Florida Atlantic University is dedicated to exploring the world's oceans and integrating the science and technology of the sea with the needs of humankind.

5759 Harvard Forest

harvardforest.fas.harvard.edu

Harvard Forest is a department of the Faculty of Arts and Sciences of Harvard University where scientists, students and collaborators explore topics ranging from conservation and environmental change to land-use history and the ways inwhich physical, biological and human systems interact to impact the earth.

5760 Hawaii Biological Survey

hbs.bishopmuseum.org

The Hawaii Biological Survey is an ongoing natural history inventory of the Hawaiian archipelago created to locate, identify and evaluate all native and non-native species of flora and fauna within the state, and maintain the referencecollections of that flora and fauna for a wide range of uses.

5761 Hawaiian Ecosystems at Risk Project

www.hear.org

The mission of the Hawaiian Ecosystem at Risk (HEAR) Project is to promote technology, methods and information to decision-makers, resource managers and the general public to aid in the fight against harmful alien species in Hawaii andthe Pacific Basin.

5762 HawkWatch International

hawkwatch.org

HawkWatch International is a non-profit organization that works to protect raptors and their environment through scientific research and public education.

5763 Hazardous Substance Research Centers

www.hsrc.org

The Hazardous Substance Research Center is a national organization that carries out an active program of basic and applied research, technology transfer and training. Their activities are conducted regionally by five multi-universitycenters, which focus on different aspects of hazardous substance management.

5764 Headwaters Science Center

www.hscbemidji.org

The Headwaters Science Center is dedicated to science education and environmental awareness. It features hands-on exhibits, a live animal collection, special events and science-related programs and demonstrations.

5765 Heartwood

heartwood.org

Heartwood is a regional network that protects forests and supports community activism in the eastern United States through education, advocacy and citizen empowerment.

5766 Horned Lizard Conservation Society

www.hornedlizards.org

The Horned Lizard Conservation Society (HLCS) is a non-profit organization devoted to protecting horned lizards throughout North America.

5767 Houston Audubon Society

houstonaudubon.org

The Houston Audubon Society works for the thoughtful conservation of the earth's natural resources by educating people to the value of the natural world; specifically the advancement of the conservation of birds and their surroundinghabitat.

5768 Illinois Recycling Association

www.illinoisrecycles.org

The Illinois Recycling Association's mission is to encourage the responsible use of resources by promoting waste reduction, re-use and recycling.

5769 Indiana Department of Natural Resources

www.in.gov/dnr

The Indianan Department of Natural Resources aims to protect, enhance, preserve and wisely use natural, cultural and recreational resources for the benefit of Indiana's citizens through professional leadership, management andeducation.

5770 Information Center for the Environment

ice.ucdavis.edu

The Information Center for the Environment (ICE) at the University of California, Davis aims to participate actively in all activities and efforts of protection, preservation and exploitation of mangrove ecosystems.

5771 Inland Seas Education Association

schoolship.org

The Inland Seas Education Association is a non-profit organization whose that provides a 'floating classroom' where people of all ages can gain first-hand training and experience in the Great Lakes ecosystem. The knowledge gainedthrough these experiences provides the leadership, understanding and commitment needed for the long-term stewardship of the Great Lakes.

5772 Institute for the Study of Society and Environment

www.isse.ucar.edu

The Institute for the Study of Society and Environment (ISSE) aims to improve societal welfare in the context of natural and changing climate and weater by conducting interdisciplinary research on societal activities related toclimate, the consequence of those activities on the atmosphere and the environment and providing effective communication of this information to decision-makers associated with weather and climate risks.

5773 International Association for Energy Economics

www.iaee.org

The International Association for Energy Economics (IAEE) provides a forum for the exchange of ideas, experience and issues among professionals interested in energy economics. IAEE's scope is worldwide, as are its members who come fromdiverse corporate, academic, scientific and government backgrounds.

5774 International Association for Environmental Hydrology

www.hydroweb.com

The International Association for Environmental Hydrology (IAEH) is a worldwide association of environmental hydrologists dedicated to the protection and cleanup of fresh water resources.

5775 International Canopy Network

internationalcanopynetwork.org

The International Canopy Network (ICAN) is devoted to facilitating the continuing interaction of people concerned with forest canopies and forest ecosystems around the world. ICAN is a non-profit organization supported by a globalcommunity of scientists, conservation advocates, canopy educators and environmental professionals.

5776 International Council for the Exploration of the Sea

www.ices.dk

The International Council for the Exploration of the Seas (ICES) is a scientific organization concerning marine ecosystems that provides the knowledge to secure the sustainable use of the seas.

5777 International Crane Foundation

www.savingcranes.org

The International Crane Foundation (ICF) works worldwide to conserve cranes and the wetland and grasslands communities on which they depend. ICF is dedicated to providing experience, knowledge, and inspiration to involve people inresolving threats to these ecosystems.

5778 International Energy Agency: Solar Heating & Cooling Programme

www.iea-shc.org

The Solar Heating and Cooling Programme was one of the frist IEA Implementing Agreements to be established. Since 1977, its 21 members have collaborated to advance active solar, passive solar and photovoltaic technologies and theirapplication in buildings.

5779 International Fund for Animal Welfare

www.ifaw.org/canada

The International Fund for Animal Welfare (IFAW) aims to improve the welfare of wild and domestic animals throughout the world by reducing commercial exploitation of animals in distress, primarily by motivating the public to preventcruelty to animals and promoting animal welfare and conservation policies that advance the well-being of both animals and people.

5780 International Geosphere-Biosphere Programme

www.igbp.net

The International Geosphere-Biosphere Programme (IGBP) aimed to coordinate international research on global-scale and regional-scale interactions between Earth's biological, chemical and physical processes and their interactions withhuman systems. The programme ended in 2015, however information still remains accessible on their website.

5781 International Ground Source Heat Pump Association

www.igshpa.org

The International Ground Source Heat Pump Association (IGSHPA) supports GHP industry research and development; promotes GHP-related current events internationally; develops and distributes internationally recognized training materials.

5782 International Institute for Industrial Environmental Economics

www.iiiee.lu.se

The International Institute for Industrial Environmental Economics (IIIEE) aims to advance knowledge on how to catalyse the transition to low-carbon and resource efficient economies and to promote sustainable solutions pursued bypublic authorities and businesses.

5783 International Institute for Sustainable Development

www.iisd.org

The International Institute for Sustainable Development (IISD) aims to champion innovation, enabling societies to live sustainably.

5784 International Otter Survival Fund

www.otter.org/Public

The International Otter Survival Fund (IOSF) is a global organization working to conserve all 13 species of otter by helping to support scientists and other workers in practical conservation, education, research, rescue andrehabilitation practices.

5785 International Primate Protection League

www.ippl.org/gibbon

The International Primate Protection League (IPPL) is dedicated to the preservation of the world's primates and maintaining a gibbon sanctuary in South Carolina.

5786 International Research Institute for Climateand Society

iri.columbia.edu

The International Research Institute for Climate and Society (IRI) aims to enhance society's capability to understand, anticipate and manage the impacts of climate in order to improve human welfare and the environment, especially indeveloping countries. This goal is conducted through strategic and applied research and education.

5787 International Rivers

www.internationalrivers.org

International Rivers works with an international network of dam-affected people, grassroots organizations, environmentalists, human rights advocates and others who are committed to stopping destructive river projects and promotingbetter options.

5788 International Society for Ecological Modelling

www.isemna.org

The International Society for Ecological Modelling (ISEM) promotes the international exchange of ideas, scientific results and general knowledge in the area of the application of systems analysis and simulation in ecology and naturalresource management.

5789 International Society of Arboriculture

2101 West Park Court 217-355-9411
PO Box 3129 888-472-8733
Champaign, IL 61826-3129 Fax: 217-355-9516
isa@isa-arbor.com
www.isa-arbor.com

Through research, technology, and education ISA is able to promote the professional practice of arboriculture and foster a greater public awareness of the benefits of trees.
Michelle Mitchell, President
Pau; Ries, President-Elect

5790 International Solar Energy Society

www.ises.org

The International Solar Energy Society aims to encourage the use and acceptance of Renewable Energy technologies; to realise a global community of industry, individuals and institutions in support of renewable energy and to create astructure to faciliate cooperation and exchange.

5791 **International Union of Forestry Research Organizations**

www.iufro.org

The International Union of Forestry Research Organizations (IUFRO) is a non-profit, non-governmental international network of forest scientists. Its objective is to promote international cooperation in forestry and forest productsresearch. IUFRO's activities are organized primarily through its 268 specialized Units in 8 technical Divisions.

5792 **International Wildlife Coalition Trust**

www.iwc.org

The International Wildlife Coalition Trust (IWCT) is a UK-based, non-profit charitable organization dedicated to public education, research, rescue, rebilitation, litigation and international treaty negotiations concerning globalwildlife and natural habitat protection issues.

5793 **International Wolf Center**

www.wolf.org

The mission of the International Wolf Center is to support the survival of wolf populations around the world by teaching about their lives, associations with other species and dynamic relationships to humans.

5794 **Iowa Department of Natural Resources**

www.iowadnr.gov

The Iowa Department of Natural Resources aims to conserve and enhance natural resources in cooperation with individuals and organizations in the state to improve quality of life and ensure a legacy for future generations.

5795 **Island Wildlife Natural Care Centre**

www.sealrescue.org

The Island Wildlife Natural Care Centre aims to rehabilitate North American wildlife, including marine mammals, with emphasis on alternative, non-toxic, non-invasive treatments; and furthering knowledge of treatments available toprofessionals in the field while educationg the public on both rehabilitation and the interaction of humans and wild animals.

5796 **Izaak Walton League of American**

www.iwla.org

The Izaak Walton League of America aims to conserve, maintain, protect and restore the soil, forest, water and other natural resources of the United States and other lands; to promote means and opportunities for education of the publicwith respect to such resources and their enjoyment and wholesome utilization.

5797 **Jane Goodall Institute**

www.janegoodall.org

The Jane Goodall Institute promotes understanding and protection of great apes and their habitat, while building on the legacy of Dr. Jane Ggoodall, to inspire individual action by young people to help animals, other people and theenvironment.

5798 **Jefferson Land Trust**

www.saveland.org

Jefferson Land Trust is a private, non-profit, grass-roots organization with a mission to conserve property and natural resources. Landowners may work with a Land Trust when they wish to permanently protect the ecological, scenic,historic or recreational qualities of land they own from inappropriate development.

5799 **Journey North**

www.learner.org/jnorth/index.html

Journey North: A Global Study of Wildlife Migration and Seasonal Change engages students in a global study of wildlife migration and seasonal change by allowing K-12 students to share their own field observations with classmates acrossNorth America.

5800 **Kentucky Department of Fish and Wildlife Resources**

fw.ky.gov

The Kentucky Department of Fish and Wildlife Resources aims to conserve and enhance fish and wildlife resources and provide opportunities for hunting, fishing, trapping, boating and other wildlife related activities.

5801 **Kentucky Water Resources Research Institute**

www.uky.edu/WaterResources/

The Kentucky Water Resources Research Institute aims to assist and stimulate academic units in the conduct of undergraduate and graduate education in water resources and water-related environmental issues.

5802 **Lake Pontchartrain Basin Foundation**

saveourlake.org

The Lake Pontchartrain Basin Foundation (LPBF) aims to restore and preserve the Lake Pontchartrain Basin for the benefit of present and future generations.

5803 **Land Conservancy of San Luis Obispo County**

lcslo.org

The Land Conservancy of San Luis Obispo County (LCSLO) pursues the protection of open space through land aquisition, conservation easements, restoration and stewardship.

5804 **Land Trust Alliance**

1250 H Street NW — 202-638-4725
Suite 600 — Fax: 202-638-4730
Washington, DC 20055 — info@lta.org
www.landtrustalliance.org

The Land Trust Alliance is a national conservation organization that works to influence the conservation movement, by promoting voluntary land conservation across the country and providing resources, leadership and training to thenation's 1,200+ non-profit, grassroots land trusts, helping them to protect important open spaces.

Andrew Bowman, President
Wendy Jackson, Executive VP

5805 **League of Conservation Voters**

www.lcv.org

The League of Conservation Voters (LCV) works to turn environmental values into national, state and local priorities. LCV advocates for sound environmental laws and policies; holds elected officials accountable for their votes andactions and elects pro-environment candidates who will champion priority issues.

5806 **Leave No Trace: Canada**

www.leavenotrace.com

The mission of the Leave No Trace (LNT) program is to promote and inspire responsible outdoor recreation through education, research and partnerships. LNT builds awareness, appreciation and respect for our wildlands.

5807 **Living on Earth**

www.loe.org

Living on Earth with Steve Curwood is a weekly environmental radio program distributed by National Public Radio that includes news, features, interviews and commentary on a broad range of ecological issues.

5808 **Lloyd Center for the Environment**

lloydcenter.org

The Lloyd Center for the Environment is a non-profit organization that provides education programs and conducts research to develop a scientific and public understanding of coastal, estaurine and watershed environments in southeasternNew England.

5809 **Long Term Ecological Research Network**

lternet.edu

The Long Term Ecological Research Network (LTER Network) aims to facilitate and conduct ecological research through the understanding of ecological pheonmena over long temporal and large spatial scales. LTER creates a legacy ofwell-designed and documented long-term experiments and observations for future generations.

5810 **Louisiana Department of Agriculture & Forestry**

www.ldaf.state.la.us

The Louisiana Department of Agriculture & Forestry is responsible for administering many of the programs and enforcing the regulations that impact every aspect of the state's agriculture and forestry industries.

5811 **Louisiana Energy & Environmental Resources & Information Center**

www.leeric.lsu.edu

The Louisiana Energy & Environmental Resource & Information Center (LEERIC) was a cooperative program that aimed to serve the information needs of Luisiana State University's faculty, staff and researchers. LEERIC also provided energyand environmental educational programs for consumers and non-college educators and students. The program is currently inactive, however their website has been archived and remains accessible.

5812 **Luke: Natural Resources Institute Finland**

www.luke.fi

Researchers and specialists working at Luke provide new solutions towards the sustainable development of the Finnish bioeconomy and the promotion of new biobased businesses.

5813 **Maine Department of Agriculture, Conservationand Forestry**

www.maine.gov/dacf

The Maine Department of Agriculture, Conservation and Forestry balances for and develops the state's various land-based, natural resources including agriculture, forests, outdoor recreation and public-access.

5814 **Maine Department of Inland Fisheries & Wildlife**

www.state.me.us/ifw

The Maine Department of Inland Fisheries & Wildlife conserves, protects and enhances the inland fisheries and wildlife resources of Maine while promoting efficiency in program management through employee involvement, intitiative,innovation and teamwork.

5815 **Mangrove.org**

mangrove.org

Mangrove.org began as a local project along the central east coast of Florida; however, now it contributes to a wide range of habitat creation and restoration programs that are international in scope.

5816 **Manomet**

125 Manomet Point Road 508-224-6521
PO Box 1770 Fax: 508-224-9220
Plymouth, MA 02345 info@manomet.org
www.manomet.org

Manomet aims to conserve natural resources for the benefit of wildlife and human populations. Through research and collaboration, Manomet builds science-based, cooperative solutions to environmental problems.
Dean H. Steeger, Chair
John Hagan, President

5817 **Marine & Environmental Research Institute**

www.merieresearch.org

The Marine & Environmental Research Institute is a non-profit scientific organization dedicated to protecting wildlife and people from the harmful impacts of toxic and chemical exposure.

5818 **Marine Technology Society**

www.mtsociety.org/home.aspx

The Marine Technology Society (MTS) aims to disseminate marine science and technical knowledge; to promote and support education for marine scientists, engineers and technicians; to advance the development of tools and proceduresrequired to explore, study and further the responsible and sustainable use of the oceans; and provide services that create a broader understanding of the relevance of marine sciences to other technologies, arts and human affairs.

5819 **Maryland Department of Natural Resources**

dnr.maryland.gov

The Maryland Department of Natural Resources hopes to help secure a sustainable future for the environment, society and economy by preserving, protecting, restoring and enhancing the state's natural resources.

5820 **Maryland Forests Association, Inc.**

www.mdforests.org

The Maryland Forest Association, Inc. (MFA) is a non-profit organization that acts as a voice for the forest, wildlife and natural resource management throughout Maryland and the tri-state area. The website acts as a tool to learnabout Maryland's issues concerning forest resources, forest land ownership, forest management and the forest products industry.

5821 **Massachusetts Department of Energy And Environmental Affairs**

www.mass.gov/eea

Massachusetts Department of Energy and Environmental Affairs aims to preserve open spaces, species habitat and working landscapes; enforce pollution laws to protect public health and natural resources; enhance the state's role inenergy conservation and production; manage fish and wildlife and provide opportunities for outdoor recreation.

5822 Medomak Valley Land Trust

www.medomakvalley.org

The Medomak Valley Land Trust is a local, private non-profit oragnization edstablished that aims to preserve the natural, recreational, scenic and productive values of the Medomak River watershed. The Trust's goals are to foster aregional perspective of the watershed and to encourage valley residents to work together to ensure that the resources they value will remain for future generations.

5823 Messinger Woods Wildlife Care & Education Center, Inc.

www.messingerwoods.org

The Messinger Woods Wildlife Care & Education Center is a non-profit organization that promotes community awareness, education and instruction; involvement and understanding; and appreciation and acceptance of wildlife in an attempt toconserve it.

5824 Michigan Department of Environmental Quality

www.michigan.gov/deq

The Michigan Department of Environmental Quality drives improvements in environmental quality for the protection of public health and natural resources to benefit current and future generations. This is attempted through effectiveadministration of agency programs and by providing for the use of innovative strategies, all while helping to foster a strong and sustainable economy.

5825 Michigan Department of Natural Resources

www.michigan.gov/dnr

The Michigan Department of Natural Resources is responsible for the stewardship of Michigan's natural resources and for the provision of outdoor recreational opportunities.

5826 Michigan Forest Association

www.michiganforests.com

The mission of the Michigan Forest Association is to promote good management on all forest land, to educate its members about good forest practices and stewardship of the land and to inform the general public about forestry issues andthe benefits of good forest management.

5827 Michigan United Conservation Clubs

www.mucc.org

Michigan United Conservation Clubs (MUCC) aims to unite citizens to conserve Michigan's natural resources and protect its outdoor heritage. MUCC works to conserve Michigan's wildlife, fisheries, waters, forest, air and soils byproviding information, education and advocacy.

5828 Midwest Renewable Energy Association

www.midwestrenew.org

The Midwest Renewable Energy Association (MREA) is a non-profit network for sharing ideas, resources and information with individuals, businesses and communities to promote a sustainable future through renewable energy and energyefficiency.

5829 Minnesota Department of Natural Resources

www.dnr.state.mn.us

The Minnesota Department of Natural Resources aims to protect and restore the state's natural environment while enhancing economic opportunities and community well-being. The DNR endorsed ecosystem-based management as its method toachieve sustainability, and uses the concept of ecosystem integrity as a benchmark to measure progress toward sustainability goals.

5830 Minnesota Pollution Control Agency

www.pca.state.mn.us

The Minnesota Pollution Control Agency (MPCA) collects data on air, water, and waste pollution in Minnesota, as well as data on regulations and permits, clean-up techniques, prevention, publications, and programs to protect Minnesota'senvironment.

5831 Missouri Department of Conservation

mdc.mo.gov

The mission of the Missouri Department of Conservation is to protect and manage the fish, forest, and wildlife resources of the state, to serve the public and facilitate their participation in resources management activities, toprovide opportunity fos all citizens to use, enjoy, and learn about fish, forest and wildlife resources.

5832 Missouri Prairie Foundation

www.moprairie.org

The Missouri Praire Foundation's mission is to preserve the Greater Praire Chicken while also restoring the vegetative and faunal balance of Missouri's grassland ecosystem.

5833 Monarch Watch

www.monarchwatch.org

Monarch Watch aims to further science education, particularly in primary and secondary school systems; to promote the conservation of Monarch butterflies; and to invlove thousands of students and adults in a cooperative study of theMonarch's spectacular fall migration.

5834 Mountain Lion Foundation

www.mountainlion.org

The Mountain Lion Foundation is a non-profit conservation and education organization dedicated to protecting the mountain lion, its wild habitat and the other wildlife that shares that habitat.

5835 NEMO: Oceanographic Data Server

archive.li/lLKXH

NEMO is a collection of data sets useful for physical oceanographers based out of Scripps Institution of Oceanography.

5836 Napa County Resource Conservation District

naparcd.org

Napa County Resource Conservation District aims to encourage and assist acceptance of individual responsibility for watershed management, including goals of enhacement of wildlife habitat; reduction of soil erosion; protection andenhacement of water quality; and promotion of land stewardship and sustainable agriculture.

5837 Nation Centers for Environmental Information

www.ngdc.noaa.gov

The National Centers for Environmental Information (NOAA) provide stewardship, products and services for geophysical data from the Sun to the Earth's sea floor; offer sceientist around the world access to global databases throughinternational exchange. Formerly known as the National Geophysical Data Center (NGDC).

5838 **National Arborists**

www.natlarb.com

National Arborists is a trade association of commercial tree care firms that develops safety and educational programs, standards of tree care practice and management information for arboricul-ture firms around the world.

5839 **National Association for Environmental Management**

www.naem.org

The National Association for Environmental Management (NAEM) aims to empower corporate leaders to advance environ-mental stewardship, create safe and healthy workplaces and pro-mote global sustainability through Environmental Health andSafety (EHS) practices.

5840 **National Association for PET Container Resources**

www.napcor.com

The National Association for PET Container Resources (NAPCOR) is the trade association for the PET plastic industry in the United States and Canada. Its mission is to facilitate PET plas-tic recycling and to promote the usage of PETpackaging.

5841 **National Association of Conservation Districts**

www.nacdnet.org

The National Association of Conservation Districts (NACD) aims to serve conservation districts by providing national leader-ship and a unified voice for natural resource conservation. The association works with landowners, organizationsand agency partners in a district to help protect the soil, water, forests, wildlife and other resources.

5842 **National Association of Environmental Professionals**

www.naep.org

The National Assocation of Environmental Professionals (NAEP) is a multi-disciplinary association dedicated to the ad-vancement of persons in the environmental profession in the US and abroad; a forum for state of the art information onenvironmental planning, research and management; a network of professional contacts and exchange on information among col-leagues in industry, government, academic and the private sector.

5843 **National Association of State Foresters**

444 N Capitol Street NW 202-624-5415
Suit 540 Fax: 202-624-5407
Washington, DC 20001 www.stateforesters.org

The National Association of State Foresters provides manage-ment assistance and protection services for more than two thirds of America's forests.

Tom Boggus, Chair
Bill O'Neill, President

5844 **National Audubon Society**

www.audubon.org

The mission of the National Audubon Society is to conserve and restor natural ecosystems, focusing on birds and other wildlife for the benefit of humanity and the earth's biological diversity.

5845 **National Center for Atmospheric Research**

ncar.ucar.edu

The National Center for Atmospheric Research (NCAR) aims to plan, organize and conduct atmospheric and related research pro-grams in collaboration with universities and other institutions; to provide state of the art research tools andfacilities to the atmo-spheric sciences community; to support and enhance university atmospheric science education and to facilitate the transfer of technology to both the public and private sectors.

5846 **National Center for Ecological Analysis and Synthesis**

www.nceas.ucsb.edu

The National Center for Ecological Analysis and Synthesis (NCEAS) aims to advance the state of ecological knowledge through the search for general patterns and principles, and to or-ganize and synthesize ecological information in amanner useful to researchers, resource managers, and policy makers addressing important environmental issues.

5847 **National Energy Foundation**

nef1.org

The National Energy Foundation (NEF) is a non-profit educa-tional organization dedicated to the development, dissemination and implementation of supplemental educational materials and programs primarily related to energy, water, naturalresources, science, conservation and the environment.

5848 **National Energy Technology Laboratory**

www.netl.doe.gov

The National Energy Technology Laboratory (NETL) is a part of the US Department of Energy national laboratory system and helps to implement a broad spectrum of energy and environmen-tal research and development programs that intend tobenefit future generations.

5849 **National Environmental Health Association**

CO

www.neha.org

The National Environmental Health Association (NEHA) aims to advance the environmental health professional for the purpose of providing a healthful environment for all.

5850 **National Gap Analysis Program**

gapanalysis.usgs.gov

The US Geological Survey Gap Analysis Program (GAP) works to ensure that common species - those that are not officially en-dangered - remain that way by idetifying the species and plant communities that are not adequately represented inexisting con-servation lands. GAP works with a wide range of government, ac-ademic, non-profit and private partners, providing them with essential data and analyses that they can use to protect the habi-tats that the survival of common species dependsupon.

5851 **National Ground Water Association**

www.ngwa.org

The National Ground Water Association (NGWA) works to pro-vide and protect the world's ground water resources; enhance the skills and credibility of all ground water professionals; develop and exchange industry knowledge and promote theground water industry and understanding of ground water resources.

5852 **National Institute of Environmental Health Sciences**

111 T.W. Alexander Drive 919-541-3345
Durham, NC 27709 Fax: 301-480-2978
webcenter@niehs.nih.gov
www.niehs.nih.gov

The National Institute of Environmental Health Sciences (NIEHS) aims to reduce the burden of human illness and dysfunc-tion from environmental causes by understanding each of these elements and how they interrelate. The NIEHS achivesthis goal through multidisciplinary biomedical research programs, pre-vention and intervention efforts and communication strategies

that encompass training, education, technology transfer and community outreach.
Linda S. Birnbaum, Director
Richard Woychik, Deputy Director

5853 **National Oceanic and Atmospheric Administration**

www.noaa.gov
The National Oceanic and Atmospheric Administration (NOAA) aims to understand and predict changes in climate, weather, oceans and the coast; to share that knowledge and information with others; and to conserve and manage coastal andmarine ecosystems and resources.

5854 **National Outdoor Leadership School**

www.nols.edu
The National Outdoor Leadership School (NOLS) is an institution that focuses on wilderness education, offering courses in Leadership, Wilderness Skills, Risk Management, Environmental Studies and Wilderness Medicine.

5855 **National Park Conservation Association**

www.npca.org
The National Parks Conservation Association (NPCA) aims to protect and enhance America's national parks.

5856 **National Renewable Energy Laboratory**

www.nrel.gov
The National Renewable Energy Laboratory (NREL) advances the science and engineering of energy efficiency, sustainable transportation and renewable power technologies, and provides the knowledge to integrate and optimize energysystems.

5857 **National Sea Grant Library**

nsgd.gso.uri.edu
The National Sea Grant Library (NSGL) was established as an archive and lending library for Sea Grant funded documents. These documents cover a wide variety of subjects, including oceanography, marine education, aquaculture, fisheries,limonology, coastal zone management, marine recreation and law. NSGL staff lends documents all over the world to aid scientists, teachers, students, fishermen and many other individuals in their reseacrh and studies.

5858 **National Wildlife Health Center**

www.nwhc.usgs.gov
The National Wildlife Health Center is a science center of the US Geological Survey dedicated to assessing the impact of disease on wildlife and to identify the role of various pathogens in contributing to wildlife losses.

5859 **National Wildlife Rehabilitators Association**

www.nwrawildlife.org
The National Wildlife Rehabilitation Association (NWRA) is a non-profit international membership organization committed to promoting and improving the integrity and professionalism of wildlife rehabilitation and contributing to thepreservation of natural ecosystems.

5860 **National Woodland Owners Association**

woodlandowners.org
The National Woodland Owners Association (NWOA) is an independent landowners group with the purpose of developing policy, legislation and representation at the national level, and providing educational and networking opportunities tolandowners throughout the country.

5861 **Native Forest Council**

forestcouncil.org
The Native Forest Council (NFC) aims to provide visionary leadership and to ensure the integrity of public land ecosystems without compromising people or forests.

5862 **Natural Energy Laboratory of Hawaii Authority: Hawaii Ocean Science & Technology Park**

nelha.hawaii.gov
The Natural Energy Laboratory of Hawaii Authority (NELHA) operates facilities at Keahole Point on Hawaii Island that pump ashore cold deep and warm surface seawater for commercial and research tenants from the private and publicsectors. Tenants utilize the seawater and NELHA's high sunlight and consistant temperatures in a wide range of aquaculture and energy projects.

5863 **Natural Environment Research Council**

www.nerc.ac.uk
The Natural Environment Research Council (NERC) is an independent UK charity which brings together people from all sectors of business, non-governmental organizations, government and the community to develop long term solutions toenvironmental issues.

5864 **Natural Environmental Research Council**

www.nerc.ac.uk
The Natural Environmental Research Council (NERC) aims to promote and support high-quality strategic and applied research, survey, long-term environmental monitoring and related post-graduate training in environmental and relatedsciences; and to generate public awareness, communicate research outcomes, encourage public engagement and dialogue, disseminate knowledge and proivide advice in relation to those activities.

5865 **Natural Resources Canada**

www.nrcan.gc.ca/home
Natural Resources Canada aims to be on the frontlines: fighting climate change, developing clean enery practices for the future, driving economic growth and creating job opportunities for Canadians.

5866 **Natural Resources Defense Council**

www.nrdc.org
The Natural Resources Defense Council (NRDC) tries to create solutions for lasting environmental change, protecting natural resources in the United States and around the world.

5867 **Nature Conservancy**

www.nature.org
The Nature Conservancy aims to preserve the plants, animals and natural communities that represent the diversity of life on Earth by protecting the lands and waters they need to survive.

5868 **Nature Saskatchewan**

www.naturesask.ca
Nature Saskatcgewan aims to promote appreciation and understanding of nature and the environment through education, conservation and research, and to protect and preserve natural ecosystems and their biodiversity.

5869 Naturenet

naturenet.net/index.php

Naturenet is a voluntary enterprise that aims to provide resources for practical nature conservation and countryside management. Based in the UK, most of the information available on Naturenet relates to the UK, particulary England.

5870 New England Wild Flower Society

www.newfs.org

The New England Wild Flower Society (NEWFS) promotes the conservation of New England's native plants to ensure healthy, biologically diverse landscapes.

5871 New England Wildlife Center

www.newildlife.com

The New England Wildlife Center is an informal hands-on science education organization that uses the practices of veterinary medical care and wildlife rehabilitation as a teaching resource for students of all ages.

5872 New Forests Project

1001 North Carolina Avenue SE 202-285-4328
Washington, DC 20003 info-newforests@theintlcenter.org
www.newforestsproject.org

The New Forests Project aims to protect, conserve and enhance the health of the Earth's ecosystems by supporting integrated grassrrots efforts to maintain and rebuild the world's forests through the promotion of agroforestry,reforestation, the protection of watersheds and the initiation of renewable energy products.

Virginia B. Foote, President
Catalina Serna-Valencia, Chief Executive Officer

5873 New Hampshire Department of Environmental Services

The New Hampshire Department of Environmental Services aims to protect, maintain and enhance environmental quality and public health in New Hampshire.

5874 New Hampshire Fish and Game Department

www.wildlife.state.nh.us

New Hampshire's Fish and Game Department aims to conserve, manage and protect the state's fish and game populations and their respective habitats, as well as inform and educate the public about these resources and provide the publicwith opportunities to use and appreciate them.

5875 New Jersey Department of Environmental Protection

www.state.nj.us/dep/

The New Jersey Department of Environmental Protection aims to assist the residents of New Jersey in preserving, restoring, sustaining, protecting and enhancing the environment to ensure the integration of high environmental quality,public health and economic vitality.

5876 New Jersey Division of Fish & Wildlife

www.state.nj.us/dep/fgw

The New Jersey Division of Fish & Wildlife aims to protect and manage the state's fish and wildlife resources to maximize their long term economic, recreational and biological values for the citizens of New Jersey.

5877 New Mexico Wilderness Alliance

www.nmwild.org

The New Mexico Wilderness Allince is dedicated to the protection, restoration, and rewilding of New Mexico's Wilderness areas by focusing on forward-looking measures to develop an active and educational wilderness constituencythroughout the state.

5878 New York Association for Reduction, Reuse and Recycling

www.nysar3.org

The New York Association for Reduction, Reuse and Recycling (NYSAR3) aims to provide statewide leadership on waste reduction, reuse and recycling issues and practices to improve the environment.

5879 New York State Department of Environmental Conservation

www.dec.ny.gov

The New York State Department of Environmental Conservation aims to conserve, imrpove and protect New York's natural resources and environment and to prevent, abate and control water, land and air pollution.

5880 North American Association for Environmental Education

www.naaee.org

The North American Association for Environmental Education is a professional association that promotes excellence in environmental education and serves environmental educators for the purpose of achieveing environmental literacy toallow present and future generationas to benefit from a safe and healthy environment.

5881 North American Lake Management Society

www.nalms.org

The North American Lake Management Society (NALMS) works to forge partnerships among citizens, scientists and professionals to foster the management and protection of lakes and reservoirs.

5882 North Carolina Coastal Federation

www.nccoast.org

The North Carolina Coastal Federation (NNCF) is a non-profit organization that seeks to protect and restore the states's coastal environment, culture and economy through citizen involvement in the management of coastal resources.

5883 North Carolina Department of Environment Quality

deq.nc.gov

The North Carolina Department of Environmental Quality aims to leadthe preservation and protection of North Carolina's natural resources by administering regulatory programs designed to protect air quality, water quality and thepublic's health.

5884 North Cascades Conservation Council

www.northcascades.org/wordpress

The North Cascades Conservation Council (NCCC) keeps government officials, environmental organizations and the general public informed about issues affecting the Greater North Cascade Ecosystem. Action is pursued through legislative,legal and public participation channels to protect the lands, waters, plants and wildlife.

5885 **Northeast Sustainable Energy Association**

www.nesea.org

The Northeast Sustainable Energy Association (NESEA) is a regional membership organization comprised of engineers, educators, builders, students, energy experts, environmental activists, transportation planners, architects, and othercitizens interested in responsible energy use. The goal is to bring clean electricity, green transportation, and healthy, efficient buildings into everyday use in order to strengthen the economy and improve the environment.

5886 **Northern Prairie Wildlife Research Center**

www.npwrc.usgs.gov

The Northern Prairie Wildlife Research Center (NPWRC) conducts integrated research to fulfill the Department of the Interior's responsibilities to the Nation's natureal resources. The NPWRC develops and disseminates scientificinformation needed to understand, conserve and manage the Nation's biological resources through focus on mid-continental plant and animal species and ecosystems of the United States.

5887 **Oceania Project**

www.oceania.org.au

The Oceania Project is a non-profit research and information organization dedicated to raising awareness about whales, dolphins, porpoises and the ocean environment.

5888 **Office of Protected Resources**

www.nmfs.noaa.gov/pr/

The Office of Protected Resources (OPR) is a program office of NOAA's NAtional Marine Fisheries Service. The program provides oversight, national policy direction and guidance on the conservation of marine mammals and endangeredspecies, and their habitats, under the jurisdiction of the Secretary of Commerce.

5889 **Ohio Environmental Protection Agency**

www.epa.state.oh.us

The Ohio Environmental Pprotection Agency has authority to implement laws and regulations regarding air and water quality standards; solid hazardous and infectious waste disposal standards; quality planning, supervision of sewagetreatment and public drinking water supplies; and cleanup of unregulated hazardous waste sites.

5890 **Ohio Wildlife Center**

www.ohiowildlifecenter.org

The Ohio Wildlife Center (OWC) is a non-profit educational organization that promotes increased appreciation and understanding of the natural environment, with particular emphasis on wildlife. OWC is supported by individuals who wishto improve their own understanding of native wild species and local wildlife issues.

5891 **Oklahoma Department of Wildlife Conservation**

www.wildlifedepartment.com

The Oklahoma Department of Wildlife Conservation aims to manage Oklahoma's wildlife resources and habitat in order to provide scientific, educational, aesthetic, economic and recreational benefits for present and future generations ofhunters, anglers and others who appreciate wildlife related activities.

5892 **Ontario Environment Network**

www.oen.ca

The Ontario Environment Network (OEN) is a non-profit, non-governmental network serving Ontario's environmental environmental community that seeks to increase awareness of these organizations and encourage discussions about means toprotect the environment.

5893 **Organization of American States: Environment**

www.oas.org/en/topics/environment.asp

The OAS supports member states in the design and implementation of policies and projects to integrate environmental priorities into poverty alleviation and socio-economic development goals.

5894 **Organization of Fish and Wildlife Information Managers**

www.ofwim.org

The Organization of Fish and Wildlife Information Managers (OFWIM) is an international non-profit organization that promotes the management and convervation of natural resources by facilitating technology and information exchange amongmanagers of fish and wildlife information.

5895 **PAWS Wildlife Rehabilitation Center & Hospital**

www.paws.org/wildlife

PAWS is a world reowned wildlife rehabiliation facility, formerly known as HOWL, the PAWS Wildlife Center receives over 5,000 injured or displaced wild animals every year. The center houses and rehabilitates these animals, and preparesthem for eventual release back into the wild.

5896 **Rachel Carson Council**

rachelcarsoncouncil.org

The Rachel Carson Council (RCC) is a clearinghouse and library with information at both scientific and layperson levels on pesticide related issues. The RCC collections contain literature searches and conservation information byexperts to educate the public. The council also produces various publications clarifying pesticide dangers and bringing alternative pest controls to the public's attention.

5897 **Renewable Fuels Association**

www.ethanolrfa.org

The Renewable Fuels Association (RFA) is comprised of companies and individuals involved in the production and use of ethanol. Ethanol is sold nationwide as a high-octane fuel that delivers improved vehicle performance while reducingemissions and improving air quality.

5898 **Renewable Natural Resources Foundation**

www.rnrf.org

The Renewable Natural Resources Foundation (RNRF) aims to advance the application of science and related disciplines in decision-making while promoting interdisciplinary collaboration to educate policymakers and the public on managingand conserving renewable natural resources.

5899 **River Systems Research Group**

boto.ocean.washington.edu

The River Systems Research Group is a project of NASA's Earth Observing System Interdisciplinary Investigation with the purpose of trying to understand the biogeochemistry, hydrology and sedimentation of the Amazon River and itsdrainage basin. Other research sites are located in Southeast Asia, Zambezi, Bhutan and Puget Sound.

5900 Snow Leopard Trust

www.snowleopard.org

The Snow Leopard Trust is dedicated to the conservation of the endangered snow leopard and its mountain ecosystem through a community-based conservation approach that is based on improved scientific understanding of snow leopardbehavior, needs, habitats and threats.

5901 Society for Conservation Biology

conbio.org

The Society for Conservation Biology (SCB) is an international professional organization dedicated to promoting the scientific study of the phenomena that affect the maintenance, loss and restoration of biological diversity.

5902 Society of Chemical Manufacturers and Affiliates (SOCMA)

1400 Crystal Drive
Suite 630
Arlington, VA 22202

571-348-5100
Fax: 571-348-5138
eo@socma.com
www.socma.com

The leading international trade association serving the small and mid-sized batch chemical manufacturers. Advocates flexible policies grounded in sound science and works to ensure that Congress and the regulatory agencies do not adopta one-size fits-all approach to the industry.ductive economy.

Jennifer L. Abril, President/CEO

5903 Steel Recycling Institute

www.recycle-steel.org

The Steel Recycling Institute promotes steel recycling and works to forge a coalition of steelmakers, can manufacturers, legislators, government officials, solid waste managers and business and consumer groups.

5904 Student Conservation Association

www.thesca.org

The Student Conservation Association (SCA) aims to build the next generation of conservation leaders and inspire lifelong stewardship of the environment by engaging young people in hands on environmental service.

5905 The Conservation Fund

www.conservationfund.org

The Conservation Fund works with private and public agencies and organizations to protect wildlife habitats, historic sites and parks.

5906 The Earth Institute: Columbia University

www.earthinstitute.columbia.edu

The Earth Institute at Columbia University blends research in the physical and social sciences, education and practical solutions to help guide its students on a path towards sustainability. Offers initiatives including water, climate,energy, urbanization, hazards & risk reduction, global health, agriculture and ecosystems.

5907 The Marine Mammal Center

www.marinemammalcenter.org

The Marine Mammal Center is working towards advancing global ocean conservation through marine mammal rescue and rehabilitation, scientific research and education.

5908 The Web Directory

www.webdirectory.com

The Web Directory is a database directory for environmental and other resources. It includes topics such as: agriculture, animals, arts, business, databases, design, disasters, education, employment, energy, forestry, generalenvironmental interest, government, health, land conservation, parks and recreation, pollution, products and services, publications, recycling, science, social science, sustainable development, transportation, vegetarianism, water resources, weatherand wildlife.

5909 UK Environmental Change Network

www.ecn.ac.uk

The Environmental Change Network aims to establish and maintain a selected network of sites within the UK from which to obtain comparable long-term datasets through the monitoring of a range of variables identified as being of majorenvironmental importance.

5910 US Department of Energy

www.energy.gov

The Department of Energy's goal is to foster a secure and reliable energy system that is environmentally and economically sustainable, to be a responsible steward of the nation's nuclear weapons and to support continued US leadershipin science and technology.

5911 US Environmental Protection Agency

1200 Pennsylvania Avenue NW
Washington, DC 20460

202-564-4700
www.epa.gov

The US Environmental Protection Agency aims to protect human health and to safeguard natural aspects of environment, including air, water and land resources.

Scott Pruitt, Administrator
Mike Flynn, Deputy Administrator

5912 US Environmental Protection Agency: Environmental Compliance Assistance Center

www.epa.gov/compliance

In partnership with state governments, tribal governments and other federal agencies, the EPA's Compliance Sector aims to assure compliance with the nation's environmental laws to help protect public health and the environment.

5913 US Environmental Protection Agency: National Estuary Program

www.epa.gov/nep

The National Estuary Program (NEP) was established in 1987 by amendments to Clean Water to identify, restore, and protect nationally significant estuaries of the United States. NEP targets a broad range of issues and engages localcommunities in the process. The program focuses not just on improving water quality in estuaries, but on maintaining the integrity entire systems, including chemical, physical and biological properties, as well as economic, recreational and aestheticvalues.

5914 US Government Accountability Office

www.gao.gov

The Government Accountability Office (GAO) supports the Congress in meeting its constitutional responsibilities and to help improve the performance and ensure the accountability of the federal government. GAO examines the use of publicfunds; evaluates federal programs and activities and provides analysis, options, recommendations and other assistance to help the Congress make effective oversight, policy and funding decisions.

5915 United States Geological Survey: Earthquake Hazards Program

earthquake.usgs.gov

The USGS Earthquake Hazards Program aims to provide and apply relevant scientific information and knowledge to reduce deaths, inhuries and property damage from earthquakes.

5916 Wisconsin Sea Grant Program

www.seagrant.wisc.edu

The Wisconsin Sea Grant Program is a statewide program of basic and applied research, education, outreach and technology dedicated to the stewardship and sustainable use of the nation's Great Lakes and ocean resources.

5917 WorldFish

www.worldfishcenter.org

WorldFish's goal is to reduce poverty and hunger by improving fisheries and aquaculture.

5918 edie.net

www.edie.net

EDIE is a free, personalized, interactive news, information and communications service for water, waste and environmental professionals around the world. With comprehensive independent coverage, powerful search facilities, e-mailalerts and discussion forums, EDIE enables the easy exchange of specialized information.

Online Databases & Clearinghouses

Environmental

5919 **AAR Bureau of Explosives**
50 F Street NW
Washington, DC 20001
BOE@aar.org
www.aar.org/boe

5920 **Asbestos Ombudsman**
401 M Street SW
A-149 C
800-368-5888
Washington, DC 20460
Answers questions about asbestos in schools.

5921 **CECA Solutions**
2737 Devonshire Place NW
202-659-0404
Suite 102
Fax: 202-659-0407
Washington, DC 20008
www.cecarf.org
Successor to Consumer Energy Council of America.
Ellen Berman, CEO
Rich Aiken, President

5922 **CHEMTREC**
American Chemistry Council
703-741-5500
800-262-8200
chemtrec@chemtrec.com
www.chemtrec.com
Critical response information for incidents involving hazardous materials.

5923 **Carbon Dioxide Information Analysis Center**
Oak Ridge National Laboratory
PO Box 2008, MS6290
Fax: 865-241-4064
Oak Ridge, TN 37831-6290
cdiac.ornl.gov
Operations to cease Sept. 30, 2017. Plans to preserve data beyond 2017 are in development.
Tom Boden, Director

5924 **Center for Environmental and Regulatory Information Systems**
Purdue University
1231 Cumberland Ave
317-494-7309
Suite A
Fax: 317-494-9727
West Layfayette, IN 47906
www.ceris.purdue.edu/ceris
Eileen Luke, Director

5925 **Center for Health, Environment & Justice**
PO Box 6806
703-237-2249
Falls Church, VA 22040-6806
info@chej.org
chej.org
Provides tools for communities to fight toxic threats.
Sharon Franklin, Chief of Operations

5926 **Center for Sustainable Systems**
University of Michigan
3012 Dana Building
734-764-1412
440 Church St
css.info@umich.edu
Ann Arbor, MI 48109-1041
css.umich.edu
Leads interdisciplinary research into systems that will support society's needs in a more sustainable manner.
Gregory A. Keoleian, Director

5927 **Clean Ocean Action**
18 Hartshorne Dr
732-872-0111
Suite 2
Fax: 732-872-8041
Highlands, NJ 07732
info@cleanoceanaction.org
www.cleanoceanaction.org
Clean Ocean Action is a broad-based coalition of over 150 conservation, community, diving, fishing, environmental, surfing, women's and business groups that works to improve and protect the waters off the New York and New Jersey coast.
Cindy Zipf, Executive Director

5928 **EPA Indoor Air Quality Information**
U.S. EPA Office of Radiation and Indoor Air
Indoor Environments Division
1200 Pennsylvania Ave NW
www.epa.gov/indoor-air-quality-iaq
Washington, DC 20460
Scott Pruitt, EPA Administrator

5929 **EPA Ozone Layer Protection**
U.S EPA
Stratospheric Protection Division
1200 Pennsylvania Ave NW
www.epa.gov/ozone-layer-protection
Washington, DC 20460
Scott Pruitt, EPA Administrator

5930 **EPA Public Information Center**
US EPA
401 M Street
202-260-7751
PM- 211B
Washington, DC 20460

5931 **EPCRA (SARA Title III) Hotline**
US EPA
401 M Street SW
202-479-2449
OS120
800-535-0202
Washington, DC 20460
Fax: 703-412-3333

5932 **Electronic Bulletin Board System**
US EPA
26 West Martin Luther King Drive
513-569-7358
Cincinnati, OH
800-258-9605
Fax: 513-569-7585
Charles W Guion

5933 **Emergency Planning and Community Right-to-Know Information Hotline**
Booz, Allen & Hamilton
1725 Jefferson Davis Highway
703-920-8977
Arlington, VA 22202
800-535-0202
Fax: 703-486-3333
Dan Kovacs, Contractor

5934 **Emission Factor Clearinghouse**
US EPA
MD-14
919-541-1000
Research Triangle Park, NC 27709
Fax: 919-541-0684
Dennis Shipman

5935 **Environmental Financing Information Network**
US EPA
EFN, WH-547
202-564-4994
401 M Street, East Tower, Room 1117
Fax: 202-565-2694
Washington, DC 20460
June Lobit

5936 **Global Change Information System**
U.S. Global Change Research Program

1800 G St NW 202-223-6262
Suite 9100 Fax: 202-223-3065
Washington, DC 20006 www.globalchange.gov
Open-source, web-based resource for global change data, information and products for use by scientists, decision makers and the public.
Dr. Michael Kuperberg, Executive Director

5937 Green Committees of Correspondence Clearinghouse
PO Box 30208 816-931-9366
Kansas City, MO 64112
Amy Belanger, Coordinator

5938 Green Lights Program
Bruce Company
1850 K Street 290 202-775-6650
Washington, DC 20006 Fax: 202-775-6680
Maria Theesen

5939 Inspector General Hotline
US EPA
1200 Pennsylvania Avenue NW
Washington, DC 20460 800-424-4000
Fax: 202-260-6976
Ed Maddox

5940 International Ground Water Modeling Center
Colorado School of Mines 303-273-3103
Golden, CO 80401 Fax: 303-273-3278
Paul van der Hijde, Director

5941 Kentucky Partners State Waste Reduction Center
University of Louisville
Ernst Hall 502-588-7260
Room 312
Louisville, KY 40292
Joyce St. Clair, Executive Director

5942 Minority Energy Information Clearinghouse
Office of Minority Economic Impact/US Energy Dept.
100 Independence Ave SW 202-586-8698
Forrestal Building, Room 5B-110 800-543-2325
Washington, DC 20585
Effie A Young, Officer

5943 Montana Natural Resource Information System
Montana State Library
1515 East 6th Avenue 406-444-3115
Helena, MT 59620 Fax: 406-444-5612
Alan Cox

5944 NYS Department of Environmental Conservation Publications, Forms, Maps
NYS Office of Communication Services
625 Broadway 518-402-8013
Albany, NY 12233-4500 Fax: 518-402-9036
www.dec.ny.gov/64.html
List of New York State Department of Environmental Conservation publications, online newsletters, bulletins, forms, maps and grant applications.

5945 National Air Toxics Information Clearinghouse
US EPA
Mail Drop 13 919-541-3586
Office of Air Quality and Standards Fax: 919-541-7674
Research Triangle Park, NC 27709
Vasu Kilaru, Database Administrator

5946 National Capital Poison Center
Georgetown Univertisy Hospital
3201 New Mexico Avenue 202-362-3867
Suite 310
Washington, DC 20016

5947 National Center for Biotechnology Information
U.S. National Library of Medicine
8600 Rockville Pike www.ncbi.nlm.nih.gov
Bethesda, MD 20894
NCBI's mission is to develop new information technologies for biomedical research.
Valerie De Crecy-Lagard, Chair

5948 National Center for Environmental Research
EPA's Office of Research and Development
1200 Pennsylvania Ave NW
MC 8722F
Washington, DC 20460
Funds research that forms scientific basis for policy decisions on environmental issues.
James H. Johnson Jr., Director

5949 National Ground Water Information Center
601 Dempsey Road 800-551-7379
Westerville, OH 43081 800-242-4965
Fax: 614-898-7786
Kevin McCray, Assistant Executive Director

5950 National Pesticide Information Retrieval System
1231 Cumberland Avenue 317-494-7309
Suite A Fax: 317-494-9727
West Lafayette, IN 4706
Virginia Walters

5951 National Pesticide Telecommunications Network
Preventive Medicine & Community Health
Texas Tech University 806-858-7378
Sciences Center 800-858-PEST
Lubbock, TX 79430 Fax: 806-743-3094
Frank L Davido

5952 National Renewable Energy Laboratory
Technical Inquiry Service
1617 Cole Boulevard 303-275-4099
Golden, CO 80401
Steve Rubin, Manager

5953 National Response Center
US Coast Guard
2100 2nd Street SW 202-267-2675
Room 2611 800-424-8802
Washington, DC 20593 Fax: 202-267-2181
Commander David Beach

5954 New York State Department of Environmental Conservation
625 Broadway 518-402-8013
Pollution Prevention Unit
Albany, NY 12233
John E Iannotti, PE

5955 Northeast Multi-Media Pollution Prevention
Northeast Waste Management Officials Association
85 Merrimac Street 617-367-8558
Boston, MA 00211
Terri Goldberg, Program Manager

5956 Nuclear Information and Resource Service
6930 Carroll Ave
Suite 340
Takoma Park, MD 20912
301-270-6477
Fax: 301-270-4291
nirs@nirs.org
www.nirs.org

Non-profit organization working for a nuclear-free, sustainable energy future.
Tim Judson, Executive Director

5957 OTS Chemical Assessment Desk
401 M Street SW
(TS-778)
Washington, DC 20460
202-260-3583
Terry O'Bryan, Executive Officer

5958 Pesticide Action Network North America
49 Powell Street
Suite 500
San Francisco, CA 94102
415-981-1771
Fax: 415-981-1991
Kathryn Gilje, Executive Director

5959 Powder River Basin Resource Council
Energy Convervation Education Committee
23 North Scott
Sheridan, WY 82801
307-672-5809
Jill Morrision, Organizer

5960 Public Information Center
US EPA
401 M Street SW
PM-211B
Washington, DC 20460
202-260-7751
Alison Cook, Director

5961 RACT/BACT/LAER Clearinghouse
Office of Air Quality Planning
Emissions Standards Division
MD-13
Research Triangle Park, NC 27709
919-541-0800
Fax: 919-541-0072
Bob Blaszczak, ESD

5962 Rachel Carson Council
rachelcarsoncouncil.org

Contains a collection of literature on the dangers of pesticides.

5963 Radon Hotline
785-532-6026
800-557-2366
Fax: 785-532-6952
radon@ksu.edu
www.epa.gov/home/epa-hotlines

5964 Records of Decision System Hotline
Computer Sciences Corporation
401 M Street SW
Room L101
Washington, DC 20460
202-260-3770
Thomas Batts

5965 Risk Communication Hotline
US EPA
401 M Street SW
W Tower, Room 425
Washington, DC 20460
202-260-5606
Fax: 202-260-9757
Ernestine Thomas

5966 Solid Waste Information Clearinghouse and Hotline
1100 Wayne Avenue, Suite 700
PO Box 7219
Silver Spring, MD 20907
800-467-9262
Fax: 301-589-7068
tvondeak@swana.org
www.swana.org
Todd von Deak, Dir Marketing/Member Service

5967 Sustainable Buildings Industry Council
National Institute of Building Sciences
1090 Vermont Ave NW
Suite 700
Washington, DC 20005
202-289-7800
Fax: 202-289-1092
nibs@nibs.org
www.nibs.org

Council of the National Institute of Building Sciences advocates for improving the performance and value of buildings through the use of sustainable design and construction strategies.
Ryan Colker, Director

5968 TNN Bulletin Board System
Office of Air Quality Planning
Standards Tech Transfer Network
Research Triangle Park, NC 27709
919-541-5616
Fax: 919-541-0824
Hersch Rorex, System Manager

5969 TOXNET
U.S. Dept. of Health & Human Services
Specialized Information Services
6707 Democracy Blvd, MSC 5467
Bethesda, MD 20892-5467
301-496-3147
888-346-3656
Fax: 301-480-3537
toxnet.nlm.nih.gov

Data network for toxicology, hazardous chemicals, environmental health and toxic releases.

5970 TSCA Assistance Information Service Hotline
Environmental Assistance Division
1200 Pennsylvania Avenue NW
Mail Code 74080
Washington, DC 20460
202-554-1404
Fax: 202-554-5603
tsca-hotline@epamail.epa.gov
The information service furnishes TSCA regulation information to the chemical industry, labor and trade organization, environmental groups and the general public. Technical as well as general information is available.
John Alter, Primary EPA

5971 Waste Exchange Clearinghouse
University of Michigan
400 Ann Street NW
Number 201-A
Grand Rapids, MI 49504
616-363-3262
Jeffery L Duphin

5972 Wastewater Treatment Information Exhange
National Small Flows Clearinghouse
West Virginia University
PO Box 6064
Morgantown, WV 56506
800-624-8301
Fax: 304-293-3161
Loukis Kissonergis

5973 Wetlands Protection Hotline
Geological Resource Consultants
1555 Wilson Boulevard
Suite 500
Arlington, VA 22209
703-527-5190
800-832-7828
John Ruffing

5974 White Lung Association
PO Box 1483
Baltimore, MD 21203
410-243-5864
Fax: 410-243-5892
James Fite, Executive Director

5975 Wisconsin Home Energy Plus Program
Home Energy +
PO Box 7970
Madison, WI 53707-7970
866-432-8947
Fax: 608-267-6931
www.homeenergyplus.wi.gov

Provides energy assistance to qualified residents.

5976 Wisconsin State Energy Office
610 North Whitney Way
2nd Floor
Madison, WI 53707
608-261-6609
Fax: 608-266-3957
oei@wisconsin.gov
www.stateenergyoffice.wi.gov

Promotes and invests in clean energy projects and assists businesses, local governments and citizens with energy-related issues.
Maria Redmond, Dir., Off. of Energy Innov.

Videos

Environmental

5977 **Acid Rain: A North American Challenge**
National Film Board of Canada
1123 Broadway 212-629-8890
Suite 307 Fax: 212-629-8502
New York, NY 10010 www.nfb.ca
Summarizes what we know today about the causes and effect of the menace of acid rain.

5978 **Adventures of the Little Koala & Friends: Laura and the Mystery Egg**
Family Home Entertaiment
15400 Sherman Way
PO Box 10124
Van Nuys, CA 91410
A cartoon exploring the topic of conservation and the protection of animals. The English dub release contains four episodes: "Laura Finds an Egg", "Conquering Mt. Breadknife", "Saving the Eucalyptus" and "Mommy Can Fly".
Noel Bloom, Founder

5979 **Air Pollution: A First Film**
Phoenix Learning Group
2349 Chaffee Dr. 314-569-0211
St. Louis, MO 63146 800-221-1274
Fax: 314-569-2834
phoenixlearninggroup.com
Program exploring the subject of air pollution such as acid rain and the solutions to this issue.
Bryan Sullivan, Executive Vice President

5980 **Basic Ecology**
Coast Community College District
1370 Adams Ave 714-438-4600
Costa Mesa, CA 92626-5429 www.cccd.edu
A film about ecology and the abiotic factors that contribute to the creation of an ecosystem.
Lori Adrian, Contact

5981 **Battle for the Trees**
National Film Board of Canada
Norman McLaren Building
3155 C"te de Liesse Rd 800-542-2164
Montreal, QC H4N-2N4 webmaster@onf.ca
www.nfb.ca
A documentary about those fighting to preserve their forests, including commentary by citizens, scientists, loggers, environmentalists and First Nations people.
Mireille Potvin, Rights Acquisitions
James Roberts, Director of Distribution

5982 **Beyond Pollution**
National Film Board of Canada
Norman McLaren Building
3155 C"te de Liesse Rd 800-542-2164
Montreal, QC H4N-2N4 webmaster@onf.ca
www.nfb.ca
A film examining the effects of the Gulf of Mexico oil spill, with interviews by environmental experts, government officials, fisherman & distributors, scientists, drilling engineers and others.
Mireille Potvin, Rights Acquisitions

5983 **Captain Planet & the Planeteers: Toxic Terror**
Turner Home Entertainment Company
1 CNN Center 404-827-1700
Atlanta, GA 30303 turner.info@turner.com
www.turner.com
Educational adventures of the Planeteers and Captain Planet exploring environmental issues such as damage to the ozone layer.
John Martin, CEO
David Levy, President

5984 **Chelyabinsk: The Most Contaminated Spot on the Planet**
Filmakers Library
3212 Duke St 703-212-8520
Alexandria, VA 22314 800-889-5937
alexanderstreet.com
The story of the Chelyabinsk atomic weapons complex, including a 1957 explosion, 1967 storm that spread radioactive dust, and the dumping of radioactive waste into a water-supply river.
Linda Gottesman, Co-President
Sue Oscar, Co-President

5985 **Children of Chernobyl**
Filmakers Library
3212 Duke St 703-212-8520
Alexandria, VA 22314 800-889-5937
alexanderstreet.com
Reveals the tragedy at Chernobyl through exclusive archival film and eyewitness accounts.
Linda Gottesman, Co-President
Sue Oscar, Co-President

5986 **Coral Cities of the Caribbean**
Nancy Sefton/Triton Productions
Earthwise Media 360-271-1584
PO Box 2593 Fax: 360-394-2168
Silverdale, WA 98383 info@earthwisevideos.com
www.earthwisevideos.com
A film taking us on a journey to the coral reefs of the Caribbean, where fish and invertebrates reside in their coral cities.
Nancy Sefton, Creative Director
Wes Nicholson, Technical Director

5987 **Cousteau - Alaska: Outrage at Valdez**
The Cousteau Society
Cousteau Society 212-532-2588
P.O.Box 506 communication@cousteau.org
Etna, NH 03750-0506 www.cousteau.org
About the impact of U.S.'s oil spill in Alaska.

5988 **Dolphins**
Freeman Films
P.O. Box 205 949-494-1055
Laguna Beach, CA 92652 Fax: 949-494-2079
contact@macfreefilms.com
macgillivrayfreeman.com
This film takes you on an underwater journey to observe the habitats and behaviors of dolphins.
Greg Macgillivray, Chairman & Film Director
Shaun Macgillivray, President & Producer

5989 **E - Is For Elephant**
TMW Media Group
#103, 2321 Abbot Kinney Blvd 310-577-8581
Venice, CA 90291 800-262-8862
general@tmwmedia.com
www.tmwmedia.com
This film explores the interdependence of all living creatures, with the focus on an elephants' life cycle, appearance and habitat.

5990 **Earth Revealed**
Annenberg Learner

PO Box 26983 202-783-0500
St. Louis, MO 63118 800-532-7637
Fax: 202-783-0333
order@learner.org
www.learner.org

A video series about the processes that shape Earth. Some topics explored are earthquakes, volcanoes, the creation of sea-floor crusts and shifting river courses.

5991 Earth's Physical Resources
The Open University

openlearn@open.ac.uk
www.open.edu

Series exploring the effectiveness of sustainable energy in the face of environmental issues. Some of the strategies discussed include wind power, biomass, hydro power, wave and tidal power, solar and geothermal power.

5992 Earthwise Media Educational Videos
Earthwise Media
PO Box 2593 360-271-1584
Silverdale, WA 98383 Fax: 360-394-2168
info@earthwisevideos.com
earthwisevideos.com

Production company specializing in environmental educational videos, multi-media presentations and computer aided learning tools.
Wes Nicholson, Technical Coordinator

5993 Ecological Realities: Natural Laws at Work
University of California
Berkeley, CA 94720 510-642-6000
webmaster@berkeley.edu
abt.ucpress.edu

A short film about a food pyramid in a marsh.

5994 Ecology: Succession
Coronet/MTI Film & Video
#212, 1990 E Lohman Ave
Las Cruces, NM 88001 800-221-1274
orders@phoenixlearninggroup.com
phoenixlearninggroup.com

A film exploring population density and its connection to the ecosystem. The focus is on the different factors that can limit population growth: climate, food shortages, predation and more.

5995 Ecology: Tree Top Insects
Kanopy Streaming
#410, 781 Beach St 415-513-1026
San Francisco, CA 94109 www.kanopystreaming.com

In this film, students explore the forest to learn about the organisms that dwell in the tree tops, most of which are insects.

5996 Ecosystems: The Florida Everglades
TMW Media Group
#103, 2321 Abbot Kinney Blvd 310-577-8581
Venice, CA 90291 800-262-8862
general@tmwmedia.com
www.tmwmedia.com

A film about the diverse ecosystems within the Florida Everglades, how they formed and how they were affected by the increase in human population. The film also looks at the measures being taken to monitor and protect the health of theEverglades.

5997 Effluents of Affluence
University of Michigan
Film Video Library
500 S State St 734-764-1817
Ann Arbor, MI 48109 Fax: 734-764-6849
mirlyn.lib.umich.edu

A film examining waste disposal methods, land fills, and metal reclamation.
Pamela Mackintosh, Coordinator

5998 Elephant Boy
London Film Productions
Ilford House
133 - 135 Oxford St londonfilmproductions@gmail.com
London W1D-2HY www.londonfilmproduction.com

British adventure film about a young Indian boy and his elephant.

5999 Empire of the Red Bear
Discovery Communications
1 Discovery Pl 240-662-2000
Silver Spring, MD 20910 corporate.discovery.com

Series about Russian wildlife, with a focus on the brown bears of the Kamchatka Peninsula.

6000 Energetics of Life
John Wiley & Sons
111 River St 201-748-6000
Hoboken, NJ 07030-5774 Fax: 201-748-6088
info@wiley.com
ca.wiley.com

Film exploring different kinds of energy such as kinetic energy, potential energy, thermodynamics and more.
Matthew Kissner, Chairman & CEO
John Kritzmacher, Chief Financial Officer

6001 Energy NOW
Energy Now
#203, 621 - 4th Ave SW
Calgary, AB T2P-0K2 energynow.ca

A magazine style TV show exploring topics of sustainable energy.

6002 Energy, The Alternatives
Media Guild

www.worldcat.org

Film about energy alternatives to fossil fuels. Some methods mentioned include harnessing the ocean's tidal cycles, harvesting the wind and developming methanol fuels.

6003 Environmental Science: Our Ozone Blanket
TMW Media Group
#103, 2321 Abbot Kinney Blvd 310-577-8581
Venice, CA 90291 800-262-8862
general@tmwmedia.com
www.tmwmedia.com

A program on the subject of science and Earth's atmosphere, exploring solutions to the damages caused to the ozone layer by CFCs.

6004 Everglades Region: An Ecological Study
John Wiley & Sons
111 River St 201-748-6000
Hoboken, NJ 07030-5774 Fax: 201-748-6088
info@wiley.com
ca.wiley.com

Film showing the ecology of the Atlantic Coastal Ridge, the Everglades, Big Cypress Swamp, and Coastal Mangrove Swamps of South Florida.

6005 Extinction in Progress
Kanopy Streaming
#410, 781 Beach St 415-513-1026
San Francisco, CA 94109 www.kanopystreaming.com

A film about the future of Haiti's natural resources, with a focus on the potential extinction of its biodiversity.
Lisa Landi, Licensing Director

6006 **Forever Wild**
Kanopy Streaming
#410, 781 Beach St 415-513-1026
San Francisco, CA 94109 www.kanopystreaming.com
A film about America's wilderness preservation efforts. The film follows those who have dedicated their time to protecting mountains, forests, deserts, prairies, and rivers from the hazzards brought on by development.
Lisa Landi, Licensing Director

6007 **Forms of Energy**
Films Media Group
132 West 31st St, 16th Fl 800-322-8755
New York, NY 10001 Fax: 800-678-3633
custserv@films.com
www.films.com
Film about different kinds of energy and their effects on objects.

6008 **Fragile Earth: Enemies of the Oak**
Oxford Scientific Films
21 Berners St, 4th fl
London W1T-3LP www.oxfordscientificfilms.tv
Film examining the economic balance within an English Oak tree, and the insect species that inhabit the tree.

6009 **From Flint: Voices of a Poisoned City**
Kanopy Streaming
#410, 781 Beach St 415-513-1026
San Francisco, CA 94109 www.kanopystreaming.com
Film about the water contamination crisis in Flint, Michigan and its detrimental affects on the health of the local people.
Lisa Landi, Licensing Director

6010 **GPN Educational Media**
Destination Education
4910 S 75th St 402-435-0110
Lincoln, NE 68516 slenzen@shopdei.com
shopgpn.com
Produces educational media - video, CD-ROM, DVD, Internet-for-16. Free previews available on line and on video. GPN offers over 1000 educational DVDs, including titles such as Animal Behavior, Bugs and Butterflies.

6011 **Glaciers: Clues to Future Climate**
TMW Media Group
#103, 2321 Abbot Kinney Blvd 310-577-8581
Venice, CA 90291 800-262-8862
general@tmwmedia.com
www.tmwmedia.com
This film presents a study of glaciers and their relevance to the irrigation of crops, hydroelectric power and underground water reservoirs. Settings discussed include Antarctica, Greenland and Iceland.

6012 **Great American Woodlots: Minnesota**
University of Maine Extension Service
420 Johnston Hall 612-625-3394
101 Pleasant St. S.E. www.extension.umn.edu
Minneapolis, MN 55455
Film about the ruffed grouse, its habitat and behaviours.

6013 **Green TV**
1125 Hayes St 415-255-4797
San Francisco, CA 94117 fgreen@greentv.org
www.greentv.org
Video production company that combines environmental journalism with dramatic wildlife and natural history footage. Some of their titles include Counting Sheep, The Forest Through The Trees, Ocean Parables, Spotted in the Woodsandmore.
Frank Green, Owner & President

6014 **Guardians of the Cliff**
Nature Episodes
www.worldcat.org
Film about Cornell University's reintroduction of the Peregrine falcon into Northeastern U.S.

6015 **Happy Campers with Miss Shirley & Friends**
Kids Express
A guide to exploring nature, made for young children.

6016 **How to Boil a Frog**
Kanopy Streaming
#410, 781 Beach St 415-513-1026
San Francisco, CA 94109 www.kanopystreaming.com
An alternative documentary about environmental problems faced by the world today. A story told through characters, this film mixes comedy with facts to make the subject more engaging. The film covers the topics of overpopulation, thewar on nature, income inequality, oil and global warming.
Lisa Landi, Licensing Director

6017 **I Walk in the Desert**
Educational Images
www.worldcat.org
Film exploring the landscape of the Southwest deserts, and the specialized plants and animals which live there.

6018 **In the Mind of Plants**
XiveTV
#21, West 14th North St
New York, NY www.xivetv.com
A film exploring plants as sentient beings, with the ability to feel and perceive their environments in unique ways.

6019 **Joe Albert's Fox Hunt**
Education Development Center
43 Foundry Ave 617-969-7100
Waltham, MA 02453-8313 Fax: 617-969-5979
www@edc.org
www.edc.org
A series about "The Pine Barrens" of New Jersey.

6020 **Kanopy Streaming**
Kanopy Streaming
#410, 781 Beach St 415-513-1026
San Francisco, CA 94109 www.kanopystreaming.com
Kanopy Streaming is a video streaming company offering many environmental science videos as part of their collection. Topics covered include pollution, climate change, environmental activism, sustainability, environment & health,nuclear power, conservation, endangered species, Marine ecosystems and more.
Lisa Landi, Licensing Director
Lauren Silagyi, Publishing Director

6021 **Last Call: Are There Limits to Growth?**
Kanopy Streaming
#410, 781 Beach St 415-513-1026
San Francisco, CA 94109 www.kanopystreaming.com
A film exploring the limits of human development in a world of finite natural resources. The scientists and authors of the book 'The Limits to Growth' send out their final message about the measures we must take to sustain ourecosytems.
Lisa Landi, Licensing Director

6022 **Legacy of an Oil Spill: Tens Years After Exxon**
The Alaska Department of Fish and Game

1255 W. 8th St
P.O. Box 115526 907-465-4100
Juneau, AK 99811-5526 dfg.webmaster@alaska.gov
www.adfg.alaska.gov
Film documenting the Exxon Valdez Oil Spill 10 years after the event, with a focus on the recovery of affected wildlife and people of the area.
Sam Cotton, Commissioner

6023 Life Off Grid
Kanopy Streaming
#410, 781 Beach St 415-513-1026
San Francisco, CA 94109 www.kanopystreaming.com
A film about the Canadians who have made the decision to live away from the cities and build their lives around renewable energy.
Lisa Landi, Licensing Director

6024 Life on a Rocky Shore
Earthwise Media
PO Box 2593 360-271-1584
Silverdale, WA 98383-2593 Fax: 360-394-2168
info@earthwisevideos.com
www.earthwisevideos.com
Film giving an introduction to the plants and animals of the Pacific Northwest's rich Intertidal Zone. The self-paced presentation uses 100 photos, video clips and graphics to illustrate the story of life in the Zone. Learn about thetides, changing bands of life, and adaptation of life in the Zone. Film covers marine biology and comes with printable teacher's guide for grades 6-12.
Wes Nicholson, Technical Coordinator

6025 Man: The Polluter
National Film Board of Canada
Norman McLaren Building
3155 C"te de Liesse Rd 800-542-2164
Montreal, QC H4N-2N4 webmaster@onf.ca
www.nfb.ca
An animated film investigating the consequences of man-made pollution, including commentary by Dr. Fred H. Knelman, Professor of Science and Human Affairs at Montreal's Concordia University.
Mireille Potvin, Rights Acquisitions

6026 Manatees, A Living Resource
Educational Images
www.worldcat.org
Film exploring manatees and the preservation efforts being made to prevent them from extinction.

6027 Microbial Ecology
Annenberg Learner
PO Box 26983 202-783-0500
St. Louis, MO 63118 800-532-7637
Fax: 202-783-0333
order@learner.org
www.learner.org
A film revealing the role microorganisms play in supporting all life forms; microorganisms are presented as being processors of oxygen, mineral nutrients for plant growth and waste materials.
Kristine Inchausti, Operations Analyst
Michele McLeod, Senior Program Officer

6028 Mitzi a Da Si
Nature Episodes
www.worldcat.org
A film examining the thermal features of Yellowstone National Park . Also covered is the subject of the Park's wildlife and their habitats.

6029 Oceans: The Mystery of the Missing Plastic
Kanopy Streaming
#410, 781 Beach St 415-513-1026
San Francisco, CA 94109 www.kanopystreaming.com
This film investigates the affects of plastics on the environment, as well as the mystery of plastic materials that have gone missing.
Lisa Landi, Licensing Director

6030 Origins
Vital Origins Productions
A film examining the affects of civilization and technology on the Earth's environment.

6031 Our Endangered Wildlife: The Massasauga Rattler
Nature Episodes
www.worldcat.org
Film examining the survival challenges faced by the Massasauga rattler as its natural habitats shrink. The focus is on a colony in a central New York wetland.

6032 Paradise Lost
National Film Board of Canada
Norman McLaren Building
3155 C"te de Liesse Rd 800-542-2164
Montreal, QC H4N-2N4 webmaster@onf.ca
www.nfb.ca
A short animation film by Evelyn Lambart capturing the need for a clean environment for all living things. The film centers on the affects of air pollution on birds, butterflies and other wild animals.
Mireille Potvin, Rights Acquisitions

6033 Queen of the Sun
Kanopy Streaming
#410, 781 Beach St 415-513-1026
San Francisco, CA 94109 www.kanopystreaming.com
A film about the challenges faced by the bee population as a result of environmental change. The film includes commentary by Beekeepers, scientists and philosophers from around the world (such as Michael Pollan, Gunther Hauk andVandana Shiva).
Lisa Landi, Licensing Director

6034 Rainbows in the Sea: A Guide to Earth's Coral Reefs
Earthwise Media
PO Box 2593 360-271-1584
Silverdale, WA 98383-2593 Fax: 360-394-2168
info@earthwisevideos.com
www.earthwisevideos.com
Showcases the wide variety of colorful fish and invertebrates living in coral reefs, how they form and what they need to blossom. The guide also includes a teacher's guide for elementary and highschool students.
28 minutes
Wes Nicholson, Technical Coordinator

6035 Return of the Dragons
Nature Episodes
www.worldcat.org
A film about alligators and alligator farming.

6036 Salt Marshes: A Special Resource
Educational Images
Video examining the ecology of salt marshes, with a focus on marsh plants, marine vegetation, animals, migrating birds, insects, fish and shellfish.

6037 Sand Dune Ecology and Formation
Educational Images
www.worldcat.org
A film exploring the formation of sand dunes and vegetation in Oregon.

6038 Science & Environment: Pollution
TMW Media Group
#103, 2321 Abbot Kinney Blvd 310-577-8581
Venice, CA 90291 800-262-8862
general@tmwmedia.com
www.tmwmedia.com
A film about the different types of pollution created by both nature as well as humans; also discussed are ways by which we may reduce waste to protect the environment.

6039 Science in Focus: Energy
Annenberg Learner
PO Box 26983 202-783-0500
St. Louis, MO 63118 800-532-7637
Fax: 202-783-0333
order@learner.org
www.learner.org
A video series of 8 one-hour programs exploring the subject of energy and its role in motion, machines, food, the human body and the universe.

6040 Seals
Media Guild
www.worldcat.org
Film discussing the management of British Isles seal population.

6041 Song of the Salish Sea: A Natural History of Northwest Waters
Earthwise Media
PO Box 2593 360-271-1584
Silverdale, WA 98383-2593 Fax: 360-394-2168
info@earthwisevideos.com
www.earthwisevideos.com
Examines the fragile habitats that make up the Strait of Georgia, Strait of Juan de Fuca and Puget Sound. DVD includes a teacher's guide, Puget Sound Beach Guide, Kids for Puget Sound Passport, and curriculums for grades 6-12.
45 minutes
Wes Nicholson, Technical Coordinator

6042 Survey of the Animal Kingdom: The Vertebrates.
Educational Images
www.worldcat.org
Video exploring creatures of aquatic environments: tunicates, lamprey, hagfish, sharks, rays, coelacanth, lungfish, ray-finned fish, sturgeon and more.

6043 The Changing Forest
A film examining the ecology of a forest near the Laurentian Shield, Quebec. We learn why the maple tree is

6044 The Chemical Kids
Filmakers Library
3212 Duke St 703-212-8520
Alexandria, VA 22314 800-889-5937
alexanderstreet.com
Alarming facts about man-made chemicals in food and water, especially how children are the most affected.
Linda Gottesman, Co-President
Sue Oscar, Co-President

6045 The Cost of Oil
Kanopy Streaming
#410, 781 Beach St 415-513-1026
San Francisco, CA 94109 www.kanopystreaming.com
A film about oil drilling in the Arctic and how it is affecting the Alaskan Inupiat people in their struggle to perserve their lifestyles and cultures.
Lisa Landi, Licensing Director

6046 The Earth at Risk Environmental Video Series
Schlessinger Video Productions
Cerebellum Corporation 415-541-9901
#406, 145 Corte Madera Town Center 866-386-0253
Corte Madera, CA 94925 Fax: 805-426-8136
customerservice@cerebellum.com
www.libraryvideocompany.com
Follows Kevin Seal in an educational series involving environmental projects, nature footage, and interviews with leading experts.

6047 The Habitable Planet: A Systems Approach to Environmental Science
Annenberg Learner
PO Box 26983 202-783-0500
St. Louis, MO 63118 800-532-7637
Fax: 202-783-0333
order@learner.org
www.learner.org
A video series containing 13 half-hour video programs about various sciences for teachers of biology, chemistry, and Earth science. The series begins with an examination of Earth's systems (geophysical, atmospheric, oceanic, andecosystems) and goes on to reveal how human activities have impacted these systems.
Kristine Inchausti, Operations Analyst
Michele McLeod, Senior Program Officer

6048 The Unnatural History of the Kakapo
Kanopy Streaming
#410, 781 Beach St 415-513-1026
San Francisco, CA 94109 www.kanopystreaming.com
Film about the endangered species of the Kakapo and scientists' efforts to save the Kakapo population from extinction.
Lisa Landi, Licensing Director

6049 The Windrifters
Nature Episodes
www.worldcat.org
Film about the re-introduction of bald eagles to the Montezuma Wildlife Refuge.

6050 The World Between the Tides: A Guide to Pacific Rocky Shores
Earthwise Media
PO Box 2593 360-271-1584
Silverdale, WA 98383-2593 Fax: 360-394-2168
info@earthwisevideos.com
www.earthwisevideos.com
A narrated journey along the intertidal area that examines harsh conditions, and how animals and plants have adapted. DVD includes teacher's guide.
23 minutes
Wes Nicholson, Technical Coordinator

6051 Tropical Rainforest
Media Guild
www.worldcat.org
Film exploring animal ecology in a rainforest environment. Also covered is a scientific research project carried out in the Los Tuxtlas Reserve (Veracruz, Mexico).

6052 Tropical Rainforests Under Fire
Educational Images

www.worldcat.org

Film about the ecology and exploitation of tropical rain forests.

6053 Unseen Life on Earth: An Introduction to Microbiology
Annenberg Learner
PO Box 26983 202-783-0500
St. Louis, MO 63118 800-532-7637
Fax: 202-783-0333
order@learner.org
www.learner.org

An educational video series on the subject of microbial functions. The series discusses the affects of microorganisms on various aspects of our lives.

6054 Walking On Oil: Alberta's Oil Sands
TMW Media Group
#103, 2321 Abbot Kinney Blvd 310-577-8581
Venice, CA 90291 800-262-8862
general@tmwmedia.com
www.tmwmedia.com

A film that examines oil deposits throughout the world, including the possibilities offered by "oil sands" as well as the dangers to the environment posed by invasive extraction processes.

6055 Warm Blooded Sea: Mammals of the Deep
Warner Home Video
Cousteau Society 212-532-2588
P.O. Box 506 communication@cousteau.org
Etna, NH 03750-0506 www.cousteau.org

A film exploring the evolution and behavior of Marine mammals such as dolphins, whales and seals. Regions explored include the South Pacific, Florida Keys, South Carolina and Argentina.

6056 Warming Warning
Media Guild

www.worldcat.org

Film covering theories about future global warming.

6057 Waters Of The World
TMW Media Group
#103, 2321 Abbot Kinney Blvd 310-577-8581
Venice, CA 90291 800-262-8862
general@tmwmedia.com
www.tmwmedia.com

Film revealing the distribution and placement of water bodies throughout the world, with a focus on the Hydrologic Cycle and major river systems of the world.

6058 Watershed: Canada's Threatened Rainforest
Media Guild

www.worldcat.org

Chronicles the expedition to Canada's Pacific Coast rainforests, covering environmental issues, complex ecosystems, and the work of conservationists.

6059 Weather Systems
TMW Media Group
#103, 2321 Abbot Kinney Blvd 310-577-8581
Venice, CA 90291 800-262-8862
general@tmwmedia.com
www.tmwmedia.com

This video series presents scientific contents in a simplified format, exploring weather and its many forms (atmosphere, air density, winds, clouds and storms) and how weather affects our lives.

6060 Wilderness Video
Wilderness Video
888 Beswick Way 541-488-9363
Ashland, OR 97520 Fax: 541-488-9363
bob@wildernessvideo.com
wildernessvideo.com

A production company offering footage and videos of nature scenes such as sunrises and sunsets, rainbows, waterfalls, storms, cities and wildlife.
Bob Glusic, Owner

Green Products & Services

General

6061 18 Rabbits Organics
31 Water St 415-922-6006
San Francisco, CA 94133 customerservice@18rabbits.com
www.18rabbits.com
Manufacturer of organic bars and granola.
Alison Seibert, Founder

6062 A.V. Olsson Trading Co., Inc.
2001 West Main St 203-969-2090
Suite 215 customerservice@avolsson.com
Stamford, CT 06902 www.avolsson.com
A.V. Olsson Trading Co. is a family-owned business focusing on the importation of fine dairy products, quality herring, and environmentally-friendly cooking and baking products.

6063 AIYA America
386 Beech Ave Unit B3 310-212-1395
Torrance, CA 90501 Fax: 310-212-1386
info@aiya-america.com
www.aiya-america.com
AIYA is Japan's leading Matcha tea producer. Matcha is the most exciting discovery of the 21st century's modern tea world. Created over 800 years ago by Buddhist monks as a meditational drink, Matcha is known today as the healthiest,rarest and most premium of all tea varieties of Japan.
Fumi Sugita, Executive General Manager

6064 Acorn Designs
5066 Mott Evans Road 607-387-3424
Trumansburg, NY 14886 800-299-3997
Fax: 607-387-5609
info@acorndesigns.org
www.acorndesigns.org
Totes and other items with wildlife and nature themes; high post-consumer recycled paper; 100% post-consumer recycled paper journals and cards. Images from nature artwork from over 30 artists.
Steve Sierigk, Owner

6065 Adventure Coffee Roasting
633 N Jasmine Place 520-247-2651
Tucson, AZ 85710 Info@AdventureCoffeeRoasting.com
www.adventurecoffeeroasting.com
Adventure Coffee Roasting encourages sustainable pesticide-free farming. They roast only certified organically grown coffee in small batches, assuring product freshness and consistency.

6066 Alexandra Avery Purely Natural Body Care
4717 SE Belmont Street 503-236-5926
Portland, OR 97215 800-669-1863
Fax: 503-234-7272
100% natural and cruelty free aromatherapy products for face and body care.
Alexandra Avery, President

6067 All Terrain
20 North Main St, Unit 1 603-763-8800
Newport, NH 03773 800-246-7328
info@allterrainco.com
www.allterrainco.com
All Terrain sells natural products to help people live more active, healthier lives. Safe and highly effective, All Terrain's products disprove the myth that if it's natural, it can't work as well as chemical-based products. Theproducts are developed by and for outdoor enthusiasts for use whether trekking in the backcountry or relaxing with family in your backyard.

6068 Allen's Naturally
PO Box 1779
Birmingham, Mi 48012 800-352-8971
www.allensnaturally.com
Making Laundry Detergents Free of Perfumes, Fragrances and Dyes for Cloth Diapering and those with MCS (Multiple Chemical Sensitivities) since 1979

6069 Allsop Home & Garden
660 North Main Street, Ste #220
PO Box 4921 866-425-5767
Ketchum, Id 83340 www.allsopgarden.com
Allsop Home & Garden is known for combining creative materials with solar power for efficient, beautiful and sustainable outdoor lighting.

6070 Alter Eco
2339 Third Street 415-701-1212
Suite 70 Fax: 415-701-1213
San Francisco, CA 94107 sales@alterecofoods.com
www.alterecofoods.com
Alter Eco is based on the premise that food is fundamental to life – and whole, healthy, delicious food can make life better for people all over the world. By working directly with the small-scale farmers who grow our quinoa, rice,sugar and cacao, helping them institute Fair Trade and Organic practices and assisting them in improving both quality of food and quality of life, they are creating a system that benefits everyone involved.
Mathieu Senard, Co-Founder/Co-CEO
Edouard Rollet, Co-Founder/Co-CEO

6071 Amy's Kitchen
PO Box 449 707-781-7535
Petaluma, CA 94953 www.amys.com
Since its inception in 1987 Amy's has created over 250 frozen meals, including pizzas, pocket sandwiches, pot pies, entrées, snacks and whole meals. In 1999, they introduced a grocery line that now includes canned soups, beans andchili as well as jarred pasta sauces and salsas.
Jack Chipman, VP of Sales
Dennis Bee, Planning Manager

6072 Ancient Harvest
1722 14th Street 310-217-8125
Suite 212 ancientharvest.com
Boulder, CO 80302
They serve up great tasting, non-GMO and organic, gluten-free foods for all, including gluten-free pasta, ancient grain blends, mac and cheese, quinoa flour, quinoa flakes and ready-to-eat polenta in a variety of inspired culinaryflavors.

6073 Andalou Naturals
7250 Redwood Blvd. 415-446-9470
Suite 208 888-898-6955
Novato, CA 94945 Fax: 415-446-9479
support@andalou.com
andalou.com
Offers skin care, hair care and body care products which are made thoughtfully and beautifully, blending advanced Fruit Stem Cell Science with natural and fair-trade ingredients, with a minimum 70% certified organic content, forvisible and healthy results.
Stacey Kelly Egide, CEO
Mark A. Egide, President

6074 Annie's
1610 5th Street 510-558-7500
Berkeley, CA 94710 800-288-1089
www.annies.com

Annie's Homegrown is a Berkeley, California-based maker of natural and organic pastas, meals and snacks.
John Foraker, CEO
Zahir Ibrahim, EVP, CFO

6075 Ark Naturals
6166 Taylor Road 239-592-9388
Suite 103 800-926-5100
Naples, FL 34109 Fax: 239-592-9338
info@arknaturals.com
www.arknaturals.com
Ark Naturals is the leading manufacturer of health, remedy and lifestyle solutions for pets from head to tail. For over 16 years, Ark Naturals has provided the most complete line of wellness and remedy products of the highest quality.
Susan D. Weiss, President

6076 Arora Creations
254 Dekalb Ave. 347-294-4815
Suite #4 info@aroracreations.com
Brooklyn, NY 11205 www.aroracreations.com
Arora Creations, Inc. launched the first-ever USDA-certified Organic Indian Grocery product line in the US market.
Dhiraj C. Arora, Founder/CEO/President

6077 Artisana Organics
810 81st Avenue 510-632-8612
Suite B 866-237-8688
Oakland, CA 94621 Fax: 510-380-6942
www.artisanaorganics.com
There passion is creating unique, delicious, healthy, gourmet food. Handmade with care, there organic foods are crafted using a temperature controlled process that preserves thé life-essential fatty acids, proteins, vitamins, andenzymes.

6078 Artistic Video
87 Tyler Avenue 631-744-5999
Sound Beach, NY 11789 888-982-4244
Fax: 631-744-5993
bobklien@movementsofmagic.com
www.movementsofmagic.com
Instructional videos and DVDs on health and fitness, alternative healing, children's programs about animals, free interactive section with articles, discussion forums, video clips, classes, instructions, Tai-Chi and other natureoriented cultures and practices.
Bob Klein, President

6079 Associated Building Maintenance Co., Inc.
2140 Priest Bridge Court 410-721-1818
Suite 3 800-721-9068
Crofton, Ma 21114 info@abmcoinc.com
www.abmcoinc.com
Associated Building Maintenance Co., Inc. is a woman-owned, contract cleaning company headquartered in Crofton, Maryland. Over 1,000 employees clean over 14 million square feet daily in the Maryland, Virginia, and Washington DC area.
Deborah Zagami, President
Harry Zagami, General Manager

6080 Aura Cacia
5398 31st Avenue 319-227-7996
Urbana, I 52345 800-437-3301
Fax: 800-717-4372
customercare@auracacia.com
www.auracacia.com
Aura Cacia makes aromatherapy accessible with innovative ready-to-use products that let even beginners realize the full benefits of our high-quality essential oils in a variety of ways that can easily be a part of any lifestyle.

6081 AusPen
99 Madison Avenue
Suite 405 Fax: 929-214-4112
New York, NY 10016 kerrie@auspen.us
www.auspen.us
Auspen supplies quality, eco-friendly refillable whiteboard markers to the general public and the education community.
Kerrie Sharpley, Founder & General Manager

6082 Aztec Secret
P.O. Box 841 775-727-8351
Pahrump, NV 89041 Fax: 775-727-1882
www.aztec-secret.com
Aztec Secret Indian Healing Clay, Jojoba Oil, Kukui Nut Oil, Tee Tree Oil and other beauty products available online and at local health food stores.

6083 BDM Holdings
7915 Jones Branch Drive 703-848-5000
McLean, VA 22102
Bennie Dibona, VP Engineering/Environment

6084 Balance of Nature
Unviersity of Chicago Press
1427 East 60th Street 773-702-7700
Chicago, IL 60637 Fax: 773-702-9756

6085 Bamboo Studio
31878 Del Obispo St. 949-951-2064
Building 118 – 336 Fax: 949-951-4726
San Juan Capistrano, CA 92675 sales@ecobambooware.com
www.ecobambooware.com
Bamboo Studio is a all-occasion dinnerware that is both disposable and reusable.

6086 Bare
38 Keyes Avenue 509-554-5540
Suite 210 Fax: 509-554-5510
San Francisco, CA 94129 info@baresnacks.com
www.baresnacks.com

6087 Barlean's
3660 Slater Road 360-384-0485
Ferndale, WA 98248 800-445-3529
questions@barleans.com
www.barleans.com
Offers flax and borage oil products.
Bruce Barlean, Owner

6088 Bee's Wrap
394 Rockydale Road 802-643-2132
Bristol, VT 05443 info@beeswrap.com
www.beeswrap.com
Offers sustainable food storage products.

6089 Begley's
3627 Briggeman Drive 714-689-0063
Los Alamitos, CA 90720 Fax: 714-242-0551
begleysbest.com
Offers earth responsible household product.
Ed Begley, Jr., Owner

6090 Bellino Fine Linens
471 South Dean Street 201-568-5255
Englewood, NJ 07631 Fax: 201-568-0155
info@bellinofinelinens.com
www.bellinofinelinens.com
BELLINO has been providing exqui- site luxury linens for the bed, bath and table for 25 years.

6091 Betty Lou's
750 SE Booth Bend Rd
McMinnville, OR 97128
503-434-5205
800-242-5205
www.bettylousinc.com
Healthy, all natural snack products; low carb, all natural, dairy, gluten, and wheat free.
Betty Lou, Owner

6092 Big Dipper Wax Works
700 South Orchard St.
Seattle, WA 98108
206-767-7322
888-826-7770
Fax: 206-938-5444
info@bigdipperwaxworks.com
www.bigdipperwaxworks.com
Hand crafted pure natural beeswax candles available in many unique styles.

6093 Big Green Cleaning Company
4860 Calle Real
Santa Barbara, CA 93110
805-692-1000
Fax: 805-967-3915
biggreen@biggreenclean.com
biggreenclean.com
Offers cleaning services.
Allen Williams, President

6094 Bio-Sun Systems
RR 2 Box 134A
Millerton, PA 16936
570-527-2200
800-847-8840
Fax: 570-537-6200
biosun@npacc.net
www.bio-sun.com
Composting toilets and modular restrooms.
Donna White, President
Al White, VP

6095 BioBag Americas, Inc.
1059 Broadway
Suite F
Dunedin, FL 34698
727-789-1646
Fax: 727-614-9746
info@biobagusa.com
biobagusa.com
BioBag provides bags and films for the collection of organic waste for the purpose of composting.

6096 Biokleen
PO Box 820689
Vancouver, WA 98682
800-477-0188
biokleenhome.com
Biokleen laundry products are triple concentrated to reduce packaging, waste and energy.
Cindy Rimer
Barry Firth

6097 Bionaturae
PO Box 98
North Franklin, CT 06254
860-642-6996
Fax: 860-642-6990
info@bionaturae.com
www.bionaturae.com
Organic Italian food.

6098 Biotta
484 East Carmel Drive
#137
Carmel, IN 46032
866-595-8917
888-524-6882
Fax: 888-816-9725
info@biottajuices.com
www.biottajuices.com
Non-GMO. Vegan. 100% pure juice.

6099 Bob's Red Mill
13521 SE Pheasant Ct
Milwaukie, OR 97222
800-349-2173
www.bobsredmill.com
Whole grain store and bakery.

6100 Bolana Enterprises, Inc.
10739 Tucker Street
Suite 270
Beltsville, MD 20705
301-595-2577
Fax: 888-750-0179
www.bolanainc.com
Bolona offer comprehensive janitorial services tailored to your organization's unique needs.

6101 Bonga Foods
24955 Paicific Coast Hwy
Suite B201
Malibu, CA 90265
310-456-1526
www.bongafoods.com
Through trading, Bonga-Baobab enables local harvesters to support themselves.

6102 Botanical Interests
660 Compton Street
Broomfield, CO 80020
303-464-6464
800-486-2647
www.botanicalinterests.com
Supplies gardeners with the highest quality seed in informative seed packets on the market.

6103 Bottled Up Designs
202 Glenrose
East Fallowfield, PA 19320
484-885-7171
www.bottledupdesigns.com
Designs recycled from reclaimed antique glass and bottles.

6104 Bragg Live Foods
Box 7
Santa Barbara, CA 93102
805-968-1020
800-446-1990
Fax: 805-968-1001
info@bragg.com
bragg.com
Paul C. Bragg, originator of Health Food Stores in America, founded the company, now run by his daughter Patricia Bragg, N.D., Ph.D., who continues to provide natural healthy products, and a library of self-help books.
Paul C. Bragg, Founder

6105 Building Maintenance Services
11 Penn Plaza
New York, NY 10001
212-714-0004
eporch@bmsllc.com
bmsbuildingservices.com
BMS provides building maintinance service, provides an environment that is clean, safe, and an enhancement to the work day.
Michael Doherty, President & CEO
Carol Gambardella, Vice President & CFO

6106 Cangles
PO Box 74
Vassar, MI 48768
877-491-5655
Service@Cangles.com
www.cangles.com
Makes jewelry out of recycled can.

6107 Celtic Sea Salt
4 Celtic Dr.
Arden, NC 28704
800-867-7258
Fax: 828-654-0529
info@selinanaturally.com
www.celticseasalt.com
Celtic Sea Salt® Brand Sea Salt is authentic, unprocessed whole salt from pristine coastal regions of the world.

6108 Cheri's Desert Harvest
1840 E. Winsett
Tucson, AZ 85719
800-743-1141
Fax: 520-623-7741
www.cherisdesertharvest.com
Cheri's all-natural products are made from fresh fruits and vegetables indigenous to the Sonoran Desert.

6109 Chia Burst
9461 Charleville Blvd.
#123
Beverly Hills, CA 90212
310-500-5119
chiabursts@yahoo.com
Supplies organic Chia seed.

6110 Chicago Vegan Foods
905 N. Ridge Ave.
Suite 7
Lombard, IL 60148
630-629-9667
info@chicagoveganfoods.com
chicagoveganfoods.com
Teese Vegan Cheese is created with the goal of mimicking cheesy-based comfort foods, minus the dairy.

6111 ChicoBag
13434 Browns Valley Drive
Chico, CA 95973
530-342-4426
888-496-6166
Fax: 530-267-5434
info@chicobag.com
www.chicobag.com
Designs long lasting reusable bags.

6112 ChildLife Essentials
8690 Hayden Place
Culver City, CA 90232
310-305-4640
800-993-0332
Fax: 310-305-4680
mailroom@childlife.net
www.childlife.net
ChildLife Essentials® provides a complete line of nutritional supplements designed specifically for infants and children.

6113 Choice Organic Tea
600 South Brandon Street
Seattle, WA 98108
206-525-0051
866-972-6879
Fax: 206-523-9750
choiceorganicteas@worldpantry.com
www.choiceorganicteas.com
A firm belief in organics, with a dedication to ensure the ethical treatment of workers who cultivate tea, and a team of dedicated employees at Choice Organic Teas, has made the company a modern day tea pioneer.

6114 Christi's Green Cleaning
Christi's Green Cleaning
Santa Cruz, CA 95060
831-406-0145
christisgreencleaning@gmail.com
www.christisgreencleaning.com
Christi's Green Cleaning uses cleaning products such as Envirox, Bon Ami, Biokleen, and Howard's Naturals which are non-toxic and environmentally friendly.

6115 Clean Conscience
4715 Broadway Street
Suite C-6
Boulder, CO 80304
303-495-2444
www.cleanconscience.com
Provides healthy home cleaning services.

6116 CleanNet USA
2010 Corporate Ridge
Suite 700
McLean, VA 22102
800-735-8838
Fax: 703-749-7719
www.cleannetusa.com
CleanNet USA® was created in response to an increasing demand for a go-to company with access to commercial cleaning service companies nationwide.

6117 Clenz Cleaning
1215 Crease St.
Philadelphia, PA 19125
215-545-0066
info@clenzphilly.com
www.clenzphilly.com
Provides cleaning service in the Greater Philadelphia area.

6118 Clif Bar & Company
1451 66th Street
Emeryville, CA 94608-1004
800-254-3227
www.clifbar.com

6119 Coconut Secret
298 Miller Ave.
Mill Valley, CA 94941
415-383-9800
888-369-3393
Fax: 415-383-9804
info@coconutsecret.com
www.coconutsecret.com
Create a low glycemic, gluten-free snack line that is safe for diabetics, using the purest, most organic, least processed ingredients.

6120 Cole's
11 Broadcommon Rd.
Bristol, RI 02809
401-396-5966
info@colestrout.com
www.colestrout.com
Cole's is the earth-friendly company dedicated to bringing you the finest, freshest foods from around the globe while preserving the delicate balance between nature and our own nutritional needs.

6121 Color Garden
1300 N Hancock
Anaheim, CA 92807
714-572-0444
Fax: 714-572-0999
inquire@colormaker.com
www.colorgarden.net
Color Garden™ pure natural food colors are 100% plant based.

6122 Colorado Mountain Jam
3573 G Rd.
Palisade, CO 81526
970-464-0745
www.plumdaisy.com
Colorado Mountain Fine Jams & Jellies mission is to offer a diverse gourmet line of jams and jellies that are as nutritious and healthy as they are delicious and pleasurable to eat.

6123 Coombs Family Farms
PO Box 117
Brattleboro, VT 05302
888-266-6271
www.coombsfamilyfarms.com
Provides maple products nad supports small family farms.

6124 Cotton Clouds
5176 S 14th Avenue
Safford, AZ 85546
520-428-7000
Fax: 520-428-6630
Yarn, patterns, books, video's, kit for weaving crochet, knitting and spinning.

6125 CureAll Cleaning Services
48B Paine Ave
Suite#2
Irvington, NJ 07111
973-251-9968
Fax: 973-251-9801
info@cureallcleaning.com
www.cureallcleaning.com
CureAll Cleaning Services, LLC is a family owned and operated company located in the northern New Jersey area.

6126 Curry Love
PO Box 25397
Los Angeles, CA 90025
888-635-8886
www.mycurrylove.com
Organic Curries

6127 DCD Cleaning Service
18895 S. Highlite
Clinton Township, MI 48035
586-343-3457
www.dcdcleaningservice.com
DCD cleaning services uses commercial products, many of which are all natural and Green Sealed certified.

6128 Dastony
PO Box 328
Glenview, IL 60025
800-518-0727
dastony.com
Dastony uses an ancient method known as stone-grinding in the production of its products.

6129 DeVita
1616 West Williams Drive
Phoenix, AZ 85027
877-2DE-VITA
devitastyle.com
DeVita Natural Skin Care and Color Cosmetics is wholly owned and operated by Cherylanne DeVita, Ph.D., President/CEO, and is a certified woman-owned business by the Women's Business Enterprise National Council (WBENC).
Cherylanne DeVita, Ph.D.,, President/CEO

6130 Delallo
6390 Route 30
Jeannette, PA 15644
877-DEL-LLO
info@DeLallo.com
www.delallo.com
Italian foods company.

6131 Denver Concierge
1450 Grove Street
Denver, CO 80204
303-975-2808
www.denverconcierge.com
Denver House Cleaning serives.
John Kitts, President
Maria Herrera, General Manager

6132 Desert Essence
PO Box 14007
Hauppauge, NY 11788
800-645-5768
CustomerCare@DesertEssence.com
www.desertessence.com
Desert Essence was founded in 1978 around a simple concept: beauty is natural, and nature is beautiful.

6133 Doctor Kracker
1100 Klein Road
Suite 200
Plano, TX 75074
972-633-1100
Fax: 972-633-1130
drkracker.com
Dr. Kracker was founded in 2003 in Dallas, Texas by a group of European and American bakers with a unique love for Artisan breads.

6134 Dr. Bronner's
1335 Park Center Drive
Vista, CA 92081
844-937-2551
Fax: 760-745-6675
info@drbronner.com
www.drbronner.com
Family-Owned and Run, Natural Product Pioneers provides high quality liquid and bar soaps

6135 DrTung's
PO Box 667
Kaneohe, HI 96744
808-239-5799
Fax: 808-239-5299
drtungs.com
Innovative Oral care products

6136 Drew's
926 Vermont Rt. 103 South
Chester, VT 05143
802-875-1184
800-228-2980
Fax: 802-875-5126
info@chefdrew.com
www.chefdrew.com
Drew's unique dressings and salsas are produced in small batches infused with authentic regional and ethnic flavors

6137 ECOBAGS
23-25 Spring Street
Suite 302
Ossining, NY 10562
914-944-4556
800-720-2247
Fax: 914-944-4609
info@ecobags.com
www.ecobags.com
Eco-Bags Products, Inc. opened for business in 1989 makes reusable bags

6138 EO Products
90 Windward Way
San Rafael, CA 94901
415-945-1900
800-570-3775
customerservice@eoproducts.com
www.eoproducts.com
Organic essential products
Max Geiser, Creative Director
Rosa Prado, Production Supervisor

6139 Earth Mama Angel Baby
9866 SE Empire Court
Clackamas, OR 97015
503-607-0607
Fax: 503-607-0667
earthmamaangelbaby.com
Provide safe, herbal alternatives for pregnant, postpartum and breastfeeding women, and babies of all ages, and to help educate people about traditional plant medicine and safe personal care.

6140 Earth Options
Solar Electric Engineering
117 Morris Street
Sebastopol, CA 95472
707-824-4150
882-198-1986
Fax: 707-542-4358
Environmental retail products.

6141 Earth Science
PO Box 1925
Corona, CA 91718
909-371-7565
800-222-6720
Fax: 909-371-0509
All-natural, environmentally sound skin and hair care products.
Kristine Schoenauer, President

6142 Earth Therapeutics
163 E. Bethpage Rd.
Plainview, NY 11803
800-789-3579
Fax: 516-454-6599
service@earththerapeutics.us
www.earththerapeutics.com

6143 Eco Touch
One Washington St.
Suite 200
Dover, NH 03820
888-375-7970
Fax: 603-319-1257
www.ecotouch.net
Rangeof car care products

6144 Eco-Dent Premium Natural Oral Care Products
PO Box 325
Twin Lakes, WI 53181
262-889-8561
Fax: 262-889-2461
ecodent@lotuspress.com
www.eco-dent.com
Natural oral care products

6145 Eco-Store
2441 Edgewater Drive
Orlando, FL 32804
407-426-9949
800-556-9949
Fax: 407-649-3148
beth@eco-store.com

Environmental home products, gifts, etc.

6146 EcoPaper
1884 Eastman Ave
Suite 107
Ventura, CA 93003
805-644-4462
www.ecopaper.com

EcoPaper makes, distributes, and sell finest environmental papers.

6147 Ecology Store
6928 Queens Boulevard
Flushing, NY 11377
718-446-4444
800-548-9660
Fax: 718-446-9860

Range of environmental products.

6148 Eden Foods
701 Tecumseh Road
Clinton, MI 49236
517-456-7424
888-424-3336
Fax: 517-456-6075
info@edenfoods.com
www.edenfoods.com

Eden Foods began in Ann Arbor in the late 1960s with friends sourcing natural food.

6149 Edison Grainery
Oakland, CA 94621
510-382-0202
Fax: 510-263-5778
service@edisongrainery.com
www.edisongrainery.com

Organic Food Ingredients and Pantry Staples.

6150 Edward & Sons
PO Box 1326
Carpinteria, CA 93014
805-684-8500
Fax: 805-684-8220
www.edwardandsons.com

Edward & Sons Trading Company, Inc. supplies innovative natural and organic vegetarian foods to stores and consumers throughout the world

6151 Effi Foods
11620 Wilshire Boulevard
Suite 900
Los Angeles, CA 90025
310-582-5938
Fax: 310-388-8798
info@effifoods.com
www.effifoods.com

EFFi Foods is a company for producing organic, holistic foods and nutraceuticals with its main focus on delivering nutritionally unprecedented snacking options with exceptional taste for people on-the-go.

Carina Ayden, Founder, Executive Director
Liz Rodriguez, Branding / Public Relations

6152 Ener-G Foods
5960 1st AVE S
Seattle, WA 98108
206-767-3928
800-331-5222
Fax: 206-764-3398
customerservice@ener-g.com
www.ener-g.com

Provide a wide range of ready-made foods and mixes that are wholesome, nutritious, risk-free and great tasting.

6153 Energy Efficient Environments
2119 Inverness Lane
Glen View, IL 60025
847-475-3005
800-336-3749

Efficient and earth-friendly devices for energy, water and light use.

6154 Environment Friendly Papers
Cherry Paper
13520 Liberty Avenue
Jamaica, NY 11419
718-297-3000
Fax: 718-297-2986
cherryop@AOL.com

100% recycled gift stationary, with original designs depicting flora and fauna of South Africa and environmental themes.

6155 Equal Exchange
50 United Drive
West Bridgewater, MA 02379
774-776-7333
Fax: 508-587-3833
orders@equalexchange.coop
equalexchange.coop

Equal Exchange's mission is to build long-term trade partnerships that are economically just and environmentally sound, to foster mutually beneficial relationships between farmers and consumers and to demonstrate, through our success,the contribution of worker co-operatives and Fair Trade to a more equitable, democratic and sustainable world.

6156 Erlander's Natural Products
Nature's Department Store
2279 Lake Avenue
Altadena, CA 91001
626-797-7004
800-562-8873
Fax: 626-798-2663

Natural olive oil-wine soap; bar and liquid roach killer from herbs, organic red zinfandel wine, 100% organic cotton pillows and mattresses, jewelry - semi-precious and costume, washing compound/non-detergent, sodium sesquicarbonate.

Leatrice Erlander, Co-Owner
Stig Erlander, Co-Owner

6157 Eton
1015 Corporation Way
Palo Alto, CA 94303
650-903-3866
800-872-2228
Fax: 650-903-3867
Info@etoncorp.com
www.etoncorp.com

Etón's vision is to harness nature's energy to power consumer products that keep people prepared, informed, entertained, and on-the-go.

6158 Executive Building Maintenance
7910 Woodmont Ave.
Suite 1310
Bethesda, MD 20814
301-657-4211
Fax: 301-657-3066
ebm@exebm.com
www.exebm.com

EBM, Inc., is a full service company offering superior cleaning and general janitorial maintenance to commercial & residential building owners, managers and construction companies.

David N. Kydd, President
Steve Chamberlain, Vice President Operations

6159 Extreme Green Cleaning
1825 North Oxnard Blvd
Suite 23
Oxnard, CA 93030
805-252-9435
extremegreencleanings.com

Cleaning services in Ventura County

6160 Fig Food Co.
PO Box 265
New York, NY 10014
855-FIG-FOOD
figfood.com

Organic food supplies

6161 Flavorganics
268 Doremus Avenue
Newark, NJ 07105
973-344-8014
Fax: 973-344-1948
flavorganics@worldpantry.com
www.flavorganics.com

Offers Organic Vanilla Extract.

6162 Florida Crystals
One North Clematis Street
Suite 200
West Palm Beach, FL 33401
561-366-5100
877-835-2828
Fax: 561-366-5158
retailproducts@floridacrystals.com
www.floridacrystals.com
Florida Crystals Corporation is a privately owned and diversified agriculture, consumer products, real estate and energy company which produces sugar.

6163 Foods Alive
4840 County Road 4
Waterloo, IN 46793
260-488-4497
www.foodsalive.com
Foods Alive is a family owned company dedicated to creating the healthiest foods.

6164 Frieling
398 York Southern Road
Fort Mill, SC 29715
803-548-2000
800-827-2582
Fax: 803-548-2060
frieling.com

6165 From The Fields
1945 East Francisco Boulevard
Suite #47 / L
San Rafael, CA 94901
415-578-2990
info@fromthefields.net
www.fromthefields.net
Makes Oragnic food like granola, porridge, oatmeal and muesli that is fresh, delicious and nourishing.

6166 From War to Peace
PO Box 4358
San Luis Obispo, CA 93403
805-545-0383
Fax: 805-888-2878
info@fromwartopeace.com
www.fromwartopeace.com
Accessories mande from recycled weapon

6167 Fruit Bliss
220 42nd Street
Brooklyn, NY 11232
646-225-6565
Fax: 718-398-2005
info@fruitbliss.com
fruitbliss.com
Deliciously juicy, organic whole fruit, sun sweetened and infused with water.

6168 FungusAmongUs
PO Box 352
Snohomish, WA 98291
360-568-3403
orders@fungusamongus.com
www.fungusamongus.com
SuppliesOrganic Mushrooms

6169 Futurebiotics
70 Commerce Drive
Hauppauge, NY 11788
631-273-6300
800-645-1721
customerservice@futurebiotics.com
www.futurebiotics.com

6170 GAIA Clean Earth Products
PO Box 1906
York, PA 17405
717-840-1638
800-726-5496
Fax: 800-726-5496
gaia@blazenet.net
Environmentally-compatible products.
Brian N Hartman, President

6171 GarbageMan
13895 Industrial Park Blvd.
Suite 100
Plymouth, MN 55441
763-269-8182
866-808-8777
Fax: 763-269-8183
email@garbagemanco.com
www.garbagemanco.com
GarbageMan, A Green Company started operations with one small truck during the spring of 2008 in Maple Grove, MN.

6172 Giusto's
344 Littlefield Avenue
South San Francisco, CA 94080
650-873-6566
888-884-1940
Fax: 650-873-2826
homebaking@giustos.com
giustos.com/landing
For three generations, the Giusto's family has been committed to providing the freshest, highest quality natural and organic products available. They offer flours, as well as an entire selection of ingredients for the home baker!

6173 GladRags
215 SE Morrison
#2000-E
Portland, OR 97214
503-282-0436
800-799-4523
hello@gladrags.com
gladrags.com
Period essential supplies

6174 GlassDharma
17900 Ocean Drive
Suite 48
Fort Bragg, CA 95437
707-964-9350
Fax: 707-964-9320
info@glassdharma.com
glassdharma.com
Manufactures glass drinking straws and accessories.
David Leonhardt, Founder

6175 Glenny's
1081 East 48th Street
Brooklyn, NY 11234
516-377-1400
Fax: 516-377-9046
Gluten-free Snacks

6176 GloryBee
120 N. Seneca Rd.
Eugene, OR 97402
800-456-7923
glorybee.com
GloryBee started in the family garage of Dick and Pat Turanski in 1975 with a dream of providing natural, healthy ingredients for the people of their town

6177 Go Green World Products, LLC
11460 N Cave Creek Road
Suite 7
Phoenix, AZ 85020
602-944-4442
866-995-4442
Fax: 602-944-4956
info@greenplanetpaints.com
www.greenplanetpaints.com
Go Green World Products offer a complete line of architectural plant and clay based paints, plant based stains and sealers/varnishes for home improvement projects.
Ted Sosnicki, President/CEO

6178 GoBIO!
RR 1
, ON L7J 2
519-853-2958
Fax: 519-853-8654
info@gobiofood.com
www.gobiofood.com
Supllies organic food

6179 Goddess Garden
6525 Gunpark Drive
Ste. 370-415
Boulder, CO 80301
303-651-3678
855-723-3786
Fax: 888-370-2878
customerservice@goddessgarden.com
www.goddessgarden.com
Oragnic product suppliers

6180 Good Boy Organics
320 Canisteo Street
Hornell, NY 14843
607-324-2200
Fax: 607-324-2388
info@goodboyorganics.com
www.goodboyorganics.com
Good Boy Organics and a growing family of delicious certified organic, non-GMO snacks and sauces

6181 Gorilly Goods
N173 W21170 Northwest Psge.
Jackson, WI 53037
262-423-8000
www.gorillygoods.com
Gorilly Goods deliver a crunchy mix of fruits and nuts, or seeds and greens, all organically grown and dehydrated raw by folks who care.

6182 Grain Millers
10400 Viking Drive
Suite 301
Eden Prairie, MN 55344
952-829-8821
800-232-6287
Fax: 952-829-8819
www.grainmillers.com
Grain Millers, Inc. sells a variety of specialized ingredients such as organic industrial alcohol, molasses, soy beans, flax and tapioca.

6183 Green Clean
PO Box 7921
Boise, ID 83707
208-345-2109
greenclean@cableone.net
www.greencleanidaho.com
Commercial & Residential Cleaning Services Using Environmentally Sensitive Products

6184 Green Clean Maine
179 Sheridan St.
Ste 200
Portland, ME 00410
207-221-6600
info@greencleanmaine.com
www.greencleanmaine.com
Green Clean for your home or small office.

6185 Green Clean, LLC
PO Box 1180
Greenbelt, MD 20768
301-486-7334
info@GreenCleanUSA.org
www.greencleanusa.org
Provide a clean, non-toxic environment for its family, friends, and employees.

6186 Green Cleaning Seattle
4615 Aurora Ave N.
Seattle, WA 98103
206-307-2270
customerservice@greencleaningseattle.com
www.greencleaningseattle.com
Seattle's 100% locally-owned & operated green home & office cleaning company.

6187 Green Foods
2220 Camino Del Sol
Oxnard, CA 93030
805-983-7470
800-777-4430
Fax: 805-983-8843
info@greenfoods.com
www.greenfoods.com
Green Foods Corporation, founded by pharmacological researcher Yoshihide Hagiwara, M.D. in 1979 is an industry leader who is dedicated to improving human health and well-being.

6188 Green Goods for the Home
333 East Grand
Suite 102
Des Moines, IA
515-309-2196
info@greengoodsforthehome.com
greengoodsforthehome.com
Green goods for home

6189 Green Guru Gear
2500 47th St
Unit 12
Boulder, CO 80301
303-258-1611
info@greengurugear.com
www.greengurugear.com
Upcycle materials into great products, provide recycling source for adventure sports, and create tangible environmental awareness.

6190 Green Home and Office
4300 Montgomery Avenue
102B
Bethesda, MD 20814
301-565-7888
Fax: 301-565-5055
info@greenhomeandoffice.net
greenhomeandoffice.net
Home and office cleaning
Merced Bermudez, Founder

6191 Green Products
221 E. Rocbaar Drive
Romeoville, IL 60446
815-407-0900
www.greenproducts.net/#
Green Products brings biobased product innovations from the fields of the farm, to the lab and ultimately to the buildings.

6192 Green Ray
115 E Putnam Avenue
Greenwich, CT 00683
203-485-1435
info@greenrayled.com
test.crmgreenrayled.com
Green Ray LED is a leading manufacturer and turn-key provider of high-quality LED lighting solutions for commercial, industrial and municipal markets.

6193 Green Roof Technology
3646 Roland Avenue
Baltimore, MD 21211
443-345-1578
Fax: 443-345-1533
info@greenroofservice.com
www.greenrooftechnology.com
Green Roof Technology are professional consultants, architects, and engineers who are specialized in the specification and design of any type of living technology especially when in ground remote locations.
Jörg Breuning, President/Founder

6194 Green Toys
4000 Bridgeway
Suite 100
Sausalito, CA 94965
415-839-9971
Fax: 415-651-9147
kelley@southardinc.com
www.greentoys.com
Recycled and oragnic toys

6195 GreenClean Colorado
6820 North Franklin Avenue
Suite 100
Loveland, CO 80538
970-663-0018
info@greencleaningcolorado.com
greencleaningcolorado.com
Green Cleaning Services from Green Clean Colorado adheres to the Reduce, Re-use and Recycle business practices.

6196 GreenIT
414 1st St. East
Suite 7
Sonoma, CA 95476
707-938-9300
info@greenit.net
www.greenit.net
Mr. Hodges established GreenIT as the first consultancy to combine those elements into a systemic and strategic approach to sustainability for Information and Communications Technology Systems.
Richard Hodges, CEO

6197 GreenShield Organic
8305 Falls of the Neuse Road
Suite 206
Raleigh, NC 27615
877-473-3650
info@greenologyproducts.com
www.greenshieldorganic.com

Greenshield Organic, a division of Greenology Products, Inc. was created by a dad on a mission to protect families from the harmful chemicals found in most cleaning products.

6198 Greenerways Organic
668 Stony Hill Road
Suite 143
Yardley, PA 19067
800-777-1603
alan@greenerdays.net
www.greenerways.com
Greener Days, is to provide affordable organic products with the belief that everyone deserves the ability to enjoy the benefits of an organic lifestyle.
Alan Neiburg, President
Jayme Bella, VP of Sales

6199 Greenpeace
564 Mission Street Box 416
San Francisco, CA 94105
510-538-7842
800-326-0959
Fax: 202-462-4517
greenpeace@npgear.com
Environmentally and socially responsible apparel, accessories and gifts.

6200 Groceries Apparel
5510 Soto St.
Unit A
Vernon, CA 90058
213-488-1002
Fax: 213-488-1102
hello@groceriesapparel.com
www.groceriesapparel.com
Apparel made from 100% organic and recyciled fabrics and dyes.
Robert W. Lohman, President/Co-Founder

6201 Guayaki
6782 Sebastopol Ave.
Suite 100
Sebastopol, CA 95472
888-482-9254
guayaki.com
The mission is to steward and restore 200,000 acres of South American Atlantic rainforest and create over 1,000 living wage jobs by 2020 by leveraging the Market Driven Restoration business model.

6202 Halo, Purely for Pets
12400 Race Track Road
Tampa, FL 33626
800-426-4256
customers@halopets.com
halopets.com
Natural pet care products are made with the finest natural ingredients available, designed to enhance your pet's well-being

6203 Handy Pantry
175 W 2700 S
Salt Lake City, UT 84115
800-735-0630
support@handypantry.com
www.handypantry.com
Handy Pantry Sprouting has been providing wholesale Certified Organic sprouting seed and sprouting supplies to natural foods retailers for over 20 years. We are proud to have tens of thousands of satisfied customers.

6204 Happy Family
40 Fulton St.
17th FL
New York, NY 10038
855-64 -APPY
parents@happyfamilybrands.com
happyfamilybrands.com
Shazi Visram, Founder & CEO
Jessica Rolph, Founding Partner & COO

6205 Heavenly Organics
106 S Green
PO Box 7
Keota, IA 52248
866-923-2184
Fax: 866-243-7096
info@heavenlyorganics.com
www.heavenlyorganics.com
Heavenly Organics is a grower, producer and worldwide distributor of premium organic food ingredients and products.
Amit Hooda, CEO
Alok Sharma, Webmaster

6206 Honey Bee Cleaners
One Waterfront Tower
419 South Street, Suite 101
Honolulu, HI 96813
808-383-9983
Fax: 808-383-9983
info@honeybeecleaners.com
www.honeybeecleaners.com
The only green commercial cleaning company accredited by Green Cleaning Institute in Hawaii.
Shota Mkheidze, President/CEO

6207 Horizon Fuel Cells Technologies
18 S. Michigan Avenue
12th floor
Chicago, IL 60603
312-757-5909
Fax: 312-757-5905
sales@horizonfuelcell.com
www.horizonfuelcell.com
Its mission is to change the game in fuel cells, by working globally on immediate commercialization, dropping technology costs, and removing the age-old hydrogen supply barriers.
George Gu, CEO
Jack Zhang, CFO

6208 Howard Products
560 Linne Road
Paso Robles, CA 93446
805-227-1000
custserv@howardproducts.com
www.howardproducts.com
Restor-A-Finish, Howard's first in an entire line of wood care products

6209 HybridLight
566 N. Dixie Dr.
Saint George, UT 84770
800-365-0350
info@hybridlight.com
hybridlight.com
Terry Peterson, Owner
Mack Peterson, Electrical Engineer

6210 Ice Chips Candy
PO Box 2401
Yelm, WA 98597
360-232-1106
866-202-6623
support@icechipscandy.com
www.icechipscandy.com
Sweet candy for diabetics

6211 Indosole
1122 Howard Street
San Francisco, CA 94103
415-570-2102
indo@indosole.com
indosole.com
Indosole's mission to salvage tires and other waste materials to give them new life as fashionable and functional goods. The soles of their shoes are derived from old tires salvaged directly from landfills, sanitized, and transformedinto brand new products manufactured in an organic process without the use of fuel powered machines.
Kyle Parsons, CEO/Founder
Kai Stober-Paul, Production Manager

6212 InterNatural Foods
1455 Broad Street
4th Floor
Bloomfield, NJ 07003
973-338-1499
Fax: 973-338-1485
www.internaturalfoods.com

Represents a variety of natural and organic food products in the U.S. marketplace.

6213 **JanCore**
610 16th St
Oakland, CA 94612
888-998-0511
Admin@JanCoreLLC.com
www.jancorellc.com
JanCore's corporate structure consists of corporate and regional management, support personnel, and an extensive service provider network that services locations throughout the state and across the country.

6214 **JaniTek Cleaning Solutions**
2735 Teepee Drive
Suite D
Stockton, CA 95205
888-833-7705
admin@janitek.net
janitek.net
JaniTek delivers a technology enhanced, superior cleaning and customer service experience.

6215 **Jason Natural Cosmetics**
8468 Warern Drive
Culver City, CA 90232
Fax: 310-838-9274
All natural cosmetics.
Jeffrey Light, President

6216 **Jovial Foods, Inc.**
PO Box 98
North Franklin, CT 06254
877-642-0644
info@jovialfoods.com
jovialfoods.com
Jovial Foods, Inc. was founded by a husband and wife team who has always been passionate about food, farming and traditions. They offer fluten free food products.
Carla , Co-Owner
Rodolfo , Co-Owner

6217 **Julian Bakery**
624 Garrison St
Suite 102
Oceanside, CA 92054
760-721-5200
www.julianbakery.com

6218 **Kettle Foods**
3125 Kettle Court SE
Salem, OR 97301
503-364-0399
Fax: 503-371-1447
www.kettlebrand.com
Vision: great taste with real, less processed foods

6219 **King's Green Cleaning**
1802 N. Shartel
Oklahoma City, OK 73103
405-549-6862
amy@kingsgreencleaning.com
kingsgreencleaning.com
Offers commercial and residential cleaning services that are safe.

6220 **Kiss My Face**
144 Main St.
Gardiner, NY 12525
845-255-0884
sales@kissmyface.com
www.kissmyface.com

6221 **Kombucha Wonder Drink**
PO Box 4244
Portland, OR 97208
503-224-7331
Fax: 503-224-2295
wonderdrink.com
Pasturised drinks

6222 **Kopali Organics**
2103 Coral Way
2nd Floor
Miami, FL 33145
305-204-7873
kopali@kopali.com
kopali.net
Organic, natural chocolates

6223 **LTC Cleaning Services**
18 Anacostia Rd. NE
Washington, DC 20019
202-642-6067
lipscomb@ltccleaningservices.com
www.ltccleaningservices.com
Certified Green Cleaning Company, uses only environmental friendly cleaning products to reduce sick leave and promote a healthy work environment.

6224 **La Preferida**
3400 W. 35th Street
Chicago, IL 60632
800-621-5422
info@lapreferida.com
www.lapreferida.com
David Brand, Quality Assurance
Juan Badillo, Sales

6225 **La Tourangelle**
125 University Avenue
Berkeley, CA 94710
510-970-9960
Fax: 510-970-9964
latourangelle.com
La Tourangelle, are an authentic & traditional family producer of specialty oils handcrafting a wide range of delicious artisan nut oils both in France and California.

6226 **Lafes Natural BodyCare**
8204 N. Lamar B-12
Austin, TX 78753
512-926-9662
800-926-5233
lafes.com
Natural personal care products

6227 **Late July Snacks**
15 Channel Center Street
#105
Boston, MA 02210
508-362-5859
info@latejuly.com
www.latejuly.com

6228 **Lifefactory**
3 Harbor Drive
Suite 200
Sausalito, CA 94965
415-729-9820
Fax: 415-520-4444
info@lifefactory.com
www.lifefactory.com

6229 **Light Mountain**
P O Box 325
Twin Lakes, WI 53181
262-889-8561
800-824-6396
lightmountain@lotuspress.com
www.light-mountain-hair-color.com
A natural hair color and conditioner product line.

6230 **Lily of the Desert**
1887 Geesling Rd.
Denton, TX 76208
940-566-9914
800-229-5459
Fax: 940-566-9925
www.lilyofthedesert.com
Founded in 1971, Lily of the Desert Organic Aloeceuticals is a family-owned vertically integrated grower, processor, and manufacturer of leading aloe vera based products.

6231 **Little Me Tea**
930 New Hope Road
Suite 11-189
Lawrenceville, GA 30045
404-375-3754
info@bigtimetea.com
littlemetea.com
Sweetented tea with fruits and veggies

6232 Living Intentions
250 S Garrard Blvd
Richmond, CA 94801
Pure food ingredients
415-824-5483
www.livingintentions.com

6233 Look Alive!
Rice Lake Products
100 27th Street NE
Minot, ND 58703
701-857-6357
800-998-7450
Fax: 701-857-6300
Environmentally safe movement devices for hunting decoys, as well as bird and pest deterring owls for home garden, boats and businesses.
Virgil Farstad, President

6234 Love Child
202B -1002 Lynham Road
Whistler, BC VON 1
604-962-5683
Fax: 604-962-5684
hello@lovechildorganics.com
lovechildorganics.com
Leah Garrad-Cole, President
John Garrad-Cole, CEO

6235 Lundberg Family Farms
5311 Midway
PO Box 369
Richvale, CA 95974
530-538-3500
www.lundberg.com
Finest qulaity of rice and rice products

6236 Made in Nature
1708 13th Street
Boulder, CO 80302
800-906-7426
www.madeinnature.com
Best-tasting, healthy organic foods.

6237 Maine Coast Sea Vegetables
3 George's Pond Road
Franklin, ME 04634
207-565-2907
Fax: 207-565-2144
info@seaveg.com
www.seaveg.com/shop/
Offer eight organically certified North Atlantic varieties of marine vegetables

6238 Manitoba Harvest
69 Eagle Drive
Winnipeg, MB R2R 1
800-665-4367
manitobaharvest.com
Manitoba Harvest Hemp Foods products are all non-gmo project verified

6239 Mass Probiotics
139 Charles Street
Boston, MA 02114
617-479-5900
golivebewell.com
Mass Probiotics, Inc. researches, develops, produces and markets a family of probiotic and prebiotic bottled beverage and supplement products under the brand name GoLive

6240 Meyenberg
PO Box 934
Turlock, CA 95381
800-891-GOAT
Fax: 209-668-4977
info@meyenberg.com
meyenberg.com
Goat milk products.

6241 Mountain Green
731 W. Fairmont Dr.
Tempe, AZ 85282
480-272-9621
info@ahealthierclean.com
mountaingreen.biz/index.aspx
Mountain Green products have cleaned family and baby laundry, kitchens and homes with concentrated formulas that are non-toxic and biodegradable

6242 Mr. Ellie Pooh
350 Wiconisco Street
Millersburg, PA 17061
347-662-6581
mrelliepooh.com
100% recycled paper products.

6243 Mrs. Leepers
1455 Broad Street
4th Floor
Bloomfield, NJ 07003
973-338-0300
winfo@worldfiner.com
mrsleepers.com
Mrs. Leepers offers a variety of Organic, Gluten Free Corn Pasta and Rice Pasta, imported from Italy for authentic taste and texture

6244 My Cleaning Service
2701 Cresmont Avenue
Baltimore, MD 21211
410-889-0505
Fax: 410-889-0553
general@mycleaningservice.com
www.mycleaningservice.com
My Cleaning Service, Inc., is women-owned businesses in Baltimore with more than 300 employees.
Kathleen Bands, Director, Marketing

6245 Nasoya Foods USA
One New England Way
Ayer, MA 01432
800-328-8638
info@nasoya-usa.com
www.nasoya.com
Produces premium vegetarian foods such as all-natural organic and all-natural tofu, Asian style wraps, shirataki noodles, Asian style noodles and Nayonaise vegan sandwich spread. The organization is dedicated to environmentallysustainable practices.
Ross Gatta, CEO

6246 Natural Value Inc.
14 Waterthrush Ct
Sacramento, CA 95831
916-836-3561
Fax: 916-914-2446
Info@NaturalValue.com
www.naturalvalue.com
To make atural and organic foods and environmentally friendly nonfood products more affordable.
Stephanie Harrison, Sales Manager
Anna Ishizaki, Sales & Marketing

6247 Natural Vitality
8500 Shoal Creek Blvd.
Building 4, Suite 208
Austin, TX 78757
866-416-9216
naturalvitality.com
To provide premium and efficacious products that have a valid and unique reason for being.

6248 Naturally Green
2710 S. Denison Ave.
San Pedro, CA 90731
800-731-5769
bryan@naturallygreencleaning.com
www.naturallygreencleaning.com
Naturally Green provides excellent organic carpet cleaning in Los Angeles with safe, natural products, using no chemicals while keeping prices affordable.

6249 Naturally It's Clean
Post Office Box 292
Westmont, IL 60559
800-375-5059
Fax: 800-809-4319
Sales@NaturallyItsClean.com
naturallyitsclean.com

Naturally It's Clean delivers the ultimate promise of natural cleaners clean and safe by using nature's most powerful cleaner, enzymes.
Mike Wallrich, Co-Founder/President
Ed Mac, SVP, Operations

6250 Nature's Baby Organics
1560-1 Newbury Rd. 818-999-2229
#284 888-902-2229
Newbury Park, CA 91320 Fax: 818-702-0110
nicole@naturesbaby.com
naturesbaby.com
Offers baby care products which contain 70% organic ingredients.

6251 Nature's Way
3051 West Maple Loop Dr.
Suite 125 800-962-8873
Lehi, UT 84043 Fax: 800-688-3303
www.naturesway.com
Manufacturer of complete vitamin, mineral, herbal products line.

6252 Naturepedic
16925 Park Circle Drive
Chagrin Falls, OH 44023 800-917-3342
cs@naturepedic.com
www.naturepedic.com
Naturepedic specializes in the design and manufacturing of quality organic mattresses for infants, toddlers, children and adults that promote natural and organic materials, a non-toxic design, fire-safety, and overall health & safety.

6253 Navitas Organics
936 B Seventh St. 415-883-8116
Box # 141 888-645-4282
Novato, CA 94945 info@navitasnaturals.com
www.navitasorganics.com
Navitas Organics is a family-owned green business headquartered in Marin County, California. They specialize in organic superfoods from around the world, and strive to be the industry leader in this fast-growing category.

6254 New Leaf Paper
510 16th Street
Suite 520 888-989-5323
Oakland, CA 94612 Fax: 415-291-9353
info@newleafpaper.com
www.newleafpaper.com
New Leaf Paper has gathered an eclectic group of people as passionate about the print and graphic design process as they are about sustainability and environmental responsibility.
Joe Fanelli, Chief Executive Officer
Leila Gilbert, Vice President, Finance

6255 NibMor
P.O. Box 6
Kennebunk, ME 04043 844-Nib-Mor1
info@nibmor.com
nibmor.com
Produces organic and natural dark chocolate bars as well as vegan drinking chocolate mixes.
Ralph Chauvin, CEO

6256 Nourish Organic Food for Healthy Skin
3740 W. 4th Avenue
Beaver Falls, PA 15010 888-385-0786
nourishorganic.com
100% USDA organic skincare and bodycare that is clinically proven to moisturize skin. Nourish is gluten-free, vegan & 100% chemical-free.

6257 Numi Organic Tea
P.O. Box 20420
Oakland, CA 94620 888-404-6864
Fax: 510-536-6864
info@numitea.com
www.numitea.com
Numi Organic Tea is a premium, Fair Trade sustainable company; specializing in unique and innovative blends of green, black, white, oolong teas.

6258 NurturMe
Freed Foods LLC 512-326-2223
PO Box 163302 info@nurturme.com
Austin, TX 78716 nurturme.com
Offers quinoa products.

6259 Nutiva
213 West Cutting Blvd
Richmond, CA 94804 800-993-4367
help@nutiva.com
nutiva.com
Nutiva offers the best Extra Virgin Organic Coconut Oil, Hemp Protein, Hemp Seed Oil and Chia Seed.
John Roulac, Founder & CEO
Neil Blomquist, Senior Advisor

6260 Old Fashioned Milk Paint
436 Main Street 978-448-6336
Groton, MA 00145 866-350-6455
Fax: 978-448-2754
anne@milkpaint.com
www.milkpaint.com
In 1974, after much experimentation, the company recreated an old Milk Paint formula to provide an authentic finish for there primary business of building reproduction furniture. Since then they have sold our paint to professionals whoare either restoring original Colonial or Shaker furniture, making reproductions, or striving for an interior design look that is both authentic and beautiful.
Anne Thibeau, President
Terri Senecal, Sales

6261 Once Again Nut Butter Collective
12 S. State St. 585-468-2535
P.O. Box 429 888-800-8075
Nunda, NY 14517 Fax: 585-468-5995
customerservice@oanb.com
www.onceagainnutbutter.com
Organic and Natural Nut Butter Manufacturer and Nut Ingredient Supplier.
Scott Owens, Employee-Owner
Robert Collins, Employee-Owner

6262 Oregon's Wild Harvest
1601 NE Hemlock Ave. 541-548-9400
Redmond, OR 97756 800-316-6869
Fax: 541-923-7235
webmaster@owharvest.com
www.oregonswildharvest.com
Oregon's Wild Harvest is an independently owned and operated herb farm in Sandy, Oregon.
Randy Buresh R.N., Co-founder, President, CVO
Pamela Martin-Buresh, Co-founder/CFO

6263 Orgain
P.O. Box 4918
Irvine, CA 92616 info@drinkorgain.com
orgain.com

6264 Organic Essence
629 Bertsch Avenue
Crescent City, CA 95531
707-465-8955
Fax: 707-465-8959
www.organic-essence.com
Organic Essence was founded in 2006 after the USDA National Organic Program allowed non-food agriculturally derived products to certify to their existing organic food standard.

6265 Organic Excellence
4727 E. Bell Road
#45-125
Phoenix, AZ 85032-2312
800-611-8331
Fax: 602-493-7917
CustomerService@OrganicExcellence.com
shop.organicexcellence.com
Organic Excellence began as a home based business in 1999. They have since grown to a worldwide company featuring high quality, chemical, fragrance, gluten and GMO free health and personal care products with the added benefits ofcertified organic herbs.

6266 Organic Gourmet
14431 Ventura Blvd.
#192
Sherman Oaks, CA 91423
800-400-7772
Fax: 818-906-7417
scenar@earthlink.net
www.organic-gourmet.com
Offers natural and organic Products for wellbeing.
Elke Heitmeyer, Founder

6267 Oriental Building Services
2526 Manana Dr.
Suite 208
Dallas, TX 75220
469-522-0001
Fax: 469-522-0003
obsusa.net
Oriental Building Services, Inc. has always believed and supported for a cleaner and safer environment. They believe that making eco-friendly change can help make a difference to your building, office, your family and the world. Notonly does it change by using eco-friendly products and techniques but uses attention to detail, care and love.

6268 PINES International, Inc.
1992 East 1400 Road
Lawrence, KS 66044
785-841-6016
800-697-4637
Fax: 785-841-1252
www.wheatgrass.com
Supply high-quality cereal grasses, grown in the soils of northeastern Kansas.

6269 Pacific Foods of Oregon
19480 SW 97th Ave.
Tualatin, OR 97062
503-692-9666
Fax: 503-692-9610
www.pacificfoods.com
Pacific food has goal- to make tasty, healthy foods with integrity.

6270 Pamela's Products
1 Carousel Lane
Ukiah, CA 95482
707-462-6605
Fax: 707-462-6642
info@pamelasproducts.com
www.pamelasproducts.com
Pamela's Products, started in 1988, is known for delicious, gluten free foods with a full line of baking mixes, cookies and snack bars.

6271 Pangea Organics
3195 Sterling Circle
Suite 200
Boulder, CO 80301
303-413-8493
877-679-5854
support@pangeaorganics.com
www.pangeaorganics.com
The skincare products are designed to be used as a platform that inspires people to lead, live, and make a living in a purposeful way.

6272 Peeled Snacks
65 15th Street
Fl 1
Brooklyn, NY 11215
212-706-2001
Fax: 646-478-9518
sales@peeledsnacks.com
peeledsnacks.com
Supplies best tasting organic, non-GMO and gluten-free ingredients and turn them into delicious snacks.
Noha Waibsnaider, Founder and CEO
Beth Kennedy, Director, Marketing

6273 Plum Organics
1485 Park Avenue
Emeryville, CA 94608
877-914-7586
info@plumorganics.com
www.plumorganics.com
Plum Organics boasts of healthful and trendy ingredients such as kale, quinoa.
Neil Grimmer, Co-Founder, CEO

6274 Polywood
1001 W. Brooklyn St.
Syracuse, IN 46567
574-457-3284
877-457-3284
Fax: 574-457-4723
corp@polywoodinc.com
www.polywoodinc.com
Low-maintenance, recyclable lumber Plywood

6275 Premier Green Cleaning Services
110 Redmond
Jackson, WY 83001
307-690-3605
premierservices@bresnan.net
www.premiergreencleaningservices.com
Green cleaning service providers

6276 Purity Organic
1625 Bush Street
Suite 3
San Francisco, CA 94109
415-440-7777
info@purityorganic.com
purityorganic.com
Supplies organic juice, coconut water and produce to market.

6277 RMC Medical Inc
7940 A State Rd
Philadephia, PA 19136
215-824-4100
800-332-0672
Fax: 215-824-1371
dan@rmcmedical.com
www.rmcmedical.com
Manufacturer of decontamination emergency response equipment.

6278 Rainbow Light Nutritional Systems
100 Avenue Tea
Santa Cruz, CA 95060
800-635-1233
Fax: 831-429-0189
www.rainbowlight.com
Rainbow Light began in 1981 by offering consumers a nutritious spirulina supplement and went on to become the first-ever food-based supplement brand.
Linda Kahler, President
Sharon Minski, VP Operation/Administration

6279 Raw Revolution
PO Box 359
Hawthorne, NY 10532
914-326-4095
www.rawrev.com
Provides irresistible, affordable, convenient superfoods using certified organic, mostly raw ingredients.

6280 Rawmio
PO Box 328
Glenview, IL 60025
800-518-0727
800-518-0727
rawmio.com
Rawmio produces handcrafted raw vegan chocolate treats

6281 Real Goods
Real Goods Solar
833 West South Boulder Road
Louisville, CO 80027
800-919-2400
www.realgoods.com
Source for simple living products designed to balance with a conscious lifestyle. Offers products that reduce energy consumption, from solar panels and wind turbines to complete solar power systems.

6282 Real Goods Trading Company
PO Box 8507
Ukiah, CA 95482
707-744-2100
800-347-0070
Fax: 707-468-9394
Recycled papers, environmental gifts and household goods.

6283 Redmond Trading Company
475 West 910 South
Heber City, UT 84032
800-367-7258
www.redmondtrading.com
Provides natural Sea-salt.

6284 Reserveage Nutrition
2255 Glades Road
Suite 342W
Boca Raton, FL 33431
800-553-1896
sales@reserveage.com
reserveage.com
ertified organic grapes direct from our Southern France vineyards.
Naomi Whittel, Founder and CEO

6285 Rustic Crust
5 Main Street
Pittsfield, NH 03263
603-435-5119
888-519-5119
info@rusticcrust.com
www.rusticcrust.com
Forzen flatbread crust

6286 Sambazon
1160 Calle Cordillera
San Clemente, CA 92673
877-726-2296
info@sambazon.com
www.sambazon.com
Make juices, smoothies, and sorbets from the finest organic ingredients. Wild harvested directly from the Amazon.

6287 Santa Barbara Olive Company
3070 Skyway Dr.
Suite 401
Santa Maria, CA 93455
805-562-1456
800-624-4896
Fax: 805-562-1464
info@sbolive.com
www.sbolive.com
Provides Gourmet olives, extra virgin olive oils, sauces and vegetable, a Santa Barbara Family Tradition since 1850.

6288 Sappo Hill Soapworks
654 Tolman Creek Road
Ashland, OR 97520
800-863-7627
www.sappohill.com
Sappo Hill makes all natural vegetable oil soaps according to traditional methods

6289 Second Renaissance Books
17 George Washington Plaza
Gaylordsville, CT 00675
800-729-6149
Fax: 860-355-7160
Editorially selected books and audio tapes. Complete selection of writing and letters by Ayn Rand.

6290 Seventh Generation
60 Lake Street
Burlington, VT 05401
800-211-4279
Fax: 802-658-1771
www.seventhgeneration.com
Formulating plant-based products that are safe and that work.

6291 Similasan
1805 Shea Center Drive
Suite 270
Highlands Ranch, CO 80129
800-240-9780
www.similasanusa.com
Similasan homeopathic products are formulated using traditional guidelines and produced according to strict Good Manufacturing Practices (GMP) by Similasan AG.

6292 Simple Squares
501 North Clinton Street
Suite 705
Chicago, IL 60654
888-966-7622
joinus@simplesquares.com
simplesquares.com
Organic nutrition bars

6293 Singing Dog Vanilla
PO Box 50042
Eugene, OR 97405
541-343-2746
888-343-0002
Fax: 541-610-1868
info@singingdogvanilla.com
www.singingdogvanilla.com
Organic vanilla lip balm, organic vanilla coffee, organic vanilla tea, organic vanilla chai, vanilla bean paste, alcohol free pure vanilla flavor and vanilla salt.

6294 Solar Service
7312 N. Milwaukee Ave.
Niles, IL 60714
847-647-9312
Fax: 847-647-9360
info@solarserviceinc.com
www.solarserviceinc.com
Solar Service is the premier solar installation company in the Midwest and among the most experienced solar providers in the United States.
Brandon Leavitt, Owner & President
Kevin Bart, System Manager

6295 Sparky Boy Enterprises
1512 Gold Avenue
Bozeman, MT 59715
406-587-5891
800-289-6656
Fax: 406-587-0223
Natural products for the home, lawn and garden.
Wayne Vinje, President

6296 St. Peter Woolen Mills
101 W. Broadway
St. Peter, MN 56082
507-934-3734
800-208-9821
spwoolen@hickorytech.net
www.woolenmill.com
Makes luxurious wool-filled comforters, mattress toppers and pillows

6297 SunRidge Farms
423 Salinas Road
Royal Oaks, CA 95076
831-786-7000
Fax: 831-786-8618
www.sunridgefarms.com
SunRidge farms are producing foods without highly processed or refined ingredients.

6298 Sunbiotics
PO Box 328
Glenview, IL 60025
800-925-0577
www.sunbiotics.com
Sunbiotics Gourmet Probiotic Snacks are delicious take on combining healthy snacks and probiotics.

6299 Sunrise Lane Products
780 Greenwich Street 212-243-4745
New York, NY 10014
Environmentally safe and cruelty-free products for home and personal care.
Rossella Mocerino, President

6300 Sunshine Solar Services
2805 Oakland Park Blvd 954-568-4876
Suite 422 info@sunshinesolarservices.com
Fort Lauderdale, FL 33306 www.sunshinesolarservices.com/index.html
Sunshine Solar Services specializes in generating solar energy in the hurricane zones of Florida and the Caribbean.

6301 Sweet Green Fields
11 Bellwether Way 360-483-4555
Suite 305 Fax: 360-483-4554
Bellingham, WA 98225 info@sweetgreenfields.com
sweetgreenfields.com
SGF produces and markets Reb-A, a great tasting, high purity, natural sweetener that is 200-350 times the sweetness of sugar.

6302 TaterPiks
1459 Depot Road 541-723-3200
Malin, OR 97632
TaterPiks - Gourmet Pickled Potatoes

6303 Teeccino Caffé, Inc.
PO Box 40829 805-966-0999
Santa Barbara, CA 93140 800-498-3434
Fax: 805-966-0522
info@teeccino.com
teeccino.com
Teeccino, America's #1 Coffee Alternative, is roasted and ground to brew and taste just like coffee

6304 The Ginger People
215 Reindollar Avenue
Marina, CA 93933 800-551-5284
Fax: 831-582-2495
info@gingerpeople.com
gingerpeople.com
Established in 1984, The Ginger People began its mission to produce the world's finest range of ginger products and ingredients

6305 The Green Catalog
Advertising Specialty Institute
www.asicentral.com
Features products that are friendly to the enviroment, designed to inspire social responsibility.

6306 The Green Life
The Green Life Store
2409 Main Street 310-392-4702
Santa Monica, CA 90405 www.thegreenlifecostore.com
Green products that are the most ecologically friendly available, for home & garden, bed & bath, children, cleaning, office, and pets.
Scott O'Brien, Owner

6307 The Hain Celestial Group
4600 Sleepytime Dr.
Boulder, CO 80301 800-434-4246
www.hain-celestial.com
The Hain Celestial Group is natural and organic food and personal care products company in North America and Europe.

6308 Thoughtful Food, Inc.
3939 West Capitol Ave. 916-372-1040
Unit F West
Sacramento, CA 95691
It's Dairy Free, Vegan and certified USDA Organic! Uses only 100% organic agave nectar which also makes it a safe choice for diabetics.
Jennifer Bielawski, CEO/Founder

6309 To-Go Ware
747 Fortress Street 530-342-4426
Chico, CA 95973 888-496-6166
info@to-goware.com
to-goware.com
To-Go Ware is committed to inspiring healthy lifestyle through food, community, and planet by providing products that are innovative safe, environmentally responsible, affordable and convenient.
Andy Keller, President/CEO
Sierra Brodleit, Marketing Manager

6310 Torie & Howard
143 West Street
Suite 121-C 888-826-9554
New Milford, CT 06776 www.torieandhoward.com
Suplly products which are delicious, tasty treats that are made in a way that is as health-friendly, eco-friendly and socially conscious as possible.

6311 Traditional Medicinals
4515 Ross Road
Sebastopol, CA 95472 800-543-4372
www.traditionalmedicinals.com
Offers a quality difference in wellness teas not found anywhere else.
Drake Sadler, Co-Founder, Chairman
Blair Kellison, CEO

6312 TreeHouse
4477 S Lamar Blvd 512-861-0712
Ste 600 888-799-5779
Austin, TX 78745 Fax: 512-900-2084
info@treehouseonline.com
treehouse.co
The construction, repair, and upgrading of homes

6313 Triangle Green Cleaning
5878 Faringdon Place 919-801-8588
#100 trianglegreencleaning@yahoo.com
Raleigh, NC 27609 www.trianglegreencleaning.com
Uses house cleaning products that are free of ammonia, phosphates, chlorine and synthetic fragrances.

6314 Tropical Valley Foods
50 Clinton Street
Plattsburgh, NY 12901 877-756-6831
Fax: 518-478-8838
chelsea@tropical-valley-foods.com
www.tropical-valley-foods.com
Tropical Valley Foods is a producer-distributor of organic and natural food products, supplying health food stores throughout the US.
Eric Bertheau, President/Owner
Jeremy , Logistics/Ops Manager

6315 TruSweets
648 Wheeling Road 334-676-1070
Wheeling, IL 60090 info@trusweets.com
www.trusweets.com
Produces flavorful sweet treats using organic ingredients.

6316 **Trujoy Sweets**
648 Wheeling Road 224-676-1070
Wheeling, IL 60090 info@trusweets.com
www.trujoysweets.com
Sweets that are made with organic ingredients, corn syrup free, no artificial colors or flavors, gluten free, vegan and kosher.

6317 **Two Bettys Green Cleaning Service**
3702 E 34th St. 612-720-8768
Minneapolis, MN 55406 info@twobettysclean.com
www.twobettysclean.com
Two Bettys Green Cleaning Company provides high quality eco-friendly green cleaning services.

6318 **USA Green Clean**
6522 Frietchie Row 301-661-6765
Columbia, MD 21045 Usagreenclean@gmail.com
usacleangreen.com
100% Green Nationwide Janitorial Cleaning Services

6319 **Valley Fresh**
1 Hormel Place
Austin, MN 55912 800-523-4635
www.valleyfresh.com
They are committed to all-natural protein that you can feel good about.

6320 **Veggie Go's**
2825 Wilderness Place
Suite 900 888-297-9426
Boulder, CO 80301 info@nakededgesnacks.com
nakededgesnacks.com

Lisa , Founder & President
John , Founder & CEO

6321 **VitalityGOODS**
5325 Gravenstein Hwy North 707-861-0386
Sebastopol, CA 95472 anne@vitalitygoods.com
www.vitalitygoods.com

Glasswares made of miron glass

6322 **Voltaic Systems**
155 Water Street 212-401-1192
Suite 410 info@voltaicsystems.com
Brooklyn, NY 11201 www.voltaicsystems.com
Voltaic Systems is a portable power company based in Brooklyn, New York.

6323 **Williams Distributors**
1801 S Cardinal Lane 262-597-9865
New Berlin, WI 53151
All natural products; nutrition, health, home care and personal care, plus water purification systems.
GL Williams, President

6324 **Wisdom Natural Brands**
1203 West San Pedro Street
Gilbert, AZ 85233 800-899-9908
info@wisdomnaturalbrands.com
www.wisdomnaturalbrands.com
Wisdom Natural Brands is the parent company of two highly respected consumer brands: SweetLeaf Sweetener and Wisdom of the Ancients herbal teas.

6325 **World Centric**
101 H Street 707-241-9190
Suite M Fax: 866-850-9732
Petaluma, CA 94952 worldcentric.org
Provides compostable food service disposables and food packaging products.

6326 **Yummy Earth**
79 N Franklin Tpke 201-857-8489
Suite 200 Fax: 201-606-8215
Ramsey, NJ 00744 support@yumearth.com
yummyearth.com

Rob Wunder, Co-Founder

6327 **Zambeezi Organic Beeswax Lip Balm**
Sambah Naturals 720-323-5975
777 Broadway info@sambahnaturals.com
Boulder, CO 80302 www.zambeezi.com
Produces lip balm with organic ingredients.
Bruce Hale, Contact

SECTION TWO:

STATISTICS & RANKINGS

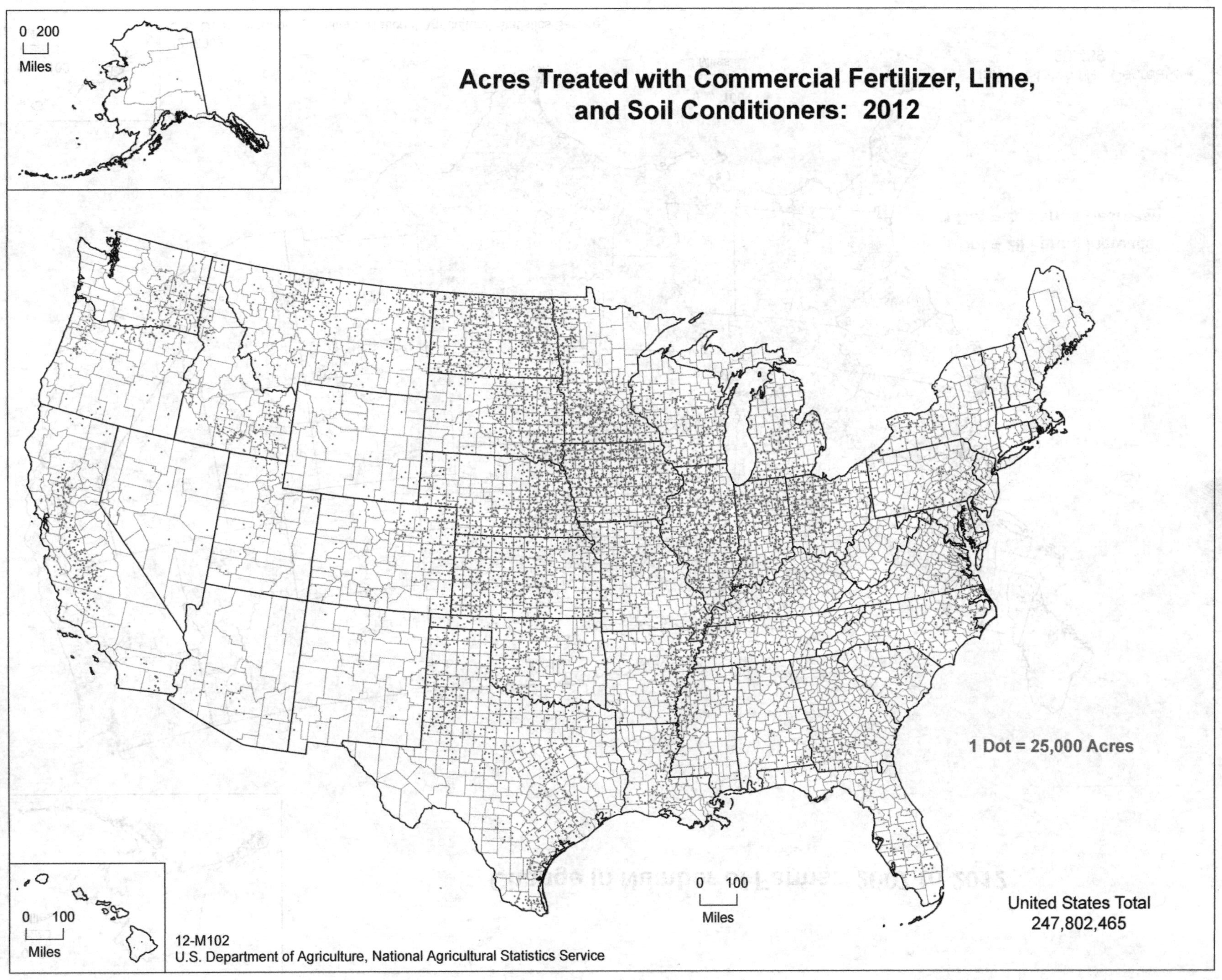
0 200
Miles
Acres Treated with Commercial Fertilizer, Lime,
and Soil Conditioners: 2012
1 Dot = 25,000 Acres
0 100
Miles
United States Total
247,802,465
0 100
Miles
12-M102
U.S. Department of Agriculture, National Agricultural Statistics Service

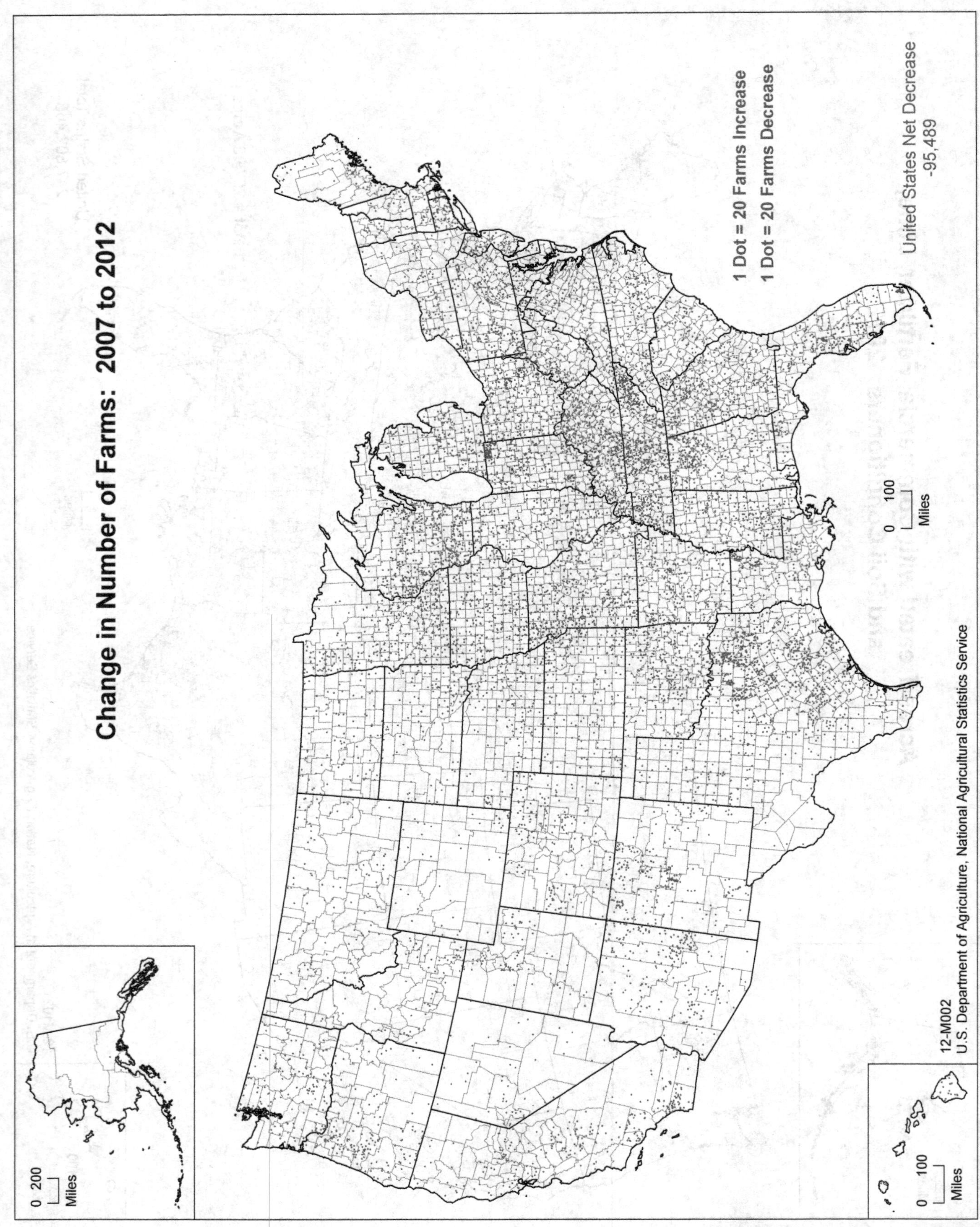

2012 Census of Agriculture

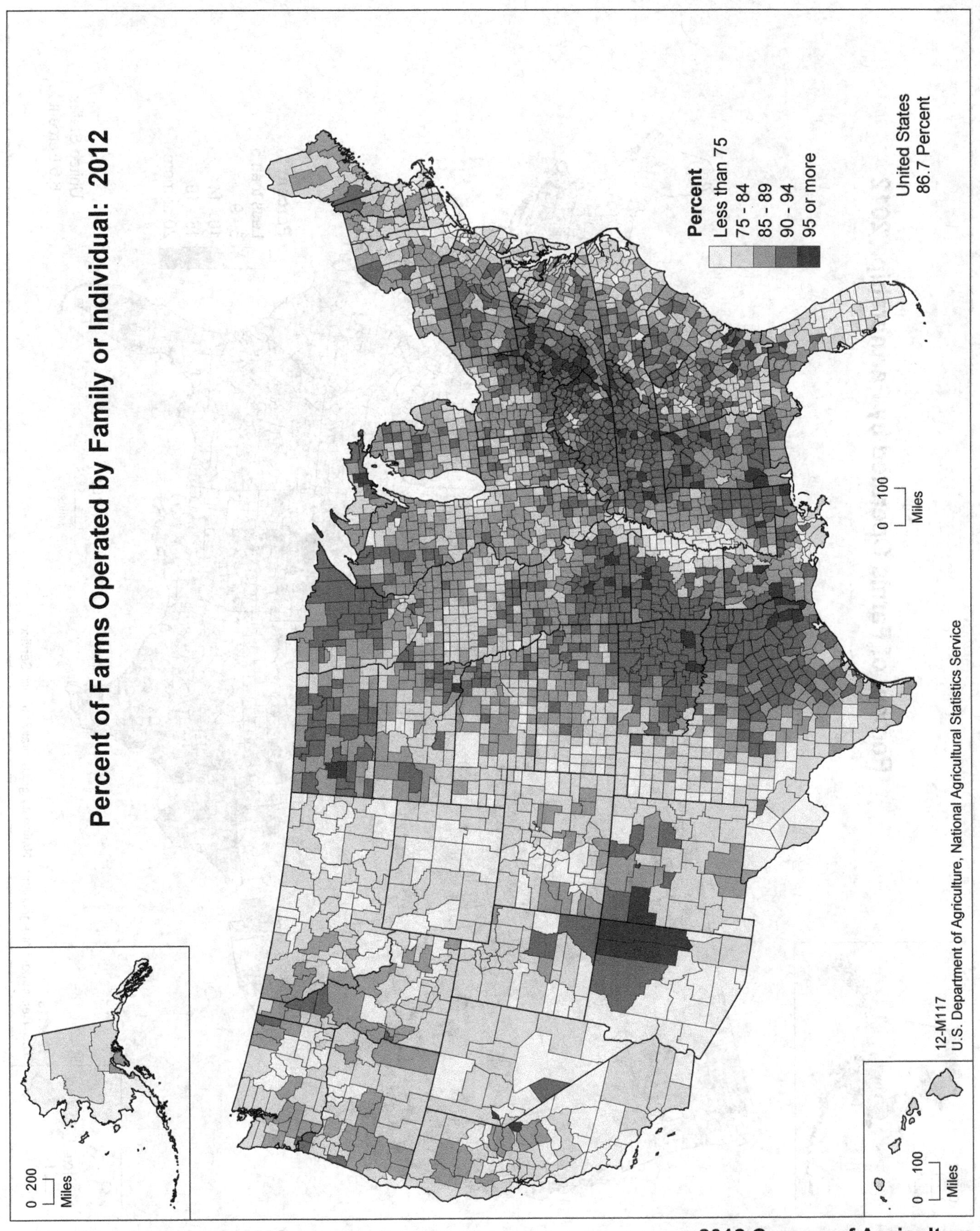
Percent of Farms Operated by Family or Individual: 2012
Percent
Less than 75
75 - 84
85 - 89
90 - 94
95 or more
United States
86.7 Percent
0 100
Miles
0 200
Miles
0 100
Miles
12-M117
U.S. Department of Agriculture, National Agricultural Statistics Service

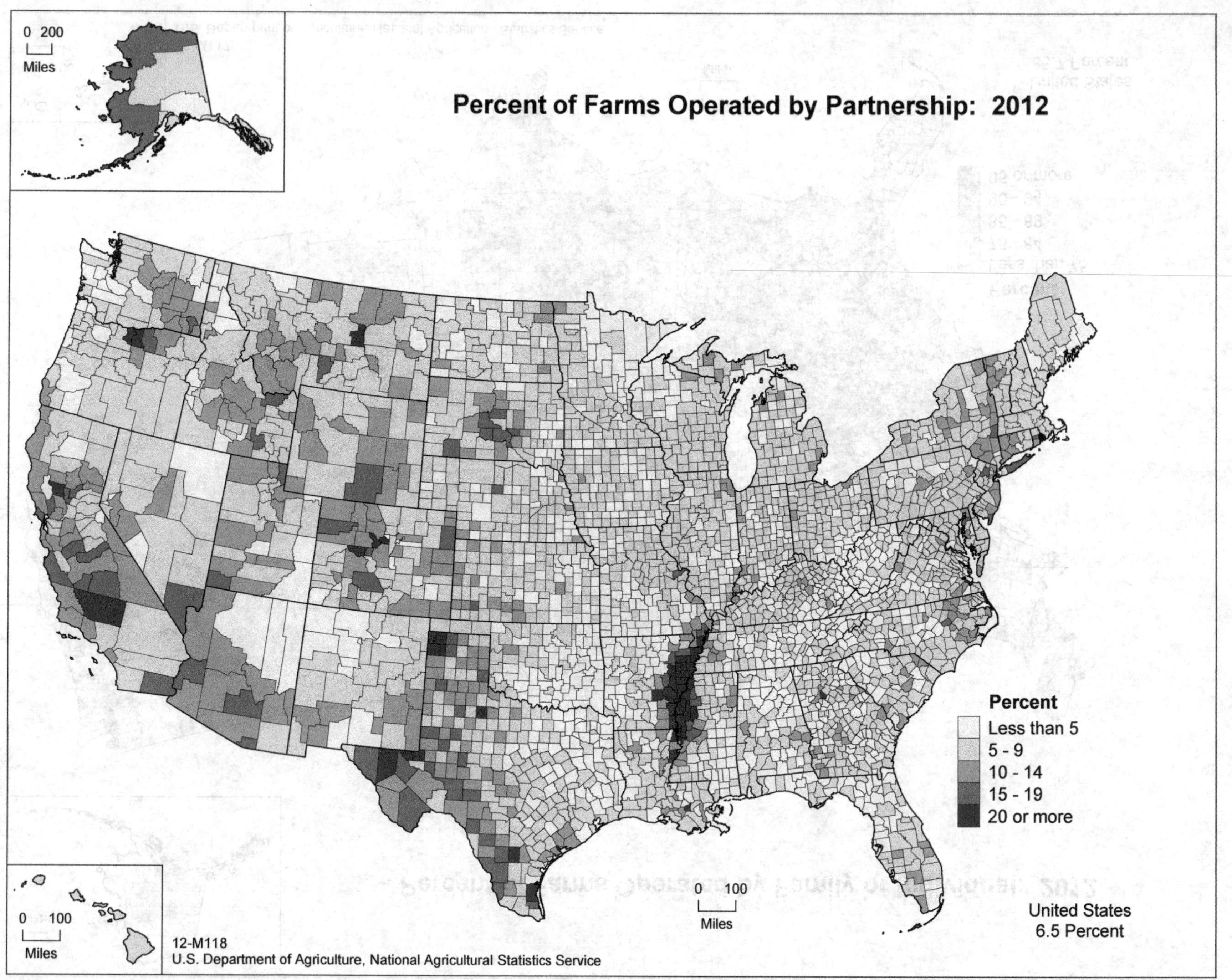

2012 Census of Agriculture

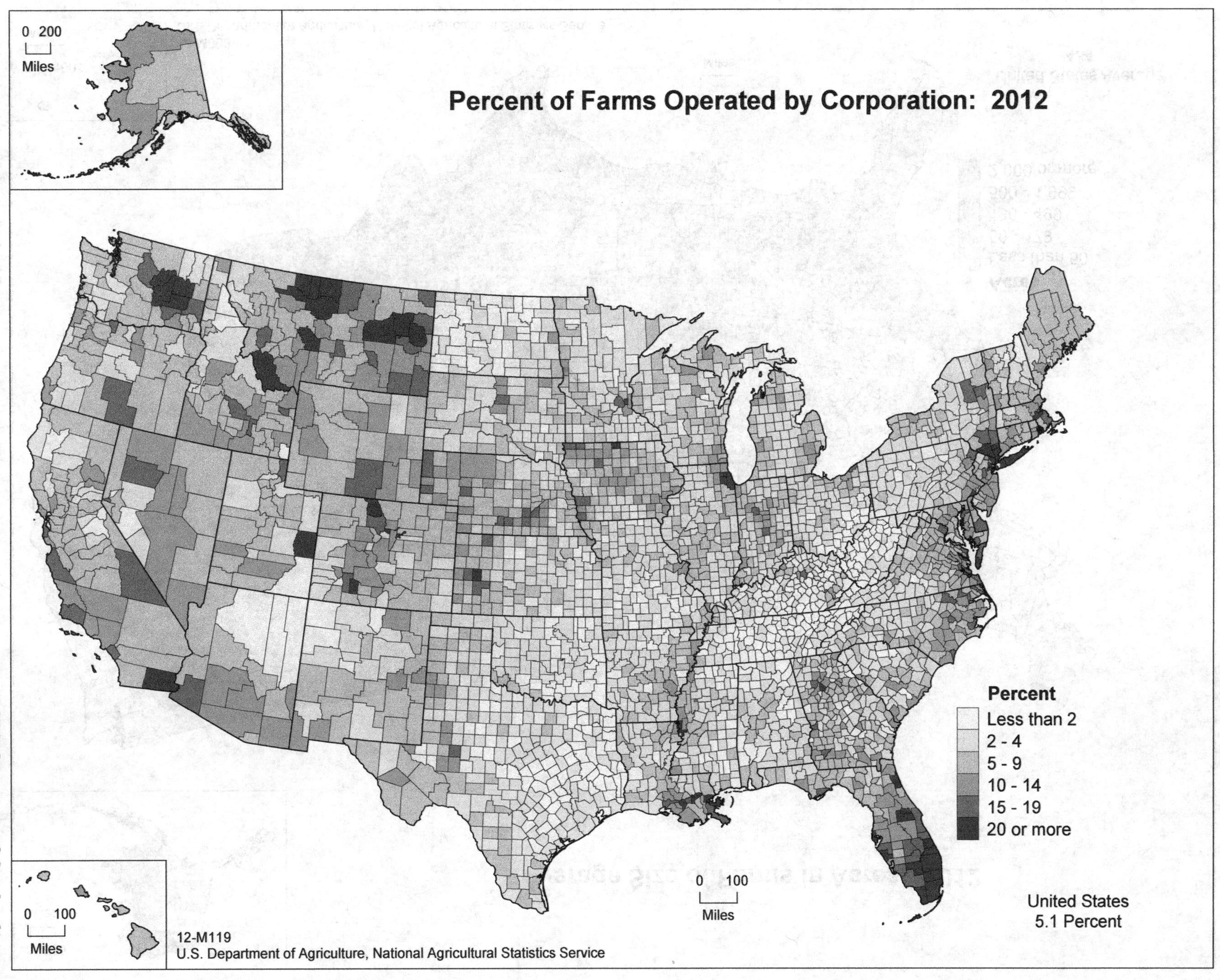
Percent of Farms Operated by Corporation: 2012
0 200
Miles
Percent
Less than 2
2 - 4
5 - 9
10 - 14
15 - 19
20 or more
0 100
Miles
United States
5.1 Percent
0 100
Miles
12-M119
U.S. Department of Agriculture, National Agricultural Statistics Service

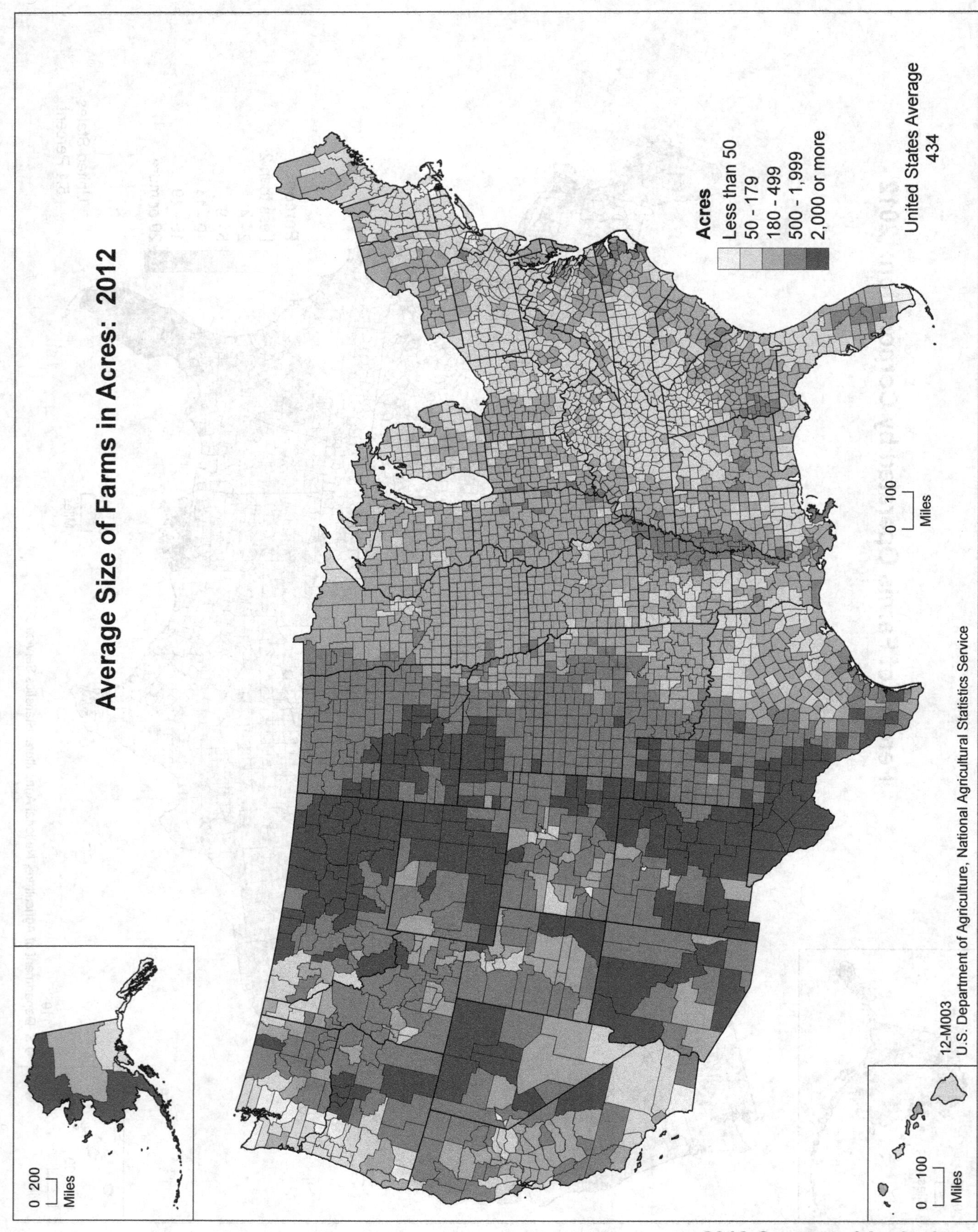

2012 Census of Agriculture

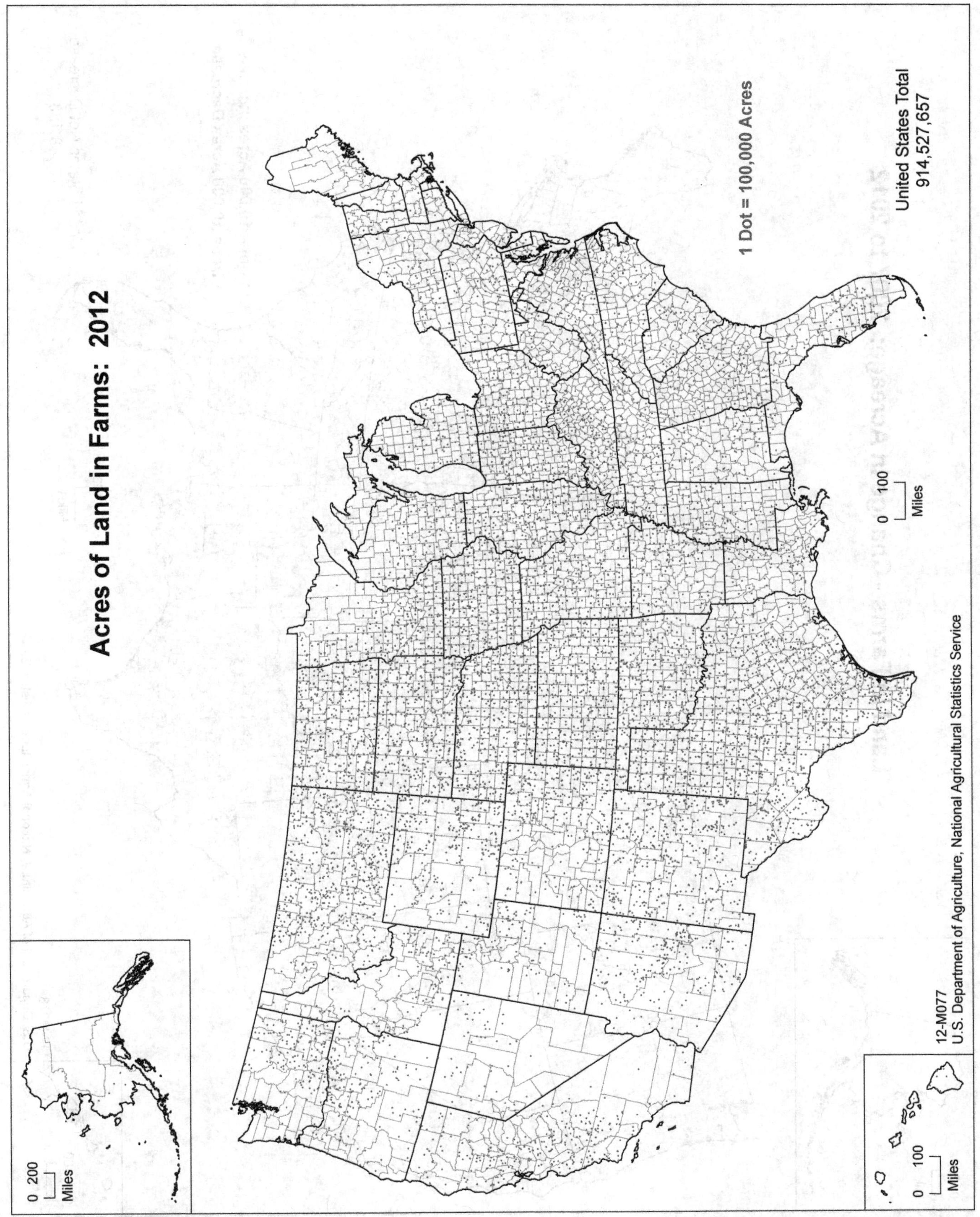
Acres of Land in Farms: 2012
1 Dot = 100,000 Acres
United States Total
914,527,657
0 100
Miles
0 200
Miles
0 100
Miles
12-M077
U.S. Department of Agriculture, National Agricultural Statistics Service

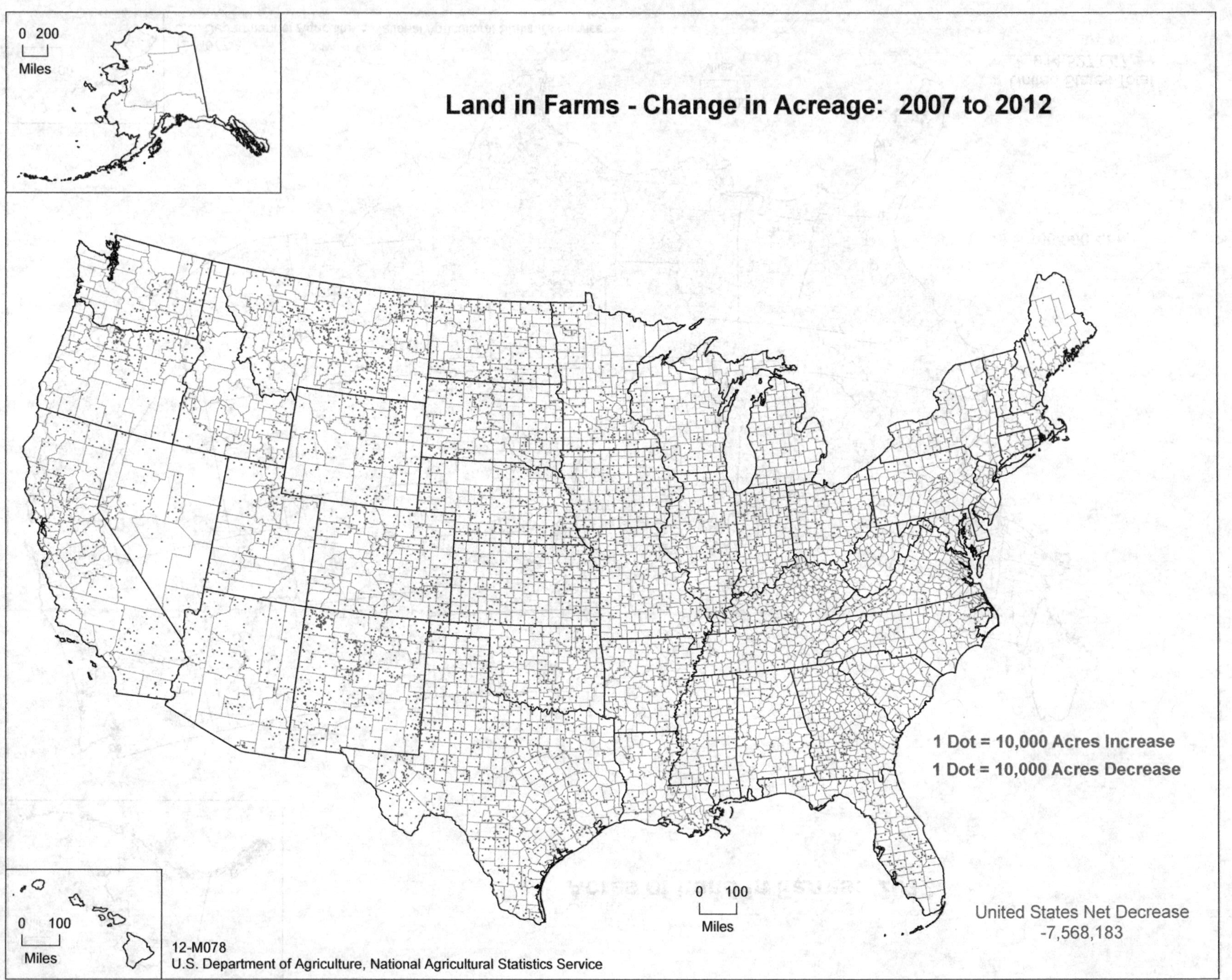

2012 Census of Agriculture

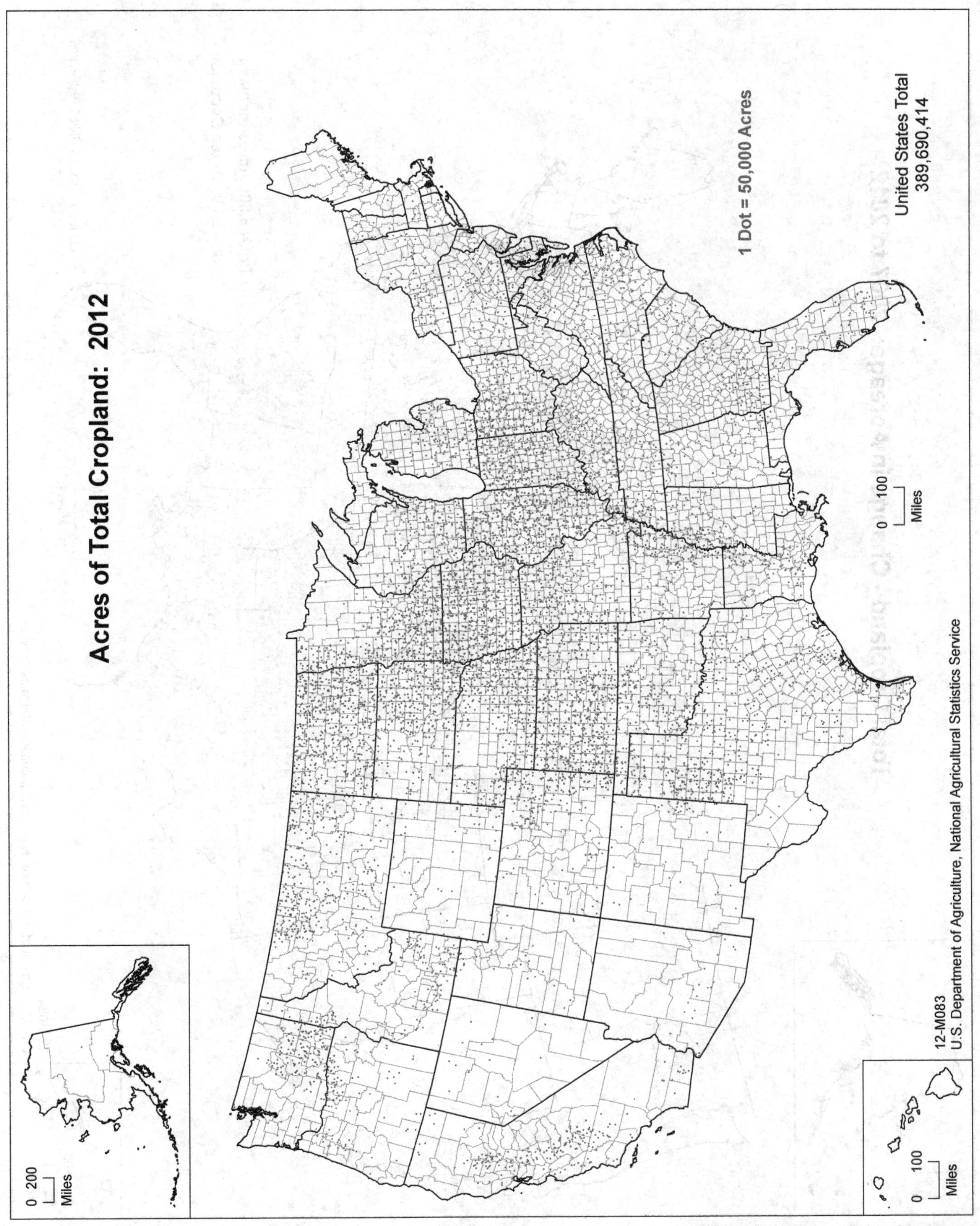

Acres of Total Cropland: 2012
1 Dot = 50,000 Acres
United States Total
389,690,414
0 100
Miles
0 200
Miles
0 100
Miles
12-M083
U.S. Department of Agriculture, National Agricultural Statistics Service

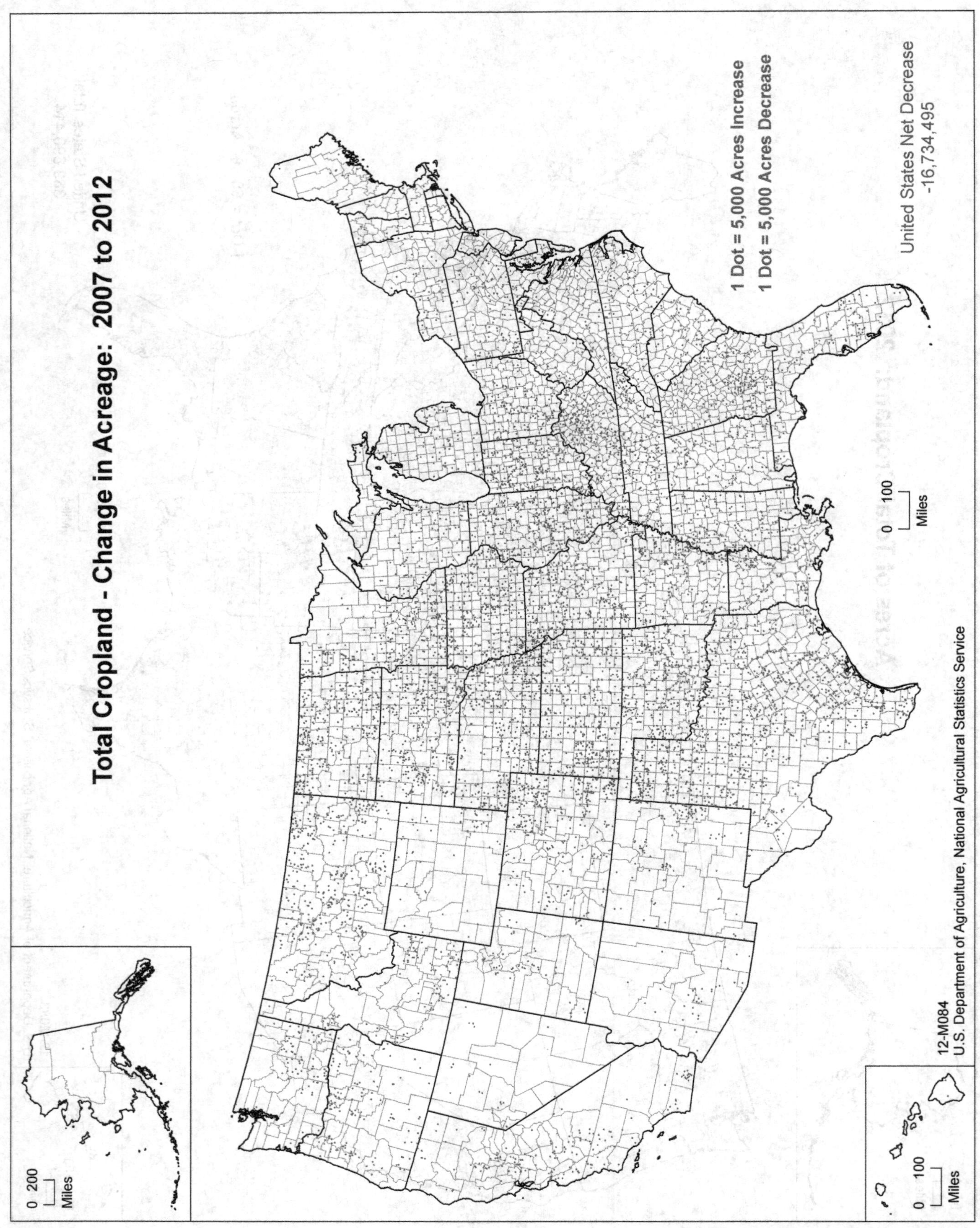
Total Cropland - Change in Acreage: 2007 to 2012
1 Dot = 5,000 Acres Increase
1 Dot = 5,000 Acres Decrease
United States Net Decrease
-16,734,495
0 100
Miles
0 200
Miles
0 100
Miles
12-M084
U.S. Department of Agriculture, National Agricultural Statistics Service
2012 Census of Agriculture

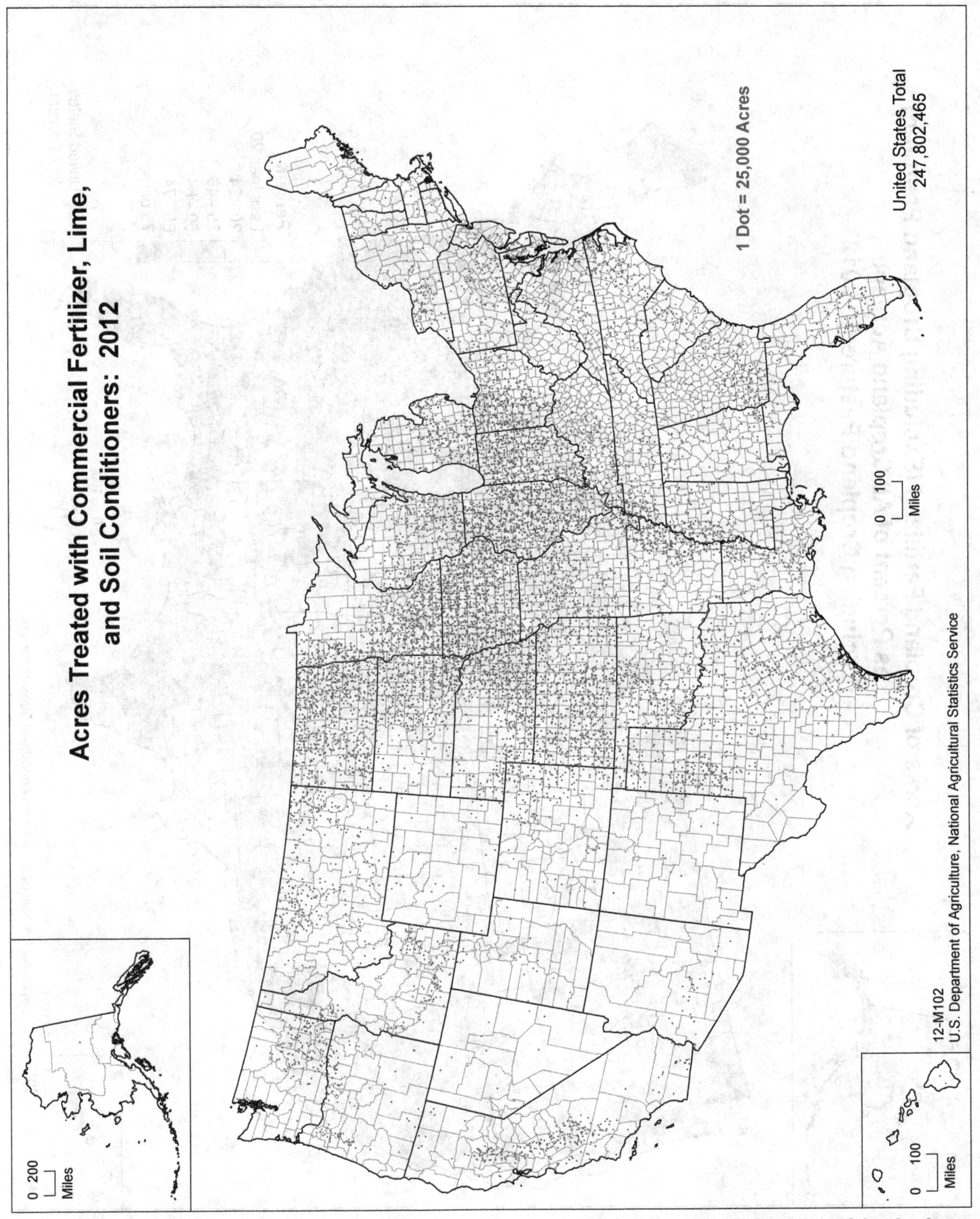

2012 Census of Agriculture

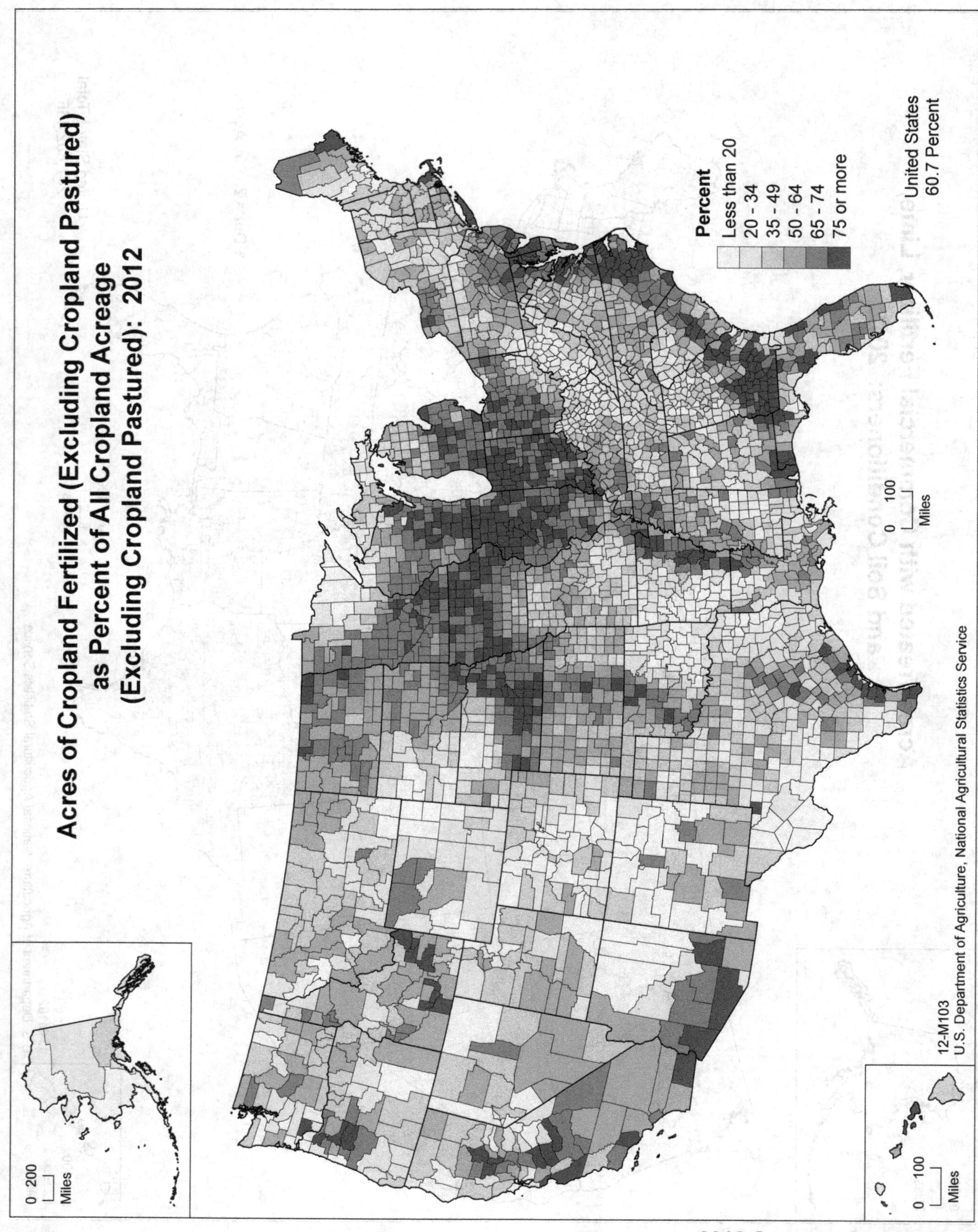
Acres of Cropland Fertilized (Excluding Cropland Pastured)
as Percent of All Cropland Acreage
(Excluding Cropland Pastured): 2012
Percent
Less than 20
20 - 34
35 - 49
50 - 64
65 - 74
75 or more
United States
60.7 Percent
0 100
Miles
0 200
Miles
0 100
Miles
12-M103
U.S. Department of Agriculture, National Agricultural Statistics Service

2012 Census of Agriculture

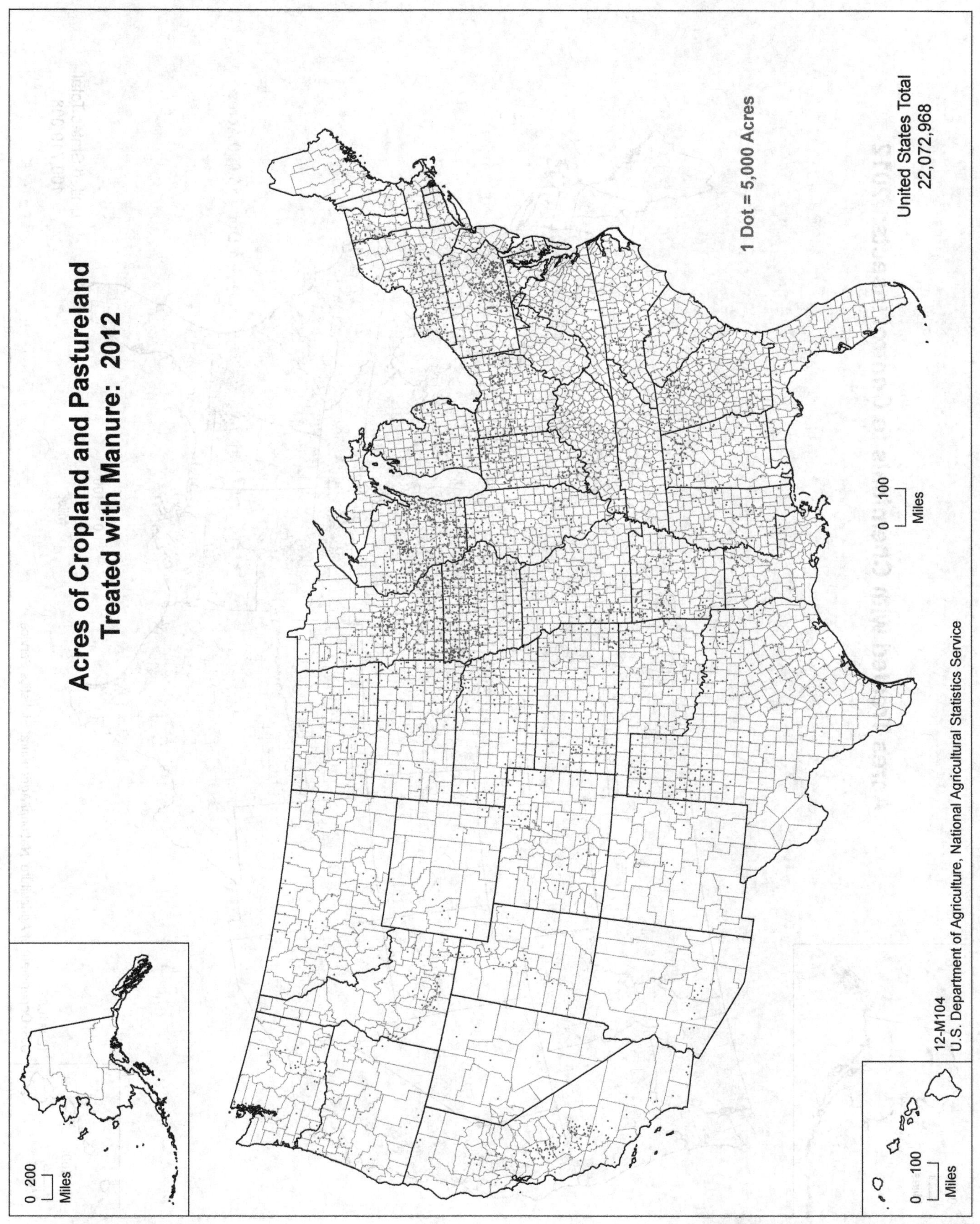

2012 Census of Agriculture

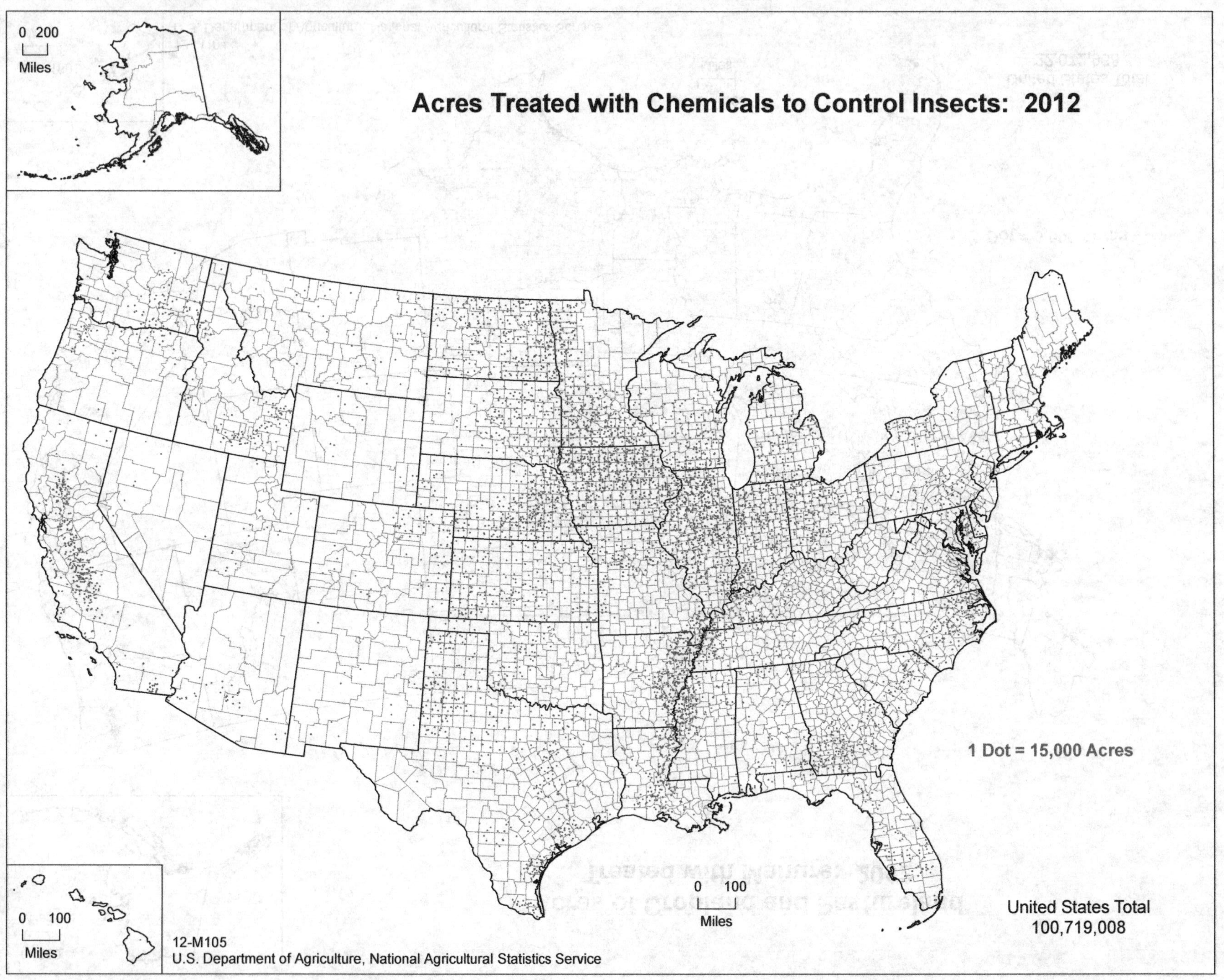
Acres Treated with Chemicals to Control Insects: 2012
0 200
Miles
1 Dot = 15,000 Acres
0 100
Miles
United States Total
100,719,008
0 100
Miles
12-M105
U.S. Department of Agriculture, National Agricultural Statistics Service

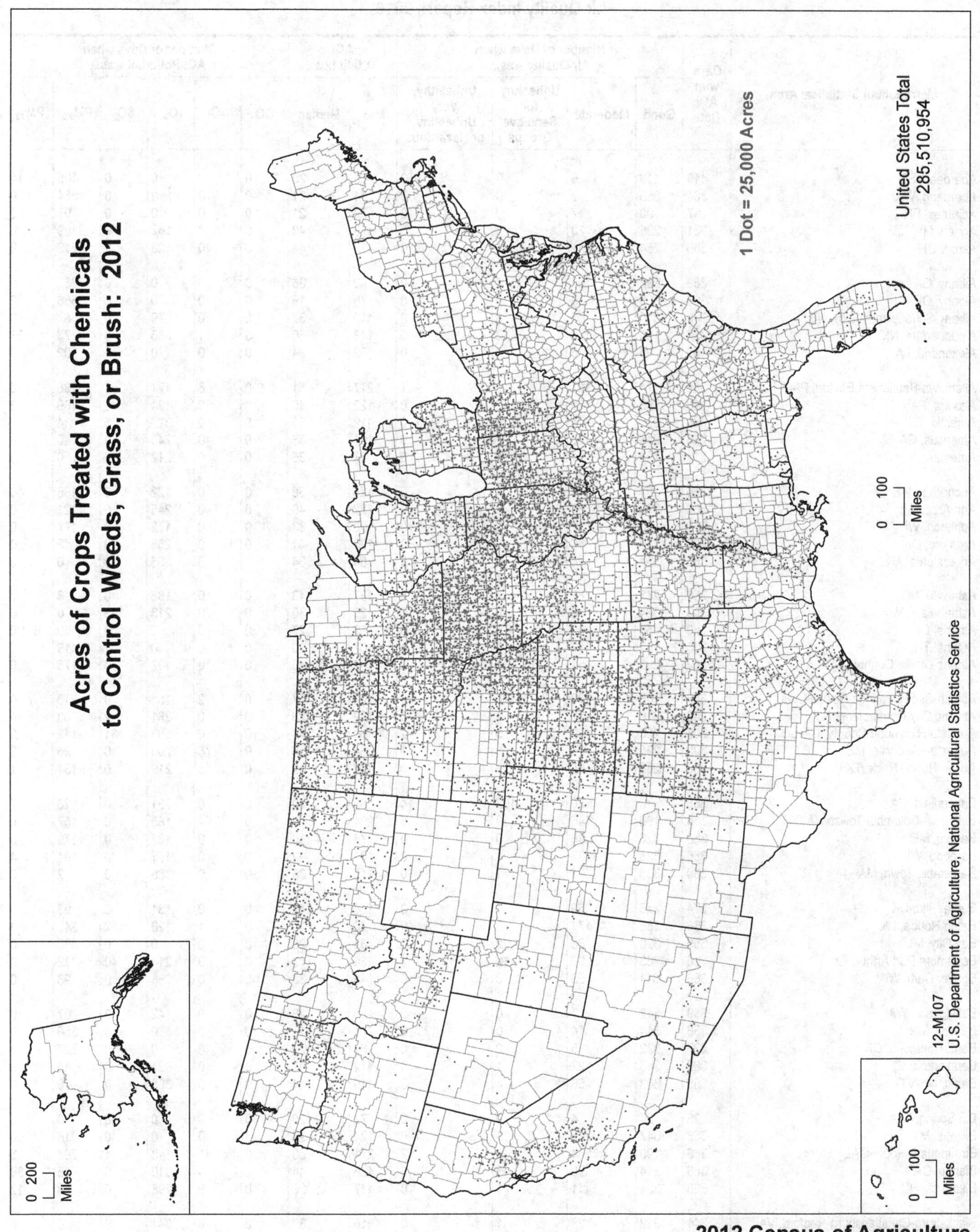

2012 Census of Agriculture

Air Quality Index Report, 2016

Metropolitan Statistical Area	Days with AQI Data	Number of Days when Air Quality was...				AQI Statistics		Number of Days when AQI Pollutant was...					
		Good	Moderate	Unhealthy for Sensitive Groups	Unhealthy, Very Unhealthy, or Hazardous	Max	Median	CO	NO_2	O_3	SO_2	$PM_{2.5}$	PM_{10}
Aberdeen, SD	119	113	6	0	0	76	20	0	0	0	0	105	14
Aberdeen, WA	364	355	9	0	0	71	21	0	0	0	0	364	0
Adjuntas, PR	97	90	7	0	0	72	21	0	0	0	0	97	0
Adrian, MI	361	286	73	2	0	119	40	0	0	162	0	199	0
Akron, OH	366	254	111	1	0	112	44	0	0	123	0	243	0
Albany, GA	363	263	100	0	0	93	36	0	0	0	0	363	0
Albany, OR	366	333	33	0	0	78	19	0	0	0	0	366	0
Albany-Schenectady-Troy, NY	366	310	53	3	0	119	37	0	0	279	0	87	0
Albuquerque, NM	366	185	178	3	0	143	50	0	1	236	0	73	56
Alexandria, LA	102	96	6	0	0	62	34	0	0	0	0	102	0
Allentown-Bethlehem-Easton, PA-NJ	366	174	181	10	1	217	51	0	6	121	1	238	0
Altoona, PA	366	285	79	2	0	122	40	0	0	194	0	169	3
Amarillo, TX	366	321	44	1	0	112	41	0	0	327	5	34	0
Americus, GA	245	218	26	1	0	101	39	0	0	245	0	0	0
Ames, IA	212	198	14	0	0	77	35	0	0	212	0	0	0
Anchorage, AK	366	251	111	4	0	128	38	0	0	122	0	156	88
Ann Arbor, MI	366	293	67	6	0	122	40	0	0	245	0	121	0
Appleton, WI	349	300	47	2	0	108	33	0	0	172	0	177	0
Ardmore, OK	298	249	46	3	0	129	41	0	0	255	0	43	0
Arkadelphia, AR	355	351	4	0	0	54	34	0	0	355	0	0	0
Asheville, NC	366	273	82	7	4	167	43	0	0	188	0	178	0
Ashtabula, OH	366	324	36	6	0	126	30	0	0	213	153	0	0
Athens, OH	60	58	2	0	0	56	27	0	0	0	0	60	0
Athens, TN	200	182	17	0	1	167	20	0	0	0	81	119	0
Athens-Clarke County, GA	362	295	61	4	2	162	40	0	0	187	0	175	0
Atlanta-Sandy Springs-Roswell, GA	366	105	229	28	4	200	57	0	2	151	0	213	0
Atlantic City-Hammonton, NJ	366	316	49	1	0	129	38	0	0	281	2	83	0
Augusta-Richmond County, GA-SC	366	256	103	5	2	166	44	0	0	193	31	142	0
Augusta-Waterville, ME	309	295	14	0	0	84	30	0	76	206	0	25	2
Austin-Round Rock, TX	366	280	85	1	0	105	42	0	15	219	0	131	1
Bakersfield, CA	366	70	180	102	14	169	80	0	0	231	0	128	7
Baltimore-Columbia-Towson, MD	366	196	146	19	5	204	49	0	24	185	0	157	0
Bangor, ME	366	320	46	0	0	75	36	0	0	187	0	179	0
Baraboo, WI	366	328	37	1	0	101	32	0	0	181	0	181	4
Barnstable Town, MA	360	336	23	1	0	115	36	0	0	358	0	2	0
Bartlesville, OK	274	215	59	0	0	100	42	0	0	181	0	93	0
Baton Rouge, LA	366	186	171	9	0	146	50	0	1	120	2	240	3
Bay City, MI	355	320	35	0	0	81	28	0	0	0	0	355	0
Beaumont-Port Arthur, TX	366	263	90	12	1	160	43	0	0	214	40	112	0
Beaver Dam, WI	366	311	52	3	0	148	36	0	0	268	0	98	0
Bellingham, WA	349	342	7	0	0	59	25	0	0	142	0	207	0
Bemidji, MN	358	344	14	0	0	71	18	0	0	0	0	358	0
Bend-Redmond, OR	327	322	5	0	0	61	22	0	0	0	0	327	0
Bennington, VT	366	343	22	1	0	112	36	0	0	321	0	45	0
Berlin, NH-VT	365	303	58	4	0	119	44	0	0	365	0	0	0
Big Spring, TX	28	24	4	0	0	72	20	0	0	0	28	0	0
Billings, MT	363	347	15	1	0	124	22	0	0	0	48	315	0
Birmingham-Hoover, AL	366	190	164	10	2	271	50	0	11	143	1	208	3
Bishop, CA	366	244	99	15	8	426	44	0	0	310	0	18	38
Bismarck, ND	366	354	11	1	0	117	33	0	6	298	0	50	12
Blacksburg-Christiansburg-Radford, VA	341	312	28	1	0	115	39	0	0	341	0	0	0
Bloomington, IL	366	309	56	1	0	108	38	0	0	290	0	76	0

Metropolitan Statistical Area	Days with AQI Data	Number of Days when Air Quality was...				AQI Statistics		Number of Days when AQI Pollutant was...					
		Good	Moderate	Unhealthy for Sensitive Groups	Unhealthy, Very Unhealthy, or Hazardous	Max	Median	CO	NO_2	O_3	SO_2	$PM_{2.5}$	PM_{10}
Bloomington, IN	357	295	59	3	0	140	36	0	0	163	0	194	0
Boise City, ID	366	218	134	13	1	155	46	0	6	151	0	205	4
Borger, TX	59	48	3	8	0	149	4	0	0	0	59	0	0
Boston-Cambridge-Newton, MA-NH	366	218	141	7	0	143	46	0	9	189	0	167	1
Boulder, CO	204	190	14	0	0	97	35	0	0	106	0	82	16
Bowling Green, KY	366	284	82	0	0	97	42	0	0	178	0	188	0
Bozeman, MT	366	339	27	0	0	97	22	16	25	0	0	325	0
Brainerd, MN	357	334	23	0	0	84	29	0	0	152	0	205	0
Branson, MO	244	235	9	0	0	61	36	0	0	214	0	30	0
Bremerton-Silverdale, WA	357	356	1	0	0	55	16	0	0	0	0	357	0
Bridgeport-Stamford-Norwalk, CT	366	223	120	16	7	185	45	0	0	163	0	203	0
Brookings, SD	365	342	22	1	0	101	34	0	0	289	0	51	25
Brownsville-Harlingen, TX	366	277	87	2	0	110	40	0	0	166	0	200	0
Brunswick, GA	343	314	27	2	0	129	35	0	0	170	0	173	0
Buffalo-Cheektowaga-Niagara Falls, NY	366	281	79	6	0	136	42	0	16	200	3	147	0
Burlington-South Burlington, VT	366	349	17	0	0	80	35	0	0	302	0	64	0
Butte-Silver Bow, MT	366	310	56	0	0	94	22	0	0	0	0	326	40
Cadillac, MI	366	324	35	7	0	126	37	0	0	313	0	53	0
Cambridge, MD	366	303	60	3	0	122	40	0	0	265	0	101	0
Canton-Massillon, OH	366	267	93	6	0	119	40	2	0	174	0	190	0
Cape Coral-Fort Myers, FL	366	324	41	1	0	105	38	0	0	249	0	116	1
Carlsbad-Artesia, NM	362	292	70	0	0	100	44	0	2	360	0	0	0
Carson City, NV	366	303	63	0	0	93	42	0	0	325	0	41	0
Casper, WY	366	333	33	0	0	80	41	0	9	350	0	5	2
Ca?on City, CO	52	52	0	0	0	50	14	0	0	0	0	0	52
Cedar Rapids, IA	366	274	90	2	0	106	40	0	0	113	19	232	2
Centralia, WA	366	355	11	0	0	66	19	0	0	0	0	366	0
Chambersburg-Waynesboro, PA	337	325	12	0	0	74	33	0	0	337	0	0	0
Champaign-Urbana, IL	366	302	64	0	0	100	39	0	0	254	0	112	0
Charleston, WV	350	295	53	2	0	119	37	31	0	158	23	138	0
Charleston-North Charleston, SC	357	307	45	3	2	158	38	0	4	169	0	182	2
Charlotte-Concord-Gastonia, NC-SC	366	227	130	7	2	156	46	0	5	253	0	108	0
Charlottesville, VA	366	322	43	1	0	122	36	0	0	175	0	191	0
Chattanooga, TN-GA	359	227	127	2	3	177	47	0	0	196	0	163	0
Cheyenne, WY	366	315	51	0	0	87	43	0	4	338	2	22	0
Chicago-Naperville-Elgin, IL-IN-WI	366	151	187	23	5	217	54	0	39	117	8	182	20
Chico, CA	366	169	181	16	0	127	52	0	0	193	0	173	0
Cincinnati, OH-KY-IN	366	166	182	18	0	140	53	0	18	134	4	207	3
Claremont-Lebanon, NH-VT	366	347	19	0	0	77	33	0	0	289	0	77	0
Clarksburg, WV	117	110	7	0	0	62	31	0	0	0	0	117	0
Clarksville, TN-KY	364	297	67	0	0	90	40	0	0	242	6	116	0
Clearlake, CA	364	357	7	0	0	74	33	0	0	362	0	2	0
Cleveland, MS	244	222	22	0	0	93	39	0	0	244	0	0	0
Cleveland, TN	115	115	0	0	0	17	1	0	0	0	115	0	0
Cleveland-Elyria, OH	366	190	152	19	5	200	50	0	8	138	39	176	5
Clinton, IA	366	176	189	1	0	108	52	0	0	66	2	298	0
Coco, PR	303	299	3	1	0	122	0	0	0	0	303	0	0
Coeur d'Alene, ID	351	325	26	0	0	83	22	0	0	0	0	351	0
College Station-Bryan, TX	73	73	0	0	0	20	1	0	0	0	73	0	0
Colorado Springs, CO	366	263	101	2	0	126	45	0	0	326	16	24	0
Columbia, MO	214	198	16	0	0	97	37	0	0	214	0	0	0
Columbia, SC	366	254	107	3	2	168	44	0	1	195	0	170	0
Columbus, GA-AL	364	264	95	5	0	148	41	0	0	157	0	207	0
Columbus, IN	366	286	75	5	0	105	40	0	6	136	0	224	0
Columbus, OH	366	264	92	10	0	126	42	0	37	186	0	142	1

Metropolitan Statistical Area	Days with AQI Data	Number of Days when Air Quality was... Good	Moderate	Unhealthy for Sensitive Groups	Unhealthy, Very Unhealthy, or Hazardous	AQI Statistics Max	Median	Number of Days when AQI Pollutant was... CO	NO_2	O_3	SO_2	$PM_{2.5}$	PM_{10}
Concord, NH	366	352	14	0	0	84	31	0	0	357	9	0	0
Cookeville, TN	122	116	6	0	0	87	29	0	0	0	0	122	0
Corning, NY	363	335	26	2	0	122	36	3	0	304	1	55	0
Corpus Christi, TX	366	307	59	0	0	93	37	0	0	259	0	107	0
Corsicana, TX	366	303	63	0	0	83	39	0	0	231	13	122	0
Corvallis, OR	194	185	9	0	0	64	15	0	0	0	0	194	0
Craig, CO	345	316	29	0	0	67	41	0	0	345	0	0	0
Crescent City, CA	49	49	0	0	0	36	13	0	0	0	0	49	0
Crestview-Fort Walton Beach-Destin, FL	366	346	20	0	0	71	36	0	0	357	0	0	9
Cullowhee, NC	271	179	83	7	2	154	45	0	0	209	0	62	0
Dallas-Fort Worth-Arlington, TX	366	217	131	17	1	174	48	0	11	241	0	113	1
Dalton, GA	261	220	40	1	0	112	44	0	0	242	0	19	0
Daphne-Fairhope-Foley, AL	279	247	32	0	0	87	37	0	0	219	0	60	0
Davenport-Moline-Rock Island, IA-IL	366	130	234	2	0	112	55	0	0	70	0	223	73
Dayton, OH	366	246	113	7	0	112	44	0	0	233	1	132	0
Decatur, AL	365	304	59	2	0	107	40	0	0	203	0	162	0
Decatur, IL	366	293	72	1	0	123	41	0	0	171	29	166	0
Deltona-Daytona Beach-Ormond Beach, FL	363	319	44	0	0	89	39	0	0	253	0	110	0
Deming, NM	360	338	19	1	2	162	17	0	0	0	0	0	360
Denver-Aurora-Lakewood, CO	366	100	240	23	3	159	60	0	90	202	1	57	16
Des Moines-West Des Moines, IA	366	312	53	1	0	138	37	0	3	131	0	231	1
Detroit-Warren-Dearborn, MI	366	148	196	22	0	147	54	0	14	107	31	188	26
Dickinson, ND	366	356	10	0	0	91	34	0	0	349	1	16	0
Dodge City, KS	366	360	6	0	0	67	16	0	0	0	0	0	366
Dothan, AL	280	265	15	0	0	97	35	0	0	213	0	67	0
Douglas, GA	23	21	2	0	0	51	35	0	0	0	0	23	0
Dover, DE	364	300	62	2	0	136	39	0	0	287	0	77	0
DuBois, PA	338	305	32	1	0	119	38	0	0	338	0	0	0
Duluth, MN-WI	366	340	25	1	0	128	33	0	0	280	0	78	8
Durango, CO	366	251	107	8	0	122	46	0	1	359	0	3	3
Durham-Chapel Hill, NC	366	267	97	2	0	119	43	0	0	169	0	197	0
Dyersburg, TN	96	95	1	0	0	55	25	0	0	0	0	96	0
Eagle Pass, TX	322	278	44	0	0	82	27	0	0	0	0	322	0
East Stroudsburg, PA	366	310	53	3	0	140	40	0	0	257	0	109	0
Eau Claire, WI	359	317	42	0	0	84	35	0	0	131	0	228	0
Effingham, IL	214	181	33	0	0	93	39	0	0	214	0	0	0
El Centro, CA	366	105	219	38	4	166	60	0	2	142	0	100	122
El Dorado, AR	366	341	24	0	1	158	4	0	0	0	246	120	0
El Paso, TX	366	198	162	6	0	147	49	0	23	190	0	152	1
Elizabethtown-Fort Knox, KY	364	248	115	1	0	101	43	0	0	96	0	268	0
Elkhart-Goshen, IN	358	265	85	8	0	131	39	0	0	134	0	224	0
Elko, NV	335	332	2	1	0	134	20	0	0	0	0	1	334
Ellensburg, WA	366	310	50	6	0	143	19	0	0	0	0	366	0
Emporia, KS	48	43	3	2	0	148	16	0	0	0	0	48	0
Erie, PA	366	295	69	2	0	129	39	0	2	234	0	130	0
Espa?ola, NM	361	303	58	0	0	80	44	0	0	359	0	2	0
Eugene, OR	366	302	63	1	0	108	34	0	0	141	0	223	2
Eureka-Arcata-Fortuna, CA	366	357	9	0	0	68	32	0	1	312	0	34	19
Evanston, WY	366	341	25	0	0	87	42	0	0	359	0	0	7
Evansville, IN-KY	366	221	137	7	1	151	45	0	0	136	27	203	0
Fairbanks, AK	366	213	94	35	24	180	37	0	3	133	1	212	17
Fairmont, WV	95	86	9	0	0	61	33	0	0	0	0	95	0
Fallon, NV	351	284	66	1	0	108	41	0	0	351	0	0	0
Fargo, ND-MN	366	324	42	0	0	86	34	0	1	207	0	138	20
Farmington, NM	366	273	91	2	0	108	44	0	7	357	0	0	2

Metropolitan Statistical Area	Days with AQI Data	Number of Days when Air Quality was...				AQI Statistics		Number of Days when AQI Pollutant was...					
		Good	Moderate	Unhealthy for Sensitive Groups	Unhealthy, Very Unhealthy, or Hazardous	Max	Median	CO	NO_2	O_3	SO_2	$PM_{2.5}$	PM_{10}
Fayetteville, NC	366	286	80	0	0	93	41	0	0	170	8	186	2
Fayetteville-Springdale-Rogers, AR-MO	366	338	28	0	0	77	38	0	0	323	0	43	0
Fernley, NV	352	282	69	1	0	101	41	0	0	352	0	0	0
Flagstaff, AZ	366	303	63	0	0	97	44	0	0	366	0	0	0
Flint, MI	364	294	61	9	0	129	38	0	0	172	0	192	0
Florence, SC	335	294	41	0	0	87	38	0	0	206	0	129	0
Florence-Muscle Shoals, AL	282	258	23	1	0	115	38	0	0	214	0	68	0
Fond du Lac, WI	189	165	21	3	0	108	38	0	0	189	0	0	0
Fort Collins, CO	366	197	161	7	1	151	50	0	0	313	0	51	2
Fort Madison-Keokuk, IA-IL-MO	113	95	18	0	0	70	32	0	0	0	0	113	0
Fort Payne, AL	348	304	43	1	0	119	40	0	0	319	0	29	0
Fort Smith, AR-OK	361	331	30	0	0	74	37	0	56	232	0	67	6
Fort Wayne, IN	366	256	107	3	0	119	42	0	3	134	0	229	0
Fresno, CA	366	92	169	80	25	190	74	0	1	211	0	139	15
Gadsden, AL	352	162	184	3	3	179	52	0	0	101	0	251	0
Gaffney, SC	172	148	23	1	0	101	41	0	0	172	0	0	0
Gainesville, FL	360	321	38	1	0	101	37	0	0	214	0	146	0
Gainesville, GA	119	103	14	1	1	155	30	0	0	0	0	119	0
Gardnerville Ranchos, NV	336	300	35	1	0	105	26	0	0	0	0	336	0
Georgetown, SC	325	322	3	0	0	62	16	0	0	0	0	0	325
Gettysburg, PA	366	284	77	5	0	119	42	0	0	290	0	76	0
Gillette, WY	366	262	103	1	0	141	43	0	0	224	0	20	122
Glenwood Springs, CO	366	328	38	0	0	84	43	0	7	353	0	4	2
Grand Island, NE	113	110	3	0	0	53	22	0	0	0	0	113	0
Grand Junction, CO	366	276	89	1	0	102	44	0	0	293	0	73	0
Grand Rapids-Wyoming, MI	366	275	81	10	0	133	40	0	0	217	1	148	0
Grants Pass, OR	366	318	48	0	0	86	29	0	0	0	0	366	0
Great Falls, MT	356	343	13	0	0	72	25	0	0	0	0	356	0
Greeley, CO	365	257	105	3	0	129	44	0	0	269	0	95	1
Green Bay, WI	366	305	56	5	0	136	35	0	0	166	0	200	0
Greenfield Town, MA	366	327	36	3	0	115	35	0	0	269	0	97	0
Greensboro-High Point, NC	366	271	91	4	0	133	42	0	0	174	0	185	7
Greenville, NC	288	242	46	0	0	100	38	0	0	155	0	133	0
Greenville-Anderson-Mauldin, SC	366	247	112	5	2	188	46	0	1	232	0	132	1
Greenwood, SC	311	285	26	0	0	87	39	0	0	311	0	0	0
Grenada, MS	109	99	10	0	0	64	31	0	0	0	0	109	0
Guayama, PR	102	91	11	0	0	70	21	0	0	0	0	101	1
Gulfport-Biloxi-Pascagoula, MS	366	309	57	0	0	97	39	0	10	193	2	161	0
Hagerstown-Martinsburg, MD-WV	355	260	91	4	0	112	43	0	0	174	0	181	0
Hailey, ID	113	98	15	0	0	92	8	0	0	0	0	113	0
Hammond, LA	117	110	7	0	0	60	28	0	0	0	0	117	0
Hanford-Corcoran, CA	366	85	207	71	3	156	70	0	0	182	0	135	49
Harrisburg-Carlisle, PA	366	234	126	6	0	116	45	0	0	165	0	201	0
Harrison, AR	365	353	12	0	0	90	36	0	0	363	0	2	0
Harrisonburg, VA	366	334	31	1	0	108	32	0	116	202	0	48	0
Hartford-West Hartford-East Hartford, CT	366	257	93	14	2	187	43	0	55	169	0	142	0
Hattiesburg, MS	336	289	47	0	0	70	35	0	0	0	0	336	0
Helena, MT	366	316	43	7	0	146	40	0	0	272	0	94	0
Hermiston-Pendleton, OR	366	321	44	1	0	112	31	0	0	106	0	260	0
Hickory-Lenoir-Morganton, NC	366	261	102	1	2	153	44	0	0	161	0	204	1
Hilo, HI	366	1	54	128	183	337	151	0	0	0	353	13	0
Hobbs, NM	364	312	52	0	0	97	41	0	1	349	0	14	0
Holland, MI	240	185	46	9	0	150	40	0	0	177	0	63	0
Homosassa Springs, FL	364	323	40	1	0	104	33	0	0	0	45	319	0
Hot Springs, AR	119	97	22	0	0	67	36	0	0	0	0	119	0

Metropolitan Statistical Area	Days with AQI Data	Number of Days when Air Quality was...				AQI Statistics		Number of Days when AQI Pollutant was...					
		Good	Moderate	Unhealthy for Sensitive Groups	Unhealthy, Very Unhealthy, or Hazardous	Max	Median	CO	NO_2	O_3	SO_2	$PM_{2.5}$	PM_{10}
Houghton, MI	51	51	0	0	0	45	8	0	0	0	0	51	0
Houma-Thibodaux, LA	366	330	36	0	0	93	37	0	0	281	0	85	0
Houston-The Woodlands-Sugar Land, TX	366	164	179	22	1	159	52	0	18	190	0	154	4
Huntington, IN	180	156	23	1	0	105	37	0	0	180	0	0	0
Huntington-Ashland, WV-KY-OH	366	246	117	3	0	129	43	0	2	125	0	239	0
Huntsville, AL	337	284	52	1	0	122	40	0	0	233	0	47	57
Idaho Falls, ID	365	332	33	0	0	67	40	0	0	296	0	69	0
Indiana, PA	366	317	45	4	0	136	38	0	0	346	20	0	0
Indianapolis-Carmel-Anderson, IN	366	197	157	12	0	143	49	0	4	125	1	234	2
Iowa City, IA	366	305	61	0	0	100	33	0	0	0	0	365	1
Ithaca, NY	361	331	28	2	0	122	36	0	0	361	0	0	0
Jackson, MS	366	251	115	0	0	100	43	0	0	134	0	232	0
Jackson, TN	115	111	4	0	0	57	25	0	0	0	0	115	0
Jackson, WY-ID	366	331	35	0	0	99	41	0	0	350	0	15	1
Jacksonville, FL	366	263	103	0	0	97	44	0	1	185	14	166	0
Jamestown, ND	366	357	9	0	0	88	9	0	0	0	34	0	332
Jamestown-Dunkirk-Fredonia, NY	366	324	39	3	0	140	37	0	0	352	3	11	0
Janesville-Beloit, WI	187	159	23	5	0	119	39	0	0	187	0	0	0
Jasper, IN	364	338	26	0	0	73	4	0	0	0	242	120	2
Jefferson City, MO	214	200	13	1	0	101	38	0	0	214	0	0	0
Johnstown, PA	365	261	104	0	0	97	43	0	5	206	2	151	1
Joplin, MO	361	319	41	1	0	110	34	0	0	191	0	0	170
Juneau, AK	305	255	50	0	0	89	20	0	0	0	0	297	8
Kahului-Wailuku-Lahaina, HI	366	348	17	1	0	130	21	0	0	0	0	366	0
Kalamazoo-Portage, MI	363	286	69	8	0	119	38	0	0	152	0	211	0
Kalispell, MT	366	327	39	0	0	77	35	0	0	229	0	87	50
Kansas City, MO-KS	366	228	131	7	0	129	46	0	14	174	1	164	13
Kapaa, HI	358	356	2	0	0	54	14	0	56	0	4	298	0
Keene, NH	366	317	48	1	0	105	36	0	0	283	0	83	0
Kennewick-Richland, WA	366	325	39	2	0	122	31	0	0	126	0	217	23
Killeen-Temple, TX	365	331	34	0	0	100	38	0	0	365	0	0	0
Kingsport-Bristol-Bristol, TN-VA	366	231	110	24	1	155	45	1	23	173	147	22	0
Kingsville, TX	153	128	25	0	0	92	28	0	0	0	0	153	0
Kinston, NC	193	171	22	0	0	97	40	0	0	193	0	0	0
Klamath Falls, OR	363	290	73	0	0	91	30	0	0	0	0	363	0
Knoxville, TN	366	197	155	11	3	169	49	0	0	248	1	106	11
Kokomo, IN	325	243	82	0	0	81	36	0	0	0	0	325	0
La Crosse-Onalaska, WI-MN	355	317	38	0	0	87	32	0	0	169	0	186	0
La Grande, OR	363	327	36	0	0	99	26	0	0	0	0	363	0
Laconia, NH	257	241	16	0	0	84	33	0	0	180	0	77	0
Lafayette, LA	366	286	80	0	0	97	42	0	0	271	0	95	0
Lafayette-West Lafayette, IN	352	277	73	2	0	101	38	0	0	156	0	196	0
Lake Charles, LA	366	239	126	1	0	112	44	0	0	102	7	257	0
Lake City, FL	345	283	62	0	0	90	38	0	0	217	0	128	0
Lake Havasu City-Kingman, AZ	357	338	19	0	0	83	18	0	0	0	0	23	334
Lakeland-Winter Haven, FL	366	320	46	0	0	90	39	0	0	235	2	129	0
Lancaster, PA	366	187	173	6	0	136	50	0	0	138	0	228	0
Lansing-East Lansing, MI	366	295	63	8	0	126	40	0	3	242	1	120	0
Laramie, WY	366	266	100	0	0	97	46	0	0	290	0	5	71
Laredo, TX	366	285	81	0	0	96	37	0	0	109	0	256	1
Las Cruces, NM	366	154	197	12	2	585	54	0	0	216	0	70	80
Las Vegas-Henderson-Paradise, NV	366	125	215	25	1	268	58	0	19	220	0	121	6
Lawrenceburg, TN	116	114	2	0	0	80	25	0	0	0	0	116	0
Lawton, OK	366	309	57	0	0	90	40	0	0	283	0	83	0
Lebanon, PA	366	189	170	7	0	122	50	0	0	119	0	247	0

Metropolitan Statistical Area	Days with AQI Data	Number of Days when Air Quality was...				AQI Statistics		Number of Days when AQI Pollutant was...					
		Good	Moderate	Unhealthy for Sensitive Groups	Unhealthy, Very Unhealthy, or Hazardous	Max	Median	CO	NO_2	O_3	SO_2	$PM_{2.5}$	PM_{10}
Lewiston, ID-WA	366	312	52	2	0	141	29	0	0	0	0	366	0
Lewiston-Auburn, ME	358	333	25	0	0	79	32	0	0	163	0	190	5
Lexington, NE	12	12	0	0	0	49	14	0	0	0	0	0	12
Lexington-Fayette, KY	366	298	67	1	0	126	40	0	27	203	4	132	0
Lima, OH	366	316	47	3	0	122	34	0	0	206	0	160	0
Lincoln, NE	267	245	22	0	0	74	36	0	0	197	7	63	0
Little Rock-North Little Rock-Conway, AR	366	257	109	0	0	100	44	0	4	163	0	199	0
Logan, UT-ID	366	271	85	10	0	129	44	0	1	227	0	136	2
Longview, TX	366	333	33	0	0	100	37	0	1	359	6	0	0
Longview, WA	363	348	15	0	0	74	18	0	0	0	0	363	0
Los Alamos, NM	51	51	0	0	0	19	6	0	0	0	0	51	0
Los Angeles-Long Beach-Anaheim, CA	366	32	226	83	25	210	75	0	28	179	0	157	2
Louisville/Jefferson County, KY-IN	366	209	138	18	1	151	48	0	8	160	0	198	0
Lubbock, TX	119	118	1	0	0	54	21	0	0	0	0	119	0
Ludington, MI	180	157	17	6	0	129	38	0	0	180	0	0	0
Lynchburg, VA	120	115	5	0	0	60	28	0	0	0	0	120	0
Macon, GA	366	267	94	5	0	147	42	0	0	138	1	227	0
Madera, CA	366	123	193	47	3	156	59	0	0	212	0	139	15
Madison, WI	366	298	65	3	0	108	38	0	0	164	5	195	2
Malone, NY	366	365	1	0	0	51	20	0	142	198	26	0	0
Manchester-Nashua, NH	366	333	30	3	0	108	37	0	0	354	0	12	0
Manitowoc, WI	188	160	21	7	0	147	37	0	0	188	0	0	0
Marietta, OH	214	189	25	0	0	90	40	0	0	214	0	0	0
Marshall, MN	356	336	19	1	0	110	30	0	0	194	0	162	0
Marshall, TX	366	328	38	0	0	76	37	0	0	228	1	136	1
Mason City, IA	350	346	4	0	0	59	15	0	0	0	0	0	350
McAlester, OK	366	307	59	0	0	83	40	0	0	244	0	122	0
McAllen-Edinburg-Mission, TX	366	289	76	1	0	114	36	0	0	179	0	184	3
Medford, OR	366	305	61	0	0	81	35	0	0	94	0	272	0
Memphis, TN-MS-AR	366	261	97	7	1	159	44	0	8	232	0	126	0
Merced, CA	366	158	173	33	2	151	53	0	0	222	0	142	2
Meridian, MS	212	203	9	0	0	71	37	0	0	212	0	0	0
Miami, OK	366	296	70	0	0	79	40	0	0	143	0	221	2
Miami-Fort Lauderdale-West Palm Beach, FL	361	203	152	5	1	164	48	0	6	75	0	241	39
Michigan City-La Porte, IN	244	205	37	2	0	112	36	0	0	169	0	75	0
Middlesborough, KY	261	236	23	1	1	161	39	0	0	234	0	27	0
Milwaukee-Waukesha-West Allis, WI	366	254	103	8	1	185	42	0	11	192	0	162	1
Minneapolis-St. Paul-Bloomington, MN-WI	366	184	177	4	1	151	50	0	6	75	1	160	124
Missoula, MT	366	166	175	25	0	139	53	0	0	42	0	324	0
Mobile, AL	366	277	87	2	0	139	41	0	0	124	9	233	0
Modesto, CA	366	147	176	40	3	164	55	0	0	196	0	164	6
Monroe, LA	344	314	30	0	0	72	36	0	0	285	0	59	0
Monroe, MI	366	349	17	0	0	68	4	0	0	0	249	117	0
Montgomery, AL	363	285	76	1	1	170	42	0	0	161	0	202	0
Montrose, CO	253	236	17	0	0	84	40	0	0	253	0	0	0
Morehead City, NC	327	308	19	0	0	93	36	0	0	327	0	0	0
Morgantown, WV	361	340	21	0	0	74	32	0	0	189	102	70	0
Morristown, TN	239	158	79	2	0	133	47	0	0	239	0	0	0
Moscow, ID	270	268	2	0	0	58	8	0	0	0	0	270	0
Moses Lake, WA	361	350	11	0	0	62	18	0	0	0	0	361	0
Mount Pleasant, TX	24	24	0	0	0	14	0	0	0	0	24	0	0
Mount Vernon, IL	285	227	58	0	0	100	39	0	0	170	0	115	0
Mount Vernon, OH	213	175	38	0	0	100	41	0	0	213	0	0	0
Mount Vernon-Anacortes, WA	366	354	12	0	0	78	32	0	1	257	0	108	0

Metropolitan Statistical Area	Days with AQI Data	Number of Days when Air Quality was... Good	Moderate	Unhealthy for Sensitive Groups	Unhealthy, Very Unhealthy, or Hazardous	AQI Statistics Max	Median	Number of Days when AQI Pollutant was... CO	NO_2	O_3	SO_2	$PM_{2.5}$	PM_{10}
Muncie, IN	230	192	37	1	0	115	39	0	0	154	0	76	0
Muscatine, IA	366	276	90	0	0	95	38	0	0	0	15	351	0
Muskegon, MI	178	138	33	5	2	159	41	0	0	178	0	0	0
Muskogee, OK	364	350	13	1	0	101	18	0	0	0	70	0	294
Myrtle Beach-Conway-North Myrtle Beach, SC-NC	137	127	8	2	0	128	27	0	0	121	16	0	0
Napa, CA	366	296	70	0	0	90	37	0	1	160	0	204	1
Naples-Immokalee-Marco Island, FL	366	336	30	0	0	87	37	0	0	233	0	133	0
Nashville-Davidson—Murfreesboro—Franklin, TN	366	235	125	5	1	217	45	0	31	155	0	180	0
New Castle, IN	119	106	13	0	0	65	28	0	0	0	0	119	0
New Castle, PA	362	331	30	1	0	112	33	0	0	345	17	0	0
New Haven-Milford, CT	366	256	96	11	3	164	44	0	24	215	0	127	0
New Orleans-Metairie, LA	366	231	124	11	0	126	46	0	3	150	55	158	0
New York-Newark-Jersey City, NY-NJ-PA	366	156	180	28	2	161	53	0	37	159	0	170	0
Niles-Benton Harbor, MI	242	181	50	11	0	140	40	0	0	174	0	68	0
Nogales, AZ	363	260	102	0	1	191	38	0	0	0	0	212	151
North Port-Sarasota-Bradenton, FL	366	297	69	0	0	97	41	0	0	218	0	148	0
Norwich-New London, CT	357	306	41	9	1	154	34	0	0	178	0	179	0
Ocala, FL	366	324	41	1	0	105	38	0	0	223	0	143	0
Odessa, TX	365	336	28	1	0	102	27	0	0	0	0	365	0
Ogden-Clearfield, UT	366	215	127	24	0	143	48	1	35	234	0	96	0
Oklahoma City, OK	366	264	99	3	0	129	44	0	23	224	0	117	2
Olympia-Tumwater, WA	349	328	21	0	0	90	27	0	0	134	0	215	0
Omaha-Council Bluffs, NE-IA	366	241	121	4	0	130	44	0	0	130	15	174	47
Orlando-Kissimmee-Sanford, FL	366	280	85	1	0	115	42	0	8	241	0	117	0
Othello, WA	346	345	1	0	0	52	14	0	0	0	0	346	0
Ottawa-Peru, IL	350	350	0	0	0	36	1	0	0	0	350	0	0
Owensboro, KY	366	233	130	2	1	156	45	0	0	86	1	279	0
Oxford, NC	213	179	34	0	0	97	41	0	0	213	0	0	0
Oxnard-Thousand Oaks-Ventura, CA	366	173	184	9	0	147	51	0	0	226	0	133	7
Paducah, KY-IL	366	256	109	1	0	115	43	0	0	101	1	264	0
Pahrump, NV	366	349	15	1	1	349	15	0	0	0	0	0	366
Palatka, FL	366	366	0	0	0	45	14	0	0	0	14	0	352
Palm Bay-Melbourne-Titusville, FL	366	332	34	0	0	84	39	0	0	278	0	88	0
Panama City, FL	366	328	38	0	0	87	38	0	0	255	0	111	0
Parkersburg-Vienna, WV	363	318	44	1	0	112	37	0	0	198	100	65	0
Payson, AZ	366	83	136	120	27	200	85	0	0	79	263	0	24
Pensacola-Ferry Pass-Brent, FL	366	304	62	0	0	97	41	0	0	262	0	104	0
Peoria, IL	366	246	108	12	0	141	43	0	0	148	50	168	0
Philadelphia-Camden-Wilmington, PA-NJ-DE-MD	366	121	225	18	2	154	57	0	6	129	3	221	7
Phoenix-Mesa-Scottsdale, AZ	366	26	265	67	7	1263	74	0	10	104	0	82	170
Pierre, SD	352	347	5	0	0	65	17	0	0	0	0	352	0
Pittsburgh, PA	366	116	220	29	1	152	58	0	0	109	18	239	0
Pittsfield, MA	355	310	45	0	0	79	27	0	0	0	0	355	0
Platteville, WI	281	251	30	0	0	78	29	0	0	0	0	281	0
Pocatello, ID	366	317	49	0	0	84	30	0	0	0	80	253	33
Ponca City, OK	361	252	106	3	0	126	43	0	0	122	5	234	0
Ponce, PR	364	341	23	0	0	70	24	4	0	0	0	88	272
Port Angeles, WA	366	328	38	0	0	69	37	0	0	238	0	128	0
Port St. Lucie, FL	366	327	39	0	0	93	39	0	0	257	0	109	0
Portland-South Portland, ME	366	327	37	2	0	108	36	0	9	280	0	73	4
Portland-Vancouver-Hillsboro, OR-WA	366	300	64	2	0	108	35	0	11	224	0	131	0
Portsmouth, OH	366	355	10	1	0	129	15	0	0	0	38	116	212
Prescott, AZ	344	295	49	0	0	90	41	0	0	344	0	0	0

Metropolitan Statistical Area	Days with AQI Data	Number of Days when Air Quality was...				AQI Statistics		Number of Days when AQI Pollutant was...					
		Good	Moderate	Unhealthy for Sensitive Groups	Unhealthy, Very Unhealthy, or Hazardous	Max	Median	CO	NO_2	O_3	SO_2	$PM_{2.5}$	PM_{10}
Price, UT	312	230	82	0	0	93	44	0	19	293	0	0	0
Prineville, OR	348	284	63	1	0	115	30	0	0	0	0	348	0
Providence-Warwick, RI-MA	366	265	95	5	1	151	44	0	32	186	0	148	0
Provo-Orem, UT	366	223	124	17	2	166	47	0	55	227	0	80	4
Pueblo, CO	128	126	2	0	0	64	20	0	0	0	0	76	52
Pullman, WA	366	359	7	0	0	84	17	0	0	0	0	366	0
Quincy, IL-MO	214	199	15	0	0	80	36	0	0	214	0	0	0
Racine, WI	197	153	35	8	1	169	42	0	0	197	0	0	0
Raleigh, NC	366	231	132	3	0	135	46	0	0	164	0	202	0
Rapid City, SD	366	289	76	1	0	101	43	0	5	241	0	44	76
Reading, PA	366	222	137	7	0	129	46	0	0	150	0	216	0
Red Bluff, CA	366	226	98	37	5	174	44	0	0	322	0	43	1
Red Wing, MN	214	202	12	0	0	87	34	0	0	214	0	0	0
Redding, CA	366	298	54	14	0	140	41	0	0	362	0	4	0
Reno, NV	366	234	125	7	0	108	46	0	13	280	0	61	12
Richmond, IN	366	363	2	1	0	106	4	0	0	0	366	0	0
Richmond, VA	366	263	99	4	0	129	43	0	8	205	1	152	0
Richmond-Berea, KY	97	87	10	0	0	90	30	0	0	0	0	97	0
Riverside-San Bernardino-Ontario, CA	366	16	189	92	69	389	90	0	23	193	0	109	41
Riverton, WY	366	305	61	0	0	84	44	0	0	335	0	31	0
Roanoke, VA	365	314	51	0	0	100	36	0	26	158	0	181	0
Rochester, MN	366	329	36	1	0	104	33	0	0	184	1	181	0
Rochester, NY	366	305	59	2	0	136	38	0	1	242	3	120	0
Rock Springs, WY	366	303	63	0	0	100	44	0	0	322	3	5	36
Rockford, IL	354	316	35	3	0	105	34	0	0	311	0	43	0
Rockland, ME	181	171	9	1	0	122	33	0	0	181	0	0	0
Rocky Mount, NC	356	305	51	0	0	97	34	0	0	173	0	183	0
Rome, GA	366	287	78	1	0	102	35	0	0	0	57	309	0
Roseburg, OR	339	325	14	0	0	65	24	0	0	0	0	339	0
Roswell, NM	48	48	0	0	0	48	12	0	0	0	0	48	0
Ruidoso, NM	51	50	1	0	0	70	9	0	0	0	0	51	0
Rutland, VT	366	320	46	0	0	87	35	0	9	230	0	127	0
Sacramento—Roseville—Arden-Arcade, CA	366	128	177	45	16	185	59	0	0	245	0	121	0
Salem, OH	365	364	1	0	0	52	1	0	0	0	305	0	60
Salem, OR	361	325	36	0	0	97	30	0	0	147	0	214	0
Salinas, CA	366	325	30	3	8	176	36	0	0	248	0	73	45
Salisbury, MD-DE	366	290	73	3	0	129	41	0	0	298	0	68	0
Salt Lake City, UT	366	201	137	23	5	166	48	0	24	256	0	83	3
San Antonio-New Braunfels, TX	366	268	92	5	1	160	43	0	5	222	0	139	0
San Diego-Carlsbad, CA	366	69	255	40	2	164	66	0	4	220	0	142	0
San Francisco-Oakland-Hayward, CA	366	216	135	13	2	154	47	0	8	154	0	204	0
San Jose-Sunnyvale-Santa Clara, CA	366	250	110	6	0	126	44	0	5	233	0	128	0
San Juan-Carolina-Caguas, PR	366	257	82	18	9	225	32	55	8	69	18	157	59
San Luis Obispo-Paso Robles-Arroyo Grande, CA	366	177	180	8	1	156	51	0	0	247	0	85	34
Sandpoint, ID	366	337	29	0	0	81	20	0	0	0	0	317	49
Sanford, NC	363	279	84	0	0	100	43	0	0	190	0	173	0
Santa Cruz-Watsonville, CA	366	347	19	0	0	72	32	0	0	245	0	121	0
Santa Fe, NM	366	301	65	0	0	90	43	0	0	363	0	3	0
Santa Maria-Santa Barbara, CA	366	264	90	9	3	315	44	0	0	250	0	79	37
Santa Rosa, CA	366	348	18	0	0	87	32	0	0	294	0	69	3
Sault Ste. Marie, MI	299	277	21	1	0	101	31	0	0	128	0	171	0
Savannah, GA	366	304	59	3	0	143	39	0	0	126	40	200	0
Sayre, PA	358	315	43	0	0	97	38	0	1	208	0	149	0
Scottsbluff, NE	87	83	4	0	0	57	19	0	0	0	0	87	0

Metropolitan Statistical Area	Days with AQI Data	Number of Days when Air Quality was...				AQI Statistics		Number of Days when AQI Pollutant was...					
		Good	Moderate	Unhealthy for Sensitive Groups	Unhealthy, Very Unhealthy, or Hazardous	Max	Median	CO	NO_2	O_3	SO_2	$PM_{2.5}$	PM_{10}
Scranton—Wilkes-Barre—Hazleton, PA	366	290	72	4	0	129	41	0	2	240	0	124	0
Seattle-Tacoma-Bellevue, WA	366	279	84	2	1	155	42	0	46	174	0	146	0
Sebastian-Vero Beach, FL	340	316	24	0	0	84	39	0	0	340	0	0	0
Sebring, FL	363	347	16	0	0	87	33	0	0	363	0	0	0
Seneca, SC	362	324	36	2	0	133	40	0	0	287	13	62	0
Sevierville, TN	358	297	58	3	0	112	44	0	0	358	0	0	0
Seymour, IN	183	146	35	2	0	129	40	0	0	183	0	0	0
Sheboygan, WI	203	166	25	10	2	164	39	0	0	203	0	0	0
Shelton, WA	366	352	14	0	0	68	20	0	0	0	0	366	0
Sheridan, WY	366	333	32	1	0	110	38	0	0	296	0	37	33
Show Low, AZ	366	301	65	0	0	90	43	0	0	352	0	0	14
Shreveport-Bossier City, LA	366	271	95	0	0	90	42	0	0	200	0	163	3
Sierra Vista-Douglas, AZ	366	281	83	2	0	141	44	0	0	319	0	3	44
Sioux City, IA-NE-SD	366	322	42	2	0	112	36	0	1	221	0	121	23
Sioux Falls, SD	366	312	52	2	0	105	38	0	2	261	0	96	7
Somerset, KY	278	246	32	0	0	90	39	0	0	210	0	68	0
Somerset, PA	357	324	32	1	0	105	36	0	0	357	0	0	0
Sonora, CA	354	223	86	38	7	164	44	0	0	354	0	0	0
South Bend-Mishawaka, IN-MI	364	246	108	10	0	129	43	0	17	150	0	197	0
Spartanburg, SC	352	241	109	2	0	126	44	0	0	130	0	222	0
Spokane-Spokane Valley, WA	366	261	103	2	0	110	41	0	0	126	0	233	7
Springfield, IL	364	319	44	1	0	105	35	0	0	321	0	43	0
Springfield, MA	366	295	65	5	1	161	39	0	5	277	0	84	0
Springfield, MO	366	313	53	0	0	71	38	0	0	177	0	188	1
Springfield, OH	366	270	90	6	0	119	42	0	0	173	3	190	0
St. Cloud, MN	366	338	28	0	0	97	30	0	0	195	0	171	0
St. George, UT	366	286	80	0	0	87	43	0	1	352	0	13	0
St. Joseph, MO-KS	366	292	74	0	0	100	40	0	0	142	0	192	32
St. Louis, MO-IL	366	180	167	17	2	159	51	0	7	148	5	200	6
St. Marys, PA	346	321	22	3	0	126	37	0	0	346	0	0	0
State College, PA	366	290	74	2	0	122	40	0	1	261	0	104	0
Steamboat Springs, CO	352	343	9	0	0	60	15	0	0	0	0	0	352
Stockton-Lodi, CA	366	138	202	25	1	166	55	0	1	140	0	221	4
Summerville, GA	242	217	25	0	0	93	42	0	0	242	0	0	0
Syracuse, NY	366	334	30	2	0	122	35	0	0	324	0	42	0
Tahlequah, OK	269	250	19	0	0	77	38	0	0	269	0	0	0
Talladega-Sylacauga, AL	117	99	18	0	0	79	35	0	0	0	0	117	0
Tallahassee, FL	365	284	79	1	1	175	41	0	0	164	0	201	0
Tampa-St. Petersburg-Clearwater, FL	366	252	108	5	1	154	45	0	0	214	15	137	0
Taos, NM	361	359	2	0	0	54	12	0	0	0	0	361	0
Terre Haute, IN	366	236	122	7	1	153	43	0	0	121	29	216	0
Texarkana, TX-AR	273	221	52	0	0	76	36	0	0	0	0	273	0
The Dalles, OR	358	322	36	0	0	77	32	0	0	121	0	237	0
Toledo, OH	366	282	79	5	0	115	40	0	0	183	32	151	0
Topeka, KS	366	335	31	0	0	87	36	0	0	328	0	33	5
Torrington, CT	365	307	50	7	1	164	38	0	0	332	0	33	0
Traverse City, MI	170	146	18	6	0	143	38	0	0	170	0	0	0
Trenton, NJ	366	256	97	12	1	151	42	0	0	225	0	141	0
Truckee-Grass Valley, CA	366	235	86	40	5	179	44	0	0	358	0	8	0
Tucson, AZ	366	201	161	4	0	119	49	0	0	240	0	15	111
Tulsa, OK	366	233	130	2	1	164	46	0	1	208	0	157	0
Tupelo, MS	238	224	14	0	0	80	39	0	0	238	0	0	0
Tuscaloosa, AL	365	224	141	0	0	100	47	0	0	90	0	275	0
Twin Falls, ID	360	353	7	0	0	67	19	0	0	0	0	360	0
Tyler, TX	366	344	21	1	0	101	37	0	5	361	0	0	0

Metropolitan Statistical Area	Days with AQI Data	Number of Days when Air Quality was...				AQI Statistics		Number of Days when AQI Pollutant was...					
		Good	Moderate	Unhealthy for Sensitive Groups	Unhealthy, Very Unhealthy, or Hazardous	Max	Median	CO	NO_2	O_3	SO_2	$PM_{2.5}$	PM_{10}
Ukiah, CA	364	334	30	0	0	66	33	0	0	181	0	181	2
Urban Honolulu, HI	366	353	13	0	0	60	31	0	1	269	0	68	28
Utica-Rome, NY	366	338	24	4	0	108	34	0	0	268	0	98	0
Valdosta, GA	327	276	51	0	0	74	33	0	0	0	0	327	0
Vallejo-Fairfield, CA	366	278	86	2	0	105	40	0	3	204	0	159	0
Vernal, UT	366	252	103	4	7	216	47	0	1	347	0	18	0
Victoria, TX	348	328	20	0	0	90	33	0	0	348	0	0	0
Vincennes, IN	359	313	42	4	0	119	35	0	0	359	0	0	0
Vineland-Bridgeton, NJ	366	301	64	1	0	136	39	0	4	237	0	125	0
Vineyard Haven, MA	350	336	12	2	0	126	35	0	0	343	0	7	0
Virginia Beach-Norfolk-Newport News, VA-NC	366	315	48	3	0	133	37	0	25	177	4	160	0
Visalia-Porterville, CA	366	80	162	102	22	177	77	0	0	221	0	138	7
Wabash, IN	347	309	33	5	0	115	35	0	0	347	0	0	0
Waco, TX	365	339	26	0	0	74	35	0	3	322	0	40	0
Walla Walla, WA	355	333	22	0	0	83	18	0	0	0	0	355	0
Walterboro, SC	343	304	36	2	1	152	34	0	0	196	0	147	0
Warner Robins, GA	352	306	44	2	0	107	33	0	0	0	0	352	0
Warren, PA	366	352	14	0	0	99	9	0	0	0	366	0	0
Washington Court House, OH	353	310	42	1	0	108	37	0	0	353	0	0	0
Washington, IN	354	351	3	0	0	82	4	0	0	0	354	0	0
Washington, NC	344	343	1	0	0	62	0	0	0	0	344	0	0
Washington-Arlington-Alexandria, DC-VA-MD-WV	366	176	174	16	0	133	51	0	19	165	0	182	0
Waterloo-Cedar Falls, IA	366	267	98	1	0	118	42	0	0	116	0	250	0
Watertown, SD	366	335	31	0	0	73	24	0	0	0	0	206	160
Watertown-Fort Atkinson, WI	201	176	21	4	0	108	40	0	0	201	0	0	0
Watertown-Fort Drum, NY	332	307	23	2	0	122	34	0	0	332	0	0	0
Wausau, WI	192	176	16	0	0	100	35	0	0	192	0	0	0
Weatherford, OK	360	357	3	0	0	64	15	0	0	0	0	0	360
Weirton-Steubenville, WV-OH	366	185	174	7	0	112	50	0	0	104	24	235	3
Wenatchee, WA	366	330	36	0	0	79	22	0	0	0	0	366	0
Wheeling, WV-OH	366	241	122	3	0	108	44	0	12	178	0	174	2
Whitewater-Elkhorn, WI	188	161	22	5	0	115	38	0	0	188	0	0	0
Wichita, KS	366	309	56	0	1	195	41	0	10	269	0	48	39
Williamsport, PA	366	335	30	1	0	108	34	0	0	353	0	0	13
Williston, ND	366	346	18	2	0	106	31	0	0	282	25	42	17
Wilmington, NC	361	331	30	0	0	90	31	0	0	172	16	173	0
Wilmington, OH	211	154	53	4	0	112	44	0	0	211	0	0	0
Winchester, VA-WV	358	302	56	0	0	90	37	0	0	175	0	183	0
Winona, MN	46	43	3	0	0	68	19	0	0	0	0	46	0
Winston-Salem, NC	366	228	135	3	0	119	45	0	5	177	0	184	0
Worcester, MA-CT	366	307	54	4	1	154	38	0	11	283	0	72	0
Yakima, WA	366	257	97	8	4	186	33	0	0	0	0	363	3
York-Hanover, PA	366	236	125	5	0	133	44	0	5	207	0	154	0
Youngstown-Warren-Boardman, OH-PA	366	239	121	6	0	143	44	0	0	191	0	174	1
Yuba City, CA	366	166	168	32	0	147	53	0	0	200	0	166	0
Yuma, AZ	366	228	124	12	2	419	46	0	0	203	0	45	118

Notes: *Dashes indicates data was not available; The Air Quality Index (AQI) is an index for reporting daily air quality. It tells you how clean or polluted your air is, and what associated health concerns you should be aware of. The AQI focuses on health effects that can happen within a few hours or days after breathing polluted air. EPA uses the AQI for six major air pollutants regulated by the Clean Air Act: CO (carbon monoxide), NO_2 (nitrogen dioxide), O_3 (ground-level ozone), SO_2 (sulfur dioxide), PM_{10} (particulate matter 10 - particles with diameters of 10 micrometers or less), $PM_{2.5}$ (particulate matter 2.5 - particles with diameters of 2.5 micrometers or less). For each of these pollutants, EPA has established national air quality standards to protect against harmful health effects.*

The AQI runs from 0 to 500. The higher the AQI value, the greater the level of air pollution and the greater the health danger. For example, an AQI value of 50 represents good air quality and little potential to affect public health, while an AQI value over 300 represents hazardous air quality. An AQI value of 100 generally corresponds to the national air quality standard for the pollutant, which is the level EPA has set to protect public health. So, AQI values below 100 are generally thought of as satisfactory. When AQI values are above 100, air quality is considered to be unhealthy-at first for certain sensitive groups of people, then for everyone as AQI values get higher. Each category corresponds to a different level of health concern. For example, when the AQI for a pollutant is between 51 and 100, the health concern is "Moderate." Here are the six levels of health concern and what they mean:

"Good" The AQI value for your community is between 0 and 50. Air quality is considered satisfactory and air pollution poses little or no risk.

"Moderate" The AQI for your community is between 51 and 100. Air quality is acceptable; however, for some pollutants there may be a moderate health concern for a very small number of individuals. For example, people who are unusually sensitive to ozone may experience respiratory symptoms.

"Unhealthy for Sensitive Groups" Certain groups of people are particularly sensitive to the harmful effects of certain air pollutants. This means they are likely to be affected at lower levels than the general public. For example, children and adults who are active outdoors and people with respiratory disease are at greater risk from exposure to ozone, while people with heart disease are at greater risk from carbon monoxide. Some people may be sensitive to more than one pollutant. When AQI values are between 101 and 150, members of sensitive groups may experience health effects. The general public is not likely to be affected when the AQI is in this range.

"Unhealthy" AQI values are between 151 and 200. Everyone may begin to experience health effects. Members of sensitive groups may experience more serious health effects.

"Very Unhealthy" AQI values between 201 and 300 trigger a health alert, meaning everyone may experience more serious health effects.

"Hazardous" AQI values over 300 trigger health warnings of emergency conditions. The entire population is more likely to be affected.

***Source:** U.S. Environmental Protection Agency, Office of Air and Radiation, Air Quality Index Report, 2016*

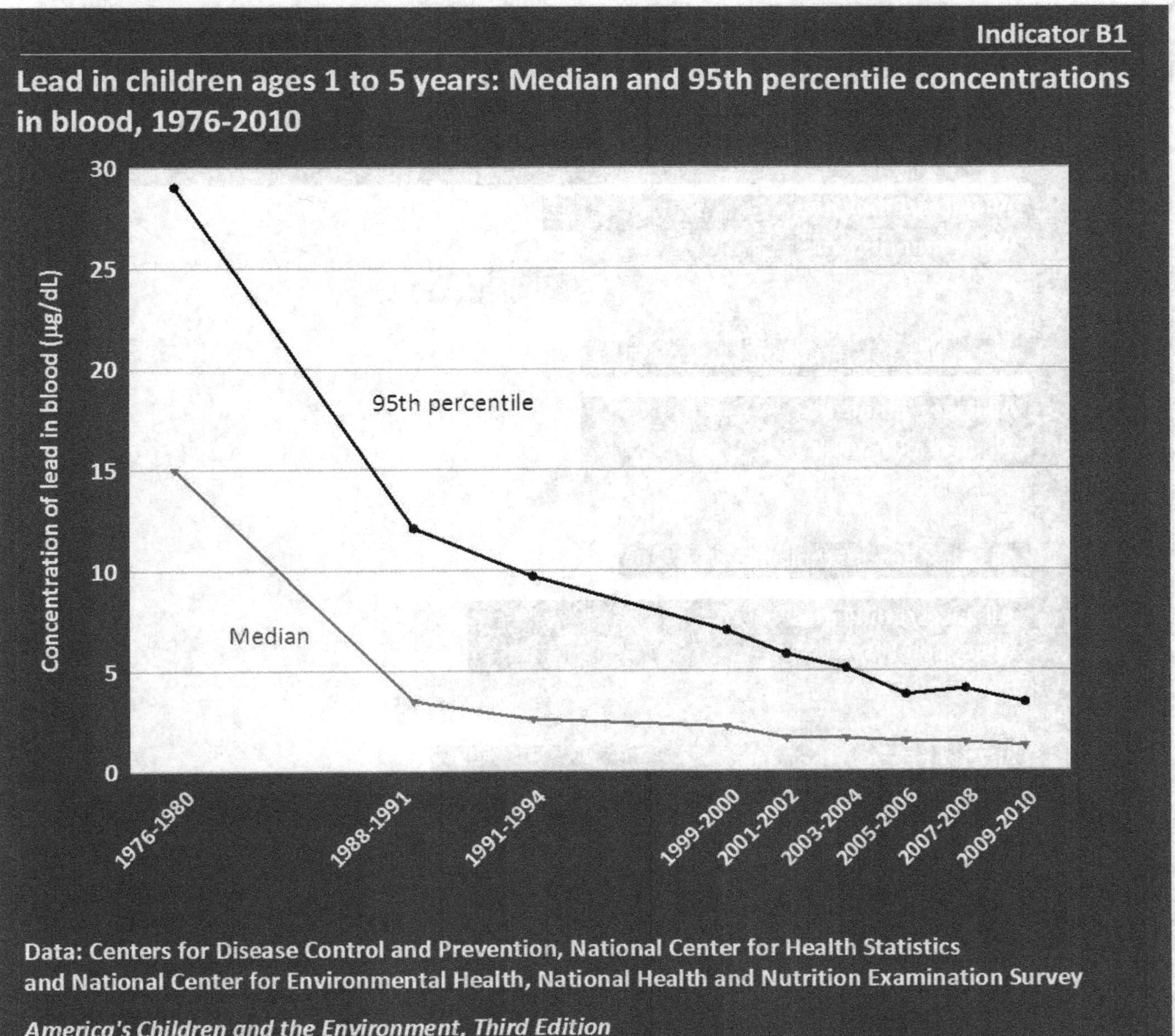
Indicator B1
Lead in children ages 1 to 5 years: Median and 95th percentile concentrations in blood, 1976-2010
Concentration of lead in blood (µg/dL)
30
25
20
15
10
5
0
95th percentile
Median
1976-1980
1988-1991
1991-1994
1999-2000
2001-2002
2003-2004
2005-2006
2007-2008
2009-2010
Data: Centers for Disease Control and Prevention, National Center for Health Statistics and National Center for Environmental Health, National Health and Nutrition Examination Survey
America's Children and the Environment, Third Edition

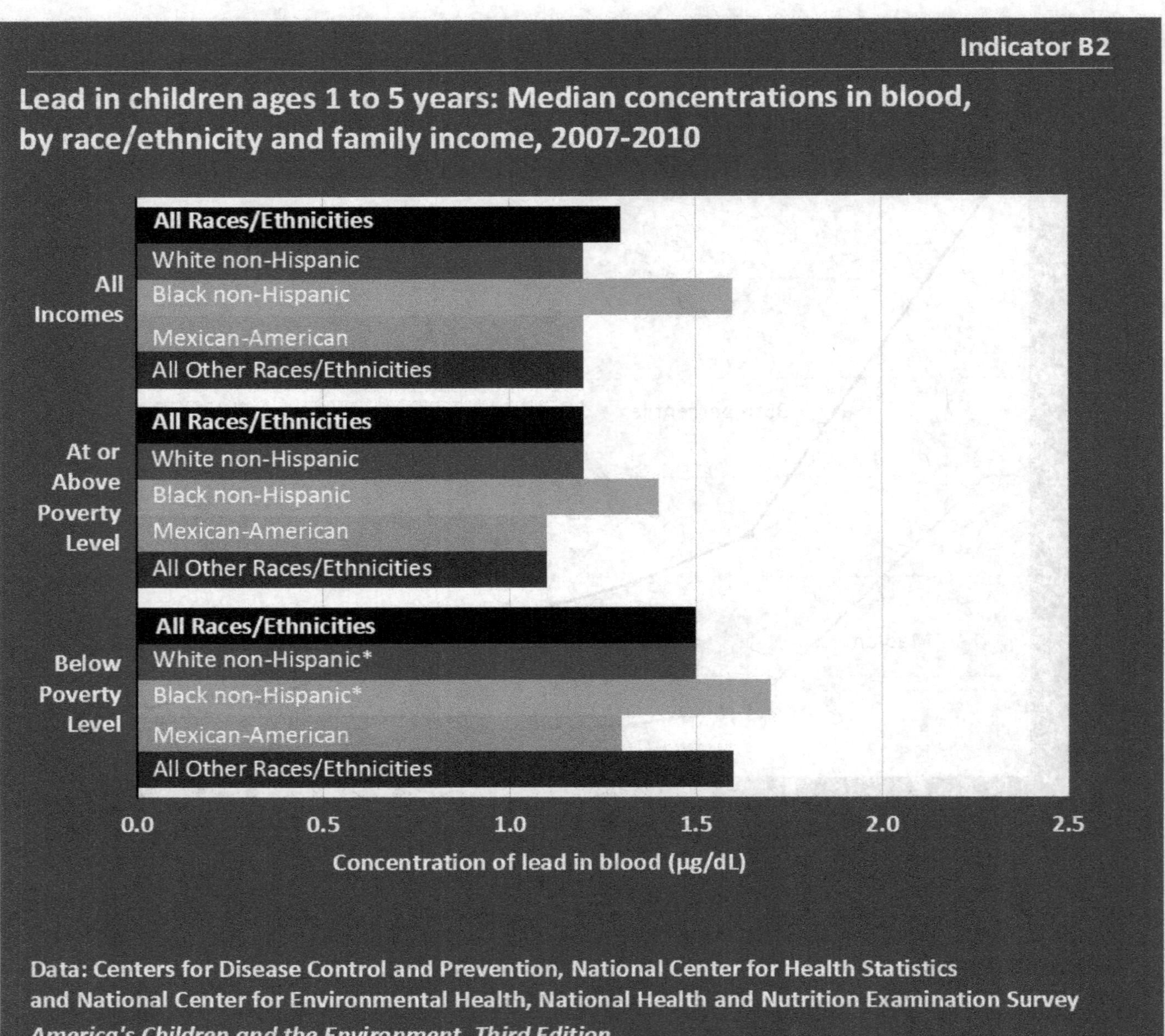
Indicator B2
Lead in children ages 1 to 5 years: Median concentrations in blood, by race/ethnicity and family income, 2007-2010
All Incomes
All Races/Ethnicities
White non-Hispanic
Black non-Hispanic
Mexican-American
All Other Races/Ethnicities
At or Above Poverty Level
All Races/Ethnicities
White non-Hispanic
Black non-Hispanic
Mexican-American
All Other Races/Ethnicities
Below Poverty Level
All Races/Ethnicities
White non-Hispanic*
Black non-Hispanic*
Mexican-American
All Other Races/Ethnicities
0.0
0.5
1.0
1.5
2.0
2.5
Concentration of lead in blood (μg/dL)
Data: Centers for Disease Control and Prevention, National Center for Health Statistics and National Center for Environmental Health, National Health and Nutrition Examination Survey
America's Children and the Environment, Third Edition

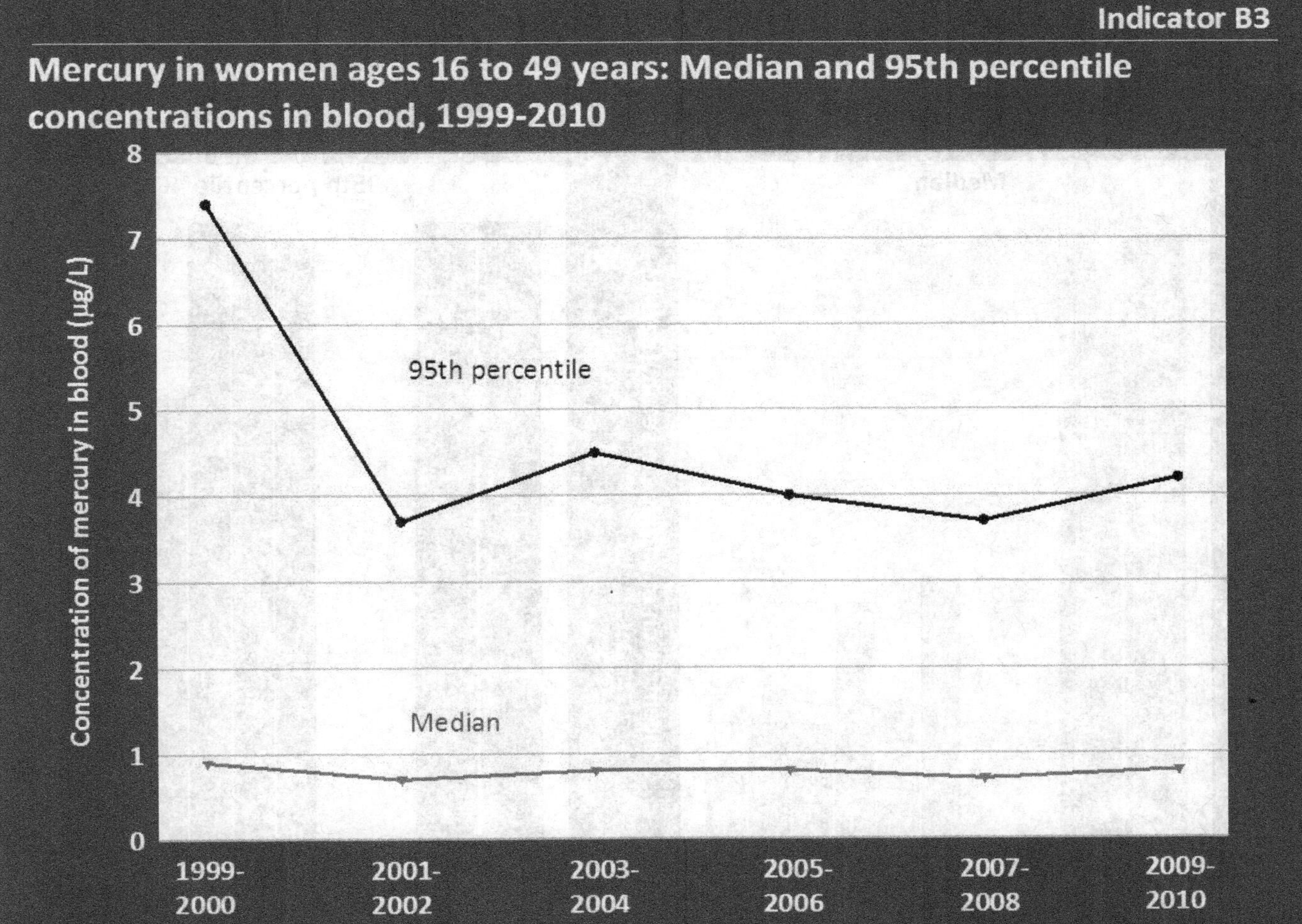

Data: Centers for Disease Control and Prevention, National Center for Health Statistics and National Center for Environmental Health, National Health and Nutrition Examination Survey

Note: To reflect exposures to women who are pregnant or may become pregnant, the estimates are adjusted for the probability (by age and race/ethnicity) that a woman gives birth.

America's Children and the Environment, Third Edition

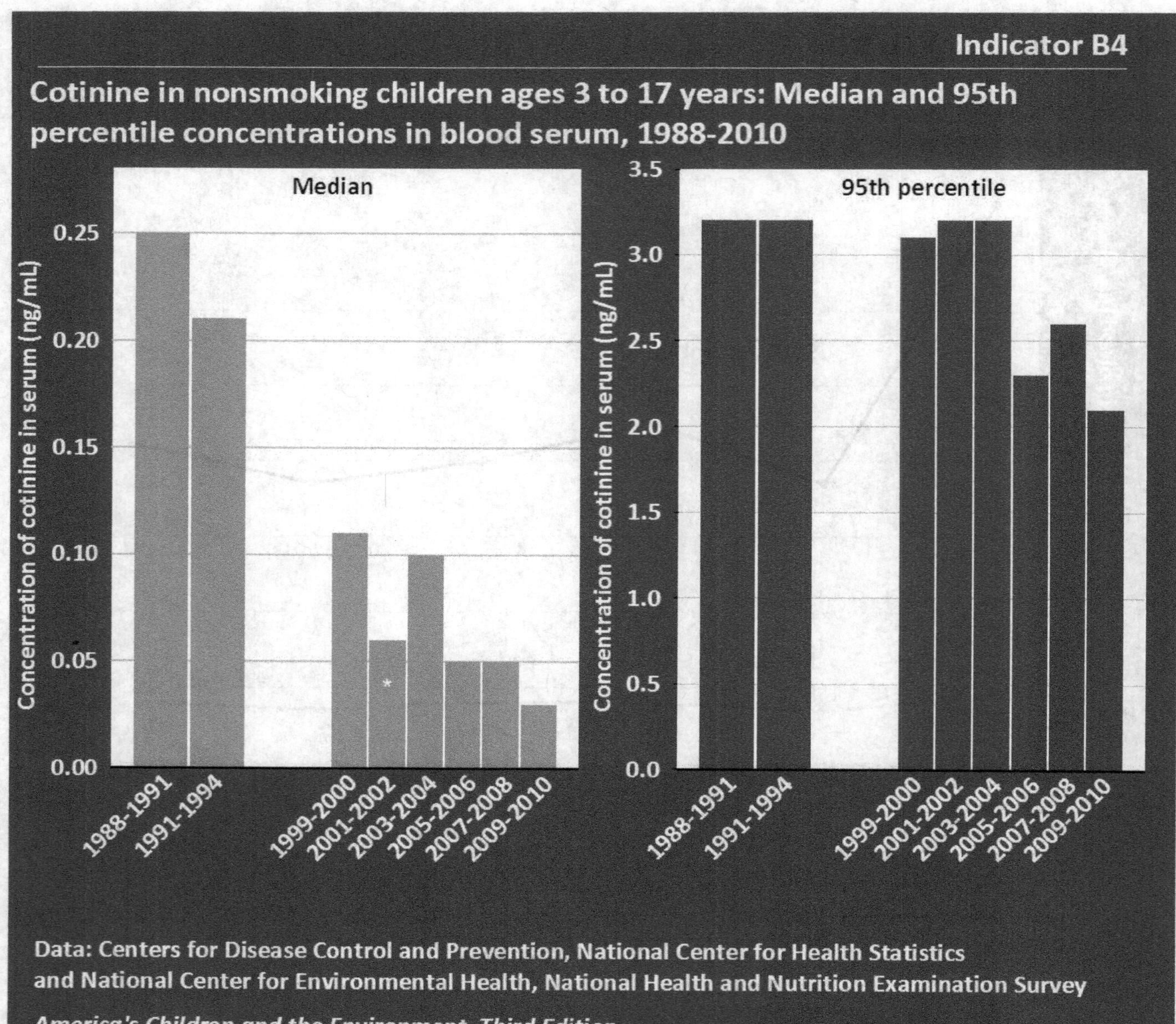
Indicator B4
Cotinine in nonsmoking children ages 3 to 17 years: Median and 95th percentile concentrations in blood serum, 1988-2010
Median
95th percentile
Concentration of cotinine in serum (ng/mL)
0.00
0.05
0.10
0.15
0.20
0.25
0.0
0.5
1.0
1.5
2.0
2.5
3.0
3.5
1988-1991
1991-1994
1999-2000
2001-2002
2003-2004
2005-2006
2007-2008
2009-2010
*
Data: Centers for Disease Control and Prevention, National Center for Health Statistics and National Center for Environmental Health, National Health and Nutrition Examination Survey
America's Children and the Environment, Third Edition

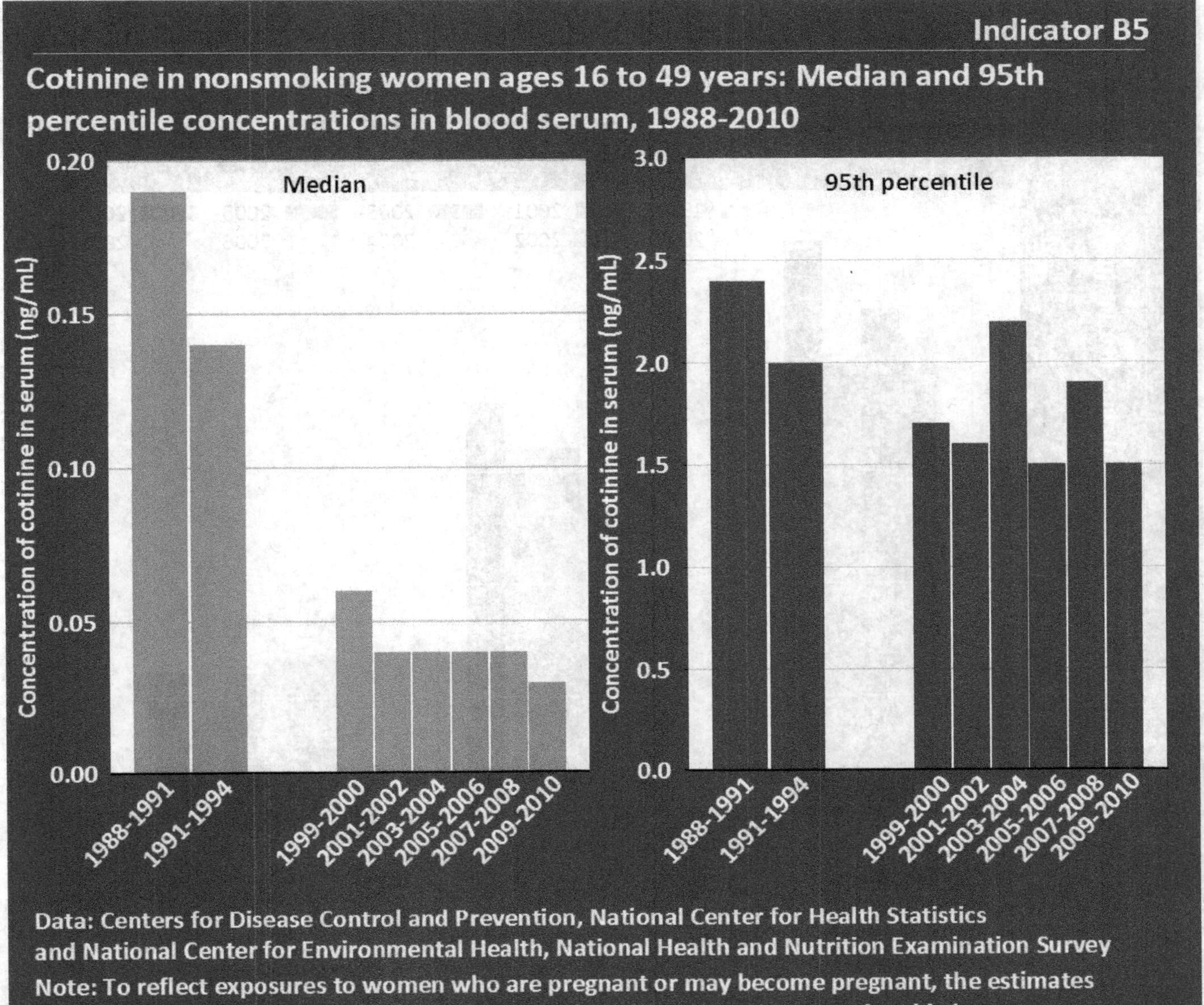
Indicator B5
Cotinine in nonsmoking women ages 16 to 49 years: Median and 95th percentile concentrations in blood serum, 1988-2010
Median
95th percentile
Concentration of cotinine in serum (ng/mL)
0.20
0.15
0.10
0.05
0.00
3.0
2.5
2.0
1.5
1.0
0.5
0.0
1988-1991
1991-1994
1999-2000
2001-2002
2003-2004
2005-2006
2007-2008
2009-2010
Data: Centers for Disease Control and Prevention, National Center for Health Statistics and National Center for Environmental Health, National Health and Nutrition Examination Survey
Note: To reflect exposures to women who are pregnant or may become pregnant, the estimates are adjusted for the probability (by age and race/ethnicity) that a woman gives birth.
America's Children and the Environment, Third Edition

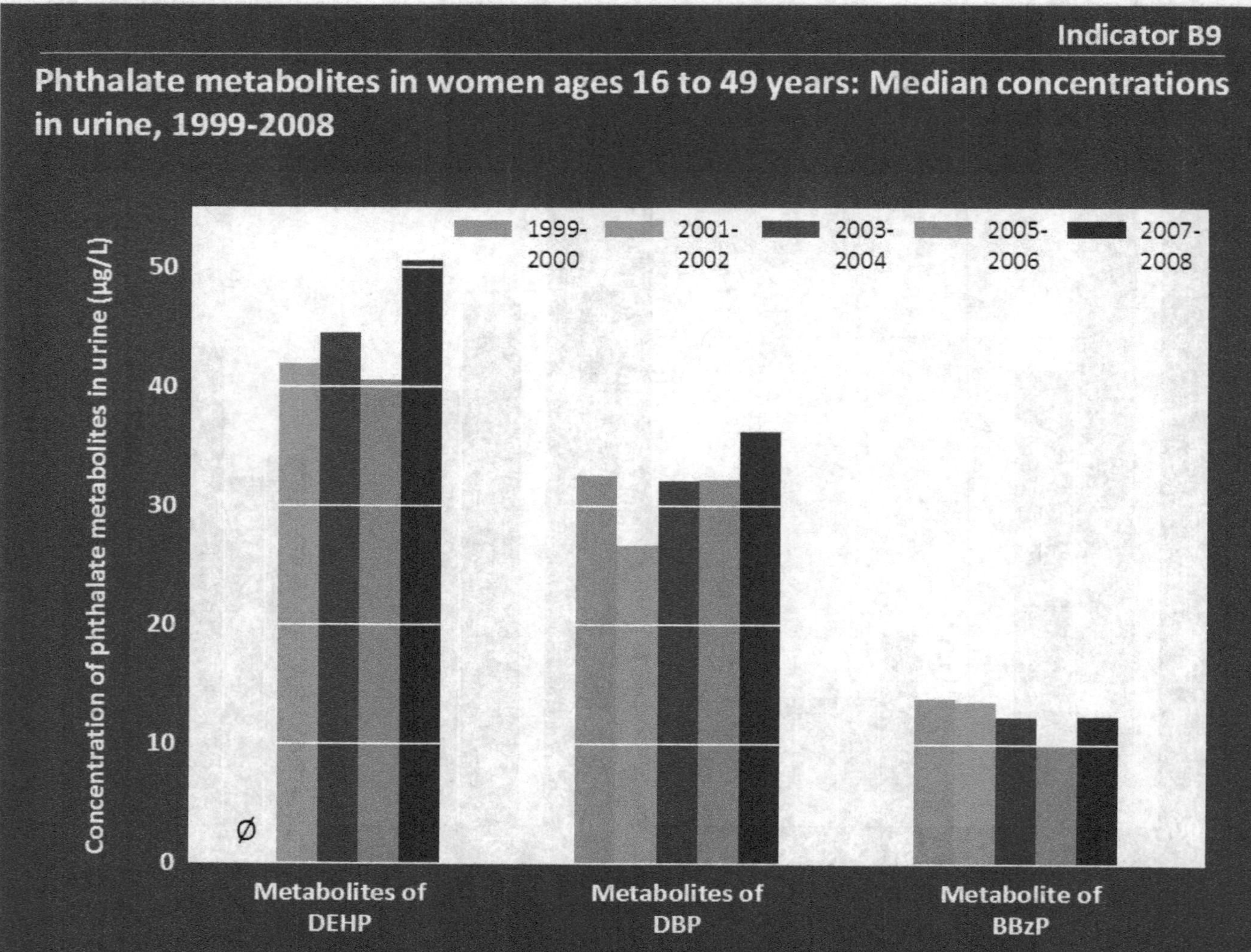
Indicator B9
Phthalate metabolites in women ages 16 to 49 years: Median concentrations in urine, 1999-2008
1999-2000
2001-2002
2003-2004
2005-2006
2007-2008
Concentration of phthalate metabolites in urine (µg/L)
50
40
30
20
10
0
Ø
Metabolites of DEHP
Metabolites of DBP
Metabolite of BBzP
Data: Centers for Disease Control and Prevention, National Center for Health Statistics and National Center for Environmental Health, National Health and Nutrition Examination Survey
Note: To reflect exposures to women who are pregnant or may become pregnant, the estimates are adjusted for the probability (by age and race/ethnicity) that a woman gives birth.
America's Children and the Environment, Third Edition

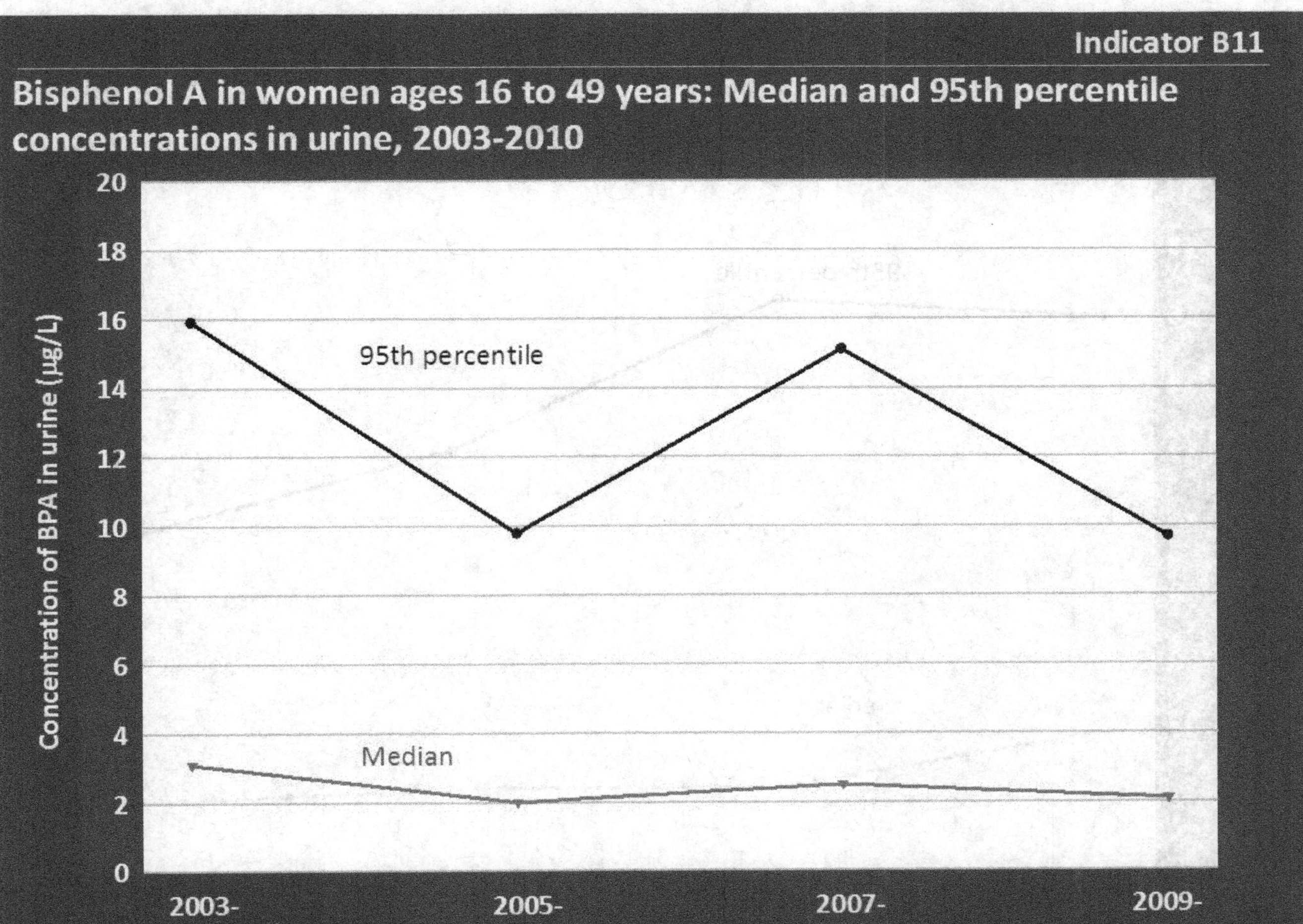

Data: Centers for Disease Control and Prevention, National Center for Health Statistics and National Center for Environmental Health, National Health and Nutrition Examination Survey

Note: To reflect exposures to women who are pregnant or may become pregnant, the estimates are adjusted for the probability (by age and race/ethnicity) that a woman gives birth.

America's Children and the Environment, Third Edition

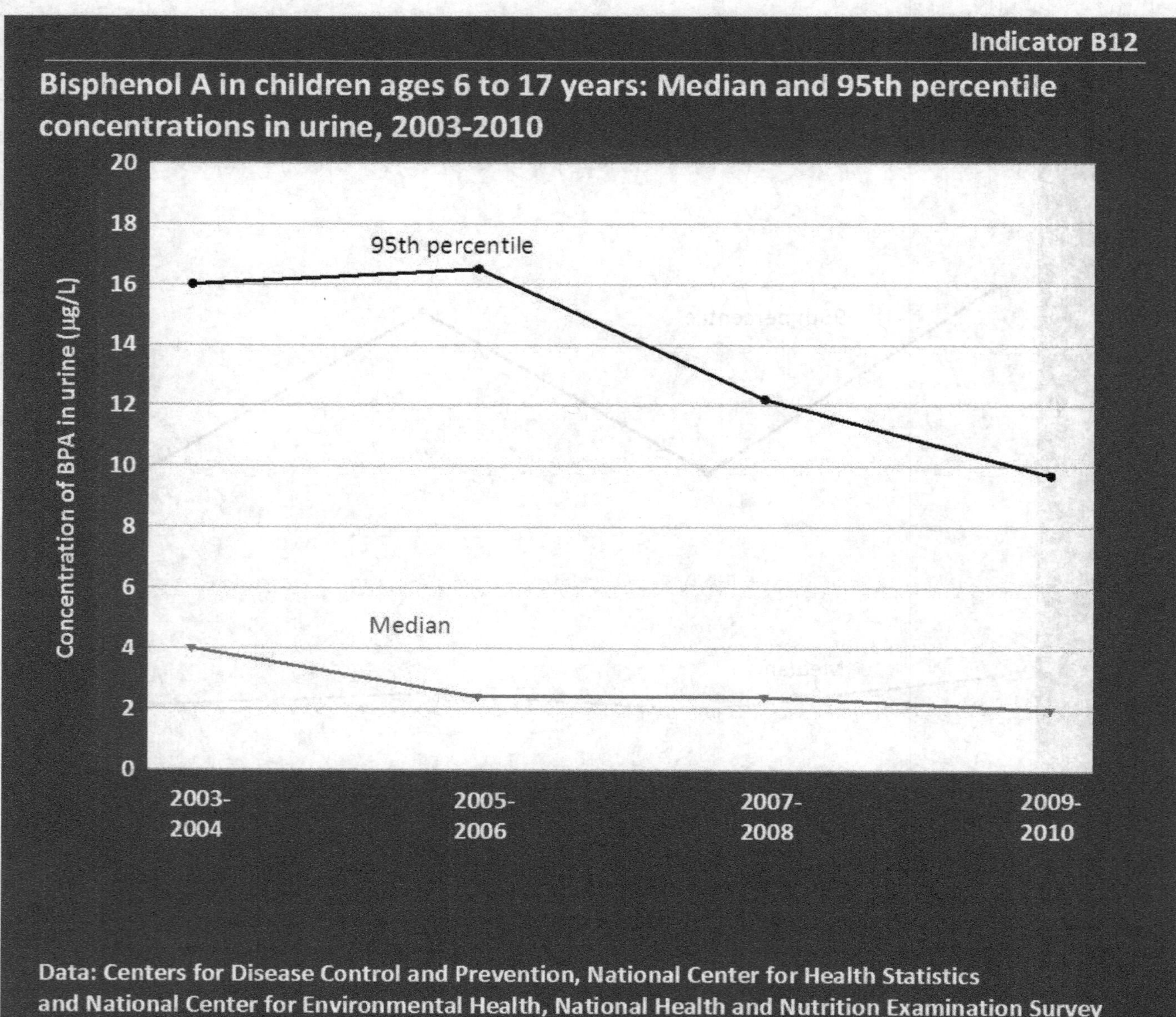
Indicator B12
Bisphenol A in children ages 6 to 17 years: Median and 95th percentile concentrations in urine, 2003-2010
Concentration of BPA in urine (µg/L)
20
18
16
14
12
10
8
6
4
2
0
95th percentile
Median
2003-2004
2005-2006
2007-2008
2009-2010
Data: Centers for Disease Control and Prevention, National Center for Health Statistics and National Center for Environmental Health, National Health and Nutrition Examination Survey
America's Children and the Environment, Third Edition

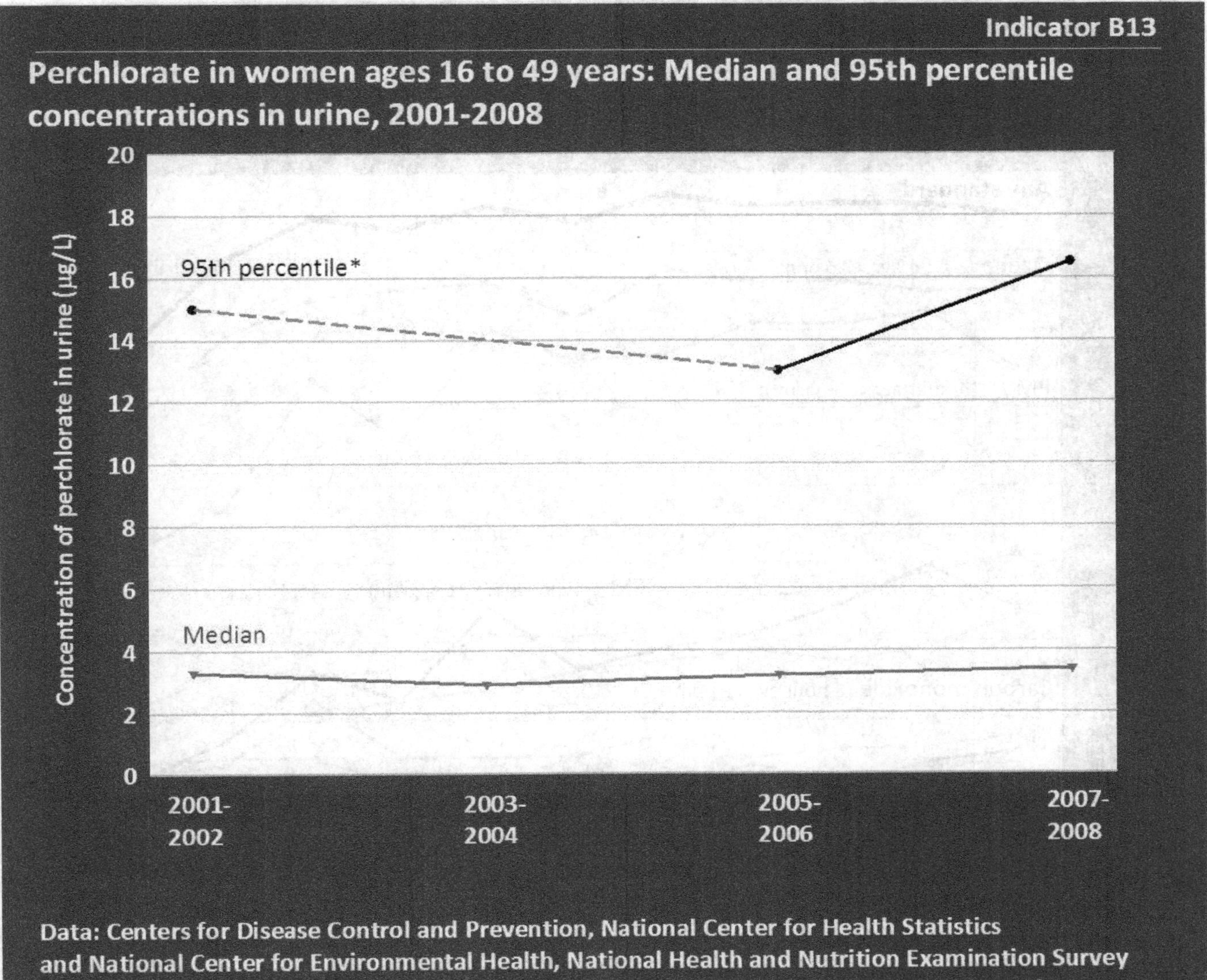
Indicator B13
Perchlorate in women ages 16 to 49 years: Median and 95th percentile concentrations in urine, 2001-2008
Concentration of perchlorate in urine (µg/L)
20
18
16
14
12
10
8
6
4
2
0
95th percentile*
Median
2001-2002
2003-2004
2005-2006
2007-2008
Data: Centers for Disease Control and Prevention, National Center for Health Statistics and National Center for Environmental Health, National Health and Nutrition Examination Survey
Note: To reflect exposures to women who are pregnant or may become pregnant, the estimates are adjusted for the probability (by age and race/ethnicity) that a woman gives birth.
America's Children and the Environment, Third Edition

Indicator E1

Percentage of children ages 0 to 17 years living in counties with pollutant concentrations above the levels of the current air quality standards, 1999-2009

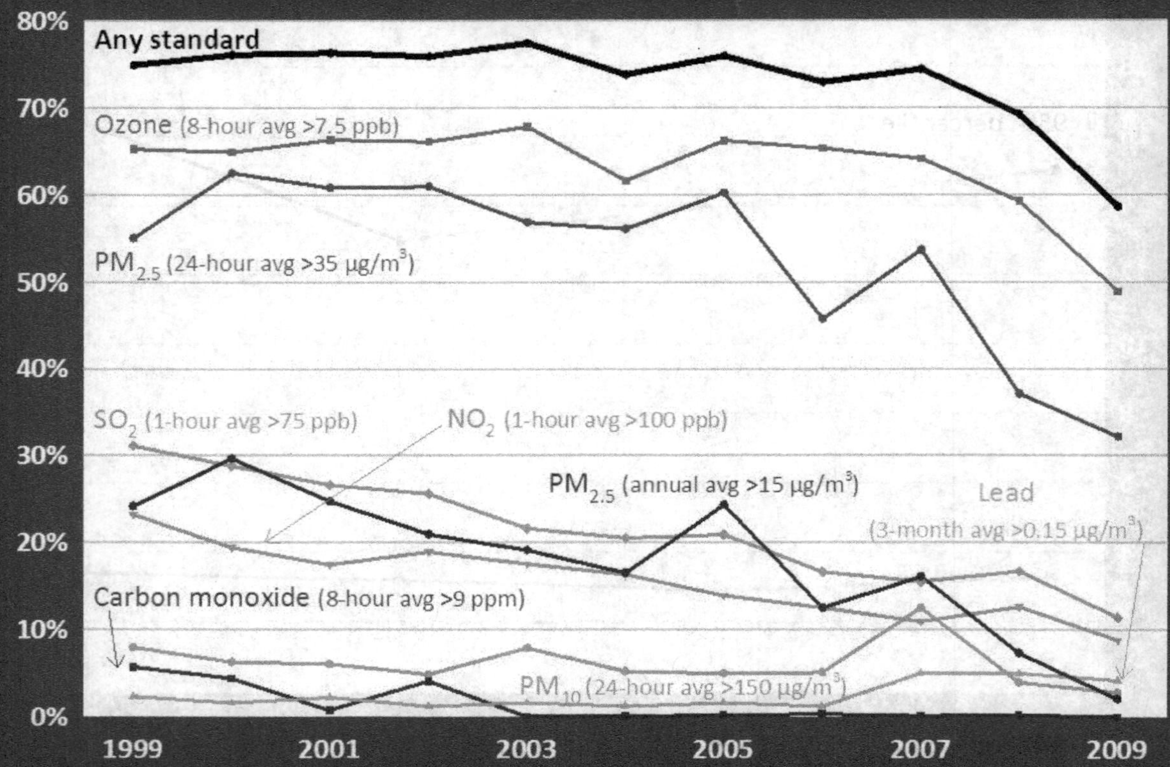

Data: U.S. Environmental Protection Agency, Office of Air and Radiation, Air Quality System

Note: EPA periodically reviews air quality standards and may change them based on updated scientific findings. Measuring concentrations above the level of a standard is not equivalent to violating the standard. The level of a standard may be exceeded on multiple days before the exceedance is considered a violation of the standard. See text for additional discussion.

America's Children and the Environment, Third Edition

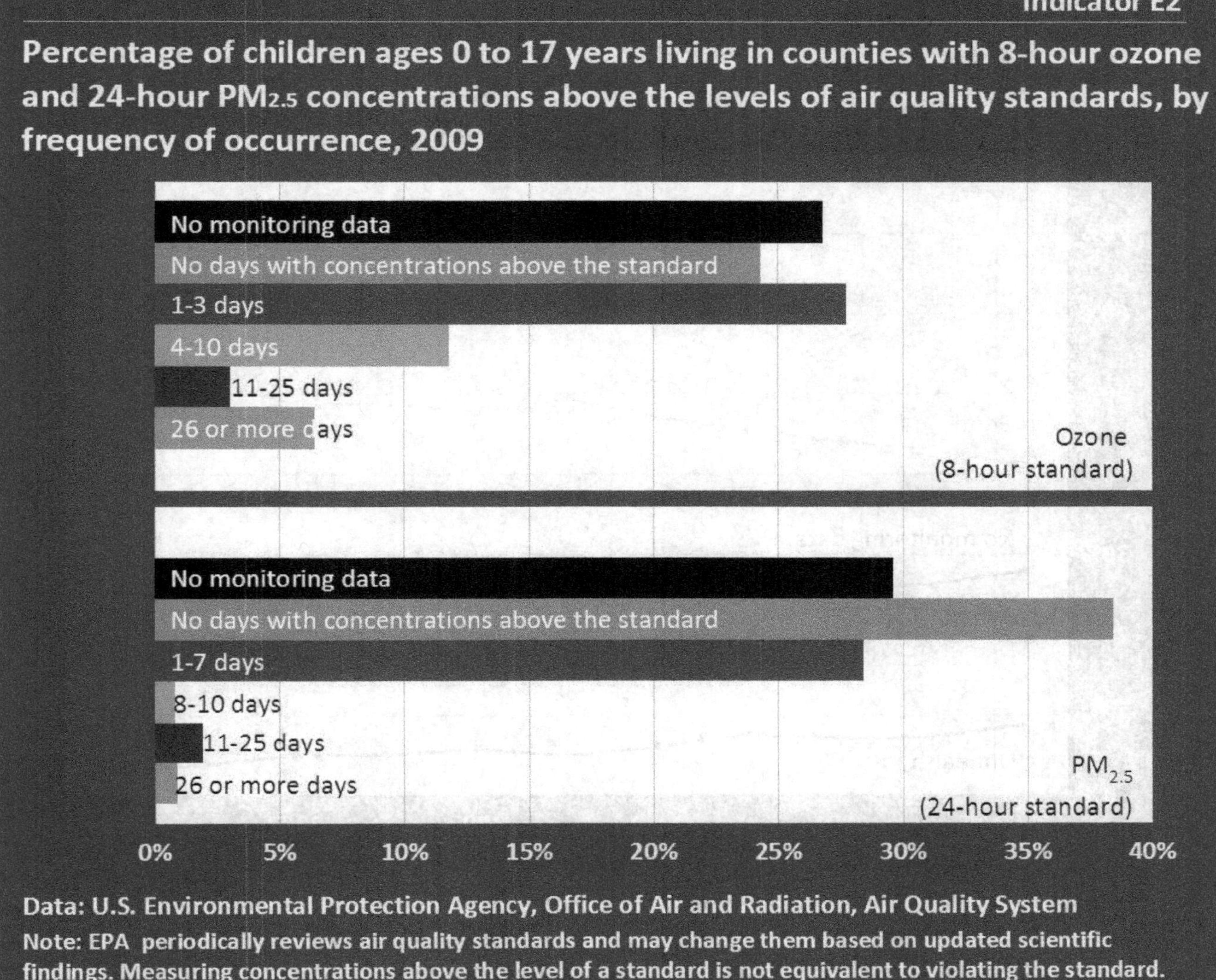
Indicator E2
Percentage of children ages 0 to 17 years living in counties with 8-hour ozone and 24-hour PM2.5 concentrations above the levels of air quality standards, by frequency of occurrence, 2009
No monitoring data
No days with concentrations above the standard
1-3 days
4-10 days
11-25 days
26 or more days
Ozone
(8-hour standard)
No monitoring data
No days with concentrations above the standard
1-7 days
8-10 days
11-25 days
26 or more days
PM2.5
(24-hour standard)
0%
5%
10%
15%
20%
25%
30%
35%
40%
Data: U.S. Environmental Protection Agency, Office of Air and Radiation, Air Quality System
Note: EPA periodically reviews air quality standards and may change them based on updated scientific findings. Measuring concentrations above the level of a standard is not equivalent to violating the standard. The level of a standard may be exceeded on multiple days before the exceedance is considered a violation of the standard. See text for additional discussion.
America's Children and the Environment, Third Edition

Percentage of days with good, moderate, or unhealthy air quality for children ages 0 to 17 years, 1999-2009

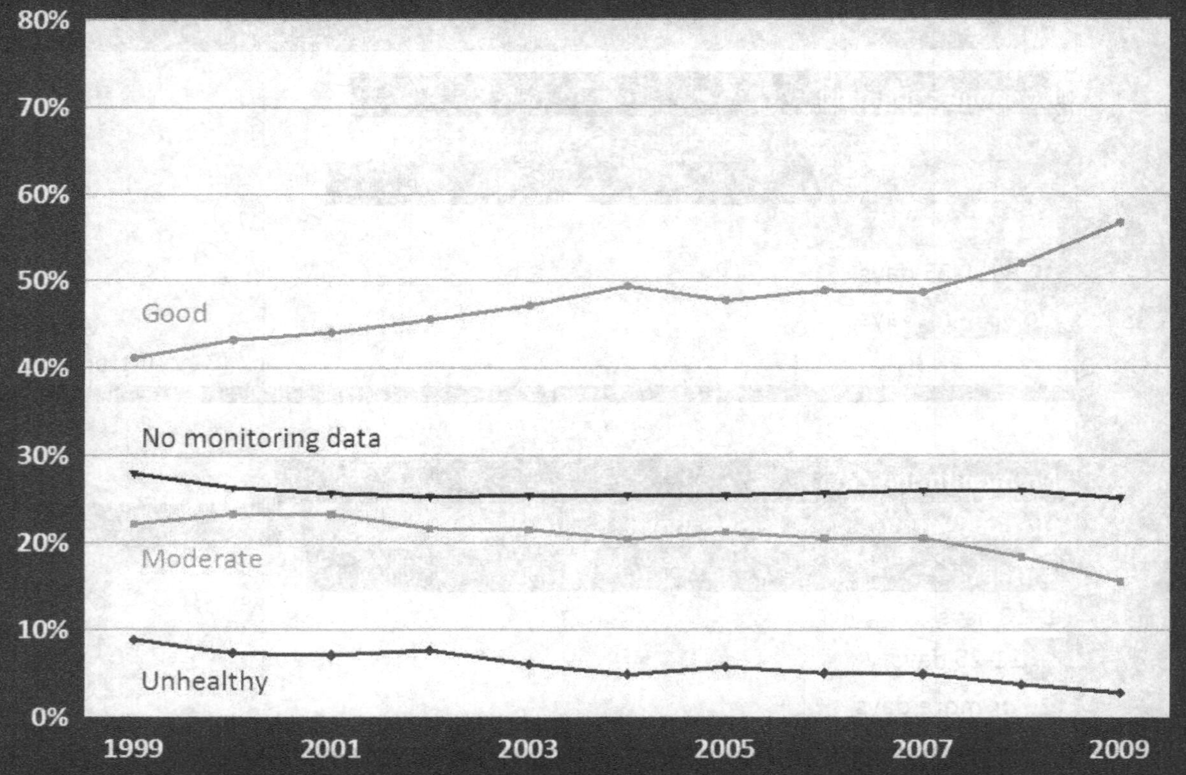

Data: U.S. Environmental Protection Agency, Office of Air and Radiation, Air Quality System

Note: Good, moderate, and unhealthy air quality are defined using EPA's Air Quality Index (AQI). The health information that supports EPA's periodic reviews of the air quality standards informs decisions on the AQI breakpoints and may change based on updated scientific findings. See text for additional discussion.

America's Children and the Environment, Third Edition

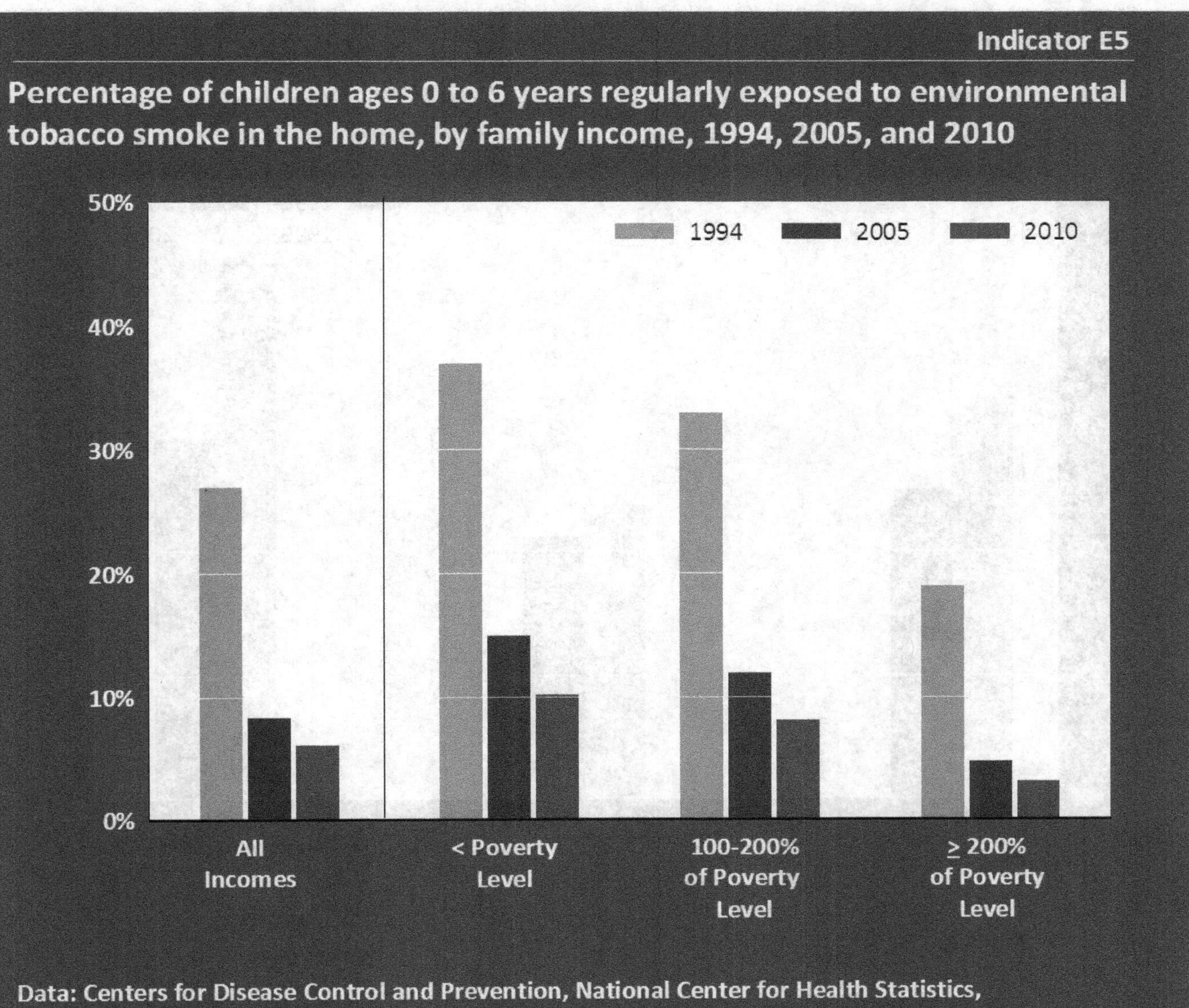
Indicator E5
Percentage of children ages 0 to 6 years regularly exposed to environmental tobacco smoke in the home, by family income, 1994, 2005, and 2010
50%
40%
30%
20%
10%
0%
1994
2005
2010
All Incomes
< Poverty Level
100-200% of Poverty Level
≥ 200% of Poverty Level
Data: Centers for Disease Control and Prevention, National Center for Health Statistics, National Health Interview Survey
America's Children and the Environment, Third Edition

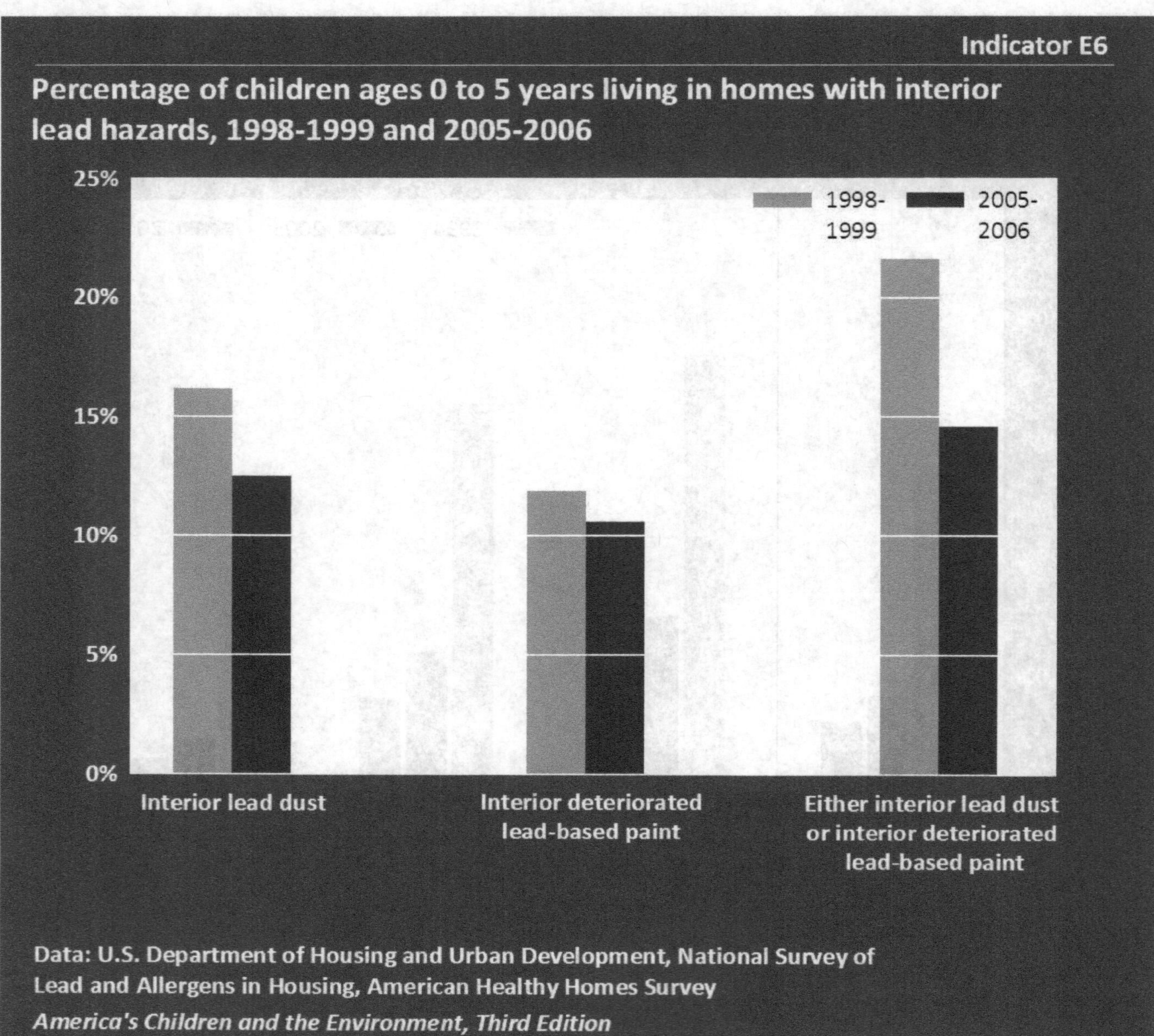
Indicator E6
Percentage of children ages 0 to 5 years living in homes with interior lead hazards, 1998-1999 and 2005-2006
25%
20%
15%
10%
5%
0%
1998-1999
2005-2006
Interior lead dust
Interior deteriorated lead-based paint
Either interior lead dust or interior deteriorated lead-based paint
Data: U.S. Department of Housing and Urban Development, National Survey of Lead and Allergens in Housing, American Healthy Homes Survey
America's Children and the Environment, Third Edition

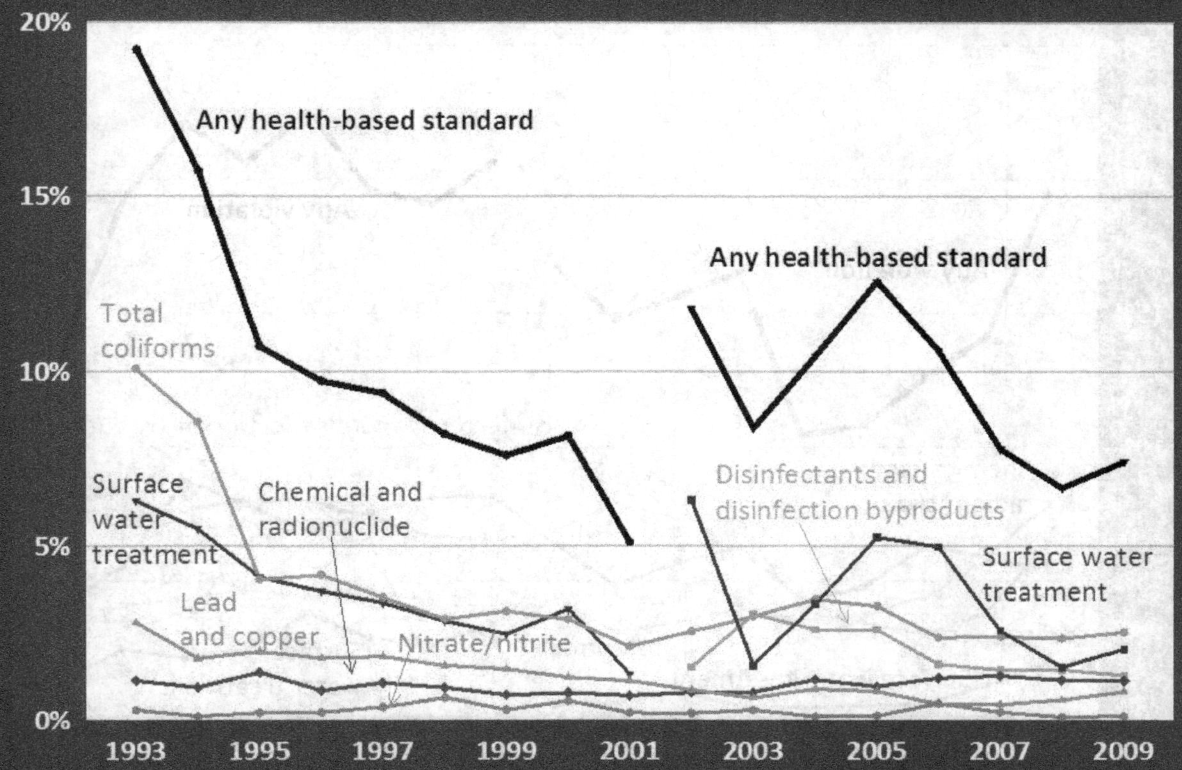

Data: U.S. Environmental Protection Agency, Office of Water, Safe Drinking Water Information System, Federal Version

Note: Breaks in lines for "Any health-based standard" and "Surface water treatment" reflect substantial regulatory changes implemented in 2002.

America's Children and the Environment, Third Edition

Indicator E8

Estimated percentage of children ages 0 to 17 years served by community water systems with violations of drinking water monitoring and reporting requirements, 1993-2009

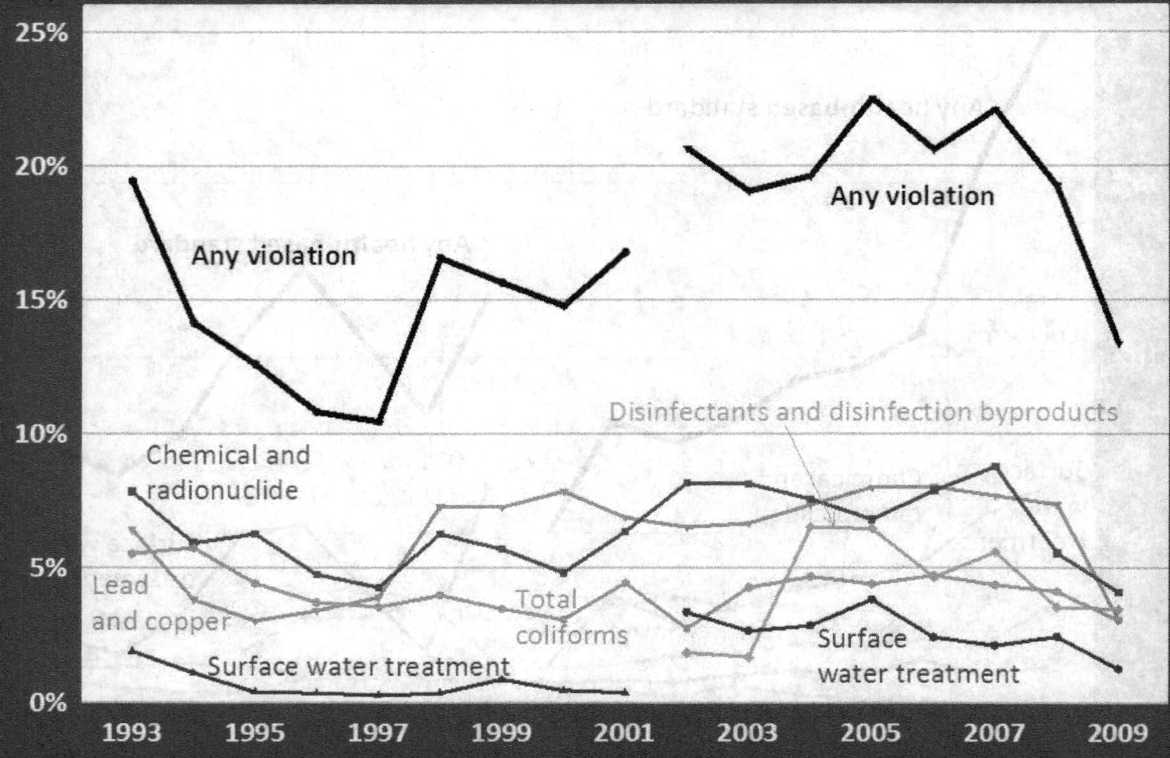

Data: U.S. Environmental Protection Agency, Office of Water, Safe Drinking Water Information System, Federal Version

Note: Breaks in lines for "Any violation" and "Surface water treatment" reflect substantial regulatory changes implemented in 2002.

America's Children and the Environment, Third Edition

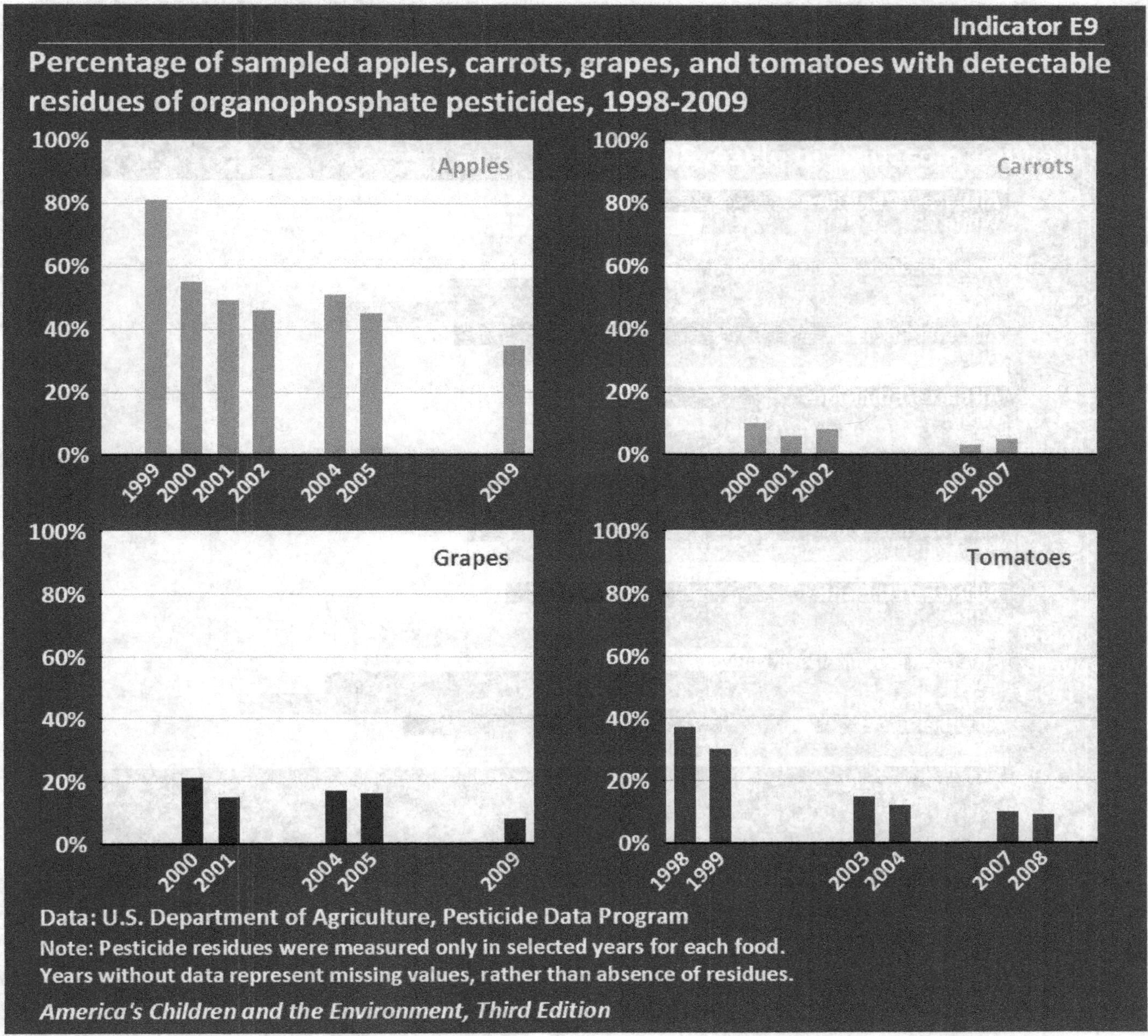
Indicator E9
Percentage of sampled apples, carrots, grapes, and tomatoes with detectable residues of organophosphate pesticides, 1998-2009
Apples
Carrots
Grapes
Tomatoes
100%
80%
60%
40%
20%
0%
1999
2000
2001
2002
2004
2005
2009
2006
2007
1998
2003
2008
Data: U.S. Department of Agriculture, Pesticide Data Program
Note: Pesticide residues were measured only in selected years for each food.
Years without data represent missing values, rather than absence of residues.
America's Children and the Environment, Third Edition

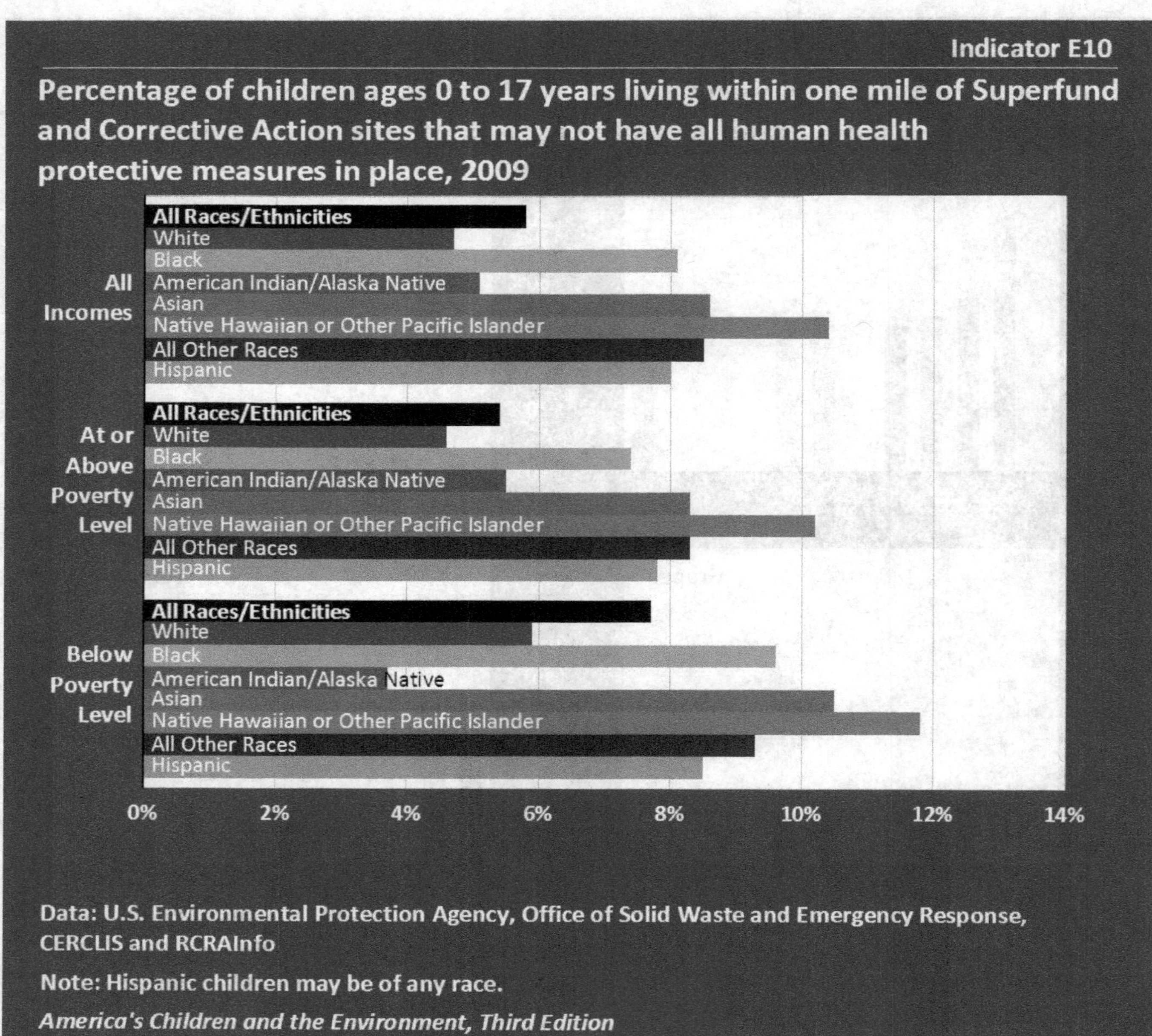
Indicator E10
Percentage of children ages 0 to 17 years living within one mile of Superfund and Corrective Action sites that may not have all human health protective measures in place, 2009
All Incomes
At or Above Poverty Level
Below Poverty Level
All Races/Ethnicities
White
Black
American Indian/Alaska Native
Asian
Native Hawaiian or Other Pacific Islander
All Other Races
Hispanic
0%
2%
4%
6%
8%
10%
12%
14%
Data: U.S. Environmental Protection Agency, Office of Solid Waste and Emergency Response, CERCLIS and RCRAInfo
Note: Hispanic children may be of any race.
America's Children and the Environment, Third Edition

Indicator E11

Distribution by race/ethnicity and family income of children living near selected contaminated lands* in 2009, compared with the distribution by race/ethnicity and income of children in the general U.S. population

All Incomes

Below Poverty Level

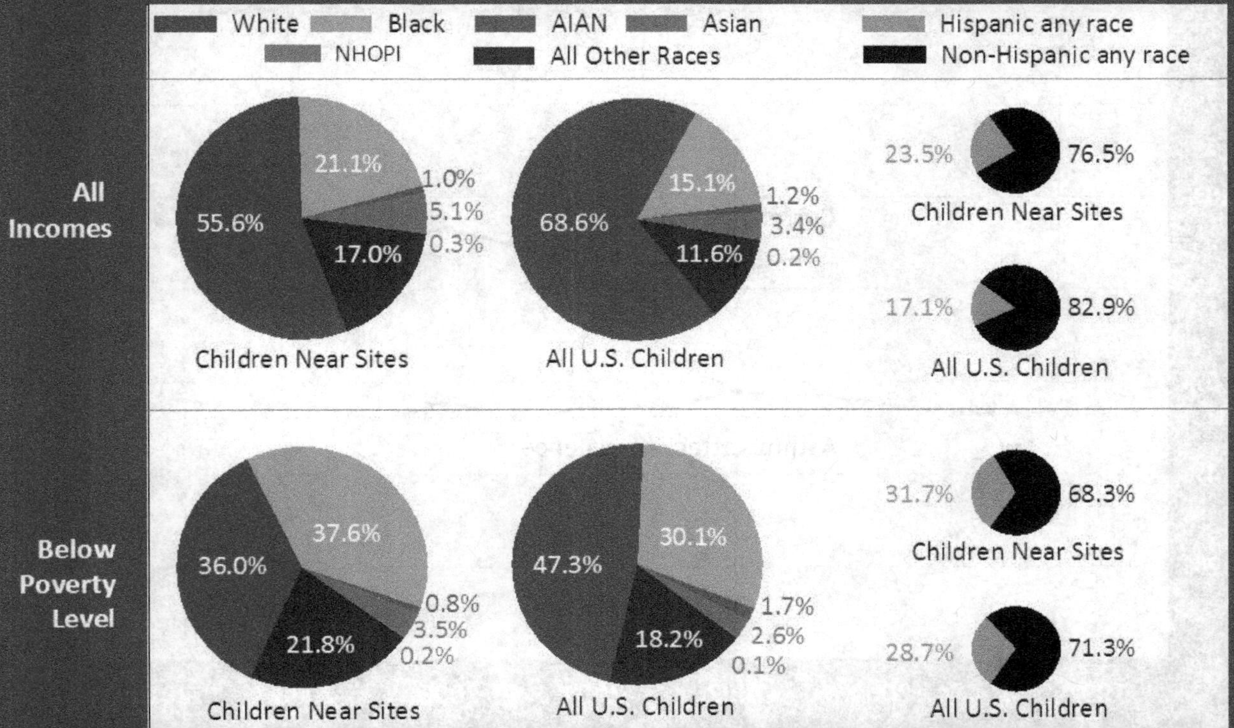

Data: U.S. EPA, Office of Solid Waste and Emergency Response, CERCLIS and RCRAInfo

Note: AIAN = American Indian/Alaska Native. NHOPI = Native Hawaiian or Other Pacific Islander. Hispanic children may be of any race.

* Within one mile of Superfund and Corrective Action sites that may not have all human health protective measures in place.

America's Children and the Environment, Third Edition

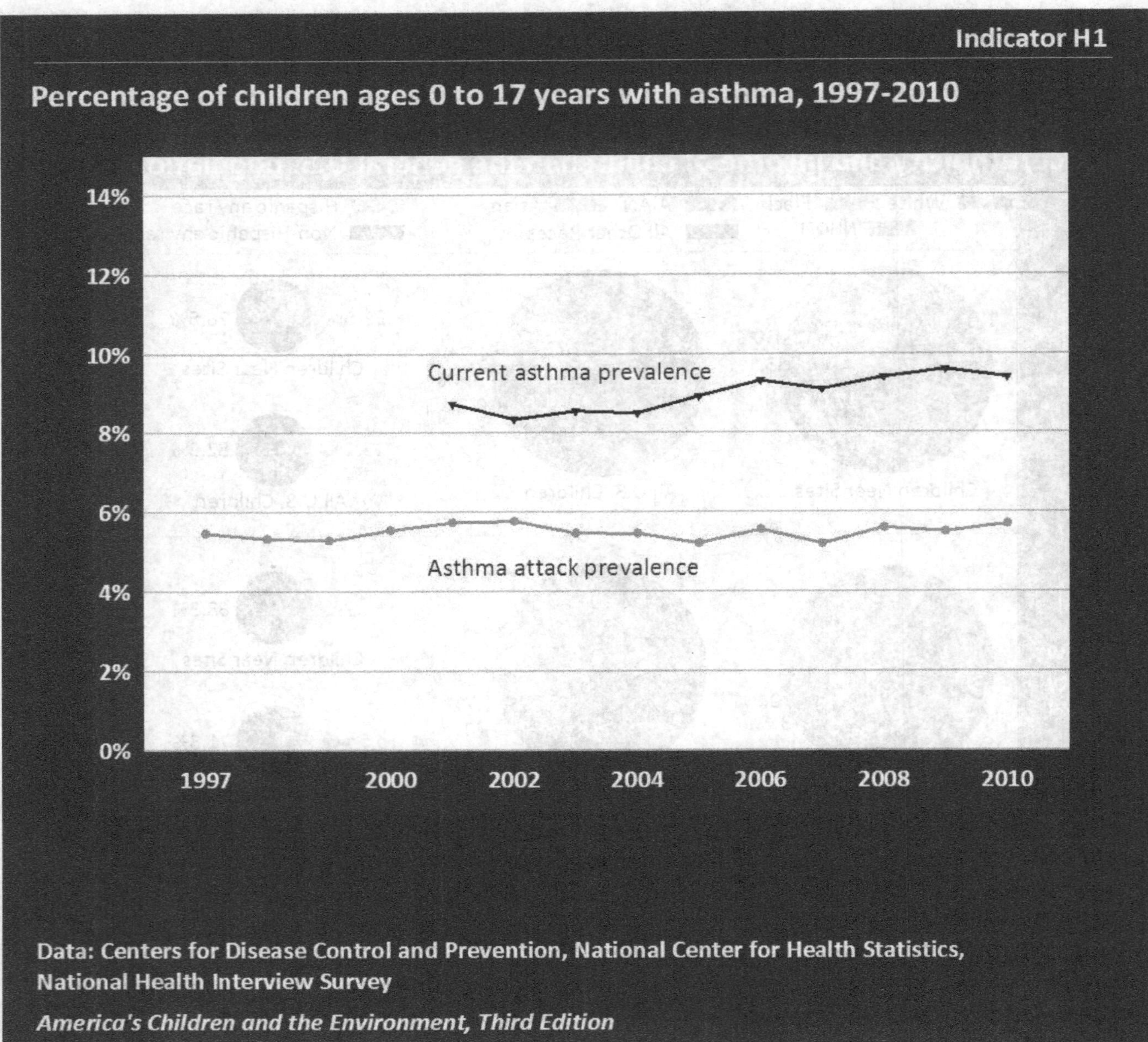
Indicator H1
Percentage of children ages 0 to 17 years with asthma, 1997-2010
14%
12%
10%
8%
6%
4%
2%
0%
Current asthma prevalence
Asthma attack prevalence
1997
2000
2002
2004
2006
2008
2010
Data: Centers for Disease Control and Prevention, National Center for Health Statistics, National Health Interview Survey
America's Children and the Environment, Third Edition

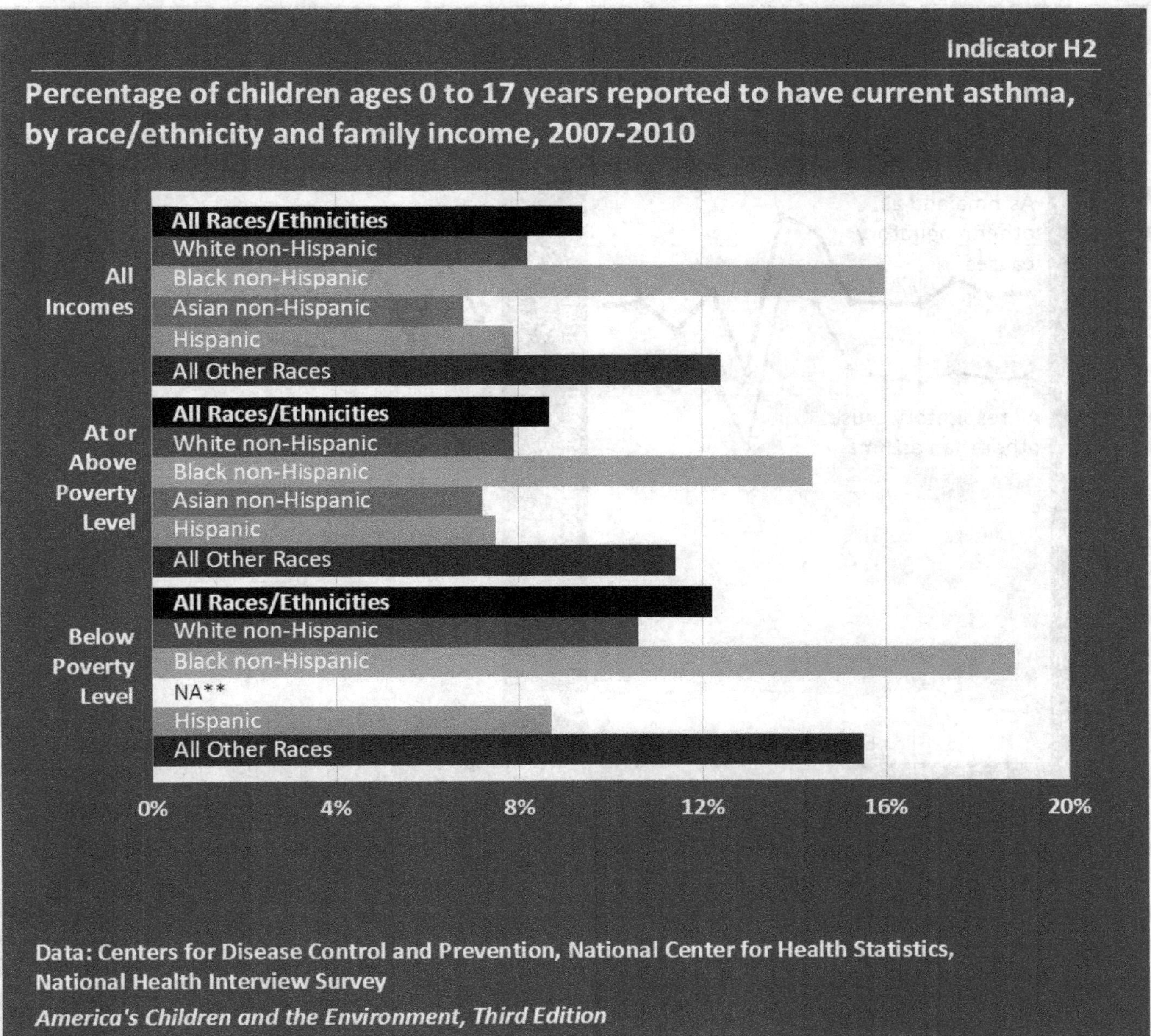
Indicator H2
Percentage of children ages 0 to 17 years reported to have current asthma, by race/ethnicity and family income, 2007-2010
All Incomes
All Races/Ethnicities
White non-Hispanic
Black non-Hispanic
Asian non-Hispanic
Hispanic
All Other Races
At or Above Poverty Level
All Races/Ethnicities
White non-Hispanic
Black non-Hispanic
Asian non-Hispanic
Hispanic
All Other Races
Below Poverty Level
All Races/Ethnicities
White non-Hispanic
Black non-Hispanic
NA**
Hispanic
All Other Races
0%
4%
8%
12%
16%
20%
Data: Centers for Disease Control and Prevention, National Center for Health Statistics, National Health Interview Survey
America's Children and the Environment, Third Edition

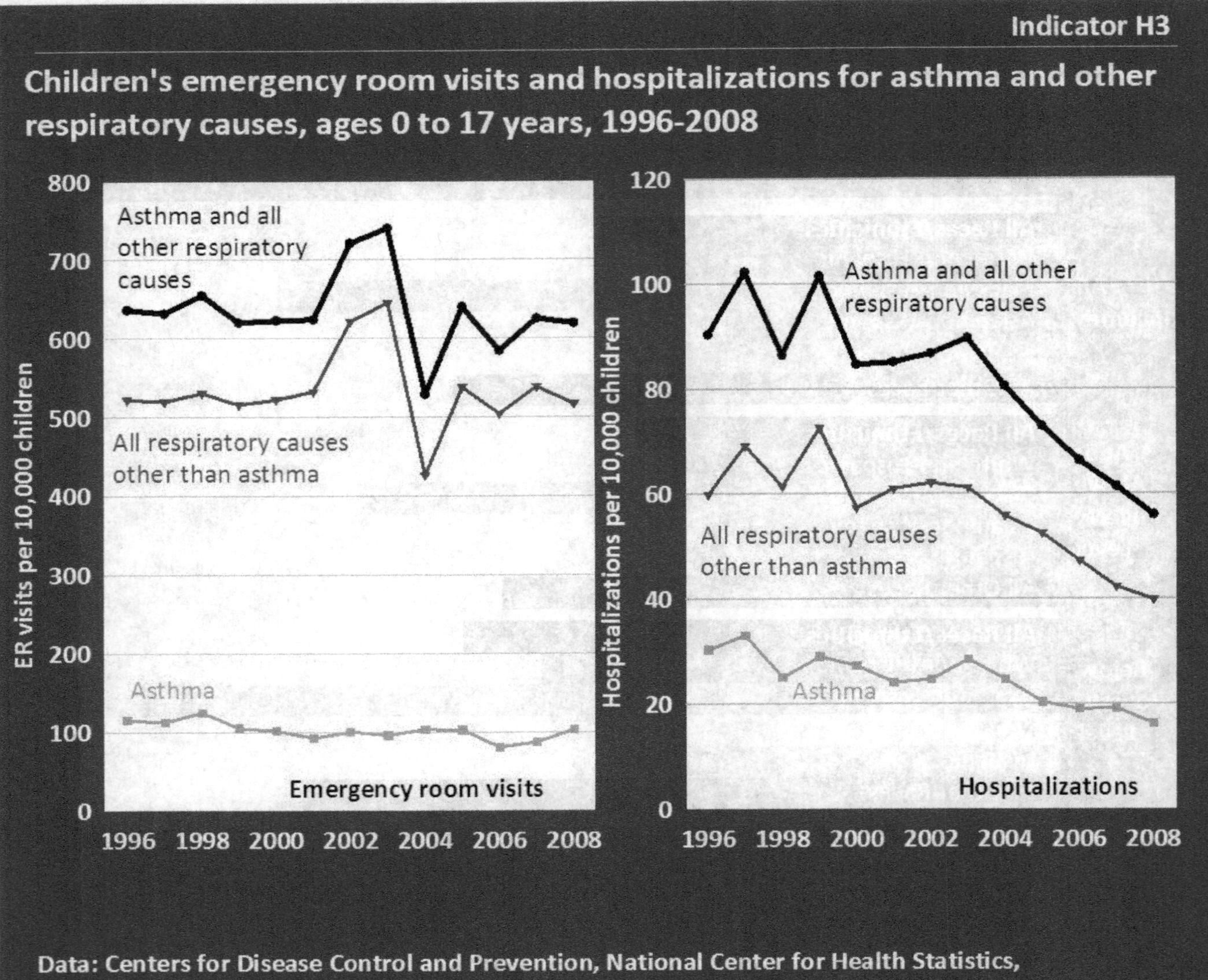
Indicator H3
Children's emergency room visits and hospitalizations for asthma and other respiratory causes, ages 0 to 17 years, 1996-2008
ER visits per 10,000 children
800
700
600
500
400
300
200
100
0
Asthma and all other respiratory causes
All respiratory causes other than asthma
Asthma
Emergency room visits
1996 1998 2000 2002 2004 2006 2008
Hospitalizations per 10,000 children
120
100
80
60
40
20
0
Asthma and all other respiratory causes
All respiratory causes other than asthma
Asthma
Hospitalizations
1996 1998 2000 2002 2004 2006 2008
Data: Centers for Disease Control and Prevention, National Center for Health Statistics, National Hospital Ambulatory Medical Care Survey (emergency room visits) and National Hospital Discharge Survey (hospitalizations)
America's Children and the Environment, Third Edition

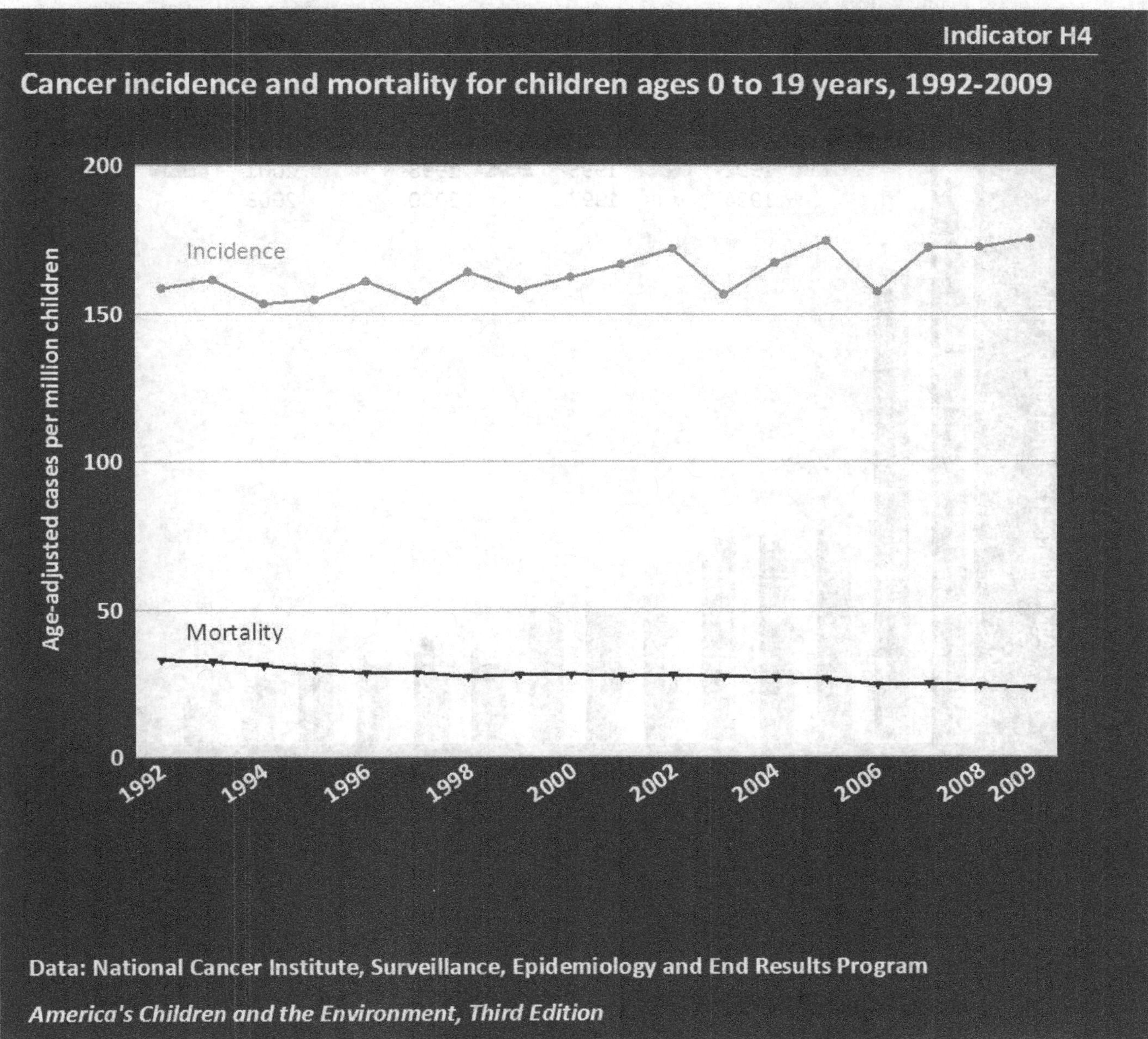
Indicator H4
Cancer incidence and mortality for children ages 0 to 19 years, 1992-2009
Age-adjusted cases per million children
200
150
100
50
0
Incidence
Mortality
1992
1994
1996
1998
2000
2002
2004
2006
2008
2009
Data: National Cancer Institute, Surveillance, Epidemiology and End Results Program
America's Children and the Environment, Third Edition

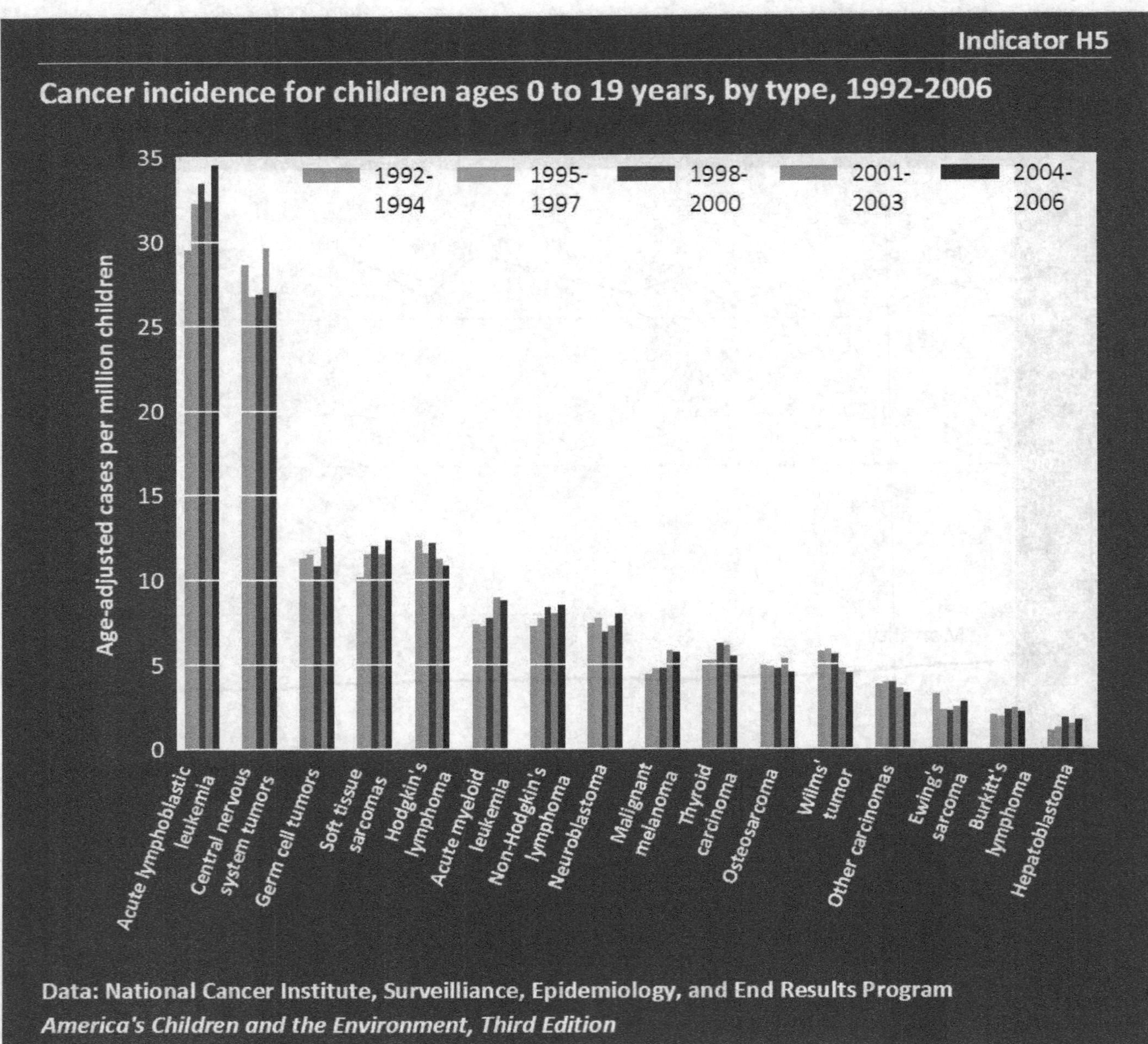
Indicator H5
Cancer incidence for children ages 0 to 19 years, by type, 1992-2006
1992-1994
1995-1997
1998-2000
2001-2003
2004-2006
Age-adjusted cases per million children
35
30
25
20
15
10
5
0
Acute lymphoblastic leukemia
Central nervous system tumors
Germ cell tumors
Soft tissue sarcomas
Hodgkin's lymphoma
Acute myeloid leukemia
Non-Hodgkin's lymphoma
Neuroblastoma
Malignant melanoma
Thyroid carcinoma
Osteosarcoma
Wilms' tumor
Other carcinomas
Ewing's sarcoma
Burkitt's lymphoma
Hepatoblastoma
Data: National Cancer Institute, Surveilliance, Epidemiology, and End Results Program
America's Children and the Environment, Third Edition

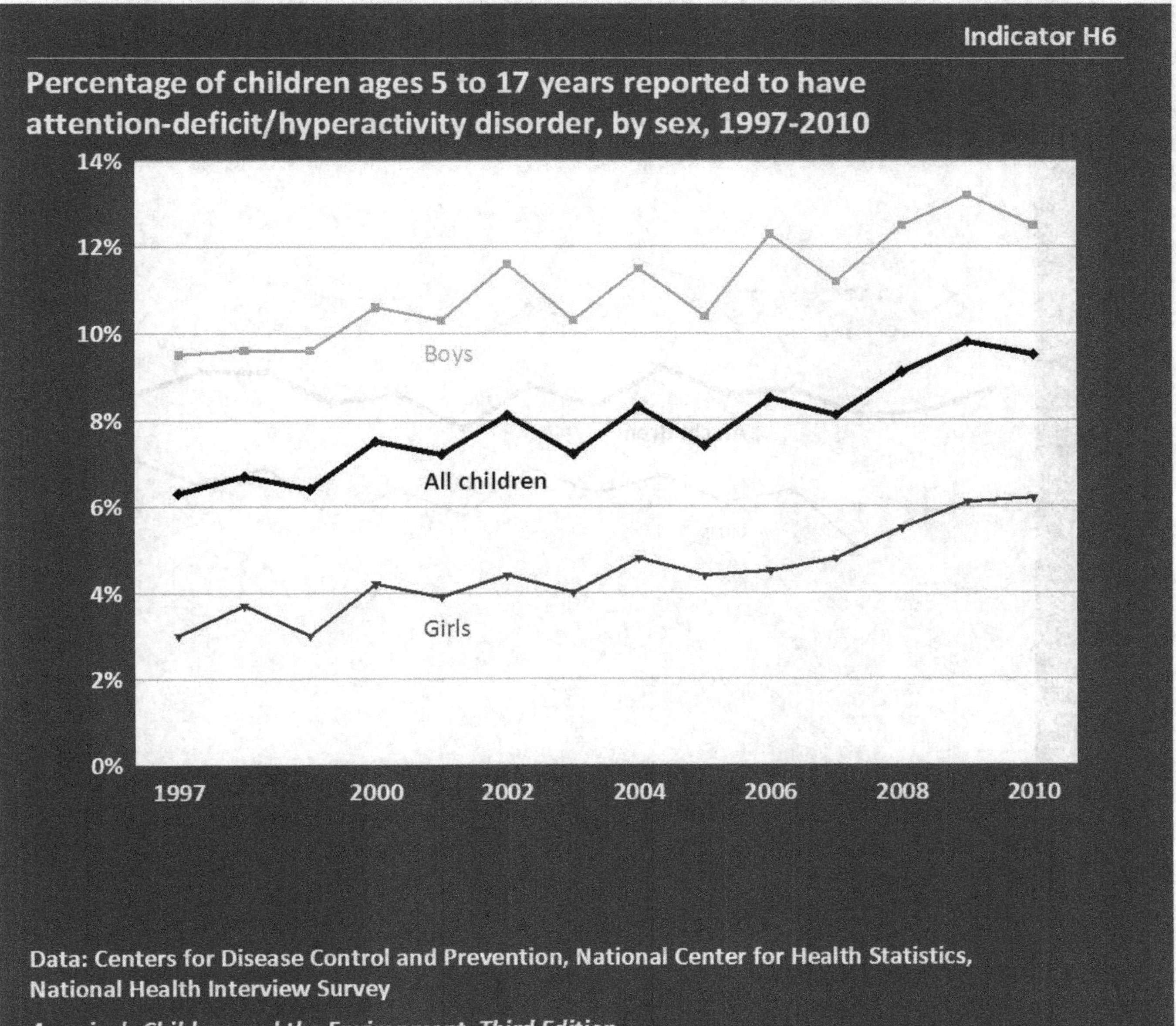
Indicator H6
Percentage of children ages 5 to 17 years reported to have attention-deficit/hyperactivity disorder, by sex, 1997-2010
14%
12%
10%
8%
6%
4%
2%
0%
Boys
All children
Girls
1997
2000
2002
2004
2006
2008
2010
Data: Centers for Disease Control and Prevention, National Center for Health Statistics, National Health Interview Survey
America's Children and the Environment, Third Edition

Percentage of children ages 5 to 17 years reported to have a learning disability, by sex, 1997-2010

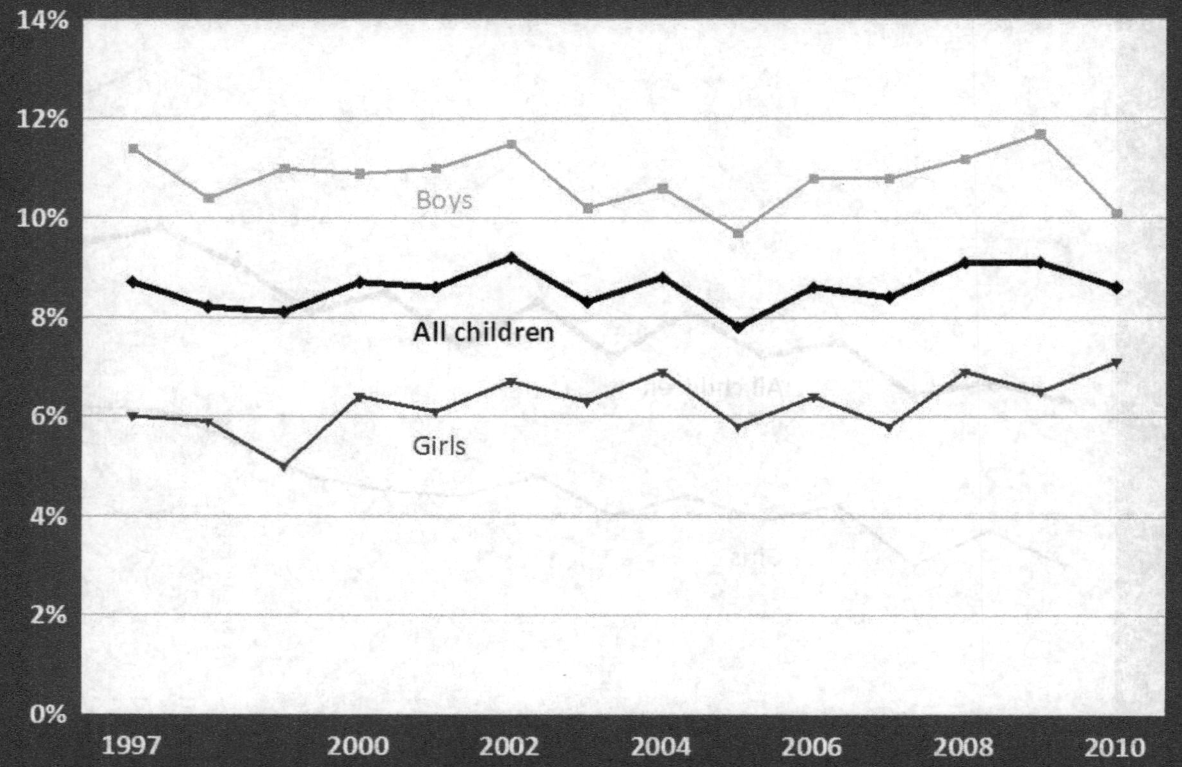

Data: Centers for Disease Control and Prevention, National Center for Health Statistics, National Health Interview Survey

America's Children and the Environment, Third Edition

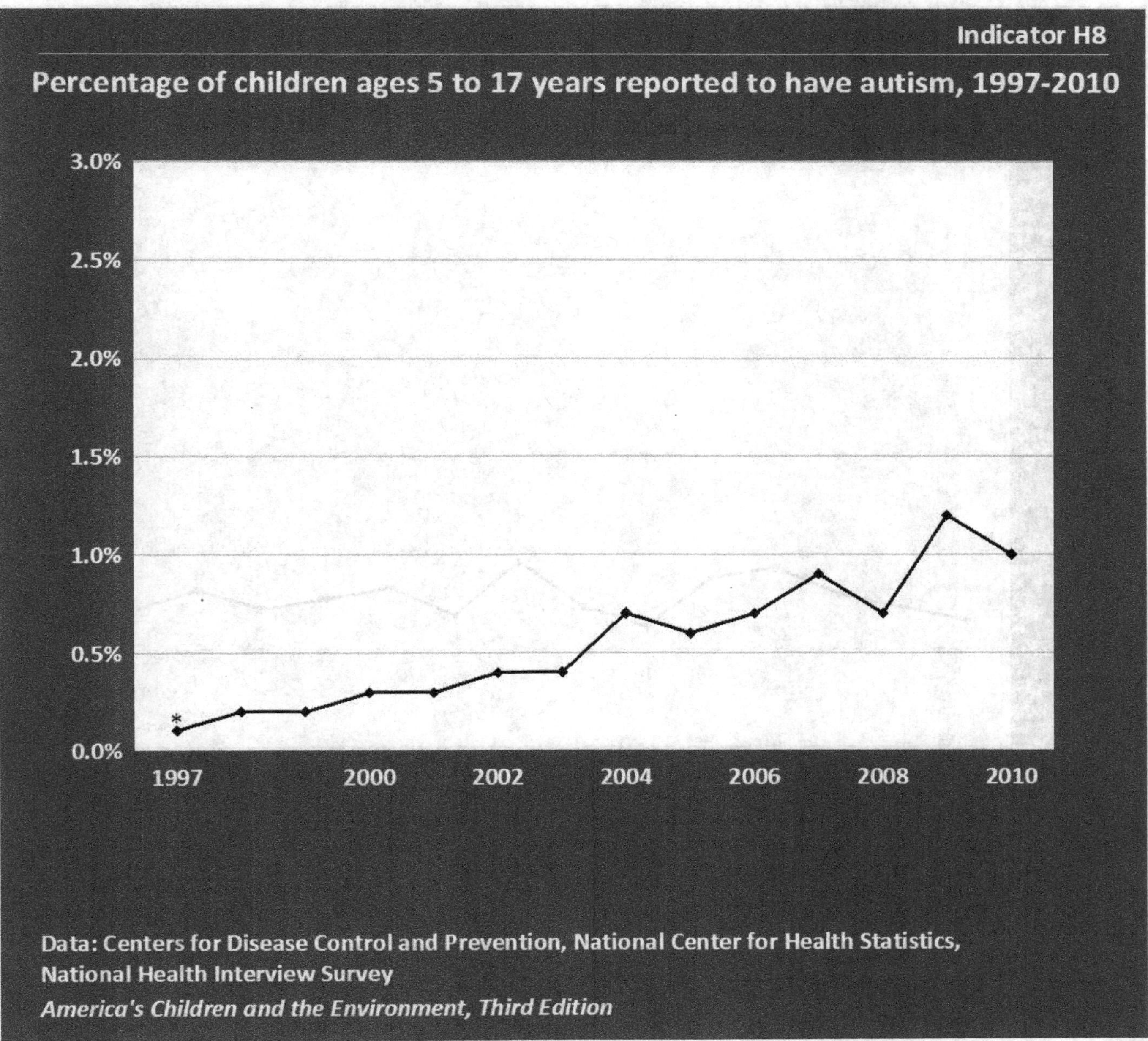
Indicator H8
Percentage of children ages 5 to 17 years reported to have autism, 1997-2010
3.0%
2.5%
2.0%
1.5%
1.0%
0.5%
0.0%
*
1997
2000
2002
2004
2006
2008
2010
Data: Centers for Disease Control and Prevention, National Center for Health Statistics, National Health Interview Survey
America's Children and the Environment, Third Edition

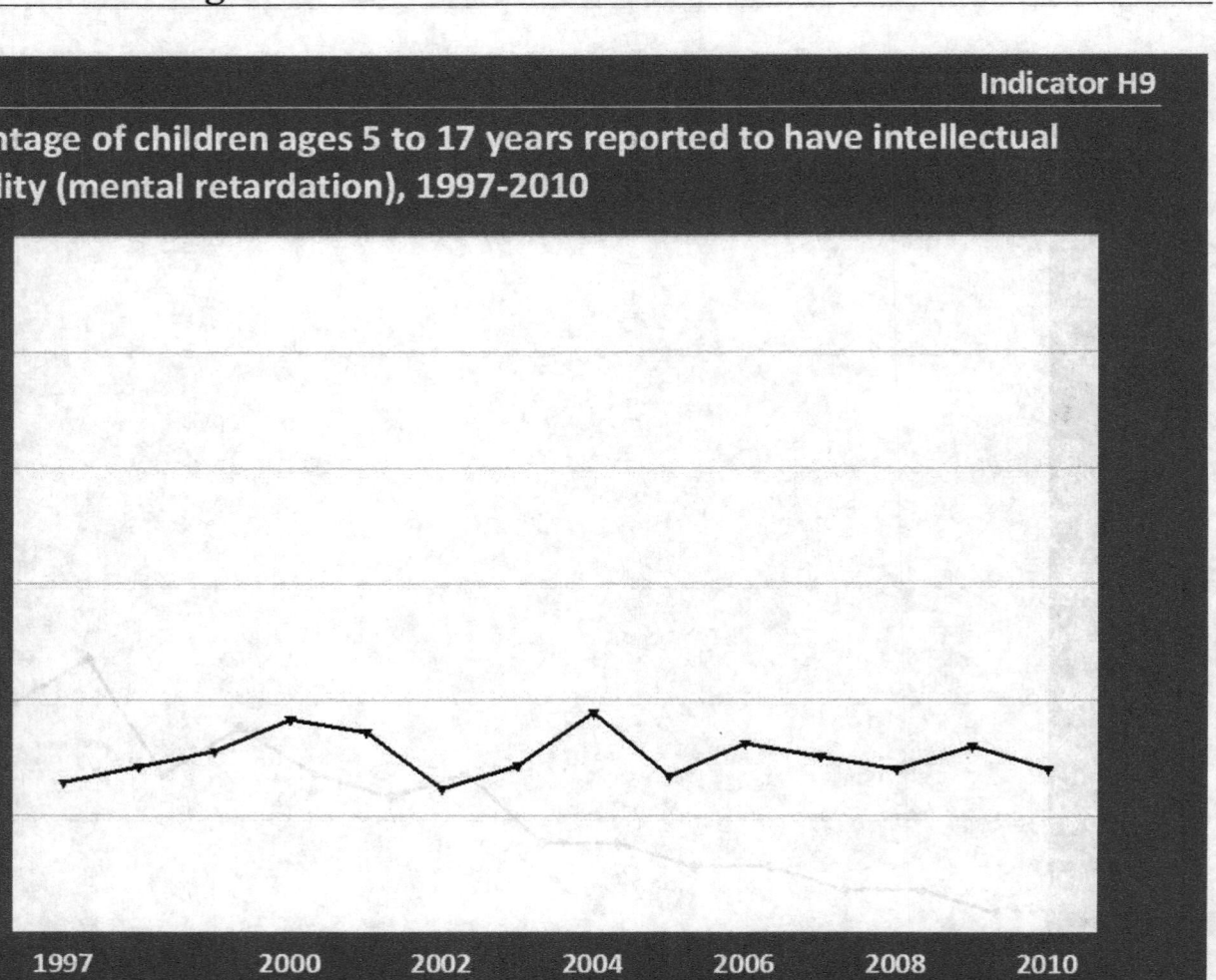

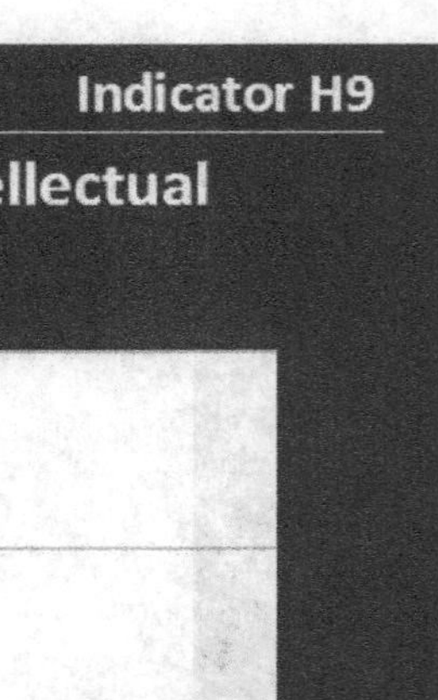

Indicator H9
Percentage of children ages 5 to 17 years reported to have intellectual disability (mental retardation), 1997-2010
3.0%
2.5%
2.0%
1.5%
1.0%
0.5%
0.0%
1997
2000
2002
2004
2006
2008
2010
Data: Centers for Disease Control and Prevention, National Center for Health Statistics, National Health Interview Survey
America's Children and the Environment, Third Edition

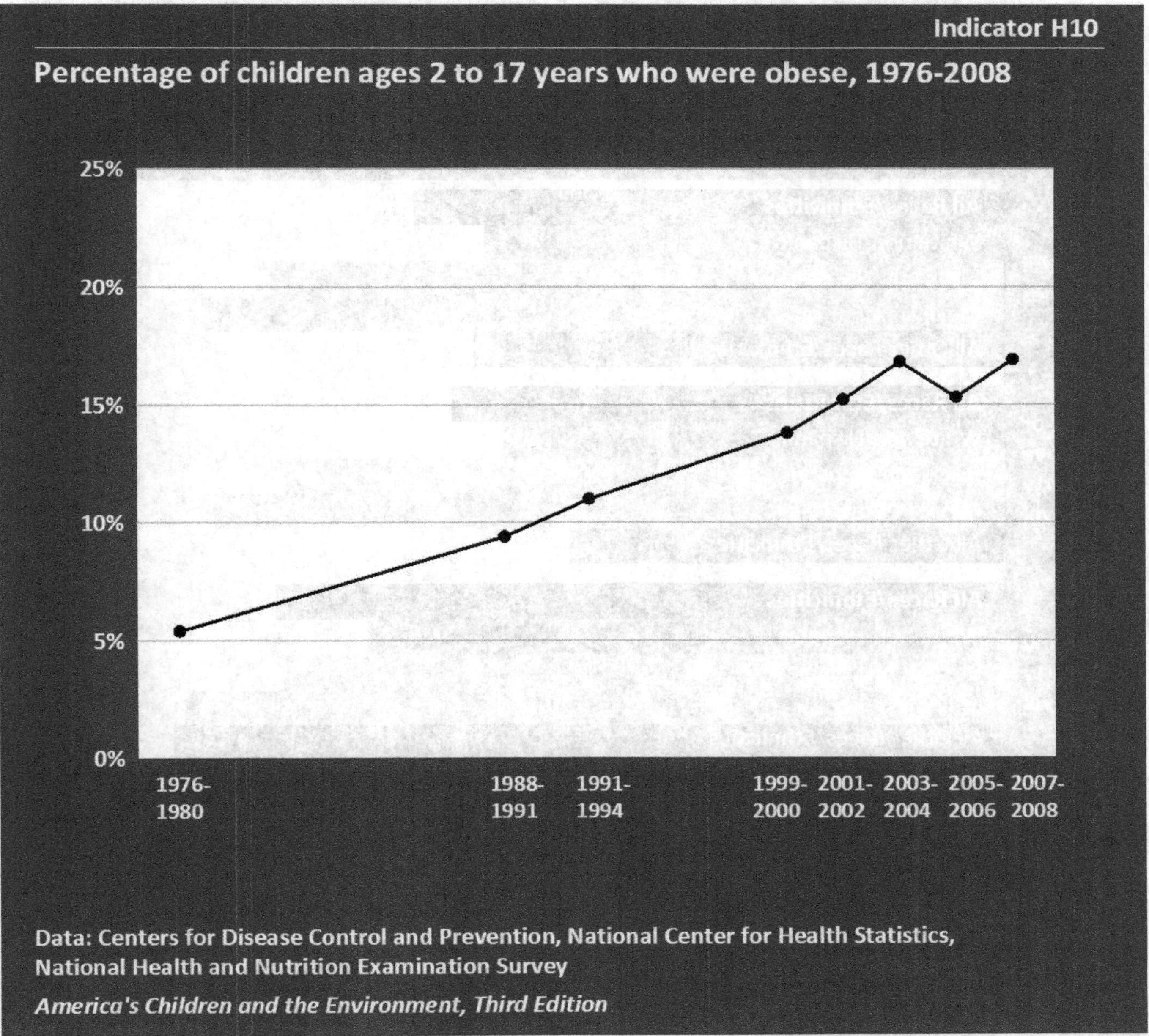
Indicator H10
Percentage of children ages 2 to 17 years who were obese, 1976-2008
25%
20%
15%
10%
5%
0%
1976-1980
1988-1991
1991-1994
1999-2000
2001-2002
2003-2004
2005-2006
2007-2008
Data: Centers for Disease Control and Prevention, National Center for Health Statistics, National Health and Nutrition Examination Survey
America's Children and the Environment, Third Edition

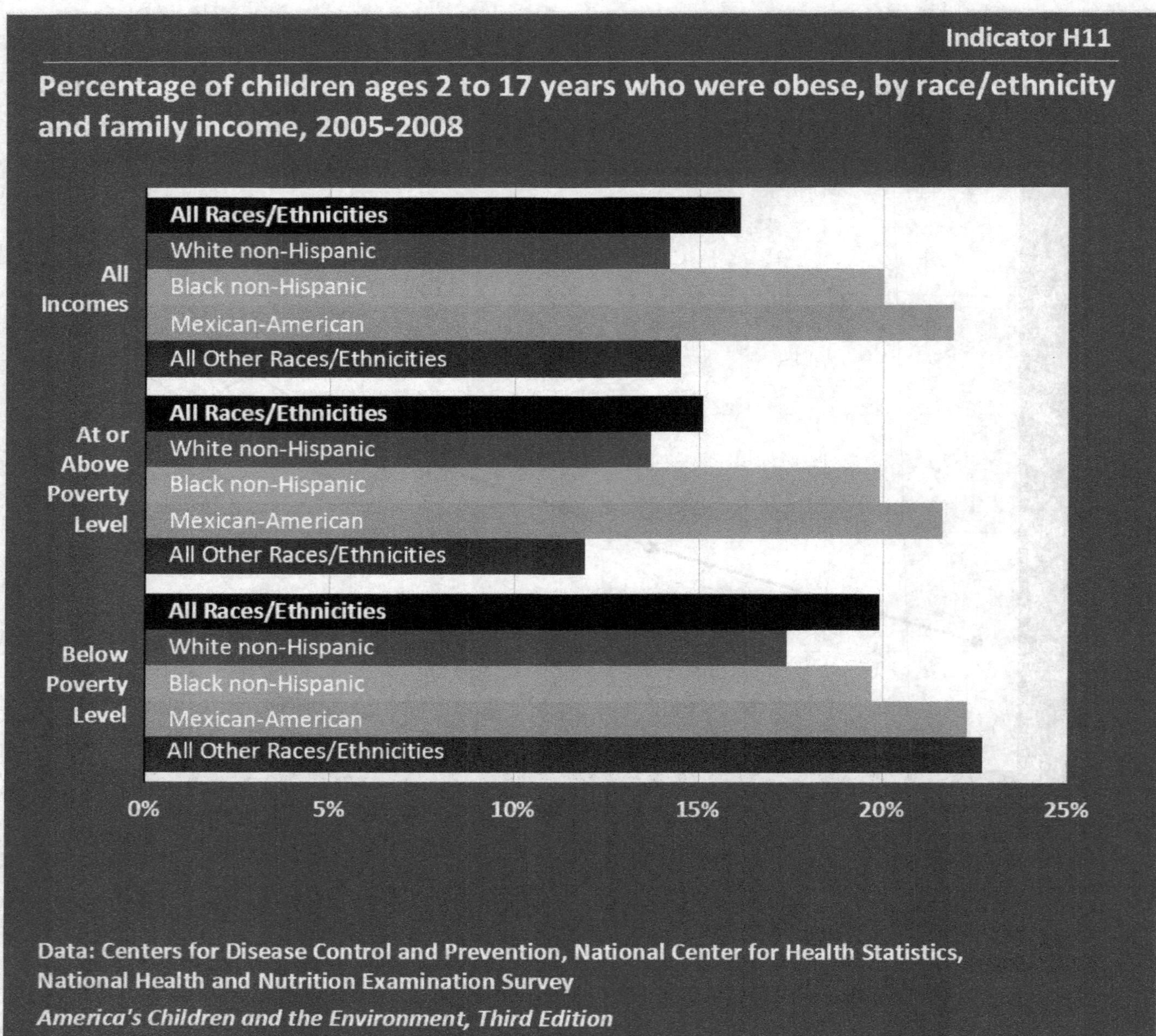
Indicator H11
Percentage of children ages 2 to 17 years who were obese, by race/ethnicity and family income, 2005-2008
All Incomes
All Races/Ethnicities
White non-Hispanic
Black non-Hispanic
Mexican-American
All Other Races/Ethnicities
At or Above Poverty Level
All Races/Ethnicities
White non-Hispanic
Black non-Hispanic
Mexican-American
All Other Races/Ethnicities
Below Poverty Level
All Races/Ethnicities
White non-Hispanic
Black non-Hispanic
Mexican-American
All Other Races/Ethnicities
0%
5%
10%
15%
20%
25%
Data: Centers for Disease Control and Prevention, National Center for Health Statistics, National Health and Nutrition Examination Survey
America's Children and the Environment, Third Edition

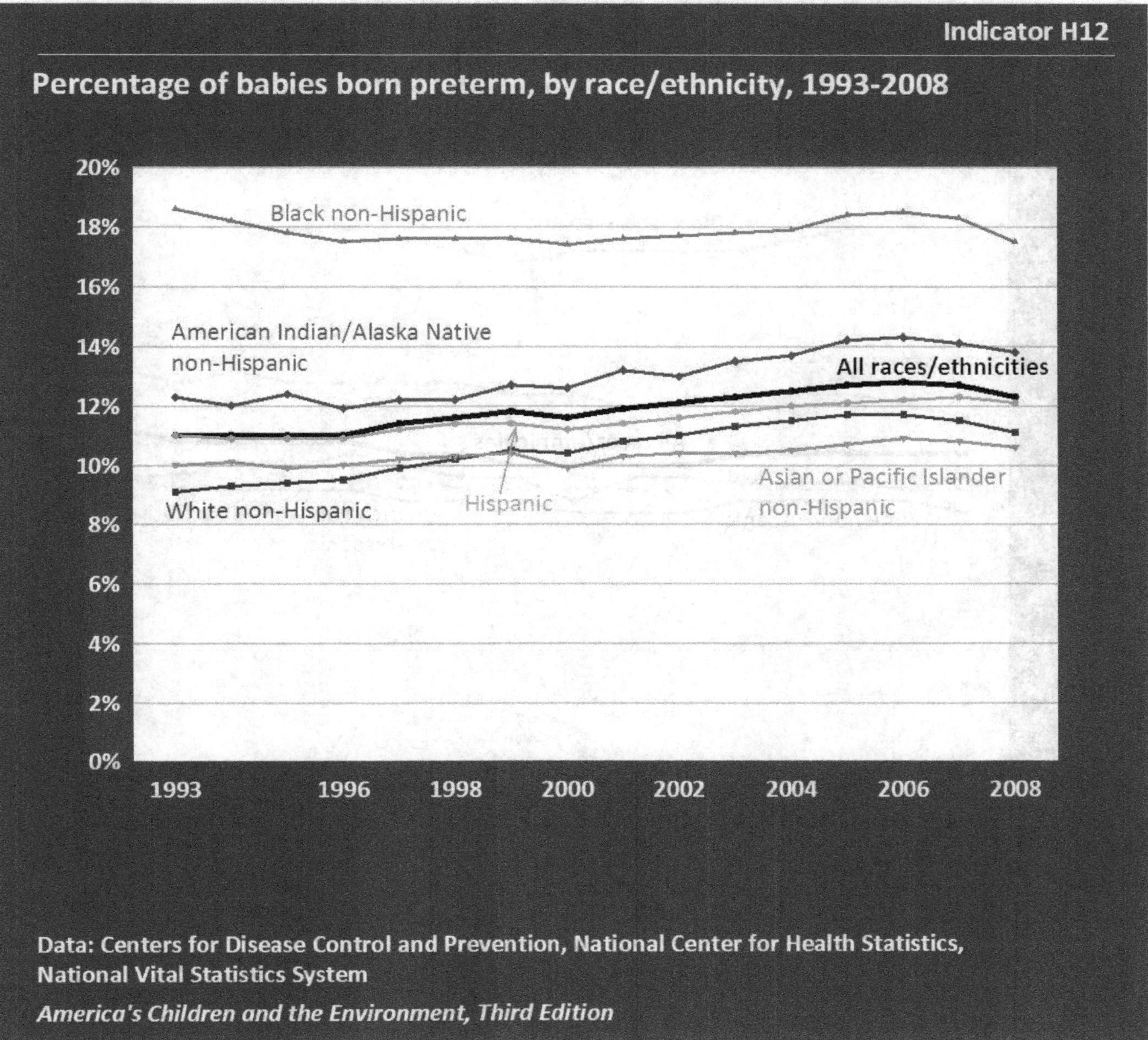
Indicator H12
Percentage of babies born preterm, by race/ethnicity, 1993-2008
20%
18%
16%
14%
12%
10%
8%
6%
4%
2%
0%
Black non-Hispanic
American Indian/Alaska Native
non-Hispanic
All races/ethnicities
Asian or Pacific Islander
non-Hispanic
White non-Hispanic
Hispanic
1993
1996
1998
2000
2002
2004
2006
2008
Data: Centers for Disease Control and Prevention, National Center for Health Statistics,
National Vital Statistics System
America's Children and the Environment, Third Edition

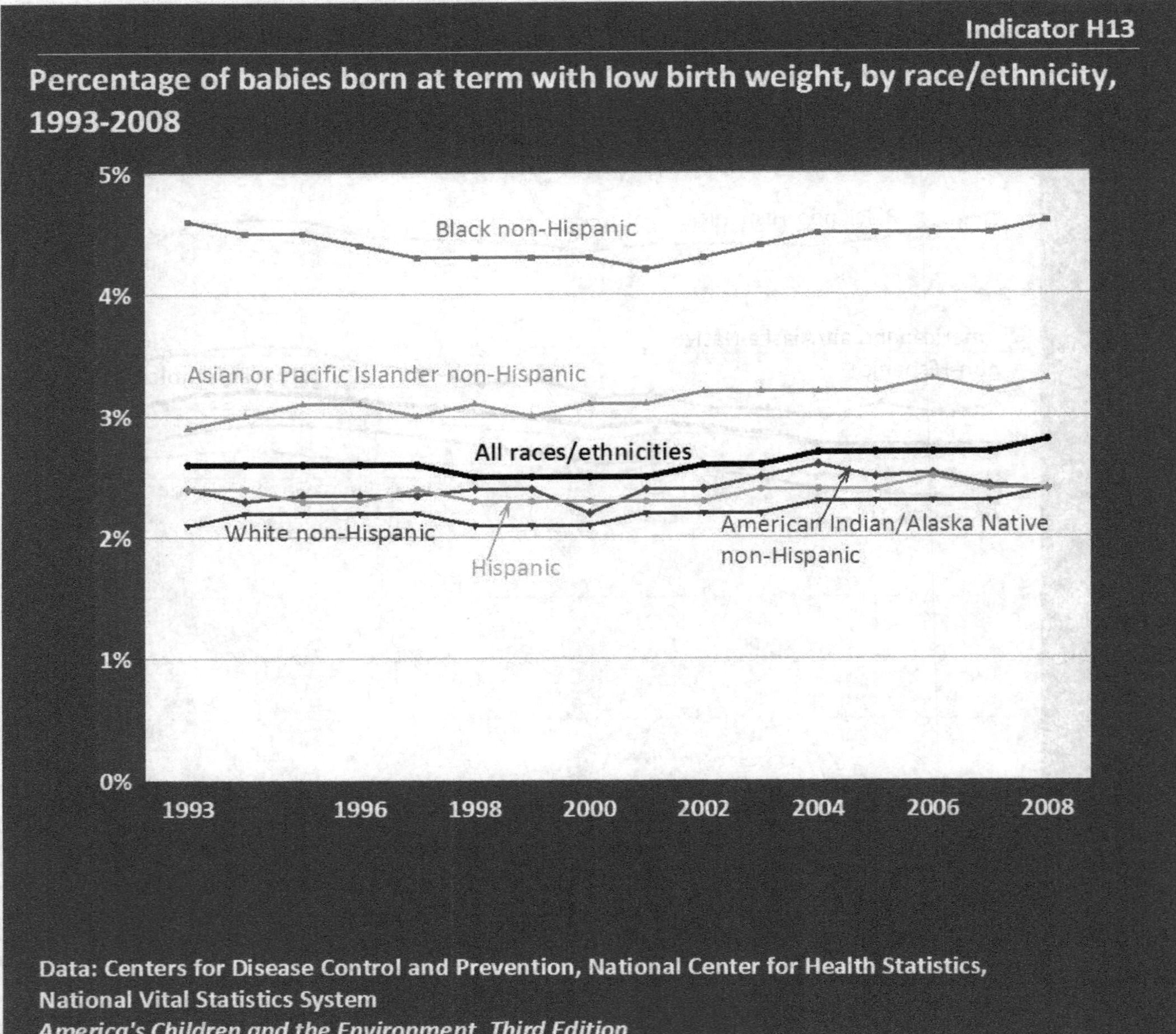
Indicator H13
Percentage of babies born at term with low birth weight, by race/ethnicity, 1993-2008
5%
4%
3%
2%
1%
0%
Black non-Hispanic
Asian or Pacific Islander non-Hispanic
All races/ethnicities
White non-Hispanic
Hispanic
American Indian/Alaska Native non-Hispanic
1993
1996
1998
2000
2002
2004
2006
2008
Data: Centers for Disease Control and Prevention, National Center for Health Statistics, National Vital Statistics System
America's Children and the Environment, Third Edition

Report on the Environment https://www.epa.gov/roe/

Drinking Water

Community water systems (CWS) are public water systems that supply water to the same population year-round. In fiscal year (FY) 2016, more than 300 million Americans (U.S. EPA, 2017a)—roughly 95 percent of the U.S. population (U.S. Census Bureau, 2017)—got at least some of their drinking water from a CWS. This indicator presents the percentage of Americans served by CWS for which states reported no violations of EPA health-based standards for more than 90 contaminants (U.S. EPA, 2017a).

Health-based standards include Maximum Contaminant Levels (MCLs), Maximum Residual Disinfection Levels (MRDLs), and Treatment Techniques (TTs). An MCL is the highest level of a contaminant that is allowed in drinking water. An MRDL is the level of a disinfectant added for water treatment that may not be exceeded at the consumer's tap without an unacceptable possibility of adverse health effects. A TT is a required treatment process (such as filtration) intended to reduce the level of a contaminant in drinking water (U.S. EPA, 2017b). TTs are adopted where it is not economically or technologically feasible to ascertain the level of a contaminant, such as microbes, where even single organisms that occur unpredictably or episodically can cause adverse health effects. Compliance with TTs may require finished water sampling, along with quantitative or descriptive measurements of process performance to gauge the efficacy of the treatment process. In general, MCL-regulated contaminants tend to have long-term rather than acute health effects, and concentrations may vary seasonally. Thus, compliance is based on averages of seasonal, quarterly, annual, or less frequent sampling.

This indicator tracks the population served by CWS for which no violations were reported to EPA annually for the period from FY 1993 to FY 2016, the latest year for which data are available. Results are reported as a percentage of the overall population served by CWS, both nationally and by EPA Region. This indicator also reports the number of persons served by systems with reported violations of standards covering surface water treatment, microbial contaminants (microorganisms that can cause disease), disinfection byproducts (chemicals that may form when disinfectants, such as chlorine, react with naturally occurring materials in water and may pose health risks), and other contaminants. The indicator is based on violations reported quarterly by states, EPA, and the Navajo Nation, who each review monitoring results for the CWS that they oversee.

What the Data Show

Of the population served by CWS nationally, the percentage served by systems for which no health-based violations were reported for the entire year increased overall from 79 percent in 1993 to 91 percent in FY 2016 (Exhibit 1). Drinking water regulations have changed in recent years. This indicator is based on reported violations of the standards in effect in any given year.

When results are broken down by EPA Region, some variability over time is evident (Exhibit 2). Between FY 1998 and FY 2016, most Regions were consistently above the national percentage. Only Region 2 remained consistently below the national percentage over the entire period of record, largely because of a small number of public water systems serving large populations.

In FY 2016, reported violations of the health-based disinfection byproducts rules (Stage 2) affected 11 million people (4 percent of the CWS-served population) (Exhibit 3). Reported violations of heath-based coliform standards affected 6 million people (2 percent of the CWS-served population), and reported violations involving surface water treatment rules were responsible for exceeding health-based standards for 4 million people (1 percent of the population served by CWS nationally).

Limitations

- Non-community water systems (typically small systems) that serve only transient populations such as restaurants or campgrounds, or serving those in a non-domestic setting for only part of their day (e.g., a school, hospital, or office building), are not included in population served figures.
- Domestic (home) use of drinking water supplied by private wells is not included. Approximately 15 percent of the U.S. population get at least some of their drinking water from private wells (U.S. EPA, 2017c).
- Bottled water, which is regulated by standards set by the Food and Drug Administration, is not included.
- National statistics based on population served can be volatile, because a single very large system can sway the results by up to 2 to 3 percent. This effect becomes more pronounced when statistics are broken down at the regional level, and still more so for a single rule.
- Some factors may lead to overstating the extent of population served by systems that violate standards. For example, the entire population served by each system in violation is reported, even though only part of the total population served may actually receive water that is out of compliance. SDWIS data does not indicate whether any, part, or all of the population served by a system receives water in violation. Therefore, there is no way to know how many, if any, people are actually drinking water in violation. In addition, violations stated on an annual basis may suggest a longer duration of violation than may be the case, as some violations may be as brief as an hour or a day.

- Other factors may lead to understating the population served by systems that violate standards. For instance, CWS that purchase water from other CWS are not always required to sample for all contaminants themselves.

- Under-reporting and late reporting of violations by states to EPA affect the ability to accurately report the national violations total. For example, EPA estimated that between 2002 and 2004, states were not reporting 38 percent of all health-based violations, which reflects a decline in the quality of violations data compared with the previous 3-year period (U.S. EPA, 2008).

- Data reviews and other quality assurance analyses indicate that the most widespread data quality problem is under-reporting of monitoring violations. Even though these violations are separate from the health-based violations covered by this indicator, failures to monitor could mask violations of TTs, MRDLs, and MCLs.

Data Sources

Data for this indicator were obtained from EPA's Safe Drinking Water Information System (U.S. EPA, 2017a) (https://www.epa.gov/ground-water-and-drinking-water/safe-drinking-water-information-system-sdwis-federal-reporting). This database contains a record of violations reported to EPA by the states or other entities that oversee public water systems, along with annual summary statistics.

References

U.S. Census Bureau. 2017. Monthly population estimates for the United States: April 1, 2010 to December 1, 2017. Accessed February 2017. https://www.census.gov/data/tables/2016/demo/popest/nation-total.html.

U.S. EPA (United States Environmental Protection Agency). 2017a. Safe Drinking Water Information System Federal Reporting Services. Accessed February 2017. https://www.epa.gov/ground-water-and-drinking-water/safe-drinking-water-information-system-sdwis-federal-reporting.

U.S. EPA. 2017b. National primary drinking water regulations. Accessed February 2017. https://www.epa.gov/ground-water-and-drinking-water/national-primary-drinking-water-regulations.

U.S. EPA. 2017c. About private water wells. Accessed February 2017. https://www.epa.gov/privatewells/about-private-water-wells.

U.S. EPA. 2008. 2006 drinking water data reliability analysis and action plan: For state reported public water system data in the EPA Safe Drinking Water Information System/Federal Version (SDWIS/FED). March 2008. https://nepis.epa.gov/.

Exhibit 1. U.S. population served by community water systems with no reported violations of EPA health-based standards, fiscal years 1993-2016

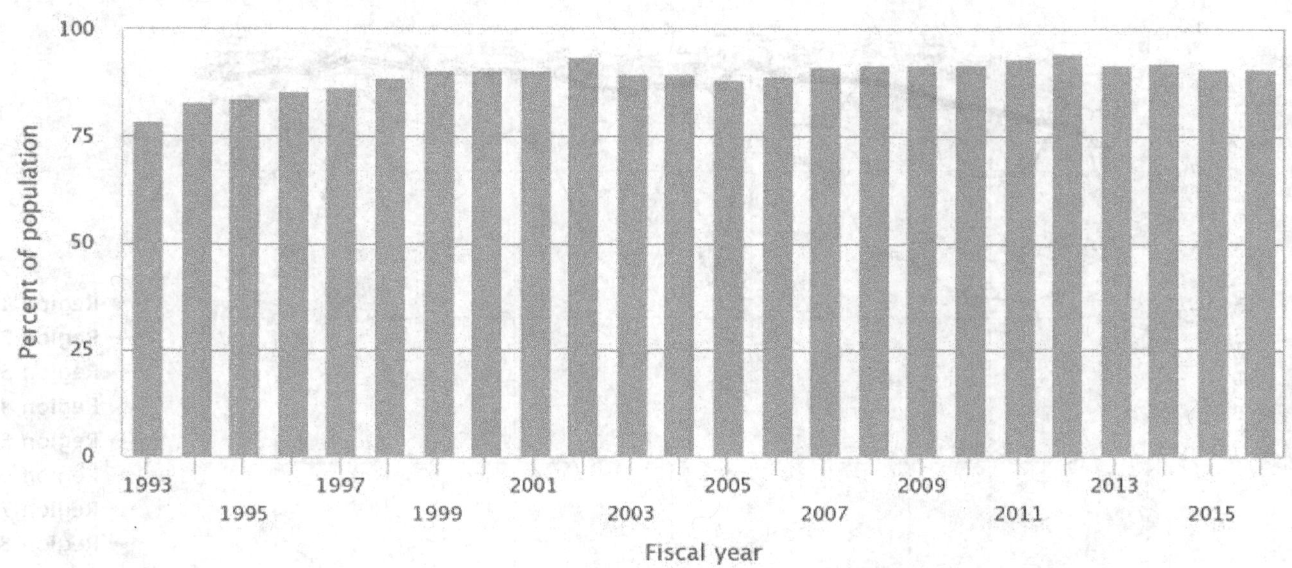

Coverage: U.S. residents served by community water systems (CWS) (approximately 95% of the total U.S. population).

Several new standards went into effect during the time period shown.

Information on the statistical significance of the trend in this exhibit is not currently available. For more information about uncertainty, variability, and statistical analysis, view the technical documentation for this indicator.

Data source: U.S. EPA, 2017a

Exhibit 2. U.S. population served by community water systems with no reported violations of EPA health-based standards, by EPA Region, fiscal years 1993-2016

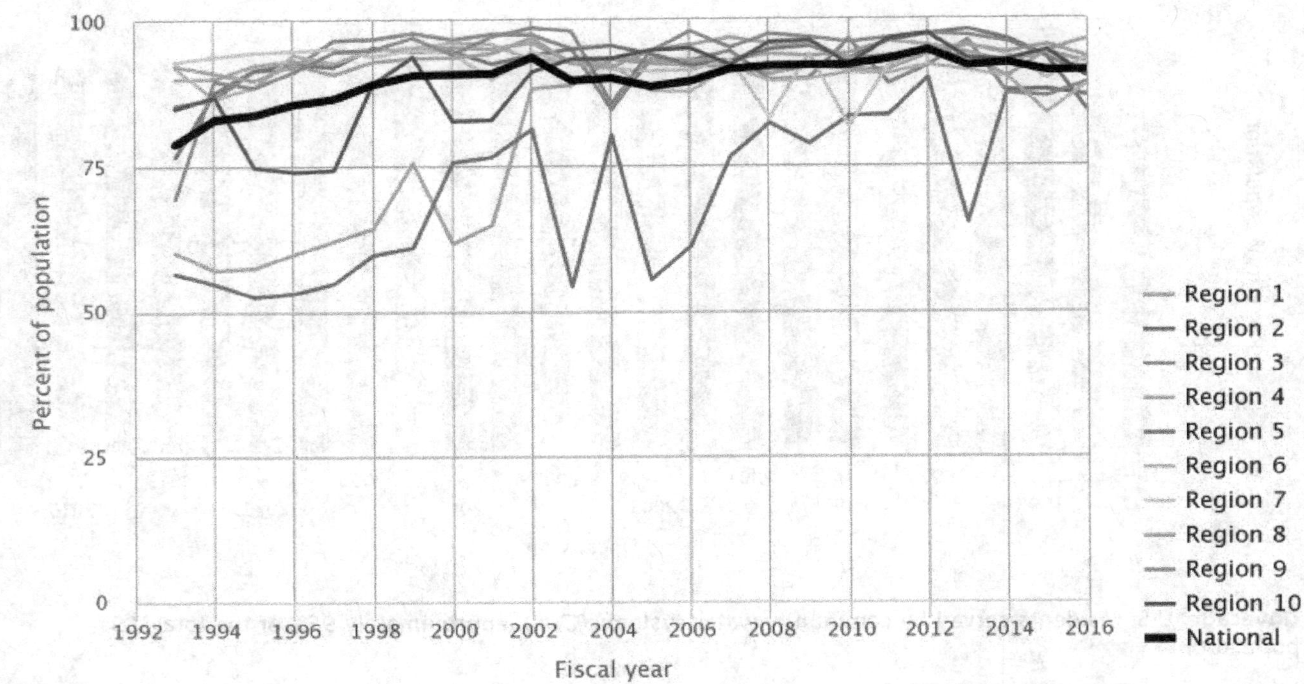

Coverage: U.S. residents served by community water systems (CWS) (approximately 95% of the total U.S. population).

Based on reported violations of the standards in effect in any given year.

Information on the statistical significance of the trends in this exhibit is not currently available. For more information about uncertainty, variability, and statistical analysis, view the technical documentation for this indicator.

Data source: U.S. EPA, 2017a

Exhibit 3. U.S. population served by community water systems with reported violations of EPA health-based standards, by type of violation, fiscal year 2016

	Population served	Percent of CWS customers
Any violation	26,956,955	8.8
Selected violations		
Stage 2 Disinfectants and Disinfection Byproducts Rules	11,135,414	3.6
Surface Water Treatment Rules	4,327,965	1.4
Total Coliform Rule	6,433,237	2.1
Arsenic	360,722	0.1
Nitrate	1,377,066	0.5

Coverage: U.S. residents served by community water systems (CWS) (approximately 95% of the total U.S. population).

Some CWS violated more than one of the selected rules.

Trend analysis has not been conducted because these data represent a single snapshot in time. For more information about uncertainty, variability, and statistical analysis, view the technical documentation for this indicator.

Data source: U.S. EPA, 2017a

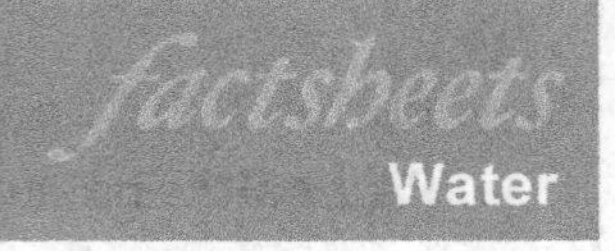

U.S. Water Supply and Distribution

Patterns of Use

All life on Earth depends on water. Human uses include drinking, bathing, crop irrigation, electricity generation, and industrial activity. For some of these uses, the available water requires treatment prior to use. Over the last century, the primary goals of water treatment have remained the same—to produce water that is biologically and chemically safe, appealing to consumers, and non-corrosive and non-scaling.

Water Uses

- In 2010, total U.S. water use was approximately 355 billion gallons per day (Bgal/d). Thermoelectric power (161 Bgal/d) and irrigation (115 Bgal/d) accounted for the largest withdrawals.[1]
- Per capita use was roughly 41% higher in western states than in eastern states in 2010, primarily due to the volume of water used for crop irrigation in the west.[1]
- In 2010, California and Texas accounted for 18% of all U.S. freshwater withdrawals, even after reducing total water use by 26% and 16%, respectively, from 2000 levels.[1,2] Florida and California accounted for 32% of saline water withdrawals.[1]

Estimated Uses of Water, 2010[1]

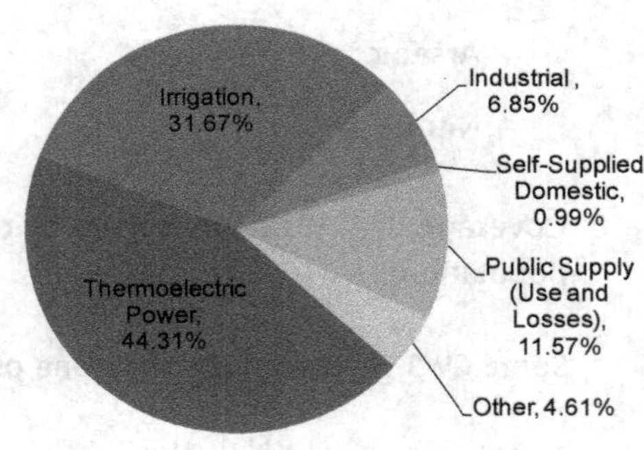

Sources of Water

- Approximately 86% of the U.S. population relied on public water supply in 2010; the remainder relies on water from domestic wells.[1]
- Surface sources account for 78% of all water withdrawals.[1]
- About 153,000 publicly owned water systems provide piped water for human consumption, of which roughly 51,000 (34%) are community water systems (CWSs).[3] 8% of all CWSs provide water to 82% of the population served.[4]
- In 2006, CWSs delivered an average of 96,000 gallons per year to each residential connection and 797,000 gallons per year to non-residential connections.[5]

Sources of Water Withdrawals[1]

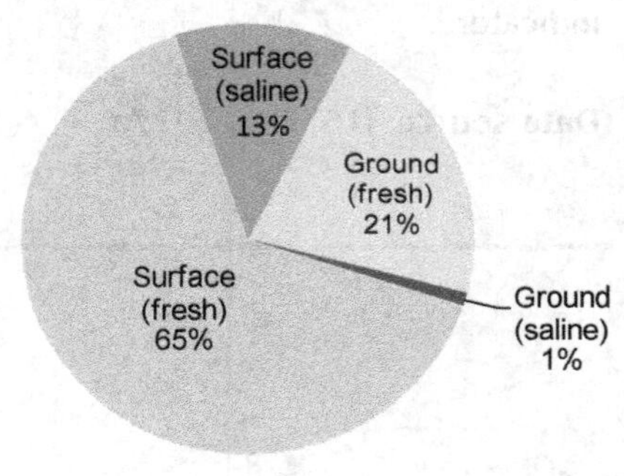

Energy Consumption

- 2% of total U.S. electricity use goes towards moving and treating water and wastewater, a 52% increase in electricity use since 1996.[4] Electricity use accounts for around 80% of municipal water processing and distribution costs.[6]
- Groundwater supply from public sources requires 2,100 kilowatt-hours per million gallons—about 31% more electricity than surface water supply, mainly due to higher raw water pumping requirements for groundwater systems.[4]
- The California State Water Project is the largest single user of energy in California, consuming 5 billion kWh per year, on average—more than 25% of the total electricity consumption for the entire state of New Mexico. In the process of delivering water from the San Francisco Bay-Delta to Southern California, the project uses 2%-3% of all electricity consumed in the state.[7]

Water Treatment

- The Safe Drinking Water Act (SDWA), enacted in 1974 and amended in 1986 and 1996, regulates contaminants in public water supplies, provides funding for infrastructure projects, protects sources of drinking water, and promotes the capacity of water systems to comply with SDWA regulations.[8]
- Typical parameters that the U.S. Environmental Protection Agency monitors for violations of drinking water standards include: microorganism, disinfectants, radionuclides, organics (e.g., volatile organic compounds and synthetic organic chemicals), and inorganics (e.g., nitrates, arsenic, radionuclides, lead, and copper).[9]
- Of all CWSs, 91% are designed to disinfect water, 23% are designed to remove or sequester iron, 13% are designed to remove or sequester manganese, and 21% are designed for corrosion control.[5]

Size Categories of Community Water Systems[3]

System Size (population served)	Number of CWSs	Population Served (millions)	% of CWSs	% of U.S. Population Served by CWSs
Very Small (25-500)	28,462	4.8	55%	2%
Small (501-3,300)	13,737	19.7	27%	7%
Medium (3,301-10,000)	4,936	28.7	10%	10%
Large (10,001-100,000)	3,802	108.8	7%	36%
Very Large (>100,000)	419	137.3	1%	46%
Total	**51,356**	**299.2**	**100%**	**100%**

Life Cycle Impacts

Infrastructure Requirements

- The 2011 Drinking Water Infrastructure Needs Survey and Assessment found that U.S. water systems need to invest $384.2 billion over the next 20 years to continue providing clean safe drinking water.[10]
- 64% ($247.5 billion) of the total national investment need is for transmission and distribution. The remaining 36% of need is for treatment ($72.5 billion), storage ($39.5 billion), source development ($20.5 billion), and other systems ($4.2 billion).[10]
- Water systems maintain more than 2 million miles of distribution mains.[11] In 2000, nearly 80% of systems were less than 40 years old, while 4% were more than 80 years old.[12] From 2001 to 2006, over 56,000 miles of distribution mains were replaced and 225,000 miles were newly added.[5]

Total 20-Year Need, by Project Type[10]

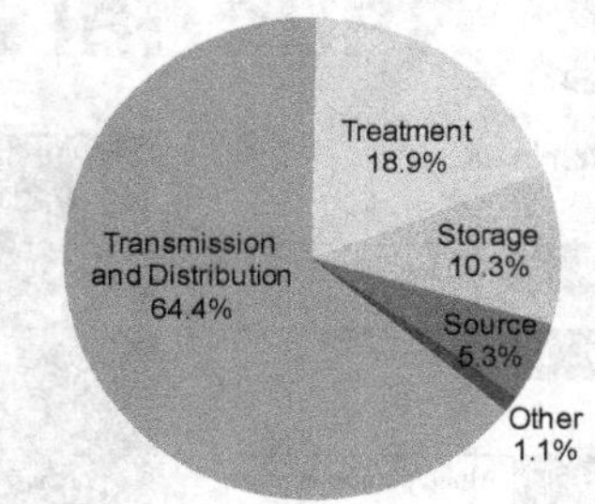

Electricity Requirements

- Supplying fresh water to public agencies required about 31 billion kWh of electricity in 2000.[6]
- One study projects electricity consumption to exceed 36 billion kWh by 2020 and 46 billion kWh by 2050. This increased production of electricity may result in environmental burdens, whose magnitude will depend directly on the fuel mix at generating facilities—fossil, nuclear, hydropower, solar, wind, and biomass.[6]
- Household appliances contribute greatly to the energy burden. Dishwashers, showers, and faucets require 0.312 kWh/gallon, 0.143 kWh/gallon, and 0.139 kWh/gallon, respectively.[13]

Projected Electricity Consumption, Public Water Supply[3,6]

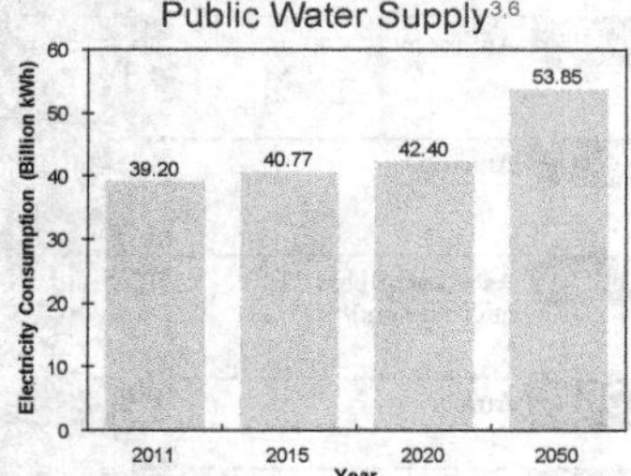

Consumptive Use

- Consumptive use is an activity that draws water from a source within a basin and returns only a portion or none of the withdrawn water to the basin. The water might have been lost to evaporation, incorporated into a product such as a beverage and shipped out of the basin, or transpired into the atmosphere through the natural action of plants and leaves.[1]
- Agriculture accounts for the largest loss of water (80-90% of total U.S. consumptive water use).[14] Of the 115 Bgal/d freshwater withdrawn for irrigation, over half is lost as a consequence of consumptive use.[1,15]
- Consumptive use for the remaining sectors — industry, thermoelectric, domestic, livestock, aquaculture, and mining — and public uses and losses total only 19%.[15] Of the 129 Bgal/d of water withdrawn for thermoelectric power in the U.S., 3% is consumed (3.5 Bgal/d).[16]
- Total freshwater consumptive use in the United States has been reported at around 100 Bgal/day.[15]

Solutions and Sustainable Alternatives

Supply Side

- Major components that offer significant energy efficiency improvement opportunities include pumping systems, pumps, and motors.[17]
- Periodic rehabilitation, repair, and replacement of water distribution infrastructure would help improve water quality and avoid leaks.[10]
- Achieve on-site energy and chemical usage efficiency to minimize the life cycle environmental impacts related to the production and distribution of energy and chemicals used in the treatment and distribution process.
- Reduce chemical usage for treatment and sludge disposal by efficient process design, recycling of sludge, and recovery and reuse of chemicals.
- On-site energy generation from renewable sources such as solar and wind.[18]
- Effective watershed management plans to protect source water are often more cost-effective and environmentally sound than treating contaminated water. For example, NYC chose to invest between $1-1.5 billion in a watershed protection project to improve the water quality in the Catskill/Delaware watershed rather than construct a new filtration plant at a capital cost of $6-8 billion.[19]
- Less than 4% of U.S. freshwater comes from brackish or saltwater, though this segment is growing. Desalination technology, such as reverse osmosis membrane filtering, unlocks large resources, but more research is needed to lower costs, energy use, and environmental impacts.[4]

Demand Side

- Better engineering practices:
  - Plumbing fixtures to reduce water consumption, e.g., high-efficiency toilets, low-flow showerheads, and faucet aerators.[20]
  - Water reuse and recycling, e.g., graywater systems and rain barrels.[20]
  - Efficient landscape irrigation practices.[20]
- Better planning and management practices:
  - Pricing and retrofit programs.[20]
  - Proper leak detection and metering.[20]
  - Residential water audit programs and public education programs.[20]

Center Pivot Irrigation System[21]

1. Maupin, M., et al. (2014) Estimated Use of Water in the United States in 2010. U.S.G.S.
2. Hutson, S., et al. (2004) Estimated Use of Water in the United States in 2000. U.S.G.S.
3. U.S. Environmental Protection Agency (EPA) (2013) Fiscal Year 2011 Drinking Water and Ground Water Statistics Report.
4. Electric Power Research Institute (2013) Electricity Use and Management in the Municipal Water Supply and Wastewater Industries.
5. U.S. EPA (2009) 2006 Community Water System Survey.
6. Electric Power Research Institute, Inc. (2002) Water & Sustainability (Volume 4): U.S. Electricity Consumption for Water Supply & Treatment – The Next Half Century. Technical Report.
7. Natural Resources Defense Council (2004) Energy Down the Drain: The Hidden Costs of California's Water Supply.
8. Tiemann, M. (2014) Safe Drinking Water Act: A Summary of the Act and Its Major Requirements. Congressional Research Service.
9. U.S. EPA (2016) "Table of Regulated Drinking Water Contaminants."
10. U.S. EPA (2013) Drinking Water Infrastructure Needs Survey and Assessment –Fifth Report.
11. American Water Works Association (2016) "Disinfection and Distribution."
12. U.S. EPA (2002) Community Water System Survey 2000.
13. Abdallah, A. and D. Rosenberg (2014) Heterogeneous Residential Water and Energy Linkages and Implications for Conservation and Management. Journal of Water Resources Planning and Management, 140(3): 288-297.
14. USDA ERS (2015) "Irrigation & Water Use Background."
15. Solley, W., et al. (1993) Estimated Use of Water in the United States in 1990. U.S. Geological Survey.
16. Diehl, T. and M. Harris (2014) Withdrawal and consumption of water by thermoelectric power plants in the United States, 2010: U.S. Geological Survey Scientific Investigations Report 2014–5184.
17. Water Research Foundation (2011) Energy Efficiency Best Practices for North American Drinking Water Utilities.
18. U.S. EPA (2016) "Energy Efficiency for Water Utilities."
19. Chichilnisky, G. and G. Heal (1998) Economic returns from the biosphere. Nature, 391: 629-630.
20. U.S. EPA (2012) "How to conserve water and use it efficiently."
21. Photo courtesy of U.S. Department of Agriculture, Natural Resources Conservation Service.

Cite as: Center for Sustainable Systems, University of Michigan. 2016. "U.S. Water Supply and Distribution Factsheet." Pub. No. CSS05-17. **August 2016**

National Primary Drinking Water Regulations

	Contaminant	MCL or TT[1] (mg/L)[2]	Potential health effects from long-term[3] exposure above the MCL	Common sources of contaminant in drinking water	Public Health Goal (mg/L)[2]
OC	Acrylamide	TT[4]	Nervous system or blood problems; increased risk of cancer	Added to water during sewage/ wastewater treatment	zero
OC	Alachlor	0.002	Eye, liver, kidney or spleen problems; anemia; increased risk of cancer	Runoff from herbicide used on row crops	zero
R	Alpha/photon emitters	15 picocuries per Liter (pCi/L)	Increased risk of cancer	Erosion of natural deposits of certain minerals that are radioactive and may emit a form of radiation known as alpha radiation	zero
IOC	Antimony	0.006	Increase in blood cholesterol; decrease in blood sugar	Discharge from petroleum refineries; fire retardants; ceramics; electronics; solder	0.006
IOC	Arsenic	0.010	Skin damage or problems with circulatory systems, and may have increased risk of getting cancer	Erosion of natural deposits; runoff from orchards; runoff from glass & electronics production wastes	0
IOC	Asbestos (fibers >10 micrometers)	7 million fibers per Liter (MFL)	Increased risk of developing benign intestinal polyps	Decay of asbestos cement in water mains; erosion of natural deposits	7 MFL
OC	Atrazine	0.003	Cardiovascular system or reproductive problems	Runoff from herbicide used on row crops	0.003
IOC	Barium	2	Increase in blood pressure	Discharge of drilling wastes; discharge from metal refineries; erosion of natural deposits	2
OC	Benzene	0.005	Anemia; decrease in blood platelets; increased risk of cancer	Discharge from factories; leaching from gas storage tanks and landfills	zero
OC	Benzo(a)pyrene (PAHs)	0.0002	Reproductive difficulties; increased risk of cancer	Leaching from linings of water storage tanks and distribution lines	zero
IOC	Beryllium	0.004	Intestinal lesions	Discharge from metal refineries and coal-burning factories; discharge from electrical, aerospace, and defense industries	0.004
R	Beta photon emitters	4 millirems per year	Increased risk of cancer	Decay of natural and man-made deposits of certain minerals that are radioactive and may emit forms of radiation known as photons and beta radiation	zero
DBP	Bromate	0.010	Increased risk of cancer	Byproduct of drinking water disinfection	zero
IOC	Cadmium	0.005	Kidney damage	Corrosion of galvanized pipes; erosion of natural deposits; discharge from metal refineries; runoff from waste batteries and paints	0.005
OC	Carbofuran	0.04	Problems with blood, nervous system, or reproductive system	Leaching of soil fumigant used on rice and alfalfa	0.04
OC	Carbon tetrachloride	0.005	Liver problems; increased risk of cancer	Discharge from chemical plants and other industrial activities	zero
D	Chloramines (as Cl_2)	MRDL=4.0[1]	Eye/nose irritation; stomach discomfort; anemia	Water additive used to control microbes	MRDLG=4[1]
OC	Chlordane	0.002	Liver or nervous system problems; increased risk of cancer	Residue of banned termiticide	zero
D	Chlorine (as Cl_2)	MRDL=4.0[1]	Eye/nose irritation; stomach discomfort	Water additive used to control microbes	MRDLG=4[1]
D	Chlorine dioxide (as ClO_2)	MRDL=0.8[1]	Anemia; infants, young children, and fetuses of pregnant women: nervous system effects	Water additive used to control microbes	MRDLG=0.8[1]
DBP	Chlorite	1.0	Anemia; infants, young children, and fetuses of pregnant women: nervous system effects	Byproduct of drinking water disinfection	0.8
OC	Chlorobenzene	0.1	Liver or kidney problems	Discharge from chemical and agricultural chemical factories	0.1
IOC	Chromium (total)	0.1	Allergic dermatitis	Discharge from steel and pulp mills; erosion of natural deposits	0.1
IOC	Copper	TT[5]; Action Level = 1.3	Short-term exposure: Gastrointestinal distress. Long-term exposure: Liver or kidney damage. People with Wilson's Disease should consult their personal doctor if the amount of copper in their water exceeds the action level	Corrosion of household plumbing systems; erosion of natural deposits	1.3
M	*Cryptosporidium*	TT[7]	Short-term exposure: Gastrointestinal illness (e.g., diarrhea, vomiting, cramps)	Human and animal fecal waste	zero

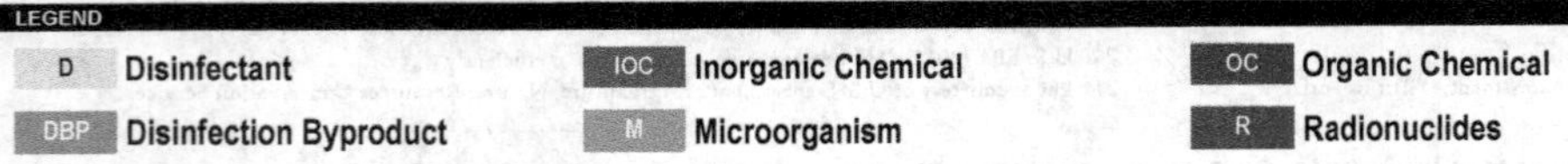

LEGEND
D Disinfectant
DBP Disinfection Byproduct
IOC Inorganic Chemical
M Microorganism
OC Organic Chemical
R Radionuclides

	Contaminant	MCL or TT[1] (mg/L)[2]	Potential health effects from long-term[3] exposure above the MCL	Common sources of contaminant in drinking water	Public Health Goal (mg/L)[2]
IOC	Cyanide (as free cyanide)	0.2	Nerve damage or thyroid problems	Discharge from steel/metal factories; discharge from plastic and fertilizer factories	0.2
OC	2,4-D	0.07	Kidney, liver, or adrenal gland problems	Runoff from herbicide used on row crops	0.07
OC	Dalapon	0.2	Minor kidney changes	Runoff from herbicide used on rights of way	0.2
OC	1,2-Dibromo-3-chloropropane (DBCP)	0.0002	Reproductive difficulties; increased risk of cancer	Runoff/leaching from soil fumigant used on soybeans, cotton, pineapples, and orchards	zero
OC	o-Dichlorobenzene	0.6	Liver, kidney, or circulatory system problems	Discharge from industrial chemical factories	0.6
OC	p-Dichlorobenzene	0.075	Anemia; liver, kidney or spleen damage; changes in blood	Discharge from industrial chemical factories	0.075
OC	1,2-Dichloroethane	0.005	Increased risk of cancer	Discharge from industrial chemical factories	zero
OC	1,1-Dichloroethylene	0.007	Liver problems	Discharge from industrial chemical factories	0.007
OC	cis-1,2-Dichloroethylene	0.07	Liver problems	Discharge from industrial chemical factories	0.07
OC	trans-1,2-Dichloroethylene	0.1	Liver problems	Discharge from industrial chemical factories	0.1
OC	Dichloromethane	0.005	Liver problems; increased risk of cancer	Discharge from drug and chemical factories	zero
OC	1,2-Dichloropropane	0.005	Increased risk of cancer	Discharge from industrial chemical factories	zero
OC	Di(2-ethylhexyl) adipate	0.4	Weight loss, liver problems, or possible reproductive difficulties	Discharge from chemical factories	0.4
OC	Di(2-ethylhexyl) phthalate	0.006	Reproductive difficulties; liver problems; increased risk of cancer	Discharge from rubber and chemical factories	zero
OC	Dinoseb	0.007	Reproductive difficulties	Runoff from herbicide used on soybeans and vegetables	0.007
OC	Dioxin (2,3,7,8-TCDD)	0.00000003	Reproductive difficulties; increased risk of cancer	Emissions from waste incineration and other combustion; discharge from chemical factories	zero
OC	Diquat	0.02	Cataracts	Runoff from herbicide use	0.02
OC	Endothall	0.1	Stomach and intestinal problems	Runoff from herbicide use	0.1
OC	Endrin	0.002	Liver problems	Residue of banned insecticide	0.002
OC	Epichlorohydrin	TT[4]	Increased cancer risk; stomach problems	Discharge from industrial chemical factories; an impurity of some water treatment chemicals	zero
OC	Ethylbenzene	0.7	Liver or kidney problems	Discharge from petroleum refineries	0.7
OC	Ethylene dibromide	0.00005	Problems with liver, stomach, reproductive system, or kidneys; increased risk of cancer	Discharge from petroleum refineries	zero
M	Fecal coliform and *E. coli*	MCL[5]	Fecal coliforms and *E. coli* are bacteria whose presence indicates that the water may be contaminated with human or animal wastes. Microbes in these wastes may cause short term effects, such as diarrhea, cramps, nausea, headaches, or other symptoms. They may pose a special health risk for infants, young children, and people with severely compromised immune systems.	Human and animal fecal waste	zero[6]
IOC	Fluoride	4.0	Bone disease (pain and tenderness of the bones); children may get mottled teeth	Water additive which promotes strong teeth; erosion of natural deposits; discharge from fertilizer and aluminum factories	4.0
M	*Giardia lamblia*	TT[7]	Short-term exposure: Gastrointestinal illness (e.g., diarrhea, vomiting, cramps)	Human and animal fecal waste	zero
OC	Glyphosate	0.7	Kidney problems; reproductive difficulties	Runoff from herbicide use	0.7
DBP	Haloacetic acids (HAA5)	0.060	Increased risk of cancer	Byproduct of drinking water disinfection	n/a[9]
OC	Heptachlor	0.0004	Liver damage; increased risk of cancer	Residue of banned termiticide	zero
OC	Heptachlor epoxide	0.0002	Liver damage; increased risk of cancer	Breakdown of heptachlor	zero
M	Heterotrophic plate count (HPC)	TT[7]	HPC has no health effects; it is an analytic method used to measure the variety of bacteria that are common in water. The lower the concentration of bacteria in drinking water, the better maintained the water system is.	HPC measures a range of bacteria that are naturally present in the environment	n/a

LEGEND

D	Disinfectant	IOC	Inorganic Chemical	OC	Organic Chemical
DBP	Disinfection Byproduct	M	Microorganism	R	Radionuclides

Contaminant		MCL or TT[1] (mg/L)[2]	Potential health effects from long-term[3] exposure above the MCL	Common sources of contaminant in drinking water	Public Health Goal (mg/L)[2]
OC	Hexachlorobenzene	0.001	Liver or kidney problems; reproductive difficulties; increased risk of cancer	Discharge from metal refineries and agricultural chemical factories	zero
OC	Hexachlorocyclopentadiene	0.05	Kidney or stomach problems	Discharge from chemical factories	0.05
IOC	Lead	TT5; Action Level=0.015	Infants and children: Delays in physical or or mental development; children could show slight deficits in attention span and learning abilities; Adults: Kidney problems; high blood pressure	Corrosion of household plumbing systems; erosion of natural deposits	zero
M	*Legionella*	TT7	Legionnaire's Disease, a type of pneumonia	Found naturally in water; multiplies in heating systems	zero
OC	Lindane	0.0002	Liver or kidney problems	Runoff/leaching from insecticide used on cattle, lumber, gardens	0.0002
IOC	Mercury (inorganic)	0.002	Kidney damage	Erosion of natural deposits; discharge from refineries and factories; runoff from landfills and croplands	0.002
OC	Methoxychlor	0.04	Reproductive difficulties	Runoff/leaching from insecticide used on fruits, vegetables, alfalfa, livestock	0.04
IOC	Nitrate (measured as Nitrogen)	10	Infants below the age of six months who drink water containing nitrate in excess of the MCL could become seriously ill and, if untreated, may die. Symptoms include shortness of breath and blue-baby syndrome.	Runoff from fertilizer use; leaching from septic tanks, sewage; erosion of natural deposits	10
IOC	Nitrite (measured as Nitrogen)	1	Infants below the age of six months who drink water containing nitrite in excess of the MCL could become seriously ill and, if untreated, may die. Symptoms include shortness of breath and blue-baby syndrome.	Runoff from fertilizer use; leaching from septic tanks, sewage; erosion of natural deposits	1
OC	Oxamyl (Vydate)	0.2	Slight nervous system effects	Runoff/leaching from insecticide used on apples, potatoes, and tomatoes	0.2
OC	Pentachlorophenol	0.001	Liver or kidney problems; increased cancer risk	Discharge from wood-preserving factories	zero
OC	Picloram	0.5	Liver problems	Herbicide runoff	0.5
OC	Polychlorinated biphenyls (PCBs)	0.0005	Skin changes; thymus gland problems; immune deficiencies; reproductive or nervous system difficulties; increased risk of cancer	Runoff from landfills; discharge of waste chemicals	zero
R	Radium 226 and Radium 228 (combined)	5 pCi/L	Increased risk of cancer	Erosion of natural deposits	zero
IOC	Selenium	0.05	Hair or fingernail loss; numbness in fingers or toes; circulatory problems	Discharge from petroleum and metal refineries; erosion of natural deposits; discharge from mines	0.05
OC	Simazine	0.004	Problems with blood	Herbicide runoff	0.004
OC	Styrene	0.1	Liver, kidney, or circulatory system problems	Discharge from rubber and plastic factories; leaching from landfills	0.1
OC	Tetrachloroethylene	0.005	Liver problems; increased risk of cancer	Discharge from factories and dry cleaners	zero
IOC	Thallium	0.002	Hair loss; changes in blood; kidney, intestine, or liver problems	Leaching from ore-processing sites; discharge from electronics, glass, and drug factories	0.0005
OC	Toluene	1	Nervous system, kidney, or liver problems	Discharge from petroleum factories	1
M	Total Coliforms	5.0 percent[8]	Coliforms are bacteria that indicate that other, potentially harmful bacteria may be present. See fecal coliforms and *E. coli*	Naturally present in the environment	zero
DBP	Total Trihalomethanes (TTHMs)	0.080	Liver, kidney or central nervous system problems; increased risk of cancer	Byproduct of drinking water disinfection	n/a[9]
OC	Toxaphene	0.003	Kidney, liver, or thyroid problems; increased risk of cancer	Runoff/leaching from insecticide used on cotton and cattle	zero
OC	2,4,5-TP (Silvex)	0.05	Liver problems	Residue of banned herbicide	0.05
OC	1,2,4-Trichlorobenzene	0.07	Changes in adrenal glands	Discharge from textile finishing factories	0.07
OC	1,1,1-Trichloroethane	0.2	Liver, nervous system, or circulatory problems	Discharge from metal degreasing sites and other factories	0.2
OC	1,1,2-Trichloroethane	0.005	Liver, kidney, or immune system problems	Discharge from industrial chemical factories	0.003
OC	Trichloroethylene	0.005	Liver problems; increased risk of cancer	Discharge from metal degreasing sites and other factories	zero

LEGEND

D Disinfectant · IOC Inorganic Chemical · OC Organic Chemical

DBP Disinfection Byproduct · M Microorganism · R Radionuclides

	Contaminant	MCL or TT[1] (mg/L)[2]	Potential health effects from long-term[3] exposure above the MCL	Common sources of contaminant in drinking water	Public Health Goal (mg/L)[2]
M	Turbidity	TT[7]	Turbidity is a measure of the cloudiness of water. It is used to indicate water quality and filtration effectiveness (e.g., whether disease-causing organisms are present). Higher turbidity levels are often associated with higher levels of disease-causing microorganisms such as viruses, parasites and some bacteria. These organisms can cause short term symptoms such as nausea, cramps, diarrhea, and associated headaches.	Soil runoff	n/a
R	Uranium	30µg/L	Increased risk of cancer, kidney toxicity	Erosion of natural deposits	zero
OC	Vinyl chloride	0.002	Increased risk of cancer	Leaching from PVC pipes; discharge from plastic factories	zero
M	Viruses (enteric)	TT[7]	Short-term exposure: Gastrointestinal illness (e.g., diarrhea, vomiting, cramps)	Human and animal fecal waste	zero
OC	Xylenes (total)	10	Nervous system damage	Discharge from petroleum factories; discharge from chemical factories	10

LEGEND

D	Disinfectant	IOC	Inorganic Chemical	OC	Organic Chemical
DBP	Disinfection Byproduct	M	Microorganism	R	Radionuclides

NOTES

1 Definitions
- Maximum Contaminant Level Goal (MCLG)—The level of a contaminant in drinking water below which there is no known or expected risk to health. MCLGs allow for a margin of safety and are non-enforceable public health goals.
- Maximum Contaminant Level (MCL)—The highest level of a contaminant that is allowed in drinking water. MCLs are set as close to MCLGs as feasible using the best available treatment technology and taking cost into consideration. MCLs are enforceable standards.
- Maximum Residual Disinfectant Level Goal (MRDLG)—The level of a drinking water disinfectant below which there is no known or expected risk to health. MRDLGs do not reflect the benefits of the use of disinfectants to control microbial contaminants.
- Maximum Residual Disinfectant Level (MRDL)—The highest level of a disinfectant allowed in drinking water. There is convincing evidence that addition of a disinfectant is necessary for control of microbial contaminants.
- Treatment Technique (TT)—A required process intended to reduce the level of a contaminant in drinking water.

2 Units are in milligrams per liter (mg/L) unless otherwise noted. Milligrams per liter are equivalent to parts per million (ppm).

3 Health effects are from long-term exposure unless specified as short-term exposure.

4 Each water system must certify annually, in writing, to the state (using third-party or manufacturers certification) that when it uses acrylamide and/or epichlorohydrin to treat water, the combination (or product) of dose and monomer level does not exceed the levels specified, as follows: Acrylamide = 0.05 percent dosed at 1 mg/L (or equivalent); Epichlorohydrin = 0.01 percent dosed at 20 mg/L (or equivalent).

5 Lead and copper are regulated by a Treatment Technique that requires systems to control the corrosiveness of their water. If more than 10 percent of tap water samples exceed the action level, water systems must take additional steps. For copper, the action level is 1.3 mg/L, and for lead is 0.015 mg/L.

6 A routine sample that is fecal coliform-positive or *E. coli*-positive triggers repeat samples--if any repeat sample is total coliform-positive, the system has an acute MCL violation. A routine sample that is total coliform-positive and fecal coliform-negative or *E. coli*-negative triggers repeat samples--if any repeat sample is fecal coliform-positive or *E. coli*-positive, the system has an acute MCL violation. See also Total Coliforms.

7 EPA's surface water treatment rules require systems using surface water or ground water under the direct influence of surface water to (1) disinfect their water, and (2) filter their water or meet criteria for avoiding filtration so that the following contaminants are controlled at the following levels:
- *Cryptosporidium*: 99 percent removal for systems that filter. Unfiltered systems are required to include Cryptosporidium in their existing watershed control provisions.
- Giardia lamblia: 99.9 percent removal/inactivation
- Viruses: 99.99 percent removal/inactivation
- *Legionella*: No limit, but EPA believes that if *Giardia* and viruses are removed/inactivated according to the treatment techniques in the surface water treatment rule, *Legionella* will also be controlled.
- Turbidity: For systems that use conventional or direct filtration, at no time can turbidity (cloudiness of water) go higher than 1 nephelolometric turbidity unit (NTU), and samples for turbidity must be less than or equal to 0.3 NTU in at least 95 percent of the samples in any month. Systems that use filtration other than conventional or direct filtration must follow state limits, which must include turbidity at no time exceeding 5 NTU.
- HPC: No more than 500 bacterial colonies per milliliter
- Long Term 1 Enhanced Surface Water Treatment; Surface water systems or ground water systems under the direct influence of surface water serving fewer than 10,000 people must comply with the applicable Long Term 1 Enhanced Surface Water Treatment Rule provisions (e.g. turbidity standards, individual filter monitoring, *Cryptosporidium* removal requirements, updated watershed control requirements for unfiltered systems).
- Long Term 2 Enhanced Surface Water Treatment; This rule applies to all surface water systems or ground water systems under the direct influence of surface water. The rule targets additional *Cryptosporidium* treatment requirements for higher risk systems and includes provisions to reduce risks from uncovered finished water storages facilities and to ensure that the systems maintain microbial protection as they take steps to reduce the formation of disinfection byproducts. (Monitoring start dates are staggered by system size. The largest systems (serving at least 100,000 people) will begin monitoring in October 2006 and the smallest systems (serving fewer than 10,000 people) will not begin monitoring until October 2008. After completing monitoring and determining their treatment bin, systems generally have three years to comply with any additional treatment requirements.)
- Filter Backwash Recycling: The Filter Backwash Recycling Rule requires systems that recycle to return specific recycle flows through all processes of the system's existing conventional or direct filtration system or at an alternate location approved by the state.

8 No more than 5.0 percent samples total coliform-positive in a month. (For water systems that collect fewer than 40 routine samples per month, no more than one sample can be total coliform-positive per month.) Every sample that has total coliform must be analyzed for either fecal coliforms or *E. coli*. If two consecutive TC-positive samples, and one is also positive for *E. coli* or fecal coliforms, system has an acute MCL violation.

9 Although there is no collective MCLG for this contaminant group, there are individual MCLGs for some of the individual contaminants:
- Haloacetic acids: dichloroacetic acid (zero); trichloroacetic acid (0.3 mg/L)
- Trihalomethanes: bromodichloromethane (zero); bromoform (zero); dibromochloromethane (0.06 mg/L)

National Secondary Drinking Water Regulation

National Secondary Drinking Water Regulations are non-enforceable guidelines regarding contaminants that may cause cosmetic effects (such as skin or tooth discoloration) or aesthetic effects (such as taste, odor, or color) in drinking water. EPA recommends secondary standards to water systems but does not require systems to comply. However, some states may choose to adopt them as enforceable standards.

Contaminant	Secondary Maximum Contaminant Level
Aluminum	0.05 to 0.2 mg/L
Chloride	250 mg/L
Color	15 (color units)
Copper	1.0 mg/L
Corrosivity	noncorrosive
Fluoride	2.0 mg/L
Foaming Agents	0.5 mg/L
Iron	0.3 mg/L
Manganese	0.05 mg/L
Odor	3 threshold odor number
pH	6.5-8.5
Silver	0.10 mg/L
Sulfate	250 mg/L
Total Dissolved Solids	500 mg/L
Zinc	5 mg/L

For More Information

EPA's Safe Drinking Water Web site:
http://www.epa.gov/safewater/

EPA's Safe Drinking Water Hotline:
(800) 426-4791

To order additional posters or other ground water and drinking water publications, please contact the National Service Center for Environmental Publications at :
(800) 490-9198, or
email: nscep@bps-lmit.com.

EPA 816-F-09-004
May 2009

Percent of population served by CWS that are receiving fluoridated water

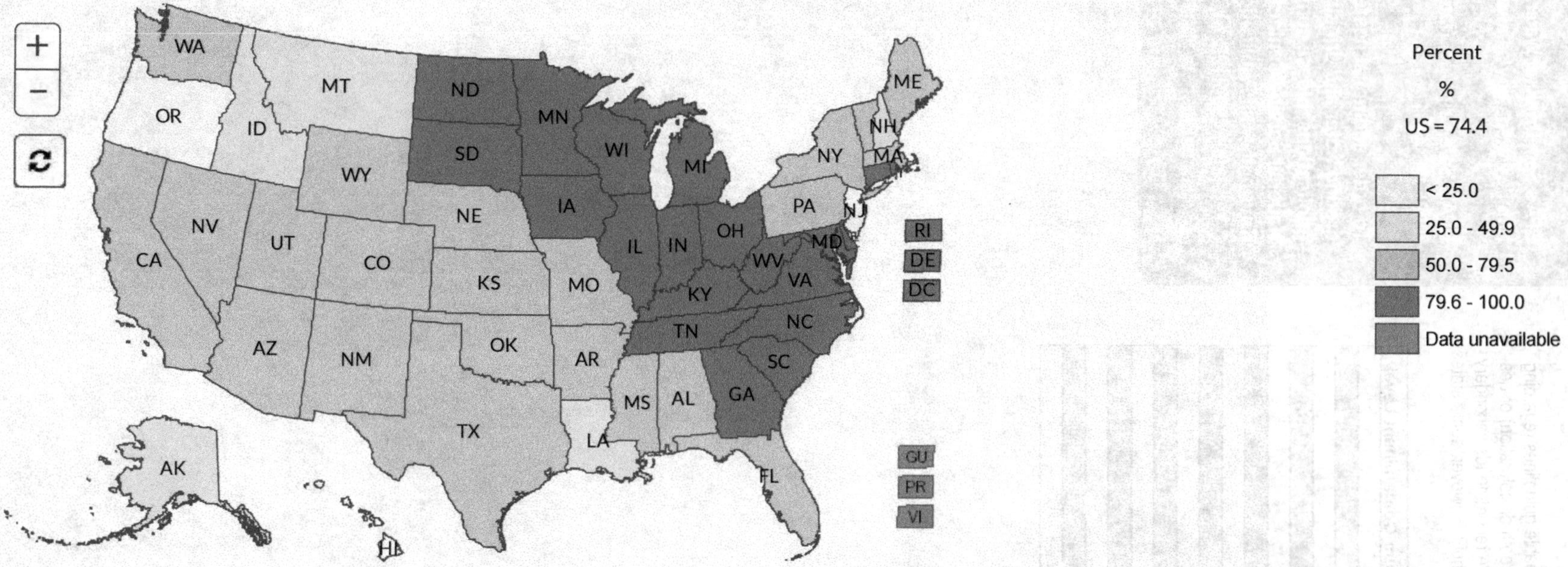

Footnotes

f	Population served by CWS exceeded the U.S. Census state population estimate; number of persons was reduced by the ratio of the population estimate to the CWS population estimate.
f,g	f: Population served by CWS exceeded the U.S. Census state population estimate; number of persons was reduced by the ratio of the population estimate to the CWS population estimate. g: Complete data were not available from WFRS; State provided additional information.

Data Source: CDC Water Fluoridation Reporting System (WFRS)

Centers for Disease Control and Prevention, National Center for Chronic Disease Prevention and Health Promotion, Division of Oral Health.Jul 20, 2017].

URL: https://nccd.cdc.gov/oralhealthdata/

Delisted Species

Species name	Date species first listed	Date species delisted	Reason delisted
Agave, Arizona (Agave arizonica) - Wherever found	5/18/1984	6/19/2006	Original Data in Error - Not a listable entity
Alligator, American (Alligator mississippiensis) - Wherever found	3/11/1967	6/4/1987	Recovered
Barberry, Truckee (Berberis (=Mahonia) sonnei) - Wherever found	12/6/1979	10/1/2003	Original Data in Error - Taxonomic revision
Bear, grizzly (Ursus arctos horribilis) - Greater Yellowstone Ecosystem DPS	7/28/1975	6/30/2017	Recovered
Bear, Louisiana black (Ursus americanus luteolus) - Wherever found	1/7/1992	3/11/2016	Recovered
Bidens, cuneate (Bidens cuneata) - Wherever found	2/17/1984	2/6/1996	Original Data in Error - Taxonomic revision
Broadbill, Guam (Myiagra freycineti) - Wherever found	8/27/1984	2/23/2004	Extinct
Butterfly, Bahama swallowtail (Heraclides andraemon bonhotei) - Wherever found	4/28/1976	8/31/1984	Original Data in Error - Act amendment
Cactus, Lloyd's hedgehog (Echinocereus lloydii) - Wherever found	11/28/1979	6/24/1999	Original Data in Error - Taxonomic revision
Cactus, spineless hedgehog (Echinocereus triglochidiatus var. inermis) - Wherever found	12/7/1979	9/22/1993	Original Data in Error - Not a listable entity
Chub, Oregon (Oregonichthys crameri) - Wherever found	10/18/1993	3/23/2015	Recovered
Cinquefoil, Robbins' (Potentilla robbinsiana) - Wherever found	9/17/1980	8/27/2002	Recovered
Cisco, longjaw (Coregonus alpenae) - Wherever found	3/11/1967	9/2/1983	Extinct
Coneflower, Tennessee purple (Echinacea tennesseensis) - Wherever found	7/5/1979	9/2/2011	Recovered
Crocodile, Morelet's (Crocodylus moreletii) - Wherever found	6/2/1970	5/23/2012	Recovered
Daisy, Maguire (Erigeron maguirei) - Wherever found	9/5/1985	2/18/2011	Recovered
Deer, Columbian white-tailed (Odocoileus virginianus leucurus) - Douglas County DPS	3/11/1967	7/24/2003	Recovered
Dove, Palau ground (Gallicolumba canifrons) - Wherever found	6/2/1970	9/12/1985	Recovered
Duck, Mexican (Anas diazi) - U.S.A. only	3/11/1967	7/25/1978	Original Data in Error - Taxonomic revision
Eagle, bald (Haliaeetus leucocephalus) - lower 48 States	3/11/1967	8/8/2007	Recovered
Falcon, American peregrine (Falco peregrinus anatum) - Wherever found	6/2/1970	8/25/1999	Recovered
Falcon, Arctic peregrine (Falco peregrinus tundrius) - Wherever found	6/2/1970	10/5/1994	Recovered
Flycatcher, Palau fantail (Rhipidura lepida) - Wherever found	6/2/1970	9/12/1985	Recovered
Fox, San Miguel Island (Urocyon littoralis littoralis) - wherever found	3/5/2004	9/12/2016	Recovered
Fox, Santa Cruz Island (Urocyon littoralis santacruzae) - wherever found	3/5/2004	9/12/2016	Recovered
Fox, Santa Rosa Island (Urocyon littoralis santarosae) - wherever found	3/5/2004	9/12/2016	Recovered
Frankenia, Johnston's (Frankenia johnstonii) - Wherever found	8/7/1984	2/11/2016	Recovered
Gambusia, Amistad (Gambusia amistadensis) - Wherever found	4/30/1980	12/4/1987	Extinct
Globeberry, Tumamoc (Tumamoca macdougalii) - Wherever found	4/29/1986	6/18/1993	Original Data in Error - New information discovered
Goldenrod, white-haired (Solidago albopilosa) - Wherever found	4/7/1988	10/11/2016	Recovered
Goose, Aleutian Canada (Branta canadensis leucopareia) - Wherever found	3/11/1967	3/20/2001	Recovered
Hedgehog cactus, purple-spined (Echinocereus engelmannii var. purpureus) - Wherever found	10/11/1979	11/27/1989	Original Data in Error - Taxonomic revision
Kangaroo, eastern gray (Macropus giganteus) - Wherever found	12/30/1974	3/9/1995	Recovered
Kangaroo, red (Macropus rufus) - Wherever found	12/30/1974	3/9/1995	Recovered
Kangaroo, western gray (Macropus fuliginosus) - Wherever found	12/30/1974	3/9/1995	Recovered
Lizard, Island night (Xantusia riversiana) - Wherever found	9/12/1977	4/1/2014	Recovered
Mallard, Mariana (Anas oustaleti) - Wherever found	12/8/1977	2/23/2004	Extinct
Milk-vetch, Rydberg (Astragalus perianus) - Wherever found	5/27/1978	9/14/1989	Original Data in Error - New information discovered
Monarch, Tinian (old world flycatcher) (Monarcha takatsukasae) - Wherever found	6/2/1970	9/21/2004	Recovered
No common name (Gahnia lanaiensis) - Wherever found	9/20/1991	5/28/2013	Original Data in Error - Taxonomic revision
Owl, Palau (Pyrroglaux podargina) - Wherever found	6/2/1970	9/12/1985	Recovered
Parakeet, scarlet-chested (Neophema splendida) - Wherever found	12/2/1970	5/5/2017	Recovered
Parakeet, turquoise (Neophema pulchella) - Wherever found	6/2/1970	5/5/2017	Recovered
Pearlymussel, Sampson's (Epioblasma sampsoni) - Wherever found	6/14/1976	1/9/1984	Extinct
Pelican, brown (Pelecanus occidentalis) - except U.S. Atlantic coast, FL, AL	6/2/1970	12/17/2009	Recovered
Pelican, brown (Pelecanus occidentalis) - U.S. Atlantic coast, FL, AL	6/2/1970	2/4/1985	Recovered
Pennyroyal, Mckittrick (Hedeoma apiculatum) - Wherever found	7/13/1982	9/22/1993	Original Data in Error - New information discovered
Pike, blue (Stizostedion vitreum glaucum) - Wherever found	3/11/1967	9/2/1983	Extinct
Pupfish, Tecopa (Cyprinodon nevadensis calidae) - Wherever found	10/13/1970	1/15/1982	Extinct
Pygmy-owl, cactus ferruginous (Glaucidium brasilianum cactorum) - AZ pop.	3/10/1997	4/14/2006	Original Data in Error - Not a listable entity
Sea lion, Steller (Eumetopias jubatus) - Eastern DPS	4/5/1990	12/4/2013	Recovered
Seal, Caribbean monk (Monachus tropicalis) - Wherever found	4/10/1979	10/28/2008	Extinct
Shagreen, Magazine Mountain (Inflectarius magazinensis) - Wherever found	4/17/1989	6/14/2013	Recovered
Shrew, Dismal Swamp southeastern (Sorex longirostris fisheri) - Wherever found	9/26/1986	2/28/2000	Original Data in Error - New information discovered
Snail, Utah valvata (Valvata utahensis) - Wherever found	12/14/1992	9/24/2010	Original Data in Error - New information discovered

Species name	Date species first listed	Date species delisted	Reason delisted
Snake, Concho water (Nerodia paucimaculata) - Wherever found	9/3/1986	11/28/2011	Recovered
Snake, Lake Erie water (Nerodia sipedon insularum) - subspecies range clarified	8/30/1999	9/15/2011	Recovered
Sparrow, dusky seaside (Ammodramus maritimus nigrescens) - Wherever found	3/11/1967	12/12/1990	Extinct
Sparrow, Santa Barbara song (Melospiza melodia graminea) - Wherever found	6/4/1973	10/12/1983	Extinct
Springsnail, Idaho (Pyrgulopsis idahoensis) - Wherever found	12/14/1992	9/5/2007	Original Data in Error - Taxonomic revision
Squirrel, Delmarva Peninsula fox (Sciurus niger cinereus) - Wherever found, except where listed as an experimental population	3/11/1967	12/16/2015	Recovered
Squirrel, Virginia northern flying (Glaucomys sabrinus fuscus) - Wherever found	7/31/1985	3/4/2013	Recovered
Sucker, Modoc (Catostomus microps) - Wherever found	6/11/1985	1/7/2016	Recovered
Sunflower, Eggert's (Helianthus eggertii) - Wherever found	5/22/1997	8/18/2005	Recovered
Treefrog, pine barrens (Hyla andersonii) - FL pop.	12/18/1977	11/22/1983	Original Data in Error - New information discovered
Trout, coastal cutthroat (Oncorhynchus clarkii clarkii) - Umpqua R.	9/13/1996	4/26/2000	Original Data in Error - Taxonomic revision
Turtle, Indian flap-shelled (Lissemys punctata punctata) - Wherever found	6/14/1976	2/29/1984	Original Data in Error - Erroneous data
Vole, Hualapai Mexican (Microtus mexicanus hualpaiensis) - Wherever found	10/1/1987	6/23/2017	Original Data in Error - Erroneous data
Whale, gray (Eschrichtius robustus) - except where listed	6/16/1994	6/16/1994	Recovered
Whale, humpback (Megaptera novaeangliae) - Brazil DPS	6/2/1970	10/11/2016	Recovered
Whale, humpback (Megaptera novaeangliae) - East Australia DPS	6/2/1970	10/11/2016	Recovered
Whale, humpback (Megaptera novaeangliae) - Gabon/Southwest Africa DPS	6/2/1970	10/11/2016	Recovered
Whale, humpback (Megaptera novaeangliae) - Hawaii DPS	6/2/1970	10/11/2016	Recovered
Whale, humpback (Megaptera novaeangliae) - Oceania DPS	6/2/1970	10/11/2016	Recovered
Whale, humpback (Megaptera novaeangliae) - Southeast Africa/Madagascar DPS	6/2/1970	10/11/2016	Recovered
Whale, humpback (Megaptera novaeangliae) - Southeastern Pacific DPS	6/2/1970	10/11/2016	Recovered
Whale, humpback (Megaptera novaeangliae) - West Australia DPS	6/2/1970	10/11/2016	Recovered
Whale, humpback (Megaptera novaeangliae) - West Indies DPS	6/2/1970	10/11/2016	Recovered
Wolf, gray (Canis lupus) - Northern Rocky Mountain DPS	3/9/1978	5/1/2017	Recovered
Woolly-star, Hoover's (Eriastrum hooveri) - Wherever found	7/19/1990	10/7/2003	Recovered

Notes: *Data as of July 24, 2017*
Source: *U.S. Fish & Wildlife Service, Threatened and Endangered Species System (TESS)*

Summary of Listed Species, Listed Populations[1] and Recovery Plans[2]

Group	United States[3]		Foreign		Total listings (U.S. and foreign)	U.S. listings with active recovery plans[2]
	Endangered	Threatened	Endangered	Threatened		
Animals						
Amphibians	20	15	8	1	44	22
Annelid Worms	0	0	0	0	0	0
Arachnids	12	0	0	0	12	12
Birds	81	20	217	18	336	87
Clams	75	14	2	0	91	71
Corals	0	6	1	16	23	0
Crustaceans	24	4	0	0	28	18
Fishes	92	72	22	6	192	105
Flatworms and Roundworms	0	0	0	0	0	0
Hydroids	0	0	0	0	0	0
Insects	73	11	4	0	88	42
Mammals	68	27	259	22	376	61
Millipedes	0	0	0	0	0	0
Reptiles	16	28	71	24	139	34
Snails	40	12	1	0	53	30
Sponges	0	0	0	0	0	0
Animal Subtotal	501	209	585	87	1,382	482
Plants						
Conifers and Cycads	1	3	0	2	6	3
Ferns and Allies	36	2	0	0	38	26
Flowering Plants	735	163	1	0	899	646
Lichens	2	0	0	0	2	2
Plant Subtotal	774	168	1	2	945	677
Grand Total	1,275	377	586	89	2,327	1,159

Notes: *Data as of July 24, 2017; (1) A listing has an E or a T in the "status" column of the tables in 50 CFR 17.11(h) or 50 CFR 17.12(h) (the "List of Endangered and Threatened Wildlife and Plants"). 19 animal species (13 in the U.S.[3] and 6 Foreign) are counted more than once in the above table, primarily because these animals have distinct population segments (each with its own individual listing status).*

The U.S. species counted more than once are:

- *Frog, mountain yellow-legged (Rana muscosa)*
- *Plover, piping (Charadrius melodus)*
- *Salamander, California tiger (Ambystoma californiense)*
- *Salmon, chinook (Oncorhynchus (=Salmo) tshawytscha)*
- *Salmon, chum (Oncorhynchus (=Salmo) keta)*
- *Salmon, coho (Oncorhynchus (=Salmo) kisutch)*
- *Salmon, sockeye (Oncorhynchus (=Salmo) nerka)*
- *Sea turtle, green (Chelonia mydas)*
- *Sea turtle, loggerhead (Caretta caretta)*
- *Steelhead (Oncorhynchus (=Salmo) mykiss)*
- *Sturgeon, Atlantic (Acipenser oxyrinchus oxyrinchus)*
- *Tern, roseate (Sterna dougallii dougallii)*
- *Wolf, gray (Canis lupus)*

The foreign species counted more than once are:

- *Caiman, broad-snouted (Caiman latirostris)*
- *Sea turtle, green (Chelonia mydas)*
- *Sea turtle, loggerhead (Caretta caretta)*
- *Shark, Scalloped Hammerhead (Sphyrna lewini)*
- *Vicuna (Vicugna vicugna)*
- *Whale, humpback (Megaptera novaeangliae)*

(2) There are a total of 603 distinct active (Draft and Final) recovery plans. Some recovery plans cover more than one species, and a few species have separate plans covering different parts of their ranges. This count includes only plans generated by the USFWS (or jointly by the USFWS and NMFS), and only listed species that occur in the United States; (3) United States listings include those populations in which the United States shares jurisdiction with another nation.

Source: *U.S. Fish & Wildlife Service, Threatened and Endangered Species System (TESS)*

Figure 1.1 Primary Energy Overview
(Quadrillion Btu)

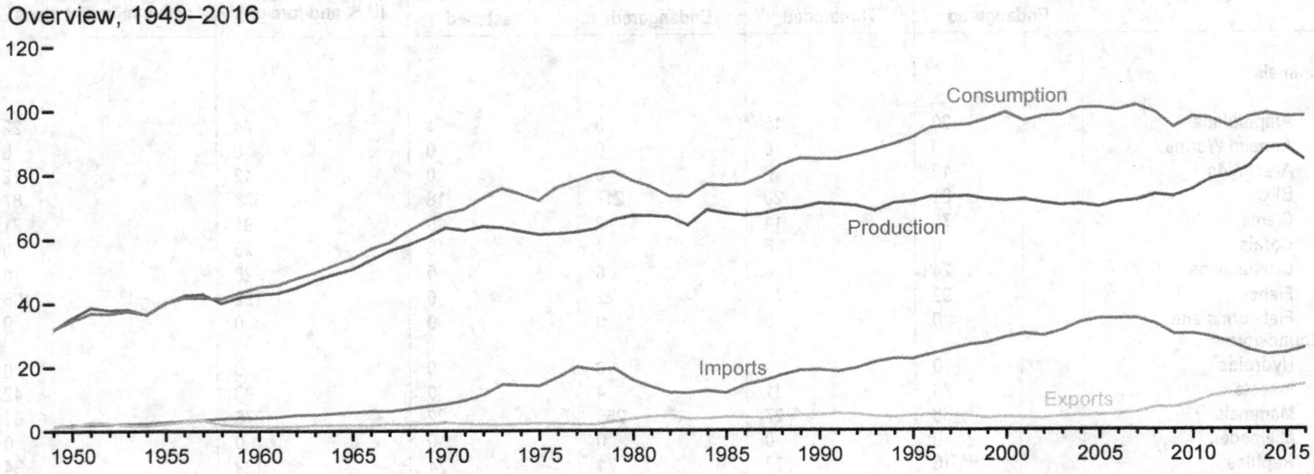

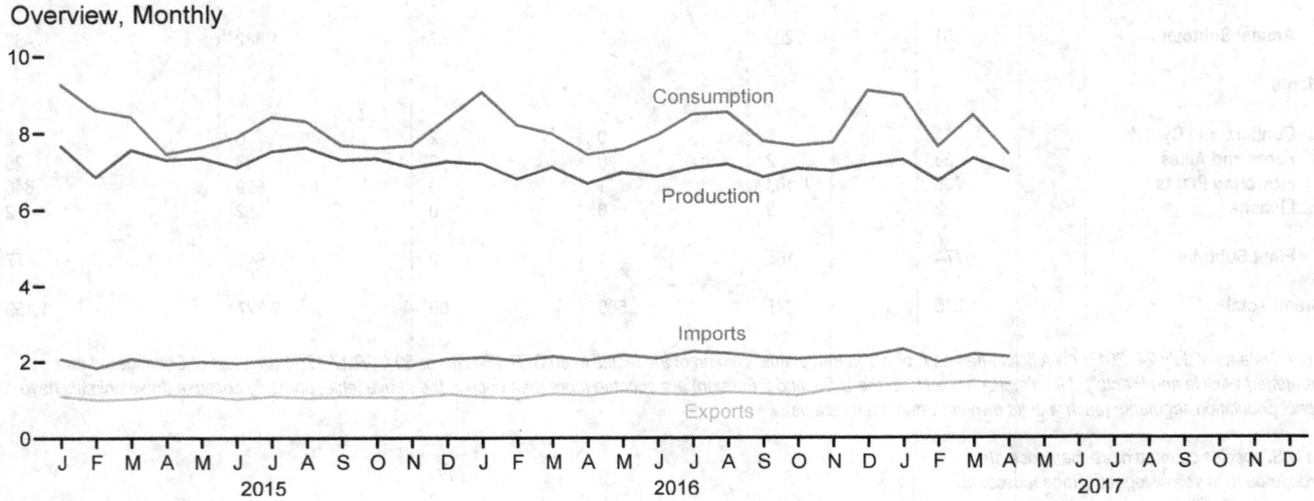

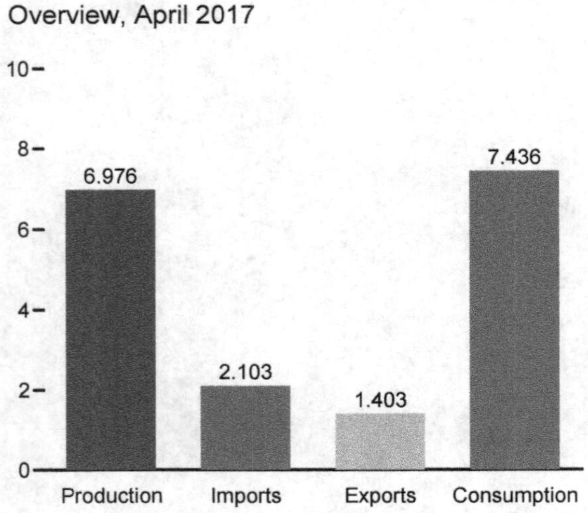

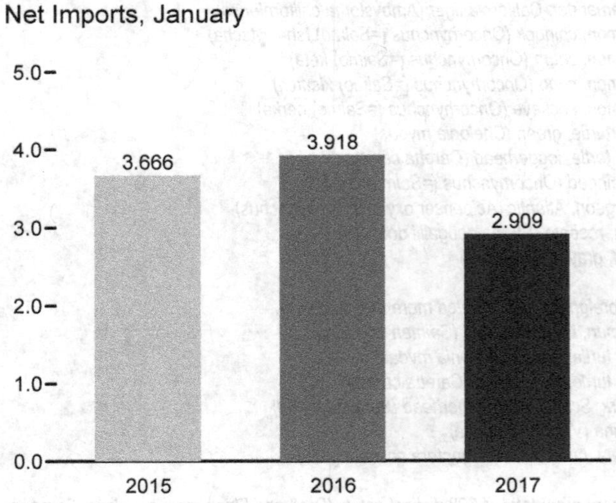

Web Page: http://www.eia.gov/totalenergy/data/monthly/#summary.
Source: Table 1.1.

Source: *U.S. Energy Information Administration, Monthly Energy Review, July 2017*

Table 1.1 Primary Energy Overview
(Quadrillion Btu)

	Production				Trade			Stock Change and Other[d]	Consumption			
	Fossil Fuels[a]	Nuclear Electric Power	Renew-able Energy[b]	Total	Imports	Exports	Net Imports[c]		Fossil Fuels[e]	Nuclear Electric Power	Renew-able Energy[b]	Total[f]
1950 Total	32.563	0.000	2.978	35.540	1.913	1.465	0.448	-1.372	31.632	0.000	2.978	34.616
1955 Total	37.364	.000	2.784	40.148	2.790	2.286	.504	-.444	37.410	.000	2.784	40.208
1960 Total	39.869	.006	2.928	42.803	4.188	1.477	2.710	-.427	42.137	.006	2.928	45.086
1965 Total	47.235	.043	3.396	50.674	5.892	1.829	4.063	-.722	50.577	.043	3.396	54.015
1970 Total	59.186	.239	4.070	63.495	8.342	2.632	5.709	-1.367	63.522	.239	4.070	67.838
1975 Total	54.733	1.900	4.687	61.320	14.032	2.323	11.709	-1.065	65.357	1.900	4.687	71.965
1980 Total	59.008	2.739	5.428	67.175	15.796	3.695	12.101	-1.210	69.828	2.739	5.428	78.067
1985 Total	57.539	4.076	6.084	67.698	11.781	4.196	7.584	1.110	66.093	4.076	6.084	76.392
1990 Total	58.560	6.104	6.040	70.704	18.817	4.752	14.065	-.284	72.332	6.104	6.040	84.484
1995 Total	57.540	7.075	6.557	71.173	22.180	4.496	17.684	2.174	77.262	7.075	6.559	91.031
2000 Total	57.366	7.862	6.102	71.330	28.865	3.962	24.904	2.583	84.735	7.862	6.104	98.817
2001 Total	58.541	8.029	5.162	71.732	30.052	3.731	26.321	-1.883	82.906	8.029	5.160	96.170
2002 Total	56.834	8.145	5.731	70.710	29.331	3.608	25.722	1.211	83.700	8.145	5.726	97.643
2003 Total	56.033	7.960	5.942	69.935	31.007	4.013	26.994	.989	83.992	7.960	5.944	97.918
2004 Total	55.942	8.223	6.063	70.228	33.492	4.351	29.141	.721	85.754	8.223	6.075	100.090
2005 Total	55.049	8.161	6.221	69.431	34.659	4.462	30.197	.560	85.709	8.161	6.233	100.188
2006 Total	55.934	8.215	6.586	70.735	34.649	4.727	29.921	-1.171	84.570	8.215	6.637	99.485
2007 Total	56.435	8.459	6.510	71.404	34.679	5.338	29.341	.270	85.927	8.459	6.523	101.015
2008 Total	57.588	8.426	7.191	73.205	32.970	6.949	26.021	-.336	83.178	8.426	7.174	98.891
2009 Total	56.669	8.355	7.620	72.645	29.690	6.920	22.770	-1.297	78.042	8.355	7.604	94.118
2010 Total	58.216	8.434	8.077	74.728	29.866	8.176	21.690	1.027	80.891	8.434	8.030	97.445
2011 Total	60.550	8.269	9.095	77.913	28.748	10.373	18.375	.553	79.447	8.269	8.999	96.842
2012 Total	62.303	8.062	8.743	79.108	27.068	11.267	15.801	-.492	77.487	8.062	8.706	94.416
2013 Total	64.201	8.244	9.250	81.696	24.623	11.788	12.835	2.627	79.440	8.244	9.276	97.157
2014 Total	69.653	8.338	9.607	87.597	23.241	12.270	10.971	-.239	80.240	8.338	9.570	98.329
2015 January	6.084	.777	.808	7.669	2.075	1.103	.972	.632	7.685	.777	.793	9.273
February	5.443	.664	.753	6.859	1.840	1.006	.834	.908	7.175	.664	.748	8.601
March	6.080	.675	.817	7.572	2.079	1.035	1.044	-.192	6.917	.675	.813	8.424
April	5.866	.625	.814	7.305	1.922	1.105	.816	-.661	6.003	.625	.812	7.460
May	5.860	.688	.807	7.355	2.000	1.110	.890	-.606	6.122	.688	.808	7.639
June	5.623	.717	.773	7.112	1.963	1.032	.930	-.145	6.386	.717	.775	7.897
July	5.978	.747	.798	7.523	2.032	1.095	.937	-.034	6.858	.747	.799	8.425
August	6.101	.757	.772	7.630	2.082	1.054	1.028	-.349	6.753	.757	.776	8.308
September	5.890	.695	.723	7.308	1.925	1.076	.849	-.475	6.237	.695	.730	7.682
October	5.956	.633	.755	7.345	1.901	1.070	.832	-.562	6.210	.633	.755	7.614
November	5.667	.630	.807	7.104	1.899	1.060	.839	-.269	6.222	.630	.804	7.674
December	5.673	.728	.862	7.264	2.076	1.156	.920	.183	6.764	.728	.857	8.367
Total	70.221	8.337	9.487	88.045	23.794	12.902	10.892	-1.572	79.330	8.337	9.471	97.365
2016 January	5.582	.758	.861	7.202	2.111	1.080	1.031	.824	R 7.433	.758	.844	R 9.057
February	5.267	.686	.852	6.805	2.022	1.038	.984	.417	R 6.658	.686	.844	8.206
March	5.495	.692	.924	7.110	2.139	1.151	.988	-.131	6.341	.692	.916	R 7.967
April	5.157	.652	.875	6.684	2.031	R 1.116	R .915	R -.160	5.902	.652	.870	R 7.438
May	5.382	.696	.887	6.965	2.169	R 1.227	R .942	R -.334	5.975	.696	.883	7.573
June	5.314	.703	.845	6.861	2.078	R 1.155	R .923	R .154	R 6.374	.703	.839	R 7.938
July	5.484	.736	.856	7.076	2.252	R 1.126	R 1.126	R .269	R 6.851	.736	.858	8.471
August	5.635	.748	.804	7.187	R 2.212	R 1.187	R 1.026	R .310	6.946	.748	.804	R 8.522
September	5.387	.684	.773	6.844	R 2.103	R 1.153	R .950	R -.023	6.295	.684	.772	7.771
October	5.612	.635	.819	7.066	R 2.065	R 1.117	R .948	-.365	6.183	.635	.813	R 7.649
November	5.497	.682	.817	6.996	2.111	R 1.255	R .856	R -.126	6.206	.682	.817	7.726
December	5.499	.749	.908	7.157	R 2.135	R 1.350	R .785	R 1.134	R 7.404	.749	.900	R 9.076
Total	65.310	8.422	10.220	83.953	R 25.429	R 13.955	R 11.474	R 1.967	R 78.569	8.422	10.161	R 97.394
2017 January	R 5.602	.765	.920	R 7.286	R 2.308	R 1.399	.909	R .753	R 7.264	.765	.897	R 8.948
February	R 5.197	.670	.866	R 6.733	R 1.966	R 1.393	.573	R .314	6.080	.670	.852	R 7.619
March	R 5.615	.681	1.023	R 7.318	R 2.176	R 1.449	R .727	R .394	6.731	.681	1.010	8.440
April	5.394	.593	.988	6.976	2.103	1.403	.700	-.240	5.842	.593	.983	7.436
4-Month Total	21.808	2.709	3.797	28.313	8.553	5.644	2.909	1.221	25.916	2.709	3.741	32.443
2016 4-Month Total	21.500	2.789	3.512	27.801	8.303	4.384	3.918	.950	26.334	2.789	3.474	32.669
2015 4-Month Total	23.473	2.741	3.192	29.405	7.916	4.249	3.666	.687	27.779	2.741	3.167	33.758

[a] Coal, natural gas (dry), crude oil, and natural gas plant liquids.
[b] See Tables 10.1–10.2c for notes on series components and estimation; and see Note, "Renewable Energy Production and Consumption," at end of Section 10.
[c] Net imports equal imports minus exports.
[d] Includes petroleum stock change and adjustments; natural gas net storage withdrawals and balancing item; coal stock change, losses, and unaccounted for; fuel ethanol stock change; and biodiesel stock change and balancing item.
[e] Coal, coal coke net imports, natural gas, and petroleum.
[f] Also includes electricity net imports.
R=Revised.

Notes: • See "Primary Energy," "Primary Energy Production," and "Primary Energy Consumption," in Glossary. • Totals may not equal sum of components due to independent rounding. • Geographic coverage is the 50 states and the District of Columbia.

Web Page: See http://www.eia.gov/totalenergy/data/monthly/#summary (Excel and CSV files) for all available annual data beginning in 1949 and monthly data beginning in 1973.

Sources: • **Production:** Table 1.2. • **Trade:** Tables 1.4a and 1.4b. • **Stock Change and Other:** Calculated as consumption minus production and net imports. • **Consumption:** Table 1.3.

Source: *U.S. Energy Information Administration, Monthly Energy Review, July 2017*

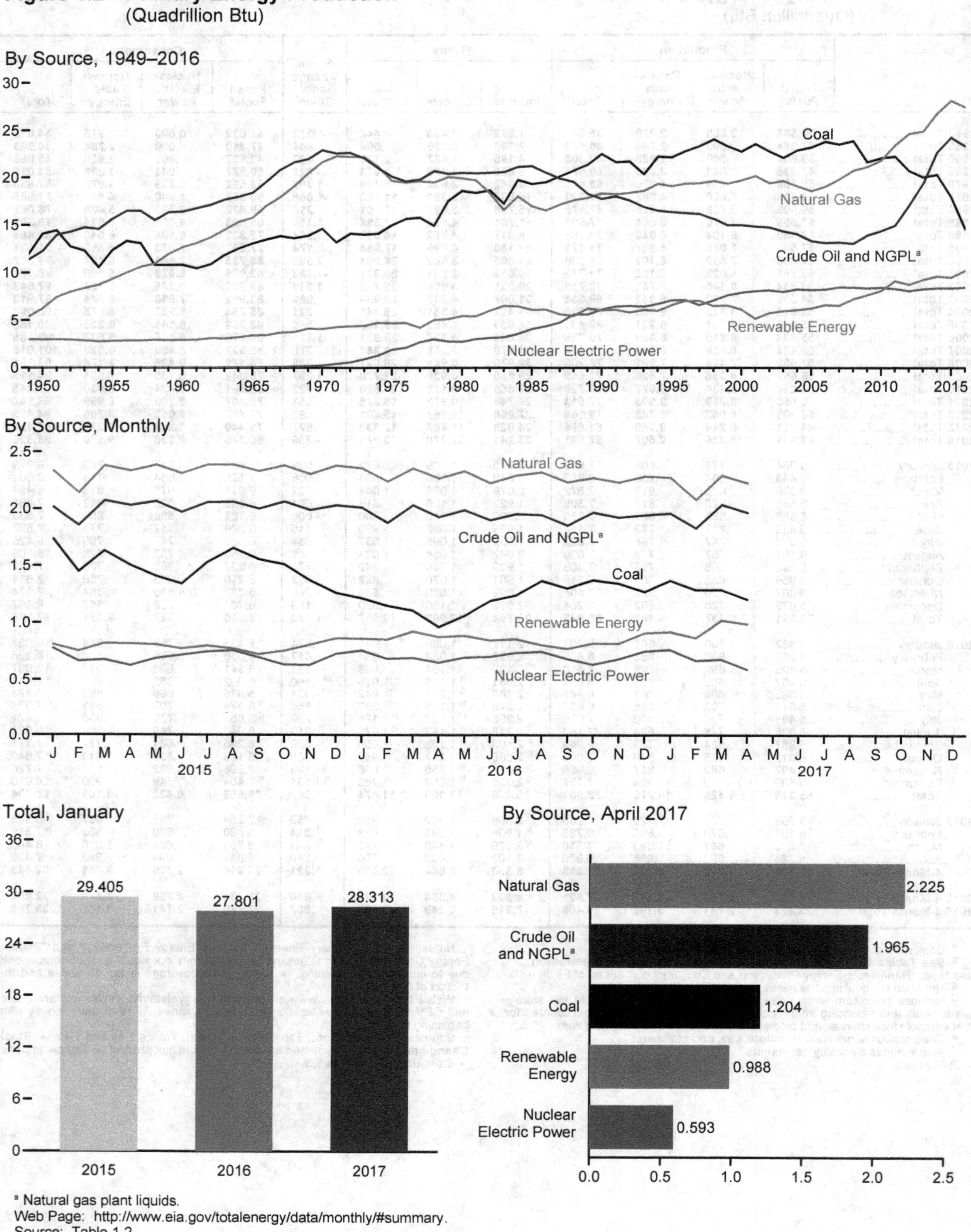

[a] Natural gas plant liquids.

Web Page: http://www.eia.gov/totalenergy/data/monthly/#summary.

Source: Table 1.2.

Source: *U.S. Energy Information Administration, Monthly Energy Review, July 2017*

Table 1.2 Primary Energy Production by Source
(Quadrillion Btu)

	Fossil Fuels					Nuclear Electric Power	Renewable Energy[a]						Total
	Coal[b]	Natural Gas (Dry)	Crude Oil[c]	NGPL[d]	Total		Hydro-electric Power[e]	Geo-thermal	Solar	Wind	Bio-mass	Total	
1950 Total	14.060	6.233	11.447	0.823	32.563	0.000	1.415	NA	NA	NA	1.562	2.978	35.540
1955 Total	12.370	9.345	14.410	1.240	37.364	.000	1.360	NA	NA	NA	1.424	2.784	40.148
1960 Total	10.817	12.656	14.935	1.461	39.869	.006	1.608	(s)	NA	NA	1.320	2.928	42.803
1965 Total	13.055	15.775	16.521	1.883	47.235	.043	2.059	.002	NA	NA	1.335	3.396	50.674
1970 Total	14.607	21.666	20.401	2.512	59.186	.239	2.634	.006	NA	NA	1.431	4.070	63.495
1975 Total	14.989	19.640	17.729	2.374	54.733	1.900	3.155	.034	NA	NA	1.499	4.687	61.320
1980 Total	18.598	19.908	18.249	2.254	59.008	2.739	2.900	.053	NA	NA	2.475	5.428	67.175
1985 Total	19.325	16.980	18.992	2.241	57.539	4.076	2.970	.097	(s)	(s)	3.016	6.084	67.698
1990 Total	22.488	18.326	15.571	2.175	58.560	6.104	3.046	.171	.059	.029	2.735	6.040	70.704
1995 Total	22.130	19.082	13.887	2.442	57.540	7.075	3.205	.152	.068	.033	3.099	6.557	71.173
2000 Total	22.735	19.662	12.358	2.611	57.366	7.862	2.811	.164	.063	.057	3.006	6.102	71.330
2001 Total	23.547	20.166	12.282	2.547	58.541	8.029	2.242	.164	.062	.070	2.624	5.162	71.732
2002 Total	22.732	19.382	12.160	2.559	56.834	8.145	2.689	.171	.060	.105	2.705	5.731	70.710
2003 Total	22.094	19.633	11.960	2.346	56.033	7.960	2.793	.173	.058	.113	2.805	5.942	69.935
2004 Total	22.852	19.074	11.550	2.466	55.942	8.223	2.688	.178	.058	.142	2.996	6.063	70.228
2005 Total	23.185	18.556	10.974	2.334	55.049	8.161	2.703	.181	.058	.178	3.101	6.221	69.431
2006 Total	23.790	19.022	10.767	2.356	55.934	8.215	2.869	.181	.061	.264	3.212	6.586	70.735
2007 Total	23.493	19.786	10.747	2.409	56.435	8.459	2.446	.186	.065	.341	3.472	6.510	71.404
2008 Total	23.851	20.703	10.614	2.419	57.588	8.426	2.511	.192	.074	.546	3.868	7.191	73.205
2009 Total	21.624	21.139	11.332	2.574	56.669	8.355	2.669	.200	.078	.721	3.953	7.620	72.645
2010 Total	22.038	21.806	11.591	2.781	58.216	8.434	2.539	.208	.090	.923	4.316	8.077	74.728
2011 Total	22.221	23.406	11.952	2.970	60.550	8.269	3.103	.212	.111	1.168	4.501	9.095	77.913
2012 Total	20.677	24.610	13.770	3.246	62.303	8.062	2.629	.212	.157	1.340	4.406	8.743	79.108
2013 Total	20.001	24.859	15.809	3.532	64.201	8.244	2.562	.214	.225	1.601	4.647	9.250	81.696
2014 Total	20.286	26.718	18.552	4.096	69.653	8.338	2.467	.214	.337	1.728	4.861	9.607	87.597
2015 January	1.734	2.334	1.662	.355	6.084	.777	.225	.018	.021	.141	.403	.808	7.669
February	1.448	2.140	1.523	.331	5.443	.664	.208	.017	.025	.139	.364	.753	6.859
March	1.628	2.380	1.695	.376	6.080	.675	.226	.018	.035	.143	.395	.817	7.572
April	1.502	2.334	1.651	.379	5.866	.625	.209	.017	.040	.167	.381	.814	7.305
May	1.409	2.385	1.679	.387	5.860	.688	.188	.018	.043	.160	.398	.807	7.355
June	1.341	2.311	1.598	.373	5.623	.717	.190	.017	.043	.125	.397	.773	7.112
July	1.531	2.389	1.669	.389	5.978	.747	.196	.018	.045	.127	.411	.798	7.523
August	1.654	2.387	1.663	.397	6.101	.757	.178	.018	.045	.122	.408	.772	7.630
September	1.555	2.332	1.616	.386	5.890	.695	.150	.016	.039	.130	.387	.723	7.308
October	1.510	2.383	1.658	.405	5.956	.633	.155	.018	.034	.153	.395	.755	7.345
November	1.373	2.305	1.596	.393	5.667	.630	.180	.018	.030	.183	.396	.807	7.104
December	1.262	2.380	1.635	.397	5.673	.728	.216	.018	.027	.187	.414	.862	7.264
Total	**17.946**	**28.061**	**19.647**	**4.567**	**70.221**	**8.337**	**2.321**	**.212**	**.426**	**1.777**	**4.751**	**9.487**	**88.045**
2016 January	1.214	[E]2.357	[E]1.631	.381	5.582	.758	.237	.019	.027	.173	.406	.861	7.202
February	1.148	[E]2.242	[E]1.518	.359	5.267	.686	.225	.018	.038	.188	.383	.852	6.805
March	1.107	[E]2.356	[E]1.627	.405	5.495	.692	.252	.019	.045	.205	.403	.924	7.110
April	.963	[E]2.267	[E]1.536	.391	5.157	.652	.237	.018	.050	.193	.377	.875	6.684
May	1.061	[E]2.331	[E]1.576	.414	5.382	.696	.236	.019	.058	.175	.398	.887	6.965
June	1.189	[E]2.225	[E]1.495	.404	5.314	.703	.213	.018	.059	.152	.403	.845	6.861
July	1.238	[E]2.292	[E]1.542	.412	5.484	.736	.198	.019	.064	.164	.412	.856	7.076
August	1.367	[E]2.322	[E]1.554	.392	5.635	.748	.180	.019	.062	.126	.416	.804	7.187
September	1.302	[E]2.233	[E]1.471	.382	5.387	.684	.152	.019	.057	.153	.392	.773	6.844
October	1.374	[E]2.271	[E]1.558	.408	5.612	.635	.161	.019	.050	.190	.399	.819	7.066
November	1.344	[E]2.230	[E]1.521	.402	5.497	.682	.175	.019	.042	.180	.401	.817	6.996
December	1.271	[E]2.285	[E]1.557	.386	5.499	.749	.210	.020	.037	.214	.427	.908	7.157
Total	**14.578**	**[E]27.412**	**[E]18.586**	**4.735**	**65.310**	**8.422**	**2.477**	**.226**	**.587**	**2.114**	**4.816**	**10.220**	**83.953**
2017 January	[R]1.369	[E]2.273	[E]1.571	.388	[R]5.602	.765	.258	.020	.036	.190	.416	.920	[R]7.286
February	[R]1.288	[RE]2.080	[RE]1.454	.375	[R]5.197	.670	.229	.018	.041	.202	.376	.866	[R]6.733
March	[R]1.287	[RE]2.292	[RE]1.615	.420	[R]5.615	.681	.281	.020	.066	.239	.417	1.023	[R]7.318
April	1.204	[E]2.225	[E]1.559	.405	5.394	.593	.272	.019	.072	.237	.388	.988	6.976
4-Month Total	**5.149**	**[E]8.870**	**[E]6.200**	**1.589**	**21.808**	**2.709**	**1.041**	**.076**	**.215**	**.867**	**1.597**	**3.797**	**28.313**
2016 4-Month Total	**4.431**	**[E]9.222**	**[E]6.312**	**1.536**	**21.500**	**2.789**	**.951**	**.074**	**.159**	**.759**	**1.568**	**3.512**	**27.801**
2015 4-Month Total	**6.312**	**9.188**	**6.532**	**1.441**	**23.473**	**2.741**	**.868**	**.070**	**.121**	**.590**	**1.543**	**3.192**	**29.405**

[a] Most data are estimates. See Tables 10.1–10.2c for notes on series components and estimation; and see Note, "Renewable Energy Production and Consumption," at end of Section 10.

[b] Beginning in 1989, includes waste coal supplied. Beginning in 2001, also includes a small amount of refuse recovery. See Table 6.1.

[c] Includes lease condensate.

[d] Natural gas plant liquids.

[e] Conventional hydroelectric power.

R=Revised. E=Estimate. NA=Not available. (s)=Less than 0.5 trillion Btu.

Notes: • See "Primary Energy Production" in Glossary. • Totals may not equal sum of components due to independent rounding. • Geographic coverage is the 50 states and the District of Columbia.

Web Page: See http://www.eia.gov/totalenergy/data/monthly/#summary (Excel and CSV files) for all available annual data beginning in 1949 and monthly data beginning in 1973.

Sources: See end of section.

Source: *U.S. Energy Information Administration, Monthly Energy Review, July 2017*

Figure 1.3 Primary Energy Consumption
(Quadrillion Btu)

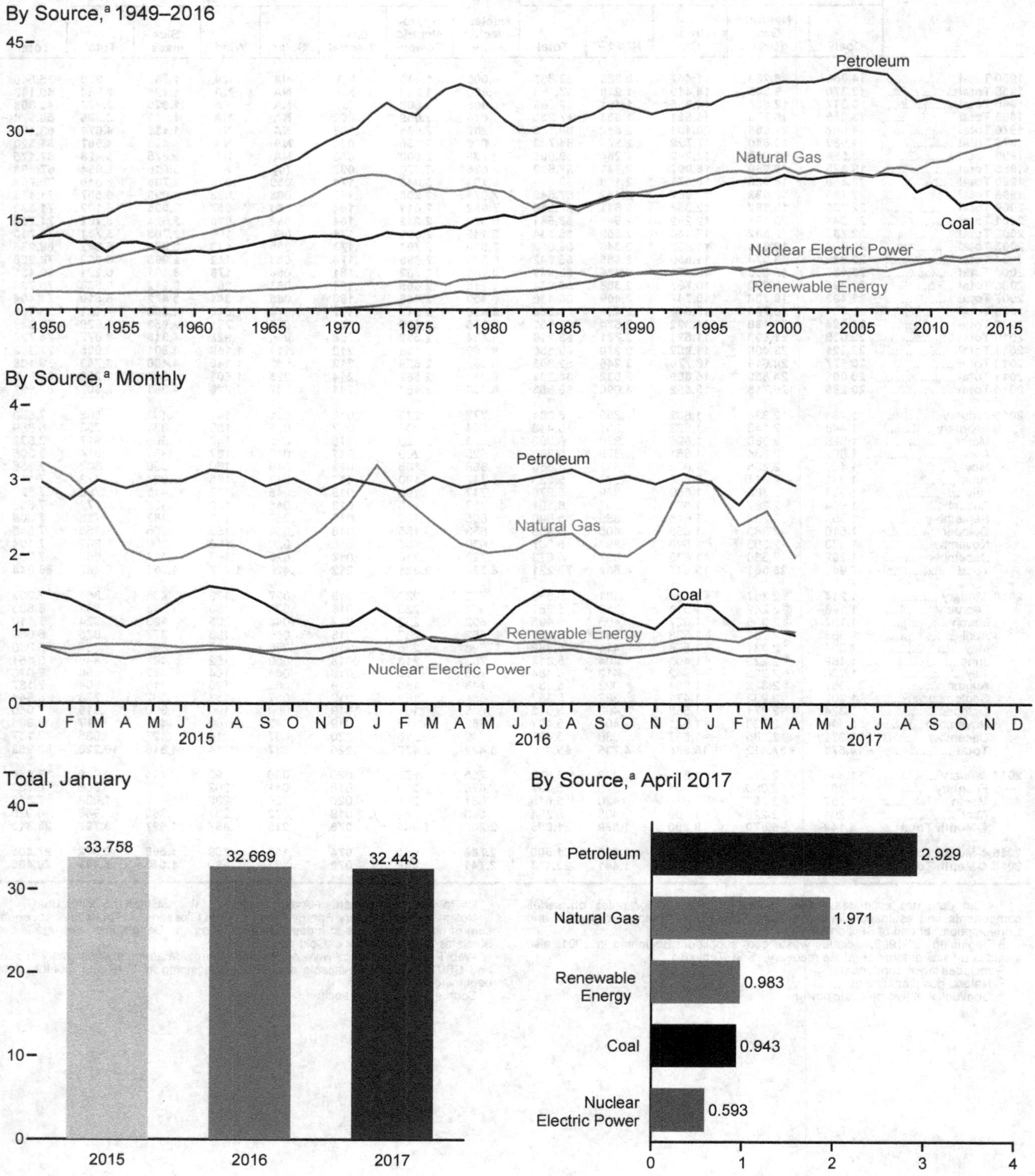

By Source,[a] 1949–2016

By Source,[a] Monthly

Total, January

By Source,[a] April 2017

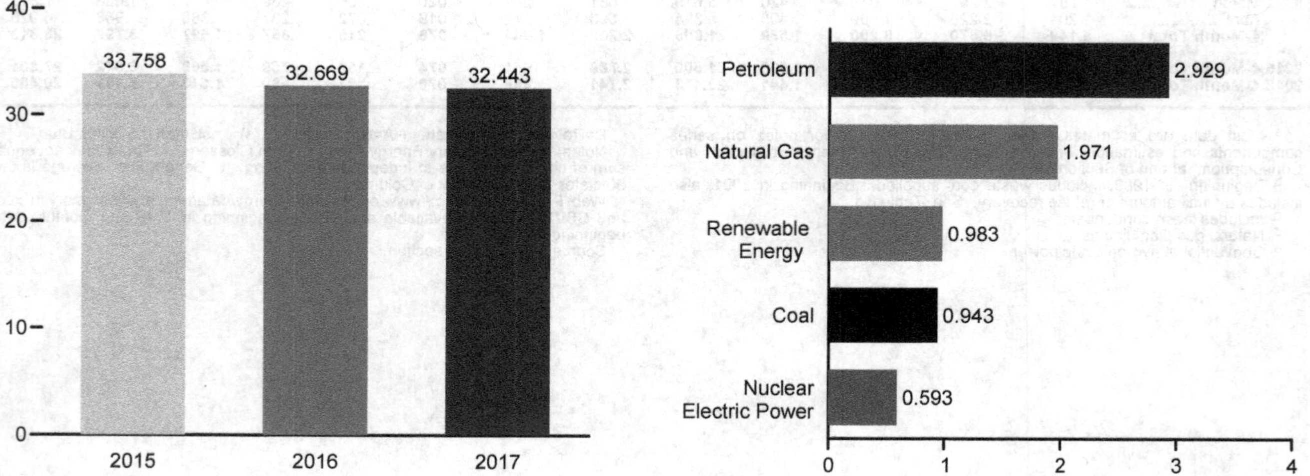

[a] Small quantities of net imports of coal coke and electricity are not shown.
Web Page: http://www.eia.gov/totalenergy/data/monthly/#summary.
Source: Table 1.3.

***Source:** U.S. Energy Information Administration, Monthly Energy Review, July 2017*

Table 1.3 Primary Energy Consumption by Source

(Quadrillion Btu)

	Fossil Fuels					Renewable Energy[a]						
	Coal	Natural Gas[b]	Petro-leum[c]	Total[d]	Nuclear Electric Power	Hydro-electric Power[e]	Geo-thermal	Solar	Wind	Bio-mass	Total	Total[f]
1950 Total	**12.347**	**5.968**	**13.315**	**31.632**	**0.000**	**1.415**	**NA**	**NA**	**NA**	**1.562**	**2.978**	**34.616**
1955 Total	**11.167**	**8.998**	**17.255**	**37.410**	**.000**	**1.360**	**NA**	**NA**	**NA**	**1.424**	**2.784**	**40.208**
1960 Total	**9.838**	**12.385**	**19.919**	**42.137**	**.006**	**1.608**	**(s)**	**NA**	**NA**	**1.320**	**2.928**	**45.086**
1965 Total	**11.581**	**15.769**	**23.246**	**50.577**	**.043**	**2.059**	**.002**	**NA**	**NA**	**1.335**	**3.396**	**54.015**
1970 Total	**12.265**	**21.795**	**29.521**	**63.522**	**.239**	**2.634**	**.006**	**NA**	**NA**	**1.431**	**4.070**	**67.838**
1975 Total	**12.663**	**19.948**	**32.732**	**65.357**	**1.900**	**3.155**	**.034**	**NA**	**NA**	**1.499**	**4.687**	**71.965**
1980 Total	**15.423**	**20.235**	**34.205**	**69.828**	**2.739**	**2.900**	**.053**	**NA**	**NA**	**2.475**	**5.428**	**78.067**
1985 Total	**17.478**	**17.703**	**30.925**	**66.093**	**4.076**	**2.970**	**.097**	**(s)**	**(s)**	**3.016**	**6.084**	**76.392**
1990 Total	**19.173**	**19.603**	**33.552**	**72.332**	**6.104**	**3.046**	**.171**	**.059**	**.029**	**2.735**	**6.040**	**84.484**
1995 Total	**20.089**	**22.671**	**34.441**	**77.262**	**7.075**	**3.205**	**.152**	**.068**	**.033**	**3.101**	**6.559**	**91.031**
2000 Total	**22.580**	**23.824**	**38.266**	**84.735**	**7.862**	**2.811**	**.164**	**.063**	**.057**	**3.008**	**6.104**	**98.817**
2001 Total	**21.914**	**22.773**	**38.190**	**82.906**	**8.029**	**2.242**	**.164**	**.062**	**.070**	**2.622**	**5.160**	**96.170**
2002 Total	**21.904**	**23.510**	**38.226**	**83.700**	**8.145**	**2.689**	**.171**	**.060**	**.105**	**2.701**	**5.726**	**97.643**
2003 Total	**22.321**	**22.831**	**38.790**	**83.992**	**7.960**	**2.793**	**.173**	**.058**	**.113**	**2.806**	**5.944**	**97.918**
2004 Total	**22.466**	**22.923**	**40.227**	**85.754**	**8.223**	**2.688**	**.178**	**.058**	**.142**	**3.008**	**6.075**	**100.090**
2005 Total	**22.797**	**22.565**	**40.303**	**85.709**	**8.161**	**2.703**	**.181**	**.058**	**.178**	**3.114**	**6.233**	**100.188**
2006 Total	**22.447**	**22.239**	**39.824**	**84.570**	**8.215**	**2.869**	**.181**	**.061**	**.264**	**3.262**	**6.637**	**99.485**
2007 Total	**22.749**	**23.663**	**39.489**	**85.927**	**8.459**	**2.446**	**.186**	**.065**	**.341**	**3.485**	**6.523**	**101.015**
2008 Total	**22.387**	**23.843**	**36.907**	**83.178**	**8.426**	**2.511**	**.192**	**.074**	**.546**	**3.851**	**7.174**	**98.891**
2009 Total	**19.691**	**23.416**	**34.959**	**78.042**	**8.355**	**2.669**	**.200**	**.078**	**.721**	**3.936**	**7.604**	**94.118**
2010 Total	**20.834**	**24.575**	**35.489**	**80.891**	**8.434**	**2.539**	**.208**	**.090**	**.923**	**4.270**	**8.030**	**97.445**
2011 Total	**19.658**	**24.955**	**34.824**	**79.447**	**8.269**	**3.103**	**.212**	**.111**	**1.168**	**4.405**	**8.999**	**96.842**
2012 Total	**17.378**	**26.089**	**34.016**	**77.487**	**8.062**	**2.629**	**.212**	**.157**	**1.340**	**4.369**	**8.706**	**94.416**
2013 Total	**18.039**	**26.805**	**34.613**	**79.440**	**8.244**	**2.562**	**.214**	**.225**	**1.601**	**4.673**	**9.276**	**97.157**
2014 Total	**17.998**	**27.383**	**34.881**	**80.240**	**8.338**	**2.467**	**.214**	**.337**	**1.728**	**4.825**	**9.570**	**98.329**
2015 January	1.498	3.223	2.966	7.685	.777	.225	.018	.021	.141	.388	.793	9.273
February	1.409	3.028	2.739	7.175	.664	.208	.017	.025	.139	.360	.748	8.601
March	1.238	2.682	2.996	6.917	.675	.226	.018	.035	.143	.391	.813	8.424
April	1.037	2.078	2.890	6.003	.625	.209	.017	.040	.167	.380	.812	7.460
May	1.206	1.923	2.995	6.122	.688	.188	.018	.043	.160	.400	.808	7.639
June	1.439	1.967	2.983	6.386	.717	.190	.017	.043	.125	.399	.775	7.897
July	1.587	2.140	3.132	6.858	.747	.196	.018	.045	.127	.413	.799	8.425
August	1.531	2.124	3.099	6.753	.757	.178	.018	.045	.122	.413	.776	8.308
September	1.351	1.968	2.917	6.237	.695	.150	.016	.039	.130	.394	.730	7.682
October	1.138	2.056	3.017	6.210	.633	.155	.018	.034	.153	.396	.755	7.614
November	1.045	2.328	2.851	6.222	.630	.180	.018	.030	.183	.393	.804	7.674
December	1.070	2.679	3.016	6.764	.728	.216	.018	.027	.187	.408	.857	8.367
Total	**15.549**	**28.196**	**35.603**	**79.330**	**8.337**	**2.321**	**.212**	**.426**	**1.777**	**4.734**	**9.471**	**97.365**
2016 January	R 1.297	3.203	2.935	R 7.433	.758	.237	.019	.027	.173	.388	.844	R 9.057
February	1.073	2.745	2.841	R 6.658	.686	.225	.018	.038	.188	.375	.844	8.206
March	.866	R 2.438	3.037	6.341	.692	.252	.019	.045	.205	.395	.916	R 7.967
April	.842	2.159	2.902	5.902	.652	.237	.018	.050	.193	.372	.870	R 7.438
May	.960	2.037	2.979	5.975	.696	.236	.019	.058	.175	.395	.883	7.573
June	R 1.317	2.073	2.985	R 6.374	.703	.213	.018	.059	.152	.397	.839	R 7.938
July	1.530	2.264	3.059	R 6.851	.736	.198	.019	.064	.164	.414	.858	8.471
August	1.521	R 2.288	3.139	6.946	.748	.180	.019	.062	.126	.417	.804	R 8.522
September	1.298	R 2.014	2.984	6.295	.684	.152	.019	.057	.153	.391	.772	7.771
October	R 1.149	1.990	3.048	6.183	.635	.161	.019	.050	.190	.394	.813	R 7.649
November	1.022	R 2.240	2.948	6.206	.682	.175	.019	.042	.180	.400	.817	7.726
December	R 1.352	R 2.970	3.085	R 7.404	.749	.210	.020	.037	.214	.419	.900	R 9.076
Total	R **14.227**	R **28.419**	**35.942**	R **78.569**	**8.422**	**2.477**	**.226**	**.587**	**2.114**	**4.756**	**10.161**	R **97.394**
2017 January	R 1.323	R 2.980	2.963	R 7.264	.765	.258	.020	.036	.190	.393	.897	R 8.948
February	R 1.022	2.393	2.666	6.080	.670	.229	.018	.041	.202	.362	.852	R 7.619
March	R 1.039	R 2.589	3.105	6.731	.681	.281	.020	.066	.239	.404	1.010	8.440
April	.943	1.971	2.929	5.842	.593	.272	.019	.072	.237	.383	.983	7.436
4-Month Total	**4.326**	**9.933**	**11.664**	**25.916**	**2.709**	**1.041**	**.076**	**.215**	**.867**	**1.542**	**3.741**	**32.443**
2016 4-Month Total	**4.078**	**10.544**	**11.715**	**26.334**	**2.789**	**.951**	**.074**	**.159**	**.759**	**1.531**	**3.474**	**32.669**
2015 4-Month Total	**5.182**	**11.011**	**11.592**	**27.779**	**2.741**	**.868**	**.070**	**.121**	**.590**	**1.518**	**3.167**	**33.758**

[a] Most data are estimates. See Tables 10.1–10.2c for notes on series components and estimation; and see Note, "Renewable Energy Production and Consumption," at end of Section 10.

[b] Natural gas only; excludes supplemental gaseous fuels. See Note 3, "Supplemental Gaseous Fuels," at end of Section 4.

[c] Petroleum products supplied, including natural gas plant liquids and crude oil burned as fuel. Does not include biofuels that have been blended with petroleum—biofuels are included in "Biomass."

[d] Includes coal coke net imports. See Tables 1.4a and 1.4b.

[e] Conventional hydroelectric power.

[f] Includes coal coke net imports and electricity net imports, which are not separately displayed. See Tables 1.4a and 1.4b.

R=Revised. NA=Not available. (s)=Less than 0.5 trillion Btu.

Notes: • See "Primary Energy Consumption" in Glossary. • See Table D1 for estimated energy consumption for 1635–1945. • Totals may not equal sum of components due to independent rounding. • Geographic coverage is the 50 states and the District of Columbia.

Web Page: See http://www.eia.gov/totalenergy/data/monthly/#summary (Excel and CSV files) for all available annual data beginning in 1949 and monthly data beginning in 1973.

Sources: See end of section.

Source: *U.S. Energy Information Administration, Monthly Energy Review, July 2017*

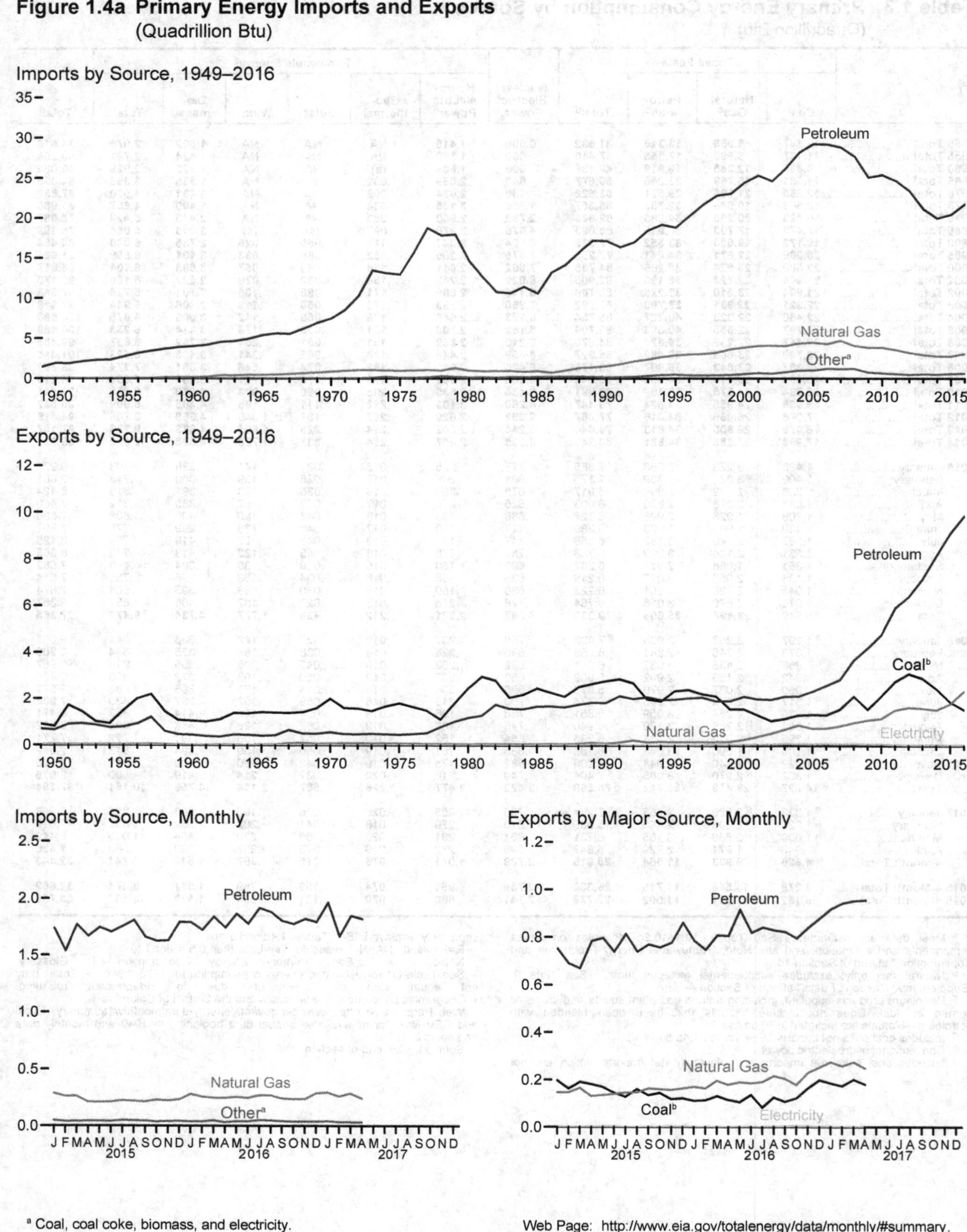

[a] Coal, coal coke, biomass, and electricity.
[b] Includes coal coke.

Web Page: http://www.eia.gov/totalenergy/data/monthly/#summary.
Sources: Tables 1.4a and 1.4b.

Source: *U.S. Energy Information Administration, Monthly Energy Review, July 2017*

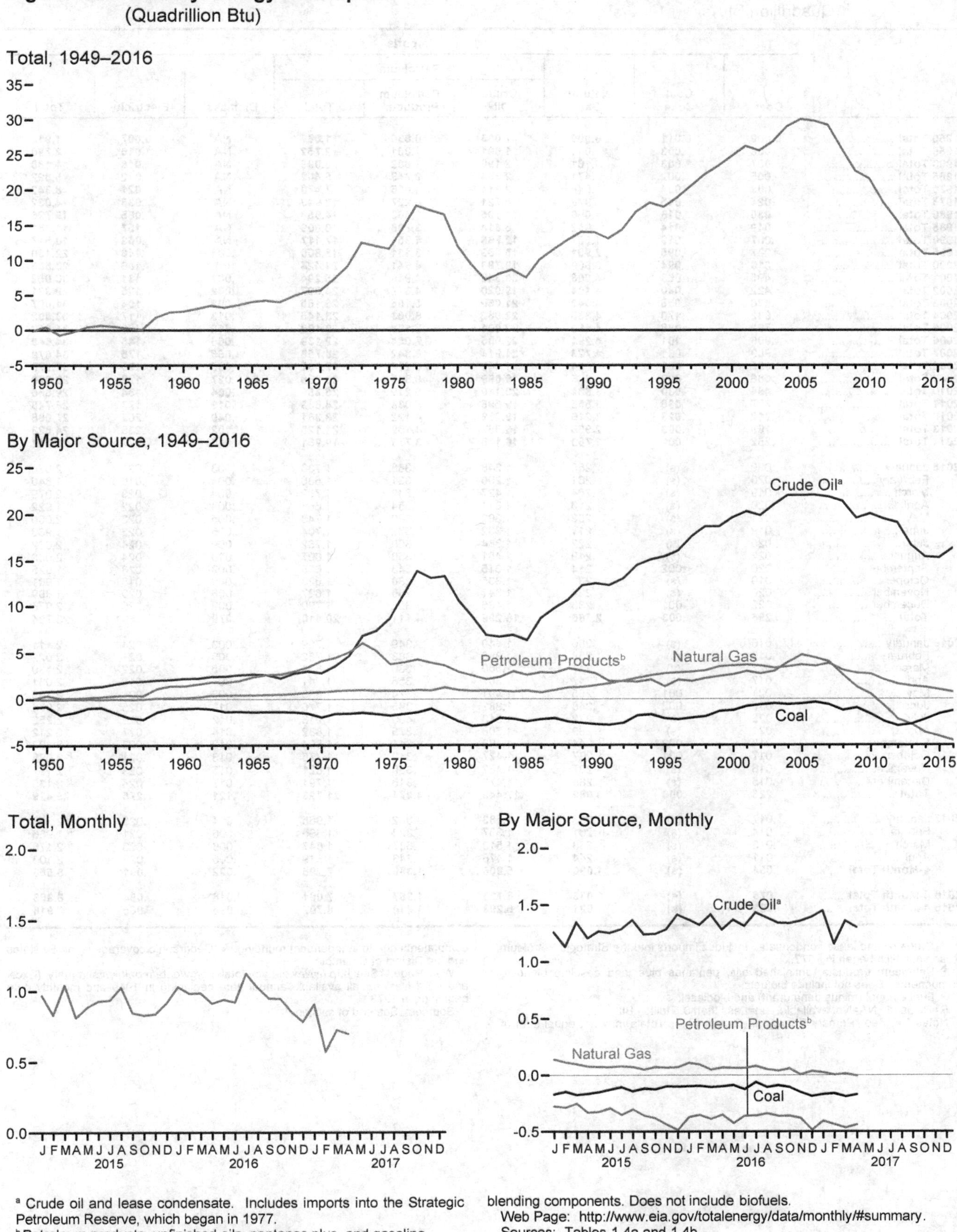

[a] Crude oil and lease condensate. Includes imports into the Strategic Petroleum Reserve, which began in 1977.
[b] Petroleum products, unfinished oils, pentanes plus, and gasoline blending components. Does not include biofuels.

Web Page: http://www.eia.gov/totalenergy/data/monthly/#summary.
Sources: Tables 1.4a and 1.4b.

Source: *U.S. Energy Information Administration, Monthly Energy Review, July 2017*

Table 1.4a Primary Energy Imports by Source

(Quadrillion Btu)

	Imports								
				Petroleum					
	Coal	Coal Coke	Natural Gas	Crude Oil[a]	Petroleum Products[b]	Total	Biomass[c]	Electricity	Total
1950 Total	**0.009**	**0.011**	**0.000**	**1.056**	**0.830**	**1.886**	**NA**	**0.007**	**1.913**
1955 Total	**.008**	**.003**	**.011**	**1.691**	**1.061**	**2.752**	**NA**	**.016**	**2.790**
1960 Total	**.007**	**.003**	**.161**	**2.196**	**1.802**	**3.999**	**NA**	**.018**	**4.188**
1965 Total	**.005**	**.002**	**.471**	**2.654**	**2.748**	**5.402**	**NA**	**.012**	**5.892**
1970 Total	**.001**	**.004**	**.846**	**2.814**	**4.656**	**7.470**	**NA**	**.021**	**8.342**
1975 Total	**.024**	**.045**	**.978**	**8.721**	**4.227**	**12.948**	**NA**	**.038**	**14.032**
1980 Total	**.030**	**.016**	**1.006**	**11.195**	**3.463**	**14.658**	**NA**	**.085**	**15.796**
1985 Total	**.049**	**.014**	**.952**	**6.814**	**3.796**	**10.609**	**NA**	**.157**	**11.781**
1990 Total	**.067**	**.019**	**1.551**	**12.766**	**4.351**	**17.117**	**NA**	**.063**	**18.817**
1995 Total	**.237**	**.095**	**2.901**	**15.669**	**3.131**	**18.800**	**.001**	**.146**	**22.180**
2000 Total	**.313**	**.094**	**3.869**	**19.783**	**4.641**	**24.424**	**(s)**	**.166**	**28.865**
2001 Total	**.495**	**.063**	**4.068**	**20.348**	**4.946**	**25.294**	**.002**	**.131**	**30.052**
2002 Total	**.422**	**.080**	**4.104**	**19.920**	**4.677**	**24.597**	**.002**	**.125**	**29.331**
2003 Total	**.626**	**.068**	**4.042**	**21.060**	**5.105**	**26.165**	**.002**	**.104**	**31.007**
2004 Total	**.682**	**.170**	**4.365**	**22.082**	**6.063**	**28.145**	**.013**	**.117**	**33.492**
2005 Total	**.762**	**.088**	**4.450**	**22.091**	**7.108**	**29.198**	**.012**	**.150**	**34.659**
2006 Total	**.906**	**.101**	**4.291**	**22.085**	**7.054**	**29.139**	**.066**	**.146**	**34.649**
2007 Total	**.909**	**.061**	**4.723**	**21.914**	**6.842**	**28.756**	**.055**	**.175**	**34.679**
2008 Total	**.855**	**.089**	**4.084**	**21.448**	**6.214**	**27.662**	**.085**	**.195**	**32.970**
2009 Total	**.566**	**.009**	**3.845**	**19.699**	**5.367**	**25.066**	**.027**	**.178**	**29.690**
2010 Total	**.484**	**.030**	**3.834**	**20.140**	**5.219**	**25.359**	**.004**	**.154**	**29.866**
2011 Total	**.327**	**.035**	**3.555**	**19.595**	**5.038**	**24.633**	**.019**	**.178**	**28.748**
2012 Total	**.212**	**.028**	**3.216**	**19.239**	**4.122**	**23.361**	**.049**	**.202**	**27.068**
2013 Total	**.199**	**.003**	**2.955**	**16.957**	**4.169**	**21.126**	**.102**	**.236**	**24.623**
2014 Total	**.252**	**.002**	**2.763**	**16.178**	**3.773**	**19.951**	**.046**	**.227**	**23.241**
2015 January	.029	(s)	.286	1.348	.388	1.736	.003	.021	2.075
February	.020	(s)	.261	1.206	.331	1.536	.004	.019	1.840
March	.019	(s)	.264	1.427	.342	1.769	.004	.023	2.079
April	.020	(s)	.210	1.311	.354	1.665	.004	.022	1.922
May	.021	(s)	.209	1.362	.380	1.743	.005	.023	2.000
June	.019	(s)	.211	1.332	.372	1.704	.006	.023	1.963
July	.025	(s)	.222	1.384	.368	1.752	.009	.024	2.032
August	.022	(s)	.219	1.451	.356	1.807	.010	.024	2.082
September	.020	.002	.214	1.315	.343	1.658	.009	.023	1.925
October	.019	(s)	.232	1.335	.288	1.623	.009	.018	1.901
November	.020	(s)	.224	1.341	.286	1.627	.008	.020	1.899
December	.022	.001	.233	1.486	.305	1.790	.009	.020	2.076
Total	**.256**	**.003**	**2.786**	**16.299**	**4.111**	**20.410**	**.079**	**.259**	**23.794**
2016 January	.016	(s)	.280	1.440	.349	1.789	.003	.024	2.111
February	.019	(s)	.258	1.388	.333	1.722	.003	.021	2.022
March	.027	(s)	.247	1.509	.330	1.839	.005	.022	2.139
April	.017	(s)	.247	1.387	.355	1.741	.007	.018	2.031
May	.021	.001	.255	1.491	.374	1.865	.008	.021	2.169
June	.015	.002	.248	1.382	.395	1.776	.013	.025	2.078
July	.022	(s)	.272	1.518	.400	1.918	.012	.028	2.252
August	.021	(s)	R .269	1.508	.375	1.882	.014	.027	R 2.212
September	.018	.002	R .244	1.463	.341	1.804	.012	.023	R 2.103
October	.017	.001	R .237	1.427	.348	1.775	.013	.021	R 2.065
November	.016	(s)	R .237	1.462	.359	1.821	.015	.023	2.111
December	.015	(s)	R .288	1.475	.316	1.791	.017	.024	R 2.135
Total	**.223**	**.006**	**R 3.082**	**17.449**	**4.274**	**21.723**	**.121**	**.275**	**R 25.429**
2017 January	.017	(s)	R .298	1.583	.382	1.965	.004	.025	R 2.308
February	.014	(s)	R .261	1.337	.328	1.665	.006	.021	R 1.966
March	.013	(s)	R .288	1.510	.337	1.847	.006	.023	R 2.176
April	.011	(s)	.244	1.476	.343	1.819	.006	.023	2.103
4-Month Total	**.054**	**(s)**	**1.090**	**5.906**	**1.389**	**7.295**	**.022**	**.091**	**8.553**
2016 4-Month Total	**.078**	**(s)**	**1.033**	**5.723**	**1.367**	**7.091**	**.018**	**.084**	**8.303**
2015 4-Month Total	**.088**	**(s)**	**1.021**	**5.293**	**1.414**	**6.707**	**.015**	**.085**	**7.916**

[a] Crude oil and lease condensate. Includes imports into the Strategic Petroleum Reserve, which began in 1977.

[b] Petroleum products, unfinished oils, pentanes plus, and gasoline blending components. Does not include biofuels.

[c] Fuel ethanol (minus denaturant) and biodiesel.

R=Revised. NA=Not available. (s)=Less than 0.5 trillion Btu.

Notes: • See "Primary Energy" in Glossary. • Totals may not equal sum of components due to independent rounding. • Geographic coverage is the 50 states and the District of Columbia.

Web Page: See http://www.eia.gov/totalenergy/data/monthly/#summary (Excel and CSV files) for all available annual data beginning in 1949 and monthly data beginning in 1973.

Sources: See end of section.

Source: *U.S. Energy Information Administration, Monthly Energy Review, July 2017*

Table 1.4b Primary Energy Exports by Source and Total Net Imports
(Quadrillion Btu)

	Exports									Net Imports[a]
				Petroleum						
	Coal	Coal Coke	Natural Gas	Crude Oil[b]	Petroleum Products[c]	Total	Biomass[d]	Electricity	Total	Total
1950 Total	0.786	0.010	0.027	0.202	0.440	0.642	NA	0.001	1.465	0.448
1955 Total	1.465	.013	.032	.067	.707	.774	NA	.002	2.286	.504
1960 Total	1.023	.009	.012	.018	.413	.431	NA	.003	1.477	2.710
1965 Total	1.376	.021	.027	.006	.386	.392	NA	.013	1.829	4.063
1970 Total	1.936	.061	.072	.029	.520	.549	NA	.014	2.632	5.709
1975 Total	1.761	.032	.074	.012	.427	.439	NA	.017	2.323	11.709
1980 Total	2.421	.051	.049	.609	.551	1.160	NA	.014	3.695	12.101
1985 Total	2.438	.028	.056	.432	1.225	1.657	NA	.017	4.196	7.584
1990 Total	2.772	.014	.087	.230	1.594	1.824	NA	.055	4.752	14.065
1995 Total	2.318	.034	.156	.200	1.776	1.976	NA	.012	4.496	17.684
2000 Total	1.528	.028	.245	.106	2.003	2.110	NA	.051	3.962	24.904
2001 Total	1.265	.033	.377	.043	1.956	1.999	(s)	.056	3.731	26.321
2002 Total	1.032	.020	.520	.019	1.963	1.982	(s)	.054	3.608	25.722
2003 Total	1.117	.018	.686	.026	2.083	2.110	.001	.082	4.013	26.994
2004 Total	1.253	.033	.862	.057	2.068	2.125	.001	.078	4.351	29.141
2005 Total	1.273	.043	.735	.067	2.276	2.344	.001	.065	4.462	30.197
2006 Total	1.264	.040	.730	.052	2.554	2.606	.005	.083	4.727	29.921
2007 Total	1.507	.036	.830	.058	2.803	2.861	.036	.069	5.338	29.341
2008 Total	2.071	.049	.972	.061	3.626	3.686	.089	.083	6.949	26.021
2009 Total	1.515	.032	1.082	.093	4.101	4.194	.035	.062	6.920	22.770
2010 Total	2.101	.036	1.147	.088	4.691	4.780	.047	.065	8.176	21.690
2011 Total	2.751	.024	1.519	.100	5.820	5.919	.108	.051	10.373	18.375
2012 Total	3.087	.024	1.633	.143	6.261	6.404	.078	.041	11.267	15.801
2013 Total	2.895	.021	1.587	.284	6.886	7.170	.076	.039	11.788	12.835
2014 Total	2.435	.023	1.528	.744	7.414	8.158	.081	.045	12.270	10.971
2015 January	.197	.002	.146	.087	.662	.749	.006	.003	1.103	.972
February	.163	.001	.146	.070	.615	.685	.006	.005	1.006	.834
March	.191	.001	.165	.077	.590	.667	.008	.003	1.035	1.044
April	.181	.002	.132	.102	.680	.782	.007	.002	1.105	.816
May	.169	.003	.135	.093	.701	.794	.007	.002	1.110	.890
June	.145	.003	.139	.076	.660	.736	.007	.002	1.032	.930
July	.128	.001	.145	.096	.715	.811	.007	.002	1.095	.937
August	.161	.001	.146	.081	.656	.737	.006	.002	1.054	1.028
September	.135	.002	.164	.070	.697	.767	.006	.002	1.076	.849
October	.144	.002	.160	.088	.667	.755	.007	.002	1.070	.832
November	.118	.002	.157	.055	.721	.775	.005	.002	1.060	.839
December	.121	.002	.163	.069	.790	.859	.008	.003	1.156	.920
Total	**1.852**	**.021**	**1.800**	**.964**	**8.153**	**9.118**	**.080**	**.031**	**12.902**	**10.892**
2016 January	.111	.001	.170	.065	.719	.784	.012	.002	1.080	1.031
February	.113	(s)	.164	.062	.683	.745	.012	.003	1.038	.984
March	.130	.001	.197	.090	.714	.804	.015	.004	1.151	.988
April	.115	.001	R.179	.102	.701	.803	.014	.003	R1.116	R.915
May	.105	.001	R.190	.117	.798	.915	.013	.003	R1.227	R.942
June	.136	.002	R.185	.066	.751	.817	.013	.002	R1.155	R.923
July	.082	.001	R.190	.084	.755	.839	.011	.002	R1.126	R1.126
August	.125	.003	R.216	.117	.710	.826	.014	.003	R1.187	R1.026
September	.107	.003	R.204	.119	.701	.820	.016	.003	R1.153	R.950
October	.122	.004	R.178	.087	.705	.792	.018	.003	R1.117	R.948
November	.164	.005	R.230	.103	.736	.838	.016	.002	R1.255	R.856
December	.199	.002	R.253	.078	.799	.877	.016	.002	R1.350	R.785
Total	**1.510**	**.025**	**R2.356**	**1.089**	**8.771**	**9.860**	**.170**	**.033**	**R13.955**	**R11.474**
2017 January	.185	.003	R.274	.132	.785	.918	.017	.002	R1.399	.909
February	.173	.001	R.257	.179	.762	.941	.017	.003	R1.393	.573
March	.201	.002	R.274	.148	.802	.950	.018	.004	R1.449	R.727
April	.181	.001	.249	.172	.780	.952	.015	.005	1.403	.700
4-Month Total	**.740**	**.007**	**1.055**	**.631**	**3.129**	**3.760**	**.067**	**.014**	**5.644**	**2.909**
2016 4-Month Total	**.469**	**.003**	**.710**	**.318**	**2.817**	**3.136**	**.054**	**.012**	**4.384**	**3.918**
2015 4-Month Total	**.731**	**.006**	**.589**	**.337**	**2.546**	**2.883**	**.027**	**.013**	**4.249**	**3.666**

[a] Net imports equal imports minus exports.
[b] Crude oil and lease condensate.
[c] Petroleum products, unfinished oils, pentanes plus, and gasoline blending components. Does not include biofuels.
[d] Beginning in 2001, includes biodiesel. Beginning in 2010, also includes fuel ethanol (minus denaturant). Beginning in 2016, also includes wood and wood-derived fuels.
R=Revised. NA=Not available. (s)=Less than 0.5 trillion Btu.

Notes: • See "Primary Energy" in Glossary. • Totals may not equal sum of components due to independent rounding. • Geographic coverage is the 50 states and the District of Columbia.
Web Page: See http://www.eia.gov/totalenergy/data/monthly/#summary (Excel and CSV files) for all available annual data beginning in 1949 and monthly data beginning in 1973.
Sources: See end of section.

Source: *U.S. Energy Information Administration, Monthly Energy Review, July 2017*

Figure 1.5 Merchandise Trade Value (Billion Dollars[a])

Imports and Exports, 1974–2016

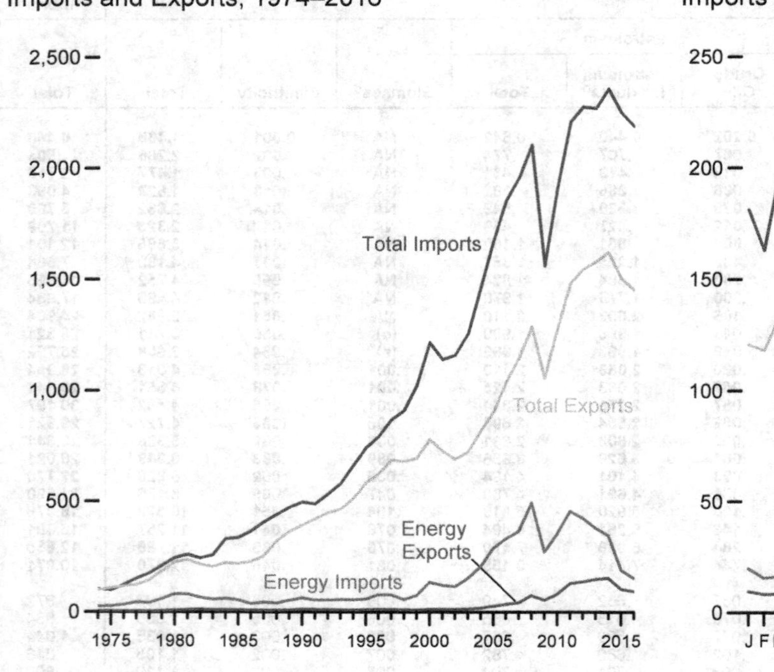

Imports and Exports, Monthly

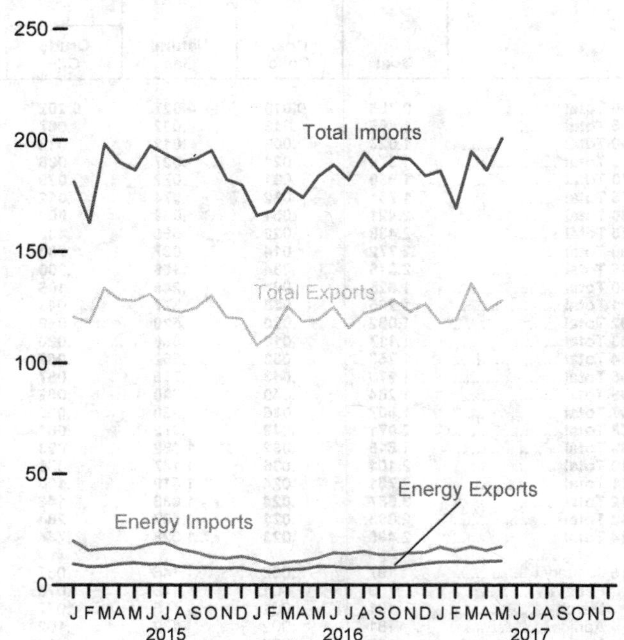

Trade Balance, 1974–2016

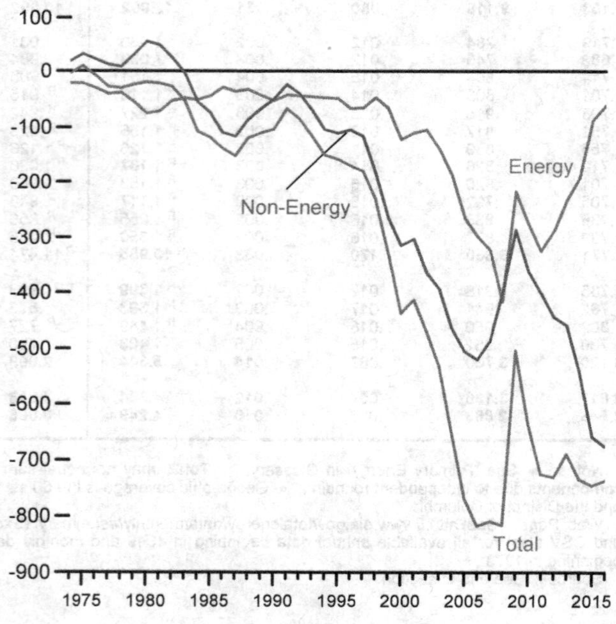

Trade Balance, Monthly

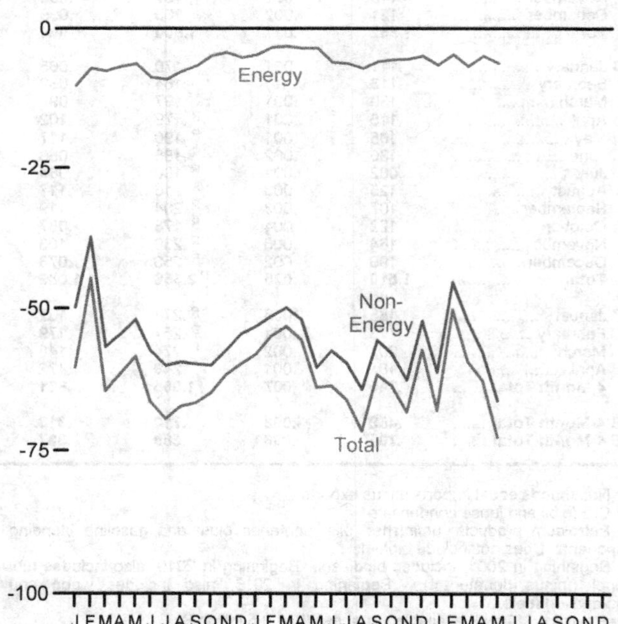

[a] Prices are not adjusted for inflation. See "Nominal Dollars" in Glossary.
Web Page: See http://www.eia.gov/totalenergy/data/monthly/#summary.
Source: Table 1.5.

Source: *U.S. Energy Information Administration, Monthly Energy Review, July 2017*

Table 1.5 Merchandise Trade Value
(Million Dollars[a])

	Petroleum[b]			Energy[c]			Non-Energy Balance	Total Merchandise		
	Exports	Imports	Balance	Exports	Imports	Balance		Exports	Imports	Balance
1974 Total	**792**	**24,668**	**-23,876**	**3,444**	**25,454**	**-22,010**	**18,126**	**99,437**	**103,321**	**-3,884**
1975 Total	**907**	**25,197**	**-24,289**	**4,470**	**26,476**	**-22,006**	**31,557**	**108,856**	**99,305**	**9,551**
1980 Total	**2,833**	**78,637**	**-75,803**	**7,982**	**82,924**	**-74,942**	**55,246**	**225,566**	**245,262**	**-19,696**
1985 Total	**4,707**	**50,475**	**-45,768**	**9,971**	**53,917**	**-43,946**	**-73,765**	**218,815**	**336,526**	**-117,712**
1990 Total	**6,901**	**61,583**	**-54,682**	**12,233**	**64,661**	**-52,428**	**-50,068**	**393,592**	**496,088**	**-102,496**
1995 Total	**6,321**	**54,368**	**-48,047**	**10,358**	**59,109**	**-48,751**	**-110,050**	**584,742**	**743,543**	**-158,801**
2000 Total	**10,192**	**119,251**	**-109,059**	**13,179**	**135,367**	**-122,188**	**-313,916**	**781,918**	**1,218,022**	**-436,104**
2001 Total	**8,868**	**102,747**	**-93,879**	**12,494**	**121,923**	**-109,429**	**-302,470**	**729,100**	**1,140,999**	**-411,899**
2002 Total	**8,569**	**102,663**	**-94,094**	**11,541**	**115,748**	**-104,207**	**-364,056**	**693,103**	**1,161,366**	**-468,263**
2003 Total	**10,209**	**132,433**	**-122,224**	**13,768**	**153,298**	**-139,530**	**-392,820**	**724,771**	**1,257,121**	**-532,350**
2004 Total	**13,130**	**179,266**	**-166,136**	**18,642**	**206,660**	**-188,018**	**-462,912**	**818,775**	**1,469,704**	**-650,930**
2005 Total	**19,155**	**250,068**	**-230,913**	**26,488**	**289,723**	**-263,235**	**-504,242**	**905,978**	**1,673,455**	**-767,477**
2006 Total	**28,171**	**299,714**	**-271,543**	**34,711**	**332,500**	**-297,789**	**-519,515**	**1,036,635**	**1,853,938**	**-817,304**
2007 Total	**33,293**	**327,620**	**-294,327**	**41,725**	**364,987**	**-323,262**	**-485,501**	**1,148,199**	**1,956,962**	**-808,763**
2008 Total	**61,695**	**449,847**	**-388,152**	**76,075**	**491,885**	**-415,810**	**-400,389**	**1,287,442**	**2,103,641**	**-816,199**
2009 Total	**44,509**	**251,833**	**-207,324**	**54,536**	**271,739**	**-217,203**	**-286,379**	**1,056,043**	**1,559,625**	**-503,582**
2010 Total	**64,753**	**333,472**	**-268,719**	**80,625**	**354,982**	**-274,357**	**-361,005**	**1,278,495**	**1,913,857**	**-635,362**
2011 Total	**[b]102,180**	**[b]431,866**	**[b]-329,686**	**128,989**	**453,839**	**-324,850**	**-400,597**	**1,482,508**	**2,207,954**	**-725,447**
2012 Total	**111,951**	**408,509**	**-296,558**	**136,054**	**423,862**	**-287,808**	**-442,638**	**1,545,821**	**2,276,267**	**-730,446**
2013 Total	**123,218**	**363,141**	**-239,923**	**147,539**	**379,758**	**-232,219**	**-457,712**	**1,578,439**	**2,268,370**	**-689,931**
2014 Total	**127,818**	**326,709**	**-198,891**	**154,498**	**347,474**	**-192,976**	**-541,506**	**1,621,874**	**2,356,356**	**-734,482**
2015 January	7,754	18,216	-10,462	9,418	19,909	-10,491	-49,802	120,880	181,173	-60,293
February	6,685	13,815	-7,130	8,189	15,545	-7,356	-37,324	118,237	162,916	-44,680
March	6,646	14,826	-8,180	8,390	16,228	-7,838	-56,685	133,664	198,187	-64,523
April	7,762	15,567	-7,805	9,448	16,469	-7,021	-54,495	128,510	190,026	-61,516
May	8,359	15,578	-7,219	9,989	16,472	-6,483	-51,865	128,161	186,509	-58,348
June	7,838	17,434	-9,596	9,260	18,309	-9,049	-57,326	130,949	197,324	-66,375
July	8,298	18,075	-9,777	9,639	19,039	-9,400	-59,978	124,201	193,579	-69,378
August	6,809	15,203	-8,394	8,241	16,147	-7,906	-59,304	122,722	189,932	-67,210
September	6,532	13,811	-7,279	7,879	14,753	-6,874	-59,744	124,853	191,470	-66,618
October	6,345	11,657	-5,312	7,703	12,644	-4,941	-59,907	130,333	195,181	-64,848
November	6,323	11,148	-4,825	7,609	11,965	-4,356	-57,274	120,522	182,152	-61,630
December	6,380	12,126	-5,746	7,692	13,018	-5,326	-54,338	120,070	179,735	-59,664
Total	**85,733**	**177,455**	**-91,722**	**103,458**	**190,501**	**-87,043**	**-658,039**	**1,503,101**	**2,248,183**	**-745,082**
2016 January	5,342	10,256	-4,914	6,549	11,380	-4,831	-53,100	107,968	165,899	-57,931
February	4,775	8,416	-3,641	5,921	9,327	-3,406	-51,348	113,363	168,117	-54,754
March	5,712	9,395	-3,683	6,970	10,164	-3,194	-49,888	125,425	178,508	-53,082
April	5,865	10,041	-4,176	7,119	10,668	-3,549	-51,902	118,645	174,096	-55,451
May	6,961	11,349	-4,388	8,412	12,013	-3,601	-60,287	119,625	183,512	-63,888
June	6,728	13,733	-7,005	8,203	14,474	-6,271	-57,339	125,098	188,708	-63,610
July	6,313	13,173	-6,860	7,665	14,151	-6,486	-59,594	115,810	181,890	-66,080
August	6,381	14,184	-7,803	7,815	15,159	-7,344	-64,173	122,529	194,046	-71,517
September	6,418	12,917	-6,499	7,740	13,827	-6,087	-55,477	124,431	185,995	-61,564
October	6,187	12,705	-6,518	7,857	13,625	-5,768	-57,815	128,440	192,023	-63,583
November	6,850	13,503	-6,653	8,818	14,445	-5,627	-62,577	123,034	191,239	-68,204
December	7,102	13,260	-6,158	9,552	14,589	-5,037	-52,093	126,642	183,772	-57,130
Total	**74,636**	**142,933**	**-68,297**	**92,623**	**153,822**	**-61,199**	**-675,595**	**1,451,011**	**2,187,805**	**-736,794**
2017 January	7,552	15,713	-8,161	10,321	17,077	-6,756	-61,104	118,004	185,863	-67,860
February	7,779	14,167	-6,388	10,522	15,293	-4,771	-45,365	119,238	169,375	-50,136
March	7,415	15,917	-8,502	10,215	17,215	-7,000	-52,086	135,663	194,750	-59,086
April	7,953	14,412	-6,459	10,537	15,558	-5,021	[R]-57,561	[R]123,765	[R]186,347	[R]-62,582
May	8,297	16,220	-7,923	10,826	17,234	-6,408	-66,168	128,025	200,602	-72,576
5-Month Total	**38,996**	**76,430**	**-37,433**	**52,422**	**82,379**	**-29,956**	**-282,284**	**624,695**	**936,936**	**-312,241**
2016 5-Month Total	**28,656**	**49,457**	**-20,802**	**34,972**	**53,551**	**-18,581**	**-266,525**	**585,026**	**870,132**	**-285,106**
2015 5-Month Total	**37,046**	**78,002**	**-40,796**	**45,263**	**84,623**	**-39,189**	**-250,171**	**629,451**	**918,810**	**-289,359**

[a] Prices are not adjusted for inflation. See "Nominal Dollars" in Glossary.
[b] Through 2010, data are for crude oil, petroleum preparations, liquefied propane and butane, and other mineral fuels. Beginning in 2011, data are for petroleum products and preparations.
[c] Petroleum, coal, natural gas, and electricity.
R=Revised.
Notes: • Monthly data are not adjusted for seasonal variations. • See Note, "Merchandise Trade Value," at end of section. • Totals may not equal sum of components due to independent rounding. • The U.S. import statistics reflect both government and nongovernment imports of merchandise from foreign countries into the U.S. customs territory, which comprises the 50 states, the District of Columbia, Puerto Rico, and the Virgin Islands.
Web Page: See http://www.eia.gov/totalenergy/data/monthly/#summary (Excel and CSV files) for all available annual and monthly data beginning in 1974.
Sources: See end of section.

Source: *U.S. Energy Information Administration, Monthly Energy Review, July 2017*

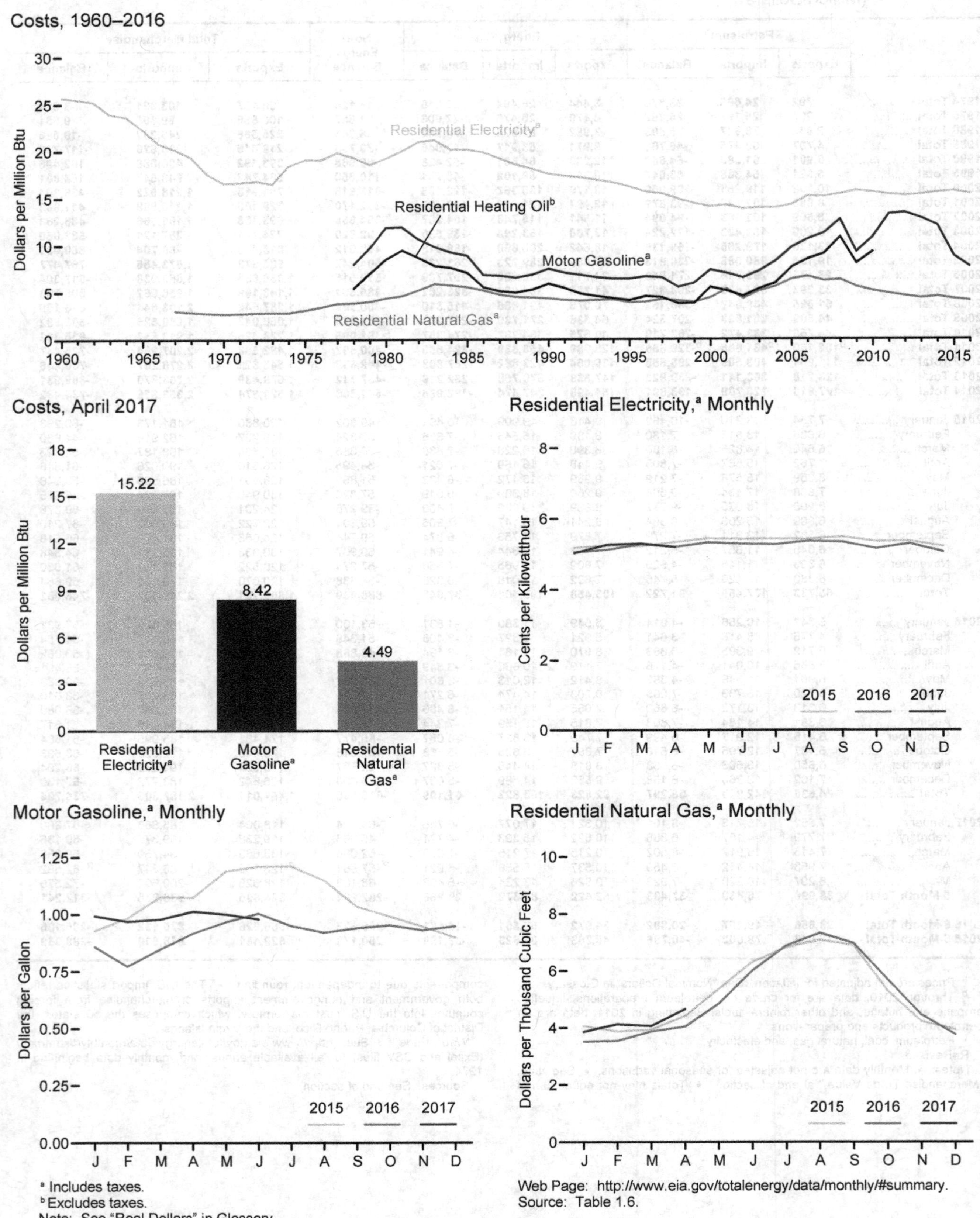

[a] Includes taxes.
[b] Excludes taxes.
Note: See "Real Dollars" in Glossary.

Web Page: http://www.eia.gov/totalenergy/data/monthly/#summary.
Source: Table 1.6.

Source: *U.S. Energy Information Administration, Monthly Energy Review, July 2017*

Table 1.6 Cost of Fuels to End Users in Real (1982–1984) Dollars

	Consumer Price Index, All Urban Consumers[a]	Motor Gasoline[b]		Residential Heating Oil[c]		Residential Natural Gas[b]		Residential Electricity[b]	
	Index 1982–1984=100	Dollars per Gallon	Dollars per Million Btu	Dollars per Gallon	Dollars per Million Btu	Dollars per Thousand Cubic Feet	Dollars per Million Btu	Cents per Kilowatthour	Dollars per Million Btu
1960 Average	**29.6**	**NA**	**NA**	**NA**	**NA**	**NA**	**NA**	**8.8**	**25.74**
1965 Average	**31.5**	**NA**	**NA**	**NA**	**NA**	**NA**	**NA**	**7.6**	**22.33**
1970 Average	**38.8**	**NA**	**NA**	**NA**	**NA**	**2.81**	**2.72**	**5.7**	**16.62**
1975 Average	**53.8**	**NA**	**NA**	**NA**	**NA**	**3.18**	**3.12**	**6.5**	**19.07**
1980 Average	**82.4**	**1.482**	**11.85**	**1.182**	**8.52**	**4.47**	**4.36**	**6.6**	**19.21**
1985 Average	**107.6**	**1.112**	**8.89**	**0.979**	**7.06**	**5.69**	**5.52**	**6.87**	**20.13**
1990 Average	**130.7**	**0.931**	**7.44**	**0.813**	**5.86**	**4.44**	**4.31**	**5.99**	**17.56**
1995 Average	**152.4**	**0.791**	**6.36**	**0.569**	**4.10**	**3.98**	**3.87**	**5.51**	**16.15**
2000 Average	**172.2**	**0.908**	**7.31**	**0.761**	**5.49**	**4.51**	**4.39**	**4.79**	**14.02**
2001 Average	**177.1**	**0.864**	**6.96**	**0.706**	**5.09**	**5.44**	**5.28**	**4.84**	**14.20**
2002 Average	**179.9**	**0.801**	**6.46**	**0.628**	**4.52**	**4.39**	**4.28**	**4.69**	**13.75**
2003 Average	**184.0**	**0.890**	**7.19**	**0.736**	**5.31**	**5.23**	**5.09**	**4.74**	**13.89**
2004 Average	**188.9**	**1.018**	**8.22**	**0.819**	**5.91**	**5.69**	**5.55**	**4.74**	**13.89**
2005 Average	**195.3**	**1.197**	**9.67**	**1.051**	**7.58**	**6.50**	**6.33**	**4.84**	**14.18**
2006 Average	**201.6**	**1.307**	**10.58**	**1.173**	**8.46**	**6.81**	**6.63**	**5.16**	**15.12**
2007 Average	**207.342**	**1.374**	**11.20**	**1.250**	**9.01**	**6.31**	**6.14**	**5.14**	**15.05**
2008 Average	**215.303**	**1.541**	**12.62**	**1.495**	**10.78**	**6.45**	**6.28**	**5.23**	**15.33**
2009 Average	**214.537**	**1.119**	**9.21**	**1.112**	**8.02**	**5.66**	**5.52**	**5.37**	**15.72**
2010 Average	**218.056**	**1.301**	**10.76**	**1.283**	**9.25**	**5.22**	**5.11**	**5.29**	**15.51**
2011 Average	**224.939**	**1.590**	**13.18**	**NA**	**NA**	**4.90**	**4.80**	**5.21**	**15.27**
2012 Average	**229.594**	**1.609**	**13.35**	**NA**	**NA**	**4.64**	**4.53**	**5.17**	**15.17**
2013 Average	**232.957**	**1.538**	**12.76**	**NA**	**NA**	**4.43**	**4.31**	**5.21**	**15.26**
2014 Average	**236.736**	**1.447**	**12.01**	**NA**	**NA**	**4.63**	**4.49**	**5.29**	**15.50**
2015 January	233.707	0.929	7.71	NA	NA	4.07	3.92	5.18	15.17
February	234.722	0.983	8.16	NA	NA	3.87	3.73	5.24	15.35
March	236.119	1.077	8.94	NA	NA	3.93	3.79	5.22	15.30
April	236.599	1.076	8.93	NA	NA	4.41	4.26	5.33	15.63
May	237.805	1.191	9.88	NA	NA	5.35	5.16	5.44	15.94
June	238.638	1.211	10.05	NA	NA	6.32	6.09	5.41	15.87
July	238.654	1.212	10.06	NA	NA	6.82	6.58	5.42	15.89
August	238.316	1.152	9.56	NA	NA	7.09	6.83	5.42	15.88
September	237.945	1.035	8.59	NA	NA	6.89	6.65	5.48	16.05
October	237.838	0.991	8.23	NA	NA	5.30	5.11	5.35	15.67
November	237.336	0.948	7.87	NA	NA	4.22	4.07	5.36	15.70
December	236.525	0.898	7.46	NA	NA	3.92	3.78	5.21	15.27
Average	**237.017**	**1.059**	**8.79**	**NA**	**NA**	**4.38**	**4.22**	**5.34**	**15.64**
2016 January	236.916	0.859	7.13	NA	NA	3.51	3.39	5.06	14.82
February	237.111	0.773	6.42	NA	NA	3.54	3.41	5.12	15.01
March	238.132	0.849	7.05	NA	NA	R 3.87	R 3.73	5.28	15.47
April	239.261	0.918	7.62	NA	NA	4.03	3.89	5.20	15.23
May	240.229	0.967	8.03	NA	NA	R 4.84	R 4.67	5.32	15.60
June	241.018	1.005	8.34	NA	NA	R 6.01	R 5.80	5.28	15.47
July	240.628	0.950	7.89	NA	NA	6.89	6.64	5.27	15.44
August	240.849	0.921	7.65	NA	NA	R 7.33	R 7.07	5.36	15.70
September	241.428	0.940	7.80	NA	NA	R 6.97	R 6.72	5.33	15.62
October	241.729	0.953	7.91	NA	NA	R 5.69	R 5.49	5.15	15.11
November	241.353	0.931	7.73	NA	NA	4.46	4.30	5.28	15.48
December	241.432	0.948	7.87	NA	NA	R 3.76	3.62	5.06	14.82
Average	**240.007**	**0.918**	**7.62**	**NA**	**NA**	R **4.20**	R **4.05**	**5.23**	**15.33**
2017 January	242.839	0.992	8.24	NA	NA	3.86	3.72	5.03	14.75
February	243.603	0.969	8.04	NA	NA	4.13	3.98	5.26	15.42
March	243.801	0.979	8.12	NA	NA	R 4.07	3.92	5.29	15.51
April	244.524	1.014	8.42	NA	NA	R 4.65	R 4.49	R 5.19	R 15.22
May	244.733	1.000	8.30	NA	NA	NA	NA	NA	NA
June	244.955	0.980	8.13	NA	NA	NA	NA	NA	NA

[a] Data are U.S. city averages for all items, and are not seasonally adjusted.
[b] Includes taxes.
[c] Excludes taxes.
R=Revised. NA=Not available.
Notes: • See "Real Dollars" in Glossary. • Fuel costs are calculated by using the Urban Consumer Price Index (CPI) developed by the Bureau of Labor Statistics. • Annual averages may not equal average of months due to independent rounding. • Geographic coverage is the 50 states and the District of Columbia.

Web Page: See http://www.eia.gov/totalenergy/data/monthly/#summary (Excel and CSV files) for all available annual data beginning in 1960 and monthly data beginning in 1995.

Sources: • **Fuel Prices:** Tables 9.4 (All Grades), 9.8, and 9.10, adjusted by the CPI; and *Monthy Energy Review*, September 2012, Table 9.8c. • **Consumer Price Index, All Urban Consumers:** U.S. Department of Labor, Bureau of Labor Statistics, series ID CUUR0000SA0. • **Conversion Factors:** Tables A1, A3, A4, and A6.

Source: *U.S. Energy Information Administration, Monthly Energy Review, July 2017*

Figure 1.7 Primary Energy Consumption and Energy Expenditures Indicators

Energy Consumption per Capita, 1949–2016

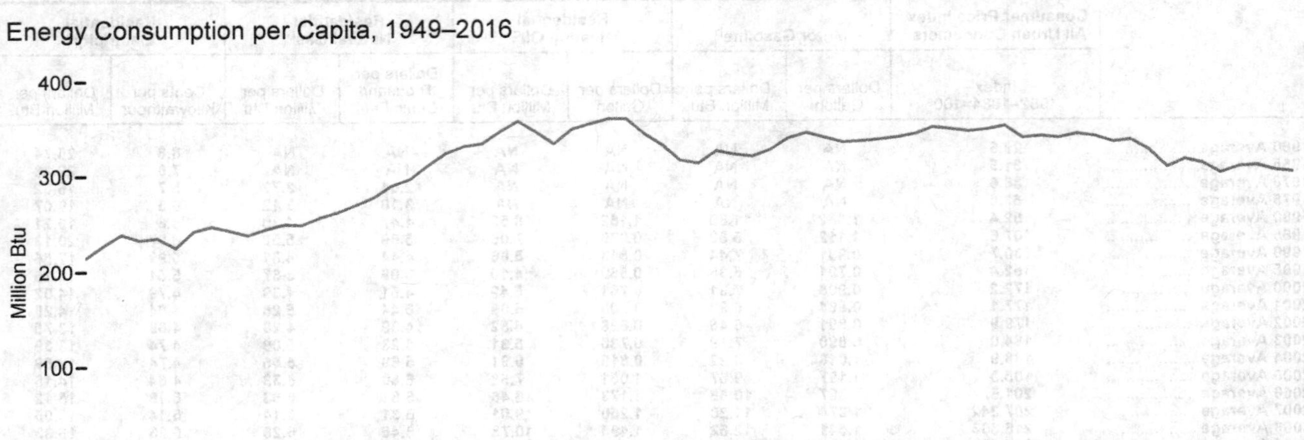

Primary Energy Consumption per Real Dollar[a] of Gross Domestic Product, 1949–2016

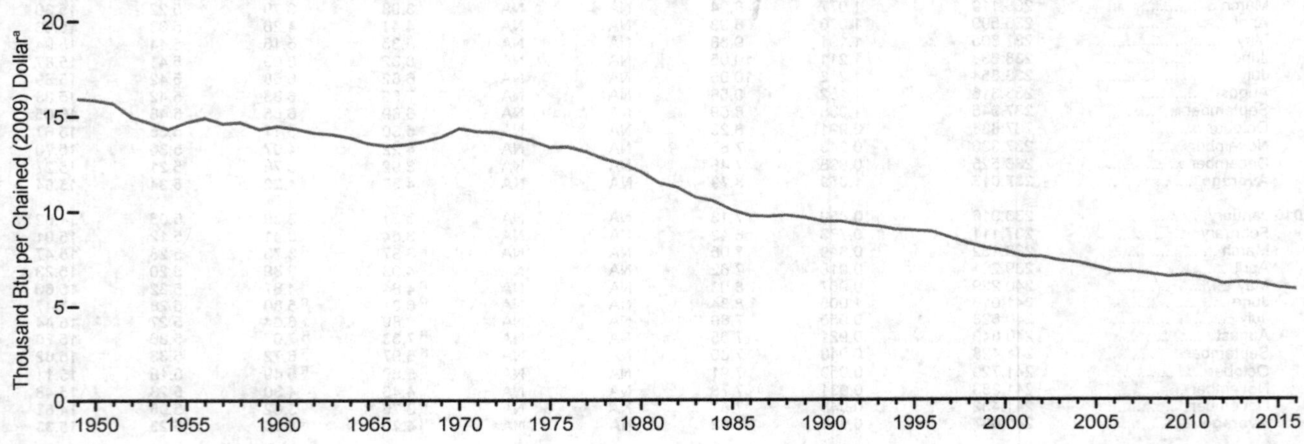

Energy Expenditures as Share of Gross Domestic Product and Gross Output,[b] 1987–2015

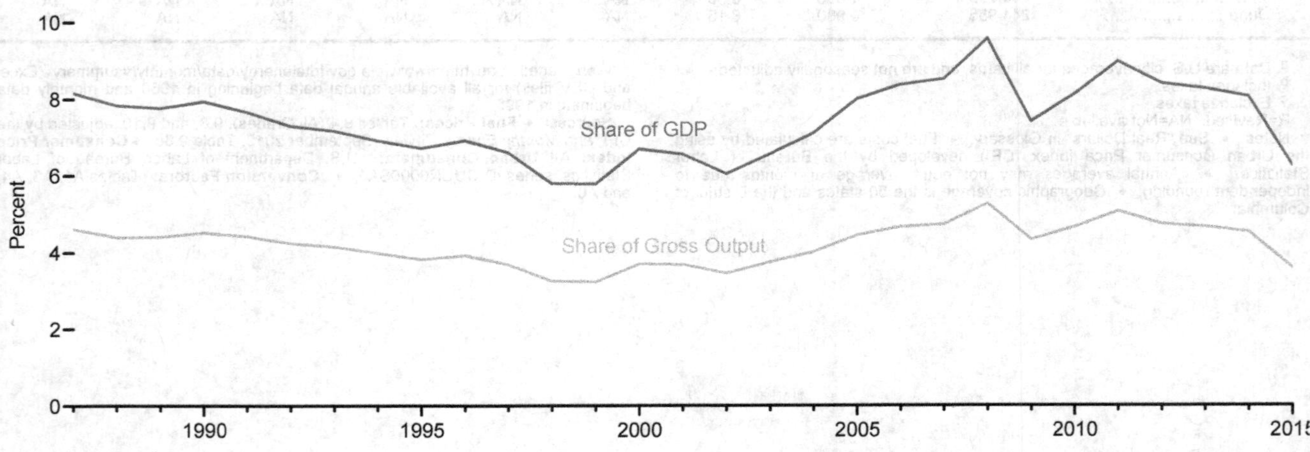

[a] See "Chained Dollars" and "Real Dollars" in Glossary.
[b] Gross output is the value of gross domestic product (GDP) plus the value of intermediate inputs used to produce GDP.

Web Page: http://www.eia.gov/totalenergy/data/monthly/#summary.
Source: Table 1.7.

***Source:** U.S. Energy Information Administration, Monthly Energy Review, July 2017*

Table 1.7 Primary Energy Consumption, Energy Expenditures, and Carbon Dioxide Emissions Indicators

	Primary Energy Consumption[a]			Energy Expenditures[b]				Carbon Dioxide Emissions[c]		
	Consumption	Consumption per Capita	Consumption per Real Dollar[d] of GDP[e]	Expenditures	Expenditures per Capita	Expenditures as Share of GDP[e]	Expenditures as Share of Gross Output[f]	Emissions	Emissions per Capita	Emissions per Real Dollar[d] of GDP[e]
	Quadrillion Btu	Million Btu	Thousand Btu per Chained (2009) Dollar[d]	Million Nominal Dollars[g]	Nominal Dollars[g]	Percent	Percent	Million Metric Tons Carbon Dioxide	Metric Tons Carbon Dioxide	Metric Tons Carbon Dioxide per Million Chained (2009) Dollars[d]
1950	34.616	227	15.85	NA	NA	NA	NA	2,382	15.6	1,091
1955	40.208	242	14.68	NA	NA	NA	NA	2,685	16.2	980
1960	45.086	250	14.50	NA	NA	NA	NA	2,914	16.1	937
1965	54.015	278	13.58	NA	NA	NA	NA	3,462	17.8	871
1970	67.838	331	14.37	82,875	404	7.7	NA	4,261	20.8	902
1975	71.965	333	13.36	171,851	796	10.2	NA	4,439	20.6	824
1980	78.067	344	12.10	374,347	1,647	13.1	NA	4,771	21.0	740
1981	76.106	332	11.50	427,898	1,865	13.3	NA	4,646	20.2	702
1982	73.099	316	11.26	426,479	1,841	12.7	NA	4,405	19.0	679
1983	72.971	312	10.74	417,617	1,786	11.5	NA	4,377	18.7	644
1984	76.632	325	10.52	[R]435,309	1,846	10.8	NA	4,614	19.6	633
1985	76.392	321	10.06	[R]438,339	[R]1,842	10.1	NA	4,600	19.3	606
1986	76.647	319	9.75	[R]384,088	[R]1,599	8.4	NA	4,608	19.2	586
1987	79.054	326	9.72	[R]397,623	[R]1,641	8.2	4.6	4,766	19.7	586
1988	82.709	338	9.76	[R]411,565	[R]1,683	7.8	4.4	4,984	20.4	588
1989	84.785	344	9.65	[R]439,046	[R]1,779	7.8	4.4	5,070	20.5	577
1990	84.484	338	9.43	[R]474,647	[R]1,901	7.9	4.5	5,039	20.2	563
1991	84.437	334	9.44	[R]472,434	[R]1,867	7.7	4.4	4,993	19.7	558
1992	85.782	334	9.26	[R]476,840	[R]1,859	7.3	4.2	5,087	19.8	549
1993	87.365	336	9.18	[R]492,267	1,894	7.2	4.2	5,185	19.9	545
1994	89.087	339	8.99	[R]504,854	1,919	6.9	4.0	5,261	20.0	531
1995	91.031	342	8.95	[R]514,622	1,933	6.7	3.8	5,323	20.0	523
1996	94.021	349	8.90	[R]560,292	2,080	6.9	3.9	5,510	20.5	522
1997	94.600	347	8.57	[R]567,960	[R]2,083	6.6	3.7	5,584	20.5	506
1998	95.018	344	8.24	[R]526,280	1,908	5.8	3.3	5,635	20.4	489
1999	96.648	346	8.01	[R]558,624	2,002	5.8	3.2	5,688	20.4	471
2000	98.817	350	7.87	[R]687,708	[R]2,437	6.7	3.7	5,868	20.8	467
2001	96.170	337	7.58	[R]696,240	[R]2,443	6.6	3.7	5,761	20.2	454
2002	97.643	339	7.56	[R]663,962	[R]2,308	6.0	3.5	5,804	20.2	450
2003	97.918	338	7.38	[R]755,068	2,603	6.6	3.8	5,853	20.2	441
2004	100.090	342	7.27	[R]871,209	[R]2,975	7.1	4.0	5,970	20.4	433
2005	100.188	339	7.04	[R]1,045,729	3,539	8.0	4.4	5,993	20.3	421
2006	99.485	333	6.81	[R]1,158,819	3,884	8.4	4.7	5,910	19.8	404
2007	101.015	335	6.79	[R]1,233,864	[R]4,096	8.5	4.7	6,000	19.9	403
2008	98.891	325	6.67	[R]1,408,750	4,633	9.6	5.3	5,809	19.1	392
2009	94.118	307	6.53	[R]1,066,275	[R]3,476	7.4	4.3	5,386	17.6	374
2010	97.445	315	6.59	[R]1,213,336	[R]3,922	8.1	4.6	5,582	18.0	378
2011	96.842	311	6.45	[R]1,392,945	[R]4,469	9.0	5.1	5,445	17.5	362
2012	94.416	301	6.15	[R]1,356,215	4,319	8.4	4.7	5,232	16.7	341
2013	97.157	307	6.22	[R]1,378,885	[R]4,361	8.3	4.7	5,360	17.0	343
2014	98.329	309	6.15	[R]1,399,486	[R]4,393	8.0	4.5	5,406	17.0	338
2015	97.365	303	5.94	[R]1,127,132	[R]3,512	[R]6.2	[R]3.6	5,259	16.4	321
2016	[R]97.394	301	5.85	NA	NA	NA	NA	[R]5,170	16.0	310

[a] See "Primary Energy Consumption" in Glossary.
[b] Expenditures include taxes where data are available.
[c] Carbon dioxide emissions from energy consumption. See Table 12.1.
[d] See "Chained Dollars" and "Real Dollars" in Glossary.
[e] See "Gross Domestic Product (GDP)" in Glossary.
[f] Gross output is the value of GDP plus the value of intermediate inputs used to produce GDP.
[g] See "Nominal Dollars" in Glossary.
R=Revised. NA=Not available.

Notes: • Data are estimates. • Geographic coverage is the 50 states and the District of Columbia.

Web Page: See http://www.eia.gov/totalenergy/data/monthly/#summary (Excel and CSV files) for all available annual data beginning in 1949.

Sources: • **Consumption:** Table 1.3. • **Consumption per Capita:** Calculated as energy consumption divided by U.S. population (see Table C1). • **Consumption per Real Dollar of GDP:** Calculated as energy consumption divided by U.S. gross domestic product in chained (2009) dollars (see Table C1). • **Expenditures:** U.S. Energy Information Administration, "State Energy Price and Expenditure Estimates, 1970 Through 2014" (June 2016), U.S. Table ET1. • **Expenditures per Capita:** Calculated as energy expenditures divided by U.S. population (see Table C1). • **Expenditures as Share of GDP:** Calculated as energy expenditures divided by U.S. gross domestic product in nominal dollars (see Table C1). • **Expenditures as Share of Gross Output:** Calculated as energy expenditures divided by U.S. gross output (see Table C1). • **Emissions:** **1949–1972**—U.S. Energy Information Administration, *Annual Energy Review 2011*, Table 11.1. **1973 forward**—Table 12.1. • **Emissions per Capita:** Calculated as carbon dioxide emissions divided by U.S. population (see Table C1). • **Emissions per Real Dollar of GDP:** Calculated as carbon dioxide emissions divided by U.S. gross domestic product in chained (2009) dollars (see Table C1).

***Source:** U.S. Energy Information Administration, Monthly Energy Review, July 2017*

Figure 1.8 Motor Vehicle Mileage, Fuel Consumption, and Fuel Economy, 1949–2015

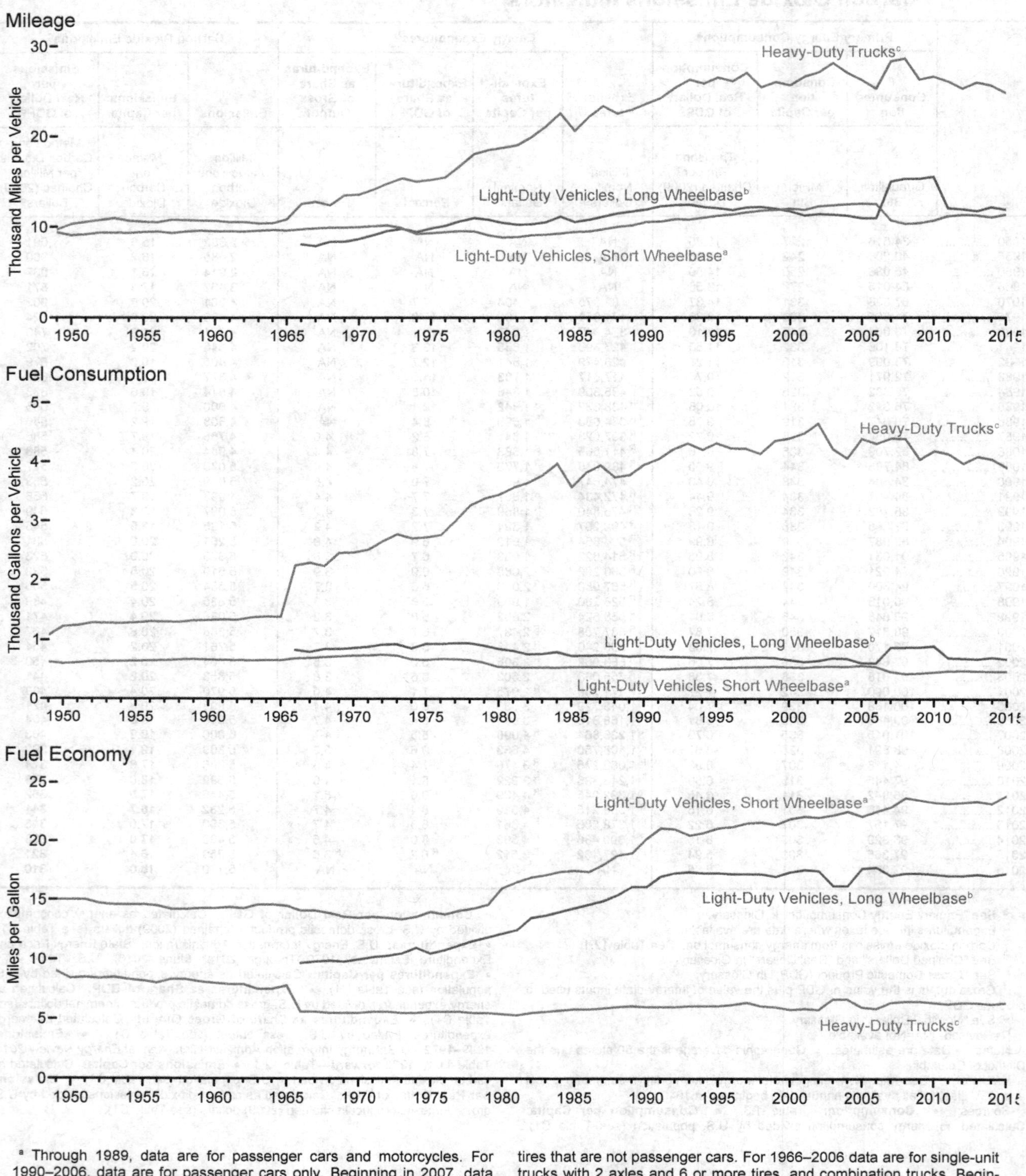

[a] Through 1989, data are for passenger cars and motorcycles. For 1990–2006, data are for passenger cars only. Beginning in 2007, data are for light-duty vehicles (passenger cars, light trucks, vans, and sport utility vehicles) with a wheelbase less than or equal to 121 inches.

[b] For 1966–2000, data are for vans, pickup trucks, and sport utility vehicles. Beginning in 2007, data are for light-duty vehicles (passenger cars, light trucks, vans, and sport utility vehicles) with a wheelbase greater than 121 inches.

[c] For 1949–1965, data are for single-unit trucks with 2 axles and 6 or more tires, combination trucks, and other vehicles with 2 axles and 4 tires that are not passenger cars. For 1966–2006 data are for single-unit trucks with 2 axles and 6 or more tires, and combination trucks. Beginning in 2007, data are for single-unit trucks with 2 axles and 6 or more tires (or a gross vehicle weight rating exceeding 10,000 pounds), and combination trucks.

Note: Through 1965, "Light-Duty Vehicles, Long Wheelbase" data are included in "Heavy-Duty Trucks."

Web Page: http://www.eia.gov/totalenergy/data/monthly/#summary.

Source: Table 1.8.

Source: *U.S. Energy Information Administration, Monthly Energy Review, July 2017*

Table 1.8 Motor Vehicle Mileage, Fuel Consumption, and Fuel Economy

	Light-Duty Vehicles, Short Wheelbase[a]			Light-Duty Vehicles, Long Wheelbase[b]			Heavy-Duty Trucks[c]			All Motor Vehicles[d]		
	Mileage	Fuel Consumption	Fuel Economy	Mileage	Fuel Consumption	Fuel Economy	Mileage	Fuel Consumption	Fuel Economy	Mileage	Fuel Consumption	Fuel Economy
	Miles per Vehicle	Gallons per Vehicle	Miles per Gallon	Miles per Vehicle	Gallons per Vehicle	Miles per Gallon	Miles per Vehicle	Gallons per Vehicle	Miles per Gallon	Miles per Vehicle	Gallons per Vehicle	Miles per Gallon
1950	9,060	603	15.0	([e])	([e])	([e])	10,316	1,229	8.4	9,321	725	12.8
1955	9,447	645	14.6	([e])	([e])	([e])	10,576	1,293	8.2	9,661	761	12.7
1960	9,518	668	14.3	([e])	([e])	([e])	10,693	1,333	8.0	9,732	784	12.4
1965	9,603	661	14.5	([e])	([e])	([e])	10,851	1,387	7.8	9,826	787	12.5
1970	9,989	737	13.5	8,676	866	10.0	13,565	2,467	5.5	9,976	830	12.0
1975	9,309	665	14.0	9,829	934	10.5	15,167	2,722	5.6	9,627	790	12.2
1980	8,813	551	16.0	10,437	854	12.2	18,736	3,447	5.4	9,458	712	13.3
1981	8,873	538	16.5	10,244	819	12.5	19,016	3,565	5.3	9,477	697	13.6
1982	9,050	535	16.9	10,276	762	13.5	19,931	3,647	5.5	9,644	686	14.1
1983	9,118	534	17.1	10,497	767	13.7	21,083	3,769	5.6	9,760	686	14.2
1984	9,248	530	17.4	11,151	797	14.0	22,550	3,967	5.7	10,017	691	14.5
1985	9,419	538	17.5	10,506	735	14.3	20,597	3,570	5.8	10,020	685	14.6
1986	9,464	543	17.4	10,764	738	14.6	22,143	3,821	5.8	10,143	692	14.7
1987	9,720	539	18.0	11,114	744	14.9	23,349	3,937	5.9	10,453	694	15.1
1988	9,972	531	18.8	11,465	745	15.4	22,485	3,736	6.0	10,721	688	15.6
1989	10,157	533	19.0	11,676	724	16.1	22,926	3,776	6.1	10,932	688	15.9
1990	10,504	520	20.2	11,902	738	16.1	23,603	3,953	6.0	11,107	677	16.4
1991	10,571	501	21.1	12,245	721	17.0	24,229	4,047	6.0	11,294	669	16.9
1992	10,857	517	21.0	12,381	717	17.3	25,373	4,210	6.0	11,558	683	16.9
1993	10,804	527	20.5	12,430	714	17.4	26,262	4,309	6.1	11,595	693	16.7
1994	10,992	531	20.7	12,156	701	17.3	25,838	4,202	6.1	11,683	698	16.7
1995	11,203	530	21.1	12,018	694	17.3	26,514	4,315	6.1	11,793	700	16.8
1996	11,330	534	21.2	11,811	685	17.2	26,092	4,221	6.2	11,813	700	16.9
1997	11,581	539	21.5	12,115	703	17.2	27,032	4,218	6.4	12,107	711	17.0
1998	11,754	544	21.6	12,173	707	17.2	25,397	4,135	6.1	12,211	721	16.9
1999	11,848	553	21.4	11,957	701	17.0	26,014	4,352	6.0	12,206	732	16.7
2000	11,976	547	21.9	11,672	669	17.4	25,617	4,391	5.8	12,164	720	16.9
2001	11,831	534	22.1	11,204	636	17.6	26,602	4,477	5.9	11,887	695	17.1
2002	12,202	555	22.0	11,364	650	17.5	27,071	4,642	5.8	12,171	719	16.9
2003	12,325	556	22.2	11,287	697	16.2	28,093	4,215	6.7	12,208	718	17.0
2004	12,460	553	22.5	11,184	690	16.2	27,023	4,057	6.7	12,200	714	17.1
2005	12,510	567	22.1	10,920	617	17.7	26,235	4,385	6.0	12,082	706	17.1
2006	12,485	554	22.5	10,920	612	17.8	25,231	4,304	5.9	12,017	698	17.2
2007	[a] 10,710	[a] 468	[a] 22.9	[b] 14,970	[b] 877	[b] 17.1	[c] 28,290	[c] 4,398	6.4	11,915	693	17.2
2008	10,290	435	23.7	15,256	880	17.3	28,573	4,387	6.5	11,631	667	17.4
2009	10,391	442	23.5	15,252	882	17.3	26,274	4,037	6.5	11,631	661	17.6
2010	10,650	456	23.3	15,474	901	17.2	26,604	4,180	6.4	11,866	681	17.4
2011	11,150	481	23.2	12,007	702	17.1	26,054	4,128	6.3	11,652	665	17.5
2012	11,262	484	23.3	11,885	694	17.1	25,255	3,973	6.4	11,707	665	17.6
2013	11,244	480	23.4	11,712	683	17.2	25,951	4,086	6.4	11,679	663	17.6
2014	11,048	476	23.2	12,138	710	17.1	25,594	4,036	6.3	11,621	666	17.5
2015[P]	11,327	475	23.9	11,855	684	17.3	24,797	3,904	6.4	11,742	656	17.9

[a] Through 1989, data are for passenger cars and motorcycles. For 1990–2006, data are for passenger cars only. Beginning in 2007, data are for light-duty vehicles (passenger cars, light trucks, vans, and sport utility vehicles) with a wheelbase less than or equal to 121 inches.

[b] For 1966–2006, data are for vans, pickup trucks, and sport utility vehicles. Beginning in 2007, data are for light-duty vehicles (passenger cars, light trucks, vans, and sport utility vehicles) with a wheelbase greater than 121 inches.

[c] For 1949–1965, data are for single-unit trucks with 2 axles and 6 or more tires, combination trucks, and other vehicles with 2 axles and 4 tires that are not passenger cars. For 1966–2006, data are for single-unit trucks with 2 axles and 6 or more tires, and combination trucks. Beginning in 2007, data are for single-unit trucks with 2 axles and 6 or more tires (or a gross vehicle weight rating exceeding 10,000 pounds), and combination trucks.

[d] Includes buses and motorcycles, which are not separately displayed.

[e] Included in "Heavy-Duty Trucks."

P=Preliminary.

Note: Geographic coverage is the 50 states and the District of Columbia.

Web Page: See http://www.eia.gov/totalenergy/data/monthly/#summary (Excel and CSV files) for all available annual data beginning in 1949.

Sources: • **Light-Duty Vehicles, Short Wheelbase: 1990–1994**—U.S. Department of Transportation, Bureau of Transportation Statistics, *National Transportation Statistics 1998,* Table 4-13. • **All Other Data: 1949–1994**—Federal Highway Administration (FHWA), *Highway Statistics Summary to 1995,* Table VM-201A. **1995 forward**—FHWA, *Highway Statistics,* annual reports, Table VM-1.

Source: *U.S. Energy Information Administration, Monthly Energy Review, July 2017*

Table 1.9 Heating Degree Days by Census Division

	New England[a]	Middle Atlantic[b]	East North Central[c]	West North Central[d]	South Atlantic[e]	East South Central[f]	West South Central[g]	Mountain[h]	Pacific[i]	United States
1950 Total	**6,794**	**6,324**	**7,027**	**7,455**	**3,521**	**3,547**	**2,277**	**6,341**	**3,906**	**5,367**
1955 Total	**6,872**	**6,231**	**6,486**	**6,912**	**3,508**	**3,513**	**2,294**	**6,704**	**4,320**	**5,246**
1960 Total	**6,828**	**6,391**	**6,908**	**7,184**	**3,780**	**4,134**	**2,767**	**6,281**	**3,799**	**5,404**
1965 Total	**7,029**	**6,393**	**6,587**	**6,932**	**3,372**	**3,501**	**2,237**	**6,086**	**3,819**	**5,146**
1970 Total	**7,022**	**6,388**	**6,721**	**7,090**	**3,452**	**3,823**	**2,558**	**6,119**	**3,726**	**5,218**
1975 Total	**6,547**	**5,892**	**6,406**	**6,880**	**2,970**	**3,437**	**2,312**	**6,260**	**4,117**	**4,905**
1980 Total	**7,071**	**6,477**	**6,975**	**6,836**	**3,378**	**3,964**	**2,494**	**5,554**	**3,539**	**5,080**
1985 Total	**6,749**	**5,971**	**6,668**	**7,262**	**2,899**	**3,660**	**2,535**	**6,059**	**3,935**	**4,889**
1990 Total	**5,987**	**5,252**	**5,780**	**6,137**	**2,307**	**2,942**	**1,968**	**5,391**	**3,603**	**4,180**
1995 Total	**6,684**	**6,093**	**6,740**	**6,911**	**2,988**	**3,648**	**2,147**	**5,101**	**3,269**	**4,640**
2000 Total	**6,625**	**5,999**	**6,315**	**6,500**	**2,905**	**3,551**	**2,153**	**4,971**	**3,460**	**4,494**
2001 Total	**6,202**	**5,541**	**5,844**	**6,221**	**2,604**	**3,327**	**2,162**	**5,004**	**3,545**	**4,257**
2002 Total	**6,234**	**5,550**	**6,128**	**6,485**	**2,664**	**3,443**	**2,292**	**5,197**	**3,510**	**4,356**
2003 Total	**6,975**	**6,258**	**6,536**	**6,593**	**2,884**	**3,559**	**2,205**	**4,817**	**3,355**	**4,544**
2004 Total	**6,709**	**5,892**	**6,178**	**6,329**	**2,715**	**3,291**	**2,041**	**5,010**	**3,346**	**4,344**
2005 Total	**6,644**	**5,950**	**6,222**	**6,213**	**2,775**	**3,380**	**1,985**	**4,896**	**3,377**	**4,348**
2006 Total	**5,885**	**5,211**	**5,703**	**5,821**	**2,475**	**3,211**	**1,802**	**4,915**	**3,557**	**4,040**
2007 Total	**6,537**	**5,756**	**6,074**	**6,384**	**2,525**	**3,187**	**2,105**	**4,939**	**3,506**	**4,268**
2008 Total	**6,434**	**5,782**	**6,677**	**7,118**	**2,712**	**3,600**	**2,125**	**5,233**	**3,566**	**4,494**
2009 Total	**6,644**	**5,922**	**6,512**	**6,841**	**2,812**	**3,536**	**2,152**	**5,139**	**3,538**	**4,481**
2010 Total	**5,934**	**5,553**	**6,185**	**6,565**	**3,167**	**3,948**	**2,449**	**5,082**	**3,624**	**4,463**
2011 Total	**6,114**	**5,483**	**6,172**	**6,565**	**2,565**	**3,343**	**2,114**	**5,322**	**3,818**	**4,312**
2012 Total	**5,561**	**4,970**	**5,356**	**5,515**	**2,306**	**2,876**	**1,650**	**4,574**	**3,411**	**3,769**
2013 Total	**6,426**	**5,838**	**6,621**	**7,135**	**2,736**	**3,648**	**2,326**	**5,273**	**3,362**	**4,465**
2014 Total	**6,675**	**6,203**	**7,194**	**7,304**	**2,951**	**3,932**	**2,422**	**4,744**	**2,774**	**4,550**
2015 January	1,336	1,260	1,334	1,266	643	835	623	818	471	890
February	1,412	1,318	1,404	1,305	666	864	498	600	334	867
March	1,101	1,002	951	802	357	445	279	484	285	584
April	588	481	454	398	131	147	55	396	295	300
May	147	100	159	215	22	37	14	268	208	119
June	84	30	45	40	1	1	0	42	26	24
July	7	4	12	12	0	0	0	24	8	6
August	8	8	24	33	0	1	0	21	13	11
September	43	27	39	50	8	13	1	78	58	32
October	459	391	365	355	143	164	42	247	111	227
November	610	529	604	650	236	312	218	686	471	445
December	725	625	775	960	279	401	357	937	619	581
Total	**6,521**	**5,775**	**6,166**	**6,088**	**2,486**	**3,220**	**2,088**	**4,600**	**2,899**	**4,086**
2016 January	1,130	1,120	1,241	1,303	659	856	564	917	568	871
February	958	901	957	936	482	573	309	621	341	628
March	757	645	670	654	240	322	180	542	393	450
April	605	515	506	425	151	162	62	383	244	310
May	254	214	221	208	58	70	17	255	179	151
June	46	22	25	28	1	0	0	42	44	21
July	4	1	3	11	0	0	0	15	19	6
August	5	1	5	17	0	0	0	31	12	6
September	69	37	40	75	2	5	1	115	65	39
October	390	317	285	304	91	89	22	265	199	197
November	672	608	582	569	290	338	155	514	331	418
December	1,057	975	1,165	1,257	478	671	445	925	626	783
Total	**5,947**	**5,356**	**5,701**	**5,786**	**2,452**	**3,086**	**1,756**	**4,624**	**3,023**	**3,878**
2017 January	1,043	973	1,082	1,211	476	578	418	962	667	767
February	907	778	775	817	323	408	209	627	495	547
March	1,042	909	834	782	347	385	147	469	394	543
April	454	340	349	401	76	93	51	405	308	248
4-Month Total	**3,445**	**3,001**	**3,040**	**3,211**	**1,222**	**1,464**	**825**	**2,464**	**1,865**	**2,105**
2016 4-Month Total	**3,450**	**3,182**	**3,375**	**3,318**	**1,532**	**1,913**	**1,115**	**2,463**	**1,547**	**2,258**
2015 4-Month Total	**4,437**	**4,061**	**4,144**	**3,773**	**1,797**	**2,290**	**1,455**	**2,298**	**1,385**	**2,641**

[a] Connecticut, Maine, Massachusetts, New Hampshire, Rhode Island, and Vermont.
[b] New Jersey, New York, and Pennsylvania.
[c] Illinois, Indiana, Michigan, Ohio, and Wisconsin.
[d] Iowa, Kansas, Minnesota, Missouri, Nebraska, North Dakota, and South Dakota.
[e] Delaware, Florida, Georgia, Maryland (and the District of Columbia), North Carolina, South Carolina, Virginia, and West Virginia.
[f] Alabama, Kentucky, Mississippi, and Tennessee.
[g] Arkansas, Louisiana, Oklahoma, and Texas.
[h] Arizona, Colorado, Idaho, Montana, Nevada, New Mexico, Utah, and Wyoming.
[i] Alaska, California, Hawaii, Oregon, and Washington.

Notes: • Degree days are relative measurements of outdoor air temperature used as an index for heating and cooling energy requirements. Heating degree days are the number of degrees that the daily average temperature falls below 65 degrees Fahrenheit (°F). Cooling degree days are the number of degrees that the daily average temperature rises above 65°F. The daily average temperature is the mean of the maximum and minimum temperatures in a 24-hour period. For example, a weather station recording an average daily temperature of 40°F would report 25 heating degree days for that day (and 0 cooling degree days). If a weather station recorded an average daily temperature of 78°F, cooling degree days for that station would be 13 (and 0 heating degree days). • Totals may not equal sum of components due to independent rounding. • Geographic coverage is the 50 states and the District of Columbia.

Web Page: See http://www.eia.gov/totalenergy/data/monthly/#summary (Excel and CSV files) for all available annual data beginning in 1949 and monthly data beginning in 1973.

Source: State-level degree day data are from U.S. Department of Commerce, National Oceanic and Atmospheric Administration, National Centers for Environmental Information. Using these state-level data, the U.S. Energy Information Administration calculates population-weighted census-division and U.S. degree day averages using state populations from the same year the degree days are measured. See methodology at http://www.eia.gov/forecasts/steo/special/pdf/2012_sp_04.pdf.

Source: *U.S. Energy Information Administration, Monthly Energy Review, July 2017*

Table 1.10 Cooling Degree Days by Census Division

	New England[a]	Middle Atlantic[b]	East North Central[c]	West North Central[d]	South Atlantic[e]	East South Central[f]	West South Central[g]	Mountain[h]	Pacific[i]	United States
1950 Total	**295**	**401**	**505**	**647**	**1,414**	**1,420**	**2,282**	**682**	**629**	**871**
1955 Total	**532**	**761**	**922**	**1,139**	**1,636**	**1,674**	**2,508**	**780**	**558**	**1,144**
1960 Total	**318**	**487**	**626**	**871**	**1,583**	**1,532**	**2,367**	**974**	**796**	**1,000**
1965 Total	**310**	**498**	**618**	**832**	**1,613**	**1,552**	**2,461**	**780**	**577**	**979**
1970 Total	**423**	**615**	**747**	**980**	**1,744**	**1,571**	**2,282**	**971**	**734**	**1,079**
1975 Total	**422**	**584**	**721**	**937**	**1,791**	**1,440**	**2,162**	**903**	**597**	**1,049**
1980 Total	**438**	**680**	**769**	**1,158**	**1,911**	**1,754**	**2,651**	**1,071**	**653**	**1,214**
1985 Total	**324**	**509**	**602**	**780**	**1,878**	**1,522**	**2,519**	**1,095**	**761**	**1,121**
1990 Total	**429**	**562**	**602**	**913**	**2,054**	**1,563**	**2,526**	**1,212**	**838**	**1,200**
1995 Total	**471**	**704**	**877**	**928**	**2,028**	**1,613**	**2,398**	**1,213**	**794**	**1,261**
2000 Total	**279**	**458**	**632**	**983**	**1,925**	**1,674**	**2,775**	**1,480**	**772**	**1,232**
2001 Total	**464**	**623**	**722**	**994**	**1,897**	**1,478**	**2,543**	**1,508**	**861**	**1,255**
2002 Total	**508**	**772**	**899**	**1,045**	**2,182**	**1,757**	**2,515**	**1,467**	**783**	**1,363**
2003 Total	**475**	**615**	**619**	**907**	**1,980**	**1,452**	**2,496**	**1,553**	**978**	**1,268**
2004 Total	**368**	**591**	**585**	**722**	**2,038**	**1,517**	**2,482**	**1,290**	**828**	**1,217**
2005 Total	**598**	**892**	**944**	**1,063**	**2,098**	**1,676**	**2,647**	**1,372**	**777**	**1,388**
2006 Total	**485**	**693**	**734**	**1,034**	**2,053**	**1,648**	**2,786**	**1,466**	**922**	**1,360**
2007 Total	**447**	**694**	**881**	**1,102**	**2,219**	**1,892**	**2,475**	**1,564**	**828**	**1,392**
2008 Total	**462**	**667**	**683**	**818**	**1,993**	**1,537**	**2,501**	**1,385**	**918**	**1,282**
2009 Total	**350**	**524**	**534**	**698**	**2,029**	**1,479**	**2,590**	**1,393**	**894**	**1,241**
2010 Total	**635**	**908**	**964**	**1,096**	**2,269**	**1,977**	**2,757**	**1,358**	**674**	**1,456**
2011 Total	**554**	**836**	**859**	**1,074**	**2,259**	**1,727**	**3,112**	**1,450**	**736**	**1,470**
2012 Total	**565**	**815**	**974**	**1,221**	**2,162**	**1,762**	**2,915**	**1,573**	**917**	**1,495**
2013 Total	**540**	**683**	**690**	**892**	**2,000**	**1,441**	**2,536**	**1,462**	**892**	**1,306**
2014 Total	**420**	**596**	**610**	**814**	**2,009**	**1,493**	**2,474**	**1,431**	**1,068**	**1,299**
2015 January	0	0	0	0	34	3	5	2	11	9
February	0	0	0	0	19	0	6	11	12	7
March	0	0	0	3	84	21	39	32	27	30
April	0	0	1	8	131	52	141	40	22	53
May	31	72	82	56	242	175	260	75	29	126
June	40	115	139	203	394	353	454	313	175	255
July	193	251	202	289	456	443	585	325	216	336
August	206	230	169	202	410	340	561	362	260	315
September	86	136	128	168	296	236	424	231	191	223
October	0	1	7	13	135	59	188	84	96	77
November	0	0	0	0	103	16	52	3	10	29
December	0	1	2	0	100	24	25	0	8	26
Total	**555**	**805**	**729**	**942**	**2,405**	**1,721**	**2,740**	**1,479**	**1,057**	**1,486**
2016 January	0	0	0	0	24	2	9	0	7	7
February	0	0	0	0	23	3	26	10	14	11
March	0	0	3	10	89	36	86	24	13	35
April	0	0	1	8	87	38	122	42	24	42
May	7	17	42	48	185	125	236	90	37	97
June	71	129	187	262	379	372	474	332	168	271
July	240	308	277	306	508	474	619	407	235	383
August	238	311	296	268	484	461	547	305	233	361
September	59	115	131	138	352	321	428	174	124	219
October	0	6	19	28	156	114	230	99	47	86
November	0	0	0	2	56	12	80	14	17	26
December	0	0	0	0	65	4	17	0	8	17
Total	**615**	**886**	**956**	**1,070**	**2,408**	**1,963**	**2,874**	**1,498**	**927**	**1,555**
2017 January	0	0	0	0	49	20	35	0	7	16
February	0	0	0	3	54	18	67	5	6	22
March	0	0	1	6	55	28	112	31	15	32
April	0	2	8	9	124	76	142	49	24	56
4-Month Total	**0**	**2**	**9**	**17**	**282**	**142**	**356**	**85**	**53**	**126**
2016 4-Month Total	**0**	**0**	**4**	**17**	**223**	**80**	**244**	**77**	**59**	**95**
2015 4-Month Total	**0**	**0**	**1**	**11**	**268**	**76**	**191**	**85**	**72**	**99**

[a] Connecticut, Maine, Massachusetts, New Hampshire, Rhode Island, and Vermont.
[b] New Jersey, New York, and Pennsylvania.
[c] Illinois, Indiana, Michigan, Ohio, and Wisconsin.
[d] Iowa, Kansas, Minnesota, Missouri, Nebraska, North Dakota, and South Dakota.
[e] Delaware, Florida, Georgia, Maryland (and the District of Columbia), North Carolina, South Carolina, Virginia, and West Virginia.
[f] Alabama, Kentucky, Mississippi, and Tennessee.
[g] Arkansas, Louisiana, Oklahoma, and Texas.
[h] Arizona, Colorado, Idaho, Montana, Nevada, New Mexico, Utah, and Wyoming.
[i] Alaska, California, Hawaii, Oregon, and Washington.

Notes: • Degree days are relative measurements of outdoor air temperature used as an index for heating and cooling energy requirements. Cooling degree days are the number of degrees that the daily average temperature rises above 65 degrees Fahrenheit (°F). Heating degree days are the number of degrees that the daily average temperature falls below 65°F. The daily average temperature is the mean of the maximum and minimum temperatures in a 24-hour period. For example, if a weather station recorded an average daily temperature of 78°F, cooling degree days for that station would be 13 (and 0 heating degree days). A weather station recording an average daily temperature of 40°F would report 25 heating degree days for that day (and 0 cooling degree days). • Totals may not equal sum of components due to independent rounding. • Geographic coverage is the 50 states and the District of Columbia.

Web Page: See http://www.eia.gov/totalenergy/data/monthly/#summary (Excel and CSV files) for all available annual data beginning in 1949 and monthly data beginning in 1973.

Source: State-level degree day data are from U.S. Department of Commerce, National Oceanic and Atmospheric Administration, National Centers for Environmental Information. Using these state-level data, the U.S. Energy Information Administration calculates population-weighted census-division and U.S. degree day averages using state populations from the same year the degree days are measured. See methodology at http://www.eia.gov/forecasts/steo/special/pdf/2012_sp_04.pdf.

Source: *U.S. Energy Information Administration, Monthly Energy Review, July 2017*

Figure 2.1 Energy Consumption by Sector
(Quadrillion Btu)

Total Consumption by End-Use Sector, 1949–2016

Industrial
Transportation
Residential
Commercial

0 10 20 30 40
1950 1955 1960 1965 1970 1975 1980 1985 1990 1995 2000 2005 2010 2015

Total Consumption by End-Use Sector, Monthly

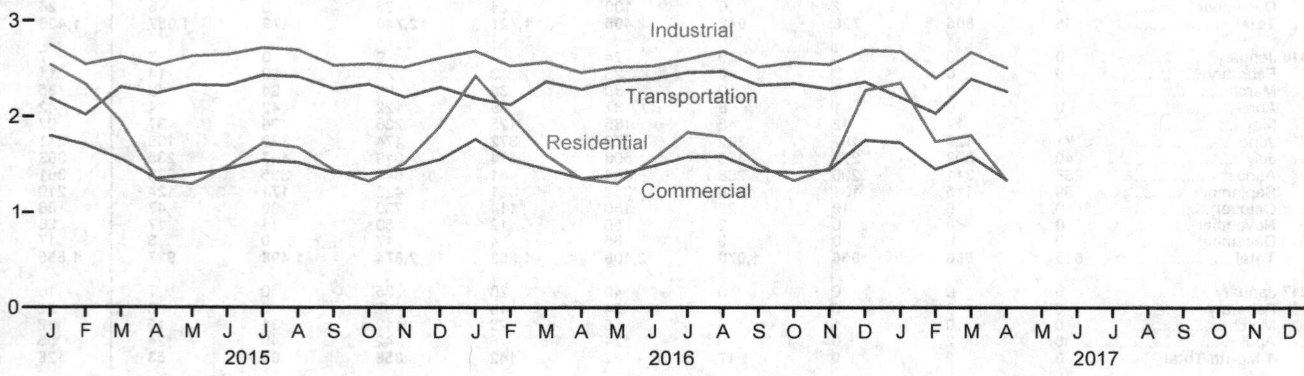

By Sector, April 2017

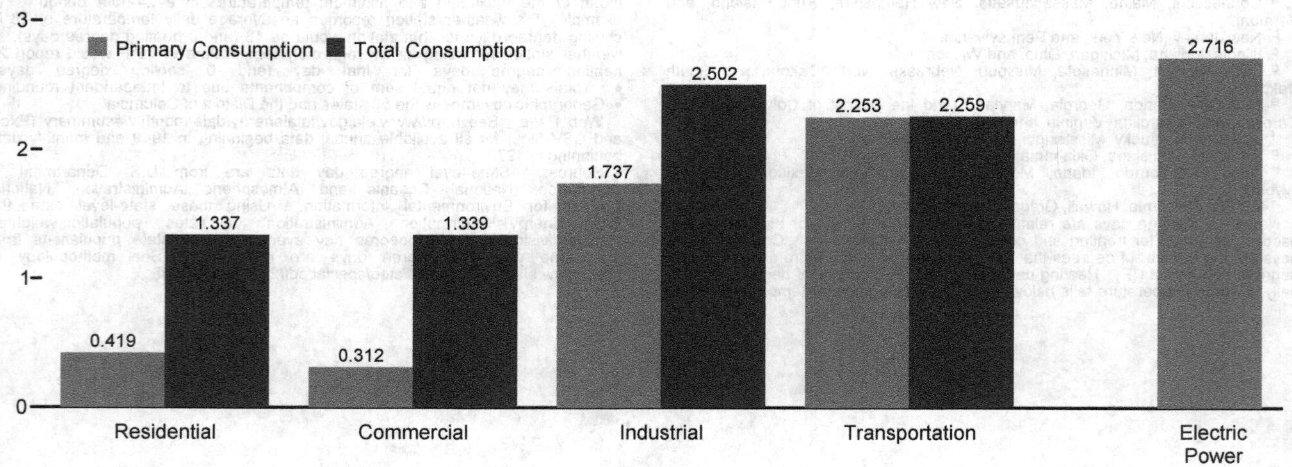

Web Page: http://www.eia.gov/totalenergy/data/monthly/#consumption.
Source: Table 2.1.

Source: *U.S. Energy Information Administration, Monthly Energy Review, July 2017*

Table 2.1 Energy Consumption by Sector
(Trillion Btu)

	End-Use Sectors								Electric Power Sector[c,d]	Balancing Item[g]	Primary Total[h]
	Residential		Commercial[a]		Industrial[b]		Transportation				
	Primary[e]	Total[f]	Primary[e]	Total[f]	Primary[e]	Total[f]	Primary[e]	Total[f]	Primary[e]		
1950 Total	4,829	5,989	2,834	3,893	13,890	16,241	8,383	8,492	4,679	(s)	34,616
1955 Total	5,608	7,278	2,561	3,895	16,103	19,485	9,474	9,550	6,461	(s)	40,208
1960 Total	6,651	9,039	2,723	4,609	16,996	20,842	10,560	10,596	8,158	(s)	45,086
1965 Total	7,279	10,639	3,177	5,845	20,148	25,098	12,399	12,432	11,012	(s)	54,015
1970 Total	8,322	13,766	4,237	8,346	22,964	29,628	16,062	16,098	16,253	(s)	67,838
1975 Total	7,990	14,813	4,059	9,492	21,434	29,413	18,210	18,245	20,270	1	71,965
1980 Total	7,439	15,753	4,105	10,578	22,595	32,039	19,659	19,697	24,269	-1	78,067
1985 Total	7,148	16,041	3,732	11,451	19,443	28,816	20,041	20,088	26,032	-4	76,392
1990 Total	6,556	16,944	3,896	13,320	21,180	31,810	22,366	22,420	d 30,495	-9	84,484
1995 Total	6,934	18,517	4,100	14,690	22,718	33,970	23,796	23,851	33,479	3	91,031
2000 Total	7,156	20,421	4,278	17,175	22,823	34,662	26,495	26,555	38,062	2	98,817
2001 Total	6,864	20,038	4,085	17,137	21,793	32,719	26,219	26,282	37,215	-6	96,170
2002 Total	6,907	20,786	4,132	17,346	21,798	32,661	26,785	26,846	38,016	5	97,643
2003 Total	7,232	21,119	4,298	17,346	21,534	32,553	26,826	26,900	38,028	-1	97,918
2004 Total	6,987	21,081	4,232	17,655	22,411	33,516	27,764	27,843	38,701	-6	100,090
2005 Total	6,901	21,613	4,052	17,853	21,410	32,442	28,199	28,280	39,626	(s)	100,188
2006 Total	6,154	20,670	3,747	17,707	21,529	32,391	28,638	28,717	39,417	(s)	99,485
2007 Total	6,589	21,519	3,922	18,253	21,363	32,385	28,771	28,858	40,371	-1	101,015
2008 Total	6,889	21,668	4,100	18,402	20,528	31,334	27,404	27,486	39,969	1	98,891
2009 Total	6,633	21,077	4,055	17,887	18,756	28,466	26,605	26,687	38,069	(s)	94,118
2010 Total	6,540	21,795	4,023	18,058	20,278	30,526	26,978	27,059	39,619	7	97,445
2011 Total	6,392	21,301	4,063	17,979	20,456	30,843	26,632	26,712	39,293	8	96,842
2012 Total	5,672	19,858	3,725	17,422	20,742	30,915	26,144	26,219	38,131	2	94,416
2013 Total	6,705	21,068	4,164	17,932	21,263	31,409	26,671	26,750	38,357	-1	97,157
2014 Total	6,990	21,429	4,380	18,255	21,407	31,643	26,917	26,996	38,629	6	98,329
2015 January	1,135	2,538	665	1,802	1,936	2,747	2,178	2,185	3,357	2	9,273
February	1,081	2,334	638	1,705	1,765	2,541	2,011	2,018	3,103	3	8,601
March	794	1,946	498	1,558	1,833	2,617	2,296	2,303	3,002	(s)	8,424
April	444	1,336	323	1,352	1,738	2,534	2,235	2,241	2,723	-2	7,460
May	303	1,295	251	1,391	1,765	2,629	2,318	2,324	3,002	(s)	7,639
June	232	1,478	216	1,452	1,752	2,646	2,312	2,318	3,383	3	7,897
July	222	1,727	219	1,543	1,814	2,719	2,424	2,431	3,741	6	8,425
August	220	1,679	222	1,520	1,800	2,692	2,405	2,412	3,655	6	8,308
September	220	1,444	221	1,414	1,706	2,533	2,280	2,286	3,251	4	7,682
October	359	1,327	307	1,407	1,734	2,546	2,329	2,335	2,886	-1	7,614
November	573	1,511	399	1,453	1,717	2,511	2,194	2,200	2,792	-1	7,674
December	777	1,901	478	1,554	1,823	2,610	2,297	2,303	2,993	-1	8,367
Total	**6,359**	**20,512**	**4,436**	**18,152**	**21,383**	**31,327**	**27,278**	**27,355**	**37,890**	**19**	**97,365**
2016 January	1,071	R 2,418	634	1,766	1,901	2,683	2,182	2,189	3,268	1	R 9,057
February	R 867	2,010	537	1,551	1,797	2,526	2,116	2,122	2,892	-3	8,206
March	607	R 1,599	409	1,452	1,809	2,562	2,355	2,361	2,794	-6	R 7,967
April	464	1,354	332	R 1,356	1,688	2,453	2,273	2,279	2,685	-5	R 7,438
May	324	1,303	268	1,392	1,698	2,513	2,361	2,367	2,925	-3	7,573
June	R 235	R 1,545	225	R 1,480	1,680	2,522	2,381	2,388	3,414	3	R 7,938
July	225	1,836	226	1,578	1,723	2,595	2,448	2,455	3,842	6	8,471
August	211	1,789	226	1,584	1,818	2,680	2,457	2,463	3,803	7	R 8,522
September	231	1,496	233	1,437	1,732	2,513	2,315	2,321	3,256	3	7,771
October	326	1,335	294	1,414	1,784	2,561	2,333	2,339	2,913	(s)	R 7,649
November	526	1,464	387	1,444	1,779	2,538	2,276	2,282	2,761	-2	7,726
December	R 996	R 2,271	R 599	1,755	1,898	2,691	2,351	2,358	3,231	1	R 9,076
Total	**R 6,082**	**20,413**	**R 4,368**	**R 18,212**	**21,308**	**30,841**	**27,849**	**27,925**	**37,784**	**3**	**R 97,394**
2017 January	R 1,029	R 2,346	611	1,726	R 1,906	R 2,678	2,190	2,197	3,211	R 1	R 8,948
February	739	R 1,739	471	1,455	1,687	2,397	2,025	2,031	2,702	-3	R 7,619
March	743	1,805	R 486	R 1,586	R 1,874	R 2,667	2,379	2,386	2,961	-3	8,440
April	419	1,337	312	1,339	1,737	2,502	2,253	2,259	2,716	(s)	7,436
4-Month Total	**2,929**	**7,227**	**1,879**	**6,106**	**7,205**	**10,244**	**8,846**	**8,872**	**11,589**	**-6**	**32,443**
2016 4-Month Total	**3,009**	**7,381**	**1,911**	**6,125**	**7,196**	**10,224**	**8,926**	**8,951**	**11,640**	**-13**	**32,669**
2015 4-Month Total	**3,454**	**8,154**	**2,124**	**6,417**	**7,272**	**10,439**	**8,720**	**8,746**	**12,186**	**2**	**33,758**

[a] Commercial sector, including commercial combined-heat-and-power (CHP) and commercial electricity-only plants.
[b] Industrial sector, including industrial combined-heat-and-power (CHP) and industrial electricity-only plants.
[c] Electricity-only and combined-heat-and-power (CHP) plants within the NAICS 22 category whose primary business is to sell electricity, or electricity and heat, to the public.
[d] Through 1988, data are for electric utilities only. Beginning in 1989, data are for electric utilities and independent power producers.
[e] See "Primary Energy Consumption" in Glossary.
[f] Total energy consumption in the end-use sectors consists of primary energy consumption, electricity retail sales, and electrical system energy losses. See Note 1, "Electrical System Energy Losses," at end of section.
[g] A balancing item. The sum of primary consumption in the five energy-use sectors equals the sum of total consumption in the four end-use sectors. However, total energy consumption does not equal the sum of the sectoral components due to the use of sector-specific conversion factors for coal and natural gas.
[h] Primary energy consumption total. See Table 1.3.

R=Revised. (s)=Less than 0.5 trillion Btu and greater than -0.5 trillion Btu.

Notes: • Data are estimates, except for the electric power sector. • See Note 2, "Classification of Power Plants Into Energy-Use Sectors," at end of Section 7. • See Note 2, "Energy Consumption Data and Surveys," at end of section. • Totals may not equal sum of components due to independent rounding. • Geographic coverage is the 50 states and the District of Columbia.

Web Page: See http://www.eia.gov/totalenergy/data/monthly/#consumption (Excel and CSV files) for all available annual data beginning in 1949 and monthly data beginning in 1973.

Sources: • **End-Use Sectors:** Tables 2.2–2.5. • **Electric Power Sector:** Table 2.6. • **Balancing Item:** Calculated as primary energy total consumption minus the sum of total energy consumption in the four end-use sectors. • **Primary Total:** Table 1.3.

Source: *U.S. Energy Information Administration, Monthly Energy Review, July 2017*

Figure 2.2 Residential Sector Energy Consumption
(Quadrillion Btu)

By Major Source, 1949–2016

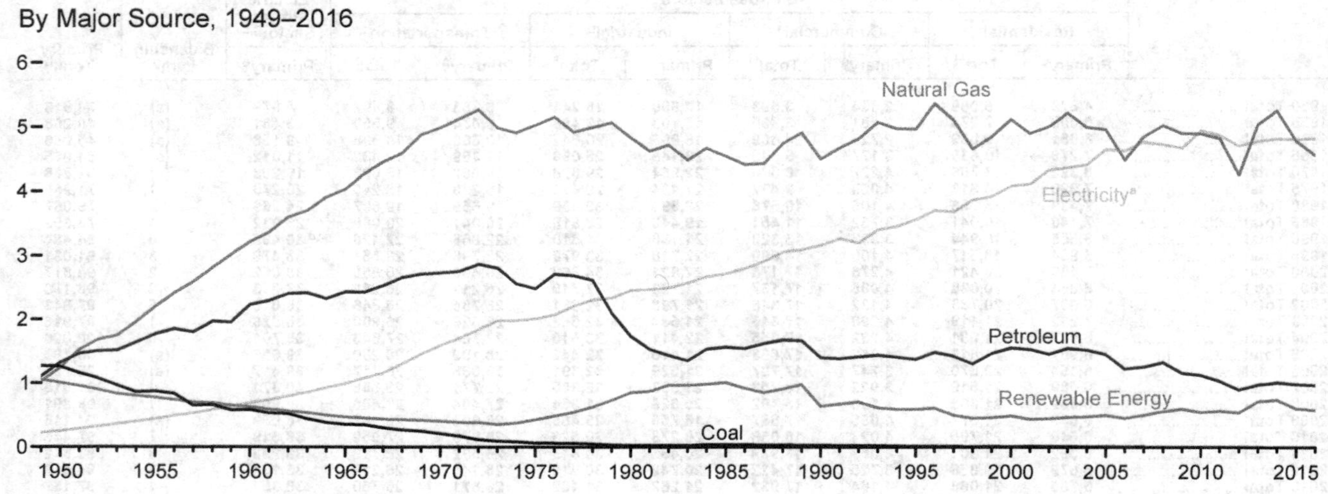

By Major Source, Monthly

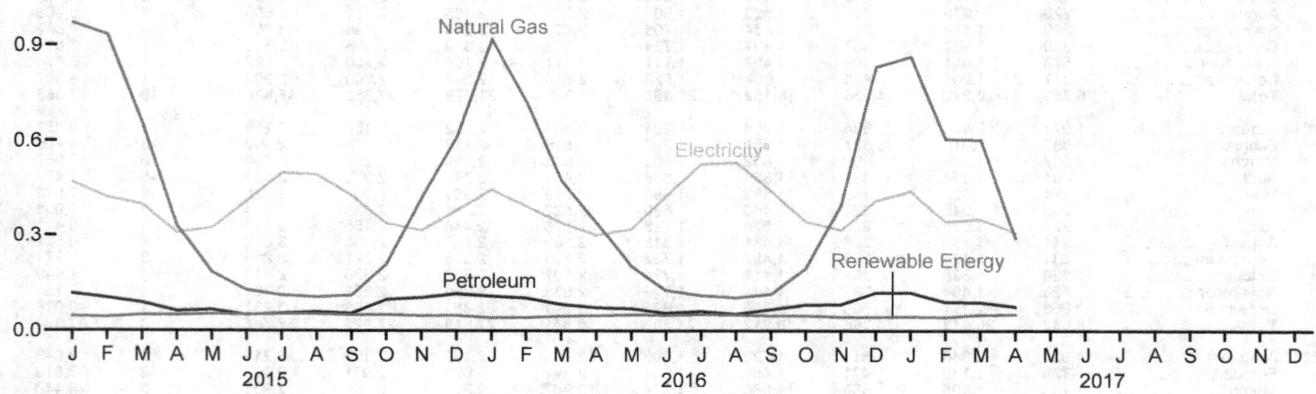

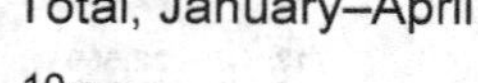

Total, January–April

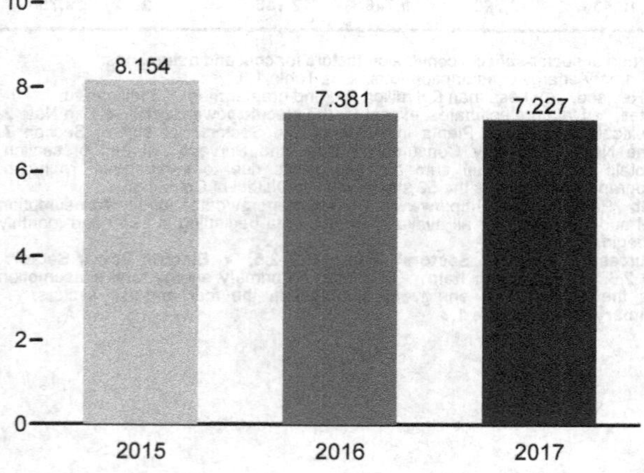

By Major Source, April 2017

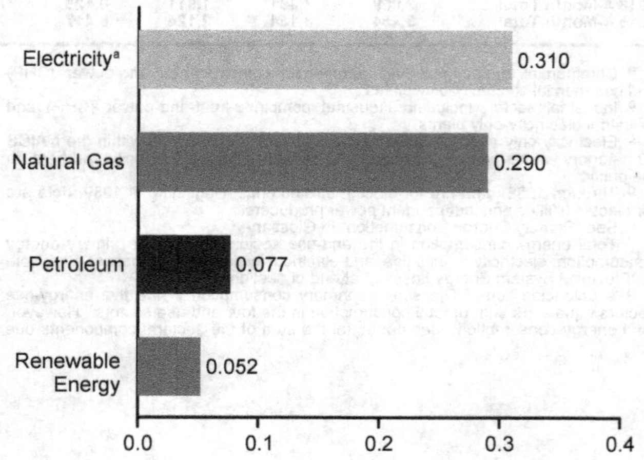

[a] Electricity retail sales.
Web Page: http://www.eia.gov/totalenergy/data/monthly/#consumption.
Source: Table 2.2.

Source: *U.S. Energy Information Administration, Monthly Energy Review, July 2017*

Table 2.2 Residential Sector Energy Consumption
(Trillion Btu)

	Primary Consumption[a]											
	Fossil Fuels				Renewable Energy[b]							
	Coal	Natural Gas[c]	Petroleum	Total	Geothermal	Solar[d]	Biomass	Total	Total Primary	Electricity Retail Sales[e]	Electrical System Energy Losses[f]	Total
1950 Total	**1,261**	**1,240**	**1,322**	**3,824**	**NA**	**NA**	**1,006**	**1,006**	**4,829**	**246**	**913**	**5,989**
1955 Total	**867**	**2,198**	**1,767**	**4,833**	**NA**	**NA**	**775**	**775**	**5,608**	**438**	**1,232**	**7,278**
1960 Total	**585**	**3,212**	**2,227**	**6,024**	**NA**	**NA**	**627**	**627**	**6,651**	**687**	**1,701**	**9,039**
1965 Total	**352**	**4,028**	**2,432**	**6,811**	**NA**	**NA**	**468**	**468**	**7,279**	**993**	**2,367**	**10,639**
1970 Total	**209**	**4,987**	**2,725**	**7,922**	**NA**	**NA**	**401**	**401**	**8,322**	**1,591**	**3,852**	**13,766**
1975 Total	**63**	**5,023**	**2,479**	**7,564**	**NA**	**NA**	**425**	**425**	**7,990**	**2,007**	**4,817**	**14,813**
1980 Total	**31**	**4,825**	**1,734**	**6,589**	**NA**	**NA**	**850**	**850**	**7,439**	**2,448**	**5,866**	**15,753**
1985 Total	**39**	**4,534**	**1,565**	**6,138**	**NA**	**NA**	**1,010**	**1,010**	**7,148**	**2,709**	**6,184**	**16,041**
1990 Total	**31**	**4,491**	**1,394**	**5,916**	**6**	**55**	**580**	**640**	**6,556**	**3,153**	**7,235**	**16,944**
1995 Total	**17**	**4,954**	**1,373**	**6,345**	**7**	**63**	**520**	**589**	**6,934**	**3,557**	**8,026**	**18,517**
2000 Total	**11**	**5,105**	**1,553**	**6,669**	**9**	**58**	**420**	**486**	**7,156**	**4,069**	**9,197**	**20,421**
2001 Total	**12**	**4,889**	**1,528**	**6,429**	**9**	**55**	**370**	**435**	**6,864**	**4,100**	**9,074**	**20,038**
2002 Total	**12**	**4,995**	**1,456**	**6,463**	**10**	**53**	**380**	**444**	**6,907**	**4,317**	**9,562**	**20,786**
2003 Total	**12**	**5,209**	**1,546**	**6,768**	**13**	**52**	**400**	**465**	**7,232**	**4,353**	**9,534**	**21,119**
2004 Total	**11**	**4,981**	**1,519**	**6,511**	**14**	**51**	**410**	**475**	**6,987**	**4,408**	**9,687**	**21,081**
2005 Total	**8**	**4,946**	**1,450**	**6,405**	**16**	**50**	**430**	**496**	**6,901**	**4,638**	**10,074**	**21,613**
2006 Total	**6**	**4,476**	**1,221**	**5,704**	**18**	**53**	**380**	**451**	**6,154**	**4,611**	**9,905**	**20,670**
2007 Total	**8**	**4,835**	**1,249**	**6,092**	**22**	**55**	**420**	**497**	**6,589**	**4,750**	**10,180**	**21,519**
2008 Total	**NA**	**5,010**	**1,324**	**6,334**	**26**	**58**	**470**	**555**	**6,889**	**4,711**	**10,068**	**21,668**
2009 Total	**NA**	**4,883**	**1,157**	**6,040**	**33**	**60**	**500**	**593**	**6,633**	**4,657**	**9,788**	**21,077**
2010 Total	**NA**	**4,878**	**1,121**	**5,999**	**37**	**65**	**440**	**541**	**6,540**	**4,933**	**10,321**	**21,795**
2011 Total	**NA**	**4,805**	**1,027**	**5,832**	**40**	**71**	**450**	**560**	**6,392**	**4,855**	**10,054**	**21,301**
2012 Total	**NA**	**4,242**	**892**	**5,134**	**40**	**79**	**420**	**539**	**5,672**	**4,690**	**9,496**	**19,858**
2013 Total	**NA**	**5,023**	**970**	**5,993**	**40**	**92**	**580**	**711**	**6,705**	**4,759**	**9,604**	**21,068**
2014 Total	**NA**	**5,242**	**1,009**	**6,251**	**40**	**109**	**590**	**739**	**6,990**	**4,801**	**9,638**	**21,429**
2015 January	NA	970	117	1,088	3	6	37	47	1,135	470	933	2,538
February	NA	933	104	1,037	3	7	34	44	1,081	423	830	2,334
March	NA	655	89	743	3	10	37	51	794	400	752	1,946
April	NA	330	63	393	3	11	36	51	444	308	584	1,336
May	NA	183	67	250	3	12	37	53	303	325	667	1,295
June	NA	128	51	179	3	13	36	52	232	410	836	1,478
July	NA	112	56	168	3	13	37	54	222	498	1,007	1,727
August	NA	106	60	166	3	13	37	54	220	493	966	1,679
September	NA	112	56	168	3	12	36	52	220	428	797	1,444
October	NA	208	99	307	3	11	37	52	359	339	630	1,327
November	NA	420	104	524	3	9	36	49	573	316	622	1,511
December	NA	611	117	728	3	8	37	49	777	381	743	1,901
Total	**NA**	**4,769**	**982**	**5,751**	**40**	**128**	**440**	**607**	**6,359**	**4,791**	**9,362**	**20,512**
2016 January	NA	R 918	110	1,028	3	8	32	43	1,071	446	901	R 2,418
February	NA	722	103	825	3	10	30	42	R 867	395	747	2,010
March	NA	475	84	559	3	13	32	48	607	342	651	R 1,599
April	NA	343	74	416	3	14	31	48	464	301	589	1,354
May	NA	203	70	273	3	16	32	51	324	321	658	1,303
June	NA	128	57	185	3	17	31	50	R 235	426	884	R 1,545
July	NA	111	62	173	3	17	32	52	225	525	1,085	1,836
August	NA	105	54	159	3	17	32	52	211	532	1,046	1,789
September	NA	115	68	R 182	3	15	31	49	231	441	824	1,496
October	NA	196	82	278	3	13	32	48	326	345	664	1,335
November	NA	398	83	481	3	11	31	45	526	317	622	1,464
December	NA	R 831	120	R 951	3	10	32	45	R 996	412	863	R 2,271
Total	**NA**	**4,543**	**967**	**R 5,509**	**40**	**161**	**373**	**573**	**R 6,082**	**4,802**	**9,528**	**20,413**
2017 January	NA	R 863	120	R 983	3	10	32	46	R 1,029	440	877	R 2,346
February	NA	604	91	695	3	11	29	43	739	345	656	R 1,739
March	NA	602	90	692	3	16	32	51	743	352	709	1,805
April	NA	290	77	367	3	18	31	52	419	310	608	1,337
4-Month Total	**NA**	**2,359**	**378**	**2,737**	**13**	**54**	**125**	**192**	**2,929**	**1,447**	**2,851**	**7,227**
2016 4-Month Total	**NA**	**2,458**	**370**	**2,828**	**13**	**45**	**123**	**181**	**3,009**	**1,484**	**2,888**	**7,381**
2015 4-Month Total	**NA**	**2,889**	**373**	**3,262**	**13**	**35**	**145**	**193**	**3,454**	**1,600**	**3,099**	**8,154**

[a] See "Primary Energy Consumption" in Glossary.
[b] See Table 10.2a for notes on series components.
[c] Natural gas only; excludes the estimated portion of supplemental gaseous fuels. See Note 3, "Supplemental Gaseous Fuels," at end of Section 4.
[d] Distributed (small-scale) solar photovoltaic (PV) electricity generation in the residential sector and distributed solar thermal energy in the residential, commercial, and industrial sectors. See Tables 10.2a and 10.5.
[e] Electricity retail sales to ultimate customers reported by electric utilities and, beginning in 1996, other energy service providers.
[f] Total losses are calculated as the primary energy consumed by the electric power sector minus the energy content of electricity retail sales. Total losses are allocated to the end-use sectors in proportion to each sector's share of total electricity retail sales. See Note 1, "Electrical System Energy Losses," at end of section.

R=Revised. NA=Not available.

Notes: • Data are estimates, except for electricity retail sales. • See Note 2, "Energy Consumption Data and Surveys," at end of section. • Totals may not equal sum of components due to independent rounding. • Geographic coverage is the 50 states and the District of Columbia.

Web Page: See http://www.eia.gov/totalenergy/data/monthly/#consumption (Excel and CSV files) for all available annual data beginning in 1949 and monthly data beginning in 1973.

Sources: See end of section.

Source: *U.S. Energy Information Administration, Monthly Energy Review, July 2017*

Figure 2.3 Commercial Sector Energy Consumption
(Quadrillion Btu)

By Major Source, 1949–2016

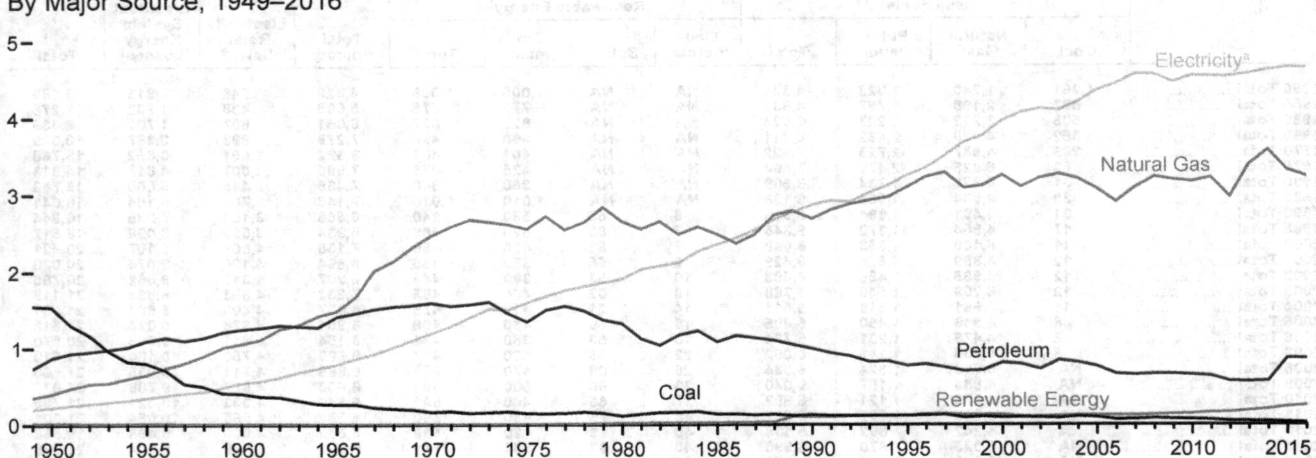

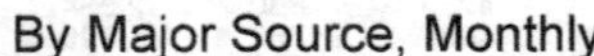

By Major Source, Monthly

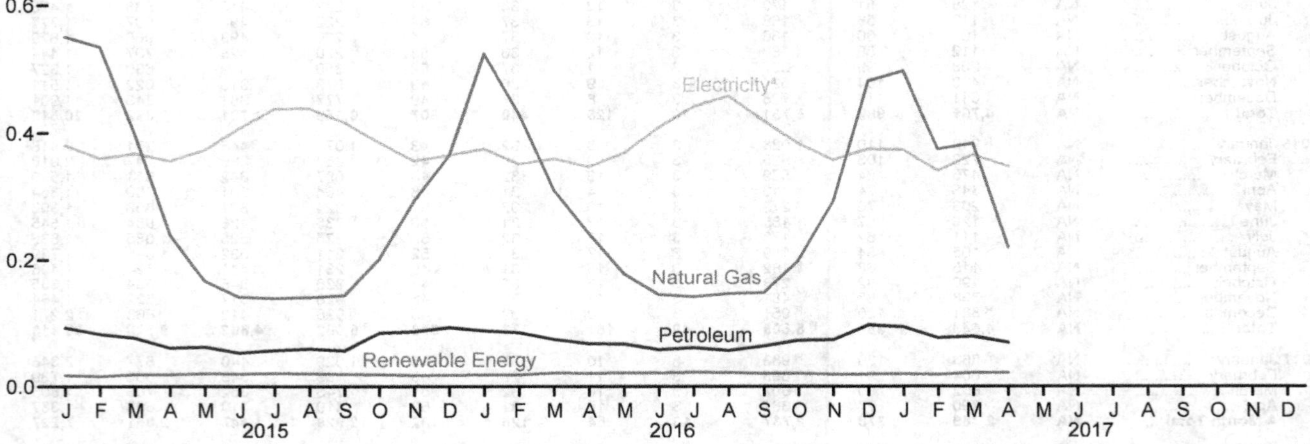

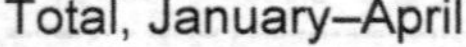

Total, January–April

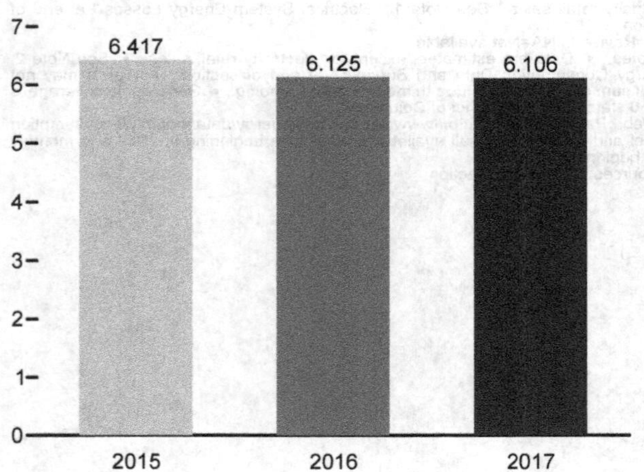

By Major Source, April 2017

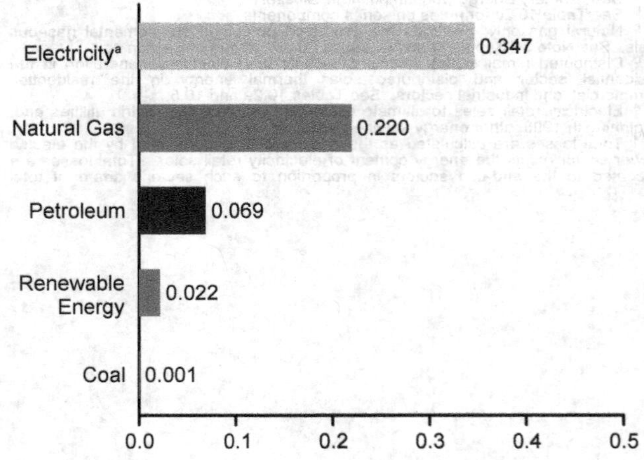

[a] Electricity retail sales.
Web Page: http://www.eia.gov/totalenergy/data/monthly/#consumption.
Source: Table 2.3.

***Source:** U.S. Energy Information Administration, Monthly Energy Review, July 2017*

Table 2.3 Commercial Sector Energy Consumption
(Trillion Btu)

	Primary Consumption[a]													
	Fossil Fuels				Renewable Energy[b]									
	Coal	Natural Gas[c]	Petroleum[d]	Total	Hydroelectric Power[e]	Geothermal	Solar[f]	Wind	Biomass	Total	Total Primary	Electricity Retail Sales[g]	Electrical System Energy Losses[h]	Total
1950 Total	**1,542**	**401**	**872**	**2,815**	**NA**	**NA**	**NA**	**NA**	**19**	**19**	**2,834**	**225**	**834**	**3,893**
1955 Total	**801**	**651**	**1,095**	**2,547**	**NA**	**NA**	**NA**	**NA**	**15**	**15**	**2,561**	**350**	**984**	**3,895**
1960 Total	**407**	**1,056**	**1,248**	**2,711**	**NA**	**NA**	**NA**	**NA**	**12**	**12**	**2,723**	**543**	**1,344**	**4,609**
1965 Total	**265**	**1,490**	**1,413**	**3,168**	**NA**	**NA**	**NA**	**NA**	**9**	**9**	**3,177**	**789**	**1,880**	**5,845**
1970 Total	**165**	**2,473**	**1,592**	**4,229**	**NA**	**NA**	**NA**	**NA**	**8**	**8**	**4,237**	**1,201**	**2,908**	**8,346**
1975 Total	**147**	**2,558**	**1,346**	**4,051**	**NA**	**NA**	**NA**	**NA**	**8**	**8**	**4,059**	**1,598**	**3,835**	**9,492**
1980 Total	**115**	**2,651**	**1,318**	**4,084**	**NA**	**NA**	**NA**	**NA**	**21**	**21**	**4,105**	**1,906**	**4,567**	**10,578**
1985 Total	**137**	**2,488**	**1,083**	**3,708**	**NA**	**NA**	**NA**	**NA**	**24**	**24**	**3,732**	**2,351**	**5,368**	**11,451**
1990 Total	**124**	**2,682**	**991**	**3,798**	**1**	**3**	**(s)**	**–**	**94**	**98**	**3,896**	**2,860**	**6,564**	**13,320**
1995 Total	**117**	**3,096**	**769**	**3,982**	**1**	**5**	**(s)**	**–**	**113**	**119**	**4,100**	**3,252**	**7,337**	**14,690**
2000 Total	**92**	**3,252**	**806**	**4,150**	**1**	**8**	**1**	**–**	**119**	**128**	**4,278**	**3,956**	**8,942**	**17,175**
2001 Total	**97**	**3,097**	**789**	**3,983**	**1**	**8**	**1**	**–**	**92**	**101**	**4,085**	**4,062**	**8,990**	**17,137**
2002 Total	**90**	**3,212**	**725**	**4,027**	**(s)**	**9**	**1**	**–**	**95**	**105**	**4,132**	**4,110**	**9,104**	**17,346**
2003 Total	**82**	**3,261**	**841**	**4,184**	**1**	**11**	**1**	**–**	**101**	**114**	**4,298**	**4,090**	**8,958**	**17,346**
2004 Total	**103**	**3,201**	**809**	**4,113**	**1**	**12**	**1**	**–**	**105**	**120**	**4,232**	**4,198**	**9,225**	**17,655**
2005 Total	**97**	**3,073**	**761**	**3,931**	**1**	**14**	**2**	**–**	**105**	**121**	**4,052**	**4,351**	**9,451**	**17,853**
2006 Total	**65**	**2,902**	**661**	**3,627**	**1**	**14**	**2**	**–**	**103**	**120**	**3,747**	**4,435**	**9,525**	**17,707**
2007 Total	**70**	**3,085**	**646**	**3,801**	**1**	**14**	**4**	**–**	**103**	**121**	**3,922**	**4,560**	**9,771**	**18,253**
2008 Total	**81**	**3,228**	**660**	**3,970**	**1**	**15**	**6**	**–**	**109**	**130**	**4,100**	**4,559**	**9,743**	**18,402**
2009 Total	**73**	**3,187**	**659**	**3,919**	**1**	**17**	**7**	**(s)**	**112**	**137**	**4,055**	**4,459**	**9,373**	**17,887**
2010 Total	**70**	**3,165**	**647**	**3,881**	**1**	**19**	**11**	**(s)**	**111**	**142**	**4,023**	**4,539**	**9,497**	**18,058**
2011 Total	**62**	**3,216**	**630**	**3,908**	**(s)**	**20**	**19**	**(s)**	**115**	**154**	**4,063**	**4,531**	**9,385**	**17,979**
2012 Total	**44**	**2,960**	**562**	**3,565**	**(s)**	**20**	**32**	**1**	**108**	**161**	**3,725**	**4,528**	**9,168**	**17,422**
2013 Total	**41**	**3,380**	**560**	**3,982**	**(s)**	**20**	**41**	**1**	**120**	**182**	**4,164**	**4,562**	**9,206**	**17,932**
2014 Total	**40**	**3,572**	**569**	**4,181**	**(s)**	**20**	**52**	**1**	**126**	**199**	**4,380**	**4,614**	**9,261**	**18,255**
2015 January	4	551	92	647	(s)	2	3	(s)	13	18	665	381	756	1,802
February	4	535	82	621	(s)	2	4	(s)	12	17	638	360	707	1,705
March	4	399	76	479	(s)	2	5	(s)	13	20	498	368	692	1,558
April	2	240	61	303	(s)	2	5	(s)	13	20	323	355	674	1,352
May	2	166	62	230	(s)	2	6	(s)	13	21	251	373	767	1,391
June	2	140	53	196	(s)	2	6	(s)	13	20	216	407	829	1,452
July	2	138	57	197	(s)	2	6	(s)	14	21	219	438	886	1,543
August	2	140	60	201	(s)	2	6	(s)	13	21	222	439	859	1,520
September	2	143	57	201	(s)	2	5	(s)	13	20	221	417	776	1,414
October	2	201	84	288	(s)	2	5	(s)	13	19	307	385	715	1,407
November	2	293	86	381	(s)	2	4	(s)	13	18	399	355	698	1,453
December	3	364	93	460	(s)	2	3	(s)	13	18	478	365	711	1,554
Total	**31**	**3,309**	**863**	**4,204**	**(s)**	**20**	**57**	**1**	**154**	**232**	**4,436**	**4,643**	**9,073**	**18,152**
2016 January	3	524	88	R 614	(s)	2	4	(s)	13	19	634	375	757	1,766
February	3	430	85	518	(s)	2	5	(s)	12	19	537	351	663	1,551
March	3	310	74	387	(s)	2	6	(s)	14	22	409	359	684	1,452
April	2	242	67	311	(s)	2	7	(s)	13	21	332	346	678	R 1,356
May	1	178	67	246	(s)	2	7	(s)	13	22	268	368	756	1,392
June	1	144	58	203	(s)	2	7	(s)	13	22	225	408	847	R 1,480
July	1	141	61	203	(s)	2	8	(s)	13	23	226	441	911	1,578
August	1	146	57	204	(s)	2	7	(s)	13	22	226	457	900	1,584
September	1	147	63	212	(s)	2	7	(s)	13	21	233	420	785	1,437
October	2	199	72	273	(s)	2	6	(s)	13	21	294	383	737	1,414
November	2	292	73	368	(s)	2	5	(s)	13	19	387	356	700	1,444
December	3	R 480	96	R 579	(s)	2	4	(s)	14	20	R 599	374	782	1,755
Total	**24**	**R 3,231**	**861**	**R 4,117**	**1**	**20**	**72**	**1**	**157**	**251**	**R 4,368**	**4,639**	**9,205**	**R 18,212**
2017 January	3	495	93	591	(s)	2	5	(s)	14	20	611	373	743	1,726
February	2	374	76	452	(s)	2	5	(s)	12	19	471	339	645	1,455
March	R 3	383	78	R 464	(s)	2	7	(s)	13	22	R 486	365	735	R 1,586
April	1	220	69	290	(s)	2	8	(s)	13	22	312	347	680	1,339
4-Month Total	**9**	**1,471**	**316**	**1,796**	**(s)**	**6**	**24**	**(s)**	**51**	**83**	**1,879**	**1,424**	**2,804**	**6,106**
2016 4-Month Total	**11**	**1,505**	**314**	**1,830**	**(s)**	**7**	**21**	**(s)**	**53**	**81**	**1,911**	**1,431**	**2,783**	**6,125**
2015 4-Month Total	**14**	**1,725**	**312**	**2,050**	**(s)**	**6**	**17**	**(s)**	**50**	**74**	**2,124**	**1,464**	**2,829**	**6,417**

[a] See "Primary Energy Consumption" in Glossary.
[b] See Table 10.2a for notes on series components and estimation.
[c] Natural gas only; excludes the estimated portion of supplemental gaseous fuels. See Note 3, "Supplemental Gaseous Fuels," at end of Section 4.
[d] Does not include biofuels that have been blended with petroleum—biofuels are included in "Biomass."
[e] Conventional hydroelectric power.
[f] Solar photovoltaic (PV) electricity net generation in the commercial sector, both utility-scale and distributed (small-scale). See Tables 10.2a and 10.5.
[g] Electricity retail sales to ultimate customers reported by electric utilities and, beginning in 1996, other energy service providers.
[h] Total losses are calculated as the primary energy consumed by the electric power sector minus the energy content of electricity retail sales. Total losses are allocated to the end-use sectors in proportion to each sector's share of total electricity retail sales. See Note 1, "Electrical System Energy Losses," at end of section.

R=Revised. NA=Not available. – =No data reported. (s)=Less than 0.5 trillion Btu.

Notes: • Data are estimates, except for coal totals beginning in 2008; hydroelectric power; solar; wind; and electricity retail sales beginning in 1979. • The commercial sector includes commercial combined-heat-and-power (CHP) and commercial electricity-only plants. See Note 2, "Classification of Power Plants Into Energy-Use Sectors," at end of Section 7. • See Note 2, "Energy Consumption Data and Surveys," at end of section. • Totals may not equal sum of components due to independent rounding. • Geographic coverage is the 50 states and the District of Columbia.

Web Page: See http://www.eia.gov/totalenergy/data/monthly/#consumption (Excel and CSV files) for all available annual data beginning in 1949 and monthly data beginning in 1973.

Sources: See end of section.

Source: *U.S. Energy Information Administration, Monthly Energy Review, July 2017*

Figure 2.4 Industrial Sector Energy Consumption
(Quadrillion Btu)

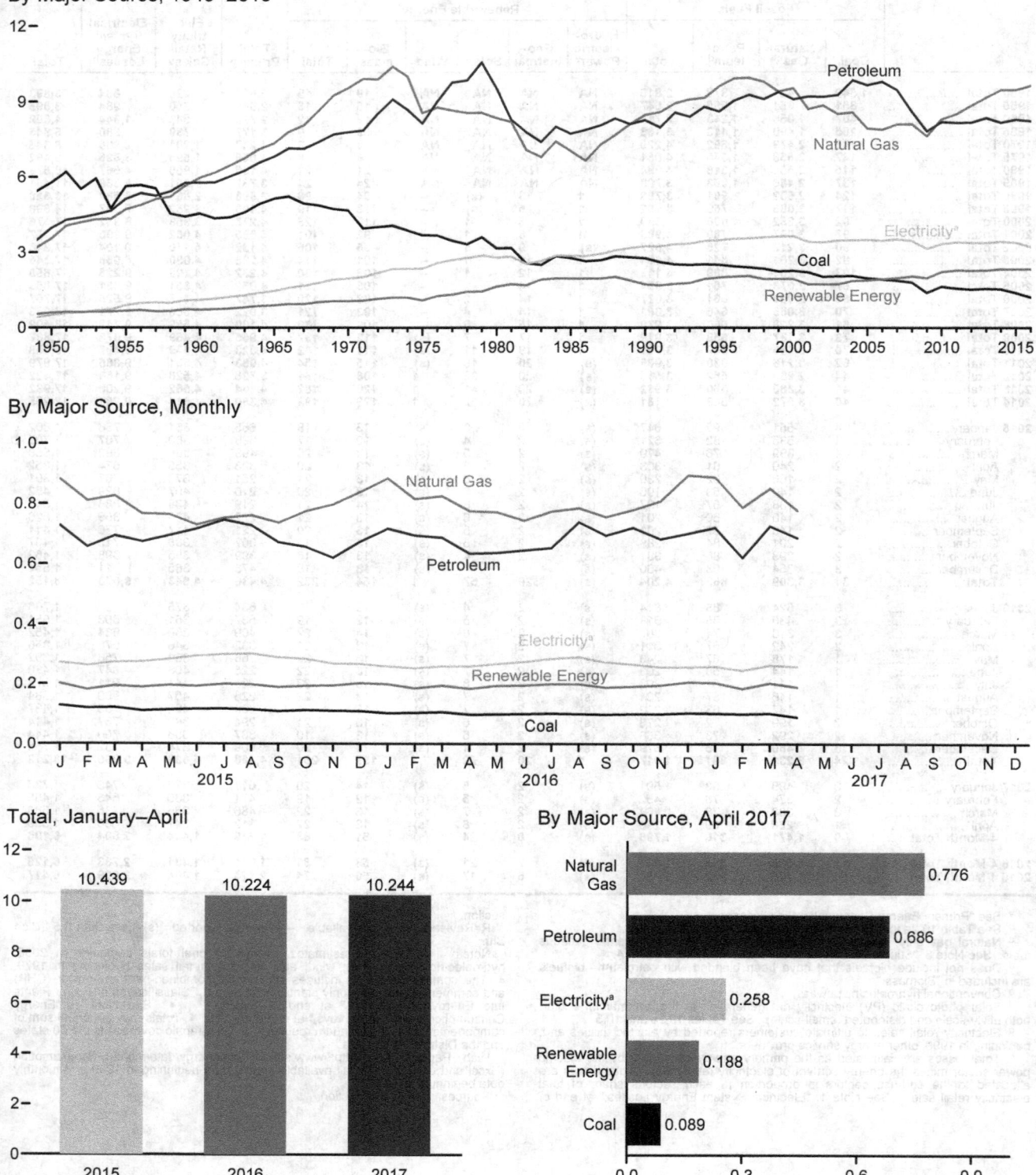

By Major Source, 1949–2016

By Major Source, Monthly

Total, January–April

By Major Source, April 2017

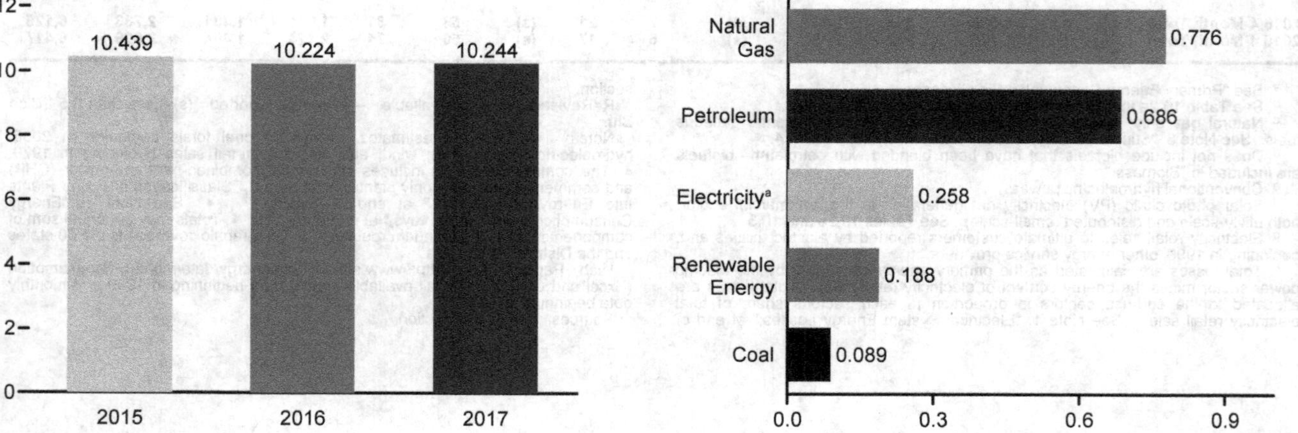

[a] Electricity retail sales.
Web Page: http://www.eia.gov/totalenergy/data/monthly/#consumption.
Source: Table 2.4.

Source: *U.S. Energy Information Administration, Monthly Energy Review, July 2017*

Table 2.4 Industrial Sector Energy Consumption
(Trillion Btu)

	Primary Consumption[a]													
	Fossil Fuels				Renewable Energy[b]									
	Coal	Natural Gas[c]	Petroleum[d]	Total[e]	Hydroelectric Power[f]	Geothermal	Solar[g]	Wind	Biomass	Total	Total Primary	Electricity Retail Sales[h]	Electrical System Energy Losses[i]	Total[e]
1950 Total	5,781	3,546	3,960	13,288	69	NA	NA	NA	532	602	13,890	500	1,852	16,241
1955 Total	5,620	4,701	5,123	15,434	38	NA	NA	NA	631	669	16,103	887	2,495	19,485
1960 Total	4,543	5,973	5,766	16,277	39	NA	NA	NA	680	719	16,996	1,107	2,739	20,842
1965 Total	5,127	7,339	6,813	19,260	33	NA	NA	NA	855	888	20,148	1,463	3,487	25,098
1970 Total	4,656	9,536	7,776	21,911	34	NA	NA	NA	1,019	1,053	22,964	1,948	4,716	29,628
1975 Total	3,667	8,532	8,127	20,339	32	NA	NA	NA	1,063	1,096	21,434	2,346	5,632	29,413
1980 Total	3,155	8,333	9,509	20,962	33	NA	NA	NA	1,600	1,633	22,595	2,781	6,664	32,039
1985 Total	2,760	7,032	7,714	17,492	33	NA	NA	NA	1,918	1,951	19,443	2,855	6,518	28,816
1990 Total	2,756	8,451	8,251	19,463	31	2	(s)	–	1,684	1,717	21,180	3,226	7,404	31,810
1995 Total	2,488	9,592	8,585	20,726	55	3	(s)	–	1,934	1,992	22,718	3,455	7,796	33,970
2000 Total	2,256	9,500	9,073	20,895	42	4	(s)	–	1,881	1,928	22,823	3,631	8,208	34,662
2001 Total	2,192	8,676	9,177	20,074	33	5	(s)	–	1,681	1,719	21,793	3,400	7,526	32,719
2002 Total	2,019	8,832	9,167	20,078	39	5	(s)	–	1,676	1,720	21,798	3,379	7,484	32,661
2003 Total	2,041	8,488	9,229	19,809	43	3	(s)	–	1,678	1,725	21,534	3,454	7,565	32,553
2004 Total	2,047	8,550	9,825	20,560	33	4	(s)	–	1,815	1,852	22,411	3,473	7,631	33,516
2005 Total	1,954	7,907	9,634	19,540	32	4	(s)	–	1,834	1,871	21,410	3,477	7,554	32,442
2006 Total	1,914	7,861	9,767	19,603	29	4	1	–	1,892	1,926	21,529	3,451	7,411	32,391
2007 Total	1,865	8,074	9,442	19,405	16	5	1	–	1,937	1,958	21,363	3,507	7,515	32,385
2008 Total	1,793	8,083	8,576	18,493	17	5	1	–	2,012	2,035	20,528	3,444	7,362	31,334
2009 Total	1,392	7,609	7,806	16,784	18	4	2	–	1,948	1,972	18,756	3,130	6,580	28,466
2010 Total	1,631	8,278	8,167	18,070	16	4	3	–	2,185	2,208	20,278	3,314	6,934	30,526
2011 Total	1,561	8,481	8,131	18,184	17	4	4	(s)	2,246	2,272	20,456	3,382	7,005	30,843
2012 Total	1,513	8,819	8,147	18,482	22	4	7	(s)	2,226	2,259	20,742	3,363	6,810	30,915
2013 Total	1,546	9,140	8,321	18,991	33	4	9	(s)	2,226	2,272	21,263	3,362	6,785	31,409
2014 Total	1,530	9,441	8,143	19,093	12	4	11	1	2,286	2,314	21,407	3,404	6,832	31,643
2015 January	128	882	728	1,735	1	(s)	1	(s)	199	201	1,936	272	539	2,747
February	119	810	657	1,585	1	(s)	1	(s)	178	180	1,765	262	515	2,541
March	121	826	694	1,640	1	(s)	1	(s)	190	193	1,833	272	512	2,617
April	110	767	674	1,549	1	(s)	1	(s)	186	189	1,738	275	521	2,534
May	114	764	695	1,570	1	(s)	1	(s)	192	195	1,765	283	581	2,629
June	116	731	716	1,560	1	(s)	1	(s)	189	192	1,752	294	599	2,646
July	117	753	746	1,615	1	(s)	1	(s)	196	199	1,814	299	605	2,719
August	115	761	728	1,602	1	(s)	1	(s)	195	197	1,800	302	591	2,692
September	109	736	672	1,517	1	(s)	1	(s)	186	189	1,706	289	538	2,533
October	112	775	656	1,542	1	(s)	1	(s)	190	193	1,734	284	528	2,546
November	110	797	620	1,524	1	(s)	1	(s)	191	193	1,717	268	526	2,511
December	109	839	675	1,622	1	(s)	1	(s)	198	201	1,823	267	520	2,610
Total	**1,380**	**9,440**	**8,260**	**19,062**	**13**	**4**	**14**	**(s)**	**2,290**	**2,321**	**21,383**	**3,366**	**6,578**	**31,327**
2016 January	R 103	884	718	1,703	1	(s)	1	(s)	196	198	1,901	259	523	2,683
February	103	815	694	1,612	1	(s)	1	(s)	182	184	1,797	252	477	2,526
March	R 106	824	687	1,616	1	(s)	1	(s)	190	194	1,809	259	494	2,562
April	R 98	775	634	1,505	1	(s)	2	(s)	180	183	1,688	259	507	2,453
May	99	R 771	636	1,505	1	(s)	2	(s)	189	193	1,698	267	548	2,513
June	100	743	644	1,487	1	(s)	2	(s)	190	193	1,680	274	568	2,522
July	101	773	652	1,525	1	(s)	2	(s)	195	199	1,723	284	588	2,595
August	99	R 785	738	1,620	1	(s)	2	(s)	195	198	1,818	290	571	2,680
September	98	R 755	694	1,546	1	(s)	2	(s)	184	187	1,732	272	509	2,513
October	99	778	720	1,594	1	(s)	1	(s)	187	190	1,784	266	512	2,561
November	99	808	682	R 1,584	1	(s)	1	(s)	192	194	1,779	256	503	2,538
December	R 103	893	700	1,694	1	(s)	1	(s)	202	205	1,898	256	536	2,691
Total	**R 1,207**	**R 9,605**	**8,198**	**18,991**	**12**	**4**	**17**	**1**	**2,283**	**2,318**	**21,308**	**3,195**	**6,339**	**30,841**
2017 January	R 101	887	720	R 1,704	1	(s)	1	(s)	200	203	R 1,906	258	514	R 2,678
February	R 99	R 787	620	R 1,504	1	(s)	1	(s)	180	183	1,687	245	465	2,397
March	101	R 849	725	R 1,673	1	(s)	2	(s)	198	202	R 1,874	263	529	R 2,667
April	89	776	686	1,550	1	(s)	2	(s)	184	188	1,737	258	507	2,502
4-Month Total	**389**	**3,299**	**2,750**	**6,430**	**5**	**1**	**7**	**(s)**	**762**	**775**	**7,205**	**1,024**	**2,015**	**10,244**
2016 4-Month Total	**409**	**3,298**	**2,732**	**6,436**	**5**	**1**	**5**	**(s)**	**748**	**759**	**7,196**	**1,029**	**2,000**	**10,224**
2015 4-Month Total	**478**	**3,284**	**2,752**	**6,509**	**5**	**1**	**4**	**(s)**	**753**	**763**	**7,272**	**1,080**	**2,086**	**10,439**

[a] See "Primary Energy Consumption" in Glossary.
[b] See Table 10.2b for notes on series components and estimation.
[c] Natural gas only; excludes the estimated portion of supplemental gaseous fuels. See Note 3, "Supplemental Gaseous Fuels," at end of Section 4.
[d] Does not include biofuels that have been blended with petroleum—biofuels are included in "Biomass."
[e] Includes coal coke net imports, which are not separately displayed. See Tables 1.4a and 1.4b.
[f] Conventional hydroelectric power.
[g] Solar photovoltaic (PV) electricity net generation in the industrial sector, both utility-scale and distributed (small-scale). See Tables 10.2b and 10.5.
[h] Electricity retail sales to ultimate customers reported by electric utilities and, beginning in 1996, other energy service providers.
[i] Total losses are calculated as the primary energy consumed by the electric power sector minus the energy content of electricity retail sales. Total losses are allocated to the end-use sectors in proportion to each sector's share of total electricity retail sales. See Note 1, "Electrical System Energy Losses," at end of section.

R=Revised. NA=Not available. – =No data reported. (s)=Less than 0.5 trillion Btu.

Notes: • Data are estimates, except for coal totals; hydroelectric power in 1949–1978 and 1989 forward; solar; wind; and electricity retail sales. • The industrial sector includes industrial combined-heat-and-power (CHP) and industrial electricity-only plants. See Note 2, "Classification of Power Plants Into Energy-Use Sectors," at end of Section 7. • See Note 2, "Energy Consumption Data and Surveys," at end of section. • Totals may not equal sum of components due to independent rounding. • Geographic coverage is the 50 states and the District of Columbia.

Web Page: See http://www.eia.gov/totalenergy/data/monthly/#consumption (Excel and CSV files) for all available annual data beginning in 1949 and monthly data beginning in 1973.

Sources: See end of section.

Source: *U.S. Energy Information Administration, Monthly Energy Review, July 2017*

Figure 2.5 Transportation Sector Energy Consumption
(Quadrillion Btu)

By Major Source, 1949–2016

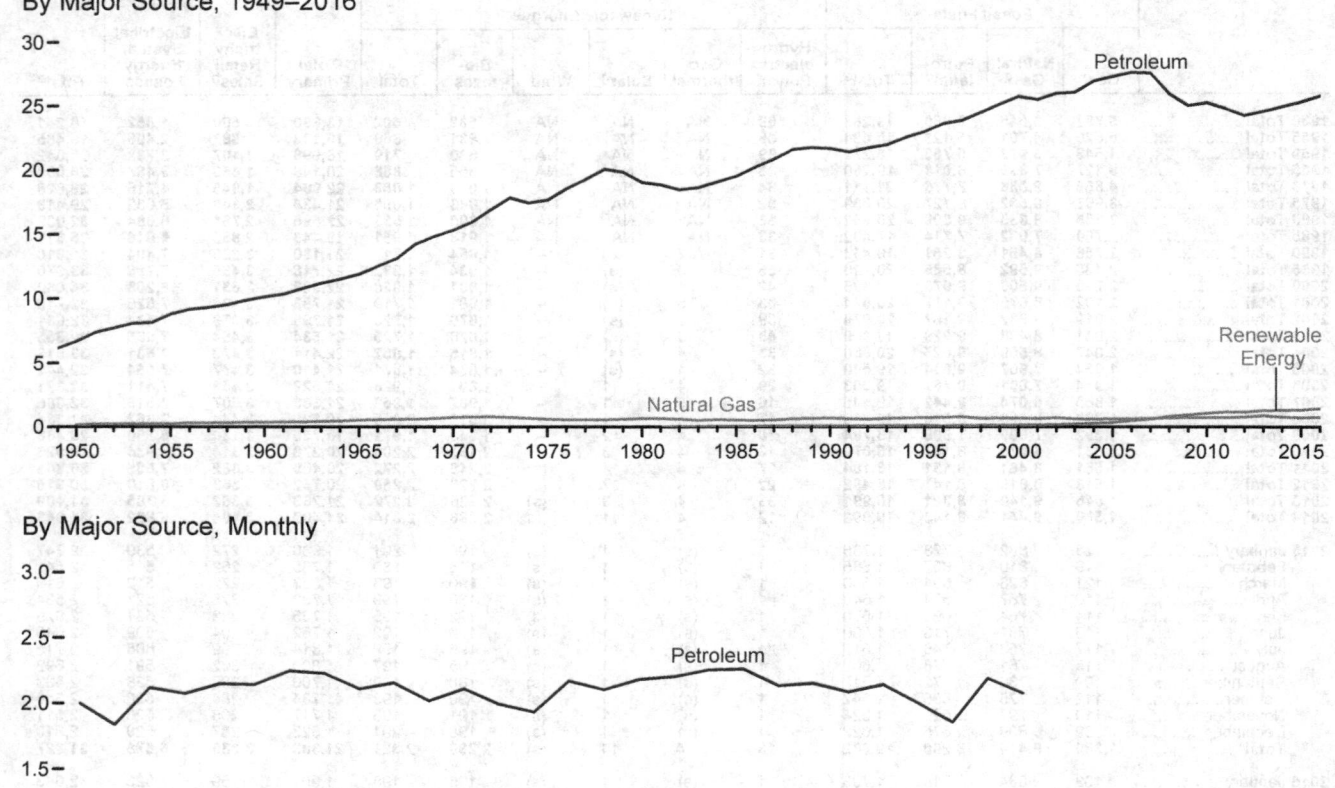

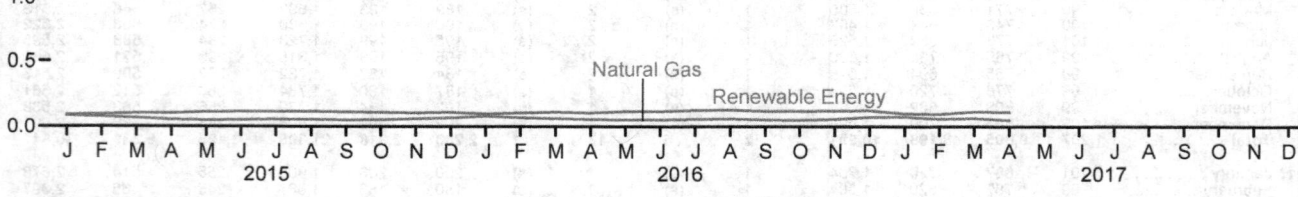

Petroleum
Renewable Energy
Natural Gas

By Major Source, Monthly

Petroleum
Natural Gas
Renewable Energy

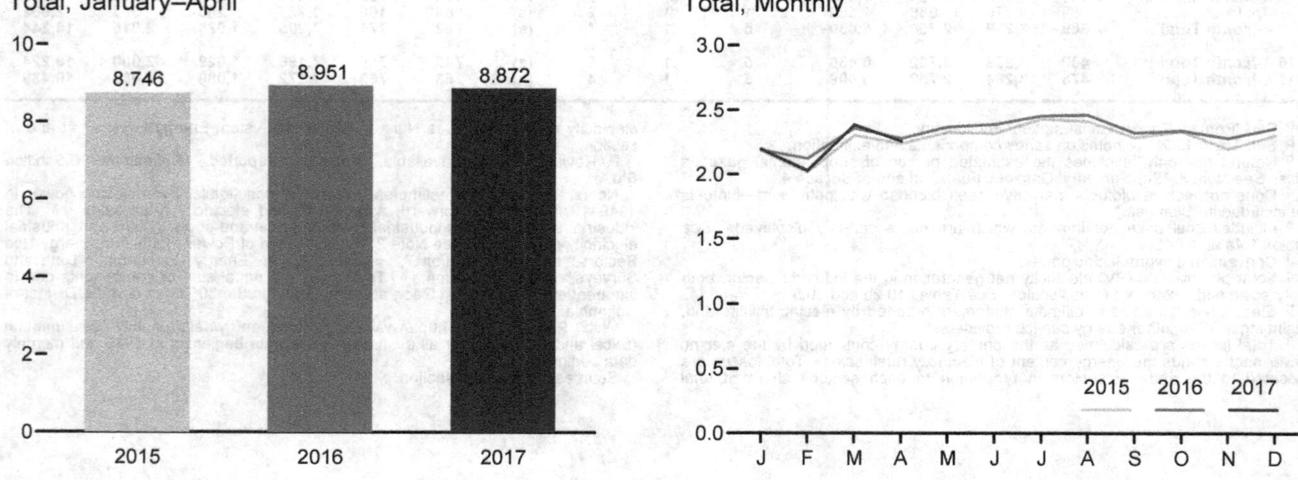

Web Page: http://www.eia.gov/totalenergy/data/monthly/#consumption.
Source: Table 2.5.

Source: *U.S. Energy Information Administration, Monthly Energy Review, July 2017*

Table 2.5 Transportation Sector Energy Consumption
(Trillion Btu)

	Primary Consumption[a]						Electricity Retail Sales[e]	Electrical System Energy Losses[f]	Total
	Fossil Fuels				Renewable Energy[b]	Total Primary			
	Coal	Natural Gas[c]	Petroleum[d]	Total	Biomass				
1950 Total	1,564	130	6,690	8,383	NA	8,383	23	86	8,492
1955 Total	421	254	8,799	9,474	NA	9,474	20	56	9,550
1960 Total	75	359	10,125	10,560	NA	10,560	10	26	10,596
1965 Total	16	517	11,866	12,399	NA	12,399	10	24	12,432
1970 Total	7	745	15,310	16,062	NA	16,062	11	26	16,098
1975 Total	1	595	17,615	18,210	NA	18,210	10	24	18,245
1980 Total	(g)	650	19,009	19,659	NA	19,659	11	27	19,697
1985 Total	(g)	519	19,472	19,992	50	20,041	14	32	20,088
1990 Total	(g)	680	21,626	22,306	60	22,366	16	37	22,420
1995 Total	(g)	724	22,959	23,683	112	23,796	17	38	23,851
2000 Total	(g)	672	25,689	26,361	135	26,495	18	42	26,555
2001 Total	(g)	658	25,419	26,077	142	26,219	20	43	26,282
2002 Total	(g)	699	25,917	26,616	170	26,785	19	42	26,846
2003 Total	(g)	627	25,969	26,596	230	26,826	23	51	26,900
2004 Total	(g)	602	26,872	27,474	290	27,764	25	54	27,843
2005 Total	(g)	624	27,236	27,860	339	28,199	26	56	28,280
2006 Total	(g)	625	27,538	28,163	475	28,638	25	54	28,717
2007 Total	(g)	663	27,505	28,169	602	28,771	28	60	28,858
2008 Total	(g)	692	25,888	26,580	825	27,404	26	56	27,486
2009 Total	(g)	715	24,955	25,670	935	26,605	27	56	26,687
2010 Total	(g)	719	25,184	25,903	1,075	26,978	26	55	27,059
2011 Total	(g)	734	24,740	25,474	1,158	26,632	26	54	26,712
2012 Total	(g)	780	24,202	24,982	1,162	26,144	25	51	26,219
2013 Total	(g)	887	24,506	25,394	1,278	26,671	26	53	26,750
2014 Total	(g)	760	24,865	25,625	1,292	26,917	26	53	26,996
2015 January	(g)	84	2,000	2,084	94	2,178	2	5	2,185
February	(g)	78	1,837	1,916	95	2,011	2	5	2,018
March	(g)	69	2,120	2,189	107	2,296	2	4	2,303
April	(g)	54	2,075	2,129	105	2,235	2	4	2,241
May	(g)	50	2,152	2,202	116	2,318	2	4	2,324
June	(g)	51	2,144	2,195	117	2,312	2	4	2,318
July	(g)	56	2,250	2,306	118	2,424	2	4	2,431
August	(g)	55	2,231	2,286	120	2,405	2	4	2,412
September	(g)	51	2,113	2,164	116	2,280	2	4	2,286
October	(g)	53	2,161	2,214	114	2,329	2	4	2,335
November	(g)	60	2,024	2,084	110	2,194	2	4	2,200
December	(g)	69	2,115	2,184	113	2,297	2	4	2,303
Total	(g)	732	25,221	25,953	1,325	27,278	26	51	27,355
2016 January	(g)	82	1,998	2,080	102	2,182	2	5	2,189
February	(g)	70	1,938	2,008	108	2,116	2	4	2,122
March	(g)	63	2,175	2,238	117	2,355	2	4	2,361
April	(g)	56	2,108	2,165	109	2,273	2	4	2,279
May	(g)	53	2,187	2,240	121	2,361	2	4	2,367
June	(g)	54	2,206	2,260	121	2,381	2	4	2,388
July	(g)	59	2,261	2,320	129	2,448	2	5	2,455
August	(g)	60	2,266	2,326	131	2,457	2	4	2,463
September	(g)	53	2,139	2,192	123	2,315	2	4	2,321
October	(g)	53	2,158	2,210	122	2,333	2	4	2,339
November	(g)	59	2,093	2,151	125	2,276	2	4	2,282
December	(g)	76	2,149	2,225	126	2,351	2	5	2,358
Total	(g)	738	25,677	26,415	1,434	27,849	26	51	27,925
2017 January	(g)	77	2,009	2,086	104	2,190	2	5	2,197
February	(g)	62	1,863	1,925	100	2,025	2	4	2,031
March	(g)	67	2,195	2,262	117	2,379	2	4	2,386
April	(g)	52	2,085	2,137	115	2,253	2	4	2,259
4-Month Total	(g)	258	8,153	8,411	436	8,846	9	17	8,872
2016 4-Month Total	(g)	271	8,218	8,490	436	8,926	9	17	8,951
2015 4-Month Total	(g)	285	8,032	8,318	402	8,720	9	18	8,746

[a] See "Primary Energy Consumption" in Glossary.
[b] See Table 10.2b for notes on series components.
[c] Natural gas only; does not include supplemental gaseous fuels—see Note 3, "Supplemental Gaseous Fuels," at end of Section 4. Data are for natural gas consumed in the operation of pipelines (primarily in compressors) and small amounts consumed as vehicle fuel—see Table 4.3.
[d] Does not include biofuels that have been blended with petroleum—biofuels are included in "Biomass."
[e] Electricity retail sales to ultimate customers reported by electric utilities and, beginning in 1996, other energy service providers.
[f] Total losses are calculated as the primary energy consumed by the electric power sector minus the energy content of electricity retail sales. Total losses are allocated to the end-use sectors in proportion to each sector's share of total electricity retail sales. See Note 1, "Electrical System Energy Losses," at end of section.
[g] Beginning in 1978, the small amounts of coal consumed for transportation are reported as industrial sector consumption.
NA=Not available.
Notes: • Data are estimates, except for coal totals through 1977; and electricity retail sales beginning in 1979. • See Note 2, "Energy Consumption Data and Surveys," at end of section. • Totals may not equal sum of components due to independent rounding. • Geographic coverage is the 50 states and the District of Columbia.
Web Page: See http://www.eia.gov/totalenergy/data/monthly/#consumption (Excel and CSV files) for all available annual data beginning in 1949 and monthly data beginning in 1973.
Sources: See end of section.

Source: *U.S. Energy Information Administration, Monthly Energy Review, July 2017*

Figure 2.6 Electric Power Sector Energy Consumption
(Quadrillion Btu)

By Major Source, 1949–2016

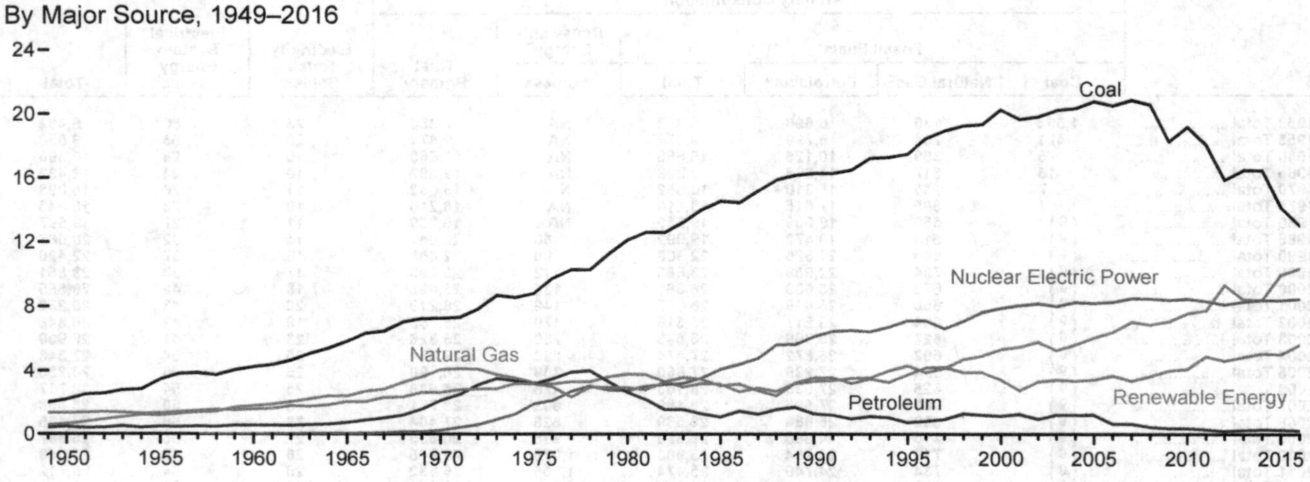

By Major Source, Monthly

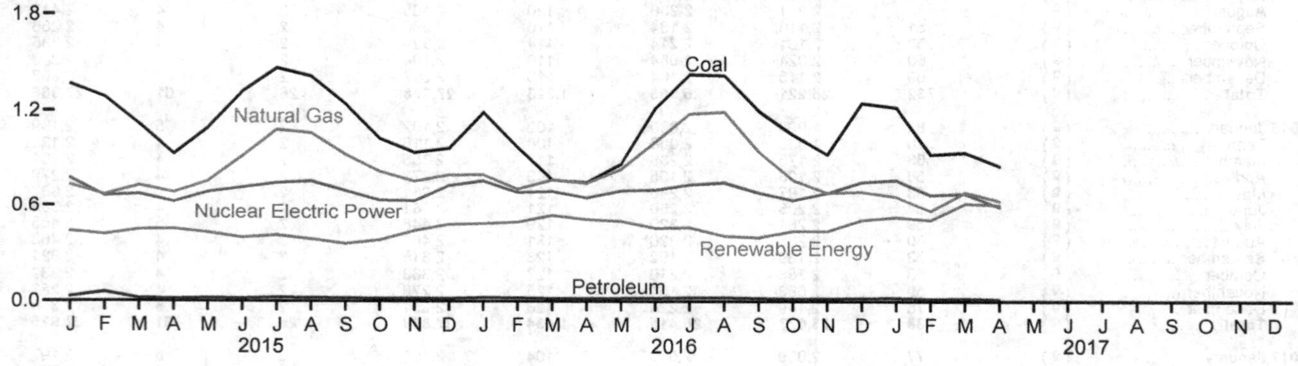

Total, January–April

By Major Source, April 2017

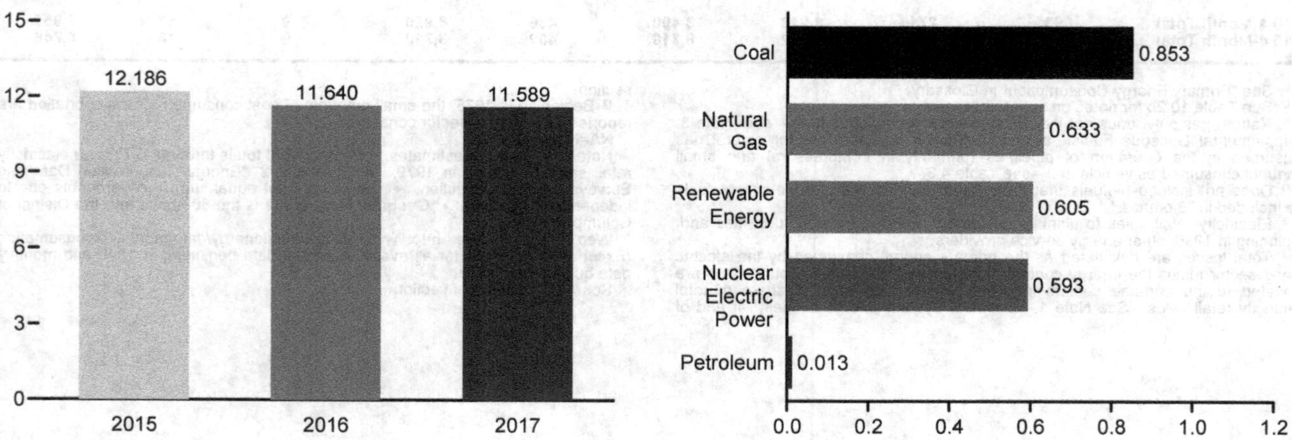

Web Page: http://www.eia.gov/totalenergy/data/monthly/#consumption.
Source: Table 2.6.

Source: *U.S. Energy Information Administration, Monthly Energy Review, July 2017*

Table 2.6 Electric Power Sector Energy Consumption
(Trillion Btu)

	Primary Consumption[a]												
	Fossil Fuels					Renewable Energy[b]							
	Coal	Natural Gas[c]	Petroleum	Total	Nuclear Electric Power	Hydroelectric Power[d]	Geothermal	Solar[e]	Wind	Biomass	Total	Electricity Net Imports[f]	Total Primary
1950 Total	**2,199**	**651**	**472**	**3,322**	**0**	**1,346**	**NA**	**NA**	**NA**	**5**	**1,351**	**6**	**4,679**
1955 Total	**3,458**	**1,194**	**471**	**5,123**	**0**	**1,322**	**NA**	**NA**	**NA**	**3**	**1,325**	**14**	**6,461**
1960 Total	**4,228**	**1,785**	**553**	**6,565**	**6**	**1,569**	**(s)**	**NA**	**NA**	**2**	**1,571**	**15**	**8,158**
1965 Total	**5,821**	**2,395**	**722**	**8,938**	**43**	**2,026**	**2**	**NA**	**NA**	**3**	**2,031**	**(s)**	**11,012**
1970 Total	**7,227**	**4,054**	**2,117**	**13,399**	**239**	**2,600**	**6**	**NA**	**NA**	**4**	**2,609**	**7**	**16,253**
1975 Total	**8,786**	**3,240**	**3,166**	**15,191**	**1,900**	**3,122**	**34**	**NA**	**NA**	**2**	**3,158**	**21**	**20,270**
1980 Total	**12,123**	**3,778**	**2,634**	**18,534**	**2,739**	**2,867**	**53**	**NA**	**NA**	**4**	**2,925**	**71**	**24,269**
1985 Total	**14,542**	**3,135**	**1,090**	**18,767**	**4,076**	**2,937**	**97**	**(s)**	**(s)**	**14**	**3,049**	**140**	**26,032**
1990 Total[g]	**16,261**	**3,309**	**1,289**	**20,859**	**6,104**	**3,014**	**161**	**4**	**29**	**317**	**3,524**	**8**	**30,495**
1995 Total	**17,466**	**4,302**	**755**	**22,523**	**7,075**	**3,149**	**138**	**5**	**33**	**422**	**3,747**	**134**	**33,479**
2000 Total	**20,220**	**5,293**	**1,144**	**26,658**	**7,862**	**2,768**	**144**	**5**	**57**	**453**	**3,427**	**115**	**38,062**
2001 Total	**19,614**	**5,458**	**1,276**	**26,348**	**8,029**	**2,209**	**142**	**6**	**70**	**337**	**2,763**	**75**	**37,215**
2002 Total	**19,783**	**5,767**	**961**	**26,511**	**8,145**	**2,650**	**147**	**6**	**105**	**380**	**3,288**	**72**	**38,016**
2003 Total	**20,185**	**5,246**	**1,205**	**26,636**	**7,960**	**2,749**	**146**	**5**	**113**	**397**	**3,411**	**22**	**38,028**
2004 Total	**20,305**	**5,595**	**1,201**	**27,101**	**8,223**	**2,655**	**148**	**6**	**142**	**388**	**3,339**	**39**	**38,701**
2005 Total	**20,737**	**6,015**	**1,222**	**27,974**	**8,161**	**2,670**	**147**	**6**	**178**	**406**	**3,406**	**85**	**39,626**
2006 Total	**20,462**	**6,375**	**637**	**27,474**	**8,215**	**2,839**	**145**	**5**	**264**	**412**	**3,665**	**63**	**39,417**
2007 Total	**20,808**	**7,005**	**648**	**28,461**	**8,459**	**2,430**	**145**	**6**	**341**	**423**	**3,345**	**107**	**40,371**
2008 Total	**20,513**	**6,829**	**459**	**27,801**	**8,426**	**2,494**	**146**	**9**	**546**	**435**	**3,630**	**112**	**39,969**
2009 Total	**18,225**	**7,022**	**382**	**25,630**	**8,355**	**2,650**	**146**	**9**	**721**	**441**	**3,967**	**116**	**38,069**
2010 Total	**19,133**	**7,528**	**370**	**27,031**	**8,434**	**2,521**	**148**	**12**	**923**	**459**	**4,064**	**89**	**39,619**
2011 Total	**18,035**	**7,712**	**295**	**26,042**	**8,269**	**3,085**	**149**	**17**	**1,167**	**437**	**4,855**	**127**	**39,293**
2012 Total	**15,821**	**9,287**	**214**	**25,322**	**8,062**	**2,606**	**148**	**40**	**1,339**	**453**	**4,586**	**161**	**38,131**
2013 Total	**16,451**	**8,376**	**255**	**25,082**	**8,244**	**2,529**	**151**	**83**	**1,600**	**470**	**4,833**	**197**	**38,357**
2014 Total	**16,427**	**8,362**	**295**	**25,085**	**8,338**	**2,454**	**151**	**165**	**1,726**	**530**	**5,026**	**182**	**38,629**
2015 January	1,366	735	29	2,130	777	224	13	11	141	45	433	18	3,357
February	1,284	670	59	2,013	664	207	12	14	139	41	412	14	3,103
March	1,116	732	18	1,865	675	225	13	19	143	43	443	19	3,002
April	928	686	17	1,630	625	208	12	22	166	40	448	20	2,723
May	1,092	758	19	1,869	688	186	13	23	160	41	423	20	3,002
June	1,319	915	19	2,252	717	189	12	23	125	44	393	21	3,383
July	1,464	1,079	23	2,566	747	195	13	24	127	48	407	21	3,741
August	1,411	1,060	21	2,492	757	177	13	25	122	48	384	22	3,655
September	1,238	924	20	2,182	695	149	11	20	130	43	354	20	3,251
October	1,025	817	17	1,860	633	154	12	17	152	41	378	16	2,886
November	936	756	18	1,710	630	179	12	16	183	44	434	18	2,792
December	960	794	17	1,771	728	214	13	14	187	47	476	17	2,993
Total	**14,138**	**9,926**	**276**	**24,341**	**8,337**	**2,308**	**148**	**228**	**1,776**	**525**	**4,985**	**227**	**37,890**
2016 January	1,189	796	23	2,007	758	236	14	14	173	45	481	21	3,268
February	969	708	21	1,698	686	224	13	22	188	43	490	17	2,892
March	763	766	18	1,548	692	250	14	25	205	43	536	18	2,794
April	748	744	18	1,510	652	236	12	27	193	40	508	15	2,685
May	863	831	19	1,713	696	235	14	33	175	40	496	19	2,925
June	1,213	1,003	20	2,236	703	212	13	33	152	42	452	23	3,414
July	1,422	1,178	24	2,625	736	197	13	38	164	45	456	25	3,842
August	1,415	1,191	24	2,630	748	180	13	36	126	46	401	24	3,803
September	1,197	943	20	2,159	684	151	14	34	153	41	393	20	3,256
October	1,048	764	16	1,828	635	160	14	29	190	39	432	18	2,913
November	923	684	17	1,625	682	175	14	25	180	40	433	21	2,761
December	1,244	690	20	1,954	749	209	15	21	214	46	505	22	3,231
Total	**12,995**	**10,299**	**240**	**23,534**	**8,422**	**2,465**	**162**	**337**	**2,112**	**509**	**5,585**	**242**	**37,784**
2017 January	1,218	660	21	1,899	765	257	14	20	189	44	525	23	3,211
February	923	568	16	1,507	670	228	13	24	202	41	507	18	2,702
March	938	688	17	1,644	681	280	14	41	238	44	618	18	2,961
April	853	633	13	1,499	593	271	14	44	237	39	605	18	2,716
4-Month Total	**3,932**	**2,549**	**68**	**6,548**	**2,709**	**1,036**	**55**	**130**	**866**	**168**	**2,255**	**77**	**11,589**
2016 4-Month Total	**3,669**	**3,014**	**80**	**6,763**	**2,789**	**946**	**53**	**88**	**758**	**171**	**2,016**	**72**	**11,640**
2015 4-Month Total	**4,693**	**2,823**	**123**	**7,638**	**2,741**	**864**	**49**	**65**	**589**	**169**	**1,736**	**72**	**12,186**

[a] See "Primary Energy Consumption" in Glossary.
[b] See Table 10.2c for notes on series components.
[c] Natural gas only; excludes the estimated portion of supplemental gaseous fuels. See Note 3, "Supplemental Gaseous Fuels," at end of Section 4.
[d] Conventional hydroelectric power.
[e] Solar photovoltaic (PV) and solar thermal electricity net generation in the electric power sector. See Tables 10.2c and 10.5.
[f] Net imports equal imports minus exports.
[g] Through 1988, data are for electric utilities only. Beginning in 1989, data are for electric utilities and independent power producers.
NA=Not available. (s)=Less than 0.5 trillion Btu.

Notes: • Data are for fuels consumed to produce electricity and useful thermal output. • The electric power sector comprises electricity-only and combined-heat-and-power (CHP) plants within the NAICS 22 category whose primary business is to sell electricity, or electricity and heat, to the public. • See Note 2, "Energy Consumption Data and Surveys," at end of section. • Totals may not equal sum of components due to independent rounding. • Geographic coverage is the 50 states and the District of Columbia.

Web Page: See http://www.eia.gov/totalenergy/data/monthly/#consumption (Excel and CSV files) for all available annual data beginning in 1949 and monthly data beginning in 1973.

Sources: See end of section.

Source: *U.S. Energy Information Administration, Monthly Energy Review, July 2017*

Table 2.7 U.S. Government Energy Consumption by Agency, Fiscal Years
(Trillion Btu)

Fiscal Year[a]	Agri-culture	Defense	Energy	GSA[b]	HHS[c]	Interior	Justice	NASA[d]	Postal Service	Trans-portation	Veterans Affairs	Other[e]	Total
1975	9.5	1,360.2	50.4	22.3	6.5	9.4	5.9	13.4	30.5	19.3	27.1	10.5	1,565.0
1976	9.3	1,183.3	50.3	20.6	6.7	9.4	5.7	12.4	30.0	19.5	25.0	11.2	1,383.4
1977	8.9	1,192.3	51.6	20.4	6.9	9.5	5.9	12.0	32.7	20.4	25.9	11.9	1,398.5
1978	9.1	1,157.8	50.1	20.4	6.5	9.2	5.9	11.2	30.9	20.6	26.8	12.4	1,360.9
1979	9.2	1,175.8	49.6	19.6	6.4	10.4	6.4	11.1	29.3	19.6	25.7	12.3	1,375.4
1980	8.6	1,183.1	47.4	18.1	6.0	8.5	5.7	10.4	27.2	19.2	24.8	12.3	1,371.2
1981	7.9	1,239.5	47.3	18.0	6.7	7.6	5.4	10.0	27.9	18.8	24.0	11.1	1,424.2
1982	7.6	1,264.5	49.0	18.1	6.4	7.4	5.8	10.1	27.5	19.1	24.2	11.6	1,451.4
1983	7.4	1,248.3	49.5	16.1	6.2	7.7	5.5	10.3	26.5	19.4	24.1	10.8	1,431.8
1984	7.9	1,292.1	51.6	16.2	6.4	8.4	6.4	10.6	27.7	19.8	24.6	10.7	1,482.5
1985	8.4	1,250.6	52.2	20.7	6.0	7.8	8.2	10.9	27.8	19.6	25.1	13.1	1,450.3
1986	6.8	1,222.8	46.9	14.0	6.2	6.9	8.6	11.2	28.0	19.4	25.0	10.8	1,406.7
1987	7.3	1,280.5	48.5	13.1	6.6	6.6	8.1	11.3	28.5	19.0	24.9	11.9	1,466.3
1988	7.8	1,165.8	49.9	12.4	6.4	7.0	9.4	11.3	29.6	18.7	26.3	15.8	1,360.3
1989	8.7	1,274.4	44.2	12.7	6.7	7.1	7.7	12.4	30.3	18.5	26.2	15.6	1,464.7
1990	9.6	1,241.7	43.5	17.5	7.1	7.4	7.0	12.4	30.6	19.0	24.9	17.5	1,438.0
1991	9.6	1,269.3	42.1	14.0	6.2	7.1	8.0	12.5	30.8	19.0	25.1	18.1	1,461.7
1992	9.1	1,104.0	44.3	13.8	6.8	7.0	7.5	12.6	31.7	17.0	25.3	15.7	1,294.8
1993	9.3	1,048.8	43.4	14.1	7.2	7.5	9.1	12.4	33.7	19.4	25.7	16.2	1,246.8
1994	9.4	977.0	42.1	14.0	7.5	7.9	10.3	12.6	35.0	19.8	25.6	17.1	1,178.2
1995	9.0	926.0	47.3	13.7	6.1	6.4	10.2	12.4	36.2	18.7	25.4	17.1	1,128.5
1996	9.1	904.5	44.6	14.5	6.6	4.3	12.1	11.5	36.4	19.6	26.8	17.7	1,107.7
1997	7.4	880.0	43.1	14.4	7.9	6.6	12.0	12.0	40.8	19.1	27.3	20.8	1,091.2
1998	7.9	837.1	31.5	14.1	7.4	6.4	15.8	11.7	39.5	18.5	27.6	19.5	1,037.1
1999	7.8	810.7	27.0	14.4	7.1	7.5	15.4	11.4	39.8	22.6	27.5	19.8	1,010.9
2000	7.4	779.1	30.5	17.6	8.0	7.8	19.7	11.1	43.3	21.2	27.0	20.3	993.1
2001	7.4	787.2	31.1	18.4	8.5	9.5	19.7	10.9	43.4	17.8	27.7	20.7	1,002.3
2002	7.2	837.5	30.7	17.5	8.0	8.2	17.7	10.7	41.6	18.3	27.7	18.4	1,043.4
2003	7.7	895.1	31.9	18.5	10.1	7.3	22.7	10.8	50.9	5.5	30.6	41.0	1,132.3
2004	7.0	960.7	31.4	18.3	8.8	8.7	17.5	9.9	50.5	5.2	29.9	44.0	1,191.7
2005	7.5	933.2	29.6	18.4	9.6	8.6	18.8	10.3	53.5	5.0	30.0	42.1	1,166.4
2006	6.8	843.7	32.9	18.2	9.3	8.1	23.5	10.2	51.8	4.6	29.3	38.1	1,076.4
2007	6.8	864.6	31.5	19.1	9.9	7.5	20.7	10.6	45.8	5.6	30.0	38.1	1,090.2
2008	6.5	910.8	32.1	18.8	10.3	7.1	19.0	10.8	47.1	7.7	29.0	R 44.1	R 1,143.2
2009	6.6	874.3	31.1	18.6	10.8	7.9	16.5	10.2	44.2	4.3	29.9	40.4	1,094.8
2010	6.8	889.9	31.7	18.8	10.4	7.3	15.7	10.1	43.3	5.7	30.2	42.9	1,112.7
2011	8.3	890.3	33.1	18.5	10.5	7.3	13.9	10.1	43.0	6.7	30.6	41.7	1,114.1
2012	6.7	828.5	30.3	16.3	10.0	6.7	15.1	8.9	40.8	5.6	29.7	40.6	1,039.3
2013	7.3	749.5	28.9	16.4	10.5	6.2	15.3	8.7	41.9	5.3	29.9	39.3	959.3
2014	6.3	730.6	29.4	17.0	9.5	6.2	15.6	8.3	43.0	5.2	31.4	39.0	941.5
2015	6.2	R 734.5	30.1	16.9	9.0	R 6.8	16.2	8.4	44.0	6.0	30.7	37.8	R 946.5
2016	R 6.2	R 709.2	R 28.9	R 15.8	R 8.7	R 6.4	R 15.6	R 8.5	R 43.9	R 6.0	R 30.3	R 37.6	R 917.2

[a] For 1975 and 1976, the U.S. Government's fiscal year was July 1 through June 30. Beginning in 1977, the U.S. Government's fiscal year is October 1 through September 30 (for example, fiscal year 2014 is October 2013 through September 2014).

[b] General Services Administration.

[c] Health and Human Services.

[d] National Aeronautics and Space Administration.

[e] Includes all U.S. government agencies not separately displayed. See http://ctsedwweb.ee.doe.gov/Annual/Report/AgencyReference.aspx for agency list.

R=Revised.

Notes: • Data in this table are developed using conversion factors that often differ from those in Tables A1–A6. • Data include energy consumed at foreign installations and in foreign operations, including aviation and ocean bunkering, primarily by the U.S. Department of Defense. U.S. Government energy use for electricity generation and uranium enrichment is excluded. • Totals may not equal sum of components due to independent rounding.

Web Page: See http://www.eia.gov/totalenergy/data/monthly/#consumption (Excel and CSV files) for all annual data beginning in 1975.

Source: U.S. Department of Energy, Office of Energy Efficiency and Renewable Energy, Federal Energy Management Program. See http://ctsedwweb.ee.doe.gov/Annual/Report/Report.aspx, "A-1 Total Site-Delivered Energy Use in All End-Use Sectors, by Federal Agency (Billion Btu)" dataset.

***Source:** U.S. Energy Information Administration, Monthly Energy Review, July 2017*

Table 2.8 U.S. Government Energy Consumption by Source, Fiscal Years
(Trillion Btu)

Fiscal Year[a]	Coal	Natural Gas[b]	Petroleum: Aviation Gasoline	Petroleum: Fuel Oil[c]	Petroleum: Jet Fuel	Petroleum: LPG[d]	Petroleum: Motor Gasoline[e]	Petroleum: Total	Other Mobility Fuels[f]	Elec-tricity	Purchased Steam and Other[g]	Total
1975	77.9	166.2	22.0	376.0	707.4	5.6	63.2	1,174.2	0.0	141.5	5.1	1,565.0
1976	71.3	151.8	11.6	329.7	610.0	4.7	60.4	1,016.4	.0	139.3	4.6	1,383.4
1977	68.4	141.2	8.8	348.5	619.2	4.1	61.4	1,042.1	.0	141.1	5.7	1,398.5
1978	66.0	144.7	6.2	332.3	601.1	3.0	60.1	1,002.9	.0	141.0	6.4	1,360.9
1979	65.1	148.9	4.7	327.1	618.6	3.7	59.1	1,013.1	.0	141.2	7.1	1,375.4
1980	63.5	147.3	4.9	307.7	638.7	3.8	56.5	1,011.6	.2	141.9	6.8	1,371.2
1981	65.1	142.2	4.6	351.3	653.3	3.5	53.2	1,066.0	.2	144.5	6.2	1,424.2
1982	68.6	146.2	3.6	349.4	672.7	3.7	53.1	1,082.5	.2	147.5	6.2	1,451.4
1983	62.4	147.8	2.6	329.5	673.4	3.8	51.6	1,060.8	.2	151.5	9.0	1,431.8
1984	65.3	157.4	1.9	342.9	693.7	3.9	51.2	1,093.6	.2	155.9	10.1	1,482.5
1985	64.8	149.9	1.9	292.6	705.7	3.8	50.4	1,054.3	.2	167.2	13.9	1,450.3
1986	63.8	140.9	1.4	271.6	710.2	3.6	45.3	1,032.1	.3	155.8	13.7	1,406.7
1987	67.0	145.6	1.0	319.5	702.3	3.6	43.1	1,069.5	.4	169.9	13.9	1,466.3
1988	60.2	144.6	6.0	284.8	617.2	2.7	41.2	951.9	.4	171.2	32.0	1,360.3
1989	48.7	152.4	.8	245.3	761.7	3.5	41.1	1,052.4	2.2	188.6	20.6	1,464.7
1990	44.3	159.4	.5	245.2	732.4	3.8	37.2	1,019.1	2.6	193.6	19.1	1,438.0
1991	45.9	154.1	.4	232.6	774.5	3.0	34.1	1,044.7	6.0	192.7	18.3	1,461.7
1992	51.7	151.2	1.0	200.6	628.2	3.0	35.6	868.4	8.4	192.5	22.5	1,294.8
1993	38.3	152.9	.7	187.0	612.4	3.5	34.5	838.1	5.8	193.1	18.6	1,246.8
1994	35.0	143.9	.6	198.5	550.7	3.2	29.5	782.6	7.7	190.9	18.2	1,178.2
1995	31.7	149.4	.3	178.4	522.3	3.0	31.9	735.9	8.4	184.8	18.2	1,128.5
1996	23.3	147.3	.2	170.5	513.0	3.1	27.6	714.4	18.7	184.0	20.1	1,107.7
1997	22.5	153.8	.3	180.0	475.7	2.6	39.0	697.6	14.5	183.6	19.2	1,091.2
1998	23.9	140.4	.2	174.5	445.5	3.5	43.0	666.8	5.9	181.4	18.8	1,037.1
1999	21.2	137.4	.1	162.1	444.7	2.4	41.1	650.4	.4	180.0	21.5	1,010.9
2000	22.7	133.8	.2	171.3	403.1	2.5	43.9	621.0	1.8	193.6	20.2	993.1
2001	18.8	133.7	.2	176.9	415.2	3.1	42.5	638.0	4.8	188.4	18.6	1,002.3
2002	16.9	133.7	.2	165.6	472.9	2.8	41.3	682.8	3.2	188.3	18.5	1,043.4
2003	18.1	135.5	.3	190.8	517.9	3.2	46.3	758.4	3.3	193.8	23.2	1,132.3
2004	17.4	135.3	.2	261.4	508.2	2.9	44.1	816.9	3.1	197.1	22.0	1,191.7
2005	17.1	135.7	.4	241.4	492.2	3.4	48.8	786.1	5.6	197.6	24.3	1,166.4
2006	23.5	132.6	.6	209.3	442.6	2.7	48.3	703.6	2.1	196.7	18.2	1,076.4
2007	20.4	131.5	.4	212.9	461.1	2.7	46.5	723.7	2.9	194.9	16.7	1,090.2
2008	20.8	[R]129.6	.4	198.4	[R]525.4	2.3	[R]49.0	[R]775.4	3.6	[R]196.1	17.7	[R]1,143.2
2009	20.3	131.7	.3	166.4	505.7	3.2	48.3	723.9	10.1	191.3	17.7	1,094.8
2010	20.0	130.1	.4	157.8	535.8	2.5	51.3	747.7	3.0	193.7	18.2	1,112.7
2011	18.5	124.7	.9	166.5	533.6	2.0	52.7	755.8	2.7	193.2	19.1	1,114.1
2012	15.9	116.2	.4	148.6	493.5	1.7	50.1	694.4	3.1	187.2	22.5	1,039.3
2013	14.3	122.5	.7	140.0	424.0	1.9	46.6	613.2	2.8	184.7	21.8	959.3
2014	13.5	125.6	.3	133.5	414.3	1.8	44.9	594.8	3.6	182.1	21.9	941.5
2015	12.6	123.3	.3	[R]134.4	418.9	1.8	46.8	[R]602.2	3.7	[R]184.4	[R]20.3	[R]946.5
2016	10.2	115.4	.3	129.7	403.9	1.7	46.5	582.2	3.6	184.5	21.4	917.2

[a] For 1975 and 1976, the U.S. Government's fiscal year was July 1 through June 30. Beginning in 1977, the U.S. Government's fiscal year is October 1 through September 30 (for example, fiscal year 2014 is October 2013 through September 2014).

[b] Natural gas, plus a small amount of supplemental gaseous fuels.

[c] Distillate fuel oil, including diesel fuel; and residual fuel oil, including Navy Special.

[d] Liquefied petroleum gases, primarily propane.

[e] Includes E10 (a mixture of 10% ethanol and 90% motor gasoline) and E15 (a mixture of 15% ethanol and 85% motor gasoline).

[f] Other types of fuel used in vehicles and equipment. Primarily includes alternative fuels such as compressed natural gas (CNG); liquefied natural gas (LNG); E85 (a mixture of 85% ethanol and 15% motor gasoline); B20 (a mixture of 20% biodiesel and 80% diesel fuel); B100 (100% biodiesel); hydrogen; and methanol.

[g] Other types of energy used in facilities. Primarily includes chilled water, but also includes small amounts of renewable energy such as wood and solar thermal.

R=Revised.

Notes: • Data in this table are developed using conversion factors that often differ from those in Tables A1–A6. • Data include energy consumed at foreign installations and in foreign operations, including aviation and ocean bunkering, primarily by the U.S. Department of Defense. U.S. Government energy use for electricity generation and uranium enrichment is excluded. • Totals may not equal sum of components due to independent rounding.

Web Page: See http://www.eia.gov/totalenergy/data/monthly/#consumption (Excel and CSV files) for all annual data beginning in 1975.

Source: U.S. Department of Energy, Office of Energy Efficiency and Renewable Energy, Federal Energy Management Program. See http://ctsedwweb.ee.doe.gov/Annual/Report/Report.aspx, "A-5 Historical Federal Energy Consumption and Cost Data by Agency and Energy Type (FY 1975 to Present)" dataset.

Source: *U.S. Energy Information Administration, Monthly Energy Review, July 2017*

Figure 3.1 Petroleum Overview
(Million Barrels per Day)

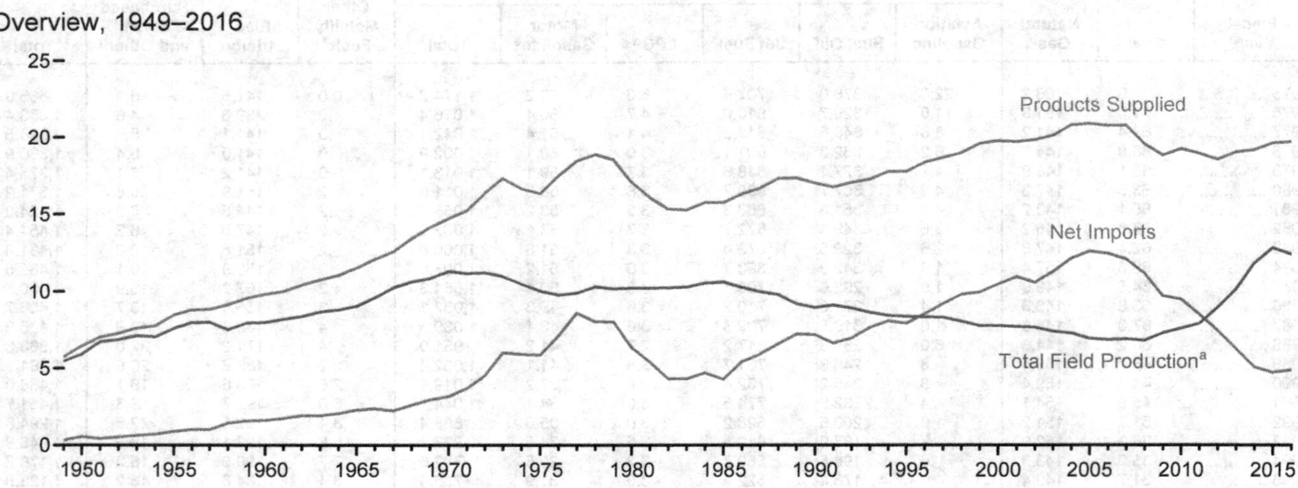

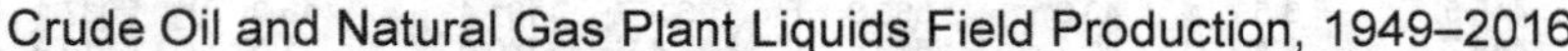

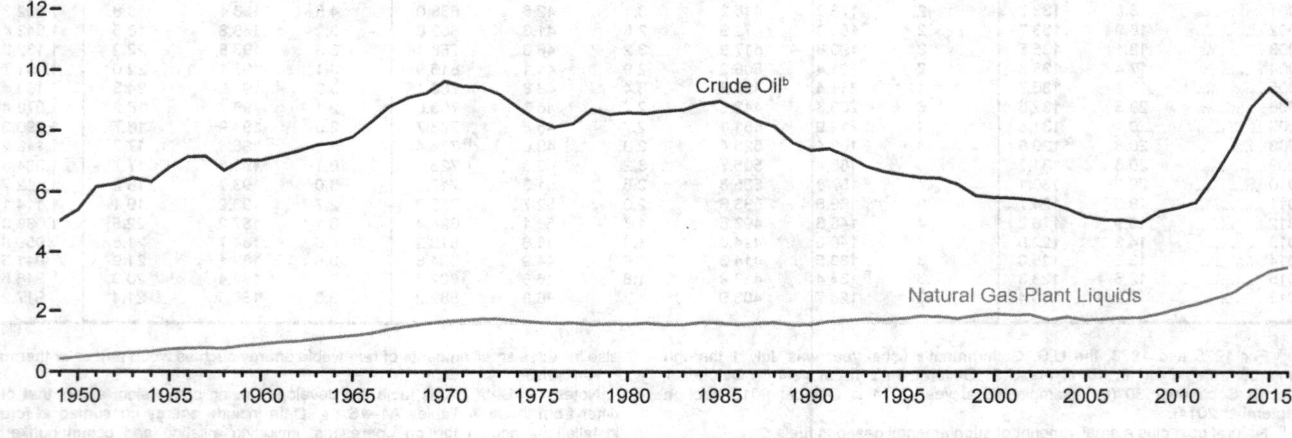

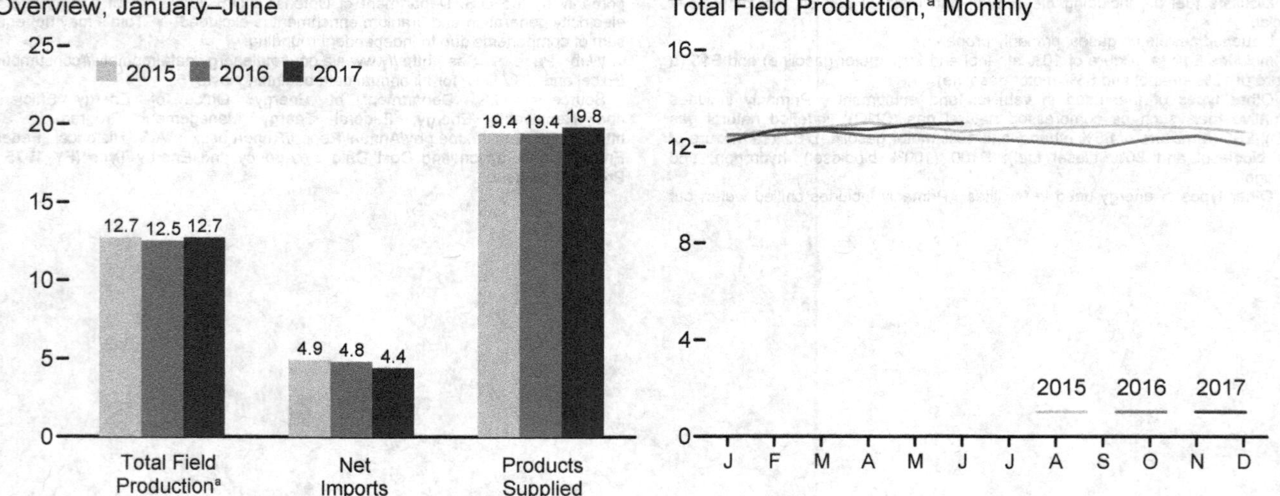

[a] Crude oil, including lease condensate, and natural gas plant liquids field production.
[b] Includes lease condensate.

Web Page: http://www.eia.gov/totalenergy/data/monthly/#petroleum.
Source: Table 3.1.

Source: *U.S. Energy Information Administration, Monthly Energy Review, July 2017*

Table 3.1 Petroleum Overview

(Thousand Barrels per Day)

	Field Production[a]					Renewable Fuels and Oxygenates[f]	Processing Gain[g]	Trade			Stock Change[j]	Adjustments[c,k]	Petroleum Products Supplied
	Crude Oil[b,c]			NGPL[e]	Total[c]			Imports[h]	Exports	Net Imports[i]			
	48 States[d]	Alaska	Total										
1950 Average	5,407	0	5,407	499	5,906	NA	2	850	305	545	-56	-51	6,458
1955 Average	6,807	0	6,807	771	7,578	NA	34	1,248	368	880	(s)	-37	8,455
1960 Average	7,034	2	7,035	929	7,965	NA	146	1,815	202	1,613	-83	-8	9,797
1965 Average	7,774	30	7,804	1,210	9,014	NA	220	2,468	187	2,281	-8	-10	11,512
1970 Average	9,408	229	9,637	1,660	11,297	NA	359	3,419	259	3,161	103	-16	14,697
1975 Average	8,183	191	8,375	1,633	10,007	NA	460	6,056	209	5,846	32	41	16,322
1980 Average	6,980	1,617	8,597	1,573	10,170	NA	597	6,909	544	6,365	140	64	17,056
1985 Average	7,146	1,825	8,971	1,609	10,581	NA	557	5,067	781	4,286	-103	200	15,726
1990 Average	5,582	1,773	7,355	1,559	8,914	NA	683	8,018	857	7,161	107	338	16,988
1995 Average	5,076	1,484	6,560	1,762	8,322	NA	774	8,835	949	7,886	-246	496	17,725
2000 Average	4,851	970	5,822	1,911	7,733	NA	948	11,459	1,040	10,419	-69	532	19,701
2001 Average	4,839	963	5,801	1,868	7,670	NA	903	11,871	971	10,900	325	501	19,649
2002 Average	4,759	985	5,744	1,880	7,624	NA	957	11,530	984	10,546	-105	529	19,761
2003 Average	4,675	974	5,649	1,719	7,369	NA	974	12,264	1,027	11,238	56	509	20,034
2004 Average	4,533	908	5,441	1,809	7,250	NA	1,051	13,145	1,048	12,097	209	542	20,731
2005 Average	4,320	864	5,184	1,717	6,901	NA	989	13,714	1,165	12,549	[l]146	509	20,802
2006 Average	4,345	741	5,086	1,739	6,825	NA	994	13,707	1,317	12,390	59	537	20,687
2007 Average	4,355	722	5,077	1,783	6,860	NA	996	13,468	1,433	12,036	-152	637	20,680
2008 Average	4,317	683	5,000	1,784	6,784	NA	993	12,915	1,802	11,114	195	803	19,498
2009 Average	4,708	645	5,353	1,910	7,263	746	979	11,691	2,024	9,667	107	224	18,771
2010 Average	4,875	600	5,475	2,074	7,549	907	1,068	11,793	2,353	9,441	39	256	19,180
2011 Average	5,085	561	5,646	2,216	7,862	1,016	1,076	11,436	2,986	8,450	-124	353	18,882
2012 Average	5,961	526	6,487	2,408	8,895	964	1,059	10,598	3,205	7,393	143	323	18,490
2013 Average	6,953	515	7,468	2,606	10,073	1,002	1,087	9,859	3,621	6,237	-133	428	18,961
2014 Average	8,267	496	8,764	3,015	11,778	1,055	1,081	9,241	4,176	5,065	262	389	19,106
2015 January	8,879	500	9,379	3,055	12,434	1,055	1,075	9,461	4,575	4,886	752	521	19,218
February	9,029	488	9,517	3,162	12,678	1,048	1,021	9,272	4,640	4,632	3	300	19,677
March	9,060	506	9,566	3,237	12,802	1,052	1,013	9,619	4,092	5,527	1,060	17	19,352
April	9,117	510	9,627	3,375	13,002	1,065	1,068	9,374	4,938	4,436	856	548	19,263
May	8,999	473	9,472	3,337	12,808	1,107	1,083	9,502	4,853	4,649	704	357	19,301
June	8,873	447	9,320	3,319	12,638	1,148	1,028	9,605	4,657	4,948	350	429	19,841
July	8,968	450	9,418	3,355	12,773	1,124	1,092	9,571	4,960	4,611	-63	462	20,126
August	8,977	408	9,384	3,419	12,803	1,103	1,099	9,858	4,507	5,351	720	294	19,930
September	8,950	472	9,423	3,437	12,860	1,090	1,046	9,358	4,851	4,507	326	241	19,418
October	8,861	497	9,358	3,489	12,847	1,104	1,040	8,842	4,617	4,225	234	519	19,500
November	8,782	523	9,304	3,498	12,803	1,117	1,065	9,151	4,903	4,248	449	361	19,144
December	8,703	522	9,225	3,417	12,642	1,124	1,108	9,742	5,266	4,476	-244	6	19,600
Average	**8,932**	**483**	**9,415**	**3,342**	**12,757**	**1,095**	**1,062**	**9,449**	**4,738**	**4,711**	**432**	**338**	**19,531**
2016 January	[E]8,678	[E]516	[E]9,194	3,303	[E]12,497	1,105	1,106	9,734	4,878	4,857	855	346	19,055
February	[E]8,639	[E]507	[E]9,147	3,329	[E]12,476	1,124	1,058	10,020	4,948	5,072	141	92	19,680
March	[E]8,663	[E]511	[E]9,174	3,509	[E]12,683	1,140	1,041	10,002	5,002	5,000	264	16	19,616
April	[E]8,458	[E]489	[E]8,947	3,504	[E]12,451	1,088	1,066	9,829	5,154	4,674	353	337	19,264
May	[E]8,377	[E]505	[E]8,882	3,593	[E]12,476	1,141	1,140	10,183	5,658	4,525	505	427	19,202
June	[E]8,241	[E]470	[E]8,711	3,618	[E]12,329	1,174	1,106	10,076	5,240	4,836	-28	327	19,799
July	[E]8,253	[E]438	[E]8,691	3,573	[E]12,264	1,174	1,184	10,507	5,209	5,298	503	296	19,712
August	[E]8,300	[E]459	[E]8,759	3,399	[E]12,158	1,184	1,142	10,311	5,114	5,196	11	462	20,131
September	[E]8,115	[E]452	[E]8,567	3,420	[E]11,987	1,159	1,117	10,194	5,250	4,944	-506	151	19,864
October	[E]8,290	[E]495	[E]8,785	3,541	[E]12,326	1,145	1,079	9,723	4,942	4,781	85	375	19,622
November	[E]8,350	[E]513	[E]8,863	3,598	[E]12,461	1,190	1,110	10,312	5,392	4,921	114	88	19,655
December	[E]8,261	[E]519	[E]8,780	3,344	[E]12,125	1,204	1,146	9,814	5,460	4,355	-743	407	19,979
Average	**[E]8,385**	**[E]490**	**[E]8,875**	**3,478**	**[E]12,352**	**1,152**	**1,108**	**10,058**	**5,188**	**4,871**	**131**	**279**	**19,631**
2017 January	[E]8,342	[E]516	[E]8,858	3,365	[E]12,223	1,166	1,125	10,698	5,691	5,007	710	424	19,234
February	[RE]8,562	[E]513	[RE]9,075	3,604	[RE]12,680	1,153	1,045	10,053	6,443	3,610	-120	[R]580	19,188
March	[RE]8,581	[E]526	[RE]9,107	3,644	[RE]12,751	1,172	1,108	10,059	5,886	4,174	-542	[R]286	20,033
April	[RE]8,557	[RE]525	[RE]9,083	[R]3,633	[RE]12,716	[R]1,138	[R]1,128	[R]10,244	[R]6,066	[R]4,178	[R]31	[R]399	[R]19,527
May	[RE]8,811	[E]510	[E]9,320	[E]3,612	[E]12,932	[E]1,087	[E]1,180	[E]10,451	[E]5,624	[E]4,827	[E]95	[RE]245	[E]20,177
June	[E]8,859	[E]461	[E]9,320	[E]3,644	[E]12,964	[E]1,077	[E]1,178	[E]9,961	[E]5,207	[E]4,753	[E]-323	[E]254	[E]20,549
6-Month Average	**[E]8,619**	**[E]509**	**[E]9,127**	**[E]3,583**	**[E]12,710**	**[E]1,132**	**[E]1,128**	**[E]10,249**	**[E]5,811**	**[E]4,438**	**[E]-22**	**[E]361**	**[E]19,792**
2016 6-Month Average	**[E]8,510**	**[E]500**	**[E]9,010**	**3,477**	**[E]12,486**	**1,129**	**1,086**	**9,974**	**5,148**	**4,825**	**353**	**258**	**19,432**
2015 6-Month Average	**8,992**	**487**	**9,479**	**3,248**	**12,727**	**1,079**	**1,048**	**9,475**	**4,624**	**4,852**	**631**	**362**	**19,437**

[a] Crude oil production on leases, and natural gas liquids (liquefied petroleum gases, pentanes plus, and a small amount of finished petroleum products) production at natural gas processing plants. Excludes what was previously classified as "Field Production" of finished motor gasoline, motor gasoline blending components, and other hydrocarbons and oxygenates; these are now included in "Adjustments."

[b] Includes lease condensate.

[c] Once a month, data for crude oil production, total field production, and adjustments are revised going back as far as the data year of the U.S. Energy Information Administration's (EIA) last published *Petroleum Supply Annual (PSA)*—these revisions are released at the same time as EIA's *Petroleum Supply Monthly*. Once a year, data for these series are revised going back as far as 10 years—these revisions are released at the same time as the PSA.

[d] United States excluding Alaska and Hawaii.

[e] Natural gas plant liquids.

[f] Renewable fuels and oxygenate plant net production.

[g] Refinery and blender net production minus refinery and blender net inputs. See Table 3.2.

[h] Includes Strategic Petroleum Reserve imports. See Table 3.3b.

[i] Net imports equal imports minus exports.

[j] A negative value indicates a decrease in stocks and a positive value indicates an increase. The current month stock change estimate is based on the change from the previous month's estimate, rather than the stocks values shown in Table 3.4. Includes crude oil stocks in the Strategic Petroleum Reserve, but excludes distillate fuel oil stocks in the Northeast Home Heating Oil Reserve. See Table 3.4.

[k] An adjustment for crude oil, hydrogen, oxygenates, renewable fuels, other hydrocarbons, motor gasoline blending components, finished motor gasoline, and distillate fuel oil. See EIA's *Petroleum Supply Monthly*, Appendix B, "PSM Explanatory Notes," for further information.

[l] Derived from the 2004 petroleum stocks value that excludes crude oil stocks on leases (1,628 million barrels), not the 2004 petroleum stocks value that includes crude oil stocks on leases (1,645 million barrels).

R=Revised. E=Estimate. NA=Not available. (s)=Less than 500 barrels per day and greater than -500 barrels per day.

Notes: • Totals may not equal sum of components due to independent rounding. • Geographic coverage is the 50 states and the District of Columbia.

Web Page: See http://www.eia.gov/totalenergy/data/monthly/#petroleum (Excel and CSV files) for all available annual data beginning in 1949 and monthly data beginning in 1973.

Sources: See end of section.

Source: *U.S. Energy Information Administration, Monthly Energy Review, July 2017*

Figure 3.2 Refinery and Blender Net Inputs and Net Production
(Million Barrels per Day)

Net Inputs and Net Production, 1949–2016

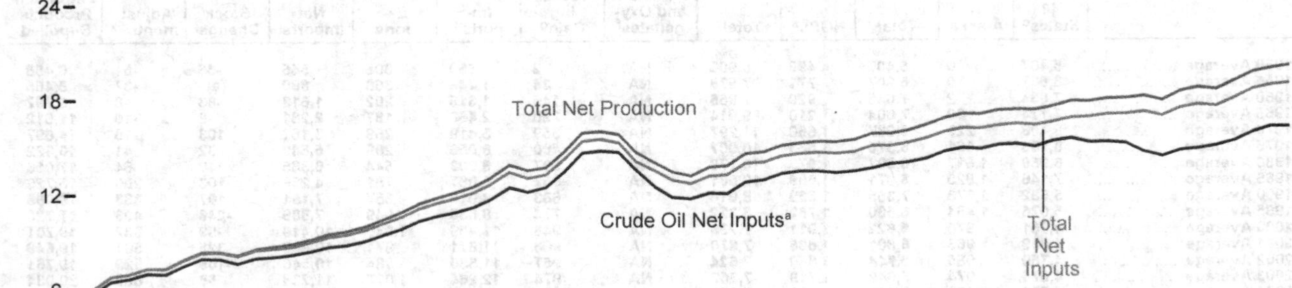

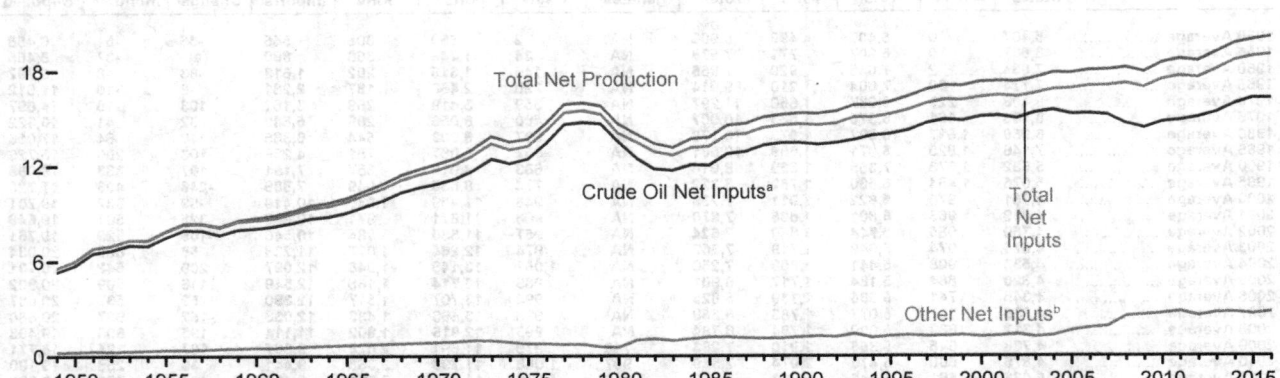

Net Production, Selected Products, 1949–2016

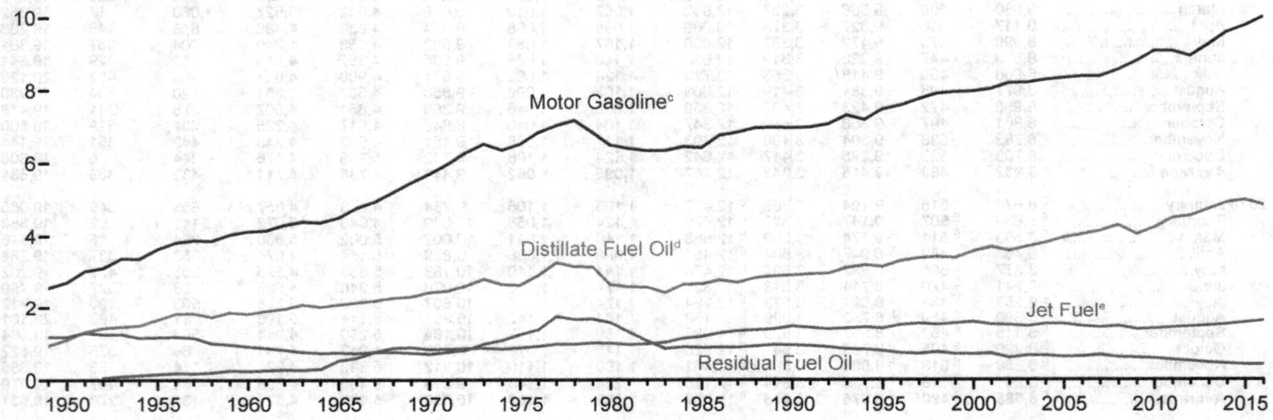

Net Inputs and Net Production, Monthly

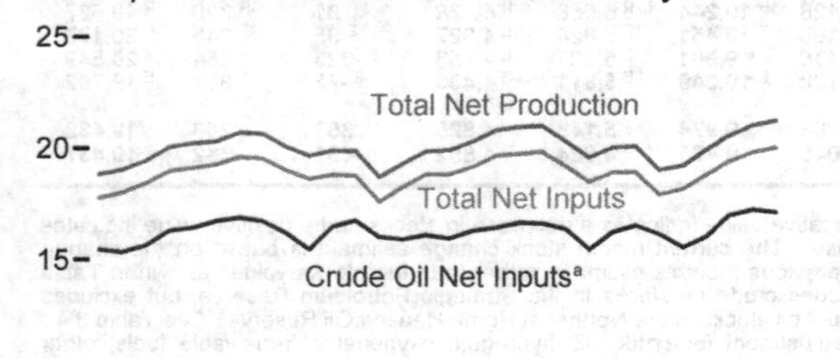

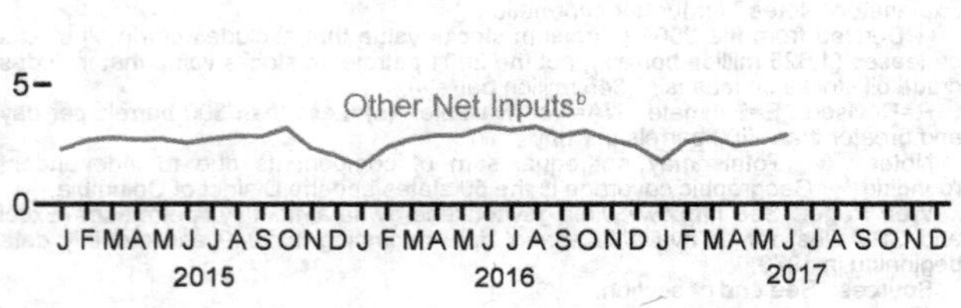

Net Production, Selected Products, Monthly

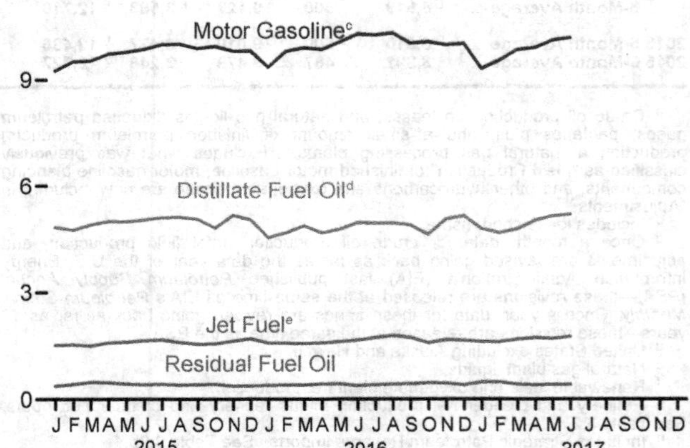

[a] Includes lease condensate.
[b] Natural gas plant liquids and other liquids.
[c] Beginning in 1993, includes fuel ethanol blended into motor gasoline.
[d] Beginning in 2009, includes renewable diesel fuel (including biodiesel) blended into distillate fuel oil.
[e] Beginning in 2005, includes kerosene-type jet fuel only.

Web Page: http://www.eia.gov/totalenergy/data/monthly/#petroleum.
Source: Table 3.2.

Source: *U.S. Energy Information Administration, Monthly Energy Review, July 2017*

Table 3.2 Refinery and Blender Net Inputs and Net Production
(Thousand Barrels per Day)

	Refinery and Blender Net Inputs[a]				Refinery and Blender Net Production[b]							
							LPG[c]					
	Crude Oil[d]	NGPL[e]	Other Liquids[f]	Total	Distillate Fuel Oil[g]	Jet Fuel[h]	Propane[i]	Total	Motor Gasoline[j]	Residual Fuel Oil	Other Products[k]	Total
1950 Average	**5,739**	**259**	**19**	**6,018**	**1,093**	**(h)**	**NA**	**80**	**2,735**	**1,165**	**947**	**6,019**
1955 Average	**7,480**	**345**	**32**	**7,857**	**1,651**	**155**	**NA**	**119**	**3,648**	**1,152**	**1,166**	**7,891**
1960 Average	**8,067**	**455**	**61**	**8,583**	**1,823**	**241**	**NA**	**212**	**4,126**	**908**	**1,420**	**8,729**
1965 Average	**9,043**	**618**	**88**	**9,750**	**2,096**	**523**	**NA**	**293**	**4,507**	**736**	**1,814**	**9,970**
1970 Average	**10,870**	**763**	**121**	**11,754**	**2,454**	**827**	**229**	**345**	**5,699**	**706**	**2,082**	**12,113**
1975 Average	**12,442**	**710**	**72**	**13,225**	**2,653**	**871**	**234**	**311**	**6,518**	**1,235**	**2,097**	**13,685**
1980 Average	**13,481**	**462**	**81**	**14,025**	**2,661**	**999**	**269**	**330**	**6,492**	**1,580**	**2,559**	**14,622**
1985 Average	**12,002**	**509**	**681**	**13,192**	**2,686**	**1,189**	**295**	**391**	**6,419**	**882**	**2,183**	**13,750**
1990 Average	**13,409**	**467**	**713**	**14,589**	**2,925**	**1,488**	**404**	**499**	**6,959**	**950**	**2,452**	**15,272**
1995 Average	**13,973**	**471**	**775**	**15,220**	**3,155**	**1,416**	**503**	**654**	**7,459**	**788**	**2,522**	**15,994**
2000 Average	**15,067**	**380**	**849**	**16,295**	**3,580**	**1,606**	**583**	**705**	**7,951**	**696**	**2,705**	**17,243**
2001 Average	**15,128**	**429**	**825**	**16,382**	**3,695**	**1,530**	**556**	**667**	**8,022**	**721**	**2,651**	**17,285**
2002 Average	**14,947**	**429**	**941**	**16,316**	**3,592**	**1,514**	**572**	**671**	**8,183**	**601**	**2,712**	**17,273**
2003 Average	**15,304**	**419**	**791**	**16,513**	**3,707**	**1,488**	**570**	**658**	**8,194**	**660**	**2,780**	**17,487**
2004 Average	**15,475**	**422**	**866**	**16,762**	**3,814**	**1,547**	**584**	**645**	**8,265**	**655**	**2,887**	**17,814**
2005 Average	**15,220**	**441**	**1,149**	**16,811**	**3,954**	**1,546**	**540**	**573**	**8,318**	**628**	**2,782**	**17,800**
2006 Average	**15,242**	**501**	**1,238**	**16,981**	**4,040**	**1,481**	**543**	**627**	**8,364**	**635**	**2,827**	**17,975**
2007 Average	**15,156**	**505**	**1,337**	**16,999**	**4,133**	**1,448**	**562**	**655**	**8,358**	**673**	**2,728**	**17,994**
2008 Average	**14,648**	**485**	**2,019**	**17,153**	**4,294**	**1,493**	**519**	**630**	**8,548**	**620**	**2,561**	**18,146**
2009 Average	**14,336**	**485**	**2,082**	**16,904**	**4,048**	**1,396**	**537**	**623**	**8,786**	**598**	**2,431**	**17,882**
2010 Average	**14,724**	**442**	**2,219**	**17,385**	**4,223**	**1,418**	**560**	**659**	**9,059**	**585**	**2,509**	**18,452**
2011 Average	**14,806**	**490**	**2,300**	**17,596**	**4,492**	**1,449**	**552**	**619**	**9,058**	**537**	**2,518**	**18,673**
2012 Average	**14,999**	**509**	**1,997**	**17,505**	**4,550**	**1,471**	**553**	**630**	**8,926**	**501**	**2,487**	**18,564**
2013 Average	**15,312**	**496**	**2,211**	**18,019**	**4,733**	**1,499**	**564**	**623**	**9,234**	**467**	**2,550**	**19,106**
2014 Average	**15,848**	**511**	**2,214**	**18,574**	**4,916**	**1,541**	**587**	**653**	**9,570**	**435**	**2,537**	**19,654**
2015 January	15,456	589	1,721	17,766	4,835	1,513	561	392	9,260	377	2,464	18,841
February	15,342	545	2,112	17,998	4,752	1,525	529	401	9,504	420	2,418	19,019
March	15,640	494	2,281	18,415	4,894	1,498	536	610	9,524	478	2,424	19,428
April	16,273	406	2,292	18,971	4,991	1,591	589	815	9,720	467	2,455	20,039
May	16,402	394	2,317	19,112	4,983	1,608	582	885	9,771	436	2,513	20,195
June	16,701	418	2,131	19,250	5,032	1,640	569	864	9,846	413	2,483	20,278
July	16,879	432	2,280	19,591	5,101	1,670	580	853	9,989	426	2,644	20,683
August	16,700	449	2,377	19,526	5,107	1,600	574	839	9,998	404	2,677	20,625
September	16,168	546	2,294	19,008	5,061	1,547	529	583	9,878	414	2,572	20,054
October	15,440	600	2,573	18,613	4,817	1,554	520	442	9,935	419	2,487	19,653
November	16,458	683	1,669	18,810	5,169	1,634	559	343	9,799	377	2,554	19,875
December	16,742	649	1,377	18,768	5,042	1,698	578	333	9,806	376	2,621	19,876
Average	**16,188**	**517**	**2,119**	**18,824**	**4,983**	**1,590**	**559**	**615**	**9,754**	**417**	**2,527**	**19,886**
2016 January	15,994	668	930	17,592	4,541	1,572	581	346	9,355	397	2,487	18,698
February	15,884	567	1,803	18,254	4,677	1,575	566	418	9,804	405	2,433	19,312
March	16,105	487	2,232	18,824	4,873	1,562	586	655	9,900	401	2,473	19,865
April	15,942	450	2,439	18,830	4,680	1,585	591	821	9,849	436	2,525	19,896
May	16,276	426	2,453	19,155	4,768	1,603	609	889	10,049	428	2,557	20,294
June	16,432	430	2,812	19,674	4,963	1,654	590	879	10,275	389	2,620	20,780
July	16,640	423	2,678	19,741	4,943	1,729	584	861	10,243	401	2,749	20,925
August	16,592	423	2,822	19,837	4,945	1,789	571	828	10,301	422	2,693	20,979
September	16,356	545	2,305	19,205	4,894	1,731	576	644	10,025	436	2,594	20,323
October	15,454	630	2,429	18,513	4,626	1,583	556	476	10,065	457	2,386	19,592
November	16,219	695	1,989	18,902	5,065	1,674	590	347	9,979	450	2,497	20,012
December	16,514	669	1,753	18,936	5,157	1,652	594	324	10,015	401	2,532	20,082
Average	**16,202**	**534**	**2,221**	**18,957**	**4,845**	**1,643**	**583**	**625**	**9,989**	**419**	**2,546**	**20,065**
2017 January	16,129	650	1,131	17,910	4,797	1,615	564	353	9,316	473	2,479	19,035
February	15,546	586	2,034	18,167	4,672	1,604	543	412	9,552	484	2,487	19,212
March	16,028	518	2,266	18,813	4,781	1,677	586	679	9,834	427	2,524	19,921
April	[R] 16,970	[R] 477	[R] 1,963	[R] 19,411	[R] 5,036	[R] 1,734	[R] 601	[R] 857	[R] 9,897	[R] 405	[R] 2,610	[R] 20,538
May	[E] 17,219	[F] 432	[RE] 2,147	[RF] 19,799	[E] 5,151	[E] 1,703	[RE] 585	[RF] 871	[E] 10,103	[E] 411	[RE] 2,740	[RE] 20,979
June	[E] 17,118	[F] 444	[E] 2,438	[F] 20,000	[E] 5,195	[E] 1,760	[E] 640	[F] 880	[E] 10,170	[E] 413	[E] 2,759	[E] 21,178
6-Month Average	[E] **16,512**	[E] **518**	[E] **1,994**	[E] **19,023**	[E] **4,941**	[E] **1,683**	[E] **587**	[E] **677**	[E] **9,814**	[E] **435**	[E] **2,601**	[E] **20,151**
2016 6-Month Average	**16,107**	**505**	**2,109**	**18,721**	**4,750**	**1,592**	**587**	**669**	**9,871**	**409**	**2,516**	**19,807**
2015 6-Month Average	**15,974**	**474**	**2,142**	**18,590**	**4,916**	**1,563**	**561**	**664**	**9,604**	**432**	**2,460**	**19,638**

[a] See "Refinery and Blender Net Inputs" in Glossary.
[b] See "Refinery and Blender Net Production" in Glossary.
[c] Liquefied petroleum gases.
[d] Includes lease condensate.
[e] Natural gas plant liquids (liquefied petroleum gases and pentanes plus).
[f] Unfinished oils (net), other hydrocarbons, and hydrogen. Beginning in 1981, also includes aviation and motor gasoline blending components (net). Beginning in 1993, also includes oxygenates (net), including fuel ethanol. Beginning in 2009, also includes renewable diesel fuel (including biodiesel).
[g] Beginning in 2009, includes renewable diesel fuel (including biodiesel) blended into distillate fuel oil.
[h] Beginning in 1965, includes kerosene-type jet fuel. (Through 1964, kerosene-type jet fuel is included with kerosene in "Other Products.") For 1952–2004, also includes naphtha-type jet fuel. (Through 1951, naphtha-type jet fuel is included in the products from which it was blended—gasoline, kerosene, and distillate fuel oil. Beginning in 2005, naphtha-type jet fuel is included in "Other Products.")
[i] Includes propylene.
[j] Finished motor gasoline. Through 1963, also includes aviation gasoline and special naphthas. Beginning in 1993, also includes fuel ethanol blended into motor gasoline.
[k] Asphalt and road oil, kerosene, lubricants, petrochemical feedstocks, petroleum coke, still gas (refinery gas), waxes, and miscellaneous products. Through 1964, also includes kerosene-type jet fuel. Beginning in 1964, also includes finished aviation gasoline and special naphthas. Beginning in 2005, also includes naphtha-type jet fuel.

R=Revised. E=Estimate. F=Forecast. NA=Not available.

Notes: • Totals may not equal sum of components due to independent rounding. • Geographic coverage is the 50 states and the District of Columbia.

Web Page: See http://www.eia.gov/totalenergy/data/monthly/#petroleum (Excel and CSV files) for all available annual data beginning in 1949 and monthly data beginning in 1973.

Sources: • **1949–1975:** Bureau of Mines, Mineral Industry Surveys, *Petroleum Statement, Annual,* annual reports. • **1976–1980:** U.S. Energy Information Administration (EIA), Energy Data Reports, *Petroleum Statement, Annual,* annual reports. • **1981–2015:** EIA, *Petroleum Supply Annual,* annual reports. • **2016 and 2017:** EIA, *Petroleum Supply Monthly,* monthly reports; and, for the current two months, *Weekly Petroleum Status Report* data system, Short-Term Integrated Forecasting System, and *Monthly Energy Review* data system calculations.

Source: *U.S. Energy Information Administration, Monthly Energy Review, July 2017*

Figure 3.3a Petroleum Trade: Overview

Overview, April 2017

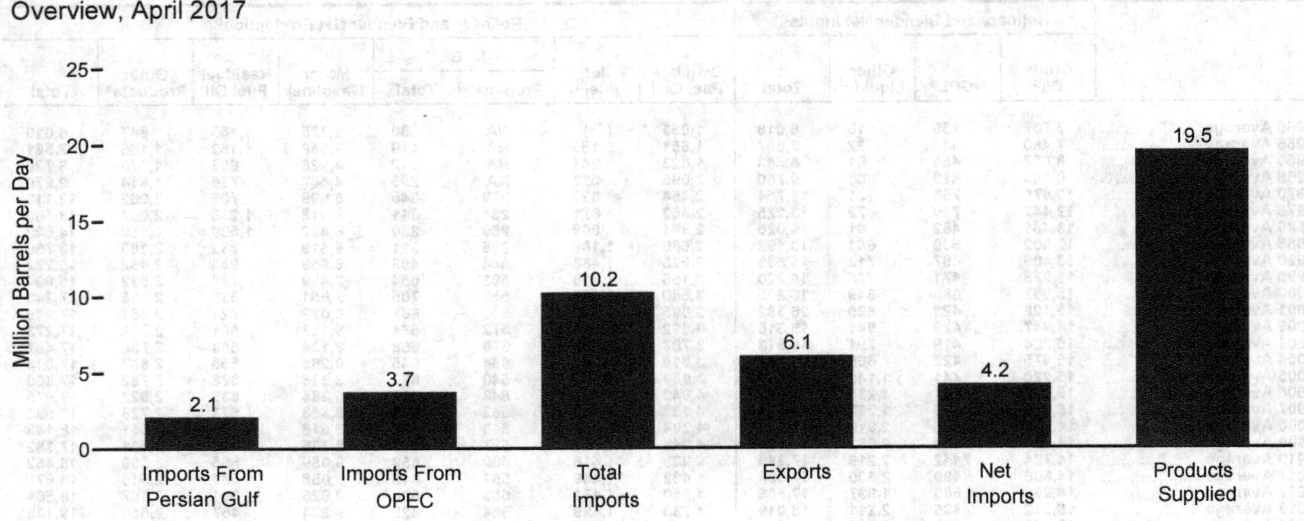

Imports From OPEC and Persian Gulf as Share of Total Imports, 1960–2016

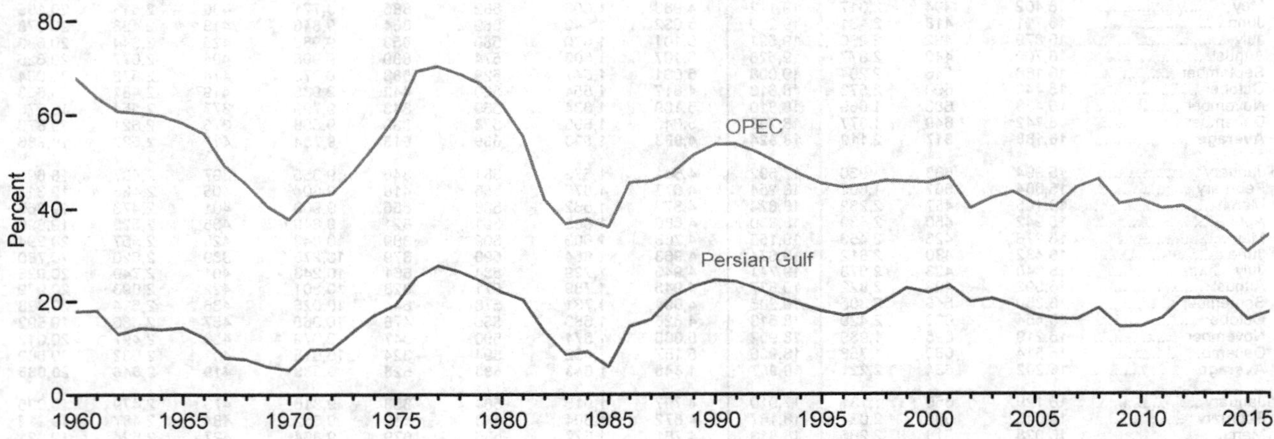

Net Imports as Share of Products Supplied, 1949–2016

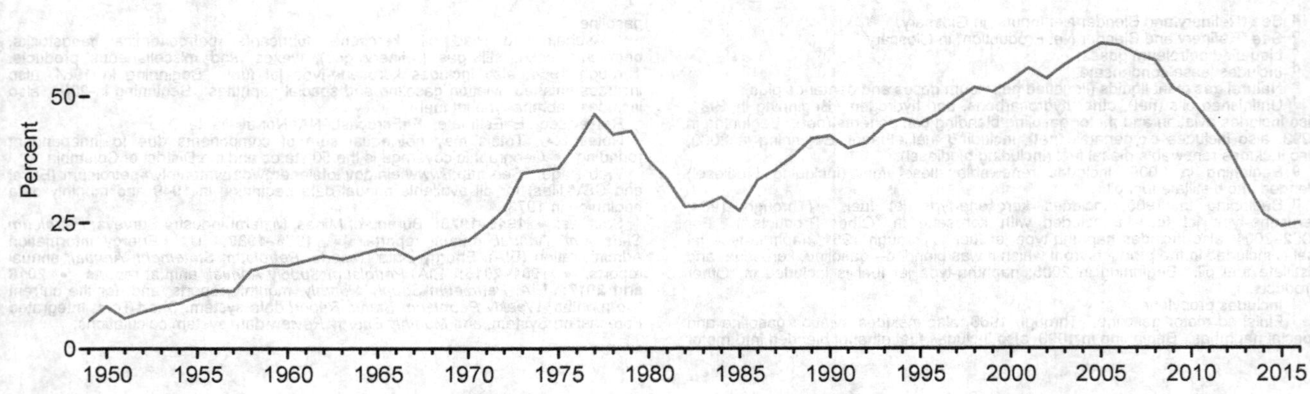

Note: OPEC=Organization of the Petroleum Exporting Countries.
Web Page: http://www.eia.gov/totalenergy/data/monthly/#petroleum.
Source: Table 3.3a.

***Source:** U.S. Energy Information Administration, Monthly Energy Review, July 2017*

Table 3.3a Petroleum Trade: Overview

	Imports From Persian Gulf[a]	Imports From OPEC[b]	Imports	Exports	Net Imports	Products Supplied	As Share of Products Supplied: Imports From Persian Gulf[a]	As Share of Products Supplied: Imports From OPEC[b]	As Share of Products Supplied: Imports	As Share of Products Supplied: Net Imports	As Share of Total Imports: Imports From Persian Gulf[a]	As Share of Total Imports: Imports From OPEC[b]
	Thousand Barrels per Day						Percent					
1950 Average	**NA**	**NA**	**850**	**305**	**545**	**6,458**	**NA**	**NA**	**13.2**	**8.4**	**NA**	**NA**
1955 Average	**NA**	**NA**	**1,248**	**368**	**880**	**8,455**	**NA**	**NA**	**14.8**	**10.4**	**NA**	**NA**
1960 Average	**326**	**1,233**	**1,815**	**202**	**1,613**	**9,797**	**3.3**	**12.6**	**18.5**	**16.5**	**17.9**	**68.0**
1965 Average	**359**	**1,439**	**2,468**	**187**	**2,281**	**11,512**	**3.1**	**12.5**	**21.4**	**19.8**	**14.5**	**58.3**
1970 Average	**184**	**1,294**	**3,419**	**259**	**3,161**	**14,697**	**1.3**	**8.8**	**23.3**	**21.5**	**5.4**	**37.8**
1975 Average	**1,165**	**3,601**	**6,056**	**209**	**5,846**	**16,322**	**7.1**	**22.1**	**37.1**	**35.8**	**19.2**	**59.5**
1980 Average	**1,519**	**4,300**	**6,909**	**544**	**6,365**	**17,056**	**8.9**	**25.2**	**40.5**	**37.3**	**22.0**	**62.2**
1985 Average	**311**	**1,830**	**5,067**	**781**	**4,286**	**15,726**	**2.0**	**11.6**	**32.2**	**27.3**	**6.1**	**36.1**
1990 Average	**1,966**	**4,296**	**8,018**	**857**	**7,161**	**16,988**	**11.6**	**25.3**	**47.2**	**42.2**	**24.5**	**53.6**
1995 Average	**1,573**	**4,002**	**8,835**	**949**	**7,886**	**17,725**	**8.9**	**22.6**	**49.8**	**44.5**	**17.8**	**45.3**
2000 Average	**2,488**	**5,203**	**11,459**	**1,040**	**10,419**	**19,701**	**12.6**	**26.4**	**58.2**	**52.9**	**21.7**	**45.4**
2001 Average	**2,761**	**5,528**	**11,871**	**971**	**10,900**	**19,649**	**14.1**	**28.1**	**60.4**	**55.5**	**23.3**	**46.6**
2002 Average	**2,269**	**4,605**	**11,530**	**984**	**10,546**	**19,761**	**11.5**	**23.3**	**58.3**	**53.4**	**19.7**	**39.9**
2003 Average	**2,501**	**5,162**	**12,264**	**1,027**	**11,238**	**20,034**	**12.5**	**25.8**	**61.2**	**56.1**	**20.4**	**42.1**
2004 Average	**2,493**	**5,701**	**13,145**	**1,048**	**12,097**	**20,731**	**12.0**	**27.5**	**63.4**	**58.4**	**19.0**	**43.4**
2005 Average	**2,334**	**5,587**	**13,714**	**1,165**	**12,549**	**20,802**	**11.2**	**26.9**	**65.9**	**60.3**	**17.0**	**40.7**
2006 Average	**2,211**	**5,517**	**13,707**	**1,317**	**12,390**	**20,687**	**10.7**	**26.7**	**66.3**	**59.9**	**16.1**	**40.2**
2007 Average	**2,163**	**5,980**	**13,468**	**1,433**	**12,036**	**20,680**	**10.5**	**28.9**	**65.1**	**58.2**	**16.1**	**44.4**
2008 Average	**2,370**	**5,954**	**12,915**	**1,802**	**11,114**	**19,498**	**12.2**	**30.5**	**66.2**	**57.0**	**18.4**	**46.1**
2009 Average	**1,689**	**4,776**	**11,691**	**2,024**	**9,667**	**18,771**	**9.0**	**25.4**	**62.3**	**51.5**	**14.4**	**40.9**
2010 Average	**1,711**	**4,906**	**11,793**	**2,353**	**9,441**	**19,180**	**8.9**	**25.6**	**61.5**	**49.2**	**14.5**	**41.6**
2011 Average	**1,861**	**4,555**	**11,436**	**2,986**	**8,450**	**18,882**	**9.9**	**24.1**	**60.6**	**44.8**	**16.3**	**39.8**
2012 Average	**2,156**	**4,271**	**10,598**	**3,205**	**7,393**	**18,490**	**11.7**	**23.1**	**57.3**	**40.0**	**20.3**	**40.3**
2013 Average	**2,009**	**3,720**	**9,859**	**3,621**	**6,237**	**18,961**	**10.6**	**19.6**	**52.0**	**32.9**	**20.4**	**37.7**
2014 Average	**1,875**	**3,237**	**9,241**	**4,176**	**5,065**	**19,106**	**9.8**	**16.9**	**48.4**	**26.5**	**20.3**	**35.0**
2015 January	1,334	2,538	9,461	4,575	4,886	19,218	6.9	13.2	49.2	25.4	14.1	26.8
February	1,433	2,794	9,272	4,640	4,632	19,677	7.3	14.2	47.1	23.5	15.5	30.1
March	1,466	2,801	9,619	4,092	5,527	19,352	7.6	14.5	49.7	28.6	15.2	29.1
April	1,532	2,734	9,374	4,938	4,436	19,263	8.0	14.2	48.7	23.0	16.3	29.2
May	1,724	3,133	9,502	4,853	4,649	19,301	8.9	16.2	49.2	24.1	18.1	33.0
June	1,617	2,869	9,605	4,657	4,948	19,841	8.1	14.5	48.4	24.9	16.8	29.9
July	1,479	2,911	9,571	4,960	4,611	20,126	7.3	14.5	47.6	22.9	15.5	30.4
August	1,247	2,750	9,858	4,507	5,351	19,930	6.3	13.8	49.5	26.8	12.7	27.9
September	1,290	2,854	9,358	4,851	4,507	19,418	6.6	14.7	48.2	23.2	13.8	30.5
October	1,519	2,899	8,842	4,617	4,225	19,500	7.8	14.9	45.3	21.7	17.2	32.8
November	1,662	3,169	9,151	4,903	4,248	19,144	8.7	16.6	47.8	22.2	18.2	34.6
December	1,773	3,274	9,742	5,266	4,476	19,600	9.0	16.7	49.7	22.8	18.2	33.6
Average	**1,507**	**2,894**	**9,449**	**4,738**	**4,711**	**19,531**	**7.7**	**14.8**	**48.4**	**24.1**	**15.9**	**30.6**
2016 January	1,520	3,052	9,734	4,878	4,857	19,055	8.0	16.0	51.1	25.5	15.6	31.4
February	1,574	3,210	10,020	4,948	5,072	19,680	8.0	16.3	50.9	25.8	15.7	32.0
March	1,820	3,576	10,002	5,002	5,000	19,616	9.3	18.2	51.0	25.5	18.2	35.8
April	1,709	3,351	9,829	5,154	4,674	19,264	8.9	17.4	51.0	24.3	17.4	34.1
May	1,933	3,642	10,183	5,658	4,525	19,202	10.1	19.0	53.0	23.6	19.0	35.8
June	1,716	3,303	10,076	5,240	4,836	19,799	8.7	16.7	50.9	24.4	17.0	32.8
July	1,793	3,803	10,507	5,209	5,298	19,712	9.1	19.3	53.3	26.9	17.1	36.2
August	1,815	3,422	10,311	5,114	5,196	20,131	9.0	17.0	51.2	25.8	17.6	33.2
September	1,982	3,572	10,194	5,250	4,944	19,864	10.0	18.0	51.3	24.9	19.4	35.0
October	1,698	3,329	9,723	4,942	4,781	19,622	8.7	17.0	49.6	24.4	17.5	34.2
November	1,703	3,567	10,312	5,392	4,921	19,655	8.7	18.1	52.5	25.0	16.5	34.6
December	1,885	3,498	9,814	5,460	4,355	19,979	9.4	17.5	49.1	21.8	19.2	35.6
Average	**1,763**	**3,445**	**10,058**	**5,188**	**4,871**	**19,631**	**9.0**	**17.5**	**51.2**	**24.8**	**17.5**	**34.2**
2017 January	2,085	3,793	10,698	5,691	5,007	19,234	10.8	19.7	55.6	26.0	19.5	35.5
February	2,013	3,445	10,053	6,443	3,610	19,188	10.5	18.0	52.4	18.8	20.0	34.3
March	1,955	3,592	10,059	5,886	4,174	20,033	9.8	17.9	50.2	20.8	19.4	35.7
April	[R]2,094	[R]3,737	[R]10,244	[R]6,066	[R]4,178	[R]19,527	[R]10.7	[R]19.1	[R]52.5	[R]21.4	[R]20.4	[R]36.5
May	NA	NA	[E]10,451	[E]5,624	[E]4,827	[E]20,177	NA	NA	[E]51.8	[E]23.9	NA	NA
June	NA	NA	[E]9,961	[E]5,207	[E]4,753	[E]20,549	NA	NA	[E]48.5	[E]23.1	NA	NA
6-Month Average	**NA**	**NA**	[E]**10,249**	[E]**5,811**	[E]**4,438**	[E]**19,792**	**NA**	**NA**	[E]**51.8**	[E]**22.4**	**NA**	**NA**
2016 6-Month Average	**1,714**	**3,358**	**9,974**	**5,148**	**4,825**	**19,432**	**8.8**	**17.3**	**51.3**	**24.8**	**17.2**	**33.7**
2015 6-Month Average	**1,518**	**2,812**	**9,475**	**4,624**	**4,852**	**19,437**	**7.8**	**14.5**	**48.7**	**25.0**	**16.0**	**29.7**

[a] Bahrain, Iran, Iraq, Kuwait, Qatar, Saudi Arabia, United Arab Emirates, and the Neutral Zone (between Kuwait and Saudi Arabia).

[b] See "Organization of the Petroleum Exporting Countries (OPEC)" in Glossary. See Table 3.3c for notes on which countries are included in the data.

R=Revised. E=Estimate. NA=Not available.

Notes: • For the feature article "Measuring Dependence on Imported Oil," published in the August 1995 *Monthly Energy Review*, see http://www.eia.gov/totalenergy/data/monthly/pdf/historical/imported_oil.pdf. • Beginning in October 1977, data include Strategic Petroleum Reserve imports. See Table 3.3b. • Annual averages may not equal average of months due to independent rounding. • U.S. geographic coverage is the 50 states and the District of Columbia. U.S. exports include shipments to U.S. territories, and imports include receipts from U.S. territories.

Web Page: See http://www.eia.gov/totalenergy/data/monthly/#petroleum (Excel and CSV files) for all available annual data beginning in 1949 and monthly data beginning in 1973.

Sources: • **1949–1975:** Bureau of Mines, Mineral Industry Surveys, *Petroleum Statement, Annual,* annual reports. • **1976–1980:** U.S. Energy Information Administration (EIA), Energy Data Reports, *Petroleum Statement, Annual,* annual reports. • **1981–2015:** EIA, *Petroleum Supply Annual,* annual reports, and unpublished revisions. • **2016 and 2017:** EIA, *Petroleum Supply Monthly,* monthly reports; and, for the current two months, *Weekly Petroleum Status Report* data system and *Monthly Energy Review* data system calculations.

Source: *U.S. Energy Information Administration, Monthly Energy Review, July 2017*

Figure 3.3b Petroleum Trade: Imports
(Million Barrels per Day)

Overview, 1949–2016

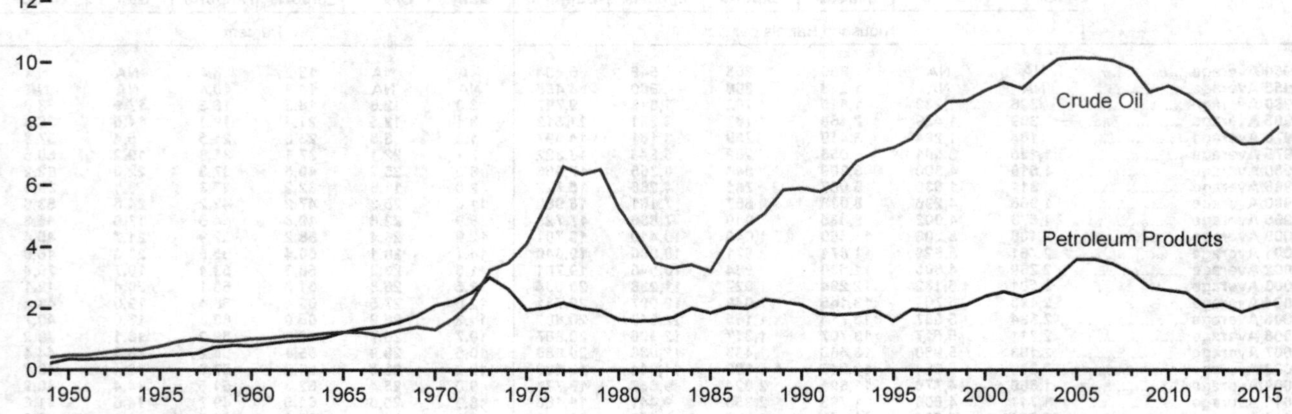

OPEC and Non-OPEC, 1960–2016

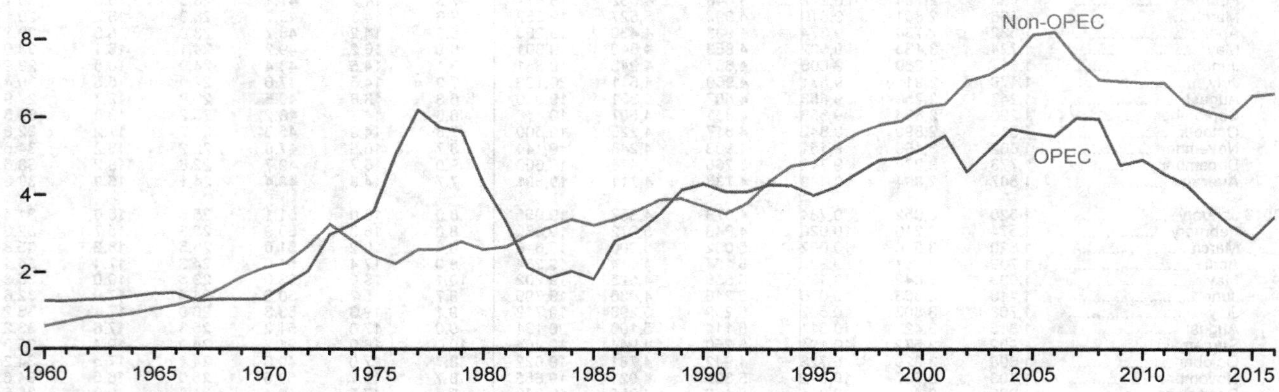

From Selected Countries, April 2017

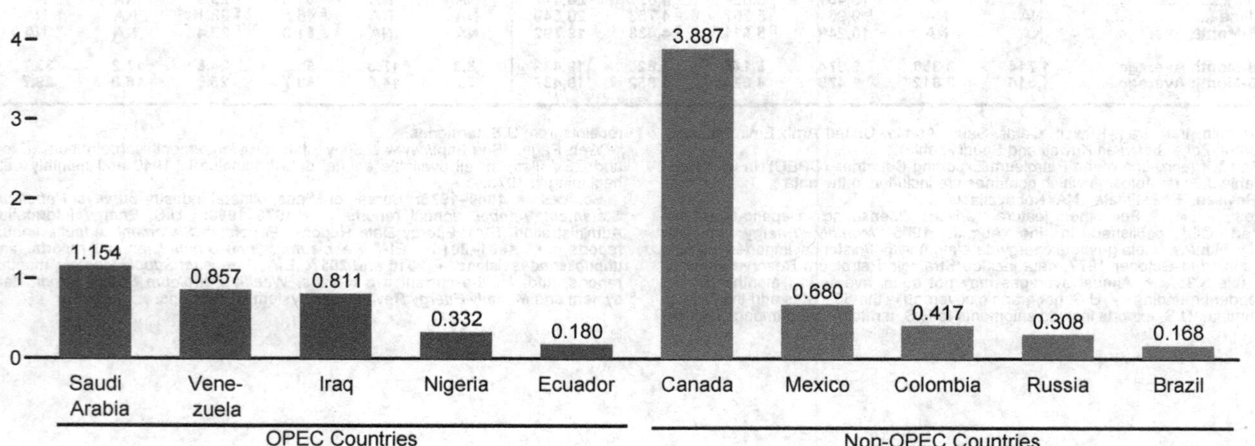

Note: OPEC=Organization of the Petroleum Exporting Countries.
Web Page: http://www.eia.gov/totalenergy/data/monthly/#petroleum.
Sources: Tables 3.3b–3.3d.

***Source:** U.S. Energy Information Administration, Monthly Energy Review, July 2017*

Table 3.3b Petroleum Trade: Imports and Exports by Type

(Thousand Barrels per Day)

	Imports										Exports		
	Crude Oil[a]		Distillate Fuel Oil	Jet Fuel[d]	LPG[b]		Motor Gasoline[f]	Residual Fuel Oil	Other[g]	Total	Crude Oil[a]	Petroleum Products	Total
	SPR[c]	Total			Propane[e]	Total							
1950 Average	--	487	7	([d])	–	–	(s)	329	27	850	95	210	305
1955 Average	--	782	12	([d])	–	–	13	417	24	1,248	32	336	368
1960 Average	--	1,015	35	34	NA	4	27	637	62	1,815	8	193	202
1965 Average	--	1,238	36	81	NA	21	28	946	119	2,468	3	184	187
1970 Average	--	1,324	147	144	26	52	67	1,528	157	3,419	14	245	259
1975 Average	--	4,105	155	133	60	112	184	1,223	144	6,056	6	204	209
1980 Average	44	5,263	142	80	69	216	140	939	130	6,909	287	258	544
1985 Average	118	3,201	200	39	67	187	381	510	550	5,067	204	577	781
1990 Average	27	5,894	278	108	115	188	342	504	705	8,018	109	748	857
1995 Average	–	7,230	193	106	102	146	265	187	708	8,835	95	855	949
2000 Average	8	9,071	295	162	161	215	427	352	938	11,459	50	990	1,040
2001 Average	11	9,328	344	148	145	206	454	295	1,095	11,871	20	951	971
2002 Average	16	9,140	267	107	145	183	498	249	1,085	11,530	9	975	984
2003 Average	–	9,665	333	109	168	225	518	327	1,087	12,264	12	1,014	1,027
2004 Average	77	10,088	325	127	209	263	496	426	1,419	13,145	27	1,021	1,048
2005 Average	52	10,126	329	190	233	328	603	530	1,609	13,714	32	1,133	1,165
2006 Average	8	10,118	365	186	228	332	475	350	1,881	13,707	25	1,292	1,317
2007 Average	7	10,031	304	217	182	247	413	372	1,885	13,468	27	1,405	1,433
2008 Average	19	9,783	213	103	185	253	302	349	1,913	12,915	29	1,773	1,802
2009 Average	56	9,013	225	81	147	182	223	331	1,635	11,691	44	1,980	2,024
2010 Average	–	9,213	228	98	121	153	134	366	1,600	11,793	42	2,311	2,353
2011 Average	–	8,935	179	69	110	135	105	328	1,686	11,436	47	2,939	2,986
2012 Average	–	8,527	126	55	116	141	44	256	1,450	10,598	67	3,137	3,205
2013 Average	–	7,730	155	84	127	148	45	225	1,471	9,859	134	3,487	3,621
2014 Average	–	7,344	195	94	108	128	49	173	1,257	9,241	351	3,824	4,176
2015 January	–	7,171	349	132	156	176	74	218	1,341	9,461	495	4,080	4,575
February	–	7,100	388	127	163	182	51	225	1,199	9,272	442	4,198	4,640
March	–	7,592	324	163	147	161	61	146	1,173	9,619	438	3,654	4,092
April	–	7,208	243	134	127	145	75	179	1,390	9,374	599	4,339	4,938
May	–	7,245	191	170	91	111	109	239	1,436	9,502	527	4,326	4,853
June	–	7,321	132	204	96	116	100	174	1,557	9,605	445	4,211	4,657
July	–	7,360	143	160	107	129	33	144	1,603	9,571	546	4,414	4,960
August	–	7,717	140	132	111	130	33	177	1,529	9,858	461	4,047	4,507
September	–	7,228	103	66	92	114	63	243	1,541	9,358	410	4,441	4,851
October	–	7,102	101	83	120	148	103	136	1,168	8,842	500	4,116	4,617
November	–	7,371	150	102	129	153	70	198	1,108	9,151	320	4,584	4,903
December	–	7,902	155	108	145	171	84	222	1,100	9,742	392	4,874	5,266
Average	**–**	**7,363**	**200**	**132**	**124**	**145**	**71**	**192**	**1,346**	**9,449**	**465**	**4,273**	**4,738**
2016 January	–	7,675	175	154	147	189	60	291	1,190	9,734	364	4,514	4,878
February	–	7,910	231	117	190	210	65	173	1,314	10,020	374	4,573	4,948
March	–	8,042	150	155	122	144	66	277	1,168	10,002	508	4,495	5,002
April	–	7,637	177	122	103	116	78	211	1,488	9,829	591	4,563	5,154
May	–	7,946	123	180	101	116	44	152	1,621	10,183	662	4,996	5,658
June	–	7,611	88	132	96	116	76	270	1,784	10,076	383	4,857	5,240
July	–	8,092	123	174	104	127	82	275	1,636	10,507	474	4,735	5,209
August	–	8,035	164	147	117	138	34	259	1,534	10,311	657	4,457	5,114
September	–	8,057	150	138	121	136	71	170	1,470	10,194	692	4,558	5,250
October	–	7,607	75	155	136	162	44	159	1,521	9,723	491	4,451	4,942
November	–	8,054	145	156	160	190	63	258	1,447	10,312	597	4,795	5,392
December	–	7,860	167	130	172	205	29	196	1,227	9,814	442	5,018	5,460
Average	**–**	**7,877**	**147**	**147**	**131**	**154**	**59**	**225**	**1,450**	**10,058**	**520**	**4,668**	**5,188**
2017 January	–	8,435	204	140	242	263	33	176	1,446	10,698	746	4,945	5,691
February	–	7,890	199	147	214	241	36	225	1,315	10,053	1,116	5,327	6,443
March	–	8,048	108	123	166	195	51	221	1,312	10,059	834	5,052	5,886
April	–	R 8,131	R 116	R 183	R 112	R 139	R 42	R 146	R 1,488	R 10,244	R 1,001	R 5,065	R 6,066
May	–	E 8,213	E 127	E 144	E 113	NA	E 33	E 248	NA	E 10,451	E 878	E 4,746	E 5,624
June	–	E 7,919	E 101	E 114	E 96	NA	E 45	E 152	NA	E 9,961	E 641	E 4,566	E 5,207
6-Month Average	**–**	**E 8,110**	**E 142**	**E 142**	**E 157**	**NA**	**E 40**	**E 195**	**NA**	**E 10,249**	**E 866**	**E 4,945**	**E 5,811**
2016 6-Month Average	**–**	**7,804**	**157**	**144**	**126**	**148**	**65**	**230**	**1,427**	**9,974**	**481**	**4,667**	**5,148**
2015 6-Month Average	**–**	**7,276**	**270**	**155**	**130**	**148**	**79**	**197**	**1,350**	**9,475**	**491**	**4,132**	**4,624**

[a] Includes lease condensate.

[b] Liquefied petroleum gases.

[c] "SPR" is the Strategic Petroleum Reserve, which began in October 1977. Through 2003, includes crude oil imports by SPR only; beginning in 2004, includes crude oil imports by SPR, and crude oil imports into SPR by others.

[d] Beginning in 1965, includes kerosene-type jet fuel. (Through 1964, kerosene-type jet fuel is included with kerosene in "Other.") For 1956–2004, also includes naphtha-type jet fuel. (Through 1955, naphtha-type jet fuel is included in "Motor Gasoline." Beginning in 2005, naphtha-type jet fuel is included in "Other.")

[e] Includes propylene.

[f] Finished motor gasoline. Through 1955, also includes naphtha-type jet fuel. Through 1963, also includes aviation gasoline and special naphthas. Through 1980, also includes motor gasoline blending components.

[g] Asphalt and road oil, aviation gasoline blending components, kerosene, lubricants, pentanes plus, petrochemical feedstocks, petroleum coke, unfinished oils, waxes, other hydrocarbons and oxygenates, and miscellaneous products. Through 1964, also includes kerosene-type jet fuel. Beginning in 1964, also includes finished aviation gasoline and special naphthas. Beginning in 1981, also includes motor gasoline blending components. Beginning in 2005, also includes naphtha-type jet fuel.

R=Revised. E=Estimate. NA=Not available. – – =Not applicable. – =No data reported. (s)=Less than 500 barrels per day.

Notes: • Totals may not equal sum of components due to independent rounding. • Geographic coverage is the 50 states and the District of Columbia.

Web Page: See http://www.eia.gov/totalenergy/data/monthly/#petroleum (Excel and CSV files) for all available annual data beginning in 1949 and monthly data beginning in 1973.

Sources: • **1949–1975:** Bureau of Mines, Mineral Industry Surveys, *Petroleum Statement, Annual*, annual reports. • **1976–1980:** U.S. Energy Information Administration (EIA), Energy Data Reports, *Petroleum Statement, Annual*, annual reports. • **1981–2015:** EIA, *Petroleum Supply Annual*, annual reports, and unpublished revisions. • **2016 and 2017:** EIA, *Petroleum Supply Monthly*, monthly reports; and, for the current two months, *Weekly Petroleum Status Report* data system and *Monthly Energy Review* data system calculations.

Source: *U.S. Energy Information Administration, Monthly Energy Review, July 2017*

Table 3.3c Petroleum Trade: Imports From OPEC Countries
(Thousand Barrels per Day)

	Algeria[a]	Angola[b]	Ecuador[c]	Iraq	Kuwait[d]	Libya[e]	Nigeria[f]	Saudi Arabia[d]	Vene-zuela	Other[g]	Total OPEC
1960 Average	(a)	(b)	(c)	22	182	(e)	(f)	84	911	34	1,233
1965 Average	(a)	(b)	(c)	16	74	42	(f)	158	994	155	1,439
1970 Average	8	(b)	(c)	–	48	47	(f)	30	989	172	1,294
1975 Average	282	(b)	57	2	16	232	762	715	702	832	3,601
1980 Average	488	(b)	27	28	27	554	857	1,261	481	577	4,300
1985 Average	187	(b)	67	46	21	4	293	168	605	439	1,830
1990 Average	280	(b)	49	518	86	–	800	1,339	1,025	199	4,296
1995 Average	234	(b)	(c)	–	218	–	627	1,344	1,480	98	4,002
2000 Average	225	(b)	(c)	620	272	R0	896	1,572	1,546	72	5,203
2001 Average	278	(b)	(c)	795	250	R0	885	1,662	1,553	105	5,528
2002 Average	264	(b)	(c)	459	228	–	621	1,552	1,398	83	4,605
2003 Average	382	(b)	(c)	481	220	–	867	1,774	1,376	61	5,162
2004 Average	452	(b)	(c)	656	250	20	1,140	1,558	1,554	70	5,701
2005 Average	478	(b)	(c)	531	243	56	1,166	1,537	1,529	47	5,587
2006 Average	657	(b)	(c)	553	185	87	1,114	1,463	1,419	38	5,517
2007 Average	670	508	(c)	484	181	117	1,134	1,485	1,361	39	5,980
2008 Average	548	513	221	627	210	103	988	1,529	1,189	26	5,954
2009 Average	493	460	185	450	182	79	809	1,004	1,063	50	4,776
2010 Average	510	393	212	415	197	70	1,023	1,096	988	3	4,906
2011 Average	358	346	206	459	191	15	818	1,195	951	16	4,555
2012 Average	242	233	180	476	305	61	441	1,365	960	9	4,271
2013 Average	115	216	236	341	328	59	281	1,329	806	10	3,720
2014 Average	110	154	215	369	311	6	92	1,166	789	23	3,237
2015 January	82	54	331	227	266	20	51	820	670	17	2,538
February	112	181	245	222	241	4	38	945	783	24	2,794
March	76	93	244	122	277	–	78	1,047	849	15	2,801
April	106	102	114	139	186	3	54	1,205	824	–	2,734
May	150	119	176	283	222	12	58	1,210	898	7	3,133
June	126	113	237	214	314	–	21	1,077	757	10	2,869
July	109	108	281	133	144	–	130	1,187	808	11	2,911
August	121	102	256	117	113	4	86	1,005	934	11	2,750
September	145	182	264	203	211	5	114	863	855	11	2,854
October	76	193	230	375	150	17	65	983	802	7	2,899
November	124	231	191	269	140	6	114	1,236	843	17	3,169
December	74	166	197	447	193	12	155	1,122	899	10	3,274
Average	**108**	**136**	**231**	**229**	**204**	**7**	**81**	**1,059**	**827**	**12**	**2,894**
2016 January	126	166	334	252	205	10	132	1,054	702	72	3,052
February	174	133	246	245	289	5	274	1,011	773	61	3,210
March	147	172	264	365	123	–	290	1,309	846	59	3,576
April	137	242	182	349	199	10	243	1,154	788	45	3,351
May	102	161	230	555	177	75	297	1,171	787	87	3,642
June	183	128	223	434	135	–	252	1,104	748	97	3,303
July	191	299	234	390	323	5	299	1,053	933	75	3,803
August	169	159	253	488	156	22	181	1,142	773	78	3,422
September	155	157	213	448	275	4	168	1,211	825	116	3,572
October	296	122	203	508	154	–	232	1,025	741	48	3,329
November	300	174	250	434	228	27	247	1,003	845	59	3,567
December	202	102	236	593	254	32	246	1,014	789	29	3,498
Average	**182**	**168**	**239**	**423**	**210**	**16**	**238**	**1,105**	**796**	**69**	**3,445**
2017 January	232	118	247	622	105	31	332	1,345	749	10	3,793
February	234	64	141	413	251	22	223	1,338	751	9	3,445
March	193	30	278	544	219	30	342	1,173	764	20	3,592
April	153	84	180	811	101	45	332	1,154	857	21	3,737
4-Month Average	**203**	**74**	**214**	**600**	**168**	**32**	**309**	**1,251**	**780**	**15**	**3,646**
2016 4-Month Average	**146**	**178**	**257**	**303**	**203**	**6**	**234**	**1,134**	**777**	**59**	**3,298**
2015 4-Month Average	**94**	**105**	**234**	**177**	**243**	**7**	**56**	**1,004**	**781**	**14**	**2,714**

[a] Algeria joined OPEC in 1969. For 1960–1968, Algeria is included in "Total Non-OPEC" on Table 3.3d.
[b] Angola joined OPEC in January 2007. For 1960–2006, Angola is included in "Total Non-OPEC" on Table 3.3d.
[c] Ecuador was a member of OPEC from 1973–1992, and rejoined OPEC in November 2007. For 1960–1972 and 1993–2007, Ecuador is included in "Total Non-OPEC" on Table 3.3d.
[d] Through 1970, includes half the imports from the Neutral Zone between Kuwait and Saudi Arabia. Beginning in 1971, imports from the Neutral Zone are reported as originating in either Kuwait or Saudi Arabia depending on the country reported to U.S. Customs.
[e] Libya joined OPEC in 1962. For 1960 and 1961, Libya is included in "Total Non-OPEC" on Table 3.3d.
[f] Nigeria joined OPEC in 1971. For 1960–1970, Nigeria is included in "Total Non-OPEC" on Table 3.3d.
[g] Includes these countries for the dates indicated: Gabon (1975–1994 and July 2016 forward), Indonesia (1962–2008 and 2016), Iran (1960 forward), Qatar (1961 forward), and United Arab Emirates (1967 forward).
– =No data reported.

Notes: • See "Organization of the Petroleum Exporting Countries (OPEC)" in Glossary. Petroleum imports not classified as "OPEC" on this table are included on Table 3.3d. • The country of origin for petroleum products may not be the country of origin for the crude oil from which the products were produced. For example, refined products imported from West European refining areas may have been produced from Middle East crude oil. • Includes imports for the Strategic Petroleum Reserve, which began in October 1977. • Totals may not equal sum of components due to independent rounding. • U.S. geographic coverage is the 50 states and the District of Columbia.

Web Page: See http://www.eia.gov/totalenergy/data/monthly/#petroleum (Excel and CSV files) for all available annual data beginning in 1960 and monthly data beginning in 1973.

Sources: • **1960–1972:** Bureau of Mines, *Minerals Yearbook,* annual reports. • **1973–1975:** Bureau of Mines, Mineral Industry Surveys, *Petroleum Statement, Annual,* annual reports. • **1976–1980:** U.S. Energy Information Administration (EIA), Energy Data Reports, *Petroleum Statement, Annual,* annual reports. • **1981–2015:** EIA, *Petroleum Supply Annual,* annual reports. • **2016 and 2017:** EIA, *Petroleum Supply Monthly,* monthly reports.

Source: *U.S. Energy Information Administration, Monthly Energy Review, July 2017*

Table 3.3d Petroleum Trade: Imports From Non-OPEC Countries
(Thousand Barrels per Day)

	Brazil	Canada	Colombia	Mexico	Nether-lands	Norway	Russia[a]	United Kingdom	U.S. Virgin Islands	Other	Total Non-OPEC
1960 Average	**1**	**120**	**42**	**16**	**NA**	**NA**	**–**	**(s)**	**NA**	**NA**	**581**
1965 Average	**–**	**323**	**51**	**48**	**1**	**–**	**–**	**(s)**	**–**	**606**	**1,029**
1970 Average	**2**	**766**	**46**	**42**	**39**	**–**	**3**	**11**	**189**	**1,027**	**2,126**
1975 Average	**5**	**846**	**9**	**71**	**19**	**17**	**14**	**14**	**406**	**1,052**	**2,454**
1980 Average	**3**	**455**	**4**	**533**	**2**	**144**	**1**	**176**	**388**	**903**	**2,609**
1985 Average	**61**	**770**	**23**	**816**	**58**	**32**	**8**	**310**	**247**	**913**	**3,237**
1990 Average	**49**	**934**	**182**	**755**	**55**	**102**	**45**	**189**	**282**	**1,128**	**3,721**
1995 Average	**8**	**1,332**	**219**	**1,068**	**15**	**273**	**25**	**383**	**278**	**1,233**	**4,833**
2000 Average	**51**	**1,807**	**342**	**1,373**	**30**	**343**	**72**	**366**	**291**	**1,581**	**6,257**
2001 Average	**82**	**1,828**	**296**	**1,440**	**43**	**341**	**90**	**324**	**268**	**1,631**	**6,343**
2002 Average	**116**	**1,971**	**260**	**1,547**	**66**	**393**	**210**	**478**	**236**	**1,649**	**6,925**
2003 Average	**108**	**2,072**	**195**	**1,623**	**87**	**270**	**254**	**440**	**288**	**1,766**	**7,103**
2004 Average	**104**	**2,138**	**176**	**1,665**	**101**	**244**	**298**	**380**	**330**	**2,008**	**7,444**
2005 Average	**156**	**2,181**	**196**	**1,662**	**151**	**233**	**410**	**396**	**328**	**2,413**	**8,127**
2006 Average	**193**	**2,353**	**155**	**1,705**	**174**	**196**	**369**	**272**	**328**	**2,446**	**8,190**
2007 Average	**200**	**2,455**	**155**	**1,532**	**128**	**142**	**414**	**277**	**346**	**1,839**	**7,489**
2008 Average	**258**	**2,493**	**200**	**1,302**	**168**	**102**	**465**	**236**	**320**	**1,416**	**6,961**
2009 Average	**309**	**2,479**	**276**	**1,210**	**140**	**108**	**563**	**245**	**277**	**1,307**	**6,915**
2010 Average	**272**	**2,535**	**365**	**1,284**	**108**	**89**	**612**	**256**	**253**	**1,112**	**6,887**
2011 Average	**253**	**2,729**	**433**	**1,206**	**100**	**113**	**624**	**159**	**186**	**1,077**	**6,881**
2012 Average	**226**	**2,946**	**433**	**1,035**	**99**	**75**	**477**	**149**	**12**	**874**	**6,327**
2013 Average	**151**	**3,142**	**389**	**919**	**89**	**54**	**460**	**147**	**–**	**786**	**6,138**
2014 Average	**160**	**3,388**	**318**	**842**	**85**	**45**	**330**	**117**	**–**	**720**	**6,004**
2015 January	236	4,010	417	831	78	11	401	140	–	799	6,923
February	138	3,942	353	784	81	58	300	88	–	733	6,478
March	170	3,899	525	875	110	52	376	83	–	727	6,818
April	232	3,849	442	714	78	37	358	111	–	820	6,640
May	108	3,562	535	663	80	108	337	138	–	838	6,369
June	255	3,625	377	856	23	66	500	134	–	898	6,736
July	222	3,488	441	755	54	87	445	142	–	1,027	6,661
August	396	3,932	339	731	22	138	509	154	–	887	7,108
September	276	3,807	292	647	53	48	369	178	–	835	6,504
October	229	3,411	221	756	32	44	307	99	–	842	5,942
November	99	3,621	402	721	39	37	320	92	–	651	5,982
December	208	4,043	390	760	38	39	219	112	–	660	6,469
Average	**215**	**3,765**	**395**	**758**	**57**	**61**	**371**	**123**	**–**	**811**	**6,554**
2016 January	168	4,111	509	710	57	58	384	115	–	569	6,683
February	148	4,201	507	539	73	61	436	71	–	773	6,810
March	112	3,882	561	657	30	143	329	141	–	571	6,426
April	160	3,558	386	788	54	89	509	149	–	784	6,478
May	110	3,571	570	676	62	44	435	106	–	967	6,541
June	194	3,485	583	739	59	113	472	168	1	958	6,773
July	158	3,436	536	733	43	108	531	92	–	1,066	6,704
August	274	3,823	534	672	31	49	479	141	–	884	6,888
September	154	3,794	500	595	67	124	406	132	–	851	6,622
October	199	3,618	346	614	107	75	483	89	–	862	6,394
November	189	4,054	368	697	74	38	419	137	–	770	6,746
December	126	4,061	397	606	60	11	318	121	–	617	6,316
Average	**166**	**3,798**	**483**	**669**	**60**	**76**	**433**	**122**	**(s)**	**806**	**6,613**
2017 January	219	4,282	345	730	75	134	348	141	–	631	6,905
February	254	4,182	401	607	81	34	319	96	–	633	6,607
March	229	4,065	338	630	47	12	379	120	–	648	6,467
April	168	3,887	417	680	62	86	308	123	–	777	6,507
4-Month Average	**217**	**4,104**	**374**	**663**	**66**	**67**	**339**	**120**	**–**	**672**	**6,623**
2016 4-Month Average	**147**	**3,937**	**491**	**675**	**53**	**88**	**413**	**120**	**–**	**672**	**6,597**
2015 4-Month Average	**195**	**3,926**	**436**	**802**	**87**	**39**	**360**	**106**	**–**	**770**	**6,722**

[a] Through 1992, may include imports from republics other than Russia in the former U.S.S.R. See "Union of Soviet Socialist Republics (U.S.S.R.)" in Glossary.

NA=Not available. – =No data reported. (s)=Less than 500 barrels per day.

Notes: • See "Organization of the Petroleum Exporting Countries (OPEC)" in Glossary. Petroleum imports not classified as "OPEC" on Table 3.3c are included on this table. • The country of origin for petroleum products may not be the country of origin for the crude oil from which the products were produced. For example, refined products imported from West European refining areas may have been produced from Middle East crude oil. • Includes imports for the Strategic Petroleum Reserve, which began in October 1977. • Totals may not equal sum of components due to independent rounding. • U.S. geographic coverage is the 50 states and the District of Columbia.

Web Page: See http://www.eia.gov/totalenergy/data/monthly/#petroleum (Excel and CSV files) for all available annual data beginning in 1960 and monthly data beginning in 1973.

Sources: • **1960–1972:** Bureau of Mines, *Minerals Yearbook,* annual reports. • **1973–1975:** Bureau of Mines, Mineral Industry Surveys, *Petroleum Statement, Annual,* annual reports. • **1976–1980:** U.S. Energy Information Administration (EIA), Energy Data Reports, *Petroleum Statement, Annual,* annual reports. • **1981–2015:** EIA, *Petroleum Supply Annual,* annual reports. • **2016 and 2017:** EIA, *Petroleum Supply Monthly,* monthly reports.

Source: *U.S. Energy Information Administration, Monthly Energy Review, July 2017*

Figure 3.4 Petroleum Stocks

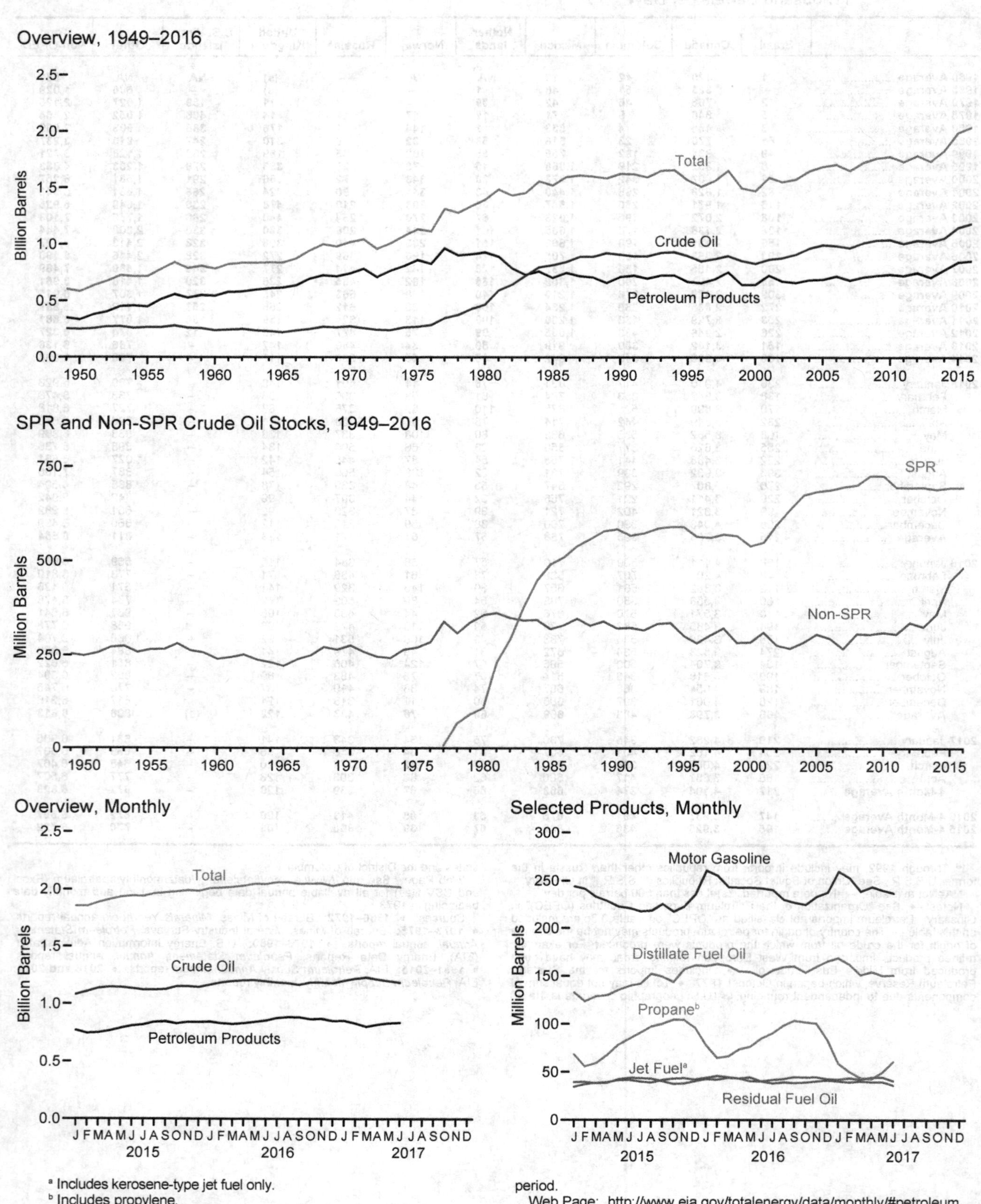

[a] Includes kerosene-type jet fuel only.
[b] Includes propylene.
Notes: • SPR=Strategic Petroleum Reserve. • Stocks are at end of period.
Web Page: http://www.eia.gov/totalenergy/data/monthly/#petroleum.
Source: Table 3.4.

***Source:** U.S. Energy Information Administration, Monthly Energy Review, July 2017*

Table 3.4 Petroleum Stocks
(Million Barrels)

	Crude Oil[a]			Distillate Fuel Oil[e]	Jet Fuel[f]	LPG[b]		Motor Gasoline[h]	Residual Fuel Oil	Other[i]	Total
	SPR[c]	Non-SPR[d]	Total			Propane[g]	Total				
1950 Year	--	248	248	72	(f)	NA	2	116	41	104	583
1955 Year	--	266	266	111	3	NA	7	165	39	123	715
1960 Year	--	240	240	138	7	NA	23	195	45	137	785
1965 Year	--	220	220	155	19	NA	30	175	56	181	836
1970 Year	--	276	276	195	28	NA	67	209	54	188	1,018
1975 Year	--	271	271	209	30	82	125	235	74	188	1,133
1980 Year	108	358	466	205	42	65	120	261	92	205	1,392
1985 Year	493	321	814	144	40	39	74	223	50	174	1,519
1990 Year	586	323	908	132	52	49	98	220	49	162	1,621
1995 Year	592	303	895	130	40	43	93	202	37	165	1,563
2000 Year	541	286	826	118	45	41	83	196	36	164	1,468
2001 Year	550	312	862	145	42	66	121	210	41	166	1,586
2002 Year	599	278	877	134	39	53	106	209	31	152	1,548
2003 Year	638	269	907	137	39	50	94	207	38	147	1,568
2004 Year	676	286	961	126	40	55	104	218	42	153	1,645
2005 Year	685	308	992	136	42	57	109	208	37	157	1,682
2006 Year	689	296	984	144	39	62	113	212	42	169	1,703
2007 Year	697	268	965	134	39	52	96	218	39	156	1,648
2008 Year	702	308	1,010	146	38	55	113	214	36	162	1,719
2009 Year	727	307	1,034	166	43	50	102	223	37	153	1,758
2010 Year	727	312	1,039	164	43	49	108	219	41	158	1,773
2011 Year	696	308	1,004	149	41	55	112	223	34	164	1,728
2012 Year	695	338	1,033	135	40	68	141	231	34	167	1,780
2013 Year	696	327	1,023	128	37	45	114	228	38	163	1,732
2014 Year	691	361	1,052	136	38	78	155	240	34	172	1,827
2015 January	691	389	1,080	133	39	68	135	244	34	185	1,850
February	691	415	1,106	124	40	56	116	241	37	187	1,850
March	691	443	1,134	129	38	59	123	233	38	187	1,883
April	691	453	1,144	130	38	68	141	229	39	188	1,909
May	692	449	1,141	135	42	78	161	223	41	187	1,931
June	694	439	1,133	140	44	85	175	221	42	187	1,941
July	695	425	1,120	142	44	91	188	218	40	188	1,939
August	695	426	1,121	153	43	98	205	218	39	183	1,962
September	695	429	1,124	149	40	100	210	225	42	180	1,971
October	695	455	1,150	144	37	105	209	217	43	177	1,979
November	695	456	1,151	157	38	104	197	223	44	182	1,992
December	695	449	1,144	161	40	96	177	235	42	184	1,985
2016 January	695	469	1,164	161	42	78	145	261	44	192	2,009
February	695	488	1,184	163	42	65	127	256	46	196	2,013
March	695	502	1,197	161	44	66	134	243	45	199	2,021
April	695	506	1,201	155	43	74	150	243	43	197	2,032
May	695	509	1,204	154	45	77	167	243	40	195	2,048
June	695	498	1,193	149	40	85	191	242	40	191	2,047
July	695	490	1,185	156	42	91	208	240	38	193	2,062
August	695	484	1,179	160	43	99	224	230	40	188	2,063
September	695	469	1,164	160	45	104	227	227	39	186	2,048
October	695	489	1,184	154	45	102	219	225	39	184	2,050
November	695	489	1,184	160	45	101	209	233	41	182	2,054
December	695	484	1,179	165	43	84	178	238	42	185	2,031
2017 January	695	504	1,200	169	42	59	145	260	40	197	2,053
February	695	524	1,218	162	44	51	134	253	40	198	2,049
March	692	538	1,229	151	42	44	130	239	41	200	2,033
April	689	R 524	R 1,213	R 155	R 45	R 43	R 138	R 244	R 40	R 200	R 2,033
May	E 685	E 513	E 1,198	E 150	E 45	E 50	RF 158	E 240	E 40	RE 199	E 2,030
June	E 682	E 502	E 1,183	E 151	E 41	E 61	F 178	E 237	E 36	E 193	E 2,020

[a] Includes lease condensate.

[b] Liquefied petroleum gases.

[c] "SPR" is the Strategic Petroleum Reserve, which began in October 1977. Crude oil stocks in the SPR include non-U.S. stocks held under foreign or commercial storage agreements.

[d] Crude oil stocks at (or in) refineries, pipelines, tank farms, and bulk terminals. Through 2004, also includes crude oil stocks on leases. Beginning in 1981, also includes stocks of Alaskan crude oil in transit by water.

[e] Excludes stocks in the Northeast Home Heating Oil Reserve. Beginning in 2009, includes renewable diesel fuel (including biodiesel) blended into distillate fuel oil.

[f] Beginning in 1965, includes kerosene-type jet fuel. (Through 1964, kerosene-type jet fuel is included with kerosene in "Other.") For 1952–2004, also includes naphtha-type jet fuel. (Through 1951, naphtha-type jet fuel is included in the products from which it was blended—gasoline, kerosene, and distillate fuel oil. Beginning in 2005, naphtha-type jet fuel is included in "Other.")

[g] Includes propylene.

[h] Includes finished motor gasoline and motor gasoline blending components; excludes oxygenates. Through 1963, also includes aviation gasoline and special naphthas.

[i] Asphalt and road oil, aviation gasoline blending components, kerosene, lubricants, pentanes plus, petrochemical feedstocks, petroleum coke, unfinished oils, waxes, miscellaneous products, oxygenates, renewable fuels, and other hydrocarbons. Through 1964, also includes kerosene-type jet fuel. Beginning in 1964, also includes finished aviation gasoline and special naphthas. Beginning in 2005, also includes naphtha-type jet fuel.

R=Revised. E=Estimate. F=Forecast. NA=Not available. – – =Not applicable.

Notes: • Stocks are at end of period. • Totals may not equal sum of components due to independent rounding. • Geographic coverage is the 50 states and the District of Columbia.

Web Page: See http://www.eia.gov/totalenergy/data/monthly/#petroleum (Excel and CSV files) for all available annual data beginning in 1949 and monthly data beginning in 1973.

Sources: • **1949–1975:** Bureau of Mines, Mineral Industry Surveys, *Petroleum Statement, Annual,* annual reports. • **1976–1980:** U.S. Energy Information Administration (EIA), Energy Data Reports, *Petroleum Statement, Annual,* annual reports. • **1981–2015:** EIA, *Petroleum Supply Annual,* annual reports. • **2016 and 2017:** EIA, *Petroleum Supply Monthly,* monthly reports; and, for the current two months, *Weekly Petroleum Status Report* data system, Short-Term Integrated Forecasting System, and *Monthly Energy Review* data system calculations.

Source: *U.S. Energy Information Administration, Monthly Energy Review, July 2017*

Figure 3.5 Petroleum Products Supplied by Type
(Million Barrels per Day)

Total Petroleum and Motor Gasoline, 1949–2016

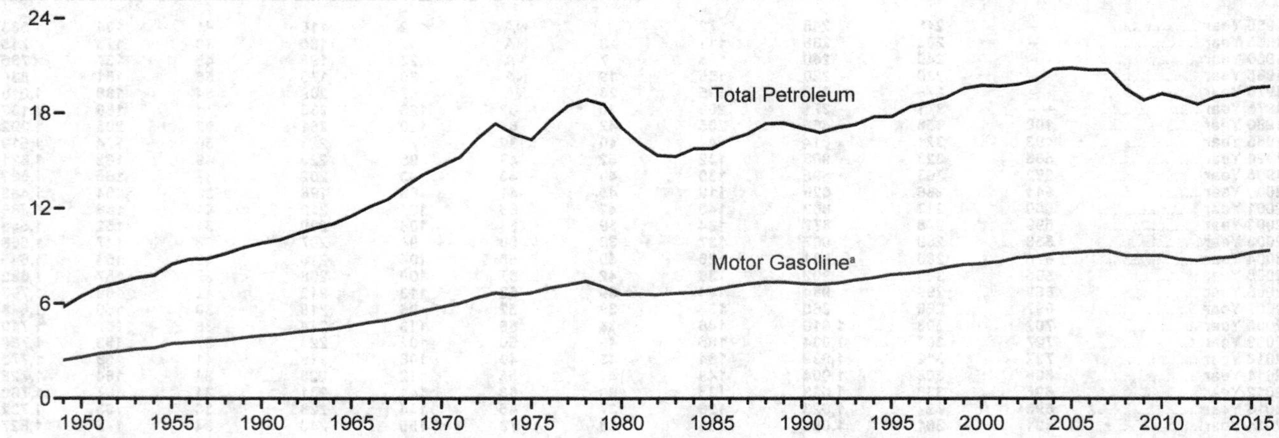

Selected Products,1949–2016

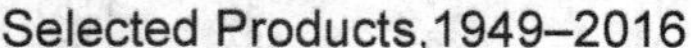

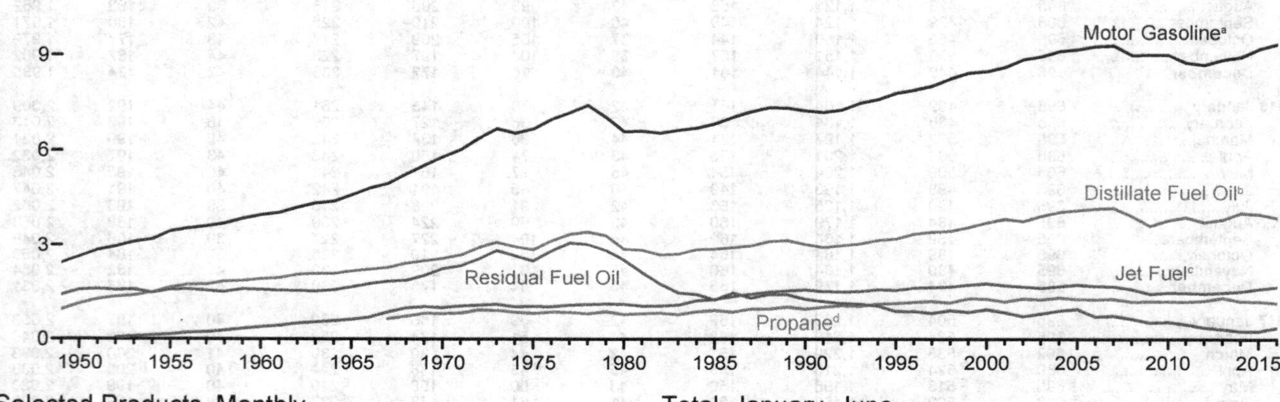

Selected Products, Monthly

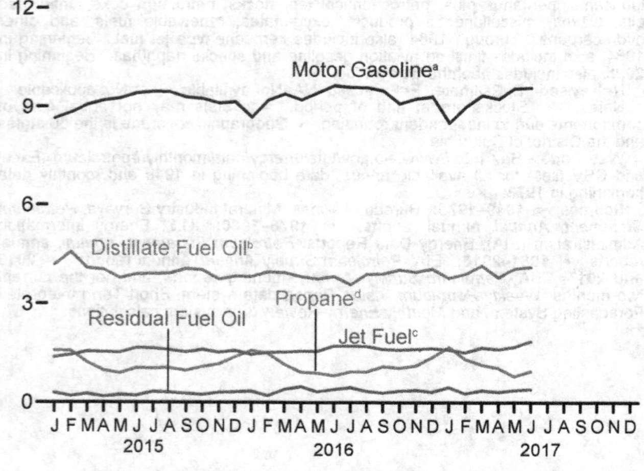

Total, January–June

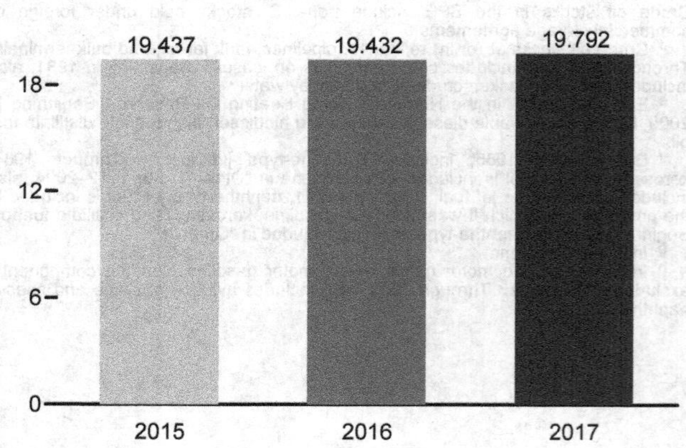

[a] Beginning in 1993, includes fuel ethanol blended into motor gasoline.
[b] Beginning in 2009, includes renewable diesel fuel (including biodiesel) blended into distillate fuel oil.
[c] Beginning in 2005, includes kerosene-type jet fuel only.
[d] Includes propylene.

Note: SPR=Strategic Petroleum Reserve.
Web Page: http://www.eia.gov/totalenergy/data/monthly/#petroleum.
Source: Table 3.5.

Source: *U.S. Energy Information Administration, Monthly Energy Review, July 2017*

Table 3.5 Petroleum Products Supplied by Type

(Thousand Barrels per Day)

	Asphalt and Road Oil	Aviation Gasoline	Distillate Fuel Oil[b]	Jet Fuel[c]	Kero-sene	LPG[a]		Lubri-cants	Motor Gasoline[e]	Petro-leum Coke	Residual Fuel Oil	Other[f]	Total
						Propane[d]	Total						
1950 Average	**180**	**108**	**1,082**	**(c)**	**323**	**NA**	**234**	**106**	**2,616**	**41**	**1,517**	**250**	**6,458**
1955 Average	**254**	**192**	**1,592**	**154**	**320**	**NA**	**404**	**116**	**3,463**	**67**	**1,526**	**366**	**8,455**
1960 Average	**302**	**161**	**1,872**	**371**	**271**	**NA**	**621**	**117**	**3,969**	**149**	**1,529**	**435**	**9,797**
1965 Average	**368**	**120**	**2,126**	**602**	**267**	**NA**	**841**	**129**	**4,593**	**202**	**1,608**	**657**	**11,512**
1970 Average	**447**	**55**	**2,540**	**967**	**263**	**776**	**1,224**	**136**	**5,785**	**212**	**2,204**	**866**	**14,697**
1975 Average	**419**	**39**	**2,851**	**1,001**	**159**	**783**	**1,333**	**137**	**6,675**	**247**	**2,462**	**1,001**	**16,322**
1980 Average	**396**	**35**	**2,866**	**1,068**	**158**	**754**	**1,469**	**159**	**6,579**	**237**	**2,508**	**1,581**	**17,056**
1985 Average	**425**	**27**	**2,868**	**1,218**	**114**	**883**	**1,599**	**145**	**6,831**	**264**	**1,202**	**1,032**	**15,726**
1990 Average	**483**	**24**	**3,021**	**1,522**	**43**	**917**	**1,556**	**164**	**7,235**	**339**	**1,229**	**1,373**	**16,988**
1995 Average	**486**	**21**	**3,207**	**1,514**	**54**	**1,096**	**1,899**	**156**	**7,789**	**365**	**852**	**1,381**	**17,725**
2000 Average	**525**	**20**	**3,722**	**1,725**	**67**	**1,235**	**2,231**	**166**	**8,472**	**406**	**909**	**1,458**	**19,701**
2001 Average	**519**	**19**	**3,847**	**1,655**	**72**	**1,142**	**2,044**	**153**	**8,610**	**437**	**811**	**1,481**	**19,649**
2002 Average	**512**	**18**	**3,776**	**1,614**	**43**	**1,248**	**2,163**	**151**	**8,848**	**463**	**700**	**1,474**	**19,761**
2003 Average	**503**	**16**	**3,927**	**1,578**	**55**	**1,215**	**2,074**	**140**	**8,935**	**455**	**772**	**1,579**	**20,034**
2004 Average	**537**	**17**	**4,058**	**1,630**	**64**	**1,276**	**2,132**	**141**	**9,105**	**524**	**865**	**1,657**	**20,731**
2005 Average	**546**	**19**	**4,118**	**1,679**	**70**	**1,229**	**2,030**	**141**	**9,159**	**515**	**920**	**1,605**	**20,802**
2006 Average	**521**	**18**	**4,169**	**1,633**	**54**	**1,215**	**2,052**	**137**	**9,253**	**522**	**689**	**1,640**	**20,687**
2007 Average	**494**	**17**	**4,196**	**1,622**	**32**	**1,235**	**2,085**	**142**	**9,286**	**490**	**723**	**1,593**	**20,680**
2008 Average	**417**	**15**	**3,945**	**1,539**	**14**	**1,154**	**1,954**	**131**	**8,989**	**464**	**622**	**1,408**	**19,498**
2009 Average	**360**	**14**	**3,631**	**1,393**	**18**	**1,160**	**2,051**	**118**	**8,997**	**427**	**511**	**1,251**	**18,771**
2010 Average	**362**	**15**	**3,800**	**1,432**	**20**	**1,160**	**2,173**	**131**	**8,993**	**376**	**535**	**1,343**	**19,180**
2011 Average	**355**	**15**	**3,899**	**1,425**	**12**	**1,153**	**2,204**	**125**	**8,753**	**361**	**461**	**1,272**	**18,882**
2012 Average	**340**	**14**	**3,741**	**1,398**	**5**	**1,175**	**2,251**	**114**	**8,682**	**360**	**369**	**1,215**	**18,490**
2013 Average	**323**	**12**	**3,827**	**1,434**	**5**	**1,275**	**2,440**	**121**	**8,843**	**354**	**319**	**1,282**	**18,961**
2014 Average	**327**	**12**	**4,037**	**1,470**	**9**	**1,167**	**2,396**	**126**	**8,921**	**347**	**257**	**1,204**	**19,106**
2015 January	200	8	4,186	1,375	3	1,580	2,814	153	8,639	404	294	1,142	19,218
February	215	8	4,559	1,445	9	1,572	2,822	123	8,829	217	195	1,255	19,677
March	222	9	4,078	1,548	11	1,228	2,419	152	9,057	377	263	1,215	19,352
April	303	14	4,027	1,527	1	966	2,261	148	9,189	377	172	1,243	19,263
May	343	13	3,778	1,519	20	890	2,238	159	9,262	383	235	1,351	19,301
June	472	12	3,897	1,654	(s)	1,053	2,326	132	9,417	407	200	1,324	19,841
July	480	18	3,901	1,650	1	1,030	2,382	156	9,470	399	325	1,343	20,126
August	510	11	3,915	1,601	2	1,042	2,291	121	9,460	412	298	1,309	19,930
September	469	11	4,063	1,534	1	970	2,196	127	9,289	283	267	1,179	19,418
October	400	14	4,014	1,614	3	1,084	2,411	145	9,245	329	236	1,090	19,500
November	287	9	3,740	1,524	1	1,169	2,557	104	9,112	306	300	1,203	19,144
December	212	9	3,831	1,578	25	1,384	2,751	130	9,148	283	317	1,317	19,600
Average	**343**	**11**	**3,995**	**1,548**	**6**	**1,162**	**2,454**	**138**	**9,178**	**349**	**259**	**1,248**	**19,531**
2016 January	200	7	3,816	1,449	-3	1,577	2,898	134	8,670	349	339	1,195	19,055
February	219	11	3,959	1,525	1	1,490	2,723	141	9,206	362	200	1,333	19,680
March	262	10	3,941	1,536	12	1,160	2,444	145	9,399	362	398	1,108	19,616
April	304	14	3,823	1,560	5	918	2,255	128	9,213	292	481	1,189	19,264
May	392	11	3,745	1,562	4	894	2,230	134	9,436	271	333	1,083	19,202
June	479	12	3,830	1,714	8	815	2,144	147	9,663	247	398	1,156	19,799
July	475	12	3,578	1,715	9	927	2,299	113	9,597	314	454	1,145	19,712
August	527	14	3,890	1,710	1	924	2,248	121	9,595	429	342	1,255	20,131
September	438	11	3,905	1,624	11	1,096	2,442	127	9,492	289	290	1,236	19,864
October	415	10	4,024	1,605	14	1,047	2,414	131	9,095	310	345	1,259	19,622
November	312	12	3,961	1,627	3	1,116	2,402	113	9,243	489	375	1,118	19,655
December	194	10	4,059	1,649	21	1,375	2,628	121	9,310	393	322	1,271	19,979
Average	**352**	**11**	**3,877**	**1,606**	**7**	**1,111**	**2,427**	**130**	**9,327**	**342**	**357**	**1,195**	**19,631**
2017 January	192	9	3,781	1,593	14	1,687	2,943	105	8,503	412	460	1,221	19,234
February	241	9	3,905	1,525	6	1,321	2,614	123	8,988	262	270	1,244	19,188
March	265	10	4,154	1,669	2	1,143	2,509	133	9,353	175	362	1,402	20,033
April	[R] 318	[R] 10	[R] 3,791	[R] 1,617	[R] 7	[R] 1,051	[R] 2,376	[R] 105	[R] 9,248	[R] 322	[R] 320	[R] 1,413	[R] 19,527
May	[RF] 400	[F] 12	[E] 4,057	[E] 1,682	[RF] 5	[E] 791	[RF] 2,218	[RF] 152	[E] 9,561	[RF] 337	[E] 365	[RE] 1,388	[E] 20,177
June	[F] 483	[F] 12	[E] 4,108	[E] 1,860	[F] 5	[E] 951	[F] 2,333	[F] 133	[E] 9,580	[F] 331	[E] 400	[E] 1,304	[E] 20,549
6-Month Average	[E] **317**	[E] **11**	[E] **3,967**	[E] **1,659**	[E] **6**	[E] **1,156**	[E] **2,498**	[E] **125**	[E] **9,207**	[E] **307**	[E] **364**	[E] **1,330**	[E] **19,792**
2016 6-Month Average	**310**	**11**	**3,851**	**1,557**	**5**	**1,141**	**2,449**	**138**	**9,263**	**314**	**359**	**1,176**	**19,432**
2015 6-Month Average	**293**	**11**	**4,081**	**1,512**	**7**	**1,211**	**2,476**	**145**	**9,067**	**363**	**227**	**1,255**	**19,437**

[a] Liquefied petroleum gases.

[b] Beginning in 2009, includes renewable diesel fuel (including biodiesel) blended into distillate fuel oil.

[c] Beginning in 1957, includes kerosene-type jet fuel. For 1952–2004, also includes naphtha-type jet fuel. (Through 1951, naphtha-type jet fuel is included in the products from which it was blended—gasoline, kerosene, and distillate fuel oil. Beginning in 2005, naphtha-type jet fuel is included in "Other.").

[d] Includes propylene.

[e] Finished motor gasoline. Through 1963, also includes special naphthas. Beginning in 1993, also includes fuel ethanol blended into motor gasoline.

[f] Pentanes plus, petrochemical feedstocks, still gas (refinery gas), waxes, and miscellaneous products. Beginning in 1964, also includes special naphthas. Beginning in 1981, also includes negative barrels per day of distillate and residual fuel oil reclassified as unfinished oils, and other products (from both primary and secondary supply) reclassified as gasoline blending components. Beginning in 1983, also includes crude oil burned as fuel. Beginning in 2005, also includes naphtha-type jet fuel.

R=Revised. E=Estimate. F=Forecast. NA=Not available. (s)=Less than 500 barrels per day and greater than -500 barrels per day.

Notes: • Petroleum products supplied is an approximation of petroleum consumption and is synonymous with the term "petroleum consumption" in Tables 3.7a–3.8c. See Note 1, "Petroleum Products Supplied and Petroleum Consumption," at end of section. • Totals may not equal sum of components due to independent rounding. • Geographic coverage is the 50 states and the District of Columbia.

Web Page: See http://www.eia.gov/totalenergy/data/monthly/#petroleum (Excel and CSV files) for all available annual data beginning in 1949 and monthly data beginning in 1973.

Sources: • **1949–1975:** Bureau of Mines, Mineral Industry Surveys, *Petroleum Statement, Annual,* annual reports. • **1976–1980:** U.S. Energy Information Administration (EIA), Energy Data Reports, *Petroleum Statement, Annual,* annual reports. • **1981–2015:** EIA, *Petroleum Supply Annual,* annual reports, and unpublished revisions. • **2016 and 2017:** EIA, *Petroleum Supply Monthly,* monthly reports; and, for the current two months, *Weekly Petroleum Status Report* data system, Short-Term Integrated Forecasting System, and *Monthly Energy Review* data system calculations.

Source: *U.S. Energy Information Administration, Monthly Energy Review, July 2017*

Figure 3.6 Heat Content of Petroleum Products Supplied by Type

Total, 1949–2016

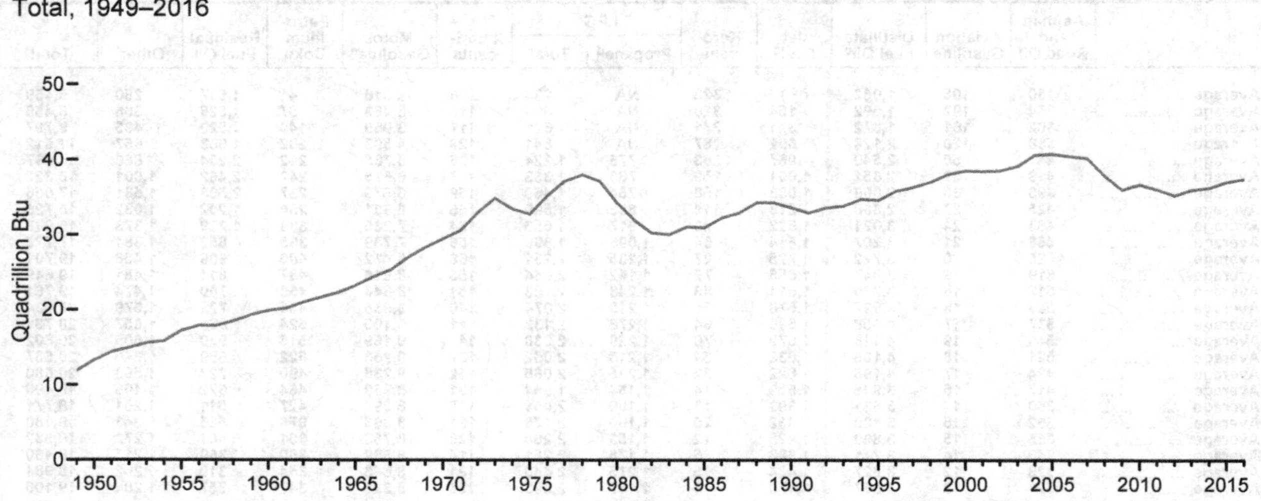

Petroleum Products Supplied as Share of Total Energy Consumption, 1949–2016

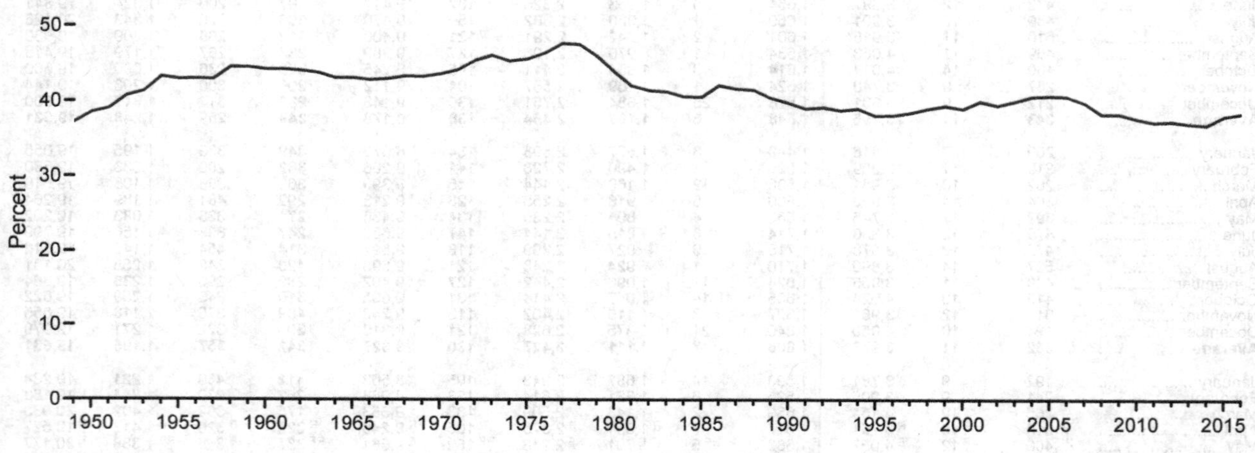

By Product, June 2017

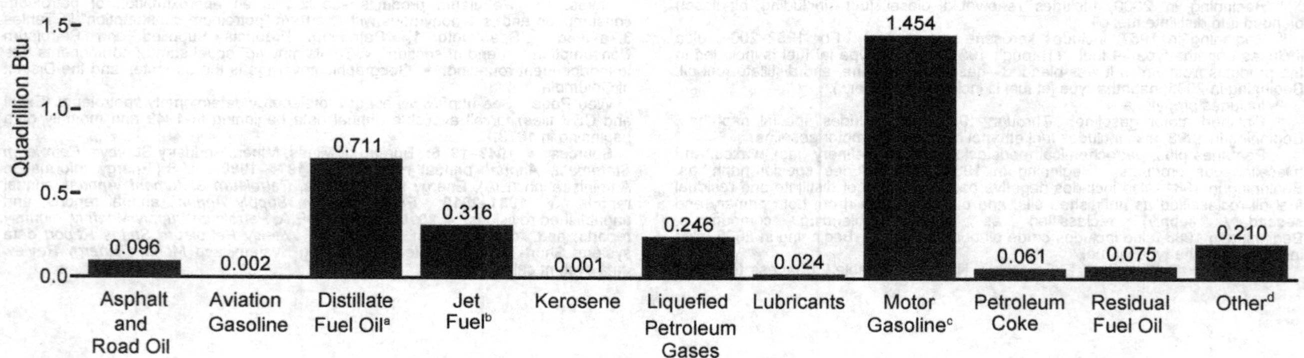

[a] Includes renewable diesel fuel (including biodiesel) blended into distillate fuel oil.
[b] Includes kerosene-type jet fuel only.
[c] Includes fuel ethanol blended into motor gasoline.
[d] All petroleum products not separately displayed.

Web Page: http://www.eia.gov/totalenergy/data/monthly/#petroleum.
Sources: Tables 1.1 and 3.6.

Source: *U.S. Energy Information Administration, Monthly Energy Review, July 2017*

Table 3.6 Heat Content of Petroleum Products Supplied by Type

(Trillion Btu)

	Asphalt and Road Oil	Aviation Gasoline	Distillate Fuel Oil[b]	Jet Fuel[c]	Kero-sene	LPG[a]		Lubri-cants	Motor Gasoline[e]	Petro-leum Coke	Residual Fuel Oil	Other[f]	Total
						Propane[d]	Total						
1950 Total	**435**	**199**	**2,300**	**(c)**	**668**	**NA**	**343**	**236**	**5,015**	**90**	**3,482**	**546**	**13,315**
1955 Total	**615**	**354**	**3,385**	**301**	**662**	**NA**	**592**	**258**	**6,640**	**147**	**3,502**	**798**	**17,255**
1960 Total	**734**	**298**	**3,992**	**739**	**563**	**NA**	**912**	**259**	**7,631**	**328**	**3,517**	**947**	**19,919**
1965 Total	**890**	**222**	**4,519**	**1,215**	**553**	**NA**	**1,232**	**286**	**8,806**	**444**	**3,691**	**1,390**	**23,246**
1970 Total	**1,082**	**100**	**5,401**	**1,973**	**544**	**1,086**	**1,689**	**301**	**11,091**	**465**	**5,057**	**1,817**	**29,521**
1975 Total	**1,014**	**71**	**6,061**	**2,047**	**329**	**1,097**	**1,807**	**304**	**12,798**	**542**	**5,649**	**2,109**	**32,732**
1980 Total	**962**	**64**	**6,110**	**2,190**	**329**	**1,059**	**1,976**	**354**	**12,648**	**522**	**5,772**	**3,278**	**34,205**
1985 Total	**1,029**	**50**	**6,098**	**2,497**	**236**	**1,236**	**2,103**	**322**	**13,098**	**582**	**2,759**	**2,152**	**30,925**
1990 Total	**1,170**	**45**	**6,422**	**3,129**	**88**	**1,284**	**2,059**	**362**	**13,872**	**745**	**2,820**	**2,839**	**33,552**
1995 Total	**1,178**	**40**	**6,812**	**3,132**	**112**	**1,534**	**2,512**	**346**	**14,834**	**802**	**1,955**	**2,837**	**34,558**
2000 Total	**1,276**	**36**	**7,927**	**3,580**	**140**	**1,734**	**2,945**	**369**	**16,167**	**895**	**2,091**	**2,979**	**38,406**
2001 Total	**1,257**	**35**	**8,170**	**3,426**	**150**	**1,598**	**2,697**	**338**	**16,386**	**961**	**1,861**	**3,056**	**38,337**
2002 Total	**1,240**	**34**	**8,020**	**3,340**	**90**	**1,747**	**2,852**	**334**	**16,829**	**1,018**	**1,605**	**3,040**	**38,401**
2003 Total	**1,220**	**30**	**8,341**	**3,265**	**113**	**1,701**	**2,748**	**309**	**16,968**	**1,000**	**1,772**	**3,264**	**39,030**
2004 Total	**1,304**	**31**	**8,642**	**3,383**	**133**	**1,791**	**2,824**	**313**	**17,333**	**1,148**	**1,990**	**3,428**	**40,528**
2005 Total	**1,323**	**35**	**8,745**	**3,475**	**144**	**1,721**	**2,682**	**312**	**17,378**	**1,125**	**2,111**	**3,318**	**40,647**
2006 Total	**1,261**	**33**	**8,831**	**3,379**	**111**	**1,701**	**2,700**	**303**	**17,531**	**1,141**	**1,581**	**3,416**	**40,289**
2007 Total	**1,197**	**32**	**8,858**	**3,358**	**67**	**1,729**	**2,733**	**313**	**17,472**	**1,072**	**1,659**	**3,313**	**40,073**
2008 Total	**1,012**	**28**	**8,346**	**3,193**	**30**	**1,620**	**2,574**	**291**	**16,865**	**1,017**	**1,432**	**2,941**	**37,728**
2009 Total	**873**	**27**	**7,661**	**2,883**	**36**	**1,624**	**2,664**	**262**	**16,750**	**937**	**1,173**	**2,611**	**35,877**
2010 Total	**878**	**27**	**8,014**	**2,963**	**41**	**1,624**	**2,821**	**291**	**16,668**	**831**	**1,228**	**2,800**	**36,561**
2011 Total	**859**	**27**	**8,217**	**2,950**	**25**	**1,614**	**2,839**	**276**	**16,191**	**801**	**1,058**	**2,676**	**35,920**
2012 Total	**827**	**25**	**7,903**	**2,901**	**11**	**1,649**	**2,912**	**254**	**16,089**	**802**	**849**	**2,558**	**35,130**
2013 Total	**783**	**22**	**8,059**	**2,969**	**11**	**1,785**	**3,167**	**268**	**16,339**	**786**	**731**	**2,677**	**35,812**
2014 Total	**793**	**22**	**8,499**	**3,042**	**19**	**1,634**	**3,090**	**280**	**16,476**	**772**	**590**	**2,518**	**36,101**
2015 January	41	1	749	242	(s)	188	313	29	1,355	76	57	202	3,065
February	40	1	736	229	1	169	281	21	1,251	37	34	200	2,832
March	46	1	729	272	2	146	266	29	1,421	71	51	213	3,101
April	60	2	697	260	(s)	111	238	27	1,395	69	32	212	2,992
May	70	2	675	267	4	106	245	30	1,453	72	46	241	3,105
June	94	2	674	281	(s)	121	247	24	1,430	74	38	227	3,091
July	99	3	697	290	(s)	123	262	29	1,486	75	63	239	3,244
August	105	2	700	281	(s)	124	252	23	1,484	78	58	229	3,212
September	93	2	703	261	(s)	112	230	23	1,410	52	50	202	3,026
October	82	2	718	284	1	129	263	27	1,450	62	46	190	3,125
November	57	1	647	259	(s)	135	270	19	1,383	56	57	207	2,956
December	44	1	685	277	4	165	302	24	1,435	53	62	233	3,121
Total	**832**	**21**	**8,411**	**3,204**	**13**	**1,627**	**3,168**	**305**	**16,952**	**776**	**595**	**2,595**	**36,870**
2016 January	41	1	682	255	(s)	188	321	25	1,360	66	66	218	3,035
February	42	2	662	251	(s)	166	280	25	1,351	64	36	230	2,943
March	54	2	705	270	2	138	266	27	1,474	68	78	203	3,148
April	61	2	661	265	1	106	238	23	1,398	53	91	211	3,005
May	81	2	670	275	1	106	242	25	1,480	51	65	199	3,090
June	95	2	663	292	1	94	225	27	1,467	45	75	206	3,097
July	98	2	640	301	2	110	248	21	1,505	60	89	209	3,174
August	109	2	695	300	(s)	110	243	23	1,505	81	67	230	3,256
September	87	2	676	276	2	126	261	23	1,441	53	55	218	3,092
October	85	2	719	282	2	124	263	25	1,426	59	67	227	3,158
November	62	2	685	277	(s)	128	252	21	1,403	90	71	197	3,059
December	40	1	726	290	4	164	287	23	1,460	74	63	230	3,199
Total	**855**	**20**	**8,184**	**3,334**	**15**	**1,560**	**3,127**	**287**	**17,269**	**765**	**821**	**2,579**	**37,256**
2017 January	39	1	676	280	2	201	324	20	1,333	78	90	222	3,066
February	45	1	631	242	1	142	255	21	1,273	45	48	203	2,764
March	54	2	743	293	(s)	136	273	25	1,467	33	71	253	3,214
April	[R]63	2	[R]656	[R]275	[R]1	[R]121	[R]249	[R]19	[R]1,404	59	60	[R]248	[R]3,036
May	[RF]82	[F]2	[E]725	[E]296	[F]1	[E]94	[F]242	[RF]29	[E]1,499	[RF]64	[E]71	[RE]232	[E]3,243
June	[F]96	[F]2	[E]711	[E]316	[F]1	[E]109	[F]246	[F]24	[E]1,454	[F]61	[E]75	[E]210	[E]3,196
6-Month Total	[E]**380**	[E]**10**	[E]**4,141**	[E]**1,703**	[E]**6**	[E]**803**	[E]**1,589**	[E]**138**	[E]**8,430**	[E]**339**	[E]**415**	[E]**1,368**	[E]**18,519**
2016 6-Month Total	**374**	**10**	**4,043**	**1,607**	**5**	**797**	**1,572**	**152**	**8,529**	**349**	**411**	**1,267**	**18,318**
2015 6-Month Total	**352**	**10**	**4,261**	**1,551**	**8**	**841**	**1,589**	**159**	**8,304**	**400**	**259**	**1,295**	**18,186**

[a] Liquefied petroleum gases.
[b] Beginning in 2009, includes renewable diesel fuel (including biodiesel) blended into distillate fuel oil.
[c] Beginning in 1957, includes kerosene-type jet fuel. For 1952–2004, also includes naphtha-type jet fuel. (Through 1951, naphtha-type jet fuel is included in the products from which it was blended—gasoline, kerosene, and distillate fuel oil. Beginning in 2005, naphtha-type jet fuel is included in "Other.").
[d] Includes propylene.
[e] Finished motor gasoline. Through 1963, also includes special naphthas. Beginning in 1993, also includes fuel ethanol blended into motor gasoline.
[f] Pentanes plus, petrochemical feedstocks, still gas (refinery gas), waxes, and miscellaneous products. Beginning in 1964, also includes special naphthas. Beginning in 1981, also includes negative barrels per day of distillate and residual fuel oil reclassified as unfinished oils, and other products (from both primary and secondary supply) reclassified as gasoline blending components. Beginning in 1983, also includes crude oil burned as fuel. Beginning in 2005, also includes naphtha-type jet fuel.

R=Revised. E=Estimate. F=Forecast. NA=Not available. (s)=Less than 0.5 trillion Btu and greater than -0.5 trillion Btu.

Notes: • Petroleum products supplied is an approximation of petroleum consumption and is synonymous with the term "petroleum consumption" in Tables 3.7a–3.8c. See Note 1, "Petroleum Products Supplied and Petroleum Consumption," at end of section. • Totals may not equal sum of components due to independent rounding. • Geographic coverage is the 50 states and the District of Columbia.

Web Page: See http://www.eia.gov/totalenergy/data/monthly/#petroleum (Excel and CSV files) for all available annual data beginning in 1949 and monthly data beginning in 1973.

Sources: See end of section.

Source: *U.S. Energy Information Administration, Monthly Energy Review, July 2017*

Figure 3.7 Petroleum Consumption by Sector

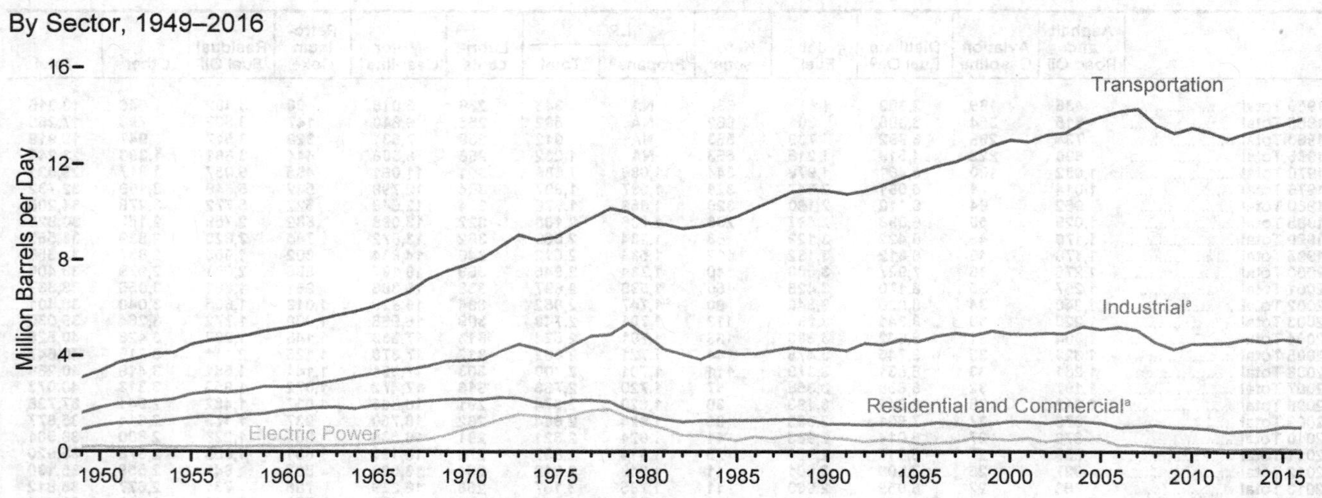

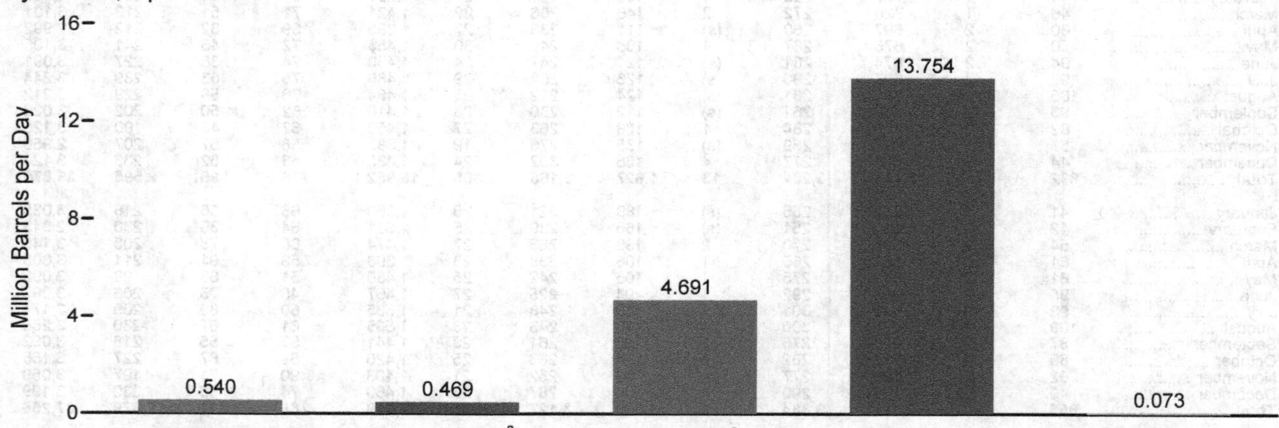

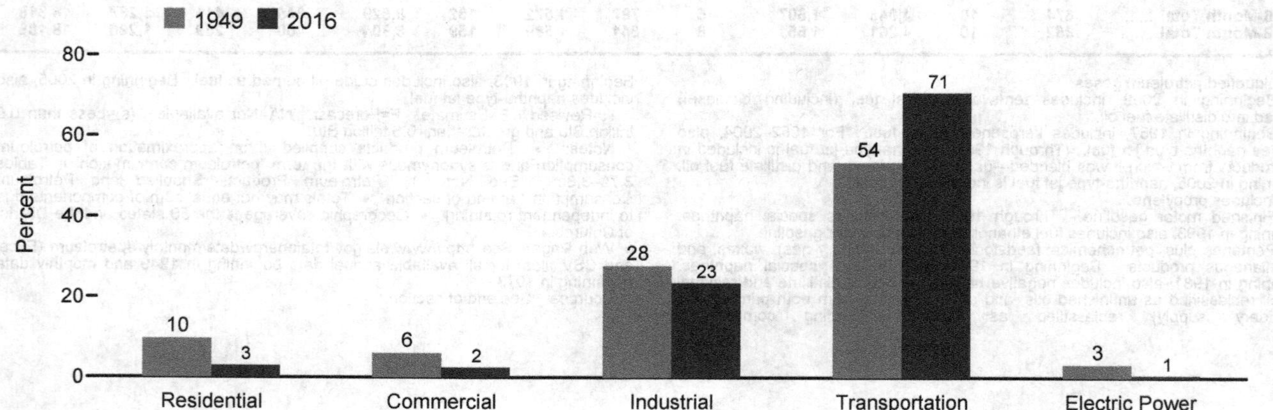

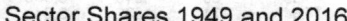

[a] Includes combined-heat-and-power plants and a small number of electricity-only plants.

Web Page: http://www.eia.gov/totalenergy/data/monthly/#petroleum.
Sources: Tables 3.7a–3.7c.

Source: *U.S. Energy Information Administration, Monthly Energy Review, July 2017*

Table 3.7a Petroleum Consumption: Residential and Commercial Sectors

(Thousand Barrels per Day)

	Residential Sector				Commercial Sector[a]						
	Distillate Fuel Oil	Kerosene	Liquefied Petroleum Gases	Total	Distillate Fuel Oil	Kerosene	Liquefied Petroleum Gases	Motor Gasoline[b,c]	Petroleum Coke	Residual Fuel Oil	Total
1950 Average	**390**	**168**	**104**	**662**	**123**	**23**	**28**	**52**	**NA**	**185**	**411**
1955 Average	**562**	**179**	**144**	**885**	**177**	**24**	**38**	**69**	**NA**	**209**	**519**
1960 Average	**736**	**171**	**217**	**1,123**	**232**	**23**	**58**	**35**	**NA**	**243**	**590**
1965 Average	**805**	**161**	**275**	**1,242**	**251**	**26**	**74**	**40**	**NA**	**281**	**672**
1970 Average	**883**	**144**	**392**	**1,419**	**276**	**30**	**102**	**45**	**NA**	**311**	**764**
1975 Average	**850**	**78**	**365**	**1,293**	**276**	**24**	**92**	**46**	**NA**	**214**	**653**
1980 Average	**617**	**51**	**222**	**890**	**243**	**20**	**63**	**56**	**NA**	**245**	**626**
1985 Average	**514**	**77**	**224**	**815**	**297**	**16**	**68**	**50**	**NA**	**99**	**530**
1990 Average	**460**	**31**	**252**	**742**	**252**	**6**	**73**	**58**	**0**	**100**	**489**
1995 Average	**426**	**36**	**282**	**743**	**225**	**11**	**78**	**10**	**(s)**	**62**	**385**
2000 Average	**424**	**46**	**395**	**865**	**230**	**14**	**107**	**23**	**(s)**	**40**	**415**
2001 Average	**427**	**46**	**375**	**849**	**239**	**15**	**102**	**20**	**(s)**	**30**	**406**
2002 Average	**404**	**29**	**384**	**817**	**209**	**8**	**101**	**24**	**(s)**	**35**	**376**
2003 Average	**438**	**34**	**389**	**861**	**233**	**9**	**112**	**32**	**(s)**	**48**	**434**
2004 Average	**433**	**41**	**364**	**839**	**221**	**10**	**108**	**23**	**(s)**	**53**	**416**
2005 Average	**402**	**40**	**366**	**809**	**210**	**10**	**94**	**24**	**(s)**	**50**	**389**
2006 Average	**335**	**32**	**318**	**685**	**189**	**7**	**88**	**26**	**(s)**	**33**	**343**
2007 Average	**342**	**21**	**345**	**708**	**181**	**4**	**87**	**32**	**(s)**	**33**	**337**
2008 Average	**354**	**10**	**394**	**758**	**181**	**2**	**113**	**24**	**(s)**	**31**	**351**
2009 Average	**276**	**13**	**391**	**680**	**187**	**2**	**99**	**28**	**(s)**	**31**	**348**
2010 Average	**266**	**14**	**379**	**659**	**185**	**2**	**100**	**28**	**(s)**	**27**	**343**
2011 Average	**248**	**9**	**347**	**604**	**186**	**2**	**100**	**24**	**(s)**	**23**	**335**
2012 Average	**228**	**4**	**286**	**518**	**168**	**1**	**98**	**21**	**(s)**	**14**	**301**
2013 Average	**233**	**4**	**336**	**573**	**163**	**(s)**	**110**	**22**	**(s)**	**11**	**306**
2014 Average	**253**	**7**	**330**	**589**	**169**	**1**	**108**	**29**	**(s)**	**3**	**311**
2015 January	424	2	345	771	277	(s)	115	[c] 195	(s)	3	590
February	405	7	346	758	265	1	115	200	(s)	3	583
March	290	9	296	595	190	1	98	205	(s)	2	496
April	181	1	277	458	118	(s)	92	208	(s)	1	419
May	175	16	274	465	114	2	91	209	(s)	1	418
June	106	(s)	285	391	69	(s)	95	213	0	1	378
July	118	1	292	411	77	(s)	97	214	0	1	389
August	147	1	281	428	96	(s)	93	214	(s)	1	404
September	144	(s)	269	414	94	(s)	89	210	(s)	1	395
October	353	2	295	650	230	(s)	98	209	(s)	2	540
November	391	1	313	706	256	(s)	104	206	(s)	3	569
December	412	19	337	768	269	3	112	207	(s)	3	593
Average	**262**	**5**	**301**	**567**	**171**	**1**	**100**	**208**	**(s)**	**2**	**481**
2016 January	378	NM	355	731	247	(s)	118	196	(s)	4	565
February	395	1	334	729	258	(s)	111	208	(s)	4	581
March	261	9	299	569	170	1	99	213	(s)	3	487
April	237	4	276	517	155	1	92	208	(s)	2	458
May	208	3	273	484	136	(s)	91	213	0	2	442
June	147	6	263	416	96	1	87	219	(s)	1	404
July	151	7	282	440	99	1	94	217	(s)	2	412
August	118	1	275	394	77	(s)	92	217	0	1	387
September	185	8	299	492	121	1	99	215	0	2	438
October	253	11	296	559	165	1	98	206	0	3	473
November	282	2	294	578	184	(s)	98	209	(s)	3	494
December	442	16	322	781	289	2	107	211	(s)	5	613
Average	**254**	**6**	**297**	**557**	**166**	**1**	**99**	**211**	**(s)**	**3**	**479**
2017 January	423	10	361	794	276	1	120	192	(s)	4	594
February	348	5	320	673	227	1	106	203	(s)	4	541
March	295	1	307	604	193	(s)	102	212	(s)	3	510
April	244	5	291	540	159	1	97	209	(s)	2	469
4-Month Average	**328**	**5**	**320**	**653**	**214**	**1**	**106**	**204**	**(s)**	**3**	**529**
2016 4-Month Average	**317**	**3**	**316**	**636**	**207**	**(s)**	**105**	**206**	**(s)**	**3**	**522**
2015 4-Month Average	**324**	**4**	**316**	**644**	**212**	**1**	**105**	**202**	**(s)**	**2**	**522**

[a] Commercial sector fuel use, including that at commercial combined-heat-and-power (CHP) and commercial electricity-only plants.

[b] Finished motor gasoline. Through 1963, also includes special naphthas. Beginning in 1993, also includes fuel ethanol blended into motor gasoline.

[c] There is a discontinuity in this time series between 2014 and 2015 due to a change in the method for allocating motor gasoline consumption to the end-use sectors. Beginning in 2015, the commercial and industrial sector shares of motor gasoline consumption are larger than in 2014, while the transportation sector share is smaller.

NA=Not available. NM=Not meaningful. (s)=Less than 500 barrels per day and greater than -500 barrels per day.

Notes: • Data are estimates. • For total petroleum consumption by all sectors, see petroleum products supplied data in Table 3.5. Petroleum products supplied is an approximation of petroleum consumption and is synonymous with the term "petroleum consumption" in Tables 3.7a–3.8c. See Note 1, "Petroleum Products Supplied and Petroleum Consumption," at end of section. • Totals may not equal sum of components due to independent rounding. • Geographic coverage is the 50 states and the District of Columbia.

Web Page: See http://www.eia.gov/totalenergy/data/monthly/#petroleum (Excel and CSV files) for all available annual data beginning in 1949 and monthly data beginning in 1973.

Sources: See end of section.

Source: *U.S. Energy Information Administration, Monthly Energy Review, July 2017*

Table 3.7b Petroleum Consumption: Industrial Sector
(Thousand Barrels per Day)

	Industrial Sector[a]									
	Asphalt and Road Oil	Distillate Fuel Oil	Kerosene	Liquefied Petroleum Gases	Lubricants	Motor Gasoline[b,c]	Petroleum Coke	Residual Fuel Oil	Other[d]	Total
1950 Average	**180**	**328**	**132**	**100**	**43**	**131**	**41**	**617**	**250**	**1,822**
1955 Average	**254**	**466**	**116**	**212**	**47**	**173**	**67**	**686**	**366**	**2,387**
1960 Average	**302**	**476**	**78**	**333**	**48**	**198**	**149**	**689**	**435**	**2,708**
1965 Average	**368**	**541**	**80**	**470**	**62**	**179**	**202**	**689**	**657**	**3,247**
1970 Average	**447**	**577**	**89**	**699**	**70**	**150**	**203**	**708**	**866**	**3,808**
1975 Average	**419**	**630**	**58**	**844**	**68**	**116**	**246**	**658**	**1,001**	**4,038**
1980 Average	**396**	**621**	**87**	**1,172**	**82**	**82**	**234**	**586**	**1,581**	**4,842**
1985 Average	**425**	**526**	**21**	**1,285**	**75**	**114**	**261**	**326**	**1,032**	**4,065**
1990 Average	**483**	**541**	**6**	**1,215**	**84**	**97**	**325**	**179**	**1,373**	**4,304**
1995 Average	**486**	**532**	**7**	**1,527**	**80**	**105**	**328**	**147**	**1,381**	**4,594**
2000 Average	**525**	**563**	**8**	**1,720**	**86**	**79**	**361**	**105**	**1,458**	**4,903**
2001 Average	**519**	**611**	**11**	**1,557**	**79**	**155**	**390**	**89**	**1,481**	**4,892**
2002 Average	**512**	**566**	**7**	**1,668**	**78**	**163**	**383**	**83**	**1,474**	**4,934**
2003 Average	**503**	**551**	**12**	**1,560**	**72**	**171**	**375**	**96**	**1,579**	**4,918**
2004 Average	**537**	**570**	**14**	**1,646**	**73**	**195**	**423**	**108**	**1,657**	**5,222**
2005 Average	**546**	**594**	**19**	**1,549**	**72**	**187**	**404**	**123**	**1,605**	**5,100**
2006 Average	**521**	**594**	**14**	**1,627**	**71**	**198**	**425**	**104**	**1,640**	**5,193**
2007 Average	**494**	**595**	**6**	**1,637**	**73**	**161**	**412**	**84**	**1,593**	**5,056**
2008 Average	**417**	**637**	**2**	**1,419**	**67**	**131**	**394**	**84**	**1,408**	**4,559**
2009 Average	**360**	**509**	**2**	**1,541**	**61**	**128**	**363**	**57**	**1,251**	**4,272**
2010 Average	**362**	**547**	**4**	**1,673**	**68**	**140**	**310**	**52**	**1,343**	**4,500**
2011 Average	**355**	**586**	**2**	**1,733**	**64**	**138**	**295**	**59**	**1,272**	**4,503**
2012 Average	**340**	**602**	**1**	**1,841**	**59**	**136**	**319**	**30**	**1,215**	**4,543**
2013 Average	**323**	**601**	**1**	**1,962**	**62**	**142**	**295**	**21**	**1,282**	**4,690**
2014 Average	**327**	**648**	**1**	**1,924**	**65**	**114**	**290**	**18**	**1,204**	**4,591**
2015 January	200	714	(s)	2,322	79	[c]132	342	17	1,142	4,948
February	215	826	1	2,329	63	135	146	8	1,255	4,977
March	222	658	1	1,996	78	138	334	16	1,215	4,660
April	303	650	(s)	1,865	76	140	330	11	1,243	4,619
May	343	466	3	1,847	82	141	330	14	1,351	4,576
June	472	543	(s)	1,919	68	144	357	12	1,324	4,838
July	480	515	(s)	1,965	80	144	335	18	1,343	4,880
August	510	486	(s)	1,890	62	144	350	17	1,309	4,769
September	469	662	(s)	1,812	65	142	222	15	1,179	4,566
October	400	444	(s)	1,989	75	141	281	14	1,090	4,434
November	287	328	(s)	2,110	54	139	264	17	1,203	4,401
December	212	396	3	2,270	67	139	239	18	1,317	4,662
Average	**343**	**555**	**1**	**2,025**	**71**	**140**	**295**	**15**	**1,248**	**4,693**
2016 January	200	583	(s)	2,391	69	132	296	22	1,195	4,888
February	219	634	(s)	2,247	72	140	306	12	1,333	4,965
March	262	651	2	2,017	74	143	304	25	1,108	4,586
April	304	515	1	1,861	66	140	229	30	1,189	4,336
May	392	451	1	1,841	69	144	214	21	1,083	4,214
June	479	504	1	1,769	76	147	185	25	1,156	4,342
July	475	326	1	1,897	58	146	251	28	1,145	4,328
August	527	535	(s)	1,855	62	146	363	21	1,255	4,765
September	438	571	1	2,015	65	145	227	17	1,236	4,715
October	415	585	2	1,992	67	139	271	21	1,259	4,751
November	312	598	(s)	1,982	58	141	440	23	1,118	4,673
December	194	532	3	2,169	62	142	340	20	1,271	4,733
Average	**352**	**540**	**1**	**2,003**	**67**	**142**	**286**	**22**	**1,195**	**4,607**
2017 January	192	521	2	2,429	54	130	355	29	1,221	4,932
February	241	601	1	2,157	64	137	215	16	1,244	4,676
March	265	741	(s)	2,070	68	143	132	23	1,402	4,844
April	318	487	1	1,960	54	141	297	20	1,413	4,691
4-Month Average	**254**	**588**	**1**	**2,156**	**60**	**137**	**250**	**22**	**1,321**	**4,789**
2016 4-Month Average	**246**	**596**	**1**	**2,129**	**70**	**139**	**284**	**22**	**1,204**	**4,692**
2015 4-Month Average	**235**	**710**	**1**	**2,125**	**74**	**136**	**291**	**13**	**1,213**	**4,798**

[a] Industrial sector fuel use, including that at industrial combined-heat-and-power (CHP) and industrial electricity-only plants.

[b] Finished motor gasoline. Through 1963, also includes special naphthas. Beginning in 1993, also includes fuel ethanol blended into motor gasoline.

[c] There is a discontinuity in this time series between 2014 and 2015 due to a change in the method for allocating motor gasoline consumption to the end-use sectors. Beginning in 2015, the commercial and industrial sector shares of motor gasoline consumption are larger than in 2014, while the transportation sector share is smaller.

[d] Pentanes plus, petrochemical feedstocks, still gas (refinery gas), waxes, and miscellaneous products. Beginning in 1964, also includes special naphthas. Beginning in 1981, also includes negative barrels per day of distillate and residual fuel oil reclassified as unfinished oils, and other products (from both primary and secondary supply) reclassified as gasoline blending components. Beginning in 1983, also includes crude oil burned as fuel. Beginning in 2005, also includes naphtha-type jet fuel.

(s)=Less than 500 barrels per day and greater than -500 barrels per day.

Notes: • Data are estimates. • For total petroleum consumption by all sectors, see petroleum products supplied data in Table 3.5. Petroleum products supplied is an approximation of petroleum consumption and is synonymous with the term "petroleum consumption" in Tables 3.7a–3.8c. See Note 1, "Petroleum Products Supplied and Petroleum Consumption," at end of section. • Totals may not equal sum of components due to independent rounding. • Geographic coverage is the 50 states and the District of Columbia.

Web Page: See http://www.eia.gov/totalenergy/data/monthly/#petroleum (Excel and CSV files) for all available annual data beginning in 1949 and monthly data beginning in 1973.

Sources: See end of section.

Source: *U.S. Energy Information Administration, Monthly Energy Review, July 2017*

Table 3.7c Petroleum Consumption: Transportation and Electric Power Sectors
(Thousand Barrels per Day)

	Transportation Sector								Electric Power Sector[a]			
	Aviation Gasoline	Distillate Fuel Oil[b]	Jet Fuel[c]	Liquefied Petroleum Gases	Lubricants	Motor Gasoline[d,e]	Residual Fuel Oil	Total	Distillate Fuel Oil[f]	Petroleum Coke	Residual Fuel Oil[g]	Total
1950 Average	**108**	**226**	**(c)**	**2**	**64**	**2,433**	**524**	**3,356**	**15**	**NA**	**192**	**207**
1955 Average	**192**	**372**	**154**	**9**	**70**	**3,221**	**440**	**4,458**	**15**	**NA**	**191**	**206**
1960 Average	**161**	**418**	**371**	**13**	**68**	**3,736**	**367**	**5,135**	**10**	**NA**	**231**	**241**
1965 Average	**120**	**514**	**602**	**23**	**67**	**4,374**	**336**	**6,036**	**14**	**NA**	**302**	**316**
1970 Average	**55**	**738**	**967**	**32**	**66**	**5,589**	**332**	**7,778**	**66**	**9**	**853**	**928**
1975 Average	**39**	**998**	**992**	**31**	**70**	**6,512**	**310**	**8,951**	**107**	**1**	**1,280**	**1,388**
1980 Average	**35**	**1,311**	**1,062**	**13**	**77**	**6,441**	**608**	**9,546**	**79**	**2**	**1,069**	**1,151**
1985 Average	**27**	**1,491**	**1,218**	**21**	**71**	**6,667**	**342**	**9,838**	**40**	**3**	**435**	**478**
1990 Average	**24**	**1,722**	**1,522**	**16**	**80**	**7,080**	**443**	**10,888**	**45**	**14**	**507**	**566**
1995 Average	**21**	**1,973**	**1,514**	**13**	**76**	**7,674**	**397**	**11,668**	**51**	**37**	**247**	**334**
2000 Average	**20**	**2,422**	**1,725**	**8**	**81**	**8,370**	**386**	**13,012**	**82**	**45**	**378**	**505**
2001 Average	**19**	**2,489**	**1,655**	**10**	**74**	**8,435**	**255**	**12,938**	**80**	**47**	**437**	**564**
2002 Average	**18**	**2,536**	**1,614**	**10**	**73**	**8,662**	**295**	**13,208**	**60**	**80**	**287**	**427**
2003 Average	**16**	**2,629**	**1,578**	**13**	**68**	**8,733**	**249**	**13,286**	**76**	**79**	**379**	**534**
2004 Average	**17**	**2,783**	**1,630**	**14**	**69**	**8,887**	**321**	**13,720**	**52**	**101**	**382**	**535**
2005 Average	**19**	**2,858**	**1,679**	**20**	**68**	**8,948**	**365**	**13,957**	**54**	**111**	**382**	**547**
2006 Average	**18**	**3,017**	**1,633**	**20**	**67**	**9,029**	**395**	**14,178**	**35**	**97**	**157**	**289**
2007 Average	**17**	**3,037**	**1,622**	**16**	**69**	**9,093**	**433**	**14,287**	**42**	**78**	**173**	**293**
2008 Average	**15**	**2,738**	**1,539**	**29**	**64**	**8,834**	**402**	**13,621**	**34**	**70**	**104**	**209**
2009 Average	**14**	**2,626**	**1,393**	**20**	**57**	**8,841**	**344**	**13,297**	**33**	**63**	**79**	**175**
2010 Average	**15**	**2,764**	**1,432**	**21**	**64**	**8,824**	**389**	**13,508**	**38**	**65**	**67**	**170**
2011 Average	**15**	**2,849**	**1,425**	**24**	**61**	**8,591**	**338**	**13,303**	**30**	**66**	**41**	**137**
2012 Average	**14**	**2,719**	**1,398**	**26**	**56**	**8,525**	**291**	**13,029**	**25**	**41**	**33**	**99**
2013 Average	**12**	**2,804**	**1,434**	**32**	**59**	**8,679**	**253**	**13,274**	**26**	**59**	**34**	**119**
2014 Average	**12**	**2,928**	**1,470**	**34**	**61**	**8,778**	**195**	**13,477**	**39**	**57**	**41**	**137**
2015 January	8	2,729	1,375	33	74	[e] 8,312	218	12,749	41	61	57	159
February	8	2,931	1,445	33	60	8,494	35	13,006	132	71	149	352
March	9	2,913	1,548	28	74	8,714	217	13,503	27	43	28	97
April	14	3,058	1,527	26	72	8,842	133	13,672	21	47	27	95
May	13	2,996	1,519	26	77	8,912	194	13,738	26	53	25	105
June	12	3,153	1,654	27	64	9,061	158	14,130	26	50	29	105
July	18	3,168	1,650	28	76	9,112	269	14,320	23	65	38	126
August	11	3,165	1,601	26	59	9,102	247	14,211	22	61	33	116
September	11	3,142	1,534	25	62	8,937	221	13,932	21	61	30	112
October	14	2,967	1,614	28	70	8,895	193	13,781	20	47	27	94
November	9	2,740	1,524	30	51	8,767	250	13,370	26	42	30	99
December	9	2,731	1,578	32	63	8,801	270	13,484	24	43	26	93
Average	**11**	**2,974**	**1,548**	**28**	**67**	**8,831**	**202**	**13,662**	**33**	**54**	**41**	**128**
2016 January	7	2,571	1,449	33	65	8,342	280	12,747	38	53	34	124
February	11	2,644	1,525	31	68	8,858	145	13,282	28	55	39	123
March	10	2,838	1,536	28	70	9,043	349	13,875	21	58	21	100
April	14	2,896	1,560	26	62	8,864	425	13,848	20	63	22	105
May	11	2,925	1,562	26	65	9,079	286	13,955	25	57	24	106
June	12	3,061	1,714	25	72	9,298	344	14,525	23	61	28	112
July	12	2,977	1,715	27	55	9,234	383	14,401	26	63	43	131
August	14	3,135	1,710	26	59	9,232	279	14,454	25	66	41	132
September	11	3,008	1,624	28	62	9,133	242	14,107	20	62	29	111
October	10	3,002	1,605	28	64	8,751	291	13,750	19	39	30	88
November	12	2,871	1,627	28	55	8,894	325	13,810	25	49	24	99
December	10	2,768	1,649	30	59	8,957	270	13,743	29	53	28	109
Average	**11**	**2,892**	**1,606**	**28**	**63**	**8,973**	**302**	**13,876**	**25**	**57**	**30**	**112**
2017 January	9	2,529	1,593	34	51	8,181	399	12,797	32	57	28	117
February	9	2,701	1,525	30	60	8,648	224	13,197	27	47	26	100
March	10	2,898	1,669	29	64	8,999	313	13,982	26	43	24	93
April	10	2,877	1,617	27	51	8,898	273	13,754	24	25	24	73
4-Month Average	**10**	**2,752**	**1,603**	**30**	**56**	**8,680**	**304**	**13,436**	**27**	**43**	**25**	**96**
2016 4-Month Average	**10**	**2,737**	**1,517**	**30**	**66**	**8,775**	**301**	**13,437**	**27**	**57**	**29**	**113**
2015 4-Month Average	**10**	**2,906**	**1,474**	**30**	**70**	**8,591**	**154**	**13,235**	**53**	**55**	**63**	**172**

[a] Electricity-only and combined-heat-and-power (CHP) plants within the NAICS 22 category whose primary business is to sell electricity, or electricity and heat, to the public. Through 1988, data are for electric utilities only; beginning in 1989, data are for electric utilities and independent power producers.

[b] Beginning in 2009, includes renewable diesel fuel (including biodiesel) blended into distillate fuel oil.

[c] Beginning in 1957, includes kerosene-type jet fuel. For 1952–2004, also includes naphtha-type jet fuel. (Through 1951, naphtha-type jet fuel is included in the products from which it was blended—gasoline, kerosene, and distillate fuel oil. Beginning in 2005, naphtha-type jet fuel is included in "Other" on Table 3.7b.)

[d] Finished motor gasoline. Through 1963, also includes special naphthas. Beginning in 1993, also includes fuel ethanol blended into motor gasoline.

[e] There is a discontinuity in this time series between 2014 and 2015 due to a change in the method for allocating motor gasoline consumption to the end-use sectors. Beginning in 2015, the commercial and industrial sector shares of motor gasoline consumption are larger than in 2014, while the transportation sector share is smaller.

[f] Fuel oil nos. 1, 2, and 4. Through 1979, data are for gas turbine and internal combustion plant use of petroleum. Through 2000, electric utility data also include small amounts of kerosene and jet fuel.

[g] Fuel oil nos. 5 and 6. Through 1979, data are for steam plant use of petroleum. Through 2000, electric utility data also include a small amount of fuel oil no. 4.

NA=Not available.

Notes: • Transportation sector data are estimates. • For total petroleum consumption by all sectors, see petroleum products supplied data in Table 3.5. Petroleum products supplied is an approximation of petroleum consumption and is synonymous with the term "petroleum consumption" in Tables 3.7a–3.8c. Other measurements of consumption by fuel type or sector may differ. For example, jet fuel product supplied may not equal jet fuel consumed by U.S-flagged aircraft. See Note 1, "Petroleum Products Supplied and Petroleum Consumption," at end of section. • Totals may not equal sum of components due to independent rounding. • Geographic coverage is the 50 states and the District of Columbia.

Web Page: See http://www.eia.gov/totalenergy/data/monthly/#petroleum (Excel and CSV files) for all available annual data beginning in 1949 and monthly data beginning in 1973.

Sources: See end of section.

Source: *U.S. Energy Information Administration, Monthly Energy Review, July 2017*

Figure 3.8a Heat Content of Petroleum Consumption by End-Use Sector, 1949–2016
(Quadrillion Btu)

Residential and Commercial[a] Sectors, Selected Products

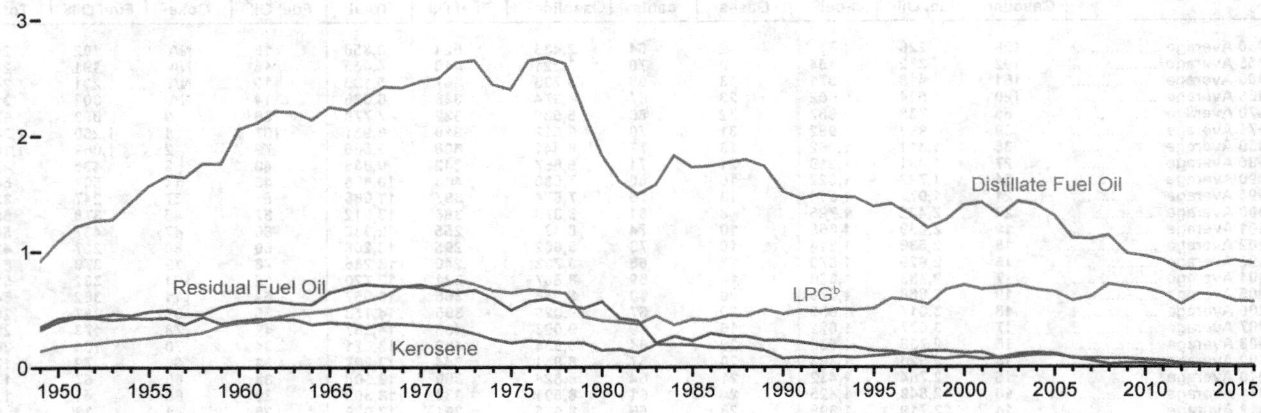

Industrial[a] Sector, Selected Products

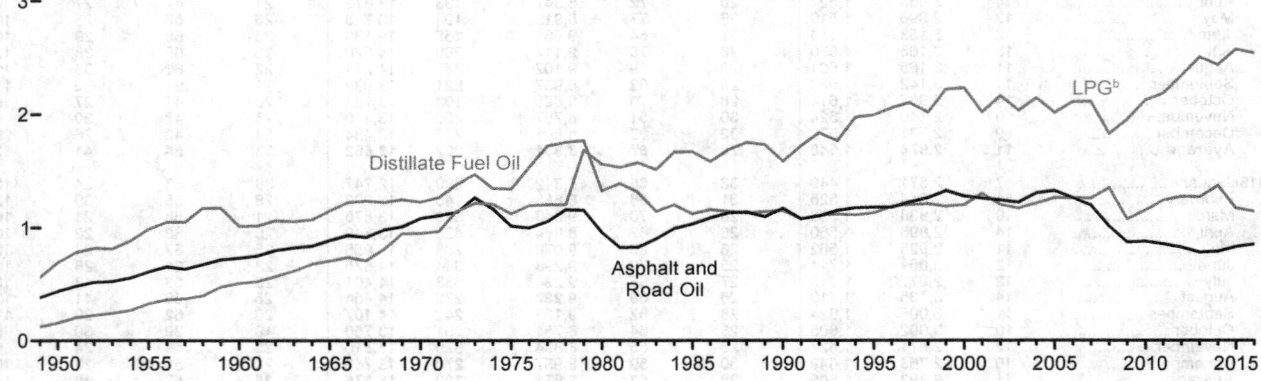

Transportation Sector, Selected Products

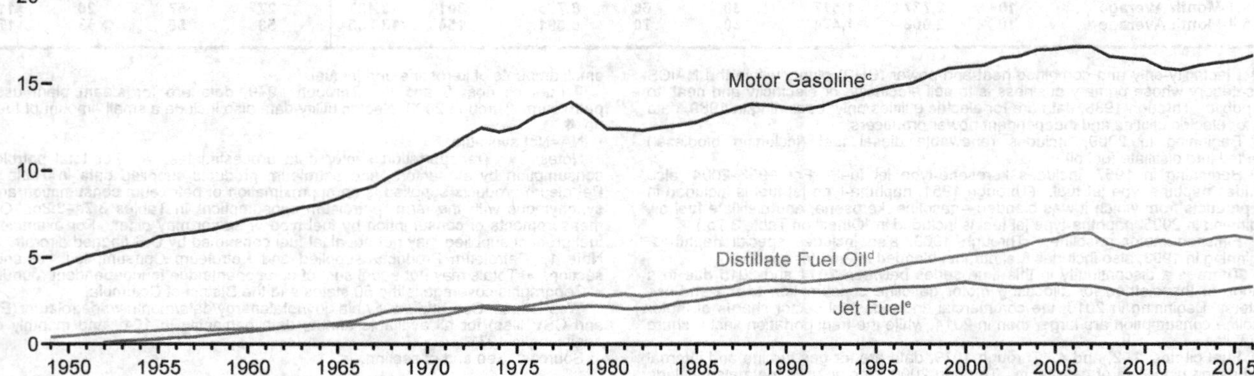

[a] Includes combined-heat-and-power plants and a small number of electricity-only plants.
[b] Liquefied petroleum gases.
[c] Beginning in 1993, includes fuel ethanol blended into motor gasoline.
[d] Beginning in 2009, includes renewable diesel fuel (including biodiesel) blended into distillate fuel oil.
[e] Beginning in 2005, includes kerosene-type jet fuel only.

Note: Petroleum products supplied is an approximation of petroleum consumption and is synonymous with the term "petroleum consumption" in Tables 3.7a–3.8c. Other measurements of consumption by fuel type or sector may differ. For example, jet fuel product supplied may not equal jet fuel consumed by U.S.-flagged aircraft.

Web Page: http://www.eia.gov/totalenergy/data/monthly/#petroleum.

Sources: Tables 3.8a–3.8c.

***Source:** U.S. Energy Information Administration, Monthly Energy Review, July 2017*

Figure 3.8b Heat Content of Petroleum Consumption by End-Use Sector, Monthly
(Quadrillion Btu)

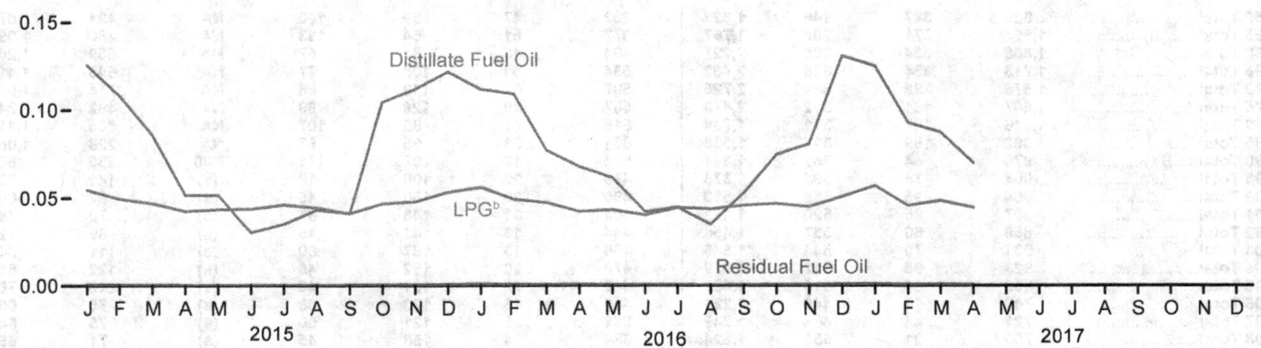

Industrial[a] Sector, Selected Products

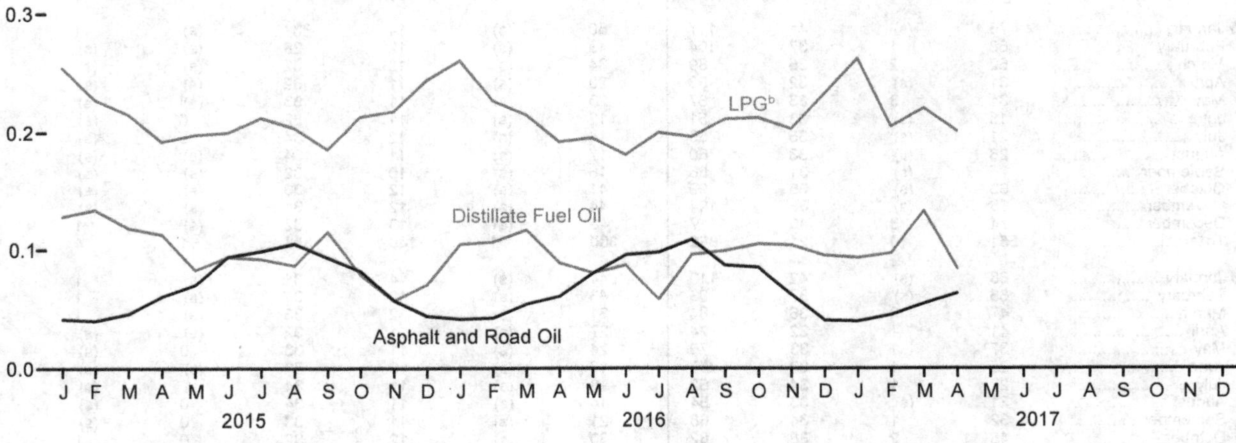

Transportation Sector, Selected Products

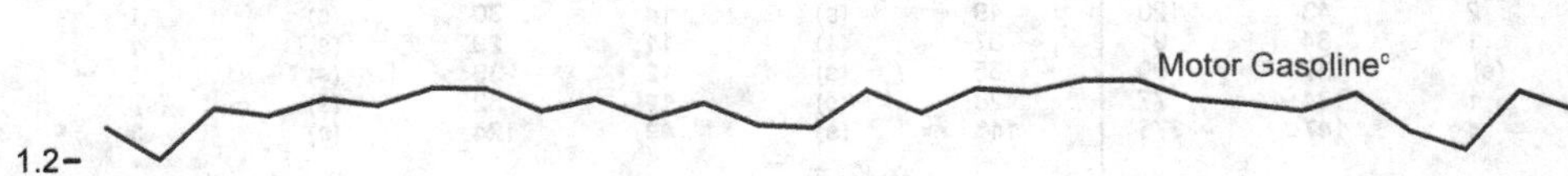

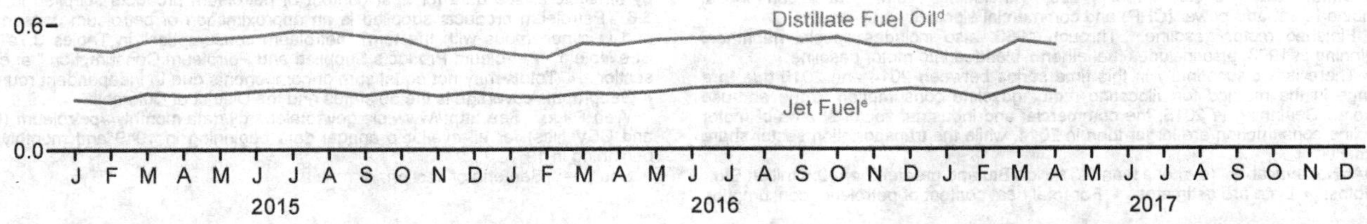

[a] Includes combined-heat-and-power plants and a small number of electricity-only plants.
[b] Liquefied petroleum gases.
[c] Includes fuel ethanol blended into motor gasoline.
[d] Includes renewable diesel fuel (including biodiesel) blended into distillate fuel oil.
[e] Includes kerosene-type jet fuel only.

Note: Petroleum products supplied is an approximation of petroleum consumption and is synonymous with the term "petroleum consumption" in Tables 3.7a–3.8c. Other measurements of consumption by fuel type or sector may differ. For example, jet fuel product supplied may not equal jet fuel consumed by U.S.-flagged aircraft.

Web Page: http://www.eia.gov/totalenergy/data/monthly/#petroleum.

Sources: Tables 3.8a–3.8c.

Source: *U.S. Energy Information Administration, Monthly Energy Review, July 2017*

Table 3.8a Heat Content of Petroleum Consumption: Residential and Commercial Sectors
(Trillion Btu)

	Residential Sector				Commercial Sector[a]						
	Distillate Fuel Oil	Kerosene	Liquefied Petroleum Gases	Total	Distillate Fuel Oil	Kerosene	Liquefied Petroleum Gases	Motor Gasoline[b,c]	Petroleum Coke	Residual Fuel Oil	Total
1950 Total	**829**	**347**	**146**	**1,322**	**262**	**47**	**39**	**100**	**NA**	**424**	**872**
1955 Total	**1,194**	**371**	**202**	**1,767**	**377**	**51**	**54**	**133**	**NA**	**480**	**1,095**
1960 Total	**1,568**	**354**	**305**	**2,227**	**494**	**48**	**81**	**67**	**NA**	**559**	**1,248**
1965 Total	**1,713**	**334**	**385**	**2,432**	**534**	**54**	**103**	**77**	**NA**	**645**	**1,413**
1970 Total	**1,878**	**298**	**549**	**2,725**	**587**	**61**	**143**	**86**	**NA**	**714**	**1,592**
1975 Total	**1,807**	**161**	**512**	**2,479**	**587**	**49**	**129**	**89**	**NA**	**492**	**1,346**
1980 Total	**1,316**	**107**	**311**	**1,734**	**518**	**41**	**88**	**107**	**NA**	**565**	**1,318**
1985 Total	**1,092**	**159**	**314**	**1,565**	**631**	**33**	**95**	**96**	**NA**	**228**	**1,083**
1990 Total	**978**	**64**	**352**	**1,394**	**536**	**12**	**102**	**111**	**0**	**230**	**991**
1995 Total	**904**	**74**	**395**	**1,373**	**478**	**22**	**109**	**18**	**(s)**	**141**	**769**
2000 Total	**904**	**95**	**555**	**1,553**	**490**	**30**	**150**	**45**	**(s)**	**92**	**807**
2001 Total	**907**	**95**	**526**	**1,528**	**508**	**31**	**143**	**37**	**(s)**	**70**	**789**
2002 Total	**859**	**60**	**537**	**1,456**	**444**	**16**	**141**	**45**	**(s)**	**80**	**726**
2003 Total	**931**	**70**	**544**	**1,546**	**496**	**19**	**157**	**60**	**(s)**	**111**	**842**
2004 Total	**923**	**85**	**512**	**1,519**	**470**	**20**	**152**	**45**	**(s)**	**122**	**810**
2005 Total	**853**	**84**	**513**	**1,450**	**447**	**22**	**131**	**46**	**(s)**	**116**	**762**
2006 Total	**709**	**66**	**446**	**1,221**	**400**	**15**	**123**	**48**	**(s)**	**75**	**662**
2007 Total	**721**	**44**	**484**	**1,249**	**381**	**9**	**121**	**60**	**(s)**	**75**	**648**
2008 Total	**750**	**21**	**553**	**1,324**	**384**	**4**	**158**	**45**	**(s)**	**71**	**663**
2009 Total	**582**	**28**	**547**	**1,157**	**395**	**4**	**139**	**52**	**(s)**	**71**	**662**
2010 Total	**562**	**29**	**530**	**1,121**	**391**	**5**	**140**	**52**	**(s)**	**62**	**650**
2011 Total	**523**	**19**	**486**	**1,027**	**391**	**3**	**141**	**44**	**(s)**	**54**	**633**
2012 Total	**482**	**8**	**402**	**892**	**355**	**1**	**138**	**39**	**(s)**	**31**	**564**
2013 Total	**491**	**8**	**470**	**970**	**344**	**1**	**154**	**40**	**(s)**	**24**	**563**
2014 Total	**533**	**14**	**462**	**1,009**	**357**	**2**	**151**	**54**	**1**	**8**	**572**
2015 January	76	(s)	41	117	50	(s)	14	[c] 31	(s)	1	95
February	66	1	37	104	43	(s)	12	28	(s)	(s)	84
March	52	2	35	89	34	(s)	12	32	(s)	(s)	78
April	31	(s)	32	63	20	(s)	11	32	(s)	(s)	63
May	31	3	33	67	20	(s)	11	33	(s)	(s)	65
June	18	(s)	33	51	12	(s)	11	32	0	(s)	55
July	21	(s)	35	56	14	(s)	12	34	0	(s)	59
August	26	(s)	33	60	17	(s)	11	34	(s)	(s)	62
September	25	(s)	31	56	16	(s)	10	32	(s)	(s)	59
October	63	(s)	35	99	41	(s)	12	33	(s)	(s)	86
November	68	(s)	36	104	44	(s)	12	31	(s)	(s)	88
December	74	3	40	117	48	(s)	13	32	(s)	1	95
Total	**551**	**10**	**421**	**982**	**360**	**1**	**140**	**383**	**1**	**4**	**889**
2016 January	68	(s)	42	110	44	(s)	14	31	(s)	1	90
February	66	(s)	37	103	43	(s)	12	31	(s)	1	87
March	47	2	36	84	31	(s)	12	33	(s)	1	76
April	41	1	32	74	27	(s)	11	32	(s)	(s)	70
May	37	1	33	70	24	(s)	11	33	0	(s)	69
June	25	1	30	57	17	(s)	10	33	(s)	(s)	60
July	27	1	34	62	18	(s)	11	34	(s)	(s)	63
August	21	(s)	33	54	14	(s)	11	34	0	(s)	59
September	32	1	34	68	21	(s)	11	33	0	(s)	65
October	45	2	35	82	30	(s)	12	32	0	1	74
November	49	(s)	34	83	32	(s)	11	32	(s)	1	75
December	79	3	38	120	52	(s)	13	33	(s)	1	99
Total	**538**	**11**	**418**	**967**	**351**	**2**	**139**	**391**	**(s)**	**6**	**888**
2017 January	76	2	43	120	49	(s)	14	30	(s)	1	95
February	56	1	34	91	37	(s)	11	29	(s)	1	78
March	53	(s)	37	90	35	(s)	12	33	(s)	1	81
April	42	1	34	77	28	(s)	11	32	(s)	(s)	71
4-Month Total	**227**	**4**	**147**	**378**	**148**	**(s)**	**49**	**124**	**(s)**	**3**	**324**
2016 4-Month Total	**221**	**2**	**147**	**370**	**145**	**(s)**	**49**	**126**	**(s)**	**2**	**323**
2015 4-Month Total	**225**	**3**	**145**	**373**	**147**	**(s)**	**48**	**123**	**(s)**	**2**	**320**

[a] Commercial sector fuel use, including that at commercial combined-heat-and-power (CHP) and commercial electricity-only plants.

[b] Finished motor gasoline. Through 1963, also includes special naphthas. Beginning in 1993, also includes fuel ethanol blended into motor gasoline.

[c] There is a discontinuity in this time series between 2014 and 2015 due to a change in the method for allocating motor gasoline consumption to the end-use sectors. Beginning in 2015, the commercial and industrial sector shares of motor gasoline consumption are larger than in 2014, while the transportation sector share is smaller.

NA=Not available. (s)=Less than 0.5 trillion Btu and greater than -0.5 trillion Btu.

Notes: • Data are estimates. • For total heat content of petroleum consumption by all sectors, see data for heat content of petroleum products supplied in Table 3.6. Petroleum products supplied is an approximation of petroleum consumption and is synonymous with the term "petroleum consumption" in Tables 3.7a–3.8c. See Note 1, "Petroleum Products Supplied and Petroleum Consumption," at end of section. • Totals may not equal sum of components due to independent rounding. • Geographic coverage is the 50 states and the District of Columbia.

Web Page: See http://www.eia.gov/totalenergy/data/monthly/#petroleum (Excel and CSV files) for all available annual data beginning in 1949 and monthly data beginning in 1973.

Sources: See end of section.

Source: *U.S. Energy Information Administration, Monthly Energy Review, July 2017*

Table 3.8b Heat Content of Petroleum Consumption: Industrial Sector
(Trillion Btu)

	Industrial Sector[a]									
	Asphalt and Road Oil	Distillate Fuel Oil	Kerosene	Liquefied Petroleum Gases	Lubricants	Motor Gasoline[b,c]	Petroleum Coke	Residual Fuel Oil	Other[d]	Total
1950 Total	435	698	274	156	94	251	90	1,416	546	3,960
1955 Total	615	991	241	323	103	332	147	1,573	798	5,123
1960 Total	734	1,016	161	507	107	381	328	1,584	947	5,766
1965 Total	890	1,150	165	712	137	342	444	1,582	1,390	6,813
1970 Total	1,082	1,226	185	953	155	288	446	1,624	1,817	7,776
1975 Total	1,014	1,339	119	1,123	149	223	540	1,509	2,109	8,127
1980 Total	962	1,324	181	1,559	182	158	516	1,349	3,278	9,509
1985 Total	1,029	1,119	44	1,664	166	218	575	748	2,152	7,714
1990 Total	1,170	1,150	12	1,582	186	185	714	411	2,839	8,251
1995 Total	1,178	1,130	15	1,990	178	200	721	337	2,837	8,587
2000 Total	1,276	1,199	16	2,228	190	150	796	241	2,979	9,075
2001 Total	1,257	1,299	23	2,014	174	295	858	203	3,056	9,179
2002 Total	1,240	1,203	14	2,160	172	309	842	190	3,040	9,170
2003 Total	1,220	1,169	24	2,028	159	324	825	220	3,264	9,233
2004 Total	1,304	1,213	28	2,141	161	371	937	249	3,428	9,832
2005 Total	1,323	1,262	39	2,009	160	355	894	281	3,318	9,641
2006 Total	1,261	1,258	30	2,104	156	374	938	239	3,416	9,777
2007 Total	1,197	1,256	13	2,106	161	302	910	193	3,313	9,452
2008 Total	1,012	1,348	4	1,823	150	246	870	194	2,941	8,588
2009 Total	873	1,073	4	1,950	135	238	805	130	2,611	7,819
2010 Total	878	1,153	7	2,121	149	260	694	120	2,800	8,183
2011 Total	859	1,236	4	2,179	142	255	663	135	2,676	8,148
2012 Total	827	1,271	2	2,335	130	252	717	70	2,558	8,163
2013 Total	783	1,266	1	2,498	138	263	663	48	2,677	8,339
2014 Total	793	1,366	3	2,430	144	210	653	41	2,518	8,157
2015 January	41	128	(s)	254	15	[c]21	65	3	202	729
February	40	134	(s)	228	11	19	26	1	200	658
March	46	118	(s)	215	15	22	63	3	213	695
April	60	113	(s)	193	14	21	61	2	212	675
May	70	83	(s)	198	15	22	63	3	241	696
June	94	94	(s)	200	12	22	66	2	227	718
July	99	92	(s)	213	15	23	64	4	239	748
August	105	87	(s)	204	12	23	67	3	229	730
September	93	115	(s)	186	12	21	41	3	202	673
October	82	80	(s)	213	14	22	54	3	190	658
November	57	57	(s)	218	10	21	49	3	207	621
December	44	71	1	244	13	22	46	4	233	676
Total	832	1,170	2	2,567	157	258	663	34	2,595	8,277
2016 January	41	104	(s)	261	13	21	57	4	218	719
February	42	106	(s)	227	13	21	55	2	230	696
March	54	116	(s)	215	14	22	58	5	203	688
April	61	89	(s)	192	12	21	43	6	211	635
May	81	81	(s)	196	13	23	41	4	199	637
June	95	87	(s)	182	14	22	35	5	206	645
July	98	58	(s)	200	11	23	48	5	209	653
August	109	96	(s)	197	12	23	69	4	230	740
September	87	99	(s)	212	12	22	42	3	218	695
October	85	105	(s)	213	13	22	52	4	227	721
November	62	104	(s)	203	11	21	81	4	197	684
December	40	95	(s)	233	12	22	65	4	230	702
Total	855	1,141	2	2,531	148	263	646	51	2,579	8,216
2017 January	39	93	(s)	262	10	20	68	6	222	721
February	45	97	(s)	206	11	19	37	3	203	621
March	54	133	(s)	221	13	22	25	4	253	726
April	63	84	(s)	202	10	21	55	4	248	687
4-Month Total	202	407	1	890	44	83	185	17	926	2,755
2016 4-Month Total	198	416	(s)	896	52	85	212	17	862	2,738
2015 4-Month Total	187	492	1	890	54	83	215	10	827	2,758

[a] Industrial sector fuel use, including that at industrial combined-heat-and-power (CHP) and industrial electricity-only plants.

[b] Finished motor gasoline. Through 1963, also includes special naphthas. Beginning in 1993, also includes fuel ethanol blended into motor gasoline.

[c] There is a discontinuity in this time series between 2014 and 2015 due to a change in the method for allocating motor gasoline consumption to the end-use sectors. Beginning in 2015, the commercial and industrial sector shares of motor gasoline consumption are larger than in 2014, while the transportation sector share is smaller.

[d] Pentanes plus, petrochemical feedstocks, still gas (refinery gas), waxes, and miscellaneous products. Beginning in 1964, also includes special naphthas. Beginning in 1981, also includes negative barrels per day of distillate and residual fuel oil reclassified as unfinished oils, and other products (from both primary and secondary supply) reclassified as gasoline blending components. Beginning in 1983, also includes crude oil burned as fuel. Beginning in 2005, also includes naphtha-type jet fuel.

(s)=Less than 0.5 trillion Btu and greater than -0.5 trillion Btu.

Notes: • Data are estimates. • For total heat content of petroleum consumption by all sectors, see data for heat content of petroleum products supplied in Table 3.6. Petroleum products supplied is an approximation of petroleum consumption and is synonymous with the term "petroleum consumption" in Tables 3.7a–3.8c. See Note 1, "Petroleum Products Supplied and Petroleum Consumption," at end of section. • Totals may not equal sum of components due to independent rounding. • Geographic coverage is the 50 states and the District of Columbia.

Web Page: See http://www.eia.gov/totalenergy/data/monthly/#petroleum (Excel and CSV files) for all available annual data beginning in 1949 and monthly data beginning in 1973.

Sources: See end of section.

Source: *U.S. Energy Information Administration, Monthly Energy Review, July 2017*

Table 3.8c Heat Content of Petroleum Consumption: Transportation and Electric Power Sectors (Trillion Btu)

	Transportation Sector								Electric Power Sector[a]			
	Aviation Gasoline	Distillate Fuel Oil[b]	Jet Fuel[c]	Liquefied Petroleum Gases	Lubricants	Motor Gasoline[d,e]	Residual Fuel Oil	Total	Distillate Fuel Oil[f]	Petroleum Coke	Residual Fuel Oil[g]	Total
1950 Total	**199**	**480**	**(c)**	**3**	**141**	**4,664**	**1,201**	**6,690**	**32**	**NA**	**440**	**472**
1955 Total	**354**	**791**	**301**	**13**	**155**	**6,175**	**1,009**	**8,799**	**32**	**NA**	**439**	**471**
1960 Total	**298**	**892**	**739**	**19**	**152**	**7,183**	**844**	**10,125**	**22**	**NA**	**530**	**553**
1965 Total	**222**	**1,093**	**1,215**	**32**	**149**	**8,386**	**770**	**11,866**	**29**	**NA**	**693**	**722**
1970 Total	**100**	**1,569**	**1,973**	**44**	**147**	**10,716**	**761**	**15,310**	**141**	**19**	**1,958**	**2,117**
1975 Total	**71**	**2,121**	**2,029**	**43**	**155**	**12,485**	**711**	**17,615**	**226**	**2**	**2,937**	**3,166**
1980 Total	**64**	**2,795**	**2,179**	**18**	**172**	**12,383**	**1,398**	**19,009**	**169**	**5**	**2,459**	**2,634**
1985 Total	**50**	**3,170**	**2,497**	**30**	**156**	**12,784**	**786**	**19,472**	**85**	**7**	**998**	**1,090**
1990 Total	**45**	**3,661**	**3,129**	**23**	**176**	**13,575**	**1,016**	**21,626**	**97**	**30**	**1,163**	**1,289**
1995 Total	**40**	**4,191**	**3,132**	**18**	**168**	**14,616**	**911**	**23,075**	**108**	**81**	**566**	**755**
2000 Total	**36**	**5,159**	**3,580**	**12**	**179**	**15,973**	**888**	**25,827**	**175**	**99**	**871**	**1,144**
2001 Total	**35**	**5,286**	**3,426**	**14**	**164**	**16,053**	**586**	**25,564**	**170**	**103**	**1,003**	**1,276**
2002 Total	**34**	**5,387**	**3,340**	**14**	**162**	**16,474**	**677**	**26,089**	**127**	**175**	**659**	**961**
2003 Total	**30**	**5,584**	**3,265**	**18**	**150**	**16,585**	**571**	**26,203**	**161**	**175**	**869**	**1,205**
2004 Total	**31**	**5,925**	**3,383**	**19**	**152**	**16,917**	**740**	**27,166**	**111**	**211**	**879**	**1,201**
2005 Total	**35**	**6,068**	**3,475**	**28**	**151**	**16,977**	**837**	**27,573**	**114**	**231**	**876**	**1,222**
2006 Total	**33**	**6,390**	**3,379**	**27**	**147**	**17,108**	**906**	**27,991**	**73**	**203**	**361**	**637**
2007 Total	**32**	**6,411**	**3,358**	**22**	**152**	**17,109**	**994**	**28,077**	**89**	**163**	**397**	**648**
2008 Total	**28**	**5,792**	**3,193**	**40**	**141**	**16,574**	**926**	**26,695**	**73**	**146**	**240**	**459**
2009 Total	**27**	**5,541**	**2,883**	**28**	**127**	**16,460**	**791**	**25,857**	**70**	**132**	**181**	**382**
2010 Total	**27**	**5,828**	**2,963**	**29**	**141**	**16,356**	**892**	**26,236**	**80**	**137**	**154**	**370**
2011 Total	**27**	**6,003**	**2,950**	**34**	**134**	**15,892**	**776**	**25,817**	**64**	**138**	**93**	**295**
2012 Total	**25**	**5,741**	**2,901**	**37**	**123**	**15,798**	**671**	**25,297**	**52**	**85**	**77**	**214**
2013 Total	**22**	**5,902**	**2,969**	**44**	**130**	**16,036**	**581**	**25,685**	**55**	**123**	**77**	**255**
2014 Total	**22**	**6,162**	**3,042**	**47**	**136**	**16,212**	**447**	**26,067**	**82**	**118**	**95**	**295**
2015 January	1	488	242	4	14	[e] 1,304	42	2,095	7	11	11	29
February	1	473	229	4	10	1,203	6	1,927	21	11	26	59
March	1	521	272	3	14	1,367	42	2,221	5	8	5	18
April	2	529	260	3	13	1,342	25	2,174	4	8	5	17
May	2	535	267	3	15	1,398	38	2,258	5	9	5	19
June	2	545	281	3	12	1,375	30	2,249	4	9	6	19
July	3	566	290	3	14	1,429	52	2,358	4	11	7	23
August	2	566	281	3	11	1,428	48	2,339	4	11	6	21
September	2	543	261	3	11	1,357	42	2,218	4	10	6	20
October	2	530	284	3	13	1,395	38	2,266	4	8	5	17
November	1	474	259	3	9	1,331	47	2,125	5	7	6	18
December	1	488	277	4	12	1,381	53	2,216	4	8	5	17
Total	**21**	**6,259**	**3,204**	**40**	**148**	**16,310**	**463**	**26,445**	**70**	**112**	**94**	**276**
2016 January	1	460	255	4	12	1,308	54	2,094	7	9	7	23
February	2	442	251	3	12	1,300	26	2,036	5	9	7	21
March	2	507	270	3	13	1,418	68	2,282	4	10	4	18
April	2	501	265	3	11	1,345	80	2,208	3	11	4	18
May	2	523	275	3	12	1,424	56	2,294	5	10	5	19
June	2	529	292	3	13	1,411	65	2,315	4	11	5	20
July	2	532	301	3	10	1,448	75	2,371	5	11	8	24
August	2	560	300	3	11	1,448	54	2,379	4	12	8	24
September	2	520	276	3	11	1,386	46	2,244	4	11	5	20
October	2	536	282	3	12	1,372	57	2,264	3	7	6	16
November	2	496	277	3	10	1,350	61	2,199	4	8	5	17
December	1	495	290	4	11	1,405	53	2,258	5	9	6	20
Total	**20**	**6,102**	**3,334**	**39**	**140**	**16,615**	**695**	**26,945**	**53**	**118**	**69**	**240**
2017 January	1	452	280	4	10	1,283	78	2,108	6	10	5	21
February	1	436	242	3	10	1,225	39	1,957	4	8	5	16
March	2	518	293	3	12	1,411	61	2,301	5	8	5	17
April	2	498	275	3	9	1,350	51	2,189	4	4	5	13
4-Month Total	**6**	**1,903**	**1,091**	**14**	**41**	**5,270**	**230**	**8,554**	**19**	**30**	**19**	**68**
2016 4-Month Total	**6**	**1,910**	**1,041**	**14**	**49**	**5,371**	**229**	**8,620**	**19**	**40**	**22**	**80**
2015 4-Month Total	**6**	**2,011**	**1,003**	**14**	**51**	**5,216**	**116**	**8,417**	**37**	**38**	**48**	**123**

[a] Electricity-only and combined-heat-and-power (CHP) plants within the NAICS 22 category whose primary business is to sell electricity, or electricity and heat, to the public. Through 1988, data are for electric utilities only; beginning in 1989, data are for electric utilities and independent power producers.

[b] Beginning in 2009, includes renewable diesel fuel (including biodiesel) blended into distillate fuel oil.

[c] Beginning in 1957, includes kerosene-type jet fuel. For 1952–2004, also includes naphtha-type jet fuel. (Through 1951, naphtha-type jet fuel is included in the products from which it was blended—gasoline, kerosene, and distillate fuel oil. Beginning in 2005, naphtha-type jet fuel is included in "Other" on Table 3.8b.)

[d] Finished motor gasoline. Through 1963, also includes special naphthas. Beginning in 1993, also includes fuel ethanol blended into motor gasoline.

[e] There is a discontinuity in this time series between 2014 and 2015 due to a change in the method for allocating motor gasoline consumption to the end-use sectors. Beginning in 2015, the commercial and industrial sector shares of motor gasoline consumption are larger than in 2014, while the transportation sector share is smaller.

[f] Fuel oil nos. 1, 2, and 4. Through 1979, data are for gas turbine and internal combustion plant use of petroleum. Through 2000, electric utility data also include small amounts of kerosene and jet fuel.

[g] Fuel oil nos. 5 and 6. Through 1979, data are for steam plant use of petroleum. Through 2000, electric utility data also include a small amount of fuel oil no. 4.

NA=Not available.

Notes: • Transportation sector data are estimates. • For total heat content of petroleum consumption by all sectors, see data for heat content of petroleum products supplied in Table 3.6. Petroleum products supplied is an approximation of petroleum consumption and is synonymous with the term "petroleum consumption" in Tables 3.7a–3.8c. Other measurements of consumption by fuel type or sector may differ. For example, jet fuel product supplied may not equal jet fuel consumed by U.S.-flagged aircraft. See Note 1, "Petroleum Products Supplied and Petroleum Consumption," at end of section. • Totals may not equal sum of components due to independent rounding. • Geographic coverage is the 50 states and the District of Columbia.

Web Page: See http://www.eia.gov/totalenergy/data/monthly/#petroleum (Excel and CSV files) for all available annual data beginning in 1949 and monthly data beginning in 1973.

Sources: See end of section.

Source: *U.S. Energy Information Administration, Monthly Energy Review, July 2017*

Figure 4.1 Natural Gas
(Trillion Cubic Feet)

Overview, 1949–2016

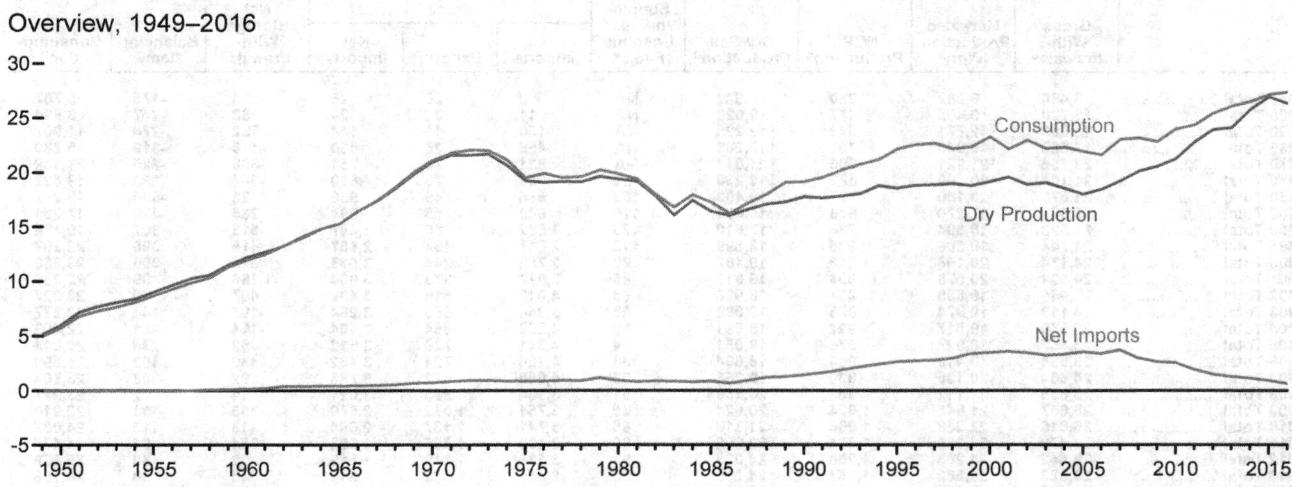

Consumption by Sector, 1949–2016

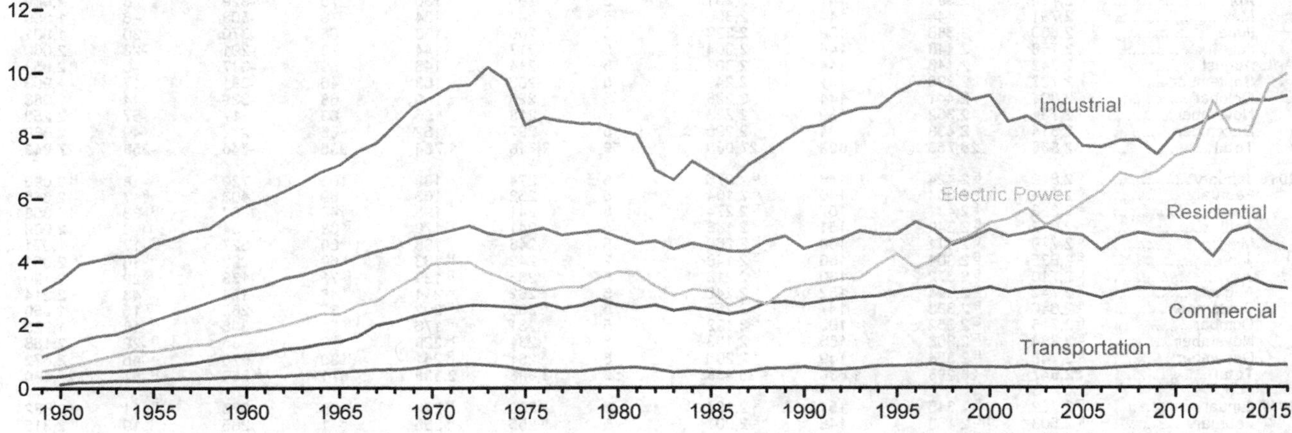

Overview, Monthly

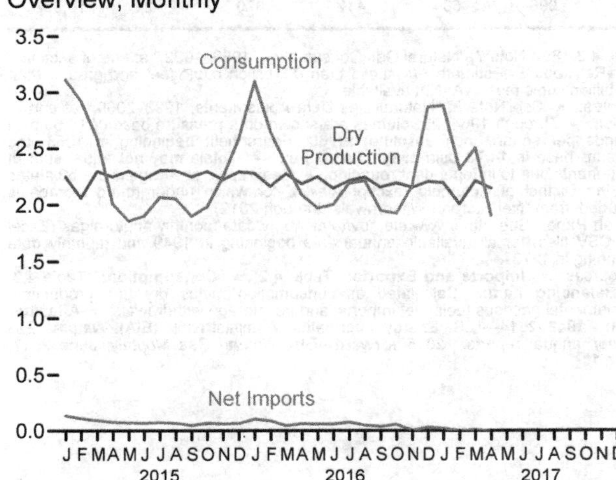

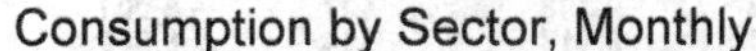

Consumption by Sector, Monthly

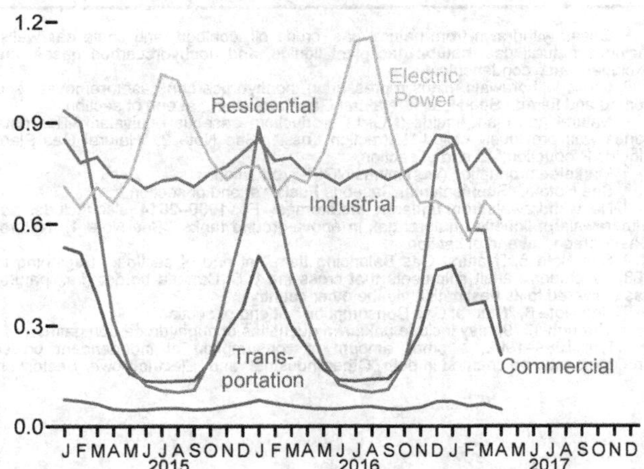

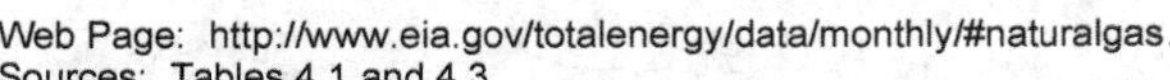

Web Page: http://www.eia.gov/totalenergy/data/monthly/#naturalgas.
Sources: Tables 4.1 and 4.3.

Source: *U.S. Energy Information Administration, Monthly Energy Review, July 2017*

Table 4.1 Natural Gas Overview
(Billion Cubic Feet)

	Gross With-drawals[a]	Marketed Production (Wet)[b]	NGPL Production[c]	Dry Gas Production[d]	Supple-mental Gaseous Fuels[e]	Trade			Net Storage With-drawals[f]	Balancing Item[g]	Consump-tion[h]
						Imports	Exports	Net Imports			
1950 Total	8,480	[i]6,282	260	[i]6,022	NA	0	26	-26	-54	-175	5,767
1955 Total	11,720	[i]9,405	377	[i]9,029	NA	11	31	-20	-68	-247	8,694
1960 Total	15,088	[i]12,771	543	[i]12,228	NA	156	11	144	-132	-274	11,967
1965 Total	17,963	[i]16,040	753	[i]15,286	NA	456	26	430	-118	-319	15,280
1970 Total	23,786	[i]21,921	906	[i]21,014	NA	821	70	751	-398	-228	21,139
1975 Total	21,104	[i]20,109	872	[i]19,236	NA	953	73	880	-344	-235	19,538
1980 Total	21,870	20,180	777	19,403	155	985	49	936	23	-640	19,877
1985 Total	19,607	17,270	816	16,454	126	950	55	894	235	-428	17,281
1990 Total	21,523	18,594	784	17,810	123	1,532	86	1,447	-513	307	[j]19,174
1995 Total	23,744	19,506	908	18,599	110	2,841	154	2,687	415	396	22,207
2000 Total	24,174	20,198	1,016	19,182	90	3,782	244	3,538	829	-306	23,333
2001 Total	24,501	20,570	954	19,616	86	3,977	373	3,604	-1,166	99	22,239
2002 Total	23,941	19,885	957	18,928	68	4,015	516	3,499	467	65	23,027
2003 Total	24,119	19,974	876	19,099	68	3,944	680	3,264	-197	44	22,277
2004 Total	23,970	19,517	927	18,591	60	4,259	854	3,404	-114	461	22,403
2005 Total	23,457	18,927	876	18,051	64	4,341	729	3,612	52	236	22,014
2006 Total	23,535	19,410	906	18,504	66	4,186	724	3,462	-436	103	21,699
2007 Total	24,664	20,196	930	19,266	63	4,608	822	3,785	192	-203	23,104
2008 Total	25,636	21,112	953	20,159	61	3,984	963	3,021	34	2	23,277
2009 Total	26,057	21,648	1,024	20,624	65	3,751	1,072	2,679	-355	-103	22,910
2010 Total	26,816	22,382	1,066	21,316	65	3,741	1,137	2,604	-13	115	24,087
2011 Total	28,479	24,036	1,134	22,902	60	3,469	1,506	1,963	-354	-94	24,477
2012 Total	29,542	25,283	1,250	24,033	61	3,138	1,619	1,519	-9	-66	25,538
2013 Total	29,523	25,562	1,357	24,206	55	2,883	1,572	1,311	546	38	26,155
2014 Total	31,405	27,498	1,608	25,890	60	2,695	1,514	1,181	-254	-283	26,593
2015 January	2,771	2,391	141	2,250	5	279	145	135	741	-18	3,113
February	2,516	2,193	129	2,063	4	254	145	109	757	-10	2,924
March	2,824	2,439	144	2,296	5	257	164	93	201	-3	2,592
April	2,750	2,391	141	2,251	5	205	130	75	-329	8	2,009
May	2,791	2,444	144	2,300	5	204	134	70	-508	-8	1,859
June	2,669	2,368	139	2,229	5	206	138	68	-370	-30	1,901
July	2,758	2,448	144	2,304	5	217	144	73	-291	-23	2,069
August	2,742	2,446	144	2,302	5	214	145	69	-317	-6	2,053
September	2,727	2,390	141	2,249	5	209	163	46	-381	-17	1,903
October	2,801	2,441	144	2,298	5	226	159	68	-339	-44	1,988
November	2,731	2,362	139	2,223	5	218	156	63	17	-57	2,250
December	2,814	2,438	144	2,295	5	227	162	66	272	-49	2,588
Total	**32,895**	**28,753**	**1,693**	**27,060**	**59**	**2,718**	**1,784**	**935**	**-546**	**-258**	**27,249**
2016 January	[E]2,819	[E]2,424	148	[E]2,275	5	274	169	105	729	[R]-18	[R]3,096
February	[E]2,668	[E]2,304	140	[E]2,164	5	252	163	89	403	[R]-7	2,655
March	[E]2,823	[E]2,431	157	[E]2,274	5	241	195	46	57	[R]-23	[R]2,358
April	[E]2,682	[E]2,340	151	[E]2,188	5	241	[R]178	[R]63	-164	[R]-3	2,089
May	[E]2,779	[E]2,411	160	[E]2,250	5	248	[R]188	[R]60	[R]-327	[R]-17	1,971
June	[E]2,635	[E]2,304	156	[E]2,148	2	242	[R]183	[R]59	-222	[R]16	[R]2,003
July	[E]2,710	[E]2,372	160	[E]2,213	5	265	[R]189	[R]76	-133	[R]29	2,190
August	[E]2,742	[E]2,394	152	[E]2,242	5	[R]262	[R]214	[R]48	-124	43	2,214
September	[E]2,640	[E]2,303	147	[E]2,155	5	[R]238	[R]202	37	-262	[R]15	1,950
October	[E]2,718	[E]2,352	160	[E]2,192	5	[R]231	[R]176	[R]55	-308	[R]-18	[R]1,925
November	[E]2,684	[E]2,308	155	[E]2,153	5	231	[R]228	[R]3	35	[R]-29	2,168
December	[E]2,748	[E]2,354	149	[E]2,205	5	[R]281	[R]251	[R]30	676	[R]-45	[R]2,872
Total	**[E]32,647**	**[E]28,295**	**1,836**	**[E]26,459**	**59**	**[R]3,006**	**[R]2,335**	**[R]671**	**[R]359**	**[R]-57**	**[R]27,490**
2017 January	[E]2,732	[E]2,345	151	[E]2,194	5	[R]290	[R]272	[R]18	675	[R]-11	[R]2,882
February	[RE]2,508	[RE]2,153	146	[RE]2,007	5	[R]255	[R]255	[R]-1	285	[R]19	[R]2,315
March	[RE]2,771	[RE]2,375	163	[RE]2,212	5	[R]281	[R]272	[R]9	275	[R]3	[R]2,504
April	[E]2,678	[E]2,305	157	[E]2,148	5	238	247	-9	-230	-6	1,907
4-Month Total	**[E]10,690**	**[E]9,178**	**617**	**[E]8,562**	**20**	**1,064**	**1,046**	**18**	**1,005**	**4**	**9,608**
2016 4-Month Total	**[E]10,993**	**[E]9,498**	**597**	**[E]8,901**	**21**	**1,007**	**704**	**303**	**1,024**	**-51**	**10,198**
2015 4-Month Total	**10,861**	**9,414**	**554**	**8,860**	**19**	**996**	**584**	**412**	**1,370**	**-24**	**10,637**

[a] Gases withdrawn from natural gas, crude oil, coalbed, and shale gas wells. Includes natural gas, natural gas plant liquids, and nonhydrocarbon gases; but excludes lease condensate.

[b] Gross withdrawals minus repressuring, nonhydrocarbon gases removed, and vented and flared. See Note 1, "Natural Gas Production," at end of section.

[c] Natural gas plant liquids (NGPL) production, gaseous equivalent. This data series was previously called "Extraction Loss." See Note 2, "Natural Gas Plant Liquids Production," at end of section.

[d] Marketed production (wet) minus NGPL production.

[e] See Note 3, "Supplemental Gaseous Fuels," at end of section.

[f] Net withdrawals from underground storage. For 1980–2014, also includes net withdrawals of liquefied natural gas in above-ground tanks. See Note 4, "Natural Gas Storage," at end of section.

[g] See Note 5, "Natural Gas Balancing Item," at end of section. Beginning in 1980, excludes transit shipments that cross the U.S.-Canada border (i.e., natural gas delivered to its destination via the other country).

[h] See Note 6, "Natural Gas Consumption," at end of section.

[i] Through 1979, may include unknown quantities of nonhydrocarbon gases.

[j] For 1989–1992, a small amount of consumption at independent power producers may be counted in both "Other Industrial" and "Electric Power Sector" on Table 4.3. See Note 7, "Natural Gas Consumption, 1989–1992," at end of section.

R=Revised. E=Estimate. (s)=Less than 0.5 billion cubic feet and greater than -0.5 billion cubic feet. NA=Not available.

Notes: • See Note 8, "Natural Gas Data Adjustments, 1993–2000," at end of section. • Through 1964, all volumes are shown on a pressure base of 14.65 psia (pounds per square inch absolute) at 60° Fahrenheit; beginning in 1965, the pressure base is 14.73 psia at 60° Fahrenheit. • Totals may not equal sum of components due to independent rounding. • Geographic coverage is the 50 states and the District of Columbia (except Alaska, for which underground storage is excluded from "Net Storage Withdrawals" through 2012).

Web Page: See http://www.eia.gov/totalenergy/data/monthly/#naturalgas (Excel and CSV files) for all available annual data beginning in 1949 and monthly data beginning in 1973.

Sources: • **Imports and Exports:** Table 4.2. • **Consumption:** Table 4.3. • **Balancing Item:** Calculated as consumption minus dry gas production, supplemental gaseous fuels, net imports, and net storage withdrawals. • **All Other Data: 1949–2014**—U.S. Energy Information Administration (EIA), *Natural Gas Annual*, annual reports. **2015 forward**—EIA, *Natural Gas Monthly*, June 2017, Table 1.

Source: *U.S. Energy Information Administration, Monthly Energy Review, July 2017*

Table 4.2 Natural Gas Trade by Country
(Billion Cubic Feet)

	Imports									Exports[a]				
	Algeria[b]	Canada[c]	Egypt[b]	Mexico[c]	Nigeria[b]	Qatar[b]	Trinidad and Tobago[b]	Other[b,d]	Total	Canada[c]	Japan[b]	Mexico[c]	Other[b,e]	Total
1950 Total	**0**	**0**	**0**	**0**	**0**	**0**	**0**	**0**	**0**	**3**	**0**	**23**	**0**	**26**
1955 Total	**0**	**11**	**0**	**(s)**	**0**	**0**	**0**	**0**	**11**	**11**	**0**	**20**	**0**	**31**
1960 Total	**0**	**109**	**0**	**47**	**0**	**0**	**0**	**0**	**156**	**6**	**0**	**6**	**0**	**11**
1965 Total	**0**	**405**	**0**	**52**	**0**	**0**	**0**	**0**	**456**	**18**	**0**	**8**	**0**	**26**
1970 Total	**1**	**779**	**0**	**(s)**	**0**	**0**	**0**	**0**	**821**	**11**	**44**	**15**	**0**	**70**
1975 Total	**5**	**948**	**0**	**0**	**0**	**0**	**0**	**0**	**953**	**10**	**53**	**9**	**0**	**73**
1980 Total	**86**	**797**	**0**	**102**	**0**	**0**	**0**	**0**	**985**	**(s)**	**45**	**4**	**0**	**49**
1985 Total	**24**	**926**	**0**	**0**	**0**	**0**	**0**	**0**	**950**	**(s)**	**53**	**2**	**0**	**55**
1990 Total	**84**	**1,448**	**0**	**0**	**0**	**0**	**0**	**0**	**1,532**	**17**	**53**	**16**	**0**	**86**
1995 Total	**18**	**2,816**	**0**	**7**	**0**	**0**	**0**	**0**	**2,841**	**28**	**65**	**61**	**0**	**154**
2000 Total	**47**	**3,544**	**0**	**12**	**13**	**46**	**99**	**21**	**3,782**	**73**	**66**	**106**	**0**	**244**
2001 Total	**65**	**3,729**	**0**	**10**	**38**	**23**	**98**	**14**	**3,977**	**167**	**66**	**141**	**0**	**373**
2002 Total	**27**	**3,785**	**0**	**2**	**8**	**35**	**151**	**8**	**4,015**	**189**	**63**	**263**	**0**	**516**
2003 Total	**53**	**3,437**	**0**	**0**	**50**	**14**	**378**	**11**	**3,944**	**271**	**66**	**343**	**0**	**680**
2004 Total	**120**	**3,607**	**0**	**0**	**12**	**12**	**462**	**46**	**4,259**	**395**	**62**	**397**	**0**	**854**
2005 Total	**97**	**3,700**	**73**	**9**	**8**	**3**	**439**	**11**	**4,341**	**358**	**65**	**305**	**0**	**729**
2006 Total	**17**	**3,590**	**120**	**13**	**57**	**0**	**389**	**0**	**4,186**	**341**	**61**	**322**	**0**	**724**
2007 Total	**77**	**3,783**	**115**	**54**	**95**	**18**	**448**	**18**	**4,608**	**482**	**47**	**292**	**2**	**822**
2008 Total	**0**	**3,589**	**55**	**43**	**12**	**3**	**267**	**15**	**3,984**	**559**	**39**	**365**	**0**	**963**
2009 Total	**0**	**3,271**	**160**	**28**	**13**	**13**	**236**	**29**	**3,751**	**701**	**31**	**338**	**3**	**1,072**
2010 Total	**0**	**3,280**	**73**	**30**	**42**	**46**	**190**	**81**	**3,741**	**739**	**33**	**333**	**32**	**1,137**
2011 Total	**0**	**3,117**	**35**	**3**	**2**	**91**	**129**	**92**	**3,469**	**937**	**18**	**499**	**52**	**1,506**
2012 Total	**0**	**2,963**	**3**	**(s)**	**0**	**34**	**112**	**26**	**3,138**	**971**	**14**	**620**	**14**	**1,619**
2013 Total	**0**	**2,786**	**0**	**1**	**3**	**7**	**70**	**17**	**2,883**	**911**	**0**	**661**	**0**	**1,572**
2014 Total	**0**	**2,635**	**0**	**1**	**0**	**0**	**43**	**16**	**2,695**	**770**	**13**	**729**	**3**	**1,514**
2015 January	0	268	0	(s)	0	0	9	2	279	73	0	69	3	145
February	0	242	0	(s)	0	0	10	2	254	78	0	65	3	145
March	0	243	0	(s)	0	0	12	3	257	90	0	74	0	164
April	0	202	0	(s)	0	0	3	0	205	53	0	77	0	130
May	0	203	0	(s)	0	0	2	0	204	45	0	87	3	134
June	0	204	0	(s)	0	0	3	0	206	45	0	91	3	138
July	0	210	0	(s)	0	0	7	0	217	40	3	101	0	144
August	0	203	0	(s)	0	0	11	0	214	41	3	101	0	145
September	0	203	0	(s)	0	0	6	0	209	60	0	100	3	163
October	0	218	0	(s)	0	0	3	6	226	57	3	98	0	159
November	0	211	0	(s)	0	0	4	3	218	61	0	92	3	156
December	0	222	0	(s)	0	0	2	3	227	59	0	100	3	162
Total	**0**	**2,626**	**0**	**1**	**0**	**0**	**71**	**20**	**2,718**	**701**	**8**	**1,054**	**20**	**1,784**
2016 January	0	262	0	(s)	0	0	12	0	274	70	0	99	0	169
February	0	242	0	(s)	0	0	10	0	252	62	0	97	3	163
March	0	232	0	(s)	0	0	9	0	241	81	0	103	10	195
April	0	237	0	(s)	0	0	5	0	241	63	0	R 105	10	R 178
May	0	243	0	(s)	0	0	5	0	248	63	0	R 116	10	R 188
June	0	234	0	(s)	0	0	8	0	242	51	0	R 116	16	R 183
July	0	259	0	(s)	0	0	6	0	265	50	0	R 123	16	R 189
August	0	R 254	0	(s)	0	0	8	0	R 262	55	0	R 136	23	R 214
September	0	R 236	0	(s)	0	0	3	0	R 238	61	0	R 127	13	R 202
October	0	R 226	0	(s)	0	0	6	0	R 231	43	0	R 130	3	R 176
November	0	R 222	0	(s)	0	0	6	3	231	75	0	R 134	20	R 228
December	0	R 272	0	(s)	0	0	9	0	R 281	97	11	R 119	23	R 251
Total	**0**	R **2,918**	**0**	**1**	**0**	**0**	**84**	**3**	R **3,006**	**771**	**11**	R **1,405**	**148**	R **2,335**
2017 January	0	R 277	0	(s)	3	0	10	0	R 290	99	11	R 136	27	R 272
February	0	R 246	0	(s)	0	0	8	0	R 255	88	4	R 130	34	R 255
March	0	R 276	0	(s)	0	0	5	0	R 281	100	0	R 140	33	R 272
April	0	233	0	(s)	0	0	5	0	238	81	7	130	29	247
4-Month Total	**0**	**1,032**	**0**	**(s)**	**3**	**0**	**29**	**0**	**1,064**	**367**	**22**	**535**	**123**	**1,046**
2016 4-Month Total	**0**	**972**	**0**	**(s)**	**0**	**0**	**35**	**0**	**1,007**	**276**	**0**	**404**	**23**	**704**
2015 4-Month Total	**0**	**954**	**0**	**(s)**	**0**	**0**	**34**	**7**	**996**	**293**	**0**	**285**	**6**	**584**

[a] Includes re-exports.
[b] As liquefied natural gas.
[c] By pipeline, except for small amounts of: liquefied natural gas (LNG) imported from Canada in 1973, 1977, 1981, and 2013 forward; LNG exported to Canada in 2007 and 2012 forward; compressed natural gas (CNG) imported from Canada in 2014 forward; CNG exported to Canada in 2013 forward; and LNG exported to Mexico beginning in 1998. See Note 9, "Natural Gas Imports and Exports," at end of section.
[d] Australia in 1997–2001 and 2004; Brunei in 2002; Equatorial Guinea in 2007; Indonesia in 1986 and 2000; Malaysia in 1999 and 2002–2005; Norway in 2008–2016; Oman in 2000–2005; Peru in 2010 and 2011; United Arab Emirates in 1996–2000; Yemen in 2010–2015; and Other (unassigned) in 2004–2015.
[e] Argentina in 2016; Barbados in 2016 and 2017; Brazil in 2010–2012, and 2014–2016; Chile in 2011, 2016, and 2017; China in 2011, 2016, and 2017; Dominican Republic in 2016 and 2017; Egypt in 2015 and 2016; India in 2010–2012, 2016, and 2017; Italy in 2016; Jordan in 2016 and 2017; Kuwait in 2016 and 2017; Malta in 2017; Pakistan in 2017; Portugal in 2012, 2016, and 2017; Russia in 2007; South Korea in 2009–2011, 2016, and 2017; Spain in 2010–2011, 2016, and 2017; Taiwan in 2015; Thailand in 2017; Turkey in 2015–2017; United Arab Emirates in 2016; and United Kingdom in 2010 and 2011.

R=Revised. (s)=Less than 500 million cubic feet.

Notes: • See Note 9, "Natural Gas Imports and Exports," at end of section. • Through 1964, all volumes are shown on a pressure base of 14.65 psia (pounds per square inch absolute) at 60° Fahrenheit; beginning in 1965, the pressure base is 14.73 psia at 60° Fahrenheit. • Totals may not equal sum of components due to independent rounding. • U.S. geographic coverage is the 50 states and the District of Columbia.

Web Page: See http://www.eia.gov/totalenergy/data/monthly/#naturalgas (Excel and CSV files) for all available annual data beginning in 1949 and monthly data beginning in 1973.

Sources: • **1949–1954:** U.S. Energy Information Administration (EIA) estimates based on Bureau of Mines, Minerals Yearbook, "Natural Gas" chapter. • **1955–1971:** Federal Power Commission data. • **1972–1987:** EIA, Form FPC-14, "Annual Report for Importers and Exporters of Natural Gas." • **1988–2014:** EIA, *Natural Gas Annual,* annual reports. • **2015 forward:** EIA, *Natural Gas Monthly,* June 2017, Tables 4 and 5; and U.S. Department of Energy, Office of Fossil Energy, "Natural Gas Imports and Exports."

Source: *U.S. Energy Information Administration, Monthly Energy Review, July 2017*

Table 4.3 Natural Gas Consumption by Sector
(Billion Cubic Feet)

	End-Use Sectors											
			Industrial					Transportation				
				Other Industrial								
	Residential	Commercial[a]	Lease and Plant Fuel	CHP[b]	Non-CHP[c]	Total	Total	Pipelines[d] and Distribution[e]	Vehicle Fuel	Total	Electric Power Sector[f,g]	Total
1950 Total	1,198	388	928	(h)	2,498	2,498	3,426	126	NA	126	629	5,767
1955 Total	2,124	629	1,131	(h)	3,411	3,411	4,542	245	NA	245	1,153	8,694
1960 Total	3,103	1,020	1,237	(h)	4,535	4,535	5,771	347	NA	347	1,725	11,967
1965 Total	3,903	1,444	1,156	(h)	5,955	5,955	7,112	501	NA	501	2,321	15,280
1970 Total	4,837	2,399	1,399	(h)	7,851	7,851	9,249	722	NA	722	3,932	21,139
1975 Total	4,924	2,508	1,396	(h)	6,968	6,968	8,365	583	NA	583	3,158	19,538
1980 Total	4,752	2,611	1,026	(h)	7,172	7,172	8,198	635	NA	635	3,682	19,877
1985 Total	4,433	2,432	966	(h)	5,901	5,901	6,867	504	NA	504	3,044	17,281
1990 Total	4,391	2,623	1,236	1,055	[i]5,963	[i]7,018	8,255	660	(s)	660	[i]3,245	[i]19,174
1995 Total	4,850	3,031	1,220	1,258	6,906	8,164	9,384	700	5	705	4,237	22,207
2000 Total	4,996	3,182	1,151	1,386	6,757	8,142	9,293	642	13	655	5,206	23,333
2001 Total	4,771	3,023	1,119	1,310	6,035	7,344	8,463	625	15	640	5,342	22,239
2002 Total	4,889	3,144	1,113	1,240	6,287	7,527	8,640	667	15	682	5,672	23,027
2003 Total	5,079	3,179	1,122	1,144	6,007	7,150	8,273	591	18	610	5,135	22,277
2004 Total	4,869	3,129	1,098	1,191	6,066	7,256	8,354	566	21	587	5,464	22,403
2005 Total	4,827	2,999	1,112	1,084	5,518	6,601	7,713	584	23	607	5,869	22,014
2006 Total	4,368	2,832	1,142	1,115	5,412	6,527	7,669	584	24	608	6,222	21,699
2007 Total	4,722	3,013	1,226	1,050	5,604	6,655	7,881	621	25	646	6,841	23,104
2008 Total	4,892	3,153	1,220	955	5,715	6,670	7,890	648	26	674	6,668	23,277
2009 Total	4,779	3,119	1,275	990	5,178	6,167	7,443	670	27	697	6,873	22,910
2010 Total	4,782	3,103	1,286	1,029	5,797	6,826	8,112	674	29	703	7,387	24,087
2011 Total	4,714	3,155	1,323	1,063	5,931	6,994	8,317	688	30	718	7,574	24,477
2012 Total	4,150	2,895	1,396	1,149	6,077	7,226	8,622	731	30	761	9,111	25,538
2013 Total	4,897	3,295	1,483	1,170	6,255	7,425	8,909	833	30	863	8,191	26,155
2014 Total	5,087	3,466	1,512	1,145	6,501	7,646	9,158	700	35	735	8,146	26,593
2015 January	937	532	132	103	616	720	852	77	3	81	711	3,113
February	902	517	121	92	569	661	782	73	3	76	648	2,924
March	633	385	135	99	564	663	798	64	3	67	709	2,592
April	319	232	132	93	516	609	741	49	3	52	664	2,009
May	177	160	135	95	509	604	739	45	3	48	734	1,859
June	124	135	131	101	475	576	706	46	3	49	886	1,901
July	108	134	135	109	483	593	728	50	3	54	1,046	2,069
August	103	135	135	110	490	601	735	50	3	53	1,027	2,053
September	108	138	132	102	477	580	712	46	3	49	895	1,903
October	201	195	135	102	512	614	749	48	3	52	792	1,988
November	406	283	130	103	536	639	770	55	3	58	732	2,250
December	591	352	135	110	565	675	810	64	3	67	769	2,588
Total	**4,610**	**3,199**	**1,587**	**1,222**	**6,313**	**7,535**	**9,121**	**666**	**39**	**706**	**9,613**	**27,249**
2016 January	887	506	E134	107	613	720	854	E76	E3	E79	771	R3,096
February	698	416	E127	100	561	661	788	E65	E3	E68	686	2,655
March	459	R299	E134	103	559	662	796	E58	E3	E61	743	R2,358
April	331	234	E129	100	520	620	749	E51	E3	E54	721	2,089
May	196	172	E133	102	510	R612	R745	E48	E3	E51	806	1,971
June	R123	139	E127	104	486	590	717	E49	E3	E52	971	R2,003
July	108	136	E131	108	508	616	747	E53	E4	E57	1,142	2,190
August	R101	141	E132	109	518	627	759	E54	E4	E58	1,155	2,214
September	111	R142	E127	104	499	603	R730	E48	E4	E51	915	1,950
October	189	192	E130	102	520	622	752	E47	E4	E51	741	R1,925
November	385	R282	E127	106	548	R653	781	E53	E4	E56	664	2,168
December	R803	R464	E130	112	621	733	863	E70	E4	E74	669	R2,872
Total	**4,391**	**R3,123**	**E1,561**	**1,257**	**R6,462**	**R7,719**	**R9,281**	**E671**	**E41**	**E712**	**9,984**	**R27,490**
2017 January	R834	R479	E129	114	613	727	856	E70	E4	E74	639	R2,882
February	584	361	E119	102	R539	R641	R760	E56	E3	E60	550	R2,315
March	582	370	E131	108	582	689	R820	E61	E4	E65	667	R2,504
April	281	212	E127	103	520	623	750	E47	E4	E50	614	1,907
4-Month Total	**2,280**	**1,422**	**E506**	**427**	**2,254**	**2,681**	**3,187**	**E234**	**E14**	**E249**	**2,470**	**9,608**
2016 4-Month Total	**2,375**	**1,454**	**E524**	**410**	**2,252**	**2,662**	**3,186**	**E249**	**E13**	**E262**	**2,921**	**10,198**
2015 4-Month Total	**2,791**	**1,666**	**519**	**388**	**2,266**	**2,653**	**3,173**	**262**	**13**	**275**	**2,733**	**10,637**

[a] All commercial sector fuel use, including that at commercial combined-heat-and-power (CHP) and commercial electricity-only plants. See Table 7.4c for CHP fuel use.
[b] Industrial combined-heat-and-power (CHP) and a small number of industrial electricity-only plants.
[c] All industrial sector fuel use other than that in "Lease and Plant Fuel" and "CHP."
[d] Natural gas consumed in the operation of pipelines, primarily in compressors. Beginning in 2009, includes line loss, which is known volumes of natural gas that are the result of leaks, damage, accidents, migration, and/or blow down.
[e] Natural gas used as fuel in the delivery of natural gas to consumers. Beginning in 2009, includes line loss, which is known volumes of natural gas that are the result of leaks, damage, accidents, migration, and/or blow down.
[f] The electric power sector comprises electricity-only and combined-heat-and-power (CHP) plants within the NAICS 22 category whose primary business is to sell electricity, or electricity and heat, to the public.
[g] Through 1988, data are for electric utilities only. Beginning in 1989, data are for electric utilities and independent power producers.
[h] Included in "Non-CHP."
[i] For 1989–1992, a small amount of consumption at independent power producers may be counted in both "Other Industrial" and "Electric Power Sector." See Note 7, "Natural Gas Consumption, 1989–1992," at end of section.

R=Revised. E=Estimate. NA=Not available. (s)=Less than 500 million cubic feet.

Notes: • Data are for natural gas, plus a small amount of supplemental gaseous fuels. See Note 3, "Supplemental Gaseous Fuels," at end of section. • See Note 8, "Natural Gas Data Adjustments, 1993–2000," at end of section. • See Note 2, "Classification of Power Plants Into Energy-Use Sectors," at end of Section 7. • Through 1964, all volumes are shown on a pressure base of 14.65 psia (pounds per square inch absolute) at 60° Fahrenheit; beginning in 1965, the pressure base is 14.73 psia at 60° Fahrenheit. • Totals may not equal sum of components due to independent rounding. • Geographic coverage is the 50 states and the District of Columbia.

Web Page: See http://www.eia.gov/totalenergy/data/monthly/#naturalgas (Excel and CSV files) for all available annual data beginning in 1949 and monthly data beginning in 1973.

Sources: • **Residential, Commercial, Lease and Plant Fuel, Other Industrial Total** and **Pipelines and Distribution: 1949–2014**—U.S. Energy Information Administration (EIA), *Natural Gas Annual (NGA),* annual reports and unpublished revisions. **2015 forward**—EIA, *Natural Gas Monthly (NGM),* June 2017, Table 2. • **Other Industrial CHP:** Table 7.4c. • **Other Industrial Non-CHP:** Calculated as other industrial total minus other industrial CHP. • **Industrial Total:** Calculated as lease and plant fuel plus other industrial total. • **Vehicle Fuel: 1990 and 1991**—EIA, NGA 2000, (November 2001), Table 95. **1992–1998**—EIA, "Alternatives to Traditional Transportation Fuels 1999" (October 1999), Table 10, and "Alternatives to Traditional Transportation Fuels 2003" (February 2004), Table 10. Data for compressed natural gas and liquefied natural gas in gasoline-equivalent gallons were converted to cubic feet by multiplying by the motor gasoline conversion factor (see Table A3) and dividing by the natural gas end-use sectors conversion factor (see Table A4). **1999–2014**—EIA, NGA, annual reports. **2015 forward**—EIA, NGM, June 2017, Table 2. • **Transportation Total:** Calculated as pipelines and distribution plus vehicle fuel. • **Electric Power Sector:** Table 7.4b. • **Total Consumption:** Calculated as the sum of residential, commercial, industrial total, transportation total, and electric power sector.

Source: *U.S. Energy Information Administration, Monthly Energy Review, July 2017*

Table 4.4 Natural Gas in Underground Storage
(Volumes in Billion Cubic Feet)

	Natural Gas in Underground Storage, End of Period			Change in Working Gas From Same Period Previous Year		Storage Activity		
	Base Gas	Working Gas	Total[a]	Volume	Percent	Withdrawals	Injections	Net[b,c]
1950 Total	NA	NA	NA	NA	NA	175	230	-54
1955 Total	863	505	1,368	40	8.7	437	505	-68
1960 Total	NA	NA	2,184	NA	NA	713	844	-132
1965 Total	1,848	1,242	3,090	83	7.2	960	1,078	-118
1970 Total	2,326	1,678	4,004	257	18.1	1,459	1,857	-398
1975 Total	3,162	2,212	5,374	162	7.9	1,760	2,104	-344
1980 Total	3,642	2,655	6,297	-99	-3.6	1,910	1,896	14
1985 Total	3,842	2,607	6,448	-270	-9.4	2,359	2,128	231
1990 Total	3,868	3,068	6,936	555	22.1	1,934	2,433	-500
1995 Total	4,349	2,153	6,503	-453	-17.4	2,974	2,566	408
2000 Total	4,352	1,719	6,071	-806	-31.9	3,498	2,684	814
2001 Total	4,301	2,904	7,204	1,185	68.9	2,309	3,464	-1,156
2002 Total	4,340	2,375	6,715	-528	-18.2	3,138	2,670	468
2003 Total	4,303	2,563	6,866	187	7.9	3,099	3,292	-193
2004 Total	4,201	2,696	6,897	133	5.2	3,037	3,150	-113
2005 Total	4,200	2,635	6,835	-61	-2.3	3,057	3,002	55
2006 Total	4,211	3,070	7,281	435	16.5	2,493	2,924	-431
2007 Total	4,234	2,879	7,113	-191	-6.2	3,325	3,133	192
2008 Total	4,232	2,840	7,073	-39	-1.4	3,374	3,340	34
2009 Total	4,277	3,130	7,407	290	10.2	2,966	3,315	-349
2010 Total	4,301	3,111	7,412	-19	-.6	3,274	3,291	-17
2011 Total	4,302	3,462	7,764	351	11.3	3,074	3,422	-348
2012 Total	4,372	3,413	7,785	-49	-1.4	2,818	2,825	-7
2013 Total	4,365	2,890	7,255	-523	-15.3	3,702	3,156	546
2014 Total	4,365	3,141	7,506	251	8.7	3,586	3,839	-253
2015 January	4,361	2,415	6,776	490	25.5	795	70	725
February	4,360	1,674	6,034	474	39.5	803	62	742
March	4,361	1,480	5,841	623	72.6	376	182	193
April	4,360	1,802	6,162	736	69.0	84	405	-321
May	4,363	2,296	6,659	748	48.3	44	542	-497
June	4,367	2,656	7,023	650	32.4	68	430	-362
July	4,372	2,933	7,305	533	22.2	96	379	-283
August	4,364	3,250	7,614	482	17.4	85	394	-309
September	4,365	3,622	7,987	435	13.7	63	435	-372
October	4,365	3,951	8,316	363	10.1	70	401	-331
November	4,368	3,935	8,303	508	14.8	214	201	12
December	4,363	3,675	8,038	534	17.0	403	138	264
Total	4,363	3,675	8,038	534	17.0	3,101	3,639	-538
2016 January	4,361	2,947	7,307	532	22.0	795	66	729
February	4,361	2,543	6,904	869	51.9	515	111	403
March	4,352	2,495	6,847	1,015	68.6	272	215	57
April	4,355	2,654	7,009	852	47.3	130	294	-164
May	4,357	2,975	7,332	679	29.5	R 75	402	R -327
June	4,360	3,194	7,554	539	20.3	94	316	-222
July	4,360	3,327	7,686	394	13.4	150	283	-133
August	4,360	3,450	7,810	200	6.2	162	286	-124
September	4,360	3,714	8,073	91	2.5	88	351	-262
October	4,362	4,021	8,383	71	1.8	78	387	-308
November	4,364	3,985	8,348	50	1.3	213	178	35
December	4,371	3,305	7,675	-370	-10.1	763	87	676
Total	4,371	3,305	7,675	-370	-10.1	R 3,335	2,977	R 359
2017 January	4,370	2,631	7,001	-316	-10.7	776	101	675
February	4,369	2,346	6,715	-197	-7.7	416	131	285
March	4,370	2,072	R 6,441	-423	R -17.0	R 443	R 167	275
April	4,371	2,301	6,671	-353	-13.3	111	341	-230
4-Month Total	– –	– –	– –	– –	– –	1,746	741	1,005
2016 4-Month Total	– –	– –	– –	– –	– –	1,711	687	1,024
2015 4-Month Total	– –	– –	– –	– –	– –	2,058	719	1,339

[a] For total underground storage capacity at the end of each calendar year, see Note 4, "Natural Gas Storage," at end of section.

[b] For 1980–2015, data differ from those shown on Table 4.1, which includes liquefied natural gas storage for that period.

[c] Positive numbers indicate that withdrawals are greater than injections. Negative numbers indicate that injections are greater than withdrawals. Net withdrawals or injections may not equal the difference between applicable ending stocks. See Note 4, "Natural Gas Storage," at end of section.

R=Revised. – – =Not applicable. NA=Not available.

Notes: • Through 1964, all volumes are shown on a pressure base of 14.65 psia (pounds per square inch absolute) at 60° Fahrenheit; beginning in 1965, the pressure base is 14.73 psia at 60° Fahrenheit. • Totals may not equal sum of components due to independent rounding. • Geographic coverage is the 50 states and the District of Columbia (except Alaska, which is excluded through 2012).

Web Page: See http://www.eia.gov/totalenergy/data/monthly/#naturalgas (Excel and CSV files) for all available annual data beginning in 1949 and monthly data beginning in 1973.

Sources: • **Storage Activity: 1949–1975**—U.S. Energy Information Administration (EIA), *Natural Gas Annual 1994, Volume 2,* Table 9. **1976–1979**—EIA, *Natural Gas Production and Consumption 1979,* Table 1. **1980–1995**—EIA, *Historical Natural Gas Annual 1930 Through 2000,* Table 11. **1996–2014**—EIA, *Natural Gas Monthly (NGM),* monthly issues. **2015 forward**—EIA, NGM, June 2017, Table 8. • **All Other Data: 1954–1974**—American Gas Association, *Gas Facts,* annual issues. **1975 and 1976**—Federal Energy Administration (FEA), Form FEA-G318-M-0, "Underground Gas Storage Report," and Federal Power Commission (FPC), Form FPC-8, "Underground Gas Storage Report." **1977 and 1978**—EIA, Form FEA-G318-M-0, "Underground Gas Storage Report," and Federal Energy Regulatory Commission (FERC), Form FERC-8, "Underground Gas Storage Report." **1979–1995**—EIA, Form EIA-191, "Underground Gas Storage Report," and FERC, Form FERC-8, "Underground Gas Storage Report." **1996–2014**—EIA, NGA, annual reports. **2015 forward**—EIA, NGM, June 2017, Table 8.

Source: *U.S. Energy Information Administration, Monthly Energy Review, July 2017*

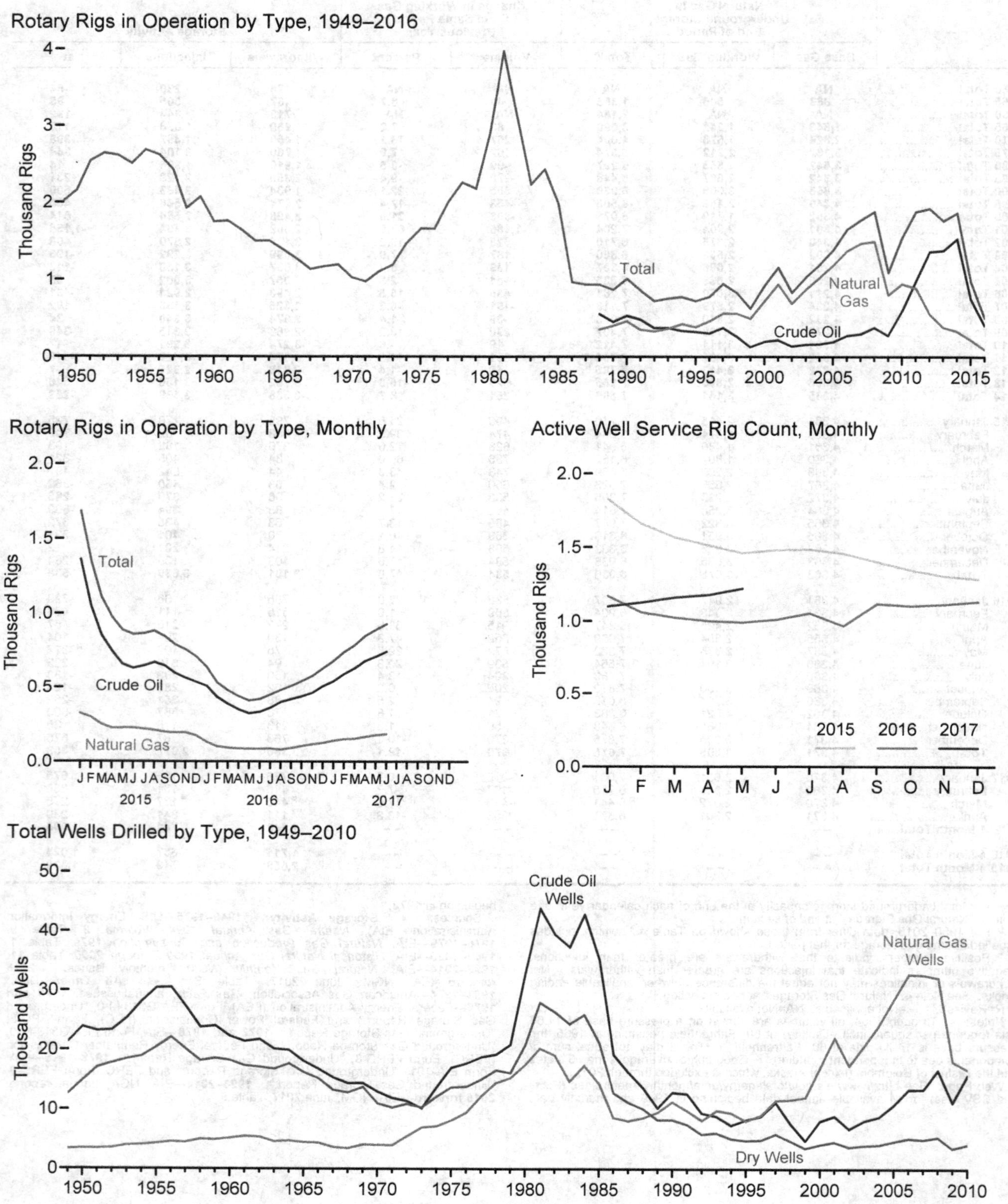

Web Page: http://www.eia.gov/totalenergy/data/monthly/#crude.
Sources: Tables 5.1 and 5.2.

Source: *U.S. Energy Information Administration, Monthly Energy Review, July 2017*

Table 5.1 Crude Oil and Natural Gas Drilling Activity Measurements
(Number of Rigs)

	Rotary Rigs in Operation[a]					Active Well Service Rig Count[c]
	By Site		By Type			
	Onshore	Offshore	Crude Oil	Natural Gas	Total[b]	
1950 Average	**NA**	**NA**	**NA**	**NA**	**2,154**	**NA**
1955 Average	**NA**	**NA**	**NA**	**NA**	**2,686**	**NA**
1960 Average	**NA**	**NA**	**NA**	**NA**	**1,748**	**NA**
1965 Average	**NA**	**NA**	**NA**	**NA**	**1,388**	**NA**
1970 Average	**NA**	**NA**	**NA**	**NA**	**1,028**	**NA**
1975 Average	**1,554**	**106**	**NA**	**NA**	**1,660**	**2,486**
1980 Average	**2,678**	**231**	**NA**	**NA**	**2,909**	**4,089**
1985 Average	**1,774**	**206**	**NA**	**NA**	**1,980**	**4,716**
1990 Average	**902**	**108**	**532**	**464**	**1,010**	**3,658**
1995 Average	**622**	**101**	**323**	**385**	**723**	**3,041**
2000 Average	**778**	**140**	**197**	**720**	**918**	**2,692**
2001 Average	**1,003**	**153**	**217**	**939**	**1,156**	**2,267**
2002 Average	**717**	**113**	**137**	**691**	**830**	**1,830**
2003 Average	**924**	**108**	**157**	**872**	**1,032**	**1,967**
2004 Average	**1,095**	**97**	**165**	**1,025**	**1,192**	**2,064**
2005 Average	**1,287**	**94**	**194**	**1,184**	**1,381**	**2,222**
2006 Average	**1,559**	**90**	**274**	**1,372**	**1,649**	**2,364**
2007 Average	**1,695**	**72**	**297**	**1,466**	**1,768**	**2,388**
2008 Average	**1,814**	**65**	**379**	**1,491**	**1,879**	**2,515**
2009 Average	**1,046**	**44**	**278**	**801**	**1,089**	**1,722**
2010 Average	**1,514**	**31**	**591**	**943**	**1,546**	**1,854**
2011 Average	**1,846**	**32**	**984**	**887**	**1,879**	**2,075**
2012 Average	**1,871**	**48**	**1,357**	**558**	**1,919**	**2,113**
2013 Average	**1,705**	**56**	**1,373**	**383**	**1,761**	**2,064**
2014 Average	**1,804**	**57**	**1,527**	**333**	**1,862**	**2,024**
2015 January	1,629	53	1,362	320	1,683	1,826
February	1,296	52	1,050	296	1,348	1,659
March	1,066	43	857	250	1,109	1,566
April	943	33	750	222	976	1,512
May	857	32	662	223	889	1,460
June	833	28	634	224	861	1,481
July	835	31	649	216	866	1,485
August	849	34	673	209	883	1,456
September	816	32	650	198	848	1,399
October	758	33	597	193	791	1,345
November	729	31	566	194	760	1,303
December	686	24	537	174	711	1,283
Average	**943**	**35**	**750**	**226**	**978**	**1,481**
2016 January	615	28	510	133	643	1,170
February	506	26	430	102	532	1,058
March	451	27	384	93	477	1,023
April	411	26	348	88	437	1,000
May	384	24	320	86	407	989
June	396	21	330	86	417	1,009
July	429	20	359	88	449	1,053
August	464	17	397	82	481	967
September	491	18	416	91	509	1,117
October	521	23	436	105	543	1,102
November	558	22	462	117	580	1,111
December	611	23	507	126	634	1,131
Average	**486**	**23**	**408**	**100**	**509**	**1,061**
2017 January	659	24	542	140	683	1,099
February	724	20	593	150	744	1,125
March	770	19	634	154	789	1,159
April	833	20	685	166	853	1,176
May	871	22	714	178	893	R1,219
June	909	22	747	184	931	NA
6-Month Average	**798**	**21**	**656**	**162**	**819**	**NA**
2016 6-Month Average	**458**	**25**	**385**	**98**	**483**	**1,042**
2015 6-Month Average	**1,115**	**40**	**896**	**257**	**1,155**	**1,584**

[a] Rotary rigs in operation are reported weekly on Fridays. Monthly data are averages of 4- or 5-week reporting periods. Multi-month data are averages of the reported weekly data over the covered months. Annual data are averages of 52- or 53-week reporting periods. Published data are rounded to the nearest whole number.

[b] Sum of rigs drilling for crude oil, rigs drilling for natural gas, and other rigs (not shown) drilling for miscellaneous purposes, such as service wells, injection wells, and stratigraphic tests. Therefore, "Total" values may not equal the sum of "Crude Oil" and "Natural Gas." "Total" values may not equal the sum of "Onshore" and "Offshore" due to independent rounding.

[c] The number of rigs doing true workovers (where tubing is pulled from the well), or doing rod string and pump repair operations, and that are, on average, crewed and working every day of the month.

R=Revised. NA=Not available.

Note: Geographic coverage is the 50 states and the District of Columbia.

Web Page: See http://www.eia.gov/totalenergy/data/monthly/#crude (Excel and CSV files) for all available annual data beginning in 1949 and monthly data beginning in 1973.

Sources: • **Rotary Rigs in Operation:** Baker Hughes, Inc., Houston, TX, "North America Rig Count," used with permission. See http://phx.corporate-ir.net/phoenix.zhtml?c=79687&p=irol-reportsother. • **Active Well Service Rig Count:** Assoc. of Energy Service Companies, Friendswood, TX. See http://www.aesc.net/AESC/Industry_Resources/Rig_Counts/AESC/Industry_Resources/Well_Service_Rig_Count.aspx?hkey=0f7d9987-7819-421e-9c4c-7e7d9323ab3c.

Source: *U.S. Energy Information Administration, Monthly Energy Review, July 2017*

Table 5.2 Crude Oil and Natural Gas Exploratory and Development Wells

	Wells Drilled												Total Footage Drilled
	Exploratory				Development				Total				
	Crude Oil	Natural Gas	Dry	Total	Crude Oil	Natural Gas	Dry	Total	Crude Oil	Natural Gas	Dry	Total	
	Number												Thousand Feet
1950 Total	**1,583**	**431**	**8,292**	**10,306**	**22,229**	**3,008**	**6,507**	**31,744**	**23,812**	**3,439**	**14,799**	**42,050**	**157,358**
1955 Total	**2,236**	**874**	**11,832**	**14,942**	**28,196**	**3,392**	**8,620**	**40,208**	**30,432**	**4,266**	**20,452**	**55,150**	**226,182**
1960 Total	**1,321**	**868**	**9,515**	**11,704**	**20,937**	**4,281**	**8,697**	**33,915**	**22,258**	**5,149**	**18,212**	**45,619**	**192,176**
1965 Total	**946**	**515**	**8,005**	**9,466**	**17,119**	**3,967**	**8,221**	**29,307**	**18,065**	**4,482**	**16,226**	**38,773**	**174,882**
1970 Total	**757**	**477**	**6,162**	**7,396**	**12,211**	**3,534**	**4,869**	**20,614**	**12,968**	**4,011**	**11,031**	**28,010**	**138,556**
1975 Total	**982**	**1,248**	**7,129**	**9,359**	**15,966**	**6,879**	**6,517**	**29,362**	**16,948**	**8,127**	**13,646**	**38,721**	**180,494**
1980 Total	**1,777**	**2,099**	**9,081**	**12,957**	**31,182**	**15,362**	**11,704**	**58,248**	**32,959**	**17,461**	**20,785**	**71,205**	**316,943**
1985 Total	**1,680**	**1,200**	**8,954**	**11,834**	**33,581**	**13,124**	**12,257**	**58,962**	**35,261**	**14,324**	**21,211**	**70,796**	**314,409**
1990 Total	**778**	**811**	**3,652**	**5,241**	**12,061**	**10,435**	**4,593**	**27,089**	**12,839**	**11,246**	**8,245**	**32,330**	**156,044**
1995 Total	**570**	**558**	**2,024**	**3,152**	**7,678**	**7,524**	**2,790**	**17,992**	**8,248**	**8,082**	**4,814**	**21,144**	**117,156**
2000 Total	**288**	**657**	**1,341**	**2,286**	**7,802**	**16,394**	**2,805**	**27,001**	**8,090**	**17,051**	**4,146**	**29,287**	**144,425**
2001 Total	**357**	**1,052**	**1,733**	**3,142**	**8,531**	**21,020**	**2,865**	**32,416**	**8,888**	**22,072**	**4,598**	**35,558**	**180,141**
2002 Total	**258**	**844**	**1,282**	**2,384**	**6,517**	**16,498**	**2,472**	**25,487**	**6,775**	**17,342**	**3,754**	**27,871**	**145,159**
2003 Total	**350**	**997**	**1,297**	**2,644**	**7,779**	**19,725**	**2,685**	**30,189**	**8,129**	**20,722**	**3,982**	**32,833**	**177,239**
2004 Total	**383**	**1,671**	**1,350**	**3,404**	**8,406**	**22,515**	**2,732**	**33,653**	**8,789**	**24,186**	**4,082**	**37,057**	**204,279**
2005 Total	**539**	**2,141**	**1,462**	**4,142**	**10,240**	**26,449**	**3,191**	**39,880**	**10,779**	**28,590**	**4,653**	**44,022**	**240,307**
2006 Total	**646**	**2,456**	**1,547**	**4,649**	**12,739**	**30,382**	**3,659**	**46,780**	**13,385**	**32,838**	**5,206**	**51,429**	**282,675**
2007 Total	**808**	**2,794**	**1,582**	**5,184**	**12,563**	**29,925**	**3,399**	**45,887**	**13,371**	**32,719**	**4,981**	**51,071**	**301,515**
2008 January	88	208	144	440	1,111	2,321	272	3,704	1,199	2,529	416	4,144	25,306
February	82	230	107	419	1,080	2,261	247	3,588	1,162	2,491	354	4,007	24,958
March	66	216	127	409	1,132	2,363	271	3,766	1,198	2,579	398	4,175	26,226
April	68	189	130	387	1,177	2,415	281	3,873	1,245	2,604	411	4,260	26,920
May	88	206	124	418	1,317	2,449	240	4,006	1,405	2,655	364	4,424	27,947
June	63	195	139	397	1,428	2,540	299	4,267	1,491	2,735	438	4,664	28,739
July	79	163	171	413	1,439	2,695	344	4,478	1,518	2,858	515	4,891	29,140
August	67	165	144	376	1,448	2,735	379	4,562	1,515	2,900	523	4,938	28,942
September	52	166	164	382	1,488	2,667	355	4,510	1,540	2,833	519	4,892	28,960
October	80	243	173	496	1,549	2,841	373	4,763	1,629	3,084	546	5,259	31,505
November	97	192	160	449	1,361	2,418	334	4,113	1,458	2,610	494	4,562	29,276
December	67	172	132	371	1,206	2,196	313	3,715	1,273	2,368	445	4,086	26,222
Total	**897**	**2,345**	**1,715**	**4,957**	**15,736**	**29,901**	**3,708**	**49,345**	**16,633**	**32,246**	**5,423**	**54,302**	**334,141**
2009 January	80	171	99	350	1,192	2,253	250	3,695	1,272	2,424	349	4,045	28,077
February	62	125	88	275	991	1,925	195	3,111	1,053	2,050	283	3,386	25,440
March	59	146	88	293	867	1,771	210	2,848	926	1,917	298	3,141	25,304
April	36	68	93	197	755	1,396	205	2,356	791	1,464	298	2,553	21,406
May	47	90	80	217	584	1,136	156	1,876	631	1,226	236	2,093	20,055
June	44	91	75	210	804	1,297	189	2,290	848	1,388	264	2,500	16,301
July	40	100	101	241	789	1,188	217	2,194	829	1,288	318	2,435	13,543
August	49	84	88	221	867	1,372	207	2,446	916	1,456	295	2,667	15,970
September	61	71	96	228	945	1,170	207	2,322	1,006	1,241	303	2,550	15,547
October	55	79	78	212	966	1,167	222	2,355	1,021	1,246	300	2,567	17,261
November	38	83	85	206	931	1,133	199	2,263	969	1,216	284	2,469	16,236
December	34	98	84	216	894	1,074	213	2,181	928	1,172	297	2,397	16,424
Total	**605**	**1,206**	**1,055**	**2,866**	**10,585**	**16,882**	**2,470**	**29,937**	**11,190**	**18,088**	**3,525**	**32,803**	**231,562**
2010 January	55	91	81	227	898	1,264	169	2,331	953	1,355	250	2,558	15,304
February	44	71	67	182	871	1,096	144	2,111	915	1,167	211	2,293	16,862
March	59	85	88	232	1,062	1,224	216	2,502	1,121	1,309	304	2,734	15,102
April	49	78	77	204	1,173	1,152	249	2,574	1,222	1,230	326	2,778	17,904
May	48	107	86	241	1,282	1,208	255	2,745	1,330	1,315	341	2,986	17,987
June	61	100	90	251	1,385	1,250	302	2,937	1,446	1,350	392	3,188	19,408
July	46	103	105	254	1,386	1,443	390	3,219	1,432	1,546	495	3,473	20,847
August	56	104	94	254	1,434	1,402	314	3,150	1,490	1,506	408	3,404	22,923
September	57	73	88	218	1,374	1,358	268	3,000	1,431	1,431	356	3,218	23,037
October	75	87	117	279	1,502	1,463	283	3,248	1,577	1,550	400	3,527	22,123
November	62	114	103	279	1,400	1,352	263	3,015	1,462	1,466	366	3,294	24,561
December	57	92	70	219	1,317	1,379	243	2,939	1,374	1,471	313	3,158	23,189
Total	**669**	**1,105**	**1,066**	**2,840**	**15,084**	**15,591**	**3,096**	**33,771**	**15,753**	**16,696**	**4,162**	**36,611**	**239,247**

Notes: • Data are estimates. • For 1960–1969, data are for well completion reports received by the American Petroleum Institute during the reporting year; for all other years, data are for well completions in a given year. • Through 1989, these well counts include only the original drilling of a hole intended to discover or further develop already discovered crude oil or natural gas resources. Other drilling activities, such as drilling an old well deeper, drilling of laterals from the original well, drilling of service and injection wells, and drilling for resources other than crude oil or natural gas are excluded. Beginning in 1990, a new well is defined as the first hole in the ground whether it is lateral or not. Due to the methodology used to estimate ultimate well counts from the available partially reported data, the counts shown on this page are frequently revised. See Note, "Crude Oil and Natural Gas Exploratory and Development Wells," at end of section. • Geographic coverage is the 50 states and the District of Columbia.

Web Page: See http://www.eia.gov/totalenergy/data/monthly/#crude (Excel and CSV files) for all available annual data beginning in 1949 and monthly data beginning in 1973.

Sources: • **1949–1965:** Gulf Publishing Company, *World Oil*, "Forecast-Review" issue. • **1966–1969:** American Petroleum Institute (API), *Quarterly Review of Drilling Statistics for the United States*, annual summaries and monthly reports. • **1970–1989:** U.S. Energy Information Administration (EIA) computations based on well reports submitted to the API. • **1990 forward:** EIA computations based on well reports submitted to IHS, Inc., Denver, CO.

Data for 2011 forward in this table have been removed while EIA evaluates the quality of the data and the estimation methodology.

Source: *U.S. Energy Information Administration, Monthly Energy Review, July 2017*

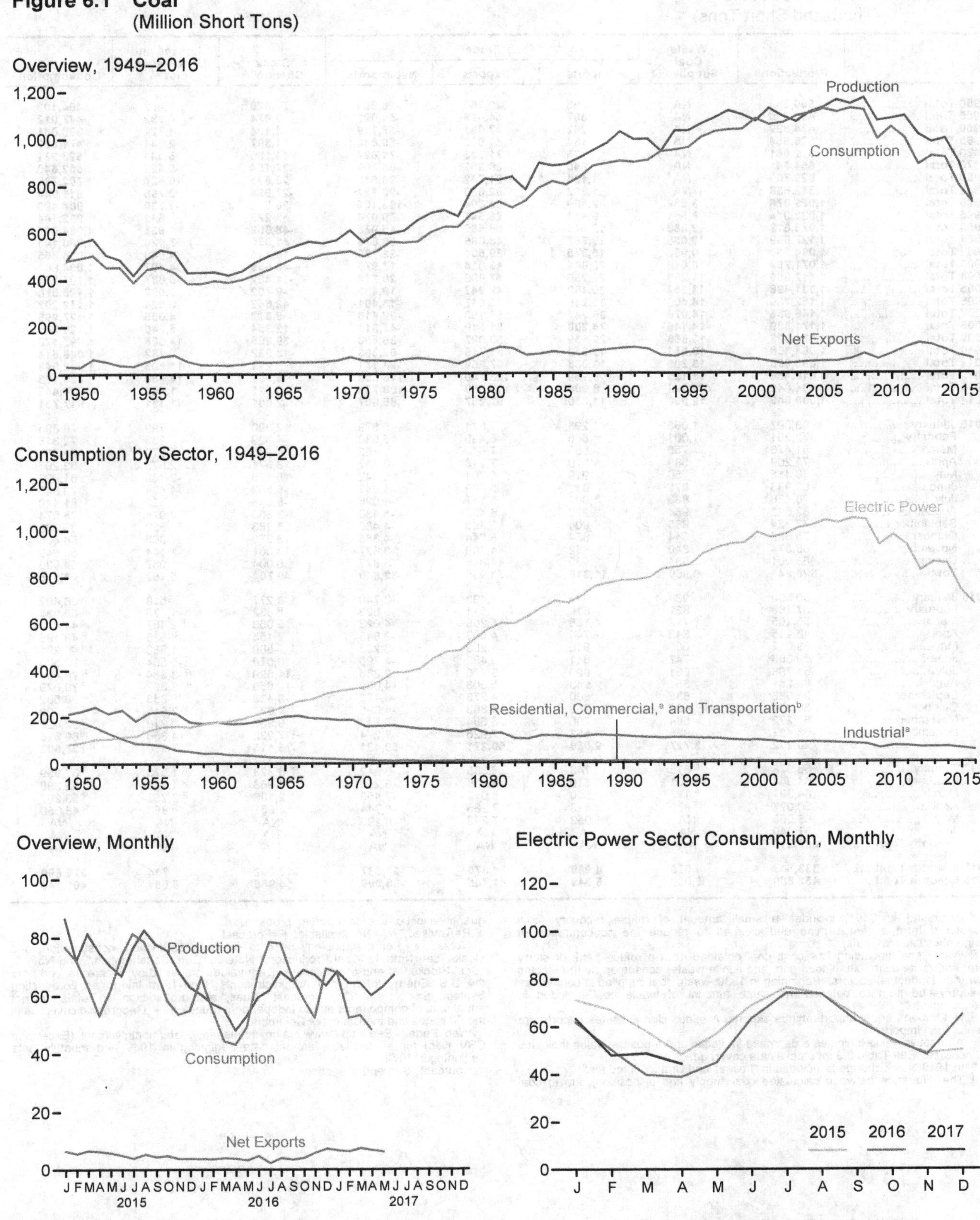

ª Includes combined-heat-and-power (CHP) plants and a small number of electricity-only-plants.

ᵇ For 1978 forward, small amounts of transportation sector use are included in "Industrial."

Web Page: http://www.eia.gov/totalenergy/data/monthly/#coal.
Sources: Tables 6.1–6.2.

Source: *U.S. Energy Information Administration, Monthly Energy Review, July 2017*

Table 6.1 Coal Overview

(Thousand Short Tons)

	Production[a]	Waste Coal Supplied[b]	Trade			Stock Change[d,e]	Losses and Unaccounted for[e,f]	Consumption
			Imports	Exports	Net Imports[c]			
1950 Total	560,388	NA	365	29,360	-28,995	27,829	9,462	494,102
1955 Total	490,838	NA	337	54,429	-54,092	-3,974	-6,292	447,012
1960 Total	434,329	NA	262	37,981	-37,719	-3,194	1,722	398,081
1965 Total	526,954	NA	184	51,032	-50,848	1,897	2,244	471,965
1970 Total	612,661	NA	36	71,733	-71,697	11,100	6,633	523,231
1975 Total	654,641	NA	940	66,309	-65,369	32,154	-5,522	562,640
1980 Total	829,700	NA	1,194	91,742	-90,548	25,595	10,827	702,730
1985 Total	883,638	NA	1,952	92,680	-90,727	-27,934	2,796	818,049
1990 Total	1,029,076	3,339	2,699	105,804	-103,104	26,542	-1,730	904,498
1995 Total	1,032,974	8,561	9,473	88,547	-79,074	-275	632	962,104
2000 Total	1,073,612	9,089	12,513	58,489	-45,976	-48,309	938	1,084,095
2001 Total	1,127,689	10,085	19,787	48,666	-28,879	41,630	7,120	1,060,146
2002 Total	1,094,283	9,052	16,875	39,601	-22,726	10,215	4,040	1,066,355
2003 Total	1,071,753	10,016	25,044	43,014	-17,970	-26,659	-4,403	1,094,861
2004 Total	1,112,099	11,299	27,280	47,998	-20,718	-11,462	6,887	1,107,255
2005 Total	1,131,498	13,352	30,460	49,942	-19,482	-9,702	9,092	1,125,978
2006 Total	1,162,750	14,409	36,246	49,647	-13,401	42,642	8,824	1,112,292
2007 Total	1,146,635	14,076	36,347	59,163	-22,816	5,812	4,085	1,127,998
2008 Total	1,171,809	14,146	34,208	81,519	-47,311	12,354	5,740	1,120,548
2009 Total	1,074,923	13,666	22,639	59,097	-36,458	39,668	14,985	997,478
2010 Total	1,084,368	13,651	19,353	81,716	-62,363	-13,039	182	1,048,514
2011 Total	1,095,628	13,209	13,088	107,259	-94,171	211	11,506	1,002,948
2012 Total	1,016,458	11,196	9,159	125,746	-116,586	6,902	14,980	889,185
2013 Total	984,842	11,279	8,906	117,659	-108,753	-38,525	1,451	924,442
2014 Total	1,000,049	12,090	11,350	97,257	-85,907	-2,601	11,101	917,731
2015 January	86,597	1,065	1,293	7,871	-6,579	2,390	1,799	76,895
February	72,251	1,001	866	6,496	-5,630	-4,929	233	72,318
March	81,476	755	850	7,612	-6,762	4,930	6,979	63,560
April	75,209	580	879	7,216	-6,337	13,571	2,673	53,207
May	70,415	756	919	6,761	-5,842	5,575	-2,169	61,923
June	66,933	872	842	5,789	-4,947	-6,552	-4,434.	73,845
July	76,476	883	1,091	5,117	-4,026	-8,638	523	81,449
August	82,623	954	970	6,409	-5,439	-3,360	2,924	78,574
September	77,724	885	904	5,388	-4,485	5,283	-529	69,369
October	75,662	544	854	5,744	-4,889	13,278	-366	58,405
November	68,574	840	882	4,709	-3,827	13,061	-1,114	53,640
December	63,001	834	969	4,846	-3,877	6,094	-1,067	54,930
Total	**896,941**	**9,969**	**11,318**	**73,958**	**-62,640**	**40,704**	**5,452**	**798,115**
2016 January	60,500	938	693	4,433	-3,740	[R]-8,277	[R]-518	[R]66,492
February	57,263	822	819	4,511	-3,693	[R]532	[R]-1,175	[R]55,036
March	55,265	719	1,186	5,208	-4,023	[R]5,063	[R]2,487	[R]44,410
April	48,115	543	740	4,583	-3,843	2,155	[R]-536	[R]43,196
May	53,012	609	910	4,209	-3,298	-889	[R]1,980	[R]49,231
June	59,388	747	641	5,432	-4,790	-10,676	[R]-1,504	[R]67,525
July	61,796	861	990	3,276	-2,286	-14,699	[R]-3,384	[R]78,454
August	68,261	851	943	5,003	-4,060	-10,656	[R]-2,322	[R]78,029
September	65,083	685	800	4,273	-3,473	-3,433	[R]-853	[R]66,582
October	68,851	483	768	4,863	-4,095	[R]4,321	[R]2,016	[R]58,902
November	67,272	584	706	6,554	-5,847	[R]9,365	[R]216	[R]52,429
December	63,427	886	652	7,926	-7,274	[R]-7,922	[R]-4,356	[R]69,316
Total	**728,232**	**8,727**	**9,850**	**60,271**	**-50,421**	[R]**-35,115**	[R]**-7,950**	[R]**729,602**
2017 January	[R]68,378	[R]875	743	7,385	-6,642	[R]-6,823	[R]1,573	[R]67,859
February	[R]64,354	[R]751	612	6,908	-6,296	[R]4,963	[R]1,449	[R]52,398
March	[R]64,301	[R]777	560	8,013	-7,453	[R]2,106	[R]2,252	[R]53,267
April	60,077	[RF]835	493	7,236	-6,744	[R]4,951	[R]867	[R]48,350
May	63,066	NA	[R]1,053	[R]7,243	[R]-6,190	NA	NA	NA
June	67,040	NA	NA	NA	NA	NA	NA	NA
6-Month Total	**387,216**	**NA**	**NA**	**NA**	**NA**	**NA**	**NA**	**NA**
2016 6-Month Total	**333,543**	**4,376**	**4,989**	**28,376**	**-23,387**	**-12,092**	**734**	**325,890**
2015 6-Month Total	**452,880**	**5,030**	**5,649**	**41,745**	**-36,096**	**14,985**	**5,081**	**401,748**

[a] Beginning in 2001, includes a small amount of refuse recovery (coal recaptured from a refuse mine and cleaned to reduce the concentration of noncombustible materials).

[b] Waste coal (including fine coal, coal obtained from a refuse bank or slurry dam, anthracite culm, bituminous gob, and lignite waste) consumed by the electric power and industrial sectors. Beginning in 1989, waste coal supplied is counted as a supply-side item to balance the same amount of waste coal included in "Consumption."

[c] Net imports equal imports minus exports. A minus sign indicates exports are greater than imports.

[d] A negative value indicates a decrease in stocks and a positive value indicates an increase. See Table 6.3 for stocks data coverage.

[e] In 1949, stock change is included in "Losses and Unaccounted for."

[f] The difference between calculated coal supply and disposition, due to coal quantities lost or to data reporting problems.

R=Revised. NA=Not available. F=Forecast.

Notes: • For methodology used to calculate production, consumption, and stocks, see Note 1, "Coal Production," Note 2, "Coal Consumption," and Note 3, "Coal Stocks," at end of section. • Data values preceded by "F" are derived from the U.S. Energy Information Administration's Short-Term Integrated Forecasting System. See Note 4, "Coal Forecast Values," at end of section. • Totals may not equal sum of components due to independent rounding. • Geographic coverage is the 50 states and the District of Columbia.

Web Page: See http://www.eia.gov/totalenergy/data/monthly/#coal (Excel and CSV files) for all available annual data beginning in 1949 and monthly data beginning in 1973.

Sources: See end of section.

Source: *U.S. Energy Information Administration, Monthly Energy Review, July 2017*

Table 6.2 Coal Consumption by Sector
(Thousand Short Tons)

	End-Use Sectors										Electric Power Sector[e,f]	Total
		Commercial			Industrial							
						Other Industrial						
	Residential	CHP[a]	Other[b]	Total	Coke Plants	CHP[c]	Non-CHP[d]	Total	Total	Transportation		
1950 Total	51,562	([g])	63,021	63,021	104,014	([h])	120,623	120,623	224,637	63,011	91,871	494,102
1955 Total	35,590	([g])	32,852	32,852	107,743	([h])	110,096	110,096	217,839	16,972	143,759	447,012
1960 Total	24,159	([g])	16,789	16,789	81,385	([h])	96,017	96,017	177,402	3,046	176,685	398,081
1965 Total	14,635	([g])	11,041	11,041	95,286	([h])	105,560	105,560	200,846	655	244,788	471,965
1970 Total	9,024	([g])	7,090	7,090	96,481	([h])	90,156	90,156	186,637	298	320,182	523,231
1975 Total	2,823	([g])	6,587	6,587	83,598	([h])	63,646	63,646	147,244	24	405,962	562,640
1980 Total	1,355	([g])	5,097	5,097	66,657	([h])	60,347	60,347	127,004	([h])	569,274	702,730
1985 Total	1,711	([g])	6,068	6,068	41,056	([h])	75,372	75,372	116,429	([h])	693,841	818,049
1990 Total	1,345	1,191	4,189	5,379	38,877	27,781	48,549	76,330	115,207	([h])	[f]782,567	904,498
1995 Total	755	1,419	3,633	5,052	33,011	29,363	43,693	73,055	106,067	([h])	850,230	962,104
2000 Total	454	1,547	2,126	3,673	28,939	28,031	37,177	65,208	94,147	([h])	985,821	1,084,095
2001 Total	481	1,448	2,441	3,888	26,075	25,755	39,514	65,268	91,344	([h])	964,433	1,060,146
2002 Total	533	1,405	2,506	3,912	23,656	26,232	34,515	60,747	84,403	([h])	977,507	1,066,355
2003 Total	551	1,816	1,869	3,685	24,248	24,846	36,415	61,261	85,509	([h])	1,005,116	1,094,861
2004 Total	512	1,917	2,693	4,610	23,670	26,613	35,582	62,195	85,865	([h])	1,016,268	1,107,255
2005 Total	378	1,922	2,420	4,342	23,434	25,875	34,465	60,340	83,774	([h])	1,037,485	1,125,978
2006 Total	290	1,886	1,050	2,936	22,957	25,262	34,210	59,472	82,429	([h])	1,026,636	1,112,292
2007 Total	353	1,927	1,247	3,173	22,715	22,537	34,078	56,615	79,331	([h])	1,045,141	1,127,998
2008 Total	([i])	2,021	1,485	3,506	22,070	21,902	32,491	54,393	76,463	([h])	1,040,580	1,120,548
2009 Total	([i])	1,798	1,412	3,210	15,326	19,766	25,549	45,314	60,641	([h])	933,627	997,478
2010 Total	([i])	1,720	1,361	3,081	21,092	24,638	24,650	49,289	70,381	([h])	975,052	1,048,514
2011 Total	([i])	1,668	1,125	2,793	21,434	22,319	23,919	46,238	67,671	([h])	932,484	1,002,948
2012 Total	([i])	1,450	595	2,045	20,751	20,065	22,773	42,838	63,589	([h])	823,551	889,185
2013 Total	([i])	1,356	595	1,951	21,474	19,761	23,294	43,055	64,529	([h])	857,962	924,442
2014 Total	([i])	1,063	824	1,887	21,297	19,076	23,870	42,946	64,243	([h])	851,602	917,731
2015 January	([i])	97	101	198	1,908	1,613	1,852	3,465	5,373	([h])	71,323	76,895
February	([i])	97	101	198	1,598	1,483	1,977	3,460	5,058	([h])	67,061	72,318
March	([i])	83	87	171	1,649	1,506	1,962	3,468	5,117	([h])	58,272	63,560
April	([i])	54	45	99	1,543	1,336	1,780	3,116	4,659	([h])	48,449	53,207
May	([i])	50	41	92	1,677	1,378	1,717	3,095	4,772	([h])	57,060	61,923
June	([i])	61	50	111	1,766	1,381	1,720	3,101	4,867	([h])	68,867	73,845
July	([i])	64	39	104	1,801	1,505	1,588	3,093	4,894	([h])	76,452	81,449
August	([i])	58	35	93	1,711	1,420	1,673	3,093	4,804	([h])	73,678	78,574
September	([i])	51	31	82	1,519	1,391	1,696	3,087	4,606	([h])	64,682	69,369
October	([i])	52	49	101	1,586	1,296	1,865	3,161	4,747	([h])	53,557	58,405
November	([i])	59	56	115	1,479	1,325	1,841	3,166	4,645	([h])	48,879	53,640
December	([i])	72	69	141	1,469	1,350	1,805	3,155	4,624	([h])	50,165	54,930
Total	([i])	**798**	**706**	**1,503**	**19,708**	**16,984**	**21,475**	**38,459**	**58,167**	([h])	**738,444**	**798,115**
2016 January	([i])	76	73	148	1,328	1,503	[R]1,543	[R]3,046	[R]4,374	([h])	61,970	[R]66,492
February	([i])	78	75	153	1,361	1,395	[R]1,639	[R]3,034	[R]4,395	([h])	50,487	[R]55,036
March	([i])	75	72	147	1,434	1,370	[R]1,672	[R]3,042	[R]4,475	([h])	39,788	[R]44,410
April	([i])	49	27	76	1,324	1,006	[R]1,806	[R]2,812	[R]4,136	([h])	38,984	[R]43,196
May	([i])	40	22	62	1,367	1,149	[R]1,671	[R]2,820	[R]4,187	([h])	44,983	[R]49,231
June	([i])	46	25	71	1,405	1,212	[R]1,594	[R]2,806	[R]4,211	([h])	63,243	[R]67,525
July	([i])	46	17	63	1,433	1,234	[R]1,588	[R]2,822	[R]4,255	([h])	74,136	[R]78,454
August	([i])	50	19	69	1,395	1,234	[R]1,574	[R]2,808	[R]4,203	([h])	73,757	[R]78,029
September	([i])	49	18	67	1,336	1,053	[R]1,759	[R]2,812	[R]4,148	([h])	62,366	[R]66,582
October	([i])	50	39	89	1,335	993	[R]1,885	[R]2,878	[R]4,213	([h])	54,601	[R]58,902
November	([i])	61	48	109	1,326	998	[R]1,894	[R]2,892	[R]4,218	([h])	48,102	[R]52,429
December	([i])	71	56	127	1,442	1,155	[R]1,734	[R]2,889	[R]4,331	([h])	64,858	[R]69,316
Total	([i])	**692**	**490**	**1,182**	**16,485**	**14,302**	[R]**20,359**	[R]**34,661**	[R]**51,146**	([h])	**677,275**	[R]**729,602**
2017 January	([i])	62	[R]76	[R]138	[R]1,431	1,288	[R]1,526	[R]2,813	[R]4,244	([h])	63,477	[R]67,859
February	([i])	50	[R]62	[R]112	[R]1,368	1,085	[R]1,739	[R]2,824	[R]4,191	([h])	48,095	[R]52,398
March	([i])	55	[R]67	[R]122	[R]1,438	1,143	1,663	2,806	[R]4,244	([h])	48,901	[R]53,267
April	([i])	37	[F]14	[F]51	[F]961	1,024	[F]1,872	[F]2,896	[F]3,857	([h])	44,441	48,350
4-Month Total	([i])	**204**	[E]**219**	[E]**424**	[E]**5,198**	**4,539**	[E]**6,799**	[E]**11,339**	[E]**16,536**	([h])	**204,914**	**221,874**
2016 4-Month Total	([i])	**278**	**247**	**525**	**5,448**	**5,274**	**6,660**	**11,933**	**17,381**	([h])	**191,228**	**209,134**
2015 4-Month Total	([i])	**331**	**335**	**666**	**6,700**	**5,938**	**7,571**	**13,509**	**20,209**	([h])	**245,105**	**265,980**

[a] Commercial combined-heat-and-power (CHP) and a small number of commercial electricity-only plants, such as those at hospitals and universities. See Note 2, "Classification of Power Plants Into Energy-Use Sectors," at end of Section 7.
[b] All commercial sector fuel use other than that in "Commercial CHP."
[c] Industrial combined-heat-and-power (CHP) and a small number of industrial electricity-only plants. See Note 2, "Classification of Power Plants Into Energy-Use Sectors," at end of Section 7.
[d] All industrial sector fuel use other than that in "Coke Plants" and "Industrial CHP."
[e] The electric power sector comprises electricity-only and combined-heat-and-power (CHP) plants within the NAICS 22 category whose primary business is to sell electricity, or electricity and heat, to the public.
[f] Through 1988, data are for electric utilities only. Beginning in 1989, data are for electric utilities and independent power producers.
[g] Included in "Commercial Other."
[h] Included in "Industrial Non-CHP."
[i] Beginning in 2008, residential coal consumption data are no longer collected by the U.S. Energy Information Administration (EIA).

R=Revised. F=Forecast.

Notes: • CHP monthly values are from Table 7.4c; electric power sector monthly values are from Table 7.4b; all other monthly values are estimates derived from collected quarterly and annual data. See Note 2, "Coal Consumption," at end of section. • Data values preceded by "F" are derived from EIA's Short-Term Integrated Forecasting System. See Note 4, "Coal Forecast Values," at end of section. • Totals may not equal sum of components due to independent rounding. • Geographic coverage is the 50 states and the District of Columbia.

Web Page: See http://www.eia.gov/totalenergy/data/monthly/#coal (Excel and CSV files) for all available annual data beginning in 1949 and monthly data beginning in 1973.

Sources: See end of section.

Source: *U.S. Energy Information Administration, Monthly Energy Review, July 2017*

Table 6.3 Coal Stocks by Sector

(Thousand Short Tons)

	Producers and Distributors	End-Use Sectors					Electric Power Sector[c,d]	Total
		Residential[a] and Commercial	Industrial			Total		
			Coke Plants	Other[b]	Total			
1950 Year	**NA**	**2,462**	**16,809**	**26,182**	**42,991**	**45,453**	**31,842**	**77,295**
1955 Year	**NA**	**998**	**13,422**	**15,880**	**29,302**	**30,300**	**41,391**	**71,691**
1960 Year	**NA**	**666**	**11,122**	**11,637**	**22,759**	**23,425**	**51,735**	**75,160**
1965 Year	**NA**	**353**	**10,640**	**13,122**	**23,762**	**24,115**	**54,525**	**78,640**
1970 Year	**NA**	**300**	**9,045**	**11,781**	**20,826**	**21,126**	**71,908**	**93,034**
1975 Year	**12,108**	**233**	**8,797**	**8,529**	**17,326**	**17,559**	**110,724**	**140,391**
1980 Year	**24,379**	**NA**	**9,067**	**11,951**	**21,018**	**21,018**	**183,010**	**228,407**
1985 Year	**33,133**	**NA**	**3,420**	**10,438**	**13,857**	**13,857**	**156,376**	**203,367**
1990 Year	**33,418**	**NA**	**3,329**	**8,716**	**12,044**	**12,044**	**156,166**	**201,629**
1995 Year	**34,444**	**NA**	**2,632**	**5,702**	**8,334**	**8,334**	**126,304**	**169,083**
2000 Year	**31,905**	**NA**	**1,494**	**4,587**	**6,081**	**6,081**	**102,296**	**140,282**
2001 Year	**35,900**	**NA**	**1,510**	**6,006**	**7,516**	**7,516**	**138,496**	**181,912**
2002 Year	**43,257**	**NA**	**1,364**	**5,792**	**7,156**	**7,156**	**141,714**	**192,127**
2003 Year	**38,277**	**NA**	**905**	**4,718**	**5,623**	**5,623**	**121,567**	**165,468**
2004 Year	**41,151**	**NA**	**1,344**	**4,842**	**6,186**	**6,186**	**106,669**	**154,006**
2005 Year	**34,971**	**NA**	**2,615**	**5,582**	**8,196**	**8,196**	**101,137**	**144,304**
2006 Year	**36,548**	**NA**	**2,928**	**6,506**	**9,434**	**9,434**	**140,964**	**186,946**
2007 Year	**33,977**	**NA**	**1,936**	**5,624**	**7,560**	**7,560**	**151,221**	**192,758**
2008 Year	**34,688**	**498**	**2,331**	**6,007**	**8,338**	**8,836**	**161,589**	**205,112**
2009 Year	**47,718**	**529**	**1,957**	**5,109**	**7,066**	**7,595**	**189,467**	**244,780**
2010 Year	**49,820**	**552**	**1,925**	**4,525**	**6,451**	**7,003**	**174,917**	**231,740**
2011 Year	**51,897**	**603**	**2,610**	**4,455**	**7,065**	**7,668**	**172,387**	**231,951**
2012 Year	**46,157**	**583**	**2,522**	**4,475**	**6,997**	**7,581**	**185,116**	**238,853**
2013 Year	**45,652**	**495**	**2,200**	**4,097**	**6,297**	**6,792**	**147,884**	**200,328**
2014 Year	**38,894**	**449**	**2,640**	**4,196**	**6,836**	**7,285**	**151,548**	**197,727**
2015 January	38,817	429	2,471	4,010	6,482	6,911	154,390	200,117
February	39,581	408	2,303	3,825	6,128	6,536	149,071	195,189
March	39,610	388	2,135	3,639	5,775	6,162	154,347	200,119
April	40,226	387	2,299	3,714	6,013	6,400	167,063	213,690
May	39,817	386	2,463	3,789	6,252	6,639	172,809	219,265
June	39,399	386	2,627	3,864	6,491	6,877	166,437	212,713
July	38,993	388	2,756	3,999	6,755	7,143	157,938	204,074
August	37,353	390	2,884	4,135	7,019	7,410	155,952	200,714
September	36,213	392	3,013	4,271	7,284	7,676	162,109	205,997
October	36,233	393	2,754	4,308	7,062	7,455	175,588	219,276
November	36,509	394	2,495	4,345	6,840	7,233	188,595	232,337
December	**35,871**	**394**	**2,236**	**4,382**	**6,618**	**7,012**	**195,548**	**238,431**
2016 January	[F]35,935	373	2,129	[R]4,231	[R]6,360	[R]6,733	187,486	[R]230,154
February	[F]36,656	353	2,022	[R]4,080	[R]6,102	[R]6,455	187,575	[R]230,686
March	[F]37,304	332	1,914	[R]3,930	[R]5,844	[R]6,176	192,269	[R]235,750
April	[F]37,808	334	1,877	[R]3,895	[R]5,772	[R]6,105	193,991	[R]237,904
May	[F]37,549	336	1,839	[R]3,860	[R]5,699	[R]6,035	193,432	[R]237,016
June	[F]37,127	337	1,802	[R]3,825	[R]5,626	[R]5,964	183,248	[R]226,339
July	[F]36,287	348	1,755	[R]3,786	[R]5,540	[R]5,889	169,465	[R]211,640
August	[F]34,719	359	1,707	[R]3,747	[R]5,454	[R]5,814	160,452	[R]200,985
September	[F]33,574	370	1,660	[R]3,708	[R]5,368	[R]5,739	158,238	[R]197,551
October	[F]33,417	367	1,665	[R]3,684	[R]5,349	[R]5,716	162,739	[R]201,873
November	[F]33,336	364	1,670	[R]3,659	[R]5,329	[R]5,694	172,208	[R]211,238
December	[F]**33,699**	**361**	**1,675**	[R]**3,635**	[R]**5,310**	[R]**5,671**	**163,946**	[R]**203,316**
2017 January	[F]33,706	[R]352	[R]1,579	[R]3,497	[R]5,076	[R]5,428	157,359	[R]196,493
February	[F]34,286	[R]344	[R]1,483	[R]3,358	[R]4,842	[R]5,185	161,985	[R]201,456
March	[F]34,719	[R]335	[R]1,388	[R]3,220	[R]4,607	[R]4,942	163,900	[R]203,561
April	[F]35,115	[F]482	[F]1,648	[F]5,031	[F]6,680	[F]7,161	166,236	208,513

[a] Through 1979, data are for the residential and commercial sectors. Beginning in 2008, data are for the commercial sector only.

[b] Through 1979, data are for manufacturing plants and the transportation sector. For 1980–2007, data are for manufacturing plants only. Beginning in 2008, data are for manufacturing plants and coal transformation/processing plants.

[c] The electric power sector comprises electricity-only and combined-heat-and-power (CHP) plants within the NAICS 22 category whose primary business is to sell electricity, or electricity and heat, to the public.

[d] Excludes waste coal. Through 1998, data are for electric utilities only. Beginning in 1999, data are for electric utilities and independent power producers.

R=Revised. NA=Not available. F=Forecast.

Notes: • Stocks are at end of period. • Electric power sector monthly values are from Table 7.5; producers and distributors monthly values are estimates derived from collected annual data; all other monthly values are estimates derived from collected quarterly values. • Data values preceded by "F" are derived from the U.S. Energy Information Administration's Short-Term Integrated Forecasting System. See Note 4, "Coal Forecast Values," at end of section. • Totals may not equal sum of components due to independent rounding. • Geographic coverage is the 50 states and the District of Columbia.

Web Page: See http://www.eia.gov/totalenergy/data/monthly/#coal (Excel and CSV files) for all available annual data beginning in 1949 and monthly data beginning in 1973.

Sources: See end of section.

Source: *U.S. Energy Information Administration, Monthly Energy Review, July 2017*

Figure 7.1 Electricity Overview
(Billion Kilowatthours)

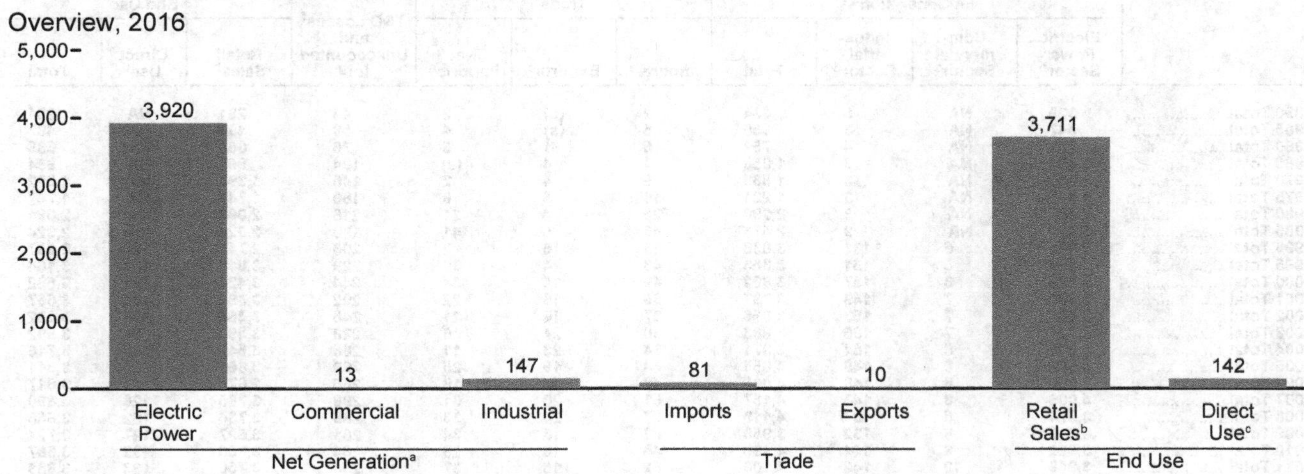

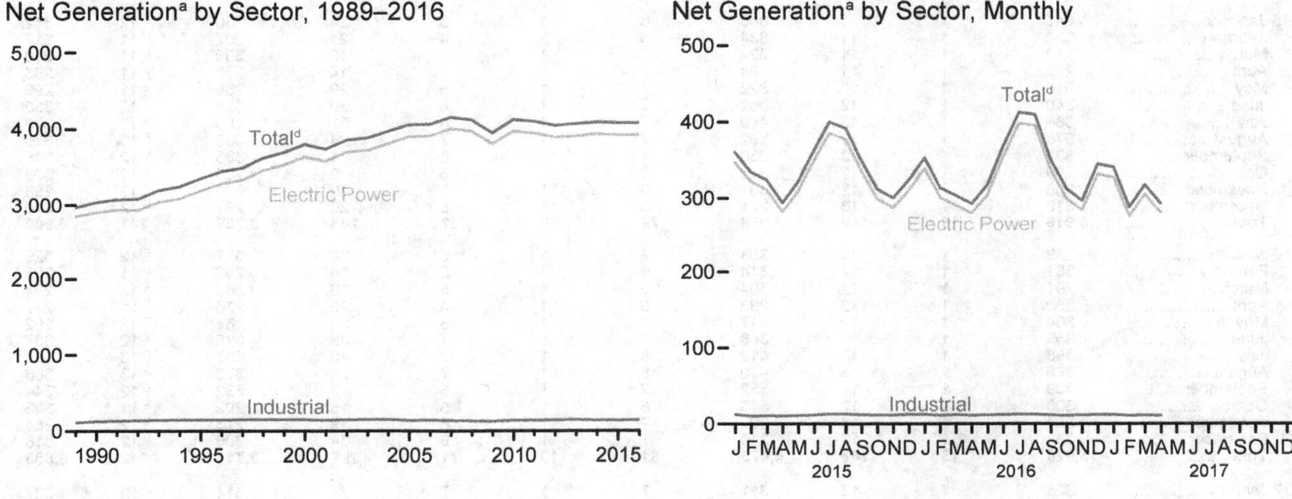

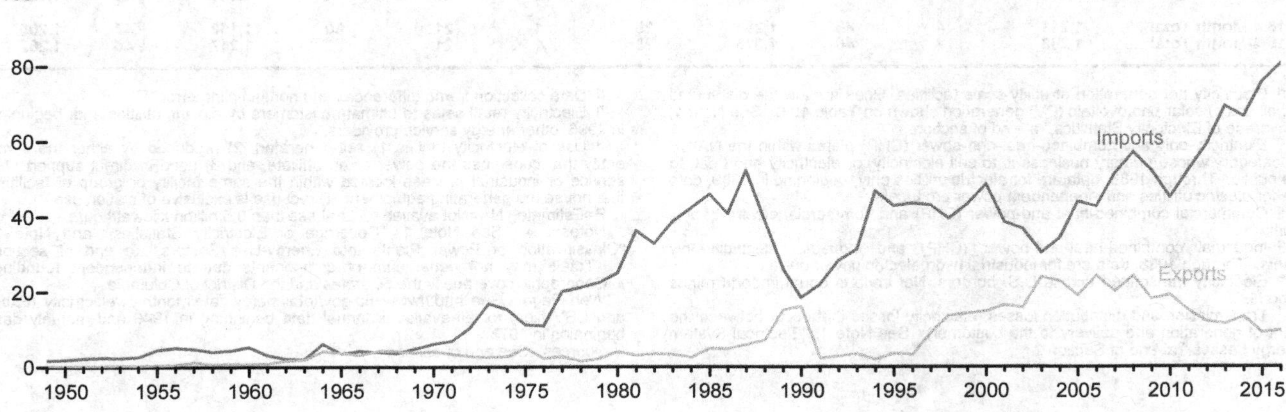

[a] Data are for utility-scale facilities.
[b] Electricity retail sales to ultimate customers reported by electric utilities and other energy service providers.
[c] See "Direct Use" in Glossary.
[d] Includes commercial sector.
Web Page: http://www.eia.gov/totalenergy/data/monthly/#electricity.
Source: Table 7.1.

Source: *U.S. Energy Information Administration, Monthly Energy Review, July 2017*

Table 7.1 Electricity Overview
(Billion Kilowatthours)

	Net Generation[a]				Trade			T&D Losses[f] and Unaccounted for[g]	End Use		
	Electric Power Sector[b]	Commercial Sector[c]	Industrial Sector[d]	Total	Imports[e]	Exports[e]	Net Imports[e]		Retail Sales[h]	Direct Use[i]	Total
1950 Total	**329**	**NA**	**5**	**334**	**2**	**(s)**	**2**	**44**	**291**	**NA**	**291**
1955 Total	**547**	**NA**	**3**	**550**	**5**	**(s)**	**4**	**58**	**497**	**NA**	**497**
1960 Total	**756**	**NA**	**4**	**759**	**5**	**1**	**5**	**76**	**688**	**NA**	**688**
1965 Total	**1,055**	**NA**	**3**	**1,058**	**4**	**4**	**(s)**	**104**	**954**	**NA**	**954**
1970 Total	**1,532**	**NA**	**3**	**1,535**	**6**	**4**	**2**	**145**	**1,392**	**NA**	**1,392**
1975 Total	**1,918**	**NA**	**3**	**1,921**	**11**	**5**	**6**	**180**	**1,747**	**NA**	**1,747**
1980 Total	**2,286**	**NA**	**3**	**2,290**	**25**	**4**	**21**	**216**	**2,094**	**NA**	**2,094**
1985 Total	**2,470**	**NA**	**3**	**2,473**	**46**	**5**	**41**	**190**	**2,324**	**NA**	**2,324**
1990 Total	**2,901**	**6**	**[c] 131**	**3,038**	**18**	**16**	**2**	**203**	**2,713**	**125**	**2,837**
1995 Total	**3,194**	**8**	**151**	**3,353**	**43**	**4**	**39**	**229**	**3,013**	**151**	**3,164**
2000 Total	**3,638**	**8**	**157**	**3,802**	**49**	**15**	**34**	**244**	**3,421**	**171**	**3,592**
2001 Total	**3,580**	**7**	**149**	**3,737**	**39**	**16**	**22**	**202**	**3,394**	**163**	**3,557**
2002 Total	**3,698**	**7**	**153**	**3,858**	**37**	**16**	**21**	**248**	**3,465**	**166**	**3,632**
2003 Total	**3,721**	**7**	**155**	**3,883**	**30**	**24**	**6**	**228**	**3,494**	**168**	**3,662**
2004 Total	**3,808**	**8**	**154**	**3,971**	**34**	**23**	**11**	**266**	**3,547**	**168**	**3,716**
2005 Total	**3,902**	**8**	**145**	**4,055**	**44**	**19**	**25**	**269**	**3,661**	**150**	**3,811**
2006 Total	**3,908**	**8**	**148**	**4,065**	**43**	**24**	**18**	**266**	**3,670**	**147**	**3,817**
2007 Total	**4,005**	**8**	**143**	**4,157**	**51**	**20**	**31**	**298**	**3,765**	**126**	**3,890**
2008 Total	**3,974**	**8**	**137**	**4,119**	**57**	**24**	**33**	**286**	**3,734**	**132**	**3,866**
2009 Total	**3,810**	**8**	**132**	**3,950**	**52**	**18**	**34**	**261**	**3,597**	**127**	**3,724**
2010 Total	**3,972**	**9**	**144**	**4,125**	**45**	**19**	**26**	**264**	**3,755**	**132**	**3,887**
2011 Total	**3,948**	**10**	**142**	**4,100**	**52**	**15**	**37**	**255**	**3,750**	**133**	**3,883**
2012 Total	**3,890**	**11**	**146**	**4,048**	**59**	**12**	**47**	**263**	**3,695**	**138**	**3,832**
2013 Total	**3,904**	**12**	**150**	**4,066**	**69**	**11**	**58**	**256**	**3,725**	**143**	**3,868**
2014 Total	**3,937**	**13**	**144**	**4,094**	**67**	**13**	**53**	**244**	**3,765**	**139**	**3,903**
2015 January	347	1	13	360	6	1	5	24	330	E 12	342
February	322	1	11	334	6	1	4	21	307	E 11	317
March	312	1	11	324	7	1	6	13	305	E 11	316
April	282	1	11	294	7	1	6	14	275	E 11	286
May	310	1	12	322	7	1	6	29	288	E 11	299
June	349	1	12	362	7	1	6	30	326	E 12	338
July	386	1	13	400	7	1	6	31	363	E 13	376
August	378	1	13	392	7	1	7	24	362	E 13	375
September	337	1	12	350	7	1	6	11	333	E 12	345
October	299	1	12	312	5	1	5	9	296	E 12	308
November	288	1	12	301	6	1	5	18	276	E 12	288
December	310	1	13	324	6	1	5	20	297	E 12	310
Total	**3,919**	**13**	**146**	**4,078**	**76**	**9**	**67**	**244**	**3,759**	**141**	**3,900**
2016 January	339	1	13	353	7	1	6	30	317	E 12	329
February	301	1	12	314	6	1	5	14	293	E 11	305
March	291	1	12	304	6	1	5	16	282	E 12	294
April	280	1	12	293	5	1	4	20	266	E 11	277
May	304	1	12	317	6	1	5	30	281	E 12	292
June	355	1	12	368	7	1	7	38	325	E 12	337
July	398	1	13	412	8	1	7	40	367	E 13	380
August	396	1	13	410	8	1	7	29	376	E 13	388
September	339	1	12	352	7	1	6	13	332	E 12	344
October	300	1	12	313	6	1	5	15	292	E 11	303
November	284	1	12	297	7	1	6	19	273	E 12	284
December	332	1	12	345	7	1	6	34	306	E 12	318
Total	**3,920**	**13**	**147**	**4,079**	**81**	**10**	**71**	**297**	**3,711**	**E 142**	**3,853**
2017 January	328	1	12	341	7	1	7	21	314	E 12	327
February	276	1	11	288	6	1	5	10	273	E 11	284
March	305	1	12	318	7	1	5	24	288	E 12	299
April	281	1	11	294	7	1	5	20	269	E 11	279
4-Month Total	**1,190**	**4**	**47**	**1,241**	**27**	**4**	**23**	**74**	**1,144**	**E 45**	**1,189**
2016 4-Month Total	**1,211**	**4**	**48**	**1,263**	**25**	**4**	**21**	**80**	**1,158**	**E 47**	**1,205**
2015 4-Month Total	**1,263**	**4**	**46**	**1,313**	**25**	**4**	**21**	**72**	**1,217**	**E 45**	**1,262**

[a] Electricity net generation at utility-scale facilities. Does not include distributed (small-scale) solar photovoltaic (PV) generation shown on Table 10.6. See Note 1, "Coverage of Electricity Statistics," at end of section.

[b] Electricity-only and combined-heat-and-power (CHP) plants within the NAICS 22 category whose primary business is to sell electricity, or electricity and heat, to the public. Through 1988, data are for electric utilities only; beginning in 1989, data are for electric utilities and independent power producers.

[c] Commercial combined-heat-and-power (CHP) and commercial electricity-only plants.

[d] Industrial combined-heat-and-power (CHP) and industrial electricity-only plants. Through 1988, data are for industrial hydroelectric power only.

[e] Electricity transmitted across U.S. borders. Net imports equal imports minus exports.

[f] Transmission and distribution losses (electricity losses that occur between the point of generation and delivery to the customer). See Note 1, "Electrical System Energy Losses," at end of Section 2.

[g] Data collection frame differences and nonsampling error.

[h] Electricity retail sales to ultimate customers by electric utilities and, beginning in 1996, other energy service providers.

[i] Use of electricity that is 1) self-generated, 2) produced by either the same entity that consumes the power or an affiliate, and 3) used in direct support of a service or industrial process located within the same facility or group of facilities that house the generating equipment. Direct use is exclusive of station use.

E=Estimate. NA=Not available. (s)=Less than 0.5 billion kilowatthours.

Notes: • See Note 1, "Coverage of Electricity Statistics," and Note 2, "Classification of Power Plants Into Energy-Use Sectors," at end of section.
• Totals may not equal sum of components due to independent rounding.
• Geographic coverage is the 50 states and the District of Columbia.

Web Page: See http://www.eia.gov/totalenergy/data/monthly/#electricity (Excel and CSV files) for all available annual data beginning in 1949 and monthly data beginning in 1973.

Sources: See end of section.

Source: *U.S. Energy Information Administration, Monthly Energy Review, July 2017*

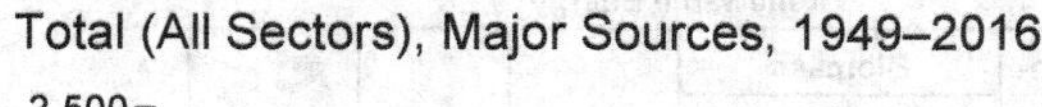

Figure 7.2 Electricity Net Generation
(Billion Kilowatthours)

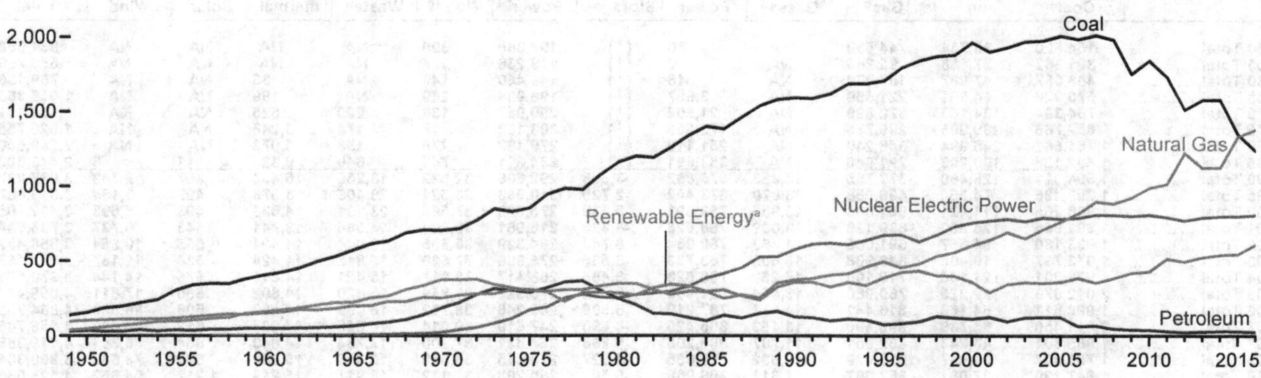

Total (All Sectors), Major Sources, Monthly

Nuclear Electric Power
Natural Gas
Coal
Renewable Energy[a]
Petroleum
J F M A M J J A S O N D J F M A M J J A S O N D J F M A M J J A S O N D
2015 2016 2017

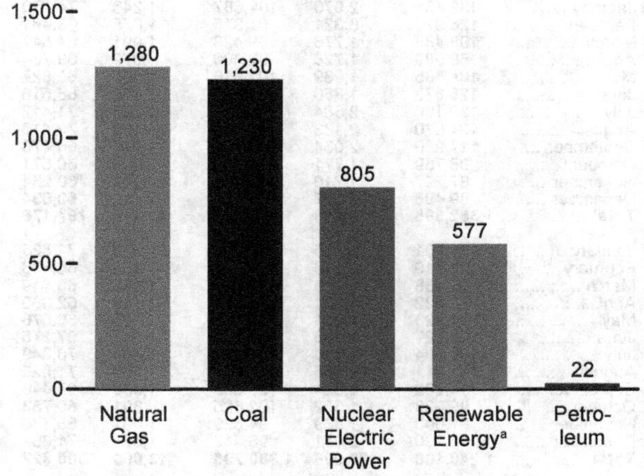

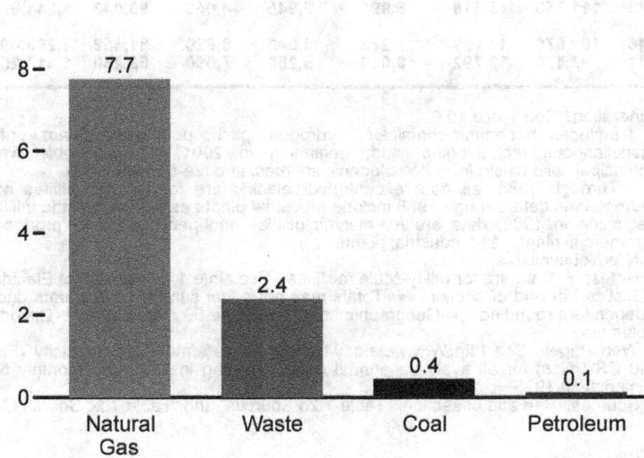

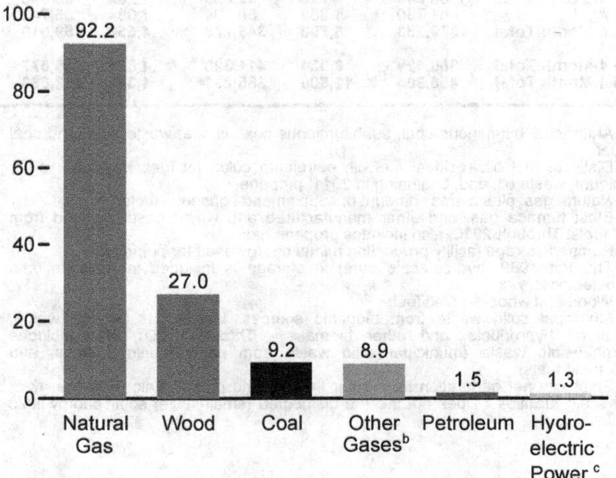

[a] Conventional hydroelectric power, wood, waste, geothermal, solar, and wind.
[b] Blast furnace gas, and other manufactured and waste gases derived from fossil fuels.
[c] Conventional hydroelectric power.
Note: Data are for utility-scale facilities.
Web Page: http://www.eia.gov/totalenergy/data/monthly/#electricity.
Sources: Tables 7.2a–7.2c.

Source: *U.S. Energy Information Administration, Monthly Energy Review, July 2017*

Table 7.2a Electricity Net Generation: Total (All Sectors)

(Sum of Tables 7.2b and 7.2c; Million Kilowatthours)

	Fossil Fuels						Renewable Energy						
							Conventional Hydroelectric Power[f]	Biomass					
	Coal[a]	Petroleum[b]	Natural Gas[c]	Other Gases[d]	Nuclear Electric Power	Hydroelectric Pumped Storage[e]		Wood[g]	Waste[h]	Geothermal	Solar[i]	Wind	Total[j]
1950 Total	154,520	33,734	44,559	NA	0	(f)	100,885	390	NA	NA	NA	NA	334,088
1955 Total	301,363	37,138	95,285	NA	0	(f)	116,236	276	NA	NA	NA	NA	550,299
1960 Total	403,067	47,987	157,970	NA	518	(f)	149,440	140	NA	33	NA	NA	759,156
1965 Total	570,926	64,801	221,559	NA	3,657	(f)	196,984	269	NA	189	NA	NA	1,058,386
1970 Total	704,394	184,183	372,890	NA	21,804	(f)	250,957	136	220	525	NA	NA	1,535,111
1975 Total	852,786	289,095	299,778	NA	172,505	(f)	303,153	18	174	3,246	NA	NA	1,920,755
1980 Total	1,161,562	245,994	346,240	NA	251,116	(f)	279,182	275	158	5,073	NA	NA	2,289,600
1985 Total	1,402,128	100,202	291,946	NA	383,691	(f)	284,311	743	640	9,325	11	6	2,473,002
1990 Total[k]	1,594,011	126,460	372,765	10,383	576,862	-3,508	292,866	32,522	13,260	15,434	367	2,789	3,037,827
1995 Total	1,709,426	74,554	496,058	13,870	673,402	-2,725	310,833	36,521	20,405	13,378	497	3,164	3,353,487
2000 Total	1,966,265	111,221	601,038	13,955	753,893	-5,539	275,573	37,595	23,131	14,093	493	5,593	3,802,105
2001 Total	1,903,956	124,880	639,129	9,039	768,826	-8,823	216,961	35,200	14,548	13,741	543	6,737	3,736,644
2002 Total	1,933,130	94,567	691,006	11,463	780,064	-8,743	264,329	38,665	15,044	14,491	555	10,354	3,858,452
2003 Total	1,973,737	119,406	649,908	15,600	763,733	-8,535	275,806	37,529	15,812	14,424	534	11,187	3,883,185
2004 Total	1,978,301	121,145	710,100	15,252	788,528	-8,488	268,417	38,117	15,421	14,811	575	14,144	3,970,555
2005 Total	2,012,873	122,225	760,960	13,464	781,986	-6,558	270,321	38,856	15,420	14,692	550	17,811	4,055,423
2006 Total	1,990,511	64,166	816,441	14,177	787,219	-6,558	289,246	38,762	16,099	14,568	508	26,589	4,064,702
2007 Total	2,016,456	65,739	896,590	13,453	806,425	-6,896	247,510	39,014	16,525	14,637	612	34,450	4,156,745
2008 Total	1,985,801	46,243	882,981	11,707	806,208	-6,288	254,831	37,300	17,734	14,840	864	55,363	4,119,388
2009 Total	1,755,904	38,937	920,979	10,632	798,855	-4,627	273,445	36,050	18,443	15,009	891	73,886	3,950,331
2010 Total	1,847,290	37,061	987,697	11,313	806,968	-5,501	260,203	37,172	18,917	15,219	1,212	94,652	4,125,060
2011 Total	1,733,430	30,182	1,013,689	11,566	790,204	-6,421	319,355	37,449	19,222	15,316	1,818	120,177	4,100,141
2012 Total	1,514,043	23,190	1,225,894	11,898	769,331	-4,950	276,240	37,799	19,823	15,562	4,327	140,822	4,047,765
2013 Total	1,581,115	27,164	1,124,836	12,853	789,016	-4,681	268,565	40,028	20,830	15,775	9,036	167,840	4,065,964
2014 Total	1,581,710	30,232	1,126,609	12,022	797,166	-6,174	259,367	42,340	21,650	15,877	17,691	181,655	4,093,606
2015 January	132,451	2,973	101,687	1,246	74,270	-551	24,138	3,717	1,725	1,362	1,155	15,162	360,455
February	126,977	6,321	91,315	1,025	63,461	-456	22,286	3,372	1,524	1,260	1,484	14,922	334,476
March	108,488	1,778	99,423	1,091	64,547	-409	24,281	3,457	1,712	1,394	2,072	15,308	324,192
April	88,989	1,728	92,806	979	59,784	-214	22,471	3,246	1,729	1,272	2,379	17,867	294,133
May	104,585	1,939	101,516	1,099	65,827	-370	20,125	3,338	1,799	1,390	2,504	17,151	322,087
June	125,673	1,860	121,478	1,118	68,516	-398	20,414	3,496	1,784	1,302	2,558	13,421	362,409
July	139,100	2,304	141,119	1,235	71,412	-513	21,014	3,806	1,989	1,357	2,627	13,675	400,419
August	134,670	2,133	139,084	1,196	72,415	-626	19,122	3,788	1,921	1,344	2,688	13,080	392,116
September	117,986	2,034	123,036	1,210	66,476	-544	16,094	3,450	1,805	1,203	2,217	13,972	350,122
October	96,759	1,771	110,005	906	60,571	-443	16,630	3,252	1,843	1,323	1,910	16,380	312,112
November	87,227	1,710	102,236	902	60,264	-285	19,338	3,418	1,902	1,334	1,730	19,682	300,653
December	89,495	1,697	109,777	1,110	69,634	-281	23,166	3,587	1,969	1,377	1,570	20,098	324,427
Total	**1,352,398**	**28,249**	**1,333,482**	**13,117**	**797,178**	**-5,091**	**249,080**	**41,929**	**21,703**	**15,918**	**24,893**	**190,719**	**4,077,601**
2016 January	113,551	2,296	109,787	1,263	72,525	-312	25,426	3,615	1,931	1,471	1,516	18,531	352,745
February	92,719	2,140	98,190	1,169	65,638	-399	24,150	3,394	1,713	1,372	2,443	20,204	313,749
March	72,138	1,766	103,791	1,241	66,149	-384	27,025	3,381	1,810	1,460	2,713	21,979	304,168
April	72,022	1,831	99,561	1,149	62,365	-452	25,475	2,909	1,819	1,340	2,949	20,745	292,836
May	81,728	1,924	110,901	977	66,576	-321	25,362	3,173	1,929	1,476	3,603	18,795	317,337
June	116,227	1,945	131,883	1,085	67,175	-497	22,902	3,414	1,829	1,364	3,610	16,318	368,418
July	136,504	2,318	151,860	1,066	70,349	-784	21,247	3,652	1,910	1,424	4,097	17,595	412,450
August	135,811	2,360	155,117	1,102	71,526	-902	19,359	3,650	1,908	1,444	3,948	13,561	410,113
September	114,282	1,924	125,639	1,050	65,448	-715	16,281	3,369	1,763	1,451	3,683	16,430	351,769
October	99,338	1,552	102,625	891	60,733	-561	17,249	3,105	1,752	1,489	3,193	20,380	312,828
November	87,000	1,839	94,529	1,001	65,179	-607	18,815	3,257	1,773	1,507	2,700	19,342	297,427
December	118,790	2,011	96,412	1,007	71,662	-753	22,538	3,584	1,932	1,620	2,299	22,991	345,238
Total	**1,240,108**	**23,906**	**1,380,295**	**13,000**	**805,327**	**-6,686**	**265,829**	**40,504**	**22,068**	**17,417**	**36,754**	**226,872**	**4,079,079**
2017 January	115,549	2,120	91,325	1,115	73,121	-418	27,704	3,451	1,891	1,541	2,206	20,350	341,072
February	87,267	1,623	78,581	1,152	64,053	-504	24,611	3,308	1,676	1,369	2,562	21,692	288,414
March	89,648	1,716	92,638	1,206	65,093	-517	30,198	3,504	1,763	1,533	4,474	25,599	317,934
April	81,789	1,332	86,234	1,084	56,743	-437	29,236	3,254	1,661	1,503	4,816	25,403	293,679
4-Month Total	**374,253**	**6,790**	**348,778**	**4,557**	**259,010**	**-1,876**	**111,750**	**13,518**	**6,991**	**5,945**	**14,058**	**93,043**	**1,241,098**
2016 4-Month Total	**350,429**	**8,034**	**411,329**	**4,821**	**266,677**	**-1,546**	**102,076**	**13,299**	**7,273**	**5,643**	**9,620**	**81,459**	**1,263,498**
2015 4-Month Total	**456,904**	**12,800**	**385,231**	**4,341**	**262,063**	**-1,631**	**93,176**	**13,792**	**6,690**	**5,288**	**7,090**	**63,259**	**1,313,256**

[a] Anthracite, bituminous coal, subbituminous coal, lignite, waste coal, and coal synfuel.

[b] Distillate fuel oil, residual fuel oil, petroleum coke, jet fuel, kerosene, other petroleum, waste oil, and, beginning in 2011, propane.

[c] Natural gas, plus a small amount of supplemental gaseous fuels.

[d] Blast furnace gas, and other manufactured and waste gases derived from fossil fuels. Through 2010, also includes propane gas.

[e] Pumped storage facility production minus energy used for pumping.

[f] Through 1989, hydroelectric pumped storage is included in "Conventional Hydroelectric Power."

[g] Wood and wood-derived fuels.

[h] Municipal solid waste from biogenic sources, landfill gas, sludge waste, agricultural byproducts, and other biomass. Through 2000, also includes non-renewable waste (municipal solid waste from non-biogenic sources, and tire-derived fuels).

[i] Electricity net generation from solar thermal and photovoltaic (PV) energy at utility-scale facilities. Does not include distributed (small-scale) solar photovoltaic generation. See Table 10.6.

[j] Includes batteries, chemicals, hydrogen, pitch, purchased steam, sulfur, miscellaneous technologies, and, beginning in 2001, non-renewable waste (municipal solid waste from non-biogenic sources, and tire-derived fuels).

[k] Through 1988, all data except hydroelectric are for electric utilities only; hydroelectric data through 1988 include industrial plants as well as electric utilities. Beginning in 1989, data are for electric utilities, independent power producers, commercial plants, and industrial plants.

NA=Not available.

Notes: • Data are for utility-scale facilities. See Note 1, "Coverage of Electricity Statistics," at end of section. • Totals may not equal sum of components due to independent rounding. • Geographic coverage is the 50 states and the District of Columbia.

Web Page: See http://www.eia.gov/totalenergy/data/monthly/#electricity (Excel and CSV files) for all available annual data beginning in 1949 and monthly data beginning in 1973.

Sources: See end of section, "Table 7.2b Sources" and "Table 7.2c Sources."

Source: *U.S. Energy Information Administration, Monthly Energy Review, July 2017*

Table 7.2b Electricity Net Generation: Electric Power Sector

(Subset of Table 7.2a; Million Kilowatthours)

	Fossil Fuels						Renewable Energy						
								Biomass					
	Coal[a]	Petroleum[b]	Natural Gas[c]	Other Gases[d]	Nuclear Electric Power	Hydroelectric Pumped Storage[e]	Conventional Hydroelectric Power[f]	Wood[g]	Waste[h]	Geothermal	Solar[i]	Wind	Total[j]
1950 Total	154,520	33,734	44,559	NA	0	(f)	95,938	390	NA	NA	NA	NA	329,141
1955 Total	301,363	37,138	95,285	NA	0	(f)	112,975	276	NA	NA	NA	NA	547,038
1960 Total	403,067	47,987	157,970	NA	518	(f)	145,833	140	NA	33	NA	NA	755,549
1965 Total	570,926	64,801	221,559	NA	3,657	(f)	193,851	269	NA	189	NA	NA	1,055,252
1970 Total	704,394	184,183	372,890	NA	21,804	(f)	247,714	136	220	525	NA	NA	1,531,868
1975 Total	852,786	289,095	299,778	NA	172,505	(f)	300,047	18	174	3,246	NA	NA	1,917,649
1980 Total	1,161,562	245,994	346,240	NA	251,116	(f)	276,021	275	158	5,073	NA	NA	2,286,439
1985 Total	1,402,128	100,202	291,946	NA	383,691	(f)	281,149	743	640	9,325	11	6	2,469,841
1990 Total[k]	1,572,109	118,864	309,486	621	576,862	-3,508	289,753	7,032	11,500	15,434	367	2,789	2,901,322
1995 Total	1,686,056	68,146	419,179	1,927	673,402	-2,725	305,410	7,597	17,986	13,378	497	3,164	3,194,230
2000 Total	1,943,111	105,192	517,978	2,028	753,893	-5,539	271,338	8,916	20,307	14,093	493	5,593	3,637,529
2001 Total	1,882,826	119,149	554,940	586	768,826	-8,823	213,749	8,294	12,944	13,741	543	6,737	3,580,053
2002 Total	1,910,613	89,733	607,683	1,970	780,064	-8,743	260,491	9,009	13,145	14,491	555	10,354	3,698,458
2003 Total	1,952,714	113,697	567,303	2,647	763,733	-8,535	271,512	9,528	13,808	14,424	534	11,187	3,721,159
2004 Total	1,957,188	114,678	627,172	3,568	788,528	-8,488	265,064	9,736	13,062	14,811	575	14,144	3,808,360
2005 Total	1,992,054	116,482	683,829	3,777	781,986	-6,558	267,040	10,570	13,031	14,692	550	17,811	3,902,192
2006 Total	1,969,737	59,708	734,417	4,254	787,219	-6,558	286,254	10,341	13,927	14,568	508	26,589	3,908,077
2007 Total	1,998,390	61,306	814,752	4,042	806,425	-6,896	245,843	10,711	14,294	14,637	612	34,450	4,005,343
2008 Total	1,968,838	42,881	802,372	3,200	806,208	-6,288	253,096	10,638	15,379	14,840	864	55,363	3,974,349
2009 Total	1,741,123	35,811	841,006	3,058	798,855	-4,627	271,506	10,738	15,954	15,009	891	73,886	3,809,837
2010 Total	1,827,738	34,679	901,389	2,967	806,968	-5,501	258,455	11,446	16,376	15,219	1,206	94,636	3,972,386
2011 Total	1,717,891	28,202	926,290	2,939	790,204	-6,421	317,531	10,733	15,989	15,316	1,727	120,121	3,948,186
2012 Total	1,500,557	20,072	1,132,791	2,984	769,331	-4,950	273,859	11,050	16,555	15,562	4,164	140,749	3,890,358
2013 Total	1,567,722	24,510	1,028,949	4,322	789,016	-4,681	265,058	12,302	16,918	15,775	8,724	167,742	3,903,715
2014 Total	1,568,774	28,043	1,033,172	3,358	797,166	-6,174	258,046	15,027	17,602	15,877	17,304	181,496	3,937,003
2015 January	131,431	2,789	93,450	394	74,270	-551	24,014	1,307	1,411	1,362	1,134	15,146	346,758
February	126,024	6,074	84,207	329	63,461	-456	22,179	1,234	1,261	1,260	1,459	14,908	322,473
March	107,471	1,644	92,110	327	64,547	-409	24,148	1,227	1,393	1,394	2,037	15,293	311,741
April	88,147	1,570	85,828	290	59,784	-214	22,331	1,025	1,402	1,272	2,338	17,850	282,197
May	103,672	1,794	94,124	338	65,827	-370	19,995	1,093	1,483	1,390	2,456	17,136	309,552
June	124,677	1,723	113,390	299	68,516	-398	20,297	1,244	1,473	1,302	2,512	13,410	349,067
July	138,060	2,185	132,266	311	71,412	-513	20,896	1,365	1,639	1,357	2,579	13,666	385,889
August	133,651	2,013	130,314	331	72,415	-626	19,030	1,410	1,587	1,344	2,639	13,070	377,856
September	117,005	1,899	114,792	331	66,476	-544	16,015	1,201	1,481	1,203	2,178	13,961	336,618
October	95,872	1,657	102,022	229	60,571	-443	16,513	1,047	1,509	1,323	1,875	16,364	299,168
November	86,362	1,583	94,132	234	60,264	-285	19,202	1,157	1,565	1,334	1,702	19,663	287,551
December	88,622	1,575	101,022	304	69,634	-281	23,017	1,254	1,620	1,377	1,545	20,080	310,423
Total	**1,340,993**	**26,505**	**1,237,656**	**3,715**	**797,178**	**-5,091**	**247,636**	**14,563**	**17,823**	**15,918**	**24,456**	**190,547**	**3,919,294**
2016 January	112,632	2,163	101,394	370	72,525	-312	25,285	1,235	1,603	1,471	1,491	18,513	339,004
February	91,856	2,013	90,441	341	65,638	-399	24,014	1,200	1,423	1,372	2,395	20,184	301,047
March	71,255	1,651	95,645	373	66,149	-384	26,873	1,148	1,461	1,460	2,664	21,957	290,840
April	71,279	1,717	91,696	330	62,365	-452	25,339	859	1,501	1,340	2,903	20,724	280,203
May	80,966	1,779	102,698	296	66,576	-321	25,226	953	1,629	1,476	3,547	18,776	304,263
June	115,375	1,817	123,467	365	67,175	-497	22,791	1,139	1,558	1,364	3,545	16,301	355,036
July	135,589	2,172	143,001	345	70,349	-784	21,140	1,289	1,595	1,424	4,024	17,578	398,363
August	134,907	2,209	146,199	346	71,526	-902	19,266	1,315	1,610	1,444	3,886	13,548	396,003
September	113,529	1,799	117,270	369	65,448	-715	16,217	1,160	1,502	1,451	3,624	16,415	338,670
October	98,633	1,429	94,516	246	60,733	-561	17,166	920	1,474	1,489	3,145	20,362	300,141
November	86,365	1,723	86,158	361	65,179	-607	18,744	973	1,498	1,507	2,660	19,324	284,484
December	118,054	1,855	87,834	327	71,662	-753	22,411	1,235	1,643	1,620	2,273	22,969	331,793
Total	**1,230,442**	**22,325**	**1,280,317**	**4,066**	**805,327**	**-6,686**	**264,470**	**13,425**	**18,496**	**17,417**	**36,157**	**226,653**	**3,919,849**
2017 January	114,723	1,991	82,815	364	73,121	-418	27,569	1,098	1,583	1,541	2,182	20,333	327,533
February	86,553	1,513	71,031	344	64,053	-504	24,488	1,076	1,397	1,369	2,533	21,675	276,093
March	88,929	1,581	84,713	382	65,093	-517	30,047	1,230	1,463	1,533	4,425	25,576	305,033
April	81,166	1,236	78,659	302	56,743	-437	29,090	1,082	1,388	1,503	4,764	25,382	281,440
4-Month Total	**371,371**	**6,321**	**317,218**	**1,392**	**259,010**	**-1,876**	**111,193**	**4,487**	**5,831**	**5,945**	**13,904**	**92,966**	**1,190,099**
2016 4-Month Total	**347,022**	**7,543**	**379,176**	**1,413**	**266,677**	**-1,546**	**101,510**	**4,442**	**5,988**	**5,643**	**9,453**	**81,379**	**1,211,094**
2015 4-Month Total	**453,072**	**12,077**	**355,595**	**1,340**	**262,063**	**-1,631**	**92,671**	**4,793**	**5,466**	**5,288**	**6,969**	**63,197**	**1,263,168**

[a] Anthracite, bituminous coal, subbituminous coal, lignite, waste coal, and coal synfuel.
[b] Distillate fuel oil, residual fuel oil, petroleum coke, jet fuel, kerosene, other petroleum, waste oil, and, beginning in 2011, propane.
[c] Natural gas, plus a small amount of supplemental gaseous fuels.
[d] Blast furnace gas, and other manufactured and waste gases derived from fossil fuels. Through 2010, also includes propane gas.
[e] Pumped storage facility production minus energy used for pumping.
[f] Through 1989, hydroelectric pumped storage is included in "Conventional Hydroelectric Power."
[g] Wood and wood-derived fuels.
[h] Municipal solid waste from biogenic sources, landfill gas, sludge waste, agricultural byproducts, and other biomass. Through 2000, also includes non-renewable waste (municipal solid waste from non-biogenic sources, and tire-derived fuels).
[i] Electricity net generation from solar thermal and photovoltaic (PV) energy at utility-scale facilities. Does not include distributed (small-scale) solar photovoltaic generation. See Table 10.6.
[j] Includes batteries, chemicals, hydrogen, pitch, purchased steam, sulfur, miscellaneous technologies, and, beginning in 2001, non-renewable waste (municipal solid waste from non-biogenic sources, and tire-derived fuels).
[k] Through 1988, data are for electric utilities only. Beginning in 1989, data are for electric utilites and independent power producers.

NA=Not available.

Notes: • Data are for utility-scale facilities. See Note 1, "Coverage of Electricity Statistics," at end of section. • The electric power sector comprises electricity-only and combined-heat-and-power (CHP) plants within the NAICS 22 category whose primary business is to sell electricity, or electricity and heat, to the public. • Totals may not equal sum of components due to independent rounding. • Geographic coverage is the 50 states and the District of Columbia.

Web Page: See http://www.eia.gov/totalenergy/data/monthly/#electricity (Excel and CSV files) for all available annual data beginning in 1949 and monthly data beginning in 1973.

Sources: See end of section.

Source: *U.S. Energy Information Administration, Monthly Energy Review, July 2017*

Table 7.2c Electricity Net Generation: Commercial and Industrial Sectors

(Subset of Table 7.2a; Million Kilowatthours)

	Commercial Sector[a]					Industrial Sector[b]							
				Biomass							Biomass		
	Coal[c]	Petroleum[d]	Natural Gas[e]	Waste[f]	Total[g]	Coal[c]	Petroleum[d]	Natural Gas[e]	Other Gases[h]	Hydroelectric Power[i]	Wood[j]	Waste[f]	Total[k]
1950 Total	NA	NA	NA	NA	NA	NA	NA	NA	NA	4,946	NA	NA	4,946
1955 Total	NA	NA	NA	NA	NA	NA	NA	NA	NA	3,261	NA	NA	3,261
1960 Total	NA	NA	NA	NA	NA	NA	NA	NA	NA	3,607	NA	NA	3,607
1965 Total	NA	NA	NA	NA	NA	NA	NA	NA	NA	3,134	NA	NA	3,134
1970 Total	NA	NA	NA	NA	NA	NA	NA	NA	NA	3,244	NA	NA	3,244
1975 Total	NA	NA	NA	NA	NA	NA	NA	NA	NA	3,106	NA	NA	3,106
1980 Total	NA	NA	NA	NA	NA	NA	NA	NA	NA	3,161	NA	NA	3,161
1985 Total	NA	NA	NA	NA	NA	NA	NA	NA	NA	3,161	NA	NA	3,161
1990 Total	796	589	3,272	812	5,837	21,107	7,008	60,007	9,641	2,975	25,379	949	130,830
1995 Total	998	379	5,162	1,519	8,232	22,372	6,030	71,717	11,943	5,304	28,868	900	151,025
2000 Total	1,097	432	4,262	1,985	7,903	22,056	5,597	78,798	11,927	4,135	28,652	839	156,673
2001 Total	995	438	4,434	1,007	7,416	20,135	5,293	79,755	8,454	3,145	26,888	596	149,175
2002 Total	992	431	4,310	1,053	7,415	21,525	4,403	79,013	9,493	3,825	29,643	846	152,580
2003 Total	1,206	423	3,899	1,289	7,496	19,817	5,285	78,705	12,953	4,222	27,988	715	154,530
2004 Total	1,340	499	3,969	1,562	8,270	19,773	5,967	78,959	11,684	3,248	28,367	797	153,925
2005 Total	1,353	375	4,249	1,657	8,492	19,466	5,368	72,882	9,687	3,195	28,271	733	144,739
2006 Total	1,310	235	4,355	1,599	8,371	19,464	4,223	77,669	9,923	2,899	28,400	572	148,254
2007 Total	1,371	189	4,257	1,599	8,273	16,694	4,243	77,580	9,411	1,590	28,287	631	143,128
2008 Total	1,261	142	4,188	1,534	7,926	15,703	3,219	76,421	8,507	1,676	26,641	821	137,113
2009 Total	1,096	163	4,225	1,748	8,165	13,686	2,963	75,748	7,574	1,868	25,292	740	132,329
2010 Total	1,111	124	4,725	1,672	8,592	18,441	2,258	81,583	8,343	1,668	25,706	869	144,082
2011 Total	1,049	89	5,487	2,315	10,080	14,490	1,891	81,911	8,624	1,799	26,691	917	141,875
2012 Total	883	196	6,603	2,319	11,301	12,603	2,922	86,500	8,913	2,353	26,725	948	146,107
2013 Total	839	124	7,154	2,567	12,234	12,554	2,531	88,733	8,531	3,463	27,691	1,346	150,015
2014 Total	595	255	7,227	2,681	12,520	12,341	1,934	86,209	8,664	1,282	27,239	1,367	144,083
2015 January	56	24	564	209	981	964	161	7,674	852	121	2,404	105	12,717
February	59	73	499	183	932	894	174	6,609	696	105	2,132	80	11,071
March	52	12	560	213	977	965	123	6,753	764	130	2,226	106	11,475
April	38	9	513	216	931	804	149	6,465	690	138	2,218	112	11,005
May	32	11	583	221	1,013	881	135	6,809	761	127	2,239	95	11,522
June	45	10	662	222	1,098	951	128	7,426	819	114	2,251	89	12,244
July	44	12	769	242	1,238	995	107	8,084	925	115	2,434	108	13,292
August	39	12	760	234	1,206	980	108	8,010	864	90	2,377	101	13,054
September	33	8	716	230	1,145	947	127	7,528	879	77	2,245	94	12,359
October	34	7	643	218	1,049	853	107	7,340	678	114	2,201	116	11,894
November	35	6	583	222	992	830	121	7,521	668	133	2,259	115	12,110
December	41	7	617	226	1,033	832	115	8,137	806	145	2,331	122	12,970
Total	**509**	**191**	**7,471**	**2,637**	**12,595**	**10,896**	**1,552**	**88,355**	**9,401**	**1,410**	**27,318**	**1,243**	**145,712**
2016 January	43	12	648	216	1,057	876	122	7,746	893	136	2,373	112	12,684
February	47	14	550	188	944	817	113	7,198	828	131	2,187	101	11,758
March	44	6	595	230	1,043	839	108	7,551	868	147	2,230	119	12,284
April	29	8	615	206	1,022	713	106	7,250	819	131	2,045	112	11,611
May	26	8	650	202	1,055	736	138	7,554	681	130	2,219	98	12,018
June	28	7	694	181	1,079	824	122	7,723	720	105	2,266	90	12,303
July	30	10	763	209	1,204	884	136	8,095	721	101	2,356	105	12,883
August	33	14	781	203	1,212	870	137	8,137	756	87	2,323	94	12,898
September	34	7	675	182	1,065	718	118	7,695	681	60	2,201	78	12,034
October	36	8	583	191	969	669	115	7,526	646	80	2,181	87	11,718
November	39	8	591	184	961	595	109	7,781	641	68	2,281	91	11,982
December	45	11	605	189	981	691	145	7,973	680	123	2,343	101	12,464
Total	**436**	**112**	**7,750**	**2,382**	**12,593**	**9,231**	**1,469**	**92,227**	**8,934**	**1,300**	**27,007**	**1,190**	**146,637**
2017 January	40	19	662	208	1,060	786	111	7,848	751	132	2,344	100	12,479
February	31	10	576	186	931	683	100	6,975	808	120	2,224	92	11,389
March	35	13	638	197	1,045	684	122	7,287	825	136	2,272	103	11,856
April	22	8	529	180	903	601	87	7,046	781	131	2,167	93	11,335
4-Month Total	**128**	**50**	**2,404**	**772**	**3,940**	**2,754**	**419**	**29,157**	**3,165**	**519**	**9,008**	**388**	**47,059**
2016 4-Month Total	**164**	**40**	**2,409**	**840**	**4,067**	**3,244**	**450**	**29,745**	**3,408**	**545**	**8,836**	**444**	**48,337**
2015 4-Month Total	**205**	**117**	**2,136**	**821**	**3,820**	**3,627**	**606**	**27,501**	**3,002**	**494**	**8,980**	**403**	**46,268**

[a] Commercial combined-heat-and-power (CHP) and commercial electricity-only plants.

[b] Industrial combined-heat-and-power (CHP) and industrial electricity-only plants.

[c] Anthracite, bituminous coal, subbituminous coal, lignite, waste coal, and coal synfuel.

[d] Distillate fuel oil, residual fuel oil, petroleum coke, jet fuel, kerosene, other petroleum, waste oil, and, beginning in 2011, propane.

[e] Natural gas, plus a small amount of supplemental gaseous fuels.

[f] Municipal solid waste from biogenic sources, landfill gas, sludge waste, agricultural byproducts, and other biomass. Through 2000, also includes non-renewable waste (municipal solid waste from non-biogenic sources, and tire-derived fuels).

[g] Includes a small amount of conventional hydroelectric power, other gases, solar photovoltaic (PV) energy, wind, wood, and other, which are not separately displayed. Does not include distributed (small-scale) solar photovoltaic generation. shown on Table 10.6.

[h] Blast furnace gas, and other manufactured and waste gases derived from fossil fuels. Through 2010, also includes propane gas.

[i] Conventional hydroelectric power.

[j] Wood and wood-derived fuels.

[k] Includes photovoltaic (PV) energy, wind, batteries, chemicals, hydrogen, pitch, purchased steam, sulfur, miscellaneous technologies, and, beginning in 2001, non-renewable waste (municipal solid waste from non-biogenic sources, and tire-derived fuels). Does not include distributed (small-scale) solar photovoltaic generation shown on Table 10.6.

NA=Not available.

Notes: • Data are for utility-scale facilities. See Note 1, "Coverage of Electricity Statistics," at end of section. • See Note 2, "Classification of Power Plants Into Energy-Use Sectors," at end of section. • Totals may not equal sum of components due to independent rounding. • Geographic coverage is the 50 states and the District of Columbia.

Web Page: See http://www.eia.gov/totalenergy/data/monthly/#electricity (Excel and CSV files) for all available annual data beginning in 1949 and monthly data beginning in 1973.

Sources: See end of section.

Source: *U.S. Energy Information Administration, Monthly Energy Review, July 2017*

Figure 7.3 Consumption of Selected Combustible Fuels for Electricity Generation

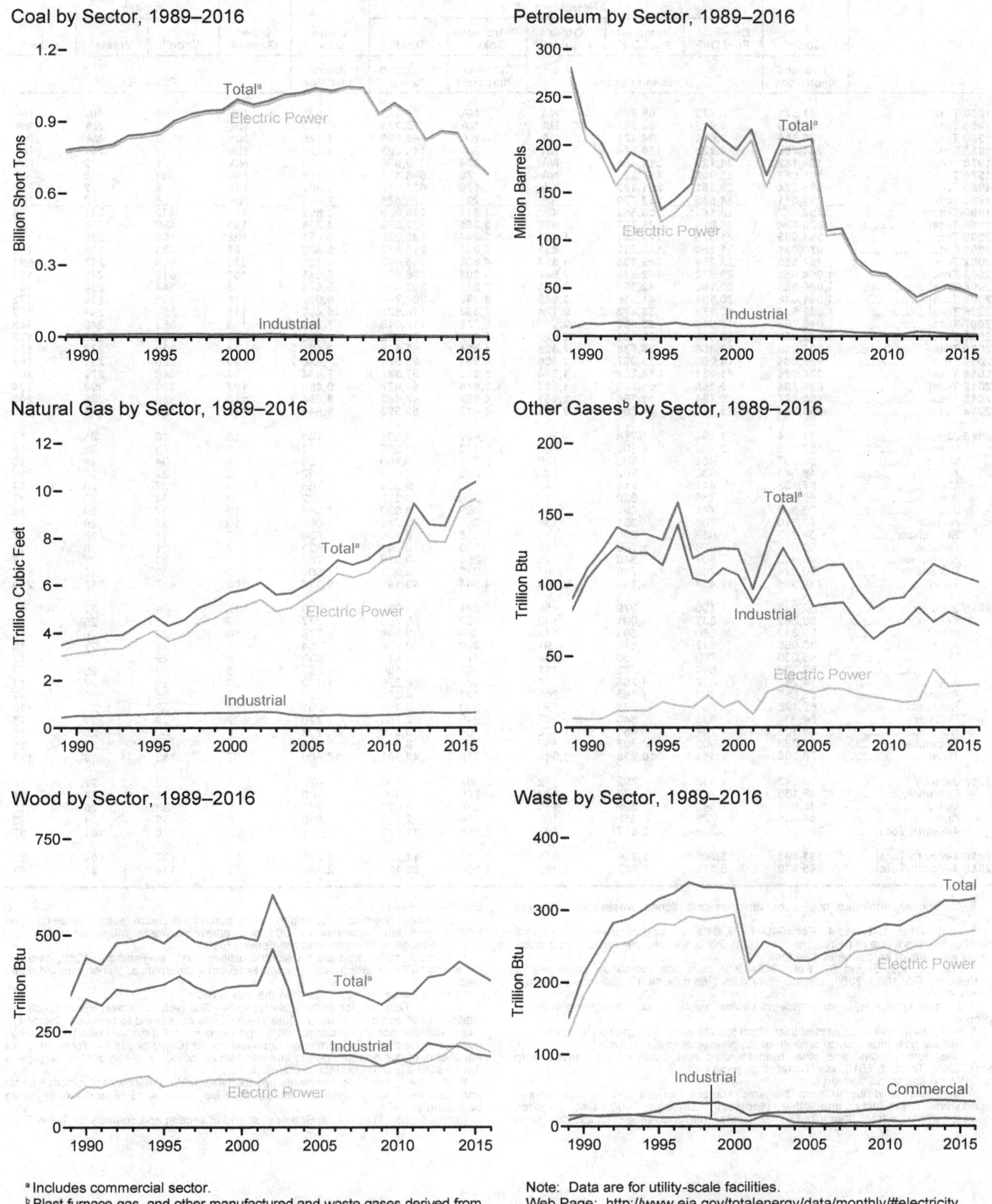

[a] Includes commercial sector.

[b] Blast furnace gas, and other manufactured and waste gases derived from fossil fuels. Through 2010, also includes propane gas.

Note: Data are for utility-scale facilities.

Web Page: http://www.eia.gov/totalenergy/data/monthly/#electricity.

Sources: Tables 7.3a–7.3c.

Source: *U.S. Energy Information Administration, Monthly Energy Review, July 2017*

Table 7.3a Consumption of Combustible Fuels for Electricity Generation: Total (All Sectors) (Sum of Tables 7.3b and 7.3c)

		Petroleum							Biomass		
	Coal[a]	Distillate Fuel Oil[b]	Residual Fuel Oil[c]	Other Liquids[d]	Petroleum Coke[e]	Total[e]	Natural Gas[f]	Other Gases[g]	Wood[h]	Waste[i]	Other[j]
	Thousand Short Tons	Thousand Barrels			Thousand Short Tons	Thousand Barrels	Billion Cubic Feet	Trillion Btu			
1950 Total	91,871	5,423	69,998	NA	NA	75,421	629	NA	5	NA	NA
1955 Total	143,759	5,412	69,862	NA	NA	75,274	1,153	NA	3	NA	NA
1960 Total	176,685	3,824	84,371	NA	NA	88,195	1,725	NA	2	NA	NA
1965 Total	244,788	4,928	110,274	NA	NA	115,203	2,321	NA	3	NA	NA
1970 Total	320,182	24,123	311,381	NA	636	338,686	3,932	NA	1	2	NA
1975 Total	405,962	38,907	467,221	NA	70	506,479	3,158	NA	(s)	2	NA
1980 Total	569,274	29,051	391,163	NA	179	421,110	3,682	NA	3	2	NA
1985 Total	693,841	14,635	158,779	NA	231	174,571	3,044	NA	8	7	NA
1990 Total[k]	792,457	18,143	190,652	437	1,914	218,800	3,692	112	442	211	36
1995 Total	860,594	19,615	95,507	680	3,355	132,578	4,738	133	480	316	42
2000 Total	994,933	31,675	143,381	1,450	3,744	195,228	5,691	126	496	330	46
2001 Total	972,691	31,150	165,312	855	3,871	216,672	5,832	97	486	228	160
2002 Total	987,583	23,286	109,235	1,894	6,836	168,597	6,126	131	605	257	191
2003 Total	1,014,058	29,672	142,518	2,947	6,303	206,653	5,616	156	519	249	193
2004 Total	1,020,523	20,163	142,088	2,856	7,677	203,494	5,675	135	344	230	183
2005 Total	1,041,448	20,651	141,518	2,968	8,330	206,785	6,036	110	355	230	173
2006 Total	1,030,556	13,174	58,473	2,174	7,363	110,634	6,462	115	350	241	172
2007 Total	1,046,795	15,683	63,833	2,917	6,036	112,615	7,089	115	353	245	168
2008 Total	1,042,335	12,832	38,191	2,822	5,417	80,932	6,896	97	339	267	172
2009 Total	934,683	12,658	28,576	2,328	4,821	67,668	7,121	84	320	272	170
2010 Total	979,684	14,050	23,997	2,056	4,994	65,071	7,680	90	350	281	184
2011 Total	934,938	11,231	14,251	1,844	5,012	52,387	7,884	91	348	279	205
2012 Total	825,734	9,285	11,755	1,565	3,675	40,977	9,485	103	390	290	204
2013 Total	860,729	9,784	11,766	1,681	4,852	47,492	8,596	115	398	298	200
2014 Total	853,634	14,465	14,704	2,363	4,412	53,593	8,544	110	431	314	200
2015 January	71,384	1,294	1,718	281	402	5,301	745	10	36	25	17
February	67,136	3,732	4,102	755	413	10,655	676	8	33	22	15
March	58,367	851	805	129	275	3,160	736	8	34	25	16
April	48,543	638	762	122	300	3,020	692	8	31	25	16
May	57,153	841	714	143	339	3,394	766	9	32	26	17
June	68,982	785	823	137	306	3,277	922	9	34	26	17
July	76,570	741	1,091	163	409	4,039	1,084	10	37	29	19
August	73,810	706	961	134	388	3,740	1,065	10	37	28	18
September	64,823	643	830	183	376	3,538	930	9	34	26	17
October	53,659	636	759	146	300	3,041	825	7	31	26	17
November	48,943	804	840	76	260	3,019	767	7	33	27	17
December	50,224	768	718	94	276	2,961	807	9	35	28	18
Total	739,594	12,438	14,124	2,363	4,044	49,145	10,017	106	407	313	204
2016 January	62,048	1,190	979	160	341	4,037	803	10	34	27	16
February	50,567	837	1,091	183	329	3,753	717	9	33	25	14
March	39,857	660	593	113	366	3,198	775	10	33	26	15
April	38,989	617	610	91	390	3,268	754	9	27	27	16
May	45,036	799	658	108	371	3,421	839	8	29	27	17
June	63,326	694	772	111	382	3,488	1,007	8	32	26	17
July	74,241	812	1,255	138	403	4,220	1,179	9	34	27	17
August	73,868	795	1,196	205	422	4,304	1,191	9	35	28	17
September	62,428	631	781	120	383	3,450	951	8	32	25	16
October	54,634	623	846	97	246	2,798	776	7	29	27	16
November	48,126	787	651	122	304	3,079	701	8	30	25	16
December	64,883	905	807	187	337	3,586	706	8	34	27	16
Total	678,005	9,351	10,238	1,636	4,275	42,601	10,400	102	382	316	193
2017 January	63,542	1,018	792	172	362	3,790	678	9	32	27	16
February	48,155	780	676	103	266	2,890	585	9	31	24	14
March	48,915	843	699	110	276	3,033	701	9	33	26	15
April	44,455	728	650	109	154	2,259	648	9	30	24	15
4-Month Total	205,067	3,369	2,817	493	1,059	11,972	2,611	36	126	101	60
2016 4-Month Total	191,461	3,305	3,274	548	1,426	14,256	3,049	38	127	104	62
2015 4-Month Total	245,430	6,515	7,387	1,287	1,390	22,137	2,850	35	134	97	63

[a] Anthracite, bituminous coal, subbituminous coal, lignite, waste coal, and coal synfuel.
[b] Fuel oil nos. 1, 2, and 4. For 1949–1979, data are for gas turbine and internal combustion plant use of petroleum. For 1980–2000, electric utility data also include small amounts of kerosene and jet fuel.
[c] Fuel oil nos. 5 and 6. For 1949–1979, data are for steam plant use of petroleum. For 1980–2000, electric utility data also include a small amount of fuel oil no. 4.
[d] Jet fuel, kerosene, other petroleum liquids, waste oil, and, beginning in 2011, propane.
[e] Petroleum coke is converted from short tons to barrels by multiplying by 5.
[f] Natural gas, plus a small amount of supplemental gaseous fuels.
[g] Blast furnace gas, and other manufactured and waste gases derived from fossil fuels. Through 2010, also includes propane gas.
[h] Wood and wood-derived fuels.
[i] Municipal solid waste from biogenic sources, landfill gas, sludge waste, agricultural byproducts, and other biomass. Through 2000, also includes non-renewable waste (municipal solid waste from non-biogenic sources, and tire-derived fuels).
[j] Batteries, chemicals, hydrogen, pitch, purchased steam, sulfur, miscellaneous technologies, and, beginning in 2001, non-renewable waste (municipal solid waste from non-biogenic sources, and tire-derived fuels).
[k] Through 1988, data are for electric utilities only. Beginning in 1989, data are for electric utilities, independent power producers, commercial plants, and industrial plants.

NA=Not available. (s)=Less than 0.5 trillion Btu.

Notes: • Data are for utility-scale facilities. See Note 1, "Coverage of Electricity Statistics," at end of section. • Data are for fuels consumed to produce electricity. Data also include fuels consumed to produce useful thermal output at a small number of electric utility combined-heat-and-power (CHP) plants. • Totals may not equal sum of components due to independent rounding. • Geographic coverage is the 50 states and the District of Columbia.

Web Page: See http://www.eia.gov/totalenergy/data/monthly/#electricity (Excel and CSV files) for all available annual data beginning in 1949 and monthly data beginning in 1973.

Sources: See "Table 7.3b Sources" at end of section and sources for Table 7.3c.

Source: *U.S. Energy Information Administration, Monthly Energy Review, July 2017*

Table 7.3b Consumption of Combustible Fuels for Electricity Generation: Electric Power Sector (Subset of Table 7.3a)

	Coal[a]	Petroleum: Distillate Fuel Oil[b]	Petroleum: Residual Fuel Oil[c]	Petroleum: Other Liquids[d]	Petroleum: Petroleum Coke[e]	Petroleum: Total[e]	Natural Gas[f]	Other Gases[g]	Biomass: Wood[h]	Biomass: Waste[i]	Other[j]
	Thousand Short Tons	Thousand Barrels			Thousand Short Tons	Thousand Barrels	Billion Cubic Feet	Trillion Btu			
1950 Total	**91,871**	**5,423**	**69,998**	**NA**	**NA**	**75,421**	**629**	**NA**	**5**	**NA**	**NA**
1955 Total	**143,759**	**5,412**	**69,862**	**NA**	**NA**	**75,274**	**1,153**	**NA**	**3**	**NA**	**NA**
1960 Total	**176,685**	**3,824**	**84,371**	**NA**	**NA**	**88,195**	**1,725**	**NA**	**2**	**NA**	**NA**
1965 Total	**244,788**	**4,928**	**110,274**	**NA**	**NA**	**115,203**	**2,321**	**NA**	**3**	**NA**	**NA**
1970 Total	**320,182**	**24,123**	**311,381**	**NA**	**636**	**338,686**	**3,932**	**NA**	**1**	**2**	**NA**
1975 Total	**405,962**	**38,907**	**467,221**	**NA**	**70**	**506,479**	**3,158**	**NA**	**(s)**	**2**	**NA**
1980 Total	**569,274**	**29,051**	**391,163**	**NA**	**179**	**421,110**	**3,682**	**NA**	**3**	**2**	**NA**
1985 Total	**693,841**	**14,635**	**158,779**	**NA**	**231**	**174,571**	**3,044**	**NA**	**8**	**7**	**NA**
1990 Total[k]	**781,301**	**16,394**	**183,285**	**25**	**1,008**	**204,745**	**3,147**	**6**	**106**	**180**	**(s)**
1995 Total	**847,854**	**18,066**	**88,895**	**441**	**2,452**	**119,663**	**4,094**	**18**	**106**	**282**	**2**
2000 Total	**982,713**	**29,722**	**138,047**	**403**	**3,155**	**183,946**	**5,014**	**19**	**126**	**294**	**1**
2001 Total	**961,523**	**29,056**	**159,150**	**374**	**3,308**	**205,119**	**5,142**	**9**	**116**	**205**	**109**
2002 Total	**975,251**	**21,810**	**104,577**	**1,243**	**5,705**	**156,154**	**5,408**	**25**	**141**	**224**	**137**
2003 Total	**1,003,036**	**27,441**	**137,361**	**1,937**	**5,719**	**195,336**	**4,909**	**30**	**156**	**216**	**136**
2004 Total	**1,012,459**	**18,793**	**138,831**	**2,511**	**7,135**	**195,809**	**5,075**	**27**	**150**	**206**	**131**
2005 Total	**1,033,567**	**19,450**	**138,337**	**2,591**	**7,877**	**199,760**	**5,485**	**24**	**166**	**205**	**116**
2006 Total	**1,022,802**	**12,578**	**56,347**	**1,783**	**6,905**	**105,235**	**5,891**	**28**	**163**	**216**	**117**
2007 Total	**1,041,346**	**15,135**	**62,072**	**2,496**	**5,523**	**107,316**	**6,502**	**27**	**165**	**221**	**117**
2008 Total	**1,036,891**	**12,318**	**37,222**	**2,608**	**5,000**	**77,149**	**6,342**	**23**	**159**	**242**	**122**
2009 Total	**929,692**	**11,848**	**27,768**	**2,110**	**4,485**	**64,151**	**6,567**	**21**	**160**	**244**	**115**
2010 Total	**971,245**	**13,677**	**23,560**	**1,848**	**4,679**	**62,477**	**7,085**	**20**	**177**	**249**	**116**
2011 Total	**928,857**	**10,961**	**13,861**	**1,655**	**4,726**	**50,105**	**7,265**	**18**	**166**	**241**	**133**
2012 Total	**820,762**	**9,000**	**11,292**	**1,339**	**2,861**	**35,937**	**8,788**	**19**	**171**	**250**	**132**
2013 Total	**855,546**	**9,511**	**11,322**	**1,488**	**4,189**	**43,265**	**7,888**	**41**	**187**	**251**	**130**
2014 Total	**848,803**	**14,052**	**14,132**	**2,157**	**4,039**	**50,537**	**7,849**	**29**	**220**	**266**	**127**
2015 January	71,028	1,253	1,685	258	369	5,040	686	3	19	21	10
February	66,799	3,610	4,052	730	388	10,333	625	2	18	19	10
March	57,999	824	778	113	255	2,988	684	2	18	21	10
April	48,230	615	742	96	271	2,811	642	2	16	21	10
May	56,820	818	699	110	320	3,225	712	3	17	22	11
June	68,609	763	807	106	288	3,115	863	3	18	22	11
July	76,179	715	1,077	142	392	3,894	1,019	2	20	25	12
August	73,431	682	947	112	369	3,589	1,001	3	20	24	11
September	64,452	624	822	162	355	3,383	870	3	17	22	11
October	53,331	616	749	123	284	2,907	768	2	15	23	11
November	48,636	787	829	57	240	2,872	709	2	17	23	11
December	49,919	749	706	76	258	2,821	744	3	19	24	11
Total	**735,433**	**12,056**	**13,893**	**2,086**	**3,789**	**46,978**	**9,322**	**29**	**215**	**268**	**127**
2016 January	61,716	1,162	962	146	319	3,863	744	3	18	23	11
February	50,256	811	1,076	163	311	3,605	662	3	18	21	10
March	39,538	643	583	103	346	3,060	717	3	17	21	10
April	38,725	596	599	82	369	3,123	698	2	13	23	11
May	44,767	777	649	72	348	3,239	781	2	14	23	11
June	63,007	674	762	88	360	3,326	946	3	17	23	11
July	73,902	786	1,244	108	381	4,043	1,116	3	18	23	11
August	73,526	763	1,185	179	399	4,123	1,127	3	19	24	11
September	62,149	610	774	97	361	3,287	891	3	17	22	10
October	54,376	598	836	58	233	2,658	719	2	14	23	10
November	47,898	761	641	101	286	2,934	641	2	14	22	10
December	64,620	876	795	148	317	3,402	645	2	18	24	11
Total	**674,481**	**9,058**	**10,105**	**1,346**	**4,031**	**40,662**	**9,688**	**30**	**196**	**272**	**127**
2017 January	63,226	977	777	149	345	3,629	615	3	16	23	11
February	47,876	756	665	81	253	2,768	529	3	16	21	9
March	48,644	813	685	92	257	2,876	643	3	18	22	10
April	44,222	704	639	94	143	2,150	592	2	15	21	10
4-Month Total	**203,967**	**3,250**	**2,766**	**416**	**998**	**11,423**	**2,380**	**10**	**65**	**87**	**40**
2016 4-Month Total	**190,235**	**3,213**	**3,219**	**494**	**1,345**	**13,650**	**2,822**	**11**	**66**	**89**	**41**
2015 4-Month Total	**244,056**	**6,302**	**7,258**	**1,198**	**1,283**	**21,172**	**2,636**	**10**	**71**	**82**	**40**

[a] Anthracite, bituminous coal, subbituminous coal, lignite, waste coal, and coal synfuel.

[b] Fuel oil nos. 1, 2, and 4. For 1949–1979, data are for gas turbine and internal combustion plant use of petroleum. For 1980–2000, electric utility data also include small amounts of kerosene and jet fuel.

[c] Fuel oil nos. 5 and 6. For 1949–1979, data are for steam plant use of petroleum. For 1980–2000, electric utility data also include a small amount of fuel oil no. 4.

[d] Jet fuel, kerosene, other petroleum liquids, waste oil, and, beginning in 2011, propane.

[e] Petroleum coke is converted from short tons to barrels by multiplying by 5.

[f] Natural gas, plus a small amount of supplemental gaseous fuels.

[g] Blast furnace gas, and other manufactured and waste gases derived from fossil fuels. Through 2010, also includes propane gas.

[h] Wood and wood-derived fuels.

[i] Municipal solid waste from biogenic sources, landfill gas, sludge waste, agricultural byproducts, and other biomass. Through 2000, also includes non-renewable waste (municipal solid waste from non-biogenic sources, and tire-derived fuels).

[j] Batteries, chemicals, hydrogen, pitch, purchased steam, sulfur, miscellaneous technologies, and, beginning in 2001, non-renewable waste (municipal solid waste from non-biogenic sources, and tire-derived fuels).

[k] Through 1988, data are for electric utilities only. Beginning in 1989, data are for electric utilities and independent power producers.

NA=Not available. (s)=Less than 0.5 trillion Btu.

Notes: • Data are for utility-scale facilities. See Note 1, "Coverage of Electricity Statistics," at end of section. • Data are for fuels consumed to produce electricity. Data also include fuels consumed to produce useful thermal output at a small number of electric utility combined-heat-and-power (CHP) plants. • The electric power sector comprises electricity-only and combined-heat-and-power (CHP) plants within the NAICS 22 category whose primary business is to sell electricity, or electricity and heat, to the public. • Totals may not equal sum of components due to independent rounding. • Geographic coverage is the 50 states and the District of Columbia.

Web Page: See http://www.eia.gov/totalenergy/data/monthly/#electricity (Excel and CSV files) for all available annual data beginning in 1949 and monthly data beginning in 1973.

Sources: See end of section.

Source: *U.S. Energy Information Administration, Monthly Energy Review, July 2017*

Table 7.3c Consumption of Selected Combustible Fuels for Electricity Generation: Commercial and Industrial Sectors (Subset of Table 7.3a)

	Commercial Sector[a]				Industrial Sector[b]						
				Biomass					Biomass		
	Coal[c]	Petroleum[d]	Natural Gas[e]	Waste[f]	Coal[c]	Petroleum[d]	Natural Gas[e]	Other Gases[g]	Wood[h]	Waste[f]	Other[i]
	Thousand Short Tons	Thousand Barrels	Billion Cubic Feet	Trillion Btu	Thousand Short Tons	Thousand Barrels	Billion Cubic Feet	Trillion Btu			
1990 Total	**417**	**953**	**28**	**15**	**10,740**	**13,103**	**517**	**104**	**335**	**16**	**36**
1995 Total	**569**	**649**	**43**	**21**	**12,171**	**12,265**	**601**	**114**	**373**	**13**	**40**
2000 Total	**514**	**823**	**37**	**26**	**11,706**	**10,459**	**640**	**107**	**369**	**10**	**45**
2001 Total	**532**	**1,023**	**36**	**15**	**10,636**	**10,530**	**654**	**88**	**370**	**7**	**44**
2002 Total	**477**	**834**	**33**	**18**	**11,855**	**11,608**	**685**	**106**	**464**	**15**	**43**
2003 Total	**582**	**894**	**38**	**19**	**10,440**	**10,424**	**668**	**127**	**362**	**13**	**46**
2004 Total	**377**	**766**	**33**	**19**	**7,687**	**6,919**	**566**	**108**	**194**	**5**	**41**
2005 Total	**377**	**585**	**34**	**20**	**7,504**	**6,440**	**518**	**85**	**189**	**5**	**46**
2006 Total	**347**	**333**	**35**	**21**	**7,408**	**5,066**	**536**	**87**	**187**	**3**	**45**
2007 Total	**361**	**258**	**34**	**19**	**5,089**	**5,041**	**554**	**88**	**188**	**4**	**41**
2008 Total	**369**	**166**	**33**	**20**	**5,075**	**3,617**	**520**	**73**	**179**	**5**	**39**
2009 Total	**317**	**190**	**34**	**23**	**4,674**	**3,328**	**520**	**62**	**160**	**4**	**42**
2010 Total	**314**	**172**	**39**	**24**	**8,125**	**2,422**	**555**	**70**	**172**	**8**	**55**
2011 Total	**347**	**137**	**47**	**31**	**5,735**	**2,145**	**572**	**74**	**182**	**7**	**57**
2012 Total	**307**	**279**	**63**	**33**	**4,665**	**4,761**	**633**	**84**	**219**	**8**	**54**
2013 Total	**513**	**335**	**67**	**36**	**4,670**	**3,892**	**642**	**74**	**210**	**11**	**50**
2014 Total	**202**	**462**	**72**	**36**	**4,629**	**2,594**	**623**	**81**	**210**	**11**	**54**
2015 January	18	34	5	3	338	227	54	7	17	1	5
February	19	95	5	3	318	228	46	6	15	1	4
March	17	19	5	3	351	153	48	6	15	1	4
April	12	15	5	3	302	194	45	6	15	1	4
May	10	15	6	3	323	154	49	6	16	1	5
June	14	14	6	3	359	148	53	7	16	1	5
July	14	16	7	3	376	129	57	8	17	1	6
August	12	18	7	3	368	133	57	7	17	1	5
September	10	9	7	3	360	146	54	7	16	1	5
October	11	8	6	3	317	127	51	5	16	1	5
November	12	8	5	3	295	139	53	5	16	1	5
December	14	9	6	3	292	131	57	6	16	1	5
Total	**163**	**260**	**70**	**35**	**3,999**	**1,907**	**625**	**77**	**191**	**10**	**58**
2016 January	14	14	6	3	319	160	53	7	16	1	4
February	15	15	5	3	296	133	50	7	15	1	3
March	14	8	5	3	304	131	52	7	15	1	4
April	11	10	5	3	254	135	50	7	14	1	4
May	9	11	6	3	260	171	53	5	15	1	4
June	10	9	6	3	310	153	54	6	16	1	4
July	11	11	7	3	328	165	57	6	16	1	4
August	12	15	7	3	330	166	57	6	16	1	4
September	12	10	6	3	267	153	54	6	15	1	4
October	13	11	5	3	246	129	52	5	15	1	4
November	13	11	5	3	215	134	55	5	16	1	4
December	15	14	6	3	249	169	56	6	16	1	4
Total	**148**	**139**	**69**	**35**	**3,376**	**1,800**	**644**	**72**	**185**	**10**	**48**
2017 January	16	31	6	3	300	130	56	6	16	1	4
February	12	16	5	3	267	106	50	7	15	1	3
March	12	22	6	3	259	135	52	7	15	1	4
April	8	14	5	3	225	96	51	6	15	1	4
4-Month Total	**48**	**83**	**22**	**11**	**1,051**	**466**	**209**	**26**	**61**	**3**	**15**
2016 4-Month Total	**54**	**47**	**22**	**12**	**1,173**	**559**	**206**	**27**	**60**	**4**	**15**
2015 4-Month Total	**65**	**163**	**20**	**11**	**1,309**	**802**	**194**	**25**	**63**	**3**	**17**

[a] Commercial combined-heat-and-power (CHP) and commercial electricity-only plants.
[b] Industrial combined-heat-and-power (CHP) and industrial electricity-only plants.
[c] Anthracite, bituminous coal, subbituminous coal, lignite, waste coal, and coal synfuel.
[d] Distillate fuel oil, residual fuel oil, petroleum coke, jet fuel, kerosene, other petroleum, waste oil, and, beginning in 2011, propane.
[e] Natural gas, plus a small amount of supplemental gaseous fuels.
[f] Municipal solid waste from biogenic sources, landfill gas, sludge waste, agricultural byproducts, and other biomass. Through 2000, also includes non-renewable waste (municipal solid waste from non-biogenic sources, and tire-derived fuels).
[g] Blast furnace gas, and other manufactured and waste gases derived from fossil fuels. Through 2010, also includes propane gas.
[h] Wood and wood-derived fuels.
[i] Batteries, chemicals, hydrogen, pitch, purchased steam, sulfur, miscellaneous technologies, and, beginning in 2001, non-renewable waste (municipal solid waste from non-biogenic sources, and tire-derived fuels).

Notes: • Data are for utility-scale facilities. See Note 1, "Coverage of Electricity Statistics," at end of section. • See Note 2, "Classification of Power Plants Into Energy-Use Sectors," at end of section. • Data are for fuels consumed to produce electricity. Through 1988, data are not available. • Totals may not equal sum of components due to independent rounding. • Geographic coverage is the 50 states and the District of Columbia.

Web Page: See http://www.eia.gov/totalenergy/data/monthly/#electricity (Excel and CSV files) for all available annual and monthly data beginning in 1989.

Sources: • **1989–1997:** U.S. Energy Information Administration (EIA), Form EIA-867, "Annual Nonutility Power Producer Report." • **1998–2000:** EIA, Form EIA-860B, "Annual Electric Generator Report—Nonutility." • **2001–2003:** EIA, Form EIA-906, "Power Plant Report." • **2004–2007:** EIA, Form EIA-906, "Power Plant Report," and Form EIA-920, "Combined Heat and Power Plant Report." • **2008 forward:** EIA, Form EIA-923, "Power Plant Operations Report."

Source: *U.S. Energy Information Administration, Monthly Energy Review, July 2017*

Figure 7.4 Consumption of Selected Combustible Fuels for Electricity Generation and Useful Thermal Output

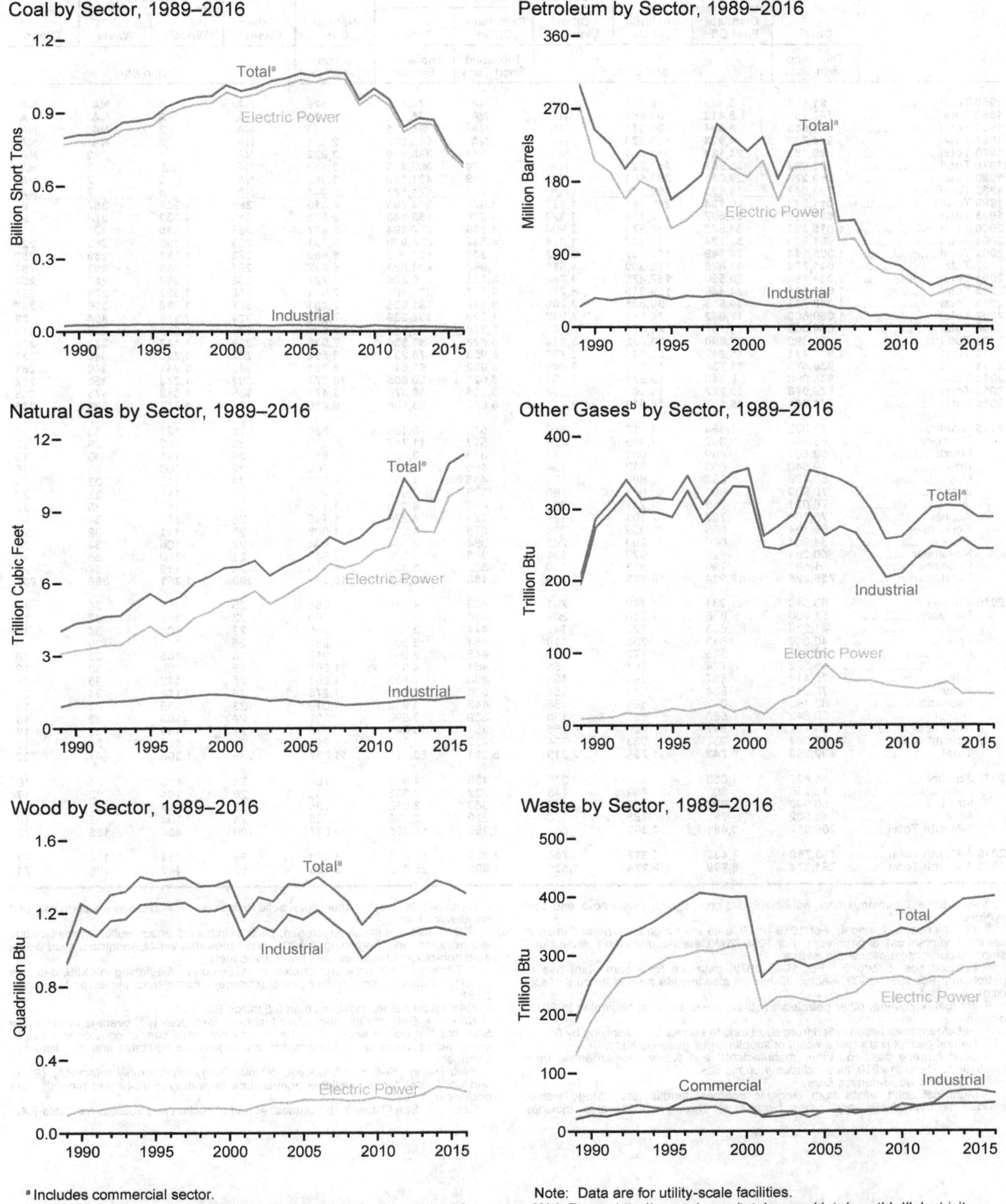

[a] Includes commercial sector.

[b] Blast furnace gas, and other manufactured and waste gases derived from fossil fuels. Through 2010, also includes propane gas.

Note: Data are for utility-scale facilities.

Web Page: http://www.eia.gov/totalenergy/data/monthly/#electricity.

Sources: Tables 7.4a–7.4c.

Source: *U.S. Energy Information Administration, Monthly Energy Review, July 2017*

Table 7.4a Consumption of Combustible Fuels for Electricity Generation and Useful Thermal Output: Total (All Sectors) (Sum of Tables 7.4b and 7.4c)

		Petroleum							Biomass		
	Coal[a]	Distillate Fuel Oil[b]	Residual Fuel Oil[c]	Other Liquids[d]	Petroleum Coke[e]	Total[e]	Natural Gas[f]	Other Gases[g]	Wood[h]	Waste[i]	Other[j]
	Thousand Short Tons	Thousand Barrels			Thousand Short Tons	Thousand Barrels	Billion Cubic Feet	Trillion Btu			
1950 Total	91,871	5,423	69,998	NA	NA	75,421	629	NA	5	NA	NA
1955 Total	143,759	5,412	69,862	NA	NA	75,274	1,153	NA	3	NA	NA
1960 Total	176,685	3,824	84,371	NA	NA	88,195	1,725	NA	2	NA	NA
1965 Total	244,788	4,928	110,274	NA	NA	115,203	2,321	NA	3	NA	NA
1970 Total	320,182	24,123	311,381	NA	636	338,686	3,932	NA	1	2	NA
1975 Total	405,962	38,907	467,221	NA	70	506,479	3,158	NA	(s)	2	NA
1980 Total	569,274	29,051	391,163	NA	179	421,110	3,682	NA	3	2	NA
1985 Total	693,841	14,635	158,779	NA	231	174,571	3,044	NA	8	7	NA
1990 Total[k]	811,538	20,194	209,081	1,332	2,832	244,765	4,346	288	1,256	257	86
1995 Total	881,012	21,697	112,168	1,322	4,590	158,140	5,572	313	1,382	374	97
2000 Total	1,015,398	34,572	156,673	2,904	4,669	217,494	6,677	356	1,380	401	109
2001 Total	991,635	33,724	177,137	1,418	4,532	234,940	6,731	263	1,182	263	229
2002 Total	1,005,144	24,749	118,637	3,257	7,353	183,409	6,986	278	1,287	289	252
2003 Total	1,031,778	31,825	152,859	4,576	7,067	224,593	6,337	294	1,266	293	262
2004 Total	1,044,798	23,520	157,478	4,764	8,721	229,364	6,727	353	1,360	282	254
2005 Total	1,065,281	24,446	156,915	4,270	9,113	231,193	7,021	348	1,353	289	237
2006 Total	1,053,783	14,655	69,846	3,396	8,622	131,005	7,404	341	1,399	300	247
2007 Total	1,069,606	17,042	74,616	4,237	7,299	132,389	7,962	329	1,336	304	239
2008 Total	1,064,503	14,137	43,477	3,765	6,314	92,948	7,689	300	1,263	328	212
2009 Total	955,190	14,800	33,672	3,218	5,828	80,830	7,938	259	1,137	333	228
2010 Total	1,001,411	15,247	26,944	2,777	6,053	75,231	8,502	262	1,226	346	237
2011 Total	956,470	11,735	16,877	2,540	6,092	61,610	8,724	282	1,241	340	261
2012 Total	845,066	9,945	13,571	2,185	5,021	50,805	10,371	302	1,273	355	252
2013 Total	879,078	10,277	14,199	2,212	6,338	58,378	9,479	305	1,318	376	236
2014 Total	871,741	15,107	16,615	2,908	5,695	63,106	9,410	304	1,378	395	236
2015 January	73,033	1,354	1,913	350	510	6,169	824	28	121	33	19
February	68,640	3,892	4,468	824	513	11,747	749	23	109	29	17
March	59,861	889	981	176	376	3,926	817	24	111	33	19
April	49,840	665	912	184	406	3,790	765	23	109	32	19
May	58,488	863	866	201	435	4,107	839	24	112	32	20
June	70,309	807	964	193	398	3,952	997	25	111	32	20
July	78,021	780	1,241	206	490	4,674	1,166	26	117	35	22
August	75,156	727	1,101	176	475	4,379	1,148	26	118	34	21
September	66,124	663	959	234	475	4,229	1,008	25	111	32	20
October	54,904	660	903	203	384	3,684	904	22	106	34	20
November	50,264	829	973	121	365	3,750	845	21	110	35	20
December	51,587	796	855	140	362	3,603	889	24	116	37	21
Total	**756,226**	**12,924**	**16,136**	**3,008**	**5,188**	**58,009**	**10,952**	**290**	**1,351**	**398**	**237**
2016 January	63,549	1,231	1,142	201	420	4,675	889	25	117	34	18
February	51,960	878	1,218	239	416	4,413	795	23	108	32	17
March	41,233	683	720	147	474	3,922	855	27	108	34	18
April	40,039	643	738	118	461	3,804	831	25	100	35	19
May	46,171	825	779	169	445	3,997	917	23	105	33	19
June	64,502	724	891	158	461	4,079	1,085	25	109	33	19
July	75,416	857	1,396	191	488	4,885	1,261	25	112	35	19
August	75,041	834	1,340	254	506	4,958	1,275	26	113	34	20
September	63,469	657	895	166	448	3,959	1,029	23	105	31	18
October	55,643	656	985	156	359	3,590	852	24	103	32	18
November	49,162	817	760	166	381	3,648	778	21	109	33	18
December	66,084	937	933	254	433	4,287	790	24	117	35	19
Total	**692,269**	**9,743**	**11,798**	**2,219**	**5,291**	**50,216**	**11,357**	**289**	**1,306**	**401**	**222**
2017 January	64,827	1,058	940	235	436	4,410	764	25	113	36	19
February	49,230	803	782	148	332	3,395	663	25	104	32	17
March	50,099	870	796	148	363	3,630	785	26	113	35	18
April	45,502	751	785	150	229	2,830	725	24	104	32	18
4-Month Total	**209,657**	**3,481**	**3,303**	**681**	**1,360**	**14,266**	**2,937**	**100**	**434**	**135**	**72**
2016 4-Month Total	**196,780**	**3,435**	**3,817**	**704**	**1,771**	**16,813**	**3,370**	**99**	**434**	**134**	**72**
2015 4-Month Total	**251,374**	**6,799**	**8,274**	**1,535**	**1,805**	**25,632**	**3,156**	**98**	**449**	**126**	**74**

[a] Anthracite, bituminous coal, subbituminous coal, lignite, waste coal, and coal synfuel.

[b] Fuel oil nos. 1, 2, and 4. For 1949–1979, data are for gas turbine and internal combustion plant use of petroleum. For 1980–2000, electric utility data also include small amounts of kerosene and jet fuel.

[c] Fuel oil nos. 5 and 6. For 1949–1979, data are for steam plant use of petroleum. For 1980–2000, electric utility data also include a small amount of fuel oil no. 4.

[d] Jet fuel, kerosene, other petroleum liquids, waste oil, and, beginning in 2011, propane.

[e] Petroleum coke is converted from short tons to barrels by multiplying by 5.

[f] Natural gas, plus a small amount of supplemental gaseous fuels.

[g] Blast furnace gas, and other manufactured and waste gases derived from fossil fuels. Through 2010, also includes propane gas.

[h] Wood and wood-derived fuels.

[i] Municipal solid waste from biogenic sources, landfill gas, sludge waste, agricultural byproducts, and other biomass. Through 2000, also includes non-renewable waste (municipal solid waste from non-biogenic sources, and tire-derived fuels).

[j] Batteries, chemicals, hydrogen, pitch, purchased steam, sulfur, miscellaneous technologies, and, beginning in 2001, non-renewable waste (municipal solid waste from non-biogenic sources, and tire-derived fuels).

[k] Through 1988, data are for electric utilities only. Beginning in 1989, data are for electric utilities, independent power producers, commercial plants, and industrial plants.

NA=Not available. (s)=Less than 0.5 trillion Btu.

Notes: • Data are for utility-scale facilities. See Note 1, "Coverage of Electricity Statistics," at end of section. • Totals may not equal sum of components due to independent rounding. • Geographic coverage is the 50 states and the District of Columbia.

Web Page: See http://www.eia.gov/totalenergy/data/monthly/#electricity (Excel and CSV files) for all available annual data beginning in 1949 and monthly data beginning in 1973.

Sources: See "Table 7.4b Sources" at end of section and sources for Table 7.4c.

Source: *U.S. Energy Information Administration, Monthly Energy Review, July 2017*

Table 7.4b Consumption of Combustible Fuels for Electricity Generation and Useful Thermal Output: Electric Power Sector (Subset of Table 7.4a)

		Petroleum							Biomass		
	Coal[a]	Distillate Fuel Oil[b]	Residual Fuel Oil[c]	Other Liquids[d]	Petroleum Coke[e]	Total[e]	Natural Gas[f]	Other Gases[g]	Wood[h]	Waste[i]	Other[j]
	Thousand Short Tons	Thousand Barrels			Thousand Short Tons	Thousand Barrels	Billion Cubic Feet	Trillion Btu			
1950 Total	91,871	5,423	69,998	NA	NA	75,421	629	NA	5	NA	NA
1955 Total	143,759	5,412	69,862	NA	NA	75,274	1,153	NA	3	NA	NA
1960 Total	176,685	3,824	84,371	NA	NA	88,195	1,725	NA	2	NA	NA
1965 Total	244,788	4,928	110,274	NA	NA	115,203	2,321	NA	3	NA	NA
1970 Total	320,182	24,123	311,381	NA	636	338,686	3,932	NA	1	2	NA
1975 Total	405,962	38,907	467,221	NA	70	506,479	3,158	NA	(s)	2	NA
1980 Total	569,274	29,051	391,163	NA	179	421,110	3,682	NA	3	2	NA
1985 Total	693,841	14,635	158,779	NA	231	174,571	3,044	NA	8	7	NA
1990 Total[k]	782,567	16,567	184,915	26	1,008	206,550	3,245	11	129	188	(s)
1995 Total	850,230	18,553	90,023	499	2,674	122,447	4,237	24	125	296	2
2000 Total	985,821	30,016	138,513	454	3,275	185,358	5,206	25	134	318	1
2001 Total	964,433	29,274	159,504	377	3,427	206,291	5,342	15	126	211	113
2002 Total	977,507	21,876	104,773	1,267	5,816	156,996	5,672	33	150	230	143
2003 Total	1,005,116	27,632	138,279	2,026	5,799	196,932	5,135	41	167	230	140
2004 Total	1,016,268	19,107	139,816	2,713	7,372	198,498	5,464	58	165	223	138
2005 Total	1,037,485	19,675	139,409	2,685	8,083	202,184	5,869	84	185	221	123
2006 Total	1,026,636	12,646	57,345	1,870	7,101	107,365	6,222	65	182	231	125
2007 Total	1,045,141	15,327	63,086	2,594	5,685	109,431	6,841	61	186	237	124
2008 Total	1,040,580	12,547	38,241	2,670	5,119	79,056	6,668	61	177	258	131
2009 Total	933,627	12,035	28,782	2,210	4,611	66,081	6,873	55	180	261	124
2010 Total	975,052	13,790	24,503	1,877	4,777	64,055	7,387	52	196	264	124
2011 Total	932,484	11,021	14,803	1,658	4,837	51,667	7,574	50	182	255	143
2012 Total	823,551	9,080	12,203	1,339	2,974	37,495	9,111	54	190	262	143
2013 Total	857,962	9,598	12,283	1,489	4,285	44,794	8,191	60	207	262	139
2014 Total	851,602	14,235	15,132	2,208	4,132	52,235	8,146	44	251	279	137
2015 January	71,323	1,272	1,754	276	379	5,198	711	4	22	23	11
February	67,061	3,683	4,182	748	397	10,599	648	4	21	20	10
March	58,272	831	857	117	264	3,126	709	3	21	22	11
April	48,449	619	819	97	281	2,941	664	3	18	22	11
May	57,060	821	777	111	330	3,360	734	4	18	23	11
June	68,867	766	883	106	298	3,248	886	3	21	23	12
July	76,452	727	1,167	142	402	4,044	1,046	3	22	26	12
August	73,678	685	1,033	113	378	3,723	1,027	4	23	25	12
September	64,682	626	910	162	363	3,516	895	4	20	23	11
October	53,557	618	845	124	292	3,049	792	3	17	24	11
November	48,879	790	911	57	252	3,020	732	3	19	25	11
December	50,165	753	792	77	268	2,964	769	4	21	25	12
Total	**738,444**	**12,193**	**14,929**	**2,131**	**3,907**	**48,787**	**9,613**	**44**	**244**	**281**	**136**
2016 January	61,970	1,169	1,042	147	329	4,002	771	4	21	25	12
February	50,487	821	1,130	174	321	3,729	686	3	21	23	11
March	39,788	647	662	108	357	3,201	743	4	20	23	11
April	38,984	600	675	83	376	3,235	721	3	15	25	12
May	44,983	781	730	72	354	3,356	806	3	16	24	12
June	63,243	679	836	89	368	3,446	971	4	19	24	12
July	74,136	792	1,324	109	389	4,172	1,142	4	20	24	12
August	73,757	769	1,274	179	408	4,263	1,155	4	21	25	12
September	62,366	614	858	98	370	3,421	915	4	18	23	11
October	54,601	603	919	58	244	2,798	741	3	15	24	11
November	48,102	764	716	101	295	3,058	664	4	17	23	11
December	64,858	886	877	155	326	3,549	669	4	20	25	12
Total	**677,275**	**9,126**	**11,043**	**1,374**	**4,137**	**42,230**	**9,984**	**44**	**222**	**287**	**137**
2017 January	63,477	985	861	162	354	3,778	639	4	19	25	12
February	48,095	759	731	85	262	2,888	550	4	18	22	10
March	48,901	816	730	92	267	2,974	667	4	20	24	11
April	44,441	707	718	94	152	2,279	614	4	18	22	10
4-Month Total	**204,914**	**3,266**	**3,041**	**434**	**1,036**	**11,920**	**2,470**	**15**	**75**	**93**	**43**
2016 4-Month Total	**191,228**	**3,238**	**3,509**	**512**	**1,382**	**14,167**	**2,921**	**15**	**76**	**95**	**45**
2015 4-Month Total	**245,105**	**6,405**	**7,612**	**1,238**	**1,322**	**21,864**	**2,733**	**15**	**81**	**87**	**43**

[a] Anthracite, bituminous coal, subbituminous coal, lignite, waste coal, and coal synfuel.

[b] Fuel oil nos. 1, 2, and 4. For 1949–1979, data are for gas turbine and internal combustion plant use of petroleum. For 1980–2000, electric utility data also include small amounts of kerosene and jet fuel.

[c] Fuel oil nos. 5 and 6. For 1949–1979, data are for steam plant use of petroleum. For 1980–2000, electric utility data also include a small amount of fuel oil no. 4.

[d] Jet fuel, kerosene, other petroleum liquids, waste oil, and, beginning in 2011, propane.

[e] Petroleum coke is converted from short tons to barrels by multiplying by 5.

[f] Natural gas, plus a small amount of supplemental gaseous fuels.

[g] Blast furnace gas, and other manufactured and waste gases derived from fossil fuels. Through 2010, also includes propane gas.

[h] Wood and wood-derived fuels.

[i] Municipal solid waste from biogenic sources, landfill gas, sludge waste, agricultural byproducts, and other biomass. Through 2000, also includes non-renewable waste (municipal solid waste from non-biogenic sources, and tire-derived fuels).

[j] Batteries, chemicals, hydrogen, pitch, purchased steam, sulfur, miscellaneous technologies, and, beginning in 2001, non-renewable waste (municipal solid waste from non-biogenic sources, and tire-derived fuels).

[k] Through 1988, data are for electric utilities only. Beginning in 1989, data are for electric utilities and independent power producers.

NA=Not available. (s)=Less than 0.5 trillion Btu.

Notes: • Data are for utility-scale facilities. See Note 1, "Coverage of Electricity Statistics," at end of section. • The electric power sector comprises electricity-only and combined-heat-and-power (CHP) plants within the NAICS 22 category whose primary business is to sell electricity, or electricity and heat, to the public. • Totals may not equal sum of components due to independent rounding. • Geographic coverage is the 50 states and the District of Columbia.

Web Page: See http://www.eia.gov/totalenergy/data/monthly/#electricity (Excel and CSV files) for all available annual data beginning in 1949 and monthly data beginning in 1973.

Sources: See end of section.

Source: *U.S. Energy Information Administration, Monthly Energy Review, July 2017*

Table 7.4c Consumption of Selected Combustible Fuels for Electricity Generation and Useful Thermal Output: Commercial and Industrial Sectors (Subset of Table 7.4a)

	Commercial Sector[a]				Industrial Sector[b]						
				Biomass					Biomass		
	Coal[c]	Petroleum[d]	Natural Gas[e]	Waste[f]	Coal[c]	Petroleum[d]	Natural Gas[e]	Other Gases[g]	Wood[h]	Waste[f]	Other[i]
	Thousand Short Tons	Thousand Barrels	Billion Cubic Feet	Trillion Btu	Thousand Short Tons	Thousand Barrels	Billion Cubic Feet	Trillion Btu			
1990 Total	**1,191**	**2,056**	**46**	**28**	**27,781**	**36,159**	**1,055**	**275**	**1,125**	**41**	**86**
1995 Total	**1,419**	**1,245**	**78**	**40**	**29,363**	**34,448**	**1,258**	**290**	**1,255**	**38**	**95**
2000 Total	**1,547**	**1,615**	**85**	**47**	**28,031**	**30,520**	**1,386**	**331**	**1,244**	**35**	**108**
2001 Total	**1,448**	**1,832**	**79**	**25**	**25,755**	**26,817**	**1,310**	**248**	**1,054**	**27**	**101**
2002 Total	**1,405**	**1,250**	**74**	**26**	**26,232**	**25,163**	**1,240**	**245**	**1,136**	**34**	**92**
2003 Total	**1,816**	**1,449**	**58**	**29**	**24,846**	**26,212**	**1,144**	**253**	**1,097**	**34**	**103**
2004 Total	**1,917**	**2,009**	**72**	**34**	**26,613**	**28,857**	**1,191**	**295**	**1,193**	**24**	**94**
2005 Total	**1,922**	**1,630**	**68**	**34**	**25,875**	**27,380**	**1,084**	**264**	**1,166**	**34**	**94**
2006 Total	**1,886**	**935**	**68**	**36**	**25,262**	**22,706**	**1,115**	**277**	**1,216**	**33**	**102**
2007 Total	**1,927**	**752**	**70**	**31**	**22,537**	**22,207**	**1,050**	**268**	**1,148**	**36**	**98**
2008 Total	**2,021**	**671**	**66**	**34**	**21,902**	**13,222**	**955**	**239**	**1,084**	**35**	**60**
2009 Total	**1,798**	**521**	**76**	**36**	**19,766**	**14,228**	**990**	**204**	**955**	**35**	**82**
2010 Total	**1,720**	**437**	**86**	**36**	**24,638**	**10,740**	**1,029**	**210**	**1,029**	**47**	**91**
2011 Total	**1,668**	**333**	**87**	**43**	**22,319**	**9,610**	**1,063**	**232**	**1,057**	**43**	**94**
2012 Total	**1,450**	**457**	**111**	**45**	**20,065**	**12,853**	**1,149**	**249**	**1,082**	**47**	**81**
2013 Total	**1,356**	**887**	**118**	**47**	**19,761**	**12,697**	**1,170**	**246**	**1,109**	**67**	**69**
2014 Total	**1,063**	**758**	**119**	**47**	**19,076**	**10,112**	**1,145**	**260**	**1,122**	**70**	**72**
2015 January	97	88	10	4	1,613	884	103	23	98	6	6
February	97	221	9	3	1,483	926	92	20	87	5	5
March	83	53	9	4	1,506	746	99	21	90	6	5
April	54	39	8	4	1,336	810	93	20	90	6	6
May	50	34	9	4	1,378	713	95	20	93	5	6
June	61	28	10	4	1,381	676	101	21	90	5	6
July	64	32	11	4	1,505	599	109	22	95	5	7
August	58	42	11	4	1,420	614	110	22	95	5	7
September	51	22	11	4	1,391	691	102	21	90	5	6
October	52	20	10	4	1,296	616	102	18	88	7	6
November	59	23	9	4	1,325	707	103	18	91	7	6
December	72	20	10	4	1,350	618	110	20	94	7	6
Total	**798**	**622**	**116**	**47**	**16,984**	**8,600**	**1,222**	**246**	**1,103**	**70**	**73**
2016 January	76	41	10	4	1,503	632	107	21	95	5	5
February	78	41	9	4	1,395	643	100	19	87	5	4
March	75	23	10	5	1,370	698	103	23	88	6	5
April	49	21	9	4	1,006	547	100	22	85	6	5
May	40	20	9	4	1,149	622	102	19	89	5	5
June	46	17	10	4	1,212	617	104	21	90	6	5
July	46	28	11	4	1,234	684	108	21	92	6	5
August	50	25	11	4	1,234	669	109	22	91	5	5
September	49	18	10	4	1,053	520	104	19	86	5	5
October	50	20	9	4	993	771	102	21	87	4	4
November	61	20	9	4	998	570	106	18	92	5	4
December	71	35	10	4	1,155	704	112	20	96	6	4
Total	**692**	**310**	**117**	**49**	**14,302**	**7,676**	**1,257**	**246**	**1,080**	**65**	**56**
2017 January	62	71	11	4	1,288	562	114	21	94	7	5
February	50	46	10	4	1,085	460	102	21	85	6	5
March	55	56	10	4	1,143	600	108	23	92	7	5
April	37	29	9	4	1,024	522	103	20	86	6	5
4-Month Total	**204**	**202**	**40**	**16**	**4,539**	**2,144**	**427**	**85**	**357**	**27**	**19**
2016 4-Month Total	**278**	**126**	**39**	**17**	**5,274**	**2,520**	**410**	**85**	**356**	**22**	**18**
2015 4-Month Total	**331**	**401**	**35**	**15**	**5,938**	**3,366**	**388**	**83**	**366**	**24**	**22**

[a] Commercial combined-heat-and-power (CHP) and commercial electricity-only plants.
[b] Industrial combined-heat-and-power (CHP) and industrial electricity-only plants.
[c] Anthracite, bituminous coal, subbituminous coal, lignite, waste coal, and coal synfuel.
[d] Distillate fuel oil, residual fuel oil, petroleum coke, jet fuel, kerosene, other petroleum, waste oil, and, beginning in 2011, propane.
[e] Natural gas, plus a small amount of supplemental gaseous fuels.
[f] Municipal solid waste from biogenic sources, landfill gas, sludge waste, agricultural byproducts, and other biomass. Through 2000, also includes non-renewable waste (municipal solid waste from non-biogenic sources, and tire-derived fuels).
[g] Blast furnace gas, and other manufactured and waste gases derived from fossil fuels. Through 2010, also includes propane gas.
[h] Wood and wood-derived fuels.
[i] Batteries, chemicals, hydrogen, pitch, purchased steam, sulfur, miscellaneous technologies, and, beginning in 2001, non-renewable waste (municipal solid waste from non-biogenic sources, and tire-derived fuels).

Notes: • Data are for utility-scale facilities. See Note 1, "Coverage of Electricity Statistics," at end of section. • See Note 2, "Classification of Power Plants Into Energy-Use Sectors," at end of section. • Totals may not equal sum of components due to independent rounding. • Geographic coverage is the 50 states and the District of Columbia.

Web Page: See http://www.eia.gov/totalenergy/data/monthly/#electricity (Excel and CSV files) for all available annual and monthly data beginning in 1989.

Sources: • **1989–1997:** U.S. Energy Information Administration (EIA), Form EIA-867, "Annual Nonutility Power Producer Report." • **1998–2000:** EIA, Form EIA-860B, "Annual Electric Generator Report—Nonutility." • **2001–2003:** EIA, Form EIA-906, "Power Plant Report." • **2004–2007:** EIA, Form EIA-906, "Power Plant Report," and Form EIA-920, "Combined Heat and Power Plant Report." • **2008 forward:** EIA, Form EIA-923, "Power Plant Operations Report."

Source: *U.S. Energy Information Administration, Monthly Energy Review, July 2017*

Figure 7.5 Stocks of Coal and Petroleum: Electric Power Sector

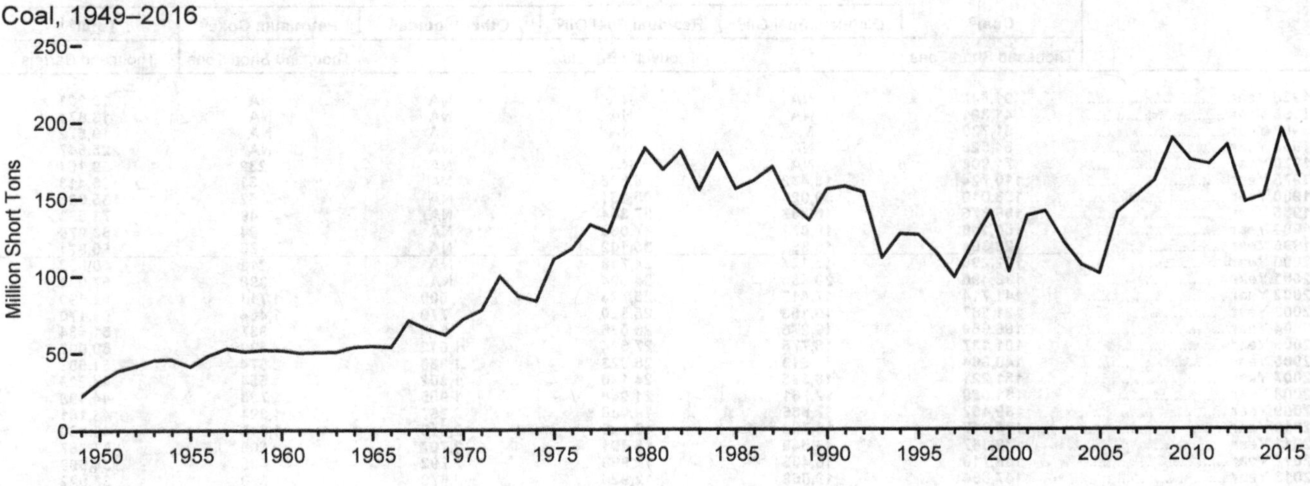

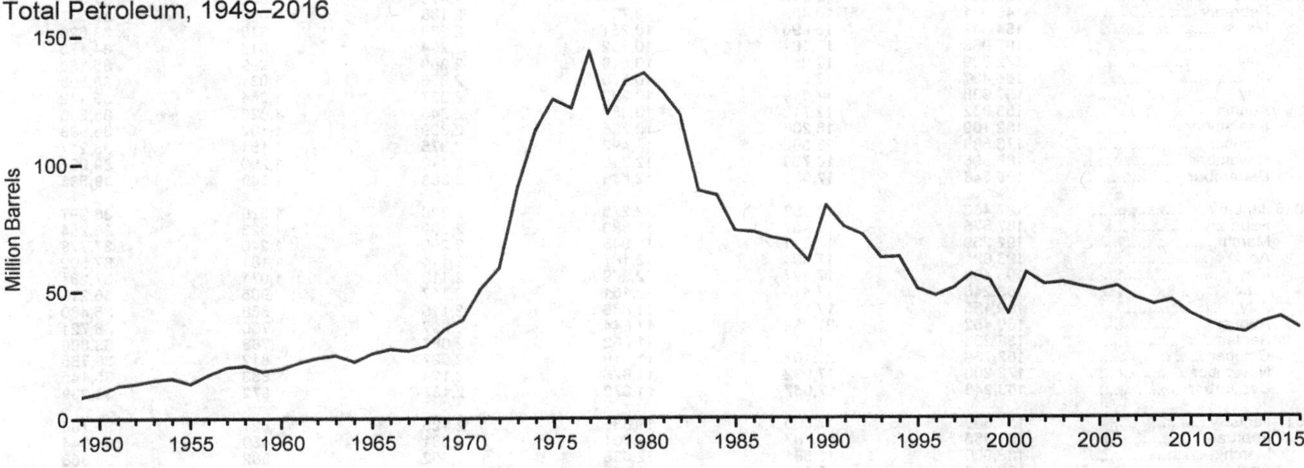

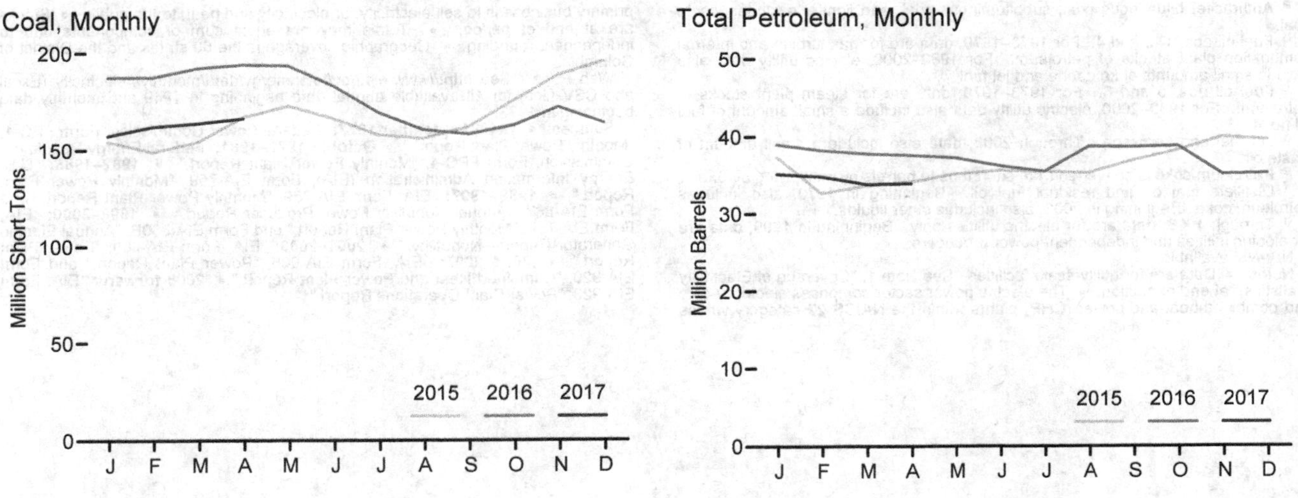

Note: Data are for utility-scale facilities.
Web Page: http://www.eia.gov/totalenergy/data/monthly/#electricity.
Source: Table 7.5.

Source: *U.S. Energy Information Administration, Monthly Energy Review, July 2017*

Table 7.5 Stocks of Coal and Petroleum: Electric Power Sector

	Coal[a]	Petroleum				
		Distillate Fuel Oil[b]	Residual Fuel Oil[c]	Other Liquids[d]	Petroleum Coke[e]	Total[e,f]
	Thousand Short Tons	Thousand Barrels			Thousand Short Tons	Thousand Barrels
1950 Year	**31,842**	**NA**	**NA**	**NA**	**NA**	**10,201**
1955 Year	**41,391**	**NA**	**NA**	**NA**	**NA**	**13,671**
1960 Year	**51,735**	**NA**	**NA**	**NA**	**NA**	**19,572**
1965 Year	**54,525**	**NA**	**NA**	**NA**	**NA**	**25,647**
1970 Year	**71,908**	**NA**	**NA**	**NA**	**239**	**39,151**
1975 Year	**110,724**	**16,432**	**108,825**	**NA**	**31**	**125,413**
1980 Year	**183,010**	**30,023**	**105,351**	**NA**	**52**	**135,635**
1985 Year	**156,376**	**16,386**	**57,304**	**NA**	**49**	**73,933**
1990 Year	**156,166**	**16,471**	**67,030**	**NA**	**94**	**83,970**
1995 Year	**126,304**	**15,392**	**35,102**	**NA**	**65**	**50,821**
2000 Year[g]	**102,296**	**15,127**	**24,748**	**NA**	**211**	**40,932**
2001 Year	**138,496**	**20,486**	**34,594**	**NA**	**390**	**57,031**
2002 Year	**141,714**	**17,413**	**25,723**	**800**	**1,711**	**52,490**
2003 Year	**121,567**	**19,153**	**25,820**	**779**	**1,484**	**53,170**
2004 Year	**106,669**	**19,275**	**26,596**	**879**	**937**	**51,434**
2005 Year	**101,137**	**18,778**	**27,624**	**1,012**	**530**	**50,062**
2006 Year	**140,964**	**18,013**	**28,823**	**1,380**	**674**	**51,583**
2007 Year	**151,221**	**18,395**	**24,136**	**1,902**	**554**	**47,203**
2008 Year	**161,589**	**17,761**	**21,088**	**1,955**	**739**	**44,498**
2009 Year	**189,467**	**17,886**	**19,068**	**2,257**	**1,394**	**46,181**
2010 Year	**174,917**	**16,758**	**16,629**	**2,319**	**1,019**	**40,800**
2011 Year	**172,387**	**16,649**	**15,491**	**2,707**	**508**	**37,387**
2012 Year	**185,116**	**16,433**	**12,999**	**2,792**	**495**	**34,698**
2013 Year	**147,884**	**16,068**	**12,926**	**2,679**	**390**	**33,622**
2014 Year	**151,548**	**18,309**	**12,764**	**2,432**	**827**	**37,643**
2015 January	154,390	18,216	12,207	2,473	892	37,355
February	149,071	16,459	9,798	2,188	850	32,697
March	154,347	16,996	10,251	2,289	818	33,626
April	167,063	17,167	10,152	2,294	912	34,173
May	172,809	17,357	10,518	2,309	999	35,180
June	166,437	17,513	10,570	2,358	1,031	35,598
July	157,938	17,519	10,263	2,337	1,064	35,442
August	155,952	17,712	10,087	2,345	1,029	35,286
September	162,109	18,286	10,766	2,339	1,102	36,898
October	175,588	18,596	11,492	2,375	1,151	38,217
November	188,595	18,738	12,310	2,440	1,290	39,937
December	**195,548**	**17,955**	**12,566**	**2,363**	**1,340**	**39,586**
2016 January	187,486	17,783	12,275	2,338	1,320	38,997
February	187,575	17,457	11,880	2,300	1,323	38,254
March	192,269	17,341	11,948	2,290	1,240	37,778
April	193,991	17,394	12,187	2,114	1,181	37,599
May	193,432	17,497	12,309	2,118	1,071	37,281
June	183,248	17,419	12,151	2,117	905	36,214
July	169,465	17,189	11,886	2,115	858	35,480
August	160,452	21,082	11,644	2,097	780	38,721
September	158,238	21,019	11,662	2,087	768	38,606
October	162,739	21,107	11,519	2,097	812	38,785
November	172,208	17,032	11,826	2,124	833	35,145
December	**163,946**	**17,057**	**11,670**	**2,153**	**872**	**35,239**
2017 January	157,359	17,065	11,839	2,125	827	35,164
February	161,985	16,767	11,701	2,081	859	34,844
March	163,900	15,561	12,036	1,852	882	33,858
April	166,236	15,492	11,825	1,852	952	33,931

[a] Anthracite, bituminous coal, subbituminous coal, and lignite; excludes waste coal.

[b] Fuel oil nos. 1, 2 and 4. For 1973–1979, data are for gas turbine and internal combustion plant stocks of petroleum. For 1980–2000, electric utility data also include small amounts of kerosene and jet fuel.

[c] Fuel oil nos. 5 and 6. For 1973–1979, data are for steam plant stocks of petroleum. For 1980–2000, electric utility data also include a small amount of fuel oil no. 4.

[d] Jet fuel and kerosene. Through 2003, data also include a small amount of waste oil.

[e] Petroleum coke is converted from short tons to barrels by multiplying by 5.

[f] Distillate fuel oil and residual fuel oil. Beginning in 1970, also includes petroleum coke. Beginning in 2002, also includes other liquids.

[g] Through 1998, data are for electric utilities only. Beginning in 1999, data are for electric utilities and independent power producers.

NA=Not available.

Notes: • Data are for utility-scale facilities. See Note 1, "Coverage of Electricity Statistics," at end of section. • The electric power sector comprises electricity-only and combined-heat-and-power (CHP) plants within the NAICS 22 category whose primary business is to sell electricity, or electricity and heat, to the public. • Stocks are at end of period. • Totals may not equal sum of components due to independent rounding. • Geographic coverage is the 50 states and the District of Columbia.

Web Page: See http://www.eia.gov/totalenergy/data/monthly/#electricity (Excel and CSV files) for all available annual data beginning in 1949 and monthly data beginning in 1973.

Sources: • **1949–September 1977:** Federal Power Commission, Form FPC-4, "Monthly Power Plant Report." • **October 1977–1981:** Federal Energy Regulatory Commission, Form FPC-4, "Monthly Power Plant Report." • **1982–1988:** U.S. Energy Information Administration (EIA), Form EIA-759, "Monthly Power Plant Report." • **1989–1997:** EIA, Form EIA-759, "Monthly Power Plant Report," and Form EIA-867, "Annual Nonutility Power Producer Report." • **1998–2000:** EIA, Form EIA-759, "Monthly Power Plant Report," and Form EIA-860B, "Annual Electric Generator Report—Nonutility." • **2001–2003:** EIA, Form EIA-906, "Power Plant Report." • **2004–2007:** EIA, Form EIA-906, "Power Plant Report," and Form EIA-920, "Combined Heat and Power Plant Report." • **2008 forward:** EIA, Form EIA-923, "Power Plant Operations Report."

Source: *U.S. Energy Information Administration, Monthly Energy Review, July 2017*

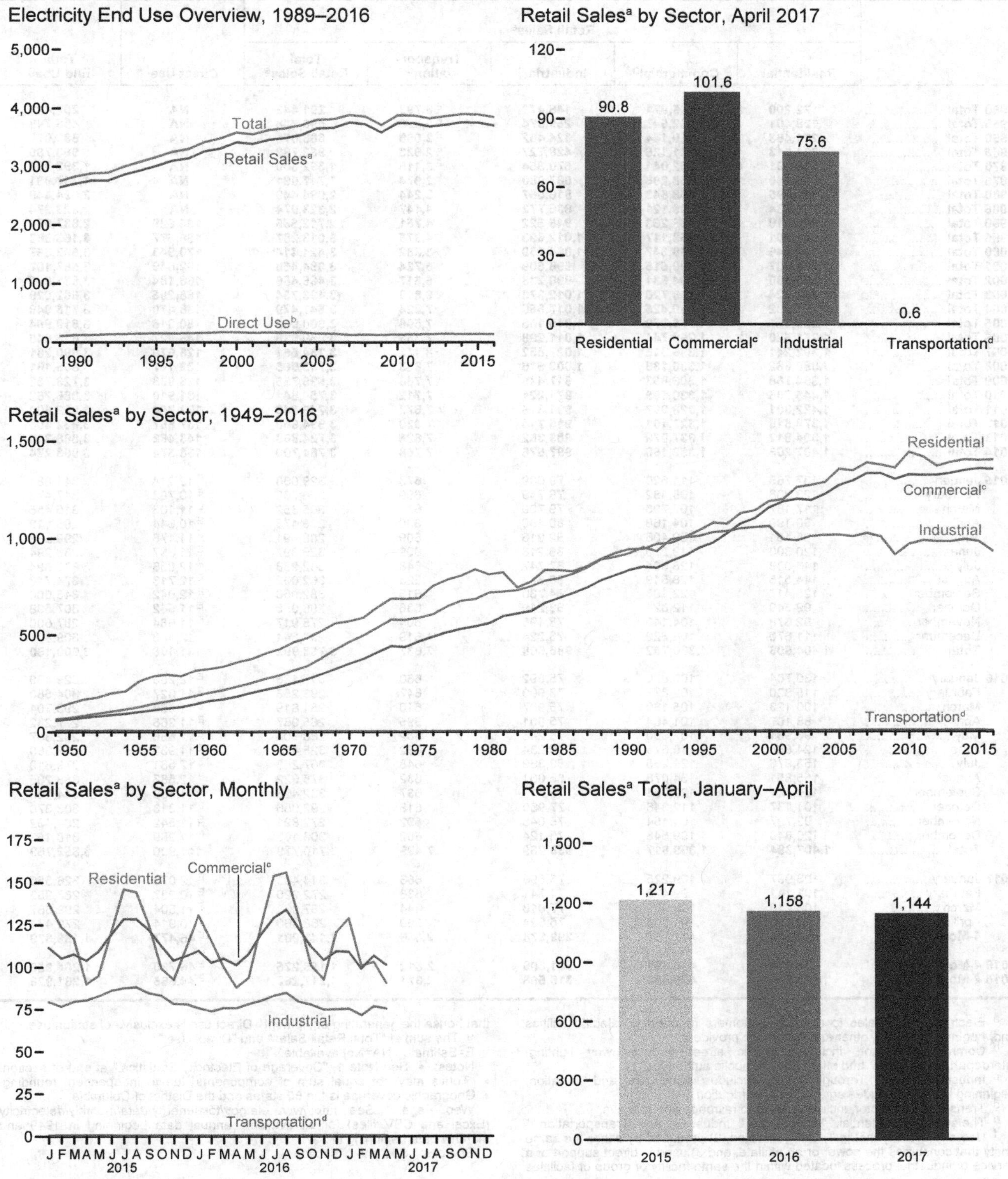

[a] Electricity retail sales to ultimate customers reported by utilities and other energy service providers.
[b] See "Direct Use" in Glossary.
[c] Commercial sector, including public street and highway lighting, interdepartmental sales, and other sales to public authorites.
[d] Transportation sector, including sales to railroads and railways.
Web Page: http://www.eia.gov/totalenergy/data/monthly/#electricity.
Source: Table 7.6.

Source: *U.S. Energy Information Administration, Monthly Energy Review, July 2017*

Table 7.6 Electricity End Use
(Million Kilowatthours)

	Retail Sales[a]						
	Residential	Commercial[b]	Industrial[c]	Transportation[d]	Total Retail Sales[e]	Direct Use[f]	Total End Use[g]
1950 Total	72,200	E 65,971	146,479	E 6,793	291,443	NA	291,443
1955 Total	128,401	E 102,547	259,974	E 5,826	496,748	NA	496,748
1960 Total	201,463	E 159,144	324,402	E 3,066	688,075	NA	688,075
1965 Total	291,013	E 231,126	428,727	E 2,923	953,789	NA	953,789
1970 Total	466,291	E 352,041	570,854	E 3,115	1,392,300	NA	1,392,300
1975 Total	588,140	E 468,296	687,680	E 2,974	1,747,091	NA	1,747,091
1980 Total	717,495	558,643	815,067	3,244	2,094,449	NA	2,094,449
1985 Total	793,934	689,121	836,772	4,147	2,323,974	NA	2,323,974
1990 Total	924,019	838,263	945,522	4,751	2,712,555	124,529	2,837,084
1995 Total	1,042,501	953,117	1,012,693	4,975	3,013,287	150,677	3,163,963
2000 Total	1,192,446	1,159,347	1,064,239	5,382	3,421,414	170,943	3,592,357
2001 Total	1,201,607	1,190,518	996,609	5,724	3,394,458	162,649	3,557,107
2002 Total	1,265,180	1,204,531	990,238	5,517	3,465,466	166,184	3,631,650
2003 Total	1,275,824	1,198,728	1,012,373	6,810	3,493,734	168,295	3,662,029
2004 Total	1,291,982	1,230,425	1,017,850	7,224	3,547,479	168,470	3,715,949
2005 Total	1,359,227	1,275,079	1,019,156	7,506	3,660,969	150,016	3,810,984
2006 Total	1,351,520	1,299,744	1,011,298	7,358	3,669,919	146,927	3,816,845
2007 Total	1,392,241	1,336,315	1,027,832	8,173	3,764,561	125,670	3,890,231
2008 Total	1,380,662	1,336,133	1,009,516	7,653	3,733,965	132,197	3,866,161
2009 Total	1,364,758	1,306,853	917,416	7,768	3,596,795	126,938	3,723,733
2010 Total	1,445,708	1,330,199	971,221	7,712	3,754,841	131,910	3,886,752
2011 Total	1,422,801	1,328,057	991,316	7,672	3,749,846	132,754	3,882,600
2012 Total	1,374,515	1,327,101	985,714	7,320	3,694,650	137,657	3,832,306
2013 Total	1,394,812	1,337,079	985,352	7,625	3,724,868	143,462	3,868,330
2014 Total	1,407,208	1,352,158	997,576	7,758	3,764,700	138,574	3,903,274
2015 January	137,765	111,620	79,609	673	329,666	E 12,214	341,881
February	123,838	105,482	76,749	699	306,768	E 10,703	317,472
March	117,167	107,796	79,709	679	305,352	E 11,103	316,455
April	90,199	104,168	80,489	620	275,475	E 10,644	286,119
May	95,161	109,406	82,916	609	288,091	E 11,178	299,268
June	120,300	119,270	86,218	609	326,397	E 11,897	338,294
July	146,038	128,504	87,747	648	362,938	E 12,956	375,894
August	144,515	128,519	88,373	625	362,032	E 12,716	374,748
September	125,417	122,195	84,730	615	332,958	E 12,042	345,000
October	99,349	112,821	83,249	636	296,055	E 11,542	307,598
November	92,678	104,140	78,495	604	275,917	E 11,684	287,600
December	111,670	106,829	78,224	619	297,344	E 12,488	309,831
Total	1,404,096	1,360,752	986,508	7,637	3,758,992	141,168	3,900,160
2016 January	130,764	109,870	75,892	660	317,186	E 12,253	329,439
February	115,820	102,877	73,909	647	293,253	E 11,327	304,580
March	100,123	105,180	75,907	610	281,819	E 11,885	293,704
April	88,107	101,464	75,801	595	265,967	E 11,265	277,232
May	93,981	107,900	78,246	582	280,708	E 11,658	292,367
June	124,888	119,673	80,234	632	325,427	E 11,933	337,360
July	153,976	129,265	83,369	648	367,258	E 12,561	379,819
August	155,851	134,078	85,061	632	375,622	E 12,583	388,205
September	129,111	122,961	79,719	637	332,428	E 11,680	344,109
October	101,137	112,346	77,960	613	292,056	E 11,313	303,370
November	92,797	104,454	75,048	592	272,891	E 11,542	284,432
December	120,840	109,548	75,124	652	306,163	E 11,989	318,153
Total	1,407,394	1,359,617	936,269	7,499	3,710,779	E 141,990	3,852,769
2017 January	128,997	109,225	75,596	666	314,483	E 12,073	326,556
February	101,141	99,478	71,741	636	272,996	E 10,987	283,982
March	103,210	106,991	77,018	644	287,863	E 11,504	299,367
April	90,780	101,566	75,624	590	268,560	E 10,914	279,474
4-Month Total	424,128	417,259	299,978	2,536	1,143,901	E 45,477	1,189,379
2016 4-Month Total	434,814	419,391	301,509	2,512	1,158,225	E 46,730	1,204,955
2015 4-Month Total	468,969	429,066	316,556	2,671	1,217,262	E 44,665	1,261,926

[a] Electricity retail sales to ultimate customers reported by electric utilities and, beginning in 1996, other energy service providers.
[b] Commercial sector, including public street and highway lighting, interdepartmental sales, and other sales to public authorities.
[c] Industrial sector. Through 2002, excludes agriculture and irrigation; beginning in 2003, includes agriculture and irrigation.
[d] Transportation sector, including sales to railroads and railways.
[e] The sum of "Residential," "Commercial," "Industrial," and "Transportation."
[f] Use of electricity that is 1) self-generated, 2) produced by either the same entity that consumes the power or an affiliate, and 3) used in direct support of a service or industrial process located within the same facility or group of facilities that house the generating equipment. Direct use is exclusive of station use.
[g] The sum of "Total Retail Sales" and "Direct Use."
E=Estimate. NA=Not available.
Notes: • See Note 1, "Coverage of Electricity Statistics," at end of section.
• Totals may not equal sum of components due to independent rounding.
• Geographic coverage is the 50 states and the District of Columbia.
Web Page: See http://www.eia.gov/totalenergy/data/monthly/#electricity (Excel and CSV files) for all available annual data beginning in 1949 and monthly data beginning in 1973.
Sources: See end of section.

Source: *U.S. Energy Information Administration, Monthly Energy Review, July 2017*

Figure 8.1 Nuclear Energy Overview

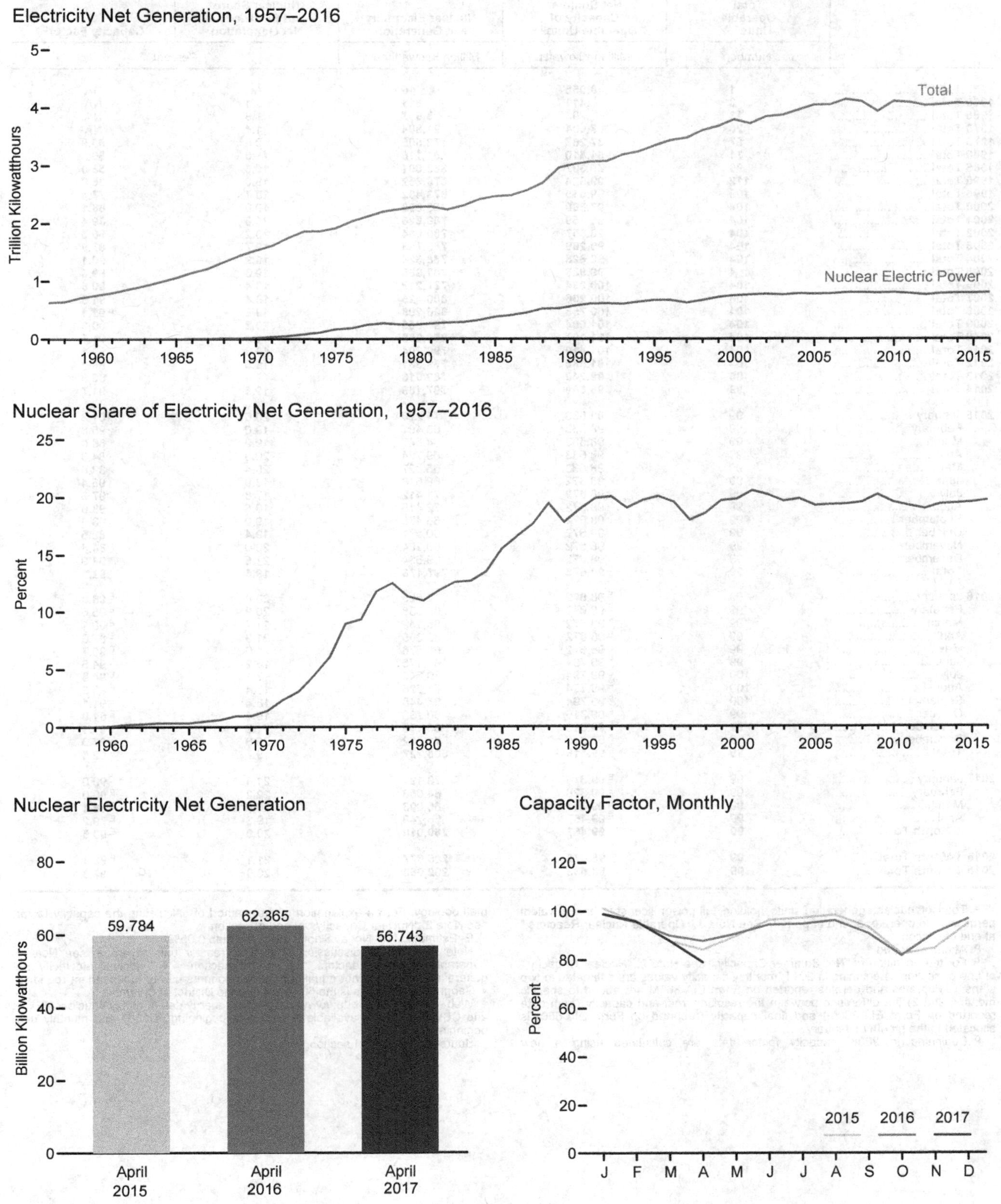

Electricity Net Generation, 1957–2016

Trillion Kilowatthours

Total

Nuclear Electric Power

Nuclear Share of Electricity Net Generation, 1957–2016

Percent

Nuclear Electricity Net Generation

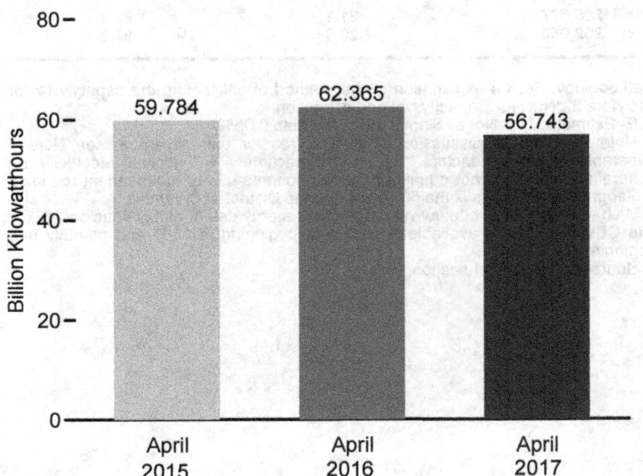

Capacity Factor, Monthly

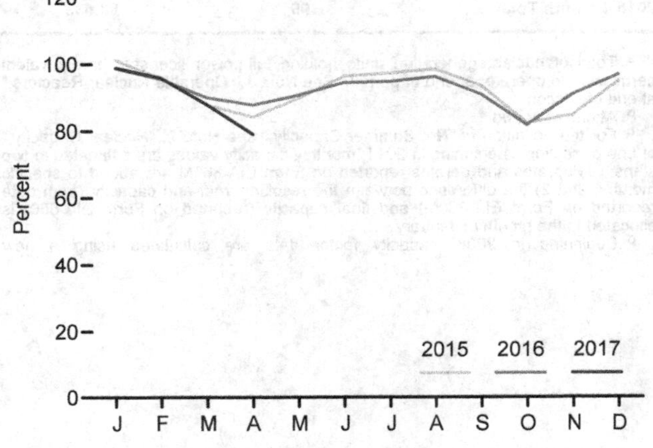

Web Page: http://www.eia.gov/totalenergy/data/monthly/#nuclear.
Sources: Tables 7.2a and 8.1.

Source: *U.S. Energy Information Administration, Monthly Energy Review, July 2017*

Table 8.1 Nuclear Energy Overview

	Total Operable Units[a,b]	Net Summer Capacity of Operable Units[b,c]	Nuclear Electricity Net Generation	Nuclear Share of Electricity Net Generation	Capacity Factor[d]
	Number	Million Kilowatts	Million Kilowatthours	Percent	
1957 Total	1	0.055	10	(s)	NA
1960 Total	3	.411	518	.1	NA
1965 Total	13	.793	3,657	.3	NA
1970 Total	20	7.004	21,804	1.4	NA
1975 Total	57	37.267	172,505	9.0	55.9
1980 Total	71	51.810	251,116	11.0	56.3
1985 Total	96	79.397	383,691	15.5	58.0
1990 Total	112	99.624	576,862	19.0	66.0
1995 Total	109	99.515	673,402	20.1	77.4
2000 Total	104	97.860	753,893	19.8	88.1
2001 Total	104	98.159	768,826	20.6	89.4
2002 Total	104	98.657	780,064	20.2	90.3
2003 Total	104	99.209	763,733	19.7	87.9
2004 Total	104	99.628	788,528	19.9	90.1
2005 Total	104	99.988	781,986	19.3	89.3
2006 Total	104	100.334	787,219	19.4	89.6
2007 Total	104	100.266	806,425	19.4	91.8
2008 Total	104	100.755	806,208	19.6	[d]91.1
2009 Total	104	101.004	798,855	20.2	90.3
2010 Total	104	101.167	806,968	19.6	91.1
2011 Total	104	[c]101.419	790,204	19.3	89.1
2012 Total	104	101.885	769,331	19.0	86.1
2013 Total	100	99.240	789,016	19.4	89.9
2014 Total	99	98.569	797,166	19.5	91.7
2015 January	99	98.533	74,270	20.6	101.3
February	99	98.533	63,461	19.0	95.8
March	99	98.533	64,547	19.9	88.0
April	99	98.533	59,784	20.3	84.3
May	99	98.533	65,827	20.4	89.8
June	99	98.672	68,516	18.9	96.4
July	99	98.672	71,412	17.8	97.3
August	99	98.672	72,415	18.5	98.6
September	99	98.672	66,476	19.0	93.6
October	99	98.672	60,571	19.4	82.5
November	99	98.672	60,264	20.0	84.8
December	99	98.672	69,634	21.5	94.9
Total	**99**	**98.672**	**797,178**	**19.6**	**92.3**
2016 January	99	[E]98.672	72,525	20.6	[E]98.8
February	99	[E]98.672	65,638	20.9	[E]95.6
March	99	[E]98.672	66,149	21.7	[E]90.1
April	99	[E]98.672	62,365	21.3	[E]87.8
May	99	[E]98.672	66,576	21.0	[E]90.7
June	99	[E]99.794	67,175	18.2	[E]94.5
July	100	[E]99.794	70,349	17.1	[E]94.8
August	100	[E]99.794	71,526	17.4	[E]96.3
September	100	[E]99.794	65,448	18.6	[E]91.1
October	99	[E]99.316	60,733	19.4	[E]81.9
November	99	[E]99.316	65,179	21.9	[E]91.1
December	99	[E]99.316	71,662	20.8	[E]97.0
Total	**99**	**[E]99.316**	**805,327**	**19.7**	**[E]92.5**
2017 January	99	[E]99.316	73,121	21.4	[E]99.0
February	99	[E]99.328	64,053	22.2	[E]96.0
March	99	[E]99.331	65,093	20.5	[E]88.1
April	99	[E]99.467	56,743	19.3	[E]79.2
4-Month Total	**99**	**[E]99.467**	**259,010**	**20.9**	**[E]90.5**
2016 4-Month Total	**99**	**[E]98.672**	**266,677**	**21.1**	**[E]93.1**
2015 4-Month Total	**99**	**98.533**	**262,063**	**20.0**	**92.3**

[a] Total of nuclear generating units holding full-power licenses, or equivalent permission to operate, at end of period. See Note 1, "Operable Nuclear Reactors," at end of section.

[b] At end of period.

[c] For the definition of "Net Summer Capacity," see Note 2, "Nuclear Capacity," at end of section. Beginning in 2011, monthly capacity values are estimated in two steps: 1) uprates and derates reported on Form EIA-860M are added to specific months; and 2) the difference between the resulting year-end capacity (from data reported on Form EIA-860M) and final capacity (reported on Form EIA-860) is allocated to the month of January.

[d] Beginning in 2008, capacity factor data are calculated using a new methodology. For an explanation of the method of calculating the capacity factor, see Note 2, "Nuclear Capacity," at end of section.

E=Estimate. NA=Not available. (s)=Less than 0.05%.

Notes: • For a discussion of nuclear reactor unit coverage, see Note 1, "Operable Nuclear Reactors," at end of section. • Nuclear electricity net generation totals may not equal sum of components due to independent rounding. • Geographic coverage is the 50 states and the District of Columbia.

Web Page: See http://www.eia.gov/totalenergy/data/monthly/#nuclear (Excel and CSV files) for all available annual data beginning in 1957 and monthly data beginning in 1973.

Sources: See end of section.

Source: *U.S. Energy Information Administration, Monthly Energy Review, July 2017*

Figure 9.1 Petroleum Prices

Crude Oil Prices, 1949–2016

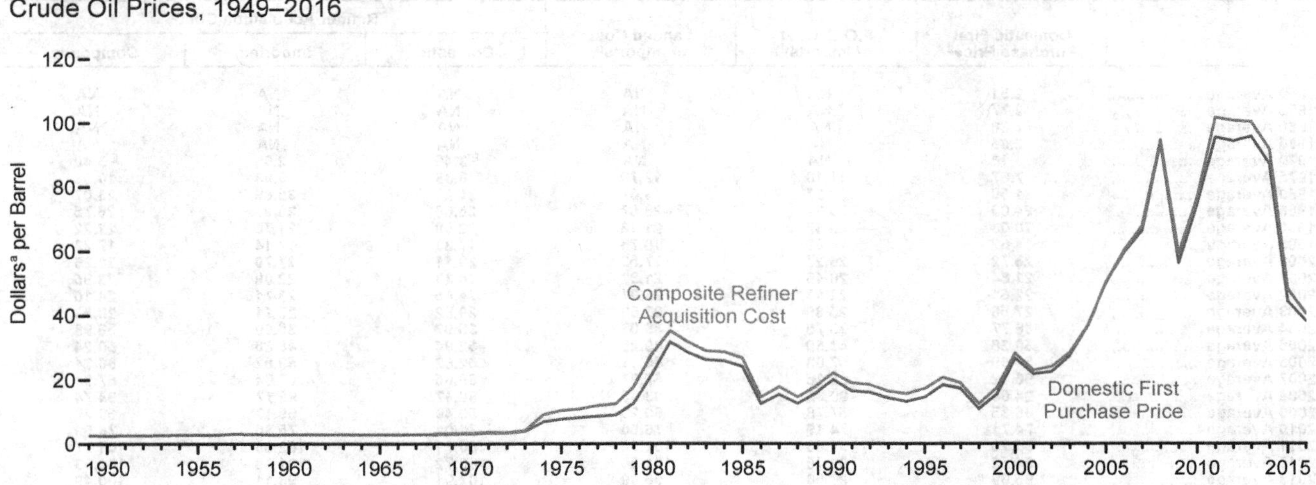

Composite Refiner Acquisition Cost, Monthly

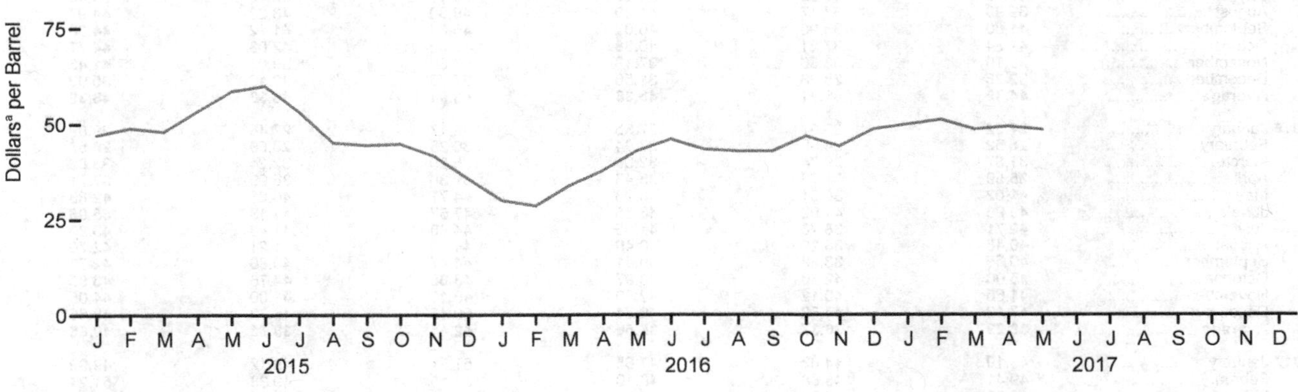

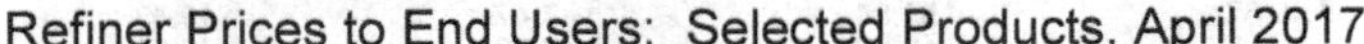

Refiner Prices to End Users: Selected Products, April 2017

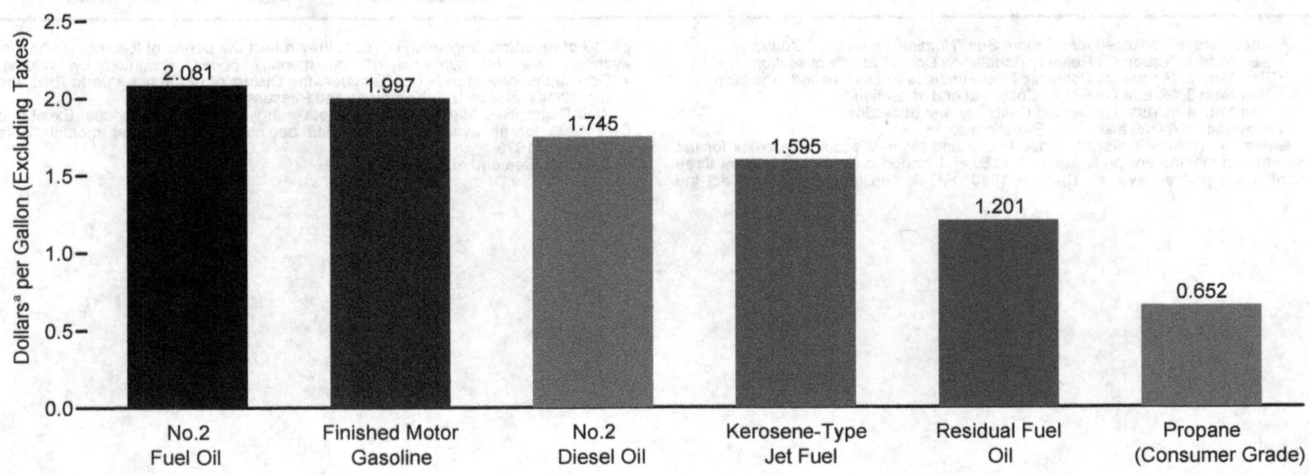

[a] Prices are not adjusted for inflation. See "Nominal Dollars" in Glossary.

Web Page: http://www.eia.gov/totalenergy/data/monthly/#prices.
Sources: Tables 9.1, 9.5, and 9.7.

Source: *U.S. Energy Information Administration, Monthly Energy Review, July 2017*

Table 9.1 Crude Oil Price Summary
(Dollars[a] per Barrel)

	Domestic First Purchase Price[c]	F.O.B. Cost of Imports[d]	Landed Cost of Imports[e]	Refiner Acquisition Cost[b]		
				Domestic	Imported	Composite
1950 Average	**2.51**	**NA**	**NA**	**NA**	**NA**	**NA**
1955 Average	**2.77**	**NA**	**NA**	**NA**	**NA**	**NA**
1960 Average	**2.88**	**NA**	**NA**	**NA**	**NA**	**NA**
1965 Average	**2.86**	**NA**	**NA**	**NA**	**NA**	**NA**
1970 Average	**3.18**	**NA**	**NA**	E **3.46**	E **2.96**	E **3.40**
1975 Average	**7.67**	**11.18**	**12.70**	**8.39**	**13.93**	**10.38**
1980 Average	**21.59**	**32.37**	**33.67**	**24.23**	**33.89**	**28.07**
1985 Average	**24.09**	**25.84**	**26.67**	**26.66**	**26.99**	**26.75**
1990 Average	**20.03**	**20.37**	**21.13**	**22.59**	**21.76**	**22.22**
1995 Average	**14.62**	**15.69**	**16.78**	**17.33**	**17.14**	**17.23**
2000 Average	**26.72**	**26.27**	**27.53**	**29.11**	**27.70**	**28.26**
2001 Average	**21.84**	**20.46**	**21.82**	**24.33**	**22.00**	**22.95**
2002 Average	**22.51**	**22.63**	**23.91**	**24.65**	**23.71**	**24.10**
2003 Average	**27.56**	**25.86**	**27.69**	**29.82**	**27.71**	**28.53**
2004 Average	**36.77**	**33.75**	**36.07**	**38.97**	**35.90**	**36.98**
2005 Average	**50.28**	**47.60**	**49.29**	**52.94**	**48.86**	**50.24**
2006 Average	**59.69**	**57.03**	**59.11**	**62.62**	**59.02**	**60.24**
2007 Average	**66.52**	**66.36**	**67.97**	**69.65**	**67.04**	**67.94**
2008 Average	**94.04**	**90.32**	**93.33**	**98.47**	**92.77**	**94.74**
2009 Average	**56.35**	**57.78**	**60.23**	**59.49**	**59.17**	**59.29**
2010 Average	**74.71**	**74.19**	**76.50**	**78.01**	**75.86**	**76.69**
2011 Average	**95.73**	**101.66**	**102.92**	**100.71**	**102.63**	**101.87**
2012 Average	**94.52**	**99.78**	**101.00**	**100.72**	**101.09**	**100.93**
2013 Average	**95.99**	**96.56**	**96.99**	**102.91**	**98.11**	**100.49**
2014 Average	**87.39**	**85.65**	**88.16**	**94.05**	**89.56**	**92.02**
2015 January	43.06	40.16	44.42	48.90	44.74	47.00
February	44.35	43.94	47.32	50.23	47.18	48.92
March	42.66	43.64	47.25	48.60	47.22	47.99
April	49.30	48.42	52.00	54.86	51.62	53.51
May	54.38	54.05	57.17	59.48	57.51	58.65
June	55.88	53.83	56.73	61.06	58.89	60.12
July	47.70	45.88	49.79	54.15	52.42	53.40
August	39.98	37.17	41.39	46.30	43.23	44.97
September	41.60	36.90	40.02	46.68	41.12	44.38
October	42.34	37.21	40.38	47.02	42.03	44.77
November	38.19	33.56	37.13	43.30	39.05	41.43
December	32.26	28.23	31.56	37.76	33.16	35.63
Average	**44.39**	**41.91**	**45.38**	**49.94**	**46.38**	**48.39**
2016 January	27.02	23.67	27.36	32.17	27.48	29.99
February	25.52	24.68	27.04	30.28	26.66	28.53
March	31.87	29.74	32.06	35.29	32.24	33.82
April	35.59	32.73	35.43	39.30	35.90	37.71
May	41.02	38.31	40.73	44.77	40.88	42.88
June	43.96	41.92	43.55	47.57	44.13	45.96
July	40.71	38.76	41.05	44.88	41.48	43.26
August	40.46	38.26	40.40	44.18	41.21	42.70
September	40.55	38.28	40.81	44.47	40.86	42.73
October	45.00	42.36	43.97	48.66	44.76	46.85
November	41.65	40.12	42.59	46.10	41.80	44.06
December	47.12	44.52	46.74	50.45	46.72	48.66
Average	**38.29**	**36.37**	**38.56**	**42.41**	**38.75**	**40.66**
2017 January	48.19	44.63	47.05	51.81	48.12	49.99
February	49.41	R 45.88	48.10	53.15	49.38	51.24
March	46.39	R 44.06	R 46.06	R 50.60	R 46.53	R 48.65
April	R 47.23	R 43.77	R 45.67	R 51.34	R 47.47	R 49.47
May	NA	NA	NA	E 49.92	E 46.68	E 48.53

[a] Prices are not adjusted for inflation. See "Nominal Dollars" in Glossary.
[b] See Note 1, "Crude Oil Refinery Acquisition Costs," at end of section.
[c] See Note 2, "Crude Oil Domestic First Purchase Prices," at end of section.
[d] See Note 3, "Crude Oil F.O.B. Costs," at end of section.
[e] See Note 4, "Crude Oil Landed Costs," at end of section.
R=Revised. NA=Not available. E=Estimate.

Notes: • Domestic first purchase prices and refinery acquisition costs for the current two months are preliminary. F.O.B. and landed costs for the current three months are preliminary. • Through 1980, F.O.B. and landed costs reflect the period of reporting; beginning in 1981, they reflect the period of loading. • Annual averages are the averages of the monthly prices, weighted by volume. • Geographic coverage is the 50 states, the District of Columbia, Puerto Rico, the Virgin Islands, and all U.S. Territories and Possessions.

Web Page: See http://www.eia.gov/totalenergy/data/monthly/#prices (Excel and CSV files) for all available annual data beginning in 1949 and monthly data beginning in 1973.

Sources: See end of section.

Source: *U.S. Energy Information Administration, Monthly Energy Review, July 2017*

Table 9.2 F.O.B. Costs of Crude Oil Imports From Selected Countries

(Dollars[a] per Barrel)

	Selected Countries							Persian Gulf Nations[b]	Total OPEC[c]	Total Non-OPEC[c]
	Angola	Colombia	Mexico	Nigeria	Saudi Arabia	United Kingdom	Venezuela			
1973 Average[d]	W	W	–	7.81	3.25	–	5.39	3.68	5.43	4.80
1975 Average	10.97	–	11.44	11.82	10.87	–	11.04	10.88	11.34	10.62
1980 Average	33.45	W	31.06	35.93	28.17	34.36	24.81	28.92	32.21	32.85
1985 Average	26.30	–	25.33	28.04	22.04	27.64	23.64	23.31	25.67	25.96
1990 Average	20.23	20.75	19.26	22.46	20.36	23.43	19.55	18.54	20.40	20.32
1995 Average	16.58	16.73	15.64	17.40	W	16.94	13.86	W	15.36	16.02
2000 Average	27.90	29.04	25.39	28.70	24.62	27.21	24.45	24.72	25.56	26.77
2001 Average	23.25	24.25	18.89	24.85	18.98	23.30	18.01	18.89	19.73	21.04
2002 Average	24.09	24.64	21.60	25.38	23.92	24.50	20.13	23.38	22.18	22.93
2003 Average	28.22	28.89	24.83	29.40	25.03	28.76	23.81	25.17	25.36	26.21
2004 Average	37.26	37.73	31.55	38.71	34.08	37.30	31.78	33.08	33.95	33.58
2005 Average	52.48	51.89	43.00	55.95	47.96	54.48	46.39	47.21	49.60	45.79
2006 Average	62.23	59.77	52.91	65.69	56.09	66.03	55.80	56.02	59.18	55.35
2007 Average	67.80	67.93	61.35	76.64	W	69.96	64.10	69.93	69.58	62.69
2008 Average	95.66	91.17	84.61	102.06	93.03	96.33	88.06	91.44	93.15	87.15
2009 Average	57.07	57.90	56.47	64.61	57.87	65.63	55.58	59.53	58.53	57.16
2010 Average	78.18	72.56	72.46	80.83	76.44	W	70.30	75.65	75.23	73.24
2011 Average	111.82	100.21	100.90	115.35	107.08	–	97.23	106.47	105.34	98.49
2012 Average	111.23	106.43	101.84	114.51	106.65	–	100.15	105.45	104.39	95.71
2013 Average	107.71	101.24	98.40	110.06	101.16	W	97.52	100.62	100.57	93.67
2014 Average	W	80.75	86.55	W	95.60	–	84.51	94.03	89.76	82.95
2015 January	–	42.49	41.19	–	48.14	–	37.99	52.21	42.64	38.89
February	W	50.79	48.12	W	47.92	–	45.85	47.70	47.31	42.43
March	W	47.25	46.89	–	50.64	–	43.51	49.75	45.54	42.63
April	W	54.95	50.49	–	58.95	–	49.03	53.33	50.55	47.41
May	W	56.30	56.80	–	61.80	–	51.99	59.55	54.95	53.59
June	W	56.42	56.78	–	58.31	–	50.34	58.57	54.06	53.70
July	W	46.62	50.71	–	W	–	44.44	50.42	46.61	45.55
August	W	42.35	40.40	–	43.38	–	35.47	43.01	38.21	36.62
September	W	W	40.50	–	44.50	–	36.23	43.87	39.81	35.06
October	W	41.56	40.18	–	42.51	–	37.77	40.68	39.33	36.02
November	–	W	36.16	–	39.87	–	31.68	38.17	33.98	33.30
December	W	28.98	30.12	W	34.75	–	24.91	33.79	29.35	27.57
Average	**W**	**47.52**	**44.90**	**W**	**47.53**	**–**	**40.73**	**46.95**	**43.25**	**41.19**
2016 January	W	W	24.12	W	26.24	–	20.73	25.73	25.05	22.66
February	W	24.91	24.50	37.83	27.46	–	22.57	26.58	27.01	23.35
March	35.33	30.47	29.01	W	34.14	–	27.31	32.32	31.37	28.35
April	W	33.57	30.79	W	37.13	–	29.07	35.67	34.08	31.92
May	W	39.00	39.04	W	42.44	W	36.65	40.55	40.51	37.04
June	49.56	41.64	42.27	48.79	45.16	–	39.33	43.77	43.73	40.22
July	45.00	36.91	39.99	W	42.11	–	35.69	40.91	39.61	38.09
August	W	36.80	38.73	W	42.48	–	37.56	40.44	40.44	36.78
September	W	40.36	38.44	W	42.31	–	36.95	40.37	40.01	37.18
October	W	40.59	42.91	W	47.10	–	40.38	45.17	44.66	40.37
November	W	39.80	39.55	W	42.50	W	38.39	41.40	42.31	38.33
December	W	45.27	45.34	W	48.79	W	44.75	47.95	47.44	42.34
Average	**42.68**	**35.28**	**36.22**	**46.20**	**39.30**	**W**	**34.71**	**38.76**	**38.51**	**34.81**
2017 January	–	47.92	45.50	W	W	–	45.94	47.61	47.30	43.27
February	W	46.97	45.91	W	R51.21	–	45.69	R50.06	R49.11	43.63
March	W	R46.05	R42.10	W	R48.50	–	R42.47	R47.80	R46.82	R41.73
April	W	46.76	44.32	W	49.91	–	44.27	48.77	47.28	41.62

[a] Prices are not adjusted for inflation. See "Nominal Dollars" in Glossary.

[b] Bahrain, Iran, Iraq, Kuwait, Qatar, Saudi Arabia, United Arab Emirates, and the Neutral Zone (between Kuwait and Saudi Arabia).

[c] See "Organization of the Petroleum Exporting Countries (OPEC)" in Glossary for exact years of each country's membership. On this table, "Total OPEC" for all years includes Algeria, Iran, Iraq, Kuwait, Libya, Nigeria, Qatar, Saudi Arabia, United Arab Emirates, and Venezuela; Angola is included in "Total OPEC" 2007 forward; Gabon is included in "Total OPEC" 1974–1995 and July 2016 forward; Ecuador is included in "Total OPEC" 1973–1992 and 2008 forward; Indonesia is included in "Total OPEC" 1973–2008 and 2016.

[d] Based on October, November, and December data only.

R=Revised. – =No data reported. W=Value withheld to avoid disclosure of individual company data.

Notes: • The Free on Board (F.O.B.) cost at the country of origin excludes all costs related to insurance and transportation. See "F.O.B. (Free on Board)" in Glossary, and Note 3, "Crude Oil F.O.B. Costs," at end of section. • Values for the current two months are preliminary. • Through 1980, prices reflect the period of reporting; beginning in 1981, prices reflect the period of loading. • Annual averages are averages of the monthly prices, including prices not published, weighted by volume. • Cargoes that are purchased on a "netback" basis, or under similar contractual arrangements whereby the actual purchase price is not established at the time the crude oil is acquired for importation into the United States, are not included in the published data until the actual prices have been determined and reported. • U.S. geographic coverage is the 50 states and the District of Columbia.

Web Page: See http://www.eia.gov/totalenergy/data/monthly/#prices (Excel and CSV files) for all available annual and monthly data beginning in 1973.

Sources: See end of section.

Source: *U.S. Energy Information Administration, Monthly Energy Review, July 2017*

Table 9.3 Landed Costs of Crude Oil Imports From Selected Countries
(Dollars[a] per Barrel)

	Selected Countries								Persian Gulf Nations[b]	Total OPEC[c]	Total Non-OPEC[c]
	Angola	Canada	Colombia	Mexico	Nigeria	Saudi Arabia	United Kingdom	Venezuela			
1973 Average[d]	**W**	**5.33**	**W**	**–**	**9.08**	**5.37**	**–**	**5.99**	**5.91**	**6.85**	**5.64**
1975 Average	**11.81**	**12.84**	**–**	**12.61**	**12.70**	**12.50**	**–**	**12.36**	**12.64**	**12.70**	**12.70**
1980 Average	**34.76**	**30.11**	**W**	**31.77**	**37.15**	**29.80**	**35.68**	**25.92**	**30.59**	**33.56**	**33.99**
1985 Average	**27.39**	**25.71**	**–**	**25.63**	**28.96**	**24.72**	**28.36**	**24.43**	**25.50**	**26.86**	**26.53**
1990 Average	**21.51**	**20.48**	**22.34**	**19.64**	**23.33**	**21.82**	**22.65**	**20.31**	**20.55**	**21.23**	**20.98**
1995 Average	**17.66**	**16.65**	**17.45**	**16.19**	**18.25**	**16.84**	**17.91**	**14.81**	**16.78**	**16.61**	**16.95**
2000 Average	**29.57**	**26.69**	**29.68**	**26.03**	**30.04**	**26.58**	**29.26**	**26.05**	**26.77**	**27.29**	**27.80**
2001 Average	**25.13**	**20.72**	**25.88**	**19.37**	**26.55**	**20.98**	**25.32**	**19.81**	**20.73**	**21.52**	**22.17**
2002 Average	**25.43**	**22.98**	**25.28**	**22.09**	**26.45**	**24.77**	**26.35**	**21.93**	**24.13**	**23.83**	**23.97**
2003 Average	**30.14**	**26.76**	**30.55**	**25.48**	**31.07**	**27.50**	**30.62**	**25.70**	**27.54**	**27.70**	**27.68**
2004 Average	**39.62**	**34.51**	**39.03**	**32.25**	**40.95**	**37.11**	**39.28**	**33.79**	**36.53**	**36.84**	**35.29**
2005 Average	**54.31**	**44.73**	**53.42**	**43.47**	**57.55**	**50.31**	**55.28**	**47.87**	**49.68**	**51.36**	**47.31**
2006 Average	**64.85**	**53.90**	**62.13**	**53.76**	**68.26**	**59.19**	**67.44**	**57.37**	**58.92**	**61.21**	**57.14**
2007 Average	**71.27**	**60.38**	**70.91**	**62.31**	**78.01**	**70.78**	**72.47**	**66.13**	**69.83**	**71.14**	**63.96**
2008 Average	**98.18**	**90.00**	**93.43**	**85.97**	**104.83**	**94.75**	**96.95**	**90.76**	**93.59**	**95.49**	**90.59**
2009 Average	**61.32**	**57.60**	**58.50**	**57.35**	**68.01**	**62.14**	**63.87**	**57.78**	**62.15**	**61.90**	**58.58**
2010 Average	**80.61**	**72.80**	**74.25**	**72.86**	**83.14**	**79.29**	**80.29**	**72.43**	**78.60**	**78.28**	**74.68**
2011 Average	**114.05**	**89.92**	**102.57**	**101.21**	**116.43**	**108.83**	**118.45**	**100.14**	**108.01**	**107.84**	**98.64**
2012 Average	**114.95**	**84.24**	**107.07**	**102.45**	**116.88**	**108.15**	**W**	**101.58**	**107.74**	**107.56**	**95.05**
2013 Average	**110.81**	**84.41**	**103.00**	**99.06**	**112.87**	**102.60**	**111.23**	**99.34**	**102.53**	**102.98**	**91.99**
2014 Average	**99.25**	**81.30**	**88.29**	**87.48**	**102.16**	**94.91**	**W**	**86.88**	**95.30**	**93.10**	**84.67**
2015 January	W	40.45	45.47	41.68	W	50.12	–	40.08	53.01	48.17	42.31
February	W	42.39	53.40	48.29	W	52.44	–	47.93	52.20	51.44	44.86
March	W	41.71	51.25	47.62	W	55.23	W	45.90	54.30	51.13	44.82
April	W	46.67	57.48	52.13	–	59.92	W	52.17	56.99	55.39	49.79
May	60.84	54.06	59.92	57.32	W	62.06	W	53.78	60.92	59.11	55.97
June	61.45	55.42	58.21	57.46	W	58.40	–	52.43	58.17	56.79	56.69
July	53.22	47.98	51.58	51.25	W	51.62	–	46.74	51.93	50.45	49.42
August	54.02	38.29	43.87	41.94	–	45.24	W	38.75	45.70	43.17	40.41
September	53.46	35.29	42.87	40.71	W	44.89	–	37.91	44.94	43.31	37.82
October	47.49	37.64	42.37	40.67	W	42.09	W	39.55	41.81	41.57	39.41
November	47.56	35.67	39.70	36.73	W	39.62	–	33.79	39.43	37.86	36.68
December	38.54	30.25	32.50	30.54	W	34.13	W	26.73	34.33	32.60	30.91
Average	**51.73**	**41.99**	**49.53**	**45.51**	**54.70**	**49.78**	**W**	**42.87**	**49.43**	**47.44**	**44.09**
2016 January	34.83	26.32	26.23	24.82	W	30.96	–	21.64	30.85	28.94	26.33
February	33.04	24.62	26.32	25.19	39.44	31.86	W	23.49	30.91	29.63	25.43
March	36.68	29.31	33.38	29.65	42.86	36.19	W	28.83	34.84	34.02	30.35
April	40.91	34.19	36.71	31.91	W	39.75	–	31.20	38.00	36.80	34.42
May	49.14	38.43	42.28	39.67	W	43.46	W	38.14	42.56	42.48	39.55
June	49.06	41.97	43.88	42.50	51.05	45.90	–	40.04	44.70	44.70	42.65
July	47.04	39.41	40.90	40.30	48.46	43.80	W	37.00	42.77	41.78	40.48
August	49.43	37.84	40.78	39.34	50.20	43.67	W	38.66	42.74	42.46	39.01
September	46.15	38.62	43.43	38.86	49.91	44.22	–	38.11	43.31	42.62	39.60
October	48.88	41.79	43.44	43.44	W	46.95	–	41.61	45.50	45.65	42.64
November	49.08	39.81	42.97	40.20	52.80	47.04	W	39.53	45.68	44.98	40.52
December	53.63	43.34	48.83	45.84	55.62	50.38	W	45.69	49.38	49.07	44.83
Average	**44.65**	**36.27**	**38.86**	**36.64**	**48.11**	**42.14**	**W**	**35.50**	**41.20**	**40.54**	**37.09**
2017 January	–	44.70	49.17	46.35	54.74	50.40	W	47.53	49.35	49.22	45.77
February	W	44.97	[R] 49.66	46.57	54.42	[R] 52.34	–	46.28	[R] 51.09	[R] 50.57	[R] 46.26
March	W	[R] 43.00	[R] 48.29	[R] 42.97	W	[R] 50.31	[R] W	[R] 43.92	[R] 49.59	[R] 48.84	[R] 43.96
April	W	42.94	48.91	44.75	W	50.77	–	45.27	49.33	48.70	43.93

[a] Prices are not adjusted for inflation. See "Nominal Dollars" in Glossary.

[b] Bahrain, Iran, Iraq, Kuwait, Qatar, Saudi Arabia, United Arab Emirates, and the Neutral Zone (between Kuwait and Saudi Arabia).

[c] See "Organization of the Petroleum Exporting Countries (OPEC)" in Glossary for exact years of each country's membership. On this table, "Total OPEC" for all years includes Algeria, Iran, Iraq, Kuwait, Libya, Nigeria, Qatar, Saudi Arabia, United Arab Emirates, and Venezuela; Angola is included in "Total OPEC" 2007 forward; Gabon is included in "Total OPEC" 1974–1995 and July 2016 forward; Ecuador is included in "Total OPEC" 1973–1992 and 2008 forward; Indonesia is included in "Total OPEC" 1973–2008 and 2016.

[d] Based on October, November, and December data only.

R=Revised. – =No data reported. W=Value withheld to avoid disclosure of individual company data.

Notes: • See "Landed Costs" in Glossary, and Note 4, "Crude Oil Landed Costs," at end of section. • Values for the current two months are preliminary. • Through 1980, prices reflect the period of reporting; beginning in 1981, prices reflect the period of loading. • Annual averages are averages of the monthly prices, including prices not published, weighted by volume. • Cargoes that are purchased on a "netback" basis, or under similar contractual arrangements whereby the actual purchase price is not established at the time the crude oil is acquired for importation into the United States, are not included in the published data until the actual prices have been determined and reported. • U.S. geographic coverage is the 50 states and the District of Columbia.

Web Page: See http://www.eia.gov/totalenergy/data/monthly/#prices (Excel and CSV files) for all available annual and monthly data beginning in 1973.

Sources: • **October 1973–September 1977:** Federal Energy Administration, Form FEA-F701-M-0, "Transfer Pricing Report." • **October 1977–December 1977:** U.S. Energy Information Administration (EIA), Form FEA-F701-M-0, "Transfer Pricing Report." • **1978–2007:** EIA, *Petroleum Marketing Annual 2008,* Table 22. • **2008 forward:** EIA, *Petroleum Marketing Monthly,* July 2017, Table 22.

Source: *U.S. Energy Information Administration, Monthly Energy Review, July 2017*

Table 9.4 Retail Motor Gasoline and On-Highway Diesel Fuel Prices

(Dollars[a] per Gallon, Including Taxes)

	Platt's / Bureau of Labor Statistics Data				U.S. Energy Information Administration Data			
	Motor Gasoline by Grade				Regular Motor Gasoline by Area Type			
	Leaded Regular	Unleaded Regular	Unleaded Premium[b]	All Grades[c]	Conventional Gasoline Areas[d]	Reformulated Gasoline Areas[e]	All Areas	On-Highway Diesel Fuel
1950 Average	**0.268**	**NA**	**NA**	**NA**	– –	– –	– –	– –
1955 Average	**.291**	**NA**	**NA**	**NA**	– –	– –	– –	– –
1960 Average	**.311**	**NA**	**NA**	**NA**	– –	– –	– –	– –
1965 Average	**.312**	**NA**	**NA**	**NA**	– –	– –	– –	– –
1970 Average	**.357**	**NA**	**NA**	**NA**	– –	– –	– –	– –
1975 Average	**.567**	**NA**	**NA**	**NA**	– –	– –	– –	– –
1980 Average	**1.191**	**1.245**	**NA**	**1.221**	– –	– –	– –	– –
1985 Average	**1.115**	**1.202**	**1.340**	**1.196**	– –	– –	– –	– –
1990 Average	**1.149**	**1.164**	**1.349**	**1.217**	**NA**	**NA**	**NA**	**NA**
1995 Average	– –	**1.147**	**1.336**	**1.205**	**1.103**	**1.163**	**1.111**	**1.109**
2000 Average	– –	**1.510**	**1.693**	**1.563**	**1.462**	**1.543**	**1.484**	**1.491**
2001 Average	– –	**1.461**	**1.657**	**1.531**	**1.384**	**1.498**	**1.420**	**1.401**
2002 Average	– –	**1.358**	**1.556**	**1.441**	**1.313**	**1.408**	**1.345**	**1.319**
2003 Average	– –	**1.591**	**1.777**	**1.638**	**1.516**	**1.655**	**1.561**	**1.509**
2004 Average	– –	**1.880**	**2.068**	**1.923**	**1.812**	**1.937**	**1.852**	**1.810**
2005 Average	– –	**2.295**	**2.491**	**2.338**	**2.240**	**2.335**	**2.270**	**2.402**
2006 Average	– –	**2.589**	**2.805**	**2.635**	**2.533**	**2.654**	**2.572**	**2.705**
2007 Average	– –	**2.801**	**3.033**	**2.849**	**2.767**	**2.857**	**2.796**	**2.885**
2008 Average	– –	**3.266**	**3.519**	**3.317**	**3.213**	**3.314**	**3.246**	**3.803**
2009 Average	– –	**2.350**	**2.607**	**2.401**	**2.315**	**2.433**	**2.353**	**2.467**
2010 Average	– –	**2.788**	**3.047**	**2.836**	**2.742**	**2.864**	**2.782**	**2.992**
2011 Average	– –	**3.527**	**3.792**	**3.577**	**3.476**	**3.616**	**3.521**	**3.840**
2012 Average	– –	**3.644**	**3.922**	**3.695**	**3.552**	**3.757**	**3.618**	**3.968**
2013 Average	– –	**3.526**	**3.843**	**3.584**	**3.443**	**3.635**	**3.505**	**3.922**
2014 Average	– –	**3.367**	**3.713**	**3.425**	**3.299**	**3.481**	**3.358**	**3.825**
2015 January	– –	2.110	2.497	2.170	2.046	2.262	2.116	2.997
February	– –	2.249	2.621	2.308	2.152	2.351	2.216	2.858
March	– –	2.483	2.867	2.544	2.352	2.697	2.464	2.897
April	– –	2.485	2.868	2.545	2.369	2.679	2.469	2.782
May	– –	2.775	3.166	2.832	2.578	3.014	2.718	2.888
June	– –	2.832	3.218	2.889	2.700	3.014	2.802	2.873
July	– –	2.832	3.252	2.893	2.666	3.061	2.794	2.788
August	– –	2.679	3.120	2.745	2.522	2.876	2.636	2.595
September	– –	2.394	2.860	2.463	2.275	2.555	2.365	2.505
October	– –	2.289	2.749	2.357	2.230	2.414	2.290	2.519
November	– –	2.185	2.640	2.249	2.088	2.304	2.158	2.467
December	– –	2.060	2.532	2.125	1.946	2.230	2.038	2.310
Average	– –	**2.448**	**2.866**	**2.510**	**2.334**	**2.629**	**2.429**	**2.707**
2016 January	– –	1.967	2.455	2.034	1.843	2.170	1.949	2.143
February	– –	1.767	2.248	1.833	1.681	1.936	1.764	1.998
March	– –	1.958	2.411	2.021	1.895	2.124	1.969	2.090
April	– –	2.134	2.585	2.196	2.027	2.293	2.113	2.152
May	– –	2.264	2.710	2.324	2.199	2.413	2.268	2.315
June	– –	2.363	2.807	2.422	2.303	2.497	2.366	2.423
July	– –	2.225	2.702	2.287	2.157	2.411	2.239	2.405
August	– –	2.155	2.629	2.218	2.119	2.300	2.178	2.351
September	– –	2.208	2.682	2.269	2.161	2.339	2.219	2.394
October	– –	2.243	2.719	2.304	2.186	2.382	2.249	2.454
November	– –	2.187	2.675	2.246	2.105	2.343	2.182	2.439
December	– –	2.230	2.698	2.289	2.192	2.385	2.254	2.510
Average	– –	**2.142**	**2.610**	**2.204**	**2.070**	**2.296**	**2.143**	**2.304**
2017 January	– –	2.351	2.815	2.409	2.285	2.482	2.349	2.580
February	– –	2.299	2.793	2.360	2.227	2.467	2.304	2.568
March	– –	2.323	2.827	2.386	2.243	2.498	2.325	2.554
April	– –	2.418	2.909	2.479	2.340	2.579	2.417	2.583
May	– –	2.386	2.894	2.448	2.303	2.577	2.391	2.560
June	– –	2.337	2.859	2.400	2.257	2.536	2.347	2.511

[a] Prices are not adjusted for inflation. See "Nominal Dollars" in Glossary.

[b] The 1981 average (available in Web file) is based on September through December data only.

[c] Also includes grades of motor gasoline not shown separately.

[d] Any area that does not require the sale of reformulated gasoline.

[e] "Reformulated Gasoline Areas" are ozone nonattainment areas designated by the U.S. Environmental Protection Agency that require the use of reformulated gasoline (RFG). Areas are reclassified each time a shift in or out of an RFG program occurs due to federal or state regulations.

NA=Not available. – – =Not applicable.

Notes: • See Note 5, "Motor Gasoline Prices," at end of section. • See "Motor Gasoline Grades," "Motor Gasoline, Conventional," "Motor Gasoline, Oxygenated," and "Motor Gasoline, Reformulated" in Glossary. • Geographic coverage: for columns 1–4, current coverage is 85 urban areas; for columns 5–7, coverage is the 50 states and the District of Columbia; for column 8, coverage is the 48 contiguous states and the District of Columbia.

Web Page: See http://www.eia.gov/totalenergy/data/monthly/#prices (Excel and CSV files) for all available annual data beginning in 1949 and monthly data beginning in 1973.

Sources: • **Motor Gasoline by Grade, Monthly Data: October 1973 forward**—U.S. Department of Labor, Bureau of Labor Statistics (BLS), *U.S. City Average Gasoline Prices.* • **Motor Gasoline by Grade, Annual Data: 1949–1973**—*Platt's Oil Price Handbook and Oilmanac, 1974,* 51st Edition. **1974 forward**—calculated by the U.S. Energy Information Administration (EIA) as simple averages of the BLS monthly data. • **Regular Motor Gasoline by Area Type:** EIA, calculated as simple averages of weighted weekly estimates from "Weekly U.S. Retail Gasoline Prices, Regular Grade." • **On-Highway Diesel Fuel:** EIA, calculated as simple averages of weighted weekly estimates from "Weekly Retail On-Highway Diesel Prices."

Source: *U.S. Energy Information Administration, Monthly Energy Review, July 2017*

Table 9.5 Refiner Prices of Residual Fuel Oil

(Dollars[a] per Gallon, Excluding Taxes)

	Residual Fuel Oil Sulfur Content Less Than or Equal to 1%		Residual Fuel Oil Sulfur Content Greater Than 1%		Average	
	Sales for Resale	Sales to End Users	Sales for Resale	Sales to End Users	Sales for Resale	Sales to End Users
1978 Average	0.293	0.314	0.245	0.275	0.263	0.298
1980 Average	.608	.675	.479	.523	.528	.607
1985 Average	.610	.644	.560	.582	.577	.610
1990 Average	.472	.505	.372	.400	.413	.444
1995 Average	.383	.436	.338	.377	.363	.392
2000 Average	.627	.708	.512	.566	.566	.602
2001 Average	.523	.642	.428	.492	.476	.531
2002 Average	.546	.640	.508	.544	.530	.569
2003 Average	.728	.804	.588	.651	.661	.698
2004 Average	.764	.835	.601	.692	.681	.739
2005 Average	1.115	1.168	.842	.974	.971	1.048
2006 Average	1.202	1.342	1.085	1.173	1.136	1.218
2007 Average	1.406	1.436	1.314	1.350	1.350	1.374
2008 Average	1.918	2.144	1.843	1.889	1.866	1.964
2009 Average	1.337	1.413	1.344	1.306	1.342	1.341
2010 Average	1.756	1.920	1.679	1.619	1.697	1.713
2011 Average	2.389	2.736	2.316	2.257	2.336	2.401
2012 Average	2.548	3.025	2.429	2.433	2.457	2.592
2013 Average	2.363	2.883	2.249	2.353	2.278	2.482
2014 Average	2.153	2.694	1.996	2.221	2.044	2.325
2015 January	.936	NA	1.038	1.192	1.023	1.264
February	1.150	NA	1.124	1.342	1.126	1.376
March	1.093	NA	1.131	1.436	1.126	1.465
April	1.124	1.704	1.114	1.465	1.114	1.516
May	1.198	NA	1.242	1.443	1.234	1.543
June	1.175	W	1.239	1.474	1.233	1.549
July	1.080	W	1.130	1.245	1.122	1.363
August	.797	W	.928	1.150	.918	1.207
September	.819	W	.856	1.063	.852	1.107
October	.812	NA	.840	1.041	.836	1.094
November	.766	W	.791	1.001	.787	1.043
December	.552	W	.639	.861	.633	.919
Average	.971	1.529	.999	1.227	.996	1.285
2016 January	.477	W	.502	.641	.499	.710
February	.475	NA	.508	.606	.504	.632
March	.582	NA	.555	.672	.558	.693
April	.633	W	.614	.734	.616	.782
May	.729	W	.722	.868	.723	.922
June	.850	W	.823	.911	.825	.983
July	.876	W	.834	.948	.835	1.030
August	.842	W	.811	.924	.815	.990
September	.846	W	.855	1.059	.854	1.076
October	.961	W	.935	1.091	.938	1.115
November	.920	NA	.907	1.040	.908	1.106
December	1.024	W	1.031	1.206	1.030	1.230
Average	.736	1.138	.746	.897	.745	.945
2017 January	1.099	W	1.121	1.249	1.119	1.309
February	1.174	W	1.115	1.243	1.121	1.291
March	1.103	W	R 1.075	1.186	R 1.077	1.239
April	1.038	W	1.039	1.147	1.039	1.201

[a] Prices are not adjusted for inflation. See "Nominal Dollars" in Glossary.

R=Revised. NA=Not available. W=Value withheld to avoid disclosure of individual company data.

Notes: • Sales for resale are those made to purchasers other than ultimate consumers. Sales to end users are those made directly to ultimate consumers, including bulk consumers (such as agriculture, industry, and electric utilities) and commercial consumers. • Values for the current month are preliminary. • Through 1982, prices are U.S. Energy Information Administration (EIA) estimates. See Note 6, "Historical Petroleum Prices," at end of section. • Geographic coverage is the 50 states and the District of Columbia.

Web Page: See http://www.eia.gov/totalenergy/data/monthly/#prices (Excel and CSV files) for all available annual data beginning in 1978 and monthly data beginning in 1982.

Sources: • **1978–2007:** EIA, *Petroleum Marketing Annual 2007,* Table 17. • **2008 forward:** EIA, *Petroleum Marketing Monthly,* July 2017, Table 16.

Source: *U.S. Energy Information Administration, Monthly Energy Review, July 2017*

Table 9.6 Refiner Prices of Petroleum Products for Resale

(Dollars[a] per Gallon, Excluding Taxes)

	Finished Motor Gasoline[b]	Finished Aviation Gasoline	Kerosene-Type Jet Fuel	Kerosene	No. 2 Fuel Oil	No. 2 Diesel Fuel	Propane (Consumer Grade)
1978 Average	**0.434**	**0.537**	**0.386**	**0.404**	**0.369**	**0.365**	**0.237**
1980 Average	**.941**	**1.128**	**.868**	**.864**	**.803**	**.801**	**.415**
1985 Average	**.835**	**1.130**	**.794**	**.874**	**.776**	**.772**	**.398**
1990 Average	**.786**	**1.063**	**.773**	**.839**	**.697**	**.694**	**.386**
1995 Average	**.626**	**.975**	**.539**	**.580**	**.511**	**.538**	**.344**
2000 Average	**.963**	**1.330**	**.880**	**.969**	**.886**	**.898**	**.595**
2001 Average	**.886**	**1.256**	**.763**	**.821**	**.756**	**.784**	**.540**
2002 Average	**.828**	**1.146**	**.716**	**.752**	**.694**	**.724**	**.431**
2003 Average	**1.002**	**1.288**	**.871**	**.955**	**.881**	**.883**	**.607**
2004 Average	**1.288**	**1.627**	**1.208**	**1.271**	**1.125**	**1.187**	**.751**
2005 Average	**1.670**	**2.076**	**1.723**	**1.757**	**1.623**	**1.737**	**.933**
2006 Average	**1.969**	**2.490**	**1.961**	**2.007**	**1.834**	**2.012**	**1.031**
2007 Average	**2.182**	**2.758**	**2.171**	**2.249**	**2.072**	**2.203**	**1.194**
2008 Average	**2.586**	**3.342**	**3.020**	**2.851**	**2.745**	**2.994**	**1.437**
2009 Average	**1.767**	**2.480**	**1.719**	**1.844**	**1.657**	**1.713**	**.921**
2010 Average	**2.165**	**2.874**	**2.185**	**2.299**	**2.147**	**2.214**	**1.212**
2011 Average	**2.867**	**3.739**	**3.014**	**3.065**	**2.907**	**3.034**	**1.467**
2012 Average	**2.929**	**3.919**	**3.080**	**3.163**	**3.031**	**3.109**	**1.033**
2013 Average	**2.812**	**3.869**	**2.953**	**3.084**	**2.966**	**3.028**	**1.048**
2014 Average	**2.618**	**3.687**	**2.763**	**2.882**	**2.741**	**2.812**	**1.165**
2015 January	1.366	2.324	1.612	1.900	1.669	1.616	.713
February	1.637	2.529	1.722	2.233	1.850	1.861	.748
March	1.770	2.801	1.731	2.098	1.847	1.815	.689
April	1.835	2.827	1.709	1.800	1.740	1.805	.566
May	2.080	3.050	1.933	1.929	1.852	1.973	.475
June	2.121	3.259	1.813	1.871	1.813	1.881	.404
July	2.072	3.217	1.655	1.701	1.654	1.729	.405
August	1.838	2.980	1.479	1.494	1.461	1.562	.402
September	1.609	2.586	1.443	1.509	1.438	1.551	.469
October	1.558	2.475	1.451	1.555	1.411	1.572	.524
November	1.426	2.385	1.400	1.554	1.356	1.456	.505
December	1.356	2.252	1.207	1.275	1.126	1.176	.499
Average	**1.726**	**2.764**	**1.592**	**1.735**	**1.565**	**1.667**	**.555**
2016 January	1.187	2.122	1.022	1.183	.976	1.015	.460
February	1.046	1.908	1.017	1.155	.948	1.043	.470
March	1.335	2.230	1.100	1.208	1.070	1.189	.497
April	1.476	2.457	1.155	1.193	1.113	1.251	.458
May	1.613	2.528	1.311	1.327	1.291	1.432	.511
June	1.643	2.591	1.428	1.445	1.404	1.531	.497
July	1.490	2.505	1.354	1.297	1.305	1.426	.476
August	1.508	2.405	1.313	1.408	1.307	1.440	.453
September	1.514	2.506	1.366	1.402	1.341	1.471	.494
October	1.568	2.551	1.471	1.580	1.443	1.592	.608
November	1.427	2.433	1.406	1.485	1.386	1.469	.588
December	1.585	2.462	1.511	1.685	1.507	1.606	.703
Average	**1.454**	**2.404**	**1.295**	**1.383**	**1.239**	**1.378**	**.523**
2017 January	1.627	2.614	1.561	1.761	1.560	1.636	.788
February	1.625	2.592	1.592	1.657	1.553	1.641	.792
March	1.634	2.618	R 1.520	1.580	1.495	1.581	R .671
April	1.723	2.741	1.545	1.572	1.499	1.627	.649

[a] Prices are not adjusted for inflation. See "Nominal Dollars" in Glossary.
[b] See Note 5, "Motor Gasoline Prices," at end of section.
R=Revised.

Notes: • Sales for resale are those made to purchasers other than ultimate consumers. Sales to end users are shown in Table 9.7; they are sales made directly to ultimate consumers, including bulk consumers (such as agriculture, industry, and electric utilities) and residential and commercial consumers. • Values for the current month are preliminary. • Through 1982, prices are U.S. Energy Information Administration (EIA) estimates. See Note 6, "Historical Petroleum Prices," at end of section. • Geographic coverage is the 50 states and the District of Columbia.

Web Page: See http://www.eia.gov/totalenergy/data/monthly/#prices (Excel and CSV files) for all available annual data beginning in 1978 and monthly data beginning in 1982.

Sources: • **1978–2007:** EIA, *Petroleum Marketing Annual 2007*, Table 4. • **2008 forward:** EIA, *Petroleum Marketing Monthly*, July 2017, Table 4.

Source: *U.S. Energy Information Administration, Monthly Energy Review, July 2017*

Table 9.7 Refiner Prices of Petroleum Products to End Users

(Dollars[a] per Gallon, Excluding Taxes)

	Finished Motor Gasoline[b]	Finished Aviation Gasoline	Kerosene-Type Jet Fuel	Kerosene	No. 2 Fuel Oil	No. 2 Diesel Fuel	Propane (Consumer Grade)
1978 Average	**0.484**	**0.516**	**0.387**	**0.421**	**0.400**	**0.377**	**0.335**
1980 Average	**1.035**	**1.084**	**.868**	**.902**	**.788**	**.818**	**.482**
1985 Average	**.912**	**1.201**	**.796**	**1.030**	**.849**	**.789**	**.717**
1990 Average	**.883**	**1.120**	**.766**	**.923**	**.734**	**.725**	**.745**
1995 Average	**.765**	**1.005**	**.540**	**.589**	**.562**	**.560**	**.492**
2000 Average	**1.106**	**1.306**	**.899**	**1.123**	**.927**	**.935**	**.603**
2001 Average	**1.032**	**1.323**	**.775**	**1.045**	**.829**	**.842**	**.506**
2002 Average	**.947**	**1.288**	**.721**	**.990**	**.737**	**.762**	**.419**
2003 Average	**1.156**	**1.493**	**.872**	**1.224**	**.933**	**.944**	**.577**
2004 Average	**1.435**	**1.819**	**1.207**	**1.160**	**1.173**	**1.243**	**.839**
2005 Average	**1.829**	**2.231**	**1.735**	**1.957**	**1.705**	**1.786**	**1.089**
2006 Average	**2.128**	**2.682**	**1.998**	**2.244**	**1.982**	**2.096**	**1.358**
2007 Average	**2.345**	**2.849**	**2.165**	**2.263**	**2.241**	**2.267**	**1.489**
2008 Average	**2.775**	**3.273**	**3.052**	**3.283**	**2.986**	**3.150**	**1.892**
2009 Average	**1.888**	**2.442**	**1.704**	**2.675**	**1.962**	**1.834**	**1.220**
2010 Average	**2.301**	**3.028**	**2.201**	**3.063**	**2.462**	**2.314**	**1.481**
2011 Average	**3.050**	**3.803**	**3.054**	**3.616**	**3.193**	**3.117**	**1.709**
2012 Average	**3.154**	**3.971**	**3.104**	**3.843**	**3.358**	**3.202**	**1.139**
2013 Average	**3.049**	**3.932**	**2.979**	**3.842**	**3.335**	**3.122**	**1.028**
2014 Average	**2.855**	**3.986**	**2.772**	**W**	**3.329**	**2.923**	**1.097**
2015 January	1.673	W	1.633	W	NA	1.819	.566
February	1.858	W	1.747	W	2.204	1.979	.671
March	2.054	W	1.766	W	2.141	1.962	.619
April	2.058	W	1.739	W	NA	1.939	.575
May	2.322	W	1.979	W	2.308	2.090	.465
June	2.374	W	1.855	W	2.321	2.021	.393
July	2.338	W	1.694	W	2.207	1.913	.405
August	2.218	W	1.516	W	2.046	1.737	.387
September	1.920	W	1.465	2.996	1.949	1.693	.468
October	1.849	W	1.473	W	NA	1.702	.479
November	1.711	W	1.424	W	1.814	1.603	.447
December	1.604	W	1.232	W	1.695	1.365	.422
Average	**2.003**	**W**	**1.629**	**W**	**2.016**	**1.819**	**.481**
2016 January	1.505	W	1.038	W	1.450	1.198	.377
February	1.332	W	1.032	W	1.407	1.185	.409
March	1.552	W	1.133	W	1.555	1.317	.481
April	1.725	W	1.187	W	1.631	1.386	.472
May	1.869	W	1.342	W	1.733	1.555	.533
June	1.961	W	1.464	W	1.861	1.661	.514
July	1.804	W	1.393	W	1.814	1.577	.491
August	1.754	W	1.330	W	NA	1.577	.460
September	1.788	W	1.394	W	1.805	1.601	.507
October	1.819	W	1.506	W	1.941	1.706	.599
November	1.759	W	1.426	W	1.787	1.599	.557
December	1.849	W	1.539	W	1.997	1.718	.666
Average	**1.730**	**W**	**1.319**	**W**	**1.716**	**1.511**	**.498**
2017 January	1.900	W	1.584	W	NA	1.747	.774
February	1.862	W	1.615	W	2.033	1.755	.814
March	1.904	W	R 1.554	W	1.909	1.699	R .657
April	1.997	W	1.595	W	2.081	1.745	.652

[a] Prices are not adjusted for inflation. See "Nominal Dollars" in Glossary.
[b] See Note 5, "Motor Gasoline Prices," at end of section.
R=Revised. NA=Not available. W=Value withheld to avoid disclosure of individual company data.

Notes: • Sales to end users are those made directly to ultimate consumers, including bulk consumers (such as agriculture, industry, and electric utilities) and residential and commercial consumers. Sales for resale are shown in Table 9.6; they are sales made to purchasers other than ultimate consumers. • Values for the current month are preliminary. • Through 1982, prices are U.S. Energy Information Administration (EIA) estimates. See Note 6, "Historical Petroleum Prices," at end of section. • Geographic coverage is the 50 states and the District of Columbia.

Web Page: See http://www.eia.gov/totalenergy/data/monthly/#prices (Excel and CSV files) for all available annual data beginning in 1978 and monthly data beginning in 1982.

Sources: • **1978–2007:** EIA, *Petroleum Marketing Annual 2007*, Table 2. • **2008 forward:** EIA, *Petroleum Marketing Monthly*, July 2017, Table 2.

Source: *U.S. Energy Information Administration, Monthly Energy Review, July 2017*

Figure 9.2 Average Retail Prices of Electricity
(Cents[a] per Kilowatthour)

By Sector, 1960–2016

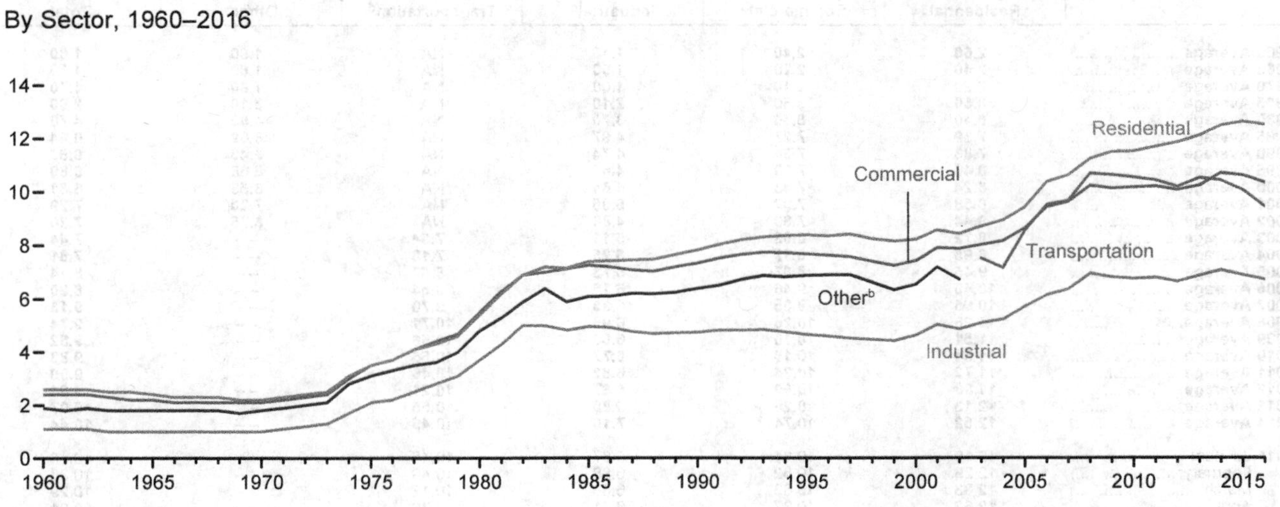

By Sector, Monthly

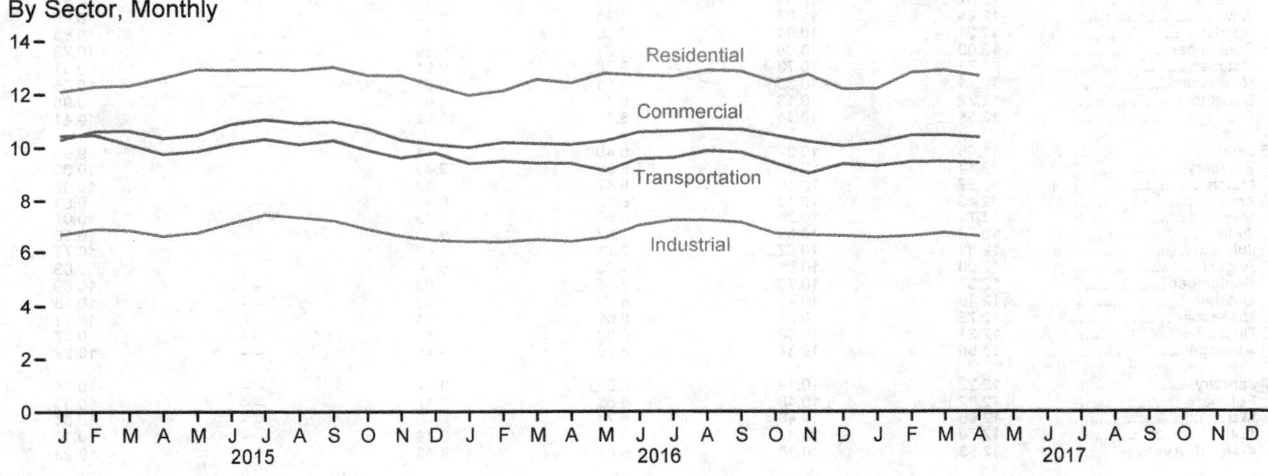

Total, January–April

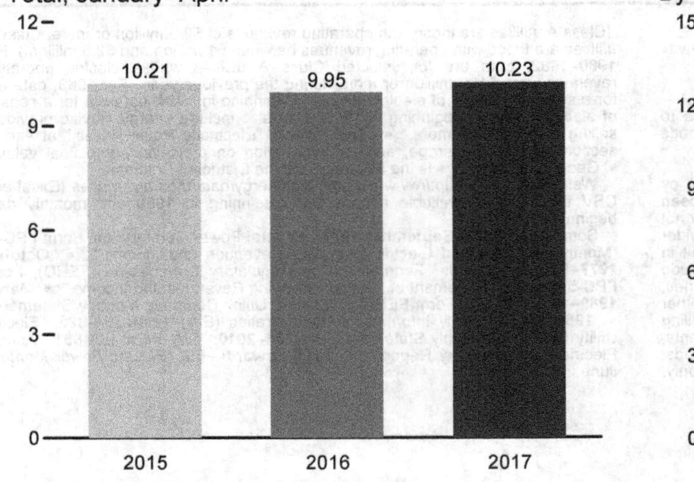

By Sector, April 2017

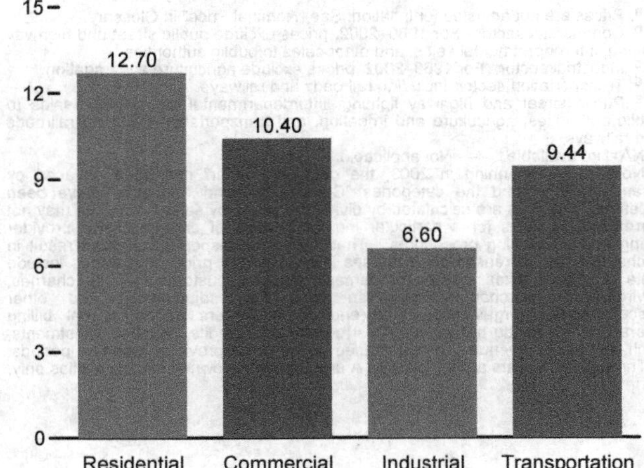

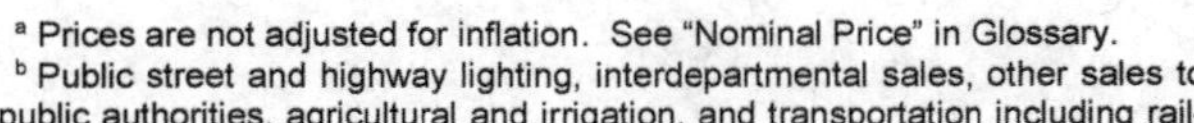

[a] Prices are not adjusted for inflation. See "Nominal Price" in Glossary.
[b] Public street and highway lighting, interdepartmental sales, other sales to public authorities, agricultural and irrigation, and transportation including railroads and railways.

Note: Includes taxes.
Web Page: http://www.eia.gov/totalenergy/data/monthly/#prices.
Source: Table 9.8.

Source: *U.S. Energy Information Administration, Monthly Energy Review, July 2017*

Table 9.8 Average Retail Prices of Electricity

(Cents[a] per Kilowatthour, Including Taxes)

	Residential	Commercial[b]	Industrial[c]	Transportation[d]	Other[e]	Total
1960 Average	**2.60**	**2.40**	**1.10**	**NA**	**1.90**	**1.80**
1965 Average	**2.40**	**2.20**	**1.00**	**NA**	**1.80**	**1.70**
1970 Average	**2.20**	**2.10**	**1.00**	**NA**	**1.80**	**1.70**
1975 Average	**3.50**	**3.50**	**2.10**	**NA**	**3.10**	**2.90**
1980 Average	**5.40**	**5.50**	**3.70**	**NA**	**4.80**	**4.70**
1985 Average	**7.39**	**7.27**	**4.97**	**NA**	**6.09**	**6.44**
1990 Average	**7.83**	**7.34**	**4.74**	**NA**	**6.40**	**6.57**
1995 Average	**8.40**	**7.69**	**4.66**	**NA**	**6.88**	**6.89**
2000 Average	**8.24**	**7.43**	**4.64**	**NA**	**6.56**	**6.81**
2001 Average	**8.58**	**7.92**	**5.05**	**NA**	**7.20**	**7.29**
2002 Average	**8.44**	**7.89**	**4.88**	**NA**	**6.75**	**7.20**
2003 Average	**8.72**	**8.03**	**5.11**	**7.54**	**– –**	**7.44**
2004 Average	**8.95**	**8.17**	**5.25**	**7.18**	**– –**	**7.61**
2005 Average	**9.45**	**8.67**	**5.73**	**8.57**	**– –**	**8.14**
2006 Average	**10.40**	**9.46**	**6.16**	**9.54**	**– –**	**8.90**
2007 Average	**10.65**	**9.65**	**6.39**	**9.70**	**– –**	**9.13**
2008 Average	**11.26**	**10.26**	**6.96**	**10.71**	**– –**	**9.74**
2009 Average	**11.51**	**10.16**	**6.83**	**10.66**	**– –**	**9.82**
2010 Average	**11.54**	**10.19**	**6.77**	**10.56**	**– –**	**9.83**
2011 Average	**11.72**	**10.24**	**6.82**	**10.46**	**– –**	**9.90**
2012 Average	**11.88**	**10.09**	**6.67**	**10.21**	**– –**	**9.84**
2013 Average	**12.13**	**10.26**	**6.89**	**10.55**	**– –**	**10.07**
2014 Average	**12.52**	**10.74**	**7.10**	**10.45**	**– –**	**10.44**
2015 January	12.10	10.31	6.67	10.45	– –	10.18
February	12.29	10.62	6.88	10.49	– –	10.36
March	12.33	10.63	6.83	10.12	– –	10.29
April	12.62	10.37	6.61	9.76	– –	10.01
May	12.93	10.47	6.74	9.87	– –	10.21
June	12.92	10.89	7.11	10.15	– –	10.64
July	12.94	11.07	7.45	10.34	– –	10.95
August	12.91	10.94	7.35	10.14	– –	10.85
September	13.03	10.98	7.21	10.29	– –	10.79
October	12.72	10.73	6.88	9.91	– –	10.31
November	12.71	10.30	6.61	9.63	– –	10.05
December	12.32	10.13	6.45	9.81	– –	9.98
Average	**12.65**	**10.64**	**6.91**	**10.09**	**– –**	**10.41**
2016 January	11.98	10.02	6.40	9.41	– –	9.96
February	12.14	10.20	6.39	9.49	– –	10.00
March	12.57	10.16	6.47	9.43	– –	10.02
April	12.43	10.13	6.40	9.41	– –	9.83
May	12.79	10.25	6.56	9.13	– –	10.07
June	12.72	10.59	7.03	9.59	– –	10.53
July	12.68	10.62	7.23	9.63	– –	10.71
August	12.90	10.71	7.23	9.89	– –	10.83
September	12.87	10.70	7.15	9.83	– –	10.69
October	12.46	10.47	6.72	9.43	– –	10.15
November	12.75	10.24	6.66	9.04	– –	10.11
December	12.21	10.08	6.63	9.40	– –	10.07
Average	**12.55**	**10.37**	**6.75**	**9.48**	**– –**	**10.28**
2017 January	12.22	10.19	6.57	9.32	– –	10.15
February	12.82	10.48	6.63	9.47	– –	10.33
March	12.90	10.48	6.74	9.48	– –	10.34
April	12.70	10.40	6.60	9.44	– –	10.10
4-Month Average	**12.63**	**10.38**	**6.63**	**9.43**	**– –**	**10.23**
2016 4-Month Average	**12.25**	**10.12**	**6.41**	**9.44**	**– –**	**9.95**
2015 4-Month Average	**12.31**	**10.48**	**6.74**	**10.22**	**– –**	**10.21**

[a] Prices are not adjusted for inflation. See "Nominal Price" in Glossary.

[b] Commercial sector. For 1960–2002, prices exclude public street and highway lighting, interdepartmental sales, and other sales to public authorities.

[c] Industrial sector. For 1960–2002, prices exclude agriculture and irrigation.

[d] Transportation sector, including railroads and railways.

[e] Public street and highway lighting, interdepartmental sales, other sales to public authorities, agriculture and irrigation, and transportation including railroads and railways.

NA=Not available. – – =Not applicable.

Notes: • Beginning in 2003, the category "Other" has been replaced by "Transportation," and the categories "Commercial" and "Industrial" have been redefined. • Prices are calculated by dividing revenue by sales. Revenue may not correspond to sales for a particular month because of energy service provider billing and accounting procedures. That lack of correspondence could result in uncharacteristic increases or decreases in the monthly prices. • Prices include state and local taxes, energy or demand charges, customer service charges, environmental surcharges, franchise fees, fuel adjustments, and other miscellaneous charges applied to end-use customers during normal billing operations. Prices do not include deferred charges, credits, or other adjustments, such as fuel or revenue from purchased power, from previous reporting periods. • Through 1979, data are for Classes A and B privately owned electric utilities only. (Class A utilities are those with operating revenues of $2.5 million or more; Class B utilities are those with operating revenues between $1 million and $2.5 million.) For 1980–1982, data are for selected Class A utilities whose electric operating revenues were $100 million or more during the previous year. For 1983, data are for a selected sample of electric utilities. Beginning in 1984, data are for a census of electric utilities. Beginning in 1996, data also include energy service providers selling to retail customers. • See Note 7, "Electricity Retail Prices," at end of section for plant coverage, and for information on preliminary and final values. • Geographic coverage is the 50 states and the District of Columbia.

Web Page: See http://www.eia.gov/totalenergy/data/monthly/#prices (Excel and CSV files) for all available annual data beginning in 1960 and monthly data beginning in 1976.

Sources: • **1960–September 1977:** Federal Power Commission, Form FPC-5, "Monthly Statement of Electric Operating Revenues and Income." • **October 1977–February 1980:** Federal Energy Regulatory Commission (FERC), Form FPC-5, "Monthly Statement of Electric Operating Revenues and Income." • **March 1980–1982:** FERC, Form FERC-5, "Electric Utility Company Monthly Statement." • **1983:** U.S. Energy Information Administration (EIA), Form EIA-826, "Electric Utility Company Monthly Statement." • **1984–2010:** EIA, Form EIA-861, "Annual Electric Power Industry Report." • **2011 forward:** EIA, *Electric Power Monthly*, June 2017, Table 5.3.

Source: *U.S. Energy Information Administration, Monthly Energy Review, July 2017*

Figure 9.3 Cost of Fossil-Fuel Receipts at Electric Generating Plants

(Dollars[a] per Million Btu, Including Taxes)

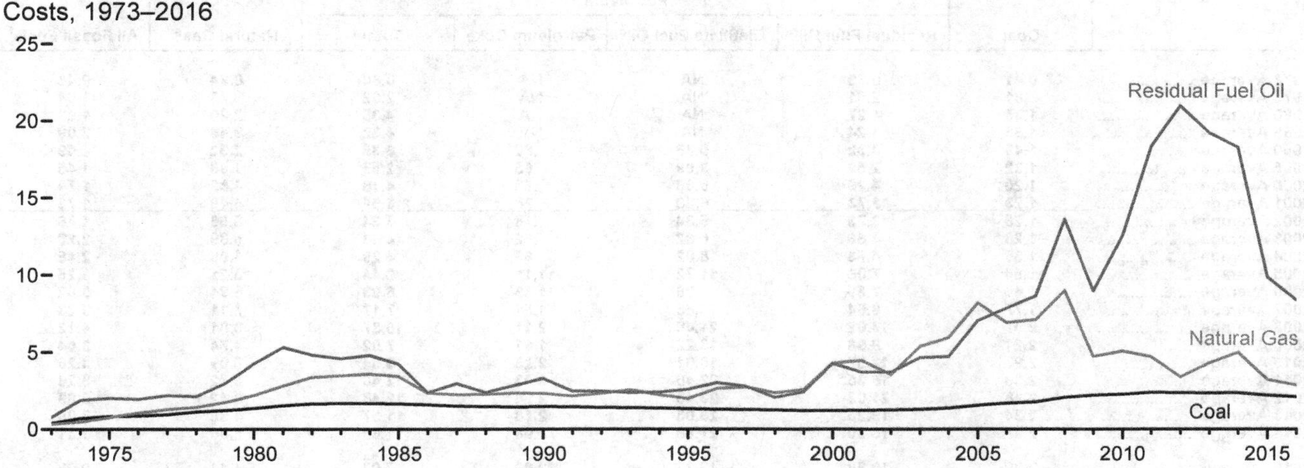

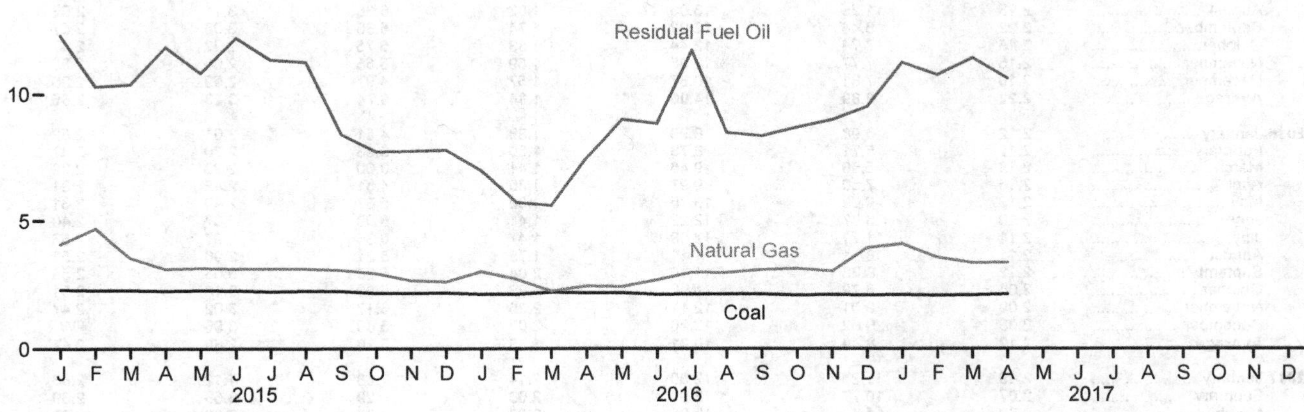

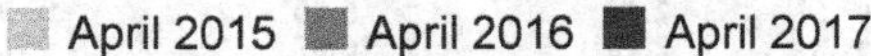

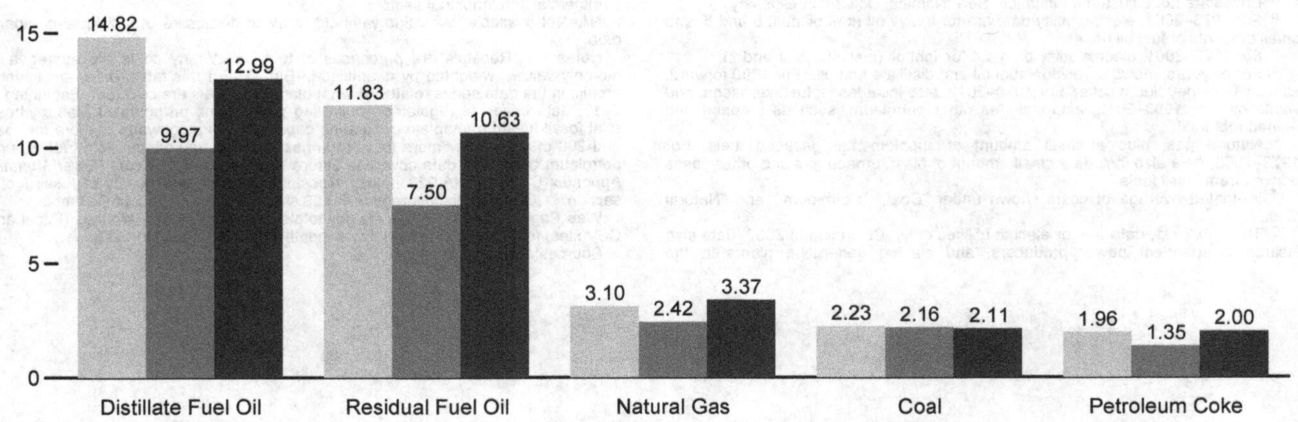

[a] Prices are not adjusted for inflation. See "Nominal Dollars" in Glossary.

Web Page: http://www.eia.gov/totalenergy/data/monthly/#prices.
Source: Table 9.9.

Source: *U.S. Energy Information Administration, Monthly Energy Review, July 2017*

Table 9.9 Cost of Fossil-Fuel Receipts at Electric Generating Plants

(Dollars[a] per Million Btu, Including Taxes)

	Coal	Petroleum				Natural Gas[e]	All Fossil Fuels[f]
		Residual Fuel Oil[b]	Distillate Fuel Oil[c]	Petroleum Coke	Total[d]		
1973 Average	**0.41**	**0.79**	**NA**	**NA**	**0.80**	**0.34**	**0.48**
1975 Average	**.81**	**2.01**	**NA**	**NA**	**2.02**	**.75**	**1.04**
1980 Average	**1.35**	**4.27**	**NA**	**NA**	**4.35**	**2.20**	**1.93**
1985 Average	**1.65**	**4.24**	**NA**	**NA**	**4.32**	**3.44**	**2.09**
1990 Average	**1.45**	**3.32**	**5.38**	**.80**	**3.35**	**2.32**	**1.69**
1995 Average	**1.32**	**2.59**	**3.99**	**.65**	**2.57**	**1.98**	**1.45**
2000 Average	**1.20**	**4.29**	**6.65**	**.58**	**4.18**	**4.30**	**1.74**
2001 Average	**1.23**	**3.73**	**6.30**	**.78**	**3.69**	**4.49**	**1.73**
2002 Average[g]	**1.25**	**3.73**	**5.34**	**.78**	**3.34**	**3.56**	**1.86**
2003 Average	**1.28**	**4.66**	**6.82**	**.72**	**4.33**	**5.39**	**2.28**
2004 Average	**1.36**	**4.73**	**8.02**	**.83**	**4.29**	**5.96**	**2.48**
2005 Average	**1.54**	**7.06**	**11.72**	**1.11**	**6.44**	**8.21**	**3.25**
2006 Average	**1.69**	**7.85**	**13.28**	**1.33**	**6.23**	**6.94**	**3.02**
2007 Average	**1.77**	**8.64**	**14.85**	**1.51**	**7.17**	**7.11**	**3.23**
2008 Average	**2.07**	**13.62**	**21.46**	**2.11**	**10.87**	**9.01**	**4.12**
2009 Average	**2.21**	**8.98**	**13.22**	**1.61**	**7.02**	**4.74**	**3.04**
2010 Average	**2.27**	**12.57**	**16.61**	**2.28**	**9.54**	**5.09**	**3.26**
2011 Average	**2.39**	**18.35**	**22.46**	**3.03**	**12.48**	**4.72**	**3.29**
2012 Average	**2.38**	**21.03**	**23.49**	**2.24**	**12.48**	**3.42**	**2.83**
2013 Average	**2.34**	**19.26**	**23.03**	**2.18**	**11.57**	**4.33**	**3.09**
2014 Average	**2.37**	**18.30**	**21.88**	**1.98**	**11.60**	**5.00**	**3.31**
2015 January	2.29	12.28	13.37	2.00	7.07	4.11	2.92
February	2.26	10.30	16.46	1.76	8.97	4.70	3.19
March	2.26	10.37	15.60	2.00	8.20	3.55	2.78
April	2.23	11.83	14.82	1.96	6.85	3.10	2.58
May	2.26	10.83	15.34	2.02	7.17	3.14	2.64
June	2.25	12.20	15.29	1.87	7.78	3.12	2.66
July	2.21	11.34	14.37	1.90	6.03	3.11	2.63
August	2.23	11.25	13.05	1.82	6.38	3.11	2.62
September	2.22	8.44	12.02	1.74	5.68	3.06	2.57
October	2.15	7.74	12.44	1.83	5.75	2.92	2.47
November	2.15	7.77	12.38	1.59	5.55	2.65	2.38
December	2.16	7.81	10.57	1.57	4.97	2.59	2.36
Average	**2.22**	**9.89**	**14.06**	**1.84**	**6.74**	**3.23**	**2.65**
2016 January	2.12	6.98	8.90	1.38	4.51	3.01	2.52
February	2.11	5.71	8.78	1.30	3.63	2.70	2.37
March	2.18	5.59	9.46	1.41	3.60	2.23	2.22
April	2.16	7.50	9.97	1.35	4.51	2.42	2.31
May	2.16	9.02	10.75	1.32	5.67	2.40	2.31
June	2.10	8.87	12.22	1.41	6.09	2.67	2.40
July	2.11	11.71	12.08	1.47	6.36	2.97	2.56
August	2.11	8.51	11.41	1.75	5.21	2.96	2.53
September	2.12	8.38	11.36	2.04	5.20	3.08	2.56
October	2.08	8.72	11.99	1.98	5.80	3.13	2.51
November	2.09	9.01	12.11	2.26	6.17	3.02	2.47
December	2.08	9.52	12.26	2.07	5.89	3.96	W
Average	**2.12**	**8.40**	**10.91**	**1.65**	**5.20**	**2.88**	**2.47**
2017 January	2.09	11.25	12.95	2.14	7.68	4.12	2.83
February	2.07	10.77	12.92	2.00	6.29	3.58	2.60
March	2.08	11.43	12.34	2.06	7.62	3.36	2.62
April	2.11	10.63	12.99	2.00	6.95	3.37	2.61
4-Month Average	**2.09**	**11.15**	**12.81**	**2.05**	**7.21**	**3.61**	**2.67**
2016 4-Month Average	**2.14**	**6.50**	**9.22**	**1.36**	**4.07**	**2.59**	**2.36**
2015 4-Month Average	**2.26**	**10.97**	**15.20**	**1.94**	**7.86**	**3.85**	**2.87**

[a] Prices are not adjusted for inflation. See "Nominal Dollars" in Glossary.

[b] For 1973–2001, electric utility data are for heavy oil (fuel oil nos. 5 and 6, and small amounts of fuel oil no. 4).

[c] For 1973–2001, electric utility data are for light oil (fuel oil nos. 1 and 2).

[d] For all years, includes residual fuel oil and distillate fuel oil. For 1990 forward, also includes petroleum coke. For 1973–2012, also includes jet fuel, kerosene, and waste oil. For 1983–2012, also includes other petroleum, such as propane and refined motor oil.

[e] Natural gas, plus a small amount of supplemental gaseous fuels. For 1973–2000, data also include a small amount of blast furnace gas and other gases derived from fossil fuels.

[f] Weighted average of costs shown under "Coal," "Petroleum," and "Natural Gas."

[g] Through 2001, data are for electric utilities only. Beginning in 2002, data also include independent power producers, and electric generating plants in the commercial and industrial sectors.

NA=Not available. W=Value withheld to avoid disclosure of individual company data.

Notes: • Receipts are purchases of fuel. • Yearly costs are averages of monthly values, weighted by quantities in Btu. • For this table, there are several breaks in the data series related to what plants and fuels are covered. Beginning in 2013, data cover all regulated generating plants; plus unregulated plants whose total fossil-fueled nameplate generating capacity is 50 megawatts or more for coal, and 200 megawatts or more for natural gas, residual fuel oil, distillate fuel oil, and petroleum coke. For data coverage before 2013, see EIA, *Electric Power Monthly*, Appendix C, Form EIA-923 notes, "Receipts and cost and quality of fossil fuels" section. • Geographic coverage is the 50 states and the District of Columbia.

Web Page: See http://www.eia.gov/totalenergy/data/monthly/#prices (Excel and CSV files) for all available annual and monthly data beginning in 1973.

Sources: See end of section.

Source: *U.S. Energy Information Administration, Monthly Energy Review, July 2017*

Figure 9.4 Natural Gas Prices
(Dollars[a] per Thousand Cubic Feet)

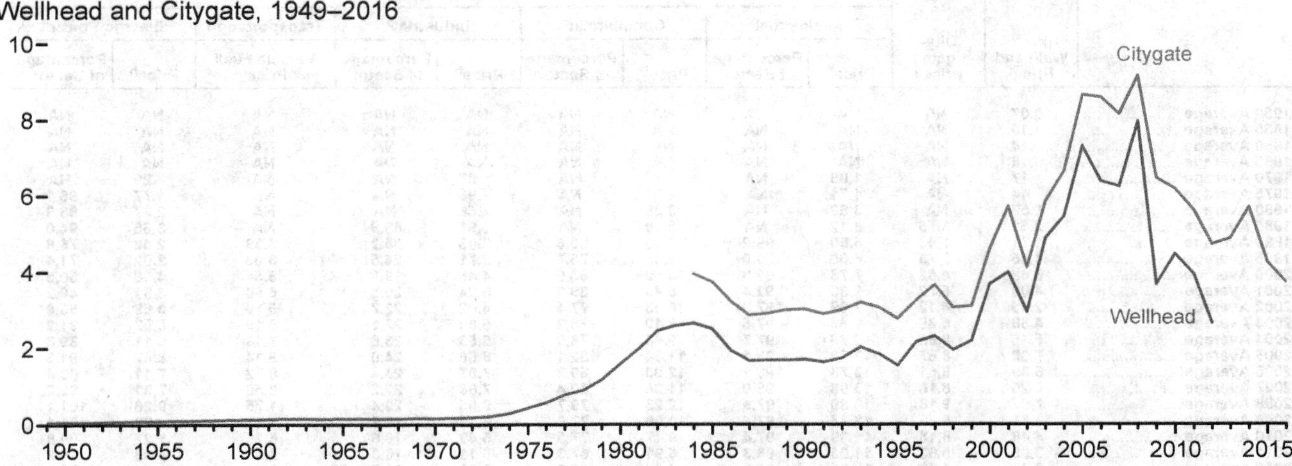

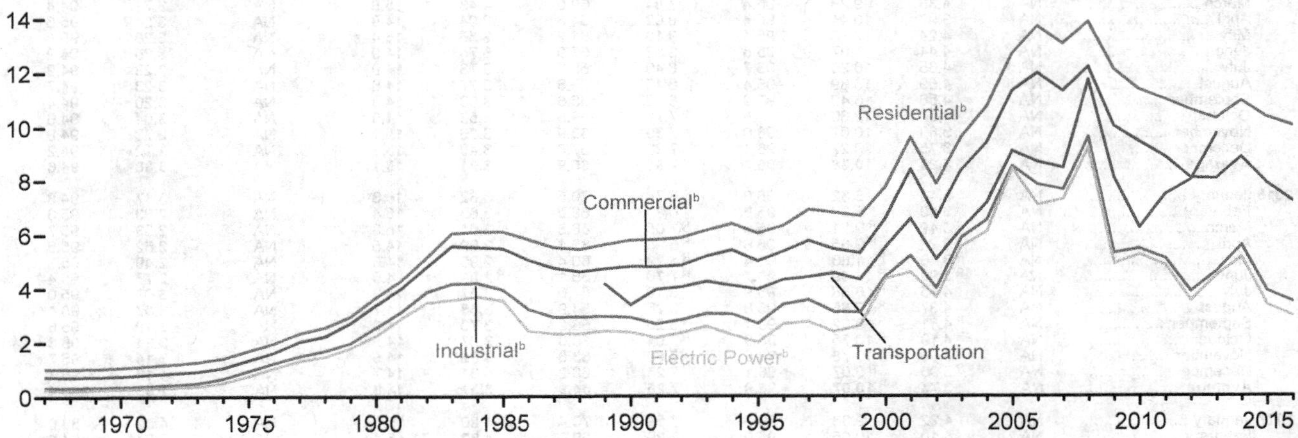

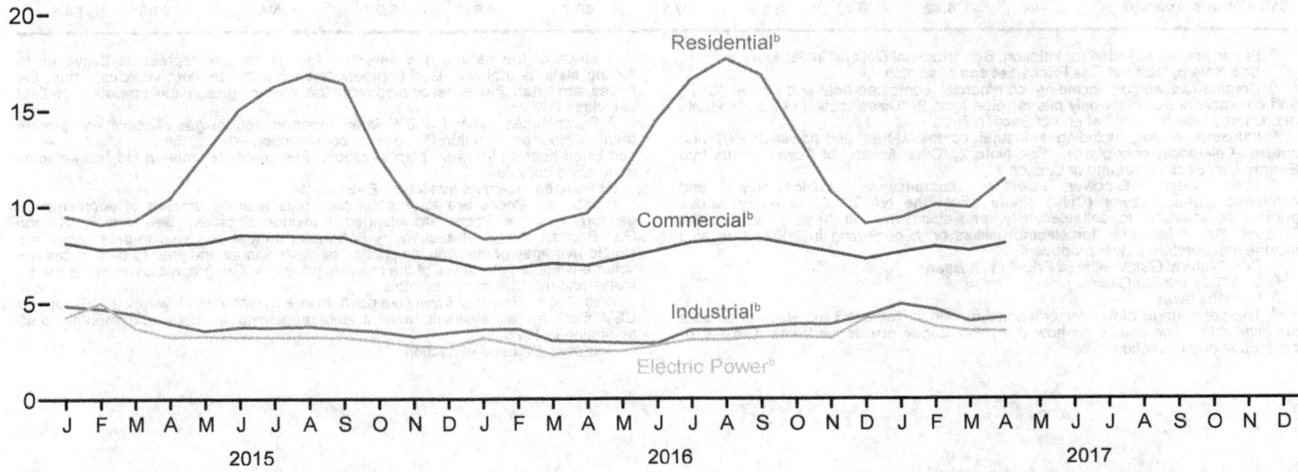

[a] Prices are not adjusted for inflation. See "Nominal Dollars" in Glossary.
[b] Includes taxes.

Web Page: http://www.eia.gov/totalenergy/data/monthly/#prices.
Source: Table 9.10.

***Source:** U.S. Energy Information Administration, Monthly Energy Review, July 2017*

Table 9.10 Natural Gas Prices
(Dollars[a] per Thousand Cubic Feet)

	Wellhead Price[f]	City-gate Price[g]	Consuming Sectors[b]								
			Residential		Commercial[c]		Industrial[d]		Transportation	Electric Power[e]	
			Price[h]	Percentage of Sector[i]	Price[h]	Percentage of Sector[i]	Price[h]	Percentage of Sector[i]	Vehicle Fuel[j] Price[h]	Price[h]	Percentage of Sector[i,k]
1950 Average	0.07	NA	NA	NA	NA	NA	NA	NA	NA	NA	NA
1955 Average	.10	NA	NA	NA	NA	NA	NA	NA	NA	NA	NA
1960 Average	.14	NA	NA	NA	NA	NA	NA	NA	NA	NA	NA
1965 Average	.16	NA	NA	NA	NA	NA	NA	NA	NA	NA	NA
1970 Average	.17	NA	1.09	NA	.77	NA	.37	NA	NA	.29	NA
1975 Average	.44	NA	1.71	NA	1.35	NA	.96	NA	NA	.77	96.1
1980 Average	1.59	NA	3.68	NA	3.39	NA	2.56	NA	NA	2.27	96.9
1985 Average	2.51	3.75	6.12	NA	5.50	NA	3.95	68.8	NA	3.55	94.0
1990 Average	1.71	3.03	5.80	99.2	4.83	86.6	2.93	35.2	3.39	2.38	76.8
1995 Average	1.55	2.78	6.06	99.0	5.05	76.7	2.71	24.5	3.98	2.02	71.4
2000 Average	3.68	4.62	7.76	92.6	6.59	63.9	4.45	19.8	5.54	4.38	50.5
2001 Average	4.00	5.72	9.63	92.4	8.43	66.0	5.24	20.8	6.60	4.61	40.2
2002 Average	2.95	4.12	7.89	97.9	6.63	77.4	4.02	22.7	5.10	[e]3.68	83.9
2003 Average	4.88	5.85	9.63	97.5	8.40	78.2	5.89	22.1	6.19	5.57	91.2
2004 Average	5.46	6.65	10.75	97.7	9.43	78.0	6.53	23.6	7.16	6.11	89.8
2005 Average	7.33	8.67	12.70	98.1	11.34	82.1	8.56	24.0	9.14	8.47	91.3
2006 Average	6.39	8.61	13.73	98.1	12.00	80.8	7.87	23.4	8.72	7.11	93.4
2007 Average	6.25	8.16	13.08	98.0	11.34	80.4	7.68	22.2	8.50	7.31	92.2
2008 Average	7.97	9.18	13.89	97.5	12.23	79.7	9.65	20.4	11.75	9.26	101.1
2009 Average	3.67	6.48	12.14	97.4	10.06	77.8	5.33	18.8	8.13	4.93	101.1
2010 Average	4.48	6.18	11.39	97.4	9.47	77.5	5.49	18.0	6.25	5.27	100.8
2011 Average	3.95	5.63	11.03	96.3	8.91	67.3	5.13	16.3	7.48	4.89	101.2
2012 Average	[E]2.66	4.73	10.65	95.8	8.10	65.2	3.88	16.2	8.04	3.54	95.5
2013 Average	NA	4.88	10.32	95.7	8.08	65.8	4.64	16.6	9.76	4.49	94.9
2014 Average	NA	5.71	10.97	95.5	8.90	65.8	5.62	15.9	NA	5.19	94.6
2015 January	NA	4.48	9.50	95.7	8.14	70.9	4.87	15.0	NA	4.31	93.6
February	NA	4.57	9.08	95.6	7.81	71.0	4.71	15.4	NA	5.02	93.7
March	NA	4.36	9.28	95.4	7.84	69.9	4.43	15.6	NA	3.71	94.4
April	NA	3.93	10.44	95.4	8.02	64.8	3.94	14.9	NA	3.24	95.6
May	NA	4.24	12.73	95.4	8.13	61.2	3.56	15.4	NA	3.28	95.5
June	NA	4.44	15.07	95.5	8.52	57.9	3.74	14.9	NA	3.25	94.9
July	NA	4.65	16.28	95.7	8.49	56.9	3.73	14.9	NA	3.23	94.9
August	NA	4.59	16.89	95.4	8.45	55.6	3.77	14.6	NA	3.23	94.7
September	NA	4.56	16.40	95.9	8.42	55.8	3.63	14.8	NA	3.20	94.4
October	NA	4.00	12.60	95.5	7.78	59.5	3.52	14.9	NA	3.04	94.6
November	NA	3.68	10.02	96.0	7.39	63.9	3.26	15.1	NA	2.78	94.8
December	NA	3.75	9.27	96.1	7.22	67.6	3.45	15.2	NA	2.72	94.2
Average	**NA**	**4.26**	**10.38**	**95.7**	**7.91**	**65.9**	**3.91**	**15.1**	**NA**	**3.38**	**94.6**
2016 January	NA	3.40	8.32	96.0	6.74	70.5	3.62	15.3	NA	3.17	94.8
February	NA	[R]3.49	8.39	95.9	6.83	69.5	3.63	15.4	NA	2.83	95.3
March	NA	3.49	[R]9.21	95.6	[R]7.05	66.8	3.04	15.3	NA	2.33	95.7
April	NA	3.22	[R]9.65	95.6	[R]6.95	65.1	2.99	14.5	NA	2.52	95.6
May	NA	[R]3.46	[R]11.63	95.4	[R]7.29	60.4	2.90	14.6	NA	2.49	95.7
June	NA	[R]3.99	[R]14.49	95.7	[R]7.70	58.1	[R]2.89	14.6	NA	2.77	95.4
July	NA	4.45	[R]16.58	95.9	8.10	57.0	3.57	14.3	NA	3.07	95.0
August	NA	4.37	[R]17.65	95.8	8.25	54.9	3.58	14.7	NA	3.07	95.1
September	NA	[R]4.61	[R]16.82	96.1	[R]8.28	56.2	3.73	14.6	NA	3.19	95.6
October	NA	[R]4.19	[R]13.75	95.9	[R]7.94	60.0	3.87	14.5	NA	3.24	95.3
November	NA	[R]3.90	10.76	96.0	7.60	63.6	3.86	14.5	NA	3.14	95.7
December	NA	[R]3.96	[R]9.07	[R]96.1	[R]7.25	68.2	4.31	14.7	NA	4.16	95.7
Average	**NA**	[R]**3.73**	[R]**10.07**	**95.9**	**7.25**	**64.9**	**3.51**	**14.8**	**NA**	**2.99**	**95.4**
2017 January	NA	4.22	9.38	96.0	7.58	[R]70.4	[R]4.90	15.0	NA	4.32	83.0
February	NA	4.10	10.05	95.9	7.89	69.0	4.62	15.1	NA	3.74	84.3
March	NA	[R]3.84	[R]9.91	95.7	[R]7.68	67.8	4.02	15.0	NA	3.52	81.5
April	NA	4.18	11.38	95.2	8.04	65.0	4.19	14.5	NA	3.49	82.4
4-Month Average	**NA**	**4.09**	**9.97**	**95.8**	**7.76**	**68.5**	**4.44**	**14.9**	**NA**	**3.77**	**82.7**
2016 4-Month Average	**NA**	**3.42**	**8.73**	**95.8**	**6.87**	**68.5**	**3.34**	**15.1**	**NA**	**2.71**	**95.4**
2015 4-Month Average	**NA**	**4.42**	**9.43**	**95.6**	**7.95**	**69.7**	**4.51**	**15.2**	**NA**	**4.06**	**94.3**

[a] Prices are not adjusted for inflation. See "Nominal Dollars" in Glossary.

[b] See Note 8, "Natural Gas Prices," at end of section.

[c] Commercial sector, including commercial combined-heat-and-power (CHP) and commercial electricity-only plants. See Note 2, "Classification of Power Plants Into Energy-Use Sectors," at end of Section 7.

[d] Industrial sector, including industrial combined-heat-and-power (CHP) and industrial electricity-only plants. See Note 2, "Classification of Power Plants Into Energy-Use Sectors," at end of Section 7.

[e] The electric power sector comprises electricity-only and combined-heat-and-power (CHP) plants within the NAICS 22 category whose primary business is to sell electricity, or electricity and heat, to the public. Through 2001, data are for electric utilities only; beginning in 2002, data also include independent power producers.

[f] See "Natural Gas Wellhead Price" in Glossary.

[g] See "Citygate" in Glossary.

[h] Includes taxes.

[i] The percentage of the sector's consumption in Table 4.3 for which price data are available. For details on how the percentages are derived, see Table 9.10 sources at end of section.

[j] Much of the natural gas delivered for vehicle fuel represents deliveries to fueling stations that are used primarily or exclusively by fleet vehicles. Thus, the prices are often those associated with the cost of gas in the operation of fleet vehicles.

[k] Percentages exceed 100% when reported natural gas receipts are greater than reported natural gas consumption—this can occur when combined-heat-and-power plants report fuel receipts related to non-electric generating activities.

R=Revised. NA=Not available. E=Estimate.

Notes: • Prices are for natural gas, plus a small amount of supplemental gaseous fuels. • Prices are intended to include all taxes. See Note 8, "Natural Gas Prices," at end of section. • Wellhead annual and year-to-date prices are simple averages of the monthly prices; all other annual and year-to-date prices are volume-weighted averages of the monthly prices. • Geographic coverage is the 50 states and the District of Columbia.

Web Page: See http://www.eia.gov/totalenergy/data/monthly/#prices (Excel and CSV files) for all available annual data beginning in 1949 and monthly data beginning in 1976.

Sources: See end of section.

Source: *U.S. Energy Information Administration, Monthly Energy Review, July 2017*

Figure 10.1 Renewable Energy Consumption
(Quadrillion Btu)

Major Sources, 1949–2016

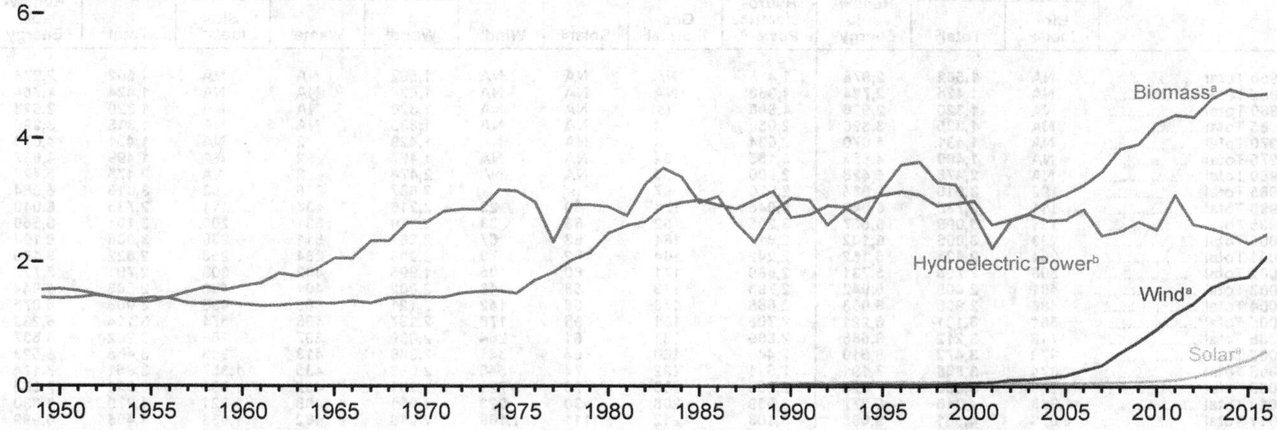

Biomass[a]
Hydroelectric Power[b]
Wind[a]
Solar[a]

By Source, 2016

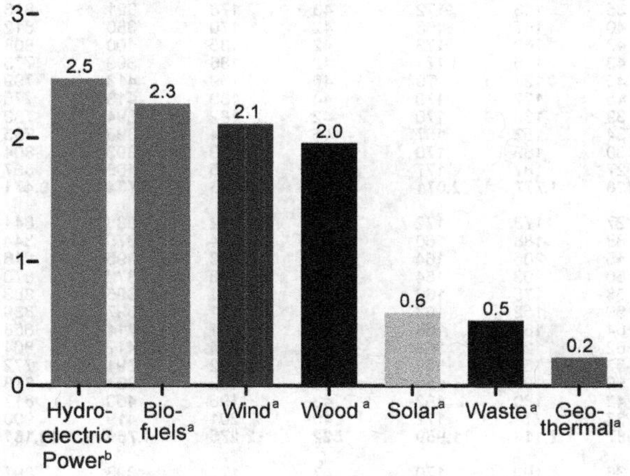

Hydroelectric Power[b]	2.5
Biofuels[a]	2.3
Wind[a]	2.1
Wood[a]	2.0
Solar[a]	0.6
Waste[a]	0.5
Geothermal[a]	0.2

By Sector, 2016

Residential	0.6
Commercial	0.3
Industrial	2.3
Transportation	1.4
Electric Power	5.6

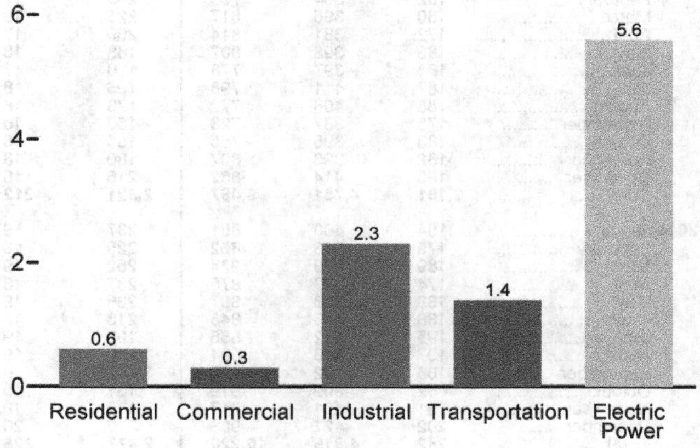

Compared With Other Resources, 1949–2016

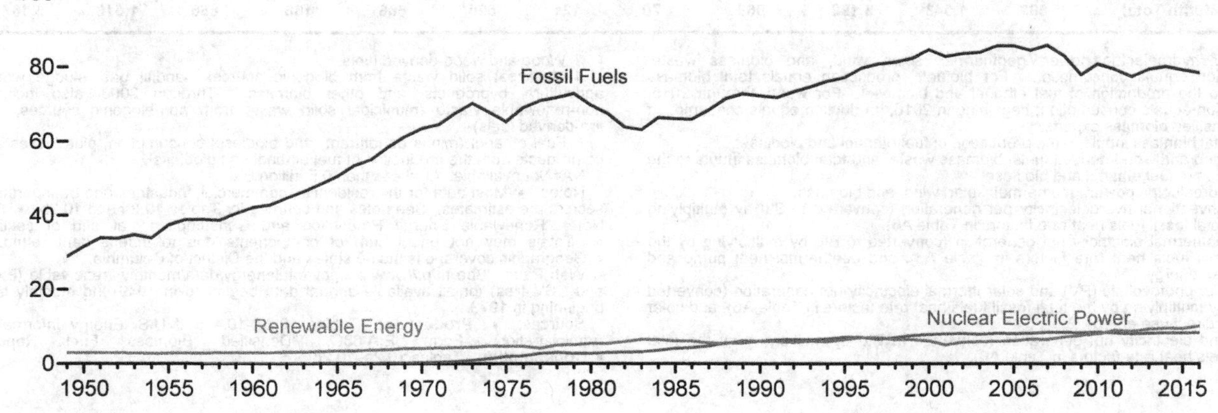

[a] See Table 10.1 for definition.
[b] Conventional hydroelectric power.

Web Page: http://www.eia.gov/totalenergy/data/monthly/#renewable.
Sources: Tables 1.3 and 10.1–10.2c.

Source: *U.S. Energy Information Administration, Monthly Energy Review, July 2017*

Table 10.1 Renewable Energy Production and Consumption by Source
(Trillion Btu)

	Production[a]			Consumption								
	Biomass		Total Renewable Energy[d]	Hydroelectric Power[e]	Geothermal[f]	Solar[g]	Wind[h]	Biomass				Total Renewable Energy
	Biofuels[b]	Total[c]						Wood[i]	Waste[j]	Biofuels[k]	Total	
1950 Total	**NA**	**1,562**	**2,978**	**1,415**	**NA**	**NA**	**NA**	**1,562**	**NA**	**NA**	**1,562**	**2,978**
1955 Total	**NA**	**1,424**	**2,784**	**1,360**	**NA**	**NA**	**NA**	**1,424**	**NA**	**NA**	**1,424**	**2,784**
1960 Total	**NA**	**1,320**	**2,928**	**1,608**	**(s)**	**NA**	**NA**	**1,320**	**NA**	**NA**	**1,320**	**2,928**
1965 Total	**NA**	**1,335**	**3,396**	**2,059**	**2**	**NA**	**NA**	**1,335**	**NA**	**NA**	**1,335**	**3,396**
1970 Total	**NA**	**1,431**	**4,070**	**2,634**	**6**	**NA**	**NA**	**1,429**	**2**	**NA**	**1,431**	**4,070**
1975 Total	**NA**	**1,499**	**4,687**	**3,155**	**34**	**NA**	**NA**	**1,497**	**2**	**NA**	**1,499**	**4,687**
1980 Total	**NA**	**2,475**	**5,428**	**2,900**	**53**	**NA**	**NA**	**2,474**	**2**	**NA**	**2,475**	**5,428**
1985 Total	**93**	**3,016**	**6,084**	**2,970**	**97**	**(s)**	**(s)**	**2,687**	**236**	**93**	**3,016**	**6,084**
1990 Total	**111**	**2,735**	**6,040**	**3,046**	**171**	**59**	**29**	**2,216**	**408**	**111**	**2,735**	**6,040**
1995 Total	**198**	**3,099**	**6,557**	**3,205**	**152**	**68**	**33**	**2,370**	**531**	**200**	**3,101**	**6,559**
2000 Total	**233**	**3,006**	**6,102**	**2,811**	**164**	**63**	**57**	**2,262**	**511**	**236**	**3,008**	**6,104**
2001 Total	**254**	**2,624**	**5,162**	**2,242**	**164**	**62**	**70**	**2,006**	**364**	**253**	**2,622**	**5,160**
2002 Total	**308**	**2,705**	**5,731**	**2,689**	**171**	**60**	**105**	**1,995**	**402**	**303**	**2,701**	**5,726**
2003 Total	**401**	**2,805**	**5,942**	**2,793**	**173**	**58**	**113**	**2,002**	**401**	**403**	**2,806**	**5,944**
2004 Total	**486**	**2,996**	**6,063**	**2,688**	**178**	**58**	**142**	**2,121**	**389**	**498**	**3,008**	**6,075**
2005 Total	**561**	**3,101**	**6,221**	**2,703**	**181**	**58**	**178**	**2,137**	**403**	**574**	**3,114**	**6,233**
2006 Total	**716**	**3,212**	**6,586**	**2,869**	**181**	**61**	**264**	**2,099**	**397**	**766**	**3,262**	**6,637**
2007 Total	**970**	**3,472**	**6,510**	**2,446**	**186**	**65**	**341**	**2,089**	**413**	**983**	**3,485**	**6,523**
2008 Total	**1,374**	**3,868**	**7,191**	**2,511**	**192**	**74**	**546**	**2,059**	**435**	**1,357**	**3,851**	**7,174**
2009 Total	**1,570**	**3,953**	**7,620**	**2,669**	**200**	**78**	**721**	**1,931**	**452**	**1,553**	**3,936**	**7,604**
2010 Total	**1,868**	**4,316**	**8,077**	**2,539**	**208**	**90**	**923**	**1,981**	**468**	**1,821**	**4,270**	**8,030**
2011 Total	**2,029**	**4,501**	**9,095**	**3,103**	**212**	**111**	**1,168**	**2,010**	**462**	**1,933**	**4,405**	**8,999**
2012 Total	**1,929**	**4,406**	**8,743**	**2,629**	**212**	**157**	**1,340**	**2,010**	**467**	**1,892**	**4,369**	**8,706**
2013 Total	**1,981**	**4,647**	**9,250**	**2,562**	**214**	**225**	**1,601**	**2,170**	**496**	**2,007**	**4,673**	**9,276**
2014 Total	**2,103**	**4,861**	**9,607**	**2,467**	**214**	**337**	**1,728**	**2,242**	**516**	**2,067**	**4,825**	**9,570**
2015 January	178	403	808	225	18	21	141	182	43	163	388	793
February	162	364	753	208	17	25	139	164	38	158	360	748
March	180	395	817	226	18	35	143	172	43	176	391	813
April	172	381	814	209	17	40	167	168	42	170	380	812
May	183	398	807	188	18	43	160	173	42	185	400	808
June	184	397	773	190	17	43	125	171	42	186	399	775
July	187	411	798	196	18	45	127	179	46	189	413	799
August	185	408	772	178	18	45	122	179	44	189	413	776
September	175	387	723	150	16	39	130	170	42	182	394	730
October	183	395	755	155	18	34	153	167	45	184	396	755
November	182	396	807	180	18	30	183	170	45	179	393	804
December	190	414	862	216	18	27	187	177	47	185	408	857
Total	**2,161**	**4,751**	**9,487**	**2,321**	**212**	**426**	**1,777**	**2,071**	**518**	**2,145**	**4,734**	**9,471**
2016 January	184	406	861	237	19	27	173	172	44	172	388	844
February	175	383	852	225	18	38	188	160	41	174	375	844
March	189	403	924	252	19	45	205	164	44	188	395	916
April	174	377	875	237	18	50	193	154	44	173	372	870
May	188	398	887	236	19	58	175	160	43	191	395	883
June	188	403	845	213	18	59	152	163	43	191	397	839
July	195	412	856	198	19	64	164	168	45	201	414	858
August	197	416	804	180	19	62	126	168	45	204	417	804
September	186	392	773	152	19	57	153	159	41	192	391	772
October	192	399	819	161	19	50	190	158	43	193	394	813
November	191	401	817	175	19	42	180	162	43	196	400	817
December	202	427	908	210	20	37	214	172	45	201	419	900
Total	**2,262**	**4,816**	**10,220**	**2,477**	**226**	**587**	**2,114**	**1,959**	**522**	**2,275**	**4,756**	**10,161**
2017 January	193	416	920	258	20	36	190	170	47	177	393	897
February	174	376	866	229	18	41	202	155	42	165	362	852
March	196	417	1,023	281	20	66	239	169	45	190	404	1,010
April	182	388	988	272	19	72	237	158	42	183	383	983
4-Month Total	**746**	**1,597**	**3,797**	**1,041**	**76**	**215**	**867**	**652**	**175**	**715**	**1,542**	**3,741**
2016 4-Month Total	**723**	**1,568**	**3,512**	**951**	**74**	**159**	**759**	**649**	**174**	**707**	**1,531**	**3,474**
2015 4-Month Total	**692**	**1,543**	**3,192**	**868**	**70**	**121**	**590**	**686**	**166**	**666**	**1,518**	**3,167**

[a] For hydroelectric power, geothermal, solar, wind, and biomass waste, production equals consumption. For biofuels, production equals total biomass inputs to the production of fuel ethanol and biodiesel. For wood, through 2015, production equals consumption; beginning in 2016, production equals consumption plus densified biomass exports.

[b] Total biomass inputs to the production of fuel ethanol and biodiesel.

[c] Wood and wood-derived fuels, biomass waste, and total biomass inputs to the production of fuel ethanol and biodiesel.

[d] Hydroelectric power, geothermal, solar, wind, and biomass.

[e] Conventional hydroelectricity net generation (converted to Btu by multiplying by the total fossil fuels heat rate factors in Table A6).

[f] Geothermal electricity net generation (converted to Btu by multiplying by the total fossil fuels heat rate factors in Table A6), and geothermal heat pump and direct use energy.

[g] Solar photovoltaic (PV) and solar thermal electricity net generation (converted to Btu by multiplying by the total fossil fuels heat rate factors in Table A6), and solar thermal direct use energy.

[h] Wind electricity net generation (converted to Btu by multiplying by the total fossil fuels heat rate factors in Table A6).

[i] Wood and wood-derived fuels.

[j] Municipal solid waste from biogenic sources, landfill gas, sludge waste, agricultural byproducts, and other biomass. Through 2000, also includes non-renewable waste (municipal solid waste from non-biogenic sources, and tire-derived fuels).

[k] Fuel ethanol (minus denaturant) and biodiesel consumption, plus losses and co-products from the production of fuel ethanol and biodiesel.

NA=Not available. (s)=Less than 0.5 trillion Btu.

Notes: • Most data for the residential, commercial, industrial, and transportation sectors are estimates. See notes and sources for Tables 10.2a and 10.2b. • See Note, "Renewable Energy Production and Consumption," at end of section. • Totals may not equal sum of components due to independent rounding. • Geographic coverage is the 50 states and the District of Columbia.

Web Page: See http://www.eia.gov/totalenergy/data/monthly/#renewable (Excel and CSV files) for all available annual data beginning in 1949 and monthly data beginning in 1973.

Sources: • **Production:** Tables 10.2a–10.4 and U.S. Energy Information Administration, Form EIA-63C, "Densified Biomass Fuel Report." • **Consumption:** Tables 10.2a–10.2c.

Source: *U.S. Energy Information Administration, Monthly Energy Review, July 2017*

Table 10.2a Renewable Energy Consumption: Residential and Commercial Sectors
(Trillion Btu)

	Residential Sector				Commercial Sector[a]								
			Biomass						Biomass				
	Geo-thermal[b]	Solar[c]	Wood[d]	Total	Hydro-electric Power[e]	Geo-thermal[b]	Solar[f]	Wind[g]	Wood[d]	Waste[h]	Fuel Ethanol[i,j]	Total	Total
1950 Total	NA	NA	1,006	1,006	NA	NA	NA	NA	19	NA	NA	19	19
1955 Total	NA	NA	775	775	NA	NA	NA	NA	15	NA	NA	15	15
1960 Total	NA	NA	627	627	NA	NA	NA	NA	12	NA	NA	12	12
1965 Total	NA	NA	468	468	NA	NA	NA	NA	9	NA	NA	9	9
1970 Total	NA	NA	401	401	NA	NA	NA	NA	8	NA	NA	8	8
1975 Total	NA	NA	425	425	NA	NA	NA	NA	8	NA	NA	8	8
1980 Total	NA	NA	850	850	NA	NA	NA	NA	21	NA	NA	21	21
1985 Total	NA	NA	1,010	1,010	NA	NA	NA	NA	24	NA	(s)	24	24
1990 Total	6	55	580	640	1	3	(s)	–	66	28	(s)	94	98
1995 Total	7	63	520	589	1	5	(s)	–	72	40	(s)	113	119
2000 Total	9	58	420	486	1	8	1	–	71	47	(s)	119	128
2001 Total	9	55	370	435	1	8	1	–	67	25	(s)	92	101
2002 Total	10	53	380	444	(s)	9	1	–	69	26	(s)	95	105
2003 Total	13	52	400	465	1	11	1	–	71	29	1	101	114
2004 Total	14	51	410	475	1	12	1	–	70	34	1	105	120
2005 Total	16	50	430	496	1	14	2	–	70	34	1	105	121
2006 Total	18	53	380	451	1	14	2	–	65	36	1	103	120
2007 Total	22	55	420	497	1	14	4	–	70	31	2	103	121
2008 Total	26	58	470	555	1	15	6	–	73	34	2	109	130
2009 Total	33	60	500	593	1	17	7	(s)	73	36	3	112	137
2010 Total	37	65	440	541	1	19	11	(s)	72	36	3	111	142
2011 Total	40	71	450	560	(s)	20	19	(s)	69	43	3	115	154
2012 Total	40	79	420	539	(s)	20	32	1	61	45	3	108	161
2013 Total	40	92	580	711	(s)	20	41	1	70	47	3	120	182
2014 Total	40	109	590	739	(s)	20	52	1	75	47	4	126	199
2015 January	3	6	37	47	(s)	2	3	(s)	7	4	[j]2	13	18
February	3	7	34	44	(s)	2	4	(s)	6	3	2	12	17
March	3	10	37	51	(s)	2	5	(s)	7	4	2	13	20
April	3	11	36	51	(s)	2	5	(s)	7	4	2	13	20
May	3	12	37	53	(s)	2	6	(s)	7	4	2	13	21
June	3	13	36	52	(s)	2	6	(s)	7	4	2	13	20
July	3	13	37	54	(s)	2	6	(s)	7	4	2	14	21
August	3	13	37	54	(s)	2	6	(s)	7	4	2	13	21
September	3	12	36	52	(s)	2	5	(s)	7	4	2	13	20
October	3	11	37	52	(s)	2	5	(s)	7	4	2	13	19
November	3	9	36	49	(s)	2	4	(s)	7	4	2	13	18
December	3	8	37	49	(s)	2	3	(s)	7	4	2	13	18
Total	40	128	440	607	(s)	20	57	1	81	47	26	154	232
2016 January	3	8	32	43	(s)	2	4	(s)	7	4	2	13	19
February	3	10	30	42	(s)	2	5	(s)	7	4	2	12	19
March	3	13	32	48	(s)	2	6	(s)	7	5	2	14	22
April	3	14	31	48	(s)	2	7	(s)	7	4	2	13	21
May	3	16	32	51	(s)	2	7	(s)	7	4	2	13	22
June	3	17	31	50	(s)	2	7	(s)	7	4	2	13	22
July	3	17	32	52	(s)	2	8	(s)	7	4	2	13	23
August	3	17	32	52	(s)	2	7	(s)	7	4	2	13	22
September	3	15	31	49	(s)	2	7	(s)	7	4	2	13	21
October	3	13	32	48	(s)	2	6	(s)	7	4	2	13	21
November	3	11	31	45	(s)	2	5	(s)	7	4	2	13	19
December	3	10	32	45	(s)	2	4	(s)	7	4	2	14	20
Total	40	161	373	573	1	20	72	1	82	49	27	157	251
2017 January	3	10	32	46	(s)	2	5	(s)	7	4	2	14	20
February	3	11	29	43	(s)	2	5	(s)	6	4	2	12	19
March	3	16	32	51	(s)	2	7	(s)	7	4	2	13	22
April	3	18	31	52	(s)	2	8	(s)	7	4	2	13	22
4-Month Total	13	54	125	192	(s)	6	24	(s)	27	16	8	51	83
2016 4-Month Total	13	45	123	181	(s)	7	21	(s)	27	17	9	53	81
2015 4-Month Total	13	35	145	193	(s)	6	17	(s)	27	15	8	50	74

[a] Commercial sector, including commercial combined-heat-and-power (CHP) and commercial electricity-only plants. See Note 2, "Classification of Power Plants Into Energy-Use Sectors," at end of Section 7.

[b] Geothermal heat pump and direct use energy.

[c] Distributed (small-scale) solar photovoltaic (PV) electricity generation in the residential sector (converted to Btu by multiplying by the fossil fuels heat rate factors in Table A6) and distributed solar thermal energy in the residential, commercial, and industrial sectors. See Table 10.5.

[d] Wood and wood-derived fuels.

[e] Conventional hydroelectricity net generation (converted to Btu by multiplying by the total fossil fuels heat rate factors in Table A6).

[f] Solar photovoltaic (PV) electricity net generation in the commercial sector (converted to Btu by multiplying by the total fossil fuels heat rate factors in Table A6), both utility-scale and distributed (small-scale). See Table 10.5.

[g] Wind electricity net generation (converted to Btu by multiplying by the total fossil fuels heat rate factors in Table A6).

[h] Municipal solid waste from biogenic sources, landfill gas, sludge waste, agricultural byproducts, and other biomass. Through 2000, also includes non-renewable waste (municipal solid waste from non-biogenic sources, and tire-derived fuels).

[i] The fuel ethanol (minus denaturant) portion of motor fuels, such as E10, consumed by the commercial sector.

[j] There is a discontinuity in this time series between 2014 and 2015 due to a change in the method for allocating motor gasoline consumption to the end-use sectors. Beginning in 2015, the commercial and industrial sector shares of fuel ethanol consumption are larger than in 2014, while the transportation sector share is smaller.

NA=Not available. – =No data reported. (s)=Less than 0.5 trillion Btu.

Notes: • Data are estimates, except for commercial sector hydroelectric power, wind, and waste. • Totals may not equal sum of components due to independent rounding. • Geographic coverage is the 50 states and the District of Columbia.

Web Page: See http://www.eia.gov/totalenergy/data/monthly/#renewable (Excel and CSV files) for all available annual data beginning in 1949 and monthly data beginning in 1973.

Sources: See end of section.

Source: *U.S. Energy Information Administration, Monthly Energy Review, July 2017*

Table 10.2b Renewable Energy Consumption: Industrial and Transportation Sectors
(Trillion Btu)

	Industrial Sector[a]										Transportation Sector		
					Biomass						Biomass		
	Hydro-electric Power[b]	Geo-thermal[c]	Solar[d]	Wind[e]	Wood[f]	Waste[g]	Fuel Ethanol[h,i]	Losses and Co-products[j]	Total	Total	Fuel Ethanol[i,k]	Bio-diesel[l]	Total[m]
1950 Total	**69**	**NA**	**NA**	**NA**	**532**	**NA**	**NA**	**NA**	**532**	**602**	**NA**	**NA**	**NA**
1955 Total	**38**	**NA**	**NA**	**NA**	**631**	**NA**	**NA**	**NA**	**631**	**669**	**NA**	**NA**	**NA**
1960 Total	**39**	**NA**	**NA**	**NA**	**680**	**NA**	**NA**	**NA**	**680**	**719**	**NA**	**NA**	**NA**
1965 Total	**33**	**NA**	**NA**	**NA**	**855**	**NA**	**NA**	**NA**	**855**	**888**	**NA**	**NA**	**NA**
1970 Total	**34**	**NA**	**NA**	**NA**	**1,019**	**NA**	**NA**	**NA**	**1,019**	**1,053**	**NA**	**NA**	**NA**
1975 Total	**32**	**NA**	**NA**	**NA**	**1,063**	**NA**	**NA**	**NA**	**1,063**	**1,096**	**NA**	**NA**	**NA**
1980 Total	**33**	**NA**	**NA**	**NA**	**1,600**	**NA**	**NA**	**NA**	**1,600**	**1,633**	**NA**	**NA**	**NA**
1985 Total	**33**	**NA**	**NA**	**NA**	**1,645**	**230**	**1**	**42**	**1,918**	**1,951**	**50**	**NA**	**50**
1990 Total	**31**	**2**	**(s)**	**–**	**1,442**	**192**	**1**	**49**	**1,684**	**1,717**	**60**	**NA**	**60**
1995 Total	**55**	**3**	**(s)**	**–**	**1,652**	**195**	**2**	**86**	**1,934**	**1,992**	**112**	**NA**	**112**
2000 Total	**42**	**4**	**(s)**	**–**	**1,636**	**145**	**1**	**99**	**1,881**	**1,928**	**135**	**NA**	**135**
2001 Total	**33**	**5**	**(s)**	**–**	**1,443**	**129**	**3**	**108**	**1,681**	**1,719**	**141**	**1**	**142**
2002 Total	**39**	**5**	**(s)**	**–**	**1,396**	**146**	**3**	**130**	**1,676**	**1,720**	**168**	**2**	**170**
2003 Total	**43**	**3**	**(s)**	**–**	**1,363**	**142**	**4**	**168**	**1,678**	**1,725**	**228**	**2**	**230**
2004 Total	**33**	**4**	**(s)**	**–**	**1,476**	**132**	**6**	**201**	**1,815**	**1,852**	**286**	**3**	**290**
2005 Total	**32**	**4**	**(s)**	**–**	**1,452**	**148**	**7**	**227**	**1,834**	**1,871**	**327**	**12**	**339**
2006 Total	**29**	**4**	**1**	**–**	**1,472**	**130**	**10**	**280**	**1,892**	**1,926**	**442**	**33**	**475**
2007 Total	**16**	**5**	**1**	**–**	**1,413**	**145**	**10**	**369**	**1,937**	**1,958**	**557**	**45**	**602**
2008 Total	**17**	**5**	**1**	**–**	**1,339**	**143**	**12**	**519**	**2,012**	**2,035**	**786**	**39**	**825**
2009 Total	**18**	**4**	**2**	**–**	**1,178**	**154**	**13**	**603**	**1,948**	**1,972**	**894**	**41**	**935**
2010 Total	**16**	**4**	**3**	**–**	**1,273**	**168**	**17**	**727**	**2,185**	**2,208**	**1,041**	**33**	**1,075**
2011 Total	**17**	**4**	**4**	**(s)**	**1,309**	**165**	**17**	**756**	**2,246**	**2,272**	**1,045**	**113**	**1,158**
2012 Total	**22**	**4**	**7**	**(s)**	**1,339**	**159**	**17**	**711**	**2,226**	**2,259**	**1,045**	**115**	**1,162**
2013 Total	**33**	**4**	**9**	**(s)**	**1,312**	**187**	**18**	**709**	**2,226**	**2,272**	**1,072**	**182**	**1,278**
2014 Total	**12**	**4**	**11**	**1**	**1,325**	**190**	**14**	**757**	**2,286**	**2,314**	**1,093**	**181**	**1,292**
2015 January	1	(s)	1	(s)	115	17	[i]1	65	199	201	[i]88	6	94
February	1	(s)	1	(s)	103	15	1	59	178	180	83	11	95
March	1	(s)	1	(s)	107	17	1	65	190	193	92	13	107
April	1	(s)	1	(s)	107	16	1	61	186	189	88	15	105
May	1	(s)	1	(s)	110	15	2	65	192	195	97	18	116
June	1	(s)	1	(s)	107	15	1	65	189	192	94	21	117
July	1	(s)	1	(s)	112	16	2	67	196	199	97	18	118
August	1	(s)	1	(s)	112	15	2	66	195	197	98	20	120
September	1	(s)	1	(s)	107	15	1	63	186	189	94	20	116
October	1	(s)	1	(s)	106	17	1	66	190	193	94	17	114
November	1	(s)	1	(s)	108	16	1	65	191	193	92	14	110
December	1	(s)	1	(s)	111	17	1	68	198	201	93	17	113
Total	**13**	**4**	**14**	**(s)**	**1,306**	**190**	**18**	**776**	**2,290**	**2,321**	**1,109**	**191**	**1,325**
2016 January	1	(s)	1	(s)	113	16	1	66	196	198	88	13	102
February	1	(s)	1	(s)	103	15	1	62	182	184	91	15	108
March	1	(s)	1	(s)	106	16	2	67	190	194	98	16	117
April	1	(s)	2	(s)	102	16	1	61	180	183	90	17	109
May	1	(s)	2	(s)	106	16	2	66	189	193	97	22	121
June	1	(s)	2	(s)	107	16	2	66	190	193	97	21	121
July	1	(s)	2	(s)	109	17	2	68	195	199	100	27	129
August	1	(s)	2	(s)	109	16	2	69	195	198	101	28	131
September	1	(s)	2	(s)	103	15	1	65	184	187	94	26	123
October	1	(s)	1	(s)	104	14	1	67	187	190	94	26	122
November	1	(s)	1	(s)	108	15	2	67	192	194	95	26	125
December	1	(s)	1	(s)	113	16	2	71	202	205	99	26	126
Total	**12**	**4**	**17**	**1**	**1,283**	**186**	**18**	**796**	**2,283**	**2,318**	**1,145**	**263**	**1,434**
2017 January	1	(s)	1	(s)	111	17	1	70	200	203	89	13	104
February	1	(s)	1	(s)	101	16	1	62	180	183	85	13	100
March	1	(s)	2	(s)	110	17	2	70	198	202	95	19	117
April	1	(s)	2	(s)	103	16	1	64	184	188	93	21	115
4-Month Total	**5**	**1**	**7**	**(s)**	**424**	**67**	**6**	**265**	**762**	**775**	**361**	**66**	**436**
2016 4-Month Total	**5**	**1**	**5**	**(s)**	**423**	**62**	**6**	**257**	**748**	**759**	**367**	**62**	**436**
2015 4-Month Total	**5**	**1**	**4**	**(s)**	**433**	**64**	**6**	**251**	**753**	**763**	**351**	**46**	**402**

[a] Industrial sector, including industrial combined-heat-and-power (CHP) and industrial electricity-only plants. See Note 2, "Classification of Power Plants Into Energy-Use Sectors," at end of Section 7.
[b] Conventional hydroelectricity net generation (converted to Btu by multiplying by the total fossil fuels heat rate factors in Table A6).
[c] Geothermal heat pump and direct use energy.
[d] Solar photovoltaic (PV) electricity net generation in the industrial sector (converted to Btu by multiplying by the total fossil fuels heat rate factors in Table A6), both utility-scale and distributed (small-scale). See Table 10.5.
[e] Wind electricity net generation (converted to Btu by multiplying by the total fossil fuels heat rate factors in Table A6).
[f] Wood and wood-derived fuels.
[g] Municipal solid waste from biogenic sources, landfill gas, sludge waste, agricultural byproducts, and other biomass. Through 2000, also includes non-renewable waste (municipal solid waste from non-biogenic sources, and tire-derived fuels).
[h] The fuel ethanol (minus denaturant) portion of motor fuels, such as E10, consumed by the industrial sector.
[i] There is a discontinuity in this time series between 2014 and 2015 due to a change in the method for allocating motor gasoline consumption to the end-use sectors. Beginning in 2015, the commercial and industrial sector shares of fuel ethanol consumption are larger than in 2014, while the transportation sector share is smaller.
[j] Losses and co-products from the production of fuel ethanol and biodiesel. Does not include natural gas, electricity, and other non-biomass energy used in the production of fuel ethanol and biodiesel—these are included in the industrial sector consumption statistics for the appropriate energy source.
[k] The fuel ethanol (minus denaturant) portion of motor fuels, such as E10 and E85, consumed by the transportation sector.
[l] Although there is biodiesel use in other sectors, all biodiesel consumption is assigned to the transportation sector.
[m] Beginning in 2009, includes imports minus stock change of other renewable diesel fuel and other renewable fuels. See "Renewable Diesel Fuel (Other)" and "Renewable Fuels (Other)" in Glossary.

NA=Not available. – =No data reported. (s)=Less than 0.5 trillion Btu.

Notes: • Data are estimates, except for industrial sector hydroelectric power in 1949–1978 and 1989 forward, and wind. • Totals may not equal sum of components due to independent rounding. • Geographic coverage is the 50 states and the District of Columbia.

Web Page: See http://www.eia.gov/totalenergy/data/monthly/#renewable (Excel and CSV files) for all available annual data beginning in 1949 and monthly data beginning in 1973.

Sources: See end of section.

Source: *U.S. Energy Information Administration, Monthly Energy Review, July 2017*

Table 10.2c Renewable Energy Consumption: Electric Power Sector

(Trillion Btu)

	Hydro-electric Power[a]	Geo-thermal[b]	Solar[c]	Wind[d]	Biomass			Total
					Wood[e]	Waste[f]	Total	
1950 Total	1,346	NA	NA	NA	5	NA	5	1,351
1955 Total	1,322	NA	NA	NA	3	NA	3	1,325
1960 Total	1,569	(s)	NA	NA	2	NA	2	1,571
1965 Total	2,026	2	NA	NA	3	NA	3	2,031
1970 Total	2,600	6	NA	NA	1	2	4	2,609
1975 Total	3,122	34	NA	NA	(s)	2	2	3,158
1980 Total	2,867	53	NA	NA	3	2	4	2,925
1985 Total	2,937	97	(s)	(s)	8	7	14	3,049
1990 Total[g]	3,014	161	4	29	129	188	317	3,524
1995 Total	3,149	138	5	33	125	296	422	3,747
2000 Total	2,768	144	5	57	134	318	453	3,427
2001 Total	2,209	142	6	70	126	211	337	2,763
2002 Total	2,650	147	6	105	150	230	380	3,288
2003 Total	2,749	146	5	113	167	230	397	3,411
2004 Total	2,655	148	6	142	165	223	388	3,339
2005 Total	2,670	147	6	178	185	221	406	3,406
2006 Total	2,839	145	5	264	182	231	412	3,665
2007 Total	2,430	145	6	341	186	237	423	3,345
2008 Total	2,494	146	9	546	177	258	435	3,630
2009 Total	2,650	146	9	721	180	261	441	3,967
2010 Total	2,521	148	12	923	196	264	459	4,064
2011 Total	3,085	149	17	1,167	182	255	437	4,855
2012 Total	2,606	148	40	1,339	190	262	453	4,586
2013 Total	2,529	151	83	1,600	207	262	470	4,833
2014 Total	2,454	151	165	1,726	251	279	530	5,026
2015 January	224	13	11	141	22	23	45	433
February	207	12	14	139	21	20	41	412
March	225	13	19	143	21	22	43	443
April	208	12	22	166	18	22	40	448
May	186	13	23	160	18	23	41	423
June	189	12	23	125	21	23	44	393
July	195	13	24	127	22	26	48	407
August	177	13	25	122	23	25	48	384
September	149	11	20	130	20	23	43	354
October	154	12	17	152	17	24	41	378
November	179	12	16	183	19	25	44	434
December	214	13	14	187	21	25	47	476
Total	2,308	148	228	1,776	244	281	525	4,985
2016 January	236	14	14	173	21	25	45	481
February	224	13	22	188	21	23	43	490
March	250	14	25	205	20	23	43	536
April	236	12	27	193	15	25	40	508
May	235	14	33	175	16	24	40	496
June	212	13	33	152	19	24	42	452
July	197	13	38	164	20	24	45	456
August	180	13	36	126	21	25	46	401
September	151	14	34	153	18	23	41	393
October	160	14	29	190	15	24	39	432
November	175	14	25	180	17	23	40	433
December	209	15	21	214	20	25	46	505
Total	2,465	162	337	2,112	222	287	509	5,585
2017 January	257	14	20	189	19	25	44	525
February	228	13	24	202	18	22	41	507
March	280	14	41	238	20	24	44	618
April	271	14	44	237	18	22	39	605
4-Month Total	1,036	55	130	866	75	93	168	2,255
2016 4-Month Total	946	53	88	758	76	95	171	2,016
2015 4-Month Total	864	49	65	589	81	87	169	1,736

[a] Conventional hydroelectricity net generation (converted to Btu by multiplying by the total fossil fuels heat rate factors in Table A6).

[b] Geothermal electricity net generation (converted to Btu by multiplying by the total fossil fuels heat rate factors in Table A6).

[c] Solar photovoltaic (PV) and solar thermal electricity net generation in the electric power sector (converted to Btu by multiplying by the total fossil fuels heat rate factors in Table A6). See Table 10.5.

[d] Wind electricity net generation (converted to Btu by multiplying by the total fossil fuels heat rate factors in Table A6).

[e] Wood and wood-derived fuels.

[f] Municipal solid waste from biogenic sources, landfill gas, sludge waste, agricultural byproducts, and other biomass. Through 2000, also includes non-renewable waste (municipal solid waste from non-biogenic sources, and tire-derived fuels).

[g] Through 1988, data are for electric utilities only. Beginning in 1989, data are for electric utilities and independent power producers.

NA=Not available. (s)=Less than 0.5 trillion Btu.

Notes: • The electric power sector comprises electricity-only and combined-heat-and-power (CHP) plants within the NAICS 22 category whose primary business is to sell electricity, or electricity and heat, to the public. • Totals may not equal sum of components due to independent rounding. • Geographic coverage is the 50 states and the District of Columbia.

Web Page: See http://www.eia.gov/totalenergy/data/monthly/#renewable (Excel and CSV files) for all available annual data beginning in 1949 and monthly data beginning in 1973.

Sources: Tables 7.2b, 7.4b, and A6.

Source: *U.S. Energy Information Administration, Monthly Energy Review, July 2017*

Table 10.3 Fuel Ethanol Overview

	Feed-stock[a]	Losses and Co-products[b]	Dena-turant[c]	Production[d]			Trade[d] Net Imports[e]	Stocks[d,f]	Stock Change[d,g]	Consumption[d]			*Consumption Minus Denaturant[h]*
	TBtu	TBtu	Mbbl	Mbbl	MMgal	TBtu	Mbbl	Mbbl	Mbbl	Mbbl	MMgal	TBtu	*TBtu*
1981 Total	**13**	**6**	**40**	**1,978**	**83**	**7**	**NA**	**NA**	**NA**	**1,978**	**83**	**7**	***7***
1985 Total	**93**	**42**	**294**	**14,693**	**617**	**52**	**NA**	**NA**	**NA**	**14,693**	**617**	**52**	***51***
1990 Total	**111**	**49**	**356**	**17,802**	**748**	**63**	**NA**	**NA**	**NA**	**17,802**	**748**	**63**	***62***
1995 Total	**198**	**86**	**647**	**32,325**	**1,358**	**115**	**387**	**2,186**	**-207**	**32,919**	**1,383**	**117**	***114***
2000 Total	**233**	**99**	**773**	**38,627**	**1,622**	**138**	**116**	**3,400**	**-624**	**39,367**	**1,653**	**140**	***137***
2001 Total	**253**	**108**	**841**	**42,028**	**1,765**	**150**	**315**	**4,298**	**898**	**41,445**	**1,741**	**148**	***144***
2002 Total	**307**	**130**	**1,019**	**50,956**	**2,140**	**182**	**306**	**6,200**	**1,902**	**49,360**	**2,073**	**176**	***171***
2003 Total	**400**	**168**	**1,335**	**66,772**	**2,804**	**238**	**292**	**5,978**	**-222**	**67,286**	**2,826**	**240**	***233***
2004 Total	**482**	**201**	**1,621**	**81,058**	**3,404**	**289**	**3,542**	**6,002**	**24**	**84,576**	**3,552**	**301**	***293***
2005 Total	**550**	**227**	**1,859**	**92,961**	**3,904**	**331**	**3,234**	**5,563**	**-439**	**96,634**	**4,059**	**344**	***335***
2006 Total	**683**	**280**	**2,326**	**116,294**	**4,884**	**414**	**17,408**	**8,760**	**3,197**	**130,505**	**5,481**	**465**	***453***
2007 Total	**907**	**368**	**3,105**	**155,263**	**6,521**	**553**	**10,457**	**10,535**	**1,775**	**163,945**	**6,886**	**584**	***569***
2008 Total	**1,286**	**518**	**4,433**	**221,637**	**9,309**	**790**	**12,610**	**14,226**	**3,691**	**230,556**	**9,683**	**821**	***800***
2009 Total	**1,503**	**602**	**5,688**	**260,424**	**10,938**	**928**	**4,720**	**16,594**	**2,368**	**262,776**	**11,037**	**936**	***910***
2010 Total	**1,823**	**726**	**6,506**	**316,617**	**13,298**	**1,127**	**-9,115**	**17,941**	**1,347**	**306,155**	**12,858**	**1,090**	***1,061***
2011 Total	**1,904**	**754**	**6,649**	**331,646**	**13,929**	**1,181**	**-24,365**	**18,238**	**297**	**306,984**	**12,893**	**1,093**	***1,065***
2012 Total	**1,801**	**709**	**6,264**	**314,714**	**13,218**	**1,120**	**-5,891**	**20,350**	**2,112**	**306,711**	**12,882**	**1,092**	***1,064***
2013 Total	**1,805**	**707**	**6,181**	**316,493**	**13,293**	**1,126**	**-5,761**	**16,424**	**-3,926**	**314,658**	**13,216**	**1,120**	***1,092***
2014 Total	**1,938**	**755**	**6,476**	**340,781**	**14,313**	**1,212**	**-18,371**	**18,739**	**2,315**	**320,095**	**13,444**	**1,139**	***1,111***
2015 January	169	65	589	29,770	1,250	106	-1,633	20,647	1,908	26,229	1,102	93	*91*
February	152	59	534	26,814	1,126	95	-1,623	21,057	410	24,781	1,041	88	*86*
March	167	65	567	29,485	1,238	105	-2,050	20,878	-179	27,614	1,160	98	*96*
April	158	61	527	27,910	1,172	99	-1,504	20,854	-24	26,430	1,110	94	*92*
May	168	65	545	29,666	1,246	106	-1,489	20,154	-700	28,877	1,213	103	*100*
June	168	65	528	29,684	1,247	106	-1,490	20,128	-26	28,220	1,185	100	*98*
July	172	66	539	30,249	1,270	108	-1,675	19,701	-427	29,001	1,218	103	*101*
August	169	65	524	29,762	1,250	106	-905	19,390	-311	29,168	1,225	104	*101*
September	162	63	519	28,571	1,200	102	-987	18,944	-446	28,030	1,177	100	*97*
October	169	66	560	29,886	1,255	106	-1,579	18,984	40	28,267	1,187	101	*98*
November	168	65	580	29,675	1,246	106	-929	20,099	1,115	27,631	1,161	98	*96*
December	176	68	624	31,081	1,305	111	-1,767	21,596	1,497	27,817	1,168	99	*96*
Total	**1,998**	**774**	**6,636**	**352,553**	**14,807**	**1,254**	**-17,632**	**21,596**	**2,857**	**332,064**	**13,947**	**1,181**	***1,153***
2016 January	171	66	615	30,319	1,273	108	-2,073	23,168	[i]1,730	26,516	1,114	94	*92*
February	162	62	583	28,678	1,204	102	-1,595	23,004	-164	27,247	1,144	97	*94*
March	174	67	600	30,812	1,294	110	-2,268	22,301	-703	29,247	1,228	104	*101*
April	158	61	554	28,059	1,178	100	-2,273	20,992	-1,309	27,095	1,138	96	*94*
May	171	66	584	30,228	1,270	108	-1,327	20,792	-200	29,101	1,222	104	*101*
June	171	66	564	30,258	1,271	108	-858	21,199	407	28,993	1,218	103	*101*
July	177	68	565	31,251	1,313	111	-1,338	21,167	-32	29,945	1,258	107	*104*
August	179	69	560	31,669	1,330	113	-1,601	21,042	-125	30,193	1,268	107	*105*
September	169	65	542	29,876	1,255	106	-2,342	20,605	-437	27,971	1,175	100	*97*
October	174	67	560	30,797	1,293	110	-3,135	20,005	-600	28,262	1,187	101	*98*
November	173	66	556	30,565	1,284	109	-2,904	19,136	-869	28,530	1,198	102	*99*
December	183	71	602	32,467	1,364	116	-2,334	19,531	395	29,738	1,249	106	*103*
Total	**2,061**	**794**	**6,885**	**364,979**	**15,329**	**1,299**	**-24,049**	**19,531**	**[i]-1,907**	**342,837**	**14,399**	**1,220**	***1,190***
2017 January	182	69	593	32,241	1,354	115	-2,507	22,633	3,102	26,632	1,119	95	*93*
February	162	62	541	28,747	1,207	102	-2,972	23,028	395	25,380	1,066	90	*88*
March	181	69	597	32,161	1,351	114	-3,044	23,759	731	28,386	1,192	101	*99*
April	166	64	540	29,500	1,239	105	-1,981	23,593	-166	27,685	1,163	99	*96*
4-Month Total	**690**	**264**	**2,271**	**122,649**	**5,151**	**436**	**-10,505**	**23,593**	**4,062**	**108,082**	**4,539**	**385**	***375***
2016 4-Month Total	**665**	**256**	**2,352**	**117,868**	**4,950**	**419**	**-8,209**	**20,992**	**-446**	**110,105**	**4,624**	**392**	***382***
2015 4-Month Total	**646**	**250**	**2,217**	**113,979**	**4,787**	**406**	**-6,811**	**20,854**	**2,115**	**105,053**	**4,412**	**374**	***365***

[a] Total corn and other biomass inputs to the production of undenatured ethanol used for fuel ethanol.

[b] Losses and co-products from the production of fuel ethanol. Does not include natural gas, electricity, and other non-biomass energy used in the production of fuel ethanol—these are included in the industrial sector consumption statistics for the appropriate energy source.

[c] The amount of denaturant in fuel ethanol produced.

[d] Includes denaturant.

[e] Through 2009, data are for fuel ethanol imports only; data for fuel ethanol exports are not available. Beginning in 2010, data are for fuel ethanol imports minus fuel ethanol (including industrial alcohol) exports.

[f] Stocks are at end of period.

[g] A negative value indicates a decrease in stocks and a positive value indicates an increase.

[h] Consumption of fuel ethanol minus denaturant. Data for fuel ethanol minus denaturant are used to develop data for "Renewable Energy/Biomass" in Tables 10.1–10.2b, as well as in Sections 1 and 2.

[i] Derived from the preliminary 2015 stocks value (21,438 thousand barrels), not the final 2015 value (21,596 thousand barrels) that is shown under "Stocks."

NA=Not available.

Notes: • Mbbl = thousand barrels. MMgal = million U.S. gallons. TBtu = trillion Btu. • Fuel ethanol data in thousand barrels are converted to million gallons by multiplying by 0.042, and are converted to Btu by multiplying by the approximate heat content of fuel ethanol—see Table A3. • Through 1980, data are not available. For 1981–1992, data are estimates. For 1993–2008, only data for feedstock, losses and co-products, and denaturant are estimates. Beginning in 2009, only data for feedstock, and losses and co-products, are estimates. • See "Denaturant," "Ethanol," "Fuel Ethanol," and "Fuel Ethanol Minus Denaturant" in Glossary. • Totals may not equal sum of components due to independent rounding. • Geographic coverage is the 50 states and the District of Columbia.

Web Page: See http://www.eia.gov/totalenergy/data/monthly/#renewable (Excel and CSV files) for all available annual and monthly data beginning in 1981.

Sources: See end of section.

Source: *U.S. Energy Information Administration, Monthly Energy Review, July 2017*

Table 10.4 Biodiesel and Other Renewable Fuels Overview

	Biodiesel													Other Renewable Fuels[f]
	Feedstock[a]	Losses and Co-products[b]	Production			Trade: Imports	Trade: Exports	Trade: Net Imports[c]	Stocks[d]	Stock Change[e]	Consumption			
	TBtu	TBtu	Mbbl	MMgal	TBtu	Mbbl	Mbbl	Mbbl	Mbbl	Mbbl	Mbbl	MMgal	TBtu	TBtu
2001 Total	**1**	**(s)**	**204**	**9**	**1**	**81**	**41**	**40**	**NA**	**NA**	**244**	**10**	**1**	**NA**
2002 Total	**1**	**(s)**	**250**	**10**	**1**	**197**	**57**	**140**	**NA**	**NA**	**390**	**16**	**2**	**NA**
2003 Total	**2**	**(s)**	**338**	**14**	**2**	**97**	**113**	**-17**	**NA**	**NA**	**322**	**14**	**2**	**NA**
2004 Total	**4**	**(s)**	**666**	**28**	**4**	**101**	**128**	**-27**	**NA**	**NA**	**639**	**27**	**3**	**NA**
2005 Total	**12**	**(s)**	**2,162**	**91**	**12**	**214**	**213**	**1**	**NA**	**NA**	**2,163**	**91**	**12**	**NA**
2006 Total	**32**	**(s)**	**5,963**	**250**	**32**	**1,105**	**856**	**250**	**NA**	**NA**	**6,213**	**261**	**33**	**NA**
2007 Total	**63**	**1**	**11,662**	**490**	**62**	**3,455**	**6,696**	**-3,241**	**NA**	**NA**	**8,422**	**354**	**45**	**NA**
2008 Total	**88**	**1**	**16,145**	**678**	**87**	**7,755**	**16,673**	**-8,918**	**NA**	**NA**	**7,228**	**304**	**39**	**NA**
2009 Total	**67**	**1**	**12,281**	**516**	**66**	**1,906**	**6,546**	**-4,640**	**711**	**711**	**[g] 7,663**	**322**	**41**	**(s)**
2010 Total	**44**	**1**	**8,177**	**343**	**44**	**564**	**2,588**	**-2,024**	**672**	**-39**	**6,192**	**260**	**33**	**(s)**
2011 Total	**125**	**2**	**23,035**	**967**	**123**	**890**	**1,799**	**-908**	**2,005**	**[h] 1,028**	**21,099**	**886**	**113**	**(s)**
2012 Total	**128**	**2**	**23,588**	**991**	**126**	**853**	**3,056**	**-2,203**	**1,984**	**-20**	**21,406**	**899**	**115**	**3**
2013 Total	**176**	**2**	**32,368**	**1,359**	**173**	**8,152**	**4,675**	**3,477**	**3,810**	**1,825**	**34,020**	**1,429**	**182**	**24**
2014 Total	**165**	**2**	**30,452**	**1,279**	**163**	**4,578**	**1,974**	**2,604**	**3,131**	**-679**	**33,735**	**1,417**	**181**	**18**
2015 January	9	(s)	1,727	73	9	372	22	350	4,032	902	1,176	49	6	(s)
February	10	(s)	1,851	78	10	526	23	503	4,245	212	2,141	90	11	1
March	13	(s)	2,326	98	12	340	191	149	4,244	(s)	2,475	104	13	2
April	14	(s)	2,568	108	14	330	240	90	4,071	-173	2,831	119	15	2
May	15	(s)	2,784	117	15	336	255	81	3,599	-471	3,337	140	18	2
June	16	(s)	2,901	122	16	673	260	413	3,063	-536	3,850	162	21	2
July	16	(s)	2,883	121	15	1,157	255	902	3,404	341	3,444	145	18	3
August	16	(s)	2,933	123	16	961	275	686	3,333	-71	3,690	155	20	2
September	13	(s)	2,479	104	13	1,062	200	862	3,021	-312	3,652	153	20	3
October	14	(s)	2,535	106	14	863	161	702	3,070	48	3,189	134	17	3
November	14	(s)	2,521	106	14	701	76	625	3,600	530	2,616	110	14	3
December	14	(s)	2,573	108	14	1,078	133	945	3,943	343	3,174	133	17	3
Total	**163**	**2**	**30,080**	**1,263**	**161**	**8,399**	**2,091**	**6,308**	**3,943**	**813**	**35,575**	**1,494**	**191**	**25**
2016 January	14	(s)	2,490	105	13	211	42	169	4,036	[i] 221	2,437	102	13	1
February	14	(s)	2,503	105	13	287	55	232	3,937	-99	2,834	119	15	2
March	15	(s)	2,829	119	15	437	234	203	3,923	-14	3,046	128	16	3
April	15	(s)	2,827	119	15	891	246	645	4,175	253	3,219	135	17	1
May	17	(s)	3,169	133	17	1,117	334	783	4,062	-113	4,065	171	22	2
June	17	(s)	3,205	135	17	1,575	220	1,355	4,735	672	3,888	163	21	3
July	18	(s)	3,330	140	18	1,681	250	1,431	4,444	-291	5,053	212	27	1
August	18	(s)	3,385	142	18	1,829	234	1,595	4,267	-177	5,157	217	28	2
September	17	(s)	3,131	132	17	1,793	150	1,643	4,212	-54	4,829	203	26	3
October	18	(s)	3,380	142	18	1,824	95	1,729	4,560	347	4,762	200	26	2
November	18	(s)	3,388	142	18	2,184	152	2,032	5,078	518	4,902	206	26	4
December	18	(s)	3,400	143	18	2,668	80	2,588	6,217	1,140	4,847	204	26	1
Total	**201**	**3**	**37,037**	**1,556**	**198**	**16,497**	**2,093**	**14,404**	**6,217**	**[i] 2,403**	**49,038**	**2,060**	**263**	**26**
2017 January	12	(s)	2,204	93	12	241	43	198	6,259	41	2,361	99	13	2
February	12	(s)	2,232	94	12	549	57	492	6,466	207	2,516	106	13	1
March	15	(s)	2,757	116	15	650	136	514	6,194	-272	3,542	149	19	3
April	16	(s)	3,014	127	16	681	283	398	5,713	-481	3,893	163	21	2
4-Month Total	**55**	**1**	**10,207**	**429**	**55**	**2,121**	**520**	**1,601**	**5,713**	**-504**	**12,313**	**517**	**66**	**9**
2016 4-Month Total	**58**	**1**	**10,648**	**447**	**57**	**1,826**	**577**	**1,249**	**4,175**	**360**	**11,537**	**485**	**62**	**7**
2015 4-Month Total	**46**	**1**	**8,472**	**356**	**45**	**1,568**	**476**	**1,092**	**4,071**	**940**	**8,623**	**362**	**46**	**5**

[a] Total vegetable oil and other biomass inputs to the production of biodiesel—calculated by multiplying biodiesel production by 5.433 million Btu per barrel. See "Biodiesel Feedstock" entry in the "Thermal Conversion Factor Source Documentation" at the end of Appendix A.

[b] Losses and co-products from the production of biodiesel. Does not include natural gas, electricity, and other non-biomass energy used in the production of biodiesel—these are included in the industrial sector consumption statistics for the appropriate energy source.

[c] Net imports equal imports minus exports.

[d] Stocks are at end of period. Includes biodiesel stocks at (or in) refineries, pipelines, and bulk terminals. Beginning in 2011, also includes stocks at biodiesel production plants.

[e] A negative value indicates a decrease in stocks and a positive value indicates an increase.

[f] Imports minus stock change of other renewable diesel fuel and other renewable fuels. See "Renewable Diesel Fuel (Other)" and "Renewable Fuels (Other)" in Glossary.

[g] In 2009, because of incomplete data coverage and differing data sources, a "Balancing Item" amount of 733 thousand barrels (653 thousand barrels in January 2009; 80 thousand barrels in February 2009) is used to balance biodiesel supply and disposition.

[h] Derived from the final 2010 stocks value for bulk terminals and biodiesel production plants (977 thousand barrels), not the final 2010 value for bulk terminals only (672 thousand barrels) that is shown under "Stocks."

[i] Derived from the preliminary 2015 stocks value (3,815 thousand barrels), not the final 2015 value (3,943 thousand barrels) that is shown under "Stocks."

NA=Not available. (s)=Less than 0.5 trillion Btu and greater than -0.5 trillion Btu.

Notes: • Mbbl = thousand barrels. MMgal = million U.S. gallons. TBtu = trillion Btu. • Biodiesel data in thousand barrels are converted to million gallons by multiplying by 0.042, and are converted to Btu by multiplying by 5.359 million Btu per barrel (the approximate heat content of biodiesel—see Table A1). • Through 2000, data are not available. Beginning in 2001, data not from U.S. Energy Information Administration (EIA) surveys are estimates. • Totals may not equal sum of components due to independent rounding. • Geographic coverage is the 50 states and the District of Columbia.

Web Page: See http://www.eia.gov/totalenergy/data/monthly/#renewable (Excel and CSV files) for all available annual and monthly data beginning in 2001.

Sources: See end of section.

Source: *U.S. Energy Information Administration, Monthly Energy Review, July 2017*

Table 10.5 Solar Energy Consumption
(Trillion Btu)

	Distributed[a] Solar Energy[b]						Utility-Scale[c] Solar Energy[b]				
		Electricity[d]					Electricity[e]				
	Heat[f]	Residential Sector	Commercial Sector	Industrial Sector	Total	Total[g]	Commercial Sector[h]	Industrial Sector[i]	Electric Power Sector[j]	Total	Total[k]
1985 Total	**NA**	**NA**	**NA**	**NA**	**NA**	**NA**	**NA**	**NA**	**(s)**	**(s)**	**(s)**
1990 Total	**55**	**(s)**	**(s)**	**(s)**	**(s)**	**55**	**–**	**–**	**4**	**4**	**59**
1995 Total	**63**	**(s)**	**(s)**	**(s)**	**1**	**63**	**–**	**–**	**5**	**5**	**68**
2000 Total	**57**	**(s)**	**1**	**(s)**	**1**	**58**	**–**	**–**	**5**	**5**	**63**
2001 Total	**55**	**(s)**	**1**	**(s)**	**1**	**56**	**–**	**–**	**6**	**6**	**62**
2002 Total	**53**	**1**	**1**	**(s)**	**2**	**54**	**–**	**–**	**6**	**6**	**60**
2003 Total	**51**	**1**	**1**	**(s)**	**2**	**53**	**–**	**–**	**5**	**5**	**58**
2004 Total	**50**	**1**	**1**	**(s)**	**2**	**53**	**–**	**–**	**6**	**6**	**58**
2005 Total	**49**	**1**	**2**	**(s)**	**3**	**52**	**–**	**–**	**6**	**6**	**58**
2006 Total	**51**	**2**	**2**	**1**	**5**	**56**	**–**	**–**	**5**	**5**	**61**
2007 Total	**53**	**2**	**4**	**1**	**7**	**59**	**–**	**–**	**6**	**6**	**65**
2008 Total	**54**	**4**	**6**	**1**	**11**	**65**	**(s)**	**–**	**9**	**9**	**74**
2009 Total	**55**	**5**	**7**	**2**	**14**	**69**	**(s)**	**–**	**9**	**9**	**78**
2010 Total	**56**	**9**	**11**	**3**	**23**	**79**	**(s)**	**(s)**	**12**	**12**	**90**
2011 Total	**58**	**13**	**19**	**4**	**36**	**93**	**1**	**(s)**	**17**	**18**	**111**
2012 Total	**59**	**20**	**30**	**7**	**57**	**116**	**1**	**(s)**	**40**	**41**	**157**
2013 Total	**61**	**31**	**38**	**9**	**78**	**139**	**3**	**(s)**	**83**	**86**	**225**
2014 Total	**62**	**47**	**49**	**11**	**107**	**169**	**4**	**(s)**	**165**	**168**	**337**
2015 January	3	3	3	1	7	10	(s)	(s)	11	11	21
February	4	3	3	1	8	11	(s)	(s)	14	14	25
March	5	5	4	1	11	16	(s)	(s)	19	19	35
April	6	6	5	1	12	17	(s)	(s)	22	22	40
May	6	6	5	1	13	19	(s)	(s)	23	23	43
June	6	6	5	1	13	19	(s)	(s)	23	24	43
July	7	7	6	1	14	20	(s)	(s)	24	24	45
August	7	7	5	1	14	20	(s)	(s)	25	25	45
September	6	6	5	1	12	18	(s)	(s)	20	21	39
October	5	6	4	1	11	16	(s)	(s)	17	18	34
November	4	5	3	1	9	14	(s)	(s)	16	16	30
December	4	4	3	1	9	13	(s)	(s)	14	15	27
Total	**63**	**65**	**53**	**14**	**132**	**194**	**4**	**(s)**	**228**	**232**	**426**
2016 January	3	5	4	1	10	13	(s)	(s)	14	14	27
February	4	6	4	1	11	15	(s)	(s)	22	23	38
March	5	8	6	1	15	20	(s)	(s)	25	25	45
April	6	9	6	2	16	22	(s)	(s)	27	27	50
May	6	10	7	2	18	24	1	(s)	33	34	58
June	6	10	7	2	19	25	1	(s)	33	34	59
July	7	11	7	2	19	26	1	(s)	38	38	64
August	7	10	7	2	19	25	1	(s)	36	37	62
September	6	9	6	2	17	22	1	(s)	34	34	57
October	5	8	5	1	15	20	(s)	(s)	29	30	50
November	4	7	4	1	12	16	(s)	(s)	25	25	42
December	4	6	4	1	11	15	(s)	(s)	21	21	37
Total	**63**	**98**	**67**	**17**	**181**	**245**	**5**	**(s)**	**337**	**343**	**587**
2017 January	3	6	4	1	12	15	(s)	(s)	20	21	36
February	4	7	5	1	14	17	(s)	(s)	24	24	41
March	5	11	7	2	19	24	(s)	(s)	41	42	66
April	6	12	7	2	21	27	(s)	(s)	44	45	72
4-Month Total	**18**	**36**	**23**	**6**	**66**	**84**	**1**	**(s)**	**130**	**131**	**215**
2016 4-Month Total	**18**	**27**	**20**	**5**	**52**	**70**	**1**	**(s)**	**88**	**90**	**159**
2015 4-Month Total	**18**	**17**	**16**	**4**	**37**	**54**	**1**	**(s)**	**65**	**66**	**121**

[a] Data are estimates for distributed (small-scale) facilities (combined generator nameplate capacity less than 1 megawatt).

[b] See "Photovoltaic Energy" and "Solar Thermal Energy" in Glossary.

[c] Data are for utility-scale facilities (combined generator nameplate capacity of 1 megawatt or more).

[d] Solar photovoltaic (PV) electricity generation at distributed (small-scale) facilities connected to the electric power grid (converted to Btu by multiplying by the fossil fuels heat rate factors in Table A6).

[e] Solar photovoltaic (PV) and solar thermal electricity net generation at utility-scale facilities (converted to Btu by multiplying by the fossil fuels heat rate factors in Table A6).

[f] Solar thermal direct use energy in the residential, commercial, and industrial sectors for all end uses, such as pool heating, hot water heating, and space heating.

[g] Data are the sum of "Distributed Solar Energy Heat" and "Distributed Solar Energy Electricity."

[h] Commercial combined-heat-and-power (CHP) and commercial electricity-only plants. See Note 2, "Classification of Power Plants Into Energy-Use Sectors," at end of Section 7.

[i] Industrial combined-heat-and-power (CHP) and industrial electricity-only plants. See Note 2, "Classification of Power Plants Into Energy-Use Sectors," at end of Section 7.

[j] Electricity-only and combined-heat-and-power (CHP) plants within the NAICS 22 category whose primary business is to sell electricity, or electricity and heat, to the public. Through 1988, data are for electric utilities only; beginning in 1989, data are for electric utilities and independent power producers.

[k] Data are the sum of "Distributed Solar Energy Total" and "Utility-Scale Solar Energy Total."

NA=Not available. – =No data reported. (s)=Less than 0.5 trillion Btu.

Notes: • Distributed (small-scale) solar energy data for all years, and utility-scale solar energy data for the current two years, are estimates. • Totals may not equal sum of components due to independent rounding. • Geographic coverage is the 50 states and the District of Columbia.

Web Page: See http://www.eia.gov/totalenergy/data/monthly/#renewable (Excel and CSV files) for all available annual and monthly data beginning in 1984.

Sources: See end of section.

Source: *U.S. Energy Information Administration, Monthly Energy Review, July 2017*

Table 10.6 Solar Electricity Net Generation
(Million Kilowatthours)

	Distributed[a] Solar Generation[b]				Utility-Scale[c] Solar Generation[b]				
	Residential Sector	Commercial Sector	Industrial Sector	Total	Commercial Sector[d]	Industrial Sector[e]	Electric Power Sector[f]	Total	Total
1985 Total	NA	NA	NA	NA	NA	NA	11	11	11
1990 Total	12	17	4	32	–	–	367	367	399
1995 Total	20	29	6	56	–	–	497	497	553
2000 Total	39	55	12	107	–	–	493	493	600
2001 Total	47	67	15	129	–	–	543	543	672
2002 Total	56	79	18	153	–	–	555	555	708
2003 Total	66	93	21	179	–	–	534	534	713
2004 Total	81	115	25	222	–	–	575	575	797
2005 Total	122	172	38	333	–	–	550	550	883
2006 Total	178	252	56	485	–	–	508	508	993
2007 Total	251	355	79	685	–	–	612	612	1,297
2008 Total	404	571	126	1,101	(s)	–	864	864	1,965
2009 Total	543	767	170	1,480	(s)	–	891	891	2,371
2010 Total	897	1,172	259	2,328	5	2	1,206	1,212	3,540
2011 Total	1,330	1,913	424	3,667	84	7	1,727	1,818	5,485
2012 Total	2,071	3,173	703	5,947	148	14	4,164	4,327	10,274
2013 Total	3,264	4,029	892	8,185	294	17	8,724	9,036	17,221
2014 Total	4,947	5,146	1,139	11,233	371	16	17,304	17,691	28,924
2015 January	340	327	80	746	20	1	1,134	1,155	1,902
February	375	356	85	816	23	1	1,459	1,484	2,299
March	536	479	119	1,134	33	2	2,037	2,072	3,206
April	609	525	129	1,264	39	2	2,338	2,379	3,643
May	676	574	144	1,394	46	2	2,456	2,504	3,898
June	693	571	144	1,408	43	2	2,512	2,558	3,966
July	741	596	150	1,487	45	2	2,579	2,627	4,114
August	746	575	147	1,468	46	2	2,639	2,688	4,156
September	679	515	135	1,330	37	2	2,178	2,217	3,547
October	618	455	125	1,198	32	2	1,875	1,910	3,107
November	515	367	100	982	27	1	1,702	1,730	2,712
December	471	349	93	914	24	1	1,545	1,570	2,484
Total	6,999	5,689	1,451	14,139	416	21	24,456	24,893	39,032
2016 January	513	409	98	1,021	23	NM	1,491	1,516	2,536
February	614	468	108	1,189	45	3	2,395	2,443	3,632
March	824	608	150	1,582	47	NM	2,664	2,713	4,295
April	939	661	164	1,763	44	NM	2,903	2,949	4,712
May	1,044	719	181	1,945	54	NM	3,547	3,603	5,548
June	1,086	723	183	1,991	62	NM	3,545	3,610	5,601
July	1,133	743	190	2,066	69	NM	4,024	4,097	6,163
August	1,100	718	186	2,004	59	NM	3,886	3,948	5,952
September	977	643	170	1,790	56	3	3,624	3,683	5,473
October	874	578	156	1,607	45	3	3,145	3,193	4,801
November	717	467	123	1,307	38	2	2,660	2,700	4,007
December	644	443	114	1,202	24	NM	2,273	2,299	3,500
Total	10,465	7,180	1,823	19,467	565	32	36,157	36,754	56,221
2017 January	682	481	120	1,282	23	NM	2,182	2,206	3,488
February	784	526	139	1,449	27	NM	2,533	2,562	4,011
March	1,142	703	210	2,054	47	2	4,425	4,474	6,529
April	1,282	760	226	2,268	50	NM	4,764	4,816	7,084
4-Month Total	3,889	2,469	695	7,054	147	NM	13,904	14,058	21,112
2016 4-Month Total	2,889	2,146	520	5,556	158	9	9,453	9,620	15,176
2015 4-Month Total	1,859	1,687	413	3,959	116	6	6,969	7,090	11,050

[a] Data are estimates for solar photovoltaic (PV) electricity generation at small-scale facilities (combined generator nameplate capacity less than 1 megawatt) connected to the electric power grid.

[b] See "Photovoltaic Energy" and "Solar Thermal Energy" in Glossary.

[c] Solar photovoltaic (PV) and solar thermal electricity net generation at utility-scale facilities (combined generator nameplate capacity of 1 megawatt or more).

[d] Commercial combined-heat-and-power (CHP) and commercial electricity-only plants. See Note 2, "Classification of Power Plants Into Energy-Use Sectors," at end of Section 7.

[e] Industrial combined-heat-and-power (CHP) and industrial electricity-only plants. See Note 2, "Classification of Power Plants Into Energy-Use Sectors," at end of Section 7.

[f] Electricity-only and combined-heat-and-power (CHP) plants within the NAICS 22 category whose primary business is to sell electricity, or electricity and heat, to the public. Through 1988, data are for electric utilities only; beginning in 1989, data are for electric utilities and independent power producers.

NA=Not available. NM=Not meaningful due to large standard error. – =No data reported. (s)=Less than 0.5 million kilowatthours.

Notes: • Distributed (small-scale) solar generation data for all years, and utility-scale solar energy data for the current two years, are estimates. • Totals may not equal sum of components due to independent rounding. • Geographic coverage is the 50 states and the District of Columbia.

Web Page: See http://www.eia.gov/totalenergy/data/monthly/#renewable (Excel and CSV files) for all available annual and monthly data beginning in 1984.

Sources: • **Distributed Solar Generation: 1989–2013**—Calculated as distributed solar energy consumption (see Table 10.5) divided by the total fossil fuels heat rate factors (see Table A6). **2014 forward**—U.S. Energy Information Administration (EIA), *Electric Power Monthly,* monthly reports, Tables 1.1, 1.2.C, 1.2.D, and 1.2.E. • **Utility-Scale Solar Generation: 1984–1988**—EIA, Form EIA-759, "Monthly Power Plant Report." **1989–1997:** EIA, Form EIA-759, "Monthly Power Plant Report," and Form EIA-867, "Annual Nonutility Power Producer Report." **1998–2000:** EIA, Form EIA-759, "Monthly Power Plant Report," and Form EIA-860B, "Annual Electric Generator Report—Nonutility." **2001–2003:** EIA, Form EIA-906, "Power Plant Report." **2004–2007:** EIA, Form EIA-906, "Power Plant Report," and Form EIA-920, "Combined Heat and Power Plant Report." **2008 forward:** EIA, Form EIA-923, "Power Plant Operations Report." • **Total:** Calculated as distributed solar generation plus utility-scale solar generation.

Source: *U.S. Energy Information Administration, Monthly Energy Review, July 2017*

Figure 11.1a World Crude Oil Production Overview
(Million Barrels per Day)

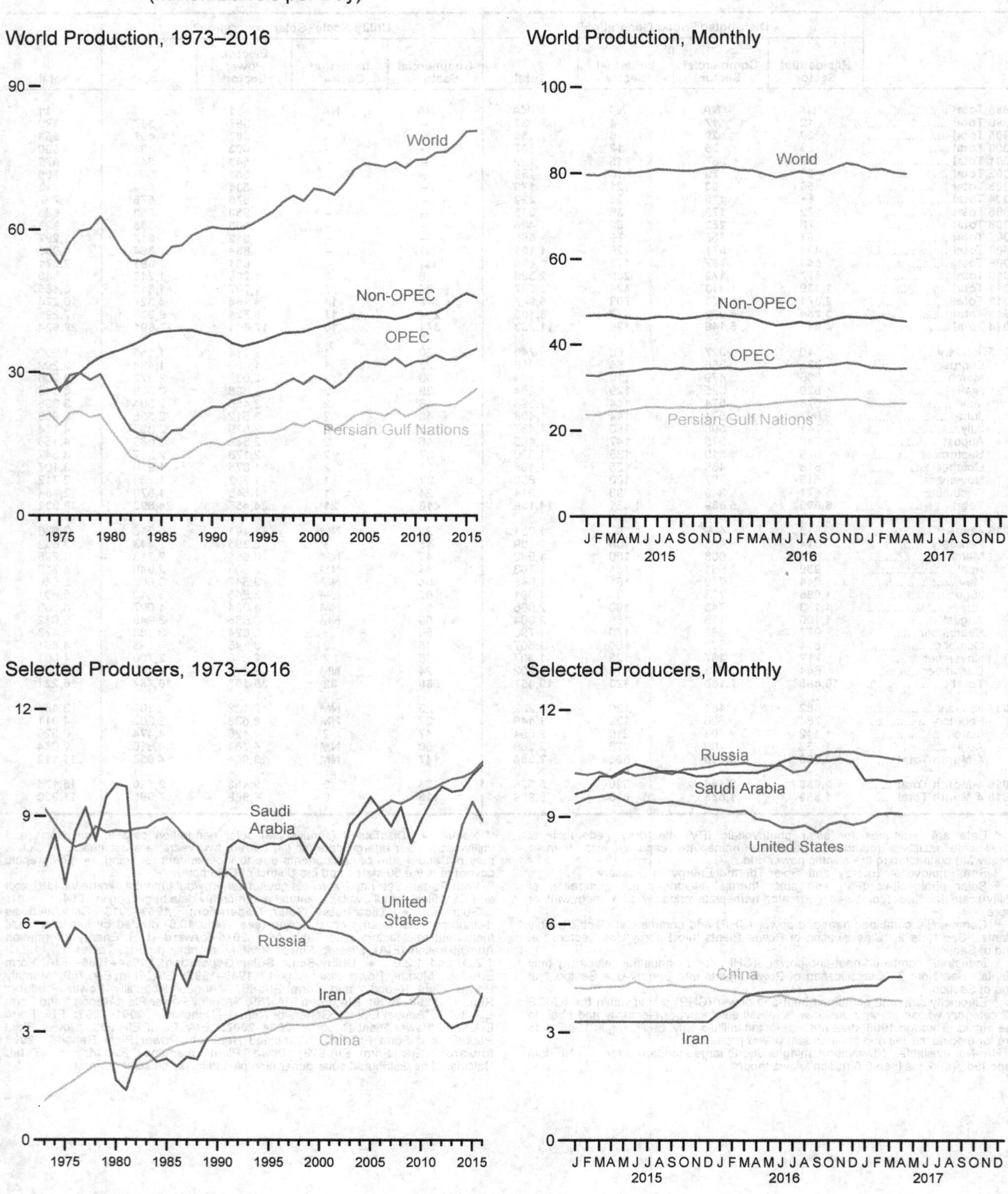

Notes: • OPEC is the Organization of the Petroleum Exporting Countries. • The Persian Gulf Nations are Bahrain, Iran, Iraq, Kuwait, Qatar, Saudi Arabia, and the United Arab Emirates. Production from the Neutral Zone between Kuwait and Saudi Arabia is included in "Persian Gulf Nations."

Web Page: http://www.eia.gov/totalenergy/data/monthly/#international.
Sources: Tables 11.1a and 11.1b.

***Source:** U.S. Energy Information Administration, Monthly Energy Review, July 2017*

Figure 11.1b World Crude Oil Production by Selected Countries
(Million Barrels per Day)

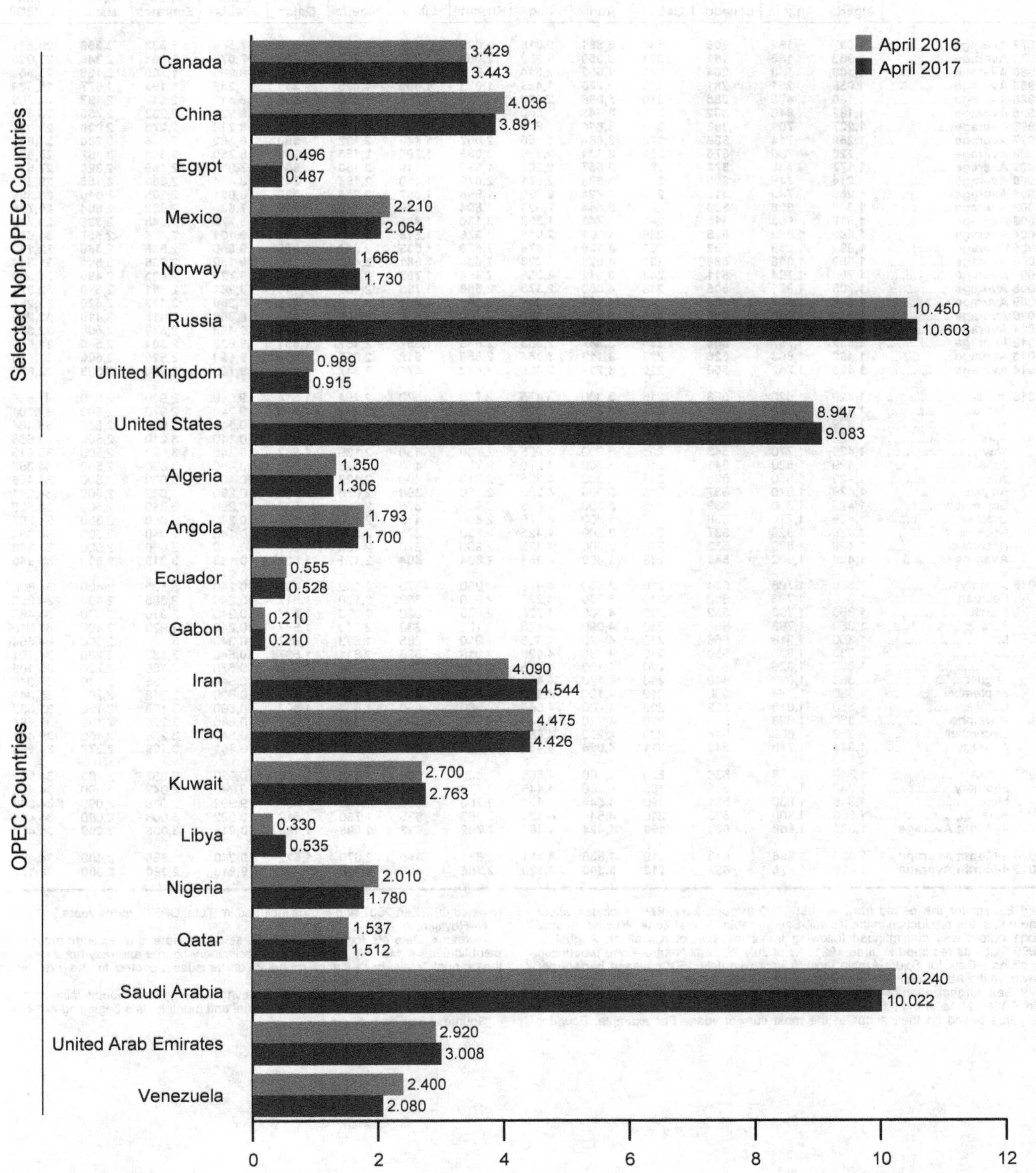

Note: OPEC is the Organization of the Petroleum Exporting Countries.
Web Page: http://www.eia.gov/totalenergy/data/monthly/#international.
Sources: Tables 11.1a and 11.1b.

Source: *U.S. Energy Information Administration, Monthly Energy Review, July 2017*

Table 11.1a World Crude Oil Production: OPEC Members
(Thousand Barrels per Day)

	Algeria	Angola	Ecuador	Gabon	Iran	Iraq	Kuwait[a]	Libya	Nigeria	Qatar	Saudi Arabia[a]	United Arab Emirates	Vene-zuela	Total OPEC[b]
1973 Average	**1,097**	**162**	**209**	**150**	**5,861**	**2,018**	**3,020**	**2,175**	**2,054**	**570**	**7,596**	**1,533**	**3,366**	**29,811**
1975 Average	**983**	**165**	**161**	**223**	**5,350**	**2,262**	**2,084**	**1,480**	**1,783**	**438**	**7,075**	**1,664**	**2,346**	**26,013**
1980 Average	**1,106**	**150**	**204**	**175**	**1,662**	**2,514**	**1,656**	**1,787**	**2,055**	**472**	**9,900**	**1,709**	**2,168**	**25,558**
1985 Average	**1,036**	**231**	**281**	**172**	**2,250**	**1,433**	**1,023**	**1,059**	**1,495**	**301**	**3,388**	**1,193**	**1,677**	**15,539**
1990 Average	**1,180**	**475**	**285**	**270**	**3,088**	**2,040**	**1,175**	**1,375**	**1,810**	**406**	**6,410**	**2,117**	**2,137**	**22,768**
1995 Average	**1,162**	**646**	**392**	**365**	**3,643**	**560**	**2,057**	**1,390**	**1,993**	**442**	**8,231**	**2,233**	**2,750**	**25,865**
1996 Average	**1,227**	**709**	**396**	**368**	**3,686**	**579**	**2,062**	**1,401**	**2,001**	**510**	**8,218**	**2,278**	**2,938**	**26,372**
1997 Average	**1,259**	**714**	**388**	**370**	**3,664**	**1,155**	**2,007**	**1,446**	**2,132**	**550**	**8,362**	**2,316**	**3,280**	**27,644**
1998 Average	**1,226**	**735**	**375**	**352**	**3,634**	**2,150**	**2,085**	**1,390**	**2,153**	**696**	**8,389**	**2,345**	**3,167**	**28,698**
1999 Average	**1,177**	**745**	**373**	**331**	**3,557**	**2,508**	**1,898**	**1,319**	**2,130**	**665**	**7,833**	**2,169**	**2,826**	**27,530**
2000 Average	**1,214**	**746**	**395**	**315**	**3,696**	**2,571**	**2,079**	**1,410**	**2,165**	**742**	**8,404**	**2,368**	**3,155**	**29,259**
2001 Average	**1,265**	**742**	**412**	**270**	**3,724**	**2,390**	**1,998**	**1,367**	**2,256**	**730**	**8,031**	**2,205**	**3,010**	**28,399**
2002 Average	**1,349**	**896**	**393**	**251**	**3,444**	**2,023**	**1,894**	**1,319**	**2,118**	**709**	**7,634**	**2,082**	**2,604**	**26,716**
2003 Average	**1,516**	**903**	**411**	**241**	**3,743**	**1,308**	**2,136**	**1,421**	**2,275**	**807**	**8,775**	**2,348**	**2,335**	**28,219**
2004 Average	**1,582**	**1,052**	**528**	**239**	**4,001**	**2,011**	**2,376**	**1,515**	**2,329**	**901**	**9,101**	**2,478**	**2,557**	**30,671**
2005 Average	**1,692**	**1,239**	**532**	**266**	**4,139**	**1,878**	**2,529**	**1,633**	**2,627**	**978**	**9,550**	**2,535**	**2,565**	**32,163**
2006 Average	**1,699**	**1,398**	**536**	**237**	**4,028**	**1,996**	**2,535**	**1,681**	**2,440**	**996**	**9,152**	**2,636**	**2,511**	**31,844**
2007 Average	**1,708**	**1,724**	**511**	**244**	**3,912**	**2,086**	**2,464**	**1,702**	**2,350**	**1,083**	**8,722**	**2,603**	**2,490**	**31,598**
2008 Average	**1,705**	**1,951**	**505**	**248**	**4,050**	**2,375**	**2,586**	**1,736**	**2,165**	**1,198**	**9,261**	**2,681**	**2,510**	**32,971**
2009 Average	**1,585**	**1,877**	**486**	**242**	**4,037**	**2,391**	**2,350**	**1,650**	**2,208**	**1,279**	**8,250**	**2,413**	**2,520**	**31,287**
2010 Average	**1,540**	**1,909**	**486**	**246**	**4,080**	**2,399**	**2,300**	**1,650**	**2,408**	**1,459**	**8,900**	**2,415**	**2,410**	**32,202**
2011 Average	**1,540**	**1,756**	**500**	**241**	**4,054**	**2,626**	**2,530**	**465**	**2,474**	**1,571**	**9,458**	**2,679**	**2,500**	**32,394**
2012 Average	**1,532**	**1,787**	**504**	**230**	**3,387**	**2,983**	**2,635**	**1,367**	**2,457**	**1,551**	**9,832**	**2,804**	**2,500**	**33,569**
2013 Average	**1,462**	**1,803**	**526**	**220**	**3,113**	**3,054**	**2,650**	**918**	**2,307**	**1,553**	**9,693**	**2,820**	**2,500**	**32,620**
2014 Average	**1,420**	**1,742**	**556**	**220**	**3,239**	**3,368**	**2,642**	**471**	**2,347**	**1,540**	**9,735**	**2,894**	**2,500**	**32,675**
2015 January	1,429	1,820	558	215	3,300	3,475	2,750	370	2,294	1,514	9,640	2,960	2,500	32,825
February	1,429	1,770	553	215	3,300	3,325	2,750	360	2,269	1,520	9,740	2,970	2,500	32,701
March	1,429	1,720	553	215	3,300	3,725	2,750	475	2,152	1,525	10,140	2,980	2,500	33,464
April	1,429	1,790	548	205	3,300	3,775	2,770	505	2,165	1,531	10,140	3,010	2,500	33,668
May	1,429	1,770	543	205	3,300	3,925	2,780	430	2,139	1,532	10,340	3,020	2,500	33,913
June	1,429	1,820	541	215	3,300	4,275	2,780	410	2,025	1,537	10,490	3,030	2,500	34,352
July	1,429	1,850	538	215	3,300	4,325	2,810	400	2,122	1,537	10,400	3,030	2,500	34,456
August	1,429	1,870	537	215	3,300	4,225	2,850	360	2,088	1,537	10,290	3,040	2,500	34,241
September	1,429	1,800	539	215	3,300	4,425	2,850	375	2,225	1,537	10,290	3,040	2,500	34,525
October	1,429	1,770	538	215	3,300	4,275	2,800	415	2,198	1,537	10,240	3,050	2,500	34,267
November	1,429	1,820	537	215	3,300	4,425	2,850	375	2,226	1,537	10,140	3,040	2,500	34,394
December	1,429	1,820	533	215	3,300	4,425	2,900	370	2,159	1,537	10,140	3,060	2,500	34,388
Average	**1,429**	**1,802**	**543**	**213**	**3,300**	**4,054**	**2,804**	**404**	**2,171**	**1,532**	**10,168**	**3,019**	**2,500**	**33,940**
2016 January	1,350	1,798	534	210	3,550	4,475	2,950	370	2,159	1,497	10,240	3,105	2,400	34,638
February	1,350	1,793	540	210	3,700	4,225	2,910	360	2,120	1,517	10,240	2,885	2,400	34,250
March	1,350	1,798	552	210	4,000	4,225	2,930	320	1,993	1,537	10,240	2,910	2,400	34,465
April	1,350	1,793	555	210	4,090	4,475	2,700	330	2,010	1,537	10,240	2,920	2,400	34,610
May	1,350	1,818	556	210	4,120	4,355	2,910	285	1,673	1,537	10,340	3,100	2,300	34,554
June	1,330	1,823	550	210	4,130	4,405	2,910	330	1,811	1,537	10,540	3,135	2,280	34,991
July	1,350	1,829	545	210	4,150	4,415	2,950	310	1,764	1,537	10,670	3,156	2,220	35,106
August	1,350	1,833	549	210	4,170	4,460	2,960	250	1,694	1,537	10,640	3,186	2,210	35,049
September	1,350	1,768	560	210	4,190	4,480	2,960	310	1,726	1,477	10,600	3,216	2,200	35,047
October	1,350	1,618	552	200	4,200	4,565	2,960	550	1,854	1,507	10,590	3,196	2,190	35,332
November	1,350	1,698	544	220	4,220	4,645	2,970	580	1,984	1,527	10,640	3,226	2,180	35,784
December	1,350	1,668	544	220	4,280	4,685	2,970	620	1,684	1,527	10,540	3,226	2,150	35,464
Average	**1,348**	**1,770**	**548**	**211**	**4,068**	**4,452**	**2,924**	**385**	**1,871**	**1,523**	**10,461**	**3,106**	**2,277**	**34,943**
2017 January	1,340	1,658	536	200	4,300	4,565	2,830	680	1,849	1,487	10,020	3,067	2,100	34,632
February	1,340	1,688	535	185	4,300	4,445	2,770	690	1,869	1,467	10,040	3,047	2,090	34,466
March	1,316	1,630	R 531	190	4,544	4,431	2,763	590	1,730	R 1,507	9,992	3,028	2,090	R 34,342
April	1,306	1,700	528	210	4,544	4,426	2,763	535	1,780	1,512	10,022	3,008	2,080	34,414
4-Month Average	**1,325**	**1,668**	**532**	**196**	**4,424**	**4,468**	**2,782**	**623**	**1,806**	**1,494**	**10,018**	**3,038**	**2,090**	**34,464**
2016 4-Month Average	**1,350**	**1,796**	**545**	**210**	**3,835**	**4,351**	**2,873**	**345**	**2,070**	**1,522**	**10,240**	**2,956**	**2,400**	**34,494**
2015 4-Month Average	**1,429**	**1,775**	**553**	**213**	**3,300**	**3,580**	**2,755**	**429**	**2,219**	**1,522**	**9,918**	**2,980**	**2,500**	**33,172**

[a] Except for the period from August 1990 through May 1991, includes about one-half of the production in the Kuwait-Saudi Arabia Neutral Zone. Kuwaiti Neutral Zone output was discontinued following Iraq's invasion of Kuwait on August 2, 1990, but was resumed in June 1991. As of July 2015 all Neutral Zone production is offline. Data for Saudi Arabia include approximately 150 thousand barrels per day from the Abu Safah field produced on behalf of Bahrain.

[b] See "Organization of the Petroleum Exporting Countries (OPEC)" in Glossary. On Tables 11.1a and 11.1b, countries are classified as "OPEC" or "Non-OPEC" in all years based on their status in the most current year. For example, Ecuador rejoined OPEC in 2007 and is thus included in "Total OPEC" for all years.

R=Revised.

Notes: • Data are for crude oil and lease condensate; they exclude natural gas plant liquids. • Monthly data are often preliminary figures and may not average to the annual totals because of rounding or because updates to the preliminary monthly data are not available.

Web Page: See http://www.eia.gov/totalenergy/data/monthly/#international (Excel and CSV files) for all available annual and monthly data beginning in 1973.

Sources: See end of section.

Source: *U.S. Energy Information Administration, Monthly Energy Review, July 2017*

Table 11.1b World Crude Oil Production: Persian Gulf Nations, Non-OPEC, and World

(Thousand Barrels per Day)

	Persian Gulf Nations[b]	Selected Non-OPEC[a] Producers									Total Non-OPEC[a]	World
		Canada	China	Egypt	Mexico	Norway	Former U.S.S.R.	Russia	United Kingdom	United States		
1973 Average	**20,668**	**1,798**	**1,090**	**165**	**465**	**32**	**8,324**	**NA**	**2**	**9,208**	**25,868**	**55,679**
1975 Average	**18,934**	**1,430**	**1,490**	**235**	**705**	**189**	**9,523**	**NA**	**12**	**8,375**	**26,816**	**52,828**
1980 Average	**17,961**	**1,435**	**2,114**	**595**	**1,936**	**486**	**11,706**	**NA**	**1,622**	**8,597**	**34,000**	**59,558**
1985 Average	**9,630**	**1,471**	**2,505**	**887**	**2,745**	**773**	**11,585**	**NA**	**2,530**	**8,971**	**38,426**	**53,965**
1990 Average	**15,278**	**1,553**	**2,774**	**873**	**2,553**	**1,630**	**10,975**	**NA**	**1,820**	**7,355**	**37,729**	**60,497**
1995 Average	**17,208**	**1,805**	**2,990**	**920**	**2,711**	**2,766**	**– –**	**5,995**	**2,489**	**6,560**	**36,569**	**62,434**
1996 Average	**17,367**	**1,837**	**3,131**	**922**	**2,944**	**3,091**	**– –**	**5,850**	**2,568**	**6,465**	**37,446**	**63,818**
1997 Average	**18,095**	**1,922**	**3,200**	**856**	**3,104**	**3,142**	**– –**	**5,920**	**2,518**	**6,452**	**38,161**	**65,806**
1998 Average	**19,337**	**1,981**	**3,198**	**834**	**3,160**	**3,011**	**– –**	**5,854**	**2,616**	**6,252**	**38,333**	**67,032**
1999 Average	**18,667**	**1,907**	**3,195**	**852**	**2,998**	**3,019**	**– –**	**6,079**	**2,684**	**5,881**	**38,437**	**65,967**
2000 Average	**19,897**	**1,977**	**3,249**	**768**	**3,104**	**3,222**	**– –**	**6,479**	**2,275**	**5,822**	**39,268**	**68,527**
2001 Average	**19,114**	**2,029**	**3,300**	**720**	**3,218**	**3,226**	**– –**	**6,917**	**2,282**	**5,801**	**39,733**	**68,132**
2002 Average	**17,824**	**2,171**	**3,390**	**715**	**3,263**	**3,131**	**– –**	**7,408**	**2,292**	**5,744**	**40,574**	**67,290**
2003 Average	**19,154**	**2,306**	**3,409**	**713**	**3,459**	**3,042**	**– –**	**8,132**	**2,093**	**5,649**	**41,242**	**69,460**
2004 Average	**20,906**	**2,398**	**3,485**	**673**	**3,476**	**2,954**	**– –**	**8,805**	**1,845**	**5,441**	**41,924**	**72,595**
2005 Average	**21,644**	**2,369**	**3,609**	**623**	**3,423**	**2,698**	**– –**	**9,043**	**1,649**	**5,184**	**41,702**	**73,866**
2006 Average	**21,377**	**2,525**	**3,673**	**535**	**3,345**	**2,491**	**– –**	**9,247**	**1,490**	**5,086**	**41,633**	**73,476**
2007 Average	**20,904**	**2,628**	**3,736**	**530**	**3,143**	**2,270**	**– –**	**9,437**	**1,498**	**5,077**	**41,578**	**73,175**
2008 Average	**22,186**	**2,579**	**3,790**	**566**	**2,839**	**2,182**	**– –**	**9,357**	**1,391**	**5,000**	**41,078**	**74,048**
2009 Average	**20,754**	**2,579**	**3,796**	**587**	**2,646**	**2,067**	**– –**	**9,495**	**1,328**	**5,353**	**41,583**	**72,869**
2010 Average	**21,589**	**2,741**	**4,078**	**568**	**2,621**	**1,871**	**– –**	**9,694**	**1,233**	**5,475**	**42,341**	**74,543**
2011 Average	**22,953**	**2,901**	**4,052**	**551**	**2,600**	**1,760**	**– –**	**9,774**	**1,026**	**5,646**	**42,230**	**74,624**
2012 Average	**23,233**	**3,138**	**4,074**	**539**	**2,593**	**1,612**	**– –**	**9,922**	**888**	**6,487**	**42,463**	**76,032**
2013 Average	**22,932**	**3,325**	**4,164**	**524**	**2,562**	**1,533**	**– –**	**10,054**	**801**	**7,468**	**43,557**	**76,177**
2014 Average	**23,469**	**3,613**	**4,208**	**517**	**2,469**	**1,562**	**– –**	**10,107**	**787**	**8,764**	**45,381**	**78,056**
2015 January	23,689	3,885	4,232	508	2,290	1,579	– –	10,231	872	9,379	46,786	79,611
February	23,655	3,906	4,218	516	2,370	1,589	– –	10,181	812	9,517	46,818	79,519
March	24,470	3,775	4,256	525	2,356	1,586	– –	10,264	867	9,566	46,959	80,422
April	24,576	3,463	4,258	503	2,235	1,614	– –	10,111	925	9,627	46,349	80,017
May	24,947	3,212	4,271	512	2,263	1,555	– –	10,270	1,016	9,472	46,095	80,009
June	25,462	3,457	4,408	504	2,283	1,596	– –	10,166	870	9,320	46,022	80,374
July	25,452	3,821	4,263	524	2,308	1,611	– –	10,213	839	9,418	46,470	80,926
August	25,292	3,922	4,278	523	2,291	1,599	– –	10,268	788	9,384	46,512	80,753
September	25,492	3,422	4,317	501	2,306	1,581	– –	10,209	862	9,423	46,026	80,551
October	25,252	3,582	4,259	517	2,314	1,685	– –	10,341	912	9,358	46,305	80,572
November	25,342	3,819	4,297	494	2,310	1,644	– –	10,361	972	9,304	46,736	81,130
December	25,412	3,866	4,275	509	2,308	1,682	– –	10,407	979	9,225	46,947	81,335
Average	**24,927**	**3,677**	**4,278**	**511**	**2,302**	**1,610**	**– –**	**10,253**	**893**	**9,415**	**46,502**	**80,442**
2016 January	25,867	3,877	4,166	498	2,294	1,657	– –	10,485	1,003	E9,194	R46,705	R81,343
February	25,527	3,797	4,133	497	2,247	1,675	– –	10,485	1,014	E9,147	R46,387	R80,637
March	25,892	3,767	4,091	497	2,249	1,632	– –	10,522	987	E9,174	R46,140	R80,605
April	26,012	3,429	4,036	496	2,210	1,666	– –	10,450	989	E8,947	R45,200	R79,810
May	26,412	2,811	3,973	495	2,207	1,608	– –	10,440	991	E8,882	R44,471	R79,025
June	26,707	3,112	4,034	495	2,213	1,480	– –	10,453	897	E8,711	R44,728	R79,719
July	26,928	3,657	3,938	494	2,192	1,762	– –	10,254	980	E8,691	R45,257	R80,363
August	27,003	3,855	3,874	493	2,179	1,603	– –	10,316	841	E8,759	R44,820	R79,869
September	26,973	3,849	3,887	493	2,146	1,430	– –	10,729	826	E8,567	R45,161	R80,208
October	27,068	3,893	3,780	492	2,135	1,766	– –	10,826	760	E8,785	R45,920	R81,252
November	27,278	4,135	3,915	491	2,105	1,785	– –	10,832	948	E8,863	R46,494	R82,278
December	27,278	3,968	3,949	491	2,067	1,706	– –	10,830	961	E8,780	R46,280	R81,744
Average	**26,583**	**3,679**	**3,981**	**494**	**2,187**	**1,648**	**– –**	**10,551**	**933**	**E8,875**	**R45,629**	**R80,571**
2017 January	26,312	4,097	3,855	490	2,054	1,660	– –	10,733	970	E8,858	R46,120	R80,752
February	26,111	4,128	3,929	489	2,051	1,709	– –	10,713	944	RE9,075	R46,460	R80,926
March	R26,306	3,607	3,903	489	2,053	R1,750	– –	10,654	945	RE9,107	R45,729	R80,071
April	26,316	3,443	3,891	487	2,064	1,730	– –	10,603	915	E9,083	45,425	79,839
4-Month Average	**26,265**	**3,814**	**3,894**	**489**	**2,056**	**1,712**	**– –**	**10,675**	**944**	**E9,029**	**45,925**	**80,389**
2016 4-Month Average	**25,828**	**3,719**	**4,107**	**497**	**2,250**	**1,657**	**– –**	**10,486**	**998**	**E9,116**	**46,111**	**80,605**
2015 4-Month Average	**24,105**	**3,756**	**4,241**	**513**	**2,312**	**1,592**	**– –**	**10,198**	**870**	**9,521**	**46,729**	**79,901**

[a] See "Organization of the Petroleum Exporting Countries (OPEC)" in Glossary. On Tables 11.1a and 11.1b, countries are classified as "OPEC" or "Non-OPEC" in all years based on their status in the most current year. For example, Ecuador rejoined OPEC in 2007 and is thus included in "Total OPEC" for all years.

[b] Bahrain, Iran, Iraq, Kuwait, Qatar, Saudi Arabia, United Arab Emirates, and the Neutral Zone (between Kuwait and Saudi Arabia).

R=Revised. NA=Not available. – – =Not applicable. E=Estimate.

Notes: • Data are for crude oil and lease condensate; they exclude natural gas plant liquids. • Monthly data are often preliminary figures and may not average to the annual totals because of rounding or because updates to the preliminary monthly data are not available. • Data for countries may not sum to World totals due to independent rounding. • U.S. geographic coverage is the 50 states and the District of Columbia.

Web Page: See http://www.eia.gov/totalenergy/data/monthly/#international (Excel and CSV files) for all available annual and monthly data beginning in 1973.

Sources: See end of section.

Source: *U.S. Energy Information Administration, Monthly Energy Review, July 2017*

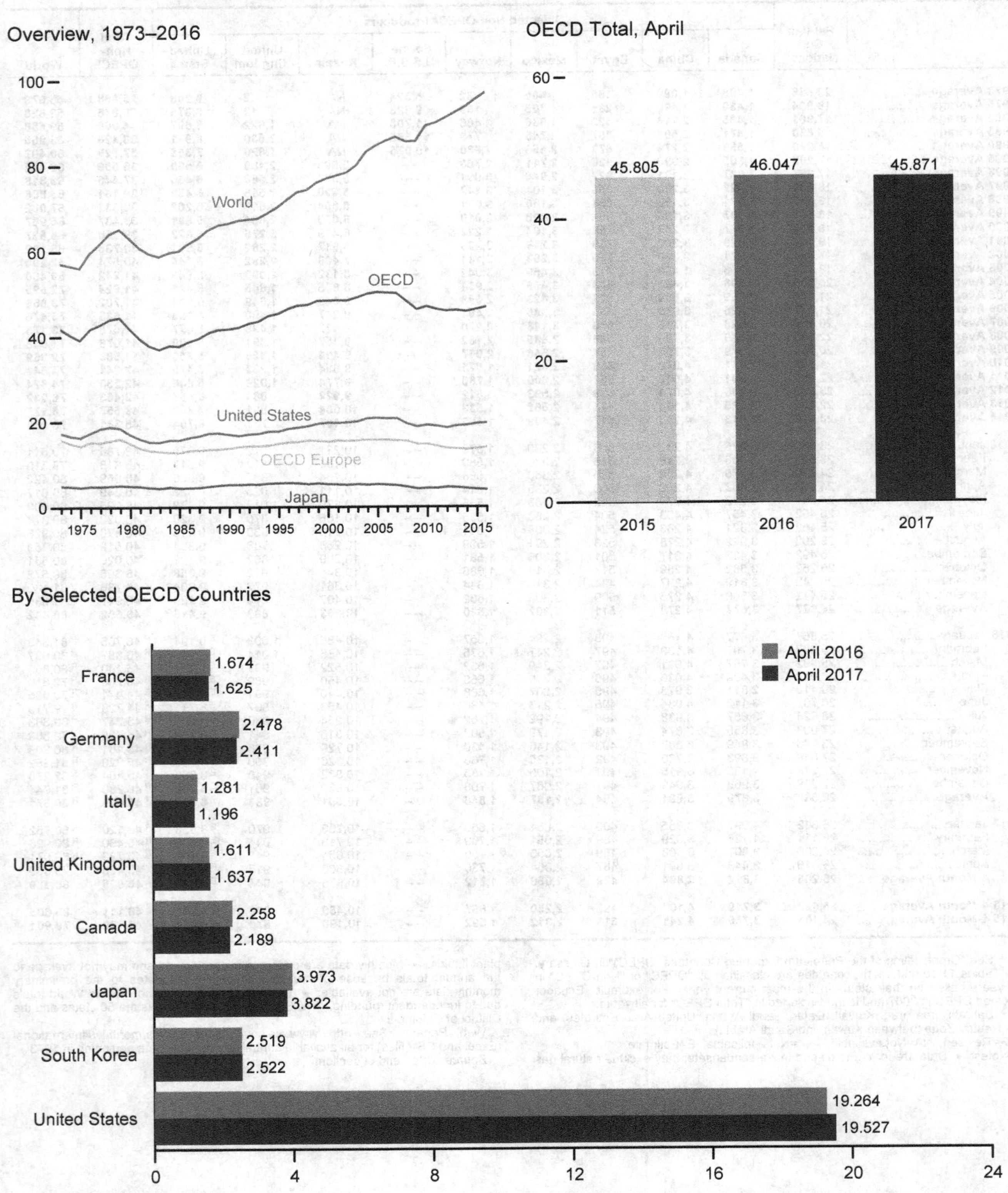

Source: *U.S. Energy Information Administration, Monthly Energy Review, July 2017*

Table 11.2 Petroleum Consumption in OECD Countries
(Thousand Barrels per Day)

	France	Germany[a]	Italy	United Kingdom	OECD Europe[b]	Canada	Japan	South Korea	United States	Other OECD[c]	OECD[d]	World
1973 Average	2,601	3,324	2,068	2,341	15,879	1,729	4,949	281	17,308	1,768	41,913	57,237
1975 Average	2,252	2,957	1,855	1,911	14,314	1,779	4,621	311	16,322	1,885	39,232	56,198
1980 Average	2,256	3,082	1,934	1,725	14,995	1,873	4,960	537	17,056	2,449	41,870	63,113
1985 Average	1,753	2,651	1,705	1,617	12,769	1,514	4,436	552	15,726	2,699	37,696	60,082
1990 Average	1,827	2,682	1,868	1,776	13,759	1,722	5,217	1,048	16,988	3,030	41,764	66,539
1995 Average	1,915	2,882	1,942	1,816	14,832	1,799	5,546	2,008	17,725	3,478	45,388	70,315
1996 Average	1,943	2,922	1,920	1,852	15,144	1,853	5,591	2,101	18,309	3,513	46,511	72,038
1997 Average	1,962	2,917	1,934	1,810	15,292	1,940	5,549	2,255	18,620	3,604	47,261	73,734
1998 Average	2,040	2,923	1,943	1,792	15,592	1,931	5,348	1,917	18,917	3,739	47,444	74,305
1999 Average	2,034	2,836	1,891	1,811	15,503	2,016	5,486	2,084	19,519	3,775	48,384	76,058
2000 Average	2,001	2,767	1,854	1,765	15,352	2,008	5,357	2,135	19,701	3,871	48,424	76,957
2001 Average	2,054	2,807	1,835	1,747	15,533	2,029	5,265	2,132	19,649	3,873	48,480	77,642
2002 Average	1,991	2,710	1,870	1,739	15,491	2,040	5,187	2,149	19,761	3,825	48,453	78,332
2003 Average	2,001	2,679	1,860	1,759	15,616	2,155	5,298	2,175	20,034	3,897	49,174	79,986
2004 Average	2,008	2,648	1,829	1,789	15,718	2,233	5,163	2,155	20,731	4,001	50,002	83,126
2005 Average	1,990	2,624	1,781	1,819	15,714	2,296	5,298	2,191	20,802	4,114	50,416	84,633
2006 Average	1,991	2,636	1,777	1,806	15,718	2,294	5,168	2,180	20,687	4,150	50,197	85,702
2007 Average	1,978	2,407	1,729	1,751	15,534	2,389	5,009	2,240	20,680	4,268	50,121	86,545
2008 Average	1,940	2,533	1,667	1,730	15,424	2,342	4,664	2,142	19,498	4,191	48,261	85,509
2009 Average	1,863	2,434	1,544	1,649	14,711	2,283	4,257	2,188	18,771	4,105	46,316	85,569
2010 Average	1,822	2,467	1,544	1,626	14,694	2,375	4,328	2,269	19,180	4,153	46,998	89,137
2011 Average	1,779	2,392	1,494	1,582	14,215	2,405	4,345	2,259	18,882	4,216	46,322	89,846
2012 Average	1,739	2,389	1,370	1,535	13,741	2,470	4,630	2,322	18,490	4,274	45,928	91,059
2013 Average	1,714	2,435	1,260	1,527	13,582	2,455	4,504	2,328	18,961	4,240	46,069	92,284
2014 Average	1,692	2,374	1,266	1,520	13,484	2,407	4,267	2,348	19,106	4,191	45,801	93,598
2015 January	1,642	2,291	1,123	1,432	12,983	2,443	4,547	2,466	19,218	4,045	45,702	NA
February	1,782	2,431	1,227	1,655	13,871	2,528	5,062	2,506	19,677	4,215	47,858	NA
March	1,691	2,388	1,219	1,478	13,484	2,339	4,530	2,403	19,352	4,213	46,321	NA
April	1,720	2,360	1,307	1,570	13,691	2,282	4,154	2,377	19,263	4,038	45,805	NA
May	1,540	2,189	1,224	1,486	13,005	2,321	3,589	2,201	19,301	4,123	44,540	NA
June	1,773	2,317	1,293	1,559	13,955	2,393	3,669	2,304	19,841	4,185	46,346	NA
July	1,809	2,390	1,391	1,495	14,143	2,441	3,791	2,289	20,126	4,278	47,069	NA
August	1,675	2,415	1,240	1,579	13,901	2,457	3,909	2,442	19,930	4,190	46,828	NA
September	1,792	2,530	1,328	1,624	14,358	2,460	3,851	2,355	19,418	4,183	46,625	NA
October	1,663	2,431	1,285	1,529	13,812	2,441	3,828	2,407	19,500	4,258	46,246	NA
November	1,497	2,393	1,250	1,580	13,415	2,405	3,969	2,522	19,144	4,211	45,666	NA
December	1,716	2,345	1,303	1,570	13,801	2,368	4,607	2,618	19,600	4,274	47,268	NA
Average	1,691	2,372	1,266	1,545	13,698	2,406	4,120	2,407	19,531	4,184	46,347	95,334
2016 January	R 1,564	2,300	R 1,108	R 1,492	R 12,877	R 2,371	R 4,345	R 2,695	19,055	R 4,089	R 45,432	NA
February	R 1,695	R 2,468	R 1,243	R 1,641	R 13,914	R 2,328	R 4,629	R 2,752	19,680	R 4,276	R 47,578	NA
March	R 1,732	R 2,475	R 1,251	R 1,538	R 13,911	R 2,304	R 4,356	R 2,533	19,616	R 4,304	R 47,023	NA
April	R 1,674	2,478	R 1,281	R 1,611	R 13,979	R 2,258	R 3,973	R 2,519	19,264	R 4,054	R 46,047	NA
May	R 1,681	2,285	R 1,246	R 1,549	R 13,639	R 2,304	R 3,579	R 2,574	19,202	R 4,133	R 45,431	NA
June	R 1,553	R 2,313	R 1,302	R 1,654	R 13,974	R 2,389	R 3,561	R 2,544	19,799	R 4,210	R 46,477	NA
July	R 1,690	2,398	R 1,305	R 1,551	R 14,057	R 2,401	R 3,779	R 2,472	19,712	R 4,101	R 46,521	NA
August	R 1,698	R 2,451	R 1,250	R 1,608	R 14,547	R 2,532	R 3,860	R 2,684	20,131	R 4,224	R 47,977	NA
September	R 1,742	R 2,426	R 1,319	R 1,646	R 14,521	R 2,455	R 3,723	R 2,642	19,864	R 4,078	R 47,282	NA
October	R 1,672	2,457	R 1,236	R 1,594	R 14,270	R 2,347	R 3,777	R 2,532	19,622	R 4,137	R 46,684	NA
November	R 1,566	2,502	R 1,206	R 1,596	R 14,057	R 2,386	R 4,158	R 2,780	19,655	R 4,211	R 47,246	NA
December	R 1,660	2,373	R 1,287	R 1,564	R 14,055	R 2,467	R 4,596	R 2,843	19,979	R 4,251	R 48,190	NA
Average	R 1,661	R 2,410	R 1,253	R 1,586	R 13,982	R 2,379	R 4,026	R 2,630	19,631	R 4,172	R 46,820	R 96,892
2017 January	R 1,738	2,273	R 1,178	R 1,445	R 13,378	R 2,350	R 4,176	R 2,665	19,234	R 3,994	R 45,798	NA
February	R 1,706	R 2,367	R 1,234	R 1,652	R 13,797	R 2,325	R 4,565	R 2,739	19,188	R 4,284	R 46,897	NA
March	R 1,709	2,569	R 1,280	R 1,492	R 14,054	R 2,376	R 4,279	R 2,668	20,033	R 4,326	R 47,736	NA
April	1,625	2,411	1,196	1,637	13,780	2,189	3,822	2,522	19,527	4,030	45,871	NA
4-Month Average	1,695	2,406	1,222	1,553	13,751	2,311	4,205	2,647	19,503	4,156	46,573	NA
2016 4-Month Average	1,666	2,429	1,220	1,569	13,664	2,315	4,324	2,623	19,401	4,180	46,506	NA
2015 4-Month Average	1,706	2,366	1,218	1,530	13,497	2,396	4,565	2,437	19,371	4,126	46,391	NA

[a] Data are for unified Germany, i.e., the former East Germany and West Germany.

[b] "OECD Europe" consists of Austria, Belgium, Denmark, Finland, France, Germany, Greece, Iceland, Ireland, Italy, Luxembourg, the Netherlands, Norway, Portugal, Spain, Sweden, Switzerland, Turkey, and the United Kingdom; for 1984 forward, Czech Republic, Hungary, Poland, and Slovakia; and, for 2000 forward, Slovenia.

[c] "Other OECD" consists of Australia, New Zealand, and the U.S. Territories; for 1984 forward, Mexico; and, for 2000 forward, Chile, Estonia, and Israel.

[d] The Organization for Economic Cooperation and Development (OECD) consists of "OECD Europe," Canada, Japan, South Korea, the United States, and "Other OECD."

R=Revised. NA=Not available.

Notes: • Totals may not equal sum of components due to independent rounding. • U.S. geographic coverage is the 50 states and the District of Columbia.

Web Page: See http://www.eia.gov/totalenergy/data/monthly/#international (Excel and CSV files) for all available annual and monthly data beginning in 1973.

Sources: • **United States:** Table 3.1. • **Chile, East Germany, Former Czechoslovakia, Hungary, Mexico, Poland, South Korea, Non-OECD Countries, U.S. Territories,** and **World: 1973–1979**—U.S. Energy Information Administration (EIA), International Energy Database. • **Countries Other Than United States: 1980–2008**—EIA, International Energy Statistics (IES). • **OECD Countries,** and **U.S. Territories: 2009 forward**—EIA, IES. • **World: 2009 forward**—EIA, International Energy Statistics Database. • **All Other Data:**—International Energy Agency (IEA), *Quarterly Oil Statistics and Energy Balances in OECD Countries*, various issues.

Source: *U.S. Energy Information Administration, Monthly Energy Review, July 2017*

Figure 11.3 Petroleum Stocks in OECD Countries
(Billion Barrels)

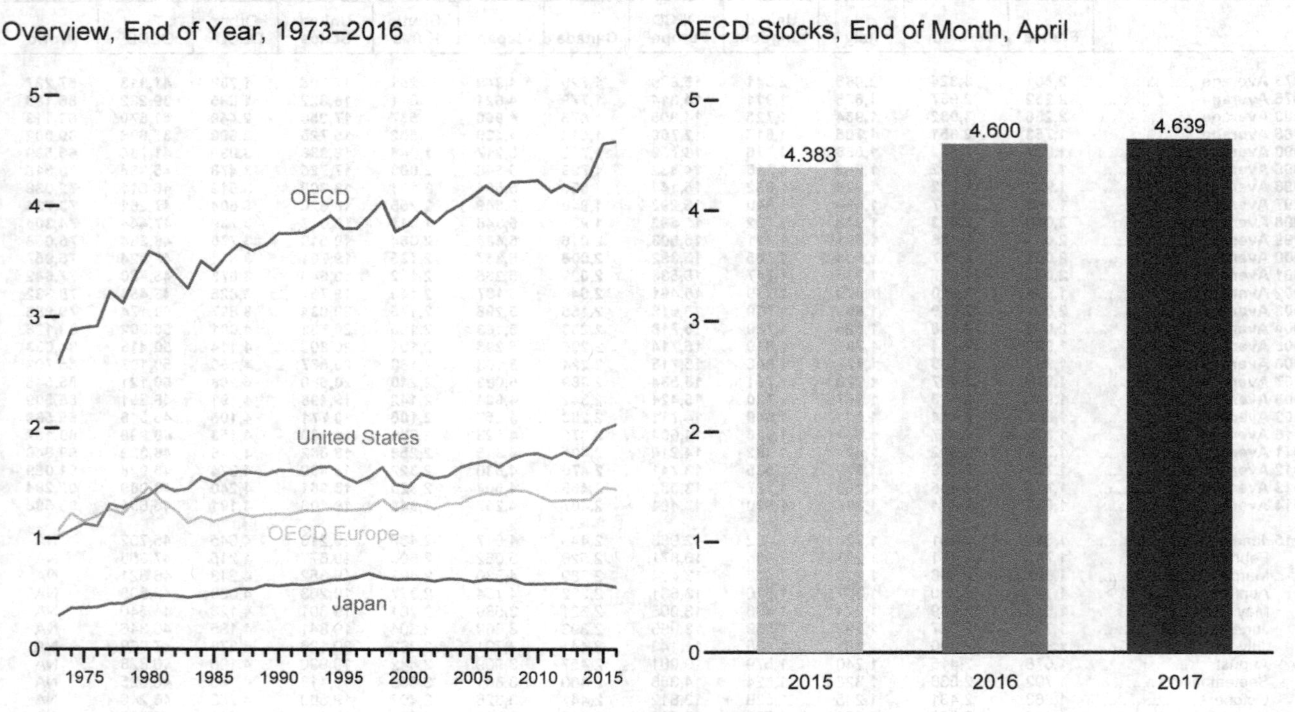

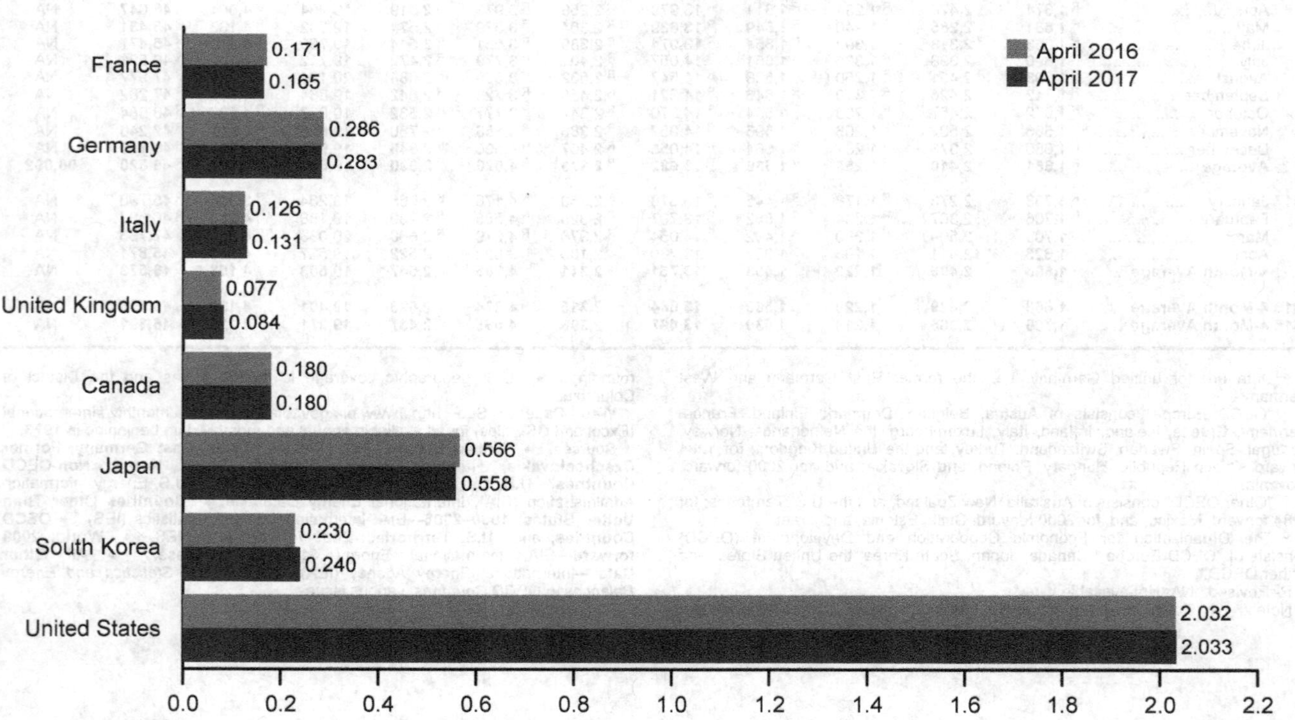

Note: OECD is the Organization for Economic Cooperation and Development.
Web Page: http://www.eia.gov/totalenergy/data/monthly/#international.
Source: Table 11.3.

Source: *U.S. Energy Information Administration, Monthly Energy Review, July 2017*

Table 11.3 Petroleum Stocks in OECD Countries

(Million Barrels)

	France	Germany[a]	Italy	United Kingdom	OECD Europe[b]	Canada	Japan	South Korea	United States	Other OECD[c]	OECD[d]
1973 Year	**201**	**181**	**152**	**156**	**1,070**	**140**	**303**	**NA**	**1,008**	**67**	**2,588**
1975 Year	**225**	**187**	**143**	**165**	**1,154**	**174**	**375**	**NA**	**1,133**	**67**	**2,903**
1980 Year	**243**	**319**	**170**	**168**	**1,464**	**164**	**495**	**NA**	**1,392**	**72**	**3,587**
1985 Year	**139**	**277**	**156**	**131**	**1,154**	**112**	**500**	**13**	**1,519**	**119**	**3,417**
1990 Year	**143**	**280**	**171**	**103**	**1,222**	**143**	**572**	**64**	**1,621**	**126**	**3,749**
1995 Year	**155**	**302**	**162**	**101**	**1,256**	**132**	**631**	**92**	**1,563**	**122**	**3,795**
1996 Year	**154**	**303**	**152**	**103**	**1,259**	**127**	**651**	**123**	**1,507**	**127**	**3,794**
1997 Year	**161**	**299**	**147**	**100**	**1,271**	**144**	**685**	**124**	**1,560**	**123**	**3,907**
1998 Year	**169**	**323**	**153**	**104**	**1,355**	**139**	**649**	**129**	**1,647**	**120**	**4,039**
1999 Year	**160**	**290**	**148**	**101**	**1,258**	**141**	**629**	**132**	**1,493**	**114**	**3,766**
2000 Year	**170**	**272**	**157**	**100**	**1,318**	**143**	**634**	**140**	**1,468**	**126**	**3,829**
2001 Year	**165**	**273**	**151**	**113**	**1,306**	**154**	**634**	**143**	**1,586**	**120**	**3,944**
2002 Year	**170**	**253**	**156**	**104**	**1,273**	**155**	**615**	**140**	**1,548**	**112**	**3,843**
2003 Year	**179**	**273**	**153**	**100**	**1,316**	**165**	**636**	**155**	**1,568**	**105**	**3,945**
2004 Year	**177**	**267**	**154**	**101**	**1,319**	**154**	**635**	**149**	**1,645**	**108**	**4,010**
2005 Year	**185**	**283**	**151**	**95**	**1,380**	**168**	**612**	**135**	**1,682**	**112**	**4,088**
2006 Year	**182**	**283**	**153**	**103**	**1,413**	**169**	**631**	**152**	**1,703**	**113**	**4,180**
2007 Year	**180**	**275**	**152**	**92**	**1,398**	**163**	**621**	**143**	**1,648**	**121**	**4,094**
2008 Year	**179**	**279**	**148**	**93**	**1,441**	**162**	**629**	**135**	**1,719**	**124**	**4,209**
2009 Year	**175**	**284**	**146**	**89**	**1,432**	**157**	**591**	**155**	**1,758**	**118**	**4,212**
2010 Year	**168**	**287**	**143**	**83**	**1,393**	**184**	**590**	**165**	**1,773**	**119**	**4,224**
2011 Year	**165**	**281**	**135**	**80**	**1,338**	**178**	**592**	**167**	**1,728**	**117**	**4,120**
2012 Year	**162**	**288**	**126**	**80**	**1,347**	**174**	**594**	**181**	**1,780**	**107**	**4,184**
2013 Year	**167**	**290**	**125**	**78**	**1,350**	**170**	**580**	**185**	**1,732**	**111**	**4,127**
2014 Year	**168**	**284**	**119**	**78**	**1,354**	**193**	**581**	**197**	**1,827**	**114**	**4,266**
2015 January	170	284	116	73	1,371	192	574	197	1,850	114	4,298
February	170	286	113	75	1,383	184	568	198	1,850	112	4,295
March	173	284	121	76	1,407	183	568	201	1,883	110	4,352
April	170	284	124	85	1,411	185	558	210	1,909	110	4,383
May	175	288	122	78	1,419	181	582	224	1,931	107	4,444
June	170	286	117	77	1,409	176	578	225	1,941	114	4,443
July	168	281	116	74	1,400	184	589	223	1,939	114	4,449
August	167	283	123	77	1,429	185	594	227	1,962	111	4,508
September	167	281	117	79	1,433	182	590	226	1,971	111	4,513
October	165	280	118	80	1,436	183	588	223	1,979	107	4,515
November	164	281	117	83	1,446	187	582	222	1,992	104	4,533
December	**168**	**285**	**117**	**81**	**1,462**	**188**	**582**	**228**	**1,985**	**109**	**4,553**
2016 January	171	287	120	83	1,486	187	580	219	2,009	112	4,593
February	169	289	123	81	1,493	183	564	233	2,013	109	4,595
March	166	289	120	77	1,478	184	560	236	2,021	111	4,590
April	171	286	126	77	1,479	180	566	230	2,032	112	4,600
May	167	289	123	81	1,487	169	574	235	2,048	115	4,626
June	167	288	121	82	1,478	175	573	238	2,047	118	4,629
July	169	290	125	75	1,498	186	577	238	2,062	121	4,681
August	167	287	130	80	1,484	186	585	233	2,063	116	4,667
September	167	285	127	78	1,467	185	587	239	2,048	115	4,640
October	163	287	128	77	1,449	190	587	238	2,050	114	4,627
November	166	283	126	80	1,454	190	573	238	2,054	107	4,616
December	**162**	**285**	**124**	**82**	**1,448**	**183**	**562**	**230**	**2,031**	**116**	**4,571**
2017 January	166	286	129	82	1,501	185	562	238	2,053	117	4,656
February	166	286	131	82	1,505	187	556	236	2,049	115	4,647
March	168	281	134	81	1,498	R185	546	238	2,033	120	R4,619
April	165	283	131	84	1,505	180	558	240	2,033	121	4,639

[a] Through December 1983, the data for Germany are for the former West Germany only. Beginning with January 1984, the data for Germany are for the unified Germany, i.e., the former East Germany and West Germany.

[b] "OECD Europe" consists of Austria, Belgium, Denmark, Finland, France, Germany, Greece, Iceland, Ireland, Italy, Luxembourg, the Netherlands, Norway, Portugal, Spain, Sweden, Switzerland, Turkey, and the United Kingdom; for 1984 forward, Czech Republic, Hungary, Poland, and Slovakia; and, for 2000 forward, Slovenia.

[c] "Other OECD" consists of Australia, New Zealand, and the U.S. Territories; for 1984 forward, Mexico; and, for 2000 forward, Chile, Estonia, and Israel.

[d] The Organization for Economic Cooperation and Development (OECD) consists of "OECD Europe," Canada, Japan, South Korea, the United States, and "Other OECD."

R=Revised. NA=Not available.

Notes: • Stocks are at end of period. • Petroleum tocks include crude oil (including strategic reserves), unfinished oils, natural gas plant liquids, and refined products. • In the United States in January 1975, 1981, and 1983, numerous respondents were added to bulk terminal and pipeline surveys, thereby affecting subsequent stocks reported. New-basis end-of-year U.S. stocks, in million barrels, would have been 1,121 in 1974, 1,425 in 1980, and 1,461 in 1982. • Totals may not equal sum of components due to independent rounding. • U.S. geographic coverage is the 50 states and the District of Columbia.

Web Page: See http://www.eia.gov/totalenergy/data/monthly/#international (Excel and CSV files) for all available annual and monthly data beginning in 1973.

Sources: • **United States:** Table 3.4. • **U.S. Territories: 1983 forward**—U.S. Energy Information Administration, International Energy Database. • **All Other Data: 1973–1982**—International Energy Agency (IEA), *Quarterly Oil Statistics and Energy Balances,* various issues. **1983**—IEA, Monthly Oil and Gas Statistics Database. **1984 forward**—IEA, Monthly Oil Data Service, July 13, 2017.

Source: *U.S. Energy Information Administration, Monthly Energy Review, July 2017*

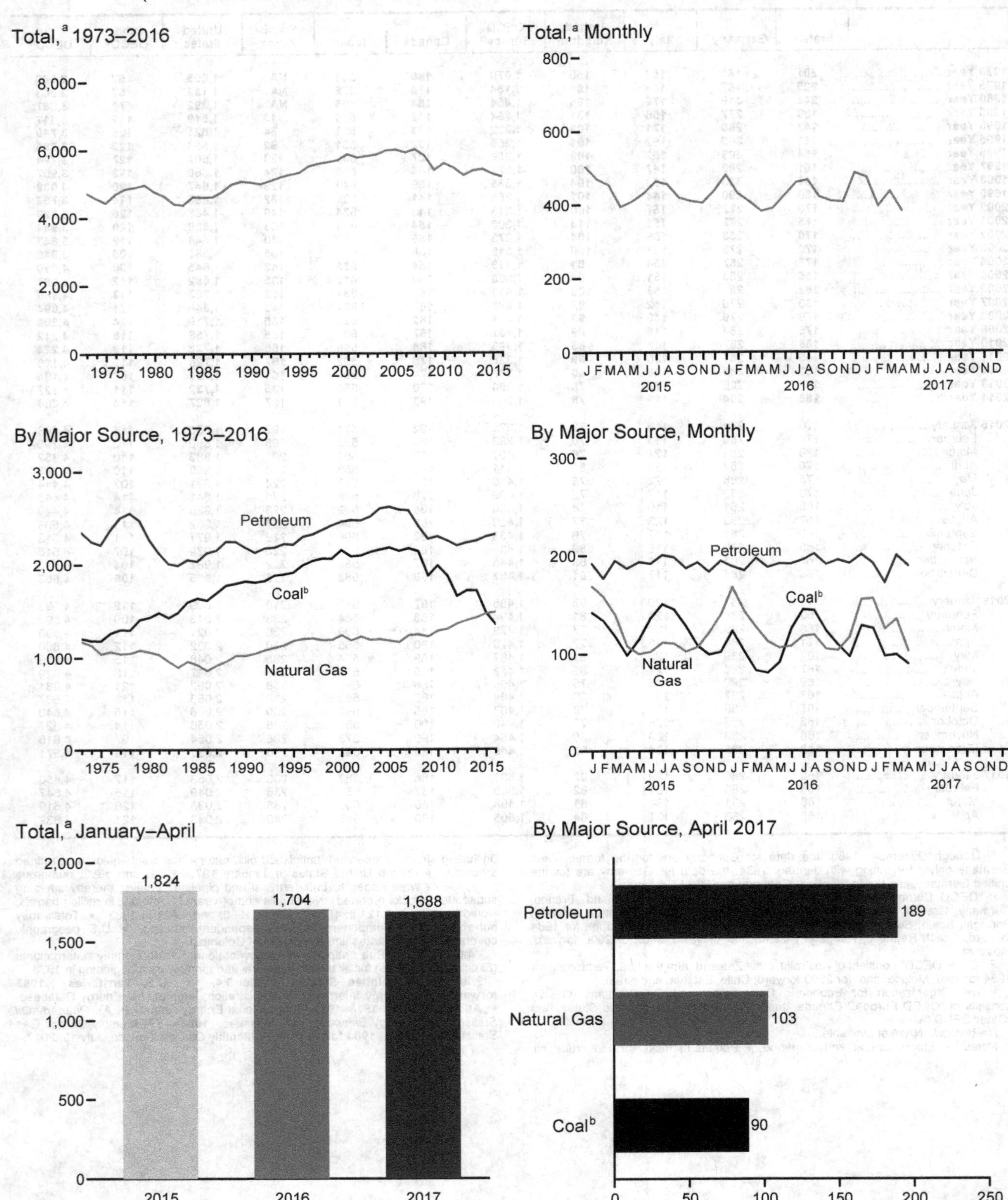

[a] Excludes emissions from biomass energy consumption.
[b] Includes coal coke net imports.

Web Page: http://www.eia.gov/totalenergy/data/monthly/#environment.
Source: Table 12.1.

Source: *U.S. Energy Information Administration, Monthly Energy Review, July 2017*

Table 12.1 Carbon Dioxide Emissions From Energy Consumption by Source
(Million Metric Tons of Carbon Dioxide[a])

	Coal[b]	Natural Gas[c]	Petroleum										Total[h,i]
			Aviation Gasoline	Distillate Fuel Oil[d]	Jet Fuel	Kero-sene	LPG[e]	Lubri-cants	Motor Gasoline[f]	Petroleum Coke	Residual Fuel Oil	Other[g]	Total	
1973 Total	**1,207**	**1,178**	**6**	**480**	**155**	**32**	**92**	**13**	**911**	**54**	**508**	**100**	**2,350**	**4,735**
1975 Total	**1,181**	**1,046**	**5**	**443**	**146**	**24**	**82**	**11**	**911**	**51**	**443**	**97**	**2,212**	**4,439**
1980 Total	**1,436**	**1,061**	**4**	**446**	**156**	**24**	**87**	**13**	**900**	**49**	**453**	**142**	**2,275**	**4,771**
1985 Total	**1,638**	**926**	**3**	**445**	**178**	**17**	**87**	**12**	**930**	**54**	**216**	**93**	**2,036**	**4,600**
1990 Total	**1,821**	**1,024**	**3**	**470**	**223**	**6**	**67**	**13**	**988**	**70**	**220**	**127**	**2,187**	**5,039**
1995 Total	**1,913**	**1,183**	**3**	**498**	**222**	**8**	**80**	**13**	**1,045**	**76**	**152**	**121**	**2,216**	**5,323**
1996 Total	**1,995**	**1,204**	**3**	**524**	**232**	**9**	**86**	**12**	**1,063**	**79**	**152**	**139**	**2,300**	**5,510**
1997 Total	**2,040**	**1,210**	**3**	**534**	**234**	**10**	**87**	**13**	**1,075**	**80**	**142**	**145**	**2,323**	**5,584**
1998 Total	**2,064**	**1,189**	**2**	**537**	**238**	**12**	**82**	**14**	**1,107**	**93**	**158**	**128**	**2,372**	**5,635**
1999 Total	**2,062**	**1,193**	**3**	**555**	**245**	**11**	**90**	**14**	**1,128**	**96**	**148**	**133**	**2,422**	**5,688**
2000 Total	**2,155**	**1,243**	**3**	**579**	**254**	**10**	**97**	**14**	**1,136**	**86**	**163**	**118**	**2,459**	**5,868**
2001 Total	**2,088**	**1,188**	**2**	**597**	**243**	**11**	**88**	**13**	**1,152**	**89**	**144**	**135**	**2,474**	**5,761**
2002 Total	**2,095**	**1,227**	**2**	**586**	**237**	**6**	**91**	**12**	**1,183**	**96**	**125**	**130**	**2,470**	**5,804**
2003 Total	**2,136**	**1,193**	**2**	**610**	**231**	**8**	**87**	**11**	**1,187**	**96**	**138**	**142**	**2,513**	**5,853**
2004 Total	**2,160**	**1,200**	**2**	**632**	**240**	**10**	**87**	**12**	**1,210**	**107**	**155**	**144**	**2,598**	**5,970**
2005 Total	**2,182**	**1,183**	**2**	**639**	**246**	**10**	**84**	**12**	**1,209**	**106**	**165**	**143**	**2,617**	**5,993**
2006 Total	**2,147**	**1,167**	**2**	**645**	**240**	**8**	**80**	**11**	**1,217**	**106**	**122**	**152**	**2,584**	**5,910**
2007 Total	**2,172**	**1,241**	**2**	**647**	**238**	**5**	**83**	**12**	**1,211**	**100**	**128**	**150**	**2,576**	**6,000**
2008 Total	**2,140**	**1,248**	**2**	**610**	**226**	**2**	**79**	**11**	**1,143**	**93**	**110**	**132**	**2,409**	**5,809**
2009 Total	**1,876**	**1,225**	**2**	**559**	**204**	**3**	**78**	**10**	**1,129**	**87**	**90**	**112**	**2,273**	**5,386**
2010 Total	**1,986**	**1,286**	**2**	**585**	**210**	**3**	**79**	**11**	**1,112**	**82**	**93**	**122**	**2,299**	**5,582**
2011 Total	**1,876**	**1,305**	**2**	**599**	**209**	**2**	**78**	**10**	**1,078**	**79**	**79**	**117**	**2,252**	**5,445**
2012 Total	**1,657**	**1,363**	**2**	**574**	**206**	**1**	**81**	**9**	**1,071**	**79**	**65**	**113**	**2,200**	**5,232**
2013 Total	**1,718**	**1,400**	**2**	**581**	**210**	**1**	**88**	**10**	**1,087**	**77**	**56**	**119**	**2,231**	**5,360**
2014 Total	**1,713**	**1,430**	**2**	**614**	**216**	**1**	**83**	**10**	**1,095**	**76**	**45**	**110**	**2,252**	**5,406**
2015 January	143	169	(s)	54	17	(s)	9	1	90	7	4	8	192	504
February	134	159	(s)	53	16	(s)	8	1	83	4	3	9	177	470
March	118	140	(s)	53	19	(s)	7	1	94	7	4	9	195	455
April	99	108	(s)	50	18	(s)	6	1	93	7	2	9	187	395
May	115	100	(s)	49	19	(s)	6	1	96	7	4	12	194	410
June	137	103	(s)	49	20	(s)	6	1	95	7	3	11	192	432
July	151	112	(s)	50	21	(s)	7	1	99	7	5	11	201	465
August	145	111	(s)	50	20	(s)	7	1	99	8	4	10	198	456
September	129	103	(s)	51	18	(s)	6	1	94	5	4	9	187	419
October	108	107	(s)	52	20	(s)	7	1	96	6	4	7	193	410
November	100	122	(s)	47	18	(s)	7	1	92	5	4	9	184	406
December	102	140	(s)	49	20	(s)	8	1	95	5	5	10	195	438
Total	**1,480**	**1,473**	**1**	**607**	**227**	**1**	**85**	**11**	**1,126**	**76**	**46**	**115**	**2,295**	**5,259**
2016 January	123	168	(s)	49	18	(s)	9	1	90	6	5	10	189	481
February	102	144	(s)	48	18	(s)	8	1	90	6	3	11	185	432
March	83	127	(s)	51	19	(s)	7	1	98	7	6	9	198	409
April	81	113	(s)	48	19	(s)	6	1	93	5	7	9	188	382
May	92	106	(s)	48	19	(s)	6	1	98	5	5	9	192	391
June	125	108	(s)	48	21	(s)	5	1	97	4	6	9	192	426
July	145	118	(s)	46	21	(s)	6	1	100	6	7	9	196	460
August	144	R 119	(s)	50	21	(s)	6	1	100	8	5	11	202	467
September	123	105	(s)	49	20	(s)	7	1	96	5	4	10	191	420
October	109	104	(s)	52	20	(s)	7	1	95	6	5	10	196	410
November	97	117	(s)	49	20	(s)	7	1	93	9	5	8	192	407
December	128	155	(s)	52	21	(s)	8	1	97	7	5	10	201	486
Total	**1,354**	**1,485**	**1**	**589**	**236**	**1**	**82**	**11**	**1,146**	**75**	**63**	**115**	**2,320**	**R 5,170**
2017 January	126	156	(s)	49	20	(s)	9	1	88	8	7	10	192	475
February	R 97	125	(s)	45	17	(s)	7	1	84	4	4	9	172	395
March	99	135	(s)	54	21	(s)	7	1	98	3	5	12	200	436
April	90	103	(s)	47	19	(s)	7	1	93	6	5	11	189	383
4-Month Total	**412**	**519**	**(s)**	**195**	**77**	**(s)**	**30**	**3**	**364**	**21**	**21**	**42**	**753**	**1,688**
2016 4-Month Total	**389**	**552**	**(s)**	**196**	**74**	**(s)**	**30**	**4**	**371**	**25**	**21**	**39**	**760**	**1,704**
2015 4-Month Total	**494**	**576**	**(s)**	**210**	**71**	**(s)**	**31**	**4**	**360**	**25**	**14**	**36**	**751**	**1,824**

[a] Metric tons of carbon dioxide can be converted to metric tons of carbon equivalent by multiplying by 12/44.
[b] Includes coal coke net imports.
[c] Natural gas, excluding supplemental gaseous fuels.
[d] Distillate fuel oil, excluding biodiesel.
[e] Liquefied petroleum gases.
[f] Finished motor gasoline, excluding fuel ethanol.
[g] Aviation gasoline blending components, crude oil, motor gasoline blending components, pentanes plus, petrochemical feedstocks, special naphthas, still gas, unfinished oils, waxes, and miscellaneous petroleum products.
[h] Includes electric power sector use of geothermal energy and non-biomass waste. See Table 12.6.
[i] Excludes emissions from biomass energy consumption. See Table 12.7.

R=Revised. (s)=Less than 0.5 million metric tons.

Notes: • Data are estimates for carbon dioxide emissions from energy consumption, including the nonfuel use of fossil fuels. See "Section 12 Methodology and Sources" at end of section. • See "Carbon Dioxide" in Glossary. • See Note 1, "Emissions of Carbon Dioxide and Other Greenhouse Gases," at end of section. • Data exclude emissions from biomass energy consumption. See Table 12.7 and Note 2, "Accounting for Carbon Dioxide Emissions From Biomass Energy Combustion," at end of section. • Totals may not equal sum of components due to independent rounding. • Geographic coverage is the 50 states and the District of Columbia.

Web Page: See http://www.eia.gov/totalenergy/data/monthly/#environment (Excel and CSV files) for all available annual and monthly data beginning in 1973.

Sources: See end of section.

Source: U.S. Energy Information Administration, Monthly Energy Review, July 2017

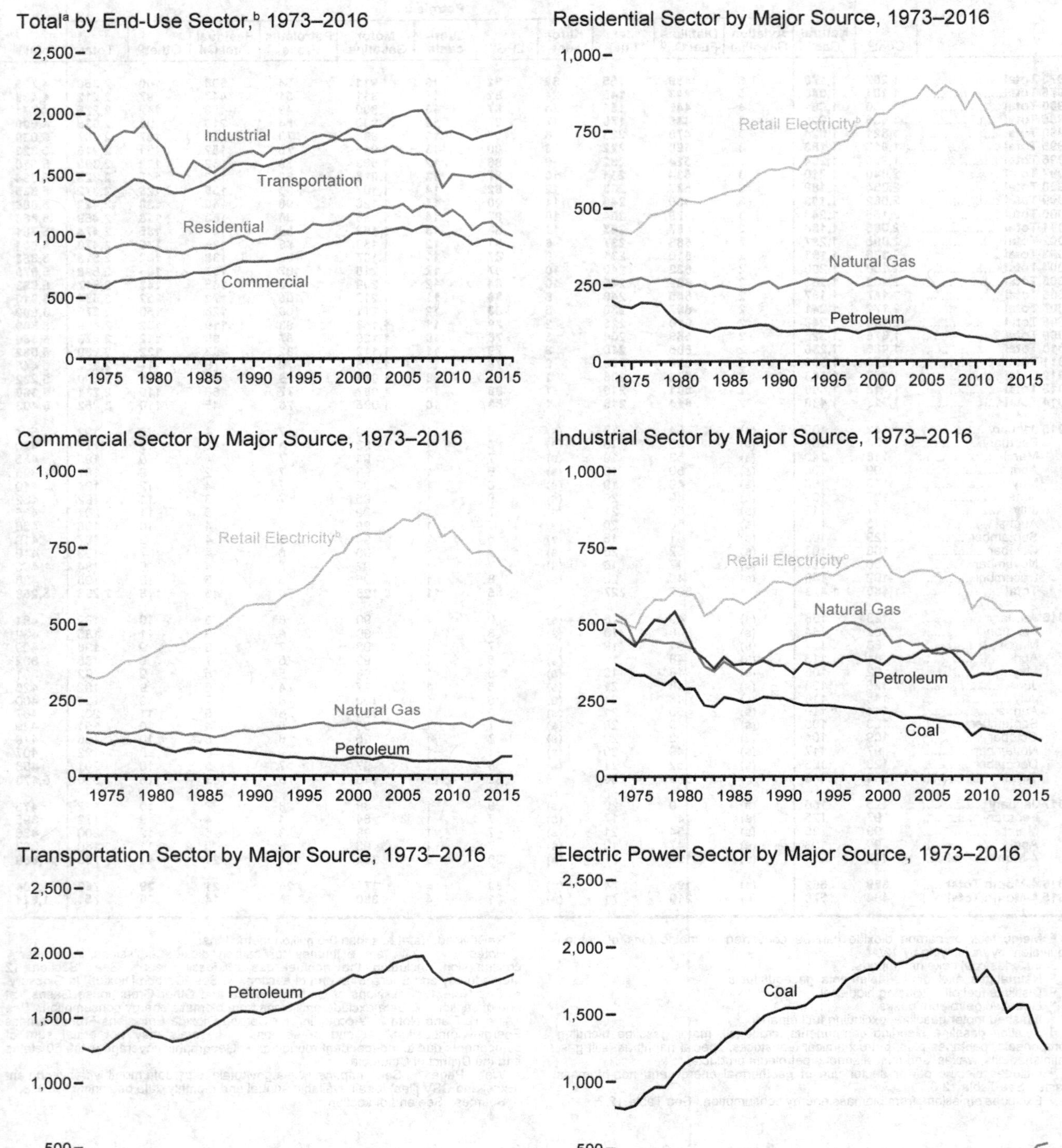

[a] Excludes emissions from biomass energy consumption.

[b] Emissions from energy consumption in the electric power sector are allocated to the end-use sectors in proportion to each sector's share of total electricity retail sales.

Web Page: http://www.eia.gov/totalenergy/data/monthly/#environment.

Sources: Tables 12.2–12.6.

Source: *U.S. Energy Information Administration, Monthly Energy Review, July 2017*

Table 12.2 Carbon Dioxide Emissions From Energy Consumption: Residential Sector

(Million Metric Tons of Carbon Dioxide[a])

	Coal	Natural Gas[b]	Petroleum				Retail Electricity[e]	Total[f]
			Distillate Fuel Oil[c]	Kerosene	LPG[d]	Total		
1973 Total	**9**	**264**	**147**	**16**	**36**	**199**	**435**	**907**
1975 Total	**6**	**266**	**132**	**12**	**32**	**176**	**419**	**867**
1980 Total	**3**	**256**	**96**	**8**	**20**	**124**	**529**	**911**
1985 Total	**4**	**241**	**80**	**11**	**20**	**111**	**553**	**909**
1990 Total	**3**	**238**	**72**	**5**	**22**	**98**	**624**	**963**
1995 Total	**2**	**263**	**66**	**5**	**25**	**96**	**678**	**1,039**
1996 Total	**2**	**284**	**68**	**6**	**30**	**104**	**710**	**1,099**
1997 Total	**2**	**270**	**64**	**7**	**29**	**99**	**719**	**1,090**
1998 Total	**1**	**247**	**56**	**8**	**27**	**91**	**759**	**1,097**
1999 Total	**1**	**257**	**60**	**8**	**33**	**102**	**762**	**1,122**
2000 Total	**1**	**271**	**66**	**7**	**35**	**108**	**805**	**1,185**
2001 Total	**1**	**259**	**66**	**7**	**33**	**106**	**805**	**1,171**
2002 Total	**1**	**265**	**63**	**4**	**34**	**101**	**835**	**1,203**
2003 Total	**1**	**276**	**68**	**5**	**34**	**108**	**847**	**1,232**
2004 Total	**1**	**264**	**67**	**6**	**32**	**106**	**856**	**1,227**
2005 Total	**1**	**262**	**62**	**6**	**32**	**101**	**897**	**1,261**
2006 Total	**1**	**237**	**52**	**5**	**28**	**85**	**869**	**1,191**
2007 Total	**1**	**257**	**53**	**3**	**31**	**86**	**897**	**1,241**
2008 Total	**NA**	**266**	**55**	**2**	**35**	**91**	**877**	**1,234**
2009 Total	**NA**	**259**	**43**	**2**	**35**	**79**	**819**	**1,157**
2010 Total	**NA**	**259**	**41**	**2**	**33**	**77**	**874**	**1,210**
2011 Total	**NA**	**255**	**38**	**1**	**31**	**70**	**823**	**1,148**
2012 Total	**NA**	**225**	**35**	**1**	**25**	**61**	**757**	**1,043**
2013 Total	**NA**	**267**	**36**	**1**	**30**	**66**	**768**	**1,100**
2014 Total	**NA**	**278**	**39**	**1**	**29**	**69**	**766**	**1,113**
2015 January	NA	51	6	(s)	3	8	72	132
February	NA	50	5	(s)	2	7	66	123
March	NA	35	4	(s)	2	6	57	98
April	NA	18	2	(s)	2	4	42	64
May	NA	10	2	(s)	2	5	49	63
June	NA	7	1	(s)	2	3	65	75
July	NA	6	2	(s)	2	4	81	90
August	NA	6	2	(s)	2	4	77	87
September	NA	6	2	(s)	2	4	64	74
October	NA	11	5	(s)	2	7	48	66
November	NA	22	5	(s)	2	7	44	74
December	NA	32	5	(s)	3	8	51	92
Total	**NA**	**253**	**40**	**1**	**27**	**68**	**714**	**1,035**
2016 January	NA	49	5	(s)	3	8	65	122
February	NA	38	5	(s)	2	7	52	98
March	NA	25	3	(s)	2	6	41	72
April	NA	18	3	(s)	2	5	38	61
May	NA	11	3	(s)	2	5	43	59
June	NA	7	2	(s)	2	4	66	77
July	NA	6	2	(s)	2	4	84	95
August	NA	6	2	(s)	2	4	84	93
September	NA	6	2	(s)	2	5	65	76
October	NA	10	3	(s)	2	6	50	66
November	NA	21	4	(s)	2	6	43	70
December	NA	44	6	(s)	2	8	62	115
Total	**NA**	**241**	**39**	**1**	**26**	**66**	**690**	**998**
2017 January	NA	46	6	(s)	3	8	63	117
February	NA	32	4	(s)	2	6	45	83
March	NA	32	4	(s)	2	6	46	84
April	NA	15	3	(s)	2	5	40	60
4-Month Total	**NA**	**125**	**17**	**(s)**	**9**	**26**	**194**	**345**
2016 4-Month Total	**NA**	**130**	**16**	**(s)**	**9**	**26**	**197**	**353**
2015 4-Month Total	**NA**	**153**	**16**	**(s)**	**9**	**26**	**237**	**416**

[a] Metric tons of carbon dioxide can be converted to metric tons of carbon equivalent by multiplying by 12/44.
[b] Natural gas, excluding supplemental gaseous fuels.
[c] Distillate fuel oil, excluding biodiesel.
[d] Liquefied petroleum gases.
[e] Emissions from energy consumption (for electricity and a small amount of useful thermal output) in the electric power sector are allocated to the end-use sectors in proportion to each sector's share of total electricity retail sales. See Tables 7.6 and 12.6.
[f] Excludes emissions from biomass energy consumption. See Table 12.7.
NA=Not available. (s)=Less than 0.5 million metric tons.

Notes: • Data are estimates for carbon dioxide emissions from energy consumption. See "Section 12 Methodology and Sources" at end of section. • See "Carbon Dioxide" in Glossary. • See Note 1, "Emissions of Carbon Dioxide and Other Greenhouse Gases," at end of section. • Data exclude emissions from biomass energy consumption. See Table 12.7 and Note 2, "Accounting for Carbon Dioxide Emissions From Biomass Energy Combustion," at end of section. • Totals may not equal sum of components due to independent rounding. • Geographic coverage is the 50 states and the District of Columbia.

Web Page: See http://www.eia.gov/totalenergy/data/monthly/#environment (Excel and CSV files) for all available annual and monthly data beginning in 1973.

Sources: See end of section.

Source: *U.S. Energy Information Administration, Monthly Energy Review, July 2017*

Table 12.3 Carbon Dioxide Emissions From Energy Consumption: Commercial Sector

(Million Metric Tons of Carbon Dioxide[a])

	Coal	Natural Gas[b]	Petroleum: Distillate Fuel Oil[c]	Petroleum: Kerosene	Petroleum: LPG[d]	Petroleum: Motor Gasoline[e]	Petroleum: Petroleum Coke	Petroleum: Residual Fuel Oil	Petroleum: Total	Retail Electricity[f]	Total[g]
1973 Total	15	141	47	5	9	6	NA	52	120	334	609
1975 Total	14	136	43	4	8	6	NA	39	100	333	583
1980 Total	11	141	38	3	6	8	NA	44	98	412	662
1985 Total	13	132	46	2	6	7	NA	18	79	480	704
1990 Total	12	142	39	1	6	8	0	18	73	566	793
1995 Total	11	164	35	2	7	1	(s)	11	56	620	851
1996 Total	12	171	35	2	8	2	(s)	11	57	643	883
1997 Total	12	174	32	2	8	3	(s)	9	54	686	926
1998 Total	9	164	31	2	7	3	(s)	7	50	724	947
1999 Total	10	165	32	2	9	2	(s)	6	51	735	960
2000 Total	9	173	36	2	9	3	(s)	7	58	783	1,022
2001 Total	9	164	37	2	9	3	(s)	6	57	797	1,027
2002 Total	9	170	32	1	9	3	(s)	6	52	795	1,026
2003 Total	8	173	36	1	10	4	(s)	9	60	796	1,037
2004 Total	10	170	34	1	10	3	(s)	10	58	815	1,053
2005 Total	9	163	33	2	8	3	(s)	9	55	841	1,069
2006 Total	6	154	29	1	8	3	(s)	6	47	835	1,043
2007 Total	7	164	28	1	8	4	(s)	6	46	861	1,078
2008 Total	8	171	28	(s)	10	3	(s)	6	47	849	1,075
2009 Total	7	169	29	(s)	9	4	(s)	6	47	784	1,007
2010 Total	7	168	29	(s)	9	3	(s)	5	46	804	1,025
2011 Total	6	171	29	(s)	9	3	(s)	4	45	768	990
2012 Total	4	157	26	(s)	9	3	(s)	2	40	731	932
2013 Total	4	179	25	(s)	10	3	(s)	2	40	736	959
2014 Total	4	190	26	(s)	10	4	(s)	1	40	736	970
2015 January	(s)	29	4	(s)	1	2	(s)	(s)	7	59	95
February	(s)	28	3	(s)	1	2	(s)	(s)	6	56	91
March	(s)	21	2	(s)	1	2	(s)	(s)	5	52	79
April	(s)	13	1	(s)	1	2	(s)	(s)	4	48	65
May	(s)	9	1	(s)	1	2	(s)	(s)	4	56	69
June	(s)	7	1	(s)	1	2	0	(s)	4	65	76
July	(s)	7	1	(s)	1	2	0	(s)	4	71	82
August	(s)	7	1	(s)	1	2	(s)	(s)	4	69	81
September	(s)	8	1	(s)	1	2	(s)	(s)	4	62	74
October	(s)	11	3	(s)	1	2	(s)	(s)	6	55	72
November	(s)	16	3	(s)	1	2	(s)	(s)	6	50	72
December	(s)	19	4	(s)	1	2	(s)	(s)	7	49	75
Total	3	176	26	(s)	9	25	(s)	(s)	61	692	932
2016 January	(s)	28	3	(s)	1	2	(s)	(s)	6	55	89
February	(s)	23	3	(s)	1	2	(s)	(s)	6	47	76
March	(s)	16	2	(s)	1	2	(s)	(s)	5	43	65
April	(s)	13	2	(s)	1	2	(s)	(s)	5	43	61
May	(s)	9	2	(s)	1	2	0	(s)	5	50	64
June	(s)	8	1	(s)	1	2	(s)	(s)	4	63	75
July	(s)	7	1	(s)	1	2	(s)	(s)	4	71	83
August	(s)	8	1	(s)	1	2	0	(s)	4	72	84
September	(s)	8	2	(s)	1	2	0	(s)	4	62	74
October	(s)	11	2	(s)	1	2	0	(s)	5	55	71
November	(s)	R 15	2	(s)	1	2	(s)	(s)	5	49	69
December	(s)	R 25	4	(s)	1	2	(s)	(s)	7	57	89
Total	2	R 171	26	(s)	9	26	(s)	(s)	61	667	902
2017 January	(s)	26	4	(s)	1	2	(s)	(s)	7	54	87
February	(s)	20	3	(s)	1	2	(s)	(s)	5	44	69
March	(s)	20	3	(s)	1	2	(s)	(s)	6	48	74
April	(s)	12	2	(s)	1	2	(s)	(s)	5	44	61
4-Month Total	1	78	11	(s)	3	8	(s)	(s)	22	190	291
2016 4-Month Total	1	80	11	(s)	3	8	(s)	(s)	22	188	291
2015 4-Month Total	1	92	11	(s)	3	8	(s)	(s)	22	215	330

[a] Metric tons of carbon dioxide can be converted to metric tons of carbon equivalent by multiplying by 12/44.
[b] Natural gas, excluding supplemental gaseous fuels.
[c] Distillate fuel oil, excluding biodiesel.
[d] Liquefied petroleum gases.
[e] Finished motor gasoline, excluding fuel ethanol.
[f] Emissions from energy consumption (for electricity and a small amount of useful thermal output) in the electric power sector are allocated to the end-use sectors in proportion to each sector's share of total electricity retail sales. See Tables 7.6 and 12.6.
[g] Excludes emissions from biomass energy consumption. See Table 12.7.
R=Revised. NA=Not available. (s)=Less than 0.5 million metric tons.

Notes: • Data are estimates for carbon dioxide emissions from energy consumption. See "Section 12 Methodology and Sources" at end of section. • See "Carbon Dioxide" in Glossary. • See Note 1, "Emissions of Carbon Dioxide and Other Greenhouse Gases," at end of section. • Data exclude emissions from biomass energy consumption. See Table 12.7 and Note 2, "Accounting for Carbon Dioxide Emissions From Biomass Energy Combustion," at end of section. • Totals may not equal sum of components due to independent rounding. • Geographic coverage is the 50 states and the District of Columbia.

Web Page: See http://www.eia.gov/totalenergy/data/monthly/#environment (Excel and CSV files) for all available annual and monthly data beginning in 1973.

Sources: See end of section.

Source: *U.S. Energy Information Administration, Monthly Energy Review, July 2017*

Table 12.4 Carbon Dioxide Emissions From Energy Consumption: Industrial Sector

(Million Metric Tons of Carbon Dioxide[a])

	Coal	Coal Coke Net Imports	Natural Gas[b]	Petroleum									Retail Elec-tricity[g]	Total[h]
				Distillate Fuel Oil[c]	Kero-sene	LPG[d]	Lubri-cants	Motor Gasoline[e]	Petroleum Coke	Residual Fuel Oil	Other[f]	Total		
1973 Total	**371**	**-1**	**536**	**106**	**11**	**44**	**7**	**18**	**52**	**144**	**100**	**483**	**515**	**1,904**
1975 Total	**336**	**2**	**440**	**97**	**9**	**39**	**6**	**16**	**51**	**117**	**97**	**431**	**490**	**1,697**
1980 Total	**289**	**-4**	**429**	**96**	**13**	**61**	**7**	**11**	**48**	**105**	**142**	**483**	**601**	**1,798**
1985 Total	**256**	**-2**	**360**	**81**	**3**	**59**	**6**	**15**	**54**	**57**	**93**	**369**	**583**	**1,566**
1990 Total	**258**	**1**	**432**	**84**	**1**	**37**	**7**	**13**	**67**	**31**	**127**	**366**	**638**	**1,695**
1995 Total	**233**	**7**	**489**	**82**	**1**	**47**	**7**	**14**	**67**	**25**	**121**	**364**	**659**	**1,751**
1996 Total	**227**	**3**	**505**	**86**	**1**	**48**	**6**	**14**	**71**	**24**	**139**	**391**	**678**	**1,803**
1997 Total	**224**	**5**	**505**	**88**	**1**	**50**	**7**	**15**	**70**	**21**	**145**	**396**	**694**	**1,824**
1998 Total	**219**	**8**	**495**	**88**	**2**	**47**	**7**	**14**	**80**	**16**	**128**	**382**	**706**	**1,809**
1999 Total	**208**	**7**	**475**	**86**	**1**	**47**	**7**	**11**	**85**	**14**	**133**	**383**	**704**	**1,778**
2000 Total	**211**	**7**	**483**	**87**	**1**	**52**	**7**	**11**	**76**	**17**	**118**	**369**	**719**	**1,788**
2001 Total	**204**	**3**	**440**	**95**	**2**	**45**	**6**	**21**	**79**	**14**	**135**	**396**	**667**	**1,711**
2002 Total	**188**	**7**	**448**	**88**	**1**	**47**	**6**	**22**	**79**	**13**	**130**	**386**	**654**	**1,683**
2003 Total	**190**	**6**	**432**	**85**	**2**	**41**	**6**	**23**	**78**	**16**	**142**	**392**	**672**	**1,692**
2004 Total	**191**	**16**	**437**	**88**	**2**	**44**	**6**	**26**	**85**	**18**	**144**	**413**	**674**	**1,731**
2005 Total	**183**	**5**	**405**	**92**	**3**	**42**	**6**	**25**	**82**	**20**	**143**	**413**	**672**	**1,678**
2006 Total	**179**	**7**	**404**	**91**	**2**	**43**	**6**	**26**	**85**	**16**	**152**	**422**	**650**	**1,662**
2007 Total	**175**	**3**	**414**	**91**	**1**	**43**	**6**	**21**	**83**	**13**	**150**	**408**	**662**	**1,661**
2008 Total	**168**	**5**	**412**	**98**	**(s)**	**32**	**6**	**17**	**78**	**13**	**132**	**376**	**642**	**1,602**
2009 Total	**131**	**-3**	**386**	**78**	**(s)**	**33**	**5**	**16**	**73**	**8**	**112**	**325**	**550**	**1,390**
2010 Total	**153**	**-1**	**421**	**84**	**1**	**35**	**6**	**17**	**68**	**6**	**122**	**338**	**587**	**1,498**
2011 Total	**146**	**1**	**431**	**90**	**(s)**	**36**	**5**	**17**	**65**	**6**	**117**	**337**	**574**	**1,489**
2012 Total	**141**	**(s)**	**447**	**93**	**(s)**	**45**	**5**	**17**	**70**	**3**	**113**	**346**	**543**	**1,477**
2013 Total	**144**	**-2**	**463**	**92**	**(s)**	**46**	**5**	**17**	**65**	**2**	**119**	**347**	**542**	**1,495**
2014 Total	**143**	**-2**	**478**	**100**	**(s)**	**42**	**5**	**14**	**64**	**2**	**110**	**337**	**543**	**1,498**
2015 January	12	(s)	45	9	(s)	5	1	1	6	(s)	8	31	42	130
February	11	(s)	41	10	(s)	5	(s)	1	2	(s)	9	28	41	121
March	11	(s)	42	9	(s)	4	1	1	6	(s)	9	30	39	122
April	10	(s)	39	8	(s)	3	1	1	6	(s)	9	29	37	115
May	11	(s)	39	6	(s)	3	1	1	6	(s)	12	29	42	121
June	11	(s)	37	7	(s)	4	(s)	1	6	(s)	11	30	47	124
July	11	(s)	38	7	(s)	4	1	2	6	(s)	11	30	48	127
August	11	(s)	39	6	(s)	4	(s)	2	7	(s)	10	28	47	125
September	10	(s)	37	8	(s)	3	(s)	1	4	(s)	9	26	43	117
October	11	(s)	39	6	(s)	4	1	1	5	(s)	7	24	40	114
November	10	(s)	40	4	(s)	4	(s)	1	5	(s)	9	24	38	112
December	10	(s)	42	5	(s)	5	(s)	1	4	(s)	10	27	36	115
Total	**129**	**-2**	**478**	**85**	**(s)**	**47**	**6**	**17**	**65**	**2**	**115**	**337**	**502**	**1,444**
2016 January	10	(s)	45	8	(s)	5	(s)	1	6	(s)	10	30	38	122
February	10	(s)	41	8	(s)	5	(s)	1	5	(s)	11	31	33	R 116
March	10	(s)	42	8	(s)	4	1	1	6	(s)	9	29	31	112
April	9	(s)	39	7	(s)	3	(s)	1	4	(s)	9	25	32	106
May	9	(s)	39	6	(s)	3	(s)	1	4	(s)	9	24	36	108
June	9	(s)	38	6	(s)	3	1	1	3	(s)	9	24	42	113
July	9	(s)	39	4	(s)	3	(s)	2	5	(s)	9	23	46	117
August	9	(s)	40	7	(s)	3	(s)	2	7	(s)	11	30	46	124
September	9	(s)	38	7	(s)	4	(s)	1	4	(s)	10	27	40	114
October	9	(s)	39	8	(s)	4	(s)	1	5	(s)	10	29	38	115
November	9	-1	41	8	(s)	4	(s)	1	8	(s)	8	29	35	114
December	10	(s)	45	7	(s)	5	(s)	1	6	(s)	10	30	39	123
Total	**113**	**-2**	**487**	**83**	**(s)**	**45**	**5**	**17**	**63**	**2**	**115**	**331**	**459**	**1,388**
2017 January	R 9	(s)	45	7	(s)	6	(s)	1	7	(s)	10	31	37	R 122
February	9	(s)	40	7	(s)	4	(s)	1	4	(s)	9	25	32	106
March	9	(s)	43	10	(s)	4	(s)	1	2	(s)	12	30	34	116
April	8	(s)	39	6	(s)	4	(s)	1	5	(s)	11	29	33	109
4-Month Total	**36**	**-1**	**167**	**30**	**(s)**	**17**	**2**	**6**	**18**	**1**	**42**	**115**	**136**	**453**
2016 4-Month Total	**38**	**(s)**	**167**	**30**	**(s)**	**17**	**2**	**6**	**21**	**1**	**39**	**116**	**135**	**456**
2015 4-Month Total	**45**	**-1**	**166**	**36**	**(s)**	**17**	**2**	**5**	**21**	**(s)**	**36**	**118**	**159**	**487**

[a] Metric tons of carbon dioxide can be converted to metric tons of carbon equivalent by multiplying by 12/44.

[b] Natural gas, excluding supplemental gaseous fuels.

[c] Distillate fuel oil, excluding biodiesel.

[d] Liquefied petroleum gases.

[e] Finished motor gasoline, excluding fuel ethanol.

[f] Aviation gasoline blending components, crude oil, motor gasoline blending components, pentanes plus, petrochemical feedstocks, special naphthas, still gas, unfinished oils, waxes, and miscellaneous petroleum products.

[g] Emissions from energy consumption (for electricity and a small amount of useful thermal output) in the electric power sector are allocated to the end-use sectors in proportion to each sector's share of total electricity retail sales. See Tables 7.6 and 12.6.

[h] Excludes emissions from biomass energy consumption. See Table 12.7.

R=Revised. (s)=Less than 0.5 million metric tons and greater than -0.5 million metric tons.

Notes: • Data are estimates for carbon dioxide emissions from energy consumption, including the nonfuel use of fossil fuels. See "Section 12 Methodology and Sources" at end of section. • See "Carbon Dioxide" in Glossary. • See Note 1, "Emissions of Carbon Dioxide and Other Greenhouse Gases," at end of section. • Data exclude emissions from biomass energy consumption. See Table 12.7 and Note 2, "Accounting for Carbon Dioxide Emissions From Biomass Energy Combustion," at end of section. • Totals may not equal sum of components due to independent rounding. • Geographic coverage is the 50 states and the District of Columbia.

Web Page: See http://www.eia.gov/totalenergy/data/monthly/#environment (Excel and CSV files) for all available annual and monthly data beginning in 1973.

Sources: See end of section.

Source: *U.S. Energy Information Administration, Monthly Energy Review, July 2017*

Table 12.5 Carbon Dioxide Emissions From Energy Consumption: Transportation Sector

(Million Metric Tons of Carbon Dioxide[a])

	Coal	Natural Gas[b]	Petroleum								Retail Electricity[f]	Total[g]
			Aviation Gasoline	Distillate Fuel Oil[c]	Jet Fuel	LPG[d]	Lubricants	Motor Gasoline[e]	Residual Fuel Oil	Total		
1973 Total	(s)	39	6	163	152	3	6	886	57	1,273	2	1,315
1975 Total	(s)	32	5	155	145	3	6	889	56	1,258	2	1,292
1980 Total	(h)	34	4	204	155	1	6	881	110	1,363	2	1,400
1985 Total	(h)	28	3	232	178	2	6	908	62	1,391	3	1,421
1990 Total	(h)	36	3	268	223	1	7	967	80	1,548	3	1,588
1995 Total	(h)	38	3	307	222	1	6	1,029	72	1,640	3	1,681
1996 Total	(h)	39	3	327	232	1	6	1,047	67	1,683	3	1,725
1997 Total	(h)	41	3	341	234	1	6	1,057	56	1,700	3	1,744
1998 Total	(h)	35	2	352	238	1	7	1,090	53	1,743	3	1,782
1999 Total	(h)	36	3	365	245	1	7	1,115	52	1,789	3	1,828
2000 Total	(h)	36	3	377	254	1	7	1,122	70	1,833	4	1,873
2001 Total	(h)	35	2	387	243	1	6	1,128	46	1,813	4	1,852
2002 Total	(h)	37	2	394	237	1	6	1,158	53	1,852	4	1,892
2003 Total	(h)	33	2	408	231	1	6	1,161	45	1,854	5	1,892
2004 Total	(h)	32	2	433	240	1	6	1,181	58	1,922	5	1,959
2005 Total	(h)	33	2	444	246	2	6	1,182	66	1,948	5	1,986
2006 Total	(h)	33	2	467	240	2	5	1,188	71	1,976	5	2,014
2007 Total	(h)	35	2	469	238	1	6	1,186	78	1,980	5	2,021
2008 Total	(h)	37	2	424	226	3	5	1,124	73	1,856	5	1,898
2009 Total	(h)	38	2	405	204	2	5	1,109	62	1,789	5	1,832
2010 Total	(h)	38	2	426	210	2	5	1,091	70	1,806	5	1,849
2011 Total	(h)	39	2	437	209	2	5	1,058	61	1,774	4	1,818
2012 Total	(h)	41	2	416	206	2	5	1,051	53	1,735	4	1,780
2013 Total	(h)	47	2	424	210	3	5	1,066	46	1,756	4	1,807
2014 Total	(h)	40	2	443	216	3	5	1,077	35	1,781	4	1,825
2015 January	(h)	4	(s)	35	17	(s)	1	87	3	143	(s)	148
February	(h)	4	(s)	34	16	(s)	(s)	80	(s)	131	(s)	136
March	(h)	4	(s)	37	19	(s)	1	91	3	152	(s)	156
April	(h)	3	(s)	38	18	(s)	(s)	89	2	148	(s)	152
May	(h)	3	(s)	38	19	(s)	1	93	3	154	(s)	157
June	(h)	3	(s)	39	20	(s)	(s)	91	2	153	(s)	157
July	(h)	3	(s)	41	21	(s)	1	95	4	161	(s)	164
August	(h)	3	(s)	41	20	(s)	(s)	95	4	160	(s)	163
September	(h)	3	(s)	39	18	(s)	(s)	90	3	151	(s)	154
October	(h)	3	(s)	38	20	(s)	(s)	93	3	155	(s)	158
November	(h)	3	(s)	34	18	(s)	(s)	88	4	145	(s)	149
December	(h)	4	(s)	35	20	(s)	(s)	92	4	151	(s)	155
Total	(h)	**39**	**1**	**449**	**227**	**3**	**5**	**1,083**	**37**	**1,806**	**4**	**1,848**
2016 January	(h)	4	(s)	33	18	(s)	(s)	87	4	143	(s)	148
February	(h)	4	(s)	32	18	(s)	(s)	86	2	139	(s)	143
March	(h)	3	(s)	36	19	(s)	(s)	94	5	156	(s)	159
April	(h)	3	(s)	36	19	(s)	(s)	89	6	151	(s)	154
May	(h)	3	(s)	38	19	(s)	(s)	95	4	157	(s)	160
June	(h)	3	(s)	38	21	(s)	(s)	94	5	158	(s)	161
July	(h)	3	(s)	38	21	(s)	(s)	96	6	162	(s)	166
August	(h)	3	(s)	40	21	(s)	(s)	96	4	162	(s)	166
September	(h)	3	(s)	37	20	(s)	(s)	92	4	153	(s)	156
October	(h)	3	(s)	38	20	(s)	(s)	91	4	155	(s)	158
November	(h)	3	(s)	35	20	(s)	(s)	89	5	150	(s)	153
December	(h)	4	(s)	35	21	(s)	(s)	93	4	154	(s)	158
Total	(h)	**39**	**1**	**437**	**236**	**2**	**5**	**1,102**	**55**	**1,840**	**4**	**1,883**
2017 January	(h)	4	(s)	32	20	(s)	(s)	85	6	144	(s)	149
February	(h)	3	(s)	31	17	(s)	(s)	81	3	133	(s)	137
March	(h)	4	(s)	37	21	(s)	(s)	94	5	157	(s)	161
April	(h)	3	(s)	36	19	(s)	(s)	90	4	149	(s)	152
4-Month Total	(h)	**14**	**(s)**	**136**	**77**	**1**	**2**	**350**	**18**	**584**	**1**	**599**
2016 4-Month Total	(h)	**14**	**(s)**	**137**	**74**	**1**	**2**	**357**	**18**	**589**	**1**	**604**
2015 4-Month Total	(h)	**15**	**(s)**	**145**	**71**	**1**	**2**	**347**	**9**	**575**	**1**	**591**

[a] Metric tons of carbon dioxide can be converted to metric tons of carbon equivalent by multiplying by 12/44.
[b] Natural gas, excluding supplemental gaseous fuels.
[c] Distillate fuel oil, excluding biodiesel.
[d] Liquefied petroleum gases.
[e] Finished motor gasoline, excluding fuel ethanol.
[f] Emissions from energy consumption (for electricity and a small amount of useful thermal output) in the electric power sector are allocated to the end-use sectors in proportion to each sector's share of total electricity retail sales. See Tables 7.6 and 12.6.
[g] Excludes emissions from biomass energy consumption. See Table 12.7.
[h] Beginning in 1978, the small amounts of coal consumed for transportation are reported as industrial sector consumption.

(s)=Less than 0.5 million metric tons.

Notes: • Data are estimates for carbon dioxide emissions from energy consumption, including the nonfuel use of fossil fuels. See "Section 12 Methodology and Sources" at end of section. • See "Carbon Dioxide" in Glossary. • See Note 1, "Emissions of Carbon Dioxide and Other Greenhouse Gases," at end of section. • Data exclude emissions from biomass energy consumption. See Table 12.7 and Note 2, "Accounting for Carbon Dioxide Emissions From Biomass Energy Combustion," at end of section. • Totals may not equal sum of components due to independent rounding. • Geographic coverage is the 50 states and the District of Columbia.

Web Page: See http://www.eia.gov/totalenergy/data/monthly/#environment (Excel and CSV files) for all available annual and monthly data beginning in 1973.

Sources: See end of section.

Source: *U.S. Energy Information Administration, Monthly Energy Review, July 2017*

Table 12.6 Carbon Dioxide Emissions From Energy Consumption: Electric Power Sector

(Million Metric Tons of Carbon Dioxide[a])

	Coal	Natural Gas[b]	Petroleum				Geo-thermal	Non-Biomass Waste[d]	Total[e]
			Distillate Fuel Oil[c]	Petroleum Coke	Residual Fuel Oil	Total			
1973 Total	812	199	20	2	254	276	NA	NA	1,286
1975 Total	824	172	17	(s)	231	248	NA	NA	1,244
1980 Total	1,137	200	12	1	194	207	NA	NA	1,544
1985 Total	1,367	166	6	1	79	86	NA	NA	1,619
1990 Total	1,548	176	7	3	92	102	(s)	6	1,831
1995 Total	1,661	228	8	8	45	61	(s)	10	1,960
1996 Total	1,752	205	8	8	50	66	(s)	10	2,033
1997 Total	1,797	219	8	10	56	75	(s)	10	2,101
1998 Total	1,828	248	10	13	82	105	(s)	10	2,192
1999 Total	1,836	260	10	11	76	97	(s)	10	2,204
2000 Total	1,927	281	13	10	69	91	(s)	10	2,310
2001 Total	1,870	290	12	11	79	102	(s)	11	2,273
2002 Total	1,890	306	9	18	52	79	(s)	13	2,288
2003 Total	1,931	278	12	18	69	98	(s)	11	2,319
2004 Total	1,943	297	8	22	69	99	(s)	11	2,350
2005 Total	1,984	319	8	24	69	101	(s)	11	2,416
2006 Total	1,954	338	5	21	28	55	(s)	12	2,358
2007 Total	1,987	372	6	17	31	54	(s)	11	2,425
2008 Total	1,959	362	5	15	19	39	(s)	12	2,373
2009 Total	1,741	373	5	13	14	33	(s)	11	2,158
2010 Total	1,828	399	6	14	12	32	(s)	11	2,270
2011 Total	1,723	409	5	14	7	26	(s)	11	2,170
2012 Total	1,511	493	4	9	6	19	(s)	11	2,034
2013 Total	1,571	444	4	13	6	23	(s)	11	2,050
2014 Total	1,569	444	6	12	7	26	(s)	11	2,050
2015 January	130	39	1	1	1	3	(s)	1	173
February	123	36	2	1	2	5	(s)	1	164
March	107	39	(s)	1	(s)	2	(s)	1	148
April	89	36	(s)	1	(s)	1	(s)	1	127
May	104	40	(s)	1	(s)	2	(s)	1	147
June	126	49	(s)	1	(s)	2	(s)	1	177
July	140	57	(s)	1	1	2	(s)	1	200
August	135	56	(s)	1	1	2	(s)	1	194
September	118	49	(s)	1	(s)	2	(s)	1	170
October	98	43	(s)	1	(s)	2	(s)	1	144
November	89	40	(s)	1	(s)	2	(s)	1	132
December	92	42	(s)	1	(s)	1	(s)	1	136
Total	1,350	527	5	11	7	24	(s)	11	1,913
2016 January	114	42	(s)	1	1	2	(s)	1	159
February	93	38	(s)	1	1	2	(s)	1	133
March	73	41	(s)	1	(s)	2	(s)	1	116
April	71	39	(s)	1	(s)	2	(s)	1	114
May	82	44	(s)	1	(s)	2	(s)	1	129
June	116	53	(s)	1	(s)	2	(s)	1	172
July	136	63	(s)	1	1	2	(s)	1	201
August	135	63	(s)	1	1	2	(s)	1	201
September	114	50	(s)	1	(s)	2	(s)	1	167
October	100	41	(s)	1	(s)	1	(s)	1	143
November	88	36	(s)	1	(s)	2	(s)	1	127
December	119	37	(s)	1	(s)	2	(s)	1	158
Total	1,241	546	4	12	5	21	(s)	11	1,821
2017 January	116	35	(s)	1	(s)	2	(s)	1	154
February	88	30	(s)	1	(s)	1	(s)	1	121
March	90	37	(s)	1	(s)	1	(s)	1	129
April	81	34	(s)	(s)	(s)	1	(s)	1	117
4-Month Total	376	135	1	3	2	6	(s)	4	520
2016 4-Month Total	350	160	1	4	2	7	(s)	4	521
2015 4-Month Total	448	150	3	4	4	10	(s)	4	612

[a] Metric tons of carbon dioxide can be converted to metric tons of carbon equivalent by multiplying by 12/44.

[b] Natural gas, excluding supplemental gaseous fuels.

[c] Distillate fuel oil, excluding biodiesel.

[d] Municipal solid waste from non-biogenic sources, and tire-derived fuels. Through 1994, also includes blast furnace gas, and other manufactured and waste gases derived from fossil fuels.

[e] Excludes emissions from biomass energy consumption. See Table 12.7.

NA=Not available. (s)=Less than 0.5 million metric tons.

Notes: • Data are estimates for carbon dioxide emissions from energy consumption. See "Section 12 Methodology and Sources" at end of section. • See "Carbon Dioxide" in Glossary. • See Note 1, "Emissions of Carbon Dioxide and Other Greenhouse Gases," at end of section. • Data exclude emissions from biomass energy consumption. See Table 12.7 and Note 2, "Accounting for Carbon Dioxide Emissions From Biomass Energy Combustion," at end of section. • Totals may not equal sum of components due to independent rounding. • Geographic coverage is the 50 states and the District of Columbia.

Web Page: See http://www.eia.gov/totalenergy/data/monthly/#environment (Excel and CSV files) for all available annual and monthly data beginning in 1973.

Sources: See end of section.

Source: U.S. Energy Information Administration, Monthly Energy Review, July 2017

Table 12.7 Carbon Dioxide Emissions From Biomass Energy Consumption

(Million Metric Tons of Carbon Dioxide[a])

	By Source					By Sector					
	Wood[b]	Biomass Waste[c]	Fuel Ethanol[d]	Bio-diesel	Total	Resi-dential	Com-mercial[e]	Indus-trial[f]	Trans-portation	Electric Power[g]	Total
1973 Total	**143**	**(s)**	**NA**	**NA**	**143**	**33**	**1**	**109**	**NA**	**(s)**	**143**
1975 Total	**140**	**(s)**	**NA**	**NA**	**141**	**40**	**1**	**100**	**NA**	**(s)**	**141**
1980 Total	**232**	**(s)**	**NA**	**NA**	**232**	**80**	**2**	**150**	**NA**	**(s)**	**232**
1985 Total	**252**	**14**	**3**	**NA**	**270**	**95**	**2**	**168**	**3**	**1**	**270**
1990 Total	**208**	**24**	**4**	**NA**	**237**	**54**	**8**	**147**	**4**	**23**	**237**
1995 Total	**222**	**30**	**8**	**NA**	**260**	**49**	**9**	**166**	**8**	**28**	**260**
1996 Total	**229**	**32**	**6**	**NA**	**266**	**51**	**10**	**170**	**6**	**30**	**266**
1997 Total	**222**	**30**	**7**	**NA**	**259**	**40**	**10**	**172**	**7**	**30**	**259**
1998 Total	**205**	**30**	**8**	**NA**	**242**	**36**	**9**	**160**	**8**	**30**	**242**
1999 Total	**208**	**29**	**8**	**NA**	**245**	**37**	**9**	**161**	**8**	**30**	**245**
2000 Total	**212**	**27**	**9**	**NA**	**248**	**39**	**9**	**161**	**9**	**29**	**248**
2001 Total	**188**	**33**	**10**	**(s)**	**231**	**35**	**9**	**147**	**10**	**31**	**231**
2002 Total	**187**	**36**	**12**	**(s)**	**235**	**36**	**9**	**144**	**12**	**35**	**235**
2003 Total	**188**	**36**	**16**	**(s)**	**240**	**38**	**9**	**141**	**16**	**37**	**240**
2004 Total	**199**	**35**	**20**	**(s)**	**255**	**38**	**10**	**151**	**20**	**36**	**255**
2005 Total	**200**	**37**	**23**	**1**	**261**	**40**	**10**	**150**	**23**	**37**	**261**
2006 Total	**197**	**36**	**31**	**2**	**266**	**36**	**9**	**151**	**33**	**38**	**266**
2007 Total	**196**	**37**	**39**	**3**	**276**	**39**	**9**	**146**	**41**	**39**	**276**
2008 Total	**193**	**39**	**55**	**3**	**290**	**44**	**10**	**139**	**57**	**40**	**290**
2009 Total	**181**	**41**	**62**	**3**	**287**	**47**	**10**	**125**	**64**	**41**	**287**
2010 Total	**186**	**42**	**73**	**2**	**303**	**41**	**10**	**136**	**74**	**42**	**303**
2011 Total	**189**	**42**	**73**	**8**	**312**	**42**	**11**	**139**	**80**	**40**	**312**
2012 Total	**189**	**42**	**73**	**8**	**312**	**39**	**10**	**141**	**80**	**42**	**312**
2013 Total	**204**	**45**	**75**	**13**	**337**	**54**	**11**	**141**	**87**	**43**	**337**
2014 Total	**210**	**47**	**76**	**13**	**346**	**55**	**12**	**142**	**88**	**49**	**346**
2015 January	17	4	6	(s)	28	4	1	12	6	4	28
February	15	3	6	1	26	3	1	11	7	4	26
March	16	4	7	1	28	4	1	12	7	4	28
April	16	4	6	1	27	3	1	12	7	4	27
May	16	4	7	1	28	4	1	12	8	4	28
June	16	4	7	2	28	3	1	12	8	4	28
July	17	4	7	1	29	4	1	12	8	4	29
August	17	4	7	1	29	4	1	12	8	4	29
September	16	4	7	1	28	3	1	11	8	4	28
October	16	4	7	1	28	4	1	12	8	4	28
November	16	4	7	1	28	3	1	12	7	4	28
December	17	4	7	1	29	4	1	12	8	4	29
Total	**194**	**47**	**79**	**14**	**334**	**41**	**14**	**141**	**90**	**48**	**334**
2016 January	16	4	6	1	27	3	1	12	7	4	27
February	15	4	6	1	26	3	1	11	7	4	26
March	15	4	7	1	28	3	1	11	8	4	28
April	14	4	6	1	26	3	1	11	7	4	26
May	15	4	7	2	28	3	1	11	8	4	28
June	15	4	7	2	28	3	1	12	8	4	28
July	16	4	7	2	29	3	1	12	9	4	29
August	16	4	7	2	29	3	1	12	9	4	29
September	15	4	7	2	27	3	1	11	8	4	27
October	15	4	7	2	27	3	1	11	8	4	27
November	15	4	7	2	28	3	1	12	8	4	28
December	16	4	7	2	29	3	1	12	9	4	29
Total	**184**	**47**	**81**	**19**	**332**	**35**	**14**	**138**	**98**	**47**	**332**
2017 January	16	4	6	1	27	3	1	12	7	4	27
February	15	4	6	1	25	3	1	11	7	4	25
March	16	4	7	1	28	3	1	12	8	4	28
April	15	4	7	2	27	3	1	11	8	4	27
4-Month Total	**61**	**16**	**26**	**5**	**108**	**12**	**5**	**46**	**30**	**15**	**108**
2016 4-Month Total	**61**	**16**	**26**	**5**	**107**	**12**	**5**	**46**	**30**	**16**	**107**
2015 4-Month Total	**64**	**15**	**25**	**3**	**108**	**14**	**4**	**47**	**27**	**16**	**108**

[a] Metric tons of carbon dioxide can be converted to metric tons of carbon equivalent by multiplying by 12/44.
[b] Wood and wood-derived fuels.
[c] Municipal solid waste from biogenic sources, landfill gas, sludge waste, agricultural byproducts, and other biomass.
[d] Fuel ethanol minus denaturant.
[e] Commercial sector, including commercial combined-heat-and-power (CHP) and commercial electricity-only plants.
[f] Industrial sector, including industrial combined-heat-and-power (CHP) and industrial electricity-only plants.
[g] The electric power sector comprises electricity-only and combined-heat-and-power (CHP) plants within the NAICS 22 category whose primary business is to sell electricity, or electricity and heat, to the public.

NA=Not available. (s)=Less than 0.5 million metric tons.

Notes: • Carbon dioxide emissions from biomass energy consumption are excluded from the energy-related carbon dioxide emissions reported in Tables 12.1–12.6. See Note 2, "Accounting for Carbon Dioxide Emissions From Biomass Energy Combustion," at end of section. • Data are estimates. See "Section 12 Methodology and Sources" at end of section. • See "Carbon Dioxide" in Glossary. • See Note 1, "Emissions of Carbon Dioxide and Other Greenhouse Gases," at end of section. • Totals may not equal sum of components due to independent rounding. • Geographic coverage is the 50 states and the District of Columbia.

Web Page: See http://www.eia.gov/totalenergy/data/monthly/#environment (Excel and CSV files) for all available annual and monthly data beginning in 1973.

Sources: See end of section.

Source: *U.S. Energy Information Administration, Monthly Energy Review, July 2017*

Environmental Revenue and Expenditures, by State

State	Revenue[1] ($/per capita)				Current Operational Expenses ($/per capita)			
	Natural Resources, Other	Park & Recreation	Sewerage	Solid Waste Management	Natural Resources, Other	Parks & Recreation	Sewerage	Solid Waste Management
Alabama	2.18	6.76	0.00	1.27	46.66	3.41	0.00	0.37
Alaska	28.15	1.73	0.00	0.00	473.61	20.11	0.00	0.00
Arizona	3.17	4.31	0.00	0.41	37.03	8.89	0.00	0.30
Arkansas	6.91	8.32	0.00	0.00	82.17	21.52	0.08	4.25
California	25.17	2.78	0.00	0.00	67.19	10.84	6.29	6.36
Colorado	3.60	1.16	0.00	0.54	46.94	14.28	0.62	0.12
Connecticut	1.82	5.18	0.00	34.30	39.03	7.61	0.00	30.58
Delaware	2.82	13.50	0.00	64.94	81.04	37.67	0.00	35.00
Florida	3.72	2.37	0.00	1.33	52.67	5.32	0.00	6.27
Georgia	4.29	11.06	0.00	0.00	38.14	17.93	0.68	0.14
Hawaii	14.59	8.07	0.00	0.00	72.15	55.42	0.01	0.00
Idaho	47.27	5.82	0.00	0.00	123.00	13.49	0.00	0.00
Illinois	1.19	0.56	0.00	0.00	16.57	5.84	0.92	2.02
Indiana	7.35	3.77	0.00	0.00	47.43	8.50	0.21	0.84
Iowa	15.90	1.45	0.00	1.41	80.07	6.85	0.23	0.75
Kansas	12.19	2.56	0.00	0.00	74.74	10.45	0.00	0.00
Kentucky	11.66	13.69	0.00	0.00	67.33	20.83	0.04	5.20
Louisiana	12.55	18.96	0.00	0.00	125.39	42.00	0.00	0.00
Maine	14.37	1.23	0.00	8.53	117.23	5.42	0.00	0.00
Maryland	2.24	4.85	19.24	0.00	60.22	15.33	18.62	3.67
Massachusetts	6.13	9.26	64.01	0.00	38.67	21.22	25.59	1.31
Michigan	4.27	0.56	0.00	0.00	27.21	9.74	0.00	0.46
Minnesota	10.94	6.46	40.57	0.00	106.16	35.74	20.99	3.08
Mississippi	11.68	2.55	0.00	0.00	79.42	16.05	0.00	0.00
Missouri	1.89	0.65	0.00	0.27	49.30	6.54	0.00	0.49
Montana	36.79	3.17	0.00	0.05	216.26	14.43	0.60	1.04
Nebraska	17.96	4.50	0.00	0.00	123.58	19.38	2.27	5.04
Nevada	3.28	2.26	0.00	0.00	34.96	6.29	0.00	2.49
New Hampshire	2.67	15.30	1.30	0.00	38.96	12.68	0.89	14.94
New Jersey	0.78	8.05	2.31	6.95	41.55	21.14	0.26	4.69
New Mexico	6.82	0.71	0.00	0.00	76.69	25.12	0.00	0.06
New York	9.46	14.00	0.00	0.01	15.12	22.50	0.00	2.28
North Carolina	4.68	1.11	0.00	0.04	42.44	12.32	0.04	1.03
North Dakota	37.28	5.46	0.00	0.00	271.04	32.63	0.00	0.00
Ohio	2.33	1.46	0.00	0.00	26.66	4.57	0.00	2.89
Oklahoma	6.39	5.95	0.00	0.39	49.68	17.55	0.00	0.16
Oregon	32.43	5.55	0.01	0.00	121.83	15.43	0.68	1.48
Pennsylvania	4.26	3.09	0.00	0.00	43.56	16.18	0.88	2.96
Rhode Island	2.99	29.31	88.22	13.26	41.40	29.37	47.33	46.89
South Carolina	5.44	3.64	0.00	0.00	38.08	15.98	0.00	0.00
South Dakota	14.01	8.57	0.00	0.00	157.25	43.27	0.00	0.00
Tennessee	2.74	5.00	0.00	0.83	42.32	12.06	0.00	0.92
Texas	1.34	1.82	0.00	2.58	30.01	4.63	0.20	1.71
Utah	5.59	0.78	0.00	1.71	59.51	13.37	0.00	0.03
Vermont	1.57	13.92	0.00	0.00	160.82	20.98	2.74	6.81
Virginia	0.28	2.76	0.00	0.00	23.97	13.46	4.76	0.12
Washington	26.31	0.33	0.00	1.40	84.66	8.65	0.00	1.34
West Virginia	20.72	8.87	1.65	0.38	95.69	26.05	0.00	5.17
Wisconsin	12.00	6.76	0.01	0.14	71.21	3.10	0.01	1.17
Wyoming	10.55	2.51	0.00	0.00	460.78	46.34	0.00	7.14

Note: *(1) Includes revenue raised through current charges only. Does not include intergovernmental revenue.*
Source: *U.S. Census Bureau, State and Local Government Finances, 2014*

Environmental Revenue and Expenditures for U.S Counties with Populations of 50,000+

County/Parish	State	Revenue[1] ($/per capita)				Current Operational Expenses ($/per capita)			
		Natural Resources, Other	Park & Recreation	Sewerage	Solid Waste Management	Natural Resources, Other	Parks & Recreation	Sewerage	Solid Waste Management
Acadia Parish	LA	0.00	1.28	0.00	0.00	9.49	2.72	0.00	81.43
Ada County	ID	9.88	0.24	0.00	24.98	10.87	0.97	0.00	17.18
Adams County	CO	0.00	6.88	0.00	1.01	5.44	28.80	0.00	0.45
Adams County	IL	0.00	0.00	0.00	0.00	0.00	0.00	0.00	0.00
Adams County	PA	0.00	0.00	0.00	0.00	15.44	19.58	0.00	0.00
Aiken County	SC	0.00	0.00	38.43	9.70	0.25	38.32	26.38	33.98
Alachua County	FL	1.12	0.00	0.00	29.58	15.93	6.61	0.00	56.94
Alamance County	NC	0.00	0.28	0.00	25.34	0.00	11.89	0.00	19.14
Alameda County	CA	0.13	0.00	0.00	0.00	22.86	0.36	0.00	0.00
Albany County	NY	0.00	16.51	5.57	0.00	0.79	14.68	54.99	0.00
Albemarle County	VA	0.00	0.00	0.13	0.00	1.10	30.24	0.00	3.70
Allegan County	MI	0.00	0.72	0.00	0.00	5.25	1.92	0.00	0.00
Allegany County	MD	0.00	0.00	109.94	4.21	14.15	7.99	156.51	19.49
Allegheny County	PA	0.00	2.76	0.00	0.00	0.22	14.33	0.00	0.00
Allen County	IN	0.00	15.50	0.29	3.15	0.86	19.62	0.29	3.30
Anderson County	SC	0.00	4.97	32.34	31.95	0.21	11.04	14.94	25.32
Anderson County	TN	0.00	0.66	0.00	2.53	2.50	0.56	0.00	18.18
Androscoggin County	ME	0.00	0.00	0.00	0.00	0.00	0.00	0.00	0.00
Anne Arundel County	MD	0.00	17.87	109.63	93.65	3.04	47.73	133.67	89.02
Anoka County	MN	0.20	10.71	0.00	12.01	2.71	30.62	0.00	11.07
Apache County	AZ	0.00	0.00	0.00	0.00	0.00	0.18	0.00	0.00
Arapahoe County	CO	0.00	1.15	0.00	0.00	0.00	28.77	0.00	0.00
Arlington County	VA	0.00	44.48	333.90	42.78	8.12	214.90	141.09	52.30
Armstrong County	PA	0.00	0.00	0.00	0.00	5.36	10.78	0.00	0.00
Aroostook County	ME	0.00	0.00	0.00	0.00	0.96	0.12	0.04	1.21
Ascension Parish	LA	0.00	0.00	0.00	0.00	63.51	21.65	10.73	0.00
Ashtabula County	OH	0.00	1.57	19.58	4.06	2.25	6.59	16.19	4.60
Atlantic County	NJ	0.00	0.12	103.41	125.62	2.01	4.20	70.31	90.97
Augusta County	VA	0.00	4.94	0.00	14.80	2.33	18.52	0.00	27.21
Baldwin County	AL	0.00	0.00	0.00	63.20	0.00	6.20	0.00	48.60
Baltimore County	MD	0.00	5.04	169.47	3.92	17.75	35.05	152.77	81.26
Bannock County	ID	1.73	0.00	0.00	44.34	10.73	0.44	0.00	27.75
Barnstable County	MA	4.58	0.00	0.00	0.00	14.34	0.00	0.00	0.00
Barrow County	GA	0.00	3.51	25.81	12.11	0.12	12.90	37.12	0.00
Bartholomew County	IN	0.00	0.32	0.85	0.00	2.53	1.55	0.09	0.00
Bartow County	GA	0.00	3.77	49.17	22.21	1.02	21.47	55.50	34.08
Bastrop County	TX	0.00	0.00	0.00	0.83	1.20	2.00	0.00	7.38
Bay County	FL	0.00	3.35	46.37	63.78	4.29	10.18	61.25	77.91
Beaufort County	SC	0.00	3.95	18.15	0.05	0.00	42.92	16.64	52.77
Beaver County	PA	0.00	0.00	0.00	0.00	0.00	9.56	0.00	2.32
Bedford County	VA	0.00	0.09	0.00	27.21	3.60	23.28	0.00	66.35
Belknap County	NH	0.00	186.30	0.00	0.00	0.00	146.14	0.00	0.00
Bell County	TX	0.00	10.16	0.00	0.00	1.99	15.97	0.00	0.02
Belmont County	OH	0.00	0.00	25.96	0.00	0.00	0.00	21.45	0.17
Benton County	AR	0.00	0.00	0.00	0.00	0.00	0.00	0.00	0.00
Benton County	OR	7.90	0.00	1.16	0.00	11.99	15.49	1.10	0.00
Benton County	WA	0.00	0.10	0.00	0.90	3.74	3.16	0.00	2.13
Bergen County	NJ	0.00	9.23	73.59	6.25	0.00	11.24	48.16	8.19
Berkeley County	SC	0.00	2.76	105.97	52.89	0.00	7.00	51.38	72.57
Berkeley County	WV	0.00	0.00	0.00	0.00	0.00	9.96	0.00	0.00
Berks County	PA	0.00	0.00	0.00	3.42	6.32	7.83	0.00	1.97
Bernalillo County	NM	0.00	1.51	0.00	7.74	1.22	18.69	0.00	13.55
Bexar County	TX	0.00	0.16	1.05	0.00	1.25	1.88	0.46	0.00
Black Hawk County	IA	0.00	3.76	1.45	0.00	0.07	13.59	0.47	0.00

County/Parish	State	Revenue[1] ($/per capita)				Current Operational Expenses ($/per capita)			
		Natural Resources, Other	Park & Recreation	Sewerage	Solid Waste Management	Natural Resources, Other	Parks & Recreation	Sewerage	Solid Waste Management
Blair County	PA	0.00	0.00	0.00	1.39	0.39	6.88	0.00	0.00
Blount County	AL	0.00	0.00	0.00	0.00	0.00	7.59	0.00	3.83
Blount County	TN	0.00	0.00	0.00	0.00	2.10	0.76	0.00	0.66
Blue Earth County	MN	0.00	2.22	0.00	0.00	45.68	7.13	0.00	25.45
Bonneville County	ID	0.00	1.15	0.00	40.37	0.19	0.00	0.00	24.40
Boone County	IL	0.00	0.00	0.00	0.00	0.00	0.00	0.00	0.00
Boone County	IN	0.00	0.00	0.00	0.00	4.70	0.00	0.05	0.00
Boone County	KY	0.00	3.63	0.00	1.94	0.00	15.16	0.00	0.00
Boone County	MO	0.00	0.00	0.00	0.00	0.39	1.94	0.53	0.38
Bossier Parish	LA	0.00	0.00	0.00	0.00	7.34	2.21	5.62	0.02
Boulder County	CO	0.00	0.68	0.23	24.80	168.03	50.99	0.28	21.22
Bowie County	TX	0.00	0.00	0.00	0.00	0.00	0.00	0.00	0.00
Box Elder County	UT	0.97	0.00	0.00	0.00	0.00	7.92	0.00	0.00
Bradford County	PA	0.00	0.00	0.00	0.00	0.00	0.00	0.00	0.00
Bradley County	TN	0.00	0.00	0.00	1.37	5.54	9.26	2.15	5.39
Brazoria County	TX	0.00	0.00	0.00	0.00	2.03	7.91	0.00	0.00
Brazos County	TX	0.00	0.00	0.00	0.17	1.47	5.59	0.00	0.28
Brevard County	FL	0.71	12.27	0.00	64.54	13.30	47.90	0.00	64.18
Bristol County	MA	0.00	0.00	0.00	0.00	0.00	0.00	0.00	0.00
Broome County	NY	0.00	10.88	0.00	40.67	5.66	26.51	0.00	30.40
Broward County	FL	2.05	10.00	37.14	30.68	13.09	37.57	21.68	28.26
Brown County	WI	0.36	9.59	0.00	34.43	9.17	49.43	0.00	35.40
Brunswick County	NC	0.00	1.94	170.89	12.98	3.69	21.06	61.15	112.69
Bucks County	PA	0.00	2.07	0.00	1.91	0.54	7.07	0.00	0.30
Bullitt County	KY	0.00	0.00	0.00	0.00	1.13	4.45	0.00	2.14
Bulloch County	GA	0.00	21.03	0.00	5.09	2.62	53.52	0.00	52.19
Buncombe County	NC	1.23	1.13	0.00	29.14	0.00	13.40	0.00	19.18
Burke County	NC	0.70	0.50	6.27	44.55	1.08	5.70	0.00	45.92
Burleigh County	ND	0.00	0.00	0.00	0.00	11.78	9.03	0.00	0.00
Burlington County	NJ	0.00	0.00	0.00	58.80	0.10	0.01	0.00	32.38
Butler County	KS	1.37	0.00	0.00	30.41	12.35	0.15	1.95	13.71
Butler County	OH	0.06	0.00	49.08	0.00	1.03	0.00	29.03	0.04
Butler County	PA	1.53	0.77	0.00	0.61	1.74	3.28	0.00	1.08
Butte County	CA	0.00	0.00	0.00	27.77	15.11	0.60	0.00	24.73
Cabarrus County	NC	0.34	5.65	0.00	3.72	1.72	18.14	0.00	3.77
Cabell County	WV	0.00	0.00	0.00	0.00	4.03	9.04	0.00	0.55
Cache County	UT	0.00	0.00	0.00	0.00	48.08	20.97	0.00	0.00
Caddo Parish	LA	0.00	0.00	0.00	0.00	0.00	14.78	0.00	0.00
Calcasieu Parish	LA	0.00	11.00	0.00	0.00	15.35	68.66	0.00	31.62
Caldwell County	NC	0.76	0.00	0.00	9.84	1.03	1.26	0.00	3.91
Calhoun County	AL	0.00	0.00	0.00	20.59	0.00	3.38	0.00	19.96
Calhoun County	MI	0.00	0.00	0.00	2.11	5.44	9.54	0.00	1.96
Calvert County	MD	0.00	34.49	54.71	100.99	36.58	195.87	46.45	101.86
Cambria County	PA	0.00	0.00	0.00	0.00	12.58	4.58	0.00	0.00
Camden County	GA	0.00	0.37	0.00	87.22	2.21	8.30	0.00	69.02
Camden County	NJ	14.12	0.52	0.00	0.00	9.18	4.96	0.00	0.53
Cameron County	TX	0.00	17.07	0.00	0.45	0.56	12.55	0.00	0.02
Campbell County	KY	0.00	1.95	0.00	0.07	0.01	5.68	0.00	0.73
Campbell County	VA	0.00	3.08	0.00	14.63	8.25	13.30	0.00	31.98
Canadian County	OK	0.00	0.00	0.00	0.00	4.20	0.00	0.00	0.00
Canyon County	ID	0.00	0.00	0.00	14.42	6.12	2.89	0.00	12.55
Cape Girardeau County	MO	0.00	0.00	0.00	0.00	0.00	4.57	0.00	0.00
Cape May County	NJ	0.00	3.21	0.00	89.85	2.75	19.54	166.80	108.73
Carbon County	PA	0.00	5.85	0.00	1.57	6.21	17.19	0.00	2.03
Carroll County	GA	0.00	6.54	0.00	22.52	1.81	21.65	0.00	43.06
Carroll County	MD	0.00	9.04	37.22	38.26	30.48	34.66	36.52	37.06

County/Parish	State	Revenue[1] ($/per capita)				Current Operational Expenses ($/per capita)			
		Natural Resources, Other	Park & Recreation	Sewerage	Solid Waste Management	Natural Resources, Other	Parks & Recreation	Sewerage	Solid Waste Management
Carteret County	NC	4.16	4.30	0.00	34.86	9.94	27.96	0.00	35.26
Carver County	MN	0.00	2.67	0.00	11.67	11.11	13.27	0.00	19.80
Cascade County	MT	0.98	27.39	0.00	13.87	9.31	47.00	0.00	11.79
Cass County	MI	0.00	0.00	0.00	0.00	5.44	2.48	0.00	0.00
Cass County	MO	0.00	0.00	0.00	0.00	0.00	0.05	0.00	0.00
Cass County	ND	0.00	0.07	0.00	0.00	112.51	5.96	0.00	0.00
Catawba County	NC	5.86	0.05	0.00	30.61	2.98	4.12	0.83	28.78
Cattaraugus County	NY	0.00	7.19	0.00	16.23	7.66	17.56	0.00	20.90
Cayuga County	NY	0.00	2.78	0.00	0.00	41.16	13.44	0.00	0.00
Cecil County	MD	0.00	1.33	63.55	57.51	20.49	19.85	56.63	75.85
Centre County	PA	0.00	0.00	0.00	0.00	12.48	0.32	0.00	1.04
Champaign County	IL	4.54	0.00	0.00	0.00	18.79	0.00	0.00	0.01
Charles County	MD	23.23	1.66	103.93	34.31	32.81	64.41	85.09	25.54
Charleston County	SC	0.00	36.49	0.00	72.18	0.00	24.69	0.00	63.23
Charlotte County	FL	0.00	12.53	137.05	103.02	55.29	71.83	201.26	105.66
Chatham County	GA	0.00	2.87	3.03	10.54	1.03	0.04	0.00	0.00
Chatham County	NC	2.98	1.14	0.28	43.03	0.00	9.37	0.00	37.63
Chautauqua County	NY	0.00	0.00	27.30	57.11	16.75	2.21	27.04	46.17
Chaves County	NM	0.00	0.00	0.00	0.00	11.34	0.00	0.00	3.69
Chelan County	WA	1.50	3.32	4.61	19.53	45.42	6.46	1.96	16.79
Chemung County	NY	0.00	2.18	31.96	20.72	16.27	27.14	45.32	20.60
Cherokee County	GA	0.00	9.30	0.00	10.17	0.68	15.01	0.00	1.30
Cherokee County	SC	0.00	0.00	0.00	0.00	0.00	0.00	0.00	40.57
Cheshire County	NH	0.00	0.00	0.00	0.00	0.83	0.00	0.00	0.00
Chester County	PA	0.00	0.18	0.00	0.00	10.13	9.78	0.00	0.00
Chesterfield County	VA	0.00	1.46	115.43	10.41	11.11	31.10	61.92	6.34
Chippewa County	WI	7.96	2.41	0.00	0.43	40.97	8.10	0.00	4.07
Chisago County	MN	0.00	0.72	0.00	0.22	14.12	5.79	0.00	7.77
Chittenden County	VT	0.00	0.00	0.00	0.00	0.00	0.00	0.00	0.00
Christian County	KY	0.00	0.00	0.00	0.00	0.04	1.32	0.00	0.50
Christian County	MO	0.00	0.00	0.00	0.00	0.00	0.00	0.00	0.00
Citrus County	FL	15.58	1.92	53.04	41.11	24.21	7.17	84.17	28.27
Clackamas County	OR	2.46	15.45	72.90	1.43	7.21	39.07	52.86	6.51
Clallam County	WA	0.80	2.79	5.28	0.54	54.46	23.56	4.62	0.72
Clark County	IN	0.00	0.00	0.00	3.42	2.88	7.80	0.15	5.57
Clark County	NV	0.00	36.92	84.54	0.00	12.93	102.58	33.96	0.00
Clark County	OH	0.00	0.00	25.06	6.00	0.00	2.99	17.88	6.03
Clark County	WA	0.96	14.44	23.25	4.86	9.39	15.52	19.78	7.44
Clay County	FL	0.00	0.02	0.00	44.91	5.87	6.44	0.00	91.99
Clay County	MN	0.00	0.00	0.00	19.12	9.04	3.38	0.00	46.63
Clay County	MO	0.00	11.07	0.00	0.00	0.00	24.64	0.00	0.00
Clayton County	GA	0.00	8.52	0.00	19.55	1.11	29.64	0.00	31.79
Clearfield County	PA	0.00	0.00	0.00	0.00	1.77	8.89	0.00	0.00
Clermont County	OH	0.00	0.00	77.94	1.79	0.00	0.00	34.51	3.81
Cleveland County	NC	0.00	0.00	0.00	61.79	0.00	0.70	0.00	47.76
Cleveland County	OK	0.00	0.00	0.00	0.00	0.00	0.00	0.00	0.00
Cobb County	GA	0.00	34.01	108.49	0.87	0.00	53.28	84.99	1.48
Cochise County	AZ	0.00	0.00	0.00	30.10	0.00	0.00	2.14	19.45
Coconino County	AZ	0.00	6.01	0.00	14.84	2.73	7.30	5.17	6.81
Coffee County	TN	0.00	0.00	0.65	1.25	5.86	0.00	0.48	27.08
Colbert County	AL	0.00	4.46	0.00	37.20	0.00	5.37	0.00	35.29
Cole County	MO	0.00	0.00	0.00	0.00	0.00	0.04	0.00	0.00
Coles County	IL	0.00	0.00	0.00	0.00	0.00	0.00	0.00	0.00
Collier County	FL	5.54	21.48	149.19	98.69	39.01	83.23	197.59	90.69
Collin County	TX	0.00	0.00	0.00	0.00	0.28	0.62	0.00	0.00

County/Parish	State	Revenue[1] ($/per capita) Natural Resources, Other	Park & Recreation	Sewerage	Solid Waste Management	Current Operational Expenses ($/per capita) Natural Resources, Other	Parks & Recreation	Sewerage	Solid Waste Management
Columbia County	FL	0.00	0.29	0.53	32.73	14.53	21.24	2.15	79.89
Columbia County	GA	0.00	5.02	109.27	0.98	1.10	10.28	46.44	3.75
Columbia County	NY	0.00	2.43	2.25	26.50	20.31	28.78	1.96	39.62
Columbia County	PA	0.00	0.00	0.00	0.00	1.67	0.94	0.00	0.00
Columbiana County	OH	0.00	0.00	15.14	0.00	0.00	0.22	13.45	0.00
Columbus County	NC	0.40	0.65	0.44	98.27	14.17	8.48	0.00	71.08
Comanche County	OK	0.00	0.00	0.00	0.00	0.00	1.70	0.00	0.00
Contra Costa County	CA	0.00	0.00	28.64	1.44	43.79	0.00	20.55	0.00
Cook County	IL	0.00	9.53	0.00	0.00	34.76	20.82	0.00	0.00
Coos County	OR	59.35	10.32	0.00	28.12	18.54	15.69	0.00	25.19
Coweta County	GA	0.00	2.75	0.00	5.10	1.28	18.68	2.91	7.97
Cowlitz County	WA	0.01	7.79	83.57	39.98	8.49	28.56	36.51	24.73
Craighead County	AR	0.00	0.00	0.00	0.00	0.00	0.00	0.00	0.00
Craven County	NC	0.00	0.65	0.00	22.35	15.27	22.15	0.00	33.25
Crawford County	AR	0.00	0.00	6.78	0.00	0.00	0.13	5.07	0.00
Crawford County	PA	0.00	0.00	0.00	0.00	3.88	4.15	0.00	3.28
Creek County	OK	0.00	0.00	0.00	0.00	0.00	2.82	0.00	0.00
Crow Wing County	MN	0.00	0.00	0.00	35.79	26.40	1.58	0.00	32.10
Cullman County	AL	0.00	17.41	0.00	52.58	0.00	17.31	0.00	51.46
Cumberland County	ME	0.00	0.00	0.00	0.00	0.49	0.00	0.00	0.00
Cumberland County	NJ	0.00	0.00	0.00	80.61	2.17	0.33	0.00	104.86
Cumberland County	NC	0.00	5.64	0.02	8.80	0.41	31.06	1.14	42.98
Cumberland County	PA	0.00	0.00	0.00	0.54	1.66	0.11	0.00	1.36
Cumberland County	TN	0.00	0.00	0.00	0.07	2.69	3.41	0.00	34.44
Curry County	NM	0.00	0.00	0.00	0.00	0.00	0.00	0.00	0.00
Cuyahoga County	OH	0.00	0.00	21.19	1.66	0.14	0.00	17.07	1.45
Dakota County	MN	0.00	1.80	0.00	15.98	12.85	22.13	0.00	17.93
Dallas County	IA	0.00	0.00	0.00	0.00	9.56	13.90	0.00	1.55
Dallas County	TX	0.00	1.39	0.00	0.00	0.00	0.81	0.00	0.00
Dane County	WI	0.64	16.88	0.00	19.03	8.20	29.61	0.00	19.37
Darke County	OH	0.00	0.00	0.00	0.00	0.00	0.00	0.00	0.00
Darlington County	SC	0.00	0.00	0.00	31.53	0.00	7.08	0.00	49.76
Dauphin County	PA	1.53	0.00	0.00	3.78	16.47	44.69	0.00	5.40
Davidson County	NC	0.00	0.77	2.72	25.45	1.18	5.54	2.65	18.08
Daviess County	KY	0.00	1.28	0.00	58.72	0.37	18.03	0.00	40.73
Davis County	UT	0.00	7.04	0.00	93.67	6.30	10.57	0.00	80.95
De Kalb County	AL	0.00	0.00	0.00	3.66	0.00	0.38	0.00	0.00
Dekalb County	GA	0.00	2.39	138.79	89.66	0.00	15.99	59.37	52.76
Dekalb County	IL	0.00	0.00	0.00	0.00	6.13	0.00	0.00	0.00
Delaware County	IN	0.00	0.96	3.02	0.00	5.41	18.16	1.50	0.00
Delaware County	OH	0.00	0.00	59.51	0.00	6.78	18.88	38.02	0.00
Delaware County	PA	0.00	0.00	0.00	0.00	0.40	2.84	0.00	15.99
Denton County	TX	0.00	0.00	0.00	0.00	0.45	0.40	0.00	0.00
Deschutes County	OR	0.00	7.32	0.00	41.98	2.73	14.00	0.00	28.18
Desoto County	MS	0.00	37.90	0.00	7.27	1.77	44.69	0.00	5.76
Dickson County	TN	0.00	0.00	0.00	41.80	3.01	0.00	0.00	58.17
Dodge County	WI	0.47	1.74	0.00	0.00	14.29	7.58	0.00	0.38
Dona Ana County	NM	0.00	0.00	3.62	0.00	3.90	0.00	6.97	0.00
Dorchester County	SC	0.00	0.00	109.37	39.38	0.00	0.07	15.40	55.65
Dougherty County	GA	0.00	0.00	0.00	43.50	1.01	4.21	0.02	34.10
Douglas County	CO	0.00	3.02	0.00	0.12	1.94	18.27	0.00	0.27
Douglas County	GA	0.00	2.73	0.00	10.83	0.05	25.21	0.00	11.10
Douglas County	KS	4.48	0.00	0.00	0.00	11.12	2.29	0.00	0.00
Douglas County	NE	0.00	0.00	0.00	0.00	24.24	5.41	0.00	0.59
Douglas County	OR	9.54	24.27	0.00	6.55	29.88	45.14	0.00	19.10
Dubuque County	IA	0.00	4.81	0.00	0.00	8.88	2.15	0.00	0.00

County/Parish	State	Revenue[1] ($/per capita)				Current Operational Expenses ($/per capita)			
		Natural Resources, Other	Park & Recreation	Sewerage	Solid Waste Management	Natural Resources, Other	Parks & Recreation	Sewerage	Solid Waste Management
Dupage County	IL	0.00	0.00	16.20	0.00	0.00	0.00	6.72	0.00
Durham County	NC	0.83	0.00	39.62	6.00	38.03	7.12	16.76	6.50
Dutchess County	NY	0.00	0.69	0.00	48.81	13.89	5.74	0.00	64.38
Eagle County	CO	0.00	0.00	0.00	58.77	0.00	12.47	0.00	46.79
Eaton County	MI	0.00	0.64	0.00	2.42	8.22	3.45	0.00	2.72
Eau Claire County	WI	5.39	3.11	0.00	8.65	18.91	8.40	0.00	10.86
Ector County	TX	0.00	6.30	0.00	0.00	0.80	8.86	0.00	0.00
Eddy County	NM	0.00	0.00	0.00	0.00	0.89	0.27	0.00	36.05
Edgecombe County	NC	0.00	0.00	0.00	36.44	0.00	0.00	0.00	36.55
El Dorado County	CA	0.00	0.46	0.00	0.94	15.47	3.95	0.00	0.00
El Paso County	CO	0.00	0.00	0.00	1.39	0.22	4.66	0.00	1.35
El Paso County	TX	0.00	0.49	0.54	0.45	0.27	8.01	0.16	0.45
Elkhart County	IN	0.00	0.99	7.34	18.35	2.97	6.86	8.55	8.56
Elko County	NV	0.00	0.27	4.62	0.00	3.03	9.61	2.08	0.00
Erie County	NY	0.00	1.38	7.65	0.00	1.02	17.87	39.15	0.00
Erie County	PA	0.00	0.00	0.00	0.00	0.00	0.00	0.00	0.00
Escambia County	FL	0.00	13.77	0.00	38.62	5.23	28.45	0.00	32.32
Essex County	NJ	0.00	15.00	0.00	47.51	0.00	16.70	0.00	35.10
Etowah County	AL	0.00	0.00	0.00	0.00	0.00	0.23	0.00	0.00
Fairbanks North Star Borough	AK	0.00	1.07	0.00	94.53	0.00	81.82	0.03	131.89
Fairfax County	VA	0.00	47.12	227.93	62.86	0.00	86.59	100.60	79.28
Fairfield County	OH	0.00	0.00	22.16	0.00	2.43	0.00	11.38	0.00
Faulkner County	AR	0.00	0.00	1.15	0.00	0.41	0.54	0.84	0.00
Fauquier County	VA	0.00	6.92	0.00	61.41	11.68	49.91	5.35	111.43
Fayette County	GA	0.00	1.73	52.62	0.88	1.01	9.30	47.28	3.17
Fayette County	PA	0.00	0.00	0.00	0.00	35.68	0.55	0.00	0.00
Flagler County	FL	0.00	1.54	1.32	14.29	3.45	17.38	1.17	14.88
Flathead County	MT	7.11	1.93	0.00	67.61	11.25	5.69	0.00	34.79
Florence County	SC	0.00	3.10	0.00	23.01	0.06	18.85	0.00	30.85
Floyd County	GA	0.00	1.43	32.96	8.21	1.42	24.80	23.85	16.08
Floyd County	IN	0.00	1.96	9.64	0.00	2.91	3.90	7.25	1.63
Fond Du Lac County	WI	0.09	10.76	0.00	0.16	13.39	25.60	0.00	1.11
Forrest County	MS	0.00	0.00	0.00	0.00	3.33	23.96	0.00	0.00
Forsyth County	GA	0.00	12.60	66.14	9.42	1.39	33.64	70.35	3.31
Forsyth County	NC	0.00	10.46	0.00	0.00	6.10	20.05	0.00	0.00
Fort Bend County	TX	1.01	0.28	0.00	0.00	11.39	2.08	0.00	0.48
Franklin County	MO	0.00	0.00	4.03	0.00	0.00	0.00	2.33	0.00
Franklin County	NC	0.52	0.00	0.00	38.37	0.00	0.72	0.00	57.75
Franklin County	OH	0.00	10.17	3.71	0.00	0.00	26.18	3.12	0.00
Franklin County	PA	0.00	0.00	0.00	0.00	0.60	0.15	0.00	0.00
Franklin County	WA	0.07	13.65	0.00	0.00	24.37	29.75	0.00	0.52
Frederick County	MD	0.00	5.13	59.58	97.60	22.39	28.37	65.75	76.56
Frederick County	VA	0.00	20.48	0.00	72.10	0.00	50.68	0.00	22.29
Fresno County	CA	0.00	1.13	8.07	13.02	11.26	2.98	7.33	12.48
Fulton County	GA	0.00	0.60	47.29	0.05	0.43	3.06	33.58	0.79
Gallatin County	MT	0.00	0.00	0.00	48.16	1.38	10.93	0.00	29.97
Galveston County	TX	0.37	1.36	0.00	0.00	6.05	8.78	0.00	0.00
Garfield County	CO	0.00	9.12	0.00	22.36	0.00	23.42	0.00	16.31
Garfield County	OK	0.00	0.00	0.00	0.00	1.46	0.00	0.00	0.00
Garland County	AR	0.00	0.00	0.00	70.41	0.00	0.15	0.00	83.37
Gaston County	NC	0.00	0.72	0.00	24.42	0.01	7.26	0.00	21.48
Genesee County	MI	0.00	4.58	0.00	0.00	2.94	15.11	0.00	0.00
Genesee County	NY	0.00	0.25	0.00	0.00	17.00	19.62	0.00	0.00
Georgetown County	SC	0.00	3.78	27.40	54.63	0.12	38.01	8.85	66.79
Gila County	AZ	0.00	0.00	0.36	27.77	1.71	2.41	0.06	7.45
Gloucester County	NJ	0.00	6.51	0.00	56.77	1.96	5.43	0.00	62.63

County/Parish	State	Revenue[1] ($/per capita) Natural Resources, Other	Park & Recreation	Sewerage	Solid Waste Management	Current Operational Expenses ($/per capita) Natural Resources, Other	Parks & Recreation	Sewerage	Solid Waste Management
Glynn County	GA	0.00	5.61	0.00	44.02	1.16	104.74	24.81	41.31
Gordon County	GA	0.00	2.36	0.00	5.82	3.02	25.25	0.00	28.21
Grady County	OK	0.00	0.00	0.00	0.00	0.00	14.37	0.00	0.00
Grafton County	NH	0.00	0.00	0.00	0.00	4.31	0.00	0.00	0.00
Grand Forks County	ND	5.36	0.00	0.00	0.00	28.10	1.47	0.00	0.00
Grand Traverse County	MI	0.00	3.86	15.67	3.13	5.62	8.16	69.88	3.38
Grant County	IN	0.00	0.00	0.00	0.00	2.07	0.00	0.25	1.44
Grant County	WA	0.25	3.55	0.00	28.15	25.71	1.76	2.73	22.71
Granville County	NC	0.22	4.14	4.27	37.79	5.15	7.73	4.46	32.63
Grays Harbor County	WA	0.01	15.11	7.17	39.91	19.51	21.00	7.40	55.44
Grayson County	TX	0.00	0.00	0.00	0.00	1.42	0.91	0.00	0.00
Greene County	MO	0.00	0.00	0.00	0.00	0.03	0.00	0.02	0.00
Greene County	OH	0.00	0.16	115.39	6.60	7.50	9.19	34.17	11.16
Greene County	TN	0.00	0.00	0.00	1.54	2.82	0.00	0.00	26.90
Greenville County	SC	0.02	9.71	15.81	13.32	0.76	28.62	12.45	22.41
Greenwood County	SC	0.00	1.15	0.00	44.58	0.00	25.91	0.00	48.35
Gregg County	TX	0.00	0.00	0.00	0.00	1.01	0.01	0.00	0.00
Grundy County	IL	0.00	0.00	0.00	0.00	0.00	0.00	0.00	0.00
Guadalupe County	TX	0.00	0.00	0.00	0.00	1.64	0.00	0.00	2.80
Guilford County	NC	0.00	1.88	0.00	0.04	0.77	5.94	0.00	2.07
Gwinnett County	GA	0.00	3.81	126.48	48.42	0.00	33.43	87.99	46.92
Hall County	GA	0.00	1.32	3.48	34.89	2.21	16.66	3.71	30.28
Hall County	NE	0.96	0.63	0.00	0.00	6.31	28.49	0.00	0.00
Hamblen County	TN	0.00	0.46	0.00	0.00	2.65	3.22	0.00	36.07
Hamilton County	IN	0.00	1.32	1.54	0.01	6.45	9.91	0.00	2.25
Hamilton County	OH	0.00	2.71	321.50	0.00	3.38	37.91	0.00	0.00
Hamilton County	TN	0.00	0.98	0.13	0.17	1.37	20.49	0.00	0.00
Hancock County	IN	0.00	0.00	0.00	1.71	4.68	3.46	16.30	0.00
Hancock County	ME	0.00	0.00	0.00	0.00	0.00	0.00	0.00	9.84
Hancock County	OH	3.15	0.00	0.00	65.39	20.19	0.00	0.00	48.56
Hanover County	VA	0.00	5.13	140.90	3.40	1.47	53.69	82.09	50.59
Hardin County	KY	0.00	0.00	0.00	41.49	0.03	0.04	0.00	34.48
Harford County	MD	0.00	3.67	53.17	50.99	6.83	75.68	57.26	58.89
Harnett County	NC	0.00	0.00	0.00	0.00	0.00	0.00	0.00	0.00
Harris County	TX	0.09	0.18	0.00	0.00	14.48	1.92	0.00	0.00
Harrison County	MS	0.00	0.00	0.00	0.00	2.04	13.09	0.00	0.00
Harrison County	WV	0.00	0.51	0.00	0.00	0.00	9.35	0.00	0.00
Hawaii County	HI	0.00	5.79	37.24	39.07	0.00	88.67	35.71	114.52
Hawkins County	TN	0.00	0.07	0.00	0.04	2.43	1.57	0.00	22.46
Hays County	TX	0.00	0.00	0.00	0.00	0.54	9.87	0.00	1.81
Haywood County	NC	0.00	0.39	0.00	81.87	6.31	3.62	0.00	62.55
Henderson County	NC	0.00	1.63	12.56	39.81	2.98	14.31	10.67	42.28
Henderson County	TX	4.00	0.00	0.00	0.00	6.79	0.00	0.00	0.00
Hendricks County	IN	0.00	0.82	2.58	0.21	4.42	3.10	2.90	0.28
Hennepin County	MN	0.00	1.67	0.00	44.10	0.00	4.02	0.00	37.14
Henrico County	VA	0.00	5.00	153.77	76.84	1.04	51.63	85.27	41.53
Henry County	GA	0.00	4.22	0.00	0.00	2.98	18.70	0.00	0.00
Hernando County	FL	0.19	3.71	68.51	14.65	7.88	14.78	74.97	39.25
Hidalgo County	TX	0.06	0.03	0.00	0.13	13.99	4.04	0.00	6.34
Highlands County	FL	4.86	0.76	0.00	34.13	37.20	13.78	0.02	81.29
Hillsborough County	FL	0.00	2.75	0.00	76.54	20.55	27.93	0.00	75.10
Hillsborough County	NH	0.00	0.00	0.00	0.00	1.01	0.00	0.00	0.00
Hinds County	MS	0.00	0.00	0.00	0.00	1.40	0.29	0.00	9.11
Horry County	SC	0.00	2.92	0.00	2.58	13.58	37.79	0.00	20.69
Houston County	AL	0.00	0.13	0.00	19.65	0.00	0.33	0.00	18.40
Houston County	GA	0.00	0.00	16.52	42.37	0.66	0.07	19.56	54.81

County/Parish	State	Revenue[1] ($/per capita)				Current Operational Expenses ($/per capita)			
		Natural Resources, Other	Park & Recreation	Sewerage	Solid Waste Management	Natural Resources, Other	Parks & Recreation	Sewerage	Solid Waste Management
Howard County	IN	0.00	0.00	0.00	0.00	3.07	1.35	4.66	3.64
Howard County	MD	0.00	59.01	99.58	65.52	19.05	112.03	31.29	73.01
Hudson County	NJ	0.00	0.45	0.00	57.30	0.00	9.72	0.00	47.28
Humboldt County	CA	0.00	2.69	0.00	5.46	8.98	6.77	0.00	5.37
Hunterdon County	NJ	0.00	12.44	0.00	0.69	2.54	18.55	0.00	0.13
Iberia Parish	LA	0.00	4.92	18.45	0.00	19.43	20.66	13.07	26.95
Imperial County	CA	0.00	0.32	0.00	11.94	20.38	4.41	0.51	29.71
Indian River County	FL	0.00	28.30	93.35	69.07	5.37	62.62	57.33	72.70
Indiana County	PA	0.00	1.00	0.00	0.00	2.55	11.89	0.00	0.36
Ingham County	MI	6.14	7.12	0.00	0.00	13.24	30.89	0.00	0.00
Iredell County	NC	0.00	2.06	0.00	46.74	0.00	7.95	0.00	29.27
Isabella County	MI	0.00	0.00	0.00	8.96	8.45	12.55	0.00	13.48
Island County	WA	5.26	0.28	5.61	70.09	16.60	21.66	5.17	69.28
Jackson County	GA	0.00	6.00	0.00	16.89	36.20	20.06	0.00	26.72
Jackson County	IL	0.00	0.00	0.00	0.00	0.00	0.00	0.00	0.00
Jackson County	MI	6.65	4.74	0.00	49.85	8.78	14.59	0.00	43.31
Jackson County	MS	0.00	4.36	0.00	0.00	1.64	28.70	0.00	9.57
Jackson County	MO	0.00	7.31	0.31	0.00	0.00	20.17	0.05	0.00
Jackson County	OR	0.00	11.30	0.00	0.00	5.81	18.96	0.00	0.44
James City County	VA	0.00	39.32	79.38	3.87	7.26	70.76	0.00	43.62
Jasper County	MO	0.00	0.00	0.00	0.00	0.00	0.00	0.00	0.00
Jefferson County	AL	0.00	0.00	224.49	1.69	0.00	0.00	87.52	4.26
Jefferson County	AR	0.00	0.00	0.00	19.95	0.11	0.36	0.00	26.27
Jefferson County	CO	0.00	0.71	0.00	0.00	1.26	18.62	0.00	0.97
Jefferson County	MO	0.00	0.00	0.00	0.00	0.00	3.88	0.00	0.00
Jefferson County	NY	0.00	0.00	0.00	16.68	12.69	1.32	0.00	21.28
Jefferson County	TN	0.00	0.00	0.00	13.78	2.49	0.00	0.00	53.89
Jefferson County	TX	0.00	21.95	0.00	0.00	1.36	33.16	0.00	0.00
Jefferson County	WV	0.00	0.00	0.00	0.00	0.00	19.26	0.00	0.00
Jefferson County	WI	0.43	13.84	0.00	0.71	12.48	23.96	0.00	1.24
Jefferson Parish	LA	0.00	9.86	56.34	46.42	74.08	63.98	84.31	66.11
Jessamine County	KY	0.00	0.00	0.00	5.27	6.57	16.83	0.00	12.44
Johnson County	IN	0.00	2.37	0.40	0.00	2.07	4.82	0.10	0.00
Johnson County	IA	0.00	0.71	0.00	0.00	2.72	10.68	0.00	4.26
Johnson County	KS	0.00	27.44	155.59	0.00	1.73	57.12	78.76	0.00
Johnson County	MO	0.00	0.00	0.00	0.00	0.00	0.00	0.00	0.00
Johnston County	NC	1.50	0.00	48.24	27.28	0.00	0.02	21.04	26.82
Jones County	MS	0.00	0.00	0.00	33.96	3.13	17.26	0.00	30.63
Josephine County	OR	7.66	7.88	0.00	1.02	20.29	9.89	0.00	1.05
Kalamazoo County	MI	0.00	3.81	0.00	0.00	0.00	14.02	0.00	0.00
Kanawha County	WV	0.00	4.12	0.00	0.00	0.00	12.31	0.00	0.00
Kane County	IL	6.19	0.00	0.00	0.11	12.44	0.00	0.00	0.64
Kankakee County	IL	0.00	0.00	0.00	0.00	0.73	0.00	0.00	0.00
Kauai County	HI	0.00	15.86	119.21	92.06	0.13	223.26	98.52	193.71
Kenai Peninsula Borough	AK	0.00	0.00	0.00	0.00	17.89	37.46	0.00	99.41
Kendall County	IL	0.00	0.00	0.00	0.00	12.29	0.00	0.00	0.00
Kennebec County	ME	0.00	0.00	0.00	0.00	0.00	0.00	0.00	0.00
Kenosha County	WI	0.06	17.15	0.00	0.75	7.72	27.38	0.00	0.00
Kent County	DE	0.00	1.92	99.25	18.35	0.56	15.19	57.99	17.05
Kent County	MI	0.00	5.99	0.00	48.07	3.66	13.47	0.00	37.82
Kenton County	KY	0.00	23.25	556.40	0.00	0.65	27.78	229.92	0.00
Kern County	CA	0.00	2.05	4.66	61.23	7.50	13.70	4.36	48.96
Kerr County	TX	0.00	0.00	0.00	0.00	4.51	2.75	0.00	0.00
Kershaw County	SC	0.00	4.89	25.51	25.16	0.02	18.18	15.10	36.40
King County	WA	5.78	3.78	207.08	6.25	19.95	20.95	68.89	7.11
Kings County	CA	0.00	0.26	0.00	0.00	15.45	18.69	0.00	0.00

County/Parish	State	Revenue[1] ($/per capita) Natural Resources, Other	Park & Recreation	Sewerage	Solid Waste Management	Current Operational Expenses ($/per capita) Natural Resources, Other	Parks & Recreation	Sewerage	Solid Waste Management
Kitsap County	WA	0.46	3.72	103.33	49.43	5.08	15.85	47.67	53.11
Klamath County	OR	9.70	0.47	0.00	62.71	18.97	7.30	0.00	59.41
Knox County	OH	0.00	0.00	32.78	0.00	7.24	0.00	19.18	1.16
Knox County	TN	0.00	0.75	0.00	0.00	1.11	23.58	0.00	9.73
Kootenai County	ID	0.00	0.43	0.00	72.74	0.50	2.19	0.00	44.26
La Crosse County	WI	0.40	4.08	0.00	96.97	17.16	7.31	0.00	91.70
La Plata County	CO	0.00	1.28	0.00	0.00	10.41	12.00	0.00	1.65
La Porte County	IN	0.00	0.02	0.00	24.95	5.41	3.55	0.00	17.23
Lackawanna County	PA	0.00	5.64	0.00	0.00	1.04	11.55	0.00	0.44
Lafayette County	MS	0.00	0.00	0.00	23.84	1.72	4.55	0.00	27.24
Lafourche Parish	LA	0.51	0.23	3.81	0.01	49.22	14.21	2.22	57.78
Lake County	CA	0.00	0.22	96.55	41.85	31.10	23.07	81.97	30.82
Lake County	FL	0.39	0.82	0.00	51.52	6.92	11.28	0.00	59.12
Lake County	IL	6.07	5.49	36.26	0.33	41.15	5.18	28.85	0.00
Lake County	IN	0.00	9.68	0.51	0.00	1.26	23.01	0.35	0.00
Lake County	OH	0.00	0.00	74.10	24.32	0.00	0.00	33.77	30.77
Lamar County	MS	0.00	0.00	0.00	0.00	4.54	12.53	0.00	24.46
Lancaster County	NE	0.00	0.00	0.00	0.00	0.00	9.14	0.00	0.00
Lancaster County	PA	0.00	0.75	0.00	0.00	8.93	2.16	0.00	0.00
Lancaster County	SC	0.00	11.82	0.00	1.35	0.00	23.91	0.00	25.37
Lane County	OR	6.90	2.73	0.00	42.66	8.63	7.55	0.00	38.45
Lapeer County	MI	0.00	1.52	0.00	0.00	7.63	4.32	0.00	0.00
Laramie County	WY	0.00	0.00	0.00	0.00	1.46	4.50	0.00	0.00
Larimer County	CO	2.37	17.70	0.00	16.59	14.88	28.22	1.09	12.50
Lasalle County	IL	0.00	0.00	0.00	0.00	0.00	1.67	0.00	0.00
Lauderdale County	AL	0.00	0.28	0.00	45.59	0.27	0.54	0.00	36.65
Lauderdale County	MS	0.00	0.00	0.00	0.00	1.67	6.78	0.00	22.57
Laurel County	KY	0.00	0.00	0.00	0.00	0.05	10.85	0.00	3.38
Laurens County	SC	0.00	0.00	0.00	29.68	0.00	2.71	0.00	28.24
Lawrence County	OH	0.00	0.00	50.71	0.00	0.00	0.00	25.02	0.00
Lawrence County	PA	0.00	0.00	0.00	0.00	0.72	2.67	0.00	1.50
Lea County	NM	0.00	38.91	0.00	0.00	1.83	80.43	0.00	13.30
Leavenworth County	KS	0.00	0.00	0.00	11.13	8.76	0.09	0.00	13.27
Lebanon County	PA	0.00	0.00	0.00	0.00	0.00	0.00	0.00	0.00
Lee County	FL	3.49	7.79	74.40	78.17	21.22	46.32	24.33	93.62
Lee County	MS	0.00	0.00	0.00	22.09	2.63	7.47	0.00	22.22
Lee County	NC	0.00	6.32	0.00	19.02	1.73	19.29	0.00	19.04
Lehigh County	PA	0.02	0.01	0.00	0.00	2.03	5.29	0.00	0.00
Lenoir County	NC	0.00	0.00	0.00	41.72	12.64	13.66	0.00	43.12
Leon County	FL	0.00	0.11	0.42	26.10	30.65	15.67	0.79	36.86
Lewis And Clark County	MT	0.00	0.00	0.00	45.61	2.72	18.77	0.00	37.84
Lewis County	WA	0.11	8.77	0.00	87.50	22.89	6.84	0.00	95.72
Lexington County	SC	0.00	0.01	0.00	7.88	4.35	0.71	0.00	31.44
Liberty County	GA	0.00	5.75	0.00	45.74	0.15	26.38	0.00	43.44
Licking County	OH	0.00	0.00	13.63	0.00	0.00	3.03	9.06	0.00
Limestone County	AL	0.00	1.04	0.00	0.00	0.00	5.56	0.00	1.93
Lincoln County	NC	0.70	0.00	26.63	41.88	3.01	14.47	16.54	46.20
Lincoln County	SD	0.00	0.00	0.00	0.00	11.70	0.56	0.00	7.99
Linn County	IA	0.00	2.48	0.00	0.00	2.36	22.21	0.00	0.12
Linn County	OR	0.00	19.91	0.00	0.00	3.28	15.63	0.00	0.00
Livingston County	MI	0.00	0.00	0.00	0.00	0.00	0.00	0.00	0.00
Livingston Parish	LA	0.00	10.93	4.18	0.00	11.08	15.85	3.14	0.00
Lonoke County	AR	0.00	0.00	0.00	0.00	0.01	0.00	0.00	9.60
Lorain County	OH	0.04	0.00	4.96	7.31	1.05	0.00	3.66	8.39
Los Angeles County	CA	0.00	0.37	6.97	4.38	19.26	28.59	5.34	2.98
Loudon County	TN	0.00	0.00	0.00	0.00	0.45	0.00	0.00	13.10

County/Parish	State	Revenue[1] ($/per capita) Natural Resources, Other	Park & Recreation	Sewerage	Solid Waste Management	Current Operational Expenses ($/per capita) Natural Resources, Other	Parks & Recreation	Sewerage	Solid Waste Management
Loudoun County	VA	0.00	44.74	0.00	16.05	3.12	89.40	4.33	13.33
Lowndes County	GA	0.00	7.23	19.14	3.18	1.20	45.31	15.83	0.61
Lowndes County	MS	0.00	0.00	0.00	0.00	6.16	19.44	0.00	0.00
Lubbock County	TX	0.00	0.00	0.00	0.00	0.79	1.83	0.00	0.00
Lucas County	OH	0.00	51.37	20.00	5.28	0.54	62.88	16.34	24.52
Luzerne County	PA	0.00	0.00	0.00	1.87	8.47	7.52	0.00	0.00
Lycoming County	PA	0.00	0.00	0.00	135.57	4.64	1.12	0.09	117.39
Lyon County	NV	0.00	2.20	63.68	0.00	0.00	15.60	8.94	0.00
Macomb County	MI	0.00	0.33	0.00	0.00	3.69	0.64	4.79	0.00
Macon County	IL	0.00	0.00	0.00	0.00	0.00	0.00	0.00	0.00
Madera County	CA	4.57	0.01	0.00	26.51	12.26	0.05	0.00	28.35
Madison County	AL	0.00	0.27	0.00	29.03	0.00	2.95	0.00	21.35
Madison County	IL	0.00	0.00	11.64	0.00	12.30	4.53	7.99	2.89
Madison County	IN	0.00	0.00	0.00	0.50	2.49	13.32	0.91	0.85
Madison County	KY	0.00	0.09	0.00	0.00	0.07	7.11	0.00	0.00
Madison County	MS	0.00	0.00	0.00	0.00	3.04	0.58	0.00	17.95
Madison County	NY	0.00	0.00	6.90	49.73	28.13	5.33	4.63	56.05
Madison County	TN	0.00	0.41	0.00	0.00	5.43	10.02	0.00	7.25
Mahoning County	OH	0.00	0.00	88.30	9.07	0.00	0.00	69.51	14.58
Manatee County	FL	0.00	9.73	170.67	107.15	29.27	47.45	95.90	91.98
Marathon County	WI	4.12	5.22	0.00	20.66	5.05	24.33	0.00	23.35
Maricopa County	AZ	0.01	1.60	0.00	0.12	6.97	2.37	0.51	1.46
Marin County	CA	0.00	12.84	53.16	0.00	31.80	89.44	38.58	7.90
Marion County	FL	0.02	3.33	39.17	8.25	10.44	13.41	11.60	42.32
Marion County	OH	0.00	0.00	17.00	0.00	1.64	0.00	15.72	25.62
Marion County	OR	0.00	0.60	2.01	67.02	1.23	0.52	2.22	58.69
Marion County	WV	0.00	4.45	0.00	0.00	0.00	34.10	0.00	0.48
Martin County	FL	0.00	10.79	91.92	122.05	46.24	57.79	52.73	117.80
Mason County	WA	16.19	0.81	30.64	42.60	34.41	7.23	23.90	41.66
Matanuska-susitna Borough	AK	0.00	11.37	1.22	64.21	0.02	26.21	2.67	47.51
Maui County	HI	0.00	2.90	282.37	83.31	0.00	165.33	152.53	113.93
Maury County	TN	0.00	0.43	0.00	19.49	1.80	11.99	0.00	38.91
Maverick County	TX	0.00	0.00	0.00	37.14	0.00	15.48	0.00	45.44
Mccracken County	KY	0.00	5.80	0.00	0.00	1.22	11.22	0.00	6.29
Mchenry County	IL	0.00	5.02	0.00	0.00	0.00	28.43	0.00	0.00
Mckinley County	NM	0.00	0.00	0.00	0.00	0.63	2.33	0.00	5.13
Mclean County	IL	0.00	0.00	0.00	0.00	0.00	6.04	0.00	0.00
Mecklenburg County	NC	0.00	2.48	14.05	12.82	9.35	38.62	0.00	9.10
Medina County	OH	0.00	0.00	77.24	49.24	1.69	0.00	66.12	37.10
Mendocino County	CA	0.00	0.19	59.01	15.65	12.06	4.79	58.34	5.44
Merced County	CA	0.00	1.19	0.00	5.84	11.99	6.68	0.00	0.00
Mercer County	NJ	0.00	19.21	0.00	113.67	0.76	30.36	0.00	100.55
Mercer County	PA	0.00	0.00	0.00	0.00	0.00	0.12	0.00	1.26
Mercer County	WV	0.00	0.00	0.00	0.00	0.00	10.41	0.00	1.02
Merrimack County	NH	0.00	0.00	0.00	0.00	4.97	0.00	0.00	0.00
Mesa County	CO	0.00	0.80	0.38	26.91	1.18	11.22	0.80	24.27
Miami County	OH	0.00	0.00	19.83	47.51	0.00	8.77	19.84	45.82
Miami-dade County	FL	0.00	18.89	118.70	98.71	32.42	106.39	70.43	95.22
Middlesex County	NJ	0.00	4.42	96.90	51.17	1.45	12.06	56.74	42.43
Milwaukee County	WI	0.00	45.05	0.00	0.00	0.00	99.54	0.00	0.00
Minnehaha County	SD	0.00	0.11	0.00	0.00	1.24	6.74	0.00	0.00
Missoula County	MT	9.05	7.35	0.00	2.63	20.36	25.43	0.00	2.30
Mobile County	AL	0.00	1.12	0.00	0.04	0.00	5.42	0.00	7.62
Mohave County	AZ	8.73	7.22	0.00	6.83	5.69	3.57	0.00	2.42
Monmouth County	NJ	0.00	11.24	0.00	42.80	2.47	29.39	0.00	49.85

County/Parish	State	Revenue[1] ($/per capita)				Current Operational Expenses ($/per capita)			
		Natural Resources, Other	Park & Recreation	Sewerage	Solid Waste Management	Natural Resources, Other	Parks & Recreation	Sewerage	Solid Waste Management
Monongalia County	WV	0.00	0.00	0.00	0.00	0.00	16.18	0.00	5.18
Monroe County	FL	0.00	9.28	0.00	225.08	20.76	19.77	3.81	209.69
Monroe County	IN	0.00	5.87	0.07	0.00	2.08	9.89	1.95	0.00
Monroe County	MI	0.00	0.18	0.00	0.00	5.17	2.93	0.00	0.00
Monroe County	NY	0.00	3.72	28.14	7.65	0.93	15.44	72.44	20.25
Monroe County	PA	0.00	0.02	0.00	0.00	21.10	16.41	0.00	0.00
Montcalm County	MI	0.00	0.21	0.00	3.04	4.88	0.32	0.00	2.80
Monterey County	CA	0.00	14.39	5.61	0.00	51.23	27.28	5.94	0.40
Montgomery County	AL	0.00	0.00	0.00	0.00	0.00	1.89	0.00	0.63
Montgomery County	MD	0.00	46.32	156.70	99.57	2.62	183.97	79.07	119.70
Montgomery County	OH	0.00	0.00	74.10	39.51	1.21	1.07	61.38	32.26
Montgomery County	PA	0.00	0.30	0.00	0.00	0.00	5.65	0.00	0.44
Montgomery County	TN	0.00	0.00	0.00	0.00	2.07	3.04	0.00	0.00
Montgomery County	TX	0.00	0.85	0.00	0.00	1.00	2.08	0.00	0.00
Montgomery County	VA	0.00	0.00	15.17	0.00	0.00	9.14	13.76	0.00
Moore County	NC	0.17	1.43	83.41	12.81	4.94	5.41	58.88	20.83
Morgan County	AL	0.00	0.00	0.00	22.50	0.00	4.79	0.00	27.72
Morgan County	IN	0.00	0.00	0.00	0.00	3.26	0.42	0.00	0.00
Morris County	NJ	0.00	25.31	0.00	76.74	1.82	78.05	0.00	73.49
Multnomah County	OR	0.00	0.00	1.13	0.00	0.31	0.00	0.64	0.00
Muskegon County	MI	0.00	3.85	105.88	13.85	0.00	3.81	50.45	12.03
Muskingum County	OH	0.00	0.00	51.63	0.00	2.35	0.00	41.26	0.00
Muskogee County	OK	0.00	0.00	0.00	0.00	0.84	0.00	0.00	0.00
Nacogdoches County	TX	0.00	1.76	0.00	0.00	1.18	14.53	0.00	0.00
Napa County	CA	0.00	0.00	202.80	0.00	104.22	3.23	97.09	0.00
Nash County	NC	1.13	0.00	2.82	21.73	3.20	5.47	7.50	21.81
Nassau County	FL	0.00	0.00	27.75	0.05	10.70	8.01	10.86	3.58
Nassau County	NY	0.00	13.28	1.25	0.00	5.14	21.72	68.90	0.00
Natrona County	WY	0.00	11.57	0.00	0.00	5.00	11.98	0.00	0.01
Navajo County	AZ	0.00	0.00	0.00	0.00	7.88	0.78	0.00	0.00
Nevada County	CA	0.00	0.07	47.08	17.61	6.37	0.00	37.98	11.98
New Castle County	DE	0.00	2.06	121.10	0.00	1.39	7.38	95.63	0.00
New Hanover County	NC	0.00	6.17	0.00	58.66	0.40	37.04	0.00	53.78
Newton County	GA	0.00	0.17	31.92	27.48	1.65	19.47	20.12	51.50
Niagara County	NY	0.00	2.29	1.45	0.81	8.36	19.26	16.34	3.25
Norfolk County	MA	0.00	1.61	0.00	0.00	0.00	1.29	0.00	0.00
Northampton County	PA	0.00	0.03	0.00	0.00	14.20	3.56	0.00	0.80
Northumberland County	PA	0.00	0.00	0.00	0.00	2.58	19.93	0.00	0.00
Nueces County	TX	0.00	2.56	0.00	0.00	0.68	11.00	0.00	0.00
Oakland County	MI	0.00	6.35	82.88	0.00	0.58	12.14	183.05	0.00
Ocean County	NJ	0.00	2.25	0.00	0.01	0.84	10.01	0.00	4.44
Oconee County	SC	0.00	4.39	0.00	15.57	0.89	21.37	0.00	47.05
Ogle County	IL	0.00	0.00	69.64	0.00	0.00	0.00	0.00	7.68
Okaloosa County	FL	2.03	6.30	11.87	40.99	5.36	70.67	60.40	39.10
Oklahoma County	OK	0.00	0.00	0.00	0.00	0.65	0.00	0.00	0.00
Oldham County	KY	0.00	3.87	0.00	0.57	1.15	14.40	0.00	4.30
Olmsted County	MN	0.00	0.00	0.57	141.37	3.46	14.11	0.32	86.70
Oneida County	NY	0.00	0.00	55.45	0.00	8.76	2.74	35.84	0.00
Onondaga County	NY	0.00	6.00	149.53	72.42	7.62	50.41	109.96	73.73
Onslow County	NC	0.00	0.93	0.00	33.50	1.95	13.13	0.00	22.77
Ontario County	NY	0.00	0.28	30.32	0.00	13.16	4.37	24.15	0.63
Orange County	CA	4.77	12.74	0.00	39.83	20.61	27.45	0.00	27.27
Orange County	FL	0.79	42.82	84.04	58.99	14.00	24.65	138.73	56.71
Orange County	NY	0.00	4.57	15.05	35.29	6.34	18.81	21.33	38.26
Orange County	NC	2.71	22.73	1.16	38.12	9.22	33.41	2.04	75.29
Orangeburg County	SC	0.00	0.00	1.31	15.82	0.00	0.00	0.00	52.73

County/Parish	State	Revenue[1] ($/per capita) Natural Resources, Other	Park & Recreation	Sewerage	Solid Waste Management	Current Operational Expenses ($/per capita) Natural Resources, Other	Parks & Recreation	Sewerage	Solid Waste Management
Osceola County	FL	0.00	10.89	0.00	12.09	7.04	38.05	0.00	9.11
Oswego County	NY	0.00	0.05	0.00	52.61	9.03	7.04	0.00	52.89
Otero County	NM	0.00	0.00	0.00	0.00	8.76	3.17	0.00	12.69
Ottawa County	MI	0.00	1.56	40.33	1.14	3.33	9.08	24.58	2.42
Otter Tail County	MN	0.00	0.00	0.00	114.70	15.77	7.25	0.00	119.11
Ouachita Parish	LA	0.08	0.98	3.28	0.00	0.05	4.38	10.10	0.00
Outagamie County	WI	0.00	0.36	0.00	90.73	14.29	5.85	0.00	118.38
Oxford County	ME	0.00	0.00	0.00	0.00	2.41	0.00	0.00	0.00
Palm Beach County	FL	2.44	12.65	45.54	185.08	26.03	49.21	46.02	139.69
Pasco County	FL	2.67	3.11	112.29	52.14	2.58	15.73	97.17	53.66
Passaic County	NJ	0.00	3.33	0.00	0.00	0.00	5.62	0.00	0.54
Paulding County	GA	0.00	3.38	79.83	5.03	2.09	15.69	63.17	5.67
Payne County	OK	0.00	0.00	0.00	0.00	3.70	9.26	0.00	0.00
Pearl River County	MS	0.00	0.00	0.00	0.00	4.07	5.00	0.00	3.21
Pender County	NC	0.00	0.73	18.49	81.72	21.60	9.69	0.94	85.44
Pennington County	SD	0.93	0.00	0.00	0.00	4.05	0.00	0.00	0.00
Penobscot County	ME	0.00	0.00	0.00	0.00	0.68	0.00	0.00	0.00
Peoria County	IL	0.00	0.00	0.00	1.53	0.00	0.00	0.00	2.04
Pickens County	SC	0.00	4.96	11.10	0.00	0.48	11.42	11.60	26.31
Pierce County	WA	0.05	11.02	86.19	4.91	16.66	23.87	39.31	7.65
Pike County	KY	0.00	0.19	0.00	78.02	0.14	12.36	0.48	44.31
Pike County	PA	0.00	0.00	0.00	0.00	58.89	3.38	0.00	0.00
Pima County	AZ	0.16	6.97	149.28	1.11	0.51	11.42	33.25	2.73
Pinal County	AZ	0.02	0.00	0.00	0.01	6.25	0.06	0.00	0.42
Pinellas County	FL	0.69	5.64	69.77	92.04	13.92	17.94	59.15	70.94
Pitt County	NC	0.00	0.00	0.00	43.81	1.23	3.46	0.00	46.02
Pittsylvania County	VA	0.00	1.06	0.00	32.03	0.55	23.47	0.00	39.82
Placer County	CA	0.02	5.93	0.00	6.47	10.38	12.48	0.00	6.05
Platte County	MO	0.00	5.10	0.00	0.00	0.00	34.11	0.00	0.00
Plymouth County	MA	0.00	0.00	0.00	0.00	0.21	0.00	0.00	0.00
Polk County	FL	0.49	0.65	0.00	58.61	8.76	12.80	0.00	41.76
Polk County	IA	0.00	30.12	2.06	0.00	14.16	23.27	0.98	0.60
Polk County	OR	1.24	0.00	0.00	0.00	9.05	0.72	0.00	0.00
Pope County	AR	0.00	0.00	0.00	0.00	0.17	0.62	0.00	0.00
Portage County	OH	0.00	0.00	67.76	27.09	0.00	0.00	36.17	17.82
Porter County	IN	0.00	2.26	0.00	0.14	1.94	7.57	0.06	0.00
Pottawatomie County	OK	0.00	0.00	0.00	0.00	0.89	0.00	0.00	0.00
Pottawattamie County	IA	0.00	0.00	0.00	0.00	13.29	11.99	0.00	2.34
Prince Georges County	MD	0.00	23.59	178.53	99.68	0.79	222.95	88.86	95.18
Prince William County	VA	0.00	28.55	138.85	40.37	0.00	63.11	88.91	32.39
Pueblo County	CO	0.00	4.76	0.00	0.00	2.28	16.83	0.00	0.00
Pulaski County	AR	0.00	0.00	0.00	11.04	0.04	0.00	0.00	9.63
Pulaski County	KY	0.00	0.66	0.00	0.00	1.46	7.22	0.00	12.42
Pulaski County	MO	0.00	0.13	0.00	0.00	0.49	11.92	0.00	0.00
Putnam County	FL	0.00	0.72	2.86	12.75	5.97	13.28	1.70	94.31
Putnam County	NY	0.00	17.66	0.00	0.14	5.63	37.09	0.00	2.30
Putnam County	TN	2.56	0.53	0.00	7.02	3.24	11.99	0.00	48.18
Putnam County	WV	0.00	7.93	0.00	0.00	0.00	9.53	0.00	0.00
Racine County	WI	0.10	2.66	0.00	0.42	5.89	9.00	0.00	0.00
Raleigh County	WV	0.00	0.00	0.00	0.00	0.00	21.00	0.00	0.00
Ramsey County	MN	0.00	7.88	0.00	0.01	1.29	18.66	0.00	38.94
Randolph County	NC	0.00	0.00	0.00	14.69	3.75	0.14	0.00	21.15
Rankin County	MS	0.00	0.00	0.00	29.42	1.82	0.97	0.00	29.70
Rapides Parish	LA	0.00	0.00	0.00	0.00	0.00	1.92	0.00	0.00
Reno County	KS	0.71	0.00	0.74	75.49	2.84	2.74	1.49	63.61
Rensselaer County	NY	0.00	0.00	41.66	0.00	2.86	2.98	26.47	0.00

County/Parish	State	Revenue[1] ($/per capita) Natural Resources, Other	Park & Recreation	Sewerage	Solid Waste Management	Current Operational Expenses ($/per capita) Natural Resources, Other	Parks & Recreation	Sewerage	Solid Waste Management
Rice County	MN	0.00	0.09	0.00	35.62	8.32	4.17	2.12	39.62
Richland County	OH	0.00	0.00	19.46	0.00	0.00	0.98	18.53	0.00
Richland County	SC	0.00	5.36	10.68	56.34	2.82	0.00	5.97	71.71
Riverside County	CA	0.00	7.07	1.60	31.22	27.95	6.05	1.52	25.02
Roane County	TN	0.00	1.59	10.35	1.97	2.37	3.98	5.31	29.23
Roanoke County	VA	0.00	54.02	0.00	0.18	0.90	87.02	0.00	55.53
Robertson County	TN	0.00	0.00	0.00	12.18	1.94	0.00	0.00	31.38
Robeson County	NC	0.00	0.20	0.00	47.51	3.99	7.38	0.00	45.65
Rock County	WI	0.80	0.79	0.00	0.00	5.71	4.08	0.00	0.00
Rock Island County	IL	0.00	13.69	0.00	0.00	0.00	28.12	0.00	0.00
Rockdale County	GA	0.00	6.80	121.97	0.81	2.30	21.65	109.43	3.74
Rockingham County	NH	0.00	0.00	0.00	0.00	0.48	0.00	0.00	0.00
Rockingham County	NC	1.85	0.00	4.80	35.21	1.74	0.10	7.21	23.03
Rockingham County	VA	0.00	9.67	34.55	74.40	1.75	17.63	23.17	49.26
Rockland County	NY	0.00	0.07	1.99	140.58	1.36	5.44	61.33	141.23
Rogers County	OK	0.00	0.00	0.00	0.00	0.00	0.00	0.00	0.00
Ross County	OH	0.00	0.00	0.74	0.00	7.41	0.00	0.98	1.52
Rowan County	NC	0.01	10.10	0.00	32.53	0.35	15.40	0.00	23.93
Rutherford County	NC	0.00	0.15	0.00	51.92	1.94	0.53	0.09	53.65
Rutherford County	TN	0.00	0.43	0.00	5.84	3.39	1.55	0.00	10.59
Rutland County	VT	0.00	0.00	0.00	0.00	0.00	0.00	0.00	0.00
Sacramento County	CA	0.00	9.56	17.47	46.68	3.12	18.33	14.86	37.56
Saginaw County	MI	0.00	0.29	0.00	1.46	2.74	31.29	0.00	2.24
Salem County	NJ	0.77	0.00	0.00	0.00	0.83	0.00	0.00	0.00
Saline County	AR	0.00	0.00	2.35	0.00	0.11	0.12	1.42	0.00
Saline County	KS	3.62	0.00	0.18	0.04	14.40	0.74	0.00	0.04
Salt Lake County	UT	0.00	6.08	0.00	10.63	6.40	90.01	0.00	10.82
San Benito County	CA	0.00	2.83	0.00	23.80	17.90	11.82	0.00	17.23
San Bernardino County	CA	0.00	4.11	4.55	53.85	19.76	8.09	0.92	28.77
San Diego County	CA	0.00	1.19	5.56	6.21	5.51	6.07	5.87	4.71
San Joaquin County	CA	0.00	2.37	4.28	29.29	17.39	8.17	5.35	26.50
San Juan County	NM	0.00	4.94	0.00	3.48	12.66	36.54	0.00	24.78
San Luis Obispo County	CA	113.19	28.75	0.00	8.85	78.77	32.20	16.21	0.66
San Mateo County	CA	0.00	2.71	6.67	4.95	6.50	13.17	4.68	2.70
Sandoval County	NM	0.00	0.00	0.00	18.10	0.00	0.00	0.00	13.63
Sangamon County	IL	0.00	0.00	0.00	0.00	0.00	0.00	0.00	0.00
Santa Barbara County	CA	0.00	13.44	22.33	55.36	30.21	23.57	10.39	45.76
Santa Clara County	CA	0.58	2.79	7.15	0.46	2.35	19.09	6.15	0.54
Santa Cruz County	CA	0.00	6.23	86.15	80.86	21.07	22.42	70.89	83.51
Santa Fe County	NM	0.00	0.00	1.63	3.30	1.16	4.79	2.17	11.68
Santa Rosa County	FL	2.62	2.02	0.00	25.81	20.11	6.00	10.95	18.09
Sarasota County	FL	44.18	6.02	125.68	44.18	62.57	63.68	47.82	89.60
Saratoga County	NY	0.00	0.00	66.14	0.00	21.06	4.17	38.05	0.00
Sarpy County	NE	0.00	4.38	12.04	28.41	1.10	11.19	4.11	14.45
Sauk County	WI	1.51	1.66	0.00	0.02	19.88	5.82	0.00	2.57
Schenectady County	NY	0.00	2.59	0.00	1.10	7.57	4.51	0.00	2.18
Schuylkill County	PA	0.00	0.00	0.00	0.00	12.96	2.28	0.00	0.00
Scott County	IA	0.00	11.80	0.00	0.00	12.86	7.21	0.00	4.77
Scott County	KY	0.00	0.00	0.00	5.54	3.10	15.76	0.00	2.61
Scott County	MN	0.00	0.82	0.00	0.00	13.83	8.78	0.00	0.00
Sebastian County	AR	0.00	5.70	0.00	0.00	0.00	10.65	0.00	0.00
Sedgwick County	KS	0.13	0.20	0.00	3.00	0.85	17.53	0.00	2.85
Seminole County	FL	0.33	2.81	63.30	27.23	6.97	16.41	44.20	56.44
Seneca County	OH	0.00	0.00	7.80	0.00	0.00	1.69	5.46	0.00
Sevier County	TN	0.00	0.00	0.00	0.24	2.99	0.00	0.00	29.08
Shasta County	CA	0.00	0.00	0.00	19.02	7.63	0.90	0.00	14.58

County/Parish	State	Revenue[1] ($/per capita) Natural Resources, Other	Park & Recreation	Sewerage	Solid Waste Management	Current Operational Expenses ($/per capita) Natural Resources, Other	Parks & Recreation	Sewerage	Solid Waste Management
Shawnee County	KS	0.00	15.68	0.00	62.57	5.39	79.58	0.00	47.67
Sheboygan County	WI	2.01	0.01	0.00	0.00	14.08	2.75	0.00	0.88
Shelby County	AL	0.00	0.00	0.00	0.00	0.00	3.32	0.00	12.07
Shelby County	TN	0.79	0.36	0.33	0.73	2.67	2.37	0.36	1.14
Sherburne County	MN	0.00	0.00	0.00	0.00	4.37	3.46	0.00	10.79
Skagit County	WA	1.86	5.00	15.04	71.32	41.10	8.62	10.33	62.78
Smith County	TX	0.00	0.00	0.00	0.00	0.78	0.00	0.00	0.59
Snohomish County	WA	0.21	4.05	0.15	63.00	2.73	10.83	18.19	49.10
Solano County	CA	0.00	1.17	0.00	9.58	5.86	2.95	0.00	0.00
Somerset County	ME	0.00	0.25	0.00	0.00	0.00	0.25	0.00	0.00
Somerset County	NJ	0.00	0.00	0.00	1.50	2.57	24.34	0.00	7.48
Somerset County	PA	0.00	0.00	0.00	0.00	19.26	6.77	0.00	0.00
Sonoma County	CA	0.00	9.19	43.22	75.94	8.95	40.43	35.96	63.06
Spalding County	GA	0.00	2.08	50.32	0.00	1.97	30.41	41.38	12.19
Spartanburg County	SC	0.00	3.18	0.00	27.14	0.00	26.55	0.00	18.02
Spokane County	WA	3.21	10.35	64.39	0.00	9.23	14.10	41.89	3.64
Spotsylvania County	VA	0.00	0.00	103.14	0.00	0.00	52.74	65.66	0.00
St Charles County	MO	0.00	13.07	0.00	0.00	0.27	28.00	0.00	0.00
St Charles Parish	LA	2.60	2.90	105.87	51.40	123.03	40.59	85.52	42.32
St Clair County	AL	0.00	0.00	0.00	0.00	0.44	0.00	0.00	0.00
St Clair County	IL	0.00	0.00	0.00	3.90	0.00	0.00	0.00	8.29
St Clair County	MI	7.83	0.11	7.31	30.30	10.34	18.13	6.97	22.47
St Croix County	WI	0.37	1.86	0.00	0.08	21.55	8.90	0.00	1.82
St Johns County	FL	13.45	39.35	64.22	85.77	7.18	78.56	34.58	86.42
St Joseph County	IN	0.03	0.02	0.00	1.82	3.76	17.29	0.00	0.00
St Landry Parish	LA	0.00	0.00	0.32	0.00	11.95	0.96	0.32	0.05
St Louis County	MN	34.46	0.00	0.00	31.01	40.30	0.15	0.00	37.46
St Louis County	MO	0.00	0.99	3.09	1.40	9.19	20.79	1.97	0.91
St Lucie County	FL	0.00	8.57	15.97	31.52	35.31	45.07	7.49	47.47
St Martin Parish	LA	0.06	1.35	3.45	0.00	14.56	3.88	3.73	0.00
St Mary Parish	LA	0.00	24.28	23.51	72.50	38.67	63.13	32.90	72.12
St Marys County	MD	0.00	30.94	128.69	3.71	16.85	76.57	38.09	33.04
St Tammany Parish	LA	0.37	5.14	17.01	1.44	14.25	17.59	11.86	5.95
Stafford County	VA	0.00	12.26	139.31	0.00	1.08	47.78	46.79	0.00
Stanislaus County	CA	0.00	4.49	0.00	12.16	7.84	14.51	0.00	8.03
Stark County	OH	0.00	0.00	56.65	0.00	0.00	0.00	38.15	0.00
Stearns County	MN	0.00	1.62	0.00	3.69	55.97	0.00	0.00	0.00
Story County	IA	0.00	0.00	0.00	0.00	5.53	7.20	0.00	3.65
Strafford County	NH	0.00	0.00	0.00	0.00	0.00	0.00	0.00	0.00
Suffolk County	NY	0.00	6.99	20.52	0.00	2.30	16.74	33.14	0.00
Sullivan County	TN	0.00	2.11	62.56	1.32	1.11	1.66	36.17	8.23
Summit County	OH	0.00	0.00	70.73	0.00	0.00	15.12	71.40	0.00
Sumner County	TN	0.00	0.00	0.00	0.00	2.50	0.01	0.00	0.00
Sumter County	FL	0.00	0.00	0.00	65.14	8.00	5.76	0.00	55.38
Sumter County	SC	0.00	0.00	0.00	0.00	0.29	22.79	0.00	0.00
Surry County	NC	0.00	0.32	0.21	26.63	2.60	8.13	0.00	30.85
Sussex County	DE	0.00	0.00	89.64	0.00	0.00	0.00	75.79	0.00
Sussex County	NJ	0.00	0.00	44.39	77.13	2.15	0.08	25.42	38.87
Sutter County	CA	0.00	0.00	0.00	0.00	28.87	6.43	0.00	0.00
Talladega County	AL	0.00	2.61	32.72	11.83	0.00	14.33	24.13	2.19
Taney County	MO	0.00	0.00	26.70	0.00	0.00	0.00	72.32	0.00
Tangipahoa Parish	LA	0.00	0.00	9.90	16.26	8.68	32.65	7.26	30.29
Tarrant County	TX	0.00	0.00	0.00	0.00	0.35	0.00	0.00	0.00
Tazewell County	IL	0.00	0.00	0.00	0.00	0.00	0.00	0.00	0.00
Tehama County	CA	0.00	0.48	2.25	0.00	18.62	4.22	2.06	0.02
Thurston County	WA	0.50	2.23	4.60	76.47	5.74	4.86	10.40	61.26

County/Parish	State	Revenue[1] ($/per capita) Natural Resources, Other	Park & Recreation	Sewerage	Solid Waste Management	Current Operational Expenses ($/per capita) Natural Resources, Other	Parks & Recreation	Sewerage	Solid Waste Management
Tippecanoe County	IN	0.00	0.31	0.74	0.05	3.14	5.05	0.23	2.58
Tipton County	TN	0.00	0.00	0.00	1.87	2.97	0.19	0.00	16.50
Tom Green County	TX	0.00	0.06	0.00	0.00	1.63	0.86	0.00	0.00
Tompkins County	NY	0.00	0.00	0.00	51.86	20.37	15.39	0.00	44.97
Tooele County	UT	0.00	0.00	0.00	0.00	0.00	32.66	0.00	0.00
Travis County	TX	0.15	0.32	0.00	0.00	3.47	7.35	0.00	0.49
Troup County	GA	0.00	8.80	0.00	23.16	0.71	70.82	0.00	15.46
Trumbull County	OH	0.00	0.00	59.09	0.00	0.00	0.00	56.74	0.00
Tulare County	CA	0.00	0.43	0.36	19.86	13.98	5.12	0.34	24.36
Tulsa County	OK	0.00	3.15	0.00	0.00	1.67	13.35	0.00	0.00
Tuolumne County	CA	0.00	4.11	0.00	23.00	9.03	19.67	0.00	18.86
Tuscaloosa County	AL	0.00	0.00	0.00	0.00	0.00	13.96	0.00	2.82
Tuscarawas County	OH	0.00	0.00	15.24	0.00	3.70	0.00	14.33	0.00
Twin Falls County	ID	12.62	0.00	0.00	28.71	12.96	6.43	0.00	35.48
Ulster County	NY	0.00	0.60	0.00	82.39	5.37	3.32	0.00	65.99
Umatilla County	OR	13.38	0.37	0.00	0.53	10.00	1.26	0.00	0.10
Union County	NJ	0.00	14.14	0.00	0.00	0.62	19.95	0.00	0.58
Union County	NC	0.00	2.29	64.80	20.26	0.00	7.99	30.70	19.93
Union County	OH	1.23	0.48	5.13	0.00	4.33	1.99	5.26	0.00
Utah County	UT	0.00	0.00	23.68	12.23	1.85	1.75	22.16	12.69
Valencia County	NM	0.00	0.00	0.00	3.30	0.00	0.00	0.00	6.69
Van Buren County	MI	0.00	0.00	0.00	0.00	7.02	0.04	0.00	0.00
Vanderburgh County	IN	0.00	4.33	0.07	0.00	1.52	14.57	0.02	0.00
Venango County	PA	0.00	0.00	0.00	0.00	11.64	5.12	0.00	0.00
Ventura County	CA	0.00	5.56	35.05	0.02	59.48	4.51	31.90	0.00
Vermilion County	IL	0.00	0.00	0.00	0.00	0.00	0.00	0.00	3.16
Vermilion Parish	LA	0.00	0.00	0.00	7.05	43.86	0.13	0.00	56.49
Vernon Parish	LA	2.15	0.00	0.00	0.00	1.65	3.57	0.00	31.46
Victoria County	TX	0.00	0.00	0.00	0.00	2.48	0.51	0.00	0.00
Vigo County	IN	0.00	0.00	0.17	1.58	5.30	9.80	0.02	0.04
Volusia County	FL	0.45	6.63	7.88	25.98	11.68	47.71	20.02	45.91
Wagoner County	OK	0.00	0.00	0.00	0.00	0.00	0.00	0.00	0.00
Wake County	NC	0.00	0.13	0.01	24.24	5.89	2.71	0.04	26.66
Walla Walla County	WA	0.97	14.00	4.53	0.00	34.71	0.62	4.04	0.65
Walton County	FL	0.00	1.30	0.00	5.69	7.57	23.94	0.00	125.35
Walton County	GA	0.00	6.39	62.72	7.91	2.40	27.31	23.89	12.84
Walworth County	WI	1.28	0.14	0.00	0.87	13.39	1.15	0.00	2.51
Ward County	ND	0.00	0.00	0.00	0.00	4.42	6.50	0.00	0.00
Warren County	KY	0.00	2.64	0.00	0.00	6.07	19.28	0.00	1.50
Warren County	NJ	0.00	0.00	0.00	56.63	4.67	0.71	0.00	47.26
Warren County	NY	0.00	1.60	0.12	0.00	18.36	18.88	0.18	0.00
Warren County	OH	0.00	0.00	37.44	0.46	0.00	0.00	30.18	0.64
Warrick County	IN	0.00	4.79	1.00	0.00	3.07	9.08	6.69	0.52
Washington County	AR	0.00	0.00	0.00	1.98	0.47	0.00	0.00	1.80
Washington County	MD	0.00	8.79	57.77	32.31	17.36	28.69	44.31	48.83
Washington County	MN	0.00	0.00	0.00	0.00	0.28	9.55	0.00	21.45
Washington County	NY	0.00	0.37	24.00	8.80	14.99	14.38	22.89	11.80
Washington County	OK	0.00	0.00	0.00	0.00	0.19	0.00	0.00	0.00
Washington County	OR	0.83	0.04	201.93	0.00	3.83	1.76	99.00	0.00
Washington County	PA	0.00	0.00	0.00	0.00	1.68	0.98	0.00	0.00
Washington County	TN	0.00	0.00	0.00	0.59	2.88	0.00	0.48	12.06
Washington County	UT	0.00	0.00	0.00	59.52	5.57	5.40	0.00	56.44
Washington County	VT	0.00	0.00	0.00	0.00	0.00	0.00	0.00	0.00
Washington County	VA	0.00	5.57	5.70	0.00	2.03	14.07	0.00	37.84
Washington County	WI	0.28	8.88	0.00	0.05	11.33	26.68	0.00	0.00
Washoe County	NV	0.00	25.28	29.54	0.00	21.04	66.40	0.00	0.00

County/Parish	State	Revenue[1] ($/per capita)				Current Operational Expenses ($/per capita)			
		Natural Resources, Other	Park & Recreation	Sewerage	Solid Waste Management	Natural Resources, Other	Parks & Recreation	Sewerage	Solid Waste Management
Washtenaw County	MI	0.03	9.37	0.00	0.00	7.13	19.21	0.00	1.45
Waukesha County	WI	0.38	13.76	0.00	3.36	5.47	30.06	0.00	6.50
Waupaca County	WI	0.23	1.73	0.00	7.91	25.56	11.74	0.00	17.98
Wayne County	IN	0.00	0.00	0.00	0.00	8.41	0.00	0.01	0.00
Wayne County	MI	1.18	0.86	58.73	0.00	0.90	7.99	57.13	0.00
Wayne County	NY	0.00	1.63	0.00	0.00	18.29	9.84	0.00	0.00
Wayne County	NC	0.00	0.00	2.72	31.74	0.00	0.72	4.07	34.57
Wayne County	OH	0.00	0.00	6.85	0.00	4.30	0.00	5.46	0.72
Wayne County	PA	0.00	0.00	0.00	0.00	20.49	7.72	0.00	54.42
Webb County	TX	0.22	2.42	0.00	0.00	0.63	3.39	1.49	0.00
Weber County	UT	0.00	0.00	0.00	0.00	0.96	55.86	0.00	0.00
Weld County	CO	0.00	0.00	0.00	3.49	5.51	1.35	0.00	0.28
Westchester County	NY	0.00	29.40	3.99	20.21	0.01	45.74	140.10	64.06
Westmoreland County	PA	0.00	0.00	0.00	0.00	0.28	7.01	0.00	0.00
Whatcom County	WA	0.26	1.68	0.00	4.47	22.80	12.16	0.00	4.54
White County	AR	0.00	0.00	0.00	0.00	0.37	0.09	0.00	0.00
Whiteside County	IL	0.00	0.00	0.00	14.63	0.00	0.00	0.00	4.62
Whitfield County	GA	0.00	0.38	0.00	46.52	1.14	7.58	0.00	52.35
Wicomico County	MD	0.00	13.21	0.00	58.99	0.88	110.70	0.00	62.06
Wilkes County	NC	0.00	1.60	0.00	31.35	7.51	12.14	0.00	25.89
Will County	IL	2.38	0.00	0.00	1.68	18.03	0.00	0.00	1.36
Williamson County	TN	0.00	19.76	0.00	3.80	1.78	49.67	0.00	20.69
Williamson County	TX	0.00	0.57	0.00	0.00	2.07	3.36	0.00	0.13
Wilson County	NC	0.00	0.00	0.00	18.01	3.24	1.04	0.00	29.30
Wilson County	TN	2.06	0.02	0.00	3.13	10.13	0.40	0.00	18.76
Windsor County	VT	0.00	0.00	0.00	0.00	0.00	0.00	0.00	0.00
Winnebago County	IL	0.00	0.00	0.00	0.00	0.00	0.00	0.00	0.00
Winnebago County	WI	0.02	1.64	0.00	50.14	8.10	10.44	0.00	47.41
Wood County	OH	0.00	0.00	0.00	16.74	4.57	2.18	0.00	18.35
Wood County	WV	0.00	0.00	0.00	0.00	0.00	3.47	0.00	0.00
Wood County	WI	7.72	5.99	0.00	0.00	15.04	25.83	0.00	0.00
Woodbury County	IA	3.40	0.00	0.00	0.00	14.08	3.20	0.00	1.87
Worcester County	MD	0.00	2.92	0.00	73.23	16.70	53.51	0.00	107.89
Wright County	MN	0.00	0.28	0.00	0.35	5.53	10.40	0.00	4.01
Yakima County	WA	0.73	0.00	0.55	34.43	12.69	0.00	1.90	28.87
Yamhill County	OR	3.16	3.67	0.50	10.57	4.01	2.46	0.40	4.35
Yavapai County	AZ	0.06	0.00	0.09	1.53	1.72	1.27	0.04	2.68
Yellowstone County	MT	0.00	26.99	0.00	3.64	2.22	3.45	0.00	3.96
Yolo County	CA	0.00	1.04	0.00	48.68	9.39	3.94	0.38	43.14
York County	ME	0.00	0.00	0.00	0.00	0.56	0.00	0.00	0.00
York County	PA	0.00	0.91	0.00	0.00	4.29	8.14	0.00	0.00
York County	SC	0.00	3.09	25.18	23.20	7.70	23.20	19.23	29.83
York County	VA	0.00	8.40	149.65	73.21	7.70	30.76	110.59	70.66
Yuba County	CA	0.00	0.00	0.00	11.68	13.68	0.03	0.00	0.03
Yuma County	AZ	0.05	0.00	0.00	0.00	2.44	0.27	2.14	2.03

Note: *(1) Includes revenue raised through current charges only. Does not include intergovernmental revenue.*
Source: *U.S. Census Bureau, State and Local Government Finances, 2014*

Environmental Revenue and Expenditures for U.S. Cities/Townships with Populations of 50,000+

City	State	Revenue[1] ($/per capita)				Current Operational Expenses ($/per capita)			
		Natural Resources, Other	Park & Recreation	Sewerage	Solid Waste Management	Natural Resources, Other	Parks & Recreation	Sewerage	Solid Waste Management
Abilene (city)	TX	0.00	5.82	100.48	106.83	0.00	56.21	91.05	84.34
Abington (township)	PA	0.00	16.06	164.83	87.62	0.00	68.05	158.94	98.95
Akron (city)	OH	0.00	4.73	319.86	60.92	0.00	28.78	227.17	208.77
Albany (city)	GA	0.00	13.42	136.03	124.79	0.00	96.86	121.32	106.67
Albany (city)	NY	0.00	11.34	0.00	106.66	0.00	38.49	0.00	81.09
Albany (city)	OR	0.00	15.12	269.80	0.00	0.00	97.25	162.27	0.00
Albuquerque (city)	NM	0.00	28.20	108.27	114.53	0.00	125.50	86.37	97.17
Alexandria (city)	VA	0.00	23.41	306.98	40.46	0.00	204.99	205.51	0.00
Allen (city)	TX	0.00	115.98	129.72	65.44	8.14	211.54	38.03	59.03
Allentown (city)	PA	0.00	13.31	86.98	122.76	0.00	43.39	78.93	243.97
Alpharetta (city)	GA	0.00	30.78	0.00	50.33	0.00	98.96	0.00	51.00
Amarillo (city)	TX	0.00	26.63	103.84	98.97	0.00	96.41	62.10	58.44
Ames (city)	IA	0.00	21.83	134.64	58.93	0.00	52.75	82.22	64.43
Amherst (town)	NY	0.00	43.69	0.02	2.46	24.01	74.20	103.67	43.73
Anaheim (city)	CA	0.00	110.36	0.00	166.70	0.00	148.74	0.00	142.26
Anchorage (municipality)	AK	0.00	8.67	164.85	103.89	0.00	28.81	80.53	69.64
Anderson (city)	IN	0.00	5.63	680.30	42.41	0.00	26.45	189.11	51.05
Ankeny (city)	IA	0.00	44.42	252.99	10.91	0.00	75.72	144.29	11.71
Ann Arbor (city)	MI	0.00	9.32	246.97	28.27	0.00	98.41	122.85	109.09
Apple Valley (city)	MN	0.00	61.05	113.85	0.00	0.00	125.56	59.24	0.10
Appleton (city)	WI	0.00	9.81	137.23	14.29	14.91	49.14	128.20	43.91
Arlington (city)	TX	0.00	36.46	164.36	5.62	0.00	78.20	111.56	1.45
Arlington Heights (village)	IL	0.00	1.72	0.00	23.36	0.00	8.29	0.00	16.18
Arvada (city)	CO	0.00	101.92	145.51	0.00	0.00	214.45	92.70	0.00
Asheville (city)	NC	0.00	37.71	35.79	29.69	0.00	132.60	25.43	53.44
Athens-Clarke County (unified govt)	GA	0.00	8.39	147.65	57.40	1.13	54.22	97.84	63.56
Atlanta (city)	GA	0.00	4.61	394.09	122.13	0.00	104.65	264.87	121.60
Auburn (city)	AL	0.00	9.89	173.39	64.69	0.00	32.86	66.36	60.11
Auburn (city)	WA	0.00	27.41	392.09	169.11	0.00	123.02	153.26	158.53
Augusta-Richmond County (consol. govt)	GA	0.00	21.83	153.36	144.89	1.33	69.96	135.82	125.56
Aurora (city)	CO	0.00	38.99	150.67	0.00	0.00	106.40	53.67	0.00
Aurora (city)	IL	0.00	9.64	16.14	9.67	0.00	29.12	12.86	9.48
Austin (city)	TX	67.96	35.73	253.62	85.99	53.40	106.04	100.24	91.44
Avondale (city)	AZ	0.00	4.19	99.99	63.18	0.00	44.07	69.26	48.26
Babylon (town)	NY	0.00	9.11	0.00	102.96	0.00	46.37	0.00	177.96
Bakersfield (city)	CA	0.00	2.97	103.82	113.58	0.00	66.99	38.93	122.83
Baltimore (city)	MD	0.00	0.27	398.80	21.13	0.00	71.01	289.30	96.08
East Baton Rouge City-Baton Rouge Parish (city/parish)	LA	0.00	24.75	325.86	158.37	1.10	49.87	181.66	157.16
Battle Creek (city)	MI	0.00	43.37	299.17	59.46	0.00	92.32	273.57	57.88
Bayonne (city)	NJ		0.00	97.95	0.00	0.00	53.82	81.03	53.43
Baytown (city)	TX	0.00	31.28	188.71	60.25	14.33	94.51	58.14	60.74
Beaumont (city)	TX	0.00	12.32	138.14	74.02	0.00	71.35	70.58	56.72
Beaverton (city)	OR	0.00	0.00	105.87	0.00	0.00	2.40	70.97	0.00
Bellevue (city)	NE	0.00	3.54	81.89	39.66	0.00	34.24	83.58	40.01
Bellevue (city)	WA	0.00	103.66	509.40	5.50	4.68	257.47	341.75	9.74
Bellingham (city)	WA	0.00	19.24	291.90	2.04	0.00	36.99	191.70	8.00
Bend (city)	OR	0.00	0.00	249.14	0.00	0.00	0.00	92.06	0.00
Bensalem (township)	PA	0.00	52.66	0.00	0.00	0.00	92.57	0.00	0.00
Berkeley (city)	CA	0.00	19.24	111.37	288.14	0.00	137.01	90.29	272.39
Berwyn (city)	IL	0.00	8.40	65.48	90.45	0.00	29.47	61.12	76.52
Bethlehem (city)	PA	0.00	26.25	168.88	29.51	0.00	61.05	150.00	57.23
Billings (city)	MT	0.00	4.04	164.68	99.28	0.00	56.04	70.55	89.25

City	State	Revenue[1] ($/per capita)				Current Operational Expenses ($/per capita)			
		Natural Resources, Other	Park & Recreation	Sewerage	Solid Waste Management	Natural Resources, Other	Parks & Recreation	Sewerage	Solid Waste Management
Birmingham (city)	AL	0.00	8.08	0.00	0.00	0.00	103.76	0.00	0.00
Bismarck (city)	ND	0.00	78.38	102.75	101.76	0.00	135.17	115.51	73.01
Blaine (city)	MN	0.00	6.70	91.96	44.27	0.00	17.90	77.19	49.35
Bloomington (city)	IL	0.00	105.66	100.00	62.40	0.00	228.58	39.27	74.06
Bloomington (city)	IN	0.00	32.97	253.92	10.99	0.00	84.98	133.75	24.16
Bloomington (city)	MN	0.00	66.59	176.54	10.14	0.00	152.73	72.93	13.74
Blue Springs (city)	MO	0.00	29.18	129.79	0.00	0.00	95.07	98.03	0.00
Boca Raton (city)	FL	27.12	79.35	198.94	80.80	220.53	352.11	177.22	73.65
Boise (city)	ID	0.18	28.91	149.30	112.95	0.15	90.57	105.67	113.09
Bolingbrook (village)	IL	0.00	100.96	64.33	0.00	0.00	137.64	40.23	70.32
Bossier City (city)	LA	0.00	3.73	166.17	68.53	0.00	46.77	67.61	57.02
Boston (city)	MA	0.00	0.00	260.89	0.00	2.97	28.19	44.81	91.47
Boulder (city)	CO	0.00	75.02	186.08	0.00	0.00	336.57	116.00	0.00
Bowie (city)	MD	0.00	21.13	52.08	0.00	0.00	118.67	53.08	99.37
Bowling Green (city)	KY	0.00	35.98	164.65	0.00	0.00	118.07	139.97	1.86
Boynton Beach (city)	FL	0.00	52.96	276.35	140.80	3.10	105.44	155.49	90.59
Bradenton (city)	FL	0.00	23.48	174.00	130.40	43.45	55.60	141.96	118.10
Brick (township)	NJ	0.00	6.89	236.71	1.98	0.03	22.66	26.28	94.44
Bridgeport (city)	CT	0.00	15.11	244.14	0.43	0.00	45.28	186.89	53.93
Bristol (city)	CT	0.00	7.18	92.77	33.42	3.09	40.73	57.27	84.76
Bristol (township)	PA	0.00	1.22	100.26	0.39	0.00	8.36	50.28	99.13
Brockton (city)	MA	0.00	6.53	196.67	79.90	0.45	12.43	91.90	69.46
Broken Arrow (city)	OK	0.00	19.02	127.61	57.28	0.00	44.58	72.84	45.42
Brookhaven (city)	GA	0.00	0.00	168.33	166.66	0.00	72.73	136.02	157.15
Brookhaven (town)	NY	0.00	8.59	0.05	105.78	0.33	39.27	0.69	111.96
Brookline (town)	MA	0.00	21.42	234.42	44.78	2.02	60.89	8.38	51.40
Brooklyn Park (city)	MN	0.00	54.47	73.85	14.04	0.00	124.80	74.71	10.29
Broomfield (city/county)	CO	0.00	75.59	118.25	0.00	0.00	203.21	82.98	3.23
Brownsville (city)	TX	0.00	6.87	124.26	71.99	0.00	49.74	75.17	26.74
Bryan (city)	TX	0.00	25.36	153.61	91.33	2.20	50.59	73.25	75.08
Buckeye (town)	AZ	0.00	10.48	101.14	70.14	0.00	49.18	69.26	62.27
Buffalo (city)	NY	0.00	0.61	244.31	73.46	0.00	29.87	146.04	157.06
Burbank (city)	CA	0.00	48.89	164.39	156.22	0.43	96.58	86.21	122.52
Burlington (city)	NC	0.00	35.90	0.00	25.01	0.00	123.20	0.00	0.00
Burnsville (city)	MN	0.00	46.49	149.38	0.00	12.20	99.89	121.55	3.49
Caldwell (city)	ID	24.83	16.98	119.76	68.21	19.27	45.30	66.70	62.46
Calumet (township)	IN	0.00	0.01	0.00	0.00	0.00	2.10	0.00	0.00
Cambridge (city)	MA	0.00	9.87	380.06	0.00	0.76	156.16	19.14	48.67
Camden (city)	NJ	0.00	0.00	95.77	0.00	0.00	12.56	72.18	59.63
Canton Charter (township)	MI	0.00	63.23	170.67	0.00	0.00	117.99	72.92	35.58
Canton (city)	OH	0.00	0.00	195.90	91.68	34.08	25.34	138.53	71.94
Cape Coral (city)	FL	0.00	46.42	240.60	0.00	17.50	97.28	127.87	0.00
Carlsbad (city)	CA	0.00	78.35	117.19	30.37	0.29	184.63	74.89	25.48
Carmel (city)	IN	0.00	107.15	31.25	0.00	0.00	138.34	55.97	0.00
Carrollton (city)	TX	0.00	29.08	96.04	60.24	7.21	64.07	2.95	42.73
Carson City (city)	NV	0.00	23.79	153.90	62.64	3.81	125.22	97.43	28.96
Cary (town)	NC	0.00	37.73	253.85	51.61	87.49	88.29	123.72	51.98
Casa Grande (city)	AZ	0.00	20.90	155.93	124.05	0.00	152.69	74.19	87.40
Casper (city)	WY	0.00	78.62	136.32	190.13	0.00	164.40	107.33	133.14
Castle Rock (town)	CO	0.00	117.42	221.30	0.00	0.00	176.73	157.48	0.00
Cedar Park (city)	TX	0.00	17.95	176.94	50.87	0.00	46.32	77.61	48.71
Cedar Rapids (city)	IA	0.00	90.55	333.57	72.49	0.00	74.00	189.43	73.35
Center (township)	IN	0.00	0.00	0.00	0.00	0.00	0.17	0.00	0.00
Champaign (city)	IL	0.00	0.00	24.39	6.53	0.00	0.00	41.25	4.46
Chandler (city)	AZ	0.00	0.00	159.59	55.20	0.00	0.00	73.93	53.45
Chapel Hill (town)	NC	0.00	11.62	36.24	6.11	0.00	98.93	26.91	68.26

City	State	Revenue[1] ($/per capita) Natural Resources, Other	Park & Recreation	Sewerage	Solid Waste Management	Current Operational Expenses ($/per capita) Natural Resources, Other	Parks & Recreation	Sewerage	Solid Waste Management
Charleston (city)	SC	0.00	41.28	51.12	0.00	0.00	112.72	21.60	40.52
Charleston (city)	WV	0.00	41.23	430.26	79.78	0.00	197.19	207.86	102.51
Charlotte (city)	NC	0.55	32.65	304.50	15.10	6.56	94.66	83.11	56.80
Chattanooga (city)	TN	0.00	5.86	473.21	40.78	4.95	110.19	248.73	108.64
Cheektowaga (town)	NY	0.00	11.17	3.86	1.65	4.54	55.07	95.89	68.91
Cherry Hill (township)	NJ	0.00	0.00	63.91	0.00	0.00	10.80	25.99	69.66
Chesapeake (city)	VA	0.17	11.40	173.00	0.65	1.48	53.32	64.59	95.83
Cheyenne (city)	WY	0.00	36.90	197.66	199.92	0.00	116.21	93.96	133.18
Chicago (city)	IL	0.00	4.22	107.37	0.00	0.11	11.27	32.93	57.59
Chicopee (city)	MA	0.00	14.30	212.10	16.61	0.00	34.64	124.98	25.24
Chula Vista (city)	CA	0.00	4.97	130.69	5.12	0.00	89.64	119.37	5.38
Cicero (town)	IL	0.00	0.00	61.32	46.86	0.00	0.00	0.00	0.00
Cincinnati (city)	OH	0.00	57.03	37.92	1.40	0.00	178.52	448.24	58.23
Clarkstown (town)	NY	0.00	22.69	0.00	0.03	27.51	71.39	9.56	103.14
Clarksville (city)	TN	0.00	7.89	191.69	0.00	0.00	47.38	91.01	0.00
Clay (town)	NY	0.00	5.40	0.00	0.00	23.73	17.61	11.24	47.05
Clay (township)	IN	0.00	0.00	0.00	0.00	0.00	0.90	0.00	0.00
Clearwater (city)	FL	1.75	80.00	343.67	187.56	112.42	226.31	157.09	190.16
Cleveland (city)	OH	0.00	6.31	57.89	10.52	0.00	99.53	44.47	62.67
Clifton (city)	NJ	0.00	2.35	105.11	4.06	7.65	15.93	80.31	77.44
Clinton Charter (township)	MI	0.00	6.45	204.51	41.79	0.00	22.57	45.58	37.91
Colerain (township)	OH	0.00	0.00	0.00	0.00	0.00	17.05	0.00	0.00
College Station (city)	TX	19.41	15.54	140.85	77.44	9.25	74.53	53.60	64.59
Colonie (town)	NY	0.00	19.86	2.57	0.10	0.17	48.14	67.92	1.96
Colorado Springs (city)	CO	0.00	4.08	159.70	0.00	0.00	31.36	67.61	0.00
Columbia (city)	MO	0.00	37.89	166.50	144.67	0.00	111.71	65.69	117.15
Columbia (city)	SC	0.00	8.01	401.71	2.19	14.32	95.10	287.45	67.84
Columbus (city)	OH	0.00	10.44	272.08	0.01	0.00	134.12	153.14	51.04
Columbus (consol. govt)	GA	0.00	18.02	153.88	52.12	4.73	66.12	68.52	62.41
Commerce (city)	CO	0.00	58.19	0.00	13.20	0.00	167.46	0.00	37.85
Concord (city)	NC	0.00	23.59	220.57	1.51	5.67	68.49	147.08	65.56
Conway (city)	AR	0.00	11.43	158.29	129.11	0.00	35.70	62.69	95.94
Coon Rapids (city)	MN	0.00	39.20	99.69	0.00	0.00	68.39	95.42	0.00
Coral Gables (city)	FL	28.05	77.69	197.65	181.94	164.66	154.76	98.13	181.90
Coral Springs (city)	FL	1.03	32.02	83.36	0.00	0.00	108.53	57.07	0.25
Corona (city)	CA	0.00	9.38	202.55	0.00	0.00	54.23	119.03	0.00
Corpus Christi (city)	TX	0.00	32.85	185.65	115.85	0.00	78.94	94.40	56.92
Corvallis (city)	OR	0.00	28.32	214.49	0.00	0.00	109.88	134.66	5.91
Council Bluffs (city)	IA	0.00	66.32	79.12	80.01	2.63	139.08	90.69	87.75
Cranston (city)	RI	0.00	0.00	253.79	0.00	0.00	31.32	199.39	0.00
Dallas (city)	TX	0.00	39.82	211.43	63.69	2.07	105.96	94.28	46.53
Daly City (city)	CA	0.00	19.66	157.70	4.45	0.00	76.29	166.47	1.29
Danbury (city)	CT	0.23	36.51	147.14	0.00	3.10	68.20	74.04	2.39
Davenport (city)	IA	0.00	43.11	195.05	52.22	0.00	114.92	145.30	49.01
Davie (town)	FL	2.29	6.59	0.00	0.00	19.75	41.36	0.00	0.00
Dayton (city)	OH	0.00	21.33	277.36	0.00	0.00	60.72	200.55	0.00
Daytona Beach (city)	FL	147.89	103.09	386.35	201.11	143.10	169.81	86.83	151.37
Dearborn (city)	MI	0.00	52.67	331.24	0.00	0.00	168.34	82.20	61.30
Dearborn Heights (city)	MI	0.00	0.00	187.82	0.00	0.00	10.23	72.41	63.76
Decatur (city)	AL	0.00	9.29	260.84	105.09	0.00	136.68	127.82	153.70
Decatur (city)	IL	0.00	0.00	71.46	17.16	0.00	15.54	40.16	0.00
Delray Beach (city)	FL	33.56	84.37	0.00	79.69	29.48	416.97	0.00	72.05
Denton (city)	TX	0.00	31.67	198.48	189.75	0.00	97.47	112.05	137.19
Denver (city/county)	CO	0.00	57.25	174.54	12.46	0.00	168.69	131.90	12.46
Des Moines (city)	IA	0.00	3.73	259.07	58.64	1.52	53.71	187.64	51.11
Des Plaines (city)	IL	0.00	0.00	76.39	69.42	0.00	0.00	43.04	82.02

City	State	Revenue[1] ($/per capita)				Current Operational Expenses ($/per capita)			
		Natural Resources, Other	Park & Recreation	Sewerage	Solid Waste Management	Natural Resources, Other	Parks & Recreation	Sewerage	Solid Waste Management
Detroit (city)	MI	0.00	3.61	759.98	67.16	2.76	38.87	380.53	36.98
Dothan (city)	AL	0.00	29.75	174.22	0.00	0.00	143.14	157.17	87.12
Dubuque (city)	IA	0.00	23.58	221.20	65.23	3.82	130.74	92.44	59.50
Duluth (city)	MN	0.00	179.69	296.44	0.00	0.00	229.95	231.35	0.00
Dupage (township)	IL	0.00	1.88	0.00	0.00	0.00	4.99	0.00	0.00
Durham (city)	NC	0.00	15.90	221.32	26.79	4.14	49.83	135.45	60.86
Eagan (city)	MN	0.00	31.99	110.25	0.00	0.00	75.40	115.23	0.00
East Hartford (town)	CT	0.00	8.47	0.00	3.06	0.06	63.04	0.00	42.52
East Orange (city)	NJ	0.00	6.85	0.00	0.00	0.00	42.38	0.00	69.15
Eau Claire (city)	WI	0.00	23.96	143.93	0.89	10.42	106.05	101.74	0.89
Eden Prairie (city)	MN	0.00	75.95	81.85	0.00	0.00	160.61	103.10	56.24
Edison (township)	NJ	0.00	1.50	110.36	0.00	0.00	26.29	31.87	12.28
Edmond (city)	OK	0.00	34.65	128.93	91.03	0.00	65.11	39.70	60.05
El Paso (city)	TX	0.00	17.17	107.09	78.47	0.00	49.17	51.11	53.18
Elgin (city)	IL	0.00	57.44	49.78	40.43	0.00	133.60	0.00	45.17
Elizabeth (city)	NJ	0.00	0.13	158.94	1.77	0.00	74.62	79.65	69.45
Elkhart (city)	IN	0.00	11.69	440.64	0.00	4.47	52.62	98.33	0.00
Elyria (city)	OH	0.00	5.21	217.17	84.80	0.00	43.34	167.98	91.92
Enid (city)	OK	0.00	7.41	100.94	96.02	0.00	41.24	65.70	63.25
Erie (city)	PA	0.00	4.32	200.31	65.85	0.00	18.24	101.45	45.05
Escondido (city)	CA	0.00	17.12	200.86	0.00	0.00	62.27	137.77	0.00
Eugene (city)	OR	0.00	32.39	219.91	0.00	0.82	151.05	170.63	11.46
Evanston (city)	IL	0.00	70.38	178.36	48.26	0.00	194.88	30.85	62.03
Evansville (city)	IN	0.02	30.46	274.98	41.02	23.29	99.79	211.38	27.48
Everett (city)	WA	0.00	44.67	325.78	21.71	0.00	138.19	228.84	7.13
Fairfield (town)	CT	0.00	18.81	90.81	0.00	16.22	67.21	76.52	61.86
Fall River (city)	MA	0.00	1.06	205.80	18.58	0.00	15.33	105.62	75.02
Fargo (city)	ND	25.41	48.64	102.60	100.81	20.05	101.93	45.33	64.82
Farmington Hills (city)	MI	0.00	54.28	125.67	0.00	0.00	87.21	42.66	43.57
Fayetteville (city)	AR	0.00	8.60	211.69	120.43	0.00	43.30	150.82	120.48
Fayetteville (city)	NC	0.00	5.64	221.99	12.37	0.48	62.64	124.05	44.64
Federal Way (city)	WA	0.00	25.84	37.18	3.20	1.57	61.58	20.88	5.01
Fishers (town)	IN	0.00	1.58	129.57	0.00	0.00	8.86	98.26	0.00
Flagstaff (city)	AZ	22.01	0.00	121.00	181.49	71.29	0.00	66.09	102.41
Flint (city)	MI	0.00	0.00	288.93	0.00	0.00	33.14	200.42	48.91
Florissant (city)	MO	0.00	27.11	0.00	0.00	0.00	78.45	3.59	0.00
Flower Mound (city)	TX	0.00	20.26	149.69	1.36	0.00	116.09	121.79	1.36
Fort Collins (city)	CO	96.79	54.65	143.85	0.00	30.09	206.37	67.89	0.00
Fort Lauderdale (city)	FL	35.41	59.62	0.00	104.16	61.02	168.46	0.00	93.62
Fort Myers (city)	FL	55.01	99.64	463.51	196.04	106.18	185.67	414.06	121.62
Fort Smith (city)	AR	0.00	11.13	138.14	172.50	0.00	39.78	85.08	123.87
Fort Wayne (city)	IN	0.00	20.68	259.06	41.18	0.00	85.41	105.26	35.64
Fort Worth (city)	TX	0.00	10.43	225.82	68.77	0.00	97.05	141.59	58.69
Framingham (town)	MA	0.00	6.45	311.90	2.93	1.61	41.35	62.87	45.70
Franklin (city)	TN	0.00	0.67	219.31	85.81	0.00	51.78	115.43	91.30
Franklin (township)	NJ	0.00	0.00	178.68	0.00	0.00	7.34	157.41	9.74
Frederick (city)	MD	0.00	44.36	137.69	1.48	0.00	124.56	115.47	51.02
Fremont (city)	CA	0.00	26.54	0.00	29.27	0.00	33.54	0.00	24.93
Fresno (city)	CA	0.00	16.87	155.98	74.94	5.13	24.53	70.43	81.56
Frisco (city)	TX	0.00	35.58	145.59	75.80	0.00	81.35	85.01	67.27
Fullerton (city)	CA	0.00	26.43	49.11	73.43	0.00	61.53	15.87	71.67
Gainesville (city)	FL	2.78	16.93	334.10	59.32	99.24	76.96	170.05	56.82
Gaithersburg (city)	MD	0.00	50.98	0.00	0.00	0.00	140.25	0.00	33.55
Garden Grove (city)	CA	0.00	7.03	111.16	0.00	0.89	41.42	27.14	0.00
Garland (city)	TX	0.00	23.72	201.00	75.12	0.00	52.57	101.61	66.38
Gary (city)	IN	0.00	7.48	307.96	52.48	0.05	16.99	195.36	68.58

City	State	Revenue[1] ($/per capita)				Current Operational Expenses ($/per capita)			
		Natural Resources, Other	Park & Recreation	Sewerage	Solid Waste Management	Natural Resources, Other	Parks & Recreation	Sewerage	Solid Waste Management
Gastonia (city)	NC	0.00	9.66	261.27	17.08	0.00	67.23	197.92	57.82
Georgetown (city)	TX	0.00	28.39	141.86	98.15	0.00	40.00	69.54	88.93
Gilbert (town)	AZ	0.00	12.38	98.58	72.87	0.00	59.34	48.75	60.08
Glendale (city)	AZ	0.00	6.26	150.35	99.63	38.54	45.90	77.93	44.51
Glendale (city)	CA	0.00	19.49	78.24	106.03	0.00	71.30	51.42	84.68
Gloucester (township)	NJ	0.00	4.97	81.15	22.90	0.00	26.19	51.26	88.26
Goodyear (city)	AZ	0.00	5.72	147.30	87.77	0.00	65.76	46.88	70.95
Grand Forks (city)	ND	0.00	92.50	197.82	151.92	0.00	33.82	85.77	108.59
Grand Island (city)	NE	0.00	15.79	169.72	48.23	0.00	71.79	101.63	33.80
Grand Junction (city)	CO	0.00	88.14	154.89	54.09	0.00	219.60	169.11	61.15
Grand Prairie (city)	TX	0.00	57.35	151.83	59.79	0.00	133.14	97.84	47.56
Grand Rapids (city)	MI	0.00	2.33	256.63	24.55	0.00	29.87	111.00	57.19
Grapevine (city)	TX	0.00	102.12	150.09	0.00	0.00	216.33	95.25	0.00
Great Falls (city)	MT	0.08	45.24	176.19	55.01	10.62	86.08	98.54	53.49
Greece (town)	NY	0.00	3.64	1.78	0.00	6.61	16.31	11.40	6.19
Greeley (city)	CO	0.00	64.11	149.31	0.00	5.41	142.00	56.44	1.55
Green Bay (city)	WI	0.22	29.89	143.78	0.48	25.56	84.95	123.41	59.85
Green (township)	OH	0.00	0.00	0.00	0.00	0.00	31.15	0.00	0.00
Greenburgh (town)	NY	0.00	18.56	0.00	0.31	0.00	77.70	7.46	43.56
Greensboro (city)	NC	0.00	71.20	197.93	63.33	6.59	176.50	121.81	110.69
Greenville (city)	NC	0.00	15.43	200.00	75.84	0.00	82.68	152.94	84.86
Greenville (city)	SC	0.00	143.24	151.43	41.46	2.15	114.25	88.50	73.19
Greenwich (town)	CT	5.32	46.62	3.15	5.27	17.76	168.77	76.90	95.46
Greenwood (city)	IN	0.00	10.75	269.38	36.98	0.00	21.47	113.93	37.69
Gresham (city)	OR	0.00	0.50	202.74	4.96	0.00	27.22	142.63	6.29
Gulfport (city)	MS	0.00	14.37	256.91	76.60	0.00	89.44	43.33	53.51
Hamden (town)	CT	0.00	0.00	0.00	0.00	0.00	12.39	0.00	0.00
Hamilton (city)	OH	0.00	17.38	223.09	59.90	0.00	43.95	147.33	51.90
Hamilton (township)	NJ	0.00	1.28	174.46	0.09	0.01	42.65	139.83	43.24
Hammond (city)	IN	0.00	56.30	229.36	72.94	0.45	111.04	230.52	70.65
Hampton (city)	VA	0.00	118.94	124.02	132.27	0.00	221.63	75.65	118.41
Harlingen (city)	TX	0.00	28.87	157.43	135.74	0.00	82.90	99.17	98.16
Harrisonburg (city)	VA	0.00	21.78	198.85	208.68	0.00	99.43	154.88	170.70
Hartford (city)	CT	0.00	0.14	0.00	0.73	0.00	11.45	0.00	19.92
Haverhill (city)	MA	0.00	0.00	130.22	0.00	0.96	22.52	161.68	54.27
Hempstead (town)	NY	0.00	7.50	0.00	12.81	12.23	78.50	0.00	112.86
Hempstead (village)	NY	0.00	0.38	0.00	65.86	0.00	46.05	2.61	51.69
Henderson (city)	NV	0.00	35.29	144.47	0.00	0.00	140.30	102.31	0.00
Hendersonville (city)	TN	0.00	18.08	0.00	73.56	0.00	47.11	0.00	87.74
Hialeah (city)	FL	0.00	0.00	122.76	63.44	28.85	36.60	150.34	76.73
High Point (city)	NC	0.00	19.77	275.10	70.98	0.00	128.32	110.00	60.40
Hillsboro (city)	OR	0.00	35.18	267.26	0.00	0.00	169.81	75.47	0.00
Hoboken (city)	NJ	0.00	0.00	0.00	0.00	4.16	20.76	0.00	88.37
Hoffman Estates (village)	IL	0.00	37.63	41.11	17.86	0.00	49.55	40.16	23.13
Hollywood (city)	FL	23.75	24.17	377.95	90.97	28.46	96.37	187.97	79.58
Honolulu (city/county)	HI	0.00	28.76	397.71	123.67	0.02	97.58	114.16	155.96
Hoover (city)	AL	0.00	12.36	45.63	0.09	0.00	94.98	24.48	76.14
Houston (city)	TX	0.00	7.55	197.63	0.92	0.00	34.63	91.66	31.02
Howell (township)	NJ	0.00	0.00	125.90	0.00	1.66	4.10	110.22	8.77
Huntersville (town)	NC	0.00	68.07	14.37	17.47	0.00	116.64	8.16	0.00
Huntington (town)	NY	0.00	39.71	14.28	105.21	28.16	68.29	23.14	186.38
Huntsville (city)	AL	0.00	54.21	181.37	58.25	3.69	113.44	87.71	0.00
Idaho Falls (city)	ID	0.07	40.86	202.74	71.03	0.00	165.58	101.11	54.40
Independence (city)	MO	0.00	28.59	182.74	0.00	0.00	89.89	127.18	0.00
Indianapolis (city)	IN	0.00	42.36	221.25	0.00	0.00	69.04	0.00	47.94

City	State	Revenue[1] ($/per capita)				Current Operational Expenses ($/per capita)			
		Natural Resources, Other	Park & Recreation	Sewerage	Solid Waste Management	Natural Resources, Other	Parks & Recreation	Sewerage	Solid Waste Management
Inglewood (city)	CA	0.00	3.54	30.84	117.42	1.59	81.40	30.25	115.62
Iowa City (city)	IA	0.00	10.50	185.97	112.21	0.00	86.62	76.17	102.54
Irvine (city)	CA	0.00	35.34	0.00	0.00	0.00	233.48	0.00	0.00
Irving (city)	TX	22.59	2.59	123.25	49.30	17.74	103.08	76.76	45.17
Irvington (township)	NJ	0.00	0.00	81.23	0.00	4.81	16.55	65.14	51.70
Islip (town)	NY	0.00	21.49	0.00	0.00	0.37	36.04	0.00	138.88
Jackson (city)	MS	0.00	14.54	97.87	70.13	0.00	88.70	97.32	66.47
Jackson (city)	TN	0.00	36.78	0.00	184.93	0.00	108.17	0.00	160.73
Jacksonville (city)	FL	0.60	9.87	272.58	73.47	39.61	95.63	105.46	81.59
Jacksonville (city)	NC	0.00	10.05	236.11	51.89	0.00	70.62	136.89	70.71
Janesville (city)	WI	0.00	31.84	139.75	83.50	6.25	63.35	118.11	88.28
Jersey City (city)	NJ	0.00	0.58	193.36	19.81	0.00	20.59	52.43	128.63
Johns Creek (city)	GA	0.00	1.46	0.00	0.00	0.00	21.17	0.00	0.00
Johnson City (city)	TN	0.00	20.01	204.82	178.95	0.00	119.00	111.76	148.25
Joliet (city)	IL	0.00	23.30	154.00	82.38	0.00	45.58	74.75	77.12
Jonesboro (city)	AR	0.00	6.44	88.48	0.87	0.00	31.63	57.06	36.82
Joplin (city)	MO	0.00	27.98	164.74	41.25	0.00	74.69	73.04	50.82
Kalamazoo (city)	MI	0.00	27.33	278.09	0.00	5.04	47.47	268.75	33.03
Kansas City (city)	MO	0.00	4.27	321.26	0.00	25.09	102.11	155.70	44.46
Kenner (city)	LA	0.00	0.00	0.00	0.00	0.00	0.00	0.00	0.00
Kennewick (city)	WA	0.00	25.14	106.95	0.00	0.00	106.13	54.62	0.00
Kenosha (city)	WI	0.00	10.08	96.65	3.09	4.37	79.54	103.15	46.69
Kent (city)	WA	0.00	23.58	334.24	4.17	1.11	112.66	261.54	0.07
Kentwood (city)	MI	0.00	4.73	0.00	0.00	0.00	34.08	8.35	1.99
Kettering (city)	OH	0.00	153.72	0.00	0.00	0.00	226.73	0.00	0.00
Killeen (city)	TX	27.36	21.03	117.20	108.66	16.15	53.63	61.27	80.14
Kingsport (city)	TN	0.00	66.12	247.85	15.69	22.29	152.16	93.35	87.31
Kirkland (city)	WA	0.00	14.46	262.97	179.44	19.99	71.46	74.62	150.13
Kissimmee (city)	FL	0.00	18.06	59.95	58.60	0.00	73.11	52.61	56.41
Knoxville (city)	TN	0.00	32.96	405.64	6.91	0.00	106.85	198.04	56.92
Kokomo (city)	IN	0.00	6.10	237.35	0.00	0.00	58.00	127.86	57.39
La Crosse (city)	WI	0.00	105.40	108.96	0.02	10.68	178.13	112.47	43.04
La Habra (city)	CA	0.00	13.65	26.17	50.78	0.00	144.17	27.18	47.18
Lafayette (city)	IN	0.00	14.58	390.99	0.03	0.67	59.86	79.66	27.10
Lafayette City (city/parish)	LA	0.00	105.33	227.00	106.12	0.00	195.47	129.34	103.41
Lake Charles (city)	LA	0.00	27.84	156.42	0.00	0.00	108.89	103.54	100.88
Lake Havasu City (city)	AZ	0.00	17.29	443.89	112.18	0.00	54.16	123.40	104.74
Lakeland (city)	FL	45.23	88.38	235.97	123.42	10.75	250.97	186.91	127.31
Lakeville (city)	MN	0.00	29.95	74.42	0.00	14.25	53.55	15.70	0.00
Lakewood (city)	CO	0.43	66.57	39.41	0.00	18.95	129.40	22.03	0.00
Lakewood (city)	OH	0.00	0.00	156.48	0.00	0.00	41.08	122.77	56.61
Lakewood (city)	WA	0.00	3.93	45.65	0.00	0.00	25.21	24.79	0.00
Lakewood (township)	NJ	0.00	0.00	40.68	0.43	0.01	13.06	37.61	74.86
Lancaster (city)	PA	0.00	2.60	222.05	66.05	14.42	100.49	172.71	67.35
Lansing (city)	MI	0.00	52.05	277.09	45.13	0.00	141.30	117.13	41.96
Laredo (city)	TX	0.00	4.22	113.98	73.75	0.00	46.74	62.67	66.24
Las Cruces (city)	NM	0.00	8.17	118.22	114.28	0.00	82.78	82.80	109.17
Las Vegas (city)	NV	0.03	11.17	98.93	88.20	4.64	76.19	94.39	7.68
Lawrence (city)	KS	0.00	26.73	193.71	119.03	1.51	86.50	104.40	98.52
Lawrence (city)	MA	0.00	0.00	118.07	0.00	0.00	7.10	19.60	46.61
Lawton (city)	OK	0.00	17.43	145.10	95.59	0.00	77.34	56.51	40.96
Layton (city)	UT	0.00	13.21	115.86	46.06	0.00	57.39	35.91	18.90
League City (city)	TX	0.00	0.00	130.93	35.86	0.00	25.52	61.74	33.44
Lees Summit (city)	MO	0.00	33.68	160.13	30.40	0.00	71.34	126.99	30.61
Lehi (city)	UT	0.00	0.84	180.97	46.70	0.00	9.60	108.13	43.52
Lenexa (city)	KS	0.00	23.08	105.21	0.00	0.00	95.96	118.65	0.00

City	State	Revenue[1] ($/per capita)				Current Operational Expenses ($/per capita)			
		Natural Resources, Other	Park & Recreation	Sewerage	Solid Waste Management	Natural Resources, Other	Parks & Recreation	Sewerage	Solid Waste Management
Lewisville (city)	TX	0.00	15.14	107.25	31.48	0.00	85.40	0.00	0.00
Lexington-Fayette (urban county govt)	KY	0.00	19.33	157.63	29.68	0.00	57.09	79.90	104.54
Lincoln (city)	NE	0.00	7.29	90.03	17.88	0.00	33.14	45.87	23.84
Little Rock (city)	AR	0.00	88.71	243.50	94.02	0.00	177.72	111.66	66.32
Livermore (city)	CA	0.00	50.31	225.73	13.10	0.00	41.37	190.81	4.41
Livonia (city)	MI	0.00	65.08	170.48	1.80	0.00	97.41	160.89	122.69
Long Beach (city)	CA	0.00	14.60	37.91	187.40	0.00	231.57	28.55	165.85
Longmont (city)	CO	0.00	77.75	162.96	70.17	0.00	137.87	110.22	61.44
Longview (city)	TX	0.00	13.98	152.34	62.73	26.24	105.32	80.67	55.87
Lorain (city)	OH	0.00	0.00	276.69	0.00	0.00	5.33	150.95	0.00
Los Angeles (city)	CA	0.00	38.45	138.09	78.87	0.00	85.46	83.82	57.76
Louisville-Jefferson County (metro govt)	KY	0.00	21.73	0.00	2.09	5.82	39.40	0.00	31.17
Loveland (city)	CO	0.00	55.35	167.54	89.07	0.00	180.75	107.22	65.27
Lowell (city)	MA	0.00	22.89	153.47	28.76	0.00	48.90	94.04	46.88
Lower Merion (township)	PA	0.00	4.36	141.87	110.14	0.00	94.76	117.93	113.26
Lubbock (city)	TX	0.00	9.71	216.80	80.13	0.00	57.99	48.29	52.45
Lynchburg (city)	VA	0.00	5.68	297.77	8.45	0.00	78.09	147.96	33.45
Lynn (city)	MA	0.00	2.28	0.00	0.00	0.02	3.51	0.00	57.11
Macomb (township)	MI	0.00	26.88	127.27	0.00	0.00	32.90	102.26	0.00
Macon (city)	GA	0.00	0.14	0.00	46.18	0.00	9.58	2.47	50.22
Madison (city)	WI	0.00	32.44	181.66	3.87	19.24	121.63	53.72	57.35
Malden (city)	MA	0.00	0.00	265.71	25.95	0.07	13.03	21.51	44.46
Manchester (city)	NH	181.86	13.13	181.90	4.19	75.44	49.63	188.30	85.95
Manchester (town)	CT	0.00	5.52	137.16	146.99	0.00	98.96	83.00	106.06
Manhattan (city)	KS	0.00	12.80	186.28	0.00	0.00	117.59	116.25	0.00
Mansfield (city)	TX	22.59	8.43	139.78	35.09	8.42	69.15	74.37	30.06
Maple Grove (city)	MN	0.00	74.20	85.52	16.82	9.11	129.27	71.63	17.16
Marietta (city)	GA	0.00	2.50	230.88	60.62	0.00	23.44	143.07	49.67
Marysville (city)	WA	0.00	15.29	241.40	95.73	10.97	34.34	50.53	43.08
Mcallen (city)	TX	0.00	16.97	104.79	119.28	0.00	122.36	9.03	95.62
Mckinney (city)	TX	0.00	5.68	142.03	45.55	0.00	48.43	95.31	41.29
Medford (city)	MA	0.00	0.00	224.65	0.00	0.10	12.12	18.72	82.65
Medford (city)	OR	0.00	29.84	138.73	0.00	0.00	57.22	86.33	0.00
Melbourne (city)	FL	34.09	38.77	229.76	4.88	11.48	102.56	153.66	0.00
Memphis (city)	TN	0.00	8.53	195.22	91.11	0.00	56.10	99.00	78.01
Menifee (city)	CA	0.00	0.00	0.00	0.00	0.00	2.55	0.00	0.00
Meriden (city)	CT	0.00	0.22	151.88	0.80	0.00	32.64	216.21	23.10
Meridian (city)	ID	0.00	5.70	143.81	0.00	0.00	43.73	78.52	0.00
Mesa (city)	AZ	0.00	27.15	143.01	102.11	0.00	108.90	46.67	69.79
Mesquite (city)	TX	15.02	13.29	134.98	68.38	4.48	71.07	42.45	49.95
Miami Beach (city)	FL	0.00	187.45	508.96	87.97	85.68	673.06	344.37	169.98
Miami (city)	FL	0.56	47.23	0.00	61.97	42.02	115.43	2.47	58.00
Miami (township)	OH	0.00	0.00	0.00	0.00	0.00	7.85	0.00	4.99
Middletown (township)	NJ	0.00	0.00	138.30	0.00	0.00	20.28	118.76	66.51
Midland (city)	TX	0.00	27.08	81.52	93.29	0.00	73.71	56.73	82.58
Midwest City (city)	OK	0.00	25.18	110.64	90.24	0.00	42.67	86.77	70.11
Milford (city)	CT	1.97	7.18	3.90	3.69	0.77	21.59	148.09	87.88
Millcreek (township)	PA	0.00	3.44	181.70	0.00	1.74	21.51	160.56	0.00
Milwaukee (city)	WI	4.45	8.60	148.54	64.89	5.89	0.00	69.18	54.45
Minneapolis (city)	MN	0.00	46.07	247.53	74.18	0.00	309.56	57.73	84.59
Minnetonka (city)	MN	13.21	59.38	145.32	0.00	19.15	127.94	99.19	0.00
Miramar (city)	FL	0.00	13.56	150.89	0.24	26.70	85.17	53.27	0.69
Mission (city)	TX	0.00	17.92	73.96	75.03	0.00	61.77	26.12	65.67
Mission Viejo (city)	CA	0.00	15.52	0.00	0.00	0.00	131.17	0.00	0.00
Missoula (city)	MT	0.00	21.60	129.26	0.00	0.00	47.95	69.76	0.00

City	State	Revenue[1] ($/per capita)				Current Operational Expenses ($/per capita)			
		Natural Resources, Other	Park & Recreation	Sewerage	Solid Waste Management	Natural Resources, Other	Parks & Recreation	Sewerage	Solid Waste Management
Mobile (city)	AL	0.00	33.82	256.31	0.00	6.78	106.83	207.47	0.00
Modesto (city)	CA	0.00	18.23	220.77	22.84	0.00	72.78	103.72	21.64
Montgomery (city)	AL	0.00	32.97	0.00	76.98	0.00	192.43	0.00	68.36
Moore (city)	OK	0.00	0.00	124.82	63.79	0.00	26.71	0.00	22.50
Mount Pleasant (town)	SC	15.37	30.93	195.60	0.05	5.01	64.37	109.04	93.08
Mount Prospect (village)	IL	0.00	0.00	51.72	46.40	0.00	7.93	32.81	78.52
Mount Vernon (city)	NY	0.00	1.17	0.79	0.01	0.00	75.05	12.30	76.21
Muncie (city)	IN	0.00	3.89	218.01	0.00	0.00	20.07	276.45	73.82
Murfreesboro (city)	TN	0.00	27.01	201.26	0.29	0.00	89.68	99.47	32.74
Nampa (city)	ID	0.00	95.46	123.51	89.49	0.00	136.09	52.88	75.33
Naperville (city)	IL	0.00	3.20	97.13	6.75	0.00	55.25	44.43	44.71
Nashua (city)	NH	0.00	0.00	124.34	30.16	4.72	51.90	72.21	84.60
Nashville-Davidson County (metro govt)	TN	4.52	27.19	181.55	8.10	4.18	125.03	92.47	31.65
New Bedford (city)	MA	0.00	4.92	209.65	0.02	2.87	29.75	121.33	51.73
New Braunfels (city)	TX	0.00	33.75	162.86	110.90	0.00	87.85	82.18	81.05
New Britain (city)	CT	0.00	35.11	116.67	25.70	2.28	128.89	66.15	64.82
New Brunswick (city)	NJ	0.00	0.00	198.86	0.00	0.00	31.69	24.28	41.92
New Haven (city)	CT	0.00	10.78	0.00	48.13	0.00	42.68	0.00	42.91
New Orleans (city)	LA	0.00	109.84	210.04	91.22	0.80	783.03	206.73	101.91
New Rochelle (city)	NY	0.00	28.89	0.00	78.13	5.68	45.33	25.52	63.29
New York (city)	NY	0.00	12.76	253.08	1.01	0.00	77.35	50.26	149.65
Newark (city)	NJ	0.00	0.00	185.44	0.00	0.00	27.35	24.08	78.78
Newport News (city)	VA	0.00	36.36	177.61	71.49	0.00	117.94	117.77	63.57
Newton (city)	MA	0.00	1.90	337.16	0.00	0.68	41.03	42.17	89.93
Noblesville (city)	IN	0.00	5.31	483.66	1.77	0.00	42.11	67.10	0.00
Norfolk (city)	VA	0.00	39.46	110.90	81.10	0.00	291.85	67.29	71.43
Normal (town)	IL	0.00	75.81	78.29	30.64	0.00	167.95	67.97	48.85
Norman (city)	OK	0.00	14.72	117.82	117.04	0.00	57.23	86.84	104.27
North Bergen (township)	NJ	0.00	5.30	220.71	3.40	0.00	33.29	139.15	96.12
North Charleston (city)	SC	0.00	4.89	35.53	0.00	0.00	63.86	34.75	72.15
North Hempstead (town)	NY	0.00	60.85	8.21	152.72	30.43	118.10	48.83	222.73
North Las Vegas (city)	NV	0.00	17.55	176.29	0.00	1.80	53.62	77.37	0.00
North Little Rock (city)	AR	0.00	21.19	200.33	11.88	0.00	87.73	177.14	74.85
Norwalk (city)	CT	0.00	10.89	173.06	0.00	0.00	49.23	90.69	0.00
Novi (city)	MI	0.00	22.22	180.36	0.00	8.34	66.18	164.77	0.00
O'fallon (city)	MO	0.00	36.35	89.61	52.53	7.65	82.31	40.77	38.72
Oak Lawn (village)	IL	0.00	0.00	48.59	55.37	0.00	8.56	29.98	56.11
Oak Park (village)	IL	0.00	0.00	63.18	59.89	0.00	0.00	45.47	56.99
Oakland (city)	CA	0.00	10.22	127.96	0.00	1.69	105.18	84.10	0.00
Ocala (city)	FL	0.00	26.64	341.40	174.23	0.00	114.66	186.50	143.84
Oceanside (city)	CA	0.00	5.57	221.91	135.95	0.00	67.31	138.36	107.57
Odessa (city)	TX	0.00	13.59	117.43	91.97	0.00	51.66	44.91	80.01
Ogden (city)	UT	0.00	21.11	207.28	73.75	0.00	81.23	151.24	56.62
Oklahoma City (city)	OK	0.00	61.23	132.39	74.22	0.00	139.15	40.29	59.47
Olathe (city)	KS	0.00	13.07	150.87	93.78	0.00	17.56	97.11	84.67
Old Bridge (township)	NJ	0.00	10.67	239.20	0.09	0.00	24.70	84.08	7.04
Omaha (city)	NE	0.00	17.42	157.73	0.00	0.09	56.78	68.32	47.88
Ontario (city)	CA	0.00	3.34	127.06	179.39	5.67	62.03	91.95	139.73
Orangetown (town)	NY	0.00	72.45	18.15	0.00	0.00	114.44	139.41	15.56
Orem (city)	UT	0.00	26.37	129.54	42.95	0.00	25.20	95.61	35.75
Orland Park (village)	IL	0.00	63.07	112.30	88.77	0.00	162.67	97.18	91.18
Orlando (city)	FL	87.12	111.03	309.05	103.51	99.86	321.71	275.94	88.64
Oshkosh (city)	WI	0.00	16.93	147.27	5.24	4.83	89.42	122.59	31.93
Overland Park (city)	KS	0.00	97.60	20.62	0.00	0.00	47.89	15.59	0.00
Owensboro (city)	KY	0.00	32.43	276.18	90.35	0.00	90.59	16.02	88.57
Oxnard (city)	CA	0.00	24.46	151.27	215.08	0.00	107.47	93.60	178.28

City	State	Revenue[1] ($/per capita): Natural Resources, Other	Revenue: Park & Recreation	Revenue: Sewerage	Revenue: Solid Waste Management	Current Operational Expenses ($/per capita): Natural Resources, Other	Current Operational Expenses: Parks & Recreation	Current Operational Expenses: Sewerage	Current Operational Expenses: Solid Waste Management
Oyster Bay (town)	NY	0.00	21.17	1.67	28.41	6.80	108.15	11.66	205.67
Palatine (village)	IL	0.00	0.00	48.73	65.01	0.00	0.00	24.95	63.79
Palm Coast (city)	FL	86.30	23.03	144.31	90.40	82.79	52.33	223.75	88.76
Palo Alto (city)	CA	0.00	86.92	523.77	454.74	0.00	397.73	445.16	421.97
Parma (city)	OH	0.00	10.49	0.00	0.00	0.00	48.33	0.00	0.00
Parsippany-troy Hills (township)	NJ	0.00	75.41	268.21	26.83	0.00	106.99	162.30	59.09
Pasadena (city)	CA	0.00	199.04	56.86	112.38	0.00	244.54	29.15	86.61
Pasadena (city)	TX	0.00	17.41	96.10	44.38	0.00	58.12	63.03	39.82
Pasco (city)	WA	0.00	18.21	132.90	0.00	19.85	70.88	88.67	0.00
Passaic (city)	NJ	0.00	0.80	75.03	2.06	0.00	19.23	67.29	64.34
Paterson (city)	NJ	0.00	0.00	56.54	2.11	0.01	25.00	6.41	58.89
Pawtucket (city)	RI	0.00	0.18	0.00	0.31	0.00	25.45	6.69	41.62
Peabody (city)	MA	0.00	40.06	191.33	0.00	0.00	59.76	14.17	60.28
Pearland (city)	TX	0.00	18.13	110.77	77.90	0.00	58.43	66.92	78.26
Pembroke Pines (city)	FL	0.12	62.44	132.80	0.00	48.75	55.34	221.50	0.00
Pensacola (city)	FL	47.35	48.09	0.62	130.96	55.00	141.52	0.00	116.27
Peoria (city)	AZ	0.00	43.73	115.54	67.75	0.00	153.11	63.37	59.97
Peoria (city)	IL	0.00	0.00	31.07	52.32	0.00	0.00	12.86	61.13
Perth Amboy (city)	NJ	0.00	7.28	184.53	0.00	0.00	27.00	97.00	53.78
Pflugerville (city)	TX	0.00	13.69	112.29	69.12	0.00	53.84	65.68	68.94
Pharr (city)	TX	0.00	10.39	79.04	33.60	0.00	29.03	41.39	31.97
Philadelphia (city)	PA	0.00	0.00	191.63	9.29	0.00	63.96	172.11	92.81
Phoenix (city)	AZ	0.00	22.53	143.28	95.11	0.44	95.93	71.06	60.49
Pike (township)	IN	0.00	0.00	0.00	0.00	0.00	0.00	0.00	0.00
Piscataway (township)	NJ	0.00	0.00	171.73	0.10	0.00	23.16	65.55	13.39
Pittsburgh (city)	PA	0.00	4.95	0.00	0.25	0.00	45.16	0.00	52.43
Plainfield (city)	NJ	0.00	0.80	209.85	212.76	0.00	13.58	119.03	178.90
Plano (city)	TX	19.44	41.19	191.55	59.17	11.31	107.38	46.33	57.15
Plantation (city)	FL	34.19	60.96	149.15	16.74	62.04	140.94	133.08	23.88
Plymouth (city)	MN	34.20	18.55	101.39	5.58	22.54	109.68	85.89	12.22
Plymouth (town)	MA	0.00	2.37	82.41	30.38	0.58	6.44	42.47	24.76
Pocatello (city)	ID	0.00	25.12	167.13	124.03	3.41	77.88	103.48	89.64
Pompano Beach (city)	FL	0.00	41.49	168.85	53.81	123.06	102.26	151.30	39.77
Pontiac (city)	MI	0.00	0.15	0.00	54.89	0.00	2.66	0.00	58.22
Port Arthur (city)	TX	0.00	1.92	143.91	143.34	0.00	52.14	84.35	124.50
Port St Lucie (city)	FL	117.31	18.20	175.85	8.90	0.00	63.50	33.17	0.00
Portland (city)	ME	0.00	31.82	332.94	23.28	0.00	140.40	233.93	58.82
Portland (city)	OR	0.00	85.16	489.74	3.68	0.00	135.30	184.99	8.65
Portsmouth (city)	VA	0.00	8.39	0.00	128.45	0.00	108.63	0.00	109.94
Providence (city)	RI	0.00	2.38	0.00	0.00	58.64	72.08	4.44	53.28
Provo (city)	UT	0.00	5.41	44.51	35.62	0.00	86.92	36.85	33.16
Pueblo (city)	CO	0.00	24.48	167.90	0.00	0.00	72.59	98.44	0.00
Quincy (city)	MA	0.10	4.84	276.10	0.00	0.00	33.28	27.25	65.76
Racine (city)	WI	0.04	13.35	209.99	10.71	6.14	109.33	178.31	64.80
Raleigh (city)	NC	0.00	55.83	283.09	50.39	0.00	152.95	111.54	65.82
Ramapo (town)	NY	0.00	29.70	0.40	8.16	0.00	81.37	19.72	24.99
Rapid City (city)	SD	0.00	110.88	155.44	123.70	0.00	196.76	60.20	92.79
Reading (city)	PA	0.00	6.62	531.62	48.69	0.00	21.18	201.62	92.68
Redding (city)	CA	0.00	10.39	248.05	214.58	0.00	66.39	136.77	228.97
Redlands (city)	CA	0.00	4.38	122.04	156.42	0.14	46.19	89.28	124.00
Redmond (city)	WA	0.00	38.53	523.52	9.88	9.83	187.30	80.96	2.87
Reno (city)	NV	0.00	17.79	240.02	0.00	0.00	47.66	147.46	0.00
Renton (city)	WA	0.00	33.46	333.78	166.24	0.00	95.76	194.71	165.05
Revere (city)	MA	0.00	0.00	13.92	0.00	0.13	7.63	23.19	60.51
Richardson (city)	TX	17.05	52.77	162.45	117.35	9.31	141.17	165.45	112.25
Richland (city)	WA	0.00	29.12	207.59	150.98	0.00	114.62	91.89	119.82

City	State	Revenue[1] ($/per capita) Natural Resources, Other	Park & Recreation	Sewerage	Solid Waste Management	Current Operational Expenses ($/per capita) Natural Resources, Other	Parks & Recreation	Sewerage	Solid Waste Management
Richmond (city)	VA	0.00	6.36	336.79	62.52	0.00	97.79	179.06	191.96
Rio Rancho (city)	NM	0.00	15.63	164.17	0.00	4.79	65.09	117.03	2.91
Riverside (city)	CA	0.00	17.90	152.90	65.72	0.00	83.91	83.36	51.48
Roanoke (city)	VA	0.00	9.87	0.00	22.00	0.00	75.32	0.70	63.71
Rochester (city)	MN	0.00	61.25	246.75	0.00	4.58	140.46	102.57	0.00
Rochester (city)	NY	0.00	10.83	0.00	122.27	0.00	64.55	2.60	170.08
Rochester Hills (city)	MI	0.00	50.74	184.26	0.00	0.00	148.12	39.40	0.00
Rock Hill (city)	SC	0.00	25.84	285.23	98.96	43.49	148.33	83.10	0.00
Rockford (city)	IL	0.00	0.00	0.00	61.61	0.00	0.00	3.87	62.18
Rockville (city)	MD	0.00	78.30	138.27	83.73	0.00	261.08	124.12	80.93
Rocky Mount (city)	NC	0.00	18.27	274.11	113.27	10.14	130.37	228.12	103.67
Rogers (city)	AR	0.00	21.07	181.10	2.77	0.00	52.71	63.47	5.08
Roseville (city)	CA	0.00	55.31	287.75	169.55	0.00	171.68	229.56	123.26
Roswell (city)	GA	0.00	0.00	15.29	89.54	2.14	108.06	10.64	93.76
Round Rock (city)	TX	0.00	27.20	175.79	15.81	0.08	80.10	65.73	1.12
Rowlett (city)	TX	0.00	14.88	183.16	79.85	8.29	55.42	32.21	55.08
Royal Oak (city)	MI	0.00	25.12	257.72	0.03	0.00	68.46	196.70	105.40
Sacramento (city)	CA	0.00	32.92	59.29	121.63	0.39	111.99	48.71	90.89
Salem (city)	OR	0.00	0.00	299.40	0.00	0.00	40.44	197.93	0.00
Salt Lake City (city)	UT	0.00	0.00	145.80	0.00	0.00	0.00	81.37	0.00
San Antonio (city)	TX	0.34	11.11	229.66	63.98	0.66	79.63	110.55	60.87
San Bernardino (city)	CA	0.00	2.65	118.10	115.76	0.00	34.08	86.02	81.56
San Diego (city)	CA	0.00	48.12	263.96	34.18	10.06	132.78	129.63	31.10
San Francisco (city/county)	CA	0.00	47.80	311.06	0.00	0.00	259.97	179.15	0.00
San Jose (city)	CA	0.00	21.32	192.36	124.79	0.00	71.35	129.53	109.97
San Marcos (city)	TX	0.00	8.90	288.24	40.58	0.00	59.31	101.08	37.25
San Mateo (city)	CA	0.00	59.35	275.83	12.68	0.00	130.34	164.71	11.66
Sandy (city)	UT	0.00	40.22	50.31	60.15	0.00	90.78	16.36	41.80
Sandy Springs (city)	GA	0.00	8.78	0.00	0.00	0.00	41.73	14.95	0.00
Sanford (city)	FL	73.83	11.49	217.87	92.29	47.87	80.50	140.96	91.91
Santa Ana (city)	CA	0.00	14.08	18.07	50.95	0.00	70.23	12.67	47.62
Santa Barbara (city)	CA	0.00	58.11	207.09	225.73	0.00	201.77	140.63	216.95
Santa Clara (city)	CA	0.00	23.55	276.97	164.79	0.00	116.17	164.19	151.07
Santa Fe (city)	NM	0.00	43.25	170.95	263.89	0.00	170.62	132.08	222.24
Santa Monica (city)	CA	0.00	245.02	226.24	256.10	0.00	361.09	141.97	247.42
Sarasota (city)	FL	1.92	190.97	374.79	188.68	56.55	250.89	206.57	155.92
Savannah (city)	GA	0.00	5.72	178.36	177.59	0.00	136.47	182.75	157.64
Schaumburg (village)	IL	0.00	5.79	36.97	0.00	0.00	34.57	32.03	56.01
Schenectady (city)	NY	0.00	16.53	164.64	79.85	0.00	27.16	111.84	66.34
Scottsdale (city)	AZ	0.00	38.19	203.32	92.33	0.00	139.14	96.94	76.45
Scranton (city)	PA	0.00	0.70	0.00	65.24	0.00	8.16	0.00	32.45
Seattle (city)	WA	0.00	62.79	499.39	239.01	21.68	223.08	113.08	185.30
Shawnee (city)	KS	0.00	19.32	0.00	0.00	0.00	64.58	25.54	0.00
Shelby Charter (township)	MI	0.00	7.10	106.38	0.00	0.00	33.85	38.32	0.00
Shoreline (city)	WA	0.00	24.34	60.35	0.00	35.22	50.97	30.16	0.00
Shreveport (city)	LA	0.00	71.70	137.04	57.86	0.00	147.03	78.53	88.95
Sioux City (city)	IA	0.00	14.13	230.16	54.62	0.00	145.22	107.38	77.12
Sioux Falls (city)	SD	0.00	1.52	163.96	63.19	0.00	112.86	59.05	40.04
Skokie (village)	IL	0.00	17.83	0.00	2.43	0.00	32.02	0.00	64.29
Smithtown (town)	NY	0.00	14.92	0.00	146.49	10.00	48.76	0.00	143.31
Smyrna (city)	GA	0.00	20.20	132.05	115.52	0.00	49.16	88.32	62.48
Somerville (city)	MA	0.00	8.12	214.83	1.98	5.02	26.45	10.20	82.66
South Bend (city)	IN	0.00	82.61	317.64	59.89	0.00	161.68	189.81	48.94
South Jordan (city)	UT	0.00	55.61	41.32	54.19	0.00	57.57	16.28	10.37
Southampton (town)	NY	0.00	42.50	0.00	32.00	0.36	156.18	1.48	39.87
Southaven (city)	MS	0.00	43.45	38.01	11.23	0.00	89.32	41.76	61.84

City	State	Revenue[1] ($/per capita)				Current Operational Expenses ($/per capita)			
		Natural Resources, Other	Park & Recreation	Sewerage	Solid Waste Management	Natural Resources, Other	Parks & Recreation	Sewerage	Solid Waste Management
Southfield (city)	MI	0.00	20.99	0.00	42.07	0.00	99.15	0.00	40.36
Sparks (city)	NV	0.00	28.52	246.77	0.00	0.00	64.86	173.34	0.00
Spokane (city)	WA	0.00	31.21	382.03	324.48	1.84	88.64	151.84	321.86
Spokane Valley (city)	WA	0.00	2.65	20.38	0.00	2.23	26.03	4.63	0.00
Springdale (city)	AR	0.00	8.19	127.81	35.94	0.00	35.75	74.93	25.31
Springfield (city)	IL	0.00	0.00	49.71	0.00	0.00	19.98	81.55	0.00
Springfield (city)	MA	0.00	5.78	0.00	28.95	0.00	55.56	0.00	60.85
Springfield (city)	MO	0.00	66.71	218.19	40.30	0.00	177.81	95.10	27.51
Springfield (city)	OH	0.00	0.00	191.27	0.00	8.66	0.00	94.30	0.00
Springfield (city)	OR	0.00	0.00	727.15	0.00	0.00	0.00	354.58	0.00
St Charles (city)	MO	0.00	29.64	164.14	0.00	0.00	70.13	116.77	0.00
St Clair Shores (city)	MI	0.00	51.29	237.31	0.00	0.00	74.01	194.15	76.77
St Cloud (city)	MN	0.00	46.38	107.44	47.19	0.00	94.80	63.97	56.55
St George (city)	UT	0.00	90.47	166.94	57.09	0.00	202.57	97.97	50.20
St Joseph (city)	MO	0.00	10.86	258.06	37.85	0.00	88.32	154.05	27.13
St Louis (city)	MO	0.00	0.95	8.24	0.00	0.00	100.07	8.54	44.79
St Paul (city)	MN	0.00	59.37	163.60	15.44	0.00	111.40	111.78	14.68
St Peters (city)	MO	0.00	117.80	90.61	137.53	0.00	178.90	65.68	140.36
St Petersburg (city)	FL	0.00	73.12	211.60	158.14	54.30	233.79	163.53	145.74
Stamford (city)	CT	0.00	15.52	193.88	12.55	2.00	20.94	101.39	90.65
Sterling Heights (city)	MI	0.00	3.57	143.09	0.00	0.00	12.66	30.30	35.66
Stockton (city)	CA	0.00	22.26	198.26	4.51	0.00	59.05	146.92	4.44
Stratford (town)	CT	0.00	12.23	196.57	6.85	0.00	27.50	115.52	77.73
Suffolk (city)	VA	0.00	9.81	161.67	70.58	0.74	73.27	32.46	66.65
Sugar Land (city)	TX	0.00	6.76	231.47	59.09	0.00	56.54	80.57	60.74
Sunrise (city)	FL	69.67	27.36	519.10	126.52	32.80	127.02	274.10	130.13
Surprise (city)	AZ	0.00	2.80	127.08	55.44	0.00	117.97	80.77	52.28
Syracuse (city)	NY	0.00	3.94	39.29	0.81	0.00	46.93	55.07	48.25
Tacoma (city)	WA	0.00	6.33	414.67	274.22	0.00	48.54	282.23	175.44
Tallahassee (city)	FL	0.00	25.85	272.99	123.59	86.22	117.16	163.75	115.64
Tampa (city)	FL	0.00	41.48	293.39	222.43	2.97	91.75	226.57	174.36
Taunton (city)	MA	0.27	0.27	189.23	42.90	4.35	19.40	75.07	31.30
Taylor (city)	MI	0.00	74.49	105.74	0.00	0.00	73.82	22.13	70.95
Taylorsville (city)	UT	0.00	0.00	23.13	0.00	0.00	3.06	14.63	0.00
Tempe (city)	AZ	0.00	20.52	231.47	83.33	0.00	25.44	116.93	88.99
Temple (city)	TX	15.28	42.04	165.97	151.25	9.91	125.74	115.16	67.07
Terre Haute (city)	IN	0.00	21.26	285.30	0.00	0.00	48.26	207.71	0.00
Thornton (city)	CO	0.00	31.79	97.04	37.61	0.00	135.55	77.70	32.24
Tigard (city)	OR	0.00	0.00	89.53	0.00	0.00	30.24	62.61	0.00
Tinley Park (village)	IL	0.00	0.49	72.31	0.00	0.00	0.00	0.00	0.00
Toledo (city)	OH	0.00	0.88	282.31	35.05	6.39	35.02	123.15	13.91
Toms River (township)	NJ	0.00	36.39	205.68	1.93	0.00	30.04	56.92	82.51
Tonawanda (town)	NY	0.00	58.36	100.59	1.45	3.85	115.65	145.69	62.29
Topeka (city)	KS	0.00	0.00	246.33	0.00	0.00	21.42	162.67	0.00
Torrance (city)	CA	0.00	31.00	21.46	76.91	0.00	115.69	25.35	73.98
Trenton (city)	NJ	0.00	0.00	149.48	0.00	0.00	11.27	121.07	96.21
Troy (city)	MI	0.00	63.69	149.83	0.00	0.00	102.36	14.46	51.36
Tucson (city)	AZ	0.00	17.33	5.91	96.46	0.00	81.51	0.00	73.76
Tulsa (city)	OK	0.00	41.84	205.04	66.45	0.00	91.83	147.06	53.35
Tuscaloosa (city)	AL	0.00	0.00	292.41	44.99	0.14	101.75	77.08	47.47
Tustin (city)	CA	0.00	10.33	0.00	0.00	0.00	37.16	0.00	0.00
Tyler (city)	TX	0.62	3.34	114.58	106.71	2.23	35.66	75.10	111.15
Union City (city)	NJ	0.00	0.00	0.00	0.00	0.00	49.37	0.84	114.43
Union (town)	NY	0.00	3.80	5.98	0.00	30.20	17.59	19.38	22.93
Union (township)	NJ	0.00	0.00	93.01	0.00	11.62	7.90	19.00	73.47
Upper Darby (township)	PA	0.00	7.02	92.93	52.82	0.00	31.17	82.87	47.85

City	State	Revenue[1] ($/per capita)				Current Operational Expenses ($/per capita)			
		Natural Resources, Other	Park & Recreation	Sewerage	Solid Waste Management	Natural Resources, Other	Parks & Recreation	Sewerage	Solid Waste Management
Utica (city)	NY	0.00	6.98	36.64	0.00	0.00	41.94	29.82	28.48
Vancouver (city)	WA	0.00	31.91	284.47	5.14	0.00	64.15	100.74	11.80
Victoria (city)	TX	0.00	7.99	178.00	75.18	0.00	80.51	66.71	46.04
Vineland (city)	NJ	0.00	0.00	155.68	60.85	0.46	10.99	137.66	53.36
Virginia Beach (city)	VA	0.00	48.89	230.94	93.70	7.55	190.81	118.50	90.96
Waco (city)	TX	0.00	41.28	166.82	126.65	0.00	141.63	61.39	91.65
Waltham (city)	MA	0.00	8.55	311.04	0.00	0.51	25.95	222.95	89.90
Warner Robins (city)	GA	0.00	5.36	80.48	109.91	0.00	29.23	69.25	110.07
Warren (city)	MI	0.00	15.33	130.90	0.00	0.00	51.19	109.70	61.67
Warwick (city)	RI	0.00	10.88	218.35	0.00	8.76	25.80	76.99	24.73
Washington Dc (city)	DC	0.00	38.48	425.24	6.68	81.22	256.18	234.70	161.34
Waterbury (city)	CT	0.00	14.92	155.36	1.28	0.00	41.63	155.50	48.44
Waterford Charter (township)	MI	0.00	9.80	195.16	0.00	0.00	21.56	190.23	0.00
Waterloo (city)	IA	0.00	40.12	187.80	59.62	0.00	102.92	103.96	48.43
Waukegan (city)	IL	0.00	0.00	30.79	2.29	0.00	0.00	17.23	63.13
Waukesha (city)	WI	0.00	23.93	135.48	0.00	21.54	71.83	143.87	44.92
Wayne (township)	IN	0.00	0.10	0.00	0.00	0.00	0.00	0.00	0.00
Wayne (township)	NJ	0.00	12.92	157.86	7.90	0.00	60.93	144.69	81.16
West Allis (city)	WI	1.42	1.65	115.85	35.86	15.82	10.51	82.72	69.53
West Bloomfield Charter (township)	MI	0.00	0.00	150.19	0.00	0.00	2.55	141.29	1.32
West Chester (township)	OH	0.00	0.00	0.00	0.00	0.00	7.92	0.00	0.00
West Des Moines (city)	IA	0.00	19.64	195.10	29.78	0.55	77.76	72.21	30.48
West Hartford (town)	CT	0.00	60.91	0.00	0.00	0.00	103.03	0.00	0.00
West Haven (city)	CT	0.00	17.30	203.35	0.24	3.55	31.82	120.59	49.80
West Jordan (city)	UT	0.00	0.67	90.98	34.94	0.00	28.47	86.45	32.81
West New York (town)	NJ	0.00	1.84	0.00	0.00	0.00	23.50	0.00	60.46
West Palm Beach (city)	FL	0.00	44.02	291.94	131.03	30.26	176.67	569.56	86.19
West Valley City (city)	UT	0.00	39.87	29.78	33.81	0.00	63.76	27.10	28.25
Westland (city)	MI	0.00	6.27	196.94	0.00	0.00	29.17	169.04	52.51
Westminster (city)	CO	0.00	92.89	156.45	0.00	2.39	183.17	54.32	2.46
Weymouth Town (city)	MA	0.00	0.00	270.13	0.00	1.83	11.20	206.84	90.54
Wheaton (city)	IL	0.00	0.00	73.80	0.00	0.00	11.11	71.06	0.00
White Plains (city)	NY	0.00	20.32	41.89	0.00	0.00	138.99	34.00	129.49
Wichita (city)	KS	0.00	10.87	151.83	2.95	3.13	69.46	72.46	3.06
Wichita Falls (city)	TX	0.00	22.39	127.19	126.66	0.00	69.12	41.61	85.68
Wilmington (city)	DE	0.00	2.65	247.43	0.00	0.00	90.66	131.43	101.62
Wilmington (city)	NC	0.00	33.87	77.51	74.20	17.73	64.62	52.42	91.66
Winston-Salem (city)	NC	0.00	29.31	212.27	52.73	0.60	58.85	89.36	103.06
Woodbridge (township)	NJ	0.00	48.53	225.87	5.37	0.00	78.55	172.94	74.89
Woodbury (city)	MN	0.00	63.30	112.88	0.00	4.37	95.09	74.78	0.00
Worcester (city)	MA	0.00	6.42	196.15	17.21	0.00	27.60	155.67	29.35
Kansas City-Wyandotte County (unified govt)	KS	0.00	8.40	179.52	52.16	0.00	38.75	133.88	42.82
Wyoming (city)	MI	0.00	3.72	213.17	0.00	0.00	51.40	168.22	5.89
Yakima (city)	WA	32.31	11.96	199.67	58.82	35.70	37.67	176.76	57.93
Yonkers (city)	NY	0.00	12.79	24.52	0.00	0.00	40.63	8.32	102.52
Youngstown (city)	OH	0.00	3.40	318.68	71.27	0.00	37.36	286.43	41.22
Ypsilanti Charter (township)	MI	0.00	18.58	0.00	0.00	0.00	42.43	0.00	51.06
Yuma (city)	AZ	0.00	32.25	210.86	36.78	0.00	117.77	154.29	39.80

Note: *(1) Includes revenue raised through current charges only. Does not include intergovernmental revenue.*
Source: *U.S. Census Bureau, State and Local Government Finances, 2014*

2. Trends in Greenhouse Gas Emissions

2.1 Recent Trends in U.S. Greenhouse Gas Emissions and Sinks

In 2015, total gross U.S. greenhouse gas emissions were 6,586.7 MMT, or million metric tons, carbon dioxide (CO_2) Eq. Total U.S. emissions have increased by 3.5 percent from 1990 to 2015, and emissions decreased from 2014 to 2015 by 2.3 percent (153.0 MMT CO_2 Eq.). The decrease in total greenhouse gas emissions between 2014 and 2015 was driven in large part by a decrease in CO_2 emissions from fossil fuel combustion. The decrease in CO_2 emissions from fossil fuel combustion was a result of multiple factors, including: (1) substitution from coal to natural gas consumption in the electric power sector; (2) warmer winter conditions in 2015 resulting in a decreased demand for heating fuel in the residential and commercial sectors; and (3) a slight decrease in electricity demand. Since 1990, U.S. emissions have increased at an average annual rate of 0.2 percent. Figure 2-1 through Figure 2-3 illustrate the overall trend in total U.S. emissions by gas, annual changes, and absolute changes since 1990. Overall, net emissions in 2015 were 11.5 percent below 2005 levels as shown in Table 2-1.

Figure 2-1: Gross U.S. Greenhouse Gas Emissions by Gas (MMT CO_2 Eq.)

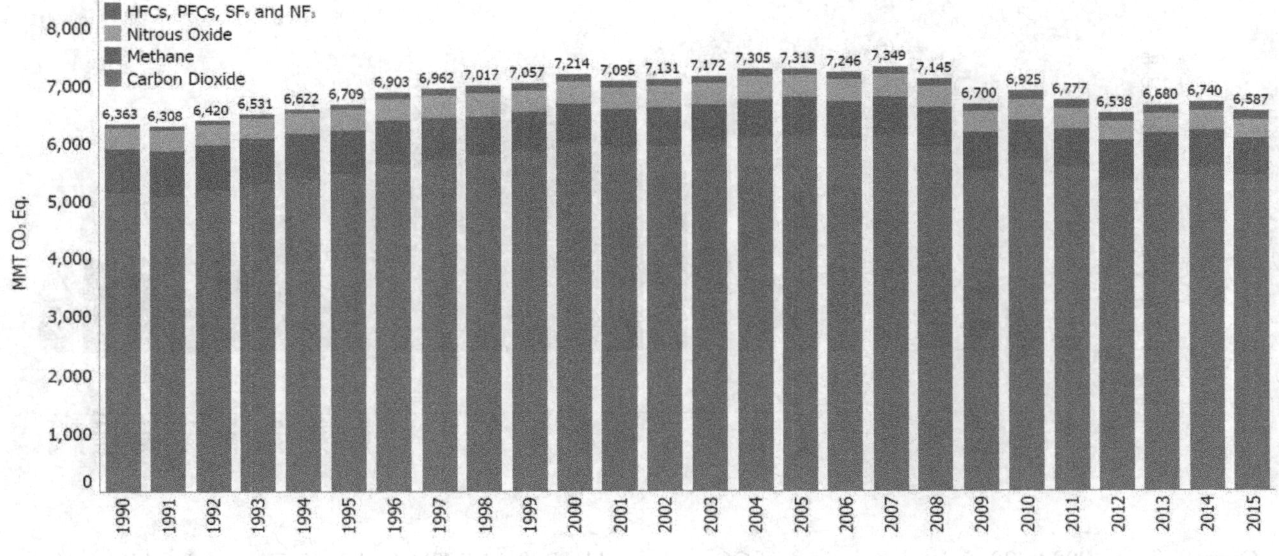

Source: *U.S. EPA, Inventory of U.S. Greenhouse Gas Emissions and Sinks: 1990–2015*

Figure 2-2: Annual Percent Change in Gross U.S. Greenhouse Gas Emissions Relative to the Previous Year

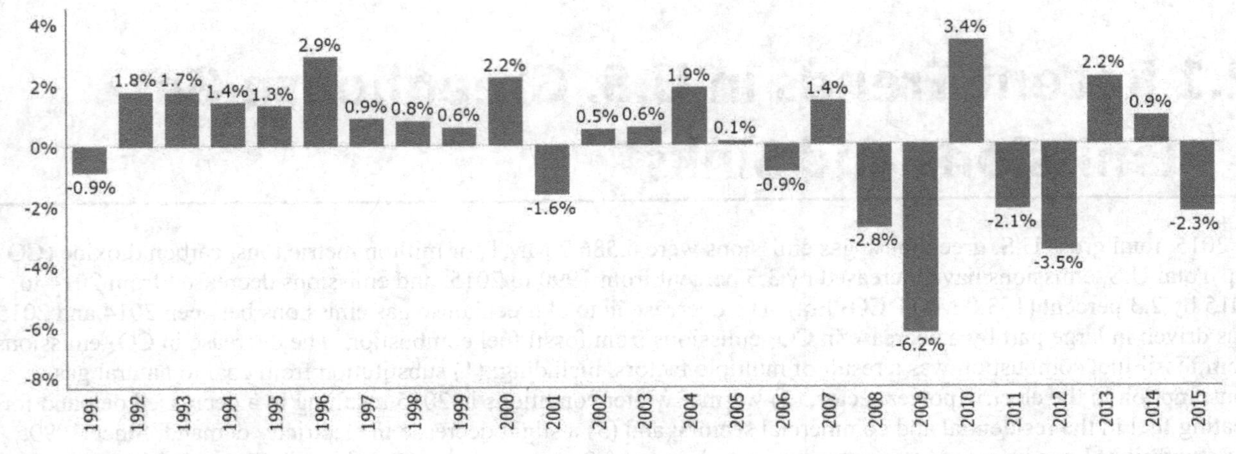

Figure 2-3: Cumulative Change in Annual Gross U.S. Greenhouse Gas Emissions Relative to 1990 (1990=0, MMT CO_2 Eq.)

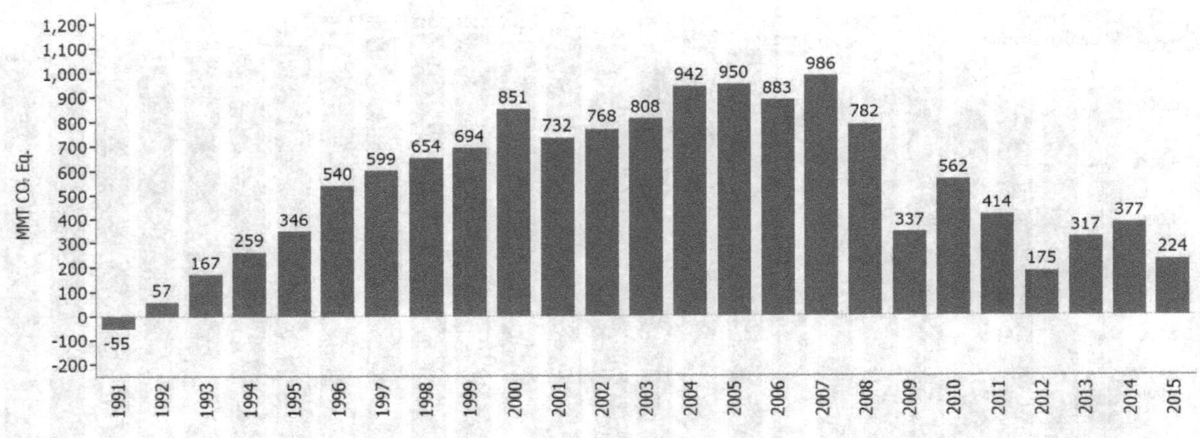

Overall, from 1990 to 2015, total emissions of CO_2 increased by 288.4 MMT CO_2 Eq. (5.6 percent), while total emissions of methane (CH_4) decreased by 125.1 MMT CO_2 Eq. (16.0 percent), and total emissions of nitrous oxide (N_2O) decreased by 24.7 MMT CO_2 Eq. (6.9 percent). During the same period, aggregate weighted emissions of hydrofluorocarbons (HFCs), perfluorocarbons (PFCs), sulfur hexafluoride (SF_6), and nitrogen trifluoride (NF_3) rose by 85.0 MMT CO_2 Eq. (85.3 percent). Despite being emitted in smaller quantities relative to the other principal greenhouse gases, emissions of HFCs, PFCs, SF_6, and NF_3 are significant because many of them have extremely high global warming potentials (GWPs), and, in the cases of PFCs, SF_6, and NF_3, long atmospheric lifetimes. Conversely, U.S. greenhouse gas emissions were partly offset by carbon (C) sequestration in managed forests, trees in urban areas, agricultural soils, landfilled yard trimmings, and coastal wetlands. These were estimated to offset 11.8 percent of total emissions in 2015.

As the largest contributor to U.S. greenhouse gas emissions, CO_2 from fossil fuel combustion has accounted for approximately 77 percent of GWP-weighted emissions for the entire time series since 1990. Emissions from this source category grew by 6.5 percent (309.4 MMT CO_2 Eq.) from 1990 to 2015 and were responsible for most of the increase in national emissions during this period. In addition, CO_2 emissions from fossil fuel combustion decreased

Source: *U.S. EPA, Inventory of U.S. Greenhouse Gas Emissions and Sinks: 1990–2015*

from 2005 levels by 697.2 MMT CO_2 Eq., a decrease of approximately 12.1 percent between 2005 and 2015. From 2014 to 2015, these emissions decreased by 2.9 percent (152.5 MMT CO_2 Eq.). Historically, changes in emissions from fossil fuel combustion have been the dominant factor affecting U.S. emission trends.

Changes in CO_2 emissions from fossil fuel combustion are influenced by many long-term and short-term factors, including population and economic growth, energy price fluctuations and market trends, technological changes, energy fuel choices, and seasonal temperatures. On an annual basis, the overall consumption and mix of fossil fuels in the United States fluctuates primarily in response to changes in general economic conditions, overall energy prices, the relative price of different fuels, weather, and the availability of non-fossil alternatives. For example, coal consumption for electricity generation is influenced by a number of factors including the relative price of coal and alternative sources, the ability to switch fuels, and longer terms trends in coal markets. Likewise, warmer winters will lead to a decrease in heating degree days and result in a decreased demand for heating fuel and electricity for heat in the residential and commercial sector, which leads to a decrease in emissions from reduced fuel use.

Energy-related CO_2 emissions also depend on the type of fuel or energy consumed and its C intensity. Producing a unit of heat or electricity using natural gas instead of coal, for example, can reduce the CO_2 emissions because of the lower C content of natural gas (see Table A-39 in Annex 2.1 for more detail on the C Content Coefficient of different fossil fuels).

A brief discussion of the year to year variability in fuel combustion emissions is provided below, beginning with 2011.

Recent trends in CO_2 emissions from fossil fuel combustion show a 3.9 percent decrease from 2011 to 2012, then a 2.6 percent and a 0.9 percent increase from 2012 to 2013 and 2013 to 2014, respectively, and a 2.9 percent decrease from 2014 to 2015. Total electricity generation remained relatively flat over that time period but emission trends generally mirror the trends in the amount of coal used to generate electricity. The consumption of coal used to generate electricity decreased by roughly 12 percent from 2011 to 2012, increased by 4 percent from 2012 to 2013, stayed relatively flat from 2013 to 2014, and decreased by 14 percent from 2014 to 2015. The overall CO_2 emission trends from fossil fuel combustion also follow closely changes in heating degree days over that time period. Heating degree days decreased by 13 percent from 2011 to 2012, increased by 18 percent from 2012 to 2013, increased by 2 percent from 2013 to 2014, and decreased by 10 percent from 2014 to 2015. The overall CO_2 emission trends from fossil fuel combustion also generally follow changes in overall petroleum use and emissions. Carbon dioxide emissions from petroleum decreased by 2.0 percent from 2011 to 2012, increased by 1.6 percent from 2012 to 2013, increased by 0.8 percent from 2013 to 2014, and increased by 1.7 percent from 2014 to 2015. The increase in petroleum CO_2 emissions from 2014 to 2015 somewhat offset emission reductions from decreased coal use in the electricity sector from 2014 to 2015.

Table 2-1 summarizes emissions and sinks from all U.S. anthropogenic sources in weighted units of MMT CO_2 Eq., while unweighted gas emissions and sinks in kilotons (kt) are provided in Table 2-2.

Table 2-1: Recent Trends in U.S. Greenhouse Gas Emissions and Sinks (MMT CO_2 Eq.)

Gas/Source	1990	2005	2011	2012	2013	2014	2015
CO_2	**5,123.0**	**6,131.8**	**5,569.5**	**5,362.1**	**5,514.0**	**5,565.5**	**5,411.4**
Fossil Fuel Combustion	4,740.3	5,746.9	5,227.1	5,024.6	5,156.5	5,202.3	5,049.8
Electricity Generation	*1,820.8*	*2,400.9*	*2,157.7*	*2,022.2*	*2,038.1*	*2,038.0*	*1,900.7*
Transportation[a]	*1,493.8*	*1,887.0*	*1,707.6*	*1,696.8*	*1,713.0*	*1,742.8*	*1,736.4*
Industrial[a]	*842.5*	*828.0*	*775.0*	*782.9*	*812.2*	*806.1*	*805.5*
Residential	*338.3*	*357.8*	*325.5*	*282.5*	*329.7*	*345.4*	*319.6*
Commercial[a]	*217.4*	*223.5*	*220.4*	*196.7*	*221.0*	*228.7*	*246.2*
U.S. Territories	*27.6*	*49.7*	*40.9*	*43.5*	*42.5*	*41.4*	*41.4*
Non-Energy Use of Fuels	117.6	138.9	109.8	106.7	123.6	119.0	125.5
Iron and Steel Production & Metallurgical Coke Production	101.5	68.0	61.1	55.4	53.3	58.6	48.9
Natural Gas Systems	37.7	30.1	35.7	35.2	38.5	42.4	42.4
Cement Production	33.5	46.2	32.2	35.3	36.4	39.4	39.9
Petrochemical Production	21.3	27.0	26.3	26.5	26.4	26.5	28.1
Lime Production	11.7	14.6	14.0	13.8	14.0	14.2	13.3
Other Process Uses of Carbonates	4.9	6.3	9.3	8.0	10.4	11.8	11.2

Source: *U.S. EPA, Inventory of U.S. Greenhouse Gas Emissions and Sinks: 1990–2015*

Ammonia Production	13.0	9.2	9.3	9.4	10.0	9.6	10.8
Incineration of Waste	8.0	12.5	10.6	10.4	10.4	10.6	10.7
Urea Fertilization	2.4	3.5	4.1	4.3	4.5	4.8	5.0
Carbon Dioxide Consumption	1.5	1.4	4.1	4.0	4.2	4.5	4.3
Liming	4.7	4.3	3.9	6.0	3.9	3.6	3.8
Petroleum Systems	3.6	3.9	4.2	3.9	3.7	3.6	3.6
Soda Ash Production and Consumption	2.8	3.0	2.7	2.8	2.8	2.8	2.8
Aluminum Production	6.8	4.1	3.3	3.4	3.3	2.8	2.8
Ferroalloy Production	2.2	1.4	1.7	1.9	1.8	1.9	2.0
Titanium Dioxide Production	1.2	1.8	1.7	1.5	1.7	1.7	1.6
Glass Production	1.5	1.9	1.3	1.2	1.3	1.3	1.3
Urea Consumption for Non-Agricultural Purposes	3.8	3.7	4.0	4.4	4.0	1.4	1.1
Phosphoric Acid Production	1.5	1.3	1.2	1.1	1.1	1.0	1.0
Zinc Production	0.6	1.0	1.3	1.5	1.4	1.0	0.9
Lead Production	0.5	0.6	0.5	0.5	0.5	0.5	0.5
Silicon Carbide Production and Consumption	0.4	0.2	0.2	0.2	0.2	0.2	0.2
Magnesium Production and Processing	+	+	+	+	+	+	+
Wood Biomass, Ethanol, and Biodiesel Consumption[b]	*219.4*	*230.7*	*276.4*	*276.2*	*299.8*	*307.1*	*291.7*
International Bunker Fuels[c]	*103.5*	*113.1*	*111.7*	*105.8*	*99.8*	*103.2*	*110.8*
CH_4	**780.8**	**680.9**	**672.1**	**666.1**	**658.8**	**659.1**	**655.7**
Enteric Fermentation	164.2	168.9	168.9	166.7	165.5	164.2	166.5
Natural Gas Systems	194.1	159.7	154.5	156.2	159.2	162.5	162.4
Landfills	179.6	134.3	119.0	120.8	116.7	116.6	115.7
Manure Management	37.2	56.3	63.0	65.6	63.3	62.9	66.3
Coal Mining	96.5	64.1	71.2	66.5	64.6	64.8	60.9
Petroleum Systems	55.5	46.0	48.0	46.4	44.5	43.0	39.9
Wastewater Treatment	15.7	16.0	15.3	15.1	14.9	14.8	14.8
Rice Cultivation	16.0	16.7	14.1	11.3	11.3	11.4	11.2
Stationary Combustion	8.5	7.4	7.1	6.6	8.0	8.1	7.0
Abandoned Underground Coal Mines	7.2	6.6	6.4	6.2	6.2	6.3	6.4
Composting	0.4	1.9	1.9	1.9	2.0	2.1	2.1
Mobile Combustion[a]	5.6	2.8	2.3	2.2	2.1	2.1	2.0
Field Burning of Agricultural Residues	0.2	0.2	0.3	0.3	0.3	0.3	0.3
Petrochemical Production	0.2	0.1	+	0.1	0.1	0.1	0.2
Ferroalloy Production	+	+	+	+	+	+	+
Silicon Carbide Production and Consumption	+	+	+	+	+	+	+
Iron and Steel Production & Metallurgical Coke Production	+	+	+	+	+	+	+
Incineration of Waste	+	+	+	+	+	+	+
International Bunker Fuels[c]	*0.2*	*0.1*	*0.1*	*0.1*	*0.1*	*0.1*	*0.1*
N_2O	**359.5**	**361.6**	**364.0**	**340.7**	**335.5**	**335.5**	**334.8**
Agricultural Soil Management	256.6	259.8	270.1	254.1	250.5	250.0	251.3
Stationary Combustion	11.9	20.2	21.3	21.4	22.9	23.4	23.1
Manure Management	14.0	16.5	17.4	17.5	17.5	17.5	17.7
Mobile Combustion[a]	41.2	35.7	22.8	20.4	18.5	16.6	15.1
Nitric Acid Production	12.1	11.3	10.9	10.5	10.7	10.9	11.6
Wastewater Treatment	3.4	4.4	4.8	4.8	4.9	4.9	5.0
Adipic Acid Production	15.2	7.1	10.2	5.5	3.9	5.4	4.3
N_2O from Product Uses	4.2	4.2	4.2	4.2	4.2	4.2	4.2
Composting	0.3	1.7	1.7	1.7	1.8	1.9	1.9
Incineration of Waste	0.5	0.4	0.3	0.3	0.3	0.3	0.3

Source: *U.S. EPA, Inventory of U.S. Greenhouse Gas Emissions and Sinks: 1990–2015*

Semiconductor Manufacture	+	0.1	0.2	0.2	0.2	0.2	0.2
Field Burning of Agricultural Residues	0.1	0.1	0.1	0.1	0.1	0.1	0.1
International Bunker Fuels[c]	*0.9*	*1.0*	*1.0*	*0.9*	*0.9*	*0.9*	*0.9*
HFCs	**46.6**	**120.0**	**154.3**	**155.9**	**159.0**	**166.7**	**173.2**
Substitution of Ozone Depleting Substances[d]	0.3	99.7	145.3	150.2	154.6	161.3	168.5
HCFC-22 Production	46.1	20.0	8.8	5.5	4.1	5.0	4.3
Semiconductor Manufacture	0.2	0.2	0.2	0.2	0.2	0.3	0.3
Magnesium Production and Processing	0.0	0.0	+	+	0.1	0.1	0.1
PFCs	**24.3**	**6.7**	**6.9**	**6.0**	**5.8**	**5.8**	**5.2**
Semiconductor Manufacture	2.8	3.2	3.4	3.0	2.8	3.2	3.2
Aluminum Production	21.5	3.4	3.5	2.9	3.0	2.5	2.0
Substitution of Ozone Depleting Substances	0.0	+	+	+	+	+	+
SF_6	**28.8**	**11.7**	**9.2**	**6.8**	**6.4**	**6.6**	**5.8**
Electrical Transmission and Distribution	23.1	8.3	6.0	4.8	4.6	4.8	4.2
Magnesium Production and Processing	5.2	2.7	2.8	1.6	1.5	1.0	0.9
Semiconductor Manufacture	0.5	0.7	0.4	0.4	0.4	0.7	0.7
NF_3	**+**	**0.5**	**0.7**	**0.6**	**0.6**	**0.5**	**0.6**
Semiconductor Manufacture	+	0.5	0.7	0.6	0.6	0.5	0.6
Total Emissions	**6,363.1**	**7,313.3**	**6,776.7**	**6,538.3**	**6,680.1**	**6,739.7**	**6,586.7**
LULUCF Emissions[e]	**10.6**	**23.0**	**19.9**	**26.1**	**19.2**	**19.7**	**19.7**
LULUCF Carbon Stock Change[f]	**(830.2)**	**(754.0)**	**(769.1)**	**(779.8)**	**(782.2)**	**(781.1)**	**(778.7)**
LULUCF Sector Net Total[g]	**(819.6)**	**(731.0)**	**(749.2)**	**(753.8)**	**(763.0)**	**(761.4)**	**(758.9)**
Net Emissions (Sources and Sinks)	**5,543.5**	**6,582.3**	**6,027.6**	**5,784.5**	**5,917.1**	**5,978.3**	**5,827.7**

Notes: Total emissions presented without LULUCF. Net emissions presented with LULUCF. Totals may not sum due to independent rounding. Parentheses indicate negative values or sequestration.

\+ Does not exceed 0.05 MMT CO_2 Eq.

[a] There was a method update in this Inventory for estimating the share of gasoline used in on-road and non-road applications. The change does not impact total U.S. gasoline consumption. It mainly results in a shift in gasoline consumption from the transportation sector to industrial and commercial sectors for 2015, creating a break in the time series. The change is discussed further in the Planned Improvements section of Chapter 3.1.

[b] Emissions from Wood Biomass, Ethanol, and Biodiesel Consumption are not included specifically in summing Energy sector totals. Net carbon fluxes from changes in biogenic carbon reservoirs are accounted for in the estimates for LULUCF.

[c] Emissions from International Bunker Fuels are not included in totals.

[d] Small amounts of PFC emissions also result from this source.

[e] LULUCF emissions include the CH_4 and N_2O emissions reported for *Peatlands Remaining Peatlands*, Forest Fires, Drained Organic Soils, Grassland Fires, and *Coastal Wetlands Remaining Coastal Wetlands*; CH_4 emissions from *Land Converted to Coastal Wetlands*; and N_2O emissions from Forest Soils and Settlement Soils.

[f] LULUCF Carbon Stock Change is the net C stock change from the following categories: *Forest Land Remaining Forest Land, Land Converted to Forest Land, Cropland Remaining Cropland, Land Converted to Cropland, Grassland Remaining Grassland, Land Converted to Grassland, Wetlands Remaining Wetlands, Land Converted to Wetlands, Settlements Remaining Settlements*, and *Land Converted to Settlements*. Refer to Table 2-8 for a breakout of emissions and removals for LULUCF by gas and source category.

[g] The LULUCF Sector Net Total is the net sum of all CH_4 and N_2O emissions to the atmosphere plus net carbon stock changes.

Table 2-2: Recent Trends in U.S. Greenhouse Gas Emissions and Sinks (kt)

Gas/Source	1990	2005	2011	2012	2013	2014	2015
CO_2	**5,123,043**	**6,131,833**	**5,569,516**	**5,362,095**	**5,514,018**	**5,565,495**	**5,411,409**
Fossil Fuel Combustion	4,740,343	5,746,942	5,227,061	5,024,643	5,156,523	5,202,300	5,049,763
Electricity Generation	*1,820,818*	*2,400,874*	*2,157,688*	*2,022,181*	*2,038,122*	*2,038,018*	*1,900,673*
Transportation[a]	*1,493,758*	*1,887,033*	*1,707,631*	*1,696,752*	*1,713,002*	*1,742,814*	*1,736,383*

Source: *U.S. EPA, Inventory of U.S. Greenhouse Gas Emissions and Sinks: 1990–2015*

Industrial[a]	*842,473*	*827,999*	*774,951*	*782,929*	*812,228*	*806,075*	*805,496*
Residential	*338,347*	*357,834*	*325,537*	*282,540*	*329,674*	*345,362*	*319,591*
Commercial[a]	*217,393*	*223,480*	*220,381*	*196,714*	*221,030*	*228,666*	*246,241*
U.S. Territories	*27,555*	*49,723*	*40,874*	*43,527*	*42,467*	*41,365*	*41,380*
Non-Energy Use of Fuels	117,585	138,913	109,756	106,750	123,645	118,995	125,526
Iron and Steel Production & Metallurgical Coke Production	101,487	68,047	61,108	55,449	53,348	58,629	48,876
Natural Gas Systems	37,732	30,076	35,662	35,203	38,457	42,351	42,351
Cement Production	33,484	46,194	32,208	35,270	36,369	39,439	39,907
Petrochemical Production	21,326	26,972	26,338	26,501	26,395	26,496	28,062
Lime Production	11,700	14,552	13,982	13,785	14,028	14,210	13,342
Other Process Uses of Carbonates	4,907	6,339	9,335	8,022	10,414	11,811	11,236
Ammonia Production	13,047	9,196	9,292	9,377	9,962	9,619	10,799
Incineration of Waste	7,950	12,469	10,564	10,379	10,398	10,608	10,676
Urea Fertilization	2,417	3,504	4,097	4,267	4,504	4,781	5,032
Carbon Dioxide Consumption	1,472	1,375	4,083	4,019	4,188	4,471	4,296
Liming	4,667	4,349	3,873	5,978	3,907	3,609	3,810
Petroleum Systems	3,553	3,927	4,192	3,876	3,693	3,567	3,567
Soda Ash Production and Consumption	2,822	2,960	2,712	2,763	2,804	2,827	2,789
Aluminum Production	6,831	4,142	3,292	3,439	3,255	2,833	2,767
Ferroalloy Production	2,152	1,392	1,735	1,903	1,785	1,914	1,960
Titanium Dioxide Production	1,195	1,755	1,729	1,528	1,715	1,688	1,635
Glass Production	1,535	1,928	1,299	1,248	1,317	1,336	1,299
Urea Consumption for Non-Agricultural Purposes	3,784	3,653	4,030	4,407	4,014	1,380	1,128
Phosphoric Acid Production	1,529	1,342	1,171	1,118	1,149	1,038	999
Zinc Production	632	1,030	1,286	1,486	1,429	956	933
Lead Production	516	553	538	527	546	459	473
Silicon Carbide Production and Consumption	375	219	170	158	169	173	180
Magnesium Production and Processing	1	3	3	2	2	2	3
Wood Biomass, Ethanol, and Biodiesel Consumption[b]	*219,413*	*230,700*	*276,413*	*276,201*	*299,785*	*307,079*	*291,735*
International Bunker Fuels[c]	*103,463*	*113,139*	*111,660*	*105,805*	*99,763*	*103,201*	*110,751*
CH_4	**31,232**	**27,238**	**26,884**	**26,643**	**26,351**	**26,366**	**26,229**
Enteric Fermentation	6,566	6,755	6,757	6,670	6,619	6,567	6,661
Natural Gas Systems	7,762	6,387	6,180	6,247	6,368	6,501	6,497
Landfills	7,182	5,372	4,760	4,834	4,669	4,663	4,628
Manure Management	1,486	2,254	2,519	2,625	2,530	2,514	2,651
Coal Mining	3,860	2,565	2,849	2,658	2,584	2,593	2,436
Petroleum Systems	2,218	1,840	1,922	1,858	1,778	1,721	1,595
Wastewater Treatment	627	639	613	604	597	592	591
Rice Cultivation	641	667	564	453	454	456	449
Stationary Combustion	339	296	283	265	320	323	280
Abandoned Underground Coal Mines	288	264	257	249	249	253	256
Composting	15	75	75	77	81	84	84
Mobile Combustion[a]	226	113	91	87	85	82	80
Field Burning of Agricultural Residues	9	8	11	11	11	11	11
Petrochemical Production	9	3	2	3	3	5	7
Ferroalloy Production	1	+	+	1	+	1	1
Silicon Carbide Production and Consumption	1	+	+	+	+	+	+

Source: *U.S. EPA, Inventory of U.S. Greenhouse Gas Emissions and Sinks: 1990–2015*

Iron and Steel Production & Metallurgical Coke Production	1	1	+	+	+	+	+
Incineration of Waste	+	+	+	+	+	+	+
International Bunker Fuels[c]	*7*	*5*	*5*	*4*	*3*	*3*	*3*
N_2O	**1,207**	**1,214**	**1,222**	**1,143**	**1,126**	**1,126**	**1,124**
Agricultural Soil Management	861	872	906	853	841	839	843
Stationary Combustion	40	68	71	72	77	78	78
Manure Management	47	55	58	59	59	59	59
Mobile Combustion[a]	138	120	77	68	62	56	51
Nitric Acid Production	41	38	37	35	36	37	39
Wastewater Treatment	11	15	16	16	16	16	17
Adipic Acid Production	51	24	34	19	13	18	14
N_2O from Product Uses	14	14	14	14	14	14	14
Composting	1	6	6	6	6	6	6
Incineration of Waste	2	1	1	1	1	1	1
Semiconductor Manufacture	+	+	1	1	1	1	1
Field Burning of Agricultural Residues	+	+	+	+	+	+	+
International Bunker Fuels[c]	*3*	*3*	*3*	*3*	*3*	*3*	*3*
HFCs	**M**	**M**	**M**	**M**	**M**	**M**	**M**
Substitution of Ozone Depleting Substances[d]	M	M	M	M	M	M	M
HCFC-22 Production	3	1	1	+	+	+	+
Semiconductor Manufacture	+	+	+	+	+	+	+
Magnesium Production and Processing	0	0	+	+	+	+	+
PFCs	**M**	**M**	**M**	**M**	**M**	**M**	**M**
Semiconductor Manufacture	M	M	M	M	M	M	M
Aluminum Production	M	M	M	M	M	M	M
Substitution of Ozone Depleting Substances	0	+	+	+	+	+	+
SF_6	**1**	**1**	**+**	**+**	**+**	**+**	**+**
Electrical Transmission and Distribution	1	+	+	+	+	+	+
Magnesium Production and Processing	+	+	+	+	+	+	+
Semiconductor Manufacture	+	+	+	+	+	+	+
NF_3	**+**	**+**	**+**	**+**	**+**	**+**	**+**
Semiconductor Manufacture	+	+	+	+	+	+	+

+ Does not exceed 0.5 kt.

M - Mixture of multiple gases

[a] There was a method update in this Inventory for estimating the share of gasoline used in on-road and non-road applications. The change does not impact total U.S. gasoline consumption. It mainly results in a shift in gasoline consumption from the transportation sector to industrial and commercial sectors for 2015, creating a break in the time series. The change is discussed further in the Planned Improvements section of Chapter 3.1.

[b] Emissions from Wood Biomass, Ethanol, and Biodiesel Consumption are not included specifically in summing Energy sector totals. Net carbon fluxes from changes in biogenic carbon reservoirs are accounted for in the estimates for LULUCF.

[c] Emissions from International Bunker Fuels are not included in totals.

[d] Small amounts of PFC emissions also result from this source.

Notes: Totals may not sum due to independent rounding. Parentheses indicate negative values or sequestration.

Emissions of all gases can be summed from each source category into a set of five sectors defined by the Intergovernmental Panel on Climate Change (IPCC). Figure 2-4 and Table 2-3 illustrate that over the twenty-six year period of 1990 to 2015, total emissions in the Energy, Industrial Processes and Product Use, and Agriculture sectors grew by 221.0 MMT CO_2 Eq. (4.1 percent), 35.5 MMT CO_2 Eq. (10.4 percent), and 27.0 MMT CO_2 Eq. (5.5 percent), respectively. Emissions from the Waste sector decreased by 59.9 MMT CO_2 Eq. (30.1 percent). Over the same period, estimates of net C sequestration for the Land Use, Land-Use Change, and Forestry sector (magnitude

Source: *U.S. EPA, Inventory of U.S. Greenhouse Gas Emissions and Sinks: 1990–2015*

of emissions plus CO_2 removals from all LULUCF categories) increased by 60.7 MMT CO_2 Eq. (7.4 percent decrease in net C sequestration).

Figure 2-4: U.S. Greenhouse Gas Emissions and Sinks by Chapter/IPCC Sector (MMT CO_2 Eq.)

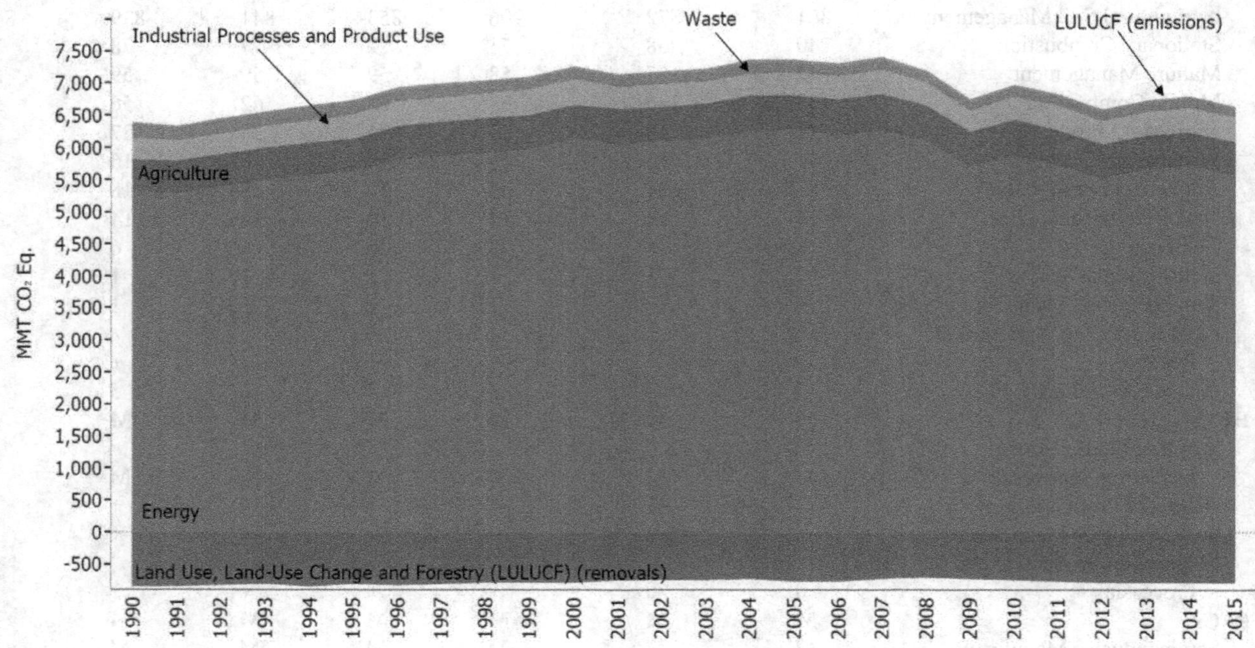

Table 2-3: Recent Trends in U.S. Greenhouse Gas Emissions and Sinks by Chapter/IPCC Sector (MMT CO_2 Eq.)

Chapter/IPCC Sector	1990	2005	2011	2012	2013	2014	2015
Energy	**5,328.1**	**6,275.3**	**5,721.2**	**5,507.0**	**5,659.1**	**5,704.9**	**5,549.1**
Fossil Fuel Combustion	4,740.3	5,746.9	5,227.1	5,024.6	5,156.5	5,202.3	5,049.8
Natural Gas Systems	231.8	189.8	190.2	191.4	197.7	204.9	204.8
Non-Energy Use of Fuels	117.6	138.9	109.8	106.7	123.6	119.0	125.5
Coal Mining	96.5	64.1	71.2	66.5	64.6	64.8	60.9
Petroleum Systems	59.0	49.9	52.2	50.3	48.2	46.6	43.4
Stationary Combustion	20.4	27.6	28.4	28.0	30.9	31.5	30.1
Mobile Combustion[a]	46.9	38.6	25.1	22.6	20.6	18.6	17.1
Incineration of Waste	8.4	12.9	10.9	10.7	10.7	10.9	11.0
Abandoned Underground Coal Mines	7.2	6.6	6.4	6.2	6.2	6.3	6.4
Industrial Processes and Product Use	**340.4**	**353.4**	**371.0**	**360.9**	**363.7**	**379.8**	**375.9**
Substitution of Ozone Depleting Substances	0.3	99.8	145.4	150.2	154.7	161.3	168.5
Iron and Steel Production & Metallurgical Coke Production	101.5	68.1	61.1	55.5	53.4	58.6	48.9
Cement Production	33.5	46.2	32.2	35.3	36.4	39.4	39.9
Petrochemical Production	21.5	27.0	26.4	26.6	26.5	26.6	28.2
Lime Production	11.7	14.6	14.0	13.8	14.0	14.2	13.3
Nitric Acid Production	12.1	11.3	10.9	10.5	10.7	10.9	11.6
Other Process Uses of Carbonates	4.9	6.3	9.3	8.0	10.4	11.8	11.2
Ammonia Production	13.0	9.2	9.3	9.4	10.0	9.6	10.8
Semiconductor Manufacture	3.6	4.7	4.9	4.5	4.1	5.0	5.0
Aluminum Production	28.3	7.6	6.8	6.4	6.2	5.4	4.8

Source: *U.S. EPA, Inventory of U.S. Greenhouse Gas Emissions and Sinks: 1990–2015*

Carbon Dioxide Consumption	1.5	1.4	4.1	4.0	4.2	4.5	4.3
HCFC-22 Production	46.1	20.0	8.8	5.5	4.1	5.0	4.3
Adipic Acid Production	15.2	7.1	10.2	5.5	3.9	5.4	4.3
N_2O from Product Uses	4.2	4.2	4.2	4.2	4.2	4.2	4.2
Electrical Transmission and Distribution	23.1	8.3	6.0	4.8	4.6	4.8	4.2
Soda Ash Production and Consumption	2.8	3.0	2.7	2.8	2.8	2.8	2.8
Ferroalloy Production	2.2	1.4	1.7	1.9	1.8	1.9	2.0
Titanium Dioxide Production	1.2	1.8	1.7	1.5	1.7	1.7	1.6
Glass Production	1.5	1.9	1.3	1.2	1.3	1.3	1.3
Urea Consumption for Non-Agricultural Purposes	3.8	3.7	4.0	4.4	4.0	1.4	1.1
Magnesium Production and Processing	5.2	2.7	2.8	1.7	1.5	1.1	1.0
Phosphoric Acid Production	1.5	1.3	1.2	1.1	1.1	1.0	1.0
Zinc Production	0.6	1.0	1.3	1.5	1.4	1.0	0.9
Lead Production	0.5	0.6	0.5	0.5	0.5	0.5	0.5
Silicon Carbide Production and Consumption	0.4	0.2	0.2	0.2	0.2	0.2	0.2
Agriculture	**495.3**	**526.4**	**541.9**	**525.9**	**516.9**	**514.7**	**522.3**
Agricultural Soil Management	256.6	259.8	270.1	254.1	250.5	250.0	251.3
Enteric Fermentation	164.2	168.9	168.9	166.7	165.5	164.2	166.5
Manure Management	51.1	72.9	80.4	83.2	80.8	80.4	84.0
Rice Cultivation	16.0	16.7	14.1	11.3	11.3	11.4	11.2
Urea Fertilization	2.4	3.5	4.1	4.3	4.5	4.8	5.0
Liming	4.7	4.3	3.9	6.0	3.9	3.6	3.8
Field Burning of Agricultural Residues	0.3	0.3	0.4	0.4	0.4	0.4	0.4
Waste	**199.3**	**158.2**	**142.6**	**144.4**	**140.4**	**140.2**	**139.4**
Landfills	179.6	134.3	119.0	120.8	116.7	116.6	115.7
Wastewater Treatment	19.1	20.4	20.1	19.9	19.8	19.7	19.7
Composting	0.7	3.5	3.5	3.7	3.9	4.0	4.0
Total Emissions[b]	**6,363.1**	**7,313.3**	**6,776.7**	**6,538.3**	**6,680.1**	**6,739.7**	**6,586.7**
Land Use, Land-Use Change, and Forestry	**(819.6)**	**(731.0)**	**(749.2)**	**(753.8)**	**(763.0)**	**(761.4)**	**(758.9)**
Forest Land	(784.3)	(729.8)	(733.8)	(723.6)	(733.5)	(731.8)	(728.7)
Cropland	2.4	(0.7)	4.0	1.3	3.1	4.0	4.7
Grassland	13.8	25.3	9.9	0.8	0.4	0.9	0.4
Wetlands	(3.9)	(5.2)	(3.9)	(4.0)	(4.0)	(4.0)	(4.1)
Settlements	(47.6)	(20.5)	(25.4)	(28.3)	(28.9)	(30.4)	(31.3)
Net Emission (Sources and Sinks)[c]	**5,543.5**	**6,582.3**	**6,027.6**	**5,784.5**	**5,917.1**	**5,978.3**	**5,827.7**

Notes: Total emissions presented without LULUCF. Net emissions presented with LULUCF.

[a] There was a method update in this Inventory for estimating the share of gasoline used in on-road and non-road applications. The change does not impact total U.S. gasoline consumption. It mainly results in a shift in gasoline consumption from the transportation sector to industrial and commercial sectors for 2015, creating a break in the time series. The change is discussed further in the Planned Improvements section of Chapter 3.1.

[b] Total emissions without LULUCF.

[c] Net emissions with LULUCF.

Notes: Totals may not sum due to independent rounding. Parentheses indicate negative values or sequestration.

Energy

Energy-related activities, primarily fossil fuel combustion, accounted for the vast majority of U.S. CO_2 emissions for the period of 1990 through 2015. Emissions from fossil fuel combustion comprise the vast majority of energy-related emissions, with CO_2 being the primary gas emitted (see Figure 2-5). Due to their relative importance, fossil fuel combustion-related CO_2 emissions are considered in detail in the Energy chapter (see Figure 2-6). In 2015,

Source: *U.S. EPA, Inventory of U.S. Greenhouse Gas Emissions and Sinks: 1990–2015*

approximately 82 percent of the energy consumed in the United States (on a Btu basis) was produced through the combustion of fossil fuels. The remaining 18 percent came from other energy sources such as hydropower, biomass, nuclear, wind, and solar energy. A discussion of specific trends related to CO_2 as well as other greenhouse gas emissions from energy consumption is presented in the Energy chapter. Energy-related activities are also responsible for CH_4 and N_2O emissions (42 percent and 12 percent of total U.S. emissions of each gas, respectively). Table 2-4 presents greenhouse gas emissions from the Energy chapter, by source and gas.

Figure 2-5: 2015 Energy Chapter Greenhouse Gas Sources (MMT CO_2 Eq.)

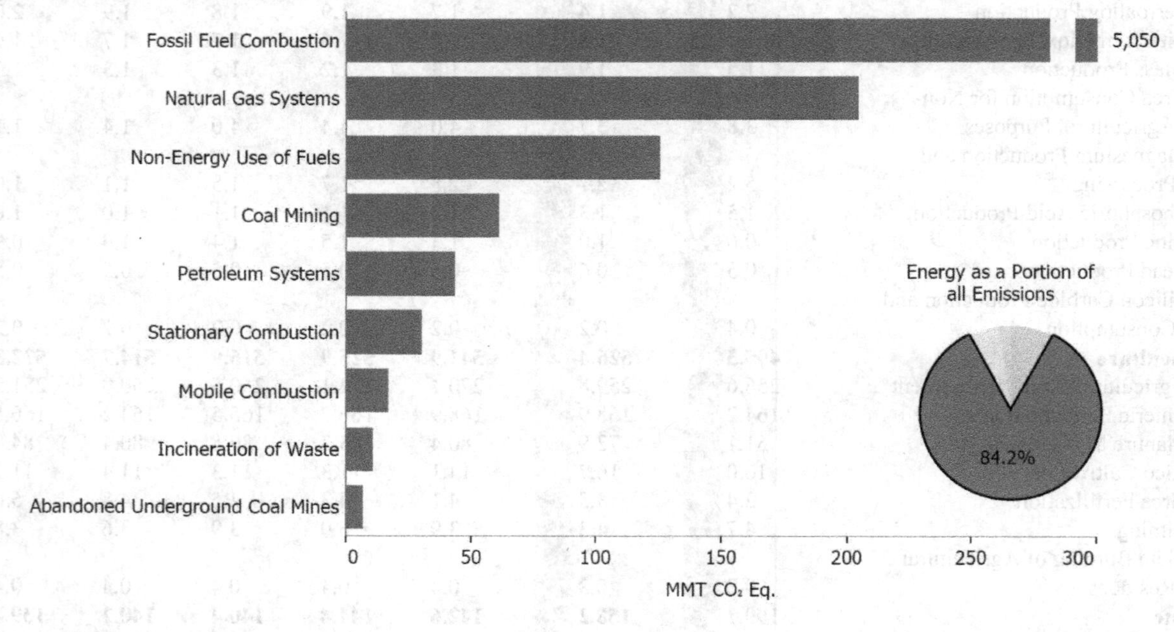

Source: *U.S. EPA, Inventory of U.S. Greenhouse Gas Emissions and Sinks: 1990–2015*

Figure 2-6: 2015 U.S. Fossil Carbon Flows (MMT CO_2 Eq.)

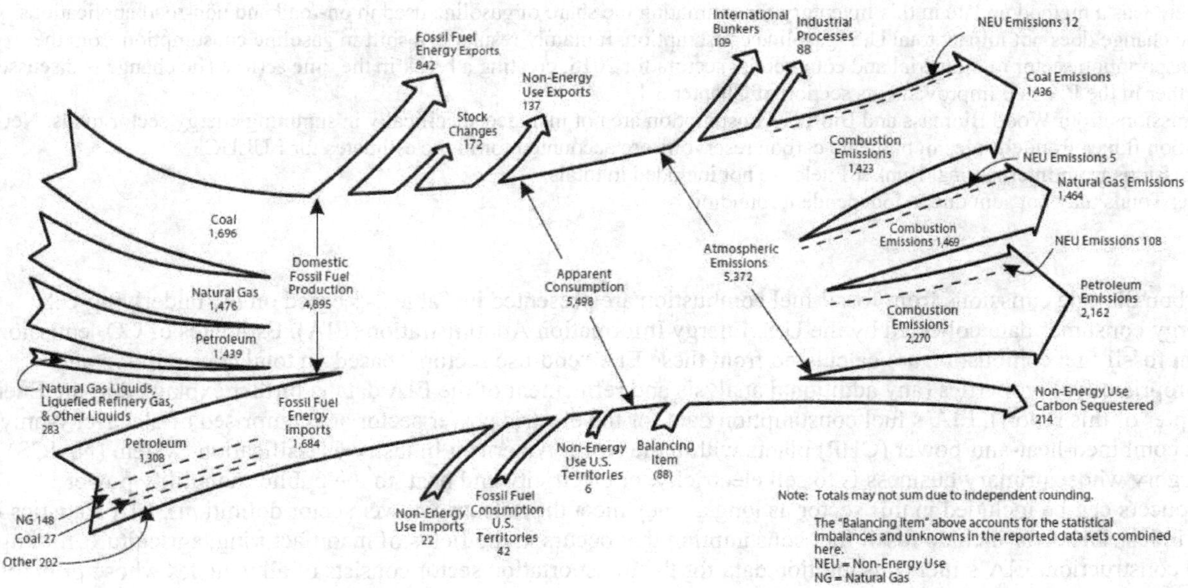

Table 2-4: Emissions from Energy (MMT CO_2 Eq.)

Gas/Source	1990	2005	2011	2012	2013	2014	2015
CO_2	**4,907.2**	**5,932.3**	**5,387.2**	**5,180.9**	**5,332.7**	**5,377.8**	**5,231.9**
Fossil Fuel Combustion	4,740.3	5,746.9	5,227.1	5,024.6	5,156.5	5,202.3	5,049.8
Electricity Generation	*1,820.8*	*2,400.9*	*2,157.7*	*2,022.2*	*2,038.1*	*2,038.0*	*1,900.7*
Transportation[a]	*1,493.8*	*1,887.0*	*1,707.6*	*1,696.8*	*1,713.0*	*1,742.8*	*1,736.4*
Industrial[a]	*842.5*	*828.0*	*775.0*	*782.9*	*812.2*	*806.1*	*805.5*
Residential	*338.3*	*357.8*	*325.5*	*282.5*	*329.7*	*345.4*	*319.6*
Commercial[a]	*217.4*	*223.5*	*220.4*	*196.7*	*221.0*	*228.7*	*246.2*
U.S. Territories	*27.6*	*49.7*	*40.9*	*43.5*	*42.5*	*41.4*	*41.4*
Non-Energy Use of Fuels	117.6	138.9	109.8	106.7	123.6	119.0	125.5
Natural Gas Systems	37.7	30.1	35.7	35.2	38.5	42.4	42.4
Incineration of Waste	8.0	12.5	10.6	10.4	10.4	10.6	10.7
Petroleum Systems	3.6	3.9	4.2	3.9	3.7	3.6	3.6
Biomass-Wood[b]	*215.2*	*206.9*	*195.2*	*194.9*	*211.6*	*217.7*	*198.7*
International Bunker Fuels[c]	*103.5*	*113.1*	*111.7*	*105.8*	*99.8*	*103.2*	*110.8*
Biofuels-Ethanol[b]	*4.2*	*22.9*	*72.9*	*72.8*	*74.7*	*76.1*	*78.9*
Biofuels-Biodiesel[b]	*0.0*	*0.9*	*8.3*	*8.5*	*13.5*	*13.3*	*14.1*
CH_4	**367.3**	**286.6**	**289.5**	**284.1**	**284.6**	**286.8**	**278.6**
Natural Gas Systems	194.1	159.7	154.5	156.2	159.2	162.5	162.4
Petroleum Systems	96.5	64.1	71.2	66.5	64.6	64.8	60.9
Coal Mining	55.5	46.0	48.0	46.4	44.5	43.0	39.9
Stationary Combustion	8.5	7.4	7.1	6.6	8.0	8.1	7.0
Abandoned Underground Coal Mines	7.2	6.6	6.4	6.2	6.2	6.3	6.4
Mobile Combustion[a]	5.6	2.8	2.3	2.2	2.1	2.1	2.0
Incineration of Waste	+	+	+	+	+	+	+
International Bunker Fuels[c]	*0.2*	*0.1*	*0.1*	*0.1*	*0.1*	*0.1*	*0.1*
N_2O	**53.6**	**56.4**	**44.4**	**42.1**	**41.7**	**40.3**	**38.6**
Stationary Combustion	11.9	20.2	21.3	21.4	22.9	23.4	23.1
Mobile Combustion[a]	41.2	35.7	22.8	20.4	18.5	16.6	15.1
Incineration of Waste	0.5	0.4	0.3	0.3	0.3	0.3	0.3

Source: *U.S. EPA, Inventory of U.S. Greenhouse Gas Emissions and Sinks: 1990–2015*

International Bunker Fuels[c]	*0.9*	*1.0*	*1.0*	*0.9*	*0.9*	*0.9*	*0.9*
Total	**5,328.1**	**6,275.3**	**5,721.2**	**5,507.0**	**5,659.1**	**5,704.9**	**5,549.1**

\+ Does not exceed 0.05 MMT CO_2 Eq.

[a] There was a method update in this Inventory for estimating the share of gasoline used in on-road and non-road applications. The change does not impact total U.S. gasoline consumption. It mainly results in a shift in gasoline consumption from the transportation sector to industrial and commercial sectors for 2015, creating a break in the time series. The change is discussed further in the Planned Improvements section of Chapter 3.1.

[b] Emissions from Wood Biomass and Biofuel Consumption are not included specifically in summing energy sector totals. Net carbon fluxes from changes in biogenic carbon reservoirs are accounted for in the estimates for LULUCF.

[c] Emissions from International Bunker Fuels are not included in totals.

Note: Totals may not sum due to independent rounding.

Carbon dioxide emissions from fossil fuel combustion are presented in Table 2-5 based on the underlying U.S. energy consumer data collected by the U.S. Energy Information Administration (EIA). Estimates of CO_2 emissions from fossil fuel combustion are calculated from these EIA "end-use sectors" based on total consumption and appropriate fuel properties (any additional analysis and refinement of the EIA data is further explained in the Energy chapter of this report). EIA's fuel consumption data for the electric power sector are comprised of electricity-only and combined-heat-and-power (CHP) plants within the North American Industry Classification System (NAICS) 22 category whose primary business is to sell electricity, or electricity and heat, to the public (nonutility power producers can be included in this sector as long as they meet they electric power sector definition). EIA statistics for the industrial sector include fossil fuel consumption that occurs in the fields of manufacturing, agriculture, mining, and construction. EIA's fuel consumption data for the transportation sector consists of all vehicles whose primary purpose is transporting people and/or goods from one physical location to another. EIA's fuel consumption data for the industrial sector consists of all facilities and equipment used for producing, processing, or assembling goods (EIA includes generators that produce electricity and/or useful thermal output primarily to support on-site industrial activities in this sector). EIA's fuel consumption data for the residential sector consist of living quarters for private households. EIA's fuel consumption data for the commercial sector consist of service-providing facilities and equipment from private and public organizations and businesses (EIA includes generators that produce electricity and/or useful thermal output primarily to support the activities at commercial establishments in this sector). Table 2-5 and Figure 2-7 summarize CO_2 emissions from fossil fuel combustion by end-use sector. Figure 2-8 further describes the total emissions from fossil fuel combustion, separated by end-use sector, including CH_4 and N_2O in addition to CO_2.

Table 2-5: CO_2 Emissions from Fossil Fuel Combustion by End-Use Sector (MMT CO_2 Eq.)

End-Use Sector	1990	2005	2011	2012	2013	2014	2015
Transportation[a]	**1,496.8**	**1,891.8**	**1,711.9**	**1,700.6**	**1,717.0**	**1,746.9**	**1,740.1**
Combustion	1,493.8	1,887.0	1,707.6	1,696.8	1,713.0	1,742.8	1,736.4
Electricity	3.0	4.7	4.3	3.9	4.0	4.1	3.7
Industrial[a]	**1,529.2**	**1,564.6**	**1,399.6**	**1,375.7**	**1,407.0**	**1,399.3**	**1,355.0**
Combustion	842.5	828.0	775.0	782.9	812.2	806.1	805.5
Electricity	686.7	736.6	624.7	592.8	594.7	593.2	549.6
Residential	**931.4**	**1,214.1**	**1,116.2**	**1,007.8**	**1,064.6**	**1,080.1**	**1,003.9**
Combustion	338.3	357.8	325.5	282.5	329.7	345.4	319.6
Electricity	593.0	856.3	790.7	725.3	734.9	734.7	684.3
Commercial[a]	**755.4**	**1,026.8**	**958.4**	**897.0**	**925.5**	**934.7**	**909.4**
Combustion	217.4	223.5	220.4	196.7	221.0	228.7	246.2
Electricity	538.0	803.3	738.0	700.3	704.5	706.0	663.1
U.S. Territories[b]	**27.6**	**49.7**	**40.9**	**43.5**	**42.5**	**41.4**	**41.4**
Total	**4,740.3**	**5,746.9**	**5,227.1**	**5,024.6**	**5,156.5**	**5,202.3**	**5,049.8**
Electricity Generation	**1,820.8**	**2,400.9**	**2,157.7**	**2,022.2**	**2,038.1**	**2,038.0**	**1,900.7**

[a] There was a method update in this Inventory for estimating the share of gasoline used in on-road and non-road applications. The change does not impact total U.S. gasoline consumption. It mainly results in a shift in gasoline consumption from the transportation sector to industrial and commercial sectors for 2015, creating a break in the time series. The change is discussed further in the Planned Improvements section of Chapter 3.1.

Source: *U.S. EPA, Inventory of U.S. Greenhouse Gas Emissions and Sinks: 1990–2015*

[b] Fuel consumption by U.S. Territories (i.e., American Samoa, Guam, Puerto Rico, U.S. Virgin Islands, Wake Island, and other U.S. Pacific Islands) is included in this report.
Notes: Combustion-related emissions from electricity generation are allocated based on aggregate national electricity consumption by each end-use sector. Totals may not sum due to independent rounding.

Figure 2-7: 2015 CO_2 Emissions from Fossil Fuel Combustion by Sector and Fuel Type (MMT CO_2 Eq.)

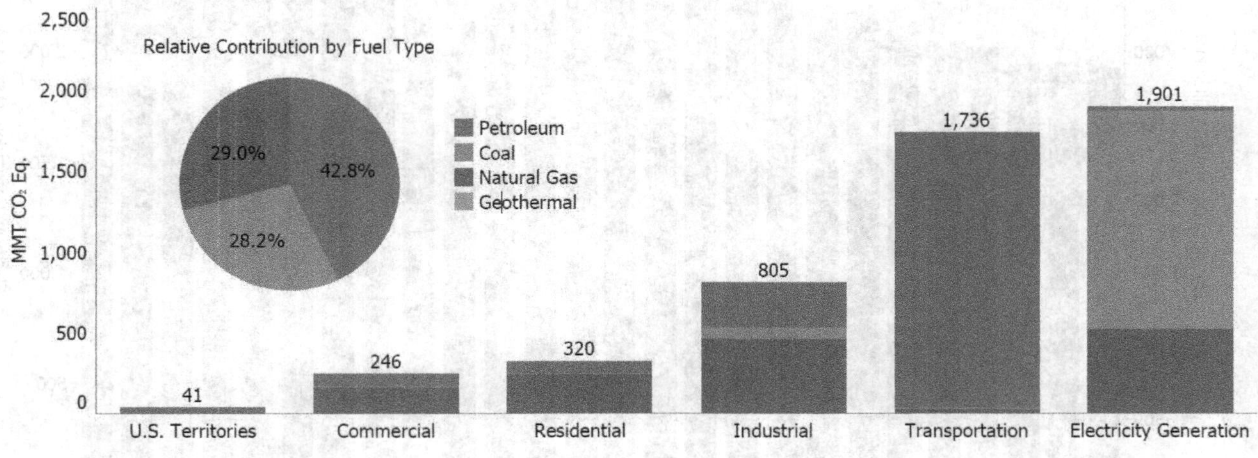

Figure 2-8: 2015 End-Use Sector Emissions of CO_2 from Fossil Fuel Combustion (MMT CO_2 Eq.)

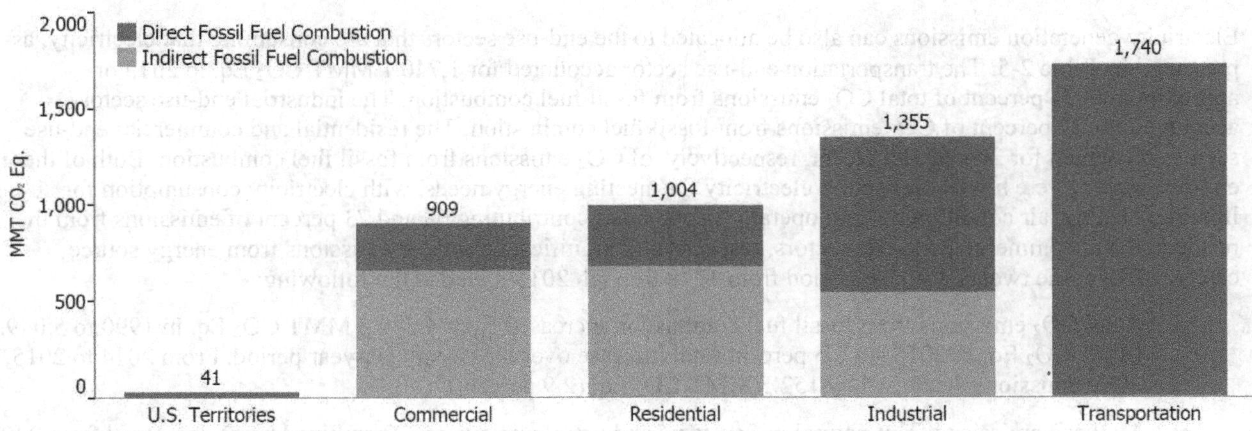

The main driver of emissions in the Energy sector is CO_2 from fossil fuel combustion. Electricity generation is the largest emitter of CO_2, and electricity generators consumed 34 percent of U.S. energy from fossil fuels and emitted 38 percent of the CO_2 from fossil fuel combustion in 2015. Changes in electricity demand and the carbon intensity of fuels used for electricity generation have a significant impact on CO_2 emissions. While emissions from the electric power sector have increased by approximately 4 percent since 1990, the carbon intensity of the electric power sector, in terms of CO_2 Eq. per QBtu has significantly decreased by 16 percent during that same timeframe. This decoupling of electricity generation and the resulting emissions is shown below in Figure 2-9.

Source: *U.S. EPA, Inventory of U.S. Greenhouse Gas Emissions and Sinks: 1990–2015*

Figure 2-9: Electricity Generation (Billion kWh) and Emissions (MMT CO_2 Eq.)

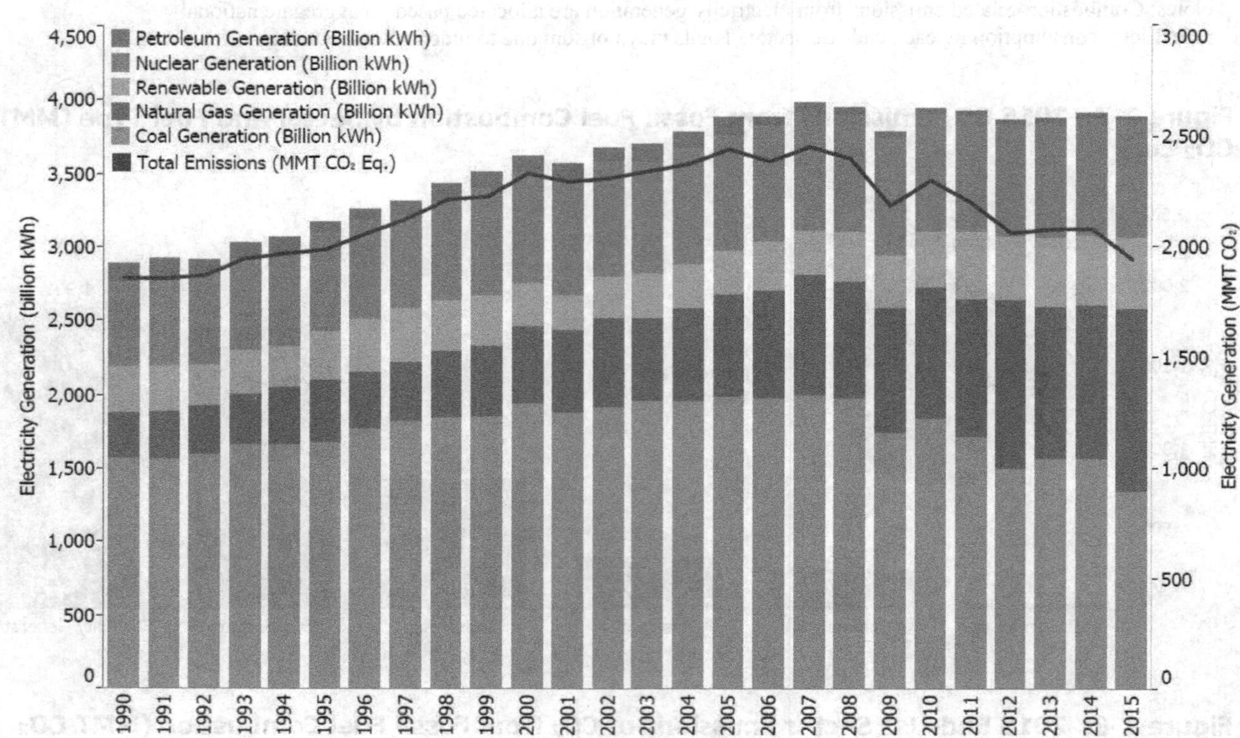

Electricity generation emissions can also be allocated to the end-use sectors that are consuming that electricity, as presented in Table 2-5. The transportation end-use sector accounted for 1,740.1 MMT CO_2 Eq. in 2015 or approximately 34 percent of total CO_2 emissions from fossil fuel combustion. The industrial end-use sector accounted for 27 percent of CO_2 emissions from fossil fuel combustion. The residential and commercial end-use sectors accounted for 20 and 18 percent, respectively, of CO_2 emissions from fossil fuel combustion. Both of these end-use sectors were heavily reliant on electricity for meeting energy needs, with electricity consumption for lighting, heating, air conditioning, and operating appliances contributing 68 and 73 percent of emissions from the residential and commercial end-use sectors, respectively. Significant trends in emissions from energy source categories over the twenty six-year period from 1990 through 2015 included the following:

- Total CO_2 emissions from fossil fuel combustion increased from 4,740.3 MMT CO_2 Eq. in 1990 to 5,049.8 MMT CO_2 Eq. in 2015 – a 6.5 percent total increase over the twenty six-year period. From 2014 to 2015, these emissions decreased by 152.5 MMT CO_2 Eq. (2.9 percent).
- Methane emissions from natural gas systems and petroleum systems (combined here) decreased from 249.5 MMT CO_2 Eq. in 1990 to 202.3 MMT CO_2 Eq. (47.2 MMT CO_2 Eq. or 18.9 percent) from 1990 to 2015. Natural gas systems CH_4 emissions decreased by 31.6 MMT CO_2 Eq. (16.3 percent) since 1990, largely due to a decrease in emissions from transmission, storage, and distribution. The decrease in transmission and storage emissions is largely due to reduced compressor station emissions (including emissions from compressors and fugitives). The decrease in distribution emissions is largely attributed to increased use of plastic piping, which has lower emissions than other pipe materials, and station upgrades at metering and regulating (M&R) stations. Petroleum systems CH_4 emissions decreased by 15.6 MMT CO_2 Eq. (or 28.1 percent) since 1990. This decrease is due primarily to decreases in emissions from associated gas venting.
- Carbon dioxide emissions from non-energy uses of fossil fuels increased by 7.9 MMT CO_2 Eq. (6.8 percent) from 1990 through 2015. Emissions from non-energy uses of fossil fuels were 125.5 MMT CO_2 Eq. in 2015, which constituted 2.3 percent of total national CO_2 emissions, approximately the same proportion as in 1990.

Source: *U.S. EPA, Inventory of U.S. Greenhouse Gas Emissions and Sinks: 1990–2015*

- Nitrous oxide emissions from stationary combustion increased by 11.2 MMT CO_2 Eq. (94.0 percent) from 1990 through 2015. Nitrous oxide emissions from this source increased primarily as a result of an increase in the number of coal fluidized bed boilers in the electric power sector.
- Nitrous oxide emissions from mobile combustion decreased by 26.1 MMT CO_2 Eq. (63.3 percent) from 1990 through 2015, primarily as a result of N_2O national emission control standards and emission control technologies for on-road vehicles.
- Carbon dioxide emissions from incineration of waste (10.7 MMT CO_2 Eq. in 2015) increased by 2.7 MMT CO_2 Eq. (34.3 percent) from 1990 through 2015, as the volume of plastics and other fossil carbon-containing materials in municipal solid waste grew.

The decrease in CO_2 emissions from fossil fuel combustion was a result of multiple factors, including: (1) substitution from coal to natural gas consumption in the electric power sector; (2) warmer winter conditions in 2015 resulting in a decreased demand for heating fuel in the residential and commercial sectors; and (3) a slight decrease in electricity demand.

Industrial Processes and Product Use

The Industrial Processes and Product Use (IPPU) chapter includes greenhouse gas emissions occurring from industrial processes and from the use of greenhouse gases in products.

Greenhouse gas emissions are produced as the by-products of many non-energy-related industrial activities. For example, industrial processes can chemically transform raw materials, which often release waste gases such as CO_2, CH_4, and N_2O. These processes are shown in Figure 2-10. Industrial processes also release HFCs, PFCs, SF_6, and NF_3 and other fluorinated compounds. In addition to the use of HFCs and some PFCs as substitutes for ozone depleting substances (ODS), fluorinated compounds such as HFCs, PFCs, SF_6, NF_3, and others are employed and emitted by a number of other industrial sources in the United States. These industries include aluminum production, HCFC-22 production, semiconductor manufacture, electric power transmission and distribution, and magnesium metal production and processing. Table 2-6 presents greenhouse gas emissions from industrial processes by source category.

Source: *U.S. EPA, Inventory of U.S. Greenhouse Gas Emissions and Sinks: 1990–2015*

Figure 2-10: 2015 Industrial Processes and Product Use Chapter Greenhouse Gas Sources (MMT CO_2 Eq.)

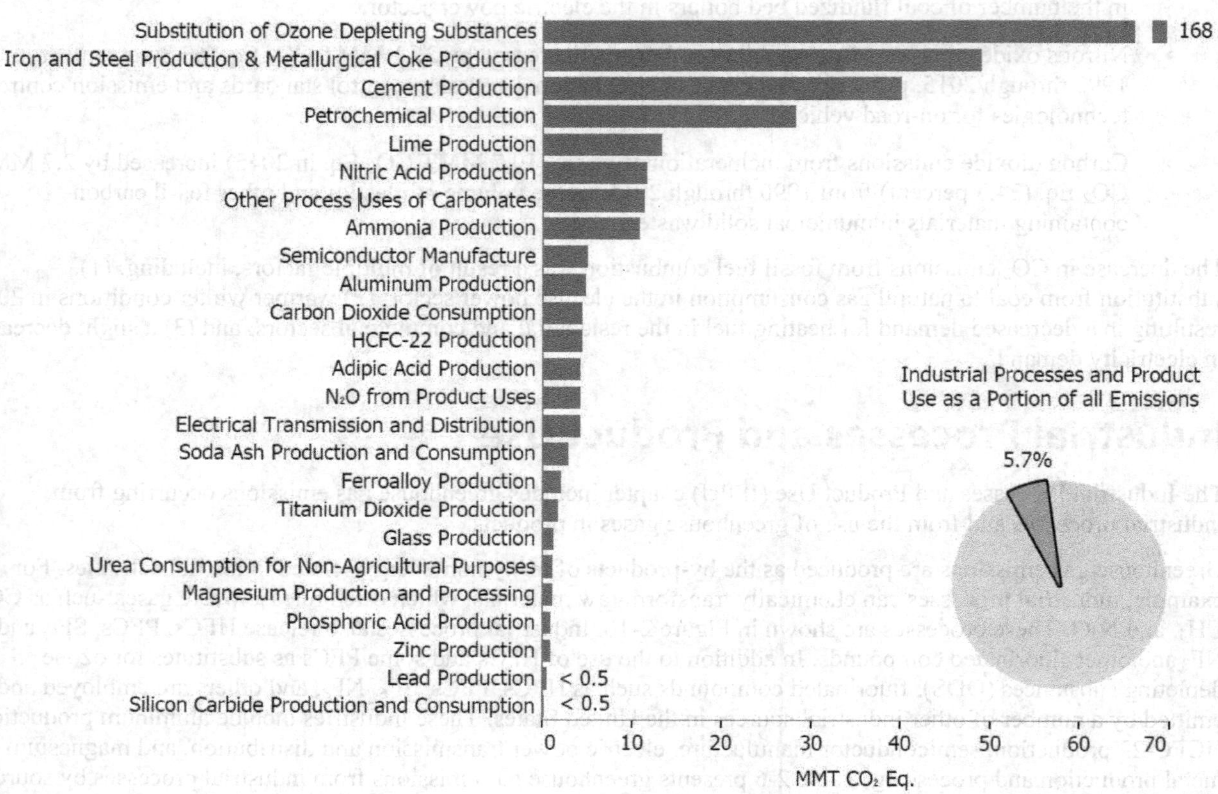

Table 2-6: Emissions from Industrial Processes and Product Use (MMT CO_2 Eq.)

Gas/Source	1990	2005	2011	2012	2013	2014	2015
CO_2	**208.8**	**191.7**	**174.3**	**171.0**	**172.9**	**179.3**	**170.7**
Iron and Steel Production & Metallurgical Coke Production	101.5	68.0	61.1	55.4	53.3	58.6	48.9
Iron and Steel Production	*99.0*	*66.0*	*59.7*	*54.9*	*51.5*	*56.6*	*46.0*
Metallurgical Coke Production	*2.5*	*2.0*	*1.4*	*0.5*	*1.8*	*2.0*	*2.8*
Cement Production	33.5	46.2	32.2	35.3	36.4	39.4	39.9
Petrochemical Production	21.3	27.0	26.3	26.5	26.4	26.5	28.1
Lime Production	11.7	14.6	14.0	13.8	14.0	14.2	13.3
Other Process Uses of Carbonates	4.9	6.3	9.3	8.0	10.4	11.8	11.2
Ammonia Production	13.0	9.2	9.3	9.4	10.0	9.6	10.8
Carbon Dioxide Consumption	1.5	1.4	4.1	4.0	4.2	4.5	4.3
Soda Ash Production and Consumption	2.8	3.0	2.7	2.8	2.8	2.8	2.8
Aluminum Production	6.8	4.1	3.3	3.4	3.3	2.8	2.8
Ferroalloy Production	2.2	1.4	1.7	1.9	1.8	1.9	2.0
Titanium Dioxide Production	1.2	1.8	1.7	1.5	1.7	1.7	1.6
Glass Production	1.5	1.9	1.3	1.2	1.3	1.3	1.3
Urea Consumption for Non-Agricultural Purposes	3.8	3.7	4.0	4.4	4.0	1.4	1.1
Phosphoric Acid Production	1.5	1.3	1.2	1.1	1.1	1.0	1.0
Zinc Production	0.6	1.0	1.3	1.5	1.4	1.0	0.9
Lead Production	0.5	0.6	0.5	0.5	0.5	0.5	0.5
Silicon Carbide Production and Consumption	0.4	0.2	0.2	0.2	0.2	0.2	0.2
Magnesium Production and Processing	+	+	+	+	+	+	+
CH_4	**0.3**	**0.1**	**0.1**	**0.1**	**0.1**	**0.2**	**0.2**

Source: *U.S. EPA, Inventory of U.S. Greenhouse Gas Emissions and Sinks: 1990–2015*

Petrochemical Production	0.2	0.1	+	0.1	0.1	0.1	0.2
Ferroalloy Production	+	+	+	+	+	+	+
Silicon Carbide Production and Consumption	+	+	+	+	+	+	+
Iron and Steel Production & Metallurgical Coke Production	+	+	+	+	+	+	+
Iron and Steel Production	+	+	+	+	+	+	+
Metallurgical Coke Production	0.0	0.0	0.0	0.0	0.0	0.0	0.0
N_2O	**31.6**	**22.8**	**25.6**	**20.4**	**19.0**	**20.8**	**20.3**
Nitric Acid Production	12.1	11.3	10.9	10.5	10.7	10.9	11.6
Adipic Acid Production	15.2	7.1	10.2	5.5	3.9	5.4	4.3
N_2O from Product Uses	4.2	4.2	4.2	4.2	4.2	4.2	4.2
Semiconductor Manufacture	+	0.1	0.2	0.2	0.2	0.2	0.2
HFCs	**46.6**	**120.0**	**154.3**	**155.9**	**159.0**	**166.7**	**173.2**
Substitution of Ozone Depleting Substances[a]	0.3	99.7	145.3	150.2	154.6	161.3	168.5
HCFC-22 Production	46.1	20.0	8.8	5.5	4.1	5.0	4.3
Semiconductor Manufacture	0.2	0.2	0.2	0.2	0.2	0.3	0.3
Magnesium Production and Processing	0.0	0.0	+	+	0.1	0.1	0.1
PFCs	**24.3**	**6.7**	**6.9**	**6.0**	**5.8**	**5.8**	**5.2**
Semiconductor Manufacture	2.8	3.2	3.4	3.0	2.8	3.2	3.2
Aluminum Production	21.5	3.4	3.5	2.9	3.0	2.5	2.0
Substitution of Ozone Depleting Substances	0.0	+	+	+	+	+	+
SF_6	**28.8**	**11.7**	**9.2**	**6.8**	**6.4**	**6.6**	**5.8**
Electrical Transmission and Distribution	23.1	8.3	6.0	4.8	4.6	4.8	4.2
Magnesium Production and Processing	5.2	2.7	2.8	1.6	1.5	1.0	0.9
Semiconductor Manufacture	0.5	0.7	0.4	0.4	0.4	0.7	0.7
NF_3	**+**	**0.5**	**0.7**	**0.6**	**0.6**	**0.5**	**0.6**
Semiconductor Manufacture	+	0.5	0.7	0.6	0.6	0.5	0.6
Total	**340.4**	**353.4**	**371.0**	**360.9**	**363.7**	**379.8**	**375.9**

+ Does not exceed 0.05 MMT CO_2 Eq.

[a] Small amounts of PFC emissions also result from this source.

Note: Totals may not sum due to independent rounding.

Overall, emissions from the IPPU sector increased by 10.4 percent from 1990 to 2015. Significant trends in emissions from IPPU source categories over the twenty-six-year period from 1990 through 2015 included the following:

- Hydrofluorocarbon and perfluorocarbon emissions from ODS substitutes have been increasing from small amounts in 1990 to 168.5 MMT CO_2 Eq. in 2015. This increase was in large part the result of efforts to phase out chlorofluorocarbons (CFCs) and other ODSs in the United States. In the short term, this trend is expected to continue, and will likely continue over the next decade as hydrochlorofluorocarbons (HCFCs), which are interim substitutes in many applications, are themselves phased-out under the provisions of the Copenhagen Amendments to the Montreal Protocol.

- Combined CO_2 and CH_4 emissions from iron and steel production and metallurgical coke production decreased by 16.6 percent to 48.9 MMT CO_2 Eq. from 2014 to 2015, and have declined overall by 52.6 MMT CO_2 Eq. (51.8 percent) from 1990 through 2015, due to restructuring of the industry, technological improvements, and increased scrap steel utilization.

- Carbon dioxide emissions from ammonia production (10.8 MMT CO_2 Eq. in 2015) decreased by 2.2 MMT CO_2 Eq. (17.2 percent) since 1990. Ammonia production relies on natural gas as both a feedstock and a fuel, and as such, market fluctuations and volatility in natural gas prices affect the production of ammonia.

- Urea consumption for non-agricultural purposes (1.1 MMT CO_2 Eq. in 2015) decreased by 2.7 MMT CO_2 Eq. (70.2 percent) since 1990. From 1990 to 2007, emissions increased by 31 percent to a peak of 4.9 MMT CO_2 Eq., before decreasing by 77 percent to 2015 levels.

- Nitrous oxide emissions from adipic acid production were 4.3 MMT CO_2 Eq. in 2015, and have decreased significantly since 1990 due to both the widespread installation of pollution control measures in the late

Source: *U.S. EPA, Inventory of U.S. Greenhouse Gas Emissions and Sinks: 1990–2015*

1990s and plant idling in the late 2000s. Emissions from adipic acid production have decreased by 72.0 percent since 1990 and by 74.8 percent since a peak in 1995.

- PFC emissions from aluminum production decreased by 90.7 percent (19.5 MMT CO_2 Eq.) from 1990 to 2015, due to both industry emission reduction efforts and lower domestic aluminum production.

Agriculture

Agricultural activities contribute directly to emissions of greenhouse gases through a variety of processes, including the following source categories: enteric fermentation in domestic livestock, livestock manure management, rice cultivation, agricultural soil management, liming, urea fertilization, and field burning of agricultural residues.

In 2015, agricultural activities were responsible for emissions of 522.3 MMT CO_2 Eq., or 7.9 percent of total U.S. greenhouse gas emissions. Methane, nitrous oxide and carbon dioxide were the primary greenhouse gases emitted by agricultural activities. Methane emissions from enteric fermentation and manure management represented approximately 25.4 percent and 10.1 percent of total CH_4 emissions from anthropogenic activities, respectively, in 2015. Agricultural soil management activities, such as application of synthetic and organic fertilizers, deposition of livestock manure, and growing N-fixing plants, were the largest source of U.S. N_2O emissions in 2015, accounting for 75.1 percent. Carbon dioxide emissions from the application of crushed limestone and dolomite (i.e., soil liming) and urea fertilization represented 0.2 percent of total CO_2 emissions from anthropogenic activities. Figure 2-11 and Table 2-7 illustrate agricultural greenhouse gas emissions by source.

Figure 2-11: 2015 Agriculture Chapter Greenhouse Gas Sources (MMT CO_2 Eq.)

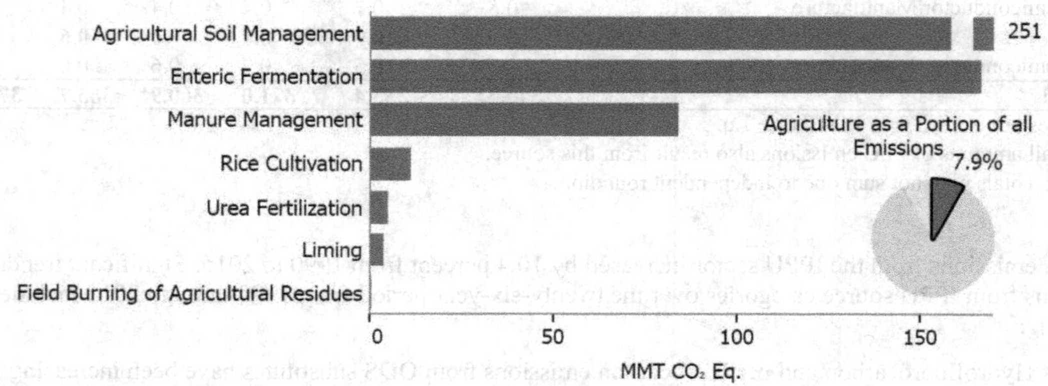

Source: *U.S. EPA, Inventory of U.S. Greenhouse Gas Emissions and Sinks: 1990–2015*

Table 2-7: Emissions from Agriculture (MMT CO_2 Eq.)

Gas/Source	1990	2005	2011	2012	2013	2014	2015
CO_2	**7.1**	**7.9**	**8.0**	**10.2**	**8.4**	**8.4**	**8.8**
Urea Fertilization	2.4	3.5	4.1	4.3	4.5	4.8	5.0
Liming	4.7	4.3	3.9	6.0	3.9	3.6	3.8
CH_4	**217.6**	**242.1**	**246.3**	**244.0**	**240.4**	**238.7**	**244.3**
Enteric Fermentation	164.2	168.9	168.9	166.7	165.5	164.2	166.5
Manure Management	37.2	56.3	63.0	65.6	63.3	62.9	66.3
Rice Cultivation	16.0	16.7	14.1	11.3	11.3	11.4	11.2
Field Burning of Agricultural Residues	0.2	0.2	0.3	0.3	0.3	0.3	0.3
N_2O	**270.6**	**276.4**	**287.6**	**271.7**	**268.1**	**267.6**	**269.1**
Agricultural Soil Management	256.6	259.8	270.1	254.1	250.5	250.0	251.3
Manure Management	14.0	16.5	17.4	17.5	17.5	17.5	17.7
Field Burning of Agricultural Residues	0.1	0.1	0.1	0.1	0.1	0.1	0.1
Total	**495.3**	**526.4**	**541.9**	**525.9**	**516.9**	**514.7**	**522.3**

Note: Totals may not sum due to independent rounding.

Some significant trends in U.S. emissions from Agriculture source categories include the following:

- Agricultural soils produced approximately 75.1 percent of N_2O emissions in the United States in 2015. Estimated emissions from this source in 2015 were 251.3 MMT CO_2 Eq. Annual N_2O emissions from agricultural soils fluctuated between 1990 and 2015, although overall emissions were 2.0 percent lower in 2015 than in 1990. Year-to-year fluctuations are largely a reflection of annual variation in weather patterns, synthetic fertilizer use, and crop production.
- Enteric fermentation is the largest anthropogenic source of CH_4 emissions in the United States. In 2015, enteric fermentation CH_4 emissions were 166.5 MMT CO_2 Eq. (25.4 percent of total CH_4 emissions), which represents an increase of 2.4 MMT CO_2 Eq. (1.5 percent) since 1990. This increase in emissions from 1990 to 2015 in enteric fermentation generally follows the increasing trends in cattle populations. From 1990 to 1995, emissions increased and then generally decreased from 1996 to 2004, mainly due to fluctuations in beef cattle populations and increased digestibility of feed for feedlot cattle. Emissions increased from 2005 to 2007, as both dairy and beef populations increased. Research indicates that the feed digestibility of dairy cow diets decreased during this period. Emissions decreased again from 2008 to 2015 as beef cattle populations again decreased.
- Liming and urea fertilization are the only source of CO_2 emissions reported in the Agriculture sector. Estimated emissions from these sources were 3.8 and 5.0 MMT CO_2 Eq., respectively. Liming and urea fertilization emissions increased by 5.6 percent and 5.3 percent, respectively, relative to 2014, and decreased by 18.4 percent and increased by 108.2 percent, respectively since 1990.
- Overall, emissions from manure management increased 64.2 percent between 1990 and 2015. This encompassed an increase of 78.3 percent for CH_4, from 37.2 MMT CO_2 Eq. in 1990 to 66.3 MMT CO_2 Eq. in 2015; and an increase of 26.6 percent for N_2O, from 14.0 MMT CO_2 Eq. in 1990 to 17.7 MMT CO_2 Eq. in 2015. The majority of the increase observed in CH_4 resulted from swine and dairy cattle manure, where emissions increased 58 and 136 percent, respectively, from 1990 to 2015. From 2014 to 2015, there was a 5.4 percent increase in total CH_4 emissions from manure management, mainly due to minor shifts in the animal populations and the resultant effects on manure management system allocations.

Land Use, Land-Use Change, and Forestry

When humans alter the terrestrial biosphere through land use, changes in land use, and land management practices, they also influence the carbon (C) stock fluxes on these lands and cause emissions of CH_4 and N_2O. Overall, managed land is a net sink for CO_2 (C sequestration) in the United States. The drivers of fluxes on managed lands include, for example, forest management practices, tree planting in urban areas, the management of agricultural

Source: *U.S. EPA, Inventory of U.S. Greenhouse Gas Emissions and Sinks: 1990–2015*

soils, the landfilling of yard trimmings and food scraps, and activities that cause changes in C stocks in coastal wetlands. The main drivers for net forest sequestration include net forest growth, increasing forest area, and a net accumulation of C stocks in harvested wood pools. The net sequestration in *Settlements Remaining Settlements,* is driven primarily by C stock gains in urban forests through net tree growth and increased urban area, as well as long-term accumulation of C in landfills from additions of yard trimmings and food scraps.

The LULUCF sector in 2015 resulted in a net increase in C stocks (i.e., net CO_2 removals) of 778.7 MMT CO_2 Eq. (Table 2-3).[1] This represents an offset of approximately 11.8 percent of total (i.e., gross) greenhouse gas emissions in 2015. Emissions of CH_4 and N_2O from LULUCF activities in 2015 were 19.7 MMT CO_2 Eq. and represent 0.3 percent of total greenhouse gas emissions.[2] Between 1990 and 2015, total C sequestration in the LULUCF sector decreased by 6.2 percent, primarily due to a decrease in the rate of net C accumulation in forests and an increase in CO_2 emissions from *Land Converted to Settlements.*

Carbon dioxide removals from C stock changes are presented in Table 2-8 along with CH_4 and N_2O emissions for LULUCF source categories. Forest fires were the largest source of CH_4 emissions from LULUCF in 2015, totaling 7.3 MMT CO_2 Eq. (292 kt of CH_4). *Coastal Wetlands Remaining Coastal Wetlands* resulted in CH_4 emissions of 3.6 MMT CO_2 Eq. (143 kt of CH_4). Grassland fires resulted in CH_4 emissions of 0.4 MMT CO_2 Eq. (16 kt of CH_4). *Peatlands Remaining Peatlands*, *Land Converted to Wetlands*, and *Drained Organic Soils* resulted in CH_4 emissions of less than 0.05 MMT CO_2 Eq. each.

Forest fires were also the largest source of N_2O emissions from LULUCF in 2015, totaling 4.8 MMT CO_2 Eq. (16 kt of N_2O). Nitrous oxide emissions from fertilizer application to settlement soils in 2015 totaled to 2.5 MMT CO_2 Eq. (8 kt of N_2O). This represents an increase of 76.6 percent since 1990. Additionally, the application of synthetic fertilizers to forest soils in 2015 resulted in N_2O emissions of 0.5 MMT CO_2 Eq. (2 kt of N_2O). Nitrous oxide emissions from fertilizer application to forest soils have increased by 455 percent since 1990, but still account for a relatively small portion of overall emissions. Grassland fires resulted in N_2O emissions of 0.4 MMT CO_2 Eq. (1 kt of N_2O). *Coastal Wetlands Remaining Coastal Wetlands* and *Drained Organic Soils* resulted in N_2O emissions of 0.1 MMT CO_2 Eq. each (less than 0.5 kt of N_2O), and *Peatlands Remaining Peatlands* resulted in N_2O emissions of less than 0.05 MMT CO_2 Eq. (see Table 2-8).

Table 2-8: U.S. Greenhouse Gas Emissions and Removals (Net Flux) from Land Use, Land-Use Change, and Forestry (MMT CO_2 Eq.)

Gas/Land-Use Category	1990	2005	2011	2012	2013	2014	2015
Carbon Stock Change[a]	**(830.2)**	**(754.0)**	**(769.1)**	**(779.8)**	**(782.2)**	**(781.1)**	**(778.7)**
Forest Land Remaining Forest Land	(697.7)	(664.6)	(670.0)	(666.9)	(670.8)	(669.3)	(666.2)
Land Converted to Forest Land	(92.0)	(81.4)	(75.8)	(75.2)	(75.2)	(75.2)	(75.2)
Cropland Remaining Cropland	(40.9)	(26.5)	(19.1)	(21.4)	(19.6)	(18.7)	(18.0)
Land Converted to Cropland	43.3	25.9	23.2	22.7	22.7	22.7	22.7
Grassland Remaining Grassland	(4.2)	5.5	(12.5)	(20.8)	(20.5)	(20.4)	(20.9)
Land Converted to Grassland	17.9	19.2	20.7	20.4	20.5	20.5	20.5
Wetlands Remaining Wetlands	(7.6)	(8.9)	(7.6)	(7.7)	(7.8)	(7.8)	(7.8)
Land Converted to Wetlands	+	+	+	+	+	+	+
Settlements Remaining Settlements	(86.2)	(91.4)	(98.7)	(99.2)	(99.8)	(101.2)	(102.1)
Land Converted to Settlements	37.2	68.4	70.7	68.3	68.3	68.3	68.3
CH_4	**6.7**	**13.3**	**11.2**	**14.9**	**11.0**	**11.3**	**11.3**
Forest Land Remaining Forest Land:							
Forest Fires	3.2	9.4	6.8	10.8	7.2	7.3	7.3
Wetlands Remaining Wetlands: Coastal Wetlands Remaining Coastal Wetlands	3.4	3.5	3.5	3.5	3.6	3.6	3.6

[1] LULUCF Carbon Stock Change is the net C stock change from the following categories: *Forest Land Remaining Forest Land, Land Converted to Forest Land, Cropland Remaining Cropland, Land Converted to Cropland, Grassland Remaining Grassland, Land Converted to Grassland, Wetlands Remaining Wetlands, Land Converted to Wetlands, Settlements Remaining Settlements,* and *Land Converted to Settlements.*

[2] LULUCF emissions include the CH_4 and N_2O emissions reported for *Peatlands Remaining Peatlands*, Forest Fires, Drained Organic Soils, Grassland Fires, and *Coastal Wetlands Remaining Coastal Wetlands*; CH_4 emissions from *Land Converted to Coastal Wetlands*; and N_2O emissions from Forest Soils and Settlement Soils.

Source: *U.S. EPA, Inventory of U.S. Greenhouse Gas Emissions and Sinks: 1990–2015*

Grassland Remaining Grassland: Grassland Fires	0.1	0.3	0.8	0.6	0.2	0.4	0.4
Forest Land Remaining Forest Land: Drained Organic Soils	+	+	+	+	+	+	+
Land Converted to Wetlands: Land Converted to Coastal Wetlands	+	+	+	+	+	+	+
Wetlands Remaining Wetlands: Peatlands Remaining Peatlands	+	+	+	+	+	+	+
N_2O	**3.9**	**9.7**	**8.7**	**11.1**	**8.2**	**8.4**	**8.4**
Forest Land Remaining Forest Land: Forest Fires	2.1	6.2	4.5	7.1	4.7	4.8	4.8
Settlements Remaining Settlements: Settlement Soils[b]	1.4	2.5	2.6	2.7	2.6	2.5	2.5
Forest Land Remaining Forest Land: Forest Soils[c]	0.1	0.5	0.5	0.5	0.5	0.5	0.5
Grassland Remaining Grassland: Grassland Fires	0.1	0.3	0.9	0.6	0.2	0.4	0.4
Wetlands Remaining Wetlands: Coastal Wetlands Remaining Coastal Wetlands	0.1	0.2	0.1	0.1	0.1	0.1	0.1
Forest Land Remaining Forest Land: Drained Organic Soils	0.1	0.1	0.1	0.1	0.1	0.1	0.1
Wetlands Remaining Wetlands: Peatlands Remaining Peatlands	+	+	+	+	+	+	+
LULUCF Emissions[d]	**10.6**	**23.0**	**19.9**	**26.1**	**19.2**	**19.7**	**19.7**
LULUCF Carbon Stock Change[a]	**(830.2)**	**(754.0)**	**(769.1)**	**(779.8)**	**(782.2)**	**(781.1)**	**(778.7)**
LULUCF Sector Net Total[e]	**(819.6)**	**(731.0)**	**(749.2)**	**(753.8)**	**(763.0)**	**(761.4)**	**(758.9)**

+ Absolute value does not exceed 0.05 MMT CO_2 Eq.

[a] LULUCF Carbon Stock Change is the net C stock change from the following categories: *Forest Land Remaining Forest Land, Land Converted to Forest Land, Cropland Remaining Cropland, Land Converted to Cropland, Grassland Remaining Grassland, Land Converted to Grassland, Wetlands Remaining Wetlands, Land Converted to Wetlands, Settlements Remaining Settlements,* and *Land Converted to Settlements.*

[b] Estimates include emissions from N fertilizer additions on both *Settlements Remaining Settlements* and *Land Converted to Settlements.*

[c] Estimates include emissions from N fertilizer additions on both *Forest Land Remaining Forest Land* and *Land Converted to Forest Land.*

[d] LULUCF emissions include the CH_4 and N_2O emissions reported for *Peatlands Remaining Peatlands*, Forest Fires, Drained Organic Soils, Grassland Fires, and *Coastal Wetlands Remaining Coastal Wetlands*; CH_4 emissions from *Land Converted to Coastal Wetlands*; and N_2O emissions from Forest Soils and Settlement Soils.

[e] The LULUCF Sector Net Total is the net sum of all CH_4 and N_2O emissions to the atmosphere plus net carbon stock changes.

Notes: Totals may not sum due to independent rounding. Parentheses indicate net sequestration.

Other significant trends from 1990 to 2015 in emissions from LULUCF categories include:

- Annual C sequestration by forest land (i.e., annual C stock accumulation in the five C pools and harvested wood products for *Forest Land Remaining Forest Land* and *Land Converted to Forest Land*) has decreased by approximately 6.1 percent since 1990. This is primarily due to decreased C stock gains in *Land Converted to Forest Land* and the harvested wood products pools within *Forest Land Remaining Forest Land.*
- Annual C sequestration from *Settlements Remaining Settlements* (which includes organic soils, urban trees, and landfilled yard trimmings and food scraps) has increased by 18.4 percent over the period from 1990 to 2015. This is primarily due to an increase in urbanized land area in the United States.
- Annual emissions from *Land Converted to Grassland* increased by approximately 14.4 percent from 1990 to 2015 due to losses in aboveground biomass, belowground biomass, dead wood, and litter C stocks from *Forest Land Converted to Grassland.*
- Annual emissions from *Land Converted to Settlements* increased by approximately 83.5 percent from 1990 to 2015 due to losses in aboveground biomass C stocks from *Forest Land Converted to Settlements* and mineral soils C stocks from *Grassland Converted to Settlements.*

Source: *U.S. EPA, Inventory of U.S. Greenhouse Gas Emissions and Sinks: 1990–2015*

Waste

Waste management and treatment activities are sources of greenhouse gas emissions (see Figure 2-12). In 2015, landfills were the third-largest source of U.S. anthropogenic CH_4 emissions, accounting for 17.6 percent of total U.S. CH_4 emissions.[3] Additionally, wastewater treatment accounts for 14.2 percent of Waste emissions, 2.3 percent of U.S. CH_4 emissions, and 1.5 percent of N_2O emissions. Emissions of CH_4 and N_2O from composting grew from 1990 to 2015, and resulted in emissions of 4.0 MMT CO_2 Eq. in 2015. A summary of greenhouse gas emissions from the Waste chapter is presented in Table 2-9.

Figure 2-12: 2015 Waste Chapter Greenhouse Gas Sources (MMT CO_2 Eq.)

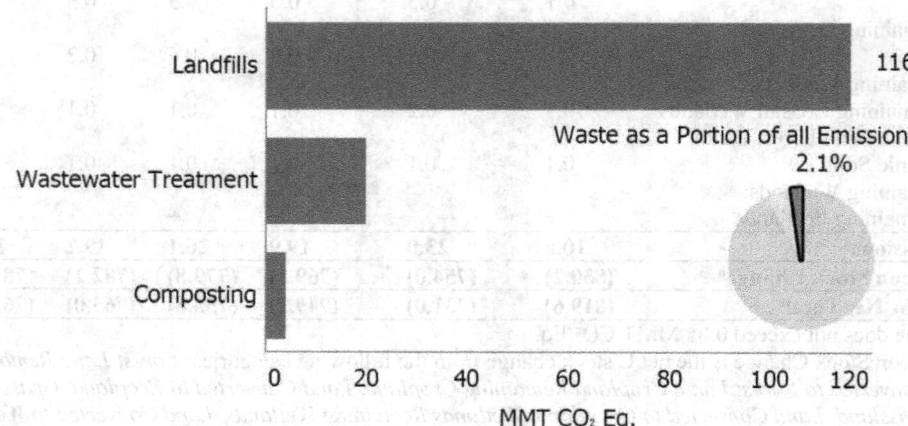

Overall, in 2015, waste activities generated emissions of 139.4 MMT CO_2 Eq., or 2.1 percent of total U.S. greenhouse gas emissions.

Table 2-9: Emissions from Waste (MMT CO_2 Eq.)

Gas/Source	1990	2005	2011	2012	2013	2014	2015
CH_4	**195.6**	**152.1**	**136.2**	**137.9**	**133.7**	**133.5**	**132.6**
Landfills	179.6	134.3	119.0	120.8	116.7	116.6	115.7
Wastewater Treatment	15.7	16.0	15.3	15.1	14.9	14.8	14.8
Composting	0.4	1.9	1.9	1.9	2.0	2.1	2.1
N_2O	**3.7**	**6.1**	**6.4**	**6.6**	**6.7**	**6.8**	**6.9**
Wastewater Treatment	3.4	4.4	4.8	4.8	4.9	4.9	5.0
Composting	0.3	1.7	1.7	1.7	1.8	1.9	1.9
Total	**199.3**	**158.2**	**142.6**	**144.4**	**140.4**	**140.2**	**139.4**

Note: Totals may not sum due to independent rounding.

Some significant trends in U.S. emissions from waste source categories include the following:

- From 1990 to 2015, net CH_4 emissions from landfills decreased by 63.8 MMT CO_2 Eq. (35.6 percent), with small increases occurring in interim years. This downward trend in emissions coincided with increased

[3] Landfills also store carbon, due to incomplete degradation of organic materials such as wood products and yard trimmings, as described in the Land Use, Land-Use Change, and Forestry chapter.

Source: *U.S. EPA, Inventory of U.S. Greenhouse Gas Emissions and Sinks: 1990–2015*

landfill gas collection and control systems, and a reduction of decomposable materials (i.e., paper and paperboard, food scraps, and yard trimmings) discarded in MSW landfills over the time series.

- Combined CH_4 and N_2O emissions from composting have generally increased since 1990, from 0.7 MMT CO_2 Eq. to 4.0 MMT CO_2 Eq. in 2015, which represents slightly more than a five-fold increase over the time series. The growth in composting since the 1990s is attributable to primarily two factors: (1) steady growth in population and residential housing, and (2) the enactment of legislation by state and local governments that discouraged the disposal of yard trimmings in landfills.
- From 1990 to 2015, CH_4 and N_2O emissions from wastewater treatment decreased by 0.9 MMT CO_2 Eq. (5.8 percent) and increased by 1.6 MMT CO_2 Eq. (47.0 percent), respectively. Methane emissions from domestic wastewater treatment have decreased since 1999 due to decreasing percentages of wastewater being treated in anaerobic systems, including reduced use of on-site septic systems and central anaerobic treatment systems. Nitrous oxide emissions from wastewater treatment processes gradually increased across the time series as a result of increasing U.S. population and protein consumption.

2.2 Emissions by Economic Sector

Throughout this report, emission estimates are grouped into five sectors (i.e., chapters) defined by the IPCC and detailed above: Energy; Industrial Processes and Product Use; Agriculture; LULUCF; and Waste. While it is important to use this characterization for consistency with UNFCCC reporting guidelines and to promote comparability across countries, it is also useful to characterize emissions according to commonly used economic sector categories: residential, commercial, industry, transportation, electricity generation, and agriculture, as well as U.S. Territories.

Using this categorization, emissions from electricity generation accounted for the largest portion (29 percent) of total U.S. greenhouse gas emissions in 2015. Transportation activities, in aggregate, accounted for the second largest portion (27 percent). Emissions from industry accounted for about 21 percent of total U.S. greenhouse gas emissions in 2015. Emissions from industry have in general declined over the past decade due to a number of factors, including structural changes in the U.S. economy (i.e., shifts from a manufacturing-based to a service-based economy), fuel switching, and efficiency improvements. The remaining 22 percent of U.S. greenhouse gas emissions were contributed by the residential, agriculture, and commercial sectors, plus emissions from U.S. Territories. The residential sector accounted for 6 percent, and primarily consisted of CO_2 emissions from fossil fuel combustion. Activities related to agriculture accounted for roughly 9 percent of U.S. emissions; unlike other economic sectors, agricultural sector emissions were dominated by N_2O emissions from agricultural soil management and CH_4 emissions from enteric fermentation, rather than CO_2 from fossil fuel combustion. The commercial sector accounted for roughly 7 percent of emissions, while U.S. Territories accounted for less than 1 percent. Carbon dioxide was also emitted and sequestered (in the form of C) by a variety of activities related to forest management practices, tree planting in urban areas, the management of agricultural soils, landfilling of yard trimmings, and changes in C stocks in coastal wetlands.

Table 2-10 presents a detailed breakdown of emissions from each of these economic sectors by source category, as they are defined in this report. Figure 2-13 shows the trend in emissions by sector from 1990 to 2015.

Source: *U.S. EPA, Inventory of U.S. Greenhouse Gas Emissions and Sinks: 1990–2015*

Figure 2-13: U.S. Greenhouse Gas Emissions Allocated to Economic Sectors (MMT CO_2 Eq.)

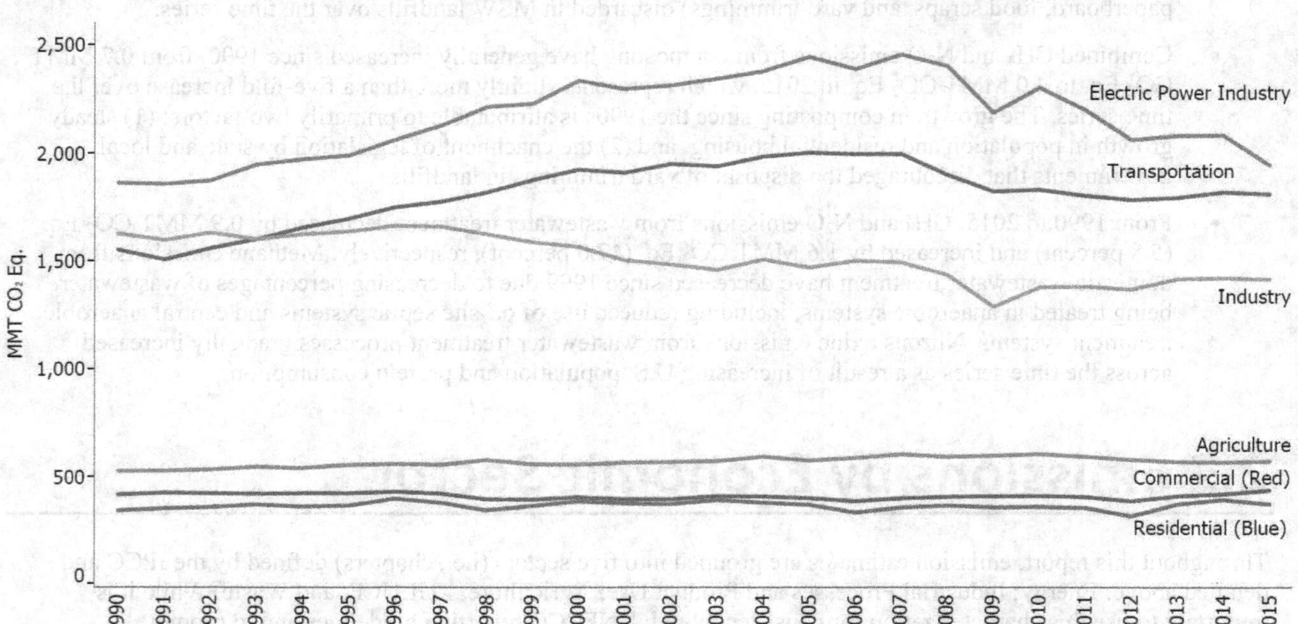

Table 2-10: U.S. Greenhouse Gas Emissions Allocated to Economic Sectors (MMT CO_2 Eq. and Percent of Total in 2015)

Sector/Source	1990	2005	2011	2012	2013	2014	2015[a]	Percent[a,b]
Electric Power Industry	**1,862.5**	**2,441.6**	**2,197.3**	**2,059.9**	**2,078.2**	**2,079.7**	**1,941.4**	**29.5%**
CO_2 from Fossil Fuel Combustion	1,820.8	2,400.9	2,157.7	2,022.2	2,038.1	2,038.0	1,900.7	28.9%
Stationary Combustion	7.7	16.5	18.0	18.2	19.5	20.0	19.9	0.3%
Incineration of Waste	8.4	12.9	10.9	10.7	10.7	10.9	11.0	0.2%
Other Process Uses of Carbonates	2.5	3.2	4.7	4.0	5.2	5.9	5.6	0.1%
Electrical Transmission and Distribution	23.1	8.3	6.0	4.8	4.6	4.8	4.2	0.1%
Transportation	**1,551.2**	**2,001.0**	**1,800.0**	**1,780.7**	**1,790.2**	**1,815.8**	**1,806.6**	**27.4%**
CO_2 from Fossil Fuel Combustion[a]	1,493.8	1,887.0	1,707.6	1,696.8	1,713.0	1,742.8	1,736.4	26.4%
Substitution of Ozone Depleting Substances	+	67.1	60.2	55.1	49.8	47.2	45.1	0.7%
Mobile Combustion[a]	45.7	36.8	23.2	20.6	18.6	16.6	15.2	0.2%
Non-Energy Use of Fuels	11.8	10.2	9.0	8.3	8.8	9.1	10.0	0.2%
Industry	**1,626.3**	**1,467.1**	**1,378.6**	**1,365.9**	**1,413.4**	**1,418.0**	**1,411.6**	**21.4%**
CO_2 from Fossil Fuel Combustion[a]	811.4	780.6	725.4	731.9	762.2	755.3	758.0	11.5%
Natural Gas Systems	231.8	189.8	190.2	191.4	197.7	204.9	204.8	3.1%
Non-Energy Use of Fuels	100.1	120.6	95.8	93.7	109.4	104.7	110.5	1.7%
Coal Mining	96.5	64.1	71.2	66.5	64.6	64.8	60.9	0.9%
Iron and Steel Production	101.5	68.1	61.1	55.5	53.4	58.6	48.9	0.7%
Petroleum Systems	59.0	49.9	52.2	50.3	48.2	46.6	43.4	0.7%
Cement Production	33.5	46.2	32.2	35.3	36.4	39.4	39.9	0.6%
Petrochemical Production	21.5	27.0	26.4	26.6	26.5	26.6	28.2	0.4%
Substitution of Ozone Depleting Substances	+	7.4	17.1	18.8	20.4	22.3	24.7	0.4%
Lime Production	11.7	14.6	14.0	13.8	14.0	14.2	13.3	0.2%
Nitric Acid Production	12.1	11.3	10.9	10.5	10.7	10.9	11.6	0.2%

Source: *U.S. EPA, Inventory of U.S. Greenhouse Gas Emissions and Sinks: 1990–2015*

Ammonia Production	13.0	9.2	9.3	9.4	10.0	9.6	10.8	0.2%
Abandoned Underground Coal Mines	7.2	6.6	6.4	6.2	6.2	6.3	6.4	0.1%
Other Process Uses of Carbonates	2.5	3.2	4.7	4.0	5.2	5.9	5.6	0.1%
HCFC-22 Production	3.6	4.7	4.9	4.5	4.1	5.0	5.0	0.1%
Semiconductor Manufacture	28.3	7.6	6.8	6.4	6.2	5.4	4.8	0.1%
Aluminum Production	1.5	1.4	4.1	4.0	4.2	4.5	4.3	0.1%
Carbon Dioxide Consumption	46.1	20.0	8.8	5.5	4.1	5.0	4.3	0.1%
Adipic Acid Production	15.2	7.1	10.2	5.5	3.9	5.4	4.3	0.1%
N_2O from Product Uses	4.2	4.2	4.2	4.2	4.2	4.2	4.2	0.1%
Stationary Combustion	4.9	4.6	3.9	3.9	3.9	3.8	3.8	0.1%
Soda Ash Production and Consumption	2.8	3.0	2.7	2.8	2.8	2.8	2.8	+
Ferroalloy Production	2.2	1.4	1.7	1.9	1.8	1.9	2.0	+
Titanium Dioxide Production	1.2	1.8	1.7	1.5	1.7	1.7	1.6	+
Mobile Combustion[a]	0.9	1.3	1.4	1.4	1.5	1.5	1.4	+
Glass Production	1.5	1.9	1.3	1.2	1.3	1.3	1.3	+
Urea Consumption for Non-Agricultural Purposes	3.8	3.7	4.0	4.4	4.0	1.4	1.1	+
Magnesium Production and Processing	5.2	2.7	2.8	1.7	1.5	1.1	1.0	+
Phosphoric Acid Production	1.5	1.3	1.2	1.1	1.1	1.0	1.0	+
Zinc Production	0.6	1.0	1.3	1.5	1.4	1.0	0.9	+
Lead Production	0.5	0.6	0.5	0.5	0.5	0.5	0.5	+
Silicon Carbide Production and Consumption	0.4	0.2	0.2	0.2	0.2	0.2	0.2	+
Agriculture	**526.7**	**574.3**	**592.0**	**577.6**	**567.5**	**566.1**	**570.3**	**8.7%**
N_2O from Agricultural Soil Management	256.6	259.8	270.1	254.1	250.5	250.0	251.3	3.8%
Enteric Fermentation	164.2	168.9	168.9	166.7	165.5	164.2	166.5	2.5%
Manure Management	51.1	72.9	80.4	83.2	80.8	80.4	84.0	1.3%
CO_2 from Fossil Fuel Combustion[a]	31.0	47.4	49.6	51.1	50.0	50.8	47.5	0.7%
Rice Cultivation	16.0	16.7	14.1	11.3	11.3	11.4	11.2	0.2%
Urea Fertilization	2.4	3.5	4.1	4.3	4.5	4.8	5.0	0.1%
Liming	4.7	4.3	3.9	6.0	3.9	3.6	3.8	0.1%
Mobile Combustion[a]	0.3	0.5	0.5	0.6	0.6	0.6	0.5	+
Field Burning of Agricultural Residues	0.3	0.3	0.4	0.4	0.4	0.4	0.4	+
Stationary Combustion	+	+	+	+	0.1	0.1	0.1	+
Commercial	**418.1**	**400.7**	**406.5**	**387.3**	**410.1**	**419.5**	**437.4**	**6.6%**
CO_2 from Fossil Fuel Combustion[a]	217.4	223.5	220.4	196.7	221.0	228.7	246.2	3.7%
Landfills	179.6	134.3	119.0	120.8	116.7	116.6	115.7	1.8%
Substitution of Ozone Depleting Substances	+	17.6	42.1	44.9	47.4	49.2	50.2	0.8%
Wastewater Treatment	15.7	16.0	15.3	15.1	14.9	14.8	14.8	0.2%
Human Sewage	3.4	4.4	4.8	4.8	4.9	4.9	5.0	0.1%
Composting	0.7	3.5	3.5	3.7	3.9	4.0	4.0	0.1%
Stationary Combustion	1.4	1.4	1.4	1.2	1.3	1.4	1.5	+
Residential	**344.9**	**370.4**	**356.3**	**318.4**	**372.6**	**393.9**	**372.7**	**5.7%**
CO_2 from Fossil Fuel Combustion	338.3	357.8	325.5	282.5	329.7	345.4	319.6	4.9%
Substitution of Ozone Depleting Substances	0.3	7.7	25.9	31.4	37.0	42.6	48.4	0.7%
Stationary Combustion	6.3	4.9	4.9	4.5	5.9	6.0	4.7	0.1%
U.S. Territories	**33.3**	**58.1**	**46.0**	**48.5**	**48.1**	**46.6**	**46.6**	**0.7%**
CO_2 from Fossil Fuel Combustion	27.6	49.7	40.9	43.5	42.5	41.4	41.4	0.6%
Non-Energy Use of Fuels	5.7	8.1	5.0	4.8	5.4	5.1	5.1	0.1%
Stationary Combustion	0.1	0.2	0.2	0.2	0.2	0.2	0.2	+
Total Emissions	**6,363.1**	**7,313.3**	**6,776.7**	**6,538.3**	**6,680.1**	**6,739.7**	**6,586.7**	**100.0%**

Source: *U.S. EPA, Inventory of U.S. Greenhouse Gas Emissions and Sinks: 1990–2015*

LULUCF Sector Net Total[c]	**(819.6)**	**(731.0)**	**(749.2)**	**(753.8)**	**(763.0)**	**(761.4)**	**(758.9)**	**(11.5%)**
Net Emissions (Sources and Sinks)	**5,543.5**	**6,582.3**	**6,027.6**	**5,784.5**	**5,917.1**	**5,978.3**	**5,827.7**	**88.5%**

Notes: Total emissions presented without LULUCF. Total net emissions presented with LULUCF.

+ Does not exceed 0.05 MMT CO_2 Eq. or 0.05 percent.

[a] There was a method update in this Inventory for estimating the share of gasoline used in on-road and non-road applications. The change does not impact total U.S. gasoline consumption. It mainly results in a shift in gasoline consumption from the transportation sector to industrial and commercial sectors for 2015, creating a break in the time series. The change is discussed further in the Planned Improvements section of Chapter 3.1.

[b] Percent of total (gross) emissions excluding emissions from LULUCF for 2015.

[c] The LULUCF Sector Net Total is the net sum of all CH_4 and N_2O emissions to the atmosphere plus net carbon stock changes.

Notes: Totals may not sum due to independent rounding. Parentheses indicate negative values or sequestration.

Emissions with Electricity Distributed to Economic Sectors

It can also be useful to view greenhouse gas emissions from economic sectors with emissions related to electricity generation distributed into end-use categories (i.e., emissions from electricity generation are allocated to the economic sectors in which the electricity is consumed). The generation, transmission, and distribution of electricity, which is the largest economic sector in the United States, accounted for 29 percent of total U.S. greenhouse gas emissions in 2015. Emissions increased by 4 percent since 1990, as electricity demand grew and fossil fuels remained the dominant energy source for generation. Electricity generation-related emissions decreased from 2014 to 2015 by 6.7 percent, primarily due to decreased CO_2 emissions from fossil fuel combustion due to an increase in natural gas consumption, and decreased coal consumption. Electricity sales to the residential and commercial end-use sectors in 2015 decreased by 0.2 percent and increased by 0.6 percent, respectively. The trend in the residential and commercial sectors can largely be attributed to warmer, less energy-intensive winter conditions compared to 2014. Electricity sales to the industrial sector in 2015 decreased by approximately 1.1 percent. Overall, in 2015, the amount of electricity generated (in kWh) decreased by 0.2 percent from the previous year. This decrease in generation contributed to a reduction in CO_2 emissions from the electric power sector of 6.7 percent, as the consumption of CO_2-intensive coal for electricity generation decreased by 13.9 percent and natural gas generation increased by 18.7 percent. The consumption of petroleum for electricity generation decreased by 6.6 percent in 2015 relative to 2014. Table 2-11 provides a detailed summary of emissions from electricity generation-related activities.

Table 2-11: Electricity Generation-Related Greenhouse Gas Emissions (MMT CO_2 Eq.)

Gas/Fuel Type or Source	1990	2005	2011	2012	2013	2014	2015
CO_2	**1,831.2**	**2,416.5**	**2,172.9**	**2,036.6**	**2,053.7**	**2,054.5**	**1,917.0**
Fossil Fuel Combustion	1,820.8	2,400.9	2,157.7	2,022.2	2,038.1	2,038.0	1,900.7
Coal	*1,547.6*	*1,983.8*	*1,722.7*	*1,511.2*	*1,571.3*	*1,569.1*	*1,350.5*
Natural Gas	*175.3*	*318.8*	*408.8*	*492.2*	*444.0*	*443.2*	*526.1*
Petroleum	*97.5*	*97.9*	*25.8*	*18.3*	*22.4*	*25.3*	*23.7*
Geothermal	*0.4*	*0.4*	*0.4*	*0.4*	*0.4*	*0.4*	*0.4*
Incineration of Waste	8.0	12.5	10.6	10.4	10.4	10.6	10.7
Other Process Uses of Carbonates	2.5	3.2	4.7	4.0	5.2	5.9	5.6
CH_4	**0.3**	**0.5**	**0.4**	**0.4**	**0.4**	**0.4**	**0.4**
Stationary Sources (Electricity Generation)	0.3	0.5	0.4	0.4	0.4	0.4	0.4
Incineration of Waste	+	+	+	+	+	+	+
N_2O	**7.8**	**16.4**	**17.9**	**18.1**	**19.4**	**19.9**	**19.8**
Stationary Sources (Electricity Generation)	7.4	16.0	17.6	17.8	19.1	19.6	19.5
Incineration of Waste	0.5	0.4	0.3	0.3	0.3	0.3	0.3
SF_6	**23.1**	**8.3**	**6.0**	**4.8**	**4.6**	**4.8**	**4.2**
Electrical Transmission and Distribution	23.1	8.3	6.0	4.8	4.6	4.8	4.2

Source: *U.S. EPA, Inventory of U.S. Greenhouse Gas Emissions and Sinks: 1990–2015*

Total	1,862.5		2,441.6		2,197.3	2,059.9	2,078.2	2,079.7	1,941.4

+ Does not exceed 0.05 MMT CO_2 Eq.

[a] Includes only stationary combustion emissions related to the generation of electricity.

Note: Totals may not sum due to independent rounding.

To distribute electricity emissions among economic end-use sectors, emissions from the source categories assigned to the electricity generation sector were allocated to the residential, commercial, industry, transportation, and agriculture economic sectors according to each economic sector's share of retail sales of electricity consumption (EIA 2017 and Duffield 2006). These source categories include CO_2 from Fossil Fuel Combustion, CH_4 and N_2O from Stationary Combustion, Incineration of Waste, Other Process Uses of Carbonates, and SF_6 from Electrical Transmission and Distribution Systems. Note that only 50 percent of the Other Process Uses of Carbonates emissions were associated with electricity generation and distributed as described; the remainder of Other Process Uses of Carbonates emissions were attributed to the industrial processes economic end-use sector.[4]

When emissions from electricity are distributed among these sectors, industrial activities account for the largest share of total U.S. greenhouse gas emissions (29.3 percent), followed closely by emissions from transportation (27.5 percent). Emissions from the residential and commercial sectors also increase substantially when emissions from electricity are included. In all sectors except agriculture, CO_2 accounts for more than 82 percent of greenhouse gas emissions, primarily from the combustion of fossil fuels.

Table 2-12 presents a detailed breakdown of emissions from each of these economic sectors, with emissions from electricity generation distributed to them. Figure 2-14 shows the trend in these emissions by sector from 1990 to 2015.

Figure 2-14: U.S. Greenhouse Gas Emissions with Electricity-Related Emissions Distributed to Economic Sectors (MMT CO_2 Eq.)

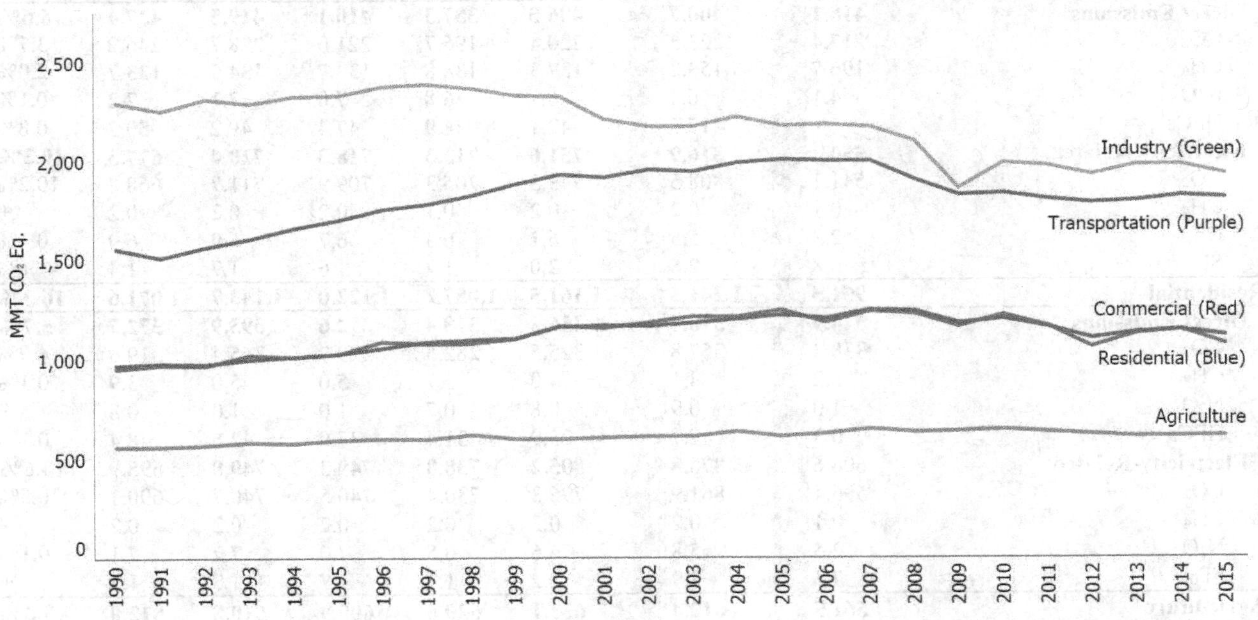

[4] Emissions were not distributed to U.S. Territories, since the electricity generation sector only includes emissions related to the generation of electricity in the 50 states and the District of Columbia.

Source: *U.S. EPA, Inventory of U.S. Greenhouse Gas Emissions and Sinks: 1990–2015*

Table 2-12: U.S. Greenhouse Gas Emissions by Economic Sector and Gas with Electricity-Related Emissions Distributed (MMT CO_2 Eq.) and Percent of Total in 2015

Sector/Gas	1990	2005	2011	2012	2013	2014	2015[a]	Percent[a,b]
Industry	**2,293.9**	**2,178.1**	**1,973.6**	**1,926.7**	**1,977.4**	**1,978.7**	**1,931.1**	**29.3%**
Direct Emissions[a]	**1,626.3**	**1,467.1**	**1,378.6**	**1,365.9**	**1,413.4**	**1,418.0**	**1,411.6**	**21.4%**
CO_2	1,159.2	1,123.7	1,030.6	1,031.6	1,081.5	1,079.3	1,079.5	16.4%
CH_4	355.4	278.4	281.9	277.1	276.3	278.5	271.5	4.1%
N_2O	35.4	26.7	29.2	24.0	22.7	24.4	23.8	0.4%
HFCs, PFCs, SF_6, and NF_3	76.3	38.2	36.8	33.1	32.9	35.7	36.8	0.6%
Electricity-Related	**667.6**	**711.0**	**595.0**	**560.8**	**564.0**	**560.7**	**519.6**	**7.9%**
CO_2	656.4	703.7	588.4	554.4	557.4	553.9	513.1	7.8%
CH_4	0.1	0.1	0.1	0.1	0.1	0.1	0.1	+
N_2O	2.8	4.8	4.9	4.9	5.3	5.4	5.3	0.1%
SF_6	8.3	2.4	1.6	1.3	1.2	1.3	1.1	+
Transportation	**1,554.4**	**2,005.9**	**1,804.3**	**1,784.7**	**1,794.3**	**1,820.0**	**1,810.4**	**27.5%**
Direct Emissions[a]	**1,551.2**	**2,001.0**	**1,800.0**	**1,780.7**	**1,790.2**	**1,815.8**	**1,806.6**	**27.4%**
CO_2	1,505.6	1,897.2	1,716.6	1,705.0	1,721.8	1,752.0	1,746.3	26.5%
CH_4	5.4	2.4	1.9	1.8	1.7	1.7	1.6	+
N_2O	40.3	34.3	21.3	18.8	16.9	15.0	13.6	0.2%
HFCs[c]	+	67.1	60.2	55.1	49.8	47.2	45.1	0.7%
Electricity-Related	**3.1**	**4.8**	**4.3**	**3.9**	**4.1**	**4.1**	**3.8**	**0.1%**
CO_2	3.1	4.8	4.3	3.9	4.0	4.1	3.8	0.1%
CH_4	+	+	+	+	+	+	+	+
N_2O	+	+	+	+	+	+	+	+
SF_6	+	+	+	+	+	+	+	+
Commercial	**968.4**	**1,217.6**	**1,158.1**	**1,100.6**	**1,128.5**	**1,139.9**	**1,114.8**	**16.9%**
Direct Emissions[a]	**418.1**	**400.7**	**406.5**	**387.3**	**410.1**	**419.5**	**437.4**	**6.6%**
CO_2	217.4	223.5	220.4	196.7	221.0	228.7	246.2	3.7%
CH_4	196.7	153.2	137.3	138.8	134.7	134.5	133.7	2.0%
N_2O	4.1	6.4	6.7	6.8	7.0	7.1	7.2	0.1%
HFCs	+	17.6	42.1	44.9	47.4	49.2	50.2	0.8%
Electricity-Related	**550.3**	**816.9**	**751.6**	**713.3**	**718.3**	**720.4**	**677.3**	**10.3%**
CO_2	541.1	808.5	743.3	705.3	709.9	711.7	668.8	10.2%
CH_4	0.1	0.2	0.2	0.1	0.2	0.2	0.2	+
N_2O	2.3	5.5	6.1	6.3	6.7	6.9	6.9	0.1%
SF_6	6.8	2.8	2.0	1.7	1.6	1.7	1.4	+%
Residential	**951.5**	**1,241.3**	**1,161.5**	**1,057.2**	**1,122.0**	**1,143.7**	**1,071.6**	**16.3%**
Direct Emissions	**344.9**	**370.4**	**356.3**	**318.4**	**372.6**	**393.9**	**372.7**	**5.7%**
CO_2	338.3	357.8	325.5	282.5	329.7	345.4	319.6	4.9%
CH_4	5.2	4.1	4.0	3.7	5.0	5.0	3.9	0.1%
N_2O	1.0	0.9	0.8	0.7	1.0	1.0	0.8	+
HFCs	0.3	7.7	25.9	31.4	37.0	42.6	48.4	0.7%
Electricity-Related	**606.6**	**870.8**	**805.2**	**738.8**	**749.3**	**749.8**	**698.9**	**10.6%**
CO_2	596.4	861.9	796.3	730.4	740.5	740.7	690.1	10.5%
CH_4	0.1	0.2	0.2	0.2	0.2	0.2	0.2	+
N_2O	2.5	5.8	6.6	6.5	7.0	7.2	7.1	0.1%
SF_6	7.5	2.9	2.2	1.7	1.7	1.7	1.5	+
Agriculture	**561.5**	**612.4**	**633.1**	**620.6**	**609.9**	**610.8**	**612.0**	**9.3%**
Direct Emissions[a]	**526.7**	**574.3**	**592.0**	**577.6**	**567.5**	**566.1**	**570.3**	**8.7%**
CO_2	38.1	55.2	57.6	61.3	58.4	59.2	56.3	0.9%
CH_4	217.7	242.3	246.5	244.2	240.6	238.9	244.5	3.7%
N_2O	270.9	276.8	288.0	272.1	268.5	268.0	269.5	4.1%
Electricity-Related	**34.8**	**38.1**	**41.1**	**43.1**	**42.4**	**44.7**	**41.7**	**0.6%**
CO_2	34.2	37.7	40.6	42.6	41.9	44.1	41.2	0.6%
CH_4	+	+	+	+	+	+	+	+
N_2O	0.1	0.3	0.3	0.4	0.4	0.4	0.4	+
SF_6	0.4	0.1	0.1	0.1	0.1	0.1	0.1	+
U.S. Territories	**33.3**	**58.1**	**46.0**	**48.5**	**48.1**	**46.6**	**46.6**	**0.7%**

Source: *U.S. EPA, Inventory of U.S. Greenhouse Gas Emissions and Sinks: 1990–2015*

Total Emissions	**6,363.1**		**7,313.3**		**6,776.7**	**6,538.3**	**6,680.1**	**6,739.7**	**6,586.7**	**100.0%**
LULUCF Sector Net Total[d]	**(819.6)**		**(731.0)**		**(749.2)**	**(753.8)**	**(763.0)**	**(761.4)**	**(758.9)**	**(11.5%)**
Net Emissions (Sources and Sinks)	**5,543.5**		**6,582.3**		**6,027.6**	**5,784.5**	**5,917.1**	**5,978.3**	**5,827.7**	**88.5%**

Notes: Total emissions presented without LULUCF. Net emissions presented with LULUCF.
+ Does not exceed 0.05 MMT CO_2 Eq. or 0.05 percent.
[a] There was a method update in this Inventory for estimating the share of gasoline used in on-road and non-road applications. The change does not impact total U.S. gasoline consumption. It mainly results in a shift in gasoline consumption from the transportation sector to industrial and commercial sectors for 2015, creating a break in the time series. The change is discussed further in the Planned Improvements section of Chapter 3.1.
[b] Percent of total gross emissions excluding emissions from LULUCF for year 2015.
[c] Includes primarily HFC-134a.
[d] The LULUCF Sector Net Total is the net sum of all CH_4 and N_2O emissions to the atmosphere plus net carbon stock changes.
Notes: Emissions from electricity generation are allocated based on aggregate electricity consumption in each end-use sector. Totals may not sum due to independent rounding.

Industry

The industry end-use sector includes CO_2 emissions from fossil fuel combustion from all manufacturing facilities, in aggregate. This end-use sector also includes emissions that are produced as a byproduct of the non-energy-related industrial process activities. The variety of activities producing these non-energy-related emissions includes CH_4 emissions from petroleum and natural gas systems, fugitive CH_4 emissions from coal mining, by-product CO_2 emissions from cement manufacture, and HFC, PFC, SF_6, and NF_3 byproduct emissions from semiconductor manufacture, to name a few. Since 1990, industrial sector emissions have declined. The decline has occurred both in direct emissions and indirect emissions associated with electricity use. In theory, emissions from the industrial end-use sector should be highly correlated with economic growth and industrial output, but heating of industrial buildings and agricultural energy consumption are also affected by weather conditions. In addition, structural changes within the U.S. economy that lead to shifts in industrial output away from energy-intensive manufacturing products to less energy-intensive products (e.g., from steel to computer equipment) also have a significant effect on industrial emissions.

Transportation

When electricity-related emissions are distributed to economic end-use sectors, transportation activities accounted for 27.5 percent of U.S. greenhouse gas emissions in 2015. The largest sources of transportation greenhouse gases in 2015 were passenger cars (41.9 percent), freight trucks (22.9 percent), light-duty trucks, which include sport utility vehicles, pickup trucks, and minivans (18.0 percent), commercial aircraft (6.6 percent), rail (2.6 percent), other aircraft (2.2 percent), pipelines (2.1 percent), and ships and boats (1.8 percent). These figures include direct CO_2, CH_4, and N_2O emissions from fossil fuel combustion used in transportation and emissions from non-energy use (i.e., lubricants) used in transportation, as well as HFC emissions from mobile air conditioners and refrigerated transport allocated to these vehicle types.

In terms of the overall trend, from 1990 to 2015, total transportation emissions increased due, in large part, to increased demand for travel. The number of vehicle miles traveled (VMT) by light-duty motor vehicles (passenger cars and light-duty trucks) increased 40 percent from 1990 to 2015,[5] as a result of a confluence of factors including population growth, economic growth, urban sprawl, and periods of low fuel prices. The decline in new light-duty vehicle fuel economy between 1990 and 2004 reflected the increasing market share of light-duty trucks, which grew

[5] VMT estimates are based on data from FHWA Highway Statistics Table VM-1 (FHWA 1996 through 2016). In 2011, FHWA changed its methods for estimating VMT by vehicle class, which led to a shift in VMT and emissions among on-road vehicle classes in the 2007 to 2015 time period. In absence of these method changes, light-duty VMT growth between 1990 and 2015 would likely have been even higher.

Source: *U.S. EPA, Inventory of U.S. Greenhouse Gas Emissions and Sinks: 1990–2015*

from about 30 percent of new vehicle sales in 1990 to 48 percent in 2004. Starting in 2005, average new vehicle fuel economy began to increase while light-duty VMT grew only modestly for much of the period. Light-duty VMT grew by less than one percent or declined each year between 2005 and 2013[6] and has since grown a faster rate (1.2 percent from 2013 to 2014, and 2.6 percent from 2014 to 2015). Average new vehicle fuel economy has improved almost every year since 2005 and the truck share decreased to about 33 percent in 2009, and has since varied from year to year between 36 percent and 43 percent. Truck share is about 43 percent of new vehicles in model year 2015 (EPA 2016a). Table 2-13 provides a detailed summary of greenhouse gas emissions from transportation-related activities with electricity-related emissions included in the totals. It is important to note that there was a change in methods between 2014 and 2015 used to estimate gasoline consumption in the transportation sector. In the absence of this change, CO_2 emissions from passenger cars, light-duty trucks, and other on-road vehicles using gasoline would likely have been higher in 2015.[7]

Almost all of the energy consumed for transportation was supplied by petroleum-based products, with more than half being related to gasoline consumption in automobiles and other highway vehicles. Other fuel uses, especially diesel fuel for freight trucks and jet fuel for aircraft, accounted for the remainder. The primary driver of transportation-related emissions was CO_2 from fossil fuel combustion, which increased by 16 percent from 1990 to 2015.[8] This rise in CO_2 emissions, combined with an increase in HFCs from close to zero emissions in 1990 to 45.1 MMT CO_2 Eq. in 2015, led to an increase in overall emissions from transportation activities of 16 percent.[9]

Table 2-13: Transportation-Related Greenhouse Gas Emissions (MMT CO_2 Eq.)

Gas/Vehicle	1990	2005	2011	2012	2013	2014	2015[a]
Passenger Cars	**656.7**	**708.7**	**774.1**	**767.7**	**763.0**	**778.4**	**758.4**
CO_2	629.3	660.1	736.9	735.5	735.5	753.7	735.7
CH_4	3.2	1.2	1.2	1.1	1.1	1.0	1.0
N_2O	24.1	15.7	12.1	10.5	9.2	7.8	6.9
HFCs	0.0	31.7	23.9	20.6	17.3	16.0	14.9
Light-Duty Trucks	**335.2**	**552.2**	**331.5**	**325.1**	**322.2**	**343.7**	**325.1**
CO_2	320.7	503.3	293.8	290.5	290.8	314.4	298.0
CH_4	1.7	0.9	0.4	0.4	0.3	0.3	0.3
N_2O	12.8	14.7	5.6	4.9	4.3	4.0	3.4
HFCs	0.0	33.3	31.7	29.3	26.7	25.0	23.4
Medium- and Heavy-Duty Trucks	**231.4**	**398.9**	**388.4**	**388.8**	**395.8**	**408.3**	**415.0**
CO_2	230.4	396.3	384.7	384.9	391.6	403.9	410.4
CH_4	0.3	0.1	0.1	0.1	0.1	0.1	0.1
N_2O	0.7	1.2	1.1	1.0	1.0	0.9	0.8
HFCs	0.0	1.2	2.5	2.8	3.1	3.4	3.6
Buses	**8.5**	**12.0**	**16.7**	**17.8**	**18.0**	**19.5**	**19.8**
CO_2	8.4	11.7	16.2	17.3	17.5	18.9	19.3
CH_4	+	+	+	+	+	+	+
N_2O	+	+	0.1	0.1	0.1	0.1	0.1
HFCs	0.0	0.3	0.4	0.4	0.4	0.4	0.4
Motorcycles	**1.8**	**1.7**	**3.6**	**4.2**	**4.0**	**3.9**	**3.7**
CO_2	1.7	1.6	3.6	4.1	3.9	3.9	3.7
CH_4	+	+	+	+	+	+	+

[6] In 2007 and 2008 light-duty VMT decreased 3 percent and 2.3 percent, respectively. Note that the decline in light-duty VMT from 2006 to 2007 is due at least in part to a change in FHWA's methods for estimating VMT. In absence of these method changes, light-duty VMT growth between 2006 and 2007 would likely have been higher. See previous footnote.

[7] There was a method update in this Inventory for estimating the share of gasoline used in on-road and non-road applications. The change does not impact total U.S. gasoline consumption. It mainly results in a shift in gasoline consumption from the transportation sector to industrial and commercial sectors for 2015, creating a break in the time series. The change is discussed further in the Planned Improvements section of Chapter 3.1.

[8] See previous footnote.

[9] See previous footnote.

Source: *U.S. EPA, Inventory of U.S. Greenhouse Gas Emissions and Sinks: 1990–2015*

N_2O	+	+	+	+	+	+	+
Commercial	**110.9**	**134.0**	**115.7**	**114.3**	**115.4**	**116.3**	**120.1**
CO_2	109.9	132.7	114.6	113.3	114.3	115.2	119.0
CH_4	0.0	0.0	0.0	0.0	0.0	0.0	0.0
N_2O	1.0	1.2	1.1	1.0	1.1	1.1	1.1
Other Aircraft[c]	**78.3**	**59.7**	**34.2**	**32.1**	**34.7**	**35.2**	**40.6**
CO_2	77.5	59.1	33.9	31.8	34.4	34.9	40.2
CH_4	0.1	0.1	+	+	+	+	+
N_2O	0.7	0.5	0.3	0.3	0.3	0.3	0.4
Ships and Boats[d]	**44.9**	**45.0**	**46.5**	**40.2**	**39.5**	**17.6**	**33.1**
CO_2	44.3	44.3	45.5	39.3	38.7	16.9	32.3
CH_4	+	+	+	+	+	+	+
N_2O	0.6	0.6	0.8	0.7	0.7	0.5	0.6
HFCs	0.0	0.1	0.1	0.1	0.1	0.1	0.1
Rail	**38.9**	**51.3**	**46.6**	**45.6**	**46.7**	**48.5**	**46.7**
CO_2	38.5	50.3	44.7	43.4	44.2	45.7	43.6
CH_4	0.1	0.1	0.1	0.1	0.1	0.1	0.1
N_2O	0.3	0.4	0.3	0.3	0.3	0.4	0.3
HFCs	0.0	0.5	1.5	1.8	2.1	2.4	2.7
Other Emissions from Electricity Generation[e]	0.1	+	+	+	+	+	+
Pipelines[f]	**36.0**	**32.4**	**38.1**	**40.5**	**46.2**	**39.4**	**38.0**
CO_2	36.0	32.4	38.1	40.5	46.2	39.4	38.0
Lubricants	**11.8**	**10.2**	**9.0**	**8.3**	**8.8**	**9.1**	**10.0**
CO_2	11.8	10.2	9.0	8.3	8.8	9.1	10.0
Total Transportation	**1,554.4**	**2,005.9**	**1,804.3**	**1,784.7**	**1,794.3**	**1,820.0**	**1,810.4**
International Bunker Fuels[g]	*104.5*	*114.2*	*112.8*	*106.8*	*100.7*	*104.2*	*111.8*
Ethanol CO_2[h]	*4.1*	*22.4*	*71.5*	*71.5*	*73.4*	*74.9*	*75.9*
Biodiesel CO_2[h]	*0.0*	*0.9*	*8.3*	*8.5*	*13.5*	*13.3*	*14.1*

+ Does not exceed 0.05 MMT CO_2 Eq.

[a] There was a method update in this Inventory for estimating the share of gasoline used in on-road and non-road applications. The change does not impact total U.S. gasoline consumption. It mainly results in a shift in gasoline consumption from the transportation sector to industrial and commercial sectors for 2015, creating a break in the time series. The change is discussed further in the Planned Improvements section of Chapter 3.1.

[b] Consists of emissions from jet fuel consumed by domestic operations of commercial aircraft (no bunkers).

[c] Consists of emissions from jet fuel and aviation gasoline consumption by general aviation and military aircraft.

[d] Fluctuations in emission estimates are associated with fluctuations in reported fuel consumption, and may reflect issues with data sources.

[e] Other emissions from electricity generation are a result of waste incineration (as the majority of municipal solid waste is combusted in "trash-to-steam" electricity generation plants), electrical transmission and distribution, and a portion of Other Process Uses of Carbonates (from pollution control equipment installed in electricity generation plants).

[f] CO_2 estimates reflect natural gas used to power pipelines, but not electricity. While the operation of pipelines produces CH_4 and N_2O, these emissions are not directly attributed to pipelines in the U.S. Inventory.

[g] Emissions from International Bunker Fuels include emissions from both civilian and military activities; these emissions are not included in the transportation totals.

[h] Ethanol and biodiesel CO_2 estimates are presented for informational purposes only. See Section 3.10 and the estimates in Land Use, Land-Use Change, and Forestry (see Chapter 6), in line with IPCC methodological guidance and UNFCCC reporting obligations, for more information on ethanol and biodiesel.

Notes: Passenger cars and light-duty trucks include vehicles typically used for personal travel and less than 8,500 lbs; medium- and heavy-duty trucks include vehicles larger than 8,500 lbs. HFC emissions primarily reflect HFC-134a. Totals may not sum due to independent rounding.

Source: *U.S. EPA, Inventory of U.S. Greenhouse Gas Emissions and Sinks: 1990–2015*

Commercial

The commercial sector is heavily reliant on electricity for meeting energy needs, with electricity consumption for lighting, heating, air conditioning, and operating appliances. The remaining emissions were largely due to the direct consumption of natural gas and petroleum products, primarily for heating and cooking needs. Energy-related emissions from the residential and commercial sectors have generally been increasing since 1990, and are often correlated with short-term fluctuations in energy consumption caused by weather conditions, rather than prevailing economic conditions. Landfills and wastewater treatment are included in this sector, with landfill emissions decreasing since 1990 and wastewater treatment emissions decreasing slightly.

Residential

The residential sector is heavily reliant on electricity for meeting energy needs, with electricity consumption for lighting, heating, air conditioning, and operating appliances. The remaining emissions were largely due to the direct consumption of natural gas and petroleum products, primarily for heating and cooking needs. Emissions from the residential sectors have generally been increasing since 1990, and are often correlated with short-term fluctuations in energy consumption caused by weather conditions, rather than prevailing economic conditions. In the long-term, this sector is also affected by population growth, regional migration trends, and changes in housing and building attributes (e.g., size and insulation).

Agriculture

The agriculture end-use sector includes a variety of processes, including enteric fermentation in domestic livestock, livestock manure management, and agricultural soil management. In 2015, agricultural soil management was the largest source of N_2O emissions, and enteric fermentation was the largest source of CH_4 emissions in the United States. This sector also includes small amounts of CO_2 emissions from fossil fuel combustion by motorized farm equipment like tractors. The agriculture sector is less reliant on electricity than the other sectors.

Box 2-1: Methodology for Aggregating Emissions by Economic Sector

In presenting the Economic Sectors in the annual *Inventory of U.S. Greenhouse Gas Emissions and Sinks*, the Inventory expands upon the standard IPCC sectors common for UNFCCC reporting. Discussing greenhouse gas emissions relevant to U.S.-specific sectors improves communication of the report's findings.

In the Electricity Generation economic sector, CO_2 emissions from the combustion of fossil fuels included in the EIA electric utility fuel consuming sector are apportioned to this economic sector. Stationary combustion emissions of CH_4 and N_2O are also based on the EIA electric utility sector. Additional sources include CO_2, CH_4, and N_2O from waste incineration, as the majority of municipal solid waste is combusted in "trash-to-steam" electricity generation plants. The Electricity Generation economic sector also includes SF_6 from Electrical Transmission and Distribution, and a portion of CO_2 from Other Process Uses of Carbonates (from pollution control equipment installed in electricity generation plants).

In the Transportation economic sector, the CO_2 emissions from the combustion of fossil fuels included in the EIA transportation fuel consuming sector are apportioned to this economic sector (additional analyses and refinement of the EIA data is further explained in the Energy chapter of this report). Emissions of CH_4 and N_2O from Mobile Combustion are also apportioned to this economic sector based on the EIA transportation fuel consuming sector. Substitution of Ozone Depleting Substances emissions are apportioned based on their specific end-uses within the source category, with emissions from transportation refrigeration/air-conditioning systems to this economic sector. Finally, CO_2 emissions from Non-Energy Uses of Fossil Fuels identified as lubricants for transportation vehicles are included in the Transportation economic sector.

For the Industry economic sector, the CO_2 emissions from the combustion of fossil fuels included in the EIA industrial fuel consuming sector, minus the agricultural use of fuel explained below, are apportioned to this economic sector. The CH_4 and N_2O emissions from stationary and mobile combustion are also apportioned to this economic sector based on the EIA industrial fuel consuming sector, minus emissions apportioned to the Agriculture

Source: *U.S. EPA, Inventory of U.S. Greenhouse Gas Emissions and Sinks: 1990–2015*

economic sector described below. Substitution of Ozone Depleting Substances emissions are apportioned based on their specific end-uses within the source category, with most emissions falling within the Industry economic sector. Additionally, all process-related emissions from sources with methods considered within the IPCC IPPU sector have been apportioned to this economic sector. This includes the process-related emissions (i.e., emissions from the actual process to make the material, not from fuels to power the plant) from such activities as Cement Production, Iron and Steel Production and Metallurgical Coke Production, and Ammonia Production. Additionally, fugitive emissions from energy production sources, such as Natural Gas Systems, Coal Mining, and Petroleum Systems are included in the Industry economic sector. A portion of CO_2 from Other Process Uses of Carbonates (from pollution control equipment installed in large industrial facilities) are also included in the Industry economic sector. Finally, all remaining CO_2 emissions from Non-Energy Uses of Fossil Fuels are assumed to be industrial in nature (besides the lubricants for transportation vehicles specified above), and are attributed to the Industry economic sector.

As agriculture equipment is included in EIA's industrial fuel consuming sector surveys, additional data is used to extract the fuel used by agricultural equipment, to allow for accurate reporting in the Agriculture economic sector from all sources of emissions, such as motorized farming equipment. Energy consumption estimates are obtained from Department of Agriculture survey data, in combination with separate EIA fuel sales reports. This supplementary data is used to apportion some of the CO_2 emissions from fossil fuel combustion, and CH_4 and N_2O emissions from stationary and mobile combustion, to the Agriculture economic sector. The other emission sources included in this economic sector are intuitive for the agriculture sectors, such as N_2O emissions from Agricultural Soils, CH_4 from Enteric Fermentation, CH_4 and N_2O from Manure Management, CH_4 from Rice Cultivation, CO_2 emissions from Liming and Urea Application, and CH_4 and N_2O from Forest Fires. Nitrous oxide emissions from the Application of Fertilizers to tree plantations (termed "forest land" by the IPCC) are also included in the Agriculture economic sector.

The Residential economic sector includes the CO_2 emissions from the combustion of fossil fuels reported for the EIA residential sector. Stationary combustion emissions of CH_4 and N_2O are also based on the EIA residential fuel consuming sector. Substitution of Ozone Depleting Substances are apportioned based on their specific end-uses within the source category, with emissions from residential air-conditioning systems to this economic sector. Nitrous oxide emissions from the Application of Fertilizers to developed land (termed "settlements" by the IPCC) are also included in the Residential economic sector.

The Commercial economic sector includes the CO_2 emissions from the combustion of fossil fuels reported in the EIA commercial fuel consuming sector data. Emissions of CH_4 and N_2O from Mobile Combustion are also apportioned to this economic sector based on the EIA transportation fuel consuming sector. Substitution of Ozone Depleting Substances emissions are apportioned based on their specific end-uses within the source category, with emissions from commercial refrigeration/air-conditioning systems apportioned to this economic sector. Public works sources including direct CH_4 from Landfills and CH_4 and N_2O from Wastewater Treatment and Composting are also included in this economic sector.

Box 2-2: Recent Trends in Various U.S. Greenhouse Gas Emissions-Related Data

Total emissions can be compared to other economic and social indices to highlight changes over time. These comparisons include: (1) emissions per unit of aggregate energy consumption, because energy-related activities are the largest sources of emissions; (2) emissions per unit of fossil fuel consumption, because almost all energy-related emissions involve the combustion of fossil fuels; (3) emissions per unit of electricity consumption, because the electric power industry—utilities and non-utilities combined—was the largest source of U.S. greenhouse gas emissions in 2015; (4) emissions per unit of total gross domestic product as a measure of national economic activity; or (5) emissions per capita.

Table 2-14 provides data on various statistics related to U.S. greenhouse gas emissions normalized to 1990 as a baseline year. These values represent the relative change in each statistic since 1990. Greenhouse gas emissions in the United States have grown at an average annual rate of 0.2 percent since 1990. Since 1990, this rate is slightly slower than that for total energy and for fossil fuel consumption, and much slower than that for electricity consumption, overall gross domestic product (GDP) and national population (see Table 2-14 and Figure 2-15). These trends vary relative to 2005, when greenhouse gas emissions, total energy and fossil fuel consumption began to peak. Greenhouse gas emissions in the United States have decreased at an average annual rate of 1.0 percent since

Source: *U.S. EPA, Inventory of U.S. Greenhouse Gas Emissions and Sinks: 1990–2015*

2005. Total energy and fossil fuel consumption have also decreased at slower rates than emissions since 2005, while electricity consumption, GDP, and national population continued to increase.

Table 2-14: Recent Trends in Various U.S. Data (Index 1990 = 100)

Variable	1990	2005	2011	2012	2013	2014	2015	Avg. Annual Change since 1990[a]	Avg. Annual Change since 2005[a]
Greenhouse Gas Emissions[b]	100	115	107	103	105	106	104	0.2%	-1.0%
Energy Consumption[c]	100	118	115	112	115	117	115	0.6%	-0.2%
Fossil Fuel Consumption[c]	100	119	110	107	110	111	110	0.4%	-0.7%
Electricity Consumption[c]	100	134	137	135	136	138	137	1.3%	0.3%
GDP[d]	100	159	168	171	174	178	183	2.5%	1.4%
Population[e]	100	118	125	126	126	127	128	1.0%	0.8%

[a] Average annual growth rate
[b] GWP-weighted values
[c] Energy-content-weighted values (EIA 2017)
[d] Gross Domestic Product in chained 2009 dollars (BEA 2017)
[e] U.S. Census Bureau (2016)

Figure 2-15: U.S. Greenhouse Gas Emissions Per Capita and Per Dollar of Gross Domestic Product

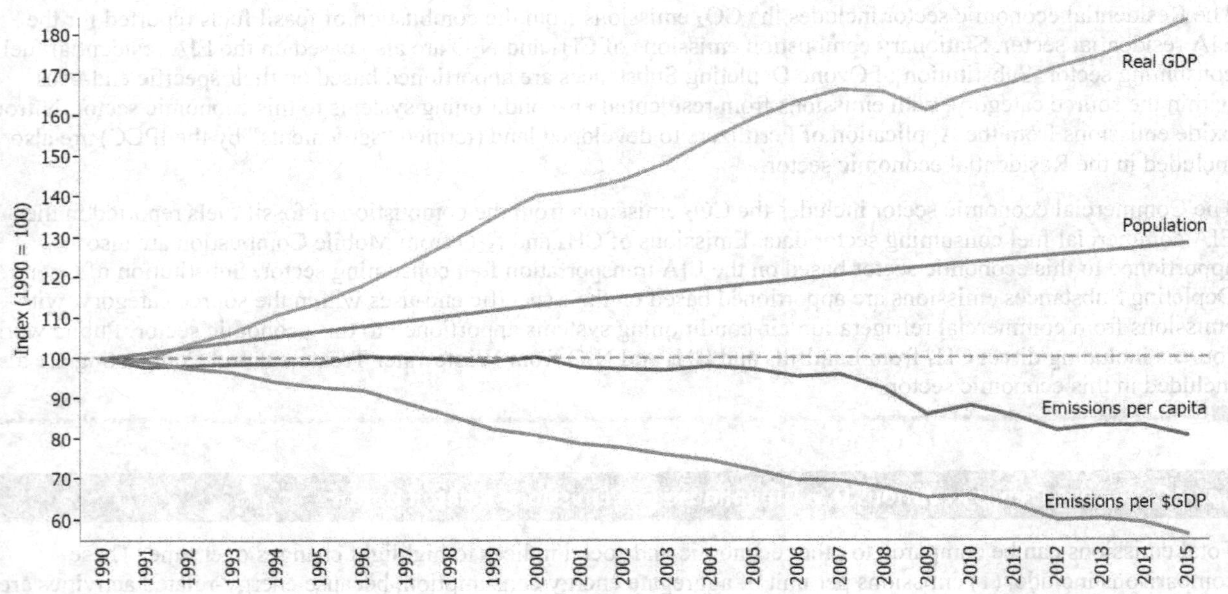

Source: BEA (2017), U.S. Census Bureau (2016), and emission estimates in this report.

Source: *U.S. EPA, Inventory of U.S. Greenhouse Gas Emissions and Sinks: 1990–2015*

2.3 Indirect Greenhouse Gas Emissions (CO, NO_x, NMVOCs, and SO_2)

The reporting requirements of the UNFCCC[10] request that information be provided on indirect greenhouse gases, which include CO, NO_x, NMVOCs, and SO_2. These gases do not have a direct global warming effect, but indirectly affect terrestrial radiation absorption by influencing the formation and destruction of tropospheric and stratospheric ozone, or, in the case of SO_2, by affecting the absorptive characteristics of the atmosphere. Additionally, some of these gases may react with other chemical compounds in the atmosphere to form compounds that are greenhouse gases. Carbon monoxide is produced when carbon-containing fuels are combusted incompletely. Nitrogen oxides (i.e., NO and NO_2) are created by lightning, fires, fossil fuel combustion, and in the stratosphere from N_2O. Non-methane volatile organic compounds—which include hundreds of organic compounds that participate in atmospheric chemical reactions (i.e., propane, butane, xylene, toluene, ethane, and many others)—are emitted primarily from transportation, industrial processes, and non-industrial consumption of organic solvents. In the United States, SO_2 is primarily emitted from coal combustion for electric power generation and the metals industry. Sulfur-containing compounds emitted into the atmosphere tend to exert a negative radiative forcing (i.e., cooling) and therefore are discussed separately.

One important indirect climate change effect of NMVOCs and NO_x is their role as precursors for tropospheric ozone formation. They can also alter the atmospheric lifetimes of other greenhouse gases. Another example of indirect greenhouse gas formation into greenhouse gases is the interaction of CO with the hydroxyl radical—the major atmospheric sink for CH_4 emissions—to form CO_2. Therefore, increased atmospheric concentrations of CO limit the number of hydroxyl molecules (OH) available to destroy CH_4.

Since 1970, the United States has published estimates of emissions of CO, NO_x, NMVOCs, and SO_2 (EPA 2015),[11] which are regulated under the Clean Air Act. Table 2-15 shows that fuel combustion accounts for the majority of emissions of these indirect greenhouse gases. Industrial processes—such as the manufacture of chemical and allied products, metals processing, and industrial uses of solvents—are also significant sources of CO, NO_x, and NMVOCs.

Table 2-15: Emissions of NO_x, CO, NMVOCs, and SO_2 (kt)

Gas/Activity	1990	2005	2011	2012	2013	2014	2015
NO_x	**21,790**	**17,443**	**12,482**	**12,038**	**11,387**	**10,810**	**9,971**
Mobile Fossil Fuel Combustion	10,862	10,295	7,294	6,871	6,448	6,024	5,417
Stationary Fossil Fuel Combustion	10,023	5,858	3,807	3,655	3,504	3,291	3,061
Oil and Gas Activities	139	321	622	663	704	745	745
Industrial Processes and Product Use	592	572	452	443	434	424	424
Forest Fires	80	239	172	276	185	188	188
Waste Combustion	82	128	73	82	91	100	100
Grassland Fires	5	21	54	39	13	27	27
Agricultural Burning	6	6	7	7	7	8	8
Waste	+	2	1	2	2	2	2
CO	**132,877**	**75,570**	**52,586**	**54,119**	**48,620**	**46,922**	**44,954**
Mobile Fossil Fuel Combustion	119,360	58,615	38,305	36,153	34,000	31,848	29,881
Forest Fires	2,832	8,486	6,136	9,815	6,655	6,642	6,642
Stationary Fossil Fuel Combustion	5,000	4,648	4,170	4,027	3,884	3,741	3,741
Waste Combustion	978	1,403	1,003	1,318	1,632	1,947	1,947
Industrial Processes and Product Use	4,129	1,557	1,229	1,246	1,262	1,273	1,273
Oil and Gas Activities	302	318	610	666	723	780	780

[10] See <http://unfccc.int/resource/docs/2013/cop19/eng/10a03.pdf>.

[11] NO_x and CO emission estimates from Field Burning of Agricultural Residues were estimated separately, and therefore not taken from EPA (2016b).

***Source:** U.S. EPA, Inventory of U.S. Greenhouse Gas Emissions and Sinks: 1990–2015*

Grassland Fires	84	358	894	657	217	442	442
Agricultural Burning	191	178	234	232	239	240	239
Waste	1	7	5	6	8	9	9
NMVOCs	**20,930**	**13,154**	**11,726**	**11,464**	**11,202**	**10,935**	**10,647**
Industrial Processes and Product Use	7,638	5,849	3,929	3,861	3,793	3,723	3,723
Mobile Fossil Fuel Combustion	10,932	5,724	4,562	4,243	3,924	3,605	3,318
Oil and Gas Activities	554	510	2,517	2,651	2,786	2,921	2,921
Stationary Fossil Fuel Combustion	912	716	599	569	539	507	507
Waste Combustion	222	241	81	94	108	121	121
Waste	673	114	38	45	51	57	57
Agricultural Burning	NA	NA	NA	NA	NA	NA	NA
SO_2	**20,935**	**13,196**	**5,877**	**5,876**	**5,874**	**4,357**	**3,448**
Stationary Fossil Fuel Combustion	18,407	11,541	5,008	5,006	5,005	3,640	2,756
Industrial Processes and Product Use	1,307	831	604	604	604	496	496
Mobile Fossil Fuel Combustion	390	180	108	108	108	93	93
Oil and Gas Activities	793	619	142	142	142	95	70
Waste Combustion	38	25	15	15	15	32	32
Waste	+	1	+	+	+	1	1
Agricultural Burning	NA	NA	NA	NA	NA	NA	NA

+ Does not exceed 0.5 kt.

NA (Not Available)

Note: Totals may not sum due to independent rounding.

Source: (EPA 2015) except for estimates from Field Burning of Agricultural Residues.

Box 2-3: Sources and Effects of Sulfur Dioxide

Sulfur dioxide (SO_2) emitted into the atmosphere through natural and anthropogenic processes affects the earth's radiative budget through its photochemical transformation into sulfate aerosols that can (1) scatter radiation from the sun back to space, thereby reducing the radiation reaching the earth's surface; (2) affect cloud formation; and (3) affect atmospheric chemical composition (e.g., by providing surfaces for heterogeneous chemical reactions). The indirect effect of sulfur-derived aerosols on radiative forcing can be considered in two parts. The first indirect effect is the aerosols' tendency to decrease water droplet size and increase water droplet concentration in the atmosphere. The second indirect effect is the tendency of the reduction in cloud droplet size to affect precipitation by increasing cloud lifetime and thickness. Although still highly uncertain the radiative forcing estimates from both the first and the second indirect effect are believed to be negative, as is the combined radiative forcing of the two (IPCC 2013).

Sulfur dioxide is also a major contributor to the formation of regional haze, which can cause significant increases in acute and chronic respiratory diseases. Once SO_2 is emitted, it is chemically transformed in the atmosphere and returns to the earth as the primary source of acid rain. Because of these harmful effects, the United States has regulated SO_2 emissions in the Clean Air Act.

Electricity generation is the largest anthropogenic source of SO_2 emissions in the United States, accounting for 59.2 percent in 2015. Coal combustion contributes nearly all of those emissions (approximately 92 percent). Sulfur dioxide emissions have decreased in recent years, primarily as a result of electric power generators switching from high-sulfur to low-sulfur coal and installing flue gas desulfurization equipment.

***Source:** U.S. EPA, Inventory of U.S. Greenhouse Gas Emissions and Sinks: 1990–2015*

Green Metro Area Rankings by Category

Metro Area	State	Air Quality[1]	Toxic Releases[2]	Superfund Sites[3]	Energy Use[4]	Motor Vehicle Use[5]	Mass Transit Use[6]	Overall Score[7]	Overall Rank[8]
Akron	OH	25	18	43	61	52	44	243	47
Albany	NY	5	33	64	72	58	18	250	52
Albuquerque	NM	53	5	51	40	17	41	207	23
Allentown	PA	57	51	71	53	16	55	303	67
Atlanta	GA	68	25	1	24	63	29	210	26
Austin	TX	11	6	1	23	21	20	82	1
Bakersfield	CA	71	70	28	12	1	63	245	51
Baltimore	MD	49	24	37	45	42	9	206	22
Baton Rouge	LA	52	74	34	13	54	69	296	64
Birmingham	AL	50	71	20	25	73	72	311	68
Boston	MA	39	11	66	49	35	7	207	23
Buffalo	NY	10	29	39	66	31	47	222	33
Charleston	SC	4	69	38	14	20	67	212	29
Charlotte	NC	38	44	55	28	55	22	242	45
Chicago	IL	62	64	29	68	12	6	241	43
Cincinnati	OH	59	52	42	48	59	53	313	70
Cleveland	OH	50	58	1	60	34	28	231	36
Columbus	OH	18	41	1	52	40	46	198	20
Dallas-Ft. Worth	TX	40	16	12	32	48	45	193	19
Dayton	OH	30	22	75	56	57	34	274	57
Denver	CO	69	43	48	57	18	8	243	47
Detroit	MI	63	65	41	64	45	65	343	75
El Paso	TX	46	26	1	27	5	43	148	8
Fresno	CA	70	2	62	15	8	42	199	21
Grand Rapids	MI	14	47	67	73	56	26	283	60
Greensboro	NC	15	35	1	33	72	31	187	17
Greenville	SC	29	32	52	26	36	75	250	52
Hartford	CT	23	17	50	62	43	36	231	36
Honolulu	HI	1	38	46	22	3	5	115	3
Houston	TX	60	72	47	16	29	27	251	54
Indianapolis	IN	47	61	32	54	69	68	331	74
Jacksonville	FL	20	55	56	8	67	37	243	47
Kansas City	MO	37	49	44	58	65	61	314	71
Knoxville	TN	47	68	45	31	66	59	316	72
Las Vegas	NV	65	40	1	38	6	30	180	16
Little Rock	AR	23	31	17	34	71	66	242	45
Los Angeles	CA	73	15	18	2	33	13	154	10
Louisville	KY	42	62	35	44	60	32	275	58
Memphis	TN	22	59	61	35	51	71	299	65
Miami	FL	43	4	24	18	38	19	146	7
Milwaukee	WI	25	42	54	74	13	24	232	39
Minneapolis-St. Paul	MN	54	50	57	75	47	10	293	63
Nashville	TN	33	53	11	36	74	48	255	55
New Orleans	LA	35	73	30	11	4	58	211	28
New York-Northern NJ	NY	61	48	63	46	2	1	221	32
Oklahoma City	OK	18	12	19	41	75	74	239	41
Omaha	NE	31	54	26	70	9	70	260	56
Orlando	FL	11	19	36	9	61	33	169	14
Oxnard	CA	58	1	33	3	19	35	149	9
Philadelphia	PA	66	39	74	47	7	11	244	50
Phoenix	AZ	74	20	14	39	23	40	210	26
Pittsburgh	PA	67	67	16	55	11	14	230	35
Portland	OR	7	30	53	20	10	12	132	5
Providence	RI	17	14	72	51	24	49	227	34
Raleigh	NC	35	9	31	30	64	38	207	23

Metro Area	State	Air Quality[1]	Toxic Releases[2]	Superfund Sites[3]	Energy Use[4]	Motor Vehicle Use[5]	Mass Transit Use[6]	Overall Score[7]	Overall Rank[8]
Richmond	VA	20	63	49	37	62	56	287	62
Riverside	CA	75	13	23	6	39	60	216	31
Rochester	NY	6	36	40	67	30	62	241	43
Sacramento	CA	64	7	27	7	14	54	173	15
Saint Louis	MO	55	56	59	50	68	23	311	68
Salt Lake City	UT	44	75	68	59	25	15	286	61
San Antonio	TX	16	28	10	21	28	17	120	4
San Diego	CA	72	8	9	1	32	16	138	6
San Francisco	CA	41	23	15	4	15	3	101	2
San Jose	CA	28	3	73	5	26	21	156	13
Seattle	WA	13	21	58	17	41	4	154	10
Springfield	MA	8	37	22	71	37	39	214	30
Syracuse	NY	2	45	65	69	46	50	277	59
Tampa-St. Petersburg	FL	27	27	60	10	50	57	231	36
Toledo	OH	9	66	1	65	44	52	237	40
Tucson	AZ	44	60	13	19	27	25	188	18
Tulsa	OK	34	57	25	42	70	73	301	66
Virginia Beach	VA	3	34	70	29	53	51	240	42
Washington	DC	56	10	21	43	22	2	154	10
Youngstown	OH	32	46	69	63	49	64	323	73

Note: *The Green Metro Index compares 75 major metropolitan areas in the U.S. on measures of environmental quality and performance appropriate to metro areas as a whole. The index is based on federal and private data for six environmental measures including: air quality, toxic releases, superfund sites, energy use, mass transit use and motor vehicle use; The figures above rank how each metro area fared in each category. Lower numbers are better; (1) Based on the percent of days the Air Quality Index (AQI) was in the "Good" range in 2016; (2) Calculated by adding the total toxic releases for each metro area and dividing by the metro area population. Data is from the Environmental Protection Agency's Toxic Release Inventory for 2015; (3) Based on the per capita number of final and proposed Superfund Sites located within each metro area. Data is from the Environmental Protection Agency's Superfund National Priorities list (data extracted 8/9/2017); (4) Based on total heating and cooling degree days per year. Data is from Weather America, A Thirty-Year Summary of Statistical Weather Data and Rankings, 2011; (5) Based on the DVMT (daily vehicle-miles of travel) per capita for each urbanized area. Data is from the Department of Transportation's Urbanized Areas: 2011 Selected Characteristics report; (6) Calculated by dividing the total total vehicle revenue miles by the population of the urbanized area. Data is from the Federal Transit Administration's 2015 National Transit Summaries and Trends report; (7) The overall score was calculated by combining the rankings of all six environmental indicators, giving equal weight to each indicator; (8) 1=best, 75=worst*

Sources: *U.S Environmental Protection Agency; U.S. Department of Transportation; Federal Transit Administration; Grey House Publishing, Weather America, A Thirty-Year Summary of Statistical Weather Data and Rankings, 2011*

Green Metro Area Overall Rankings

Metro Area	State	Overall Rank[1]	Overall Score[2]
Austin	TX	1	82
San Francisco	CA	2	101
Honolulu	HI	3	115
San Antonio	TX	4	120
Portland	OR	5	132
San Diego	CA	6	138
Miami	FL	7	146
El Paso	TX	8	148
Oxnard	CA	9	149
Washington	DC	10	154
Seattle	WA	10	154
Los Angeles	CA	10	154
San Jose	CA	13	156
Orlando	FL	14	169
Sacramento	CA	15	173
Las Vegas	NV	16	180
Greensboro	NC	17	187
Tucson	AZ	18	188
Dallas-Ft. Worth	TX	19	193
Columbus	OH	20	198
Fresno	CA	21	199
Baltimore	MD	22	206
Boston	MA	23	207
Raleigh	NC	23	207
Albuquerque	NM	23	207
Atlanta	GA	26	210
Phoenix	AZ	26	210
New Orleans	LA	28	211
Charleston	SC	29	212
Springfield	MA	30	214
Riverside	CA	31	216
New York-Northern NJ	NY	32	221
Buffalo	NY	33	222
Providence	RI	34	227
Pittsburgh	PA	35	230
Cleveland	OH	36	231
Hartford	CT	36	231
Tampa-St. Petersburg	FL	36	231
Milwaukee	WI	39	232
Toledo	OH	40	237
Oklahoma City	OK	41	239
Virginia Beach	VA	42	240
Chicago	IL	43	241
Rochester	NY	43	241
Charlotte	NC	45	242
Little Rock	AR	45	242
Denver	CO	47	243
Jacksonville	FL	47	243
Akron	OH	47	243
Philadelphia	PA	50	244
Bakersfield	CA	51	245
Albany	NY	52	250
Greenville	SC	52	250
Houston	TX	54	251
Nashville	TN	55	255

Metro Area	State	Overall Rank[1]	Overall Score[2]
Omaha	NE	56	260
Dayton	OH	57	274
Louisville	KY	58	275
Syracuse	NY	59	277
Grand Rapids	MI	60	283
Salt Lake City	UT	61	286
Richmond	VA	62	287
Minneapolis-St. Paul	MN	63	293
Baton Rouge	LA	64	296
Memphis	TN	65	299
Tulsa	OK	66	301
Allentown	PA	67	303
Saint Louis	MO	68	311
Birmingham	AL	68	311
Cincinnati	OH	70	313
Kansas City	MO	71	314
Knoxville	TN	72	316
Youngstown	OH	73	323
Indianapolis	IN	74	331
Detroit	MI	75	343

Note: *The Green Metro Index compares 75 major metropolitan areas in the U.S. on measures of environmental quality and performance appropriate to metro areas as a whole. The index is based on federal data for six environmental measures including: air quality, toxic releases, superfund sites, energy use, mass transit use and motor vehicle use; (1) A lower number indicates better environmental quality or performance; (2) The overall score was calculated by combining the rankings of all six environmental indicators, giving equal weight to each indicator.*
Sources: *U.S Environmental Protection Agency; U.S. Department of Transportation; Federal Transit Administration; Grey House Publishing, Weather America, A Thirty-Year Summary of Statistical Weather Data and Rankings, 2011*

Broad Land Cover/Use

The contiguous 48 states, Hawaii, Puerto Rico, and the U.S. Virgin Islands cover over 1.94 billion acres of land and water; about 71 percent of this area is non-Federal rural land – nearly 1.4 billion acres.

Non-Federal rural lands are predominantly forest land (413 million acres), rangeland (406 million acres), and cropland (363 million acres).

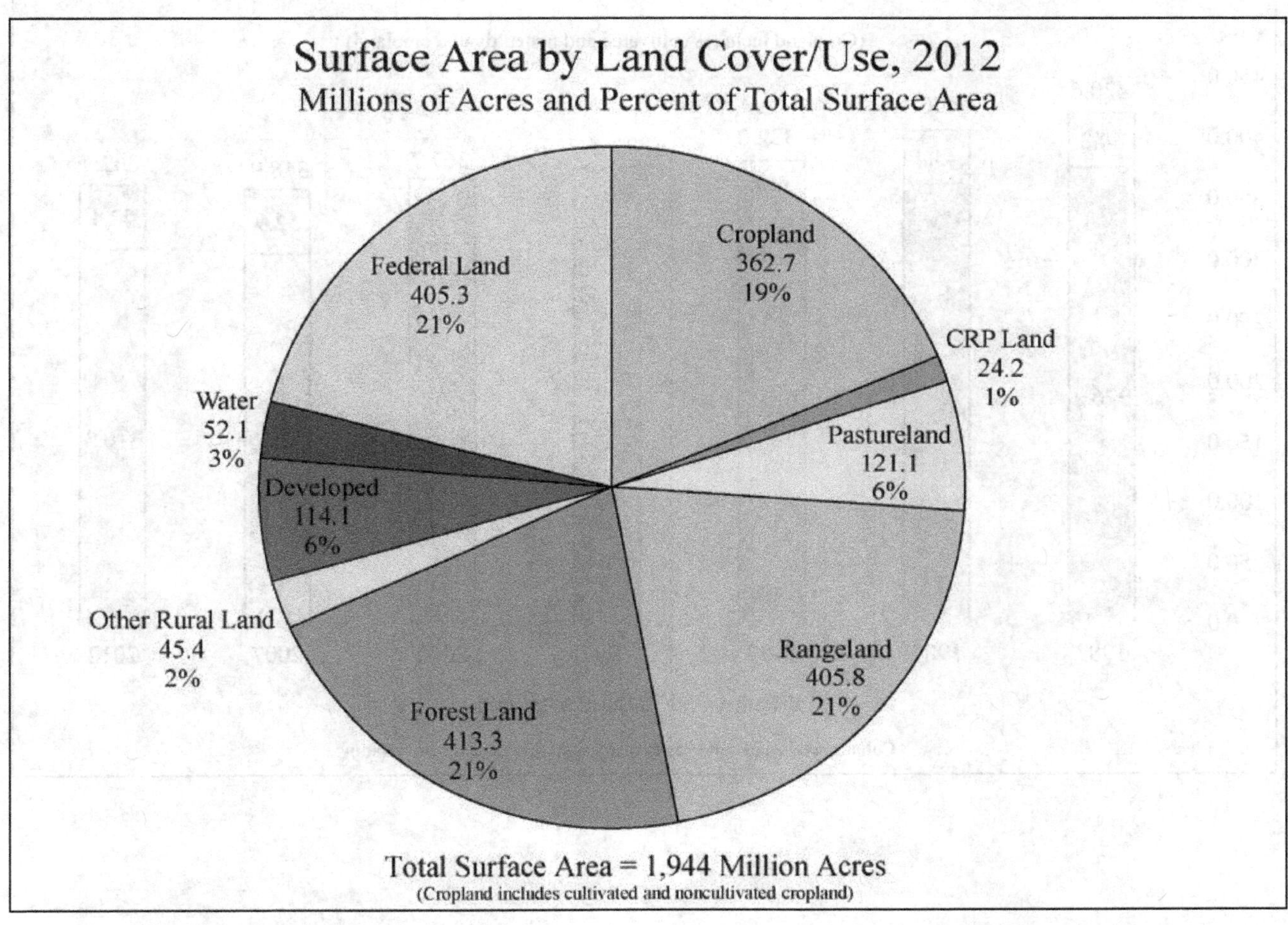

Source: *U.S. Department of Agriculture, 2012 National Resources Inventory, Summary Report, August 2015*

Cropland

Cropland acreage increased by about 4 million acres from 2007 to 2012 after a steady decline over the previous 25 years. The increase was a little over 1 percent from 359 to 363 million acres. Most of the gain came from land coming out of the Conservation Reserve Program counterbalanced to some degree by losses of cropland to development and other rural land.

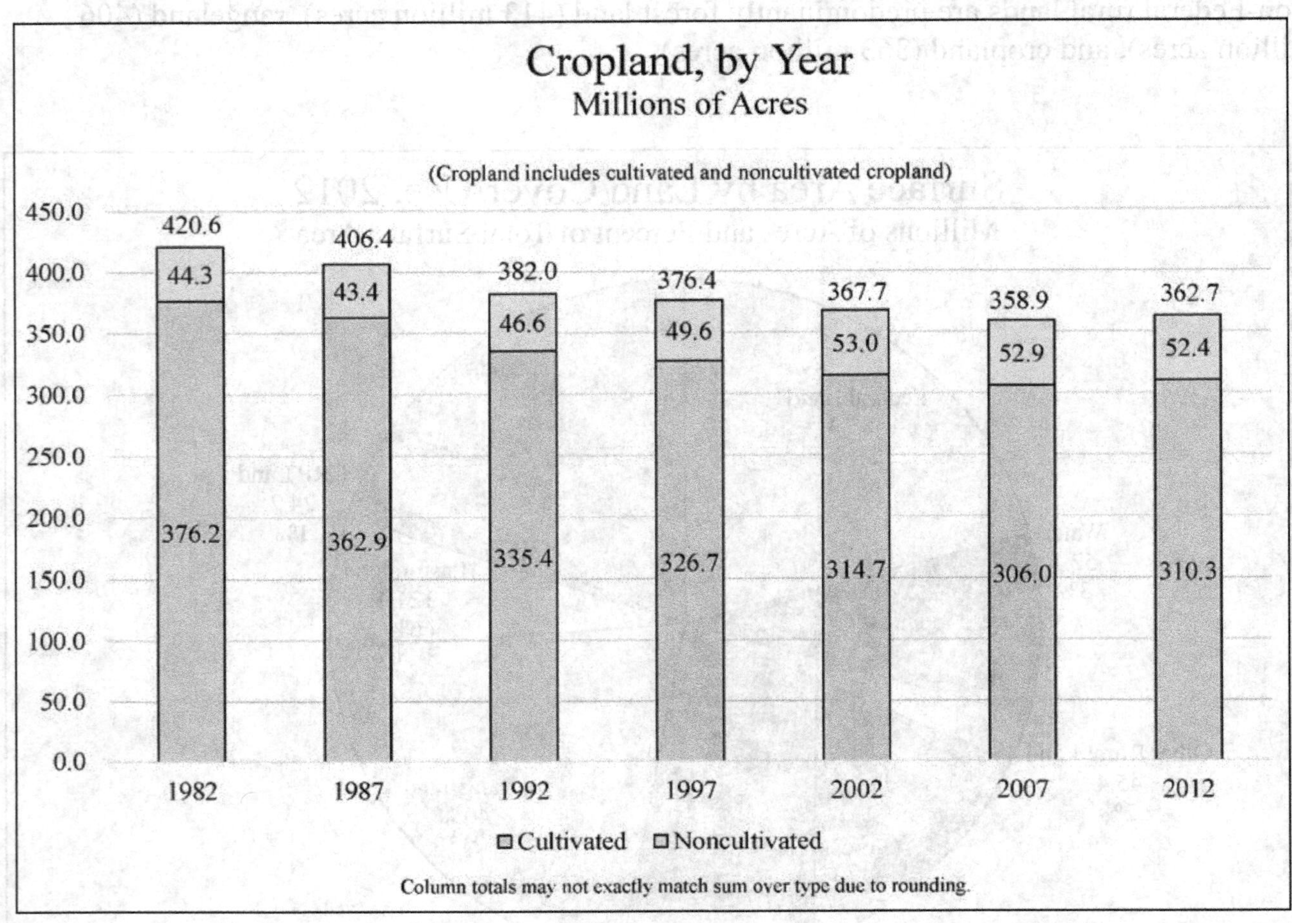

Source: *U.S. Department of Agriculture, 2012 National Resources Inventory, Summary Report, August 2015*

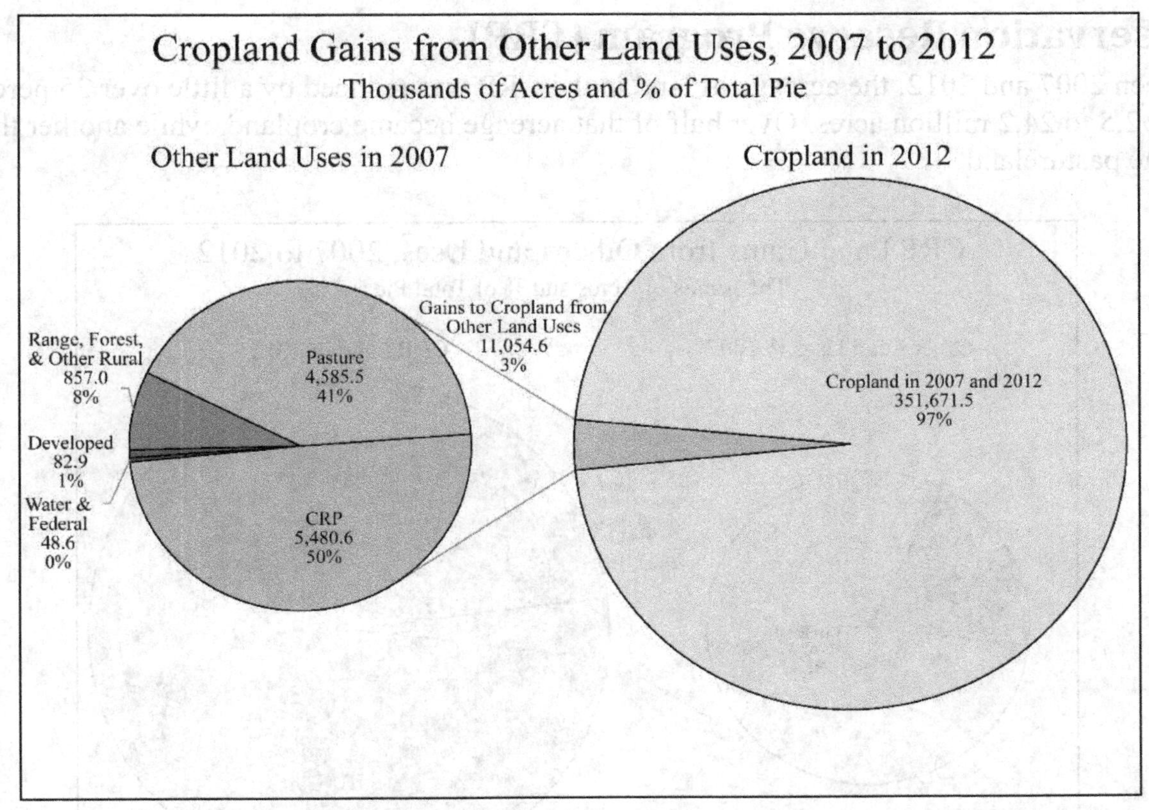

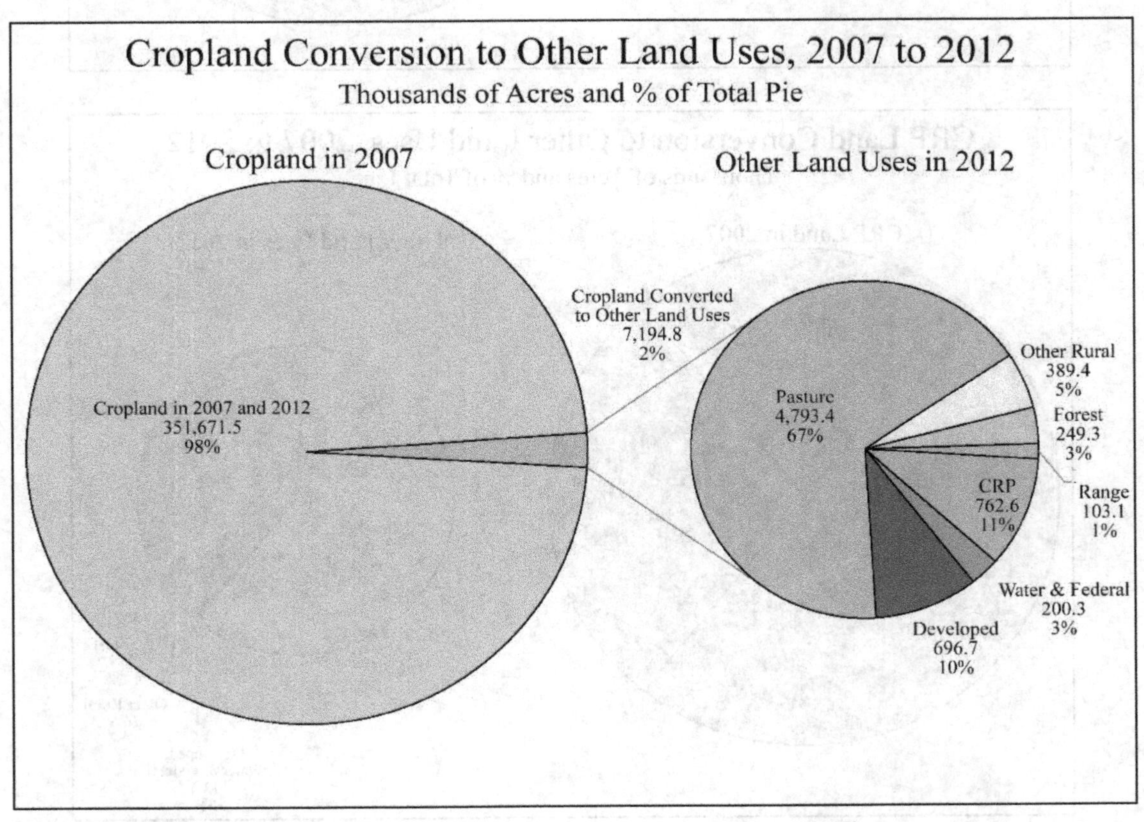

Source: *U.S. Department of Agriculture, 2012 National Resources Inventory, Summary Report, August 2015*

Conservation Reserve Program (CRP)

Between 2007 and 2012, the acreage of land in the CRP was reduced by a little over 25 percent, from 32.5 to 24.2 million acres. Over half of that acreage became cropland, while another third became pastureland

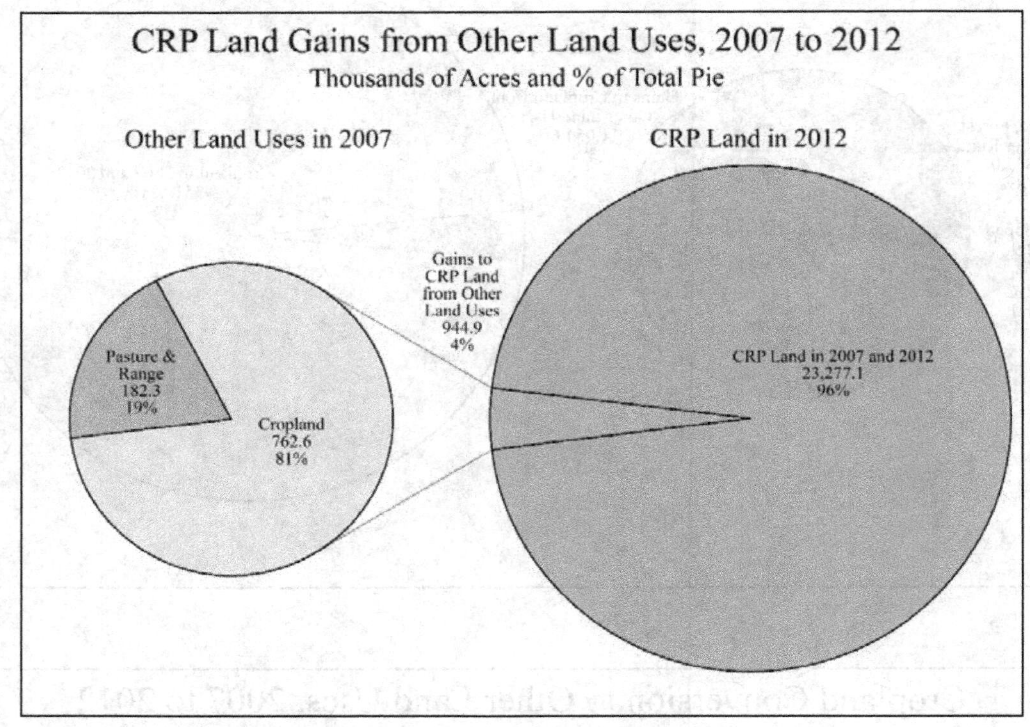

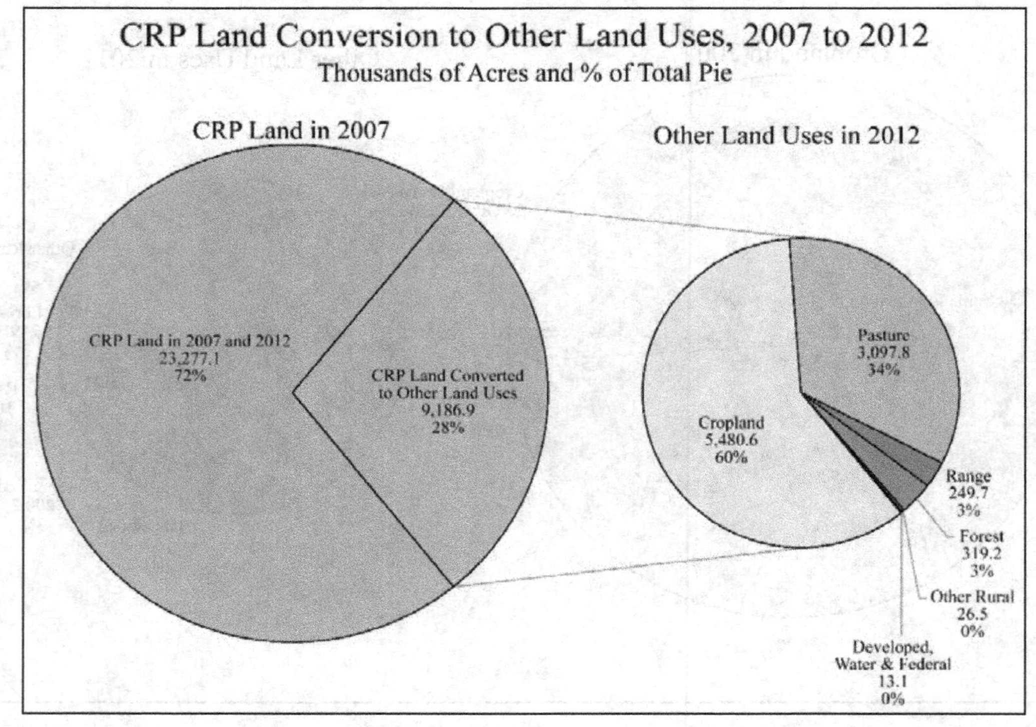

Source: *U.S. Department of Agriculture, 2012 National Resources Inventory, Summary Report, August 2015*

Development

About 44 million acres of land were newly developed between 1982 and 2012, bringing the total to about 114 million acres; that represents a 59 percent increase. Thus, more than 37 percent of developed land in the 48 conterminous states, Hawaii, Puerto Rico and the Virgin Islands was developed during the last 30 years.

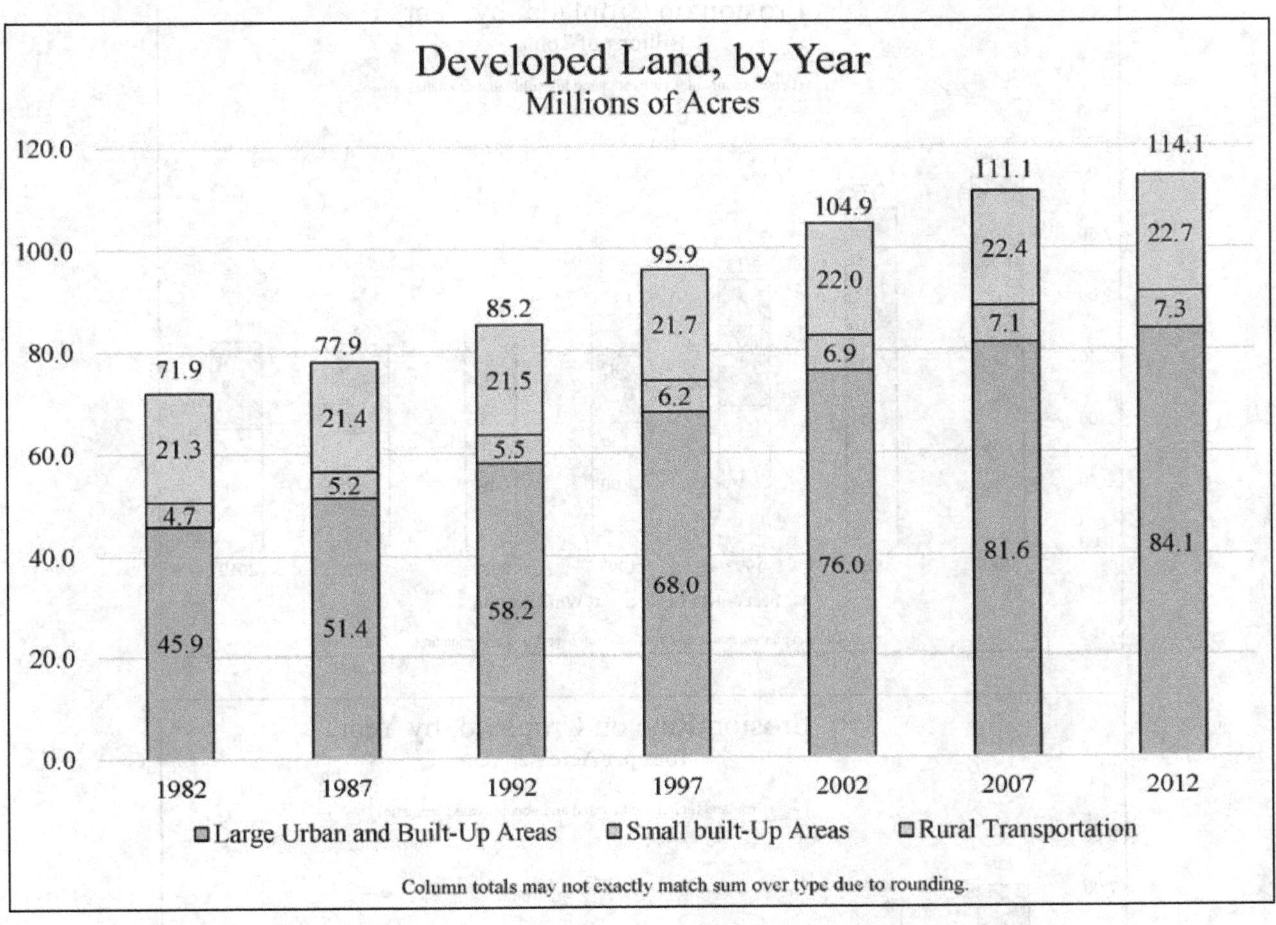

Source: *U.S. Department of Agriculture, 2012 National Resources Inventory, Summary Report, August 2015*

Erosion

Soil erosion on cropland decreased 44 percent between 1982 and 2012. Water (sheet and rill) erosion declined from 1.59 billion tons per year to .96 billion tons per year, and erosion due to wind decreased from 1.38 billion tons per year to .71 billion tons per year. (See charts below and maps on the next page).

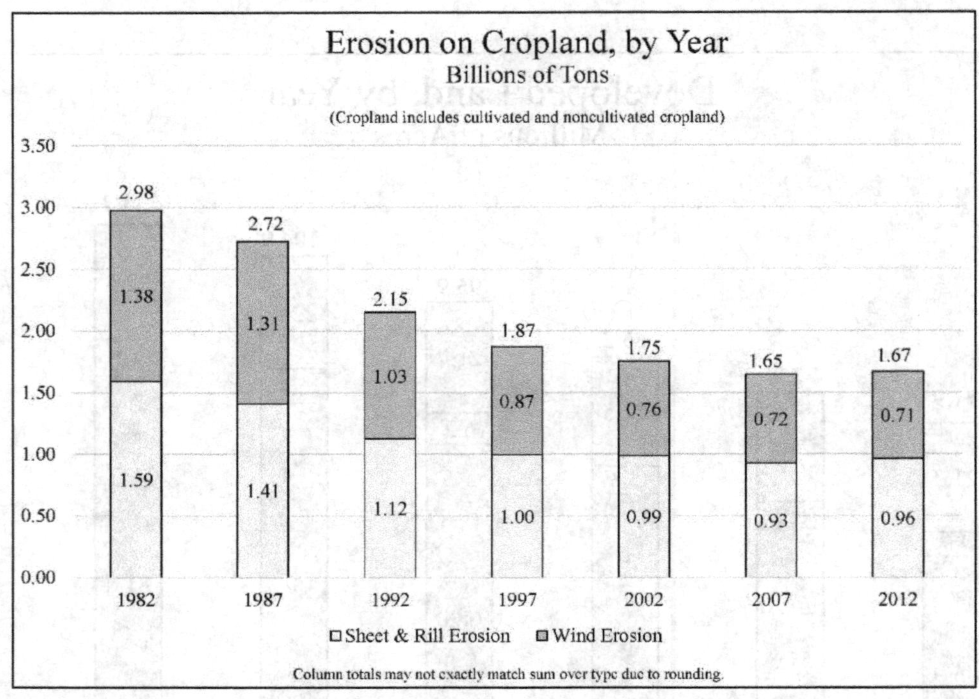

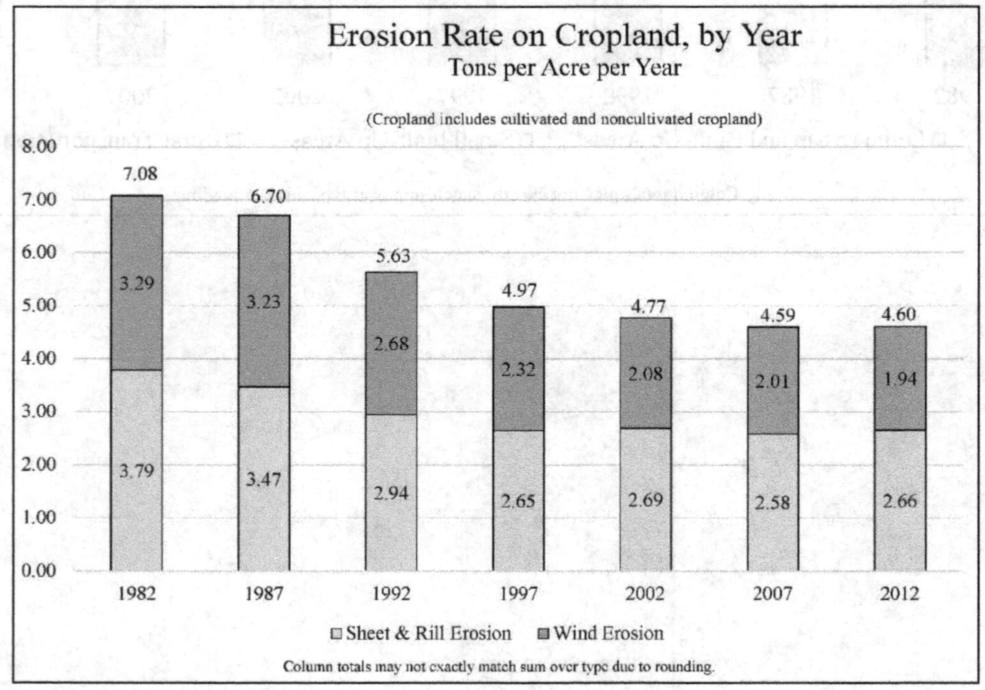

Source: *U.S. Department of Agriculture, 2012 National Resources Inventory, Summary Report, August 2015*

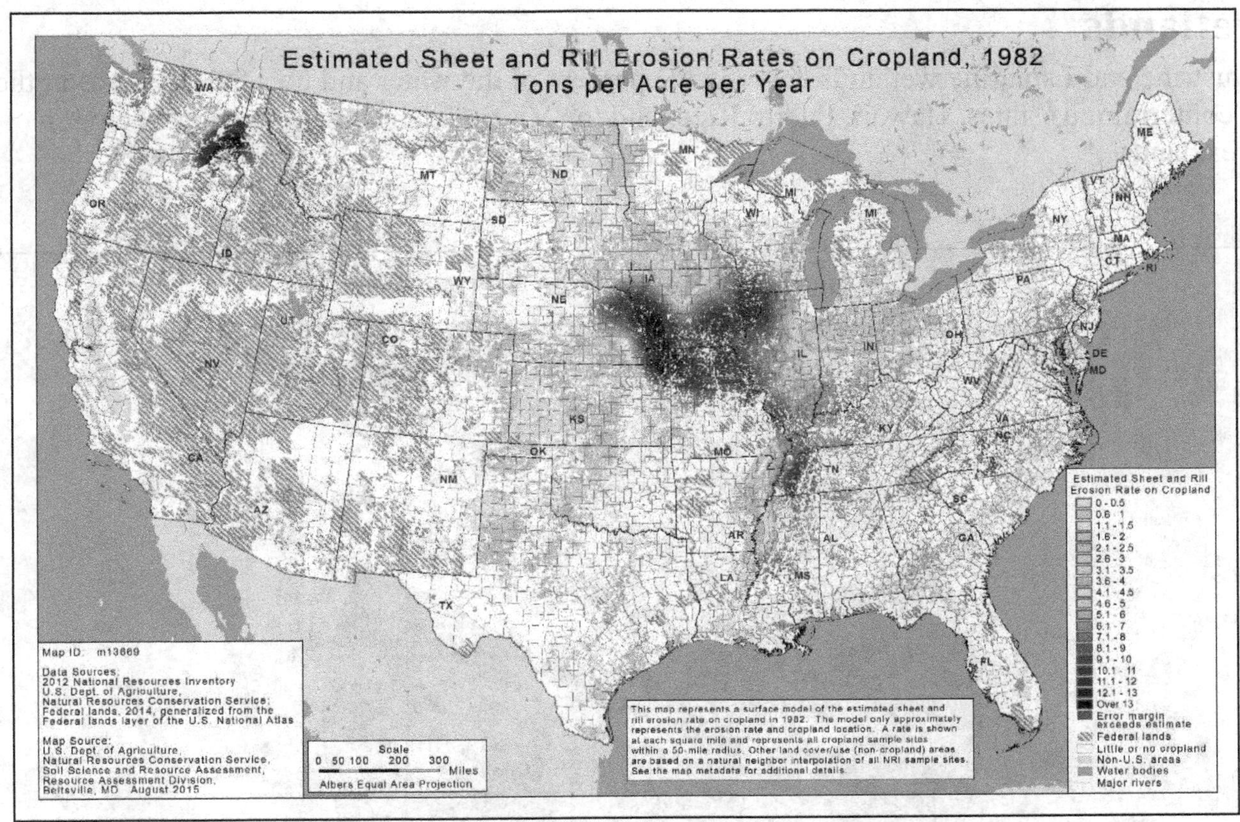

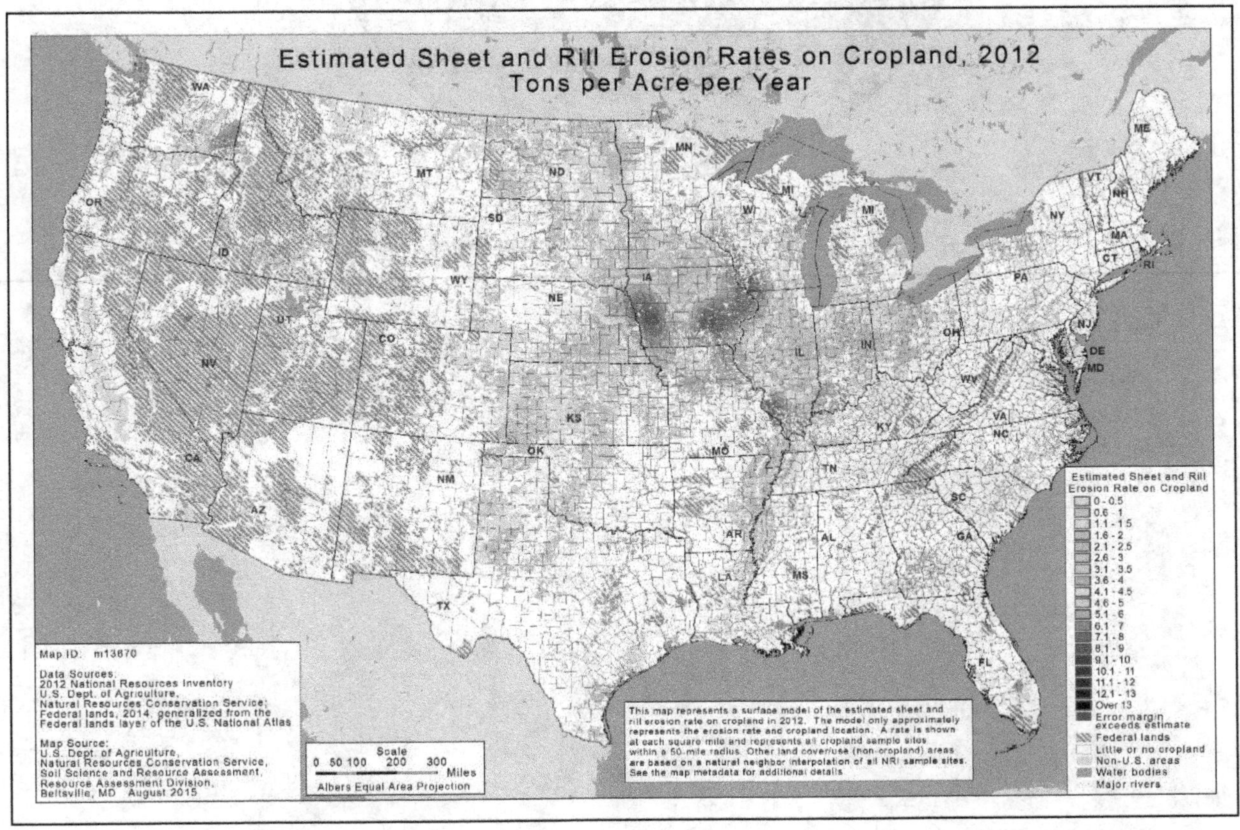

Source: *U.S. Department of Agriculture, 2012 National Resources Inventory, Summary Report, August 2015*

Wetlands

Palustrine and Estuarine wetlands covered 7.2 percent of the water and non-federal lands in the 48 conterminous states, Hawaii, Puerto Rico, and the Virgin Islands, with over half being in forest lands.

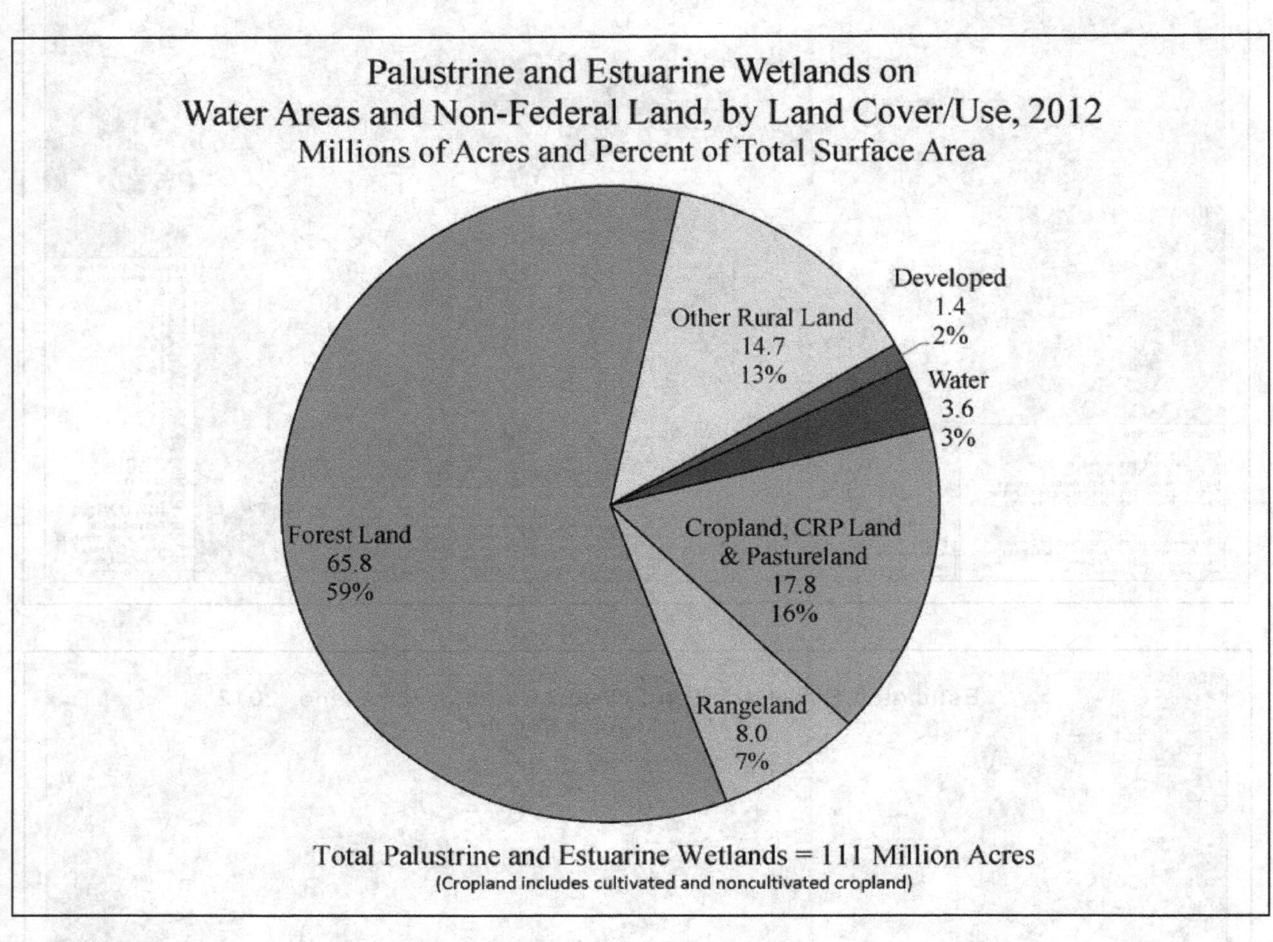

Source: *U.S. Department of Agriculture, 2012 National Resources Inventory, Summary Report, August 2015*

Broad Land Cover/Use

Land use is surprisingly dynamic, with annual shifts in and out of different uses. Examining net change in land use reveals general trends, but masks the real extent of land use change over time. In agriculture there are frequent shifts in the use of land among cropland, pastureland, rangeland, and forest land. Each time land changes use, it may affect erosion potential, contiguity of habitat, hydrologic features of the landscape, or other natural processes or functions.

Key Definitions

Water Areas

A broad land cover/use category comprising water bodies and streams that are permanent open water.

Non-Federal Land

Most NRI estimates pertain only to non-Federal rural lands; non-Federal lands include privately owned lands, tribal and trust lands, and lands controlled by State and local governments.

Developed Land

The NRI category of developed land differs from that used by some other data collection entities. For the NRI, the intent is to identify which lands have been removed from the rural land base, while other studies are interested in human populations (e.g., Census of Population) and housing units (e.g., American Housing Survey). The NRI developed land category includes (a) large tracts of urban and built-up land; (b) small tracts of built-up land of less than 10 acres; and (c) land outside of these built-up areas that is in a rural transportation corridor (roads, railroads, and associated rights-of-way).

Cropland and Pastureland

These definitions are provided in Chapter 4.

Conservation Reserve Program (CRP) Land

This definition is provided in chapter 4.

Source: *U.S. Department of Agriculture, 2012 National Resources Inventory, Summary Report, August 2015*

Rangeland

A broad land cover/use category on which the climax or potential plant cover is composed principally of native grasses, grasslike plants, forbs or shrubs suitable for grazing and browsing, and introduced forage species that are managed like rangeland. This would include areas where introduced hardy and persistent grasses, such as crested wheatgrass, are planted and such practices as deferred grazing, burning, chaining, and rotational grazing are used, with little or no chemicals or fertilizer being applied. Grasslands, savannas, many wetlands, some deserts, and tundra are considered to be rangeland. Certain communities of low forbs and shrubs, such as mesquite, chaparral, mountain shrub, and pinyon-juniper, are also included as rangeland.

Forest Land

A broad land cover/use category that is at least 10 percent stocked by single-stemmed woody species of any size that will be at least 4 meters (13 feet) tall at maturity. Also included is land bearing evidence of natural regeneration of tree cover (cut over forest or abandoned farmland) and not currently developed for non-forest use. Ten percent stocked, when viewed from a vertical direction, equates to an areal canopy cover of leaves and branches of 25 percent or greater. The minimum area for classification as forest land is 1 acre, and the area must be at least 100 feet wide.

Other Rural Land

A broad land cover/use category that includes farmsteads and other land in farms, barren land, marshland, and permanent snow-ice.

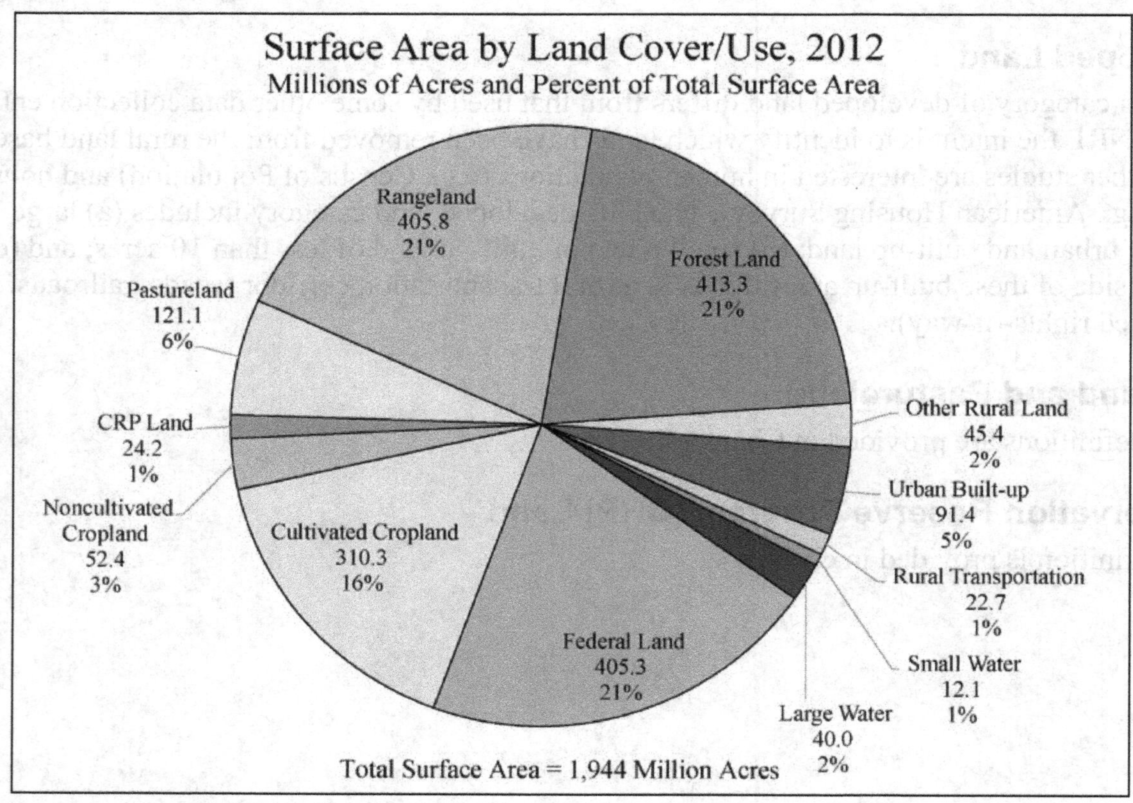

Source: *U.S. Department of Agriculture, 2012 National Resources Inventory, Summary Report, August 2015*

Change in Broad Land Cover/Use

The land cover/use change tables (3 – 9) show estimates of both gross change from one category to another between the two specific years, as well as net change from the initial year to the subsequent year along the bottom. Along the primary diagonal of each of these tables is an estimate of the acreage that was in the same land cover/use category in both years. Under each estimate is the margin of error, as discussed further in chapter 7.

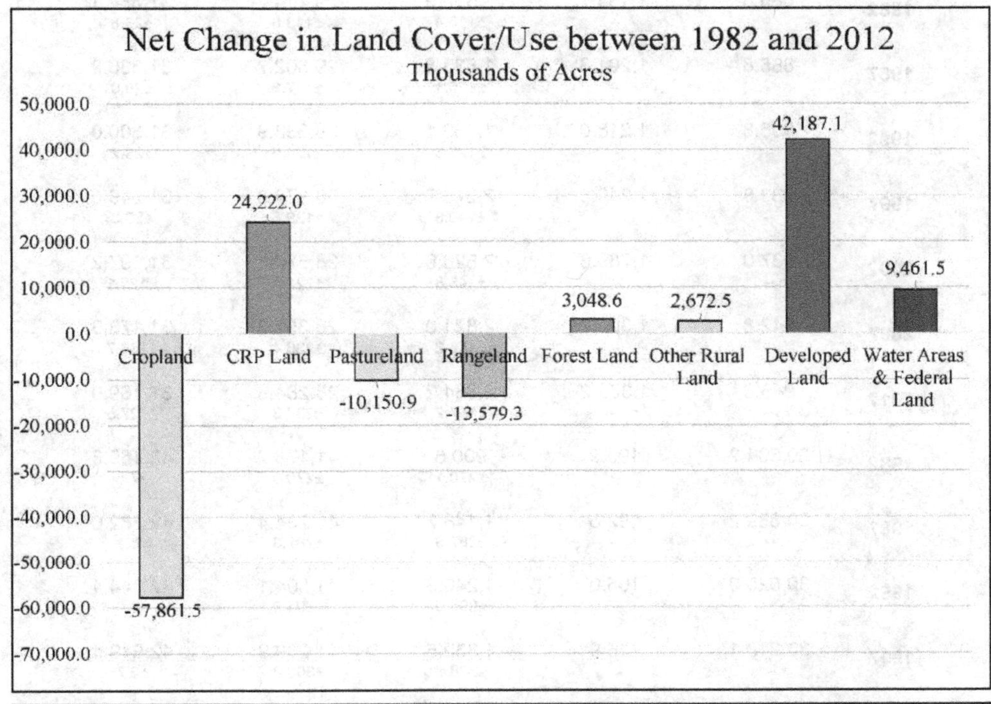

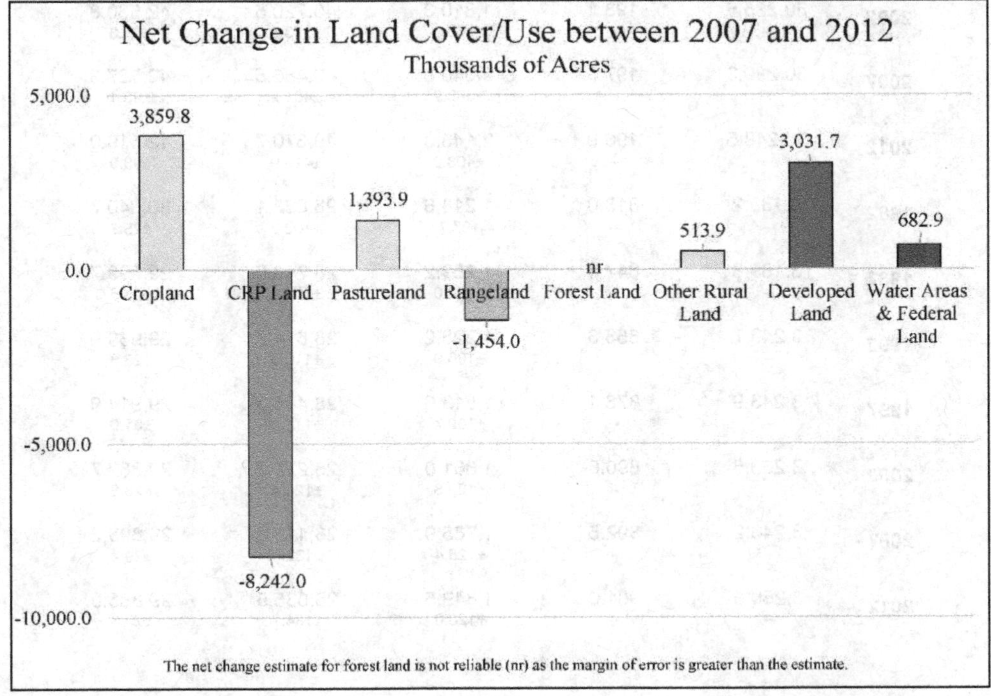

Source: *U.S. Department of Agriculture, 2012 National Resources Inventory, Summary Report, August 2015*

Table 1 - Surface area of non-Federal and Federal land and water areas, by State and year
In thousands of acres, with margins of error

State	Year	Federal land	Water areas	Non-Federal Land			Total surface area
				Developed	Rural	Total	
Alabama	1982	885.0 --	1,184.7 --	1,639.9 ±115.4	29,714.2 ±113.8	31,354.1 ±28.8	33,423.8 --
	1987	885.8 --	1,201.8 --	1,833.5 ±120.1	29,502.7 ±117.3	31,336.2 ±28.0	33,423.8 --
	1992	905.8 --	1,218.0 --	1,966.1 ±129.8	29,333.9 ±124.9	31,300.0 ±28.2	33,423.8 --
	1997	933.8 --	1,240.5 --	2,276.7 ±140.8	28,972.8 ±139.5	31,249.5 ±28.3	33,423.8 --
	2002	937.0 --	1,289.6 --	2,626.6 ±143.8	28,570.6 ±221.1	31,197.2 ±125.1	33,423.8 --
	2007	942.8 --	1,302.7 --	2,821.0 ±156.2	28,357.3 ±236.4	31,178.3 ±126.7	33,423.8 --
	2012	945.6 --	1,309.2 --	2,884.2 ±157.2	28,284.8 ±237.3	31,169.0 ±127.5	33,423.8 --
Arizona	1982	30,604.2 --	190.9 --	990.6 ±270.1	41,178.7 ±270.0	42,169.3 ±7.8	72,964.4 --
	1987	30,389.2 --	192.6 --	1,148.2 ±287.6	41,234.4 ±287.3	42,382.6 ±8.1	72,964.4 --
	1992	30,025.0 --	195.0 --	1,240.3 ±295.0	41,504.1 ±294.9	42,744.4 ±9.0	72,964.4 --
	1997	30,218.1 --	196.9 --	1,339.5 ±308.8	41,209.9 ±308.8	42,549.4 ±9.7	72,964.4 --
	2002	30,235.5 --	198.1 --	1,810.3 ±365.0	40,720.5 ±373.8	42,530.8 ±98.3	72,964.4 --
	2007	30,239.3 --	197.8 --	2,040.8 ±393.2	40,486.5 ±401.2	42,527.3 ±98.1	72,964.4 --
	2012	30,248.5 --	196.9 --	2,148.3 ±408.2	40,370.7 ±416.9	42,519.0 ±98.0	72,964.4 --
Arkansas	1982	3,183.2 --	813.0 --	1,218.6 ±97.7	28,822.1 ±102.3	30,040.7 ±28.3	34,036.9 --
	1987	3,189.8 --	847.4 --	1,259.2 ±102.0	28,740.5 ±107.4	29,999.7 ±28.5	34,036.9 --
	1992	3,243.7 --	853.3 --	1,325.2 ±106.0	28,614.7 ±110.5	29,939.9 ±28.6	34,036.9 --
	1997	3,243.9 --	878.1 --	1,513.6 ±109.7	28,401.3 ±115.2	29,914.9 ±31.0	34,036.9 --
	2002	3,263.6 --	890.6 --	1,661.0 ±120.8	28,221.7 ±126.4	29,882.7 ±28.6	34,036.9 --
	2007	3,246.2 --	892.5 --	1,785.9 ±126.4	28,112.3 ±132.9	29,898.2 ±29.4	34,036.9 --
	2012	3,250.9 --	901.0 --	1,849.5 ±128.0	28,035.5 ±134.7	29,885.0 ±29.3	34,036.9 --

***Source:** U.S. Department of Agriculture, 2012 National Resources Inventory, Summary Report, August 2015*

Table 1 - Surface area of non-Federal and Federal land and water areas, by State and year
In thousands of acres, with margins of error

State	Year	Federal land	Water areas	Non-Federal Land			Total surface area
				Developed	Rural	Total	
California	1982	45,865.1 --	1,804.0 --	4,076.6 ±345.6	49,764.5 ±352.8	53,841.1 ±40.1	101,510.2 --
	1987	45,888.3 --	1,809.8 --	4,335.9 ±358.5	49,476.2 ±365.3	53,812.1 ±39.9	101,510.2 --
	1992	46,511.3 --	1,812.4 --	4,835.4 ±368.9	48,351.1 ±372.1	53,186.5 ±39.0	101,510.2 --
	1997	46,542.0 --	1,804.2 --	5,360.4 ±372.3	47,803.6 ±375.8	53,164.0 ±40.1	101,510.2 --
	2002	47,088.1 --	1,816.6 --	5,771.5 ±407.4	46,834.0 ±403.6	52,605.5 ±27.9	101,510.2 --
	2007	47,295.1 --	1,823.3 --	6,096.6 ±410.6	46,295.2 ±408.1	52,391.8 ±28.0	101,510.2 --
	2012	47,384.1 --	1,825.8 --	6,255.0 ±415.7	46,045.3 ±413.0	52,300.3 ±28.8	101,510.2 --
Caribbean	1982	87.5 --	46.2 --	286.8 ±29.8	1,886.6 ±29.3	2,173.4 ±2.7	2,307.1 --
	1987	80.2 --	46.8 --	335.6 ±29.3	1,844.5 ±28.8	2,180.1 ±3.2	2,307.1 --
	1992	82.7 --	47.1 --	414.0 ±31.3	1,763.3 ±31.1	2,177.3 ±3.2	2,307.1 --
	1997	83.4 --	46.9 --	531.6 ±30.4	1,645.2 ±29.9	2,176.8 ±3.3	2,307.1 --
	2002	84.4 --	47.0 --	561.0 ±34.6	1,614.7 ±41.5	2,175.7 ±32.4	2,307.1 --
	2007	84.4 --	47.1 --	581.5 ±35.4	1,594.1 ±43.1	2,175.6 ±32.5	2,307.1 --
	2012	84.9 --	48.3 --	598.6 ±35.7	1,575.3 ±43.9	2,173.9 ±32.6	2,307.1 --
Colorado	1982	23,501.4 --	323.8 --	1,203.5 ±106.1	41,595.8 ±124.1	42,799.3 ±55.8	66,624.5 --
	1987	23,634.1 --	325.1 --	1,346.9 ±138.5	41,318.4 ±149.2	42,665.3 ±55.6	66,624.5 --
	1992	23,711.3 --	324.4 --	1,492.0 ±149.4	41,096.8 ±157.8	42,588.8 ±55.5	66,624.5 --
	1997	23,884.6 --	325.2 --	1,597.1 ±164.1	40,817.6 ±171.6	42,414.7 ±55.2	66,624.5 --
	2002	23,964.7 --	319.0 --	1,778.1 ±193.4	40,562.7 ±191.8	42,340.8 ±18.1	66,624.5 --
	2007	24,027.8 --	319.5 --	1,889.3 ±201.9	40,387.9 ±200.1	42,277.2 ±18.3	66,624.5 --
	2012	24,076.0 --	323.3 --	1,927.1 ±204.0	40,298.1 ±201.6	42,225.2 ±18.2	66,624.5 --

Source: *U.S. Department of Agriculture, 2012 National Resources Inventory, Summary Report, August 2015*

Table 1 - Surface area of non-Federal and Federal land and water areas, by State and year
In thousands of acres, with margins of error

State	Year	Federal land	Water areas	Non-Federal Land			Total surface area
				Developed	Rural	Total	
Connecticut	1982	8.5 --	125.2 --	840.8 ±32.2	2,220.2 ±34.1	3,061.0 ±5.3	3,194.7 --
	1987	13.1 --	125.1 --	892.7 ±32.7	2,163.8 ±34.3	3,056.5 ±5.4	3,194.7 --
	1992	13.3 --	126.1 --	937.0 ±34.0	2,118.3 ±35.6	3,055.3 ±5.3	3,194.7 --
	1997	14.5 --	126.4 --	981.7 ±32.7	2,072.1 ±34.3	3,053.8 ±5.1	3,194.7 --
	2002	14.9 --	126.4 --	1,036.6 ±36.5	2,016.8 ±38.2	3,053.4 ±5.1	3,194.7 --
	2007	14.9 --	126.6 --	1,069.0 ±37.1	1,984.2 ±38.8	3,053.2 ±5.3	3,194.7 --
	2012	15.3 --	127.1 --	1,081.5 ±37.2	1,970.8 ±39.0	3,052.3 ±5.2	3,194.7 --
Delaware	1982	23.7 --	301.4 --	159.4 ±26.3	1,049.0 ±26.8	1,208.4 ±2.6	1,533.5 --
	1987	23.6 --	301.6 --	176.6 ±28.7	1,031.7 ±29.1	1,208.3 ±2.6	1,533.5 --
	1992	23.6 --	301.7 --	193.8 ±29.9	1,014.4 ±30.1	1,208.2 ±2.7	1,533.5 --
	1997	23.6 --	302.0 --	215.2 ±31.3	992.7 ±31.3	1,207.9 ±2.9	1,533.5 --
	2002	23.9 --	302.5 --	250.5 ±34.8	956.6 ±33.9	1,207.1 ±4.5	1,533.5 --
	2007	24.0 --	303.5 --	278.5 ±37.9	927.5 ±37.5	1,206.0 ±3.8	1,533.5 --
	2012	24.3 --	303.8 --	291.5 ±39.7	913.9 ±39.5	1,205.4 ±3.7	1,533.5 --
Florida	1982	3,626.5 --	3,094.6 --	2,812.8 ±234.4	27,999.8 ±231.6	30,812.6 ±66.1	37,533.7 --
	1987	3,659.0 --	3,099.9 --	3,130.3 ±243.0	27,644.5 ±241.4	30,774.8 ±66.7	37,533.7 --
	1992	3,821.2 --	3,129.4 --	3,735.0 ±265.3	26,848.1 ±260.3	30,583.1 ±61.7	37,533.7 --
	1997	3,838.9 --	3,129.2 --	4,406.2 ±280.6	26,159.4 ±284.7	30,565.6 ±57.5	37,533.7 --
	2002	3,849.0 --	3,150.1 --	4,925.1 ±297.5	25,609.5 ±309.7	30,534.6 ±30.4	37,533.7 --
	2007	3,875.9 --	3,178.3 --	5,345.3 ±321.9	25,134.2 ±336.0	30,479.5 ±32.1	37,533.7 --
	2012	3,880.0 --	3,170.5 --	5,496.2 ±330.8	24,987.0 ±344.4	30,483.2 ±32.0	37,533.7 --

Source: *U.S. Department of Agriculture, 2012 National Resources Inventory, Summary Report, August 2015*

Table 1 - Surface area of non-Federal and Federal land and water areas, by State and year
In thousands of acres, with margins of error

State	Year	Federal land	Water areas	Non-Federal Land			Total surface area
				Developed	Rural	Total	
Georgia	1982	2,049.0 --	935.7 --	2,238.2 ±119.8	32,517.6 ±118.9	34,755.8 ±22.9	37,740.5 --
	1987	2,056.1 --	941.9 --	2,483.7 ±132.9	32,258.8 ±131.8	34,742.5 ±23.1	37,740.5 --
	1992	2,074.7 --	978.4 --	2,927.0 ±142.3	31,760.4 ±143.5	34,687.4 ±23.7	37,740.5 --
	1997	2,074.6 --	1,004.4 --	3,707.1 ±158.0	30,954.4 ±160.1	34,661.5 ±25.7	37,740.5 --
	2002	2,072.9 --	1,039.5 --	4,216.9 ±200.4	30,411.2 ±202.4	34,628.1 ±29.4	37,740.5 --
	2007	2,081.8 --	1,062.2 --	4,526.2 ±213.5	30,070.3 ±214.7	34,596.5 ±31.7	37,740.5 --
	2012	2,084.0 --	1,077.2 --	4,631.6 ±219.6	29,947.7 ±221.6	34,579.3 ±31.3	37,740.5 --
Hawaii	1982	407.2 --	23.0 --	166.4 ±32.0	3,526.4 ±31.8	3,692.8 ±4.3	4,123.0 --
	1987	473.7 --	23.1 --	171.0 ±32.4	3,455.2 ±32.1	3,626.2 ±4.2	4,123.0 --
	1992	475.4 --	22.9 --	193.5 ±35.4	3,431.2 ±35.2	3,624.7 ±4.2	4,123.0 --
	1997	446.9 --	22.9 --	200.9 ±35.2	3,452.3 ±34.9	3,653.2 ±4.2	4,123.0 --
	2002	453.4 --	23.0 --	217.2 ±37.9	3,429.4 ±37.6	3,646.6 ±4.0	4,123.0 --
	2007	605.7 --	23.1 --	224.4 ±39.5	3,269.8 ±39.1	3,494.2 ±4.0	4,123.0 --
	2012	610.7 --	23.1 --	241.9 ±41.1	3,247.3 ±40.5	3,489.2 ±4.0	4,123.0 --
Idaho	1982	33,243.4 --	543.6 --	558.7 ±49.3	19,141.8 ±53.6	19,700.5 ±13.6	53,487.5 --
	1987	33,040.1 --	546.4 --	621.3 ±52.0	19,279.7 ±56.0	19,901.0 ±13.6	53,487.5 --
	1992	33,128.4 --	549.1 --	675.1 ±59.7	19,134.9 ±62.4	19,810.0 ±13.2	53,487.5 --
	1997	33,415.9 --	551.1 --	770.2 ±66.7	18,750.3 ±68.5	19,520.5 ±13.2	53,487.5 --
	2002	33,440.4 --	552.1 --	821.4 ±67.9	18,673.6 ±68.6	19,495.0 ±9.9	53,487.5 --
	2007	33,445.6 --	554.6 --	888.3 ±71.6	18,599.0 ±72.2	19,487.3 ±10.7	53,487.5 --
	2012	33,448.8 --	555.8 --	913.7 ±72.4	18,569.2 ±72.9	19,482.9 ±10.7	53,487.5 --

Source: *U.S. Department of Agriculture, 2012 National Resources Inventory, Summary Report, August 2015*

Table 1 - Surface area of non-Federal and Federal land and water areas, by State and year In thousands of acres, with margins of error

State	Year	Federal land	Water areas	Non-Federal Land			Total surface area
				Developed	Rural	Total	
Illinois	1982	476.5 --	735.2 --	2,626.2 ±121.0	32,220.8 ±126.7	34,847.0 ±26.8	36,058.7 --
	1987	477.2 --	731.4 --	2,763.8 ±125.7	32,086.3 ±132.3	34,850.1 ±24.9	36,058.7 --
	1992	492.6 --	727.3 --	2,858.5 ±128.7	31,980.3 ±132.7	34,838.8 ±23.4	36,058.7 --
	1997	490.8 --	722.8 --	3,096.2 ±123.7	31,748.9 ±124.6	34,845.1 ±22.9	36,058.7 --
	2002	493.0 --	736.0 --	3,228.3 ±134.4	31,601.4 ±134.8	34,829.7 ±21.7	36,058.7 --
	2007	499.6 --	742.3 --	3,355.2 ±142.8	31,461.6 ±142.1	34,816.8 ±21.7	36,058.7 --
	2012	502.1 --	747.1 --	3,415.6 ±147.0	31,393.9 ±146.3	34,809.5 ±22.1	36,058.7 --
Indiana	1982	469.9 --	351.8 --	1,781.1 ±88.5	20,555.6 ±92.1	22,336.7 ±19.1	23,158.4 --
	1987	468.9 --	360.9 --	1,897.6 ±90.3	20,431.0 ±94.9	22,328.6 ±18.7	23,158.4 --
	1992	470.1 --	364.6 --	2,002.6 ±98.4	20,321.1 ±102.4	22,323.7 ±18.2	23,158.4 --
	1997	468.8 --	362.9 --	2,191.7 ±110.2	20,135.0 ±114.2	22,326.7 ±18.4	23,158.4 --
	2002	475.1 --	370.1 --	2,333.1 ±115.9	19,980.1 ±119.2	22,313.2 ±17.1	23,158.4 --
	2007	476.9 --	378.1 --	2,456.0 ±121.9	19,847.4 ±124.7	22,303.4 ±18.3	23,158.4 --
	2012	479.3 --	385.3 --	2,522.0 ±124.4	19,771.8 ±127.1	22,293.8 ±20.0	23,158.4 --
Iowa	1982	174.5 --	457.9 --	1,637.6 ±97.8	33,746.5 ±96.5	35,384.1 ±18.9	36,016.5 --
	1987	175.6 --	461.5 --	1,663.9 ±102.5	33,715.5 ±103.0	35,379.4 ±19.2	36,016.5 --
	1992	175.3 --	473.5 --	1,693.0 ±102.9	33,674.7 ±103.1	35,367.7 ±19.3	36,016.5 --
	1997	199.1 --	479.8 --	1,767.7 ±105.5	33,569.9 ±105.6	35,337.6 ±19.8	36,016.5 --
	2002	208.2 --	489.8 --	1,841.6 ±108.7	33,476.9 ±108.8	35,318.5 ±16.7	36,016.5 --
	2007	211.9 --	495.5 --	1,904.4 ±115.1	33,404.7 ±114.8	35,309.1 ±16.7	36,016.5 --
	2012	214.2 --	501.2 --	1,942.1 ±116.6	33,359.0 ±116.0	35,301.1 ±16.9	36,016.5 --

Source: *U.S. Department of Agriculture, 2012 National Resources Inventory, Summary Report, August 2015*

Table 1 - Surface area of non-Federal and Federal land and water areas, by State and year
In thousands of acres, with margins of error

State	Year	Federal land	Water areas	Non-Federal Land			Total surface area
				Developed	Rural	Total	
Kansas	1982	474.9 --	516.4 --	1,736.8 ±69.4	49,932.7 ±73.7	51,669.5 ±19.3	52,660.8 --
	1987	475.6 --	516.9 --	1,764.0 ±69.1	49,904.3 ±74.3	51,668.3 ±19.1	52,660.8 --
	1992	485.6 --	516.4 --	1,864.6 ±73.1	49,794.2 ±77.7	51,658.8 ±19.8	52,660.8 --
	1997	491.8 --	526.8 --	1,962.8 ±70.5	49,679.4 ±77.0	51,642.2 ±20.8	52,660.8 --
	2002	492.2 --	536.2 --	2,036.1 ±75.8	49,596.3 ±79.3	51,632.4 ±20.3	52,660.8 --
	2007	483.3 --	551.3 --	2,093.0 ±84.3	49,533.2 ±89.1	51,626.2 ±22.1	52,660.8 --
	2012	469.4 --	555.3 --	2,123.4 ±86.2	49,512.7 ±91.3	51,636.1 ±21.8	52,660.8 --
Kentucky	1982	1,043.4 --	600.4 --	1,139.9 ±72.0	23,079.7 ±74.7	24,219.6 ±30.2	25,863.4 --
	1987	1,089.2 --	602.6 --	1,331.4 ±81.5	22,840.2 ±85.5	24,171.6 ±30.0	25,863.4 --
	1992	1,132.8 --	618.2 --	1,489.8 ±85.1	22,622.6 ±90.2	24,112.4 ±31.1	25,863.4 --
	1997	1,142.1 --	626.7 --	1,720.8 ±96.6	22,373.8 ±102.6	24,094.6 ±30.2	25,863.4 --
	2002	1,261.9 --	637.8 --	1,953.7 ±93.4	22,010.0 ±99.2	23,963.7 ±16.1	25,863.4 --
	2007	1,271.2 --	644.8 --	2,062.8 ±96.0	21,884.6 ±101.1	23,947.4 ±17.0	25,863.4 --
	2012	1,273.5 --	648.2 --	2,116.6 ±95.9	21,825.1 ±99.7	23,941.7 ±17.1	25,863.4 --
Louisiana	1982	1,047.7 --	4,348.5 --	1,252.4 ±52.7	24,728.2 ±68.0	25,980.6 ±42.0	31,376.8 --
	1987	1,106.4 --	4,409.1 --	1,396.7 ±52.9	24,464.6 ±63.7	25,861.3 ±41.7	31,376.8 --
	1992	1,175.9 --	4,446.3 --	1,484.8 ±60.3	24,269.8 ±69.7	25,754.6 ±43.3	31,376.8 --
	1997	1,177.8 --	4,439.7 --	1,627.2 ±65.6	24,132.1 ±75.9	25,759.3 ±47.8	31,376.8 --
	2002	1,229.1 --	4,475.4 --	1,755.7 ±71.5	23,916.6 ±83.6	25,672.3 ±44.0	31,376.8 --
	2007	1,228.2 --	4,564.2 --	1,838.1 ±69.6	23,746.3 ±83.3	25,584.4 ±46.7	31,376.8 --
	2012	1,244.4 --	4,576.2 --	1,900.5 ±66.8	23,655.7 ±80.5	25,556.2 ±48.2	31,376.8 --

Source: *U.S. Department of Agriculture, 2012 National Resources Inventory, Summary Report, August 2015*

Table 1 - Surface area of non-Federal and Federal land and water areas, by State and year
In thousands of acres, with margins of error

State	Year	Federal land	Water areas	Non-Federal Land			Total surface area
				Developed	Rural	Total	
Maine	1982	151.4 --	1,289.6 --	503.9 ±68.3	19,021.3 ±89.1	19,525.2 ±68.0	20,966.2 --
	1987	178.0 --	1,290.6 --	549.5 ±73.6	18,948.1 ±95.8	19,497.6 ±67.9	20,966.2 --
	1992	182.3 --	1,291.2 --	592.0 ±77.5	18,900.7 ±100.8	19,492.7 ±68.1	20,966.2 --
	1997	192.5 --	1,290.9 --	700.0 ±86.1	18,782.8 ±109.5	19,482.8 ±68.2	20,966.2 --
	2002	201.4 --	1,291.1 --	789.0 ±89.9	18,684.7 ±111.7	19,473.7 ±68.1	20,966.2 --
	2007	206.3 --	1,290.8 --	843.1 ±93.6	18,626.0 ±116.2	19,469.1 ±68.1	20,966.2 --
	2012	206.5 --	1,291.3 --	866.9 ±98.4	18,601.5 ±121.1	19,468.4 ±68.2	20,966.2 --
Maryland	1982	154.7 --	1,670.1 --	976.4 ±115.7	5,068.7 ±114.5	6,045.1 ±7.6	7,869.9 --
	1987	155.1 --	1,672.5 --	1,063.1 ±118.6	4,979.2 ±117.4	6,042.3 ±7.4	7,869.9 --
	1992	162.1 --	1,674.2 --	1,132.6 ±122.3	4,901.0 ±121.3	6,033.6 ±7.7	7,869.9 --
	1997	162.1 --	1,676.6 --	1,320.9 ±125.5	4,710.3 ±125.1	6,031.2 ±7.8	7,869.9 --
	2002	164.9 --	1,678.4 --	1,411.4 ±124.8	4,615.2 ±125.0	6,026.6 ±8.5	7,869.9 --
	2007	165.5 --	1,680.0 --	1,483.2 ±128.9	4,541.2 ±128.4	6,024.4 ±8.7	7,869.9 --
	2012	168.2 --	1,681.1 --	1,514.6 ±129.2	4,506.0 ±128.5	6,020.6 ±8.8	7,869.9 --
Massachusetts	1982	85.3 --	371.2 --	1,117.2 ±63.1	3,765.3 ±63.2	4,882.5 ±15.1	5,339.0 --
	1987	88.8 --	371.5 --	1,231.1 ±66.1	3,647.6 ±66.5	4,878.7 ±14.8	5,339.0 --
	1992	89.8 --	373.5 --	1,371.3 ±66.3	3,504.4 ±67.1	4,875.7 ±14.5	5,339.0 --
	1997	89.8 --	373.1 --	1,592.1 ±68.8	3,284.0 ±71.1	4,876.1 ±13.8	5,339.0 --
	2002	91.1 --	372.9 --	1,675.5 ±66.8	3,199.5 ±68.1	4,875.0 ±13.8	5,339.0 --
	2007	91.3 --	372.2 --	1,734.7 ±67.7	3,140.8 ±70.3	4,875.5 ±13.9	5,339.0 --
	2012	73.6 --	371.9 --	1,766.4 ±74.1	3,127.1 ±77.0	4,893.5 ±13.8	5,339.0 --

Source: U.S. Department of Agriculture, 2012 National Resources Inventory, Summary Report, August 2015

Table 1 - Surface area of non-Federal and Federal land and water areas, by State and year
In thousands of acres, with margins of error

State	Year	Federal land	Water areas	Non-Federal Land			Total surface area
				Developed	Rural	Total	
Michigan	1982	3,099.4 --	1,148.0 --	2,853.7 ±133.9	30,248.1 ±132.9	33,101.8 ±36.0	37,349.2 --
	1987	3,132.9 --	1,145.8 --	3,065.2 ±143.2	30,005.3 ±141.3	33,070.5 ±35.9	37,349.2 --
	1992	3,179.7 --	1,150.2 --	3,334.1 ±150.5	29,685.2 ±147.0	33,019.3 ±35.9	37,349.2 --
	1997	3,179.7 --	1,149.8 --	3,712.4 ±161.5	29,307.3 ±161.4	33,019.7 ±35.4	37,349.2 --
	2002	3,188.4 --	1,160.7 --	4,016.9 ±161.6	28,983.2 ±167.6	33,000.1 ±23.7	37,349.2 --
	2007	3,198.0 --	1,170.2 --	4,180.5 ±162.3	28,800.5 ±166.8	32,981.0 ±25.3	37,349.2 --
	2012	3,202.8 --	1,176.0 --	4,219.4 ±161.7	28,751.0 ±167.3	32,970.4 ±24.7	37,349.2 --
Minnesota	1982	3,402.4 --	3,169.4 --	1,716.4 ±75.1	45,721.7 ±85.1	47,438.1 ±32.7	54,009.9 --
	1987	3,416.7 --	3,177.0 --	1,840.5 ±80.3	45,575.7 ±89.5	47,416.2 ±31.7	54,009.9 --
	1992	3,410.8 --	3,180.0 --	1,952.3 ±85.2	45,466.8 ±94.8	47,419.1 ±31.6	54,009.9 --
	1997	3,412.0 --	3,177.9 --	2,176.3 ±96.0	45,243.7 ±103.4	47,420.0 ±31.7	54,009.9 --
	2002	3,427.1 --	3,184.5 --	2,289.8 ±99.2	45,108.5 ±109.3	47,398.3 ±32.6	54,009.9 --
	2007	3,407.6 --	3,187.9 --	2,371.9 ±104.6	45,042.5 ±113.3	47,414.4 ±33.2	54,009.9 --
	2012	3,434.4 --	3,190.7 --	2,415.1 ±105.6	44,969.7 ±113.2	47,384.8 ±33.7	54,009.9 --
Mississippi	1982	1,519.2 --	724.8 --	1,142.5 ±94.2	27,140.8 ±97.8	28,283.3 ±29.6	30,527.3 --
	1987	1,558.2 --	795.3 --	1,217.4 ±95.5	26,956.4 ±104.7	28,173.8 ±36.1	30,527.3 --
	1992	1,635.6 --	834.2 --	1,294.1 ±96.3	26,763.4 ±106.2	28,057.5 ±35.7	30,527.3 --
	1997	1,653.4 --	862.6 --	1,499.9 ±107.8	26,511.4 ±121.6	28,011.3 ±36.2	30,527.3 --
	2002	1,677.6 --	894.8 --	1,667.2 ±119.0	26,287.7 ±133.5	27,954.9 ±36.5	30,527.3 --
	2007	1,685.0 --	890.7 --	1,783.8 ±133.6	26,167.8 ±146.7	27,951.6 ±37.4	30,527.3 --
	2012	1,685.3 --	856.0 --	1,858.8 ±140.0	26,127.2 ±149.6	27,986.0 ±35.3	30,527.3 --

Source: *U.S. Department of Agriculture, 2012 National Resources Inventory, Summary Report, August 2015*

Table 1 - Surface area of non-Federal and Federal land and water areas, by State and year In thousands of acres, with margins of error

State	Year	Federal land	Water areas	Non-Federal Land			Total surface area
				Developed	Rural	Total	
Missouri	1982	1,999.6 --	767.4 --	2,169.1 ±95.2	39,677.8 ±97.2	41,846.9 ±19.4	44,613.9 --
	1987	1,969.4 --	799.0 --	2,277.2 ±99.3	39,568.3 ±99.9	41,845.5 ±21.1	44,613.9 --
	1992	1,983.8 --	814.1 --	2,395.3 ±102.8	39,420.7 ±104.2	41,816.0 ±21.4	44,613.9 --
	1997	2,000.5 --	827.8 --	2,634.4 ±114.1	39,151.2 ±113.6	41,785.6 ±20.5	44,613.9 --
	2002	2,009.8 --	848.2 --	2,796.7 ±119.3	38,959.2 ±114.0	41,755.9 ±18.4	44,613.9 --
	2007	2,016.3 --	866.0 --	2,927.1 ±123.9	38,804.5 ±118.2	41,731.6 ±19.3	44,613.9 --
	2012	2,018.7 --	874.3 --	2,992.9 ±127.4	38,728.0 ±121.5	41,720.9 ±19.8	44,613.9 --
Montana	1982	26,865.1 --	1,054.6 --	829.6 ±92.1	65,360.7 ±105.0	66,190.3 ±51.5	94,110.0 --
	1987	26,775.4 --	1,053.3 --	840.3 ±91.9	65,441.0 ±105.3	66,281.3 ±51.5	94,110.0 --
	1992	26,681.8 --	1,044.2 --	892.6 ±97.9	65,491.4 ±113.4	66,384.0 ±48.4	94,110.0 --
	1997	26,756.5 --	1,033.2 --	953.6 ±102.6	65,366.7 ±116.4	66,320.3 ±44.8	94,110.0 --
	2002	26,779.9 --	1,035.5 --	990.4 ±106.6	65,304.2 ±117.4	66,294.6 ±33.5	94,110.0 --
	2007	26,843.3 --	1,038.4 --	1,045.9 ±116.0	65,182.4 ±126.5	66,228.3 ±33.1	94,110.0 --
	2012	26,983.6 --	1,042.9 --	1,069.8 ±120.1	65,013.7 ±130.6	66,083.5 ±32.9	94,110.0 --
Nebraska	1982	515.3 --	473.4 --	1,040.0 ±101.8	47,480.9 ±107.1	48,520.9 ±19.6	49,509.6 --
	1987	521.8 --	481.2 --	1,053.0 ±104.3	47,453.6 ±109.3	48,506.6 ±19.2	49,509.6 --
	1992	589.2 --	483.2 --	1,070.4 ±109.3	47,366.8 ±114.5	48,437.2 ±19.3	49,509.6 --
	1997	587.3 --	487.4 --	1,117.1 ±111.9	47,317.8 ±116.8	48,434.9 ±18.8	49,509.6 --
	2002	586.9 --	492.1 --	1,145.8 ±112.4	47,284.8 ±118.0	48,430.6 ±20.4	49,509.6 --
	2007	582.8 --	494.9 --	1,175.9 ±112.1	47,256.0 ±117.3	48,431.9 ±21.1	49,509.6 --
	2012	581.2 --	497.7 --	1,189.9 ±111.6	47,240.8 ±117.8	48,430.7 ±22.5	49,509.6 --

Source: *U.S. Department of Agriculture, 2012 National Resources Inventory, Summary Report, August 2015*

Table 1 - Surface area of non-Federal and Federal land and water areas, by State and year
In thousands of acres, with margins of error

State	Year	Federal land	Water areas	Non-Federal Land			Total surface area
				Developed	Rural	Total	
Nevada	1982	59,448.6 --	393.0 --	226.9 ±54.4	10,694.6 ±56.1	10,921.5 ±6.6	70,763.1 --
	1987	59,356.9 --	399.5 --	267.3 ±61.7	10,739.4 ±64.5	11,006.7 ±6.6	70,763.1 --
	1992	59,448.0 --	400.5 --	296.8 ±62.4	10,617.8 ±65.4	10,914.6 ±6.6	70,763.1 --
	1997	59,500.4 --	400.8 --	319.3 ±64.9	10,542.6 ±67.7	10,861.9 ±6.1	70,763.1 --
	2002	59,520.5 --	400.4 --	461.6 ±84.7	10,380.6 ±86.4	10,842.2 ±16.1	70,763.1 --
	2007	59,469.8 --	401.1 --	527.6 ±95.8	10,364.6 ±97.5	10,892.2 ±16.1	70,763.1 --
	2012	59,478.6 --	401.6 --	555.0 ±97.9	10,327.9 ±98.8	10,882.9 ±16.4	70,763.1 --
New Hampshire	1982	725.8 --	232.3 --	402.1 ±43.1	4,580.8 ±46.3	4,982.9 ±12.0	5,941.0 --
	1987	726.2 --	232.5 --	499.2 ±56.5	4,483.1 ±59.3	4,982.3 ±11.9	5,941.0 --
	1992	755.3 --	233.3 --	561.6 ±58.5	4,390.8 ±61.4	4,952.4 ±12.0	5,941.0 --
	1997	763.7 --	234.3 --	629.0 ±62.6	4,314.0 ±65.7	4,943.0 ±12.0	5,941.0 --
	2002	779.2 --	234.3 --	670.2 ±61.2	4,257.3 ±65.8	4,927.5 ±11.1	5,941.0 --
	2007	788.2 --	234.6 --	714.5 ±65.5	4,203.7 ±69.8	4,918.2 ±11.0	5,941.0 --
	2012	801.8 --	234.7 --	728.7 ±65.6	4,175.8 ±69.9	4,904.5 ±11.0	5,941.0 --
New Jersey	1982	156.3 --	553.7 --	1,177.4 ±68.0	3,328.2 ±71.4	4,505.6 ±9.4	5,215.6 --
	1987	159.1 --	555.5 --	1,385.1 ±72.8	3,115.9 ±77.3	4,501.0 ±9.2	5,215.6 --
	1992	169.4 --	558.7 --	1,454.2 ±71.4	3,033.3 ±75.5	4,487.5 ±9.4	5,215.6 --
	1997	169.4 --	562.0 --	1,652.5 ±75.2	2,831.7 ±78.3	4,484.2 ±8.5	5,215.6 --
	2002	175.0 --	562.9 --	1,771.5 ±78.6	2,706.2 ±81.9	4,477.7 ±8.4	5,215.6 --
	2007	176.7 --	563.5 --	1,824.6 ±80.0	2,650.8 ±83.3	4,475.4 ±8.7	5,215.6 --
	2012	177.6 --	563.6 --	1,848.0 ±79.9	2,626.4 ±83.6	4,474.4 ±9.3	5,215.6 --

Source: *U.S. Department of Agriculture, 2012 National Resources Inventory, Summary Report, August 2015*

Table 1 - Surface area of non-Federal and Federal land and water areas, by State and year
In thousands of acres, with margins of error

State	Year	Federal land	Water areas	Non-Federal Land			Total surface area
				Developed	Rural	Total	
New Mexico	1982	25,459.1 --	162.4 --	713.7 ±96.3	51,488.1 ±99.0	52,201.8 ±16.0	77,823.3 --
	1987	25,987.5 --	163.0 --	778.8 ±103.0	50,894.0 ±107.4	51,672.8 ±16.1	77,823.3 --
	1992	26,251.5 --	159.2 --	836.8 ±113.5	50,575.8 ±117.2	51,412.6 ±16.2	77,823.3 --
	1997	26,262.3 --	164.4 --	1,009.4 ±124.1	50,387.2 ±127.5	51,396.6 ±15.7	77,823.3 --
	2002	26,344.2 --	166.9 --	1,224.7 ±155.6	50,087.5 ±157.5	51,312.2 ±16.2	77,823.3 --
	2007	26,349.0 --	167.0 --	1,285.1 ±161.2	50,022.2 ±163.9	51,307.3 ±16.1	77,823.3 --
	2012	26,355.1 --	166.9 --	1,327.9 ±163.4	49,973.4 ±166.5	51,301.3 ±16.1	77,823.3 --
New York	1982	234.4 --	1,392.3 --	2,831.9 ±122.1	26,950.5 ±124.5	29,782.4 ±19.5	31,409.1 --
	1987	233.8 --	1,393.7 --	2,938.4 ±128.1	26,843.2 ±130.4	29,781.6 ±19.5	31,409.1 --
	1992	224.0 --	1,399.7 --	3,084.0 ±132.9	26,701.4 ±134.7	29,785.4 ±19.8	31,409.1 --
	1997	232.5 --	1,404.4 --	3,429.6 ±142.9	26,342.6 ±144.8	29,772.2 ±21.2	31,409.1 --
	2002	214.0 --	1,416.6 --	3,671.9 ±152.4	26,106.6 ±155.4	29,778.5 ±23.8	31,409.1 --
	2007	212.0 --	1,421.3 --	3,783.2 ±152.8	25,992.6 ±154.6	29,775.8 ±23.4	31,409.1 --
	2012	212.5 --	1,423.5 --	3,844.2 ±154.8	25,928.9 ±157.2	29,773.1 ±22.7	31,409.1 --
North Carolina	1982	2,037.0 --	2,734.4 --	2,359.2 ±109.8	26,578.7 ±103.5	28,937.9 ±16.4	33,709.3 --
	1987	2,191.8 --	2,751.1 --	2,782.5 ±120.9	25,983.9 ±114.4	28,766.4 ±17.2	33,709.3 --
	1992	2,362.6 --	2,758.3 --	3,255.0 ±144.0	25,333.4 ±139.6	28,588.4 ±17.7	33,709.3 --
	1997	2,363.5 --	2,766.6 --	3,735.2 ±166.8	24,844.0 ±165.2	28,579.2 ±20.3	33,709.3 --
	2002	2,371.0 --	2,780.2 --	4,391.4 ±196.2	24,166.7 ±194.6	28,558.1 ±21.4	33,709.3 --
	2007	2,377.9 --	2,788.7 --	4,663.9 ±203.1	23,878.8 ±202.2	28,542.7 ±20.7	33,709.3 --
	2012	2,380.8 --	2,795.4 --	4,802.6 ±208.5	23,730.5 ±207.7	28,533.1 ±21.2	33,709.3 --

Source: *U.S. Department of Agriculture, 2012 National Resources Inventory, Summary Report, August 2015*

Table 1 - Surface area of non-Federal and Federal land and water areas, by State and year In thousands of acres, with margins of error

State	Year	Federal land	Water areas	Non-Federal Land			Total surface area
				Developed	Rural	Total	
North Dakota	1982	1,706.1 --	1,034.6 --	894.6 ±65.2	41,615.4 ±92.0	42,510.0 ±45.0	45,250.7 --
	1987	1,722.2 --	1,031.9 --	903.1 ±65.9	41,593.5 ±92.0	42,496.6 ±45.3	45,250.7 --
	1992	1,764.0 --	1,031.0 --	916.4 ±64.9	41,539.3 ±91.6	42,455.7 ±45.1	45,250.7 --
	1997	1,763.9 --	1,162.9 --	944.2 ±65.4	41,379.7 ±91.4	42,323.9 ±44.8	45,250.7 --
	2002	1,765.3 --	1,206.8 --	956.6 ±71.1	41,322.0 ±73.4	42,278.6 ±17.7	45,250.7 --
	2007	1,771.7 --	1,208.2 --	966.5 ±73.1	41,304.3 ±74.8	42,270.8 ±18.5	45,250.7 --
	2012	1,766.0 --	1,258.3 --	1,012.5 ±76.4	41,213.9 ±78.9	42,226.4 ±18.9	45,250.7 --
Ohio	1982	298.8 --	391.9 --	2,862.3 ±119.5	22,891.8 ±120.0	25,754.1 ±17.7	26,444.8 --
	1987	295.8 --	396.1 --	3,067.0 ±122.6	22,685.9 ±123.6	25,752.9 ±17.3	26,444.8 --
	1992	321.1 --	400.3 --	3,335.6 ±134.0	22,387.8 ±135.4	25,723.4 ±17.5	26,444.8 --
	1997	323.2 --	400.3 --	3,705.2 ±147.0	22,016.1 ±148.3	25,721.3 ±18.9	26,444.8 --
	2002	330.9 --	411.0 --	3,920.0 ±145.3	21,782.9 ±148.8	25,702.9 ±14.6	26,444.8 --
	2007	336.6 --	419.0 --	4,109.9 ±152.2	21,579.3 ±156.5	25,689.2 ±16.2	26,444.8 --
	2012	359.1 --	423.6 --	4,178.3 ±155.3	21,483.8 ±159.6	25,662.1 ±16.1	26,444.8 --
Oklahoma	1982	1,071.2 --	1,002.7 --	1,493.5 ±90.4	41,170.7 ±100.1	42,664.2 ±28.2	44,738.1 --
	1987	1,058.3 --	1,019.2 --	1,569.6 ±89.5	41,091.0 ±98.2	42,660.6 ±25.2	44,738.1 --
	1992	1,057.9 --	1,041.4 --	1,635.0 ±95.8	41,003.8 ±102.3	42,638.8 ±28.8	44,738.1 --
	1997	1,175.8 --	1,051.4 --	1,784.2 ±107.8	40,726.7 ±113.1	42,510.9 ±29.8	44,738.1 --
	2002	1,183.0 --	1,073.2 --	1,948.8 ±116.6	40,533.1 ±122.6	42,481.9 ±33.3	44,738.1 --
	2007	1,185.0 --	1,088.9 --	2,077.2 ±117.6	40,387.0 ±123.2	42,464.2 ±31.9	44,738.1 --
	2012	1,186.0 --	1,097.0 --	2,187.3 ±117.4	40,267.8 ±123.9	42,455.1 ±32.5	44,738.1 --

Source: *U.S. Department of Agriculture, 2012 National Resources Inventory, Summary Report, August 2015*

Table 1 - Surface area of non-Federal and Federal land and water areas, by State and year
In thousands of acres, with margins of error

State	Year	Federal land	Water areas	Non-Federal Land			Total surface area
				Developed	Rural	Total	
Oregon	1982	31,852.3 --	834.1 --	978.2 ±102.5	28,496.4 ±103.0	29,474.6 ±41.2	62,161.0 --
	1987	31,923.9 --	834.7 --	1,070.0 ±113.2	28,332.4 ±111.4	29,402.4 ±40.0	62,161.0 --
	1992	32,095.0 --	710.1 --	1,148.9 ±117.4	28,207.0 ±113.7	29,355.9 ±40.2	62,161.0 --
	1997	32,153.6 --	846.5 --	1,257.3 ±124.1	27,903.6 ±121.7	29,160.9 ±40.1	62,161.0 --
	2002	32,087.1 --	849.4 --	1,325.5 ±132.1	27,899.0 ±136.0	29,224.5 ±19.4	62,161.0 --
	2007	32,094.6 --	850.3 --	1,410.7 ±134.3	27,805.4 ±137.7	29,216.1 ±19.2	62,161.0 --
	2012	32,108.5 --	851.0 --	1,429.4 ±134.8	27,772.1 ±138.2	29,201.5 ±19.5	62,161.0 --
Pennsylvania	1982	672.8 --	469.2 --	2,766.7 ±102.5	25,086.5 ±110.5	27,853.2 ±19.2	28,995.2 --
	1987	674.1 --	470.5 --	2,947.7 ±111.7	24,902.9 ±121.1	27,850.6 ±19.6	28,995.2 --
	1992	676.8 --	473.4 --	3,378.1 ±129.1	24,466.9 ±136.3	27,845.0 ±19.2	28,995.2 --
	1997	676.8 --	474.8 --	3,914.2 ±145.4	23,929.4 ±151.0	27,843.6 ±18.5	28,995.2 --
	2002	677.0 --	479.5 --	4,167.3 ±155.6	23,671.4 ±158.8	27,838.7 ±37.5	28,995.2 --
	2007	677.3 --	482.5 --	4,330.0 ±165.0	23,505.4 ±168.0	27,835.4 ±37.3	28,995.2 --
	2012	679.9 --	483.7 --	4,410.5 ±166.9	23,421.1 ±170.6	27,831.6 ±37.5	28,995.2 --
Rhode Island	1982	8.6 --	151.9 --	171.1 ±12.7	481.7 ±13.0	652.8 ±2.4	813.3 --
	1987	8.8 --	151.7 --	180.8 ±13.6	472.0 ±14.0	652.8 ±2.3	813.3 --
	1992	9.4 --	152.0 --	198.2 ±14.0	453.7 ±14.3	651.9 ±2.3	813.3 --
	1997	6.1 --	151.9 --	204.8 ±14.1	450.5 ±14.4	655.3 ±2.2	813.3 --
	2002	3.9 --	152.0 --	219.3 ±14.5	438.1 ±14.7	657.4 ±2.4	813.3 --
	2007	4.0 --	152.1 --	227.7 ±15.8	429.5 ±16.0	657.2 ±2.4	813.3 --
	2012	4.0 --	152.1 --	231.0 ±15.4	426.2 ±15.7	657.2 ±2.4	813.3 --

***Source:** U.S. Department of Agriculture, 2012 National Resources Inventory, Summary Report, August 2015*

Table 1 - Surface area of non-Federal and Federal land and water areas, by State and year
In thousands of acres, with margins of error

State	Year	Federal land	Water areas	Non-Federal Land			Total surface area
				Developed	Rural	Total	
South Carolina	1982	1,009.8 --	783.0 --	1,361.1 ±79.6	16,785.4 ±82.3	18,146.5 ±19.5	19,939.3 --
	1987	1,006.7 --	792.4 --	1,527.6 ±91.1	16,612.6 ±92.1	18,140.2 ±19.4	19,939.3 --
	1992	1,013.7 --	795.4 --	1,753.8 ±100.3	16,376.4 ±101.7	18,130.2 ±19.9	19,939.3 --
	1997	1,013.7 --	798.3 --	2,115.5 ±106.6	16,011.8 ±109.5	18,127.3 ±20.1	19,939.3 --
	2002	1,028.2 --	810.4 --	2,423.5 ±102.0	15,677.2 ±104.4	18,100.7 ±17.4	19,939.3 --
	2007	1,046.8 --	819.4 --	2,595.3 ±107.5	15,477.8 ±110.0	18,073.1 ±18.3	19,939.3 --
	2012	1,050.9 --	825.3 --	2,692.0 ±107.1	15,371.1 ±109.2	18,063.1 ±18.4	19,939.3 --
South Dakota	1982	2,693.9 --	876.6 --	810.0 ±64.2	44,977.5 ±67.4	45,787.5 ±14.8	49,358.0 --
	1987	2,729.4 --	883.9 --	815.8 ±66.5	44,928.9 ±69.9	45,744.7 ±14.7	49,358.0 --
	1992	2,771.2 --	886.2 --	868.4 ±91.4	44,832.2 ±94.9	45,700.6 ±15.1	49,358.0 --
	1997	2,771.2 --	890.8 --	919.4 ±101.1	44,776.6 ±104.8	45,696.0 ±14.7	49,358.0 --
	2002	2,773.8 --	890.8 --	935.1 ±104.2	44,758.3 ±106.8	45,693.4 ±15.3	49,358.0 --
	2007	2,776.1 --	892.4 --	954.1 ±107.4	44,735.4 ±110.6	45,689.5 ±15.2	49,358.0 --
	2012	2,782.6 --	893.9 --	961.7 ±108.4	44,719.8 ±111.5	45,681.5 ±15.3	49,358.0 --
Tennessee	1982	1,289.6 --	752.5 --	1,656.4 ±102.9	23,275.1 ±108.0	24,931.5 ±22.8	26,973.6 --
	1987	1,311.3 --	754.4 --	1,893.9 ±110.1	23,014.0 ±113.9	24,907.9 ±21.6	26,973.6 --
	1992	1,309.6 --	762.7 --	2,180.2 ±115.5	22,721.1 ±119.8	24,901.3 ±20.4	26,973.6 --
	1997	1,309.6 --	767.6 --	2,630.8 ±131.5	22,265.6 ±136.4	24,896.4 ±21.0	26,973.6 --
	2002	1,384.4 --	776.4 --	2,831.1 ±140.1	21,981.7 ±140.5	24,812.8 ±10.7	26,973.6 --
	2007	1,391.0 --	782.4 --	3,025.5 ±151.4	21,774.7 ±152.7	24,800.2 ±12.1	26,973.6 --
	2012	1,406.3 --	787.5 --	3,115.8 ±154.9	21,664.0 ±156.2	24,779.8 ±11.8	26,973.6 --

Source: *U.S. Department of Agriculture, 2012 National Resources Inventory, Summary Report, August 2015*

Table 1 - Surface area of non-Federal and Federal land and water areas, by State and year
In thousands of acres, with margins of error

State	Year	Federal land	Water areas	Non-Federal Land			Total surface area
				Developed	Rural	Total	
Texas	1982	2,823.9 --	3,779.0 --	5,188.0 ±190.0	159,261.0 ±195.0	164,449.0 ±44.7	171,051.9 --
	1987	2,867.9 --	3,921.3 --	5,703.2 ±206.3	158,559.5 ±207.1	164,262.7 ±48.3	171,051.9 --
	1992	2,965.0 --	4,044.4 --	6,249.0 ±243.1	157,793.5 ±239.1	164,042.5 ±49.9	171,051.9 --
	1997	2,966.6 --	4,124.7 --	6,922.4 ±257.8	157,038.2 ±258.8	163,960.6 ±47.1	171,051.9 --
	2002	3,021.2 --	4,160.2 --	7,749.1 ±275.6	156,121.4 ±280.6	163,870.5 ±46.6	171,051.9 --
	2007	3,053.8 --	4,206.2 --	8,490.9 ±287.6	155,301.0 ±297.1	163,791.9 ±55.1	171,051.9 --
	2012	3,086.7 --	4,235.2 --	8,936.6 ±312.7	154,793.4 ±325.3	163,730.0 ±58.3	171,051.9 --
Utah	1982	34,290.0 --	1,506.4 --	454.8 ±90.5	18,087.7 ±112.2	18,542.5 ±39.5	54,338.9 --
	1987	34,007.7 --	2,095.3 --	496.8 ±99.0	17,739.1 ±119.4	18,235.9 ±39.4	54,338.9 --
	1992	34,204.8 --	1,525.4 --	556.0 ±109.6	18,052.7 ±127.5	18,608.7 ±39.2	54,338.9 --
	1997	34,607.8 --	1,539.6 --	633.7 ±120.4	17,557.8 ±136.9	18,191.5 ±39.6	54,338.9 --
	2002	34,824.1 --	1,539.5 --	735.2 ±130.7	17,240.1 ±151.4	17,975.3 ±31.7	54,338.9 --
	2007	34,835.8 --	1,539.5 --	816.3 ±138.8	17,147.3 ±158.6	17,963.6 ±31.8	54,338.9 --
	2012	34,842.0 --	1,540.1 --	866.6 ±141.7	17,090.2 ±161.3	17,956.8 ±32.0	54,338.9 --
Vermont	1982	315.8 --	267.3 --	263.8 ±24.8	5,306.7 ±33.5	5,570.5 ±16.9	6,153.6 --
	1987	348.4 --	267.8 --	305.7 ±25.7	5,231.7 ±33.0	5,537.4 ±16.9	6,153.6 --
	1992	368.5 --	268.2 --	334.2 ±26.7	5,182.7 ±34.2	5,516.9 ±16.8	6,153.6 --
	1997	395.1 --	267.4 --	347.2 ±26.8	5,143.9 ±34.9	5,491.1 ±16.7	6,153.6 --
	2002	440.1 --	267.7 --	370.5 ±28.0	5,075.3 ±29.8	5,445.8 ±5.3	6,153.6 --
	2007	452.6 --	268.1 --	389.3 ±30.1	5,043.6 ±31.9	5,432.9 ±5.5	6,153.6 --
	2012	455.6 --	268.7 --	398.9 ±31.5	5,030.4 ±33.1	5,429.3 ±5.8	6,153.6 --

Source: *U.S. Department of Agriculture, 2012 National Resources Inventory, Summary Report, August 2015*

Table 1 - Surface area of non-Federal and Federal land and water areas, by State and year
In thousands of acres, with margins of error

State	Year	Federal land	Water areas	Non-Federal Land			Total surface area
				Developed	Rural	Total	
Virginia	1982	2,290.9 --	1,883.1 --	1,829.8 ±107.5	21,083.3 ±106.8	22,913.1 ±13.1	27,087.1 --
	1987	2,308.8 --	1,884.8 --	2,069.6 ±108.2	20,823.9 ±107.1	22,893.5 ±13.3	27,087.1 --
	1992	2,329.1 --	1,892.2 --	2,270.2 ±115.2	20,595.6 ±114.0	22,865.8 ±13.6	27,087.1 --
	1997	2,330.8 --	1,893.2 --	2,608.5 ±110.2	20,254.6 ±110.0	22,863.1 ±14.5	27,087.1 --
	2002	2,347.7 --	1,898.1 --	2,865.0 ±109.4	19,976.3 ±112.1	22,841.3 ±42.0	27,087.1 --
	2007	2,353.8 --	1,905.6 --	3,051.6 ±109.7	19,776.1 ±112.4	22,827.7 ±42.0	27,087.1 --
	2012	2,354.4 --	1,910.5 --	3,158.2 ±112.8	19,664.0 ±117.5	22,822.2 ±42.4	27,087.1 --
Washington	1982	12,401.1 --	1,569.9 --	1,613.8 ±148.4	28,450.5 ±156.3	30,064.3 ±20.8	44,035.3 --
	1987	12,420.6 --	1,570.7 --	1,694.9 ±149.4	28,349.1 ±156.7	30,044.0 ±20.5	44,035.3 --
	1992	12,424.6 --	1,570.2 --	1,920.4 ±163.3	28,120.1 ±169.8	30,040.5 ±21.0	44,035.3 --
	1997	12,426.2 --	1,570.7 --	2,173.0 ±179.4	27,865.4 ±185.4	30,038.4 ±19.5	44,035.3 --
	2002	12,512.0 --	1,575.1 --	2,359.8 ±185.8	27,588.4 ±191.4	29,948.2 ±21.9	44,035.3 --
	2007	12,536.7 --	1,576.7 --	2,490.2 ±180.8	27,431.7 ±185.8	29,921.9 ±22.0	44,035.3 --
	2012	12,546.2 --	1,579.4 --	2,540.5 ±180.7	27,369.2 ±184.8	29,909.7 ±21.8	44,035.3 --
West Virginia	1982	1,137.0 --	160.3 --	633.0 ±44.7	13,577.9 ±48.3	14,210.9 ±9.1	15,508.2 --
	1987	1,150.5 --	161.0 --	675.9 ±46.7	13,520.8 ±50.2	14,196.7 ±9.1	15,508.2 --
	1992	1,240.8 --	164.7 --	759.5 ±51.7	13,343.2 ±54.3	14,102.7 ±8.8	15,508.2 --
	1997	1,241.5 --	168.0 --	961.4 ±60.5	13,137.3 ±63.6	14,098.7 ±9.4	15,508.2 --
	2002	1,257.2 --	175.1 --	1,076.2 ±60.4	12,999.7 ±62.7	14,075.9 ±10.2	15,508.2 --
	2007	1,267.5 --	176.7 --	1,126.5 ±62.3	12,937.5 ±64.4	14,064.0 ±10.4	15,508.2 --
	2012	1,270.2 --	177.2 --	1,147.0 ±61.0	12,913.8 ±63.1	14,060.8 ±10.4	15,508.2 --

Source: *U.S. Department of Agriculture, 2012 National Resources Inventory, Summary Report, August 2015*

Table 1 - Surface area of non-Federal and Federal land and water areas, by State and year
In thousands of acres, with margins of error

State	Year	Federal land	Water areas	Non-Federal Land			Total surface area
				Developed	Rural	Total	
Wisconsin	1982	1,775.4 --	1,290.5 --	1,984.5 ±102.5	30,869.6 ±111.3	32,854.1 ±29.0	35,920.0 --
	1987	1,782.3 --	1,292.4 --	2,098.3 ±109.2	30,747.0 ±118.1	32,845.3 ±30.5	35,920.0 --
	1992	1,810.4 --	1,290.9 --	2,222.9 ±113.2	30,595.8 ±121.5	32,818.7 ±29.2	35,920.0 --
	1997	1,811.5 --	1,286.6 --	2,406.7 ±122.9	30,415.2 ±130.0	32,821.9 ±29.7	35,920.0 --
	2002	1,812.1 --	1,290.4 --	2,549.2 ±139.5	30,268.3 ±145.4	32,817.5 ±29.5	35,920.0 --
	2007	1,819.0 --	1,294.7 --	2,685.4 ±148.4	30,120.9 ±154.0	32,806.3 ±28.9	35,920.0 --
	2012	1,824.5 --	1,299.1 --	2,752.6 ±152.0	30,043.8 ±157.4	32,796.4 ±29.6	35,920.0 --
Wyoming	1982	29,505.1 --	466.5 --	537.5 ±67.5	32,093.7 ±65.8	32,631.2 ±14.5	62,602.8 --
	1987	29,504.8 --	468.4 --	580.9 ±68.7	32,048.7 ±69.9	32,629.6 ±15.4	62,602.8 --
	1992	29,552.5 --	469.4 --	592.3 ±70.6	31,988.6 ±72.1	32,580.9 ±15.6	62,602.8 --
	1997	29,566.3 --	469.4 --	624.4 ±73.2	31,942.7 ±75.9	32,567.1 ±15.7	62,602.8 --
	2002	29,546.4 --	471.4 --	644.7 ±75.0	31,940.3 ±76.9	32,585.0 ±19.2	62,602.8 --
	2007	29,559.8 --	474.7 --	732.4 ±118.6	31,835.9 ±120.4	32,568.3 ±20.5	62,602.8 --
	2012	29,558.8 --	477.5 --	754.1 ±119.9	31,812.4 ±121.9	32,566.5 ±21.1	62,602.8 --
Total	1982	398,167.5 --	49,752.4 --	71,925.4 ±756.8	1,424,297.3 ±830.8	1,496,222.7 ±210.2	1,944,142.6 --
	1987	398,699.0 --	50,821.9 --	77,941.7 ±836.4	1,416,680.0 ±903.9	1,494,621.7 ±209.3	1,944,142.6 --
	1992	400,989.0 --	50,536.5 --	85,169.9 ±970.6	1,407,447.2 ±1,007.1	1,492,617.1 ±205.1	1,944,142.6 --
	1997	402,555.9 --	51,062.4 --	95,901.2 ±1,016.4	1,394,623.1 ±1,059.9	1,490,524.3 ±219.6	1,944,142.6 --
	2002	404,112.7 --	51,546.3 --	104,875.6 ±1,186.5	1,383,608.0 ±1,209.5	1,488,483.6 ±284.5	1,944,142.6 --
	2007	404,786.4 --	51,912.1 --	111,080.8 ±1,238.1	1,376,363.3 ±1,259.6	1,487,444.1 ±280.5	1,944,142.6 --
	2012	405,278.4 --	52,103.0 --	114,112.5 ±1,271.6	1,372,648.7 ±1,295.2	1,486,761.2 ±271.4	1,944,142.6 --

Source: *U.S. Department of Agriculture, 2012 National Resources Inventory, Summary Report, August 2015*

Table 1 - Surface area of non-Federal and Federal land and water areas, by State and year
In thousands of acres, with margins of error

State	Year	Federal land	Water areas	Non-Federal Land			Total surface area
				Developed	Rural	Total	

Notes:
• Acreages for Federal land, water areas, and total surface area are established through geospatial processes and administrative records; therefore, statistical margins of error are not applicable and shown as a dashed line (--).

Source: U.S. Department of Agriculture, 2012 National Resources Inventory, Summary Report, August 2015

Table 2 - Land Cover/use of non-Federal rural land, by State and year
In thousands of acres, with margins of error

State	Year	Cropland	CRP land	Pastureland	Rangeland	Forest land	Other rural land	Total rural land
Alabama	1982	4,474.3 ±179.7	--	3,789.4 ±199.2	70.3 ±53.4	20,855.8 ±184.0	524.4 ±77.1	29,714.2 ±113.8
	1987	3,947.7 ±187.8	207.5 --	3,641.3 ±169.7	70.4 ±51.9	21,143.4 ±178.0	492.4 ±71.2	29,502.7 ±117.3
	1992	3,130.0 ±190.9	528.8 --	3,761.1 ±161.4	70.3 ±51.9	21,235.8 ±180.9	607.9 ±84.5	29,333.9 ±124.9
	1997	2,916.3 ±209.7	522.2 --	3,556.2 ±150.0	71.6 ±52.9	21,312.5 ±199.0	594.0 ±76.3	28,972.8 ±139.5
	2002	2,499.7 ±193.1	466.1 --	3,482.1 ±216.2	68.8 ±143.3	21,541.6 ±245.1	512.3 ±104.8	28,570.6 ±221.1
	2007	2,239.4 ±184.5	330.7 --	3,473.1 ±196.5	68.8 ±143.3	21,665.6 ±240.2	579.7 ±111.7	28,357.3 ±236.4
	2012	2,322.5 ±217.4	309.0 --	3,193.4 ±246.3	68.8 ±143.3	21,759.7 ±236.9	631.4 ±112.4	28,284.8 ±237.3
Arizona	1982	1,245.3 ±140.8	--	81.6 ±50.4	33,179.3 ±937.2	4,709.5 ±928.6	1,963.0 ±528.6	41,178.7 ±270.0
	1987	1,233.0 ±139.8	0.0 --	74.7 ±39.4	33,212.8 ±931.5	4,688.6 ±930.2	2,025.3 ±536.8	41,234.4 ±287.3
	1992	1,215.0 ±137.0	0.0 --	78.5 ±34.4	33,593.2 ±962.1	4,569.1 ±948.6	2,048.3 ±516.5	41,504.1 ±294.9
	1997	1,212.8 ±136.7	0.0 --	72.5 ±33.5	33,252.0 ±1,010.7	4,490.1 ±957.6	2,182.5 ±510.4	41,209.9 ±308.8
	2002	936.1 ±151.4	0.0 --	72.4 ±52.2	33,200.1 ±1,188.7	4,359.0 ±971.0	2,152.9 ±559.6	40,720.5 ±373.8
	2007	902.5 ±142.7	0.0 --	71.5 ±50.3	33,031.6 ±1,186.8	4,341.2 ±967.6	2,139.7 ±546.5	40,486.5 ±401.2
	2012	890.1 ±149.9	0.0 --	62.0 ±47.7	32,958.0 ±1,191.0	4,342.8 ±968.3	2,117.8 ±544.3	40,370.7 ±416.9
Arkansas	1982	8,043.0 ±444.2	--	5,581.0 ±326.4	15.3 ±15.3	14,865.9 ±451.2	316.9 ±41.8	28,822.1 ±102.3
	1987	7,915.7 ±437.3	95.4 --	5,553.4 ±321.4	15.3 ±15.3	14,831.2 ±452.2	329.5 ±39.5	28,740.5 ±107.4
	1992	7,675.0 ±440.5	227.8 --	5,489.6 ±322.2	11.4 ±13.5	14,870.9 ±451.5	340.0 ±40.0	28,614.7 ±110.5
	1997	7,586.4 ±433.3	230.4 --	5,270.9 ±296.0	11.4 ±13.5	14,941.0 ±458.2	361.2 ±52.3	28,401.3 ±115.2
	2002	7,505.3 ±456.8	162.2 --	5,241.1 ±313.1	20.1 ±56.0	14,918.8 ±463.7	374.2 ±62.1	28,221.7 ±126.4
	2007	7,301.9 ±442.8	134.3 --	5,224.5 ±332.7	20.1 ±56.0	15,040.6 ±485.3	390.9 ±66.9	28,112.3 ±132.9
	2012	7,142.0 ±446.1	115.1 --	5,296.3 ±337.6	20.1 ±56.0	15,067.7 ±480.3	394.3 ±63.0	28,035.5 ±134.7

Source: *U.S. Department of Agriculture, 2012 National Resources Inventory, Summary Report, August 2015*

Table 2 - Land Cover/use of non-Federal rural land, by State and year
In thousands of acres, with margins of error

State	Year	Cropland	CRP land	Pastureland	Rangeland	Forest land	Other rural land	Total rural land
California	1982	10,507.6 ±556.5	--	1,263.8 ±207.9	20,772.3 ±1,142.4	14,952.0 ±765.2	2,268.8 ±438.1	49,764.5 ±352.8
	1987	10,240.2 ±609.8	68.9 --	1,365.2 ±241.0	20,518.6 ±1,185.2	14,986.3 ±790.5	2,297.0 ±445.7	49,476.2 ±365.3
	1992	10,003.9 ±575.7	185.0 --	1,086.8 ±238.3	19,930.4 ±1,105.9	14,776.5 ±793.5	2,368.5 ±432.6	48,351.1 ±372.1
	1997	9,682.5 ±607.2	173.0 --	1,041.2 ±237.1	19,887.0 ±1,139.7	14,556.1 ±792.9	2,463.8 ±430.8	47,803.6 ±375.8
	2002	9,401.3 ±657.7	188.9 --	1,222.0 ±263.8	19,121.2 ±1,038.8	14,362.7 ±703.8	2,537.9 ±575.5	46,834.0 ±403.6
	2007	9,187.8 ±658.4	139.4 --	1,163.0 ±298.3	19,011.2 ±1,053.1	14,207.7 ±703.0	2,586.1 ±559.2	46,295.2 ±408.1
	2012	9,139.2 ±653.3	90.2 --	1,185.1 ±193.4	18,891.3 ±1,068.2	14,166.5 ±691.6	2,573.0 ±577.5	46,045.3 ±413.0
Caribbean	1982	402.0 ±30.1	--	764.9 ±45.7	147.9 ±18.0	525.9 ±41.5	45.9 ±12.6	1,886.6 ±29.3
	1987	371.1 ±28.9	0.0 --	751.6 ±41.9	144.2 ±18.2	526.1 ±40.9	51.5 ±12.0	1,844.5 ±28.8
	1992	356.2 ±33.4	0.0 --	686.2 ±37.0	137.5 ±16.9	527.2 ±37.3	56.2 ±11.3	1,763.3 ±31.1
	1997	354.4 ±30.3	0.0 --	452.7 ±28.9	138.4 ±17.8	637.6 ±39.7	62.1 ±13.3	1,645.2 ±29.9
	2002	338.9 ±34.3	0.0 --	418.0 ±33.3	134.4 ±23.4	655.8 ±45.0	67.6 ±17.4	1,614.7 ±41.5
	2007	257.9 ±42.5	0.0 --	443.5 ±46.9	129.1 ±24.2	700.0 ±51.9	63.6 ±15.2	1,594.1 ±43.1
	2012	237.9 ±50.8	0.0 --	370.0 ±45.8	127.0 ±23.7	792.2 ±56.1	48.2 ±14.2	1,575.3 ±43.9
Colorado	1982	10,650.6 ±626.2	--	1,077.0 ±130.7	25,447.3 ±762.9	3,750.9 ±438.9	670.0 ±141.1	41,595.8 ±124.1
	1987	9,746.7 ±654.0	1,113.8 --	1,077.8 ±129.7	24,949.7 ±772.3	3,717.6 ±437.9	712.8 ±152.3	41,318.4 ±149.2
	1992	8,912.0 ±606.2	1,912.6 --	1,122.5 ±139.4	24,865.3 ±777.2	3,548.4 ±454.0	736.0 ±135.2	41,096.8 ±157.8
	1997	8,804.2 ±590.6	1,890.1 --	1,129.6 ±138.2	24,791.5 ±761.3	3,485.4 ±448.8	716.8 ±138.5	40,817.6 ±171.6
	2002	8,243.2 ±581.3	2,203.0 --	946.6 ±177.5	25,013.4 ±709.1	3,396.1 ±422.5	760.4 ±175.3	40,562.7 ±191.8
	2007	7,787.5 ±561.4	2,446.6 --	1,044.6 ±195.0	24,956.6 ±701.6	3,380.3 ±425.3	772.3 ±173.1	40,387.9 ±200.1
	2012	7,953.0 ±544.0	2,125.9 --	1,268.7 ±214.2	24,821.0 ±711.6	3,370.5 ±426.2	759.0 ±164.4	40,298.1 ±201.6

Source: *U.S. Department of Agriculture, 2012 National Resources Inventory, Summary Report, August 2015*

Table 2 - Land Cover/use of non-Federal rural land, by State and year
In thousands of acres, with margins of error

State	Year	Cropland	CRP land	Pastureland	Rangeland	Forest land	Other rural land	Total rural land
Connecticut	1982	233.7	--	122.0	0.0	1,761.0	103.5	2,220.2
		±38.9		±25.4	--	±59.3	±22.5	±34.1
	1987	220.3	0.0	122.3	0.0	1,719.9	101.3	2,163.8
		±35.4	--	±28.3	--	±56.5	±22.3	±34.3
	1992	215.8	0.0	110.9	0.0	1,692.6	99.0	2,118.3
		±34.6	--	±21.3	--	±55.8	±20.2	±35.6
	1997	197.5	0.0	104.3	0.0	1,674.8	95.5	2,072.1
		±32.9	--	±21.0	--	±53.4	±19.1	±34.3
	2002	175.9	0.0	109.3	0.0	1,633.8	97.8	2,016.8
		±32.3	--	±21.9	--	±54.9	±18.9	±38.2
	2007	173.2	0.0	96.7	0.0	1,613.8	100.5	1,984.2
		±31.2	--	±21.2	--	±58.5	±19.3	±38.8
	2012	173.0	0.0	90.6	0.0	1,604.2	103.0	1,970.8
		±31.6	--	±21.9	--	±60.4	±19.5	±39.0
Delaware	1982	520.1	--	34.4	0.0	374.5	120.0	1,049.0
		±37.4		±11.4	--	±42.6	±25.9	±26.8
	1987	513.2	0.0	28.5	0.0	370.8	119.2	1,031.7
		±36.4	--	±9.6	--	±44.5	±25.8	±29.1
	1992	502.5	0.8	25.5	0.0	364.4	121.2	1,014.4
		±37.1	--	±7.7	--	±43.3	±25.2	±30.1
	1997	485.8	0.8	24.0	0.0	356.9	125.2	992.7
		±35.0	--	±8.8	--	±40.3	±25.0	±31.3
	2002	459.9	1.3	26.1	0.0	347.0	122.3	956.6
		±36.0	--	±7.6	--	±38.3	±26.6	±33.9
	2007	417.1	1.8	33.4	0.0	339.9	135.3	927.5
		±37.6	--	±9.7	--	±37.7	±29.6	±37.5
	2012	410.8	0.5	33.3	0.0	340.5	128.8	913.9
		±38.1	--	±11.8	--	±39.0	±27.0	±39.5
Florida	1982	3,577.7	--	4,388.8	4,299.9	13,374.5	2,358.9	27,999.8
		±237.8		±246.0	±327.2	±359.7	±316.5	±231.6
	1987	3,202.0	93.7	4,682.1	3,958.2	13,327.0	2,381.5	27,644.5
		±253.6	--	±289.7	±336.8	±371.5	±318.5	±241.4
	1992	3,051.0	123.9	4,598.1	3,408.9	13,280.9	2,385.3	26,848.1
		±268.3	--	±303.3	±301.9	±366.7	±329.7	±260.3
	1997	2,783.3	120.0	4,518.8	3,122.3	13,200.2	2,414.8	26,159.4
		±273.5	--	±334.9	±317.1	±374.9	±335.9	±284.7
	2002	2,902.9	88.5	4,015.5	2,819.1	13,317.2	2,466.3	25,609.5
		±301.3	--	±323.8	±318.4	±379.5	±332.5	±309.7
	2007	2,829.0	63.1	3,838.1	2,608.2	13,177.0	2,618.8	25,134.2
		±341.2	--	±335.0	±309.1	±347.2	±322.5	±336.0
	2012	2,848.2	50.2	3,780.7	2,571.0	13,175.5	2,561.4	24,987.0
		±303.1	--	±293.0	±308.4	±345.1	±328.5	±344.4

Source: *U.S. Department of Agriculture, 2012 National Resources Inventory, Summary Report, August 2015*

Table 2 - Land Cover/use of non-Federal rural land, by State and year
In thousands of acres, with margins of error

State	Year	Cropland	CRP land	Pastureland	Rangeland	Forest land	Other rural land	Total rural land
Georgia	1982	6,592.8 ±213.9	--	2,937.1 ±174.2	0.0 --	22,063.8 ±374.4	923.9 ±116.5	32,517.6 ±118.9
	1987	5,938.4 ±207.3	301.8 --	2,929.6 ±154.9	0.0 --	22,193.6 ±356.9	895.4 ±111.8	32,258.8 ±131.8
	1992	5,201.2 ±256.3	593.7 --	3,039.2 ±167.5	0.0 --	22,047.7 ±388.9	878.6 ±106.9	31,760.4 ±143.5
	1997	4,758.5 ±190.6	595.3 --	2,891.5 ±167.1	0.0 --	21,849.5 ±375.6	859.6 ±121.8	30,954.4 ±160.1
	2002	4,421.9 ±218.6	310.0 --	2,807.3 ±200.6	0.0 --	22,005.1 ±379.0	866.9 ±120.6	30,411.2 ±202.4
	2007	4,174.1 ±265.4	231.0 --	2,825.8 ±227.6	0.0 --	21,916.7 ±373.6	922.7 ±134.2	30,070.3 ±214.7
	2012	4,188.1 ±283.5	218.8 --	2,750.7 ±235.2	0.0 --	21,807.6 ±410.2	982.5 ±132.2	29,947.7 ±221.6
Hawaii	1982	284.6 ±73.5	--	59.9 ±21.9	1,078.2 ±122.8	1,620.9 ±157.2	482.8 ±168.7	3,526.4 ±31.8
	1987	280.3 ±71.2	0.0 --	50.6 ±22.0	1,064.9 ±124.4	1,592.4 ±157.9	467.0 ±168.3	3,455.2 ±32.1
	1992	259.5 ±69.9	0.0 --	52.0 ±21.8	1,074.4 ±127.6	1,583.6 ±159.9	461.7 ±171.1	3,431.2 ±35.2
	1997	229.6 ±59.9	0.0 --	53.7 ±22.3	1,070.6 ±128.1	1,599.4 ±152.3	499.0 ±165.5	3,452.3 ±34.9
	2002	146.4 ±51.5	0.0 --	84.1 ±22.7	1,101.6 ±110.0	1,595.0 ±160.9	502.3 ±180.3	3,429.4 ±37.6
	2007	100.2 ±60.7	0.0 --	87.2 ±22.4	1,075.5 ±105.7	1,525.8 ±154.1	481.1 ±179.7	3,269.8 ±39.1
	2012	85.7 ±58.0	0.0 --	87.4 ±22.9	1,069.8 ±103.9	1,526.9 ±156.6	477.5 ±179.8	3,247.3 ±40.5
Idaho	1982	6,508.2 ±320.2	--	1,234.6 ±159.5	6,908.8 ±370.0	4,104.1 ±342.5	386.1 ±82.0	19,141.8 ±53.6
	1987	6,163.8 ±310.3	448.0 --	1,239.9 ±144.2	6,826.3 ±359.4	4,194.8 ±341.3	406.9 ±79.0	19,279.7 ±56.0
	1992	5,715.5 ±317.1	822.4 --	1,252.8 ±157.0	6,793.7 ±360.9	4,133.5 ±344.5	417.0 ±80.0	19,134.9 ±62.4
	1997	5,535.6 ±315.8	784.2 --	1,273.4 ±150.1	6,656.7 ±371.9	4,076.1 ±338.9	424.3 ±79.9	18,750.3 ±68.5
	2002	5,412.4 ±338.5	787.5 --	1,296.2 ±171.8	6,632.5 ±365.1	4,106.5 ±325.8	438.5 ±111.4	18,673.6 ±68.6
	2007	5,277.4 ±353.1	806.7 --	1,308.8 ±187.4	6,627.2 ±376.4	4,107.5 ±329.8	471.4 ±115.2	18,599.0 ±72.2
	2012	5,384.5 ±335.2	566.3 --	1,420.0 ±195.8	6,624.8 ±381.3	4,099.1 ±331.0	474.5 ±114.9	18,569.2 ±72.9

Source: *U.S. Department of Agriculture, 2012 National Resources Inventory, Summary Report, August 2015*

Table 2 - Land Cover/use of non-Federal rural land, by State and year
In thousands of acres, with margins of error

State	Year	Cropland	CRP land	Pastureland	Rangeland	Forest land	Other rural land	Total rural land
Illinois	1982	24,752.5 ±264.4	--	3,180.5 ±226.3	0.0 --	3,626.1 ±175.5	661.7 ±34.3	32,220.8 ±126.7
	1987	24,719.8 ±258.7	120.7 --	2,937.3 ±211.0	0.0 --	3,647.7 ±174.5	660.8 ±37.5	32,086.3 ±132.3
	1992	24,139.8 ±252.1	706.2 --	2,774.1 ±207.4	0.0 --	3,707.4 ±174.1	652.8 ±37.9	31,980.3 ±132.7
	1997	24,061.2 ±216.1	725.6 --	2,519.8 ±189.6	0.0 --	3,804.7 ±165.9	637.6 ±44.3	31,748.9 ±124.6
	2002	24,133.7 ±230.8	655.4 --	2,233.5 ±183.5	0.0 --	3,929.7 ±172.7	649.1 ±57.8	31,601.4 ±134.8
	2007	23,883.8 ±224.4	677.2 --	2,236.0 ±173.2	0.0 --	3,992.7 ±173.0	671.9 ±62.1	31,461.6 ±142.1
	2012	23,920.8 ±241.3	554.4 --	2,220.6 ±189.9	0.0 --	4,024.0 ±175.6	674.1 ±64.1	31,393.9 ±146.3
Indiana	1982	13,818.3 ±188.1	--	2,201.4 ±120.9	0.0 --	3,812.2 ±141.7	723.7 ±69.0	20,555.6 ±92.1
	1987	13,890.4 ±197.8	143.5 --	1,901.6 ±111.8	0.0 --	3,824.9 ±141.7	670.6 ±66.7	20,431.0 ±94.9
	1992	13,560.0 ±201.9	413.1 --	1,843.8 ±112.5	0.0 --	3,824.4 ±143.1	679.8 ±73.5	20,321.1 ±102.4
	1997	13,453.1 ±224.4	377.9 --	1,842.3 ±109.9	0.0 --	3,811.2 ±144.2	650.5 ±63.6	20,135.0 ±114.2
	2002	13,355.5 ±228.3	239.5 --	1,907.0 ±152.6	0.0 --	3,847.5 ±150.0	630.6 ±83.4	19,980.1 ±119.2
	2007	13,258.2 ±239.2	194.9 --	1,842.7 ±141.4	0.0 --	3,900.3 ±150.1	651.3 ±78.4	19,847.4 ±124.7
	2012	13,308.2 ±232.4	153.3 --	1,736.2 ±152.3	0.0 --	3,938.0 ±153.3	636.1 ±81.1	19,771.8 ±127.1
Iowa	1982	26,375.9 ±259.1	--	4,539.5 ±191.4	0.0 --	1,911.0 ±147.9	920.1 ±59.6	33,746.5 ±96.5
	1987	25,661.1 ±249.5	1,243.4 --	3,950.5 ±197.5	0.0 --	1,980.5 ±147.7	880.0 ±58.4	33,715.5 ±103.0
	1992	24,898.9 ±235.9	2,089.8 --	3,708.5 ±197.6	0.0 --	2,117.4 ±155.7	860.1 ±56.6	33,674.7 ±103.1
	1997	25,212.6 ±227.0	1,739.0 --	3,534.9 ±180.0	0.0 --	2,215.6 ±161.0	867.8 ±59.4	33,569.9 ±105.6
	2002	25,370.6 ±241.8	1,507.8 --	3,423.8 ±179.1	0.0 --	2,321.3 ±161.2	853.4 ±73.9	33,476.9 ±108.8
	2007	25,474.7 ±226.7	1,427.3 --	3,266.8 ±164.6	0.0 --	2,356.6 ±148.5	879.3 ±82.8	33,404.7 ±114.8
	2012	25,968.2 ±254.7	1,030.6 --	3,104.5 ±207.9	0.0 --	2,358.6 ±158.6	897.1 ±85.7	33,359.0 ±116.0

Source: *U.S. Department of Agriculture, 2012 National Resources Inventory, Summary Report, August 2015*

Table 2 - Land Cover/use of non-Federal rural land, by State and year In thousands of acres, with margins of error

State	Year	Cropland	CRP land	Pastureland	Rangeland	Forest land	Other rural land	Total rural land
Kansas	1982	29,122.8 ±400.4	--	2,122.9 ±147.4	16,427.5 ±344.8	1,571.2 ±108.8	688.3 ±63.4	49,932.7 ±73.7
	1987	28,496.6 ±395.8	645.7 --	2,173.0 ±140.1	16,332.1 ±342.5	1,574.7 ±110.3	682.2 ±63.9	49,904.3 ±74.3
	1992	26,535.2 ±406.1	2,867.3 --	2,292.1 ±141.8	15,753.0 ±334.9	1,658.1 ±111.3	688.5 ±57.0	49,794.2 ±77.7
	1997	26,485.8 ±413.6	2,848.8 --	2,319.1 ±141.0	15,659.8 ±346.5	1,666.2 ±108.4	699.7 ±59.4	49,679.4 ±77.0
	2002	26,458.3 ±363.6	2,625.5 --	2,414.8 ±196.0	15,694.7 ±339.3	1,688.9 ±107.0	714.1 ±71.5	49,596.3 ±79.3
	2007	25,606.2 ±394.2	3,164.7 --	2,566.7 ±207.4	15,686.8 ±368.8	1,746.2 ±128.8	762.6 ±89.5	49,533.2 ±89.1
	2012	25,834.1 ±486.9	2,352.8 --	2,967.0 ±275.9	15,808.1 ±376.3	1,790.1 ±133.5	760.6 ±83.3	49,512.7 ±91.3
Kentucky	1982	5,928.6 ±155.9	--	5,943.6 ±158.6	0.0 --	10,521.2 ±174.9	686.3 ±64.3	23,079.7 ±74.7
	1987	5,447.8 ±179.4	204.4 --	5,911.7 ±160.8	0.0 --	10,568.7 ±193.0	707.6 ±65.7	22,840.2 ±85.5
	1992	5,097.2 ±165.2	423.3 --	5,892.0 ±139.0	0.0 --	10,640.1 ±203.5	570.0 ±54.7	22,622.6 ±90.2
	1997	5,191.9 ±145.5	332.2 --	5,686.0 ±124.3	0.0 --	10,701.1 ±202.2	462.6 ±40.3	22,373.8 ±102.6
	2002	5,346.2 ±292.7	272.7 --	5,237.2 ±265.6	0.0 --	10,614.0 ±190.1	539.9 ±74.3	22,010.0 ±99.2
	2007	5,213.0 ±291.1	285.8 --	5,280.8 ±292.0	0.0 --	10,588.1 ±187.0	516.9 ±97.2	21,884.6 ±101.1
	2012	5,463.4 ±258.5	169.1 --	5,070.8 ±260.8	0.0 --	10,611.0 ±175.2	510.8 ±91.2	21,825.1 ±99.7
Louisiana	1982	6,333.8 ±220.5	--	2,322.8 ±156.1	214.4 ±41.2	13,019.6 ±231.2	2,837.6 ±151.4	24,728.2 ±68.0
	1987	6,178.4 ±189.1	42.3 --	2,285.3 ±155.8	212.6 ±39.4	12,856.3 ±228.1	2,889.7 ±149.7	24,464.6 ±63.7
	1992	5,821.6 ±196.4	155.9 --	2,392.5 ±138.6	213.0 ±36.5	12,798.0 ±234.0	2,888.8 ±143.2	24,269.8 ±69.7
	1997	5,511.9 ±176.0	140.4 --	2,512.2 ±143.0	202.4 ±34.0	12,888.1 ±227.6	2,877.1 ±151.3	24,132.1 ±75.9
	2002	5,275.6 ±167.2	202.7 --	2,430.0 ±170.1	203.8 ±33.5	12,936.0 ±247.5	2,868.5 ±143.4	23,916.6 ±83.6
	2007	5,060.4 ±187.7	241.8 --	2,486.8 ±202.4	212.7 ±34.7	12,877.3 ±251.6	2,867.3 ±136.3	23,746.3 ±83.3
	2012	4,943.2 ±184.5	191.2 --	2,549.5 ±214.9	211.0 ±36.9	12,867.5 ±244.1	2,893.3 ±137.6	23,655.7 ±80.5

Source: *U.S. Department of Agriculture, 2012 National Resources Inventory, Summary Report, August 2015*

Table 2 - Land Cover/use of non-Federal rural land, by State and year
In thousands of acres, with margins of error

State	Year	Cropland	CRP land	Pastureland	Rangeland	Forest land	Other rural land	Total rural land
Maine	1982	517.4 ±116.9	--	311.3 ±60.2	0.0 --	17,633.3 ±192.7	559.3 ±137.7	19,021.3 ±89.1
	1987	503.6 ±113.6	0.0 --	264.8 ±53.3	0.0 --	17,635.7 ±187.7	544.0 ±133.8	18,948.1 ±95.8
	1992	447.4 ±85.2	35.6 --	213.3 ±61.6	0.0 --	17,648.8 ±194.0	555.6 ±117.0	18,900.7 ±100.8
	1997	422.1 ±81.7	29.7 --	178.8 ±51.1	0.0 --	17,661.0 ±212.1	491.2 ±121.5	18,782.8 ±109.5
	2002	384.7 ±92.1	29.7 --	184.7 ±41.1	0.0 --	17,606.2 ±228.2	479.4 ±156.5	18,684.7 ±111.7
	2007	362.6 ±96.8	29.7 --	181.5 ±46.5	0.0 --	17,564.7 ±234.6	487.5 ±171.8	18,626.0 ±116.2
	2012	353.1 ±92.5	29.7 --	167.1 ±49.6	0.0 --	17,564.9 ±236.1	486.7 ±172.2	18,601.5 ±121.1
Maryland	1982	1,763.5 ±91.7	--	540.5 ±44.7	0.0 --	2,427.5 ±111.5	337.2 ±30.6	5,068.7 ±114.5
	1987	1,706.5 ±86.4	1.1 --	562.4 ±36.8	0.0 --	2,394.5 ±107.1	314.7 ±31.1	4,979.2 ±117.4
	1992	1,642.5 ±84.7	18.8 --	557.5 ±37.4	0.0 --	2,370.5 ±108.3	311.7 ±30.7	4,901.0 ±121.3
	1997	1,576.8 ±84.1	19.1 --	475.9 ±33.6	0.0 --	2,327.4 ±102.6	311.1 ±32.2	4,710.3 ±125.1
	2002	1,472.6 ±91.6	13.9 --	455.5 ±54.5	0.0 --	2,343.4 ±107.2	329.8 ±25.9	4,615.2 ±125.0
	2007	1,402.3 ±90.7	17.2 --	467.3 ±56.3	0.0 --	2,306.4 ±107.8	348.0 ±26.0	4,541.2 ±128.4
	2012	1,386.6 ±91.2	5.9 --	462.0 ±53.9	0.0 --	2,299.1 ±106.6	352.4 ±28.0	4,506.0 ±128.5
Massachusetts	1982	293.2 ±51.0	--	192.2 ±36.7	0.0 --	3,036.7 ±105.7	243.2 ±34.6	3,765.3 ±63.2
	1987	281.5 ±51.5	0.0 --	166.0 ±32.5	0.0 --	2,949.9 ±103.1	250.2 ±35.1	3,647.6 ±66.5
	1992	260.1 ±52.3	0.0 --	163.5 ±32.2	0.0 --	2,839.2 ±102.4	241.6 ±35.9	3,504.4 ±67.1
	1997	264.4 ±53.2	0.0 --	128.7 ±26.7	0.0 --	2,666.7 ±103.0	224.2 ±34.7	3,284.0 ±71.1
	2002	248.8 ±52.9	0.0 --	136.0 ±32.7	0.0 --	2,596.3 ±104.2	218.4 ±32.2	3,199.5 ±68.1
	2007	223.1 ±45.7	0.0 --	147.4 ±31.8	0.0 --	2,559.2 ±106.5	211.1 ±32.3	3,140.8 ±70.3
	2012	218.8 ±44.2	0.0 --	148.7 ±31.4	0.0 --	2,549.6 ±109.8	210.0 ±31.5	3,127.1 ±77.0

Source: *U.S. Department of Agriculture, 2012 National Resources Inventory, Summary Report, August 2015*

Table 2 - Land Cover/use of non-Federal rural land, by State and year
In thousands of acres, with margins of error

State	Year	Cropland	CRP land	Pastureland	Rangeland	Forest land	Other rural land	Total rural land
Michigan	1982	9,363.0 ±264.3	--	3,065.2 ±177.0	0.0 --	15,901.8 ±277.5	1,918.1 ±136.9	30,248.1 ±132.9
	1987	9,240.4 ±248.7	54.6 --	2,741.6 ±183.5	0.0 --	16,097.0 ±262.8	1,871.7 ±140.8	30,005.3 ±141.3
	1992	8,927.9 ±249.5	237.1 --	2,575.1 ±164.9	0.0 --	16,106.9 ±260.3	1,838.2 ±137.5	29,685.2 ±147.0
	1997	8,475.6 ±264.8	321.3 --	2,273.5 ±138.5	0.0 --	16,378.6 ±257.8	1,858.3 ±137.0	29,307.3 ±161.4
	2002	8,111.6 ±264.8	258.4 --	2,376.8 ±146.5	0.0 --	16,628.8 ±249.2	1,607.6 ±134.2	28,983.2 ±167.6
	2007	7,927.8 ±290.4	191.1 --	2,356.2 ±220.0	0.0 --	16,644.0 ±216.6	1,681.4 ±131.9	28,800.5 ±166.8
	2012	7,994.6 ±294.5	125.4 --	2,273.3 ±218.0	0.0 --	16,648.6 ±219.9	1,709.1 ±137.8	28,751.0 ±167.3
Minnesota	1982	22,940.0 ±487.7	--	3,886.2 ±254.9	0.0 --	16,252.2 ±608.2	2,643.3 ±201.5	45,721.7 ±85.1
	1987	22,335.6 ±484.0	778.3 --	3,637.5 ±248.7	0.0 --	16,146.2 ±622.8	2,678.1 ±200.8	45,575.7 ±89.5
	1992	21,301.2 ±467.8	1,810.5 --	3,468.6 ±211.3	0.0 --	16,214.1 ±620.1	2,672.4 ±197.8	45,466.8 ±94.8
	1997	21,355.2 ±490.8	1,543.7 --	3,481.9 ±187.9	0.0 --	16,265.4 ±601.7	2,597.5 ±190.9	45,243.7 ±103.4
	2002	21,131.1 ±523.3	1,424.7 --	3,607.3 ±310.0	0.0 --	16,323.8 ±570.9	2,621.6 ±191.0	45,108.5 ±109.3
	2007	20,834.6 ±525.9	1,441.9 --	3,748.5 ±321.8	0.0 --	16,370.8 ±582.7	2,646.7 ±197.4	45,042.5 ±113.3
	2012	21,069.0 ±483.7	1,079.2 --	3,757.7 ±291.9	0.0 --	16,389.2 ±584.7	2,674.6 ±197.0	44,969.7 ±113.2
Mississippi	1982	7,408.1 ±267.5	--	3,986.5 ±216.5	0.0 --	15,407.1 ±313.9	339.1 ±37.4	27,140.8 ±97.8
	1987	6,644.0 ±255.8	294.2 --	3,893.2 ±215.9	0.0 --	15,797.0 ±315.9	328.0 ±36.3	26,956.4 ±104.7
	1992	5,730.5 ±245.9	765.3 --	3,941.2 ±210.4	0.0 --	16,000.2 ±317.9	326.2 ±35.7	26,763.4 ±106.2
	1997	5,360.8 ±231.5	797.6 --	3,700.5 ±177.5	0.0 --	16,282.3 ±301.8	370.2 ±44.9	26,511.4 ±121.6
	2002	4,930.1 ±241.1	783.9 --	3,380.9 ±210.4	0.0 --	16,784.0 ±301.5	408.8 ±66.7	26,287.7 ±133.5
	2007	4,726.7 ±227.3	729.6 --	3,302.4 ±197.7	0.0 --	16,942.2 ±300.7	466.9 ±76.2	26,167.8 ±146.7
	2012	4,774.7 ±242.2	604.3 --	3,124.5 ±175.6	0.0 --	17,145.2 ±294.8	478.5 ±76.1	26,127.2 ±149.6

Source: *U.S. Department of Agriculture, 2012 National Resources Inventory, Summary Report, August 2015*

Table 2 - Land Cover/use of non-Federal rural land, by State and year
In thousands of acres, with margins of error

State	Year	Cropland	CRP land	Pastureland	Rangeland	Forest land	Other rural land	Total rural land
Missouri	1982	14,905.8 ±285.6	--	12,434.5 ±352.2	123.6 ±44.3	11,537.8 ±297.7	676.1 ±54.9	39,677.8 ±97.2
	1987	14,293.2 ±278.6	572.1 --	12,067.8 ±344.7	89.2 ±38.1	11,878.0 ±305.7	668.0 ±50.6	39,568.3 ±99.9
	1992	13,234.2 ±308.9	1,605.2 --	11,736.5 ±307.6	84.7 ±38.7	12,106.5 ±306.8	653.6 ±51.5	39,420.7 ±104.2
	1997	13,530.4 ±279.3	1,606.6 --	10,877.1 ±294.9	72.4 ±38.9	12,428.3 ±303.2	636.4 ±51.1	39,151.2 ±113.6
	2002	13,555.9 ±299.5	1,488.4 --	10,716.2 ±346.1	48.1 ±57.6	12,500.3 ±325.2	650.3 ±70.8	38,959.2 ±114.0
	2007	13,422.2 ±279.8	1,463.7 --	10,696.3 ±343.0	53.8 ±61.2	12,474.0 ±309.3	694.5 ±83.9	38,804.5 ±118.2
	2012	13,956.0 ±265.6	1,107.2 --	10,347.0 ±294.9	46.9 ±61.8	12,571.1 ±303.9	699.8 ±78.2	38,728.0 ±121.5
Montana	1982	17,129.7 ±877.0	--	3,134.7 ±328.7	38,088.9 ±1,006.1	5,950.5 ±576.7	1,056.9 ±214.0	65,360.7 ±105.0
	1987	16,211.1 ±849.4	1,485.4 --	3,200.9 ±245.7	37,540.3 ±1,015.4	5,954.5 ±572.6	1,048.8 ±206.8	65,441.0 ±105.3
	1992	15,077.8 ±877.1	2,779.5 --	3,411.4 ±315.9	37,246.8 ±998.4	5,952.9 ±582.5	1,023.0 ±204.8	65,491.4 ±113.4
	1997	15,145.0 ±869.8	2,720.9 --	3,558.0 ±365.9	36,959.9 ±974.0	5,948.0 ±568.9	1,034.9 ±211.9	65,366.7 ±116.4
	2002	14,397.6 ±868.1	3,261.5 --	3,786.7 ±383.8	36,938.2 ±1,020.4	5,930.8 ±526.7	989.4 ±211.6	65,304.2 ±117.4
	2007	13,978.2 ±859.7	3,315.4 --	3,988.2 ±422.9	36,967.5 ±1,021.4	5,917.4 ±530.9	1,015.7 ±211.6	65,182.4 ±126.5
	2012	14,457.0 ±878.3	2,360.1 --	4,444.4 ±454.4	36,908.8 ±1,020.0	5,831.7 ±558.0	1,011.7 ±194.9	65,013.7 ±130.6
Nebraska	1982	20,327.2 ±449.1	--	1,944.2 ±130.8	23,635.3 ±488.8	846.4 ±99.2	727.8 ±47.6	47,480.9 ±107.1
	1987	19,986.9 ±402.8	590.2 --	1,903.6 ±140.7	23,373.8 ±463.0	858.9 ±100.5	740.2 ±51.4	47,453.6 ±109.3
	1992	19,299.9 ±402.2	1,361.7 --	1,877.0 ±138.2	23,220.1 ±461.6	859.8 ±102.4	748.3 ±53.0	47,366.8 ±114.5
	1997	19,511.0 ±403.5	1,244.8 --	1,787.9 ±122.2	23,151.7 ±456.1	877.4 ±101.9	745.0 ±58.4	47,317.8 ±116.8
	2002	19,585.2 ±403.6	1,101.0 --	1,814.6 ±134.7	23,154.9 ±445.0	862.7 ±94.8	766.4 ±64.9	47,284.8 ±118.0
	2007	19,568.8 ±417.8	1,198.3 --	1,794.7 ±140.0	23,081.4 ±463.9	849.0 ±96.5	763.8 ±80.9	47,256.0 ±117.3
	2012	19,979.1 ±405.2	816.4 --	1,821.5 ±162.7	23,003.5 ±486.7	831.9 ±92.6	788.4 ±101.2	47,240.8 ±117.8

Source: *U.S. Department of Agriculture, 2012 National Resources Inventory, Summary Report, August 2015*

Table 2 - Land Cover/use of non-Federal rural land, by State and year
In thousands of acres, with margins of error

State	Year	Cropland	CRP land	Pastureland	Rangeland	Forest land	Other rural land	Total rural land
Nevada	1982	869.8 ±167.1	--	279.3 ±87.6	8,795.6 ±212.0	388.5 ±136.6	361.4 ±90.8	10,694.6 ±56.1
	1987	843.2 ±170.3	0.0 --	291.6 ±89.8	8,840.8 ±215.5	396.9 ±136.5	366.9 ±96.2	10,739.4 ±64.5
	1992	771.8 ±164.2	1.4 --	286.8 ±88.0	8,818.6 ±201.8	396.8 ±137.0	342.4 ±99.9	10,617.8 ±65.4
	1997	700.2 ±157.2	2.4 --	282.6 ±91.0	8,890.9 ±197.2	318.0 ±118.5	348.5 ±95.2	10,542.6 ±67.7
	2002	687.0 ±161.3	0.0 --	257.5 ±79.4	8,767.7 ±224.9	324.4 ±125.5	344.0 ±84.3	10,380.6 ±86.4
	2007	659.7 ±154.9	0.0 --	223.9 ±75.2	8,800.9 ±233.1	319.7 ±124.1	360.4 ±87.8	10,364.6 ±97.5
	2012	629.4 ±153.6	0.0 --	233.2 ±77.0	8,777.0 ±229.5	320.8 ±124.3	367.5 ±89.3	10,327.9 ±98.8
New Hampshire	1982	158.9 ±27.9	--	149.7 ±33.4	0.0 --	4,125.0 ±69.4	147.2 ±28.9	4,580.8 ±46.3
	1987	145.8 ±28.0	0.0 --	135.4 ±32.0	0.0 --	4,046.9 ±71.4	155.0 ±27.8	4,483.1 ±59.3
	1992	139.7 ±26.8	0.0 --	128.6 ±31.5	0.0 --	3,961.0 ±75.0	161.5 ±28.6	4,390.8 ±61.4
	1997	131.8 ±26.3	0.0 --	121.8 ±32.5	0.0 --	3,913.5 ±80.8	146.9 ±25.9	4,314.0 ±65.7
	2002	123.5 ±26.5	0.0 --	119.7 ±26.4	0.0 --	3,862.8 ±79.6	151.3 ±29.9	4,257.3 ±65.8
	2007	119.5 ±26.9	0.0 --	115.8 ±24.5	0.0 --	3,822.3 ±84.7	146.1 ±28.7	4,203.7 ±69.8
	2012	118.3 ±26.5	0.0 --	118.8 ±25.1	0.0 --	3,790.6 ±83.6	148.1 ±28.9	4,175.8 ±69.9
New Jersey	1982	803.7 ±60.5	--	219.4 ±37.9	0.0 --	1,917.6 ±65.5	387.5 ±44.2	3,328.2 ±71.4
	1987	687.9 ±56.1	0.0 --	175.8 ±26.6	0.0 --	1,871.7 ±70.3	380.5 ±43.2	3,115.9 ±77.3
	1992	650.9 ±52.3	0.5 --	159.9 ±26.9	0.0 --	1,848.7 ±73.2	373.3 ±44.0	3,033.3 ±75.5
	1997	589.5 ±52.1	0.5 --	129.7 ±19.8	0.0 --	1,746.2 ±69.5	365.8 ±43.6	2,831.7 ±78.3
	2002	529.2 ±54.5	0.0 --	127.2 ±23.6	0.0 --	1,675.5 ±72.2	374.3 ±46.4	2,706.2 ±81.9
	2007	496.0 ±51.1	0.0 --	141.2 ±25.6	0.0 --	1,648.0 ±74.3	365.6 ±45.9	2,650.8 ±83.3
	2012	482.8 ±49.2	0.0 --	144.9 ±25.9	0.0 --	1,636.3 ±75.7	362.4 ±45.3	2,626.4 ±83.6

Source: *U.S. Department of Agriculture, 2012 National Resources Inventory, Summary Report, August 2015*

Table 2 - Land Cover/use of non-Federal rural land, by State and year In thousands of acres, with margins of error

State	Year	Cropland	CRP land	Pastureland	Rangeland	Forest land	Other rural land	Total rural land
New Mexico	1982	2,410.6 ±165.6	--	187.1 ±176.2	42,331.5 ±983.0	5,542.3 ±800.8	1,016.6 ±289.8	51,488.1 ±99.0
	1987	1,953.6 ±183.3	425.5 --	222.6 ±176.6	41,776.6 ±988.2	5,390.1 ±786.1	1,125.6 ±324.3	50,894.0 ±107.4
	1992	1,891.5 ±187.2	481.8 --	231.3 ±176.0	41,263.5 ±902.9	5,540.8 ±767.1	1,166.9 ±330.5	50,575.8 ±117.2
	1997	1,864.9 ±174.4	467.2 --	235.1 ±179.1	40,918.9 ±962.3	5,748.8 ±811.2	1,152.3 ±333.4	50,387.2 ±127.5
	2002	1,555.3 ±190.0	594.1 --	268.5 ±183.1	40,928.4 ±986.9	5,613.8 ±874.1	1,127.4 ±370.5	50,087.5 ±157.5
	2007	1,526.8 ±199.3	547.3 --	265.7 ±179.1	40,932.1 ±978.9	5,581.2 ±870.3	1,169.1 ±380.0	50,022.2 ±163.9
	2012	1,537.8 ±199.5	406.0 --	431.2 ±178.4	40,704.0 ±970.0	5,616.8 ±896.2	1,277.6 ±398.1	49,973.4 ±166.5
New York	1982	5,854.7 ±232.3	--	3,846.3 ±159.4	0.0 --	16,596.9 ±213.6	652.6 ±71.1	26,950.5 ±124.5
	1987	5,689.6 ±225.8	18.4 --	3,418.9 ±165.1	0.0 --	16,917.6 ±223.3	798.7 ±72.0	26,843.2 ±130.4
	1992	5,554.4 ±212.4	55.8 --	3,075.5 ±146.7	0.0 --	17,249.2 ±240.5	766.5 ±66.9	26,701.4 ±134.7
	1997	5,336.9 ±223.1	53.8 --	2,734.0 ±136.1	0.0 --	17,480.0 ±246.3	737.9 ±71.8	26,342.6 ±144.8
	2002	5,225.6 ±201.1	51.1 --	2,641.0 ±158.9	0.0 --	17,441.1 ±245.9	747.8 ±68.5	26,106.6 ±155.4
	2007	5,005.5 ±220.0	41.5 --	2,695.9 ±185.0	0.0 --	17,483.6 ±237.6	766.1 ±69.6	25,992.6 ±154.6
	2012	5,122.6 ±227.4	28.2 --	2,509.7 ±191.4	0.0 --	17,486.0 ±217.0	782.4 ±69.4	25,928.9 ±157.2
North Carolina	1982	6,711.3 ±256.6	--	1,965.6 ±113.5	0.0 --	17,149.8 ±289.7	752.0 ±96.1	26,578.7 ±103.5
	1987	6,383.0 ±272.5	31.6 --	1,992.0 ±129.5	0.0 --	16,805.4 ±265.2	771.9 ±94.6	25,983.9 ±114.4
	1992	5,970.3 ±255.5	139.5 --	2,018.0 ±119.4	0.0 --	16,433.5 ±274.6	772.1 ±95.9	25,333.4 ±139.6
	1997	5,686.8 ±248.8	131.2 --	2,055.9 ±123.8	0.0 --	16,166.3 ±270.3	803.8 ±93.0	24,844.0 ±165.2
	2002	5,449.5 ±237.3	75.3 --	1,978.3 ±162.7	0.0 --	15,813.8 ±291.0	849.8 ±97.7	24,166.7 ±194.6
	2007	5,290.6 ±231.4	87.7 --	1,925.5 ±160.0	0.0 --	15,649.5 ±289.4	925.5 ±101.5	23,878.8 ±202.2
	2012	5,149.3 ±258.2	54.4 --	1,973.4 ±169.3	0.0 --	15,631.3 ±293.6	922.1 ±105.4	23,730.5 ±207.7

Source: *U.S. Department of Agriculture, 2012 National Resources Inventory, Summary Report, August 2015*

Table 2 - Land Cover/use of non-Federal rural land, by State and year
In thousands of acres, with margins of error

State	Year	Cropland	CRP land	Pastureland	Rangeland	Forest land	Other rural land	Total rural land
North Dakota	1982	27,056.9 ±390.3	--	1,175.4 ±157.3	11,529.9 ±383.4	462.5 ±85.6	1,390.7 ±121.4	41,615.4 ±92.0
	1987	27,111.4 ±373.3	531.6 --	1,125.9 ±127.7	10,978.5 ±386.5	461.0 ±85.5	1,385.1 ±108.3	41,593.5 ±92.0
	1992	24,750.9 ±388.2	2,897.6 --	1,109.4 ±140.1	10,925.9 ±396.8	456.9 ±85.1	1,398.6 ±108.9	41,539.3 ±91.6
	1997	24,967.5 ±351.1	2,801.9 --	1,018.9 ±139.4	10,748.4 ±395.8	452.5 ±81.6	1,390.5 ±116.1	41,379.7 ±91.4
	2002	24,247.6 ±373.7	3,197.6 --	1,068.1 ±190.2	10,970.3 ±395.6	449.5 ±81.2	1,388.9 ±110.1	41,322.0 ±73.4
	2007	24,056.4 ±420.9	3,209.6 --	1,239.5 ±208.2	10,912.9 ±401.8	447.7 ±80.8	1,438.2 ±134.9	41,304.3 ±74.8
	2012	24,769.7 ±432.6	2,036.6 --	1,693.9 ±256.3	10,812.5 ±414.2	446.3 ±81.5	1,454.9 ±111.0	41,213.9 ±78.9
Ohio	1982	12,398.8 ±166.2	--	2,790.9 ±144.5	0.0 --	6,711.8 ±181.1	990.3 ±66.3	22,891.8 ±120.0
	1987	12,289.0 ±176.7	57.3 --	2,479.5 ±125.6	0.0 --	6,939.6 ±205.5	920.5 ±72.3	22,685.9 ±123.6
	1992	11,881.3 ±161.0	307.2 --	2,353.0 ±129.8	0.0 --	6,960.0 ±215.7	886.3 ±56.9	22,387.8 ±135.4
	1997	11,613.1 ±196.3	323.3 --	2,065.9 ±154.5	0.0 --	7,060.9 ±204.9	952.9 ±48.6	22,016.1 ±148.3
	2002	11,287.4 ±208.3	254.3 --	2,264.5 ±149.8	0.0 --	7,140.6 ±215.0	836.1 ±83.4	21,782.9 ±148.8
	2007	11,060.0 ±224.2	226.2 --	2,320.9 ±165.5	0.0 --	7,077.3 ±217.4	894.9 ±88.8	21,579.3 ±156.5
	2012	11,098.9 ±229.4	159.2 --	2,253.0 ±163.6	0.0 --	7,098.8 ±214.5	873.9 ±93.8	21,483.8 ±159.6
Oklahoma	1982	11,585.5 ±325.9	--	7,212.6 ±217.6	14,751.2 ±406.5	7,211.4 ±274.6	410.0 ±49.5	41,170.7 ±100.1
	1987	10,955.3 ±348.0	585.2 --	7,573.9 ±196.8	14,183.3 ±410.1	7,361.4 ±284.1	431.9 ±50.4	41,091.0 ±98.2
	1992	10,114.1 ±348.0	1,158.4 --	7,816.3 ±217.5	13,923.7 ±417.4	7,535.6 ±294.9	455.7 ±50.1	41,003.8 ±102.3
	1997	9,743.7 ±348.3	1,137.1 --	7,988.9 ±208.7	13,833.2 ±420.8	7,585.8 ±285.9	438.0 ±48.4	40,726.7 ±113.1
	2002	9,108.9 ±383.6	1,014.4 --	8,419.8 ±293.5	13,859.3 ±435.1	7,678.9 ±248.3	451.8 ±56.6	40,533.1 ±122.6
	2007	8,831.0 ±401.6	1,058.2 --	8,490.0 ±254.5	13,814.3 ±401.9	7,700.6 ±237.8	492.9 ±66.4	40,387.0 ±123.2
	2012	8,769.3 ±422.2	804.2 --	8,752.4 ±323.1	13,696.4 ±399.8	7,750.4 ±282.7	495.1 ±70.1	40,267.8 ±123.9

Source: *U.S. Department of Agriculture, 2012 National Resources Inventory, Summary Report, August 2015*

Table 2 - Land Cover/use of non-Federal rural land, by State and year
In thousands of acres, with margins of error

State	Year	Cropland	CRP land	Pastureland	Rangeland	Forest land	Other rural land	Total rural land
Oregon	1982	4,307.4 ±303.9	--	2,004.6 ±262.8	9,248.1 ±600.8	12,419.1 ±430.4	517.2 ±117.1	28,496.4 ±103.0
	1987	3,912.9 ±327.5	393.3 --	1,980.6 ±257.7	9,157.6 ±602.4	12,369.0 ±438.2	519.0 ±118.8	28,332.4 ±111.4
	1992	3,724.9 ±326.8	522.9 --	1,969.1 ±250.5	9,143.4 ±612.1	12,338.0 ±464.6	508.7 ±108.7	28,207.0 ±113.7
	1997	3,705.7 ±314.4	482.7 --	1,905.9 ±232.2	8,979.7 ±614.4	12,261.6 ±468.6	568.0 ±116.3	27,903.6 ±121.7
	2002	3,638.9 ±328.8	443.9 --	1,779.3 ±227.6	9,065.1 ±591.5	12,357.3 ±468.9	614.5 ±121.8	27,899.0 ±136.0
	2007	3,521.9 ±316.8	520.0 --	1,757.9 ±221.4	9,029.2 ±582.0	12,339.2 ±465.5	637.2 ±122.9	27,805.4 ±137.7
	2012	3,491.2 ±307.2	493.2 --	1,809.0 ±227.6	9,002.8 ±585.6	12,329.0 ±461.4	646.9 ±119.2	27,772.1 ±138.2
Pennsylvania	1982	5,891.9 ±253.1	--	2,636.1 ±154.2	0.0 --	15,614.8 ±274.4	943.7 ±91.0	25,086.5 ±110.5
	1987	5,756.4 ±255.5	15.4 --	2,482.1 ±175.5	0.0 --	15,695.1 ±283.8	953.9 ±90.6	24,902.9 ±121.1
	1992	5,585.7 ±255.5	92.2 --	2,320.0 ±158.6	0.0 --	15,550.9 ±284.8	918.1 ±88.2	24,466.9 ±136.3
	1997	5,464.3 ±262.6	90.3 --	1,902.3 ±153.6	0.0 --	15,593.3 ±301.8	879.2 ±95.5	23,929.4 ±151.0
	2002	5,136.9 ±283.0	43.0 --	2,042.6 ±167.7	0.0 --	15,679.4 ±300.1	769.5 ±118.0	23,671.4 ±158.8
	2007	4,985.2 ±263.9	51.3 --	2,012.7 ±179.7	0.0 --	15,643.2 ±299.5	813.0 ±106.2	23,505.4 ±168.0
	2012	5,038.1 ±272.2	26.1 --	1,905.4 ±167.2	0.0 --	15,603.1 ±307.9	848.4 ±108.3	23,421.1 ±170.6
Rhode Island	1982	27.6 ±8.1	--	34.2 ±12.0	0.0 --	395.9 ±19.2	24.0 ±8.4	481.7 ±13.0
	1987	26.7 ±7.6	0.0 --	32.2 ±11.2	0.0 --	391.9 ±20.8	21.2 ±8.4	472.0 ±14.0
	1992	22.7 ±6.5	0.0 --	25.1 ±8.7	0.0 --	383.2 ±20.1	22.7 ±8.5	453.7 ±14.3
	1997	18.9 ±6.4	0.0 --	26.9 ±7.6	0.0 --	381.8 ±19.6	22.9 ±8.4	450.5 ±14.4
	2002	17.9 ±7.5	0.0 --	26.2 ±7.5	0.0 --	372.8 ±19.6	21.2 ±7.7	438.1 ±14.7
	2007	17.7 ±6.6	0.0 --	25.3 ±7.2	0.0 --	364.5 ±20.4	22.0 ±7.4	429.5 ±16.0
	2012	17.2 ±6.6	0.0 --	23.7 ±6.9	0.0 --	361.4 ±20.0	23.9 ±7.7	426.2 ±15.7

Source: *U.S. Department of Agriculture, 2012 National Resources Inventory, Summary Report, August 2015*

Table 2 - Land Cover/use of non-Federal rural land, by State and year In thousands of acres, with margins of error

State	Year	Cropland	CRP land	Pastureland	Rangeland	Forest land	Other rural land	Total rural land
South Carolina	1982	3,536.6 ±122.7	--	1,173.6 ±122.0	0.0 --	11,362.5 ±172.7	712.7 ±72.8	16,785.4 ±82.3
	1987	3,284.4 ±120.2	95.1 --	1,145.4 ±110.3	0.0 --	11,368.5 ±164.9	719.2 ±77.6	16,612.6 ±92.1
	1992	2,942.9 ±105.9	265.6 --	1,156.5 ±108.3	0.0 --	11,293.6 ±167.2	717.8 ±80.8	16,376.4 ±101.7
	1997	2,552.4 ±100.2	262.5 --	1,166.7 ±100.1	0.0 --	11,275.5 ±175.1	754.7 ±81.9	16,011.8 ±109.5
	2002	2,385.4 ±107.6	186.6 --	1,085.4 ±148.9	0.0 --	11,256.5 ±196.1	763.3 ±85.6	15,677.2 ±104.4
	2007	2,215.8 ±150.0	162.4 --	1,104.3 ±164.5	0.0 --	11,173.0 ±226.7	822.3 ±87.6	15,477.8 ±110.0
	2012	2,186.8 ±159.9	97.4 --	1,078.4 ±168.2	0.0 --	11,165.0 ±234.7	843.5 ±85.8	15,371.1 ±109.2
South Dakota	1982	17,093.0 ±304.9	--	2,658.8 ±234.3	23,225.2 ±438.2	565.9 ±113.8	1,434.6 ±135.3	44,977.5 ±67.4
	1987	17,669.0 ±371.3	360.8 --	2,225.9 ±207.1	22,668.9 ±448.9	567.2 ±111.3	1,437.1 ±133.4	44,928.9 ±69.9
	1992	16,580.8 ±367.6	1,755.6 --	2,135.8 ±194.2	22,359.2 ±450.0	561.8 ±109.1	1,439.0 ±132.4	44,832.2 ±94.9
	1997	16,860.9 ±357.3	1,685.9 --	2,046.7 ±172.2	22,168.3 ±464.4	550.7 ±109.7	1,464.1 ±139.2	44,776.6 ±104.8
	2002	17,177.8 ±375.4	1,298.3 --	2,006.8 ±266.0	22,252.5 ±458.8	561.9 ±108.8	1,461.0 ±145.9	44,758.3 ±106.8
	2007	17,081.9 ±357.7	1,343.0 --	1,960.0 ±278.4	22,296.6 ±450.0	567.2 ±110.5	1,486.7 ±143.4	44,735.4 ±110.6
	2012	17,627.5 ±376.8	671.3 --	2,073.0 ±300.8	22,267.6 ±453.0	576.0 ±110.2	1,504.4 ±140.1	44,719.8 ±111.5
Tennessee	1982	5,501.5 ±161.8	--	5,250.0 ±202.3	0.0 --	12,048.3 ±280.1	475.3 ±59.8	23,275.1 ±108.0
	1987	5,279.1 ±153.4	172.9 --	5,045.3 ±207.0	0.0 --	12,059.8 ±278.7	456.9 ±54.1	23,014.0 ±113.9
	1992	4,750.0 ±144.2	438.5 --	5,053.8 ±192.7	0.0 --	12,036.4 ±268.3	442.4 ±50.5	22,721.1 ±119.8
	1997	4,538.4 ±174.5	374.8 --	4,885.1 ±212.1	0.0 --	11,945.5 ±261.4	521.8 ±54.9	22,265.6 ±136.4
	2002	4,501.7 ±211.5	223.1 --	4,801.5 ±271.6	0.0 --	11,928.6 ±264.3	526.8 ±66.4	21,981.7 ±140.5
	2007	4,315.9 ±198.6	223.0 --	4,753.9 ±260.4	0.0 --	11,888.7 ±280.4	593.2 ±69.2	21,774.7 ±152.7
	2012	4,544.0 ±201.8	160.5 --	4,438.1 ±259.9	0.0 --	11,897.8 ±299.4	623.6 ±71.6	21,664.0 ±156.2

Source: *U.S. Department of Agriculture, 2012 National Resources Inventory, Summary Report, August 2015*

Table 2 - Land Cover/use of non-Federal rural land, by State and year
In thousands of acres, with margins of error

State	Year	Cropland	CRP land	Pastureland	Rangeland	Forest land	Other rural land	Total rural land
Texas	1982	33,495.2 ±694.7	--	16,812.1 ±450.5	94,422.7 ±921.2	12,685.1 ±249.5	1,845.9 ±161.2	159,261.0 ±195.0
	1987	31,435.6 ±712.0	1,586.8 --	16,583.9 ±483.3	93,786.7 ±974.4	13,242.7 ±288.8	1,923.8 ±169.5	158,559.5 ±207.1
	1992	28,524.1 ±711.7	3,979.9 --	16,583.1 ±506.1	93,231.7 ±1,008.5	13,455.7 ±283.6	2,019.0 ±161.3	157,793.5 ±239.1
	1997	27,183.1 ±704.8	3,905.2 --	16,000.0 ±465.7	93,777.0 ±942.5	14,061.8 ±306.0	2,111.1 ±173.5	157,038.2 ±258.8
	2002	25,803.3 ±738.2	4,021.7 --	16,161.5 ±505.1	94,003.8 ±957.8	13,970.0 ±351.8	2,161.1 ±161.7	156,121.4 ±280.6
	2007	24,319.3 ±733.8	4,020.4 --	16,488.4 ±486.3	94,084.2 ±961.1	14,050.6 ±377.9	2,338.1 ±179.0	155,301.0 ±297.1
	2012	23,895.6 ±742.0	3,222.6 --	17,577.1 ±468.0	93,739.9 ±959.1	13,991.1 ±396.1	2,367.1 ±176.6	154,793.4 ±325.3
Utah	1982	2,053.8 ±286.1	--	530.2 ±83.2	11,353.5 ±663.5	2,261.3 ±468.2	1,888.9 ±481.5	18,087.7 ±112.2
	1987	1,930.5 ±313.6	149.9 --	591.2 ±90.7	11,091.4 ±656.0	2,247.1 ±469.6	1,729.0 ±483.6	17,739.1 ±119.4
	1992	1,828.0 ±316.6	222.3 --	642.0 ±99.2	11,256.3 ±650.5	2,210.1 ±462.5	1,894.0 ±480.6	18,052.7 ±127.5
	1997	1,643.1 ±313.2	216.4 --	650.6 ±102.3	10,826.3 ±683.5	2,324.9 ±526.6	1,896.5 ±478.3	17,557.8 ±136.9
	2002	1,580.9 ±311.0	177.8 --	620.8 ±109.0	10,700.4 ±698.2	2,293.7 ±546.5	1,866.5 ±531.2	17,240.1 ±151.4
	2007	1,487.2 ±314.5	169.8 --	609.2 ±89.4	10,715.4 ±704.4	2,285.1 ±546.5	1,880.6 ±528.0	17,147.3 ±158.6
	2012	1,454.1 ±314.8	178.1 --	651.7 ±116.1	10,622.4 ±708.5	2,308.6 ±555.6	1,875.3 ±534.3	17,090.2 ±161.3
Vermont	1982	641.6 ±55.7	--	442.0 ±50.5	0.0 --	4,139.0 ±70.8	84.1 ±16.6	5,306.7 ±33.5
	1987	637.0 ±64.0	0.0 --	377.5 ±48.1	0.0 --	4,135.6 ±71.0	81.6 ±15.9	5,231.7 ±33.0
	1992	621.7 ±63.6	0.0 --	346.5 ±38.2	0.0 --	4,130.3 ±68.3	84.2 ±18.5	5,182.7 ±34.2
	1997	592.4 ±62.7	0.0 --	337.7 ±38.3	0.0 --	4,124.7 ±69.8	89.1 ±21.0	5,143.9 ±34.9
	2002	560.2 ±61.2	0.0 --	319.7 ±41.3	0.0 --	4,102.2 ±71.5	93.2 ±20.0	5,075.3 ±29.8
	2007	545.5 ±62.2	0.0 --	312.8 ±42.6	0.0 --	4,072.2 ±74.3	113.1 ±26.1	5,043.6 ±31.9
	2012	532.2 ±63.4	0.0 --	320.2 ±42.1	0.0 --	4,049.9 ±74.8	128.1 ±32.7	5,030.4 ±33.1

Source: *U.S. Department of Agriculture, 2012 National Resources Inventory, Summary Report, August 2015*

Table 2 - Land Cover/use of non-Federal rural land, by State and year
In thousands of acres, with margins of error

State	Year	Cropland	CRP land	Pastureland	Rangeland	Forest land	Other rural land	Total rural land
Virginia	1982	3,457.6 ±171.8	--	3,298.9 ±158.9	0.0 --	13,708.9 ±229.4	617.9 ±53.9	21,083.3 ±106.8
	1987	3,167.4 ±180.1	24.2 --	3,273.9 ±153.7	0.0 --	13,778.6 ±226.1	579.8 ±55.3	20,823.9 ±107.1
	1992	2,950.5 ±177.8	74.8 --	3,264.0 ±151.8	0.0 --	13,729.0 ±218.1	577.3 ±51.0	20,595.6 ±114.0
	1997	2,935.3 ±181.3	70.3 --	3,051.0 ±162.8	0.0 --	13,618.6 ±211.9	579.4 ±46.3	20,254.6 ±110.0
	2002	2,878.7 ±190.6	35.1 --	3,015.9 ±184.9	0.0 --	13,490.8 ±207.5	555.8 ±61.8	19,976.3 ±112.1
	2007	2,784.7 ±190.2	31.4 --	2,987.8 ±179.9	0.0 --	13,365.7 ±205.5	606.5 ±64.0	19,776.1 ±112.4
	2012	2,784.9 ±186.8	28.4 --	2,941.6 ±188.5	0.0 --	13,295.1 ±219.7	614.0 ±69.7	19,664.0 ±117.5
Washington	1982	7,635.0 ±415.6	--	1,311.5 ±179.9	6,011.7 ±371.9	12,839.9 ±401.0	652.4 ±109.8	28,450.5 ±156.3
	1987	7,161.6 ±417.3	452.9 --	1,338.9 ±199.2	5,978.9 ±360.2	12,767.5 ±395.2	649.3 ±107.0	28,349.1 ±156.7
	1992	6,594.2 ±404.6	1,012.3 --	1,328.1 ±214.1	5,888.7 ±354.9	12,648.2 ±389.9	648.6 ±101.4	28,120.1 ±169.8
	1997	6,536.7 ±404.1	1,016.9 --	1,181.6 ±178.9	5,884.3 ±353.0	12,553.0 ±390.8	692.9 ±97.9	27,865.4 ±185.4
	2002	6,297.2 ±414.4	1,191.6 --	1,080.4 ±130.2	5,890.0 ±377.9	12,416.6 ±383.6	712.6 ±117.8	27,588.4 ±191.4
	2007	5,894.4 ±373.8	1,432.3 --	1,080.2 ±127.7	5,946.4 ±390.6	12,337.0 ±384.4	741.4 ±117.6	27,431.7 ±185.8
	2012	5,831.1 ±360.8	1,306.5 --	1,215.1 ±152.2	5,951.0 ±396.7	12,298.8 ±384.4	766.7 ±117.2	27,369.2 ±184.8
West Virginia	1982	1,085.2 ±86.6	--	1,879.1 ±118.7	0.0 --	10,374.2 ±158.8	239.4 ±38.1	13,577.9 ±48.3
	1987	985.1 ±80.9	0.6 --	1,737.0 ±113.2	0.0 --	10,546.8 ±157.5	251.3 ±40.5	13,520.8 ±50.2
	1992	903.6 ±77.4	0.6 --	1,621.5 ±110.4	0.0 --	10,529.7 ±150.7	287.8 ±52.4	13,343.2 ±54.3
	1997	852.0 ±79.0	0.0 --	1,519.2 ±103.8	0.0 --	10,507.7 ±145.3	258.4 ±38.1	13,137.3 ±63.6
	2002	802.4 ±90.9	0.6 --	1,479.6 ±111.1	0.0 --	10,453.9 ±135.6	263.2 ±75.9	12,999.7 ±62.7
	2007	752.0 ±88.5	0.6 --	1,447.7 ±119.9	0.0 --	10,432.7 ±130.6	304.5 ±80.6	12,937.5 ±64.4
	2012	719.1 ±89.9	0.0 --	1,424.1 ±134.6	0.0 --	10,429.0 ±148.6	341.6 ±87.4	12,913.8 ±63.1

Source: U.S. Department of Agriculture, 2012 National Resources Inventory, Summary Report, August 2015

Table 2 - Land Cover/use of non-Federal rural land, by State and year
In thousands of acres, with margins of error

State	Year	Cropland	CRP land	Pastureland	Rangeland	Forest land	Other rural land	Total rural land
Wisconsin	1982	11,467.4 ±286.8	--	3,552.5 ±185.3	0.0 --	14,275.5 ±234.7	1,574.2 ±136.5	30,869.6 ±111.3
	1987	11,340.2 ±312.0	218.1 --	3,228.9 ±200.9	0.0 --	14,364.3 ±240.2	1,595.5 ±138.2	30,747.0 ±118.1
	1992	10,835.3 ±290.3	660.1 --	3,123.9 ±212.8	0.0 --	14,378.0 ±238.5	1,598.5 ±133.1	30,595.8 ±121.5
	1997	10,606.6 ±305.7	661.9 --	3,054.4 ±213.1	0.0 --	14,479.6 ±263.0	1,612.7 ±129.0	30,415.2 ±130.0
	2002	10,273.2 ±284.4	602.7 --	3,113.8 ±234.8	0.0 --	14,595.7 ±270.2	1,682.9 ±153.3	30,268.3 ±145.4
	2007	10,160.4 ±293.8	524.2 --	3,079.7 ±220.4	0.0 --	14,690.1 ±277.1	1,666.5 ±147.3	30,120.9 ±154.0
	2012	10,364.9 ±285.4	297.2 --	3,027.2 ±210.7	0.0 --	14,697.9 ±275.0	1,656.6 ±150.4	30,043.8 ±157.4
Wyoming	1982	2,523.9 ±303.2	--	738.5 ±362.0	27,277.8 ±420.0	1,079.0 ±283.3	474.5 ±198.2	32,093.7 ±65.8
	1987	2,361.0 ±329.0	129.0 --	835.1 ±365.7	27,165.9 ±436.6	1,082.6 ±281.6	475.1 ±197.3	32,048.7 ±69.9
	1992	2,200.0 ±332.6	251.4 --	919.1 ±379.6	27,007.3 ±460.7	1,086.2 ±282.0	524.6 ±231.3	31,988.6 ±72.1
	1997	2,131.9 ±339.9	246.9 --	1,066.4 ±405.7	26,992.6 ±470.2	1,078.5 ±276.9	426.4 ±172.1	31,942.7 ±75.9
	2002	2,205.2 ±301.7	279.6 --	790.5 ±311.6	27,173.2 ±421.9	1,077.4 ±245.9	414.4 ±199.0	31,940.3 ±76.9
	2007	2,148.3 ±285.0	282.9 --	733.3 ±319.8	27,168.4 ±435.9	1,079.3 ±248.4	423.7 ±206.1	31,835.9 ±120.4
	2012	2,159.5 ±297.8	196.5 --	809.9 ±323.0	27,073.2 ±440.6	1,083.5 ±248.1	489.8 ±222.0	31,812.4 ±121.9
Total	1982	420,587.6 ±2,087.1	--	131,288.9 ±1,352.8	419,356.2 ±3,274.4	410,288.6 ±2,578.8	42,776.0 ±1,139.2	1,424,297.3 ±830.8
	1987	406,375.0 ±2,026.7	13,753.6 --	127,407.7 ±1,361.4	413,937.0 ±3,254.8	412,263.5 ±2,752.0	42,943.2 ±1,203.8	1,416,680.0 ±903.9
	1992	382,001.1 ±1,985.1	33,982.7 --	125,817.6 ±1,250.0	410,221.0 ±3,143.4	412,188.5 ±2,776.2	43,236.3 ±1,133.0	1,407,447.2 ±1,007.1
	1997	376,360.8 ±2,046.7	32,694.8 --	120,692.7 ±1,294.3	408,067.3 ±3,226.8	413,330.8 ±2,798.9	43,476.7 ±1,122.9	1,394,623.1 ±1,059.9
	2002	367,675.1 ±2,080.0	31,763.4 --	119,294.3 ±1,586.6	407,761.6 ±3,334.3	413,709.5 ±2,579.2	43,404.1 ±1,369.6	1,383,608.0 ±1,209.5
	2007	358,866.3 ±2,009.3	32,464.0 --	119,744.1 ±1,468.5	407,230.9 ±3,447.5	413,123.4 ±2,541.0	44,934.6 ±1,377.5	1,376,363.3 ±1,259.6
	2012	362,726.1 ±1,933.0	24,222.0 --	121,138.0 ±1,334.2	405,776.9 ±3,419.6	413,337.2 ±2,593.2	45,448.5 ±1,343.0	1,372,648.7 ±1,295.2

***Source:** U.S. Department of Agriculture, 2012 National Resources Inventory, Summary Report, August 2015*

Table 2 - Land Cover/use of non-Federal rural land, by State and year
In thousands of acres, with margins of error

State	Year	Cropland	CRP land	Pastureland	Rangeland	Forest land	Other rural land	Total rural land

Notes:
• Acreages for Conservation Reserve Program (CRP) land are established through geospatial processes and administrative records; therefore, statistical margins of error are not applicable and shown as a dashed line (--). CRP was not implemented until 1985.
• Cropland includes cultivated and non-cultivated cropland.
• When the estimate is 0.0, margins of error are not applicable and shown as a dashed line (--).
• Estimates in red = STOP, these estimates are not reliable. The margin of error is equal to or greater than the estimate so the confidence interval includes zero.

Source: *U.S. Department of Agriculture, 2012 National Resources Inventory, Summary Report, August 2015*

Superfund National Priorities List

St.	City/Area	Site Name	Status	Date	Score[1]
AK	Adak	Adak Naval Air Station	Final	05/31/1994	51.37
AK	Anchorage	Fort Richardson (USARMY)	Final	05/31/1994	50.00
AK	Anchorage	Standard Steel & Metal Salvage Yard (USDOT)	Deleted	09/30/2002	46.25
AK	Fairbanks	Arctic Surplus	Deleted	09/25/2006	42.24
AK	Fairbanks North Star Borough	Fort Wainwright	Final	08/30/1990	42.40
AK	Fairbanks North Star Borough	Eielson Air Force Base	Final	11/21/1989	48.14
AK	Fairbanks North Star Borough	Alaska Battery Enterprises	Deleted	07/26/1996	30.98
AK	Greater Anchorage Borough	Elmendorf Air Force Base	Final	08/30/1990	45.91
AK	Thorne Bay	Salt Chuck Mine	Final	03/04/2010	50.00
AL	Anniston	Anniston Army Depot (Southeast Industrial Area)	Final	03/13/1989	51.91
AL	Axis	Stauffer Chemical Co. (LeMoyne Plant)	Final	09/21/1984	32.34
AL	Birmingham	35th Avenue	Proposed	09/22/2014	50.00
AL	Bucks	Stauffer Chemical Co. (Cold Creek Plant)	Final	09/21/1984	46.77
AL	Childersburg	Alabama Army Ammunition Plant	Final	07/22/1987	36.83
AL	Greenville	Mowbray Engineering Co.	Deleted	12/30/1993	53.67
AL	Headland	American Brass	Final	05/10/1999	55.61
AL	Huntsville	Redstone Arsenal (USARMY/NASA)	Final	05/31/1994	50.00
AL	Leeds	Interstate Lead Co. (ILCO)	Final	06/10/1986	42.86
AL	Limestone, Morgan	Triana/Tennessee River	Final	09/08/1983	61.42
AL	McIntosh	Ciba-Geigy Corp. (McIntosh Plant)	Final	09/21/1984	53.42
AL	McIntosh	Olin Corp. (McIntosh Plant)	Final	09/21/1984	39.71
AL	Montgomery	T.H. Agriculture & Nutrition Co. (Montgomery Plant)	Final	08/30/1990	44.46
AL	Montgomery	Capitol City Plume	Proposed	05/11/2000	50.00
AL	Perdido	Perdido Ground Water Contamination	Final	09/08/1983	30.29
AL	Saraland	Redwing Carriers, Inc. (Saraland)	Deleted	09/28/2015	30.83
AL	Vincent	Alabama Plating Company, Inc.	Final	09/18/2012	30.20
AR	Birta, Ola	Midland Products	Final	06/10/1986	30.77
AR	Edmondson	Gurley Pit	Deleted	11/06/2003	40.13
AR	El Dorado	Popile, Inc.	Final	10/14/1992	50.03
AR	Ft. Smith	Industrial Waste Control	Deleted	04/07/2008	30.31
AR	Jacksonville	Vertac, Inc.	Final	09/08/1983	65.46
AR	Jacksonville	Rogers Road Municipal Landfill	Deleted	10/12/2010	29.64
AR	Jacksonville	Jacksonville Municipal Landfill	Deleted	03/14/2000	29.64
AR	Mena	Mid-South Wood Products	Final	09/08/1983	45.87
AR	Newport	Cecil Lindsey	Deleted	09/22/1989	35.60
AR	Norphlet	MacMillan Ring Free Oil	Final	05/12/2014	50.00
AR	Omaha	Arkwood, Inc.	Final	03/31/1989	28.95
AR	Paragould	Monroe Auto Equipment Co. (Paragould Pit)	Deleted	09/29/2014	46.01
AR	Plainview	Mountain Pine Pressure Treating	Final	07/22/1999	41.93
AR	Reader	Ouachita Nevada Wood Treater	Final	05/11/2000	50.00
AR	Walnut Ridge	Frit Industries	Deleted	10/14/1997	39.47
AR	West Helena	Cedar Chemical Corporation	Final	09/18/2012,	
AR	West Memphis	South 8th Street Landfill	Deleted	09/28/2004	50.27
AS	Taputimu	Taputimu Farm	Deleted	03/07/1986,	
AZ	Avondale, Goodyear	Phoenix-Goodyear Airport Area	Final	09/08/1983	45.91
AZ	Chandler	Williams Air Force Base	Final	11/21/1989	37.93
AZ	Dewey-Humboldt	Iron King Mine - Humboldt Smelter	Final	09/03/2008	52.69
AZ	Glendale	Luke Air Force Base	Deleted	04/22/2002	37.93
AZ	Globe	Mountain View Mobile Home Estates	Deleted	04/18/1988,	
AZ	Hassayampa	Hassayampa Landfill	Final	07/22/1987	42.79
AZ	Phoenix	Motorola, Inc. (52nd Street Plant)	Final	10/04/1989	40.83
AZ	Phoenix	Nineteenth Avenue Landfill	Deleted	09/25/2006	54.27
AZ	Scottsdale	Indian Bend Wash Area	Final	09/08/1983	42.24
AZ	St. David	Apache Powder Co.	Final	08/30/1990	39.09
AZ	Tucson	Tucson International Airport Area	Final	09/08/1983	57.80
AZ	Yuma	Yuma Marine Corps Air Station	Final	02/21/1990	32.24

St.	City/Area	Site Name	Status	Date	Score[1]
CA	Alameda	Alameda Naval Air Station	Final	07/22/1999	50.00
CA	Alhambra	San Gabriel Valley (Area 3)	Final	05/08/1984	28.90
CA	Alviso	South Bay Asbestos Area	Final	06/10/1986	44.68
CA	Arvin	Brown & Bryant, Inc. (Arvin Plant)	Final	10/04/1989	53.36
CA	Baldwin Park Area	San Gabriel Valley (Area 2)	Final	05/08/1984	42.24
CA	Barstow	Barstow Marine Corps Logistics Base	Final	11/21/1989	37.93
CA	Casmalia	Casmalia Resources	Final	09/13/2001	30.00
CA	Clear Lake	Sulphur Bank Mercury Mine	Final	08/30/1990	44.42
CA	Cloverdale	MGM Brakes	Final	09/08/1983	34.70
CA	Coalinga	Coalinga Asbestos Mine	Deleted	04/24/1998	45.55
CA	Concord	Concord Naval Weapons Station	Final	12/16/1994	50.00
CA	Crescent City	Del Norte Pesticide Storage	Deleted	09/18/2002	35.79
CA	Cupertino	Intersil Inc./Siemens Components	Final	08/30/1990	28.90
CA	Davis	Frontier Fertilizer	Final	05/31/1994	35.04
CA	Davis	Laboratory for Energy-Related Health Research/Old Campus Landfill (USDOE)	Final	05/31/1994	50.00
CA	El Monte	San Gabriel Valley (Area 1)	Final	05/08/1984	42.24
CA	El Toro	El Toro Marine Corps Air Station	Final	02/21/1990	37.43
CA	Fillmore	Pacific Coast Pipe Lines	Final	10/04/1989	46.01
CA	Fresno	Industrial Waste Processing	Final	08/30/1990	51.13
CA	Fresno	Fresno Municipal Sanitary Landfill	Final	10/04/1989	35.57
CA	Fresno	T.H. Agriculture & Nutrition Co.	Deleted	08/21/2006	42.24
CA	Fresno County	Atlas Asbestos Mine	Final	09/21/1984	45.55
CA	Fullerton	McColl	Final	09/08/1983	41.77
CA	Glen Avon Heights	Stringfellow	Final	09/08/1983,	
CA	Glendale	San Fernando Valley (Area 3)	Deleted	10/12/2004	42.24
CA	Glendale, Los Angeles	San Fernando Valley (Area 2)	Final	06/10/1986	42.24
CA	Hoopa	Celtor Chemical Works	Deleted	09/30/2003	30.31
CA	Idria	New Idria Mercury Mine	Final	09/16/2011	31.66
CA	Imperial	Stoker Company	Proposed	07/29/1991	70.94
CA	Jackson	Argonaut Mine	Final	09/09/2016	58.31
CA	Kern County	Edwards Air Force Base	Final	08/30/1990	33.62
CA	La Puente	San Gabriel Valley (Area 4)	Final	05/08/1984	28.90
CA	Lathrop	Sharpe Army Depot	Final	07/22/1987	42.24
CA	Livermore	Lawrence Livermore National Laboratory (Site 300) (USDOE)	Final	08/30/1990	31.58
CA	Livermore	Lawrence Livermore Laboratory (USDOE)	Final	07/22/1987	42.24
CA	Los Angeles	Del Amo	Final	09/05/2002	47.12
CA	Los Angeles	San Fernando Valley (Area 1)	Final	06/10/1986	42.24
CA	Los Angeles	San Fernando Valley (Area 4)	Final	06/10/1986	35.57
CA	Malaga	Purity Oil Sales, Inc.	Final	09/08/1983	43.27
CA	Marina	Fort Ord	Final	02/21/1990	42.24
CA	Markleeville	Leviathan Mine	Final	05/11/2000	50.00
CA	Maywood	Pemaco Maywood	Final	01/19/1999	45.23
CA	Merced	Castle Air Force Base (6 Areas)	Final	07/22/1987	37.93
CA	Modesto	Modesto Ground Water Contamination	Final	03/31/1989	28.90
CA	Monterey Park	Operating Industries, Inc., Landfill	Final	06/10/1986	57.22
CA	Mountain View	Fairchild Semiconductor Corp. (Mountain View Plant)	Final	02/11/1991	31.94
CA	Mountain View	Spectra-Physics, Inc.	Final	02/11/1991	37.20
CA	Mountain View	CTS Printex, Inc.	Final	02/21/1990	33.62
CA	Mountain View	Jasco Chemical Corp.	Final	10/04/1989	35.36
CA	Mountain View	Teledyne Semiconductor	Final	07/22/1987	35.35
CA	Mountain View	Intel Corp. (Mountain View Plant)	Final	06/10/1986	29.76
CA	Mountain View	Raytheon Corp.	Final	06/10/1986	29.76
CA	Nevada City	Lava Cap Mine	Final	01/19/1999	33.66
CA	Oakland	AMCO Chemical	Final	09/29/2003	50.00
CA	Oroville	Koppers Co., Inc. (Oroville Plant)	Final	09/21/1984	33.73
CA	Oroville	Western Pacific Railroad Co.	Deleted	08/29/2001	39.79
CA	Oroville	Louisiana-Pacific Corp.	Deleted	11/21/1996	33.73
CA	Oxnard	Halaco Engineering Company	Final	09/19/2007	58.31
CA	Palo Alto	Hewlett-Packard (620-640 Page Mill Road)	Final	02/21/1990	29.76

St.	City/Area	Site Name	Status	Date	Score[1]
CA	Pasadena	Jet Propulsion Laboratory (NASA)	Final	10/14/1992	50.00
CA	Paso Robles	Klau/Buena Vista Mine	Final	04/19/2006	50.00
CA	Petaluma	Sola Optical USA, Inc.	Deleted	10/31/2013	33.39
CA	Porterville	Beckman Instruments (Porterville Plant)	Final	06/10/1986	34.21
CA	Rancho Cordova	Aerojet General Corp.	Final	09/08/1983	54.63
CA	Redding	Iron Mountain Mine	Final	09/08/1983	56.16
CA	Rialto	Rockets, Fireworks, and Flares (RFF)	Final	09/23/2009	50.00
CA	Richmond	United Heckathorn Co.	Final	03/14/1990	38.49
CA	Richmond	Liquid Gold Oil Corp.	Deleted	09/11/1996	43.32
CA	Riverbank	Riverbank Army Ammunition Plant	Final	02/21/1990	63.94
CA	Riverside	Alark Hard Chrome	Final	12/01/2000	50.50
CA	Riverside	March Air Force Base	Final	11/21/1989	31.94
CA	Rogue River - Siskiyou National Forest	Blue Ledge Mine	Final	09/16/2011	50.28
CA	Sacramento	Mather Air Force Base	Final	07/22/1987	28.90
CA	Sacramento	McClellan Air Force Base (Ground Water Contamination)	Final	07/22/1987	57.93
CA	Sacramento	Sacramento Army Depot	Final	07/22/1987	44.46
CA	Sacramento	Jibboom Junkyard	Deleted	09/10/1991	28.94
CA	Salinas	Crazy Horse Sanitary Landfill	Final	08/30/1990	37.93
CA	Salinas	Firestone Tire & Rubber Co. (Salinas Plant)	Deleted	04/21/2005	45.91
CA	San Bernardino	Newmark Ground Water Contamination	Final	03/31/1989	35.57
CA	San Bernardino	Norton Air Force Base	Final	07/22/1987	39.65
CA	San Diego County	Camp Pendleton Marine Corps Base	Final	11/21/1989	33.79
CA	San Francisco	Treasure Island Naval Air Station - Hunters Point Annex	Final	11/21/1989	48.77
CA	San Jose	Lorentz Barrel & Drum Co.	Final	10/04/1989	33.94
CA	Santa Clara	Synertek, Inc. (Building 1)	Final	10/04/1989	31.94
CA	Santa Clara	Applied Materials	Final	07/22/1987	31.94
CA	Santa Clara	National Semiconductor Corp.	Final	07/22/1987	35.57
CA	Santa Clara	Intel Corp. (Santa Clara III)	Final	06/10/1986	31.94
CA	Santa Clara	Intel Magnetics	Final	06/10/1986	31.94
CA	Santa Fe Springs	Waste Disposal, Inc.	Final	07/22/1987	34.60
CA	Scotts Valley	Watkins-Johnson Co. (Stewart Dvision Plant)	Final	08/30/1990	28.90
CA	Selma	Selma Treating Co.	Final	09/08/1983	48.83
CA	Solano County	Travis Air Force Base	Final	11/21/1989	29.49
CA	South Gate	Jervis B. Webb Co.	Final	05/10/2012	45.76
CA	South Gate	Southern Avenue Industrial Area	Final	05/10/2012	50.00
CA	South Gate	Cooper Drum Company	Final	06/14/2001	50.00
CA	South San Jose	Fairchild Semiconductor Corp. (South San Jose Plant)	Final	10/04/1989	44.46
CA	Stockton	McCormick & Baxter Creosoting Co.	Final	10/14/1992	74.86
CA	Sunnyvale	Advanced Micro Devices, Inc. (Building 915)	Final	08/30/1990	31.94
CA	Sunnyvale	TRW Microwave, Inc. (Building 825)	Final	02/21/1990	31.94
CA	Sunnyvale	Moffett Naval Air Station	Final	07/22/1987	29.49
CA	Sunnyvale	Monolithic Memories	Final	07/22/1987	35.57
CA	Sunnyvale	Advanced Micro Devices, Inc.	Final	06/10/1986	37.93
CA	Sunnyvale	Westinghouse Electric Corp. (Sunnyvale Plant)	Final	06/10/1986	39.93
CA	Torrance	Montrose Chemical Corp.	Final	10/04/1989	32.10
CA	Tracy	Tracy Defense Depot (USARMY)	Final	08/30/1990	37.16
CA	Turlock	Valley Wood Preserving, Inc.	Final	03/31/1989	32.01
CA	Ukiah	Coast Wood Preserving	Final	09/08/1983	44.73
CA	Victorville	George Air Force Base	Final	02/21/1990	33.62
CA	Visalia	Southern California Edison Co. (Visalia Poleyard)	Deleted	09/25/2009	48.91
CA	Weed	J.H. Baxter & Co.	Final	10/04/1989	34.78
CA	Westminster	Ralph Gray Trucking Co.	Deleted	09/28/2004	35.04
CA	Whittier	Omega Chemical Corporation	Final	01/19/1999	30.94
CO	Adams County	Rocky Mountain Arsenal (USARMY)	Final	07/22/1987	58.15
CO	Arapahoe County	Lowry Landfill	Final	09/21/1984	48.36
CO	Boulder County	Marshall Landfill	Final	09/08/1983,	
CO	Canon City	Lincoln Park	Final	09/21/1984	31.31
CO	Commerce City	Sand Creek Industrial	Deleted	12/20/1996	59.65
CO	Commerce City	Woodbury Chemical Co.	Deleted	03/22/1993	44.87
CO	Creede	Nelson Tunnel/Commodore Waste Rock	Final	09/03/2008	48.03

St.	City/Area	Site Name	Status	Date	Score[1]
CO	Denver	Vasquez Boulevard and I-70	Final	07/22/1999	50.00
CO	Denver	Chemical Sales Co.	Final	08/30/1990	37.93
CO	Denver	Broderick Wood Products	Final	09/21/1984	35.13
CO	Denver	Denver Radium Site	Final	09/08/1983	44.11
CO	Golden	Rocky Flats Plant (USDOE)	Final	10/04/1989	64.32
CO	Gunnison National Forest	Standard Mine	Final	09/14/2005	50.00
CO	Idaho Springs	Central City, Clear Creek	Final	09/08/1983	51.39
CO	Leadville	California Gulch	Final	09/08/1983	55.84
CO	Minturn, Redcliff	Eagle Mine	Final	06/10/1986	47.19
CO	Pitkin County	Smuggler Mountain	Deleted	09/23/1999	31.31
CO	Pueblo	Colorado Smelter	Final	12/11/2014	50.00
CO	Rio Grande County	Summitville Mine	Final	05/31/1994	50.00
CO	Salida	Smeltertown Site	Proposed	02/07/1992	58.56
CO	San Juan	Bonita Peak Mining District	Final	09/09/2016	50.00
CO	Uravan	Uravan Uranium Project (Union Carbide Corp.)	Final	06/10/1986	43.53
CO	Ward	Captain Jack Mill	Final	09/29/2003	50.56
CO	Waterton	Air Force Plant PJKS	Final	11/21/1989	42.93
CT	Barkhamsted	Barkhamsted-New Hartford Landfill	Final	10/04/1989	38.05
CT	Beacon Falls	Beacon Heights Landfill	Final	09/08/1983	46.77
CT	Canterbury	Yaworski Waste Lagoon	Final	09/08/1983	36.72
CT	Cheshire	Cheshire Ground Water Contamination	Deleted	07/02/1997	35.57
CT	Durham	Durham Meadows	Final	10/04/1989	33.94
CT	East Windsor	Broad Brook Mill	Proposed	12/01/2000	54.35
CT	Naugatuck Borough	Laurel Park, Inc.	Final	09/08/1983,	
CT	New London	New London Submarine Base	Final	08/30/1990	36.53
CT	Norwalk	Kellogg-Deering Well Field	Final	09/21/1984	39.92
CT	Plainfield	Gallup's Quarry	Final	10/04/1989	46.29
CT	Southington	Old Southington Landfill	Final	09/21/1984	54.35
CT	Southington	Solvents Recovery Service of New England	Final	09/08/1983	44.93
CT	Sterling	Revere Textile Prints Corp.	Deleted	09/02/1994	41.06
CT	Stratford	Raymark Industries, Inc.	Final	04/25/1995,	
CT	Vernon	Precision Plating Corp.	Final	10/04/1989	49.10
CT	Waterbury	Scovill Industrial Landfill	Final	07/27/2000	50.00
CT	Wolcott	Nutmeg Valley Road	Deleted	09/23/2005	42.69
CT	Woodstock	Linemaster Switch Corp.	Final	02/21/1990	33.71
DC	Washington	Washington Navy Yard	Final	07/28/1998	48.57
DE	Cheswold	Chem-Solv, Inc.	Final	08/30/1990	37.93
DE	Delaware City	Standard Chlorine of Delaware, Inc.	Final	07/22/1987	35.42
DE	Delaware City	Delaware City PVC Plant	Final	09/08/1983	30.55
DE	Dover	Dover Gas Light Co.	Final	10/04/1989	35.57
DE	Dover	Dover Air Force Base	Final	03/13/1989	35.89
DE	Dover	Wildcat Landfill	Deleted	03/14/2003	30.61
DE	Kent County	Coker's Sanitation Service Landfills	Deleted	08/02/2011	52.15
DE	Kirkwood	Harvey & Knott Drum, Inc.	Final	09/08/1983	30.77
DE	Laurel	Sussex County Landfill No. 5	Deleted	09/28/2001	28.90
DE	Millsboro	NCR Corp. (Millsboro Plant)	Final	07/22/1987	38.21
DE	Millsboro	Millsboro TCE	Proposed	09/23/2009	50.00
DE	Mount Pleasant	Sealand Limited	Deleted	07/01/1997	33.10
DE	New Castle	Halby Chemical Co.	Final	06/10/1986	30.90
DE	New Castle County	Army Creek Landfill	Final	09/08/1983	69.92
DE	New Castle County	Delaware Sand & Gravel Landfill	Final	09/08/1983	46.60
DE	New Castle County	Tybouts Corner Landfill	Final	09/08/1983,	
DE	New Castle County	New Castle Spill	Deleted	06/12/1996	38.33
DE	New Castle County	New Castle Steel	Deleted	03/17/1989	30.40
DE	Newport	Koppers Co., Inc. (Newport Plant)	Final	08/30/1990	33.56
DE	Newport	E.I. du Pont de Nemours & Co., Inc. (Newport Pigment Plant Landfill)	Final	02/21/1990	51.91
DE	Smyrna	Tyler Refrigeration Pit	Deleted	03/29/2004	33.94
FL	Baldwin	Yellow Water Road Dump	Deleted	05/18/1999	30.26
FL	Brandon	Sydney Mine Sludge Ponds	Final	10/04/1989	38.93

St.	City/Area	Site Name	Status	Date	Score[1]
FL	Cantonment	Dubose Oil Products Co.	Deleted	10/01/2004	34.18
FL	Clermont	Tower Chemical Co.	Final	09/08/1983	44.03
FL	Cottondale	Sapp Battery Salvage	Final	09/08/1983	47.70
FL	Davie	Davie Landfill	Deleted	08/21/2006	57.86
FL	Deland	Sherwood Medical Industries	Final	09/08/1983	39.83
FL	Duval County	Hipps Road Landfill	Deleted	02/27/2012	31.94
FL	Fort Lauderdale	Florida Petroleum Reprocessors	Final	03/06/1998	50.00
FL	Fort Lauderdale	Wingate Road Municipal Incinerator Dump	Final	10/04/1989	31.72
FL	Fort Lauderdale	Hollingsworth Solderless Terminal	Final	09/08/1983	44.53
FL	Gainesville	Cabot/Koppers	Final	09/21/1984	36.69
FL	Galloway	Alpha Chemical Corp.	Deleted	06/28/1995	43.24
FL	Hialeah	B&B Chemical Co., Inc.	Deleted	08/05/2014	35.35
FL	Hialeah	Standard Auto Bumper Corp.	Deleted	10/26/2007	42.79
FL	Hialeah	Northwest 58th Street Landfill	Deleted	10/11/1996	49.43
FL	Homestead	Homestead Air Force Base	Final	08/30/1990	42.40
FL	Indiantown	Florida Steel Corp.	Final	09/08/1983	45.92
FL	Jacksonville	Fairfax St. Wood Treaters	Final	09/18/2012	50.00
FL	Jacksonville	Kerr-McGee Chemical Corp - Jacksonville	Final	03/04/2010	70.71
FL	Jacksonville	Cecil Field Naval Air Station	Final	11/21/1989	31.99
FL	Jacksonville	Jacksonville Naval Air Station	Final	11/21/1989	32.08
FL	Jacksonville	Pickettville Road Landfill	Final	09/08/1983	42.94
FL	Lake Alfred	Callaway & Son Drum Service	Deleted	08/04/2009	46.22
FL	Lake Park	Trans Circuits, Inc.	Final	02/04/2000	50.00
FL	Lake Park	BMI-Textron	Deleted	11/18/2002	35.34
FL	Lakeland	Landia Chemical Company	Final	05/11/2000	50.00
FL	Live Oak	Brown Wood Preserving	Deleted	09/22/1995	45.51
FL	Longwood	General Dynamics Longwood	Final	09/29/2010	50.00
FL	Madison	Madison County Sanitary Landfill	Final	08/30/1990	37.93
FL	Marianna	United Metals, Inc.	Final	04/30/2003	33.73
FL	Medley	Pepper Steel & Alloys, Inc.	Final	09/21/1984	31.92
FL	Miami	Continental Cleaners	Final	03/15/2012	50.00
FL	Miami	Airco Plating Co.	Final	02/21/1990	42.47
FL	Miami	Miami Drum Services	Final	09/08/1983	53.56
FL	Miami	Anaconda Aluminum Co./Milgo Electronics Corp.	Deleted	07/09/1998	31.03
FL	Miami	Gold Coast Oil Corp.	Deleted	10/09/1996	57.80
FL	Miami	Varsol Spill	Deleted	09/01/1988	44.46
FL	Milton	Whiting Field Naval Air Station	Final	05/31/1994	50.00
FL	Mount Pleasant	Parramore Surplus	Deleted	02/21/1989	37.61
FL	North Miami	Munisport Landfill	Deleted	09/24/1999	32.37
FL	North Miami Beach	Anodyne, Inc.	Final	02/21/1990	31.03
FL	Orlando	Chevron Chemical Co. (Ortho Division)	Final	05/31/1994	50.00
FL	Orlando	City Industries, Inc.	Final	10/04/1989	32.00
FL	Palm Bay	Harris Corp. (Palm Bay Plant)	Final	07/22/1987	35.57
FL	Panama City	Tyndall Air Force Base	Final	04/01/1997	50.00
FL	Pembroke Park	Petroleum Products Corp.	Final	07/22/1987	40.11
FL	Pensacola	Escambia Wood - Pensacola	Final	12/16/1994	50.00
FL	Pensacola	Pensacola Naval Air Station	Final	11/21/1989	42.40
FL	Pensacola	Agrico Chemical Co.	Final	10/04/1989	44.98
FL	Pensacola	American Creosote Works (Pensacola Plant)	Final	09/08/1983	58.41
FL	Pensacola	Beulah Landfill	Deleted	06/22/1998	38.17
FL	Plant City	Schuylkill Metals Corp.	Deleted	08/22/2001	59.16
FL	Pompano Beach	Flash Cleaners	Final	09/03/2008	50.00
FL	Pompano Beach	Chemform, Inc.	Deleted	07/28/2000	37.93
FL	Pompano Beach	Wilson Concepts of Florida, Inc.	Deleted	04/04/1995	37.93
FL	Port Salerno	Solitron Microwave	Final	07/28/1998	50.00
FL	Princeton	Woodbury Chemical Co. (Princeton Plant)	Deleted	11/27/1995	39.43
FL	Quincy	Post and Lumber Preserving Co. Inc.	Proposed	09/09/2016	36.33
FL	Ruskin	JJ Seifert Machine	Final	03/04/2010	50.00
FL	Sanford	Sanford Dry Cleaners	Final	09/29/2010	50.00

St.	City/Area	Site Name	Status	Date	Score[1]
FL	Seffner	Taylor Road Landfill	Final	09/08/1983	51.37
FL	Tampa	Raleigh Street Dump	Final	04/09/2009	50.00
FL	Tampa	Alaric Area Ground Water Plume	Final	12/01/2000	41.91
FL	Tampa	Southern Solvents, Inc.	Final	07/27/2000	50.00
FL	Tampa	MRI Corp (Tampa)	Final	12/23/1996	37.62
FL	Tampa	Stauffer Chemical Co (Tampa)	Final	12/23/1996	59.81
FL	Tampa	Helena Chemical Co. (Tampa Plant)	Final	10/14/1992	30.19
FL	Tampa	Peak Oil Co./Bay Drum Co.	Final	06/10/1986	58.15
FL	Tampa	Reeves Southeastern Galvanizing Corp.	Final	09/08/1983	58.75
FL	Tampa	Kassauf-Kimerling Battery Disposal	Deleted	10/02/2000	53.42
FL	Tampa	Sixty-Second Street Dump	Deleted	10/01/1999	49.09
FL	Tampa	Tri-City Oil Conservationist, Inc.	Deleted	09/01/1988	39.30
FL	Tarpon Springs	Stauffer Chemical Co. (Tarpon Springs)	Final	05/31/1994	50.00
FL	Temple Terrace	Normandy Park Apartments	Proposed	02/13/1995	49.98
FL	Thonotosassa	Arkla Terra Property	Final	04/09/2009	50.00
FL	Vero Beach	Piper Aircraft Corp./Vero Beach Water & Sewer Department	Final	02/21/1990	31.13
FL	Warrington	Pioneer Sand Co.	Deleted	02/08/1993	51.97
FL	Whitehouse	Whitehouse Oil Pits	Final	09/08/1983	52.58
FL	Whitehouse	Coleman-Evans Wood Preserving Co.	Deleted	05/27/2014	46.18
FL	Zellwood	Zellwood Ground Water Contamination	Final	09/08/1983	51.91
FM	Palikir	PCB Wastes	Deleted	03/07/1986,	
GA	Albany	Marine Corps Logistics Base	Final	11/21/1989	44.65
GA	Albany	Firestone Tire & Rubber Co. (Albany Plant)	Final	10/04/1989	30.08
GA	Albany	T.H. Agriculture & Nutrition Co. (Albany Plant)	Final	03/31/1989	40.93
GA	Athens	Luminous Processes, Inc.	Deleted	12/30/1982,	
GA	Augusta	Alternate Energy Resources	Final	04/19/2006	50.00
GA	Augusta	Peach Orchard Road PCE Ground Water Plume	Final	09/14/2005	50.00
GA	Augusta	Monsanto Corp. (Augusta Plant)	Deleted	03/09/1998	35.65
GA	Brunswick	Brunswick Wood Preserving	Final	04/01/1997	54.49
GA	Brunswick	LCP Chemicals Georgia	Final	06/17/1996,	
GA	Brunswick	Hercules 009 Landfill	Final	09/21/1984	52.58
GA	Brunswick	Terry Creek Dredge Spoil Areas/Hercules Outfall	Proposed	04/01/1997	50.18
GA	Camilla	Camilla Wood Preserving Company	Final	07/28/1998	50.00
GA	Cedartown	Diamond Shamrock Corp. Landfill	Final	08/30/1990	35.60
GA	Cedartown	Cedartown Industries, Inc.	Deleted	09/19/2006	42.00
GA	Cedartown	Cedartown Municipal Landfill	Deleted	03/10/1999	33.62
GA	Fort Valley	Woolfolk Chemical Works, Inc.	Final	08/30/1990	42.24
GA	Houston County	Robins Air Force Base (Landfill #4/Sludge Lagoon)	Final	07/22/1987	51.66
GA	Kensington	Mathis Brothers Landfill (South Marble Top Road)	Final	03/31/1989	30.78
GA	Macon	Macon Naval Ordnance Plant	Final	05/24/2013	48.97
GA	Macon	Armstrong World Industries	Final	09/16/2011	50.00
GA	Peach County	Powersville Site	Deleted	11/01/2010	35.53
GA	Tifton	Marzone Inc./Chevron Chemical Co.	Final	10/04/1989	30.26
GU	Ordot	Ordot Landfill	Final	09/08/1983,	
GU	Yigo	Andersen Air Force Base	Final	10/14/1992	50.00
HI	Honolulu County	Del Monte Corp. (Oahu Plantation)	Final	12/16/1994	50.00
HI	Oahu	Naval Computer and Telecommunications Area Master Station Eastern Pacific	Final	05/31/1994	50.00
HI	Oahu	Schofield Barracks (USARMY)	Deleted	08/10/2000	28.90
HI	Pearl Harbor	Pearl Harbor Naval Complex	Final	10/14/1992	70.82
IA	Atlantic	PCE Former Dry Cleaner	Final	04/07/2016	50.00
IA	Camanche	Lawrence Todtz Farm	Final	06/10/1986	52.11
IA	Cedar Rapids	Electro-Coatings, Inc.	Final	10/04/1989	42.24
IA	Charles City	Shaw Avenue Dump	Final	07/22/1987	30.01
IA	Charles City	White Farm Equipment Co. Dump	Deleted	10/30/2000	43.40
IA	Charles City	LaBounty Site	Deleted	10/06/1993	70.73
IA	Council Bluffs	Aidex Corp.	Deleted	10/21/1993,	
IA	Des Moines	Railroad Avenue Groundwater Contamination	Final	09/05/2002	50.00
IA	Des Moines	Des Moines TCE	Final	09/08/1983	42.28
IA	Dubuque	Peoples Natural Gas Co.	Final	08/30/1990	46.24

St.	City/Area	Site Name	Status	Date	Score[1]
IA	Fairfield	Fairfield Coal Gasification Plant	Final	08/30/1990	38.05
IA	Hospers	Farmers' Mutual Cooperative	Deleted	11/13/2001	33.74
IA	Kellogg	Midwest Manufacturing/North Farm	Final	06/10/1986	32.04
IA	Keokuk	Sheller-Globe Corp. Disposal	Deleted	09/24/2001	33.66
IA	Mason City	Mason City Coal Gasification Plant	Final	12/16/1994	69.33
IA	Mason City	Northwestern States Portland Cement Co.	Deleted	08/31/1995	57.80
IA	Middletown	Iowa Army Ammunition Plant	Final	08/30/1990	29.73
IA	Orange City	Vogel Paint & Wax Co.	Final	06/10/1986	31.45
IA	Ottumwa	John Deere (Ottumwa Works Landfills)	Deleted	01/22/2001	42.32
IA	Red Oak	Red Oak City Landfill	Deleted	09/26/2005	34.13
IA	Sergeant Bluff	Mid-America Tanning Co.	Deleted	09/24/2004	47.91
IA	Waterloo	Waterloo Coal Gasification Plant	Proposed	10/14/1992	50.00
IA	West Point	E.I. du Pont de Nemours & Co., Inc. (County Road X23)	Deleted	09/25/1995	46.01
ID	Idaho Falls	Idaho National Engineering Laboratory (USDOE)	Final	11/21/1989	51.91
ID	Lemhi County	Blackbird Mine	Proposed	05/10/1993	50.00
ID	Mountain Home	Mountain Home Air Force Base	Final	08/30/1990	57.80
ID	Pocatello	Eastern Michaud Flats Contamination	Final	08/30/1990	57.80
ID	Pocatello	Pacific Hide & Fur Recycling Co.	Deleted	11/04/1999	42.30
ID	Pocatello	Union Pacific Railroad Co.	Deleted	09/22/1997	53.47
ID	Rathdrum	Arrcom (Drexler Enterprises)	Deleted	12/23/1992	29.28
ID	Smelterville	Bunker Hill Mining & Metallurgical Complex	Final	09/08/1983	54.76
ID	Soda Springs	Monsanto Chemical Co. (Soda Springs Plant)	Final	08/30/1990	54.77
ID	Soda Springs	Kerr-McGee Chemical Corp. (Soda Springs Plant)	Final	10/04/1989	51.91
ID	St. Maries	St. Maries Creosote	Proposed	12/01/2000	50.00
ID	Yellow Pine	Stibnite/Yellow Pine Mining Area	Proposed	09/13/2001	50.00
IL	Antioch	H.O.D. Landfill	Final	02/21/1990	34.68
IL	Beckemeyer	Circle Smelting Corp	Proposed	06/17/1996	70.71
IL	Belvidere	MIG/Dewane Landfill	Final	08/30/1990	49.91
IL	Belvidere	Parsons Casket Hardware Co.	Final	07/22/1987	55.58
IL	Belvidere	Belvidere Municipal Landfill	Deleted	02/09/2015	28.62
IL	Byron	Byron Salvage Yard	Final	09/08/1983	33.93
IL	Cahokia, Sauget	Sauget Area 1	Proposed	09/13/2001	50.00
IL	Calumet City	Estech General Chemical Company	Final	09/30/2015	30.00
IL	Carterville	Sangamo Electric Dump/Crab Orchard National Wildlife Refuge (USDOI)	Final	07/22/1987	43.70
IL	Chicago	Lake Calumet Cluster	Final	03/04/2010	30.00
IL	Danville	Hegeler Zinc	Final	04/27/2005	50.00
IL	DePue	DePue/New Jersey Zinc/Mobil Chemical Corp.	Final	05/10/1999	70.71
IL	DuPage County	Kerr-McGee (Kress Creek/West Branch of DuPage River)	Final	02/11/1991	39.05
IL	DuPage County, West Chicago	Kerr-McGee (Residential Areas)	Final	08/30/1990	38.15
IL	East Cape Girardeau	Ilada Energy Co.	Deleted	01/08/2001	34.21
IL	Fairmont City	Old American Zinc Plant	Final	04/07/2016	30.00
IL	Galena	Bautsch-Gray Mine	Final	09/18/2012	48.97
IL	Galesburg	Galesburg/Koppers Co.	Final	09/08/1983	34.78
IL	Granite City	Jennison-Wright Corporation	Final	06/17/1996	40.30
IL	Granite City	NL Industries/Taracorp Lead Smelter	Final	06/10/1986	38.11
IL	Greenup	A & F Materials Reclaiming, Inc.	Deleted	06/11/2012	55.49
IL	Hartford	Chemetco	Final	03/04/2010	30.00
IL	Hillsboro	Eagle Zinc Co Div T L Diamond	Final	09/19/2007	50.00
IL	Joliet	Amoco Chemicals (Joliet Landfill)	Final	02/21/1990	39.44
IL	Joliet	Joliet Army Ammunition Plant (Load-Assembly-Packing Area)	Final	03/13/1989	35.23
IL	Joliet	Joliet Army Ammunition Plant (Manufacturing Area)	Final	07/22/1987	32.08
IL	La Salle	Matthiessen and Hegeler Zinc Company	Final	09/29/2003	50.00
IL	La Salle	LaSalle Electric Utilities	Final	09/08/1983	42.06
IL	Lawrenceville	Indian Refinery-Texaco Lawrenceville	Final	12/01/2000	56.67
IL	Lemont	Lenz Oil Service, Inc.	Final	10/04/1989	42.33
IL	Libertyville	Petersen Sand & Gravel	Deleted	02/11/1991	38.43
IL	Marshall	Velsicol Chemical Corp. (Marshall Plant)	Final	09/08/1983	48.78
IL	Morristown	Acme Solvents Reclaiming, Inc. (Morristown Plant)	Final	09/08/1983	31.98
IL	Ottawa	Ottawa Radiation Areas	Final	10/14/1992	50.00

St.	City/Area	Site Name	Status	Date	Score[1]
IL	Pembroke Township	Cross Brothers Pail Recycling (Pembroke)	Final	09/08/1983	42.04
IL	Quincy	Adams County Quincy Landfills 2&3	Final	08/30/1990	34.21
IL	Rantoul	Chanute Air Force Base	Proposed	12/01/2000	48.30
IL	Rockford	Interstate Pollution Control, Inc.	Final	03/31/1989	46.01
IL	Rockford	Southeast Rockford Ground Water Contamination	Final	03/31/1989	42.24
IL	Rockford	Pagel's Pit	Final	06/10/1986	45.91
IL	Rockton	Beloit Corp.	Final	08/30/1990	52.08
IL	Sandoval	Sandoval Zinc Company	Final	09/16/2011	30.00
IL	Sauget	Sauget Area 2	Proposed	09/13/2001	50.00
IL	Savanna	Savanna Army Depot Activity	Final	03/13/1989	42.20
IL	South Elgin	Tri-County Landfill Co./Waste Management of Illinois, Inc.	Final	03/31/1989	42.76
IL	Taylor Springs	ASARCO Taylor Springs	Final	09/27/2006	30.00
IL	Taylorville	Central Illinois Public Service Co.	Final	08/30/1990	28.95
IL	Warrenville	DuPage County Landfill/Blackwell Forest	Final	02/21/1990	35.57
IL	Wauconda	Wauconda Sand & Gravel	Final	09/08/1983	53.42
IL	Waukegan	Yeoman Creek Landfill	Final	03/31/1989	33.23
IL	Waukegan	Johns-Manville Corp.	Final	09/08/1983	38.20
IL	Waukegan	Outboard Marine Corp.	Final	09/08/1983,	
IL	West Chicago	Kerr-McGee (Sewage Treatment Plant)	Deleted	04/22/2013	35.20
IL	West Chicago	Kerr-McGee (Reed-Keppler Park)	Deleted	02/08/2010	39.51
IL	Woodstock	Woodstock Municipal Landfill	Final	10/04/1989	50.10
IN	Bloomington	Bennett Stone Quarry	Final	09/21/1984	32.55
IN	Bloomington	Lemon Lane Landfill	Final	09/08/1983	29.31
IN	Bloomington	Neal's Landfill (Bloomington)	Final	09/08/1983	42.93
IN	Claypool	Lakeland Disposal Service, Inc.	Final	03/31/1989	34.10
IN	Columbia City	Wayne Waste Oil	Final	09/08/1983	42.33
IN	Columbus	Columbus Old Municipal Landfill #1	Deleted	01/24/2014	45.31
IN	Columbus	Tri-State Plating	Deleted	07/14/1997	29.28
IN	East Chicago	U.S. Smelter and Lead Refinery, Inc.	Final	04/09/2009	58.31
IN	Elkhart	North Shore Drive	Final	09/22/2014	50.00
IN	Elkhart	Lane Street Ground Water Contamination	Final	09/23/2009	40.53
IN	Elkhart	Lusher Street Ground Water Contamination	Final	03/19/2008	50.00
IN	Elkhart	Conrail Rail Yard (Elkhart)	Final	08/30/1990	42.24
IN	Elkhart	Himco Dump	Final	02/21/1990	42.31
IN	Elkhart	Main Street Well Field	Final	09/08/1983	42.49
IN	Evansville	Jacobsville Neighborhood Soil Contamination	Final	07/22/2004	35.52
IN	Fort Wayne	Fort Wayne Reduction Dump	Final	06/10/1986	42.47
IN	Garden City	Garden City Ground Water Plume	Final	12/12/2013	50.00
IN	Gary	Gary Development Landfill	Final	09/16/2011	30.00
IN	Gary	MIDCO II	Final	06/10/1986	30.16
IN	Gary	Lake Sandy Jo (M&M Landfill)	Final	09/08/1983	38.21
IN	Gary	MIDCO I	Final	09/08/1983	46.44
IN	Gary	Ninth Avenue Dump	Final	09/08/1983	40.32
IN	Griffith	American Chemical Service, Inc.	Final	09/21/1984	34.98
IN	Hancock County	Poer Farm	Deleted	02/11/1991	37.38
IN	Indianapolis	West Vermont Drinking Water Contamination	Final	09/09/2016	50.00
IN	Indianapolis	Keystone Corridor Ground Water Contamination	Final	12/12/2013	50.00
IN	Indianapolis	Reilly Tar & Chemical Corp. (Indianapolis Plant)	Final	09/21/1984	34.03
IN	Indianapolis	Riverside Ground Water Contamination	Proposed	04/07/2016	50.00
IN	Indianapolis	Southside Sanitary Landfill	Deleted	07/03/1997	41.94
IN	Indianapolis	Carter Lee Lumber Co.	Deleted	07/09/1996	35.40
IN	Kokomo	Kokomo Contaminated Ground Water Plume	Final	03/26/2015	50.00
IN	Kokomo	Continental Steel Corp.	Final	03/31/1989	31.85
IN	La Porte	Fisher-Calo	Final	09/08/1983	52.05
IN	Lafayette	Tippecanoe Sanitary Landfill, Inc	Final	08/30/1990	42.24
IN	Lebanon	Wedzeb Enterprises, Inc.	Deleted	09/10/1991	31.27
IN	Marion	Marion (Bragg) Dump	Final	09/08/1983	35.25
IN	Martinsville	Pike and Mulberry Streets PCE Plume	Final	05/24/2013	50.00
IN	Michigan City	Waste, Inc., Landfill	Deleted	10/20/2008	50.63

St.	City/Area	Site Name	Status	Date	Score[1]
IN	Mishawaka	Douglass Road/Uniroyal, Inc., Landfill	Final	03/31/1989	36.61
IN	Osceola	Galen Myers Dump/Drum Salvage	Final	03/31/1989	42.24
IN	Seymour	Seymour Recycling Corp.	Final	09/08/1983,	
IN	South Bend	Beck's Lake	Final	12/12/2013	50.00
IN	South Bend	Whiteford Sales & Service Inc./Nationalease	Deleted	09/06/1996	51.87
IN	Spencer	Neal's Dump (Spencer)	Deleted	10/04/1999	36.55
IN	Terre Haute	Elm Street Ground Water Contamination	Final	03/07/2007	50.00
IN	Terre Haute	International Minerals & Chemicals Corp. (Terre Haute East Plant)	Deleted	02/11/1991	57.80
IN	Vincennes	Prestolite Battery Division	Final	10/04/1989	40.63
IN	Westville	Cam-Or Inc.	Final	03/06/1998	58.91
IN	Zionsville	Northside Sanitary Landfill, Inc.	Final	09/21/1984	46.04
IN	Zionsville	Envirochem Corp.	Final	09/08/1983	46.44
KS	Arkansas City	Arkansas City Dump	Deleted	03/01/1996,	
KS	Cherokee County	Cherokee County	Final	09/08/1983	58.15
KS	Colby	Ace Services	Final	09/29/1995	50.00
KS	Cowley County	Strother Field Industrial Park	Final	06/10/1986	33.62
KS	Delavan	Tri-County Public Airport	Proposed	07/27/2000	50.00
KS	El Dorado	Pester Refinery Co.	Final	03/31/1989	30.16
KS	Great Bend	Plating, Inc.	Final	03/19/2008	50.00
KS	Hutchinson	Obee Road	Final	07/22/1987	33.62
KS	Iola	Former United Zinc & Associated Smelters	Final	05/24/2013	50.00
KS	Johnson County	Doepke Disposal (Holliday)	Final	09/08/1983	47.46
KS	Junction City	Fort Riley	Final	08/30/1990	33.79
KS	Olathe	Chemical Commodities, Inc.	Final	05/31/1994	50.00
KS	Topeka	Hydro-Flex Inc.	Deleted	11/09/1993	42.79
KS	Wichita	29th & Mead Ground Water Contamination	Deleted	04/29/1996	35.35
KS	Wichita	Big River Sand Co.	Deleted	10/14/1992	32.56
KS	Wichita	Johns' Sludge Pond	Deleted	01/06/1992	35.94
KS	Wichita Heights	57th and North Broadway Streets Site	Final	10/14/1992	50.00
KS	Wright	Wright Ground Water Contamination	Final	06/17/1996	50.00
KY	Auburn	Caldwell Lace Leather Co., Inc.	Final	08/30/1990	34.21
KY	Brooks	Smith's Farm	Final	06/10/1986	32.69
KY	Brooks	A.L. Taylor (Valley of Drums)	Deleted	05/17/1996,	
KY	Calvert City	Airco	Final	09/21/1984	33.29
KY	Calvert City	B.F. Goodrich	Final	09/08/1983	33.01
KY	Dayhoit	National Electric Coil Co./Cooper Industries	Final	10/14/1992	50.00
KY	Hawesville	National Southwire Aluminum Co.	Deleted	10/05/2015	50.00
KY	Hillsboro	Maxey Flats Nuclear Disposal	Final	06/10/1986	31.71
KY	Howe Valley	Howe Valley Landfill	Deleted	07/26/1996	36.73
KY	Island	Brantley Landfill	Final	02/21/1990	52.73
KY	Jefferson County	Distler Farm	Final	09/08/1983	34.62
KY	Louisville	Lee's Lane Landfill	Deleted	04/25/1996	39.52
KY	Maceo	Green River Disposal, Inc.	Final	08/30/1990	29.12
KY	Mayfield	General Tire & Rubber Co. (Mayfield Landfill)	Deleted	10/27/2000	32.94
KY	Newport	Newport Dump	Deleted	06/03/1996	37.63
KY	Olaton	Fort Hartford Coal Co. Stone Quarry	Final	08/30/1990	43.84
KY	Paducah	Paducah Gaseous Diffusion Plant (USDOE)	Final	05/31/1994	56.95
KY	Peewee Valley	Red Penn Sanitation Co. Landfill	Deleted	09/14/2001	38.10
KY	Shepherdsville	Tri-City Disposal Co.	Final	03/31/1989	33.82
KY	West Point	Distler Brickyard	Final	09/08/1983	44.77
LA	Abbeville	Gulf Coast Vacuum Services	Deleted	07/23/2001	42.78
LA	Abbeville	D.L. Mud, Inc.	Deleted	03/07/2000	32.37
LA	Abbeville	PAB Oil & Chemical Service, Inc.	Deleted	01/03/2000	38.94
LA	Alexandria	Ruston Foundry	Deleted	07/13/2010	43.17
LA	Ascension Parish	Dutchtown Treatment Plant	Deleted	11/16/1999	36.41
LA	Bayou Sorrel	Bayou Sorrel	Deleted	09/29/1997	34.69
LA	Bogalusa	Colonial Creosote	Final	09/30/2015	50.00
LA	Bossier City	Highway 71/72 Refinery	Proposed	02/13/1995	50.00
LA	Darrow	Old Inger Oil Refinery	Deleted	08/12/2008,	
LA	Denham Springs	Combustion, Inc.	Final	08/30/1990	33.79

St.	City/Area	Site Name	Status	Date	Score[1]
LA	Doyline	Louisiana Army Ammunition Plant	Final	03/13/1989	30.26
LA	Grand Cheniere	Mallard Bay Landing Bulk Plant	Deleted	09/19/2005	48.55
LA	Houma	Delta Shipyard	Final	09/22/2014	48.05
LA	Jennings	SBA Shipyard	Final	09/09/2016	50.00
LA	Jennings	EVR-Wood Treating/Evangeline Refining Company	Final	09/18/2012	48.20
LA	Lake Charles	Gulf State Utilities-North Ryan Street	Proposed	02/13/1995	50.43
LA	Madisonville	Madisonville Creosote Works	Final	12/23/1996	48.01
LA	Marion	Marion Pressure Treating	Final	02/04/2000	50.00
LA	New Orleans	Agriculture Street Landfill	Final	12/16/1994	50.00
LA	Ponchatoula	Delatte Metals	Deleted	08/08/2005	50.00
LA	Scotlandville	Petro-Processors of Louisiana, Inc.	Final	09/21/1984	41.44
LA	Scotlandville	Devil's Swamp Lake	Proposed	03/08/2004	50.00
LA	Slaughter	Central Wood Preserving Co.	Deleted	09/18/2009	48.53
LA	Slidell	Bayou Bonfouca	Final	09/08/1983	29.78
LA	Slidell	Southern Shipbuilding	Deleted	06/16/1998	50.00
LA	Sorrento	Cleve Reber	Deleted	12/30/1997	48.80
LA	Winnfield	American Creosote Works, Inc. (Winnfield Plant)	Final	10/14/1992	50.70
MA	Acton	W.R. Grace & Co., Inc. (Acton Plant)	Final	09/08/1983	59.31
MA	Amesbury	Microfab Inc (Former)	Proposed	09/09/2016	50.00
MA	Ashland	Nyanza Chemical Waste Dump	Final	09/08/1983	69.22
MA	Attleboro	Walton & Lonsbury Inc.	Final	05/24/2013	58.30
MA	Attleboro, Norton	Shpack Landfill	Final	06/10/1986	29.45
MA	Bedford	Hanscom Field/Hanscom Air Force Base	Final	05/31/1994	50.00
MA	Bedford	Naval Weapons Industrial Reserve Plant	Final	05/31/1994	50.00
MA	Billerica	Iron Horse Park	Final	09/21/1984	42.93
MA	Bridgewater	Cannon Engineering Corp. (CEC)	Deleted	09/24/2013	39.89
MA	Concord	Nuclear Metals, Inc.	Final	06/14/2001	58.31
MA	Danvers	Creese & Cook Tannery (Former)	Final	05/24/2013	60.57
MA	Dartmouth	Re-Solve, Inc.	Final	09/08/1983	47.71
MA	Fairhaven	Atlas Tack Corp.	Final	02/21/1990	42.60
MA	Falmouth	Otis Air National Guard Base/Camp Edwards	Final	11/21/1989	45.92
MA	Fort Devens	Fort Devens	Final	11/21/1989	42.24
MA	Franklin	BJAT LLC	Final	09/30/2015	41.91
MA	Groveland	Groveland Wells	Final	09/08/1983	40.74
MA	Haverhill	Haverhill Municipal Landfill	Final	06/10/1986	30.29
MA	Holbrook	Baird & McGuire	Final	09/08/1983	66.35
MA	Lanesboro	Rose Disposal Pit	Final	06/10/1986	33.03
MA	Lowell	Silresim Chemical Corp.	Final	09/08/1983	42.72
MA	Mansfield	Hatheway and Patterson Company	Final	09/05/2002	56.60
MA	Natick	Natick Laboratory Army Research, Development, and Engineering Center	Final	05/31/1994	50.00
MA	New Bedford	Sullivan's Ledge	Final	09/21/1984	32.77
MA	New Bedford	New Bedford Site	Final	09/08/1983,	
MA	Norwood	Norwood PCBs	Deleted	05/31/2011	29.43
MA	Palmer	PSC Resources	Final	09/08/1983	38.66
MA	Pittsfield	GE - Housatonic River	Proposed	09/25/1997	70.71
MA	Plymouth	Plymouth Harbor/Cannon Engineering Corp.	Deleted	11/19/1993	54.82
MA	Salem	Salem Acres	Deleted	07/23/2001	34.94
MA	Sudbury	Fort Devens-Sudbury Training Annex	Deleted	01/29/2002	35.57
MA	Tewksbury	Sutton Brook Disposal Area	Final	06/14/2001	57.12
MA	Tyngsborough	Charles-George Reclamation Trust Landfill	Final	09/08/1983	47.20
MA	Walpole	Blackburn and Union Privileges	Final	05/31/1994	50.00
MA	Watertown	Materials Technology Laboratory (USARMY)	Deleted	11/21/2006	48.57
MA	Westborough	Hocomonco Pond	Final	09/08/1983	44.80
MA	Weymouth	South Weymouth Naval Air Station	Final	05/31/1994	50.00
MA	Wilmington	Olin Chemical	Final	04/19/2006	50.00
MA	Woburn	Industri-Plex	Final	09/08/1983	72.42
MA	Woburn	Wells G&H	Final	09/08/1983	42.71
MD	Aberdeen	Aberdeen Proving Ground (Michaelsville Landfill)	Final	10/04/1989	31.09
MD	Abingdon	Bush Valley Landfill	Final	03/31/1989	40.30

St.	City/Area	Site Name	Status	Date	Score[1]
MD	Annapolis	Middletown Road Dump	Deleted	04/18/1988	29.36
MD	Anne Arundel County	Curtis Bay Coast Guard Yard	Final	09/05/2002	50.00
MD	Baltimore	Kane & Lombard Street Drums	Final	06/10/1986	30.15
MD	Baltimore	68th Street Dump	Proposed	04/30/2003	50.00
MD	Baltimore	Chemical Metals Industries, Inc.	Deleted	12/30/1982,	
MD	Beltsville	Beltsville Agricultural Research Center (USDA)	Final	05/31/1994	50.00
MD	Brandywine	Brandywine DRMO	Final	05/10/1999	50.15
MD	Camp Springs	Andrews Air Force Base	Final	05/10/1999	50.00
MD	Cecil County	Ordnance Products, Inc.	Final	09/25/1997	32.15
MD	Cumberland	Limestone Road	Final	09/08/1983	30.54
MD	Dundalk	Sauer Dump	Final	03/15/2012	50.00
MD	Edgewood	Aberdeen Proving Ground (Edgewood Area)	Final	02/21/1990	53.57
MD	Elkton	Dwyer Property Ground Water Plume	Final	03/10/2011	50.00
MD	Elkton	Spectron, Inc.	Final	05/31/1994	51.42
MD	Elkton	Sand, Gravel and Stone	Final	09/08/1983	41.08
MD	Fort Detrick	Fort Detrick Area B Ground Water	Final	04/09/2009	49.52
MD	Hagerstown	Central Chemical (Hagerstown)	Final	09/25/1997	50.00
MD	Harmans	Mid-Atlantic Wood Preservers, Inc.	Deleted	07/18/2000	42.31
MD	Hollywood	Southern Maryland Wood Treating	Deleted	04/05/2005	34.21
MD	Indian Head	Indian Head Naval Surface Warfare Center	Final	09/29/1995	50.00
MD	Odenton	Fort George G. Meade	Final	07/28/1998	51.44
MD	St. Mary's County	Patuxent River Naval Air Station	Final	05/31/1994	50.00
MD	Woodlawn	Woodlawn County Landfill	Final	07/22/1987	48.13
ME	Augusta	O'Connor	Deleted	07/22/2014	31.86
ME	Brooksville	Callahan Mine	Final	09/05/2002	50.00
ME	Brunswick	Brunswick Naval Air Station	Final	07/22/1987	43.38
ME	Corinna	Eastland Woolen Mill	Final	07/22/1999	70.71
ME	Gray	McKin Co.	Final	09/08/1983	60.97
ME	Kittery	Portsmouth Naval Shipyard	Final	05/31/1994	50.00
ME	Leeds	Leeds Metal	Final	09/18/2012	32.25
ME	Limestone	Loring Air Force Base	Final	02/21/1990	34.49
ME	Meddybemps	Eastern Surplus	Final	06/17/1996	50.00
ME	Plymouth	West Site/Hows Corners	Final	09/29/1995	50.00
ME	Saco	Saco Municipal Landfill	Final	02/21/1990	29.49
ME	Saco	Saco Tannery Waste Pits	Deleted	09/29/1999	43.19
ME	South Hope	Union Chemical Co., Inc.	Final	10/04/1989	32.11
ME	Washburn	Pinette's Salvage Yard	Deleted	09/30/2002	33.98
ME	Windham	Keddy Mill	Final	05/12/2014	50.00
ME	Winthrop	Winthrop Landfill	Final	09/08/1983	35.62
MI	Adrian	Anderson Development Co.	Deleted	01/26/1996	31.02
MI	Albion	Albion-Sheridan Township Landfill	Final	10/04/1989	33.79
MI	Albion	McGraw Edison Corp.	Final	09/08/1983	33.42
MI	Allegan	Rockwell International Corp. (Allegan Plant)	Final	07/22/1987	52.15
MI	Battle Creek	Verona Well Field	Final	09/08/1983	46.86
MI	Bay City	Bay City Middlegrounds	Proposed	02/13/1995	50.00
MI	Belding	H & K Sales	Deleted	05/21/1998,	
MI	Benton Harbor	Aircraft Components (D & L Sales)	Final	06/17/1996,	
MI	Brighton	Rasmussen's Dump	Final	09/08/1983	31.80
MI	Bronson	North Bronson Industrial Area	Final	06/10/1986	33.93
MI	Buchanan	Electrovoice	Final	09/21/1984	35.36
MI	Cadillac	Kysor Industrial Corp.	Final	10/04/1989	33.94
MI	Cadillac	Northernaire Plating	Final	09/08/1983	57.93
MI	Charlevoix	Charlevoix Municipal Well	Deleted	12/02/1993	37.94
MI	Clare	Clare Water Supply	Final	09/21/1984	38.43
MI	Dalton Township	Duell & Gardner Landfill	Final	09/08/1983	34.68
MI	Dalton Township	Ott/Story/Cordova Chemical Co.	Final	09/08/1983	53.41
MI	Davisburg	Springfield Township Dump	Final	09/08/1983	51.97
MI	Detroit	Carter Industrials, Inc.	Deleted	03/25/1997	37.79
MI	Filer City	Packaging Corp. of America	Final	09/08/1983	51.91

St.	City/Area	Site Name	Status	Date	Score[1]
MI	Gibraltar	DSC McLouth Steel Gibraltar Plant	Final	03/26/2015	50.00
MI	Grand Ledge	Parsons Chemical Works, Inc.	Final	03/31/1989	31.32
MI	Grand Rapids	State Disposal Landfill, Inc.	Final	02/21/1990	42.24
MI	Grand Rapids	H. Brown Co., Inc.	Final	06/10/1986	39.88
MI	Grand Rapids	Butterworth #2 Landfill	Final	09/08/1983	50.31
MI	Grand Rapids	Folkertsma Refuse	Deleted	04/10/1996	33.12
MI	Grandville	Organic Chemicals, Inc.	Final	09/08/1983	32.93
MI	Green Oak Township	Spiegelberg Landfill	Deleted	06/13/2011	53.61
MI	Greilickville	Grand Traverse Overall Supply Co.	Final	09/08/1983	35.53
MI	Hartford	Burrows Sanitation	Deleted	07/14/2015	30.59
MI	Highland	Hi-Mill Manufacturing Co.	Final	02/21/1990	49.54
MI	Holland	Waste Management of Michigan (Holland Lagoons)	Deleted	01/14/2013	37.20
MI	Houghton County	Torch Lake	Final	06/10/1986	46.72
MI	Howard Township	U.S. Aviex	Final	09/08/1983	33.66
MI	Howell	Shiawassee River	Final	09/08/1983	31.01
MI	Ionia	American Anodco, Inc.	Final	03/31/1989	57.99
MI	Ionia	Ionia City Landfill	Final	09/08/1983	31.31
MI	Iosco County	Wurtsmith Air Force Base	Proposed	01/18/1994	50.00
MI	Kalamazoo	Allied Paper, Inc./Portage Creek/Kalamazoo River	Final	08/30/1990	36.41
MI	Kalamazoo	Michigan Disposal Service (Cork Street Landfill)	Final	02/21/1990	37.93
MI	Kalamazoo	Roto-Finish Co., Inc.	Final	06/10/1986	40.70
MI	Kalamazoo	Auto Ion Chemicals, Inc.	Final	09/08/1983	32.07
MI	Kent City	Kent City Mobile Home Park	Deleted	03/20/1995	33.62
MI	Kentwood	Kentwood Landfill	Final	09/08/1983	35.39
MI	Lake Ann	Metal Working Shop	Deleted	12/23/1992	28.82
MI	Lansing	Barrels, Inc.	Final	10/04/1989	42.24
MI	Lansing	Adam's Plating	Final	03/31/1989	29.64
MI	Lansing	Motor Wheel, Inc.	Final	06/10/1986	48.91
MI	Macomb Township	South Macomb Disposal Authority (Landfills #9 and #9A)	Final	06/10/1986	33.67
MI	Mancelona Township	Tar Lake	Final	09/08/1983	48.55
MI	Marquette	Cliff/Dow Dump	Deleted	11/17/2000	34.50
MI	Metamora	Metamora Landfill	Final	09/21/1984	35.51
MI	Muskegon	Peerless Plating Co.	Final	08/30/1990	43.94
MI	Muskegon	Kaydon Corp.	Final	02/21/1990	34.21
MI	Muskegon	Bofors Nobel, Inc.	Final	03/31/1989	53.42
MI	Muskegon	Thermo-Chem, Inc.	Final	06/10/1986	53.36
MI	Muskegon Heights	SCA Independent Landfill	Final	09/08/1983	34.75
MI	Oscoda	Hedblum Industries	Final	09/08/1983	37.29
MI	Oshtemo Township	K&L Avenue Landfill	Final	09/08/1983	38.10
MI	Ossineke	Ossineke Ground Water Contamination	Deleted	01/31/1996	33.78
MI	Otisville	Forest Waste Products	Final	09/08/1983	38.64
MI	Park Township	Southwest Ottawa County Landfill	Final	09/08/1983	39.66
MI	Pere Marquette Township	Mason County Landfill	Deleted	09/09/1999	34.18
MI	Petoskey	Petoskey Municipal Well Field	Final	09/08/1983	42.68
MI	Pleasant Plains Township	Wash King Laundry	Final	09/08/1983	40.03
MI	Rochester Hills	J & L Landfill	Final	03/31/1989	31.65
MI	Rose Center	Cemetery Dump	Deleted	04/19/1995	34.16
MI	Rose Township	Rose Township Dump	Final	09/08/1983	50.92
MI	Sault Sainte Marie	Cannelton Industries, Inc.	Final	08/30/1990	30.16
MI	Sparta Township	Sparta Landfill	Final	09/08/1983	32.00
MI	St. Clair Shores	Ten-Mile Drain	Final	09/29/2010	48.88
MI	St. Joseph	Bendix Corp./Allied Automotive	Final	02/21/1990	37.27
MI	St. Louis	Gratiot County Golf Course	Final	03/04/2010	29.54
MI	St. Louis	Gratiot County Landfill	Final	09/08/1983,	
MI	St. Louis	Velsicol Chemical Corp.(Michigan)	Final	09/08/1983	52.29
MI	St. Louis	Gratiot County Golf Course	Deleted	09/08/1983	40.22
MI	Sturgis	Sturgis Municipal Wells	Final	09/21/1984	42.24
MI	Swartz Creek	Berlin & Farro	Deleted	06/24/1998	66.74
MI	Temperance	Novaco Industries	Deleted	07/14/1998	38.20

St.	City/Area	Site Name	Status	Date	Score[1]
MI	Traverse City	Avenue E Ground Water Contamination	Deleted	03/20/2007	31.19
MI	Utica	G&H Landfill	Final	09/08/1983	49.09
MI	Utica	Liquid Disposal, Inc.	Final	09/08/1983	63.28
MI	Whitehall	Muskegon Chemical Co.	Final	02/21/1990	34.19
MI	Whitehall	Whitehall Municipal Wells	Deleted	02/11/1991	35.45
MI	Wyandotte	Lower Ecorse Creek Dump	Deleted	07/01/2005,	
MI	Wyoming	Spartan Chemical Co.	Final	09/08/1983	41.05
MI	Wyoming Township	Chem Central	Final	09/08/1983	38.20
MN	Adrian	Adrian Municipal Well Field	Deleted	12/30/1992	33.62
MN	Andover	South Andover Site	Final	09/08/1983	35.41
MN	Andover	Waste Disposal Engineering	Deleted	06/05/1996	50.92
MN	Baxter, Brainerd	Burlington Northern (Brainerd/Baxter Plant)	Final	09/08/1983	46.77
MN	Baytown Township	Baytown Township Ground Water Plume	Final	12/16/1994	35.62
MN	Bemidji	Kummer Sanitary Landfill	Deleted	04/26/1996	35.57
MN	Brooklyn Center	Joslyn Manufacturing & Supply Co.	Final	09/21/1984	44.30
MN	Burnsville	Freeway Sanitary Landfill	Final	06/10/1986	45.91
MN	Cannon Falls	Dakhue Sanitary Landfill	Deleted	07/24/1995	42.24
MN	Cass Lake	St. Regis Paper Co.	Final	09/21/1984	52.88
MN	Dakota County	Pine Bend Sanitary Landfill	Deleted	06/23/1998	52.11
MN	East Bethel Township	East Bethel Demolition Landfill	Deleted	05/07/1996	28.75
MN	Fairview Township	Agate Lake Scrapyard	Deleted	08/01/1997	29.68
MN	Faribault	Nutting Truck & Caster Co.	Final	09/21/1984	37.87
MN	Fridley	Fridley Commons Park Well Field	Final	01/19/1999	50.00
MN	Fridley	Naval Industrial Reserve Ordnance Plant	Final	11/21/1989	30.83
MN	Fridley	Kurt Manufacturing Co.	Final	06/10/1986	31.41
MN	Fridley	FMC Corp. (Fridley Plant)	Final	09/08/1983	65.50
MN	Fridley	Boise Cascade/Onan Corp./Medtronics, Inc.	Deleted	02/15/1995	50.06
MN	Hermantown	Arrowhead Refinery Co.	Final	09/21/1984	43.75
MN	LaGrand Township	LaGrand Sanitary Landfill	Deleted	10/23/1997	37.51
MN	Lake Elmo	Washington County Landfill	Deleted	05/16/1996	42.24
MN	Lehillier	Lehillier/Mankato Site	Final	09/08/1983	42.49
MN	Long Prairie	Long Prairie Ground Water Contamination	Final	06/10/1986	31.94
MN	Minneapolis	South Minneapolis Residential Soil Contamination	Final	09/19/2007	44.58
MN	Minneapolis	General Mills/Henkel Corp.	Final	09/21/1984	36.28
MN	Minneapolis	Whittaker Corp.	Deleted	02/11/1999	40.03
MN	Minneapolis	Twin Cities Air Force Reserve Base (Small Arms Range Landfill)	Deleted	12/16/1996	33.62
MN	Minneapolis	Union Scrap Iron & Metal Co.	Deleted	09/10/1991	42.63
MN	Morris	Morris Arsenic Dump	Deleted	03/07/1986	38.27
MN	New Brighton	MacGillis & Gibbs/Bell Lumber & Pole Co.	Final	09/21/1984	48.33
MN	New Brighton	New Brighton/Arden Hills/TCAAP (USARMY)	Final	09/08/1983	59.16
MN	Oak Grove Township	Oak Grove Sanitary Landfill	Deleted	10/17/1996	43.40
MN	Oakdale	Oakdale Dump	Final	09/08/1983	55.71
MN	Oronoco	Olmsted County Sanitary Landfill	Deleted	02/15/1995	40.70
MN	Perham	Perham Arsenic Site	Final	09/21/1984	37.98
MN	Pine Bend	Koch Refining Co./N-Ren Corp.	Deleted	06/15/1995	31.14
MN	Rosemount	University of Minnesota (Rosemount Research Center)	Deleted	02/06/2001	45.91
MN	Sebeka	Ritari Post & Pole	Final	07/22/1987	29.81
MN	St. Augusta Township	St. Augusta Sanitary Landfill/Engen Dump	Deleted	11/14/1996	33.85
MN	St. Louis County	St. Louis River Site	Final	09/21/1984	32.08
MN	St. Louis Park	Reilly Tar & Chemical Corp. (St. Louis Park Plant)	Final	09/08/1983,	
MN	St. Louis Park	NL Industries/Taracorp/Golden Auto	Deleted	05/21/1998	39.97
MN	St. Paul	Koppers Coke	Final	09/08/1983	55.05
MN	Waite Park	Waite Park Wells	Final	06/10/1986	31.94
MN	Windom	Windom Dump	Deleted	10/06/2000	38.17
MO	Amazonia	Wheeling Disposal Service Co., Inc., Landfill	Deleted	10/30/2000	48.58
MO	Annapolis	Annapolis Lead Mine	Final	07/22/2004	56.67
MO	Bridgeton	Westlake Landfill	Final	08/30/1990	29.85
MO	Caledonia	Washington County Lead District - Furnace Creek	Final	03/10/2011	50.00
MO	Cape Girardeau	Missouri Electric Works	Final	02/21/1990	31.20

St.	City/Area	Site Name	Status	Date	Score[1]
MO	Cape Girardeau	Kem-Pest Laboratories	Deleted	09/20/2001	33.89
MO	Desloge	Big River Mine Tailings/St. Joe Minerals Corp.	Final	10/14/1992	84.91
MO	Ellisville	Ellisville Site	Final	09/08/1983,	
MO	Fredericktown	Madison County Mines	Final	09/29/2003	58.41
MO	Granby	Newton County Mine Tailings	Final	09/29/2003	50.00
MO	Imperial	Minker/Stout/Romaine Creek	Final	09/08/1983	36.78
MO	Independence	Lake City Army Ammunition Plant (Northwest Lagoon)	Final	07/22/1987	33.62
MO	Jasper County	Oronogo-Duenweg Mining Belt	Final	08/30/1990	46.20
MO	Jefferson County	Southwest Jefferson County Mining	Final	09/23/2009	70.71
MO	Joplin	Newton County Wells	Final	07/27/2000	50.00
MO	Kansas City	Conservation Chemical Co.	Final	10/04/1989	29.85
MO	Liberty	Lee Chemical	Final	06/10/1986	46.81
MO	Malden	Bee Cee Manufacturing Co.	Final	06/10/1986	28.59
MO	Moscow Mills	Shenandoah Stables	Deleted	09/25/2001	30.09
MO	Neosho	Pools Prairie	Final	09/17/1999	50.00
MO	New Haven	Riverfront	Final	12/01/2000	50.00
MO	North Kansas City	Armour Road	Final	05/10/1999	50.00
MO	Oak Grove Village	Oak Grove Village Well	Final	09/05/2002	50.00
MO	Old Mines	Washington County Lead District - Old Mines	Final	03/19/2008	76.81
MO	Potosi	Washington County Lead District - Potosi	Final	03/19/2008	50.00
MO	Republic	Solid State Circuits, Inc.	Final	06/10/1986	37.93
MO	Richwoods	Washington County Lead District - Richwoods	Final	03/19/2008	76.81
MO	Rogersville	Compass Plaza Well TCE	Final	03/15/2012	50.00
MO	Sikeston	Quality Plating	Final	06/10/1986	40.70
MO	Springfield	Fulbright Landfill	Final	09/08/1983	40.60
MO	Springfield	North-U Drive Well Contamination	Deleted	09/08/1994	28.90
MO	St. Charles County	Weldon Spring Former Army Ordnance Works	Final	02/21/1990	30.26
MO	St. Charles County	Weldon Spring Quarry/Plant/Pits (USDOE/Army)	Final	07/22/1987	58.60
MO	St. Louis County	St. Louis Airport/Hazelwood Interim Storage/Futura Coatings Co.	Final	10/04/1989	38.31
MO	Times Beach	Times Beach	Deleted	09/25/2001	40.08
MO	Valley Park	Valley Park TCE	Final	06/10/1986	35.57
MO	Verona	Syntex Facility	Final	09/08/1983	43.78
MO	Vienna	Vienna Wells	Final	09/29/2010	50.00
MP	Garapan	PCB Warehouse	Deleted	03/07/1986,	
MS	Canton	Southeastern Wood Preserving	Final	03/15/2012	48.03
MS	Clarksdale	Red Panther Chemical Company	Final	09/16/2011	39.43
MS	Columbia	Newsom Brothers/Old Reichhold Chemicals, Inc.	Deleted	09/27/2000	45.70
MS	Columbus	Kerr-McGee Chemical Corp - Columbus	Final	09/16/2011	52.47
MS	Flowood	Sonford Products	Final	03/07/2007	31.66
MS	Flowood	Flowood Site	Deleted	02/16/1996,	
MS	Greenville	Walcotte Chemical Co. Warehouses	Deleted	12/30/1982,	
MS	Gulfport	Chemfax, Inc.	Final	03/15/2012	38.40
MS	Hattiesburg	Davis Timber Company	Final	07/27/2000	48.57
MS	Louisville	American Creosote Works, Inc.	Final	09/13/2001	62.20
MS	Picayune	Picayune Wood Treating	Final	07/22/2004	51.03
MS	Wesson	Potter Co.	Proposed	05/10/1993	50.00
MT	Anaconda	Anaconda Co. Smelter	Final	09/08/1983	58.71
MT	Barker	Barker Hughesville Mining District	Final	09/13/2001	50.00
MT	Basin	Basin Mining Area	Final	10/22/1999	61.15
MT	Billings	Lockwood Solvent Ground Water Plume	Final	12/01/2000	45.69
MT	Black Eagle	ACM Smelter and Refinery	Final	03/10/2011	54.26
MT	Bozeman	Idaho Pole Co.	Final	06/10/1986	38.29
MT	Butte	Montana Pole and Treating	Final	07/22/1987	33.03
MT	Columbia Falls	Anaconda Aluminum Co Columbia Falls Reduction Plant	Final	09/09/2016	68.39
MT	Columbus	Mouat Industries	Final	06/10/1986	31.66
MT	East Helena	East Helena Site	Final	09/21/1984	61.65
MT	Helena, Rimini	Upper Tenmile Creek Mining Area	Final	10/22/1999	50.00
MT	Libby	Libby Asbestos	Final	10/24/2002,	
MT	Libby	Libby Ground Water Contamination	Final	09/08/1983	37.67

St.	City/Area	Site Name	Status	Date	Score[1]
MT	Livingston	Burlington Northern Livingston Shop Complex	Proposed	08/23/1994	50.00
MT	Milltown	Milltown Reservoir Sediments	Final	09/08/1983	43.78
MT	Missoula	Smurfit-Stone Mill	Proposed	05/24/2013	50.00
MT	Neihart	Carpenter Snow Creek Mining District	Final	09/13/2001	50.00
MT	Silver Bow Creek	Silver Bow Creek/Butte Area	Final	09/08/1983	63.76
MT	Superior	Flat Creek IMM	Final	09/23/2009	51.33
NC	Aberdeen	Aberdeen Contaminated Ground Water	Final	09/03/2008	50.00
NC	Aberdeen	Geigy Chemical Corp. (Aberdeen Plant)	Final	10/04/1989	33.02
NC	Aberdeen	Aberdeen Pesticide Dumps	Final	03/31/1989	52.70
NC	Arden	Blue Ridge Plating Company	Final	09/14/2005	38.67
NC	Ashe County	Ore Knob Mine	Final	09/23/2009	50.00
NC	Asheville	CTS of Asheville, Inc.	Final	03/15/2012	38.40
NC	Belmont	Jadco-Hughes Facility	Final	06/10/1986	42.00
NC	Castle Hayne	Reasor Chemical Company	Final	09/05/2002	32.14
NC	Charlotte	Ram Leather Care	Final	09/29/2003	40.43
NC	Charlotte	Martin-Marietta, Sodyeco, Inc.	Deleted	01/20/2012	51.93
NC	Concord	Bypass 601 Ground Water Contamination	Final	06/10/1986	37.93
NC	Cordova	Charles Macon Lagoon & Drum Storage	Final	07/22/1987	47.10
NC	East Flat Rock	General Electric Co/Shepherd Farm	Final	12/16/1994	70.71
NC	Fayetteville	Cape Fear Wood Preserving	Final	07/22/1987	34.09
NC	Fayetteville	Carolina Transformer Co.	Final	07/22/1987	33.76
NC	Gastonia	Hemphill Road TCE	Final	12/12/2013	50.00
NC	Gastonia	Davis Park Road TCE	Final	01/19/1999	33.50
NC	Havelock	Cherry Point Marine Corps Air Station	Final	12/16/1994	70.71
NC	Hazelwood	Benfield Industries, Inc.	Final	10/04/1989	31.67
NC	Jacksonville	ABC One Hour Cleaners	Final	03/31/1989	29.11
NC	Maco	Potter's Septic Tank Service Pits	Final	03/31/1989	29.14
NC	Morrisville	Koppers Co., Inc. (Morrisville Plant)	Final	03/31/1989	41.89
NC	Navassa	Kerr-McGee Chemical Corp - Navassa	Final	03/04/2010	50.00
NC	North Belmont	North Belmont PCE	Final	07/22/1999	50.00
NC	Onslow County	Camp Lejeune Military Reservation	Final	10/04/1989	33.13
NC	Oxford	Cristex Drum	Final	12/12/2013	48.00
NC	Oxford	JFD Electronics/Channel Master	Final	10/04/1989	39.03
NC	Raleigh	Ward Transformer	Final	04/30/2003	50.00
NC	Raleigh	North Carolina State University (Lot 86, Farm Unit #1)	Final	06/10/1986	48.36
NC	Riegelwood	Wright Chemical Corporation	Final	03/10/2011	48.03
NC	Roxboro	GMH Electronics	Final	09/23/2009	50.00
NC	Salisbury	National Starch & Chemical Corp.	Final	10/04/1989	46.51
NC	Shelby	Celanese Corp. (Shelby Fiber Operations)	Final	06/10/1986	48.98
NC	Statesville	Sigmon's Septic Tank Service	Final	04/27/2005	30.03
NC	Statesville	FCX, Inc. (Statesville Plant)	Final	02/21/1990	37.93
NC	Swannanoa	Chemtronics, Inc.	Final	09/08/1983	30.16
NC	Warrenton	PCB Spills	Deleted	03/07/1986,	
NC	Washington	FCX, Inc. (Washington Plant)	Final	03/31/1989	40.39
NC	Waynesville	Barber Orchard	Final	09/13/2001	70.71
NC	Wilmington	Horton Iron and Metal	Final	09/16/2011	48.03
NC	Wilmington	New Hanover County Airport Burn Pit	Deleted	09/20/2012	39.39
NC	Yadkinville	Holcomb Creosote Co	Final	09/18/2012	48.00
ND	Lidgerwood, Rutland, Wyndmere	Arsenic Trioxide Site	Deleted	07/05/1996,	
ND	Minot	Minot Landfill	Deleted	04/01/1997	33.58
NE	Bruno	Bruno Co-op Association/Associated Properties	Final	06/17/1996	50.00
NE	Columbus	10th Street Site	Final	08/30/1990	28.90
NE	Grand Island	Parkview Well	Final	04/19/2006	50.00
NE	Grand Island	Cleburn Street Well	Final	10/14/1992	50.00
NE	Hall County	Cornhusker Army Ammunition Plant	Final	07/22/1987	51.13
NE	Hastings	West Highway 6 & Highway 281	Final	04/19/2006	50.00
NE	Hastings	Garvey Elevator	Final	09/14/2005	50.00
NE	Hastings	Hastings Ground Water Contamination	Final	06/10/1986	42.24
NE	Lindsay	Lindsay Manufacturing Co.	Final	10/04/1989	47.91
NE	Mead	Nebraska Ordnance Plant (Former)	Final	08/30/1990	31.94

St.	City/Area	Site Name	Status	Date	Score[1]
NE	Norfolk	Iowa-Nebraska Light & Power Co	Final	04/07/2016	40.80
NE	Norfolk	Sherwood Medical Co.	Final	10/14/1992	50.00
NE	Ogallala	Ogallala Ground Water Contamination	Final	12/16/1994	50.00
NE	Omaha	Omaha Lead	Final	04/30/2003	50.00
NE	Valley	Old HWY 275 and N 288th Street	Proposed	09/09/2016	50.00
NE	Waverly	Waverly Ground Water Contamination	Deleted	11/20/2006	37.93
NE	York	PCE Southeast Contamination	Final	05/12/2014	43.33
NE	York	PCE/TCE Northeast Contamination	Final	05/12/2014	50.00
NH	Barrington	Tibbetts Road	Final	06/10/1986	41.09
NH	Berlin	Chlor-Alkali Facility (Former)	Final	09/14/2005	30.54
NH	Conway	Kearsarge Metallurgical Corp.	Final	09/21/1984	38.45
NH	Dover	Dover Municipal Landfill	Final	09/08/1983	36.98
NH	Epping	Keefe Environmental Services	Final	09/08/1983	65.19
NH	Farmington	Collins & Aikman Plant (Former)	Final	12/12/2013	50.00
NH	Kingston	Ottati & Goss/Kingston Steel Drum	Final	09/08/1983	53.41
NH	Londonderry	Auburn Road Landfill	Final	09/08/1983	36.30
NH	Londonderry	Tinkham Garage	Final	09/08/1983	43.24
NH	Londonderry	Town Garage/Radio Beacon	Deleted	07/21/2014	31.94
NH	Merrimack	New Hampshire Plating Co.	Final	10/14/1992	50.00
NH	Milford	Fletcher's Paint Works & Storage	Final	03/31/1989	35.39
NH	Milford	Savage Municipal Water Supply	Final	09/21/1984	37.52
NH	Nashua	Sylvester	Final	09/08/1983,	
NH	Nashua	Mohawk Tannery	Proposed	05/11/2000	52.40
NH	Newington, Portsmouth	Pease Air Force Base	Final	02/21/1990	39.42
NH	North Hampton	Coakley Landfill	Final	06/10/1986	29.16
NH	Peterborough	South Municipal Water Supply Well	Final	09/21/1984	35.64
NH	Plaistow	Beede Waste Oil	Final	12/23/1996	70.71
NH	Raymond	Mottolo Pig Farm	Final	07/22/1987	40.70
NH	Somersworth	Somersworth Sanitary Landfill	Final	09/08/1983	65.56
NH	Troy	Troy Mills Landfill	Final	09/29/2003	50.00
NJ	Alexandria Township	Crown Vantage Landfill	Deleted	08/28/2015	50.00
NJ	Asbury Park	M&T Delisa Landfill	Deleted	03/21/1991	32.27
NJ	Atlantic County	Federal Aviation Administration Technical Center	Final	08/30/1990	39.65
NJ	Bayville	Denzer & Schafer X-Ray Co.	Deleted	12/29/1998	40.36
NJ	Berkley Township	Beachwood/Berkley Wells	Deleted	01/06/1992	42.24
NJ	Beverly	Cosden Chemical Coatings Corp.	Final	07/22/1987	33.86
NJ	Boonton	Pepe Field	Deleted	07/11/2003	33.83
NJ	Bound Brook	Brook Industrial Park	Final	10/04/1989	58.12
NJ	Bound Brook	American Cyanamid Co.	Final	09/08/1983	50.28
NJ	Brick Township	Brick Township Landfill	Final	09/08/1983	58.13
NJ	Bridgeport	Chemical Leaman Tank Lines, Inc.	Final	09/21/1984	47.53
NJ	Bridgeport	Bridgeport Rental & Oil Services	Final	09/08/1983	60.73
NJ	Byram	Mansfield Trail Dump	Final	03/10/2011	50.00
NJ	Camden	Martin Aaron, Inc.	Final	07/22/1999	50.00
NJ	Camden, Gloucester City	Welsbach & General Gas Mantle (Camden Radiation)	Final	06/17/1996	41.46
NJ	Carlstadt	Scientific Chemical Processing	Final	09/08/1983	55.97
NJ	Chatham Township	Rolling Knolls Landfill	Final	09/29/2003	58.31
NJ	Chester Township	Combe Fill South Landfill	Final	09/08/1983	45.22
NJ	Cinnaminson Township	Cinnaminson Township (Block 702) Ground Water Contamination	Final	06/10/1986	37.93
NJ	Colts Neck	Naval Weapons Station Earle (Site A)	Final	08/30/1990	29.65
NJ	Dover	Dover Municipal Well 4	Final	09/08/1983	28.90
NJ	East Brunswick Township	Fried Industries	Final	06/10/1986	33.61
NJ	East Rutherford	Universal Oil Products (Chemical Division)	Final	09/08/1983	54.63
NJ	Edgewater	Quanta Resources	Final	09/05/2002	50.00
NJ	Edison Township	Chemical Insecticide Corp.	Final	08/30/1990	37.93
NJ	Edison Township	Kin-Buc Landfill	Final	09/08/1983	50.64
NJ	Edison Township	Renora, Inc.	Deleted	03/20/2000	40.44
NJ	Egg Harbor Township	Delilah Road	Deleted	10/13/2009	49.33
NJ	Elizabeth	Chemical Control	Final	09/08/1983	47.13

St.	City/Area	Site Name	Status	Date	Score[1]
NJ	Evesham Township	Ellis Property	Final	09/08/1983	34.62
NJ	Fair Lawn	Fair Lawn Well Field	Final	09/08/1983	42.49
NJ	Fairfield	Unimatic Manufacturing Corporation	Final	05/12/2014	50.00
NJ	Fairfield	Caldwell Trucking Co.	Final	09/08/1983	58.30
NJ	Florence	Roebling Steel Co.	Final	09/08/1983	41.02
NJ	Florence Township	Florence Land Recontouring, Inc., Landfill	Deleted	05/13/2004	47.39
NJ	Franklin Borough	Metaltec/Aerosystems	Final	09/08/1983	48.95
NJ	Franklin Township	Franklin Burn	Final	06/17/1996	40.67
NJ	Franklin Township	Higgins Disposal	Final	08/30/1990	30.87
NJ	Franklin Township	Higgins Farm	Final	03/31/1989	30.47
NJ	Franklin Township	Myers Property	Final	09/08/1983	33.83
NJ	Freehold Township	Lone Pine Landfill	Final	09/08/1983	66.33
NJ	Galloway Township	Emmell's Septic Landfill	Final	07/22/1999	50.00
NJ	Galloway Township	Mannheim Avenue Dump	Deleted	08/27/2007	36.56
NJ	Galloway Township	Pomona Oaks Residential Wells	Deleted	05/07/1998	31.94
NJ	Garfield	Garfield Ground Water Contamination	Final	09/16/2011,	
NJ	Gibbsboro	Sherwin-Williams/Hilliards Creek	Final	03/19/2008	50.00
NJ	Gibbsboro	United States Avenue Burn	Final	07/22/1999	50.00
NJ	Gibbsboro	Route 561 Dump	Proposed	07/28/1998	50.00
NJ	Gibbstown	Hercules, Inc. (Gibbstown Plant)	Final	09/08/1983	40.36
NJ	Glen Ridge	Glen Ridge Radium Site	Deleted	09/02/2009	49.14
NJ	Gloucester Township	GEMS Landfill	Final	09/08/1983	68.53
NJ	Hamilton Township	D'Imperio Property	Final	09/08/1983	55.79
NJ	Hillsborough	Krysowaty Farm	Deleted	02/22/1989	55.14
NJ	Hoboken	Grand Street Mercury	Deleted	09/18/2007,	
NJ	Howell Township	Zschiegner Refining	Final	03/06/1998	50.00
NJ	Howell Township	Bog Creek Farm	Final	09/08/1983	43.23
NJ	Jackson Township	Jackson Township Landfill	Deleted	09/13/1995	38.11
NJ	Jamesburg, South Brunswick Township	JIS Landfill	Final	09/08/1983	45.14
NJ	Jersey City	PJP Landfill	Final	09/08/1983	28.73
NJ	Jobstown	Kauffman & Minteer, Inc.	Final	03/31/1989	28.51
NJ	Kearny	Standard Chlorine	Final	09/19/2007	50.00
NJ	Kearny	Diamond Head Oil Refinery Div.	Final	09/05/2002	30.00
NJ	Kingwood Township	De Rewal Chemical Co.	Final	09/21/1984	35.72
NJ	Lakehurst	Naval Air Engineering Center	Final	07/22/1987	50.53
NJ	Linden	LCP Chemicals Inc.	Final	07/28/1998	50.00
NJ	Lodi	Lodi Municipal Well	Deleted	12/29/1998	33.39
NJ	Mantua Township	Helen Kramer Landfill	Final	09/08/1983	72.66
NJ	Manville	Federal Creosote	Deleted	06/18/2014	50.00
NJ	Marlboro Township	Burnt Fly Bog	Final	09/08/1983	59.16
NJ	Maywood, Rochelle Park	Maywood Chemical Co.	Final	09/08/1983	51.19
NJ	Middlesex	Middlesex Sampling Plant (USDOE)	Final	01/19/1999	50.00
NJ	Milford	Curtis Specialty Papers, Inc.	Final	09/23/2009	50.00
NJ	Millington	Asbestos Dump	Deleted	07/12/2010	39.61
NJ	Millville	Nascolite Corp.	Final	09/21/1984	51.13
NJ	Minotola	South Jersey Clothing Co.	Final	10/04/1989	42.24
NJ	Minotola	Garden State Cleaners Co.	Final	03/31/1989	28.90
NJ	Monroe Township	Monroe Township Landfill	Deleted	02/03/1994	42.37
NJ	Montclair, West Orange	Montclair/West Orange Radium Site	Deleted	09/02/2009	49.14
NJ	Montgomery Township	Montgomery Township Housing Development	Final	09/08/1983	37.93
NJ	Morganville	Imperial Oil Co., Inc./Champion Chemicals	Final	09/08/1983	33.87
NJ	Mount Holly	Landfill & Development Co.	Final	09/21/1984	33.62
NJ	Mount Olive Township	Combe Fill North Landfill	Deleted	06/02/2004	47.79
NJ	Newark	Pierson's Creek	Final	09/22/2014	47.99
NJ	Newark	Riverside Industrial Park	Final	05/24/2013	50.00
NJ	Newark	White Chemical Corp.	Final	09/25/1991,	
NJ	Newark	Diamond Alkali Co.	Final	09/21/1984	35.40
NJ	Newfield Borough	Shieldalloy Corp.	Final	09/21/1984	58.75
NJ	Oakland	Witco Chemical Corp. (Oakland Plant)	Deleted	09/29/1995	30.63

St.	City/Area	Site Name	Status	Date	Score[1]
NJ	Old Bridge Township	Global Sanitary Landfill	Final	03/31/1989	45.92
NJ	Old Bridge Township	CPS/Madison Industries	Final	09/08/1983	69.73
NJ	Old Bridge Township	Evor Phillips Leasing	Final	09/08/1983	36.64
NJ	Old Bridge Township, Sayreville	Raritan Bay Slag	Final	11/04/2009	50.00
NJ	Orange	U.S. Radium Corp.	Final	09/08/1983	37.79
NJ	Parsippany, Troy Hills	Sharkey Landfill	Final	09/08/1983	48.85
NJ	Pedricktown	NL Industries	Final	09/08/1983	52.96
NJ	Pemberton Township	Lang Property	Final	09/08/1983	48.89
NJ	Pemberton Township	Fort Dix (Landfill Site)	Deleted	09/24/2012	37.40
NJ	Pennsauken Township	Puchack Well Field	Final	03/06/1998	50.00
NJ	Pennsauken Township	Swope Oil & Chemical Co.	Final	09/08/1983	35.68
NJ	Piscataway	Chemsol, Inc.	Final	09/08/1983	42.69
NJ	Pitman	Lipari Landfill	Final	09/08/1983	75.60
NJ	Pleasant Plains	Reich Farms	Final	09/08/1983	53.48
NJ	Pleasantville	Price Landfill	Final	09/08/1983,	
NJ	Plumstead Township	Goose Farm	Final	09/08/1983	47.71
NJ	Plumstead Township	Wilson Farm	Deleted	09/08/2009	33.93
NJ	Plumstead Township	Hopkins Farm	Deleted	08/27/2002	34.09
NJ	Plumstead Township	Pijak Farm	Deleted	03/03/1997	43.48
NJ	Plumstead Township	Spence Farm	Deleted	03/03/1997	45.87
NJ	Ringwood Borough	Ringwood Mines/Landfill	Final	09/08/1983	52.58
NJ	Rockaway Township	Picatinny Arsenal (USARMY)	Final	02/21/1990	42.92
NJ	Rockaway Township	Radiation Technology, Inc.	Final	09/21/1984	42.56
NJ	Rockaway Township	Rockaway Borough Well Field	Final	09/08/1983	42.34
NJ	Rockaway Township	Rockaway Township Wells	Final	09/08/1983	28.90
NJ	Rocky Hill Borough	Rocky Hill Municipal Well	Final	09/08/1983	37.93
NJ	Saddle Brook Township	Curcio Scrap Metal, Inc.	Final	07/22/1987	34.37
NJ	Sayreville	Atlantic Resources Corporation	Final	09/05/2002	50.00
NJ	Sayreville	Horseshoe Road	Final	09/29/1995	51.37
NJ	Sayreville	Sayreville Landfill	Deleted	09/29/2011	37.05
NJ	Shamong Township	Ewan Property	Final	09/21/1984	50.19
NJ	South Brunswick	South Brunswick Landfill	Deleted	02/27/1998	53.42
NJ	South Kearny	Syncon Resins	Final	09/08/1983	43.43
NJ	South Plainfield	Woodbrook Road Dump	Final	04/30/2003	50.00
NJ	South Plainfield	Cornell Dubilier Electronics, Inc.	Final	07/28/1998	50.27
NJ	Sparta Township	A. O. Polymer	Final	09/08/1983	28.91
NJ	Swainton	Williams Property	Final	09/08/1983	40.45
NJ	Tabernacle Township	Tabernacle Drum Dump	Deleted	05/08/2008	36.83
NJ	Thorofare	Matteo & Sons, Inc.	Final	09/27/2006	50.00
NJ	Toms River	Ciba-Geigy Corp.	Final	09/08/1983	50.33
NJ	Upper Deerfield Township	Upper Deerfield Township Sanitary Landfill	Deleted	06/09/2000	33.62
NJ	Upper Freehold Township	Friedman Property	Deleted	03/07/1986	33.88
NJ	Vineland	Former Kil-Tone Company	Final	04/07/2016	65.29
NJ	Vineland	Iceland Coin Laundry Area Ground Water Plume	Final	10/22/1999	30.30
NJ	Vineland	Vineland Chemical Co., Inc.	Final	09/21/1984	59.16
NJ	Vineland	Vineland State School	Deleted	05/07/1998	40.84
NJ	Voorhees Township	Cooper Road	Deleted	02/22/1989	36.79
NJ	Wall Township	White Swan Cleaners/Sun Cleaners Area Ground Water Contamination	Final	09/23/2004	41.63
NJ	Wall Township	Monitor Devices, Inc./Intercircuits, Inc.	Final	06/10/1986	41.93
NJ	Wall Township	Waldick Aerospace Devices, Inc.	Final	06/10/1986	44.86
NJ	Wallington Borough	Industrial Latex Corp.	Deleted	04/21/2003	32.38
NJ	Warren County	Pohatcong Valley Ground Water Contamination	Final	03/31/1989	28.90
NJ	Wayne Township	W.R. Grace & Co., Inc./Wayne Interim Storage Site (USDOE)	Deleted	09/30/2012	47.14
NJ	West Orange/Orange	Orange Valley Regional Ground Water Contamination	Final	09/18/2012	50.00
NJ	Wharton Borough	Dayco Corp./L.E. Carpenter Co.	Final	07/22/1987	46.13
NJ	Winslow Township	Lightman Drum Company	Final	10/22/1999	42.03
NJ	Winslow Township	King of Prussia	Final	09/08/1983	47.19
NJ	Woodland Township	Woodland Route 532 Dump	Final	09/21/1984	34.98
NJ	Woodland Township	Woodland Route 72 Dump	Final	09/21/1984	31.17

St.	City/Area	Site Name	Status	Date	Score[1]
NJ	Woodridge Borough	Ventron/Velsicol	Final	09/21/1984	51.38
NJ	Woolwich Township	Matlack, Inc.	Final	05/24/2013	45.54
NJ	Wrightstown	McGuire Air Force Base #1	Final	10/22/1999	47.20
NM	Albuquerque	Fruit Avenue Plume	Final	10/22/1999	50.00
NM	Albuquerque	AT&SF (Albuquerque)	Final	12/16/1994	50.00
NM	Albuquerque	South Valley	Final	09/08/1983,	
NM	Carrizozo	Cimarron Mining Corp.	Final	10/04/1989	38.93
NM	Church Rock	United Nuclear Corp.	Final	09/08/1983	30.36
NM	Clovis	AT & SF (Clovis)	Deleted	03/17/2003	33.62
NM	Espanola	North Railroad Avenue Plume	Final	01/19/1999	50.00
NM	Farmington	Lee Acres Landfill (USDOI)	Final	08/30/1990	39.37
NM	Grants	Grants Chlorinated Solvents Plume	Final	07/22/2004	50.00
NM	Laguna Pueblo	Jackpile-Paguate Uranium Mine	Final	12/12/2013	50.00
NM	Las Cruces	Griggs & Walnut Ground Water Plume	Final	06/14/2001	50.00
NM	Lemitar	Cal West Metals (USSBA)	Deleted	12/20/1996	59.37
NM	Los Lunas	Pagano Salvage	Deleted	10/14/1992	35.57
NM	Milan	Homestake Mining Co.	Final	09/08/1983	34.21
NM	Prewitt	Prewitt Abandoned Refinery	Final	08/30/1990	44.24
NM	Questa	Chevron Questa Mine	Final	09/16/2011	50.00
NM	Roswell	Lea and West Second Street	Final	04/07/2016	50.00
NM	Roswell	McGaffey and Main Groundwater Plume	Final	09/05/2002	50.00
NM	Silver City	Cleveland Mill	Deleted	07/23/2001	40.37
NM	Socorro	Eagle Picher Carefree Battery	Final	09/19/2007	50.00
NV	Churchill County, Lyon County	Carson River Mercury Site	Final	08/30/1990	39.07
NV	Yerington	Anaconda Copper Mine	Proposed	09/09/2016	50.00
NY	Amenia	Sarney Farm	Final	06/10/1986	33.20
NY	Aurelius, Fleming, Springport	Cayuga County Ground Water Contamination	Final	09/05/2002	50.00
NY	Batavia	Batavia Landfill	Deleted	11/29/2005	50.18
NY	Bohemia	BioClinical Laboratories, Inc.	Deleted	09/09/1994	32.91
NY	Brant	Wide Beach Development	Deleted	08/30/1994	56.58
NY	Brewster	Brewster Well Field	Final	09/08/1983	37.93
NY	Brooklyn	Gowanus Canal	Final	03/04/2010	50.00
NY	Brooklyn, Queens	Newtown Creek	Final	09/29/2010	50.00
NY	Byron	Byron Barrel & Drum	Final	06/10/1986	37.27
NY	Caledonia	Jones Chemicals, Inc.	Final	02/21/1990	33.62
NY	Carthage	Crown Cleaners of Watertown, Inc.	Final	09/05/2002	49.00
NY	Central Islip	MacKenzie Chemical Works, Inc.	Final	09/13/2001	50.00
NY	Cheektowaga	Pfohl Brothers Landfill	Deleted	09/22/2008	50.11
NY	Clayville	Ludlow Sand & Gravel	Deleted	12/02/2013	36.88
NY	Cold Springs	Marathon Battery Corp.	Deleted	10/18/1996	30.27
NY	Colonie	Mercury Refining, Inc.	Final	09/08/1983	44.58
NY	Conklin	Conklin Dumps	Deleted	04/25/1997	33.93
NY	Copiague	Action Anodizing, Plating, & Polishing Corp.	Deleted	09/29/1995	34.72
NY	Cortland	Rosen Brothers Scrap Yard/Dump	Final	03/31/1989	51.35
NY	Dayton	Peter Cooper Corporation (Markhams)	Deleted	09/20/2010	30.00
NY	Deer Park	SMS Instruments, Inc.	Deleted	09/13/2010	37.32
NY	Dutchess	Wappinger Creek	Final	09/09/2016	50.00
NY	East Farmingdale	Circuitron Corp.	Final	03/31/1989	54.27
NY	East Fishkill	Shenandoah Road Ground Water Contamination	Final	06/14/2001	50.00
NY	Ellenville	Ellenville Scrap Iron and Metal	Final	09/05/2002	50.27
NY	Elmira	Facet Enterprises, Inc.	Final	09/08/1983	46.67
NY	Farmingdale	Liberty Industrial Finishing	Final	06/10/1986	50.65
NY	Farmingdale	Preferred Plating Corp.	Final	06/10/1986	35.06
NY	Farmingdale	Tronic Plating Co., Inc.	Deleted	10/15/2001	45.14
NY	Farmingdale	Kenmark Textile Corp.	Deleted	05/01/1995	31.72
NY	Franklin Square	Genzale Plating Co.	Final	07/22/1987	33.79
NY	Fulton	Fulton Terminals	Final	09/08/1983	36.50
NY	Garden City	Old Roosevelt Field Contaminated Ground Water Area	Final	05/11/2000	50.00
NY	Glen Cove	Li Tungsten Corp.	Final	10/14/1992	50.00

St.	City/Area	Site Name	Status	Date	Score[1]
NY	Glen Cove	Mattiace Petrochemical Co., Inc.	Final	03/31/1989	31.90
NY	Glenwood Landing	Applied Environmental Services	Final	06/10/1986	41.15
NY	Gowanda	Peter Cooper	Final	03/06/1998	50.00
NY	Great Neck	Stanton Cleaners Area Ground Water Contamination	Final	05/10/1999	35.76
NY	Hamilton	C & J Disposal Leasing Co. Dump	Deleted	09/20/1994	35.10
NY	Hauppauge	Computer Circuits	Final	05/10/1999	50.00
NY	Hempstead	Pasley Solvents & Chemicals, Inc.	Deleted	09/26/2011	39.65
NY	Hewlett	Peninsula Boulevard Ground Water Plume	Final	07/22/2004	50.00
NY	Hicksville	Hooker Chemical & Plastics Corp./Ruco Polymer Corp.	Final	06/10/1986	41.60
NY	Hicksville	Anchor Chemicals	Deleted	09/30/1999	37.20
NY	High Falls	Mohonk Road Industrial Plant	Final	01/19/1999	50.00
NY	Hillburn	Hudson Technologies, Inc.	Proposed	05/11/2000	50.00
NY	Holbrook	Goldisc Recordings, Inc.	Final	06/10/1986	33.39
NY	Holley	Diaz Chemical Corporation	Final	07/22/2004	50.00
NY	Hopewell Junction	Hopewell Precision Area Contamination	Final	04/27/2005	50.00
NY	Horseheads	Kentucky Avenue Well Field	Final	09/08/1983	39.65
NY	Hudson River	Hudson River PCBs	Final	09/21/1984	54.66
NY	Hyde Park	Jones Sanitation	Deleted	09/23/2005	52.52
NY	Islip	Islip Municipal Sanitary Landfill	Final	03/31/1989	33.39
NY	Le Roy	Lehigh Valley Railroad	Final	01/19/1999	50.00
NY	Lincklaen	Solvent Savers	Final	09/08/1983	34.78
NY	Lisbon	Sealand Restoration, Inc.	Final	08/30/1990	29.36
NY	Little Valley	Little Valley	Final	06/17/1996,	
NY	Lockport	Eighteenmile Creek	Final	03/15/2012	50.00
NY	Malta	Malta Rocket Fuel Area	Final	07/22/1987	33.62
NY	Massena	General Motors (Central Foundry Division)	Final	09/21/1984	40.71
NY	Maybrook	Nepera Chemical Co., Inc.	Final	06/10/1986	39.87
NY	Mineola, North Hempstead	Jackson Steel	Deleted	09/26/2016	50.00
NY	Moira	York Oil Co.	Final	09/08/1983	47.70
NY	Nassau	Dewey Loeffel Landfill	Final	03/10/2011	50.00
NY	New Cassel/Hicksville	New Cassel/Hicksville Ground Water Contamination	Final	09/16/2011	50.00
NY	New York City	Radium Chemical Co., Inc.	Deleted	03/24/1995,	
NY	Newburgh	Consolidated Iron and Metal	Deleted	12/03/2014	50.00
NY	Niagara Falls	Forest Glen Mobile Home Subdivision	Final	11/21/1989,	
NY	Niagara Falls	Hooker (S Area)	Final	09/08/1983	51.62
NY	Niagara Falls	Hooker (Hyde Park)	Deleted	10/23/2013	34.77
NY	Niagara Falls	Love Canal	Deleted	09/30/2004	52.23
NY	Niagara Falls	Hooker (102nd Street)	Deleted	08/05/2004	30.48
NY	North Hempstead	Fulton Avenue	Final	03/06/1998	33.08
NY	North Sea	North Sea Municipal Landfill	Deleted	09/27/2005	33.74
NY	Noyack, Sag Harbor	Rowe Industries Ground Water Contamination	Final	07/22/1987	31.94
NY	Old Bethpage	Claremont Polychemical	Final	06/10/1986	31.62
NY	Olean	Olean Well Field	Final	09/08/1983	44.46
NY	Oswego	Pollution Abatement Services	Final	09/08/1983,	
NY	Oyster Bay	Old Bethpage Landfill	Final	09/08/1983	58.83
NY	Oyster Bay	Syosset Landfill	Deleted	04/28/2005	54.27
NY	Plattekill	Hertel Landfill	Final	06/10/1986	33.62
NY	Plattsburgh	Plattsburgh Air Force Base	Final	11/21/1989	30.34
NY	Port Crane	Tri-Cities Barrel Co., Inc.	Final	10/04/1989	44.06
NY	Port Jefferson Station	Lawrence Aviation Industries, Inc.	Final	02/04/2000	50.00
NY	Port Jervis	Carroll & Dubies Sewage Disposal	Final	02/21/1990	33.74
NY	Port Washington	Port Washington Landfill	Final	09/08/1983	45.46
NY	Ramapo	Ramapo Landfill	Final	09/08/1983	44.73
NY	Ridgewood	Wolff-Alport Chemical Company	Final	05/12/2014	50.00
NY	Rome	Griffiss Air Force Base	Final	07/22/1987	34.20
NY	Romulus	Seneca Army Depot	Final	08/30/1990	35.52
NY	Saratoga Springs	Niagara Mohawk Power Corp. (Saratoga Spings Plant)	Final	02/21/1990	35.48
NY	Sidney	Sidney Landfill	Final	03/31/1989	29.36
NY	Sidney Center	Richardson Hill Road Landfill/Pond	Final	07/22/1987	34.86

St.	City/Area	Site Name	Status	Date	Score[1]
NY	Smithtown	Smithtown Ground Water Contamination	Final	01/19/1999	50.00
NY	South Cairo	American Thermostat Co.	Final	09/08/1983	33.61
NY	South Glens Falls	GE Moreau	Final	09/08/1983	58.21
NY	Syracuse	Onondaga Lake	Final	12/16/1994	50.00
NY	Town of Bedford	Katonah Municipal Well	Deleted	03/20/2000	35.35
NY	Town of Champion	Black River PCBs	Final	09/29/2010	48.03
NY	Town of Colesville	Colesville Municipal Landfill	Final	06/10/1986	30.26
NY	Town of Granby	Clothier Disposal	Deleted	02/08/1996	34.48
NY	Town of Hyde Park	Haviland Complex	Final	06/10/1986	33.62
NY	Town of Johnstown	Johnstown City Landfill	Final	06/10/1986	48.36
NY	Town of Shelby	FMC Corp. (Dublin Road Landfill)	Final	06/10/1986	32.90
NY	Town of Vestal	Robintech, Inc./National Pipe Co.	Final	06/10/1986	30.75
NY	Town of Volney	Volney Municipal Landfill	Final	06/10/1986	32.89
NY	Upton	Brookhaven National Laboratory (USDOE)	Final	11/21/1989	39.92
NY	Vestal	Vestal Water Supply Well 1-1	Final	09/08/1983	37.93
NY	Vestal	Vestal Water Supply Well 4-2	Deleted	09/30/1999	42.24
NY	Vestal	BEC Trucking	Deleted	10/14/1992	30.75
NY	Village of Endicott	Endicott Village Well Field	Final	06/10/1986	35.57
NY	Village of Hoosick Falls	Saint-Gobain Performance Plastics	Proposed	09/09/2016	50.00
NY	Village of Narrowsburg	Cortese Landfill	Final	06/10/1986	32.11
NY	Village of Sidney	GCL Tie and Treating Inc.	Final	05/31/1994	48.54
NY	Village of Suffern	Suffern Village Well Field	Deleted	05/28/1993	35.57
NY	Warwick	Warwick Landfill	Deleted	07/06/2001	29.41
NY	Wellsville	Sinclair Refinery	Final	09/08/1983	53.90
NY	West Winfield	Hiteman Leather	Deleted	02/13/2012	50.00
NY	Wheatfield	Niagara County Refuse	Deleted	07/30/2004	39.85
OH	Ashtabula	Fields Brook	Final	09/08/1983	44.95
OH	Beavercreek	Lammers Barrel	Final	09/29/2003	69.33
OH	Circleville	Bowers Landfill	Deleted	10/29/1997	50.49
OH	Cleveland	Chemical & Minerals Reclamation	Deleted	12/30/1982,	
OH	Columbus	Air Force Plant 85	Proposed	01/18/1994	50.00
OH	Copley	Copley Square Plaza	Final	04/27/2005	50.00
OH	Darke County	Arcanum Iron & Metal	Deleted	08/31/2001	62.26
OH	Dayton	Behr Dayton Thermal System VOC Plume	Final	04/09/2009	50.00
OH	Dayton	North Sanitary Landfill	Final	05/31/1994	50.00
OH	Dayton	Wright-Patterson Air Force Base	Final	10/04/1989	57.85
OH	Dayton	Sanitary Landfill Co. (Industrial Waste Disposal Co., Inc.)	Final	06/10/1986	35.57
OH	Dayton	Powell Road Landfill	Final	09/21/1984	31.62
OH	Deerfield Township	Summit National	Final	09/08/1983	52.28
OH	Dover	Reilly Tar & Chemical Corp. (Dover Plant)	Final	08/30/1990	31.38
OH	Dover	Dover Chemical Corp.	Proposed	05/10/1993	50.00
OH	Elyria	Republic Steel Corp. Quarry	Deleted	11/12/2002	29.85
OH	Fernald	Feed Materials Production Center (USDOE)	Final	11/21/1989	57.56
OH	Franklin Township	Coshocton Landfill	Deleted	10/07/1998	39.14
OH	Gnadenhutten	Alsco Anaconda	Deleted	11/05/2001	42.94
OH	Hamilton	Chem-Dyne	Final	09/08/1983,	
OH	Hamilton	Armco Inc., Hamilton Plant	Proposed	04/30/2003	69.34
OH	Hamilton Township	E.H. Schilling Landfill	Final	09/08/1983	34.56
OH	Hannibal	Ormet Corp.	Final	07/22/1987	46.44
OH	Ironton	Allied Chemical & Ironton Coke	Final	09/08/1983	47.05
OH	Jackson Township	Fultz Landfill	Final	09/08/1983	39.42
OH	Jefferson Township	Laskin/Poplar Oil Co.	Deleted	09/05/2000	35.95
OH	Kings Mills	Peters Cartridge Factory	Final	09/18/2012	50.00
OH	Kingsville	Big D Campground	Final	09/08/1983	30.77
OH	Marietta	Van Dale Junkyard	Final	06/10/1986	33.03
OH	Marion Township	Little Scioto River	Final	09/23/2009	48.03
OH	Miamisburg	Mound Plant (USDOE)	Final	11/21/1989	34.61
OH	Milford	Milford Contaminated Aquifer	Final	03/10/2011	50.00
OH	Minerva	TRW, Inc. (Minerva Plant)	Final	03/31/1989	38.08
OH	Moraine	South Dayton Dump & Landfill	Proposed	09/23/2004	48.63

St.	City/Area	Site Name	Status	Date	Score[1]
OH	New Carlisle	New Carlisle Landfill	Final	04/09/2009	46.40
OH	New Lyme	New Lyme Landfill	Final	09/08/1983	31.19
OH	Painesville	Diamond Shamrock Corp. (Painesville Works)	Proposed	05/10/1993	50.00
OH	Reading	Pristine, Inc.	Final	09/08/1983	35.25
OH	Riverside	Valley Pike VOCs	Final	09/09/2016	50.00
OH	Rock Creek	Old Mill	Final	09/08/1983	35.95
OH	Salem	Nease Chemical	Final	09/08/1983	47.19
OH	South Point	South Point Plant	Final	09/21/1984	46.33
OH	St. Clairsville	Buckeye Reclamation	Final	09/08/1983	35.10
OH	Troy	West Troy Contaminated Aquifer	Final	09/18/2012	50.00
OH	Troy	East Troy Contaminated Aquifer	Final	09/03/2008	50.00
OH	Troy	Miami County Incinerator	Final	09/21/1984	57.84
OH	Troy	United Scrap Lead Co., Inc.	Final	09/21/1984	58.15
OH	Uniontown	Industrial Excess Landfill	Final	06/10/1986	51.13
OH	West Chester	Skinner Landfill	Final	09/08/1983	30.23
OH	Zanesville	Zanesville Well Field	Final	09/08/1983	35.59
OK	Ardmore	Imperial Refining Company	Deleted	09/19/2013	30.00
OK	Bartlesville	National Zinc Corp.	Proposed	05/10/1993	50.00
OK	Collinsville	Tulsa Fuel and Manufacturing	Final	01/19/1999	50.00
OK	Creek County	Wilcox Oil Company	Final	12/12/2013	50.00
OK	Criner	Hardage/Criner	Final	09/08/1983	51.01
OK	Cushing	Hudson Refinery	Final	07/22/1999	29.34
OK	Cyril	Oklahoma Refining Co.	Final	02/21/1990	46.01
OK	Oklahoma City	Tinker Air Force Base (Soldier Creek/Building 3001)	Final	07/22/1987	42.24
OK	Oklahoma City	Mosley Road Sanitary Landfill	Deleted	09/26/2013	38.06
OK	Oklahoma City	Double Eagle Refinery Co.	Deleted	08/21/2008	30.83
OK	Oklahoma City	Fourth Street Abandoned Refinery	Deleted	08/21/2008	30.67
OK	Oklahoma City	Tenth Street Dump/Junkyard	Deleted	11/21/2000	30.98
OK	Ottawa County	Tar Creek (Ottawa County)	Final	09/08/1983	58.15
OK	Sand Springs	Sand Springs Petrochemical Complex	Deleted	03/17/2000	28.86
OK	Tulsa	Compass Industries (Avery Drive)	Deleted	07/18/2002	36.57
OR	Albany	Teledyne Wah Chang	Final	09/08/1983	54.27
OR	Astoria	Astoria Marine Construction Company	Proposed	03/10/2011	50.00
OR	Clackamas	Northwest Pipe & Casing/Hall Process Co	Final	10/14/1992	51.09
OR	Corvallis	United Chrome Products, Inc.	Final	09/21/1984	31.07
OR	Cottage Grove	Black Butte Mine	Final	03/04/2010	50.00
OR	Hermiston	Umatilla Army Depot (Lagoons)	Final	07/22/1987	31.31
OR	Joseph	Joseph Forest Products	Deleted	11/04/1999	32.60
OR	Klamath Falls	North Ridge Estates	Final	09/16/2011,	
OR	Lake County	Fremont National Forest/White King and Lucky Lass Uranium Mines (USDA)	Final	04/25/1995	50.00
OR	Portland	Portland Harbor	Final	12/01/2000	50.00
OR	Portland	McCormick & Baxter Creosoting Co. (Portland Plant)	Final	05/31/1994	50.00
OR	Portland	Harbor Oil	Deleted	06/05/2014	48.00
OR	Portland	Gould, Inc.	Deleted	09/30/2002	32.12
OR	Portland	Allied Plating, Inc.	Deleted	11/14/1994	39.25
OR	Riddle	Formosa Mine	Final	09/19/2007	50.00
OR	Sheridan	Taylor Lumber and Treating	Final	06/14/2001	71.78
OR	The Dalles	Union Pacific Railroad Co. Tie-Treating Plant	Final	08/30/1990	37.93
OR	The Dalles	Martin-Marietta Aluminum Co.	Deleted	07/05/1996	43.70
OR	Troutdale	Reynolds Metals Company	Final	12/16/1994	70.71
PA	Ambler	BoRit Asbestos	Final	04/09/2009	50.00
PA	Ambler	Ambler Asbestos Piles	Deleted	12/27/1996	34.47
PA	Antis Township, Logan Township	Delta Quarries & Disposal, Inc./Stotler Landfill	Final	03/31/1989	41.08
PA	Bally Borough	Bally Ground Water Contamination	Final	07/22/1987	37.93
PA	Bloomsburg	Safety Light Corporation	Final	04/27/2005	70.71
PA	Bridgeton Township	Boarhead Farms	Final	03/31/1989	39.92
PA	Bridgewater Township	Bendix Flight Systems Division	Final	07/22/1987	33.74
PA	Bruin Borough	Bruin Lagoon	Deleted	09/18/1997	73.11
PA	Buffalo Township	Hranica Landfill	Deleted	09/18/1997	51.94

St.	City/Area	Site Name	Status	Date	Score[1]
PA	Chambersburg	Letterkenny Army Depot (SE Area)	Final	07/22/1987	34.21
PA	Chester	Wade (ABM)	Deleted	03/23/1989	36.63
PA	Columbia	UGI Columbia Gas Plant	Final	05/31/1994	50.78
PA	Coraopolis	Breslube-Penn, Inc	Final	06/17/1996	50.00
PA	Croydon	Croydon TCE	Final	06/10/1986	31.60
PA	Cumberland Township	Westinghouse Elevator Co. Plant	Final	06/10/1986	36.37
PA	Darby Township	Lower Darby Creek Area	Final	06/14/2001	50.00
PA	Delaware County	Austin Avenue Radiation Site	Deleted	04/18/2002,	
PA	Denver	Berkley Products Co. Dump	Deleted	03/19/2007	30.00
PA	Douglassville	Douglassville Disposal	Final	09/08/1983	55.18
PA	Doylestown	Chem-Fab	Final	03/19/2008	50.00
PA	Dublin Borough	Dublin TCE Site	Final	08/30/1990	28.90
PA	Eagleville	Moyers Landfill	Deleted	05/27/2014	37.62
PA	East Conventry Township	Recticon/Allied Steel Corp.	Final	10/04/1989	32.06
PA	East Whiteland Township	Foote Mineral Co.	Final	10/14/1992	50.00
PA	Elizabethtown	Elizabethtown Landfill	Final	03/31/1989	28.98
PA	Emmaus Borough	Rodale Manufacturing Co., Inc.	Final	10/14/1992	50.00
PA	Erie	Mill Creek Dump	Final	09/21/1984	49.31
PA	Erie	Presque Isle	Deleted	02/13/1989	40.59
PA	Exton	A.I.W. Frank/Mid-County Mustang	Final	10/04/1989	42.40
PA	Falls Creek	Jackson Ceramix	Final	09/14/2005	30.22
PA	Foster Township	C & D Recycling	Final	07/22/1987	43.92
PA	Frackville	Metropolitan Mirror and Glass Co., Inc.	Deleted	08/16/2005	34.33
PA	Franklin County	Letterkenny Army Depot (PDO Area)	Final	03/13/1989	37.51
PA	Girard Township	Lord-Shope Landfill	Final	09/08/1983	38.89
PA	Glen Rock	AMP, Inc. (Glen Rock Facility)	Deleted	10/02/1996	39.03
PA	Grove City	Osborne Landfill	Final	09/08/1983	54.60
PA	Hamburg	Price Battery	Final	04/27/2005	37.86
PA	Harleysville	Baghurst Drive	Final	09/22/2014	50.00
PA	Harrison Township	Lindane Dump	Final	09/08/1983	51.62
PA	Hatboro	Raymark	Final	10/04/1989	53.42
PA	Hatfield	North Penn - Area 2	Final	10/04/1989	35.57
PA	Haverford	Havertown PCP	Final	09/08/1983	38.34
PA	Heidelberg Township	Ryeland Road Arsenic	Final	07/22/2004	60.30
PA	Hellertown	Hellertown Manufacturing Co.	Final	03/31/1989	51.91
PA	Hereford Township	Crossley Farm	Final	10/14/1992	29.66
PA	Hermitage	River Road Landfill (Waste Management, Inc.)	Deleted	01/29/2004	43.12
PA	Hickory Township	Sharon Steel Corp (Farrell Works Disposal Area)	Final	07/28/1998	50.00
PA	Hometown	Eastern Diversified Metals	Final	10/04/1989	31.02
PA	Honeybrook Township	Walsh Landfill	Final	09/21/1984	33.64
PA	Hopewell Township	York County Solid Waste and Refuse Authority Landfill	Deleted	02/14/2005	44.26
PA	Jackson Township	Whitmoyer Laboratories	Final	06/10/1986	46.25
PA	Jefferson Borough	Resin Disposal	Deleted	10/21/2003	37.69
PA	Kimberton Borough	Kimberton	Final	09/08/1983	29.44
PA	King of Prussia	Stanley Kessler	Final	09/08/1983	33.89
PA	Lansdale	North Penn - Area 6	Final	03/31/1989	35.57
PA	Lansdowne	Lansdowne Radiation Site	Deleted	09/10/1991,	
PA	Lock Haven	Drake Chemical	Final	09/08/1983	38.52
PA	Longswamp Township	Berks Sand Pit	Final	09/21/1984	32.02
PA	Lower Pottsgrove Township	Occidental Chemical Corp./Firestone Tire & Rubber Co.	Final	10/04/1989	45.91
PA	Lower Providence Township	Commodore Semiconductor Group	Final	10/04/1989	42.35
PA	Lower Salford Township	Salford Quarry	Final	09/23/2009	50.00
PA	Lower Windsor Township	Modern Sanitation Landfill	Final	06/10/1986	33.93
PA	Maitland	Jacks Creek/Sitkin Smelting & Refining, Inc.	Final	10/04/1989	40.37
PA	Malvern	Malvern TCE	Final	09/08/1983	46.69
PA	Marcus Hook	East Tenth Street	Proposed	01/18/1994	67.68
PA	McAdoo Borough	McAdoo Associates	Deleted	12/13/2001,	
PA	Mechanicsburg	Navy Ships Parts Control Center	Final	05/31/1994	50.00
PA	Middletown	Middletown Air Field	Deleted	07/10/1997	35.69

St.	City/Area	Site Name	Status	Date	Score[1]
PA	Montgomery Township	North Penn - Area 5	Final	03/31/1989	35.57
PA	Mountain Top	Foster Wheeler Energy Corporation/Church Road TCE	Proposed	04/09/2009	50.00
PA	Nesquehoning	Tonolli Corp.	Final	10/04/1989	46.58
PA	Neville Island	Ohio River Park	Final	08/30/1990	42.24
PA	Newlin Township	Strasburg Landfill	Final	03/31/1989	30.71
PA	Nockamixon Township	Revere Chemical Co.	Final	07/22/1987	31.31
PA	North Wales	North Penn - Area 7	Final	03/31/1989	35.57
PA	North Whitehall Township	Heleva Landfill	Final	09/08/1983	50.23
PA	Old Forge Borough	Lackawanna Refuse	Deleted	09/28/1999	36.57
PA	Old Forge Borough	Lehigh Electric & Engineering Co.	Deleted	03/07/1986	30.26
PA	Palmerton	Palmerton Zinc Pile	Final	09/08/1983	42.93
PA	Paoli	Paoli Rail Yard	Final	08/30/1990	32.18
PA	Parker	Craig Farm Drum	Deleted	09/30/2013	28.72
PA	Philadelphia	Franklin Slag Pile (MDC)	Final	09/05/2002	50.20
PA	Philadelphia	Metal Banks	Final	09/08/1983	33.23
PA	Philadelphia	Publicker Industries Inc.	Deleted	11/01/2000	59.06
PA	Philadelphia	Enterprise Avenue	Deleted	03/07/1986	40.80
PA	Pittston	Butler Mine Tunnel	Final	07/22/1987	49.51
PA	Pocono Summit	Route 940 Drum Dump	Deleted	11/30/2000	44.06
PA	Richland Township	Watson Johnson Landfill	Final	09/13/2001	70.71
PA	Sadsburyville	Old Wilmington Road Ground Water Contamination	Final	02/04/2000	50.00
PA	Saegertown	Saegertown Industrial Area	Final	02/21/1990	33.62
PA	Scott Township	Aladdin Plating	Deleted	11/16/2001	35.57
PA	Seven Valleys	Old City of York Landfill	Final	09/08/1983	33.93
PA	Sharon	Westinghouse Electric Corp. (Sharon Plant)	Final	08/30/1990	41.33
PA	Shoemakersville	Brown's Battery Breaking	Final	06/10/1986	37.34
PA	Souderton	North Penn - Area 1	Final	03/31/1989	35.57
PA	South Whitehall Township	Novak Sanitary Landfill	Final	10/04/1989	42.31
PA	Spring Township	Berks Landfill	Deleted	11/14/2008	46.10
PA	Springettsbury Township	East Mount Zion	Final	09/21/1984	41.01
PA	State College Borough	Centre County Kepone	Final	09/08/1983	45.09
PA	Straban Township	Hunterstown Road	Final	06/10/1986	48.27
PA	Straban Township	Shriver's Corner	Final	06/10/1986	46.13
PA	Stroudsburg	Butz Landfill	Final	03/31/1989	32.00
PA	Stroudsburg	Brodhead Creek	Deleted	07/23/2001	31.09
PA	Taylor Borough	Taylor Borough Dump	Deleted	09/30/1999	30.94
PA	Terry Township	Bell Landfill	Final	10/04/1989	34.79
PA	Tobyhanna	Tobyhanna Army Depot	Final	08/30/1990	37.93
PA	Trainer	Metro Container Corporation	Final	03/15/2012	50.00
PA	Union Township	Keystone Sanitation Landfill	Final	07/22/1987	33.76
PA	Upper Macungie Township	Dorney Road Landfill	Final	09/21/1984	46.10
PA	Upper Macungie Township	Reeser's Landfill	Deleted	05/31/1990	30.35
PA	Upper Merion Township	Crater Resources, Inc./Keystone Coke Co./Alan Wood Steel Co.	Final	10/14/1992	50.00
PA	Upper Merion Township	Henderson Road	Final	09/21/1984	41.69
PA	Upper Merion Township	Tysons Dump	Final	09/21/1984	63.10
PA	Upper Saucon Township	Voortman Farm	Deleted	05/31/1989	28.62
PA	Valley Township	MW Manufacturing	Final	06/10/1986	46.44
PA	Warminster	Fischer & Porter Co.	Final	09/08/1983	29.07
PA	Warminster Township	Naval Air Development Center (8 Waste Areas)	Final	10/04/1989	57.93
PA	Weisenberg Township	Hebelka Auto Salvage Yard	Deleted	09/20/1999	31.94
PA	West Caln Township	William Dick Lagoons	Final	07/22/1987	36.64
PA	West Caln Township	Blosenski Landfill	Final	09/08/1983	30.57
PA	West Hazleton	Valmont TCE	Final	09/13/2001	43.16
PA	Westline	Westline Site	Deleted	10/14/1992	31.71
PA	Williams Township	Industrial Lane	Final	09/21/1984	42.47
PA	Williamsport	Avco Lycoming (Williamsport Division)	Final	02/21/1990	42.24
PA	Willow Grove	Willow Grove Naval Air and Air Reserve Station	Final	09/29/1995	50.00
PA	Worcester	North Penn - Area 12	Final	02/21/1990	28.90
PA	Worman	CryoChem, Inc.	Final	10/04/1989	28.58

St.	City/Area	Site Name	Status	Date	Score[1]
PR	Almirante Norte Ward	V&M/Albaladejo	Deleted	10/22/2001	50.00
PR	Arecibo	Pesticide Warehouse I	Final	09/27/2006	50.00
PR	Barceloneta	Upjohn Facility	Final	09/21/1984	41.92
PR	Barceloneta	RCA Del Caribe	Deleted	06/17/2005	31.14
PR	Bo. Cambalache	The Battery Recycling Company	Proposed	09/09/2016	56.66
PR	Cabo Rojo	Cabo Rojo Ground Water Contamination	Final	03/10/2011	50.00
PR	Caguas	Hormigas Ground Water Plume	Final	03/10/2011	50.00
PR	Candeleria Ward	Scorpio Recycling, Inc.	Final	02/04/2000	50.00
PR	Cidra	Cidra Ground Water Contamination	Final	07/22/2004	50.00
PR	Corozal	Corozal Well	Final	03/15/2012	50.00
PR	Dorado	Dorado Ground Water Contamination	Final	09/09/2016	50.00
PR	Florida Afuera	Barceloneta Landfill	Deleted	10/03/2011	41.11
PR	Jobos	Fibers Public Supply Wells	Final	09/21/1984	35.34
PR	Juana Diaz	GE Wiring Devices	Deleted	10/16/2000	31.24
PR	Juncos	Juncos Landfill	Final	09/08/1983	32.57
PR	Manati	Pesticide Warehouse III	Final	04/30/2003	50.00
PR	Maunabo	Maunabo Area Ground Water Contamination	Final	09/27/2006	50.00
PR	Rio Abajo	Frontera Creek	Deleted	12/29/1998	43.07
PR	Rio Abajo Ward	Vega Baja Solid Waste Disposal	Final	07/22/1999	50.37
PR	Sabana Seca	Naval Security Group Activity	Deleted	10/07/1998	34.28
PR	San German	San German Ground Water Contamination	Final	03/19/2008	50.00
PR	Utuado	Papelera Puertorriquena, Inc.	Final	09/23/2009	34.69
PR	Vega Alta	Vega Alta Public Supply Wells	Final	09/21/1984	42.24
PR	Vieques	Atlantic Fleet Weapons Training Area - Vieques	Final	02/11/2005,	
RI	Burrillville	Western Sand & Gravel	Final	09/08/1983	51.35
RI	Coventry	Picillo Farm	Final	09/08/1983,	
RI	Cumberland, Lincoln	Peterson/Puritan, Inc.	Final	09/08/1983	40.10
RI	Glocester	Davis (GSR) Landfill	Deleted	08/13/1999	38.89
RI	Johnston	Central Landfill	Final	06/10/1986	46.71
RI	Newport	Newport Naval Education/Training Center	Final	11/21/1989	32.25
RI	North Kingstown	Davisville Naval Construction Battalion Center	Final	11/21/1989	34.52
RI	North Providence	Centredale Manor Restoration Project	Final	02/04/2000	70.71
RI	North Smithfield	Landfill & Resource Recovery, Inc. (L&RR)	Final	09/08/1983	49.58
RI	North Smithfield	Stamina Mills, Inc.	Final	09/08/1983	34.07
RI	Smithfield	Davis Liquid Waste	Final	09/08/1983	47.25
RI	South Kingstown	West Kingston Town Dump/URI Disposal Area	Final	10/14/1992	50.00
RI	South Kingstown	Rose Hill Regional Landfill	Final	10/04/1989	38.11
SC	Aiken	Savannah River Site (USDOE)	Final	11/21/1989	47.70
SC	Barnwell	Shuron Inc.	Final	12/23/1996	68.26
SC	Beaufort	Kalama Specialty Chemicals	Final	09/21/1984	57.90
SC	Beaufort	Independent Nail Co.	Deleted	04/03/1995	57.90
SC	Burton	Wamchem, Inc.	Final	09/21/1984	47.70
SC	Cayce	Lexington County Landfill Area	Final	10/04/1989	37.93
SC	Cayce	SCRDI Dixiana	Final	09/08/1983	40.70
SC	Charleston	Koppers Co., Inc. (Charleston Plant)	Final	12/16/1994	50.00
SC	Columbia	SCRDI Bluff Road	Final	09/08/1983,	
SC	Columbia	Palmetto Recycling, Inc.	Deleted	10/13/2000	29.46
SC	Dixiana	Palmetto Wood Preserving	Final	09/21/1984	38.43
SC	Fairfax	Helena Chemical Co. Landfill	Final	02/21/1990	33.89
SC	Florence	Koppers Co., Inc. (Florence Plant)	Deleted	09/13/2013	51.27
SC	Fort Lawn	Carolawn, Inc.	Final	09/08/1983	32.04
SC	Fountain Inn	Beaunit Corp. (Circular Knit & Dye)	Final	02/21/1990	32.44
SC	Gaffney	Medley Farm Drum Dump	Final	03/31/1989	31.58
SC	Greenville	US Finishing/Cone Mills	Final	09/16/2011	50.00
SC	Greer	Aqua-Tech Environmental Inc. (Groce Laboratories)	Final	12/16/1994	50.00
SC	Greer	Elmore Waste Disposal	Final	03/31/1989	31.45
SC	Jefferson	Brewer Gold Mine	Final	04/27/2005	50.00
SC	McCormick	Barite Hill/Nevada Goldfields	Final	04/09/2009	50.00
SC	North Charleston	Macalloy Corporation	Final	02/04/2000	50.00

St.	City/Area	Site Name	Status	Date	Score[1]
SC	Parris Island	Parris Island Marine Corps Recruit Depot	Final	12/16/1994	50.00
SC	Pickens	Sangamo Weston, Inc./Twelve-Mile Creek/Lake Hartwell PCB Contamination	Final	02/21/1990	37.63
SC	Pontiac	Townsend Saw Chain Co.	Final	02/21/1990	35.94
SC	Rantoules	Geiger (C & M Oil)	Deleted	01/06/2014	32.25
SC	Rock Hill	Rock Hill Chemical Co.	Final	02/21/1990	40.29
SC	Rock Hill	Leonard Chemical Co., Inc.	Final	09/21/1984	47.10
SC	Simpsonville	Para-Chem Southern, Inc.	Final	08/30/1990	32.94
SC	Simpsonville	Golden Strip Septic Tank Service	Deleted	09/10/1998	40.30
SC	Travelers Rest	Rochester Property	Deleted	10/09/2007	36.72
SD	Lead	Gilt Edge Mine	Final	12/01/2000	50.00
SD	Rapid City	Ellsworth Air Force Base	Final	08/30/1990	33.62
SD	Sioux Falls	Williams Pipe Line Co. Disposal Pit	Deleted	04/02/1999	42.24
SD	Whitewood	Whitewood Creek	Deleted	08/13/1996,	
TN	Alamo	Alamo Contaminated Ground Water	Final	09/16/2011	50.00
TN	Arlington	Arlington Blending & Packaging	Final	07/22/1987	39.03
TN	Chattanooga	Tennessee Products	Final	09/29/1995,	
TN	Chattanooga	Amnicola Dump	Deleted	04/30/1996	40.91
TN	Collierville	Walker Machine Products, Inc.	Final	05/12/2014	50.00
TN	Collierville	Smalley-Piper	Final	04/27/2005	50.00
TN	Collierville	Carrier Air Conditioning Co.	Final	02/21/1990	48.91
TN	Gallaway	Gallaway Pits	Deleted	04/29/1996	30.77
TN	Harriman	Clinch River Corporation	Final	05/24/2013	48.03
TN	Jackson	American Creosote Works, Inc. (Jackson Plant)	Final	06/10/1986	35.22
TN	Jackson	ICG Iselin Railroad Yard	Deleted	01/07/2002	50.00
TN	Knoxville	Smokey Mountain Smelters	Final	09/29/2010	50.00
TN	Lawrenceburg	Murray-Ohio Dump	Final	09/08/1983	46.44
TN	Lewisburg	Lewisburg Dump	Deleted	02/21/1996	33.45
TN	Memphis	Memphis Defense Depot (DLA)	Final	10/14/1992	58.06
TN	Memphis	Former Custom Cleaners	Proposed	09/09/2016	50.00
TN	Memphis	North Hollywood Dump	Deleted	12/31/1997,	
TN	Milan	Milan Army Ammunition Plant	Final	07/22/1987	58.15
TN	Moscow	Chemet Co.	Deleted	10/09/1996	50.00
TN	Oak Ridge	Oak Ridge Reservation (USDOE)	Final	11/21/1989	51.13
TN	Rossville	Ross Metals Inc.	Final	04/01/1997	37.65
TN	Toone	Velsicol Chemical Corp. (Hardeman County)	Final	09/08/1983	47.71
TN	Waynesboro	Mallory Capacitor Co.	Final	10/04/1989	29.44
TN	Wrigley	Wrigley Charcoal Plant	Final	03/31/1989	36.14
TX	Azle	Sandy Beach Road Ground Water Plume	Final	09/14/2005	50.00
TX	Bell County	Rockwool Industries Inc.	Final	09/29/1998	48.00
TX	Bridge City	Bailey Waste Disposal	Deleted	10/15/2007	53.42
TX	Bridge City	Triangle Chemical Co.	Deleted	04/08/1997	28.75
TX	Burnet	Main Street Ground Water Plume	Final	09/30/2015	50.00
TX	Channelview	San Jacinto River Waste Pits	Final	03/19/2008	50.00
TX	Conroe	Conroe Creosoting Company	Final	09/29/2003	48.00
TX	Conroe	United Creosoting Co.	Final	09/21/1984	37.29
TX	Corpus Christi	Brine Service Company	Final	09/05/2002	50.00
TX	Crosby	French, Ltd.	Final	09/08/1983	63.33
TX	Crosby	Sikes Disposal Pits	Final	09/08/1983	61.62
TX	Crystal City	Crystal City Airport	Deleted	03/23/1995	32.26
TX	Dallas	RSR Corp.	Final	09/29/1995	50.00
TX	Deer Park	Patrick Bayou	Final	09/05/2002	47.83
TX	Donna	Donna Reservoir and Canal System	Final	03/19/2008	50.00
TX	Fort Worth	Air Force Plant #4 (General Dynamics)	Final	08/30/1990	39.92
TX	Fort Worth	Pesses Chemical Co.	Deleted	09/28/1995	28.86
TX	Freeport	Gulfco Marine Maintenance	Final	04/30/2003	50.00
TX	Friendswood	Brio Refining, Inc.	Deleted	12/28/2006	50.38
TX	Friendswood	Dixie Oil Processors, Inc.	Deleted	08/21/2006	34.21
TX	Grand Prairie	Bio-Ecology Systems, Inc.	Deleted	08/05/1996	35.06
TX	Greenville	Old ESCO Manufacturing	Final	09/03/2008	40.81

St.	City/Area	Site Name	Status	Date	Score[1]
TX	Happy	North East 2nd Street (formerly Attebury Grain Storage Facility)	Final	04/09/2009	32.33
TX	Hempstead	Sheridan Disposal Services	Final	03/31/1989	30.16
TX	Highlands	Highlands Acid Pit	Final	09/08/1983	37.77
TX	Houston	Jones Road Ground Water Plume	Final	09/29/2003	46.50
TX	Houston	Many Diversified Interests, Inc.	Final	01/19/1999	32.07
TX	Houston	Sol Lynn/Industrial Transformers	Final	03/31/1989	39.65
TX	Houston	North Cavalcade Street	Final	06/10/1986	37.08
TX	Houston	South Cavalcade Street	Final	06/10/1986	38.69
TX	Houston	Geneva Industries/Fuhrmann Energy	Final	09/21/1984	59.46
TX	Houston	Crystal Chemical Co.	Final	09/08/1983	60.90
TX	Houston	Harris (Farley Street)	Deleted	04/18/1988	33.94
TX	Ingleside	Falcon Refinery	Final	09/16/2011	50.00
TX	Jasper	Hart Creosoting Company	Final	07/22/1999	48.00
TX	Jasper	Jasper Creosoting Company Inc.	Final	07/28/1998	50.00
TX	Jefferson County	State Marine of Port Arthur	Deleted	02/06/2012	48.00
TX	Karnack	Longhorn Army Ammunition Plant	Final	08/30/1990	39.83
TX	Kermit	Highway 18 Ground Water	Proposed	09/09/2016	50.00
TX	La Marque	Motco, Inc.	Final	09/08/1983,	
TX	Leon Valley	Bandera Road Ground Water Plume	Final	03/07/2007	50.00
TX	Levelland	State Road 114 Ground Water Plume	Final	10/22/1999	42.41
TX	Liberty County	Petro-Chemical Systems, Inc. (Turtle Bayou)	Final	06/10/1986	29.94
TX	Live Oak	Eldorado Chemical Co.,, Inc.	Final	09/09/2016	38.85
TX	Longview	Garland Creosoting	Final	10/22/1999	49.10
TX	Midland	West County Road 112 Ground Water	Final	03/10/2011	50.00
TX	Odessa	Midessa Ground Water Plume	Final	03/19/2008	50.00
TX	Odessa	East 67th Street Ground Water Plume	Final	03/07/2007	50.00
TX	Odessa	Sprague Road Ground Water Plume	Final	09/25/1997	43.21
TX	Odessa	Odessa Chromium #1	Final	06/10/1986	42.24
TX	Odessa	Odessa Chromium #2 (Andrews Highway)	Deleted	07/19/2004	42.24
TX	Pantex Village	Pantex Plant (USDOE)	Final	05/31/1994	51.22
TX	Pasadena	US Oil Recovery	Final	09/18/2012	50.00
TX	Perryton	City of Perryton Well No. 2	Final	01/19/1999	50.00
TX	Point Comfort	ALCOA (Point Comfort)/Lavaca Bay	Final	02/23/1994	50.00
TX	Port Arthur	Palmer Barge Line	Deleted	02/06/2012	50.00
TX	Port Neches	Star Lake Canal	Final	07/27/2000	50.00
TX	San Antonio	R & H Oil Company	Proposed	06/14/2001	50.00
TX	Terrell	Van der Horst USA Corporation	Final	03/04/2010	48.00
TX	Texarkana	Lone Star Army Ammunition Plant	Final	07/22/1987	31.85
TX	Texarkana	Koppers Co., Inc. (Texarkana Plant)	Final	06/10/1986	31.31
TX	Texarkana	Texarkana Wood Preserving Co.	Final	06/10/1986	40.19
TX	Texas City	Malone Service Company, Inc.	Final	06/14/2001	50.00
TX	Texas City	Tex-Tin Corp.	Final	09/18/1998	50.00
TX	Waskom	Stewco, Inc.	Deleted	10/04/1995	48.86
TX	Willow Park	Circle Court Ground Water Plume	Final	09/18/2012	50.00
UT	Bountiful	Intermountain Waste Oil Refinery	Final	05/11/2000	50.00
UT	Bountiful, Woods Cross	Bountiful/Woods Cross 5th South PCE Plume	Final	09/13/2001	50.00
UT	Eureka	Eureka Mills	Final	09/05/2002	50.00
UT	Magna	Kennecott (North Zone)	Proposed	01/18/1994	59.18
UT	Midvale	Midvale Slag	Deleted	04/08/2015	42.47
UT	Midvale	Sharon Steel Corp. (Midvale Tailings)	Deleted	09/24/2004	41.85
UT	Monticello	Monticello Mill Tailings (USDOE)	Final	11/21/1989	35.86
UT	Monticello	Monticello Radioactively Contaminated Properties	Deleted	02/28/2000	35.03
UT	Murray City	Murray Smelter	Proposed	01/18/1994	86.60
UT	Ogden	Hill Air Force Base	Final	07/22/1987	49.94
UT	Ogden	Ogden Defense Depot (DLA)	Final	07/22/1987	45.10
UT	Salt Lake City	700 South 1600 East PCE Plume	Final	05/24/2013	50.00
UT	Salt Lake City	Wasatch Chemical Co. (Lot 6)	Final	02/11/1991	49.91
UT	Salt Lake City	Utah Power & Light/American Barrel Co.	Final	10/04/1989	37.93
UT	Salt Lake City	Portland Cement (Kiln Dust 2 & 3)	Final	06/10/1986	54.40
UT	Salt Lake City	Petrochem Recycling Corp./Ekotek, Inc.	Deleted	06/30/2003	62.81

St.	City/Area	Site Name	Status	Date	Score[1]
UT	Salt Lake City	Rose Park Sludge Pit	Deleted	06/30/2003,	
UT	Sandy City	Davenport and Flagstaff Smelters	Final	04/30/2003	32.50
UT	Stockton	Jacobs Smelter	Final	02/04/2000	50.00
UT	Summit County	Richardson Flat Tailings	Proposed	02/07/1992	50.23
UT	Tooele	Tooele Army Depot (North Area)	Final	08/30/1990	53.95
UT	Tooele	International Smelting and Refining	Deleted	10/11/2011	58.31
UT	Tooele County	U.S. Magnesium	Final	11/04/2009	59.18
UT	Woods Cross	Five Points PCE Plume	Final	09/19/2007	50.00
VA	Buckingham	Buckingham County Landfill	Final	10/04/1989	40.70
VA	Chesapeake	St. Juliens Creek Annex (U.S. Navy)	Final	07/27/2000	50.00
VA	Chesterfield County	C & R Battery Co., Inc.	Final	07/22/1987	46.44
VA	Chesterfield County	Defense General Supply Center (DLA)	Final	07/22/1987	33.85
VA	Chuckatuck	Saunders Supply Co.	Final	10/04/1989	36.88
VA	Culpeper	Culpeper Wood Preservers, Inc.	Final	10/04/1989	45.91
VA	Dahlgren	Naval Surface Warfare - Dahlgren	Final	10/14/1992	50.03
VA	Farrington	H & H Inc., Burn Pit	Final	03/31/1989	33.71
VA	Frederick County	Rhinehart Tire Fire Dump	Deleted	09/30/2005	30.57
VA	Front Royal	Avtex Fibers, Inc.	Final	06/10/1986	35.39
VA	Hampton	Langley Air Force Base/NASA Langley Research Center	Final	05/31/1994	50.00
VA	Montross	Arrowhead Associates, Inc./Scovill Corp.	Final	02/21/1990	37.15
VA	Newport News	Fort Eustis (US Army)	Final	12/16/1994	50.00
VA	Newtown	Greenwood Chemical Co.	Final	07/22/1987	53.17
VA	Norfolk	Norfolk Naval Base (Sewells Point Naval Complex)	Final	04/01/1997	50.00
VA	Piney River	U.S. Titanium	Final	09/08/1983	34.78
VA	Pittsylvania County	First Piedmont Corp. Rock Quarry (Route 719)	Final	07/22/1987	30.16
VA	Portsmouth	Peck Iron and Metal	Final	11/04/2009	48.52
VA	Portsmouth	Norfolk Naval Shipyard	Final	07/22/1999	50.00
VA	Portsmouth	Abex Corp.	Final	08/30/1990	36.53
VA	Portsmouth	Atlantic Wood Industries, Inc.	Final	02/21/1990	37.14
VA	Quantico	Marine Corps Combat Development Command	Final	05/31/1994	50.00
VA	Richmond	Rentokil, Inc. (Virginia Wood Preserving Division)	Final	03/31/1989	30.34
VA	Roanoke County	Matthews Electroplating	Deleted	01/19/1989,	
VA	Salem	Dixie Caverns County Landfill	Deleted	09/28/2001	35.27
VA	Saltville	Saltville Waste Disposal Ponds	Final	09/08/1983	29.52
VA	Selma	Kim-Stan Landfill	Final	07/22/1999	50.00
VA	Spotsylvania County	L.A. Clarke & Son	Final	06/10/1986	34.24
VA	Sterling	Hidden Lane Landfill	Final	03/19/2008	50.00
VA	Suffolk	Former Nansemond Ordnance Depot	Final	07/22/1999	70.71
VA	Suffolk	Suffolk City Landfill	Deleted	01/24/1995	35.76
VA	Virginia Beach	Naval Amphibious Base Little Creek	Final	05/10/1999	50.00
VA	Williamsburg	Naval Weapons Station Yorktown - Cheatham Annex	Final	12/01/2000	49.27
VA	York County	Chisman Creek	Final	09/08/1983	47.19
VA	Yorktown	Naval Weapons Station - Yorktown	Final	10/14/1992	50.00
VI	Christiansted	Island Chemical Corp./Virgin Islands Chemical Corp.	Deleted	10/16/2009	50.00
VI	Tutu	Tutu Wellfield	Final	09/29/1995	50.00
VT	Bennington	Jard Company, Inc.	Final	09/22/2014	58.31
VT	Bennington	Bennington Municipal Sanitary Landfill	Final	03/31/1989	49.07
VT	Bennington	Tansitor Electronics, Inc.	Deleted	09/29/1999	35.72
VT	Burlington	Pine Street Canal	Final	09/08/1983,	
VT	Corinth	Pike Hill Copper Mine	Final	07/22/2004	50.00
VT	Lyndon	Parker Sanitary Landfill	Final	02/21/1990	52.29
VT	Lyndon	Darling Hill Dump	Deleted	09/29/1999	43.92
VT	Pownal	Pownal Tannery	Final	01/19/1999	50.00
VT	Rockingham	BFI Sanitary Landfill (Rockingham)	Final	10/04/1989	41.92
VT	Springfield	Old Springfield Landfill	Final	09/08/1983	34.79
VT	Strafford	Elizabeth Mine	Final	06/14/2001	50.00
VT	Vershire	Ely Copper Mine	Final	09/13/2001	50.00
VT	Williston	Commerce Street Plume	Final	04/27/2005	48.48
VT	Woodford	Burgess Brothers Landfill	Final	03/31/1989	52.58

St.	City/Area	Site Name	Status	Date	Score[1]
WA	Bainbridge Island	Wyckoff Co./Eagle Harbor	Final	07/22/1987	32.55
WA	Bellingham	Oeser Co	Final	09/25/1997	69.34
WA	Benton County	Hanford 100-Area (USDOE)	Final	10/04/1989	46.38
WA	Benton County	Hanford 200-Area (USDOE)	Final	10/04/1989	69.05
WA	Benton County	Hanford 300-Area (USDOE)	Final	10/04/1989	65.23
WA	Benton County	Hanford 1100-Area (USDOE)	Deleted	09/30/1996	36.34
WA	Bremerton	Bremerton Gasworks	Final	05/10/2012	50.00
WA	Bremerton	Puget Sound Naval Shipyard Complex	Final	05/31/1994	50.00
WA	Bremerton	Bangor Ordnance Disposal (USNAVY)	Final	07/22/1987	30.42
WA	Brush Prairie	Toftdahl Drums	Deleted	12/23/1988	40.22
WA	Centralia	Centralia Municipal Landfill	Final	08/30/1990	36.36
WA	Chehalis	Hamilton/Labree Roads Ground Water Contamination	Final	07/27/2000	37.65
WA	Chehalis	American Crossarm & Conduit Co.	Final	10/04/1989	30.44
WA	Everson	Northwest Transformer	Deleted	09/28/1999	33.82
WA	Everson	Northwest Transformer (South Harkness Street)	Deleted	09/26/1997	30.56
WA	Freeman	Grain Handling Facility at Freeman	Final	09/30/2015	50.00
WA	Indian Island	Port Hadlock Detachment (USNAVY)	Deleted	06/14/2005	50.00
WA	Kent	Seattle Municipal Landfill (Kent Highlands)	Final	08/30/1990	52.19
WA	Kent	Midway Landfill	Final	06/10/1986	54.27
WA	Kent	Western Processing Co., Inc.	Final	09/08/1983	58.63
WA	Keyport	Naval Undersea Warfare Station (4 Areas)	Final	10/04/1989	33.60
WA	Kitsap County	Jackson Park Housing Complex (USNAVY)	Final	05/31/1994	50.00
WA	Lakewood	Lakewood	Final	09/08/1983	42.49
WA	Loomis	Silver Mountain Mine	Deleted	09/22/1997	29.98
WA	Manchester	Old Navy Dump/Manchester Laboratory (USEPA/NOAA)	Final	05/31/1994	50.00
WA	Maple Valley	Queen City Farms	Final	09/21/1984	34.38
WA	Marysville	Tulalip Landfill	Deleted	09/18/2002	50.00
WA	Mead	Kaiser Aluminum (Mead Works)	Final	09/08/1983	38.07
WA	Mica	Mica Landfill	Final	06/10/1986	34.64
WA	Moses Lake	Moses Lake Wellfield Contamination	Final	10/14/1992	50.00
WA	Neah Bay	Makah Reservation Warmhouse Beach Dump	Final	12/12/2013	50.00
WA	North Bonneville	Hamilton Island Landfill (USA/COE)	Deleted	05/25/1995	51.97
WA	Pasco	Pasco Sanitary Landfill	Final	02/21/1990	44.46
WA	Pierce County	Hidden Valley Landfill (Thun Field)	Final	03/31/1989	37.93
WA	Pierce County	Commencement Bay, Near Shore/Tide Flats	Final	09/08/1983	42.20
WA	Renton	Quendall Terminals	Final	04/19/2006	50.00
WA	Renton	Pacific Car & Foundry Co.	Final	02/21/1990	42.33
WA	Seattle	Lockheed West Seattle	Final	03/07/2007	50.00
WA	Seattle	Lower Duwamish Waterway	Final	09/13/2001	50.00
WA	Seattle	Pacific Sound Resources	Final	05/31/1994	70.71
WA	Seattle	Harbor Island (Lead)	Final	09/08/1983	34.60
WA	Silverdale	Bangor Naval Submarine Base	Final	08/30/1990	55.91
WA	Spokane	North Market Street	Final	08/30/1990	32.61
WA	Spokane	General Electric Co. (Spokane Shop)	Final	10/04/1989	57.80
WA	Spokane	Northside Landfill	Final	06/10/1986	28.90
WA	Spokane	Colbert Landfill	Final	09/08/1983	41.59
WA	Spokane	Old Inland Pit	Deleted	08/31/1999	29.35
WA	Spokane	Spokane Junkyard/Associated Properties	Deleted	09/23/1997	50.00
WA	Spokane County	Fairchild Air Force Base (4 Waste Areas)	Final	03/13/1989	31.98
WA	Spokane County	Greenacres Landfill	Final	09/21/1984	28.90
WA	Tacoma	American Lake Gardens/McChord AFB	Final	09/21/1984	28.90
WA	Tacoma	Commencement Bay, South Tacoma Channel	Final	09/08/1983	54.63
WA	Tacoma	McChord Air Force Base (Wash Rack/Treatment Area)	Deleted	09/26/1996	42.24
WA	Tacoma	Fort Lewis (Landfill No. 5)	Deleted	05/22/1995	33.79
WA	Tillicum	Fort Lewis Logistics Center	Final	11/21/1989	35.48
WA	Tumwater	Palermo Well Field Ground Water Contamination	Final	04/01/1997	50.00
WA	Vancouver	Boomsnub/Airco	Final	04/25/1995,	
WA	Vancouver	Vancouver Water Station #1 Contamination	Final	05/31/1994	50.00
WA	Vancouver	Vancouver Water Station #4 Contamination	Final	10/14/1992	50.00

St.	City/Area	Site Name	Status	Date	Score[1]
WA	Vancouver	Frontier Hard Chrome, Inc.	Final	09/08/1983	57.93
WA	Vancouver	ALCOA (Vancouver Smelter)	Deleted	09/30/1996	57.80
WA	Vancouver	Bonneville Power Administration Ross Complex (USDOE)	Deleted	09/23/1996	53.67
WA	Wellpinit	Midnite Mine	Final	05/11/2000	50.00
WA	Whidbey Island	Naval Air Station, Whidbey Island (Ault Field)	Final	02/21/1990	47.58
WA	Whidbey Island	Naval Air Station, Whidbey Island (Seaplane Base)	Deleted	09/21/1995	39.64
WA	Yakima	FMC Corp. (Yakima)	Final	09/08/1983	38.80
WA	Yakima	Yakima Plating Co.	Deleted	08/23/1994	37.93
WA	Yakima	Pesticide Lab (Yakima)	Deleted	09/01/1993	29.33
WI	Algoma	Algoma Municipal Landfill	Final	07/22/1987	39.99
WI	Appleton	N.W. Mauthe Co., Inc.	Final	03/31/1989,	
WI	Ashippun	Oconomowoc Electroplating Co., Inc.	Final	09/21/1984	31.86
WI	Ashland	Ashland/Northern States Power Lakefront	Final	09/05/2002	50.00
WI	Blooming Grove	Madison Metropolitan Sewerage District Lagoons	Final	02/21/1990	32.65
WI	Brookfield	Waste Management of Wisconsin, Inc. (Brookfield Sanitary Landfill)	Final	08/30/1990	28.90
WI	Brookfield	Master Disposal Service Landfill	Final	09/21/1984	47.49
WI	Caledonia	Hunts Disposal Landfill	Final	07/22/1987	31.02
WI	Cedarburg	Amcast Industrial Corporation	Final	09/23/2009	46.86
WI	Cleveland Township	Mid-State Disposal, Inc. Landfill	Final	09/21/1984	35.23
WI	Daniels	Penta Wood Products	Final	06/17/1996	50.00
WI	DePere	Better Brite Plating Chrome & Zinc Shops	Final	08/30/1990	48.91
WI	Delavan	Delavan Municipal Well #4	Final	09/21/1984	28.90
WI	Dunn	City Disposal Corp. Landfill	Final	09/21/1984	36.84
WI	Eau Claire	National Presto Industries, Inc.	Final	06/10/1986	42.39
WI	Eau Claire	Eau Claire Municipal Well Field	Deleted	05/27/2014	35.57
WI	Eau Claire	Waste Research & Reclamation Co.	Deleted	02/05/1993	32.13
WI	Excelsior	Sauk County Landfill	Final	10/04/1989	34.21
WI	Fond Du Lac County	Ripon City Landfill	Final	05/31/1994	39.04
WI	Franklin	Fadrowski Drum Disposal	Deleted	09/06/2005	31.08
WI	Franklin Township	Lemberger Transport & Recycling	Final	09/21/1984	34.58
WI	Germantown	Omega Hills North Landfill	Deleted	12/11/1996	58.54
WI	Green Bay	Fox River NRDA/PCB Releases	Proposed	07/28/1998	50.00
WI	Harrison	Schmalz Dump	Final	09/21/1984	48.92
WI	Janesville	Janesville Ash Beds	Final	09/21/1984	57.90
WI	Janesville	Janesville Old Landfill	Final	09/21/1984	57.93
WI	Kohler	Kohler Co. Landfill	Final	09/21/1984	42.93
WI	La Prairie Township	Wheeler Pit	Deleted	04/20/2004	57.80
WI	Medford	Scrap Processing Co., Inc.	Final	09/21/1984	34.24
WI	Menomonee Falls	Lauer I Sanitary Landfill	Final	09/21/1984	42.69
WI	Middleton	Refuse Hideaway Landfill	Final	10/14/1992	34.67
WI	Milwaukee	Moss-American Co., Inc. (Kerr-McGee Oil Co.)	Final	09/21/1984	32.14
WI	Muskego	Muskego Sanitary Landfill	Final	09/21/1984	51.91
WI	Onalaska	Onalaska Municipal Landfill	Final	09/21/1984	42.47
WI	Sheboygan	Sheboygan Harbor & River	Final	06/10/1986	33.79
WI	Sparta	Northern Engraving Co.	Deleted	10/29/1997	38.75
WI	Spencer	Spickler Landfill	Final	07/22/1987	44.24
WI	Stoughton	Hagen Farm	Final	07/22/1987	32.06
WI	Stoughton	Stoughton City Landfill	Final	06/10/1986	35.79
WI	Tomah	Tomah Municipal Sanitary Landfill	Final	03/31/1989	45.91
WI	Tomah	Tomah Armory	Final	07/22/1987	30.63
WI	Tomah	Tomah Fairgrounds	Deleted	08/20/2001	32.87
WI	Wausau	Wausau Ground Water Contamination	Final	06/10/1986	28.91
WI	Whitelaw	Lemberger Landfill, Inc.	Final	06/10/1986	34.07
WI	Williamstown	Hechimovich Sanitary Landfill	Final	03/31/1989	47.91
WV	Clarksburg	North 25th Street Glass and Zinc	Final	09/09/2016	48.03
WV	Fairmont	Big John Salvage - Hoult Road	Final	07/27/2000	48.57
WV	Fairmont	Sharon Steel Corp (Fairmont Coke Works)	Final	12/23/1996	57.08
WV	Follansbee	Follansbee	Deleted	01/16/2004	33.77
WV	Leetown	Leetown Pesticide	Deleted	08/29/1996	36.72

St.	City/Area	Site Name	Status	Date	Score[1]
WV	Mineral County	Allegany Ballistics Laboratory (USNAVY)	Final	05/31/1994	50.00
WV	Morgantown	Ordnance Works Disposal Areas	Final	06/10/1986	35.62
WV	Moundsville	Hanlin-Allied-Olin	Final	07/22/1999	53.98
WV	Nitro	Fike Chemical, Inc.	Final	09/08/1983	36.30
WV	Point Pleasant	West Virginia Ordnance (USARMY)	Final	09/08/1983,	
WV	Ravenswood	Ravenswood PCE Ground Water Plume	Final	09/23/2004	50.00
WV	Vienna	Vienna Tetrachloroethene	Final	10/22/1999	50.00
WY	Cheyenne	F.E. Warren Air Force Base	Final	02/21/1990	39.23
WY	Evansville	Mystery Bridge Rd/U.S. Highway 20	Final	08/30/1990	32.10
WY	Laramie	Baxter/Union Pacific Tie Treating	Deleted	12/06/1999	37.24

***Notes:** (1) Federal Register Hazard Rankings System (HRS) score. The HRS is a model that is used to evaluate the relative threats to human health and the environment posed by actual or potential releases of hazardous substances, pollutants, and contaminants. The HRS criteria take into account the population at risk, the hazard potential of the substances, as well as the potential for contamination of drinking water supplies, direct human contact, destruction of sensitive ecosystems, damage to natural resources affecting the human food chain, contamination of surface water used for recreation or potable water consumption, and contamination of ambient air. The higher the score, the higher the potential threat to human health or the environment.*

***Source:** U.S. Environmental Protection Agency, CERCLIS Hazardous Waste Sites, August 10, 2017*

2015 ATSDR Substance Priority List

2015 Rank	Substance Name	Totals Points	2013 Rank	CAS Number[1]
1	ARSENIC	1671.6	1	007440-38-2
2	LEAD	1529.4	2	007439-92-1
3	MERCURY	1458.6	3	007439-97-6
4	VINYL CHLORIDE	1358.9	4	000075-01-4
5	POLYCHLORINATED BIPHENYLS	1345.1	5	001336-36-3
6	BENZENE	1327.6	6	000071-43-2
7	CADMIUM	1318.8	7	007440-43-9
8	BENZO(A)PYRENE	1304.4	8	000050-32-8
9	POLYCYCLIC AROMATIC HYDROCARBONS	1279.1	9	130498-29-2
10	BENZO(B)FLUORANTHENE	1249.7	10	000205-99-2
11	CHLOROFORM	1202.4	11	000067-66-3
12	AROCLOR 1260	1190.0	12	011096-82-5
13	DDT, P,P'-	1182.0	13	000050-29-3
14	AROCLOR 1254	1171.3	14	011097-69-1
15	DIBENZO(A,H)ANTHRACENE	1155.6	15	000053-70-3
16	TRICHLOROETHYLENE	1153.4	16	000079-01-6
17	CHROMIUM,, HEXAVALENT	1146.8	17	018540-29-9
18	DIELDRIN	1142.9	18	000060-57-1
19	PHOSPHORUS, WHITE	1141.3	19	007723-14-0
20	HEXACHLOROBUTADIENE	1128.2	20	000087-68-3
21	DDE, P,P'-	1125.9	21	000072-55-9
22	CHLORDANE	1125.6	22	000057-74-9
23	AROCLOR 1242	1124.7	24	053469-21-9
24	COAL TAR CREOSOTE	1124.4	23	008001-58-9
25	ALDRIN	1114.6	25	000309-00-2
26	DDD, P,P'-	1113.1	26	000072-54-8
27	AROCLOR 1248	1104.5	27	012672-29-6
28	HEPTACHLOR	1100.6	28	000076-44-8
29	AROCLOR	1099.5	29	012767-79-2
30	BENZIDINE	1091.2	30	000092-87-5
31	ACROLEIN	1088.5	31	000107-02-8
32	TOXAPHENE	1087.8	32	008001-35-2
33	TETRACHLOROETHYLENE	1076.7	33	000127-18-4
34	HEXACHLOROCYCLOHEXANE, GAMMA-	1075.1	34	000058-89-9
35	CYANIDE	1069.8	35	000057-12-5
36	HEXACHLOROCYCLOHEXANE, BETA-	1053.4	36	000319-85-7
37	DISULFOTON	1047.2	38	000298-04-4
38	BENZO(A)ANTHRACENE	1046.0	38	000056-55-3
39	1,2-DIBROMOETHANE	1041.7	39	000106-93-4
40	ENDRIN	1037.6	40	000072-20-8
41	DIAZINON	1036.6	41	000333-41-5
42	HEXACHLOROCYCLOHEXANE, DELTA-	1034.8	42	000319-86-8
43	BERYLLIUM	1031.0	43	007440-41-7
44	ENDOSULFAN	1027.7	44	000115-29-7
45	AROCLOR 1221	1027.0	45	011104-28-2
46	1,2-DIBROMO-3-CHLOROPROPANE	1025.7	46	000096-12-8
47	HEPTACHLOR EPOXIDE	1020.7	47	001024-57-3
48	ENDOSULFAN, ALPHA	1018.0	48	000959-98-8
49	CIS-CHLORDANE	1015.6	49	005103-71-9
50	CARBON TETRACHLORIDE	1012.1	50	000056-23-5
51	COBALT	1012.0	51	007440-48-4
52	AROCLOR 1016	1011.5	52	012674-11-2
53	DDT, O,P'-	1007.8	53	000789-02-6
54	PENTACHLOROPHENOL	1007.2	54	000087-86-5
55	METHOXYCHLOR	1005.9	55	000072-43-5

2015 Rank	Substance Name	Totals Points	2013 Rank	CAS Number[1]
56	ENDOSULFAN SULFATE	1003.3	56	001031-07-8
57	NICKEL	995.7	57	007440-02-0
58	DI-N-BUTYL PHTHALATE	994.6	58	000084-74-2
59	ENDRIN KETONE	991.6	59	053494-70-5
60	DIBROMOCHLOROPROPANE	982.9	60	067708-83-2
61	BENZO(K)FLUORANTHENE	969.8	61	000207-08-9
62	TRANS-CHLORDANE	967.7	62	005103-74-2
63	ENDOSULFAN, BETA	967.1	63	033213-65-9
64	XYLENES, TOTAL	964.6	64	001330-20-7
65	CHLORPYRIFOS	963.8	65	002921-88-2
66	CHROMIUM(VI) TRIOXIDE	960.0	66	001333-82-0
67	AROCLOR 1232	957.9	67	011141-16-5
68	ENDRIN ALDEHYDE	957.4	68	007421-93-4
69	METHANE	952.7	69	000074-82-8
70	3,3'-DICHLOROBENZIDINE	940.4	70	000091-94-1
71	2-HEXANONE	940.2	71	000591-78-6
72	2,3,7,8-TETRACHLORODIBENZO-P-DIOXIN	939.8	72	001746-01-6
73	BENZOFLUORANTHENE	935.6	73	056832-73-6
74	TOLUENE	917.9	74	000108-88-3
75	ZINC	915.5	75	007440-66-6
76	PENTACHLOROBENZENE	906.8	76	000608-93-5
77	DI(2-ETHYLHEXYL)PHTHALATE	905.0	77	000117-81-7
78	CHROMIUM	895.6	78	007440-47-3
79	AROCLOR 1240	888.3	79	071328-89-7
80	NAPHTHALENE	877.4	80	000091-20-3
81	2,4,6-TRINITROTOLUENE	877.4	81	000118-96-7
82	1,1-DICHLOROETHENE	875.8	82	000075-35-4
83	BROMODICHLOROETHANE	866.3	83	000683-53-4
84	2,4,6-TRICHLOROPHENOL	866.0	84	000088-06-2
85	BIS(2-CHLOROETHYL) ETHER	865.9	85	000111-44-4
86	DDD, O,P'-	865.7	86	000053-19-0
87	HYDRAZINE	860.9	87	000302-01-2
88	METHYLENE CHLORIDE	860.0	88	000075-09-2
89	2,4-DINITROPHENOL	858.1	89	000051-28-5
90	4,4'-METHYLENEBIS(2-CHLOROANILINE)	857.3	90	000101-14-4
91	1,2-DICHLOROETHANE	852.7	91	000107-06-2
92	THIOCYANATE	845.9	92	000302-04-5
93	HEXACHLOROBENZENE	843.5	93	000118-74-1
94	ASBESTOS	840.8	94	001332-21-4
95	RADIUM-226	832.8	95	013982-63-3
96	RDX (Cyclonite)	831.9	96	000121-82-4
97	URANIUM	831.3	97	007440-61-1
98	2,4-DINITROTOLUENE	830.7	98	000121-14-2
99	ETHION	829.9	99	000563-12-2
100	RADIUM	827.2	100	007440-14-4
101	4,6-DINITRO-O-CRESOL	827.0	101	000534-52-1
102	THORIUM	823.9	102	007440-29-1
103	DIMETHYLARSINIC ACID	821.2	103	000075-60-5
104	CHLORINE	820.3	104	007782-50-5
105	1,3,5-TRINITROBENZENE	818.5	105	000099-35-4
106	RADON	818.3	106	010043-92-2
107	HEXACHLOROCYCLOHEXANE, ALPHA-	815.5	107	000319-84-6
108	RADIUM-228	815.1	108	015262-20-1
109	THORIUM-230	813.6	109	014269-63-7
110	URANIUM-235	812.0	110	015117-96-1
111	THORIUM-228	810.1	111	014274-82-9
112	URANIUM-234	809.5	112	013966-29-5
113	RADON-222	809.2	113	014859-67-7
114	COAL TARS	808.0	115	008007-45-2

2015 Rank	Substance Name	Totals Points	2013 Rank	CAS Number[1]
115	METHYLMERCURY	807.8	116	022967-92-6
116	1,1,1-TRICHLOROETHANE	807.6	114	000071-55-6
117	N-NITROSODI-N-PROPYLAMINE	807.1	117	000621-64-7
118	COPPER	806.5	118	007440-50-8
119	CHRYSOTILE ASBESTOS	806.1	119	012001-29-5
120	PLUTONIUM-239	805.9	120	015117-48-3
121	POLONIUM-210	805.5	121	013981-52-7
122	PLUTONIUM-238	805.2	122	013981-16-3
123	LEAD-210	805.0	123	014255-04-0
124	AMOSITE ASBESTOS	804.2	125	012172-73-5
124	PLUTONIUM	804.2	125	007440-07-5
124	STRONTIUM-90	804.2	125	010098-97-2
127	RADON-220	804.1	128	022481-48-7
128	CHLOROBENZENE	803.9	124	000108-90-7
129	AMERICIUM-241	803.8	129	086954-36-1
130	ETHYLBENZENE	802.8	130	000100-41-4
131	AZINPHOS-METHYL	802.5	132	000086-50-0
132	BARIUM	802.1	131	007440-39-3
133	CHLORDECONE	802.1	133	000143-50-0
134	NEPTUNIUM-237	801.9	134	013994-20-2
135	HYDROGEN CYANIDE	801.7	135	000074-90-8
136	PLUTONIUM-240	801.4	136	014119-33-6
137	1,2,3-TRICHLOROBENZENE	800.1	137	000087-61-6
138	FLUORANTHENE	799.6	138	000206-44-0
139	MANGANESE	798.3	139	007439-96-5
140	S,S,S-TRIBUTYL PHOSPHOROTRITHIOATE	797.6	140	000078-48-8
141	CHRYSENE	791.3	141	000218-01-9
142	2,4,5-TRICHLOROPHENOL	790.3	142	000095-95-4
143	POLYBROMINATED BIPHENYLS	784.2	143	067774-32-7
144	DICOFOL	783.8	144	000115-32-2
145	SELENIUM	775.9	145	007782-49-2
146	1,1,2,2-TETRACHLOROETHANE	775.6	146	000079-34-5
147	HEPTACHLORODIBENZO-P-DIOXIN	773.4	147	037871-00-4
148	PARATHION	773.3	148	000056-38-2
149	HEXACHLOROCYCLOHEXANE, TECHNICAL GRADE	772.9	149	000608-73-1
150	TRICHLOROFLUOROETHANE	772.3	150	027154-33-2
151	BROMINE	770.0	151	007726-95-6
152	AROCLOR 1268	764.4	152	011100-14-4
153	1,3-BUTADIENE	760.9	153	000106-99-0
154	HEPTACHLORODIBENZOFURAN	755.2	154	038998-75-3
155	TRIFLURALIN	754.2	155	001582-09-8
156	1,2,3,4,6,7,8,9-OCTACHLORODIBENZOFURAN	742.6	156	039001-02-0
157	AMMONIA	741.1	157	007664-41-7
158	2-METHYLNAPHTHALENE	726.5	158	000091-57-6
159	2,3,4,7,8-PENTACHLORODIBENZOFURAN	723.3	160	057117-31-4
160	1,4-DICHLOROBENZENE	723.2	159	000106-46-7
161	1,1-DICHLOROETHANE	721.8	161	000075-34-3
162	NALED	720.4	162	000300-76-5
163	1,1,2-TRICHLOROETHANE	719.3	163	000079-00-5
164	HEXACHLOROCYCLOPENTADIENE	717.9	164	000077-47-4
165	1,2-DIPHENYLHYDRAZINE	717.6	165	000122-66-7
166	PHORATE	715.0	166	000298-02-2
167	TRICHLOROETHANE	712.1	167	025323-89-1
168	ACENAPHTHENE	710.0	168	000083-32-9
169	TETRACHLOROBIPHENYL	709.1	169	026914-33-0
170	OXYCHLORDANE	705.4	170	027304-13-8
171	PALLADIUM	705.3	171	007440-05-3
172	CRESOL, PARA-	703.0	172	000106-44-5

2015 Rank	Substance Name	Totals Points	2013 Rank	CAS Number[1]
173	GAMMA-CHLORDENE	701.9	173	056641-38-4
174	INDENO(1,2,3-CD)PYRENE	701.9	174	000193-39-5
175	TETRACHLOROPHENOL	696.9	175	025167-83-3
176	1,2-DICHLOROBENZENE	696.4	176	000095-50-1
177	1,2-DICHLOROETHENE, TRANS-	691.7	177	000156-60-5
178	CHLOROETHANE	687.0	178	000075-00-3
179	ALUMINUM	686.0	179	007429-90-5
180	P-XYLENE	685.9	181	000106-42-3
181	PHENOL	685.7	180	000108-95-2
182	CARBON MONOXIDE	682.3	182	000630-08-0
183	CARBON DISULFIDE	681.6	183	000075-15-0
184	2,4-DIMETHYLPHENOL	679.0	184	000105-67-9
185	DIBENZOFURAN	675.5	185	000132-64-9
186	ACETONE	672.6	186	000067-64-1
187	HEXACHLOROETHANE	669.2	187	000067-72-1
188	BUTYL METHYL PHTHALATE	667.4	188	034006-76-3
189	CHLOROMETHANE	664.8	189	000074-87-3
190	HEXACHLORODIBENZOFURAN	659.7	190	055684-94-1
191	BUTYL BENZYL PHTHALATE	657.3	191	000085-68-7
192	HYDROGEN SULFIDE	656.2	192	007783-06-4
193	DICHLORVOS	655.3	193	000062-73-7
194	DIBENZOFURANS, CHLORINATED	652.8	194	042934-53-2
195	CRESOL, ORTHO-	652.2	195	000095-48-7
196	HEXACHLORODIBENZO-P-DIOXIN	651.2	196	034465-46-8
197	VANADIUM	649.8	197	007440-62-2
198	N-NITROSODIMETHYLAMINE	648.2	198	000062-75-9
199	1,2,4-TRICHLOROBENZENE	646.3	199	000120-82-1
200	ETHOPROP	643.4	200	013194-48-4
201	TETRACHLORODIBENZO-P-DIOXIN	641.0	201	041903-57-5
202	BROMOFORM	634.2	202	000075-25-2
203	PENTACHLORODIBENZOFURAN	631.2	203	030402-15-4
204	1,3-DICHLOROBENZENE	627.6	204	000541-73-1
205	PENTACHLORODIBENZO-P-DIOXIN	625.4	205	036088-22-9
206	N-NITROSODIPHENYLAMINE	624.6	206	000086-30-6
207	2,3,7,8-TETRACHLORODIBENZOFURAN	618.7	207	051207-31-9
208	2,4-DICHLOROPHENOL	618.0	208	000120-83-2
209	2,3-DIMETHYLNAPHTHALENE	617.6	209	000581-40-8
210	1,4-DIOXANE	614.8	210	000123-91-1
211	FLUORINE	613.2	211	007782-41-4
212	CESIUM-137	609.9	212	010045-97-3
212	CHROMIC ACID	609.9	212	007738-94-5
214	NITRITE	608.9	214	014797-65-0
215	2-BUTANONE	607.9	215	000078-93-3
216	1,2-DICHLOROETHYLENE	607.6	216	000540-59-0
217	POTASSIUM-40	607.5	217	013966-00-2
218	DINITROTOLUENE	607.2	218	025321-14-6
219	COAL TAR PITCH	605.2	220	065996-93-2
220	SILVER	604.9	219	007440-22-4
221	THORIUM-227	604.9	222	015623-47-9
222	NITRATE	604.9	221	014797-55-8
223	ARSENIC ACID	604.3	223	007778-39-4
224	FORMALDEHYDE	604.2	224	000050-00-0
225	ARSENIC TRIOXIDE	603.8	225	001327-53-3
226	BENZOPYRENE	603.4	226	073467-76-2
227	CHLORDANE, TECHNICAL	602.5	227	012789-03-6
228	STROBANE	602.5	228	008001-50-1
229	4-AMINOBIPHENYL	602.4	229	000092-67-1
229	PYRETHRUM	602.4	229	008003-34-7

2015 Rank	Substance Name	Totals Points	2013 Rank	CAS Number[1]
231	ARSINE	602.4	231	007784-42-1
232	DIMETHOATE	602.4	231	000060-51-5
233	BIS(CHLOROMETHYL) ETHER	601.9	New	000542-88-1
233	CARBOPHENOTHION	601.9	233	000786-19-6
235	ALPHA-CHLORDENE	601.4	234	056534-02-2
235	IODINE-131	601.4	234	010043-66-0
235	MERCURIC CHLORIDE	601.4	234	007487-94-7
235	SODIUM ARSENITE	601.4	234	007784-46-5
235	URANIUM-233	601.4	234	013968-55-3
240	ANTIMONY	601.0	239	007440-36-0
241	DIBROMOCHLOROMETHANE	599.4	240	000124-48-1
242	CRESOLS	596.7	241	001319-77-3
243	DICHLOROBENZENE	594.8	242	025321-22-6
244	2,4-D ACID	594.3	243	000094-75-7
245	2-CHLOROPHENOL	590.5	244	000095-57-8
246	BUTYLATE	589.9	245	002008-41-5
247	DIMETHYL FORMAMIDE	585.2	247	000068-12-2
248	PHENANTHRENE	584.7	246	000085-01-8
249	4-NITROPHENOL	579.3	248	000100-02-7
250	DIURON	578.7	249	000330-54-1
251	TETRACHLOROETHANE	576.4	250	025322-20-7
252	DICHLOROETHANE	567.3	251	001300-21-6
253	ETHYL ETHER	564.9	252	000060-29-7
254	DIMETHYLANILINE	561.7	253	000121-69-7
255	PYRENE	560.9	254	000129-00-0
256	1,3-DICHLOROPROPENE, CIS-	560.5	255	010061-01-5
257	1,2,3,4,6,7,8-HEPTACHLORODIBENZO-P-DIOXIN	558.6	256	035822-46-9
258	PHOSPHINE	555.3	257	007803-51-2
259	TRICHLOROBENZENE	554.8	258	012002-48-1
260	2,6-DINITROTOLUENE	554.0	259	000606-20-2
261	FLUORIDE ION	548.9	260	016984-48-8
262	1,2,3,4,6,7,8-HEPTACHLORODIBENZOFURAN	548.5	261	067562-39-4
263	PENTAERYTHRITOL TETRANITRATE	548.1	262	000078-11-5
264	1,3-DICHLOROPROPENE, TRANS-	547.6	263	010061-02-6
265	ACRYLONITRILE	543.0	264	000107-13-1
266	BIS(2-ETHYLHEXYL)ADIPATE	542.3	265	000103-23-1
267	1,2-DICHLOROETHENE, CIS-	540.8	271	000156-59-2
268	CARBAZOLE	539.8	266	000086-74-8
269	METOLACHLOR	538.2	267	051218-45-2
270	2-CHLOROANILINE	538.0	268	000095-51-2
271	1,2,3-TRICHLOROPROPANE	535.9	269	000096-18-4
272	CARBARYL	535.4	270	000063-25-2
273	STYRENE	527.9	272	000100-42-5
274	METHYL ISOBUTYL KETONE	527.3	273	000108-10-1
275	THALLIUM	524.5	274	007440-28-0

***Notes:** Substances were assigned the same rank when two (or more) substances received equivalent total scores; (1) CAS Number = Chemical Abstracts Service registry number*

The Comprehensive Environmental Response, Compensation, and Liability Act (CERCLA) section 104 (i), as amended by the Superfund Amendments and Reauthorization Act (SARA), requires ATSDR and the EPA to prepare a list, in order of priority, of substances that are most commonly found at facilities on the National Priorities List (NPL) and which are determined to pose the most significant potential threat to human health due to their known or suspected toxicity and potential for human exposure at these NPL sites. CERCLA also requires this list to be revised periodically to reflect additional information on hazardous substances. This substance priority list is revised and published on a 2-year basis, with a yearly informal review and revision. Each substance on the list is a candidate to become the subject of a toxicological profile prepared by ATSDR. The listing algorithm prioritizes substances based on frequency of occurrence at NPL sites, toxicity, and potential for human exposure to the substances found at NPL sites. It should be noted that this priority list is not a list of "most toxic" substances, but rather a prioritization of substances based on a combination of their frequency, toxicity, and potential for human exposure at NPL sites. Thus, it is possible for substances with low toxicity but high NPL frequency of occurrence and exposure to be on this priority list. The objective of this priority list is to rank substances across all NPL hazardous waste sites to provide guidance in selecting which substances will be the subject of toxicological profiles prepared by ATSDR.

***Source:** Center for Disease Control, Agency for Toxic Substances and Disease Registry, 2015 ATDSR Substance Priority List*

TRI On-site and Off-site Reported Disposed of or Otherwise Released (in pounds), for Facilities in All Industries, for All Chemicals, by State, U.S., 2015

State	Total On-site Disposal or Other Releases[1]	Total Off-site Disposal or Other Releases[2]	Total On- and Off-site Disposal or Other Releases
Alabama	71,816,034	12,738,854	84,554,888
Alaska	585,741,121	697,831	586,438,952
Arizona	84,034,799	1,485,679	85,520,478
Arkansas	29,376,736	3,317,302	32,694,038
California	26,860,552	4,401,580	31,262,132
Colorado	21,672,773	5,545,296	27,218,069
Connecticut	777,622	741,722	1,519,344
Delaware	4,603,520	1,576,778	6,180,298
District of Columbia	21,602	558	22,159
Florida	55,744,871	4,786,604	60,531,475
Georgia	52,861,061	3,377,973	56,239,034
Hawaii	2,401,098	168,480	2,569,578
Idaho	46,491,341	487,441	46,978,782
Illinois	75,266,308	40,227,664	115,493,972
Indiana	87,205,884	48,854,987	136,060,871
Iowa	28,717,916	6,599,674	35,317,590
Kansas	15,780,697	2,762,046	18,542,742
Kentucky	54,406,982	7,938,362	62,345,344
Louisiana	130,909,037	9,583,315	140,492,352
Maine	6,826,794	2,625,472	9,452,265
Maryland	6,361,116	1,718,603	8,079,719
Massachusetts	1,479,982	1,916,167	3,396,149
Michigan	46,444,838	26,359,604	72,804,441
Minnesota	21,440,281	4,642,048	26,082,329
Mississippi	61,698,535	3,223,521	64,922,056
Missouri	70,372,156	5,118,976	75,491,133
Montana	37,324,638	1,060,913	38,385,552
Nebraska	19,126,323	1,803,666	20,929,989
Nevada	318,703,631	4,833,650	323,537,281
New Hampshire	326,267	145,027	471,294
New Jersey	6,800,991	67,763,241	74,564,232
New Mexico	19,381,318	3,048,012	22,429,329
New York	11,770,012	3,526,505	15,296,517
North Carolina	40,598,670	21,749,898	62,348,568
North Dakota	36,948,347	9,962,795	46,911,141
Ohio	84,369,691	22,006,589	106,376,280
Oklahoma	24,852,502	2,107,072	26,959,574
Oregon	14,853,611	1,269,076	16,122,687
Pennsylvania	38,630,516	27,296,043	65,926,559
Rhode Island	293,938	166,604	460,542
South Carolina	31,040,348	7,946,304	38,986,653
South Dakota	6,354,844	84,776	6,439,620
Tennessee	72,437,576	12,917,792	85,355,368
Texas	189,792,702	44,424,856	234,217,558
Utah	227,367,455	1,846,081	229,213,536
Vermont	210,277	144,527	354,804
Virginia	35,048,544	3,679,762	38,728,307
Washington	21,891,094	4,051,239	25,942,333
West Virginia	25,545,217	5,915,253	31,460,470
Wisconsin	19,213,865	12,885,611	32,099,476
Wyoming	17,945,818	2,571,313	20,517,132
American Samoa	58,478	0	58,478
Guam	467,033	0	467,033
Northern Mariana Islands	5,545	0	5,545
Puerto Rico	1,897,218	187,034	2,084,252

State	Total On-site Disposal or Other Releases[1]	Total Off-site Disposal or Other Releases[2]	Total On- and Off-site Disposal or Other Releases
Virgin Islands	15,986	9	15,995
Total U.S.	2,892,586,109	464,290,183	3,356,876,292

Notes: *TRI = Toxic Release Inventory; Reporting year (RY) 2015 is the most recent TRI data available. Facilities reporting to TRI were required to submit RY 2015 data to EPA by July 1, 2016. TRI Explorer is using an updated data set (released to the public in March 2017). This dataset includes revisions for the years 1988 to 2015 processed by EPA, after the National Analysis Dataset was released. Revisions submitted to EPA after this time are not reflected in TRI Explorer reports.*

(1) On-site Disposal or Other Releases include Underground Injection to Class I Wells (Section 5.4.1), RCRA Subtitle C Landfills (5.5.1A), Other Landfills (5.5.1B), Fugitive or Non-point Air Emissions (5.1), Stack or Point Air Emissions (5.2), Surface Water Discharges (5.3), Underground Injection to Class II-V Wells (5.4.2), Land Treatment/Application Farming (5.5.2), RCRA Subtitle C Surface Impoundments (5.5.3A), Other Surface Impoundments (5.5.3B), and Other Land Disposal (5.5.4). Off-site Disposal or Other Releases include from Section 6.2 Class I Underground Injection Wells (M81), Class II-V Underground Injection Wells (M82, M71), RCRA Subtitle C Landfills (M65), Other Landfills (M64, M72), Storage Only (M10), Solidification/Stabilization - Metals and Metal Category Compounds only (M41 or M40), Wastewater Treatment (excluding POTWs) - Metals and Metal Category Compounds only (M62 or M61), RCRA Subtitle C Surface Impoundments (M66), Other Surface Impoundments (M67, M63), Land Treatment (M73), Other Land Disposal (M79), Other Off-site Management (M90), Transfers to Waste Broker - Disposal (M94, M91), and Unknown (M99) and, from Section 6.1 Transfers to POTWs (metals and metal category compounds only).

(2) Off-site disposal or other releases show only net off-site disposal or other releases, that is, off-site disposal or other releases transferred to other TRI facilities reporting such transfers as on-site disposal or other releases are not included to avoid double counting.

This report may not include all states in the US. A state may not be included in this report for two reasons: 1) there are no facilities reporting to TRI in the particular state; or 2) the facilities reporting to TRI in the particular state did not report to TRI for the user-specified selection criteria.

Users of TRI information should be aware that TRI data reflect releases and other waste management activities of chemicals, not whether (or to what degree) the public has been exposed to those chemicals. Release estimates alone are not sufficient to determine exposure or to calculate potential adverse effects on human health and the environment. TRI data, in conjunction with other information, can be used as a starting point in evaluating exposures that may result from releases and other waste management activities which involve toxic chemicals. The determination of potential risk depends upon many factors, including the toxicity of the chemical, the fate of the chemical, and the amount and duration of human or other exposure to the chemical after it is released.

Source: *U.S. Environmental Protection Agency, TRI Explorer, August 10, 2017*

TRI On-site and Off-site Reported Disposed of or Otherwise Released (in grams), for Facilities in All Industries, Dioxin and Dioxin-like Compounds, by State, U.S., 2015

State	Total On-site Disposal or Other Releases[1]	Total Off-site Disposal or Other Releases[2]	Total On- and Off-site Disposal or Other Releases
Alabama	241.989	106.831	348.820
Alaska	0.864	0.000	0.864
Arizona	20.540	35.420	55.960
Arkansas	52.485	0.531	53.017
California	49.273	78.667	127.940
Colorado	16.191	0.577	16.768
Connecticut	0.561	0.000	0.561
Delaware	7.208	346.063	353.271
Florida	267.769	0.645	268.414
Georgia	123.345	1.482	124.827
Hawaii	0.681	0.968	1.649
Idaho	6.881	9.760	16.641
Illinois	19.346	80.823	100.169
Indiana	238.041	309.175	547.216
Iowa	20.313	11.183	31.497
Kansas	181.522	19,344.313	19,525.835
Kentucky	138.370	4,264.488	4,402.858
Louisiana	154.545	397.650	552.195
Maine	5.095	4.643	9.738
Maryland	5.005	4.359	9.364
Massachusetts	1.587	0.000	1.587
Michigan	2,606.777	1,692.012	4,298.789
Minnesota	17.799	177.084	194.884
Mississippi	1,706.740	0.130	1,706.870
Missouri	36.757	0.000	36.757
Montana	8.339	1.230	9.569
Nebraska	4.979	0.000	4.979
Nevada	2.673	0.514	3.187
New Hampshire	0.186	0.000	0.186
New Jersey	1.909	40.406	42.315
New Mexico	4.782	0.523	5.304
New York	9.582	2.583	12.164
North Carolina	89.767	2.783	92.549
North Dakota	17.494	0.000	17.494
Ohio	538.060	140.731	678.791
Oklahoma	46.820	39.030	85.850
Oregon	8.543	6.578	15.121
Pennsylvania	39.958	2.300	42.258
South Carolina	39.334	4.565	43.899
South Dakota	12.669	0.000	12.669
Tennessee	1,090.632	47.722	1,138.354
Texas	8,239.268	25,039.313	33,278.581
Utah	18,839.921	521.009	19,360.930
Virginia	14.583	13.717	28.300
Washington	22.941	170.374	193.315
West Virginia	497.135	31.436	528.571
Wisconsin	35.073	983.613	1,018.686
Wyoming	19.550	0.000	19.550
Guam	0.658	0.000	0.658
Puerto Rico	2.463	0.000	2.463
Virgin Islands	0.906	0.000	0.906
Total U.S.	35,507.907	53,915.229	89,423.136

***Notes:** TRI = Toxic Release Inventory; Reporting year (RY) 2015 is the most recent TRI data available. Facilities reporting to TRI were required to submit RY 2015 data to EPA by July 1, 2016. TRI Explorer is using an updated data set (released to* *the public in March 2017). This dataset includes revisions for the years 1988 to 2015 processed by EPA, after the National Analysis Dataset was released. Revisions submitted to EPA after this time are not reflected in TRI Explorer reports.*

(1) On-site Disposal or Other Releases include Underground Injection to Class I Wells (Section 5.4.1), RCRA Subtitle C Landfills (5.5.1A), Other Landfills (5.5.1B), Fugitive or Non-point Air Emissions (5.1), Stack or Point Air Emissions (5.2), Surface Water Discharges (5.3), Underground Injection to Class II-V Wells (5.4.2), Land Treatment/Application Farming (5.5.2), RCRA Subtitle C Surface Impoundments (5.5.3A), Other Surface Impoundments (5.5.3B), and Other Land Disposal (5.5.4). Off-site Disposal or Other Releases include from Section 6.2 Class I Underground Injection Wells (M81), Class II-V Underground Injection Wells (M82, M71), RCRA Subtitle C Landfills (M65), Other Landfills (M64, M72), Storage Only (M10), Solidification/Stabilization - Metals and Metal Category Compounds only (M41 or M40), Wastewater Treatment (excluding POTWs) - Metals and Metal Category Compounds only (M62 or M61), RCRA Subtitle C Surface Impoundments (M66), Other Surface Impoundments (M67, M63), Land Treatment (M73), Other Land Disposal (M79), Other Off-site Management (M90), Transfers to Waste Broker - Disposal (M94, M91), and Unknown (M99) and, from Section 6.1 Transfers to POTWs (metals and metal category compounds only).

(2) Off-site disposal or other releases show only net off-site disposal or other releases, that is, off-site disposal or other releases transferred to other TRI facilities reporting such transfers as on-site disposal or other releases are not included to avoid double counting.

This report may not include all states in the US. A state may not be included in this report for two reasons: 1) there are no facilities reporting to TRI in the particular state; or 2) the facilities reporting to TRI in the particular state did not report to TRI for the user-specified selection criteria.

Users of TRI information should be aware that TRI data reflect releases and other waste management activities of chemicals, not whether (or to what degree) the public has been exposed to those chemicals. Release estimates alone are not sufficient to determine exposure or to calculate potential adverse effects on human health and the environment. TRI data, in conjunction with other information, can be used as a starting point in evaluating exposures that may result from releases and other waste management activities which involve toxic chemicals. The determination of potential risk depends upon many factors, including the toxicity of the chemical, the fate of the chemical, and the amount and duration of human or other exposure to the chemical after it is released.

***Source:** U.S. Environmental Protection Agency, TRI Explorer, August 10, 2017*

TRI On-site and Off-site Reported Disposed of or Otherwise Released (in pounds), for Facilities in All Industries, for All Chemicals, Top 75 Counties, 2015

Rank	County	State	Total On-site Disposal or Other Releases[1]	Total Off-site Disposal or Other Releases[2]	Total On- and Off-site Disposal or Other Releases
1	Northwest Arctic	Alaska	542,092,725	1	542,092,725
2	Salt Lake	Utah	207,370,938	821,914	208,192,852
3	Humboldt	Nevada	120,854,049	55,908	120,909,957
4	Lander	Nevada	67,895,056	2,586	67,897,642
5	Hudson	New Jersey	80,944	65,708,937	65,789,881
6	Gila	Arizona	52,519,281	442,616	52,961,897
7	White Pine	Nevada	43,915,373	71	43,915,444
8	Harris	Texas	34,497,992	8,146,232	42,644,223
9	Lake	Indiana	23,601,806	18,774,538	42,376,344
10	Brazoria	Texas	39,005,131	491,703	39,496,833
11	Mercer	North Dakota	25,269,616	12,764,198	38,033,813
12	Eureka	Nevada	36,573,159	58,896	36,632,054
13	Elko	Nevada	31,444,646	286,728	31,731,374
14	Jefferson	Texas	12,463,656	18,026,375	30,490,032
15	Juneau	Alaska	29,951,063	0	29,951,063
16	Escambia	Florida	28,847,725	82,762	28,930,487
17	Wayne	Michigan	7,698,067	19,795,135	27,493,203
18	Humphreys	Tennessee	24,547,945	94,380	24,642,325
19	Nueces	Texas	13,892,838	10,343,774	24,236,612
20	Harrison	Mississippi	23,203,858	23,290	23,227,148
21	Reynolds	Missouri	23,092,649	9,828	23,102,477
22	Shoshone	Idaho	23,039,114	620	23,039,734
23	St Charles	Louisiana	22,133,413	3,011	22,136,424
24	Washington	Illinois	20,903,695	9,773	20,913,468
25	Iron	Missouri	20,243,511	120,423	20,363,934
26	Ascension Parish	Louisiana	19,775,517	198,523	19,974,040
27	Silver Bow	Montana	18,421,275	52,324	18,473,599
28	Spencer	Indiana	17,541,930	921,608	18,463,538
29	Peoria	Illinois	1,309,410	16,584,931	17,894,341
30	Will	Illinois	15,146,926	2,374,635	17,521,561
31	Monroe	Mississippi	15,394,372	171,847	15,566,219
32	Jefferson Parish	Louisiana	12,109,155	2,989,285	15,098,440
33	Calhoun	Texas	12,833,215	589,978	13,423,193
34	Marquette	Michigan	12,594,821	180,265	12,775,086
35	Marion	Indiana	1,749,740	10,919,672	12,669,412
36	Rosebud	Montana	12,204,005	161,095	12,365,100
37	Allegheny	Pennsylvania	4,110,410	7,618,185	11,728,595
38	Sandusky	Ohio	11,612,469	61,878	11,674,347
39	Carroll	Kentucky	6,665,404	4,842,781	11,508,185
40	Allen	Ohio	10,956,634	499,678	11,456,313
41	Mobile	Alabama	5,938,118	4,890,479	10,828,597
42	Tooele	Utah	10,428,997	394,166	10,823,162
43	Benton	Washington	9,898,107	841,698	10,739,805
44	Ouachita Parish	Louisiana	10,718,646	4,381	10,723,027
45	Montgomery	Virginia	10,163,819	182,212	10,346,031
46	East Baton Rouge Parish	Louisiana	5,775,459	4,570,183	10,345,642
47	Sumter	Alabama	10,255,759	5,466	10,261,225
48	Rutherford	North Carolina	780,654	9,166,980	9,947,634
49	Pershing	Nevada	9,838,010	20,842	9,858,852
50	Indiana	Pennsylvania	9,333,031	30,570	9,363,601
51	Fairbanks North Star Boro	Alaska	8,683,799	462,633	9,146,432
52	Cook	Illinois	2,945,082	6,141,346	9,086,427
53	Kern	California	8,860,338	28,918	8,889,256
54	Jefferson	Alabama	5,156,925	3,369,251	8,526,176
55	Sullivan	Tennessee	8,085,853	428,969	8,514,822

Rank	County	State	Total On-site Disposal or Other Releases[1]	Total Off-site Disposal or Other Releases[2]	Total On- and Off-site Disposal or Other Releases
56	Shelby	Tennessee	3,339,129	5,033,115	8,372,244
57	Calcasieu Parish	Louisiana	7,940,160	219,607	8,159,768
58	Coshocton	Ohio	6,857,442	1,242,135	8,099,577
59	Ashtabula	Ohio	7,774,664	79,871	7,854,535
60	Greenlee	Arizona	7,751,621	43,707	7,795,328
61	Orange	Texas	5,304,795	2,340,128	7,644,923
62	Grant	New Mexico	7,623,733	5,090	7,628,823
63	Montgomery	Tennessee	5,394,146	2,187,726	7,581,872
64	Richmond	Georgia	7,494,165	9,313	7,503,479
65	Lee	Iowa	6,538,087	949,604	7,487,691
66	Pima	Arizona	7,368,580	115,952	7,484,532
67	Iberville Parish	Louisiana	5,619,496	1,740,795	7,360,291
68	San Juan	New Mexico	4,586,089	2,563,549	7,149,637
69	Victoria	Texas	6,949,061	150,640	7,099,701
70	Harrison	West Virginia	6,874,777	3,002	6,877,778
71	Caribou	Idaho	6,675,845	1,193	6,677,038
72	Calcasieu	Louisiana	6,515,623	111,950	6,627,573
73	Nye	Nevada	6,523,644	44,066	6,567,710
74	Oliver	North Dakota	5,017,611	1,511,060	6,528,671
75	Cuyahoga	Ohio	3,613,360	2,893,040	6,506,399

Notes: *TRI = Toxic Release Inventory; Reporting year (RY) 2015 is the most recent TRI data available. Facilities reporting to TRI were required to submit RY 2015 data to EPA by July 1, 2016. TRI Explorer is using an updated data set (released to the public in March 2017). This dataset includes revisions for the years 1988 to 2015 processed by EPA, after the National Analysis Dataset was released. Revisions submitted to EPA after this time are not reflected in TRI Explorer reports.*

(1) On-site Disposal or Other Releases include Underground Injection to Class I Wells (Section 5.4.1), RCRA Subtitle C Landfills (5.5.1A), Other Landfills (5.5.1B), Fugitive or Non-point Air Emissions (5.1), Stack or Point Air Emissions (5.2), Surface Water Discharges (5.3), Underground Injection to Class II-V Wells (5.4.2), Land Treatment/Application Farming (5.5.2), RCRA Subtitle C Surface Impoundments (5.5.3A), Other Surface Impoundments (5.5.3B), and Other Land Disposal (5.5.4). Off-site Disposal or Other Releases include from Section 6.2 Class I Underground Injection Wells (M81), Class II-V Underground Injection Wells (M82, M71), RCRA Subtitle C Landfills (M65), Other Landfills (M64, M72), Storage Only (M10), Solidification/Stabilization - Metals and Metal Category Compounds only (M41 or M40), Wastewater Treatment (excluding POTWs) - Metals and Metal Category Compounds only (M62 or M61), RCRA Subtitle C Surface Impoundments (M66), Other Surface Impoundments (M67, M63), Land Treatment (M73), Other Land Disposal (M79), Other Off-site Management (M90), Transfers to Waste Broker - Disposal (M94, M91), and Unknown (M99) and, from Section 6.1 Transfers to POTWs (metals and metal category compounds only).

(2) Off-site disposal or other releases show only net off-site disposal or other releases, that is, off-site disposal or other releases transferred to other TRI facilities reporting such transfers as on-site disposal or other releases are not included to avoid double counting.

This report may not include all states in the US. A state may not be included in this report for two reasons: 1) there are no facilities reporting to TRI in the particular state; or 2) the facilities reporting to TRI in the particular state did not report to TRI for the user-specified selection criteria.

Users of TRI information should be aware that TRI data reflect releases and other waste management activities of chemicals, not whether (or to what degree) the public has been exposed to those chemicals. Release estimates alone are not sufficient to determine exposure or to calculate potential adverse effects on human health and the environment. TRI data, in conjunction with other information, can be used as a starting point in evaluating exposures that may result from releases and other waste management activities which involve toxic chemicals. The determination of potential risk depends upon many factors, including the toxicity of the chemical, the fate of the chemical, and the amount and duration of human or other exposure to the chemical after it is released.

Source: *U.S. Environmental Protection Agency, TRI Explorer, August 10, 2017*

TRI On-site and Off-site Reported Disposed of or Otherwise Released (in grams), for Facilities in All Industries, Dioxin and Dioxin-like Compounds, Top 75 Counties, 2015

Rank	County	State	Total On-site Disposal or Other Releases[1]	Total Off-site Disposal or Other Releases[2]	Total On- and Off-site Disposal or Other Releases
1	Harris	Texas	29.426	25,036.699	25,066.125
2	Linn	Kansas	176.764	19,344.300	19,521.064
3	Tooele	Utah	18,826.673	513.920	19,340.593
4	Brazoria	Texas	5,720.180	0.000	5,720.180
5	Marshall	Kentucky	20.221	3,986.786	4,007.006
6	Midland	Michigan	2,489.883	0.000	2,489.883
7	Nueces	Texas	2,373.510	0.000	2,373.510
8	Branch	Michigan	89.040	1,692.012	1,781.052
9	Harrison	Mississippi	1,361.418	0.061	1,361.479
10	Humphreys	Tennessee	1,040.724	0.029	1,040.752
11	Sheboygan	Wisconsin	11.232	943.146	954.379
12	Ashtabula	Ohio	486.253	0.000	486.253
13	Mason	West Virginia	481.320	0.000	481.320
14	New Castle	Delaware	7.208	346.068	353.276
15	San Patricio	Texas	4.062	324.706	328.768
16	Allen	Indiana	6.225	304.850	311.075
17	Monroe	Mississippi	296.782	0.000	296.782
18	Barren	Kentucky	1.084	270.164	271.248
19	Iberville Parish	Louisiana	14.584	219.535	234.119
20	Clay	Florida	230.225	0.000	230.225
21	Dakota	Minnesota	2.367	176.791	179.158
22	Calcasieu	Louisiana	20.840	128.532	149.372
23	Tuscarawas	Ohio	6.668	126.660	133.328
24	Wabash	Indiana	97.160	0.000	97.160
25	Tuscaloosa	Alabama	94.669	0.000	94.669
26	Cowlitz	Washington	6.753	85.021	91.774
27	Pike	Alabama	84.200	0.000	84.200
28	Pierce	Washington	1.027	81.875	82.902
29	Porter	Indiana	74.750	0.000	74.750
30	Butler	Kentucky	72.450	0.000	72.450
31	St Clair	Alabama	3.321	56.950	60.271
32	Los Angeles	California	3.449	53.686	57.135
33	Catawba	North Carolina	52.136	0.000	52.136
34	Greene	Georgia	51.110	0.000	51.110
35	East Baton Rouge Parish	Louisiana	35.694	13.447	49.141
36	Etowah	Alabama	0.531	44.669	45.200
37	Cass	Texas	43.670	0.000	43.670
38	Kern	California	32.533	10.921	43.454
39	Cook	Illinois	2.625	39.590	42.215
40	Racine	Wisconsin	1.465	40.592	42.057
41	Peoria	Illinois	0.614	41.233	41.847
42	Creek	Oklahoma	2.057	39.030	41.087
43	Maricopa	Arizona	5.106	35.420	40.526
44	Mccurtain	Oklahoma	39.104	0.000	39.104
45	Blount	Tennessee	9.343	23.290	32.633
46	Putnam	Indiana	32.113	0.000	32.113
47	St Charles Parish	Louisiana	8.068	21.854	29.923
48	Kemper	Mississippi	29.092	0.000	29.092
49	Orange	Texas	27.384	1.311	28.695
50	Calcasieu Parish	Louisiana	23.096	5.404	28.500
51	Tyler	West Virginia	1.383	26.290	27.673
52	Iberville	Louisiana	25.912	0.000	25.912
53	San Bernardino	California	10.217	14.046	24.262
54	Bergen	New Jersey	0.000	21.484	21.484
55	Richmond	Georgia	21.266	0.077	21.342

Rank	County	State	Total On-site Disposal or Other Releases[1]	Total Off-site Disposal or Other Releases[2]	Total On- and Off-site Disposal or Other Releases
56	Scott	Iowa	7.359	11.130	18.489
57	York	South Carolina	18.146	0.000	18.146
58	Sullivan	Tennessee	17.864	0.051	17.915
59	Lucas	Ohio	17.118	0.000	17.118
60	Camden	New Jersey	1.432	15.594	17.025
61	Henderson	Kentucky	15.531	0.000	15.531
62	Fulton	Georgia	15.360	0.000	15.360
63	Escambia	Alabama	15.356	0.000	15.356
64	Ascension Parish	Louisiana	9.071	5.096	14.167
65	Mercer	North Dakota	14.121	0.000	14.121
66	Ashley	Arkansas	13.057	0.000	13.057
67	Maury	Tennessee	1.411	11.629	13.040
68	Jefferson	Arkansas	12.483	0.000	12.483
69	Columbus	North Carolina	9.709	2.611	12.321
70	Loudon	Tennessee	0.754	11.557	12.311
71	Pueblo	Colorado	10.741	0.000	10.741
72	Kootenai	Idaho	0.520	9.760	10.280
73	Yankton	South Dakota	10.248	0.000	10.248
74	Ashland	Wisconsin	10.071	0.000	10.071
75	Apache	Arizona	9.974	0.000	9.974

Notes: *TRI = Toxic Release Inventory; Reporting year (RY) 2015 is the most recent TRI data available. Facilities reporting to TRI were required to submit RY 2015 data to EPA by July 1, 2016. TRI Explorer is using an updated data set (released to the public in March 2017). This dataset includes revisions for the years 1988 to 2015 processed by EPA, after the National Analysis Dataset was released. Revisions submitted to EPA after this time are not reflected in TRI Explorer reports.*

(1) On-site Disposal or Other Releases include Underground Injection to Class I Wells (Section 5.4.1), RCRA Subtitle C Landfills (5.5.1A), Other Landfills (5.5.1B), Fugitive or Non-point Air Emissions (5.1), Stack or Point Air Emissions (5.2), Surface Water Discharges (5.3), Underground Injection to Class II-V Wells (5.4.2), Land Treatment/Application Farming (5.5.2), RCRA Subtitle C Surface Impoundments (5.5.3A), Other Surface Impoundments (5.5.3B), and Other Land Disposal (5.5.4). Off-site Disposal or Other Releases include from Section 6.2 Class I Underground Injection Wells (M81), Class II-V Underground Injection Wells (M82, M71), RCRA Subtitle C Landfills (M65), Other Landfills (M64, M72), Storage Only (M10), Solidification/Stabilization - Metals and Metal Category Compounds only (M41 or M40), Wastewater Treatment (excluding POTWs) - Metals and Metal Category Compounds only (M62 or M61), RCRA Subtitle C Surface Impoundments (M66), Other Surface Impoundments (M67, M63), Land Treatment (M73), Other Land Disposal (M79), Other Off-site Management (M90), Transfers to Waste Broker - Disposal (M94, M91), and Unknown (M99) and, from Section 6.1 Transfers to POTWs (metals and metal category compounds only).

(2) Off-site disposal or other releases show only net off-site disposal or other releases, that is, off-site disposal or other releases transferred to other TRI facilities reporting such transfers as on-site disposal or other releases are not included to avoid double counting.

This report may not include all states in the US. A state may not be included in this report for two reasons: 1) there are no facilities reporting to TRI in the particular state; or 2) the facilities reporting to TRI in the particular state did not report to TRI for the user-specified selection criteria.

Users of TRI information should be aware that TRI data reflect releases and other waste management activities of chemicals, not whether (or to what degree) the public has been exposed to those chemicals. Release estimates alone are not sufficient to determine exposure or to calculate potential adverse effects on human health and the environment. TRI data, in conjunction with other information, can be used as a starting point in evaluating exposures that may result from releases and other waste management activities which involve toxic chemicals. The determination of potential risk depends upon many factors, including the toxicity of the chemical, the fate of the chemical, and the amount and duration of human or other exposure to the chemical after it is released.

Source: *U.S. Environmental Protection Agency, TRI Explorer, August 10, 2017*

TRI On-site and Off-site Reported Disposed of or Otherwise Released (in pounds), for Facilities in All Industries, for All Chemicals, Top 75 Zipcodes, 2015

Rank	Zip	City	State	Total On-site Disposal or Other Releases[1]	Total Off-site Disposal or Other Releases[2]	Total On- and Off-site Disposal or Other Releases
1	99752	Kotzebue	Alaska	542,092,725	1	542,092,725
2	84006	Bingham Canyon	Utah	164,191,739	43,129	164,234,868
3	89414	Golconda	Nevada	120,200,748	14,680	120,215,428
4	89822	Carlin	Nevada	64,669,743	301,745	64,971,488
5	07032	Kearny	New Jersey	25	64,945,214	64,945,238
6	89319	Ruth	Nevada	42,363,749	0	42,363,749
7	84044	Magna	Utah	42,352,986	209	42,353,195
8	89820	Battle Mountain	Nevada	39,620,421	0	39,620,421
9	77511	Alvin	Texas	33,250,963	0	33,250,963
10	58523	Beulah	North Dakota	24,914,416	7,704,865	32,619,281
11	99801	Juneau	Alaska	31,865,370	0	31,865,370
12	65440	Boss	Missouri	31,405,386	73,478	31,478,864
13	85135	Hayden	Arizona	30,336,141	142	30,336,283
14	89821	Crescent Valley	Nevada	28,301,067	2,562	28,303,629
15	32533	Cantonment	Florida	28,283,350	12,540	28,295,890
16	37134	New Johnsonville	Tennessee	22,735,355	74	22,735,429
17	46402	Gary	Indiana	21,764,881	828,467	22,593,348
18	39571	Pass Christian	Mississippi	21,686,207	23,070	21,709,277
19	85532	Claypool	Arizona	21,222,236	434,110	21,656,345
20	62257	Marissa	Illinois	20,884,482	9,773	20,894,255
21	70070	Luling	Louisiana	20,288,488	187	20,288,675
22	47635	Rockport	Indiana	17,524,285	921,608	18,445,893
23	59701	Butte	Montana	18,420,628	0	18,420,628
24	46312	East Chicago	Indiana	575,296	17,674,040	18,249,337
25	83846	Mullan	Idaho	17,031,531	589	17,032,120
26	77641	Port Arthur	Texas	7,287	16,370,000	16,377,287
27	77536	Deer Park	Texas	15,486,687	835,108	16,321,795
28	39746	Hamilton	Mississippi	15,187,380	0	15,187,380
29	60436	Joliet	Illinois	13,669,536	1,503,052	15,172,588
30	70734	Geismar	Louisiana	14,779,475	189,641	14,969,116
31	59323	Colstrip	Montana	12,204,005	161,002	12,365,007
32	70094	Westwego	Louisiana	12,103,808	9,017	12,112,825
33	49814	Champion	Michigan	12,066,958	46	12,067,004
34	41045	Ghent	Kentucky	6,622,819	4,714,005	11,336,824
35	45804	Lima	Ohio	10,880,863	265,548	11,146,410
36	77979	Port Lavaca	Texas	10,724,701	376,705	11,101,406
37	43464	Vickery	Ohio	10,968,603	18,705	10,987,308
38	46231	Indianapolis	Indiana	12,084	10,822,624	10,834,708
39	71280	Sterlington	Louisiana	10,719,636	4,381	10,724,017
40	84029	Grantsville	Utah	10,352,491	281,625	10,634,117
41	35459	Emelle	Alabama	10,255,200	5,105	10,260,305
42	24141	Radford	Virginia	10,131,074	9,704	10,140,778
43	78380	Robstown	Texas	8,928,714	1,170,099	10,098,813
44	61615	Peoria	Illinois	1	9,922,232	9,922,233
45	89419	Lovelock	Nevada	9,704,358	20,842	9,725,200
46	99352	Richland	Washington	9,368,069	6,144	9,374,213
47	78407	Corpus Christi	Texas	2,582,572	6,340,728	8,923,300
48	70805	Baton Rouge	Louisiana	4,786,299	4,001,989	8,788,289
49	99737	Delta Junction	Alaska	8,640,052	310	8,640,362
50	70346	Donaldsonville	Louisiana	8,352,632	0	8,352,632
51	37660	Kingsport	Tennessee	8,203,028	30,635	8,233,663
52	70665	Sulphur	Louisiana	8,004,490	150,074	8,154,564
53	48120	Dearborn	Michigan	625,729	7,500,751	8,126,479
54	71052	Mansfield	Louisiana	8,098,236	0	8,098,236
55	93206	Buttonwillow	California	8,038,645	83	8,038,728

Rank	Zip	City	State	Total On-site Disposal or Other Releases[1]	Total Off-site Disposal or Other Releases[2]	Total On- and Off-site Disposal or Other Releases
56	28114	Mooresboro	North Carolina	770,174	7,167,186	7,937,361
57	85540	Morenci	Arizona	7,751,621	43,707	7,795,328
58	44004	Ashtabula	Ohio	7,659,124	48,179	7,707,303
59	61607	Peoria	Illinois	1,035,626	6,572,864	7,608,490
60	37040	Clarksville	Tennessee	5,394,146	2,187,726	7,581,872
61	63633	Centerville	Missouri	7,142,650	4,158	7,146,808
62	77905	Victoria	Texas	6,943,561	133,830	7,077,391
63	26366	Haywood	West Virginia	6,847,759	0	6,847,759
64	83276	Soda Springs	Idaho	6,675,845	916	6,676,761
65	97812	Arlington	Oregon	6,459,358	25,110	6,484,468
66	43812	Coshocton	Ohio	5,234,401	1,238,344	6,472,744
67	52627	Fort Madison	Iowa	6,398,886	12,605	6,411,490
68	70669	Westlake	Louisiana	6,367,927	37,735	6,405,662
69	82001	Cheyenne	Wyoming	6,205,665	0	6,205,665
70	55308	Becker	Minnesota	6,174,262	37	6,174,299
71	36513	Calvert	Alabama	3,157,874	3,005,811	6,163,685
72	58530	Center	North Dakota	5,017,611	1,060,792	6,078,403
73	15104	Braddock	Pennsylvania	105,361	5,929,180	6,034,541
74	88252	Jal	New Mexico	6,030,673	0	6,030,673
75	15748	Homer City	Pennsylvania	5,946,062	30,109	5,976,170

Notes: *TRI = Toxic Release Inventory; Reporting year (RY) 2015 is the most recent TRI data available. Facilities reporting to TRI were required to submit RY 2015 data to EPA by July 1, 2016. TRI Explorer is using an updated data set (released to the public in March 2017). This dataset includes revisions for the years 1988 to 2015 processed by EPA, after the National Analysis Dataset was released. Revisions submitted to EPA after this time are not reflected in TRI Explorer reports.*

(1) On-site Disposal or Other Releases include Underground Injection to Class I Wells (Section 5.4.1), RCRA Subtitle C Landfills (5.5.1A), Other Landfills (5.5.1B), Fugitive or Non-point Air Emissions (5.1), Stack or Point Air Emissions (5.2), Surface Water Discharges (5.3), Underground Injection to Class II-V Wells (5.4.2), Land Treatment/Application Farming (5.5.2), RCRA Subtitle C Surface Impoundments (5.5.3A), Other Surface Impoundments (5.5.3B), and Other Land Disposal (5.5.4). Off-site Disposal or Other Releases include from Section 6.2 Class I Underground Injection Wells (M81), Class II-V Underground Injection Wells (M82, M71), RCRA Subtitle C Landfills (M65), Other Landfills (M64, M72), Storage Only (M10), Solidification/Stabilization - Metals and Metal Category Compounds only (M41 or M40), Wastewater Treatment (excluding POTWs) - Metals and Metal Category Compounds only (M62 or M61), RCRA Subtitle C Surface Impoundments (M66), Other Surface Impoundments (M67, M63), Land Treatment (M73), Other Land Disposal (M79), Other Off-site Management (M90), Transfers to Waste Broker - Disposal (M94, M91), and Unknown (M99) and, from Section 6.1 Transfers to POTWs (metals and metal category compounds only).

(2) Off-site disposal or other releases show only net off-site disposal or other releases, that is, off-site disposal or other releases transferred to other TRI facilities reporting such transfers as on-site disposal or other releases are not included to avoid double counting.

This report may not include all states in the US. A state may not be included in this report for two reasons: 1) there are no facilities reporting to TRI in the particular state; or 2) the facilities reporting to TRI in the particular state did not report to TRI for the user-specified selection criteria.

Users of TRI information should be aware that TRI data reflect releases and other waste management activities of chemicals, not whether (or to what degree) the public has been exposed to those chemicals. Release estimates alone are not sufficient to determine exposure or to calculate potential adverse effects on human health and the environment. TRI data, in conjunction with other information, can be used as a starting point in evaluating exposures that may result from releases and other waste management activities which involve toxic chemicals. The determination of potential risk depends upon many factors, including the toxicity of the chemical, the fate of the chemical, and the amount and duration of human or other exposure to the chemical after it is released.

Source: *U.S. Environmental Protection Agency, TRI Explorer, August 10, 2017*

TRI On-site and Off-site Reported Disposed of or Otherwise Released (in grams), for Facilities in All Industries, Dioxin and Dioxin-like Compounds, Top 75 Zipcodes, 2015

Rank	Zip	City	State	Total On-site Disposal or Other Releases[1]	Total Off-site Disposal or Other Releases[2]	Total On- and Off-site Disposal or Other Releases
1	77571	La Porte	Texas	20.100	24,776.441	24,796.541
2	66767	Prescott	Kansas	176.743	19,344.300	19,521.043
3	84029	Grantsville	Utah	18,826.673	513.920	19,340.593
4	77541	Freeport	Texas	5,719.450	0.000	5,719.450
5	42029	Calvert City	Kentucky	20.221	3,986.786	4,007.006
6	48667	Midland	Michigan	2,489.883	0.000	2,489.883
7	78380	Robstown	Texas	2,371.012	0.000	2,371.012
8	49036	Coldwater	Michigan	89.040	1,692.012	1,781.052
9	39571	Pass Christian	Mississippi	1,361.418	0.061	1,361.479
10	37134	New Johnsonville	Tennessee	1,038.705	0.029	1,038.734
11	53081	Sheboygan	Wisconsin	11.232	943.146	954.379
12	44004	Ashtabula	Ohio	486.253	0.000	486.253
13	25253	Letart	West Virginia	480.320	0.000	480.320
14	19809	Wilmington	Delaware	6.635	345.979	352.614
15	46774	New Haven	Indiana	6.225	304.850	311.075
16	39746	Hamilton	Mississippi	296.782	0.000	296.782
17	42141	Glasgow	Kentucky	1.084	270.164	271.248
18	77536	Deer Park	Texas	1.301	238.392	239.693
19	70764	Plaquemine	Louisiana	14.566	219.535	234.100
20	32091	Starke	Florida	230.225	0.000	230.225
21	55068	Rosemount	Minnesota	1.811	176.791	178.602
22	70669	Westlake	Louisiana	42.980	133.936	176.916
23	44683	Uhrichsville	Ohio	6.668	126.660	133.328
24	46992	Wabash	Indiana	97.160	0.000	97.160
25	35188	Woodstock	Alabama	94.500	0.000	94.500
26	98632	Longview	Washington	6.753	85.021	91.774
27	36079	Troy	Alabama	84.200	0.000	84.200
28	98421	Tacoma	Washington	1.027	81.875	82.902
29	46304	Chesterton	Indiana	74.750	0.000	74.750
30	42261	Morgantown	Kentucky	72.450	0.000	72.450
31	35987	Steele	Alabama	3.000	56.950	59.950
32	91746	La Puente	California	0.171	53.686	53.857
33	30642	Greensboro	Georgia	51.110	0.000	51.110
34	28601	Hickory	North Carolina	50.713	0.000	50.713
35	70805	Baton Rouge	Louisiana	34.801	13.447	48.248
36	35903	Gadsden	Alabama	0.531	44.669	45.200
37	75572	Queen City	Texas	43.670	0.000	43.670
38	60411	Chicago Heights	Illinois	2.084	39.590	41.674
39	61615	Peoria	Illinois	0.002	41.233	41.235
40	74066	Sapulpa	Oklahoma	2.057	39.030	41.087
41	85338	Goodyear	Arizona	1.860	35.420	37.280
42	53403	Racine	Wisconsin	1.318	31.954	33.272
43	37701	Alcoa	Tennessee	9.343	23.290	32.633
44	46135	Greencastle	Indiana	32.113	0.000	32.113
45	93561	Tehachapi	California	32.103	0.000	32.103
46	39358	Scooba	Mississippi	29.092	0.000	29.092
47	77015	Houston	Texas	6.057	21.865	27.923
48	26146	Friendly	West Virginia	1.383	26.290	27.673
49	70079	Norco	Louisiana	5.633	20.610	26.242
50	77632	Orange	Texas	26.031	0.000	26.031
51	70765	Plaquemine	Louisiana	25.912	0.000	25.912
52	74728	Broken Bow	Oklahoma	22.436	0.000	22.436
53	07407	Elmwood Park	New Jersey	0.000	21.484	21.484
54	30906	Augusta	Georgia	21.016	0.004	21.020
55	29704	Catawba	South Carolina	18.038	0.000	18.038

Rank	Zip	City	State	Total On-site Disposal or Other Releases[1]	Total Off-site Disposal or Other Releases[2]	Total On- and Off-site Disposal or Other Releases
56	37660	Kingsport	Tennessee	17.864	0.051	17.915
57	43616	Oregon	Ohio	17.118	0.000	17.118
58	08103	Camden	New Jersey	1.432	15.594	17.025
59	74764	Valliant	Oklahoma	16.668	0.000	16.668
60	30344	Atlanta	Georgia	15.360	0.000	15.360
61	42420	Henderson	Kentucky	14.689	0.000	14.689
62	70734	Geismar	Louisiana	9.358	5.096	14.454
63	71635	Crossett	Arkansas	13.057	0.000	13.057
64	38474	Mount Pleasant	Tennessee	1.411	11.629	13.040
65	28456	Riegelwood	North Carolina	9.709	2.611	12.321
66	37774	Loudon	Tennessee	0.754	11.557	12.311
67	52802	Davenport	Iowa	0.594	11.130	11.724
68	93501	Mojave	California	0.430	10.921	11.352
69	92337	Fontana	California	0.110	10.876	10.986
70	83854	Post Falls	Idaho	0.520	9.760	10.280
71	57078	Yankton	South Dakota	10.248	0.000	10.248
72	54806	Ashland	Wisconsin	10.071	0.000	10.071
73	36426	Brewton	Alabama	9.714	0.000	9.714
74	82201	Wheatland	Wyoming	9.656	0.000	9.656
75	81004	Pueblo	Colorado	9.574	0.000	9.574

Notes: *TRI = Toxic Release Inventory; Reporting year (RY) 2015 is the most recent TRI data available. Facilities reporting to TRI were required to submit RY 2015 data to EPA by July 1, 2016. TRI Explorer is using an updated data set (released to the public in March 2017). This dataset includes revisions for the years 1988 to 2015 processed by EPA, after the National Analysis Dataset was released. Revisions submitted to EPA after this time are not reflected in TRI Explorer reports.*

(1) On-site Disposal or Other Releases include Underground Injection to Class I Wells (Section 5.4.1), RCRA Subtitle C Landfills (5.5.1A), Other Landfills (5.5.1B), Fugitive or Non-point Air Emissions (5.1), Stack or Point Air Emissions (5.2), Surface Water Discharges (5.3), Underground Injection to Class II-V Wells (5.4.2), Land Treatment/Application Farming (5.5.2), RCRA Subtitle C Surface Impoundments (5.5.3A), Other Surface Impoundments (5.5.3B), and Other Land Disposal (5.5.4). Off-site Disposal or Other Releases include from Section 6.2 Class I Underground Injection Wells (M81), Class II-V Underground Injection Wells (M82, M71), RCRA Subtitle C Landfills (M65), Other Landfills (M64, M72), Storage Only (M10), Solidification/Stabilization - Metals and Metal Category Compounds only (M41 or M40), Wastewater Treatment (excluding POTWs) - Metals and Metal Category Compounds only (M62 or M61), RCRA Subtitle C Surface Impoundments (M66), Other Surface Impoundments (M67, M63), Land Treatment (M73), Other Land Disposal (M79), Other Off-site Management (M90), Transfers to Waste Broker - Disposal (M94, M91), and Unknown (M99) and, from Section 6.1 Transfers to POTWs (metals and metal category compounds only).

(2) Off-site disposal or other releases show only net off-site disposal or other releases, that is, off-site disposal or other releases transferred to other TRI facilities reporting such transfers as on-site disposal or other releases are not included to avoid double counting.

This report may not include all states in the US. A state may not be included in this report for two reasons: 1) there are no facilities reporting to TRI in the particular state; or 2) the facilities reporting to TRI in the particular state did not report to TRI for the user-specified selection criteria.

Users of TRI information should be aware that TRI data reflect releases and other waste management activities of chemicals, not whether (or to what degree) the public has been exposed to those chemicals. Release estimates alone are not sufficient to determine exposure or to calculate potential adverse effects on human health and the environment. TRI data, in conjunction with other information, can be used as a starting point in evaluating exposures that may result from releases and other waste management activities which involve toxic chemicals. The determination of potential risk depends upon many factors, including the toxicity of the chemical, the fate of the chemical, and the amount and duration of human or other exposure to the chemical after it is released.

Source: *U.S. Environmental Protection Agency, TRI Explorer, August 10, 2017*

Introduction

U.S. Environmental Protection Agency (EPA) has collected and reported data on the generation and disposition of waste in the United States for more than 30 years. We use this information to measure the success of waste reduction and recycling programs across the country and characterize our national waste stream. These facts and figures are current through calendar year 2014.

In 2014, in the United States, about 258 million tons (U.S. short tons unless specified) of municipal solid waste (MSW) were generated. Over 89 million tons of MSW were recycled and composted, equivalent to a 34.6 percent recycling rate (see Figure 1 and Figure 2). In addition, over 33 million tons of MSW were combusted with energy recovery and 136 million tons were landfilled (see Table 1).

Food

Nationally, the composting of food rose from1.84 million tons in 2013 (5.0 percent of food) to 1.94 million tons in 2014 (5.1 percent of food).

Recycling and composting of MSW results in greenhouse gas (GHG) emissions reduction. In 2014, the 89 million tons of MSW recycled and composted provided an annual reduction of over 181 million metric tons of carbon dioxide equivalent ($MMTCO_2E$) emissions, comparable to the annual emissions from over 38 million passenger cars.[1]

As the title for the annual report suggests, EPA is thinking beyond waste. Sustainable Materials Management (SMM) refers to the use and reuse of materials in the most productive and sustainable way across their entire life cycle. SMM conserves resources, reduces waste, slows climate change and minimizes the environmental impacts of the materials we use.

Figure 1. MSW Generation Rates, 1960 to 2014

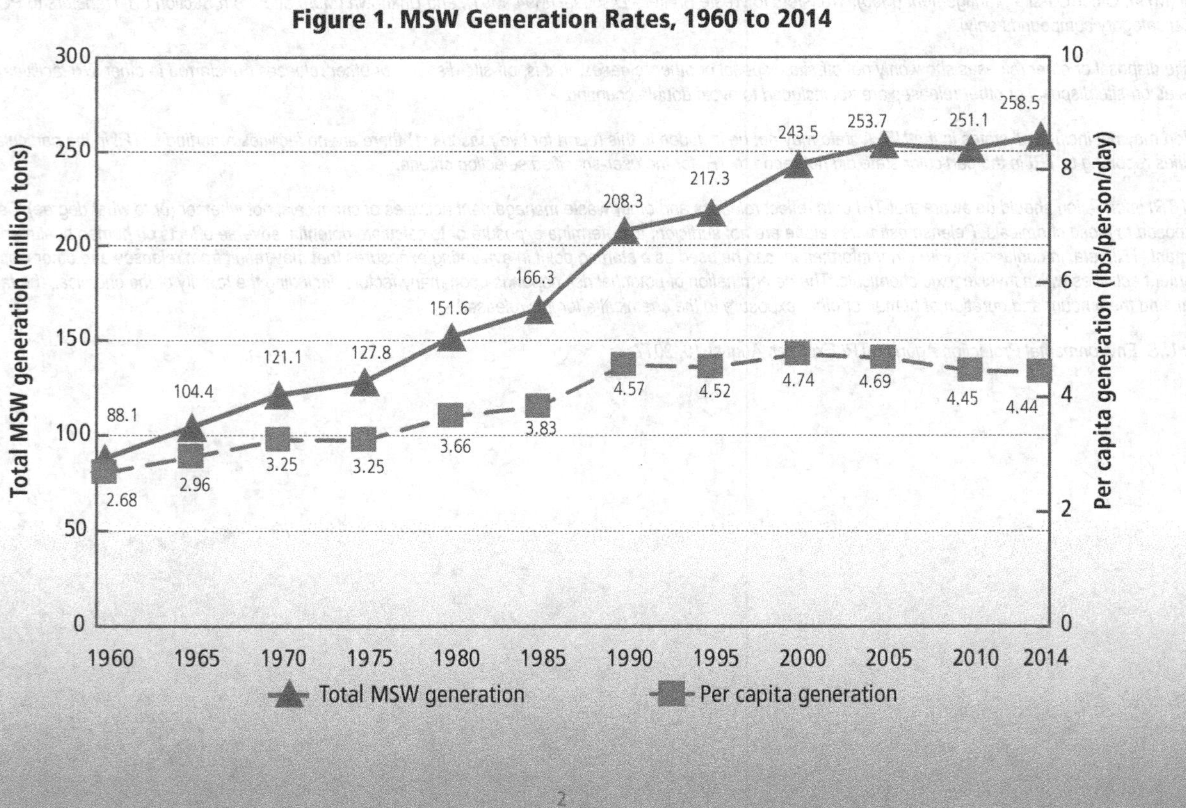

2

Source: U.S. EPA, Advancing Sustainable Materials Management: 2014 Fact Sheet, November 2016

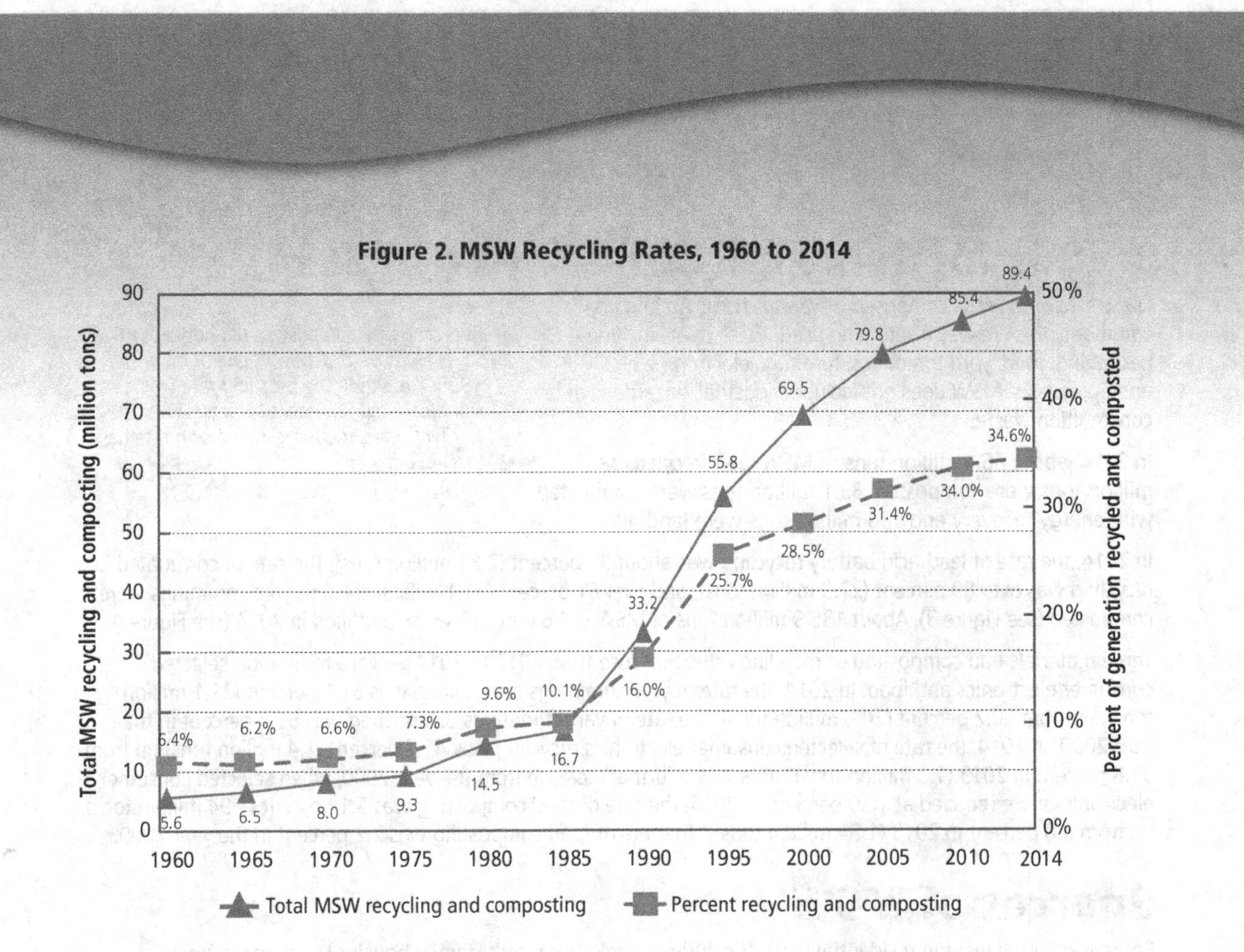

The sustainable management of natural capital has become increasingly important with expanding demand for finite resources on the global scale. For economic growth to reliably continue, responsible use of natural resources must consider the environmental and human health impacts. Considering the entire life cycle of the needed materials, businesses are able to reduce environmental and human health risk while enhancing and sustaining their value proposition.

According to the United Nations Environment Programme, International Resources Panel (UNEP IRP), "data suggest that while long-run relative decoupling of material extraction from GDP [gross domestic product] can be observed at a global level, this relative decoupling is not sufficient to prevent a persistent increasing trend in absolute resource extraction. Indeed, in contrast to the long-run relative decoupling trend over the 20th century, recent years' data suggest that resource extraction has begun to increase at a faster rate than GDP, suggestive of 'recoupling'."[2] In a subsequent report, the UNEP IRP expands upon these observations: "the material intensity of the world economy has been increasing for the past decade, driven by the great acceleration that has occurred since the year 2000. Globally, more material per unit of GDP is now required. Production has shifted from very material-efficient countries to countries that have low material efficiency, resulting in an overall decline in material efficiency."[3]

3

Source: *U.S. EPA, Advancing Sustainable Materials Management: 2014 Fact Sheet, November 2016*

Trends in Municipal Solid Waste in 2014

Our trash, or MSW, is comprised of various items Americans commonly throw away after being used. These items include packaging, food, yard trimmings, furniture, electronics, tires and appliances. MSW does not include industrial, hazardous or construction waste.

Recycling and composting did not exceed 15 percent of total MSW generation until 1990. Growth in the recycling rate was significant over the next 15 years. Over the last five years, the recycling growth rate has leveled off.

In 2014, about 66.4 million tons of MSW were recyled, 23 million tons were composted, 33.1 million tons were combusted with energy recovery and 136 million tons were landfilled.

In 2014, the rate of lead-acid battery recycling was about 99 percent (2.81 million tons). The rate of corrugated box recycling was over 89 percent (27.3 million tons), and over 61 percent (21.1 million tons) of yard trimmings were composted (see Figure 3). About 135.9 million tons of MSW (52.6 percent) were landfilled in 2014 (see Figure 4).

Three materials had composting or recycling rates that rose from 2013 to 2014 — yard trimmings, selected consumer electronics and food. In 2014, the rate of yard trimmings composting was 61.1 percent (21.1 million tons), up from 60.2 percent (20.6 million tons). The rate of yard trimmings composting was 51.7 percent in the year 2000. In 2014, the rate of selected consumer electronics recycling was 41.7 percent (1.4 million tons) up from 37.8 percent in 2013 (1.3 million tons).[4] This was a further increase from the year 2000, when selected consumer electronics were recycled at 10.0 percent. In 2014, the rate of food composting was 5.1 percent (1.94 million tons), up from 5.0 percent in 2013 (1.84 million tons).[5] The rate of food composting was 2.2 percent in the year 2000.

Sources of MSW

Sources of MSW include residential waste (including waste from multi-family housing) and waste from commercial and institutional locations, such as businesses, schools and hospitals.

Over the last few decades, the generation, recycling, composting, combustion with energy recovery and landfilling of MSW changed substantially. Solid waste generation per person per day peaked in 2000. The 4.4 pounds per person per day in 2014 is about the same as in 2013, and is one of the lowest rates since before 1990. The recycling and composting rate has increased from less than 10 percent of generated MSW in1980 to over 34 percent in 2014. Combustion with energy recovery increased from less than two percent of generation in 1980 to 12.8 percent in 2014. Landfilling of waste decreased from 89 percent in 1980 to under 53 percent in 2014.

4

Source: *U.S. EPA, Advancing Sustainable Materials Management: 2014 Fact Sheet, November 2016*

Figure 3. Recycling and Composting Rates of Selected Products, 2014*

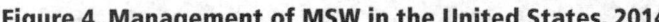

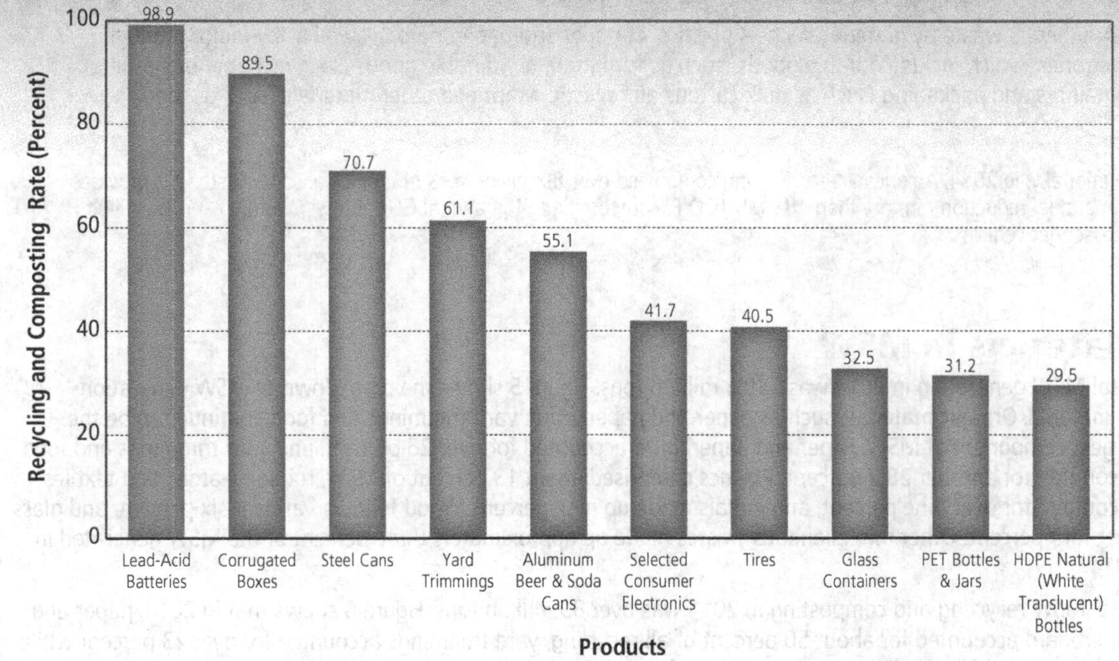
100
80
60
40
20
0
Recycling and Composting Rate (Percent)
98.9
89.5
70.7
61.1
55.1
41.7
40.5
32.5
31.2
29.5
Lead-Acid Batteries
Corrugated Boxes
Steel Cans
Yard Trimmings
Aluminum Beer & Soda Cans
Selected Consumer Electronics
Tires
Glass Containers
PET Bottles & Jars
HDPE Natural (White Translucent) Bottles
Products

*Does not include combustion with energy recovery.

Figure 4. Management of MSW in the United States, 2014

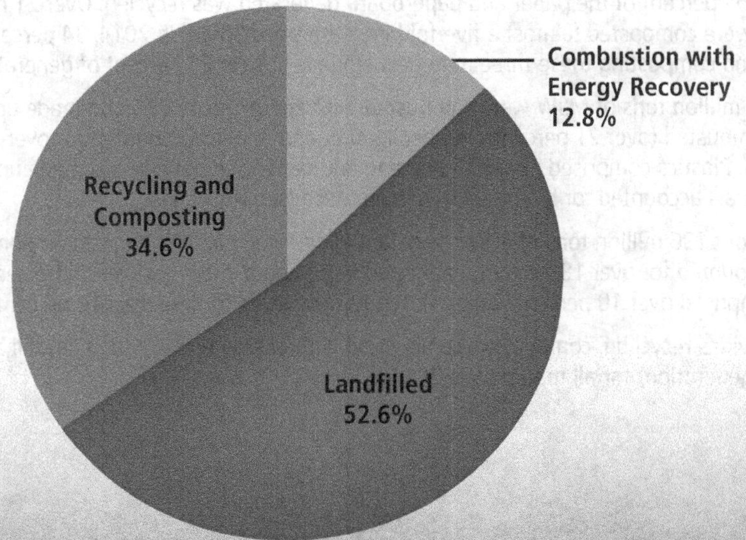
Combustion with Energy Recovery 12.8%
Recycling and Composting 34.6%
Landfilled 52.6%

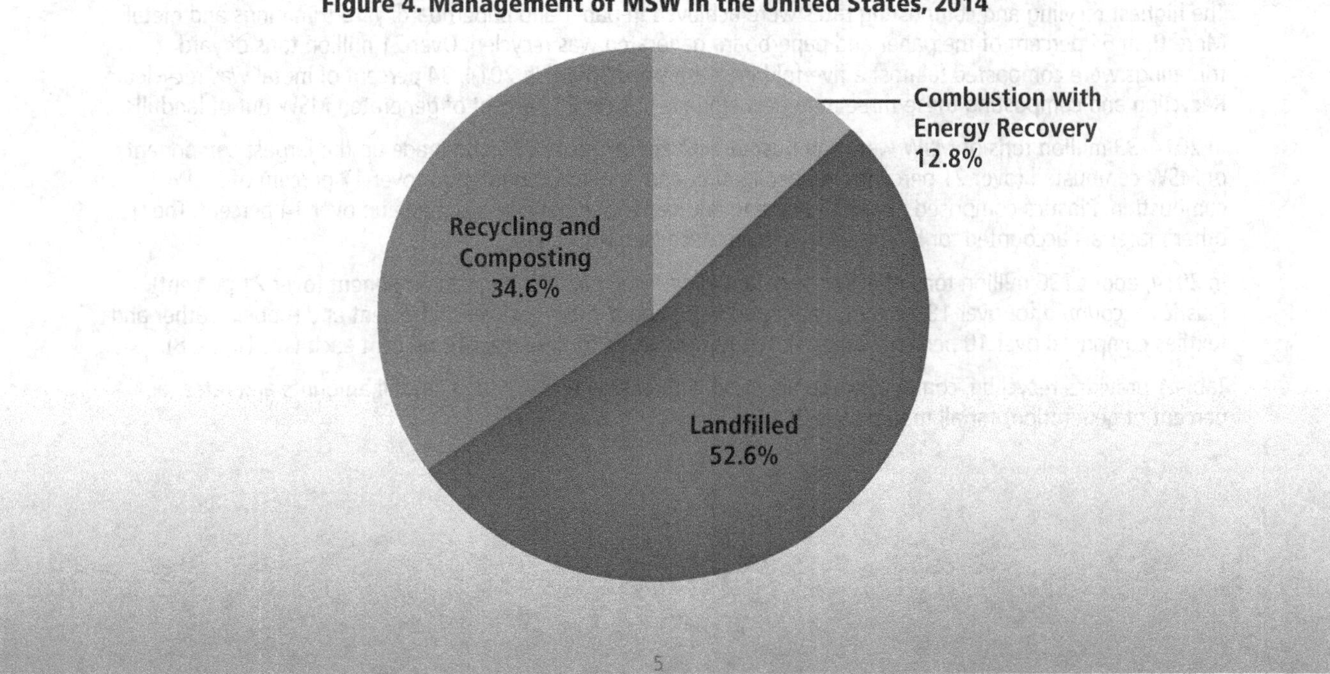

5

Source: *U.S. EPA, Advancing Sustainable Materials Management: 2014 Fact Sheet, November 2016*

Analyzing MSW

EPA analyzes waste by material, such as plastics, or paper and paperboard, as well as by major product categories, which include durable goods (such as furniture), nondurable goods (such as paper or clothing), containers and packaging (such as milk cartons and plastic wrap) and other materials (such as food).

Nationally, in 2014, Americans recycled and composted over 89 million tons of municipal solid waste. This provides an annual reduction of more than 181 $MMTCO_2E$, comparable to the annual GHG emissions from over 38 million passenger vehicles.

Materials in MSW

Total MSW generation in 2014 was 258.5 million tons. Figure 5 shows the breakdown of MSW generation by material. Organic materials such as paper and paperboard, yard trimmings and food continued to be the largest component of MSW. Paper and paperboard accounted for over 26 percent, and yard trimmings and food accounted for another 28.2 percent. Plastics comprised about 13 percent of MSW; rubber, leather, and textiles accounted for over nine percent; and metals made up nine percent. Wood followed at over six percent, and glass over four percent. Other miscellaneous wastes made up approximately three percent of the MSW generated in 2014.

Total MSW recycling and composting in 2014 was over 89 million tons. Figure 6 shows that in 2014, paper and paperboard accounted for about 50 percent of all recycling, yard trimmings accounted for over 23 percent while food accounted for another two percent. Metals comprised about nine percent and glass, plastic and wood made up about three percent each. Other miscellaneous materials made up about six percent of MSW recycling and composting.

The highest recyling and composting rates were achieved in paper and paperboard, yard trimmings and metals. More than 64 percent of the paper and paperboard generated was recycled. Over 21 million tons of yard trimmings were composted (almost a five-fold increase since 1990). In 2014, 34 percent of metal was recycled. Recycling and composting these three materials alone kept over 28 percent of generated MSW out of landfills.

In 2014, 33 million tons of MSW were combusted with energy recovery. Food made up the largest component of MSW combusted (over 21 percent). Rubber, leather and textiles accounted for over 17 percent of MSW combustion. Plastics comprised about 15 percent; and paper and paperboard made up over 14 percent. The other materials accounted for less than 10 percent each (see Figure 7).

In 2014, about 136 million tons of MSW were landfilled. Food was the largest component (over 21 percent). Plastics accounted for over 18 percent, paper and paperboard made up over 14 percent and rubber, leather and textiles comprised over 10 percent. Other materials accounted for less than 10 percent each (see Figure 8).

Table 1 provides recycling, composting, combustion with energy recovery and landfill amounts and rates (as percent of generation) for all materials in 2014.

Source: U.S. EPA, *Advancing Sustainable Materials Management: 2014 Fact Sheet*, November 2016

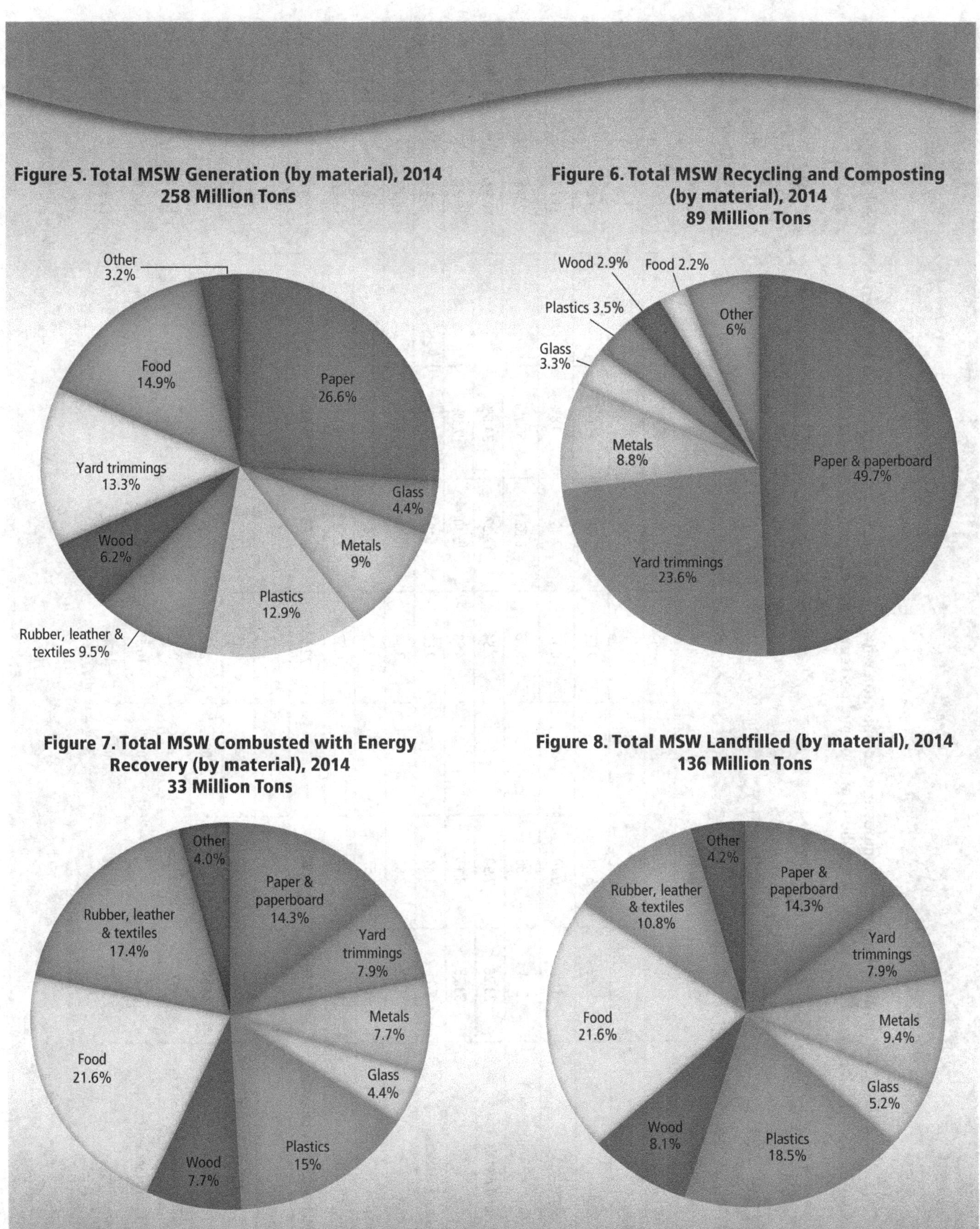

Source: *U.S. EPA, Advancing Sustainable Materials Management: 2014 Fact Sheet, November 2016*

Table 1. Generation, Recycling, Composting, Combustion with Energy Recovery and Landfilling of Materials in MSW, 2014*
(in millions of tons and percent of generation of each material)

Material	Weight Generated	Weight Recycled	Weight Composted	Weight Combusted with Energy Recovery	Weight Landfilled	Recycling as Percent of Generation	Composting as Percent of Generation	Combustion as Percent of Generation	Landfilling as Percent of Generation
Paper and paperboard	68.61	44.40		4.74	19.47	64.7%		6.9%	28.4%
Glass	11.48	2.99		1.45	7.04	26.0%		12.6%	61.3%
Metals									
Steel	17.69	5.84		2.02	9.83	33.0%		11.4%	55.6%
Aluminum	3.53	0.70		0.47	2.36	19.8%		13.3%	66.9%
Other nonferrous metals†	2.04	1.36		0.05	0.63	66.7%		2.5%	30.9%
Total metals	**23.26**	**7.90**		**2.54**	**12.82**	**34.0%**		**10.9%**	**55.1%**
Plastics	33.25	3.17		4.98	25.10	9.5%		15.0%	75.5%
Rubber and leather	8.21	1.44		2.62	4.15	17.5%		31.9%	50.5%
Textiles	16.22	2.62		3.14	10.46	16.2%		19.4%	64.5%
Wood	16.12	2.57		2.54	11.01	15.9%		15.8%	68.3%
Other materials	4.44	1.29		0.57	2.58	29.1%		12.8%	58.1%
Total materials in products	**181.59**	**66.38**		**22.58**	**92.63**	**36.6%**		**12.4%**	**51.0%**
Other wastes									
Food, other‡	38.40		1.94	7.15	29.31		5.1%	18.6%	76.3%
Yard trimmings	34.50		21.08	2.63	10.79		61.1%	7.6%	31.3%
Miscellaneous inorganic wastes	3.97			0.78	3.19			19.6%	80.4%
Total other wastes	**76.87**		**23.02**	**10.56**	**43.29**		**29.9%**	**13.7%**	**56.3%**
Total municipal solid waste	**258.46**	**66.38**	**23.02**	**33.14**	**135.92**	**25.7%**	**8.9%**	**12.8%**	**52.6%**

* Includes waste from residential, commercial and institutional sources.
† Includes lead from lead-acid batteries.
‡ Includes collection of other MSW organics for composting.

Details might not add to totals due to rounding.
Negligible = Less than 5,000 tons or 0.05 percent.

8

Source: *U.S. EPA, Advancing Sustainable Materials Management: 2014 Fact Sheet, November 2016*

Products in MSW

The breakdown of the 258 million tons of MSW generated in 2014 by product category follows. Containers and packaging made up the largest portion of MSW generated: 29.7 percent, or over 76 million tons. Nondurable and durable goods each made up about 20 percent (over 52 million tons) each. Food made up 14.9 percent (38.4 million tons), yard trimmings made up 13.3 percent (34.5 million tons) and other wastes made up 1.5 percent (4 million tons).

Table 2 shows the generation, recycling, composting, combustion with energy recovery and landfilling of materials in the product categories, by weight and as percent of generation. This table shows that the recycling of containers and packaging was the highest of the four product categories, with over 51 percent of the generated materials recycled. Paper products, steel and aluminum were the most recycled materials by percentage in this category. Over 75 percent of paper and paperboard containers and packaging was recycled. Over 72 percent of steel packaging (mostly cans) was recycled. The recycling rate for aluminum packaging was almost 39 percent, including over 55 percent of aluminum beverage cans.

Over 32 percent of glass containers was recycled, while over 26 percent of wood packaging (mostly wood pallets) was recycled. Almost 15 percent of plastic containers and packaging was recycled—mostly from soft drink, milk and water bottles. Plastic bottles were the most recycled plastic products. Polyethylene terephthalate (PET) bottles and jars were recycled at over 31 percent. Recycling of high density polyethylene (HDPE) natural (white translucent) bottles was estimated at over 29 percent (see 2014 data tables).

Nondurable goods generally last less than three years. Overall recycling of nondurable goods was about 33 percent in 2014. Newspapers/mechanical papers and other paper products were the most recycled nondurable goods. Newspapers/mechanical papers include newspapers, directories, inserts, and some advertisement and direct mail printing. Sixty-eight percent of newspapers/mechanical papers were recycled. Collectively, the recycling of other paper products such as office paper and magazines was over 44 percent in 2014. Clothing, footwear and other textile products are included in the nondurable goods category. These products were recycled at a rate of over 17 percent.

Every ton of office paper recycled can save the energy equivalent of 322 gallons of gasoline consumed.

Overall, 18 percent of durable goods was recycled in 2014. Due to the high rate of lead recycling from lead-acid batteries, nonferrous metals (other than aluminum) had one of the highest recycling rates. With an almost 99 percent recycling rate, lead-acid batteries continued to be one of the most recycled products. Recycling of steel in all durable goods was over 27 percent, with high rates of recycling from appliances and other miscellaneous items. Recycling of selected consumer electronics (ranging from TVs, computers and cell phones to fax machines) was over 41 percent (see Figure 3).

Measured by percentage of generation, products with the highest recycling rates in 2014 were lead-acid batteries (98.9 percent), corrugated boxes (89.5 percent), steel cans (70.7 percent), newspapers/mechanical papers (68.2 percent), yard trimmings (61.1 percent), major appliances (58.3 percent), aluminum cans (55.1 percent), mixed paper (44.4 percent), selected consumer electronics (41.7 percent), and tires (40.5 percent) (see 2014 data tables).

Recycling just one ton of aluminum cans conserves more than 152 million Btu, the equivalent of 1,024 gallons of gasoline or 21 barrels of oil consumed.

9

Source: *U.S. EPA, Advancing Sustainable Materials Management: 2014 Fact Sheet, November 2016*

Table 2. Generation, Recycling, Composting, Combustion with Energy Recovery and Landfilling of Materials in MSW, 2014*
(in millions of tons and percent of generation of each product)

Products	Weight Generated	Weight Recycled	Weight Composted	Weight Combusted with Energy Recovery	Weight Landfilled	Recycling as Percent of Generation	Composting as Percent of Generation	Combustion as Percent of Generation	Landfilling as Percent of Generation
Durable goods									
Steel	15.52	4.26		1.90	9.36	27.4%		12.2%	60.3%
Aluminum	1.52	Not Available		0.21	1.31	Not Available		13.8%	86.2%
Other non-ferrous metals†	2.04	1.36		0.05	0.63	66.7%		2.5%	30.9%
Glass	2.28	Negligible		0.23	2.05	Negligible		10.1%	89.9%
Plastics	12.15	0.91		1.28	9.96	7.5%		10.5%	82.0%
Rubber and leather	7.12	1.44		2.41	3.27	20.2%		33.8%	45.9%
Wood	6.39	Negligible		1.14	5.25	Negligible		17.8%	82.2%
Textiles	3.96	0.49		1.16	2.31	12.4%		29.3%	58.3%
Other materials	1.67	1.29		0.03	0.35	77.2%		1.8%	21.0%
Total durable goods	**52.65**	**9.75**		**8.41**	**34.49**	**18.5%**		**16.0%**	**65.5%**
Nondurable goods									
Paper and paperboard	29.47	14.91		2.85	11.71	50.6%		9.7%	39.7%
Plastics	6.78	0.14		1.31	5.33	2.1%		19.3%	78.6%
Rubber and leather	1.09	Negligible		0.21	0.88	Negligible		19.3%	80.7%
Textiles	11.95	2.13		1.92	7.90	17.8%		16.1%	66.1%
Other materials	2.98	Negligible		0.58	2.40	Negligible		19.5%	80.5%
Total nondurable goods	**52.27**	**17.18**		**6.87**	**28.22**	**32.9%**		**13.1%**	**54.0%**

(table continued...)

10

Source: *U.S. EPA, Advancing Sustainable Materials Management: 2014 Fact Sheet, November 2016*

Table 2. Generation, Recycling, Composting, Combustion with Energy Recovery and Landfilling of Materials in MSW, 2014*
(in millions of tons and percent of generation of each product) (...table continued)

Products	Weight Generated	Weight Recycled	Weight Composted	Weight Combusted with Energy Recovery	Weight Landfilled	Recycling as Percent of Generation	Composting as Percent of Generation	Combustion as Percent of Generation	Landfilling as Percent of Generation
Containers and packaging									
Steel	2.17	1.58		0.12	0.47	72.8%		5.5%	21.7%
Aluminum	1.81	0.70		0.22	0.89	38.7%		12.2%	49.2%
Glass	9.20	2.99		1.22	4.99	32.5%		13.3%	54.2%
Paper and paperboard	39.13	29.49		1.89	7.75	75.4%		4.8%	19.8%
Plastics	14.32	2.12		2.39	9.81	14.8%		16.7%	68.5%
Wood	9.73	2.57		1.40	5.76	26.4%		14.4%	59.2%
Other materials	0.31	Negligible		0.06	0.25	Negligible		19.4%	80.6%
Total containers and packaging	**76.67**	**39.45**		**7.30**	**29.92**	**51.5%**		**9.5%**	**39.0%**
Other wastes									
Food, other‡	38.40		1.94	7.15	29.31		5.1%	18.6%	76.3%
Yard trimmings	34.50		21.08	2.63	10.79		61.1%	7.6%	31.3%
Miscellaneous inorganic wastes	3.97			0.78	3.19			19.6%	80.4%
Total other wastes	**76.87**		**23.02**	**10.56**	**43.29**		**29.9%**	**13.7%**	**56.3%**
Total municipal solid waste	**258.46**	**66.38**	23.02	**33.14**	**135.92**	**25.7%**	**8.9%**	**12.8%**	**52.6%**

* Includes waste from residential, commercial and institutional sources.

† Includes lead from lead-acid batteries.

‡ Includes collection of other MSW organics for composting.Details might not add to totals due to rounding. Negligible = less than 5,000 tons or 0.05 percent.

11

Source: *U.S. EPA, Advancing Sustainable Materials Management: 2014 Fact Sheet, November 2016*

Combustion with Energy Recovery

Most of the MSW combustion in the U.S. incorporates recovery of an energy product (generally steam or electricity).

- In 2014, about 33.1 million tons (12.8 percent) of materials were combusted for energy recovery (see Table 3).
- From 1990 to 2000, the quantity of MSW combusted with energy recovery increased over 13 percent to about 34 million tons.
- MSW combustion for energy recovery has decreased from about 34 million tons in 2000 to 33.1 million tons in 2014.

Landfilling of MSW

While the number of U.S. landfills has steadily declined over the years, the average landfill size has increased. At the national level, landfill capacity appears to be sufficient for our current practices—although it is limited in some areas.

- Since 1990, the total amount of MSW going to landfills dropped by 9.3 million tons, from 145.3 million to 136 million tons in 2014 (see Table 3).
- The net per capita 2014 landfilling rate (after recycling, composting and combustion with energy recovery) was 2.3 pounds per day, lower than the 3.2 per capita rate in 1990 (see Table 4).
- From 1985 to 1995 there was a rapid rise in the cost to manage MSW going to landfills, followed by a steady decrease from 1995 to 2004. Since 2004, there has been a steady increase in landfill tipping fees (see Figure 9). The tipping fees are expressed in constant 2014 dollars.

Source: *U.S. EPA, Advancing Sustainable Materials Management: 2014 Fact Sheet, November 2016*

Table 3. Generation, Recycling, Composting, Combustion with Energy Recovery and Landfilling of MSW, 1960 to 2014 (in millions of tons)

Activity	1960	1970	1980	1990	2000	2005	2010	2012	2013	2014
Generation	88.1	121.1	151.6	208.3	243.5	253.7	251.1	251.8	255.0	258.5
Recycling	5.6	8.0	14.5	29.0	53.0	59.2	65.3	65.6	65.1	66.4
Composting*	neg.	neg.	neg.	4.2	16.5	20.6	20.2	21.3	22.4	23.0
Combustion with energy recovery†	0.0	0.5	2.8	29.8	33.7	31.7	29.3	32.5	33.2	33.1
Landfilling and other disposal‡	82.5	112.6	134.3	145.3	140.3	142.2	136.3	132.4	134.3	136.0

* Composting of yard trimmings, food and other MSW organic material. Does not include backyard composting.

† Includes combustion of MSW in mass burn or refuse-derived fuel form, and combustion with energy recovery of source separated materials in MSW (e.g., wood pallets, tire-derived fuel).

‡ Landfilling after recycling, composting and combustion with energy recovery. Includes combustion without energy recovery.

Details might not add to totals due to rounding.

neg. Negligible = less than 5,000 tons or 0.05 percent.

Table 4. Generation, Recycling, Composting, Combustion with Energy Recovery and Landfilling of MSW, 1960 to 2014 (in pounds per person per day)

Activity	1960	1970	1980	1990	2000	2005	2010	2012	2013	2014
Generation	2.7	3.3	3.7	4.6	4.7	4.7	4.4	4.4	4.4	4.4
Recycling	0.2	0.2	0.4	0.6	1.0	1.1	1.1	1.1	1.1	1.1
Composting*	neg.	neg.	neg.	0.1	0.3	0.4	0.4	0.4	0.4	0.4
Combustion with energy recovery†	0.0	neg.	0.1	0.7	0.7	0.6	0.5	0.6	0.6	0.6
Landfilling and other disposal‡	2.5	3.1	3.2	3.2	2.7	2.6	2.4	2.3	2.3	2.3
Population (In millions)	180.0	204.0	227.3	249.9	281.4	296.4	309.1	313.9	316.1	318.9

* Composting of yard trimmings, food and other MSW organic material. Does not include backyard composting.

† Includes combustion of MSW in mass burn or refuse-derived fuel form, and combustion with energy recovery of source separated materials in MSW (e.g., wood pallets, tire-derived fuel).

‡ Landfilling after recycling, composting and combustion with energy recovery. Includes combustion without energy recovery.

Details might not add to totals due to rounding.

neg. Negligible = less than 5,000 tons or 0.05 percent.

13

Source: *U.S. EPA, Advancing Sustainable Materials Management: 2014 Fact Sheet, November 2016*

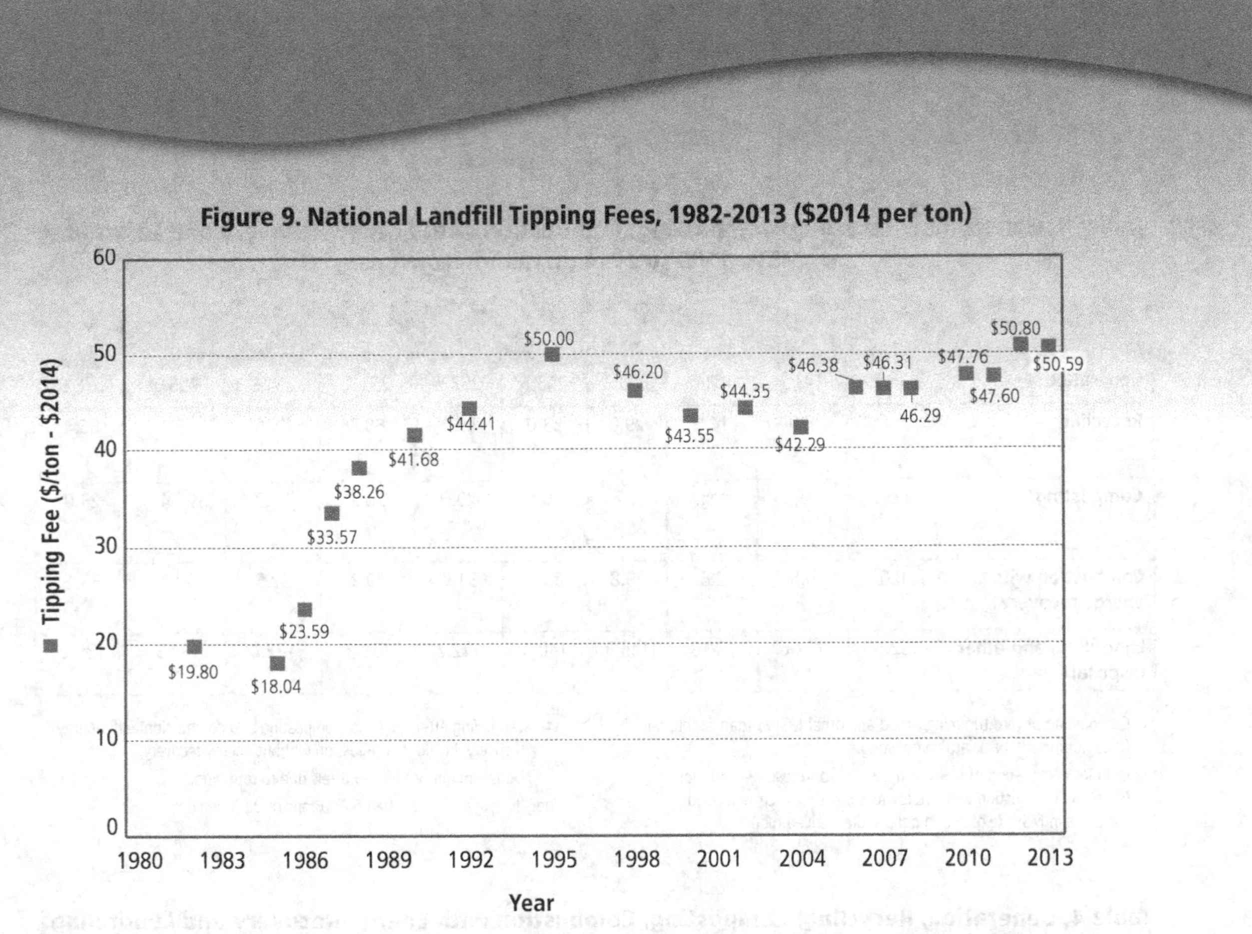

National mean annual landfill tipping fees were normalized to constant $2014 using the consumer price index (CPI) from the Bureau of Labor Statistics to allow meaningful comparisons. This figure shows an average increase from 1985 to 1995 of $3.15 per year followed by a steady decrease of $0.77 per year followed by an increase of $0.83 from 2004 to 2013.

Source: National Solid Wastes Management Association (NSWMA) Municipal Solid Waste Landfill Facts. October 2011. Data from 1985 to 2010. Waste & Recycling News, 2013 Landfill Tipping Fee Survey. Spring 2013. Data for 2012 and 2013.

The Benefits of Recycling and Composting

The energy and GHG benefits of recycling, composting and combustion with energy recovery shown in Table 5 are calculated using EPA's WARM (Waste Reduction Model) methodology (see: https://www.epa.gov/warm). WARM calculates and totals GHG emissions of baseline and alternative waste management practices, including source reduction, recycling, composting, combustion and landfilling. Paper and paperboard recycling, at about 44.4 million tons, resulted in a reduction of over 138 MMTCO$_2$E in 2014. This reduction is equivalent to removing over 29 million cars from the road for one year.

> Recycling and composting over 89 million tons of MSW saved over 1.1 quadrillion BTU of energy in 2014. That's the same amount of energy consumed by over 25 million U.S. households per year.

In 2014, over 89 million tons of MSW were recycled and composted. These activities provided an annual reduction of more than 181 MMTCO$_2$E comparable to removing the emissions from over 38 million passenger vehicles from the road in one year.

14

Source: *U.S. EPA, Advancing Sustainable Materials Management: 2014 Fact Sheet, November 2016*

Table 5. Greenhouse Gas Benefits Associated with Recycling and Composting of Specific Materials, 2014* (in millions of tons recycled and composted, $MMTCO_2E$ and in numbers of cars taken off the road per year)

Material	Weight Recycled and Composted (millions of tons)	GHG Benefits $MMTCO_2E$	Numbers of Cars Taken Off the Road per Year
Paper and paperboard	44.4	138.4	29.2 million
Glass	2.99	0.8	175 thousand
Metals			
Steel	5.84	10.6	2.2 million
Aluminum	0.7	6.4	1.3 million
Other nonferrous metals†	1.36	5.9	1.25 million
Total metals	**7.9**	**22.9**	**4.8 million**
Plastics	3.17	3.2	670 thousand
Rubber and leather‡	1.44	0.5	114 thousand
Textiles	2.62	6.2	1.3 million
Wood	2.57	6.3	1.3 million
Other wastes			
Food, other^	1.94	0.3	72 thousand
Yard trimmings	21.08	3.1	651 thousand

* Includes materials from residential, commercial and institutional sources.

† Includes lead from lead-acid batteries. Other nonferrous metals calculated in WARM as mixed metals.

‡ Recycling only includes rubber from tires.

^ Includes collection of other MSW organics for composting.

These calculations do not include an additional 1.29 million tons of MSW recycled that could not be addressed in the WARM model. $MMTCO_2E$ is million metric tons of carbon dioxide equivalent.

Source: WARM model Version 14 (https://www.epa.gov/warm)

Composting Collection Programs[6,7]

- About 3,560 community composting programs were documented in 2014—an increase from 3,227 in 2002.
- Food composting collection programs served over 2.8 million households in 2014.

15

Source: *U.S. EPA, Advancing Sustainable Materials Management: 2014 Fact Sheet, November 2016*

MSW Generation and Household Spending

Over the years, the change in the amount of MSW generated typically imitated trends in how much money U.S. households spent on goods and services. Personal Consumer Expenditures (PCE) measure U.S. household spending on goods and services such as food, clothing, vehicles and recreation services. PCE accounts for approximately 70 percent of U.S. Gross Domestic Product, a key indicator of economic growth. PCE adjusted for inflation is referred to as real PCE. This metric is more useful in making comparisons over time because it normalizes the value of a dollar by considering how much a dollar could purchase in the past versus today. Figure 10 explores the relationship between MSW generated and real PCE since 1960.

Figure 10 is an indexed graph showing the relative changes in real PCE, MSW generated and MSW generated per capita over time. It is indexed to allow all three of these metrics to be shown on the same graph and compare their relative rates of change since 1960. The indexed value indicates the change in the value of the data since 1960. For example, if for a given year the value is three, then the data value for that year would be three times the 1960 value. In this case, if the 1960 value was 200, then the resulting year's value would be 600. The 2014 MSW per capita generation indexed value is 1.7, which means MSW per capita generation has increased by 70 percent since 1960.

Figure 10 shows that real PCE has increased at a faster rate than MSW generation, and the disparity has become even more distinct since the mid 1990s. This metric indicates the amount of MSW generated per dollar spent is falling. In other words, the U.S. economy has been able to enjoy dramatic increases in household spending on consumer goods and services without the societal impact of similarly increasing MSW generation rates. This figure also shows that the MSW generated per capita leveled off in the early-to-mid 2000s and has since fallen. This is important because as population continues to grow, it will be necessary for MSW generated per capita to continue to fall to maintain or decrease the total amount of MSW generated as a country.

Figure 10. Indexed MSW Generated and Real PCE over Time (1960-2014)

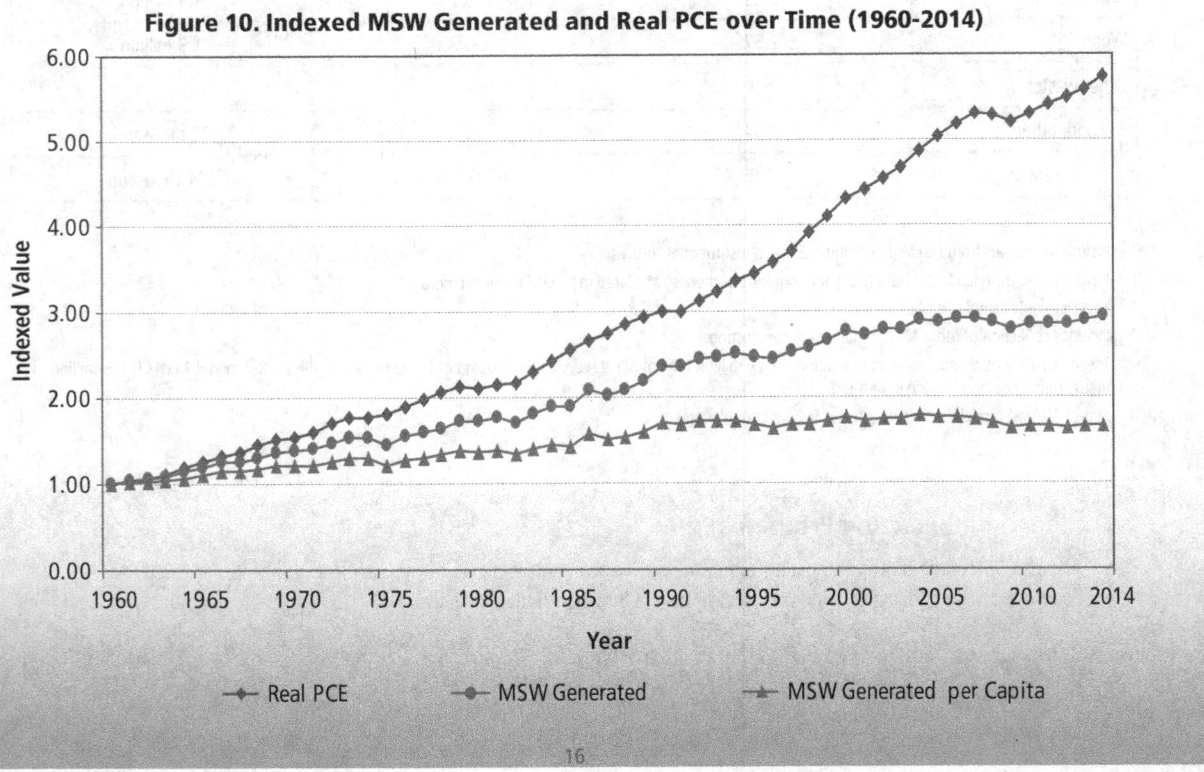

Source: *U.S. EPA, Advancing Sustainable Materials Management: 2014 Fact Sheet, November 2016*

Construction and Demolition (C&D) Debris Generation Results

C&D debris is a type of waste which is not included in MSW. Materials included in C&D are steel, wood products, drywall and plaster, brick, clay tile, asphalt shingles, concrete and asphalt concrete. These materials are used in building as well as road and bridge sectors. The generation estimate represents C&D amounts from construction, renovation and demolition activities for buildings, roads and bridges.

In 2014, 534 million tons of C&D debris were generated. Figure 11 shows the 2014 generation composition for C&D. Concrete was the largest portion (70 percent), followed by asphalt concrete (14 percent). Wood products made up seven percent and the other products accounted for nine percent combined. The 2014 generation estimates are presented in more detail in Table 6. As shown in Figure 12, demolition represented over 90 percent of total C&D debris generation as opposed to construction which represented under 10 percent.

Figure 11. C&D Generation Composition by Material, 2014
534 Million Tons (before recycling)

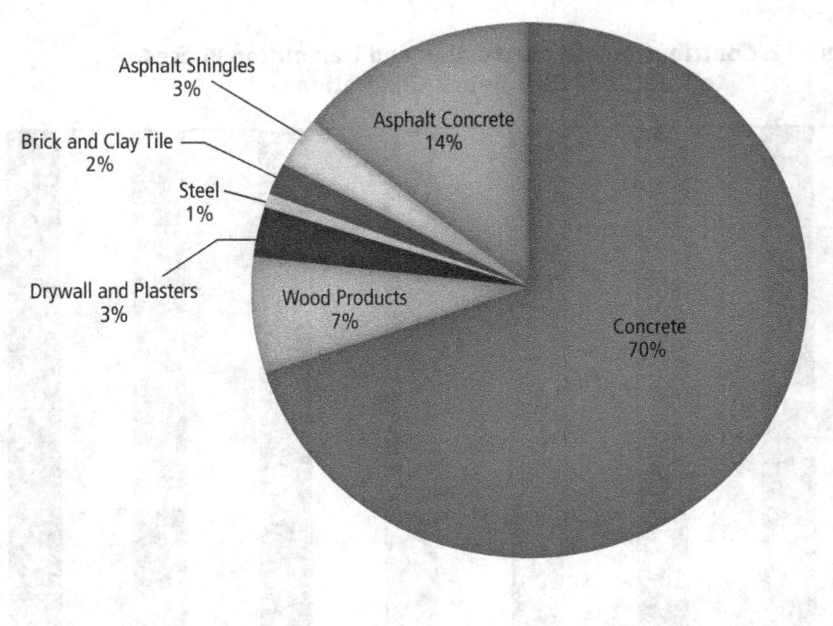

17

Source: U.S. EPA, *Advancing Sustainable Materials Management: 2014 Fact Sheet*, November 2016

Table 6. C&D Debris Generation by Material and Activity (million tons)

	Waste During Construction	Demolition Debris	Total C&D Debris
	2014	2014	2014
Concrete	21.7	353.6	375.3
Wood Products	2.9	35.8	38.7
Drywall and Plasters	3.3	10.3	13.6
Steel	0.0	4.3	4.3
Brick and Clay Tile	0.2	11.8	12.0
Asphalt Shingles	0.8	12.7	13.5
Asphalt Concrete	0.0	76.6	76.6
Total	**28.9**	**505.1**	**534.0**

Figure 12. Contribution of Construction and Demolition Phases to Total 2014 C&D Debris Generation

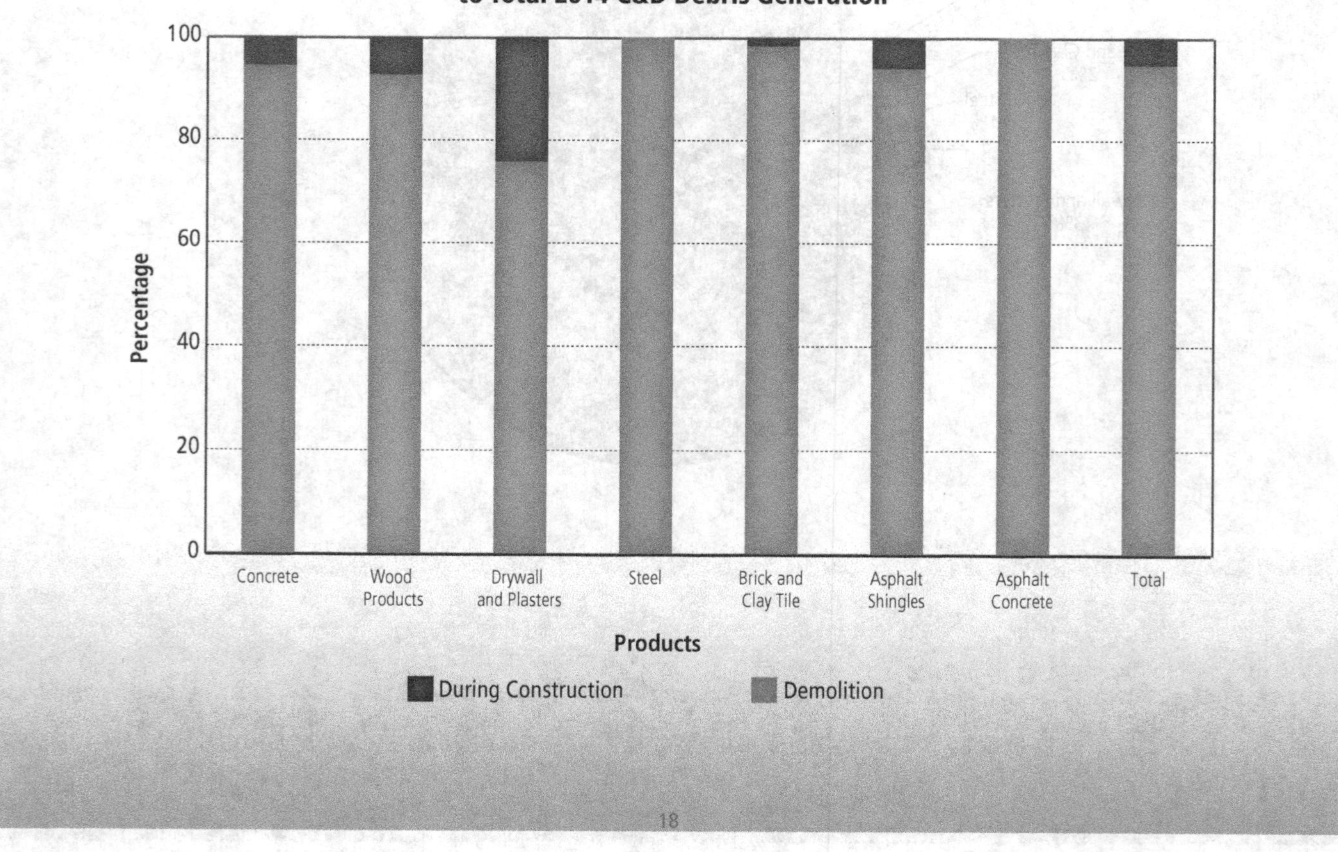

18

Source: U.S. EPA, Advancing Sustainable Materials Management: 2014 Fact Sheet, November 2016

Table 7 displays the amount of C&D debris generation from buildings, roads and bridges and other structures for each material. The other structures category includes communication, power, transportation, sewer and waste disposal, water supply, conservation and development and manufacturing infrastructure. In 2014, roads and bridges contributed significantly more to C&D debris generation than buildings and other structures, and concrete made up the largest share of C&D debris generation for all three categories.[8]

Table 7. C&D Debris Generation by Source (million tons)

	Buildings	Roads and Bridges	Other
	2014	2014	2014
Concrete	84.8	157.4	133.1
Wood Products[a]	37.3		1.4
Drywall and Plasters	13.6		
Steel[b]	4.4		
Brick and Clay Tile	12.0		
Asphalt Shingles	13.5		
Asphalt Concrete		76.6	
Total	**165.6**	**234.0**	**134.5**

[a] Wood consumption in buildings also includes some lumber consumed for the construction of other structures. Data were not available to allocate lumber consumption for non-residential and unspecified uses between buildings and other structures except for railroad ties. Since non-residential buildings such as barns, warehouses and small commercial buildings are assumed to consume a greater amount of lumber than other structures, the amount of lumber for construction remaining after the amount for railroad ties is split out, is included in the buildings source category.

[b] Steel consumption in buildings also includes steel consumed for the construction of roads and bridges. Data were not available to allocate steel consumption across different sources, but buildings are assumed to consume the largest portion of steel for construction.

Thinking Beyond Waste

EPA is helping change the way our society protects the environment and conserves resources for future generations by thinking beyond recycling, composting, combustion with energy recovery and landfilling. Building on the familiar concept of Reduce, Reuse, Recycle, the Agency is employing a systemic approach that seeks to reduce materials use and associated environmental impacts over their entire life cycle, called sustainable materials management (SMM). This process starts with extraction of natural resources and material processing through product design and manufacturing, then the product use stage, followed by collection/processing and final end of life. By examining how materials are used throughout their life cycle, an SMM approach seeks to use materials in the most productive way with an emphasis on using fewer materials and products, reducing toxic chemicals and environmental impacts throughout the material's life cycle and assuring we have sufficient resources to meet today's needs and those of the future. Data on MSW generation, recycling, composting, combustion with energy recovery and landfilling is an important starting point for the full SMM approach.

Source: *U.S. EPA, Advancing Sustainable Materials Management: 2014 Fact Sheet, November 2016*

Resources

The data summarized in this fact sheet characterizes the MSW stream as a whole by using a materials flow methodology that relies on a mass balance approach. EPA recognizes that there are several approaches to measuring material flows (e.g. volume). To be consistent, EPA reports the materials quantities in tons in the current fact sheet but will continue to explore options for alternative measurement quantifications to describe materials management in the U.S.

EPA has consistently used materials flow analysis (MFA) to allow for comparison of data over the last three decades. EPA recognizes this methodology differs from other methodologies that also estimate generation of MSW and other waste data. EPA will continue to work with stakeholders to identify methodologies and additional publically available data to improve our national understanding of materials flow in the U.S.

The following provides an example of how the materials flow methodology is used in the fact sheet. To determine the amounts of paper recycled, information is gathered on the amounts processed by paper mills and made into new paper on a national basis plus recycled paper exported, instead of counting paper collected for recycling on a state-by-state basis. Using data gathered from industry associations, businesses and government sources, such as the U.S. Department of Commerce and the U.S. Census Bureau we estimate tons of materials and products generated, recycled, composted, combusted with energy recovery and landfilled. Other sources of data, such as waste characterizations and research reports performed by governments, industry or the press, supplement these data. The data on C&D debris generated summarized in this report is also developed using a materials flow methodology.

The benefits of MSW recycling and composting, such as elimination of GHG emissions, are calculated using EPA's WARM methodology. WARM calculates and totals GHG emissions of baseline and alternative waste management practices including source reduction, recycling, composting, combustion and landfilling. The model calculates emissions in metric tons of carbon equivalent (MTCE), metric tons of carbon dioxide equivalent ($MTCO_2E$) and energy units (million Btu) across a wide range of material types commonly found in MSW. EPA developed GHG emissions reduction factors through a life-cycle assessment methodology. Please see: https://www.epa.gov/warm.

The 2014 data tables and Summaries of the MSW characterization methodology and WARM are available on the EPA website along with information about waste reduction, recycling and sustainable materials management.

Please see:

https://www.epa.gov/smm/advancing-sustainable-materials-management-facts-and-figures-report
https://www.epa.gov/recycle

https://www.epa.gov/smm

20

Source: *U.S. EPA, Advancing Sustainable Materials Management: 2014 Fact Sheet, November 2016*

Endnotes

1. All benefit calculations in the fact sheet are derived from WARM version 14. Source: Waste Reduction Model (WARM). U.S. Environmental Protection Agency. https://www.epa.gov/warm.
2. UNEP (2016) *Resource Efficiency: Potential and Economic Implications. A report of the International Resource Panel.* Ekins, P., Hughes, N., et al., p. 15. https://www.env.go.jp/press/files/jp/102839.pdf
3. UNEP (2016). *Global Material Flows and Resource Productivity. An Assessment Study of the UNEP International Resource Panel.* H. Schandl, M. Fischer-Kowalski, J. West, S. Giljum, M. Dittrich, N. Eisenmenger, A. Geschke, M. Lieber, H. P. Wieland, A. Schaffartzik, F. Krausmann, S. Gierlinger, K. Hosking, M. Lenzen, H. Tanikawa, A. Miatto, and T. Fishman. Paris, United Nations Environment Programme, p. 16.
4. "Electronic Products Generation and Recycling in the United States, 2013 and 2014" U.S. Environmental Protection Agency (2016). https://www.epa.gov/smm/studies-summary-tables-and-data-related-advancing-sustainable-materials-management-report
5. "Food Waste Management in the United States, 2014" U.S. Environmental Protection Agency (2016). https://www.epa.gov/smm/studies-summary-tables-and-data-related-advancing-sustainable-materials-management-report
6. Source for 2002 community composting program data: "The State of Garbage In America." Simmons, Phil, Scott M. Kaufman, and Nickolas J. Themelis. *BioCycle* 47, no. 4, p. 26 (2006). Sources for 2014 data: "State of Composting in the U.S.: What, Why, Where & How." Institute for Local Self-Reliance (2014); *Advancing Sustainable Materials Management: Facts and Figures 2013.* U.S. Environmental Protection Agency (2015). https://www.epa.gov/smm/advancing-sustainable-materials-management-facts-and-figures-report
7. Sources for food composting collection programs: "Residential Food Waste Collection in the U.S. — BioCycle Nationwide Survey." Supplemental tables. *BioCycle* 54, no. 3, p. 23 (2013); *Advancing Sustainable Materials Management: Facts and Figures 2013.* U.S. Environmental Protection Agency (2015). https://www.epa.gov/smm/advancing-sustainable-materials-management-facts-and-figures-report
8. "Construction and Demolition Debris Generation in the United States, 2014" U.S. Environmental Protection Agency (2016). https://www.epa.gov/smm/studies-summary-tables-and-data-related-advancing-sustainable-materials-management-report

21

Source: *U.S. EPA, Advancing Sustainable Materials Management: 2014 Fact Sheet, November 2016*

Table 1. Materials Generated* in the Municipal Waste Stream, 1960 to 2014
(In thousands of tons and percent of total generation)

Materials	Thousands of Tons									
	1960	1970	1980	1990	2000	2005	2010	2012	2013	2014
Paper and Paperboard	29,990	44,310	55,160	72,730	87,740	84,840	71,310	68,620	68,560	68,610
Glass	6,720	12,740	15,130	13,100	12,770	12,540	11,520	11,590	11,540	11,480
Metals										
Ferrous	10,300	12,360	12,620	12,640	14,150	15,210	16,920	16,940	17,720	17,690
Aluminum	340	800	1,730	2,810	3,190	3,330	3,510	3,510	3,500	3,530
Other Nonferrous	180	670	1,160	1,100	1,600	1,860	2,020	1,980	2,010	2,040
Total Metals	*10,820*	*13,830*	*15,510*	*16,550*	*18,940*	*20,400*	22,450	22,430	23,230	23,260
Plastics	390	2,900	6,830	17,130	25,550	29,380	31,400	31,920	32,620	33,250
Rubber and Leather	1,840	2,970	4,200	5,790	6,670	7,290	7,750	8,100	8,350	8,210
Textiles	1,760	2,040	2,530	5,810	9,480	11,510	13,220	14,500	15,320	16,220
Wood	3,030	3,720	7,010	12,210	13,570	14,790	15,710	15,820	15,770	16,120
Other **	70	770	2,520	3,190	4,000	4,290	4,710	4,570	4,440	4,440
Total Materials in Products	54,620	83,280	108,890	146,510	178,720	185,040	178,070	177,550	179,830	181,590
Other Wastes										
Food	12,200	12,800	13,000	23,860	30,700	32,930	35,740	36,430	37,060	38,400
Yard Trimmings	20,000	23,200	27,500	35,000	30,530	32,070	33,400	33,960	34,200	34,500
Miscellaneous Inorganic Wastes	1,300	1,780	2,250	2,900	3,500	3,690	3,840	3,900	3,930	3,970
Total Other Wastes	33,500	37,780	42,750	61,760	64,730	68,690	72,980	74,290	75,190	76,870
Total MSW Generated - Weight	88,120	121,060	151,640	208,270	243,450	253,730	251,050	251,840	255,020	258,460

Materials	Percent of Total Generation									
	1960	1970	1980	1990	2000	2005	2010	2012	2013	2014
Paper and Paperboard	34.0%	36.6%	36.4%	34.9%	36.0%	33.4%	28.4%	27.2%	26.9%	26.5%
Glass	7.6%	10.5%	10.0%	6.3%	5.2%	4.9%	4.6%	4.6%	4.5%	4.4%
Metals										
Ferrous	11.7%	10.2%	8.3%	6.1%	5.8%	6.0%	6.7%	6.7%	6.9%	6.8%
Aluminum	0.4%	0.7%	1.1%	1.3%	1.3%	1.3%	1.4%	1.4%	1.4%	1.4%
Other Nonferrous	0.2%	0.6%	0.8%	0.5%	0.7%	0.7%	0.8%	0.8%	0.8%	0.8%
Total Metals	*12.3%*	*11.4%*	*10.2%*	*7.9%*	*7.8%*	*8.0%*	*8.9%*	*8.9%*	*9.1%*	*9.0%*
Plastics	0.4%	2.4%	4.5%	8.2%	10.5%	11.6%	12.5%	12.7%	12.8%	12.9%
Rubber and Leather	2.1%	2.5%	2.8%	2.8%	2.7%	2.9%	3.1%	3.2%	3.3%	3.2%
Textiles	2.0%	1.7%	1.7%	2.8%	3.9%	4.5%	5.3%	5.8%	6.0%	6.3%
Wood	3.4%	3.1%	4.6%	5.9%	5.6%	5.8%	6.3%	6.3%	6.2%	6.2%
Other **	0.1%	0.6%	1.7%	1.5%	1.6%	1.7%	1.9%	1.8%	1.7%	1.7%
Total Materials in Products	62.0%	68.8%	71.8%	70.3%	73.4%	72.9%	70.9%	70.5%	70.5%	70.3%
Other Wastes										
Food	13.8%	10.6%	8.6%	11.5%	12.6%	13.0%	14.2%	14.5%	14.5%	14.9%
Yard Trimmings	22.7%	19.2%	18.1%	16.8%	12.5%	12.6%	13.3%	13.5%	13.4%	13.3%
Miscellaneous Inorganic Wastes	1.5%	1.5%	1.5%	1.4%	1.4%	1.5%	1.5%	1.5%	1.5%	1.5%
Total Other Wastes	38.0%	31.2%	28.2%	29.7%	26.6%	27.1%	29.1%	29.5%	29.5%	29.7%
Total MSW Generated - %	100.0%	100.0%	100.0%	100.0%	100.0%	100.0%	100.0%	100.0%	100.0%	100.0%

* Generation before materials recycling, composting, combustion with energy recovery, or landfilling. Does not include construction & demolition debris, industrial process wastes, or certain other wastes. Details may not add to totals due to rounding.

** Includes electrolytes in batteries and fluff pulp, feces, and urine in disposable diapers.

Source: *U.S. EPA, Advancing Sustainable Materials Management: 2014 Tables and Figures, December 2016*

Table 2. Materials Recycled and Composted* in Municipal Solid Waste, 1960 to 2014

(In thousands of tons and percent of generation of each material)

Materials	Thousands of Tons									
	1960	1970	1980	1990	2000	2005	2010	2012	2013	2014
Paper and Paperboard	5,080	6,770	11,740	20,230	37,560	41,960	44,570	44,360	43,400	44,400
Glass	100	160	750	2,630	2,880	2,590	3,130	3,210	3,150	2,990
Metals										
Ferrous	50	150	370	2,230	4,680	5,020	5,800	5,590	5,870	5,840
Aluminum	Neg.	10	310	1,010	860	690	680	710	700	700
Other Nonferrous	Neg.	320	540	730	1,060	1,280	1,440	1,390	1,370	1,360
Total Metals	*50*	*480*	*1,220*	*3,970*	*6,600*	*6,990*	7,920	7,690	7,940	7,900
Plastics	Neg.	Neg.	20	370	1,480	1,780	2,500	2,790	2,990	3,170
Rubber and Leather	330	250	130	370	820	1,050	1,440	1,500	1,490	1,440
Textiles	50	60	160	660	1,320	1,830	2,050	2,290	2,380	2,620
Wood	Neg.	Neg.	Neg.	130	1,370	1,830	2,280	2,410	2,470	2,570
Other **	Neg.	300	500	680	980	1,210	1,370	1,310	1,300	1,290
Total Materials in Products	5,610	8,020	14,520	29,040	53,010	59,240	65,260	65,560	65,120	66,380
Other Wastes										
Food	Neg.	Neg.	Neg.	Neg.	680	690	970	1,740	1,840	1,940
Yard Trimmings	Neg.	Neg.	Neg.	4,200	15,770	19,860	19,200	19,590	20,600	21,080
Miscellaneous Inorganic Wastes	Neg.	Neg.	Neg.	Neg.	Neg.	Neg.	Neg.	Neg.	Neg.	Neg.
Total Other Wastes	Neg.	Neg.	Neg.	4,200	16,450	20,550	20,170	21,330	22,440	23,020
Total MSW Recycled and Composted - Weight	5,610	8,020	14,520	33,240	69,460	79,790	85,430	86,890	87,560	89,400
Materials	**Percent of Generation of Each Material**									
	1960	1970	1980	1990	2000	2005	2010	2012	2013	2014
Paper and Paperboard	16.9%	15.3%	21.3%	27.8%	42.8%	49.5%	62.5%	64.6%	63.3%	64.7%
Glass	1.5%	1.3%	5.0%	20.1%	22.6%	20.7%	27.2%	27.7%	27.3%	26.0%
Metals										
Ferrous	0.5%	1.2%	2.9%	17.6%	33.1%	33.0%	34.3%	33.0%	33.1%	33.0%
Aluminum	Neg.	1.3%	17.9%	35.9%	27.0%	20.7%	19.4%	20.2%	20.0%	19.8%
Other Nonferrous	Neg.	47.8%	46.6%	66.4%	66.3%	68.8%	71.3%	70.2%	68.2%	66.7%
Total Metals	*0.5%*	*3.5%*	*7.9%*	*24.0%*	*34.8%*	*34.3%*	35.3%	34.3%	34.2%	34.0%
Plastics	Neg.	Neg.	0.3%	2.2%	5.8%	6.1%	8.0%	8.7%	9.2%	9.5%
Rubber and Leather	17.9%	8.4%	3.1%	6.4%	12.3%	14.4%	18.6%	18.5%	17.8%	17.5%
Textiles	2.8%	2.9%	6.3%	11.4%	13.9%	15.9%	15.5%	15.8%	15.5%	16.2%
Wood	Neg.	Neg.	Neg.	1.1%	10.1%	12.4%	14.5%	15.2%	15.7%	15.9%
Other **	Neg.	39.0%	19.8%	21.3%	24.5%	28.2%	29.1%	28.7%	29.3%	29.1%
Total Materials in Products	10.3%	9.6%	13.3%	19.8%	29.7%	32.0%	36.6%	36.9%	36.2%	36.6%
Other Wastes										
Food, Other^	Neg.	Neg.	Neg.	Neg.	2.2%	2.1%	2.7%	4.8%	5.0%	5.1%
Yard Trimmings	Neg.	Neg.	Neg.	12.0%	51.7%	61.9%	57.5%	57.7%	60.2%	61.1%
Miscellaneous Inorganic Wastes	Neg.	Neg.	Neg.	Neg.	Neg.	Neg.	Neg.	Neg.	Neg.	Neg.
Total Other Wastes	Neg.	Neg.	Neg.	6.8%	25.4%	29.9%	27.6%	28.7%	29.8%	29.9%
Total MSW Recycled and Composted - %	6.4%	6.6%	9.6%	16.0%	28.5%	31.4%	34.0%	34.5%	34.3%	34.6%

* Recycling and composting of postconsumer wastes; does not include converting/fabrication scrap. Details may not add to totals due to rounding.

** Collection of electrolytes in batteries; probably not recycled.

Neg = Less than 5,000 tons or 0.05 percent.

^ Includes paper and mixed MSW for composting.

Source: *U.S. EPA, Advancing Sustainable Materials Management: 2014 Tables and Figures, December 2016*

Table 3. Materials Combusted with Energy Recovery* in the Municipal Waste Stream, 1960 to 2014

(In thousands of tons and percent of total combusted)

Materials	Thousands of Tons									
	1960	1970	1980	1990	2000	2005	2010	2012	2013	2014
Paper and Paperboard		150	860	8,930	9,730	7,800	4,740	4,770	4,990	4,740
Glass		60	300	1,810	1,790	1,660	1,360	1,480	1,450	1,450
Metals										
Ferrous		60	250	1,690	1,610	1,640	1,810	2,020	2,040	2,020
Aluminum		0	30	300	390	410	440	470	460	470
Other Nonferrous		0	20	60	50	50	60	60	50	50
Total Metals		60	300	2,050	2,050	2,100	2,310	2,550	2,550	2,540
Plastics		0	140	2,980	4,120	4,330	4,530	4,990	4,910	4,980
Rubber and Leather		10	70	830	1,970	2,110	1,910	2,350	2,710	2,620
Textiles		10	50	880	1,880	2,110	2,270	2,790	3,030	3,140
Wood		10	150	2,080	2,290	2,270	2,310	2,550	2,500	2,540
Other **		0	30	410	540	510	540	590	580	570
Total Materials in Products		300	1,900	19,970	24,370	22,890	19,970	22,070	22,720	22,580
Other Wastes										
Food		50	260	4,060	5,820	5,870	6,150	6,830	6,970	7,150
Yard Trimmings		90	550	5,240	2,860	2,220	2,510	2,830	2,690	2,630
Miscellaneous Inorganic Wastes		10	50	490	680	670	680	770	780	780
Total Other Wastes		150	860	9,790	9,360	8,760	9,340	10,430	10,440	10,560
Total MSW Combusted - Weight		450	2,760	29,760	33,730	31,650	29,310	32,500	33,160	33,140

Materials	Percent of Total Combusted									
	1960	1970	1980	1990	2000	2005	2010	2012	2013	2014
Paper and Paperboard		33.3%	31.2%	30.0%	28.8%	24.6%	16.2%	14.7%	15.0%	14.3%
Glass		13.3%	10.9%	6.1%	5.3%	5.2%	4.6%	4.6%	4.4%	4.4%
Metals										
Ferrous		13.3%	9.0%	5.7%	4.8%	5.2%	6.2%	6.2%	6.2%	6.1%
Aluminum		0.0%	1.1%	1.0%	1.2%	1.3%	1.5%	1.4%	1.4%	1.4%
Other Nonferrous		0.0%	0.7%	0.2%	0.1%	0.1%	0.2%	0.2%	0.2%	0.2%
Total Metals		13.3%	10.8%	6.9%	6.1%	6.6%	7.9%	7.8%	7.8%	7.7%
Plastics		Neg.	5.1%	10.0%	12.2%	13.7%	15.5%	15.4%	14.8%	15.0%
Rubber and Leather		2.2%	2.5%	2.8%	5.9%	6.7%	6.5%	7.2%	8.2%	7.9%
Textiles		2.2%	1.8%	2.9%	5.6%	6.7%	7.7%	8.6%	9.1%	9.5%
Wood		2.2%	5.4%	7.0%	6.8%	7.2%	7.9%	7.8%	7.5%	7.7%
Other **		Neg.	1.1%	1.4%	1.6%	1.6%	1.8%	1.8%	1.7%	1.7%
Total Materials in Products		66.6%	68.8%	67.1%	72.3%	72.3%	68.1%	67.9%	68.5%	68.1%
Other Wastes										
Food		11.1%	9.4%	13.6%	17.3%	18.5%	21.0%	21.0%	21.0%	21.6%
Yard Trimmings		20.0%	20.0%	17.6%	8.5%	7.0%	8.6%	8.7%	8.1%	7.9%
Miscellaneous Inorganic Wastes		2.3%	1.8%	1.7%	1.9%	2.1%	2.3%	2.4%	2.4%	2.4%
Total Other Wastes		33.4%	31.2%	32.9%	27.7%	27.7%	31.9%	32.1%	31.5%	31.9%
Total MSW Combusted with Energy Recovery- %		100.0%	100.0%	100.0%	100.0%	100.0%	100.0%	100.0%	100.0%	100.0%

* Products and materials combusted with energy recovery estimated at percentage total MSW after recycling and composting. In 2014, 19.6 percent of MSW after recycling and composting was combusted with energy recovery except for major appliances, tires, and lead-acid batteries (see Table 16). No combustion with energy recovery in 1960 (see Table 35). Does not include construction & demolition debris, industrial process wastes, or certain other wastes. Details may not add to totals due to rounding.

** Includes electrolytes in batteries and fluff pulp, feces, and urine in disposable diapers.

Source: *U.S. EPA, Advancing Sustainable Materials Management: 2014 Tables and Figures, December 2016*

Table 4. Materials Landfilled* in the Municipal Waste Stream, 1960 to 2014
(In thousands of tons and percent of total landfilled)

Materials	Thousands of Tons									
	1960	1970	1980	1990	2000	2005	2010	2012	2013	2014
Paper and Paperboard	24,910	37,390	42,560	43,570	40,450	35,080	22,000	19,490	20,170	19,470
Glass	6,620	12,520	14,080	8,660	8,100	8,290	7,030	6,900	6,940	7,040
Metals										
Ferrous	10,250	12,150	12,000	8,720	7,860	8,550	9,310	9,330	9,810	9,830
Aluminum	340	790	1,390	1,500	1,940	2,230	2,390	2,330	2,340	2,360
Other Nonferrous	180	350	600	310	490	530	520	530	590	630
Total Metals	*10,770*	*13,290*	*13,990*	*10,530*	*10,290*	*11,310*	12,220	12,190	12,740	12,820
Plastics	390	2,900	6,670	13,780	19,950	23,270	24,370	24,140	24,720	25,100
Rubber and Leather	1,510	2,710	4,000	4,590	3,880	4,130	4,400	4,250	4,150	4,150
Textiles	1,710	1,970	2,320	4,270	6,280	7,570	8,900	9,420	9,910	10,460
Wood	3,030	3,710	6,860	10,000	9,910	10,690	11,120	10,860	10,800	11,010
Other **	70	470	1,990	2,100	2,480	2,570	2,800	2,670	2,560	2,580
Total Materials in Products	49,010	74,960	92,470	97,500	101,340	102,910	92,840	89,920	91,990	92,630
Other Wastes										
Food	12,200	12,750	12,740	19,800	24,200	26,370	28,620	27,860	28,250	29,310
Yard Trimmings	20,000	23,110	26,950	25,560	11,900	9,990	11,690	11,540	10,910	10,790
Miscellaneous Inorganic Wastes	1,300	1,770	2,200	2,410	2,820	3,020	3,160	3,130	3,150	3,190
Total Other Wastes	33,500	37,630	41,890	47,770	38,920	39,380	43,470	42,530	42,310	43,290
Total MSW Landfilled - Weight	82,510	112,590	134,360	145,270	140,260	142,290	136,310	132,450	134,300	135,920

Materials	Percent of Total Landfilled									
	1960	1970	1980	1990	2000	2005	2010	2012	2013	2014
Paper and Paperboard	30.2%	33.2%	31.7%	30.0%	28.8%	24.7%	16.1%	14.7%	15.0%	14.3%
Glass	8.0%	11.1%	10.5%	6.0%	5.8%	5.8%	5.1%	5.2%	5.2%	5.2%
Metals										
Ferrous	12.4%	10.8%	8.9%	6.0%	5.6%	6.0%	6.8%	7.0%	7.3%	7.2%
Aluminum	0.4%	0.7%	1.0%	1.0%	1.4%	1.6%	1.8%	1.8%	1.7%	1.7%
Other Nonferrous	0.2%	0.3%	0.4%	0.2%	0.3%	0.3%	0.4%	0.4%	0.5%	0.5%
Total Metals	*13.0%*	*11.8%*	*10.3%*	*7.2%*	*7.3%*	*7.9%*	9.0%	9.2%	9.5%	9.4%
Plastics	0.5%	2.6%	5.0%	9.5%	14.2%	16.4%	17.9%	18.2%	18.4%	18.5%
Rubber and Leather	1.8%	2.4%	3.0%	3.2%	2.8%	2.9%	3.2%	3.2%	3.1%	3.1%
Textiles	2.1%	1.7%	1.7%	2.9%	4.5%	5.3%	6.5%	7.1%	7.4%	7.7%
Wood	3.7%	3.3%	5.1%	6.9%	7.1%	7.5%	8.2%	8.2%	8.0%	8.1%
Other **	0.1%	0.4%	1.5%	1.4%	1.8%	1.8%	2.1%	2.0%	1.9%	1.9%
Total Materials in Products	59.4%	66.6%	68.8%	67.1%	72.3%	72.3%	68.1%	67.9%	68.5%	68.2%
Other Wastes										
Food	14.8%	11.3%	9.5%	13.6%	17.3%	18.5%	21.0%	21.0%	21.0%	21.6%
Yard Trimmings	24.2%	20.5%	20.1%	17.6%	8.5%	7.0%	8.6%	8.7%	8.1%	7.9%
Miscellaneous Inorganic Wastes	1.6%	1.6%	1.6%	1.7%	1.9%	2.2%	2.3%	2.4%	2.4%	2.3%
Total Other Wastes	40.6%	33.4%	31.2%	32.9%	27.7%	27.7%	31.9%	32.1%	31.5%	31.8%
Total MSW Landfilled - %	100.0%	100.0%	100.0%	100.0%	100.0%	100.0%	100.0%	100.0%	100.0%	100.0%

* Landfilling after recycling, composting, and combustion with energy recovery. Does not include construction & demolition debris, industrial process wastes, or certain other wastes. Details may not add to totals due to rounding.

** Includes electrolytes in batteries and fluff pulp, feces, and urine in disposable diapers.

Source: *U.S. EPA, Advancing Sustainable Materials Management: 2014 Tables and Figures, December 2016*

Table 5. Paper and Paperboard Products In MSW, 2014
(In thousands of tons and percent of generation)

Product Category	Generation (Thousand tons)	Recycled (Thousand tons)	Recycled (Percent of generation)	Combusted with Energy Recovery (Thousand tons)	Landfilled (Thousand tons)
Nondurable Goods					
Newspapers/Mechanical Papers†	7,620	5,200	68.2%	470	1,950
Books	830				
Magazines	1,260				
Office-type Papers*	4,530				
Standard Mail**	4,050				
Other Commercial Printing	2,190				
Tissue Paper and Towels	3,640				
Paper Plates and Cups	1,380				
Other Nonpackaging Paper***	3,970				
Subtotal Nondurable Goods excluding Newspaper/Mechanical Papers§	21,850	9,710	44.4%	2,380	9,760
Total Paper and Paperboard Nondurable Goods	29,470	14,910	50.6%	2,850	11,710
Containers and Packaging					
Corrugated Boxes	30,490	27,280	89.5%	630	2,580
Gable Top/Aseptic Cartons‡	590				
Folding Cartons	5,410				
Other Paperboard Packaging	70				
Bags and Sacks	880				
Other Paper Packaging	1,690				
Subtotal Containers and Packaging excluding Corrugated Boxes§	8,640	2,210	25.6%	1,260	5,170
Total Paper and Paperboard Containers and Packaging	39,130	29,490	75.4%	1,890	7,750
Total Paper and Paperboard^	**68,600**	**44,400**	**64.7%**	**4,740**	**19,460**

† Starting in 2010, newsprint and groundwood inserts expanded to include directories and other mechanical papers previously counted as Other Commercial Printing.

* High-grade papers such as copy paper and printer paper; both residential and commercial.

** Formerly called Third Class Mail by the U.S. Postal Service.

*** Includes paper in games and novelties, cards, etc.

§ Valid default values for separating out paper and paperboard sub-categories for recovery and discards were not available.

‡ Includes milk, juice, and other products packaged in gable top cartons and liquid food aseptic cartons.

^ Table 5 does not include 10,000 tons of paper used in durable goods (Table 1).

Neg. = Less than 5,000 tons or 0.05 percent.

Source: *U.S. EPA, Advancing Sustainable Materials Management: 2014 Tables and Figures, December 2016*

Table 6. Glass Products in MSW, 2014
(In thousands of tons and percent of generation)

Product Category	Generation	Recycled		Combusted with Energy Recovery	Landfilled
	(Thousand tons)	(Thousand tons)	(Percent of generation)	(Thousand tons)	(Thousand tons)
Durable Goods*	2,280	Neg.	Neg.	230	2,050
Containers and Packaging					
Beer and Soft Drink Bottles**	5,370	2,120	39.5%	640	3,180
Wine and Liquor Bottles	1,790	570	31.8%	240	1,140
Other Bottles and Jars	2,040	300	14.7%	340	1,790
Total Glass Containers	9,200	2,990	32.5%	1,220	6,110
Total Glass	**11,480**	**2,990**	**26.0%**	**1,450**	**8,390**

Glass as a component of appliances, furniture, consumer electronics, etc.
Includes carbonated drinks and non-carbonated water, teas, flavored drinks, and ready-to-drink alcoholic coolers and cocktails.
Neg. = Less than 5,000 tons or 0.05 percent.
Details may not add to totals due to rounding.

Source: *U.S. EPA, Advancing Sustainable Materials Management: 2014 Tables and Figures, December 2016*

Table 7. Metal Products in MSW, 2014

(In thousands of tons and percent of generation)

Product Category	Generation	Recycled		Combusted with Energy Recovery	Landfilled
	(Thousand tons)	(Thousand tons)	(Percent of generation)	(Thousand tons)	(Thousand tons)
Durable Goods					
Ferrous Metals*	15,520	4,260	27.4%	1,900	9,360
Aluminum**	1,520	NA	NA	210	1,310
Lead†	1,380	1,360	99%		20
Other Nonferrous Metals‡	660	Neg.	Neg.	50	610
Total Metals in Durable Goods	**19,080**	**5,620**	**29.5%**	**2,160**	**11,300**
Nondurable Goods					
Aluminum	200	NA	NA	40	160
Containers and Packaging					
Steel					
Cans	1,670	1,180	70.7%	100	390
Other Steel Packaging	500	400	80.0%	20	80
Total Steel Packaging	**2,170**	**1,580**	**72.8%**	**120**	**470**
Aluminum					
Beer and Soft Drink Cans§	1,270	700	55.1%	110	460
Other Cans	130	NA	NA	30	100
Foil and Closures	410	NA	NA	80	330
Total Aluminum Packaging	**1,810**	**700**	**38.7%**	**220**	**890**
Total Metals in Containers and Packaging	**3,980**	**2,280**	**57.3%**	**340**	**1,360**
Total Metals	23,260	7,900	34.0%	2,540	12,820
Ferrous	17,690	5,840	33.0%	2,020	9,830
Aluminum	3,530	700	19.8%	170	2,360
Other nonferrous	2,040	1,360	66.7%	50	630

* Ferrous metals (iron and steel) in appliances, furniture, tires, and miscellaneous durables.
** Aluminum in appliances, furniture, and miscellaneous durables.
† Lead in lead-acid batteries.
‡ Other nonferrous metals in appliances and miscellaneous durables.
§ Aluminum can recycling does not include used beverage cans imported to produce new beverage cans.
NA = Not Available
Details may not add to totals due to rounding.

Source: *U.S. EPA, Advancing Sustainable Materials Management: 2014 Tables and Figures, December 2016*

Table 8. Plastics in Products In MSW, 2014
(In thousands of tons and percent of generation by resin)

Product Category	Generation	Recycled		Combusted with energy Recovery	Landfilled
	(Thousand tons)	(Thousand tons)	(Percent of generation)	(Thousand tons)	(Thousand tons)
Durable Goods					
PET	540				
HDPE	1,340				
PVC	200				
LDPE/LLDPE	1,990				
PP	3,960				
PS	730				
Other resins	3,390				
Total Plastics in Durable Goods	**12,150**	**910**	**7.5%**	**1,280**	**9,960**
Nondurable Goods‡					
Plastic Plates and Cups§					
LDPE/LLDPE	20				
PLA	20				
PP	140				
PS	840				
Subtotal Plastic Plates and Cups	1,020	Neg.	Neg.	200	820
Trash Bags					
HDPE	200				
LDPE/LLDPE	800				
Subtotal Trash Bags	1,000			200	800
All other nondurables*					
PET	660				
HDPE	570				
PVC	250				
LDPE/LLDPE	1,240				
PLA	30				
PP	1,290				
PS	200				
Other resins	520				
Subtotal All Other Nondurables	4,760	140	2.9%	910	3,710
Total Plastics in Nondurable Goods, by resin					
PET	660				
HDPE	770				
PVC	250				
LDPE/LLDPE	2,060				
PLA	50				
PP	1,430				
PS	1,040				
Other resins	520				
Total Plastics in Nondurable Goods	**6,780**	**140**	**2.1%**	**1,310**	**5,330**

Source: *U.S. EPA, Advancing Sustainable Materials Management: 2014 Tables and Figures, December 2016*

Table 8. Plastics in Products In MSW, 2014
(In thousands of tons and percent of generation by resin)

Product Category	Generation	Recycled		Combusted with energy Recovery	Landfilled
	(Thousand tons)	(Thousand tons)	(Percent of generation)	(Thousand tons)	(Thousand tons)
Plastic Containers & Packaging					
Bottles and Jars**					
PET	2,920	910	31.2%	390	1,620
Natural Bottles†					
HDPE	780	230	29.5%	110	440
Other plastic containers					
HDPE	1,480	320	21.6%		
PVC	20	Neg.			
LDPE/LLDPE	40	Neg.			
PP	230	40	17.4%		
PS	80	Neg.			
Subtotal Other Containers	**1,850**	**360**	**19.5%**	**290**	**1,200**
Bags, sacks, & wraps					
HDPE	760	50	6.6%		
PVC	50				
LDPE/LLDPE	2,530	450	17.8%		
PP	560				
PS	150				
Subtotal Bags, Sacks, & Wraps	**4,050**	**500**	**12.3%**	**700**	**2,850**
Other Plastics Packaging‡					
PET	950	60	6.3%		
HDPE	700	10	1.4%		
PVC	320	Neg.			
LDPE/LLDPE	1,090	Neg.			
PLA	10	Neg.			
PP	930	20	2.2%		
PS	330	30	9.1%		
Other resins	390	Neg.			
Subtotal Other Packaging	**4,720**	**120**	**2.5%**	**900**	**3,700**
Total Plastics in Containers & Packaging, by resin					
PET	3,870	970	25.1%		
HDPE	3,720	610	16.4%		
PVC	390	Neg.			
LDPE/LLDPE	3,660	450	12.3%		
PLA	10	Neg.			
PP	1,720	60	3.5%		
PS	560	30	5.4%		
Other resins	390	Neg.			
Total Plastics in Containers & Packaging	**14,320**	**2,120**	**14.8%**	**2,390**	**9,810**

Source: *U.S. EPA, Advancing Sustainable Materials Management: 2014 Tables and Figures, December 2016*

Table 8. Plastics in Products In MSW, 2014
(In thousands of tons and percent of generation by resin)

Product Category	Generation	Recycled		Combusted with energy Recovery	Landfilled
	(Thousand tons)	(Thousand tons)	(Percent of generation)	(Thousand tons)	(Thousand tons)
Total Plastics in MSW, by resin					
PET	5,070	970	19.1%		
HDPE	5,830	610	10.5%		
PVC	840	Neg.			
LDPE/LLDPE	7,710	450	5.8%		
PLA	60	Neg.			
PP	7,110	60	0.8%		
PS	2,330	30	1.3%		
Other resins	4,300	1,050	24.4%		
Total Plastics in MSW	**33,250**	**3,170**	**9.5%**	**4,980**	**25,100**

‡ Nondurable goods other than containers and packaging.

§ Due to source data aggregation, PET cups are included in "Other Plastic Packaging".

* All other nondurables include plastics in disposable diapers, clothing, footwear, etc.

** Injection stretch blow molded PET containers as identified in *Report on Postconsumer PET Container Recycling Activity in 2014*. National Association for PET Container Resources. Recycling includes caps, lids, and other material collected with PET bottles and jars.

† White translucent homopolymer bottles as defined in the *2014 United States National Postconsumer Plastics Bottles Recycling Report*. American Chemistry Council and the Association of Postconsumer Plastic Recyclers.

Neg. = negligible, less than 5,000 tons
HDPE = High density polyethylene
LDPE = Low density polyethylene
LLDPE = Linear low density polyethylene

‡ Other plastic packaging includes coatings, closures, lids, PET cups, caps, clamshells, egg cartons, produce baskets, trays, shapes, loose fill, etc.

PP caps and lids recycled with PET bottles and jars are included in the recycling estimate for PET bottles and jars.
Other resins include commingled/undefined plastic packaging recycling.
Some detail of recycling by resin omitted due to lack of data.

Source: *U.S. EPA, Advancing Sustainable Materials Management: 2014 Tables and Figures, December 2016*

Table 9. Rubber and Leather Products In MSW, 2014
(In thousands of tons and percent of generation)

Product Category	Generation (Thousand tons)	Recycled (Thousand tons)	Recycled (Percent of generation)	Combusted with energy Recovery (Thousand tons)	Landfilled (Thousand tons)
Durable Goods					
Rubber in Tires*	3,550	1,440	40.6%	1,960	150
Other Durables**	3,570	Neg.	Neg.	450	3,120
Total Rubber & Leather					
Durable Goods	7,120	1,440	20.2%	2,410	3,270
Nondurable Goods					
Clothing and Footwear	830	Neg.	Neg.	160	670
Other Nondurables	260	Neg.	Neg.	50	210
Total Rubber & Leather					
Nondurable Goods	1,090	Neg.	Neg.	210	880
Total Rubber & Leather	8,210	1,440	17.5%	2,620	4,150

* Automobile and truck tires. Does not include other materials in tires.

** Includes carpets and rugs and other miscellaneous durables.

Neg. = Less than 5,000 tons or 0.05 percent.

Details may not add to totals due to rounding.

Source: *U.S. EPA, Advancing Sustainable Materials Management: 2014 Tables and Figures, December 2016*

Table 10. Products Generated* in the Municipal Waste Stream, 1960 to 2014
(In thousands of tons and percent of total generation)

Products	Thousands of Tons									
	1960	1970	1980	1990	2000	2005	2010	2012	2013	2014
Durable Goods	9,920	14,660	21,800	29,810	38,870	45,060	49,350	50,890	52,520	52,650
(Detail in Table 14)										
Nondurable Goods	17,330	25,060	34,420	52,170	64,010	63,650	53,250	51,430	51,540	52,270
(Detail in Table 18)										
Containers and Packaging	27,370	43,560	52,670	64,530	75,840	76,330	75,470	75,230	75,770	76,670
Detail in Table 22)										
Total Product** Wastes	54,620	83,280	108,890	146,510	178,720	185,040	178,070	177,550	179,830	181,590
Other Wastes										
Food	12,200	12,800	13,000	23,860	30,700	32,930	35,740	36,430	37,060	38,400
Yard Trimmings	20,000	23,200	27,500	35,000	30,530	32,070	33,400	33,960	34,200	34,500
Miscellaneous Inorganic Wastes	1,300	1,780	2,250	2,900	3,500	3,690	3,840	3,900	3,930	3,970
Total Other Wastes	33,500	37,780	42,750	61,760	64,730	68,690	72,980	74,290	75,190	76,870
Total MSW Generated - Weight	88,120	121,060	151,640	208,270	243,450	253,730	251,050	251,840	255,020	258,460

Products	Percent of Total Generation									
	1960	1970	1980	1990	2000	2005	2010	2012	2013	2014
Durable Goods	11.3%	12.1%	14.4%	14.3%	16.0%	17.8%	19.7%	20.2%	20.6%	20.4%
(Detail in Table 14)										
Nondurable Goods	19.7%	20.7%	22.7%	25.0%	26.3%	25.1%	21.2%	20.4%	20.2%	20.2%
(Detail in Table 18)										
Containers and Packaging	31.1%	36.0%	34.7%	31.0%	31.2%	30.1%	30.1%	29.9%	29.7%	29.7%
(Detail in Table 23)										
Total Product** Wastes	62.0%	68.8%	71.8%	70.3%	73.4%	72.9%	70.9%	70.5%	70.5%	70.3%
Other Wastes										
Food	13.8%	10.6%	8.6%	11.5%	12.6%	13.0%	14.2%	14.5%	14.5%	14.9%
Yard Trimmings	22.7%	19.2%	18.1%	16.8%	12.5%	12.6%	13.3%	13.5%	13.4%	13.3%
Miscellaneous Inorganic Wastes	1.5%	1.5%	1.5%	1.4%	1.4%	1.5%	1.5%	1.5%	1.5%	1.5%
Total Other Wastes	38.0%	31.2%	28.2%	29.7%	26.6%	27.1%	29.1%	29.5%	29.5%	29.7%
Total MSW Generated - %	100.0%	100.0%	100.0%	100.0%	100.0%	100.0%	100.0%	100.0%	100.0%	100.0%

* Generation before materials recycling, composting, combustion with energy recovery, or landfilling. Does not include construction & demolition debris, industrial process wastes, or certain other wastes. Details may not add to totals due to rounding.

** Other than food products.

Source: *U.S. EPA, Advancing Sustainable Materials Management: 2014 Tables and Figures, December 2016*

Table 11. Products Recycled and Composted* in the Municipal Waste Stream, 1960 to 2014

(In thousands of tons and percent of total generation)

Products	Thousands of Tons									
	1960	1970	1980	1990	2000	2005	2010	2012	2013	2014
Durable Goods	350	940	1,360	3,460	6,580	7,970	9,390	9,530	9,660	9,750
(Detail in Table 15)										
Nondurable Goods	2,390	3,730	4,670	8,800	17,560	19,770	19,190	17,270	16,410	17,180
(Detail in Table 19)										
Containers and Packaging	2,870	3,350	8,490	16,780	28,870	31,500	36,680	38,760	39,050	39,450
Detail in Table 24)										
Total Product** Wastes	5,610	8,020	14,520	29,040	53,010	59,240	65,260	65,560	65,120	66,380
Other Wastes										
Food, Other^	Neg.	Neg.	Neg.	Neg.	680	690	970	1,740	1,840	1,940
Yard Trimmings	Neg.	Neg.	Neg.	4,200	15,770	19,860	19,200	19,590	20,600	21,080
Miscellaneous Inorganic Wastes	Neg.	Neg.	Neg.	Neg.	Neg.	Neg.	Neg.	Neg.	Neg.	Neg.
Total Other Wastes	Neg.	Neg.	Neg.	4,200	16,450	20,550	20,170	21,330	22,440	23,020
Total MSW Recycled and Composted - Weight	5,610	8,020	14,520	33,240	69,460	79,790	85,430	86,890	87,560	89,400

Products	Percent of Total Generation									
	1960	1970	1980	1990	2000	2005	2010	2012	2013	2014
Durable Goods	3.5%	6.4%	6.2%	11.6%	16.9%	17.7%	19.0%	18.7%	18.4%	18.5%
(Detail in Table 15)										
Nondurable Goods	13.8%	14.9%	13.6%	16.9%	27.4%	31.1%	36.0%	33.6%	31.8%	32.9%
(Detail in Table 19)										
Containers and Packaging	10.5%	7.7%	16.1%	26.0%	38.1%	41.3%	48.6%	51.5%	51.5%	51.5%
(Detail in Table 25)										
Total Product** Wastes	10.3%	9.6%	13.3%	19.8%	29.7%	32.0%	36.6%	36.9%	36.2%	36.6%
Other Wastes										
Food, Other^	Neg.	Neg.	Neg.	Neg.	2.2%	2.1%	2.7%	4.8%	5.0%	5.1%
Yard Trimmings	Neg.	Neg.	Neg.	12.0%	51.7%	61.9%	57.5%	57.7%	60.2%	61.1%
Miscellaneous Inorganic Wastes	Neg.	Neg.	Neg.	Neg.	Neg.	Neg.	Neg.	Neg.	Neg.	Neg.
Total Other Wastes	Neg.	Neg.	Neg.	6.8%	25.4%	29.9%	27.6%	28.7%	29.8%	29.9%
Total MSW Recycled and Composted - %	6.4%	6.6%	9.6%	16.0%	28.5%	31.4%	34.0%	34.5%	34.3%	34.6%

* Recycling and composting of postconsumer wastes; does not include converting/fabrication scrap. Details may not add to totals due to rounding.

** Other than food products.

^ Includes collection of soiled paper and mixed MSW for composting.

Neg. = Less than 5,000 tons or 0.05 percent.

Source: *U.S. EPA, Advancing Sustainable Materials Management: 2014 Tables and Figures, December 2016*

Table 12. Products Combusted with Energy Recovery* in the Municipal Waste Stream, 1960 to 2014

(In thousands of tons and percent of total combusted)

Products	Thousands of Tons									
	1960	1970	1980	1990	2000	2005	2010	2012	2013	2014
Durable Goods		60	440	4,480	6,260	6,750	7,070	8,150	8,490	8,410
(Detail in Table 16)										
Nondurable Goods		90	580	7,380	9,000	7,980	6,030	6,740	6,960	6,870
(Detail in Table 20)										
Containers and Packaging		150	880	8,110	9,110	8,160	6,870	7,180	7,270	7,300
Detail in Table 26)										
Total Product** Wastes		300	1,900	19,970	24,370	22,890	19,970	22,070	22,720	22,580
Other Wastes										
Food		50	260	4,060	5,820	5,870	6,150	6,830	6,970	7,150
Yard Trimmings		90	550	5,240	2,860	2,220	2,510	2,830	2,690	2,630
Miscellaneous Inorganic Wastes		10	50	490	680	670	680	770	780	780
Total Other Wastes		150	860	9,790	9,360	8,760	9,340	10,430	10,440	10,560
Total MSW Combusted with Energy Recovery - Weight		450	2,760	29,760	33,730	31,650	29,310	32,500	33,160	33,140

Products	Percent of Total Combusted									
	1960	1970	1980	1990	2000	2005	2010	2012	2013	2014
Durable Goods		13.3%	15.9%	15.1%	18.6%	21.3%	24.1%	25.1%	25.6%	25.4%
(Detail in Table 16)										
Nondurable Goods		19.9%	21.0%	24.8%	26.7%	25.2%	20.6%	20.7%	21.0%	20.7%
(Detail in Table 20)										
Containers and Packaging		33.3%	31.9%	27.3%	27.0%	25.8%	23.4%	22.1%	21.9%	22.0%
(Detail in Table 27)										
Total Product** Wastes		66.6%	68.8%	67.1%	72.3%	72.3%	68.1%	67.9%	68.5%	68.1%
Other Wastes										
Food		11.1%	9.4%	13.6%	17.3%	18.5%	21.0%	21.0%	21.0%	21.6%
Yard Trimmings		20.0%	20.0%	17.6%	8.5%	7.0%	8.6%	8.7%	8.1%	7.9%
Miscellaneous Inorganic Wastes		2.3%	1.8%	1.7%	1.9%	2.1%	2.3%	2.4%	2.4%	2.4%
Total Other Wastes		33.4%	31.2%	32.9%	27.7%	27.7%	31.9%	32.1%	31.5%	31.9%
Total MSW Combusted with Energy Recovery - %		100.0%	100.0%	100.0%	100.0%	100.0%	100.0%	100.0%	100.0%	100.0%

* Products and materials combusted with energy recovery estimated at percentage total MSW after recycling and composting. In 2014, 19.6 percent of MSW after recycling and composting was combusted with energy recovery. Does not include construction & demolition debris, industrial process wastes, or certain other wastes. Details may not add to totals due to rounding.

** Other than food products.

Neg. = Less than 5,000 tons or 0.05 percent.

Source: *U.S. EPA, Advancing Sustainable Materials Management: 2014 Tables and Figures, December 2016*

Table 13. Products Landfilled* in the Municipal Waste Stream, 1960 to 2014
(In thousands of tons and percent of total landfilled)

Products	Thousands of Tons									
	1960	1970	1980	1990	2000	2005	2010	2012	2013	2014
Durable Goods	9,570	13,660	20,000	21,870	26,030	30,340	32,890	33,210	34,370	34,490
(Detail in Table 17										
Nondurable Goods	14,940	21,240	29,170	35,990	37,450	35,900	28,030	27,420	28,170	28,220
(Detail in Table 21)										
Containers and Packaging	24,500	40,060	43,300	39,640	37,860	36,670	31,920	29,290	29,450	29,920
Detail in Table 28)										
Total Product** Wastes	49,010	74,960	92,470	97,500	101,340	102,910	92,840	89,920	91,990	92,630
Other Wastes										
Food	12,200	12,750	12,740	19,800	24,200	26,370	28,620	27,860	28,250	29,310
Yard Trimmings	20,000	23,110	26,950	25,560	11,900	9,990	11,690	11,540	10,910	10,790
Miscellaneous Inorganic Wastes	1,300	1,770	2,200	2,410	2,820	3,020	3,160	3,130	3,150	3,190
Total Other Wastes	33,500	37,630	41,890	47,770	38,920	39,380	43,470	42,530	42,310	43,290
Total MSW Landfilled - Weight	82,510	112,590	134,360	145,270	140,260	142,290	136,310	132,450	134,300	135,920

Products	Percent of Total Landfilled									
	1960	1970	1980	1990	2000	2005	2010	2012	2013	2014
Durable Goods	11.6%	12.1%	14.9%	15.0%	18.6%	21.3%	24.1%	25.1%	25.6%	25.4%
(Detail in Table 17)										
Nondurable Goods	18.1%	18.9%	21.7%	24.8%	26.7%	25.2%	20.6%	20.7%	21.0%	20.8%
(Detail in Table 21)										
Containers and Packaging	29.7%	35.6%	32.2%	27.3%	27.0%	25.8%	23.4%	22.1%	21.9%	22.0%
(Detail in Table 29)										
Total Product** Wastes	59.4%	66.6%	68.8%	67.1%	72.3%	72.3%	68.1%	67.9%	68.5%	68.2%
Other Wastes										
Food	14.8%	11.3%	9.5%	13.6%	17.3%	18.5%	21.0%	21.0%	21.0%	21.6%
Yard Trimmings	24.2%	20.5%	20.1%	17.6%	8.5%	7.0%	8.6%	8.7%	8.1%	7.9%
Miscellaneous Inorganic Wastes	1.6%	1.6%	1.6%	1.7%	1.9%	2.1%	2.3%	2.4%	2.4%	2.3%
Total Other Wastes	40.6%	33.4%	31.2%	32.9%	27.7%	27.7%	31.9%	32.1%	31.5%	31.8%
Total MSW Landfilled - %	100.0%	100.0%	100.0%	100.0%	100.0%	100.0%	100.0%	100.0%	100.0%	100.0%

* Landfilling after recycling, composting, and combustion with energy recovery. Does not include construction & demolition debris, industrial process wastes, or certain other wastes. Details may not add to totals due to rounding.

** Other than food products.

Neg. = Less than 5,000 tons or 0.05 percent.

Source: *U.S. EPA, Advancing Sustainable Materials Management: 2014 Tables and Figures, December 2016*

Table 14. Products Generated* in the Municipal Waste Stream, 1960 to 2014 (With Detail On Durable Goods)

(In thousands of tons and percent of total generation)

Products	Thousands of Tons									
	1960	1970	1980	1990	2000	2005	2010	2012	2013	2014
Durable Goods										
Major Appliances	1,630	2,170	2,950	3,310	3,640	3,610	4,020	4,190	4,470	4,650
Small Appliances**				460	1,040	1,180	1,830	1,950	1,950	1,960
Furniture and Furnishings	2,150	2,830	4,760	6,790	8,120	9,340	10,820	11,500	11,620	11,860
Carpets and Rugs**				1,660	2,460	2,960	3,720	3,860	3,820	3,730
Rubber Tires	1,120	1,890	2,720	3,610	4,930	4,910	5,130	5,540	5,760	5,560
Batteries, Lead-Acid	Neg.	820	1,490	1,510	2,280	2,750	3,020	2,890	2,860	2,840
Miscellaneous Durables										
Selected Consumer Electronics***					1,900	2,630	3,120	3,310	3,360	3,360
Other Miscellaneous Durables					14,500	17,680	17,690	17,650	18,680	18,690
Total Miscellaneous Durables	5,020	6,950	9,880	12,470	16,400	20,310	20,810	20,960	22,040	22,050
Total Durable Goods	9,920	14,660	21,800	29,810	38,870	45,060	49,350	50,890	52,520	52,650
Nondurable Goods	17,330	25,060	34,420	52,170	64,010	63,650	53,250	51,430	51,540	52,270
(Detail in Table 18)										
Containers and Packaging	27,370	43,560	52,670	64,530	75,840	76,330	75,470	75,230	75,770	76,670
(Detail in Table 22)										
Total Product Wastes†	54,620	83,280	108,890	146,510	178,720	185,040	178,070	177,550	179,830	181,590
Other Wastes										
Food	12,200	12,800	13,000	23,860	30,700	32,930	35,740	36,430	37,060	38,400
Yard Trimmings	20,000	23,200	27,500	35,000	30,530	32,070	33,400	33,960	34,200	34,500
Miscellaneous Inorganic Wastes	1,300	1,780	2,250	2,900	3,500	3,690	3,840	3,900	3,930	3,970
Total Other Wastes	33,500	37,780	42,750	61,760	64,730	68,690	72,980	74,290	75,190	76,870
Total MSW Generated - Weight	88,120	121,060	151,640	208,270	243,450	253,730	251,050	251,840	255,020	258,460

Products	Percent of Total Generation									
	1960	1970	1980	1990	2000	2005	2010	2012	2013	2014
Durable Goods										
Major Appliances	1.8%	1.8%	1.9%	1.6%	1.5%	1.4%	1.6%	1.7%	1.8%	1.8%
Small Appliances**				0.2%	0.4%	0.5%	0.7%	0.8%	0.8%	0.8%
Furniture and Furnishings	2.4%	2.3%	3.1%	3.3%	3.3%	3.7%	4.3%	4.6%	4.6%	4.6%
Carpets and Rugs**				0.8%	1.0%	1.2%	1.5%	1.5%	1.5%	1.4%
Rubber Tires	1.3%	1.6%	1.8%	1.7%	2.0%	1.9%	2.0%	2.2%	2.3%	2.2%
Batteries, Lead-Acid	Neg.	0.7%	1.0%	0.7%	0.9%	1.1%	1.2%	1.1%	1.1%	1.1%
Miscellaneous Durables										
Selected Consumer Electronics***					0.8%	1.0%	1.2%	1.3%	1.3%	1.3%
Other Miscellaneous Durables					6.0%	7.0%	7.0%	7.0%	7.3%	7.2%
Total Miscellaneous Durables	5.7%	5.7%	6.5%	6.0%	6.7%	8.0%	8.3%	8.3%	8.6%	8.5%
Total Durable Goods	11.3%	12.1%	14.4%	14.3%	16.0%	17.8%	19.7%	20.2%	20.6%	20.4%
Nondurable Goods	19.7%	20.7%	22.7%	25.0%	26.3%	25.1%	21.2%	20.4%	20.2%	20.2%
(Detail in Table 18)										
Containers and Packaging	31.1%	36.0%	34.7%	31.0%	31.2%	30.1%	30.1%	29.9%	29.7%	29.7%
(Detail in Table 23)										
Total Product Wastes†	62.0%	68.8%	71.8%	70.3%	73.4%	72.9%	70.9%	70.5%	70.5%	70.3%
Other Wastes										
Food	13.8%	10.6%	8.6%	11.5%	12.6%	13.0%	14.2%	14.5%	14.5%	14.9%
Yard Trimmings	22.7%	19.2%	18.1%	16.8%	12.5%	12.6%	13.3%	13.5%	13.4%	13.3%
Miscellaneous Inorganic Wastes	1.5%	1.5%	1.5%	1.4%	1.4%	1.5%	1.5%	1.5%	1.5%	1.5%
Total Other Wastes	38.0%	31.2%	28.2%	29.7%	26.6%	27.1%	29.1%	29.5%	29.5%	29.7%
Total MSW Generated - %	100.0%	100.0%	100.0%	100.0%	100.0%	100.0%	100.0%	100.0%	100.0%	100.0%

* Generation before materials recycling, composting, combustion with energy recovery, or landfilling. Does not include construction & demolition debris, industrial process wastes, or certain other wastes. Details may not add to totals due to rounding.

** Not estimated separately prior to 1990. † Other than food products. Neg. = Less than 5,000 tons or 0.05 percent.

*** Not estimated separately prior to 2000. In 2014, the consumer electronics generation method was revised for 2010 through 2014. See https://www.epa.gov/smm/studies-summary-tables-and-data-related-advancing-sustainable-materials-management-report for further information.

Source: *U.S. EPA, Advancing Sustainable Materials Management: 2014 Tables and Figures, December 2016*

Table 15. Products Recycled and Composted* in the Municipal Waste Stream, 1960 to 2014 (With Detail On Durable Goods)

(In thousands of tons and percent of total generation)

Products	Thousands of Tons									
	1960	1970	1980	1990	2000	2005	2010	2012	2013	2014
Durable Goods										
Major Appliances	10	50	130	1,070	2,000	2,420	2,610	2,680	2,620	2,710
Small Appliances**				10	20	20	120	120	120	120
Furniture and Furnishings	Neg.	Neg.	Neg.	Neg.	Neg.	Neg.	10	10	10	10
Carpets and Rugs**				Neg.	190	250	270	290	240	210
Rubber Tires	330	250	150	440	1,290	1,640	2,270	2,330	2,330	2,250
Batteries, Lead-Acid	Neg.	620	1,040	1,470	2,130	2,640	2,980	2,860	2,830	2,810
Miscellaneous Durables										
Selected Consumer Electronics***					190	360	650	1,000	1,270	1,400
Other Miscellaneous Durables					760	640	480	240	240	240
Total Miscellaneous Durables	10	20	40	470	950	1,000	1,130	1,240	1,510	1,640
Total Durable Goods	350	940	1,360	3,460	6,580	7,970	9,390	9,530	9,660	9,750
Nondurable Goods	2,390	3,730	4,670	8,800	17,560	19,770	19,190	17,270	16,410	17,180
(Detail in Table 19)										
Containers and Packaging	2,870	3,350	8,490	16,780	28,870	31,500	36,680	38,760	39,050	39,450
(Detail in Table 24)										
Total Product Wastes†	5,610	8,020	14,520	29,040	53,010	59,240	65,260	65,560	65,120	66,380
Other Wastes										
Food, Other^	Neg.	Neg.	Neg.	Neg.	680	690	970	1,740	1,840	1,940
Yard Trimmings	Neg.	Neg.	Neg.	4,200	15,770	19,860	19,200	19,590	20,600	21,080
Miscellaneous Inorganic Wastes	Neg.	Neg.	Neg.	Neg.	Neg.	Neg.	Neg.	Neg.	Neg.	Neg.
Total Other Wastes	Neg.	Neg.	Neg.	4,200	16,450	20,550	20,170	21,330	22,440	23,020
Total MSW Recycled and Composted - Weight	5,610	8,020	14,520	33,240	69,460	79,790	85,430	86,890	87,560	89,400

Products	Percent of Total Generation									
	1960	1970	1980	1990	2000	2005	2010	2012	2013	2014
Durable Goods										
Major Appliances	0.6%	2.3%	4.4%	32.3%	54.9%	67.0%	64.9%	64.0%	58.6%	58.3%
Small Appliances**				2.2%	1.9%	1.7%	6.6%	6.2%	6.2%	6.1%
Furniture and Furnishings	Neg.	Neg.	Neg.	Neg.	Neg.	Neg.	0.1%	0.1%	0.1%	0.1%
Carpets and Rugs**				Neg.	7.7%	8.4%	7.3%	7.5%	6.3%	5.6%
Rubber Tires	29.5%	13.2%	5.5%	12.2%	26.2%	33.4%	44.2%	42.1%	40.5%	40.5%
Batteries, Lead-Acid	Neg.	75.6%	69.8%	97.4%	93.4%	96.0%	98.7%	99.0%	99.0%	98.9%
Miscellaneous Durables										
Selected Consumer Electronics***					10.0%	13.7%	20.8%	30.2%	37.8%	41.7%
Other Miscellaneous Durables					5.2%	3.6%	2.7%	1.4%	1.3%	1.3%
Total Miscellaneous Durables	0.2%	0.3%	0.4%	3.8%	5.8%	4.9%	5.4%	5.9%	6.9%	7.4%
Total Durable Goods	3.5%	6.4%	6.2%	11.6%	16.9%	17.7%	19.0%	18.7%	18.4%	18.5%
Nondurable Goods	13.8%	14.9%	13.6%	16.9%	27.4%	31.1%	36.0%	33.6%	31.8%	32.9%
(Detail in Table 19)										
Containers and Packaging	10.5%	7.7%	16.1%	26.0%	38.1%	41.3%	48.6%	51.5%	51.5%	51.5%
(Detail in Table 25)										
Total Product Wastes†	10.3%	9.6%	13.3%	19.8%	29.7%	32.0%	36.6%	36.9%	36.2%	36.6%
Other Wastes										
Food, Other^	Neg.	Neg.	Neg.	Neg.	2.2%	2.1%	2.7%	4.8%	5.0%	5.1%
Yard Trimmings	Neg.	Neg.	Neg.	12.0%	51.7%	61.9%	57.5%	57.7%	60.2%	61.1%
Miscellaneous Inorganic Wastes	Neg.	Neg.	Neg.	Neg.	Neg.	Neg.	Neg.	Neg.	Neg.	Neg.
Total Other Wastes	Neg.	Neg.	Neg.	6.8%	25.4%	29.9%	27.6%	28.7%	29.8%	29.9%
Total MSW Recycled and Composted - %	6.4%	6.6%	9.6%	16.0%	28.5%	31.4%	34.0%	34.5%	34.3%	34.6%

* Recycling and composting of postconsumer wastes; does not include converting/fabrication scrap. Details may not add to totals due to rounding.

** Not estimated separately prior to 1990. † Other than food products.

*** Not estimated separately prior to 2000.

^ Includes collection of soiled paper and mixed MSW for composting.

Neg. = Less than 5,000 tons or 0.05 percent.

Source: *U.S. EPA, Advancing Sustainable Materials Management: 2014 Tables and Figures, December 2016*

Table 16. Products Combusted with Energy Recovery* in the Municipal Waste Stream, 1960 to 2014 (With Detail On Durable Goods)

(In thousands of tons and percent of total combusted)

Products	Thousands of Tons									
	1960	1970	1980	1990	2000	2005	2010	2012	2013	2014
Durable Goods										
Major Appliances±§		0	0	0	0	0	0	0	0	0
Small Appliances**				90	200	200	310	360	370	370
Furniture and Furnishings		Neg.	90	1,150	1,570	1,700	1,910	2,270	2,300	2,320
Carpets and Rugs**				290	440	490	610	710	710	690
Rubber Tires§		Neg.	30	400	2,260	2,390	2,000	2,580	3,190	3,080
Batteries, Lead-Acid±		0	0	0	0	0	0	0	0	0
Miscellaneous Durables										
Selected Consumer Electronics										
Other Miscellaneous Durables										
Total Miscellaneous Durables§		60	320	2,550	1,790	1,970	2,240	2,230	1,920	1,950
Total Durable Goods		60	440	4,480	6,260	6,750	7,070	8,150	8,490	8,410
Nondurable Goods		90	580	7,380	9,000	7,980	6,030	6,740	6,960	6,870
(Detail in Table 20)										
Containers and Packaging		150	880	8,110	9,110	8,160	6,870	7,180	7,270	7,300
(Detail in Table 26)										
Total Product Wastes†		300	1,900	19,970	24,370	22,890	19,970	22,070	22,720	22,580
Other Wastes										
Food		50	260	4,060	5,820	5,870	6,150	6,830	6,970	7,150
Yard Trimmings		90	550	5,240	2,860	2,220	2,510	2,830	2,690	2,630
Miscellaneous Inorganic Wastes		10	50	490	680	670	680	770	780	780
Total Other Wastes		150	860	9,790	9,360	8,760	9,340	10,430	10,440	10,560
Total MSW Combusted with Energy Recovery - Weight		450	2,760	29,760	33,730	31,650	29,310	32,500	33,160	33,140

Products	Percent of Total Combusted									
	1960	1970	1980	1990	2000	2005	2010	2012	2013	2014
Durable Goods										
Major Appliances±§		0.0%	0.0%	0.0%	0.0%	0.0%	0.0%	0.0%	0.0%	0.0%
Small Appliances**				0.3%	0.6%	0.6%	1.1%	1.1%	1.1%	1.1%
Furniture and Furnishings		Neg.	3.3%	3.9%	4.7%	5.4%	6.5%	7.0%	7.0%	7.0%
Carpets and Rugs**				1.0%	1.3%	1.5%	2.1%	2.2%	2.1%	2.1%
Rubber Tires§		Neg.	1.1%	1.3%	6.7%	7.6%	6.8%	7.9%	9.6%	9.3%
Batteries, Lead-Acid±		0.0%	0.0%	0.0%	0.0%	0.0%	0.0%	0.0%	0.0%	0.0%
Miscellaneous Durables										
Selected Consumer Electronics										
Other Miscellaneous Durables										
Total Miscellaneous Durables§		13.3%	11.6%	8.6%	5.3%	6.2%	7.6%	6.9%	5.8%	5.9%
Total Durable Goods		13.3%	15.9%	15.1%	18.6%	21.3%	24.1%	25.1%	25.6%	25.4%
Nondurable Goods		19.9%	21.0%	24.8%	26.7%	25.2%	20.6%	20.7%	21.0%	20.7%
(Detail in Table 20)										
Containers and Packaging		33.3%	31.9%	27.3%	27.0%	25.8%	23.4%	22.1%	21.9%	22.0%
(Detail in Table 27)										
Total Product Wastes†		66.6%	68.8%	67.1%	72.3%	72.3%	68.1%	67.9%	68.5%	68.1%

Source: *U.S. EPA, Advancing Sustainable Materials Management: 2014 Tables and Figures, December 2016*

Table 16. Products Combusted with Energy Recovery* in the Municipal Waste Stream, 1960 to 2014 (With Detail On Durable Goods)

(In thousands of tons and percent of total combusted)

Products	Percent of Total Combusted									
	1960	1970	1980	1990	2000	2005	2010	2012	2013	2014
Other Wastes										
Food		11.1%	9.4%	13.6%	17.3%	18.5%	21.0%	21.0%	21.0%	21.6%
Yard Trimmings		20.0%	20.0%	17.6%	8.5%	7.0%	8.6%	8.7%	8.1%	7.9%
Miscellaneous Inorganic Wastes		2.3%	1.8%	1.7%	1.9%	2.1%	2.3%	2.4%	2.4%	2.4%
Total Other Wastes		33.4%	31.2%	32.9%	27.7%	27.7%	31.9%	32.1%	31.5%	31.9%
Total MSW Combusted with Energy Recovery - %		100.0%	100.0%	100.0%	100.0%	100.0%	100.0%	100.0%	100.0%	100.0%

* Products and materials combusted with energy recovery estimated at percentage total MSW after recycling and composting. In 2014, 19.6 percent of MSW after recycling and composting was combusted with energy recovery. Does not include construction & demolition debris, industrial process wastes, or certain other wastes. Details may not add to totals due to rounding.

** Not estimated separately prior to 1990.

Neg. = Less than 5,000 tons or 0.05 percent.

† Other than food products.

§ Tires: tires to fuel based on industry percentage estimates applied to tire generation. Total Miscellaneous Durables: calculated as difference between total durable goods going to combustion and individual durable goods shown. The amounts of consumer electronics going to combustion with energy recovery are not available and are included in Total Miscellaneous Durables.

± Energy Recovery Council, 2016. Major appliances and lead-acid batteries are not accepted at waste-to-energy facilities.

Source: *U.S. EPA, Advancing Sustainable Materials Management: 2014 Tables and Figures, December 2016*

Table 17. Products Landfilled* in the Municipal Waste Stream, 1960 to 2014 (With Detail On Durable Goods)

(In thousands of tons and percent of total landfilled)

Products	Thousands of Tons									
	1960	1970	1980	1990	2000	2005	2010	2012	2013	2014
Durable Goods										
Major Appliances	1,620	2,120	2,820	2,240	1,640	1,190	1,410	1,510	1,850	1,940
Small Appliances**				360	820	960	1,400	1,470	1,460	1,470
Furniture and Furnishings	2,150	2,830	4,670	5,640	6,550	7,640	8,900	9,220	9,310	9,530
Carpets and Rugs**				1,370	1,830	2,220	2,840	2,860	2,870	2,830
Rubber Tires	790	1,640	2,540	2,770	1,380	880	860	630	240	230
Batteries, Lead-Acid		200	450	40	150	110	40	30	30	30
Miscellaneous Durables										
Selected Consumer Electronics***										
Other Miscellaneous Durables										
Total Miscellaneous Durables	5,010	6,870	9,520	9,450	13,660	17,340	17,440	17,490	18,610	18,460
Total Durable Goods	9,570	13,660	20,000	21,870	26,030	30,340	32,890	33,210	34,370	34,490
Nondurable Goods	14,940	21,240	29,170	35,990	37,450	35,900	28,030	27,420	28,170	28,220
(Detail in Table 21)										
Containers and Packaging	24,500	40,060	43,300	39,640	37,860	36,670	31,920	29,290	29,450	29,920
(Detail in Table 28)										
Total Product Wastes†	49,010	74,960	92,470	97,500	101,340	102,910	92,840	89,920	91,990	92,630
Other Wastes										
Food	12,200	12,750	12,740	19,800	24,200	26,370	28,620	27,860	28,250	29,310
Yard Trimmings	20,000	23,110	26,950	25,560	11,900	9,990	11,690	11,540	10,910	10,790
Miscellaneous Inorganic Wastes	1,300	1,770	2,200	2,410	2,820	3,020	3,160	3,130	3,150	3,190
Total Other Wastes	33,500	37,630	41,890	47,770	38,920	39,380	43,470	42,530	42,310	43,290
Total MSW Landfilled- Weight	82,510	112,590	134,360	145,270	140,260	142,290	136,310	132,450	134,300	135,920

Products	Percent of Total Landfilled									
	1960	1970	1980	1990	2000	2005	2010	2012	2013	2014
Durable Goods										
Major Appliances	2.0%	1.9%	2.1%	1.5%	1.2%	0.8%	1.0%	1.1%	1.4%	1.4%
Small Appliances**				0.2%	0.6%	0.7%	1.0%	1.1%	1.1%	1.1%
Furniture and Furnishings	2.6%	2.5%	3.5%	3.9%	4.7%	5.4%	6.5%	7.0%	6.9%	7.0%
Carpets and Rugs**				0.9%	1.3%	1.5%	2.1%	2.2%	2.1%	2.1%
Rubber Tires	1.0%	1.5%	1.9%	1.9%	1.0%	0.6%	0.6%	0.5%	0.2%	0.2%
Batteries, Lead-Acid	Neg.	0.2%	0.3%	0.1%	0.1%	0.1%	0.1%	0.0%	0.0%	0.0%
Miscellaneous Durables										
Selected Consumer Electronics***										
Other Miscellaneous Durables										
Total Miscellaneous Durables	6.1%	6.1%	7.1%	6.5%	9.7%	12.2%	12.8%	13.2%	13.9%	13.6%
Total Durable Goods	11.6%	12.1%	14.9%	15.0%	18.6%	21.3%	24.1%	25.1%	25.6%	25.4%
Nondurable Goods	18.1%	18.9%	21.7%	24.8%	26.7%	25.2%	20.6%	20.7%	21.0%	20.8%
(Detail in Table 21)										
Containers and Packaging	29.7%	35.6%	32.2%	27.3%	27.0%	25.8%	23.4%	22.1%	21.9%	22.0%
(Detail in Table 29)										
Total Product Wastes†	59.4%	66.6%	68.8%	67.1%	72.3%	72.3%	68.1%	67.9%	68.5%	68.2%
Other Wastes										
Food	14.8%	11.3%	9.5%	13.6%	17.3%	18.5%	21.0%	21.0%	21.0%	21.6%
Yard Trimmings	24.2%	20.5%	20.1%	17.6%	8.5%	7.0%	8.6%	8.7%	8.1%	7.9%
Miscellaneous Inorganic Wastes	1.6%	1.6%	1.6%	1.7%	1.9%	2.2%	2.3%	2.4%	2.4%	2.3%
Total Other Wastes	40.6%	33.4%	31.2%	32.9%	27.7%	27.7%	31.9%	32.1%	31.5%	31.8%
Total MSW Landfilled - %	100.0%	100.0%	100.0%	100.0%	100.0%	100.0%	100.0%	100.0%	100.0%	100.0%

* Landfilling after recycling, composting, and combustion with energy recovery. Details may not add to totals due to rounding.

** Not estimated separately prior to 1990.

*** The amount of consumer electronics going to combustion with energy recovery versus landfilling are not available. These products are included in Total Miscellaneous Durables.

† Other than food products.

Neg. = Less than 5,000 tons or 0.05 percent.

Source: *U.S. EPA, Advancing Sustainable Materials Management: 2014 Tables and Figures, December 2016*

Table 18. Products Generated* in the Municipal Waste Stream, 1960 to 2014 (With Detail on Nondurable Goods)

(In thousands of tons and percent of generation of each product)

Products	Thousands of Tons									
	1960	1970	1980	1990	2000	2005	2010	2012	2013	2014
Durable Goods	9,920	14,660	21,800	29,810	38,870	45,060	49,350	50,890	52,520	52,650
(Detail in Table 14)										
Nondurable Goods										
Newspapers/Mechanical Papers†	7,110	9,510	11,050	13,430	14,790	12,790	9,880	8,380	8,050	7,620
Directories†**				610	680	660	-	-	-	-
Other Paper Nondurable Goods										
Books and Magazines	1,920	2,470	3,390							
Books**				970	1,240	1,100	990	860	850	830
Magazines**				2,830	2,230	2,580	1,590	1,470	1,410	1,260
Office-Type Papers***	1,520	2,650	4,000	6,410	7,420	6,620	5,260	4,750	4,770	4,530
Standard Mail§				3,820	5,570	5,830	4,340	4,150	4,150	4,050
Other Commercial Printing†	1,260	2,130	3,120	4,460	7,380	6,440	2,480	2,130	1,870	2,190
Tissue Paper and Towels	1,090	2,080	2,300	2,960	3,220	3,460	3,490	3,510	3,620	3,640
Paper Plates and Cups	270	420	630	650	960	1,160	1,350	1,290	1,320	1,380
Other Nonpackaging Paper	2,700	3,630	4,230	3,840	4,250	4,490	4,190	4,010	3,940	3,970
Total Other Paper Nondurable Goods							23,690	22,170	21,930	21,850
Disposable Diapers	Neg.	350	1,930	2,700	3,230	3,410	3,700	3,590	3,540	3,560
Plastic Plates and Cups§			190	650	870	930	890	1,060	1,010	1,020
Trash Bags**				780	850	1,060	980	1,020	980	1,000
Clothing and Footwear	1,360	1,620	2,170	4,010	6,470	7,890	9,100	10,310	11,120	12,150
Towels, Sheets and Pillowcases**				710	820	980	1,290	1,290	1,280	1,270
Other Miscellaneous Nondurables	100	200	1,410	3,340	4,030	4,250	3,720	3,610	3,630	3,800
Total Nondurable Goods	17,330	25,060	34,420	52,170	64,010	63,650	53,250	51,430	51,540	52,270
Containers and Packaging	27,370	43,560	52,670	64,530	75,840	76,330	75,470	75,230	75,770	76,670
(Detail in Table 22)										
Total Product Wastes‡	54,620	83,280	108,890	146,510	178,720	185,040	178,070	177,550	179,830	181,590
Other Wastes	33,500	37,780	42,750	61,760	64,730	68,690	72,980	74,290	75,190	76,870
Total MSW Generated - Weight	88,120	121,060	151,640	208,270	243,450	253,730	251,050	251,840	255,020	258,460

Products	Percent of Generation of Each Product									
	1960	1970	1980	1990	2000	2005	2010	2012	2013	2014
Durable Goods	11.3%	12.1%	14.4%	14.3%	16.0%	17.8%	19.7%	20.2%	20.6%	20.4%
(Detail in Table 14)										
Nondurable Goods										
Newspapers/Mechanical Papers†	8.1%	7.9%	7.3%	6.4%	6.1%	5.0%	3.9%	3.3%	3.2%	2.9%
Directories†**				0.3%	0.3%	0.3%	-	-	-	-
Other Paper Nondurable Goods										
Books and Magazines	2.2%	2.0%	2.2%							
Books**				0.5%	0.5%	0.4%	0.4%	0.3%	0.3%	0.3%
Magazines**				1.4%	0.9%	1.0%	0.6%	0.6%	0.6%	0.5%
Office-Type Papers***	1.7%	2.2%	2.6%	3.1%	3.0%	2.6%	2.1%	1.9%	1.9%	1.8%
Standard Mail§				1.8%	2.3%	2.3%	1.7%	1.6%	1.6%	1.6%
Other Commercial Printing†	1.4%	1.8%	2.1%	2.1%	3.0%	2.5%	1.0%	0.8%	0.7%	0.8%
Tissue Paper and Towels	1.2%	1.7%	1.5%	1.4%	1.3%	1.4%	1.4%	1.4%	1.4%	1.4%
Paper Plates and Cups	0.3%	0.3%	0.4%	0.3%	0.4%	0.5%	0.5%	0.5%	0.5%	0.5%
Other Nonpackaging Paper	3.1%	3.0%	2.8%	1.8%	1.7%	1.8%	1.7%	1.6%	1.5%	1.5%
Total Other Paper Nondurable Goods							9.4%	8.8%	8.6%	8.4%
Disposable Diapers	Neg.	0.3%	1.3%	1.3%	1.3%	1.3%	1.5%	1.4%	1.4%	1.4%
Plastic Plates and Cups§			0.1%	0.3%	0.4%	0.4%	0.4%	0.4%	0.4%	0.4%
Trash Bags**				0.4%	0.3%	0.4%	0.4%	0.4%	0.4%	0.4%

Source: *U.S. EPA, Advancing Sustainable Materials Management: 2014 Tables and Figures, December 2016*

Table 18. Products Generated* in the Municipal Waste Stream, 1960 to 2014 (With Detail on Nondurable Goods)

(In thousands of tons and percent of generation of each product)

Products	Percent of Generation of Each Product									
	1960	1970	1980	1990	2000	2005	2010	2012	2013	2014
Clothing and Footwear	1.5%	1.3%	1.4%	1.9%	2.7%	3.1%	3.6%	4.1%	4.4%	4.7%
Towels, Sheets and Pillowcases**				0.3%	0.3%	0.4%	0.5%	0.5%	0.5%	0.5%
Other Miscellaneous Nondurables	0.1%	0.2%	0.9%	1.6%	1.7%	1.7%	1.5%	1.4%	1.4%	1.5%
Total Nondurables	19.7%	20.7%	22.7%	25.0%	26.3%	25.1%	21.2%	20.4%	20.2%	20.2%
Containers and Packaging	31.1%	36.0%	34.7%	31.0%	31.2%	30.1%	30.1%	29.9%	29.7%	29.7%
(Detail in Table 23)										
Total Product Wastes‡	62.0%	68.8%	71.8%	70.3%	73.4%	72.9%	70.9%	70.5%	70.5%	70.3%
Other Wastes	38.0%	31.2%	28.2%	29.7%	26.6%	27.1%	29.1%	29.5%	29.5%	29.7%
Total MSW Generated - %	100.0%	100.0%	100.0%	100.0%	100.0%	100.0%	100.0%	100.0%	100.0%	100.0%

* Generation before materials recycling, composting, combustion with energy recovery, or landfilling. Does not include construction & demolition debris, industrial process wastes, or certain other wastes. Details may not add to totals due to rounding.

† Starting in 2010, newsprint and groundwood inserts expanded to include directories and other mechanical papers previously counted as Other Commercial Printing.

** Not estimated separately prior to 1990.

*** High-grade paper such as printer paper; generated in both commercial and residential sources.

§ Standard Mail: Not estimated separately prior to 1990. Formerly called Third Class Mail and Standard (A) Mail by the U.S. Postal Service.

§ Plastic Plates and Cups: Not estimated separately prior to 1980.

‡ Other than food products.

\- Detailed data not available.

Neg. = Less than 5,000 tons or 0.05 percent.

Source: *U.S. EPA, Advancing Sustainable Materials Management: 2014 Tables and Figures, December 2016*

Table 19. Products Recycled and Composted* in Municipal Solid Waste, 1960 to 2014 (With Detail on Nondurable Goods)

(In thousands of tons and percent of generation of each product)

Products	Thousands of Tons									
	1960	1970	1980	1990	2000	2005	2010	2012	2013	2014
Durable Goods	350	940	1,360	3,460	6,580	7,970	9,390	9,530	9,660	9,750
(Detail in Table 15)										
Nondurable Goods										
Newspapers/Mechanical Papers†	1,820	2,250	3,020	5,110	8,720	9,360	7,070	5,870	5,390	5,200
Directories†**				50	120	120	-	-	-	-
Other Paper Nondurable Goods										
Books and Magazines	100	260	280							
Books**				100	240	270	-	-	-	-
Magazines**				300	710	960	-	-	-	-
Office-Type Papers***	250	710	870	1,700	4,090	4,110	-	-	-	-
Standard Mail§				200	1,830	2,090	-	-	-	-
Other Commercial Printing†	130	340	350	700	810	1,440	-	-	-	-
Tissue Paper and Towels	Neg.	Neg.	Neg.	Neg.	Neg.	Neg.	-	-	-	-
Paper Plates and Cups	Neg.	Neg.	Neg.	Neg.	Neg.	Neg.	-	-	-	-
Other Nonpackaging Paper	40	110	Neg.	Neg.	Neg.	Neg.	-	-	-	-
Total Other Paper Nondurable Goods							10,650	9,570	9,060	9,710
Disposable Diapers				Neg.	Neg.	Neg.	Neg.	Neg.	Neg.	Neg.
Plastic Plates and Cups§			Neg.	Neg.	Neg.	Neg.	Neg.	Neg.	Neg.	Neg.
Trash Bags**				Neg.	Neg.	Neg.	Neg.	Neg.	Neg.	Neg.
Clothing and Footwear	50	60	150	520	900	1,250	1,250	1,470	1,600	1,900
Towels, Sheets and Pillowcases**				120	140	170	220	230	230	230
Other Miscellaneous Nondurables	Neg.	Neg.	Neg.	Neg.	Neg.	Neg.	Neg.	130	130	140
Total Nondurable Goods	2,390	3,730	4,670	8,800	17,560	19,770	19,190	17,270	16,410	17,180
Containers and Packaging	2,870	3,350	8,490	16,780	28,870	31,500	36,680	38,760	39,050	39,450
(Detail in Table 24)										
Total Product Wastes‡	5,610	8,020	14,520	29,040	53,010	59,240	65,260	65,560	65,120	66,380
Other Wastes	Neg.	Neg.	Neg.	4,200	16,450	20,550	20,170	21,330	22,440	23,020
Total MSW Recycled and Composted - Weight	5,610	8,020	14,520	33,240	69,460	79,790	85,430	86,890	87,560	89,400

Products	Percent of Generation of Each Product									
	1960	1970	1980	1990	2000	2005	2010	2012	2013	2014
Durable Goods	3.5%	6.4%	6.2%	11.6%	16.9%	17.7%	19.0%	18.7%	18.4%	18.5%
(Detail in Table 15)										
Nondurable Goods										
Newspapers/Mechanical Papers†	25.6%	23.7%	27.3%	38.0%	59.0%	73.2%	71.6%	70.0%	67.0%	68.2%
Directories†**				8.2%	17.6%	18.2%	-	-	-	-
Other Paper Nondurable Goods										
Books and Magazines	5.2%	10.5%	8.3%							
Books**				10.3%	19.4%	24.5%	-	-	-	-
Magazines**				10.6%	31.8%	37.2%	-	-	-	-
Office-Type Papers***	16.4%	26.8%	21.8%	26.5%	55.1%	62.1%	-	-	-	-
Standard Mail§				5.2%	32.9%	35.8%	-	-	-	-
Other Commercial Printing†	10.3%	16.0%	11.2%	15.7%	11.0%	22.4%	-	-	-	-
Tissue Paper and Towels	Neg.	Neg.	Neg.	Neg.	Neg.	Neg.	-	-	-	-
Paper Plates and Cups	Neg.	Neg.	Neg.	Neg.	Neg.	Neg.	-	-	-	-
Other Nonpackaging Paper	1.5%	3.0%	Neg.	Neg.	Neg.	Neg.	-	-	-	-
Total Other Paper Nondurable Goods							45.0%	43.2%	41.3%	44.4%

Source: *U.S. EPA, Advancing Sustainable Materials Management: 2014 Tables and Figures, December 2016*

Table 19. Products Recycled and Composted* in Municipal Solid Waste, 1960 to 2014 (With Detail on Nondurable Goods)

(In thousands of tons and percent of generation of each product)

Products	Percent of Generation of Each Product									
	1960	1970	1980	1990	2000	2005	2010	2012	2013	2014
Disposable Diapers				Neg.	Neg.	Neg.	Neg.	Neg.	Neg.	Neg.
Plastic Plates and Cups§			Neg.	Neg.	Neg.	Neg.	Neg.	Neg.	Neg.	Neg.
Trash Bags**				Neg.	Neg.	Neg.	Neg.	Neg.	Neg.	Neg.
Clothing and Footwear	Neg.	Neg.	Neg.	13.0%	13.9%	15.8%	13.7%	14.3%	14.4%	15.6%
Towels, Sheets and Pillowcases**				16.9%	17.1%	17.3%	17.1%	17.8%	18.0%	18.1%
Other Miscellaneous Nondurables	Neg.	Neg.	Neg.	Neg.	Neg.	Neg.	Neg.	Neg.	3.6%	3.7%
Total Nondurables	13.8%	14.9%	13.6%	16.9%	27.4%	31.1%	36.0%	33.6%	31.8%	32.9%
Containers and Packaging	10.5%	7.7%	16.1%	26.0%	38.1%	41.3%	48.6%	51.5%	51.5%	51.5%
(Detail in Table 25)										
Total Product Wastes‡	10.3%	9.6%	13.3%	19.8%	29.7%	32.0%	36.6%	36.9%	36.2%	36.6%
Other Wastes	Neg.	Neg.	Neg.	6.8%	25.4%	29.9%	27.6%	28.7%	29.8%	29.9%
Total MSW Recycled and Composted - %	6.4%	6.6%	9.6%	16.0%	28.5%	31.4%	34.0%	34.5%	34.3%	34.6%

* Recycling and composting of postconsumer wastes; does not include converting/fabrication scrap. Details may not add to totals due to rounding.

† Starting in 2010, newsprint and groundwood inserts expanded to include directories and other mechanical papers previously counted as Other Commercial Printing.

** Not estimated separately prior to 1990.

*** High-grade paper such as printer paper; generated in both commercial and residential sources.

§ Standard Mail: Not estimated separately prior to 1990. Formerly called Third Class Mail and Standard (A) Mail by the U.S. Postal Service.

§ Plastic Plates and Cups: Not estimated separately prior to 1980.

‡ Other than food products.

\- Detailed data not available.

Neg. = Less than 5,000 tons or 0.05 percent.

Source: *U.S. EPA, Advancing Sustainable Materials Management: 2014 Tables and Figures, December 2016*

Table 20. Products Combusted with Energy Recovery* in Municipal Solid Waste, 1960 to 2014 (With Detail on Nondurable Goods)

(In thousands of tons and percent of total combusted)

Products	Thousands of Tons									
	1960	1970	1980	1990	2000	2005	2010	2012	2013	2014
Durable Goods	0	60	440	4,480	6,260	6,750	7,070	8,150	8,490	8,410
(Detail in Table 16)										
Nondurable Goods										
Newspapers/Mechanical Papers†	0	30	160	1,420	1,180	620	500	490	530	470
Directories†**				100	110	100	-	-	-	-
Other Paper Nondurable Goods										
Books and Magazines	0	10	60							
Books**				150	190	150	-	-	-	-
Magazines**				430	290	290	-	-	-	-
Office-Type Papers***	0	10	60	800	650	460	-	-	-	-
Standard Mail§				620	730	680	-	-	-	-
Other Commercial Printing†	0	10	60	640	1,270	910	-	-	-	-
Tissue Paper and Towels	0	10	50	500	620	630	-	-	-	-
Paper Plates and Cups	0	Neg.	10	110	190	210	-	-	-	-
Other Nonpackaging Paper	0	10	80	650	820	820	-	-	-	-
Total Other Paper Nondurable Goods							2,310	2,480	2,550	2,380
Disposable Diapers		Neg.	30	460	630	620	650	710	700	690
Plastic Plates and Cups§			Neg.	110	170	170	160	210	200	200
Trash Bags**				130	160	190	170	200	190	200
Clothing and Footwear	0	10	50	590	1,080	1,210	1,390	1,750	1,890	2,010
Towels, Sheets and Pillowcases**				100	130	150	190	210	210	200
Other Miscellaneous Nondurables	0	Neg.	20	570	780	770	660	690	690	720
Total Nondurables	0	90	580	7,380	9,000	7,980	6,030	6,740	6,960	6,870
Containers and Packaging	0	150	880	8,110	9,110	8,160	6,870	7,180	7,270	7,300
(Detail in Table 26)										
Total Product Wastes‡	0	300	1,900	19,970	24,370	22,890	19,970	22,070	22,720	22,580
Other Wastes	0	150	860	9,790	9,360	8,760	9,340	10,430	10,440	10,560
Total MSW Combusted with Energy Recovery - Weight	0	450	2,760	29,760	33,730	31,650	29,310	32,500	33,160	33,140

Products	Percent of Total Combusted									
	1960	1970	1980	1990	2000	2005	2010	2012	2013	2014
Durable Goods		13.3%	15.9%	15.1%	18.6%	21.3%	24.1%	25.1%	25.6%	25.4%
(Detail in Table 16)										
Nondurable Goods										
Newspapers/Mechanical Papers†		6.7%	5.8%	4.8%	3.5%	2.0%	1.7%	1.5%	1.6%	1.4%
Directories†**				0.3%	0.3%	0.3%	-	-	-	-
Other Paper Nondurable Goods										
Books and Magazines		2.2%	2.2%							
Books**				0.5%	0.6%	0.5%	-	-	-	-
Magazines**				1.4%	0.9%	0.9%	-	-	-	-
Office-Type Papers***		2.2%	2.2%	2.7%	1.8%	1.4%	-	-	-	-
Standard Mail§				2.1%	2.2%	2.1%	-	-	-	-
Other Commercial Printing†		2.2%	2.2%	2.2%	3.8%	2.9%	-	-	-	-

Source: *U.S. EPA, Advancing Sustainable Materials Management: 2014 Tables and Figures, December 2016*

Table 20. Products Combusted with Energy Recovery* in Municipal Solid Waste, 1960 to 2014
(With Detail on Nondurable Goods)
(In thousands of tons and percent of total combusted)

Products	Percent of Total Combusted								
	1960	1970	1980	1990	2000	2005	2010	2012	2013	2014
Tissue Paper and Towels		2.2%	1.8%	1.7%	1.8%	2.0%	-	-	-	-
Paper Plates and Cups		Neg.	0.4%	0.4%	0.6%	0.7%	-	-	-	-
Other Nonpackaging Paper		2.2%	2.8%	2.2%	2.4%	2.6%	-	-	-	-
Total Other Paper Nondurable Goods							7.9%	7.6%	7.7%	7.2%
Disposable Diapers		Neg.	1.1%	1.5%	1.9%	2.0%	2.2%	2.2%	2.1%	2.1%
Plastic Plates and Cups§			Neg.	0.4%	0.5%	0.5%	0.5%	0.6%	0.6%	0.6%
Trash Bags**				0.4%	0.5%	0.6%	0.6%	0.6%	0.6%	0.6%
Clothing and Footwear		2.2%	1.8%	2.0%	3.2%	3.8%	4.7%	5.4%	5.7%	6.1%
Towels, Sheets and Pillowcases**				0.3%	0.4%	0.5%	0.7%	0.7%	0.6%	0.6%
Other Miscellaneous Nondurables		Neg.	0.7%	1.9%	2.3%	2.4%	2.3%	2.1%	2.1%	2.1%
Total Nondurables		19.9%	21.0%	24.8%	26.7%	25.2%	20.6%	20.7%	21.0%	20.7%
Containers and Packaging		33.3%	31.9%	27.3%	27.0%	25.8%	23.4%	22.1%	21.9%	22.0%
(Detail in Table 27)										
Total Product Wastes‡		66.6%	68.8%	67.1%	72.3%	72.3%	68.1%	67.9%	68.5%	68.1%
Other Wastes		33.4%	31.2%	32.9%	27.7%	27.7%	31.9%	32.1%	31.5%	31.9%
Total MSW Combusted with Energy Recovery - %		100.0%	100.0%	100.0%	100.0%	100.0%	100.0%	100.0%	100.0%	100.0%

* Products and materials combusted with energy recovery estimated at percentage total MSW after recovery for recycling and composting. In 2014, 19.6 percent of MSW after recycling and composting was combusted with energy recovery. Does not include construction & demolition debris, industrial process wastes, or certain other wastes. Details may not add to totals due to rounding.

† Starting in 2010, newsprint and groundwood inserts expanded to include directories and other mechanical papers previously counted as Other Commercial Printing.

** Not estimated separately prior to 1990.

*** High-grade paper such as printer paper; generated in both commercial and residential sources.

§ Standard Mail: Not estimated separately prior to 1990. Formerly called Third Class Mail and Standard (A) Mail by the U.S. Postal Service.

§ Plastic Plates and Cups: Not estimated separately prior to 1980.

‡ Other than food products.

\- Detailed data not available.

Neg. = Less than 5,000 tons or 0.05 percent.

Source: *U.S. EPA, Advancing Sustainable Materials Management: 2014 Tables and Figures, December 2016*

Table 21. Products Landfilled* in Municipal Solid Waste, 1960 to 2014 (With Detail on Nondurable Goods)

(In thousands of tons and percent of total landfilled)

Products	Thousands of Tons									
	1960	1970	1980	1990	2000	2005	2010	2012	2013	2014
Durable Goods	9,570	13,660	20,000	21,870	26,030	30,340	32,890	33,210	34,370	34,490
(Detail in Table 17)										
Nondurable Goods										
Newspapers/Mechanical Papers†	5,290	7,230	7,870	6,900	4,890	2,810	2,310	2,020	2,130	1,950
Directories†**				460	450	440	-	-	-	-
Other Paper Nondurable Goods										
Books and Magazines	1,820	2,200	3,050							
Books**				720	810	680	-	-	-	-
Magazines**				2,100	1,230	1,330	-	-	-	-
Office-Type Papers***	1,270	1,930	3,070	3,910	2,680	2,050	-	-	-	-
Standard Mail§				3,000	3,010	3,060	-	-	-	-
Other Commercial Printing†	1,130	1,780	2,710	3,120	5,300	4,090	-	-	-	-
Tissue Paper and Towels	1,090	2,070	2,250	2,460	2,600	2,830	-	-	-	-
Paper Plates and Cups	270	420	620	540	770	950	-	-	-	-
Other Nonpackaging Paper	2,660	3,510	4,150	3,190	3,430	3,670	-	-	-	-
Total Other Paper Nondurable Goods							10,730	10,120	10,320	9,760
Disposable Diapers		350	1,900	2,240	2,600	2,790	3,050	2,880	2,840	2,870
Plastic Plates and Cups§			190	540	700	760	730	850	810	820
Trash Bags**				650	690	870	810	820	790	800
Clothing and Footwear	1,310	1,550	1,970	2,900	4,490	5,430	6,460	7,090	7,630	8,240
Towels, Sheets and Pillowcases**				490	550	660	880	850	840	840
Other Miscellaneous Nondurables	100	200	1,390	2,770	3,250	3,480	3,060	2,790	2,810	2,940
Total Nondurables	14,940	21,240	29,170	35,990	37,450	35,900	28,030	27,420	28,170	28,220
Containers and Packaging	24,500	40,060	43,300	39,640	37,860	36,670	31,920	29,290	29,450	29,920
(Detail in Table 28)										
Total Product Wastes‡	49,010	74,960	92,470	97,500	101,340	102,910	92,840	89,920	91,990	92,630
Other Wastes	33,500	37,630	41,890	47,770	38,920	39,380	43,470	42,530	42,310	43,290
Total MSW Landfilled - Weight	82,510	112,590	134,360	145,270	140,260	142,290	136,310	132,450	134,300	135,920

Products	Percent of Total Landfilled									
	1960	1970	1980	1990	2000	2005	2010	2012	2013	2014
Durable Goods	11.6%	12.1%	14.9%	15.1%	18.6%	21.3%	24.1%	25.1%	25.6%	25.4%
(Detail in Table 17)										
Nondurable Goods										
Newspapers/Mechanical Papers†	6.4%	6.4%	5.9%	4.7%	3.5%	2.0%	1.7%	1.5%	1.6%	1.4%
Directories†**				0.3%	0.3%	0.3%	-	-	-	-
Other Paper Nondurable Goods										
Books and Magazines	2.2%	2.0%	2.3%							
Books**				0.5%	0.6%	0.5%	-	-	-	-
Magazines**				1.4%	0.9%	0.9%	-	-	-	-
Office-Type Papers***	1.5%	1.7%	2.3%	2.7%	1.9%	1.4%	-	-	-	-
Standard Mail§				2.1%	2.1%	2.1%	-	-	-	-

Source: *U.S. EPA, Advancing Sustainable Materials Management: 2014 Tables and Figures, December 2016*

Table 21. Products Landfilled* in Municipal Solid Waste, 1960 to 2014 (With Detail on Nondurable Goods)

(In thousands of tons and percent of total landfilled)

Products	Percent of Total Landfilled									
	1960	1970	1980	1990	2000	2005	2010	2012	2013	2014
Other Commercial Printing†	1.4%	1.6%	2.0%	2.1%	3.8%	2.9%	-	-	-	-
Tissue Paper and Towels	1.3%	1.8%	1.7%	1.7%	1.9%	2.0%	-	-	-	-
Paper Plates and Cups	0.3%	0.4%	0.5%	0.4%	0.5%	0.7%	-	-	-	-
Other Nonpackaging Paper	3.2%	3.1%	3.1%	2.2%	2.4%	2.6%	-	-	-	-
Total Other Paper Nondurable Goods							7.9%	7.6%	7.7%	7.2%
Disposable Diapers	Neg.	0.3%	1.4%	1.5%	1.9%	2.0%	2.2%	2.2%	2.1%	2.1%
Plastic Plates and Cups§			0.1%	0.4%	0.5%	0.5%	0.5%	0.6%	0.6%	0.6%
Trash Bags**				0.4%	0.5%	0.6%	0.6%	0.6%	0.6%	0.6%
Clothing and Footwear	1.6%	1.4%	1.5%	2.0%	3.2%	3.8%	4.7%	5.4%	5.7%	6.1%
Towels, Sheets and Pillowcases**				0.3%	0.4%	0.5%	0.6%	0.7%	0.6%	0.6%
Other Miscellaneous Nondurables	0.1%	0.2%	1.0%	1.9%	2.3%	2.4%	2.3%	2.1%	2.1%	2.2%
Total Nondurables	18.1%	18.9%	21.7%	24.8%	26.7%	25.2%	20.6%	20.7%	21.0%	20.8%
Containers and Packaging	29.7%	35.6%	32.2%	27.3%	27.0%	25.8%	23.4%	22.1%	21.9%	22.0%
(Detail in Table 29)										
Total Product Wastes‡	59.4%	66.6%	68.8%	67.1%	72.3%	72.3%	68.1%	67.9%	68.5%	68.2%
Other Wastes	40.6%	33.4%	31.2%	32.9%	27.7%	27.7%	31.9%	32.1%	31.5%	31.8%
Total MSW Landfilled - %	100.0%	100.0%	100.0%	100.0%	100.0%	100.0%	100.0%	100.0%	100.0%	100.0%

* Landfilling after recycling, composting, and combustion with energy recovery. Does not include construction & demolition debris, industrial process wastes, or certain other wastes. Details may not add to totals due to rounding.

† Starting in 2010, newsprint and groundwood inserts expanded to include directories and other mechanical papers previously counted as Other Commercial Printing.

** Not estimated separately prior to 1990.

*** High-grade paper such as printer paper; generated in both commercial and residential sources.

§ Standard Mail: Not estimated separately prior to 1990. Formerly called Third Class Mail and Standard (A) Mail by the U.S. Postal Service.

§ Plastic Plates and Cups: Not estimated separately prior to 1980.

‡ Other than food products.

\- Detailed data not available.

Neg. = Less than 5,000 tons or 0.05 percent.

Source: *U.S. EPA, Advancing Sustainable Materials Management: 2014 Tables and Figures, December 2016*

Table 22. Products Generated* in the Municipal Waste Stream, 1960 to 2014 (With Detail on Containers and Packaging)
(In thousands of tons)

Products	Thousands of Tons									
	1960	1970	1980	1990	2000	2005	2010	2012	2013	2014
Durable Goods	9,920	14,660	21,800	29,810	38,870	45,060	49,350	50,890	52,520	52,650
(Detail in Table 14)										
Nondurable Goods	17,330	25,060	34,420	52,170	64,010	63,650	53,250	51,430	51,540	52,270
(Detail in Table 18)										
Containers and Packaging										
Glass Packaging										
Beer and Soft Drink Bottles**	1,400	5,580	6,740	5,640	5,710	6,540	5,670	5,580	5,420	5,370
Wine and Liquor Bottles	1,080	1,900	2,450	2,030	1,910	1,630	1,700	1,820	1,740	1,790
Other Bottles & Jars	3,710	4,440	4,780	4,160	3,420	2,290	1,990	2,000	2,100	2,040
Total Glass Packaging	6,190	11,920	13,970	11,830	11,040	10,460	9,360	9,400	9,260	9,200
Steel Packaging										
Beer and Soft Drink Cans	640	1,570	520	150	Neg.	Neg.	Neg.	Neg.	Neg.	Neg.
Cans	3,760	3,540	2,850	2,540	2,630	2,130	2,300	1,850	1,870	1,670
Other Steel Packaging	260	270	240	200	240	240	440	380	530	500
Total Steel Packaging	4,660	5,380	3,610	2,890	2,870	2,370	2,740	2,230	2,400	2,170
Aluminum Packaging										
Beer and Soft Drink Cans	Neg.	100	850	1,550	1,520	1,450	1,370	1,300	1,270	1,270
Other Cans	Neg.	60	40	20	50	80	70	120	120	130
Foil and Closures	170	410	380	330	380	400	460	430	410	410
Total Aluminum Packaging	170	570	1,270	1,900	1,950	1,930	1,900	1,850	1,800	1,810
Paper & Paperboard Pkg										
Corrugated Boxes	7,330	12,760	17,080	24,010	30,210	30,930	29,050	29,480	30,050	30,490
Other Paper & Paperboard Pkg										
Gable Top/Aseptic Cartons‡			790	510	550	500	-	-	-	-
Folding Cartons			3,820	4,300	5,820	5,530	-	-	-	-
Other Paperboard Packaging	3,840	4,830	230	290	200	160	-	-	-	-
Bags and Sacks			3,380	2,440	1,490	1,120	-	-	-	-
Wrapping Papers			200	110	Neg.	Neg.	-	-	-	-
Other Paper Packaging	2,940	3,810	850	1,020	1,670	1,400	-	-	-	-
Subtotal Other Paper & Paperboard Pkg	*6,780*	*8,640*	*9,270*	*8,670*	*9,730*	*8,710*	*8,630*	*8,530*	*8,510*	*8,640*
Total Paper & Board Pkg	14,110	21,400	26,350	32,680	39,940	39,640	37,680	38,010	38,560	39,130
Plastics Packaging										
PET Bottles and Jars			260	430	1,720	2,540	2,670	2,790	2,880	2,920
HDPE Natural Bottles			230	530	690	800	800	780	780	780
Other Containers	60	910	890	1,430	1,740	1,420	1,830	1,850	1,830	1,850
Bags and Sacks			390	940	1,650	1,640	770	-	-	-
Wraps			840	1,530	2,550	2,810	3,160	-	-	-
Subtotal Bags, Sacks, and Wraps			*1,230*	*2,470*	*4,200*	*4,450*	*3,930*	*3,810*	*3,780*	*4,050*
Other Plastics Packaging	60	1,180	790	2,040	2,840	3,210	4,450	4,550	4,710	4,720
Total Plastics Packaging	120	2,090	3,400	6,900	11,190	12,420	13,680	13,780	13,980	14,320
Other Packaging										
Wood Packaging	2,000	2,070	3,940	8,180	8,610	9,230	9,770	9,610	9,410	9,680
Other Misc. Packaging	120	130	130	150	240	280	340	350	360	360
Total Containers & Pkg	27,370	43,560	52,670	64,530	75,840	76,330	75,470	75,230	75,770	76,670
Total Product Wastes†	54,620	83,280	108,890	146,510	178,720	185,040	178,070	177,550	179,830	181,590
Other Wastes										
Food	12,200	12,800	13,000	23,860	30,700	32,930	35,740	36,430	37,060	38,400
Yard Trimmings	20,000	23,200	27,500	35,000	30,530	32,070	33,400	33,960	34,200	34,500
Miscellaneous Inorganic Wastes	1,300	1,780	2,250	2,900	3,500	3,690	3,840	3,900	3,930	3,970
Total Other Wastes	33,500	37,780	42,750	61,760	64,730	68,690	72,980	74,290	75,190	76,870
Total MSW Generated - Weight	88,120	121,060	151,640	208,270	243,450	253,730	251,050	251,840	255,020	258,460

* Generation before materials recycling, composting, combustion with energy recovery, or landfilling. Details may not add to totals due to rounding.

** Includes carbonated drinks and non-carbonated water, teas, flavored drinks, and ready-to-drink alcoholic coolers and cocktails.

‡ Includes milk, juice, and other products packaged in gable top cartons and liquid food aseptic cartons.

† Other than food products. Neg. = Less than 5,000 tons or 0.05 percent. NA = Not Available - Detailed data not available.

Source: *U.S. EPA, Advancing Sustainable Materials Management: 2014 Tables and Figures, December 2016*

Table 23. Products Generated* in the Municipal Waste Stream, 1960 to 2014 (With Detail on Containers and Packaging)

(In percent of total generation)

Products	Percent of Total Generation									
	1960	1970	1980	1990	2000	2005	2010	2012	2013	2014
Durable Goods	11.3%	12.1%	14.4%	14.3%	16.0%	17.8%	19.7%	20.2%	20.6%	20.4%
(Detail in Table 14)										
Nondurable Goods	19.7%	20.7%	22.7%	25.0%	26.3%	25.1%	21.2%	20.4%	20.2%	20.2%
(Detail in Table 18)										
Containers and Packaging										
Glass Packaging										
Beer and Soft Drink Bottles**	1.6%	4.6%	4.4%	2.7%	2.3%	2.6%	2.3%	2.2%	2.1%	2.1%
Wine and Liquor Bottles	1.2%	1.6%	1.6%	1.0%	0.8%	0.6%	0.7%	0.7%	0.7%	0.7%
Other Bottles & Jars	4.2%	3.7%	3.2%	2.0%	1.4%	0.9%	0.8%	0.8%	0.8%	0.8%
Total Glass Packaging	7.0%	9.8%	9.2%	5.7%	4.5%	4.1%	3.7%	3.7%	3.6%	3.6%
Steel Packaging										
Beer and Soft Drink Cans	0.7%	1.3%	0.3%	0.1%	Neg.	Neg.	Neg.	Neg.	Neg.	Neg.
Cans	4.3%	2.9%	1.9%	1.2%	1.1%	0.8%	0.9%	0.7%	0.7%	0.6%
Other Steel Packaging	0.3%	0.2%	0.2%	0.1%	0.1%	0.1%	0.2%	0.2%	0.2%	0.2%
Total Steel Packaging	5.3%	4.4%	2.4%	1.4%	1.2%	0.9%	1.1%	0.9%	0.9%	0.8%
Aluminum Packaging										
Beer and Soft Drink Cans	Neg.	0.1%	0.6%	0.7%	0.6%	0.6%	0.5%	0.5%	0.5%	0.5%
Other Cans	Neg.	Neg.	Neg.	Neg.	Neg.	Neg.	0.03%	0.05%	0.05%	0.05%
Foil and Closures	0.2%	0.3%	0.3%	0.2%	0.2%	0.2%	0.2%	0.2%	0.2%	0.2%
Total Aluminum Packaging	0.2%	0.5%	0.8%	0.9%	0.8%	0.8%	0.8%	0.7%	0.7%	0.7%
Paper & Paperboard Pkg										
Corrugated Boxes	8.3%	10.5%	11.3%	11.5%	12.4%	12.2%	11.6%	11.7%	11.8%	11.8%
Other Paper & Paperboard Pkg										
Gable Top/Aseptic Cartons‡			0.5%	0.2%	0.2%	0.2%	-	-	-	-
Folding Cartons			2.5%	2.1%	2.4%	2.2%	-	-	-	-
Other Paperboard Packaging	4.4%	4.0%	0.2%	0.1%	0.1%	0.1%	-	-	-	-
Bags and Sacks			2.2%	1.2%	0.6%	0.4%	-	-	-	-
Wrapping Papers			0.1%	0.1%	Neg.	Neg.	-	-	-	-
Other Paper Packaging	3.3%	3.1%	0.6%	0.5%	0.7%	0.6%	-	-	-	-
Subtotal Other Paper & Paperboard Pkg							*3.4%*	*3.4%*	*3.3%*	*3.3%*
Total Paper & Board Pkg	16.0%	17.7%	17.4%	15.7%	16.4%	15.6%	15.0%	15.1%	15.1%	15.1%
Plastics Packaging										
PET Bottles and Jars			0.2%	0.2%	0.7%	1.0%	1.1%	1.1%	1.1%	1.1%
HDPE Natural Bottles			0.2%	0.3%	0.3%	0.3%	0.3%	0.3%	0.3%	0.3%
Other Containers	0.1%	0.8%	0.6%	0.7%	0.7%	0.6%	0.7%	0.7%	0.7%	0.7%
Bags and Sacks			0.3%	0.5%	0.7%	0.6%	0.3%	-	-	-
Wraps			0.6%	0.7%	1.0%	1.1%	1.3%	-	-	-
Subtotal Bags, Sacks, and Wraps			*0.8%*	*1.2%*	*1.7%*	*1.8%*	*1.6%*	*1.5%*	*1.5%*	*1.6%*
Other Plastics Packaging	0.1%	1.0%	0.5%	1.0%	1.2%	1.3%	1.8%	1.8%	1.8%	1.8%
Total Plastics Packaging	0.1%	1.7%	2.2%	3.3%	4.6%	4.9%	5.4%	5.5%	5.5%	5.5%
Other Packaging										
Wood Packaging	2.3%	1.7%	2.6%	3.9%	3.5%	3.6%	3.9%	3.8%	3.7%	3.7%
Other Misc. Packaging	0.1%	0.1%	0.1%	0.1%	0.1%	0.1%	0.1%	0.1%	0.1%	0.1%
Total Containers & Pkg	31.1%	36.0%	34.7%	31.0%	31.2%	30.1%	30.1%	29.9%	29.7%	29.7%
Total Product Wastes†	62.0%	68.8%	71.8%	70.3%	73.4%	72.9%	70.9%	70.5%	70.5%	70.3%
Other Wastes										
Food	13.8%	10.6%	8.6%	11.5%	12.6%	13.0%	14.2%	14.5%	14.5%	14.9%
Yard Trimmings	22.7%	19.2%	18.1%	16.8%	12.5%	12.6%	13.3%	13.5%	13.4%	13.3%
Miscellaneous Inorganic Wastes	1.5%	1.5%	1.5%	1.4%	1.4%	1.5%	1.5%	1.5%	1.5%	1.5%
Total Other Wastes	38.0%	31.2%	28.2%	29.7%	26.6%	27.1%	29.1%	29.5%	29.5%	29.7%
Total MSW Recycled and Composted - %	100.0%	100.0%	100.0%	100.0%	100.0%	100.0%	100.0%	100.0%	100.0%	100.0%

* Generation before materials recycling, composting, combustion with energy recovery, or landfilling. Details may not add to totals due to rounding.

** Includes carbonated drinks and non-carbonated water, teas, flavored drinks, and ready-to-drink alcoholic coolers and cocktails.

‡ Includes milk, juice, and other products packaged in gable top cartons and liquid food aseptic cartons.

† Other than food products.

Neg. = Less than 5,000 tons or 0.05 percent.

Source: *U.S. EPA, Advancing Sustainable Materials Management: 2014 Tables and Figures, December 2016*

Table 24. Products Recycled and Composted* in Municipal Solid Waste, 1960 to 2014 (With Detail on Containers and Packaging)

(In thousands of tons)

Products	Thousands of Tons									
	1960	1970	1980	1990	2000	2005	2010	2012	2013	2014
Durable Goods	350	940	1,360	3,460	6,580	7,970	9,390	9,530	9,660	9,750
(Detail in Table 15)										
Nondurable Goods	2,390	3,730	4,670	8,800	17,560	19,770	19,190	17,270	16,410	17,180
(Detail in Table 19)										
Containers and Packaging										
Glass Packaging										
Beer and Soft Drink Bottles**	90	140	730	1,890	1,530	2,000	2,350	2,290	2,240	2,120
Wine and Liquor Bottles	10	10	20	210	430	250	540	620	600	570
Other Bottles & Jars	Neg.	Neg.	Neg.	520	920	340	240	300	310	300
Total Glass Packaging	100	150	750	2,620	2,880	2,590	3,130	3,210	3,150	2,990
Steel Packaging										
Beer and Soft Drink Cans	10	20	50	40	Neg.	Neg.				
Cans	20	60	150	590	1,530	1,340	1,540	1,310	1,320	1,180
Other Steel Packaging	Neg.	Neg.	Neg.	60	160	160	350	300	420	400
Total Steel Packaging	30	80	200	690	1,690	1,500	1,890	1,610	1,740	1,580
Aluminum Packaging										
Beer and Soft Drink Cans	Neg.	10	320	990	830	650	680	710	700	700
Other Cans	Neg.	Neg.	Neg.	Neg.	Neg.	Neg.	NA	NA	NA	NA
Foil and Closures	Neg.	Neg.	Neg.	20	30	40	NA	NA	NA	NA
Total Aluminum Pkg	Neg.	10	320	1,010	860	690	680	710	700	700
Paper & Paperboard Pkg										
Corrugated Boxes	2,520	2,760	6,390	11,530	20,330	22,100	24,690	26,810	26,590	27,280
Other Paper & Paperboard Pkg										
Gable Top/Aseptic Cartons‡			Neg.	Neg.	Neg.	Neg.	-	-	-	-
Folding Cartons			520	340	410	1,190	-	-	-	-
Other Paperboard Packaging			Neg.	Neg.	Neg.	Neg.	-	-	-	-
Bags and Sacks			Neg.	200	300	320	-	-	-	-
Wrapping Papers			Neg.	Neg.	Neg.	Neg.	-	-	-	-
Other Paper Packaging	220	350	300	Neg.	Neg.	Neg.	-	-	-	-
Subtotal Other Paper & Paperboard Pkg							2,160	2,110	2,360	2,210
Total Paper & Board Pkg	2,740	3,110	7,210	12,070	21,040	23,610	26,850	28,920	28,950	29,490
Plastics Packaging										
PET Bottles and Jars			10	140	380	590	780	860	900	910
HDPE Natural Bottles			Neg.	20	210	230	220	220	220	230
Other Containers	Neg.	Neg.	Neg.	20	170	140	300	310	330	360
Bags and Sacks										
Wraps										
Subtotal Bags, Sacks, and Wraps			Neg.	60	180	230	450	440	510	500
Other Plastics Packaging	Neg.	Neg.	Neg.	20	90	90	100	70	80	120
Total Plastics Packaging	Neg.	Neg.	10	260	1,030	1,280	1,850	1,900	2,040	2,120
Other Packaging										
Wood Packaging	Neg.	Neg.	Neg.	130	1,370	1,830	2,280	2,410	2,470	2,570
Other Misc. Packaging	Neg.	Neg.	Neg.	Neg.	Neg.	Neg.	Neg.	Neg.	Neg.	Neg.
Total Containers & Pkg	2,870	3,350	8,490	16,780	28,870	31,500	36,680	38,760	39,050	39,450
Total Product Wastes†	5,610	8,020	14,520	29,040	53,010	59,240	65,260	65,560	65,120	66,380

Source: *U.S. EPA, Advancing Sustainable Materials Management: 2014 Tables and Figures, December 2016*

Table 24. Products Recycled and Composted* in Municipal Solid Waste, 1960 to 2014 (With Detail on Containers and Packaging)

(In thousands of tons)

Products	Thousands of Tons									
	1960	1970	1980	1990	2000	2005	2010	2012	2013	2014
Other Wastes										
Food, Other^	Neg.	Neg.	Neg.	Neg.	680	690	970	1,740	1,840	1,940
Yard Trimmings	Neg.	Neg.	Neg.	4,200	15,770	19,860	19,200	19,590	20,600	21,080
Miscellaneous Inorganic Wastes	Neg.	Neg.	Neg.	Neg.	Neg.	Neg.	Neg.	Neg.	Neg.	Neg.
Total Other Wastes	Neg.	Neg.	Neg.	4,200	16,450	20,550	20,170	21,330	22,440	23,020
Total MSW Recycled and Composted - Weight	5,610	8,020	14,520	33,240	69,460	79,790	85,430	86,890	87,560	89,400

* Recycling and composting of postconsumer wastes; does not include converting/fabrication scrap. Details may not add to totals due to rounding.
** Includes carbonated drinks and non-carbonated water, teas, flavored drinks, and ready-to-drink alcoholic coolers and cocktails.
‡ Includes milk, juice, and other products packaged in gable top cartons and liquid food aseptic cartons.
† Other than food products.
^ Includes collection of soiled paper and mixed MSW for composting.
Neg. = Less than 5,000 tons or 0.05 percent. NA = Not Available - Detailed data not available.

Source: U.S. EPA, Advancing Sustainable Materials Management: 2014 Tables and Figures, December 2016

Table 25. Products Recycled and Composted* in Municipal Solid Waste, 1960 to 2014 (With Detail on Containers and Packaging)

(In percent of generation of each product)

Products	Percent of Generation of Each Product									
	1960	1970	1980	1990	2000	2005	2010	2012	2013	2014
Durable Goods	3.5%	6.4%	6.2%	11.6%	16.9%	17.7%	19.0%	18.7%	18.4%	18.5%
(Detail in Table 15)										
Nondurable Goods	13.8%	14.9%	13.6%	16.9%	27.4%	31.1%	36.0%	33.6%	31.8%	32.9%
(Detail in Table 19)										
Containers and Packaging										
Glass Packaging										
Beer and Soft Drink Bottles**	6.4%	2.5%	10.8%	33.5%	26.8%	30.6%	41.4%	41.0%	41.3%	39.5%
Wine and Liquor Bottles	Neg.	Neg.	Neg.	10.3%	22.5%	15.3%	31.8%	34.1%	34.5%	31.8%
Other Bottles & Jars	Neg.	Neg.	Neg.	12.5%	26.9%	14.8%	12.1%	15.0%	14.8%	14.7%
Total Glass Packaging	1.6%	1.3%	5.4%	22.1%	26.1%	24.8%	*33.4%*	*34.1%*	*34.0%*	*32.5%*
Steel Packaging										
Beer and Soft Drink Cans	1.6%	1.3%	9.6%	26.7%	Neg.	Neg.				
Cans	Neg.	1.7%	5.3%	23.2%	58.2%	62.9%	67.0%	70.8%	70.6%	70.7%
Other Steel Packaging	Neg.	Neg.	Neg.	30.0%	66.7%	66.7%	79.5%	78.9%	79.2%	80.0%
Total Steel Packaging	Neg.	1.5%	5.5%	23.9%	58.9%	63.3%	*69.0%*	*72.2%*	*72.5%*	*72.8%*
Aluminum Packaging										
Beer and Soft Drink Cans	Neg.	10.0%	37.6%	63.9%	54.6%	44.8%	49.6%	54.6%	55.1%	55.1%
Other Cans	Neg.	Neg.	Neg.	Neg.	Neg.	Neg.	NA	NA	NA	NA
Foil and Closures	Neg.	Neg.	Neg.	6.1%	7.9%	10.0%	NA	NA	NA	NA
Total Aluminum Pkg	Neg.	1.8%	25.2%	53.2%	44.1%	35.8%	*35.8%*	*38.4%*	*38.9%*	*38.7%*
Paper & Paperboard Pkg										
Corrugated Boxes	34.4%	21.6%	37.4%	48.0%	67.3%	71.5%	85.0%	90.9%	88.5%	89.5%
Other Paper & Paperboard Pkg										
Gable Top/Aseptic Cartons‡			Neg.	Neg.	Neg.	Neg.	-	-	-	-
Folding Cartons			Neg.	Neg.	7.0%	21.5%	-	-	-	-
Other Paperboard Packaging			Neg.	Neg.	Neg.	Neg.	-	-	-	-
Bags and Sacks			Neg.	Neg.	20.1%	28.6%	-	-	-	-
Wrapping Papers			Neg.	Neg.	Neg.	Neg.	-	-	-	-
Other Paper Packaging	7.5%	9.2%	35.3%	Neg.	Neg.	Neg.	-	-	-	-
Subtotal Other Paper & Paperboard Pkg							25.0%	24.7%	27.7%	25.6%
Total Paper & Board Pkg	19.4%	14.5%	27.4%	36.9%	52.7%	59.6%	*71.3%*	*76.1%*	*75.1%*	*75.4%*
Plastics Packaging										
PET Bottles and Jars			3.8%	32.6%	22.1%	23.2%	29.2%	30.8%	31.3%	31.2%
HDPE Natural Bottles			Neg.	3.8%	30.4%	28.8%	27.5%	28.2%	28.2%	29.5%
Other Containers	Neg.	Neg.	Neg.	1.4%	9.8%	9.9%	16.4%	16.8%	18.0%	19.5%
Bags and Sacks										
Wraps										
Subtotal Bags, Sacks, and Wraps			Neg.	2.4%	4.3%	5.2%	11.5%	11.5%	13.5%	12.3%
Other Plastics Packaging	Neg.	Neg.	Neg.	1.0%	3.2%	2.8%	2.2%	1.5%	1.7%	2.5%
Total Plastics Packaging	Neg.	Neg.	Neg.	3.8%	9.2%	10.3%	*13.5%*	*13.8%*	*14.6%*	*14.8%*
Other Packaging										
Wood Packaging	Neg.	Neg.	Neg.	1.6%	15.9%	19.8%	23.3%	25.1%	26.2%	26.5%
Other Misc. Packaging	Neg.	Neg.	Neg.	Neg.	Neg.	Neg.	Neg.	Neg.	Neg.	Neg.
Total Containers & Pkg	10.5%	7.7%	16.1%	26.0%	38.1%	41.3%	48.6%	51.5%	51.5%	51.5%
Total Product Wastes†	10.3%	9.6%	13.3%	19.8%	29.7%	32.0%	36.6%	36.9%	36.2%	36.6%

Source: *U.S. EPA, Advancing Sustainable Materials Management: 2014 Tables and Figures, December 2016*

Table 25. Products Recycled and Composted* in Municipal Solid Waste, 1960 to 2014 (With Detail on Containers and Packaging)

(In percent of generation of each product)

Products	Percent of Generation of Each Product									
	1960	1970	1980	1990	2000	2005	2010	2012	2013	2014
Other Wastes										
Food, Other^	Neg.	Neg.	Neg.	Neg.	2.2%	2.1%	2.7%	4.8%	5.0%	5.1%
Yard Trimmings	Neg.	Neg.	Neg.	12.0%	51.7%	61.9%	57.5%	57.7%	60.2%	61.1%
Miscellaneous Inorganic Wastes	Neg.	Neg.	Neg.	Neg.	Neg.	Neg.	Neg.	Neg.	Neg.	Neg.
Total Other Wastes	Neg.	Neg.	Neg.	6.8%	25.4%	29.9%	27.6%	28.7%	29.8%	29.9%
Total MSW Recycled and Composted - %	6.4%	6.6%	9.6%	16.0%	28.5%	31.4%	34.0%	34.5%	34.3%	34.6%

* Recycling and composting of postconsumer wastes; does not include converting/fabrication scrap. Details may not add to totals due to rounding.
** Includes carbonated drinks and non-carbonated water, teas, flavored drinks, and ready-to-drink alcoholic coolers and cocktails.
‡ Includes milk, juice, and other products packaged in gable top cartons and liquid food aseptic cartons.
† Other than food products.
^ Includes collection of soiled paper and mixed MSW for composting.
Neg. = Less than 5,000 tons or 0.05 percent. NA = Not Available - Detailed data not available.

Source: *U.S. EPA, Advancing Sustainable Materials Management: 2014 Tables and Figures, December 2016*

Table 26. Products Combusted with Energy Recovery* in Municipal Solid Waste, 1960 to 2014 (With Detail on Containers and Packaging) (In thousands of tons)

Products	Thousands of Tons									
	1960	1970	1980	1990	2000	2005	2010	2012	2013	2014
Durable Goods	0	60	440	4,480	6,260	6,750	7,070	8,150	8,490	8,410
(Detail in Table 16)										
Nondurable Goods	0	90	580	7,380	9,000	7,980	6,030	6,740	6,960	6,870
(Detail in Table 20)										
Containers and Packaging										
Glass Packaging										
Beer and Soft Drink Bottles**	0	20	120	640	810	830	590	650	630	640
Wine and Liquor Bottles	0	10	50	310	290	250	210	240	230	240
Other Bottles & Jars	0	20	100	620	490	350	310	330	350	340
Total Glass Packaging	0	50	270	1,570	1,590	1,430	1,110	1,220	1,210	1,220
Steel Packaging										
Beer and Soft Drink Cans	0	10	10	20	Neg.	Neg.	Neg.	Neg.	Neg.	Neg.
Cans	0	10	50	330	210	140	130	110	110	100
Other Steel Packaging	0	Neg.	Neg.	20	20	10	20	20	20	20
Total Steel Packaging	0	20	60	370	230	150	150	130	130	120
Aluminum Packaging										
Beer and Soft Drink Cans	0	Neg.	10	100	130	150	120	120	110	110
Other Cans	0	Neg.	Neg.	Neg.	10	10	10	20	20	30
Foil and Closures	0	Neg.	10	50	70	70	80	80	80	80
Total Aluminum Pkg	0	Neg.	20	150	210	230	210	220	210	220
Paper & Paperboard Pkg										
Corrugated Boxes	0	40	210	2,120	1,920	1,610	770	530	690	630
Other Paper & Paperboard Pkg										
Gable Top/Aseptic Cartons‡			20	90	110	90	-	-	-	-
Folding Cartons			70	670	1,050	790	-	-	-	-
Other Paperboard Packaging	0	20	Neg.	50	40	30	-	-	-	-
Bags and Sacks			70	380	230	150	-	-	-	-
Wrapping Papers			Neg.	20	Neg.	Neg.	-	-	-	-
Other Paper Packaging	0	10	10	170	320	250	-	-	-	-
Subtotal Other Paper & Paperboard Pkg							1,150	1,260	1,220	1,260
Total Paper & Board Pkg	0	70	380	3,500	3,670	2,920	1,920	1,790	1,910	1,890
Plastics Packaging										
PET Bottles and Jars			Neg.	50	260	350	330	380	390	390
HDPE Natural Bottles			Neg.	90	90	100	100	110	110	110
Other Containers	0	Neg.	20	240	300	230	270	300	300	290
Bags and Sacks										
Wraps										
Subtotal Bags, Sacks, and Wraps			30	410	780	770	620	660	650	700
Other Plastics Packaging	0	Neg.	20	340	530	570	770	880	920	900
Total Plastics Packaging	0	Neg.	70	1,130	1,960	2,020	2,090	2,330	2,370	2,390

Source: *U.S. EPA, Advancing Sustainable Materials Management: 2014 Tables and Figures, December 2016*

Table 26. Products Combusted with Energy Recovery* in Municipal Solid Waste, 1960 to 2014 (With Detail on Containers and Packaging)

(In thousands of tons)

Products	Thousands of Tons									
	1960	1970	1980	1990	2000	2005	2010	2012	2013	2014
Other Packaging										
Wood Packaging	0	10	80	1,370	1,400	1,350	1,330	1,420	1,370	1,390
Other Misc. Packaging	0	Neg.	Neg.	20	50	60	60	70	70	70
Total Containers & Pkg	0	150	880	8,110	9,110	8,160	6,870	7,180	7,270	7,300
Total Product Wastes†	0	300	1,900	19,970	24,370	22,890	19,970	22,070	22,720	22,580
Other Wastes										
Food	0	50	260	4,060	5,820	5,870	6,150	6,830	6,970	7,150
Yard Trimmings	0	90	550	5,240	2,860	2,220	2,510	2,830	2,690	2,630
Miscellaneous Inorganic Wastes	0	10	50	490	680	670	680	770	780	780
Total Other Wastes	0	150	860	9,790	9,360	8,760	9,340	10,430	10,440	10,560
Total MSW Combusted with Energy Recovery - Weight	0	450	2,760	29,760	33,730	31,650	29,310	32,500	33,160	33,140

* Products and materials combusted with energy recovery estimated at percentage total MSW after recovery for recycling and composting. In 2014, 19.6 percent of MSW after recycling and composting was combusted with energy recovery. Details may not add to totals due to rounding.

** Includes carbonated drinks and non-carbonated water, teas, flavored drinks, and ready-to-drink alcoholic coolers and cocktails.

‡ Includes milk, juice, and other products packaged in gable top cartons and liquid food aseptic cartons.

† Other than food products.

Neg. = Less than 5,000 tons or 0.05 percent. NA = Not Available - Detailed data not available.

Source: *U.S. EPA, Advancing Sustainable Materials Management: 2014 Tables and Figures, December 2016*

Table 27. Products Combusted with Energy Recovery* in Municipal Solid Waste, 1960 to 2014 (With Detail on Containers and Packaging)

(In percent of total combusted)

Products	Percent of Total Combusted									
	1960	1970	1980	1990	2000	2005	2010	2012	2013	2014
Durable Goods		13.3%	15.9%	15.1%	18.6%	21.3%	24.1%	25.1%	25.6%	25.4%
(Detail in Table 16)										
Nondurable Goods		19.9%	21.0%	24.8%	26.7%	25.2%	20.6%	20.7%	21.0%	20.7%
(Detail in Table 20)										
Containers and Packaging										
Glass Packaging										
Beer and Soft Drink Bottles**		4.5%	4.3%	2.2%	2.4%	2.6%	2.0%	2.0%	1.9%	2.0%
Wine and Liquor Bottles		2.2%	1.8%	1.0%	0.8%	0.8%	0.7%	0.8%	0.7%	0.7%
Other Bottles & Jars		4.4%	3.6%	2.1%	1.5%	1.1%	1.1%	1.0%	1.0%	1.0%
Total Glass Packaging		11.1%	9.8%	5.3%	4.7%	4.5%	3.8%	3.8%	3.6%	3.7%
Steel Packaging										
Beer and Soft Drink Cans		2.2%	0.4%	0.1%	Neg.	Neg.	Neg.	Neg.	Neg.	Neg.
Cans		2.2%	1.8%	1.1%	0.6%	0.5%	0.4%	0.3%	0.3%	0.3%
Other Steel Packaging		Neg.	Neg.	0.1%	0.1%	0.0%	0.1%	0.1%	0.1%	0.1%
Total Steel Packaging		4.4%	2.2%	1.2%	0.7%	0.5%	0.5%	0.4%	0.4%	0.4%
Aluminum Packaging										
Beer and Soft Drink Cans		Neg.	0.4%	0.3%	0.4%	0.5%	0.4%	0.4%	0.3%	0.3%
Other Cans		Neg.	Neg.	Neg.	Neg.	Neg.	Neg.	0.1%	0.1%	0.1%
Foil and Closures		Neg.	0.4%	0.2%	0.2%	0.2%	0.3%	0.2%	0.2%	0.2%
Total Aluminum Pkg		Neg.	0.7%	0.5%	0.6%	0.7%	0.7%	0.7%	0.6%	0.6%
Paper & Paperboard Pkg										
Corrugated Boxes		8.9%	7.6%	7.1%	5.7%	5.1%	2.6%	1.6%	2.1%	1.9%
Other Paper & Paperboard Pkg										
Gable Top/Aseptic Cartons‡			0.7%	0.3%	0.3%	0.3%	-	-	-	-
Folding Cartons			2.5%	2.3%	3.1%	2.5%	-	-	-	-
Other Paperboard Packaging		4.5%	Neg.	0.2%	0.1%	0.1%	-	-	-	-
Bags and Sacks			2.5%	1.3%	0.7%	0.4%	-	-	-	-
Wrapping Papers			Neg.	0.1%	Neg.	Neg.	-	-	-	-
Other Paper Packaging		2.2%	0.4%	0.6%	1.0%	0.8%	-	-	-	-
Subtotal Other Paper & Paperboard Pkg							3.9%	3.9%	3.7%	3.8%
Total Paper & Board Pkg		15.6%	13.8%	11.8%	10.9%	9.2%	6.6%	5.5%	5.8%	5.7%
Plastics Packaging										
PET Bottles and Jars			Neg.	0.2%	0.8%	1.1%	1.1%	1.2%	1.2%	1.2%
HDPE Natural Bottles			Neg.	0.3%	0.3%	0.3%	0.4%	0.3%	0.3%	0.3%
Other Containers		Neg.	0.7%	0.8%	0.9%	0.7%	0.9%	0.9%	0.9%	0.9%
Bags and Sacks										
Wraps										
Subtotal Bags, Sacks, and Wraps			1.1%	1.4%	2.3%	2.4%	2.1%	2.0%	2.0%	2.1%
Other Plastics Packaging		Neg.	0.7%	1.1%	1.5%	1.8%	2.6%	2.7%	2.8%	2.7%
Total Plastics Packaging		Neg.	2.5%	3.8%	5.8%	6.4%	7.1%	7.1%	7.2%	7.2%
Other Packaging										
Wood Packaging		2.2%	2.9%	4.6%	4.2%	4.3%	4.5%	4.4%	4.1%	4.2%
Other Misc. Packaging		Neg.	Neg.	0.1%	0.1%	0.2%	0.2%	0.2%	0.2%	0.2%
Total Containers & Pkg		33.3%	31.9%	27.3%	27.0%	25.8%	23.4%	22.1%	21.9%	22.0%
Total Product Wastes†		66.6%	68.8%	67.1%	72.3%	72.3%	68.1%	67.9%	68.5%	68.1%

Source: *U.S. EPA, Advancing Sustainable Materials Management: 2014 Tables and Figures, December 2016*

Table 27. Products Combusted with Energy Recovery* in Municipal Solid Waste, 1960 to 2014 (With Detail on Containers and Packaging)
(In percent of total combusted)

Products	Percent of Total Combusted									
	1960	1970	1980	1990	2000	2005	2010	2012	2013	2014
Other Wastes										
Food		11.1%	9.4%	13.6%	17.3%	18.5%	21.0%	21.0%	21.0%	21.6%
Yard Trimmings		20.0%	20.0%	17.6%	8.5%	7.0%	8.6%	8.7%	8.1%	7.9%
Miscellaneous Inorganic Wastes		2.3%	1.8%	1.7%	1.9%	2.1%	2.3%	2.4%	2.4%	2.4%
Total Other Wastes		33.4%	31.2%	32.9%	27.7%	27.7%	31.9%	32.1%	31.5%	31.9%
Total MSW Combusted with Energy Recovery - %		100.0%	100.0%	100.0%	100.0%	100.0%	100.0%	100.0%	100.0%	100.0%

* Products and materials combusted with energy recovery estimated at percentage total MSW after recovery for recycling and composting. In 2014, 19.6 percent of MSW after recycling and composting was combusted with energy recovery. Details may not add to totals due to rounding.

** Includes carbonated drinks and non-carbonated water, teas, flavored drinks, and ready-to-drink alcoholic coolers and cocktails.

‡ Includes milk, juice, and other products packaged in gable top cartons and liquid food aseptic cartons.

† Other than food products.

Neg. = Less than 5,000 tons or 0.05 percent. NA = Not Available - Detailed data not available.

Source: *U.S. EPA, Advancing Sustainable Materials Management: 2014 Tables and Figures, December 2016*

Table 28. Products Landfilled* in Municipal Solid Waste, 1960 to 2014 (With Detail on Containers and Packaging)

(In thousands of tons)

Products	Thousands of Tons									
	1960	1970	1980	1990	2000	2005	2010	2012	2013	2014
Durable Goods	9,570	13,660	20,000	21,870	26,030	30,340	32,890	33,210	34,370	34,490
(Detail in Table 17)										
Nondurable Goods	14,940	21,240	29,170	35,990	37,450	35,900	28,030	27,420	28,170	28,220
(Detail in Table 21)										
Containers and Packaging										
Glass Packaging										
Beer and Soft Drink Bottles**	1,310	5,420	5,890	3,110	3,370	3,710	2,730	2,640	2,550	2,610
Wine and Liquor Bottles	1,070	1,880	2,380	1,510	1,190	1,130	950	960	910	980
Other Bottles & Jars	3,710	4,420	4,680	3,020	2,010	1,600	1,440	1,370	1,440	1,400
Total Glass Packaging	*6,090*	*11,720*	*12,950*	*7,640*	*6,570*	*6,440*	*5,120*	*4,970*	*4,900*	*4,990*
Steel Packaging										
Beer and Soft Drink Cans	630	1,540	460	90	Neg.	Neg.	Neg.	Neg.	Neg.	Neg.
Cans	3,740	3,470	2,650	1,620	890	650	630	430	440	390
Other Steel Packaging	260	270	240	120	60	70	70	60	90	80
Total Steel Packaging	*4,630*	*5,280*	*3,350*	*1,830*	*950*	*720*	*700*	*490*	*530*	*470*
Aluminum Packaging										
Beer and Soft Drink Cans	Neg.	90	520	460	560	650	570	470	460	460
Other Cans	Neg.	60	40	20	40	70	60	100	100	100
Foil and Closures	170	410	370	260	280	290	380	350	330	330
Total Aluminum Pkg	*170*	*560*	*930*	*740*	*880*	*1,010*	*1,010*	*920*	*890*	*890*
Paper & Paperboard Pkg										
Corrugated Boxes	4,810	9,960	10,480	10,360	7,960	7,220	3,590	2,140	2,770	2,580
Other Paper & Paperboard Pkg										
Gable Top/Aseptic Cartons‡			770	420	440	410	-	-	-	-
Folding Cartons			3,230	3,290	4,360	3,550	-	-	-	-
Other Paperboard Packaging	3,840	4,810	230	240	160	130	-	-	-	-
Bags and Sacks			3,310	1,860	960	650	-	-	-	-
Wrapping Papers			200	90	Neg.	Neg.	-	-	-	-
Other Paper Packaging	2,720	3,450	540	850	1,350	1,150	-	-	-	-
Subtotal Other Paper & Paperboard Pkg							5,320	5,160	4,930	5,170
Total Paper & Board Pkg	*11,370*	*18,220*	*18,760*	*17,110*	*15,230*	*13,110*	*8,910*	*7,300*	*7,700*	*7,750*
Plastics Packaging										
PET Bottles and Jars			250	240	1,080	1,600	1,560	1,550	1,590	1,620
HDPE Natural Bottles			230	420	390	470	480	450	450	440
Other Containers	60	910	870	1,170	1,270	1,050	1,260	1,240	1,200	1,200
Bags and Sacks										
Wraps										
Subtotal Bags, Sacks, and Wraps			1,200	2,000	3,240	3,450	2,860	2,710	2,620	2,850
Other Plastics Packaging	60	1,180	770	1,680	2,220	2,550	3,580	3,600	3,710	3,700
Total Plastics Packaging	*120*	*2,090*	*3,320*	*5,510*	*8,200*	*9,120*	*9,740*	*9,550*	*9,570*	*9,810*
Other Packaging										
Wood Packaging	2,000	2,060	3,860	6,680	5,840	6,050	6,160	5,780	5,570	5,720
Other Misc. Packaging	120	130	130	130	190	220	280	280	290	290
Total Containers & Pkg	24,500	40,060	43,300	39,640	37,860	36,670	31,920	29,290	29,450	29,920
Total Product Wastes†	49,010	74,960	92,470	97,500	101,340	102,910	92,840	89,920	91,990	92,630

Source: *U.S. EPA, Advancing Sustainable Materials Management: 2014 Tables and Figures, December 2016*

Table 28. Products Landfilled* in Municipal Solid Waste, 1960 to 2014 (With Detail on Containers and Packaging)
(In thousands of tons)

Products	Thousands of Tons									
	1960	1970	1980	1990	2000	2005	2010	2012	2013	2014
Other Wastes										
Food	12,200	12,750	12,740	19,800	24,200	26,370	28,620	27,860	28,250	29,310
Yard Trimmings	20,000	23,110	26,950	25,560	11,900	9,990	11,690	11,540	10,910	10,790
Miscellaneous Inorganic Wastes	1,300	1,770	2,200	2,410	2,820	3,020	3,160	3,130	3,150	3,190
Total Other Wastes	33,500	37,630	41,890	47,770	38,920	39,380	43,470	42,530	42,310	43,290
Total MSW Landfilled - Weight	82,510	112,590	134,360	145,270	140,260	142,290	136,310	132,450	134,300	135,920

* Landfilling after recycling, composting, and combustion with energy recovery. Does not include construction & demolition debris, industrial process wastes, or certain other wastes. Details may not add to totals due to rounding.

** Includes carbonated drinks and non-carbonated water, teas, flavored drinks, and ready-to-drink alcoholic coolers and cocktails.

‡ Includes milk, juice, and other products packaged in gable top cartons and liquid food aseptic cartons.

† Other than food products.

Neg. = Less than 5,000 tons or 0.05 percent. NA = Not Available - Detailed data not available.

Source: U.S. EPA, *Advancing Sustainable Materials Management: 2014 Tables and Figures, December 2016*

Table 29. Products Landfilled* in Municipal Solid Waste, 1960 to 2014 (With Detail on Containers and Packaging)

(In percent of total landfilled)

Products	Percent of Total Landfilled									
	1960	1970	1980	1990	2000	2005	2010	2012	2013	2014
Durable Goods	11.6%	12.1%	14.9%	15.0%	18.6%	21.3%	24.1%	25.1%	25.6%	25.4%
(Detail in Table 17)										
Nondurable Goods	18.1%	18.9%	21.7%	24.8%	26.7%	25.2%	20.6%	20.7%	21.0%	20.8%
(Detail in Table 21)										
Containers and Packaging										
Glass Packaging										
Beer and Soft Drink Bottles**	1.6%	4.8%	4.4%	2.1%	2.4%	2.6%	2.0%	2.0%	1.9%	2.0%
Wine and Liquor Bottles	1.3%	1.7%	1.8%	1.0%	0.8%	0.8%	0.7%	0.8%	0.7%	0.7%
Other Bottles & Jars	4.5%	3.9%	3.5%	2.1%	1.5%	1.1%	1.1%	1.0%	1.0%	1.0%
Total Glass Packaging	*7.4%*	*10.4%*	*9.6%*	*5.3%*	*4.7%*	*4.5%*	*3.8%*	*3.8%*	*3.6%*	*3.7%*
Steel Packaging										
Beer and Soft Drink Cans	0.8%	1.4%	0.3%	0.1%	Neg.	Neg.	Neg.	Neg.	Neg.	Neg.
Cans	4.5%	3.1%	2.0%	1.1%	0.6%	0.5%	0.5%	0.3%	0.3%	0.3%
Other Steel Packaging	0.3%	0.2%	0.2%	0.1%	0.1%	0.0%	0.1%	0.1%	0.1%	0.1%
Total Steel Packaging	*5.6%*	*4.7%*	*2.5%*	*1.3%*	*0.7%*	*0.5%*	*0.6%*	*0.4%*	*0.4%*	*0.4%*
Aluminum Packaging										
Beer and Soft Drink Cans	Neg.	0.1%	0.4%	0.3%	0.4%	0.5%	0.4%	0.4%	0.3%	0.3%
Other Cans	Neg.	0.1%	0.0%	0.0%	Neg.	Neg.	Neg.	0.1%	0.1%	0.1%
Foil and Closures	0.2%	0.4%	0.3%	0.2%	0.2%	0.2%	0.3%	0.2%	0.2%	0.2%
Total Aluminum Pkg	*0.2%*	*0.5%*	*0.7%*	*0.5%*	*0.6%*	*0.7%*	*0.7%*	*0.7%*	*0.6%*	*0.6%*
Paper & Paperboard Pkg										
Corrugated Boxes	5.8%	8.8%	7.8%	7.1%	5.7%	5.1%	2.6%	1.6%	2.1%	1.9%
Other Paper & Paperboard Pkg										
Gable Top/Aseptic Cartons‡			0.6%	0.3%	0.3%	0.3%	-	-	-	-
Folding Cartons			2.4%	2.3%	3.1%	2.5%	-	-	-	-
Other Paperboard Packaging	4.7%	4.3%	0.2%	0.2%	0.1%	0.1%	-	-	-	-
Bags and Sacks			2.5%	1.3%	0.7%	0.4%	-	-	-	-
Wrapping Papers			0.1%	0.1%	Neg.	Neg.	-	-	-	-
Other Paper Packaging	3.3%	3.1%	0.4%	0.6%	1.0%	0.8%	-	-	-	-
Subtotal Other Paper & Paperboard Pkg							3.9%	3.9%	3.7%	3.8%
Total Paper & Board Pkg	*13.8%*	*16.2%*	*14.0%*	*11.8%*	*10.9%*	*9.2%*	*6.5%*	*5.5%*	*5.8%*	*5.7%*
Plastics Packaging										
PET Bottles and Jars			0.2%	0.2%	0.8%	1.1%	1.1%	1.2%	1.2%	1.2%
HDPE Natural Bottles			0.2%	0.3%	0.3%	0.3%	0.4%	0.3%	0.3%	0.3%
Other Containers	0.1%	0.8%	0.6%	0.8%	0.9%	0.7%	0.9%	0.9%	0.9%	0.9%
Bags and Sacks										
Wraps										
Subtotal Bags, Sacks, and Wraps			0.9%	1.4%	2.3%	2.4%	2.1%	2.0%	2.0%	2.1%
Other Plastics Packaging	0.1%	1.0%	0.6%	1.2%	1.5%	1.8%	2.6%	2.7%	2.8%	2.7%
Total Plastics Packaging	*0.1%*	*1.9%*	*2.5%*	*3.8%*	*5.8%*	*6.4%*	*7.1%*	*7.1%*	*7.2%*	*7.2%*
Other Packaging										
Wood Packaging	2.4%	1.8%	2.9%	4.6%	4.2%	4.3%	4.5%	4.4%	4.1%	4.2%
Other Misc. Packaging	0.1%	0.1%	0.1%	0.1%	0.1%	0.2%	0.2%	0.2%	0.2%	0.2%
Total Containers & Pkg	29.7%	35.6%	32.2%	27.3%	27.0%	25.8%	23.4%	22.1%	21.9%	22.0%
Total Product Wastes†	59.4%	66.6%	68.8%	67.1%	72.3%	72.3%	68.1%	67.9%	68.5%	68.2%
Other Wastes										
Food	14.8%	11.3%	9.5%	13.6%	17.3%	18.5%	21.0%	21.0%	21.0%	21.6%
Yard Trimmings	24.2%	20.5%	20.1%	17.6%	8.5%	7.0%	8.6%	8.7%	8.1%	7.9%
Miscellaneous Inorganic Wastes	1.6%	1.6%	1.6%	1.7%	1.9%	2.2%	2.3%	2.4%	2.4%	2.3%
Total Other Wastes	40.6%	33.4%	31.2%	32.9%	27.7%	27.7%	31.9%	32.1%	31.5%	31.8%
Total MSW Landfilled - %	100.0%	100.0%	100.0%	100.0%	100.0%	100.0%	100.0%	100.0%	100.0%	100.0%

* Landfilling after recycling, composting, and combustion with energy recovery. Does not include construction & demolition debris, industrial process wastes, or certain other wastes. Details may not add to totals due to rounding.

** Includes carbonated drinks and non-carbonated water, teas, flavored drinks, and ready-to-drink alcoholic coolers and cocktails.

‡ Includes milk, juice, and other products packaged in gable top cartons and liquid food aseptic cartons.

† Other than food products.

Neg. = Less than 5,000 tons or 0.05 percent. NA = Not Available - Detailed data not available.

Source: *U.S. EPA, Advancing Sustainable Materials Management: 2014 Tables and Figures, December 2016*

Table 30. Selected Examples of Source Reduction Practices

Source Reduction Practice	MSW Product Categories			
	Durable Goods	Nondurable Goods	Containers & Packaging	Organics (Wood, Yard Waste, Food, etc.)
Product or Packaging Redesign				
Materials reduction	▪ Downgauge metals in appliances	▪ Paperless purchase orders ▪ Concentrated products	▪ Container lightweighting ▪ Right size packaging ▪ Eliminate unnecessary layers of packaging ▪ Refillable/reusable containers, including use of flexible pouches for refills for rigid containers	▪ Xeriscaping ▪ Just in time ordering / inventory control ▪ Adjust menus to reduce frequently uneaten or wasted items
Materials substitution	▪ Use of composites in appliances and electronic circuitry		▪ Replace rigid or heavy packaging with lighter or more compact options, e.g., cereal in bags. coffee in brick packs ▪ Use life cycle data to choose material with lower lifecycle impact	
Lengthen Life	▪ High mileage tires ▪ Electronic components reduce moving parts	▪ Regular servicing ▪ Consider purchasing warranties to make repair more affordable ▪ Extend warranties	▪ Design for secondary use ▪ Design for upgrades (e.g., add computer memory or processing capacity, battery upgrades) ▪ Reusable packaging	▪ Clearer label information on food expiration date ▪ Avoid spoilage by changing: – Packaging – Storage and transportation – Supply chain management
Consumer Practices				
	▪ Purchase long lived products ▪ Regular servicing ▪ Repair ▪ Buying less stuff	▪ Repair ▪ Duplex printing ▪ Sharing ▪ Reduce unwanted mail ▪ Purchasing concentrated products ▪ Buying less stuff	▪ Purchasing products in bulk (less packaging) ▪ Reusable bags and containers ▪ Buying less stuff	▪ Food donation ▪ Avoid spoilage by monitoring and tracking food and purchases and use ▪ Reduce over-purchasing ▪ Proper food storage and preparation ▪ Repurposing (e.g., older bread can be made into croutons) ▪ Backyard composting ▪ Vermi-composting ▪ Grasscycling
Reuse				
By Design	▪ Document materials and methods for disassembly/ repair/reuse ▪ Use materials and systems that exhibit modularity, and standardization to facilitate reuse and repair – Minimize connections between parts and/or make connections more accessible for ease of repair and replacement of parts	▪ Reusable shipping or mailing envelopes	▪ Reusable pallets ▪ Returnable secondary packaging ▪ Reusable/refillable dispensers for cleaning products ▪ Reusable service ware in food service ▪ Use durable reusable water bottles instead of disposable bottles	

Source: *U.S. EPA, Advancing Sustainable Materials Management: 2014 Tables and Figures, December 2016*

Table 30. Selected Examples of Source Reduction Practices

Source Reduction Practice	MSW Product Categories			
	Durable Goods	Nondurable Goods	Containers & Packaging	Organics (Wood, Yard Waste, Food, etc.)
	– Mechanical connections with bolts and screws instead of glues, to facilitate repair – Minimize connections to increase ease of repair or part replacement – Provide adequate tolerances to allow for removal and replacement or repair of parts without affecting adjacent components			
Secondary	▪ Borrow or rent for temporary use ▪ Give to charity ▪ Buy or sell at garage sales	▪ Donate clothing, books ▪ Waste paper scratch pads	▪ Loosefill ▪ Grocery sacks ▪ Dairy containers ▪ Glass and plastic bottles and jars	
Reduce/Eliminate Toxins				
	▪ Eliminate PCBs	▪ Soy or waterbased inks ▪ Waterbased solvents ▪ Reduce mercury	▪ Replace lead foil on wine bottles ▪ Replace BPA-containing plastic products, liners, and coatings with alternative materials	

Source: *U.S. EPA, Advancing Sustainable Materials Management: 2014 Tables and Figures, December 2016*

Table 31. Residential Food Collection and Composting Programs in the U.S., 2014

State	Households Served	State	Households Served
California	1,339,076	New York	101,306
Colorado	54,113	Ohio	73,889
Iowa	39,630	Oregon	216,686
Maryland	18,350	Pennsylvania	580
Massachusetts	13,050	Texas	134,000
Michigan	63,000	Vermont	2,700
Minnesota	85,752	Washington	682,436
New Jersey	9,600	Wisconsin	600
Total U.S. Households Served			**2,848,368**
Total U.S. Households			**117,259,427** **2.4%**

BioCycle January 2015. Residential Food Waste Collection in the U.S. — *BioCycle* Nationwide Survey. Additional web search to supplement *BioCycle* survey.

Source: *U.S. EPA, Advancing Sustainable Materials Management: 2014 Tables and Figures, December 2016*

Table 32. Material Recovery Facilities (MRF), 2014*

Region	Number	Estimated Throughput (tpd)
NORTHEAST	175	29,792
SOUTH	238	45,375
MIDWEST	231	28,003
WEST	153	37,176
U.S. Total	**797**	**140,346**

*Number of facilities and throughput include bale and ship operations receiving fiber, mainly OCC, that bale and ship with no additional processing.
Source: Governmental Advisory Associates, Inc. Data provided December 2014.

Source: *U.S. EPA, Advancing Sustainable Materials Management: 2014 Tables and Figures, December 2016*

Table 33. Municipal Waste-To-Energy Projects, 2014

Region	Number Operational	Design Capacity (tpd)
NORTHEAST	38	44,415
SOUTH	21	32,004
MIDWEST	14	11,524
WEST	7	7,310
U.S. Total*	80	95,253

* Excludes 4 inactive facilities (representing another 996 tpd capacity).
WTE includes mass burn, modular, and refuse-derived fuel combustion facilities.
Source: "The 2014 ERC Directory of Waste-to-Energy Facilities." Energy Recovery Council (ERC). May 2014.

Source: *U.S. EPA, Advancing Sustainable Materials Management: 2014 Tables and Figures, December 2016*

Table 34. Landfill Facilities, 2014

Region	Number of Landfills
NORTHEAST	166
SOUTH	680
MIDWEST	381
WEST	729
U.S. Total	1,908

Source: State environmental websites.

Source: *U.S. EPA, Advancing Sustainable Materials Management: 2014 Tables and Figures, December 2016*

Table 35. Generation, Recycling, Composting, Combustion with Energy Recovery, and Landfilling of Municipal Solid Waste, 1960 to 2014

(In thousands of tons and percent of total generation)

	Thousands of Tons									
	1960	1970	1980	1990	2000	2005	2010	2012	2013	2014
Generation	88,120	121,060	151,640	208,270	243,450	253,730	251,050	251,840	255,020	258,460
Recycling	5,610	8,020	14,520	29,040	53,010	59,240	65,260	65,560	65,120	66,380
Composting*	Neg.	Neg.	Neg.	4,200	16,450	20,550	20,170	21,330	22,440	23,020
Combustion with energy recovery**	0	450	2,760	29,760	33,730	31,650	29,310	32,500	33,160	33,140
Discards to landfill, other disposal†	82,510	112,590	134,360	145,270	140,260	142,290	136,310	132,450	134,300	135,920
	Pounds per Person per Day									
	1960	1970	1980	1990	2000	2005	2010	2012	2013	2014
Generation	2.68	3.25	3.66	4.57	4.74	4.69	4.45	4.40	4.42	4.44
Recycling	0.17	0.22	0.35	0.64	1.03	1.10	1.16	1.14	1.13	1.14
Composting*	Neg.	Neg.	Neg.	0.09	0.32	0.38	0.36	0.37	0.39	0.40
Combustion with energy recovery**	0.00	0.01	0.07	0.65	0.66	0.59	0.52	0.57	0.57	0.57
Discards to landfill, other disposal†	2.51	3.02	3.24	3.19	2.73	2.62	2.41	2.32	2.33	2.33
Population (thousands)	179,979	203,984	227,255	249,907	281,422	296,410	309,051	313,914	316,129	318,857

	Percent of Total Generation									
	1960	1970	1980	1990	2000	2005	2010	2012	2013	2014
Generation	100.0%	100.0%	100.0%	100.0%	100.0%	100.0%	100.0%	100.0%	100.0%	100.0%
Recycling	6.4%	6.6%	9.6%	14.0%	21.8%	23.3%	26.0%	26.0%	25.5%	25.7%
Composting*	Neg.	Neg.	Neg.	2.0%	6.7%	8.1%	8.0%	8.5%	8.8%	8.9%
Combustion with energy recovery**	0.0%	0.3%	1.8%	14.2%	13.9%	12.5%	11.7%	12.9%	13.0%	12.8%
Landfilling and other disposal†	93.6%	93.1%	88.6%	69.8%	57.6%	56.1%	54.3%	52.6%	52.7%	52.6%

* Composting of yard trimmings, food and other MSW organic material. Does not include backyard composting.

** Includes combustion with energy recovery of MSW in mass burn or refuse-derived fuel form, and combustion with energy recovery of source separated materials in MSW (e.g., wood pallets and tire-derived fuel). 2014 includes 29,540 MSW, 520 wood, and 3,080 tires (1,000 tons).

† Landfilling after recycling and composting minus combustion with energy recovery. Includes combustion without energy recovery.

Details may not add to totals due to rounding.

Source: *U.S. EPA, Advancing Sustainable Materials Management: 2014 Tables and Figures, December 2016*

Figure 1. Municipal Solid Waste in the Universe of Subtitle D Wastes

Subtitle D Wastes

The Subtitle D Waste included in this report as Municipal Solid Waste (MSW), which includes:

- Containers and packaging such as soft drink bottles and corrugated boxes
- Durable goods such as furniture and appliances
- Nondurable goods such as newspapers, trash bags, and clothing
- Other wastes such as food and yard trimmings.

Subtitle D Wastes not included as MSW in this report are:

- Municipal sludges
- Industrial nonhazardous process wastes
- Construction and demolition debris*
- Land clearing debris
- Transportation parts and equipment
- Agricultural wastes
- Oil and gas wastes
- Mining wastes
- Auto bodies
- Fats, grease, and oils

*Combustion and demolition debris generation is included in this report, but is outside of the scope of MSW.

Source: *U.S. EPA, Advancing Sustainable Materials Management: 2014 Tables and Figures, December 2016*

Figure 2. Definition of Terms

The materials flow methodology produces an estimate of total municipal solid waste (MSW) generation in the United States, by material categories and by product categories.

The term ***generation*** as used in this report refers to the weight of materials and products as they enter the waste management system from residential, commercial, institutional and industrial sources and before recycling, composting, combustion or landfilling take place. Preconsumer (industrial) scrap is not included in the generation estimates. Source reduction activities (e.g., backyard composting of yard trimmings) take place ahead of generation.

Source reduction as used in this report refers to activities that reduce the amount of wastes before they enter the municipal solid waste management system. Reuse is a source reduction activity involving the recovery or reapplication of a package, used product, or material in a manner that retains its original form or identity. Reuse of products such as refillable glass bottles, reusable plastic food storage containers, or refurbished wood pallets is considered to be source reduction, not recycling.

Recycling as used in this report is defined as the recovery of useful materials, such as paper, glass, plastic, metals, construction and demolition (C&D) debris and organics from the waste stream (e.g. MSW), along with the transformation of the materials to make new products to reduce the amount of virgin raw materials needed to meet consumer demands. For recycled products, recycling equals reported purchases of postconsumer collected material (e.g., glass cullet, old newspapers) plus net exports (if any) of the material. Thus, recycling of old corrugated containers (OCC) is the sum of OCC purchases by paper mills plus net exports of OCC. If recycling as reported by a data source includes converting or fabrication (preconsumer) scrap, the preconsumer scrap is not counted towards the recycling estimates in this report. Imported secondary materials are not counted in recycling estimates in this report. For some materials, additional uses, such as glass used for highway construction or newspapers used to make insulation, are added into the recycling totals.

Composting is the decomposition of organic materials by aerobic microorganisms. Composting facilities manage the amount of moisture, amount of oxygen and mixture of organic materials for optimal composting conditions. The composting process emits heat, water vapor and biogenic carbon dioxide, reducing the raw organic materials in mass and volume to create compost.[1] Composting of materials as estimated in this report includes yard trimmings, food waste and mixed MSW containing food waste.

Combustion with energy recovery, often called "waste-to-energy," as used in this report refers to confined and controlled burning with energy recovery, which not only decreases the volume of solid waste destined for landfills, but can also recover energy from the waste burning process.

Landfilling as used in this report refers to the MSW remaining after recycling, composting and combustion with energy recovery. These materials presumably would be landfilled in a discrete area of land or excavation that receives household waste. Some MSW however, is littered, stored or disposed onsite, or burned onsite, particularly in rural areas. No good estimates for these other disposal practices are available, but the total amounts of MSW involved are presumed to be small.

For the analysis of municipal solid waste in this report, products are divided into three basic categories: durable goods, nondurable goods, and containers and packaging. The durable goods and nondurable goods categories generally follow the definitions of the U.S. Department of Commerce.

Durable goods are those products that last three years or more. Products in this category include major and small appliances, furniture and furnishings, carpets and rugs, tires, lead-acid batteries, consumer electronics, and other miscellaneous durables.

Nondurable goods are those products that last less than three years. Products in this category include newspapers, books, magazines, office papers, directories, mail, other commercial printing, tissue paper and towels, paper and plastic plates and cups, trash bags, disposable diapers, clothing and footwear, towels, sheets and pillowcases, other nonpackaging paper, and other miscellaneous nondurables.

Containers and packaging are assumed to be discarded the same year the products they contain are purchased. Products in this category include bottles, containers, corrugated boxes, milk cartons, folding cartons, bags, sacks, and wraps, wood packaging, and other miscellaneous packaging.

---

[1] Platt, B., Goldstein, N. 2014. State of Composting in the U.S. *BioCycle* 55(6): 19. http://www.biocycle.net/2014/07/16/state-of-composting-in-the-us/.

Source: *U.S. EPA, Advancing Sustainable Materials Management: 2014 Tables and Figures, December 2016*

Figure 3. Paper and Paperboard Products Generated in MSW, 2014

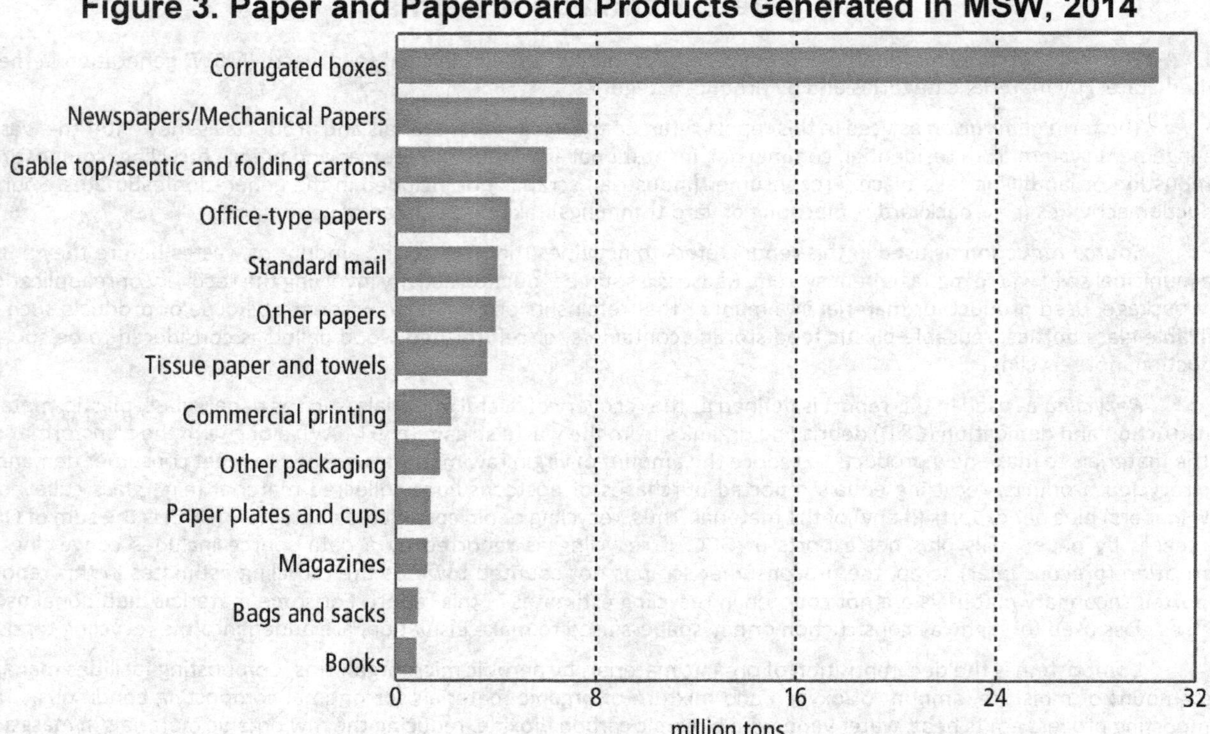

Figure 4. Paper and Paperboard Generation and Recycling, 1960 to 2014

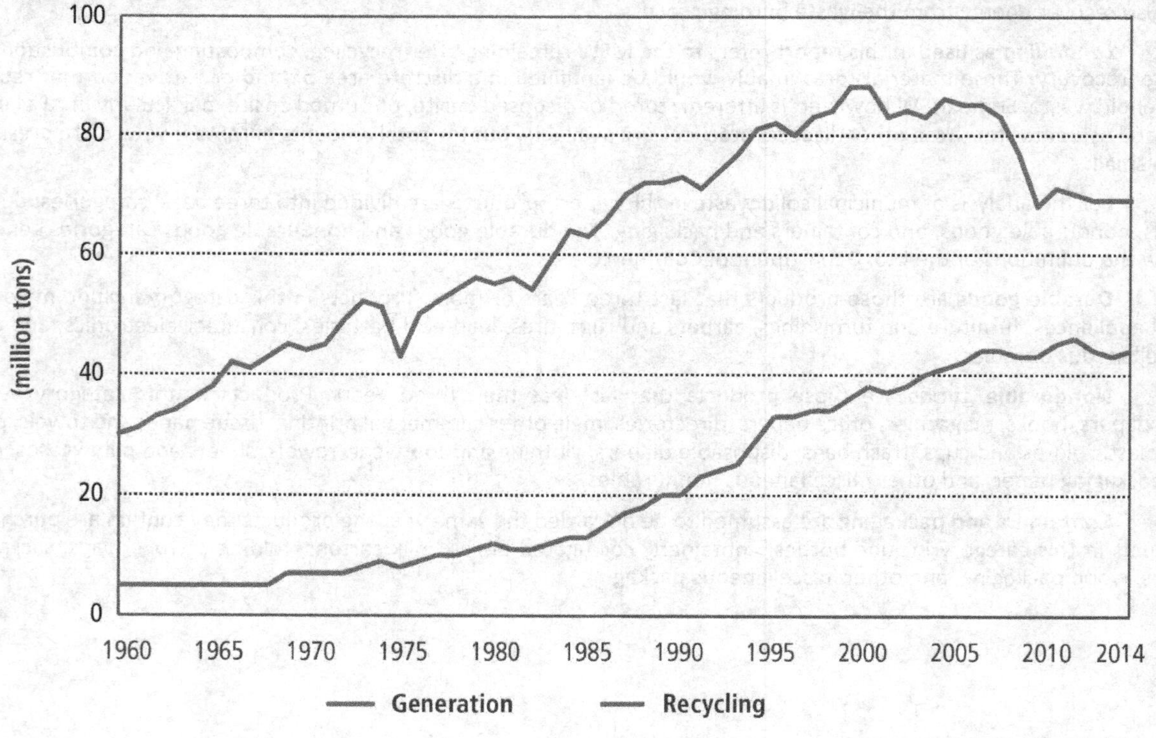

Source: U.S. EPA, *Advancing Sustainable Materials Management: 2014 Tables and Figures, December 2016*

Figure 5. Glass Products Generated in MSW, 2014

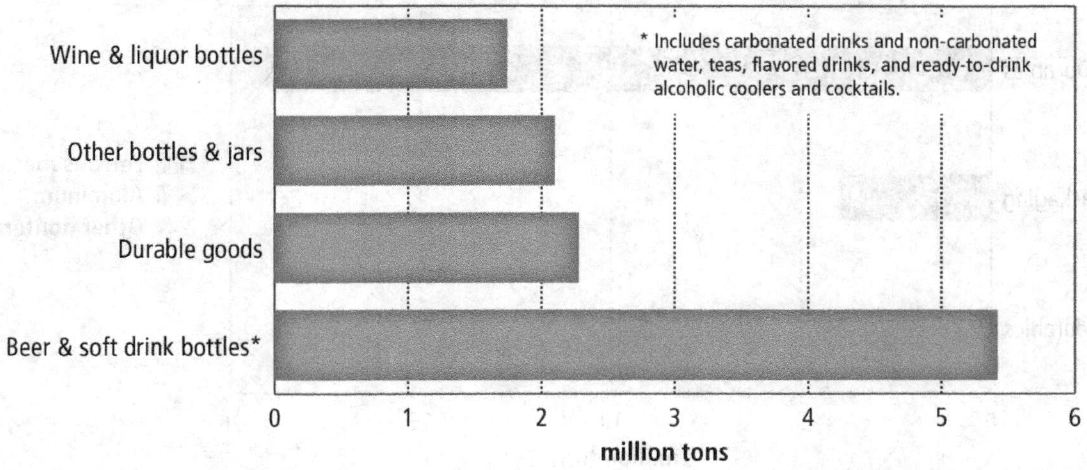

Wine & liquor bottles
Other bottles & jars
Durable goods
Beer & soft drink bottles*

0 1 2 3 4 5 6
million tons

* Includes carbonated drinks and non-carbonated water, teas, flavored drinks, and ready-to-drink alcoholic coolers and cocktails.

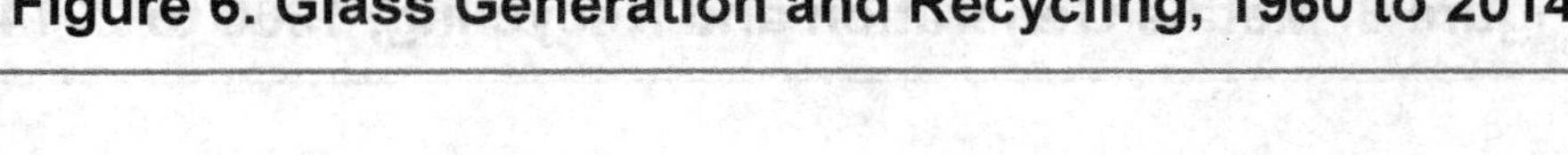

Figure 6. Glass Generation and Recycling, 1960 to 2014

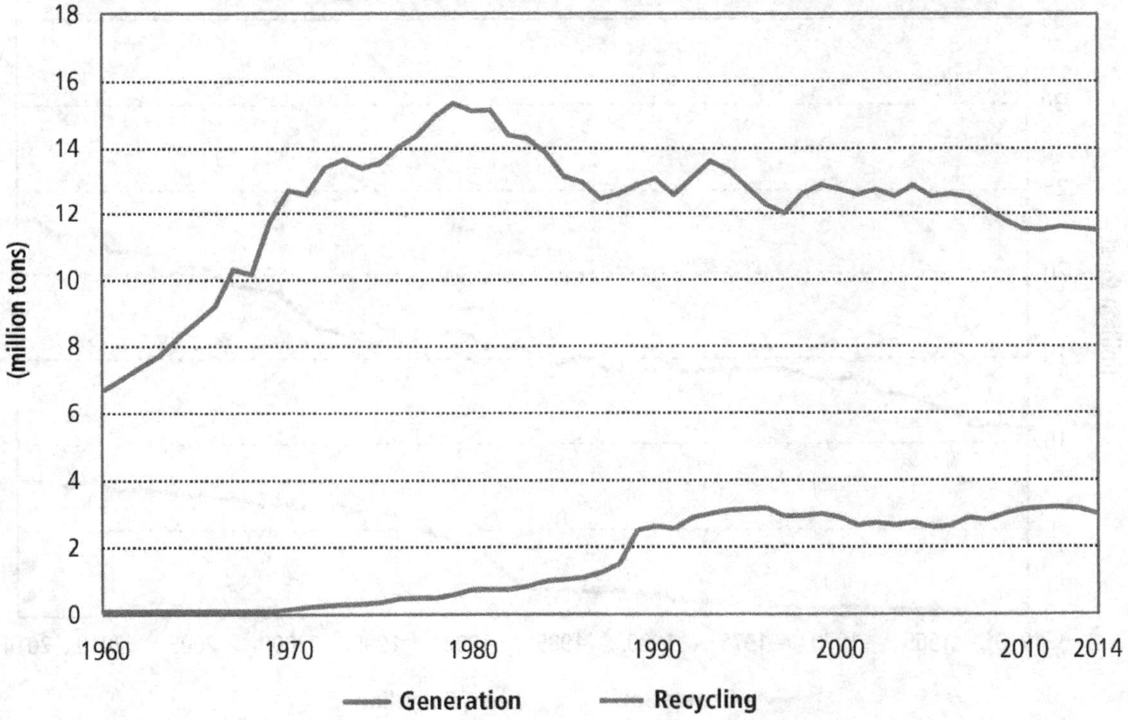

(million tons)
18 16 14 12 10 8 6 4 2 0
1960 1970 1980 1990 2000 2010 2014

Generation — Recycling

Source: U.S. EPA, *Advancing Sustainable Materials Management: 2014 Tables and Figures, December 2016*

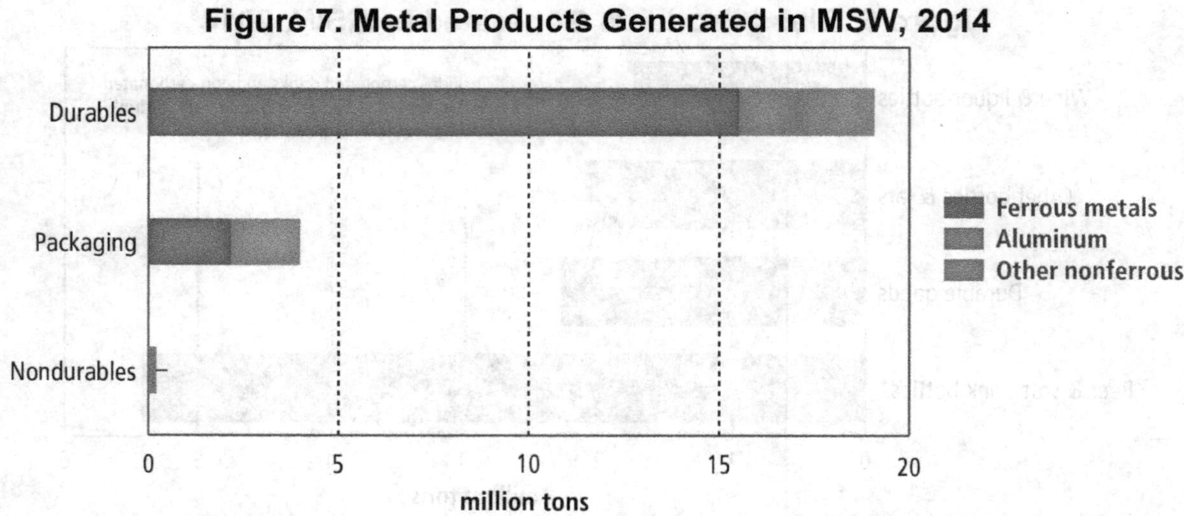

Figure 7. Metal Products Generated in MSW, 2014

Durables
Packaging
Nondurables
0
5
10
15
20
million tons
Ferrous metals
Aluminum
Other nonferrous

Figure 8. Metals Generation and Recycling, 1960 to 2014

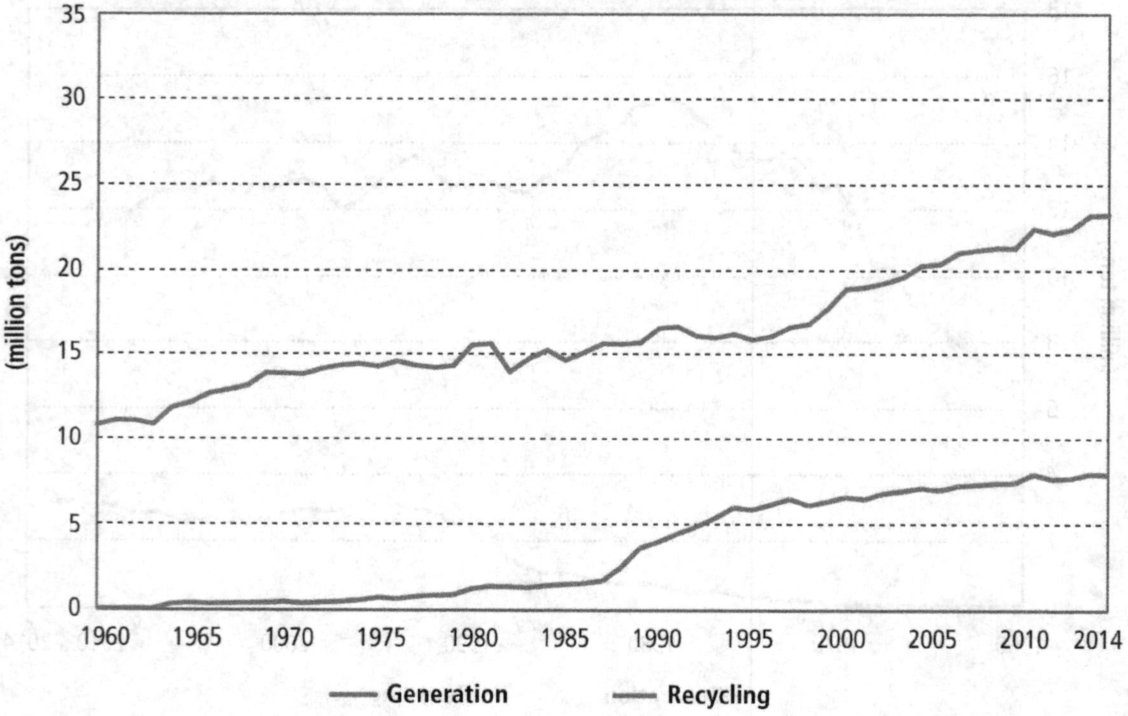

35
30
25
20
15
10
5
0
(million tons)
1960
1965
1970
1975
1980
1985
1990
1995
2000
2005
2010
2014
Generation
Recycling

Source: *U.S. EPA, Advancing Sustainable Materials Management: 2014 Tables and Figures, December 2016*

Figure 9. Plastics Products Generated in MSW, 2014

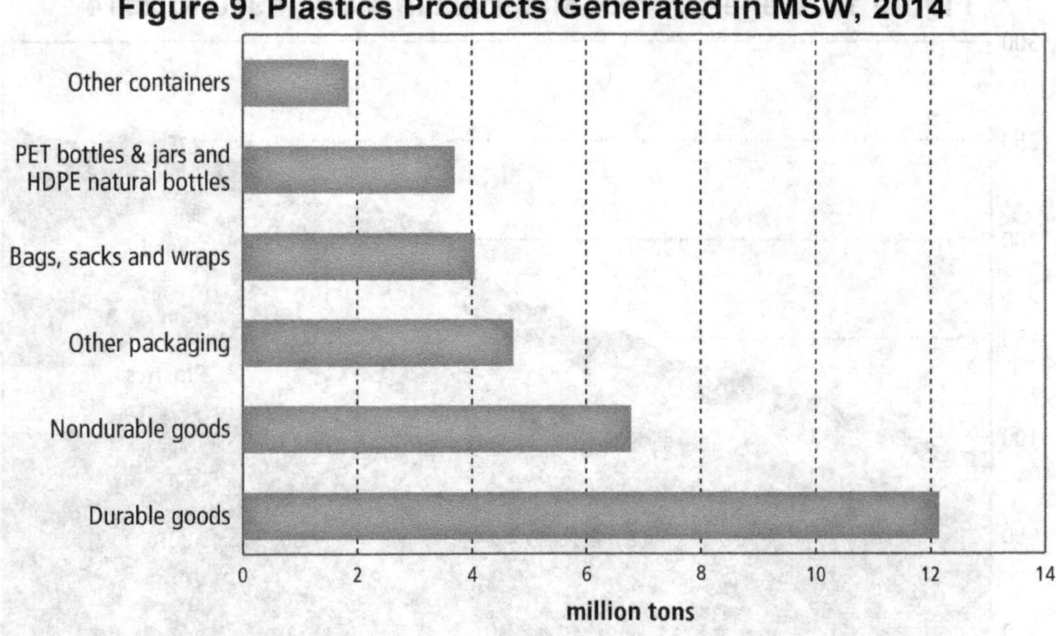

Figure 10. Plastics Generation and Recycling, 1960 to 2014

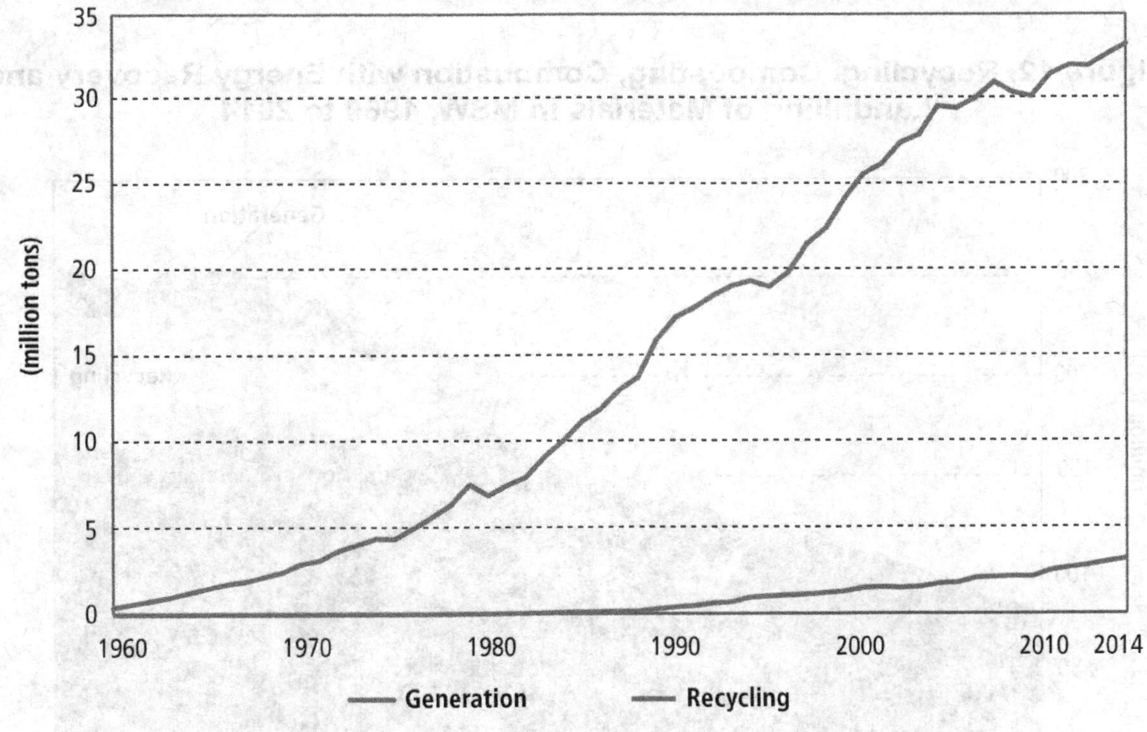

Source: *U.S. EPA, Advancing Sustainable Materials Management: 2014 Tables and Figures, December 2016*

Figure 11. Generation of Materials in MSW, 1960 to 2014

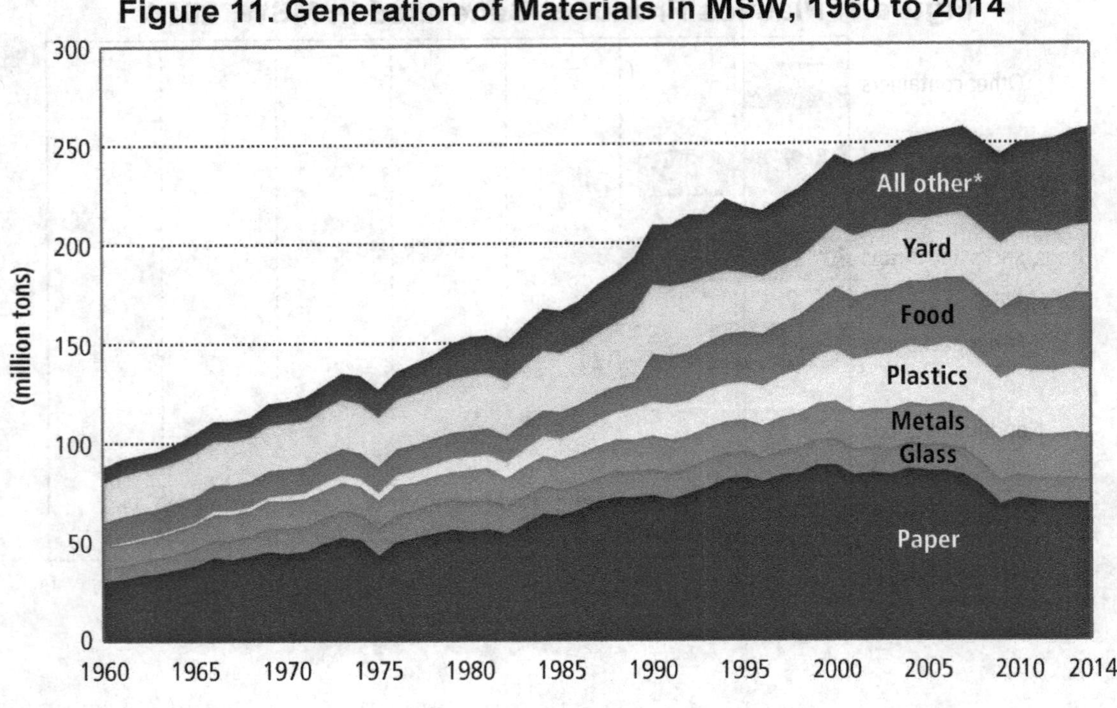

* "All other" includes primarily wood, rubber and leather, and textiles.

Figure 12. Recycling, Composting, Combustion with Energy Recovery and Landfilling of Materials in MSW, 1960 to 2014

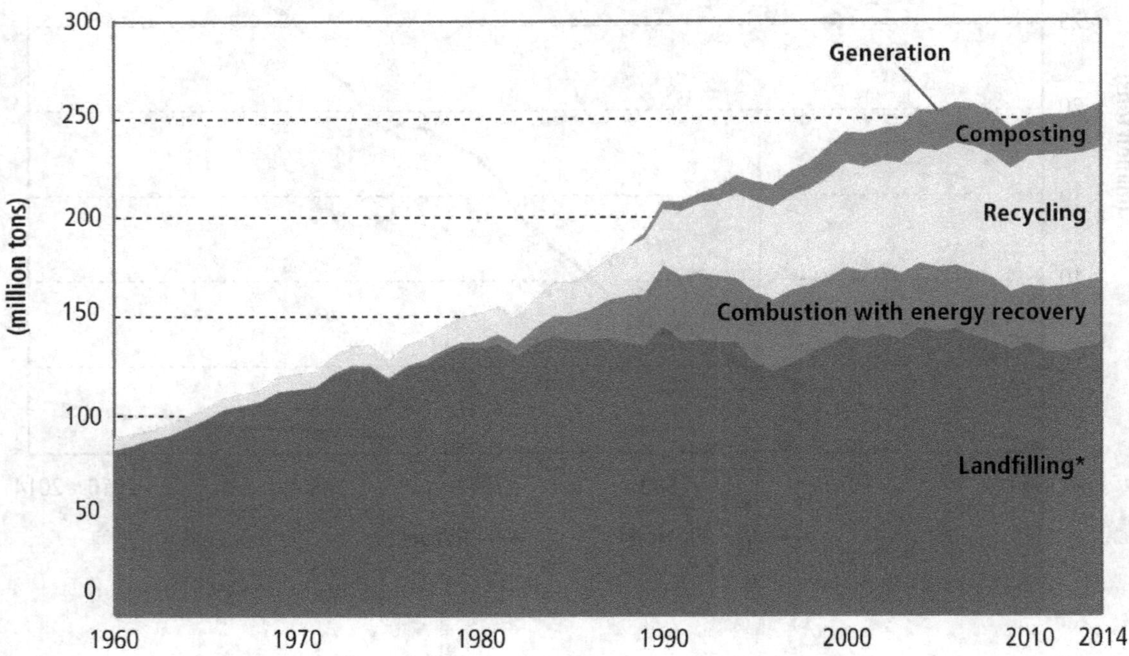

*Landfilling after composting, recycling and combustion with energy recovery. Includes combustion without energy recovery.

Source: *U.S. EPA, Advancing Sustainable Materials Management: 2014 Tables and Figures, December 2016*

Figure 13. Materials Recycling and Composting in MSW,* 2014
(89.4 Million tons)

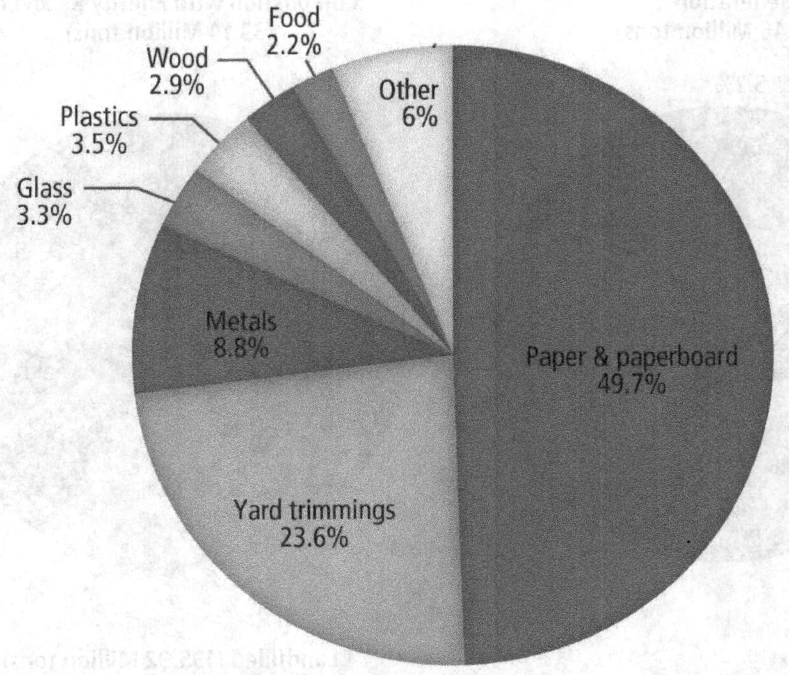

* In percent by weight of total recycling and composting

Source: *U.S. EPA, Advancing Sustainable Materials Management: 2014 Tables and Figures, December 2016*

Figure 14. Materials Generated, Combusted with Energy Recovery and Landfilled in MSW, 2014

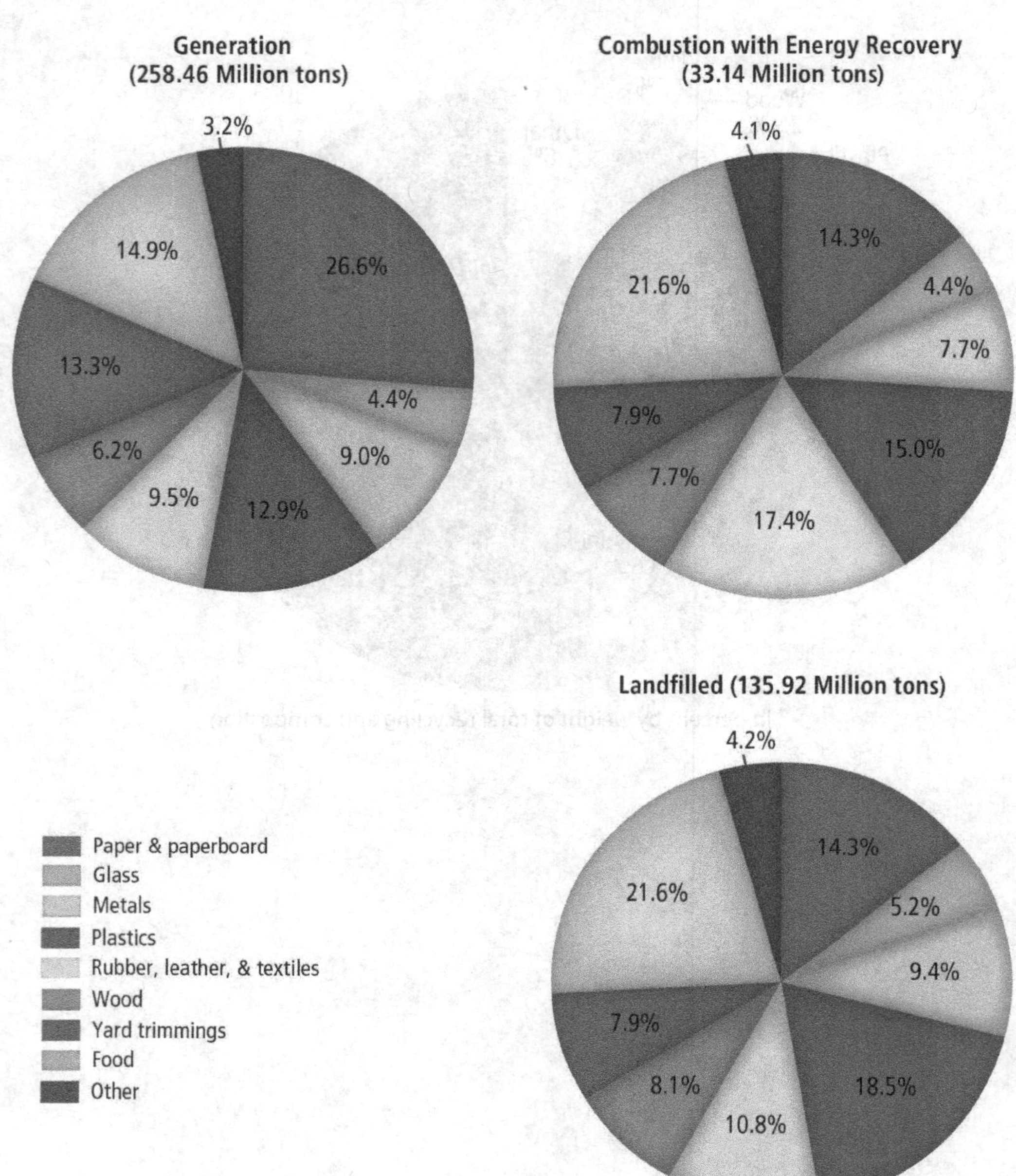

Source: U.S. EPA, Advancing Sustainable Materials Management: 2014 Tables and Figures, December 2016

Figure 15. Generation of Products in MSW, 1960 to 2014

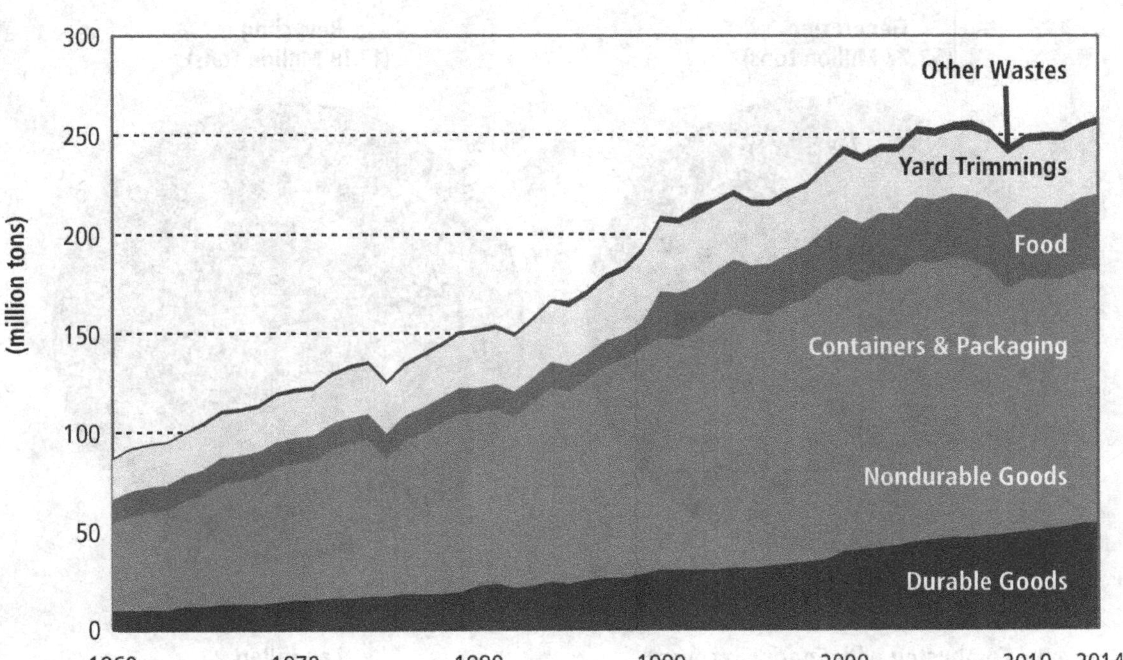

Source: *U.S. EPA, Advancing Sustainable Materials Management: 2014 Tables and Figures, December 2016*

Figure 16. Nondurable Goods Generated, Recycled, Combusted with Energy Recovery and Landfilled in Municipal Solid Waste, 2014

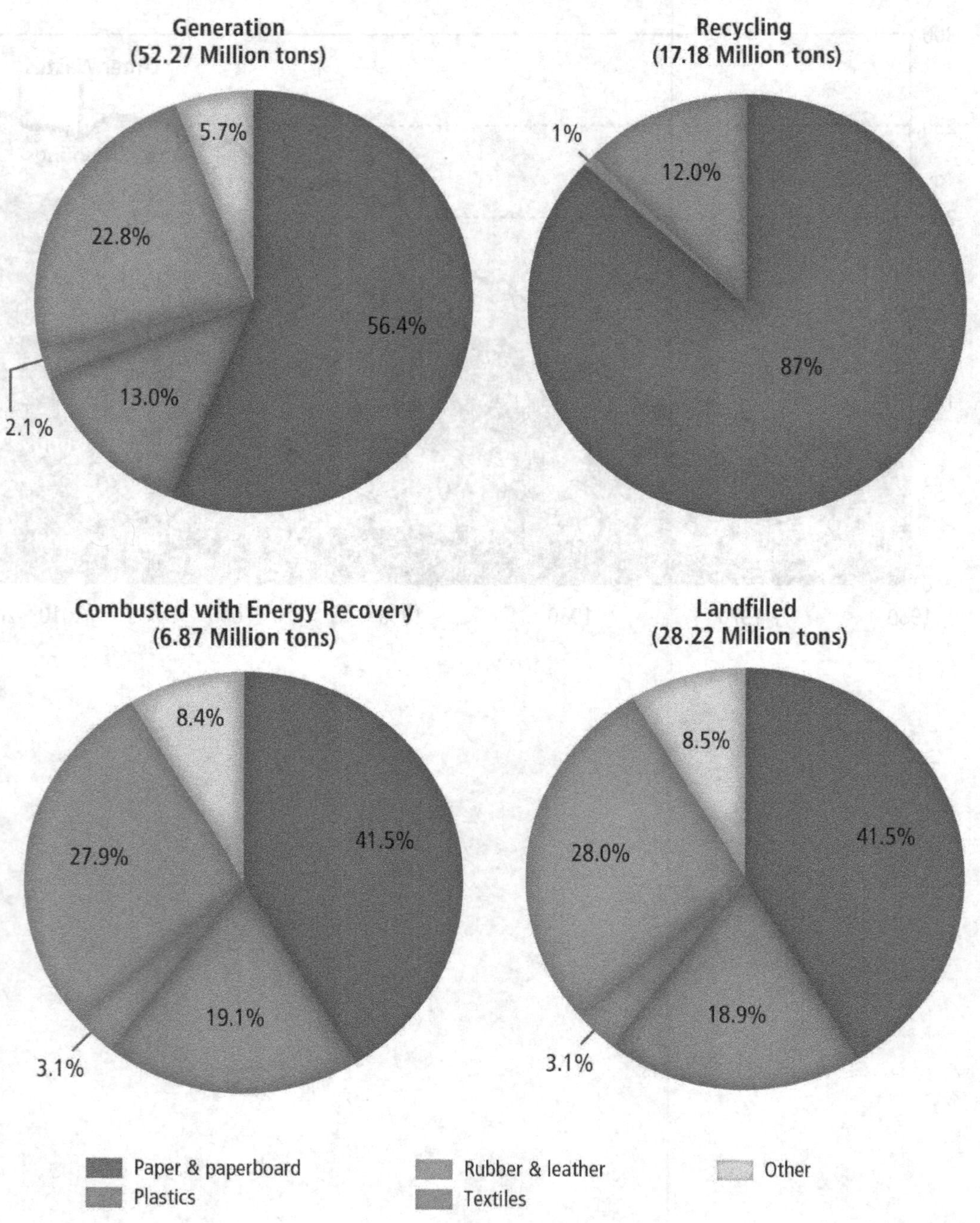

Source: *U.S. EPA, Advancing Sustainable Materials Management: 2014 Tables and Figures, December 2016*

Figure 17. Containers and Packaging Materials Generated, Recycled, Combusted with Energy Recovery and Landfilled in Municipal Solid Waste, 2014

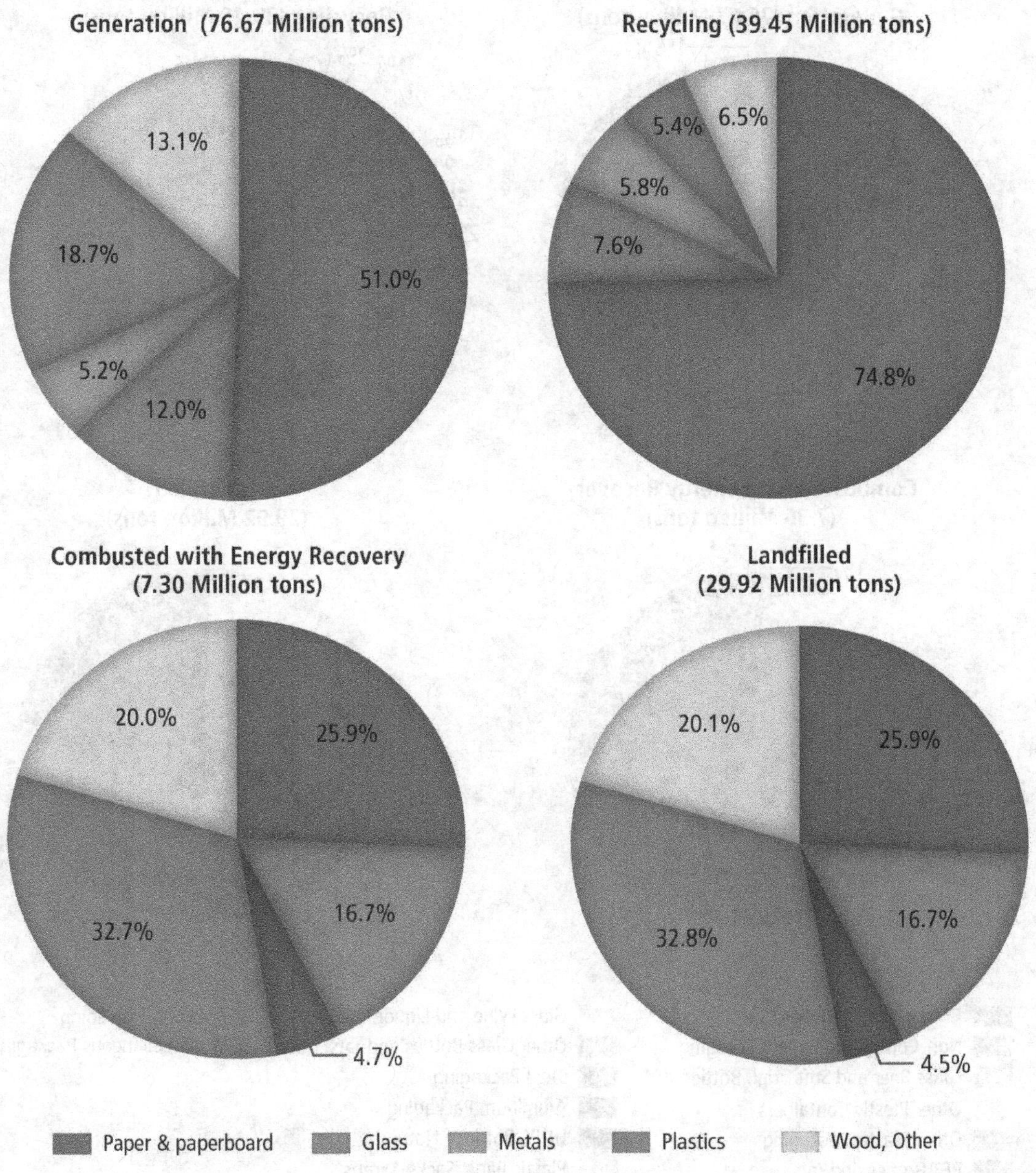

Source: *U.S. EPA, Advancing Sustainable Materials Management: 2014 Tables and Figures, December 2016*

Figure 18. Containers and Packaging Generated, Recycled, Combusted with Energy Recovery and Landfilled in Municipal Solid Waste, 2014

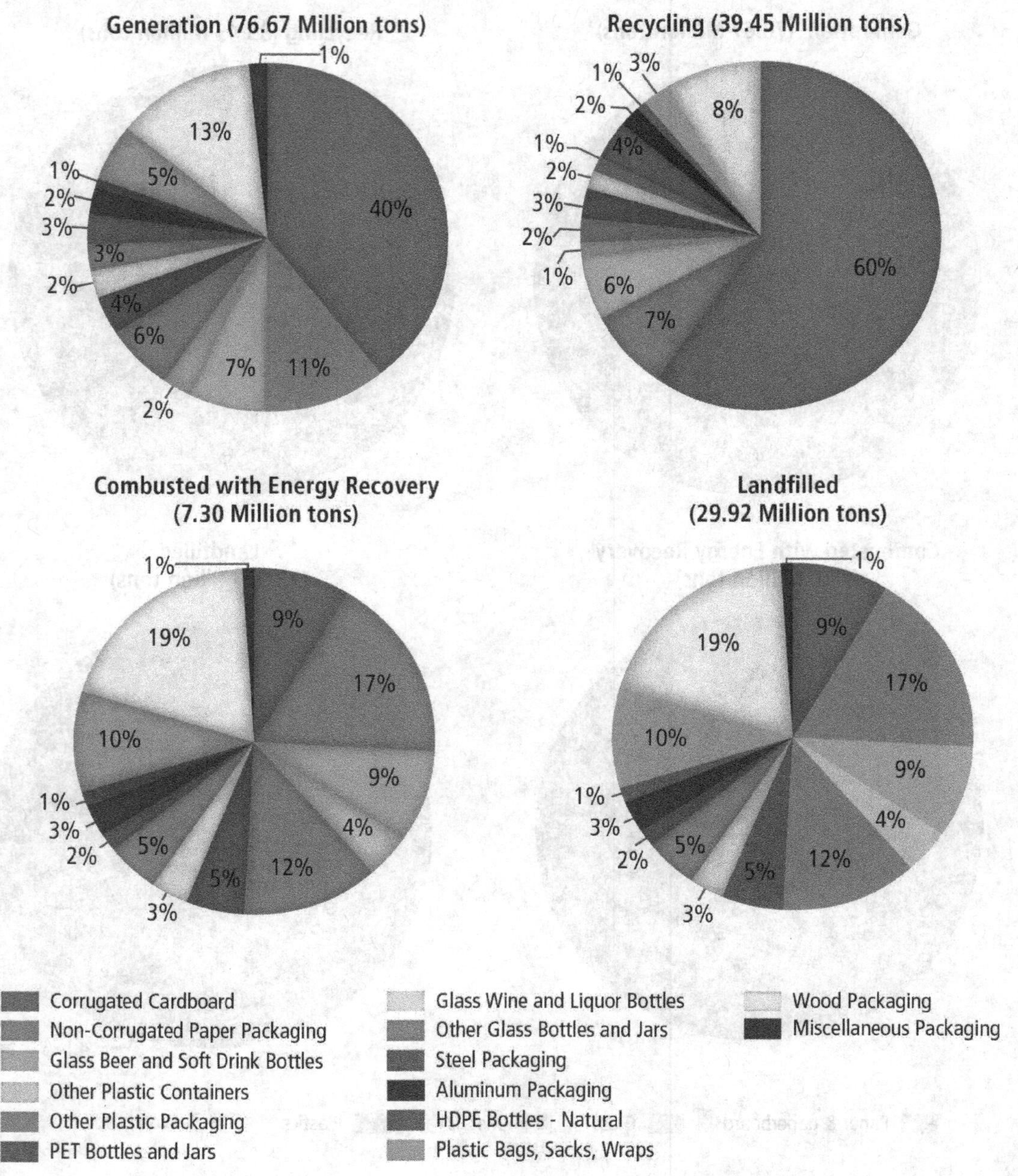

Source: *U.S. EPA, Advancing Sustainable Materials Management: 2014 Tables and Figures, December 2016*

Figure 19. Diagram of Solid Waste Management

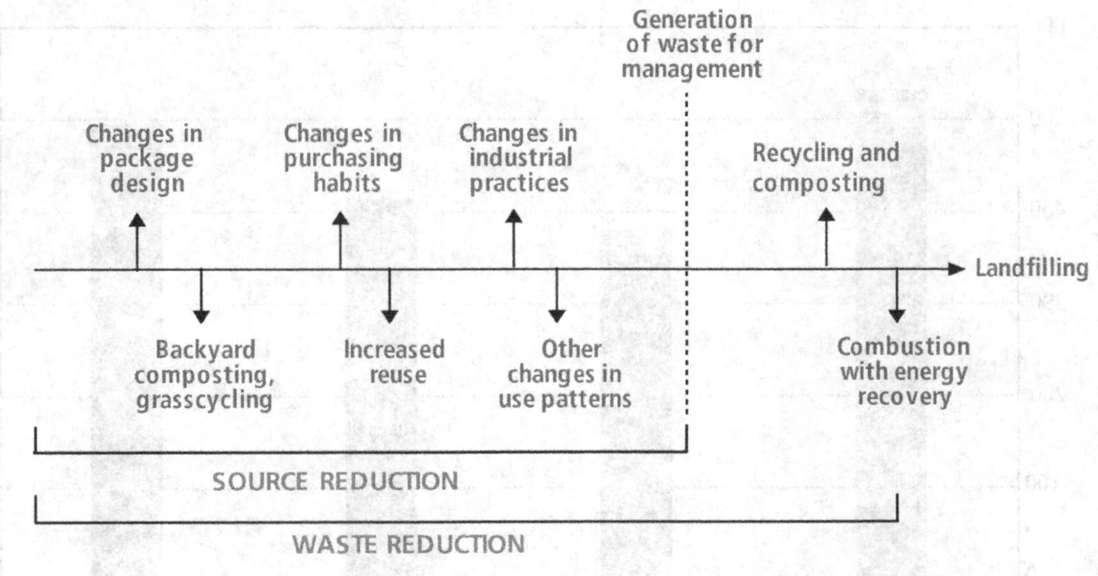

Figure 20. States with Bottle Deposit Rules

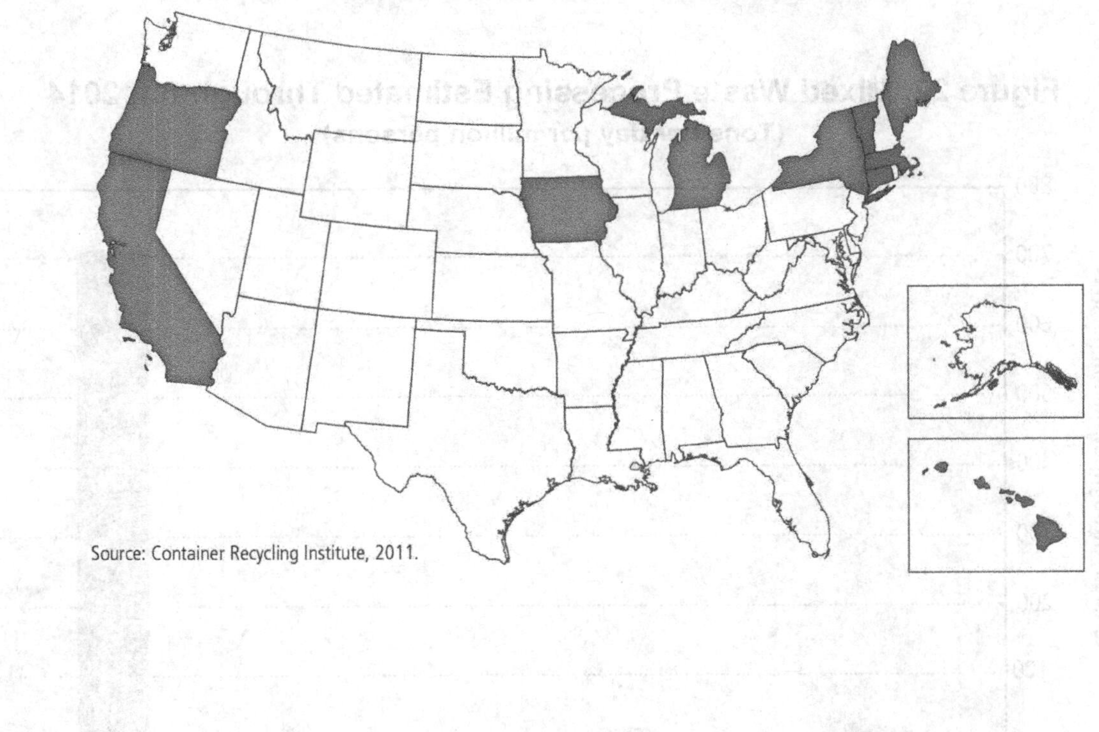

Source: *U.S. EPA, Advancing Sustainable Materials Management: 2014 Tables and Figures, December 2016*

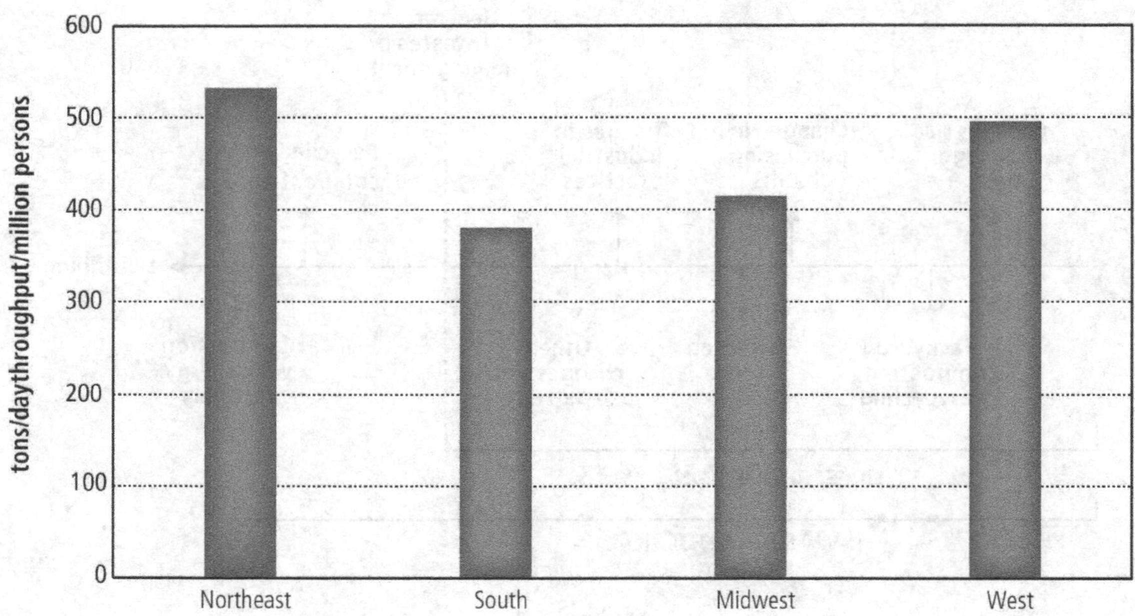

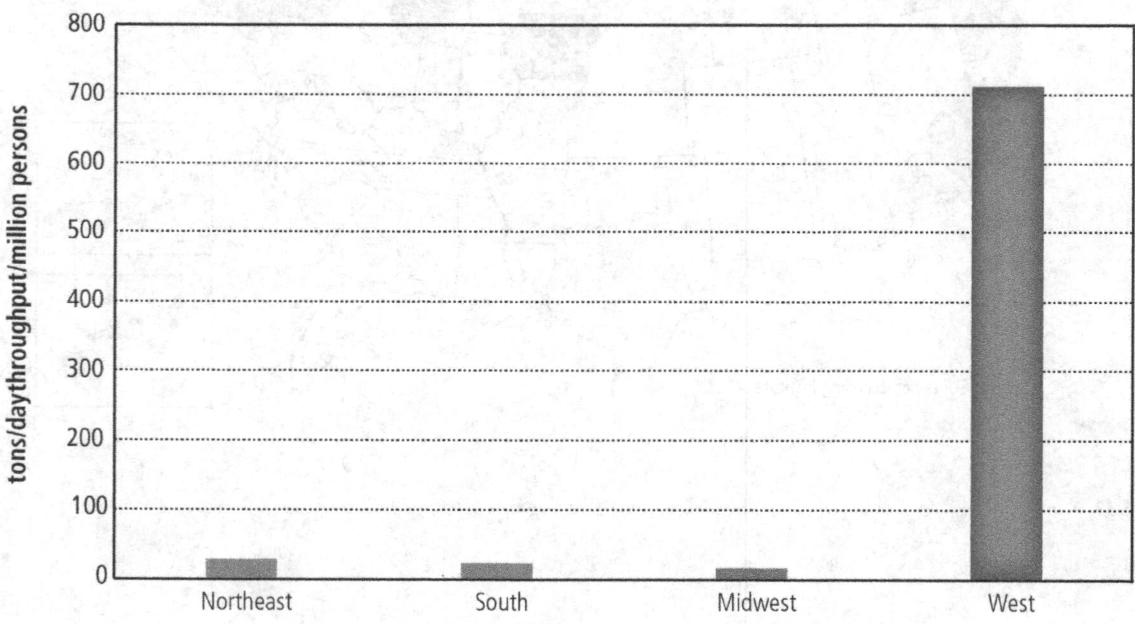

Source: *U.S. EPA, Advancing Sustainable Materials Management: 2014 Tables and Figures, December 2016*

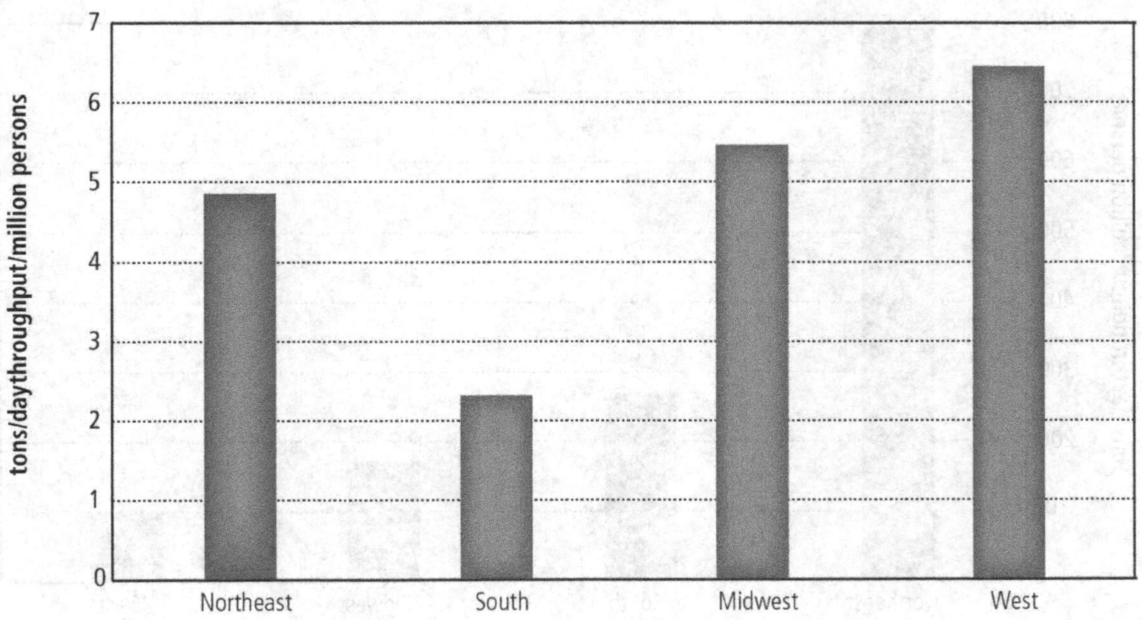

Source: U.S. Census Bureau; BioCycle, November 2011, Medina County, Ohio and West Wendover, Nevada websites.

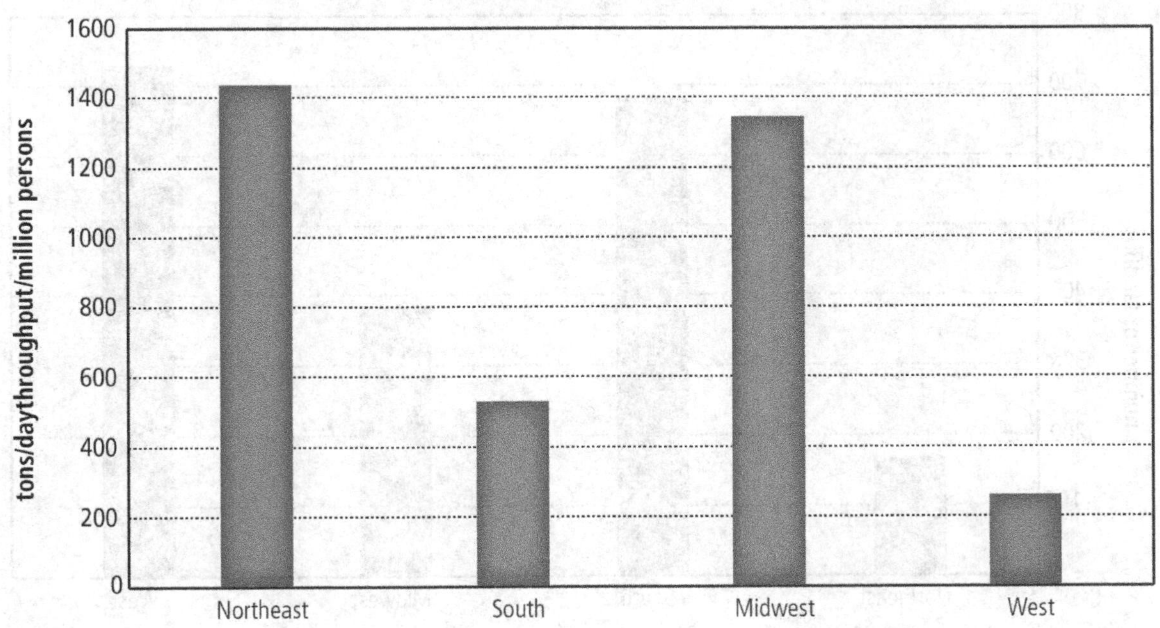

Source: Institute for Local Self-Reliance. July 2014 "State of Composting in the U.S." Facilities composting yard trimmings. Includes data for 48 states. An Internet search provided information for Alaska, Hawaii, Louisiana, Nevada, New Hampshire, Oklahoma, and West Virginia.

Source: *U.S. EPA, Advancing Sustainable Materials Management: 2014 Tables and Figures, December 2016*

Figure 25. Municipal Waste-To-Energy Capacity, 2014

(Capacity in tons per million persons)

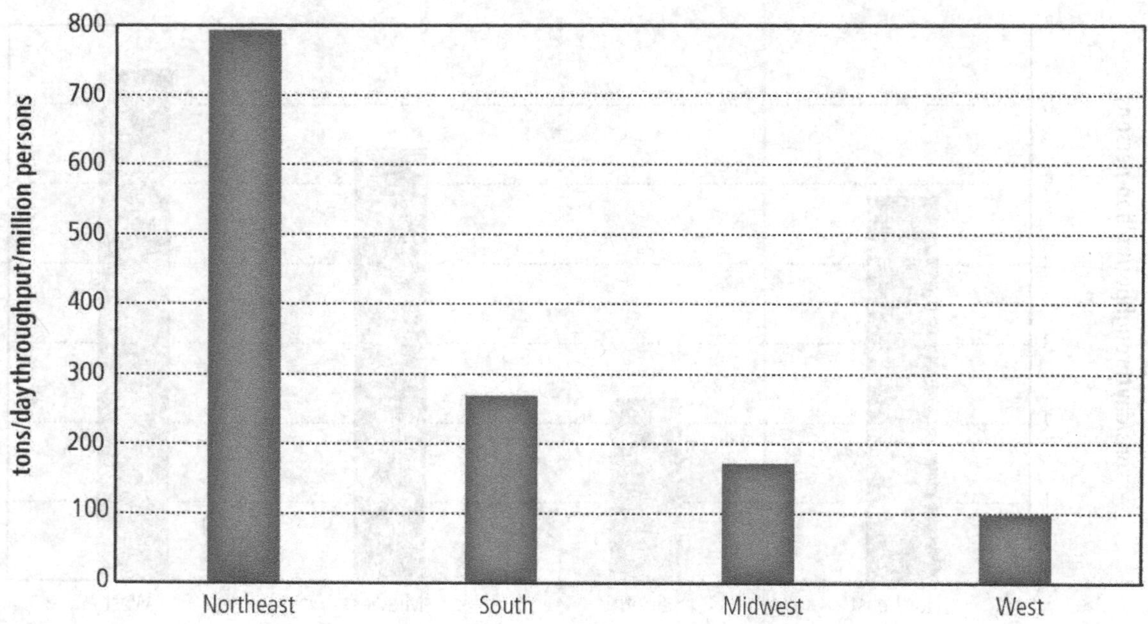

Source: U.S. Census Bureau, Energy Recovery Council (ERC). May 2014.

Figure 26. Number of Landfills in the U.S., 2014

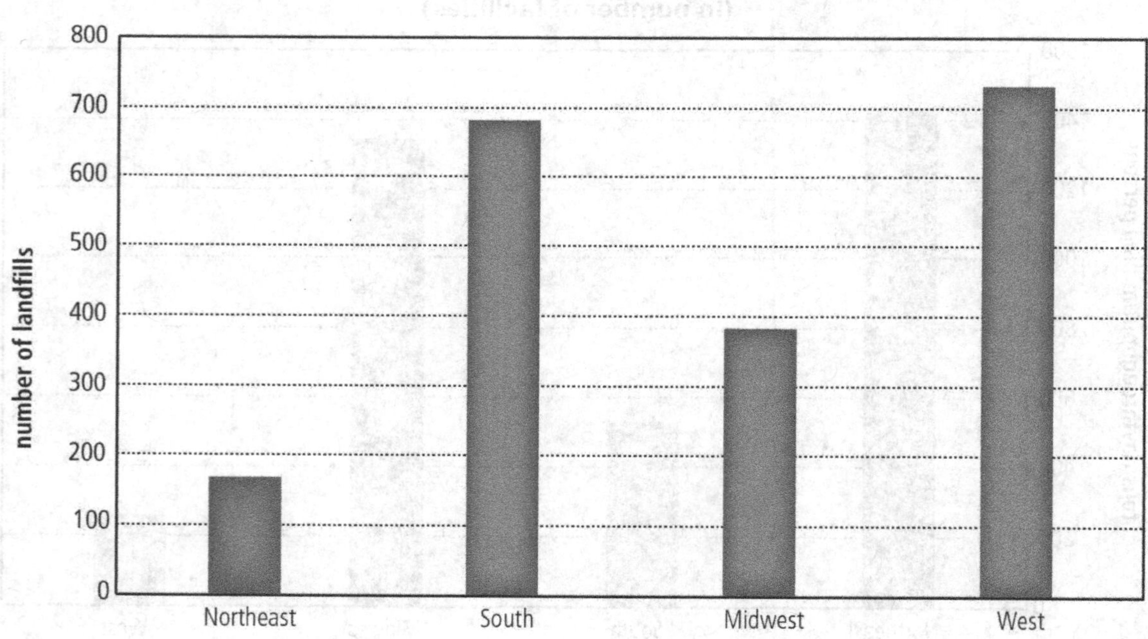

Source: State environmental websites.

Source: *U.S. EPA, Advancing Sustainable Materials Management: 2014 Tables and Figures, December 2016*

1 Introduction

1.1 Purpose of Report

The U.S. Environmental Protection Agency (EPA) is responsible for regulating the production and use of pesticides in the United States under the Federal Insecticide, Fungicide, and Rodenticide Act (FIFRA) and the Federal Food, Drug, and Cosmetic Act (FFDCA). This report provides economic information on the U.S. sectors that produce and use pesticides covered by these federal regulatory statutes and programs. Economic profile information covers a variety of topics, particularly the pesticide market with respect to dollar values and quantities of active ingredient. The EPA Office of Pesticide Programs has issued such market reports since 1979 (EPA 1979). The intended audience of this document includes those entities seeking an overview of sales and usage in the pesticide industry, which may include federal and state agencies, researchers, academia, and the general public.

Neither EPA nor any other federal agency has a program devoted specifically to collecting information for the purpose of estimating the overall pesticide market in terms of dollars spent and quantities of active ingredients used on an annual basis. Therefore, this information must be compiled from external sources (see Data Sources). The data in this report represent approximate values rather than precise values with known statistical properties.

This report is intended only to present objective economic profile and trend information reflecting the best information available to EPA on pesticide sales and use. It does not interpret, offer conclusions, or make inferences about the data. Detailed analysis of causal factors or implications, such as potential impacts on human health, the environment, or the economy, falls beyond the scope of this report.

We caution the reader not to infer too much from changes in the amount of pesticides used from year to year. Changes in the amount of pesticides used are not necessarily correlated with changes in the level of pest control or changes in the human health and environmental risks associated with pesticide use. Yearly variation in pesticide sales may reflect for example, changes in survey methodology, changes in the price of pesticides, or the introduction and adoption of new pesticide/chemistries with associated higher prices. Similarly, yearly variation in pounds of pesticides applied may be influenced by factors such as survey methodology, pesticide pricing, increased usage of newer pesticide chemistries with similar toxicity at reduced application rates, or changes in application methodology (*e.g.,* seed treatment vs. post emergence applications).

1.2 Data Sources

The agency based its estimates of pesticide usage and expenditures on data from public and proprietary databases and market research reports that have met EPA requirements for environmental data as evidenced by their documented quality systems, including prescribed quality assurance and quality control activities to ensure the quality of the data (EPA 2008). Public data sources include several reports developed by the United States Department of Agriculture's National Agricultural Statistics Service (USDA/NASS). These publications cover a broad range of pesticide sales and usage information. The associated data quality measures for each report are published on the USDA/NASS website *(https://www.nass.usda.gov/Publications/Methodology_and_Data_Quality)*. Proprietary data sources include agricultural and non-agricultural pesticide survey data and research reports of pesticide usage statistics collected and sold by private market research firms. The survey methodology is documented in the firms' quality assurance documents, and results are deemed statistically valid by the Agency's standards. These data, produced by well-known organizations, also serve pesticide registrants and other private sector firms analysing the U.S. and world pesticide markets. The methods used by the various public and proprietary data sources vary from large statistically based grower/user samples or panels to use of more limited interview/survey approaches of growers, applicators, pesticide suppliers, and pest management consultants. No single source provides data on all use sites. Each source and its method were considered on their merits when judging the usefulness and relevance to making annual market estimates

Source: *U.S. EPA, Pesticide Industry Sales and Usage, 2008-2012 Market Estimate, Released 2017*

for this report. Comparisons across data sources were done where appropriate. Data presented in this report are merged, averaged, and rounded so that the presented information is not proprietary, business confidential, or trade secret.

It should be noted that additional pesticide usage may have occurred that is not included in this document because the available studies do not survey all sites (*e.g.,* small acreage crops). Furthermore, usage data on a particular site may be noted in data sources, but not quantified, because of small sample size or other factors. In these instances, usage data associated with the site are not reported in this document, and may therefore underestimate actual usage. Lack of reported usage data for a pesticide or use site does not imply zero usage.

This report presents data at both the producer and user levels. Producer level data are obtained by surveying companies that manufacture and formulate pesticides to determine the amount of pesticides sold in a given year in terms of dollars and pounds active ingredient (a.i.) by pesticide type (see Sections 2.1 and 3.1). User level data are obtained by surveying persons or businesses that purchase and apply pesticides, such as farmers, commercial pesticide applicators, and homeowners to determine the amount of pesticides applied in a given year in terms of dollars and pounds a.i. (see Sections 2.2 – 2.3, 3.2 – 3.7, and 4).

1.3 Scope of Report

This report profiles the U.S. pesticide industry, on an annual basis, for the years 2008-2012. Data were estimated using several different parameters (e.g., pesticide type, pesticide group, market sector) and appear in tabular form. The scope of the report is largely inclusive of the U.S. pesticide industry and includes data on expenditures (sales in dollars), volume (pounds applied), firms, individuals involved in production and use of pesticides, number of pesticides, and number of certified applicators, among other topics. Data on expenditures and sales are reported in nominal terms for the year indicated (*i.e.,* not adjusted or indexed for inflation). Data on pesticide usage are reported only as pounds applied and not acres treated. The report includes graphical representations of the data where useful for illustration purposes.

Following the Introduction (Section 1), Section 2 of the report summarizes world and U.S. pesticide expenditures, and Section 3 summarizes world and U.S. pesticide usage. Section 4 presents summary-level information on pesticide users and producers.

1.4 Data Reporting Changes

Since the last publication of this report (EPA 2011), there have been several changes in data sources and calculation methods used to derive the estimates of pesticide usage and expenditures. These changes were the result of discontinued private market research data sources and the availability of more current data that more accurately reflected pesticide sales and usage statistics for the reported timeframes.

The previous proprietary source of data for producer level expenditures on pesticides and pounds of pesticide applied in the world and U.S. markets has been discontinued and has been replaced with a new source. Thus, the grouping and trends in these data (Sections 2.1 and 3.1) may vary slightly from those reported in previous versions of this document. Additionally, in previous versions of this report, some user level data were updated by calculating a percent change in the market and applying that percent change to the values presented in previous reports. In this report, no data are extrapolated with the exception of the 2009 Industrial/Commercial/ Government category values. Because of a lack of data, the 2009 values are an average of the 2012 and 2007 values for this category. All data presented are based on the best available estimates for each reported year. Not all of the included data sources for user level data report yearly; therefore, data are only reported for years for which data are available. Several studies used to determine the cost and quantity of non-agricultural pesticide use have also been discontinued. Therefore, in order to update this report, the

Source: *U.S. EPA, Pesticide Industry Sales and Usage, 2008-2012 Market Estimate, Released 2017*

values in these categories were calculated differently than in previous versions. In order to maintain continuity in the data, and to prevent the false appearance of changes in usage patterns, the values for 2005 and 2007 were recalculated using the same methods and sources used to update this report, and thus vary slightly from the values reported for these timeframes in previous versions of this publication.

Source: *U.S. EPA, Pesticide Industry Sales and Usage, 2008-2012 Market Estimate, Released 2017*

2 2008 - 2012 Sales

2.1 World and U.S. Pesticide Expenditures

World pesticide expenditures at the producer level totalled nearly $56 billion in 2012 (see Figure 2.1). Between 2008 and 2012, expenditures on herbicides consistently accounted for the largest portion of total expenditures in all years (approximately 45%), followed by expenditures on insecticides, fungicides, and other pesticides, respectively (see Table 2.1).

U.S. pesticide expenditures at the producer level totalled nearly $9 billion in 2012 (see Figure 2.1). Between 2008 and 2012, U.S. expenditures accounted for 18-16% of total world pesticide expenditures. Most recently, in 2012, U.S. expenditures accounted for 21% of world expenditures on herbicides (including plant growth regulators [PGRs]), 14% of world expenditures on insecticides, 10% of world expenditures on fungicides, and 23% of world expenditures on fumigants (Table 2.1). Figure 2.1 displays the distribution of pesticide expenditures by pesticide type in the U.S. and world markets. See Section 2.2 for a more detailed look at U.S. expenditures on pesticides from 2008 to 2012.

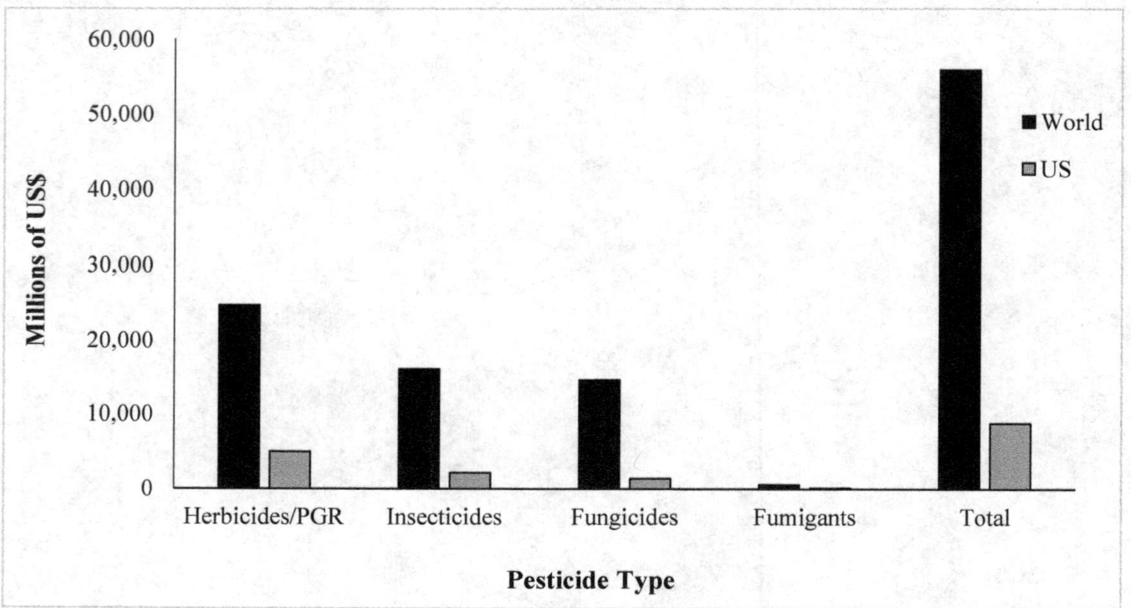

Figure 2.1. World and U.S. Pesticide Expenditures at Producer Level by Pesticide Type, 2012 Estimates

Source: Phillips McDougall, AgriService (2008-2012). (*http://phillipsmcdougall.co.uk/agriservice/*)

Source: *U.S. EPA, Pesticide Industry Sales and Usage, 2008-2012 Market Estimate, Released 2017*

Table 2.1. World and U.S. Pesticide Expenditures at the Producer Level by Pesticide Type, 2008 - 2012 Estimates

Year and Pesticide Type	World Market		U.S. Market		U.S. Percentage of World Market
	Millions of $	%	Millions of $	%	
2012					
Herbicides/PGR*	24,727	44	5,115	58	21
Insecticides	16,023	29	2,184	25	14
Fungicides	14,565	26	1,430	16	10
Fumigants	606	1	137	2	23
Total	55,921		8,866		16
2011					
Herbicides/PGR	23,322	44	4,904	58	21
Insecticides	15,055	28	2,125	25	14
Fungicides	13,898	26	1,348	16	10
Fumigants	554	1	145	2	26
Total	52,829		8,522		16
2010					
Herbicides/PGR	21,131	45	4,755	58	23
Insecticides	13,356	28	2,038	25	15
Fungicides	12,106	26	1,232	15	10
Fumigants	578	1	138	2	24
Total	47,171		8,163		17
2009					
Herbicides/PGR	21,376	46	5,058	59	24
Insecticides	12,382	27	2,009	23	16
Fungicides	11,692	25	1,166	14	10
Fumigants	557	1	122	1	22
Total	46,007		8,355		18
2008					
Herbicides/PGR	23,516	48	5,364	63	23
Insecticides	12,486	26	1,882	22	15
Fungicides	12,249	25	1,186	14	10
Fumigants	591	1	123	1	21
Total	48,842		8,555		18

*Source: Phillips McDougall, AgriService (2008-2012). (*http://phillipsmcdougall.co.uk/agriservice/*)**Note:** Insecticide and fungicide values include seed treatment uses. Totals may not be exact due to rounding. Table data do not cover wood preservatives, specialty biocides, chlorine/hypochlorites, vertebrate pesticides or other chemicals used as pesticides (e.g., sulfur and petroleum oil).*

*PGR – Plant Growth Regulator

***Source:** U.S. EPA, Pesticide Industry Sales and Usage, 2008-2012 Market Estimate, Released 2017*

2.2 User Expenditures on Conventional Pesticides in the United States

U.S. expenditures at the user level for conventional pesticides totalled nearly $14 billion in 2012 and nearly $13 billion in 2009 (see Figure 2.2 and Table 2.2). Conventional pesticides are defined here as all active ingredients other than biological pesticides and antimicrobial pesticides. Pesticides included in the estimates are herbicides (including PGRs), insecticides, fungicides, fumigants, sulfur and oils, and other pesticides. Other pesticides include chemicals that may be used as pesticides but are not primarily produced as pesticides for the agricultural market (*e.g.,* sulfuric acid and phosphoric acid), as well as rodenticides and repellents used in the home and industrial markets. The estimates exclude expenditures on wood preservatives and specialty biocides, which are discussed separately in section 3.7 of this report.

Increases in spending in the agricultural sector on all pesticide types, as well as increases in spending in the home and garden sector on insecticides, fungicides, and other pesticides, resulted in an overall increase in total pesticide expenditures in 2012. Expenditures in the agriculture sector accounted for approximately two-thirds of total pesticide expenditures in both 2012 and 2009. Within the agricultural sector, the majority of pesticide expenditures were on herbicides, which accounted for approximately 59% of the market in 2012 and 63% in 2009. In the remaining sectors, the majority of expenditures were on insecticides, which accounted for approximately 80% of expenditures in the home and garden sector and 50% of expenditures in the industrial/commercial/governmental sector in both 2009 and 2012 (see Table 2.2). Figure 2.2 displays the distribution of expenditures by pesticide type and sector in 2012.

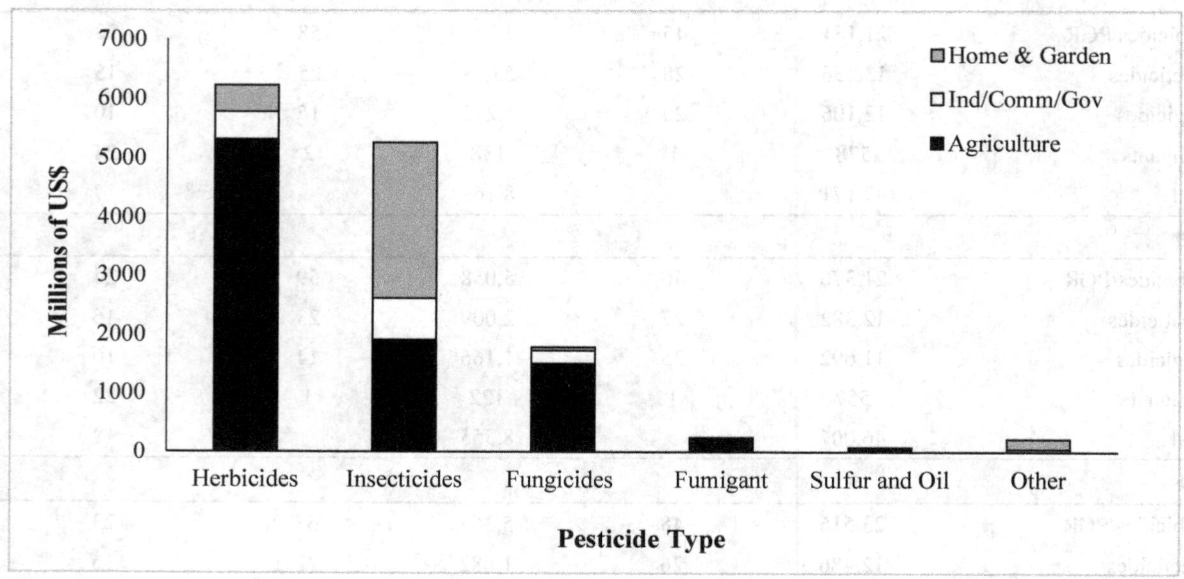

Figure 2.2. User Expenditures on Pesticides in the United States by Pesticide Type and Market Sector, 2012 Estimates

Sources: Agricultural Market Research Proprietary Data (2005-2012).
Non-Agricultural Market Research Proprietary Data (2005-2012)
USDA/NASS Quick Stats (*http://www.nass.usda.gov/Quick_Stats/*)

Source: *U.S. EPA, Pesticide Industry Sales and Usage, 2008-2012 Market Estimate, Released 2017*

Table 2.2. User Expenditures on Conventional Pesticides in the United States by Pesticide Type and Market Sector - 2012, 2009, 2007, and 2005 Estimates

Year and Market Sector	Herbicides/ PGR		Insecticides		Fungicides		Fumigant		Sulfur and Oil[1]		Other[2]		Total	
	Mil $	%	Mil $	%	Mil $	%	Mil $	%	Mil $	%	Mil $	%	Mil $	%
2012														
Agriculture[3]	5,313	85	1,909	36	1,499	84	245	100	82	100	7	3	9,055	66
Ind/Comm/Gov	460	7	700	13	230	13	—	—	—	—	40	18	1,430	10
Home & Garden	450	7	2,650	50	55	3	—	—	—	—	175	79	3,330	24
Total	6,223		5,259		1,784		245		82		222		13,815	
2009														
Agriculture[3]	5,192	85	1,618	34	1,128	79	229	100	70	100	4	2	8,241	64
Ind/Comm/Gov[4]	470	8	708	15	248	17	—	—	—	—	35	18	1,490	12
Home & Garden	475	8	2,500	52	50	4	—	—	—	—	155	80	3,180	25
Total	6,147		4,833		1,443		229		70		189		12,911	
2007*														
Agriculture[3]	4,135	82	1,428	31	820	73	227	100	66	100	6	4	6,682	59
Ind/Comm/Gov	480	10	715	15	265	23	—	—	—	—	30	20	1,490	13
Home & Garden	420	8	2,500	54	45	4	—	—	—	—	115	76	3,080	27
Total	5,035		4,643		1,130		227		66		151		11,252	
2005*														
Agriculture[3]	4,352	84	1,314	31	699	70	197	100	63	100	5	3	6,630	61
Ind/Comm/Gov	460	9	675	16	260	26	—	—	—	—	30	21	1,425	13
Home & Garden	395	8	2,200	53	40	4	—	—	—	—	109	76	2,744	25
Total	5,207		4,189		999		197		63		144		10,799	

Sources: Agricultural Market Research Proprietary Data (2005-2012).
Non-Agricultural Market Research Proprietary Data (2005-2012)
USDA/NASS Quick Stats (*http://www.nass.usda.gov/Quick_Stats/*)

Note: *Includes the cost of insecticides, herbicides, fungicides, and other pesticides, excluding the cost of custom application. Insecticide and fungicide values include seed treatment uses. Totals may not be exact due to rounding.*

1 "Sulfur and Oil" includes sulfur, petroleum distillate, and petroleum oil.

2 "Other" includes chemicals used as pesticides which are not primarily produced as pesticides for the agricultural market (e.g., sulfuric acid and phosphoric acid) as well as rodenticides and repellant use in the home and industrial markets. It does not cover specialty biocides or wood preservatives.

3 USDA/NASS data incorporated into agricultural expenditures to account for malathion expenditures in the Boll Weevil Eradication Program (BWEP).

4 Due to lack of data, the values presented for 2009 for the Industrial/Commercial/ Government category are an average of the 2012 and 2007 values. This value may over or underestimate actual 2009 usage, due to fluctuations in annual usage.

* Updated values for 2007 and 2005 presented for continuity. See Data Reporting Changes.

Source: *U.S. EPA, Pesticide Industry Sales and Usage, 2008-2012 Market Estimate, Released 2017*

2.3 Pesticide Farm Expenditures in the United States

Pesticides are a significant component of total farm production expenditures and an important element of farm budgeting and management. Farm expenditures includes the cost of pesticides (as reported in sections 2.1 and 2.2 of this report) as well as the cost of pesticide application. Based on available USDA/NASS Census of Agriculture data, which is published every five years, U.S. pesticide expenditures in 2007 and 2012 totalled 4.2% and 5% of total farm expenditures, respectively (see Table 2.3). Both farm expenditures and pesticide expenditures increased in 2012. Total farm production expenditures include all farm-related expenses. Pesticide expenses include insecticides, herbicides, fungicides, and other pesticides, including costs of custom application.

Table 2.3. Pesticide Farm Expenditures in the United States

Expenditure (Million $)	2012	2007
Total	$328,900	$241,000
Pesticides	$16,500	$10,000
Crop	$14,900	$8,900
Livestock	$1,600	$1,100
Pesticides as % of Total	5%	4.2%

Source: USDA/NASS. 2007 and 2012. Census of Agriculture: United States Summary and State Data, Volume 1, Part 51 (*"http://www.agcensus.usda.gov/Publications/2007 and http://www.agcensus.usda.gov/Publications/2012*).

Note: *Pesticide expenses include insecticides, herbicides, fungicides, and other pesticides, including cost of custom application.*

Source: *U.S. EPA, Pesticide Industry Sales and Usage, 2008-2012 Market Estimate, Released 2017*

3 2008 - 2012 Usage

3.1 World and U.S. Pesticide Usage

World pesticide usage at the producer level totalled nearly 6 billion pounds annually in both 2011 and 2012 (see Figure 3.1 and Table 3.1). Between 2008 and 2012, herbicides accounted for the largest portion of global usage (approximately 50% annually in all years), followed by fumigants, insecticides, and fungicides, respectively.

U.S. pesticide usage totalled over 1.1 billion pounds annually in both 2011 and 2012, with herbicides accounting for nearly 50% of total U.S. pesticide usage in 2011 and nearly 60% of usage in 2012 (see Table 3. 1). On average across all reported years (2008-2012), U.S. pesticide use accounted for approximately 23% of total pounds of pesticides applied, 25% of total pounds of herbicides applied, 43% of total pounds of fumigants applied, 12% of fungicides applied, and 6% of insecticides applied worldwide. Figure 3.1 displays the distribution of pounds of pesticides applied at the producer level by pesticide type in 2012. For a more detailed look at U.S. pesticide usage, see tables 3.2 through 3.7.

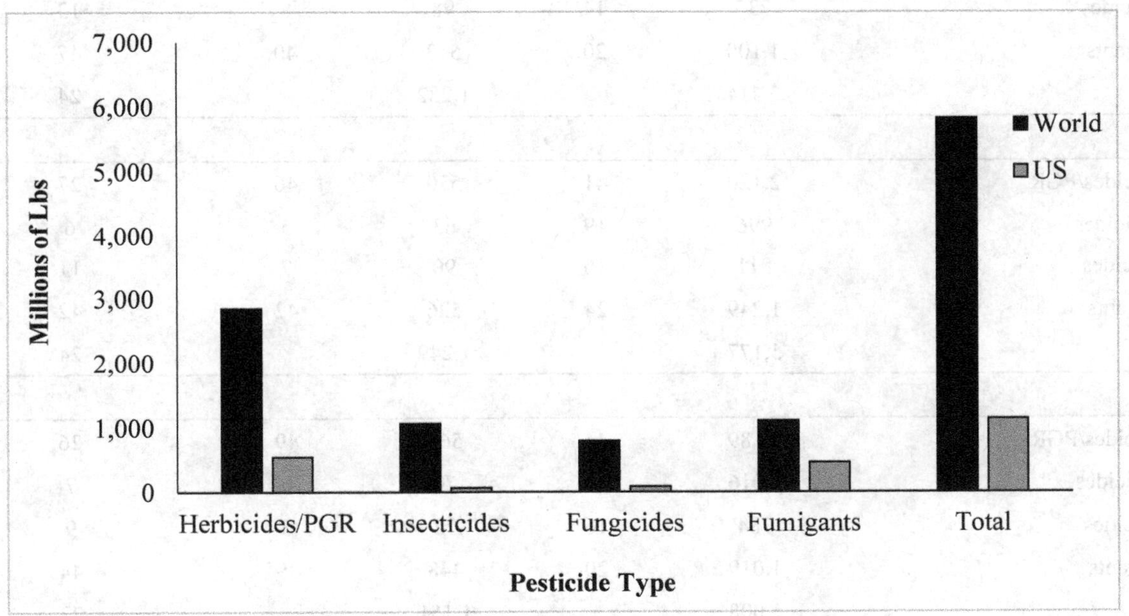

Figure 3.1. World and U.S. Pesticide Amounts of Active Ingredient at Producer Level by Pesticide Type, 2012 Estimates

Source: Phillips McDougall, AgriService, (2008-2012). (*http://phillipsmcdougall.co.uk/agriservice/*).

Source: *U.S. EPA, Pesticide Industry Sales and Usage, 2008-2012 Market Estimate, Released 2017*

Table 3.1. World and U.S. Amount of Pesticide Active Ingredient Used at the Producer Level by Pesticide Type 2008 - 2012 Estimates

Year and Pesticide Type	World Market		U.S. Market		U.S. Percentage of World Market
	Mil lbs	%	Mil lbs	%	
2012					
Herbicides/PGR	2,847	49	678	57	24
Insecticides	1,065	18	64	5	6
Fungicides	799	14	105	9	13
Fumigants	1,110	19	435	37	39
Total	5,821		1,182		20
2011					
Herbicides/PGR	2,508	46	609	48	24
Insecticides	1,070	20	62	5	6
Fungicides	735	14	98	8	13
Fumigants	1,100	20	513	40	47
Total	5,414		1,282		24
2010					
Herbicides/PGR	2,120	41	570	46	27
Insecticides	996	19	63	5	6
Fungicides	811	16	90	7	11
Fumigants	1,249	24	526	42	42
Total	5,177		1,249		24
2009					
Herbicides/PGR	2,189	44	560	49	26
Insecticides	1,016	20	70	6	7
Fungicides	784	16	72	6	9
Fumigants	1,019	20	448	39	44
Total	5,008		1,151		23
2008					
Herbicides/PGR	2,083	43	540	48	26
Insecticides	972	20	63	6	6
Fungicides	737	15	80	7	11
Fumigants	1,058	22	452	40	43
Total	4,850		1,135		23

Source: Phillips McDougall, AgriService, (2008-2012). (*http://phillipsmcdougall.co.uk/agriservice/*).

Note: *Insecticide and fungicide values include seed treatment uses. Totals may not be exact due to rounding. Table data do not cover wood preservatives, specialty biocides, chlorine/hypochlorites, vertebrate pesticides, or other chemicals used as pesticides (e.g., sulfur and petroleum oil).*

Source: *U.S. EPA, Pesticide Industry Sales and Usage, 2008-2012 Market Estimate, Released 2017*

3.2 Pesticide Usage in the United States: Conventional

Pesticide usage in the agricultural sector accounted for nearly 90% of the total pesticide usage between 2005 and 2012, with the two non-agricultural sectors (industry/commercial/government and home & garden) cumulatively accounting for the remaining percent of the total use in each year (see Figure 3.2 and Table 3.2). Usage in the agriculture sector also accounted for the majority of the total usage of each pesticide type. On average across all reported years (2008-2012), approximately 90% of herbicides, 85% of fungicides, 60% of insecticides, 100% of sulfur and oil, and approximately 60% of other pesticides applied in the U.S. were applied in the agricultural sector. Within all sectors, the majority of usage in 2012 was from herbicides, which accounted for approximately 62% of pesticides applied in the agricultural sector, 54% of pesticides applied in the professional sector, and 47% of pesticides applied in the home and garden sector. Figure 3.2 displays the distribution of usage by pesticide type and sector in 2012. Table 3.2 shows the breakout of conventional pesticide usage at the user level by pesticide type and market sector. Pesticide usage is reported as pounds applied and does not reflect acres treated.

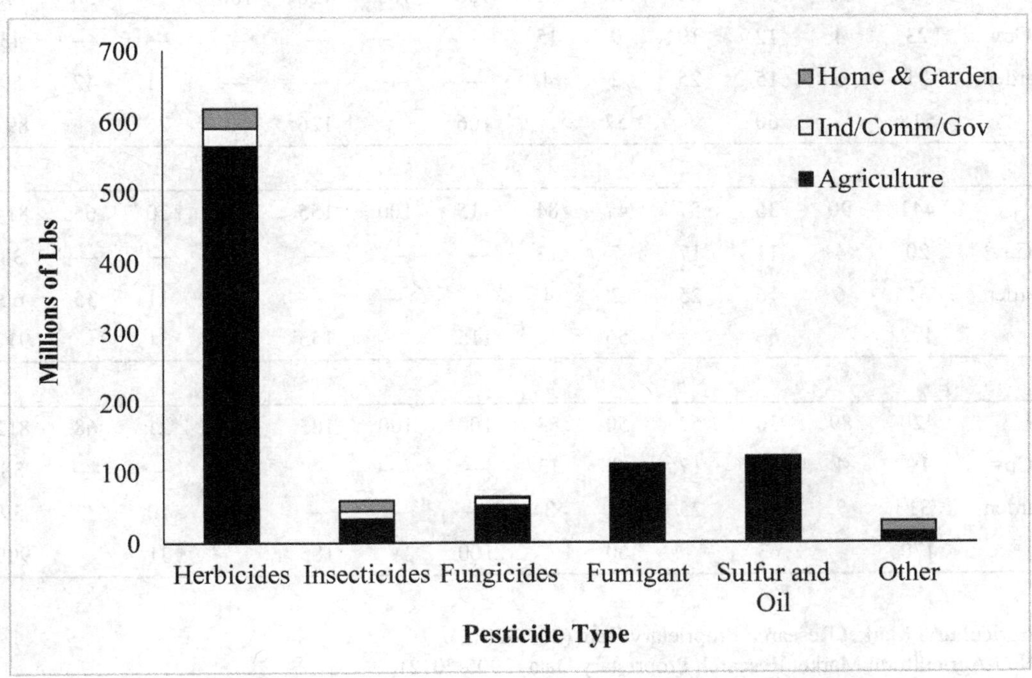

Figure 3.2. Conventional Pesticide Active Ingredient Usage in the United States by Pesticide Type and Market Sector, 2012 Estimates.

Sources: Agricultural Market Research Proprietary Data (2005-2012).
Non-Agricultural Market Research Proprietary Data (2005-2012)
USDA/NASS Quick Stats (*http://www.nass.usda.gov/Quick_Stats/*)

***Source:** U.S. EPA, Pesticide Industry Sales and Usage, 2008-2012 Market Estimate, Released 2017*

Table 3.2. Conventional Pesticide Active Ingredient Usage in the United States by Pesticide Type and Market Sector, 2012, 2009, 2007, and 2005 Estimates

Year and Market Sector	Herbicides/ PGR		Insecticides		Fungicides		Fumigant		Sulfur and Oil[1]		Other [2]		Total	
	Mil lbs	%	Mil lbs	%	Mil lbs	%	Mil lbs	%	Mil lbs	%	Mil lbs	%	Mil lbs	%
2012														
Agriculture[3]	564	91	34	57	53	82	111	100	122	100	15	50	899	89
Ind/Comm/Gov	26	4	12	20	10	15	—	—	—	—	—	—	48	5
Home & Garden	28	5	14	23	2	3	—	—	—	—	15	50	59	6
Total	618		60		65		111		122		30		1,006	
2009														
Agriculture[3]	464	90	33	55	46	81	106	100	126	100	15	58	790	89
Ind/Comm/Gov[4]	23	4	12	19	9	15	—	—	—	—	—	—	43	5
Home & Garden	31	6	15	25	2	4	—	—	—	—	11	42	59	7
Total	518		60		57		106		126		26		892	
2007*														
Agriculture[3]	441	90	36	57	47	84	115	100	155	100	20	65	814	89
Ind/Comm/Gov[3]	20	4	11	17	7	13	—	—	—	—	—	—	38	4
Home & Garden	31	6	16	25	2	4	—	—	—	—	11	35	60	7
Total	492		63		56		115		155		31		912	
2005*														
Agriculture[3]	420	89	36	57	50	83	100	100	185	100	21	68	812	89
Ind/Comm/Gov	19	4	11	17	8	13	—	—	—	—	—	—	38	4
Home & Garden	31	7	16	25	2	3	—	—	—	—	10	32	59	6
Total	470		63		60		100		185		31		909	

Sources: Agricultural Market Research Proprietary Data (2005-2012).
Non-Agricultural Market Research Proprietary Data (2005-2012)

USDA/NASS Quick Stats (*http://www.nass.usda.gov/Quick_Stats/*)

Note: *Insecticide and fungicide values include seed treatment uses. Totals may not be exact due to rounding.*

1 "Sulfur and Oil" includes sulfur, petroleum distillate, and petroleum oil.

2 "Other" includes chemicals used as pesticides which are not primarily produced as pesticides for the agricultural market (e.g., sulfuric acid and phosphoric acid) as well as rodenticides and repellant use in the home and industrial markets. It does not cover specialty biocides or wood preservatives.

3 USDA/NASS data incorporated into agricultural expenditures to account for malathion expenditures in the Boll Weevil Eradication Program (BWEP).

4 Due to lack of data, the values presented for 2009 are an average of the 2012 and 2007 values for the Industrial/Commercial/ Government category. This value may over or underestimate actual 2009 usage, due to fluctuations in annual usage.

* Updated values for 2007 and 2005 presented for continuity. See Data Reporting Changes.

Source: *U.S. EPA, Pesticide Industry Sales and Usage, 2008-2012 Market Estimate, Released 2017*

3.3 Share of U.S. Conventional Pesticide Active Ingredient Usage in the Agricultural and Non-Agricultural Market Sectors

Table 3.3 shows the agricultural and non-agricultural market share of total conventional pesticides consumed in 2012, 2009, 2007, and 2005. The agricultural sector accounts for nearly 90% of the total amount of conventional pesticides used in all years.

Table 3.3. Share of U.S. Conventional Pesticide Active Ingredient Usage in the Agricultural and Non-Agricultural Market Sectors: 2012, 2009, 2007, and 2005 Estimates

Year	U. S.	Agricultural Market Sector		Non-Agricultural Market Sector	
	Mil lbs	Mil lbs	% of U.S.	Mil lbs	% of U.S.
2012	854	762	89	92	11
2009	735	649	88	86	12
2007*	726	639	88	87	12
2005*	693	606	87	87	13

Source: EPA estimates based on Table 3.2.

***Note:** Table data excludes sulfur and oil, other chemicals used as pesticides (e.g., sulfuric acid and insect repellents), as well as wood preservatives, specialty biocides, and chlorine/hypochlorites.*

* Updated values for 2007 and 2005 presented for continuity.

3.4 Most Commonly Used Conventional Pesticide Active Ingredients in the U.S. Agricultural Market Sector

Table 3.4 shows the 25 most commonly used conventional pesticide active ingredients in the agricultural sector in 2012, and their ranking and usage range in selected earlier years. Glyphosate was the most used active ingredient in 2012 (270 million to 290 million pounds used), as it has been since 2001. Twelve of the top 25 active ingredients used in the agricultural sector in 2012 are herbicides; four are fungicides; two are insecticides; five are fumigants; and two are plant growth regulators. These rankings rely on the estimated pounds of conventional pesticides used in the agricultural sector, taken from public and proprietary databases. As noted previously, data only reflect pounds applied and not acres treated. Absence of a pesticide from this list should not be construed as lack of importance in agricultural crop production.

__Source:__ U.S. EPA, Pesticide Industry Sales and Usage, 2008-2012 Market Estimate, Released 2017

Table 3.4. Most Commonly Used Conventional Pesticide Active Ingredients in the Agricultural Market Sector in 2012, and their Rankings and Usage Rate Range in 2012, 2009, 2007, and 2005 Estimates (Ranked by Range‡ in Millions of Pounds of Active Ingredient)

Active Ingredient	Type	2012		2009		2007*		2005*	
		Rank	Range	Rank	Range	Rank	Range	Rank	Range
Glyphosate	H	1	270-290	1	209-229	1	170-190	1	147-167
Atrazine	H	2	64-74	2	59-69	2	70-80	2	66-76
Metolachlor-S	H	3	34-44	6	24-34	4	27-37	5	25-35
Dichloropropene	Fum	4	32-42	4	27-37	6	24-34	4	28-38
2,4-D	H	5	30-40	5	24-34	7	22-32	7	21-31
Metam	Fum	6	30-40	3	30-40	3	48-58	3	36-46
Acetochlor	H	7	28-38	7	23-33	5	25-35	6	24-34
Metam Potassium	Fum	8	16-26	8	14-24	13	6-10	—	0-3
Chloropicrin	Fum	9	8-18	9	6-16	9	5-15	10	5-15
Chlorothalonil	F	10	6-16	11	6-10	12	6-10	13	6-10
Pendimethalin	H	11	6-16	10	6-16	10	6-10	9	5-15
Ethephon	PGR	12	7-11	12	6-10	11	6-10	11	7-11
Mancozeb	F	13	5-9	16	3-7	19	3-7	16	5-9
Chlorpyrifos	I	14	4-8	13	5-9	14	6-10	15	5-9
Metolachlor	H	15	4-8	22	1-5	—	0-4	—	0-3
Hydrated Lime	F	16	3-7	15	4-8	20	2-6	—	1-5
Propanil	H	17	3-7	17	3-7	18	3-7	18	3-7
Dicamba	H	18	3-7	25	1-5	—	1-5	22	1-5
Trifluralin	H	19	3-7	18	3-7	17	4-8	14	6-10
Decan-1-ol	PGR	20	3-7	—	1-5	—	1-5	—	0-4
Copper Hydroxide	F	21	3-7	20	2-6	15	5-9	12	7-11
Acephate	I	22	2-6	—	1-5	22	1-5	23	1-5
Paraquat	H	23	2-6	—	1-5	25	1-5	24	1-5
Methyl Bromide	Fum	24	2-6	14	5-9	8	8-18	8	9-19
Glufosinate	H	25	2-6	—	1-5	—	1-5	—	0-4

Sources: Agricultural Market Research Proprietary Data, (2007, 2009, and 2012).
USDA/NASS Quick Stats (*http://www.nass.usda.gov/Quick_Stats/*)

Note: *This list is limited to conventional pesticides, and does not include sulfur, petroleum oil, and other chemicals used as pesticides (e.g., sulfuric acid and insect repellents), wood preservatives, specialty biocides, or chlorine/hypochlorites. H indicates herbicide; I, insecticide; Fum, fumigant; F, fungicide; and PGR, plant growth regulator. A dash (—) indicates that the pesticide was not one of the 25 most commonly used (pesticides) in the given year.*

‡ Values presented as a range to retain the proprietary nature of the data. Ranking based on actual values.
* Updated values for 2007 and 2005 presented for continuity.

Source: *U.S. EPA, Pesticide Industry Sales and Usage, 2008-2012 Market Estimate, Released 2017*

3.5 Most Commonly Used Conventional Pesticide Active Ingredients in the U.S. Non-Agricultural Market Sector

Tables 3.5 and 3.6 show the 10 most commonly used conventional pesticide active ingredients in the two non-agricultural sectors (home & garden and industry/commercial/government) for 2012, and their rank and usage range in 2009. In 2012, six of the top 10 active ingredients used in the home and garden sector are herbicides, and four are insecticides. Five of the top 10 active ingredients used in the industry/commercial/government sector in 2012 are herbicides, one is a fungicide, and four are insecticides. Because some applicators apply pesticides in both markets, there may be some usage reported in one market that may have occurred in the other. The rankings are based on non-agricultural market research proprietary data and present the best available data.

Table 3.5. Most Commonly Used Conventional Pesticide Active Ingredients in the Home and Garden Market Sector in 2012, and their Rankings and Usage Rate Range in 2012, and 2009 Estimates (Ranked by Range‡ in Millions of Pounds of Active Ingredient)

Active Ingredient	Type	2012		2009	
		Rank	Range	Rank	Range
2,4-D	H	1	7-9	1	8-11
Glyphosate	H	2	4-6	2	5-8
*MCPP	H	3	2-4	4	4-6
Pendimethalin	H	4	2-4	5	3-5
Carbaryl	I	5	2-4	3	4-6
Acephate	I	6	1-3	10	<1
Permethrin and other pyrethroids	I	7	1-3	6	2-4
Dicamba	H	8	1-3	7	1-3
*MCPA	H	9	1-3	—	—
Malathion	I	10	1-3	6	2-4

Sources: Non-Agricultural Market Research Proprietary Data, (2012 and 2009).
USDA/NASS Quick Stats (*http://www.nass.usda.gov/Quick_Stats/*)

***Note:** H indicates herbicide, and I indicates insecticide. A dash (—) indicates that an estimate is not available.*

*MCPP - Methylchlorophenoxypropionic acid
*MCPA - 2-methyl-4-chlorophenoxyacetic acid
‡ Values presented as a range to retain the proprietary nature of the data. Ranking based on actual values.

***Source:** U.S. EPA, Pesticide Industry Sales and Usage, 2008-2012 Market Estimate, Released 2017*

Table 3.6. Most Commonly Used Conventional Pesticide Active Ingredients in the Industry/ Commercial/ Government Market Sector in 2012 and their Rankings and Usage Rate Range in 2012, and 2009 Estimates (Ranked by Range‡ in Millions of Pounds of Active Ingredient)

Active Ingredient	Type	2012		2009	
		Rank	Range	Rank	Range
Glyphosate	H	1	7-9	1	4-6
Chlorothalonil	F	2	5-7	3	2-4
2,4-D	H	3	4-6	2	3-5
Pendimethalin	H	4	2-4	4	1-3
Prodiamine	H	5	0-2	12	0-2
Sulfuryl fluoride	I	6	0-2	7	1-3
Acephate	I	7	0-2	13	0-2
Simazine	H	8	0-2	24	0-2
*Bti	I	9	0-2	43	0-2
Bifenthrin	I	10	0-2	34	0-2

Source: EPA estimates based on Non-Agricultural Market Research Proprietary Data (2012 and 2009).

Note: *H indicates herbicide, I indicates insecticide, and F indicates fungicide.*

* *Bacillus thuringiensis serotype israelensis*
‡ *Values presented as a range to retain the proprietary nature of the data. Ranking based on actual values.*

3.6 Organophosphate Insecticides Usage in the United States

Since the passage of the Food Quality Protection Act (FQPA) in 1996, this class of conventional pesticides has been a primary focus of EPA reregistration and registration review activities. Table 3.7 compares usage of all active ingredients from 2000 to 2012 with all organophosphate (OP) insecticide usage over the same time period. This time period is displayed to provide a broad view of the decreasing trend in OP usage due in part to EPA action. OP insecticides with the most usage include acephate, chlorpyrifos, malathion, naled, phorate, dicrotophos, phosmet, dimethoate, terbufos, ethoprophos, and tetrachlorvinphos (see Table 3.8). For more information on the active ingredients included in this pesticide class and their registration status, refer to U.S. EPA's Office of Pesticide Programs Special Docket EPA-HQ-OPP-2007-0151 at *www.regulations.gov*.

The estimates of organophosphate insecticide usage rely on public and proprietary databases. The amount of OP insecticides used in the U.S. has declined more than 70% since 2000, from an estimated 70 million pounds to 20 million pounds in 2012 (see Table 3.8 and Figure 3.3). OP usage as a percentage of total insecticide use has decreased from 71% in 2000 to 33% in 2012. The decrease in OP usage reflects a shift in usage to other classes of pesticides (i.e., pyrethroids, neonicotinoids, and other new chemistries) because of the phasing out and use restrictions placed on OP insecticides as a result of pesticide registration review. The decrease also reflects reduced malathion usage due to the gradual completion of the Boll Weevil Eradication Program (BWEP).

Source: *U.S. EPA, Pesticide Industry Sales and Usage, 2008-2012 Market Estimate, Released 2017*

Table 3.7. Organophosphate Insecticide Active Ingredients Usage in the United States All Market Sectors, 2000–2012 Estimates

Year	All Insecticides[1]	Organophosphate Insecticides	
	Mil lbs	Mil lbs	% of All Insecticides
2000	99	70	71
2001	102	54	53
2002	90	47	52
2003	84	41	48
2004	77	40	52
2005	69	33	48
2006	66	30	46
2007	64	27	42
2008	65	28	43
2009	60	23	38
2010	56	21	38
2011	56	22	39
2012	60	20	33

Source: Agricultural Market Research Proprietary Data (2000-2012).
Non-Agricultural Market Research Proprietary Data (2000-2012)
USDA/NASS Quick Stats (*http://www.nass.usda.gov/Quick_Stats/*)

[1] Table data only includes conventional insecticides.

Source: *U.S. EPA, Pesticide Industry Sales and Usage, 2008-2012 Market Estimate, Released 2017*

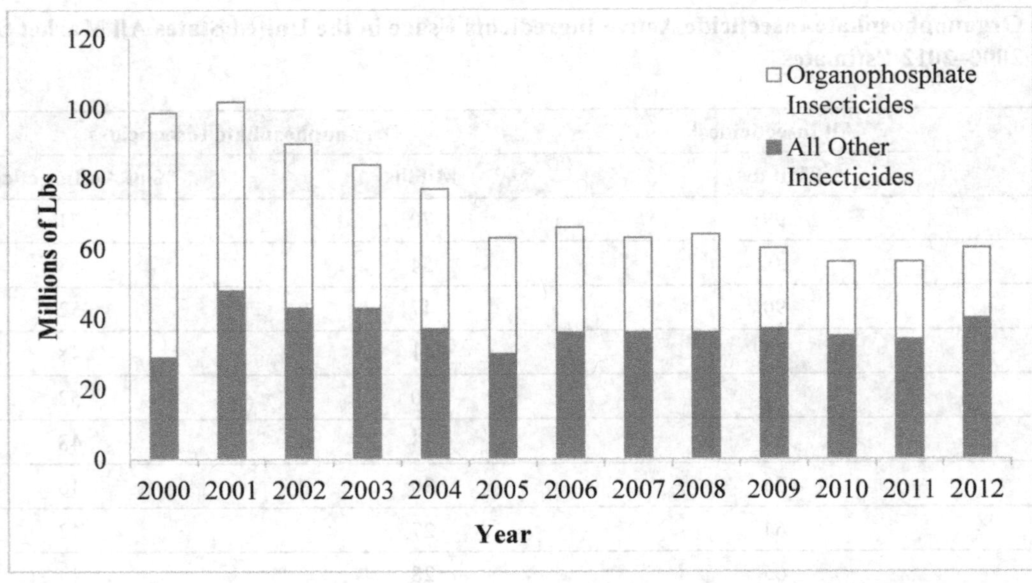

Figure 3.3. Total Amount of Organophosphate and All Other Insecticide Active Ingredients Usage in the United States in All Market Sectors, 2000–2012

Source: Agricultural Market Research Proprietary Data (2000-2012).
Non-Agricultural Market Research Proprietary Data (2000-2012)
USDA/NASS Quick Stats (*http://www.nass.usda.gov/Quick_Stats/*)

Table 3.8. Most Commonly Used Organophosphate Insecticide Active Ingredients, All Market Sectors, 2005, 2007, 2009, and 2012 Estimates (Ranked by Range in Millions of Pounds of Active Ingredient)

Active Ingredient	2012		2009		2007*		2005*	
	Rank	Range	Rank	Range	Rank	Range	Rank	Range
Chlorpyrifos	1	5-8	1	6-9	1	6-9	2	6-9
Acephate	2	5-8	2	3-6	3	3-6	3	3-5
Malathion	3	1-4	3	2-5	2	5-7	1	10-13
Naled	4	1-2	4	1-2	4	1-2	5	1-2
Phorate	5	1-2	6	<1	7	1-2	6	1-2
Dicrotophos	6	1-2	7	<1	5	1-2	7	1-2
Dimethoate	7	<1	8	<1	9	<1	9	<1
Terbufos	8	<1	9	<1	8	<1	—	—
Phosmet	9	<1	5	<1	6	1-2	4	1-3
Ethoprophos	10	<1	—	—	—	—	—	—

Source: Agricultural Market Research Proprietary Data (2005-2012).
Non-Agricultural Market Research Proprietary Data (2005-2012)
USDA/NASS Quick Stats (*http://www.nass.usda.gov/Quick_Stats/*)

***Note:** A dash (—) indicates that the organophosphate pesticide was not one of the 10 most commonly used in the given year.*

* Updated values for 2007 and 2005 presented for continuity.

***Source:** U.S. EPA, Pesticide Industry Sales and Usage, 2008-2012 Market Estimate, Released 2017*

3.7 Pesticide Usage in the United States: Specialty Biocides and Wood Preservatives

Table 3.9 shows the total amount of specialty biocides and wood preservatives by end-use market in the United States in 2012. Specialty biocides include water treatment chemicals (recreational and industrial), disinfectants and sanitizers, waterborne wood preservatives, and products for other uses such as use in adhesives, sealants, and leather. Water treatment chemicals accounted for most specialty biocide usage in 2012, approximately 50%, followed by waterborne wood preservatives, which account for approximately 35% of the total amount of specialty biocides usage.

Table 3.9. Specialty Biocides Used in the United States by End-Use Market, 2012 Estimates

Year and End Use Market	Total	
	Mil lbs	%
2012		
Recreational and Industrial Water Treatment[1]	285	47
Disinfectants and Sanitizers[2]	45	7
Other Specialty Biocides[3]	60	10
Waterborne Wood Preservatives	212	35
Total	602	100

Source: Kline & Company, Specialty Biocides, 2012

Note: *Totals may not be exact due to rounding.*

1 "Recreational and Industrial Water Treatment" does not include hypochlorite or chlorine use.

2 "Disinfectants and Sanitizers" includes industrial/institutional applications and household cleaning products, and does not include hypochlorite or chlorine use.

3 "Other Specialty Biocides" includes biocides for adhesives and sealants, leather, synthetic latex polymers, metalworking fluids, paints and coatings, petroleum products, plastics, mineral slurries, textiles, and antifoulants.

Source: *U.S. EPA, Pesticide Industry Sales and Usage, 2008-2012 Market Estimate, Released 2017*

4 Producers and Users

4.1 Pesticide Producers and Users in 2012

Table 4.1 lists 2012 estimates of the number of firms that are designated as pesticide producers, formulators, distributors, and establishments. Table 4.2 lists 2012 estimates of the number of exterminating and pest control firms and certified pesticide applicators. Table 4.3 lists 2012 estimates of farm land, acres harvested, and the number of farms using pesticides and fertilizers. Table 4.4 lists 2011 estimates of the number of households using pesticides.

Table 4.1. Number of U.S. Pesticide Producers, Formulators, and Distributors

Major Pesticide Producers	12
Other Pesticide Producers	100
Major Pesticide Formulators	120–150
Other Pesticide Formulators	1,550
Distributors	24,686
Establishments	42,160

Source: EPA Estimates

Note: *Entities may operate as both a producer and a formulator. This may result in the number of entities being overestimated.*

Table 4.2. Number of Exterminating and Pest Control Firms and Number of Certified Applicators

Exterminating and Pest Control Firms	23,413
Private[1] Certified Applicators	474,525
Commercial[2] Certified Applicators	425,086
Certified Applicators that Work for Federal Agencies	4,007

Sources: Kline & Company, Global Professional Pest Management Markets for Pesticides, 2012
Washington State University, Certification Plan and Reporting Database (CPARD), 2012
USDA, Office of Pest Management Policy (OPMP), Personal Communication, 2016

1 Private certified applicators refer primarily to farmers or other persons producing an agricultural commodity and using restricted-use pesticides (RUPs).

2 Commercial certified applicators refer to professional pesticide applicators.

Source: *U.S. EPA, Pesticide Industry Sales and Usage, 2008-2012 Market Estimate, Released 2017*

Table 4.3. Land in Farms, Land Harvested, Number of Farms, and Farms Using Pesticides

Land in Farms (acres)	915 million
Land in Production (acres)	390 million
Land Harvested (acres)	315 million
Total Number of Farms	2.109 million
Total Number of Farms with Cropland	1.552 million
Total Number of Farms with Harvested Cropland	1.289 million
Number of Farms Using Chemicals for:	
Insects on Crops/Hay	361,286
Nematodes	58,865
Diseases on Crops/Orchards	121,682
Weed/Grass/Brush	794,320
Defoliation/Fruit Thinning	53,200
Any or all of the above	999,806
Any or all of the above plus fertilizer	1,187,446

Source: USDA/NASS. 2012. Census of Agriculture: United States Summary and State Data, Volume 1, Part 51 (*http://www.agcensus.usda.gov/Publications/2012*).

Table 4.4. Number of U.S. Households Using Pesticides by Pesticide Type

Pesticide Type	Households
Insecticides	82 million
Fungicides	16 million
Herbicides	52 million
Repellents	57 million
Disinfectants	66 million
Any Pesticides	88 million

Sources: EPA estimates based on the 2012 Kline & Company study and 2010 U.S. Census Bureau population estimate

***Source:** U.S. EPA, Pesticide Industry Sales and Usage, 2008-2012 Market Estimate, Released 2017*

5 Glossary

ACTIVE INGREDIENT (a.i.): The chemical or substance component of a pesticide product intended to kill, repel, attract, mitigate, or control a pest, or that acts as a plant growth regulator, desiccant, or nitrogen stabilizer. The remainder of a formulated pesticide product consists of one or more "inert ingredients" (*e.g.,* water, solvents, emulsifiers, surfactants, clay, and propellants), which are there for reasons other than pesticidal activity.

AGRICULTURAL SECTOR (OR MARKET): Pesticides applied by owner/operators and custom/commercial applicators to farms and facilities involved in the production of raw agricultural commodities, principally food, fiber, and tobacco; includes non-crop and post-harvest use as well as crop and field applications.

CERTIFIED APPLICATOR: A person who is authorized to apply "restricted-use" pesticides as a result of meeting requirements for certification under FIFRA-mandated programs. Applicator certification programs are conducted by states, territories, and tribes in accordance with national standards set by EPA. "Restricted-use pesticides" may be used only by or under the direct supervision of specially trained and certified applicators.

COMMERCIAL APPLICATOR: A person applying pesticides as part of a business, applying pesticides for hire, or applying pesticides as part of his or her job with another (not for hire) type of business, organization, or agency. Commercial applicators often are certified, but need to be so only if they apply restricted-use pesticides.

CONVENTIONAL PESTICIDES: Conventional pesticides are all active ingredients other than biological pesticides and antimicrobial pesticides. Conventional active ingredients are generally produced synthetically, *i.e.,* are synthetic chemicals that prevent, mitigate, destroy, or repel any pest; or that act as a plant growth regulator, desiccant, defoliant or nitrogen stabilizer.

ECONOMIC SECTORS (OR MARKETS): In this report, estimates of quantities used and user expenditures for pesticides are broken out separately for the three general economic user sectors (or markets) as follows: agriculture, industrial/commercial/governmental, and home and garden. These three sectors/markets are defined elsewhere in this glossary.

ESTABLISHMENT: The term "establishment" means any place where a pesticide or device or active ingredient used in producing a pesticide is produced, or held, for distribution or sale.

FDA: The U.S. Food and Drug Administration, a branch of the U.S. Department of Health and Human Services, is involved in regulation of pesticides in the United States, particularly in the enforcement of tolerances in food and feed products.

FFDCA: Federal Food, Drug, and Cosmetic Act, the law that controls pesticide residues in food and feed.

FIFRA: Federal Insecticide, Fungicide, and Rodenticide Act, the law that generally controls pesticide sale and use.

FQPA: The Food Quality Protection Act (FQPA) of 1996 amended the Federal Insecticide, Fungicide, and Rodenticide Act (FIFRA) and the Federal Food, Drug, and Cosmetic Act (FFDCA).

HOME AND GARDEN SECTOR (OR MARKET): Involves pesticides applied by homeowners to homes and gardens, including lawns and single- and multiple-unit housing. Does not include pesticides for home and garden applications by professional applicators.

INDUSTRIAL/COMMERCIAL/GOVERNMENTAL USER SECTOR (OR MARKET): Involves pesticides applied by professional applicators (by owners/operators/employees and custom/commercial applicators) to industrial, commercial, and governmental facilities, buildings, sites, and land, plus custom/commercial applications to homes and gardens, including lawns. May also be referred to as the "professional market" for pesticides.

Source: *U.S. EPA, Pesticide Industry Sales and Usage, 2008-2012 Market Estimate, Released 2017*

NON-AGRICULTURAL SECTORS: General term referring to a combination of the home and garden and industrial/commercial/governmental sectors.

OTHER PESTICIDES: Chemicals registered as pesticides but that are produced and marketed mostly for other purposes (*i.e.,* multi-use chemicals). Notable examples are rodenticides, repellents, sulfur, petroleum products (*e.g.,* kerosene, oils, and distillates), salt, and sulfuric acid.

PESTICIDE: May be used to refer to an active ingredient (as defined above) or formulated pesticide product registered under FIFRA.

PESTICIDE USAGE: Refers to actual applications of pesticides, generally in terms of quantity applied or units treated.

PRIVATE APPLICATOR: A category of applicator certification for farmers and/or employees, such that they can legally apply restricted-use pesticides or supervise others doing so who are not certified.

PRODUCER LEVEL: Data covering companies that manufacture and formulate pesticides.

PROFESSIONAL MARKET: Sales of pesticides for application to industrial/commercial/governmental sector and to homes and gardens, by certified/commercial applicators.

PROPRIETARY DATA, AGRICULTURAL AND NON-AGRICULTURAL: Pesticide industry marketing research data that EPA purchases from private data research companies. These data are for EPA use only and cannot be divulged without vendor consent.

SPECIALTY BIOCIDES: Specialty biocides include biocides used for water treatment chemicals (recreational and industrial), disinfectants and sanitizers, waterborne wood preservatives, and products for other uses such as use in adhesives, sealants, and leather.

TOLERANCE: The maximum amount of a pesticide allowable in a food or feed product before it is considered adulterated, usually specified in parts per million.

USDA/NASS: The U.S. Department of Agriculture, National Agricultural Statistics Service. Publicly available data on U.S. agricultural pesticide use (www.nass.usda.gov).

USER LEVEL: Data covering persons or businesses that purchase and apply pesticides, such as farmers, commercial pesticide applicators, and homeowners.

WOOD PRESERVATIVES: Pesticide active ingredients intended to prevent wood degradation problems due to insects, fungal rot, or other pests.

Source: *U.S. EPA, Pesticide Industry Sales and Usage, 2008-2012 Market Estimate, Released 2017*

Recycling Profiles of 100 Major U.S. Cities

City	State	System Type	Voluntary	Materials Collected	Plastic Types
Akron	OH	curbside	no	all metal food, beverage cans, aluminum trays, aluminum foil, glass bottles, jars of any color, rigid plastics marked #1 thru #7 such as milk jugs, plastic bottles, newspapers, magazines, junk mail, and cardboard (corrugated only)	#1, #2, #3, #4, #5, #6, #7
Albuquerque	NM	curbside, drop-off	yes	newspapers, magazines, and shopping catalogs; junk mail and home office paper; tin/steel (small pieces/containers); aluminum cans; all plastic bottles and jugs with a neck or screw top; #1 - #7 plastic bottles or tubs; corrugated cardboard (flattened and bundled)	#1, #2, #3, #4, #5, #6, #7
Anaheim	CA	curbside, drop-off	yes	plastic bottles/containers, aluminum/tin cans, glass bottles and jars (lids off), bi-metal cans, cardboard/Kraft paper, newspapers, computer paper, white/color ledger paper, coated stock, office papers, magazines, mixed paper, cereal boxes (without lining), egg/milk cartons, aluminum foil, laundry bottles, drink boxes	#1, #2, #3, #4, #5, #6, *7
Anchorage	AK	curbside, drop-off	yes	mixed paper: newspapers, magazines, junk mail, flattened cardboard, paper bags, paper egg cartons, file folders, phonebooks, cereal boxes, copy paper; aluminum and tin/steel cans; plastic bottles (PET #1 bottles with a neck); plastic jugs (HDPE #2 jugs with a neck, no yogurt tubs); plastic bags and film: newspaper sleeves, grocery bags, shrink wrap, glass bottles and jars	#1, #2
Arlington	TX	curbside, drop-off	yes	newspapers, magazines, phone books, junk mail and envelopes, office paper, corrugated cardboard (flattened), paper bags, jars/bottles (clear, brown and green), plastic jugs/tubs and bottles, aerosol cans, plastic bags, aluminum/steel/tin cans, pots and pans	#1, #2
Atlanta	GA	curbside	yes	all paper products (except boxes/paper with food contamination), shredded paper (in clear plastic bags), glass bottles/jars (lids removed & placed in recycling), all hard plastic #1-7, aluminum/steel/tin cans, aerosol cans, cardboard (dry and broken down), books	#1, #2, #3, #4, #5, #6, #7
Aurora	CO	curbside, drop-off	yes	the city does not have a public trash collection system, and therefore does not provide recycling services directly. However, most of the private companies that are registered to collect trash in Aurora also provide their customers curbside recycling services. Programs vary. Cartons can now be recycled in these programs.	#1, #2, #3, #4, #5, #6, #7
Austin	TX	curbside	yes	newspapers, magazines, catalogs, junk mail, office paper; aluminum, steel and tin cans; glass bottles and jars, all colors; rigid plastic (#1 through #7); corrugated cardboard; boxboard (cereal and beverage boxes)	#1, #2, #3, #4, #5, #6, #7
Babylon	NY	drop-off, scheduled curbside	yes	plastics/glass, computer paper, telephone books, junk mail, metal/aluminum cans, polystyrene, newspapers, cardboard, concrete, tires, (waste oil, batteries, car batteries-drop-off only) Also accepted are bicycles for the adopt-a-bike program.	#1, #2, #3, #4, #5, #6, #7
Bakersfield	CA	curbside, drop-off	yes	newspaper, cardboard, cereal-type boxes, junk mail, plastics #1-7, office paper, magazines, aluminum/steel/tin cans, phone books, glass bottles and jars	#1, #2, #3, #4, #5, #6, #7
Baltimore	MD	curbside, drop-off	yes	glass jars/bottles (brown, clear or green), aluminum/steel/tin cans, rigid plastic #1-5, empty aerosol cans, newspapers, magazines, telephone books, ad mail, cardboard/boxes, paper (all colors and types), cartons waxed), books	#1, #2, #3, #4, #5
Baton Rouge	LA	curbside, drop-off	yes	newspaper, magazines, scrap paper, cardboard, glass, plastics with a 1 - 7 inside the triangular recycle symbol, milk cartons, juice boxes, detergent refill containers, aluminum/tin/metal alloy cans and metal lids	#1, #2, #3, #4, #5, #6, #7
Birmingham	AL	curbside, drop-off	yes	glass (all types); mixed paper (cereal boxes, box packaged foods, phone books, magazines, office paper, junk mail, etc.); newspaper; corrugated cardboard (broken down); aluminum, steel and tin cans; plastics #1 thru #7; At drop-off—cell phones; printer and ink toner cartridges; batteries (rechargeable and single-use). E-waste: computers, monitors (no TV's) printers, peripherals, other plug-in electronics	#1, #2, #3, #4, #5, #6, #7

City	State	System Type	Voluntary	Materials Collected	Plastic Types
Boston	MA	curbside, drop-off	yes	newspaper (with inserts); magazines/catalogs; junk mail (remove free samples; plastic envelope window is ok); white and colored paper/brown bags; telephone books; flattened food boxes; paperback books; milk and juice cartons; juice/soy milk boxes; cardboard boxes; pizza boxes (empty); glass bottles/jars; tin and aluminum cans, foil, and pie plates; all plastic containers (no motor oil or chemical containers); cardboard/spiral cans; rigid plastics	#1, #2, #3, #4, #5, #6, #7
Brookhaven	NY	curbside, drop-off	no	glass bottles (clear and colored), aluminum/bimetallic/ tin cans, aerosol spray cans, plastic, aluminum foil/containers, newspapers, Kraft & PC paper, corrugated cardboard cartons, mixed low grade paper, phone books	#1, #2, #3, #4, #5, #6, #7
Buffalo	NY	curbside	yes	paper (newspaper, office paper, cardboard, and other paper types); glass bottles and jars (clear and colored); aluminum and steel cans; plastics (all household, rigid, jugs and bottles)	#1, #2, #3, #4, #5, #6, #7
Charlotte	NC	curbside, drop-off	yes	all glass containers, paper, shopping catalogs, milk and juice cartons, newspapers and inserts, cardboard, plastics #1-5 and #7, liquor bottles, spiral paper cans, aluminum/steel/tin cans, telephone books, office paper	#1, #2, #3, #4, #5, #7
Chesapeake	VA	curbside, drop-off	yes	food & beverage containers (OJ containers, shelf stable soup/ almond milk containers); aluminum and steel cans; pie plates and foil; glass jars and bottles; newspapers; #1 and #2 plastic bottles; gift wrapping paper; cardboard (flattened); cereal boxes, paper towel rolls, etc.	#1, #2
Chicago	IL	curbside, drop-off	yes	city-served blue cart program (clean paper, newspaper, magazines, junk mail, cardboard, clean food boxes, phone books, catalogs, brown paper bags, gift wrap (no bows/ribbons), glass jars and bottles, empty aluminum/tin/steel cans, empty aerosol cans, rinsed aluminum foil and pie plates, milk, juice, plastic bottles and containers #1-5 and 7)	#1, #2, #3, #4, #5, #7
Cincinnati	OH	curbside, drop-off	yes	newspaper; office paper; junk mail and envelopes; cardboard (broken down 3' X 3'); paperboard (such as cereal boxes); brown paper bags; magazines; plastic bottles and jugs only; aluminum and steel cans; empty aerosol cans (remove lids and tips); glass bottles and jars (remove lids); cartons	#1, #2, #3, #4, #5, #6, #7
Cleveland	OH	curbside (pilot program), drop-off	yes	glass bottles and jars (rinsed), metal cans (rinsed), plastic containers, newspapers, mixed paper, cardboard (flattened)	#1, #2, #3, #4, #5, #6, #7
Colorado Springs	CO	drop-off	yes	magazines, glass, plastic bags, aluminum, appliances, tires, electronics, metals, motor oil, automotive batteries, paint, hazardous chemicals	#1, #2, #3, #4, #5, #6, #7
Columbus	OH	curbside, drop-off	yes	newspaper, including all inserts; magazines, catalogs and telephone books; mail, scrap paper and envelopes (windows ok); brown paper bags; paperboard (such as cereal or snack boxes); cardboard boxes (flattened); bottles and jars; plastic bottles (any); glass bottles and jars; aluminum/tin/steel cans; aerosol cans	#1, #2, #3, #4, #5, #6, #7
Corpus Christi	TX	curbside, drop-off	yes	newspapers (with ads and inserts); junk mail and envelopes, magazines, catalogs and phone books, paperboard boxes (like cereal boxes), shoe boxes and other similar paper; corrugated cardboard (flattened to less than 2ft square); aluminum, tin and steel; plastic bottles and containers, #1-7; No glass being recycled at this time	#1, #2, #3, #4, #5, #6, #7
Dallas	TX	curbside, drop-off	yes	newspapers and inserts, mixed paper, magazines, junk mail, home/ office paper, cardboard & boxboard, glass containers, plastic bottles, aluminum cans, steel/tin food cans, empty aerosol cans, cartons	#1, #2, #3, #4, #5, #7
Denver	CO	curbside, drop-off	yes	newspapers and inserts, mixed paper, magazines, junk mail, home/office paper, glass containers, aluminum cans, steel/tin food cans, cardboard (flattened and no larger than 2ft x 2ft), phone books, plastic bottles/jars/containers #1-7, empty aerosol cans	#1, #2, #3, #4, #5, #6, #7
Des Moines	IA	curbside, drop-off	yes	glass bottles and jars, wire hangers, newspapers and inserts, brown paper bags, corrugated cardboard, junk mail, contained shredded paper, telephone books, magazines, catalogs, paperback books, folders and window envelopes, aluminum/tin cans, plastic containers (with twist off tops)	plastic containers (with twist off tops)

City	State	System Type	Voluntary	Materials Collected	Plastic Types
Detroit	MI	drop-off, pick-up (select communities/businesses)	yes	newspaper; mixed paper (items that CAN NOT be recycled are: tissue paper, receipts, napkins, wrapping paper, and paper towel); glossy paper; books; cardboard and clean chipboard; glass; all metals; plastic (#1 and #2 plastics together, and #4, #5, #6, and #7 plastics together); Styrofoam; aseptic containers; batteries; computers and electronics; # 1, #2, and #4 plastic bags	#1, #2, #4, #5, #6, #7
El Paso	TX	curbside, drop-off	no	corrugated cardboard, brown paper bags, newspapers and inserts, magazines, junk mail, white/colored bond paper, computer paper, plastic (lids removed), aluminum/steel/tin cans, aluminum foil and pie plates, copper, brass, iron, aluminum, (No Glass)	#1, #2, #3, #4, #5, #6, #7
Fort Wayne	IN	curbside	yes	newspapers, magazines, catalogs, cardboard, fiberboard, phonebooks, paperback books, plastic #1-7, glass (brown, clear, green), cans (aluminum, bi-metal, tin, steel), aluminum foil and pie pans	#1, #2, #3, #4, #5, #6, #7
Fort Worth	TX	curbside	yes	paper, cardboard, catalogs, envelopes, junk mail, magazines, newspapers (all sections), paper bags, telephone books, aluminum cans/baking tins, steel/tin food cans/lids, empty aerosol cans, steel paint cans (empty), glass bottles and jars, pots/pans, plastic bottles/cups/jars	#1, #2, #3, #4, #5, #6, #7
Fremont	CA	curbside, drop-off	yes	newspapers and inserts, most white/colored paper, magazines, junk mail, brown paper bags, catalogs, window envelopes, paper egg cartons, telephone books, flattened cereal/cracker/shoe boxes, glass bottles and jars, plastic containers, aluminum/steel/tin cans, yard waste, food scraps	#1, #2, #3, #4, #5, #6, #7
Fresno	CA	curbside, drop-off	no	aluminum/tin/aerosol cans, small appliances, cardboard, catalogs, chipboard, glass bottles and jars (all colors), junk mail (including envelopes), magazines, newspapers and inserts, plastic bottles (clear/green plastic soda and water bottles, plastic containers, phone books, yard waste	#1, #2, #3, #4, #5, #7
Garland	TX	curbside, drop-off	yes	newspapers and inserts, magazines, aluminum/steel/tin cans, empty aerosol cans, glass bottles and jars (lids removed), plastic, corrugated cardboard, junk mail, brown paper bags, telephone books, white office/computer paper, chipboard	#1, #2, #3, #4, #5, #7
Glendale	AZ	curbside, drop-off	yes	aluminum cans/foil/foil baking pans, empty aerosol cans, cardboard, cartons, chipboard (without inserts), magazines, junk mail, catalogs, brown paper bags, telephone directories, newspapers and inserts, plastic containers, steel/tin cans (all rinsed, clean and dry)	#1, #2, #3, #4, #5, #6, #7
Grand Rapids	MI	curbside, drop-off (at participating locations)	yes	aluminum/steel cans, glass bottles and jars (all colors), plastic bottles, newspapers and inserts, junk mail, corrugated cardboard, magazines, telephone books, white ledger paper, cereal boxes (with liners removed), colored/mixed paper	#1, #2, #3, #4, #5, #6, #7
Greensboro	NC	curbside, drop-off	yes	plastic bottles and jugs, newspapers, magazines, all aluminum beverage cans/pans/foil, office paper, mail, notebook paper, corrugated cardboard, chipboard, brown/gray egg cartons, all steel beverage and food cans, glass (all colors, shapes and sizes), aerosol cans (empty)	#1, #2, #3, #4, #5, #6, #7
Hempstead	NY	curbside, drop-off	yes	newspapers and inserts (tied or paper bagged), magazines, catalogs, box board, cans, all rigid plastic, bottles/glass, aluminum foil/pans/cans, corrugated cardboard (flattened and tied)	#1, #2, #4, #5, #6
Hialeah	FL	curbside	yes	newspapers, aluminum/steel/tin cans, plastics, glass bottles and jars, plastic coated cardboard, six-pack rings, milk and juice containers	#1, #2, #3, #4, #5, #6, #7
Honolulu	HI	drop-off, curbside	yes	newspaper (inserts and magazines removed), corrugated cardboard (flattened), office paper, glass bottles and jars (no lids), aluminum/ steel cans, plastic containers (no tops), grass, tree and hedge trimmings, christmas trees	#1, #2
Houston	TX	curbside, drop-off	no	newspapers, magazines, telephone books, aluminum and tin cans, junk mail, corrugated cardboard, plastic soft drink/milk/water containers, used oil, #6 plastic accepted at select drop-off centers only	#1, #2, #3, #4, #5, #7

City	State	System Type	Voluntary	Materials Collected	Plastic Types
Indianapolis	IN	curbside (varies by community), drop-off	yes	glass; #1-#7 plastics; aluminum, tin, and steel beverage and food cans; newspapers; cardboard and magazines; phone books; empty aerosol cans	#1, #2, #3, #4, #5, #6, #7
Islip	NY	curbside	yes	newspapers, magazines, junk mail, tin/beverage cans, plastic, bottles/glass, corrugated cardboard	#1, #2
Jacksonville	FL	curbside	yes	plastic, glass bottles and jars, metal and aluminum cans, empty aerosol cans, newspapers and inserts, magazines, catalogs, phone books, paperboard cartons, brown paper bags, corrugated cardboard	#1, #2, #3, #4, #5, #6, #7
Jersey City	NJ	curbside, drop-off	no	all glass, cans, plastics, milk and juice containers, as well as drink boxes, mixed newspaper, magazines, junk mail, office paper, telephone books, cardboard boxes, corrugated and laundry detergent boxes	#1, #2, #3, #4, #5, #6, #7
Kansas City	MO	curbside, drop-off	yes	aluminum cans, household (dry cell) batteries, corrugated cardboard, clothing (dry), foil/pie pans, glass bottles (accepted at drop-off locations), magazines, newspapers, mixed office paper, paperboard, plastic bottles, tin cans, telephone books, scrap metal, yard waste	#1, #2, #3, #4, #5, #6, #7
Las Vegas	NV	curbside, drop-off	yes	newspaper, magazines, mixed paper, glass/plastic containers, aluminum/tin cans and scrap, copper, radiators, corrugated cardboard, phone books, dry/clean clothing and shoes	#1, #2, #3, #4, #5, #6, #7
Lexington-Fayette	KY	curbside	no	boxboard, brown paper bags, catalogs, corrugated cardboard, magazines, newspapers/inserts, office paper, telephone books, junk mail, empty aerosol cans, aluminum/steel cans, plastic bottles/jugs only, glass bottles and jars (blue, brown, clear, and green)	#1, #2
Lincoln	NE	drop-off, curbside (private collection)	yes	newspaper, glass containers, aluminum/steel/tin cans, paperboard and corrugated cardboard, mixed residential paper, plastic	#1, #2, #3, #4, #5
Long Beach	CA	curbside, drop-off	yes	glass, aluminum, steel, tin, plastic, clean polystyrene (Styrofoam(r)), empty aerosol and paint cans, mixed paper, bundled newspapers, corrugated cardboard, used motor oil (collected by request only)	#1, #2, #3, #4, #5, #6, #7
Los Angeles	CA	curbside, drop-off	yes	paper, all cardboard boxes and chipboard, all aluminum, tin, metal, and bi-metal cans, pie tins, clean aluminum foils; empty paint and aerosol cans with caps removed, and wire hangers, all glass bottles and jars, plastics 1 through 7, clean polystyrene (Styrofoam®)	#1, #2, #3, #4, #5, #6, #7
Louisville	KY	curbside, drop-off	yes	junk mail, brown paper bags, telephone books, magazines, catalogs, newspapers and inserts, flattened cardboard, glass bottles and jars (clear, brown, green and blue) aluminum/steel/tin cans, empty aerosol cans, aluminum foil/pie and cake pans, plastic, office paper and envelopes	#1, #2, #3, #4, #5, #6, #7
Lubbock	TX	drop-off	yes	glass (clear and colored), plastic, aluminum and beverage cans, tin food cans, corrugated cardboard, newspaper (no inserts), computer paper (green bar or shredded), white ledger paper, yard waste, used motor oil (under 5 gallons)	#1, #2
Madison	WI	curbside, drop-off	no	newspapers, corrugated cardboard, magazines, catalogs, brown paper bags, telephone books, glass bottles and jars only, aluminum/tin/steel cans, plastic containers, empty paint cans, #1 clam shells and blister packs, metal pots/pans	#1, #2, #3, #4, #5, #6, #7
Memphis	TN	curbside, drop-off	yes	aluminum/steel cans, empty aerosol cans, plastic bottles, glass bottles and jars (clear, brown and green), newspapers and inserts, magazines, telephone books, office paper, junk mail, white/colored paper, envelopes, manila folders, stationery, yard waste	#1, #2
Mesa	AZ	curbside, drop-off	yes	aluminum, cardboard, chipboard, glass food and beverage jars and bottles, metal cans, newspapers, magazines, mixed paper, plastic bottles/jugs/jars, telephone books	#1, #2, #3, #4, #5, #6, #7
Miami	FL	curbside	yes	glass/narrow neck plastic bottles, aluminum/steel cans, magazines, office/mixed paper, corrugated cardboard, white goods, yard trash, tires	only narrow-neck plastic containers

City	State	System Type	Voluntary	Materials Collected	Plastic Types
Milwaukee	WI	curbside	yes	plastic, glass jars and bottles (all colors), aluminum containers/foil/pans, bulky #2 plastics (like 5-gallon buckets), cartons, metal pots/pans, newspaper, magazines, catalogs, phone books, steel food cans, empty aerosol cans	#1, #2, #4, #5
Minneapolis	MN	curbside, drop-off	yes	dry boxboard, office paper, mail, cans, corrugated cardboard, glass, household batteries, magazines, newspapers, telephone books, plastic bottles, cartons	#1, #2, #3, #4, #5, #6, #7
Mobile	AL	drop-off	yes	plastic beverage containers, aluminum beverage cans, steel cans, corrugated cardboard, newspapers, magazines, junk mail, telephone books, computer paper, cereal boxes, glass jars (brown/amber, green/blue and clear), styrofoam packing peanuts, pine straw	#1, #2
Montgomery	AL	drop-off	yes	aluminum, paper, cardboard; additional programs for recycling: rechercheable batteries, tires, used motor oil, christmas trees, mobile phones, plastic bags, shredded paper	#1, #2
Nashville	TN	curbside, drop-off (glass must be dropped off)	yes	paper (newspaper, magazines, junk mail, phone books, paperback books, paperboard, cereal boxes, freezer food boxes); cardboard, aluminum and steel cans, plastic containers (plastic bottles, and dairy containers labeled #1 through #7); glass bottles should be taken to one of the drop-off or convenience centers or arrange for separate curbside collection	#1, #2, #3, #4, #5, #6, #7
New Orleans	LA	curbside, drop-off (glass must be dropped off)	yes	newspapers, magazines, telephone books, catalogs, brown paper bags, plastic, aluminum/steel/tin cans, glass, clean, unsoiled corrugated boxes	#1, #2, #3, #4, #5, #6, #7
New York	NY	curbside, drop-off	no	paper, mail and envelopes, wrapping paper, smooth cardboard, paper bags, cardboard egg cartons and trays, newspapers, magazines, catalogs, phone books, softcover books, corrugated cardboard, metal cans, aluminum foil, household metals, bulk metal (metal furniture, cabinets, large appliances, etc.), glass bottles and jars, plastic bottles and jugs, milk cartons and juice boxes, leaf program (fall)	na
Newark	NJ	curbside, drop-off	no	glass bottles and jars, cans, bottles, corrugated cardboard, newspapers, magazines, mixed high-grade white paper, aluminum and bimetal cans, used motor oil, leaves, plastic: milk jugs, soda bottles, water bottles, juice bottles and laundry detergent containers	na
Norfolk	VA	curbside, drop-off	yes	aluminum cans/pie plates/foil, glass bottles and jars, corrugated cardboard and chipboard (flattened), phone books, unwanted mail, household batteries, newspapers, plastic soda/water bottles, plastic milk/water/detergent jugs, steel cans, mixed office paper	na
North Hempstead	NY	curbside, drop-off	yes	newspapers/inserts, magazines, direct mail, catalogs, construction/wrapping paper, index/greeting cards, paperback books, plastic, food/beverage cans, aluminum foil/pie tins, glass (clear and colored)	#1, #2, #4, #5, #6
Oakland	CA	curbside, drop-off	yes	glass bottles and jars, plastic bottles and jugs, tin and aluminum cans/foil/pie plates, milk cartons, empty spray cans, empty and dry metal latex paint containers, newspapers, catalogs, magazines, paper egg cartons, holiday trees (seasonal)	na
Oklahoma City	OK	curbside, drop-off	yes	plastic milk jugs and beverage bottles, aluminum and steel food and beverage cans, glass food and beverage jars and bottles, newspapers and inserts, paper bags, magazines	#1, #2, #3, #4, #5, #6, #7
Omaha	NE	curbside, drop-off	yes	newspapers and inserts, magazines, catalogs, telephone books, junk mail, detergent boxes, wrapping paper, paperback books, office/school paper, plastic, glass bottles and jars (drop-off only), aluminum/steel/tin cans, corrugated cardboard	#1, #2, #3, #5
Oyster Bay	NY	curbside, drop-off	yes	newspapers and inserts (tied and separated), mixed paper and magazines (tied and separated); food and beverage cans, plastics (rigid only), bottles/glass	na

City	State	System Type	Voluntary	Materials Collected	Plastic Types
Philadelphia	PA	curbside, drop-off	no	mixed paper (newspapers including inserts, junk mail, envelopes, telephone books, magazines and catalogs, cereal type boxes - no liners, home office paper, stationery and other clean paper); metal cans, aluminum cans, empty aerosol cans (no caps), empty paint cans (air dried), paint can lids (separated from the paint cans), glass bottles and jars, plastic and cardboard, (clean foam #6 materials ok for drop-off)	#1, #2, #3, #4, #5, #6, #7
Phoenix	AZ	curbside, drop-off	yes	telephone books, plastic, food/glass bottles/jars, office paper, newspapers, magazines, cardboard, chipboard, milk/juice cartons, juice boxes, junk mail, aluminum cans/pie plates/foil, steel cans, metal hangers, scrap metal, aerosol cans, shredded paper (placed in clear bags)	#1, #2, #3, #4, #5, #6, #7
Pittsburgh	PA	curbside, drop-off	no	plastic/metal containers, newspapers and inserts, corrugated cardboard, magazines, catalogs, glossy paper, white office paper, glass (clear and colored), all metal cans, empty aerosol and paint cans, aluminum foil/containers, plastic bottles, jugs, and jars (no lids/caps)	#1, #2, #3, #4, #5
Plano	TX	curbside, drop-off	yes	newspapers, magazines, catalogs, junk mail, telephone books, brown paper bags, chipboard/ boxboard, corrugated cardboard boxes, aluminum/ steel/tin cans, plastic, aerosol cans, glass jars/ containers/dishes/drinking glasses/vases (any color), office paper	#1, #2, #3, #4, #5, #6, #7
Portland	OR	curbside, drop-off	no	newspapers, scrap paper, glass bottles and jars, magazines, corrugated cardboard, Kraft paper, plastic bottles (including milk jugs), steel/tin cans, used motor oil (in jugs)	na
Raleigh	NC	curbside, drop-off	yes	newspapers and inserts, magazines, catalogs, junk mail, food and beverage cans, plastic, glass food and beverage containers, aseptic boxes, aluminum foil/trays/ cans (clean), phone books	#1, #2, #3, #4, #5, #7
Richmond	VA	curbside, drop-off	yes	newspapers, mixed paper, aluminum cans/foil, steel cans, glass bottles and jars, milk cartons, juice boxes, plastic, cardboard	#1, #2
Riverside	CA	curbside, drop-off	yes	aluminum/tin cans, glass, polystyrene, newspapers, white office paper, computer paper, cardboard, magazines, junk mail; C.U.R.E. program: gas run equipment, air conditioners, refrigerators, car batteries, appliances, electronics	#1, #2, #3, #4, #5, #6, #7
Rochester	NY	curbside	no	newspapers and inserts, magazines, glossy catalogs, corrugated cardboard, laundry baskets, glass, CD jewel cases, plastic food and beverage containers, milk/juice cartons, empty aerosol cans, aluminum/tin/bi-metal cans, durable kitchen cookware	#1, #2, #3, #4, #5, #6, #7
Sacramento	CA	curbside	yes	glass bottles and jars (all colors), newspapers, junk mail, envelopes, telephone books, magazines, catalogs, brown paper bags, paper egg cartons, shoe boxes, computer/colored paper, paper 6-pk containers and boxes, cardboard, aluminum/tin cans, plastic	#1, #2, #3, #4, #5, #6, #7
Saint Louis	MO	curbside, drop-off	yes	aluminum cans, glass bottles and jars (clear, green and brown), newspapers and inserts, magazines, thin catalogs, steel food cans, plastic bottles and jugs, paperboard, office paper, corrugated cardboard	#1, #2, #3, #4, #5, #7
Saint Paul	MN	curbside, drop-off	yes	newspapers/inserts, mail, envelopes, magazines, catalogs, office/school paper, boxboard, corrugated cardboard boxes, glass bottles and jars (clear/colors), metal cans/lids, jar lids, bottle caps, aluminum foil/trays, good clothes/linens	#1, #2, #4, #5, #7
Saint Petersburg	FL	curbside, drop-off	yes	mixed paper; newspapers; glass and plastic bottles; metal/aluminum cans; food and beverage cartons; corrugated cardboard boxes (flattened); drop-off: appliances, mixed metal, yard waste	#1, #2, #3, #4, #5, #6, #7
San Antonio	TX	curbside, drop-off	yes	paper (ad circulars, catalogs, carbonless paper, dry goods packaging with liners removed, envelopes, file folders, cardboard, junk mail, magazines, newspapers, office paper, paperback books, paper bags, paper towel/toilet paper cores, phone books, non-metallic gift wrap); plastics (#1 through #7); glass (bottles and jars all colors); metal (aluminum, steel and tin beverage and food cans)	#1, #2, #3, #4, #5, #6, #7

City	State	System Type	Voluntary	Materials Collected	Plastic Types
San Diego	CA	curbside, drop-off	no	glass bottles and jars, empty aerosol cans, plastic bottles and jars, cardboard, aluminum cans, paper bags, aluminum foil, foil trays, bagged shredded paper, newspapers, metal cans, phone books, paper or frozen food boxes, mail and magazines, paper and catalogs	#1, #2, #3, #4, #5, #7
San Francisco	CA	curbside, drop-off	no	paper, envelopes (windows okay), corrugated cardboard, aluminum cans and foil, cereal boxes (without lining), glass bottles and jars, egg cartons (paper only), plastic (rigid and hard), junk mail and brochures, spray cans (must be empty), magazines, steel (tin) cans, newspapers, phone books, wrapping paper	#1, #2, #3, #4, #5, #6, #7
San Jose	CA	curbside	yes	metal cans, milk and juice cartons, glass bottles and jars (brown, clear and green), plastic, carbonless paper, cardboard, catalogs, envelopes, junk mail, magazines, newspapers and inserts, paper bags, polystyrene, scrap metals, textiles	#1, #2, #3, #4, #5, #6, #7
Santa Ana	CA	curbside, drop-off	yes	newspaper, mixed/white paper, cardboard, junk mail, magazines, telephone books, cereal/tissue boxes, glass/plastic bottles and jars, aluminum/steel/tin cans, empty aerosol cans, pie tins, plastic milk containers	na
Scottsdale	AZ	curbside, drop-off	yes	aseptic boxes, corrugated cardboard/chipboard, glass (clear, green, amber), magazines, telephone books, aluminum/steel/tin cans, empty aerosol cans, newspapers/inserts, junk mail, brown paper bags, plastic jugs/bottles, clean aluminum foil	#1, #2, #3, #4, #5, #6, #7
Seattle	WA	curbside, drop-off	yes	cardboard, magazines, junk mail, envelopes, aseptic packaging, telephone books, glass bottles and jars (all colors), steel/tin cans, plastic bottles and jars with necks/tubs/jugs, milk and juice cartons, aluminum, used motor oil	sorted by type not resin code or #
Shreveport	LA	curbside, drop-off	yes	paper; plastic and glass bottles; metal cans; magazines; cardboard; corrugated boxes; newspaper; catalogs; detergent bottles	#1, #2, #3, #4, #5, #6, #7
Stockton	CA	curbside, drop-off	yes	aluminum beverage containers, steel/tin cans, glass bottles/jars, plastic, newspapers, telephone books	#1, #2
Tampa	FL	curbside	yes	glass bottles and jars (all colors), newspapers, aluminum/steel cans, milk and juice cartons made from paper, plastic containers, phone books, paperback books, cardboard, foil pie tins, empty aerosol cans	#1, #2, #3, #4, #5, #6, #7
Toledo	OH	curbside	yes	junk mail, paper, boxboard, corrugated cardboard, newspapers, magazines, milk/juice cartons, glass bottles, tin and aluminum cans	#1, #2, #3, #4, #5, #6, #7
Tucson	AZ	curbside, drop-off	yes	white/colored paper, envelopes, junk mail, magazines, catalogs, paperboard/chipboard, phone books, fiberboard, cartons, newspapers, brown paper bags, corrugated cardboard, plastic, steel/tin cans, aluminum cans/foil/baking pans, glass food/beverage containers	#1, #2, #3, #4, #5, #6, #7
Tulsa	OK	curbside, drop-off	yes	glass jars and bottles (green, brown and clear), plastic #1-7, aluminum/steel cans, newspapers and inserts, magazines, office paper, box board	#1, #2, #3, #4, #5, #6, #7
Virginia Beach	VA	curbside, drop-off	yes	newspapers, cardboard, chipboard, junk mail, catalogs, magazines, telephone books, glass bottles and jars with lids removed (clear, green and brown), plastic bottles with a neck or spout only, aluminum/steel/tin cans	#1, #2
Washington	DC	curbside	yes	glass jars and bottles; metals (aluminum pie plates, tin, aluminum and steel cans); aerosol cans; plastic bottles (all narrow-necked or screw-topped bottles marked with a #1 through #7); paper (white and colored papers, envelopes, forms, file folders, tablets, junk mail, cereal boxes, shoeboxes, wrapping paper, shredded paper/mail, catalogs, magazines, paperback books and phone books); newspaper (including inserts); corrugated cardboard; brown paper bags	#1, #2, #3, #4, #5, #6, #7
Wichita	KS	curbside (private-no public trash collection)	yes	aluminum cans; appliances; batteries; books; carpet pad; catalogs; cellular phones; clothes hangers; clothing; computers; curbside recycling; eyeglasses; furniture; glass; hazardous materials; hearing aids; magazines; medication; metal; motor oil; packaging material; paper items; phone directories; plastics; printer cartridges; televisions; tires; unsolicited mail; wood and yard waste; Items collected vary according to service provider.	#1, #2, #3, #4, #5, #6, #7

Source: *Independent research by the editors, June 2017*

Occupational and Environmental Exposures Capable of Causing Illness

Common Name/Synonym	Primary Name	AOEC Code[1]	Use[2]	Asth-magen[3]	Asthma Detail[3]
1,1,1,2-Tetrafluoroethane	1,1,1,2-Tetrafluoroethane	190.156			
1,1,1-Trichloroethane	Methyl Chloroform	190.08	S		
1,1,2-Trichloroethane	1,1,2-Trichloroethane	190.12	S		
1,1-Azobisformamide	Azodicarbamide	260.18		Yes	Rs
1,2,3-Trihydroxybenzene	1,2,3-Trihydroxybenzene	180.06			
1,2,4-Benzenetricarboxylic Acid 1,2-Anhydride	Trimellitic Anhydride	151.03		Yes	Rs
1,2,4-Triazole-3-carboxamide	Ribavirin	321.32			
1,2,4-Trichlorobenzene	1,2,4-Trichlorobenzene	201.02			
1,2-benzenedicarboxaldehyde	Ortho-phthalaldehyde	120.1			R
1,2-Benzisothiazol-3(2H)one	Saccharin	320.38			R
1,2-Dibromoethane	Ethylene Dibromide	191.01	P		
1,2-Dichloroethane	Ethylene Dichloride	190.07	S		
1,2-Dichloroethylene	1,2-Dichloroethylene	190.06	S		
1,2-Dichloropropane	Propylene Dichloride	190.11	S		
1,2-Ethanediol	Ethylene Glycol	80.011			
1,3-Butylene Glycol	1,3-Butylene Glycol	80.04			
1,3-Dichloro-1,1,2,2,3-pentafluoropropane	1,3-Dichloro-1,1,2,2,3-pentafluoropropane	192.022			
1,3-Dichloro-2-Propanol	1,3-Dichloro-2-Propanol	190.17			
1,3-Dihydroxy-2-propanone	Dihydroxyacetone	130.08			
1,4-?-D-Glucan glucohydrolase	Amyloglucosidase	324.11		Yes	Rs
1,4-Benzenediamine	1,4-Benzenediamine	251.061			R
1,4-Dioxane	Dioxane	100.04	S		
1,5-Naphthylene Ester Isocyanic Acid	Naphthalene Diisocyanate	221.03		Yes	G
1,6-Diisocyanato-Hexane	Hexamethylene Diisocyanate	221.04		Yes	G
1,6-Hexanediamine	Hexamethylenediamine	232.1			R
1-Allyl-3-Methoxy-4-Hydroxybenzene	Eugenol	100.07		Yes	Rs
1-beta-D-ribofuranosyl-1H-1,2,4-triazole-3-carboxamide	Ribavirin	321.32			
1-Bromo-3-chloro-5,5-dimethylhydantoin	1-Bromo-3-chloro-5,5-dimethylhydantoin	191.04			R
1-Butanol	N-Butyl Alcohol	70.04	S		
1-Chloro-2,3-Epoxypropane	Epichlorohydrin	110.01			
1-Hydroxy-2-methoxybenzene	Guaiacol	100.09			
1-Methyl-2-Pyrrolidinone	1-Methyl-2-Pyrrolidinone	260.12			
1-Pentanol	Amyl Alcohol	70.02			
1-Propanol	Propyl Alcohol	70.08	S		
1-Propyl Chloride	Chloropropane	190.05	S		
2,3,7,8-TCDD	2,3,7,8-Tetrachlorodibenzodioxin	200.041	P		
2,3,7,8-Tetrachlorodibenzodioxin	2,3,7,8-Tetrachlorodibenzodioxin	200.041	P		
2,4,5-T	2,4,5-T	200.011	P		
2,4,6-Trinitrophenol	Picric Acid	250.09			
2,4-D	2,4-D	200.012	P		
2,6-Dichlorobenzonitrile	2,6-Dichlorobenzonitrile	200.1	P		
2-Aminoethanol	Monoethanolamine	231.01		Yes	Rs
2-Aminopropane	Isopropylamine	230.03			
2-Butanone	Methyl Ethyl Ketone	130.03	S		
2-Butoxyethanol	2-Butoxyethanol	91.03	S		R
2-Chloroacetophenone	Mace	320.27			
2-Chloroethanol	Beta-Chloroethyl Alcohol	70.03			
2-Chloroethylphosphonic Acid	Ethephon	291.12	P		
2-Ethoxyethanol	Ethylene Glycol Monoethyl Ether	91.02	S		
2-Ethoxyethyl Acetate	2-Ethoxyethyl Acetate	141.05			
2-Ethylhexyl Nitrate	2-Ethylhexyl Nitrate	260.31			
2-Furanmethanol	Furfuryl Alcohol	70.09			R
2-Hydroxyethanethiol	Mercaptoethanol	310.04			
2-Hydroxypropyl Acrylate	2-Hydroxypropyl Acrylate	142.09			
2-Methylpropane	Isobutane	60.04			

Common Name/Synonym	Primary Name	AOEC Code[1]	Use[2]	Asthmagen[3]	Asthma Detail[3]
2-Naphthylamine	Beta-Naphthylamine	251.05			
2-Nitropropane	2-Nitropropane	260.141			
2-Oxetanone	Beta-Propiolactone	320.04			
2-Pentanone	Methyl Propyl Ketone	130.1			
2-Propanol	Isopropyl Alcohol	70.06	S		
2-Propanone	Acetone	130.01	S		
2-Propen-1-ol	Allyl Alcohol	70.01			
2-Propenal	Acrolein	120.02			
2-Thiocarbamide	2-Thiocarbamide	310.071			
3,3'-Dichlorobenzidene & Salts	3,3'-Dichlorobenzidene & Salts	250.13			
3,3-Dichloro-1,1,1,2,2-pentafluoropropane	3,3-Dichloro-1,1,1,2,2-pentafluoropropane	192.021			
3-Amino-5-mercapto-1,2,4-triazole	3-Amino-5-mercapto-1,2,4-triazole	260.3		Yes	Rs
3-Dimethylamino Propylamine	3-Dimethylamino Propylamine	232.05			R
3-DMAPA	3-Dimethylamino Propylamine	232.05			R
3-mercaptopropionate	3-mercaptopropionate	310.13			
3-mercaptopropionic Acid	3-mercaptopropionic Acid	310.12			
3-thiopropionic Acid	3-mercaptopropionic Acid	310.12			
4,4'-Methylenebis(2-Chloroaniline)	4,4'-Methylenebis(2-Chloroaniline)	250.03			
4,4-Aminodiphenyl	Benzidine	251.03			
4,4-Diaminodiphenylmethane	Methylenedianiline	250.16			
4-Hydroxyaniline	Para-Aminophenol	251.01			
4-Methyl-2-Pentanone	Methyl Isobutyl Ketone	130.04	S		
4-PC	4-Phenylcyclohexene	60.11			
4-Phenylcyclohexene	4-Phenylcyclohexene	60.11			
5-chloro-2-(2,4-dichlorohydroxy) phenol	5-chloro-2-(2,4-dichlorohydroxy) phenol	181.03		Yes	Rs
5-Nonanone	Butyl Ketone	130.06	S		
7 ACA	7-aminocephalosporanic acid	321.064			R
7-Amino-3-thiomethyl-3-cephalosporanic acid	7-Amino-3-thiomethyl-3-cephalosporanic acid	321.065			R
7-aminocephalosporanic acid	7-aminocephalosporanic acid	321.064			R
7CTD	Tosyalate dihydrate	321.069			R
7TACA	7-Amino-3-thiomethyl-3-cephalosporanic acid	321.065			R
8-Hydroxyquinoline	8-Hydroxyquinoline	250.02			
8-Quinolinol	8-Hydroxyquinoline	250.02			
90% Uncured methacrylate ester monomers	Optigard	142.13			
?-lactalbumin	?-lactalbumin	380.23		Yes	Rs
Abiruana	Pouteria glomerata	373.08		Yes	Rs
Abrasives, NOS	Abrasives, NOS	10.01			
ABS Copolymer	Acrylonitrile-Butadiene-Styrene Copolymer	270.29			R
Acacia	Gum Arabic	372.01		Yes	Rs
Acarian	Acarian	382.11		Yes	
Acephate	Acephate	291.11	P		R
Acetaldehyde	Acetaldehyde	120.01			
Acetamide	Acetamide	260.01			
Acetates, NOS	Acetates, NOS	141			
Acetic Acid	Glacial Acetic Acid	50.34		Yes	Rrs
Acetic Acid Ethyl Ester	Ethyl Acetate	141.03	S		
Acetic Anhydride	Acetic Anhydride	151.09			
Acetic Ether	Ethyl Acetate	141.03	S		
Acetic Oxide	Acetic Anhydride	151.09			
Acetone	Acetone	130.01	S		
Acetonitrile	Acetonitrile	210.01			
Acetophenone	Mace	320.27			
Acetylene	Acetylene	60.01			
Acetylene Dichloride	1,2-Dichloroethylene	190.06	S		
Acetylene Trichloride	Trichloroethylene	190.13	S		
Acid & Base Mixture	Acid & Base Mixture	50.33			
Acid Solder	Acid Solder	50.26			
Acid Stripper	Acid Stripper	50.25			
Acids, Bases, Oxidizers, NOS	Acids, Bases, Oxidizers, NOS	50			

Common Name/Synonym	Primary Name	AOEC Code[1]	Use[2]	Asth-magen[3]	Asthma Detail[3]
Acridine	Acridine	250.15			
Acrolein	Acrolein	120.02			
Acrylamide	Acrylamide	260.02			
Acrylate	Acrylic Monomer	142.01			
Acrylates, NOS	Acrylates, NOS	142			
Acrylic Acid	Acrylic Acid	150.08			R
Acrylic Acid Butyl Ester	Butyl Acrylate	142.02			R
Acrylic Acid Polymer	Acrylics	270.01			
Acrylic Acid, 1,1,1-(Trihydroxymethyl) Propane Triester	Trimethylolpropane Triacrylate	142.08			
Acrylic Acid, 2(Diethylamino)ethyl Ester	Diethylaminoethyl Acrylate	142.06			
Acrylic Acid, 2-Hydroxypropylester	2-Hydroxypropyl Acrylate	142.09			
Acrylic Aldehyde	Acrolein	120.02			
Acrylic Amide	Acrylamide	260.02			
Acrylic capstock pellets	Acrylic capstock pellets	270.43			
Acrylic Monomer	Acrylic Monomer	142.01			
Acrylic Resins	Acrylics	270.01			
Acrylics	Acrylics	270.01			
Acrylonitrile	Acrylonitrile	210.02			
Acrylonitrile-Butadiene-Styrene Copolymer	Acrylonitrile-Butadiene-Styrene Copolymer	270.29			
Acrylonitrile-Butadiene-Styrene-Polyvinyl Chloride	Acrylonitrile-Butadiene-Styrene-Polyvinyl Chloride	270.3			
Actibon	Activated Carbon	10.041			
Activated Carbon	Activated Carbon	10.041			
Activol	Para-Aminophenol	251.01			
Adding Machine	Keyboard Use	360.02			
Adhesive, Epoxy	Adhesive, Epoxy	110.06		Yes	G
Adhesive, NOS	Glues, NOS	320.11			
Aerosolized Pentamidine	Pentamidine	321.23			
Aflotoxins	Aflotoxins	391.091			
African Maple, ayous, wawa, abeche, or samba	Triplochiton Scleroxylon	373.09		Yes	Rs
African Zebrawood	Microberlinia brazzavillensis	373.13		Yes	Rs
Agent Orange	Agent Orange	200.01	P		
AIDS Exposure	HIV Exposure	390.08			
Air Bag Discharge Products	Air Bag Discharge Products	320.44			
Air Freshener	Air Freshener	320.42			
Air Pollutants, Indoor	Air Pollutants, Indoor	320.01			
Air Pollutants, Indoor, from Building Renovation	Indoor Air Pollutants from Building Renovation	320.33			
Air Pollutants, Outdoor	Air Pollutants, Outdoor	320.02			
Air Pressure, Changes	Air Pressure, Changes	350.07			
Albuterol Aerosol	Salbutamol	321.31		Yes	Rs
Alcalase	Bacillus Subtilis Enzymes	324.01		Yes	Rs
Alcalaser	Protease	324.011		Yes	Rs
Alcohol	Ethanol	70.05	S		
Alcohols, NOS	Alcohols, NOS	70	S		
Aldehydes, NOS	Aldehydes, NOS	120			
Aldrin	Aldrin	280.01	P		
Alicyclic Hydrocarbons, NOS	Alicyclic Hydrocarbons, NOS	60.002			
Aliphatic Hydrocarbons, NOS	Aliphatic Hydrocarbons, NOS	60.001			
Alkyd Resins	Alkyd Resins	270.21			
Alkyl Dimethyl Benzyl Ammonium Chloride	Alkyl Dimethyl Benzyl Ammonium Chloride	322.3219		Yes	Rs
Alkylcyanoacrylates, NOS	Cyanoacrylates, NOS	142.07		Yes	Rs
Allyl Alcohol	Allyl Alcohol	70.01			
Allylguaiacol	Eugenol	100.07		Yes	Rs
Almond Shell Dust (Prunus dulcis)	Almond Shell Dust (Prunus dulcis)	370.71		Yes	Rs
Alpha Amylase	Fungal Amylase	324.09		Yes	Rs
alpha Amylase (bacterial)	alpha Amylase (bacterial)	324.16		Yes	Rs
alpha Amylase (pancreatic)	alpha Amylase (pancreatic)	324.17		Yes	Rs
Alpha Lactalbumin	Alpha Lactalbumin	380.101		Yes	Rs
Alpha-Chlorotoluene	Benzyl Chloride	200.02			

Common Name/Synonym	Primary Name	AOEC Code[1]	Use[2]	Asth-magen[3]	Asthma Detail[3]
Alpha-Naphthylamine	Alpha-Naphthylamine	251.04			
Alternaria	Alternaria	391.12		Yes	Rs
Alternaria Aleternata	Alternaria	391.12		Yes	Rs
Alternaria Alternata Toxin	Alternaria	391.12		Yes	Rs
Alternaria spp	Alternaria	391.12		Yes	Rs
Alumina	Aluminum Oxide	20.02		Yes	Rs
Aluminum	Aluminum	20.011		Yes	Rs
Aluminum Chloride	Aluminum Chloride	20.012		Yes	Rs
Aluminum Compounds	Aluminum Compounds	20.01		Yes	Rs
Aluminum Hydroxide	Aluminum Hydroxide	50.3			
Aluminum Oxide	Aluminum Oxide	20.02		Yes	Rs
Aluminum Oxide, Corundum	Aluminum Oxide, Corundum	20.021		Yes	Rs
Aluminum Phosphide	Aluminum Phosphide	40.31	P		
Amaranth	Amaranth	252.01			
Amino Acids, NOS	Amino Acids, NOS	250.19			
Amino Resins	Amino Resins	270.22			
Aminobenzene	Aniline	250.01			
Aminoethyl Ethanolamine	Aminoethyl Ethanolamine	231.03		Yes	Rs
Aminophen	Aniline	250.01			
Ammonia	Ammonium Hydroxide, NOS	322.07		Yes	Rrs
Ammonia Solution (10%)	Ammonia Solution (10%)	322.09		Yes	Rs
Ammonia Solution (29%)	Ammonia Solution (29%)	322.08		Yes	Rs
Ammonia Solution, NOS	Ammonium Hydroxide, NOS	322.07		Yes	Rrs
Ammonia, Household	Ammonia Solution (10%)	322.09		Yes	Rs
Ammonium Bichromate	Ammonium Bichromate	22.02		Yes	Rs
Ammonium bifluoride	Ammonium bifluoride	40.34			
Ammonium Chloride	Ammonium Chloride	52.031			
Ammonium chloroplatinate	Ammonium Hexachloroplatinate (IV)	24.01		Yes	Rs
Ammonium Hexachloroplatinate (IV)	Ammonium Hexachloroplatinate (IV)	24.01		Yes	Rs
Ammonium Hydroxide, NOS	Ammonium Hydroxide, NOS	322.07		Yes	Rrs
Ammonium Persulfate	Ammonium Persulfate	52.04			
Ammonium Phosphate	Ammonium Phosphate	40.32	P		
Ammonium Salts	Ammonium Salts	52.03			
Ammonium Sulfate	Ammonium Sulfate	52.05			
Ampicillin	Ampicillin	321.041		Yes	G
Amprolium	Amprolium	321.11		Yes	Rs
AMT	3-Amino-5-mercapto-1,2,4-triazole	260.3		Yes	Rs
Amyl Acetate	Amyl Acetate	141.01			
Amyl Alcohol	Amyl Alcohol	70.02			
Amyl Nitrite	Amyl Nitrite	260.27			
Amylase and protease	Flaviastase	324.06		Yes	Rs
Amyloglucosidase	Amyloglucosidase	324.11		Yes	Rs
Ananase	Bromelain	324.07		Yes	Rs
Anesthetic Ethers, NOS	Anesthetic Ethers, NOS	190.155			R
Anesthetic Gases, Halogenated	Anesthetic Gases, Halogenated	190.154			R
Anesthetic Gases, NOS	Anesthetic Gases, NOS	320.03			
Anhydride, NOS	Anhydride, NOS	151			
Anhydrous Ammonia	Anhydrous Ammonia	52.011		Yes	Rr
Aniline	Aniline	250.01			
Aniline Dyes, NOS	Aniline Dyes, NOS	251			
Animal Material, NOS	Animal Material, NOS	380			R
Animal Material, NOS (see specific animals)	Animal Material, NOS	380			R
Anisakis simplex	Anisakis simplex	382.26		Yes	Rs
Anthracene	Anthracene	161.01			
Antifreeze	Antifreeze	80.01			
Antigens, Animal	Antigens, Animal	380.01			
Antigens, Animal (see specific animals)	Antigens, Animal	380.01			
Antimony	Antimony	20.031			

Common Name/Synonym	Primary Name	AOEC Code[1]	Use[2]	Asth-magen[3]	Asthma Detail[3]
Antimony Compounds	Antimony Compounds	20.03			
Antimony Hydride	Antimony Hydride	20.04			
Arabidopsis Thaliana	Arabidopsis Thaliana	370.52		Yes	Rs
Argan Powder	Argan Powder	370.81		Yes	Rs
Argon	Argon	40.01			
Arochlor	Polychlorinated Biphenyls	200.07			
Aromatic Hydrocarbons, NOS	Aromatic Hydrocarbons, NOS	160	S		
Aromatic Solvents, NOS	Aromatic Hydrocarbons, NOS	160	S		
Arsenic	Arsenic	20.051			
Arsenic Compounds	Arsenic Compounds	20.05			
Arsine	Arsine	20.06			
Arthropod, NOS	Insect, NOS	382			
Asbestos, Amosite	Asbestos, Amosite	10.021			
Asbestos, Chrysotile	Asbestos, Chrysotile	10.023			
Asbestos, Crocidolite	Asbestos, Crocidolite	10.024			
Asbestos, NOS	Asbestos, NOS	10.02			
Asbestos, Tremolite	Asbestos, Tremolite	10.025			
Ash, NOS	Ash, NOS	10.16			
Ashwood, Ash, American Ash, or White Ash	Fraxinus Americana	373.17		Yes	Rs
Aspergillus	Aspergillus	391.02			
Aspergillus Flavus	Aspergillus Flavus	391.021			
Aspergillus Fumigatus	Aspergillus Fumigatus	391.022			
Aspergillus Glaucus	Aspergillus Glaucus	391.023			
Aspergillus Niger	Aspergillus Niger	391.024			
Aspergillus Versicolor	Aspergillus Versicolor	391.025			
Asphalt	Asphalt	61.07			
Asphyxiant Gases, NOS	Asphyxiant Gases, NOS	40.25			
Assault, Physical	Assault, Physical	353.12			
Astral Oil	Astral Oil	61.032	S		
Atorvastatin powder	Atorvastatin powder	321.37			
Augmentin	Augmentin	321.044			
Auramine	Auramine	251.02			
Australian Sheep Blowfly	Sheep Blowfly	382.12		Yes	Rs
Auto Accident	Motor Vehicle Accident	353.05			
Avian Material, NOS	Avian Material, NOS	380.16			
Ayruvedic Medications	Ayruvedic Medications	321.35			
Azabenzene	Pyridine	250.14			
Azine	Pyridine	250.14			
Aziridine	Ethylenimine	260.101			
Azo Compounds, NOS	Azo Compounds, NOS	252			
Azo Dyes, NOS	Azo Compounds, NOS	252			
Azobisformamide	Azodicarbamide	260.18		Yes	Rs
Azodicarbamide	Azodicarbamide	260.18		Yes	Rs
B-Galactosidase	Lactase	324.14			
B-Mercaptoethanol	Mercaptoethanol	310.04			
Baby's Breath	Baby's Breath	370.17		Yes	
Bacillus lichenformis	Bacillus lichenformis	324.012			
Bacillus licheniformis enzyme	Protease	324.011		Yes	Rs
Bacillus licheniformis enzyme	Esperase	324.1		Yes	Rs
Bacillus Subtilis enzyme	Protease	324.011		Yes	Rs
Bacillus Subtilis Enzymes	Bacillus Subtilis Enzymes	324.01		Yes	Rs
Bacillus Thurigiensis	Bacillus Thurigiensis	390.14	P		
Bacteria	Infectious Agents, NOS	390.07			
Balfourodendron Riedelianum	Pau Marfim	373.18		Yes	
Baquacil	Polyhexamethylene Biguanide	260.29	P		
Barium	Barium	20.071			
Barium Compounds	Barium Compounds	20.07			
Barn Dust	Manure	380.02			
Barn Mite	Barn Mite	382.15		Yes	

Common Name/Synonym	Primary Name	AOEC Code[1]	Use[2]	Asthmagen[3]	Asthma Detail[3]
Barometric Pressure, Changes	Air Pressure, Changes	350.07			
Bat Guano	Bat Guano	380.12		Yes	
Baygon	Propoxur	292.04	P		
BCDMH	1-Bromo-3-chloro-5,5-dimethylhydantoin	191.04			R
BCME	Bis Chloromethyl Ether	100.01			
Bee Moth	Bee Moth	382.05		Yes	
Bee Sting	Venom	380.05			
Bending	Posture, Body - Dynamic	362.03			
Benlate Fungicide	Benomyl	260.03	P		
Benomyl	Benomyl	260.03	P		
Benzalkonium Chloride Quats in cleaning agents, NOS	Benzalkonium Chloride, NOS	322.321		Yes	Rs
Benzalkonium Chloride, NOS	Benzalkonium Chloride, NOS	322.321		Yes	Rs
Benzamide	N,N-diethyl-m-toluamide	260.26	P		
Benzene	Benzene	160.01	S		
Benzenediamine	Benzenediamine	251.06			R
Benzenediazonium Chloride	Diazonium Chloride	252.031		Yes	Rs
Benzidine	Benzidine	251.03			
Benzoic Acid	Benzoic Acid	150.02			
Benzol	Benzene	160.01	S		
Benzoyl Chloride	Benzoyl Chloride	200.09			
Benzoyl Peroxide	Benzoyl Peroxide	50.27			
Benzyl Chloride	Benzyl Chloride	200.02			
Benzyl-C10-16-alkyldimethyl, chlorides	Benzyl-C10-16-alkyldimethyl, chlorides	322.3211		Yes	Rs
Benzyl-C12-16-alkyldimethyl ammonium, chlorides	Benzyl-C12-16-alkyldimethyl ammonium, chlorides	322.3222		Yes	Rs
Benzyl-C12-18-alkyldimethyl ammonium, chlorides	Benzyl-C12-18-alkyldimethyl ammonium, chlorides	322.3221		Yes	Rs
Benzyl-C16-18-alkyldimethyl ammonium, chlorides	Benzyl-C16-18-alkyldimethyl ammonium, chlorides	322.3223		Yes	Rs
Benzyldimethylstearylammonium Chloride	Benzyldimethylstearylammonium Chloride	322.3215		Yes	Rs
Beryllium	Beryllium	20.081			
Beryllium Compounds	Beryllium Compounds	20.08			
Beta-Chloroethyl Alcohol	Beta-Chloroethyl Alcohol	70.03			
Beta-Galactosidase	Lactase	324.14			
Beta-glucanase	Beta-glucanase	324.22		Yes	Rs
Beta-Lactosidase	Lactase	324.14			
Beta-mercaptopropionic Acid	3-mercaptopropionic Acid	310.12			
Beta-Naphthylamine	Beta-Naphthylamine	251.05			
Beta-Propiolactone	Beta-Propiolactone	320.04			
Beta-thiopropionic Acid	3-mercaptopropionic Acid	310.12			
Bioaerosols	Microorganisms, NOS	390			
Bis 2-Chloroethyl Ether	Dichloroethyl Ether	100.03			
Bis Chloromethyl Ether	Bis Chloromethyl Ether	100.01			
Bis-2-Chloroethyl Sulfide	Mustard Gas	190.16			
Bismuth	Bismuth	20.091			
Bismuth Compounds	Bismuth Compounds	20.09			
Bisphenol A diglycidyl ether (BADGE)	Bisphenol A diglycidyl ether (BADGE)	110.08		Yes	Rs
Bitrex	Denatonium Benzoate	320.37			
Black GR	Rifazol Black GR	325.08		Yes	Rs
Bleach	Sodium Hypochlorite	322.1		Yes	Rs
Bleach plus Acid (mixture)	Bleach plus Acid (mixture)	322.11			R
Bleach plus Ammonia (Mixture)	Bleach plus Ammonia (Mixture)	322.12			R
Bleaching Powder	Calcium Hypochloride	322.13			
Blood Exposure (Unknown Infection Status)	Body Fluid Exposure (Unknown Infection Status)	390.16			
Bloodworm	Bloodworm	382.18			
Bodily Reaction	Bodily Reaction	360.07			
Body Fluid Exposure (Unknown Infection Status)	Body Fluid Exposure (Unknown Infection Status)	390.16			
Boric Acid	Boric Acid	20.101			
Boron	Boron	20.102			
Boron Compounds	Boron Compounds	20.1			
Boron Hydride	Diborane	20.11			

Common Name/Synonym	Primary Name	AOEC Code[1]	Use[2]	Asthmagen[3]	Asthma Detail[3]
Borrelium Virus	Borrelium Virus	390.15			
Bovine Serum Albumin	Bovine Serum Albumin	380.13		Yes	Rs
BPL	Beta-Propiolactone	320.04			
Brass	Brass	20.43			
Brazil Ginseng	Brazil Ginseng	370.53		Yes	Rs
Brazilian Ginseng	Brazil Ginseng	370.53		Yes	Rs
Brazing, NOS	Brazing, NOS	23.002			
Brick Oil	Creosote	180.01			
Brilliant Orange 3R	Rifazol Brilliant Orange 3R	325.07		Yes	Rs
Brilliant Yellow 160	Remazol Brilliant Yellow 4GL	325.27			R
Bromelain	Bromelain	324.07		Yes	Rs
Bromelin	Bromelain	324.07		Yes	Rs
Brominated Fluorocarbon	Brominated Fluorocarbon	192.03			
Brominated Pesticides, NOS	Brominated Pesticides, NOS	191	P		
Bromine	Bromine	30.01			
Bromomethane	Methyl Bromide	191.03	P		
Bt	Bacillus Thurigiensis	390.14	P		
BTC 776	BTC 776	322.3218		Yes	Rs
BTC 927	BTC 927	322.3212		Yes	Rs
Buckwheat	Buckwheat	371.01		Yes	G
Building Renovation	Indoor Air Pollutants from Building Renovation	320.33			
Burning Fume	Welding, NOS	23.001			
Burnt Lime	Calcium Oxide	50.05			
Butadiene & Styrene	Butadiene & Styrene	271.01			
Butyl Acetate	Butyl Acetate	141.02	S		
Butyl Acrylate	Butyl Acrylate	142.02			R
Butyl Ketone	Butyl Ketone	130.06	S		
Butyl-Cellosolve	2-Butoxyethanol	91.03	S		R
C. Carnea	Chrysoperla Carnea	382.22		Yes	
C.I. Pigment Red 48:1	Red BBN	325.22		Yes	Rs
C.I. Reactive Black 5	Remazol Black B	325.11			R
C.I. Reactive Blue 203	Remazol Marine Blue GG	325.24			R
C.I. Reactive Yellow 145	Rifafix Yellow 3 RN	325.06		Yes	Rs
C.I. Reactive Yellow 39	Lanasol Yellow 4G	325.09		Yes	Rs
Cabreuva	Cabreuva	373.23		Yes	
Cacoon Seed	Cacoon Seed	370.32		Yes	
Caddis Flies	Caddis Flies	382.27		Yes	Rs
Cadmium	Cadmium	20.121			
Cadmium Compounds	Cadmium Compounds	20.12			
Cadmium Salts	Cadmium Salts	20.122			
Caesalpinia Echinata	Fernambouc	373.16		Yes	
Calcium Bisulfite	Calcium Bisulfite	50.03			
Calcium Carbide	Calcium Carbide	50.36			
Calcium Carbonate	Calcium Carbonate	50.35			
Calcium Chloride	Calcium Chloride	41.01			
Calcium Cyanamide	Calcium Cyanamide	260.04			
Calcium Hypochloride	Calcium Hypochloride	322.13			
Calcium Oxide	Calcium Oxide	50.05			
Calcium Salts, NOS	Calcium Salts, NOS	40.02			
Calculator	Keyboard Use	360.02			
California Redwood	California Redwood	373.02		Yes	
Camphor Oil	Camphor Oil	320.48			R
Cannabis dust (marijuana and hemp)	Cannabis dust (marijuana and hemp)	370.62		Yes	Rs
Cannabis smoke	Cannabis smoke	330.05		Yes	Rs
Capsicum	Capsicum	370.35			
Captafol	Captafol	320.081		Yes	Rs
Captan	Captan	260.05	P		
Car Accident	Motor Vehicle Accident	353.05			

Common Name/Synonym	Primary Name	AOEC Code[1]	Use[2]	Asth-magen[3]	Asthma Detail[3]
Car Crash	Motor Vehicle Accident	353.05			
Carbamate Pesticides, NOS	Carbamate Pesticides, NOS	292	P		
Carbaryl	Carbaryl	292.02	P		
Carbazotic Acid	Picric Acid	250.09			
Carbinol	Methanol	70.07	S		
Carbolic Acid	Phenol	180.04			
Carbon Black	Carbon Black	10.042			
Carbon Dioxide	Carbon Dioxide	40.03			
Carbon Disulfide	Carbon Disulfide	310.01			
Carbon Monoxide	Carbon Monoxide	40.04			
Carbon Tetrachloride	Carbon Tetrachloride	190.01	S		
Carbonless Paper	Carbonless Paper	320.05			
Carbopol	Carbopol, NOS	270.36			
Carbopol, NOS	Carbopol, NOS	270.36			
Carborundum	Silicon Carbide	10.18			
Carene	Carene	60.21		Yes	Rs
Carmine	Carmine	320.24			
Carminic Acid	Carmine	320.24			
Carpet Dust	Carpet Dust	320.35			
Carpet Fibers	Carpet Dust	320.35			
Carrying	Lifting	361.02			
Casein	Casein	380.11		Yes	Rs
Cash Register Use	Keyboard Use	360.02			
Castor Bean	Castor Bean	370.13		Yes	
Cat	Cat	380.22		Yes	Rs
Catalysts, NOS	Enzymes, NOS	324			
Caught In or Between Objects	Caught In or Between Objects	353.1			
Caustic Soda	Sodium Hydroxide	50.18			
Ceclor	Ceclor	321.26			
Cedar of Lebanon	Cedar of Lebanon	373.03		Yes	
Cedrus Libani	Cedar of Lebanon	373.03		Yes	
Cefaclor	Ceclor	321.26			
Cefadroxil	Cefadroxil	321.061			R
Ceftazidine	Ceftazidine	321.062			R
Ceiba Pentandra Gaertner	Kapok	370.43		Yes	
Celery	Celery	370.011			
Cellosolve	Ethylene Glycol Monoethyl Ether	91.02	S		
Cellulase	Cellulase	324.19		Yes	Rs
Cement Dust	Cement Dust	10.03			R
Central American Walnut	Juglans Olanchana	373.11		Yes	Rs
Cephalexin	Cephalexin	321.063			R
Cephalosporins	Cephalosporins	321.06			R
Ceratitis capitata	Ceratitis capitata	382.3		Yes	Rs
Cerium	Cerium	20.131			
Cerium Compounds	Cerium Compounds	20.13			
Cetalkonium Chloride	Cetalkonium Chloride	322.3217		Yes	Rs
Cetane	Cetane	61.1			
CFC	Chlorofluorocarbon, NOS	192.02			
Chamomile	Chamomile	370.54		Yes	Rs
Champignon flies	Champignon flies	382.29		Yes	Rs
Chemical Dust, NOS	Chemicals, NOS	320.06			
Chemicals, NOS	Chemicals, NOS	320.06			
Chemicals, Unknown	Chemicals, NOS	320.06			
Chemotherapeutic Drugs	Chemotherapeutic Drugs	321.01			
Chicken	Chicken	380.07		Yes	
Chicory	Cichorium intybus	370.18		Yes	Rs
Chil-Perm CP-30	Chil-Perm CP-30	320.31	S		
Chloramide	Chloramine	30.09			R
Chloramine	Chloramine	30.09			R

Common Name/Synonym	Primary Name	AOEC Code[1]	Use[2]	Asthmagen[3]	Asthma Detail[3]
Chloramine compounds, NOS	Chloramine compounds, NOS	30.09			
Chloramine T	Chloramine T	260.21		Yes	Rs
Chlorbenzol	Chlorobenzene	201.04	S		
Chlordane	Chlordane	280.02	P		
Chlorex	Dichloroethyl Ether	100.03			
Chlorhexidine	Chlorhexidine	200.08		Yes	Rs
Chlorimide	Dichloramine	30.1			R
Chlorinated Benzenes, NOS	Chlorinated Benzenes, NOS	201			
Chlorinated Dibenzodioxins	Chlorinated Dibenzodioxins	200.04			
Chlorinated Dibenzodioxins (except TCDD)	Chlorinated Dibenzodioxins	200.04	P		
Chlorinated Hydrocarbons, NOS	Chlorinated Hydrocarbons, NOS	190	S		
Chlorinated Naphthalene	Chlorinated Naphthalene	200.03			
Chlorinated Phenols, NOS	Chlorinated Phenols, NOS	181			
Chlorinated Solvents, NOS	Chlorinated Hydrocarbons, NOS	190	S		
Chlorine	Chlorine	30.02		Yes	Rrs
Chlorine Dioxide	Chlorine Dioxide	30.06			
Chlorine Trifluoride	Chlorine Trifluoride	30.05			
Chlorobenzene	Chlorobenzene	201.04	S		
Chlorobutadiene	Chloroprene	190.04			
Chlorodiphenyl	Polychlorinated Biphenyls	200.07			
Chloroethane	Chloroethane	190.02	S		
Chloroethene	Vinyl Chloride Monomer	190.14			
Chlorofluorocarbon, NOS	Chlorofluorocarbon, NOS	192.02			
Chloroform	Chloroform	190.03			
Chloromethyl Ether	Bis Chloromethyl Ether	100.01			
Chloromethyl Methyl Ether	Chloromethyl Methyl Ether	100.02			
Chlorophenoxy Herbicides, NOS	Chlorophenoxy Herbicides, NOS	200.11	P		
Chlorophora Excelsa	Iroko	373.05		Yes	
Chloropicrin	Chloropicrin	260.06	P		
Chloroprene	Chloroprene	190.04			
Chloropropane	Chloropropane	190.05	S		
Chlorothalonil	Chlorothalonil	210.03	P	Yes	Rs
Chlorous Acid	Chlorous Acid	30.07			
Chlorpyrifos	Chlorpyrifos	291.05	P		R
Chorella Algae	Chorella Algae	370.36		Yes	
Chromic Acid	Chromic Acid	22.04		Yes	Rs
Chromium Compounds	Chromium Compounds	20.14		Yes	Rs
Chromium Metal	Chromium Metal	20.141		Yes	Rs
Chromium, Hexavalent, NOS	Chromium, Hexavalent, NOS	22		Yes	Rs
Chromium, Not Hexavalent	Chromium, Not Hexavalent	20.142		Yes	Rs
Chrysonilia sitophilia	Chrysonilia sitophilia	390.111		Yes	Rs
Chrysoperla Carnea	Chrysoperla Carnea	382.22		Yes	
Chymotrypsin	Chymotrypsin	324.2			R
Cibachrome Brilliant Scarlet 3R	Cibachrome Brilliant Scarlet 3R	325.03		Yes	Rs
Cichorium intybus	Cichorium intybus	370.18		Yes	Rs
Cidex	Glutaraldehyde	120.051		Yes	Rs
Cidex OPA	Ortho-phthalaldehyde	120.1			R
Cigarette Smoke	Cigarette Smoke	330.01			R
Cimetidine	Cimetidine	321.17		Yes	Rs
Cinnamene	Styrene	160.04	S	Yes	Rs
Cinnamic Aldehyde	Cinnamic Aldehyde	120.08			
Cinnamic Oil	Cinnamon Oil	120.089			
Cinnamomum Zeylanicum	Cinnamon	373.22		Yes	
Cinnamon	Cinnamon	373.22		Yes	
Citric Acid	Citric Acid	50.07			
Clam	Clam	381.1		Yes	
Clandestine Drug laboratory	Methamphetamine Laboratory	320.4			
Clay	Clay	10.051			

Common Name/Synonym	Primary Name	AOEC Code[1]	Use[2]	Asth-magen[3]	Asthma Detail[3]
Clay 347	Clay	10.051			
Clay, NOS	Clay, NOS	10.05			
Cleaner, Citric	Cleaner, Citric	322.36			
Cleaners, Abrasive	Cleaners, Abrasive	322.14			
Cleaners, Acid	Cleaners, Acid	322.15			
Cleaners, Carpet	Cleaners, Carpet	322.16			
Cleaners, Caustic (excluding Lye)	Cleaners, Caustic (excluding Lye)	322.17			
Cleaners, Detergent, NOS	Cleaners, Detergent, NOS	322.18			
Cleaners, Disinfectant, NOS	Cleaners, Disinfectant, NOS	322.19			
Cleaners, Drain	Cleaners, Drain	322.2			
Cleaners, Floor Stripping	Cleaners, Floor Stripping	322.21			
Cleaners, Graffiti Removing	Cleaners, Graffiti Removing	322.22	S		
Cleaners, Household, General Purpose	Cleaners, Household, General Purpose	322.04			
Cleaners, Laundry Soap/Detergent	Cleaners, Laundry Soap/Detergent	322.23			
Cleaners, Lye	Cleaners, Lye	322.24			
Cleaners, Oven	Cleaners, Oven	322.25			
Cleaners, Pine Oil	Cleaners, Pine Oil	322.26			
Cleaners, Solvent-Based	Cleaners, Solvent-Based	322.06	S		
Cleaners, Tile	Cleaners, Tile	322.27			
Cleaners, Toilet Bowl	Cleaners, Toilet Bowl	322.28			
Cleaners, Wallpaper	Cleaners, Wallpaper	322.29			
Cleaning Fluids, Photocopier	Cleaning Fluids, Photocopier	322.03			
Cleaning Fluids/Spot Removers	Cleaning Fluids/Spot Removers	322.3	S		
Cleaning Materials, NOS	Cleaning Materials, NOS	322			
Cleaning Mixtures (excluding Bleach plus Acid or Ammonia)	Cleaning Mixtures (excluding Bleach plus Acid or Ammonia)	322.31			
Clove Oil	Oil of Clove	160.06			
CMME	Chloromethyl Methyl Ether	100.02			
CO	Carbon Monoxide	40.04			
Coal	Coal	10.06			
Coal Naphtha	Benzene	160.01	S		
Coal Tar	Polycyclic Aromatic Hydrocarbons, NOS	161			
Coal Tar Oil	Creosote	180.01			
Coating, Epoxy	Paint, Epoxy	110.05			
Cobalt	Cobalt	20.151		Yes	Rs
Cobalt Compounds	Cobalt Compounds	20.15		Yes	G
Cocabolla	Cocabolla	373.04		Yes	
Cockroach	Cockroach	382.28			
Cocoa	Cocoa Bean	370.47			
Cocoa Bean	Cocoa Bean	370.47			
Cocobolo	Cocabolla	373.04		Yes	
Coconut	Coconut	370.009			
Codeine	Codeine	321.182		Yes	Rs
Coffee Bean	Coffee Bean	370.12		Yes	
Coke Oven Emissions	Polycyclic Aromatic Hydrocarbons, NOS	161			
Cold	Cold	350.02			
Colistin	Colistin	321.34		Yes	Rs
Collodion	Collodion	270.39			
Collodium	Collodion	270.39			
Colophony	Colophony	23.05		Yes	G
Color Index No. 0-16	Rifazol Brilliant Orange 3R	325.07		Yes	Rs
Color Index No. 0-20	Rifacion Orange HE 2G	325.05		Yes	Rs
Color Index No. BK-5	Rifazol Black GR	325.08		Yes	Rs
Colorado Potato Beetle	Leptinotarsa Decemlineata	382.23		Yes	
Combustion Products, NOS	Smoke, NOS	330.03			
Computer Keyboard	Keyboard Use	360.02			
Computer Mouse Use	Keyboard Use	360.02			
Concrete, wet	Concrete, wet	10.24			
Contact Pressure	Contact Pressure	360.01			

Common Name/Synonym	Primary Name	AOEC Code[1]	Use[2]	Asth-magen[3]	Asthma Detail[3]
Contaminated Well Water due to Hydrofracking	Contaminated Well Water due to Hydrofracking	170.1			
Coolants	Lubricants, NOS	320.14			
Copper	Copper	20.161			
Copper Compounds	Copper Compounds	20.16			
Copper Phthalocyanine	Copper Phthalocyanine	20.49			
Copper Sulfate	Copper Sulfate	20.51			
Copper Sulfate (Anhydrous)	Copper Sulfate	20.51			
Corn Dust	Corn Dust	370.51			
Corn Mint Oil	Corn Mint Oil	320.47			R
Corn Starch	Corn Starch	371.06			
Corrosive Preventative	Corrosive Preventative	60.23			
Cosmetics, NOS	Cosmetics, NOS	320.28			R
Cosmetology Chemicals, NOS	Cosmetics, NOS	320.28			R
Cotton Dust	Cotton Dust	370.02			
Coumarin	Coumarin	321.03			
Cow Dander	Cow Dander	380.041		Yes	
Crab	Crab	381.02		Yes	G
Creosote	Creosote	180.01			
Cresol	Cresol	180.02			
Cresylic Acid	Cresol	180.02			
Cricket	Cricket	382.04		Yes	
Crotonaldehyde	Crotonaldehyde	120.09			
CRT Radiation	Radiation, Electromagnetic	352.01			
Crude oil	Crude oil	170.04			
Cuprilinic Blue	Copper Phthalocyanine	20.49			
Cutting fluid, soy based	Cutting fluid, soy based	170.08			
Cutting Oils	Cutting Oils	170.01		Yes	G
Cutting or Piercing Object, Except Blood-Contam. Sharps	Cutting or Piercing Object, Except Blood-Contam. Sharps	353.11			
Cuttlefish	Cuttlefish	381.06		Yes	
Cyanides, NOS	Cyanides, NOS	211			
Cyanoacrylates, NOS	Cyanoacrylates, NOS	142.07		Yes	Rs
Cyanurotramide	Melamine	260.28			
Cyclohexane	Cyclohexane	60.14	S		
Cyclohexanediamine_(1,2-diaminocyclohexane)	Cyclohexanediamine_(1,2-diaminocyclohexane)	60.25			R
Cyclohexanone	Cyclohexanone	130.07	S		
Cyclohexylamine	Cyclohexylamine	230.06			
Cyclopentadiene	Cyclopentadiene	60.13			
Cyclophosphamide	Cyclophosphamide	321.29			
Cytoxan	Cyclophosphamide	321.29			
D-Limonene	D-Limonene	60.18	S		R
Dalbergia Retusa	Cocabolla	373.04		Yes	
Dander, Animal (NOS)	Dander, Animal (NOS)	380.04			
Daphnia	Daphnia	382.1		Yes	
DCB	Dichlorobenzene	201.01	P		
DDT	DDT	280.03	P		
DEA (Diethanolamine)	Diethanolamine	231.041		Yes	Rs
DEA (Diethylaniline)	Diethylaniline	250.18			
DEET	N,N-diethyl-m-toluamide	260.26	P		
Degreaser, NOS	Degreaser, NOS	171.04			
Denatonium Benzoate	Denatonium Benzoate	320.37			
Deodorizer, Aerosol	Air Freshener	320.42			
Dermasorb	Dimethyl Sulfoxide	310.14			
DHA	Dihydroxyacetone	130.08			
di-Halo	1-Bromo-3-chloro-5,5-dimethylhydantoin	191.04			R
Diacetyl	Diacetyl	130.09			
Diacetyl morphine	Diacetyl morphine	321.185		Yes	Rs
Dialkyl Methyl Benzyl Ammonium Chloride	Dialkyl Methyl Benzyl Ammonium Chloride	322.3213		Yes	Rs
Diamines, NOS	Diamines, NOS	233			
Diatomaceous Earth	Silica, Amorphous	10.12			

Common Name/Synonym	Primary Name	AOEC Code[1]	Use[2]	Asth-magen[3]	Asthma Detail[3]
Diazinon	Diazinon	291.03	P		R
Diazomethane	Diazomethane	260.23			
Diazonium Chloride	Diazonium Chloride	252.031		Yes	Rs
Diazonium Salt, NOS	Diazonium Salt, NOS	252.03			R
Diazonium Tetrafluoroborate	Diazonium Tetrafluoroborate	252.032		Yes	Rs
Diborane	Diborane	20.11			
Dichlobenil	2,6-Dichlorobenzonitrile	200.1	P		
Dichloramine	Dichloramine	30.1			R
Dichlorobenzene	Dichlorobenzene	201.01	P		
Dichlorodiphenyltrichloroethane	DDT	280.03	P		
Dichloroethyl Ether	Dichloroethyl Ether	100.03			
Dichloromethane	Methylene Chloride	190.09	S		
Dichloromethyl Ether	Bis Chloromethyl Ether	100.01			
Dichlorosilane	Dichlorosilane	40.27			
Dichlorvos	Dichlorvos	291.1	P		R
Dicumyl-peroxide	Dicumyl-peroxide	50.141		Yes	Rs
Didecyl Dimethyl Ammonium Chloride	Didecyl Dimethyl Ammonium Chloride	322.323		Yes	Rs
Dieldrin	Dieldrin	280.04	P		
Diesel Exhaust	Diesel Exhaust	331.01			R
Diesel Fuel	Diesel Fuel	61.06	S		
Diesel Oil	Diesel Oil	61.061	S		
Diethanolamine	Diethanolamine	231.041		Yes	Rs
Diethyl Ether	Ethyl Ether	100.05			
Diethyl Formamide	Diethyl Formamide	260.24	S		
Diethyl Silicate	Diethyl Silicate	140.02			
Diethyl Sulfate	Diethyl Sulfate	310.02			
Diethylamine	Diethylamine	230.02			
Diethylaminoethyl Acrylate	Diethylaminoethyl Acrylate	142.06			
Diethylaniline	Diethylaniline	250.18			
Diethylene Glycol	Diethylene Glycol	80.02			
Diethylenediamine	Piperazine	260.19		Yes	Rs
Diethylenetriamine	Diethylenetriamine	232.07			
Diethyltoluamide	N,N-diethyl-m-toluamide	260.26	P		
Difluoroethane	Difluoroethane	192.05			
Dihydroxyacetone	Dihydroxyacetone	130.08			
Diisocyanates, NOS	Diisocyanates, NOS	221		Yes	G
Dimethoate	Dimethoate	291.07	P		R
Dimethyl dicarbonate	Dimethyl dicarbonate	40.35			
Dimethyl Ethyl Benzyl Ammonium Chloride	Dimethyl Ethyl Benzyl Ammonium Chloride	322.3214		Yes	Rs
Dimethyl Ketone	Acetone	130.01	S		
Dimethyl Methane	Propane	60.2			
Dimethyl Sulfate	Dimethyl Sulfate	310.03			
Dimethyl Sulfide	Dimethyl Sulfide	165.01			
Dimethyl Sulfoxide	Dimethyl Sulfoxide	310.14			
Dimethylacetamide	N,N-Dimethylacetamide	260.07			
Dimethylamine	Dimethylamine	230.04			
Dimethylaminoethanol	Dimethylethanolamine	231.042		Yes	Rs
Dimethylbenzene	Xylene	160.03	S		
Dimethylethanolamine	Dimethylethanolamine	231.042		Yes	Rs
Dimethylhydrazine	Dimethylhydrazine	260.09			
Dinitro-o-Cresol	Dinitro-o-Cresol	250.06			
Dinitrobenzene	Dinitrobenzene	250.05			
Dinitrobenzol	Dinitrobenzene	250.05			
Dinitrol	Dinitro-o-Cresol	250.06			
Dinitrophenol	Dinitrophenol	250.12			
Dinitrotoluene	Dinitrotoluene	250.07			
Dinitrotoluol	Dinitrotoluene	250.07			
Dioctylphthalate	Dioctylphthalate	140.03			

Common Name/Synonym	Primary Name	AOEC Code[1]	Use[2]	Asth-magen[3]	Asthma Detail[3]
Dioscorea Batatas	Dioscorea Batatas	370.39		Yes	
Diospyros Crassiflora	Ebony	373.2		Yes	
Dioxane	Dioxane	100.04	S		
Dioxin	Chlorinated Dibenzodioxins	200.04			
Dipentene	Limonene	60.05	S		
Diphenylmethane Diisocyanate	Methylene Bisphenyl Diisocyanate	221.02		Yes	G
Dipropylene Glycol Methyl Ether	Dipropylene Glycol Methyl Ether	90.011	S		
Disinfectants, NOS	Disinfectants, NOS	50.28			
DMAC	N,N-Dimethylacetamide	260.07			
DMDC	Dimethyl dicarbonate	40.35			
DMF	N,N-Dimethylformamide	260.08	S		
DMN	N-Nitrosodimethylamine	240.01			
DMNA	N-Nitrosodimethylamine	240.01			
DMS	Dimethyl sulfide	165.01			
DMSO	Dimethyl Sulfoxide	310.14			
DNOC	Dinitro-o-Cresol	250.06			
DNT	Dinitrotoluene	250.07			
Dodecanedioic Acid	Dodecanedioic Acid	270.4		Yes	Rs
Dodecyl-dimethyl-benzylammonium Chloride	Dodecyl-dimethyl-benzylammonium Chloride	322.3216		Yes	Rs
Dodecylphenol	Dodecylphenol	180.08			
Drawing compound	Drawing compound	170.07			
Drilling mud, mineral oil based	Drilling mud, mineral oil based	168.02			
Drilling Mud, NOS	Drilling Mud, NOS	168			
Drilling mud, oil based NOS	Drilling mud, oil based NOS	168.04			
Drilling mud, synthetic based	Drilling mud, synthetic based	168.05			
Drilling mud, vegetable oil based	Drilling mud, vegetable oil based	168.03			
Drilling mud, water based	Drilling mud, water based	168.01			
Drimaren Brilliant Blue K-BL	Drimaren Brilliant Blue K-BL	325.04		Yes	Rs
Drimaren Brilliant Yellow-K-3GL	Drimaren Brilliant Yellow K-3GL	325.02		Yes	Rs
Drimarene Brilliant Blue K-BL	Drimaren Brilliant Blue K-BL	325.04		Yes	Rs
Drimarene Brilliant Yellow K-3GL	Drimaren Brilliant Yellow K-3GL	325.02		Yes	Rs
Drosophila melanogaster	Drosophila melanogaster	382.07		Yes	Rs
Dry Air	Humidity, Low	350.04			
Dry Cleaning Fluid, NOS	Dry Cleaning Fluid, NOS	322.34	S		
Drywall Mud	Drywall Mud	10.23			
Dursban	Chlorpyrifos	291.05	P		R
Dust, NOS	Dust, NOS	10			
Dye Intermediates, NOS	Dyes, NOS	250.17			
Dyes, NOS	Dyes, NOS	250.17			
E-cigarette emissions	Electronic cigarette emissions	320.49			
E. Kuehniella	Ephestia Kuehniella	382.25		Yes	
Eastern White Cedar	Eastern White Cedar	373.19		Yes	G
Ebony	Ebony	373.2		Yes	
Echinodorus Larva	Fish Feed	381.09		Yes	
EDB	Ethylene Dibromide	191.01	P		
EDTA/Edetic Acid	Ethylenediamine Tetraacetic Acid	232.08			
EGBE	2-Butoxyethanol	91.03	S		R
EGEE	Ethylene Glycol Monoethyl Ether	91.02	S		
Egg Lysozyme	Lysozyme	324.08		Yes	Rs
Egg Protein	Egg Protein	380.06		Yes	G
EGME	Ethylene Glycol Monomethyl Ether	91.01	S		
Electrical Shock	Electrical Shock	353.01			
Electricity	Electrical Shock	353.01			
Electromagnetic Fields	Radiation, Electromagnetic	352.01			
Electronic cigarette emissions	Electronic cigarette emissions	320.49			
Electroplating Chemicals, NOS	Electroplating Chemicals, NOS	320.07			
ELF	Radiation, Electromagnetic	352.01			
Embalming fluid, NOS	Embalming fluid, NOS	120.2			

Common Name/Synonym	Primary Name	AOEC Code[1]	Use[2]	Asth-magen[3]	Asthma Detail[3]
EMF	Radiation, Electromagnetic	352.01			
Enamel Thinner	Thinner	171.02	S		
endo-1,4-Xylanase (from Trichoderma viride)	endo-1,4-Xylanase (from Trichoderma viride)	324.122		Yes	Rs
Endotoxin	Endotoxin	391.13			
Endrin	Endrin	280.05	P		
Enflurane	Enflurane	190.151		Yes	Rs
Engine Exhaust	Engine Exhaust	331.02			
Engineered Stone Countertop Dust	Engineered Stone Dust	10.136			
Environmental electronic cigarette emissions	Electronic cigarette emissions	320.49			
Environmental Tobacco Smoke	Cigarette Smoke	330.01			R
Enzymes, NOS	Enzymes, NOS	324			
Ephestia Kuehniella	Ephestia Kuehniella	382.25		Yes	
Epichlorohydrin	Epichlorohydrin	110.01			
Epigallocatechin gallate	Tea	370.14		Yes	Rs
EPO 60	EPO 60	232.06		Yes	Rs
Epoxies	Epoxy Resins	110.02		Yes	G
Epoxy Resin Hardeners	Epoxy Resins	110.02		Yes	G
Epoxy Resins	Epoxy Resins	110.02		Yes	G
Ergonomic Factors, NOS	Ergonomic Factors, NOS	360			
Esperase	Esperase	324.1		Yes	Rs
Estrogens	Estrogens	321.02			
Ethane Trichloride	1,1,2-Trichloroethane	190.12	S		
Ethanedioic Acid	Oxalic Acid	150.03			
Ethanol	Ethanol	70.05	S		
Ethanol Ethylene Diamine	Aminoethyl Ethanolamine	231.03		Yes	Rs
Ethanolamines, NOS	Ethanolamines, NOS	231		Yes	Rs
Ethephon	Ethephon	291.12	P		
Ether	Ethyl Ether	100.05			
Ethidium Bromide	Ethidium Bromide	250.171			
Ethine	Acetylene	60.01			
Ethoxyethane	Ethyl Ether	100.05			
Ethyl 2-hydroxypropionate	Ethyl lactate	140.07			
Ethyl Acetate	Ethyl Acetate	141.03	S		
Ethyl acetone	Methyl Propyl Ketone	130.1			
Ethyl Acrylate	Ethyl Acrylate	142.05			
Ethyl Alcohol	Ethanol	70.05	S		
Ethyl Benzene	Ethyl Benzene	160.07	S		
Ethyl Chloride	Chloroethane	190.02	S		
Ethyl Ether	Ethyl Ether	100.05			
Ethyl lactate	Ethyl lactate	140.07			
Ethyl Methacrylate	Ethyl Methacrylate	142.03			R
Ethyl Methyl Ether	Ethyl Methyl Ether	100.06			
Ethyl Oxide	Ethyl Ether	100.05			
Ethyl Sulfate	Diethyl Sulfate	310.02			
Ethylene Chlorohydrin	Beta-Chloroethyl Alcohol	70.03			
Ethylene Dibromide	Ethylene Dibromide	191.01	P		
Ethylene Dichloride	Ethylene Dichloride	190.07	S		
Ethylene Glycol	Ethylene Glycol	80.011			
Ethylene Glycol Ethers, NOS	Ethylene Glycol Ethers, NOS	91	S		
Ethylene Glycol Monobutyl Ether	2-Butoxyethanol	91.03	S		R
Ethylene Glycol Monoethyl Ether	Ethylene Glycol Monoethyl Ether	91.02	S		
Ethylene Glycol Monomethyl Ether	Ethylene Glycol Monomethyl Ether	91.01	S		
Ethylene Oxide	Ethylene Oxide	110.03		Yes	Rr
Ethylenediamine	Ethylenediamine	232.01		Yes	Rs
Ethylenediamine Tetraacetic Acid	Ethylenediamine Tetraacetic Acid	232.08			
Ethylenimine	Ethylenimine	260.101			
Ethyne	Acetylene	60.01			
ETO	Ethylene Oxide	110.03		Yes	Rr
ETS	Cigarette Smoke	330.01			R

Common Name/Synonym	Primary Name	AOEC Code[1]	Use[2]	Asth-magen[3]	Asthma Detail[3]
Eucalyptus Oil	Eucalyptus Oil	320.36			R
Eucalyptus Scent	Eucalyptus Oil	320.36			R
Eugenol	Eugenol	100.07		Yes	Rs
European Corn Borer	Ostrinia Nubilalis	382.24		Yes	
Exercise	Exercise	360.06			
Exhaust, NOS	Exhaust, NOS	331			
Explosion	Explosion	353.02			
Extranase	Bromelain	324.07		Yes	Rs
Extremely Low Frequency Elctromagnetic Radiation	Radiation, Electromagnetic	352.01			
Fabric, NOS	Fabric, NOS	270.44			
Fall From Height	Fall, NOS	353.03			
Fall, NOS	Fall, NOS	353.03			
Fats	Oils, NOS	170.03			
FC 113	Trichlorotrifluoroethane	192.04			
FD&C Red No. 2	Amaranth	252.01			
Feldspar Dust	Feldspar Dust	10.131			
Fenamiphos	Nemacur	291.06	P		R
Fenthion	Fenthion	291.13	P	Yes	Rs
Fenugreek	Fenugreek	370.42		Yes	
Fernambouc	Fernambouc	373.16		Yes	
Ferric Chloride	Ferric Chloride	20.201			
Fertilizers, NOS	Fertilizers, NOS	320.09			
Fiberglass	Fiberglass	10.091			
Fibrous Glass	Fiberglass	10.091			
Ficam	Ficam	292.03	P		
Fingerprint Powder	Fingerprint Powder	320.34			
Fire Extinguisher Discharge	Fire Extinguisher Discharge	320.1			
Fire retardant	Halon	320.101			
Fish Feed	Fish Feed	381.09		Yes	
Fish Feed, Mosquito Larva	Fish Feed	381.09		Yes	
Fixer	Photo Developing Chemicals, NOS	320.17			
Flaviastase	Flaviastase	324.06		Yes	Rs
Floor Finish	Floor Wax	322.35			
Floor Wax	Floor Wax	322.35			
Flour, NOS	Flour, NOS	371		Yes	G
Fluazinam	Fluazinam	320.082		Yes	Rs
Flumetsulam	N-(2,6-difluorophenyl)-5-methyl-(1,2,4) triazolo (1,5-a) pyrimidine-2-sulfonomide	320.131	P		
Fluorescent Lamp Phosphor	Fluorescent Lamp Phosphor	40.33			
Fluorine	Fluorine	30.03			R
Fluorocarbons, NOS	Fluorocarbons, NOS	192			
Fluosilicic Acid	Hydrofluosilicic Acid	50.44			
Fluxes, NOS	Fluxes, NOS	40.05			
Fly Ash	Fly Ash	10.07			
Forceful Movements, NOS	Forceful Movements, NOS	361.01			
Formaldehyde	Formaldehyde	120.03		Yes	G
Formalin	Formaldehyde	120.03		Yes	G
Formates, NOS	Formates, NOS	140.01			
Formic Acid	Formic Acid	150.01			
Fowl Mite	Fowl Mite	382.14		Yes	
Fraxinus Americana	Fraxinus Americana	373.17		Yes	Rs
Freesia	Freesia	370.3		Yes	
Freon, Heated	Freon, Heated	192.06		Yes	Rs
Freon, NOS	Freon, NOS	192.01			
Freon, Unheated	Freon, Unheated	192.07			
Frog	Frog	380.09		Yes	
Fruit Fly	Drosophila melanogaster	382.07		Yes	Rs
Fruit Juices	Fruit Juices	370.05			

Common Name/Synonym	Primary Name	AOEC Code[1]	Use[2]	Asth-magen[3]	Asthma Detail[3]
Fulvin P/G	Griseofulvin	321.27			
Fumes, NOS	Smoke, NOS	330.03			
Fungal Amylase	Fungal Amylase	324.09		Yes	Rs
Fungal Amyloglucosidase	Amyloglucosidase	324.11		Yes	Rs
Fungal Hemicellulase	Fungal Hemicellulase	324.12		Yes	Rs
Fungi, NOS	Mold, NOS	391.01			R
Fungicide, NOS	Fungicide, NOS	320.08	P		
Furfural	Furfural	120.04			
Furfuryl Alcohol	Furfuryl Alcohol	70.09			R
Furfuryl alcohol mixed with a catalyst	Furfuryl alcohol mixed with a catalyst	70.092		Yes	Rs
Garlic Dust	Garlic Dust	370.21		Yes	
Garlon 4	Garlon 4	260.25	P		
Gas Metal Arc Welding on Uncoated Mild Steel	Gas Metal Arc Welding on Uncoated Mild Steel	23.07		Yes	Rs
Gasoline	Gasoline	61.04	S		
Gasoline Exhaust	Engine Exhaust	331.02			
Germanium	Germanium	20.171			
Germanium Compounds	Germanium Compounds	20.17			
Glacial Acetic Acid	Glacial Acetic Acid	50.34		Yes	Rrs
Glues, NOS	Glues, NOS	320.11			
Glutaraldehyde	Glutaraldehyde	120.051		Yes	Rs
Gluten	Gluten	371.02		Yes	G
Glyceryl Trinitrate	Nitroglycerin	261.01			
Glycol Compound and Benzyl Compound	Glycol Compound and Benzyl Compound	321.21		Yes	Rs
Glycol Ethers, NOS	Glycol Ethers, NOS	90	S		
Glycol Monoethyl Ether Acetate	2-Ethoxyethyl Acetate	141.05			
Glyphosate	Glyphosate	320.132			
Gold	Gold	20.181			
Gold Compounds	Gold Compounds	20.18			
Gonystylus Bancanus	Gonystylus Bancanus	373.14		Yes	Rs
Grain Alcohol	Ethanol	70.05	S		
Grain Dust	Grain Dust	370.03		Yes	G
Grain Mite	Grain Mite	382.16		Yes	
Grain Parasite	Grain Mite	382.16		Yes	
Granite	Granite	11.01			
Granola, NOS	Granola, NOS	370.002			
Graphite	Graphite	10.08			
Grass Cuttings	Grass Cuttings	370.07			
Greases	Oils, NOS	170.03			
Green Beans	Green Beans	370.37		Yes	
Green Coffee Bean	Coffee Bean	370.12		Yes	G
Green Lacewing	Chrysoperla Carnea	382.22		Yes	
Grinding Dust	Abrasives, NOS	10.01			
Gripping, Forceful	Gripping, Forceful	361.03			
Gris-PEG	Griseofulvin	321.27			
Grisactin-Ultra	Griseofulvin	321.27			
Griseofulvin	Griseofulvin	321.27			
Guaiacol	Guaiacol	100.09			
Guar	Guar	372.04		Yes	
Guinea Pig Antigens	Guinea Pig Antigens	380.17		Yes	G
Gum Acacia	Gum Arabic	372.01		Yes	Rs
Gum Arabic	Gum Arabic	372.01		Yes	Rs
Gutta-percha	Gutta-percha	372.06		Yes	
Gypsophilia Paniculata	Baby's Breath	370.17		Yes	
Gypsum	Gypsum	10.171			
Gypsum, NOS	Gypsum, NOS	10.17			
H2S	Hydrogen Sulfide	40.06			
Habanolide	Habanolide	320.43			
Hair Products	Hair Products	320.12			
Hair Solutions	Hair Products	320.12			

Common Name/Synonym	Primary Name	AOEC Code[1]	Use[2]	Asth-magen[3]	Asthma Detail[3]
Hair Spray	Hair Products	320.12			
Halon	Halon	320.101			
Halothane	Halothane	190.153			R
Halowax	Chlorinated Naphthalene	200.03			
Hand-Arm Posture	Posture, Upper Extremity	362.01			
Hand-Arm Vibration	Vibration, Regional	354.01			
Handwriting	Gripping, Forceful	361.03			
Haptachlorine	Heptachlor	280.08	P		
Hard Metal	Tungsten Compounds	20.52			
Hardwood, Tropical, NOS	Hardwood, Tropical, NOS	373.24			
Hay	Hay	370.08			
Hazard Not On File	Hazard Not On File	0			
HBR	Hydrobromic Acid	50.09			
HCFC-225ca	3,3-Dichloro-1,1,1,2,2-pentafluoropropane	192.021			
HCFC-225cb	1,3-Dichloro-1,1,2,2,3-pentafluoropropane	192.022			
HCL	Hydrochloric Acid	50.1		Yes	Rr
HCN	Hydrogen Cyanide	211.01			
HDI	Hexamethylene Diisocyanate	221.04		Yes	G
HDI Prepolymers	Prepolymer of Hexamethylene diisocyanate	221.08		Yes	Rs
Heat	Heat	350.03			
Heat Shrink Wrapping	Heat Shrink Wrapping	326.02			R
Heated Electrostatic Polyester Paint	Polyethylene Terephthalate/Polybutylene Terephthalate	270.25		Yes	Rs
Heavy Lifting	Lifting	361.02			
Heavy Metals, NOS	Heavy Metals, NOS	20.46			
Hemicellulase (from Aspergillus niger)	Hemicellulase (from Aspergillus niger)	324.121		Yes	Rs
Henna	Henna	370.27		Yes	
Hepatitis B	Hepatitis B	390.09			
Hepatitis C	Hepatitis C	390.12			
Heptachlor	Heptachlor	280.08	P		
Heptane	Heptane	60.03	S		
Herbal Tea, NOS	Herbal Tea, NOS	370.001			R
Herbicides, NOS	Herbicides, NOS	320.13	P		
Heroin	Diacetyl morphine	321.185		Yes	Rs
Hexachlorobenzene	Hexachlorobenzene	201.03	P		
Hexachlorophene	Hexachlorophene	181.02		Yes	Rs
Hexahydrophthalic Anhydride	Hexahydrophthalic Anhydride	151.08		Yes	Rs
Hexamethylene Diisocyanate	Hexamethylene Diisocyanate	221.04		Yes	G
Hexamethylenediamine	Hexamethylenediamine	232.1			R
Hexamethylenetetramine	Hexamethylenetetramine	232.02			R
Hexane	Hexane	60.02	S		
Hexone	Methyl Isobutyl Ketone	130.04	S		
Hexylene Glycol	Hexylene Glycol	80.03			
HF	Hydrofluoric Acid	50.11			
High Force	Forceful Movements, NOS	361.01			
High Temperature	Heat	350.03			
Himic Anhydride	Himic Anhydride	151.07		Yes	Rs
Histoplasma Capsulatum	Histoplasma Capsulatum	390.03			
HIV Exposure	HIV Exposure	390.08			
Honeybee	Honeybee	382.08		Yes	
Hops	Hops	370.16		Yes	
Hot Liquid	Heat	350.03			
Hot Tub Fumes, NOS	Hot Tub Fumes, NOS	327.04			
Hoya	Hoya	381.04			R
Humidity, High	Humidity, High	350.05			
Humidity, Low	Humidity, Low	350.04			
Hydralazine	Hydralazine	321.14		Yes	Rs
Hydrated Lime	Hydrated Lime	50.051			
Hydraulics	Lubricants, NOS	320.14			

Common Name/Synonym	Primary Name	AOEC Code[1]	Use[2]	Asthmagen[3]	Asthma Detail[3]
Hydrazine	Hydrazine	260.11			
Hydrazine Derivatives	Hydrazine Derivatives	260.119			
Hydrazoic Acid	Hydrazoic Acid	50.08			
Hydrobromic Acid	Hydrobromic Acid	50.09			
Hydrocarbons, NOS	Hydrocarbons, NOS	170			
Hydrochloric Acid	Hydrochloric Acid	50.1		Yes	Rr
Hydrocodone	Hydrocodone	321.187		Yes	Rs
Hydrofluoric Acid	Hydrofluoric Acid	50.11			
Hydrofluosilicic Acid	Hydrofluosilicic Acid	50.44			
Hydrogen Bromide	Hydrobromic Acid	50.09			
Hydrogen Chloride	Hydrochloric Acid	50.1		Yes	Rr
Hydrogen Cyanide	Hydrogen Cyanide	211.01			
Hydrogen Fluoride	Hydrofluoric Acid	50.11			
Hydrogen gas	Hydrogen gas	40.36			
Hydrogen Peroxide	Hydrogen Peroxide	50.12			
Hydrogen Sulfate	Sulfuric Acid	50.24		Yes	Rr
Hydrogen Sulfide	Hydrogen Sulfide	40.06			
Hydroquinone	Hydroquinone	180.03			
Hydroxybenzene	Phenol	180.04			
Hypoxia	Hypoxia	353.04			
ILA Soap	Cleaners, Solvent-Based	322.06	S		
Imbuia	Imbuia	373.26		Yes	Rs
Imidacloprid	Imidacloprid	320.451	P		
Imipenem	Imipenem	321.2			
Incense Smoke	Incense Smoke	330.07			
Incinerator Fume, NOS	Incinerator Fume, NOS	330.04			
Indium	Indium	20.191			
Indium Compounds	Indium Compounds	20.19			
Indoor Air Pollutants from Building Renovation	Indoor Air Pollutants from Building Renovation	320.33			
Infectious Agents, NOS	Infectious Agents, NOS	390.07			
Inflamen	Bromelain	324.07		Yes	Rs
Infrared Light	Infrared Light	352.05			
INH	Isonicotinic Acid Hydrazide	321.13		Yes	Rs
Inks containing 30% acrylic acid, 30% hydroxy-propanoic acid CAS# 79-33-4, 25% bronze po	Inks containing 30% acrylic acid, 30% hydroxy-propanoic acid CAS# 79-33-4, 25% bronze po	170.021		Yes	Rs
Inks, NOS	Inks, NOS	170.02			
Inorganic Acids, NOS	Acids, Bases, Oxidizers, NOS	50			
Inorganic Compounds, NOS	Inorganic Compounds, NOS	40			
Inorganic Dust, NOS	Dust, NOS	10			
Insect Bite, NOS	Insect Bite, NOS	382.21			
Insect, NOS	Insect, NOS	382			
Insecticides, NOS	Insecticides, NOS	320.45	P		
Iodine	Iodine	30.04			
Iodophors	Iodophors	322.05			
IPDI	Isophorone Diisocyanate	221.05		Yes	Rs
Ipecac	Ipecacuanha	321.16			R
Ipecacuanha	Ipecacuanha	321.16			R
IR	Infrared Light	352.05			
IR Light	Infrared Light	352.05			
Irgasan	5-chloro-2-(2,4-dichlorohydroxy) phenol	181.03		Yes	Rs
Iroko	Iroko	373.05		Yes	
Iron	Iron	20.202			
Iron Compounds	Iron Compounds	20.2			
Irritant Gases, NOS	Irritant Gases, NOS	40.24			
Isoamyl Nitrite	Amyl Nitrite	260.27			
Isobutane	Isobutane	60.04			
Isocyanates, NOS	Isocyanates, NOS	220			
Isofenphos	Pyrfon	291.09	P		R

Common Name/Synonym	Primary Name	AOEC Code[1]	Use[2]	Asth-magen[3]	Asthma Detail[3]
Isoflurane	Isoflurane	190.157		Yes	Rs
Isolyzer	Isolyzer	120.05		Yes	Rs
Isoniazid	Isonicotinic Acid Hydrazide	321.13		Yes	Rs
Isonicotinic Acid Hydrazide	Isonicotinic Acid Hydrazide	321.13		Yes	Rs
Isononanoyl Oxybenzene Sulfonate	Isononanoyl Oxybenzene Sulfonate	322.331			
Isooctane	Isooctane	60.12			
Isophorone diamine	Isophorone diamine	232.09			R
Isophorone Diisocyanate	Isophorone Diisocyanate	221.05		Yes	Rs
Isophthalic Acid Chloride	Isophthaloyl Chloride	200.05			
Isophthaloyl Chloride	Isophthaloyl Chloride	200.05			
Isopropanol	Isopropyl Alcohol	70.06	S		
Isopropyl Alcohol	Isopropyl Alcohol	70.06	S		
Isopropylamine	Isopropylamine	230.03			
Jalapeno Pepper	Jalapeno Pepper	370.46			
Jet Exhaust	Jet Exhaust	331.03			
Jet Fuel	Jet Fuel	61.05	S		
Job Control	Stress	360.04			
Job Demand	Stress	360.04			
Joint replacement, elevated chromium	Joint replacement, elevated chromium	20.601			
Joint replacement, elevated cobalt	Joint replacement, elevated cobalt	20.602			
Joint replacement, toxicity NOS	Joint replacement, toxicity NOS	20.6			
Juglans Olanchana	Juglans Olanchana	373.11		Yes	Rs
Kanechlor	Polychlorinated Biphenyls	200.07			
Kaolin	Clay	10.051			
Kapok	Kapok	370.43		Yes	
Karaya	Karaya	372.03		Yes	
Kejaat	Kejaat	373.12		Yes	
Kerosene	Kerosene	61.031	S		
Kerosine	Kerosene	61.031	S		
Ketones, NOS	Ketones, NOS	130	S		
Kevlar	Poly (P-Phenylenediamine)	270.35			
Key Punching	Keyboard Use	360.02			
Keyboard and Mouse Use	Keyboard Use	360.02			
Keyboard Use	Keyboard Use	360.02			
Kneeling	Posture, Body - Static	362.02			
KOH	Potassium Hydroxide	50.17			
Kotibe	Kotibe	373.21		Yes	
L. Caesar Larva	L. Caesar Larva	382.19		Yes	
L. Decemlineata	Leptinotarsa Decemlineata	382.23		Yes	
Laboratory Animals, NOS (see specific animals)	Animal Material, NOS	380			R
Lacquer	Lacquer	171.07			
Lacquer Thinner	Thinner	171.02	S		
Lactase	Lactase	324.14			
lactic acid, ethyl ester	Ethyl lactate	140.07			
Lactoserum	Lactoserum	380.1		Yes	Rs
Lanasol Blue 3G	Lanasol Blue 3G	325.29			R
Lanasol Blue 3R	Lanasol Blue 3G	325.29			R
Lanasol Brown G	Lanasol Brown G	325.3			R
Lanasol Orange G	Lanasol Orange G	325.33			R
Lanasol Orange R	Lanasol Orange R	325.16			R
Lanasol Red 2G	Lanasol Red 2G	325.31			R
Lanasol Red 5B	Lanasol Red 5B	325.14			R
Lanasol Red B	Lanasol Red B	325.13			R
Lanasol Red G	Lanasol Red G	325.15			R
Lanasol Scarlet 2R	Lanasol Scarlet 2R	325.32			R
Lanasol Yellow 4G	Lanasol Yellow 4G	325.09		Yes	Rs
Laser cutting, stainless	Laser cutting, stainless	23.011			
Lasers	Lasers	352.02			
Latex Gloves, NOS	Latex, Natural Rubber	270.02		Yes	G

Common Name/Synonym	Primary Name	AOEC Code[1]	Use[2]	Asth-magen[3]	Asthma Detail[3]
Latex, Natural Rubber	Latex, Natural Rubber	270.02		Yes	G
Latex, Synthetic	Latex, Synthetic	270.03			
Lathyrus Sativus	Lathyrus Sativus	370.29		Yes	
Lauryl Dimethyl Benzyl Ammonium Chloride	Dodecyl-dimethyl-benzylammonium Chloride	322.3216		Yes	Rs
Leachate	Leachate	323.02			
Lead, Inorganic Compounds	Lead, Inorganic Compounds	20.21			
Lead, Metal	Lead, Metal	20.211			
Lead, Organic	Lead, Organic	20.221			
Lead, Organic Compounds	Lead, Organic Compounds	20.22			
Lead-based Paint	Lead-based Paint	20.212			
Leather Dust	Leather Dust	380.03			
Leptinotarsa Decemlineata	Leptinotarsa Decemlineata	382.23		Yes	
Lesser Mealworm	Lesser Mealworm	382.09		Yes	
Levafix Black 5-GA	Levafix Black 5-GA	325.18			R
Levafix Black EB	Remazol Black B	325.11			R
Levafix Black EG	Levafix Black EG	325.17			R
Levafix Brilliant Blue K-BL	Drimaren Brilliant Blue K-BL	325.04		Yes	Rs
Levafix Brilliant Yellow E36	Levafix Brilliant Yellow E36	325.01		Yes	Rs
Levafix Golden Yellow E-3GA	Levafix Goldgelb E-3GA	325.2			R
Levafix Goldgelb E-3GA	Levafix Goldgelb E-3GA	325.2			R
Levafix Marinblau E-2BA	Levafix Marinblau E-2BA	325.19			R
Levafix Orange	Levafix Orange	325.12		Yes	Rs
Lifting	Lifting	361.02			
Lightning Powder	Fingerprint Powder	320.34			
Lime	Calcium Oxide	50.05			
Lime Chloride	Calcium Hypochloride	322.13			
Limonene	Limonene	60.05	S		
Limonium Tataricum	Limonium Tataricum	370.38		Yes	
Lindane	Lindane	280.06	P		
Linseed Oil	Linseed Oil	60.15			
Linseed Oilcake	Linseed Oilcake	60.24		Yes	Rs
Lipase	Lipase	324.21		Yes	Rs
Local Vibration	Vibration, Regional	354.01			
Locust	Locust	382.02		Yes	
Losartan	Losartan	321.36			R
Low Temperature	Cold	350.02			
LPG	Propane	60.2			
Lubricants, NOS	Lubricants, NOS	320.14			
Lycopodium	Lycopodium	370.25		Yes	
Lye	Sodium Hydroxide	50.18			
Lysozyme	Lysozyme	324.08		Yes	Rs
m-Delphene	N,N-diethyl-m-toluamide	260.26	P		
Mace	Mace	320.27			
Magenta	Magenta	251.07			
Magnesium	Magnesium	20.231			
Magnesium Aluminum Silicate	Magnesium Aluminum Silicate	20.232			R
Magnesium Compounds	Magnesium Compounds	20.23			
Mahogany	Mahogany	373.07		Yes	
Malathion	Malathion	291.01	P		R
Maleic Anhydride	Maleic Anhydride	151.02		Yes	Rs
Malt	Malt	370.56		Yes	Rs
Man-Made Mineral Fibers	Man-Made Mineral Fibers	10.092			
Man-Made Mineral Fibers, NOS	Man-Made Mineral Fibers, NOS	10.09			
Manganese	Manganese	20.241			
Manganese Compounds	Manganese Compounds	20.24			
Manure	Manure	380.02			
MAP	Ammonium Phosphate	40.32	P		
Marijuana dust	changed to 370.62	330.05			

Common Name/Synonym	Primary Name	AOEC Code[1]	Use[2]	Asth-magen[3]	Asthma Detail[3]
Marijuana dust	Cannabis dust (marijuana and hemp)	370.62		Yes	Rs
Marijuana plant	Cannabis dust (marijuana and hemp)	370.62		Yes	Rs
Marijuana Smoke	Cannabis Smoke	330.05		Yes	Rs
Marinblau E-2BA	Levafix Marinblau E-2BA	325.19			R
Maxatase	Bacillus Subtilis Enzymes	324.01		Yes	Rs
Maxataser	Protease	324.011		Yes	Rs
MBK	Methyl N-Butyl Ketone	130.05	S		
MDA	Methylenedianiline	250.16			
MDI	Methylene Bisphenyl Diisocyanate	221.02		Yes	G
ME-MDA	4,4'-Methylenebis(2-Chloroaniline)	250.03			
Mechanical Pressure	Contact Pressure	360.01			
Med fly	Ceratitis capitata	382.3		Yes	Rs
Mediterranean Fruit Fly	Ceratitis capitata	382.3		Yes	Rs
MEK	Methyl Ethyl Ketone	130.03	S		
MEK Peroxide	MEK Peroxide	130.02			
Melamine	Melamine	260.28			
Menta Arvensis Piperadcens	Corn Mint Oil	320.47			R
Mental Factors	Stress	360.04			
Menthol	Menthol	370.61			R
Mercaptans, NOS	Mercaptans, NOS	311			
Mercaptoethanol	Mercaptoethanol	310.04			
Mercaptopropionic Acid	3-mercaptopropionic Acid	310.12			
Mercuric Chloride	Mercuric Chloride	20.251			
Mercuric Salts	Mercuric Salts	20.252			
Mercury, Inorganic Compounds	Mercury, Inorganic Compounds	20.25			
Mercury, Organic	Mercury, Organic	20.261			
Mercury, Organic Compounds	Mercury, Organic Compounds	20.26			
Mesentericopeptidase	Esperase	324.1		Yes	Rs
Metal Carbonyls	Metal Carbonyls	20.44			
Metal Dust, NOS	Metal Dust, NOS	21			
Metal Fumes, NOS	Metal Fumes, NOS	20			
Metal Polish, Tarnish Remover, or Preventative	Metal Polish, Tarnish Remover, or Preventative	322.02			
Metal Working Fluids	Cutting Oils	170.01		Yes	G
Metallic Oxides, NOS	Metal Fumes, NOS	20			
Metals, NOS	Metals, NOS	20.47			
Metam Sodium	Sodium N-methyldithiocarbamate	292.01	P		
Methamidophos	Acephate	291.11	P		R
Methamphetamine Laboratory	Methamphetamine Laboratory	320.4			
Methane	Methane	60.06			
Methanol	Methanol	70.07	S		
Methaoxyethanol	Ethylene Glycol Monomethyl Ether	91.01	S		
Methoxychlor	Methoxychlor	280.07	P		
Methoxyflurane	Methoxyflurane	190.152			R
Methoxymethane	Ethyl Methyl Ether	100.06			
Methyl 2-Hydroxybenzoate Acrylate Acid	Methyl Salicylate	140.05			R
Methyl Alcohol	Methanol	70.07	S		
Methyl Blue	Methyl Blue	325.1		Yes	Rs
Methyl Bromide	Methyl Bromide	191.03	P		
Methyl Carbinol	Ethanol	70.05	S		
Methyl Cellosolve	Ethylene Glycol Monomethyl Ether	91.01	S		
Methyl Chloroform	Methyl Chloroform	190.08	S		
Methyl Dichlorosilane	Methyl Dichlorosilane	40.271			
Methyl Ester Isocyanic Acid	Methyl Isocyanate	220.01			
Methyl Ethyl Ketone	Methyl Ethyl Ketone	130.03	S		
Methyl Ethyl Ketone Peroxide	MEK Peroxide	130.02			
Methyl Isobutyl Ketone	Methyl Isobutyl Ketone	130.04	S		
Methyl Isocyanate	Methyl Isocyanate	220.01			
Methyl Isothiocyanate	Methyl Isothiocyanate	220.02	P		

Common Name/Synonym	Primary Name	AOEC Code[1]	Use[2]	Asth-magen[3]	Asthma Detail[3]
Methyl Mercury due to Fish Consumption	Methyl Mercury, Organic	20.262			
Methyl Mercury, Organic	Methyl Mercury, Organic	20.262			
Methyl Methacrylate	Methyl Methacrylate	142.04		Yes	Rs
Methyl N-Butyl Ketone	Methyl N-Butyl Ketone	130.05	S		
Methyl Propyl Ketone	Methyl Propyl Ketone	130.1			
Methyl Pyrrolidone	Methyl Pyrrolidone	260.121			
Methyl Salicylate	Methyl Salicylate	140.05			R
Methyl Sulfoxide	Dimethyl Sulfoxide	310.14			
Methyl Tertiary Butyl Ether	Methyl Tertiary Butyl Ether	100.08			
Methyl Tetrahydrophthalic Anhydride	Methyl Tetrahydrophthalic Anhydride	151.05		Yes	Rs
Methyl-4-Isopropenyl Cyclohexene-1	Limonene	60.05	S		
Methylbenzene	Toluene	160.02	S		
Methylcatechol	Guaiacol	100.09			
Methyldopa	Methyldopa	321.09		Yes	Rs
Methylene Bisphenyl Diisocyanate	Methylene Bisphenyl Diisocyanate	221.02		Yes	G
Methylene Chloride	Methylene Chloride	190.09	S		
Methylene Dichloride	Methylene Chloride	190.09	S		
Methylenedianiline	Methylenedianiline	250.16			
Methylphenol	Cresol	180.02			
Methylstyrene	Vinyl Toluene	160.08	S		
Methylthiomethane	Dimethyl sulfide	165.01			
Methylvinylbenzene	Vinyl Toluene	160.08	S		
Mexican Bean Weevil	Mexican Bean Weevil	382.06		Yes	
MGK 264	N-Octyl Bicycloheptene Dicarboximide	320.3	P		
MIBK	Methyl Isobutyl Ketone	130.04	S		
MIC	Methyl Isocyanate	220.01			
Mice	Mice	380.14		Yes	G
Micotil	Micotil	321.3			
Microberlinia brazzavillensis	Microberlinia brazzavillensis	373.13		Yes	Rs
Microorganisms, NOS	Microorganisms, NOS	390			
Mineral Naphtha	Benzene	160.01	S		
Mineral Oil	Mineral Oil	60.07			
Mineral Oil Mist	Mineral Oil	60.07			
Mineral Spirits	Petroleum Spirits	61.011	S		
Mineral Thinner	Naptha	61.012	S		
Mineral Turpentine	Naptha	61.012	S		
Mineral Wool	Rockwool	10.093			
MINT X Rodent repellant trash bags	MINT X Rodent repellant trash bags	320.5			R
Mites, NOS	Mites, NOS	382.13		Yes	G
Mitoxantrone	Mitoxantrone	321.011		Yes	Rs
Mixed DCB	Mixed DCB	201.011	P		
Mixture of Hydrogen Peroxide and Peroxyacetic Acid	Mixture of Hydrogen Peroxide and Peroxyacetic Acid	50.48		Yes	Rs
Mixture of Prepolymer of Polymethylene Polyphenylisocyanate (PPI) and 4,4'-Methylenediphen	Mixture of Prepolymer of Polymethylene Polyphenylisocyanate (PPI) and 4,4'-Methylenediphen	221.09		Yes	Rs
MMMF	Man-Made Mineral Fibers	10.092			
MMMF, NOS	Man-made Mineral Fibers, NOS	10.09			
MOCA	4,4'-Methylenebis(2-Chloroaniline)	250.03			
Moisture	Humidity, High	350.05			
Mold, NOS	Mold, NOS	391.01			R
Molybdenum	Molybdenum	20.271			
Molybdenum Compounds	Molybdenum Compounds	20.27			
Monoammonium Phosphate	Ammonium Phosphate	40.32	P		
Monobromomethane	Methyl Bromide	191.03	P		
Monochloroethane	Chloroethane	190.02	S		
Monochloroethylene	Vinyl Chloride Monomer	190.14			
Monoethanolamine	Monoethanolamine	231.01		Yes	Rs
Morphine	Morphine	321.181		Yes	Rs
Mosquito Bite	Insect Bite, NOS	382.21			
Motor Oil, Synthetic	Motor Oil, Synthetic	170.05			

Common Name/Synonym	Primary Name	AOEC Code[1]	Use[2]	Asth-magen[3]	Asthma Detail[3]
Motor Vehicle Accident	Motor Vehicle Accident	353.05			
MPK	Methyl Propyl Ketone	130.1			
MTBE	Methyl Tertiary Butyl Ether	100.08			
Multiple Chemicals	Chemicals, NOS	320.06			
Multiple Solvents	Solvents, NOS	171	S		
Muramidase	Lysozyme	324.08		Yes	Rs
Muriatic Acid	Hydrochloric Acid	50.1		Yes	Rr
Mushrooms, NOS	Mushrooms, NOS	391.1			R
Mustard Gas	Mustard Gas	190.16			
Mustargen	Mustargen HCL	321.28			
Mustargen HCL	Mustargen HCL	321.28			
Mycotoxins	Mycotoxins	391.09			
Mylar	Polyethylene Terephthalate	270.26			
Myrocarpus Fastigiatus Fr. All.	Cabreuva	373.23		Yes	
N,N-diethyl-3-methyl-	N,N-diethyl-m-toluamide	260.26	P		
N,N-diethyl-m-toluamide	N,N-diethyl-m-toluamide	260.26	P		
N,N-Diethylethanamine	Triethylamine	230.05			
N,N-Dimethylacetamide	N,N-Dimethylacetamide	260.07			
N,N-Dimethylethanolamine	Dimethylethanolamine	231.042		Yes	Rs
N,N-Dimethylformamide	N,N-Dimethylformamide	260.08	S		
N,N-Dimethylnitrosamine	N-Nitrosodimethylamine	240.01			
N-(2,6-difluorophenyl)-5-methyl-(1,2,4) triazolo (1,5-a) pyrimidine-2-sulfonomide	N-(2,6-difluorophenyl)-5-methyl-(1,2,4) triazolo (1,5-a) pyrimidine-2-sulfonomide	320.131	P		
N-Amyl Acetate	Amyl Acetate	141.01			
N-Amyl Alcohol	Amyl Alcohol	70.02			
N-Butyl Acetate	Butyl Acetate	141.02	S		
N-Butyl Acrylate	Butyl Acrylate	142.02			R
N-Butyl Alcohol	N-Butyl Alcohol	70.04	S		
N-Butyl Mercaptan	N-Butyl Mercaptan	311.01			
N-Butylamine	N-Butylamine	230.01			
N-Chloropropane	Chloropropane	190.05	S		
N-Heptane	Heptane	60.03	S		
N-Hexane	Hexane	60.02	S		
N-Hexyl Acrylate	N-Hexyl Acrylate	142.12			
N-Methylmorpholine	N-Methylmorpholine	260.2			R
N-Nitrosodimethylamine	N-Nitrosodimethylamine	240.01			
N-Octyl Bicycloheptene Dicarboximide	N-Octyl Bicycloheptene Dicarboximide	320.3	P		
N-Pentane	Pentane	60.19	S		
N-Pentyl Acetate	Amyl Acetate	141.01			
N2O	Nitrous Oxide	40.09			
NaClO	Sodium Hypochlorite	322.1		Yes	Rs
Nacre Dust	Nacre Dust	370.22			R
Nail Care Products	Nail Care Products	320.41			
NaOH	Sodium Hydroxide	50.18			
Naphtha	Naphtha	61.02	S		
Naphthalene	Naphthalene	160.05			
Naphthalene Diisocyanate	Naphthalene Diisocyanate	221.03		Yes	G
Naphthalin	Naphthalene	160.05			
Naptha	Naptha	61.012	S		
Natural Gas	Natural Gas	60.08			
Navy Blue HER	Navy Blue HER	325.21			R
NCR Paper	Carbonless Paper	320.05			
NDI	Naphthalene Diisocyanate	221.03		Yes	G
Nemacur	Nemacur	291.06	P		R
Neoprene	Neoprene	271.02			
Neosar	Cyclophosphamide	321.29			
Nerve Gas	Nerve Gas	291.04			
Nesorgordonia Papaverifera	Kotibe	373.21		Yes	

Common Name/Synonym	Primary Name	AOEC Code[1]	Use[2]	Asth-magen[3]	Asthma Detail[3]
Neurospora	Neurospora	390.11		Yes	Rs
New Carpet Odor	4-Phenylcyclohexene	60.11			
New Mexico Range Moth Caterpillar	New Mexico Range Moth Caterpillar	382.2		Yes	
Nickel	Nickel	20.281		Yes	Rs
Nickel Compounds	Nickel Compounds	20.28		Yes	Rs
Nicotine Sulfate	Nicotine Sulfate	260.13	P		
Ninhydrin	Ninhydrin	320.25			
Nitramine	Tetryl	250.1			
Nitric Acid	Nitric Acid	50.13			
Nitric Oxide	Nitric Oxide	40.081			
Nitrobenzene	Nitrobenzene	250.04			
Nitrobenzol	Nitrobenzene	250.04			
Nitroethane	Nitroethane	260.142			
Nitrogen	Nitrogen	40.07			
Nitrogen chloride	Trichloramine	30.11		Yes	Rs
Nitrogen Dioxide	Nitrogen Dioxide	40.082			
Nitrogen Mustard Hydrochloride	Mustargen HCL	321.28			
Nitrogen Mustard, NOS	Nitrogen Mustard, NOS	50.061			
Nitrogen Oxide	Nitric Oxide	40.081			
Nitrogen Oxides, NOS	Nitrogen Oxides, NOS	40.08			
Nitroglycerin	Nitroglycerin	261.01			
Nitromethane	Nitromethane	260.143			
Nitroparaffins	Nitroparaffins	260.14			
Nitrophenol	Nitrophenol	250.11			
Nitrous Oxide	Nitrous Oxide	40.09			
NO	Nitric Oxide	40.081			
No. 1 Fuel Oil	Kerosene	61.031	S		
No. 2 Fuel Oil	No. 2 Fuel Oil	61.062	S		
NO2	Nitrogen Dioxide	40.082			
Noise	Noise	350.01			
Nonoxynol	Nonoxynol	320.461			
Nonylphenol polyethylene glycol ether	Nonylphenol polyethylene glycol ether	90.013			
Nuclear Reactor Release	Nuclear Reactor Release	351.02			
NuSpraylok	Glues, NOS	320.11			
Nylon	Nylon	270.17			
Nylon Flock	Nylon Flock	10.22			R
o-methoxyphenol	Guaiacol	100.09			
O. Nubilalis	Ostrinia Nubilalis	382.24		Yes	
Oak	Quercus	373.06		Yes	Rs
Octacide 264	N-Octyl Bicycloheptene Dicarboximide	320.3	P		
Octopus	Octopus	381.12		Yes	Rs
Odors	Odors	320.15			
Off gassing of fracking tanks	Off gassing of hydraulic fracturing holding tanks	170.09			
Off gassing of hydraulic fracturing holding tanks	Off gassing of hydraulic fracturing holding tanks	170.09			
Oil Dispersants, NOS	Oil Dispersants, NOS	320.193			
Oil Mist	Cutting Oils	170.01		Yes	G
Oil of Clove	Oil of Clove	160.06			
Oil of Mirbane	Nitrobenzene	250.04			
Oil of Wintergreen	Methyl Salicylate	140.05			R
Oil Orange SS	Oil Orange SS	252.02			
Oils, NOS	Oils, NOS	170.03			
Oils, Vegetable	Oils, Vegetable	370.34			
Omite	Propargite	310.06	P		
Omite Cr	Omite Cr	310.061	P		
OPA	Ortho-phthalaldehyde	120.1			R
Opiate Compounds	Opiate Compounds	321.18		Yes	Rs
Optigard	Optigard	142.13			
Orange 3R	Rifazol Brilliant Orange 3R	325.07		Yes	Rs
Orange HE 2G	Rifacion Orange HE 2G	325.05		Yes	Rs

Common Name/Synonym	Primary Name	AOEC Code[1]	Use[2]	Asth-magen[3]	Asthma Detail[3]
Organic Chemicals, NOS	Hydrocarbons, NOS	170			
Organic Dusts, NOS	Organic Dusts, NOS	370.003			
Organic Phosphates, Nonpesticide	Organic Phosphates, Nonpesticide	300			
Organochlorine Insecticides, NOS	Organochlorine Pesticides, NOS	280	P		
Organochlorine Pesticides, NOS	Organochlorine Pesticides, NOS	280	P		
Organophosphate Pesticides, NOS	Organophosphate Pesticides, NOS	291	P		R
Orthene	Acephate	291.11	P		R
Ortho-phthalaldehyde	Ortho-phthalaldehyde	120.1			R
Orthophenylphenol	Orthophenylphenol	180.07	P		R
Osmium	Osmium	20.291			
Osmium Compounds	Osmium Compounds	20.29			
Ostrinia Nubilalis	Ostrinia Nubilalis	382.24		Yes	
Oxacyclohexedecen-2-one	Habanolide	320.43			
Oxalic Acid	Oxalic Acid	150.03			
Oxycide	Mixture of Hydrogen Peroxide and Peroxyacetic Acid	50.48		Yes	Rs
Oxycodone	Oxycodone	321.186		Yes	Rs
Oxygen Deficiency	Hypoxia	353.04			
Oxygen Propane Torch	Oxygen Propane Torch	23.012			
Oxygen, Liquid	Oxygen, Liquid	40.1			
Ozone	Ozone	40.11			
P-Dichlorobenzene	Dichlorobenzene	201.01	P		
P-Dihydroxybenzene	Hydroquinone	180.03			
P-Hydroxyphenol	Hydroquinone	180.03			
P-Mentha-1,8-Diene	Limonene	60.05	S		
PAH	Polycyclic Aromatic Hydrocarbons, NOS	161			
Paint Thinner	Thinner	171.02	S		
Paint, Acrylic	Acrylics	270.01			
Paint, Epoxy	Paint, Epoxy	110.05			
Paint, Latex	Paint, Latex	171.05			
Paint, NOS	Paint, NOS	171.01	S		
Paint, Oil-Based	Paint, Oil-Based	171.06			
Pancreatic amylase	alpha Amylase (pancreatic)	324.17		Yes	Rs
Pancreatin	Pancreatin	324.05		Yes	Rs
PAP	Para-Aminophenol	251.01			
Papain	Papain	324.03		Yes	Rs
Papaverine	Papaverine	321.184		Yes	Rs
Paper Dust	Paper Dust	370.01			
Paprika	Paprika	370.31		Yes	
Para-Aminophenol	Para-Aminophenol	251.01			
Paraffin	Paraffin	60.09			
Paraffin Oil	Mineral Oil	60.07			
Paraffin Wax	Paraffin	60.09			
Paraformaldehyde	Paraformaldehyde	120.06		Yes	G
Paraldehyde	Paraldehyde	120.07			
Paraquat	Paraquat	260.15	P		
Parasites, NOS	Parasites, NOS	382.17			
Parathion	Parathion	291.02	P		R
Pau Marfim	Pau Marfim	373.18		Yes	
PCBs	Polychlorinated Biphenyls	200.07			
PCP	Pentachlorophenol	181.01			
PE, NOS	Polyethylene, NOS	270.06			
Pectin	Pectin	370.23		Yes	Rs
Pectinase	Pectinase	324.6		Yes	Rs
Penicillamine	Penicillamine	321.05		Yes	Rs
Penicillins	Penicillins	321.042		Yes	G
Penicillium	Penicillium	391.03		Yes	Rs
Pentachloronitrobenzene	Pentachloronitrobenzene	200.06	P		
Pentachlorophenol	Pentachlorophenol	181.01			

Common Name/Synonym	Primary Name	AOEC Code[1]	Use[2]	Asth-magen[3]	Asthma Detail[3]
Pentaerythritol Tetrakis	3-mercaptopropionate	310.13			
Pentaerythritol Tetranitrate	Pentaerythritol Tetranitrate	261.02			
Pentamidine	Pentamidine	321.23			
Pentane	Pentane	60.19	S		
Pepper Spray	Capsicum	370.35			
Peppermint (mentha piperita)	Menthol	370.61			R
Pepsin A	Pepsin A	324.04		Yes	G
Pepsin B (pig stomach)	Pepsin B (pig stomach)	324.041		Yes	Rs
Pepsin, NOS	Pepsin, NOS	324.04		Yes	G
Peptidase (from enterobacterium Serratia)	Peptidase (from enterobacterium Serratia)	324.18		Yes	Rs
Perc	Perchlorethylene	190.1	S		
Perchlorethylene	Perchlorethylene	190.1	S		
Perchlorobenzene Fungicide	Hexachlorobenzene	201.03	P		
Perchloroethylene	Perchlorethylene	190.1	S		
Perfume, NOS	Perfume, NOS	320.23			
Perlite	Perlite	10.15			
Peroxidase Catalyst	Peroxidase Catalyst	324.13			
Peroxide 2-Butanone	MEK Peroxide	130.02			
Peroxides	Peroxides	50.14			
Peroxyacetic Acid	Peroxyacetic Acid	50.42			R
Persulfate Salts	Persulfate Salts	40.26		Yes	G
Pesticides, NOS	Pesticides, NOS	320.16	P		
PETN	Pentaerythritol Tetranitrate	261.02			
Petrochemicals, NOS	Hydrocarbons, NOS	170			
Petrol	Gasoline	61.04	S		
Petrolatum Liquid	Mineral Oil	60.07			
Petroleum Distillates, NOS	Petroleum Fractions, NOS	61	S		
Petroleum Fractions, NOS	Petroleum Fractions, NOS	61	S		
Petroleum Naphtha	Naphtha	61.02	S		
Petroleum Spirits	Petroleum Spirits	61.011	S		
PFA	Polyfunctional aziridine	260.102		Yes	Rs
Pharmaceuticals, NOS	Pharmaceuticals, NOS	321			
Phenol	Phenol	180.04			
Phenol Formaldehyde Resin	Phenol Formaldehyde Resin	120.11		Yes	Rs
Phenolic Resins	Phenolics	270.04			
Phenolics	Phenolics	270.04			
Phenols, NOS	Phenols, NOS	180			
Phenyl Chloride	Chlorobenzene	201.04	S		
Phenylamine	Aniline	250.01			
Phenylene Diamine	Benzenediamine	251.06			R
Phenylglycine Acid Chloride	Phenylglycine Acid Chloride	321.07		Yes	Rs
Phenylmethane	Toluene	160.02	S		
Phosgene	Phosgene	40.12			
Phosphate Ester, NOS	Phosphate Ester, NOS	140.06			
Phosphine	Phosphine	40.13	P		
Phosphoric Acid	Phosphoric Acid	50.15			
Phosphorodithioic acid	Phosphorodithoic acid	291.15			
Phosphorodithoic acid	Phosphorodithoic acid	291.15			
Phosphorus Bromide	Phosphorus Bromide	50.32			
Phosphorus Pentasulfide	Phosphorus Pentasulfide	40.14			
Phosphorus Sulfide	Phosphorus Pentasulfide	40.14			
Phosphorus Tribromide	Phosphorus Bromide	50.32			
Phosphorus Trichloride	Phosphorus Trichloride	50.16			
Phostoxin	Aluminum Phosphide	40.31	P		
Photo Developer, Black & White	Photo Developer, Black & White	180.031			
Photo Developer, Color	Photo Developing Chemicals, NOS	320.17			
Photo Developing Chemicals, NOS	Photo Developing Chemicals, NOS	320.17			
Phthalate Ester	Phthalate Ester	140.04			

Common Name/Synonym	Primary Name	AOEC Code[1]	Use[2]	Asth-magen[3]	Asthma Detail[3]
Phthalic Acid Anhydride	Phthalic Anhydride	151.01		Yes	Rs
Phthalic Aldehyde	Ortho-phthalaldehyde	120.1			R
Phthalic Anhydride	Phthalic Anhydride	151.01		Yes	Rs
Phthaloyl Chloride	Isophthaloyl Chloride	200.05			
Physical Factors, NOS	Physical Factors, NOS	350			
Phytase	Phytase	324.23		Yes	Rs
Pickle Processing (Unknown Causal Agent)	Pickle Processing (Unknown Causal Agent)	326.01			
Picric Acid	Picric Acid	250.09			
Pig	Pig	380.08		Yes	
Pig stomach pepsin	New code 324.041	324.04			
Pigeon Droppings	Pigeon Droppings	380.21			
Pinching	Gripping, Forceful	361.03			
Pine Wood Dust	Pine Wood Dust	373.25			
Pinellia Ternata	Pinellia Ternata	370.4		Yes	
Piperacillin	Piperacillin	321.043		Yes	Rs
Piperazine	Piperazine	260.19		Yes	Rs
Piperazine Citrate	Piperazine Citrate	260.192		Yes	Rs
Piperazine Hydrochloride	Piperazine Hydrochloride	260.191		Yes	Rs
Piperonyl Butoxide	Piperonyl Butoxide	290.01	P		
Plant Material, NOS	Plant Material, NOS	370.004			
Plant Waste	Grass Cuttings	370.07			
Plasmopara	Plasmopara	391.05			
Plasmopara Viticola	Plasmopara	391.05			
Plaster	Plaster	10.1			
Plaster of Paris	Plaster of Paris	10.172			
Plastic Dust	Plastic Dust	10.143			
Plastic Smoke	Plastic Smoke	330.02			
Plasticizers	Plasticizers	270.13			
Plastics, NOS	Polymers, NOS	270			
Plastics, Pre-Polymer	Polymers, NOS	270			
Platinum	Platinum	20.301			
Platinum Compounds	Platinum Compounds	20.3			
Plexiglass	Polymethyl Methacrylate	142.11		Yes	Rs
Plexiglass Dust	New code is 142.11	270.18			
Plutonium	Plutonium	351.01			
PMMA	Polymethyl Methacrylate	142.11		Yes	Rs
PNA	Polycyclic Aromatic Hydrocarbons, NOS	161			
Poison Ivy	Poisonous Plants	370.06			
Poison Oak	Poisonous Plants	370.06			
Poison Sumac	Poisonous Plants	370.06			
Poisonous Plants	Poisonous Plants	370.06			
Pollen	Pollen	370.1			
Pollution from Acts of Terrorism/War	World Trade Center Pollution	320.39			
Poly (P-Phenylenediamine)	Poly (P-Phenylenediamine)	270.35			
Polyamide Fibers	Nylon Flock	10.22			R
Polyamine EPO 60	EPO 60	232.06		Yes	Rs
Polyamines, NOS	Polyamines, NOS	232			
Polybutadiene	Polybutadiene	270.42			
Polycarbamate	Polycarbamate	270.071			
Polychlorinated Biphenyls	Polychlorinated Biphenyls	200.07			
Polychlorobutadiene	Polychlorobutadiene	271.021			
Polychloroprene	Neoprene	271.02			
Polycyclic Aromatic Hydrocarbons, NOS	Polycyclic Aromatic Hydrocarbons, NOS	161			
Polydimethyl Siloxane	Polydimethyl Siloxane	270.031			
Polyester Resin	Polyester Resin	270.05			
Polyethylamine	Polyethylamine	230.07			
Polyethylene Glycol Stearates	Polyethylene Glycol Stearates	320.192			
Polyethylene Terephthalate	Polyethylene Terephthalate	270.26			
Polyethylene Terephthalate/Polybutylene Terephthalate	Polyethylene Terephthalate/Polybutylene Terephthalate	270.25		Yes	Rs

Common Name/Synonym	Primary Name	AOEC Code[1]	Use[2]	Asth-magen[3]	Asthma Detail[3]
Polyethylene, Heated	Polyethylene, Heated	270.31			R
Polyethylene, NOS	Polyethylene, NOS	270.06			
Polyethylene, Unheated	Polyethylene, Unheated	270.32			
Polyfunctional aziridine	Polyfunctional aziridine	260.102		Yes	Rs
Polyhexamethylene Biguanide	Polyhexamethylene Biguanide	260.29	P		
Polyimides	Polyimides	270.19			
Polymer Fume	Plastic Smoke	330.02			
Polymers, NOS	Polymers, NOS	270			
Polymethyl Methacrylate	Polymethyl Methacrylate	142.11		Yes	Rs
Polymethyl Methacrylate	Polymethyl Methacrylate	142.11		Yes	Rs
Polymethylene Polyphenylisocyanate	Polymethylene Polyphenylisocyanate	221.06		Yes	G
Polynuclear Aromatics	Polycyclic Aromatic Hydrocarbons, NOS	161			
Polypropylene, Heated	Polypropylene, Heated	270.33		Yes	Rs
Polypropylene, NOS	Polypropylene, NOS	270.24			
Polypropylene, Unheated	Polypropylene, Unheated	270.34			
Polystyrene	Polystyrene	270.2			
Polysulphide Polymer Adhesive	Polysulphide Polymer Adhesive	320.111			
Polytetrafluoroethylene	Polytetrafluoroethylene	270.12			
Polytetrafluoroethylene, Thermal Decomposition Products	Polytetrafluoroethylene, Thermal Decomposition Products	270.37			
Polyurethane	Polyurethane	270.079			
Polyurethane Coating	Polyurethane Coating	270.073			
Polyvinyl Alcohol	Polyvinyl Alcohol	270.08			
Polyvinyl Butyral Resins	Polyvinylbutyral	270.28			
Polyvinyl chloride (Fibrex)	Polyvinyl chloride (Fibrex)	270.093			
Polyvinyl Chloride (heated)	Polyvinyl Chloride (heated)	270.091		Yes	Rs
Polyvinyl Chloride (Non-heated)	Polyvinyl Chloride (Non-heated)	270.092		Yes	Rs
Polyvinyl Chloride Dust	Polyvinyl Chloride Dust	10.141			
Polyvinyl Chloride, Thermal Decomposition Products	Polyvinyl Chloride, Thermal Decomposition Products	270.38		Yes	Rs
Polyvinyl Pyrrolidone	Polyvinyl Pyrrolidone	270.14			
Polyvinylbutyral	Polyvinylbutyral	270.28			
Poppers	Amyl Nitrite	260.27			
Porcelain	Porcelain	10.11			
Portland Cement	Cement Dust	10.03			R
Posture, Body - Dynamic	Posture, Body - Dynamic	362.03			
Posture, Body - Static	Posture, Body - Static	362.02			
Posture, NOS	Posture, NOS	362			
Posture, Upper Extremity	Posture, Upper Extremity	362.01			
Potassium Aluminum Tetrafluoride (KALF4)	Potassium Aluminum Tetrafluoride (KALF4)	20.014		Yes	Rs
Potassium Aluminum Tetrafluoride (KALF4)	Potassium Aluminum Tetrafluoride (KALF4)	20.014		Yes	Rs
Potassium Bicarbonate	Potassium Bicarbonate	50.19			
Potassium Carbonate	Potassium Carbonate	50.41			
Potassium Chlorate	Potassium Chlorate	40.16			
Potassium Cyanide	Potassium Cyanide	211.02			
Potassium Dichromate	Potassium Dichromate	22.01			
Potassium Hydroxide	Potassium Hydroxide	50.17			
Potassium Nitrate	Potassium Nitrate	42.01			
Potassium Permanganate	Potassium Permanganate	50.39			
Potassium Salts, NOS	Potassium Salts, NOS	40.15			
Potroom exposures in primary aluminum production	Potroom exposures in primary aluminum production	20.013		Yes	Rs
Pouteria glomerata	Pouteria glomerata	373.08		Yes	Rs
Pouteria glomerata	Pouteria glomerata	373.1		Yes	Rs
PPI	Polymethylene Polyphenylisocyanate	221.06		Yes	G
Prawn	Prawn	381.03		Yes	G
Prepolymer of Hexamethylene diisocyanate	Prepolymer of Hexamethylene diisocyanate	221.08		Yes	Rs
Prepolymer of toluene diisocyanate	Prepolymer of toluene diisocyanate	221.07		Yes	Rs
Printing Chemicals, NOS	Printing Chemicals, NOS	320.29			
Producer Gas Residue	Polycyclic Aromatic Hydrocarbons, NOS	161			
Prolonged Position	Posture, Body - Static	362.02			

Common Name/Synonym	Primary Name	AOEC Code[1]	Use[2]	Asth-magen[3]	Asthma Detail[3]
Pronase	Pronase	324.24		Yes	Rs
Propane	Propane	60.2			
Propane Exhaust	Propane Exhaust	331.04			
Propanol	Isopropyl Alcohol	70.06	S		
Propargite	Propargite	310.06			
Propenamide	Acrylamide	260.02			
Propenenitrile	Acrylonitrile	210.02			
Propetamphos	Safrotin	291.08	P		R
Propionic Acid	Propionic Acid	310.15			
Propoxur	Propoxur	292.04	P		
Propyl Alcohol	Propyl Alcohol	70.08	S		
Propyl Hydride	Propane	60.2			
Propylene Dichloride	Propylene Dichloride	190.11	S		
Propylene Glycol Ethers	Propylene Glycol Ethers	90.012	S		
Propylene Oxide	Propylene Oxide	110.07			
Protease	Protease	324.011		Yes	Rs
Proteolytic Enzymes, NOS	Enzymes, NOS	324			
Protozoa Giardia	Protozoa Giardia	390.13			
Proventil	Salbutamol	321.31		Yes	Rs
Psychological Factors	Stress	360.04			
Psyllium	Psyllium	321.08		Yes	Rs
Pteridine	Pteridine	250.2			
Pterocarpus Angolensis	Kejaat	373.12		Yes	
PTFE	Polytetrafluoroethylene	270.12			
Pulling	Forceful Movements, NOS	361.01			
Pulp Mill Effluent	Pulp Mill Effluent	370.006			
purple top	Super Sani-Cloth Germicidal Disposable wipe				
Pushing	Forceful Movements, NOS	361.01			
PVA	Polyvinyl Alcohol	270.08			
PVC (heated)	Polyvinyl Chloride (heated)	270.091		Yes	Rs
PVC (Non-heated)	Polyvinyl Chloride (Non-heated)	270.092		Yes	Rs
PVC Dust	Polyvinyl Chloride Dust	10.141			
Pyrethrins	Pyrethrins	320.181	P		R
Pyrethroids	Pyrethroids	320.182	P		R
Pyrfon	Pyrfon	291.09	P		R
Pyridine	Pyridine	250.14			
Pyrogallic Acid	1,2,3-Trihydroxybenzene	180.06			
Pyrogallol	1,2,3-Trihydroxybenzene	180.06			
Pyromellitic Acid Dianhydride	Pyromellitic Dianhydride	151.04		Yes	Rs
Pyromellitic Dianhydride	Pyromellitic Dianhydride	151.04		Yes	Rs
Quartz Dust	Quartz Dust	10.132			
Quartz Surfacing Products	Engineered Stone Countertop Dust	10.136			
Quaternary ammonium compounds in cleaning agents	Benzalkonium Chloride, NOS	322.321		Yes	Rs
Quaternary Ammonium Compounds, NOS	Quaternary Ammonium Compounds, NOS	322.32			
Quercus	Quercus	373.06		Yes	Rs
Quicklime	Calcium Oxide	50.05			
Quillaja Bark	Quillaja Bark	373.15		Yes	Rs
Quinone	Quinone	180.05			
Rabbit Antigens	Rabbit Antigens	380.15		Yes	
Radiation, Electromagnetic	Radiation, Electromagnetic	352.01			
Radiation, Ionizing, NOS	Radiation, Ionizing, NOS	351			
Radiation, Microwave	Radiation, Microwave	352.03			
Radiation, Nonionizing, NOS	Radiation, Nonionizing, NOS	352			
Radiation, Ultraviolet	Radiation, Ultraviolet	352.04			
Radio Frequency Radiation	Radiation, Microwave	352.03			
Radiographic Fixative	Radiographic Fixative	320.32			R
Radioisotopes	Therapeutic Radiation	351.04			
Radon	Radon	351.03			

Common Name/Synonym	Primary Name	AOEC Code[1]	Use[2]	Asthmagen[3]	Asthma Detail[3]
Ramin	Gonystylus Bancanus	373.14		Yes	Rs
Raspberries	Fruit Juices	370.05			
Rat Antigens	Rat Antigens	380.18		Yes	G
Rat Feces	Rat Feces	380.2			
Reactice Red 78	Lanasol Scarlet 2R	325.32			R
Reactive Blue 114	Drimaren Brilliant Blue K-BL	325.04		Yes	Rs
Reactive Blue 171	Navy Blue HER	325.21			R
Reactive Blue 50	Lanasol Blue 3G	325.29			R
Reactive Brown 47	Lanasol Brown G	325.3			R
Reactive Dyes, NOS	Reactive Dyes, NOS	325			R
Reactive Orange 29	Lanasol Orange G	325.33			R
Reactive Orange 67	Levafix Goldgelb E-3GA	325.2			R
Reactive Orange 68	Lanasol Orange R	325.16			R
Reactive Orange 82	Remazol Brilliant Orange FR	325.26			R
Reactive Red 116	Lanasol Red 2G	325.31			R
Reactive Red 65	Lanasol Red B	325.13			R
Reactive Red 66	Lanasol Red 5B	325.14			R
Reactive Red 83	Lanasol Red G	325.15			R
Reactive Yellow 107	Remazol Gold Yellow RNL	325.25			R
Red BBN	Red BBN	325.22		Yes	Rs
Red HE 3B	Red HE 3B	325.23			R
Red Soft Coral	Red Soft Coral	381.05		Yes	
Refined Petroleum Solvent	Refined Petroleum Solvent	61.013	S		
Refractory Ceramic Fiber	Refractory Ceramic Fiber	10.094			
Remazol Black B	Remazol Black B	325.11			R
Remazol Black GF	Remazol Black B	325.11			R
Remazol Black GR	Rifazol Black GR	325.08		Yes	Rs
Remazol Brilliant Orange 3R	Rifazol Brilliant Orange 3R	325.07		Yes	Rs
Remazol Brilliant Orange FR	Remazol Brilliant Orange FR	325.26			R
Remazol Brilliant Yellow 4GL	Remazol Brilliant Yellow 4GL	325.27			R
Remazol Gold Yellow RNL	Remazol Gold Yellow RNL	325.25			R
Remazol Marine Blue GG	Remazol Marine Blue GG	325.24			R
Remazol Navy Blue GG	Remazol Marine Blue GG	325.24			R
Rennet	Rennet	324.25		Yes	Rs
Repetitive Lifting	Lifting	361.02			
Repetitive Motion	Repetitive Motion	360.03			
Repetitive Trauma	Repetitive Motion	360.03			
Resin containing furfuryl alcohol	Resin containing furfuryl alcohol	70.091		Yes	Rs
Resin Systems, NOS	Resin Systems, NOS	270.15			
Resins, NOS	Resins, NOS	270.151			
Rhodium	Rhodium	20.53		Yes	Rs
Ribavirin	Ribavirin	321.32			
Rice Dust	Rice Dust	370.48		Yes	Rs
Rice Flour	Rice Flour	371.07			
Rifacion Orange HE 2G	Rifacion Orange HE 2G	325.05		Yes	Rs
Rifafix Yellow 3 RN	Rifafix Yellow 3 RN	325.06		Yes	Rs
Rifazol Black GR	Rifazol Black GR	325.08		Yes	Rs
Rifazol Brilliant Orange 3R	Rifazol Brilliant Orange 3R	325.07		Yes	Rs
Rizolipase	Lipase	324.21		Yes	Rs
Road Pitch	Asphalt	61.07			
Road Tar	Asphalt	61.07			
Rock, NOS	Rock, NOS	11			
Rockwool	Rockwool	10.093			
Roofing Tar	Asphalt	61.07			
Rose Hips	Rose Hips	370.19		Yes	
Rotating Shifts	Stress	360.04			
Round Up	Glyphosate	320.132			
Rubber Dust	Rubber Dust	10.142			
Rubber, NOS	Rubber, NOS	271			

Common Name/Synonym	Primary Name	AOEC Code[1]	Use[2]	Asth-magen[3]	Asthma Detail[3]
Rust Inhibitor	Rust Inhibitor	60.22			
Rye Dust	Rye Dust	370.49			
Rye Flour	Rye Flour	371.03		Yes	G
Saccharin	Saccharin	320.38			R
Safrotin	Safrotin	291.08	P		R
Salbutamol	Salbutamol	321.31		Yes	Rs
Salbutamol Intermediate	Glycol Compound and Benzyl Compound	321.21		Yes	Rs
Salicylate	Salicylic Acid	321.25			
Salicylic Acid	Salicylic Acid	321.25			
Salmo salar	Salmon	381.13		Yes	Rs
Salmon	Salmon	381.13		Yes	Rs
SBR	Butadiene & Styrene	271.01			
Scopthalmus maximus	Turbot	381.14		Yes	Rs
Screw Worm Fly	Screw Worm Fly	382.03		Yes	
Sec-Propyl Alcohol	Isopropyl Alcohol	70.06	S		
Selenium	Selenium	20.311			
Selenium Compounds	Selenium Compounds	20.31			
Senna	Senna Plant	321.19		Yes	Rs
Senna laxative	Senna laxative	321.191			R
Senna plant	Senna plant	321.19		Yes	Rs
Sequoia Sempervirens	California Redwood	373.02		Yes	
Sericin	Sericin	370.26		Yes	
Serralysin	Peptidase (from enterobacterium Serratia)	324.18		Yes	Rs
Sesame Seed Dust	Sesame Seed Dust	370.45			
Sevin	Carbaryl	292.02	P		
Sevoflurane	Sevoflurane	190.158		Yes	Rs
Sewage	Sewer Water	323.03			
Sewer Gas	Sewer Gas	40.061			
Sewer Water	Sewer Water	323.03			
Shale	Shale	61.08			
Shark Cartilage	Shark Cartilage	381.11			R
Sharps	HIV Exposure	390.08			
Sheep Blowfly	Sheep Blowfly	382.12		Yes	Rs
Shellfish	Shellfish	381.01			
Shrimp	Shrimp Meal	381.07		Yes	
Shrimp Meal	Shrimp Meal	381.07		Yes	
Sick Building	Air Pollutants, Indoor	320.01			
Silage Microorganisms, NOS	Silage Microorganisms, NOS	391.11			
Silica Flour	Quartz Dust	10.132			
Silica Sand	Silica, Cystalline	10.133			
Silica, Amorphous	Silica, Amorphous	10.12			
Silica, Crystalline	Silica, Crystalline	10.133			
Silica, Crystalline, NOS	Silica, Crystalline, NOS	10.13			
Silica, Vitreous	Silica, Vitreous	10.135			
Silicon Carbide	Silicon Carbide	10.18			
Silicon Dioxide	Silica, Crystalline	10.133			
Silicone	Silicone	270.1			
Silicone Fluid	Silicone	270.1			
Silicone Rubber	Silicone	270.1			
Silkworm	Silkworm	382.01		Yes	
Silkworm Larva	Silkworm	382.01		Yes	
Siloxanes	Silicone	270.1			
Silver	Silver	20.321			
Silver Compounds	Silver Compounds	20.32			
Silver Sulfate	Silver Sulfate	20.322			
Sitting	Posture, Body - Static	362.02			
Skin Contact	Contact Pressure	360.01			
Slime Mold	Slime Mold	391.06			

Common Name/Synonym	Primary Name	AOEC Code[1]	Use[2]	Asth-magen[3]	Asthma Detail[3]
Slime Mold Dictyostelium Discoideum	Slime Mold	391.06			
Slip, Trip, or Fall on Same Level	Fall, NOS	353.03			
Smoke Inhalation	Smoke, NOS	330.03			
Smoke, Lead-Containing	Smoke, Lead-Containing	330.06			
Smoke, NOS	Smoke, NOS	330.03			
Snake Bite	Venom	380.05			
Snappers	Amyl Nitrite	260.27			
SO2	Sulfur Dioxide	40.201			
Soap, excluding Laundry Soap/Detergent	Soap, excluding Laundry Soap/Detergent	322.01			
Soapbark	Quillaja Bark	373.15		Yes	Rs
Soda Ash	Soda Ash	50.211			
Sodium Azide	Sodium Azide	211.04			
Sodium Benzoate	Sodium Benzoate	50.31			
Sodium Bisulfate	Sodium Bisulfate	50.4			
Sodium Bisulfite	Sodium Bisulfite	40.18			
Sodium Borohydride	Sodium Borohydride	40.29			
Sodium Carbonate	Sodium Carbonate	50.21			
Sodium Carboxymethyl Cellulose	Sodium Carboxymethyl Cellulose	270.11			
Sodium Caseinate	Casein	380.11		Yes	Rs
Sodium Chloride	Sodium Chloride	41.02			
Sodium Chlorite	Sodium Chlorite	30.08			
Sodium Cyanide	Sodium Cyanide	211.03			
Sodium Dichromate	Sodium Dichromate	22.03			
Sodium dioxide	Sodium dioxide	50.451			
Sodium dithionite	Sodium hydrosulfite	40.37			
Sodium hydrosulfite	Sodium hydrosulfite	40.37			
Sodium Hydroxide	Sodium Hydroxide	50.18			
Sodium Hypochlorite	Sodium Hypochlorite	322.1		Yes	Rs
Sodium Metabisulfite	Sodium Metabisulfite	40.28		Yes	Rs
Sodium Metasilicate	Sodium Metasilicate	50.22			
Sodium N-methyldithiocarbamate	Sodium N-methyldithiocarbamate	292.01	P		
Sodium Nitrate	Sodium Nitrate	42.02			
Sodium Oxide	Sodium Oxide	50.45			
Sodium Salts, NOS	Sodium Salts, NOS	40.17			
Sodium Silicate	Sodium Silicate	50.23			
Sodium Sulfide	Sodium Sulfide	40.19			
Sodium Sulfite	Sodium Bisulfite	40.18			
Sodium Tripolyphosphate	Sodium Tripolyphosphate	50.38			
Soldering flux (heated) Alkyl Aryl Polyether Alcohol/Polypropylene Glycol Mixt.	Soldering flux (heated) Alkyl Aryl Polyether Alcohol/Polypropylene Glycol	70.1		Yes	Rs
Soldering Flux (heated) Zinc Chloride/Ammonium Chloride	Soldering Flux (heated) Zinc Chloride/Ammonium Chloride	23.08		Yes	Rs
Soldering Flux, NOS	Soldering Flux, NOS	23.04			
Soldering, NOS	Soldering, NOS	23.1			
Soluble Halogenated Platinum Compounds, NOS	Soluble Halogenated Platinum Compounds, NOS	24		Yes	G
Solvent Naphtha	Naptha	61.012	S		
Solvents, NOS	Solvents, NOS	171	S		
Sour gas	Sour gas	60.081			
Soya Flour	Soya Flour	371.05		Yes	G
Soybean Lecithin	Soybean Lecithin	370.41		Yes	
Soybean Lectin	Soybean Lecithin	370.41		Yes	
Spider Bite	Insect Bite, NOS	382.21			
Spiramycin	Spiramycin	321.1		Yes	Rs
Spirits of Turpentine	Turpentine	60.1	S	Yes	Rs
Stachybotrys	Stachybotrys	391.07			
Standing	Posture, Body - Static	362.02			
Staph Aureus	Staph Aureus	390.071			
Steam	Heat	350.03			
Stearic Acid	Stearic Acid	150.05			
Stibine	Antimony Hydride	20.04			

Common Name/Synonym	Primary Name	AOEC Code[1]	Use[2]	Asth-magen[3]	Asthma Detail[3]
Stick Welding	Stick Welding	23.09			
Stoddard Solvent	Stoddard Solvent	61.014	S		
Stooping	Posture, Body - Dynamic	362.03			
Stress	Stress	360.04			
Stripper	Stripper	171.03	S		
Strontium	Strontium	20.501			
Strontium Compounds	Strontium Compounds	20.5			
Struck Against/Struck By Objects or Persons	Struck Against/Struck By Objects or Persons	353.09			
Struck by Falling Object	Struck by Falling Object	353.08			
Struck by Motor Vehicle (Road)	Struck by Motor Vehicle (Road)	353.06			
Struck by Vehicle or Equipment (Non-road)	Struck by Vehicle or Equipment (Non-road)	353.07			
Struck By/Against Object as Result of Fall	Fall, NOS	353.03			
Strychnine	Strychnine	260.16	P		
Styrene	Styrene	160.04	S	Yes	Rs
Styrene Monomer	Styrene	160.04	S	Yes	Rs
Styrene-Butadiene Copolymer	Butadiene & Styrene	271.01			
Styrene-Maleic Anhydride Polymer	Styrene-Maleic Anhydride Resin	270.23			
Styrene-Maleic Anhydride Resin	Styrene-Maleic Anhydride Resin	270.23			
Subtilisin	Bacillus Subtilis Enzymes	324.01		Yes	Rs
Subtilisin	Protease	324.011		Yes	Rs
Subtilisins	Bacillus Subtilis Enzymes	324.01			
Suffocation	Hypoxia	353.04			
Sulfites, NOS	Sulfites, NOS	310.1			
Sulfonates, NOS	Sulfonates, NOS	322.33			
Sulfur (multiple codes use this spelling only)	Sulphur				
Sulfur Chloride	Sulfur Chloride	40.22			
Sulfur Dioxide	Sulfur Dioxide	40.201			
Sulfur Gas	Sulfur Gas	40.21			
Sulfur Hydrocarbons, NOS	Sulfur Hydrocarbons, NOS	165			
Sulfur Monochloride	Sulfur Chloride	40.22			
Sulfur Oxides, NOS	Sulfur Oxides, NOS	40.2			
Sulfur, Elemental	Sulfur, Elemental	10.21	P		
Sulfuric Acid	Sulfuric Acid	50.24		Yes	Rr
Sulfuric Acid Diethyl Ester	Diethyl Sulfate	310.02			
Sulfuric Acid Dimethyl Ester	Dimethyl Sulfate	310.03			
Sunflower	Sunflower	370.2		Yes	
Surfactant-Specific amines	Surfactant-Specific amines	320.191		Yes	Rs
Surfactants, NOS	Surfactants, NOS	320.19			
Synonym	Primary Name	AOEC Exposur	P=Pes	Yes	Rs=Se
Talc	Talc	12			
Talc, Fibrous	Talc, Fibrous	12.01			
Talc, Nonasbestiform	Talc, Nonasbestiform	12.02			
Tall Oil, Crude	Tall Oil, Crude	110.041		Yes	Rs
Tall Oil, Fatty Acids	Tall Oil, Fatty Acids	110.043			R
Tall Oil, Rosin	Tall Oil, Rosin	110.042		Yes	Rs
Tanganyika Aningre	Pouteria glomerata	373.1		Yes	Rs
Tannic Acid	Tannic Acid	150.06			
Tar Camphor	Naphthalene	160.05			
Tartaric Acid	Tartaric Acid	150.07			
TCE	Trichloroethylene	190.13	S		
TDI	Toluene Diisocyanate	221.01		Yes	G
TDI Prepolymers	Prepolymer of toluene diisocyanate	221.07		Yes	Rs
Tea	Tea	370.14		Yes	Rs
Tear Gas	Mace	320.27			
Teflon	Polytetrafluoroethylene	270.12			
Teflon, Thermal Decomposition Products	Polytetrafluoroethylene, Thermal Decomposition Products	270.37			

Common Name/Synonym	Primary Name	AOEC Code[1]	Use[2]	Asth-magen[3]	Asthma Detail[3]
Tellurium	Tellurium	20.331			
Tellurium Compounds	Tellurium Compounds	20.33			
Terpene	Terpene	60.17	S		R
Terra Cotta	Terra Cotta	10.052			
Tetrachloro-Isophthalonitrile	Chlorothalonil	210.03	P	Yes	Rs
Tetrachloroethylene	Perchlorethylene	190.1	S		
Tetrachloromethane	Carbon Tetrachloride	190.01	S		
Tetrachlorophthalic Anhydride	Tetrachlorophthalic Anhydride	151.06		Yes	Rs
Tetracycline	Tetracycline	321.12		Yes	Rs
Tetraethyl Lead	Tetraethyl Lead	20.222			
Tetrahydrofuran	Tetrahydrofuran	60.16			
Tetramethrin	Tetramethrin	320.183	P	Yes	Rs
Tetrazene	Tetrazene	260.22		Yes	Rs
Tetryl	Tetryl	250.1			
Textile Dust, NOS	Textile Dust, NOS	320.22			
Thallium Compounds	Thallium Salts	40.23	P		
Thallium Salts	Thallium Salts	40.23	P		
Thapsia Garganica L	Thapsigargin	370.33			
Thapsigargin	Thapsigargin	370.33			
Theatrical Fog, Glycol-Based	Theatrical Fog, Glycol-Based	320.21			
Theatrical Fog, NOS	Theatrical Fog, NOS	320.2			
Thebaine	Thebaine	321.183		Yes	Rs
Theophylline	Theophylline	321.24			
Therapeutic Radiation	Therapeutic Radiation	351.04			
Thermal cutting of stainless steel	Thermal cutting of stainless steel	23.011			
Thermal Energy	Heat	350.03			
Thermophilic Actinomyces	Thermophilic Actinomyces	390.05			
Thiamine	Thiamine	370.6		Yes	Rs
Thinner	Thinner	171.02	S		
Thioglycol	Mercaptoethanol	310.04			
Thiophosphoric Anhydride	Phosphorus Pentasulfide	40.14			
Thiourea	Thiourea	310.07			
Thiram	Thiuram	310.08			
Thiuram	Thiuram	310.08			
Thorium	Thorium	20.341			
Thorium Compounds	Thorium Compounds	20.34			
THU	Thiourea	310.07			
Thuja Occidentalis	Eastern White Cedar	373.19		Yes	G
Thuja Plicata	Western Red Cedar	373.01		Yes	G
Thyme	Thyme	370.007		Yes	Rs
Thymol	Thymol	370.005			R
Thymus Vulgaris	Thyme	370.007		Yes	Rs
Tilmicosin Phosphate	Micotil	321.3			
Tin, Inorganic	Tin, Inorganic	20.351			
Tin, Inorganic Compounds	Tin, Inorganic Compounds	20.35			
Tin, Organic	Tin, Organic	20.361			R
Tin, Organic Compounds	Tin, Organic Compounds	20.36			R
Titanium	Titanium	20.481			
Titanium Compounds	Titanium Compounds	20.48			
TMA	Trimellitic Anhydride	151.03		Yes	Rs
TMPTA	Trimethylolpropane Triacrylate	142.08			
TNT	Trinitrotoluene	250.08			
Tobacco Leaf	Tobacco Leaf	370.15		Yes	G
Toluene	Toluene	160.02	S		
Toluene Diisocyanate	Toluene Diisocyanate	221.01		Yes	G
Toluene-2,4-Diisocyanate	Toluene Diisocyanate	221.01		Yes	G
Toluol	Toluene	160.02	S		
Tomato	Tomato	370.55			R
Toner, Copier	Toner, Copier	10.04			

Common Name/Synonym	Primary Name	AOEC Code[1]	Use[2]	Asthmagen[3]	Asthma Detail[3]
Tooth Enamel Dust	Tooth Enamel Dust	10.19			R
Tosyalate dihydrate	Tosyalate dihydrate	321.069			R
Tragacanth	Tragacanth	372.02		Yes	
Transmission Fluid	Lubricants, NOS	320.14			
Trauma, Acute, NOS	Trauma, Acute, NOS	353			
Traumanase	Bromelain	324.07		Yes	Rs
Trental	Trental	321.22			
Triazines, NOS	Triazines, NOS	260.17	P		
Tributyl Tin Oxide	Tributyl Tin Oxide	20.363	P	Yes	Rs
Trichloramine	Trichloramine	30.11		Yes	Rs
Trichloroacetic Acid	Trichloroacetic Acid	50.43			
Trichloroethylene	Trichloroethylene	190.13	S		
Trichloromethane	Chloroform	190.03			
Trichloronitromethane	Chloropicrin	260.06	P		
Trichlorotrifluoroethane	Trichlorotrifluoroethane	192.04			
Trichoderma	Trichoderma	391.08			
Trichoderma Koningii	Trichoderma	391.08			
Triclosan	5-chloro-2-(2,4-dichlorohydroxy) phenol	181.03		Yes	Rs
Tricresyl phosphate	Tricresyl phosphate	291.14			
Triethanolamine	Triethanolamine	231.02		Yes	Rs
Triethylamine	Triethylamine	230.05			
Triethylenetetramine	Triethylenetetramine	232.03		Yes	Rs
Trifluoroacetic Acid	Trifluoroacetic Acid	50.37			
Trifluorotrichloroethane	Trichlorotrifluoroethane	192.04			
Triglycidyl Isocyanurate	Triglycidyl Isocyanurate	270.41		Yes	Rs
Trimellitic Anhydride	Trimellitic Anhydride	151.03		Yes	Rs
Trimethylhexane-1,6-diamine/Isophorondiamine Mixture	Trimethylhexane-1,6-diamine/Isophorondiamine Mixture	232.04		Yes	Rs
Trimethylhexanediamine/Isophorondiamine Mixture	Trimethylhexane-1,6-diamine/Isophorondiamine Mixture	232.04		Yes	Rs
Trimethylolpropane Triacrylate	Trimethylolpropane Triacrylate	142.08			
Trimethylolpropane Triacrylate/2-Hydroxypropyl Acrylate	Trimethylolpropane Triacrylate/2-Hydroxypropyl Acrylate	142.1		Yes	Rs
Trinitroglycerin	Nitroglycerin	261.01			
Trinitrotoluene	Trinitrotoluene	250.08			
Trinitrotoluol	Trinitrotoluene	250.08			
Triplochiton Scleroxylon	Triplochiton Scleroxylon	373.09		Yes	Rs
Tris	Tris	300.01			
Tris 2,3-Dibromopropyl Phosphate	Tris	300.01			
Trisodium Phosphate	Trisodium Phosphate	50.2			
Trout	Trout	381.08		Yes	Rs
Trypsin	Trypsin	324.02		Yes	Rs
Tuberculosis	Tuberculosis	390.1			
Tungsten Carbide	Tungsten Carbide	20.37		Yes	Rs
Tungsten Carbide/Cobalt	Tungsten Carbide/Cobalt	20.451		Yes	Rs
Tungsten Compounds	Tungsten Compounds	20.52			
Turbot	Turbot	381.14		Yes	Rs
Turpentine	Turpentine	60.1	S	Yes	Rs
Twisting	Posture, Body - Dynamic	362.03			
Tylosin Tartrate	Tylosin Tartrate	321.15		Yes	Rs
Typewriter	Keyboard Use	360.02			
Typing	Keyboard Use	360.02			
Ultrasound	Ultrasound	350.06			
Unspecified Solvents	Solvents, NOS	171	S		
Upper Extremity Awkward Positions	Posture, Upper Extremity	362.01			
Uranium	Uranium	20.54			
Uranium	Uranium	351.05			
Urea Formaldehyde	Urea Formaldehyde	270.16			R
Urea Formaldehyde Resin	Urea Formaldehyde Resin	270.16		Yes	Rs
Urea Formaldehyde Resin	Urea Formaldehyde Resin	270.161		Yes	Rs
Urethane	Urethane	270.07			

Common Name/Synonym	Primary Name	AOEC Code[1]	Use[2]	Asth-magen[3]	Asthma Detail[3]
Urethane Enamel Paint	Urethane Enamel Paint	270.072			
UV Light	Radiation, Ultraviolet	352.04			
UV Radiation	Radiation, Ultraviolet	352.04			
Vanadium	Vanadium	20.381			
Vanadium Compounds	Vanadium Compounds	20.38			
Vanadium Hydroxide Oxide Phosphate	Vanadium Hydroxide Oxide Phosphate	40.3			
Vancomycin	Vancomycin	321.33		Yes	Rs
Vapam	Sodium N-methyldithiocarbamate	292.01	P		
Vaping emissions	Electronic cigarette emissions	320.49			
Varethane Paint	Polyurethane Coating	270.073			
Varnish	Lacquer	171.07			
Varnish Makers' & Painters' Naphtha	Naptha	61.012	S		
Varsol	Naptha	61.012	S		
VDT Keyboard	Keyboard Use	360.02			
VDT Radiation	Radiation, Electromagnetic	352.01			
VDT Screen/Visual	VDT Screen/Visual	360.05			
VDT Typing	Keyboard Use	360.02			
Vegetable Dust	Vegetable Dust	370.04			
Vegetable Juices	Fruit Juices	370.05			
Velcorin	Dimethyl dicarbonate	40.35			
Venom	Venom	380.05			
Ventilation, Inadequate	Air Pollutants, Indoor	320.01			
Vermiculite	Vermiculite	10.2			
Vetch	Vicia Sativa	370.11		Yes	
Vibration, NOS	Vibration, NOS	354			
Vibration, Regional	Vibration, Regional	354.01			
Vibration, Whole Body	Vibration, Whole Body	354.02			
Vicia Sativa	Vicia Sativa	370.11		Yes	
Vinegar	Vinegar	50.46			R
Vinyl Acetate	Vinyl Acetate	141.04			
Vinyl Carbinol	Allyl Alcohol	70.01			
Vinyl Chloride Monomer	Vinyl Chloride Monomer	190.14			
Vinyl Cyanide	Acrylonitrile	210.02			
Vinyl Dust	Polyvinyl Chloride Dust	10.141			
Vinyl Fumes	Plastic Smoke	330.02			
Vinyl Monomer	Vinyl Chloride Monomer	190.14			
Vinyl Plastic Wrap	Vinyl Plastic Wrap	270.27			
Vinyl Toluene	Vinyl Toluene	160.08	S		
Vinyl Trichloride	1,1,2-Trichloroethane	190.12	S		
Vinyl, NOS	Vinyl, NOS	10.14			
Vinylbenzene	Styrene	160.04	S	Yes	Rs
Violence, Other than Physical Assault	Violence, Other than Physical Assault	353.13			
Violence, Physical Assault	Assault, Physical	353.12			
Virazole	Ribavirin	321.32			
Viruses	Infectious Agents, NOS	390.07			
VM & P Naphtha	Naptha	61.012	S		
VOC, NOS	Hydrocarbons, NOS	170			
Walking	Walking	360.08			
Waste water treatment chemicals	Waste water treatment chemicals	50.47			
Waste, Hazardous	Waste, Hazardous	323.01			
Waste, Hazardous Acid	Waste, Hazardous	323.01			
Waste, NOS	Waste, NOS	323			
Waste, Treated Human Sludge	Waste, Treated Human Sludge	323.04			
Water Chlorination Byproducts	Water Chlorination Byproducts	327.01			
Water Contamination, Inorganic	Water Contamination, Inorganic	327.02			
Water Contamination, NOS	Water Contamination, NOS	327			
Water Contamination, Organic	Water Contamination, Organic	327.03			
Waxes, NOS	Waxes, NOS	170.06			

Common Name/Synonym	Primary Name	AOEC Code[1]	Use[2]	Asth-magen[3]	Asthma Detail[3]
Weeping Fig	Weeping Fig	370.24		Yes	
Welding Freon	Freon, Heated	192.06		Yes	Rs
Welding Fume, Copper/Nickel	Welding Fume, Copper/Nickel	23.03			
Welding Fume, Galvanized Metal	Welding Fume, Galvanized Metal	23.06			
Welding Fume, Iron or Steel	Welding Fume, Iron or Steel	23.02			
Welding Fume, NOS	Welding Fume, NOS	23			
Welding Fume, Stainless Steel	Welding Fume, Stainless Steel	23.01		Yes	G
Welding, NOS	Welding, NOS	23.001			
Western Red Cedar	Western Red Cedar	373.01		Yes	G
Wet Weather	Humidity, High	350.05			
Wheat Dust	Wheat Dust	370.5			
Wheat Flour	Wheat Flour	371.04		Yes	G
White Oil	Mineral Oil	60.07			
White Spirits	Petroleum Spirits	61.011	S		
White Tar	Naphthalene	160.05			
Wood Alcohol	Methanol	70.07	S		
Wood Ash	Ash, NOS	10.16			
Wood Bark, NOS	Wood Dust, NOS	373			
Wood Dust, NOS	Wood Dust, NOS	373			
Wood Spirits	Methanol	70.07	S		
Wool Dust	Wool Dust	370.44			
Word Processing	Keyboard Use	360.02			
World Trade Center Dust	World Trade Center Pollution	320.39			
World Trade Center Pollution	World Trade Center Pollution	320.39			
X-Ray Developer	X-Ray Developer	180.032			
Xrays	Therapeutic Radiation	351.04			
Xylanase (from Thermomyces lanuginosis)	Xylanase (from Thermomyces lanuginosis)	324.123		Yes	Rs
Xylanase (Medical literature uses this as a synonym)	Fungal Hemicullulase	324.12		Yes	Rs
Xylene	Xylene	160.03	S		
Xylol	Xylene	160.03	S		
Yeast	Yeast	370.28			
Yellow 3 RN	Rifafix Yellow 3 RN	325.06		Yes	Rs
Yellow 3R	Yellow 3R	325.28			R
Yellow 4GL	Remazol Brilliant Yellow 4GL	325.27			R
Yellow GR	Yellow 3R	325.28			R
Zeolite	Zeolite	324.15			
Zinc	Zinc	20.391			R
Zinc Chloride	Zinc Chloride	20.4			
Zinc Compounds	Zinc Compounds	20.39			R
Zinc Oxide	Zinc Oxide	20.393		Yes	Rs
Zirconium	Zirconium	20.411			
Zirconium Compounds	Zirconium Compounds	20.41			

Note: *(1) Association of Occupational & Environmental Clinics code; (2) S=Solvent, P=Pesticide; (3) A supplemental designation for asthmagens (indicated by an "A") is included on the list. Formal criteria for the asthmagen designation were first established for sensitizer-induced asthma in 2002, and for irritant-induced asthma (Reactive Airways Dysfunction Syndrome (RADS) in 2008. These criteria were developed in collaboration with experts in occupational and pulmonary medicine. An * in the asthmagen designation field means that specific substances within this generic category meet the AOEC criteria for an asthmagen. There are many other specific substances within this category that have not been studied as to whether or not they cause asthma. Clinicians evaluating patients with exposure to other substances in this category should have a high level of suspicion that specific substances within this category that have not been studied may also cause asthma. Exposures designated with an "A" for asthmagen are further classified by which criteria they meet. Exposures reviewed and meeting criteria for sensitizer-induced asthma are designated "Rs"; those reviewed and meeting criteria for RADS are designated "Rr"; those reviewed and not meeting either set of criteria are designated "R". Should any exposures be reviewed and determined to meet both criteria they will be designated "Rrs". Substances that are generally accepted as asthmagens are designated "G".*

The Association of Occupational and Environmental Clinics (AOEC) Exposure Code List was first developed in 1994, for use by AOEC members in order to help systematically identify both existing and emerging occupational and environmental health concerns. The AOEC Exposure Code List includes a wide range of exposures including not only chemicals but exposures to metals, dusts, plants, animals etc. as well as physical hazards e.g. falls, lifting, repetitive strains, etc. Neither the AOEC exposure code list nor the asthmagen designations are considered an official document of any governmental agency.

Source: *Association of Occupational & Environmental Clinics, August 12, 2017*

Serum Cotinine (1999 – 2010)

Metabolite of nicotine (component of tobacco smoke)

Geometric mean and selected percentiles of serum concentrations (in ng/mL) for the ***non-smoking U.S. population from the National Health and Nutrition Examination Survey.

	Survey years	Geometric mean (95% conf. interval)	50th Percentile (95% conf. interval)	75th Percentile (95% conf. interval)	90th Percentile (95% conf. interval)	95th Percentile (95% conf. interval)	Sample size
Race/ethnicity							
Mexican Americans	99-00	*	**< LOD**	**.140** (.110-.180)	**.506** (.370-.726)	**1.21** (.900-1.70)	2241
	01-02**	**.060** (<LOD-.084)	**< LOD**	**.160** (.080-.310)	**.730** (.480-1.19)	**2.12** (1.19-2.96)	1878
	03-04	**.054** (.043-.068)	**.030** (.020-.050)	**.120** (.080-.180)	**.690** (.430-1.00)	**2.65** (1.87-3.57)	1707
	05-06	**.047** (.038-.059)	**.030** (.020-.040)	**.100** (.070-.150)	**.500** (.370-.730)	**1.54** (.830-2.49)	1807
	07-08	**.044** (.033-.057)	**.030** (.020-.040)	**.080** (.060-.120)	**.480** (.290-.880)	**1.59** (1.00-3.07)	1412
	09-10	**.038** (.032-.045)	**.020** (.020-.030)	**.060** (.050-.080)	**.360** (.230-.640)	**1.35** (.710-2.25)	1615
Non-Hispanic blacks	99-00	**.175** (.153-.201)	**.131** (.111-.150)	**.505** (.400-.625)	**1.43** (1.21-1.75)	**2.34** (1.84-3.50)	1333
	01-02**	**.164** (.137-.197)	**.130** (.110-.160)	**.580** (.450-.770)	**1.77** (1.55-2.05)	**3.15** (2.50-4.30)	1602
	03-04	**.144** (.104-.198)	**.120** (.080-.180)	**.520** (.350-.770)	**1.54** (1.20-2.14)	**2.77** (2.18-3.54)	1704
	05-06	**.114** (.085-.153)	**.080** (.060-.120)	**.440** (.240-.690)	**1.42** (.900-2.03)	**2.45** (1.70-3.70)	1630
	07-08	**.094** (.079-.112)	**.060** (.050-.090)	**.320** (.250-.390)	**1.19** (.980-1.46)	**2.37** (1.75-2.88)	1244
	09-10	**.095** (.074-.122)	**.070** (.050-.090)	**.320** (.210-.540)	**1.33** (.900-2.05)	**2.85** (1.97-3.60)	1129
Non-Hispanic whites	99-00	*	**.050** (<LOD-.073)	**.216** (.154-.312)	**.950** (.621-1.40)	**1.92** (1.48-3.02)	1950
	01-02**	**.052** (<LOD-.068)	**< LOD**	**.120** (.090-.180)	**.800** (.570-1.11)	**1.88** (1.48-2.30)	2847
	03-04	**.066** (.050-.087)	**.040** (.030-.070)	**.180** (.120-.300)	**.920** (.620-1.32)	**2.01** (1.70-2.49)	2500
	05-06	**.049** (.042-.056)	**.030** (.030-.040)	**.100** (.080-.130)	**.530** (.330-.800)	**1.27** (.980-1.62)	2404
	07-08	**.056** (.043-.073)	**.040** (.030-.050)	**.130** (.080-.240)	**.750** (.440-1.27)	**1.70** (1.24-2.54)	2485
	09-10	**.037** (.033-.043)	**.020** (.020-.030)	**.070** (.050-.080)	**.350** (.240-.560)	**1.06** (.780-1.60)	2743

Limit of detection (LOD, see Data Analysis section) for Survey years 99-00, 01-02, 03-04, 05-06, 07-08, and 09-10 are 0.05, 0.05, 0.015, 0.015, 0.015, and 0.015 respectively.
< LOD means less than the limit of detection, which may vary for some chemicals by year and by individual sample.
*Not calculated: proportion of results below limit of detection was too high to provide a valid result.
**In the 2001-2002 survey period, 83% of measurements had an LOD of 0.015 ng/mL, and 17% had an LOD of 0.05 ng/mL.
***Non-smoking is defined as a serum cotinine concentration of 10 ng/mL or less.

Biomonitoring Summary

http://www.cdc.gov/biomonitoring/Cotinine_BiomonitoringSummary.html

Factsheet

http://www.cdc.gov/biomonitoring/Cotinine_FactSheet.html

Source: *Centers for Disease Control & Prevention, Fourth National Report on Human Exposure to Environmental Chemicals, Updated Tables, January 2017*

Serum Cotinine (2011 - 2012)

Metabolite of nicotine (component of tobacco smoke)

Geometric mean and selected percentiles of serum concentrations (in ng/mL) for the **non-smoking** U.S. population from the National Health and Nutrition Examination Survey.

	Survey years	Geometric mean (95% conf. interval)	50th Percentile (95% conf. interval)	75th Percentile (95% conf. interval)	90th Percentile (95% conf. interval)	95th Percentile (95% conf. interval)	Sample size
Total	11-12	*	**.020** (.018-.023)	**.059** (.049-.072)	**.356** (.263-.500)	**1.30** (.882-1.60)	6108
Age group							
3-11 years	11-12	**.058** (.045-.074)	**.031** (.024-.045)	**.172** (.100-.313)	**1.02** (.627-1.94)	**2.49** (1.56-3.36)	1348
12-19 years	11-12	**.049** (.040-.061)	**.025** (.020-.037)	**.147** (.083-.235)	**.711** (.520-1.06)	**1.47** (1.05-2.29)	990
20 years and older	11-12	*	**.019** (.016-.020)	**.047** (.040-.053)	**.210** (.176-.263)	**.835** (.566-1.38)	3770
Gender							
Males	11-12	**.041** (.037-.045)	**.023** (.020-.026)	**.076** (.065-.095)	**.530** (.397-.715)	**1.76** (1.35-2.42)	2903
Females	11-12	*	**.019** (.016-.021)	**.048** (.040-.059)	**.244** (.189-.314)	**.819** (.572-1.31)	3205
Race/ethnicity							
Mexican Americans	11-12	**.033** (.027-.042)	**.021** (.016-.027)	**.055** (.040-.081)	**.230** (.106-.386)	**.668** (.349-2.07)	886
Non-Hispanic blacks	11-12	**.076** (.054-.107)	**.045** (.032-.071)	**.259** (.127-.513)	**1.10** (.678-2.02)	**2.86** (1.46-4.20)	1576
Non-Hispanic whites	11-12	*	**.017** (<LOD-.020)	**.048** (.039-.061)	**.277** (.207-.363)	**1.10** (.627-1.50)	1841
All Hispanics	11-12	**.033** (.028-.040)	**.021** (.017-.026)	**.054** (.041-.074)	**.233** (.123-.387)	**.834** (.377-2.37)	1587
Asians	11-12	**.030** (.026-.035)	**.023** (.020-.027)	**.046** (.037-.058)	**.123** (.083-.201)	**.308** (.201-.594)	878

Limit of detection (LOD, see Data Analysis section) for Survey year 11-12 is 0.015.
< LOD means less than the limit of detection, which may vary for some chemicals by year and by individual sample.
* Not calculated: proportion of results below limit of detection was too high to provide a valid result.
**Non-smoking is defined as a serum cotinine of 10 ng/mL or less.

Biomonitoring Summary

http://www.cdc.gov/biomonitoring/Cotinine_BiomonitoringSummary.html

Factsheet

http://www.cdc.gov/biomonitoring/Cotinine_FactSheet.html

Source: *Centers for Disease Control & Prevention, Fourth National Report on Human Exposure to Environmental Chemicals, Updated Tables, January 2017*

Urinary NNAL (4-(methylnitrosamino)-1-(3-pyridyl)-1-butanol) (2007 – 2010)

Metabolite of (4-(methylnitrosamino)-1-(3-pyridyl)-1-butanone) (NNK)

Geometric mean and selected percentiles of urine concentrations (in pg/mL) for the ****non-smoking** U.S. population from the National Health and Nutrition Examination Survey.

	Survey years	Geometric mean (95% conf. interval)	50th Percentile (95% conf. interval)	75th Percentile (95% conf. interval)	90th Percentile (95% conf. interval)	95th Percentile (95% conf. interval)	Sample size
Total	07-08	*	**< LOD**	**2.80** (2.20-3.70)	**11.1** (8.80-14.4)	**24.5** (18.0-30.4)	5212
	09-10	*	**< LOD**	**1.90** (1.60-2.40)	**7.30** (6.40-8.50)	**16.7** (13.9-19.6)	6067
Age group							
6-11 years	07-08	*	**1.30** (.600-2.60)	**8.50** (4.70-13.8)	**31.4** (17.5-49.8)	**60.6** (37.1-75.7)	875
	09-10	*	**.600** (<LOD-1.00)	**3.10** (2.20-5.00)	**15.5** (10.4-22.8)	**29.3** (18.1-59.4)	937
12-19 years	07-08	*	**1.20** (.600-2.10)	**5.00** (3.80-9.20)	**20.0** (11.9-27.5)	**39.1** (20.6-60.9)	843
	09-10	*	**.900** (<LOD-1.50)	**3.70** (2.70-5.20)	**12.5** (6.90-25.5)	**29.1** (13.9-51.4)	1004
20 years and older	07-08	*	**< LOD**	**2.10** (1.70-2.50)	**8.20** (6.90-9.80)	**16.6** (13.9-21.5)	3494
	09-10	*	**< LOD**	**1.60** (1.30-1.90)	**6.10** (5.10-6.90)	**13.1** (10.7-15.8)	4126
Gender							
Males	07-08	*	**< LOD**	**3.80** (3.00-4.50)	**12.6** (10.6-15.0)	**27.5** (18.9-38.1)	2463
	09-10	*	**< LOD**	**2.40** (1.90-3.00)	**8.30** (7.20-9.90)	**19.3** (15.2-22.5)	2903
Females	07-08	*	**< LOD**	**2.10** (1.50-2.90)	**9.70** (7.10-13.6)	**21.6** (16.6-28.0)	2749
	09-10	*	**< LOD**	**1.60** (1.30-1.90)	**6.50** (4.70-8.80)	**14.0** (10.7-19.0)	3164
Race/ethnicity							
Mexican Americans	07-08	*	**< LOD**	**2.00** (1.20-3.10)	**6.90** (4.90-9.00)	**13.9** (10.8-17.3)	1206
	09-10	*	**< LOD**	**1.60** (1.20-2.20)	**4.90** (3.70-7.00)	**11.1** (5.70-18.4)	1476
Non-Hispanic blacks	07-08	*	**.800** (<LOD-1.90)	**4.90** (3.60-6.30)	**14.0** (11.6-17.2)	**26.1** (18.5-33.2)	1057
	09-10	**1.81** (1.30-2.54)	**1.40** (<LOD-2.40)	**5.90** (3.80-8.10)	**18.9** (11.7-26.1)	**34.0** (18.9-61.9)	1004
Non-Hispanic whites	07-08	*	**< LOD**	**2.80** (1.90-4.10)	**11.9** (8.20-17.7)	**27.5** (19.6-35.4)	2047
	09-10	*	**< LOD**	**1.80** (1.40-2.40)	**6.80** (5.40-8.40)	**15.2** (11.9-19.3)	2514

Limit of detection (LOD, see Data Analysis section) for Survey years 07-08 and 09-10 are 0.6 and 0.6 respectively.
< LOD means less than the limit of detection, which may vary for some chemicals by year and by individual sample.
* Not calculated: proportion of results below limit of detection was too high to provide a valid result.
**Non-smoking is defined as a serum cotinine concentration of 10 ng/mL or less.

Biomonitoring Summary

http://www.cdc.gov/biomonitoring/NNAL_BiomonitoringSummary.html

Factsheet

http://www.cdc.gov/biomonitoring/NNAL_FactSheet.html

Source: *Centers for Disease Control & Prevention, Fourth National Report on Human Exposure to Environmental Chemicals, Updated Tables, January 2017*

Urinary NNAL (4-(methylnitrosamino)-1-(3-pyridyl)-1-butanol) (2011 - 2012)

Metabolite of (4-(methylnitrosamino)-1-(3-pyridyl)-1-butanone) (NNK)

Geometric mean and selected percentiles of urine concentrations (in pg/mL) for the **non-smoking U.S. population from the National Health and Nutrition Examination Survey.

	Survey years	Geometric mean (95% conf. interval)	50th Percentile (95% conf. interval)	75th Percentile (95% conf. interval)	90th Percentile (95% conf. interval)	95th Percentile (95% conf. interval)	Sample size
Total	11-12	*	**.800** (.700-.900)	**2.30** (2.00-2.60)	**7.40** (6.10-8.90)	**15.7** (11.7-21.0)	5486
Age group							
6-11 years	11-12	**1.91** (1.57-2.32)	**1.30** (1.10-1.70)	**5.10** (3.80-7.30)	**21.1** (11.5-31.9)	**36.7** (20.1-60.2)	955
12-19 years	11-12	**1.53** (1.35-1.73)	**1.30** (1.10-1.40)	**3.10** (2.20-4.30)	**10.8** (7.60-14.4)	**19.3** (13.2-27.0)	949
20 years and older	11-12	*	**.700** (.600-.900)	**2.00** (1.80-2.20)	**5.70** (4.80-6.80)	**11.7** (10.0-14.9)	3582
Gender							
Males	11-12	**1.32** (1.23-1.41)	**1.00** (.900-1.10)	**2.80** (2.40-3.10)	**9.80** (7.60-11.2)	**19.5** (13.5-26.4)	2616
Females	11-12	*	**.700** (.600-.800)	**1.90** (1.70-2.20)	**5.70** (4.60-7.20)	**12.4** (9.00-18.5)	2870
Race/ethnicity							
Mexican Americans	11-12	**1.12** (.956-1.30)	**.900** (.700-1.20)	**1.90** (1.50-2.50)	**5.30** (3.70-7.40)	**9.50** (7.70-15.0)	775
Non-Hispanic blacks	11-12	**1.98** (1.57-2.48)	**1.60** (1.30-2.10)	**5.10** (3.30-8.70)	**15.9** (9.40-28.8)	**30.4** (18.5-46.7)	1393
Non-Hispanic whites	11-12	*	**.800** (.600-.900)	**2.10** (1.80-2.40)	**6.70** (5.30-8.50)	**14.4** (11.4-20.4)	1679
Asians	11-12	*	**.600** (<LOD-.700)	**1.20** (1.00-1.50)	**2.80** (1.90-3.80)	**5.00** (3.40-6.80)	814

Limit of detection (LOD, see Data Analysis section) for Survey year 11-12 is 0.6.
< LOD means less than the limit of detection, which may vary for some chemicals by year and by individual sample.
* Not calculated: proportion of results below limit of detection was too high to provide a valid result.
**Non-smoking is defined as a serum cotinine of 10 ng/mL or less.

Biomonitoring Summary

http://www.cdc.gov/biomonitoring/NNAL_BiomonitoringSummary.html

Factsheet

http://www.cdc.gov/biomonitoring/NNAL_FactSheet.html

***Source:** Centers for Disease Control & Prevention, Fourth National Report on Human Exposure to Environmental Chemicals, Updated Tables, January 2017*

Urinary NNAL (4-(methylnitrosamino)-1-(3-pyridyl)-1-butanol) (creatinine corrected) (2007 – 2010)

Metabolite of (4-(methylnitrosamino)-1-(3-pyridyl)-1-butanone) (NNK)

Geometric mean and selected percentiles of urine concentrations (in pg/mg of creatinine) for the **non-smoking U.S. population from the National Health and Nutrition Examination Survey.

	Survey years	Geometric mean (95% conf. interval)	50th Percentile (95% conf. interval)	75th Percentile (95% conf. interval)	90th Percentile (95% conf. interval)	95th Percentile (95% conf. interval)	Sample size
Total	07-08	*	**< LOD**	**2.79** (2.31-3.50)	**10.3** (7.36-14.0)	**20.5** (16.4-27.5)	5210
	09-10	*	**< LOD**	**2.05** (1.88-2.28)	**6.40** (5.71-7.41)	**14.6** (11.5-17.3)	6066
Age group							
6-11 years	07-08	*	**2.15** (1.38-3.22)	**10.7** (5.95-17.9)	**38.3** (21.2-57.1)	**60.9** (46.4-72.1)	875
	09-10	*	**1.19** (<LOD-1.52)	**4.25** (2.88-6.37)	**19.2** (11.0-28.8)	**37.2** (22.9-53.0)	936
12-19 years	07-08	*	**1.14** (.710-1.75)	**4.40** (2.59-7.36)	**14.2** (10.5-23.1)	**29.2** (15.6-41.9)	841
	09-10	*	**1.05** (<LOD-1.26)	**3.08** (1.96-4.37)	**10.0** (6.02-15.2)	**20.7** (12.3-30.2)	1004
20 years and older	07-08	*	**< LOD**	**2.34** (2.00-2.73)	**6.82** (5.49-8.65)	**15.1** (11.8-17.7)	3494
	09-10	*	**< LOD**	**1.84** (1.71-2.00)	**5.21** (4.57-6.07)	**11.4** (8.42-14.1)	4126
Gender							
Males	07-08	*	**< LOD**	**2.98** (2.39-3.71)	**10.5** (7.57-12.9)	**20.9** (15.7-29.0)	2462
	09-10	*	**< LOD**	**2.00** (1.86-2.25)	**6.61** (6.00-7.83)	**15.1** (11.7-19.8)	2902
Females	07-08	*	**< LOD**	**2.67** (2.14-3.37)	**9.87** (6.79-14.9)	**20.0** (15.7-27.9)	2748
	09-10	*	**< LOD**	**2.09** (1.82-2.36)	**6.15** (4.88-8.21)	**12.7** (9.26-17.3)	3164
Race/ethnicity							
Mexican Americans	07-08	*	**< LOD**	**2.16** (1.55-3.00)	**5.91** (4.32-8.30)	**13.3** (8.36-17.9)	1205
	09-10	*	**< LOD**	**1.73** (1.36-2.11)	**5.00** (3.72-6.84)	**10.0** (6.79-14.7)	1476
Non-Hispanic blacks	07-08	*	**.960** (<LOD-1.42)	**3.70** (2.50-5.31)	**11.5** (9.18-14.2)	**20.8** (14.5-28.8)	1056
	09-10	**1.40** (.982-2.01)	**1.21** (<LOD-2.06)	**3.96** (2.78-5.99)	**12.2** (7.29-20.3)	**23.4** (14.3-35.4)	1003
Non-Hispanic whites	07-08	*	**< LOD**	**2.93** (2.22-4.00)	**11.4** (7.22-17.1)	**23.9** (17.1-32.0)	2047
	09-10	*	**< LOD**	**1.96** (1.82-2.15)	**6.09** (5.00-7.83)	**14.7** (10.0-18.2)	2514

< LOD means less than the limit of detection for the urine levels not corrected for creatinine.
* Not calculated: proportion of results below limit of detection was too high to provide a valid result.
**Non-smoking is defined as a serum cotinine concentration of 10 ng/mL or less.

Biomonitoring Summary

http://www.cdc.gov/biomonitoring/NNAL_BiomonitoringSummary.html

Factsheet

http://www.cdc.gov/biomonitoring/NNAL_FactSheet.html

Source: *Centers for Disease Control & Prevention, Fourth National Report on Human Exposure to Environmental Chemicals, Updated Tables, January 2017*

Urinary NNAL (4-(methylnitrosamino)-1-(3-pyridyl)-1-butanol) (creatinine corrected) (2011 - 2012)

Metabolite of (4-(methylnitrosamino)-1-(3-pyridyl)-1-butanone) (NNK)

Geometric mean and selected percentiles of urine concentrations (in pg/mg of creatinine) for the **non-smoking** U.S. population from the National Health and Nutrition Examination Survey.

	Survey years	Geometric mean (95% conf. interval)	50th Percentile (95% conf. interval)	75th Percentile (95% conf. interval)	90th Percentile (95% conf. interval)	95th Percentile (95% conf. interval)	Sample size
Total	11-12	*	**1.06** (1.00-1.14)	**2.47** (2.14-2.72)	**6.57** (5.24-8.25)	**14.3** (11.7-18.4)	5483
Age group							
6-11 years	11-12	**2.57** (2.13-3.10)	**1.91** (1.60-2.47)	**5.93** (4.21-8.49)	**23.5** (13.7-31.6)	**39.1** (23.5-59.0)	954
12-19 years	11-12	**1.45** (1.31-1.60)	**1.14** (1.05-1.25)	**3.40** (2.50-3.99)	**9.14** (5.71-13.4)	**18.4** (12.2-22.2)	949
20 years and older	11-12	*	**1.00** (.938-1.08)	**2.12** (1.91-2.42)	**5.00** (4.26-6.18)	**10.5** (8.56-13.0)	3580
Gender							
Males	11-12	**1.19** (1.10-1.29)	**.984** (.909-1.05)	**2.38** (2.08-2.68)	**7.36** (5.60-9.33)	**15.2** (11.5-21.4)	2615
Females	11-12	*	**1.18** (1.04-1.30)	**2.48** (2.17-2.86)	**5.67** (4.69-8.21)	**13.5** (10.3-18.0)	2868
Race/ethnicity							
Mexican Americans	11-12	**1.15** (.985-1.35)	**1.03** (.860-1.22)	**1.94** (1.67-2.35)	**4.72** (3.51-6.74)	**9.93** (6.46-15.9)	775
Non-Hispanic blacks	11-12	**1.50** (1.18-1.91)	**1.31** (1.02-1.63)	**3.70** (2.36-6.09)	**11.5** (6.69-19.0)	**19.7** (11.5-33.7)	1392
Non-Hispanic whites	11-12	*	**1.04** (.984-1.14)	**2.47** (2.06-2.79)	**5.94** (5.14-7.72)	**16.1** (11.5-18.9)	1677
Asians	11-12	*	**.972** (<LOD-1.17)	**1.82** (1.56-2.24)	**3.57** (2.86-4.79)	**5.71** (4.29-8.57)	814

< LOD means less than the limit of detection for the urine levels not corrected for creatinine.
* Not calculated: proportion of results below limit of detection was too high to provide a valid result.
**Non-smoking is defined as a serum cotinine of 10 ng/mL or less.

Biomonitoring Summary

http://www.cdc.gov/biomonitoring/NNAL_BiomonitoringSummary.html

Factsheet

http://www.cdc.gov/biomonitoring/NNAL_FactSheet.html

Source: *Centers for Disease Control & Prevention, Fourth National Report on Human Exposure to Environmental Chemicals, Updated Tables, January 2017*

Urinary Bisphenol A (2003 – 2010)

Geometric mean and selected percentiles of urine concentrations (in µg/L) for the U.S. population from the National Health and Nutrition Examination Survey.

	Survey years	Geometric mean (95% conf. interval)	50th Percentile (95% conf. interval)	75th Percentile (95% conf. interval)	90th Percentile (95% conf. interval)	95th Percentile (95% conf. interval)	Sample size
Total	03-04	**2.64** (2.38-2.94)	**2.80** (2.50-3.10)	**5.50** (5.00-6.20)	**10.6** (9.40-12.0)	**16.0** (14.4-17.2)	2517
	05-06	**1.90** (1.79-2.02)	**2.00** (1.90-2.00)	**3.70** (3.50-3.90)	**7.00** (6.40-7.60)	**11.5** (10.0-13.6)	2548
	07-08	**2.08** (1.92-2.26)	**2.10** (1.90-2.30)	**4.10** (3.60-4.60)	**7.70** (6.80-8.70)	**13.0** (10.0-15.6)	2604
	09-10	**1.83** (1.72-1.94)	**1.90** (1.70-2.00)	**3.50** (3.30-3.80)	**6.60** (6.00-7.20)	**9.60** (8.50-11.3)	2749
Age group							
6-11 years	03-04	**3.55** (2.95-4.29)	**3.80** (2.70-5.00)	**6.90** (6.00-8.30)	**12.6** (9.50-15.1)	**16.0** (11.5-23.3)	314
	05-06	**2.86** (2.52-3.24)	**2.70** (2.30-2.90)	**5.00** (4.40-5.80)	**13.5** (9.30-16.8)	**22.8** (13.6-34.6)	356
	07-08	**2.48** (2.21-2.77)	**2.40** (1.90-3.00)	**4.50** (3.70-5.50)	**7.60** (6.30-9.50)	**13.4** (8.80-17.8)	389
	09-10	**1.81** (1.55-2.10)	**1.70** (1.50-2.00)	**3.40** (3.00-4.00)	**6.50** (4.30-9.70)	**9.20** (6.50-15.1)	415
12-19 years	03-04	**3.74** (3.31-4.22)	**4.30** (3.60-4.60)	**7.80** (6.50-9.00)	**13.5** (11.8-15.2)	**16.5** (15.2-20.9)	715
	05-06	**2.42** (2.18-2.68)	**2.40** (2.10-2.70)	**4.30** (3.90-5.20)	**8.40** (6.50-10.8)	**11.9** (10.7-14.8)	702
	07-08	**2.45** (2.14-2.80)	**2.40** (2.10-2.60)	**4.40** (3.60-5.50)	**9.70** (7.30-11.9)	**12.2** (9.70-19.0)	401
	09-10	**2.11** (1.86-2.40)	**2.20** (1.90-2.40)	**3.80** (3.20-4.50)	**6.90** (4.70-10.8)	**11.1** (6.90-21.0)	420
20 years and older	03-04	**2.41** (2.15-2.72)	**2.60** (2.30-2.80)	**5.10** (4.50-5.70)	**9.50** (8.10-11.3)	**15.2** (12.4-18.1)	1488
	05-06	**1.75** (1.62-1.89)	**1.80** (1.70-2.00)	**3.40** (3.10-3.70)	**6.40** (5.80-7.50)	**10.7** (8.80-12.1)	1490
	07-08	**1.99** (1.82-2.18)	**2.00** (1.80-2.30)	**3.90** (3.40-4.60)	**7.40** (6.60-8.50)	**13.2** (9.10-15.7)	1814
	09-10	**1.79** (1.67-1.93)	**1.80** (1.60-2.00)	**3.50** (3.30-3.70)	**6.50** (6.00-7.20)	**9.60** (8.30-11.3)	1914
Gender							
Males	03-04	**2.92** (2.63-3.24)	**3.20** (2.70-3.60)	**6.10** (5.40-6.60)	**10.4** (9.50-11.6)	**16.0** (12.7-17.6)	1229
	05-06	**2.09** (1.92-2.28)	**2.10** (2.00-2.30)	**3.70** (3.40-4.20)	**7.70** (6.80-9.30)	**12.8** (10.1-15.8)	1270
	07-08	**2.20** (2.01-2.41)	**2.10** (1.90-2.40)	**4.00** (3.60-4.70)	**8.10** (6.70-9.70)	**14.0** (8.70-20.8)	1294
	09-10	**1.94** (1.82-2.07)	**1.90** (1.70-2.00)	**3.70** (3.40-4.10)	**6.90** (5.90-7.90)	**10.9** (8.40-13.5)	1399
Females	03-04	**2.41** (2.11-2.75)	**2.50** (2.20-2.80)	**5.00** (4.20-6.20)	**10.6** (8.70-12.5)	**15.9** (13.5-20.1)	1288
	05-06	**1.74** (1.55-1.95)	**1.80** (1.60-2.00)	**3.70** (3.10-4.00)	**6.20** (5.80-7.60)	**10.4** (7.70-14.7)	1278
	07-08	**1.97** (1.80-2.16)	**2.00** (1.80-2.20)	**4.10** (3.60-4.60)	**7.40** (6.80-8.20)	**12.0** (9.60-14.1)	1310
	09-10	**1.73** (1.60-1.87)	**1.80** (1.60-2.00)	**3.40** (3.20-3.70)	**6.50** (5.60-7.10)	**9.20** (8.00-11.2)	1350
Race/ethnicity							
Mexican Americans	03-04	**2.58** (2.15-3.08)	**2.60** (2.10-3.20)	**5.20** (4.40-6.50)	**9.90** (7.30-13.9)	**15.4** (10.2-19.7)	613
	05-06	**2.05** (1.75-2.40)	**2.00** (1.70-2.40)	**3.60** (3.00-4.20)	**6.90** (5.40-10.1)	**12.2** (8.00-15.6)	637
	07-08	**2.09** (1.94-2.26)	**2.00** (1.80-2.30)	**3.80** (3.30-4.30)	**7.10** (6.10-8.60)	**11.7** (7.70-14.6)	531
	09-10	**1.92** (1.69-2.19)	**2.10** (1.80-2.30)	**3.50** (3.10-4.10)	**6.50** (5.20-7.50)	**9.00** (6.90-16.2)	566
Non-Hispanic blacks	03-04	**4.24** (3.73-4.82)	**4.30** (3.80-5.10)	**8.20** (7.10-9.80)	**14.2** (11.7-16.9)	**20.6** (14.9-25.2)	652
	05-06	**2.50** (2.25-2.77)	**2.70** (2.30-3.00)	**4.60** (4.00-5.00)	**8.00** (6.80-9.30)	**11.3** (8.90-14.2)	678
	07-08	**2.66** (2.38-2.97)	**2.80** (2.60-3.10)	**5.40** (4.40-6.40)	**9.10** (7.50-10.4)	**13.3** (10.0-15.1)	597
	09-10	**2.51** (2.22-2.83)	**2.60** (2.30-3.00)	**4.40** (3.80-5.00)	**7.30** (6.10-8.80)	**10.3** (7.90-13.6)	516
Non-Hispanic whites	03-04	**2.51** (2.26-2.79)	**2.70** (2.50-3.00)	**5.20** (4.70-5.80)	**9.60** (8.30-10.9)	**15.1** (12.6-16.7)	1092
	05-06	**1.76** (1.62-1.91)	**1.80** (1.60-2.00)	**3.50** (3.20-3.80)	**6.80** (5.90-7.60)	**11.0** (8.80-13.7)	1038
	07-08	**2.06** (1.87-2.27)	**2.00** (1.80-2.30)	**4.00** (3.40-4.70)	**7.80** (6.70-8.90)	**13.7** (9.80-16.1)	1077
	09-10	**1.73** (1.60-1.87)	**1.70** (1.60-1.90)	**3.40** (3.10-3.70)	**6.40** (5.40-7.60)	**9.20** (8.20-11.2)	1206

Limit of detection (LOD, see Data Analysis section) for Survey years 03-04, 05-06, 07-08 and 09-10 are 0.4, 0.4, 0.4, and 0.4 respectively.

Biomonitoring Summary

http://www.cdc.gov/biomonitoring/BisphenolA_BiomonitoringSummary.html

Factsheet

http://www.cdc.gov/biomonitoring/BisphenolA_FactSheet.html

Source: *Centers for Disease Control & Prevention, Fourth National Report on Human Exposure to Environmental Chemicals, Updated Tables, January 2017*

Urinary Bisphenol A (2011 - 2014)

Geometric mean and selected percentiles of urine concentrations (in µg/L) for the U.S. population from the National Health and Nutrition Examination Survey.

	Survey years	Geometric mean (95% conf. interval)	50th Percentile (95% conf. interval)	75th Percentile (95% conf. interval)	90th Percentile (95% conf. interval)	95th Percentile (95% conf. interval)	Sample size
Total	11-12	**1.51** (1.41-1.62)	**1.40** (1.30-1.60)	**3.00** (2.70-3.30)	**5.60** (4.90-6.50)	**9.40** (7.70-11.2)	2489
	13-14	**1.28** (1.20-1.36)	**1.30** (1.20-1.40)	**2.50** (2.40-2.70)	**4.90** (4.10-5.60)	**7.70** (6.80-8.30)	2686
Age group							
6-11 years	11-12	**1.58** (1.41-1.78)	**1.50** (1.30-1.70)	**3.10** (2.60-3.50)	**6.70** (5.10-8.00)	**8.70** (6.20-21.4)	396
	13-14	**1.43** (1.30-1.59)	**1.40** (1.30-1.60)	**2.90** (2.30-3.40)	**4.40** (4.10-5.20)	**8.00** (5.20-10.2)	409
12-19 years	11-12	**1.69** (1.42-2.00)	**1.70** (1.30-2.10)	**3.30** (2.80-4.00)	**6.90** (4.80-7.90)	**10.0** (7.10-13.0)	388
	13-14	**1.28** (1.16-1.41)	**1.20** (1.10-1.40)	**2.40** (1.90-2.70)	**4.60** (3.30-5.20)	**6.80** (5.20-8.10)	462
20 years and older	11-12	**1.48** (1.35-1.61)	**1.40** (1.20-1.60)	**2.90** (2.50-3.30)	**5.40** (4.70-6.30)	**9.30** (7.30-12.2)	1705
	13-14	**1.26** (1.18-1.35)	**1.30** (1.20-1.40)	**2.50** (2.40-2.80)	**4.90** (4.10-6.00)	**7.80** (6.80-8.60)	1815
Gender							
Males	11-12	**1.64** (1.49-1.81)	**1.50** (1.40-1.70)	**3.20** (2.70-3.70)	**6.00** (5.00-7.70)	**9.50** (7.80-11.2)	1259
	13-14	**1.43** (1.30-1.58)	**1.40** (1.30-1.60)	**2.80** (2.40-3.20)	**5.30** (4.30-6.60)	**8.30** (6.80-10.3)	1285
Females	11-12	**1.39** (1.25-1.55)	**1.30** (1.20-1.50)	**2.80** (2.40-3.20)	**5.20** (4.30-6.30)	**8.50** (6.50-13.4)	1230
	13-14	**1.15** (1.05-1.26)	**1.20** (1.10-1.30)	**2.30** (2.00-2.60)	**4.20** (3.80-5.20)	**7.20** (5.60-8.10)	1401
Race/ethnicity							
Mexican Americans	11-12	**1.45** (1.30-1.63)	**1.40** (1.20-1.60)	**2.80** (2.30-3.10)	**5.00** (4.20-6.50)	**7.70** (5.90-9.70)	316
	13-14	**1.28** (1.06-1.53)	**1.30** (1.00-1.70)	**2.50** (2.10-2.80)	**4.10** (3.50-4.90)	**5.60** (4.60-7.30)	438
Non-Hispanic blacks	11-12	**2.12** (1.88-2.38)	**2.00** (1.80-2.40)	**4.10** (3.40-4.60)	**7.10** (5.70-8.10)	**11.4** (8.10-14.3)	665
	13-14	**1.83** (1.62-2.07)	**1.90** (1.50-2.20)	**3.60** (3.20-4.10)	**6.80** (5.70-7.80)	**9.80** (7.70-12.9)	609
Non-Hispanic whites	11-12	**1.46** (1.34-1.58)	**1.30** (1.20-1.50)	**2.90** (2.50-3.20)	**5.40** (4.60-6.60)	**8.90** (6.90-13.4)	813
	13-14	**1.22** (1.13-1.31)	**1.30** (1.10-1.40)	**2.40** (2.20-2.70)	**4.40** (3.90-5.90)	**7.40** (6.40-8.30)	988
All Hispanics	11-12	**1.48** (1.25-1.74)	**1.40** (1.20-1.70)	**2.80** (2.20-3.40)	**5.70** (4.20-7.30)	**9.10** (6.50-14.1)	571
	13-14	**1.31** (1.18-1.46)	**1.30** (1.10-1.50)	**2.60** (2.20-2.80)	**4.10** (3.70-4.70)	**6.10** (4.90-7.50)	690
Asians	11-12	**1.03** (.863-1.23)	**.900** (.800-1.10)	**1.80** (1.50-2.20)	**4.00** (2.40-6.40)	**7.30** (3.90-11.9)	352
	13-14	**.782** (.646-.948)	**.800** (.700-.900)	**1.40** (1.00-1.80)	**2.40** (1.80-3.30)	**3.60** (2.40-12.1)	289

Limit of detection (LOD, see Data Analysis section) for Survey years 11-12 and 13-14 are 0.4 and 0.2, respectively.

Biomonitoring Summary

http://www.cdc.gov/biomonitoring/BisphenolA_BiomonitoringSummary.html

Factsheet

http://www.cdc.gov/biomonitoring/BisphenolA_FactSheet.html

Source: *Centers for Disease Control & Prevention, Fourth National Report on Human Exposure to Environmental Chemicals, Updated Tables, January 2017*

Urinary Bisphenol A (creatinine corrected) (2003 – 2010)

Geometric mean and selected percentiles of urine concentrations (in µg/g of creatinine) for the U.S. population from the National Health and Nutrition Examination Survey.

	Survey years	Geometric mean (95% conf. interval)	50th Percentile (95% conf. interval)	75th Percentile (95% conf. interval)	90th Percentile (95% conf. interval)	95th Percentile (95% conf. interval)	Sample size
Total	03-04	**2.58** (2.36-2.82)	**2.50** (2.31-2.80)	**4.29** (3.88-4.75)	**7.67** (6.62-8.66)	**11.2** (9.78-12.4)	2514
	05-06	**1.86** (1.79-1.92)	**1.71** (1.64-1.79)	**3.01** (2.86-3.20)	**5.73** (5.29-6.36)	**9.70** (8.31-10.9)	2548
	07-08	**2.10** (1.95-2.25)	**1.95** (1.84-2.03)	**3.45** (3.02-3.83)	**6.09** (5.10-7.45)	**10.0** (7.48-13.2)	2604
	09-10	**1.91** (1.79-2.04)	**1.76** (1.67-1.84)	**3.06** (2.80-3.33)	**5.33** (4.68-6.06)	**8.03** (6.94-10.0)	2749
Age group							
6-11 years	03-04	**4.32** (3.63-5.14)	**4.29** (3.63-5.23)	**7.14** (5.83-9.56)	**12.2** (9.84-14.8)	**15.7** (12.2-23.2)	314
	05-06	**3.14** (2.79-3.54)	**2.80** (2.55-3.06)	**5.04** (4.46-5.71)	**15.6** (8.15-22.4)	**24.6** (19.9-48.5)	356
	07-08	**3.05** (2.73-3.41)	**2.69** (2.38-3.12)	**5.06** (4.33-5.60)	**11.9** (6.30-17.4)	**20.8** (12.7-26.3)	389
	09-10	**2.36** (2.09-2.65)	**2.18** (2.00-2.53)	**3.70** (3.14-4.29)	**5.97** (4.57-9.15)	**9.57** (6.52-13.7)	415
12-19 years	03-04	**2.80** (2.52-3.11)	**2.74** (2.35-3.22)	**4.74** (4.21-5.09)	**7.79** (6.41-8.87)	**11.8** (8.05-14.2)	713
	05-06	**1.80** (1.67-1.95)	**1.65** (1.50-1.76)	**2.73** (2.41-2.98)	**5.71** (4.07-7.50)	**8.52** (6.94-12.2)	702
	07-08	**1.90** (1.72-2.10)	**1.69** (1.50-2.00)	**2.94** (2.38-3.60)	**5.10** (4.17-6.82)	**7.72** (5.32-13.9)	401
	09-10	**1.70** (1.47-1.95)	**1.60** (1.34-1.88)	**2.63** (2.11-3.58)	**4.47** (3.76-6.19)	**6.71** (4.40-17.8)	420
20 years and older	03-04	**2.39** (2.17-2.64)	**2.36** (2.15-2.59)	**3.93** (3.44-4.33)	**6.64** (5.97-7.74)	**10.0** (9.01-11.4)	1487
	05-06	**1.75** (1.67-1.84)	**1.64** (1.56-1.75)	**2.84** (2.67-3.08)	**5.38** (4.89-5.87)	**8.54** (7.58-9.77)	1490
	07-08	**2.04** (1.90-2.20)	**1.92** (1.79-2.03)	**3.36** (2.91-3.78)	**6.02** (4.88-7.48)	**9.32** (7.48-12.1)	1814
	09-10	**1.90** (1.76-2.05)	**1.76** (1.66-1.84)	**3.04** (2.76-3.24)	**5.33** (4.67-6.11)	**8.00** (6.97-10.0)	1914
Gender							
Males	03-04	**2.38** (2.15-2.63)	**2.31** (2.08-2.70)	**4.19** (3.81-4.64)	**7.10** (6.41-8.28)	**9.94** (9.06-11.7)	1228
	05-06	**1.68** (1.57-1.80)	**1.56** (1.45-1.64)	**2.73** (2.43-3.14)	**5.27** (4.64-6.04)	**8.40** (6.81-11.4)	1270
	07-08	**1.85** (1.71-2.01)	**1.77** (1.57-1.91)	**2.97** (2.59-3.33)	**5.41** (4.47-7.51)	**9.52** (6.29-13.4)	1294
	09-10	**1.74** (1.62-1.87)	**1.60** (1.48-1.72)	**2.76** (2.53-2.96)	**5.00** (4.16-5.86)	**7.50** (6.22-9.00)	1399
Females	03-04	**2.78** (2.50-3.08)	**2.68** (2.40-2.94)	**4.41** (3.81-5.15)	**7.93** (6.48-10.2)	**12.4** (9.29-18.2)	1286
	05-06	**2.04** (1.95-2.14)	**1.85** (1.76-2.02)	**3.21** (2.98-3.39)	**6.47** (5.51-7.50)	**9.86** (8.62-11.8)	1278
	07-08	**2.36** (2.17-2.57)	**2.14** (1.98-2.33)	**3.77** (3.43-4.31)	**6.67** (5.41-7.83)	**10.5** (7.45-15.2)	1310
	09-10	**2.09** (1.92-2.27)	**1.93** (1.80-2.15)	**3.33** (2.94-3.84)	**5.49** (4.87-6.74)	**8.80** (6.47-12.5)	1350
Race/ethnicity							
Mexican Americans	03-04	**2.34** (2.02-2.71)	**2.38** (2.00-2.65)	**3.85** (3.24-4.55)	**7.09** (5.00-9.04)	**10.9** (8.50-14.3)	612
	05-06	**1.84** (1.66-2.04)	**1.62** (1.45-1.84)	**2.99** (2.56-3.60)	**6.00** (4.51-8.00)	**10.3** (6.84-14.9)	637
	07-08	**2.04** (1.86-2.24)	**1.88** (1.72-2.11)	**3.33** (2.96-3.95)	**5.68** (5.05-6.59)	**8.90** (6.30-11.8)	531
	09-10	**1.91** (1.71-2.13)	**1.76** (1.67-1.87)	**3.13** (2.63-3.57)	**5.51** (4.72-6.97)	**8.71** (5.86-14.4)	566
Non-Hispanic blacks	03-04	**2.92** (2.58-3.32)	**2.95** (2.51-3.27)	**4.90** (4.07-6.13)	**8.64** (7.53-9.63)	**11.9** (10.2-13.3)	651
	05-06	**1.76** (1.62-1.90)	**1.68** (1.53-1.92)	**2.82** (2.67-3.04)	**4.56** (3.85-5.43)	**6.81** (5.00-9.27)	678
	07-08	**2.06** (1.91-2.23)	**2.03** (1.83-2.25)	**3.24** (2.86-3.78)	**5.71** (5.15-6.54)	**8.59** (6.54-10.9)	597
	09-10	**1.82** (1.65-2.01)	**1.70** (1.56-1.89)	**2.90** (2.39-3.17)	**4.94** (4.02-6.03)	**6.74** (5.95-8.09)	516
Non-Hispanic whites	03-04	**2.58** (2.37-2.81)	**2.55** (2.32-2.80)	**4.30** (3.93-4.67)	**7.58** (6.32-8.87)	**11.0** (9.34-12.4)	1091
	05-06	**1.85** (1.75-1.96)	**1.70** (1.60-1.82)	**3.08** (2.78-3.31)	**5.80** (5.13-6.72)	**9.77** (7.87-11.5)	1038
	07-08	**2.15** (1.97-2.35)	**1.97** (1.84-2.11)	**3.50** (3.04-3.95)	**6.44** (5.04-8.00)	**10.9** (7.47-14.5)	1077
	09-10	**1.94** (1.79-2.10)	**1.78** (1.67-1.92)	**3.16** (2.80-3.59)	**5.45** (4.67-6.94)	**8.55** (6.73-10.0)	1206

Biomonitoring Summary

http://www.cdc.gov/biomonitoring/BisphenolA_BiomonitoringSummary.html

Factsheet

http://www.cdc.gov/biomonitoring/BisphenolA_FactSheet.html

Source: *Centers for Disease Control & Prevention, Fourth National Report on Human Exposure to Environmental Chemicals, Updated Tables, January 2017*

Urinary Bisphenol A (creatinine corrected) (2011 - 2014)

Geometric mean and selected percentiles of urine concentrations (in µg/g of creatinine) for the U.S. population from the National Health and Nutrition Examination Survey.

	Survey years	Geometric mean (95% conf. interval)	50th Percentile (95% conf. interval)	75th Percentile (95% conf. interval)	90th Percentile (95% conf. interval)	95th Percentile (95% conf. interval)	Sample size
Total	11-12	**1.72** (1.61-1.84)	**1.58** (1.46-1.71)	**2.86** (2.62-3.01)	**4.62** (4.12-5.65)	**8.24** (6.47-11.0)	2487
	13-14	**1.28** (1.18-1.39)	**1.21** (1.11-1.32)	**2.12** (1.92-2.33)	**3.88** (3.46-4.24)	**5.09** (4.65-5.96)	2684
Age group							
6-11 years	11-12	**2.27** (1.97-2.62)	**2.00** (1.78-2.16)	**3.33** (2.93-3.75)	**7.94** (4.71-12.4)	**14.0** (6.45-47.5)	395
	13-14	**1.81** (1.68-1.96)	**1.80** (1.52-2.03)	**3.10** (2.63-3.46)	**4.48** (4.00-4.96)	**7.03** (5.00-9.92)	409
12-19 years	11-12	**1.64** (1.44-1.87)	**1.48** (1.13-1.98)	**2.88** (2.21-3.23)	**4.50** (3.37-8.16)	**8.74** (3.57-18.4)	388
	13-14	**1.04** (.887-1.21)	**.932** (.809-1.19)	**1.71** (1.33-2.03)	**2.69** (2.28-3.33)	**3.99** (3.29-4.67)	462
20 years and older	11-12	**1.68** (1.57-1.80)	**1.55** (1.43-1.68)	**2.75** (2.54-3.00)	**4.55** (4.00-5.39)	**7.73** (5.73-10.0)	1704
	13-14	**1.27** (1.16-1.39)	**1.21** (1.11-1.30)	**2.09** (1.90-2.31)	**3.88** (3.33-4.37)	**5.09** (4.58-5.97)	1813
Gender							
Males	11-12	**1.54** (1.40-1.69)	**1.37** (1.20-1.59)	**2.55** (2.21-2.94)	**4.38** (3.75-6.00)	**8.24** (6.01-11.0)	1258
	13-14	**1.20** (1.11-1.31)	**1.12** (.988-1.25)	**1.95** (1.78-2.24)	**3.75** (3.25-4.29)	**4.91** (4.42-7.02)	1284
Females	11-12	**1.91** (1.76-2.08)	**1.75** (1.57-1.97)	**2.93** (2.73-3.24)	**4.94** (4.27-6.24)	**8.13** (6.00-11.1)	1229
	13-14	**1.36** (1.23-1.51)	**1.28** (1.17-1.43)	**2.25** (2.03-2.48)	**3.94** (3.27-4.48)	**5.18** (4.50-6.07)	1400
Race/ethnicity							
Mexican Americans	11-12	**1.64** (1.49-1.80)	**1.46** (1.32-1.64)	**2.70** (2.34-3.01)	**4.50** (3.45-7.00)	**7.37** (4.76-11.4)	316
	13-14	**1.30** (1.16-1.45)	**1.27** (1.05-1.57)	**2.25** (1.97-2.50)	**3.57** (3.04-3.98)	**4.25** (3.93-4.83)	438
Non-Hispanic blacks	11-12	**1.65** (1.48-1.84)	**1.50** (1.30-1.71)	**2.63** (2.11-3.17)	**4.82** (3.82-6.24)	**7.23** (5.98-10.7)	665
	13-14	**1.35** (1.25-1.46)	**1.32** (1.13-1.46)	**2.17** (1.96-2.35)	**3.89** (3.24-4.27)	**5.00** (4.40-6.01)	609
Non-Hispanic whites	11-12	**1.77** (1.64-1.92)	**1.64** (1.49-1.78)	**2.90** (2.65-3.08)	**4.60** (4.05-6.00)	**9.00** (6.11-12.3)	811
	13-14	**1.28** (1.14-1.44)	**1.21** (1.06-1.38)	**2.13** (1.85-2.42)	**3.94** (3.33-4.56)	**5.60** (4.65-6.53)	987
All Hispanics	11-12	**1.66** (1.44-1.90)	**1.47** (1.28-1.70)	**2.80** (2.39-3.14)	**4.82** (3.67-7.00)	**7.69** (5.76-9.62)	571
	13-14	**1.30** (1.19-1.43)	**1.25** (1.09-1.42)	**2.20** (1.92-2.47)	**3.61** (3.13-3.98)	**4.54** (4.03-4.89)	690
Asians	11-12	**1.38** (1.25-1.52)	**1.32** (1.16-1.40)	**2.11** (1.84-2.50)	**4.04** (2.80-6.25)	**7.42** (4.38-12.1)	352
	13-14	**.990** (.847-1.16)	**.918** (.778-1.05)	**1.62** (1.39-1.97)	**2.71** (2.09-4.00)	**4.44** (2.71-10.0)	288

Biomonitoring Summary

http://www.cdc.gov/biomonitoring/BisphenolA_BiomonitoringSummary.html

Factsheet

http://www.cdc.gov/biomonitoring/BisphenolA_FactSheet.html

Source: *Centers for Disease Control & Prevention, Fourth National Report on Human Exposure to Environmental Chemicals, Updated Tables, January 2017*

Urinary Triclosan (2003 – 2010)

Geometric mean and selected percentiles of urine concentrations (in µg/L) for the U.S. population from the National Health and Nutrition Examination Survey.

	Survey years	Geometric mean (95% conf. interval)	50th Percentile (95% conf. interval)	75th Percentile (95% conf. interval)	90th Percentile (95% conf. interval)	95th Percentile (95% conf. interval)	Sample size
Total	03-04	**13.0** (11.6-14.6)	**9.20** (7.90-10.9)	**47.4** (38.2-58.4)	**249** (188-304)	**461** (383-522)	2517
	05-06	**18.5** (16.1-21.3)	**15.1** (11.8-18.5)	**76.2** (57.9-97.6)	**334** (279-402)	**655** (573-739)	2548
	07-08	**15.3** (13.5-17.4)	**12.1** (10.2-13.8)	**57.2** (46.1-65.9)	**225** (176-288)	**494** (371-615)	2604
	09-10	**14.5** (12.6-16.6)	**10.7** (8.80-12.6)	**51.2** (39.4-67.7)	**238** (200-284)	**483** (398-569)	2749
Age group							
6-11 years	03-04	**8.16** (6.20-10.8)	**6.00** (4.00-8.50)	**20.7** (14.3-31.6)	**123** (36.4-163)	**157** (113-380)	314
	05-06	**12.8** (9.89-16.7)	**10.3** (8.30-17.2)	**35.4** (23.9-65.8)	**97.6** (67.4-181)	**246** (99.5-462)	356
	07-08	**11.8** (7.57-18.2)	**9.80** (6.70-13.9)	**27.7** (14.8-52.2)	**98.5** (40.5-364)	**296** (67.4-826)	389
	09-10	**10.9** (9.35-12.8)	**9.90** (7.10-11.9)	**28.3** (22.1-35.5)	**95.5** (71.5-117)	**200** (114-474)	415
12-19 years	03-04	**14.5** (11.0-19.1)	**10.3** (8.20-13.1)	**39.0** (26.5-86.4)	**304** (134-566)	**655** (310-890)	715
	05-06	**18.8** (14.9-23.8)	**15.4** (11.0-21.0)	**67.5** (45.3-100)	**330** (174-461)	**566** (389-707)	702
	07-08	**18.2** (13.8-23.8)	**13.8** (9.40-20.1)	**63.2** (38.7-110)	**296** (144-395)	**401** (308-853)	401
	09-10	**11.7** (9.89-13.8)	**8.80** (7.30-10.9)	**30.2** (24.3-40.6)	**165** (56.7-289)	**301** (220-431)	420
20 years and older	03-04	**13.6** (12.0-15.3)	**9.60** (8.20-11.5)	**51.7** (39.6-65.7)	**261** (198-317)	**472** (406-522)	1488
	05-06	**19.3** (16.4-22.6)	**15.5** (11.8-19.4)	**84.3** (61.0-114)	**366** (289-462)	**738** (583-864)	1490
	07-08	**15.4** (13.7-17.3)	**12.3** (10.1-14.4)	**60.1** (48.5-69.0)	**225** (185-286)	**504** (378-573)	1814
	09-10	**15.5** (12.9-18.5)	**11.1** (8.60-14.2)	**61.8** (41.8-86.0)	**262** (214-327)	**544** (415-621)	1914
Gender							
Males	03-04	**16.2** (13.4-19.6)	**11.7** (9.30-14.8)	**84.9** (50.6-111)	**317** (231-433)	**574** (461-716)	1229
	05-06	**21.3** (17.6-25.7)	**17.6** (11.9-23.2)	**103** (69.9-143)	**446** (366-488)	**738** (601-873)	1270
	07-08	**15.2** (12.9-17.9)	**12.3** (9.50-15.3)	**60.6** (45.8-72.8)	**236** (159-338)	**467** (367-636)	1294
	09-10	**14.8** (12.7-17.4)	**10.9** (8.60-13.3)	**55.1** (40.4-77.5)	**243** (214-295)	**455** (327-600)	1399
Females	03-04	**10.6** (9.29-12.1)	**7.60** (6.10-9.10)	**33.2** (27.1-39.4)	**144** (96.5-250)	**380** (258-430)	1288
	05-06	**16.2** (13.9-18.8)	**12.6** (10.1-15.6)	**58.7** (41.5-81.9)	**226** (169-304)	**513** (310-773)	1278
	07-08	**15.5** (12.6-18.9)	**12.0** (9.90-14.1)	**52.1** (37.1-74.4)	**210** (133-367)	**504** (285-648)	1310
	09-10	**14.2** (12.0-16.8)	**10.5** (8.70-12.6)	**50.0** (34.4-63.8)	**235** (149-302)	**488** (332-661)	1350
Race/ethnicity							
Mexican Americans	03-04	**14.6** (10.6-20.1)	**8.80** (5.40-17.5)	**65.4** (32.8-127)	**357** (225-456)	**597** (372-992)	613
	05-06	**26.7** (21.2-33.7)	**18.7** (13.5-25.5)	**196** (99.4-269)	**668** (475-759)	**866** (750-1180)	637
	07-08	**17.1** (12.9-22.6)	**11.8** (8.40-17.8)	**67.4** (42.5-106)	**358** (208-474)	**556** (363-856)	531
	09-10	**14.9** (12.2-18.3)	**10.2** (8.20-12.8)	**54.7** (33.3-86.5)	**345** (260-494)	**691** (443-1180)	566
Non-Hispanic blacks	03-04	**14.4** (11.4-18.2)	**11.1** (8.70-16.1)	**37.6** (30.2-58.0)	**203** (87.5-341)	**450** (254-750)	652
	05-06	**17.3** (13.3-22.4)	**14.0** (10.4-19.0)	**59.2** (37.7-98.3)	**258** (138-460)	**541** (273-1190)	678
	07-08	**13.7** (11.7-16.1)	**11.3** (8.80-13.9)	**41.4** (28.9-49.6)	**150** (93.5-265)	**480** (190-757)	597
	09-10	**12.8** (10.8-15.0)	**9.30** (7.70-11.7)	**34.3** (24.0-44.6)	**168** (88.4-263)	**451** (202-959)	516
Non-Hispanic whites	03-04	**12.9** (11.2-14.9)	**9.20** (7.40-11.0)	**49.2** (37.8-63.4)	**245** (163-334)	**461** (383-527)	1092
	05-06	**17.5** (14.9-20.6)	**15.1** (10.9-19.0)	**74.3** (54.1-90.3)	**288** (231-366)	**569** (462-693)	1038
	07-08	**15.0** (12.6-17.7)	**12.3** (9.80-14.5)	**59.6** (41.9-73.4)	**197** (147-266)	**408** (296-537)	1077
	09-10	**14.0** (11.8-16.7)	**10.5** (8.30-12.9)	**51.7** (33.1-79.2)	**216** (174-266)	**431** (301-565)	1206

Limit of detection (LOD, see Data Analysis section) for Survey years 03-04, 05-06, 07-08 and 09-10 are 2.3, 2.3, 2.3, and 2.3 respectively.

Biomonitoring Summary

http://www.cdc.gov/biomonitoring/Triclosan_BiomonitoringSummary.html

Factsheet

http://www.cdc.gov/biomonitoring/Triclosan_FactSheet.html

Source: *Centers for Disease Control & Prevention, Fourth National Report on Human Exposure to Environmental Chemicals, Updated Tables, January 2017*

Urinary Triclosan (2011 - 2014)

Geometric mean and selected percentiles of urine concentrations (in µg/L) for the U.S. population from the National Health and Nutrition Examination Survey.

	Survey years	Geometric mean (95% conf. interval)	50th Percentile (95% conf. interval)	75th Percentile (95% conf. interval)	90th Percentile (95% conf. interval)	95th Percentile (95% conf. interval)	Sample size
Total	11-12	**11.8** (10.6-13.1)	**7.10** (6.10-7.90)	**41.6** (30.2-59.5)	**267** (207-332)	**553** (429-722)	2489
	13-14	**9.78** (9.01-10.6)	**6.30** (5.70-7.20)	**33.9** (29.1-39.1)	**172** (138-208)	**379** (324-431)	2686
Age group							
6-11 years	11-12	**7.18** (5.73-9.01)	**5.00** (3.40-7.30)	**17.2** (10.4-21.8)	**77.6** (28.9-184)	**184** (78.7-393)	396
	13-14	**8.24** (6.70-10.1)	**6.10** (4.80-8.00)	**22.9** (15.3-33.5)	**73.8** (52.7-96.0)	**124** (91.2-204)	409
12-19 years	11-12	**10.1** (7.70-13.3)	**5.80** (4.70-7.50)	**25.5** (15.1-38.9)	**156** (73.5-286)	**489** (171-1550)	388
	13-14	**7.96** (6.81-9.31)	**6.00** (4.80-7.40)	**19.7** (15.4-25.3)	**85.7** (37.2-183)	**224** (122-325)	462
20 years and older	11-12	**12.7** (11.2-14.4)	**7.60** (6.40-8.50)	**57.4** (37.0-75.8)	**298** (243-388)	**594** (437-845)	1705
	13-14	**10.3** (9.32-11.3)	**6.40** (5.60-7.50)	**39.3** (32.4-48.5)	**203** (147-270)	**420** (350-529)	1815
Gender							
Males	11-12	**11.6** (10.1-13.1)	**6.40** (5.30-7.50)	**41.6** (28.1-58.7)	**320** (211-388)	**566** (392-722)	1259
	13-14	**9.95** (8.75-11.3)	**6.40** (5.20-8.50)	**34.7** (29.3-40.6)	**172** (126-215)	**372** (297-479)	1285
Females	11-12	**12.0** (10.2-14.0)	**7.60** (6.20-8.60)	**42.2** (25.7-75.8)	**242** (188-286)	**545** (380-855)	1230
	13-14	**9.63** (8.41-11.0)	**6.20** (5.60-7.10)	**31.7** (24.9-42.5)	**173** (112-240)	**384** (302-528)	1401
Race/ethnicity							
Mexican Americans	11-12	**12.6** (8.98-17.8)	**7.20** (4.70-11.7)	**47.6** (21.9-82.7)	**411** (151-628)	**628** (393-1250)	316
	13-14	**8.65** (5.55-13.5)	**5.20** (2.60-12.2)	**31.9** (15.4-68.0)	**191** (79.5-346)	**488** (180-822)	438
Non-Hispanic blacks	11-12	**10.5** (9.08-12.2)	**6.70** (5.70-8.40)	**29.9** (22.4-40.0)	**169** (106-278)	**475** (278-718)	665
	13-14	**8.34** (7.54-9.23)	**5.50** (4.40-6.60)	**24.9** (18.9-32.6)	**145** (68.6-209)	**304** (204-509)	609
Non-Hispanic whites	11-12	**11.7** (10.0-13.7)	**7.00** (5.60-8.00)	**44.6** (24.4-75.8)	**248** (184-392)	**552** (365-759)	813
	13-14	**10.0** (8.95-11.3)	**6.40** (5.60-8.00)	**34.7** (29.2-43.1)	**148** (122-210)	**350** (253-438)	988
All Hispanics	11-12	**13.4** (11.6-15.5)	**7.50** (6.40-9.30)	**48.3** (33.2-75.5)	**411** (264-518)	**861** (536-1040)	571
	13-14	**9.14** (6.95-12.0)	**6.00** (3.70-9.50)	**29.6** (17.9-44.3)	**208** (131-325)	**583** (325-737)	690
Asians	11-12	**11.7** (7.75-17.8)	**7.30** (3.80-15.1)	**42.9** (18.6-125)	**274** (117-433)	**453** (235-636)	352
	13-14	**11.5** (9.24-14.3)	**6.20** (4.30-9.10)	**71.5** (25.2-121)	**294** (212-428)	**594** (384-740)	289

Limit of detection (LOD, see Data Analysis section) for Survey years 11-12 and 13-14 are 2.3 and 1.7, respectively.

Biomonitoring Summary

http://www.cdc.gov/biomonitoring/Triclosan_BiomonitoringSummary.html

Factsheet

http://www.cdc.gov/biomonitoring/Triclosan_FactSheet.html

Source: *Centers for Disease Control & Prevention, Fourth National Report on Human Exposure to Environmental Chemicals, Updated Tables, January 2017*

Urinary Triclosan (creatinine corrected) (2003 – 2010)

Geometric mean and selected percentiles of urine concentrations (in µg/g of creatinine) for the U.S. population from the National Health and Nutrition Examination Survey.

	Survey years	Geometric mean (95% conf. interval)	50th Percentile (95% conf. interval)	75th Percentile (95% conf. interval)	90th Percentile (95% conf. interval)	95th Percentile (95% conf. interval)	Sample size
Total	03-04	**12.7** (11.5-14.1)	**9.48** (8.22-10.4)	**43.9** (33.8-60.6)	**212** (172-241)	**368** (294-463)	2514
	05-06	**18.0** (16.0-20.3)	**13.0** (11.5-16.1)	**73.2** (57.3-91.6)	**304** (240-364)	**532** (434-674)	2548
	07-08	**15.5** (13.7-17.5)	**12.4** (10.6-14.2)	**50.4** (40.2-59.8)	**233** (171-300)	**443** (330-559)	2604
	09-10	**15.1** (13.2-17.4)	**10.9** (9.41-12.4)	**49.4** (37.0-67.3)	**256** (191-322)	**454** (352-557)	2749
Age group							
6-11 years	03-04	**9.93** (7.43-13.3)	**7.55** (4.72-13.4)	**25.1** (15.3-35.6)	**116** (39.9-236)	**236** (115-336)	314
	05-06	**14.1** (10.8-18.5)	**13.5** (7.97-18.5)	**38.6** (26.0-54.1)	**108** (62.4-169)	**241** (108-598)	356
	07-08	**14.5** (9.47-22.1)	**13.0** (8.00-17.5)	**33.1** (17.5-72.4)	**132** (52.7-331)	**331** (131-599)	389
	09-10	**14.2** (12.4-16.4)	**12.0** (8.84-15.0)	**37.1** (27.0-47.3)	**129** (89.1-155)	**300** (148-469)	415
12-19 years	03-04	**10.9** (8.32-14.2)	**7.45** (5.48-10.7)	**31.8** (21.9-61.1)	**193** (90.7-318)	**356** (169-580)	713
	05-06	**14.0** (11.0-17.8)	**11.1** (8.68-13.6)	**51.0** (33.0-73.4)	**193** (125-306)	**385** (203-739)	702
	07-08	**14.1** (11.0-18.1)	**11.0** (7.87-14.4)	**50.2** (27.1-78.8)	**206** (95.3-293)	**378** (238-571)	401
	09-10	**9.38** (7.86-11.2)	**7.71** (5.71-9.21)	**23.2** (17.3-29.3)	**153** (63.0-201)	**247** (166-379)	420
20 years and older	03-04	**13.4** (12.0-15.1)	**10.0** (8.89-11.4)	**50.0** (36.0-73.8)	**224** (186-272)	**385** (308-506)	1487
	05-06	**19.3** (16.9-22.0)	**13.7** (11.6-17.0)	**86.1** (64.0-109)	**343** (262-411)	**581** (440-718)	1490
	07-08	**15.8** (14.0-17.8)	**12.6** (10.7-14.5)	**52.3** (43.8-64.6)	**244** (186-309)	**484** (336-568)	1814
	09-10	**16.4** (13.7-19.6)	**11.5** (9.63-14.8)	**57.1** (38.4-80.2)	**279** (202-364)	**504** (372-601)	1914
Gender							
Males	03-04	**13.2** (11.3-15.6)	**9.21** (6.86-12.1)	**73.1** (45.8-85.9)	**237** (175-294)	**384** (294-506)	1228
	05-06	**17.1** (14.1-20.7)	**12.4** (10.0-18.5)	**82.6** (58.2-109)	**308** (232-368)	**472** (355-721)	1270
	07-08	**12.8** (10.9-15.0)	**10.0** (8.12-13.0)	**45.7** (32.1-57.3)	**191** (132-241)	**330** (253-456)	1294
	09-10	**13.3** (11.3-15.7)	**9.21** (7.40-11.7)	**43.9** (33.5-67.4)	**230** (178-276)	**345** (276-429)	1399
Females	03-04	**12.2** (10.6-14.2)	**9.54** (8.45-10.4)	**32.3** (26.2-46.6)	**182** (138-217)	**336** (225-480)	1286
	05-06	**19.0** (16.1-22.6)	**13.8** (11.7-16.7)	**64.0** (47.6-89.8)	**301** (209-434)	**619** (418-898)	1278
	07-08	**18.5** (15.6-22.0)	**14.4** (12.4-16.8)	**55.3** (38.5-77.0)	**300** (182-435)	**571** (359-729)	1310
	09-10	**17.1** (14.6-20.1)	**12.3** (10.7-14.8)	**50.6** (37.0-71.3)	**300** (187-422)	**556** (422-668)	1350
Race/ethnicity							
Mexican Americans	03-04	**13.3** (9.38-18.8)	**9.18** (5.45-13.9)	**66.7** (28.8-112)	**292** (151-432)	**453** (263-1150)	612
	05-06	**24.1** (19.3-29.9)	**17.6** (13.3-22.8)	**154** (96.4-242)	**440** (379-601)	**736** (601-818)	637
	07-08	**16.6** (12.2-22.6)	**12.6** (8.51-16.5)	**60.1** (39.6-80.3)	**325** (182-475)	**637** (368-828)	531
	09-10	**14.8** (12.1-18.2)	**9.38** (7.63-12.4)	**45.4** (32.2-110)	**352** (244-458)	**578** (402-737)	566
Non-Hispanic blacks	03-04	**9.94** (7.92-12.5)	**7.74** (5.50-10.0)	**30.2** (25.6-37.3)	**132** (78.0-213)	**260** (127-513)	651
	05-06	**12.2** (9.47-15.6)	**9.50** (7.64-11.8)	**41.0** (23.3-77.4)	**179** (106-243)	**352** (203-674)	678
	07-08	**10.6** (8.91-12.7)	**8.34** (6.47-10.1)	**28.6** (22.3-36.7)	**120** (71.0-203)	**266** (151-407)	597
	09-10	**9.23** (7.62-11.2)	**6.62** (5.63-8.18)	**22.7** (16.9-29.1)	**136** (63.6-240)	**356** (180-689)	516
Non-Hispanic whites	03-04	**13.3** (11.6-15.1)	**9.82** (8.11-11.5)	**47.0** (34.3-67.7)	**213** (160-272)	**358** (276-480)	1091
	05-06	**18.4** (16.0-21.2)	**13.5** (11.6-17.0)	**73.4** (56.8-97.0)	**282** (231-343)	**472** (367-699)	1038
	07-08	**15.6** (13.1-18.7)	**13.0** (10.7-14.8)	**50.4** (35.9-65.9)	**222** (129-303)	**418** (262-586)	1077
	09-10	**15.8** (13.1-19.0)	**11.4** (9.41-14.8)	**52.0** (37.0-71.3)	**242** (159-323)	**410** (317-547)	1206

Biomonitoring Summary

http://www.cdc.gov/biomonitoring/Triclosan_BiomonitoringSummary.html

Factsheet

http://www.cdc.gov/biomonitoring/Triclosan_FactSheet.html

Source: *Centers for Disease Control & Prevention, Fourth National Report on Human Exposure to Environmental Chemicals, Updated Tables, January 2017*

Urinary Triclosan (creatinine corrected) (2011 - 2014)

Geometric mean and selected percentiles of urine concentrations (in µg/g of creatinine) for the U.S. population from the National Health and Nutrition Examination Survey.

	Survey years	Geometric mean (95% conf. interval)	50th Percentile (95% conf. interval)	75th Percentile (95% conf. interval)	90th Percentile (95% conf. interval)	95th Percentile (95% conf. interval)	Sample size
Total	11-12	**13.4** (11.8-15.1)	**8.39** (6.79-10.0)	**49.3** (37.4-57.5)	**309** (229-404)	**642** (508-788)	2487
	13-14	**9.83** (9.00-10.7)	**6.90** (6.27-7.65)	**29.9** (25.1-34.4)	**173** (138-207)	**358** (292-425)	2684
Age group							
6-11 years	11-12	**10.3** (8.18-12.9)	**6.70** (5.62-9.06)	**22.4** (16.3-31.7)	**103** (54.5-153)	**235** (113-333)	395
	13-14	**10.4** (8.61-12.6)	**8.97** (6.62-11.5)	**23.4** (18.4-36.1)	**78.1** (57.0-125)	**184** (81.2-268)	409
12-19 years	11-12	**9.84** (7.85-12.4)	**5.83** (4.95-7.23)	**26.3** (19.0-37.8)	**182** (65.0-399)	**421** (182-647)	388
	13-14	**6.46** (5.24-7.96)	**5.11** (4.39-5.93)	**15.7** (10.0-21.8)	**53.6** (33.2-105)	**153** (102-289)	462
20 years and older	11-12	**14.4** (12.4-16.7)	**9.06** (7.41-11.2)	**54.3** (43.9-75.0)	**364** (246-514)	**660** (536-817)	1704
	13-14	**10.4** (9.44-11.4)	**7.17** (6.32-8.26)	**34.4** (29.3-41.6)	**202** (162-234)	**408** (296-531)	1813
Gender							
Males	11-12	**10.8** (9.49-12.2)	**6.40** (5.24-8.53)	**37.4** (26.8-49.4)	**226** (153-309)	**536** (311-656)	1258
	13-14	**8.36** (7.44-9.41)	**5.74** (4.80-6.67)	**26.7** (22.6-31.8)	**143** (111-195)	**296** (216-426)	1284
Females	11-12	**16.5** (13.8-19.6)	**10.8** (8.44-12.7)	**53.3** (44.2-75.0)	**381** (273-539)	**746** (614-900)	1229
	13-14	**11.5** (10.0-13.1)	**8.08** (6.70-9.23)	**34.4** (25.1-42.2)	**205** (150-253)	**419** (294-573)	1400
Race/ethnicity							
Mexican Americans	11-12	**14.2** (10.4-19.5)	**8.29** (6.10-12.4)	**62.5** (31.8-111)	**399** (163-536)	**536** (271-900)	316
	13-14	**8.82** (5.50-14.1)	**6.08** (3.08-13.4)	**25.5** (15.9-61.3)	**147** (68.8-340)	**425** (142-659)	438
Non-Hispanic blacks	11-12	**8.18** (7.09-9.44)	**5.52** (4.66-6.27)	**21.5** (16.7-29.9)	**130** (74.3-222)	**365** (229-461)	665
	13-14	**6.16** (5.30-7.15)	**4.27** (3.52-4.93)	**16.7** (12.7-21.3)	**107** (66.1-125)	**218** (116-284)	609
Non-Hispanic whites	11-12	**14.2** (12.1-16.7)	**8.95** (6.79-11.7)	**51.9** (39.1-69.1)	**311** (180-569)	**675** (508-817)	811
	13-14	**10.6** (9.78-11.5)	**7.78** (6.67-9.09)	**33.0** (26.4-40.2)	**178** (128-215)	**339** (247-420)	987
All Hispanics	11-12	**15.0** (13.0-17.3)	**8.58** (6.52-11.4)	**70.8** (40.8-98.6)	**449** (320-514)	**647** (506-913)	571
	13-14	**9.07** (6.64-12.4)	**6.08** (3.75-11.0)	**24.7** (17.0-55.6)	**197** (114-322)	**462** (322-619)	690
Asians	11-12	**15.7** (10.2-24.2)	**10.5** (6.05-17.4)	**51.8** (23.6-142)	**333** (127-609)	**575** (381-719)	352
	13-14	**14.6** (11.5-18.6)	**8.00** (5.74-13.3)	**100** (39.3-151)	**406** (247-528)	**659** (419-917)	288

Biomonitoring Summary

http://www.cdc.gov/biomonitoring/Triclosan_BiomonitoringSummary.html

Factsheet

http://www.cdc.gov/biomonitoring/Triclosan_FactSheet.html

Source: *Centers for Disease Control & Prevention, Fourth National Report on Human Exposure to Environmental Chemicals, Updated Tables, January 2017*

Urinary Total Arsenic (2003 – 2010)

Geometric mean and selected percentiles of urine concentrations (in µg /L) for the U.S. population from the National Health and Nutrition Examination Survey.

	Survey years	Geometric mean (95% conf. interval)	50th Percentile (95% conf. interval)	75th Percentile (95% conf. interval)	90th Percentile (95% conf. interval)	95th Percentile (95% conf. interval)	Sample size
Total	03-04	**8.30** (7.19-9.57)	**7.70** (6.90-8.90)	**16.0** (14.1-18.7)	**37.4** (31.6-43.5)	**65.4** (48.7-83.3)	2557
	05-06	**9.29** (8.05-10.7)	**8.65** (7.48-9.99)	**17.1** (14.9-20.6)	**41.1** (33.3-49.7)	**66.7** (53.7-87.0)	2576
	07-08	**8.10** (7.44-8.83)	**7.49** (6.90-8.12)	**14.9** (13.2-17.0)	**33.3** (29.8-38.7)	**50.8** (42.3-65.1)	2605
	09-10	**9.28** (8.47-10.2)	**8.15** (7.20-8.98)	**18.0** (15.3-20.8)	**44.6** (39.0-55.1)	**85.6** (64.7-114)	2860
Age group							
6-11 years	03-04	**7.08** (5.66-8.84)	**6.80** (5.90-7.70)	**10.9** (8.90-14.2)	**24.6** (13.8-61.8)	**46.9** (17.5-178)	290
	05-06	**7.19** (5.81-8.90)	**6.96** (5.32-8.88)	**11.5** (9.19-16.0)	**19.6** (13.1-51.5)	**34.1** (19.6-58.5)	355
	07-08	**6.85** (5.98-7.83)	**6.40** (5.74-7.23)	**10.8** (9.75-12.3)	**22.5** (16.9-34.7)	**41.0** (21.1-52.8)	390
	09-10	**6.63** (5.74-7.66)	**5.94** (5.14-7.19)	**10.8** (9.37-12.5)	**26.0** (18.2-33.4)	**37.7** (27.8-65.6)	378
12-19 years	03-04	**8.55** (7.34-9.97)	**8.10** (6.80-9.40)	**15.2** (12.2-17.8)	**30.5** (23.1-40.4)	**46.1** (32.9-62.5)	725
	05-06	**8.19** (6.87-9.77)	**7.92** (6.37-9.50)	**14.0** (11.6-18.1)	**28.2** (22.9-32.9)	**41.9** (32.7-48.0)	701
	07-08	**7.09** (6.17-8.14)	**6.87** (5.88-7.86)	**11.4** (9.41-13.7)	**20.4** (16.1-26.6)	**38.2** (21.6-53.3)	373
	09-10	**6.45** (5.58-7.47)	**6.11** (5.26-6.89)	**10.8** (8.59-13.7)	**25.9** (16.2-32.9)	**38.8** (27.8-55.1)	454
20 years and older	03-04	**8.41** (7.25-9.77)	**7.90** (7.00-9.10)	**17.0** (15.0-19.7)	**40.5** (34.9-46.2)	**66.2** (51.2-93.1)	1542
	05-06	**9.76** (8.43-11.3)	**9.12** (7.85-10.4)	**18.9** (15.8-22.9)	**44.2** (35.2-56.1)	**71.4** (57.7-98.3)	1520
	07-08	**8.43** (7.70-9.22)	**7.94** (7.09-8.67)	**16.2** (14.5-18.6)	**35.2** (30.4-42.3)	**59.0** (44.2-75.6)	1842
	09-10	**10.2** (9.14-11.3)	**8.75** (7.95-9.81)	**20.4** (17.2-24.1)	**52.1** (42.4-66.1)	**93.1** (74.2-127)	2028
Gender							
Males	03-04	**9.50** (8.34-10.8)	**8.90** (7.70-9.80)	**17.6** (15.2-20.1)	**41.6** (32.5-52.8)	**65.8** (48.7-95.4)	1281
	05-06	**10.1** (8.61-11.8)	**8.95** (8.05-10.0)	**18.3** (15.5-22.9)	**40.8** (31.0-52.6)	**63.7** (46.4-78.7)	1271
	07-08	**9.25** (8.28-10.3)	**8.50** (7.37-9.53)	**17.0** (14.6-19.4)	**36.0** (32.1-44.2)	**62.5** (44.3-84.6)	1318
	09-10	**10.1** (9.06-11.3)	**8.80** (7.80-9.75)	**20.4** (16.1-23.9)	**47.4** (42.1-64.1)	**89.1** (71.6-114)	1401
Females	03-04	**7.30** (6.02-8.84)	**6.90** (5.90-8.30)	**15.0** (11.3-19.5)	**33.4** (26.5-41.7)	**60.5** (40.8-77.1)	1276
	05-06	**8.60** (7.38-10.0)	**8.18** (6.64-9.97)	**15.9** (13.7-19.9)	**41.5** (32.2-53.7)	**72.6** (54.8-122)	1305
	07-08	**7.14** (6.51-7.82)	**6.54** (6.09-7.14)	**12.7** (11.6-14.4)	**30.1** (26.0-34.0)	**49.1** (40.1-57.5)	1287
	09-10	**8.55** (7.44-9.83)	**7.63** (6.45-8.62)	**15.8** (13.1-19.9)	**41.5** (31.7-55.5)	**81.5** (54.3-132)	1459
Race/ethnicity							
Mexican Americans	03-04	**9.29** (8.12-10.6)	**9.20** (8.10-10.3)	**16.2** (13.5-19.9)	**34.4** (24.0-60.5)	**68.2** (41.3-111)	618
	05-06	**9.55** (8.54-10.7)	**9.11** (7.99-10.3)	**15.6** (14.0-17.1)	**29.2** (21.4-56.8)	**67.6** (41.7-81.4)	652
	07-08	**8.98** (8.13-9.92)	**8.84** (7.80-9.48)	**15.4** (12.3-19.7)	**35.2** (25.0-46.0)	**53.0** (44.2-77.4)	510
	09-10	**8.47** (7.30-9.84)	**7.96** (6.87-9.08)	**13.9** (11.3-17.7)	**34.7** (25.0-53.2)	**60.9** (49.3-78.7)	613
Non-Hispanic blacks	03-04	**11.6** (9.50-14.1)	**10.4** (7.90-11.8)	**21.5** (14.9-34.4)	**43.5** (36.2-61.8)	**78.0** (43.6-141)	722
	05-06	**11.0** (8.60-14.0)	**9.55** (6.99-13.3)	**21.9** (14.9-28.9)	**44.9** (31.1-71.4)	**82.3** (49.2-164)	692
	07-08	**10.5** (9.40-11.7)	**9.21** (8.22-10.4)	**18.4** (16.1-21.5)	**42.4** (32.9-52.8)	**65.6** (45.5-112)	585
	09-10	**10.9** (9.46-12.5)	**9.26** (7.70-11.4)	**21.7** (17.6-24.2)	**49.1** (32.2-81.7)	**84.8** (51.3-174)	546
Non-Hispanic whites	03-04	**7.12** (6.13-8.27)	**7.00** (6.10-7.90)	**13.7** (11.3-15.8)	**29.0** (22.6-35.9)	**53.1** (38.4-65.6)	1074
	05-06	**8.66** (7.20-10.4)	**8.05** (6.52-9.66)	**16.3** (13.4-20.6)	**40.8** (29.4-50.2)	**58.5** (46.0-88.0)	1041
	07-08	**6.98** (6.31-7.71)	**6.46** (5.93-7.29)	**12.4** (11.3-14.3)	**28.3** (21.6-32.6)	**42.1** (32.3-50.0)	1088
	09-10	**8.18** (7.46-8.96)	**7.24** (6.46-8.21)	**14.8** (12.7-17.4)	**38.9** (31.7-44.4)	**66.3** (49.3-88.7)	1224

Limit of detection (LOD, see Data Analysis section) for Survey years 03-04, 05-06, 07-08 and 09-10 are 0.74, 0.74, 0.74, and 0.74 respectively.

Biomonitoring Summary

http://www.cdc.gov/biomonitoring/Arsenic_BiomonitoringSummary.html

Factsheet

http://www.cdc.gov/biomonitoring/Arsenic_FactSheet.html

Source: *Centers for Disease Control & Prevention, Fourth National Report on Human Exposure to Environmental Chemicals, Updated Tables, January 2017*

Urinary Total Arsenic (2011 - 2014)

Geometric mean and selected percentiles of urine concentrations (in µg As/L) for the U.S. population from the National Health and Nutrition Examination Survey.

	Survey years	Geometric mean (95% conf. interval)	50th Percentile (95% conf. interval)	75th Percentile (95% conf. interval)	90th Percentile (95% conf. interval)	95th Percentile (95% conf. interval)	Sample size
Total	11-12	**6.85** (5.85-8.02)	**6.09** (5.22-7.12)	**13.0** (10.9-16.6)	**32.0** (25.9-39.0)	**52.5** (41.9-66.2)	2504
	13-14	**6.29** (5.58-7.08)	**5.82** (5.10-6.69)	**11.7** (10.5-13.2)	**26.6** (23.7-30.1)	**46.0** (37.5-56.1)	2662
Age group							
6-11 years	11-12	**6.02** (5.03-7.19)	**5.50** (4.58-6.56)	**10.5** (7.93-14.1)	**30.1** (16.7-46.5)	**53.0** (37.5-70.3)	399
	13-14	**5.21** (4.57-5.95)	**4.78** (4.27-5.57)	**8.79** (7.52-10.3)	**17.1** (12.4-25.3)	**29.0** (17.9-47.7)	402
12-19 years	11-12	**6.01** (4.45-8.11)	**5.26** (3.95-7.47)	**10.9** (7.74-16.9)	**25.9** (16.6-44.0)	**44.0** (25.9-153)	390
	13-14	**5.79** (4.96-6.75)	**5.33** (4.83-5.91)	**9.40** (8.44-11.8)	**22.0** (17.4-28.1)	**44.1** (27.0-90.8)	451
20 years and older	11-12	**7.09** (6.03-8.33)	**6.31** (5.32-7.45)	**13.6** (11.3-18.3)	**33.2** (26.7-39.5)	**52.5** (41.9-77.3)	1715
	13-14	**6.49** (5.72-7.36)	**6.12** (5.22-7.06)	**12.1** (10.9-14.2)	**27.9** (24.1-32.1)	**48.0** (37.5-57.5)	1809
Gender							
Males	11-12	**7.69** (6.35-9.31)	**6.84** (5.33-8.59)	**15.4** (11.7-19.7)	**33.5** (27.7-41.9)	**56.5** (42.2-78.0)	1262
	13-14	**6.67** (5.97-7.46)	**6.37** (5.68-7.12)	**11.7** (10.8-13.0)	**27.0** (22.3-32.5)	**48.5** (33.3-57.5)	1316
Females	11-12	**6.14** (5.22-7.22)	**5.42** (4.79-6.25)	**11.6** (9.85-13.7)	**29.0** (22.5-38.2)	**50.6** (37.5-79.8)	1242
	13-14	**5.94** (5.18-6.80)	**5.38** (4.68-6.28)	**11.2** (9.49-13.7)	**26.0** (21.8-31.1)	**43.6** (36.0-55.8)	1346
Race/ethnicity							
Mexican Americans	11-12	**7.12** (5.73-8.84)	**6.94** (5.34-8.70)	**12.2** (9.84-16.5)	**24.2** (18.4-35.7)	**44.0** (23.8-70.3)	317
	13-14	**5.73** (5.01-6.56)	**5.64** (4.93-6.47)	**9.19** (8.10-10.2)	**17.5** (11.2-36.6)	**36.6** (15.4-73.0)	453
Non-Hispanic blacks	11-12	**9.31** (7.19-12.0)	**8.18** (6.16-10.8)	**17.9** (13.1-25.3)	**46.8** (28.8-76.5)	**82.1** (53.1-107)	669
	13-14	**8.17** (6.87-9.72)	**6.99** (6.01-8.20)	**14.9** (10.9-18.2)	**30.7** (25.5-38.2)	**59.8** (40.0-79.0)	579
Non-Hispanic whites	11-12	**5.89** (4.92-7.06)	**5.08** (4.56-6.06)	**10.8** (8.48-15.5)	**26.3** (20.3-34.9)	**43.2** (34.9-56.0)	820
	13-14	**5.67** (4.88-6.59)	**5.30** (4.40-6.62)	**11.0** (9.16-12.7)	**22.4** (17.6-29.9)	**39.0** (30.8-50.6)	985
All Hispanics	11-12	**7.62** (6.63-8.76)	**7.32** (6.31-8.35)	**13.7** (11.7-16.6)	**25.8** (21.2-29.8)	**45.6** (28.7-55.8)	573
	13-14	**6.16** (5.24-7.22)	**5.93** (5.02-6.82)	**10.4** (9.11-11.9)	**20.2** (14.2-30.1)	**37.5** (24.1-57.9)	701
Asians	11-12	**16.7** (14.7-18.9)	**14.9** (12.8-19.0)	**39.0** (33.2-44.8)	**83.2** (61.4-108)	**117** (88.4-145)	353
	13-14	**12.1** (10.4-14.1)	**11.5** (9.08-13.6)	**30.8** (23.2-37.0)	**70.7** (52.5-90.8)	**126** (79.2-181)	292

Limit of detection (LOD, see Data Analysis section) for Survey year 11-12 and 13-14 are 1.25 and 0.26.

Biomonitoring Summary

http://www.cdc.gov/biomonitoring/Arsenic_BiomonitoringSummary.html

Factsheet

http://www.cdc.gov/biomonitoring/Arsenic_FactSheet.html

Source: *Centers for Disease Control & Prevention, Fourth National Report on Human Exposure to Environmental Chemicals, Updated Tables, January 2017*

Urinary Total Arsenic (creatinine corrected) (2003 – 2010)

Geometric mean and selected percentiles of urine concentrations (in µg /g of creatinine) for the U.S. population from the National Health and Nutrition Examination Survey.

	Survey years	Geometric mean (95% conf. interval)	50th Percentile (95% conf. interval)	75th Percentile (95% conf. interval)	90th Percentile (95% conf. interval)	95th Percentile (95% conf. interval)	Sample size
Total	03-04	**8.24** (7.07-9.59)	**7.04** (5.93-8.51)	**14.1** (11.6-17.2)	**30.4** (26.0-38.7)	**50.4** (40.3-64.5)	2557
	05-06	**9.15** (7.93-10.6)	**7.70** (6.55-8.98)	**15.2** (11.7-19.4)	**35.1** (26.5-44.7)	**62.8** (44.7-85.0)	2576
	07-08	**8.46** (7.78-9.21)	**7.06** (6.56-7.74)	**13.8** (12.5-15.2)	**28.9** (24.2-36.7)	**49.0** (38.8-70.5)	2605
	09-10	**9.90** (9.06-10.8)	**7.90** (6.98-8.97)	**17.6** (15.4-20.2)	**45.2** (36.6-53.3)	**80.8** (60.5-94.4)	2860
Age group							
6-11 years	03-04	**8.25** (6.58-10.3)	**7.18** (5.93-9.45)	**11.7** (9.10-16.3)	**22.2** (12.0-69.5)	**40.1** (14.7-188)	290
	05-06	**8.88** (7.05-11.2)	**7.87** (6.19-9.42)	**11.8** (9.32-18.9)	**24.5** (13.0-62.8)	**45.4** (22.9-80.9)	355
	07-08	**8.87** (8.06-9.77)	**7.53** (6.73-7.88)	**13.4** (10.2-16.0)	**26.7** (19.9-34.0)	**37.2** (28.6-71.4)	390
	09-10	**8.97** (7.93-10.2)	**7.42** (6.70-8.32)	**11.0** (9.90-14.0)	**33.5** (17.0-54.6)	**60.8** (36.6-84.9)	378
12-19 years	03-04	**6.11** (5.23-7.13)	**5.06** (4.47-6.04)	**9.66** (7.44-11.2)	**17.8** (12.0-26.0)	**27.8** (20.7-35.9)	725
	05-06	**6.30** (5.56-7.14)	**5.19** (4.80-6.19)	**9.62** (8.12-11.1)	**19.4** (13.9-25.8)	**28.0** (21.9-33.2)	701
	07-08	**5.50** (4.91-6.16)	**4.96** (4.25-5.40)	**7.69** (6.09-9.31)	**16.8** (10.8-21.1)	**22.5** (16.8-29.1)	373
	09-10	**6.06** (5.34-6.87)	**4.95** (4.39-5.81)	**9.18** (7.00-11.0)	**19.2** (14.5-21.3)	**28.4** (20.8-35.7)	454
20 years and older	03-04	**8.64** (7.38-10.1)	**7.47** (6.20-9.01)	**15.4** (12.7-18.8)	**33.8** (27.3-41.2)	**53.9** (45.4-64.5)	1542
	05-06	**9.75** (8.46-11.2)	**8.22** (6.98-9.75)	**17.0** (12.8-21.3)	**41.0** (29.6-52.5)	**68.4** (52.8-89.7)	1520
	07-08	**9.00** (8.20-9.88)	**7.55** (6.79-8.53)	**14.9** (13.1-17.1)	**32.5** (25.8-41.0)	**59.4** (41.0-86.2)	1842
	09-10	**10.8** (9.71-12.0)	**8.73** (7.69-9.71)	**20.1** (16.5-24.2)	**50.8** (40.5-59.7)	**87.3** (70.0-105)	2028
Gender							
Males	03-04	**8.00** (6.81-9.40)	**6.75** (5.66-8.35)	**13.7** (11.0-18.0)	**28.7** (25.1-36.4)	**45.6** (35.3-62.1)	1281
	05-06	**8.26** (7.09-9.63)	**7.16** (5.87-8.54)	**12.9** (10.2-18.0)	**28.8** (22.9-36.3)	**46.1** (35.1-66.5)	1271
	07-08	**8.30** (7.49-9.18)	**6.79** (6.39-7.61)	**13.2** (11.8-15.2)	**28.9** (23.5-38.5)	**47.7** (35.7-68.1)	1318
	09-10	**9.21** (8.55-9.93)	**7.22** (6.43-8.67)	**17.0** (14.9-18.6)	**41.8** (35.4-47.9)	**66.9** (52.0-81.5)	1401
Females	03-04	**8.47** (7.12-10.1)	**7.33** (6.10-8.75)	**14.4** (11.7-17.7)	**32.3** (24.2-46.6)	**58.4** (42.8-75.0)	1276
	05-06	**10.1** (8.72-11.7)	**8.29** (7.23-9.87)	**17.4** (13.0-21.4)	**43.8** (29.2-61.5)	**74.1** (55.0-96.2)	1305
	07-08	**8.63** (7.91-9.41)	**7.13** (6.53-8.33)	**14.1** (12.3-16.9)	**27.9** (24.1-37.0)	**51.4** (39.7-83.3)	1287
	09-10	**10.6** (9.36-12.0)	**8.38** (7.40-9.41)	**18.6** (14.9-23.9)	**50.8** (35.1-72.9)	**87.8** (66.8-109)	1459
Race/ethnicity							
Mexican Americans	03-04	**8.61** (7.33-10.1)	**7.76** (6.30-9.44)	**12.6** (10.2-15.9)	**24.0** (17.7-34.8)	**42.4** (24.8-62.4)	618
	05-06	**8.98** (7.89-10.2)	**7.48** (6.72-8.87)	**12.8** (11.0-16.3)	**28.1** (21.1-35.5)	**49.1** (31.0-108)	652
	07-08	**8.88** (7.71-10.2)	**7.38** (6.51-8.63)	**14.1** (10.6-17.8)	**28.6** (22.5-35.3)	**48.2** (31.1-75.7)	510
	09-10	**8.88** (7.87-10.0)	**7.62** (6.69-8.45)	**13.2** (10.7-17.2)	**31.4** (23.7-38.5)	**49.8** (37.5-68.9)	613
Non-Hispanic blacks	03-04	**8.31** (6.99-9.88)	**6.88** (5.66-8.41)	**13.8** (11.5-17.0)	**27.6** (17.9-56.0)	**54.3** (27.5-120)	722
	05-06	**7.96** (6.40-9.92)	**6.48** (5.21-8.30)	**13.4** (10.0-18.6)	**32.5** (18.7-66.5)	**71.4** (35.6-98.8)	692
	07-08	**7.72** (6.98-8.54)	**6.60** (6.01-7.56)	**13.4** (11.5-15.4)	**25.7** (22.1-30.0)	**42.7** (31.4-60.3)	585
	09-10	**8.67** (7.54-9.98)	**7.26** (5.96-9.02)	**15.6** (12.4-21.3)	**38.7** (31.5-48.7)	**63.9** (43.1-102)	546
Non-Hispanic whites	03-04	**7.50** (6.25-9.01)	**6.32** (5.28-7.96)	**12.5** (9.86-17.1)	**26.8** (21.8-32.0)	**40.0** (31.3-53.9)	1074
	05-06	**9.01** (7.57-10.7)	**7.68** (6.18-9.56)	**14.3** (11.1-20.8)	**31.9** (24.1-46.1)	**59.4** (37.9-96.2)	1041
	07-08	**7.82** (7.05-8.68)	**6.72** (6.00-7.54)	**12.5** (11.1-13.9)	**24.6** (19.6-32.3)	**43.1** (29.1-64.0)	1088
	09-10	**9.14** (8.35-10.0)	**7.10** (6.43-8.06)	**15.8** (13.7-18.4)	**40.9** (30.4-50.8)	**66.4** (50.9-90.0)	1224

Biomonitoring Summary

http://www.cdc.gov/biomonitoring/Arsenic_BiomonitoringSummary.html

Factsheet

http://www.cdc.gov/biomonitoring/Arsenic_FactSheet.html

Source: *Centers for Disease Control & Prevention, Fourth National Report on Human Exposure to Environmental Chemicals, Updated Tables, January 2017*

Urinary Total Arsenic (creatinine corrected) (2011 - 2014)

Geometric mean and selected percentiles of urine concentrations (in µg As/g of creatinine) for the U.S. population from the National Health and Nutrition Examination Survey.

	Survey years	Geometric mean (95% conf. interval)	50th Percentile (95% conf. interval)	75th Percentile (95% conf. interval)	90th Percentile (95% conf. interval)	95th Percentile (95% conf. interval)	Sample size
Total	11-12	**7.77** (6.85-8.81)	**6.39** (5.57-7.24)	**13.7** (11.5-16.5)	**30.8** (24.6-38.6)	**50.4** (38.2-70.1)	2502
	13-14	**7.27** (6.62-7.99)	**6.10** (5.39-6.88)	**11.9** (10.5-13.5)	**27.6** (23.8-32.8)	**52.0** (43.5-60.9)	2661
Age group							
6-11 years	11-12	**8.63** (7.26-10.3)	**6.87** (5.84-8.00)	**12.3** (9.58-15.5)	**27.7** (17.7-57.7)	**91.2** (26.2-129)	398
	13-14	**7.78** (7.08-8.54)	**6.91** (5.91-7.65)	**12.5** (10.3-13.6)	**17.7** (16.1-21.1)	**29.9** (20.4-52.1)	402
12-19 years	11-12	**5.75** (4.49-7.36)	**4.69** (3.70-5.73)	**8.73** (6.26-13.3)	**22.1** (11.5-52.6)	**34.9** (21.1-159)	390
	13-14	**5.24** (4.53-6.06)	**4.21** (3.61-4.61)	**7.92** (5.75-10.3)	**17.6** (12.6-23.0)	**30.5** (20.3-54.1)	451
20 years and older	11-12	**8.04** (7.07-9.14)	**6.52** (5.88-7.69)	**14.8** (12.1-18.8)	**32.4** (25.2-39.8)	**49.7** (38.2-70.1)	1714
	13-14	**7.58** (6.87-8.36)	**6.39** (5.66-7.29)	**12.4** (10.9-14.7)	**31.0** (26.0-37.9)	**54.0** (47.9-66.1)	1808
Gender							
Males	11-12	**7.20** (6.15-8.43)	**6.13** (5.18-7.23)	**12.5** (10.5-15.2)	**28.3** (20.2-34.9)	**50.4** (33.3-69.6)	1261
	13-14	**6.69** (6.07-7.38)	**5.55** (4.96-6.26)	**10.9** (9.50-12.5)	**26.0** (19.5-30.6)	**47.9** (36.5-55.3)	1315
Females	11-12	**8.35** (7.40-9.42)	**6.64** (6.12-7.37)	**15.0** (12.2-19.1)	**33.1** (26.1-41.4)	**50.7** (39.8-79.0)	1241
	13-14	**7.88** (7.03-8.82)	**6.67** (5.82-7.78)	**13.1** (10.9-15.6)	**31.3** (24.9-39.4)	**54.1** (46.3-68.3)	1346
Race/ethnicity							
Mexican Americans	11-12	**8.00** (6.85-9.36)	**6.91** (6.07-7.98)	**11.9** (9.05-14.6)	**26.1** (16.7-39.4)	**40.8** (24.0-70.1)	317
	13-14	**6.54** (5.70-7.51)	**5.83** (5.08-6.54)	**8.97** (7.32-11.6)	**17.1** (12.6-20.8)	**29.2** (15.1-72.2)	453
Non-Hispanic blacks	11-12	**7.24** (5.51-9.51)	**5.83** (4.65-7.96)	**13.5** (9.02-19.0)	**28.8** (21.5-46.3)	**55.4** (31.6-87.1)	669
	13-14	**6.23** (5.25-7.39)	**4.86** (4.24-6.22)	**10.3** (8.03-13.4)	**22.7** (17.8-29.1)	**37.4** (25.8-70.5)	579
Non-Hispanic whites	11-12	**7.13** (6.05-8.39)	**5.72** (5.05-6.70)	**12.4** (10.3-15.4)	**28.4** (21.7-37.5)	**46.5** (33.1-75.8)	818
	13-14	**7.01** (6.25-7.87)	**5.87** (5.13-6.88)	**11.6** (9.92-13.7)	**27.5** (21.6-35.8)	**49.5** (40.8-55.3)	984
All Hispanics	11-12	**8.53** (7.74-9.40)	**7.60** (6.84-8.42)	**12.8** (11.2-14.1)	**25.3** (20.8-30.8)	**37.5** (28.2-50.6)	573
	13-14	**6.87** (6.08-7.76)	**6.26** (5.36-6.89)	**10.3** (8.75-11.9)	**18.7** (14.3-24.0)	**28.7** (18.9-50.7)	701
Asians	11-12	**22.3** (19.1-26.1)	**20.1** (16.3-25.2)	**39.4** (32.2-61.0)	**100** (73.2-129)	**162** (114-202)	353
	13-14	**19.0** (16.1-22.5)	**15.2** (13.0-19.2)	**41.9** (31.1-59.2)	**95.0** (74.2-131)	**137** (111-229)	292

Biomonitoring Summary

http://www.cdc.gov/biomonitoring/Arsenic_BiomonitoringSummary.html

Factsheet

http://www.cdc.gov/biomonitoring/Arsenic_FactSheet.html

Source: *Centers for Disease Control & Prevention, Fourth National Report on Human Exposure to Environmental Chemicals, Updated Tables, January 2017*

Blood Lead (1999 – 2010)

Geometric mean and selected percentiles of blood concentrations (in µg/dL) for the U.S. population from the National Health and Nutrition Examination Survey.

	Survey years	Geometric mean (95% conf. interval)	50th Percentile (95% conf. interval)	75th Percentile (95% conf. interval)	90th Percentile (95% conf. interval)	95th Percentile (95% conf. interval)	Sample size
Total	99-00	**1.66** (1.60-1.72)	**1.60** (1.60-1.70)	**2.50** (2.40-2.60)	**3.80** (3.60-4.00)	**5.00** (4.70-5.50)	7970
	01-02	**1.45** (1.39-1.51)	**1.40** (1.40-1.50)	**2.20** (2.10-2.30)	**3.40** (3.20-3.60)	**4.50** (4.20-4.70)	8945
	03-04	**1.43** (1.36-1.50)	**1.40** (1.30-1.50)	**2.10** (2.10-2.20)	**3.20** (3.10-3.30)	**4.20** (3.90-4.40)	8373
	05-06	**1.29** (1.23-1.36)	**1.27** (1.20-1.34)	**2.01** (1.91-2.11)	**3.05** (2.86-3.22)	**3.91** (3.64-4.18)	8407
	07-08	**1.27** (1.21-1.34)	**1.22** (1.18-1.30)	**1.90** (1.80-2.00)	**2.80** (2.67-2.96)	**3.70** (3.50-3.90)	8266
	09-10	**1.12** (1.08-1.16)	**1.07** (1.03-1.12)	**1.70** (1.62-1.77)	**2.58** (2.45-2.71)	**3.34** (3.14-3.57)	8793
Age group							
1-5 years	99-00	**2.23** (1.96-2.53)	**2.20** (1.90-2.50)	**3.40** (2.80-3.90)	**4.90** (4.00-6.60)	**7.00** (6.10-8.30)	723
	01-02	**1.70** (1.55-1.87)	**1.60** (1.50-1.80)	**2.50** (2.20-2.90)	**4.20** (3.50-5.20)	**5.80** (4.70-6.90)	898
	03-04	**1.77** (1.60-1.95)	**1.70** (1.50-1.90)	**2.50** (2.30-2.80)	**3.90** (3.30-4.60)	**5.10** (4.10-6.60)	911
	05-06	**1.46** (1.36-1.57)	**1.43** (1.34-1.55)	**2.10** (1.97-2.20)	**2.98** (2.72-3.32)	**3.80** (3.49-4.54)	968
	07-08	**1.51** (1.37-1.66)	**1.43** (1.30-1.60)	**2.20** (1.98-2.31)	**3.20** (2.65-3.85)	**4.10** (3.40-5.19)	817
	09-10	**1.17** (1.08-1.26)	**1.15** (1.03-1.27)	**1.70** (1.50-1.87)	**2.39** (2.08-2.65)	**3.37** (2.63-4.11)	836
6-11 years	99-00	**1.51** (1.36-1.66)	**1.40** (1.30-1.60)	**2.10** (1.80-2.50)	**3.30** (2.80-3.80)	**4.50** (3.40-6.20)	905
	01-02	**1.25** (1.14-1.36)	**1.20** (1.00-1.30)	**1.70** (1.60-2.00)	**2.80** (2.50-3.10)	**3.70** (3.00-4.70)	1044
	03-04	**1.25** (1.12-1.39)	**1.20** (1.10-1.40)	**1.80** (1.50-2.10)	**2.60** (2.10-3.10)	**3.30** (2.50-4.60)	856
	05-06	**1.02** (.948-1.10)	**.970** (.890-1.01)	**1.40** (1.28-1.55)	**2.06** (1.80-2.72)	**3.00** (2.26-3.81)	934
	07-08	**.988** (.914-1.07)	**.960** (.880-1.07)	**1.31** (1.22-1.49)	**1.90** (1.70-2.11)	**2.50** (2.10-2.88)	1011
	09-10	**.838** (.792-.887)	**.810** (.740-.840)	**1.13** (1.06-1.21)	**1.64** (1.45-1.84)	**2.01** (1.88-2.25)	1009
12-19 years	99-00	**1.10** (1.04-1.17)	**1.10** (1.00-1.20)	**1.50** (1.40-1.70)	**2.30** (2.10-2.40)	**2.90** (2.70-3.00)	2135
	01-02	**.942** (.899-.986)	**.900** (.900-1.00)	**1.30** (1.20-1.40)	**2.00** (1.90-2.10)	**2.70** (2.40-2.90)	2231
	03-04	**.946** (.878-1.02)	**.900** (.800-1.00)	**1.30** (1.20-1.40)	**1.90** (1.70-2.10)	**2.60** (2.20-3.00)	2081
	05-06	**.797** (.746-.852)	**.740** (.690-.790)	**1.08** (.990-1.20)	**1.69** (1.50-1.85)	**2.23** (1.98-2.46)	1996
	07-08	**.800** (.744-.859)	**.760** (.720-.820)	**1.04** (.980-1.16)	**1.50** (1.35-1.70)	**1.90** (1.70-2.32)	1074
	09-10	**.680** (.636-.727)	**.660** (.590-.700)	**.910** (.840-.990)	**1.29** (1.19-1.43)	**1.72** (1.52-1.86)	1183
20 years and older	99-00	**1.75** (1.68-1.81)	**1.70** (1.60-1.80)	**2.60** (2.50-2.70)	**3.90** (3.70-4.10)	**5.20** (4.80-5.60)	4207
	01-02	**1.56** (1.49-1.62)	**1.60** (1.50-1.60)	**2.30** (2.30-2.40)	**3.60** (3.40-3.70)	**4.60** (4.30-5.00)	4772
	03-04	**1.52** (1.45-1.60)	**1.50** (1.40-1.60)	**2.30** (2.20-2.40)	**3.30** (3.20-3.50)	**4.30** (4.00-4.60)	4525
	05-06	**1.41** (1.34-1.48)	**1.41** (1.33-1.48)	**2.17** (2.04-2.31)	**3.22** (3.05-3.43)	**4.12** (3.82-4.38)	4509
	07-08	**1.38** (1.31-1.46)	**1.34** (1.26-1.42)	**2.06** (1.94-2.18)	**3.00** (2.80-3.14)	**3.90** (3.68-4.23)	5364
	09-10	**1.23** (1.19-1.28)	**1.20** (1.14-1.25)	**1.85** (1.78-1.93)	**2.77** (2.60-2.93)	**3.57** (3.29-3.84)	5765
Gender							
Males	99-00	**2.01** (1.93-2.09)	**1.90** (1.90-2.00)	**2.90** (2.80-3.00)	**4.50** (4.10-4.80)	**6.00** (5.50-6.50)	3913
	01-02	**1.78** (1.71-1.86)	**1.80** (1.70-1.80)	**2.70** (2.50-2.80)	**3.90** (3.80-4.10)	**5.40** (5.00-5.50)	4339
	03-04	**1.69** (1.62-1.75)	**1.60** (1.50-1.70)	**2.50** (2.40-2.60)	**3.70** (3.40-3.90)	**4.80** (4.50-5.20)	4132
	05-06	**1.52** (1.42-1.62)	**1.49** (1.41-1.58)	**2.30** (2.12-2.51)	**3.48** (3.20-3.75)	**4.36** (4.04-4.76)	4092
	07-08	**1.47** (1.39-1.56)	**1.40** (1.32-1.50)	**2.17** (2.00-2.30)	**3.21** (3.01-3.53)	**4.41** (4.10-4.88)	4147
	09-10	**1.31** (1.25-1.36)	**1.26** (1.20-1.32)	**1.96** (1.89-2.03)	**2.93** (2.72-3.15)	**3.84** (3.54-4.39)	4366
Females	99-00	**1.37** (1.32-1.43)	**1.30** (1.30-1.40)	**2.00** (1.90-2.10)	**3.10** (2.90-3.30)	**4.00** (3.80-4.20)	4057
	01-02	**1.19** (1.14-1.25)	**1.20** (1.10-1.20)	**1.80** (1.70-1.90)	**2.60** (2.50-2.80)	**3.60** (3.10-4.00)	4606
	03-04	**1.22** (1.14-1.31)	**1.20** (1.10-1.30)	**1.80** (1.70-2.00)	**2.70** (2.50-3.00)	**3.50** (3.10-3.80)	4241
	05-06	**1.11** (1.05-1.17)	**1.06** (.980-1.15)	**1.73** (1.61-1.84)	**2.59** (2.44-2.74)	**3.25** (3.12-3.44)	4315
	07-08	**1.11** (1.06-1.16)	**1.09** (1.00-1.14)	**1.64** (1.54-1.74)	**2.41** (2.35-2.50)	**3.00** (2.81-3.20)	4119
	09-10	**.966** (.929-1.01)	**.940** (.890-.970)	**1.43** (1.36-1.53)	**2.18** (2.08-2.30)	**2.81** (2.63-2.93)	4427

Limit of detection (LOD, see Data Analysis section) for Survey years 99-00, 01-02, 03-04, 05-06, 07-08, and 09-10 are 0.3, 0.3, 0.28, 0.25, 0.25, and 0.25 respectively.

Biomonitoring Summary

http://www.cdc.gov/biomonitoring/Lead_BiomonitoringSummary.html

Factsheet

http://www.cdc.gov/biomonitoring/Lead_FactSheet.html

Source: *Centers for Disease Control & Prevention, Fourth National Report on Human Exposure to Environmental Chemicals, Updated Tables, January 2017*

Blood Lead (1999 – 2010)

Geometric mean and selected percentiles of blood concentrations (in µg/dL) for the U.S. population from the National Health and Nutrition Examination Survey.

	Survey years	Geometric mean (95% conf. interval)	50th Percentile (95% conf. interval)	75th Percentile (95% conf. interval)	90th Percentile (95% conf. interval)	95th Percentile (95% conf. interval)	Sample size
Race/ethnicity							
Mexican Americans	99-00	**1.83** (1.75-1.91)	**1.80** (1.70-1.90)	**2.80** (2.60-2.90)	**4.20** (3.90-4.60)	**5.80** (5.10-6.60)	2742
	01-02	**1.46** (1.34-1.60)	**1.50** (1.30-1.60)	**2.30** (2.10-2.60)	**3.60** (3.40-4.20)	**5.40** (4.40-6.70)	2268
	03-04	**1.55** (1.43-1.69)	**1.50** (1.40-1.60)	**2.30** (2.10-2.50)	**3.50** (2.90-4.20)	**4.90** (3.90-6.40)	2085
	05-06	**1.29** (1.21-1.38)	**1.26** (1.15-1.36)	**2.00** (1.87-2.20)	**3.16** (2.79-3.58)	**4.22** (3.47-5.36)	2236
	07-08	**1.25** (1.15-1.36)	**1.20** (1.10-1.31)	**1.88** (1.70-2.06)	**2.81** (2.60-3.20)	**3.92** (3.20-5.00)	1712
	09-10	**1.14** (1.03-1.28)	**1.04** (.940-1.18)	**1.76** (1.52-1.99)	**2.93** (2.63-3.30)	**3.92** (3.60-4.69)	1966
Non-Hispanic blacks	99-00	**1.87** (1.75-2.00)	**1.80** (1.70-2.00)	**2.80** (2.60-3.00)	**4.30** (4.00-4.60)	**5.70** (5.20-6.10)	1842
	01-02	**1.65** (1.52-1.80)	**1.60** (1.40-1.70)	**2.60** (2.30-2.90)	**4.20** (3.80-4.70)	**5.80** (5.30-6.50)	2219
	03-04	**1.69** (1.52-1.89)	**1.60** (1.40-1.80)	**2.60** (2.20-3.00)	**4.10** (3.50-4.70)	**5.30** (4.60-6.60)	2293
	05-06	**1.39** (1.26-1.53)	**1.31** (1.19-1.45)	**2.16** (1.95-2.42)	**3.48** (3.19-3.80)	**4.65** (4.21-5.14)	2193
	07-08	**1.39** (1.30-1.48)	**1.30** (1.20-1.42)	**2.10** (2.00-2.20)	**3.22** (3.08-3.50)	**4.50** (4.00-4.80)	1746
	09-10	**1.24** (1.18-1.30)	**1.19** (1.12-1.25)	**1.87** (1.76-1.99)	**2.90** (2.68-3.18)	**3.86** (3.57-4.29)	1593
Non-Hispanic whites	99-00	**1.62** (1.55-1.69)	**1.60** (1.50-1.70)	**2.40** (2.30-2.50)	**3.60** (3.40-3.90)	**5.00** (4.40-5.70)	2716
	01-02	**1.43** (1.37-1.48)	**1.40** (1.30-1.50)	**2.20** (2.10-2.20)	**3.20** (3.10-3.40)	**4.20** (3.90-4.50)	3806
	03-04	**1.37** (1.32-1.43)	**1.30** (1.30-1.40)	**2.10** (2.00-2.10)	**3.00** (2.80-3.20)	**3.90** (3.60-4.30)	3478
	05-06	**1.28** (1.19-1.37)	**1.27** (1.17-1.38)	**1.97** (1.86-2.14)	**2.99** (2.73-3.25)	**3.82** (3.41-4.20)	3310
	07-08	**1.24** (1.16-1.33)	**1.20** (1.10-1.30)	**1.86** (1.72-2.00)	**2.70** (2.54-2.90)	**3.50** (3.20-3.89)	3461
	09-10	**1.10** (1.04-1.16)	**1.07** (1.00-1.15)	**1.67** (1.59-1.76)	**2.49** (2.35-2.63)	**3.14** (2.99-3.36)	3760

Limit of detection (LOD, see Data Analysis section) for Survey years 99-00, 01-02, 03-04, 05-06, 07-08, and 09-10 are 0.3, 0.3, 0.28, 0.25, 0.25, and 0.25 respectively.

Biomonitoring Summary

http://www.cdc.gov/biomonitoring/Lead_BiomonitoringSummary.html

Factsheet

http://www.cdc.gov/biomonitoring/Lead_FactSheet.html

Source: *Centers for Disease Control & Prevention, Fourth National Report on Human Exposure to Environmental Chemicals, Updated Tables, January 2017*

Blood Lead (2011 - 2014)

Geometric mean and selected percentiles of blood concentrations (in µg/dL) for the U.S. population from the National Health and Nutrition Examination Survey.

	Survey years	Geometric mean (95% conf. interval)	50th Percentile (95% conf. interval)	75th Percentile (95% conf. interval)	90th Percentile (95% conf. interval)	95th Percentile (95% conf. interval)	Sample size
Total	11-12	**.973** (.916-1.04)	**.930** (.880-.980)	**1.52** (1.41-1.61)	**2.38** (2.17-2.61)	**3.16** (2.77-3.68)	7920
	13-14	**.858** (.813-.906)	**.830** (.780-.870)	**1.32** (1.24-1.42)	**2.10** (1.96-2.30)	**2.81** (2.49-3.14)	5215
Age group							
1-5 years	11-12	**.970** (.877-1.07)	**.950** (.870-1.04)	**1.34** (1.20-1.65)	**2.26** (1.88-2.65)	**2.91** (2.41-3.83)	713
	13-14	**.782** (.705-.869)	**.740** (.680-.800)	**1.08** (.940-1.24)	**1.58** (1.33-1.90)	**2.24** (1.68-2.64)	818
6-11 years	11-12	**.681** (.623-.744)	**.640** (.600-.700)	**.930** (.820-1.05)	**1.34** (1.14-1.60)	**1.89** (1.36-2.94)	1048
	13-14	**.567** (.529-.607)	**.530** (.500-.570)	**.760** (.700-.820)	**1.13** (1.01-1.23)	**1.42** (1.21-1.83)	1075
12-19 years	11-12	**.554** (.511-.601)	**.530** (.490-.570)	**.740** (.660-.830)	**1.09** (.960-1.19)	**1.31** (1.16-1.65)	1129
	13-14	**.506** (.464-.551)	**.460** (.420-.500)	**.670** (.600-.750)	**1.13** (.870-1.53)	**1.69** (1.27-2.06)	627
20 years and older	11-12	**1.09** (1.03-1.16)	**1.05** (1.00-1.12)	**1.67** (1.56-1.79)	**2.56** (2.33-2.77)	**3.36** (2.98-3.93)	5030
	13-14	**.967** (.921-1.02)	**.940** (.900-.980)	**1.45** (1.37-1.55)	**2.26** (2.09-2.49)	**3.03** (2.65-3.55)	2695
Gender							
Males	11-12	**1.13** (1.06-1.21)	**1.07** (1.01-1.14)	**1.74** (1.63-1.88)	**2.73** (2.48-3.01)	**3.68** (3.18-4.22)	3968
	13-14	**.994** (.919-1.08)	**.940** (.890-1.00)	**1.48** (1.35-1.61)	**2.41** (2.07-2.90)	**3.47** (2.89-4.32)	2587
Females	11-12	**.842** (.796-.890)	**.820** (.780-.860)	**1.30** (1.22-1.39)	**1.98** (1.83-2.22)	**2.59** (2.32-2.94)	3952
	13-14	**.746** (.715-.777)	**.730** (.700-.760)	**1.19** (1.11-1.28)	**1.86** (1.69-2.02)	**2.33** (2.24-2.42)	2628
Race/ethnicity							
Mexican Americans	11-12	**.838** (.767-.916)	**.780** (.690-.880)	**1.27** (1.15-1.40)	**2.05** (1.81-2.36)	**3.06** (2.34-3.59)	1077
	13-14	**.746** (.685-.813)	**.690** (.650-.750)	**1.17** (1.10-1.28)	**1.88** (1.61-2.04)	**2.38** (2.03-2.74)	969
Non-Hispanic blacks	11-12	**.998** (.947-1.05)	**.910** (.850-.990)	**1.53** (1.45-1.60)	**2.58** (2.31-2.91)	**3.72** (3.04-4.58)	2195
	13-14	**.871** (.787-.963)	**.830** (.720-.940)	**1.39** (1.27-1.48)	**2.17** (2.00-2.38)	**3.03** (2.48-4.00)	1119
Non-Hispanic whites	11-12	**.993** (.914-1.08)	**.960** (.880-1.03)	**1.56** (1.40-1.73)	**2.43** (2.11-2.74)	**3.14** (2.67-3.85)	2493
	13-14	**.882** (.820-.950)	**.870** (.800-.920)	**1.34** (1.24-1.48)	**2.20** (1.94-2.48)	**2.97** (2.43-3.58)	1848
All Hispanics	11-12	**.855** (.793-.922)	**.820** (.750-.880)	**1.27** (1.18-1.39)	**2.00** (1.86-2.23)	**2.84** (2.41-3.34)	1931
	13-14	**.742** (.695-.793)	**.690** (.660-.730)	**1.14** (1.08-1.24)	**1.80** (1.62-1.99)	**2.36** (2.03-2.72)	1481
Asians	11-12	**1.15** (1.06-1.24)	**1.14** (1.02-1.26)	**1.70** (1.56-1.86)	**2.56** (2.36-2.72)	**3.28** (2.80-3.65)	1005
	13-14	**1.01** (.923-1.11)	**1.02** (.900-1.19)	**1.48** (1.35-1.66)	**2.25** (2.06-2.39)	**2.67** (2.37-2.86)	510

Limit of detection (LOD, see Data Analysis section) for Survey year 11-12 and 13-14 are 0.25 and 0.07.

Biomonitoring Summary

http://www.cdc.gov/biomonitoring/Lead_BiomonitoringSummary.html

Factsheet

http://www.cdc.gov/biomonitoring/Lead_FactSheet.html

Source: *Centers for Disease Control & Prevention, Fourth National Report on Human Exposure to Environmental Chemicals, Updated Tables, January 2017*

Urinary Lead (1999 – 2010)

Geometric mean and selected percentiles of urine concentrations (in µg/L) for the U.S. population from the National Health and Nutrition Examination Survey.

	Survey years	Geometric mean (95% conf. interval)	50th Percentile (95% conf. interval)	75th Percentile (95% conf. interval)	90th Percentile (95% conf. interval)	95th Percentile (95% conf. interval)	Sample size
Total	99-00	**.766** (.708-.828)	**.800** (.800-.900)	**1.40** (1.30-1.50)	**2.20** (2.00-2.30)	**2.90** (2.60-3.30)	2465
	01-02	**.677** (.637-.718)	**.700** (.700-.800)	**1.20** (1.20-1.30)	**2.00** (1.90-2.20)	**2.70** (2.50-2.80)	2690
	03-04	**.636** (.595-.680)	**.640** (.580-.690)	**1.04** (.960-1.12)	**1.73** (1.52-1.86)	**2.29** (2.03-2.62)	2558
	05-06	**.554** (.523-.587)	**.570** (.540-.600)	**.990** (.910-1.05)	**1.58** (1.44-1.73)	**2.14** (1.94-2.45)	2576
	07-08	**.493** (.467-.520)	**.500** (.470-.530)	**.850** (.790-.910)	**1.38** (1.23-1.58)	**1.97** (1.75-2.17)	2627
	09-10	**.458** (.441-.476)	**.470** (.450-.480)	**.790** (.750-.830)	**1.24** (1.11-1.38)	**1.65** (1.46-1.84)	2848
Age group							
6-11 years	99-00	**1.07** (.955-1.20)	**1.10** (.900-1.30)	**1.50** (1.40-1.70)	**2.40** (1.80-3.10)	**3.40** (2.40-5.00)	340
	01-02	**.753** (.661-.857)	**.800** (.600-.900)	**1.20** (1.10-1.40)	**2.10** (1.60-2.40)	**2.60** (2.10-3.70)	368
	03-04	**.795** (.671-.941)	**.790** (.640-.900)	**1.35** (.970-1.86)	**2.27** (1.62-4.09)	**3.33** (2.23-4.41)	290
	05-06	**.508** (.447-.579)	**.510** (.440-.560)	**.740** (.620-.980)	**1.33** (1.00-1.86)	**1.90** (1.33-2.60)	355
	07-08	**.494** (.411-.593)	**.520** (.410-.590)	**.790** (.660-.900)	**1.23** (.980-1.73)	**1.90** (1.51-2.18)	394
	09-10	**.443** (.399-.493)	**.460** (.430-.490)	**.710** (.630-.820)	**1.09** (.880-1.33)	**1.40** (1.06-1.82)	378
12-19 years	99-00	**.659** (.579-.749)	**.700** (.600-.800)	**1.10** (.900-1.30)	**1.80** (1.40-2.20)	**2.20** (1.90-2.80)	719
	01-02	**.564** (.526-.605)	**.600** (.500-.600)	**1.00** (.800-1.10)	**1.60** (1.40-1.70)	**2.00** (1.80-2.40)	762
	03-04	**.604** (.553-.660)	**.630** (.570-.680)	**.920** (.810-1.02)	**1.32** (1.14-1.80)	**1.86** (1.44-2.29)	725
	05-06	**.472** (.421-.530)	**.490** (.450-.540)	**.780** (.710-.830)	**1.19** (1.10-1.45)	**1.65** (1.34-1.80)	701
	07-08	**.386** (.346-.431)	**.380** (.350-.410)	**.640** (.560-.720)	**1.03** (.870-1.24)	**1.38** (1.09-1.91)	376
	09-10	**.320** (.283-.361)	**.320** (.270-.370)	**.530** (.460-.630)	**.830** (.710-1.10)	**1.16** (.860-1.37)	451
20 years and older	99-00	**.752** (.691-.818)	**.800** (.700-.900)	**1.40** (1.30-1.50)	**2.20** (2.00-2.40)	**2.90** (2.60-3.30)	1406
	01-02	**.688** (.641-.738)	**.700** (.700-.800)	**1.20** (1.20-1.30)	**2.00** (1.90-2.30)	**2.80** (2.50-2.90)	1560
	03-04	**.625** (.579-.674)	**.620** (.560-.700)	**1.04** (.960-1.11)	**1.70** (1.52-1.80)	**2.21** (2.04-2.49)	1543
	05-06	**.574** (.539-.612)	**.600** (.560-.640)	**1.02** (.970-1.13)	**1.65** (1.53-1.81)	**2.21** (1.99-2.57)	1520
	07-08	**.512** (.485-.540)	**.530** (.490-.560)	**.900** (.820-.950)	**1.49** (1.29-1.64)	**2.01** (1.78-2.33)	1857
	09-10	**.486** (.465-.507)	**.490** (.470-.520)	**.830** (.780-.880)	**1.32** (1.16-1.46)	**1.71** (1.52-2.03)	2019
Gender							
Males	99-00	**.923** (.822-1.04)	**.900** (.900-1.00)	**1.60** (1.40-1.80)	**2.50** (2.20-2.90)	**3.40** (2.90-3.80)	1227
	01-02	**.808** (.757-.862)	**.800** (.800-.900)	**1.40** (1.30-1.50)	**2.50** (2.20-2.70)	**3.20** (2.90-3.50)	1335
	03-04	**.731** (.680-.785)	**.730** (.680-.800)	**1.17** (1.07-1.27)	**2.03** (1.78-2.22)	**2.66** (2.33-2.91)	1281
	05-06	**.672** (.638-.707)	**.690** (.620-.760)	**1.16** (1.04-1.28)	**1.78** (1.60-2.00)	**2.45** (2.00-2.97)	1271
	07-08	**.560** (.518-.606)	**.570** (.530-.620)	**.930** (.840-1.02)	**1.63** (1.36-1.97)	**2.30** (1.97-3.07)	1327
	09-10	**.527** (.491-.566)	**.540** (.480-.580)	**.880** (.820-.960)	**1.41** (1.25-1.58)	**1.83** (1.62-2.21)	1398
Females	99-00	**.642** (.589-.701)	**.700** (.600-.800)	**1.20** (1.10-1.30)	**1.90** (1.60-2.20)	**2.40** (2.10-3.00)	1238
	01-02	**.573** (.535-.613)	**.600** (.600-.600)	**1.10** (1.00-1.10)	**1.60** (1.50-1.80)	**2.20** (1.90-2.40)	1355
	03-04	**.558** (.506-.616)	**.540** (.480-.620)	**.920** (.820-1.04)	**1.49** (1.24-1.75)	**1.82** (1.59-2.30)	1277
	05-06	**.461** (.425-.499)	**.460** (.430-.510)	**.810** (.730-.880)	**1.27** (1.17-1.46)	**1.86** (1.54-2.17)	1305
	07-08	**.436** (.412-.461)	**.430** (.400-.480)	**.760** (.690-.830)	**1.22** (1.05-1.34)	**1.67** (1.44-1.81)	1300
	09-10	**.400** (.378-.424)	**.420** (.390-.440)	**.690** (.660-.740)	**1.05** (.990-1.13)	**1.42** (1.26-1.59)	1450

Limit of detection (LOD, see Data Analysis section) for Survey years 99-00, 01-02, 03-04, 05-06, 07-08, and 09-10 are 0.1, 0.1, 0.33, 0.1, 0.1, and 0.1 respectively.

Biomonitoring Summary

http://www.cdc.gov/biomonitoring/Lead_BiomonitoringSummary.html

Factsheet

http://www.cdc.gov/biomonitoring/Lead_FactSheet.html

Source: *Centers for Disease Control & Prevention, Fourth National Report on Human Exposure to Environmental Chemicals, Updated Tables, January 2017*

Urinary Lead (1999 – 2010)

Geometric mean and selected percentiles of urine concentrations (in µg/L) for the U.S. population from the National Health and Nutrition Examination Survey.

	Survey years	Geometric mean (95% conf. interval)	50th Percentile (95% conf. interval)	75th Percentile (95% conf. interval)	90th Percentile (95% conf. interval)	95th Percentile (95% conf. interval)	Sample size
Race/ethnicity							
Mexican Americans	99-00	**1.02** (.915-1.13)	**1.10** (.900-1.20)	**1.80** (1.60-1.90)	**2.90** (2.50-3.40)	**4.30** (3.10-5.40)	884
	01-02	**.833** (.745-.931)	**.900** (.700-1.00)	**1.50** (1.20-1.70)	**2.50** (2.00-2.90)	**3.30** (2.70-3.80)	683
	03-04	**.815** (.710-.935)	**.840** (.700-.990)	**1.31** (1.18-1.59)	**2.19** (1.86-2.50)	**2.66** (2.13-3.97)	618
	05-06	**.729** (.653-.815)	**.770** (.680-.860)	**1.32** (1.15-1.59)	**2.22** (1.81-2.64)	**3.08** (2.50-4.03)	652
	07-08	**.607** (.528-.698)	**.610** (.530-.690)	**.990** (.890-1.21)	**1.76** (1.37-2.17)	**2.29** (1.82-2.80)	515
	09-10	**.546** (.483-.618)	**.520** (.460-.580)	**.930** (.800-1.09)	**1.66** (1.34-1.89)	**2.16** (1.80-2.87)	613
Non-Hispanic blacks	99-00	**1.11** (1.00-1.23)	**1.10** (1.00-1.20)	**1.90** (1.50-2.10)	**3.00** (2.40-3.50)	**4.20** (3.30-5.70)	568
	01-02	**.940** (.833-1.06)	**.900** (.800-1.00)	**1.60** (1.30-1.80)	**2.70** (2.10-3.40)	**3.70** (2.90-4.80)	667
	03-04	**.848** (.729-.986)	**.850** (.710-1.00)	**1.40** (1.10-1.72)	**2.14** (1.78-2.64)	**2.82** (2.31-3.89)	723
	05-06	**.666** (.604-.734)	**.660** (.590-.760)	**1.09** (.980-1.18)	**1.62** (1.42-1.85)	**2.24** (1.65-2.90)	692
	07-08	**.618** (.558-.685)	**.620** (.560-.690)	**1.01** (.920-1.13)	**1.56** (1.38-1.90)	**2.06** (1.88-2.60)	589
	09-10	**.560** (.522-.601)	**.550** (.490-.600)	**.910** (.830-1.01)	**1.53** (1.26-1.71)	**1.96** (1.68-2.80)	544
Non-Hispanic whites	99-00	**.695** (.625-.773)	**.700** (.700-.900)	**1.30** (1.10-1.40)	**2.00** (1.80-2.40)	**2.70** (2.30-3.10)	822
	01-02	**.610** (.572-.651)	**.700** (.600-.700)	**1.10** (1.10-1.20)	**1.90** (1.70-2.00)	**2.40** (2.30-2.60)	1132
	03-04	**.591** (.556-.628)	**.590** (.540-.650)	**.960** (.910-.990)	**1.52** (1.40-1.75)	**2.14** (1.78-2.51)	1074
	05-06	**.520** (.477-.566)	**.540** (.490-.580)	**.950** (.820-1.05)	**1.53** (1.30-1.76)	**2.07** (1.78-2.45)	1041
	07-08	**.452** (.422-.485)	**.460** (.430-.490)	**.780** (.700-.880)	**1.23** (1.03-1.50)	**1.79** (1.58-1.97)	1095
	09-10	**.431** (.406-.458)	**.450** (.410-.480)	**.750** (.690-.820)	**1.11** (1.05-1.24)	**1.51** (1.39-1.67)	1225

Limit of detection (LOD, see Data Analysis section) for Survey years 99-00, 01-02, 03-04, 05-06, 07-08, and 09-10 are 0.1, 0.1, 0.33, 0.1, 0.1, and 0.1 respectively.

Biomonitoring Summary

http://www.cdc.gov/biomonitoring/Lead_BiomonitoringSummary.html

Factsheet

http://www.cdc.gov/biomonitoring/Lead_FactSheet.html

Source: *Centers for Disease Control & Prevention, Fourth National Report on Human Exposure to Environmental Chemicals, Updated Tables, January 2017*

Urinary Lead (2011 - 2014)

Geometric mean and selected percentiles of urine concentrations (in µg/L) for the U.S. population from the National Health and Nutrition Examination Survey.

	Survey years	Geometric mean (95% conf. interval)	50th Percentile (95% conf. interval)	75th Percentile (95% conf. interval)	90th Percentile (95% conf. interval)	95th Percentile (95% conf. interval)	Sample size
Total	11-12	**.360** (.328-.396)	**.370** (.340-.400)	**.650** (.580-.720)	**1.05** (.980-1.17)	**1.49** (1.26-1.75)	2504
	13-14	**.277** (.257-.298)	**.290** (.270-.300)	**.500** (.480-.530)	**.840** (.780-.900)	**1.17** (1.01-1.41)	2664
Age group							
6-11 years	11-12	**.346** (.292-.410)	**.370** (.300-.440)	**.610** (.540-.770)	**1.12** (.830-1.51)	**1.54** (1.28-1.85)	399
	13-14	**.222** (.192-.258)	**.240** (.200-.270)	**.390** (.330-.450)	**.630** (.560-.810)	**.870** (.710-1.09)	402
12-19 years	11-12	**.259** (.219-.305)	**.260** (.220-.340)	**.470** (.380-.530)	**.720** (.540-.900)	**.970** (.720-1.17)	390
	13-14	**.201** (.166-.245)	**.220** (.190-.260)	**.360** (.290-.440)	**.550** (.450-.700)	**.750** (.570-.880)	451
20 years and older	11-12	**.381** (.348-.416)	**.390** (.360-.420)	**.680** (.640-.730)	**1.11** (1.01-1.21)	**1.58** (1.28-1.90)	1715
	13-14	**.297** (.280-.315)	**.300** (.290-.320)	**.540** (.510-.580)	**.900** (.820-.980)	**1.27** (1.08-1.55)	1811
Gender							
Males	11-12	**.414** (.367-.466)	**.420** (.380-.460)	**.730** (.640-.800)	**1.16** (.990-1.47)	**1.73** (1.33-2.18)	1262
	13-14	**.315** (.295-.337)	**.320** (.290-.340)	**.580** (.520-.620)	**.940** (.840-1.08)	**1.48** (1.15-1.92)	1318
Females	11-12	**.316** (.282-.355)	**.320** (.290-.360)	**.580** (.500-.660)	**.970** (.830-1.14)	**1.31** (1.15-1.41)	1242
	13-14	**.245** (.222-.269)	**.260** (.240-.280)	**.460** (.430-.480)	**.720** (.670-.790)	**1.00** (.870-1.16)	1346
Race/ethnicity							
Mexican Americans	11-12	**.372** (.320-.431)	**.380** (.320-.480)	**.670** (.550-.780)	**1.17** (.820-1.58)	**1.67** (1.17-2.18)	317
	13-14	**.277** (.240-.319)	**.290** (.250-.320)	**.480** (.440-.580)	**.890** (.690-1.15)	**1.21** (.930-1.97)	453
Non-Hispanic blacks	11-12	**.431** (.385-.483)	**.440** (.370-.520)	**.730** (.660-.830)	**1.15** (1.00-1.39)	**1.64** (1.39-1.87)	669
	13-14	**.371** (.320-.429)	**.380** (.310-.440)	**.620** (.530-.730)	**1.09** (.830-1.34)	**1.45** (1.24-1.72)	581
Non-Hispanic whites	11-12	**.346** (.311-.385)	**.360** (.330-.390)	**.610** (.540-.700)	**1.02** (.920-1.16)	**1.38** (1.14-1.85)	820
	13-14	**.267** (.245-.290)	**.280** (.260-.300)	**.500** (.450-.540)	**.820** (.730-.920)	**1.16** (.950-1.60)	985
All Hispanics	11-12	**.372** (.327-.423)	**.370** (.320-.420)	**.670** (.590-.750)	**1.15** (.950-1.31)	**1.51** (1.18-2.13)	573
	13-14	**.270** (.239-.305)	**.280** (.240-.320)	**.480** (.440-.540)	**.820** (.690-.930)	**1.17** (.940-1.47)	701
Asians	11-12	**.383** (.341-.429)	**.380** (.350-.460)	**.690** (.620-.790)	**1.15** (.950-1.32)	**1.38** (1.21-1.72)	353
	13-14	**.257** (.230-.287)	**.290** (.240-.350)	**.470** (.410-.510)	**.710** (.560-.790)	**.890** (.750-.980)	292

Limit of detection (LOD, see Data Analysis section) for Survey year 11-12 and 13-14 are 0.08 and 0.03.

Biomonitoring Summary

http://www.cdc.gov/biomonitoring/Lead_BiomonitoringSummary.html

Factsheet

http://www.cdc.gov/biomonitoring/Lead_FactSheet.html

Source: *Centers for Disease Control & Prevention, Fourth National Report on Human Exposure to Environmental Chemicals, Updated Tables, January 2017*

Urinary Lead (creatinine corrected) (1999 – 2010)

Geometric mean and selected percentiles of urine concentrations (in µg/g of creatinine) for the U.S. population from the National Health and Nutrition Examination Survey.

	Survey years	Geometric mean (95% conf. interval)	50th Percentile (95% conf. interval)	75th Percentile (95% conf. interval)	90th Percentile (95% conf. interval)	95th Percentile (95% conf. interval)	Sample size
Total	99-00	**.721** (.700-.742)	**.701** (.677-.725)	**1.11** (1.05-1.15)	**1.70** (1.62-1.85)	**2.38** (2.22-2.79)	2465
	01-02	**.639** (.603-.677)	**.635** (.588-.676)	**1.03** (.963-1.08)	**1.52** (1.43-1.61)	**2.03** (1.89-2.22)	2689
	03-04	**.632** (.603-.662)	**.622** (.594-.655)	**.979** (.920-1.03)	**1.49** (1.33-1.64)	**1.97** (1.73-2.26)	2558
	05-06	**.546** (.520-.573)	**.530** (.510-.560)	**.860** (.810-.900)	**1.27** (1.15-1.37)	**1.71** (1.50-1.89)	2576
	07-08	**.514** (.482-.548)	**.500** (.460-.530)	**.800** (.720-.880)	**1.30** (1.23-1.42)	**1.85** (1.73-1.96)	2627
	09-10	**.488** (.466-.512)	**.470** (.440-.500)	**.760** (.710-.810)	**1.16** (1.08-1.28)	**1.53** (1.41-1.62)	2848
Age group							
6-11 years	99-00	**1.17** (.975-1.41)	**1.06** (.918-1.22)	**1.55** (1.22-1.97)	**2.71** (1.67-4.66)	**4.66** (1.97-18.0)	340
	01-02	**.918** (.841-1.00)	**.870** (.800-.933)	**1.27** (1.12-1.43)	**2.33** (1.59-3.64)	**3.64** (1.89-5.56)	368
	03-04	**.926** (.812-1.06)	**.914** (.781-1.03)	**1.45** (1.17-1.72)	**2.14** (1.62-3.47)	**3.47** (2.19-5.31)	290
	05-06	**.628** (.563-.701)	**.590** (.530-.680)	**.870** (.770-.940)	**1.29** (1.03-1.82)	**1.96** (1.32-2.42)	355
	07-08	**.643** (.543-.763)	**.630** (.530-.730)	**1.02** (.770-1.24)	**1.50** (1.24-2.02)	**2.04** (1.70-2.58)	394
	09-10	**.604** (.551-.662)	**.580** (.520-.650)	**.870** (.780-1.00)	**1.32** (1.09-1.51)	**1.60** (1.38-1.75)	378
12-19 years	99-00	**.496** (.460-.535)	**.469** (.408-.508)	**.709** (.655-.828)	**1.11** (.981-1.28)	**1.65** (1.15-2.79)	719
	01-02	**.404** (.380-.428)	**.375** (.342-.400)	**.603** (.541-.702)	**.990** (.882-1.18)	**1.41** (1.07-1.63)	762
	03-04	**.432** (.404-.461)	**.404** (.383-.436)	**.623** (.551-.730)	**.938** (.828-1.06)	**1.23** (1.09-1.35)	725
	05-06	**.363** (.333-.395)	**.340** (.310-.360)	**.510** (.460-.600)	**.800** (.690-.930)	**1.07** (.940-1.23)	701
	07-08	**.302** (.270-.337)	**.290** (.250-.340)	**.430** (.400-.490)	**.670** (.550-.790)	**.900** (.700-1.09)	376
	09-10	**.299** (.273-.328)	**.290** (.260-.320)	**.420** (.370-.490)	**.620** (.550-.760)	**.880** (.740-1.01)	451
20 years and older	99-00	**.720** (.683-.758)	**.712** (.667-.739)	**1.10** (1.02-1.18)	**1.69** (1.53-1.87)	**2.31** (2.15-2.62)	1406
	01-02	**.658** (.617-.703)	**.652** (.608-.702)	**1.05** (.992-1.11)	**1.51** (1.40-1.61)	**2.00** (1.85-2.19)	1559
	03-04	**.641** (.606-.679)	**.633** (.605-.670)	**.988** (.917-1.04)	**1.47** (1.28-1.63)	**1.94** (1.72-2.12)	1543
	05-06	**.573** (.548-.600)	**.570** (.530-.600)	**.890** (.850-.960)	**1.32** (1.22-1.41)	**1.77** (1.53-1.94)	1520
	07-08	**.545** (.513-.579)	**.530** (.490-.570)	**.840** (.760-.910)	**1.36** (1.27-1.49)	**1.92** (1.78-2.08)	1857
	09-10	**.514** (.489-.539)	**.500** (.460-.530)	**.790** (.730-.840)	**1.22** (1.10-1.35)	**1.57** (1.46-1.71)	2019
Gender							
Males	99-00	**.720** (.679-.763)	**.693** (.645-.734)	**1.10** (.992-1.22)	**1.68** (1.50-2.09)	**2.43** (2.15-3.03)	1227
	01-02	**.639** (.607-.673)	**.638** (.586-.686)	**1.01** (.957-1.08)	**1.55** (1.41-1.61)	**2.06** (1.88-2.43)	1334
	03-04	**.615** (.588-.644)	**.593** (.561-.639)	**.914** (.862-.977)	**1.44** (1.25-1.53)	**2.00** (1.71-2.28)	1281
	05-06	**.551** (.522-.582)	**.530** (.510-.580)	**.830** (.770-.910)	**1.25** (1.13-1.39)	**1.77** (1.42-2.20)	1271
	07-08	**.501** (.471-.534)	**.490** (.450-.530)	**.750** (.700-.810)	**1.29** (1.15-1.49)	**1.88** (1.71-1.98)	1327
	09-10	**.481** (.458-.505)	**.450** (.430-.490)	**.740** (.690-.800)	**1.15** (1.04-1.29)	**1.56** (1.37-1.70)	1398
Females	99-00	**.722** (.681-.765)	**.707** (.667-.746)	**1.11** (1.05-1.18)	**1.74** (1.50-2.02)	**2.38** (2.03-2.88)	1238
	01-02	**.639** (.594-.688)	**.625** (.571-.682)	**1.03** (.946-1.11)	**1.50** (1.39-1.61)	**1.98** (1.85-2.15)	1355
	03-04	**.648** (.601-.698)	**.649** (.604-.718)	**1.03** (.938-1.10)	**1.56** (1.34-1.73)	**1.96** (1.72-2.20)	1277
	05-06	**.541** (.507-.577)	**.530** (.500-.580)	**.880** (.820-.940)	**1.28** (1.12-1.41)	**1.64** (1.38-1.91)	1305
	07-08	**.527** (.489-.568)	**.500** (.470-.550)	**.840** (.740-.960)	**1.34** (1.23-1.47)	**1.79** (1.56-2.08)	1300
	09-10	**.495** (.466-.526)	**.480** (.450-.520)	**.780** (.710-.830)	**1.20** (1.08-1.32)	**1.52** (1.39-1.62)	1450

Biomonitoring Summary

http://www.cdc.gov/biomonitoring/Lead_BiomonitoringSummary.html

Factsheet

http://www.cdc.gov/biomonitoring/Lead_FactSheet.html

Source: *Centers for Disease Control & Prevention, Fourth National Report on Human Exposure to Environmental Chemicals, Updated Tables, January 2017*

Urinary Lead (creatinine corrected) (1999 – 2010)

Geometric mean and selected percentiles of urine concentrations (in µg/g of creatinine) for the U.S. population from the National Health and Nutrition Examination Survey.

	Survey years	Geometric mean (95% conf. interval)	50th Percentile (95% conf. interval)	75th Percentile (95% conf. interval)	90th Percentile (95% conf. interval)	95th Percentile (95% conf. interval)	Sample size
Race/ethnicity							
Mexican Americans	99-00	**.940** (.876-1.01)	**.887** (.796-1.03)	**1.43** (1.37-1.58)	**2.38** (2.08-2.77)	**3.46** (2.78-4.18)	884
	01-02	**.810** (.731-.898)	**.774** (.702-.893)	**1.29** (1.09-1.44)	**2.05** (1.75-2.50)	**2.78** (2.56-3.33)	682
	03-04	**.755** (.681-.838)	**.708** (.612-.851)	**1.18** (1.09-1.31)	**1.86** (1.50-2.26)	**2.31** (1.98-2.92)	618
	05-06	**.686** (.638-.737)	**.680** (.620-.740)	**1.00** (.930-1.13)	**1.63** (1.39-1.88)	**2.20** (1.77-3.20)	652
	07-08	**.607** (.514-.717)	**.590** (.500-.690)	**.970** (.770-1.19)	**1.56** (1.25-2.07)	**2.20** (1.78-2.46)	515
	09-10	**.573** (.526-.623)	**.540** (.470-.610)	**.950** (.780-1.06)	**1.59** (1.41-1.82)	**2.02** (1.82-2.40)	613
Non-Hispanic blacks	99-00	**.722** (.659-.790)	**.671** (.583-.753)	**1.11** (.988-1.20)	**2.00** (1.56-2.51)	**2.83** (2.20-3.88)	568
	01-02	**.644** (.559-.742)	**.608** (.510-.710)	**.962** (.853-1.20)	**1.79** (1.36-2.33)	**2.75** (2.04-3.98)	667
	03-04	**.609** (.529-.701)	**.569** (.492-.698)	**.900** (.793-1.03)	**1.48** (1.11-1.97)	**2.24** (1.65-2.88)	723
	05-06	**.483** (.459-.508)	**.470** (.440-.490)	**.740** (.670-.820)	**1.18** (1.06-1.29)	**1.60** (1.37-1.85)	692
	07-08	**.452** (.414-.492)	**.440** (.400-.490)	**.710** (.610-.780)	**1.13** (.930-1.33)	**1.57** (1.21-1.88)	589
	09-10	**.444** (.417-.473)	**.420** (.390-.470)	**.680** (.600-.740)	**1.07** (.940-1.18)	**1.51** (1.18-1.65)	544
Non-Hispanic whites	99-00	**.696** (.668-.725)	**.677** (.645-.718)	**1.07** (.997-1.14)	**1.66** (1.50-1.83)	**2.31** (1.94-2.82)	822
	01-02	**.615** (.579-.654)	**.621** (.571-.667)	**1.00** (.933-1.07)	**1.46** (1.37-1.52)	**1.88** (1.62-2.03)	1132
	03-04	**.623** (.592-.655)	**.618** (.587-.657)	**.971** (.914-1.03)	**1.44** (1.25-1.61)	**1.85** (1.64-2.10)	1074
	05-06	**.541** (.500-.585)	**.530** (.490-.580)	**.850** (.790-.920)	**1.24** (1.12-1.37)	**1.62** (1.37-1.94)	1041
	07-08	**.506** (.466-.550)	**.490** (.460-.540)	**.790** (.700-.880)	**1.27** (1.15-1.42)	**1.81** (1.59-1.96)	1095
	09-10	**.482** (.448-.518)	**.460** (.430-.500)	**.740** (.690-.820)	**1.15** (1.01-1.30)	**1.46** (1.32-1.59)	1225

Biomonitoring Summary

http://www.cdc.gov/biomonitoring/Lead_BiomonitoringSummary.html

Factsheet

http://www.cdc.gov/biomonitoring/Lead_FactSheet.html

Source: *Centers for Disease Control & Prevention, Fourth National Report on Human Exposure to Environmental Chemicals, Updated Tables, January 2017*

Urinary Lead (creatinine corrected) (2011 - 2014)

Geometric mean and selected percentiles of urine concentrations (in µg/g of creatinine) for the U.S. population from the National Health and Nutrition Examination Survey.

	Survey years	Geometric mean (95% conf. interval)	50th Percentile (95% conf. interval)	75th Percentile (95% conf. interval)	90th Percentile (95% conf. interval)	95th Percentile (95% conf. interval)	Sample size
Total	11-12	**.409** (.380-.440)	**.396** (.374-.418)	**.634** (.583-.675)	**1.00** (.878-1.16)	**1.51** (1.24-1.71)	2502
	13-14	**.320** (.302-.339)	**.313** (.294-.331)	**.519** (.491-.554)	**.823** (.756-.907)	**1.16** (1.00-1.30)	2663
Age group							
6-11 years	11-12	**.494** (.430-.567)	**.459** (.414-.529)	**.708** (.559-.930)	**1.18** (.884-1.56)	**1.56** (1.12-2.22)	398
	13-14	**.331** (.297-.370)	**.313** (.273-.370)	**.500** (.452-.571)	**.833** (.667-.938)	**1.07** (.905-1.34)	402
12-19 years	11-12	**.247** (.218-.281)	**.224** (.206-.264)	**.385** (.317-.429)	**.541** (.440-.667)	**.667** (.513-1.03)	390
	13-14	**.182** (.160-.208)	**.169** (.142-.194)	**.276** (.225-.330)	**.457** (.339-.640)	**.640** (.438-.908)	451
20 years and older	11-12	**.433** (.402-.466)	**.414** (.389-.437)	**.660** (.619-.712)	**1.05** (.929-1.22)	**1.61** (1.28-1.87)	1714
	13-14	**.346** (.331-.363)	**.337** (.321-.353)	**.554** (.505-.592)	**.861** (.789-.935)	**1.23** (1.04-1.46)	1810
Gender							
Males	11-12	**.388** (.346-.436)	**.377** (.338-.418)	**.590** (.524-.658)	**.987** (.833-1.17)	**1.51** (1.16-1.89)	1261
	13-14	**.315** (.293-.339)	**.303** (.278-.327)	**.486** (.440-.541)	**.758** (.692-.913)	**1.16** (.956-1.58)	1317
Females	11-12	**.430** (.405-.457)	**.416** (.385-.444)	**.667** (.626-.709)	**1.03** (.905-1.21)	**1.49** (1.21-1.71)	1241
	13-14	**.325** (.303-.348)	**.325** (.308-.336)	**.545** (.500-.580)	**.864** (.785-.929)	**1.18** (.970-1.33)	1346
Race/ethnicity							
Mexican Americans	11-12	**.418** (.370-.471)	**.409** (.356-.462)	**.667** (.598-.716)	**1.05** (.822-1.25)	**1.32** (1.16-1.54)	317
	13-14	**.316** (.283-.352)	**.319** (.278-.336)	**.500** (.450-.589)	**.845** (.720-1.04)	**1.16** (.908-1.36)	453
Non-Hispanic blacks	11-12	**.335** (.301-.374)	**.316** (.269-.357)	**.529** (.464-.598)	**.906** (.770-1.07)	**1.34** (1.06-1.55)	669
	13-14	**.282** (.251-.317)	**.275** (.237-.316)	**.455** (.398-.515)	**.750** (.611-.920)	**.977** (.836-1.21)	581
Non-Hispanic whites	11-12	**.419** (.378-.465)	**.404** (.369-.439)	**.642** (.559-.722)	**.966** (.826-1.22)	**1.62** (1.16-2.00)	818
	13-14	**.329** (.306-.353)	**.317** (.293-.344)	**.541** (.486-.589)	**.860** (.750-.933)	**1.23** (.983-1.60)	984
All Hispanics	11-12	**.416** (.377-.460)	**.401** (.366-.442)	**.641** (.561-.694)	**1.02** (.851-1.24)	**1.40** (1.16-1.65)	573
	13-14	**.301** (.276-.328)	**.307** (.269-.327)	**.473** (.438-.508)	**.795** (.667-.882)	**1.07** (.882-1.24)	701
Asians	11-12	**.511** (.453-.577)	**.512** (.440-.588)	**.829** (.706-.980)	**1.28** (1.05-1.57)	**1.61** (1.40-2.22)	353
	13-14	**.403** (.360-.451)	**.417** (.342-.503)	**.619** (.549-.708)	**.929** (.767-1.03)	**1.12** (.955-1.33)	292

Biomonitoring Summary

http://www.cdc.gov/biomonitoring/Lead_BiomonitoringSummary.html

Factsheet

http://www.cdc.gov/biomonitoring/Lead_FactSheet.html

Source: *Centers for Disease Control & Prevention, Fourth National Report on Human Exposure to Environmental Chemicals, Updated Tables, January 2017*

Blood Total Mercury (2003 – 2010)

Geometric mean and selected percentiles of blood concentrations (in µg/L) for the U.S. population from the National Health and Nutrition Examination Survey.

	Survey years	Geometric mean (95% conf. interval)	50th Percentile (95% conf. interval)	75th Percentile (95% conf. interval)	90th Percentile (95% conf. interval)	95th Percentile (95% conf. interval)	Sample size
Total	03-04	**.797** (.703-.903)	**.800** (.700-.900)	**1.70** (1.50-1.90)	**3.30** (2.90-3.90)	**4.90** (4.30-5.50)	8373
	05-06	**.863** (.787-.946)	**.830** (.760-.920)	**1.66** (1.48-1.93)	**3.20** (2.87-3.54)	**4.64** (4.17-5.25)	8407
	07-08	**.769** (.689-.859)	**.740** (.660-.830)	**1.48** (1.29-1.69)	**2.95** (2.46-3.59)	**4.64** (3.74-5.79)	8266
	09-10	**.863** (.792-.941)	**.790** (.730-.880)	**1.68** (1.49-1.91)	**3.43** (3.07-3.84)	**5.13** (4.57-5.67)	8793
Age group							
1-5 years	03-04	**.326** (.285-.372)	**.300** (.300-.300)	**.500** (.500-.700)	**1.00** (.800-1.60)	**1.80** (1.30-2.50)	911
	05-06	*	**< LOD**	**.500** (.470-.550)	**.940** (.820-1.24)	**1.43** (1.25-1.59)	968
	07-08	*	**< LOD**	**.440** (.380-.540)	**.830** (.620-1.12)	**1.32** (.960-2.40)	817
	09-10	*	**< LOD**	**.490** (.430-.590)	**.890** (.740-1.08)	**1.30** (1.08-1.52)	836
6-11 years	03-04	**.419** (.363-.484)	**.400** (.400-.500)	**.700** (.700-.900)	**1.30** (1.00-1.60)	**1.90** (1.40-3.50)	856
	05-06	*	**.410** (.330-.460)	**.740** (.630-1.00)	**1.43** (1.21-1.87)	**2.34** (1.53-3.42)	934
	07-08	*	**.380** (.340-.440)	**.700** (.600-.790)	**1.21** (.970-1.36)	**1.56** (1.34-1.80)	1011
	09-10	*	**.360** (<LOD-.400)	**.670** (.590-.770)	**1.22** (1.05-1.45)	**1.88** (1.43-2.61)	1009
12-19 years	03-04	**.490** (.418-.574)	**.500** (.400-.600)	**1.00** (.800-1.20)	**1.80** (1.40-2.30)	**2.60** (2.10-3.30)	2081
	05-06	**.513** (.461-.570)	**.460** (.390-.530)	**.850** (.740-1.04)	**1.66** (1.31-1.98)	**2.41** (2.12-2.90)	1996
	07-08	**.469** (.426-.516)	**.440** (.390-.490)	**.800** (.670-.970)	**1.55** (1.30-1.72)	**2.05** (1.77-2.34)	1074
	09-10	**.534** (.473-.602)	**.450** (.370-.540)	**.910** (.770-1.11)	**2.04** (1.53-2.55)	**3.01** (2.53-3.63)	1183
20 years and older	03-04	**.979** (.860-1.12)	**1.00** (.800-1.10)	**2.00** (1.70-2.30)	**3.80** (3.20-4.40)	**5.40** (4.60-6.70)	4525
	05-06	**1.06** (.967-1.15)	**1.03** (.930-1.15)	**1.98** (1.73-2.22)	**3.64** (3.33-4.01)	**5.31** (4.82-5.67)	4509
	07-08	**.944** (.833-1.07)	**.890** (.780-1.03)	**1.73** (1.47-2.09)	**3.41** (2.82-4.17)	**5.32** (4.32-6.72)	5364
	09-10	**1.04** (.956-1.14)	**.970** (.870-1.08)	**2.00** (1.80-2.20)	**3.96** (3.55-4.27)	**5.75** (5.14-6.50)	5765
Gender							
Males	03-04	**.814** (.714-.927)	**.800** (.700-.900)	**1.80** (1.50-2.00)	**3.70** (3.20-4.30)	**5.40** (4.60-6.50)	4132
	05-06	**.864** (.783-.954)	**.810** (.720-.940)	**1.69** (1.48-2.01)	**3.30** (2.86-3.73)	**4.83** (4.08-5.45)	4092
	07-08	**.809** (.709-.923)	**.760** (.670-.850)	**1.56** (1.31-1.81)	**3.21** (2.72-4.06)	**5.16** (4.12-6.97)	4147
	09-10	**.883** (.810-.962)	**.790** (.730-.870)	**1.75** (1.54-2.02)	**3.84** (3.35-4.26)	**5.65** (5.13-6.34)	4366
Females	03-04	**.781** (.689-.886)	**.800** (.700-.900)	**1.60** (1.40-1.80)	**3.00** (2.50-3.50)	**4.40** (3.60-5.30)	4241
	05-06	**.864** (.791-.943)	**.850** (.770-.920)	**1.63** (1.44-1.89)	**3.09** (2.75-3.46)	**4.51** (4.01-5.28)	4315
	07-08	**.748** (.677-.827)	**.720** (.660-.810)	**1.42** (1.24-1.60)	**2.70** (2.27-3.27)	**3.93** (3.17-5.16)	4119
	09-10	**.845** (.772-.924)	**.800** (.720-.880)	**1.61** (1.43-1.81)	**3.13** (2.76-3.48)	**4.43** (4.04-5.11)	4427
Race/ethnicity							
Mexican Americans	03-04	**.563** (.472-.672)	**.600** (.500-.700)	**1.00** (.800-1.30)	**1.90** (1.60-2.40)	**3.00** (2.20-3.80)	2085
	05-06	**.597** (.524-.679)	**.580** (.490-.670)	**1.04** (.870-1.24)	**1.70** (1.40-2.12)	**2.58** (1.96-3.31)	2236
	07-08	**.594** (.536-.658)	**.580** (.520-.670)	**1.03** (.900-1.17)	**1.73** (1.49-2.04)	**2.48** (2.10-2.91)	1712
	09-10	**.613** (.571-.659)	**.580** (.540-.630)	**1.01** (.890-1.15)	**1.63** (1.47-1.90)	**2.45** (2.03-2.93)	1966
Non-Hispanic blacks	03-04	**.877** (.753-1.02)	**.900** (.800-1.00)	**1.60** (1.40-1.80)	**3.00** (2.30-4.00)	**4.40** (3.30-6.00)	2293
	05-06	**.823** (.697-.972)	**.800** (.670-.940)	**1.50** (1.21-1.92)	**2.72** (2.14-3.59)	**4.09** (3.22-5.16)	2193
	07-08	**.766** (.711-.825)	**.780** (.710-.830)	**1.32** (1.23-1.42)	**2.25** (1.99-2.58)	**3.42** (2.74-3.90)	1746
	09-10	**.928** (.805-1.07)	**.900** (.800-1.02)	**1.67** (1.38-1.96)	**2.93** (2.20-4.21)	**4.56** (3.34-6.69)	1593
Non-Hispanic whites	03-04	**.776** (.655-.919)	**.800** (.700-.900)	**1.70** (1.40-2.00)	**3.20** (2.60-3.90)	**4.70** (4.00-5.60)	3478
	05-06	**.891** (.801-.992)	**.870** (.770-1.00)	**1.74** (1.50-2.10)	**3.37** (2.88-3.76)	**4.76** (4.18-5.37)	3310
	07-08	**.743** (.651-.847)	**.720** (.620-.820)	**1.43** (1.18-1.70)	**2.79** (2.33-3.41)	**4.18** (3.57-4.83)	3461
	09-10	**.856** (.766-.957)	**.790** (.690-.920)	**1.70** (1.46-1.98)	**3.43** (2.94-3.94)	**4.92** (4.30-5.65)	3760

Limit of detection (LOD, see Data Analysis section) for Survey years 03-04, 05-06, 07-08 and 09-10 are 0.2, 0.33, 0.33, and 0.33 respectively.
< LOD means less than the limit of detection, which may vary for some chemicals by year and by individual sample.
* Not calculated: proportion of results below limit of detection was too high to provide a valid result.

Biomonitoring Summary

http://www.cdc.gov/biomonitoring/Mercury_BiomonitoringSummary.html

Factsheet

http://www.cdc.gov/biomonitoring/Mercury_FactSheet.html

Source: *Centers for Disease Control & Prevention, Fourth National Report on Human Exposure to Environmental Chemicals, Updated Tables, January 2017*

Blood Total Mercury (2011 - 2014)

Geometric mean and selected percentiles of blood concentrations (in µg/L) for the U.S. population from the National Health and Nutrition Examination Survey.

	Survey years	Geometric mean (95% conf. interval)	50th Percentile (95% conf. interval)	75th Percentile (95% conf. interval)	90th Percentile (95% conf. interval)	95th Percentile (95% conf. interval)	Sample size
Total	11-12	**.703** (.617-.801)	**.640** (.580-.730)	**1.38** (1.14-1.72)	**2.87** (2.39-3.62)	**4.40** (3.50-5.71)	7920
	13-14	**.683** (.621-.751)	**.620** (.540-.690)	**1.29** (1.14-1.46)	**2.65** (2.32-3.08)	**4.36** (3.65-4.97)	5215
Age group							
1-5 years	11-12	**.262** (.237-.291)	**.250** (.220-.270)	**.390** (.340-.450)	**.680** (.540-.880)	**.990** (.790-1.21)	713
	13-14	*	< LOD	**.410** (.370-.450)	**.810** (.710-.990)	**1.21** (1.05-1.48)	818
6-11 years	11-12	**.330** (.287-.379)	**.320** (.280-.360)	**.530** (.480-.600)	**.930** (.780-1.20)	**1.40** (1.02-2.17)	1048
	13-14	*	**.300** (<LOD-.360)	**.570** (.470-.680)	**1.12** (.980-1.36)	**1.62** (1.38-2.19)	1075
12-19 years	11-12	**.411** (.355-.476)	**.370** (.320-.450)	**.680** (.590-.800)	**1.32** (1.08-1.75)	**2.25** (1.46-2.87)	1129
	13-14	**.412** (.367-.463)	**.350** (.310-.420)	**.630** (.530-.750)	**1.20** (.900-1.67)	**1.87** (1.30-2.38)	627
20 years and older	11-12	**.863** (.753-.990)	**.790** (.690-.940)	**1.68** (1.36-2.12)	**3.35** (2.71-4.31)	**5.02** (3.94-6.96)	5030
	13-14	**.814** (.736-.900)	**.740** (.650-.850)	**1.54** (1.36-1.71)	**3.08** (2.73-3.56)	**4.88** (4.36-5.21)	2695
Gender							
Males	11-12	**.712** (.623-.815)	**.650** (.570-.730)	**1.40** (1.17-1.72)	**3.00** (2.44-3.91)	**4.94** (3.50-6.79)	3968
	13-14	**.688** (.617-.767)	**.620** (.530-.720)	**1.30** (1.12-1.54)	**2.76** (2.36-3.34)	**4.52** (3.65-5.23)	2587
Females	11-12	**.694** (.609-.791)	**.640** (.580-.740)	**1.36** (1.09-1.75)	**2.81** (2.28-3.50)	**4.03** (3.29-5.08)	3952
	13-14	**.678** (.617-.745)	**.610** (.530-.700)	**1.27** (1.14-1.42)	**2.56** (2.17-3.08)	**4.15** (3.37-4.93)	2628
Race/ethnicity							
Mexican Americans	11-12	**.483** (.424-.550)	**.480** (.400-.560)	**.810** (.720-.900)	**1.44** (1.16-1.63)	**1.90** (1.57-2.19)	1077
	13-14	**.487** (.433-.547)	**.430** (.390-.510)	**.760** (.690-.870)	**1.41** (1.14-1.69)	**1.98** (1.70-2.38)	969
Non-Hispanic blacks	11-12	**.679** (.542-.852)	**.630** (.500-.790)	**1.24** (.880-1.72)	**2.45** (1.84-3.14)	**3.80** (2.70-5.37)	2195
	13-14	**.699** (.614-.796)	**.650** (.570-.750)	**1.20** (1.08-1.40)	**2.30** (1.65-2.96)	**3.34** (2.35-5.93)	1119
Non-Hispanic whites	11-12	**.688** (.582-.813)	**.630** (.550-.750)	**1.38** (1.09-1.82)	**2.83** (2.18-3.82)	**4.25** (3.02-6.24)	2493
	13-14	**.672** (.598-.755)	**.620** (.520-.720)	**1.30** (1.12-1.51)	**2.61** (2.18-3.08)	**4.15** (3.35-4.98)	1848
All Hispanics	11-12	**.612** (.527-.710)	**.590** (.490-.700)	**1.08** (.890-1.33)	**1.96** (1.60-2.68)	**3.03** (2.37-3.86)	1931
	13-14	**.551** (.486-.624)	**.490** (.420-.580)	**.910** (.820-1.10)	**1.76** (1.44-2.12)	**2.59** (2.06-3.14)	1481
Asians	11-12	**1.86** (1.58-2.19)	**2.30** (1.84-2.64)	**4.32** (3.71-5.21)	**7.71** (6.38-8.79)	**10.3** (8.85-12.0)	1005
	13-14	**1.72** (1.46-2.03)	**1.77** (1.42-2.26)	**3.92** (3.35-4.55)	**7.78** (6.39-9.16)	**9.99** (9.16-13.7)	510

Limit of detection (LOD, see Data Analysis section) for Survey year 11-12 and 13-14 are 0.16 and 0.28.
< LOD means less than the limit of detection, which may vary for some chemicals by year and by individual sample.
* Not calculated: proportion of results below limit of detection was too high to provide a valid result.

Biomonitoring Summary

http://www.cdc.gov/biomonitoring/Mercury_BiomonitoringSummary.html

Factsheet

http://www.cdc.gov/biomonitoring/Mercury_FactSheet.html

Source: *Centers for Disease Control & Prevention, Fourth National Report on Human Exposure to Environmental Chemicals, Updated Tables, January 2017*

Urinary Mercury (2003 – 2010)

Geometric mean and selected percentiles of urine concentrations (in µg/L) for the U.S. population from the National Health and Nutrition Examination Survey.

	Survey years	Geometric mean (95% conf. interval)	50th Percentile (95% conf. interval)	75th Percentile (95% conf. interval)	90th Percentile (95% conf. interval)	95th Percentile (95% conf. interval)	Sample size
Total	03-04	**.447** (.406-.492)	**.420** (.360-.480)	**1.00** (.870-1.14)	**2.08** (1.78-2.42)	**3.19** (2.76-3.55)	2538
	05-06	**.468** (.426-.514)	**.460** (.410-.510)	**1.03** (.900-1.12)	**2.11** (1.88-2.36)	**2.94** (2.58-3.26)	2578
	07-08	**.443** (.408-.482)	**.440** (.400-.470)	**.880** (.760-1.00)	**1.74** (1.62-1.96)	**2.66** (2.29-3.08)	2634
	09-10	*	**.400** (.360-.450)	**.850** (.770-.910)	**1.53** (1.30-1.81)	**2.42** (2.07-2.72)	2865
Age group							
6-11 years	03-04	**.254** (.213-.304)	**.200** (.160-.250)	**.440** (.330-.580)	**1.16** (.610-1.61)	**1.96** (1.13-2.97)	287
	05-06	**.333** (.267-.416)	**.320** (.250-.390)	**.650** (.470-.840)	**1.32** (.930-1.88)	**2.18** (1.28-3.40)	355
	07-08	**.301** (.260-.347)	**.290** (.230-.340)	**.520** (.430-.620)	**1.03** (.770-1.23)	**1.87** (1.03-3.48)	398
	09-10	*	**.260** (.220-.320)	**.510** (.430-.620)	**1.03** (.730-1.31)	**1.58** (1.18-1.88)	379
12-19 years	03-04	**.358** (.313-.408)	**.330** (.290-.370)	**.700** (.530-.840)	**1.60** (1.14-2.52)	**2.93** (1.88-3.66)	722
	05-06	**.372** (.286-.486)	**.350** (.270-.470)	**.740** (.580-.920)	**1.61** (.970-2.81)	**2.59** (1.40-4.45)	703
	07-08	**.364** (.326-.406)	**.380** (.320-.450)	**.590** (.550-.650)	**1.24** (.830-1.71)	**1.82** (1.41-2.29)	375
	09-10	*	**.290** (.230-.360)	**.530** (.470-.630)	**1.09** (.890-1.31)	**1.73** (1.28-2.31)	455
20 years and older	03-04	**.495** (.442-.555)	**.480** (.410-.570)	**1.12** (.930-1.29)	**2.20** (1.85-2.65)	**3.33** (2.76-3.88)	1529
	05-06	**.505** (.468-.545)	**.510** (.460-.560)	**1.11** (1.04-1.16)	**2.23** (1.97-2.50)	**3.11** (2.64-3.37)	1520
	07-08	**.477** (.435-.523)	**.470** (.430-.520)	**.970** (.850-1.10)	**1.89** (1.69-2.20)	**2.82** (2.33-3.56)	1861
	09-10	*	**.450** (.390-.510)	**.890** (.810-1.00)	**1.66** (1.40-2.01)	**2.53** (2.21-2.84)	2031
Gender							
Males	03-04	**.433** (.405-.463)	**.400** (.350-.460)	**.940** (.840-1.05)	**1.88** (1.63-2.18)	**2.68** (2.34-3.05)	1266
	05-06	**.464** (.411-.523)	**.450** (.400-.520)	**.980** (.860-1.11)	**2.03** (1.57-2.48)	**3.00** (2.48-3.37)	1270
	07-08	**.457** (.417-.501)	**.460** (.400-.520)	**.880** (.780-1.01)	**1.68** (1.53-1.77)	**2.40** (2.11-2.76)	1326
	09-10	*	**.410** (.340-.480)	**.860** (.750-.950)	**1.46** (1.29-1.66)	**2.21** (1.93-2.53)	1404
Females	03-04	**.460** (.396-.534)	**.430** (.330-.530)	**1.07** (.870-1.28)	**2.26** (1.77-2.90)	**3.54** (2.76-4.31)	1272
	05-06	**.472** (.424-.525)	**.470** (.390-.550)	**1.07** (.900-1.19)	**2.14** (1.84-2.50)	**2.89** (2.60-3.38)	1308
	07-08	**.431** (.388-.478)	**.430** (.380-.460)	**.870** (.710-1.05)	**1.88** (1.55-2.38)	**2.92** (2.27-4.17)	1308
	09-10	*	**.390** (.360-.450)	**.840** (.730-.940)	**1.61** (1.29-2.03)	**2.61** (2.16-3.12)	1461
Race/ethnicity							
Mexican Americans	03-04	**.416** (.340-.509)	**.360** (.280-.430)	**.960** (.700-1.23)	**2.19** (1.39-3.24)	**3.16** (1.99-6.30)	619
	05-06	**.451** (.369-.551)	**.420** (.310-.560)	**1.01** (.780-1.25)	**2.22** (1.48-2.64)	**3.00** (2.27-4.01)	651
	07-08	**.409** (.349-.480)	**.370** (.330-.450)	**.780** (.700-.950)	**1.82** (1.26-1.97)	**2.55** (1.87-3.08)	514
	09-10	*	**.350** (.280-.430)	**.670** (.520-.890)	**1.53** (1.06-1.84)	**2.29** (1.81-2.76)	615
Non-Hispanic blacks	03-04	**.476** (.413-.549)	**.430** (.360-.530)	**.890** (.770-1.00)	**1.96** (1.60-2.31)	**3.09** (2.03-4.89)	713
	05-06	**.453** (.384-.533)	**.450** (.380-.550)	**.890** (.710-1.13)	**1.78** (1.34-2.29)	**2.57** (2.21-3.15)	691
	07-08	**.478** (.411-.556)	**.460** (.380-.540)	**.910** (.770-1.06)	**1.85** (1.42-2.41)	**2.76** (1.97-4.19)	589
	09-10	*	**.410** (.340-.490)	**.840** (.650-1.08)	**1.66** (1.34-1.95)	**2.64** (1.88-3.30)	546
Non-Hispanic whites	03-04	**.441** (.382-.509)	**.420** (.330-.520)	**1.01** (.840-1.23)	**2.08** (1.67-2.46)	**3.24** (2.67-3.60)	1066
	05-06	**.459** (.409-.513)	**.440** (.400-.510)	**1.00** (.860-1.12)	**2.07** (1.77-2.40)	**2.81** (2.47-3.37)	1044
	07-08	**.431** (.378-.493)	**.430** (.380-.480)	**.880** (.700-1.07)	**1.71** (1.50-2.18)	**2.70** (2.18-3.59)	1100
	09-10	*	**.390** (.330-.470)	**.850** (.750-.950)	**1.52** (1.26-2.01)	**2.42** (1.93-2.85)	1225

Limit of detection (LOD, see Data Analysis section) for Survey years 03-04, 05-06, 07-08 and 09-10 are 0.14, 0.11, 0.08, and 0.08 respectively.
* Not calculated: proportion of results below limit of detection was too high to provide a valid result.

Biomonitoring Summary

http://www.cdc.gov/biomonitoring/Mercury_BiomonitoringSummary.html

Factsheet

http://www.cdc.gov/biomonitoring/Mercury_FactSheet.html

Source: *Centers for Disease Control & Prevention, Fourth National Report on Human Exposure to Environmental Chemicals, Updated Tables, January 2017*

Urinary Mercury (2011 - 2014)

Geometric mean and selected percentiles of urine concentrations (in µg/L) for the U.S. population from the National Health and Nutrition Examination Survey.

	Survey years	Geometric mean (95% conf. interval)	50th Percentile (95% conf. interval)	75th Percentile (95% conf. interval)	90th Percentile (95% conf. interval)	95th Percentile (95% conf. interval)	Sample size
Total	11-12	**.324** (.285-.368)	**.320** (.280-.370)	**.660** (.580-.770)	**1.37** (1.15-1.59)	**1.83** (1.62-2.14)	2507
	13-14	**.246** (.221-.273)	**.200** (.170-.240)	**.470** (.400-.570)	**1.07** (.900-1.22)	**1.64** (1.35-1.96)	2666
Age group							
6-11 years	11-12	**.241** (.206-.283)	**.220** (.190-.270)	**.450** (.390-.530)	**.930** (.680-1.36)	**1.37** (.990-2.03)	401
	13-14	*	**< LOD**	**.220** (.150-.310)	**.560** (.340-.840)	**.890** (.640-1.10)	401
12-19 years	11-12	**.257** (.212-.312)	**.270** (.220-.340)	**.490** (.390-.600)	**.840** (.650-1.24)	**1.31** (.920-1.75)	390
	13-14	*	**< LOD**	**.240** (.200-.310)	**.560** (.400-.860)	**1.02** (.610-1.81)	452
20 years and older	11-12	**.346** (.303-.396)	**.340** (.290-.400)	**.720** (.620-.850)	**1.49** (1.20-1.67)	**1.93** (1.67-2.29)	1716
	13-14	**.274** (.246-.305)	**.240** (.200-.280)	**.540** (.450-.630)	**1.16** (1.00-1.33)	**1.76** (1.44-2.04)	1813
Gender							
Males	11-12	**.342** (.293-.399)	**.330** (.290-.380)	**.670** (.580-.810)	**1.34** (1.03-1.67)	**1.91** (1.54-2.51)	1260
	13-14	**.243** (.219-.268)	**.200** (.170-.220)	**.480** (.390-.600)	**1.07** (.840-1.33)	**1.55** (1.28-1.96)	1319
Females	11-12	**.307** (.262-.360)	**.300** (.250-.360)	**.660** (.540-.770)	**1.37** (1.17-1.54)	**1.82** (1.54-2.14)	1247
	13-14	**.249** (.218-.284)	**.210** (.170-.260)	**.470** (.390-.570)	**1.07** (.820-1.27)	**1.75** (1.25-2.26)	1347
Race/ethnicity							
Mexican Americans	11-12	**.301** (.261-.348)	**.300** (.200-.400)	**.620** (.510-.680)	**1.25** (.910-1.53)	**1.75** (1.32-2.25)	317
	13-14	**.229** (.198-.265)	**.160** (.150-.210)	**.450** (.300-.620)	**1.12** (.780-1.35)	**1.47** (.970-2.38)	454
Non-Hispanic blacks	11-12	**.360** (.316-.410)	**.360** (.320-.400)	**.670** (.570-.800)	**1.33** (1.06-1.60)	**1.99** (1.48-3.06)	671
	13-14	**.279** (.228-.340)	**.250** (.190-.320)	**.530** (.400-.690)	**1.10** (.900-1.49)	**1.82** (1.11-2.48)	580
Non-Hispanic whites	11-12	**.308** (.260-.365)	**.290** (.260-.360)	**.630** (.510-.810)	**1.37** (1.09-1.64)	**1.77** (1.49-2.14)	819
	13-14	**.240** (.211-.271)	**.200** (.160-.230)	**.460** (.370-.580)	**1.06** (.840-1.24)	**1.64** (1.24-2.04)	988
All Hispanics	11-12	**.330** (.299-.364)	**.330** (.270-.390)	**.680** (.610-.760)	**1.30** (1.15-1.53)	**1.98** (1.61-2.42)	574
	13-14	**.239** (.207-.276)	**.180** (.150-.240)	**.460** (.360-.620)	**1.14** (.800-1.35)	**1.57** (1.24-2.15)	702
Asians	11-12	**.430** (.351-.527)	**.450** (.330-.580)	**.910** (.750-1.12)	**1.69** (1.31-2.06)	**2.41** (1.77-3.53)	355
	13-14	**.313** (.269-.363)	**.270** (.220-.340)	**.620** (.520-.710)	**1.18** (.890-1.66)	**1.78** (1.20-3.10)	291

Limit of detection (LOD, see Data Analysis section) for Survey year 11-12 and 13-14 are 0.05 and 0.13.
< LOD means less than the limit of detection, which may vary for some chemicals by year and by individual sample.
* Not calculated: proportion of results below limit of detection was too high to provide a valid result.

Biomonitoring Summary

http://www.cdc.gov/biomonitoring/Mercury_BiomonitoringSummary.html

Factsheet

http://www.cdc.gov/biomonitoring/Mercury_FactSheet.html

Source: *Centers for Disease Control & Prevention, Fourth National Report on Human Exposure to Environmental Chemicals, Updated Tables, January 2017*

Urinary Mercury (creatinine corrected) (2003 – 2010)

Geometric mean and selected percentiles of urine concentrations (in µg/g of creatinine) for the U.S. population from the National Health and Nutrition Examination Survey.

	Survey years	Geometric mean (95% conf. interval)	50th Percentile (95% conf. interval)	75th Percentile (95% conf. interval)	90th Percentile (95% conf. interval)	95th Percentile (95% conf. interval)	Sample size
Total	03-04	**.443** (.404-.486)	**.447** (.392-.498)	**.909** (.785-1.00)	**1.65** (1.40-1.86)	**2.35** (1.88-2.85)	2537
	05-06	**.460** (.414-.511)	**.450** (.410-.510)	**.870** (.790-1.00)	**1.63** (1.44-1.75)	**2.26** (2.12-2.50)	2578
	07-08	**.462** (.425-.502)	**.450** (.400-.490)	**.820** (.750-.960)	**1.57** (1.38-1.73)	**2.32** (2.00-2.89)	2634
	09-10	*	**.409** (.367-.459)	**.793** (.691-.893)	**1.43** (1.24-1.67)	**2.09** (1.79-2.39)	2865
Age group							
6-11 years	03-04	**.297** (.246-.358)	**.276** (.208-.347)	**.485** (.391-.630)	**1.25** (.667-1.79)	**1.79** (1.11-2.61)	286
	05-06	**.411** (.323-.524)	**.390** (.290-.500)	**.710** (.510-.960)	**1.30** (.990-2.12)	**2.55** (1.38-3.50)	355
	07-08	**.393** (.351-.440)	**.350** (.300-.440)	**.630** (.540-.770)	**1.15** (.860-1.50)	**1.68** (1.18-2.99)	398
	09-10	*	**.357** (.306-.406)	**.632** (.500-.750)	**1.04** (.863-1.26)	**1.62** (1.19-1.98)	379
12-19 years	03-04	**.255** (.225-.289)	**.217** (.196-.275)	**.464** (.376-.535)	**1.06** (.714-1.39)	**1.67** (1.13-2.03)	722
	05-06	**.286** (.230-.356)	**.260** (.200-.320)	**.500** (.380-.660)	**1.09** (.660-1.70)	**1.76** (1.11-2.67)	703
	07-08	**.284** (.251-.320)	**.280** (.230-.300)	**.500** (.400-.550)	**.890** (.620-1.08)	**1.18** (.980-1.36)	375
	09-10	*	**.226** (.202-.287)	**.481** (.429-.553)	**.917** (.736-1.18)	**1.41** (1.12-1.62)	455
20 years and older	03-04	**.508** (.455-.566)	**.525** (.447-.616)	**1.00** (.875-1.09)	**1.76** (1.46-2.11)	**2.54** (2.04-3.00)	1529
	05-06	**.503** (.461-.549)	**.510** (.470-.550)	**.940** (.850-1.07)	**1.69** (1.50-1.86)	**2.31** (2.12-2.54)	1520
	07-08	**.507** (.463-.555)	**.500** (.450-.550)	**.940** (.810-1.02)	**1.69** (1.51-2.01)	**2.56** (2.09-3.17)	1861
	09-10	*	**.454** (.395-.517)	**.861** (.731-.988)	**1.51** (1.29-1.85)	**2.15** (1.88-2.57)	2031
Gender							
Males	03-04	**.365** (.333-.400)	**.362** (.309-.417)	**.696** (.620-.784)	**1.31** (1.18-1.44)	**1.87** (1.51-2.30)	1266
	05-06	**.380** (.336-.431)	**.390** (.330-.440)	**.740** (.600-.890)	**1.27** (1.09-1.47)	**1.73** (1.62-1.85)	1270
	07-08	**.408** (.374-.445)	**.390** (.350-.450)	**.730** (.650-.810)	**1.22** (1.11-1.36)	**1.69** (1.54-2.11)	1326
	09-10	*	**.337** (.298-.391)	**.675** (.585-.802)	**1.19** (1.06-1.29)	**1.50** (1.33-1.78)	1404
Females	03-04	**.532** (.472-.599)	**.545** (.455-.652)	**1.06** (.969-1.21)	**1.88** (1.64-2.30)	**2.77** (2.12-3.56)	1271
	05-06	**.552** (.494-.617)	**.540** (.490-.620)	**1.09** (.850-1.27)	**1.96** (1.72-2.14)	**2.78** (2.35-3.17)	1308
	07-08	**.520** (.469-.576)	**.490** (.460-.540)	**.960** (.820-1.11)	**1.92** (1.58-2.24)	**2.83** (2.24-3.50)	1308
	09-10	*	**.475** (.423-.552)	**.890** (.771-1.07)	**1.81** (1.43-2.09)	**2.57** (2.09-2.94)	1461
Race/ethnicity							
Mexican Americans	03-04	**.384** (.307-.480)	**.365** (.280-.455)	**.768** (.619-.990)	**1.62** (1.23-2.16)	**2.32** (1.78-4.01)	618
	05-06	**.425** (.337-.536)	**.400** (.310-.490)	**.840** (.560-1.29)	**1.82** (1.30-2.47)	**2.63** (2.22-3.20)	651
	07-08	**.409** (.350-.479)	**.380** (.310-.480)	**.790** (.690-.850)	**1.55** (1.08-1.98)	**2.03** (1.55-2.70)	514
	09-10	*	**.333** (.272-.400)	**.660** (.494-.861)	**1.29** (1.02-1.54)	**1.95** (1.52-2.89)	615
Non-Hispanic blacks	03-04	**.343** (.301-.391)	**.306** (.265-.368)	**.587** (.522-.687)	**1.28** (.964-1.63)	**2.13** (1.41-2.87)	713
	05-06	**.328** (.285-.378)	**.320** (.270-.370)	**.610** (.470-.780)	**1.15** (.930-1.40)	**1.64** (1.29-1.96)	691
	07-08	**.350** (.303-.404)	**.330** (.280-.380)	**.590** (.490-.690)	**1.10** (.840-1.46)	**1.85** (1.13-2.77)	589
	09-10	*	**.317** (.259-.393)	**.582** (.500-.659)	**1.05** (.900-1.30)	**1.55** (1.18-1.96)	546
Non-Hispanic whites	03-04	**.463** (.400-.537)	**.476** (.385-.588)	**.970** (.800-1.07)	**1.67** (1.32-2.11)	**2.40** (1.88-2.90)	1066
	05-06	**.475** (.426-.531)	**.490** (.440-.540)	**.890** (.820-1.02)	**1.61** (1.42-1.75)	**2.23** (1.98-2.50)	1044
	07-08	**.481** (.423-.546)	**.480** (.390-.540)	**.890** (.750-1.03)	**1.58** (1.34-2.02)	**2.49** (1.89-3.18)	1100
	09-10	*	**.434** (.370-.500)	**.833** (.689-1.04)	**1.50** (1.26-1.87)	**2.12** (1.80-2.64)	1225

* Not calculated: proportion of results below limit of detection was too high to provide a valid result.

Biomonitoring Summary

http://www.cdc.gov/biomonitoring/Mercury_BiomonitoringSummary.html

Factsheet

http://www.cdc.gov/biomonitoring/Mercury_FactSheet.html

Source: *Centers for Disease Control & Prevention, Fourth National Report on Human Exposure to Environmental Chemicals, Updated Tables, January 2017*

Urinary Mercury (creatinine corrected) (2011 - 2014)

Geometric mean and selected percentiles of urine concentrations (in µg/g of creatinine) for the U.S. population from the National Health and Nutrition Examination Survey.

	Survey years	Geometric mean (95% conf. interval)	50th Percentile (95% conf. interval)	75th Percentile (95% conf. interval)	90th Percentile (95% conf. interval)	95th Percentile (95% conf. interval)	Sample size
Total	11-12	**.367** (.333-.405)	**.353** (.306-.394)	**.676** (.623-.754)	**1.33** (1.13-1.50)	**1.75** (1.49-2.32)	2505
	13-14	**.283** (.260-.309)	**.270** (.250-.290)	**.571** (.511-.644)	**1.20** (1.05-1.36)	**1.61** (1.47-1.81)	2665
Age group							
6-11 years	11-12	**.345** (.298-.398)	**.306** (.276-.344)	**.537** (.441-.613)	**1.08** (.884-1.43)	**1.62** (1.07-2.34)	400
	13-14	*	< LOD	**.429** (.310-.529)	**.750** (.563-.897)	**1.11** (.713-1.72)	401
12-19 years	11-12	**.246** (.219-.277)	**.221** (.190-.269)	**.405** (.368-.453)	**.735** (.571-1.11)	**1.21** (.742-1.49)	390
	13-14	*	< LOD	**.257** (.200-.281)	**.580** (.391-.735)	**.846** (.580-1.07)	452
20 years and older	11-12	**.393** (.351-.439)	**.383** (.330-.437)	**.750** (.673-.805)	**1.38** (1.17-1.63)	**1.95** (1.50-2.48)	1715
	13-14	**.318** (.291-.349)	**.304** (.281-.333)	**.644** (.561-.741)	**1.32** (1.13-1.47)	**1.76** (1.50-1.88)	1812
Gender							
Males	11-12	**.320** (.278-.368)	**.294** (.267-.358)	**.558** (.478-.667)	**1.11** (.791-1.44)	**1.57** (1.21-2.00)	1259
	13-14	**.242** (.223-.263)	**.231** (.206-.259)	**.476** (.429-.542)	**.902** (.779-1.11)	**1.31** (1.13-1.49)	1318
Females	11-12	**.418** (.374-.466)	**.409** (.355-.453)	**.800** (.706-.900)	**1.46** (1.29-1.65)	**2.00** (1.63-2.60)	1246
	13-14	**.330** (.297-.367)	**.315** (.273-.356)	**.692** (.600-.822)	**1.44** (1.18-1.68)	**1.83** (1.60-2.12)	1347
Race/ethnicity							
Mexican Americans	11-12	**.339** (.288-.399)	**.286** (.225-.393)	**.641** (.433-.789)	**1.17** (1.00-1.42)	**1.70** (1.31-2.24)	317
	13-14	**.261** (.231-.295)	**.237** (.209-.273)	**.516** (.409-.709)	**1.04** (.810-1.48)	**1.62** (1.11-2.55)	454
Non-Hispanic blacks	11-12	**.280** (.245-.320)	**.261** (.224-.294)	**.467** (.411-.529)	**.896** (.638-1.14)	**1.43** (1.10-1.57)	671
	13-14	**.211** (.169-.264)	**.202** (.152-.269)	**.409** (.333-.516)	**.794** (.643-1.10)	**1.34** (.880-1.52)	580
Non-Hispanic whites	11-12	**.372** (.323-.428)	**.364** (.294-.433)	**.700** (.619-.805)	**1.35** (1.05-1.63)	**1.75** (1.41-2.48)	817
	13-14	**.295** (.269-.323)	**.278** (.257-.310)	**.602** (.516-.689)	**1.27** (1.08-1.45)	**1.64** (1.46-1.82)	987
All Hispanics	11-12	**.369** (.342-.399)	**.331** (.283-.384)	**.674** (.612-.772)	**1.24** (1.13-1.44)	**1.86** (1.47-2.92)	574
	13-14	**.267** (.237-.300)	**.237** (.214-.273)	**.541** (.448-.634)	**1.07** (.837-1.36)	**1.61** (1.24-1.86)	702
Asians	11-12	**.577** (.473-.705)	**.562** (.467-.700)	**1.16** (.872-1.44)	**1.82** (1.54-2.00)	**2.29** (1.90-3.12)	355
	13-14	**.488** (.422-.565)	**.475** (.373-.600)	**.917** (.779-1.06)	**1.88** (1.35-2.19)	**2.57** (1.88-4.24)	291

< LOD means less than the limit of detection for the urine levels not corrected for creatinine.
* Not calculated: proportion of results below limit of detection was too high to provide a valid result.

Biomonitoring Summary

http://www.cdc.gov/biomonitoring/Mercury_BiomonitoringSummary.html

Factsheet

http://www.cdc.gov/biomonitoring/Mercury_FactSheet.html

Source: *Centers for Disease Control & Prevention, Fourth National Report on Human Exposure to Environmental Chemicals, Updated Tables, January 2017*

Urinary Nitrate (2001 - 2010)

Geometric mean and selected percentiles of urine concentrations (in mg/L) for the U.S. population from the National Health and Nutrition Examination Survey.

	Survey years	Geometric mean (95% conf. interval)	50th Percentile (95% conf. interval)	75th Percentile (95% conf. interval)	90th Percentile (95% conf. interval)	95th Percentile (95% conf. interval)	Sample size
Total	01-02	**48.2** (46.2-50.3)	**49.0** (46.0-52.0)	**78.0** (73.0-83.0)	**100** (100-130)	**140** (130-150)	1617
	05-06	**42.7** (39.6-46.1)	**47.8** (44.4-51.2)	**74.6** (69.8-79.4)	**108** (101-114)	**133** (125-144)	7697
	07-08	**46.3** (44.6-48.1)	**50.3** (48.4-52.0)	**76.0** (72.7-79.1)	**110** (104-116)	**138** (132-146)	7629
	09-10	**40.7** (38.9-42.7)	**43.3** (41.1-45.8)	**68.7** (65.5-72.5)	**98.5** (93.4-102)	**126** (114-137)	2844
Age group							
6-11 years	01-02	**62.2** (53.8-71.8)	**68.0** (58.0-79.0)	**94.0** (84.0-100)	**130** (100-160)	**150** (120-380)	374
	05-06	**51.2** (47.4-55.4)	**54.7** (51.9-58.2)	**79.2** (72.8-87.2)	**113** (101-128)	**141** (120-158)	1054
	07-08	**55.2** (51.7-58.9)	**60.2** (56.1-64.3)	**84.5** (80.1-92.5)	**117** (107-135)	**149** (132-189)	1143
	09-10	**46.8** (43.2-50.6)	**50.3** (45.5-58.2)	**73.2** (70.2-79.1)	**98.7** (86.7-112)	**119** (98.0-186)	377
12-19 years	01-02	**57.4** (53.5-61.6)	**66.0** (60.0-69.0)	**91.0** (86.0-95.0)	**120** (100-130)	**150** (130-160)	827
	05-06	**52.5** (48.5-56.8)	**57.5** (52.3-62.6)	**84.2** (79.9-88.4)	**119** (111-124)	**144** (129-153)	2106
	07-08	**55.5** (51.5-59.7)	**56.8** (51.9-61.5)	**84.1** (76.2-94.5)	**119** (107-133)	**144** (133-162)	1135
	09-10	**44.6** (41.0-48.4)	**48.0** (43.3-54.9)	**75.2** (70.0-79.4)	**106** (91.6-119)	**133** (106-163)	452
20 years and older	01-02	**45.4** (43.3-47.5)	**49.0** (46.0-52.0)	**78.0** (73.0-83.0)	**100** (100-130)	**140** (130-150)	1617
	05-06	**40.5** (37.4-43.9)	**45.0** (41.3-48.3)	**71.7** (67.1-77.4)	**105** (98.0-113)	**129** (122-142)	4537
	07-08	**44.2** (42.5-45.9)	**48.1** (46.0-49.7)	**73.2** (70.1-76.5)	**107** (101-113)	**135** (128-146)	5351
	09-10	**39.6** (37.4-41.9)	**42.3** (39.4-44.8)	**66.4** (62.3-71.9)	**97.2** (91.9-102)	**124** (113-144)	2015
Gender							
Males	01-02	**57.5** (54.6-60.6)	**63.0** (59.0-67.0)	**89.0** (83.0-94.0)	**130** (100-140)	**150** (140-170)	1335
	05-06	**48.4** (44.6-52.6)	**52.7** (48.3-57.8)	**79.4** (72.8-86.5)	**110** (103-121)	**136** (123-152)	3765
	07-08	**51.9** (49.9-54.1)	**56.1** (53.8-58.0)	**79.5** (75.7-83.5)	**112** (105-119)	**137** (131-149)	3839
	09-10	**44.9** (41.8-48.2)	**46.0** (43.1-49.7)	**73.3** (67.9-77.1)	**105** (95.6-112)	**133** (117-159)	1401
Females	01-02	**40.7** (38.4-43.2)	**43.0** (41.0-48.0)	**72.0** (68.0-76.0)	**100** (98.0-120)	**130** (120-150)	1483
	05-06	**37.9** (35.1-40.8)	**42.0** (38.2-46.0)	**69.2** (65.5-73.4)	**104** (96.6-110)	**130** (124-140)	3932
	07-08	**41.4** (39.3-43.7)	**43.9** (41.5-46.3)	**71.3** (67.5-74.8)	**108** (99.8-115)	**138** (132-149)	3790
	09-10	**37.1** (34.9-39.5)	**40.3** (36.4-43.9)	**65.9** (62.0-69.8)	**92.2** (88.4-98.5)	**117** (101-130)	1443
Race/ethnicity							
Mexican Americans	01-02	**53.2** (48.7-58.2)	**59.0** (52.0-66.0)	**84.0** (79.0-91.0)	**120** (100-150)	**160** (130-180)	707
	05-06	**47.8** (44.7-51.2)	**52.4** (49.9-56.2)	**77.9** (75.1-83.1)	**113** (104-120)	**148** (133-156)	1972
	07-08	**48.7** (45.0-52.6)	**51.9** (47.4-56.7)	**75.6** (69.7-81.3)	**111** (100-122)	**148** (127-164)	1505
	09-10	**41.3** (39.3-43.5)	**43.5** (41.2-46.4)	**66.4** (61.0-73.9)	**92.6** (86.5-99.7)	**111** (94.4-132)	611
Non-Hispanic blacks	01-02	**53.8** (47.8-60.5)	**58.0** (51.0-64.0)	**84.0** (77.0-93.0)	**120** (100-130)	**140** (130-170)	680
	05-06	**45.9** (42.1-50.0)	**50.4** (46.6-54.9)	**75.0** (68.8-80.8)	**101** (95.3-110)	**127** (114-148)	2078
	07-08	**47.5** (45.0-50.3)	**50.3** (48.6-52.5)	**74.7** (71.9-77.3)	**105** (97.1-116)	**134** (125-150)	1707
	09-10	**39.0** (36.5-41.7)	**44.1** (41.6-46.3)	**65.4** (61.5-69.6)	**94.2** (86.6-101)	**121** (101-141)	544
Non-Hispanic whites	01-02	**46.3** (44.1-48.6)	**51.0** (47.0-53.0)	**81.0** (78.0-85.0)	**120** (100-130)	**140** (130-150)	1228
	05-06	**41.2** (37.6-45.2)	**46.2** (41.3-50.6)	**73.3** (67.3-80.1)	**107** (98.2-115)	**129** (122-142)	3056
	07-08	**45.0** (42.7-47.5)	**49.2** (46.1-52.6)	**75.5** (70.5-80.0)	**108** (101-116)	**134** (128-140)	3190
	09-10	**39.8** (37.2-42.6)	**42.1** (39.1-45.2)	**68.4** (63.0-73.5)	**95.6** (89.8-100)	**119** (106-131)	1215

Limit of detection (LOD, see Data Analysis section) for Survey years 01-02, 05-06, 07-08, and 09-10 are 0.7, 0.7, 0.7, and 0.7 respectively.

Source: *Centers for Disease Control & Prevention, Fourth National Report on Human Exposure to Environmental Chemicals, Updated Tables, January 2017*

Urinary Nitrate (2011 - 2014)

Geometric mean and selected percentiles of urine concentrations (in mg/L) for the U.S. population from the National Health and Nutrition Examination Survey.

	Survey years	Geometric mean (95% conf. interval)	50th Percentile (95% conf. interval)	75th Percentile (95% conf. interval)	90th Percentile (95% conf. interval)	95th Percentile (95% conf. interval)	Sample size
Total	11-12	**41.8** (39.7-44.1)	**44.5** (42.3-47.2)	**71.5** (68.1-76.4)	**108** (99.3-116)	**133** (119-156)	2467
	13-14	**40.8** (38.8-42.9)	**42.2** (39.6-45.7)	**72.2** (67.8-78.7)	**107** (101-112)	**136** (123-151)	2644
Age group							
6-11 years	11-12	**47.4** (43.3-52.0)	**54.1** (49.2-61.3)	**78.6** (74.3-84.0)	**99.8** (93.2-113)	**121** (104-141)	394
	13-14	**44.7** (41.0-48.8)	**47.3** (42.3-51.7)	**79.2** (68.9-86.0)	**119** (95.8-138)	**151** (124-189)	398
12-19 years	11-12	**43.3** (37.4-50.1)	**50.4** (39.8-58.3)	**71.5** (66.5-78.0)	**107** (91.9-121)	**135** (108-183)	384
	13-14	**46.5** (40.8-53.0)	**51.1** (42.5-59.3)	**83.4** (72.9-89.6)	**112** (92.5-120)	**122** (115-134)	449
20 years and older	11-12	**41.0** (38.7-43.5)	**43.4** (40.8-46.2)	**70.1** (66.1-75.7)	**110** (98.7-117)	**135** (117-164)	1689
	13-14	**39.6** (37.6-41.8)	**40.7** (38.2-44.1)	**70.2** (64.2-76.1)	**107** (101-111)	**136** (120-153)	1797
Gender							
Males	11-12	**46.9** (43.3-50.8)	**48.4** (43.6-53.0)	**76.2** (69.9-81.7)	**114** (101-124)	**150** (116-175)	1251
	13-14	**43.6** (40.1-47.4)	**45.3** (41.0-50.6)	**73.1** (64.3-83.5)	**108** (99.8-113)	**141** (118-157)	1313
Females	11-12	**37.4** (34.4-40.7)	**41.2** (36.4-46.0)	**67.9** (60.6-73.7)	**101** (89.8-114)	**120** (113-145)	1216
	13-14	**38.2** (36.1-40.5)	**39.2** (37.5-41.7)	**71.4** (67.8-74.8)	**107** (99.8-112)	**134** (120-141)	1331
Race/ethnicity							
Mexican Americans	11-12	**41.1** (36.9-45.8)	**45.9** (40.4-51.3)	**65.9** (61.8-70.9)	**89.8** (78.4-108)	**112** (89.8-159)	313
	13-14	**42.0** (36.0-49.0)	**45.3** (35.4-56.6)	**72.0** (61.7-83.4)	**111** (93.0-134)	**136** (111-163)	451
Non-Hispanic blacks	11-12	**44.9** (41.5-48.6)	**47.6** (41.6-52.3)	**73.8** (67.8-79.8)	**107** (97.1-117)	**139** (116-150)	663
	13-14	**46.4** (42.4-50.9)	**50.0** (44.9-54.4)	**73.6** (66.4-80.6)	**105** (92.1-119)	**135** (107-172)	574
Non-Hispanic whites	11-12	**41.0** (38.0-44.1)	**43.6** (39.6-47.9)	**71.9** (66.7-78.0)	**110** (96.1-117)	**132** (115-169)	810
	13-14	**39.3** (36.6-42.3)	**40.2** (37.6-43.9)	**71.9** (64.5-80.9)	**107** (95.9-111)	**128** (114-145)	976
All Hispanics	11-12	**41.0** (36.7-45.7)	**44.4** (40.2-48.9)	**67.2** (60.9-73.9)	**95.3** (82.9-113)	**120** (97.0-159)	566
	13-14	**41.1** (36.8-45.8)	**44.4** (39.0-50.5)	**70.0** (62.7-76.7)	**107** (94.2-116)	**138** (120-153)	699
Asians	11-12	**50.2** (43.7-57.6)	**50.8** (45.8-57.5)	**84.0** (72.1-91.9)	**146** (121-171)	**238** (142-380)	341
	13-14	**44.4** (38.9-50.7)	**45.2** (36.6-53.0)	**91.6** (76.2-99.5)	**150** (114-183)	**189** (139-282)	291

Limit of detection (LOD, see Data Analysis section) for Survey year 11-12 and 13-14 are 0.7 and 0.7, respectively.

Source: *Centers for Disease Control & Prevention, Fourth National Report on Human Exposure to Environmental Chemicals, Updated Tables, January 2017*

Urinary Nitrate (creatinine corrected) (2001 - 2010)

Geometric mean and selected percentiles of urine concentrations (in mg/g of creatinine) for the U.S. population from the National Health and Nutrition Examination Survey.

	Survey years	Geometric mean (95% conf. interval)	50th Percentile (95% conf. interval)	75th Percentile (95% conf. interval)	90th Percentile (95% conf. interval)	95th Percentile (95% conf. interval)	Sample size
Total	01-02	**49.8** (47.7-51.9)	**46.9** (44.2-49.6)	**63.8** (61.2-67.7)	**90.9** (84.3-98.8)	**120** (111-128)	1616
	05-06	**42.6** (40.2-45.1)	**42.4** (40.1-44.7)	**59.7** (55.8-64.1)	**85.5** (81.3-91.3)	**113** (106-118)	7697
	07-08	**47.7** (45.9-49.7)	**46.0** (44.0-48.3)	**66.5** (62.4-70.5)	**98.0** (92.3-102)	**127** (119-135)	7628
	09-10	**43.7** (42.1-45.3)	**42.3** (41.0-43.7)	**60.2** (57.6-63.0)	**88.5** (83.3-96.1)	**115** (104-127)	2843
Age group							
6-11 years	01-02	**72.0** (66.1-78.4)	**66.0** (62.6-70.4)	**87.0** (80.2-97.7)	**129** (96.5-144)	**144** (130-235)	374
	05-06	**60.8** (57.4-64.5)	**57.3** (53.6-60.6)	**76.5** (70.9-82.1)	**109** (95.0-123)	**134** (121-164)	1054
	07-08	**70.2** (65.7-74.9)	**65.9** (62.4-69.5)	**89.0** (83.2-96.5)	**128** (112-152)	**173** (140-216)	1143
	09-10	**64.2** (58.8-70.0)	**60.2** (56.3-63.3)	**80.7** (68.9-96.1)	**107** (96.1-124)	**127** (105-202)	376
12-19 years	01-02	**44.8** (43.4-46.2)	**43.8** (42.6-45.0)	**56.2** (52.2-59.7)	**73.2** (65.2-85.1)	**93.4** (79.0-104)	826
	05-06	**39.8** (37.8-41.9)	**38.1** (36.3-40.3)	**51.8** (47.7-56.0)	**70.6** (63.1-78.8)	**88.9** (79.4-103)	2106
	07-08	**43.4** (41.3-45.5)	**40.5** (38.6-43.5)	**56.0** (52.7-59.2)	**76.6** (69.0-86.2)	**98.0** (85.4-121)	1134
	09-10	**41.7** (39.3-44.4)	**39.7** (38.3-41.7)	**54.0** (48.4-57.4)	**73.4** (61.0-86.1)	**88.5** (71.0-117)	452
20 years and older	01-02	**48.3** (45.9-50.9)	**46.9** (44.2-49.6)	**63.8** (61.2-67.7)	**90.9** (84.3-98.8)	**120** (111-128)	1616
	05-06	**41.4** (38.9-43.9)	**41.0** (38.8-43.7)	**58.6** (54.8-63.1)	**85.3** (80.2-91.0)	**111** (105-116)	4537
	07-08	**46.5** (44.6-48.4)	**44.7** (42.5-47.0)	**65.0** (60.7-69.2)	**96.1** (90.0-102)	**125** (117-132)	5351
	09-10	**42.2** (40.3-44.2)	**41.0** (39.6-42.5)	**58.6** (55.4-62.2)	**87.7** (81.0-98.5)	**116** (103-133)	2015
Gender							
Males	01-02	**47.6** (44.7-50.7)	**46.1** (43.4-48.7)	**61.3** (58.0-64.5)	**86.7** (77.1-97.3)	**114** (97.3-125)	1335
	05-06	**40.1** (37.5-42.9)	**39.5** (36.7-42.8)	**55.3** (51.6-59.5)	**77.2** (70.7-83.0)	**95.9** (89.6-102)	3765
	07-08	**44.6** (42.8-46.6)	**42.8** (40.7-45.1)	**60.6** (58.1-64.4)	**85.6** (81.1-91.3)	**111** (101-121)	3839
	09-10	**41.0** (38.9-43.1)	**39.1** (37.6-40.6)	**54.6** (52.2-58.1)	**83.3** (74.6-90.0)	**103** (96.1-122)	1400
Females	01-02	**51.9** (49.9-54.1)	**51.2** (48.4-53.0)	**69.1** (66.7-71.2)	**100** (91.7-111)	**129** (118-140)	1481
	05-06	**45.1** (42.8-47.6)	**45.0** (42.4-47.4)	**64.4** (60.0-69.6)	**96.8** (87.8-105)	**128** (117-134)	3932
	07-08	**51.0** (48.9-53.2)	**50.0** (47.5-52.7)	**72.3** (67.8-76.8)	**107** (101-116)	**146** (129-163)	3789
	09-10	**46.5** (44.4-48.7)	**46.5** (44.8-48.4)	**64.2** (60.5-69.4)	**96.6** (83.3-106)	**121** (106-152)	1443
Race/ethnicity							
Mexican Americans	01-02	**50.9** (45.7-56.8)	**48.1** (44.9-51.4)	**67.4** (60.3-77.6)	**97.3** (85.7-117)	**135** (100-161)	707
	05-06	**44.6** (42.6-46.7)	**44.0** (42.2-45.3)	**60.4** (58.1-62.9)	**89.9** (82.0-95.4)	**120** (111-128)	1972
	07-08	**48.7** (45.1-52.7)	**47.0** (43.5-50.5)	**64.8** (59.7-69.9)	**93.5** (88.9-101)	**128** (108-156)	1505
	09-10	**43.4** (40.5-46.5)	**42.2** (39.7-45.9)	**58.2** (54.7-61.3)	**86.2** (77.1-92.5)	**104** (90.8-122)	611
Non-Hispanic blacks	01-02	**38.7** (36.3-41.3)	**38.0** (34.6-41.3)	**53.5** (50.3-57.4)	**70.3** (64.9-79.3)	**91.7** (78.9-100)	679
	05-06	**32.9** (30.9-35.0)	**31.9** (29.8-34.1)	**45.4** (41.5-49.6)	**64.0** (60.1-68.0)	**81.2** (75.3-89.6)	2078
	07-08	**35.9** (34.2-37.7)	**34.8** (33.3-36.6)	**49.0** (44.8-53.6)	**69.1** (63.5-77.4)	**87.8** (78.1-97.4)	1706
	09-10	**31.4** (28.9-34.0)	**32.2** (29.7-34.5)	**43.3** (40.8-47.3)	**59.9** (54.8-69.7)	**77.1** (62.2-98.3)	543
Non-Hispanic whites	01-02	**51.4** (49.4-53.4)	**49.1** (46.9-51.5)	**66.9** (64.2-69.4)	**95.2** (87.7-100)	**124** (115-132)	1227
	05-06	**43.7** (40.8-46.8)	**43.9** (40.8-46.8)	**61.4** (56.5-66.2)	**85.5** (80.6-91.9)	**110** (102-116)	3056
	07-08	**49.0** (46.7-51.4)	**47.4** (44.9-50.5)	**68.2** (63.3-73.1)	**98.3** (91.2-105)	**126** (118-135)	3190
	09-10	**44.7** (42.7-46.9)	**43.8** (41.5-46.1)	**62.0** (58.6-64.7)	**87.7** (83.3-96.1)	**106** (103-117)	1215

Source: *Centers for Disease Control & Prevention, Fourth National Report on Human Exposure to Environmental Chemicals, Updated Tables, January 2017*

Urinary Nitrate (creatinine corrected) (2011 - 2014)

Geometric mean and selected percentiles of urine concentrations (in mg/g of creatinine) for the U.S. population from the National Health and Nutrition Examination Survey.

	Survey years	Geometric mean (95% conf. interval)	50th Percentile (95% conf. interval)	75th Percentile (95% conf. interval)	90th Percentile (95% conf. interval)	95th Percentile (95% conf. interval)	Sample size
Total	11-12	**47.8** (45.3-50.4)	**46.0** (43.7-49.2)	**67.4** (62.6-71.5)	**103** (88.7-117)	**137** (117-153)	2465
	13-14	**47.2** (45.2-49.4)	**46.3** (43.2-49.4)	**66.2** (62.9-70.2)	**97.3** (91.0-104)	**123** (116-133)	2643
Age group							
6-11 years	11-12	**68.0** (63.3-73.1)	**66.4** (60.9-68.7)	**87.3** (81.2-95.6)	**122** (110-132)	**144** (124-156)	393
	13-14	**67.1** (62.3-72.2)	**63.2** (59.4-67.1)	**83.6** (72.4-95.2)	**118** (99.1-145)	**159** (110-230)	398
12-19 years	11-12	**42.2** (39.6-44.9)	**41.5** (38.7-43.8)	**54.0** (51.2-57.7)	**69.1** (63.6-77.1)	**86.9** (69.1-104)	384
	13-14	**42.2** (39.7-44.8)	**41.9** (37.2-44.7)	**52.8** (47.9-58.1)	**69.2** (61.0-82.0)	**85.6** (72.6-107)	449
20 years and older	11-12	**46.8** (44.0-49.8)	**44.9** (41.7-47.9)	**66.8** (60.5-73.0)	**105** (87.4-122)	**142** (116-165)	1688
	13-14	**46.3** (44.2-48.5)	**45.2** (42.5-48.2)	**66.0** (62.8-70.2)	**97.4** (90.5-105)	**123** (113-136)	1796
Gender							
Males	11-12	**44.1** (41.8-46.6)	**43.8** (40.8-45.9)	**59.8** (57.0-62.4)	**87.1** (76.9-98.4)	**109** (98.4-120)	1250
	13-14	**43.7** (41.4-46.2)	**42.5** (38.9-45.6)	**59.8** (55.7-65.5)	**84.0** (78.6-94.3)	**110** (99.1-128)	1312
Females	11-12	**51.6** (47.9-55.5)	**50.0** (45.8-54.0)	**76.5** (68.9-85.1)	**120** (98.1-143)	**151** (132-170)	1215
	13-14	**50.9** (48.2-53.7)	**50.5** (47.1-53.5)	**71.6** (67.8-75.7)	**107** (95.6-113)	**135** (118-156)	1331
Race/ethnicity							
Mexican Americans	11-12	**46.4** (41.0-52.6)	**43.6** (38.9-49.7)	**62.4** (52.7-78.0)	**86.4** (72.1-124)	**110** (84.0-203)	313
	13-14	**48.1** (43.4-53.2)	**48.3** (46.0-50.9)	**67.3** (62.1-72.0)	**99.3** (83.0-116)	**128** (100-169)	451
Non-Hispanic blacks	11-12	**35.0** (33.2-36.9)	**34.3** (32.1-36.3)	**47.5** (44.0-51.3)	**69.2** (62.2-78.1)	**89.3** (77.1-102)	663
	13-14	**35.5** (33.4-37.8)	**33.8** (32.0-35.9)	**46.2** (43.5-49.7)	**67.3** (60.4-75.0)	**87.3** (76.6-95.6)	574
Non-Hispanic whites	11-12	**50.1** (47.2-53.2)	**49.0** (45.7-52.3)	**68.9** (63.8-79.4)	**107** (91.1-129)	**144** (121-154)	808
	13-14	**48.6** (46.3-50.9)	**47.9** (44.8-51.4)	**67.8** (62.9-72.5)	**97.4** (89.5-105)	**122** (109-136)	975
All Hispanics	11-12	**45.8** (42.4-49.5)	**44.1** (41.7-46.2)	**61.5** (55.4-69.3)	**85.2** (78.5-95.6)	**115** (86.4-159)	566
	13-14	**45.9** (43.1-48.9)	**46.1** (43.1-48.3)	**65.5** (61.0-68.6)	**95.4** (85.0-105)	**126** (105-137)	699
Asians	11-12	**67.2** (61.9-72.9)	**62.9** (56.3-68.8)	**106** (93.3-118)	**178** (153-216)	**247** (203-318)	341
	13-14	**69.6** (62.2-78.0)	**62.7** (52.5-76.8)	**101** (85.2-132)	**168** (140-194)	**200** (173-261)	291

Source: *Centers for Disease Control & Prevention, Fourth National Report on Human Exposure to Environmental Chemicals, Updated Tables, January 2017*

UV Index for 58 U.S. Cities

City	State	Clear Sky UV Index					UV Index Forecast				
		Extreme	Very High	High	Moderate	Low	Extreme	Very High	High	Moderate	Low
Albuquerque	NM	86	107	32	107	33	58	112	42	100	53
Anchorage	AK	0	0	3	126	236	0	0	1	105	259
Atlanta	GA	40	137	45	125	18	3	133	35	101	93
Atlantic City	NJ	0	117	66	78	104	0	75	65	87	138
Baltimore	MD	2	119	62	83	99	0	76	65	85	139
Billings	MT	0	79	65	83	138	0	52	72	92	149
Bismarck	ND	0	58	76	86	145	0	20	82	105	158
Boise	ID	3	103	55	85	119	0	78	69	87	131
Boston	MA	0	88	66	84	127	0	48	74	82	161
Buffalo	NY	0	85	70	79	131	0	29	88	87	161
Burlington	VT	0	68	78	76	143	0	22	77	88	178
Charleston	SC	33	153	36	133	10	3	134	47	110	71
Charleston	WV	7	123	61	81	93	0	75	62	73	155
Cheyenne	WY	15	115	62	70	103	2	89	68	90	116
Chicago	IL	0	101	59	83	122	0	33	77	105	150
Cleveland	OH	0	100	66	79	120	0	43	81	95	146
Concord	NH	0	85	68	79	133	0	34	66	112	153
Dallas	TX	50	129	44	131	11	5	118	54	98	90
Denver	CO	34	100	66	73	92	7	96	76	85	101
Des Moines	IA	0	105	59	83	118	0	63	61	115	126
Detroit	MI	0	93	63	83	126	0	23	85	107	150
Dover	DE	0	120	63	84	98	0	74	65	90	136
Hartford	CT	0	99	64	80	122	0	51	65	95	154
Honolulu	HI	156	124	83	2	0	138	125	87	15	0
Houston	TX	81	122	52	110	0	9	148	42	104	62
Indianapolis	IN	2	118	62	77	106	0	63	64	104	134
Jackson	MS	56	134	35	140	0	12	132	39	116	66
Jacksonville	FL	56	144	41	124	0	26	141	43	121	34
Las Vegas	NV	44	109	61	93	58	7	113	77	92	76
Little Rock	AR	28	135	52	104	46	1	113	52	93	106
Los Angeles	CA	71	110	44	116	24	35	121	53	108	48
Louisville	KY	8	123	60	85	89	0	81	63	88	133
Memphis	TN	22	140	50	101	52	1	114	58	86	106
Miami	FL	125	107	64	69	0	75	139	56	91	4
Milwaukee	WI	0	90	61	84	130	0	26	82	98	159
Minneapolis	MN	0	74	69	83	139	0	21	75	103	166
Mobile	AL	70	129	47	119	0	27	137	50	109	42
New Orleans	LA	82	121	49	113	0	37	135	46	105	42
New York	NY	0	110	62	82	111	0	57	72	91	145
Norfolk	VA	6	132	65	81	81	0	105	53	80	127
Oklahoma City	OK	25	135	49	96	60	1	108	54	109	93
Omaha	NE	0	107	61	80	117	0	62	58	118	127
Philadelphia	PA	0	116	62	80	107	0	64	65	99	137
Phoenix	AZ	76	108	41	120	20	29	122	54	108	52
Pittsburgh	PA	1	112	61	80	111	0	52	68	82	163
Portland	ME	0	71	74	80	140	0	25	75	108	157
Portland	OR	0	64	79	88	134	0	39	70	83	173
Providence	RI	0	95	67	82	121	0	52	69	91	153
Raleigh	NC	16	133	61	89	66	0	106	51	89	119
Saint Louis	MO	6	124	59	84	92	0	72	72	104	117
Salt Lake City	UT	27	107	62	72	97	7	98	58	90	112
San Francisco	CA	4	112	85	83	81	0	98	84	84	99
San Juan	PR	203	105	57	0	0	176	118	68	2	1
Seattle	WA	0	33	92	94	146	0	18	69	90	188
Sioux Falls	SD	0	93	56	87	129	0	57	51	109	148

City	State	Clear Sky UV Index					UV Index Forecast				
		Extreme	Very High	High	Moderate	Low	Extreme	Very High	High	Moderate	Low
Tampa	FL	90	124	53	98	0	36	145	58	111	15
Washington	DC	2	120	62	85	96	0	80	65	83	137
Wichita	KS	10	126	63	78	88	1	96	55	105	108

Notes: *Figures are the number of days in each exposure category; The days may not add up to 365 due to missing data.*

The UV Index is a next day forecast of the amount of skin damaging UV radiation expected to reach the earth's surface at the time when the sun is highest in the sky (solar noon). The amount of UV radiation reaching the surface is primarily related to the elevation of the sun in the sky, the amount of ozone in the stratosphere, and the amount of clouds present. The UV Index can range from 0 (when it is night time) to 15 or 16 (in the tropics at high elevations under clear skies). UV radiation is greatest when the sun is highest in the sky and rapidly decreases as the sun approaches the horizon. The higher the UV Index, the greater the dose rate of skin damaging (and eye damaging) UV radiation. Consequently, the higher the UV Index, the smaller the time it takes before skin damage occurs.

Source: *NOAA, Climate Prediction Center, UV Index: Annual Time Series, 2015*

Acronyms & Abbreviations

A

A&I: Alternative and Innovative (Wastewater Treatment System)

AA: Accountable Area; Adverse Action; Advices of Allowance; Assistant Administrator; Associate Administrator; Atomic Absorption

AAEE: American Academy of Environmental Engineers

AANWR: Alaskan Arctic National Wildlife Refuge

AAP: Asbestos Action Program

AAPCO: American Association of Pesticide Control Officials

AARC: Alliance for Acid Rain Control

ABEL: EPA's computer model for analyzing a violator's ability to pay a civil penalty.

ABES: Alliance for Balanced Environmental Solutions

AC: Actual Commitment. Advisory Circular

A&C: Abatement and Control

ACA: American Conservation Association

ACBM: Asbestos-Containing Building Material

ACE: Alliance for Clean Energy

ACE: Any Credible Evidence

ACEEE: American Council for an Energy Efficient Economy

ACFM: Actual Cubic Feet Per Minute

ACL: Alternate Concentration Limit. Analytical Chemistry Laboratory

ACM: Asbestos-Containing Material

ACP: Agriculture Control Program (Water Quality Management); ACP: Air Carcinogen Policy

ACQUIRE: Aquatic Information Retrieval

ACQR: Air Quality Control Region

ACS: American Chemical Society

ACT: Action

ACTS: Asbestos Contractor Tracking System

ACWA: American Clean Water Association

ACWM: Asbestos-Containing Waste Material

ADABA: Acceptable Data Base

ADB: Applications Data Base

ADI: Acceptable Daily Intake

ADP: AHERA Designated Person; Automated Data Processing

ADQ: Audits of Data Quality

ADR: Alternate Dispute Resolution

ADSS: Air Data Screening System

ADT: Average Daily Traffic

AEA: Atomic Energy Act

AEC: Associate Enforcement Counsels

AEE: Alliance for Environmental Education

AEERL: Air and Energy Engineering Research Laboratory

AEM: Acoustic Emission Monitoring

AERE: Association of Environmental and Resource Economists

AES: Auger Electron Spectrometry

AFA: American Forestry Association

AFCA: Area Fuel Consumption Allocation

AFCEE: Air Force Center for Environmental Excellence

AFS: AIRS Facility Subsystem

AFUG: AIRS Facility Users Group

AH: Allowance Holders

AHERA: Asbestos Hazard Emergency Response Act

AHU: Air Handling Unit

AI: Active Ingredient

AIC: Active to Inert Conversion

AICUZ: Air Installation Compatible Use Zones

AID: Agency for International Development

AIHC: American Industrial Health Council

AIP: Auto Ignition Point

AIRMON: Atmospheric Integrated Research Monitoring Network

AIRS: Aerometric Information Retrieval System

AL: Acceptable Level

ALA: Delta-Aminolevulinic Acid

ALA-O: Delta-Aminolevulinic Acid Dehydrates

ALAPO: Association of Local Air Pollution Control Officers

ALARA: As Low As Reasonably Achievable

ALC: Application Limiting Constituent

ALJ: Administrative Law Judge

ALMS: Atomic Line Molecular Spectroscopy

ALR: Action Leakage Rate

AMBIENS: Atmospheric Mass Balance of Industrially Emitted and Natural Sulfur

AMOS: Air Management Oversight System

AMPS: Automatic Mapping and Planning System

AMSA: Association of Metropolitan Sewer Agencies

ANC: Acid Neutralizing Capacity

ANPR: Advance Notice of Proposed Rulemaking

ANRHRD: Air, Noise, & Radiation Health Research Division/ORD

ANSS: American Nature Study Society

AOAC: Association of Official Analytical Chemists

AOC: Abnormal Operating Conditions

AOD: Argon-Oxygen Decarbonization

AOML: Atlantic Oceanographic and Meteorological Laboratory

AP: Accounting Point

APA: Administrative Procedures Act

APCA: Air Pollution Control Association

APCD: Air Pollution Control District

APDS: Automated Procurement Documentation System

APHA: American Public Health Association

APRAC: Urban Diffusion Model for Carbon Monoxide from Motor Vehicle Traffic

APTI: Air Pollution Training Institute

APWA: American Public Works Association

AQ-7: Non-reactive Pollutant Modelling

AQCCT: Air-Quality Criteria and Control Techniques

AQCP: Air Quality Control Program

AQCR: Air-Quality Control Region

AQD: Air-Quality Digest

AQDHS: Air-Quality Data Handling System

AQDM: Air-Quality Display Model

AQMA: Air-Quality Maintenance Area

AQMD: Air Quality Management District

AQMP: Air-Quality Maintenance Plan; Air-Quality Management Plan

AQSM: Air-Quality Simulation Model

AQTAD: Air-Quality Technical Assistance Demonstration

AR: Administrative Record

A&R: Air and Radiation

ARA: Assistant Regional Administrator; Associate Regional Administrator

ARAC: Acid Rain Advisory Committee

ARAR: Applicable or Relevant and Appropriate Standards, Limitations, Criteria, and Requirements

ARB: Air Resources Board

ARC: Agency Ranking Committee

ARCC: American Rivers Conservation Council

ARCS: Alternative Remedial Contract Strategy

ARG: American Resources Group

ARIP: Accidental Release Information Program

ARL: Air Resources Laboratory

ARM: Air Resources Management

ARNEWS: Acid Rain National Early Warning Systems

ARO: Alternate Regulatory Option

ARRP: Acid Rain Research Program

ARRPA: Air Resources Regional Pollution Assessment Model

ARS: Agricultural Research Service

ARZ: Auto Restricted Zone

AS: Area Source

ASC: Area Source Category

ASDWA: Association of State Drinking Water Administrators

ASHAA: Asbestos in Schools Hazard Abatement Act

ASHRAE: American Society of Heating, Refrigerating, and Air-Conditioning Engineers

ASIWCPA: Association of State and Interstate Water Pollution Control Administrators

ASMDHS: Airshed Model Data Handling System

ASRL: Atmospheric Sciences Research Laboratory

AST: Advanced Secondary (Wastewater) Treatment

ASTHO: Association of State and Territorial Health Officers

ASTM: American Society for Testing and Materials

ASTSWMO: Association of State and Territorial Solid Waste Management Officials

AT: Advanced Treatment. Alpha Track Detection

ATERIS: Air Toxics Exposure and Risk Information System

ATS: Action Tracking System; Allowance Tracking System

ATSDR: Agency for Toxic Substances and Disease Registry

ATTF: Air Toxics Task Force

AUSM: Advanced Utility Simulation Model

A/WPR: Air/Water Pollution Report

AWRA: American Water Resources Association

AWT: Advanced Wastewater Treatment

AWWA: American Water Works Association

AWWARF: American Water Works Association Research Foundation.

B

BAA: Board of Assistance Appeals

BAC: Bioremediation Action Committee; Biotechnology Advisory Committee

BACM: Best Available Control Measures

BACT: Best Available Control Technology

BADT: Best Available Demonstrated Technology

BAF: Bioaccumulation Factor

BaP: Benzo(a)Pyrene

BAP: Benefits Analysis Program

BART: Best Available Retrofit Technology

BASIS: Battelle's Automated Search Information System

BAT: Best Available Technology

BATEA: Best Available Treatment Economically Achievable

BCT: Best Control Technology

BCPCT: Best Conventional Pollutant Control Technology

BDAT: Best Demonstrated Achievable Technology

BDCT: Best Demonstrated Control Technology

BDT: Best Demonstrated Technology

BEJ: Best Engineering Judgement. Best Expert Judgment

BF: Bonafide Notice of Intent to Manufacture or Import (IMD/OTS)

BID: Background Information Document. Buoyancy Induced Dispersion

BIOPLUME: Model to Predict the Maximum Extent of Existing Plumes

BMP: Best Management Practice(s)

BMR: Baseline Monitoring Report

BO: Budget Obligations

BOA: Basic Ordering Agreement (Contracts)

BOD: Biochemical Oxygen Demand. Biological Oxygen Demand

BOF: Basic Oxygen Furnace

BOP: Basic Oxygen Process

BOPF: Basic Oxygen Process Furnace

BOYSNC: Beginning of Year Significant Non-Compliers

BP: Boiling Point

BPJ: Best Professional Judgment

BPT: Best Practicable Technology. Pest Practicable Treatment

BPWTT: Best Practical Wastewater Treatment Technology

BRI: Building-Related Illness

BRS: Bibliographic Retrieval Service

BSI: British Standards Institute

BSO: Benzene Soluble Organics

BTZ: Below the Treatment Zone

BUN: Blood Urea Nitrogen

C

CA: Citizen Act. Competition Advocate. Cooperative Agreements. Corrective Action

CAA: Clean Air Act; Compliance Assurance Agreement

CAAA: Clean Air Act Amendments

CAER: Community Awareness and Emergency Response

CAFE: Corporate Average Fuel Economy

CAFO: Concentrated Animal Feedlot; Consent Agreement/Final Order

CAG: Carcinogenic Assessment Group

CAIR: Clean Air Interstate Rule: Comprehensive Assessment of Information Rule

CALINE: California Line Source Model

CAM: Compliance Assurance Monitoring rule; Compliance Assurance Monitoring

CAMP: Continuous Air Monitoring Program

CAN: Common Account Number

CAO: Corrective Action Order

CAP: Corrective Action Plan. Cost Allocation Procedure. Criteria Air Pollutant

CAPMoN: Canadian Air and Precipitation Monitoring Network

CAR: Corrective Action Report

CAS: Center for Automotive Safety; Chemical Abstract Service

CASAC: Clean Air Scientific Advisory Committee

CASLP: Conference on Alternative State and Local Practices

CASTNet: Clean Air Status and Trends Network

CATS: Corrective Action Tracking System

CAU: Carbon Adsorption Unit; Command Arithmetic Unit

CB: Continuous Bubbler

CBA: Chesapeake Bay Agreement. Cost Benefit Analysis

CBD: Central Business District

CBEP: Community Based Environmental Project

CBI: Compliance Biomonitoring Inspection; Confidential Business Information

CBOD: Carbonaceous Biochemical Oxygen Demand

CBP: Chesapeake Bay Program; County Business Patterns

CCA: Competition in Contracting Act

CCAA: Canadian Clean Air Act

CCAP: Center for Clean Air Policy; Climate Change Action Plan

CCEA: Conventional Combustion Environmental Assessment

CCHW: Citizens Clearinghouse for Hazardous Wastes

CCID: Confidential Chemicals Identification System

CCMS/NATO: Committee on Challenges of a Modern Society/North Atlantic Treaty Organization

CCP: Composite Correction Plan

CC/RTS: Chemical Collection/ Request Tracking System

CCTP: Clean Coal Technology Program

CD: Climatological Data

CDB: Consolidated Data Base

CDBA: Central Data Base Administrator

CDBG: Community Development Block Grant

CDD: Chlorinated dibenzo-p-dioxin

CDF: Chlorinated dibenzofuran

CDHS: Comprehensive Data Handling System

CDI: Case Development Inspection

CDM: Climatological Dispersion Model; Comprehensive Data Management

CDMQC: Climatological Dispersion Model with Calibration and Source Contribution

CDNS: Climatological Data National Summary

CDP: Census Designated Places

CDS: Compliance Data System

CE: Categorical Exclusion. Conditionally Exempt Generator

CEA: Cooperative Enforcement Agreement; Cost and Economic Assessment

CEAT: Contractor Evidence Audit Team

CEARC: Canadian Environmental Assessment Research Council

CEB: Chemical Element Balance

CEC: Commission for Environmental Cooperation

CECATS: CSB Existing Chemicals Assessment Tracking System

CEE: Center for Environmental Education

CEEM: Center for Energy and Environmental Management

CEI: Compliance Evaluation Inspection

CELRF: Canadian Environmental Law Research Foundation

CEM: Continuous Emission Monitoring

CEMS: Continuous Emission Monitoring System

CEPA: Canadian Environmental Protection Act

CEPP: Chemical Emergency Preparedness Plan

CEQ: Council on Environmental Quality

CERCLA: Comprehensive Environmental Response, Compensation, and Liability Act (1980)

CERCLIS: Comprehensive Environmental Response, Compensation, and Liability Information System

CERT: Certificate of Eligibility

CESQG: Conditionally Exempt Small Quantity Generator

CEST: Community Environmental Service Teams

CF: Conservation Foundation

CFC: Chlorofluorocarbons

CFM: Chlorofluoromethanes

CFR: Code of Federal Regulations

CHABA: Committee on Hearing and Bio-Acoustics

CHAMP: Community Health Air Monitoring Program

CHEMNET: Chemical Industry Emergency Mutual Aid Network

CHESS: Community Health and Environmental Surveillance System

CHIP: Chemical Hazard Information Profiles

CI: Compression Ignition. Confidence Interval

CIAQ: Council on Indoor Air Quality

CIBL: Convective Internal Boundary Layer

CICA: Competition in Contracting Act

CICIS: Chemicals in Commerce Information System

CIDRS: Cascade Impactor Data Reduction System

CIMI: Committee on Integrity and Management Improvement

CIS: Chemical Information System. Contracts Information System

CKD: Cement Kiln Dust

CKRC: Cement Kiln Recycling Coalition

CLC: Capacity Limiting Constituents

CLEANS: Clinical Laboratory for Evaluation and Assessment of Toxic Substances

CLEVER: Clinical Laboratory for Evaluation and Validation of Epidemiologic Research

CLF: Conservation Law Foundation

CLI: Consumer Labelling Initiative

CLIPS: Chemical List Index and Processing System

CLP: Contract Laboratory Program

CM: Corrective Measure

CMA: Chemical Manufacturers Association

CMB: Chemical Mass Balance

CME: Comprehensive Monitoring Evaluation

CMEL: Comprehensive Monitoring Evaluation Log

CMEP: Critical Mass Energy Project

CNG: Compressedd Natural Gas

COCO: Contractor-Owned/ Contractor-Operated

COD: Chemical Oxygen Demand

COH: Coefficient Of Haze

CPDA: Chemical Producers and Distributor Association

CPF: Carcinogenic Potency Factor

CPO: Certified Project Officer

CQA: Construction Quality Assurance

CR: Continuous Radon Monitoring

CROP: Consolidated Rules of Practice

CRP: Child-Resistant Packaging; Conservation Reserve Program

CRR: Center for Renewable Resources

CRSTER: Single Source Dispersion Model

CSCT: Committee for Site Characterization

CSGWPP: Comprehensive State Ground Water Protection Program

CSI: Common Sense Initiative; Compliance Sampling Inspection

CSIN: Chemical Substances Information Network

CSMA: Chemical Specialties Manufacturers Association

CSO: Combined Sewer Overflow

CSPA: Council of State Planning Agencies

CSRL: Center for the Study of Responsive Law

CTARC: Chemical Testing and Assessment Research Commission

CTG: Control Techniques Guidelines

CTSA: Cleaner TechnologiesSubstitutess Assessment

CV: Chemical Vocabulary

CVS: Constant Volume Sampler

CW: Continuous working-level monitoring

CWA: Clean Water Act (aka FWPCA)

CWAP: Clean Water Action Project

CWTC: Chemical Waste Transportation Council

CZMA: Coastal Zone Management Act

CZARA: Coastal Zone Management Act Reauthorization Amendments

D

DAPSS: Document and Personnel Security System (IMD)

DBP: Disinfection By-Product

DCI: Data Call-In

DCO: Delayed Compliance Order

DCO: Document Control Officer

DDT: DichloroDiphenylTrichloroethane

DERs: Data Evaluation Records

DES: Diethylstilbesterol

DfE: Design for the Environment

DI: Diagnostic Inspection

DMR: Discharge Monitoring Report

DNA: Deoxyribonucleic acid

DNAPL: Dense Non-Aqueous Phase Liquid

DO: Dissolved Oxygen

DOW: Defenders Of Wildlife

DPA: Deepwater Ports Act

DPD: Method of Measuring Chlorine Residual in Water

DQO: Data Quality Objective

DRE: Destruction and Removal Efficiency

DRES: Dietary Risk Evaluation System

DRMS: Defense Reutilization and Marketing Service

DRR: Data Review Record

DS: Dichotomous Sampler

DSAP: Data Self Auditing Program

DSCF: Dry Standard Cubic Feet

DSCM: Dry Standard Cubic Meter

DSS: Decision Support System; Domestic Sewage Study

DT: Detectors (radon) damaged or lost; Detention Time

DU: Decision Unit. Ducks Unlimited; Dobson Unit

DUC: Decision Unit Coordinator

DWEL: Drinking Water Equivalent Level

DWS: Drinking Water Standard

DWSRF: Drinking Water State Revolving Fund

E

EA: Endangerment Assessment; Enforcement Agreement; Environmental Action; Environmental Assessment;. Environmental Audit

EAF: Electric Arc Furnaces

EAG: Exposure Assessment Group

EAO: Emergency Administrative Order

EAP: Environmental Action Plan

Acronyms & Abbreviations

EAR: Environmental Auditing Roundtable

EASI: Environmental Alliance for Senior Involvement

EB: Emissions Balancing

EC: Emulsifiable Concentrate; Environment Canada; Effective Concentration

ECA: Economic Community for Africa

ECAP: Employee Counselling and Assistance Program

ECD: Electron Capture Detector

ECHH: Electro-Catalytic Hyper-Heaters

ECHO: Enforcement and Compliance History Online

ECL: Environmental Chemical Laboratory

ECOS: Environmental Council of the States

ECR: Enforcement Case Review

ECRA: Economic Cleanup Responsibility Act

ED: Effective Dose

EDA: Emergency Declaration Area

EDB: Ethylene Dibromide

EDC: Ethylene Dichloride

EDD: Enforcement Decision Document

EDF: Environmental Defense Fund

EDRS: Enforcement Document Retrieval System

EDS: Electronic Data System; Energy Data System

EDTA: Ethylene Diamine Triacetic Acid

EDX: Electronic Data Exchange

EDZ: Emission Density Zoning

EEA: Energy and Environmental Analysis

EECs: Estimated Environmental Concentrations

EER: Excess Emission Report

EERL: Eastern Environmental Radiation Laboratory

EERU: Environmental Emergency Response Unit

EESI: Environment and Energy Study Institute

EESL: Environmental Ecological and Support Laboratory

EETFC: Environmental Effects, Transport, and Fate Committee

EF: Emission Factor

EFO: Equivalent Field Office

EFTC: European Fluorocarbon Technical Committee

EGR: Exhaust Gas Recirculation

EH: Redox Potential

EHC: Environmental Health Committee

EHS: Extremely Hazardous Substance

EI: Emissions Inventory

EIA: Environmental Impact Assessment. Economic Impact Assessment

EIL: Environmental Impairment Liability

EIR: Endangerment Information Report; Environmental Impact Report

EIS: Environmental Impact Statement; Environmental Inventory System

EIS/AS: Emissions Inventory System/Area Source

EIS/PS: Emissions Inventory System/Point Source

EJ: Environmental Justice

EKMA: Empirical Kinetic Modeling Approach

EL: Exposure Level

ELI: Environmental Law Institute

ELR: Environmental Law Reporter

EM: Electromagnetic Conductivity

EMAP: Environmental Mapping and Assessment Program

EMAS: Enforcement Management and Accountability System

EMR: Environmental Management Report

EMS: Enforcement Management System

EMSL: Environmental Monitoring Support Systems Laboratory

EMTS: Environmental Monitoring Testing Site; Exposure Monitoring Test Site

EnPA: Environmental Performance Agreement

EO: Ethylene Oxide

EOC: Emergency Operating Center

EOF: Emergency Operations Facility (RTP)

EOP: End Of Pipe

EOT: Emergency Operations Team

EP: Earth Protectors; Environmental Profile; End-use Product; Experimental Product; Extraction Procedure

EPAA: Environmental Programs Assistance Act

EPAAR: EPA Acquisition Regulations

EPCA: Energy Policy and Conservation Act

EPACT: Environmental Policy Act

EPACASR: EPA Chemical Activities Status Report

EPCRA: Emergency Planning and Community Right to Know Act

EPD: Emergency Planning District

EPI: Environmental Policy Institute

EPIC: Environmental Photographic Interpretation Center

EPNL: Effective Perceived Noise Level

EPRI: Electric Power Research Institute

EPTC: Extraction Procedure Toxicity Characteristic

EQIP: Environmental Quality Incentives Program

ER: Ecosystem Restoration; Electrical Resistivity

ERA: Economic Regulatory Agency

ERAMS: Environmental Radiation Ambient Monitoring System

ERC: Emergency Response Commission. Emissions Reduction Credit, Environmental Research Center

ERCS: Emergency Response Cleanup Services

ERDA: Energy Research and Development Administration

ERD&DAA: Environmental Research, Development and Demonstration Authorization Act

ERL: Environmental Research Laboratory

ERNS: Emergency Response Notification System

ERP: Enforcement Response Policy

ERT: Emergency Response Team

ERTAQ: ERT Air Quality Model

ES: Enforcement Strategy

ESA: Endangered Species Act. Environmentally Sensitive Area

ESC: Endangered Species Committee

ESCA: Electron Spectroscopy for Chemical Analysis

ESCAP: Economic and Social Commission for Asia and the Pacific

ESECA: Energy Supply and Environmental Coordination Act

ESH: Environmental Safety and Health

ESP: Electrostatic Precipitators

ET: Emissions Trading

ETI: Environmental Technology Initiative

ETP: Emissions Trading Policy

ETS: Emissions Tracking System; Environmental Tobacco Smoke

ETV: Environmental Technology Verification Program

EUP: End-Use Product; Experimental Use Permit

EWCC: Environmental Workforce Coordinating Committee

EXAMS: Exposure Analysis Modeling System

ExEx: Expected Exceedance

F

FACA: Federal Advisory Committee Act

FAN: Fixed Account Number

FATES: FIFRA and TSCA Enforcement System

FBC: Fluidized Bed Combustion

FCC: Fluid Catalytic Converter

FCCC: Framework Convention on Climate Change

FCCU: Fluid Catalytic Cracking Unit

FCO: Federal Coordinating Officer (in disaster areas); Forms Control Officer

FDF: Fundamentally Different Factors

FDL: Final Determination Letter

FDO: Fee Determination Official

FE: Fugitive Emissions

FEDS: Federal Energy Data System

FEFx: Forced Expiratory Flow

FEIS: Fugitive Emissions Information System

FEL: Frank Effect Level

FEPCA: Federal Environmental Pesticide Control Act; enacted as amendments to FIFRA.

FERC: Federal Energy Regulatory Commission

FES: Factor Evaluation System

FEV: Forced Expiratory Volume

FEV1: Forced Expiratory Volume—one second; Front End Volatility Index

FF: Federal Facilities

FFAR: Fuel and Fuel Additive Registration

FFDCA: Federal Food, Drug, and Cosmetic Act

FFEO: Federal Facilities Enforcement Office

FFF: Firm Financial Facility

FFFSG: Fossil-Fuel-Fired Steam Generator

FFIS: Federal Facilities Information System

FFP: Firm Fixed Price

FGD: Flue-Gas Desulfurization

FID: Flame Ionization Detector

FIFRA: Federal Insecticide, Fungicide, and Rodenticide Act

FIM: Friable Insulation Material

FINDS: Facility Index System

FIP: Final Implementation Plan

FIPS: Federal Information Procedures System

FIT: Field Investigation Team

FLETC: Federal Law Enforcement Training Center

FLM: Federal Land Manager

FLP: Flash Point

FLPMA: Federal Land Policy and Management Act

FMAP: Financial Management Assistance Project

F/M: Food to Microorganism Ratio

FML: Flexible Membrane Liner

FMP: Facility Management Plan

FMP: Financial Management Plan

FMS: Financial Management System

FMVCP: Federal Motor Vehicle Control Program

FOE: Friends Of the Earth

FOIA: Freedom Of Information Act

FOISD: Fiber Optic Isolated Spherical Dipole Antenna

FONSI: Finding Of No Significant Impact

FORAST: Forest Response to Anthropogenic Stress

FP: Fine Particulate

FPA: Federal Pesticide Act

FPAS: Foreign Purchase Acknowledgement Statements

FPD: Flame Photometric Detector

FPEIS: Fine Particulate Emissions Information System

FPM: Federal Personnel Manual

FPPA: Federal Pollution Prevention Act

FPR: Federal Procurement Regulation

FPRS: Federal Program Resources Statement; Formal Planning and Supporting System

FQPA: Food Quality Protection Act

FR: Federal Register. Final Rulemaking

FRA: Federal Register Act

FREDS: Flexible Regional Emissions Data System

FRES: Forest Range Environmental Study

FRM: Federal Reference Methods

FRN: Federal Register Notice. Final Rulemaking Notice

FRS: Formal Reporting System

FS: Feasibility Study

FSA: Food Security Act

FSS: Facility Status Sheet; Federal Supply Schedule

FTP: Federal Test Procedure (for motor vehicles)

FTS: File Transfer Service

FTTS: FIFRA/TSCA Tracking System

FUA: Fuel Use Act

FURS: Federal Underground Injection Control Reporting System

FVMP: Federal Visibility Monitoring Program

FWCA: Fish and Wildlife Coordination Act

FWPCA: Federal Water Pollution and Control Act (aka CWA). Federal Water Pollution and Control Administration

FY: Fiscal Year

G

GAAP: Generally Accepted Accounting Principles

GAC: Granular Activated Carbon

GACT: Granular Activated Carbon Treatment

GAW: Global Atmospheric Watch

GCC: Global Climate Convention

GC/MS: Gas Chromatograph/ Mass Spectograph

GCVTC: Grand Canyon Visibility Transport Commission

GCWR: Gross Combination Weight Rating

GDE: Generic Data Exemption

GEI: Geographic Enforcement Initiative

GEMI: Global Environmental Management Initiative

GEMS: Global Environmental Monitoring System; Graphical Exposure Modeling System

GEP: Good Engineering Practice

GFF: Glass Fiber Filter

GFO: Grant Funding Order

GFP: Government-Furnished Property

GICS: Grant Information and Control System

GIS: Geographic Information Systems; Global Indexing System

GLC: Gas Liquid Chromatography

GLERL: Great Lakes Environmental Research Laboratory

GLNPO: Great Lakes National Program Office

GLP: Good Laboratory Practices

GLWQA: Great Lakes Water Quality Agreement

GMCC: Global Monitoring for Climatic Change

G/MI: Grams per mile

GOCO: Government-Owned/ Contractor-Operated

GOGO: Government-Owned/ Government-Operated

GOP: General Operating Procedures

GOPO: Government-Owned/ Privately-Operated

GPAD: Gallons-per-acre per-day

GPG: Grams-per-Gallon

GPR: Ground-Penetrating Radar

GPRA: Government Performance and Results Act

GPS: Groundwater Protection Strategy

GR: Grab Radon Sampling

GRAS: Generally Recognized as Safe

GRCDA: Government Refuse Collection and Disposal Association

GRGL: Groundwater Residue Guidance Level

GT: Gas Turbine

GTN: Global Trend Network

GTR: Government Transportation Request

GVP: Gasoline Vapor Pressure

GVW: Gross Vehicle Weight

GVWR: Gross Vehicle Weight Rating

GW: Grab Working-Level Sampling. Groundwater

GWDR: Ground Water Disinfection Rule

GWM: Groundwater Monitoring

GWP: Global Warming Potential

GWPC: Ground Water Protection Council

GWPS: Groundwater Protection Standard; Groundwater Protection Strategy

H

HA: Health Advisory

HAD: Health Assessment Document

HAP: Hazardous Air Pollutant

HAPEMS: Hazardous Air Pollutant Enforcement Management System

HAPPS: Hazardous Air Pollutant Prioritization System

HATREMS: Hazardous and Trace Emissions System

HAZMAT: Hazardous Materials

HAZOP: Hazard and Operability Study

HBFC: Hydrobromofluorocarbon

HC: Hazardous Constituents; Hydrocarbon

HCCPD: Hexachlorocyclo-pentadiene

HCFC: Hydrochlorofluorocarbon

HCP: Hypothermal Coal Process

HDD: Heavy-Duty Diesel

HDDT: Heavy-duty Diesel Truck

HDDV: Heavy-Duty Diesel Vehicle

HDE: Heavy-Duty Engine

HDG: Heavy-Duty Gasoline-Powered Vehicle

HDGT: Heavy-Duty Gasoline Truck

HDGV: Heavy-Duty Gasoline Vehicle

HDPE: High Density Polyethylene

HDT: Highest Dose Tested in a study. Heavy-Duty Truck

HDV: Heavy-Duty Vehicle

HEAL: Human Exposure Assessment Location

HECC: House Energy and Commerce Committee

HEI: Health Effects Institute

HEM: Human Exposure Modeling

HEPA: High-Efficiency Particulate Air

HEPA: Highly Efficient Particulate Air Filter

HERS: Hyperion Energy Recovery System

HFC: Hydrofluorocarbon

HHDDV: Heavy Heavy-Duty Diesel Vehicle

HHE: Human Health and the Environment

HHV: Higher Heating Value

HI: Hazard Index

HI-VOL: High-Volume Sampler

HIWAY: A Line Source Model for Gaseous Pollutants

HLRW: High Level Radioactive Waste

HMIS: Hazardous Materials Information System

HMS: Highway Mobile Source

HMTA: Hazardous Materials Transportation Act

HMTR: Hazardous Materials Transportation Regulations

HOC: Halogenated Organic Carbons

HON: Hazardous Organic NESHAP

HOV: High-Occupancy Vehicle

HP: Horse Power

HPLC: High-Performance Liquid Chromatography

HPMS: Highway Performance Monitoring System

HPV: High Priority Violator

HQCDO: Headquarters Case Development Officer

HRS: Hazardous Ranking System

HRUP: High-Risk Urban Problem

HSDB: Hazardous Substance Data Base

HSL: Hazardous Substance List

HSWA: Hazardous and Solid Waste Amendments

HT: Hypothermally Treated

HTP: High Temperature and Pressure

HVAC: Heating, Ventilation, and Air-Conditioning system

HVIO: High Volume Industrial Organics

HW: Hazardous Waste

HWDMS: Hazardous Waste Data Management System

HWGTF: Hazardous Waste Groundwater Task Force; Hazardous Waste Groundwater Test Facility

HWIR: Hazardous Waste Identification Rule

HWLT: Hazardous Waste Land Treatment

HWM: Hazardous Waste Management

HWRTF: Hazardous Waste Restrictions Task Force

HWTC: Hazardous Waste Treatment Council

I

I/A: Innovative/Alternative

IA: Interagency Agreement

IAAC: Interagency Assessment Advisory Committee

IADN: Integrated Atmospheric Deposition Network

IAG: Interagency Agreement

IAP: Incentive Awards Program. Indoor Air Pollution

IAQ: Indoor Air Quality

IARC: International Agency for Research on Cancer

IATDB: Interim Air Toxics Data Base

IBSIN: Innovations in Building Sustainable Industries

IBT: Industrial Biotest Laboratory

IC: Internal Combustion

ICAIR: Interdisciplinary Planning and Information Research

ICAP: Inductively Coupled Argon Plasma

ICB: Information Collection Budget

ICBN: International Commission on the Biological Effects of Noise

ICCP: International Climate Change Partnership

ICE: Industrial Combustion Emissions Model. Internal Combustion Engine

ICP: Inductively Coupled Plasma

ICR: Information Collection Request

ICRE: Ignitability, Corrosivity, Reactivity, Extraction

ICRP: International Commission on Radiological Protection

ICRU: International Commission of Radiological Units and Measurements

ICS: Incident Command System. Institute for Chemical Studies; Intermittent Control Strategies.; Intermittent Control System

ICWM: Institute for Chemical Waste Management

IDEA: Integrated Data for Enforcement Analysis

IDLH: Immediately Dangerous to Life and Health

IEB: International Environment Bureau

IEMP: Integrated Environmental Management Project

IES: Institute for Environmental Studies

IFB: Invitation for Bid

IFCAM: Industrial Fuel Choice Analysis Model

IFCS: International Forum on Chemical Safety

IFIS: Industry File Information System

IFMS: Integrated Financial Management System

IFPP: Industrial Fugitive Process Particulate

IGCC: Integrated Gasification Combined Cycle

IGCI: Industrial Gas Cleaning Institute

IIS: Inflationary Impact Statement

IINERT: In-Place Inactivation and Natural Restoration Technologies

IJC: International Joint Commission (on Great Lakes)

I/M: Inspection/Maintenance

IMM: Intersection Midblock Model

IMPACT: Integrated Model of Plumes and Atmosphere in Complex Terrain

IMPROVE: Interagency Monitoring of Protected Visual Environment

INPUFF: Gaussian Puff Dispersion Model

INT: Intermittent

IOB: Iron Ore Beneficiation

IOU: Input/Output Unit

IPCS: International Program on Chemical Safety

IP: Inhalable Particles

IPM: Inhalable Particulate Matter. Integrated Pest Management

IPP: Implementation Planning Program. Integrated Plotting Package; Inter-media Priority Pollutant (document); Independent Power Producer

IPCC: Intergovernmental Panel on Climate Change

IPM: Integrated Pest Management

IRG: Interagency Review Group

IRLG: Interagency Regulatory Liaison Group (Composed of EPA, CPSC, FDA, and OSHA)

IRIS: Instructional Resources Information System. Integrated Risk Information System

IRM: Intermediate Remedial Measures

IRMC: Inter-Regulatory Risk Management Council

IRP: Installation Restoration Program

IRPTC: International Register of Potentially Toxic Chemicals

IRR: Institute of Resource Recovery

IRS: International Referral Systems

IS: Interim Status

ISAM: Indexed Sequential File Access Method

ISC: Industrial Source Complex

ISCL: Interim Status Compliance Letter

ISCLT: Industrial Source Complex Long Term Model

ISCST: Industrial Source Complex Short Term Model

ISD: Interim Status Document

ISE: Ion-specific electrode

ISMAP: Indirect Source Model for Air Pollution

ISO: International Organization for Standardization

ISPF: (IBM) Interactive System Productivity Facility

ISS: Interim Status Standards

ITC: Innovative Technology Council

ITC: Interagency Testing Committee

ITRC: Interstate Technology Regulatory Coordination

ITRD: Innovative Treatment Remediation Demonstration

IUP: Intended Use Plan

IUR: Inventory Update Rule

IWC: In-Stream Waste Concentration

IWS: Ionizing Wet Scrubber

J

JAPCA: Journal of Air Pollution Control Association

JCL: Job Control Language

JEC: Joint Economic Committee

JECFA: Joint Expert Committee of Food Additives

JEIOG: Joint Emissions Inventory Oversight Group

JLC: Justification for Limited Competition

JMPR: Joint Meeting on Pesticide Residues

JNCP: Justification for Non-Competitive Procurement

JOFOC: Justification for Other Than Full and Open Competition

JPA: Joint Permitting Agreement

JSD: Jackson Structured Design

JSP: Jackson Structured Programming

JTU: Jackson Turbidity Unit

L

LAA: Lead Agency Attorney

LADD: Lifetime Average Daily Dose; Lowest Acceptable Daily Dose

LAER: Lowest Achievable Emission Rate

LAI: Laboratory Audit Inspection

LAMP: Lake Acidification Mitigation Project

LC: Lethal Concentration. Liquid Chromatography

LCA: Life Cycle Assessment

LCD: Local Climatological Data

LCL: Lower Control Limit

LCM: Life Cycle Management

LCRS: Leachate Collection and Removal System

LD: Land Disposal. Light Duty

LD L0: The lowest dosage of a toxic substance that kills test organisms.

LDAR: Leak Detection and Repair

LDC: London Dumping Convention

LDCRS: Leachate Detection, Collection, and Removal System

LDD: Light-Duty Diesel

LDDT: Light-Duty Diesel Truck

LDDV: Light-Duty Diesel Vehicle

LDGT: Light-Duty Gasoline Truck

LDIP: Laboratory Data Integrity Program

LDR: Land Disposal Restrictions

LDRTF: Land Disposal Restrictions Task Force

LDS: Leak Detection System

LDT: Lowest Dose Tested. Light-Duty Truck

LDV: Light-Duty Vehicle

LEL: Lowest Effect Level. Lower Explosive Limit

LEP: Laboratory Evaluation Program

LEPC: Local Emergency Planning Committee

LERC: Local Emergency Response Committee

LEV: Low Emissions Vehicle

LFG: Landfill Gas

LFL: Lower Flammability Limit

LGR: Local Governments Reimbursement Program

LHDDV: Light Heavy-Duty Diesel Vehicle

LI: Langelier Index

LIDAR: Light Detection and Ranging

LIMB: Limestone-Injection Multi-Stage Burner

LLRW: Low Level Radioactive Waste

LMFBR: Liquid Metal Fast Breeder Reactor

LMOP: Landfill Methane Outreach Program

LNAPL: Light Non-Aqueous Phase Liquid

LOAEL: Lowest-Observed-Adverse-Effect-Level

LOD: Limit of Detection

LQER: Lesser Quantity Emission Rates

LQG: Large Quantity Generator

LRTAP: Long Range Transboundary Air Pollution

LUIS: Label Use Information System

M

MAC: Mobile Air Conditioner

MACT: Maximum Achievable Control Technology

MAPSIM: Mesoscale Air Pollution Simulation Model

MATC: Maximum Acceptable Toxic Concentration

MBAS: Methylene-Blue-Active Substances

MCL: Maximum Contaminant Level

MCLG: Maximum Contaminant Level Goal

MCS: Multiple Chemical Sensitivity

MDL: Method Detection Limit

MEC: Model Energy Code

MEI: Maximally (or most) Exposed Individual

MEP: Multiple Extraction Procedure

MHDDV: Medium Heavy-Duty Diesel Vehicle

MOBILE5A: Mobile Source Emission Factor Model

MOE: Margin Of Exposure

MOS: Margin of Safety

MP: Manufacturing-use Product; Melting Point

MPCA: Microbial Pest Control Agent

MPI: Maximum Permitted Intake

MPN: Maximum Possible Number

MPWC: Multiprocess Wet Cleaning

MRBMA: Mercury-Containing and Rechargeable Battery Management Act

MRF: Materials Recovery Facility

MRID: Master Record Identification number

MRL: Maximum-Residue Limit (Pesticide Tolerance)

MSW: Municipal Solid Waste

MTBE: Methyl tertiary butyl ether

MTD: Maximum Tolerated Dose

MUP: Manufacturing-Use Product

MUTA: Mutagenicity

MWC: Machine Wet Cleaning

N

NAA: Nonattainment Area

NAAEC: North American Agreement on Environmental Cooperation

NAAQS: National Ambient Air Quality Standards

NACA: National Agricultural Chemicals Association

NACEPT: National Advisory Council for Environmental Policy and Technology

NADP/NTN: National Atmospheric Deposition Program/National Trends Network

NAMS: National Air Monitoring Stations

NAPAP: National Acid Precipitation Assessment Program

NAPL: Non-Aqueous Phase Liquid

NAPS: National Air Pollution Surveillance

NARA: National Agrichemical Retailers Association

NARSTO: North American Research Strategy for Tropospheric Ozone

NAS: National Academy of Sciences

NASA: National Aeronautics and Space Administration

NASDA: National Association of State Departments of Agriculture

NCAMP: National Coalition Against the Misuse of Pesticides

NCEPI: National Center for Environmental Publications and Information

NCWS: Non-Community Water System

NEDS: National Emissions Data System

NEIC: National Enforcement Investigations Center

NEPA: National Environmental Policy Act

NEPI: National Environmental Policy Institute

NEPPS: National Environmental Performance Partnership System

NESHAP: National Emission Standard for Hazardous Air Pollutants

NIEHS: National Institute for Environmental Health Sciences

NETA: National Environmental Training Association

NFRAP: No Further Remedial Action Planned

NICT: National Incident Coordination Team

NIOSH: National Institute of Occupational Safety and Health

NIPDWR: National Interim Primary Drinking Water Regulations

NISAC: National Industrial Security Advisory Committee

NMHC: Nonmethane Hydrocarbons

NMOC: Non-Methane Organic Component

NMVOC: Non-methane Volatile Organic Chemicals

NO: Nitric Oxide

NOý: Nitrogen Dioxide

NOA: Notice of Arrival

NOAA: National Oceanographic and Atmospheric Agency

NOAC: Nature of Action Code

NOAEL: No Observable Adverse Effect Level

NOEL: No Observable Effect Level

NOIC: Notice of Intent to Cancel

NOIS: Notice of Intent to Suspend

N_2O: Nitrous Oxide

NOV: Notice of Violation

NO_x: Nitrogen Oxides

NORM: Naturally Occurring Radioactive Material

NPCA: National Pest Control Association

NPDES: National Pollutant Discharge Elimination System

NPHAP: National Pesticide Hazard Assessment Program

NPIRS: National Pesticide Information Retrieval System

NPMS: National Performance Measures Strategy

NPTN: National Pesticide Telecommunications Network

NRD: Natural Resource Damage

NRDC: Natural Resources Defense Council

NSDWR: National Secondary Drinking Water Regulations

NSEC: National System for Emergency Coordination

NSEP: National System for Emergency Preparedness

NSPS: New Source Performance Standards

NSR: New Source Review

NSR/PSD: National Source Review/Prevention of Significant Deterioration

NTI: National Toxics Inventory

NTIS: National Technical Information Service

NTNCWS: Non-Transient Non-Community Water System

NTP: National Toxicology Program

NTU: Nephlometric Turbidity Unit

O

O_3: Ozone

OAQPS: Office of Air Quality Planning and Standards

OCD: Offshore and Coastal Dispersion

ODP: Ozone-Depleting Potential

ODS: Ozone-Depleting Substances

OECA: Office of Enforcement and Compliance Assurance

OECD: Organization for Economic Cooperation and Development

OF: Optional Form

OI: Order for Information

OLC: Office of Legal Counsel

OLTS: On Line Tracking System

O&M: Operations and Maintenance

ORE: Office of Regulatory Enforcement

ORM: Other Regulated Material

ORP: Oxidation-Reduction Potential

OTAG: Ozone Transport Assessment Group

OTC: Ozone Transport Commission

OTIS: Online Tracking Information System

OTR: Ozone Transport Region

P

P2: Pollution Prevention

PAG: Pesticide Assignment Guidelines

PAH: Polynuclear Aromatic Hydrocarbons

PAI: Performance Audit Inspection (CWA); Pure Active Ingredient compound

PAM: Pesticide Analytical Manual

PAMS: Photochemical Assessment Monitoring Stations

PAT: Permit Assistance Team (RCRA)

PATS: Pesticide Action Tracking System; Pesticides Analytical Transport Solution

Pb: Lead

PBA: Preliminary Benefit Analysis (BEAD)

PCA: Principle Component Analysis

PCB: Polychlorinated Biphenyl

PCE: Perchloroethylene

PCM: Phase Contrast Microscopy

PCN: Policy Criteria Notice

PCO: Pest Control Operator

PCSD: President's Council on Sustainable Development

PDCI: Product Data Call-In

PFC: Perfluorated Carbon

PFCRA: Program Fraud Civil Remedies Act

PHC: Principal Hazardous Constituent

PHI: Pre-Harvest Interval

PHSA: Public Health Service Act

PI: Preliminary Injunction. Program Information

PIC: Products of Incomplete Combustion

PIGS: Pesticides in Groundwater Strategy

PIMS: Pesticide Incident Monitoring System

PIN: Pesticide Information Network

PIN: Procurement Information Notice

PIP: Public Involvement Program

PIPQUIC: Program Integration Project Queries Used in Interactive Command

PIRG: Public Interest Research Group

PIRT: Pretreatment Implementation Review Task Force

PIT: Permit Improvement Team

PITS: Project Information Tracking System

PLIRRA: Pollution Liability Insurance and Risk Retention Act

PLM: Polarized Light Microscopy

PLUVUE: Plume Visibility Model

PM: Particulate Matter

PMAS: Photochemical Assessment Monitoring Stations

$PM_{2.5}$: Particulate Matter Smaller than 2.5 Micrometers in Diameter

PM_{10}: Particulate Matter (nominally 10m and less)

PM_{15}: Particulate Matter (nominally 15m and less)

PMEL: Pacific Marine Environmental Laboratory

PMN: Premanufacture Notification

PMNF: Premanufacture Notification Form

PMR: Pollutant Mass Rate

PMR: Proportionate Mortality Ratio

PMRS: Performance Management and Recognition System

PMS: Program Management System

PNA: Polynuclear Aromatic Hydrocarbons

PO: Project Officer

POC: Point Of Compliance

POE: Point Of Exposure

POGO: Privately-Owned/ Government-Operated

POHC: Principal Organic Hazardous Constituent

POI: Point Of Interception

POLREP: Pollution Report

POM: Particulate Organic Matter. Polycyclic Organic Matter

POP: Persistent Organic Pollutant

POR: Program of Requirements

POTW: Publicly Owned Treatment Works

POV: Privately Owned Vehicle

PP: Program Planning

PPA: Planned Program Accomplishment

PPB: Parts Per Billion

PPE: Personal Protective Equipment

PPG: Performance Partnership Grant

PPIC: Pesticide Programs Information Center

PPIS: Pesticide Product Information System; Pollution Prevention Incentives for States

PPMAP: Power Planning Modeling Application Procedure

PPM/PPB: Parts per million/ parts per billion

PPSP: Power Plant Siting Program

PPT: Parts Per Trillion

PPTH: Parts Per Thousand

PQUA: Preliminary Quantitative Usage Analysis

PR: Pesticide Regulation Notice; Preliminary Review

PRA: Paperwork Reduction Act; Planned Regulatory Action

PRATS: Pesticides Regulatory Action Tracking System

PRC: Planning Research Corporation

PRI: Periodic Reinvestigation

PRM: Prevention Reference Manuals

PRN: Pesticide Registration Notice

PRP: Potentially Responsible Party

PRZM: Pesticide Root Zone Model

PS: Point Source

PSAM: Point Source Ambient Monitoring

PSC: Program Site Coordinator

PSD: Prevention of Significant Deterioration

PSES: Pretreatment Standards for Existing Sources

PSI: Pollutant Standards Index; Pounds Per Square Inch; Pressure Per Square Inch

PSIG: Pressure Per Square Inch Gauge

PSM: Point Source Monitoring

PSNS: Pretreatment Standards for New Sources

PSU: Primary Sampling Unit

PTDIS: Single Stack Meteorological Model in EPA UNAMAP Series

PTE: Potential to Emit

PTFE: Polytetrafluoroethylene (Teflon)

PTMAX: Single Stack Meteorological Model in EPA UNAMAP series

PTPLU: Point Source Gaussian Diffusion Model

PUC: Public Utility Commission

PV: Project Verification

PVC: Polyvinyl Chloride

PWB: Printed Wiring Board

PWS: Public Water Supply/ System

PWSS: Public Water Supply System

Q

QAC: Quality Assurance Coordinator

QA/QC: Quality Assistance/ Quality Control

QAMIS: Quality Assurance Management and Information System

QAO: Quality Assurance Officer

QAPP: Quality Assurance Program (or Project) Plan

QAT: Quality Action Team

QBTU: Quadrillion British Thermal Units

QC: Quality Control

QCA: Quiet Communities Act

QCI: Quality Control Index

QCP: Quiet Community Program

QL: Quantification Limit

QNCR: Quarterly Noncompliance Report

QUA: Qualitative Use Assessment

QUIPE: Quarterly Update for Inspector in Pesticide Enforcement

R

RA: Reasonable Alternative; Regulatory Alternatives; Regulatory Analysis; Remedial Action; Resource Allocation; Risk Analysis; Risk Assessment

RAATS: RCRA Administrate Action Tracking System

RAC: Radiation Advisory Committee. Raw Agricultural Commodity; Regional Asbestos Coordinator. Response Action Coordinator

RACM: Reasonably Available Control Measures

RACT: Reasonably Available Control Technology

RAD: Radiation Adsorbed Dose (unit of measurement of radiation absorbed by humans)

RADM: Random Walk Advection and Dispersion Model; Regional Acid Deposition Model

RAM: Urban Air Quality Model for Point and Area Source in EPA UNAMAP Series

RAMP: Rural Abandoned Mine Program

RAMS: Regional Air Monitoring System

RAP: Radon Action Program; Registration Assessment Panel; Remedial Accomplishment Plan; Response Action Plan

RAPS: Regional Air Pollution Study

RARG: Regulatory Analysis Review Group

RAS: Routine Analytical Service

RAT: Relative Accuracy Test

RB: Request for Bid

RBAC: Re-use Business Assistance Center

RBC: Red Blood Cell

RC: Responsibility Center

RCC: Radiation Coordinating Council

RCDO: Regional Case Development Officer

RCO: Regional Compliance Officer

RCP: Research Centers Program

RCRA: Resource Conservation and Recovery Act

RCRIS: Resource Conservation and Recovery Information System

RD/RA: Remedial Design/ Remedial Action

R&D: Research and Development

RD&D: Research, Development and Demonstration

RDF: Refuse-Derived Fuel

RDNA: Recombinant DNA

RDU: Regional Decision Units

RDV: Reference Dose Values

RE: Reasonable Efforts; Reportable Event

REAP: Regional Enforcement Activities Plan

REE: Rare Earth Elements

REEP: Review of Environmental Effects of Pollutants

RECLAIM: Regional Clean Air Initiatives Marker

RED: Reregistration Eligibility Decision Document

REDA: Recycling Economic Development Advocate

ReFIT: Reinvention for Innovative Technologies

REI: Restricted Entry Interval

REM: (Roentgen Equivalent Man)

REM/FIT: Remedial/Field Investigation Team

REMS: RCRA Enforcement Management System

REP: Reasonable Efforts Program

REPS: Regional Emissions Projection System

RESOLVE: Center for Environmental Conflict Resolution

RF: Response Factor

RFA: Regulatory Flexibility Act

RFB: Request for Bid

RfC: Reference Concentration

RFD: Reference Dose Values

RFI: Remedial Field Investigation

RFP: Reasonable Further Programs. Request for Proposal

RHRS: Revised Hazard Ranking System

RI: Reconnaissance Inspection

RI: Remedial Investigation

RIA: Regulatory Impact Analysis; Regulatory Impact Assessment

RIC: Radon Information Center

RICC: Retirement Information and Counseling Center

RICO: Racketeer Influenced and Corrupt Organizations Act

RI/FS: Remedial Investigation/ Feasibility Study

RIM: Regulatory Interpretation Memorandum

RIN: Regulatory Identifier Number

RIP: RCRA Implementation Plan

RISC: Regulatory Information Service Center

RJE: Remote Job Entry

RLL: Rapid and Large Leakage (Rate)

RMCL: Recommended Maximum Contaminant Level (this phrase being discontinued in favor of MCLG)

RMDHS: Regional Model Data Handling System

RMIS: Resources Management Information System

RMP: Risk Management Plan

RNA: Ribonucleic Acid

ROADCHEM: Roadway Version that Includes Chemical Reactions of BI, NO_2, and O_3

ROADWAY: A Model to Predict Pollutant Concentrations Near a Roadway

ROC: Record Of Communication

RODS: Records Of Decision System

ROG: Reactive Organic Gases

ROLLBACK: A Proportional Reduction Model

ROM: Regional Oxidant Model

ROMCOE: Rocky Mountain Center on Environment

ROP: Rate of Progress; Regional Oversight Policy

ROPA: Record Of Procurement Action

ROSA: Regional Ozone Study Area

RP: Radon Progeny Integrated Sampling. Respirable Particulates. Responsible Party

RPAR: Rebuttable Presumption Against Registration

RPM: Reactive Plume Model. Remedial Project Manager

RQ: Reportable Quantities

RRC: Regional Response Center

RRT: Regional Response Team; Requisite Remedial Technology

RS: Registration Standard

RSCC: Regional Sample Control Center

RSD: Risk-Specific Dose

RSE: Removal Site Evaluation

RTCM: Reasonable Transportation Control Measure

RTDF: Remediation Technologies Development Forum

RTDM: Rough Terrain Diffusion Model

RTECS: Registry of Toxic Effects of Chemical Substances

RTM: Regional Transport Model

RTP: Research Triangle Park

RUP: Restricted Use Pesticide

RVP: Reid Vapor Pressure

RWC: Residential Wood Combustion

S

S&A: Sampling and Analysis. Surveillance and Analysis

SAB: Science Advisory Board

SAC: Suspended and Cancelled Pesticides

SAEWG: Standing Air Emissions Work Group

SAIC: Special-Agents-In-Charge

SAIP: Systems Acquisition and Implementation Program

SAMI: Southern Appalachian Mountains Initiative

SAMWG: Standing Air Monitoring Work Group

SANE: Sulfur and Nitrogen Emissions

SANSS: Structure and Nomenclature Search System

SAP: Scientific Advisory Panel

SAR: Start Action Request. Structural Activity Relationship (of a qualitative assessment)

SARA: Superfund Amendments and Reauthorization Act of 1986

SAROAD: Storage and Retrieval Of Aerometric Data

SAS: Special Analytical Service. Statistical Analysis System

SASS: Source Assessment Sampling System

SAV: Submerged Aquatic Vegetation

SBC: Single Breath Cannister

SC: Sierra Club

SCAP: Superfund Consolidated Accomplishments Plan

SCBA: Self-Contained Breathing Apparatus

SCC: Source Classification Code

SCD/SWDC: Soil or Soil and Water Conservation District

SCFM: Standard Cubic Feet Per Minute

SCLDF: Sierra Club Legal Defense Fund

SCR: Selective Catalytic Reduction

SCRAM: State Consolidated RCRA Authorization Manual

SCRC: Superfund Community Relations Coordinator

SCS: Supplementary Control Strategy/System

SCSA: Soil Conservation Society of America

SCSP: Storm and Combined Sewer Program

SCW: Supercritical Water Oxidation

SDC: Systems Decision Plan

SDWA: Safe Drinking Water Act

SDWIS: Safe Drinking Water Information System

SBS: Sick Building Syndrome

SEA: State Enforcement Agreement

SEA: State/EPA Agreement

SEAM: Surface, Environment, and Mining

SEAS: Strategic Environmental Assessment System

SEDS: State Energy Data System

SEGIP: State Environmental Goals and Improvement Project

SEIA: Socioeconomic Impact Analysis

SEM: Standard Error of the Means

SEP: Standard Evaluation Procedures

SEP: Supplementary Environmental Project

SEPWC: Senate Environment and Public Works Committee

SERC: State Emergency Planning Commission

SES: Secondary Emissions Standard

SETAC: Society for Environmental Toxicology and Chemistry

SETS: Site Enforcement Tracking System

SF: Standard Form. Superfund

SFA: Spectral Flame Analyzers

SFDS: Sanitary Facility Data System

SFFAS: Superfund Financial Assessment System

SFIP: Sector Facility Indexing Project

SFIREG: State FIFRA Issues Research and Evaluation Group

SFS: State Funding Study

SHORTZ: Short Term Terrain Model

SHWL: Seasonal High Water Level

SI: International System of Units. Site Inspection. Surveillance Index. Spark Ignition

SIC: Standard Industrial Classification

SICEA: Steel Industry Compliance Extension Act

SIMS: Secondary Ion-Mass Spectrometry

SIP: State Implementation Plan

SITE: Superfund Innovative Technology Evaluation

SLAMS: State/Local Air Monitoring Station

SLN: Special Local Need

SLSM: Simple Line Source Model

SMART: Simple Maintenance of ARTS

SMCL: Secondary Maximum Contaminant Level

SMCRA: Surface Mining Control and Reclamation Act

SME: Subject Matter Expert

SMO: Sample Management Office

SMOA: Superfund Memorandum of Agreement

SMP: State Management Plan

SMR: Standardized Mortality Ratio

SMSA: Standard Metropolitan Statistical Area

SNA: System Network Architecture

SNAAQS: Secondary National Ambient Air Quality Standards

SNAP: Significant New Alternatives Project; Significant Noncompliance Action Program

SNARL: Suggested No Adverse Response Level

SNC: Significant Noncompliers

SNUR: Significant New Use Rule

SO_2: Sulfur Dioxide

SOC: Synthetic Organic Chemicals

SOCMI: Synthetic Organic Chemicals Manufacturing Industry

SOFC: Solid Oxide Fuel Cell

SOTDAT: Source Test Data

SOW: Scope Of Work

SPAR: Status of Permit Application Report

SPCC: Spill Prevention, Containment, and Countermeasure

SPE: Secondary Particulate Emissions

SPF: Structured Programming Facility

SPI: Strategic Planning Initiative

SPLMD: Soil-pore Liquid Monitoring Device

SPMS: Strategic Planning and Management System; Special Purpose Monitoring Stations

SPOC: Single Point Of Contact

SPS: State Permit System

SPSS: Statistical Package for the Social Sciences

SPUR: Software Package for Unique Reports

SQBE: Small Quantity Burner Exemption

SQG: Small Quantity Generator

SR: Special Review

SRAP: Superfund Remedial Accomplishment Plan

SRC: Solvent-Refined Coal

SRF: State Revolving Fund

SRM: Standard Reference Method

SRP: Special Review Procedure

SRR: Second Round Review. Submission Review Record

SRTS: Service Request Tracking System

SS: Settleable Solids. Superfund Surcharge. Suspended Solids

SSA: Sole Source Aquifer

SSAC: Soil Site Assimilated Capacity

SSC: State Superfund Contracts

SSD: Standards Support Document

SSEIS: Standard Support and Environmental Impact Statement; Stationary Source Emissions and Inventory System.

SSI: Size Selective Inlet

SSMS: Spark Source Mass Spectrometry

SSO: Sanitary Sewer Overflow; Source Selection Official

SSRP: Source Reduction Review Project

SSTS: Section Seven Tracking System

SSURO: Stop Sale, Use and Removal Order

STALAPCO: State and Local Air-Pollution Control Officials

STAPPA: State and Territorial Air Pollution

STAR: Stability Wind Rose. State Acid Rain Projects

STARS: Strategic Targeted Activities for Results System

STEL: Short Term Exposure Limit

STEM: Scanning Transmission-Electron Microscope

STN: Scientific and Technical Information Network

STORET: Storage and Retrieval of Water-Related Data

STP: Sewage Treatment Plant. Standard Temperature and Pressure

STTF: Small Town Task Force (EPA)

SUP: Standard Unit of Processing

SURE: Sulfate Regional Experiment Program

SV: Sampling Visit; Significant Violater

SW: Slow Wave

SWAP: Source Water Assessment Program

SWARF: Waste from Metal Grinding Process

SWC: Settlement With Conditions

SWDA: Solid Waste Disposal Act

SWIE: Southern Waste Information Exchange

SWMU: Solid Waste Management Unit

SWPA: Source Water Protection Area

SWQPPP: Source Water Quality Protection Partnership Petitions

SWTR: Surface Water Treatment Rule

SYSOP: Systems Operator

T

TAD: Technical Assistance Document

TAG: Technical Assistance Grant

TALMS: Tunable Atomic Line Molecular Spectroscopy

TAMS: Toxic Air Monitoring System

TAMTAC: Toxic Air Monitoring System Advisory Committee

TAP: Technical Assistance Program

TAPDS: Toxic Air Pollutant Data System

TAS: Tolerance Assessment System

TBT: Tributyltin

TC: Target Concentration. Technical Center. Toxicity Characteristics. Toxic Concentration:

TCDD: Dioxin (Tetrachlorodibenzo-p-dioxin)

TCDF: Tetrachlorodi-benzofurans

TCE: Trichloroethylene

TCF: Total Chlorine Free

TCLP: Total Concentrate Leachate Procedure. Toxicity Characteristic Leachate Procedure

TCM: Transportation Control Measure

TCP: Transportation Control Plan; Trichloropropane;

TCRI: Toxic Chemical Release Inventory

TD: Toxic Dose

TDS: Total Dissolved Solids

TEAM: Total Exposure Assessment Model

TEC: Technical Evaluation Committee

TED: Turtle Excluder Devices

TEG: Tetraethylene Glycol

TEGD: Technical Enforcement Guidance Document

TEL: Tetraethyl Lead

TEM: Texas Episodic Model

TEP: Typical End-use Product. Technical Evaluation Panel

TERA: TSCA Environmental Release Application

TES: Technical Enforcement Support

TEXIN: Texas Intersection Air Quality Model

TGO: Total Gross Output

TGAI: Technical Grade of the Active Ingredient

TGP: Technical Grade Product

THC: Total Hydrocarbons

THM: Trihalomethane

TI: Temporary Intermittent

TI: Therapeutic Index

TIBL: Thermal Internal Boundary Layer

TIC: Technical Information Coordinator. Tentatively Identified Compounds

TIM: Technical Information Manager

TIP: Technical Information Package

TIP: Transportation Improvement Program

TIS: Tolerance Index System

TISE: Take It Somewhere Else

TITC: Toxic Substance Control Act Interagency Testing Committee

TLV: Threshold Limit Value

TLV-C: TLV-Ceiling

TLV-STEL: TLV-Short Term Exposure Limit

TLV-TWA: TLV-Time Weighted Average

TMDL: Total Maximum Daily Limit; Total Maximum Daily Load

TMRC: Theoretical Maximum Residue Contribution

TNCWS: Transient Non-Community Water System

TNT: Trinitrotoluene

TO: Task Order

TOA: Trace Organic Analysis

TOC: Total Organic Carbon/ Compound

TOX: Tetradichloroxylene

TP: Technical Product; Total Particulates

TPC: Testing Priorities Committee

TPI: Technical Proposal Instructions

TPQ: Threshold Planning Quantity

TPSIS: Transportation Planning Support Information System

TPTH: Triphenyltinhydroxide

TPY: Tons Per Year

TQM: Total Quality Management

T-R: Transformer-Rectifier

TRC: Technical Review Committee

TRD: Technical Review Document

TRI: Toxic Release Inventory

TRIP: Toxic Release Inventory Program

TRIS: Toxic Chemical Release Inventory System

TRLN: Triangle Research Library Network

TRO: Temporary Restraining Order

TSA: Technical Systems Audit

TSCA: Toxic Substances Control Act

TSCATS: TSCA Test Submissions Database

TSCC: Toxic Substances Coordinating Committee

TSD: Technical Support Document

TSDF: Treatment, Storage, and Disposal Facility

TSDG: Toxic Substances Dialogue Group

TSI: Thermal System Insulation

TSM: Transportation System Management

TSO: Time Sharing Option

TSP: Total Suspended Particulates

TSS: Total Suspended (non-filterable) Solids

TTFA: Target Transformation Factor Analysis

TTHM: Total Trihalomethane

TTN: Technology Transfer Network

TTO: Total Toxic Organics

TTY: Teletypewriter

TVA: Tennessee Valley Authority

TVOC: Total Volatile Organic Compounds

TWA: Time Weighted Average

TWS: Transient Water System

TZ: Treatment Zone

U

UAC: User Advisory Committee

UAM: Urban Airshed Model

UAO: Unilateral Administrative Order

UAPSP: Utility Acid Precipitation Study Program

UAQI: Uniform Air Quality Index

UARG: Utility Air Regulatory Group

UCC: Ultra Clean Coal

UCCI: Urea-Formaldehyde Foam Insulation

UCL: Upper Control Limit

UDMH: Unsymmetrical Dimethyl Hydrazine

UEL: Upper Explosive Limit

UF: Uncertainty Factor

UFL: Upper Flammability Limit

ug/m^3: Micrograms Per Cubic Meter

UIC: Underground Injection Control

ULEV: Ultra Low Emission Vehicles

UMTRCA: Uranium Mill Tailings Radiation Control Act

UNAMAP: Users' Network for Applied Modeling of Air Pollution

UNECE: United Nations Economic Commission for Europe

UNEP: United Nations Environment Program

USC: Unified Soil Classification

USDA: United States Department of Agriculture

USDW: Underground Sources of Drinking Water

USFS: United States Forest Service

UST: Underground Storage Tank

UTM: Universal Transverse Mercator

UTP: Urban Transportation Planning

UV: Ultraviolet

UVA, UVB, UVC: Ultraviolet Radiation Bands

UZM: Unsaturated Zone Monitoring

V

VALLEY: Meteorological Model to Calculate Concentrations on Elevated Terrain

VCM: Vinyl Chloride Monomer

VCP: Voluntary Cleanup Program

VE: Visual Emissions

VEO: Visible Emission Observation

VHS: Vertical and Horizontal Spread Model

VHT: Vehicle-Hours of Travel

VISTTA: Visibility Impairment from Sulfur Transformation and Transport in the Atmosphere

VKT: Vehicle Kilometers Traveled

VMT: Vehicle Miles Traveled

VOC: Volatile Organic Compounds

VOS: Vehicle Operating Survey

VOST: Volatile Organic Sampling Train

VP: Vapor Pressure

VSD: Virtually Safe Dose

VSI: Visual Site Inspection

VSS: Volatile Suspended Solids

W

WA: Work Assignment

WADTF: Western Atmospheric Deposition Task Force

WAP: Waste Analysis Plan

WAVE: Water Alliances for Environmental Efficiency

WB: Wet Bulb

WCED: World Commission on Environment and Development

WDROP: Distribution Register of Organic Pollutants in Water

WENDB: Water Enforcement National Data Base

WERL: Water Engineering Research Laboratory

WET: Whole Effluent Toxicity test

WHO: World Health Organization

WHP: Wellhead Protection Program

WHPA: Wellhead Protection Area

WHWT: Water and Hazardous Waste Team

WICEM: World Industry Conference on Environmental Management

WL: Warning Letter; Working Level (radon measurement)

WLA/TMDL: Wasteload Allocation/Total Maximum Daily Load

WLM: Working Level Months

WMO: World Meteorological Organization

WP: Wettable Powder

WPCF: Water Pollution Control Federation

WQS: Water Quality Standard

WRC: Water Resources Council

WRDA: Water Resources Development Act

WRI: World Resources Institute

WS: Work Status

WSF: Water Soluble Fraction

WSRA: Wild and Scenic Rivers Act

WSTB: Water Sciences and Technology Board

WSTP: Wastewater Sewage Treatment Plant

WWEMA: Waste and Wastewater Equipment Manufacturers Association

WWF: World Wildlife Fund

WWTP: Wastewater Treatment Plant

WWTU: Wastewater Treatment Unit

Z

ZEV: Zero Emissions Vehicle

ZHE: Zero Headspace Extractor

ZOI: Zone Of Incorporation

ZRL: Zero Risk Level

Note: *Some acronyms have more than one meaning. Multiple meanings are listed, separated by semi-colons.*

Source: *U.S. Environmental Protection Agency, "Terms of Environment"*

Glossary of Environmental Terms

A

Abandoned Well: A well whose use has been permanently discontinued or which is in a state of such disrepair that it cannot be used for its intended purpose.

Abatement: Reducing the degree or intensity of, or eliminating, pollution.

Abatement Debris: Waste from remediation activities.

Absorbed Dose: In exposure assessment, the amount of a substance that penetrates an exposed organism's absorption barriers (e.g. skin, lung tissue, gastrointestinal tract) through physical or biological processes. The term is synonymous with internal dose.

Absorption: The uptake of water , other fluids, or dissolved chemicals by a cell or an organism (as tree roots absorb dissolved nutrients in soil.)

Absorption Barrier: Any of the exchange sites of the body that permit uptake of various substances at different rates (e.g. skin, lung tissue, and gastrointestinal-tract wall)

Accident Site: The location of an unexpected occurrence, failure or loss, either at a plant or along a transportation route, resulting in a release of hazardous materials.

Acclimatization: The physiological and behavioral adjustments of an organism to changes in its environment.

Acid: A corrosive solution with a pH less than 7.

Acid Aerosol: Acidic liquid or solid particles small enough to become airborne. High concentrations can irritate the lungs and have been associated with respiratory diseases like asthma.

Acid Deposition: A complex chemical and atmospheric phenomenon that occurs when emissions of sulfur and nitrogen compounds and other substances are transformed by chemical processes in the atmosphere, often far from the original sources, and then deposited on earth in either wet or dry form. The wet forms, popularly called "acid rain," can fall to earth as rain, snow, or fog. The dry forms are acidic gases or particulates.

Acid Mine Drainage: Drainage of water from areas that have been mined for coal or other mineral ores. The water has a low pH because of its contact with sulfur-bearing material and is harmful to aquatic organisms.

Acid Neutralizing Capacity: Measure of ability of a base (e.g. water or soil) to resist changes in pH.

Acid Rain: (See: acid deposition.)

Acidic: The condition of water or soil that contains a sufficient amount of acid substances to lower the pH below 7.0.

Action Levels: 1. Regulatory levels recommended by EPA for enforcement by FDA and USDA when pesticide residues occur in food or feed commodities for reasons other than the direct application of the pesticide. As opposed to "tolerances" which are established for residues occurring as a direct result of proper usage, action levels are set for inadvertent residues resulting from previous legal use or accidental contamination. 2. In the Superfund program, the existence of a contaminant concentration in the environment high enough to warrant action or trigger a response under SARA and the National Oil and Hazardous Substances Contingency Plan. The term is also used in other regulatory programs. (See: tolerances.)

Activated Carbon: A highly adsorbent form of carbon used to remove odors and toxic substances from liquid or gaseous emissions. In waste treatment, it is used to remove dissolved organic matter from waste drinking water. It is also used in motor vehicle evaporative control systems.

Activated Sludge: Product that results when primary effluent is mixed with bacteria-laden sludge and then agitated and aerated to promote biological treatment, speeding the breakdown of organic matter in raw sewage undergoing secondary waste treatment.

Activator: A chemical added to a pesticide to increase its activity.

Active Ingredient: In any pesticide product, the component that kills, or otherwise controls, target pests. Pesticides are regulated primarily on the basis of active ingredients.

Activity Plans: Written procedures in a school's asbestos-management plan that detail the steps a Local Education Agency (LEA) will follow in performing the initial and additional cleaning, operation and maintenance-program tasks; periodic surveillance; and reinspection required by the Asbestos Hazard Emergency Response Act (AHERA).

Acute Effect: An adverse effect on any living organism which results in severe symptoms that develop rapidly; symptoms often subside after the exposure stops.

Acute Exposure: A single exposure to a toxic substance which may result in severe biological harm or death. Acute exposures are usually characterized as lasting no longer than a day, as compared to longer, continuing exposure over a period of time.

Acute Toxicity: The ability of a substance to cause severe biological harm or death soon after a single exposure or dose. Also, any poisonous effect resulting from a single short-term exposure to a toxic substance. (See: chronic toxicity, toxicity.)

Adaptation: Changes in an organism's physiological structure or function or habits that allow it to survive in new surroundings.

Add-on Control Device: An air pollution control device such as carbon absorber or incinerator that reduces the pollution in an exhaust gas. The control device usually does not affect the process being controlled and thus is "add-on" technology, as opposed to a scheme to control pollution through altering the basic process itself.

Adequately Wet: Asbestos containing material that is sufficiently mixed or penetrated with liquid to prevent the release of particulates.

Administered Dose: In exposure assessment, the amount of a substance given to a test subject (human or animal) to determine dose-response relationships. Since exposure to chemicals is usually inadvertent, this quantity is often called potential dose.

Administrative Order: A legal document signed by EPA directing an individual, business, or other entity to take corrective action or refrain from an activity. It describes the violations and actions to be taken, and can be enforced in court. Such orders may be issued, for example, as a result of an administrative complaint whereby the respondent is ordered to pay a penalty for violations of a statute.

Administrative Order On Consent: A legal agreement signed by EPA and an individual, business, or other entity through which the violator agrees to pay for correction of violations, take the required corrective or cleanup actions, or refrain from an activity. It describes the actions to be taken, may be subject to a comment period, applies to civil actions, and can be enforced in court.

Administrative Procedures Act: A law that spells out procedures and requirements related to the promulgation of regulations.

Administrative Record: All documents which EPA considered or relied on in selecting the response action at a Superfund site, culminating in the record of decision for remedial action or, an action memorandum for removal actions.

Adsorption: Removal of a pollutant from air or water by collecting the pollutant on the surface of a solid material; e.g., an advanced method of treating waste in which activated carbon removes organic matter from waste-water.

Adulterants: Chemical impurities or substances that by law do not belong in a food, or pesticide.

Adulterated: 1. Any pesticide whose strength or purity falls below the quality stated on its label. 2. A food, feed, or product that contains illegal pesticide residues.

Advanced Treatment: A level of wastewater treatment more stringent than secondary treatment; requires an 85-percent reduction in conventional pollutant concentration or a significant reduction in non-conventional pollutants. Sometimes called tertiary treatment.

Advanced Wastewater Treatment: Any treatment of sewage that goes beyond the secondary or biological water treatment stage and includes the removal of nutrients such as phosphorus and nitrogen and a high percentage of suspended solids. (See primary, secondary treatment.)

Adverse Effects Data: FIFRA requires a pesticide registrant to submit data to EPA on any studies or other information regarding unreasonable adverse effects of a pesticide at any time after its registration.

Advisory: A non-regulatory document that communicates risk information to those who may have to make risk management decisions.

Aerated Lagoon: A holding and/or treatment pond that speeds up the natural process of biological decomposition of organic waste by stimulating the growth and activity of bacteria that degrade organic waste.

Aeration: A process which promotes biological degradation of organic matter in water. The process may be passive (as when waste is exposed to air), or active (as when a mixing or bubbling device introduces the air).

Aeration Tank: A chamber used to inject air into water.

Aerobic: Life or processes that require, or are not destroyed by, the presence of oxygen. (See: anaerobic.)

Aerobic Treatment: Process by which microbes decompose complex organic compounds in the presence of oxygen and use the liberated energy for reproduction and growth. (Such processes include extended aeration, trickling filtration, and rotating biological contactors.)

Aerosol: 1. Small droplets or particles suspended in the atmosphere, typically containing sulfur. They are usually emitted naturally (e.g. in volcanic eruptions) and as the result of anthropogenic (human) activities such as burning fossil fuels. 2. The pressurized gas used to propel substances out of a container.

Aerosol: A finely divided material suspended in air or other gaseous environment.

Affected Landfill: Under the Clean Air Act, landfills that meet criteria for capacity, age, and emissions rates set by the EPA. They are required to collect and combust their gas emissions.

Affected Public: 1.The people who live and/or work near a hazardous waste site. 2. The human population adversely impacted following exposure to a toxic pollutant in food, water, air, or soil.

Afterburner: In incinerator technology, a burner located so that the combustion gases are made to pass through its flame in order to remove smoke and odors. It may be attached to or be separated from the incinerator proper.

Age Tank: A tank used to store a chemical solution of known concentration for feed to a chemical feeder. Also called a day tank.

Agent: Any physical, chemical, or biological entity that can be harmful to an organism (synonymous with stressors.)

Agent Orange: A toxic herbicide and defoliant used in the Vietnam conflict, containing 2,4,5-trichlorophen-oxyacetic acid (2,4,5-T) and 2-4 dichlorophenoxyacetic acid (2,4-D) with trace amounts of dioxin.

Agricultural Pollution: Farming wastes, including runoff and leaching of pesticides and fertilizers; erosion and dust from plowing; improper disposal of animal manure and carcasses; crop residues, and debris.

Agricultural Waste: Poultry and livestock manure, and residual materials in liquid or solid form generated from the production and marketing of poultry, livestock or fur-bearing animals; also includes grain, vegetable, and fruit harvest residue.

Agroecosystem: Land used for crops, pasture, and livestock; the adjacent uncultivated land that supports other vegetation and wildlife; and the associated atmosphere, the underlying soils, groundwater, and drainage networks.

AHERA Designated Person (ADP): A person designated by a Local Education Agency to ensure that the AHERA requirements for asbestos management and abatement are properly implemented.

Air Binding: Situation where air enters the filter media and harms both the filtration and backwash processes.

Air Changes Per Hour (ACH): The movement of a volume of air in a given period of time; if a house has one air change per hour, it means that the air in the house will be replaced in a one-hour period.

Air Cleaning: Indoor-air quality-control strategy to remove various airborne particulates and/or gases from the air. Most common methods are particulate filtration, electrostatic precipitation, and gas sorption.

Air Contaminant: Any particulate matter, gas, or combination thereof, other than water vapor. (See: air pollutant.)

Air Curtain: A method of containing oil spills. Air bubbling through a perforated pipe causes an upward water flow that slows the spread of oil. It can also be used to stop fish from entering polluted water.

Air Exchange Rate: The rate at which outside air replaces indoor air in a given space.

Air Gap: Open vertical gap or empty space that separates drinking water supply to be protected from another water system in a treatment plant or other location. The open gap protects the drinking water from contamination by backflow or back siphonage.

Air Handling Unit: Equipment that includes a fan or blower, heating and/or cooling coils, regulator controls, condensate drain pans, and air filters.

Air Mass: A large volume of air with certain meteorological or polluted characteristics—e.g., a heat inversion or smogginess—while in one location. The characteristics can change as the air mass moves away.

Air Monitoring: (See: monitoring.)

Air/Oil Table: The surface between the vadose zone and ambient oil; the pressure of oil in the porous medium is equal to atmospheric pressure.

Air Padding: Pumping dry air into a container to assist with the withdrawal of liquid or to force a liquefied gas such as chlorine out of the container.

Air Permeability: Permeability of soil with respect to air. Important to the design of soil-gas surveys. Measured in darcys or centimeters-per-second.

Air Plenum: Any space used to convey air in a building, furnace, or structure. The space above a suspended ceiling is often used as an air plenum.

Air Pollutant: Any substance in air that could, in high enough concentration, harm man, other animals, vegetation, or material. Pollutants may include almost any natural or artificial composition of airborne matter capable of being airborne. They may be in the form of solid particles, liquid droplets, gases, or in combination thereof. Generally, they fall into two main groups: (1) those emitted directly from identifiable sources and (2) those produced in the air by interaction between two or more primary pollutants, or by reaction with normal atmospheric constituents, with or without photoactivation. Exclusive of pollen, fog, and dust, which are of natural origin, about 100 contaminants have been identified. Air pollutants are often grouped in categories for ease in classification; some of he categories are: solids, sulfur compounds, volatile organic chemicals, particulate matter, nitrogen compounds, oxygen compounds, halogen compounds, radioactive compound, and odors.

Air Pollution: The presence of contaminants or pollutant substances in the air that interfere with human health or welfare, or produce other harmful environmental effects.

Air Pollution Control Device: Mechanism or equipment that cleans emissions generated by a source (e.g. an incinerator, industrial smokestack, or an automobile exhaust system) by removing pollutants that would otherwise be released to the atmosphere.

Air Pollution Episode: A period of abnormally high concentration of air pollutants, often due to low winds and temperature inversion, that can cause illness and death. (See: episode, pollution.)

Air Quality Control Region:

Air Quality Criteria: The levels of pollution and lengths of exposure above which adverse health and welfare effects may occur.

Air Quality Standards: The level of pollutants prescribed by regulations that are not be exceeded during a given time in a defined area.

Air Sparging: Injecting air or oxygen into an aquifer to strip or flush volatile contaminants as air bubbles up through The ground water and is captured by a vapor extraction system.

Air Stripping: A treatment system that removes volatile organic compounds (VOCs) from contaminated ground water or surface water by forcing an airstream through the water and causing the compounds to evaporate.

Air Toxics: Any air pollutant for which a national ambient air quality standard (NAAQS) does not exist (i.e. excluding ozone, carbon monoxide, PM-10, sulfur dioxide, nitrogen oxide) that may reasonably be anticipated to cause cancer; respiratory, cardiovascular, or developmental effects; reproductive dysfunctions, neurological disorders, heritable gene mutations, or other serious or irreversible chronic or acute health effects in humans.

Airborne Particulates: Total suspended particulate matter found in the atmosphere as solid particles or liquid droplets. Chemical composition of particulates varies widely, depending on location and time of year. Sources of airborne particulates include: dust, emissions from industrial processes, combustion products from the burning of wood and coal, combustion products associated with motor vehicle or non-road engine exhausts, and reactions to gases in the atmosphere.

Airborne Release: Release of any pollutant into the air.

Alachlor: A herbicide, marketed under the trade name Lasso, used mainly to control weeds in corn and soybean fields.

Alar: Trade name for daminozide, a pesticide that makes apples redder, firmer, and less likely to drop off trees before growers are ready to pick them. It is also used to a lesser extent on peanuts, tart cherries, concord grapes, and other fruits.

Aldicarb: An insecticide sold under the trade name Temik. It is made from ethyl isocyanate.

Algae: Simple rootless plants that grow in sunlit waters in proportion to the amount of available nutrients. They can affect water quality adversely by lowering the dissolved oxygen in the water. They are food for fish and small aquatic animals.

Algal Blooms: Sudden spurts of algal growth, which can affect water quality adversely and indicate potentially hazardous changes in local water chemistry.

Algicide: Substance or chemical used specifically to kill or control algae.

Aliquot: A measured portion of a sample taken for analysis. One or more aliquots make up a sample. (See: duplicate.)

Alkaline: The condition of water or soil which contains a sufficient amount of alkali substance to raise the pH above 7.0.

Alkalinity: The capacity of bases to neutralize acids. An example is lime added to lakes to decrease acidity.

Allergen: A substance that causes an allergic reaction in individuals sensitive to it.

Alluvial: Relating to and/or sand deposited by flowing water.

Alternate Method: Any method of sampling and analyzing for an air or water pollutant that is not a reference or equivalent method but that has been demonstrated in specific cases-to EPA's satisfaction-to produce results adequate for compliance monitoring.

Alternative Compliance: A policy that allows facilities to choose among methods for achieving emission-reduction or risk-reduction instead of command-and control regulations that specify standards and how to meet them. Use of a theoretical emissions bubble over a facility to cap the amount of pollution emitted while allowing the company to choose where and how (within the facility) it complies.(See: bubble, emissions trading.)

Alternative Fuels: Substitutes for traditional liquid, oil-derived motor vehicle fuels like gasoline and diesel. Includes mixtures of alcohol-based fuels with gasoline, methanol, ethanol, compressed natural gas, and others.

Alternative Remedial Contract Strategy Contractors: Government contractors who provide project management and technical services to support remedial response activities at National Priorities List sites.

Ambient Air: Any unconfined portion of the atmosphere: open air, surrounding air.

Ambient Air Quality Standards: (See: Criteria Pollutants and National Ambient Air Quality Standards.)

Ambient Measurement: A measurement of the concentration of a substance or pollutant within the immediate environs of an organism; taken to relate it to the amount of possible exposure.

Ambient Medium: Material surrounding or contacting an organism (e.g. outdoor air, indoor air, water, or soil, through which chemicals or pollutants can reach the organism. (See: biological medium, environmental medium.)

Ambient Temperature: Temperature of the surrounding air or other medium.

Amprometric Titration: A way of measuring concentrations of certain substances in water using an electric current that flows during a chemical reaction.

Anaerobic: A life or process that occurs in, or is not destroyed by, the absence of oxygen.

Anaerobic Decomposition: Reduction of the net energy level and change in chemical composition of organic matter caused by microorganisms in an oxygen-free environment.

Animal Dander: Tiny scales of animal skin, a common indoor air pollutant.

Animal Studies: Investigations using animals as surrogates for humans with the expectation that the results are pertinent to humans.

Anisotropy: In hydrology, the conditions under which one or more hydraulic properties of an aquifer vary from a reference point.

Annular Space, Annulus: The space between two concentric tubes or casings, or between the casing and the borehole wall.

Antagonism: Interference or inhibition of the effect of one chemical by the action of another.

Antarctic "Ozone Hole": Refers to the seasonal depletion of ozone in the upper atmosphere above a large area of Antarctica. (See: Ozone Hole.)

Anti-Degradation Clause: Part of federal air quality and water quality requirements prohibiting deterioration where pollution levels are above the legal limit.

Anti-Microbial: An agent that kills microbes.

Applicable or Relevant and Appropriate Requirements (ARARs): Any state or federal statute that pertains to protection of human life and the environment in addressing specific conditions or use of a particular cleanup technology at a Superfund site,

Applied Dose: In exposure assessment, the amount of a substance in contact with the primary absorption boundaries of an organism (e.g. skin, lung tissue, gastrointestinal track) and available for absorption.

Aqueous: Something made up of water.

Aqueous Solubility: The maximum concentration of a chemical that will dissolve in pure water at a reference temperature.

Aquifer: An underground geological formation, or group of formations, containing water. Are sources of groundwater for wells and springs.

Aquifer Test: A test to determine hydraulic properties of an aquifer.

Aquitard: Geological formation that may contain groundwater but is not capable of transmitting significant quantities of it under normal hydraulic gradients. May function as confining bed.

Architectural Coatings: Coverings such as paint and roof tar that are used on exteriors of buildings.

Area of Review: In the UIC program, the area surrounding an injection well that is reviewed during the permitting process to determine if flow between aquifers will be induced by the injection operation.

Area Source: Any source of air pollution that is released over a relatively small area but which cannot be classified as a point source. Such sources may include vehicles and other small engines, small businesses and household activities, or biogenic sources such as a forest that releases hydrocarbons.

Aromatics: A type of hydrocarbon, such as benzene or toluene, with a specific type of ring structure. Aromatics are sometimes added to gasoline in order to increase octane. Some aromatics are toxic.

Arsenicals: Pesticides containing arsenic.

Artesian (Aquifer or Well): Water held under pressure in porous rock or soil confined by impermeable geological formations.

Asbestos: A mineral fiber that can pollute air or water and cause cancer or asbestosis when inhaled. EPA has banned or severely restricted its use in manufacturing and construction.

Asbestos Abatement: Procedures to control fiber release from asbestos-containing materials in a building or to remove them entirely, including removal, encapsulation, repair, enclosure, encasement, and operations and maintenance programs.

Asbestos Assessment: In the asbestos-in-schools program, the evaluation of the physical condition and potential for damage of all friable asbestos containing materials and thermal insulation systems.

Asbestos Program Manager: A building owner or designated representative who supervises all aspects of the facility asbestos management and control program.

Asbestos-Containing Waste Materials (ACWM): Mill tailings or any waste that contains commercial asbestos and is generated by a source covered by the Clean Air Act Asbestos NESHAPS.

Asbestosis: A disease associated with inhalation of asbestos fibers. The disease makes breathing progressively more difficult and can be fatal.

Ash: The mineral content of a product remaining after complete combustion.

Assay: A test for a specific chemical, microbe, or effect.

Assessment Endpoint: In ecological risk assessment, an explicit expression of the environmental value to be protected; includes both an ecological entity and specific attributed thereof. entity (e.g. salmon are a valued ecological entity; reproduction and population maintenance—the attribute—form an assessment endpoint.)

Assimilation: The ability of a body of water to purify itself of pollutants.

Assimilative Capacity: The capacity of a natural body of water to receive wastewaters or toxic materials without deleterious effects and without damage to aquatic life or humans who consume the water.

Association of Boards of Certification: An international organization representing boards which certify the operators of waterworks and wastewater facilities.

Attainment Area: An area considered to have air quality as good as or better than the national ambient air quality standards as defined in the Clean Air Act. An area may be an attainment area for one pollutant and a non-attainment area for others.

Attenuation: The process by which a compound is reduced in concentration over time, through absorption, adsorption, degradation, dilution, and/or transformation. an also be the decrease with distance of sight caused by attenuation of light by particulate pollution.

Attractant: A chemical or agent that lures insects or other pests by stimulating their sense of smell.

Attrition: Wearing or grinding down of a substance by friction. Dust from such processes contributes to air pollution.

Availability Session: Informal meeting at a public location where interested citizens can talk with EPA and state officials on a one-to-one basis.

Available Chlorine: A measure of the amount of chlorine available in chlorinated lime, hypochlorite compounds, and other materials used as a source of chlorine when compared with that of liquid or gaseous chlorines.

Avoided Cost: The cost a utility would incur to generate the next increment of electric capacity using its own resources; many landfill gas projects' buy back rates are based on avoided costs.

A-Scale Sound Level: A measurement of sound approximating the sensitivity of the human ear, used to note the intensity or annoyance level of sounds.

B

Back Pressure: A pressure that can cause water to backflow into the water supply when a user's waste water system is at a higher pressure than the public system.

Backflow/Back Siphonage: A reverse flow condition created by a difference in water pressures that causes water to flow back into the distribution pipes of a drinking water supply from any source other than the intended one.

Background Level: 1. The concentration of a substance in an environmental media (air, water, or soil) that occurs naturally or is not the result of human activities. 2. In exposure assessment the concentration of a substance in a defined control area, during a fixed period of time before, during, or after a data-gathering operation..

Backwashing: Reversing the flow of water back through the filter media to remove entrapped solids.

Backyard Composting: Diversion of organic food waste and yard trimmings from the municipal waste stream by composting hem in one's yard through controlled decomposition of organic matter by bacteria and fungi into a humus-like product. It is considered source reduction, not recycling, because the composted materials never enter the municipal waste stream.

Barrel Sampler: Open-ended steel tube used to collect soil samples.

BACT - Best Available Control Technology: An emission limitation based on the maximum degree of emission reduction (considering energy, environmental, and economic impacts) achievable through application of production processes and available methods, systems, and techniques. BACT does not permit emissions in excess of those allowed under any applicable Clean Air Act provisions. Use of the BACT concept is allowable on a case by case basis for major new or modified emissions sources in attainment areas and applies to each regulated pollutant.

Bacteria: (Singular: bacterium) Microscopic living organisms that can aid in pollution control by metabolizing organic matter in sewage, oil spills or other pollutants. However, bacteria in soil, water or air can also cause human, animal and plant health problems.

Bactericide: A pesticide used to control or destroy bacteria, typically in the home, schools, or hospitals.

Baffle: A flat board or plate, deflector, guide, or similar device constructed or placed in flowing water or slurry systems to cause more uniform flow velocities to absorb energy and to divert, guide, or agitate liquids.

Baffle Chamber: In incinerator design, a chamber designed to promote the settling of fly ash and coarse particulate matter by changing the direction and/or reducing the velocity of the gases produced by the combustion of the refuse or sludge.

Baghouse Filter: Large fabric bag, usually made of glass fibers, used to eliminate intermediate and large (greater than 20 PM in diameter) particles. This device operates like the bag of an electric vacuum cleaner, passing the air and smaller particles while entrapping the larger ones.

Bailer: A pipe with a valve at the lower end, used to remove slurry from the bottom or side of a well as it is being drilled, or to collect groundwater samples from wells or open boreholes. 2. A tube of varying length.

Baling: Compacting solid waste into blocks to reduce volume and simplify handling.

Ballistic Separator: A machine that sorts organic from inorganic matter for composting.

Band Application: The spreading of chemicals over, or next to, each row of plants in a field.

Banking: A system for recording qualified air emission reductions for later use in bubble, offset, or netting transactions. (See: emissions trading.)

Bar Screen: In wastewater treatment, a device used to remove large solids.

Barrier Coating(s): A layer of a material that obstructs or prevents passage of something through a surface that is to be protected; e.g., grout, caulk, or various sealing compounds; sometimes used with polyurethane membranes to prevent corrosion or oxidation of metal surfaces, chemical impacts on various materials, or, for example, to prevent radon infiltration through walls, cracks, or joints in a house.

Basal Application: In pesticides, the application of a chemical on plant stems or tree trunks just above the soil line.

Basalt: Consistent year-round energy use of a facility; also refers to the minimum amount of electricity supplied continually to a facility.

Bean Sheet: Common term for a pesticide data package record.

Bed Load: Sediment particles resting on or near the channel bottom that are pushed or rolled along by the flow of water.

BEN: EPA's computer model for analyzing a violator's economic gain from not complying with the law.

Bench-scale Tests: Laboratory testing of potential cleanup technologies (See: treatability studies.)

Benefit-Cost Analysis: An economic method for assessing the benefits and costs of achieving alternative health-based standards at given levels of health protection.

Benthic/Benthos: An organism that feeds on the sediment at the bottom of a water body such as an ocean, lake, or river.

Bentonite: A colloidal clay, expansible when moist, commonly used to provide a tight seal around a well casing.

Beryllium: An metal hazardous to human health when inhaled as an airborne pollutant. It is discharged by machine shops, ceramic and propellant plants, and foundries.

Best Available Control Measures (BACM): A term used to refer to the most effective measures (according to EPA guidance) for controlling small or dispersed particulates and other emissions from sources such as roadway dust, soot and ash from woodstoves and open burning of rush, timber, grasslands, or trash.

Best Available Control Technology (BACT): For any specific source, the currently available technology producing the greatest reduction of air pollutant emissions,taking into account energy, environmental, economic, and other costs.

Best Available Control Technology (BACT): The most stringent technology available for controlling emissions; major sources are required to use BACT, unless it can be demonstrated that it is not feasible for energy, environmental, or economic reasons.

Best Demonstrated Available Technology (BDAT): As identified by EPA, the most effective commercially available means of treating specific types of hazardous waste. The BDATs may change with advances in treatment technologies.

Best Management Practice (BMP): Methods that have been determined to be the most effective, practical means of preventing or reducing pollution from non-point sources.

Bimetal: Beverage containers with steel bodies and aluminum tops; handled differently from pure aluminum in recycling.

Bioaccumulants: Substances that increase in concentration in living organisms as they take in contaminated air, water, or food because the substances are very slowly metabolized or excreted. (See: biological magnification.)

Bioassay: A test to determine te relative strength of a substance by comparing its effect on a test organism with that of a standard preparation.

Bioavailabiliity: Degree of ability to be absorbed and ready to interact in organism metabolism.

Biochemical Oxygen Demand (BOD): A measure of the amount of oxygen consumed in the biological processes that break down organic matter in water. The greater the BOD, the greater the degree of pollution.

Bioconcentration: The accumulation of a chemical in tissues of a fish or other organism to levels greater than in the surrounding medium.

Biodegradable: Capable of decomposing under natural conditions.

Biodiversity: Refers to the variety and variability among living organisms and the ecological complexes in which they occur. Diversity can be defined as the number of different items and their relative frequencies. For biological diversity, these items are organized at many levels, ranging from complete ecosystems to the biochemical structures that are the molecular basis of heredity. Thus, the term encompasses different ecosystems, species, and genes.

Biological Contaminants: Living organisms or derivates (e.g. viruses, bacteria, fungi, and mammal and bird antigens) that can cause harmful health effects when inhaled, swallowed, or otherwise taken into the body.

Biological Control: In pest control, the use of animals and organisms that eat or otherwise kill or out-compete pests.

Biological Integrity: The ability to support and maintain balanced, integrated, functionality in the natural habitat of a given region. Concept is applied primarily in drinking water management.

Biological Magnification: Refers to the process whereby certain substances such as pesticides or heavy metals move up the food chain, work their way into rivers or lakes, and are eaten by aquatic organisms such as fish, which in turn are eaten by large birds, animals or humans. The substances become concentrated in tissues or internal organs as they move up the chain. (See: bioaccumulants.)

Biological Measurement: A measurement taken in a biological medium. For exposure assessment, it is related to the measurement is taken to related it to the established internal dose of a compound.

Biological Medium: One of the major component of an organism; e.g. blood, fatty tissue, lymph nodes or breath, in which chemicals can be stored or transformed. (See: ambient medium, environmental medium.)

Biological Oxidation: Decomposition of complex organic materials by microorganisms. Occurs in self-purification of water bodies and in activated sludge wastewater treatment.

Biological Oxygen Demand (BOD): An indirect measure of the concentration of biologically degradable material present in organic wastes. It usually reflects the amount of oxygen consumed in five days by biological processes breaking down organic waste.

Biological pesticides: Certain microorganism, including bacteria, fungi, viruses, and protozoa that are effective in controlling pests. These agents usually do not have toxic effects on animals and people and do not leave toxic or persistent chemical residues in the environment.

Biological Stressors: Organisms accidentally or intentionally dropped into habitats in which they do not evolve naturally; e.g. gypsy moths, Dutch elm disease, certain types of algae, and bacteria.

Biological Treatment: A treatment technology that uses bacteria to consume organic waste.

Biologically Effective Dose: The amount of a deposited or absorbed compound reaching the cells or target sites where adverse effect occur, or where the chemical interacts with a membrane.

Biologicals: Vaccines, cultures and other preparations made from living organisms and their products, intended for use in diagnosing, immunizing, or treating humans or animals, or in related research.

Biomass: All of the living material in a given area; often refers to vegetation.

Biome: Entire community of living organisms in a single major ecological area. (See: biotic community.)

Biomonitoring: 1. The use of living organisms to test the suitability of effluents for discharge into receiving waters and to test the quality of such waters downstream from the discharge. 2. Analysis of blood, urine, tissues, etc. to measure chemical exposure in humans.

Bioremediation: Use of living organisms to clean up oil spills or remove other pollutants from soil, water, or wastewater; use of organisms such as non-harmful insects to remove agricultural pests or counteract diseases of trees, plants, and garden soil.

Biosensor: Analytical device comprising a biological recognition element (e.g. enzyme, receptor, DNA, antibody, or microorganism) in intimate contact with an electrochemical, optical, thermal, or acoustic signal transducer that together permit analyses of chemical properties or quantities. Shows potential development in some areas, including environmental monitoring.

Biosphere: The portion of Earth and its atmosphere that can support life.

Biostabilizer: A machine that converts solid waste into compost by grinding and aeration.

Biota: The animal and plant life of a given region.

Biotechnology: Techniques that use living organisms or parts of organisms to produce a variety of products (from medicines to industrial enzymes) to improve plants or animals or to develop microorganisms to remove toxics from bodies of water, or act as pesticides.

Biotic Community: A naturally occurring assemblage of plants and animals that live in the same environment and are mutually sustaining and interdependent. (See: biome.)

Biotransformation: Conversion of a substance into other compounds by organisms; includes biodegredation.

Blackwater: Water that contains animal, human, or food waste.

Blood Products: Any product derived from human blood, including but not limited to blood plasma, platelets, red or white corpuscles, and derived licensed products such as interferon.

Bloom: A proliferation of algae and/or higher aquatic plants in a body of water; often related to pollution, especially when pollutants accelerate growth.

BOD5: The amount of dissolved oxygen consumed in five days by biological processes breaking down organic matter.

Body Burden: The amount of a chemical stored in the body at a given time, especially a potential toxin in the body as the result of exposure.

Bog: A type of wetland that accumulates appreciable peat deposits. Bogs depend primarily on precipitation for their water source, and are usually acidic and rich in plant residue with a conspicuous mat of living green moss.

Boiler: A vessel designed to transfer heat produced by combustion or electric resistance to water. Boilers may provide hot water or steam.

Boom: 1. A floating device used to contain oil on a body of water. 2. A piece of equipment used to apply pesticides from a tractor or truck.

Borehole: Hole made with drilling equipment.

Botanical Pesticide: A pesticide whose active ingredient is a plant-produced chemical such as nicotine or strychnine. Also called a plant-derived pesticide.

Bottle Bill: Proposed or enacted legislation which requires a returnable deposit on beer or soda containers and provides for retail store or other redemption. Such legislation is designed to discourage use of throw-away containers.

Bottom Ash: The non-airborne combustion residue from burning pulverized coal in a boiler; the material which falls to the bottom of the boiler and is removed mechanically; a concentration of non-combustible materials, which may include toxics.

Bottom Land Hardwoods: Forested freshwater wetlands adjacent to rivers in the southeastern United States, especially valuable for wildlife breeding, nesting and habitat.

Bounding Estimate: An estimate of exposure, dose, or risk that is higher than that incurred by the person in the population with the currently highest exposure, dose, or risk. Bounding estimates are useful in developing statements that exposures, doses, or risks are not greater than an estimated value.

Brackish: Mixed fresh and salt water.

Breakpoint Chlorination: Addition of chlorine to water until the chlorine demand has been satisfied.

Breakthrough: A crack or break in a filter bed that allows the passage of floc or particulate matter through a filter; will cause an increase in filter effluent turbidity.

Breathing Zone: Area of air in which an organism inhales.

Brine Mud: Waste material, often associated with well-drilling or mining, composed of mineral salts or other inorganic compounds.

British Thermal Unit: Unit of heat energy equal to the amount of heat required to raise the temperature of one pound of water by one degree Fahrenheit at sea level.

Broadcast Application: The spreading of pesticides over an entire area.

Brownfields: Abandoned, idled, or under used industrial and commercial facilities/sites where expansion or redevelopment is complicated by real or perceived environmental contamination. They can be in urban, suburban, or rural areas. EPA's Brownfields initiative helps communities mitigate potential health risks and restore the economic viability of such areas or properties.

Bubble: A system under which existing emissions sources can propose alternate means to comply with a set of emissions limitations; under the bubble concept, sources can control more than required at one emission point where control costs are relatively low in return for a comparable relaxation of controls at a second emission point where costs are higher.

Bubble Policy: (See: emissions trading.)

Buffer: A solution or liquid whose chemical makeup is such that it minimizes changes in pH when acids or bases are added to it.

Buffer Strips: Strips of grass or other erosion-resisting vegetation between or below cultivated strips or fields.

Building Cooling Load: The hourly amount of heat that must be removed from a building to maintain indoor comfort (measured in British thermal units (Btus).

Building Envelope: The exterior surface of a building's construction—the walls, windows, floors, roof, and floor. Also called building shell.

Building Related Illness: Diagnosable illness whose cause and symptoms can be directly attributed to a specific pollutant source within a building (e.g. Legionnaire's disease, hypersensitivity, pneumonitis.) (See: sick building syndrome.)

Bulk Sample: A small portion (usually thumbnail size) of a suspect asbestos-containing building material collected by an asbestos inspector for laboratory analysis to determine asbestos content.

Bulky Waste: Large items of waste materials, such as appliances, furniture, large auto parts, trees, stumps.

Burial Ground (Graveyard): A disposal site for radioactive waste materials that uses earth or water as a shield.

Buy-Back Center: Facility where individuals or groups bring reyclables in return for payment.

By-product: Material, other than the principal product, generated as a consequence of an industrial process or as a breakdown product in a living system.

C

Cadmium (Cd): A heavy metal that accumulates in the environment.

Cancellation: Refers to Section 6 (b) of the Federal Insecticide, Fungicide and Rodenticide Act (FIFRA) which authorizes cancellation of a pesticide registration if unreasonable adverse effects to the environment and public health develop when a product is used according to widespread and commonly recognized practice, or if its labeling or other material required to be submitted does not comply with FIFRA provisions.

Cap: A layer of clay, or other impermeable material installed over the top of a closed landfill to prevent entry of rainwater and minimize leachate.

Capacity Assurance Plan: A statewide plan which supports a state's ability to manage the hazardous waste generated within its boundaries over a twenty year period.

Capillary Action: Movement of water through very small spaces due to molecular forces called capillary forces.

Capillary Fringe: The porous material just above the water table which may hold water by capillarity (a property of surface tension that draws water upwards) in the smaller void spaces.

Capillary Fringe: The zone above he water table within which the porous medium is saturated by water under less than atmospheric pressure.

Capture Efficiency: The fraction of organic vapors generated by a process that are directed to an abatement or recovery device.

Carbon Absorber: An add-on control device that uses activated carbon to absorb volatile organic compounds from a gas stream. (The VOCs are later recovered from the carbon.)

Carbon Adsorption: A treatment system that removes contaminants from ground water or surface water by forcing it through tanks containing activated carbon treated to attract the contaminants.

Carbon Monoxide (CO): A colorless, odorless, poisonous gas produced by incomplete fossil fuel combustion.

Carbon Tetrachloride (CC14): Compound consisting of one carbon atom ad four chlorine atoms, once widely used as a industrial raw material, as a solvent, and in the production of

CFCs. Use as a solvent ended when it was discovered to be carcinogenic.

Carboxyhemoglobin: Hemoglobin in which the iron is bound to carbon monoxide(CO) instead of oxygen.

Carcinogen: Any substance that can cause or aggravate cancer.

Carrier: 1.The inert liquid or solid material in a pesticide product that serves as a delivery vehicle for the active ingredient. Carriers do not have toxic properties of their own. 2. Any material or system that can facilitate the movement of a pollutant into the body or cells.

Carrying Capacity: 1. In recreation management, the amount of use a recreation area can sustain without loss of quality. 2. In wildlife management, the maximum number of animals an area can support during a given period.

CAS Registration Number: A number assigned by the Chemical Abstract Service to identify a chemical.

Case Study: A brief fact sheet providing risk, cost, and performance information on alternative methods and other pollution prevention ideas, compliance initiatives, voluntary efforts, etc.

Cask: A thick-walled container (usually lead) used to transport radioactive material. Also called a coffin.

Catalyst: A substance that changes the speed or yield of a chemical reaction without being consumed or chemically changed by the chemical reaction.

Catalytic Converter: An air pollution abatement device that removes pollutants from motor vehicle exhaust, either by oxidizing them into carbon dioxide and water or reducing them to nitrogen.

Catalytic Incinerator: A control device that oxidizes volatile organic compounds (VOCs) by using a catalyst to promote the combustion process. Catalytic incinerators require lower temperatures than conventional thermal incinerators, thus saving fuel and other costs.

Categorical Exclusion: A class of actions which either individually or cumulatively would not have a significant effect on the human environment and therefore would not require preparation of an environmental assessment or environmental impact statement under the National Environmental Policy Act (NEPA).

Categorical Pretreatment Standard: A technology-based effluent limitation for an industrial facility discharging into a municipal sewer system. Analogous in stringency to Best Availability Technology (BAT) for direct dischargers.

Cathodic Protection: A technique to prevent corrosion of a metal surface by making it the cathode of an electrochemical cell.

Cavitation: The formation and collapse of gas pockets or bubbles on the blade of an impeller or the gate of a valve; collapse of these pockets or bubbles drives water with such force that it can cause pitting of the gate or valve surface.

Cells: 1. In solid waste disposal, holes where waste is dumped, compacted, and covered with layers of dirt on a daily basis. 2. The smallest structural part of living matter capable of functioning as an independent unit.

Cementitious: Densely packed and nonfibrous friable materials.

Central Collection Point: Location were a generator of regulated medical waste consolidates wastes originally generated at various locations in his facility. The wastes are gathered together for treatment on-site or for transportation elsewhere for treatment and/or disposal. This term could also apply to community hazardous waste collections, industrial and other waste management systems.

Centrifugal Collector: A mechanical system using centrifugal force to remove aerosols from a gas stream or to remove water from sludge.

CERCLIS: The federal Comprehensive Environmental Response, Compensation, and Liability Information System is a database that includes all sites which have been nominated for investigation by the Superfund program.

Channelization: Straightening and deepening streams so water will move faster, a marsh-drainage tactic that can interfere with waste assimilation capacity, disturb fish and wildlife habitats, and aggravate flooding.

Characteristic: Any one of the four categories used in defining hazardous waste: ignitability, corrosivity, reactivity, and toxicity.

Characterization of Ecological Effects: Part of ecological risk assessment that evaluates ability of a stressor to cause adverse effects under given circumstances.

Characterization of Exposure: Portion of an ecological risk assessment that evaluates interaction of a stressor with one or more ecological entities.

Check-Valve Tubing Pump: Water sampling tool also referred to as a water Pump.

Chemical Case: For purposes of review and regulation, the grouping of chemically similar pesticide active ingredients (e.g. salts and esters of the same chemical) into chemical cases.

Chemical Compound: A distinct and pure substance formed by the union or two or more elements in definite proportion by weight.

Chemical Element: A fundamental substance comprising one kind of atom; the simplest form of matter.

Chemical Oxygen Demand (COD): A measure of the oxygen required to oxidize all compounds, both organic and inorganic, in water.

Chemical Stressors: Chemicals released to the environment through industrial waste, auto emissions, pesticides, and other human activity that can cause illnesses and even death in plants and animals.

Chemical Treatment: Any one of a variety of technologies that use chemicals or a variety of chemical processes to treat waste.

Chemnet: Mutual aid network of chemical shippers and contractors that assigns a contracted emergency response company to provide technical support if a representative of the firm whose chemicals are involved in an incident is not readily available.

Chemosterilant: A chemical that controls pests by preventing reproduction.

Chemtrec: The industry-sponsored Chemical Transportation Emergency Center; provides information and/or emergency assistance to emergency responders.

Child Resistant Packaging (CRP): Packaging that protects children or adults from injury or illness resulting from accidental contact with or ingestion of residential pesticides that meet or exceed specific toxicity levels. Required by FIFRA regulations. Term is also used for protective packaging of medicines.

Chiller: A device that generates a cold liquid that is circulated through an air-handling unit's cooling coil to cool the air supplied to the building.

Chilling Effect: The lowering of the Earth's temperature because of increased particles in the air blocking the sun's rays. (See: greenhouse effect.)

Chisel Plowing: Preparing croplands by using a special implement that avoids complete inversion of the soil as in conventional plowing. Chisel plowing can leave a protective cover or crops residues on the soil surface to help prevent erosion and improve filtration.

Chlorinated Hydrocarbons: 1. Chemicals containing only chlorine, carbon, and hydrogen. These include a class of persistent, broad-spectrum insecticides that linger in the environment and accumulate in the food chain. Among them are DDT, aldrin, dieldrin, heptachlor, chlordane, lindane, endrin, Mirex, hexachloride, and toxaphene. Other examples include TCE, used as an industrial solvent. 2. Any chlorinated organic compounds including chlorinated solvents such as dichloromethane, trichloromethylene, chloroform.

Chlorinated Solvent: An organic solvent containing chlorine atoms(e.g. methylene chloride and 1,1,1-trichloromethane). Uses of chlorinated solvents are include aerosol spray containers, in highway paint, and dry cleaning fluids.

Chlorination: The application of chlorine to drinking water, sewage, or industrial waste to disinfect or to oxidize undesirable compounds.

Chlorinator: A device that adds chlorine, in gas or liquid form, to water or sewage to kill infectious bacteria.

Chlorine-Contact Chamber: That part of a water treatment plant where effluent is disinfected by chlorine.

Chlorofluorocarbons (CFCs): A family of inert, nontoxic, and easily liquefied chemicals used in refrigeration, air conditioning, packaging, insulation, or as solvents and aerosol propellants. Because CFCs are not destroyed in the lower atmosphere they drift into the upper atmosphere where their chlorine components destroy ozone. (See: fluorocarbons.)

Chlorophenoxy: A class of herbicides that may be found in domestic water supplies and cause adverse health effects.

Chlorosis: Discoloration of normally green plant parts caused by disease, lack of nutrients, or various air pollutants.

Cholinesterase: An enzyme found in animals that regulates nerve impulses by the inhibition of acetylcholine. Cholinesterase inhibition is associated with a variety of acute symptoms such as nausea, vomiting, blurred vision, stomach cramps, and rapid heart rate.

Chromium: (See: heavy metals.)

Chronic Effect: An adverse effect on a human or animal in which symptoms recur frequently or develop slowly over a long period of time.

Chronic Exposure: Multiple exposures occurring over an extended period of time or over a significant fraction of an animal's or human's lifetime (Usually seven years to a lifetime.)

Chronic Toxicity: The capacity of a substance to cause long-term poisonous health effects in humans, animals, fish, and other organisms. (See: acute toxicity.)

Circle of Influence: The circular outer edge of a depression produced in the water table by the pumping of water from a well. (See: cone of depression.)

Cistern: Small tank or storage facility used to store water for a home or farm; often used to store rain water.

Clarification: Clearing action that occurs during wastewater treatment when solids settle out. This is often aided by centrifugal action and chemically induced coagulation in wastewater.

Clarifier: A tank in which solids settle to the bottom and are subsequently removed as sludge.

Class I Area: Under the Clean Air Act. a Class I area is one in which visibility is protected more stringently than under the national ambient air quality standards; includes national parks, wilderness areas, monuments, and other areas of special national and cultural significance.

Class I Substance: One of several groups of chemicals with an ozone depletion potential of 0.2 or higher, including CFCS, Halons, Carbon Tetrachloride, and Methyl Chloroform (listed in the Clean Air Act), and HBFCs and Ethyl Bromide (added by EPA regulations). (See: Global warming potential.)

Class II Substance: A substance with an ozone depletion potential of less than 0.2. All HCFCs are currently included in this classification. (See: Global warming potential.)

Clay Soil: Soil material containing more than 40 percent clay, less than 45 percent sand, and less than 40 percent silt.

Clean Coal Technology: Any technology not in widespread use prior to the Clean Air Act Amendments of 1990. This Act will achieve significant reductions in pollutants associated with the burning of coal.

Clean Fuels: Blends or substitutes for gasoline fuels, including compressed natural gas, methanol, ethanol, and liquified petroleum gas.

Cleaner Technologies Substitutes Assessment: A document that systematically evaluates the relative risk, performance, and cost trade-offs of technological alternatives; serves as a repository for all the technical data (including methodology and results) developed by a DfE or other pollution prevention or education project.

Cleanup: Actions taken to deal with a release or threat of release of a hazardous substance that could affect humans and/or the environment. The term "cleanup" is sometimes used interchangeably with the terms remedial action, removal action, response action, or corrective action.

Clear Cut: Harvesting all the trees in one area at one time, a practice that can encourage fast rainfall or snowmelt runoff, erosion, sedimentation of streams and lakes, and flooding, and destroys vital habitat.

Clear Well: A reservoir for storing filtered water of sufficient quantity to prevent the need to vary the filtration rate with variations in demand. Also used to provide chlorine contact time for disinfection.

Climate Change (also referred to as 'global climate change'): The term 'climate change' is sometimes used to refer to all forms of climatic inconsistency, but because the Earth's climate is never static, the term is more properly used to imply a significant change from one climatic condition to another. In some cases, 'climate change' has been used synonymously with the term, 'global warming'; scientists however, tend to use the term in the wider sense to also include natural changes in climate. (See: global warming.)

Cloning: In biotechnology, obtaining a group of genetically identical cells from a single cell; making identical copies of a gene.

Closed-Loop Recycling: Reclaiming or reusing wastewater for non-potable purposes in an enclosed process.

Closure: The procedure a landfill operator must follow when a landfill reaches its legal capacity for solid ceasing acceptance of solid waste and placing a cap on the landfill site.

Co-fire: Burning of two fuels in the same combustion unit; e.g., coal and natural gas, or oil and coal.

Coagulation: Clumping of particles in wastewater to settle out impurities, often induced by chemicals such as lime, alum, and iron salts.

Coal Cleaning Technology: A precombustion process by which coal is physically or chemically treated to remove some of its sulfur so as to reduce sulfur dioxide emissions.

Coal Gasification: Conversion of coal to a gaseous product by one of several available technologies.

Coastal Zone: Lands and waters adjacent to the coast that exert an influence on the uses of the sea and its ecology, or whose uses and ecology are affected by the sea.

Code of Federal Regulations (CFR): Document that codifies all rules of the executive departments and agencies of the federal government. It is divided into fifty volumes, known as titles. Title 40 of the CFR (referenced as 40 CFR) lists all environmental regulations.

Coefficient of Haze (COH): A measurement of visibility interference in the atmosphere.

Cogeneration: The consecutive generation of useful thermal and electric energy from the same fuel source.

Coke Oven: An industrial process which converts coal into coke, one of the basic materials used in blast furnaces for the conversion of iron ore into iron.

Cold Temperature CO: A standard for automobile emissions of carbon monoxide (CO) emissions to be met at a low temperature (i.e. 20 degrees Fahrenheit). Conventional automobile catalytic converters are not efficient in cold weather until they warm up.

Coliform Index: A rating of the purity of water based on a count of fecal bacteria.

Coliform Organism: Microorganisms found in the intestinal tract of humans and animals. Their presence in water indicates fecal pollution and potentially adverse contamination by pathogens.

Collector: Public or private hauler that collects nonhazardous waste and recyclable materials from residential, commercial, institutional and industrial sources. (See: hauler.)

Collector Sewers: Pipes used to collect and carry wastewater from individual sources to an interceptor sewer that will carry it to a treatment facility.

Colloids: Very small, finely divided solids (that do not dissolve) that remain dispersed in a liquid for a long time due to their small size and electrical charge.

Combined Sewer Overflows: Discharge of a mixture of storm water and domestic waste when the flow capacity of a sewer system is exceeded during rainstorms.

Combined Sewers: A sewer system that carries both sewage and storm-water runoff. Normally, its entire flow goes to a waste treatment plant, but during a heavy storm, the volume of water may be so great as to cause overflows of untreated mixtures of storm water and sewage into receiving waters. Storm-water runoff may also carry toxic chemicals from industrial areas or streets into the sewer system.

Combustion: 1. Burning, or rapid oxidation, accompanied by release of energy in the form of heat and light. 2. Refers to controlled burning of waste, in which heat chemically alters organic compounds, converting into stable inorganics such as carbon dioxide and water.

Combustion Chamber: The actual compartment where waste is burned in an incinerator.

Combustion Product: Substance produced during the burning or oxidation of a material.

Command Post: Facility located at a safe distance upwind from an accident site, where the on-scene coordinator, responders, and technical representatives make response decisions, deploy manpower and equipment, maintain liaison with news media, and handle communications.

Command-and-Control Regulations: Specific requirements prescribing how to comply with specific standards defining acceptable levels of pollution.

Comment Period: Time provided for the public to review and comment on a proposed EPA action or rulemaking after publication in the Federal Register.

Commercial Waste: All solid waste emanating from business establishments such as stores, markets, office buildings, restaurants, shopping centers, and theaters.

Commercial Waste Management Facility: A treatment, storage, disposal, or transfer facility which accepts waste from a variety of sources, as compared to a private facility which normally manages a limited waste stream generated by its own operations.

Commingled Recyclables: Mixed recyclables that are collected together.

Comminuter: A machine that shreds or pulverizes solids to make waste treatment easier.

Comminution: Mechanical shredding or pulverizing of waste. Used in both solid waste management and wastewater treatment.

Common Sense Initiative: Voluntary program to simplify environmental regulation to achieve cleaner, cheaper, smarter results, starting with six major industry sectors.

Community: In ecology, an assemblage of populations of different species within a specified location in space and time. Sometimes, a particular subgrouping may be specified, such as the fish community in a lake or the soil arthropod community in a forest.

Community Relations: The EPA effort to establish two-way communication with the public to create understanding of EPA programs and related actions, to ensure public input into decision-making processes related to affected communities, and to make certain that the Agency is aware of and responsive to public concerns. Specific community relations activities are required in relation to Superfund remedial actions.

Community Water System: A public water system which serves at least 15 service connections used by year-round residents or regularly serves at least 25 year-round residents.

Compact Fluorescent Lamp (CFL): Small fluorescent lamps used as more efficient alternatives to incandescent lighting. Also called PL, CFL, Twin-Tube, or BIAX lamps.

Compaction: Reduction of the bulk of solid waste by rolling and tamping.

Comparative Risk Assessment: Process that generally uses the judgement of experts to predict effects and set priorities among a wide range of environmental problems.

Complete Treatment: A method of treating water that consists of the addition of coagulant chemicals, flash mixing, coagulation-flocculation, sedimentation, and filtration. Also called conventional filtration.

Compliance Coal: Any coal that emits less than 1.2 pounds of sulfur dioxide per million Btu when burned. Also known as low sulfur coal.

Compliance Coating: A coating whose volatile organic compound content does not exceed that allowed by regulation.

Compliance Cycle: The 9-year calendar year cycle, beginning January 1, 1993, during which public water systems must monitor. Each cycle consists of three 3-year compliance periods.

Compliance Monitoring: Collection and evaluation of data, including self-monitoring reports, and verification to show whether pollutant concentrations and loads contained in permitted discharges are in compliance with the limits and conditions specified in the permit.

Compliance Schedule: A negotiated agreement between a pollution source and a government agency that specifies dates and procedures by which a source will reduce emissions and, thereby, comply with a regulation.

Composite Sample: A series of water samples taken over a given period of time and weighted by flow rate.

Compost: The relatively stable humus material that is produced from a composting process in which bacteria in soil mixed with garbage and degradable trash break down the mixture into organic fertilizer.

Composting: The controlled biological decomposition of organic material in the presence of air to form a humus-like material. Controlled methods of composting include mechanical mixing and aerating, ventilating the materials by dropping them through a vertical series of aerated chambers, or placing the compost in piles out in the open air and mixing it or turning it periodically.

Composting Facilities: 1. An offsite facility where the organic component of municipal solid waste is decomposed under controlled conditions; 2.an aerobic process in which organic materials are ground or shredded and then decomposed to humus in windrow piles or in mechanical digesters, drums, or similar enclosures.

Compressed Natural Gas (CNG): An alternative fuel for motor vehicles; considered one of the cleanest because of low hydrocarbon emissions and its vapors are relatively non-ozone producing. However, vehicles fueled with CNG do emit a significant quantity of nitrogen oxides.

Concentration: The relative amount of a substance mixed with another substance. An example is five ppm of carbon monoxide in air or 1 mg/l of iron in water.

Condensate: 1.Liquid formed when warm landfill gas cools as it travels through a collection system. 2. Water created by cooling steam or water vapor.

Condensate Return System: System that returns the heated water condensing within steam piping to the boiler and thus saves energy.

Conditional Registration: Under special circumstances, the Federal Insecticide, Fungicide, and Rodenticide Act (FIFRA) permits registration of pesticide products that is "conditional" upon the submission of additional data. These special circumstances include a finding by the EPA Administrator that a new product or use of an existing pesticide will not significantly increase the risk of unreasonable adverse effects. A product containing a new (previously unregistered) active ingredient may be conditionally registered only if the Administrator finds that such conditional registration is in the public interest, that a reasonable time for conducting the additional studies has not elapsed, and the use of the pesticide for the period of conditional registration will not present an unreasonable risk.

Conditionally Exempt Generators (CE): Persons or enterprises which produce less than 220 pounds of hazardous waste per month. Exempt from most regulation, they are required merely to determine whether their waste is hazardous, notify appropriate state or local agencies, and ship it by an authorized transporter to a permitted facility for proper disposal. (See : small quantity generator.)

Conductance: A rapid method of estimating the dissolved solids content of water supply by determining the capacity of a water sample to carry an electrical current. Conductivity is a measure of the ability of a solution to carry and electrical current.

Conductivity: A measure of the ability of a solution to carry an electrical current.

Cone of Depression: A depression in the water table that develops around a pumped well.

Cone of Influence: The depression, roughly conical in shape, produced in a water table by the pumping of water from a well.

Cone Penterometer Testing (CPT): A direct push system used to measure lithology based on soil penetration resistance. Sensors in the tip of the cone of the DP rod measure tip resistance and side-wall friction, transmitting electrical signals to digital processing equipment on the ground surface. (See: direct push.)

Confidential Business Information (CBI): Material that contains trade secrets or commercial or financial information that has been claimed as confidential by its source (e.g. a pesticide or new chemical formulation registrant). EPA has special procedures for handling such information.

Confidential Statement of Formula (CSF): A list of the ingredients in a new pesticide or chemical formulation. The list is submitted at the time for application for registration or change in formulation.

Confined Aquifer: An aquifer in which ground water is confined under pressure which is significantly greater than atmospheric pressure.

Confluent Growth: A continuous bacterial growth covering all or part of the filtration area of a membrane filter in which the bacteria colonies are not discrete.

Consent Decree: A legal document, approved by a judge, that formalizes an agreement reached between EPA and potentially responsible parties (PRPs) through which PRPs will conduct all or part of a cleanup action at a Superfund site; cease or correct actions or processes that are polluting the environment; or otherwise comply with EPA initiated regulatory enforcement actions to resolve the contamination at the Superfund site involved. The consent decree describes the actions PRPs will take and may be subject to a public comment period.

Conservation: Preserving and renewing, when possible, human and natural resources. The use, protection, and improvement of natural resources according to principles that will ensure their highest economic or social benefits.

Conservation Easement: Easement restricting a landowner to land uses that that are compatible with long-term conservation and environmental values.

Constituent(s) of Concern: Specific chemicals that are identified for evaluation in the site assessment process

Construction and Demolition Waste: Waste building materials, dredging materials, tree stumps, and rubble resulting from construction, remodeling, repair, and demolition of homes, commercial buildings and other structures and pavements. May contain lead, asbestos, or other hazardous substances.

Construction Ban: If, under the Clean Air Act, EPA disapproves an area's planning requirements for correcting nonattainment, EPA can ban the construction or modification of any major stationary source of the pollutant for which the area is in nonattainment.

Consumptive Water Use: Water removed from available supplies without return to a water resources system, e.g. water used in manufacturing, agriculture, and food preparation.

Contact Pesticide: A chemical that kills pests when it touches them, instead of by ingestion. Also, soil that contains the minute skeletons of certain algae that scratch and dehydrate waxy-coated insects.

Contaminant: Any physical, chemical, biological, or radiological substance or matter that has an adverse effect on air, water, or soil.

Contamination: Introduction into water, air, and soil of microorganisms, chemicals, toxic substances, wastes, or wastewater in a concentration that makes the medium unfit for its next intended use. Also applies to surfaces of objects, buildings, and various household and agricultural use products.

Contamination Source Inventory: An inventory of contaminant sources within delineated State Water-Protection Areas. Targets likely sources for further investigation.

Contingency Plan: A document setting out an organized, planned, and coordinated course of action to be followed in case of a fire, explosion, or other accident that releases toxic chemicals, hazardous waste, or radioactive materials that threaten human health or the environment. (See: National Oil and Hazardous Substances Contingency Plan.)

Continuous Discharge: A routine release to the environment that occurs without interruption, except for infrequent shutdowns for maintenance, process changes, etc.

Continuous Sample: A flow of water, waste or other material from a particular place in a plant to the location where samples are collected for testing. May be used to obtain grab or composite samples.

Contour Plowing: Soil tilling method that follows the shape of the land to discourage erosion.

Contour Strip Farming: A kind of contour farming in which row crops are planted in strips, between alternating strips of close-growing, erosion-resistant forage crops.

Contract Labs: Laboratories under contract to EPA, which analyze samples taken from waste, soil, air, and water or carry out research projects.

Control Technique Guidelines (CTG): EPA documents designed to assist state and local pollution authorities to achieve and maintain air quality standards for certain sources (e.g. organic emissions from solvent metal cleaning known as degreasing) through reasonably available control technologies (RACT).

Controlled Reaction: A chemical reaction under temperature and pressure conditions maintained within safe limits to produce a desired product or process.

Conventional Filtration: (See: complete treatment.)

Conventional Pollutants: Statutorily listed pollutants understood well by scientists. These may be in the form of organic waste, sediment, acid, bacteria, viruses, nutrients, oil and grease, or heat.

Conventional Site Assessment: Assessment in which most of the sample analysis and interpretation of data is completed off-site; process usually requires repeated mobilization of equipment and staff in order to fully determine the extent of contamination.

Conventional Systems: Systems that have been traditionally used to collect municipal wastewater in gravity sewers and convey it to a central primary or secondary treatment plant prior to discharge to surface waters.

Conventional Tilling: Tillage operations considered standard for a specific location and crop and that tend to bury the crop residues; usually considered as a base for determining the cost effectiveness of control practices.

Conveyance Loss: Water loss in pipes, channels, conduits, ditches by leakage or evaporation.

Cooling Electricity Use: Amount of electricity used to meet the building cooling load. (See: building cooling load.)

Cooling Tower: A structure that helps remove heat from water used as a coolant; e.g., in electric power generating plants.

Cooling Tower: Device which dissipates the heat from water-cooled systems by spraying the water through streams of rapidly moving air.

Cooperative Agreement: An assistance agreement whereby EPA transfers money, property, services or anything of value to a state, university, non-profit, or not-for-profit organization for the accomplishment of authorized activities or tasks.

Core: The uranium-containing heart of a nuclear reactor, where energy is released.

Core Program Cooperative Agreement: An assistance agreement whereby EPA supports states or tribal governments with funds to help defray the cost of non-item-specific administrative and training activities.

Corrective Action: EPA can require treatment, storage and disposal (TSDF) facilities handling hazardous waste to undertake corrective actions to clean up spills resulting from failure to follow hazardous waste management procedures or other mistakes. The process includes cleanup procedures designed to guide TSDFs toward in spills.

Corrosion: The dissolution and wearing away of metal caused by a chemical reaction such as between water and the pipes, chemicals touching a metal surface, or contact between two metals.

Corrosive: A chemical agent that reacts with the surface of a material causing it to deteriorate or wear away.

Cost/Benefit Analysis: A quantitative evaluation of the costs which would have incurred by implementing an environmental regulation versus the overall benefits to society of the proposed action.

Cost Recovery: A legal process by which potentially responsible parties who contributed to contamination at a Superfund site can be required to reimburse the Trust Fund for money spent during any cleanup actions by the federal government.

Cost Sharing: A publicly financed program through which society, as a beneficiary of environmental protection, shares part of the cost of pollution control with those who must actually install the controls. In Superfund, for example, the government may pay part of the cost of a cleanup action with those responsible for the pollution paying the major share.

Cost-Effective Alternative: An alternative control or corrective method identified after analysis as being the best available in terms of reliability, performance, and cost. Although costs are one important consideration, regulatory and compliance analysis does not require EPA to choose the least expensive alternative. For example, when selecting or approving a method for cleaning up a Superfund site, the Agency balances costs with the long-term effectiveness of the methods proposed and the potential danger posed by the site.

Cover Crop: A crop that provides temporary protection for delicate seedlings and/or provides a cover canopy for seasonal soil protection and improvement between normal crop production periods.

Cover Material: Soil used to cover compacted solid waste in a sanitary landfill.

Cradle-to-Grave or Manifest System: A procedure in which hazardous materials are identified and followed as they are produced, treated, transported, and disposed of by a series of permanent, linkable, descriptive documents (e.g. manifests). Commonly referred to as the cradle-to-grave system.

Criteria: Descriptive factors taken into account by EPA in setting standards for various pollutants. These factors are used to determine limits on allowable concentration levels, and to limit the number of violations per year. When issued by EPA, the criteria provide guidance to the states on how to establish their standards.

Criteria Pollutants: The 1970 amendments to the Clean Air Act required EPA to set National Ambient Air Quality Standards for certain pollutants known to be hazardous to human health. EPA has identified and set standards to protect human health and welfare for six pollutants: ozone, carbon monoxide, total suspended particulates, sulfur dioxide, lead, and nitrogen oxide. The term, "criteria pollutants" derives from the requirement that EPA must describe the characteristics and potential health and welfare effects of these pollutants. It is on the basis of these criteria that standards are set or revised.

Critical Effect: The first adverse effect, or its known precursor, that occurs as a dose rate increases. Designation is based on evaluation of overall database.

Crop Consumptive Use: The amount of water transpired during plant growth plus what evaporated from the soil surface and foliage in the crop area.

Crop Rotation: Planting a succession of different crops on the same land rea as opposed to planting the same crop time after time.

Cross Contamination: The movement of underground contaminants from one level or area to another due to invasive subsurface activities.

Cross-Connection: Any actual or potential connection between a drinking water system and an unapproved water supply or other source of contamination.

Crumb Rubber: Ground rubber fragments the size of sand or silt used in rubber or plastic products, or processed further into reclaimed rubber or asphalt products.

Cryptosporidium: A protozoan microbe associated with the disease cryptosporidiosis in man. The disease can be transmitted through ingestion of drinking water, person-to-person contact, or other pathways, and can cause acute diarrhea, abdominal pain, vomiting, fever, and can be fatal as it was in the Milwaukee episode.

Cubic Feet Per Minute (CFM): A measure of the volume of a substance flowing through air within a fixed period of time. With regard to indoor air, refers to the amount of air, in cubic feet, that is exchanged with outdoor air in a minute's time; i.e. the air exchange rate.

Cullet: Crushed glass.

Cultural Eutrophication: Increasing rate at which water bodies "die" by pollution from human activities.

Cultures and Stocks: Infectious agents and associated biologicals including cultures from medical and pathological laboratories; cultures and stocks of infectious agents from research and industrial laboratories; waste from the production of biologicals; discarded live and attenuated vaccines; and culture dishes and devices used to transfer, inoculate, and mix cultures. (See: regulated medical waste.)

Cumulative Ecological Risk Assessment: Consideration of the total ecological risk from multiple stressors to a given eco-zone.

Cumulative Exposure: The sum of exposures of an organism to a pollutant over a period of time.

Cumulative Working Level Months (CWLM): The sum of lifetime exposure to radon working levels expressed in total working level months.

Curb Stop: A water service shutoff valve located in a water service pipe near the curb and between the water main and the building.

Curbside Collection: Method of collecting recyclable materials at homes, community districts or businesses.

Cutie-Pie: An instrument used to measure radiation levels.

Cuttings: Spoils left by conventional drilling with hollow stem auger or rotary drilling equipment.

Cyclone Collector: A device that uses centrifugal force to remove large particles from polluted air.

D

Data Call-In: A part of the Office of Pesticide Programs (OPP) process of developing key required test data, especially on the long-term, chronic effects of existing pesticides, in advance of scheduled Registration Standard reviews. Data Call-In from manufacturers is an adjunct of the Registration Standards program intended to expedite re-registration.

Data Quality Objectives (DQOs): Qualitative and quantitative statements of the overall level of uncertainty that a decision-maker will accept in results or decisions based on environmental data. They provide the statistical framework for planning and managing environmental data operations consistent with user's needs.

Day Tank: Another name for deaerating tank. (See: age tank.)

DDT: The first chlorinated hydrocarbon insecticide chemical name: Dichloro-Diphenyl-Trichloroethane. It has a half-life of 15 years and can collect in fatty tissues of certain animals. EPA banned registration and interstate sale of DDT for virtually all but emergency uses in the United States in 1972 because of its persistence in the environment and accumulation in the food chain.

Dead End: The end of a water main which is not connected to other parts of the distribution system.

Deadmen: Anchors drilled or cemented into the ground to provide additional reactive mass for DP sampling rigs.

Glossary of Environmental Terms

Decant: To draw off the upper layer of liquid after the heaviest material (a solid or another liquid) has settled.

Decay Products: Degraded radioactive materials, often referred to as "daughters" or "progeny"; radon decay products of most concern from a public health standpoint are polonium-214 and polonium-218.

Dechlorination: Removal of chlorine from a substance.

Decomposition: The breakdown of matter by bacteria and fungi, changing the chemical makeup and physical appearance of materials.

Decontamination: Removal of harmful substances such as noxious chemicals, harmful bacteria or other organisms, or radioactive material from exposed individuals, rooms and furnishings in buildings, or the exterior environment.

Deep-Well Injection: Deposition of raw or treated, filtered hazardous waste by pumping it into deep wells, where it is contained in the pores of permeable subsurface rock.

Deflocculating Agent: A material added to a suspension to prevent settling.

Defluoridation: The removal of excess flouride in drinking water to prevent the staining of teeth.

Defoliant: An herbicide that removes leaves from trees and growing plants.

Degasification: A water treatment that removes dissolved gases from the water.

Degree-Day: A rough measure used to estimate the amount of heating required in a given area; is defined as the difference between the mean daily temperature and 65 degrees Fahrenheit. Degree-days are also calculated to estimate cooling requirements.

Delegated State: A state (or other governmental entity such as a tribal government) that has received authority to administer an environmental regulatory program in lieu of a federal counterpart. As used in connection with NPDES, UIC, and PWS programs, the term does not connote any transfer of federal authority to a state.

Delist: Use of the petition process to have a facility's toxic designation rescinded.

Demand-side Waste Management: Prices whereby consumers use purchasing decisions to communicate to product manufacturers that they prefer environmentally sound products packaged with the least amount of waste, made from recycled or recyclable materials, and containing no hazardous substances.

Demineralization: A treatment process that removes dissolved minerals from water.

Denitrification: The biological reduction of nitrate to nitrogen gas by denitrifying bacteria in soil.

Dense Non-Aqueous Phase Liquid (DNAPL): Non-aqueous phase liquids such as chlorinated hydrocarbon solvents or petroleum fractions with a specific gravity greater than 1.0 that sink through the water column until they reach a confining layer. Because they are at the bottom of aquifers instead of floating on the water table, typical monitoring wells do not indicate their presence.

Density: A measure of how heavy a specific volume of a solid, liquid, or gas is in comparison to water. depending on the chemical.

Depletion Curve: In hydraulics, a graphical representation of water depletion from storage-stream channels, surface soil, and groundwater. A depletion curve can be drawn for base flow, direct runoff, or total flow.

Depressurization: A condition that occurs when the air pressure inside a structure is lower that the air pressure outdoors. Depressurization can occur when household appliances such as fireplaces or furnaces, that consume or exhaust house air, are not supplied with enough makeup air. Radon may be drawn into a house more rapidly under depressurized conditions.

Dermal Absorption/Penetration: Process by which a chemical penetrates the skin and enters the body as an internal dose.

Dermal Exposure: Contact between a chemical and the skin.

Dermal Toxicity: The ability of a pesticide or toxic chemical to poison people or animals by contact with the skin. (See: contact pesticide.)

DES: A synthetic estrogen, diethylstilbestrol is used as a growth stimulant in food animals. Residues in meat are thought to be carcinogenic.

Desalination: [Desalinization] (1) Removing salts from ocean or brackish water by using various technologies. (2) Removal of salts from soil by artificial means, usually leaching.

Desiccant: A chemical agent that absorbs moisture; some desiccants are capable of drying out plants or insects, causing death.

Design Capacity: The average daily flow that a treatment plant or other facility is designed to accommodate.

Design Value: The monitored reading used by EPA to determine an area's air quality status; e.g., for ozone, the fourth highest reading measured over the most recent three years is the design value.

Designated Pollutant: An air pollutant which is neither a criteria nor hazardous pollutant, as described in the Clean Air Act, but for which new source performance standards exist. The Clean Air Act does require states to control these pollutants, which include acid mist, total reduced sulfur (TRS), and fluorides.

Designated Uses: Those water uses identified in state water quality standards that must be achieved and maintained as required under the Clean Water Act. Uses can include cold water fisheries, public water supply, and irrigation.

Designer Bugs: Popular term for microbes developed through biotechnology that can degrade specific toxic chemicals at their source in toxic waste dumps or in ground water.

Destination Facility: The facility to which regulated medical waste is shipped for treatment and destruction, incineration, and/or disposal.

Destratification: Vertical mixing within a lake or reservoir to totally or partially eliminate separate layers of temperature, plant, or animal life.

Destroyed Medical Waste: Regulated medical waste that has been ruined, torn apart, or mutilated through thermal treatment, melting, shredding, grinding, tearing, or breaking, so that it is no longer generally recognized as medical waste, but has not yet been treated (excludes compacted regulated medical waste).

Destruction and Removal Efficiency (DRE): A percentage that represents the number of molecules of a compound removed or destroyed in an incinerator relative to the number of molecules entering the system (e.g. a DRE of 99.99 percent means that 9,999 molecules are destroyed for every 10,000 that enter; 99.99 percent is known as "four nines." For some pollutants, the RCRA removal requirement may be as stringent as "six nines").

Destruction Facility: A facility that destroys regulated medical waste.

Desulfurization: Removal of sulfur from fossil fuels to reduce pollution.

Detectable Leak Rate: The smallest leak (from a storage tank), expressed in terms of gallons- or liters-per-hour, that a test can reliably discern with a certain probability of detection or false alarm.

Detection Criterion: A predetermined rule to ascertain whether a tank is leaking or not. Most volumetric tests use a threshold value as the detection criterion. (See: volumetric tank tests.)

Detection Limit: The lowest concentration of a chemical that can reliably be distinguished from a zero concentration.

Detention Time: 1. The theoretical calculated time required for a small amount of water to pass through a tank at a given rate of flow. 2. The actual time that a small amount of water is in a settling basin, flocculating basin, or rapid-mix chamber. 3. In storage reservoirs, the length of time water will be held before being used.

Detergent: Synthetic washing agent that helps to remove dirt and oil. Some contain compounds which kill useful bacteria and encourage algae growth when they are in wastewater that reaches receiving waters.

Development Effects: Adverse effects such as altered growth, structural abnormality, functional deficiency, or death observed in a developing organism.

Dewater: 1. Remove or separate a portion of the water in a sludge or slurry to dry the sludge so it can be handled and disposed of. 2. Remove or drain the water from a tank or trench.

Diatomaceous Earth (Diatomite): A chalk-like material (fossilized diatoms) used to filter out solid waste in wastewater treatment plants; also used as an active ingredient in some powdered pesticides.

Diazinon: An insecticide. In 1986, EPA banned its use on open areas such as sod farms and golf courses because it posed a danger to migratory birds. The ban did not apply to agricultural, home lawn or commercial establishment uses.

Dibenzofurans: A group of organic compounds, some of which are toxic.

Dicofol: A pesticide used on citrus fruits.

Diffused Air: A type of aeration that forces oxygen into sewage by pumping air through perforated pipes inside a holding tank.

Diffusion: The movement of suspended or dissolved particles (or molecules) from a more concentrated to a less concentrated area. The process tends to distribute the particles or molecules more uniformly.

Digester: In wastewater treatment, a closed tank; in solid-waste conversion, a unit in which bacterial action is induced and accelerated in order to break down organic matter and establish the proper carbon to nitrogen ratio.

Digestion: The biochemical decomposition of organic matter, resulting in partial gasification, liquefaction, and mineralization of pollutants.

Dike: A low wall that can act as a barrier to prevent a spill from spreading.

Diluent: Any liquid or solid material used to dilute or carry an active ingredient.

Dilution Ratio: The relationship between the volume of water in a stream and the volume of incoming water. It affects the ability of the stream to assimilate waste.

Dimictic: Lakes and reservoirs that freeze over and normally go through two stratifications and two mixing cycles a year.

Dinocap: A fungicide used primarily by apple growers to control summer diseases. EPA proposed restrictions on its use in 1986 when laboratory tests found it caused birth defects in rabbits.

Dinoseb: A herbicide that is also used as a fungicide and insecticide. It was banned by EPA in 1986 because it posed the risk of birth defects and sterility.

Dioxin: Any of a family of compounds known chemically as dibenzo-p-dioxins. Concern about them arises from their potential toxicity as contaminants in commercial products. Tests on laboratory animals indicate that it is one of the more toxic anthropogenic (man-made) compounds.

Direct Discharger: A municipal or industrial facility which introduces pollution through a defined conveyance or system such as outlet pipes; a point source.

Direct Filtration: A method of treating water which consists of the addition of coagulent chemicals, flash mixing, coagulation, minimal flocculation, and filtration. Sedimentation is not uses.

Direct Push: Technology used for performing subsurface investigations by driving, pushing, and/or vibrating small-diameter hollow steel rods into the ground/ Also known as direct drive, drive point, or push technology.

Direct Runoff: Water that flows over the ground surface or through the ground directly into streams, rivers, and lakes.

Discharge: Flow of surface water in a stream or canal or the outflow of ground water from a flowing artesian well, ditch, or spring. Can also apply tp discharge of liquid effluent from a facility or to chemical emissions into the air through designated venting mechanisms.

Disinfectant: A chemical or physical process that kills pathogenic organisms in water, air, or on surfaces. Chlorine is often used to disinfect sewage treatment effluent, water supplies, wells, and swimming pools.

Disinfectant By-Product: A compound formed by the reaction of a disinfenctant such as chlorine with organic material in the water supply; a chemical byproduct of the disinfection process..

Disinfectant Time: The time it takes water to move from the point of disinfectant application (or the previous point of residual disinfectant measurement) to a point before or at the point where the residual disinfectant is measured. In pipelines, the time is calculated by dividing the internal volume of the pipe by he maximum hourly flow rate; within mixing basins and storage reservoirs it is determined by tracer studies of an equivalent demonstration.

Dispersant: A chemical agent used to break up concentrations of organic material such as spilled oil.

Displacement Savings: Saving realized by displacing purchases of natural gas or electricity from a local utility by using landfill gas for power and heat.

Disposables: Consumer products, other items, and packaging used once or a few times and discarded.

Disposal: Final placement or destruction of toxic, radioactive, or other wastes; surplus or banned pesticides or other chemicals; polluted soils; and drums containing hazardous materials from removal actions or accidental releases. Disposal may be accomplished through use of approved secure landfills, surface impoundments, land farming, deep-well injection, ocean dumping, or incineration.

Disposal Facilities: Repositories for solid waste, including landfills and combustors intended for permanent containment or destruction of waste materials. Excludes transfer stations and composting facilities.

Dissolved Oxygen (DO): The oxygen freely available in water, vital to fish and other aquatic life and for the prevention of odors. DO levels are considered a most important indicator of a water body's ability to support desirable aquatic life. Secondary and advanced waste treatment are generally designed to ensure adequate DO in waste-receiving waters.

Dissolved Solids: Disintegrated organic and inorganic material in water. Excessive amounts make water unfit to drink or use in industrial processes.

Distillation: The act of purifying liquids through boiling, so that the steam or gaseous vapors condense to a pure liquid. Pollutants and contaminants may remain in a concentrated residue.

Disturbance: Any event or series of events that disrupt ecosystem, community, or population structure and alters the physical environment.

Diversion: 1. Use of part of a stream flow as water supply. 2. A channel with a supporting ridge on the lower side constructed across a slope to divert water at a non-erosive velocity to sites where it can be used and disposed of.

Diversion Rate: The percentage of waste materials diverted from traditional disposal such as landfilling or incineration to be recycled, composted, or re-used.

DNA Hybridization: Use of a segment of DNA, called a DNA probe, to identify its complementary DNA; used to detect specific genes.

Dobson Unit (DU): Units of ozone level measurement. measurement of ozone levels. If, for example, 100 DU of ozone were brought to the earth's surface they would form a layer one millimeter thick. Ozone levels vary geographically, even in the absence of ozone depletion.

Domestic Application: Pesticide application in and around houses, office buildings, motels, and other living or working areas.(See: residential use.)

Dosage/Dose: 1. The actual quantity of a chemical administered to an organism or to which it is exposed. 2. The amount of a substance that reaches a specific tissue (e.g. the liver). 3. The amount of a substance available for interaction with metabolic processes after crossing the outer boundary of an organism. (See: absorbed dose, administered dose, applied dose, potential dose.)

Dose Equivalent: The product of the absorbed dose from ionizing radiation and such factors as account for biological differences due to the type of radiation and its distribution in the body in the body.

Dose Rate: In exposure assessment, dose per time unit (e.g. mg/day), sometimes also called dosage.

Dose Response: Shifts in toxicological responses of an individual (such as alterations in severity) or populations (such as alterations in incidence) that are related to changes in the dose of any given substance.

Dose Response Curve: Graphical representation of the relationship between the dose of a stressor and the biological response thereto.

Dose-Response Assessment: 1. Estimating the potency of a chemical. 2. In exposure assessment, the process of determining the relationship between the dose of a stressor and a specific biological response. 3. Evaluating the quantitative relationship between dose and toxicological responses.

Dose-Response Relationship: The quantitative relationship between the amount of exposure to a substance and the extent of toxic injury or disease produced.

Dosimeter: An instrument to measure dosage; many so-called dosimeters actually measure exposure rather than dosage. Dosimetry is the process or technology of measuring and/or estimating dosage.

DOT Reportable Quantity: The quantity of a substance specified in a U.S. Department of Transportation regulation that triggers labeling, packaging and other requirements related to shipping such substances.

Downgradient: The direction that groundwater flows; similar to "downstream" for surface water.

Downstream Processors: Industries dependent on crop production (e.g. canneries and food processors).

DP Hole: Hole in the ground made with DP equipment. (See: direct push.)

Draft: 1. The act of drawing or removing water from a tank or reservoir. 2. The water which is drawn or removed.

Draft Permit: A preliminary permit drafted and published by EPA; subject to public review and comment before final action on the application.

Drainage: Improving the productivity of agricultural land by removing excess water from the soil by such means as ditches or subsurface drainage tiles.

Drainage Basin: The area of land that drains water, sediment, and dissolved materials to a common outlet at some point along a stream channel.

Drainage Well: A well drilled to carry excess water off agricultural fields. Because they act as a funnel from the surface to the groundwater below. Drainage wells can contribute to groundwater pollution.

Drawdown: 1. The drop in the water table or level of water in the ground when water is being pumped from a well. 2. The amount of water used from a tank or reservoir. 3. The drop in the water level of a tank or reservoir.

Dredging: Removal of mud from the bottom of water bodies. This can disturb the ecosystem and causes silting that kills aquatic life. Dredging of contaminated muds can expose biota to heavy metals and other toxics. Dredging activities may be subject to regulation under Section 404 of the Clean Water Act.

Drilling Fluid: Fluid used to lubricate the bit and convey drill cuttings to the surface with rotary drilling equipment. Usually composed of bentonite slurry or muddy water. Can become contaminated, leading to cross contamination, and may require special disposal. Not used with DP methods

Drinking Water Equivalent Level: Protective level of exposure related to potentially non-carcinogenic effects of chemicals that are also known to cause cancer.

Drinking Water State Revolving Fund: The Fund provides capitalization grants to states to develop drinking water revolving loan funds to help finance system infrastructure improvements, assure source-water protection, enhance operation and management of drinking-water systems, and otherwise promote local water-system compliance and protection of public health.

Drive Casing: Heavy duty steel casing driven along with the sampling tool in cased DP systems. Keeps the hole open between sampling runs and is not removed until last sample has been collected.

Drive Point Profiler: An exposed groundwater DP system used to collect multiple depth-discrete groundwater samples. Ports in the tip of the probe connect to an internal stainless steel or teflon tube that extends to the surface. Samples are collected via suction or airlift methods. Deionized water is pumped down through the ports to prevent plugging while driving the tool to the next sampling depth.

Drop-off: Recyclable materials collection method in which individuals bring them to a designated collection site.

Dual-Phase Extraction: Active withdrawal of both liquid and gas phases from a well usually involving the use of a vacuum pump.

Dump: A site used to dispose of solid waste without environmental controls.

Duplicate: A second aliquot or sample that is treated the same as the original sample in order to determine the precision of the analytical method. (See: aliquot.)

Dustfall Jar: An open container used to collect large particles from the air for measurement and analysis.

Dynamometer. A device used to place a load on an engine and measure its performance.

Dystrophic Lakes: Acidic, shallow bodies of water that contain much humus and/or other organic matter; contain many plants but few fish.

E

Ecological Entity: In ecological risk assessment, a general term referring to a species, a group of species, an ecosystem function or characteristic, or a specific habitat or biome.

Ecological/Environmental Sustainability: Maintenance of ecosystem components and functions for future generations.

Ecological Exposure: Exposure of a non-human organism to a stressor.

Ecological Impact: The effect that a man-caused or natural activity has on living organisms and their non-living (abiotic) environment.

Ecological Indicator: A characteristic of an ecosystem that is related to, or derived from, a measure of biotic or abiotic variable, that can provide quantitative information on ecological structure and function. An indicator can contribute to a measure of integrity and sustainability.

Ecological Integrity: A living system exhibits integrity if, when subjected to disturbance, it sustains and organizes self-correcting ability to recover toward a biomass end-state that is normal for that system. End-states other than the pristine or naturally whole may be accepted as normal and good.

Ecological Risk Assessment: The application of a formal framework, analytical process, or model to estimate the effects of human actions(s) on a natural resource and to interpret the significance of those effects in light of the uncertainties identified in each component of the assessment process. Such analysis includes initial hazard identification, exposure and dose-response assessments, and risk characterization.

Ecology: The relationship of living things to one another and their environment, or the study of such relationships.

Economic Poisons: Chemicals used to control pests and to defoliate cash crops such as cotton.

Ecosphere: The "bio-bubble" that contains life on earth, in surface waters, and in the air. (See: biosphere.)

Ecosystem: The interacting system of a biological community and its non-living environmental surroundings.

Ecosystem Structure: Attributes related to the instantaneous physical state of an ecosystem; examples include species population density, species richness or evenness, and standing crop biomass.

Ecotone: A habitat created by the juxtaposition of distinctly different habitats; an edge habitat; or an ecological zone or boundary where two or more ecosystems meet.

Effluent: Wastewater—treated or untreated—that flows out of a treatment plant, sewer, or industrial outfall. Generally refers to wastes discharged into surface waters.

Effluent Guidelines: Technical EPA documents which set effluent limitations for given industries and pollutants.

Effluent Limitation: Restrictions established by a state or EPA on quantities, rates, and concentrations in wastewater discharges.

Effluent Standard: (See: effluent limitation.)

Ejector: A device used to disperse a chemical solution into water being treated.

Electrodialysis: A process that uses electrical current applied to permeable membranes to remove minerals from water. Often used to desalinize salty or brackish water.

Electromagnetic Geophysical Methods: Ways to measure subsurface conductivity via low-frequency electromagnetic induction.

Electrostatic Precipitator (ESP): A device that removes particles from a gas stream (smoke) after combustion occurs. The ESP imparts an electrical charge to the particles, causing them to adhere to metal plates inside the precipitator. Rapping on the plates causes the particles to fall into a hopper for disposal.

Eligible Costs: The construction costs for wastewater treatment works upon which EPA grants are based.

EMAP Data: Environmental monitoring data collected under the auspices of the Environmental Monitoring and Assessment Program. All EMAP data share the common attribute of being of known quality, having been collected in the context of explicit data quality objectives (DQOs) and a consistent quality assurance program.

Emergency and Hazardous Chemical Inventory: An annual report by facilities having one or more extremely hazardous substances or hazardous chemicals above certain weight limits.

Emergency (Chemical): A situation created by an accidental release or spill of hazardous chemicals that poses a threat to the safety of workers, residents, the environment, or property.

Emergency Episode: (See: air pollution episode.)

Emergency Exemption: Provision in FIFRA under which EPA can grant temporary exemption to a state or another federal agency to allow the use of a pesticide product not registered for that particular use. Such actions involve unanticipated and/or severe pest problems where there is not time or interest by a manufacturer to register the product for that use. (Registrants cannot apply for such exemptions.)

Emergency Removal Action: 1. Steps take to remove contaminated materials that pose imminent threats to local residents (e.g. removal of leaking drums or the excavation of explosive waste.) 2. The state record of such removals.

Emergency Response Values: Concentrations of chemicals, published by various groups, defining acceptable levels for short-term exposures in emergencies.

Emergency Suspension: Suspension of a pesticide product registration due to an imminent hazard. The action immediately halts distribution, sale, and sometimes actual use of the pesticide involved.

Emission: Pollution discharged into the atmosphere from smokestacks, other vents, and surface areas of commercial or industrial facilities; from residential chimneys; and from motor vehicle, locomotive, or aircraft exhausts.

Emission Cap: A limit designed to prevent projected growth in emissions from existing and future stationary sources from eroding any mandated reductions. Generally, such provisions require that any emission growth from facilities under the restrictions be offset by equivalent reductions at other facilities under the same cap. (See: emissions trading.)

Emission Factor: The relationship between the amount of pollution produced and the amount of raw material processed. For example, an emission factor for a blast furnace making iron would be the number of pounds of particulates per ton of raw materials.

Emission Inventory: A listing, by source, of the amount of air pollutants discharged into the atmosphere of a community; used to establish emission standards.

Emission Standard: The maximum amount of air polluting discharge legally allowed from a single source, mobile or stationary.

Emissions Trading: The creation of surplus emission reductions at certain stacks, vents or similar emissions sources and the use of this surplus to meet or redefine pollution requirements applicable to other emissions sources. This allows one source to increase emissions when another source reduces them, maintaining an overall constant emission level. Facilities that reduce emissions substantially may "bank" their "credits" or sell them to other facilities or industries.

Emulsifier: A chemical that aids in suspending one liquid in another. Usually an organic chemical in an aqueous solution.

Encapsulation: The treatment of asbestos-containing material with a liquid that covers the surface with a protective coating or embeds fibers in an adhesive matrix to prevent their release into the air.

Enclosure: Putting an airtight, impermeable, permanent barrier around asbestos-containing materials to prevent the release of asbestos fibers into the air.

End User: Consumer of products for the purpose of recycling. Excludes products for re-use or combustion for energy recovery.

End-of-the-pipe: Technologies such as scrubbers on smokestacks and catalytic convertors on automobile tailpipes that reduce emissions of pollutants after they have formed.

End-use Product: A pesticide formulation for field or other end use. The label has instructions for use or application to control pests or regulate plant growth. The term excludes products used to formulate other pesticide products.

Endangered Species: Animals, birds, fish, plants, or other living organisms threatened with extinction by anthropogenic (man-caused) or other natural changes in their environment. Requirements for declaring a species endangered are contained in the Endangered Species Act.

Endangerment Assessment: A study to determine the nature and extent of contamination at a site on the National Priorities List and the risks posed to public health or the environment. EPA or the state conducts the study when a legal action is to be taken to direct potentially responsible parties to clean up a site or pay for it. An endangerment assessment supplements a remedial investigation.

Endrin: A pesticide toxic to freshwater and marine aquatic life that produces adverse health effects in domestic water supplies.

Energy Management System: A control system capable of monitoring environmental and system loads and adjusting HVAC operations accordingly in order to conserve energy while maintaining comfort.

Energy Recovery: Obtaining energy from waste through a variety of processes (e.g. combustion).

Enforceable Requirements: Conditions or limitations in permits issued under the Clean Water Act Section 402 or 404 that, if violated, could result in the issuance of a compliance order or initiation of a civil or criminal action under federal or applicable state laws. If a permit has not been issued, the term includes any requirement which, in the Regional Administrator's judgement, would be included in the permit when issued. Where no permit applies, the term includes any requirement which the RA determines is necessary for the best practical waste treatment technology to meet applicable criteria.

Enforcement: EPA, state, or local legal actions to obtain compliance with environmental laws, rules, regulations, or agreements and/or obtain penalties or criminal sanctions for violations. Enforcement procedures may vary, depending on the requirements of different environmental laws and related implementing regulations. Under CERCLA, for example, EPA will seek to require potentially responsible parties to clean up a Superfund site, or pay for the cleanup, whereas under the Clean Air Act the Agency may invoke sanctions against cities failing to meet ambient air quality standards that could prevent certain types of construction or federal funding. In other situations, if investigations by EPA and state agencies uncover willful violations, criminal trials and penalties are sought.

Enforcement Decision Document (EDD): A document that provides an explanation to the public of EPA's selection of the cleanup alternative at enforcement sites on the National Priorities List. Similar to a Record of Decision.

Engineered Controls: Method of managing environmental and health risks by placing a barrier between the contamination and the rest of the site, thus limiting exposure pathways.

Enhanced Inspection and Maintenance (I&M): An improved automobile inspection and maintenance program—aimed at reducing automobile emissions—-that contains, at a minimum, more vehicle types and model years, tighter inspection, and better management practices. It may also include annual computerized or centralized inspections, under-the-hood inspection—for signs of tampering with pollution control equipment—and increased repair waiver cost.

Enrichment: The addition of nutrients (e.g. nitrogen, phosphorus, carbon compounds) from sewage effluent or agricultural runoff to surface water, greatly increases the growth potential for algae and other aquatic plants.

Entrain: To trap bubbles in water either mechanically through turbulence or chemically through a reaction.

Environment: The sum of all external conditions affecting the life, development and survival of an organism.

Environmental Assessment: An environmental analysis prepared pursuant to the National Environmental Policy Act to determine whether a federal action would significantly affect the environment and thus require a more detailed environmental impact statement.

Environmental Audit: An independent assessment of the current status of a party's compliance with applicable environmental requirements or of a party's environmental compliance policies, practices, and controls.

Environmental/Ecological Risk: The potential for adverse effects on living organisms associated with pollution of the environment by effluents, emissions, wastes, or accidental chemical releases; energy use; or the depletion of natural resources.

Environmental Equity/Justice: Equal protection from environmental hazards for individuals, groups, or communities regardless of race, ethnicity, or economic status. This applies to the development, implementation, and enforcement of environmental laws, regulations, and policies, and implies that no population of people should be forced to shoulder a disproportionate share of negative environmental impacts of pollution or environmental hazard due to a lack of political or economic strength levels.

Environmental Exposure: Human exposure to pollutants originating from facility emissions. Threshold levels are not necessarily surpassed, but low-level chronic pollutant exposure is one of the most common forms of environmental exposure (See: threshold level).

Environmental Fate: The destiny of a chemical or biological pollutant after release into the environment.

Environmental Fate Data: Data that characterize a pesticide's fate in the ecosystem, considering factors that foster its degradation (light, water, microbes), pathways and resultant products.

Environmental Impact Statement: A document required of federal agencies by the National Environmental Policy Act for major projects or legislative proposals significantly affecting the environment. A tool for decision making, it describes the positive and negative effects of the undertaking and cites alternative actions.

Environmental Indicator: A measurement, statistic or value that provides a proximate gauge or evidence of the effects of environmental management programs or of the state or condition of the environment.

Environmental Justice: The fair treatment of people of all races, cultures, incomes, and educational levels with respect to the development and enforcement of environmental laws, regulations, and policies.

Environmental Lien: A charge, security, or encumbrance on a property's title to secure payment of cost or debt arising from response actions, cleanup, or other remediation of hazardous substances or petroleum products.

Environmental Medium: A major environmental category that surrounds or contacts humans, animals, plants, and other organisms (e.g. surface water, ground water, soil or air) and through which chemicals or pollutants move. (See: ambient medium, biological medium.)

Environmental Monitoring for Public Access and Community Tracking: Joint EPA, NOAA, and USGS program to provide timely and effective communication of environmental data and information through improved and updated technology solutions that support timely environmental monitoring reporting, interpreting, and use of the information for the benefit of the public. (See: real-time monitoring.)

Environmental Response Team: EPA experts located in Edison, N.J., and Cincinnati, OH, who can provide around-the-clock technical assistance to EPA regional offices and states during all types of hazardous waste site emergencies and spills of hazardous substances.

Environmental Site Assessment: The process of determining whether contamination is present on a parcel of real property.

Environmental Sustainability: Long-term maintenance of ecosystem components and functions for future generations.

Environmental Tobacco Smoke: Mixture of smoke from the burning end of a cigarette, pipe, or cigar and smoke exhaled by the smoker. (See: passive smoking/secondhand smoke.)

Epidemiology: Study of the distribution of disease, or other health-related states and events in human populations, as related to age, sex, occupation, ethnicity, and economic status in order to identify and alleviate health problems and promote better health.

Epilimnion: Upper waters of a thermally stratified lake subject to wind action.

Episode (Pollution): An air pollution incident in a given area caused by a concentration of atmospheric pollutants under meteorological conditions that may result in a significant increase in illnesses or deaths. May also describe water pollution events or hazardous material spills.

Equilibrium: In relation to radiation, the state at which the radioactivity of consecutive elements within a radioactive series is neither increasing nor decreasing.

Equivalent Method: Any method of sampling and analyzing for air pollution which has been demonstrated to the EPA Administrator's satisfaction to be, under specific conditions, an acceptable alternative to normally used reference methods.

Erosion: The wearing away of land surface by wind or water, intensified by land-clearing practices related to farming, residential or industrial development, road building, or logging.

Established Treatment Technologies: Technologies for which cost and performance data are readily available. (See: Innovative treatment technologies.)

Estimated Environmental Concentration: The estimated pesticide concentration in an ecosystem.

Estuary: Region of interaction between rivers and near-shore ocean waters, where tidal action and river flow mix fresh and salt water. Such areas include bays, mouths of rivers, salt marshes, and lagoons. These brackish water ecosystems shelter and feed marine life, birds, and wildlife. (See: wetlands.)

Ethanol: An alternative automotive fuel derived from grain and corn; usually blended with gasoline to form gasohol.

Ethylene Dibromide (EDB): A chemical used as an agricultural fumigant and in certain industrial processes. Extremely toxic and found to be a carcinogen in laboratory animals, EDB has been banned for most agricultural uses in the United States.

Eutrophic Lakes: Shallow, murky bodies of water with concentrations of plant nutrients causing excessive production of algae. (See: dystrophic lakes.)

Eutrophication: The slow aging process during which a lake, estuary, or bay evolves into a bog or marsh and eventually disappears. During the later stages of eutrophication the water body is choked by abundant plant life due to higher levels of nutritive compounds such as nitrogen and phosphorus. Human activities can accelerate the process.

Evaporation Ponds: Areas where sewage sludge is dumped and dried.

Evapotranspiration: The loss of water from the soil both by evaporation and by transpiration from the plants growing in the soil.

Exceedance: Violation of the pollutant levels permitted by environmental protection standards.

Exclusion: In the asbestos program, one of several situations that permit a Local Education Agency (LEA) to delete one or more of the items required by the Asbestos Hazard Emergency Response Act (AHERA); e.g. records of previous asbestos sample collection and analysis may be used by the accredited inspector in lieu of AHERA bulk sampling.

Exclusionary Ordinance: Zoning that excludes classes of persons or businesses from a particular neighborhood or area.

Exempt Solvent: Specific organic compounds not subject to requirements of regulation because they are deemed by EPA to be of negligible photochemical reactivity.

Exempted Aquifer: Underground bodies of water defined in the Underground Injection Control program as aquifers that are potential sources of drinking water though not being used as such, and thus exempted from regulations barring underground injection activities.

Exemption: A state (with primacy) may exempt a public water system from a requirement involving a Maximum Contaminant Level (MCL), treatment technique, or both, if the system cannot comply due to compelling economic or other factors, or because the system was in operation before the requirement or MCL was instituted; and the exemption will not create a public health risk. (See: variance.)

Exotic Species: A species that is not indigenous to a region.

Experimental Use Permit: Obtained by manufacturers for testing new pesticides or uses thereof whenever they conduct experimental field studies to support registration on 10 acres or more of land or one acre or more of water.

Experimental Use Permit: A permit granted by EPA that allows a producer to conduct tests of a new pesticide, product and/or use outside the laboratory. The testing is usually done on ten or more acres of land or water surface.

Explosive Limits: The amounts of vapor in the air that form explosive mixtures; limits are expressed as lower and upper limits and give the range of vapor concentrations in air that will explode if an ignition source is present.

Exports : In solid waste program, municipal solid waste and recyclables transported outside the state or locality where they originated.

Exposure: The amount of radiation or pollutant present in a given environment that represents a potential health threat to living organisms.

Exposure Assessment: Identifying the pathways by which toxicants may reach individuals, estimating how much of a chemical an individual is likely to be exposed to, and estimating the number likely to be exposed.

Exposure Concentration: The concentration of a chemical or other pollutant representing a health threat in a given environment.

Exposure Indicator: A characteristic of the environment measured to provide evidence of the occurrence or magnitude of a response indicator's exposure to a chemical or biological stress.

Exposure Level: The amount (concentration) of a chemical at the absorptive surfaces of an organism.

Exposure Pathway: The path from sources of pollutants via, soil, water, or food to man and other species or settings.

Exposure Route: The way a chemical or pollutant enters an organism after contact; i.e. by ingestion, inhalation, or dermal absorption.

Exposure-Response Relationship: The relationship between exposure level and the incidence of adverse effects.

Extraction Procedure (EP Toxic): Determining toxicity by a procedure which simulates leaching; if a certain concentration of a toxic substance can be leached from a waste, that waste is considered hazardous, i.e."EP Toxic."

Extraction Well: A discharge well used to remove groundwater or air.

Extremely Hazardous Substances: Any of 406 chemicals identified by EPA as toxic, and listed under SARA Title III. The list is subject to periodic revision.

F

Fabric Filter: A cloth device that catches dust particles from industrial emissions.

Facilities Plans: Plans and studies related to the construction of treatment works necessary to comply with the Clean Water Act or RCRA. A facilities plan investigates needs and provides information on the cost-effectiveness of alternatives, a recommended plan, an environmental assessment of the recommendations, and descriptions of the treatment works, costs, and a completion schedule.

Facility Emergency Coordinator: Representative of a facility covered by environmental law (e.g, a chemical plant) who participates in the emergency reporting process with the Local Emergency Planning Committee (LEPC).

Facultative Bacteria: Bacteria that can live under aerobic or anaerobic conditions.

Feasibility Study: 1. Analysis of the practicability of a proposal; e.g., a description and analysis of potential cleanup alternatives for a site such as one on the National Priorities List. The feasibility study usually recommends selection of a cost-effective alternative. It usually starts as soon as the remedial investigation is underway; together, they are commonly referred to as the "RI/FS". 2. A small-scale investigation of a problem to ascertain whether a proposed research approach is likely to provide useful data.

Fecal Coliform Bacteria: Bacteria found in the intestinal tracts of mammals. Their presence in water or sludge is an indicator of pollution and possible contamination by pathogens.

Federal Implementation Plan: Under current law, a federally implemented plan to achieve attainment of air quality standards, used when a state is unable to develop an adequate plan.

Federal Motor Vehicle Control Program: All federal actions aimed at controlling pollution from motor vehicles by such efforts as establishing and enforcing tailpipe and evaporative emission standards for new vehicles, testing methods development, and guidance to states operating inspection and maintenance programs. Federally designated area that is required to meet and maintain federal ambient air quality standards. May include nearby locations in the same state or nearby states that share common air pollution problems.

Feedlot: A confined area for the controlled feeding of animals. Tends to concentrate large amounts of animal waste that cannot be absorbed by the soil and, hence, may be carried to nearby streams or lakes by rainfall runoff.

Fen: A type of wetland that accumulates peat deposits. Fens are less acidic than bogs, deriving most of their water from groundwater rich in calcium and magnesium. (See: wetlands.)

Ferrous Metals: Magnetic metals derived from iron or steel; products made from ferrous metals include appliances, furniture, containers, and packaging like steel drums and barrels. Recycled products include processing tin/steel cans, strapping, and metals from appliances into new products.

FIFRA Pesticide Ingredient: An ingredient of a pesticide that must be registered with EPA under the Federal Insecticide, Fungicide, and Rodenticide Act. Products making pesticide claims must register under FIFRA and may be subject to labeling and use requirements.

Fill: Man-made deposits of natural soils or rock products and waste materials.

Filling: Depositing dirt, mud or other materials into aquatic areas to create more dry land, usually for agricultural or commercial development purposes, often with ruinous ecological consequences.

Filter Strip: Strip or area of vegetation used for removing sediment, organic matter, and other pollutants from runoff and wastewater.

Filtration: A treatment process, under the control of qualified operators, for removing solid (particulate) matter from water by means of porous media such as sand or a man-made filter; often used to remove particles that contain pathogens.

Financial Assurance for Closure: Documentation or proof that an owner or operator of a facility such as a landfill or other waste repository is capable of paying the projected costs of closing the facility and monitoring it afterwards as provided in RCRA regulations.

Finding of No Significant Impact: A document prepared by a federal agency showing why a proposed action would not have a significant impact on the environment and thus would not require preparation of an Environmental Impact Statement. An FNSI is based on the results of an environmental assessment.

Finished Water: Water is "finished" when it has passed through all the processes in a water treatment plant and is ready to be delivered to consumers.

First Draw: The water that comes out when a tap is first opened, likely to have the highest level of lead contamination from plumbing materials.

Fix a Sample: A sample is "fixed" in the field by adding chemicals that prevent water quality indicators of interest in the sample from changing before laboratory measurements are made.

Fixed-Location Monitoring: Sampling of an environmental or ambient medium for pollutant concentration at one location continuously or repeatedly.

Flammable: Any material that ignites easily and will burn rapidly.

Flare: A control device that burns hazardous materials to prevent their release into the environment; may operate continuously or intermittently, usually on top of a stack.

Flash Point: The lowest temperature at which evaporation of a substance produces sufficient vapor to form an ignitable mixture with air.

Floc: A clump of solids formed in sewage by biological or chemical action.

Flocculation: Process by which clumps of solids in water or sewage aggregate through biological or chemical action so they can be separated from water or sewage.

Floodplain: The flat or nearly flat land along a river or stream or in a tidal area that is covered by water during a flood.

Floor Sweep: Capture of heavier-than-air gases that collect at floor level.

Flow Rate: The rate, expressed in gallons -or liters-per-hour, at which a fluid escapes from a hole or fissure in a tank. Such measurements are also made of liquid waste, effluent, and surface water movement.

Flowable: Pesticide and other formulations in which the active ingredients are finely ground insoluble solids suspended in a liquid. They are mixed with water for application.

Flowmeter: A gauge indicating the velocity of wastewater moving through a treatment plant or of any liquid moving through various industrial processes.

Flue Gas: The air coming out of a chimney after combustion in the burner it is venting. It can include nitrogen oxides, carbon oxides, water vapor, sulfur oxides, particles and many chemical pollutants.

Flue Gas Desulfurization: A technology that employs a sorbent, usually lime or limestone, to remove sulfur dioxide from the gases produced by burning fossil fuels. Flue gas desulfurization is current state-of-the art technology for major SO_2 emitters, like power plants.

Fluidized: A mass of solid particles that is made to flow like a liquid by injection of water or gas is said to have been fluidized. In water treatment, a bed of filter media is fluidized by backwashing water through the filter.

Fluidized Bed Incinerator: An incinerator that uses a bed of hot sand or other granular material to transfer heat directly to waste. Used mainly for destroying municipal sludge.

Flume: A natural or man-made channel that diverts water.

Fluoridation: The addition of a chemical to increase the concentration of fluoride ions in drinking water to reduce the incidence of tooth decay.

Fluorides: Gaseous, solid, or dissolved compounds containing fluorine that result from industrial processes. Excessive amounts in food can lead to fluorosis.

Fluorocarbons (FCs): Any of a number of organic compounds analogous to hydrocarbons in which one or more hydrogen atoms are replaced by fluorine. Once used in the United States as a propellant for domestic aerosols, they are now found mainly in coolants and some industrial processes. FCs containing chlorine are called chlorofluorocarbons (CFCs). They are believed to be modifying the ozone layer in the stratosphere, thereby allowing more harmful solar radiation to reach the Earth's surface.

Flush: 1. To open a cold-water tap to clear out all the water which may have been sitting for a long time in the pipes. In new homes, to flush a system means to send large volumes of water gushing through the unused pipes to remove loose particles of solder and flux. 2. To force large amounts of water through a system to clean out piping or tubing, and storage or process tanks.

Flux: 1. A flowing or flow. 2. A substance used to help metals fuse together.

Fly Ash: Non-combustible residual particles expelled by flue gas.

Fogging: Applying a pesticide by rapidly heating the liquid chemical so that it forms very fine droplets that resemble smoke or fog. Used to destroy mosquitoes, black flies, and similar pests.

Food Chain: A sequence of organisms, each of which uses the next, lower member of the sequence as a food source.

Food Processing Waste: Food residues produced during agricultural and industrial operations.

Food Waste: Uneaten food and food preparation wastes from residences and commercial establishments such as grocery stores, restaurants, and produce stands, institutional cafeterias and kitchens, and industrial sources like employee lunchrooms.

Food Web: The feeding relationships by which energy and nutrients are transferred from one species to another.

Formaldehyde: A colorless, pungent, and irritating gas, CH20, used chiefly as a disinfectant and preservative and in synthesizing other compounds like resins.

Formulation: The substances comprising all active and inert ingredients in a pesticide.

Fossil Fuel: Fuel derived from ancient organic remains; e.g. peat, coal, crude oil, and natural gas.

Fracture: A break in a rock formation due to structural stresses; e.g. faults, shears, joints, and planes of fracture cleavage.

Free Product: A petroleum hydrocarbon in the liquid free or non aqueous phase. (See: non-aqueous phase liquid.)

Freeboard: 1. Vertical distance from the normal water surface to the top of a confining wall. 2. Vertical distance from the sand surface to the underside of a trough in a sand filter.

Fresh Water: Water that generally contains less than 1,000 milligrams-per-liter of dissolved solids.

Friable: Capable of being crumbled, pulverized, or reduced to powder by hand pressure.

Friable Asbestos: Any material containing more than one-percent asbestos, and that can be crumbled or reduced to powder by hand pressure. (May include previously non-friable material which becomes broken or damaged by mechanical force.)

Fuel Economy Standard: The Corporate Average Fuel Economy Standard (CAFE) effective in 1978. It enhanced the national fuel conservation effort imposing a miles-per-gallon floor for motor vehicles.

Fuel Efficiency: The proportion of energy released by fuel combustion that is converted into useful energy.

Fuel Switching: 1. A precombustion process whereby a low-sulfur coal is used in place of a higher sulfur coal in a power plant to reduce sulfur dioxide emissions. 2. Illegally using leaded gasoline in a motor vehicle designed to use only unleaded.

Fugitive Emissions: Emissions not caught by a capture system.

Fume: Tiny particles trapped in vapor in a gas stream.

Fumigant: A pesticide vaporized to kill pests. Used in buildings and greenhouses.

Functional Equivalent: Term used to describe EPA's decision-making process and its relationship to the environmental review conducted under the National Environmental Policy Act (NEPA). A review is considered functionally equivalent when it addresses the substantive components of a NEPA review.

Fungicide: Pesticides which are used to control, deter, or destroy fungi.

Fungistat: A chemical that keeps fungi from growing.

Fungus (Fungi): Molds, mildews, yeasts, mushrooms, and puffballs, a group of organisms lacking in chlorophyll (i.e. are not photosynthetic) and which are usually non-mobile, filamentous, and multicellular. Some grow in soil, others attach themselves to decaying trees and other plants whence they obtain nutrients. Some are pathogens, others stabilize sewage and digest composted waste.

Furrow Irrigation: Irrigation method in which water travels through the field by means of small channels between each groups of rows.

Future Liability: Refers to potentially responsible parties' obligations to pay for additional response activities beyond those specified in the Record of Decision or Consent Decree.

G

Game Fish: Species like trout, salmon, or bass, caught for sport. Many of them show more sensitivity to environmental change than "rough" fish.

Garbage: Animal and vegetable waste resulting from the handling, storage, sale, preparation, cooking, and serving of foods.

Gas Chromatograph/Mass Spectrometer: Instrument that identifies the molecular composition and concentrations of various chemicals in water and soil samples.

Gasahol: Mixture of gasoline and ethanol derived from fermented agricultural products containing at least nine percent ethanol. Gasohol emissions contain less carbon monoxide than those from gasoline.

Gasification: Conversion of solid material such as coal into a gas for use as a fuel.

Gasoline Volatility: The property of gasoline whereby it evaporates into a vapor. Gasoline vapor is a mixture of volatile organic compounds.

General Permit: A permit applicable to a class or category of dischargers.

General Reporting Facility: A facility having one or more hazardous chemicals above the 10,000 pound threshold for planning quantities. Such facilities must file MSDS and emergency inventory information with the SERC, LEPC, and local fire departments.

Generally Recognized as Safe (GRAS): Designation by the FDA that a chemical or substance (including certain pesticides) added to food is considered safe by experts, and so is exempted from the usual FFDCA food additive tolerance requirements.

Generator: 1. A facility or mobile source that emits pollutants into the air or releases hazardous waste into water or soil. 2. Any person, by site, whose act or process produces regulated medical waste or whose act first causes such waste to become subject to regulation. Where more than one person (e.g. doctors with separate medical practices) are located in the same building, each business entity is a separate generator.

Genetic Engineering: A process of inserting new genetic information into existing cells in order to modify a specific organism for the purpose of changing one of its characteristics.

Genotoxic: Damaging to DNA; pertaining to agents known to damage DNA.

Geographic Information System (GIS): A computer system designed for storing, manipulating, analyzing, and displaying data in a geographic context.

Geological Log: A detailed description of all underground features (depth, thickness, type of formation) discovered during the drilling of a well.

Geophysical Log: A record of the structure and composition of the earth encountered when drilling a well or similar type of test hold or boring.

Geothermal/Ground Source Heat Pump: These heat pumps are underground coils to transfer heat from the ground to the inside of a building. (See: heat pump; water source heat pump)

Germicide: Any compound that kills disease-causing microorganisms.

Giardia Lamblia: Protozoan in the feces of humans and animals that can cause severe gastrointestinal ailments. It is a common contaminant of surface waters.

Glass Containers: For recycling purposes, containers like bottles and jars for drinks, food, cosmetics and other products. When being recycled, container glass is generally separated into color categories for conversion into new containers, construction materials or fiberglass insulation.

Global Warming: An increase in the near surface temperature of the Earth. Global warming has occurred in the distant past as the result of natural influences, but the term is most often used to refer to the warming predicted to occur as a result of increased emissions of greenhouse gases. Scientists generally agree that the Earth's surface has warmed by about 1 degree Fahrenheit in the past 140 years. The Intergovernmental Panel on Climate Change (IPCC) recently concluded that increased concentrations of greenhouse gases are causing an increase in the Earth's surface temperature and that increased concentrations of sulfate aerosols have led to relative cooling in some regions, generally over and downwind of heavily industrialized areas. (See: climate change)

Global Warming Potential: The ratio of the warming caused by a substance to the warming caused by a similar mass of carbon dioxide. CFC-12, for example, has a GWP of 8,500, while water has a GWP of zero. (See: Class I Substance and Class II Substance.)

Glovebag: A polyethylene or polyvinyl chloride bag-like enclosure affixed around an asbestos-containing source (most often thermal system insulation) permitting the material to be removed while minimizing release of airborne fibers to the surrounding atmosphere.

Gooseneck: A portion of a water service connection between the distribution system water main and a meter. Sometimes called a pigtail.

Grab Sample: A single sample collected at a particular time and place that represents the composition of the water, air, or soil only at that time and place.

Grain Loading: The rate at which particles are emitted from a pollution source. Measurement is made by the number of grains per cubic foot of gas emitted.

Granular Activated Carbon Treatment: A filtering system often used in small water systems and individual homes to remove organics. Also used by municipal water treatment plantsd. GAC can be highly effective in lowering elevated levels of radon in water.

Grasscycling: Source reduction activities in which grass clippings are left on the lawn after mowing.

Grassed Waterway: Natural or constructed watercourse or outlet that is shaped or graded and established in suitable vegetation for the disposal of runoff water without erosion.

Gray Water: Domestic wastewater composed of wash water from kitchen, bathroom, and laundry sinks, tubs, and washers.

Greenhouse Effect: The warming of the Earth's atmosphere attributed to a buildup of carbon dioxide or other gases; some scientists think that this build-up allows the sun's rays to heat the Earth, while making the infra-red radiation atmosphere opaque to infra-red radiation, thereby preventing a counterbalancing loss of heat.

Greenhouse Gas: A gas, such as carbon dioxide or methane, which contributes to potential climate change.

Grinder Pump: A mechanical device that shreds solids and raises sewage to a higher elevation through pressure sewers.

Gross Alpha/Beta Particle Activity: The total radioactivity due to alpha or beta particle emissions as inferred from measurements on a dry sample.

Gross Power-Generation Potential: The installed power generation capacity that landfill gas can support.

Ground Cover: Plants grown to keep soil from eroding.

Ground Water: The supply of fresh water found beneath the Earth's surface, usually in aquifers, which supply wells and springs. Because ground water is a major source of drinking water, there is growing concern over contamination from leaching agricultural or industrial pollutants or leaking underground storage tanks.

Ground Water Under the Direct Influence (UDI) of Surface Water: Any water beneath the surface of the ground with: 1. significant occurence of insects or other microorganisms, algae, or large-diameter pathogens; 2. significant and relatively rapid shifts in water characteristics such as turbidity, temperature, conductivity, or pH which closely correlate to climatological or surface water conditions. Direct influence is determined for individual sources in accordance with criteria established by a state.

Ground-Penetrating Radar: A geophysical method that uses high frequency electromagnetic waves to obtain subsurface information.

Ground-Water Discharge: Ground water entering near coastal waters which has been contaminated by landfill leachate, deep well injection of hazardous wastes, septic tanks, etc.

Ground-Water Disinfection Rule: A 1996 amendment of the Safe Drinking Water Act requiring EPA to promulgate national primary drinking water regulations requiring disinfection as for all public water systems, including surface waters and ground water systems.

Gully Erosion: Severe erosion in which trenches are cut to a depth greater than 30 centimeters (a foot). Generally, ditches deep enough to cross with farm equipment are considered gullies.

H

Habitat: The place where a population (e.g. human, animal, plant, microorganism) lives and its surroundings, both living and non-living.

Habitat Indicator: A physical attribute of the environment measured to characterize conditions necessary to support an organism, population, or community in the absence of pollutants; e.g. salinity of estuarine waters or substrate type in streams or lakes.

Half-Life: 1. The time required for a pollutant to lose one-half of its original coconcentrationor example, the biochemical half-life of DDT in the environment is 15 years. 2. The time required for half of the atoms of a radioactive element to undergo self-transmutation or decay (half-life of radium is 1620 years). 3. The time required for the elimination of half a total dose from the body.

Halogen: A type of incandescent lamp with higher energy-efficiency that standard ones.

Halon: Bromine-containing compounds with long atmospheric lifetimes whose breakdown in the stratosphere causes depletion of ozone. Halons are used in firefighting.

Hammer Mill: A high-speed machine that uses hammers and cutters to crush, grind, chip, or shred solid waste.

Hard Water: Alkaline water containing dissolved salts that interfere with some industrial processes and prevent soap from sudsing.

Hauler: Garbage collection company that offers complete refuse removal service; many will also collect recyclables.

Hazard: 1. Potential for radiation, a chemical or other pollutant to cause human illness or injury. 2. In the pesticide program, the inherent toxicity of a compound. Hazard identification of a given substances is an informed judgment based on verifiable toxicity data from animal models or human studies.

Hazard Assessment: Evaluating the effects of a stressor or determining a margin of safety for an organism by comparing the concentration which causes toxic effects with an estimate of exposure to the organism.

Hazard Communication Standard: An OSHA regulation that requires chemical manufacturers, suppliers, and importers to assess the hazards of the chemicals that they make, supply, or import, and to inform employers, customers, and workers of these hazards through MSDS information.

Hazard Evaluation: A component of risk evaluation that involves gathering and evaluating data on the types of health injuries or diseases that may be produced by a chemical and on the conditions of exposure under which such health effects are produced.

Hazard Identification: Determining if a chemical or a microbe can cause adverse health effects in humans and what those effects might be.

Hazard Quotient: The ratio of estimated site-specific exposure to a single chemical from a site over a specified period to the estimated daily exposure level, at which no adverse health effects are likely to occur.

Hazard Ratio: A term used to compare an animal's daily dietary intake of a pesticide to its LD 50 value. A ratio greater than 1.0 indicates that the animal is likely to consume an a dose amount which would kill 50 percent of animals of the same species. (See: LD 50 /Lethal Dose.)

Hazardous Air Pollutants: Air pollutants which are not covered by ambient air quality standards but which, as defined in the Clean Air Act, may present a threat of adverse human health effects or adverse environmental effects.Such pollutants include asbestos, beryllium, mercury, benzene, coke oven emissions, radionuclides, and vinyl chloride.

Hazardous Chemical: An EPA designation for any hazardous material requiring an MSDS under OSHA's Hazard Communication Standard. Such substances are capable of producing fires and explosions or adverse health effects like cancer and dermatitis. Hazardous chemicals are distinct from hazardous waste.(See: Hazardous Waste.)

Hazardous Ranking System: The principal screening tool used by EPA to evaluate risks to public health and the environment associated with abandoned or uncontrolled hazardous waste sites. The HRS calculates a score based on the potential of hazardous substances spreading from the site through the air, surface water, or ground water, and on other factors such as density and proximity of human population. This score is the primary factor in deciding if the site should be on the National Priorities List and, if so, what ranking it should have compared to other sites on the list.

Hazardous Substance: 1. Any material that poses a threat to human health and/or the environment. Typical hazardous substances are toxic, corrosive, ignitable, explosive, or chemically reactive. 2. Any substance designated by EPA to be reported if a designated quantity of the substance is spilled in the waters of the United States or is otherwise released into the environment.

Hazardous Waste: By-products of society that can pose a substantial or potential hazard to human health or the environment when improperly managed. Possesses at least one of four characteristics (ignitability, corrosivity, reactivity, or toxicity), or appears on special EPA lists.

Hazardous Waste Landfill: An excavated or engineered site where hazardous waste is deposited and covered.

Hazardous Waste Minimization: Reducing the amount of toxicity or waste produced by a facility via source reduction or environmentally sound recycling.

Hazards Analysis: Procedures used to (1) identify potential sources of release of hazardous materials from fixed facilities or transportation accidents; (2) determine the vulnerability of a geographical area to a release of hazardous materials; and (3) compare hazards to determine which present greater or lesser risks to a community.

Hazards Identification: Providing information on which facilities have extremely hazardous substances, what those chemicals are, how much there is at each facility, how the chemicals are stored, and whether they are used at high temperatures.

Headspace: The vapor mixture trapped above a solid or liquid in a sealed vessel.

Health Advisory Level: A non-regulatory health-based reference level of chemical traces (usually in ppm) in drinking water at which there are no adverse health risks when ingested over various periods of time. Such levels are established for one day, 10 days, long-term and life-time exposure periods. They contain a wide margin of safety.

Health Assessment: An evaluation of available data on existing or potential risks to human health posed by a Superfund site. The Agency for Toxic Substances and Disease Registry (ATSDR) of the Department of Health and Human Services (DHHS) is required to perform such an assessment at every site on the National Priorities List.

Heat Island Effect: A "dome" of elevated temperatures over an urban area caused by structural and pavement heat fluxes, and pollutant emissions.

Heat Pump: An electric device with both heating and cooling capabilities. It extracts heat from one medium at a lower (the heat source) temperature and transfers it to another at a higher temperature (the heat sink), thereby cooling the first and warming the second. (See: geothermal, water source heat pump.)

Heavy Metals: Metallic elements with high atomic weights; (e.g. mercury, chromium, cadmium, arsenic, and lead); can damage living things at low concentrations and tend to accumulate in the food chain.

Heptachlor: An insecticide that was banned on some food products in 1975 and in all of them 1978. It was allowed for use in seed treatment until 1983. More recently it was found in milk and other dairy products in Arkansas and Missouri where dairy cattle were illegally fed treated seed.

Herbicide: A chemical pesticide designed to control or destroy plants, weeds, or grasses.

Herbivore: An animal that feeds on plants.

Heterotrophic Organisms: Species that are dependent on organic matter for food.

High End Exposure (dose) Estimate: An estimate of exposure, or dose level received anyone in a defined population that is greater than the 90th percentile of all individuals in that population, but less than the exposure at the highest percentile in that population. A high end risk descriptor is an estimate of the risk level for such individuals. Note that risk is based on a combination of exposure and susceptibility to the stressor.

High Intensity Discharge: A generic term for mercury vapor, metal halide, and high pressure sodium lamps and fixtures.

High-Density Polyethylene: A material used to make plastic bottles and other products that produces toxic fumes when burned.

High-Level Nuclear Waste Facility: Plant designed to handle disposal of used nuclear fuel, high-level radioactive waste, and plutonium waste.

High-Level Radioactive Waste (HLRW): Waste generated in core fuel of a nuclear reactor, found at nuclear reactors or by nuclear fuel reprocessing; is a serious threat to anyone who comes near the waste without shielding. (See: low-level radioactive waste.)

High-Line Jumpers: Pipes or hoses connected to fire hydrants and laid on top of the ground to provide emergency water service for an isolated portion of a distribution system.

High-Risk Community: A community located within the vicinity of numerous sites of facilities or other potential sources of envienvironmental exposure/health hazards which may result in high levels of exposure to contaminants or pollutants.

High-to-Low-Dose Extrapolation: The process of prediction of low exposure risk to humans and animals from the measured high-exposure-high-risk data involving laboratory animals.

Highest Dose Tested: The highest dose of a chemical or substance tested in a study.

Holding Pond: A pond or reservoir, usually made of earth, built to store polluted runoff.

Holding Time: The maximum amount of time a sample may be stored before analysis.

Hollow Stem Auger Drilling: Conventional drilling method that uses augurs to penetrate the soil. As the augers are rotated, soil cuttings are conveyed to the ground surface via augur spirals. DP tools can be used inside the hollow augers.

Homeowner Water System: Any water system which supplies piped water to a single residence.

Homogeneous Area: In accordance with Asbestos Hazard and Emergency Response Act (AHERA) definitions, an area of surfacing materials, thermal surface insulation, or miscellaneous material that is uniform in color and texture.

Hood Capture Efficiency: Ratio of the emissions captured by a hood and directed into a control or disposal device, expressed as a percent of all emissions.

Host: 1. In genetics, the organism, typically a bacterium, into which a gene from another organism is transplanted. 2. In medicine, an animal infected or parasitized by another organism.

Household Hazardous Waste: Hazardous products used and disposed of by residential as opposed to industrial consumers. Includes paints, stains, varnishes, solvents, pesticides, and other materials or products containing volatile chemicals that can catch fire, react or explode, or that are corrosive or toxic.

Household Waste (Domestic Waste): Solid waste, composed of garbage and rubbish, which normally originates in a private home or apartment house. Domestic waste may contain a significant amount of toxic or hazardous waste.

Human Equivalent Dose: A dose which, when administered to humans, produces an effect equal to that produced by a dose in animals.

Human Exposure Evaluation: Describing the nature and size of the population exposed to a substance and the magnitude and duration of their exposure.

Human Health Risk: The likelihood that a given exposure or series of exposures may have damaged or will damage the health of individuals.

Hydraulic Conductivity: The rate at which water can move through a permeable medium. (i.e. the coefficient of permeability.)

Hydraulic Gradient: In general, the direction of groundwater flow due to changes in the depth of the water table.

Hydrocarbons (HC): Chemical compounds that consist entirely of carbon and hydrogen.

Hydrogen Sulfide (H2S): Gas emitted during organic decomposition. Also a by-product of oil refining and burning. Smells like rotten eggs and, in heavy concentration, can kill or cause illness.

Hydrogeological Cycle: The natural process recycling water from the atmosphere down to (and through) the earth and back to the atmosphere again.

Hydrogeology: The geology of ground water, with particular emphasis on the chemistry and movement of water.

Hydrologic Cycle: Movement or exchange of water between the atmosphere and earth.

Hydrology: The science dealing with the properties, distribution, and circulation of water.

Hydrolysis: The decomposition of organic compounds by interaction with water.

Hydronic: A ventilation system using heated or cooled water pumped through a building.

Hydrophilic: Having a strong affinity for water.

Glossary of Environmental Terms

Hydrophobic: Having a strong aversion for water.

Hydropneumatic: A water system, usually small, in which a water pump is automatically controlled by the pressure in a compressed air tank.

Hypersensitivity Diseases: Diseases characterized by allergic responses to pollutants; diseases most clearly associated with indoor air quality are asthma, rhinitis, and pneumonic hypersensitivity.

Hypolimnion: Bottom waters of a thermally stratified lake. The hypolimnion of a eutrophic lake is usually low or lacking in oxygen.

Hypoxia/Hypoxic Waters: Waters with dissolved oxygen concentrations of less than 2 ppm, the level generally accepted as the minimum required for most marine life to survive and reproduce.

I

Identification Code or EPA I.D. Number: The unique code assigned to each generator, transporter, and treatment, storage, or disposal facility by regulating agencies to facilitate identification and tracking of chemicals or hazardous waste.

Ignitable: Capable of burning or causing a fire.

IM240: A high-tech, transient dynamometer automobile emissions test that takes up to 240 seconds.

Imhoff Cone: A clear, cone-shaped container used to measure the volume of settleable solids in a specific volume of water.

Immediately Dangerous to Life and Health (IDLH): The maximum level to which a healthy individual can be exposed to a chemical for 30 minutes and escape without suffering irreversible health effects or impairing symptoms. Used as a "level of concern." (See: level of concern.)

Imminent Hazard: One that would likely result in unreasonable adverse effects on humans or the environment or risk unreasonable hazard to an endangered species during the time required for a pesticide registration cancellation proceeding.

Imminent Threat: A high probability that exposure is occurring.

Immiscibility: The inability of two or more substances or liquids to readily dissolve into one another, such as soil and water. Immiscibility The inability of two or more substances or liquids to readily dissolve into one another, such as soil and water.

Impermeable: Not easily penetrated. The property of a material or soil that does not allow, or allows only with great difficulty, the movement or passage of water.

Imports: Municipal solid waste and recyclables that have been transported to a state or locality for processing or final disposition (but that did not originate in that state or locality).

Impoundment: A body of water or sludge confined by a dam, dike, floodgate, or other barrier.

In Situ: In its original place; unmoved unexcavated; remaining at the site or in the subsurface.

In-Line Filtration: Pre-treatment method in which chemicals are mixed by the flowing water; commonly used in pressure filtration installations. Eliminates need for flocculation and sedimentation.

In-Situ Flushing: Introduction of large volumes of water, at times supplemented with cleaning compounds, into soil, waste, or ground water to flush hazardous contaminants from a site.

In-Situ Oxidation: Technology that oxidizes contaminants dissolved in ground water, converting them into insoluble compounds.

In-Situ Stripping: Treatment system that removes or "strips" volatile organic compounds from contaminated ground or surface water by forcing an airstream through the water and causing the compounds to evaporate.

In-Situ Vitrification: Technology that treats contaminated soil in place at extremely high temperatures, at or more than 3000 degrees Fahrenheit.

In Vitro: Testing or action outside an organism (e.g. inside a test tube or culture dish.)

In Vivo: Testing or action inside an organism.

Incident Command Post: A facility located at a safe distance from an emergency site, where the incident commander, key staff, and technical representatives can make decisions and deploy emergency manpower and equipment.

Incident Command System (ICS): The organizational arrangement wherein one person, normally the Fire Chief of the impacted district, is in charge of an integrated, comprehensive emergency response organization and the emergency incident site, backed by an Emergency Operations Center staff with resources, information, and advice.

Incineration: A treatment technology involving destruction of waste by controlled burning at high temperatures; e.g., burning sludge to remove the water and reduce the remaining residues to a safe, non-burnable ash that can be disposed of safely on land, in some waters, or in underground locations.

Incineration at Sea: Disposal of waste by burning at sea on specially-designed incinerator ships.

Incinerator: A furnace for burning waste under controlled conditions.

Incompatible Waste: A waste unsuitable for mixing with another waste or material because it may react to form a hazard.

Indemnification: In the pesticide program, legal requirement that EPA pay certain end-users, dealers, and distributors for the cost of stock on hand at the time a pesticide registration is suspended.

Indicator: In biology, any biological entity or processes, or community whose characteristics show the presence of specific environmental conditions. 2. In chemistry, a substance that shows a visible change, usually of color, at a desired point in a chemical reaction. 3.A device that indicates the result of a measurement; e.g. a pressure gauge or a moveable scale.

Indirect Discharge: Introduction of pollutants from a non-domestic source into a publicly owned waste-treatment system. Indirect dischargers can be commercial or industrial facilities whose wastes enter local sewers.

Indirect Source: Any facility or building, property, road or parking area that attracts motor vehicle traffic and, indirectly, causes pollution.

Indoor Air: The breathable air inside a habitable structure or conveyance.

Indoor Air Pollution: Chemical, physical, or biological contaminants in indoor air.

Indoor Climate: Temperature, humidity, lighting, air flow and noise levels in a habitable structure or conveyance. Indoor climate can affect indoor air pollution.

Industrial Pollution Prevention: Combination of industrial source reduction and toxic chemical use substitution.

Industrial Process Waste: Residues produced during manufacturing operations.

Industrial Sludge: Semi-liquid residue or slurry remaining from treatment of industrial water and wastewater.

Industrial Source Reduction: Practices that reduce the amount of any hazardous substance, pollutant, or contaminant entering any waste stream or otherwise released into the environment. Also reduces the threat to public health and the environment associated with such releases. Term includes equipment or technology modifications, substitution of raw materials, and improvements in housekeeping, maintenance, training or inventory control.

Industrial Waste: Unwanted materials from an industrial operation; may be liquid, sludge, solid, or hazardous waste.

Inert Ingredient: Pesticide components such as solvents, carriers, dispersants, and surfactants that are not active against target pests. Not all inert ingredients are innocuous.

Inertial Separator: A device that uses centrifugal force to separate waste particles.

Infectious Agent: Any organism, such as a pathogenic virus, parasite, or or bacterium, that is capable of invading body tissues, multiplying, and causing disease.

Infectious Waste: Hazardous waste capable of causing infections in humans, including: contaminated animal waste; human blood and blood products; isolation waste, pathological waste; and discarded sharps (needles, scalpels or broken medical instruments).

Infiltration: 1. The penetration of water through the ground surface into sub-surface soil or the penetration of water from the soil into sewer or other pipes through defective joints, connections, or manhole walls. 2. The technique of applying large volumes of waste water to land to penetrate the surface and percolate through the underlying soil. (See: percolation.)

Infiltration Gallery: A sub-surface groundwater collection system, typically shallow in depth, constructed with open-jointed or perforated pipes that discharge collected water into a watertight chamber from which the water is pumped to treatment facilities and into the distribution system. Usually located close to streams or ponds.

Infiltration Rate: The quantity of water that can enter the soil in a specified time interval.

Inflow: Entry of extraneous rain water into a sewer system from sources other than infiltration, such as basement drains, manholes, storm drains, and street washing.

Influent: Water, wastewater, or other liquid flowing into a reservoir, basin, or treatment plant.

Information Collection Request (ICR): A description of information to be gathered in connection with rules, proposed rules, surveys, and guidance documents that contain information-gathering requirements. The ICR describes what information is needed, why it is needed, how it will be collected, and how much collecting it will cost. The ICR is submitted by the EPA to the Office of Management and Budget (OMB) for approval.

Information File: In the Superfund program, a file that contains accurate, up-to-date documents on a Superfund site. The file is usually located in a public building (school, library, or city hall) convenient for local residents.

Inhalable Particles: All dust capable of entering the human respiratory tract.

Initial Compliance Period (Water): The first full three-year compliance period which begins at least 18 months after promulgation.

Injection Well: A well into which fluids are injected for purposes such as waste disposal, improving the recovery of crude oil, or solution mining.

Injection Zone: A geological formation receiving fluids through a well.

Innovative Technologies: New or inventive methods to treat effectively hazardous waste and reduce risks to human health and the environment.

Innovative Treatment Technologies: Technologies whose routine use is inhibited by lack of data on performance and cost. (See: Established treatment technologies.)

Inoculum: 1. Bacteria or fungi injected into compost to start biological action. 2. A medium containing organisms, usually bacteria or a virus, that is introduced into cultures or living organisms.

Inorganic Chemicals: Chemical substances of mineral origin, not of basically carbon structure.

Insecticide: A pesticide compound specifically used to kill or prevent the growth of insects.

Inspection and Maintenance (I/M): 1. Activities to ensure that vehicles' emission controls work properly. 2. Also applies to wastewater treatment plants and other anti-pollution facilities and processes.

Institutional Waste: Waste generated at institutions such as schools, libraries, hospitals, prisons, etc.

Instream Use: Water use taking place within a stream channel; e.g., hydro-electric power generation, navigation, water quality improvement, fish propagation, recreation.

Integrated Exposure Assessment: Cumulative summation (over time) of the magnitude of exposure to a toxic chemical in all media.

Integrated Pest Management (IPM): A mixture of chemical and other, non-pesticide, methods to control pests.

Integrated Waste Management: Using a variety of practices to handle municipal solid waste; can include source reduction, recycling, incineration, and landfilling.

Interceptor Sewers: Large sewer lines that, in a combined system, control the flow of sewage to the treatment plant. In a storm, they allow some of the sewage to flow directly into a receiving stream, thus keeping it from overflowing onto the streets. Also used in separate systems to collect the flows from main and trunk sewers and carry them to treatment points.

Interface: The common boundary between two substances such as a water and a solid, water and a gas, or two liquids such as water and oil.

Interfacial Tension: The strength of the film separating two immiscible fluids (e.g. oil and water) measured in dynes per, or millidynes per centimeter.

Interim (Permit) Status: Period during which treatment, storage and disposal facilities coming under RCRA in 1980 are temporarily permitted to operate while awaiting a permanent permit. Permits issued under these circumstances are usually called "Part A" or "Part B" permits.

Internal Dose: In exposure assessment, the amount of a substance penetrating the absorption barriers (e.g. skin, lung tissue, gastrointestinal tract) of an organism through either physical or biological processes. (See: absorbed dose)

Interstate Carrier Water Supply: A source of water for drinking and sanitary use on planes, buses, trains, and ships operating in more than one state. These sources are federally regulated.

Interstate Commerce Clause: A clause of the U.S. Constitution which reserves to the federal government the right to regulate the conduct of business across state lines. Under this clause, for example, the U.S. Supreme Court has ruled that states may not inequitably restrict the disposal of out-of-state wastes in their jurisdictions.

Interstate Waters: Waters that flow across or form part of state or international boundaries; e.g. the Great Lakes, the Mississippi River, or coastal waters.

Interstitial Monitoring: The continuous surveillance of the space between the walls of an underground storage tank.

Intrastate Product: Pesticide products once registered by states for sale and use only in the state. All intrastate products have been converted to full federal registration or canceled.

Inventory (TSCA): Inventory of chemicals produced pursuant to Section 8 (b) of the Toxic Substances Control Act.

Inversion: A layer of warm air that prevents the rise of cooling air and traps pollutants beneath it; can cause an air pollution episode.

Ion: An electrically charged atom or group of atoms.

Ion Exchange Treatment: A common water-softening method often found on a large scale at water purification plants that remove some organics and radium by adding calcium oxide or calcium hydroxide to increase the pH to a level where the metals will precipitate out.

Ionization Chamber: A device that measures the intensity of ionizing radiation.

Ionizing Radiation: Radiation that can strip electrons from atoms; e.g. alpha, beta, and gamma radiation.

IRIS: EPA's Integrated Risk Information System, an electronic data base containing the Agency's latest descriptive and quantitative regulatory information on chemical constituents.

Irradiated Food: Food subject to brief radioactivity, usually gamma rays, to kill insects, bacteria, and mold, and to permit storage without refrigeration.

Irradiation: Exposure to radiation of wavelengths shorter than those of visible light (gamma, x-ray, or ultra- violet), for medical purposes, to sterilize milk or other foodstuffs, or to induce polymerization of monomers or vulcanization of rubber.

Irreversible Effect: Effect characterized by the inability of the body to partially or fully repair injury caused by a toxic agent.

Irrigation: Applying water or wastewater to land areas to supply the water and nutrient needs of plants.

Irrigation Efficiency: The amount of water stored in the crop root zone compared to the amount of irrigation water applied.

Irrigation Return Flow: Surface and subsurface water which leaves the field following application of irrigation water.

Irritant: A substance that can cause irritation of the skin, eyes, or respiratory system. Effects may be acute from a single high level exposure, or chronic from repeated low-level exposures to such compounds as chlorine, nitrogen dioxide, and nitric acid.

Isoconcentration: More than one sample point exhibiting the same isolate concentration.

Isopleth: The line or area represented by an isoconcentration.

Isotope: A variation of an element that has the same atomic number of protons but a different weight because of the number of neutrons. Various isotopes of the same element may have different radioactive behaviors, some are highly unstable..

Isotropy: The condition in which the hydraulic or other properties of an aquifer are the same in all directions.

J

Jar Test: A laboratory procedure that simulates a water treatment plant's coagulation/flocculation units with differing chemical doses, mix speeds, and settling times to estimate the minimum or ideal coagulant dose required to achieve certain water quality goals.

Joint and Several Liability: Under CERCLA, this legal concept relates to the liability for Superfund site cleanup and other costs on the part of more than one potentially responsible party (i.e. if there were several owners or users of a site that became contaminated over the years, they could all be considered potentially liable for cleaning up the site.)

K

Karst: A geologic formation of irregular limestone deposits with sinks, underground streams, and caverns.

Kinetic Energy: Energy possessed by a moving object or water body.

Kinetic Rate Coefficient: A number that describes the rate at which a water constituent such as a biochemical oxygen demand or dissolved oxygen rises or falls, or at which an air pollutant reacts.

L

Laboratory Animal Studies: Investigations using animals as surrogates for humans.

Lagoon: 1. A shallow pond where sunlight, bacterial action, and oxygen work to purify wastewater; also used for storage of wastewater or spent nuclear fuel rods. 2. Shallow body of water, often separated from the sea by coral reefs or sandbars.

Land Application: Discharge of wastewater onto the ground for treatment or reuse. (See: irrigation.)

Land Ban: Phasing out of land disposal of most untreated hazardous wastes, as mandated by the 1984 RCRA amendments.

Land Disposal Restrictions: Rules that require hazardous wastes to be treated before disposal on land to destroy or immobilize hazardous constituents that might migrate into soil and ground water.

Land Farming (of Waste): A disposal process in which hazardous waste deposited on or in the soil is degraded naturally by microbes.

Landfills: 1. Sanitary landfills are disposal sites for non-hazardous solid wastes spread in layers, compacted to the smallest practical volume, and covered by material applied at the end of each operating day. 2. Secure chemical landfills are disposal sites for hazardous waste, selected and designed to minimize the chance of release of hazardous substances into the environment.

Glossary of Environmental Terms

Landscape: The traits, patterns, and structure of a specific geographic area, including its biological composition, its physical environment, and its anthropogenic or social patterns. An area where interacting ecosystems are grouped and repeated in similar form.

Landscape Characterization: Documentation of the traits and patterns of the essential elements of the landscape.

Landscape Ecology: The study of the distribution patterns of communities and ecosystems, the ecological processes that affect those patterns, and changes in pattern and process over time.

Landscape Indicator: A measurement of the landscape, calculated from mapped or remotely sensed data, used to describe spatial patterns of land use and land cover across a geographic area. Landscape indicators may be useful as measures of certain kinds of environmental degradation such as forest fragmentation.

Langelier Index (LI): An index reflecting the equilibrium pH of a water with respect to calcium and alkalinity; used in stabilizing water to control both corrosion and scale deposition.

Large Quantity Generator: Person or facility generating more than 2200 pounds of hazardous waste per month. Such generators produce about 90 percent of the nation's hazardous waste, and are subject to all RCRA requirements.

Large Water System: A water system that services more than 50,000 customers.

Laser Induced Fluorescence: A method for measuring the relative amount of soil and/or groundwater with an in-situ sensor.

Latency: Time from the first exposure of a chemical until the appearance of a toxic effect.

Lateral Sewers: Pipes that run under city streets and receive the sewage from homes and businesses, as opposed to domestic feeders and main trunk lines.

Laundering Weir: Sedimention basin overflow weir.

LC 50/Lethal Concentration: Median level concentration, a standard measure of toxicity. It tells how much of a substance is needed to kill half of a group of experimental organisms in a given time. (See: LD 50.)

LD 50/ Lethal Dose: The dose of a toxicant or microbe that will kill 50 percent of the test organisms within a designated period. The lower the LD 50, the more toxic the compound.

Ldlo: Lethal dose low; the lowest dose in an animal study at which lethality occurs.

Leachate: Water that collects contaminants as it trickles through wastes, pesticides or fertilizers. Leaching may occur in farming areas, feedlots, and landfills, and may result in hazardous substances entering surface water, ground water, or soil.

Leachate Collection System: A system that gathers leachate and pumps it to the surface for treatment.

Leaching: The process by which soluble constituents are dissolved and filtered through the soil by a percolating fluid. (See: leachate.)

Lead (Pb): A heavy metal that is hazardous to health if breathed or swallowed. Its use in gasoline, paints, and plumbing compounds has been sharply restricted or eliminated by federal laws and regulations. (See: heavy metals.)

Lead Service Line: A service line made of lead which connects the water to the building inlet and any lead fitting connected to it.

Legionella: A genus of bacteria, some species of which have caused a type of pneumonia called Legionaires Disease.

Lethal Concentration 50: Also referred to as LC50, a concentration of a pollutant or effluent at which 50 percent of the test organisms die; a common measure of acute toxicity.

Lethal Dose 50: Also referred to as LD50, the dose of a toxicant that will kill 50 percent of test organisms within a designated period of time; the lower the LD 50, the more toxic the compound.

Level of Concern (LOC): The concentration in air of an extremely hazardous substance above which there may be serious immediate health effects to anyone exposed to it for short periods

Life Cycle of a Product: All stages of a product's development, from extraction of fuel for power to production, marketing, use, and disposal.

Lifetime Average Daily Dose: Figure for estimating excess lifetime cancer risk.

Lifetime Exposure: Total amount of exposure to a substance that a human would receive in a lifetime (usually assumed to be 70 years).

Lift: In a sanitary landfill, a compacted layer of solid waste and the top layer of cover material.

Lifting Station: (See: pumping station.)

Light Non-Aqueous Phase Liquid (LNAPL): A non-aqueous phase liquid with a specific gravity less than 1.0. Because the specific gravity of water is 1.0, most LNAPLs float on top of the water table. Most common petroleum hydrocarbon fuels and lubricating oils are LNAPLs.

Light-Emitting Diode: A long-lasting illumination technology used for exit signs which requires very little power

Limestone Scrubbing: Use of a limestone and water solution to remove gaseous stack-pipe sulfur before it reaches the atmosphere.

Limit of Detection (LOD): The minimum concentration of a substance being analyzed test that has a 99 percent probability of being identified.

Limited Degradation: An environmental policy permitting some degradation of natural systems but terminating at a level well beneath an established health standard.

Limiting Factor: A condition whose absence or excessive concentration, is incompatible with the needs or tolerance of a species or population and which may have a negative influence on their ability to thrive.

Limnology: The study of the physical, chemical, hydrological, and biological aspects of fresh water bodies.

Lindane: A pesticide that causes adverse health effects in domestic water supplies and is toxic to freshwater fish and aquatic life.

Liner: 1. A relatively impermeable barrier designed to keep leachate inside a landfill. Liner materials include plastic and dense clay. 2. An insert or sleeve for sewer pipes to prevent leakage or infiltration.

Lipid Solubility: The maximum concentration of a chemical that will dissolve in fatty substances. Lipid soluble substances are insoluble in water. They will very selectively disperse through the environment via uptake in living tissue.

Liquefaction: Changing a solid into a liquid.

Liquid Injection Incinerator: Commonly used system that relies on high pressure to prepare liquid wastes for incineration by breaking them up into tiny droplets to allow easier combustion.

List: Shorthand term for EPA list of violating facilities or firms debarred from obtaining government contracts because they violated certain sections of the Clean Air or Clean Water Acts. The list is maintained by The Office of Enforcement and Compliance Monitoring.

Listed Waste: Wastes listed as hazardous under RCRA but which have not been subjected to the Toxic Characteristics Listing Process because the dangers they present are considered self-evident.

Lithology: Mineralogy, grain size, texture, and other physical properties of granular soil, sediment, or rock.

Litter: 1. The highly visible portion of solid waste carelessly discarded outside the regular garbage and trash collection and disposal system. 2. leaves and twigs fallen from forest trees.

Littoral Zone: 1. That portion of a body of fresh water extending from the shoreline lakeward to the limit of occupancy of rooted plants. 2. A strip of land along the shoreline between the high and low water levels.

Local Education Agency (LEA): In the asbestos program, an educational agency at the local level that exists primarily to operate schools or to contract for educational services, including primary and secondary public and private schools. A single, unaffiliated school can be considered an LEA for AHERA purposes.

Local Emergency Planning Committee (LEPC): A committee appointed by the state emergency response commission, as required by SARA Title III, to formulate a comprehensive emergency plan for its jurisdiction.

Low Density Polyethylene (LOPE): Plastic material used for both rigid containers and plastic film applications.

Low Emissivity (low-E) Windows: New window technology that lowers the amount of energy loss through windows by inhibiting the transmission of radiant heat while still allowing sufficient light to pass through.

Low NO_x Burners: One of several combustion technologies used to reduce emissions of Nitrogen Oxides (NO_x.)

Low-Level Radioactive Waste (LLRW): Wastes less hazardous than most of those associated with a nuclear reactor; generated by hospitals, research laboratories, and certain industries. The Department of Energy, Nuclear Regulatory Commission, and EPA share responsibilities for managing them. (See: high-level radioactive wastes.)

Lower Detection Limit: The smallest signal above background noise an instrument can reliably detect.

Lower Explosive Limit (LEL): The concentration of a compound in air below which the mixture will not catch on fire.

Lowest Acceptable Daily Dose: The largest quantity of a chemical that will not cause a toxic effect, as determined by animal studies.

Lowest Achievable Emission Rate: Under the Clean Air Act, the rate of emissions that reflects (1) the most stringent emission limitation in the implementation plan of any state for such source unless the owner or operator demonstrates such limitations are not achievable; or (2) the most stringent emissions limitation achieved in practice, whichever is more stringent. A proposed new or modified source may not emit pollutants in excess of existing new source standards.

Lowest Observed Adverse Effect Level (LOAEL): The lowest level of a stressor that causes statistically and biologically significant differences in test samples as compared to other samples subjected to no stressor.

M

Macropores: Secondary soil features such as root holes or desiccation cracks that can create significant conduits for movement of NAPL and dissolved contaminants, or vapor-phase contaminants.

Magnetic Separation: Use of magnets to separate ferrous materials from mixed municipal waste stream.

Major Modification: This term is used to define modifications of major stationary sources of emissions with respect to Prevention of Significant Deterioration and New Source Review under the Clean Air Act.

Major Stationary Sources: Term used to determine the applicability of Prevention of Significant Deterioration and new source regulations. In a nonattainment area, any stationary pollutant source with potential to emit more than 100 tons per year is considered a major stationary source. In PSD areas the cutoff level may be either 100 or 250 tons, depending upon the source.

Majors: Larger publicly owned treatment works (POTWs) with flows equal to at least one million gallons per day (mgd) or servicing a population equivalent to 10,000 persons; certain other POTWs having significant water quality impacts. (See: minors.)

Man-Made (Anthropogenic) Beta Particle and Photon Emitters: All radionuclides emitting beta particles and/or photons listed in Maximum Permissible Body Burdens and Maximum Permissible Concentrations of Radonuclides in Air and Water for Occupational Exposure.

Management Plan: Under the Asbestos Hazard Emergency Response Act (AHERA), a document that each Local Education Agency is required to prepare, describing all activities planned and undertaken by a school to comply with AHERA regulations, including building inspections to identify asbestos-containing materials, response actions, and operations and maintenance programs to minimize the risk of exposure.

Managerial Controls: Methods of nonpoint source pollution control based on decisions about managing agricultural wastes or application times or rates for agrochemicals.

Mandatory Recycling: Programs which by law require consumers to separate trash so that some or all recyclable materials are recovered for recycling rather than going to landfills.

Manifest: A one-page form used by haulers transporting waste that lists EPA identification numbers, type and quantity of waste, the generator it originated from, the transporter that shipped it, and the storage or disposal facility to which it is being shipped. It includes copies for all participants in the shipping process.

Manifest System: Tracking of hazardous waste from "cradle-to-grave" (generation through disposal) with accompanying documents known as manifests.(See: cradle to grave.)

Manual Separation: Hand sorting of recyclable or compostable materials in waste.

Manufacturer's Formulation: A list of substances or component parts as described by the maker of a coating, pesticide, or other product containing chemicals or other substances.

Manufacturing Use Product: Any product intended (labeled) for formulation or repackaging into other pesticide products.

Margin of Safety: Maximum amount of exposure producing no measurable effect in animals (or studied humans) divided by the actual amount of human exposure in a population.

Margin of Exposure (MOE): The ratio of the no-observed adverse-effect-level to the estimated exposure dose.

Marine Sanitation Device: Any equipment or process installed on board a vessel to receive, retain, treat, or discharge sewage.

Marsh: A type of wetland that does not accumulate appreciable peat deposits and is dominated by herbaceous vegetation. Marshes may be either fresh or saltwater, tidal or non-tidal. (See: wetlands.)

Material Category: In the asbestos program, broad classification of materials into thermal surfacing insulation, surfacing material, and miscellaneous material.

Material Safety Data Sheet (MSDS): A compilation of information required under the OSHA Communication Standard on the identity of hazardous chemicals, health, and physical hazards, exposure limits, and precautions. Section 311 of SARA requires facilities to submit MSDSs under certain circumstances.

Material Type: Classification of suspect material by its specific use or application; e.g., pipe insulation, fireproofing, and floor tile.

Materials Recovery Facility (MRF): A facility that processes residentially collected mixed recyclables into new products available for market.

Maximally (or Most) Exposed Individual: The person with the highest exposure in a given population.

Maximum Acceptable Toxic Concentration: For a given ecological effects test, the range (or geometric mean) between the No Observable Adverse Effect Level and the Lowest Observable Adverse Effects Level.

Maximum Available Control Technology (MACT): The emission standard for sources of air pollution requiring the maximum reduction of hazardous emissions, taking cost and feasibility into account. Under the Clean Air Act Amendments of 1990, the MACT must not be less than the average emission level achieved by controls on the best performing 12 percent of existing sources, by category of industrial and utility sources.

Maximum Contaminant Level: The maximum permissible level of a contaminant in water delivered to any user of a public system. MCLs are enforceable standards.

Maximum Contaminant Level Goal (MCLG): Under the Safe Drinking Water Act, a non-enforceable concentration of a drinking water contaminant, set at the level at which no known or anticipated adverse effects on human health occur and which allows an adequate safety margin. The MCLG is usually the starting point for determining the regulated Maximum Contaminant Level. (See: maximum contaminant level.)

Maximum Exposure Range: Estimate of exposure or dose level received by an individual in a defined population that is greater than the 98th percentile dose for all individuals in that population, but less than the exposure level received by the person receiving the highest exposure level.

Maximum Residue Level: Comparable to a U.S. tolerance level, the Maximum Residue Level the enforceable limit on food pesticide levels in some countries. Levels are set by the Codex Alimentarius Commission, a United Nations agency managed and funded jointly by the World Health Organization and the Food and Agriculture Organization.

Maximum Tolerated Dose: The maximum dose that an animal species can tolerate for a major portion of its lifetime without significant impairment or toxic effect other than carcinogenicity.

Measure of Effect/ Measurement Endpoint: A measurable characteristic of ecological entity that can be related to an assessment endpoint; e.g. a laboratory test for eight species meeting certain requirements may serve as a measure of effect for an assessment endpoint, such as survival of fish, aquatic, invertebrate or algal species under acute exposure.

Measure of Exposure: A measurable characteristic of a stressor (such as the specific amount of mercury in a body of water) used to help quantify the exposure of an ecological entity or individual organism.

Mechanical Aeration: Use of mechanical energy to inject air into water to cause a waste stream to absorb oxygen.

Mechanical Separation: Using mechanical means to separate waste into various components.

Mechanical Turbulence: Random irregularities of fluid motion in air caused by buildings or other nonthermal, processes.

Media: Specific environments—air, water, soil—which are the subject of regulatory concern and activities.

Medical Surveillance: A periodic comprehensive review of a worker's health status; acceptable elements of such surveillance program are listed in the Occupational Safety and Health Administration standards for asbestos.

Medical Waste: Any solid waste generated in the diagnosis, treatment, or immunization of human beings or animals, in research pertaining thereto, or in the production or testing of biologicals, excluding hazardous waste identified or listed under 40 CFR Part 261 or any household waste as defined in 40 CFR Sub-section 261.4 (b)(1).

Medium-size Water System: A water system that serves 3,300 to 50,000 customers.

Meniscus: The curved top of a column of liquid in a small tube.

Mercury (Hg): Heavy metal that can accumulate in the environment and is highly toxic if breathed or swallowed. (See:heavy metals.)

Mesotrophic: Reservoirs and lakes which contain moderate quantities of nutrients and are moderately productive in terms of aquatic animal and plant life.

Metabolites: Any substances produced by biological processes, such as those from pesticides.

Metalimnion: The middle layer of a thermally stratified lake or reservoir. In this layer there is a rapid decrease in temperature with depth. Also called thermocline.

Methane: A colorless, nonpoisonous, flammable gas created by anaerobic decomposition of organic compounds. A major component of natural gas used in the home.

Methanol: An alcohol that can be used as an alternative fuel or as a gasoline additive. It is less volatile than gasoline; when blended with gasoline it lowers the carbon monoxide emissions but increases hydrocarbon emissions. Used as pure fuel, its emissions are less ozone-forming than those from gasoline. Poisonous to humans and animals if ingested.

Method 18: An EPA test method which uses gas chromatographic techniques to measure the concentration of volatile organic compounds in a gas stream.

Method 24: An EPA reference method to determine density, water content and total volatile content (water and VOC) of coatings.

Method 25: An EPA reference method to determine the VOC concentration in a gas stream.

Method Detection Limit (MDL): See limit of detection.

Methoxychlor: Pesticide that causes adverse health effects in domestic water supplies and is toxic to freshwater and marine aquatic life.

Methyl Orange Alkalinity: A measure of the total alkalinity in a water sample in which the color of methyl orange reflects the change in level.

Microbial Growth: The amplification or multiplication of microorganisms such as bacteria, algae, diatoms, plankton, and fungi.

Microbial Pesticide: A microorganism that is used to kill a pest, but is of minimum toxicity to humans.

Microclimate: 1. Localized climate conditions within an urban area or neighborhood. 2. The climate around a tree or shrub or a stand of trees.

Microenvironmental Method: A method for sequentially assessing exposure for a series of microenvironments that can be approximated by constant concentrations of a stressor.

Microenvironments: Well-defined surroundings such as the home, office, or kitchen that can be treated as uniform in terms of stressor concentration.

Million-Gallons Per Day (MGD): A measure of water flow.

Minimization: A comprehensive program to minimize or eliminate wastes, usually applied to wastes at their point of origin. (See: waste minimization.)

Mining of an Aquifer: Withdrawal over a period of time of ground water that exceeds the rate of recharge of the aquifer.

Mining Waste: Residues resulting from the extraction of raw materials from the earth.

Minor Source: New emissions sources or modifications to existing emissions sources that do not exceed NAAQS emission levels.

Minors: Publicly owned treatment works with flows less than 1 million gallons per day. (See: majors.)

Miscellaneous ACM: Interior asbestos-containing building material or structural components, members or fixtures, such as floor and ceiling tiles; does not include surfacing materials or thermal system insulation.

Miscellaneous Materials: Interior building materials on structural components, such as floor or ceiling tiles.

Miscible Liquids: Two or more liquids that can be mixed and will remain mixed under normal conditions.

Missed Detection: The situation that occurs when a test indicates that a tank is "tight" when in fact it is leaking.

Mist: Liquid particles measuring 40 to 500 micrometers (pm), are formed by condensation of vapor. By comparison, fog particles are smaller than 40 micrometers (pm).

Mitigation: Measures taken to reduce adverse impacts on the environment.

Mixed Funding: Settlements in which potentially responsible parties and EPA share the cost of a response action.

Mixed Glass: Recovered container glass not sorted into categories (e.g. color, grade).

Mixed Liquor: A mixture of activated sludge and water containing organic matter undergoing activated sludge treatment in an aeration tank.

Mixed Metals: Recovered metals not sorted into categories such as aluminum, tin, or steel cans or ferrous or non-ferrous metals.

Mixed Municipal Waste: Solid waste that has not been sorted into specific categories (such as plastic, glass, yard trimmings, etc.)

Mixed Paper: Recovered paper not sorted into categories such as old magazines, old newspapers, old corrugated boxes, etc.

Mixed Plastic: Recovered plastic unsorted by category.

Mobile Incinerator Systems: Hazardous waste incinerators that can be transported from one site to another.

Mobile Source: Any non-stationary source of air pollution such as cars, trucks, motorcycles, buses, airplanes, and locomotives.

Model Plant: A hypothetical plant design used for developing economic, environmental, and energy impact analyses as support for regulations or regulatory guidelines; first step in exploring the economic impact of a potential NSPS.

Modified Bin Method: Way of calculating the required heating or cooling for a building based on determining how much energy the system would use if outdoor temperatures were within a certain temperature interval and then multiplying the energy use by the time the temperature interval typically occurs.

Modified Source: The enlargement of a major stationary pollutant sources is often referred to as modification, implying that more emissions will occur.

Moisture Content: 1.The amount of water lost from soil upon drying to a constant weight, expressed as the weight per unit of dry soil or as the volume of water per unit bulk volume of the soil. For a fully saturated medium, moisture content indicates the porosity. 2. Water equivalent of snow on the ground; an indicator of snowmelt flood potential.

Molecule: The smallest division of a compound that still retains or exhibits all the properties of the substance.

Molten Salt Reactor: A thermal treatment unit that rapidly heats waste in a heat-conducting fluid bath of carbonate salt.

Monitoring: Periodic or continuous surveillance or testing to determine the level of compliance with statutory requirements and/or pollutant levels in various media or in humans, plants, and animals.

Monitoring Well: 1. A well used to obtain water quality samples or measure groundwater levels. 2. A well drilled at a hazardous waste management facility or Superfund site to collect ground-water samples for the purpose of physical, chemical, or biological analysis to determine the amounts, types, and distribution of contaminants in the groundwater beneath the site.

Monoclonal Antibodies (Also called MABs and MCAs): 1. Man-made (anthropogenic) clones of a molecule, produced in quantity for medical or research purposes. 2. Molecules of living organisms that selectively find and attach to other molecules to which their structure conforms exactly. This could also apply to equivalent activity by chemical molecules.

Monomictic: Lakes and reservoirs which are relatively deep, do not freeze over during winter, and undergo a single stratification and mixing cycle during the year (usually in the fall).

Montreal Protocol: Treaty, signed in 1987, governs stratospheric ozone protection and research, and the production and use of ozone-depleting substances. It provides for the end of production of ozone-depleting substances such as CFCS. Under the Protocol, various research groups continue to assess the ozone layer. The Multilateral Fund provides resources to developing nations to promote the transition to ozone-safe technologies.

Moratorium: During the negotiation process, a period of 60 to 90 days during which EPA and potentially responsible parties may reach settlement but no site response activities can be conducted.

Morbidity: Rate of disease incidence.

Mortality: Death rate.

Most Probable Number: An estimate of microbial density per unit volume of water sample, based on probability theory.

Muck Soils: Earth made from decaying plant materials.

Mudballs: Round material that forms in filters and gradually increases in size when not removed by backwashing.

Mulch: A layer of material (wood chips, straw, leaves, etc.) placed around plants to hold moisture, prevent weed growth, and enrich or sterilize the soil.

Multi-Media Approach: Joint approach to several environmental media, such as air, water, and land.

Multiple Chemical Sensitivity: A diagnostic label for people who suffer multi-system illnesses as a result of contact with, or proximity to, a variety of airborne agents and other substances.

Multiple Use: Use of land for more than one purpose; e.g., grazing of livestock, watershed and wildlife protection, recreation, and timber production. Also applies to use of bodies of water for recreational purposes, fishing, and water supply.

Multistage Remote Sensing: A strategy for landscape characterization that involves gathering and analyzing information at several geographic scales, ranging from generalized levels of detail at the national level through high levels of detail at the local scale.

Municipal Discharge: Discharge of effluent from waste water treatment plants which receive waste water from households, commercial establishments, and industries in the coastal drainage basin. Combined sewer/separate storm overflows are included in this category.

Municipal Sewage: Wastes (mostly liquid) orginating from a community; may be composed of domestic wastewaters and/or industrial discharges.

Municipal Sludge: Semi-liquid residue remaining from the treatment of municipal water and wastewater.

Municipal Solid Waste: Common garbage or trash generated by industries, businesses, institutions, and homes.

Mutagen/Mutagenicity: An agent that causes a permanent genetic change in a cell other than that which occurs during normal growth. Mutagenicity is the capacity of a chemical or physical agent to cause such permanent changes.

N

National Ambient Air Quality Standards (NAAQS): Standards established by EPA that apply for outdoor air throughout the country. (See: criteria pollutants, state implementation plans, emissions trading.)

National Emissions Standards for Hazardous Air Pollutants (NESHAPS): Emissions standards set by EPA for an air pollutant not covered by NAAQS that may cause an increase in fatalities or in serious, irreversible, or incapacitating illness. Primary standards are designed to protect human health, secondary standards to protect public welfare (e.g. building facades, visibility, crops, and domestic animals).

National Environmental Performance Partnership Agreements: System that allows states to assume greater responsibility for environmental programs based on their relative ability to execute them.

National Estuary Program: A program established under the Clean Water Act Amendments of 1987 to develop and implement conservation and management plans for protecting estuaries and restoring and maintaining their chemical, physical, and biological integrity, as well as controlling point and nonpoint pollution sources.

National Municipal Plan: A policy created in 1984 by EPA and the states in 1984 to bring all publicly owned treatment works (POTWs) into compliance with Clean Water Act requirements.

National Oil and Hazardous Substances Contingency Plan (NOHSCP/NCP): The federal regulation that guides determination of the sites to be corrected under both the Superfund program and the program to prevent or control spills into surface waters or elsewhere.

National Pollutant Discharge Elimination System (NPDES): A provision of the Clean Water Act which prohibits discharge of pollutants into waters of the United States unless a special permit is issued by EPA, a state, or, where delegated, a tribal government on an Indian reservation.

National Priorities List (NPL): EPA's list of the most serious uncontrolled or abandoned hazardous waste sites identified for possible long-term remedial action under Superfund. The list is based primarily on the score a site receives from the Hazard Ranking System. EPA is required to update the NPL at least once a year. A site must be on the NPL to receive money from the Trust Fund for remedial action.

National Response Center: The federal operations center that receives notifications of all releases of oil and hazardous substances into the environment; open 24 hours a day, is operated by the U.S. Coast Guard, which evaluates all reports and notifies the appropriate agency.

National Response Team (NRT): Representatives of 13 federal agencies that, as a team, coordinate federal responses to nationally significant incidents of pollution—an oil spill, a major chemical release, or a - superfund response action—and provide advice and technical assistance to the responding agency(ies) before and during a response action.

National Secondary Drinking Water Regulations: Commonly referred to as NSDWRs.

Navigable Waters: Traditionally, waters sufficiently deep and wide for navigation by all, or specified vessels; such waters in the United States come under federal jurisdiction and are protected by certain provisions of the Clean Water Act.

Necrosis: Death of plant or animal cells or tissues. In plants, necrosis can discolor stems or leaves or kill a plant entirely.

Negotiations (Under Superfund): After potentially responsible parties are identified for a site, EPA coordinates with them to reach a settlement that will result in the PRP paying for or conducting the cleanup under EPA supervision. If negotiations fail, EPA can order the PRP to conduct the cleanup or EPA can pay for the cleanup using Superfund monies and then sue to recover the costs.

Nematocide: A chemical agent which is destructive to nematodes.

Nephelometric: Method of of measuring turbidity in a water sample by passing light through the sample and measuring the amount of the light that is deflected.

Netting: A concept in which all emissions sources in the same area that owned or controlled by a single company are treated as one large source, thereby allowing flexibility in controlling individual sources in order to meet a single emissions standard. (See: bubble.)

Neutralization: Decreasing the acidity or alkalinity of a substance by adding alkaline or acidic materials, respectively.

New Source: Any stationary source built or modified after publication of final or proposed regulations that prescribe a given standard of performance.

New Source Performance Standards (NSPS): Uniform national EPA air emission and water effluent standards which limit the amount of pollution allowed from new sources or from modified existing sources.

New Source Review (NSR): A Clean Air Act requirement that State Implementation Plans must include a permit review that applies to the construction and operation of new and modified stationary sources in nonattainment areas to ensure attainment of national ambient air quality standards.

Nitrate: A compound containing nitrogen that can exist in the atmosphere or as a dissolved gas in water and which can have harmful effects on humans and animals. Nitrates in water can cause severe illness in infants and domestic animals. A plant nutrient and inorganic fertilizer, nitrate is found in septic systems, animal feed lots, agricultural fertilizers, manure, industrial waste waters, sanitary landfills, and garbage dumps.

Nitric Oxide (NO): A gas formed by combustion under high temperature and high pressure in an internal combustion engine; it is converted by sunlight and photochemical processes in ambient air to nitrogen oxide. NO is a precursor of ground-level ozone pollution, or smog..

Nitrification: The process whereby ammonia in wastewater is oxidized to nitrite and then to nitrate by bacterial or chemical reactions.

Nitrilotriacetic Acid (NTA): A compound now replacing phosphates in detergents.

Nitrite: 1. An intermediate in the process of nitrification. 2. Nitrous oxide salts used in food preservation.

Nitrogen Dioxide (NO_2): The result of nitric oxide combining with oxygen in the atmosphere; major component of photochemical smog.

Nitrogen Oxide (NO_x): The result of photochemical reactions of nitric oxide in ambient air; major component of photochemical smog. Product of combustion from transportation and stationary sources and a major contributor to the formation of ozone in the troposphere and to acid deposition.

Nitrogenous Wastes: Animal or vegetable residues that contain significant amounts of nitrogen.

Nitrophenols: Synthetic organopesticides containing carbon, hydrogen, nitrogen, and oxygen.

No Further Remedial Action Planned: Determination made by EPA following a preliminary assessment that a site does not pose a significant risk and so requires no further activity under CERCLA.

No Observable Adverse Effect Level (NOAEL): An exposure level at which there are no statistically or biologically significant increases in the frequency or severity of adverse effects between the exposed population and its appropriate control; some effects may be produced at this level, but they are not considered as adverse, or as precurors to adverse effects. In an experiment with several NOAELs, the regulatory focus is primarily on the highest one, leading to the common usage of the term NOAEL as the highest exposure without adverse effects.

No Till: Planting crops without prior seedbed preparation, into an existing cover crop, sod, or crop residues, and eliminating subsequent tillage operations.

No-Observed-Effect-Level (NOEL): Exposure level at which there are no statistically or biological significant differences in the frequency or severity of any effect in the exposed or control populations.

Noble Metal: Chemically inactive metal such as gold; does not corrode easily.

Noise: Product-level or product-volume changes occurring during a test that are not related to a leak but may be mistaken for one.

Non-Aqueous Phase Liquid (NAPL): Contaminants that remain undiluted as the original bulk liquid in the subsurface, e.g. spilled oil. (See: fee product.)

Non-Attainment Area: Area that does not meet one or more of the National Ambient Air Quality Standards for the criteria pollutants designated in the Clean Air Act.

Non-Binding Allocations of Responsibility (NBAR): A process for EPA to propose a way for potentially responsible parties to allocate costs among themselves.

Non-Community Water System: A public water system that is not a community water system; e.g. the water supply at a camp site or national park.

Non-Compliance Coal: Any coal that emits greater than 3.0 pounds of sulfur dioxide per million BTU when burned. Also known as high-sulfur coal.

Non-Contact Cooling Water: Water used for cooling which does not come into direct contact with any raw material, product, byproduct, or waste.

Non-Conventional Pollutant: Any pollutant not statutorily listed or which is poorly understood by the scientific community.

Non-Degradation: An environmental policy which disallows any lowering of naturally occurring quality regardless of preestablished health standards.

Non-Ferrous Metals: Nonmagnetic metals such as aluminum, lead, and copper. Products made all or in part from such metals include containers, packaging, appliances, furniture, electronic equipment and aluminum foil.

Non-ionizing Electromagnetic Radiation: 1. Radiation that does not change the structure of atoms but does heat tissue and may cause harmful biological effects. 2. Microwaves, radio waves, and low-frequency electromagnetic fields from high-voltage transmission lines.

Non-Methane Hydrocarbon (NMHC): The sum of all hydrocarbon air pollutants except methane; significant precursors to ozone formation.

Non-Methane Organic Gases (NMOG): The sum of all organic air pollutants. Excluding methane; they account for aldehydes, ketones, alcohols, and other pollutants that are not hydrocarbons but are precursors of ozone.

Non-Point Sources: Diffuse pollution sources (i.e. without a single point of origin or not introduced into a receiving stream from a specific outlet). The pollutants are generally carried off the land by storm water. Common non-point sources are agriculture, forestry, urban, mining, construction, dams, channels, land disposal, saltwater intrusion, and city streets.

Non-potable: Water that is unsafe or unpalatable to drink because it contains pollutants, contaminants, minerals, or infective agents.

Non-Road Emissions: Pollutants emitted by combustion engines on farm and construction equipment, gasoline-powered lawn and garden equipment, and power boats and outboard motors.

Non-Transient Non-Community Water System: A public water system that regularly serves at least 25 of the same non-resident persons per day for more than six months per year.

Nondischarging Treatment Plant: A treatment plant that does not discharge treated wastewater into any stream or river. Most are pond systems that dispose of the total flow they receive by means of evaporation or percolation to groundwater, or facilities that dispose of their effluent by recycling or reuse (e.g. spray irrigation or groundwater discharge).

Nonfriable Asbestos-Containing Materials: Any material containing more than one percent asbestos (as determined by Polarized Light Microscopy) that, when dry, cannot be crumbled, pulverized, or reduced to powder by hand pressure.

Nonhazardous Industrial Waste: Industrial process waste in wastewater not considered municipal solid waste or hazardous waste under RARA.

Notice of Deficiency: An EPA request to a facility owner or operator requesting additional information before a preliminary decision on a permit application can be made.

Notice of Intent to Cancel: Notification sent to registrants when EPA decides to cancel registration of a product containing a pesticide.

Notice of Intent to Deny: Notification by EPA of its preliminary intent to deny a permit application.

Notice of Intent to Suspend: Notification sent to a pesticide registrant when EPA decides to suspend product sale and distribution because of failure to submit requested data in a timely and/or acceptable manner, or because of imminent hazard. (See: emergency suspension.)

Nuclear Reactors and Support Facilities: Uranium mills, commercial power reactors, fuel reprocessing plants, and uranium enrichment facilities.

Nuclear Winter: Prediction by some scientists that smoke and debris rising from massive fires of a nuclear war could block sunlight for weeks or months, cooling the earth's surface and producing climate changes that could, for example, negatively affect world agricultural and weather patterns.

Nuclide: An atom characterized by the number of protons, neturons, and energy in the nucleus.

Nutrient: Any substance assimilated by living things that promotes growth. The term is generally applied to nitrogen and phosphorus in wastewater, but is also applied to other essential and trace elements.

Nutrient Pollution: Contamination of water resources by excessive inputs of nutrients. In surface waters, excess algal production is a major concern.

O

Ocean Discharge Waiver: A variance from Clean Water Act requirements for discharges into marine waters.

Odor Threshold: The minimum odor of a water or air sample that can just be detected after successive dilutions with odorless water. Also called threshold odor.

OECD Guidelines: Testing guidelines prepared by the Organization of Economic and Cooperative Development of the United Nations. They assist in preparation of protocols for studies of toxicology, environmental fate, etc.

Off-Site Facility: A hazardous waste treatment, storage or disposal area that is located away from the generating site.

Office Paper: High grade papers such as copier paper, computer printout, and stationary almost entirely made of uncoated chemical pulp, although some ground wood is used. Such waste is also generated in homes, schools, and elsewhere.

Offsets: A concept whereby emissions from proposed new or modified stationary sources are balanced by reductions from existing sources to stabilize total emissions. (See: bubble, emissions trading, netting)

Offstream Use: Water withdrawn from surface or groundwater sources for use at another place.

Oil and Gas Waste: Gas and oil drilling muds, oil production brines, and other waste associated with exploration for, development and production of crude oil or natural gas.

Oil Desulfurization: Widely used precombustion method for reducing sulfur dioxide emissions from oil-burning power plants. The oil is treated with hydrogen, which removes some of the sulfur by forming hydrogen sulfide gas.

Oil Fingerprinting: A method that identifies sources of oil and allows spills to be traced to their source.

Oil Spill: An accidental or intentional discharge of oil which reaches bodies of water. Can be controlled by chemical dispersion, combustion, mechanical containment, and/or adsorption. Spills from tanks and pipelines can also occur away from water bodies, contaminating the soil, getting into sewer systems and threatening underground water sources.

Oligotrophic Lakes: Deep clear lakes with few nutrients, little organic matter and a high dissolved-oxygen level.

On-Scene Coordinator (OSC): The predesignated EPA, Coast Guard, or Department of Defense official who coordinates and directs Superfund removal actions or Clean Water Act oil- or hazardous-spill response actions.

On-Site Facility: A hazardous waste treatment, storage or disposal area that is located on the generating site.

Onboard Controls: Devices placed on vehicles to capture gasoline vapor during refueling and route it to the engines when the vehicle is starting so that it can be efficiently burned.

Onconogenicity: The capacity to induce cancer.

One-hit Model: A mathematical model based on the biological theory that a single "hit" of some minimum critical amount of a carcinogen at a cellular target such as DNA can start an irreversible series events leading to a tumor.

Opacity: The amount of light obscured by particulate pollution in the air; clear window glass has zero opacity, a brick wall is 100 percent opaque. Opacity is an indicator of changes in performance of particulate control systems.

Open Burning: Uncontrolled fires in an open dump.

Open Dump: An uncovered site used for disposal of waste without environmental controls. (See: dump.)

Operable Unit: Term for each of a number of separate activities undertaken as part of a Superfund site cleanup. A typical operable unit would be removal of drums and tanks from the surface of a site.

Operating Conditions: Conditions specified in a RCRA permit that dictate how an incinerator must operate as it burns different waste types. A trial burn is used to identify operating conditions needed to meet specified performance standards.

Operation and Maintenance: 1. Activities conducted after a Superfund site action is completed to ensure that the action is effective. 2. Actions taken after construction to ensure that facilities constructed to treat waste water will be properly operated and maintained to achieve normative efficiency levels and prescribed effluent limitations in an optimum manner. 3. On-going asbestos management plan in a school or other public building, including regular inspections, various methods of maintaining asbestos in place, and removal when necessary.

Operator Certification: Certification of operators of community and nontransient noncommunity water systems, asbestos specialists, pesticide applicators, hazardous waste transporter, and other such specialists as required by the EPA or a state agency implementing an EPA-approved environmental regulatory program.

Optimal Corrosion Control Treatment: An erosion control treatment that minimizes the lead and copper concentrations at users' taps while also ensuring that the treatment does not cause the water system to violate any national primary drinking water regulations.

Oral Toxicity: Ability of a pesticide to cause injury when ingested.

Organic: 1. Referring to or derived from living organisms. 2. In chemistry, any compound containing carbon.

Organic Chemicals/Compounds: Naturally occuring (animal or plant-produced or synthetic) substances containing mainly carbon, hydrogen, nitrogen, and oxygen.

Organic Matter: Carbonaceous waste contained in plant or animal matter and originating from domestic or industrial sources.

Organism: Any form of animal or plant life.

Organophosphates: Pesticides that contain phosphorus; short-lived, but some can be toxic when first applied.

Organophyllic: A substance that easily combines with organic compounds.

Organotins: Chemical compounds used in anti-foulant paints to protect the hulls of boats and ships, buoys, and pilings from marine organisms such as barnacles.

Original AHERA Inspection/Original Inspection/Inspection: Examination of school buildings arranged by Local Education Agencies to identify asbestos-containing-materials, evaluate their condition, and take samples of materials suspected to contain asbestos; performed by EPA-accredited inspectors.

Original Generation Point: Where regulated medical or other material first becomes waste.

Osmosis: The passage of a liquid from a weak solution to a more concentrated solution across a semipermeable membrane that allows passage of the solvent (water) but not the dissolved solids.

Other Ferrous Metals: Recyclable metals from strapping, furniture, and metal found in tires and consumer electronics but does not include metals found in construction materials or cars, locomotives, and ships. (See: ferrous metals.)

Other Glass: Recyclable glass from furniture, appliances, and consumer electronics. Does not include glass from transportation products (cars trucks or shipping containers) and construction or demolition debris. (See: glass.)

Other Nonferrous Metals: Recyclable nonferrous metals such as lead, copper, and zinc from appliances, consumer electronics, and nonpackaging aluminum products. Does not include nonferrous metals from industrial applications and construction and demolition debris. (See: nonferrous metals.)

Other Paper: For Recyclable paper from books, third-class mail, commercial printing, paper towels, plates and cups; and other nonpackaging paper such as posters, photographic papers, cards and games, milk cartons, folding boxes, bags, wrapping paper, and paperboard. Does not include wrapping paper or shipping cartons.

Other Plastics: Recyclable plastic from appliances, eating utensils, plates, containers, toys, and various kinds of equipment. Does not include heavy-duty plastics such as yielding materials.

Other Solid Waste: Recyclable nonhazardous solid wastes, other than municipal solid waste, covered under Subtitle D of RARA. (See: solid waste.)

Other Wood: Recyclable wood from furniture, consumer electronics cabinets, and other nonpackaging wood products. Does not include lumber and tree stumps recovered from construction and demolition activities, and industrial process waste such as shavings and sawdust.

Outdoor Air Supply: Air brought into a building from outside.

Outfall: The place where effluent is discharged into receiving waters.

Overburden: Rock and soil cleared away before mining.

Overdraft: The pumping of water from a groundwater basin or aquifer in excess of the supply flowing into the basin; results in a depletion or "mining" of the groundwater in the basin. (See: groundwater mining)

Overfire Air: Air forced into the top of an incinerator or boiler to fan the flames.

Overflow Rate: One of the guidelines for design of the settling tanks and clarifers in a treatment plant; used by plant operators to determine if tanks and clarifiers are over or under-used.

Overland Flow: A land application technique that cleanses waste water by allowing it to flow over a sloped surface. As the water flows over the surface, contaminants are absorbed and the water is collected at the bottom of the slope for reuse.

Oversized Regulated Medical Waste: Medical waste that is too large for plastic bags or standard containers.

Overturn: One complete cycle of top to bottom mixing of previously stratified water masses. This phenomenon may occur in spring or fall, or after storms, and results in uniformity of chemical and physical properties of water at all depths.

Oxidant: A collective term for some of the primary constituents of photochemical smog.

Oxidation Pond: A man-made (anthropogenic) body of water in which waste is consumed by bacteria, used most frequently with other waste-treatment processes; a sewage lagoon.

Oxidation: The chemical addition of oxygen to break down pollutants or organizac waste; e.g., destruction of chemicals such as cyanides, phenols, and organic sulfur compounds in sewage by bacterial and chemical means.

Oxidation-Reduction Potential: The electric potential required to transfer electrons from one compound or element (the oxidant) to another compound (the reductant); used as a qualitative measure of the state of oxidation in water treatment systems.

Oxygenated Fuels: Gasoline which has been blended with alcohols or ethers that contain oxygen in order to reduce carbon monoxide and other emissions.

Oxygenated Solvent: An organic solvent containing oxygen as part of the molecular structure. Alcohols and ketones are oxygenated compounds often used as paint solvents.

Ozonation/Ozonator: Application of ozone to water for disinfection or for taste and odor control. The ozonator is the device that does this.

Ozone (O_3): Found in two layers of the atmosphere, the stratosphere and the troposphere. In the stratosphere (the atmospheric layer 7 to 10 miles or more above the earth's surface) ozone is a natural form of oxygen that provides a protective layer shielding the earth from ultraviolet radiation.In the troposphere (the layer extending up 7 to 10 miles from the earth's surface), ozone is a chemical oxidant and major component of photochemical smog. It can seriously impair the respiratory system and is one of the most wide- spread of all the criteria pollutants for which the Clean Air Act required EPA to set standards. Ozone in the troposphere is produced through complex chemical reactions of nitrogen oxides, which are among the primary pollutants emitted by combustion sources; hydrocarbons, released into the atmosphere through the combustion, handling and processing of petroleum products; and sunlight.

Ozone Depletion: Destruction of the stratospheric ozone layer which shields the earth from ultraviolet radiation harmful to life. This destruction of ozone is caused by the breakdown of certain chlorine and/or bromine containing compounds (chlorofluorocarbons or halons), which break down when they reach the stratosphere and then catalytically destroy ozone molecules.

Ozone Hole: A thinning break in the stratospheric ozone layer. Designation of amount of such depletion as an "ozone hole" is made when the detected amount of depletion exceeds fifty percent. Seasonal ozone holes have been observed over both the Antarctic and Arctic regions, part of Canada, and the extreme northeastern United States.

Ozone Layer: The protective layer in the atmosphere, about 15 miles above the ground, that absorbs some of the sun's ultraviolet rays, thereby reducing the amount of potentially harmful radiation that reaches the earth's surface.

P

Packaging: The assembly of one or more containers and any other components necessary to ensure minimum compliance with a program's storage and shipment packaging requirements. Also, the containers, etc. involved.

Packed Bed Scrubber: An air pollution control device in which emissions pass through alkaline water to neutralize hydrogen chloride gas.

Packed Tower: A pollution control device that forces dirty air through a tower packed with crushed rock or wood chips while liquid is sprayed over the packing material. The pollutants in the air stream either dissolve or chemically react with the liquid.

Packer: An inflatable gland, or balloon, used to create a temporary seal in a borehole, probe hole, well, or drive casing. It is made of rubber or non-reactive materials.

Palatable Water: Water, at a desirable temperature, that is free from objectionable tastes, odors, colors, and turbidity.

Pandemic: A widespread epidemic throughout an area, nation or the world.

Paper: In the recycling business, refers to products and materials, including newspapers, magazines, office papers, corrugated containers, bags and some paperboard packaging that can be recycled into new paper products.

Paper Processor/Plastics Processor: Intermediate facility where recovered paper or plastic products and materials are sorted, decontaminated, and prepared for final recycling.

Parameter: A variable, measurable property whose value is a determinant of the characteristics of a system; e.g. temperature, pressure, and density are parameters of the atmosphere.

Paraquat: A standard herbicide used to kill various types of crops, including marijuana. Causes lung damage if smoke from the crop is inhaled..

Parshall Flume: Device used to measure the flow of water in an open channel.

Part A Permit, Part B Permit: (See: Interim Permit Status.)

Participation Rate: Portion of population participating in a recycling program.

Particle Count: Results of a microscopic examination of treated water with a special "particle counter" that classifies suspended particles by number and size.

Particulate Loading: The mass of particulates per unit volume of air or water.

Particulates: 1. Fine liquid or solid particles such as dust, smoke, mist, fumes, or smog, found in air or emissions. 2. Very small solids suspended in water; they can vary in size, shape, density and electrical charge and can be gathered together by coagulation and flocculation.

Partition Coefficient: Measure of the sorption phenomenon, whereby a pesticide is divided between the soil and water phase; also referred to as adsorption partition coefficient.

Parts Per Billion (ppb)/Parts Per Million (ppm): Units commonly used to express contamination ratios, as in establishing the maximum permissible amount of a contaminant in water, land, or air.

Passive Smoking/Secondhand Smoke: Inhalation of others' tobacco smoke.

Passive Treatment Walls: Technology in which a chemical reaction takes place when contaminated ground water comes in contact with a barrier such as limestone or a wall containing iron filings.

Pathogens: Microorganisms (e.g., bacteria, viruses, or parasites) that can cause disease in humans, animals and plants.

Pathway: The physical course a chemical or pollutant takes from its source to the exposed organism.

Pay-As-You-Throw/Unit-Based Pricing: Systems under which residents pay for municipal waste management and disposal services by weight or volume collected, not a fixed fee.

Peak Electricity Demand: The maximum electricity used to meet the cooling load of a building or buildings in a given area.

Peak Levels: Levels of airborne pollutant contaminants much higher than average or occurring for short periods of time in response to sudden releases.

Percent Saturatiuon: The amount of a substance that is dissolved in a solution compared to the amount that could be dissolved in it.

Perched Water: Zone of unpressurized water held above the water table by impermeable rock or sediment.

Percolating Water: Water that passes through rocks or soil under the force of gravity.

Percolation: 1. The movement of water downward and radially through subsurface soil layers, usually continuing downward to ground water. Can also involve upward movement of water. 2. Slow seepage of water through a filter.

Performance Bond: Cash or securities deposited before a landfill operating permit is issued, which are held to ensure that all requirements for operating ad subsequently closing the landfill are faithful performed. The money is returned to the owner after proper closure of the landfill is completed. If contamination or other problems appear at any time during operation, or upon closure, and are not addressed, the owner must forfeit all or part of the bond which is then used to cover clean-up costs.

Performance Data (For Incinerators): Information collected, during a trial burn, on concentrations of designated organic compounds and pollutants found in incinerator emissions. Data analysis must show that the incinerator meets performance standards under operating conditions specified in the RCRA permit. (See: trial burn; performance standards.)

Performance Standards: 1. Regulatory requirements limiting the concentrations of designated organic compounds, particulate matter, and hydrogen chloride in emissions from incinerators. 2. Operating standards established by EPA for various permitted pollution control systems, asbestos inspections, and various program operations and maintenance requirements.

Periphyton: Microscopic underwater plants and animals that are firmly attached to solid surfaces such as rocks, logs, and pilings.

Permeability: The rate at which liquids pass through soil or other materials in a specified direction.

Permissible Dose: The dose of a chemical that may be received by an individual without the expectation of a significantly harmful result.

Permissible Exposure Limit: Also referred to as PEL, federal limits for workplace exposure to contaminants as established by OSHA.

Permit: An authorization, license, or equivalent control document issued by EPA or an approved state agency to implement the requirements of an environmental regulation; e.g. a permit to operate a wastewater treatment plant or to operate a facility that may generate harmful emissions.

Persistence: Refers to the length of time a compound stays in the environment, once introduced. A compound may persist for less than a second or indefinitely.

Persistent Pesticides: Pesticides that do not break down chemically or break down very slowly and remain in the environment after a growing season.

Personal Air Samples: Air samples taken with a pump that is directly attached to the worker with the collecting filter and cassette placed in the worker's breathing zone (required under OSHA asbestos standards and EPA worker protection rule).

Personal Measurement: A measurement collected from an individual's immediate environment.

Personal Protective Equipment: Clothing and equipment worn by pesticide mixers, loaders and applicators and re-entry workers, hazmat emergency responders, workers cleaning up Superfund sites, et. al., which is worn to reduce their exposure to potentially hazardous chemicals and other pollutants.

Pest: An insect, rodent, nematode, fungus, weed or other form of terrestrial or aquatic plant or animal life that is injurious to health or the environment.

Pest Control Operator: Person or company that applies pesticides as a business (e.g. exterminator); usually describes household services, not agricultural applications.

Pesticide: Substances or mixture there of intended for preventing, destroying, repelling, or mitigating any pest. Also, any substance or mixture intended for use as a plant regulator, defoliant, or desiccant.

Pesticide Regulation Notice: Formal notice to pesticide registrants about important changes in regulatory policy, procedures, regulations.

Pesticide Tolerance: The amount of pesticide residue allowed by law to remain in or on a harvested crop. EPA sets these levels well below the point where the compounds might be harmful to consumers.

PETE (Polyethylene Terepthalate): Thermoplastic material used in plastic soft drink and rigid containers.

Petroleum: Crude oil or any fraction thereof that is liquid under normal conditions of temperature and pressure. The term includes petroleum-based substances comprising a complex blend of hydrocarbons derived from crude oil through the process of separation, conversion, upgrading, and finishing, such as motor fuel, jet oil, lubricants, petroleum solvents, and used oil.

Petroleum Derivatives: Chemicals formed when gasoline breaks down in contact with ground water.

pH: An expression of the intensity of the basic or acid condition of a liquid; may range from 0 to 14, where 0 is the most acid and 7 is neutral. Natural waters usually have a pH between 6.5 and 8.5.

Pharmacokinetics: The study of the way that drugs move through the body after they are swallowed or injected.

Phenolphthalein Alkalinity: The alkalinity in a water sample measured by the amount of standard acid needed to lower the pH to a level of 8.3 as indicated by the change of color of the phenolphthalein from pink to clear.

Phenols: Organic compounds that are byproducts of petroleum refining, tanning, and textile, dye, and resin manufacturing. Low concentrations cause taste and odor problems in water; higher concentrations can kill aquatic life and humans.

Phosphates: Certain chemical compounds containing phosphorus.

Phosphogypsum Piles (Stacks): Principal byproduct generated in production of phosphoric acid from phosphate rock. These piles may generate radioactive radon gas.

Phosphorus: An essential chemical food element that can contribute to the eutrophication of lakes and other water bodies. Increased phosphorus levels result from discharge of phosphorus-containing materials into surface waters.

Phosphorus Plants: Facilities using electric furnaces to produce elemental phosphorous for commercial use, such as high grade phosphoric acid, phosphate-based detergent, and organic chemicals use.

Photochemical Oxidants: Air pollutants formed by the action of sunlight on oxides of nitrogen and hydrocarbons.

Photochemical Smog: Air pollution caused by chemical reactions of various pollutants emitted from different sources. (See: photochemical oxidants.)

Photosynthesis: The manufacture by plants of carbohydrates and oxygen from carbon dioxide mediated by chlorophyll in the presence of sunlight.

Physical and Chemical Treatment: Processes generally used in large-scale wastewater treatment facilities. Physical processes may include air-stripping or filtration. Chemical treatment includes coagulation, chlorination, or ozonation. The term can also refer to treatment of toxic materials in surface and ground waters, oil spills, and some methods of dealing with hazardous materials on or in the ground.

Phytoplankton: That portion of the plankton community comprised of tiny plants; e.g. algae, diatoms.

Phytoremediation: Low-cost remediation option for sites with widely dispersed contamination at low concentrations.

Phytotoxic: Harmful to plants.

Phytotreatment: The cultivation of specialized plants that absorb specific contaminants from the soil through their roots or foliage. This reduces the concentration of contaminants in the soil, but incorporates them into biomasses that may be released back into the environment when the plant dies or is harvested.

Picocuries Per Liter pCi/L): A unit of measure for levels of radon gas; becquerels per cubic meter is metric equivalent.

Piezometer: A nonpumping well, generally of small diameter, for measuring the elevation of a water table.

Pilot Tests: Testing a cleanup technology under actual site conditions to identify potential problems prior to full-scale implementation.

Plankton: Tiny plants and animals that live in water.

Plasma Arc Reactors: devices that use an electric arc to thermally decompose organic and inorganic materials at ultra-high temperatures into gases and a vitrified slag residue. A plasma arc reactor can operate as any of the following:

- integral component of chemical, fuel, or electricty production systems, processing high or medium value organic compounds into a synthetic gas used as a fuel

- materials recovery device, processing scrap to recover metal from the slag
- destruction or incineration system, processing waste materials into slag and gases ignited inside of a secondary combustion chamber that follows the reactor

Plasmid: A circular piece of DNA that exists apart from the chromosome and replicates independently of it. Bacterial plasmids carry information that renders the bacteria resistant to antibiotics. Plasmids are often used in genetic engineering to carry desired genes into organisms.

Plastics: Non-metallic chemoreactive compounds molded into rigid or pliable construction materials, fabrics, etc.

Plate Tower Scrubber: An air pollution control device that neutralizes hydrogen chloride gas by bubbling alkaline water through holes in a series of metal plates.

Plug Flow: Type of flow the occurs in tanks, basins, or reactors when a slug of water moves through without ever dispersing or mixing with the rest of the water flowing through.

Plugging: Act or process of stopping the flow of water, oil, or gas into or out of a formation through a borehole or well penetrating that formation.

Plume: 1. A visible or measurable discharge of a contaminant from a given point of origin. Can be visible or thermal in water, or visible in the air as, for example, a plume of smoke. 2 The area of radiation leaking from a damaged reactor. 3. Area downwind within which a release could be dangerous for those exposed to leaking fumes.

Plutonium: A radioactive metallic element chemically similar to uranium.

PM-10/PM-2.5: PM 10 is measure of particles in the atmosphere with a diameter of less than ten or equal to a nominal 10 micrometers. PM-2.5 is a measure of smaller particles in the air. PM-10 has been the pollutant particulate level standard against which EPA has been measuring Clean Air Act compliance. On the basis of newer scientific findings, the Agency is considering regulations that will make PM-2.5 the new "standard".

Pneumoconiosis: Health conditions characterized by permanent deposition of substantial amounts of particulate matter in the lungs and by the tissue reaction to its presence; can range from relatively harmless forms of sclerosis to the destructive fibrotic effect of silicosis.

Point Source: A stationary location or fixed facility from which pollutants are discharged; any single identifiable source of pollution; e.g. a pipe, ditch, ship, ore pit, factory smokestack.

Point-of-Contact Measurement of Exposure: Estimating exposure by measuring concentrations over time (while the exposure is taking place) at or near the place where it is occurring.

Point-of-Disinfectant Application: The point where disinfectant is applied and water downstream of that point is not subject to recontamination by surface water runoff.

Point-of-Use Treatment Device: Treatment device applied to a single tap to reduce contaminants in the drinking water at the one faucet.

Pollen: The fertilizing element of flowering plants; background air pollutant.

Pollutant: Generally, any substance introduced into the environment that adversely affects the usefulness of a resource or the health of humans, animals, or ecosystems..

Pollutant Pathways: Avenues for distribution of pollutants. In most buildings, for example, HVAC systems are the primary pathways although all building components can interact to affect how air movement distributes pollutants.

Pollutant Standard Index (PSI): Indicator of one or more pollutants that may be used to inform the public about the potential for adverse health effects from air pollution in major cities.

Pollution: Generally, the presence of a substance in the environment that because of its chemical composition or quantity prevents the functioning of natural processes and produces undesirable environmental and health effects.Under the Clean Water Act, for example, the term has been defined as the man-made or man-induced alteration of the physical, biological, chemical, and radiological integrity of water and other media.

Pollution Prevention: 1. Identifying areas, processes, and activities which create excessive waste products or pollutants in order to reduce or prevent them through, alteration, or eliminating a process. Such activities, consistent with the Pollution Prevention Act of 1990, are conducted across all EPA programs and can involve cooperative efforts with such agencies as the Departments of Agriculture and Energy. 2. EPA has initiated a number of voluntary programs in which industrial, or commercial or "partners" join with EPA in promoting activities that conserve energy, conserve and protect water supply, reduce emissions or find ways of utilizing them as energy resources, and reduce the waste stream. Among these are: Agstar, to reduce methane emissions through manure management. Climate Wise, to lower industrial greenhouse-gas emissions and energy costs. Coalbed Methane Outreach, to boost methane recovery at coal mines. Design for the Environment, to foster including environmental considerations in product design and processes. Energy Star programs, to promote energy efficiency in commercial and residential buildings, office equipment, transformers, computers, office equipment, and home appliances. Environmental Accounting, to help businesses identify environmental costs and factor them into management decision making. Green Chemistry, to promote and recognize cost-effective breakthroughs in chemistry that prevent pollution. Green Lights, to spread the use of energy-efficient lighting technologies. Indoor Environments, to reduce risks from indoor-air pollution. Landfill Methane Outreach, to develop landfill gas-to-energy projects. Natural Gas Star, to reduce methane emissions from the natural gas industry. Ruminant Livestock Methane, to reduce methane emissions from ruminant livestock. Transportation Partners, to reduce carbon dioxide emissions from the transportation sector. Voluntary Aluminum Industrial Partnership, to reduce perfluorocarbon emissions from the primary aluminum industry. WAVE, to promote efficient water use in the lodging industry. Wastewi$e, to reduce business-generated solid waste through prevention, reuse, and recycling. (See: Common Sense Initiative and Project XL.)

Polychlorinated Biphenyls: A group of toxic, persistent chemicals used in electrical transformers and capacitors for insulating purposes, and in gas pipeline systems as lubricant. The sale and new use of these chemicals, also known as PCBs, were banned by law in 1979.

Portal-of-Entry Effect: A local effect produced in the tissue or organ of first contact between a toxicant and the biological system.

Polonium: A radioactive element that occurs in pitchblende and other uranium-containing ores.

Polyelectrolytes: Synthetic chemicals that help solids to clump during sewage treatment.

Polymer: A natural or synthetic chemical structure where two or more like molecules are joined to form a more complex molecular structure (e.g. polyethylene in plastic).

Polyvinyl Chloride (PVC): A tough, environmentally indestructible plastic that releases hydrochloric acid when burned.

Population: A group of interbreeding organisms occupying a particular space; the number of humans or other living creatures in a designated area.

Population at Risk: A population subgroup that is more likely to be exposed to a chemical, or is more sensitive to the chemical, than is the general population.

Porosity: Degree to which soil, gravel, sediment, or rock is permeated with pores or cavities through which water or air can move.

Post-Chlorination: Addition of chlorine to plant effluent for disinfectant purposes after the effluent has been treated.

Post-Closure: The time period following the shutdown of a waste management or manufacturing facility; for monitoring purposes, often considered to be 30 years.

Post-Consumer Materials/Waste: Recovered materials that are diverted from municipal solid waste for the purpose of collection, recycling, and disposition.

Post-Consumer Recycling: Use of materials generated from residential and consumer waste for new or similar purposes; e.g. converting wastepaper from offices into corrugated boxes or newsprint.

Potable Water: Water that is safe for drinking and cooking.

Potential Dose: The amount of a compound contained in material swallowed, breathed, or applied to the skin.

Potentially Responsible Party (PRP): Any individual or company—including owners, operators, transporters or generators—potentially responsible for, or contributing to a spill or other contamination at a Superfund site. Whenever possible, through administrative and legal actions, EPA requires PRPs to clean up hazardous sites they have contaminated.

Potentiation: The ability of one chemical to increase the effect of another chemical.

Potentiometric Surface: The surface to which water in an aquifer can rise by hydrostatic pressure.

Precautionary Principle: When information about potential risks is incomplete, basing decisions about the best ways to manage or reduce risks on a preference for avoiding unnecessary health risks instead of on unnecessary economic expenditures.

Pre-Consumer Materials/Waste: Materials generated in manufacturing and converting processes such as manufacturing scrap and trimmings and cuttings. Includes print overruns, overissue publications, and obsolete inventories.

Pre-Harvest Interval: The time between the last pesticide application and harvest of the treated crops.

Prechlorination: The addition of chlorine at the headworks of a treatment plant prior to other treatment processes. Done mainly for disinfection and control of tastes, odors, and aquatic growths, and to aid in coagulation and settling,

Precipitate: A substance separated from a solution or suspension by chemical or physical change.

Precipitation: Removal of hazardous solids from liquid waste to permit safe disposal; removal of particles from airborne emissions as in rain (e.g. acid precipitation).

Precipitator: Pollution control device that collects particles from an air stream.

Precursor: In photochemistry, a compound antecedent to a pollutant. For example, volatile organic compounds (VOCs) and nitric oxides of nitrogen react in sunlight to form ozone or other photochemical oxidants. As such, VOCs and oxides of nitrogen are precursors.

Preliminary Assessment: The process of collecting and reviewing available information about a known or suspected waste site or release.

Prescriptive: Water rights which are acquired by diverting water and putting it to use in accordance with specified procedures; e.g. filing a request with a state agency to use unused water in a stream, river, or lake.

Pressed Wood Products: Materials used in building and furniture construction that are made from wood veneers, particles, or fibers bonded together with an adhesive under heat and pressure.

Pressure Sewers: A system of pipes in which water, wastewater, or other liquid is pumped to a higher elevation.

Pressure, Static: In flowing air, the total pressure minus velocity pressure, pushing equally in all directions.

Pressure, Total: In flowing air, the sum of the static and velocity pressures.

Pressure, Velocity: In flowing air, the pressure due to velocity and density of air.

Pretreatment: Processes used to reduce, eliminate, or alter the nature of wastewater pollutants from non-domestic sources before they are discharged into publicly owned treatment works (POTWs).

Prevalent Level Samples: Air samples taken under normal conditions (also known as ambient background samples).

Prevalent Levels: Levels of airborne contaminant occurring under normal conditions.

Prevention of Significant Deterioration (PSD): EPA program in which state and/or federal permits are required in order to restrict emissions from new or modified sources in places where air quality already meets or exceeds primary and secondary ambient air quality standards.

Primacy: Having the primary responsibility for administering and enforcing regulations.

Primary Drinking Water Regulation: Applies to public water systems and specifies a contaminant level, which, in the judgment of the EPA Administrator, will not adversely affect human health.

Primary Effect: An effect where the stressor acts directly on the ecological component of interest, not on other parts of the ecosystem. (See: secondary effect.)

Primary Standards: National ambient air quality standards designed to protect human health with an adequate margin for safety. (See: National Ambient Air Quality Standards, secondary standards.)

Primary Treatment: First stage of wastewater treatment in which solids are removed by screening and settling.

Primary Waste Treatment: First steps in wastewater treatment; screens and sedimentation tanks are used to remove most materials that float or will settle. Primary treatment removes about 30 percent of carbonaceous biochemical oxygen demand from domestic sewage.

Principal Organic Hazardous Constituents (POHCs): Hazardous compounds monitored during an incinerator's trial burn, selected for high concentration in the waste feed and difficulty of combustion.

Prions: Microscopic particles made of protein that can cause disease.

Prior Appropriation: A doctrine of water law that allocates the rights to use water on a first-come, first-served basis.

Probability of Detection : The likelihood, expressed as a percentage, that a test method will correctly identify a leaking tank.

Process Variable: A physical or chemical quantity which is usually measured and controlled in the operation of a water treatment plant or industrial plant.

Process Verification: Verifying that process raw materials, water usage, waste treatment processes, production rate and other facts relative to quantity and quality of pollutants contained in discharges are substantially described in the permit application and the issued permit.

Process Wastewater: Any water that comes into contact with any raw material, product, byproduct, or waste.

Process Weight: Total weight of all materials, including fuel, used in a manufacturing process; used to calculate the allowable particulate emission rate.

Producers: Plants that perform photosynthesis and provide food to consumers.

Product Level: The level of a product in a storage tank.

Product Water: Water that has passed through a water treatment plant and is ready to be delivered to consumers.

Products of Incomplete Combustion (PICs): Organic compounds formed by combustion. Usually generated in small amounts and sometimes toxic, PICs are heat-altered versions of the original material fed into the incinerator (e.g. charcoal is a P.I.C. from burning wood).

Project XL: An EPA initiative to give states and the regulated community the flexibility to develop comprehensive strategies as alternatives to multiple current regulatory requirements in order to exceed compliance and increase overall environmental benefits.

Propellant: Liquid in a self-pressurized pesticide product that expels the active ingredient from its container.

Proportionate Mortality Ratio (PMR): The number of deaths from a specific cause in a specific period of time per 100 deaths from all causes in the same time period.

Proposed Plan: A plan for a site cleanup that is available to the public for comment.

Proteins: Complex nitrogenous organic compounds of high molecular weight made of amino acids; essential for growth and repair of animal tissue. Many, but not all, proteins are enzymes.

Protocol: A series of formal steps for conducting a test.

Protoplast: A membrane-bound cell from which the outer wall has been partially or completely removed. The term often is applied to plant cells.

Protozoa: One-celled animals that are larger and more complex than bacteria. May cause disease.

Public Comment Period: The time allowed for the public to express its views and concerns regarding an action by EPA (e.g. a Federal Register Notice of proposed rule-making, a public notice of a draft permit, or a Notice of Intent to Deny).

Public Health Approach: Regulatory and voluntary focus on effective and feasible risk management actions at the national and community level to reduce human exposures and risks, with priority given to reducing exposures with the biggest impacts in terms of the number affected and severity of effect.

Public Health Context: The incidence, prevalence, and severity of diseases in communities or populations and the factors that account for them, including infections, exposure to pollutants, and other exposures or activities.

Public Hearing: A formal meeting wherein EPA officials hear the public's views and concerns about an EPA action or proposal. EPA is required to consider such comments when evaluating its actions. Public hearings must be held upon request during the public comment period.

Public Notice: 1. Notification by EPA informing the public of Agency actions such as the issuance of a draft permit or scheduling of a hearing. EPA is required to ensure proper public notice, including publication in newspapers and broadcast over radio and television stations. 2. In the safe drinking water program, water suppliers are required to publish and broadcast notices when pollution problems are discovered.

Public Water System: A system that provides piped water for human consumption to at least 15 service connections or regularly serves 25 individuals.

Publicly Owned Treatment Works (POTWs): A waste-treatment works owned by a state, unit of local government, or Indian tribe, usually designed to treat domestic wastewaters.

Pumping Station: Mechanical device installed in sewer or water system or other liquid-carrying pipelines to move the liquids to a higher level.

Pumping Test: A test conducted to determine aquifer or well characteristics.

Purging: Removing stagnant air or water from sampling zone or equipment prior to sample collection.

Putrefaction: Biological decomposition of organic matter; associated with anaerobic conditions.

Putrescible: Able to rot quickly enough to cause odors and attract flies.

Pyrolysis: Decomposition of a chemical by extreme heat.

Q

Qualitative Use Assessment: Report summarizing the major uses of a pesticide including percentage of crop treated, and amount of pesticide used on a site.

Quality Assurance/Quality Control: A system of procedures, checks, audits, and corrective actions to ensure that all EPA research design and performance, environmental monitoring and sampling, and other technical and reporting activities are of the highest achievable quality.

Quench Tank: A water-filled tank used to cool incinerator residues or hot materials during industrial processes.

R

Radiation: Transmission of energy though space or any medium. Also known as radiant energy.

Radiation Standards: Regulations that set maximum exposure limits for protection of the public from radioactive materials.

Radio Frequency Radiation: (See non-ionizing electromagnetic radiation.)

Radioactive Decay: Spontaneous change in an atom by emission of of charged particles and/or gamma rays; also known as radioactive disintegration and radioactivity.

Radioactive Substances: Substances that emit ionizing radiation.

Radioactive Waste: Any waste that emits energy as rays, waves, streams or energetic particles. Radioactive materials are often mixed with hazardous waste, from nuclear reactors, research institutions, or hospitals.

Radioisotopes: Chemical variants of radioactive elements with potentially oncogenic, teratogenic, and mutagenic effects on the human body.

Radionuclide: Radioactive particle, man-made (anthropogenic) or natural, with a distinct atomic weight number. Can have a long life as soil or water pollutant.

Radius of Vulnerability Zone: The maximum distance from the point of release of a hazardous substance in which the airborne concentration could reach the level of concern under specified weather conditions.

Radius of Influence: 1. The radial distance from the center of a wellbore to the point where there is no lowering of the water table or potentiometric surface (the edge of the cone of depression); 2. the radial distance from an extraction well that has adequate air flow for effective removal of contaminants when a vacuum is applied to the extraction well.

Radon: A colorless naturally occurring, radioactive, inert gas formed by radioactive decay of radium atoms in soil or rocks.

Radon Daughters/Radon Progeny: Short-lived radioactive decay products of radon that decay into longer-lived lead isotopes that can attach themselves to airborne dust and other particles and, if inhaled, damage the linings of the lungs.

Radon Decay Products: A term used to refer collectively to the immediate products of the radon decay chain. These include Po-218, Pb-214, Bi-214, and Po-214, which have an average combined half-life of about 30 minutes.

Rainbow Report: Comprehensive document giving the status of all pesticides now or ever in registration or special reviews. Known as the "rainbow report" because chapters are printed on different colors of paper.

Rasp: A machine that grinds waste into a manageable material and helps prevent odor.

Raw Agricultural Commodity: An unprocessed human food or animal feed crop (e.g., raw carrots, apples, corn, or eggs.)

Raw Sewage: Untreated wastewater and its contents.

Raw Water: Intake water prior to any treatment or use.

Re-entry: (In indoor air program) Refers to air exhausted from a building that is immediately brought back into the system through the air intake and other openings.

Reactivity: Refers to those hazardous wastes that are normally unstable and readily undergo violent chemical change but do not explode.

Reaeration: Introduction of air into the lower layers of a reservoir. As the air bubbles form and rise through the water, the oxygen dissolves into the water and replenishes the dissolved oxygen. The rising bubbles also cause the lower waters to rise to the surface where they take on oxygen from the atmosphere.

Real-Time Monitoring: Monitoring and measuring environmental developments with technology and communications systems that provide time-relevant information to the public in an easily understood format people can use in day-to-day decision-making about their health and the environment.

Reasonable Further Progress: Annual incremental reductions in air pollutant emissions as reflected in a State Implementation Plan that EPA deems sufficient to provide for the attainment of the applicable national ambient air quality standards by the statutory deadline.

Reasonable Maximum Exposure: The maximum exposure reasonably expected to occur in a population.

Reasonable Worst Case: An estimate of the individual dose, exposure, or risk level received by an individual in a defined population that is greater than the 90th percentile but less than that received by anyone in the 98th percentile in the same population.

Reasonably Available Control Measures (RACM): A broadly defined term referring to technological and other measures for pollution control.

Reasonably Available Control Technology (RACT): Control technology that is reasonably available, and both technologically and economically feasible. Usually applied to existing sources in nonattainment areas; in most cases is less stringent than new source performance standards.

Recarbonization: Process in which carbon dioxide is bubbled into water being treated to lower the pH.

Receiving Waters: A river, lake, ocean, stream or other watercourse into which wastewater or treated effluent is discharged.

Receptor: Ecological entity exposed to a stressor.

Recharge: The process by which water is added to a zone of saturation, usually by percolation from the soil surface; e.g., the recharge of an aquifer.

Recharge Area: A land area in which water reaches the zone of saturation from surface infiltration, e.g., where rainwater soaks through the earth to reach an aquifer.

Recharge Rate: The quantity of water per unit of time that replenishes or refills an aquifer.

Reclamation: (In recycling) Restoration of materials found in the waste stream to a beneficial use which may be for purposes other than the original use.

Recombinant Bacteria: A microorganism whose genetic makeup has been altered by deliberate introduction of new genetic elements. The offspring of these altered bacteria also contain these new genetic elements; i.e. they "breed true."

Recombinant DNA: The new DNA that is formed by combining pieces of DNA from different organisms or cells.

Recommended Maximum Contaminant Level (RMCL): The maximum level of a contaminant in drinking water at which no known or anticipated adverse effect on human health would occur, and that includes an adequate margin of safety. Recommended levels are nonenforceable health goals. (See: maximum contaminant level.)

Reconstructed Source: Facility in which components are replaced to such an extent that the fixed capital cost of the new components exceeds 50 percent of the capital cost of constructing a comparable brand-new facility. New-source performance standards may be applied to sources reconstructed after the proposal of the standard if it is technologically and economically feasible to meet the standards.

Reconstruction of Dose: Estimating exposure after it has occurred by using evidence within an organism such as chemical levels in tissue or fluids.

Record of Decision (ROD): A public document that explains which cleanup alternative(s) will be used at National Priorities List sites where, under CERCLA, Trust Funds pay for the cleanup.

Recovery Rate: Percentage of usable recycled materials that have been removed from the total amount of municipal solid waste generated in a specific area or by a specific business.

Recycle/Reuse: Minimizing waste generation by recovering and reprocessing usable products that might otherwise become waste (.i.e. recycling of aluminum cans, paper, and bottles, etc.).

Recycling and Reuse Business Assistance Centers: Located in state solid-waste or economic-development agencies, these centers provide recycling businesses with customized and targeted assistance.

Recycling Economic Development Advocates: Individuals hired by state or tribal economic development offices to focus financial, marketing, and permitting resources on creating recycling businesses.

Recycling Mill: Facility where recovered materials are remanufactured into new products.

Recycling Technical Assistance Partnership National Network: A national information-sharing resource designed to help businesses and manufacturers increase their use of recovered materials.

Red Bag Waste: (See: infectious waste.)

Red Border: An EPA document undergoing review before being submitted for final management decision-making.

Red Tide: A proliferation of a marine plankton toxic and often fatal to fish, perhaps stimulated by the addition of nutrients. A tide can be red, green, or brown, depending on the coloration of the plankton.

Redemption Program: Program in which consumers are monetarily compensated for the collection of recyclable materials, generally through prepaid deposits or taxes on beverage containers. In some states or localities legislation has enacted redemption programs to help prevent roadside litter. (See: bottle bill.)

Reduction: The addition of hydrogen, removal of oxygen, or addition of electrons to an element or compound.

Reentry Interval: The period of time immediately following the application of a pesticide during which unprotected workers should not enter a field.

Reference Dose (RfD): The RfD is a numerical estimate of a daily oral exposure to the human population, including sensitive subgroups such as children, that is not likely to cause harmful effects during a lifetime. RfDs are generally used for health effects that are thought to have a threshold or low dose limit for producing effects.

Glossary of Environmental Terms

Reformulated Gasoline: Gasoline with a different composition from conventional gasoline (e.g., lower aromatics content) that cuts air pollutants.

Refueling Emissions: Emissions released during vehicle re-fueling.

Refuse: (See: solid waste.)

Refuse Reclamation: Conversion of solid waste into useful products; e.g., composting organic wastes to make soil conditioners or separating aluminum and other metals for recycling.

Regeneration: Manipulation of cells to cause them to develop into whole plants.

Regional Response Team (RRT): Representatives of federal, local, and state agencies who may assist in coordination of activities at the request of the On-Scene Coordinator before and during a significant pollution incident such as an oil spill, major chemical release, or Superfund response.

Registrant: Any manufacturer or formulator who obtains registration for a pesticide active ingredient or product.

Registration: Formal listing with EPA of a new pesticide before it can be sold or distributed. Under the Federal Insecticide, Fungicide, and Rodenticide Act, EPA is responsible for registration (pre-market licensing) of pesticides on the basis of data demonstrating no unreasonable adverse effects on human health or the environment when applied according to approved label directions.

Registration Standards: Published documents which include summary reviews of the data available on a pesticide's active ingredient, data gaps, and the Agency's existing regulatory position on the pesticide.

Regulated Asbestos-Containing Material (RACM): Friable asbestos material or nonfriable ACM that will be or has been subjected to sanding, grinding, cutting, or abrading or has crumbled, or been pulverized or reduced to powder in the course of demolition or renovation operations.

Regulated Medical Waste: Under the Medical Waste Tracking Act of 1988, any solid waste generated in the diagnosis, treatment, or immunization of human beings or animals, in research pertaining thereto, or in the production or testing of biologicals. Included are cultures and stocks of infectious agents; human blood and blood products; human pathological body wastes from surgery and autopsy; contaminated animal carcasses from medical research; waste from patients with communicable diseases; and all used sharp implements, such as needles and scalpels, and certain unused sharps. (See: treated medical waste; untreated medical waste; destroyed medical waste.)

Relative Ecological Sustainability: Ability of an ecosystem to maintain relative ecological integrity indefinitely.

Relative Permeability: The permeability of a rock to gas, NAIL, or water, when any two or more are present.

Relative Risk Assessment: Estimating the risks associated with different stressors or management actions.

Release: Any spilling, leaking, pumping, pouring, emitting, emptying, discharging, injecting, escaping, leaching, dumping, or disposing into the environment of a hazardous or toxic chemical or extremely hazardous substance.

Remedial Action (RA): The actual construction or implementation phase of a Superfund site cleanup that follows remedial design.

Remedial Design: A phase of remedial action that follows the remedial investigation/feasibility study and includes development of engineering drawings and specifications for a site cleanup.

Remedial Investigation: An in-depth study designed to gather data needed to determine the nature and extent of contamination at a Superfund site; establish site cleanup criteria; identify preliminary alternatives for remedial action; and support technical and cost analyses of alternatives. The remedial investigation is usually done with the feasibility study. Together they are usually referred to as the "RI/FS".

Remedial Project Manager (RPM): The EPA or state official responsible for overseeing on-site remedial action.

Remedial Response: Long-term action that stops or substantially reduces a release or threat of a release of hazardous substances that is serious but not an immediate threat to public health.

Remediation: 1. Cleanup or other methods used to remove or contain a toxic spill or hazardous materials from a Superfund site; 2. for the Asbestos Hazard Emergency Response program, abatement methods including evaluation, repair, enclosure, encapsulation, or removal of greater than 3 linear feet or square feet of asbestos-containing materials from a building.

Remote Sensing: The collection and interpretation of information about an object without physical contact with the object; e.g., satellite imaging, aerial photography, and open path measurements.

Removal Action: Short-term immediate actions taken to address releases of hazardous substances that require expedited response. (See: cleanup.)

Renewable Energy Production Incentive (REPI): Incentive established by the Energy Policy Act available to renewable energy power projects owned by a state or local government or nonprofit electric cooperative.

Repeat Compliance Period: Any subsequent compliance period after the initial one.

Reportable Quantity (RQ): Quantity of a hazardous substance that triggers reports under CERCLA. If a substance exceeds its RQ, the release must be reported to the National Response Center, the SERC, and community emergency coordinators for areas likely to be affected.

Repowering: Rebuilding and replacing major components of a power plant instead of building a new one.

Representative Sample: A portion of material or water that is as nearly identical in content and consistency as possible to that in the larger body of material or water being sampled.

Reregistration: The reevaluation and relicensing of existing pesticides originally registered prior to current scientific and regulatory standards. EPA reregisters pesticides through its Registration Standards Program.

Reserve Capacity: Extra treatment capacity built into solid waste and wastewater treatment plants and interceptor sewers to accommodate flow increases due to future population growth.

Reservoir: Any natural or artificial holding area used to store, regulate, or control water.

Residential Use: Pesticide application in and around houses, office buildings, apartment buildings, motels, and other living or working areas.

Residential Waste: Waste generated in single and multi-family homes, including newspapers, clothing, disposable tableware, food packaging, cans, bottles, food scraps, and yard trimmings other than those that are diverted to backyard composting. (See: Household hazardous waste.)

Residual: Amount of a pollutant remaining in the environment after a natural or technological process has taken place; e.g., the sludge remaining after initial wastewater treatment, or particulates remaining in air after it passes through a scrubbing or other process.

Residual Risk: The extent of health risk from air pollutants remaining after application of the Maximum Achievable Control Technology (MACT).

Residual Saturation: Saturation level below which fluid drainage will not occur.

Residue: The dry solids remaining after the evaporation of a sample of water or sludge.

Resistance: For plants and animals, the ability to withstand poor environmental conditions or attacks by chemicals or disease. May be inborn or acquired.

Resource Recovery: The process of obtaining matter or energy from materials formerly discarded.

Response Action: 1. Generic term for actions taken in response to actual or potential health-threatening environmental events such as spills, sudden releases, and asbestos abatement/management problems. 2. A CERCLA-authorized action involving either a short-term removal action or a long-term removal response. This may include but is not limited to: removing hazardous materials from a site to an EPA-approved hazardous waste facility for treatment, containment or treating the waste on-site, identifying and removing the sources of ground-water contamination and halting further migration of contaminants. 3. Any of the following actions taken in school buildings in response to AHERA to reduce the risk of exposure to asbestos: removal, encapsulation, enclosure, repair, and operations and maintenance. (See: cleanup.)

Responsiveness Summary: A summary of oral and/or written public comments received by EPA during a comment period on key EPA documents, and EPA's response to those comments.

Restoration: Measures taken to return a site to pre-violation conditions.

Restricted Entry Interval: The time after a pesticide application during which entry into the treated area is restricted.

Restricted Use: A pesticide may be classified (under FIFRA regulations) for restricted use if it requires special handling because of its toxicity, and, if so, it may be applied only by trained, certified applicators or those under their direct supervision.

Restriction Enzymes: Enzymes that recognize specific regions of a long DNA molecule and cut it at those points.

Retrofit: Addition of a pollution control device on an existing facility without making major changes to the generating plant. Also called backfit.

Reuse: Using a product or component of municipal solid waste in its original form more than once; e.g., refilling a glass bottle that has been returned or using a coffee can to hold nuts and bolts.

Reverse Osmosis: A treatment process used in water systems by adding pressure to force water through a semi-permeable membrane. Reverse osmosis removes most drinking water contaminants. Also used in wastewater treatment. Large-scale reverse osmosis plants are being developed.

Reversible Effect: An effect which is not permanent; especially adverse effects which diminish when exposure to a toxic chemical stops.

Ribonucleic Acid (RNA): A molecule that carries the genetic message from DNA to a cellular protein-producing mechanism.

Rill: A small channel eroded into the soil by surface runoff; can be easily smoothed out or obliterated by normal tillage.

Ringlemann Chart: A series of shaded illustrations used to measure the opacity of air pollution emissions, ranging from light grey through black; used to set and enforce emissions standards.

Riparian Habitat: Areas adjacent to rivers and streams with a differing density, diversity, and productivity of plant and animal species relative to nearby uplands.

Riparian Rights: Entitlement of a land owner to certain uses of water on or bordering the property, including the right to prevent diversion or misuse of upstream waters. Generally a matter of state law.

Risk: A measure of the probability that damage to life, health, property, and/or the environment will occur as a result of a given hazard.

Risk (Adverse) for Endangered Species: Risk to aquatic species if anticipated pesticide residue levels equal one-fifth of LD10 or one-tenth of LC50; risk to terrestrial species if anticipated pesticide residue levels equal one-fifth of LC10 or one-tenth of LC50.

Risk Assessment: Qualitative and quantitative evaluation of the risk posed to human health and/or the environment by the actual or potential presence and/or use of specific pollutants.

Risk Characterization: The last phase of the risk assessment process that estimates the potential for adverse health or ecological effects to occur from exposure to a stressor and evaluates the uncertainty involved.

Risk Communication: The exchange of information about health or environmental risks among risk assessors and managers, the general public, news media, interest groups, etc.

Risk Estimate: A description of the probability that organisms exposed to a specific dose of a chemical or other pollutant will develop an adverse response, e.g., cancer.

Risk Factor: Characteristics (e.g., race, sex, age, obesity) or variables (e.g., smoking, occupational exposure level) associated with increased probability of a toxic effect.

Risk for Non-Endangered Species: Risk to species if anticipated pesticide residue levels are equal to or greater than LC50.

Risk Management: The process of evaluating and selecting alternative regulatory and non-regulatory responses to risk. The selection process necessarily requires the consideration of legal, economic, and behavioral factors.

Risk-based Targeting: The direction of resources to those areas that have been identified as having the highest potential or actual adverse effect on human health and/or the environment.

Risk-Specific Dose: The dose associated with a specified risk level.

River Basin: The land area drained by a river and its tributaries.

Rodenticide: A chemical or agent used to destroy rats or other rodent pests, or to prevent them from damaging food, crops, etc.

Rotary Kiln Incinerator: An incinerator with a rotating combustion chamber that keeps waste moving, thereby allowing it to vaporize for easier burning.

Rough Fish: Fish not prized for sport or eating, such as gar and suckers. Most are more tolerant of changing environmental conditions than are game or food species.

Route of Exposure: The avenue by which a chemical comes into contact with an organism, e.g., inhalation, ingestion, dermal contact, injection.

Rubbish: Solid waste, excluding food waste and ashes, from homes, institutions, and workplaces.

Run-Off: That part of precipitation, snow melt, or irrigation water that runs off the land into streams or other surface-water. It can carry pollutants from the air and land into receiving waters.

Running Losses: Evaporation of motor vehicle fuel from the fuel tank while the vehicle is in use.

S

Sacrifical Anode: An easily corroded material deliberately installed in a pipe or intake to give it up (sacrifice it) to corrosion while the rest of the water supply facility remains relatively corrosion-free.

Safe: Condition of exposure under which there is a practical certainty that no harm will result to exposed individuals.

Safe Water: Water that does not contain harmful bacteria, toxic materials, or chemicals, and is considered safe for drinking even if it may have taste, odor, color, and certain mineral problems.

Safe Yield: The annual amount of water that can be taken from a source of supply over a period of years without depleting that source beyond its ability to be replenished naturally in "wet years."

Safener: A chemical added to a pesticide to keep it from injuring plants.

Salinity: The percentage of salt in water.

Salt Water Intrusion: The invasion of fresh surface or ground water by salt water. If it comes from the ocean it may be called sea water intrusion.

Salts: Minerals that water picks up as it passes through the air, over and under the ground, or from households and industry.

Salvage: The utilization of waste materials.

Sampling Frequency: The interval between the collection of successive samples.

Sanctions: Actions taken by the federal government for failure to provide or implement a State Implementation Plan (SIP). Such action may include withholding of highway funds and a ban on construction of new sources of potential pollution.

Sand Filters: Devices that remove some suspended solids from sewage. Air and bacteria decompose additional wastes filtering through the sand so that cleaner water drains from the bed.

Sanitary Landfill: (See: landfills.)

Sanitary Sewers: Underground pipes that carry off only domestic or industrial waste, not storm water.

Sanitary Survey: An on-site review of the water sources, facilities, equipment, operation and maintenance of a public water system to evaluate the adequacy of those elements for producing and distributing safe drinking water.

Sanitary Water (Also known as gray water): Water discharged from sinks, showers, kitchens, or other non-industrial operations, but not from commodes.

Sanitation: Control of physical factors in the human environment that could harm development, health, or survival.

Saprolite: A soft, clay-rich, thoroughly decomposed rock formed in place by chemical weathering of igneous or metamorphic rock. Forms in humid, tropical, or subtropical climates.

Saprophytes: Organisms living on dead or decaying organic matter that help natural decomposition of organic matter in water.

Saturated Zone: The area below the water table where all open spaces are filled with water under pressure equal to or greater than that of the atmosphere.

Saturation: The condition of a liquid when it has taken into solution the maximum possible quantity of a given substance at a given temperature and pressure.

Science Advisory Board (SAB): A group of external scientists who advise EPA on science and policy.

Scrap: Materials discarded from manufacturing operations that may be suitable for reprocessing.

Scrap Metal Processor: Intermediate operating facility where recovered metal is sorted, cleaned of contaminants, and prepared for recycling.

Screening: Use of screens to remove coarse floating and suspended solids from sewage.

Screening Risk Assessment: A risk assessment performed with few data and many assumptions to identify exposures that should be evaluated more carefully for potential risk.

Scrubber: An air pollution device that uses a spray of water or reactant or a dry process to trap pollutants in emissions.

Secondary Drinking Water Regulations: Non-enforceable regulations applying to public water systems and specifying the maximum contamination levels that, in the judgment of EPA, are required to protect the public welfare. These regulations apply to any contaminants that may adversely affect the odor or appearance of such water and consequently may cause people served by the system to discontinue its use.

Secondary Effect: Action of a stressor on supporting components of the ecosystem, which in turn impact the ecological component of concern. (See: primary effect.)

Secondary Materials: Materials that have been manufactured and used at least once and are to be used again.

Secondary Standards: National ambient air quality standards designed to protect welfare, including effects on soils, water, crops, vegetation, man-made (anthropogenic) materials, animals, wildlife, weather, visibility, and climate; damage to property; transportation hazards; economic values, and personal comfort and well-being.

Secondary Treatment: The second step in most publicly owned waste treatment systems in which bacteria consume the organic parts of the waste. It is accomplished by bringing together waste, bacteria, and oxygen in trickling filters or in the activated sludge process. This treatment removes floating and settleable solids and about 90 percent of the oxygen-demanding substances and suspended solids. Disinfection is the final stage of secondary treatment. (See: primary, tertiary treatment.)

Secure Chemical Landfill: (See:landfills.)

Secure Maximum Contaminant Level: Maximum permissible level of a contaminant in water delivered to the free flowing outlet of the ultimate user, or of contamination resulting from corrosion of piping and plumbing caused by water quality.

Glossary of Environmental Terms

Sediment: Topsoil, sand, and minerals washed from the land into water, usually after rain or snow melt.

Sediment Yield: The quantity of sediment arriving at a specific location.

Sedimentation: Letting solids settle out of wastewater by gravity during treatment.

Sedimentation Tanks: Wastewater tanks in which floating wastes are skimmed off and settled solids are removed for disposal.

Sediments: Soil, sand, and minerals washed from land into water, usually after rain. They pile up in reservoirs, rivers and harbors, destroying fish and wildlife habitat, and clouding the water so that sunlight cannot reach aquatic plants. Careless farming, mining, and building activities will expose sediment materials, allowing them to wash off the land after rainfall.

Seed Protectant: A chemical applied before planting to protect seeds and seedlings from disease or insects.

Seepage: Percolation of water through the soil from unlined canals, ditches, laterals, watercourses, or water storage facilities.

Selective Pesticide: A chemical designed to affect only certain types of pests, leaving other plants and animals unharmed.

Semi-Confined Aquifer: An aquifer partially confined by soil layers of low permeability through which recharge and discharge can still occur.

Semivolatile Organic Compounds: Organic compounds that volatilize slowly at standard temperature (20 degrees C and 1 atm pressure).

Senescence: The aging process. Sometimes used to describe lakes or other bodies of water in advanced stages of eutrophication. Also used to describe plants and animals.

Septic System: An on-site system designed to treat and dispose of domestic sewage. A typical septic system consists of tank that receives waste from a residence or business and a system of tile lines or a pit for disposal of the liquid effluent (sludge) that remains after decomposition of the solids by bacteria in the tank and must be pumped out periodically.

Septic Tank: An underground storage tank for wastes from homes not connected to a sewer line. Waste goes directly from the home to the tank. (See: septic system.)

Service Connector: The pipe that carries tap water from a public water main to a building.

Service Line Sample: A one-liter sample of water that has been standing for at least 6 hours in a service pipeline and is collected according to federal regulations.

Service Pipe: The pipeline extending from the water main to the building served or to the consumer's system.

Set-Back: Setting a thermometer to a lower temperature when the building is unoccupied to reduce consumption of heating energy. Also refers to setting the thermometer to a higher temperature during unoccupied periods in the cooling season.

Settleable Solids: Material heavy enough to sink to the bottom of a wastewater treatment tank.

Settling Chamber: A series of screens placed in the way of flue gases to slow the stream of air, thus helping gravity to pull particles into a collection device.

Settling Tank: A holding area for wastewater, where heavier particles sink to the bottom for removal and disposal.

7Q10: Seven-day, consecutive low flow with a ten year return frequency; the lowest stream flow for seven consecutive days that would be expected to occur once in ten years.

Sewage: The waste and wastewater produced by residential and commercial sources and discharged into sewers.

Sewage Lagoon: (See: lagoon.)

Sewage Sludge: Sludge produced at a Publicly Owned Treatment Works, the disposal of which is regulated under the Clean Water Act.

Sewer: A channel or conduit that carries wastewater and storm-water runoff from the source to a treatment plant or receiving stream. "Sanitary" sewers carry household, industrial, and commercial waste. "Storm" sewers carry runoff from rain or snow. "Combined" sewers handle both.

Sewerage: The entire system of sewage collection, treatment, and disposal.

Shading Coefficient: The amount of the sun's heat transmitted through a given window compared with that of a standard 1/8- inch-thick single pane of glass under the same conditions.

Sharps: Hypodermic needles, syringes (with or without the attached needle), Pasteur pipettes, scalpel blades, blood vials, needles with attached tubing, and culture dishes used in animal or human patient care or treatment, or in medical, research or industrial laboratories. Also included are other types of broken or unbroken glassware that were in contact with infectious agents, such as used slides and cover slips, and unused hypodermic and suture needles, syringes, and scalpel blades.

Shock Load: The arrival at a water treatment plant of raw water containing unusual amounts of algae, colloidal matter. color, suspended solids, turbidity, or other pollutants.

Short-Circuiting: When some of the water in tanks or basins flows faster than the rest; may result in shorter contact, reaction, or settling times than calculated or presumed.

Sick Building Syndrome: Building whose occupants experience acute health and/or comfort effects that appear to be linked to time spent therein, but where no specific illness or cause can be identified. Complaints may be localized in a particular room or zone, or may spread throughout the building. (See: building-related illness.)

Signal: The volume or product-level change produced by a leak in a tank.

Signal Words: The words used on a pesticide label—Danger, Warning, Caution—to indicate level of toxicity.

Significant Deterioration: Pollution resulting from a new source in previously "clean" areas. (See: prevention of significant deterioration.)

Significant Municipal Facilities: Those publicly owned sewage treatment plants that discharge a million gallons per day or more and are therefore considered by states to have the potential to substantially affect the quality of receiving waters.

Significant Non-Compliance: (See significant violations.)

Significant Potential Source of Contamination: A facility or activity that stores, uses, or produces compounds with potential for significant contaminating impact if released into the source water of a public water supply.

Significant Violations: Violations by point source dischargers of sufficient magnitude or duration to be a regulatory priority.

Silt: Sedimentary materials composed of fine or intermediate-sized mineral particles.

Silviculture: Management of forest land for timber.

Single-Breath Canister: Small one-liter canister designed to capture a single breath. Used in air pollutant ingestion research.

Sink: Place in the environment where a compound or material collects.

Sinking: Controlling oil spills by using an agent to trap the oil and sink it to the bottom of the body of water where the agent and the oil are biodegraded.

SIP Call: EPA action requiring a state to resubmit all or part of its State Implementation Plan to demonstrate attainment of the require national ambient air quality standards within the statutory deadline. A SIP Revision is a revision of a SIP altered at the request of EPA or on a state's initiative. (See: State Implementation Plan.)

Site: An area or place within the jurisdiction of the EPA and/or a state.

Site Assessment Program: A means of evaluating hazardous waste sites through preliminary assessments and site inspections to develop a Hazard Ranking System score.

Site Inspection: The collection of information from a Superfund site to determine the extent and severity of hazards posed by the site. It follows and is more extensive than a preliminary assessment. The purpose is to gather information necessary to score the site, using the Hazard Ranking System, and to determine if it presents an immediate threat requiring prompt removal.

Site Safety Plan: A crucial element in all removal actions, it includes information on equipment being used, precautions to be taken, and steps to take in the event of an on-site emergency.

Siting: The process of choosing a location for a facility.

Skimming: Using a machine to remove oil or scum from the surface of the water.

Slow Sand Filtration: Passage of raw water through a bed of sand at low velocity, resulting in substantial removal of chemical and biological contaminants.

Sludge: A semi-solid residue from any of a number of air or water treatment processes; can be a hazardous waste.

Sludge Digester: Tank in which complex organic substances like sewage sludges are biologically dredged. During these reactions, energy is released and much of the sewage is converted to methane, carbon dioxide, and water.

Slurry: A watery mixture of insoluble matter resulting from some pollution control techniques.

Small Quantity Generator (SQG-sometimes referred to as "Squeegee"): Persons or enterprises that produce 220-2200 pounds per month of hazardous waste; they are required to keep more records than conditionally exempt generators. The largest category of hazardous waste generators, SQGs, include automotive shops, dry cleaners, photographic developers, and many other small businesses. (See: conditionally exempt generators.)

Smelter: A facility that melts or fuses ore, often with an accompanying chemical change, to separate its metal content. Emissions cause pollution. "Smelting" is the process involved.

Smog: Air pollution typically associated with oxidants. (See: photochemical smog.)

Smoke: Particles suspended in air after incomplete combustion.

Soft Detergents: Cleaning agents that break down in nature.

Soft Water: Any water that does not contain a significant amount of dissolved minerals such as salts of calcium or magnesium.

Soil Adsorption Field: A sub-surface area containing a trench or bed with clean stones and a system of piping through which treated sewage may seep into the surrounding soil for further treatment and disposal.

Soil and Water Conservation Practices: Control measures consisting of managerial, vegetative, and structural practices to reduce the loss of soil and water.

Soil Conditioner: An organic material like humus or compost that helps soil absorb water, build a bacterial community, and take up mineral nutrients.

Soil Erodibility: An indicator of a soil's susceptibility to raindrop impact, runoff, and other erosive processes.

Soil Gas: Gaseous elements and compounds in the small spaces between particles of the earth and soil. Such gases can be moved or driven out under pressure.

Soil Moisture: The water contained in the pore space of the unsaturated zone.

Soil Sterilant: A chemical that temporarily or permanently prevents the growth of all plants and animals,

Solder: Metallic compound used to seal joints between pipes. Until recently, most solder contained 50 percent lead. Use of solder containing more than 0.2 percent lead in pipes carrying drinking water is now prohibited.

Sole-Source Aquifer: An aquifer that supplies 50-percent or more of the drinking water of an area.

Solid Waste: Non-liquid, non-soluble materials ranging from municipal garbage to industrial wastes that contain complex and sometimes hazardous substances. Solid wastes also include sewage sludge, agricultural refuse, demolition wastes, and mining residues. Technically, solid waste also refers to liquids and gases in containers.

Solid Waste Disposal: The final placement of refuse that is not salvaged or recycled.

Solid Waste Management: Supervised handling of waste materials from their source through recovery processes to disposal.

Solidification and Stabilization: Removal of wastewater from a waste or changing it chemically to make it less permeable and susceptible to transport by water.

Solubility: The amount of mass of a compound that will dissolve in a unit volume of solution. Aqueous Solubility is the maximum concentration of a chemical that will dissolve in pure water at a reference temperature.

Soot: Carbon dust formed by incomplete combustion.

Sorption: The action of soaking up or attracting substances; process used in many pollution control systems.

Source Area: The location of liquid hydrocarbons or the zone of highest soil or groundwater concentrations, or both, of the chemical of concern.

Source Characterization Measurements: Measurements made to estimate the rate of release of pollutants into the environment from a source such as an incinerator, landfill, etc.

Source Reduction: Reducing the amount of materials entering the waste stream from a specific source by redesigning products or patterns of production or consumption (e.g., using returnable beverage containers). Synonymous with waste reduction.

Source Separation: Segregating various wastes at the point of generation (e.g., separation of paper, metal and glass from other wastes to make recycling simpler and more efficient).

Source-Water Protection Area: The area delineated by a state for a Public Water Supply or including numerous such suppliers, whether the source is ground water or surface water or both.

Sparge or Sparging: Injection of air below the water table to strip dissolved volatile organic compounds and/or oxygenate ground water to facilitate aerobic biodegradation of organic compounds.

Special Local-Needs Registration: Registration of a pesticide product by a state agency for a specific use that is not federally registered. However, the active ingredient must be federally registered for other uses. The special use is specific to that state and is often minor, thus may not warrant the additional cost of a full federal registration process. SLN registration cannot be issued for new active ingredients, food-use active ingredients without tolerances, or for a canceled registration. The products cannot be shipped across state lines.

Special Review: Formerly known as Rebuttable Presumption Against Registration (RPAR), this is the regulatory process through which existing pesticides suspected of posing unreasonable risks to human health, non-target organisms, or the environment are referred for review by EPA. Such review requires an intensive risk/benefit analysis with opportunity for public comment. If risk is found to outweigh social and economic benefits, regulatory actions can be initiated, ranging from label revisions and use-restriction to cancellation or suspended registration.

Special Waste: Items such as household hazardous waste, bulky wastes (refrigerators, pieces of furniture, etc.) tires, and used oil.

Species: 1. A reproductively isolated aggregate of interbreeding organisms having common attributes and usually designated by a common name.2. An organism belonging to belonging to such a category.

Specific Conductance: Rapid method of estimating the dissolved solid content of a water supply by testing its capacity to carry an electrical current.

Specific Yield: The amount of water a unit volume of saturated permeable rock will yield when drained by gravity.

Spill Prevention, Containment, and Countermeasures Plan (SPCP): Plan covering the release of hazardous substances as defined in the Clean Water Act.

Spoil: Dirt or rock removed from its original location—destroying the composition of the soil in the process—as in strip-mining, dredging, or construction.

Sprawl: Unplanned development of open land.

Spray Tower Scrubber: A device that sprays alkaline water into a chamber where acid gases are present to aid in neutralizing the gas.

Spring: Ground water seeping out of the earth where the water table intersects the ground surface.

Spring Melt/Thaw: The process whereby warm temperatures melt winter snow and ice. Because various forms of acid deposition may have been stored in the frozen water, the melt can result in abnormally large amounts of acidity entering streams and rivers, sometimes causing fish kills.

Stabilization: Conversion of the active organic matter in sludge into inert, harmless material.

Stabilization Ponds: (See: lagoon.)

Stable Air: A motionless mass of air that holds, instead of dispersing, pollutants.

Stack: A chimney, smokestack, or vertical pipe that discharges used air.

Stack Effect: Air, as in a chimney, that moves upward because it is warmer than the ambient atmosphere.

Stack Effect: Flow of air resulting from warm air rising, creating a positive pressure area at the top of a building and negative pressure area at the bottom. This effect can overpower the mechanical system and disrupt building ventilation and air circulation.

Stack Gas: (See: flue gas.)

Stage II Controls: Systems placed on service station gasoline pumps to control and capture gasoline vapors during refuelling.

Stagnation: Lack of motion in a mass of air or water that holds pollutants in place.

Stakeholder: Any organization, governmental entity, or individual that has a stake in or may be impacted by a given approach to environmental regulation, pollution prevention, energy conservation, etc.

Standard Industrial Classification Code: Also known as SIC Codes, a method of grouping industries with similar products or services and assigning codes to these groups.

Standard Sample: The part of finished drinking water that is examined for the presence of coliform bacteria.

Standards: Norms that impose limits on the amount of pollutants or emissions produced. EPA establishes minimum standards, but states are allowed to be stricter.

Start of a Response Action: The point in time when there is a guarantee or set-aside of funding by EPA, other federal agencies, states or Principal Responsible Parties in order to begin response actions at a Superfund site.

State Emergency Response Commission (SERC): Commission appointed by each state governor according to the requirements of SARA Title III. The SERCs designate emergency planning districts, appoint local emergency planning committees, and supervise and coordinate their activities.

State Environmental Goals and Indication Project: Program to assist state environmental agencies by providing technical and financial assistance in the development of environmental goals and indicators.

State Implementation Plans (SIP): EPA approved state plans for the establishment, regulation, and enforcement of air pollution standards.

State Management Plan: Under FIFRA, a state management plan required by EPA to allow states, tribes, and U.S. territories the flexibility to design and implement ways to protect ground water from the use of certain pesticides.

Static Water Depth: The vertical distance from the centerline of the pump discharge down to the surface level of the free pool while no water is being drawn from the pool or water table.

Static Water Level: 1. Elevation or level of the water table in a well when the pump is not operating. 2. The level or elevation to which water would rise in a tube connected to an artesian aquifer or basin in a conduit under pressure.

Stationary Source: A fixed-site producer of pollution, mainly power plants and other facilities using industrial combustion processes. (See: point source.)

Sterilization: The removal or destruction of all microorganisms, including pathogenic and other bacteria, vegetative forms, and spores.

Sterilizer: One of three groups of anti-microbials registered by EPA for public health uses. EPA considers an antimicrobial to be a sterilizer when it destroys or eliminates all forms of bacteria, viruses, and fungi and their spores. Because spores are considered the most difficult form of microorganism to destroy, EPA considers the term sporicide to be synonymous with sterilizer.

Storage: Temporary holding of waste pending treatment or disposal, as in containers, tanks, waste piles, and surface impoundments.

Storm Sewer: A system of pipes (separate from sanitary sewers) that carries water runoff from buildings and land surfaces.

Stratification: Separating into layers.

Stratigraphy: Study of the formation, composition, and sequence of sediments, whether consolidated or not.

Stratosphere: The portion of the atmosphere 10-to-25 miles above the earth's surface.

Stressors: Physical, chemical, or biological entities that can induce adverse effects on ecosystems or human health.

Strip-Cropping: Growing crops in a systematic arrangement of strips or bands that serve as barriers to wind and water erosion.

Strip-Mining: A process that uses machines to scrape soil or rock away from mineral deposits just under the earth's surface.

Structural Deformation: Distortion in walls of a tank after liquid has been added or removed.

Subchronic: Of intermediate duration, usually used to describe studies or periods of exposure lasting between 5 and 90 days.

Subchronic Exposure: Multiple or continuous exposures lasting for approximately ten percent of an experimental species lifetime, usually over a three-month period.

Submerged Aquatic Vegetation: Vegetation that lives at or below the water surface; an important habitat for young fish and other aquatic organisms.

Subwatershed: Topographic perimeter of the catchment area of a stream tributary.

Sulfur Dioxide (SO_2): A pungent, colorless, gasformed primarily by the combustion of fossil fuels; becomes a pollutant when present in large amounts.

Sump: A pit or tank that catches liquid runoff for drainage or disposal.

Superchlorination: Chlorination with doses that are deliberately selected to produce water free of combined residuals so large as to require dechlorination.

Supercritical Water: A type of thermal treatment using moderate temperatures and high pressures to enhance the ability of water to break down large organic molecules into smaller, less toxic ones. Oxygen injected during this process combines with simple organic compounds to form carbon dioxide and water.

Superfund: The program operated under the legislative authority of CERCLA and SARA that funds and carries out EPA solid waste emergency and long-term removal and remedial activities. These activities include establishing the National Priorities List, investigating sites for inclusion on the list, determining their priority, and conducting and/or supervising cleanup and other remedial actions.

Superfund Innovative Technology Evaluation (SITE) Program: EPA program to promote development and use of innovative treatment and site characterization technologies in Superfund site cleanups.

Supplemental Registration: An arrangement whereby a registrant licenses another company to market its pesticide product under the second company's registration.

Supplier of Water: Any person who owns or operates a public water supply.

Surface Impoundment: Treatment, storage, or disposal of liquid hazardous wastes in ponds.

Surface Runoff: Precipitation, snow melt, or irrigation water in excess of what can infiltrate the soil surface and be stored in small surface depressions; a major transporter of non-point source pollutants in rivers, streams, and lakes..

Surface Uranium Mines: Strip mining operations for removal of uranium-bearing ore.

Surface Water: All water naturally open to the atmosphere (rivers, lakes, reservoirs, ponds, streams, impoundments, seas, estuaries, etc.)

Surface-Water Treatment Rule: Rule that specifies maximum contaminant level goals for Giardia lamblia, viruses, and Legionella and promulgates filtration and disinfection requirements for public water systems using surface-water or ground-water sources under the direct influence of surface water. The regulations also specify water quality, treatment, and watershed protection criteria under which filtration may be avoided.

Surfacing ACM: Asbestos-containing material that is sprayed or troweled on or otherwise applied to surfaces, such as acoustical plaster on ceilings and fireproofing materials on structural members.

Surfacing Material: Material sprayed or troweled onto structural members (beams, columns, or decking) for fire protection; or on ceilings or walls for fireproofing, acoustical or decorative purposes. Includes textured plaster, and other textured wall and ceiling surfaces.

Surfactant: A detergent compound that promotes lathering.

Surrogate Data: Data from studies of test organisms or a test substance that are used to estimate the characteristics or effects on another organism or substance.

Surveillance System: A series of monitoring devices designed to check on environmental conditions.

Susceptibility Analysis: An analysis to determine whether a Public Water Supply is subject to significant pollution from known potential sources.

Suspect Material: Building material suspected of containing asbestos; e.g., surfacing material, floor tile, ceiling tile, thermal system insulation.

Suspended Loads: Specific sediment particles maintained in the water column by turbulence and carried with the flow of water.

Suspended Solids: Small particles of solid pollutants that float on the surface of, or are suspended in, sewage or other liquids. They resist removal by conventional means.

Suspension: Suspending the use of a pesticide when EPA deems it necessary to prevent an imminent hazard resulting from its continued use. An emergency suspension takes effect immediately; under an ordinary suspension a registrant can request a hearing before the suspension goes into effect. Such a hearing process might take six months.

Suspension Culture: Cells growing in a liquid nutrient medium.

Swamp: A type of wetland dominated by woody vegetation but without appreciable peat deposits. Swamps may be fresh or salt water and tidal or non-tidal. (See: wetlands.)

Synergism: An interaction of two or more chemicals that results in an effect greater than the sum of their separate effects.

Synthetic Organic Chemicals (SOCs): Man-made (anthropogenic) organic chemicals. Some SOCs are volatile; others tend to stay dissolved in water instead of evaporating.

System With a Single Service Connection: A system that supplies drinking water to consumers via a single service line.

Systemic Pesticide: A chemical absorbed by an organism that interacts with the organism and makes the organism toxic to pests.

T

Tail Water: The runoff of irrigation water from the lower end of an irrigated field.

Tailings: Residue of raw material or waste separated out during the processing of crops or mineral ores.

Tailpipe Standards: Emissions limitations applicable to mobile source engine exhausts.

Tampering: Adjusting, negating, or removing pollution control equipment on a motor vehicle.

Technical Assistance Grant (TAG): As part of the Superfund program, Technical Assistance Grants of up to $50,000 are provided to citizens' groups to obtain assistance in interpreting information related to clean-ups at Superfund sites or those proposed for the National Priorities List. Grants are used by such groups to hire technical advisors to help them understand the site-related technical information for the duration of response activities.

Technical-Grade Active Ingredient (TGA): A pesticide chemical in pure form as it is manufactured prior to being formulated into an end-use product (e.g. wettable powders, granules, emulsifiable concentrates). Registered manufactured products composed of such chemicals are known as Technical Grade Products.

Technology-Based Limitations: Industry-specific effluent limitations based on best available preventive technology applied to a discharge when it will not cause a violation of water quality standards at low stream flows. Usually applied to discharges into large rivers.

Technology-Based Standards: Industry-specific effluent limitations applicable to direct and indirect sources which are developed on a category-by-category basis using statutory factors, not including water-quality effects.

Teratogen: A substance capable of causing birth defects.

Teratogenesis: The introduction of nonhereditary birth defects in a developing fetus by exogenous factors such as physical or chemical agents acting in the womb to interfere with normal embryonic development.

Terracing: Dikes built along the contour of sloping farm land that hold runoff and sediment to reduce erosion.

Tertiary Treatment: Advanced cleaning of wastewater that goes beyond the secondary or biological stage, removing nutrients such as phosphorus, nitrogen, and most BOD and suspended solids.

Theoretical Maximum Residue Contribution: The theoretical maximum amount of a pesticide in the daily diet of an average person. It assumes that the diet is composed of all food items for which there are tolerance-level residues of the pesticide. The TMRC is expressed as milligrams of pesticide/kilograms of body weight/day.

Therapeutic Index: The ratio of the dose required to produce toxic or lethal effects to the dose required to produce nonadverse or therapeutic response.

Thermal Pollution: Discharge of heated water from industrial processes that can kill or injure aquatic organisms.

Thermal Stratification: The formation of layers of different temperatures in a lake or reservoir.

Thermal System Insulation (TSI): Asbestos-containing material applied to pipes, fittings, boilers, breeching, tanks, ducts, or other interior structural components to prevent heat loss or gain or water condensation.

Thermal Treatment: Use of elevated temperatures to treat hazardous wastes. (See: incineration; pyrolysis.)

Thermocline: The middle layer of a thermally stratified lake or reservoir. In this layer, there is a rapid decrease in temperatures in a lake or reservoir.

Threshold: The lowest dose of a chemical at which a specified measurable effect is observed and below which it is not observed.

Threshold: The dose or exposure level below which a significant adverse effect is not expected.

Threshold Level: Time-weighted average pollutant concentration values, exposure beyond which is likely to adversely affect human health. (See: environmental exposure)

Threshold Limit Value (TLV): The concentration of an airborne substance to which an average person can be repeatedly exposed without adverse effects. TLVs may be expressed in three ways: (1) TLV-TWA—Time weighted average, based on an allowable exposure averaged over a normal 8-hour workday or 40-hour work- week; (2) TLV-STEL—Short-term exposure limit or maximum concentration for a brief specified period of time, depending on a specific chemical (TWA must still be met); and (3) TLV-C—Ceiling Exposure Limit or maximum exposure concentration not to be exceeded under any circumstances. (TWA must still be met.)

Threshold Odor: (See: Odor threshold)

Threshold Planning Quantity: A quantity designated for each chemical on the list of extremely hazardous substances that triggers notification by facilities to the State Emergency Response Commission that such facilities are subject to emergency planning requirements under SARA Title III.

Thropic Levels: A functional classification of species that is based on feeding relationships (e.g. generally aquatic and terrestrial green plants comprise the first thropic level, and herbivores comprise the second.)

Tidal Marsh: Low, flat marshlands traversed by channels and tidal hollows, subject to tidal inundation; normally, the only vegetation present is salt-tolerant bushes and grasses. (See: wetlands.)

Tillage: Plowing, seedbed preparation, and cultivation practices.

Time-weighted Average (TWA): In air sampling, the average air concentration of contaminants during a given period.

Tire Processor: Intermediate operating facility where recovered tires are processed in preparation for recycling.

Tires: As used in recycling, passenger car and truck tires (excludes airplane, bus, motorcycle and special service military, agricultural, off-the-road and-slow speed industrial tires). Car and truck tires are recycled into rubber products such as trash cans, storage containers, rubberized asphalt or used whole for playground and reef construction.

Tolerance Petition: A formal request to establish a new tolerance or modify an existing one.

Tolerances: Permissible residue levels for pesticides in raw agricultural produce and processed foods. Whenever a pesticide is registered for use on a food or a feed crop, a tolerance (or exemption from the tolerance requirement) must be established. EPA establishes the tolerance levels, which are enforced by the Food and Drug Administration and the Department of Agriculture.

Tonnage: The amount of waste that a landfill accepts, usually expressed in tons per month. The rate at which a landfill accepts waste is limited by the landfill's permit.

Topography: The physical features of a surface area including relative elevations and the position of natural and man-made (anthropogenic) features.

Total Dissolved Phosphorous: The total phosphorous content of all material that will pass through a filter, which is determined as orthophosphate without prior digestion or hydrolysis. Also called soluble P. or ortho P.

Total Dissolved Solids (TDS): All material that passes the standard glass river filter; now called total filtrable residue. Term is used to reflect salinity.

Total Petroleum Hydrocarbons (TPH): Measure of the concentration or mass of petroleum hydrocarbon constituents present in a given amount of soil or water. The word "total" is a misnomer—few, if any, of the procedures for quantifying hydrocarbons can measure all of them in a given sample. Volatile ones are usually lost in the process and not quantified and non-petroleum hydrocarbons sometimes appear in the analysis.

Total Recovered Petroleum Hydrocarbon: A method for measuring petroleum hydrocarbons in samples of soil or water.

Total Suspended Particles (TSP): A method of monitoring airborne particulate matter by total weight.

Total Suspended Solids (TSS): A measure of the suspended solids in wastewater, effluent, or water bodies, determined by tests for "total suspended non-filterable solids." (See: suspended solids.)

Toxaphene: Chemical that causes adverse health effects in domestic water supplies and is toxic to fresh water and marine aquatic life.

Toxic Chemical: Any chemical listed in EPA rules as "Toxic Chemicals Subject to Section 313 of the Emergency Planning and Community Right-to-Know Act of 1986."

Toxic Chemical Release Form: Information form required of facilities that manufacture, process, or use (in quantities above a specific amount) chemicals listed under SARA Title III.

Toxic Chemical Use Substitution: Replacing toxic chemicals with less harmful chemicals in industrial processes.

Toxic Cloud: Airborne plume of gases, vapors, fumes, or aerosols containing toxic materials.

Toxic Concentration: The concentration at which a substance produces a toxic effect.

Toxic Dose: The dose level at which a substance produces a toxic effect.

Toxic Pollutants: Materials that cause death, disease, or birth defects in organisms that ingest or absorb them. The quantities and exposures necessary to cause these effects can vary widely.

Toxic Release Inventory: Database of toxic releases in the United States compiled from SARA Title III Section 313 reports.

Toxic Substance: A chemical or mixture that may present an unreasonable risk of injury to health or the environment.

Toxic Waste: A waste that can produce injury if inhaled, swallowed, or absorbed through the skin.

Toxicant: A harmful substance or agent that may injure an exposed organism.

Toxicity: The degree to which a substance or mixture of substances can harm humans or animals. Acute toxicity involves harmful effects in an organism through a single or short-term exposure. Chronic toxicity is the ability of a substance or mixture of substances to cause harmful effects over an extended period, usually upon repeated or continuous exposure sometimes lasting for the entire life of the exposed organism. Subchronic toxicity is the ability of the substance to cause effects for more than one year but less than the lifetime of the exposed organism.

Toxicity Assessment: Characterization of the toxicological properties and effects of a chemical, with special emphasis on establishment of dose-response characteristics.

Toxicity Testing: Biological testing (usually with an invertebrate, fish, or small mammal) to determine the adverse effects of a compound or effluent.

Toxicological Profile: An examination, summary, and interpretation of a hazardous substance to determine levels of exposure and associated health effects.

Transboundary Pollutants: Air pollution that travels from one jurisdiction to another, often crossing state or international boundaries. Also applies to water pollution.

Transfer Station: Facility where solid waste is transferred from collection vehicles to larger trucks or rail cars for longer distance transport.

Transient Water System: A non-community water system that does not serve 25 of the same nonresidents per day for more than six months per year.

Transmission Lines: Pipelines that transport raw water from its source to a water treatment plant, then to the distribution grid system.

Transmissivity: The ability of an aquifer to transmit water.

Transpiration: The process by which water vapor is lost to the atmosphere from living plants. The term can also be applied to the quantity of water thus dissipated.

Transportation Control Measures (TCMs): Steps taken by a locality to reduce vehicular emission and improve air quality by reducing or changing the flow of traffic; e.g. bus and HOV lanes, carpooling and other forms of ride-shairing, public transit, bicycle lanes.

Transporter: Hauling firm that picks up properly packaged and labeled hazardous waste from generators and transports it to designated facilities for treatment, storage, or disposal. Transporters are subject to EPA and DOT hazardous waste regulations.

Trash: Material considered worthless or offensive that is thrown away. Generally defined as dry waste material, but in common usage it is a synonym for garbage, rubbish, or refuse.

Trash-to-Energy Plan: Burning trash to produce energy.

Treatability Studies: Tests of potential cleanup technologies conducted in a laboratory (See: bench-scale tests.)

Treated Regulated Medical Waste: Medical waste treated to substantially reduce or eliminate its pathogenicity, but that has not yet been destroyed.

Treated Wastewater: Wastewater that has been subjected to one or more physical, chemical, and biological processes to reduce its potential of being health hazard.

Treatment: (1) Any method, technique, or process designed to remove solids and/or pollutants from solid waste, waste-streams, effluents, and air emissions. (2) Methods used to change the biological character or composition of any regulated medical waste so as to substantially reduce or eliminate its potential for causing disease.

Treatment Plant: A structure built to treat wastewater before discharging it into the environment.

Treatment, Storage, and Disposal Facility: Site where a hazardous substance is treated, stored, or disposed of. TSD facilities are regulated by EPA and states under RCRA.

Tremie: Device used to place concrete or grout under water.

Trial Burn: An incinerator test in which emissions are monitored for the presence of specific organic compounds, particulates, and hydrogen chloride.

Trichloroethylene (TCE): A stable, low boiling-point colorless liquid, toxic if inhaled. Used as a solvent or metal degreasing agent, and in other industrial applications.

Trickle Irrigation: Method in which water drips to the soil from perforated tubes or emitters.

Trickling Filter: A coarse treatment system in which wastewater is trickled over a bed of stones or other material covered with bacteria that break down the organic waste and produce clean water.

Trihalomethane (THM): One of a family of organic compounds named as derivative of methane. THMs are generally by-products of chlorination of drinking water that contains organic material.

Troposhpere: The layer of the atmosphere closest to the earth's surface.

Trust Fund (CERCLA): A fund set up under the Comprehensive Environmental Response, Compensation and Liability Act (CERCLA) to help pay for cleanup of hazardous waste sites and for legal action to force those responsible for the sites to clean them up.

Tube Settler: Device using bundles of tubes to let solids in water settle to the bottom for removal by conventional sludge collection means; sometimes used in sedimentation basins and clarifiers to improve particle removal.

Tuberculation: Development or formation of small mounds of corrosion products on the inside of iron pipe. These tubercules roughen the inside of the pipe, increasing its resistance to water flow.

Tundra: A type of treeless ecosystem dominated by lichens, mosses, grasses, and woody plants. Tundra is found at high latitudes (arctic tundra) and high altitudes (alpine tundra). Arctic tundra is underlain by permafrost and is usually water saturated. (See: wetlands.)

Turbidimeter: A device that measures the cloudiness of suspended solids in a liquid; a measure of the quantity of suspended solids.

Turbidity: 1. Haziness in air caused by the presence of particles and pollutants. 2. A cloudy condition in water due to suspended silt or organic matter.

U

Ultra Clean Coal (UCC): Coal that is washed, ground into fine particles, then chemically treated to remove sulfur, ash, silicone, and other substances; usually briquetted and coated with a sealant made from coal.

Ultraviolet Rays: Radiation from the sun that can be useful or potentially harmful. UV rays from one part of the spectrum (UV-A) enhance plant life. UV rays from other parts of the spectrum (UV-B) can cause skin cancer or other tissue damage. The ozone layer in the atmosphere partly shields us from ultraviolet rays reaching the earth's surface.

Uncertainty Factor: One of several factors used in calculating the reference dose from experimental data. UFs are intended to account for (1) the variation in sensitivity among humans; (2) the uncertainty in extrapolating animal data to humans; (3) the uncertainty in extrapolating data obtained in a study that covers less than the full life of the exposed animal or human; and (4) the uncertainty in using LOAEL data rather than NOAEL data.

Unconfined Aquifer: An aquifer containing water that is not under pressure; the water level in a well is the same as the water table outside the well.

Underground Injection Control (UIC): The program under the Safe Drinking Water Act that regulates the use of wells to pump fluids into the ground.

Underground Injection Wells: Steel- and concrete-encased shafts into which hazardous waste is deposited by force and under pressure.

Underground Sources of Drinking Water: Aquifers currently being used as a source of drinking water or those capable of supplying a public water system. They have a total dissolved solids content of 10,000 milligrams per liter or less, and are not "exempted aquifers." (See: exempted aquifer.)

Underground Storage Tank (UST): A tank located at least partially underground and designed to hold gasoline or other petroleum products or chemicals.

Unreasonable Risk: Under the Federal Insecticide, Fungicide, and Rodenticide Act (FIFRA), "unreasonable adverse effects" means any unreasonable risk to man or the environment, taking into account the medical, economic, social, and environmental costs and benefits of any pesticide.

Unsaturated Zone: The area above the water table where soil pores are not fully saturated, although some water may be present.

Upper Detection Limit: The largest concentration that an instrument can reliably detect.

Uranium Mill Tailings Piles: Former uranium ore processing sites that contain leftover radioactive materials (wastes), including radium and unrecovered uranium.

Uranium Mill-Tailings Waste Piles: Licensed active mills with tailings piles and evaporation ponds created by acid or alkaline leaching processes.

Urban Runoff: Storm water from city streets and adjacent domestic or commercial properties that carries pollutants of various kinds into the sewer systems and receiving waters.

Urea-Formaldehyde Foam Insulation: A material once used to conserve energy by sealing crawl spaces, attics, etc.; no longer used because emissions were found to be a health hazard.

Use Cluster: A set of competing chemicals, processes, and/or technologies that can substitute for one another in performing a particular function.

Used Oil: Spent motor oil from passenger cars and trucks collected at specified locations for recycling (not included in the category of municipal solid waste).

User Fee: Fee collected from only those persons who use a particular service, as compared to one collected from the public in general.

Utility Load: The total electricity demand for a utility district.

V

Vadose Zone: The zone between land surface and the water table within which the moisture content is less than saturation (except in the capillary fringe) and pressure is less than atmospheric. Soil pore space also typically contains air or other gases. The capillary fringe is included in the vadose zone. (See: Unsaturated Zone.)

Valued Environmental Attributes/Components: Those aspects(components/processes/functions) of ecosystems, human health, and environmental welfare considered to be important and potentially at risk from human activity or natural hazards. Similar to the term "valued environmental components" used in environmental impact assessment.

Vapor: The gas given off by substances that are solids or liquids at ordinary atmospheric pressure and temperatures.

Vapor Capture System: Any combination of hoods and ventilation system that captures or contains organic vapors so they may be directed to an abatement or recovery device.

Vapor Dispersion: The movement of vapor clouds in air due to wind, thermal action, gravity spreading, and mixing.

Vapor Plumes: Flue gases visible because they contain water droplets.

Vapor Pressure: A measure of a substance's propensity to evaporate, vapor pressure is the force per unit area exerted by vapor in an equilibrium state with surroundings at a given pressure. It increases exponentially with an increase in temperature. A relative measure of chemical volatility, vapor pressure is used to calculate water partition coefficients and volatilization rate constants.

Vapor Recovery System: A system by which the volatile gases from gasoline are captured instead of being released into the atmosphere.

Variance: Government permission for a delay or exception in the application of a given law, ordinance, or regulation.

Vector: 1. An organism, often an insect or rodent, that carries disease. 2. Plasmids, viruses, or bacteria used to transport genes into a host cell. A gene is placed in the vector; the vector then "infects" the bacterium.

Vegetative Controls: Non-point source pollution control practices that involve vegetative cover to reduce erosion and minimize loss of pollutants.

Vehicle Miles Travelled (VMT): A measure of the extent of motor vehicle operation; the total number of vehicle miles travelled within a specific geographic area over a given period of time.

Ventilation Rate: The rate at which indoor air enters and leaves a building. Expressed as the number of changes of outdoor air per unit of time (air changes per hour (ACH), or the rate at which a volume of outdoor air enters in cubic feet per minute (CFM).

Ventilation/Suction: The act of admitting fresh air into a space in order to replace stale or contaminated air; achieved by blowing air into the space. Similarly, suction represents the admission of fresh air into an interior space by lowering the pressure outside of the space, thereby drawing the contaminated air outward.

Venturi Scrubbers: Air pollution control devices that use water to remove particulate matter from emissions.

Vinyl Chloride: A chemical compound, used in producing some plastics, that is believed to be oncogenic.

Virgin Materials: Resources extracted from nature in their raw form, such as timber or metal ore.

Viscosity: The molecular friction within a fluid that produces flow resistance.

Volatile: Any substance that evaporates readily.

Volatile Liquids: Liquids which easily vaporize or evaporate at room temperature.

Volatile Organic Compound (VOC): Any organic compound that participates in atmospheric photochemical reactions except those designated by EPA as having negligible photochemical reactivity.

Volatile Solids: Those solids in water or other liquids that are lost on ignition of the dry solids at 550ø centigrade.

Volatile Synthetic Organic Chemicals: Chemicals that tend to volatilize or evaporate.

Volume Reduction: Processing waste materials to decrease the amount of space they occupy, usually by compacting, shredding, incineration, or composting.

Volumetric Tank Test: One of several tests to determine the physical integrity of a storage tank; the volume of fluid in the tank is measured directly or calculated from product-level changes. A marked drop in volume indicates a leak.

Vulnerability Analysis: Assessment of elements in the community that are susceptible to damage if hazardous materials are released.

Vulnerable Zone: An area over which the airborne concentration of a chemical accidentally released could reach the level of concern.

W

Waste: 1. Unwanted materials left over from a manufacturing process. 2. Refuse from places of human or animal habitation.

Waste Characterization: Identification of chemical and microbiological constituents of a waste material.

Waste Exchange: Arrangement in which companies exchange their wastes for the benefit of both parties.

Waste Feed: The continuous or intermittent flow of wastes into an incinerator.

Waste Generation: The weight or volume of materials and products that enter the waste stream before recycling, composting, landfilling, or combustion takes place. Also can represent the amount of waste generated by a given source or category of sources.

Waste Load Allocation: 1. The maximum load of pollutants each discharger of waste is allowed to release into a particular waterway. Discharge limits are usually required for each specific water quality criterion being, or expected to be, violated. 2. The portion of a stream's total assimilative capacity assigned to an individual discharge.

Waste Minimization: Measures or techniques that reduce the amount of wastes generated during industrial production processes; term is also applied to recycling and other efforts to reduce the amount of waste going into the waste stream.

Waste Piles: Non-containerized, lined or unlined accumulations of solid, nonflowing waste.

Waste Reduction: Using source reduction, recycling, or composting to prevent or reduce waste generation.

Waste Stream: The total flow of solid waste from homes, businesses, institutions, and manufacturing plants that is recycled, burned, or disposed of in landfills, or segments thereof such as the "residential waste stream" or the "recyclable waste stream."

Waste Treatment Lagoon: Impoundment made by excavation or earth fill for biological treatment of wastewater.

Waste Treatment Plant: A facility containing a series of tanks, screens, filters and other processes by which pollutants are removed from water.

Waste Treatment Stream: The continuous movement of waste from generator to treater and disposer.

Waste-Heat Recovery: Recovering heat discharged as a byproduct of one process to provide heat needed by a second process.

Waste-to-Energy Facility/Municipal-Waste Combustor: Facility where recovered municipal solid waste is converted into a usable form of energy, usually via combustion.

Wastewater: The spent or used water from a home, community, farm, or industry that contains dissolved or suspended matter.Water Pollution: The presence in water of enough harmful or objectionable material to damage the water's quality.

Wastewater Infrastructure: The plan or network for the collection, treatment, and disposal of sewage in a community. The level of treatment will depend on the size of the community, the type of discharge, and/or the designated use of the receiving water.

Wastewater Operations and Maintenance: Actions taken after construction to ensure that facilities constructed to treat wastewater will be operated, maintained, and managed to reach prescribed effluent levels in an optimum manner.

Wastewater Treatment Plan: A facility containing a series of tanks, screens, filters, and other processes by which pollutants are removed from water. Most treatments include chlorination to attain safe drinking water standards.

Water Purveyor: A public utility, mutual water company, county water district, or municipality that delivers drinking water to customers.

Water Quality Criteria: Levels of water quality expected to render a body of water suitable for its designated use. Criteria are based on specific levels of pollutants that would make the water harmful if used for drinking, swimming, farming, fish production, or industrial processes.

Water Quality Standards: State-adopted and EPA-approved ambient standards for water bodies. The standards prescribe the use of the water body and establish the water quality criteria that must be met to protect designated uses.

Water Quality-Based Limitations: Effluent limitations applied to dischargers when mere technology-based limitations would cause violations of water quality standards. Usually applied to discharges into small streams.

Water Quality-Based Permit: A permit with an effluent limit more stringent than one based on technology performance. Such limits may be necessary to protect the designated use of receiving waters (e.g. recreation, irrigation, industry or water supply).

Water Solubility: The maximum possible concentration of a chemical compound dissolved in water. If a substance is water soluble it can very readily disperse through the environment.

Water Storage Pond: An impound for liquid wastes designed to accomplish some degree of biochemical treatment.

Water Supplier: One who owns or operates a public water system.

Water Supply System: The collection, treatment, storage, and distribution of potable water from source to consumer.

Water Table: The level of groundwater.

Water Treatment Lagoon: An impound for liquid wastes designed to accomplish some degree of biochemical treatment.

Water Well: An excavation where the intended use is for location, acquisition, development, or artificial recharge of ground water.

Water-Soluble Packaging: Packaging that dissolves in water; used to reduce exposure risks to pesticide mixers and loaders.

Water-Source Heat Pump: Heat pump that uses wells or heat exchangers to transfer heat from water to the inside of a building. Most such units use ground water. (See: groundsource heat pump; heat pump.)

Waterborne Disease Outbreak: The significant occurence of acute illness associated with drinking water from a public water system that is deficient in treatment, as determined by appropriate local or state agencies.

Watershed: The land area that drains into a stream; the watershed for a major river may encompass a number of smaller watersheds that ultimately combine at a common point.

Watershed Approach: A coordinated framework for environmental management that focuses public and private efforts on the highest priority problems within hydrologically-defined geographic areas taking into consideration both ground and surface water flow.

Watershed Area: A topographic area within a line drawn connecting the highest points uphill of a drinking waterintake into which overland flow drains.

Weight of Scientific Evidence: Considerations in assessing the interpretation of published information about toxicity—quality of testing methods, size and power of study design, consistency of results across studies, and biological plausibility of exposure-response relationships and statistical associations.

Weir: 1. A wall or plate placed in an open channel to measure the flow of water. 2. A wall or obstruction used to control flow from settling tanks and clarifiers to ensure a uniform flow rate and avoid short-circuiting. (See: short-circuiting.)

Well: A bored, drilled, or driven shaft, or a dug hole whose depth is greater than the largest surface dimension and whose purpose is to reach underground water supplies or oil, or to store or bury fluids below ground.

Well Field: Area containing one or more wells that produce usable amounts of water or oil.

Well Injection: The subsurface emplacement of fluids into a well.

Well Monitoring: Measurement by on-site instruments or laboratory methods of well water quality.

Well Plug: A watertight, gastight seal installed in a bore hole or well to prevent movement of fluids.

Well Point: A hollow vertical tube, rod, or pipe terminating in a perforated pointed shoe and fitted with a fine-mesh screen.

Wellhead Protection Area: A protected surface and subsurface zone surrounding a well or well field supplying a public water system to keep contaminants from reaching the well water.

Wetlands: An area that is saturated by surface or ground water with vegetation adapted for life under those soil conditions, as swamps, bogs, fens, marshes, and estuaries.

Wettability: The relative degree to which a fluid will spread into or coat a solid surface in the presence of other immiscible fluids.

Wettable Powder: Dry formulation that must be mixed with water or other liquid before it is applied.

Wheeling: The transmission of electricity owned by one entity through the facilities owned by another (usually a utility).

Whole-Effluent-Toxicity Tests: Tests to determine the toxicity levels of the total effluent from a single source as opposed to a series of tests for individual contaminants.

Wildlife Refuge: An area designated for the protection of wild animals, within which hunting and fishing are either prohibited or strictly controlled.

Wire-to-Wire Efficiency: The efficiency of a pump and motor together.

Wood Packaging: Wood products such as pallets, crates, and barrels.

Wood Treatment Facility: An industrial facility that treats lumber and other wood products for outdoor use. The process employs chromated copper arsenate, which is regulated as a hazardous material.

Wood-Burning-Stove Pollution: Air pollution caused by emissions of particulate matter, carbon monoxide, total suspended particulates, and polycyclic organic matter from wood-burning stoves.

Working Level (WL): A unit of measure for documenting exposure to radon decay products, the so-called "daughters." One working level is equal to approximately 200 picocuries per liter.

Working Level Month (WLM): A unit of measure used to determine cumulative exposure to radon.

X

Xenobiota: Any biotum displaced from its normal habitat; a chemical foreign to a biological system.

Y

Yard Waste: The part of solid waste composed of grass clippings, leaves, twigs, branches, and other garden refuse.

Yellow-Boy: Iron oxide flocculant (clumps of solids in waste or water); usually observed as orange-yellow deposits in surface streams with excess iron content. (See: floc, flocculation.)

Yield: The quantity of water (expressed as a rate of flow or total quantity per year) that can be collected for a given use from surface or groundwater sources.

Z

Zero Air: Atmospheric air purified to contain less than 0.1 ppm total hydrocarbons.

Zooplankton: Small (often microscopic) free-floating aquatic plants or animals.

Zone of Saturation: The layer beneath the surface of the land containing openings that may fill with water.

Source: *U.S. Environmental Protection Agency, "Terms of Environment"*

A

Entry Name Index

B

Entry Name Index

C

E

H

I

J

K

L

M

N

O

P

Q

R

S

T

U

Alabama

Alaska

Arizona

Arkansas

California

Colorado

Connecticut

Delaware

District of Columbia

Florida

Georgia

Hawaii

Idaho

Illinois

Indiana

Iowa

Kansas

Kentucky

Louisiana

Maine

Maryland

Massachusetts

Michigan

Minnesota

Mississippi

Missouri

Montana

Nebraska

Nevada

New Hampshire

New Jersey

New Mexico

New York

North Carolina

North Dakota

Ohio

Oklahoma

Oregon

Pennsylvania

Rhode Island

South Carolina

South Dakota

Tennessee

Texas

Utah

Vermont

Virginia

Washington

West Virginia

Wisconsin

Wyoming

Canada

Acid rain (*See also:* Air pollution; Water pollution)

Agricultural Engineering

Agricultural conservation (*See also:* Soil conservation)

Agricultural ecology (*See also*: Agricultural conservation)

Agriculture (*See also:* Sustainable agriculture)

Air pollution (*See also:* Acid rain; Aerosols; Pollution, Environmental effects of)

Air quality (*See also:* Air pollution)

Alcohol as fuel

Alternative fuels

Animal conservation

Animal ecology

Aquaculture

Aquatic ecology (*See also:* Marine ecology)

Architecture and energy conservation

Arctic ecology

Arid regions

Coral reef ecology

Dolphins

Drinking water

Ecological preserves

Ecology (*See also:* Conservation of natural resources)

Electricity

Elephants

Endangered species, Animals

Endangered species, Plants

Energy conservation

Energy consumption

Energy conversion

Energy economics

Energy management

Energy policy

Energy resources (*See also:* Biomass energy)

Energy technology

Environmental chemistry (*See also:* Air pollution)

Environmental compliance

Environmental design

Environmental economics (*See also:* Energy economics)

Environmental education

Environmental engineering (*See also:* Environmental design)

Environmental ethics

Environmental finances

Environmental health (*See also:* Air pollution)

Environmental impact analysis

Environmental monitoring

Environmental policy

Environmental protection

Environmental quality

Environmental sciences

Estuaries

Fertilizers

Fire ecology

Fish feeding and feeds

Fish habitat

Fish populations

Fish reproduction and growth

Fisheries

Fishery management

Fishery policy

Fishes

Food science and technology

Forest ecology

Forest management (*See also:* Fire ecology)

Forests and forestry (*See also:* National forests)

Fuels (*See also:* Biomass energy)

Geographic information systems

Geothermal resources

Glaciology

Global warming

Great Lakes

Groundwater

Habitat, Ecology

Hazardous substances

Hazardous waste

Hazardous waste management

Human ecology (*See also:* Conservation of natural resources)

Hydrocarbons

Hydrogen as fuel

Hydrology

Industrial hygiene

Industrial safety

Inhalation toxicology

Lake renewal

Lakes

Land use (*See also:* Agricultural conservation)

Land use and development

Law, Environmental (*See also:* Acid rain; Air pollution)

Litter (Trash)

Livestock

Marine biology (*See also:* Marine ecology)

Marine ecology (*See also:* Coral reef ecology)

Marine engineering

Marine industries (*See also:* Marine resources)

Marine mammals (*See also:* Dolphins; Whales)

Marine pollution

Marine resources

Marine sciences

Maritime law

Materials testing

Mines and mineral resources

Mountain ecology

Municipal waste

National forests (*See also:* Forests and forestry)

National parks and reserves (*See also:* Parks)

Natural products

Natural resources

Natural resources development

Noise pollution

Nuclear energy

Nuclear engineering

Nuclear safety

Occupational diseases

Ocean

Ocean engineering

Oceanography

Oil pollution

Organic gardening

Ornithology

Ozone

Supplemental material on these subjects can be found in the Statistics & Rankings section beginning on page 521

Parks (*See also:* National parks and reserves)

Pest control, Integrated

Pesticides

Pesticides and the environment

Petroleum

Plant communities

Plant conservation

Plants, Protection of (*See also:* Plant conservation)

Plastics

Polar regions (*See also:* Arctic ecology)

Pollution (*See also:* Air pollution)

Pollution control

Pollution, Environmental effects of

Population

Prairie ecology

Public awareness/information programs

Pulp and paper technology

Radiation effects

Radioactive pollution (*See also:* Radioactive wastes)

Radioactive wastes (*See also:* Hazardous waste management)

Radon

Rain forest

Recreation areas

Recycling (*See also:* Energy conservation)

Renewable energy sources (*See also:* Solar energy, Wind energy)

Renewable natural resources

Reservoirs (*See also:* Water resources)

Subject Index

Tropical ecology (*See also:* Ecology, Tropical)

Tropical forestry

Underground storage

Urban wildlife

Vegetation mapping

Waste disposal

Waste management

Waste products (*See also:* Recycling [Waste, etc.])

Waste treatment

Wastewater treatment

Water conservation (*See also:* Water quality control)

Water pollution (*See also:* Acid rain)

Water quality (*See also:* Water pollution; Water quality control)

Water quality control (*See also:* Water reclamation)

Water reclamation (*See also:* Water use)

Water resources (*See also:* Groundwater; Reservoirs)

Water treatment (*See also:* Water reclamation)

Water use (*See also:* Water reclamation)

Waterfowl

Watersheds

Wetlands (*See also:* Estuaries)

Whales

Wilderness area

Wildlife (*See also:* Animal ecology; Wildlife management)

Wildlife management

Wind energy

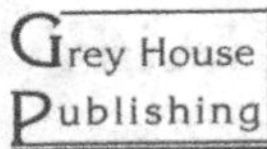

2017 Title List

Visit www.GreyHouse.com for Product Information, Table of Contents, and Sample Pages.

General Reference

An African Biographical Dictionary
America's College Museums
American Environmental Leaders: From Colonial Times to the Present
Encyclopedia of African-American Writing
Encyclopedia of Constitutional Amendments
An Encyclopedia of Human Rights in the United States
Encyclopedia of Invasions & Conquests
Encyclopedia of Prisoners of War & Internment
Encyclopedia of Religion & Law in America
Encyclopedia of Rural America
Encyclopedia of the Continental Congress
Encyclopedia of the United States Cabinet, 1789-2010
Encyclopedia of War Journalism
Encyclopedia of Warrior Peoples & Fighting Groups
The Environmental Debate: A Documentary History
The Evolution Wars: A Guide to the Debates
From Suffrage to the Senate: America's Political Women
Gun Debate: An Encyclopedia of Gun Control & Gun Rights
Political Corruption in America
Privacy Rights in the Digital Era
The Religious Right: A Reference Handbook
Speakers of the House of Representatives, 1789-2009
This is Who We Were: 1880-1900
This is Who We Were: A Companion to the 1940 Census
This is Who We Were: In the 1900s
This is Who We Were: In the 1910s
This is Who We Were: In the 1920s
This is Who We Were: In the 1940s
This is Who We Were: In the 1950s
This is Who We Were: In the 1960s
This is Who We Were: In the 1970s
This is Who We Were: In the 1980s
This is Who We Were: In the 1990s
U.S. Land & Natural Resource Policy
The Value of a Dollar 1600-1865: Colonial Era to the Civil War
The Value of a Dollar: 1860-2014
Working Americans 1770-1869 Vol. IX: Revolutionary War to the Civil War
Working Americans 1880-1999 Vol. I: The Working Class
Working Americans 1880-1999 Vol. II: The Middle Class
Working Americans 1880-1999 Vol. III: The Upper Class
Working Americans 1880-1999 Vol. IV: Their Children
Working Americans 1880-2015 Vol. V: Americans At War
Working Americans 1880-2005 Vol. VI: Women at Work
Working Americans 1880-2006 Vol. VII: Social Movements
Working Americans 1880-2007 Vol. VIII: Immigrants
Working Americans 1880-2009 Vol. X: Sports & Recreation
Working Americans 1880-2010 Vol. XI: Inventors & Entrepreneurs
Working Americans 1880-2011 Vol. XII: Our History through Music
Working Americans 1880-2012 Vol. XIII: Education & Educators
Working Americans 1880-2016 Vol. XIV: Industry Through the Ages
World Cultural Leaders of the 20th & 21st Centuries

Education Information

Charter School Movement
Comparative Guide to American Elementary & Secondary Schools
Complete Learning Disabilities Directory
Educators Resource Directory
Special Education: Policy and Curriculum Development

Health Information

Comparative Guide to American Hospitals
Complete Directory for Pediatric Disorders
Complete Directory for People with Chronic Illness
Complete Directory for People with Disabilities
Complete Mental Health Directory
Diabetes in America: Analysis of an Epidemic
Directory of Health Care Group Purchasing Organizations
HMO/PPO Directory
Medical Device Market Place
Older Americans Information Directory

Business Information

Complete Television, Radio & Cable Industry Directory
Directory of Business Information Resources
Directory of Mail Order Catalogs
Directory of Venture Capital & Private Equity Firms
Environmental Resource Handbook
Food & Beverage Market Place
Grey House Homeland Security Directory
Grey House Performing Arts Directory
Grey House Safety & Security Directory
Hudson's Washington News Media Contacts Directory
New York State Directory
Sports Market Place Directory

Statistics & Demographics

American Tally
America's Top-Rated Cities
America's Top-Rated Smaller Cities
Ancestry & Ethnicity in America
The Asian Databook
Comparative Guide to American Suburbs
The Hispanic Databook
Profiles of America
"Profiles of" Series - State Handbooks
Weather America

Financial Ratings Series

TheStreet Ratings' Guide to Bond & Money Market Mutual Funds
TheStreet Ratings' Guide to Common Stocks
TheStreet Ratings' Guide to Exchange-Traded Funds
TheStreet Ratings' Guide to Stock Mutual Funds
TheStreet Ratings' Ultimate Guided Tour of Stock Investing
Weiss Ratings' Consumer Guides
Weiss Ratings' Financial Literary Basic Guides
Weiss Ratings' Guide to Banks
Weiss Ratings' Guide to Credit Unions
Weiss Ratings' Guide to Health Insurers
Weiss Ratings' Guide to Life & Annuity Insurers
Weiss Ratings' Guide to Property & Casualty Insurers

Bowker's Books In Print® Titles

American Book Publishing Record® Annual
American Book Publishing Record® Monthly
Books In Print®
Books In Print® Supplement
Books Out Loud™
Bowker's Complete Video Directory™
Children's Books In Print®
El-Hi Textbooks & Serials In Print®
Forthcoming Books®
Law Books & Serials In Print™
Medical & Health Care Books In Print™
Publishers, Distributors & Wholesalers of the US™
Subject Guide to Books In Print®
Subject Guide to Children's Books In Print®

Canadian General Reference

Associations Canada
Canadian Almanac & Directory
Canadian Environmental Resource Guide
Canadian Parliamentary Guide
Canadian Venture Capital & Private Equity Firms
Financial Post Directory of Directors
Financial Services Canada
Governments Canada
Health Guide Canada
The History of Canada
Libraries Canada
Major Canadian Cities

SALEM PRESS

2017 Title List

Visit www.SalemPress.com for Product Information, Table of Contents, and Sample Pages.

Science, Careers & Mathematics

Ancient Creatures
Applied Science
Applied Science: Engineering & Mathematics
Applied Science: Science & Medicine
Applied Science: Technology
Biomes and Ecosystems
Careers in The Arts: Fine, Performing & Visual
Careers in Building Construction
Careers in Business
Careers in Chemistry
Careers in Communications & Media
Careers in Environment & Conservation
Careers in Financial Services
Careers in Healthcare
Careers in Hospitality & Tourism
Careers in Human Services
Careers in Law, Criminal Justice & Emergency Services
Careers in Manufacturing
Careers in Overseas Jobs
Careers in Physics
Careers in Sales, Insurance & Real Estate
Careers in Science & Engineering
Careers in Sports & Fitness
Careers in Technology Services & Repair
Computer Technology Innovators
Contemporary Biographies in Business
Contemporary Biographies in Chemistry
Contemporary Biographies in Communications & Media
Contemporary Biographies in Environment & Conservation
Contemporary Biographies in Healthcare
Contemporary Biographies in Hospitality & Tourism
Contemporary Biographies in Law & Criminal Justice
Contemporary Biographies in Physics
Earth Science
Earth Science: Earth Materials & Resources
Earth Science: Earth's Surface and History
Earth Science: Physics & Chemistry of the Earth
Earth Science: Weather, Water & Atmosphere
Encyclopedia of Energy
Encyclopedia of Environmental Issues
Encyclopedia of Environmental Issues: Atmosphere and Air Pollution
Encyclopedia of Environmental Issues: Ecology and Ecosystems
Encyclopedia of Environmental Issues: Energy and Energy Use
Encyclopedia of Environmental Issues: Policy and Activism
Encyclopedia of Environmental Issues: Preservation/Wilderness Issues
Encyclopedia of Environmental Issues: Water and Water Pollution
Encyclopedia of Global Resources
Encyclopedia of Global Warming
Encyclopedia of Mathematics & Society
Encyclopedia of Mathematics & Society: Engineering, Tech, Medicine
Encyclopedia of Mathematics & Society: Great Mathematicians
Encyclopedia of Mathematics & Society: Math & Social Sciences
Encyclopedia of Mathematics & Society: Math Development/Concepts
Encyclopedia of Mathematics & Society: Math in Culture & Society
Encyclopedia of Mathematics & Society: Space, Science, Environment
Encyclopedia of the Ancient World
Forensic Science
Geography Basics
Internet Innovators
Inventions and Inventors
Magill's Encyclopedia of Science: Animal Life
Magill's Encyclopedia of Science: Plant life
Notable Natural Disasters
Principles of Astronomy
Principles of Biology
Principles of Chemistry
Principles of Physical Science
Principles of Physics
Principles of Research Methods
Principles of Sustainability
Science and Scientists
Solar System
Solar System: Great Astronomers
Solar System: Study of the Universe
Solar System: The Inner Planets
Solar System: The Moon and Other Small Bodies
Solar System: The Outer Planets
Solar System: The Sun and Other Stars
World Geography

Literature

American Ethnic Writers
Classics of Science Fiction & Fantasy Literature
Critical Approaches: Feminist
Critical Approaches: Multicultural
Critical Approaches: Moral
Critical Approaches: Psychological
Critical Insights: Authors
Critical Insights: Film
Critical Insights: Literary Collection Bundles
Critical Insights: Themes
Critical Insights: Works
Critical Survey of Drama
Critical Survey of Graphic Novels: Heroes & Super Heroes
Critical Survey of Graphic Novels: History, Theme & Technique
Critical Survey of Graphic Novels: Independents/Underground Classics
Critical Survey of Graphic Novels: Manga
Critical Survey of Long Fiction
Critical Survey of Mystery & Detective Fiction
Critical Survey of Mythology and Folklore: Heroes and Heroines
Critical Survey of Mythology and Folklore: Love, Sexuality & Desire
Critical Survey of Mythology and Folklore: World Mythology
Critical Survey of Poetry
Critical Survey of Poetry: American Poets
Critical Survey of Poetry: British, Irish & Commonwealth Poets
Critical Survey of Poetry: Cumulative Index
Critical Survey of Poetry: European Poets
Critical Survey of Poetry: Topical Essays
Critical Survey of Poetry: World Poets
Critical Survey of Science Fiction & Fantasy
Critical Survey of Shakespeare's Plays
Critical Survey of Shakespeare's Sonnets
Critical Survey of Short Fiction
Critical Survey of Short Fiction: American Writers
Critical Survey of Short Fiction: British, Irish, Commonwealth Writers
Critical Survey of Short Fiction: Cumulative Index
Critical Survey of Short Fiction: European Writers
Critical Survey of Short Fiction: Topical Essays
Critical Survey of Short Fiction: World Writers
Critical Survey of World Literature
Critical Survey of Young Adult Literature
Cyclopedia of Literary Characters
Cyclopedia of Literary Places
Holocaust Literature
Introduction to Literary Context: American Poetry of the 20th Century
Introduction to Literary Context: American Post-Modernist Novels
Introduction to Literary Context: American Short Fiction
Introduction to Literary Context: English Literature
Introduction to Literary Context: Plays
Introduction to Literary Context: World Literature
Magill's Literary Annual 2015
Magill's Survey of American Literature
Magill's Survey of World Literature
Masterplots
Masterplots II: African American Literature
Masterplots II: American Fiction Series
Masterplots II: British & Commonwealth Fiction Series
Masterplots II: Christian Literature
Masterplots II: Drama Series
Masterplots II: Juvenile & Young Adult Literature, Supplement
Masterplots II: Nonfiction Series
Masterplots II: Poetry Series
Masterplots II: Short Story Series
Masterplots II: Women's Literature Series
Notable African American Writers
Notable American Novelists
Notable Playwrights
Notable Poets
Recommended Reading: 600 Classics Reviewed
Short Story Writers

2017 Title List

Visit www.SalemPress.com for Product Information, Table of Contents, and Sample Pages.

History and Social Science

The 2000s in America
50 States
African American History
Agriculture in History
American First Ladies
American Heroes
American Indian Culture
American Indian History
American Indian Tribes
American Presidents
American Villains
America's Historic Sites
Ancient Greece
The Bill of Rights
The Civil Rights Movement
The Cold War
Countries, Peoples & Cultures
Countries, Peoples & Cultures: Central & South America
Countries, Peoples & Cultures: Central, South & Southeast Asia
Countries, Peoples & Cultures: East & South Africa
Countries, Peoples & Cultures: East Asia & the Pacific
Countries, Peoples & Cultures: Eastern Europe
Countries, Peoples & Cultures: Middle East & North Africa
Countries, Peoples & Cultures: North America & the Caribbean
Countries, Peoples & Cultures: West & Central Africa
Countries, Peoples & Cultures: Western Europe
Defining Documents: American Revolution
Defining Documents: American West
Defining Documents: Ancient World
Defining Documents: Civil Rights
Defining Documents: Civil War
Defining Documents: Court Cases
Defining Documents: Dissent & Protest
Defining Documents: Emergence of Modern America
Defining Documents: Exploration & Colonial America
Defining Documents: Immigration & Immigrant Communities
Defining Documents: Manifest Destiny
Defining Documents: Middle Ages
Defining Documents: Nationalism & Populism
Defining Documents: Native Americans
Defining Documents: Postwar 1940s
Defining Documents: Reconstruction
Defining Documents: Renaissance & Early Modern Era
Defining Documents: 1920s
Defining Documents: 1930s
Defining Documents: 1950s
Defining Documents: 1960s
Defining Documents: 1970s
Defining Documents: The 17th Century
Defining Documents: The 18th Century
Defining Documents: Vietnam War
Defining Documents: Women
Defining Documents: World War I
Defining Documents: World War II
The Eighties in America
Encyclopedia of American Immigration
Encyclopedia of Flight
Encyclopedia of the Ancient World
Fashion Innovators
The Fifties in America
The Forties in America
Great Athletes
Great Athletes: Baseball
Great Athletes: Basketball
Great Athletes: Boxing & Soccer
Great Athletes: Cumulative Index
Great Athletes: Football
Great Athletes: Golf & Tennis
Great Athletes: Olympics
Great Athletes: Racing & Individual Sports
Great Events from History: 17th Century
Great Events from History: 18th Century
Great Events from History: 19th Century
Great Events from History: 20th Century (1901-1940)
Great Events from History: 20th Century (1941-1970)
Great Events from History: 20th Century (1971-2000)
Great Events from History: 21st Century (2000-2016)
Great Events from History: African American History
Great Events from History: Cumulative Indexes
Great Events from History: LGBTG
Great Events from History: Middle Ages
Great Events from History: Modern Scandals
Great Events from History: Renaissance & Early Modern Era
Great Lives from History: 17th Century
Great Lives from History: 18th Century
Great Lives from History: 19th Century
Great Lives from History: 20th Century
Great Lives from History: 21st Century (2000-2016)
Great Lives from History: American Women
Great Lives from History: Ancient World
Great Lives from History: Asian & Pacific Islander Americans
Great Lives from History: Cumulative Indexes
Great Lives from History: Incredibly Wealthy
Great Lives from History: Inventors & Inventions
Great Lives from History: Jewish Americans
Great Lives from History: Latinos
Great Lives from History: Notorious Lives
Great Lives from History: Renaissance & Early Modern Era
Great Lives from History: Scientists & Science
Historical Encyclopedia of American Business
Issues in U.S. Immigration
Magill's Guide to Military History
Milestone Documents in African American History
Milestone Documents in American History
Milestone Documents in World History
Milestone Documents of American Leaders
Milestone Documents of World Religions
Music Innovators
Musicians & Composers 20th Century
The Nineties in America
The Seventies in America
The Sixties in America
Survey of American Industry and Careers
The Thirties in America
The Twenties in America
United States at War
U.S. Court Cases
U.S. Government Leaders
U.S. Laws, Acts, and Treaties
U.S. Legal System
U.S. Supreme Court
Weapons and Warfare
World Conflicts: Asia and the Middle East

Health

Addictions & Substance Abuse
Adolescent Health & Wellness
Cancer
Complementary & Alternative Medicine
Community & Family Health
Genetics & Inherited Conditions
Health Issues
Infectious Diseases & Conditions
Magill's Medical Guide
Nutrition
Nursing
Psychology & Behavioral Health
Psychology Basics

2017 Title List

Visit **www.HWWilsonInPrint.com** for Product Information, Table of Contents and Sample Pages

Current Biography
Current Biography Cumulative Index 1946-2013
Current Biography Monthly Magazine
Current Biography Yearbook: 2003
Current Biography Yearbook: 2004
Current Biography Yearbook: 2005
Current Biography Yearbook: 2006
Current Biography Yearbook: 2007
Current Biography Yearbook: 2008
Current Biography Yearbook: 2009
Current Biography Yearbook: 2010
Current Biography Yearbook: 2011
Current Biography Yearbook: 2012
Current Biography Yearbook: 2013
Current Biography Yearbook: 2014
Current Biography Yearbook: 2015
Current Biography Yearbook: 2016

Core Collections
Children's Core Collection
Fiction Core Collection
Graphic Novels Core Collection
Middle & Junior High School Core
Public Library Core Collection: Nonfiction
Senior High Core Collection
Young Adult Fiction Core Collection

The Reference Shelf
Aging in America
American Military Presence Overseas
The Arab Spring
The Brain
The Business of Food
Campaign Trends & Election Law
Conspiracy Theories
The Digital Age
Dinosaurs
Embracing New Paradigms in Education
Faith & Science
Families: Traditional and New Structures
The Future of U.S. Economic Relations: Mexico, Cuba, and Venezuela
Global Climate Change
Graphic Novels and Comic Books
Guns in America
Immigration
Immigration in the U.S.
Internet Abuses & Privacy Rights
Internet Safety
LGBTQ in the 21st Century
Marijuana Reform
The News and its Future
The Paranormal
Politics of the Ocean
Prescription Drug Abuse
Racial Tension in a "Postracial" Age
Reality Television
Representative American Speeches: 2008-2009
Representative American Speeches: 2009-2010
Representative American Speeches: 2010-2011
Representative American Speeches: 2011-2012
Representative American Speeches: 2012-2013
Representative American Speeches: 2013-2014
Representative American Speeches: 2014-2015
Representative American Speeches: 2015-2016
Representative American Speeches: 2016-2017
Rethinking Work
Revisiting Gender
Robotics
Russia
Social Networking
Social Services for the Poor
Space Exploration & Development
Sports in America
The Supreme Court
The Transformation of American Cities
U.S. Infrastructure
U.S. National Debate Topic: Educational Reform
U.S. National Debate Topic: Surveillance
U.S. National Debate Topic: The Ocean
U.S. National Debate Topic: Transportation Infrastructure
Whistleblowers

Readers' Guide
Abridged Readers' Guide to Periodical Literature
Readers' Guide to Periodical Literature

Indexes
Index to Legal Periodicals & Books
Short Story Index
Book Review Digest

Sears List
Sears List of Subject Headings
Sears: Lista de Encabezamientos de Materia

Facts About Series
Facts About American Immigration
Facts About China
Facts About the 20th Century
Facts About the Presidents
Facts About the World's Languages

Nobel Prize Winners
Nobel Prize Winners: 1901-1986
Nobel Prize Winners: 1987-1991
Nobel Prize Winners: 1992-1996
Nobel Prize Winners: 1997-2001

World Authors
World Authors: 1995-2000
World Authors: 2000-2005

Famous First Facts
Famous First Facts
Famous First Facts About American Politics
Famous First Facts About Sports
Famous First Facts About the Environment
Famous First Facts: International Edition

American Book of Days
The American Book of Days
The International Book of Days

Monographs
American Reformers
The Barnhart Dictionary of Etymology
Celebrate the World
Guide to the Ancient World
Indexing from A to Z
The Poetry Break
Radical Change: Books for Youth in a Digital Age

Wilson Chronology
Wilson Chronology of Asia and the Pacific
Wilson Chronology of Human Rights
Wilson Chronology of Ideas
Wilson Chronology of the Arts
Wilson Chronology of the World's Religions
Wilson Chronology of Women's Achievements